CHILD DEVELOPMENT

LAURA E. BERK

CUSTOM EDITION FOR KAPLAN UNIVERSITY

Taken from:

Child Development, Eighth Edition
by Laura E. Berk

KAPLAN UNIVERSITY

Custom Publishing

New York Boston San Francisco
London Toronto Sydney Tokyo Singapore Madrid
Mexico City Munich Paris Cape Town Hong Kong Montreal

Cover Art: Courtesy of PhotoDisc/Getty Images.

Taken from:

Child Development, Eighth Edition
by Laura E. Berk

Published by Allyn and Bacon
Boston, Massachusetts 02116

This special edition published in cooperation with Pearson Custom Publishing.

Printed in the United States of America

10 9

2008420093

CG

Pearson
Custom Publishing
is a division of

PEARSON

www.pearsonhighered.com

ISBN 10: 0-558-03741-0
ISBN 13: 978-0-558-03741-3

About the Author

Laura E. Berk is a distinguished professor of psychology at Illinois State University, where she has taught child and human development to both undergraduate and graduate students for more than three decades. She received her bachelor's degree in psychology from the University of California, Berkeley, and her master's and doctoral degrees in child development and educational psychology from the University of Chicago. She has been a visiting scholar at Cornell University, UCLA, Stanford University, and the University of South Australia.

Berk has published widely on the effects of school environments on children's development, the development of private speech, and most recently, the role of make-believe play in development. Her research has been funded by the U.S. Office of Education and the National Institute of Child Health and Human Development. It has appeared in many prominent journals, including *Child Development, Developmental Psychology, Merrill-Palmer Quarterly, Journal of Abnormal Child Psychology, Development and Psychopathology,* and *Early Childhood Research Quarterly.* Her empirical studies have attracted the attention of the general public, leading to contributions to *Psychology Today* and *Scientific American.* She has also been featured on National Public Radio's Morning Edition and in *Parents Magazine, Wondertime,* and *Readers' Digest.*

Berk has served as research editor for *Young Children* and consulting editor for *Early Childhood Research Quarterly* and the *Journal of Cognitive Education and Psychology.* She is a frequent contributor to edited volumes on early childhood development, having recently authored chapters on the importance of parenting, on make-believe play and self-regulation, and on the kindergarten child. She has also written the chapter on development for *The Many Faces of Psychological Research in the Twenty-First Century* (Society for the Teaching of Psychology), the chapter on social development for *The Chicago Companion to the Child,* the article on Vygotsky for the *Encyclopedia of Cognitive Science,* and the chapter on storytelling as a teaching strategy for *Voices of Experience: Memorable Talks from the National Institute on the Teaching of Psychology* (Association for Psychological Science).

Berk's books include *Private Speech: From Social Interaction to Self-Regulation, Scaffolding Children's Learning: Vygotsky and Early Childhood Education,* and *Landscapes of Development: An Anthology of Readings.* In addition to *Child Development,* she is author of the best-selling texts *Infants, Children, and Adolescents; Development Through the Lifespan;* and *Exploring Lifespan Development,* published by Allyn and Bacon. Her book for parents and teachers is *Awakening Children's Minds: How Parents and Teachers Can Make a Difference.*

Berk is active in work for children's causes. In addition to service in her home community, she is a member of the national board of directors and chair of the central region advisory board of Jumpstart, a nonprofit organization that provides one-to-one literacy intervention to thousands of low-income preschoolers across the United States, using college and university students as interveners. Berk is a fellow of the American Psychological Association, Division 7: Developmental Psychology.

Features at a Glance

Biology and Environment

From Research to Practice

Cultural Influences

Social Issues

Applying What We Know

Contents

A Personal Note to Students

My more than thirty years of teaching child development have brought me in contact with thousands of students like you—students with diverse majors, future goals, interests, and needs. Some are affiliated with my own field, psychology, but many come from other related fields—education, sociology, anthropology, family studies, social service, nursing, and biology, to name just a few. Each semester, my students' aspirations have proven to be as varied as their fields of study. Many look toward careers in applied work with children—teaching, caregiving, nursing, counseling, social work, school psychology, and program administration. Some plan to teach child development, and a few want to do research. Most hope someday to become parents, whereas others are already parents who come with a desire to better understand and rear their children. And almost all arrive with a deep curiosity about how they themselves developed from tiny infants into the complex human beings they are today.

My goal in preparing this eighth edition of *Child Development* is to provide a textbook that meets the instructional goals of your course as well as your personal interests and needs. To achieve these objectives, I have grounded this book in a carefully selected body of classic and current theory and research. In addition, the text highlights the interacting contributions of biology and environment to the developing child, explains how the research process helps solve real-world problems, illustrates commonalities and differences between ethnic groups and cultures, discusses the broader social contexts in which children develop, and pays special attention to policy issues that are crucial for safeguarding children's well-being in today's world. I have also provided a unique pedagogical program that will assist you in mastering information, integrating various aspects of development, critically examining controversial issues, and applying what you have learned.

I hope that learning about child development will be as rewarding for you as I have found it over the years. I would like to know what you think about both the field of child development and this book. I welcome your comments; please feel free to send them to me at Department of Psychology, Box 4620, Illinois State University, Normal, IL 61790, or care of the publisher, who will forward them to me.

Laura E. Berk

Preface for Instructors

My decision to write *Child Development* was inspired by a wealth of professional and personal experiences. First and foremost were the interests and needs of thousands of students of child development in my classes in more than three decades of college teaching. I aimed for a text that is intellectually stimulating, that provides depth as well as breadth of coverage, that portrays the complexities of child development with clarity and excitement, and that is relevant and useful in building a bridge from theory and research to children's everyday lives.

Today, *Child Development* reaches around the globe, with editions published in six languages: English, Chinese, Georgian, Japanese, Russian, and Spanish. Instructor and student enthusiasm for the book not only has been among my greatest sources of pride and satisfaction, but also has inspired me to rethink and improve each edition. I am honored and humbled to have entrusted to me the awesome responsibility of introducing the field of child development to so many students.

The twenty years since *Child Development* first appeared have been a period of unprecedented expansion and change in theory and research. This eighth edition represents these rapid transformations, with a wealth of new content and teaching tools:

- *Diverse pathways of change are highlighted.* Investigators have reached broad consensus that variations in biological makeup, everyday tasks, and the people who support children in mastery of those tasks lead to wide individual differences in children's paths of change and resulting competencies. This edition pays more attention to variability in development and to recent theories—including ecological, sociocultural, and dynamic systems—that attempt to explain it. Multicultural and cross-cultural findings, including international comparisons, are enhanced throughout the text and in revised and expanded Cultural Influences boxes.

- *The complex, bidirectional relationship between biology and environment is given greater attention.* Accumulating evidence on development of the brain, motor skills, cognitive and language competencies, temperament, and developmental problems underscores the way biological factors emerge in, are modified by, and share power with experience. The interconnection between biology and environment is revisited throughout the text narrative and in the Biology and Environment boxes with new and updated topics.

- *Inclusion of interdisciplinary research is expanded.* The move toward viewing thoughts, feelings, and behavior as an integrated whole, affected by a wide array of influences in biology, social context, and culture, has motivated developmental researchers to strengthen their ties with other fields of psychology and with other disciplines. Topics and findings included in this edition increasingly reflect the contributions of educational psychology, social psychology, health psychology, clinical psychology, neuropsychology, biology, pediatrics, sociology, anthropology, social welfare, and other fields.

- *The links among theory, research, and applications—a theme of this book since its inception—are strengthened.* As researchers intensify their efforts to generate findings relevant to real-life situations, I have placed even greater weight on social policy issues and sound theory- and research-based practices. Further applications are provided in the Applying What We Know tables, which give students concrete ways of building bridges between their learning and the real world.

- *Expanded coverage of Canadian content offers an integrated North American representation of the field.* With its contemporary North American perspective, the text greatly expands students' opportunity to learn more about social and cultural contexts for development and the powerful impact of public policies—especially in the realms of health and education—on children's lives. Canadian research and examples are included throughout the text.

- *The role of active student learning is made more explicit.* A new **TAKE A MOMENT...** feature, built into the chapter narrative, asks students to think deeply and critically or to engage in an exercise or application as they read. Ask Yourself questions at the end of each major section have been thoroughly revised and expanded to promote four approaches to engaging actively with the subject matter: *Review, Apply, Connect,* and *Reflect.* This feature assists students in thinking about what they have learned from multiple vantage points.

Text Philosophy

The basic approach of this book has been shaped by my own professional and personal history as a teacher, researcher, and parent. It consists of seven philosophical ingredients that I regard as essential for students to emerge from a course with a thorough understanding of child development:

1. **An understanding of major theories and the strengths and shortcomings of each.** The first chapter begins by emphasizing that only knowledge of multiple theories can do justice to the richness of child development. In each topical domain, I present a variety of theoretical perspectives, indicate how each highlights previously overlooked facets of development, and discuss research

that evaluates it. If one or two theories have emerged as especially prominent in a particular area, I indicate why, in terms of the theory's broad explanatory power. Consideration of contrasting theories also serves as the context for an evenhanded analysis of many controversial issues throughout the text.

2. **An appreciation of research strategies for investigating child development.** To evaluate theories, students need a firm grounding in research methods and designs. I devote an entire chapter to a description and critique of research strategies. Throughout the book, numerous studies are discussed in sufficient detail for students to use what they have learned to critically assess the findings, conclusions, and implications of research.
3. **Knowledge of both the sequence of child development and the processes that underlie it.** Students are provided with a description of the organized sequence of development along with processes of change. An understanding of process—how complex combinations of biological and environmental events produce development—has been the focus of most recent research. Accordingly, the text reflects this emphasis. But new information about the timetable of change has also emerged. In many ways, children have proved to be far more competent than they were believed to be in the past. Current evidence on the sequence and timing of development, along with its implications for process, is presented throughout the book.
4. **An appreciation of the impact of context and culture on child development.** A wealth of research indicates that children live in rich physical and social contexts that affect all aspects of development. In each chapter, the student travels to distant parts of the world as I review a growing body of cross-cultural evidence. The text narrative also discusses many findings on socioeconomically and ethnically diverse children within the United States and Canada, and children with varying abilities and disabilities. Besides highlighting the role of immediate settings, such as family, neighborhood, and school, I underscore the impact of larger social structures—societal values, laws, and government programs—on children's well-being.
5. **An understanding of the joint contributions of biology and environment to development.** The field recognizes more powerfully than ever before the interaction of hereditary/constitutional and environmental factors—that these contributions to development combine in complex ways and cannot be separated in a simple manner. Numerous examples of how biological dispositions can be maintained as well as transformed by social contexts are presented throughout the book.
6. **A sense of the interdependency of all aspects of development—physical, cognitive, emotional, and social.** Every chapter takes an integrated approach to understanding children. I show how physical, cognitive, emotional, and social development are interwoven. Within the text narrative and in a special series of Ask Yourself *Connect* questions at the end of major sections, students are referred to other parts of the book to deepen their grasp of relationships among various aspects of change.
7. **An appreciation of the interrelatedness of theory, research, and applications.** Throughout this book, I emphasize that theories of child development and the research stimulated by them provide the foundation for sound, effective practices with children. The links among theory, research, and applications are reinforced by an organizational format in which theory and research are presented first, followed by practical implications. In addition, a current focus in the field—harnessing child development knowledge to shape social policies that support children's needs—is reflected in every chapter. The text addresses the current condition of children in the United States, Canada, and around the world, and shows how theory and research have sparked successful interventions.

New Coverage in the Eighth Edition

Child development is a fascinating and ever-changing field of study, with constantly emerging new discoveries and refinements in existing knowledge. The eighth edition represents this burgeoning contemporary literature, with more than 1,800 new citations. Cutting-edge topics throughout the text underscore the book's major themes. Here is a sampling:

- **Chapter 1:** Updated Biology and Environment box on resilience • New, applied examples of the contributions of behaviorism and social learning theory • Introduction to developmental cognitive neuroscience as a new area of investigation • Updated section on public policies and child development
- **Chapter 2:** New examples of research using systematic observation, structured interviews, and correlational designs • Expanded and updated section on psychophysiological methods of assessing brain functioning, including EEG, ERPs, fMRI, PET, and NIROT • New Biology and Environment box on prenatal iron deficiency, brain development, and memory impairments in infants of diabetic mothers, illustrating the use of ERPs to study atypical brain and cognitive functioning • Revised section on sequential designs, including a new example • Expanded discussion of ethics and the use of deception in research with children
- **Chapter 3:** Inclusion of both germline and somatic mutation, with implications for modifiability of the genotype and gene-environment interaction • New evidence on genetic treatment of disease • Updated research on fetal sensory and behavioral capacities • Updated Biology and Environment box on the prenatal environment and health in later life • Expanded and updated

consideration of a wide range of teratogens • Inclusion of the new designation for harmful effects of prenatal alcohol exposure—fetal alcohol spectrum disorder—and its associated three diagnoses: fetal alcohol syndrome (FAS), partial fetal alcohol syndrome (PFAS), and alcohol-related neurodevelopmental disorder (ARND) • Enhanced discussion of the impact of maternal infectious disease on the developing organism, with special attention to AIDS, cytomegalovirus, and herpes simplex 2 • New evidence on the long-term consequences of emotional stress during pregnancy • New findings on oxygen deprivation during childbirth, head-cooling treatment to reduce brain injury, and developmental consequences • Updated discussion of preterm and low-birth-weight infants, including long-term developmental outcomes for very low-birth-weight babies • Updated Social Issues: Health box on health care and other policies for parents and newborn babies, including cross-national infant mortality rates and the importance of generous parental leave

- **Chapter 4:** New findings on contributions of sleep to infant learning and memory • Updated Biology and Environment box on sudden infant death syndrome, including protective sleeping practices • New research on infant crying, including a nurse home-visiting program to reduce colic • Expanded and updated section on newborn imitation, including the role of mirror neurons in the human capacity for imitation and other social abilities • New research on fetal and newborn pain perception • New findings on babies' capacity to statistically analyze the speech stream • New Biology and Environment box on "tuning in" to familiar speech, faces, and music • Expanded and updated section on intermodal perception, including its contributions to all aspects of psychological development • New research on infants born with cataracts and children adopted from Romanian orphanages, bearing on the question of whether infancy is a sensitive period of development
- **Chapter 5:** Updated findings on youth sports, including gender differences in participation and consequences for development • New statistics and evidence on teenage use of performance-enhancing drugs • Expanded treatment of brain development in childhood and adolescence • New findings on development of handedness • Revised and updated section on overweight and obesity, including rapid increase in developing nations, contributing factors—low education and income, parental feeding practices, childhood sleep, television viewing, physical activity, and the broader cultural environment—and prevention and treatment • New Biology and Environment box on low-level lead exposure and children's development • New evidence on implications of pubertal timing for psychological adjustment in adolescence and adulthood • Discussion of the Internet as a hazardous "sex educator," including adolescents' exposure to pornography on the Internet • Updated statistics and evidence on sexually transmitted disease, including international comparisons and teenagers' understanding of modes of transmission • New evidence on the long-term consequences of adolescent parenthood and on prevention strategies • New Social Issues box on intergenerational continuity in adolescent parenthood
- **Chapter 6:** New evidence on infants' understanding of object permanence, including brain-wave findings • New research on development of categorization in toddlerhood and early childhood • New findings on cultural influences on development of drawing, operational thought, and cognitive maps • New findings on the influence of schooling on development of propositional thought • Updated findings on relationships of the imaginary audience and personal fable to adolescent adjustment • Expanded and updated research on adolescent decision making • Enhanced discussion of infants' physical knowledge, with emphasis on sensitivity to basic principles of object support • New research on the controversy over whether babies have basic number concepts, including brain-wave findings and cross-cultural evidence • Expanded consideration of preschoolers' biological knowledge, including growth, inheritance, illness, and death
- **Chapter 7:** Updated coverage of connectionism, including constructivist connectionist models • New Social Issues box on enhancing cognitive control through preschool education • Revised and updated Biology and Environment box on children with attention-deficit hyperactivity disorder • Enhanced consideration of fuzzy trace theory, gains in gist memory, and why certain memory inaccuracies increase while others decrease with age • Revised and updated discussion of development of autobiographical memory, with new research on cultural variations in parent–child conversations about past events • Updated Biology and Environment box on infantile amnesia • New research on factors that affect the accuracy of children's eyewitness memory • New findings on development of metacognition, including age-related gains in ability to discriminate good from bad reasoning • Updated evidence on contributions of phonological awareness to emergent literacy and reading progress • Updated research on early development of counting and math concepts, including estimation • Recent research on factors that support scientific reasoning
- **Chapter 8:** Updated From Research to Practice box on emotional intelligence • Inclusion of the most recent edition of the Bayley Scales of Infant and Toddler Development (Bayley-III) • Updated consideration of adoption studies confirming the joint contributions of heredity and environment to IQ • New findings on cultural bias in testing, with special attention to adult communication

styles • Revised and expanded Social Issues box on high-stakes testing • New research on early intervention for low-income children, including Early Head Start • Summary of factors contributing to the enduring impact of outstanding early intervention programs—the High/Scope Perry Preschool Project, the Chicago Child–Parent Centers, and the Carolina Abecedarian Project

- **Chapter 9:** New evidence on factors accounting for the sensitive period, or younger-age advantage, for language learning • Expanded attention to information-processing theories of language development, including connectionist models • New evidence on infant visual language discrimination, with implications for bilingual development • New research on the facilitating role of child-directed speech in early language progress • Impact of cochlear implants on language development in deaf-born babies • Updated findings on the contributions of joint attention, infant pointing, and other preverbal gestures to early language development • Expanded consideration of young children's strategies for word learning, including the shape bias • Inclusion of the emergentist coalition model, a new account of how children figure out word meanings • New research on toddlers' sensitivity to grammatical structures in comprehension • Updated research on the impact of parental reformulations of children's errors on grammatical development • Enhanced discussion of narrative development, including the supportive role of make-believe play • Expanded section on bilingual development, including effects on brain and cognitive development
- **Chapter 10:** Revised and updated Biology and Environment box on parental depression and child development, including both maternal and paternal depression • Updated section on emotions and health, with expanded coverage of stress reactivity, cortisol levels, and problematic development among Romanian orphanage children • New research on school-age children's capacity to distinguish between feeling and expressing emotions, with implications for emotional self-regulation • New research on the self-regulatory dimension of temperament—effortful control—and consequences for children's cognitive and social competence • Enhanced consideration of cultural variations in sensitive caregiving, with implications for attachment security • New research on the joint contribution of infant characteristics and parental sensitivity to attachment security • Expanded section on fathers' involvement with infants, including cultural variations • Enhanced discussion of the influence of attachment quality on later development • Updated Social Issues box on the influence of quality of child care and long child-care hours on attachment and later development
- **Chapter 11:** Updated section on development of self-awareness and self-recognition in the first two years, with new research on cultural variations • New evidence on preschoolers' developing awareness of an enduring self—a self persisting over time • New findings on social experiences contributing to young children's theory of mind, with special emphasis on parent–child conversations about mental states • Updated Biology and Environment box on "mindblindnesss" and autism • Updated section on development of self-concept, including contributions of parent–child communication and culture • New research on cultural and gender differences in children's self-esteem • New research on identity statuses, cognitive styles, and adjustment • Revised Social Issues box on adolescent suicide, with evidence on the impact of cultural disintegration and community powerlessness on high suicide rates among Native American and Canadian Aboriginal youths • Updated Cultural Influences box on identity development among ethnic minority youths • New findings on development of racial and ethnic prejudices and strategies for reducing children's prejudices
- **Chapter 12:** Expanded treatment of the biological roots of human morality, with special attention to an evolved prosocial capacity resulting from our evolutionary history of group living • New research on parenting, child temperament, and conscience development • Updated Cultural Influences box on ethnic differences in the consequences of physical punishment • Updated research on cultural variations in considering an actor's intentions in judging the morality of truthfulness and lying • Revised evaluation of Kohlberg's stages, including issues raised by a pragmatic approach to moral judgment • New research on situational influences on care-based moral reasoning • Revised and expanded section on the domain approach to moral understanding, including coordination of moral, social-conventional, and personal concerns during middle childhood and adolescence • New research on the distinction between proactive and reactive aggression • Updated findings on gender differences in aggression from toddlerhood to adolescence • New findings on the implications of proactive and reactive aggression for social-cognitive deficits and distortions, which act to sustain aggression • Evaluations of zero tolerance policies in schools, including consideration of why they fail to reduce youth aggression and other forms of misconduct
- **Chapter 13:** New research on the rigidity of gender stereotypes in early childhood and increasing gender-stereotype flexibility during the school years • New findings of parents' differential communication with boys and girls in gender-stereotyped activities • New research on cultural variations in gender typing within gender-segregated peer groups • Updated evidence on gender-typing in the media, with special attention to young children's picture books • New findings on implications of the cognitive changes that lead up to gender

constancy (gender stability and gender consistency) for children's gender stereotyping • Updated research on sex differences in verbal, spatial, and mathematical abilities, including contributing factors • New research on the widening gender gap in reading and writing achievement with age, including possible contributing factors • Updated evidence on sex differences in depression, with special attention to the role of a feminine gender identity

- **Chapter 14:** New findings on the harmful impact of parental psychological control on children's adjustment • New findings on special challenges in parenting adolescents in immigrant families and in risky neighborhoods • Expanded consideration of ethnic variations in child-rearing beliefs and practices • New research on effects of parenting on sibling relationships in middle childhood • New evidence on development of children in gay and lesbian families • Updated sections on divorce and remarriage and children's development • Expanded and updated section on consequences of child maltreatment, including new findings on central nervous system damage
- **Chapter 15:** New findings on friendship, including resemblance between friends and contributions of friendship to adjustment • Updated findings on peer acceptance, including its implications for bullying and victimization • Revised and updated Social Issues box on bullies and their victims • New findings on implications of attachment to parents for quality of friendship and romantic ties • Updated evidence on relationship of heavy TV viewing in childhood and early adolescence to later aggressive acts • New findings on the impact of TV viewing on children and adolescents' gender stereotyped attitude and behaviors • New evidence on children's developing understanding of the Internet's technical complexity, with consequences for their knowledge of its social risks • Expanded treatment of the impact of computer use on academic achievement, with special attention to Web access • New research on adolescents' use of the Internet for communication, including benefits and risks • New findings on gains in academic and social skills associated with Montessori preschool education • New Social Issues box on benefits of school recess • New evidence on contributions of social maturity to school readiness • Updated cross-national comparisons of U.S. and Canadian students' academic achievement

Pedagogical Features

Maintaining a highly accessible writing style—one that is lucid and engaging without being simplistic—continues to be one of my major goals. I frequently converse with students, encouraging them to relate what they read to their own lives. In doing so, I hope to make the study of child development involving and pleasurable.

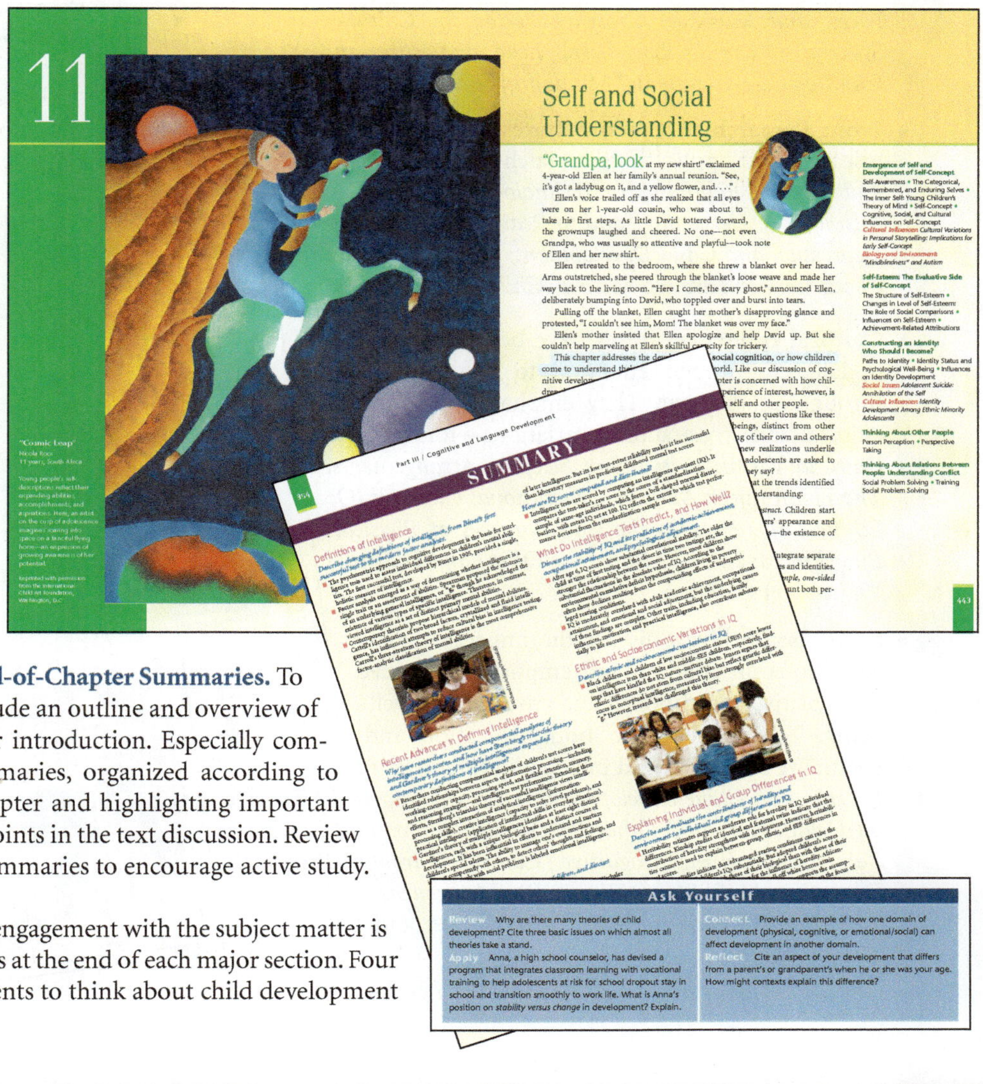

- **Chapter Introductions and End-of-Chapter Summaries.** To provide a helpful preview, I include an outline and overview of chapter content in each chapter introduction. Especially comprehensive end-of-chapter summaries, organized according to the major divisions of each chapter and highlighting important terms, remind students of key points in the text discussion. Review questions are included in the summaries to encourage active study.

- **Ask Yourself Questions.** Active engagement with the subject matter is also supported by study questions at the end of each major section. Four types of questions prompt students to think about child development in diverse ways: ***Review*** questions help students recall and comprehend information they have just read. ***Apply*** questions encourage the application of knowledge to controversial issues and problems faced by children, parents, and professionals who work with them. ***Connect*** questions help students build an image of the whole child by integrating what they have learned across age periods and domains of development. ***Reflect*** questions help make the study of child development personally meaningful by asking students to reflect on their own development. Each question is answered on the text's MyDevelopmentLab website.

- **Take a Moment . . .** This new active-learning feature, built into the text narrative, asks students to "take a moment" to think about an important point, integrate information on children's development, or engage in an exercise or an application to clarify a challenging concept. **TAKE A MOMENT. . .** highlights and reinforces the text's strength in conversing with and actively engaging the student in learning and in inspiring critical thinking.

Four types of thematic boxes accentuate the philosophical themes of this book:

- **Biology and Environment** boxes highlight the growing attention to the complex, bidirectional relationship between biology and environment during development. Examples include *Brain Plasticity: Insights from Research on Brain-Damaged Children and Adults; "Tuning In" to Familiar Speech, Faces, and Music: A Sensitive Period for Culture-Specific Learning; Low-Level Lead Exposure and Children's Development; "Mindblindness" and Autism.*

- **From Research to Practice** boxes integrate theory, research, and applications on such topics as *The Pros and Cons of Reproductive Technologies; Speech–Gesture Mismatches: Using the Hand to Read the Mind; Parental Depression and Child Development;* and *Children Learn About Gender Through Mother–Child Conversations.*

- **Cultural Influences** boxes have been expanded and updated to deepen attention to culture threaded throughout the text. They emphasize both multicultural and cross-cultural variations—for example, *Cultural Variation in Infant Sleeping Arrangements; The Flynn Effect: Massive Generational Gains in IQ; Ethnic Differences in the Consequences of Physical Punishment;* and *The Impact of Ethnic and Political Violence on Children.*

- **Social Issues** boxes discuss the impact of social conditions on children and emphasize the need for sensitive social policies to ensure their well-being. Topics related to both education and health are addressed and include *Welfare Reform, Poverty, and Child Development; A Cross-National Perspective on Health Care and Other Policies for Parents and Newborn Babies; Enhancing Cognitive Control Through Preschool Education; High-Stakes Testing; Two Approaches to Bilingual Education: Canada and the United States;* and *Bullies and Their Victims.*

- **Applying What We Know Tables.** In this feature, I summarize research-based applications on many issues, speaking directly to students as parents or future parents and to those pursuing different careers or areas of study, such as teaching, health care, counseling, or social work. They include: *Soothing a Crying Baby; Communicating with Adolescents About Sexual Issues; Supporting Emergent Literacy in Early Childhood;* and *Regulating TV and Computer Use.*

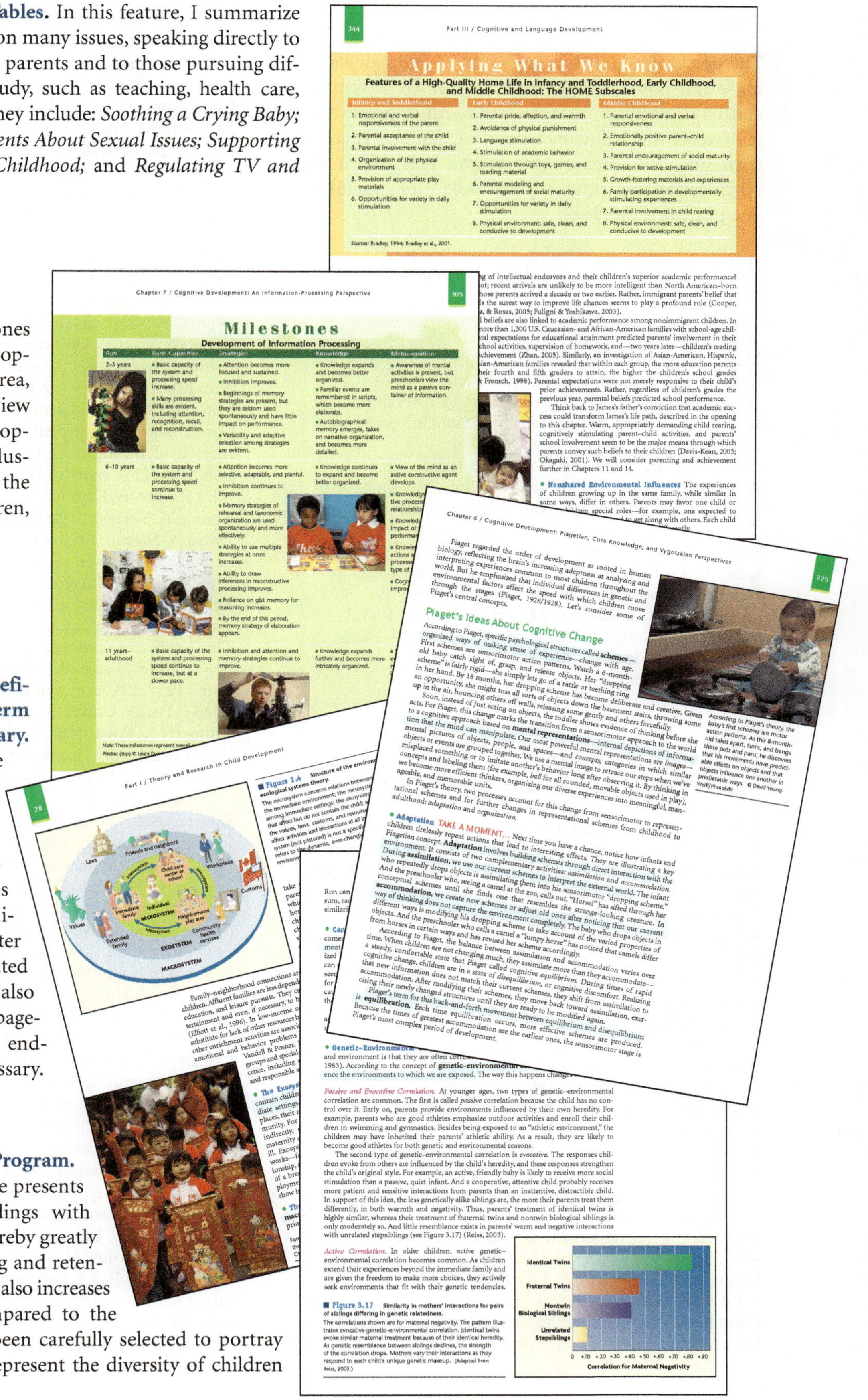

- **Milestones Tables.** Milestones tables summarize major developments within each topical area, providing a convenient overview of the chronology of development. They are beautifully illustrated with many photos of the attainments of infants, children, and adolescents.

- **In-Text Key Terms with Definitions, End-of-Chapter Term List, and End-of-Book Glossary.** Mastery of terms that make up the central vocabulary of the field is promoted through in-text highlighting of key-term and concept definitions, which encourages students to review the terminology of the field in greater depth by rereading related information. Key terms also appear in an end-of-chapter page-referenced term list and an end-of-book page-referenced glossary.

- **Enhanced Art and Photo Program.** A thoroughly revised art style presents concepts and research findings with clarity and attractiveness, thereby greatly aiding student understanding and retention. The illustration program also increases the number of photos compared to the previous edition. Each has been carefully selected to portray the text discussion and to represent the diversity of children around the world.

Acknowledgments

The dedicated contributions of many individuals helped make this book a reality and contributed to refinements and improvements in each edition. An impressive cast of reviewers provided many helpful suggestions, constructive criticisms, and encouragement and enthusiasm for the organization and content of the book. I am grateful to each one of them.

Reviewers for the First through Seventh Editions

Martha W. Alibali, University of Wisconsin, Madison
Daniel Ashmead, Vanderbilt University
Margarita Azmitia, University of California, Santa Cruz
Catherine L. Bagwell, University of Richmond
Lorraine Bahrick, Florida International University
Lynne Baker-Ward, North Carolina State University
David Baskind, Delta College
Carole R. Beal, University of Massachusetts
Rebecca S. Bigler, The University of Texas, Austin
Dana W. Birnbaum, University of Maine at Orono
Kathryn N. Black, Purdue University
Paul Bloom, Yale University
James H. Bodle, College of Mount Saint Joseph
Cathryn L. Booth, University of Washington
J. Paul Boudreau, University of Prince Edward Island
Sam Boyd, University of Central Arkansas
Darlene A. Brodeur, Acadia University
Celia A. Brownell, University of Pittsburgh
M. Michele Burnette, Community College of Allegheny County
Toni A. Campbell, San Jose State University
M. Beth Casey, Boston College
Robert Cohen, University of Memphis
John Condry, Cornell University
Robert Coplan, Carleton University
Rhoda Cummings, University of Nevada, Reno
James L. Dannemiller, University of Wisconsin, Madison
Zoe Ann Davidson, Alabama A & M University
Darlene DeSantis, West Chester University
Nancy Digdon, Grant MacEwan College
Rebecca Eder, Bryn Mawr College
Richard Ely, Boston University
Claire Etaugh, Bradley University
Bill Fabricius, Arizona State University
Beverly Fagot, University of Oregon
Francine Favretto, University of Maryland
Larry Fenson, San Diego State University
Jayne Gackenbach, Grant MacEwan College
James Garbarino, Cornell University
Jane F. Gaultney, University of North Carolina, Charlotte
John C. Gibbs, The Ohio State University
Peter Gordon, University of Pittsburgh
Katherine Green, Millersville University
Craig H. Hart, Brigham Young University
Joyce A. Hemphill, University of Wisconsin, Madison
Kenneth Hill, Saint Mary's University, Halifax
Alice S. Honig, Syracuse University
Carla L. Hudson Kam, University of California, Berkeley
Janis Jacobs, Pennsylvania State University
Scott P. Johnson, New York University
Katherine Kipp, University of Georgia
Paul Klaczynski, The Pennsylvania State University
Mareile Koenig, George Washington University Hospital
Claire Kopp, Claremont Graduate School
Beth Kurtz-Costes, University of North Carolina, Chapel Hill
Gary W. Ladd, Arizona State University
Daniel Lapsley, Ball State University
Frank Laycock, Oberlin College
Elise Lehman, George Mason University
Mary D. Leinbach, University of Oregon
Richard Lerner, Tufts University
Marc Lewis, Ontario Institute for Studies in Education, University of Toronto
Wilma M. Marshall, Douglas College
Robert S. Marvin, University of Virginia
Ashley E. Maynard, University of Hawaii
Tom McBride, Princeton University
Carolyn J. Mebert, University of New Hampshire
Gary B. Melton, University of Nebraska, Lincoln
Mary Evelyn Moore, Illinois State University
Lois Muir, University of Wisconsin, La Crosse
John P. Murray, Kansas State University
Bonnie K. Nastasi, State University of New York at Albany
David A. Nelson, Brigham Young University
Larry Nucci, University of Illinois at Chicago
Peter Ornstein, University of North Carolina
Randall Osbourne, Indiana University East
Carol Pandey, Pierce College, Los Angeles
Thomas S. Parish, Kansas State University
B. Kay Pasley, Colorado State University
Kathy Pezdek, Claremont Graduate School
Ellen F. Potter, University of South Carolina at Columbia
Kimberly K. Powlishta, Northern Illinois University
Kathleen Preston, Humboldt State University
Bud Protinsky, Virginia Polytechnic Institute and State University
Daniel Reschly, Iowa State University
Rosemary Rosser, University of Arizona
Alan Russell, Flinders University
Jane Ann Rysberg, California State University, Chico
Phil Schoggen, Cornell University
Maria E. Sera, University of Iowa
Beth Shapiro, Emory University
Susan Siaw, California State Polytechnic University
Linda Siegel, University of British Columbia
Barbara B. Simon, Midlands Technical College
Robert Siegler, Carnegie Mellon University
Gregory J. Smith, Dickinson College
Robert J. Sternberg, Yale University
Harold Stevenson, University of Michigan
Daniel Swingley, University of Pennsylvania
Doug Symons, Acadia University
Ross A. Thompson, University of California, Davis
Barbara A. Tinsley, University of Illinois at Urbana–Champaign
Kim F. Townley, University of Kentucky
Tracy Vaillancourt, McMaster University
Janet Valadez, Pan American University
Susan K. Walker, University of Maryland
Amye R. Warren, University of Tennessee at Chattanooga
Yiyuan Xu, University of Hawaii

Reviewers for the Eighth Edition

Ellen Altermatt, Hanover College
Rebecca S. Bigler, The University of Texas, Austin
Lori Camparo, Whittier College
M. Beth Casey, Boston College
Robert Cohen, University of Memphis
Teddi Deka, Missouri Western State University
Laura DeRose, Adelphi University
John C. Gibbs, The Ohio State University
Suzanne Gurland, Middlebury College
Nina Howe, Concordia University
Scott P. Johnson, New York University
Patricia K. Kerig, Miami University of Ohio
Catherine Massey, Slippery Rock University
Brad Morris, Grand Valley State University
Geoff Navara, Trend University
David A. Nelson, Brigham Young University
Simone Nguyen, University of North Carolina, Wilmington
Stephen Reznick, University of North Carolina, Chapel Hill
Leher Singh, Boston University
Doug Symons, Acadia University
Lorraine Taylor, University of North Carolina, Chapel Hill
Tracy Vaillancourt, McMaster University
Cecilia Wainryb, University of Utah
Wenfan Yan, Indiana University of Pennsylvania
Laura Zimmermann, Shenandoah University

My sincere appreciation, also, to the faculty focus group participants, who gathered in April, 2007, to discuss the unique needs of the child development course and to make recommendations for the new edition: Rebecca S. Bigler, The University of Texas at Austin; Heather A. Bouchey, University of Vermont; M. Beth Casey, Boston College; Robert Coplan, Carleton University; Scott P. Johnson, New York University; Michael P. Maratsos, University of Minnesota; David A. Nelson, Brigham Young University; Kimberly Saudino, Boston University; and Daniel Swingley, University of Pennsylvania.

I would like to extend special thanks to William L. Roberts, Thompson Rivers University, for invaluable assistance in preparing a new edition that speaks to both American and Canadian students. For many long months, Bill regularly took time from his demanding schedule to provide me with information on the current status of children and families in Canada and on public policies and programs aimed at protecting and supporting the development of Canadian children. Bill's contributions have greatly enriched the cultural and public policy content of the text. It has been a pleasure to get to know and work with him.

Colleagues and students at Illinois State University aided my research and contributed significantly to the text's supplements. Richard Payne, Department of Politics and Government, Illinois State University, is a kind and devoted friend with whom I have shared many profitable discussions about the writing process, the condition of children and families, and other topics that have significantly influenced my perspective on child development and social policy. Sara Harris joined me in preparing the Instructor's Resource Manual and the "Explorations in Child Development" and "Window on Child Development" DVD Guides, bringing to these tasks enthusiasm, imagination, depth of knowledge, and impressive writing skill. Sara also proofread the Test Bank, PowerPoint Presentation, and Grade Aid Study Guide Practice Tests with great care and attention to detail. Claire Christensen's outstanding, dedicated work in gathering and organizing library materials, revising the Grade Aid, and developing plans for the "Explorations in Child Development" DVD is much appreciated.

The supplements package also benefited from the talents and diligence of several other individuals. Gillian Wark of Simon Fraser University and Anoosha Aghakhani of the University of Calgary adapted several features of the Instructor's Resource Manual for its Canadian edition. Nina Hnatov and Jessica Carloni authored an extensive Test Bank and set of Practice Tests. Diana Murphy designed and wrote a highly attractive PowerPoint presentation.

Michelle Limoges, Acquisitions Editor, brought skillful and caring attention to the multifaceted task of coordinating the eighth edition—arranging for manuscript reviews, text supplements, photo illustrations, and other essential tasks. Judy Ashkenaz, development editor, worked closely with me as I wrote each chapter, making sure that every thought and concept would be precisely expressed and well developed. Her keen editing skills and impressive knowledge of children's issues made the editing a learning experience and pleasure.

Donna Simons, Senior Production Administrator, coordinated the complex production tasks that resulted in this beautiful eighth edition. I am grateful for her keen aesthetic sensibilities, attention to detail, flexibility, efficiency, and thoughtfulness. I thank Sarah Evertson for obtaining the photographs that so aptly illustrate the text narrative. Margaret Pinette, Bill Heckman, and Lisa Peachey Flanagan provided outstanding copyediting and proofreading.

A final word of gratitude goes to my family, whose love, patience, and understanding have enabled me to be wife, mother, teacher, researcher, and text author at the same time. My sons, David and Peter, grew up with my child development texts, passing from childhood to adolescence and then to adulthood as successive editions were written. David has a special connection with the books' subject matter as an elementary school teacher, and Peter is now an experienced attorney and newly married to his vivacious, caring, and talented Melissa. All three continue to enrich my understanding through reflections on events and progress in their own lives. My husband, Ken, willingly made room for yet another time-consuming endeavor in our life together and communicated his belief in its importance in a great many unspoken, caring ways.

Laura E. Berk

Supplementary Materials

Instructor Supplements

A variety of teaching tools is available to assist instructors in organizing lectures, planning demonstrations and examinations, and ensuring student comprehension.

MyDevelopmentLab This interactive and instructive multimedia resource can be used as a supplement to a classroom course or to completely administer an online course. Prepared in collaboration with Laura Berk, MyDevelopmentLab includes a variety of assessments that enable continuous evaluation of students' learning. Extensive video footage, multimedia simulations, biographies of major figures in the field, and interactive activities that are unique to *Child Development* are also included. Among new MyDevelopmentLab features, "Careers in Child Development" explains how knowledge of child development is essential for a wide range of career paths, and "Classic Studies in Child Development" focuses on key historical research that profoundly advanced the field. The power of MyDevelopmentLab lies in its design as an all-inclusive teaching and learning tool. For a sampling of its rich content, contact your Pearson publisher's representative.

Instructor's Classroom Kit, Volumes I and II A comprehensive instructional resource, this classroom kit includes all print supplements. Supplements for Chapters 1 to 7 are in Volume I; those for Chapters 8 to 15 are in Volume II. Organized by chapter, each volume contains the Instructor's Resource Manual, Test Bank, Grade Aid Study Guide with Practice Tests, and slides from the PowerPoint presentation.

- ***Instructor's Resource Manual (IRM)*** This thoroughly revised IRM can be used by first-time or experienced instructors to enrich classroom experiences. Each chapter includes a Chapter-at-a-Glance grid, Brief Chapter Summary, Learning Objectives, detailed Lecture Outlines, Lecture Enhancements, Learning Activities, Ask Yourself questions with answers, Suggested Student Readings, Transparencies list, and Media Materials list.
- ***Test Bank.*** The Test Bank contains over 1,850 multiple-choice and essay questions, each of which is page-referenced to chapter content and classified by type (factual, applied, or conceptual). Each chapter also includes a selection of essay questions and sample answers.
- ***Grade Aid with Practice Tests*** This helpful study guide offers Chapter Summaries, Learning Objectives, Study Questions organized according to major headings in the text, Crossword Puzzles for mastering important terms, and two multiple-choice Practice Tests per chapter.
- ***PowerPoint Presentation*** The PowerPoint presentation contains illustrations and outlines of key topics for each chapter from the text, presented in a clear and visually attractive format.

Computerized Test Bank. This computerized version of the test bank, in easy-to-use TestGen software, lets you prepare tests for printing as well as for network and online testing. It has full editing capability. Test items are also available in CourseCompass, Blackboard, and WebCT formats.

Transparencies. Over 200 full-color transparencies taken from the text and other sources are referenced in the Instructor's Resource Manual for the most appropriate use in your classroom presentations.

"Explorations in Child Development" DVD. This new DVD is over two hours in length and contains more than 30 two- to eight-minute narrated segments, designed for effective classroom use, that illustrate the many theories, concepts, and milestones of child development. New additions include segments on children's drawing, high-quality child care, adopted children and their families, gender identity and stereotyping, delinquency and juvenile justice, and much more. "Explorations in Child Development" DVD and DVD Guide are available to instructors who adopt the text for in-class use and are also available as a student supplement for free when packaged with the text. The DVD Guide helps students use the DVD in conjunction with the textbook, deepening their understanding and applying what they have learned to everyday life.

"A Window on Child Development" Running Observational Footage DVD. This video provides more than two hours of unscripted footage on many aspects of child development. Examples of content include early language learning, make-believe play, moral reasoning in middle childhood, and friendship and popularity in adolescence. "A Window on Child Development" DVD and DVD Guide are available to instructors who adopt the text for in-class use and are also available as a student supplement for free when packaged with the text.

Student Supplements

Beyond the study aids found in the textbook, Pearson offers a number of supplements for students:

MyDevelopmentLab This interactive and instructive multimedia resource is an all-inclusive learning tool. Prepared in collaboration with Laura Berk, MyDevelopmentLab engages users and reinforces learning through controlled assessments, extensive video footage, multimedia simulations, biographies of major figures in the field, and interactive activities that are unique to Child Development. In addition, "Careers in Child Development," explains how knowledge of child development is essential for a wide range of career paths, and "Classic Studies in Child Development" focuses on key historical research that profoundly advanced the field. Easy to use, MyDevelopmentLab meets the individual learning needs of every student. For a sampling of its rich content, visit www.mydevelopmentlab.com.

Grade Aid with Practice Tests. This helpful study guide offers Chapter Summaries, Learning Objectives, Study Questions organized according to major headings in the text, Suggested Student Readings, Crossword Puzzles for mastering important terms, and two multiple-choice Practice Tests per chapter.

Emerging Adulthood Booklet. This revised mini-chapter details the most current theory and research on this new period of development, which intervenes between adolescence and full assumption of adult roles. It is also available as an appendix to the text on MyDevelopmentLab. Updates to the Eighth Edition include: Expanded attention to SES and ethnic variations in the experience of emerging adulthood • Updated research on cognitive changes • Enhanced consideration of identity development • New findings on changing conceptions of close relationships and the process of forging a romantic partnership • Enhanced attention to gender and ethnic differences in career development • Expanded discussion of the parent–emerging adult relationship.

Milestones Study Cards. Adapted from the popular Milestones Tables featured in the text, these colorfully illustrated study cards outline key developmental attainments in an easy-to-use, chronological organization that assists students in integrating the various domains of development and constructing a vision of the whole developing child.

About the Cover and Chapter-Opening Art

I would like to extend grateful acknowledgments to the International Museum of Children's Art, Oslo, Norway, and to the International Child Art Foundation, Washington, D.C., for the exceptional cover image and chapter-opening art, which depict the talents, concerns, and viewpoints of child and adolescent artists from around the world. The awe-inspiring collection of children's art gracing this text expresses family, school, and community themes; good times and personal triumphs; profound appreciation for beauty; and great depth of emotion. I am pleased to share this window into children's creativity, insightfulness, sensitivity, and compassion with readers.

1

"Market"
Radwa Gamal Mohamed Abd el Hameed
13 years, Egypt

This portrayal of an open-air market captures the diverse activities related to commerce, transportation, resources, and culture that make up village life. As the theories reviewed in this chapter reveal, a similarly complex blend of genetic, family, community, and societal forces influences child development.

History, Theory, and Applied Directions

Not long ago, I left my Midwestern home to live for a year near the small city in northern California where I spent my childhood. One morning, I visited the neighborhood where I grew up—a place I had not seen since I was 12 years old.

I stood at the entrance to my old schoolyard. Buildings and grounds that had looked large to me as a child now seemed strangely small. I peered through the window of my first-grade classroom. The desks were no longer arranged in rows but grouped in intimate clusters. Computers rested against the far wall, near where I once sat. I walked my old route home from school, the distance shrunken by my longer stride. I stopped in front of my best friend Kathryn's house, where we once drew sidewalk pictures, crossed the street to play kickball, and produced plays in the garage. In place of the small shop where I had purchased penny candy stood a child-care center, filled with the voices and vigorous activity of toddlers and preschoolers.

As I walked, I reflected on early experiences that contributed to who I am and what I am like today—weekends helping my father in his downtown clothing shop, the year my mother studied to become a high school teacher, moments of companionship and rivalry with my sister and brother, Sunday outings to museums and the seashore, and visits to my grandmother's house, where I became someone extra special.

As I passed the homes of my childhood friends, I thought of what I knew about the course of their lives. Kathryn, star pupil and president of our sixth-grade class—today a successful corporate lawyer and mother of two. Shy, withdrawn Phil, cruelly teased because of his cleft lip—now owner of a thriving chain of hardware stores and member of the city council. Julio, immigrant from Mexico who joined our class in third grade—today director of an elementary school bilingual education program and single parent of an adopted Mexican boy. And finally, my next-door neighbor Rick, who picked fights at recess, struggled with reading, repeated fourth grade, dropped out of high school, and (so I heard) moved from one job to another over the following ten years.

As you begin this course in child development, perhaps you, too, are wondering about some of the same questions that crossed my mind during that nostalgic neighborhood walk:

- In what ways are children's home, school, and neighborhood experiences the same today as they were in generations past, and in what ways are they different?
- How are the infant's and young child's perceptions of the world the same as the adult's, and how are they different?

- What determines the features that humans have in common and those that make each of us unique—physically, mentally, and behaviorally?
- How did Julio, transplanted at age 8 to a new culture, master its language and customs and succeed in its society, yet remain strongly identified with his ethnic community?
- Why do some of us, like Kathryn and Rick, retain the same styles of responding that characterized us as children, whereas others, like Phil, change in essential ways?
- How do cultural changes—employed mothers, child care, divorce, smaller families, and new technologies—affect children's characteristics?

These are central questions addressed by **child development,** an area of study devoted to understanding constancy and change from conception through adolescence. Child development is part of a larger, interdisciplinary field known as **developmental science,** which includes all changes we experience throughout the lifespan (Lerner, 2006). Great diversity characterizes the interests and concerns of the thousands of investigators who study child development. But all have a common goal: to describe and identify those factors that influence the consistencies and changes in young people during the first two decades of life.

The Field of Child Development

Look again at the questions just listed, and you will see that they are not only of scientific interest. Each has *applied,* or practical, importance as well. In fact, scientific curiosity is just one factor that led child development to become the exciting field of study it is today. Research about development has also been stimulated by social pressures to better the lives of children. For example, the beginning of public education in the early part of the twentieth century led to a demand for knowledge about what and how to teach children of different ages. Pediatricians' interest in improving children's health required an understanding of physical growth and nutrition. The social service profession's desire to treat children's anxieties and behavior problems required information about personality and social development. And parents have continually asked for advice about child-rearing practices and experiences that would promote the well-being of their child.

Our large storehouse of information about child development is *interdisciplinary.* It has grown through the combined efforts of people from many fields. Because of the need to solve everyday problems concerning children, researchers from psychology, sociology, anthropology, biology, and neuroscience have joined forces with professionals from education, family studies, medicine, public health, and social service—to name just a few. The field of child development, as it exists today, is a monument to the contributions of these many disciplines. Its body of knowledge is not just scientifically important but relevant and useful.

Domains of Development

To make the vast, interdisciplinary study of human constancy and change more orderly and convenient, development often is divided into three broad domains: *physical, cognitive,* and *emotional and social.* Refer to Figure 1.1 for a description and illustration of each. In this book, we will largely consider the domains of development in the order just mentioned. Yet the domains are not really distinct. Rather, they combine in an integrated, holistic fashion to yield the living, growing child. Furthermore, each domain influences and is influenced by the others. For example, in Chapter 4, you will see that new motor capacities, such as reaching, sitting, crawling, and walking (physical), contribute greatly to infants' understanding of their surroundings (cognitive). When babies think and act more competently, adults stimulate them more with games, language, and expressions of delight at their new achievements (emotional and social). These enriched experiences, in turn, promote all aspects of development.

Emotional and Social Development
Changes in emotional communication, self-understanding, knowledge about other people, interpersonal skills, friendships, intimate relationships, and moral reasoning and behavior

Physical Development
Changes in body size, proportions, appearance, functioning of body systems, perceptual and motor capacities, and physical health

Cognitive Development
Changes in intellectual abilities, including attention, memory, academic and everyday knowledge, problem solving, imagination, creativity, and language

■ **Figure 1.1** **Major domains of development.**
The three domains are not really distinct. Rather, they overlap and interact. *Photos:* (left) © Jim Commentucci/Syracuse Newspapers/The Image Works; (middle) © Jose Luis Pelaez, Inc./CORBIS; (right) © David Young-Wolff/PhotoEdit

You will encounter instances of the interwoven nature of all domains on almost every page of this book. Also, look for the *Ask Yourself* feature at the end of major sections, designed to deepen your understanding and inspire new insights. Within it, I have included *Review* questions, which help you recall and think about information you have just read; *Apply* questions, which encourage you to apply your knowledge to controversial issues and problems faced by parents, teachers, and children; *Connect* questions, which help you form a coherent, unified picture of child development; and *Reflect* questions, which invite you to reflect on your own development and that of people you know well.

Periods of Development

Besides distinguishing and integrating the three domains, another dilemma arises in discussing development: how to divide the flow of time into sensible, manageable parts. Researchers usually use the following age periods, as each brings new capacities and social expectations that serve as important transitions in major theories:

1. *The prenatal period: from conception to birth.* In this nine-month period, the most rapid time of change, a one-celled organism is transformed into a human baby with remarkable capacities for adjusting to life in the surrounding world.
2. *Infancy and toddlerhood: from birth to 2 years.* This period brings dramatic changes in the body and brain that support the emergence of a wide array of motor, perceptual, and intellectual capacities; the beginnings of language; and first intimate ties to others. Infancy spans the first year; toddlerhood spans the second, during which children take their first independent steps, marking a shift to greater autonomy.

Child development is so dramatic that researchers divide it into periods. These brothers and sisters in Niger, shown here with their parents and their grown sister (at left), illustrate, from left, early childhood, infancy, middle childhood, toddlerhood, and adolescence. © Uwe Ommer/*1,000 Families*—Taschen

3. *Early childhood: from 2 to 6 years.* The body becomes longer and leaner, motor skills are refined, and children become more self-controlled and self-sufficient. Make-believe play blossoms, supporting every aspect of psychological development. Thought and language expand at an astounding pace, a sense of morality becomes evident, and children establish ties with peers.
4. *Middle childhood: from 6 to 11 years.* Children learn about the wider world and master new responsibilities that increasingly resemble those they will perform as adults. Hallmarks of this period are improved athletic abilities, participation in organized games with rules, more logical thought processes, mastery of basic literacy skills, and advances in self-understanding, morality, and friendship.
5. *Adolescence: from 11 to 18 years.* This period initiates the transition to adulthood. Puberty leads to an adult-sized body and sexual maturity. Thought becomes abstract and idealistic, and schooling is increasingly directed toward preparation for higher education and the world of work. Young people begin to establish autonomy from the family and define personal values and goals.

For many contemporary youths in industrialized nations, the transition to adult roles has become increasingly prolonged—so much so that some researchers have posited a new period of development called *emerging adulthood,* which spans ages 18 to 25. Although emerging adults have moved beyond adolescence, they have not yet fully assumed adult roles. Rather, during higher education and sometimes beyond, these young people intensify their exploration of options in love, career, and personal values before making enduring commitments. Because the period of emerging adulthood surfaced only during the past few decades, researchers have just begun to study it (Arnett, 2000, 2003; Arnett & Tanner, 2006). Perhaps it is *your* period of development. In later chapters, we will touch on milestones of emerging adulthood, which build on adolescent attainments. To find out more about this period, consult the mini-chapter entitled "Emerging Adulthood," available as a supplement to this text.

With this introduction in mind, let's turn to some basic issues that have captivated, puzzled, and sparked debate among child development theorists. Then our discussion will trace the emergence of the field and survey major theories.

Basic Issues

Research on child development did not begin until the late nineteenth and early twentieth centuries. But ideas about how children grow and change have a much longer history. As these speculations combined with research, they inspired the construction of *theories* of development. A **theory** is an orderly, integrated set of statements that describes, explains, and predicts behavior. For example, a good theory of infant–caregiver attachment would (1) *describe* the behaviors of babies around 6 to 8 months of age as they seek the affection and comfort of a familiar adult, (2) *explain* how and why infants develop this strong desire to bond with a caregiver, and (3) *predict* the consequences of this emotional bond for future relationships.

Theories are vital tools for two reasons. First, they provide organizing frameworks for our observations of children. In other words, they *guide and give meaning* to what we see. Second, theories that are verified by research often serve as a sound basis for practical action. Once a theory helps us *understand* development, we are in a much better position *to know how to improve* the welfare and treatment of children.

As we will see later, theories are influenced by cultural values and belief systems of their times. But theories differ in one important way from mere opinion and belief: A theory's continued existence depends on *scientific verification.* In other words, every theory must be tested using a fair set of research procedures agreed on by the scientific community, and its findings must endure, or be replicated over time. (We will consider research strategies in Chapter 2.)

Within the field of child development, many theories offer very different ideas about what children are like and how they change. The study of child development provides no ultimate truth because investigators do not always agree on the meaning of what they see. Also, children are complex beings; they change physically, cognitively, emotionally, and socially. No single theory has been able to incorporate and explain all these aspects. But the existence of many theories helps advance knowledge as researchers continually try to support, contradict, and integrate these different points of view.

Although there are many theories, we can easily organize them by looking at the stand they take on three basic issues: (1) Is the course of development continuous or discontinuous? (2) Does one course of development characterize all children, or are there many possible courses? (3) Are genetic or environmental factors more important in influencing development? Let's look closely at each of these issues.

Continuous or Discontinuous Development?

Recently, the mother of 20-month-old Angelo reported to me with amazement that her young son had pushed a toy car across the living room floor while making a motorlike sound, "Brmmmm, brmmmm," for the first time. When he hit a nearby wall with a bang, Angelo let go of the car, exclaimed, "C'ash," and laughed heartily.

"How come Angelo can pretend, but he couldn't a few months ago?" queried his mother. "And I wonder what 'Brrmmmm, brmmmm' and 'Crash!' mean to Angelo? Does he understand motorlike sounds and collision the same way I do?"

Angelo's mother has raised a puzzling issue about development: How can we best describe the differences in capacities and behavior between small infants, young children, adolescents, and adults? As Figure 1.2 illustrates, major theories recognize two possibilities.

One view holds that infants and preschoolers respond to the world in much the same way adults do. The difference between the immature and mature being is simply one of *amount* or *complexity.* For example, little Angelo's thinking might be just as logical and well-organized as our own. Perhaps (as his mother reports) he can sort objects into simple categories, recognize whether he has more of one kind than another, and remember where he left his favorite toy at child care the week before. Angelo's only limitation may be that he cannot perform these skills with as much information and precision as we can. If this is so, then Angelo's development is **continuous**—a process of gradually adding more of the same types of skills that were there to begin with.

According to a second view, Angelo's thoughts, emotions, and behavior differ considerably from those of adults. His development is **discontinuous**—a process in which new ways of understanding and responding to the world emerge at specific times. From this perspective, Angelo is not yet able to organize objects or remember and interpret experiences as we do. Instead, he will move through a series of developmental steps, each with unique features, until he reaches the highest level of functioning.

■ Figure 1.2
Is development continuous or discontinuous?
(a) Some theorists believe that development is a smooth, continuous process. Children gradually add more of the same types of skills. (b) Other theorists think that development takes place in discontinuous stages. Children change rapidly as they step up to a new level of development and then change very little for a while. With each step, the child interprets and responds to the world in a qualitatively different way.

(a) **Continuous Development** (b) **Discontinuous Development**

Theories that accept the discontinuous perspective regard development as taking place in **stages**—qualitative changes in thinking, feeling, and behaving that characterize specific periods of development. In stage theories, development is much like climbing a staircase, with each step corresponding to a more mature, reorganized way of functioning. The stage concept also assumes that children undergo periods of rapid transformation as they step up from one stage to the next, alternating with plateaus during which they stand solidly within a stage. In other words, change is fairly sudden rather than gradual and ongoing.

Does development actually occur in a neat, orderly sequence of stages? This ambitious assumption has faced significant challenges. Later in this chapter, we will review some influential stage theories.

One Course of Development or Many?

Stage theorists assume that people everywhere follow the same sequence of development. For example, in the domain of cognition, a stage theorist might try to identify the common biological and environmental influences that lead children to represent their world through language and make-believe play in early childhood, to think more logically in middle childhood, and to reason more systematically and abstractly in adolescence.

At the same time, the field of child development is becoming increasingly aware that children grow up in distinct **contexts**—unique combinations of personal and environmental circumstances that can result in different paths of change. For example, a shy child who fears social encounters develops in very different contexts from those of a sociable agemate who readily seeks out other people (Kagan, 2003). Children in non-Western village societies encounter experiences in their families and communities that differ sharply from those of children in large Western cities. These different circumstances foster different cognitive capacities, social skills, and feelings about the self and others (Shweder et al., 2006).

Will this toddler's tantrums extend into a lifelong pattern of difficult behavior? Some theorists, who stress the importance of heredity, emphasize stability—that she will remain hard to manage. Others believe that stability arises from early experiences—how the mother handles her child's emotional outbursts. Still others believe that change is possible if new experiences support it.
© Bubbles Photolibrary/Alamy

As you will see, contemporary theorists regard the contexts that mold development as many-layered and complex. On the personal side, these include heredity and biological makeup. On the environmental side, they include both immediate settings—home, child-care center, school, and neighborhood—and circumstances more remote from children's everyday lives: community resources, societal values and priorities, and historical time period. Finally, researchers today are more conscious than ever before of cultural diversity in development.

Relative Influence of Nature and Nurture?

In addition to describing the course of development, each theory takes a stand on a major question about its underlying causes: Are genetic or environmental factors more important in influencing development? This is the age-old **nature–nurture controversy.** By *nature,* we mean inborn biological givens—the hereditary information we receive from our parents at the moment of conception. By *nurture,* we mean the complex forces of the physical and social world that influence our biological makeup and psychological experiences before and after birth.

Although all theories grant at least some role to both nature and nurture, they vary in emphasis. Consider the following question: Is the older child's ability to think in more complex ways largely the result of an inborn timetable of growth, or is it primarily influenced by stimulation from parents and teachers?

Do children acquire language because they are genetically predisposed to do so or because parents intensively teach them from an early age? And what accounts for the vast individual differences among children—in height, weight, physical coordination, intelligence, personality, and social skills? Is nature or nurture more responsible?

A theory's position on the roles of nature and nurture affects how it explains individual differences. Some theorists emphasize *stability*—that children who are high or low in a characteristic (such as verbal ability, anxiety, or sociability) will remain so at later ages. These theorists typically stress the importance of *heredity.* If they regard environment as important, they usually point to *early experiences* as establishing a lifelong pattern of behavior. Powerful negative events in the first few years, they argue, cannot be fully overcome by later, more positive ones (Bowlby, 1980; Johnson, 2000; Sroufe, 2005). Other theorists, taking a more optimistic view, emphasize that *change* is possible and even likely if new experiences support it (Greenspan & Shanker, 2004; Lester, Masten, & McEwen, 2006).

Throughout this book, you will see that investigators disagree, often sharply, on the question of *stability or change.* Their answers have great applied significance. If you believe that development is largely due to nature, then providing experiences aimed at promoting change would seem to be of little value. If, on the other hand, you are convinced of the supreme importance of early experience, then you would intervene as soon as possible, offering high-quality stimulation and support to ensure that children develop at their best. Finally, if you think that environment is profoundly influential throughout development, you would provide assistance any time children or adolescents face difficulties, in the belief that, with the help of favorable life circumstances, they can recover from early negative events.

A Balanced Point of View

So far, we have discussed the basic issues of child development in terms of extremes—solutions favoring one side or the other. But as we trace the unfolding of the field in the rest of this chapter, you will see that the positions of many theorists have softened. Today, some theorists believe that both continuous and discontinuous changes occur. Many acknowledge that development has both universal features and features unique to each individual and his or her contexts. And a growing number regard heredity and environment as inseparably interwoven, each affecting the potential of the other to modify the child's traits and capacities (Cole, 2006; Gottlieb, Wahlsten, & Lickliter, 2006; Huttenlocher, 2002; Lerner, 2006; Rutter, 2007). We will discuss these new ideas about nature and nurture in Chapter 3.

Finally, as you will see later in this book, the relative impact of early and later experiences varies greatly from one domain of development to another and even—as the Biology and Environment box on pages 10–11 indicates—across individuals! Because of the complex network of factors contributing to human change and the challenge of isolating the effects of each, many theoretical viewpoints have gathered research support. Although debate continues, this circumstance has also sparked more balanced visions of child development.

Ask Yourself

Review Why are there many theories of child development? Cite three basic issues on which almost all theories take a stand.

Apply Anna, a high school counselor, has devised a program that integrates classroom learning with vocational training to help adolescents at risk for school dropout stay in school and transition smoothly to work life. What is Anna's position on *stability versus change* in development? Explain.

Connect Provide an example of how one domain of development (physical, cognitive, or emotional/social) can affect development in another domain.

Reflect Cite an aspect of your development that differs from a parent's or grandparent's when he or she was your age. How might contexts explain this difference?

▪ Biology *and* Environment ▪

Resilient Children

John and his best friend Gary grew up in a rundown, crime-ridden inner-city neighborhood. By age 10, each had experienced years of family conflict followed by parental divorce. Reared for the rest of childhood and adolescence in mother-headed households, John and Gary rarely saw their fathers. Both dropped out of high school and were in and out of trouble with the police.

Then their paths diverged. By age 30, John had fathered two children with women he never married, had spent time in prison, was unemployed, and drank alcohol heavily. In contrast, Gary had returned to finish high school, had studied auto mechanics at a community college, and became manager of a gas station and repair shop. Married with two children, he had saved his earnings and bought a home. He was happy, healthy, and well-adapted to life.

A wealth of evidence shows that environmental risks—poverty, negative family interactions, parental divorce, job loss, mental illness, and drug abuse—predispose children to future problems (Masten & Gewirtz, 2006; Sameroff, 2006). Why did Gary "beat the odds" and come through unscathed?

New evidence on **resilience**—the ability to adapt effectively in the face of threats to development—is receiving increasing attention as investigators look for ways to protect young people from the damaging effects of stressful life conditions (Masten & Powell, 2003). This interest has been inspired by several long-term studies on the relationship of life stressors in childhood to competence and adjustment in adolescence and adulthood (Fergusson & Horwood, 2003; Garmezy, 1993; Masten et al., 1995; Werner, 2001). In each study, some individuals were shielded from negative outcomes, whereas others had lasting problems. Four broad factors offered protection from the damaging effects of stressful life events.

Personal Characteristics of Children

A child's biologically endowed characteristics can reduce exposure to risk or lead to experiences that compensate for early stressful events. High intelligence and socially valued talents (in music or athletics, for example) increase the chances that a child will have rewarding experiences in school and in the community that offset the impact of a stressful home life. Temperament is particularly powerful. Children who have easygoing, sociable dispositions and who can readily inhibit negative emotions and impulses tend to have an optimistic outlook on life and a special capacity to adapt to change—qualities that elicit positive responses from others. In contrast, emotionally reactive and irritable children often tax the patience of people around them (Mathiesen & Prior, 2006; Werner, 2005; Wong et al., 2006). For example, both John and Gary moved several times during their childhoods. Each time, John became anxious and angry. Gary looked forward to making new friends and exploring a new neighborhood.

A Warm Parental Relationship

A close relationship with at least one parent who provides warmth, appropriately high expectations, monitoring of the child's activities, and an organized home environment fosters resilience (Masten & Shaffer, 2006). But this factor (as well as the next one) is not independent of children's personal characteristics. Children

Historical Foundations

Contemporary theories of child development are the result of centuries of change in Western cultural values, philosophical thinking about children, and scientific progress. To understand the field as it exists today, we must return to its early beginnings—to ideas about children that long preceded scientific child study but that linger as important forces in current theory and research.

Medieval Times

Historical artifacts and writings show that childhood was regarded as a separate period of life as early as medieval Europe—the sixth through the fifteenth centuries. Medieval painters often depicted children wearing loose, comfortable gowns, playing games, and looking up to adults. Written texts contained terms that distinguished children under age 7 or 8 from other people and that recognized even young teenagers as not fully mature. By the fourteenth century, manuals offering advice on many aspects of child care, including health, feeding, clothing, and games, were common (Alexandre-Bidon & Lett, 1997; Lett, 1997). Laws recognized that children needed protection from people who might mistreat them, and courts exercised leniency with lawbreaking youths because of their tender years (Hanawalt, 1993).

In sum, in medieval times, if not before, clear awareness existed of children as vulnerable beings. Religious writings, however, contained contradictory depictions of children's basic

who are relaxed, socially responsive, and able to deal with change are easier to rear and more likely to enjoy positive relationships with parents and other people. At the same time, some children may develop more attractive dispositions as a result of parental warmth and attention (Conger & Conger, 2002).

Social Support Outside the Immediate Family

The most consistent asset of resilient children is a strong bond with a competent, caring adult. For children who do not have a close bond with either parent, a grandparent, aunt, uncle, or teacher who forms a special relationship with the child can promote resilience (Masten & Reed, 2002). Gary received support from his grandfather, who listened to Gary's concerns and helped him solve problems. In addition, Gary's grandfather had a stable marriage and work life and handled stressors skillfully. Consequently, he served as a model of effective coping.

Associations with rule-abiding peers who value school achievement are also linked to resilience. But children who have positive relationships with adults are far more likely to establish these supportive peer ties.

Community Resources and Opportunities

Community supports—good schools, convenient and affordable health care and social services, libraries, and recreation centers—foster both parents' and children's well-being. In addition, opportunities to participate in community life help older children and adolescents overcome adversity. Extracurricular activities at school, religious youth groups, scouting, and other organizations teach important social skills, such as cooperation, leadership, and contributing to others' welfare. As participants acquire these competencies, they gain in self-reliance, self-esteem and community commitment (Benson et al., 2006). As a college student, Gary volunteered for Habitat for Humanity, joining a team building affordable housing in low-income neighborhoods. Community involvement offered Gary additional opportunities to form meaningful relationships, which further strengthened his resilience.

Research on resilience highlights the complex connections between heredity and environment. Armed with positive characteristics, which stem from innate endowment, favorable rearing experiences, or both, children and adolescents take action to reduce stressful situations.

But when many risks pile up, they are increasingly difficult to overcome (Luthar, 2006). To inoculate children against the negative effects of risk, interventions must not only reduce risks but also enhance children's protective relationships at home, in school, and in the community. This means attending to both the person and the environment—strengthening children's capacities while also reducing hazardous experiences.

This child's special relationship with his grandmother promotes resilience. By providing social support, she helps him cope with stress and solve problems constructively. © Tom Stewart/Corbis

nature, sometimes portraying them as possessed by the devil and in need of purification, at other times as innocent and close to angels (Hanawalt, 2003). Both ideas foreshadowed later views of childhood.

The Reformation

In the sixteenth century, the Puritan belief in original sin gave rise to the view that children were born evil and stubborn and had to be civilized (Shahar, 1990). Harsh, restrictive child-rearing practices were recommended to tame the depraved child. Children were dressed in stiff, uncomfortable clothing that held them in adultlike postures, and disobedient students were routinely beaten by their schoolmasters. But although punitiveness was the prevailing child-rearing philosophy, love and affection for their children prevented most Puritan parents from using extremely repressive measures (Moran & Vinovskis, 1986).

As the Puritans emigrated from England to North America, they brought the belief that child rearing was one of their most important obligations. Although they continued to regard the child's soul as tainted by original sin, they tried to teach their sons and daughters to use reason to tell right from wrong (Clarke-Stewart, 1998). The Puritans were the first to devise special reading materials for children that instructed them in religious and moral ideals. As they trained their children in self-reliance and self-control, Puritan parents gradually adopted a moderate balance between severity and permissiveness (Pollock, 1987).

As early as medieval times, adults viewed childhood as a distinct developmental period. The children in this fourteenth-century image, painted in a book of songs, are dressed in loose, comfortable gowns as they play a lively game of Blind Man's Bluff. © The Art Archive/ Bibliothèque Universitaire de Médecine, Montpellier/Dagli Orti

Philosophies of the Enlightenment

The seventeenth-century Enlightenment brought new philosophies that emphasized ideals of human dignity and respect. Conceptions of childhood were more humane than those of the past.

• John Locke The writings of British philosopher John Locke (1632–1704) served as the forerunner of a twentieth-century perspective that we will discuss shortly: behaviorism. Locke viewed the child as a **tabula rasa**—Latin for "blank slate." According to this idea, children begin as nothing at all; their characters are shaped entirely by experience. Locke (1690/1892) saw parents as rational tutors who can mold the child in any way they wish through careful instruction, effective example, and rewards for good behavior. He was ahead of his time in recommending child-rearing practices that present-day research supports—for example, the use of praise and approval as rewards, rather than money or sweets. He also opposed physical punishment: "The child repeatedly beaten in school cannot look upon books and teachers without experiencing fear and anger." Locke's philosophy led to a change from harshness toward children to kindness and compassion.

Look carefully at Locke's ideas, and you will see that he regarded development as *continuous:* Adultlike behaviors are gradually built up through the warm, consistent teachings of parents. His view of the child as a tabula rasa led him to champion *nurture*—the power of the environment to shape the child. And his faith in nurture suggests the possibility of *many courses of development* and of *change at later ages* due to new experiences. Finally, Locke's philosophy characterizes children as doing little to influence their own destiny, which is written on "blank slates" by others. This vision of a passive child has been discarded. All contemporary theories view children as active, purposeful beings who make sense of their world and contribute substantially to their own development.

• Jean-Jacques Rousseau In the eighteenth century, French philosopher Jean-Jacques Rousseau (1712–1778) introduced a new view of childhood. Children, Rousseau (1762/1955) claimed, are not blank slates and empty containers to be filled by adult instruction. Instead, they are **noble savages,** naturally endowed with a sense of right and wrong and with an innate plan for orderly, healthy growth. Unlike Locke, Rousseau believed that children's built-in moral sense and unique ways of thinking and feeling would only be harmed by adult training. His was a child-centered philosophy in which adults should be receptive to the child's needs at each of four stages: infancy, childhood, late childhood, and adolescence.

Rousseau's philosophy includes two influential concepts. The first is the concept of *stage,* which we discussed earlier. The second is the concept of **maturation,** which refers to a genetically determined, naturally unfolding course of growth. In contrast to Locke, Rousseau saw children as determining their own destinies. And he took a different stand on basic developmental issues. And he viewed development as a *discontinuous, stagewise* process that follows a *single, unified course* mapped out by *nature.*

Scientific Beginnings

The study of child development evolved quickly in the late nineteenth and early twentieth centuries. Early observations of children were soon followed by improved methods and theories. Each advance contributed to the firm foundation on which the field rests today.

• Darwin: Forefather of Scientific Child Study A century after Rousseau, British naturalist Charles Darwin (1809–1882) joined an expedition to distant parts of the world, where he observed infinite variation among plant and animal species. He also saw that within a species, no two individuals are exactly alike. From these observations, he constructed his famous *theory of evolution.*

The theory emphasized two related principles: *natural selection* and *survival of the fittest.* Darwin explained that certain species survive in particular parts of the world because they have characteristics that fit with, or are adapted to, their surroundings. Other species die off because they are not as well-suited to their environments. Individuals within a species who best meet the environments' survival requirements live long enough to reproduce and pass their more beneficial characteristics to future generations. Darwin's emphasis on the adaptive value of physical characteristics and behavior eventually found its way into important twentieth-century theories.

During his explorations, Darwin discovered that early prenatal growth is strikingly similar in many species. Other scientists concluded from Darwin's observation that the development of the human child follows the same general plan as the evolution of the human species. Although this belief eventually proved inaccurate, efforts to chart parallels between child growth and human evolution prompted researchers to make careful observations of all aspects of children's behavior. Out of these first attempts to document an idea about development, scientific child study was born.

• **The Baby Biographies** TAKE A MOMENT... Imagine yourself as a forerunner in the field of child development, confronted with studying children for the first time. How might you go about this challenging task? Scientists of the late nineteenth and early twentieth centuries did what most of us would probably do—they selected a child of their own or of a close relative. Then, beginning in early infancy, they jotted down day-by-day descriptions and impressions of the child's behavior. By the 1890s, these baby biographies were being published regularly. In the following excerpt from one, the author reflects on the birth of her young niece:

> Its first act is a cry, not of wrath, . . . nor a shout of joy, . . . but a snuffling, and then a long, thin tearless *á—á*, with the timbre of a Scotch bagpipe, purely automatic, but of discomfort. With this monotonous and dismal cry, with its red, shriveled, parboiled skin . . . , it is not strange that, if the mother . . . has not come to love her child before birth, there is a brief interval occasionally dangerous to the child before the maternal instinct is fully aroused.
>
> It cannot be denied that this unflattering description is fair enough, and our baby was no handsomer than the rest of her kind. . . . Yet she did not lack admirers. I have never noticed that women (even those who are not mothers) mind a few little aesthetic defects, . . . with so many counterbalancing charms in the little warm, soft, living thing. (Shinn, 1900, pp. 20–21)

Can you tell from this passage why the baby biographies have sometimes been upheld as examples of how *not* to study children? These first investigators tended to be emotionally invested in the infants they observed, and they seldom began with a clear idea of what they wanted to find out. Not surprisingly, many of their records were eventually discarded as biased. Nevertheless, the baby biographies were a step in the right direction. Two nineteenth-century theorists, Darwin (1877) and German biologist William Preyer (1882/1888), contributed to these early records of children's behavior. Preyer, especially, set high standards for making observations, recording what he saw immediately and checking the accuracy of his notes against those of a second observer (Cairns, 1998). These are the same standards that today's researchers use when observing children. As a result of the biographers' pioneering efforts, the child became a common focus of scientific research.

• **The Normative Period** G. Stanley Hall (1844–1924), one of the most influential American psychologists of the early twentieth century, is generally regarded as the founder of the child study movement (Cairns & Cairns, 2006). Inspired by Darwin's work, Hall and his well-known student Arnold Gesell (1880–1961) developed theories based on evolutionary ideas. These early leaders regarded child development as a *maturational process*—a genetically determined series of events that unfold automatically, much like a flower (Gesell, 1933; Hall, 1904).

Hall and Gesell are remembered less for their one-sided theories than for their intensive efforts to describe all aspects of child development. This launched the **normative approach,** in which measures of behavior are taken on large numbers of individuals and age-related averages are computed to represent typical development. Using this procedure, Hall constructed elaborate questionnaires asking children of different ages almost everything they could tell about themselves—interests, fears, imaginary playmates, dreams, friendships, everyday knowledge, and more. Similarly, through observations and parental interviews, Gesell collected detailed normative information on the motor achievements, social behaviors, and personality characteristics of infants and children.

Gesell was also among the first to make knowledge about child development meaningful to parents by informing them of what to expect at each age. If, as he believed, the timetable of development is the product of millions of years of evolution, then children are naturally knowledgeable about their needs. His child-rearing advice, in the tradition of Rousseau, recommended sensitivity to children's cues (Thelen & Adolph, 1992). Along with Benjamin Spock's *Baby and Child Care,* Gesell's books became a central part of a rapidly expanding child development literature for parents (see the From Research to Practice box on the following page).

• **The Mental Testing Movement** While Hall and Gesell were developing their theories and methods in the United States, French psychologist Alfred Binet (1857–1911) was also taking a normative approach to child development, but for a different reason. In the early 1900s, Binet and his colleague Theodore Simon were asked by Paris school officials to find a way to identify children with learning problems who needed to be placed in special classes. To address these practical educational concerns, Binet and Simon constructed the first successful intelligence test.

Binet began with a well-developed theory of intelligence. In contrast to earlier views, which reduced intelligence to simple elements of reaction time and sensitivity to physical stimuli, he captured the complexity of children's thinking. Binet defined intelligence as good judgment, planning, and critical reflection (Sternberg & Jarvin, 2003). Then he created age-graded test items that directly measured these abilities.

In 1916, at Stanford University, Binet's test was adapted for use with English-speaking children. Since then, the English version has been known as the *Stanford-Binet Intelligence Scale.* Besides providing a score that could successfully predict school achievement, the Binet test sparked tremendous interest in individual differences in development. Comparisons of the scores of children who vary in gender, ethnicity, birth order, family background, and other characteristics became a major focus of research. And intelligence tests rose quickly to the forefront of the nature–nurture controversy.

• **James Mark Baldwin: Early Developmental Theorist** A final important figure, long overlooked in the history of child development, is American psychologist James Mark Baldwin (1861–1934), who carried out his innovative work in both Canada and the United States. Baldwin (1897) was a theorist and a keen observer of children's behavior whose rich interpretations of development are experiencing a revival today. He believed that children's understanding of their physical and social worlds develops through a sequence of stages, beginning with the simplest behavior patterns of the newborn infant and concluding with the adult's capacity to think abstractly and reflectively (Cairns, 1998).

Yet in Baldwin's view, neither the child nor the environment controlled development. Instead, he granted nature and nurture equal importance. Children, he argued, actively revise their ways of thinking about the world, but they also learn through habit, or by copying others' behaviors. As development proceeds, the child and her social surroundings influence each other, forming an inseparable, interwoven network.

Consider these ideas, and you will see why Baldwin (1895) argued that heredity and environment should not be viewed as distinct, opposing forces. Instead, he claimed, most human characteristics are "due to both causes working together" (p. 77). As we turn now to an overview of modern theories of child development, you will find Baldwin's ideas represented in several, especially the more recent ones.

Ask Yourself

Review Imagine a debate between John Locke and Jean-Jacques Rousseau on the nature–nurture controversy. Summarize the argument that each historical figure is likely to present.

Connect What do the ideas of Rousseau, Darwin, and Hall have in common?

Reflect Find out whether your parents read Gesell, Spock, or other parenting advice books when you were growing up. What questions about child rearing most concerned them? Do you think today's parents have concerns that differ from those of your parents? Explain.

▪ *From* Research *to* Practice ▪

Social Change and the Popular Literature on Parenting

Almost all parents—especially new ones—feel a need for sound advice on how to rear their children. To meet this need, experts have long been communicating with the general public through a wide variety of popular books and magazines. Before the 1970s, publications emphasized the central role of mothers in healthy child development. In the 1980s, fathers were encouraged to share in the full range of child-rearing responsibilities as research revealed that they influence all aspects of psychological development. Around that time, information about nonparental child care appeared. Experts reassured employed mothers that their babies did not require their continuous presence and offered advice on how to select good child care (Young, 1990).

From the mid-1990s to the present, an increasing number of books have responded to concerns over the consequences of social change for parents' and children's well-being. More working parents complained of overly demanding lives and reported spending less time with their children in joint mealtimes, conversations, play, and other leisure activities. At the same time, many parents reported worrisome changes in their children, including reduced engagement in school and increases in emotional and behavior problems (Berk, 2005; Vandivere, Gallagher, & Moore, 2004). And in one nationally representative survey of U.S. parents, more than half judged the job that they were doing in rearing their children as "fair" or "poor." Many of these respondents believed that parents of previous generations had done better (Public Agenda, 2002). Few felt that they knew what to do to rear their children effectively.

In *Awakening Children's Minds,* Laura Berk (2004) points out that parents' efforts to rear competent, well-adjusted children are complicated by both unfavorable cultural influences (such as scarcity of high-quality child care and harmful media messages) and a contradictory parenting-advice literature. Whereas some parenting manuals assert that parents are all-powerful, others grant supremacy to children's biological makeup. In the face of these incompatible messages, many parents come to doubt their own importance and retreat from engagement with their children. Berk argues that in view of the many factors in U.S. society that threaten children's development, parenting today not only matters, but matters more than ever.

In a similar vein, James Garbarino and Claire Bedard (2002), in *Parents Under Siege,* address issues of youth antagonism and violence, including recent heinous crimes resulting in family and school maimings and murders. Because multiple factors—an impulsive, explosive temperament, unfavorable school experiences, and antisocial peer influences—contribute to these tragedies, parents are not to blame for them. But, Garbarino and Bedard emphasize, parents nevertheless bear considerable responsibility. Often, they are unaware of everyday experiences that lead their youngster down the path to antisocial acts.

Experts writing for contemporary parents often emphasize the importance of increased adult involvement in children's lives. Much research shows that parents, though not all-powerful, profoundly influence their children's development. © Tetra Images/Alamy

In terms of solutions, most experts writing for parents affirm the need for greater adult involvement in children's lives. Berk (2004) shows how essential cognitive, moral, and social capacities emerge from parent–child communication in such everyday activities as a bedtime story, a homework assignment, an episode of make-believe play, or a family dinner. Garbarino and Bedard (2002) make a case for "empowered parenting," in which parents consider their youngsters' strengths and limitations while closely monitoring and, when necessary, intervening in the social environment. They also admonish parents to provide a "moral compass of character" by insisting that children meet standards for personal achievement and caring for others. And in *The Ten Basic Principles of Good Parenting,* Laurence Steinberg (2004) aims to restore in parents a philosophy of good child rearing by outlining ten research-based parenting strategies that help children become kind, secure, and competent. These include: be loving, establish rules and set limits, treat your child with respect, and foster independence by helping your child think through decisions.

Yet increasingly, popular advice has underscored that parents cannot do the job alone—they need the help of a caring community and society. **TAKE A MOMENT...** As you study child development, select one or more popular books on parenting and evaluate their advice on the basis of what you have learned. How is the growing agreement of experts with the African proverb, "It takes a village to raise a child," consistent with the focus of current theories on *contexts* for development, described later in this chapter?

Mid-Twentieth-Century Theories

In the mid-twentieth century, the field of child development expanded into a legitimate discipline. Specialized research centers and professional societies devoted to the scientific study of children were founded. A leader among these is the Society for Research in Child Development (SRCD), established in 1933 to promote interdisciplinary research, dissemination of information, and applications of research findings. The society's inaugural membership of 425 grew rapidly. Today, approximately 5,500 researchers, applied professionals, and students from more than 50 countries are members.

As child development attracted increasing interest, a variety of theories emerged, each of which continues to have followers today. In these theories, the European concern with the child's inner thoughts and feelings contrasts sharply with the North American academic focus on scientific precision and concrete, observable behavior.

The Psychoanalytic Perspective

By the 1930s and 1940s, parents were increasingly seeking professional help in dealing with children's emotional difficulties. The earlier normative movement had answered the question, What are children like? Now another question had to be addressed: How and why do children become the way they are? To treat psychological problems, psychiatrists and social workers turned to an emerging approach to personality development that emphasized the unique history of each child.

According to the **psychoanalytic perspective,** children move through a series of stages in which they confront conflicts between biological drives and social expectations. How these conflicts are resolved determines the person's ability to learn, to get along with others, and to cope with anxiety. Among the many individuals who contributed to the psychoanalytic perspective, two were especially influential: Sigmund Freud, founder of the psychoanalytic movement, and Erik Erikson.

Freud's Theory Freud (1856–1939), a Viennese physician, sought a cure for emotionally troubled adults by having them talk freely about painful events of their childhoods. Working with these remembrances, Freud examined the unconscious motivations of his patients and constructed his **psychosexual theory,** which emphasizes that how parents manage their child's sexual and aggressive drives in the first few years is crucial for healthy personality development.

In Freud's theory, three parts of the personality—id, ego, and superego—become integrated during a sequence of five stages, summarized in Table 1.1. The *id,* the largest portion of the mind, is the source of basic biological needs and desires. The *ego,* the conscious, rational part of personality, emerges in early infancy to redirect the id's impulses so they are discharged in acceptable ways. For example, aided by the ego, the hungry baby of a few months of age stops crying when he sees his mother warm a bottle or unfasten her clothing to nurse him. And the more competent preschooler goes into the kitchen and gets a snack on her own.

Between 3 and 6 years of age, the *superego,* or conscience, develops through interactions with parents, who insist that children conform to the values of society. Now the ego faces the increasingly complex task of reconciling the demands of the id, the external world, and conscience (Freud, 1923/1974). For example, when the ego is tempted to gratify an id impulse by hitting a playmate to get an attractive toy, the superego may warn that such behavior is wrong. The ego must decide which of the two forces (id or superego) will win this inner struggle or work out a compromise, such as asking for a turn with the toy. According to Freud, the relations established between id, ego, and superego during the preschool years determine the individual's basic personality.

Freud (1938/1973) believed that during childhood, sexual impulses shift their focus from the oral to the anal to the genital regions of the body. In each stage, parents walk a fine line between permitting too much or too little gratification of their child's basic needs. If parents strike an appropriate balance, then children grow into well-adjusted adults with the capacity for mature sexual behavior and investment in family life.

Table 1.1 Freud's Psychosexual Stages

Psychosexual Stage	Approximate Age	Description
Oral	Birth–1 year	The new ego directs the baby's sucking activities toward breast or bottle. If oral needs are not met appropriately, the individual may develop such habits as thumb sucking, fingernail biting, and pencil chewing in childhood and overeating and smoking later in life.
Anal	1–3 years	Toddlers and preschoolers enjoy holding and releasing urine and feces. Toilet training becomes a major issue between parent and child. If parents insist that children be trained before they are ready, or if they make too few demands, conflicts about anal control may appear in the form of extreme orderliness and cleanliness or messiness and disorder.
Phallic	3–6 years	As preschoolers take pleasure in genital stimulation, Freud's Oedipus conflict for boys and Electra conflict for girls arise: Children feel a sexual desire for the other-sex parent and hostility toward the same-sex parent. To avoid punishment and loss of parental love, they suppress these impulses and, instead, adopt the same-sex parent's characteristics and values. As a result, the superego is formed, and children feel guilty whenever they violate its standards.
Latency	6–11 years	Sexual instincts die down, and the superego develops further. The child acquires new social values from adults and same-sex peers outside the family.
Genital	Adolescence	With puberty, the sexual impulses of the phallic stage reappear. If development has been successful during earlier stages, it leads to marriage, mature sexuality, and the birth and rearing of children. This stage extends through adulthood.

Freud's theory was the first to stress the influence of the early parent–child relationship on development. But his perspective was eventually criticized. First, it overemphasized the influence of sexual feelings in development. Second, because it was based on the problems of sexually repressed, well-to-do adults in nineteenth-century Victorian society, it did not apply in other cultures. Finally, Freud had not studied children directly.

• **Erikson's Theory** Several of Freud's followers took what was useful from his theory and improved on his vision. The most important of these neo-Freudians is Erik Erikson (1902–1994), who expanded the picture of development at each stage. In his **psychosocial theory,** Erikson emphasized that in addition to mediating between id impulses and superego demands, the ego makes a positive contribution to development, acquiring attitudes and skills at each stage that make the individual an active, contributing member of society. A basic psychosocial conflict, which is resolved along a continuum from positive to negative, determines healthy or maladaptive outcomes at each stage. As Table 1.2 on page 18 shows, Erikson's first five stages parallel Freud's stages, but Erikson added three adult stages. He was one of the first to recognize the lifespan nature of development.

Unlike Freud, Erikson pointed out that normal development must be understood in relation to each culture's life situation. For example, in the 1940s, he observed that Yurok Indians of the northwest coast of the United States deprived babies of breastfeeding for the first 10 days after birth and instead fed them a thin soup. At age 6 months, infants were abruptly weaned—if necessary, by having the

Children of the Lacandon Mayan people of southern Mexico look on as their father makes souvenir arrows similar to those of their ancestors. The Lacandon—descendants of hunter-gatherers and subsistence farmers who lived in isolation for hundreds of years—teach many ancient skills and traditions to each new generation, including tool making, unique agricultural techniques, mythological stories, and dream interpretation. As Erikson recognized, these children's development can be understood only in relation to their distinct culture. © Danita Delmont/Alamy

Table 1.2 Erikson's Psychosocial Stages, with Corresponding Psychosexual Stages Indicated

Erik Erikson

Psychosocial Stage	Period of Development	Description
Basic trust versus mistrust (Oral)	Birth–1 year	From warm, responsive care, infants gain a sense of trust, or confidence, that the world is good. Mistrust occurs when infants have to wait too long for comfort or are handled harshly.
Autonomy versus shame and doubt (Anal)	1–3 years	Using new mental and motor skills, children want to choose and decide for themselves. Parents can foster autonomy by permitting reasonable free choice and not forcing or shaming the child.
Initiative versus guilt (Phallic)	3–6 years	Through make-believe play, children experiment with the kind of person they can become. Initiative—a sense of ambition and responsibility—develops when parents support their child's new sense of purpose. The danger is that parents will demand too much self-control, which leads to overcontrol, meaning too much guilt.
Industry versus inferiority (Latency)	6–11 years	At school, children develop the capacity to work and cooperate with others. Inferiority develops when negative experiences at home, at school, or with peers lead to feelings of incompetence.
Identity versus identity confusion (Genital)	Adolescence	The adolescent tries to answer the questions, Who am I, and what is my place in society? By exploring values and vocational goals, the young person forms a personal identity. The negative outcome is confusion about future adult roles.
Intimacy versus isolation	Young adulthood	Young people work on establishing intimate ties to others. Because of earlier disappointments, some individuals cannot form close relationships and remain isolated.
Generativity versus stagnation	Middle adulthood	Generativity means giving to the next generation through child rearing, caring for other people, or productive work. The person who fails in these ways feels an absence of meaningful accomplishment.
Integrity versus despair	Old age	In this final stage, individuals reflect on the kind of person they have been. Integrity results from feeling that life was worth living as it happened. Old people who are dissatisfied with their lives fear death.

mother leave for a few days. From our cultural vantage point, this deliberate deprivation seems cruel. But Erikson explained that because the Yurok depended on salmon, which fill the river just once a year, the development of considerable self-restraint was essential for survival. In this way, he showed that child rearing can be understood only in relation to the competencies valued and needed by a child's society.

• **Contributions and Limitations of the Psychoanalytic Perspective** A special strength of the psychoanalytic perspective is its emphasis on the individual's unique life history as worthy of study and understanding. Consistent with this view, psychoanalytic theorists accept the *clinical,* or *case study, method,* which synthesizes information from a variety of sources into a detailed picture of the personality of a single child. (We will discuss this method further in Chapter 2.) Psychoanalytic theory has also inspired a wealth of research on many aspects of emotional and social development, including infant–caregiver attachment, aggression, sibling relationships, child-rearing practices, morality, gender roles, and adolescent identity.

Despite its extensive contributions, the psychoanalytic perspective is no longer in the mainstream of child development research. Psychoanalytic theorists may have become isolated from the rest of the field because they were so strongly committed to in-depth study of individual children that they failed to consider other methods. In addition, many psychoanalytic ideas, such as psychosexual stages and ego functioning, are so vague that they are difficult or impossible to test empirically (Crain, 2005; Thomas, 2005). Nevertheless, Erikson's broad outline of change captures the essence of psychosocial attainments at each age period. Consequently, we will return to it in later chapters.

Behaviorism and Social Learning Theory

As the psychoanalytic perspective gained in prominence, child study was also influenced by a very different perspective. According to **behaviorism,** directly observable events—stimuli and responses—are the appropriate focus of study. North American behaviorism began in the early twentieth century with the work of psychologist John Watson (1878–1958), who, rejecting the psychoanalytic concern with the unseen workings of the mind, set out to create an objective science of psychology.

• **Traditional Behaviorism** Watson was inspired by Russian physiologist Ivan Pavlov's studies of animal learning. Pavlov knew that dogs release saliva as an innate reflex when they are given food. But he noticed that his dogs started salivating before they tasted any food—when they saw the trainer who usually fed them. The dogs, Pavlov reasoned, must have learned to associate a neutral stimulus (the trainer) with another stimulus (food) that produces a reflexive response (salivation). Because of this association, the neutral stimulus alone could bring about a response resembling the reflex. Eager to test this idea, Pavlov successfully taught dogs to salivate at the sound of a bell by pairing it with the presentation of food. He had discovered *classical conditioning.*

Watson wanted to find out if classical conditioning could be applied to children's behavior. In a historic experiment, he taught Albert, an 11-month-old infant, to fear a neutral stimulus—a soft white rat—by presenting it several times with a sharp, loud sound, which naturally scared the baby. Little Albert, who at first had reached out eagerly to touch the furry rat, began to cry and turn his head away at the sight of it (Watson & Raynor, 1920). In fact, Albert's fear was so intense that researchers eventually challenged the ethics of studies like this one. Consistent with Locke's tabula rasa, Watson concluded that environment is the supreme force in development and that adults can mold children's behavior by carefully controlling stimulus–response associations. He viewed development as a continuous process, consisting of a gradual increase with age in the number and strength of these associations.

Another form of behaviorism was American psychologist B. F. Skinner's (1904–1990) *operant conditioning theory.* According to Skinner, the frequency of a behavior can be increased by following it with a wide variety of *reinforcers*—food, drink, praise, a friendly smile, or a new toy—or decreased through *punishment,* such as disapproval or withdrawal of privileges. As a result of Skinner's work, operant conditioning became a broadly applied learning principle. We will consider these conditioning principles further when we explore the infant's learning capacities in Chapter 4.

• **Social Learning Theory** Psychologists wondered whether behaviorism might offer a more direct and effective explanation of the development of children's social behavior than the less precise concepts of psychoanalytic theory. This sparked approaches that built on the principles of conditioning, offering expanded views of how children and adults acquire new responses.

Several kinds of **social learning theory** emerged. The most influential, devised by Canadian-born psychologist Albert Bandura (1925–), emphasized *modeling,* otherwise known as *imitation* or *observational learning,* as a powerful source of development. The baby who claps her hands after her mother does so, the child who angrily hits a playmate in the same way that he has been punished at home, and the teenager who wears the same clothes and hairstyle as her friends at school are all displaying observational learning. In his early work, Bandura found that diverse factors affect children's motivation to imitate—their own history of reinforcement or punishment for the behavior, the promise of future reinforcement or punishment, and even vicarious reinforcement or punishment (observing the model being reinforced or punished).

Bandura's work continues to influence much research on children's social development. But today, like the field of child development as a whole, his theory stresses the importance of

Social learning theory recognizes that children acquire many skills through modeling. By observing and imitating her mother's behavior, this Vietnamese preschooler is becoming a skilled user of chopsticks. © Margot Granitsas/ The Image Works

cognition, or thinking. Bandura has shown that children's ability to listen, remember, and abstract general rules from complex sets of observed behaviors affects their imitation and learning. In fact, the most recent revision of Bandura's (1992, 2001) theory places such strong emphasis on how children think about themselves and other people that he calls it a *social-cognitive* rather than a social learning approach.

In Bandura's revised view, children gradually become more selective in what they imitate. From watching others engage in self-praise and self-blame and through feedback about the worth of their own actions, children develop *personal standards* for behavior and a *sense of self-efficacy*—the belief that their own abilities and characteristics will help them succeed. These cognitions guide responses in particular situations (Bandura, 1999, 2001). For example, imagine a parent who often remarks, "I'm glad I kept working on that task, even though it was hard," who explains the value of persistence, and who encourages it by saying, "I know you can do a good job on that homework!" Soon the child starts to view herself as hardworking and high-achieving and selects people with these characteristics as models. In this way, as children acquire attitudes, values, and convictions about themselves, they control their own learning and behavior.

• Contributions and Limitations of Behaviorism and Social Learning Theory Behaviorism and social learning theory have had a major impact on practices with children. **Behavior modification** consists of procedures that combine conditioning and modeling to eliminate undesirable behaviors and increase desirable responses. It has been used to relieve a wide range of serious developmental problems, such as persistent aggression, language delays, and extreme fears (Martin & Pear, 2007).

Behavior modification is also effective in dealing with common, everyday difficulties, including poor time management; unwanted habits such as nail biting and thumb sucking; and anxiety over such recurrent events as test taking, public speaking, and medical and dental treatments. In one study, researchers reduced 4- and 5-year-olds' unruliness in a preschool classroom by reinforcing them with tokens (which they could exchange for candy) when they behaved appropriately and punishing them by taking away tokens when they screamed, threw objects, attacked other children, or refused to comply with a teacher's request (Conyers et al., 2004). In another investigation, children with acute burn injuries played a virtual reality game while nurses engaged in the painful process of changing their bandages. Visual images and sound effects delivered through a headset made the children feel as if they were in a fantasy world. As the game reinforced children's concentration and pleasure, it distracted them from the medical procedure, causing their pain and anxiety to drop sharply compared with dressing changes in which the game was unavailable (Das et al., 2005).

Nevertheless, many theorists believe that behaviorism and social learning theory offer too narrow a view of important environmental influences. These extend beyond immediate reinforcements, punishments, and modeled behaviors to children's rich physical and social worlds. Behaviorism and social learning theory have also been criticized for underestimating children's contributions to their own development. Bandura, with his emphasis on cognition, is unique among theorists whose work grew out of the behaviorist tradition in granting children an active role in their own learning.

Piaget's Cognitive-Developmental Theory

If one individual has influenced the contemporary field of child development more than any other, it is Swiss cognitive theorist Jean Piaget (1896–1980). North American investigators had been aware of Piaget's work since 1930. But they did not grant it much attention until the 1960s, mainly because Piaget's ideas were at odds with behaviorism, which dominated North American psychology during the middle of the twentieth century (Cairns & Cairns, 2006). Piaget did not believe that children's learning depends on reinforcers, such as rewards from adults. According to his **cognitive-developmental theory,** children actively construct knowledge as they manipulate and explore their world.

• Piaget's Stages Piaget's view of development was greatly influenced by his early training in biology. Central to his theory is the biological concept of *adaptation* (Piaget, 1971). Just as

Table 1.3 Piaget's Stages of Cognitive Development

Stage	Period of Development	Description
Sensorimotor	Birth–2 years	Infants "think" by acting on the world with their eyes, ears, hands, and mouth. As a result, they invent ways of solving sensorimotor problems, such as pulling a lever to hear the sound of a music box, finding hidden toys, and putting objects into and taking them out of containers.
Preoperational	2–7 years	Preschool children use symbols to represent their earlier sensorimotor discoveries. Development of language and make-believe play takes place. However, thinking lacks the logic of the two remaining stages.
Concrete operational	7–11 years	Children's reasoning becomes logical and better organized. School-age children understand that a certain amount of lemonade or play dough remains the same even after its appearance changes. They also organize objects into hierarchies of classes and subclasses. However, thinking falls short of adult intelligence. It is not yet abstract.
Formal operational	11 years on	The capacity for abstract, systematic thinking enables adolescents, when faced with a problem, to start with a hypothesis, deduce testable inferences, and isolate and combine variables to see which inferences are confirmed. Adolescents can also evaluate the logic of verbal statements without referring to real-world circumstances.

© Bettmann/CORBIS

Jean Piaget

structures of the body are adapted to fit with the environment, so structures of the mind develop to better fit with, or represent, the external world. In infancy and early childhood, Piaget claimed, children's understanding is different from adults'. For example, he believed that young babies do not realize that an object hidden from view—a favorite toy or even the mother—continues to exist. He also concluded that preschoolers' thinking is full of faulty logic. For example, children younger than age 7 commonly say that the amount of liquid changes when it is poured into a different-shaped container. According to Piaget, children eventually revise these incorrect ideas in their ongoing efforts to achieve an *equilibrium,* or balance, between internal structures and information they encounter in their everyday worlds.

In Piaget's theory, as the brain develops and children's experiences expand, they move through four broad stages, each characterized by qualitatively distinct ways of thinking. Table 1.3 provides a brief description of Piaget's stages. Cognitive development begins in the *sensorimotor stage* with the baby's use of the senses and movements to explore the world. These action patterns evolve into the symbolic but illogical thinking of the preschooler in the *preoperational stage.* Then cognition is transformed into the more organized, logical reasoning of the school-age child in the *concrete operational stage.* Finally, in the *formal operational stage,* thought becomes the abstract, systematic reasoning system of the adolescent and adult.

In Piaget's preoperational stage, preschool children use symbols to represent their earlier sensorimotor discoveries. Language and make-believe play develop rapidly. These 4-year-olds create an imaginative play scene with dress-up clothes and the assistance of a cooperative family pet. © Tom McCarthy/ImageState

Piaget devised special methods for investigating how children think. Early in his career, he carefully observed his three infant children and presented them with everyday problems, such as an attractive object that could be grasped, mouthed, kicked, or searched for. From their responses, Piaget derived his ideas about cognitive changes during the first two years. To study childhood and adolescent thought, Piaget adapted the clinical method of psychoanalysis, conducting open-ended *clinical interviews* in which a child's initial response to a task served as the basis for Piaget's next question. We will look more closely at this technique in Chapter 2.

● **Contributions and Limitations of Piaget's Theory** Piaget convinced the field that children are active learners whose minds consist of

In Piaget's concrete operational stage, school-age children think in an organized, logical fashion about concrete objects. These 6- and 7-year-olds making pizza dough understand that the amount of dough remains the same after they change its shape from a ball to a flattened circle. © Richard Hutchings/ CORBIS

rich structures of knowledge. Besides investigating children's understanding of the physical world, Piaget explored their reasoning about the social world. His stages have sparked a wealth of research on children's conceptions of themselves, other people, and human relationships. In practical terms, Piaget's theory encouraged the development of educational philosophies and programs that emphasize children's discovery learning and direct contact with the environment.

Despite Piaget's overwhelming contributions, his theory has been challenged. Research indicates that Piaget underestimated the competencies of infants and preschoolers. We will see in Chapter 6 that when young children are given tasks scaled down in difficulty and relevant to their everyday experiences, their understanding appears closer to that of the older child and adult than Piaget assumed. This discovery has led many researchers to conclude that the maturity of children's thinking may depend on their familiarity with the task presented and the complexity of knowledge sampled. Furthermore, many studies show that children's performance on Piagetian problems can be improved with training—findings that call into question Piaget's assumption that discovery learning rather than adult teaching is the best way to foster development (Klahr & Nigam, 2004; Siegler & Svetina, 2006). Critics also point out that Piaget's stagewise account pays insufficient attention to social and cultural influences—and the resulting wide variation in thinking that exists among children of the same age.

Today, the field of child development is divided over its loyalty to Piaget's ideas. Those who continue to find merit in Piaget's stages often accept a modified view—one in which changes in children's thinking take place more gradually than Piaget believed (Case, 1998; Demetriou et al., 2002; Fischer & Bidell, 2006; Halford & Andrews, 2006). Among those who disagree with Piaget's stage sequence, some have embraced an approach that emphasizes continuous gains in children's cognition: information processing. And still others have been drawn to theories that highlight the role of children's social and cultural contexts. We take up these approaches in the next section.

Ask Yourself

Review What aspect of behaviorism made it attractive to critics of the psychoanalytic perspective? How did Piaget's theory respond to a major limitation of behaviorism?

Apply A 4-year-old becomes frightened of the dark and refuses to go to sleep at night. How would a psychoanalyst and a behaviorist differ in their views of how this problem developed?

Connect Although social learning theory focuses on social development and Piaget's theory on cognitive development, each has enhanced our understanding of other domains. Mention an additional domain addressed by each theory.

Reflect Illustrate Bandura's ideas by describing a personal experience in which you observed and received feedback from another person that strengthened your self-efficacy—belief that your abilities and characteristics will help you succeed.

Recent Theoretical Perspectives

New ways of understanding children are constantly emerging—questioning, building on, and enhancing the discoveries of earlier theories. Today, a burst of fresh approaches and research emphases is broadening our understanding of children's development.

Information Processing

In the 1970s and 1980s, researchers turned to the field of cognitive psychology for ways to understand the development of children's thinking. The design of digital computers that use mathematically specified steps to solve problems suggested to psychologists that the human mind might also be viewed as a symbol-manipulating system through which information flows—a perspective called **information processing** (Klahr & MacWhinney, 1998; Munakata, 2006). From the time information is presented to the senses at *input* until it emerges as a behavioral response at *output,* information is actively coded, transformed, and organized.

• **Concern with Rigor and Precision** Information-processing researchers often use flowcharts to map the precise steps individuals use to solve problems and complete tasks, much like the plans devised by programmers to get computers to perform a series of "mental operations" (Siegler & Alibali, 2005). To see the usefulness of this approach, let's look at an example.

In a study of problem solving, a researcher provided a pile of blocks varying in size, shape, and weight and asked school-age children to build a bridge across a "river" (painted on a floor mat) that was too wide for any single block to span (Thornton, 1999). Figure 1.3 shows one solution to the problem: Two planklike blocks span the water, each held in place by the counterweight of heavy blocks on the bridge's towers. Whereas older children easily built successful bridges, only one 5-year-old did. Careful tracking of her efforts revealed that she repeatedly tried unsuccessful strategies, such as pushing two planks together and pressing down on their ends to hold them in place. But eventually, her experimentation triggered the idea of using the blocks as counterweights. Her mistaken procedures helped her understand why the counterweight approach worked. These findings show how a child's actions within a task can facilitate problem solving. Although this child had no prior understanding of counterweight and balance, she arrived at just as effective a solution as older children, who started with considerable task-relevant knowledge.

Many information-processing models exist. Some, like the one just considered, track children's mastery of one or a few tasks. Others describe the human cognitive system as a whole (Atkinson & Shiffrin, 1968; Lockhart & Craik, 1990). These general models are used as guides for asking questions about broad age changes in children's thinking: Does a child's ability to solve problems become more organized and "planful" with age? What strategies do younger and older children use to remember new information, and how do those strategies affect children's recall?

The information-processing approach is also being used to clarify the processing of social information. For example, flowcharts exist that track the steps children use to solve social problems (such as how to enter an ongoing play group) and acquire gender-linked preferences and behaviors (Crick & Dodge, 1994; Liben & Bigler, 2002). If we can identify how social problem solving and gender stereotyping arise in childhood, then we can design interventions that promote more favorable social development.

Like Piaget's theory, the information-processing approach views children as actively making sense of their experiences and as modifying their own thinking in response to environmental demands (Halford, 2005; Munakata, 2006). But unlike Piaget's theory, it does not divide development into stages. Rather, the thought processes studied—perception, attention, memory, categorization of information, planning, problem solving, and comprehension of written and spoken prose—are regarded as similar at all ages but present to a lesser or greater extent. Therefore, the view of development is one of continuous change.

A great strength of the information-processing approach is its commitment to rigorous research methods. Because it has provided precise accounts of how children of different ages engage in many aspects of thinking, its findings have led to teaching methods that help children approach academic tasks in more advanced ways (Blumenfeld, Marx, & Harris, 2006). But information processing has fallen short in some respects. It has been better at analyzing

Figure 1.3

Information-processing flowchart showing the steps that a 5-year-old used to solve a bridge-building problem.

Her task was to use blocks varying in size, shape, and weight, some of which were planklike, to construct a bridge across a "river" (painted on a floor mat) too wide for any single block to span. The child discovered how to counterweight and balance the bridge. The arrows reveal that even after building a successful counterweight, she returned to earlier, unsuccessful strategies, which seemed to help her understand why the counterweight approach worked. (Adapted from Thornton, 1999.)

thinking into its components than at putting them back together into a comprehensive theory. And it virtually ignores aspects of children's cognition that are not linear and logical, such as imagination and creativity (Birney et al., 2005).

• **Developmental Cognitive Neuroscience** Over the past two decades, as information-processing research has expanded, a new area of investigation has arisen, called **developmental cognitive neuroscience.** It brings together researchers from psychology, biology, neuroscience, and medicine to study the relationship between changes in the brain and the developing child's cognitive processing and behavior patterns.

Improved methods for analyzing brain activity while children perform various tasks have greatly enhanced knowledge of relationships between brain functioning, cognitive capacities, and behavior (Johnson, 2005; Westermann et al., 2007). Armed with these brain-imaging techniques (which we will consider in Chapter 5), neuroscientists are tackling questions like these: How do specific experiences at various ages influence the growth and organization of the young child's brain? What transformations in the brain make it harder for adolescents and adults than for children to acquire a second language?

Neuroscientists are making rapid progress in identifying the types of experiences that support or undermine brain development at various ages. They are also clarifying the brain bases of many learning and behavior disorders, and they are contributing to effective treatments for children with disabilities by examining the impact of various intervention techniques on both brain functioning and behavior (Munakata, Casey, & Diamond, 2004). Although much remains to be discovered, developmental cognitive neuroscience is already transforming our understanding of development and yielding major practical applications. An advantage of having many theories is that they encourage researchers to attend to previously neglected dimensions of children's lives. The final four perspectives we will discuss all focus on *contexts* for development. The first of these views emphasizes that the development of many capacities is influenced by our long evolutionary history.

Ethology and Evolutionary Developmental Psychology

Ethology is concerned with the adaptive, or survival, value of behavior and its evolutionary history (Hinde, 1992). Its roots can be traced to the work of Darwin. Two European zoologists, Konrad Lorenz (1952) and Niko Tinbergen (1973), laid its modern foundations. Watching diverse animal species in their natural habitats, Lorenz and Tinbergen observed behavior patterns that promote survival. The best known of these is *imprinting,* the early following behavior of certain baby birds, such as geese, which ensures that the young will stay close to the mother and be fed and protected from danger. Imprinting takes place during an early, restricted period of development. If the mother goose is absent during this time but an object resembling her in important features is present, young goslings may imprint on it instead.

Observations of imprinting led to a major concept in child development: the *critical period.* It refers to a limited time during which the child is biologically prepared to acquire certain adaptive behaviors but needs the support of an appropriately stimulating environment. Many researchers have conducted studies to find out whether complex cognitive and social behaviors must be learned during certain periods. For example, if children are deprived of adequate food or physical and social stimulation during their early years, will their intelligence be impaired? If language is not mastered during early childhood, is the child's capacity to acquire it reduced?

Ethology focuses on the adaptive, or survival, value of behavior and on similarities between human behavior and that of other species, especially our primate relatives. Observing this chimpanzee mother cuddling her 8-day-old infant helps us understand the human–infant caregiver relationship. AP Images

In later chapters, we will discover that the term *sensitive period* applies better to human development than the strict notion of a critical period (Bornstein, 1989). A **sensitive period** is a time that is optimal for certain capacities to emerge and in which the individual is especially responsive to environmental influences. However, its boundaries are less well-defined than those of a critical period. Development can occur later, but it is harder to induce.

Inspired by observations of imprinting, British psychoanalyst John Bowlby (1969) applied ethological theory to the understanding of the human infant–caregiver relationship. He argued that infant smiling, babbling, grasping, and crying are built-in social signals that encourage the caregiver to approach, care for, and interact with the baby. By keeping the parent near, these behaviors help ensure that the infant will be fed, protected from danger, and provided with stimulation and affection necessary for healthy growth. The development of attachment in human infants is far more complex than imprinting in baby birds; it is a lengthy process that leads the baby to form a deep affectionate tie with the caregiver (Thompson, 2006). In Chapter 10, we will consider how infant, caregiver, and family context contribute to attachment and how attachment influences later development.

Observations by ethologists have shown that many aspects of children's social behavior, including emotional expressions, aggression, cooperation, and social play, resemble those of our primate relatives. Recently, researchers have extended this effort in a new area of research called **evolutionary developmental psychology.** It seeks to understand the adaptive value of species-wide cognitive, emotional, and social competencies as those competencies change with age (Geary, 2006b). Evolutionary developmental psychologists ask questions like these: What role does the newborn's visual preference for facelike stimuli play in survival? Does it support older infants' capacity to distinguish familiar caregivers from unfamiliar people? Why do children play in gender-segregated groups? What do they learn from such play that might lead to adult gender-typed behaviors, such as male dominance and female investment in caregiving?

As these examples suggest, evolutionary psychologists are not just concerned with the genetic and biological roots of development. They recognize that humans' large brain and extended childhood resulted from the need to master an increasingly complex environment, so they are also interested in learning (Bjorklund & Blasi, 2005). And they realize that today's lifestyles differ so radically from those of our evolutionary ancestors that certain evolved behaviors (such as life-threatening risk taking in adolescents and male-to-male violence) are no longer adaptive (Blasi & Bjorklund, 2003). By clarifying the origins and development of such behaviors, evolutionary developmental psychology may help spark more effective interventions.

In sum, evolutionary psychologists want to understand the entire *organism–environment system.* The next contextual perspective we will discuss, Vygotsky's sociocultural theory, serves as an excellent complement to the evolutionary viewpoint because it highlights social and cultural dimensions of children's experiences.

Vygotsky's Sociocultural Theory

The field of child development has recently seen a dramatic increase in studies addressing the cultural context of children's lives. Investigations that make comparisons across cultures, and between ethnic groups within cultures, provide insight into whether developmental pathways apply to all children or are limited to particular environmental conditions (Cole, 2005).

Today, much research is examining the relationship of *culturally specific beliefs and practices* to development. The contributions of Russian psychologist Lev Vygotsky (1896–1934) have played a major role in this trend. Vygotsky's (1934/1987) perspective, known as **sociocultural theory,** focuses on how *culture*—the values, beliefs, customs, and skills of a social group—is transmitted to the next generation. According to Vygotsky, *social interaction*—in particular, cooperative dialogues between children and more knowledgeable members of society—is necessary for children to acquire the ways of thinking and behaving that make up a community's culture (Rowe & Wertsch, 2002). Vygotsky believed that as adults and more-expert peers help children master culturally meaningful activities, the communication between them becomes part of children's thinking. As children internalize the features of these dialogues, they can use the language within them to guide their own thought and actions and to acquire new skills (Berk & Harris, 2003). The young child instructing herself while working a puzzle or preparing a table for dinner has begun to produce the same kind of guiding comments that an adult previously used to help her master important tasks.

Lev Vygotsky, pictured here with his daughter, believed many cognitive processes and skills are socially transferred from more knowledgeable members of society to children. Vygotsky's sociocultural theory helps explain the wide cultural variation in cognitive competencies. Courtesy of James V. Wertsch, Washington University in St. Louis

With her mother's guidance, this Navajo child learns to use a vertical weaving loom. According to Vygotsky's sociocultural theory, social interaction between children and more knowledgeable members of their culture leads to ways of thinking and behaving essential for success in that culture. © Paul Chesley/Getty Images/Stone

Vygotsky's theory has been especially influential in the study of children's cognition. Vygotsky agreed with Piaget that children are active, constructive beings. But whereas Piaget emphasized children's independent efforts to make sense of their world, Vygotsky viewed cognitive development as a *socially mediated process,* in which children depend on assistance from adults and more-expert peers as they tackle new challenges.

In Vygotsky's theory, children undergo certain stagewise changes. For example, when they acquire language, they gain in ability to participate in dialogues with others, and mastery of culturally valued competencies surges forward. When children enter school, they spend much time discussing language, literacy, and other academic concepts—experiences that encourage them to reflect on their own thinking (Bodrova & Leong, 2007; Kozulin, 2003). As a result, they gain dramatically in reasoning and problem solving.

At the same time, Vygotsky stressed that dialogues with experts lead to continuous changes in cognition that vary greatly from culture to culture. Consistent with this view, a major finding of cross-cultural research is that cultures select different tasks for children's learning (Rogoff, 2003). Social interaction surrounding those tasks leads to competencies essential for success in a particular culture. For example, in industrialized nations, teachers help people learn to read, drive a car, or use a computer. Among the Zinacanteco Indians of southern Mexico, adult experts guide young girls as they master complicated weaving techniques (Greenfield, 2004; Greenfield, Maynard, & Childs, 2000). In Brazil and other developing nations, child candy sellers with little or no schooling develop sophisticated mathematical abilities as the result of buying candy from wholesalers, pricing it in collaboration with adults and experienced peers, and bargaining with customers on city streets (Saxe, 1988). And as the research reported in the Cultural Influences box on the following page indicates, adults encourage culturally valued skills in children at a remarkably early age.

Research stimulated by Vygotsky's theory reveals that children in every culture develop unique strengths. But Vygotsky's emphasis on culture and social experience led him to neglect the biological side of development. Although he recognized the importance of heredity and brain growth, he said little about their role in cognitive change. Furthermore, Vygotsky's focus on social transmission of knowledge meant that, compared with other theorists, he placed less emphasis on children's capacity to shape their own development. Followers of Vygotsky stress that children actively participate in the conversations and social activities from which their development springs. From these joint experiences, they not only acquire culturally valued practices but also modify and transform those practices (Rogoff, 1998, 2003). Contemporary sociocultural theorists grant the individual and society balanced, mutually influential roles.

Ecological Systems Theory

Urie Bronfenbrenner (1917–2005) is responsible for an approach that has moved to the forefront of the field over the past two decades because it offers the most differentiated and complete account of contextual influences on children's development. **Ecological systems theory** views the child as developing within a complex *system* of relationships affected by multiple levels of the surrounding environment. Because the child's biologically influenced dispositions join with environmental forces to mold development, Bronfenbrenner recently characterized his perspective as a *bioecological model* (Bronfenbrenner, 2005; Bronfenbrenner & Morris, 2006).

Bronfenbrenner envisioned the environment as a series of nested structures, including but also extending beyond home, school, and neighborhood settings in which children spend their everyday lives (see Figure 1.4 on page 28). Each layer of the environment is viewed as having a powerful impact on development.

• **The Microsystem** The innermost level of the environment, the **microsystem,** consists of activities and interaction patterns in the child's immediate surroundings. Bronfenbrenner

Cultural Influences

!Kung Infancy: Acquiring Culture

Interactions between caregivers and infants take different forms in different cultures. Through those interactions, adults start to transmit their society's values and skills to the next generation, channeling the course of future development.

Focusing on a culture very different from our own, researchers studied how caregivers respond to infants' play with objects among the !Kung, a hunting-and-gathering society living in the desert regions of Botswana, Africa (Bakeman et al., 1990). Daily foraging missions take small numbers of adults several miles from the campground, but most obtain enough food to contribute to group survival by working only three out of every seven days. A mobile way of life also prevents the !Kung from collecting many possessions that require extensive care and maintenance. Adults have many free hours to relax around the campfire, and they spend it in intense social contact with one another and with children (Draper & Cashdan, 1988).

In this culture of intimate social bonds and minimal property, objects are valued as things to be shared, not as personal possessions. This message is conveyed to !Kung children at a very early age. Between 6 and 12 months, grandmothers start to train babies in the importance of exchanging objects by guiding them in handing beads to relatives. The child's first words generally include *i* ("Here, take this") and *na* ("Give it to me").

In !Kung society, no toys are made for infants. Instead, natural objects, such as twigs, grass, stones, and nutshells, are always available, along with cooking implements. However, adults do not encourage babies to play with these objects. In fact, adults are unlikely to interact with infants while they are exploring objects independently. But when a baby offers an object to another person, adults become highly responsive, encouraging and vocalizing much more than at other times. Thus, the !Kung cultural emphasis on the interpersonal rather than physical aspects of existence is reflected in how adults interact with the very youngest members of their community.

!Kung children grow up in a hunting-and-gathering society in which possessions are a burden rather than an asset. From an early age, children experience warm social contact with adults and are taught the importance of sharing. Here a !Kung baby enjoys a close, affectionate exchange with his grandmother.

TAKE A MOMENT... When you next have a chance, observe the conditions under which parents in your own society respond to infants' involvement with objects. How is parental responsiveness linked to cultural values? How does it compare with findings on the !Kung?

emphasized that to understand child development at this level, we must keep in mind that all relationships are *bidirectional:* Adults affect children's behavior, but children's biologically and socially influenced characteristics—their physical attributes, personalities, and capacities—also affect adults' behavior. For example, a friendly, attentive child is likely to evoke positive, patient reactions from parents, whereas an irritable or distractible child is more likely to receive impatience, restriction, and punishment. When these reciprocal interactions occur often over time, they have an enduring impact on development (Collins et al., 2000; Crockenberg & Leerkes, 2003b).

At the same time, *third parties*—other individuals in the microsystem—affect the quality of any two-person relationship. If they are supportive, interaction is enhanced. For example, when parents encourage one another in their child-rearing roles, each engages in more effective parenting. In contrast, when a marriage is tense and hostile, parents often interfere with one another's child-rearing efforts, are less responsive to children's needs, and criticize, express anger, and punish (Cox, Paley, & Harter, 2001; McHale et al., 2002). Similarly, children can affect their parents' relationship in powerful ways. For example, as Chapter 14 will reveal, divorce is often associated with lasting adjustment problems. Yet long before the marital breakup, some children were impulsive and defiant. These behaviors may have contributed to, as well as been caused by, their parents' marital problems (Strohschein, 2005).

• **The Mesosystem** The second level of Bronfenbrenner's model, the **mesosystem,** encompasses connections between microsystems, such as home, school, neighborhood, and child-care center. For example, a child's academic progress depends not just on activities that

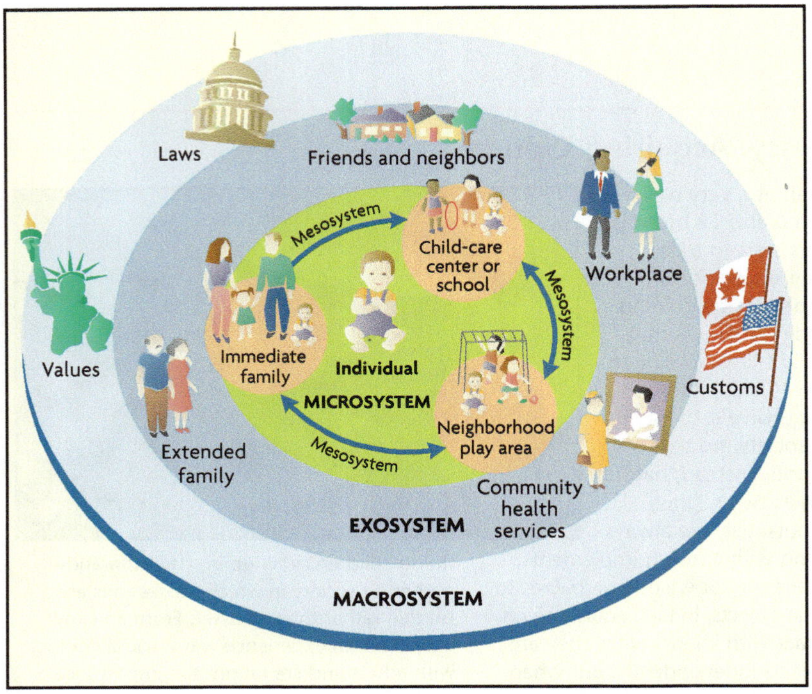

Figure 1.4 Structure of the environment in ecological systems theory.

The *microsystem* concerns relations between the child and the immediate environment; the *mesosystem,* connections among immediate settings; the *exosystem,* social settings that affect but do not contain the child; and the *macrosystem,* the values, laws, customs, and resources of the culture that affect activities and interactions at all inner layers. The *chronosystem* (not pictured) is not a specific context. Instead, it refers to the dynamic, ever-changing nature of the person's environment.

take place in classrooms. It is also promoted by parent involvement in school life and the extent to which academic learning is carried over into the home (Gershoff & Aber, 2006). Similarly, parent–child interaction at home is likely to affect caregiver–child interaction in the child-care setting, and vice versa. Each relationship is more likely to support development when there are links, in the form of visits and cooperative exchanges of information, between home and child care.

Family–neighborhood connections are especially important for economically disadvantaged children. Affluent families are less dependent on their immediate surroundings for social support, education, and leisure pursuits. They can afford to transport their children to lessons and entertainment and even, if necessary, to better-quality schools in distant parts of the community (Elliott et al., 1996). In low-income neighborhoods, in-school and after-school programs that substitute for lack of other resources by providing child care and art, music, sports, scouting, and other enrichment activities are associated with improved school performance and a reduction in emotional and behavior problems in middle childhood (Peters, Petrunka, & Arnold, 2003; Vandell & Posner, 1999). Neighborhood organizations, such as religious youth groups and special-interest clubs, contribute to favorable development in adolescence, including self-confidence, school achievement, educational aspirations, and responsible social behavior (Gonzales et al., 1996; Kerestes & Youniss, 2003).

• **The Exosystem** The **exosystem** consists of social settings that do not contain children but that nevertheless affect children's experiences in immediate settings. These can be formal organizations, such as parents' workplaces, their religious institutions, and health and welfare services in the community. For example, parents' work settings can support child rearing and, indirectly, enhance development through flexible work schedules, paid maternity and paternity leave, and sick leave for parents whose children are ill. Exosystem supports also can be informal, such as parents' social networks—friends and extended-family members who provide advice, companionship, and even financial assistance. Research confirms the negative impact of a breakdown in exosystem activities. Families who are affected by unemployment or are socially isolated, with few personal or community-based ties, show increased rates of conflict and child abuse (Werkele & Wolfe, 2003).

• **The Macrosystem** The outermost level of Bronfenbrenner's model, the **macrosystem,** consists of cultural values, laws, customs, and resources. The priority that the macrosystem gives to children's needs affects the support

Family–neighborhood connections—at the level of the mesosystem in ecological systems theory—enhance development. These children proudly carry traditional banners in a Chinese New Year parade in Vancouver, British Columbia. © PhotoBliss/Alamy

they receive at inner levels of the environment. For example, in countries that require generous workplace benefits for employed parents and set high standards for the quality of child care, children are more likely to have favorable experiences in their immediate settings. As you will see later in this chapter and in other parts of this book, such programs are far less available in the United States than in Canada and other industrialized nations (Children's Defense Fund, 2005; Waldfogel, 2001).

• **An Ever-Changing System** According to Bronfenbrenner, the environment is not a static force that affects children in a uniform way. Instead, it is ever-changing. Important life events, such as the birth of a sibling, the beginning of school, a move to a new neighborhood, or parents' divorce, modify existing relationships between children and their environments, producing new conditions that affect development. In addition, the timing of environmental change affects its impact. The arrival of a new sibling has very different consequences for a homebound toddler than for a school-age child with many relationships and activities beyond the family.

Bronfenbrenner called the temporal dimension of his model the **chronosystem** (the prefix *chrono-* means "time"). Changes in life events can be imposed on the child, as in the examples just given. Alternatively, they can arise from within the child, since as children get older they select, modify, and create many of their own settings and experiences. How they do so depends on their physical, intellectual, and personality characteristics and their environmental opportunities. Therefore, in ecological systems theory, development is neither controlled by environmental circumstances nor driven solely by inner dispositions. Rather, children are both products and producers of their environments: The child and the environment form a network of interdependent effects. Notice how our discussion of resilient children on pages 10–11 illustrates this idea. You will see many more examples throughout this book.

New Directions: Development as a Dynamic System

Today, researchers recognize both consistency and variability in children's development and want to do a better job of explaining variation. Consequently, a new wave of theorists has adopted a **dynamic systems perspective.** According to this view, the child's mind, body, and physical and social worlds form an *integrated system* that guides mastery of new skills. The system is *dynamic*, or constantly in motion. A change in any part of it—from brain growth to physical and social surroundings—disrupts the current organism–environment relationship. When this happens, the child actively reorganizes her behavior so the components of the system work together again but in a more complex, effective way (Fischer & Bidell, 2006; Spencer & Schöner, 2003; Thelen & Smith, 2006).

Researchers adopting a dynamic systems perspective try to find out just how children attain new levels of organization by studying their behavior while they are in transition (Thelen & Corbetta, 2002). For example, when presented with an attractive toy, how does a 3-month-old baby who shows many, varied movements discover how to reach for it? On hearing a new word, how does a 2-year-old figure out the category of objects or events to which it refers?

Dynamic systems theorists acknowledge that a common human genetic heritage and basic regularities in children's physical and social worlds yield certain universal, broad outlines of development. But biological makeup, everyday tasks, and the people who support children in mastery of those tasks vary greatly, leading to wide individual differences in specific skills. Even when children master the same skills, such as walking, talking, or adding and subtracting, they often do so in unique ways. And because children build competencies by engaging in real activities in real contexts, different skills vary in maturity within the same child. From this perspective, development cannot be characterized as a single line of change. As Figure 1.5 shows, it is more like a web of fibers branching out in many directions, each representing a different skill area

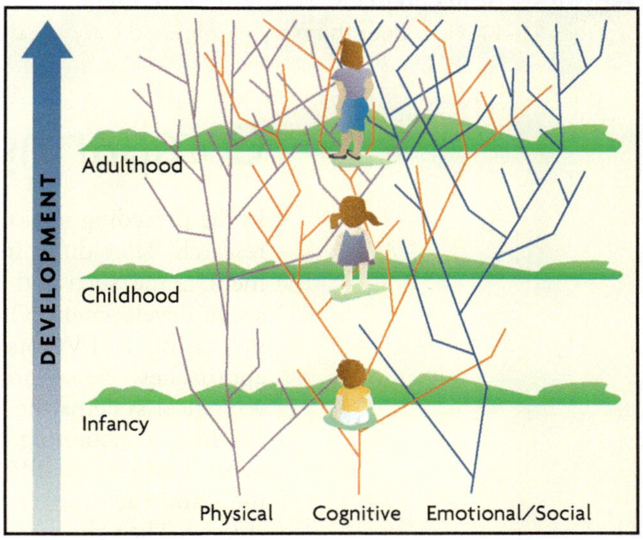

■ **Figure 1.5** **The dynamic systems view of development.** Rather than envisioning a single line of stagewise or continuous change (refer to Figure 1.2 on page 7), dynamic systems theorists conceive of development as a web of fibers branching out in many directions. Each strand in the web represents a skill within the major domains of development—physical, cognitive, and emotional/social. The differing directions of the strands signify possible variations in paths and outcomes as the child masters skills necessary to participate in diverse contexts. The interconnections of the strands at each row of "hills" portray stagelike changes—periods of major transformation in which various skills work together as a functioning whole. As the web expands, skills become more numerous, complex, and effective. (Adapted from Fischer & Bidell, 2006.)

The dynamic systems perspective views the child's mind, body, and physical and social worlds as a continually reorganizing, integrated system. A change in any part of the system disrupts the current organism–environment relationship. As he experiences the physical, cognitive, and emotional changes of early adolescence, this boy and his father must devise new, more mature ways of relating to one another.
© Bonnie Kamin/PhotoEdit

that may undergo continuous and stagewise transformations (Fischer & Bidell, 2006).

The dynamic systems view has been inspired by other scientific disciplines, especially biology and physics. It also draws on information-processing and contextual theories—evolutionary developmental psychology, sociocultural theory, and ecological systems theory. Dynamic systems research is still in its early stages. The perspective has largely been applied to children's motor and cognitive skills, but some investigators have drawn on it to explain emotional and social development as well (Campos, Frankel, & Camras, 2004; Fogel & Garvey, 2007; Lewis, 2000). Consider the young teenager, whose body and reasoning powers are changing massively and who also is confronting the challenges of secondary school. Researchers following parent–child interaction over time found that the transition to adolescence disrupted family communication. It became unstable and variable for several years—a mix of positive, neutral, and negative exchanges. Gradually, as parent and adolescent devised new, more mature ways of relating to one another, the system reorganized and stabilized. Once again, interaction became predictable and mostly positive (Granic et al., 2003).

As dynamic systems research illustrates, today investigators are tracking and analyzing development in all its complexity. In doing so, they hope to move closer to an all-encompassing approach to understanding change.

Ask Yourself

Review Explain how each recent theoretical perspective regards children as active contributors to their own development.

Apply Mario wants to find out precisely how children of different ages recall stories. Anna is interested in how adult–child communication in different cultures influences children's storytelling. Which theoretical perspective has Mario probably chosen? How about Anna? Explain.

Connect Return to the Biology and Environment box on pages 10–11. How does the story of John and Gary illustrate bidirectional influences within the microsystem, as described in ecological systems theory?

Reflect To illustrate the chronosystem in ecological systems theory, select an important event from your childhood, such as a move to a new neighborhood, a class with an inspiring teacher, or parental divorce. How did the event affect you? How might its impact have differed had you been five years younger? How about five years older?

Comparing Child Development Theories

In the preceding sections, we reviewed major theoretical perspectives in child development research. They differ in many respects. First, they focus on different domains of development. Some, such as the psychoanalytic perspective and ethology, emphasize emotional and social development. Others, such as Piaget's cognitive-developmental theory, information processing, and Vygotsky's sociocultural theory, stress changes in thinking. The remaining approaches—behaviorism, social learning theory, evolutionary developmental psychology, ecological systems theory, and the dynamic systems perspective—discuss many aspects of children's functioning. Second, every theory contains a point of view about child development. **TAKE A MOMENT...** As we conclude our review of theoretical perspectives, identify the stand each theory takes on the controversial issues presented at the beginning of this chapter. Then check your analysis against Table 1.4.

Table 1.4 Stances of Major Theories on Basic Issues in Child Development

Theory	Continuous or Discontinuous Development?	One Course of Development or Many?	Nature or Nurture as More Important?
Psychoanalytic perspective	*Discontinuous:* Psychosexual and psychosocial development takes place in stages.	*One course:* Stages are assumed to be universal.	*Both nature and nurture:* Innate impulses are channeled and controlled through child-rearing experiences. *Early experiences* set the course of later development.
Behaviorism and social learning theory	*Continuous:* Development involves an increase in learned behaviors.	*Many possible courses:* Behaviors reinforced and modeled may vary from child to child.	*Emphasis on nurture:* Development results from conditioning and modeling. *Both early and later experiences* are important.
Piaget's cognitive-developmental theory	*Discontinuous:* Cognitive development takes place in stages.	*One course:* Stages are assumed to be universal.	*Both nature and nurture:* Development occurs as the brain matures and children exercise their innate drive to discover reality in a generally stimulating environment. *Both early and later experiences* are important.
Information processing	*Continuous:* Children gradually improve in perception, attention, memory, and problem-solving skills.	*One course:* Changes studied characterize most or all children.	*Both nature and nurture:* Children are active, sense-making beings who modify their thinking as the brain develops and they confront new environmental demands. *Both early and later experiences* are important.
Ethology and evolutionary developmental psychology	*Both continuous and discontinuous:* Children gradually develop a wider range of adaptive behaviors. Sensitive periods occur, in which qualitatively distinct capacities emerge fairly suddenly.	*One course:* Adaptive behaviors and sensitive periods apply to all members of a species.	*Both nature and nurture:* Evolution and heredity influence behavior, and learning lends greater flexibility and adaptiveness to it. In sensitive periods, *early experiences* set the course of later development.
Vygotsky's sociocultural theory	*Both continuous and discontinuous:* Language acquisition and schooling lead to stagewise changes. Dialogues with more expert members of society also lead to continuous changes that vary from culture to culture.	*Many possible courses:* Socially mediated changes in thought and behavior vary from culture to culture.	*Both nature and nurture:* Heredity, brain growth, and dialogues with more expert members of society jointly contribute to development. *Both early and later experiences* are important.
Ecological systems theory	*Not specified.*	*Many possible courses:* Children's characteristics join with environmental forces at multiple levels to mold development in unique ways.	*Both nature and nurture:* Children's characteristics and the reactions of others affect each other in a bidirectional fashion. Layers of the environment influence child-rearing experiences. *Both early and later experiences* are important.
Dynamic systems perspective	*Both continuous and discontinuous:* Change in the system is always ongoing. Stagelike transformations occur as children reorganize their behavior so components of the system work as a functioning whole.	*Many possible courses:* Biological makeup, everyday tasks, and social experiences vary, yielding wide individual differences in specific skills.	*Both nature and nurture:* The child's mind, body, and physical and social surroundings form an integrated system that guides mastery of new skills. *Both early and later experiences* are important.

Finally, we have seen that every theory has strengths and limitations. Perhaps you find that you are attracted to some theories, but you have doubts about others. As you read more about child development in later chapters, you may find it useful to keep a notebook in which you test your theoretical likes and dislikes against the evidence. Don't be surprised if you revise your ideas many times, just as theorists have done throughout the past century. By the end of this course, you will have built your own personal perspective on child development. Very likely, it will be an *eclectic position,* or blend of several theories because every viewpoint we have considered has contributed to what we know about children.

Applied Directions: Child Development and Social Policy

In recent years, the field of child development has become increasingly concerned with applying its vast knowledge base to solving pressing social problems. Today, we know much more than ever before about family, school, and community contexts that foster physically healthy and cognitively and socially competent children. Yet a nation's values, policies, and programs powerfully affect children's experiences in these immediate contexts.

Social policy is any planned set of actions by a group, institution, or governing body directed at attaining a social goal. When widespread social problems arise, nations attempt to solve them through a special type of social policy called **public policy**—laws and government programs aimed at improving current conditions. Return to Bronfenbrenner's ecological systems theory, and note how the concept of the macrosystem suggests that sound public policies are essential for protecting children's well-being. For example, when poverty increases and families become homeless, a country might decide to build more low-cost housing, raise the minimum wage, and increase welfare benefits. When reports indicate that many children are not achieving well in school, federal and state or provincial governments might grant more tax money to school districts, strengthen teacher preparation, and make sure that help reaches children who need it most at the earliest possible age.

U.S. and Canadian public policies safeguarding children and youths have lagged behind policies in other developed nations. A striking indicator is that about 18 percent of U.S. and 12 percent of Canadian children are poor—rates that climb to 32 percent for Native-American children, 34 percent for African-American and Hispanic children, and as high as 30 to 40 percent for Canadian Aboriginal children,[1] depending on the specific poverty measure used (Statistics Canada, 2007a, 2007h). Families hit hardest are parents under age 25 with young children. For single mothers with infants and preschoolers, the poverty rate in the United States is nearly 50 percent, in Canada 30 percent (Canada Campaign 2000, 2007; U.S. Census Bureau, 2007b).

Of all Western nations, the United States has the highest percentage of extremely poor children. More than 6 percent of U.S. children live in deep poverty (well below the poverty threshold, the income level judged necessary for a minimum living standard), compared with 2.5 percent in Canada. However, these circumstances are worrisome in both countries because the earlier poverty begins, the deeper it is, and the longer it lasts, the more devastating are its effects. Children of poverty are more likely than other children to suffer from lifelong poor physical health, persistent deficits in cognitive development and academic achievement, high school dropout, mental illness, and antisocial behavior (Aber, Jones, & Raver, 2007; Dearing, McCartney, & Taylor, 2006; Ryan, Fauth, & Brooks-Gunn, 2006).

In Los Angeles, a 4-year-old waits to receive a "back-to-school" give-away from an organization that provides new clothing, shoes, and school supplies to poverty-stricken children. The program's goal of meeting children's material needs helps counter their underprivileged home lives, which—combined with unfavorable school and community conditions—put children at risk for academic and social problems. AP Images/Kevork Djansezian

As Table 1.5 reveals, the United States does not rank well on any key measure of children's health and well-being. Canada fares somewhat better, devoting considerably more of its resources to education and health. For example, all Canadian citizens have access to government-funded health care.

The problems of children and youths extend beyond the indicators in Table 1.5. The United States is the only industrialized nation in the world that does not have a universal, publicly funded health-care system. Hence,

[1] Aboriginal peoples in Canada include three groups: (1) First Nations, or Native Canadian peoples; (2) Inuit, most of whom live in northern Canada; and (3) Métis, or mixed-blood people of both Native Canadian and European descent.

Table 1.5 How Do the United States and Canada Compare to Other Nations on Indicators of Children's Health and Well-Being?

Indicator	U.S. Rank[a]	Canadian Rank[a]	Some Countries the United States and Canada Trail
Childhood poverty (among 23 industrialized nations considered)	23rd	16th	Czech Republic, Germany, Norway, Sweden, Spain[b]
Infant deaths in the first year of life (worldwide)	26th	16th	Hong Kong, Ireland, Singapore, Spain
Teenage birth rate (among 28 industrialized nations considered)	28th	21st	*For Canada:* Albania, Australia, Czech Republic, Denmark, Poland, Netherlands *For the U.S.:* Iceland, Portugal, Hungary, Slovak Republic
Public expenditures on education as a percentage of gross domestic product[c] (among 22 industrialized nations considered)	10th	6th	*For Canada:* Israel, Sweden *For the U.S.:* Australia, France, New Zealand, Sweden
Public expenditures on early childhood education and child care as a percentage of gross domestic product[c] (among 14 industrialized nations considered)	9th	14th	Austria, Germany, Italy, Netherlands, France, Sweden
Public expenditures on health as a percentage of gross domestic product[c] (among 22 industrialized nations considered)	16th	4th	*For Canada:* France, Iceland, Switzerland *For the U.S.:* Austria, Australia, Hungary, New Zealand

[a]1 = highest, or best, rank.

[b]U.S. and Canadian childhood poverty and, especially, depth of poverty in the United States greatly exceed poverty rates in these nations. For example, the poverty rate is 6 percent in the Czech Republic, 4 percent in Norway, and 2.5 percent in Sweden.

[c]Gross domestic product is the value of all goods and services produced by a nation during a specified time period. It provides an overall measure of a nation's wealth.

Sources: Luxembourg Income Study, 2005; OECD, 2006; Perie et al., 2000; UNICEF, 2001; U.S. Census Bureau, 2007b; U.S. Department of Education, 2007.

approximately 11 percent of U.S. children—most of them in low-income families—have no health insurance (National Coalition on Health Care, 2007). Furthermore, both the United States and Canada have been slow to move toward national standards and funding for child care. In both countries, affordable child care is in short supply, and much of it is substandard in quality (Goelman et al., 2000; Muenchow & Marsland, 2007; OECD, 2006). In families affected by divorce, weak enforcement of child support payments heightens poverty in mother-headed households. By the time they finish high school, many North American non-college-bound young people do not have the vocational preparation they need to contribute fully to society. And by ages 18 to 20, about 11 percent of U.S. and Canadian adolescents have not yet earned a high school diploma (Bushnik, Barr-Telford, & Bussiére, 2004; U.S. Department of Education, 2007). Most high school dropouts are from low-income families and have a long history of poor academic achievement, lack of interest in schoolwork, and low academic self-esteem. Those who do not return to finish their education are at risk for lifelong poverty.

Why have attempts to help children and youths been difficult to realize in the United States and (to a lesser extent) Canada? A complex set of cultural, political, and economic forces is involved.

Culture and Public Policies

TAKE A MOMENT... Consider the question, Who should be responsible for rearing young children? How would you answer it? Here are some typical responses from my students: "If parents decide to have a baby, then they should be ready to care for it." "Most people are not happy about others intruding into family life." "If parents work hard, then they won't need government assistance." These statements reflect a widely held opinion in North America—that the care and rearing of young children, and paying for that care, are the duty of parents, and only parents. This view has a long history—one in which independence, self-reliance, and the privacy of family life emerged as central North American values (Halfon & McLearn, 2002). It is one reason, among others, that the public has been slow to endorse government-supported benefits for all families, such as high-quality child care. And it has also contributed to the large number of U.S. and Canadian children who remain poor, even though their parent or parents are gainfully employed (Gruendel & Aber, 2007; Pohl, 2002; Statistics Canada, 2007a).

Consider our discussion so far, and you will see that it reflects cultural variation in values that strongly influence public policies: the extent to which *individualism* versus *collectivism* prevails. In **individualistic societies,** people think of themselves as separate entities and are largely concerned with their own personal needs. In **collectivist societies,** people define themselves as part of a group and stress group goals over individual goals (Triandis, 1995). Although individualism tends to increase as cultures become more complex, cross-national differences remain. The United States is strongly individualistic, while Canada falls in between the United States and most Western European nations, which lean toward collectivism.

Furthermore, less consensus exists among North American than among European citizens on issues of child and family policy, resulting in fewer and more limited programs—ones that usually target only the most economically disadvantaged and leave many needy children unserved (Ripple & Zigler, 2003). And good social programs are expensive; they must compete for a fair share of a country's economic resources. Children can easily remain unrecognized because they cannot vote or speak out to protect their own interests, as adult citizens do. Instead, they must rely on the goodwill of others to make them an important government priority.

Without vigilance from child advocates, policies directed at solving one social problem can work at cross-purposes with children's well-being, leaving them in dire straits or worsening their condition. Consider, for example, welfare reforms aimed at returning welfare recipients to the work force. As the Social Issues box on the following page makes clear, these policies can help or harm children, depending on whether they lift a family out of poverty.

Contributions of Child Development Research

As the evidence in the Social Issues box suggests, for a policy to be effective in meeting children's needs, research must guide it at every step—during design, implementation, and evaluation of the program. Events of the 1960s and 1970s initiated the current trend toward greater involvement of child development researchers in the policy process (Phillips & Styfco, 2007).

For example, in 1965, research on the importance of early experiences for children's intellectual development played a major role in the founding of Project Head Start, the largest educational and family-services intervention program for poverty-stricken preschool children in the United States. In Chapter 8, we will see that several decades of research on the long-term benefits of Head Start helped the program survive, contributed to recent increased government support, and inspired the Aboriginal Head Start Program in Canada. In another instance, findings on the severe impact of malnutrition on early brain development stimulated government-sponsored supplemental food programs. Since the 1970s, the U.S. Special Supplemental Food Program for Women, Infants, and Children (WIC) and the Canadian Prenatal Nutrition Program (CPNP) have supplied poverty-stricken women and their young children with food packages, nutrition education, breastfeeding support, and referral to health and social services.

As researchers examined the impact of child and family services, they saw how settings remote from children's daily lives affect their well-being. As a result, investigators broadened their focus to include wider social contexts, such as workplace, community, mass media, and government. They also addressed the impact of societal changes on children, including high rates of poverty, divorce, family violence, teenage parenthood, maternal employment, and nonparental child care. All these efforts have helped to refine existing policies, inspire new initiatives, and expand our understanding of child development.

Between 1960 and 2000, the number of policy-relevant articles in *Child Development,* one of the field's leading scientific journals, increased fivefold (Phillips & Styfco, 2007). The field of child development now recognizes that sound public policy is among the most powerful tools for preventing developmental problems and enhancing children's quality of life.

Social Issues

Welfare Reform, Poverty, and Child Development

In the mid-1990s, the United States and Canada both changed their welfare policies, instituting welfare-to-work programs that ended decades of guaranteed government financial aid to needy families. In these new systems, recipients must go to work or face reduced or terminated benefits. The goal is to encourage families on welfare to become self-sufficient. The U.S. program is strictly time-limited. A family can be on welfare for only 24 continuous months, with a lifetime limit of 60 months, and the states can further restrict these benefits. For example, a state can prevent payments from increasing if recipients have more children, and it can deny teenage single mothers any benefits.

Canadian welfare policies, while also strongly employment focused, are more flexible. In Ontario, for example, welfare recipients must actively look for a job, participate in community volunteer work while acquiring work skills, and take any paid work offered if they are physically capable of performing it. In contrast to the U.S. policy, however, a Canadian family's benefits increase if family size increases, although several provinces have reduced these payments (National Forum on Welfare to Work, 2004).

Until recently, most evaluations of welfare-to-work focused on declines in the number of families on the welfare rolls. By these standards, welfare-to-work seemed to be a resounding success. But as researchers looked more closely, they found that some people made successful transitions to financial independence—typically, those who had more schooling and fewer mental health problems. Others, however, had difficulty meeting work requirements, lost their benefits, and fell deeper into poverty. Consequently, as welfare caseloads declined, the incomes of the poorest single-mother families dropped sharply (Lindsey & Martin, 2003).

Designers of welfare-to-work assumed it would be beneficial for children. But moving off welfare without increasing family income poses serious risks to child development. In one study, mothers who left welfare and also left poverty engaged in more positive parenting and had preschoolers who showed more favorable cognitive development, compared with working mothers whose incomes remained below the poverty threshold. Among these mothers, harsh, coercive parenting remained high (Smith et al., 2001).

This mother, who lives with her young daughter in public housing, depends on welfare benefits to make ends meet. Since the mid-1990s, the United States has cut back on programs guaranteeing aid to needy families, making it difficult for poverty-stricken parents to meet their children's physical, cognitive, and emotional needs.
© Dan Atkin/Alamy

In other research, families who moved from welfare to a combination of welfare and work experienced a greater reduction in young children's behavior problems than families who moved to total reliance on work (Dunifon, Kalil, & Danziger, 2003; Gennetian & Morris, 2003). Why was the welfare–work combination so beneficial? Most welfare recipients must take unstable jobs with erratic work hours and minimal or no benefits. Working while retaining some welfare support probably gave mothers an added sense of economic stability. In the United States, it also sustained government-provided health insurance (Medicaid), a major source of U.S. parents' worry about leaving welfare (Slack et al., 2007). The resulting reduction of financial anxiety seemed to enhance children's adjustment.

In sum, welfare reform promotes children's development only when it results in a more adequate standard of living. Punitive aspects of welfare-to-work that reduce or cut off benefits push families deeper into poverty, with destructive consequences for children's well-being. Because of a shortage of affordable child care in the United States and Canada (care for one child can consume 50 percent or more of a minimum-wage earner's income), mothers of young children are least able to earn enough by working. Yet poverty is most harmful to development when it occurs early in life (see page 32).

Welfare policies in other Western nations do not just encourage parents to be better providers. They also protect children from the damaging effects of poverty. France, for example, guarantees most of its citizens a modest minimum income. Single parents receive an extra amount during their child's first three years—a benefit that acknowledges a special need for income support during this period. Government-funded, high-quality child care begins at age 3, enabling mothers to go to work knowing that their children's development is supported (Duncan & Brooks-Gunn, 2000).

Canada offers working parents more generous tax refunds than are available in the United States. Still, widespread poverty in both nations underscores the need for more effective poverty prevention policies—ones that help poor families rear children while they move toward financial independence.

Looking Toward the Future

The Children's Defense Fund is the most vigorous interest group working for the well-being of children in the United States. This poster dramatizes the fact that millions of U.S. children have no health insurance. Courtesy of Children's Defense Fund

Policies aimed at fostering children's development can be justified on two grounds. The first is that children are the future—the parents, workers, and citizens of tomorrow. Investing in children yields valuable returns to a nation's economy and quality of life (Heckman & Masterov, 2004).

Second, child-oriented policies can be defended on humanitarian grounds—children's basic rights as human beings. In 1989, the United Nations General Assembly, with the assistance of experts from many child-related fields, drew up the *Convention on the Rights of the Child,* a legal agreement among nations that commits each cooperating country to work toward guaranteeing environments that foster children's development, protect them from harm, and enhance their community participation and self-determination. Examples of rights include the highest attainable standard of health; an adequate standard of living; free and compulsory education; a happy, understanding, and loving family life; protection from all forms of abuse and neglect; and freedom of thought, conscience, and religion, subject to appropriate parental guidance and national law.

Canada's Parliament ratified the Convention in 1991. Although the United States played a key role in drawing up the Convention, it is one of only two countries in the world whose legislature has not yet ratified it. (The other is war-torn Somalia, which currently does not have a recognized national government.) U.S. individualism has stood in the way. Opponents maintain that the Convention's provisions would shift the burden of child rearing from the family to the state (Melton, 2005).

Although the worrisome state of many children and families persists, efforts are being made to improve their condition. Throughout this book, we will discuss many successful programs that could be expanded. Also, growing awareness of the gap between what we know and what we do to better children's lives has led experts in child development to join with concerned citizens as advocates for more effective policies. As a result, several influential interest groups devoted to the well-being of children have emerged.

In the United States, the most vigorous of these groups is the Children's Defense Fund. This private, nonprofit organization founded by Marian Wright Edelman in 1973 engages in research, public education, legal action, drafting of legislation, congressional testimony, and community organizing. Among its publications is *The State of America's Children,* which provides a comprehensive analysis of children's condition, including government-sponsored programs that serve children and families and proposals for improving those programs. To learn more about the Children's Defense Fund, visit its website at *www.childrensdefense.org.*

In 1991, Canada initiated a public education movement, called Campaign 2000, to build nationwide awareness of the extent and consequences of child poverty and to lobby government representatives for improved policies benefiting children. Diverse organizations—including professional, religious, health, and labor groups at national, provincial, and community levels—have joined forces to work toward campaign goals. These

Campaign 2000 is Canada's public education movement aimed at building national awareness of the extent of child poverty and the need to improve policies benefiting children. This Campaign 2000 poster calls for a national poverty reduction strategy. Courtesy of Campaign 2000—End Child & Family Poverty in Canada, www.campaign2000.ca

include raising basic living standards so no child lives in poverty, ensuring each child affordable, appropriate housing, and strengthening child care and other community resources that assist families in rearing children. Consult *www.campaign2000.ca* to explore the work of Campaign 2000, including its annual *Report Card on Child Poverty in Canada.*

Finally, more researchers are collaborating with community and government agencies to enhance the social relevance of their investigations. They are also doing a better job of disseminating their findings to the public in easily understandable, compelling ways, through television documentaries, newspaper stories, magazine articles, websites, and direct reports to government officials (Gruendel & Aber, 2007). As a result, they are helping to create the sense of immediacy about the condition of children and families that is necessary to spur a society into action.

Ask Yourself

Review Explain why both strong advocacy and policy-relevant research are vital for designing and implementing public policies that meet children's needs.

Apply Check your local newspaper or one or two national news magazines to see how often articles on the condition of children and families appear. Why is it important for researchers to communicate with the general public about children's needs?

Connect Give an example of how cultural values and economic decisions affect child-oriented public policies. What level of Bronfenbrenner's ecological systems theory contains these influences?

Reflect Do you agree with the widespread North American sentiment that government should not become involved in family life? Explain.

SUMMARY

The Field of Child Development

What is the field of child development, and what factors stimulated expansion of the field?

- **Child development** is a field devoted to understanding human constancy and change from conception through adolescence. It is part of the larger, interdisciplinary field **developmental science,** which includes changes throughout the lifespan.
- Child development research has been stimulated by both scientific curiosity and social pressures to improve the lives of children.

How is child development typically divided into domains and periods?

- Child development often is divided into three broad domains: (1) physical, (2) cognitive, and (3) emotional and social. These domains are not really distinct; they form an integrated whole.
- Researchers generally segment child development into five periods, each bringing new capacities and social expectations that serve as important transitions in major theories: (1) the prenatal period (conception to birth), (2) infancy and toddlerhood (birth to 2 years), (3) early childhood (2 to 6 years), (4) middle childhood (6 to 11 years), and (5) adolescence (11 to 18 years). Many contemporary youths in industrialized nations experience an additional period of development, emerging adulthood (18 to 25 years), in which they engage in further exploration before fully assuming adult roles.

Basic Issues

Identify three basic issues on which child development theories take a stand.

- Almost all child development **theories** take a stand on three controversial issues: (1) Is development a **continuous** process, or is it **discontinuous,** taking place in discrete, qualitatively distinct **stages**? (2) Does one general course of development characterize all children, or do many possible courses exist, depending on the **contexts** in which children grow up? (3) Does development depend more on genetic or environmental factors—the **nature–nurture controversy**—and is it stable or open to change?
- Contemporary theorists take a balanced stand on these issues, recognizing that answers may vary across domains of development and even, as research on **resilience** illustrates, across individuals.

Historical Foundations

Describe major historical influences on current theories of child development.

- Contemporary theories of child development have roots as far back as medieval times, when childhood was already regarded as a separate phase of life. In the sixteenth and seventeenth centuries, the Puritan conception of original sin led to a harsh philosophy of child rearing. The Enlightenment brought more humane ideas about treatment of children.
- Locke's notion of the child as a **tabula rasa,** provided the philosophical basis for twentieth-century behaviorism, while Rousseau's idea that children are **noble savages** included the concepts of stage and **maturation.**
- A century later, Darwin's theory emphasized the adaptive value of physical characteristics and behavior and stimulated scientific child study.
- Efforts to observe children directly began in the late nineteenth and early twentieth centuries with baby biographies. Soon after, Hall and Gesell introduced the **normative approach,** which produced a large body of descriptive facts about children.
- Binet and Simon constructed the first successful intelligence test, which sparked interest in individual differences in development and led to a heated controversy over nature versus nurture. Baldwin's theory was ahead of its time in granting nature and nurture equal importance and regarding children and their social surroundings as mutually influential.

Mid-Twentieth-Century Theories

What theories influenced the study of child development in the mid-twentieth century?

- In the 1930s and 1940s, psychiatrists and social workers turned to the **psychoanalytic perspective** for help in treating children's emotional and behavior problems. In Freud's **psychosexual theory,** children move through five stages, during which three parts of the personality—*id, ego,* and *superego*—become integrated.
- Erikson's **psychosocial theory** builds on Freud's theory by emphasizing the ego as a positive force in development, the development of culturally relevant attitudes and skills, and the lifespan nature of development.
- As the psychoanalytic perspective gained in prominence, **behaviorism** emerged in an effort to create an objective science of psychology. Skinner's operant conditioning theory emphasizes the role of reinforcement and punishment in increasing or decreasing the frequency of a behavior.

© Margot Granitsas/The Image Works

- Bandura's **social learning theory,** focuses on modeling as the major means through which children acquire new responses. Its most recent revision, which stresses the role of cognition in children's imitation and learning, is described as a social-cognitive approach. Behaviorism and social learning theory gave rise to **behavior modification** to eliminate undesirable behaviors and increase desirable responses.
- Piaget's **cognitive-developmental theory** emphasizes that children actively construct knowledge as they manipulate and explore their world. According to Piaget, children move through four stages, beginning with the baby's sensorimotor action patterns and ending with the elaborate, abstract reasoning system of the adolescent and adult. Piaget's theory has stimulated a wealth of research on children's thinking and encouraged educational programs that emphasize discovery learning.

Recent Theoretical Perspectives

Describe recent theoretical perspectives on child development.

- **Information processing** views the mind as a complex, symbol-manipulating system, much like a computer. This approach helps researchers understand exactly what children of different ages do when faced with tasks and problems. Information processing has led to teaching interventions that help children approach tasks in more advanced ways.
- Over the past two decades, researchers in **developmental cognitive neuroscience** have begun to study the relationship between changes in the brain and the developing child's cognitive processing and behavior patterns. They have made progress in identifying the types of experiences to which the brain is sensitive at various ages and in clarifying the brain bases of many learning and behavior disorders.
- Four perspectives emphasize contexts for development. **Ethology** stresses the evolutionary origins and adaptive value of behavior and inspired the **sensitive period** concept. In **evolutionary developmental psychology,** researchers have extended this emphasis, seeking to understand the adaptiveness of species-wide competencies as they change over time.
- Vygotsky's **sociocultural theory,** which views cognitive development as a socially mediated process, has enhanced our understanding of cultural variation. Through cooperative dialogues with more expert members of society, children use language to guide their own thought and actions and acquire culturally relevant knowledge and skills.
- Bronfenbrenner's **ecological systems theory** views the child as developing within a complex system of relationships affected by multiple, nested layers of the environment—**microsystem, mesosystem, exosystem,** and **macrosystem.** The **chronosystem** represents the dynamic, ever-changing nature of children and their experiences.

© Photo Bliss/Alamy

- Inspired by ideas in other sciences and recent perspectives in child development, a new wave of theorists has adopted a **dynamic systems perspective** to account for wide variation in development. According to this view, the mind, body, and physical and social worlds form an integrated system that guides mastery of new skills. A change in any part of the system prompts the child to reorganize her behavior so the various components work together again, but in a more complex, effective way.

Comparing Child Development Theories

Identify the stand taken by each major theory on the basic issues of child development.

- Theories that are major forces in child development research vary in their focus on different domains of development, in their view of development, and in their strengths and limitations. (For a full summary, see Table 1.4 on page 31.)

Applied Directions: Child Development and Social Policy

Explain the importance of social policies for safeguarding children's well-being, and cite factors that affect the policy-making process, noting the role of child development research.

- The field of child development has become increasingly concerned with applying its vast knowledge base to solving pressing social problems. When widespread problems arise, nations attempt to solve them through a

© Dan Atkin/Alamy

special type of **social policy** called **public policy.** Favorable laws and government programs are essential for safeguarding children's well-being. U.S. and (to a lesser extent) Canadian public policies favoring children and youths have lagged behind policies in other developed nations.

- One important factor influencing public policies is the extent to which a society's values are **individualistic** (emphasizing individual needs) or **collectivist.** Other factors are a nation's economic resources and the role of organizations and individuals that advocate for children's needs.
- Policy-relevant research helps refine existing policies, forge new policy directions, and expand our understanding of child development.

IMPORTANT TERMS AND CONCEPTS

behavior modification (p. 20)
behaviorism (p. 19)
child development (p. 4)
chronosystem (p. 29)
cognitive-developmental theory (p. 20)
collectivist society (p. 34)
contexts (p. 8)
continuous development (p. 7)
developmental cognitive neuroscience (p. 24)
developmental science (p. 4)
discontinuous development (p. 7)
dynamic systems perspective (p. 29)
ecological systems theory (p. 26)
ethology (p. 24)
evolutionary developmental psychology (p. 25)
exosystem (p. 28)
individualistic society (p. 34)
information processing (p. 22)
macrosystem (p. 28)
maturation (p. 12)
mesosystem (p. 27)
microsystem (p. 26)
nature–nurture controversy (p. 8)
noble savage (p. 12)
normative approach (p. 13)
psychoanalytic perspective (p. 16)
psychosexual theory (p. 16)
psychosocial theory (p. 17)
public policy (p. 32)
resilience (p. 10)
sensitive period (p. 24)
social learning theory (p. 19)
social policy (p. 32)
sociocultural theory (p. 25)
stage (p. 8)
tabula rasa (p. 12)
theory (p. 6)

2

"Future Is Fun"
Francisca Candra
10 years, Indonesia

This young artist envisions the future as a dazzling array of people, vehicles, and buildings within a vivid, fanciful natural environment. Research strategies provide insights into how best to protect, nourish, and encourage children so they will thrive—now and in the world of the future.

Research Strategies

As my colleague Ron crossed the street between his academic department and our laboratory school, his face reflected apprehension. After weeks of planning, Ron was ready to launch his study on the development of children's peer relations. From his own school years, he recalled the anguish of several classmates who were taunted and shunned by peers. Ron thought his research could help rejected children, many of whom go on to lead troubled lives. So he was puzzled by a request to appear before the school's research committee.

The meeting included teachers and administrators charged with evaluating research proposals for their ethical integrity. A third-grade teacher spoke up: "Ron, I see the value of your work, but frankly, I'm concerned about your asking my students to indicate which classmates they like most and which they like least. I've got a couple of kids who are soundly disliked, and I'm doing my best to keep the lid on the situation. There's also an immigrant West Indian child who's new to my classroom, and she's being ostracized because of the way she dresses and speaks. If you come in and start sensitizing my class to whom they like and dislike, the children are going to share these opinions. Unfortunately, I think your study could promote conflict and negative interaction!"

Imagine Ron's dismay at the prospect of abandoning his research. This chapter looks at the research process—the many challenges investigators face as they plan and implement studies of children. By the time Ron arrived at the laboratory school, prepared to collect his data, he had already traveled a long and arduous path. First, he had spent many weeks developing a researchable idea, based on theory and prior knowledge of children's peer relations. Next, he had chosen an appropriate research strategy, which involved two main tasks. First, he had selected from a variety of *research methods*—participants' specific activities, such as taking tests, answering questionnaires, responding to interviews, or being observed. Second, he had decided on a *research design*—an overall plan for his study that would permit the best test of his research idea. Finally, Ron had scrutinized his procedures for any possible harm they might cause to participants.

Still, as Ron approached a committee charged with protecting the welfare of research participants, he faced an ethical dilemma. Research, whether on animals or humans, must meet certain standards that protect participants from stressful treatment. Because of children's immaturity and vulnerability, extra precautions must be taken to ensure that their rights are not violated. In the final section of this chapter, you will learn how Ron resolved the committee's challenge to the ethical integrity of his research.

From Theory to Hypothesis

In Chapter 1, we saw how theories structure the research process by identifying important research concerns and, occasionally, preferred methods for collecting data. We also discussed how theories guide the application of findings to real-life circumstances and practices with children. In fact, research usually begins with a prediction drawn from a theory, called a **hypothesis.** Think back to the various child development theories presented in Chapter 1. Many hypotheses can be drawn from any one of them that, once tested, would reflect on the accuracy of the theory.

Sometimes research pits a hypothesis taken from one theory against a hypothesis taken from another. For example, a theorist emphasizing the role of maturation in development would predict that adult encouragement will have little effect on the age at which children utter their first words, learn to count, or tie their shoes. A sociocultural theorist, in contrast, would speculate that these skills can be promoted through adult teaching.

At other times, research tests predictions drawn from a single theory. For example, ecological systems theory suggests that providing isolated, divorced mothers with social supports will lead them to be more patient with their children. An ethologist might hypothesize that an infant's cry will stimulate strong physiological arousal in adults who hear it, motivating them to soothe and protect a suffering baby.

Occasionally, little or no theory exists on a topic of interest. In these instances, the investigator may start with a *research question,* such as, Have recent world events—the U.S war in Iraq and a global rise in terrorism—heightened children's fears and anxieties? Which teenagers are heavy users of Internet communication—e-mail, instant messaging, and chat rooms? Are they sociable young people with many friends, or lonely individuals with few in-person social supports? Hypotheses and research questions offer investigators vital guidance as they settle on research methods and research designs.

At this point, you may be wondering, Why learn about research strategies? Why not leave these matters to research specialists and concentrate on what is already known about the child and how that knowledge can be applied? There are two reasons. First, each of us must be a wise and critical consumer of knowledge. Knowing the strengths and limitations of various research strategies is important in separating dependable information from misleading results. Second, individuals who work directly with children may be in a unique position to build bridges between research and practice by conducting studies, either on their own or in partnership with experienced investigators. Community agencies such as schools, mental health facilities, and parks and recreation programs sometimes collaborate with researchers in designing, implementing, and evaluating interventions aimed at enhancing children's development (Lerner, Fisher, & Weinberg, 2000). To broaden these efforts, a basic understanding of the research process is essential.

How can classrooms be designed to foster young children's optimal learning? What teaching strategies best promote reading readiness? Collaborations between researchers and teachers are well-suited for designing studies aimed at answering these questions. © Michael Newman/PhotoEdit

Common Methods of Gathering Information

How does a researcher choose a basic approach to gathering information about children? Common methods include systematic observation, self-reports (such as questionnaires and interviews), clinical or case studies of a single child, and ethnographies of the life circumstances of a specific group of children. As you read about these methods, you may find it helpful to refer to Table 2.1, which summarizes the strengths and limitations of each.

Table 2.1 Strengths and Limitations of Common Information-Gathering Methods

Method	Description	Strengths	Limitations
Systematic Observation			
Naturalistic observation	Observation of behavior in natural contexts	Reflects participants' everyday behaviors.	Cannot control conditions under which participants are observed. Accuracy of observations may be reduced by observer influence and observer bias.
Structured observation	Observation of behavior in a laboratory, where conditions are the same for all participants	Grants each participant an equal opportunity to display the behavior of interest. Permits study of behaviors rarely seen in everyday life.	May not yield observations typical of participants' behavior in everyday life. Accuracy of observations may be reduced by observer influence and observer bias.
Self-Reports			
Clinical interview	Flexible interviewing procedure in which the investigator obtains a complete account of the participant's thoughts	Comes as close as possible to the way participants think in everyday life. Great breadth and depth of information can be obtained in a short time.	May not result in accurate reporting of information. Flexible procedure makes comparing individuals' responses difficult.
Structured interview, questionnaires, and tests	Self-report instruments in which each participant is asked the same questions in the same way	Permits comparisons of participants' responses and efficient data collection. Researchers can specify answer alternatives that participants might not think of in an open-ended interview.	Does not yield the same depth of information as a clinical interview. Responses are still subject to inaccurate reporting.
Psychophysiological Methods	Methods that measure the relationship between physiological processes and behavior	Reveals which central nervous system structures contribute to development and individual differences in certain competencies. Helps infer the perceptions, thoughts, and emotions of infants and young children, who cannot report them clearly.	Cannot reveal with certainty the meaning of autonomic or brain activity. Many factors besides those of interest to the researcher can influence a physiological response.
Clinical, or Case Study, Method	A full picture of one individual's psychological functioning, obtained by combining interviews, observations, test scores, and sometimes psychophysiological assessments	Provides rich, descriptive insights into factors that affect development.	May be biased by researchers' theoretical preferences. Findings cannot be applied to individuals other than the participant.
Ethnography	Participant observation of a culture or distinct social group; by making extensive field notes, the researcher tries to capture the culture's unique values and social processes	Provides a more complete description than can be derived from a single observational visit, interview, or questionnaire.	May be biased by researchers' values and theoretical preferences. Findings cannot be applied to individuals and settings other than the ones studied.

Systematic Observation

Observations of the behavior of children, and of the adults who are important in their lives, can be made in different ways. One approach is to go into the field, or natural environment, and record the behavior of interest—a method called **naturalistic observation.**

A study of preschoolers' responses to their peers' distress provides a good example of this technique (Farver & Branstetter, 1994). Observing 3- and 4-year-olds in child-care centers, the

In naturalistic observation, the researcher goes into the field and records the behavior of interest. This researcher, who is observing children at a summer camp, might be focusing on their playmate choices, cooperation, helpfulness, or conflicts. A limitation of this method is that some children have more opportunities than others to display certain behaviors in everyday life. © Bob Daemmrich/The Image Works

researchers recorded each instance of crying and the reactions of nearby children—whether they ignored, watched, or commented on the child's unhappiness; scolded or teased; or shared, helped, or expressed sympathy. Caregiver behaviors—explaining why a child was crying, mediating conflict, or offering comfort—were noted to see if adult sensitivity was related to children's caring responses. A strong relationship emerged. The great strength of naturalistic observation is that investigators can see directly the everyday behaviors they hope to explain.

Naturalistic observation also has a major limitation: Not all children have the same opportunity to display a particular behavior in everyday life. In the study just mentioned, some children might have witnessed a child crying more often than others or been exposed to more cues for positive social responses from caregivers. For this reason, they might have displayed more compassion.

Researchers commonly deal with this difficulty by making **structured observations,** in which the investigator sets up a laboratory situation that evokes the behavior of interest so that every participant has an equal opportunity to display the response. In one study, 2-year-olds' emotional reactions to harm that they thought they had caused were observed by asking them to take care of a rag doll that had been modified so its leg would fall off when the child picked it up. To make the child feel at fault, once the leg detached, an adult "talked for" the doll by saying, "Ow!" Researchers recorded children's facial expressions of sadness and concern for the injured doll, efforts to help the doll, and body tension—responses that indicated remorse and a desire to make amends for the mishap. In addition, mothers were asked to engage in brief conversations about emotions with their children (Garner, 2003). Toddlers whose mothers more often explained the causes and consequences of emotion were more likely to express concern for the injured doll.

Structured observation permits greater control over the research situation than does naturalistic observation. In addition, the method is especially useful for studying behaviors—such as parent–child or friendship interactions—that investigators rarely have an opportunity to see in everyday life. For example, to compare friendship quality of aggressive and nonaggressive children, researchers had nearly one hundred 10-year-old boys come to a laboratory, each accompanied by his best friend. The pairs were observed as they played a board game and jointly solved scrambled-word puzzles. The aggressive boys and their friends more often violated game rules, cheated while working on the puzzles by looking at an answer key, and encouraged each other to engage in these dishonest acts. In addition, observers rated these boys' interactions as angrier and less cooperative than the interactions of nonaggressive boys and their friends (Bagwell & Coie, 2004). The researchers concluded that rather than being warm and supportive, aggressive boys' close peer ties provide a context in which they practice hostility and other negative behaviors, which may contribute to increased antisocial behavior.

In this study, antisocial boys' laboratory interactions were probably similar to their natural behaviors. The boys acted negatively even though they knew they were being observed. But the great disadvantage of structured observations is that most of the time, we cannot be certain that participants behave in the laboratory as they do in their natural environments.

• **Collecting Systematic Observations** The procedures used to collect systematic observations vary, depending on the research problem posed. Occasionally investigators choose to record the entire stream of behavior—everything the participant says and does over a certain time period. In one study, researchers wanted to find out whether maternal sensitivity in infancy and early childhood contribute to readiness for formal schooling at age 6 (Hirsh-Pasek & Burchinal, 2006). Between age 6 months and 4½ years, the investigators periodically videotaped mother–child 15-minute play sessions. Then they rated each session for maternal positive emotion, support, stimulating play, and respect for the child's autonomy—ingredients of sensitivity that did predict better language and academic progress when the children reached kindergarten.

In other studies, information on only one or a few kinds of behavior is needed, permitting more efficient procedures. In these instances, a common approach is **event sampling,** in which the observer records all instances of a particular behavior during a specified time period. In the study of preschoolers' responses to their peers' distress reported earlier, the researchers used event sampling by recording each instance in which a child cried, followed by other children's reactions.

Another way to observe efficiently is **time sampling.** In this procedure, the researcher records whether certain behaviors occur during a sample of short intervals. First, a checklist of the target behaviors is prepared. Then the observation period is divided into a series of brief time segments. For example, a half-hour observation period might be divided into 120 fifteen-second intervals. The observer watches the target person and checks off behaviors during each interval, repeating this process until the observation period is complete. Recently, my collaborators and I used time sampling to find out how parents and children spent time while visiting a community children's museum. Our observers followed more than one hundred parent–child pairs for 10 minutes each, checking off parent and child behaviors during 20 thirty-second intervals. Findings revealed that, on average, parents and children were jointly engaged in the museum's exhibits during 45 percent of the intervals. During an additional 30 percent, parents remained nearby, closely observing their children's activities (Mann, Braswell, & Berk, 2005). Clearly, the museum afforded parents many opportunities to interact with and learn about their children.

Researchers have devised ingenious ways of observing children's difficult-to-capture behaviors. For example, to record instances of bullying, a group of investigators set up video cameras overlooking a classroom and a playground and had fourth to sixth graders wear small remote microphones and pocket-sized transmitters (Craig, Pepler, & Atlas, 2000). Results revealed that bullying occurred often—at rates of 2.4 episodes per hour in the classroom and 4.5 episodes per hour on the playground. Yet only 15 to 18 percent of the time did teachers take steps to stop the harassment. We will return to the topic of bullying in Chapter 15.

• **Limitations of Systematic Observation** A major problem with systematic observation is **observer influence**—the effects of the observer on the behavior studied. The presence of a watchful, unfamiliar individual may cause both children and adults to react in unnatural ways. For children under age 7 or 8, observer influence is generally limited to the first session or two. Young children cannot stop "being themselves" for long, and they quickly get used to the observer's presence. But older children and adults often engage in more socially desirable behavior when they know that they are being observed. In these instances, researchers can regard participants' responses as an indication of the best behavior they can display under the circumstances.

To minimize observer influence, an adaptation period, in which observers visit the research setting so participants can get used to their presence, can be helpful. Another approach is to ask individuals who are part of the child's natural environment to do the observing. For example, in several studies, parents have been trained to record their children's behavior. Besides reducing the impact of an unfamiliar observer, this method limits the amount of time needed to gather observations, as some information can take a long time to obtain. In one such study, researchers wanted to know how preschool and young school-age children's TV watching affected their other home activities (Huston et al., 1999). To find out, every other month they telephoned parents for a detailed report of children's time use during the previous 24 hours. Findings indicated that the more children watched entertainment TV (cartoons and general-audience programs), the less time they spent reading, doing educational activities (such as art, music, and puzzles), and interacting with adults and peers.

Another serious danger is **observer bias.** When observers are aware of the purposes of a study, they may see and record what they expect to see rather than what participants actually do. Therefore, people who have no knowledge of the investigator's hypotheses—or who at least have little personal investment in them—are best suited to collect the observations.

Finally, although systematic observation provides invaluable information on how children and adults behave, it conveys little about the reasoning that underlies their behavior. For this kind of information, researchers must turn to self-report techniques.

Self-Reports: Interviews and Questionnaires

Self-reports ask research participants to provide information on their perceptions, thoughts, abilities, feelings, attitudes, beliefs, and past experiences. They range from relatively unstructured clinical interviews, the method used by Piaget to study children's thinking, to highly structured interviews, questionnaires, and tests.

• **Clinical Interviews** In a **clinical interview,** researchers use a flexible, conversational style to probe for the participant's point of view. In the following example, Piaget questioned a 3-year-old child about his understanding of dreams:

> *Where does the dream come from?*—I think you sleep so well that you dream.—*Does it come from us or from outside?*—From outside.—*When you are in bed and you dream, where is the dream?*—In my bed, under the blanket. I don't really know. If it was in my stomach, the bones would be in the way and I shouldn't see it.—*Is the dream there when you sleep?*—Yes, it is in the bed beside me. (Piaget, 1926/1930, pp. 97–98)

Although a researcher conducting clinical interviews with more than one child would typically ask the same first question to establish a common task, individualized prompts are used to provide a fuller picture of each child's reasoning (Ginsburg, 1997).

The clinical interview has two major strengths. First, it permits people to display their thoughts in terms that are as close as possible to the way they think in everyday life. Second, the clinical interview can provide a large amount of information in a fairly brief period. For example, in an hour-long session, we can obtain a wide range of child-rearing information from a parent—far more than we could capture by observing for the same amount of time.

• **Limitations of Clinical Interviews** A major limitation of the clinical interview has to do with the accuracy with which people report their thoughts, feelings, and experiences. Some participants, wishing to please the interviewer, may make up answers that do not represent their actual thinking. When asked about past events, some may have trouble recalling exactly what happened. And because the clinical interview depends on verbal ability and expressiveness, it may underestimate the capacities of individuals who have difficulty putting their thoughts into words. Skillful interviewers minimize these problems by wording questions carefully. They also watch for cues indicating that the participant may not have clearly understood a question or may need extra time to feel comfortable in the interview situation.

Interviews on certain topics are particularly vulnerable to distortion. In a few instances, researchers have been able to compare parents' and children's descriptions of past events with information gathered years earlier, at the time the events occurred. Reports of psychological states and family processes obtained on the two occasions showed little or no agreement (Henry et al., 1994). Parents often recall their child's development in glowing terms, reporting faster progress, fewer childhood problems, and child-rearing practices more in line with current expert advice than with records of behavior (Yarrow, Campbell, & Burton, 1970). Interviews that focus on current rather than past information and on specific characteristics rather than global judgments show a better match with observations and other sources of information. Even so, parents are far from perfect in describing their practices and their children's personalities, preferences, and cognitive abilities (Miller & Davis, 1992; Rothbart & Bates, 2006; Waschbusch, Daleiden, & Drabman, 2000).

Finally, as mentioned in Chapter 1, the clinical interview has been criticized because of its flexibility. When questions are phrased differently for each participant, variations in responses may reflect the manner of interviewing rather than real differences in the way individuals think about a topic. To reduce this problem, researchers can use a second self-report method, the structured interview.

• **Structured Interviews, Tests, and Questionnaires** In a **structured interview,** each individual is asked the same set of questions in the same way. This approach eliminates the possibility that an interviewer might press and prompt some participants more than others. In addition, structured interviews are much more efficient than clinical interviews. Answers are briefer, and researchers can obtain written responses from an entire group of children or group of parents at the same time. Also, by listing answer alternatives, researchers can specify the activities and behaviors of interest—ones that participants might not think of in an open-ended clinical interview. For example, when parents were asked what they considered "the most important thing for children to prepare them for life," 62 percent checked "to think for themselves" when this alternative appeared on a list. Yet only 5 percent thought of it during a clinical interview (Schwarz, 1999).

Nevertheless, structured interviews do not yield the same depth of information as a clinical interview. And they can still be affected by the problem of inaccurate reporting.

Psychophysiological Methods

Researchers' desire to uncover the biological bases of perceptual, cognitive, and emotional responses has led to the use of **psychophysiological methods,** which measure the relationship between physiological processes and behavior. Investigators who rely on these methods want to find out which central nervous system structures contribute to development and individual differences. Psychophysiological methods also help investigators infer the perceptions, thoughts, and emotions of infants and young children, who cannot report their psychological experiences clearly.

Involuntary activities of the autonomic nervous system[1]—changes in heart rate, blood pressure, respiration, pupil dilation, electrical conductance of the skin, and stress hormone levels—are highly sensitive to psychological state. For example, heart rate can be used to infer whether an infant is staring blankly at a stimulus (heart rate is stable), processing information (heart rate slows during concentration), or experiencing distress (heart rate rises). Heart rate variations are also linked to certain emotions, such as interest, fear, anger, and sadness (Fox & Card, 1998; Hastings, Zahn-Waxler, & Usher, 2007). And as Chapter 10 will reveal, distinct patterns of autonomic activity are related to aspects of temperament, such as shyness and sociability (Kagan & Fox, 2006).

Autonomic indicators have been enriched by diverse measures of brain functioning, described in Table 2.2 on page 48. Among these methods, the two most frequently used detect changes in *electrical activity* in the cerebral cortex—the brain's outer layers, which play a central role in complex mental functions, including attention, perception, memory, language, reasoning, planning, and problem solving. In an *electroencephalogram (EEG)*, researchers examine brain-wave patterns for stability and organization—signs of mature functioning of the cortex. And as a child processes a particular stimulus, *event-related potentials (ERPs)* detect the general location of cortical activity—a technique often used to study preverbal infants' responsiveness to various stimuli, the impact of experience on development of regions of the cerebral cortex, and atypical brain functioning in children at risk for learning and emotional problems (DeBoer, Scott, & Nelson, 2007; deRegnier, 2005). For example, different wave patterns appear when 3-month-olds from English-speaking homes hear passages in English, Italian, and Dutch, suggesting that the infants can discriminate the intonation patterns of the three languages and indicating the brain regions involved (Shafer, Shucard, & Jaeger, 1999). And as the Biology and Environment box on pages 50–51 illustrates, ERP findings are clarifying the impact of deficient prenatal nutrition on early brain development and cognitive functioning.

Neuroimaging techniques, which yield detailed, three-dimensional computerized pictures of the entire brain and its active areas, provide the

In preparing for an EEG, a researcher applies gel to electrodes before attaching them to a baby's scalp. This method records the stability and organization of electrical brain-wave activity in the cerebral cortex. It can also be used to measure ERPs, the frequency and amplitude of brain waves in particular areas of the cerebral cortex in response to specific stimuli, such as music or speech.

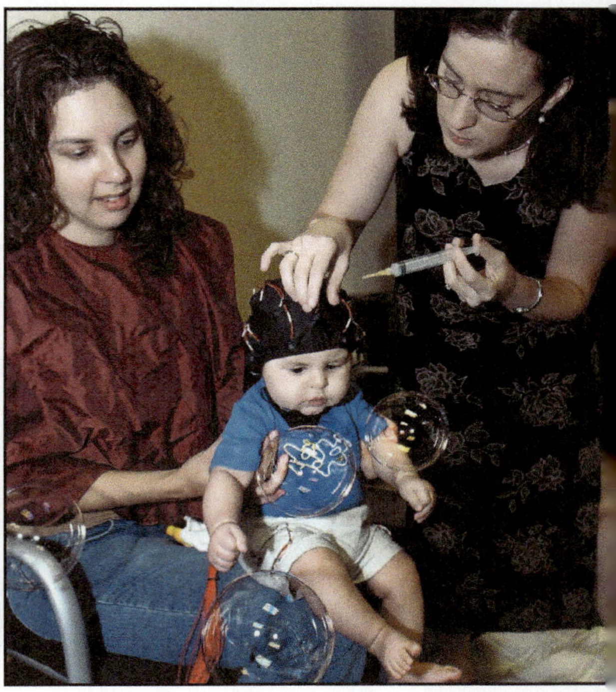

[1]The autonomic nervous system, which regulates involuntary actions, is divided into two parts: (1) the *sympathetic nervous system,* which mobilizes energy to deal with threatening situations (as when your heart rate rises in response to a fear-arousing event), and (2) the *parasympathetic nervous system,* which acts to conserve energy (as when your heart rate slows as you focus on an interesting stimulus).

Table 2.2 Methods for Measuring Brain Functioning

Method	Description
Electroencephalogram (EEG)	Electrodes, usually embedded in a head cap or net, are attached to the scalp with conductive gel to record the stability and organization of electrical brain-wave activity in the brain's outer layers—the cerebral cortex.
Event-related potentials (ERPs)	Using the EEG, the frequency and amplitude of brain waves in response to particular stimuli (such as a picture, music, or speech) are recorded in multiple areas of the cerebral cortex. Enables study of brain function "online," as cognition is occurring, but limited to identifying general (rather than precise) regions of stimulus-induced activity. Can be used with infants and young children, who may sit on the parent's lap or move within a limited range during testing.
Functional magnetic resonance imaging (fMRI)	While the person lies quietly inside a tunnel-shaped apparatus that creates a magnetic field, a scanner magnetically detects increased blood flow and oxygen metabolism in precise areas of the brain as the individual processes particular stimuli. The result is a computerized moving picture of "online" activity anywhere in the brain (not just its outer layers). Not appropriate for children younger than age 5 to 6, who cannot remain still during testing. Cost of equipment and testing is much higher than that of EEG and ERPs.
Positron emission tomography (PET)	After injection or inhalation of a radioactive substance, the individual quietly lies inside a tunnel-shaped apparatus with a scanner that emits fine streams of X-rays, which detect increased blood flow and oxygen metabolism in areas of the brain while the person processes particular stimuli. As with fMRI, the result is a computerized moving picture of "online" activity anywhere in the brain, but not appropriate for children younger than age 5 to 6, and high in cost.
Near-infrared optical topography (NIROT)	Using thin, flexible optical fibers attached to the scalp, infrared (invisible) light is beamed at the brain; its absorption by areas of the cerebral cortex varies with changes in blood flow and oxygen metabolism. The optical fibers detect these light-absorption variations while the individual processes particular stimuli, yielding a computerized moving picture of "online" activity in specific areas of the cerebral cortex (but not throughout the brain). Unlike fMRI and PET, an infant or child can sit on the parent's lap and move within limited range.

Sources: Taga et al., 2003; Nelson, Thomas, & de Haan, 2006.

most precise information about which brain regions are specialized for certain capacities and about abnormalities in brain functioning. In both *positron emission tomography (PET)* and *functional magnetic resonance imaging (fMRI),* the child lies inside a tunnel-like apparatus. But unlike PET, fMRI does not depend on X-ray photography, which requires injection of a radioactive substance. Rather, when a child is exposed to a stimulus, fMRI detects increases in blood flow and oxygen metabolism throughout the brain magnetically, yielding a colorful, moving picture of parts of the brain used to perform a given activity (see Figure 2.1 for an example).

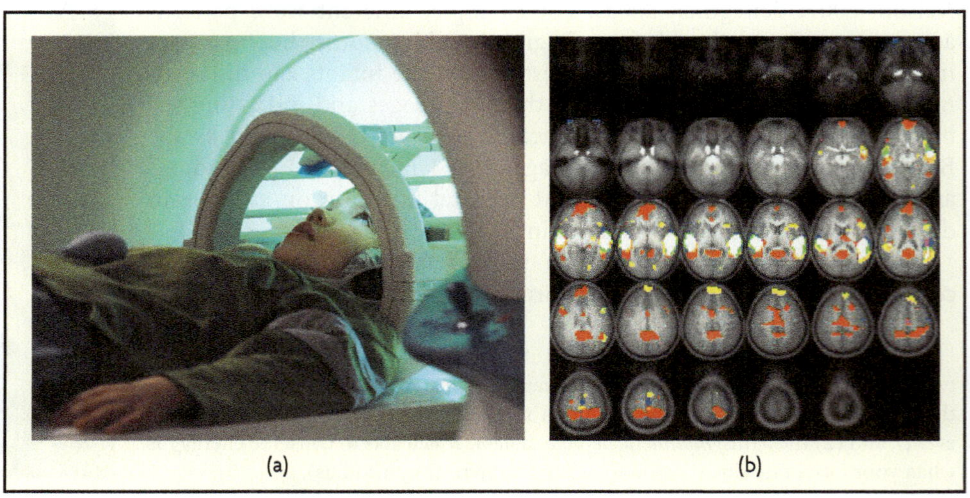

■ **Figure 2.1 Functional magnetic resonance imaging (fMRI).**
(a) This 6-year-old is part of a study that uses fMRI to find out how his brain processes light and motion. (b) The fMRI image shows which areas of the boy's brain are active while he views changing visual stimuli. *Photos:* (left) AP/Wide World Photos; (right) © Scott K. Holland

PET and fMRI are not suitable for infants and young children because they require that the child remain as motionless as possible on a narrow plank in an enclosed space filled with the noise of the surrounding machine for an extended time—often up to an hour (Nelson, Thomas, & de Haan, 2006). A new brain-imaging method that works well in infancy and early childhood is *near-infrared optical topography (NIROT),* in which infrared (invisible) light is beamed at regions of the cerebral cortex to measure blood flow and oxygen metabolism while the child attends to a stimulus (refer again to Table 2.2). Because the apparatus consists only of thin, flexible optical fibers attached to the scalp using a head cap (see Figure 2.2), a baby can sit on the parent's lap (Taga et al., 2003). Unlike PET and fMRI, which map activity changes throughout the brain, NIROT is limited to examining the functioning of the cerebral cortex. It has been used to study the responsiveness of the young brain to various sensory stimuli (sights, sounds, and odors) in both typically developing babies and babies with neurological abnormalities (Homae et al., 2006; Meek, 2002).

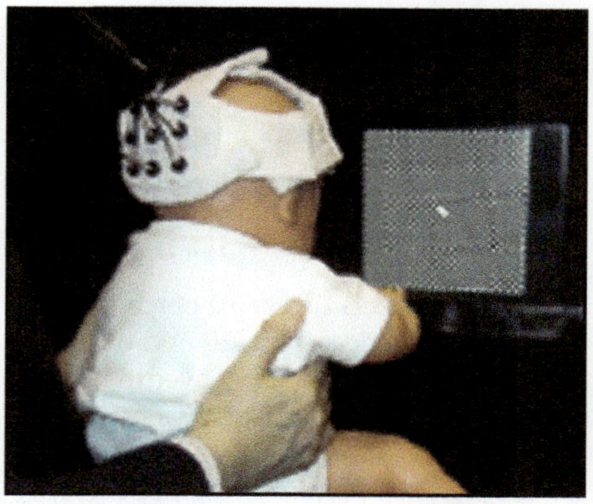

Figure 2.2 **Near-infrared optical topography (NIROT).**
A 2-month-old is held in a sitting position on his parent's lap so he can look at a visual stimulus. Using NIROT, optical fibers are attached to the baby's scalp, enabling infrared light to be beamed at areas of the cerebral cortex, which yields images of active areas as he processes the stimulus. During testing, the baby can move freely within a limited range. (From G. Taga, K. Asakawa, A. Maki, Y. Konishi, & H. Koisumi, 2003, "Brain Imaging in Awake Infants by Near-Infrared Optical Topography," *Proceedings of the National Academy of Sciences, 100,* p. 10723. Reprinted by permission.) Courtesy of Gentaro Taga, University of Tokyo.

Psychophysiological methods are powerful tools for uncovering relationships between the brain and psychological development. But like all research methods, they have limitations. Even though a stimulus produces a consistent pattern of autonomic or brain activity, investigators cannot be certain that an infant or child has processed it in a certain way. Second, many factors can influence a physiological response (Kagan, 2006). A researcher who takes a change in heart rate, respiration, or brain activity as an indicator of information processing or emotional state must make sure that the change was not due instead to hunger, boredom, fatigue, or body movements. Third, children often do not perform as well while attached to electrodes or lying in an fMRI scanner as they do outside the apparatus. Finally, a child's fearful reaction to the equipment affects physiological measures. Preparing children by taking them through a simulated experience can ease their apprehension (Davidson, Thomas, & Casey, 2003; Rosenberg et al., 1997). Without such efforts, detection of correspondences between physiological and psychological reactions is difficult.

The Clinical, or Case Study, Method

An outgrowth of psychoanalytic theory, the **clinical, or case study, method** brings together a wide range of information on one child, including interviews, observations, test scores, and sometimes psychophysiological measures. The aim is to obtain as complete a picture as possible of that child's psychological functioning and the experiences that led up to it.

The clinical method is well-suited to studying the development of certain types of individuals who are few in number but vary widely in characteristics. For example, the method has been used to find out what contributes to the accomplishments of *prodigies*—extremely gifted children who attain adult competence in a field before age 10 (Moran & Gardner, 2006). Consider Adam, a boy who read, wrote, and composed musical pieces before he was out of diapers. By age 4, Adam was deeply involved in mastering human symbol systems—French, German, Russian, Sanskrit, Greek, the computer programming language BASIC, ancient hieroglyphs, music, and mathematics. Adam's parents provided a home rich in stimulation and reared him with affection, firmness, and humor. They searched for schools in which he could both develop his abilities and form rewarding social relationships. He graduated from college at age 18 and continued to pursue musical composition (Goldsmith, 2000). Would Adam have realized his potential without the chance combination of his special gift and nurturing, committed parents? Probably not, researchers concluded (Feldman, 2004).

Using the clinical, or case study, method, this researcher combines interviews with the mother and observations and testing of the child to construct an in-depth picture of one child's psychological functioning. A major limitation is that investigators' theoretical preferences may bias what they see and conclude. © Spencer Grant/PhotoEdit

Biology *and* Environment

Prenatal Iron Deficiency, Brain Development, and Memory Impairments in Infants of Diabetic Mothers: Findings of ERP Research

Diabetes affects nearly 10 percent of North Americans age 20 and older—a rate that has risen sharply over the past quarter century as a result of widespread overweight and obesity. Increasingly prevalent among all sectors of the population, diabetes nevertheless is at least twice as likely to affect low-income ethnic minority as white adults. Today, about 5 percent of pregnant mothers are diabetic—a 50 percent increase over the past decade. Most had the disease before becoming pregnant; others developed it during pregnancy (Canadian Diabetes Association, 2007; U.S. Department of Health and Human Services, 2007b). In either case, their newborn babies are at risk for long-term developmental problems.

In the early weeks of pregnancy, when organs are forming, a diabetic mother's out-of-control blood sugar (glucose) increases the risk of birth defects. Later in pregnancy, excess blood glucose causes the fetus to be "overfed" and to grow unusually large, often causing birth complications. Furthermore, to metabolize this flood of maternal glucose, the fetus secretes abnormally high levels of insulin—a circumstance that greatly increases demand for oxygen. To extract extra oxygen from the mother's system, the fetus increases production of oxygen-carrying red blood cells. This expanding red blood-cell mass requires extra iron, which the fetus can obtain only by taxing its own iron stores in the liver, muscles, heart, and brain.

In animal research on maternal diabetes, by late pregnancy iron stores decline sharply in the brain's temporal lobes (located on each side of the brain, just above the ears), which house structures centrally involved in memory development—specifically, the *hippocampus,* which plays a crucial role in the formation of new memories. Prenatal iron depletion interferes with growth of brain cells and their connections, permanently reducing the size and altering the structure of the hippocampus in laboratory rats (deUngria et al., 2000).

In human research, diabetic mothers bear children who, at school age, tend to score lower than their agemates on intelligence tests (Rizzo, 1997). Is prenatal iron deficiency and resulting early damage to the brain's memory areas responsible? In a series of studies, Charles Nelson (2007) and his collaborators used ERPs to assess young infants' memory performance, focusing on a particular slow brain wave in the temporal lobes believed to reflect memory processing.

Typically developing newborns come to recognize their mother's voice through repeated exposure during pregnancy; they suck more on a nipple to hear a recording of it than the voice of an unfamiliar woman (DeCasper & Spence, 1988). In a comparison of newborns of diabetic mothers likely to have a brain iron deficiency (based on a measure of body iron stores) with normal-iron controls, ERPs were recorded as the babies listened to sound clips of their mother's or a stranger's voice (Sidappa et al., 2004). The controls showed a distinctive ERP slow brain wave to each stimulus, indicating recognition of the mother's voice. The brain iron–deficient babies showed no difference in ERP brain waves to the two stimuli, suggesting memory impairment of prenatal origin.

Do these memory deficits persist beyond the newborn period—evidence that diabetes-linked prenatal brain damage has lasting consequences? At 6 months, the researchers recorded ERPs while infants alternately viewed a videotaped image of their mother's face and that of an unfamiliar woman. Consistent with the newborn findings, control infants responded with distinct ERP slow waves in the temporal lobes to the two faces, while infants of diabetic mothers displayed no difference. Even after months of experience, they could not recognize their mother's facial image (Nelson et al., 2000).

At an 8-month follow-up, babies were given a more challenging memory task. After feeling a novel object (an unusually shaped wooden block) held beneath an apron so they could not see it, the infants were tested visually: They viewed photos of the novel

The clinical method yields richly detailed case narratives that offer valuable insights into the many factors affecting development. Nevertheless, like all other methods, it has drawbacks. Because information often is collected unsystematically and subjectively, researchers' theoretical preferences may bias their observations and interpretations. In addition, investigators cannot assume that their conclusions apply, or generalize, to anyone other than the child studied (Stanovich, 2004). Even when patterns emerge across several cases, it is wise to confirm them with other research strategies.

Methods for Studying Culture

To study the impact of culture, researchers adjust the methods just considered or tap procedures specially devised for cross-cultural and multicultural research. Which approach investigators choose depends on their research goals (Triandis, 1998).

Sometimes researchers are interested in characteristics that are believed to be universal but that vary in degree from one society to the next. These investigators might ask, Do parents make greater maturity demands of children in some cultures than in others? How strong

object interspersed with photos of familiar objects (Nelson et al., 2003). Again, infants of diabetic mothers showed no ERP evidence of distinguishing the novel object from other stimuli. The control babies, in contrast, responded to the novel object with a stronger temporal-lobe ERP slow wave, suggesting a ready ability to recognize the novel stimulus, even when presented in a different sensory modality (see Figure 2.3).

Nelson and his colleagues have followed their research participants through the preschool years, amassing additional ERP evidence for poorer memory (especially more rapid forgetting) in children born to diabetic mothers than in controls (deRegnier et al., 2007). The ERP findings highlight a previously hidden pregnancy complication: As a result of iron depletion in critical brain areas, a diabetic pregnancy places the fetus at risk for lasting memory deficits and, thus, for long-term learning and academic problems. The researchers believe that damage to the hippocampus, located deep inside the temporal lobes, is responsible—a hypothesis they hope to pursue as new methods making possible fMRIs on babies become available.

Nelson's research underscores the need to find more effective ways of intervening with iron supplementation in diabetic pregnancies, as well as the importance of sufficient dietary iron for every expectant mother and her developing fetus. Diabetes prevention is also vital, through weight control, increased exercise, and improved diet beginning in childhood—topics we take up in Chapter 5.

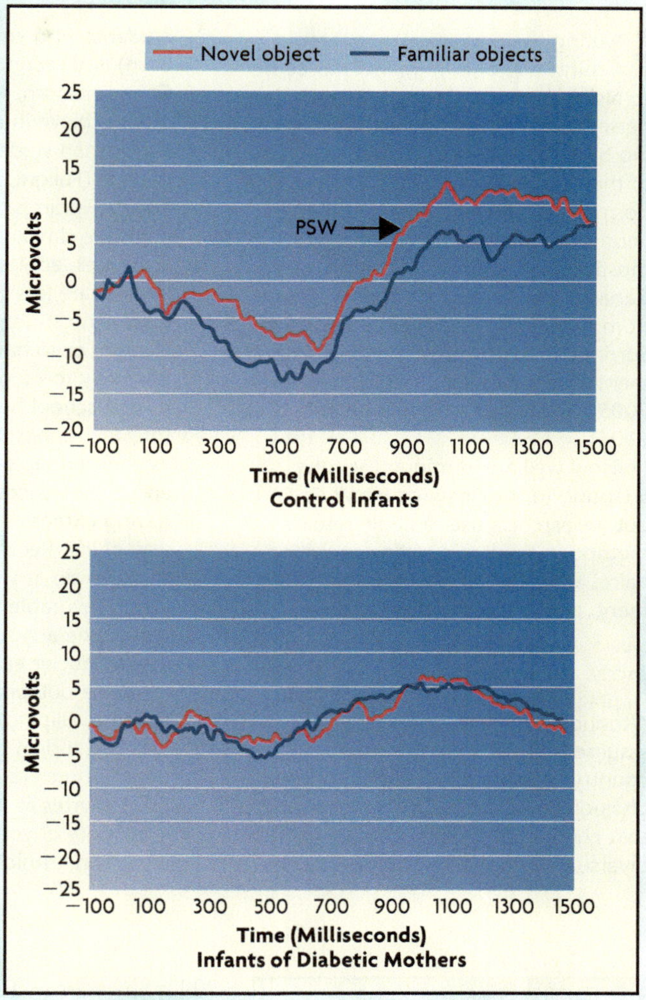

Figure 2.3 **ERPs recorded over the left temporal lobe as 8-month-old infants of diabetic mothers and controls viewed familiar and novel objects.**

After infants explored a novel object by touch, they were tested visually: They viewed photos of the novel object interspersed with photos of familiar objects. Control infants responded with a greater ERP positive slow wave (PSW) to the novel object than the familiar object, suggesting that they recognized the novel stimulus. The infants of diabetic mothers, in contrast, showed no ERP evidence of distinguishing novel from familiar stimuli. (From C. A. Nelson, S. Wewerka, A. J. Borscheid, R.-A. deRegnier, & M. K. Georgieff, 2003, "Electrophysiologic evidence of impaired cross-modal recognition memory in 8-month-old infants of diabetic mothers," *Journal of Pediatrics*, 142, pp. 575–582. Copyright © 2003 Elsevier. Reprinted by permission.)

are gender stereotypes in different nations? In each instance, several cultural groups will be compared, and all participants must be questioned or observed in the same way. Therefore, researchers draw on the self-report and observational procedures we have already considered, adapting them through translation so they can be understood in each cultural context. For example, to study cultural variation in parenting practices, the same questionnaire, asking for ratings on such items as "I often hug and kiss my child" or "I scold my child when his/her behavior does not meet my expectations," is given to all participants (Wu et al., 2002).

At other times, researchers want to uncover the *cultural meanings* of children's and adults' behaviors by becoming as familiar as possible with their way of life. To achieve this goal, investigators rely on a method borrowed from the field of anthropology—**ethnography.** Like the clinical method, ethnographic research is a descriptive, qualitative technique. But instead of aiming to understand a single individual, it is directed at understanding a culture or a distinct social group through *participant observation.* Typically, the researcher spends months and sometimes years in the cultural community, participating in its daily life. Extensive field notes are gathered, consisting of a mix of observations, self-reports from members of the culture, and careful interpretations by the investigator (Miller, Hengst, & Wang,

Cultural Influences

Immigrant Youths: Amazing Adaptation

During the past quarter century, a rising tide of immigrants has come to North America, fleeing war and persecution in their homelands or seeking better life chances. Today, one-fifth of the U.S. youth population has foreign-born parents; nearly one-third of these youths are foreign-born themselves, mostly from Asia and Latin America. In Canada, too, immigrant youths—mostly from Asia, Africa, the Middle East, and Europe—are the fastest-growing segment of the population (Service Canada, 2005; Suarez-Orozco, Todorova, & Qin, 2006).

How well are immigrant youths adapting to their new country? To find out, researchers use multiple research methods—academic testing, questionnaires assessing psychological adjustment, and in-depth ethnographies.

Academic Achievement and Adjustment

Although educators and laypeople often assume that the transition to a new country has a negative impact on psychological well-being, evidence reveals that children of immigrant parents from diverse countries adapt amazingly well. Students who are first-generation (foreign-born) and second-generation (U.S.– or Canadian-born, with immigrant parents) often achieve in school as well as or better than students of native-born parents (Fuligni, 2004; Saucier et al., 2002). Findings on psychological adjustment are similar. Compared with their agemates, adolescents from immigrant families are less likely to commit delinquent and violent acts, to use drugs and alcohol, or to have early sex. They are also less likely to be obese or to have missed school because of illness. And they feel as positively about themselves as young people with native-born parents. These successes do not depend on having extensive time to adjust to a new way of life. Recently arrived high school students do as well in school and report just as favorable self-esteem as those who came at younger ages (Fuligni, 1998; Saucier et al., 2002).

These outcomes are strongest for Chinese, Filipino, Japanese, Korean, and East Indian youths, less dramatic for other ethnicities (Fuligni, 2004; Louie, 2001; Portes & Rumbaut, 2005). And a minority of young people—especially of certain ethnicities, including Cambodians and Laotians—deviate from these favorable patterns, showing high rates of school failure and dropout, delinquency, teenage parenthood, and drug use (Zhou & Xiong, 2005). Variations in parental economic resources and education contribute to these trends. Still, many first- and second-generation youths from ethnic groups that face considerable financial hardship (such as Mexican and Vietnamese) are successful (Fuligni & Yoshikawa, 2003). Factors other than income are responsible—notably, family values and strong ethnic-community ties.

Family and Community Influences

Ethnographies reveal that immigrant parents view education as the surest way to improve life chances (Goldenberg et al., 2001; Louie, 2001). Aware of the challenges their children face, they typically emphasize trying hard. They remind their children that, because educational opportunities were not available in their native countries, they themselves are often limited to menial jobs.

Adolescents from immigrant families internalize their parents' valuing of education, endorsing it more strongly than agemates with native-born

2003; Shweder et al., 2006). Later, these notes are put together into a description of the community that tries to capture its unique values and social processes.

The basic assumption of the ethnographic method is that entering into close contact with a social group will allow researchers to understand the beliefs and behaviors of its members in a way that is not possible with an observational visit, interview, or questionnaire. Some ethnographies take in many aspects of children's experience, as one researcher did in describing what it is like to grow up in a small American town. Others focus on one or a few settings, such as home, school, or neighborhood life (LeVine et al., 1994; Peshkin, 1978, 1997; Valdés, 1998). And still others are limited to a particular practice, such as uncovering cultural and religious influences on children's make-believe play. For example, ethnographic findings reveal that East Indian Hindu parents encourage preschoolers to communicate with "invisible" characters. They regard this activity as linked to *karma* (the cycle of birth and death) and believe that the child may be remembering a past life. In contrast, Christian fundamentalist parents often discourage children from pretending to be

This Western ethnographer is spending months living among the Efe people of the Republic of Congo. Here he observes a group of young children sharing food. Among the Efe, cooperation and generosity are highly valued and encouraged from an early age. © Ed Tronick/Anthro-Photo

This Hmong girl from southeast Asia performs a cultural dance at an ethnic festival in St. Paul, Minnesota, where many Hmong immigrants have settled. Cultural values that engender allegiance to family and community promote high achievement and protect many immigrant youths from involvement in risky behaviors. © Steve Skjold/PhotoEdit

parents (Asakawa, 2001; Fuligni, 2004). Because minority ethnicities usually stress allegiance to family and community over individual goals, first- and second-generation young people often feel a strong sense of obligation to their parents. They view school success as both their own and their parents' success and as an important way of repaying their parents for the hardships they have endured (Bacallao & Smokowski, 2007; Fuligni, Yip, & Tseng, 2002). Both family relationships and school achievement protect these youths from delinquency, early pregnancy, drug use, and other risky behaviors (see the Biology and Environment box on resilient children on pages 10–11 in Chapter 1).

Immigrant parents of successful youths typically develop close ties to an ethnic community, which exerts additional control through a high consensus on values and constant monitoring of young people's activities. The comments capture the power of these family and community forces:

> *Thuy Trang, age 14, from Vietnam, middle-school Student of the Year:* When my parents first emigrated from Vietnam, they spent every waking hour working hard to support a family. They have sacrificed for me, and I am willing to do anything for them.

> *Elizabeth, age 16, from Vietnam, straight-A student, like her two older sisters:* My parents know pretty much all the kids in the neighborhood. . . . Everybody here knows everybody else. It's hard to get away with much. (Zhou & Bankston, 1998, pp. 93, 130)

> *Juan, teenager from Mexico:* A really big part of the Hispanic population [is] being close to family, and the family being a priority all the time. I hate people who say, "Why do you want to go to a party where your family's at? Don't you want to get away from them?" You know, I don't really get tired of them. I've always been really close to them. That connection to my parents, that trust that you can talk to them, that makes me Mexican. (Bacallao & Smokowski, 2007, p. 62)

The experiences of high-achieving, well-adjusted immigrant youths are not problem-free. Adolescents who had arrived in Canada within the previous five years described their first year as "very difficult" because they did not yet speak either English or French—Canada's two official languages—and felt socially isolated (Hanvey & Kunz, 2000). Young immigrants also encounter racial and ethnic prejudices and experience tensions between family values and the new culture—challenges we will take up in Chapter 11. In the long term, however, family and community cohesion, supervision, and high expectations promote favorable outcomes.

unreal characters, believing that such play promotes dangerous spiritual ideas and deceitful behavior (Taylor & Carlson, 2000). As the Cultural Influences box above illustrates, researchers may use ethnography to supplement traditional self-report and observational methods if they suspect that cultural differences reflect unique meanings.

Ethnographers strive to minimize their own influence on the culture they are studying by becoming part of it. Nevertheless, as with clinical studies, investigators' cultural values and theoretical commitments sometimes lead them to observe selectively or misinterpret what they see. Finally, the findings of ethnographic studies cannot be assumed to generalize beyond the people and settings in which the research was conducted.

Ask Yourself

Review Why might a researcher choose structured observation over naturalistic observation? How about the reverse? What might lead the researcher to opt for clinical interviewing over systematic observation?

Apply A researcher wants to study the thoughts and feelings of children who have a parent on active duty in the military. Which method is best suited for investigating this question? Why?

Connect What strengths and limitations do the clinical (or case study) method and ethnography have in common?

Reliability and Validity: Keys to Scientifically Sound Research

Once investigators choose their research methods, they must ensure that their procedures provide trustworthy information. To be acceptable to the scientific community, self-reports, observations, and physiological measures must be both *reliable* and *valid*—two keys to scientifically sound research.

Reliability

Suppose you and a research partner go into an elementary school classroom and record how attentive and cooperative each child is. But although you are simultaneously rating the same children, you and your partner come up with very different judgments. Or perhaps you question a group of children about their interests, but a week later, when you ask them again, they give you very different answers. **Reliability** refers to the consistency, or repeatability, of measures of behavior. To be reliable, observations and evaluations of peoples' actions cannot be unique to a single observer. Instead, observers must agree on what they see. And an interview, test, or questionnaire, when given again within a short time (before participants could reasonably be expected to change their opinions or develop new responses), must yield similar results on both occasions.

Researchers determine the reliability of data in various ways. In observational research, observers are asked to evaluate the same behaviors, and agreement between them—called *inter-rater reliability*—is obtained. Reliability of self-report and psychophysiological data can be demonstrated by comparing children's responses to the same measures on separate occasions, an approach called *test–retest reliability.* In the case of self-reports, researchers can also compare children's answers on different forms of the same test or questionnaire. And if necessary, reliability can be estimated from a single testing session by comparing children's answers on different halves of the test.

Because clinical and ethnographic studies do not yield quantitative scores that can be matched with those of another observer or test form, other procedures must be used to determine the reliability of these methods. After examining the qualitative records, one or more judges can see if they agree with the researcher that the patterns and themes identified are grounded in evidence and are plausible (Silverman, 2006).

Validity

For research methods to have high **validity,** they must accurately measure characteristics that the researcher set out to measure. **TAKE A MOMENT...** After thinking about this idea, can you come up with an example that shows why reliability is essential for valid research? Methods that are implemented carelessly, unevenly, and inconsistently cannot possibly represent what an investigator originally intended to study.

But to guarantee validity, researchers must go further. They often examine the content of observations and self-reports to make sure all behaviors of interest are included. For example, a test intended to measure fifth-grade children's knowledge of mathematics would not

To relax this child before a research session, an adult allowed him to build freely with blocks—an activity he enjoys greatly. Making the boy feel at ease helps ensure internal validity—the accuracy of research findings. It may also foster external validity, the extent to which findings generalize to other situations, such as home or preschool. © Bob Daemmrich/The Image Works

be valid if it contained only addition problems but no subtraction, multiplication, or division problems (Miller, 2007). Another approach is to see how effective a method is in predicting behavior we would reasonably expect it to predict. If scores on a math test are valid, they should be related to how well children do on their math assignments in school or even to how quickly and accurately they can make change in a game of Monopoly.

As we turn now to research designs, you will discover that the concept of validity can also be applied more broadly: to the overall accuracy of research findings and conclusions. In setting up an investigation, researchers must safeguard two types of validity. The first, **internal validity,** is the degree to which *conditions internal to the design of the study* permit an accurate test of the researcher's hypothesis or question. If, during any phase of the investigation—selecting participants, choosing research settings and tasks, and implementing procedures—participants' behavior is influenced by factors unrelated to the hypothesis, then the accuracy of the results is in doubt. Second, researchers must consider **external validity,** the degree to which their *findings generalize to settings and participants outside the original study.* Ensuring that samples, tasks, and contexts for conducting research represent the real-world people and situations that the investigator aims to understand is key to this type of accuracy.

Ask Yourself

Review Explain why, although a research method must be reliable to be valid, reliability *does not guarantee* validity.

Apply In studying the development of attention in school-age children, a researcher wonders whether to make naturalistic observations or structured observations. Which approach is best for ensuring internal validity? How about external validity? Why?

Connect Why is it better for a researcher to use multiple methods rather than just one method to test a hypothesis or answer a research question?

General Research Designs

In deciding on a research design, investigators choose a way of setting up a study that permits them to test their hypotheses with the greatest certainty possible. Two main types of designs are used in all research on human behavior: *correlational* and *experimental.*

Correlational Design

In a **correlational design,** researchers gather information on individuals, generally in natural life circumstances, and make no effort to alter their experiences. Then they look at relationships between participants' characteristics and their behavior or development. Suppose we want to answer such questions as, Do parents' styles of interacting with their children have any bearing on children's intelligence? Does attending a child-care center promote children's friendliness with peers? How do child abuse and neglect affect children's self-esteem and relationships with peers? In these and many other instances, the conditions of interest are difficult or impossible to arrange and control and must be studied as they currently exist.

The correlational design offers a way of examining relationships between variables. But correlational studies have one major limitation: We cannot infer cause and effect. For example, if we were to find that parental interaction is related to children's intelligence, we would not know whether parents' behavior actually *causes* intellectual differences among children. In fact, the opposite is possible. The behaviors of highly intelligent children may be so attractive that they cause parents to interact more favorably. Or a third variable that we did not even consider, such as the amount of noise and distraction in the home, may cause changes in both parental interaction and children's intelligence.

Do parents' styles of interacting with their children affect their children's academic performance and peer relations? Researchers can use a correlational design to examine the relationship between parenting styles and children's development, but it will not permit them to infer cause and effect. © Ed Bock/CORBIS

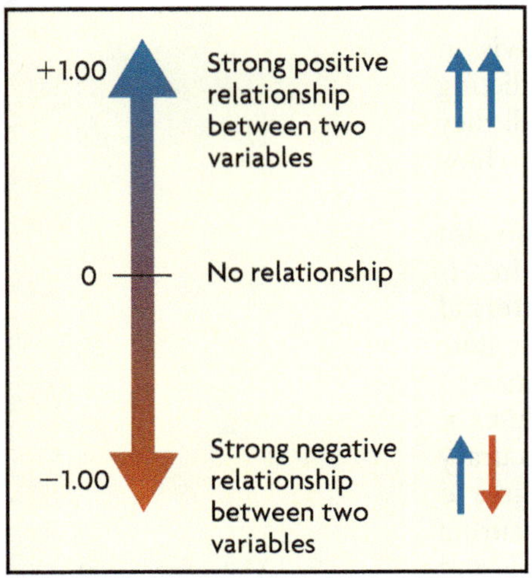

Figure 2.4 The meaning of correlation coefficients.
The magnitude of the number indicates the *strength* of the relationship. The sign of the number (+ or −) indicates the *direction* of the relationship.

In correlational studies, and in other types of research designs, investigators often examine relationships between variables by using a **correlation coefficient**—a number that describes how two measures, or variables, are associated with each other. Although other statistical approaches to examining relationships also exist, we will encounter the correlation coefficient in discussing research findings throughout this book. So let's look at what it is and how it is interpreted. A correlation coefficient can range in value from +1.00 to −1.00. The *magnitude, or size, of the number* shows the *strength of the relationship.* A zero correlation indicates no relationship; the closer the value is to either +1.00 or −1.00, the stronger the relationship (see Figure 2.4). For instance, a correlation of −.78 is high, −.52 is moderate, and −.18 is low. Note, however, that correlations of +.52 and −.52 are equally strong. The *sign of the number* refers to the *direction of the relationship.* A positive sign (+) means that as one variable *increases,* the other also *increases.* A negative sign (−) indicates that as one variable *increases,* the other *decreases.*

Let's look at some examples of how a correlation coefficient works. One researcher reported a +.55 correlation between a measure of maternal language stimulation and the size of children's vocabularies at age 2 years (Hoff, 2003). This is a moderate correlation, which indicates that mothers who spoke more to their toddlers had children who were more advanced in language development. In two other studies, child-rearing practices were related to children's compliance in consistent ways. First, the extent to which mothers were warm and sensitive during a play session correlated positively (+.34) with 2-year-olds' willingness to comply with their mother's directive to clean up toys (Feldman & Klein, 2003). Second, the extent to which mothers spoke harshly, interrupted, and controlled their 4-year-olds' play correlated negatively with children's compliance, at −.31 for boys and −.42 for girls (Smith et al., 2004). These moderate correlations revealed that the more mothers expressed affection and support, the more their children cooperated. And the more mothers restricted and coerced, the less the children cooperated (see Figure 2.5 for visual portrayals of these relationships).

All these investigations found correlations between parenting and young children's behavior. **TAKE A MOMENT...** Are you tempted to conclude that the maternal behaviors influenced children's responses? Although the researchers in these studies suspected this was so, they could not be sure of cause and effect. Can you think of other possible explanations? Finding a relationship in a correlational study does suggest that tracking down its cause—with a more powerful experimental strategy, if possible—would be worthwhile.

Figure 2.5 A positive and a negative correlation.
A researcher reported that maternal warmth and sensitivity were positively correlated with children's willingness to comply with their mother's directive to clean up toys (a). A second researcher reported that maternal restriction and coercion were negatively correlated with children's compliance (b). Each dot represents a participant's score on the two variables—maternal behavior and child compliance. Both correlations are moderate in strength because the pattern of dots deviates from a straight line, which would be a perfect correlation. Notice how in the positive correlation, as maternal warmth *increases,* child compliance tends to *increase.* In the negative correlation, as maternal restriction *increases,* child compliance tends to *decrease.* If a pattern of dots shows no upward or downward trend, then the correlation is near zero, indicating little or no relationship between the two variables.

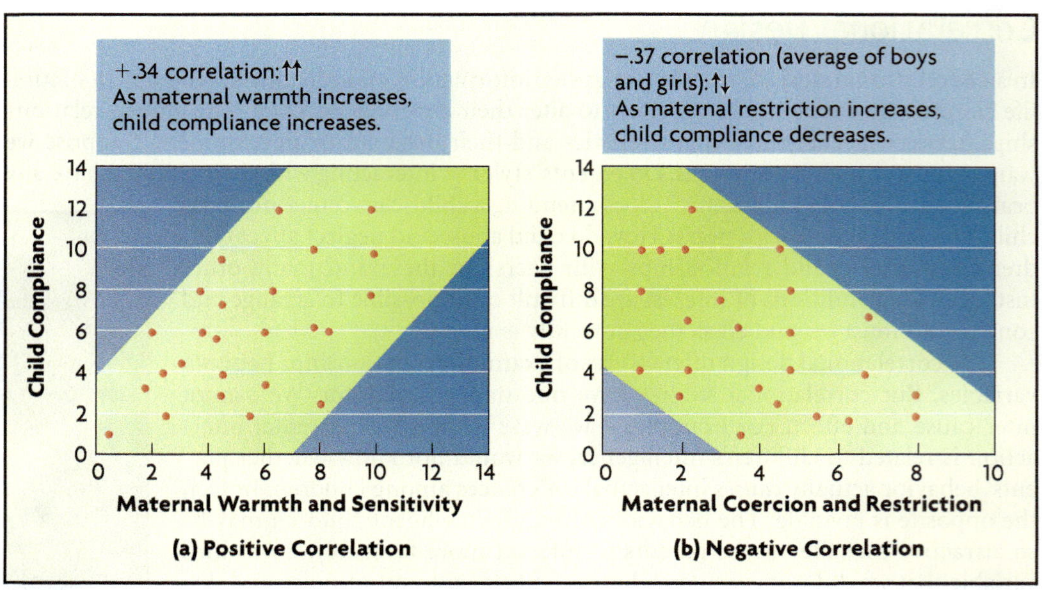

Experimental Design

An **experimental design** permits inferences about cause and effect because researchers use an evenhanded procedure to assign people to two or more treatment conditions. In an experiment, the events and behaviors of interest are divided into two types: independent and dependent variables. The **independent variable** is the one the investigator expects to cause changes in another variable. The **dependent variable** is the one the investigator expects to be influenced by the independent variable. Cause-and-effect relationships can be detected because the researcher directly *controls* or *manipulates* changes in the independent variable by exposing participants to the treatment conditions. Then the researcher compares their performance on measures of the dependent variable.

In one **laboratory experiment,** researchers explored the impact of adults' angry interactions on children's adjustment (El-Sheikh, Cummings, & Reiter, 1996). They hypothesized that the way angry encounters end (independent variable) affects children's emotional reactions (dependent variable). Four- and 5-year-olds were brought one at a time to a laboratory, accompanied by their mothers. One group was exposed to an *unresolved-anger treatment,* in which two adult actors entered the room and argued but did not work out their disagreements. The other group witnessed a *resolved-anger treatment,* in which the adults ended their disputes by apologizing and compromising. As Figure 2.6 shows, when they witnessed a follow-up adult conflict, more children in the resolved-anger treatment showed a decline in distress, as measured by fewer anxious facial expressions, less freezing in place, and less seeking of closeness to their mothers. The experiment revealed that anger resolution can reduce the stressful impact of adult conflict on children.

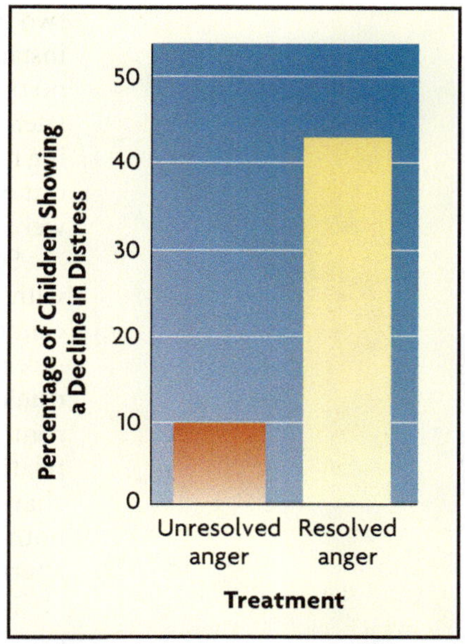

Figure 2.6 **Does the way adults end their angry encounters affect children's emotional reactions?**

A laboratory experiment revealed that children who had previously witnessed adults resolving their disputes by apologizing and compromising were more likely to decline in distress when witnessing subsequent adult conflicts than were children who witnessed adults leaving their arguments unresolved. Notice in this graph that only 10 percent of children in the unresolved-anger treatment declined in distress (see bar on left), whereas 42 percent of children in the resolved-anger treatment did so (see bar on right). (Adapted from El-Sheikh, Cummings, & Reiter, 1996.)

In experimental studies, investigators must take special precautions to control for participants' characteristics that could reduce the internal validity of their findings. For example, in the study just described, if a greater number of children from homes high in parental conflict ended up in the unresolved-anger treatment, we could not tell what produced the results—the independent variable or the children's backgrounds. Parental conflict and the treatment conditions would be **confounding variables**—so closely associated that their effects on an outcome cannot be distinguished. To protect against this problem, researchers engage in **random assignment** of participants to treatment conditions. By using an unbiased procedure, such as drawing numbers out of a hat or flipping a coin, investigators increase the chances that participants' characteristics will be equally distributed across treatment groups.

Sometimes researchers combine random assignment with another technique called **matching.** In this procedure, participants are measured ahead of time on the factor in question—in our example, exposure to parental conflict. Then children high and low on that factor are assigned in equal numbers to each treatment condition. In this way, the experimental groups are deliberately matched, or made equivalent, on characteristics that are likely to distort the results.

Modified Experimental Designs

Most experiments are conducted in laboratories, where researchers can achieve the maximum possible control over treatment conditions. But, as we have already indicated, findings obtained in laboratories often have limited external validity: They may not apply to everyday situations. In **field experiments,** researchers capitalize on opportunities to randomly assign participants to treatment conditions in natural settings. In the experiment we just considered, we can conclude that the emotional climate established by adults affects children's behavior in the laboratory. But does it have the same effect in daily life?

Another study helps answer this question (Yarrow, Scott, & Waxler, 1973). This time, the research was carried out in a child-care center. A caregiver deliberately interacted differently with two groups of preschoolers. In one condition (the *nurturant treatment*), she modeled many instances of warmth and helpfulness. In the second condition (the *control,* because it involved no treatment), she behaved as usual, with no special emphasis on concern for others. Two weeks later, the researchers created several situations that called for helpfulness. For example, a visiting mother asked each child to watch her baby for a few moments, but the baby's toys had fallen out of the playpen. The investigators found that children exposed to the nurturant treatment were much more likely than those in the control condition to return toys to the baby.

See the Social Issues box on the following page for an additional example of field research, with important implications for how best to foster children's intelligence. Often researchers cannot randomly assign participants and manipulate conditions in the real world, as these investigators were able to do. Sometimes they can compromise by conducting **natural, or quasi-, experiments,** comparing treatments that already exist, such as different family environments, schools, child-care centers, and preschool programs. These studies differ from correlational research only in that groups of people are carefully chosen to ensure that their characteristics are as much alike as possible. Occasionally, the same participants experience both treatments. In this way, investigators do their best to avoid confounding variables and alternative explanations for treatment effects.

Natural experiments permit researchers to examine the impact of many conditions that cannot be experimentally manipulated for ethical reasons—for example, the influence of premature birth, grade retention, or child maltreatment on development (Sameroff & MacKenzie, 2003). In one such study, maltreated and nonmaltreated 8- to 12-year-olds were enrolled in the same summer camp and, therefore, were observed and questioned under similar social conditions. When asked to complete stories about parenting that tapped themes of conflict, discipline, autonomy, and affection, maltreated children gave responses that were less elaborate and more negative than those of their nonmaltreated counterparts. Furthermore, peers rated maltreated children as more disruptive, more aggressive, and less cooperative (see Figure 2.7). Not surprisingly, peers strongly disliked these youngsters. Finally, children who represented their parents negatively in stories were especially likely to display maladaptive social behaviors (Shields, Ryan, & Cicchetti, 2001). The investigators concluded that maltreated children's internalized, unfavorable parenting images probably contribute to their poor social adjustment. And their poor adjustment reduces their access to the healing effects of warm, enjoyable relationships with peers. Despite intriguing findings like these, natural experiments cannot achieve the precision and rigor of true experimental research.

To help you compare the correlational and experimental designs we have discussed, Table 2.3 on page 60 summarizes their strengths and limitations. Now let's take a close look at designs for studying development.

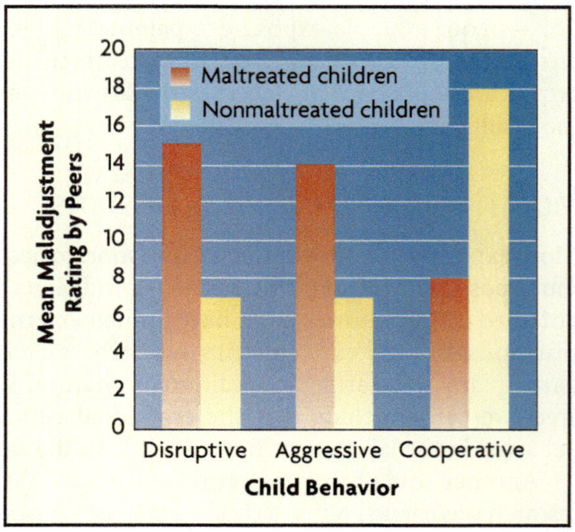

Figure 2.7 **A natural, or quasi-, experiment on the relationship of child maltreatment to children's social adjustment.** Researchers brought maltreated and nonmaltreated children together at a summer camp so they could be observed under similar conditions. After only a short time together, peers consistently rated maltreated children as less well-adjusted—more disruptive, more aggressive, and less cooperative. (Adapted from Shields, Ryan, & Cicchetti, 2001.)

▪ Social Issues ▪

Can Musical Experiences Enhance Intelligence?

In a 1993 experiment, researchers reported that college students who listened to a Mozart sonata for a few minutes just before taking a test of spatial reasoning abilities did better on the test than students who took the test after listening to relaxation instructions or sitting in silence (Rauscher, Shaw, & Ky, 1993). Strains of Mozart, the investigators concluded, seem to induce changes in the brain that "warm up" neural connections, thereby improving thinking. But the gain in performance, widely publicized as the "Mozart effect," lasted only 15 minutes and proved difficult to replicate. Rather than involving a real change in ability, Mozart seemed to improve arousal and mood, yielding better concentration on the test (Schellenberg et al., 2007).

Despite mounting evidence that the Mozart effect was uncertain at best, the media and politicians were enthralled with the idea that a brief exposure of the brain to classical music in infancy, when neural connections are forming rapidly, might yield lifelong intellectual benefits. Soon the states of Georgia, Tennessee, and South Dakota began providing free CDs containing classical music for every newborn baby leaving the hospital. Yet no studies of the Mozart effect have ever been conducted on infants! And an experiment with school-age children failed to demonstrate any intellectual gains as a result of simply listening to music (McKelvie & Low, 2002).

Research suggests that to produce lasting gains in mental-test scores, interventions must be long-lasting and involve children's active participation. Consequently, Glenn Schellenberg (2004) wondered, Can music lessons enhance intelligence? Children who take music lessons must practice regularly, exhibit extended focused attention, read music, memorize lengthy musical passages, understand diverse musical structures, and master technical skills. These experiences might foster cognitive processing, particularly during childhood, when regions of the brain are taking on specialized functions and are highly sensitive to environmental influences.

In a field experiment, Schellenberg recruited 132 six-year-olds—children just old enough for formal lessons. First, the children took an intelligence test and were rated on social maturity, permitting the researchers to see whether music lessons would affect some aspects of development but not others. Next, the children were randomly assigned to one of four experimental conditions. Two were music groups; one received piano lessons and the other voice lessons. The third group took drama lessons—a condition that shed light on whether intellectual gains were unique to musical experiences. The fourth group—a no-lessons control—was offered music lessons the following year. All music and drama instruction took place at the prestigious Royal Conservatory of Music in Toronto, where experienced teachers taught the children in small groups. After 36 weeks of lessons, a longitudinal follow-up was conducted: The children's intelligence and social maturity were assessed again.

All four groups gained in mental-test performance, probably because the participants had just entered grade school, which usually leads to an increase in intelligence test scores (see Chapter 8). But the two music groups consistently gained more than the control groups (see Figure 2.8). Their advantage, though just a few points, extended across many mental abilities, including verbal and spatial skills and speed of thinking. At the same time, only the drama group improved in social maturity; the music and no-lessons control groups showed no change.

When children take music lessons, they gain in mental test performance compared to children who take drama lessons or no lessons at all. To make music, they must engage in diverse intellectual skills: reading notation, memorizing passages, analyzing structures, and mastering technical skills. © Danita Delimont/Alamy

In sum, active, sustained musical experiences can lead to small increases in intelligence among 6-year-olds that do not arise from comparable drama lessons. But other enrichment activities with similar properties, such as reading, science, math, and chess programs, may confer similar benefits. All demand that children invest far more time and effort than they would in listening to a Mozart sonata. Nevertheless—despite absence of evidence to support their claims—music companies persist in selling CDs entitled "Tune Your Brain with Mozart," "Music for Accelerating Learning," and "Mozart for Newborns: A Bright Beginning."

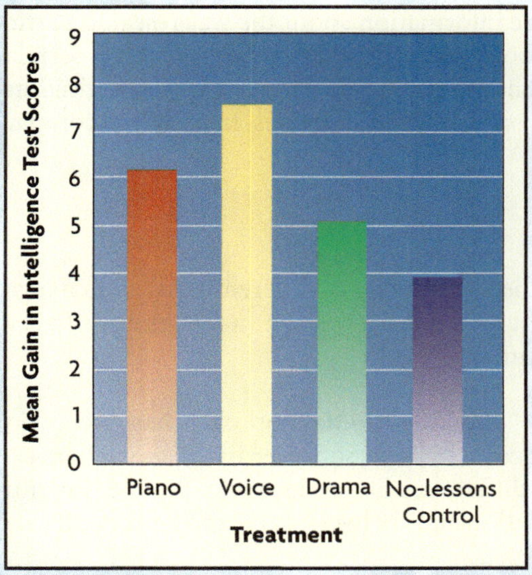

Figure 2.8 **Music lessons promote gains in intelligence.** In a field experiment comparing 36 weeks of piano and voice lessons with drama lessons and a no-lessons control, children in the two groups receiving music lessons showed slightly greater gains in intelligence test performance. (Adapted from Schellenberg, 2004.)

Table 2.3 Strengths and Limitations of General Research Designs

Design	Description	Strengths	Limitations
Correlational design	The investigator obtains information on participants without altering their experiences.	Permits study of relationships between variables.	Does not permit inferences about cause-and-effect relationships.
Laboratory experiment	Under controlled laboratory conditions, the investigator manipulates an independent variable and looks at its effect on a dependent variable; requires random assignment of participants to treatment conditions.	Permits inferences about cause-and-effect relationships.	Findings may not generalize to the real world.
Field experiment	The investigator randomly assigns participants to treatment conditions in natural settings.	Permits generalization of experimental findings to the real world.	Control over the treatment is generally weaker than in a laboratory experiment.
Natural, or quasi-, experiment	The investigator compares already existing treatments in the real world, carefully selecting groups of participants to ensure that their characteristics are as much alike as possible.	Permits study of many real-world conditions that cannot be experimentally manipulated.	Findings may be due to variables other than the treatment.

Ask Yourself

Review Why are natural experiments less precise than laboratory and field experiments?

Apply A researcher compares children who went to summer leadership camps with children who attended athletic camps. She finds that those who attended leadership camps are friendlier. Should the investigator tell parents that sending children to leadership camps will cause them to be more sociable? Why or why not?

Connect Reread the description of the study of aggressive boys and their friendships on page 44. What type of design did the researchers use, and why?

Reflect Design a study to investigate whether time devoted to adult–child picture-book reading in the preschool years contributes to reading readiness at school entry. List steps you will take to protect the internal and external validity of your investigation.

Designs for Studying Development

Scientists interested in child development require information about the way research participants change over time. To answer questions about development, they must extend correlational and experimental approaches to include measurements at different ages. Longitudinal and cross-sectional designs are special *developmental research* strategies. In each, age comparisons form the basis of the research plan.

The Longitudinal Design

In a **longitudinal design,** participants are studied repeatedly at different ages, and changes are noted as they get older. The time spanned may be relatively short (a few months to several years) or very long (a decade or even a lifetime).

• Advantages of the Longitudinal Design The longitudinal approach has two major strengths. First, because it tracks the performance of each person over time, researchers can identify common patterns as well as individual differences in development. Second, longitudinal studies permit investigators to examine relationships between early and later events and behaviors. Let's illustrate these ideas.

A group of researchers wondered whether children who display extreme personality styles—either angry and explosive or shy and withdrawn—retain the same dispositions when they become adults. In addition, the researchers wanted to know what kinds of experiences promote stability or change in personality and what consequences explosiveness and shyness have for long-term adjustment. To answer these questions, the researchers delved into the archives of the Guidance Study, a well-known longitudinal investigation that was initiated in 1928 at the University of California, Berkeley, and continued for several decades (Caspi, Elder, & Bem, 1987, 1988).

Results revealed that the two personality styles were moderately stable. Between ages 8 and 30, a good number of individuals remained the same, whereas others changed substantially. When stability did occur, it appeared to be due to a "snowballing effect," in which children evoked responses from adults and peers that acted to maintain their dispositions. Explosive youngsters were likely to be treated with anger, whereas shy children were apt to be ignored. As a result, the two types of children came to view their social worlds differently. Explosive children regarded others as hostile; shy children regarded them as unfriendly (Caspi & Roberts, 2001). Together, these factors led explosive children to sustain or increase their unruliness and shy children to continue to withdraw.

Persistence of extreme personality styles affected many areas of adult adjustment. For men, the results of early explosiveness were most apparent in their work lives, in the form of conflicts with supervisors, frequent job changes, and unemployment. Because few women in this sample of an earlier generation worked after marriage, their family lives were most affected. Explosive girls grew up to be hotheaded wives and mothers who were especially prone to divorce. Sex differences in the long-term consequences of shyness were even greater. Men who had been withdrawn in childhood were delayed in marrying, becoming fathers, and developing careers. However, because a withdrawn, unassertive style was socially acceptable for females in the mid-twentieth century, women who had shy personalities showed no special adjustment problems.

• **Problems in Conducting Longitudinal Research** Despite their strengths, longitudinal investigations pose a number of problems that can compromise both internal and external validity. **Biased sampling**—the failure to enlist participants who represent the population of interest—is a common problem. People who willingly participate in research that requires them to be observed and tested over many years are likely to have distinctive characteristics—at the very least, a special appreciation for the scientific value of research. As a result, we cannot easily generalize from them to the rest of the population. Furthermore, longitudinal samples generally become more biased as the investigation proceeds because of **selective attrition.** Participants may move away or drop out for other reasons, and the ones who remain are likely to differ in important ways from the ones who do not continue.

The very experience of being repeatedly observed, interviewed, and tested can also interfere with a study's validity. Children and adults may gradually be alerted to their own thoughts, feelings, and actions, think about them, and revise them in ways that have little to do with age-related change. In addition, with repeated testing, participants may become "test-wise." Their performance may improve as a result of **practice effects**—better test-taking skills and increased familiarity with the test—not because of factors commonly associated with development.

The most widely discussed threat to the validity of longitudinal findings is cultural–historical change, commonly called **cohort effects.** Longitudinal studies examine the development of *cohorts*—children developing in the same time period who are influenced by particular cultural and historical conditions. Results based on one cohort may not apply to children developing at other times. For example, look back at the findings on female shyness described in the previous section, which were gathered in the 1950s. Today's shy young women tend to be poorly adjusted—a difference that may be due to changes in

Children who were victims of the December 2004 tsunami in Indonesia participate in art therapy to help them cope with the loss of family members. This powerfully destructive historical event is a cohort effect, with profound consequences for development. © Lynsey Addario/CORBIS

gender roles in Western societies. Shy adults, whether male or female, feel more depressed, have fewer social supports, and may do less well in educational and career attainment than their agemates (Caspi, 2000; Caspi et al., 2003). Similarly, a longitudinal study of social development would probably result in quite different findings if it were carried out in the first decade of the twenty-first century, around the time of World War II, or during the Great Depression of the 1930s.

Cohort effects don't just operate broadly on an entire generation. They also occur when specific experiences influence some children but not others in the same generation. For example, children who witnessed the terrorist attacks of September 11, 2001 (either because they were near Ground Zero or because they saw injury and death on TV), or who lost a parent in the disaster were far more likely than other children to display persistent emotional problems, including intense fear, anxiety, and depression—difficulties still evident two years later (Pfeffer et al., 2007; Saylor et al., 2003). A study of one New York City sample suggested that as many as one-fourth of the city's children had been traumatized by the event (Hoven et al., 2005).

Finally, changes occurring within the field of child development may create problems for longitudinal research covering an extended time period. Theories and methods constantly change, and those that first inspired a longitudinal study may become outdated. For this reason, as well as the others just mentioned, many recent longitudinal studies span only a few months or years. Although short-term longitudinal research does not yield the same breadth of information as long-term studies, it does spare researchers some formidable obstacles.

The Cross-Sectional Design

The length of time it takes for many behaviors to change, even in limited longitudinal studies, has led researchers to turn to a more convenient strategy for studying development. In the **cross-sectional design,** groups of people differing in age are studied at the same point in time.

• **Advantages of the Cross-Sectional Design** The cross-sectional design is an efficient strategy for describing age-related trends. And because participants are measured only once, researchers need not be concerned about such difficulties as selective attrition, practice effects, or changes in the field that might make the findings obsolete by the time the study is complete.

An investigation in which students in grades 3, 6, 9, and 12 filled out a questionnaire asking about their sibling relationships provides a good illustration (Buhrmester & Furman, 1990). Findings revealed that sibling interaction was characterized by greater equality and less power assertion with age. Also, feelings of sibling companionship declined during adolescence. The researchers thought that several factors contributed to these age differences. As later-born children become more competent and independent, they no longer need, and are probably less willing to accept, direction from older siblings. And as adolescents move from psychological dependence on the family to greater involvement with peers, they may have less time and emotional need to invest in siblings. As you will see in Chapter 14, subsequent research has confirmed these intriguing ideas about the development of sibling relationships.

• **Problems in Conducting Cross-Sectional Research** Despite its convenience, cross-sectional research does not provide evidence about development at the level at which it actually occurs: the individual. For example, in the cross-sectional study of sibling relationships just discussed, comparisons are limited to age-group averages. We cannot tell if important individual differences exist. Indeed, longitudinal findings reveal that adolescents vary considerably in the changing quality of their sibling relationships. Although many become more distant, others become more supportive and intimate, still others more rivalrous and antagonistic (Branje et al., 2004; Dunn, Slomkowski, & Beardsall, 1994; Whiteman & Loken, 2006).

Cross-sectional studies—especially those that cover a wide age span—have another problem. Like longitudinal research, they can be threatened by cohort effects. For example, comparisons of 5-year-old cohorts and 15-year-old cohorts—groups born and reared in different years—may not really represent age-related changes. Instead, they may reflect unique experiences associated with the time period in which the age groups were growing up.

Improving Developmental Designs

Researchers have devised ways of building on the strengths and minimizing the weaknesses of longitudinal and cross-sectional approaches. Several modified developmental designs have resulted.

• Sequential Designs To overcome some of the limitations of traditional developmental designs, investigators sometimes use **sequential designs,** in which they conduct several similar cross-sectional or longitudinal studies (called *sequences*) at varying times. As the illustration in Figure 2.9 reveals, some sequential designs combine longitudinal and cross-sectional strategies, an approach that has three advantages:

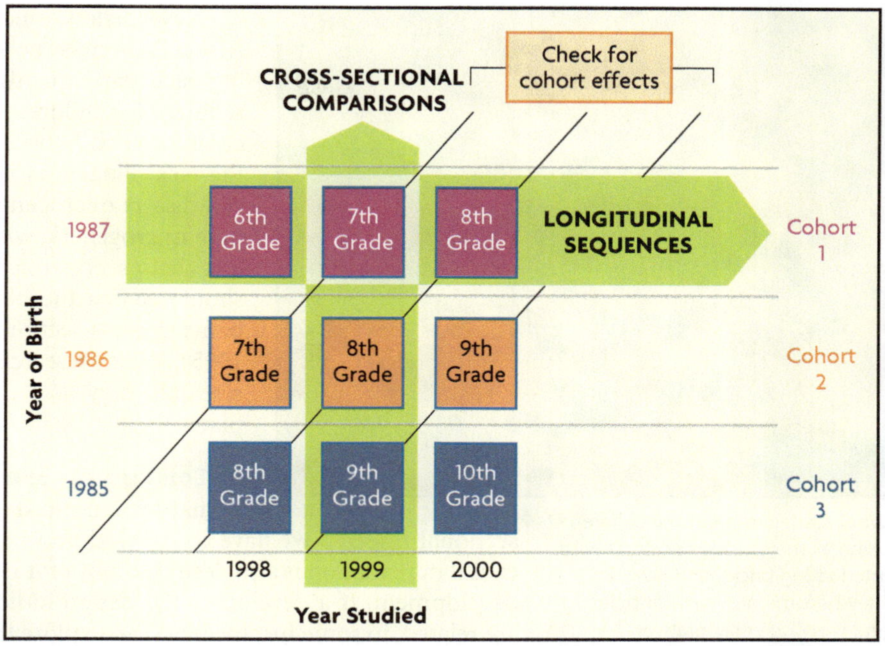

Figure 2.9 Example of a sequential design. Three cohorts, born in 1985 (blue), 1986 (pink), and 1987 (green), respectively, are followed longitudinally for three years. Testing the cohorts in overlapping grades enables researchers to check for cohort effects by comparing participants born in different years when they reach the same grade (see diagonals). In a study using this design, same-grade adolescents who were members of different cohorts scored similarly on a questionnaire assessing family harmony, indicating no cohort effects. By following each cohort for just three years, the investigator could infer a developmental trend across five years, from sixth to tenth grade.

- We can find out whether cohort effects are operating by comparing participants of the same age who were born in different years. In Figure 2.9, for example, we can compare the longitudinal samples at seventh, eighth, and ninth grades. If they do not differ, we can rule out cohort effects.
- We can make both longitudinal and cross-sectional comparisons. If outcomes are similar, we can be especially confident about the findings.
- The design is efficient. In our example, we can find out about change over a five-year period by following each cohort for three years.

In a study that used the design in Figure 2.9, researchers wanted to find out if family harmony changed as young people experienced the dramatic physical and psychological changes of adolescence (Baer, 2002). A questionnaire assessing emotional bonding among family members was given to three adolescent cohorts, each born a year apart. In longitudinal follow-ups, each cohort again responded to the questionnaire during the following two years.

Findings for the three cohorts converged: All reported (1) a slight decline in family harmony with grade and (2) similar levels of family harmony as they reached the same grade, confirming that there were no cohort effects. Therefore, the researchers concluded that family closeness diminishes steadily from sixth to tenth grade, noting, however, that the change is mild—not enough to threaten supportive family ties. **TAKE A MOMENT...** Turn back to our discussion of parent–adolescent communication as a dynamic system on pages 29–30 in Chapter 1 and our consideration of adolescent sibling relationships on page 62. How are those results helpful in interpreting the outcomes of the sequential study just described?

• Examining Microcosms of Development In the examples of developmental research we have discussed, observations of children are fairly widely spaced. When we observe once a year or every few years, we can describe change, but we cannot easily capture the processes that produce it. The **microgenetic design,** an adaptation of the longitudinal approach, presents children with a novel task and follows their mastery over a series of closely spaced sessions. Within this "microcosm" of development, researchers observe how change occurs (Kuhn, 1995; Siegler & Crowley, 1991). The microgenetic design is especially useful for studying cognitive development—for example, the strategies children use to acquire new knowledge in reading, mathematics, and science (Siegler, 2002, 2006). As you will see in Chapter 4, the microgenetic design has also been used to trace infants' mastery of motor skills.

What strategies are these children using as they jointly construct with interlocking bricks, and how do they become proficient at building and working collaboratively? A microgenetic design, which permits researchers to follow children's mastery of a challenging task, is uniquely suited to answering these questions. © Bob Daemmrich/The Image Works

Nevertheless, microgenetic studies are difficult to carry out. Researchers must pore over hours of recorded information, analyzing each participant's behavior many times. In addition, the time required for children to change is hard to anticipate. It depends on a careful match between the child's capabilities and the demands of the task. Finally, as in other longitudinal research, practice effects can distort microgenetic findings. As a check, researchers can compare microgenetic with cross-sectional observations. If new behaviors that emerge microgenetically reflect typical development, they should match the behaviors displayed by more advanced participants in cross-sectional studies, who are observed only once (Kuhn, 1995). When researchers overcome the challenges of microgenetic research, they reap the benefits of seeing development as it takes place.

• Combining Experimental and Developmental Designs Perhaps you noticed that all the examples of longitudinal and cross-sectional research we have considered permit only correlational, not causal, inferences. Yet causal information is also desirable, both for testing theories and for finding ways to enhance development. If a developmental design indicates that children's experiences and behavior are related, in some instances we can explore the causal link by experimentally manipulating the experiences. If, as a result, development is enhanced, then we have strong evidence for a causal association between experiences and behavior. Today, research that combines an experimental strategy with either a longitudinal or a cross-sectional approach is increasingly common. For a summary of the strengths and limitations of developmental research designs, refer to Table 2.4.

Table 2.4 Strengths and Limitations of Developmental Research Designs

Design	Description	Strengths	Limitations
Longitudinal design	The investigator studies the same group of participants repeatedly at different ages.	Permits study of common patterns and individual differences in development and relationships between early and later events and behaviors.	Age-related changes may be distorted because of biased sampling, selective attrition, practice effects, and cohort effects. Theoretical and methodological changes in the field can make findings obsolete.
Cross-sectional design	The investigator studies groups of participants differing in age at the same time.	More efficient than the longitudinal design. Not plagued by selective attrition, practice effects, or theoretical and methodological changes in the field.	Does not permit study of individual developmental trends. Age differences may be distorted because of cohort effects.
Sequential design	The investigator conducts several similar cross-sectional or longitudinal studies (called sequences) at varying times.	When the design includes longitudinal sequences, permits both longitudinal and cross-sectional comparisons. Also reveals cohort effects. Permits tracking of age-related changes more efficiently than the longitudinal design.	May have the same problems as longitudinal and cross-sectional strategies, but the design itself helps identify difficulties.
Microgenetic design	The investigator presents children with a novel task and follows their mastery over a series of closely spaced sessions.	Offers insights into how change occurs.	Requires intensive study of participants' moment-by-moment behaviors; the time required for participants to change is difficult to anticipate; practice effects may distort developmental trends.

Ask Yourself

Review Explain how cohort effects can distort the findings of both longitudinal and cross-sectional studies. How does the sequential design reveal cohort effects?

Apply A researcher wants to know whether children enrolled in child-care centers in the first few years of life do as well in school as those who are not in child care. Which developmental design is appropriate for answering this question? Explain.

Connect Review the study on music lessons and intelligence reported in the Social Issues box on page 59. Explain how it combines an experimental with a developmental design. What advantage does this approach offer?

Reflect Suppose a researcher asks you to enroll your baby in a 10-year longitudinal study. What factors would lead you to agree and stay involved? Do your answers shed light on why longitudinal studies often have biased samples? Explain.

Ethics in Research on Children

Research into human behavior creates ethical issues because, unfortunately, the quest for scientific knowledge can sometimes exploit people. When children take part in research, the ethical concerns are especially complex. Children are more vulnerable than adults to physical and psychological harm. In addition, immaturity makes it difficult or impossible for children to evaluate for themselves what participation in research will mean. For these reasons, special ethical guidelines for research on children have been developed by the federal government, by funding agencies, and by research-oriented associations such as the American Psychological Association (2002), the Canadian Psychological Association (2000), and the Society for Research in Child Development (1993).

Table 2.5 presents a summary of children's basic research rights. **TAKE A MOMENT...** Once you have examined them, think back to the ethical controversy faced by my colleague Ron, described at the beginning of this chapter. Then read about the following research situations, each of which also poses a serious ethical dilemma. What precautions do you think should be taken in each instance? Is either so threatening to children's well-being that it should not be carried out?

- In a study of moral development, a researcher wants to assess children's ability to resist temptation by videotaping their behavior without their knowledge. She promises 7-year-olds a prize for solving difficult puzzles but tells them not to look at a classmate's correct solutions, which are deliberately placed at the back of the room. Informing children ahead of time that cheating is being studied or that their behavior is being monitored will destroy the purpose of the study.

Table 2.5 Children's Research Rights

Research Right	Description
Protection from harm	Children have the right to be protected from physical or psychological harm in research. If in doubt about the harmful effects of research, investigators should seek the opinion of others. When harm seems possible, investigators should find other means for obtaining the desired information or abandon the research.
Informed consent	All research participants, including children, have the right to have explained to them, in language appropriate to their level of understanding, all aspects of the research that may affect their willingness to participate. When children are participants, informed consent of parents as well as others who act on the child's behalf (such as school officials) should be obtained, preferably in writing. Children, and the adults responsible for them, have the right to discontinue participation in the research at any time.
Privacy	Children have the right to concealment of their identity on all information collected in the course of research. They also have this right with respect to written reports and any informal discussions about the research.
Knowledge of results	Children have the right to be informed of the results of research in language that is appropriate to their level of understanding.
Beneficial treatments	If experimental treatments believed to be beneficial are under investigation, children in control groups have the right to alternative beneficial treatments if they are available.

Sources: American Psychological Association, 2002; Canadian Psychological Association, 2000; Society for Research in Child Development, 1993.

- A researcher is interviewing fifth graders about their experiences with bullying. A girl describes being victimized by an older sibling, but the behavior is not severe enough to warrant a report of abuse to child welfare authorities. Although the girl is unhappy, she wants to handle the problem on her own. If the researcher alerts the girl's parents to provide protection and help, he will violate his promise to keep participants' responses private.

Did you find it difficult to evaluate these examples? Virtually every organization that has devised ethical principles for research has concluded that conflicts arising in research situations do not have simple right or wrong answers. The ultimate responsibility for the ethical integrity of research lies with the investigator. But researchers are advised—and often required—to seek advice from others. Committees for this purpose (like the one that evaluated Ron's research) exist in colleges, universities, and other institutions. These *institutional review boards (IRBs)* assess proposed studies on the basis of a **risks-versus-benefits ratio,** which involves weighing the costs to participants in terms of inconvenience and possible psychological or physical injury against the study's value for advancing knowledge and improving conditions of life.

Ron's procedures, the school's research committee claimed, might not offer children sufficient **protection from harm.** If there are any risks to the safety and welfare of participants that the research does not justify, then preference is always given to the research participants. Vulnerability to harm, as the From Research to Practice box on the following page reveals, varies with children's age and characteristics. Occasionally, further inquiry can help resolve perplexing ethical dilemmas. In Ron's case, he provided the research committee with findings showing that asking elementary school children to identify disliked peers does not cause them to interact less frequently or more negatively with those children (Bell-Dolan, Foster, & Sikora, 1989). At the same time, Ron agreed to take special precautions when requesting such information. He promised to ask all the children to keep their comments confidential. He also arranged to conduct the study at a time when classmates had limited opportunity to interact with one another—just before a school vacation (Bell-Dolan & Wessler, 1994). With these safeguards in place, the committee approved Ron's research.

The ethical principle of **informed consent**—people's right to have all aspects of a study explained to them that might affect their willingness to participate—requires special interpretation when participants cannot fully appreciate the research goals and activities. Parental consent is meant to protect the safety of children whose ability to decide is not yet fully mature. In addition, researchers should obtain the agreement of other individuals who act on children's behalf, such as institutional officials when research is conducted in schools, child-care centers, or hospitals. This is especially important when studies include special groups, such as abused children, whose parents may not always represent their best interests (refer again to the From Research to Practice box).

As soon as children are old enough to appreciate the purpose of the research, and certainly by 7 years of age, their own informed consent should be obtained in addition to parental consent. Around age 7, changes in children's thinking permit them to better understand basic scientific principles and the needs of others. Researchers should respect and enhance these new capacities by giving school-age children a full explanation of research activities in language they can understand (Fisher, 1993). Careful attention to informed consent helps resolve dilemmas about revealing children's responses to parents, teachers, or other authorities when those responses suggest that the child's welfare is in danger. Children can be told in advance that if they report that someone is harming them, the researcher will tell an appropriate adult to take action to ensure the child's safety (Mishna, Antle, & Regehr, 2004).

Finally, all ethical guidelines advise that special precautions be taken in the use of deception and concealment, as occurs when researchers observe children from behind one-way mirrors, give them false feedback about their performance, or do not tell them the truth regarding the real subject of the research. By their very nature, studies involving deception breach the research right to make a fully informed decision about participation. Furthermore, deception can be particularly disturbing to children, who rely on a basic faith in the honesty of adults to feel secure.

Nevertheless, when revealing the purpose of a study would compromise internal validity, deception may be necessary. Its appropriateness depends on whether a study's potential benefits to society are great enough to justify infringing on informed consent and risking other harm (Fisher, 2005). In one controversial investigation, researchers planned to study children's formation of stereotypes and prejudices against a visible minority group by having

▪ *From* Research *to* Practice ▪

Children's Research Risks: Developmental and Individual Differences

Researchers interested in children face formidable challenges in defining their ethical responsibilities. Compared with adults, children are less capable of benefiting from research experiences. Furthermore, most risks children encounter are psychological rather than physical (as in medical research) and therefore difficult to anticipate and even detect (Thompson, 1992). Consider, for example, 7-year-old Henry, who did not want to answer a researcher's questions about how he feels about his younger brother, who has physical disabilities. Because Henry's parents told him they had given permission for his participation, he did not feel free to say no. Or take 11-year-old Isabelle, who tried to solve a problem but failed. Despite the researcher's assurances that the task was set up to be impossible, Isabelle ended up doubting her own competence.

How can we make sure that children are subjected to the least research risk possible? One valuable resource is our expanding knowledge of age-related capacities and individual differences. Research risks vary with development in complex ways. Some risks decrease with age, others increase, and still others occur at many or all ages (Thompson, 1990). And because of their personal characteristics and life circumstances, some children are more vulnerable to harm than others.

Age Differences

Research plans for younger children typically receive the most scrutiny because their limited cognitive competencies restrict their ability to make reasoned decisions and resist violations of their rights. In addition, as Henry's predicament illustrates, young children's limited social power can make it hard to refuse participation. In research that examined children's understanding of research procedures, 9-year-olds had great difficulty identifying their research rights and recognizing violations of those rights. Even 12-year-olds struggled to grasp their rights to decline participation, be protected from harm, and be given the study's results (Bruzzese & Fisher, 2003). And regardless of age, most children and adolescents thought that withdrawing from a study would have negative consequences and felt external pressure to continue. For example, they believed the researcher would be unhappy if they stopped (Ondrusek et al., 1998). But if researchers briefly name and explain each research right, comprehension improves, especially among adolescents.

Although this 10-year-old responds to the researcher's questions, she may not know why she is being interviewed, or realize that she has the right to withdraw from the study without negative consequences. Because children have difficulty understanding the research process, extra steps must be taken to protect their research rights. © Stockbyte/Getty Images

Whereas young children often fail to comprehend the research process, older children are more susceptible to procedures that threaten the way they view themselves. As middle childhood brings greater sensitivity to others' evaluations, giving false negative feedback or inducing failure (as happened to Isabelle) becomes more stressful. In adolescence, when questioning of authority is common, young people may be better at sizing up and rejecting researchers' deceptive evaluations (Thompson, 1992).

Children's Unique Characteristics

At times, children's backgrounds and experiences introduce vulnerabilities. For example, in certain ethnic minority communities, where deference to authority, maintaining pleasant relationships, and meeting the needs of a guest (the researcher) are highly valued, children and parents may be likely to consent when they would rather not do so (Fisher et al., 2002). In other circumstances, such as child maltreatment, parents are not necessarily good advocates for their children's rights. The consent of an additional adult invested in the child's welfare—a relative, teacher, or therapist—may be necessary to protect the child. And in some cases, such as teenagers who are substance abusers or delinquents, parents may be so eager to get them into contact with professionals that they are willing to agree to almost any research, with little forethought (Drotar et al., 2000).

Finding ways to reconcile the risks-versus-benefits conflicts we have considered is vital because research on children is of great value to society. As institutional review boards evaluate each study, participants' age and unique characteristics should be central to the discussion. Children and adolescents need clear, age-appropriate explanations of their rights, reminders of those rights as the research proceeds, and invitations to ask questions about anything they do not understand (Kon & Klug, 2006). And their decision should be the final word in most investigations, even though this standard is not mandatory in current guidelines.

most students in summer school classes wear red T-shirts (the "majority") and several children in each class wear yellow T-shirts (the "minority"), without giving the children any reason for the groupings (Brown & Bigler, 2002). At the end of the summer session, the children would be asked to rate the likeability of each of their classmates, and to rate each group on positive and negative traits ("friendly," "smart," "dirty," "mean").

At first, teachers refused to allow the study, arguing that students assigned to the "minority" group could be psychologically harmed. But the investigators countered that millions of racial and ethnic minority children and children with disabilities are placed in a similar position every day, and that it would be of great value to the mostly white participants to better understand the consequences of being a minority group member (Bigler, 2007). As a result, the teachers allowed the research to go forward.

When deception is used with adults, **debriefing,** in which the researcher provides a full account and justification of the activities, occurs after the research session is over. Debriefing should also be done with children, and in the study just described, it seemed to work well. Still, young children often lack the cognitive skills to understand the reasons for deceptive procedures, and despite explanations, they may leave the research situation with their belief in the honesty of adults undermined. Ethical standards permit deception in research with children if investigators satisfy institutional committees that nondeceptive alternatives do not offer sufficient scientific controls to test the hypothesis under investigation. Nevertheless, because deception may have serious emotional consequences for some youngsters, many child development specialists believe that researchers should use it only if the risk of harm is minimal.

Ask Yourself

Review Explain why researchers must consider children's age-related capacities to ensure that they are protected from harm and have freely consented to research.

Apply As a researcher was engaged in naturalistic observation of preschoolers' play, one child said, "Stop watching me!" Referring to the research rights listed in Table 2.5, indicate how the researcher should respond, and why.

Connect In the experiment on music lessons and intelligence reported in the Social Issues box on page 59, why was it ethically important for the researchers to offer music lessons to the no-lessons control group during the year after completion of the study?

Reflect Would you approve the study on stereotyping and prejudice, in which summer-school students (without being given an explanation) wore colored T-shirts that identified them as members of "majority" and "minority" groups? Explain. What ethical safeguards do you regard as vital in conducting research that requires deception of children to ensure internal validity?

SUMMARY

From Theory to Hypothesis

Describe the role of theories, hypotheses, and research questions in the research process.

© Michael Newman/PhotoEdit

- Research usually begins with a **hypothesis,** a prediction about behavior drawn from a theory. When little or no theory exists on a topic of interest, investigators begin with a research question. On the basis of the hypothesis or question, the investigator selects research methods (specific activities of participants) and a research design (overall plan for the study).

Common Methods of Gathering Information

Describe research methods commonly used to study children, noting strengths and limitations of each.

- **Naturalistic observations,** gathered in children's everyday environments, permit researchers to see directly the everyday behaviors they hope to explain. In contrast, **structured observations** in laboratories give every participant an equal opportunity to display the behaviors of interest.
- Depending on the researcher's purpose, observations can preserve participants' entire stream of behavior, or they can be limited to one or a few behaviors, as in **event sampling** and **time sampling. Observer influence** and **observer bias** can reduce the accuracy of observational findings.
- Self-reports include the **clinical interview,** a flexible, open-ended method that permits participants to express their thoughts in ways similar to their thinking in everyday life. **Structured interviews,** tests, and questionnaires are more efficient, permitting researchers to ask about activities and behaviors that participants might not think of mentioning in an open-ended interview. Both approaches depend on participants' ability and willingness to engage in accurate reporting.
- **Psychophysiological methods** help researchers uncover the biological bases of children's perceptual, cognitive, and emotional responses. Among measures of brain functioning, electroencephalogram (EEG) and event-related potentials

(ERPs) detect changes in electrical activity in the cerebral cortex. Neuroimaging techniques, such as positron emission tomography (PET) and functional magnetic resonance imaging (fMRI), yield the most precise information about brain region specialization and abnormalities in brain functioning. Near infrared optical topography (NIROT) is well-suited for use with infants and young children. However, investigators cannot be sure that a child demonstrating a particular pattern of autonomic or brain activity has actually processed a stimulus in a certain way.

- The **clinical,** or **case study, method** provides an in-depth understanding of a single child's development and psychological functioning. But collection of information may be unsystematic and subjective, and researchers cannot generalize beyond the child studied.
- Child development researchers have adapted observational and self-report methods to permit direct comparisons of cultures. To uncover the cultural meanings of children's and adults' behaviors, they rely on **ethnography,** engaging in participant observation. But investigators' cultural values and theoretical commitments may lead them to observe selectively or misinterpret what they see.

Reliability and Validity: Keys to Scientifically Sound Research

Explain how reliability and validity apply to research methods and to the overall accuracy of research findings and conclusions.

- **Reliability** refers to the consistency, or repeatability, of measures of behavior. In observational research, inter-rater reliability is determined by having observers evaluate the same behaviors. For self-report and psychophysiological measures, test–retest reliability is determined. In clinical and ethnographic research, reliability involves assessing whether the patterns and themes identified by the researcher are grounded in evidence and are plausible.
- A research method has high **validity** if, after examining its content and relationships with other measures of behavior, the researcher finds that it reflects what it was intended to measure. The concept of validity can also be applied to the overall accuracy of research findings and conclusions. In designing a study, investigators must ensure **internal validity**—that conditions internal to the design permit an accurate test of the hypothesis or question. They must also consider **external validity**—the degree to which findings generalize to settings and participants outside the original study.

General Research Designs

Distinguish correlational and experimental research designs, noting strengths and limitations of each.

- A **correlational design** examines relationships between variables without altering people's experiences. The **correlation coefficient** is often used to measure the association between variables. Although correlational studies do not permit cause-and-effect inferences, their use is justified when it is difficult or impossible to control the variables of interest.
- An **experimental design** permits cause-and-effect inferences. Researchers manipulate an **independent variable** by exposing groups of participants to two or more treatment conditions, then determine the effect of this variable on a **dependent variable. Random assignment** and **matching** ensure that characteristics of participants and treatment conditions do not operate as **confounding variables,** reducing the internal validity of experimental findings.
- **Laboratory experiments** usually achieve a high degree of control, but their findings may not apply to everyday life. In **field experiments,** researchers randomly assign participants to treatment conditions in the real world. Some investigators conduct **natural,** or **quasi-, experiments,** comparing existing treatments involving groups of people whose characteristics are as much alike as possible. This approach is less precise and rigorous than a true experimental design.

Designs for Studying Development

Describe designs for studying development, noting strengths and limitations of each.

- In the **longitudinal design,** participants are studied repeatedly at different ages to identify common patterns as well as individual differences in development, and the relationship between early and later events and behaviors. Problems include **biased sampling, selective attrition, practice effects,** and changes in accepted theories and methods during long-term studies. **Cohort effects**—difficulty generalizing to children growing up during different time periods—also threaten the validity of longitudinal findings.
- In the **cross-sectional design,** groups of participants differing in age are studied at the same time—an efficient approach that avoids such problems as selective attrition, practice effects, theoretical and methodological changes in the field. But it is limited to comparisons of age-group averages and, like longitudinal research, can be threatened by cohort effects.
- Modified developmental designs overcome some limitations of longitudinal and cross-sectional research. The **sequential design** allows researchers to test for cohort effects, make longitudinal and cross-sectional comparisons, and gather information about development efficiently. In the **microgenetic design,** researchers track change as it occurs to gain insights into processes of development. However, the time required for children to change is hard to anticipate, and practice effects can bias findings.

© Bob Daemmrich/The Image Works

Ethics in Research on Children

What special ethical issues arise in doing research on children?

- Because of their immaturity, children are especially vulnerable to harm and often cannot evaluate the risks and benefits of research. Ethical principles and institutional review boards (IRBs) that weigh research in terms of a **risks-versus-benefits ratio** help safeguard children's rights and afford them **protection from harm.** In addition to parental consent and agreement of others who act on children's behalf, researchers should seek the **informed consent** of children age 7 and older. The use of deception, though sometimes necessary, is especially risky with children because **debriefing** can undermine their faith in the trustworthiness of adults.

IMPORTANT TERMS AND CONCEPTS

biased sampling (p. 61)
clinical interview (p. 46)
clinical, or case study, method (p. 49)
cohort effects (p. 61)
confounding variables (p. 57)
correlation coefficient (p. 56)
correlational design (p. 55)
cross-sectional design (p. 62)
debriefing (p. 68)
dependent variable (p. 57)
ethnography (p. 51)
event sampling (p. 45)
experimental design (p. 57)
external validity (p. 55)
field experiment (p. 57)
hypothesis (p. 42)
independent variable (p. 57)
informed consent (p. 66)
internal validity (p. 55)
laboratory experiment (p. 57)
longitudinal design (p. 60)
matching (p. 57)
microgenetic design (p. 63)
natural, or quasi-, experiment (p. 58)
naturalistic observation (p. 43)
observer bias (p. 45)
observer influence (p. 45)
practice effects (p. 61)
protection from harm (p. 66)
psychophysiological methods (p. 47)
random assignment (p. 57)
reliability (p. 54)
risks-versus-benefits ratio (p. 66)
selective attrition (p. 61)
sequential design (p. 63)
structured interview (p. 46)
structured observation (p. 44)
time sampling (p. 45)
validity (p. 54)

3

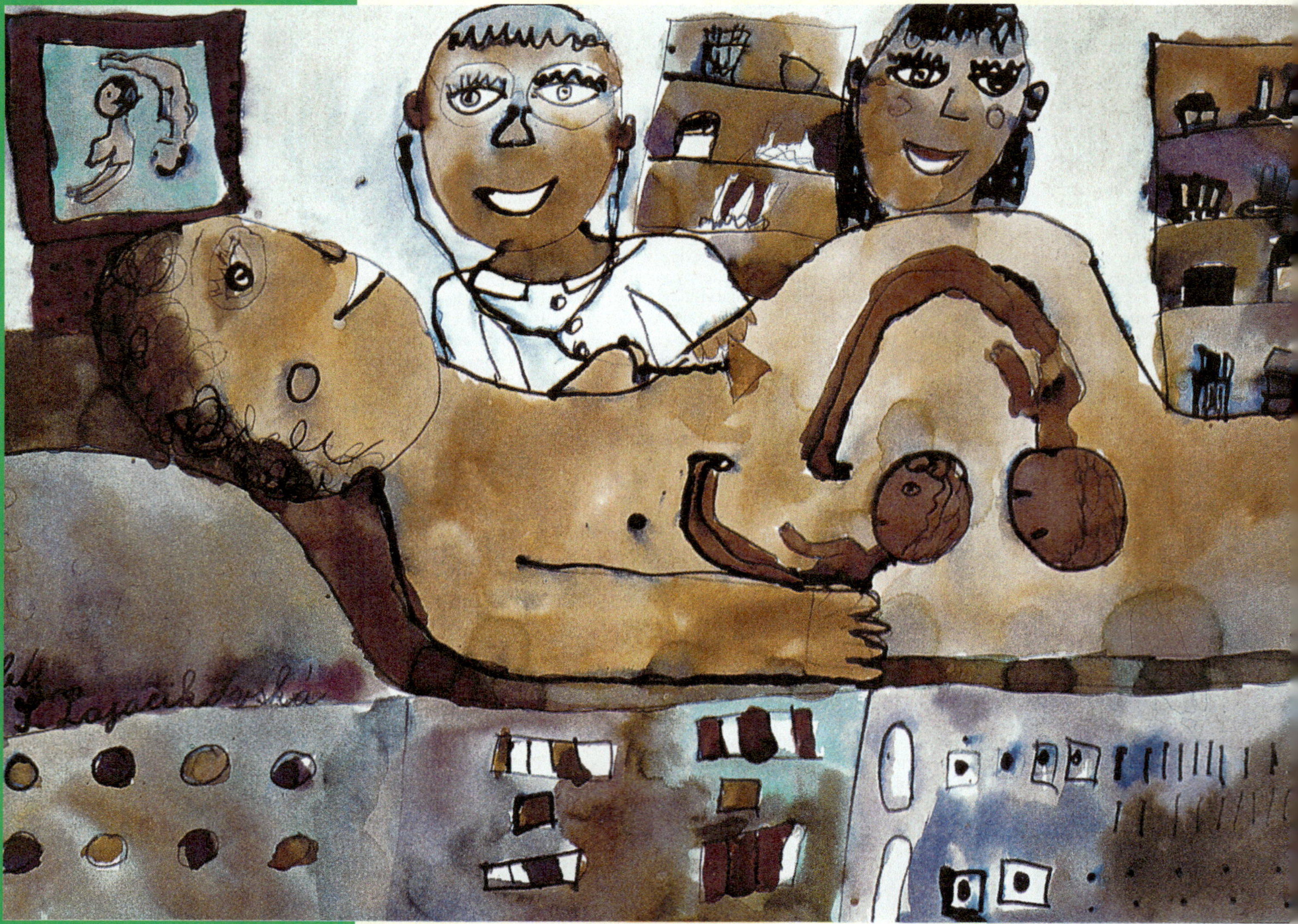

"Mother at the Specialist's"
Sonja Zajcikovska
7 years, Former Czechoslovakia

This artist's portrait of her twin siblings, floating within her mother's protective womb and surrounded by an optimistic world, captures the myriad influences on children's development. From the very beginning, a complex blend of genetic and environmental forces contributes to children's growth, advancing capacities, and well-being.

Biological Foundations, Prenatal Development, and Birth

"It's a girl," announces the doctor, holding up the squalling little creature as her new parents gaze with amazement at their miraculous creation.

"A girl! We've named her Sarah!" exclaims the proud father to eager relatives waiting for news of their new family member.

As we join these parents in thinking about how this wondrous being came into existence and imagining her future, we are struck by many questions. How could this baby, equipped with everything necessary for life outside the womb, have developed from the union of two tiny cells? What ensures that Sarah will, in due time, roll over, walk, talk, make friends, imagine, and create—just like other typically developing children born before her? Why is she a girl and not a boy, dark-haired rather than blond, calm and cuddly instead of wiry and energetic? What difference will it make that Sarah is given a name and place in one family, community, nation, and culture rather than another?

To answer these questions, we begin by considering genetic foundations. Because nature has prepared us for survival, all humans have features in common. Yet each of us is also unique. TAKE A MOMENT... Think about several children you know well, and jot down the most obvious physical and behavioral similarities between them and their parents. Did you find that one child shows combined features of both parents, another resembles just one parent, whereas a third is not like either parent? These directly observable characteristics are called **phenotypes.** They depend in part on the individual's **genotype**—the complex blend of genetic information that determines our species and influences all our unique characteristics. Yet phenotypes, as our discussion will show, are also affected by environmental influences—ones that begin even before conception.

Next, we trace prenatal development, the most rapid period of growth, during which complex transactions between heredity and environment profoundly affect children's health and well-being. Then we turn to the drama of birth and to the problems of infants who are born underweight or too early.

As our discussion proceeds, some findings about the influence of nature and nurture may surprise you. For example, many people believe that when children inherit unfavorable characteristics, not much can be done to help them. Others are convinced that the damage done to a child by a harmful environment can easily be corrected. We will see that neither of these assumptions is true. In the final section of this chapter, we take up the question of how nature and nurture work together to shape the course of development.

Genetic Foundations

Each of us is made up of trillions of units called *cells.* Within every cell is a control center, or *nucleus,* containing rodlike structures called **chromosomes,** which store and transmit genetic information. Their number varies from species to species—48 for chimpanzees, 64 for horses, 40 for mice, and 46 for human beings. Human chromosomes come in 23 matching pairs (an exception is the XY pair in males, which we will discuss shortly). Each member of a pair corresponds to the other in size, shape, and genetic functions, with one chromosome inherited from the mother and the other from the father (see Figure 3.1).

The Genetic Code

Chromosomes are made up of a chemical substance called **deoxyribonucleic acid,** or **DNA.** As Figure 3.2 shows, DNA is a long double-stranded molecule that looks like a twisted ladder. Each rung of the ladder consists of a pair of chemical substances called *bases.* Although the bases always pair up in the same way across the ladder rungs—A with T, C with G—they can occur in any order along its sides. It is this sequence of base pairs that provides genetic instructions. A **gene** is a segment of DNA along the length of the chromosome. Genes can be of different lengths—perhaps 100 to several thousand ladder rungs long. An estimated 20,000 to 25,000 genes lie along the human chromosomes (International Human Genome Sequencing Consortium, 2004).

We share some of our genetic makeup with even the simplest organisms, such as bacteria and molds, and most of it with other mammals, especially primates. Between 98 and 99 percent of chimpanzee and human DNA is identical. This means that only a small portion of our heredity is responsible for the traits that make us human, from our upright gait to our extraordinary language and cognitive capacities. And the genetic variation from one human to the next is even less! Individuals around the world are about 99.1 percent genetically identical (Gibbons, 1998; Gibbons et al., 2004). Only a tiny quantity of DNA contributes to human variation in traits and capacities.

A unique feature of DNA is that it can duplicate itself through a process called **mitosis.** This special ability permits a single cell, formed at conception, to develop into a complex human being composed of a great many cells. Refer again to Figure 3.2, and you will see that during mitosis, the chromosomes copy themselves. As a result, each new body cell contains the same number of chromosomes and the identical genetic information.

Genes accomplish their task by sending instructions for making a rich assortment of proteins to the *cytoplasm,* the area surrounding the cell nucleus. Proteins, which trigger chemical reactions throughout the body, are the biological foundation on which our characteristics are built. How do humans, with far fewer genes than scientists once thought (only twice as many as the worm or fly), manage to develop into such complex beings? The answer lies in

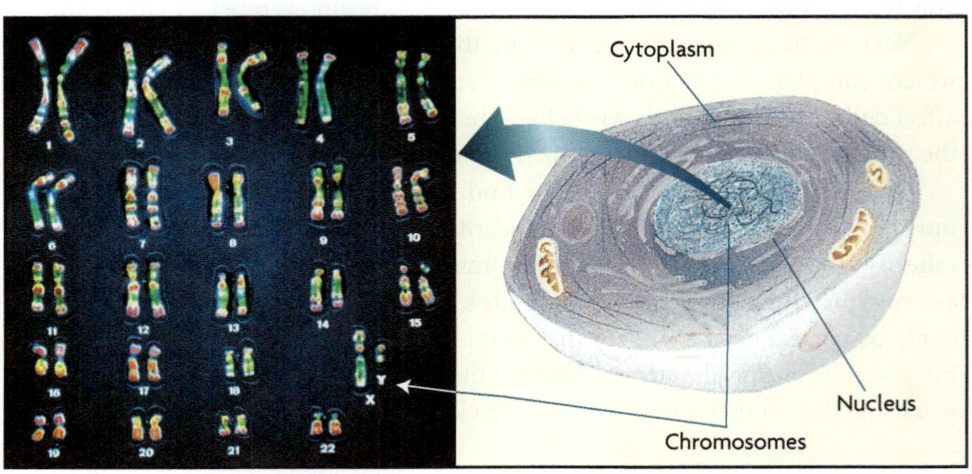

■ **Figure 3.1** **A karyotype, or photograph, of human chromosomes.** The 46 chromosomes shown here were isolated from a human cell, stained, greatly magnified, and arranged in pairs according to decreasing size of the upper "arm" of each chromosome. The twenty-third pair, XY, reveals that the cell donor is a male. In a female, this pair would be XX. © CNRI/Science Photo Library/Photo Researchers, Inc.

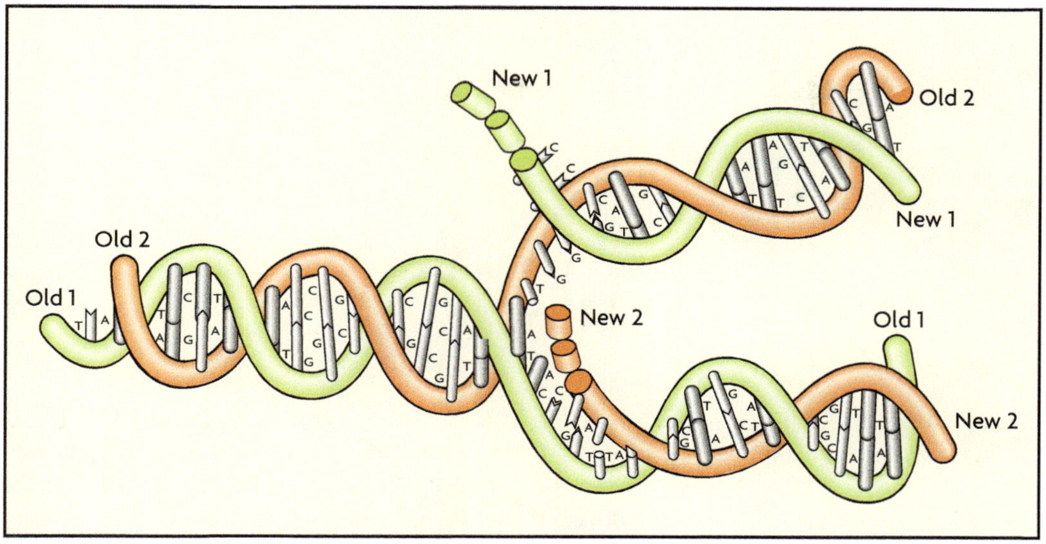

■ Figure 3.2 DNA's ladder-like structure.
This figure shows that the pairings of bases across the rungs of the ladder are very specific: Adenine (A) always appears with thymine (T), and cytosine (C) always appears with guanine (G). Here, the DNA ladder duplicates by splitting down the middle of its ladder rungs. Each free base picks up a new complementary partner from the area surrounding the cell nucleus.

the proteins our genes make, which break up and reassemble in staggering variety—about 10 to 20 million altogether. Simpler species have far fewer proteins. Furthermore, the communication system between the cell nucleus and cytoplasm, which fine-tunes gene activity, is more intricate in humans than in simpler organisms. Within the cell, a wide range of environmental factors modify gene expression (Lashley, 2007). So even at this microscopic level, biological events are the result of *both* genetic and nongenetic forces.

The Sex Cells

New individuals are created when two special cells called **gametes,** or sex cells—the sperm and ovum—combine. A gamete contains only 23 chromosomes, half as many as a regular body cell. Gametes are formed through a cell division process called **meiosis,** which halves the number of chromosomes normally present in body cells. When sperm and ovum unite at fertilization, the cell that results, called a **zygote,** will again have 46 chromosomes.

The steps involved in meiosis are shown in Figure 3.3 on page 74. First, chromosomes pair up, and each one copies itself. Then a special event called **crossing over** occurs, in which chromosomes next to each other break at one or more points along their length and exchange segments, so that genes from one are replaced by genes from another. This shuffling of genes creates new hereditary combinations. Next, the chromosome pairs separate into different cells, but chance determines which member of each pair will gather with others and end up in the same gamete. Finally, each chromosome leaves its partner and becomes part of a gamete containing only 23 chromosomes instead of the usual 46.

These events make the likelihood extremely low—about 1 in 700 trillion—that nontwin offspring of the same two parents will be genetically identical (Gould & Keeton, 1996). Therefore, meiosis helps us understand why siblings differ, even though they also have features in common because their genotypes come from the same pool of parental genes. The genetic variability produced by meiosis is important in an evolutionary sense: Because it generates offspring that vary in phenotype, it increases the chances that at least some members of a species will cope with ever-changing environments and will survive.

In the male, four sperm are produced when meiosis is complete. Also, the cells from which sperm arise are produced continuously throughout life. For this reason, a healthy man can father a child at any age after sexual maturity. In the female, meiosis results in just one ovum; the remaining genetic material degenerates. In addition, the female is born with all her ova already present in her ovaries, and she can bear children for only three to four decades. Still, there are plenty of female sex cells. About 1 to 2 million are present at birth, 40,000 remain at adolescence, and approximately 350 to 450 will mature during a woman's childbearing years (Moore & Persaud, 2008).

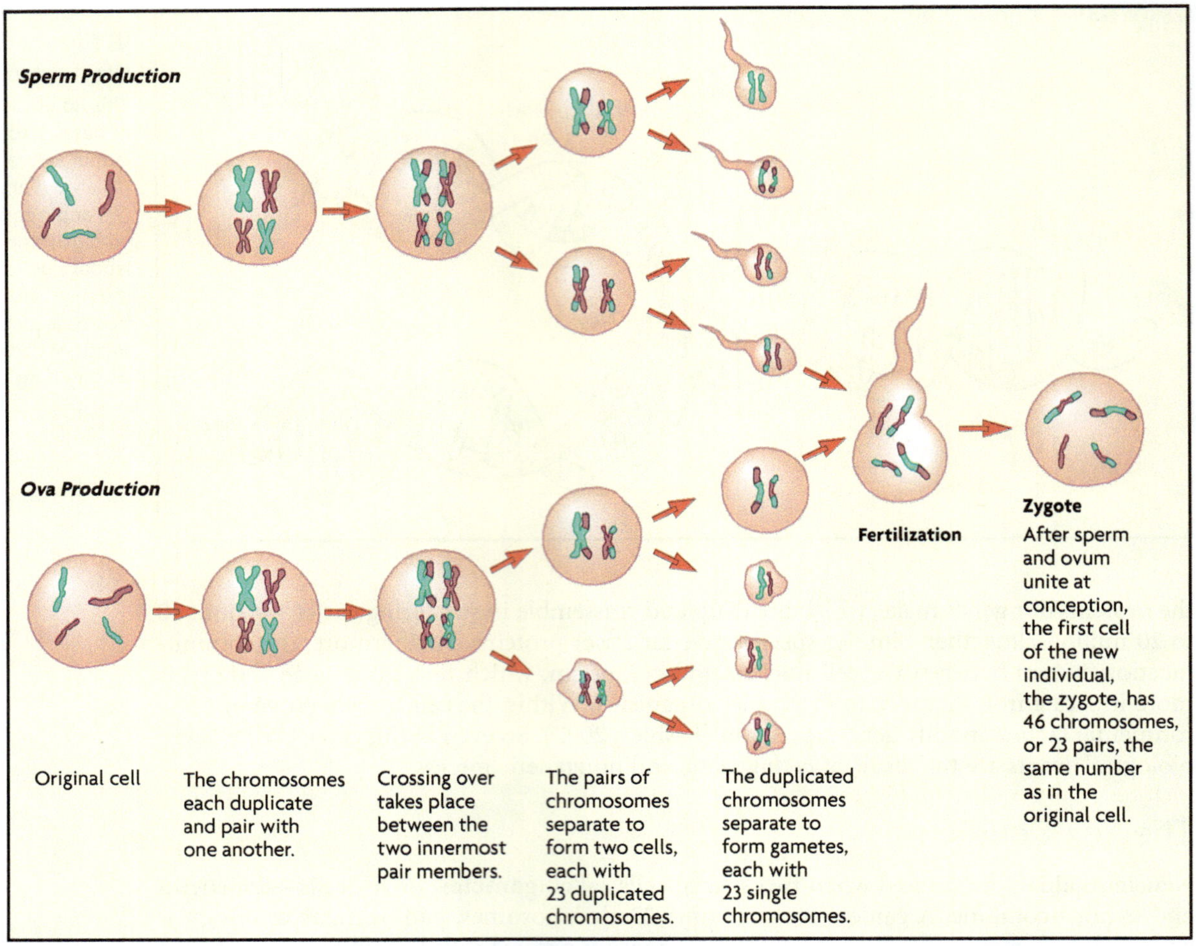

Figure 3.3 **The cell division process of meiosis, leading to gamete formation.** (Here, original cells are depicted with 2 rather than the full complement of 23 pairs.) Meiosis creates gametes with only half the usual number of chromosomes. When sperm and ovum unite at conception, the first cell of the new individual (the zygote) has the correct, full number of chromosomes.

Boy or Girl?

Return to Figure 3.1 and note the 22 matching pairs of chromosomes, which geneticists number from longest (1) to shortest (22). These are called **autosomes** (meaning *not* sex chromosomes). The twenty-third pair consists of **sex chromosomes.** In females, this pair is called XX; in males, it is called XY. The X is a relatively large chromosome, whereas the Y is short and carries little genetic material. When gametes form in males, the X and Y chromosomes separate into different sperm cells. The gametes that form in females all carry an X chromosome. Therefore, the sex of the new organism is determined by whether an X-bearing or a Y-bearing sperm fertilizes the ovum. In fact, scientists have isolated three genes on the Y chromosome that are crucial for male sexual development—one that switches on the production of male hormones and two involved in the formation of male sex organs. But they also know that other genes, some known and some yet to be discovered, are involved in the development of sexual characteristics (Bhagavath & Layman, 2007; Cotinot et al., 2002).

Multiple Offspring

Sometimes a zygote that has started to duplicate separates into two clusters of cells that develop into two individuals. These are called **identical,** or **monozygotic, twins** because they have the same genetic makeup. The frequency of identical twins is the same around the world—about 1 in every 330 births (Hall, 2003). Animal research has uncovered a variety of environmental influences that prompt this type of twinning, including temperature changes, variation in oxygen levels, and late fertilization of the ovum. In a minority of cases, the identical twinning runs in families, suggesting a genetic influence (Lashley, 2007).

Fraternal, or **dizygotic, twins,** the most common type of multiple birth, result from the release and fertilization of two ova. Fraternal twins are genetically no more alike than ordinary siblings. Table 3.1 summarizes genetic and environmental factors that increase the chances of giving birth to fraternal twins. Older maternal age, fertility drugs, and in vitro fertilization (to be discussed shortly) are major causes of the dramatic rise in fraternal twinning and other multiple births in industrialized nations over the past several decades (Machin, 2005; Russell et al., 2003). Currently, fraternal twins account for 1 in about every 60 births in the United States and 1 in every 50 births in Canada (Statistics Canada, 2007c; U.S. Department of Health and Human Services, 2007a).

These identical, or monozygotic, twins were created when a duplicating zygote separated into two clusters of cells, and two individuals with the same genetic makeup developed. © Laura Dwight Photography

Patterns of Genetic Inheritance

Two forms of each gene occur at the same place on the chromosomes, one inherited from the mother and one from the father. Each form of a gene is called an **allele.** If the alleles from both parents are alike, the child is **homozygous** and will display the inherited trait. If the alleles differ, then the child is **heterozygous,** and relationships between the alleles determine the trait that will appear.

• Dominant–Recessive Relationships In many heterozygous pairings, **dominant–recessive inheritance** occurs: Only one allele affects the child's characteristics. It is called *dominant;* the second allele, which has no effect, is called *recessive.* Hair color is an example. The allele for dark hair is dominant (we can represent it with a capital *D*), whereas the one for blond hair is recessive (symbolized by a lowercase *b*). A child who inherits a homozygous pair of dominant alleles *(DD)* and a child who inherits a heterozygous pair *(Db)* will both be dark-haired, even though their genotypes differ. Blond hair can result only from having two recessive alleles *(bb).* Still, heterozygous individuals with just one recessive allele *(Db)* can pass that trait to their children. Therefore, they are called **carriers** of the trait.

Table 3.1 Maternal Factors Linked to Fraternal Twinning

Factor	Description
Ethnicity	Occurs in 4 per 1,000 births among Asians, 8 per 1,000 births among whites, 12 to 16 per 1,000 births among blacks[a]
Family history of twinning	Occurs more often among women whose mothers and sisters have given birth to fraternal twins, suggesting a genetic influence
Age	Rises with maternal age, peaking between 35 and 39 years, and then rapidly falls
Nutrition	Occurs less often among women with poor diets; occurs more often among women who are tall and overweight or of normal weight as opposed to slight body build
Number of births	Is more likely with each additional birth
Fertility drugs and in vitro fertilization	Is more likely with fertility hormones and in vitro fertilization (see pages 84–85), which also increase the chances of bearing triplets, quadruplets, or quintuplets

[a]Worldwide rates, not including multiple births resulting from use of fertility drugs.

Sources: Bortolus et al., 1999; Hall, 2003; Lashley, 2007.

Table 3.2 Examples of Dominant and Recessive Characteristics

Dominant	Recessive
Dark hair	Blond hair
Normal hair	Pattern baldness
Curly hair	Straight hair
Nonred hair	Red hair
Facial dimples	No dimples
Normal hearing	Some forms of deafness
Normal vision	Nearsightedness
Farsightedness	Normal vision
Normal vision	Congenital eye cataracts
Normally pigmented skin	Albinism
Double-jointedness	Normal joints
Type A blood	Type O blood
Type B blood	Type O blood
Rh-positive blood	Rh-negative blood

Note: Many normal characteristics that were previously thought to result from dominant–recessive inheritance, such as eye color, are now regarded as due to multiple genes. For the characteristics listed here, there seems to be general agreement that the simple dominant–recessive relationship holds.

Source: McKusick, 2007.

Some human characteristics and disorders that follow the rules of dominant–recessive inheritance are listed in Table 3.2 and Table 3.3, respectively. As you can see, many disabilities and diseases are the product of recessive alleles. One of the most frequently occurring recessive disorders is *phenylketonuria,* or *PKU,* which affects the way the body breaks down proteins contained in many foods. Infants born with two recessive alleles lack an enzyme that converts one of the basic amino acids that make up proteins (phenylalanine) into a byproduct essential for body functioning (tyrosine). Without this enzyme, phenylalanine quickly builds to toxic levels that damage the central nervous system. By 1 year, infants with PKU are permanently mentally retarded.

Despite its potentially damaging effects, PKU provides an excellent illustration of the fact that inheriting unfavorable genes does not always lead to an untreatable condition. All U.S. states and Canadian provinces require that each newborn be given a blood test for PKU. If the disease is found, doctors place the baby on a diet low in phenylalanine. Children who receive this treatment nevertheless take slightly more time to process information and show mild deficits in certain cognitive skills, such as memory, planning, decision making, and problem solving, because even small amounts of phenylalanine interfere with brain functioning (Antshel, 2003; Channon, Mockler, & Lee, 2005; Christ et al., 2006). But as long as dietary treatment begins early and continues, children with PKU usually attain an average level of intelligence and have a normal lifespan.

In dominant–recessive inheritance, if we know the genetic makeup of the parents, we can predict the percentage of children in a family who are likely to display or carry a trait. Figure 3.4 illustrates this for PKU. Notice that for a child to inherit the condition, each parent must have a recessive allele *(p)*. As the figure also shows, a single gene can affect more than one trait. Because of their inability to convert phenylalanine into tyrosine (which is responsible for pigmentation), children with PKU usually have light hair and blue eyes. Furthermore, children vary in the degree to which phenylalanine accumulates in their tissues and in the extent to which they respond to treatment. This is due to the action of **modifier genes,** which enhance or dilute the effects of other genes.

Only rarely are serious diseases due to dominant alleles. Think about why this is so. Children who inherit the dominant allele always develop the disorder. They seldom live long enough to reproduce, so the harmful dominant allele is eliminated from the family's heredity in a single generation. Some dominant disorders, however, do persist. One is *Huntington disease,* a condition in which the central nervous system degenerates. Why has this disorder endured? Its symptoms usually do not appear until age 35 or later, after the person has passed on the dominant allele to his or her children.

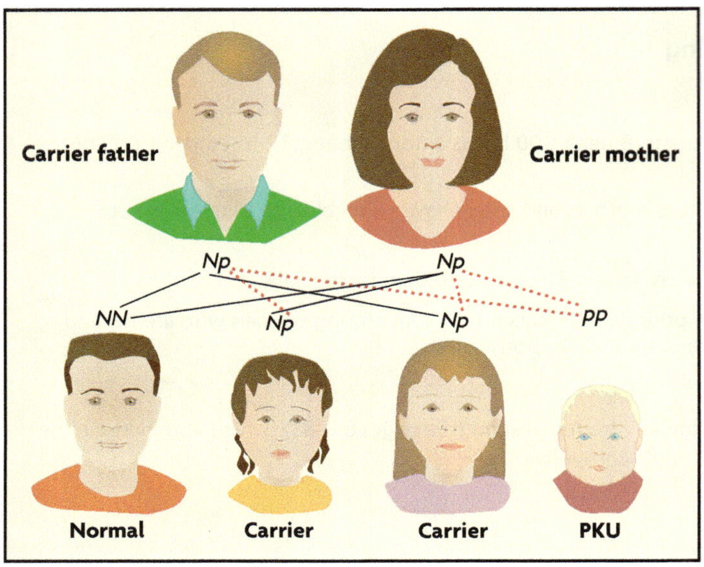

Figure 3.4 Dominant–recessive mode of inheritance, as illustrated by PKU.

When both parents are heterozygous carriers of the recessive gene *(p)*, we can predict that 25 percent of their offspring are likely to be normal *(NN)*, 50 percent are likely to be carriers *(Np)*, and 25 percent are likely to inherit the disorder *(pp)*. Notice that the PKU-affected child, in contrast to his siblings, has light hair. The recessive gene for PKU affects more than one trait. It also leads to fair coloring.

Table 3.3 Examples of Dominant and Recessive Diseases

Disease	Description	Mode of Inheritance	Incidence	Treatment
Autosomal Diseases				
Cooley's anemia	Pale appearance, retarded physical growth, and lethargic behavior begin in infancy.	Recessive	1 in 500 births to parents of Mediterranean descent	Frequent blood transfusion; death from complications usually occurs by adolescence.
Cystic fibrosis	Lungs, liver, and pancreas secrete large amounts of thick mucus, leading to breathing and digestive difficulties.	Recessive	1 in 2,000 to 2,500 Caucasian births; 1 in 16,000 births to North Americans of African descent	Bronchial drainage, prompt treatment of respiratory infection, dietary management. Advances in medical care allow survival with good life quality into adulthood.
Phenylketonuria (PKU)	Inability to metabolize the amino acid phenylalanine, contained in many proteins, causes severe central nervous system damage in the first year of life.	Recessive	1 in 8,000 births	Placing the child on a special diet results in average intelligence and normal lifespan. Subtle deficits in memory, planning, decision making, and problem solving are often present.
Sickle cell anemia	Abnormal sickling of red blood cells causes oxygen deprivation, pain, swelling, and tissue damage. Anemia and susceptibility to infections, especially pneumonia, occur.	Recessive	1 in 400 to 600 births to North Americans of African descent	Blood transfusions, painkillers, prompt treatment of infection. No known cure; 50 percent die by age 55.
Tay-Sachs disease	Central nervous system degeneration, with onset at about 6 months, leads to poor muscle tone, blindness, deafness, and convulsions.	Recessive	1 in 3,600 births to Jews of European descent and to French Canadians	None. Death by 3 to 4 years of age.
Huntington disease	Central nervous system degeneration leads to muscular coordination difficulties, mental deterioration, and personality changes. Symptoms usually do not appear until age 35 or later.	Dominant	1 in 18,000 to 25,000 births to North Americans	None. Death 10 to 20 years after symptom onset.
Marfan syndrome	Tall, slender build; thin, elongated arms and legs; and heart defects and eye abnormalities, especially of the lens. Excessive lengthening of the body results in a variety of skeletal defects.	Dominant	1 in 5,000 to 10,000 births	Correction of heart and eye defects sometimes possible. Death from heart failure in young adulthood is common.
X-Linked Diseases				
Duchenne muscular dystrophy	Degenerative muscle disease. Abnormal gait, loss of ability to walk between 7 and 13 years of age.	Recessive	1 in 3,000 to 5,000 male births	None. Death from respiratory infection or weakening of the heart muscle usually occurs in adolescence.
Hemophilia	Blood fails to clot normally. Can lead to severe internal bleeding and tissue damage.	Recessive	1 in 4,000 to 7,000 male births	Blood transfusions. Safety precautions to prevent injury.
Diabetes insipidus	Insufficient production of the hormone vasopressin results in excessive thirst and urination. Dehydration can cause central nervous system damage.	Recessive	1 in 2,500 male births	Hormone replacement.

Note: For recessive disorders, carrier status can be detected in prospective parents through a blood test or genetic analyses. For all disorders listed, prenatal diagnosis is available (see page 83).

Sources: Kliegman et al., 2008; Lashley, 2007; McKusick, 2007.

Incomplete Dominance In some heterozygous circumstances, the dominant–recessive relationship does not hold completely. Instead, we see **incomplete dominance,** a pattern of inheritance in which both alleles are expressed in the phenotype, resulting in a combined trait, or one that is intermediate between the two.

The *sickle cell trait,* a heterozygous condition present in many black Africans, provides an example. *Sickle cell anemia* (see Table 3.3 on page 77) occurs in full form when a child inherits two recessive alleles. They cause the usually round red blood cells to become sickle (crescent-moon) shaped, especially under low-oxygen conditions. The sickled cells clog the blood vessels and block the flow of blood, causing intense pain, swelling, and tissue damage. Despite medical advances that today allow 85 percent of affected children to survive to adulthood, North Americans with sickle cell anemia have an average life expectancy of only 55 years (Driscoll, 2007). Heterozygous individuals are protected from the disease under most circumstances. However, when they experience oxygen deprivation—for example, at high altitudes or after intense physical exercise—the single recessive allele asserts itself, and a temporary, mild form of the illness occurs.

The sickle cell allele is common among black Africans for a special reason. Carriers of it are more resistant to malaria than are individuals with two alleles for normal red blood cells. In Africa, where malaria is common, these carriers survived and reproduced more frequently than others, leading the gene to be maintained in the black population. In regions of the world where the risk of malaria is low, the frequency of the gene is declining. For example, compared with 20 percent of black Africans, only 8 percent of African Americans are carriers. The carrier rate is believed to be slightly higher in Canada than in the United States because a greater proportion of African Canadians are recent immigrants (Goldbloom, 2004).

X-Linked Inheritance Males and females have an equal chance of inheriting recessive disorders carried on the autosomes, such as PKU and sickle cell anemia. But when a harmful allele is carried on the X chromosome, **X-linked inheritance** applies. Males are more likely to be affected because their sex chromosomes do not match. In females, any recessive allele on one X chromosome has a good chance of being suppressed by a dominant allele on the other X. But the Y chromosome is only about one-third as long and therefore lacks many corresponding alleles to override those on the X. A well-known example is *hemophilia,* a disorder in which the blood fails to clot normally. Figure 3.5 shows its greater likelihood of inheritance by male children whose mothers carry the abnormal allele.

Besides X-linked disorders, many other sex differences reveal the male to be at a disadvantage. Rates of miscarriage, infant and childhood deaths, birth defects, learning disabilities, behavior disorders, and mental retardation all are greater for boys (Butler & Meaney, 2005). It is possible that these sex differences can be traced to the genetic code. The female, with two X chromosomes, benefits from a greater variety of genes. Nature, however, seems to have adjusted for the male's disadvantage. Worldwide, about 105 boys are born for every 100 girls, and judging from miscarriage and abortion statistics, an even greater number of boys are conceived (Pyeritz, 1998).

Nevertheless, in recent decades, the proportion of male births has declined in many industrialized countries, including the United States, Canada, and European nations (Jongbloet et al., 2001). Some researchers attribute this trend to a rise in stressful living conditions, which heighten spontaneous abortions, especially of male fetuses. In a test of this hypothesis, male-to-female birth ratios in East Germany were examined over the 54-year period between 1946 and 1999. The ratio was lowest in 1991, the year that the country's economy collapsed (Catalano, 2003). Similarly, in a California study spanning the decade of the 1990s, the percentage of male fetal deaths increased in months in which unemployment (a major stressor) also rose above its typical level (Catalano et al., 2005).

Figure 3.5 X-linked inheritance.

In the example shown here, the allele on the father's X chromosome is normal. The mother has one normal and one abnormal recessive allele on her X chromosomes. By looking at the possible combinations of the parents' alleles, we can predict that 50 percent of these parents' male children are likely to have the disorder, and 50 percent of their female children are likely to be carriers of it.

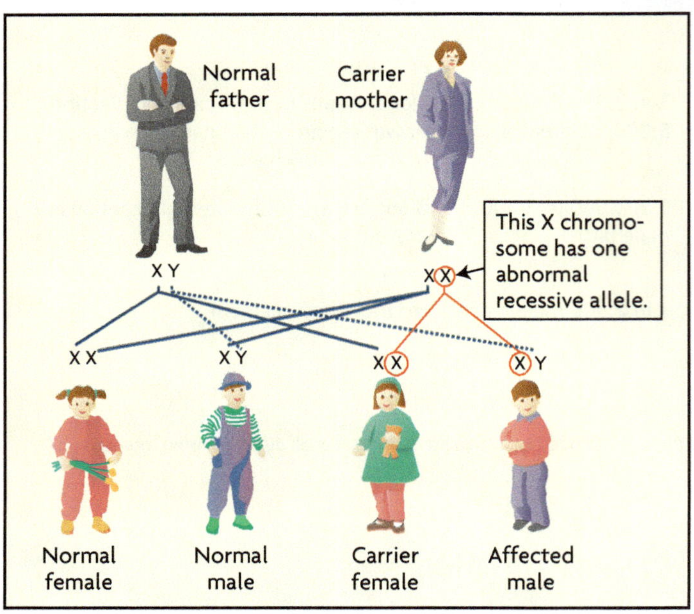

• Genomic Imprinting More than 1,000 human characteristics follow the rules of dominant–recessive and incomplete-dominance inheritance (McKusick, 2007). In these cases, whichever parent contributes a gene to the new individual, the gene responds in the same way. Geneticists, however, have identified exceptions. In **genomic imprinting,** alleles are *imprinted,* or chemically marked, so that one pair member (either the mother's or the father's) is activated, regardless of its makeup. The imprint is often temporary; it may be erased in the next generation, and it may not occur in all individuals (Everman & Cassidy, 2000).

An eighth grader, who has fragile X syndrome, enjoys a hug from a supportive teammate after middle school football practice. The disorder, tied to gene damage on the X chromosome, causes a range of deficits—from mild learning disabilities to severe mental retardation. On that spectrum, this 14-year-old falls in the middle. AP Images/The Herald, Dan Bates

Imprinting helps us understand certain puzzling genetic patterns. For example, children are more likely to develop diabetes if their father, rather than their mother, suffers from it. And people with asthma or hay fever tend to have mothers, not fathers, with the illness. Imprinting is involved in several childhood cancers and in *Prader-Willi syndrome,* a disorder with symptoms of mental retardation and severe obesity (Benarroch et al., 2007). It may also explain why Huntington disease, when inherited from the father, tends to emerge earlier and progress more rapidly (Navarrete, Martinez, & Salamanca, 1994).

Genetic imprinting can also operate on the sex chromosomes, as *fragile X syndrome*—the most common inherited cause of mental retardation—reveals. In this disorder, which affects about 1 in 4,000 males and 1 in 6,000 females, an abnormal repetition of a sequence of DNA bases occurs in a special spot on the X chromosome, damaging a particular gene. The defective gene at the fragile site is expressed only when it is passed from mother to child. Because the disorder is X-linked, males are more severely affected (Reiss & Dant, 2003). Females usually have a normally functioning gene on their other X chromosome (inherited from the father) that partially compensates for the abnormal gene.

EEG and fMRI research on children with fragile X syndrome reveals reduced size, structural abnormalities, and atypical activity in many areas of the cerebral cortex (Kabakus et al., 2006). Intellectual deficits range from mild learning disabilities to severe mental retardation. Certain physical features, such as enlarged ears, a long face with a prominent chin, and (in males) enlarged testicles are common. Fragile X has also been linked to 2 to 3 percent of cases of *autism,* a serious disorder usually diagnosed in early childhood that involves impaired social interaction, delayed or absent language and communication, and repetitive motor behavior (Goodlin-Jones et al., 2004).

• Mutation Although less than 3 percent of pregnancies result in the birth of a baby with a hereditary abnormality, these children account for about 20 percent of infant deaths and contribute substantially to lifelong impaired physical and mental functioning (U.S. Department of Health and Human Services, 2006). How are harmful genes created in the first place? The answer is **mutation,** a sudden but permanent change in a segment of DNA. A mutation may affect only one or two genes, or it may involve many genes, as in the chromosomal disorders we will discuss shortly. Some mutations occur spontaneously, simply by chance. Others are caused by hazardous environmental agents.

Although nonionizing forms of radiation—electromagnetic waves and microwaves—have no demonstrated impact on DNA, ionizing (high-energy) radiation is an established cause of mutation. Women who receive repeated doses before conception are more likely to miscarry or to give birth to children with hereditary defects. The incidence of genetic abnormalities, such as physical malformations and childhood cancer, is also higher in children whose fathers are exposed to radiation in their occupation. However, infrequent and mild exposure to radiation does not cause genetic damage (Jacquet, 2004). Rather, high doses over a long period impair DNA.

The examples just given illustrate *germline mutation,* which takes place in the cells that give rise to gametes. When the affected individual mates, the defective DNA is passed on to the next generation. In a second type, called *somatic mutation,* normal body cells mutate, an event that can occur at any time of life. The DNA defect appears in every cell derived from the affected body cell, eventually becoming widespread enough to cause disease or disability.

It is easy to see how disorders that run in families can result from germline mutation. But somatic mutation may be involved in these disorders as well. Some people harbor a genetic susceptibility that causes certain body cells to mutate easily in the presence of triggering events (Weiss, 2005). This helps explain why some individuals develop serious illnesses (such as cancer) as a result of smoking, exposure to pollutants, or psychological stress, while others do not.

• **Polygenic Inheritance** So far, we have discussed patterns of inheritance in which people either do or do not display a trait. These cut-and-dried individual differences are much easier to trace to their genetic origins than are characteristics that vary on a continuum among people, such as height, weight, intelligence, and personality. These traits are due to **polygenic inheritance,** in which many genes determine the characteristic in question. Polygenic inheritance is complex, and much about it is still unknown. In the final section of this chapter, we will discuss how researchers infer the influence of heredity on human attributes when they do not know the precise patterns of inheritance.

Chromosomal Abnormalities

Besides harmful recessive alleles, abnormalities of the chromosomes are a major cause of serious developmental problems. Most chromosomal defects result from mistakes occurring during meiosis, when the ovum and sperm are formed. A chromosome pair does not separate properly, or part of a chromosome breaks off. Because these errors involve far more DNA than problems due to single genes, they usually produce many physical and mental symptoms.

• **Down Syndrome** The most common chromosomal disorder, occurring in 1 out of every 1,000 live births, is *Down syndrome.* In 95 percent of cases, it results from a failure of the twenty-first pair of chromosomes to separate during meiosis, so the new individual inherits three of these chromosomes rather than the normal two. For this reason, Down syndrome is sometimes called *trisomy 21.* In other, less frequent forms, an extra twenty-first chromosome is attached to part of another chromosome (called *translocation* pattern). Or an error occurs during the early stages of mitosis, causing some but not all body cells to have the defective chromosomal makeup (called *mosaic* pattern) (Saitta & Zackai, 2005). Because less genetic material is involved in the mosaic type, symptoms of the disorder are less extreme.

The boy on the right has facial features typical of children with Down syndrome. Despite his impaired intellectual development, he is doing well because he is growing up in a stimulating home where he is loved and accepted and receives attention from family members.

The consequences of Down syndrome include mental retardation, memory and speech problems, limited vocabulary, and slow motor development. Brain-imaging studies reveal a reduction in size of the brain, which is more pronounced in certain regions of the cerebral cortex (Pinter et al., 2001). Affected individuals also have distinct physical features—a short, stocky build, a flattened face, a protruding tongue, almond-shaped eyes, and (in 50 percent of cases) an unusual crease running across the palm of the hand. In addition, infants with Down syndrome are often born with eye cataracts, hearing loss, and heart and intestinal defects. Because of medical advances, fewer individuals with Down syndrome die early than was the case in the past. Many survive into their fifties and a few into their sixties to eighties (Roizen & Patterson, 2003). However, more than half of affected individuals who live past age 40 show symptoms of Alzheimer's disease, the most common form of dementia (Menendez, 2005). Genes on chromosome 21 are linked to this disorder.

Caring for a baby with Down syndrome poses extra challenges for parents. Facial deformities often lead to breathing and feeding difficulties. Also, these infants smile less readily, show poor eye-to-eye contact, have weak muscle tone, and explore objects less persistently (Slonims & McConachie, 2006). But when parents encourage them to engage with their surroundings, Down syndrome children develop more favorably. They also benefit from infant and preschool intervention programs, although emotional, social, and motor skills improve more than intellectual performance (Carr, 2002). Clearly, environmental factors affect how well children with Down syndrome fare.

As Table 3.4 shows, the risk of bearing a Down syndrome baby rises dramatically with maternal age. Why is this so? Geneticists believe that the ova, present in the woman's body since her own prenatal period, weaken over time. As a result, chromosomes do not separate properly as they complete the process of meiosis at conception. But in about 5 to 10 percent of cases, the extra genetic material originates with the father. The reasons for this mutation are unknown. Some studies suggest a role for advanced paternal age, while others show no age effects (Dzurova & Pikhart, 2005; Fisch et al., 2003; Sherman et al., 2005).

Table 3.4 Risk of Giving Birth to a Baby with Down Syndrome, by Maternal Age

Maternal Age	Risk
20	1 in 1,900 births
25	1 in 1,200
30	1 in 900
33	1 in 600
36	1 in 280
39	1 in 130
42	1 in 65
45	1 in 30
48	1 in 15

Note: The risk of giving birth to a baby with Down syndrome after age 35 has increased slightly over the past 20 years, due to improved medical interventions during pregnancy and consequent greater likelihood of a Down syndrome fetus surviving to be liveborn.

Sources: Adapted from Halliday et al., 1995; Meyers et al., 1997.

• **Abnormalities of the Sex Chromosomes** Disorders of the autosomes other than Down syndrome usually disrupt development so severely that miscarriage occurs. When such babies are born, they rarely survive beyond early childhood. In contrast, abnormalities of the sex chromosomes usually lead to fewer problems. In fact, sex chromosome disorders often are not recognized until adolescence when, in some deviations, puberty is delayed. The most common problems involve the presence of an extra chromosome (either X or Y) or the absence of one X in females (see Table 3.5).

A variety of myths about individuals with sex chromosome disorders have been discredited by research. For example, as is evident from Table 3.5, males with *XYY syndrome* are not necessarily more aggressive and antisocial than XY males. And most children with sex chromosome disorders do not suffer from mental retardation. Instead, their intellectual problems are usually very specific. Verbal difficulties—for example, with reading and vocabulary—are common among girls with *triple X syndrome* and boys with *Klinefelter syndrome,* both of whom inherit an extra X chromosome. In contrast, girls with *Turner syndrome,* who are missing an X, have trouble with spatial relationships—for example, drawing pictures, telling right from left, following travel directions, and noticing changes in facial expressions (Kesler, 2007; Lawrence et al., 2003; Simpson et al., 2003). Brain-imaging research confirms that adding to or subtracting from the usual number of X chromosomes alters development of certain regions of the cerebral cortex and other brain structures, yielding particular intellectual deficits (Cutter et al., 2006; Itti et al., 2006).

Table 3.5 Sex Chromosomal Disorders

Disorder	Description	Incidence	Treatment
XYY syndrome	Extra Y chromosome. Above-average height, large teeth, and sometimes severe acne. Intelligence, male sexual development, and fertility are normal.	1 in 1,000 male births	No special treatment necessary.
Triple X syndrome (XXX)	Extra X chromosome. Tallness and impaired verbal intelligence. Female sexual development and fertility are normal.	1 in 500 to 1,250 female births	Special education to treat verbal ability problems.
Klinefelter syndrome (XXY)	Extra X chromosome. Tallness, body fat distribution resembling that of females, incomplete development of sex characteristics at puberty, sterility, and impaired verbal intelligence.	1 in 900 male births	Hormone therapy at puberty to stimulate development of sex characteristics; special education to treat verbal ability problems.
Turner syndrome (XO)	Missing X chromosome. Short stature, webbed neck, thyroid and heart abnormalities, incomplete development of sex characteristics at puberty, sterility, and impaired spatial intelligence.	1 in 2,500 to 8,000 female births	Hormone therapy in childhood to stimulate physical growth and at puberty to promote development of sex characteristics; special education to treat spatial ability problems.

Sources: Geerts, Steyaert, & Fryns, 2003; Kesler, 2007; Saitta & Zackai, 2005; Simpson et al., 2003.

Ask Yourself

Review Explain the genetic origins of PKU and Down syndrome. Cite evidence indicating that both heredity and environment contribute to the development of children with these disorders.

Review Using your knowledge of genetic imprinting and X-linked inheritance, explain why males are more vulnerable than females to miscarriage, infant death, genetic disorders, and other problems.

Apply Gilbert's genetic makeup is homozygous for dark hair. Jan's is homozygous for blond hair. What color is Gilbert's hair? How about Jan's? What proportion of their children are likely to be dark-haired? Explain.

Connect Referring to ecological systems theory (Chapter 1), explain why parents of children with genetic disorders often experience increased stress. What factors, within and beyond the family, can help these parents support their children's development?

Reproductive Choices

In the past, many couples with genetic disorders in their families chose not to bear children rather than risk the birth of an abnormal baby. Today, genetic counseling and prenatal diagnosis help people make informed decisions about conceiving, carrying a pregnancy to term, or adopting a child.

Genetic Counseling

Genetic counseling is a communication process designed to help couples understand genetic principles, genetic testing, and prevention of genetic disorders; assess their chances of giving birth to a baby with a hereditary disorder; and choose the best course of action in view of risks and family goals (Resta et al., 2006). Individuals likely to seek counseling are those who have had difficulties bearing children—for example, repeated miscarriages—or who know that genetic problems exist in their families. In addition, women who delay childbearing past age 35 are often candidates for genetic counseling. After this time, the overall rate of chromosomal abnormalities rises sharply, from 1 in every 190 to as many as 1 in every 20 pregnancies at age 43 (Wille et al., 2004). However, because younger mothers give birth in far greater numbers than older mothers, they bear the majority of babies with genetic defects. As a result, some experts argue that maternal needs, not age, should determine referral for genetic counseling (Berkowitz, Roberts, & Minkoff, 2006).

If a family history of mental retardation, psychological disorders, physical defects, or inherited diseases exists, the genetic counselor interviews the couple and prepares a *pedigree*, a picture of the family tree in which affected relatives are identified. The pedigree is used to estimate the likelihood that parents will have an abnormal child, using the genetic principles discussed earlier in this chapter. For many disorders, blood tests or genetic analyses can reveal whether the parent is a carrier of the harmful gene. Carrier detection is possible for all the recessive diseases listed in Table 3.3 on page 77, as well as others, and for fragile X syndrome.

When all the relevant information is in, the genetic counselor helps people consider appropriate options. These include taking a chance and conceiving, adopting a child, or choosing from a variety of reproductive technologies (see the From Research to Practice box on pages 84–85).

Prenatal Diagnosis and Fetal Medicine

If couples who might bear an abnormal child decide to conceive, several **prenatal diagnostic methods**—medical procedures that permit detection of problems before birth—are available (see Table 3.6). Women of advanced maternal age are prime candidates for *amniocentesis* or *chorionic villus sampling* (see Figure 3.6 on page 86). Except for *maternal blood* *analysis*, however, prenatal diagnosis should not be used routinely, since other methods pose some risk of injuring the developing organism.

Prenatal diagnosis has led to advances in fetal medicine. For example, by inserting a needle into the uterus, doctors can administer drugs to the fetus. Surgery has been performed to repair such problems as heart, lung, and diaphragm malformations, urinary tract obstructions, and neural defects (Hanson, Corbet, & Ballard, 2005). Fetuses with blood disorders have been given blood transfusions. And those with immune deficiencies have received bone marrow transplants that succeeded in creating a normally functioning immune system (Williams, 2006).

These techniques frequently result in complications, the most common being premature labor and miscarriage (Flake, 2003). Yet parents may be willing to try almost any option, even one with only a slim chance of success. Currently, the medical profession is struggling with how to help parents make informed decisions about fetal surgery.

Advances in *genetic engineering* also offer new hope for correcting hereditary defects. As part of the Human Genome Project—an ambitious international research program aimed at deciphering the chemical makeup of human genetic material (genome)—researchers have mapped the sequence of all human DNA base pairs. Using that information, they are "annotating" the genome—identifying all its genes and their functions, including their protein products and what these products do. A major goal is to understand the estimated 4,000 human disorders, both those due to single genes and those resulting from a complex interplay of multiple genes and environmental factors.

Table 3.6 Prenatal Diagnostic Methods

Method	Description
Amniocentesis	The most widely used technique. A hollow needle is inserted through the abdominal wall to obtain a sample of fluid in the uterus. Cells are examined for genetic defects. Can be performed by the 14th week after conception; 1 to 2 more weeks are required for test results. Small risk of miscarriage.
Chorionic villus sampling	A procedure that can be used if results are desired or needed very early in pregnancy. A thin tube is inserted into the uterus through the vagina, or a hollow needle is inserted through the abdominal wall. A small plug of tissue is removed from the end of one or more chorionic villi, the hairlike projections on the membrane surrounding the developing organism. Cells are examined for genetic defects. Can be performed at 9 weeks after conception, and results are available within 24 hours. Entails a slightly greater risk of miscarriage than amniocentesis. Also associated with a small risk of limb deformities, which increases the earlier the procedure is performed.
Fetoscopy	A small tube with a light source at one end is inserted into the uterus to inspect the fetus for defects of the limbs and face. Also allows a sample of fetal blood to be obtained, permitting diagnosis of such disorders as hemophilia and sickle cell anemia, as well as neural defects (see below). Usually performed between 15 and 18 weeks after conception but can be done as early as 5 weeks. Entails some risk of miscarriage.
Ultrasound	High-frequency sound waves are beamed at the uterus; their reflection is translated into a picture on a video screen that reveals the size, shape, and placement of the fetus. By itself, permits assessment of fetal age, detection of multiple pregnancies, and identification of gross physical defects. Also used to guide amniocentesis, chorionic villus sampling, and fetoscopy. When used five or more times, may increase the chances of low birth weight.
Maternal blood analysis	By the second month of pregnancy, some of the developing organism's cells enter the maternal bloodstream. An elevated level of alpha-fetoprotein may indicate kidney disease, abnormal closure of the esophagus, or neural tube defects, such as anencephaly (absence of most of the brain) and spina bifida (bulging of the spinal cord from the spinal column). Isolated cells can be examined for genetic defects.
Preimplantation genetic diagnosis	After in vitro fertilization and duplication of the zygote into a cluster of about 8 to 10 cells, 1 or 2 cells are removed and examined for hereditary defects. Only if that sample is free of detectable genetic disorders is the fertilized ovum implanted in the woman's uterus.

Sources: Bianchi, 2005; Kumar & O'Brien, 2004; Moore & Persaud, 2008; Sermon, Van Steirteghem, & Liebaers, 2004.

▪ *From* Research *to* Practice ▪

The Pros and Cons of Reproductive Technologies

Some couples decide not to risk pregnancy because of a family history of genetic disease. Many others—in fact, one-sixth of all couples who try to conceive—discover that they are sterile. And some never-married adults and gay and lesbian partners want to bear children. Today, increasing numbers of individuals are turning to alternative methods of conception—technologies that, although they fulfill the wish of parenthood, have become the subject of heated debate.

Donor Insemination and In Vitro Fertilization

For several decades, *donor insemination*—injection of sperm from an anonymous man into a woman—has been used to overcome male reproductive difficulties. In recent years, it has also enabled women without a male partner to become pregnant. Donor insemination is 70 to 80 percent successful, resulting in about 30,000 to 50,000 births in North America each year (Reynolds et al., 2003; Wright et al., 2004).

In vitro fertilization is another reproductive technology that has become increasingly common. Since the first "test tube" baby was born in England in 1978, 1 percent of all children in developed countries—about 40,000 babies in the United States and 3,500 in Canada—have been conceived through this technique annually (Jackson, Gibson, & Wu, 2004; Sutcliffe, 2002). With in vitro fertilization, a woman is given hormones that stimulate the ripening of several ova. These are removed surgically and placed in a dish of nutrients, to which sperm are added. Once an ovum is fertilized and begins to duplicate into several cells, it is injected into the mother's uterus.

By mixing and matching gametes, pregnancies can be brought about when either or both partners have a reproductive problem. Usually, in vitro fertilization is used to treat women whose fallopian tubes are permanently damaged. But a recently developed technique permits a single sperm to be injected directly into an ovum, thereby overcoming most male fertility problems. And a "sex sorter" method helps ensure that couples who carry X-linked diseases (which usually affect males) have a daughter. Fertilized ova and sperm can even be frozen and stored in embryo banks for use at some future time, thereby guaranteeing healthy zygotes should age or illness lead to fertility problems.

The overall success rate of in vitro fertilization is about 30 percent. However, success declines steadily with age, from 40 percent in women younger than age 35 to 7 percent in women age 43 and older (Wright et al., 2004).

Children conceived through these methods may be genetically unrelated to one or both of their parents. In addition, most parents who used in vitro fertilization do not tell their children about their origins, even though health professionals usually encourage them to do so. Does lack of genetic ties or secrecy surrounding these techniques interfere with parent–child relationships? Perhaps because of a strong desire for parenthood, caregiving tends to be somewhat warmer for young children conceived through donor insemination or in vitro fertilization. And in vitro infants are as securely attached to their parents, and in vitro children and adolescents as well adjusted, as their counterparts who were naturally conceived (Golombok & MacCallum, 2003; Golombok et al., 2004; Punamaki, 2006).

Although donor insemination and in vitro fertilization have many benefits, serious questions have arisen about their use. Most U.S. states and Canadian provinces have few legal guidelines for these procedures. As a result, donors are not always screened for genetic or sexually transmitted diseases. In many countries, including the United States and Canada, doctors are not required to keep records of donor characteristics (Richards, 2004). Canada, however, does retain a file on donor identities, permitting contact only in cases of serious disease, where knowledge of the child's genetic background might be helpful for medical reasons (Bioethics Consultative Committee, 2003). Another concern is that the in vitro "sex sorter" method will lead to parental sex selection, thereby eroding the moral value that boys and girls are equally precious.

Finally, more than 50 percent of in vitro procedures result in multiple births. Most are twins, but 9 percent are triplets and higher-order multiples. Consequently, among in vitro babies, the rate of low birth weight is 2.6 times higher than in the general population (Jackson, Gibson, & Wu, 2004). Risk of major birth defects also doubles because of many factors, including drugs used to induce ripening of ova and to maintain the pregnancy and delays in fertilizing ova outside the womb (Machin, 2005). In sum, in vitro fertilization poses greater risks than natural conception to infant survival and healthy development.

Surrogate Motherhood

An even more controversial form of medically assisted conception is *surrogate motherhood.* Typically in this procedure, sperm from a man whose wife is infertile are used to inseminate a woman, called a

Already, thousands of genes have been identified, including those involved in hundreds of diseases, such as cystic fibrosis; Duchenne muscular dystrophy; Huntington disease; Marfan syndrome; heart, digestive, blood, eye, and nervous system abnormalities; and many forms of cancer (National Institutes of Health, 2007). As a result, new treatments are being explored, such as *gene therapy*—correcting genetic abnormalities by delivering DNA carrying a functional gene to the cells. In recent experiments, gene therapy relieved symptoms in hemophilia patients and in

surrogate, who is paid a fee for her childbearing services. In return, the surrogate agrees to turn the baby over to the man (who is the natural father). The child is then adopted by his wife.

Although most of these arrangements proceed smoothly, those that end up in court highlight serious risks for all concerned. In one case, both parties rejected the infant with severe disabilities that resulted from the pregnancy. In several others, the surrogate mother wanted to keep the baby, or the couple changed their minds during the pregnancy. These children came into the world in the midst of conflict that threatened to last for years.

Because surrogacy usually involves the wealthy as contractors for infants and the less economically advantaged as surrogates, it may promote exploitation of financially needy women. In addition, most surrogates already have children of their own, who may be deeply affected by the pregnancy. Knowledge that their mother would give away a baby for profit may cause these children to worry about the security of their own family circumstances.

Fertility drugs and in vitro fertilization often lead to multiple fetuses. Although these sextuplets are healthy, reproductive technologies can pose grave ethical dilemmas. When three or more fetuses fill the womb, pregnancy complications may be so severe that doctors recommend aborting one or more to save the others.
AP Images/The Holland Sentinel, Dennis P. J. Geppert

New Reproductive Frontiers

Reproductive technologies are evolving faster than societies can weigh the ethics of these procedures. Doctors have used donor ova from younger women in combination with in vitro fertilization to help postmenopausal women become pregnant. Most recipients are in their forties, but several women in their fifties and sixties have given birth. These cases raise questions about bringing children into the world whose parents may not live to see them reach adulthood. Based on U.S. life expectancy data, 1 in 3 mothers and 1 in 2 fathers having a baby at age 55 will die before their child enters college (U.S. Census Bureau, 2007b).

Currently, experts are debating other reproductive options. At donor banks, customers can select ova or sperm on the basis of physical characteristics and even IQ. And scientists are devising ways to alter the DNA of human ova, sperm, and embryos to protect against hereditary disorders—techniques that could be used to engineer other desired characteristics. Many worry that these practices are dangerous steps toward selective breeding through "designer babies"—controlling offspring traits by manipulating genetic makeup.

Furthermore, scientists have successfully cloned (made multiple copies of) fertilized ova in sheep, cattle, and monkeys, and they are working on effective ways to do so in humans. By providing extra ova for injection, cloning might improve the success rate of in vitro fertilization. But it also opens the possibility of mass-producing genetically identical people. Therefore, it is widely condemned.

Although new reproductive technologies permit many barren couples to rear healthy newborn babies, laws are needed to regulate such practices. In Australia, New Zealand, Sweden, and Switzerland, individuals conceived with donated gametes have a right to information about their genetic origins (Frith, 2001). Pressure from those working in the field of assisted reproduction may soon lead to similar policies in the United States and Canada. Australia, Canada, and the Netherlands prohibit any genetic alteration of human gametes, with other nations following suit (Bernier & Grégoire, 2004). But some scientists argue that this total ban is too restrictive because it interferes with serving therapeutic needs.

In the case of surrogate motherhood, the ethical problems are so complex that 18 U.S. states have sharply restricted the practice, and Australia, Canada, and many European nations have banned it, arguing that the status of a baby should not be a matter of commercial arrangement and that a part of the body should not be rented or sold (Chen, 2003; McGee, 1997). Denmark, France, and Great Britain have prohibited in vitro fertilization for women past menopause (Bioethics Consultative Committee, 2003). At present, nothing is known about the psychological consequences of being a product of these procedures. Research on how such children grow up, including what they know and how they feel about their origins, is important for weighing the pros and cons of these techniques.

patients with severe immune system dysfunction. A few, however, experienced serious side effects (Relph, Harrington, & Pandha, 2004). In another approach, called *proteomics*, scientists modify gene-specified proteins involved in disease (Bradshaw & Burlingame, 2005).

Genetic treatments seem some distance in the future for most single-gene defects, however, and even farther off for diseases involving multiple genes that combine in complex ways with one another and the environment. Fortunately, 95 percent of fetuses examined through

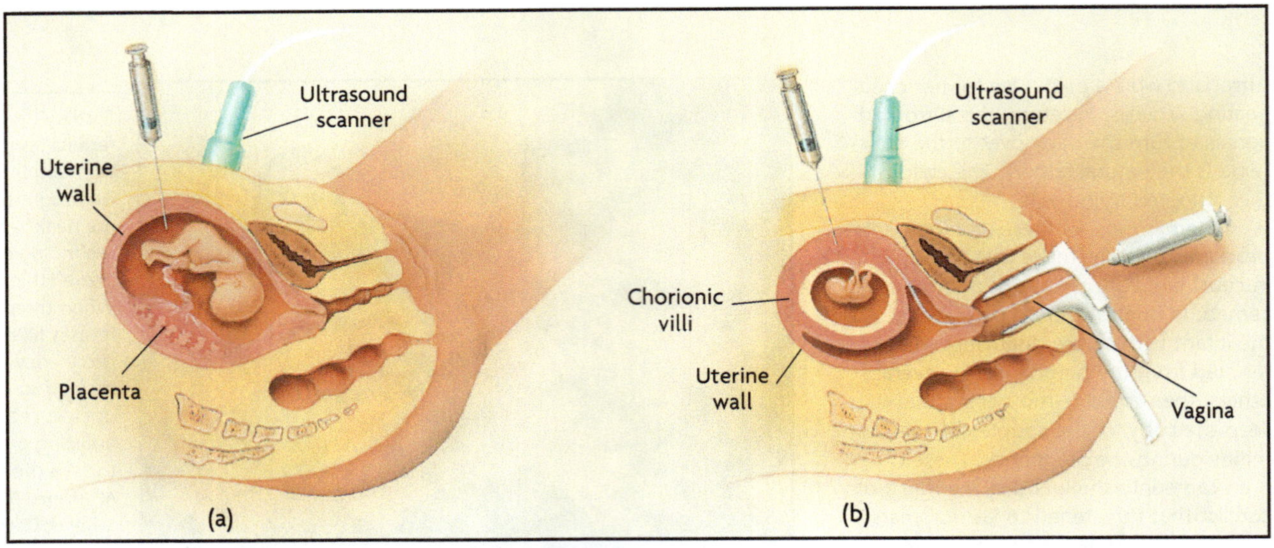

Figure 3.6 **Amniocentesis and chorionic villus sampling.**
Today, hundreds of defects and diseases can be detected before birth using these two procedures. (a) In amniocentesis, a hollow needle is inserted through the abdominal wall into the uterus during the fourteenth week after conception or later. Fluid is withdrawn, and fetal cells are cultured, a process that takes about one to two weeks. (b) Chorionic villus sampling can be performed much earlier in pregnancy, at nine weeks after conception, and results are available within 24 hours. Two approaches to obtaining a sample of chorionic villus are shown: inserting a thin tube through the vagina into the uterus and inserting a needle through the abdominal wall. In both amniocentesis and chorionic villus sampling, an ultrasound scanner is used for guidance. (From K. L. Moore and T. V. N. Persaud, 2008, *Before We Are Born, 7th ed.*, p. 69. Copyright © 2008, with permission from Elsevier, Inc.)

prenatal diagnosis are normal (Moore & Persaud, 2008). The availability of such tests allows many individuals whose family history would have caused them to avoid pregnancy to bear healthy children.

Ask Yourself

Review Why is genetic counseling called a *communication process?* Who should seek it?

Review Describe the ethical pros and cons of fetal surgery, surrogate motherhood, and postmenopausal-assisted childbearing.

Apply Imagine that you must counsel a couple considering in vitro fertilization using donor ova to overcome infertility. What medical and ethical risks would you raise?

Reflect Imagine that you are a woman who is a carrier of fragile X syndrome but who wants to have children. Would you become pregnant, adopt, use a surrogate mother, or give up your desire for parenthood? Explain. If you became pregnant, would you opt for prenatal diagnosis? Explain your decisions.

Prenatal Development

The sperm and ovum that unite to form the new individual are uniquely suited for the task of reproduction. The ovum is a tiny sphere, measuring 1/175 inch in diameter, that is barely visible to the naked eye as a dot the size of the period at the end of this sentence. But in its microscopic world, it is a giant—the largest cell in the human body. The ovum's size makes it a perfect target for the much smaller sperm, which measure only 1/500 inch.

Conception

About once every 28 days, in the middle of a woman's menstrual cycle, an ovum bursts from one of her *ovaries*, two walnut-sized organs located deep inside her abdomen, and is drawn into one of two *fallopian tubes*—long, thin structures that lead to the hollow, soft-lined uterus (see Figure 3.7). While the ovum is traveling, the spot on the ovary from which it was released, now called the *corpus luteum*, secretes hormones that prepare the lining of the uterus to receive a fertilized ovum. If pregnancy does not occur, the corpus luteum shrinks, and the lining of the uterus is discarded two weeks later with menstruation.

The male produces sperm in vast numbers—an average of 300 million a day. In the final process of maturation, each sperm develops a tail that permits it to swim long distances, upstream in the female reproductive tract, through the *cervix* (opening of the uterus), and into the fallopian tube, where fertilization usually takes place. The journey is difficult, and many sperm die. Only 300 to 500 reach the ovum, if one happens to be present. Sperm live for up to 6 days and can lie in wait for the ovum, which survives for only 1 day after being released into the fallopian tube. However, most conceptions result from intercourse during a 3-day period—on the day of or during the 2 days preceding ovulation (Wilcox, Weinberg, & Baird, 1995).

With conception, the story of prenatal development begins to unfold. The vast changes that take place during the 38 weeks of pregnancy are usually divided into three periods: (1) the period of the zygote, (2) the period of the embryo, and (3) the period of the fetus. As we look at what happens in each, you may find it useful to refer to the Milestones table on page 88.

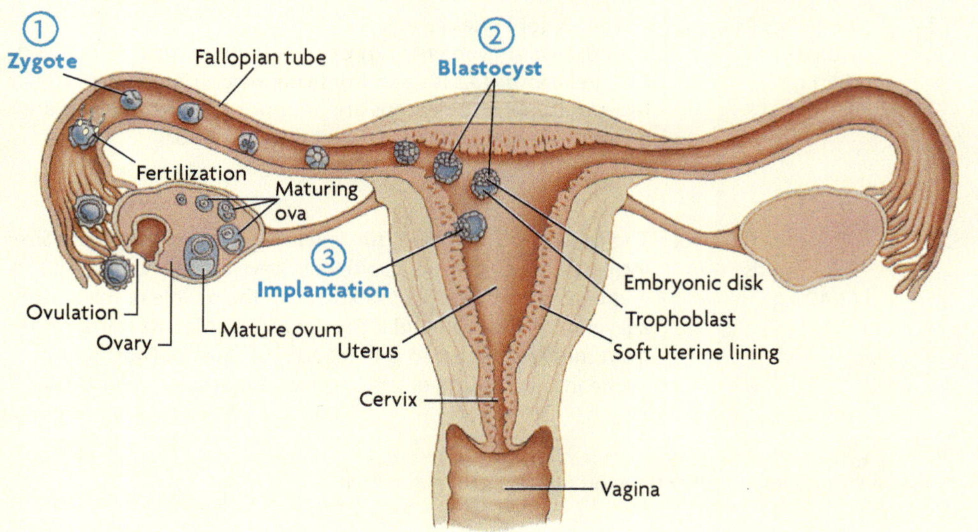

① **Zygote**
As the zygote moves down the fallopian tube, it duplicates, at first slowly and then more rapidly.

② **Blastocyst**
By the fourth day it forms a hollow, fluid-filled ball, called a blastocyst. The inner cells, called the embryonic disk, will become the new organism. The outer cells, or trophoblast, will provide protective covering.

③ **Implantation**
At the end of the first week, the blastocyst begins to implant in the uterine lining.

Figure 3.7 **Female reproductive organs, showing fertilization, early cell duplication, and implantation.**
(From K. L. Moore and T. V. N. Persaud, 2003, *Before We Are Born, 6th ed.*, p. 87. Copyright © 2003, with permission from Elsevier, Inc.)

Milestones

Prenatal Development

Trimester	Period	Weeks	Length and Weight	Major Events
First	Zygote	1		The one-celled zygote multiplies and forms a blastocyst.
	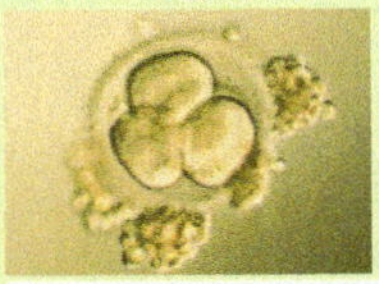	2		The blastocyst burrows into the uterine lining. Structures that feed and protect the developing organism begin to form—*amnion, chorion, yolk sac, placenta,* and *umbilical cord.*
	Embryo	3–4	¼ inch (6 mm)	A primitive brain and spinal cord appear. Heart, muscles, ribs, backbone, and digestive tract begin to develop.
	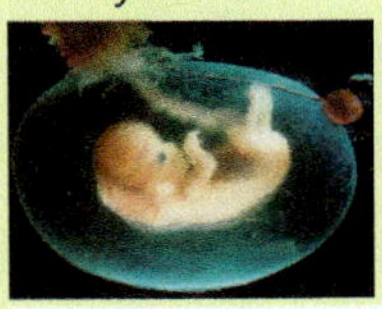	5–8	1 inch (2.5 cm); ⅐ ounce (4 g)	Many external body structures (face, arms, legs, toes, fingers) and internal organs form. The sense of touch begins to develop, and the embryo can move.
	Fetus 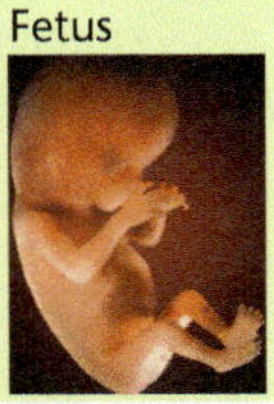	9–12	3 inches (7.6 cm); less than 1 ounce (28 g)	Rapid increase in size begins. Nervous system, organs, and muscles become organized and connected, and new behavioral capacities (kicking, thumb sucking, mouth opening, and rehearsal of breathing) appear. External genitals are well-formed, and the fetus's sex is evident.
Second	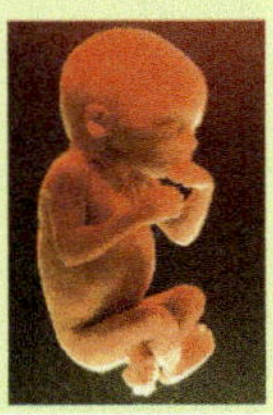	13–24	12 inches (30 cm); 1.8 pounds (820 g)	The fetus continues to enlarge rapidly. In the middle of this period, fetal movements can be felt by the mother. Vernix and lanugo keep the fetus's skin from chapping in the amniotic fluid. Most of the brain's neurons are present by 24 weeks. Eyes are sensitive to light, and the fetus reacts to sound.
Third	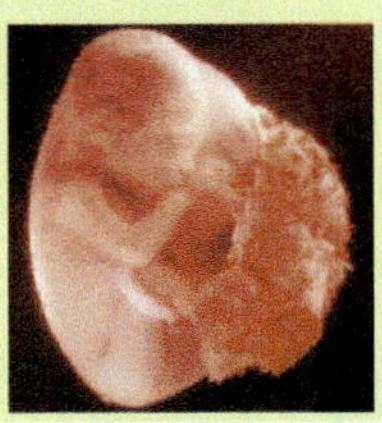	25–38	20 inches (50 cm); 7.5 pounds (3,400 g)	The fetus has a chance of survival if born during this time. Size increases. Lungs mature. Rapid brain development causes sensory and behavioral capacities to expand. In the middle of this period, a layer of fat is added under the skin. Antibodies are transmitted from mother to fetus to protect against disease. Most fetuses rotate into an upside-down position in preparation for birth.

Source: Moore & Persaud, 2008. *Photos* (from top to bottom): © Claude Cortier/Photo Researchers, Inc.; © G. Moscoso/Photo Researchers, Inc.; © John Watney/Photo Researchers, Inc.; © James Stevenson/Photo Researchers, Inc.; © Lennart Nilsson, *A Child Is Born*/Bonniers

The Period of the Zygote

The period of the zygote lasts about two weeks, from fertilization until the tiny mass of cells drifts down and out of the fallopian tube and attaches itself to the wall of the uterus. The zygote's first cell duplication is long and drawn out; it is not complete until about 30 hours after conception. Gradually, new cells are added at a faster rate. By the fourth day, 60 to 70 cells exist that form a hollow, fluid-filled ball called a *blastocyst* (refer again to Figure 3.7). The cells on the inside, called the *embryonic disk,* will become the new organism; the thin outer ring of cells, termed the *trophoblast,* will provide protective covering and nourishment.

• **Implantation** Between the seventh and ninth days, *implantation* occurs: The blastocyst burrows deep into the uterine lining where, surrounded by the woman's nourishing blood, it

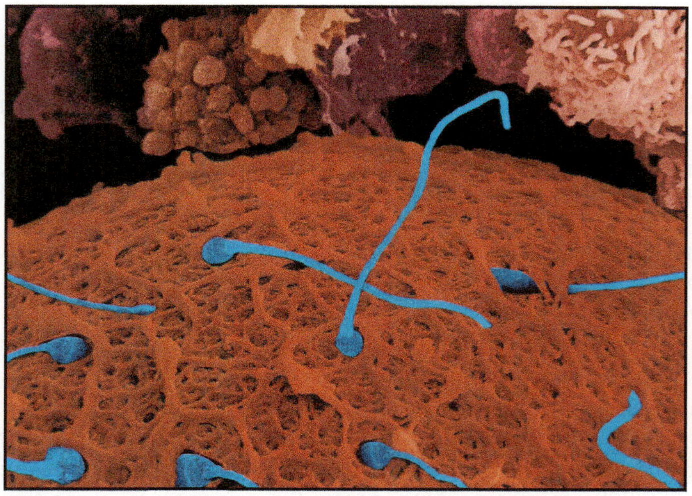

Conception. In this photo taken with the aid of a powerful microscope, sperm have completed their journey up the female reproductive tract and are beginning to penetrate the surface of the enormous-looking ovum, the largest cell in the human body. When one of the sperm successfully fertilizes the ovum, the resulting zygote will begin to duplicate. © Jack Burns/Ace/Phototake

Period of the zygote: seventh to ninth day. The fertilized ovum duplicates at an increasingly rapid rate, forming a hollow ball of cells, or blastocyst, by the fourth day after fertilization. Here the blastocyst, magnified thousands of times, burrows into the uterine lining between the seventh and ninth day. © Lennart Nilsson, *A Child Is Born*/Bonniers

starts to grow in earnest. At first, the trophoblast (protective outer layer) multiplies fastest. It forms a membrane, called the **amnion,** that encloses the developing organism in *amniotic fluid*. The amnion helps keep the temperature of the prenatal world constant and provides a cushion against any jolts caused by the woman's movement. A *yolk sac* emerges that produces blood cells until the developing liver, spleen, and bone marrow are mature enough to take over this function (Moore & Persaud, 2008).

The events of these first two weeks are delicate and uncertain. As many as 30 percent of zygotes do not survive this period. In some, the sperm and ovum do not join properly. In others, for some unknown reason, cell duplication never begins. By preventing implantation in these cases, nature eliminates most prenatal abnormalities (Sadler, 2006).

• The Placenta and Umbilical Cord By the end of the second week, cells of the trophoblast form another protective membrane—the **chorion,** which surrounds the amnion. From the chorion, tiny hairlike *villi*, or blood vessels, emerge.[1] As these villi burrow into the uterine wall, a special organ called the *placenta* starts to develop. By bringing the mother's and the embryo's blood close together, the **placenta** permits food and oxygen to reach the developing organism and waste products to be carried away. A membrane forms that allows these substances to be exchanged but prevents the mother's and the embryo's blood from mixing directly.

The placenta is connected to the developing organism by the **umbilical cord.** In the period of the zygote, the cord first appears as a primitive body stalk, but during the course of pregnancy, it grows to a length of 1 to 3 feet. The umbilical cord contains one large vein that delivers blood loaded with nutrients and two arteries that remove waste products. The force of blood flowing through the cord keeps it firm, much like a garden hose, so it seldom tangles while the embryo, like a space-walking astronaut, floats freely in its fluid-filled chamber (Moore & Persaud, 2008).

By the end of the period of the zygote, the developing organism has found food and shelter in the uterus. Already, it is a very complex being. These dramatic beginnings take place before most mothers know they are pregnant.

[1]Recall from Table 3.6 on page 83 that *chorionic villus sampling* is the prenatal diagnostic method that can be performed earliest, at nine weeks after conception. In this procedure, tissues from the ends of the villi are removed and examined for genetic abnormalities.

The Period of the Embryo

The period of the **embryo** lasts from implantation through the eighth week of pregnancy. During these brief six weeks, the most rapid prenatal changes take place, as the groundwork is laid for all body structures and internal organs. Because all parts of the body are forming, the embryo is especially vulnerable to interference with healthy development. But the short time span of embryonic growth helps limit opportunities for serious harm.

• Last Half of the First Month In the first week of this period, the embryonic disk forms three layers of cells: (1) the *ectoderm,* which will become the nervous system and skin; (2) the *mesoderm,* from which will develop the muscles, skeleton, circulatory system, and other internal organs; and (3) the *endoderm,* which will become the digestive system, lungs, urinary tract, and glands. These three layers give rise to all parts of the body.

At first, the nervous system develops fastest. The ectoderm folds to form a *neural tube,* or primitive spinal cord. At 3½ weeks, the top swells to form the brain. Production of *neurons* (nerve cells that store and transmit information) begins deep inside the neural tube at the astounding pace of more than 250,000 per minute. Once formed, neurons travel along tiny threads to their permanent locations, where they will form the major parts of the brain (Nelson, Thomas, & de Haan, 2006).

While the nervous system is developing, the heart begins to pump blood, and muscles, backbone, ribs, and digestive tract appear. At the end of the first month, the curled embryo—only ¼ inch long—consists of millions of organized groups of cells with specific functions.

• The Second Month In the second month, growth continues rapidly. The eyes, ears, nose, jaw, and neck form. Tiny buds become arms, legs, fingers, and toes. Internal organs are more distinct: The intestines grow, the heart develops separate chambers, and the liver and spleen take over production of blood cells so the yolk sac is no longer needed. Changing body proportions cause the embryo's posture to become more upright. Now 1 inch long and ⅐ ounce in weight, the embryo can sense its world. It responds to touch, particularly in the mouth area and on the soles of the feet. And it can move, although its tiny flutters are still too light to be felt by the mother (Moore & Persaud, 2008).

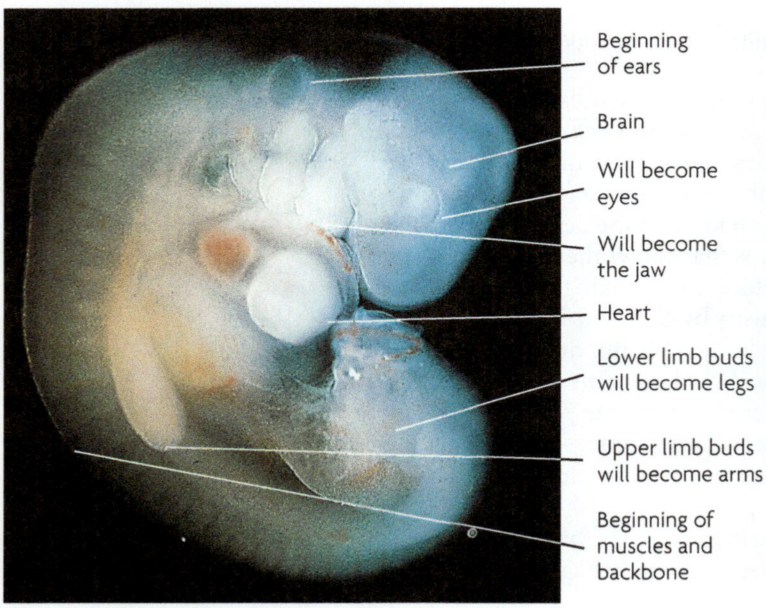

Period of the embryo: fourth week. Although this 4-week-old embryo is only ¼ inch long, many body structures have begun to form. © Lennart Nilsson, *A Child Is Born*/Bonniers

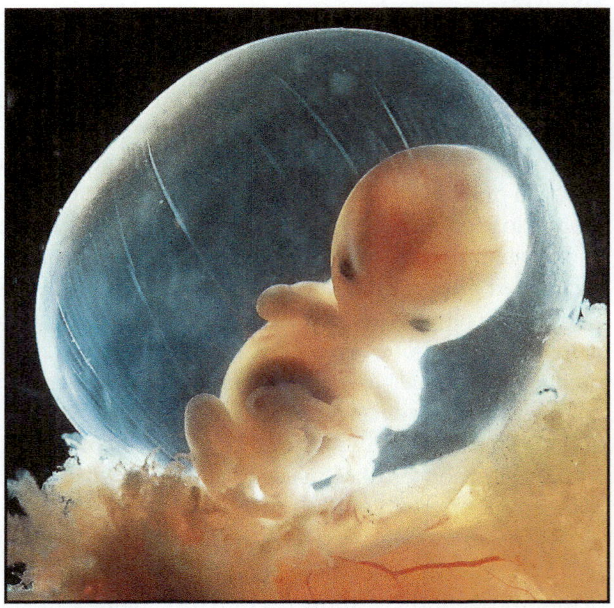

Period of the embryo: seventh week. The embryo's posture is more upright. Body structures—eyes, nose, arms, legs, and internal organs—are more distinct. The embryo now responds to touch and can also move, though at less than 1 inch long and 1 ounce in weight, it is still too tiny to be felt by the mother. © Lennart Nilsson, *A Child Is Born*/Bonniers

The Period of the Fetus

The period of the **fetus,** from the ninth week to the end of pregnancy, is the longest prenatal period. During this "growth and finishing" phase, the organism increases rapidly in size, especially from the ninth to the twentieth week.

• The Third Month In the third month, the organs, muscles, and nervous system start to become organized and connected. When the brain signals, the fetus kicks, bends its arms, forms a fist, curls its toes, opens its mouth, and even sucks its thumb. The tiny lungs begin to expand and contract in an early rehearsal of breathing movements. By the twelfth week, the external genitals are well-formed, and the sex of the fetus is evident with ultrasound (Sadler, 2006). Other finishing touches appear, such as fingernails, toenails, tooth buds, and eyelids that open and close. The heartbeat is now stronger and can be heard through a stethoscope.

Prenatal development is often divided into *trimesters,* or three equal time periods. At the end of the third month, the first trimester is complete.

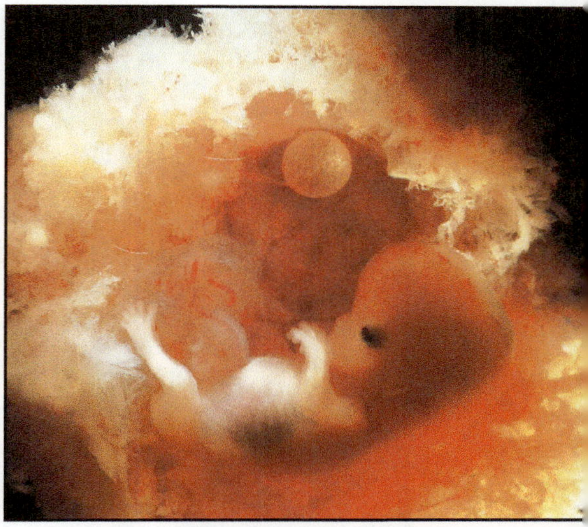

Period of the fetus: eleventh week. The brain and muscles are better connected. The fetus can kick, bend its arms, open and close its hands and mouth, and suck its thumb. Notice the yolk sac, which produces blood cells. As pregnancy advances, it shrinks, and the internal organs take over this function.
© Lennart Nilsson, *A Child Is Born*/ Bonniers

• The Second Trimester By the middle of the second trimester, between 17 and 20 weeks, the new being has grown large enough that the mother can feel its movements. A white, cheeselike substance called **vernix** covers the skin, protecting it from chapping during the long months spent in the amniotic fluid. White, downy hair called **lanugo** also covers the entire body, helping the vernix stick to the skin.

At the end of the second trimester, many organs are well-developed. Also, most of the brain's billions of neurons are in place; few will be produced after this time. However, *glial cells,* which support and feed the neurons, continue to increase at a rapid rate throughout the remaining months of pregnancy, as well as after birth. Consequently, brain weight increases tenfold from the twentieth week until birth (Roelfsema et al., 2004).

Brain growth means new behavioral capacities. The 20-week-old fetus can be stimulated as well as irritated by sounds. If a doctor looks inside the uterus with fetoscopy (refer again to Table 3.6), fetuses try to shield their eyes from the light with their hands, indicating that sight has begun to emerge (Moore & Persaud, 2008). Still, a fetus born at this time cannot survive. Its lungs are too immature, and the brain cannot yet control breathing movements or body temperature.

• The Third Trimester During the final trimester, a fetus born early has a chance of survival. The point at which the baby can first survive, called the **age of viability,** occurs sometime between 22 and 26 weeks (Moore & Persaud, 2008). A baby born between the seventh and eighth months, however, usually needs oxygen assistance to breathe. Although the brain's respiratory center is now mature, tiny air sacs in the lungs are not yet ready to inflate and exchange carbon dioxide for oxygen.

During the last three months, the brain continues to make great strides. The *cerebral cortex,* the seat of human intelligence, enlarges. Convolutions and grooves in its surface appear, permitting a dramatic increase in surface area without extensive increase in head size. As a result, maximum prenatal brain growth occurs, yet the full-term baby's head does not become too large to pass through the birth canal. As neurological organization improves, the fetus spends more time awake. At 20 weeks, fetal heart rate reveals no periods of alertness. But by 28 weeks, fetuses are awake about 11 percent of the time, a figure that rises to 16 percent just before birth (DiPietro et al., 1996). Between 30 and 34 weeks, fetuses show rhythmic alternations between sleep and wakefulness that gradually increase in organization (Rivkees, 2003). Around this time, synchrony between fetal heart rate and motor activity peaks: A rise in heart rate is usually followed within 5 seconds by a burst of motor activity (DiPietro et al., 2006). These are clear signs that coordinated neural networks are beginning to form in the brain.

By the end of pregnancy, the fetus takes on the beginnings of a personality. Higher fetal activity in the last weeks of pregnancy predicts a more active infant in the first month of life—a relationship that, for boys, persists into early childhood (Groome et al., 1999). Fetal activity is linked in other ways to infant temperament. In one study, more active fetuses during the third trimester became 1-year-olds who could better handle frustration and 2-year-olds who

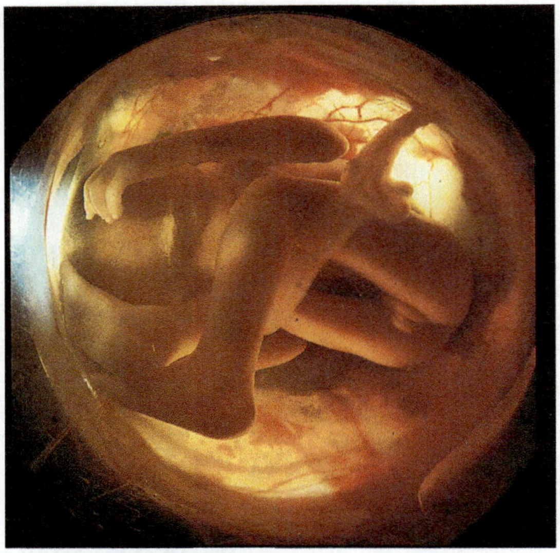

Period of the fetus: twenty-second week. This fetus is almost 1 foot long and weighs slightly more than 1 pound. Its movements can easily be felt by the mother and other family members, by placing a hand on her abdomen. The fetus has reached the age of viability: If born, it has a slim chance of surviving. © Lennart Nilsson, *A Child Is Born*/Bonniers

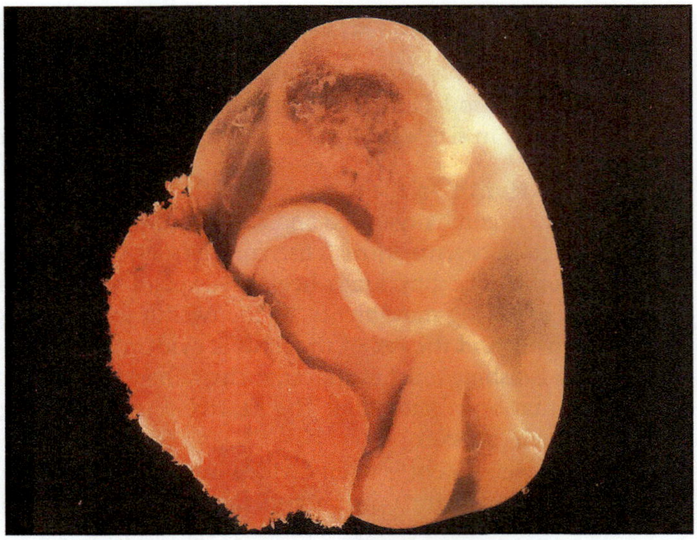

Period of the fetus: thirty-sixth week. This fetus fills the uterus. To provide it with nourishment, the umbilical cord and placenta have grown large. Notice the vernix—a cheeselike substance on the skin that protects it from chapping. The fetus has accumulated a layer of fat to assist with temperature regulation after birth. In two more weeks, it will be full term. © Lennart Nilsson, *A Child Is Born*/Bonniers

were less fearful, in that they more readily interacted with toys and with an unfamiliar adult in a laboratory (DiPietro et al., 2002). Perhaps fetal activity level is an indicator of healthy neurological development, which fosters adaptability in childhood. The relationships just described, however, are only modest. As you will see in Chapter 10, sensitive caregiving can modify the temperaments of children who have difficulty adapting to new experiences.

The third trimester also brings greater responsiveness to external stimulation. Between 23 and 30 weeks, connections form between the cerebral cortex and brain regions involved in pain sensitivity. By this time, painkillers should be used in any surgical procedures (Lee et al., 2005). And by 28 weeks, fetuses blink their eyes in reaction to nearby sounds (Kisilevsky & Low, 1998; Saffran, Werker, & Werner, 2006).

Within the next six weeks, fetuses distinguish the tone and rhythm of different voices and sounds: They show systematic heart rate changes in response to a male versus a female speaker, to the mother's voice versus a stranger's, and to a simple familiar melody (descending tones) versus an unfamiliar melody (ascending tones) (Granier-Deferre et al., 2003; Huotilainen et al., 2005; Kisilevsky et al., 2003; Lecanuet et al., 1993). And in one clever study, mothers read aloud Dr. Seuss's lively book *The Cat in the Hat* each day during the last six weeks of pregnancy. After birth, their infants learned to turn on recordings of the mother's voice by sucking on nipples. They sucked hardest to hear *The Cat in the Hat*—the sound they had come to know while still in the womb (DeCasper & Spence, 1986).

TAKE A MOMENT... On the basis of these findings, would you recommend that expectant mothers provide fetuses with certain kinds of stimulation to enhance later mental development? Notice how risky it is to draw such conclusions. First, specific forms of fetal stimulation, such as reading aloud or playing classical music, are unlikely to have a long-lasting impact on cognitive development because of the developing child's constantly changing capacities and experiences, which can override the impact of fetal stimulation (Lecanuet, Granier-Deferre, & DeCasper, 2005). Second, although ordinary stimulation contributes to the functioning of sensory systems, excessive input can be dangerous. For example, animal studies indicate that a sensitive period (see page 24 in Chapter 1) exists in which the fetal ear is highly susceptible to injury. During that time, prolonged exposure to sounds that are harmless to the mature ear can permanently damage fetal inner-ear structures (Rubel & Ryals, 1982, 1983).

In the final three months, the fetus gains more than 5 pounds and grows 7 inches. As it fills the uterus, it gradually moves less often. In addition, brain development, which enables the organism to inhibit behavior, contributes to this decline in physical activity (DiPietro et al., 1996). In the eighth month, a layer of fat is added to assist with temperature regulation. The fetus also receives antibodies from the mother's blood to protect against illnesses, since the newborn's own immune system will not work well until several months after birth. In the last weeks, most fetuses assume an upside-down position, partly because of the shape of the uterus and also because the head is heavier than the feet. Growth slows, and birth is about to take place.

Ask Yourself

Review Why is the period of the embryo regarded as the most dramatic prenatal period? Why is the period of the fetus called the "growth and finishing" phase?

Apply Amy, two months pregnant, wonders how the developing organism is being fed and what parts of the body have formed. "I don't look pregnant yet, so does that mean not much development has taken place?" she asks. How would you respond to Amy?

Connect How is brain development related to fetal capacities and behavior? What implications do individual differences in fetal behavior have for the baby's temperament after birth?

Prenatal Environmental Influences

Although the prenatal environment is far more constant than the world outside the womb, many factors can affect the embryo and fetus. In the following sections, you will see that there is much that parents—and society as a whole—can do to create a safe environment for development before birth.

Teratogens

The term **teratogen** refers to any environmental agent that causes damage during the prenatal period. Scientists chose this label (from the Greek word *teras,* meaning "malformation" or "monstrosity") because they first learned about harmful prenatal influences from cases in which babies had been profoundly damaged. Yet the harm done by teratogens is not always simple and straightforward. It depends on the following factors:

- *Dose.* As we discuss particular teratogens, you will see that larger doses over longer time periods usually have more negative effects.
- *Heredity.* The genetic makeup of the mother and that of the developing organism play an important role. Some individuals are better able than others to withstand harmful environments.
- *Other negative influences.* The presence of several negative factors at once, such as poor nutrition, lack of medical care, and additional teratogens, can worsen the impact of a single harmful agent.
- *Age.* The effects of teratogens vary with the age of the organism at time of exposure. To understand this last idea, think of the *sensitive period* concept. Recall that a sensitive period is a limited time span in which a part of the body or a behavior is biologically prepared to develop rapidly. During that time, it is especially sensitive to its surroundings. If the environment is harmful, then damage occurs, and recovery is difficult and sometimes impossible.

Figure 3.8 on page 94 summarizes prenatal sensitive periods. Look at it carefully, and you will see that some parts of the body, such as the brain and eye, have long sensitive periods. Other sensitive periods, such as those for the limbs and palate, are much shorter. Figure 3.8 also indicates that we can make some general statements about the timing of harmful influences: In the *period of the zygote,* before implantation, teratogens rarely have any impact. If they do, the tiny mass of cells is usually so damaged that it dies. The *embryonic period* is the time when serious defects are most likely to occur because the foundations for all body parts are being laid down. During the *fetal period,* teratogenic damage is usually minor. However, organs such as the brain, ears, eyes, teeth, and genitals can still be strongly affected.

The effects of teratogens go beyond immediate physical damage. Some health outcomes are subtle and delayed. As the Biology and Environment box on pages 96–97 illustrates, they may not show up for decades. Furthermore, psychological consequences may occur indirectly, as a result of physical damage. For example, a defect resulting from drugs the mother took during pregnancy can affect others' reactions to the child as well as the child's ability to explore the environment. These experiences, in turn, can have far-reaching consequences for cognitive, emotional, and social development.

Notice how an important idea about development discussed in Chapter 1 is at work here: *bidirectional influences* between child and environment. Now let's look at what scientists have discovered about a variety of teratogens.

• Prescription and Nonprescription Drugs In the early 1960s, the world learned a tragic lesson about drugs and prenatal development. At that time, a sedative called *thalidomide* was widely available in Canada, Europe, and South America. When taken by mothers 4 to 6 weeks after conception, thalidomide produced gross deformities of the embryo's developing arms and legs and, less frequently, damage to the ears, heart, kidneys, and genitals. About 7,000 infants worldwide were affected (Moore & Persaud, 2008). As children exposed to thalidomide grew older, many scored below average in intelligence. Perhaps the drug damaged the central nervous system directly. Or the conditions in which these severely deformed youngsters were reared may have impaired their intellectual development.

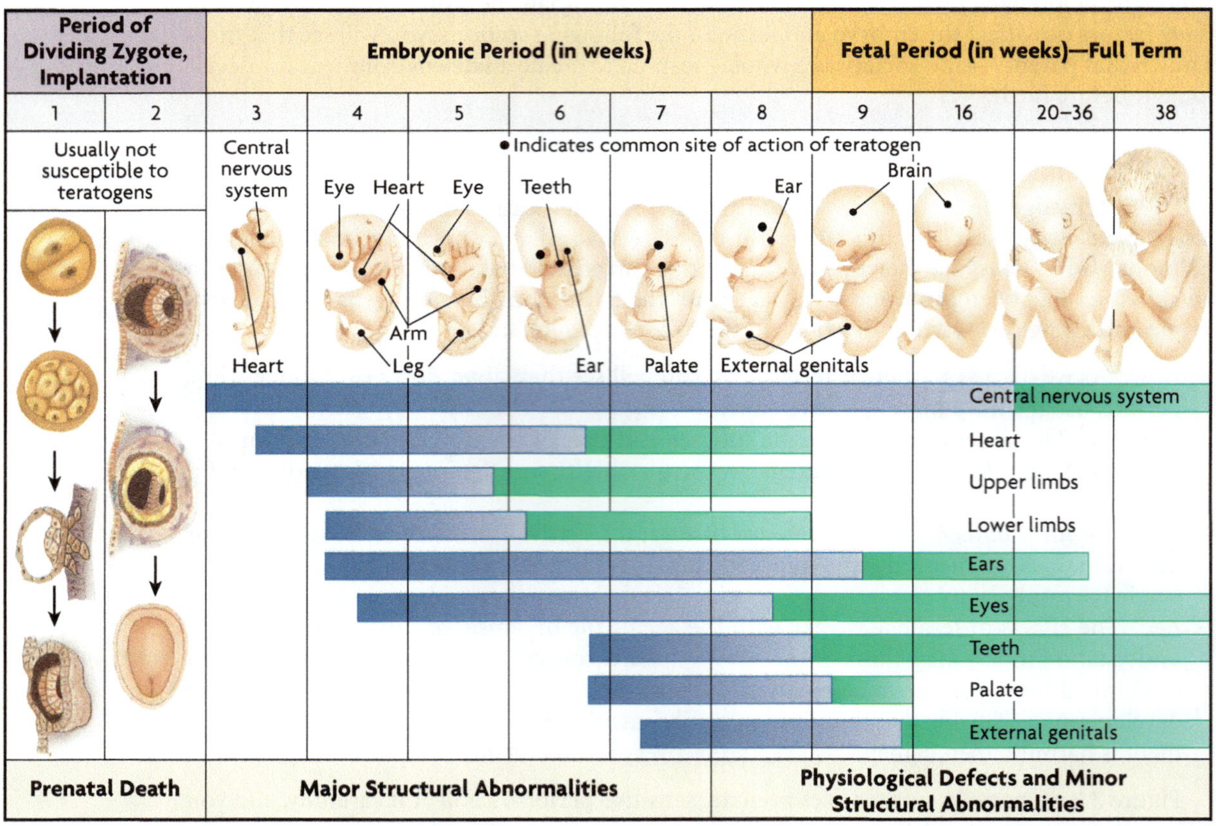

■ Figure 3.8 Sensitive periods in prenatal development.

Each organ or structure has a sensitive period, during which its development may be disturbed. Blue horizontal bars indicate highly sensitive periods. Green horizontal bars indicate periods that are somewhat less sensitive to teratogens, although damage can occur. (From K. L. Moore and T. V. N. Persaud, 2008, *Before We Are Born, 7th ed.*, p. 313. Copyright © 2008, with permission from Elsevier, Inc.)

Another medication, a synthetic hormone called *diethylstilbestrol (DES),* was widely prescribed between 1945 and 1970 to prevent miscarriages. As daughters of these mothers reached adolescence and young adulthood, they showed unusually high rates of cancer of the vagina, malformations of the uterus, and infertility. When they tried to have children, their pregnancies more often resulted in prematurity, low birth weight, and miscarriage than those of non-DES-exposed women. Young men showed an increased risk of genital abnormalities and cancer of the testes (Hammes & Laitman, 2003; Palmer et al., 2001).

Currently, the most widely used potent teratogen is a vitamin A derivative called *Accutane,* used to treat severe acne (also known by the generic name *isotretinoin*). Exposure during the first trimester of pregnancy results in extensive damage to the developing organism, including abnormalities of the eye, ear, skull, brain, heart, central nervous system, and immune system. Hundreds of thousands of U.S. and Canadian women of childbearing age take Accutane, and the number of prescriptions is increasing. Accutane's packaging warns users to avoid pregnancy by using two methods of birth control, but many women do not heed this advice (Honein, Paulozzi, & Erickson, 2001). Despite its established harmful effects, more than 2,300 reports of drug-exposed pregnancies have occurred in the United States alone. Although the number of babies born with Accutane-caused malformations is not known, at least 162 documented American cases exist (Andresen, 2006).

Indeed, any drug with a molecule small enough to penetrate the placental barrier can enter the embryonic or fetal bloodstream. Nevertheless, many pregnant women continue to take over-the-counter medications without consulting their doctors. Aspirin is one of the most common. Several studies suggest that regular aspirin use is linked to low birth weight, infant death around the time of birth, poorer motor development, and lower intelligence test scores in early childhood, although other research fails to confirm these findings (Barr et al., 1990; Kozer et al., 2003; Streissguth et al., 1987). Coffee, tea, cola, and cocoa contain another frequently consumed drug, caffeine. Heavy caffeine intake (more than three cups of coffee per day) is associated with low birth weight, miscarriage, and newborn withdrawal symptoms, such as irritability and vomiting (Klebanoff et al., 2002; Vik et al., 2003). And antidepressant medication taken during the third trimester is linked to increased risk of birth complications, including low birth weight and respiratory distress (Oberlander et al., 2006).

Because children's lives are involved, we must take findings like these seriously. At the same time, we cannot be sure that these frequently used drugs actually cause the problems mentioned. Often mothers take more than one drug. If the embryo or fetus is injured, it is hard to tell which drug might be responsible or whether other factors correlated with drug taking are really at fault. Until we have more information, the safest course for pregnant women is to cut down on or avoid such drugs entirely. Unfortunately, many women do not know that they are pregnant during the early weeks of the embryonic period, when exposure to teratogens can be of greatest threat.

• **Illegal Drugs** The use of highly addictive mood-altering drugs, such as cocaine and heroin, has become more widespread, especially in poverty-stricken inner-city areas, where these drugs provide a temporary escape from a daily life of hopelessness. Nearly 4 percent of North American pregnant women take these substances (British Columbia Reproductive Care Program, 2003; U.S. Department of Health and Human Services, 2007c).

Babies born to users of cocaine, heroin, or methadone (a less addictive drug used to wean people away from heroin) are at risk for a wide variety of problems, including prematurity, low birth weight, physical defects, breathing difficulties, and death at or around the time of birth (Behnke et al., 2001; Schuetze & Eiden, 2006; Walker, Rosenberg, & Balaban-Gil, 1999). In addition, these infants are born drug-addicted. They often are feverish and irritable and have trouble sleeping, and their cries are abnormally shrill and piercing—a common symptom among stressed newborns (Bauer et al., 2005). When mothers with many problems of their own must care for these babies, who are difficult to calm, cuddle, and feed, behavior problems are likely to persist.

Throughout the first year, heroin- and methadone-exposed infants are less attentive to the environment than nonexposed babies, and their motor development is slow. After infancy, some children get better, whereas others remain jittery and inattentive. The kind of parenting

Biology *and* Environment

The Prenatal Environment and Health in Later Life

When Michael entered the world 55 years ago, six weeks premature and weighing only 4 pounds, the doctor delivering him wasn't sure he would make it. Michael not only survived but enjoyed good health until his mid-forties, when, during a routine medical checkup, he was diagnosed with high blood pressure and type 2 diabetes. Michael had no apparent risk factors for these conditions: He wasn't overweight, didn't smoke, and didn't eat high-fat foods. Nor did the illnesses run in his family. Could the roots of Michael's health problems date back to his prenatal development?

Increasing evidence suggests that prenatal environmental factors—ones that are not toxic (as are tobacco or alcohol) but rather fairly subtle, such as the flow of nutrients and hormones across the placenta—can affect an individual's health decades later.

Low Birth Weight and Heart Disease, Stroke, and Diabetes

Carefully controlled animal experiments reveal that a poorly nourished, underweight fetus experiences changes in body structure and function that result in cardiovascular disease in adulthood (Franco et al., 2002). To explore this relationship in humans, researchers tapped public records, gathering information on the birth weights of 15,000 British men and women and the occurrence of disease in middle adulthood. Those weighing less than 5 pounds at birth had a 50 percent greater chance of dying of heart disease and stroke, even after income, education, and a variety of health risks were controlled. The connection between birth weight and cardiovascular disease was strongest for people whose weight-to-length ratio at birth was very low—a sign of prenatal growth stunting (Godfrey & Barker, 2000; Martyn, Barker, & Osmond, 1996).

In other large-scale studies, a consistent link between low birth weight and heart disease, stroke, and diabetes in middle adulthood emerged—for both sexes and in diverse countries, including Finland, India, Jamaica, the Netherlands, and the United States (Barker et al., 2002; Fowden, Giussani, & Forhead, 2005; Roseboom, de Rooij, & Painter, 2006). Smallness itself does not cause later health problems; rather, researchers believe, complex factors associated with it are involved.

Some speculate that a poorly nourished fetus diverts large amounts of blood to the brain, causing organs in the abdomen, such as the liver and kidneys (involved in controlling cholesterol and blood pressure), to be undersized (Hales & Ozanne, 2003).

Prenatal environmental factors—even subtle ones such as the flow of nutrients and hormones across the placenta—can affect an individual's health in later life. This newborn girl's high birth weight places her at increased risk for breast, digestive, and lymphatic cancers in adulthood. © David Young-Wolff/PhotoEdit

they receive may explain why problems last for some but not for others (Cosden, Peerson, & Elliott, 1997).

Evidence on cocaine suggests that some prenatally exposed babies develop lasting difficulties. Cocaine constricts the blood vessels, causing oxygen delivery to the developing organism to fall for 15 minutes following a high dose. It also can alter the production and functioning of neurons and the chemical balance in the fetus's brain. These effects may contribute to an array of cocaine-associated physical defects, including eye, bone, genital, urinary tract, kidney, and heart deformities; brain hemorrhages and seizures; and severe growth retardation (Covington et al., 2002; Feng, 2005; Mayes, 1999). Several studies report perceptual, motor, attention, memory, language, and impulse control problems in infancy that persist into the preschool and school years (Dennis et al., 2006; Lester et al., 2003; Linares et al., 2006; Noland et al., 2005; Singer et al., 2004).

But other investigations reveal no major negative effects of prenatal cocaine exposure (Behnke et al., 2006; Frank et al., 2005; Hurt et al., 2005). These contradictory findings indicate how difficult it is to isolate the precise damage caused by illegal drugs. Cocaine users vary greatly in the amount, potency, and purity of the cocaine they ingest. Also, they often take several drugs, display other high-risk behaviors, suffer from poverty and other stresses, and engage in insensitive caregiving. The joint impact of these factors worsens outcomes for

The result is heightened later risk for heart disease and stroke. In the case of diabetes, inadequate prenatal nutrition may permanently impair functioning of the pancreas, leading blood sugar (glucose) to rise beyond control as the person ages (Wu et al., 2004). Yet another hypothesis, supported by both animal and human research, is that the malfunctioning placentas of some expectant mothers permit high levels of stress hormones to reach the fetus, which retard fetal growth, increase fetal blood pressure, and promote excess blood sugar, predisposing the developing person to later disease (Stocker, Arch, & Cawthorne, 2005).

Finally, prenatally growth-stunted babies often gain excessive weight in childhood, once they have access to plentiful food. This excess weight usually persists, greatly magnifying the risk of diabetes (Hyppönen, Power, & Smith, 2003).

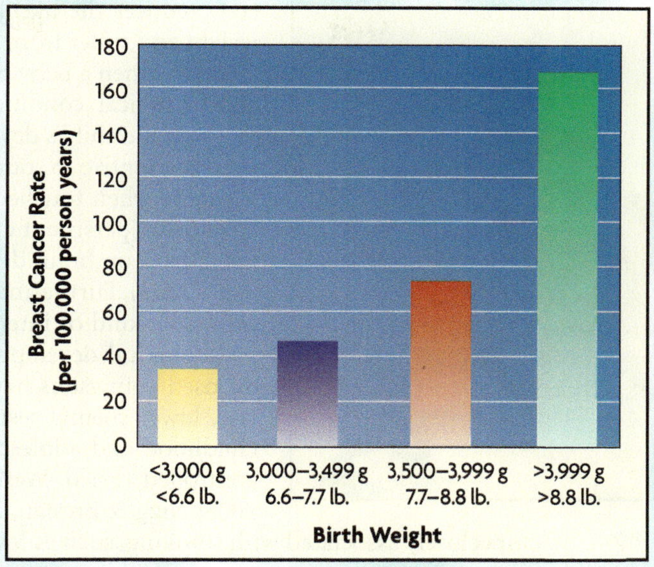

■ Figure 3.9
Relationship of birth weight to breast cancer risk in adulthood.
In a study of more than 2,000 British births with follow-ups in adulthood, birth weight predicted breast cancer incidence after many other prenatal and postnatal health risks were controlled. The breast cancer risk was especially high for women whose birth weights were greater than 3,999 grams, or 8.8 pounds. (Adapted from dos Santos Silva et al., 2004.)

High Birth Weight and Breast Cancer

The other prenatal growth extreme—high birth weight—is related to breast cancer, the most common malignancy in adult women (Ahlgren et al., 2004; Andersson et al., 2001; Vatten et al., 2002). In one study of more than 2,000 British women, high birth weight—especially weight above 8.8 pounds—was associated with a greatly increased incidence of breast cancer, even after other cancer risks were controlled (see Figure 3.9) (dos Santos Silva et al., 2004). Researchers suspect that the culprit is excessive estrogen in the overweight expectant mother, which promotes large fetal size and alters the makeup of beginning breast tissue so that it may more readily respond to estrogen in adulthood by becoming malignant.

High birth weight is also associated with increases in digestive and lymphatic cancers in both men and women (McCormack et al., 2005). As yet, the reasons are unclear.

Prevention

The relationships between prenatal development and later-life illnesses emerging in research do not mean that the illnesses are inevitable. Prenatal environmental conditions *influence* adult health, and the steps people take to protect their health can prevent prenatal risks from becoming reality. Researchers advise individuals who were low-weight at birth to get regular medical checkups and to be attentive to diet, weight, fitness, and stress—controllable factors that contribute to heart disease and type 2 diabetes. And high-birth-weight women should be conscientious about breast self-exams and mammograms, which permit early detection—and, in many instances, cure—of breast cancer.

children (Jones, 2006). But researchers have yet to determine exactly what accounts for findings of cocaine-related damage in some studies but not in others.

Another illegal drug, marijuana, is used more widely than heroin and cocaine. Studies examining its relationship to low birth weight and prematurity reveal mixed findings (Fried, 1993). Several researchers have linked prenatal marijuana exposure to smaller head size (a measure of brain growth); to sleep, attention, and memory difficulties in childhood; and to poorer problem-solving performance in adolescence (Dahl et al., 1995; Goldschmidt et al., 2004; Gray et al., 2005; Huizink & Mulder, 2006). As with cocaine, however, lasting consequences are not well-established. Overall, the effects of illegal drugs are far less consistent than the impact of two legal substances to which we now turn: tobacco and alcohol.

• **Tobacco** Although smoking has declined in Western nations, an estimated 17 percent of U.S. and 20 percent of Canadian women smoke during their pregnancies (Health Canada, 2005; U.S. Department of Health and Human Services, 2007c). The best-known effect of smoking during the prenatal period is low birth weight. But the likelihood of other serious consequences, such as miscarriage, prematurity, impaired heart rate and breathing during sleep, infant death, and asthma and cancer later in childhood, is also increased (Franco et al., 2000; Jaakkola & Gissler, 2004). The more cigarettes a mother smokes, the greater the chances

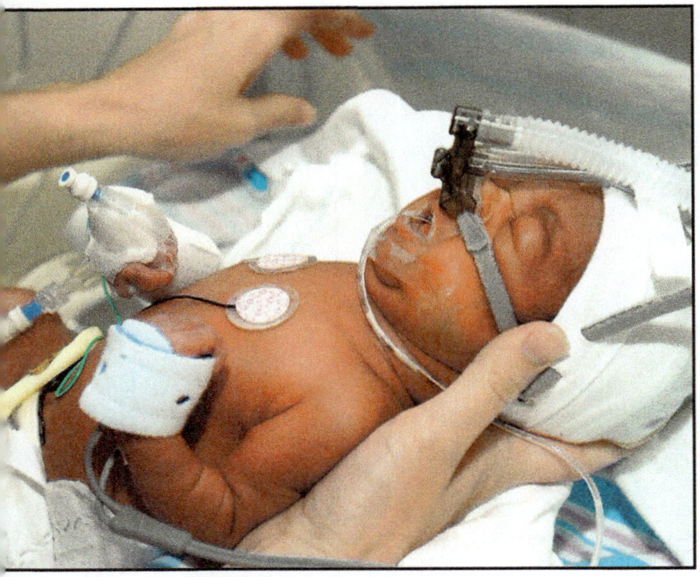

This 3-day-old infant, born many weeks before his due date, is underweight and breathes with the aid of a respirator. Prematurity and low birth weight can result from a variety of environmental influences during pregnancy, including maternal drug use and cigarette smoking. Babies born early and underweight are at increased risk for later physical, emotional, and behavior problems and learning deficits. © Chet Gordon/The Image Works

that her baby will be affected. And if a pregnant woman stops smoking at any time, even during the third trimester, she immediately reduces the likelihood that her infant will be born underweight and suffer from future problems (Klesges et al., 2001).

Even when a baby of a smoking mother appears to be born in good physical condition, slight behavioral abnormalities may threaten the child's development. Newborns of smoking mothers are less attentive to sounds, display more muscle tension, are more excitable when touched and visually stimulated, and more often have colic (persistent crying)—findings that suggest subtle negative effects on brain development (Law et al., 2003; Sondergaard et al., 2002). Furthermore, an unresponsive, restless baby may not evoke the kind of interaction from adults that promotes healthy psychological development. Some studies report that prenatally exposed youngsters have shorter attention spans, poorer memories, lower mental test scores, and more behavior problems in childhood and adolescence, after many other factors have been controlled (Fried, Watkinson, & Gray, 2003; Huizink & Mulder, 2006; Nigg & Breslau, 2007; Thapar et al., 2003). However, other factors closely associated with smoking, such as lower maternal education and income levels, may contribute to these outcomes (Huijbregts et al., 2006).

Exactly how can smoking harm the fetus? Nicotine, the addictive substance in tobacco, constricts blood vessels, lessens blood flow to the uterus, and causes the placenta to grow abnormally. This reduces the transfer of nutrients, so the fetus gains weight poorly. Also, nicotine raises the concentration of carbon monoxide in the bloodstreams of both mother and fetus. Carbon monoxide displaces oxygen from red blood cells, damaging the central nervous system and slowing body growth in the fetuses of laboratory animals (Friedman, 1996). Similar effects may occur in humans.

From one-third to one-half of nonsmoking pregnant women are "passive smokers" because their husbands, relatives, or co-workers use cigarettes. Passive smoking is also related to low birth weight, infant death, childhood respiratory illnesses, and possible long-term impairments in attention and learning (Hanke, Sobala, & Kalinka, 2004; Makin, Fried, & Watkinson, 1991; Pattenden et al., 2006). Clearly, expectant mothers should avoid smoke-filled environments.

• **Alcohol** In his moving book *The Broken Cord,* Michael Dorris (1989), a Dartmouth University anthropology professor, described what it was like to rear his adopted son Abel (called Adam in the book), whose biological mother died of alcohol poisoning shortly after his birth. A Sioux Indian, Abel was born with **fetal alcohol spectrum disorder (FASD),** a term that encompasses a range of physical, mental, and behavioral outcomes caused by prenatal alcohol exposure. As Table 3.7 shows, children with FASD are given one of three diagnoses, which vary in severity:

1. **Fetal alcohol syndrome (FAS),** distinguished by (a) slow physical growth, (b) a pattern of three facial abnormalities (short eyelid openings; a thin upper lip; a smooth or flattened philtrum, or indentation running from the bottom of the nose to the center of the upper lip), and (c) brain injury, evident in a small head and impairment in at least three areas of functioning—for example, memory, language and communication, attention span and activity level (overactivity), planning and reasoning, motor coordination, or social skills. Other defects—of the eyes, ears, nose, throat, heart, genitals, urinary tract, or immune system—may also be present. Abel was diagnosed as having FAS. As is typical for this disorder, his mother drank heavily throughout pregnancy.
2. **Partial fetal alcohol syndrome (p-FAS),** characterized by (a) two of the three facial abnormalities just mentioned and (b) brain injury, again evident in at least three areas of impaired functioning. Mothers of children with p-FAS generally drank alcohol in smaller quantities, and children's defects vary with the timing and length of alcohol exposure.

Table 3.7 Fetal Alcohol Spectrum Disorder: Criteria for Diagnosis

	Diagnostic Category		
Criteria	**FAS**	**p-FAS**	**ARND**
Slow physical growth	Yes	No	No
Facial abnormalities: • Short eyelid openings • Thin upper lip • Smooth or flattened philtrum	All three are present	Two of the three are present	None are present
Brain injury	Impairment in a minimum of three areas of functioning	Impairment in a minimum of three areas of functioning	Impairment in a minimum of three areas of functioning

Source: Loock et al., 2005.

Furthermore, recent evidence suggests that paternal alcohol use around the time of conception may induce genetic alterations, thereby contributing to symptoms (Abel, 2004).

3. **Alcohol-related neurodevelopmental disorder (ARND),** in which at least three areas of mental functioning are impaired, despite typical physical growth and absence of facial abnormalities. Again, prenatal alcohol exposure, though confirmed, is less pervasive than in FAS (Chudley et al., 2005; Loock et al., 2005).

Even when provided with enriched diets, FAS babies fail to catch up in physical size during infancy or childhood. Mental impairment associated with all three FASD diagnoses is also permanent: In his teens and twenties, Abel Dorris had trouble concentrating and keeping a routine job, and he suffered from poor judgment. For example, he would buy something and not wait for change, or wander off in the middle of a task. He died in 1991, at age 23, after being hit by a car.

The more alcohol a woman consumes during pregnancy, the poorer the child's motor coordination, speed of information processing, attention, reasoning, and intelligence and achievement test scores during the preschool and school years (Burden, Jacobson, & Jacobson, 2005; Korkman, Kettunen, & Autti-Raemoe, 2003; Mattson, Calarco, & Lang, 2006). In adolescence and early adulthood, FASD is associated with persisting attention and motor-coordination deficits, poor school performance, trouble with the law, inappropriate sexual behavior, alcohol and drug abuse, and lasting mental health problems (Barr et al., 2006; Connor et al., 2006; Howell et al., 2006; Streissguth et al., 2004).

How does alcohol produce its devastating effects? First, it interferes with cell duplication and migration in the primitive neural tube. EEG and fMRI research reveals reduced brain size, damage to many brain structures, and abnormalities in brain functioning, including the electrical and chemical activity involved in transferring messages from one part of the brain to another (Riley, McGee, & Sowell, 2004; Spadoni et al., 2007). Second, the body uses large quantities of oxygen to metabolize alcohol. A pregnant woman's heavy drinking draws away oxygen that the developing organism needs for cell growth.

About 25 percent of U.S. and 15 percent of Canadian mothers report drinking some

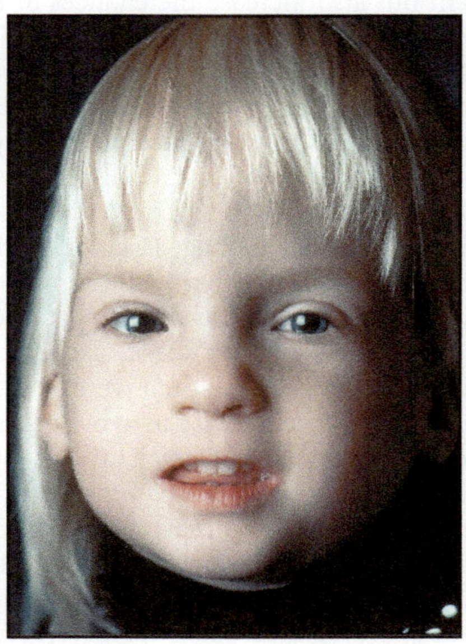

Left photo: This toddler's mother drank heavily during pregnancy. Her widely spaced eyes, thin upper lip, and short eyelid openings are typical of fetal alcohol syndrome (FAS). *Right photo:* This 11-year-old girl also has the facial abnormalities of FAS and shows the slow physical growth that accompanies the disorder. *Left:* © George Steinmetz; *right:* © David Young-Wolff/PhotoEdit

alcohol during their pregnancies. As with heroin and cocaine, alcohol abuse is higher in poverty-stricken women. On some Native-American and Canadian First Nations reservations, the incidence of FAS is as high as 10 to 20 percent (Dell & Roberts, 2005; Silverman et al., 2001; U.S. Department of Health and Human Services, 2007c). Unfortunately, when affected girls later become pregnant, the poor judgment caused by the syndrome often prevents them from understanding why they should avoid alcohol themselves. Thus, the tragic cycle is likely to be repeated in the next generation.

How much alcohol is safe during pregnancy? Even mild drinking, less than one drink per day, is associated with reduced head size and body growth among children followed into adolescence (Jacobson et al., 2004; Martinez-Frias et al., 2004). Recall that other factors—both genetic and environmental—can make some fetuses more vulnerable to teratogens. Therefore, no amount of alcohol is safe. Couples planning a pregnancy and expectant mothers should avoid alcohol entirely.

• **Radiation** Earlier we saw that ionizing radiation can cause mutation, damaging the DNA in ova and sperm. When mothers are exposed to radiation during pregnancy, the embryo or fetus can suffer additional harm. Defects due to radiation were tragically apparent in the children born to pregnant Japanese women who survived the atomic bombing of Hiroshima and Nagasaki during World War II. Similar abnormalities surfaced in the nine months following the 1986 Chernobyl, Ukraine, nuclear power plant accident. After each disaster, the incidence of miscarriage and of babies born with underdeveloped brains, physical deformities, and slow physical growth rose dramatically (Hoffmann, 2001; Schull, 2003).

Even when a radiation-exposed baby seems normal, problems may appear later. For example, even low-level radiation, resulting from industrial leakage or medical X-rays, can increase the risk of childhood cancer (Fattibene et al., 1999). In middle childhood, prenatally exposed Chernobyl children showed abnormal EEG brain-wave activity, lower intelligence test scores, and rates of language and emotional disorders two to three times greater than those of nonexposed Russian children (Kolominsky, Igumnov, & Drozdovitch, 1999; Loganovskaja & Loganovsky, 1999).

This child's mother was just a few weeks pregnant during the Chernobyl nuclear power plant disaster. Radiation exposure probably is responsible for his limb deformities. He is also at risk for low intelligence and language and emotional disorders. © Sergei Guneyev/Time & Life Pictures/Getty Images

• **Environmental Pollution** In industrialized nations, an astounding number of potentially dangerous chemicals are released into the environment. More than 75,000 are in common use in the United States, and many new pollutants are introduced each year. When 10 newborns were randomly selected from U.S. hospitals for analysis of umbilical cord blood, researchers uncovered a startling array of industrial contaminants—287 in all! They concluded that many babies are "born polluted" by chemicals that not only impair prenatal development but also increase the chances of life-threatening diseases and health problems later on (Houlihan et al., 2005).

One established teratogen is *mercury.* In the 1950s, an industrial plant released waste containing high levels of mercury into a bay providing food and water for the town of Minamata, Japan. Many children born at the time displayed physical deformities, mental retardation, abnormal speech, difficulty in chewing and swallowing, and uncoordinated movements. High levels of prenatal mercury exposure disrupt production and migration of neurons, causing widespread brain damage (Clarkson, Magos, & Myers, 2003; Hubbs-Tait et al., 2005). In the Faroe Islands of Northern Europe, where increased mercury exposure results from seafood diets that include pilot-whale meat, mercury concentration in umbilical-cord blood and tissue predicted deficits in speed of cognitive processing and motor, attention, and verbal test performance when children were assessed at age 7 and again at age 14 (Debes et al., 2006). Pregnant women are wise to avoid eating long-lived predatory fish, including swordfish, albacore tuna, and shark, which are heavily contaminated with mercury.

For many years, *polychlorinated biphenyls (PCBs)* were used to insulate electrical equipment, until research showed that, like mercury, they found their way into waterways and entered the food supply. In Taiwan, prenatal exposure to very high levels of PCBs in rice oil resulted in low birth weight, discolored skin, deformities of the gums and nails, EEG brain-wave abnormalities, and delayed cognitive development (Chen & Hsu, 1994; Chen et al., 1994). Steady, low-level PCB exposure is also harmful. Women who frequently ate PCB-contaminated fish, compared with those who ate little or no fish, had infants with lower birth weights, smaller heads, more intense physiological reactions to stress, persisting attention and memory difficulties, and lower intelligence test scores in childhood (Jacobson & Jacobson, 2003; Stewart et al., 2000; Walkowiak et al., 2001).

Another teratogen, *lead,* is present in paint flaking off the walls of old buildings and in certain materials used in industrial occupations. High levels of prenatal lead exposure are consistently related to prematurity, low birth weight, brain damage, and a wide variety of physical defects. Even low levels may be dangerous. In some studies, affected babies showed slightly poorer mental and motor development. In one investigation, unfavorable effects—in the form of increased delinquent and antisocial behaviors—were evident in adolescence (Bellinger, 2005; Dietrich et al., 2001).

• Maternal Disease Five percent of women catch an infectious disease while pregnant. Most of these illnesses, such as the common cold, seem to have no impact on the embryo or fetus. However, as Table 3.8 indicates, certain diseases can cause extensive damage.

Viruses. Rubella, otherwise known as three-day, or German, measles, is a well-known teratogen. In the mid-1960s, a worldwide epidemic of rubella led to the birth of more than 20,000 North American babies with serious defects. Consistent with the sensitive-period concept, the greatest damage occurs when rubella strikes during the embryonic period. More than 50 percent of infants whose mothers become ill during that time show eye cataracts; deafness; heart, genital, urinary, and intestinal defects; and mental retardation (Eberhart-Phillips, Frederick, & Baron, 1993). Infection during the fetal period is less likely to be harmful, but low birth weight, hearing loss, and bone defects may still occur. And the brain abnormalities resulting from prenatal rubella increase the risk of severe mental illness, especially schizophrenia, in adulthood (Brown, 2006).

Because vaccination against rubella in infancy and childhood is now routine, new disease outbreaks are unlikely in industrialized nations (Hyde et al., 2006). But an estimated 100,000

Table 3.8 Effects of Some Infectious Diseases During Pregnancy

Disease	Miscarriage	Physical Malformations	Mental Retardation	Low Birth Weight and Prematurity
Viral				
Acquired immune deficiency syndrome (AIDS)	0	?	+	?
Chicken pox	0	+	+	+
Cytomegalovirus	+	+	+	+
Herpes simplex 2 (genital herpes)	+	+	+	+
Mumps	+	?	0	0
Rubella (German measles)	+	+	+	+
Bacterial				
Chlamydia	+	?	0	+
Syphilis	+	+	+	?
Tuberculosis	+	?	+	+
Parasitic				
Malaria	+	0	0	+
Toxoplasmosis	+	+	+	+

+ = established finding, 0 = no present evidence, ? = possible effect that is not clearly established.

Sources: Jones, Lopez, & Wilson, 2003; Kliegman et al., 2008; Mardh, 2002; O'Rahilly & Müller, 2001.

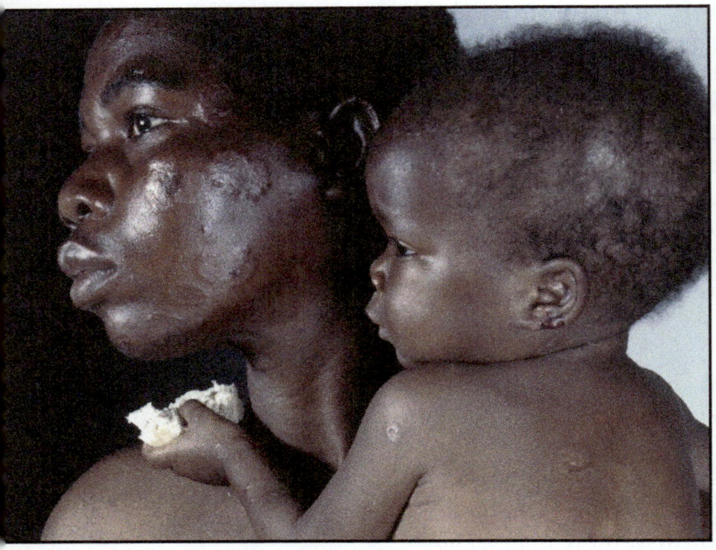

This South African mother and infant have AIDS. Both have extensive ringworm skin rashes. Antiviral drugs that have dramatically reduced prenatal AIDS transmission in Western nations are not widely available in Africa, where most new infections occur, more than half affecting women. © Dr. M. A. Ansary/ Photo Researchers, Inc.

cases of prenatal infection continue to occur worldwide, almost all in developing countries in Africa and Asia with weak or absent immunization programs (Robinson et al., 2006).

The *human immunodeficiency virus (HIV)*, which can lead to *acquired immune deficiency syndrome (AIDS)*, a disease that destroys the immune system, has infected increasing numbers of women over the past two decades. Currently, women account for about one-fourth of cases in North America, Western Europe, and East Asia. Although the incidence of AIDS has declined in industrialized nations, the disease is rampant in developing countries, where 95 percent of new infections occur, more than half of which affect women. In South Africa, for example, one-fourth of all pregnant women are HIV-positive (Kasmauski & Jaret, 2003; Quinn & Overbaugh, 2005). HIV-infected expectant mothers pass the deadly virus to the fetus 20 to 30 percent of the time.

AIDS progresses rapidly in infants. By 6 months, weight loss, diarrhea, and repeated respiratory illnesses are common. The virus also causes brain damage, as indicated by seizures, gradual loss in brain weight, and delayed mental and motor development. Most prenatal AIDS babies survive for only five to eight months after the appearance of these symptoms (O'Rahilly & Müller, 2001). The antiviral drug zidovudine (ZDV) reduces prenatal AIDS transmission by as much as 95 percent, with no harmful consequences of drug treatment for children (Culnane et al., 1999). It has led to a dramatic decline in prenatally acquired AIDS in Western nations, but ZVD is not widely available in impoverished regions of the world (United Nations, 2006).

As Table 3.8 reveals, the developing organism is especially sensitive to the family of herpes viruses, for which no vaccine or treatment exists. Among these, *cytomegalovirus* (the most frequent prenatal infection, transmitted through respiratory or sexual contact) and *herpes simplex 2* (which is sexually transmitted) are especially dangerous. In both, the virus invades the mother's genital tract, infecting babies either during pregnancy or at birth. Both diseases often have no symptoms, very mild symptoms, or symptoms with which people are unfamiliar, thereby increasing the likelihood of contagion. Pregnant women who are not in a mutually monogamous relationship are at greatest risk.

Bacterial and Parasitic Diseases. Table 3.8 also includes several bacterial and parasitic diseases. Among the most common is *toxoplasmosis*, caused by a parasite found in many animals. Pregnant women may become infected from eating raw or undercooked meat or from contact with the feces of infected cats. About 40 percent of women who have the disease transmit it to the developing organism. If it strikes during the first trimester, it is likely to cause eye and brain damage. Later infection is linked to mild visual and cognitive impairments. And about 80 percent of affected newborns with no obvious signs of damage develop learning or visual disabilities in later life (Jones, Lopez, & Wilson, 2003). Expectant mothers can avoid toxoplasmosis by making sure that the meat they eat is well-cooked, having pet cats checked for the disease, and turning over care of litter boxes to other family members.

Other Maternal Factors

Besides exposure to teratogens, maternal exercise, nutrition, and emotional well-being affect the embryo and fetus. In addition, many expectant parents wonder how a mother's age affects the course of pregnancy. We examine each of these factors in the following sections.

• **Exercise** In healthy, physically fit women, regular moderate exercise, such as walking, swimming, biking, or an aerobic workout, is related to increased birth weight (Leiferman & Evenson, 2003). However, very frequent, vigorous, extended exercise—working up a sweat for more than 30 minutes, four or five days a week, especially late in pregnancy—results in lower birth weight than in healthy controls (Clapp et al., 2002; Pivarnik, 1998). Hospital-sponsored childbirth education programs frequently offer exercise classes and suggest appropriate routines that help women prepare for labor and delivery.

During the last trimester, when the abdomen grows very large, mothers often must cut back on exercise. Most women, however, do not engage in sufficient moderate exercise during pregnancy to promote their own and their baby's health (Poudevigne & O'Connor, 2006). An expectant mother who remains fit experiences fewer physical discomforts, such as back pain, upward pressure on the chest, or difficulty breathing in the final weeks.

Nutrition During the prenatal period, when children are growing more rapidly than at any other time, they depend totally on the mother for nutrients. A healthy diet that results in a maternal weight gain of 25 to 30 pounds (10 to 13.5 kilograms) helps ensure the health of mother and baby.

Consequences of Prenatal Malnutrition. During World War II, a severe famine occurred in the Netherlands, giving scientists a rare opportunity to study the impact of nutrition on prenatal development. Findings revealed that the sensitive-period concept operates with nutrition, just as it does with teratogens. Women affected by the famine during the first trimester were more likely to have miscarriages or give birth to babies with physical defects. When women were past the first trimester, fetuses usually survived, but many were born underweight and had small heads (Stein et al., 1975).

We now know that prenatal malnutrition can cause serious damage to the central nervous system. The poorer the mother's diet, the greater the loss in brain weight, especially if malnutrition occurred during the last trimester. During that time, the brain is increasing rapidly in size; for it to reach its full potential, the mother must have a diet high in all the basic nutrients (Morgane et al., 1993). An inadequate diet during pregnancy can also distort the structure of other organs, including the liver, kidney, and pancreas, resulting in lifelong health problems (refer again to the Biology and Environment box on pages 96–97).

Because poor nutrition suppresses development of the immune system, prenatally malnourished babies frequently catch respiratory illnesses (Chandra, 1991). In addition, they often are irritable and unresponsive to stimulation. Like drug-addicted newborns, they have a high-pitched cry that is particularly distressing to their caregivers. In poverty-stricken families, these effects quickly combine with a stressful home life. With age, low intelligence test scores and serious learning problems become more apparent (Pollitt, 1996).

Prevention and Treatment. Many studies show that providing pregnant women with adequate food has a substantial impact on the health of their babies. Yet the growth demands of the prenatal period require more than just increased quantity of food. Vitamin–mineral enrichment is also crucial.

For example, taking a folic acid supplement around the time of conception reduces by more than 70 percent abnormalities of the neural tube, such as *anencephaly* and *spina bifida* (see Table 3.6 on page 83) (MCR Vitamin Study Research Group, 1991). In addition, adequate folic acid intake during the last 10 weeks of pregnancy cuts in half the risk of premature delivery and low birth weight (Scholl, Heidiger, & Belsky, 1996). Because of these findings, U.S. and Canadian government guidelines recommend that all women of childbearing age consume 0.4 milligrams of folic acid per day. For women who have previously had a pregnancy affected by neural tube defect, the recommended amount is 4 milligrams of folate per day beginning one month before conception and continuing through the first trimester, with some experts recommending 5 milligrams (dosage must be carefully monitored, as excessive intake can be harmful) (American Academy of Pediatrics, 2006). About half of North American pregnancies are unplanned, so government regulations mandate that bread, flour, rice, pasta, and other grain products be fortified with folic acid.

Other vitamins and minerals also have established benefits. Enriching women's diets with calcium helps prevent maternal high blood pressure and premature births. Adequate magnesium

An instructor leads a nutrition class for poor urban women and their children in Madras, India. By promoting a proper diet during pregnancy, the class helps prevent prenatal malnutrition. Mothers also learn how breastfeeding can protect their newborn babies' healthy growth. © David H. Wells/Corbis

and zinc reduce the risk of many prenatal and birth complications (Durlach, 2004; Kontic-Vucinic, Sulovic, & Radunovic, 2006). Fortifying table salt with iodine virtually eradicates *cretinism,* a condition of stunted growth and cognitive impairment, caused by prenatal iodine deficiency, that is a common cause of mental retardation in the developing world (Maberly, Haxton, & van der Haar, 2003). And sufficient vitamin C and iron beginning early in pregnancy promote growth of the placenta and healthy birth weight (Christian, 2003). Nevertheless, a supplement program should complement, not replace, efforts to improve maternal diets during pregnancy. For women who do not get enough food or an adequate variety of foods, multivitamin tablets are a necessary, but not a sufficient, intervention.

When poor nutrition continues throughout pregnancy, infants usually require more than dietary improvement. In response to their tired, restless behavior, parents tend to be less sensitive and stimulating. The babies, in turn, become even more passive and withdrawn. Successful interventions must break this cycle of apathetic caregiver–baby interaction. Some do so by teaching parents how to interact effectively with their infants; others focus on stimulating infants to promote active engagement with their physical and social surroundings (Grantham-McGregor et al., 1994; Grantham-McGregor, Schofield, & Powell, 1987).

Although prenatal malnutrition is highest in poverty-stricken regions of the world, it is not limited to developing countries. The U.S. Special Supplemental Food Program for Women, Infants, and Children (WIC), which provides food packages and nutrition education to low-income pregnant women, reaches about 90 percent of those who qualify because of their extremely low incomes. But many U.S. women who need nutrition intervention are not eligible for WIC (U.S. Department of Agriculture, 2005b). The Canadian Prenatal Nutrition Program (CPNP), which provides counseling, social support, access to health care, and shelter, as well as food to all pregnant women in need, regardless of income, reaches nearly 10 percent of expectant mothers in Canada (Health Canada, 2006a).

• **Emotional Stress** When women experience severe emotional stress during pregnancy, their babies are at risk for a wide variety of difficulties. Intense anxiety is associated with higher rates of miscarriage, prematurity, low birth weight, infant respiratory and digestive illnesses and sleep disturbances, and irritability during the first three years (Field et al., 2007; Mulder et al., 2002; Wadhwa, Sandman, & Garite, 2001). It is also related to several commonly occurring physical defects, such as cleft lip and palate, heart deformities, and pyloric stenosis (tightening of the infant's stomach outlet, which must be treated surgically) (Carmichael & Shaw, 2000).

How can maternal stress affect the developing organism? **TAKE A MOMENT...** To understand this process, list the changes you sensed in your own body the last time you were under stress. When we experience fear and anxiety, stimulant hormones released into our bloodstream cause us to be "poised for action." Large amounts of blood are sent to parts of the body involved in the defensive response—the brain, the heart, and muscles in the arms, legs, and trunk. Blood flow to other organs, including the uterus, is reduced. As a result, the fetus is deprived of a full supply of oxygen and nutrients.

Stress hormones also cross the placenta, causing a dramatic rise in fetal heart rate and activity level (Monk et al., 2000, 2004). They may permanently alter fetal neurological functioning as well, thereby heightening stress reactivity in later life (Graham et al., 1999; Monk et al., 2003). In one study, researchers identified mothers who had been directly exposed to the September 11, 2001, World Trade Center collapse during their pregnancies. At age 9 months, their babies were tested for saliva concentrations of *cortisol,* a hormone involved in regulating the stress response. Infants whose mothers had reacted to the disaster with severe anxiety had cortisol levels that were abnormally low—a symptom of reduced physiological capacity to manage stress (Yehuda et al., 2005). Consistent with this finding, maternal emotional stress during pregnancy predicts anxiety, short attention span, anger, aggression, and overactivity among preschool and school-age children, above and beyond the impact of other risks, such as maternal smoking during pregnancy, low birth weight, postnatal maternal anxiety, and low SES (de Weerth & Buitelaar, 2005; Gutteling et al., 2006; Van den Bergh, 2004).

But stress-related prenatal complications are greatly reduced when mothers have partners, other family members, and friends who offer support (Federenko & Wadhwa, 2004). The link between social support and positive pregnancy outcomes is particularly strong for low-income women, who often lead highly stressful lives (Hoffman & Hatch, 1996). Enhancing supportive social networks for pregnant mothers can help prevent prenatal complications.

• **Maternal Age and Previous Births** Over the past quarter century, first births to women in their thirties have increased more than threefold, and those to women in their early forties have doubled. Many more couples are putting off childbearing until their careers are well-established and they know they can support a child. Recall that women who delay having children until their thirties or forties face increased risk of infertility, miscarriage, and babies born with chromosomal defects. Are other pregnancy complications also more common among older mothers? Research consistently indicates that healthy women in their thirties have about the same rates of prenatal and birth problems as those in their twenties (Bianco et al., 1996; Dildy et al., 1996; Prysak, Lorenz, & Kisly, 1995). Thereafter, as Figure 3.10 shows, complication rates increase, with a sharp rise among women age 50 to 55—an age at which, because of menopause and aging reproductive organs, few women can conceive naturally (Salihu et al., 2003).

In the case of teenage mothers, does physical immaturity cause prenatal problems? Again, research shows that it does not. As we will see in Chapter 5, nature tries to ensure that once a girl can conceive, she is physically ready to carry and give birth to a baby. Infants born to teenagers have a higher rate of problems, but not directly because of maternal age. Most pregnant teenagers come from low-income backgrounds, where stress, poor nutrition, and health problems are common. Also, many are afraid to seek medical care or, in the United States, do not have access to care because they lack health insurance (U.S. Department of Health and Human Services, 2007c).

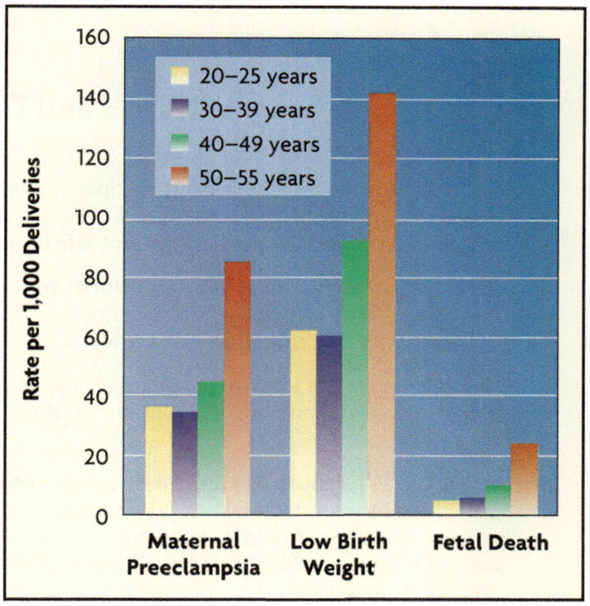

Figure 3.10 **Relationship of maternal age to prenatal and birth complications.**

Complications increase after age 40, with a sharp rise between 50 and 55 years. Preeclampsia (also known as toxemia) is a serious disorder of the second and third trimesters involving high blood pressure, sudden weight gains, headaches, and swelling of the face, hands, and feet. Without immediate treatment, the condition progresses rapidly and is a leading cause of maternal and infant illness and death. Similarly, low birth weight greatly increases the risk of infant death and health problems. (Adapted from Salihu et al., 2003.)

As we conclude our discussion of the prenatal environment, refer to Applying What We Know on page 106, which summarizes "do's and don'ts" for a healthy pregnancy. Public education about these vital precautions can greatly reduce prenatal health problems and their long-term negative consequences. The Canadian Institute of Child Health, a national nonprofit organization devoted to improving the health of Canada's children and youths, disseminates information to the public on how to foster prenatal health. It also advocates for safe, supportive care during childbirth—our next topic.

Ask Yourself

Review Why is it difficult to determine the effects of many environmental agents, such as drugs and pollution, on the embryo and fetus?

Apply Nora, pregnant for the first time, has heard about the teratogenic impact of alcohol and tobacco. But she still believes that a few cigarettes and a glass of wine a day won't be harmful. Provide Nora with research-based reasons for not smoking or drinking.

Connect List teratogens and other maternal factors that affect brain development during the prenatal period. Using Figure 3.8 on page 94, explain why the central nervous system is often affected when the prenatal environment is compromised.

Reflect A recent survey reported that only 24 percent of women of childbearing age knew that taking a daily folic acid supplement around the time of conception reduces the incidence of neural tube defects (U.S. Department of Health and Human Services, 2004). Were you aware of the prenatal effects of folic acid? If you had to choose five environmental influences in a campaign aimed at promoting healthy prenatal development, which ones would you choose, and why?

Applying What We Know

Do's and Don'ts for a Healthy Pregnancy

Do	Don't
Do make sure that you have been vaccinated against infectious diseases that are dangerous to the embryo and fetus, such as rubella, before you get pregnant. Most vaccinations are not safe during pregnancy.	Don't take any drugs without consulting your doctor.
Do see a doctor as soon as you suspect that you are pregnant—within a few weeks after a missed menstrual period—and continue to get regular medical checkups throughout pregnancy.	Don't smoke. If you have already smoked during part of your pregnancy, cut down or (better yet) quit. If other members of your family smoke, ask them to quit or to smoke outside.
Do obtain literature from your doctor, library, or bookstore about prenatal development, and ask your doctor about anything that concerns you.	Don't drink alcohol from the time you decide to get pregnant.
Do eat a well-balanced diet and take vitamin–mineral supplements, as prescribed by your doctor, both prior to and during pregnancy. On average, a woman should increase her intake by 100 calories a day in the first trimester, 265 in the second, and 430 in the third. Gain 25 to 30 pounds gradually.	Don't engage in activities that might expose your embryo or fetus to environmental hazards, such as radiation or chemical pollutants. If you work in an occupation that involves these agents, ask for a safer assignment or leave of absence.
Do keep physically fit through moderate exercise. If possible, join a special exercise class for expectant mothers.	Don't engage in activities that might expose your embryo or fetus to harmful infectious diseases. For example, to avoid toxoplasmosis, do not eat undercooked meat, handle cat litter, or garden in areas frequented by cats.
Do avoid emotional stress. If you are a single parent, find a relative or friend on whom you can count for emotional support.	Don't choose pregnancy as a time to go on a diet.
Do get plenty of rest. An overtired mother is at risk for complications.	Don't gain too much weight during pregnancy. An excessive weight gain is associated with complications.
Do enroll in a prenatal and childbirth education class with your partner or other companion. When parents know what to expect, the nine months before birth can be one of the most joyful times of life.	

Childbirth

It is not surprising that childbirth is often referred to as labor. It is the hardest physical work that a woman may ever do. A complex series of hormonal exchanges between mother and fetus initiates the process, which divides naturally into three stages (see Figure 3.11):

1. *Dilation and effacement of the cervix.* This is the longest stage of labor, lasting an average of 12 to 14 hours with a first birth and 4 to 6 hours with later births. Contractions of the uterus gradually become more frequent and powerful, causing the cervix, or uterine opening, to widen and thin to nothing, forming a clear channel from the uterus into the birth canal, or vagina.
2. *Delivery of the baby.* Once the cervix is fully open, the baby is ready to be born. This second stage is much shorter than the first, lasting about 50 minutes for a first baby and 20 minutes with later births. Strong contractions of the uterus continue, but the mother also feels a natural urge to squeeze and push with her abdominal muscles. As she does so with each contraction, she forces the baby down and out.
3. *Birth of the placenta.* Labor comes to an end with a few final contractions and pushes. These cause the placenta to separate from the wall of the uterus and be delivered in about 5 to 10 minutes.

The Baby's Adaptation to Labor and Delivery

At first glance, labor and delivery seem like a dangerous ordeal for the baby. The strong uterine contractions expose the head to a great deal of pressure, and they squeeze the placenta and the umbilical cord repeatedly. Each time, the baby's supply of oxygen is temporarily reduced.

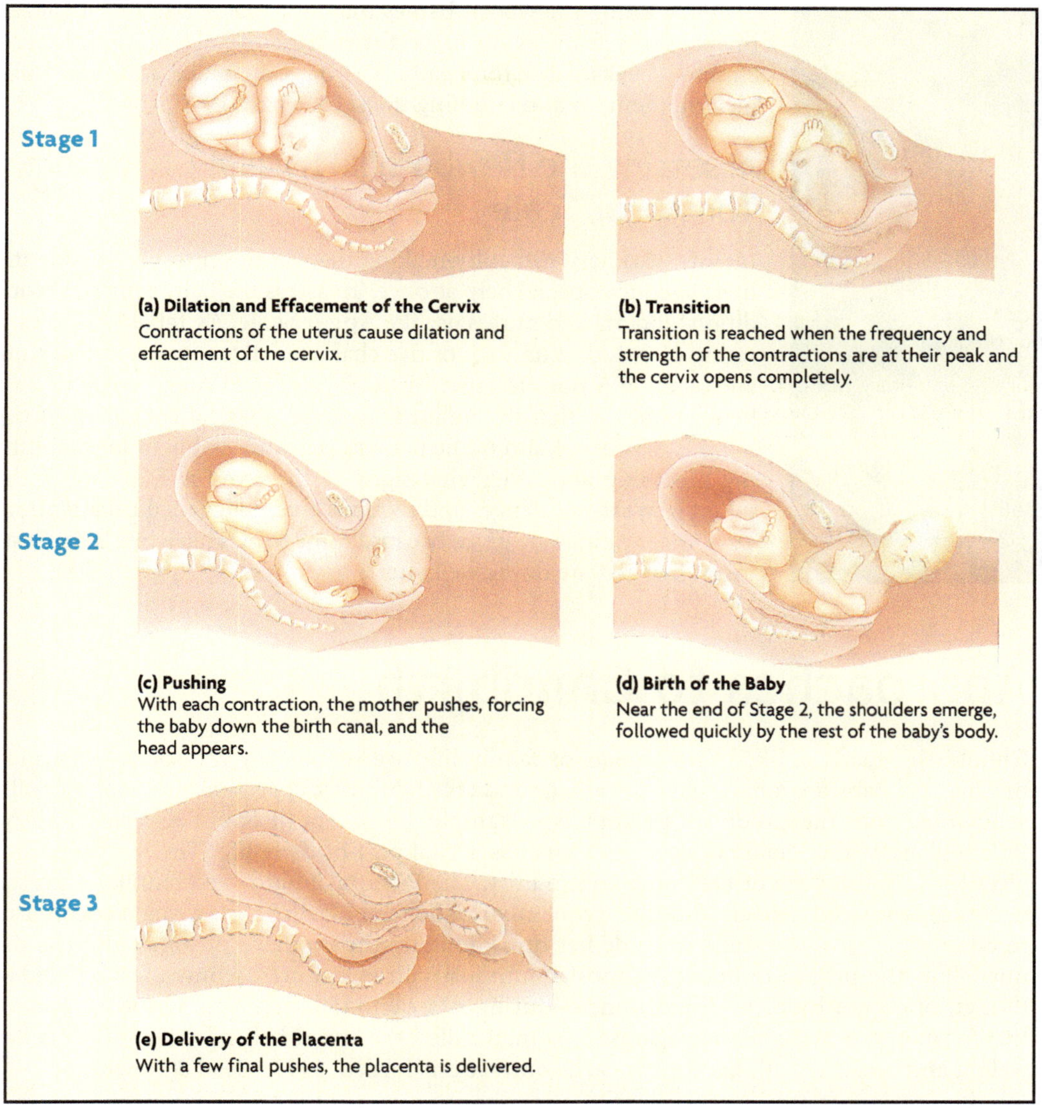

(a) Dilation and Effacement of the Cervix
Contractions of the uterus cause dilation and effacement of the cervix.

(b) Transition
Transition is reached when the frequency and strength of the contractions are at their peak and the cervix opens completely.

(c) Pushing
With each contraction, the mother pushes, forcing the baby down the birth canal, and the head appears.

(d) Birth of the Baby
Near the end of Stage 2, the shoulders emerge, followed quickly by the rest of the baby's body.

(e) Delivery of the Placenta
With a few final pushes, the placenta is delivered.

■ Figure 3.11
The three stages of labor.

Fortunately, healthy babies are well-equipped to withstand these traumas. The force of the contractions causes the infant to produce high levels of stress hormones. But in contrast to high stress levels during pregnancy, which can endanger the baby, the infant's production of stress hormones during childbirth is adaptive. It helps the baby withstand oxygen deprivation by sending a rich supply of blood to the brain and heart. In addition, stress hormones prepare the baby to breathe by causing the lungs to absorb any remaining fluid and by expanding the bronchial tubes (passages leading to the lungs). Finally, stress hormones arouse infants into alertness so they are born wide awake, ready to interact with their world (Lagercrantz & Slotkin, 1986).

The Newborn Baby's Appearance

Parents are often surprised at the odd-looking newborn—a far cry from the storybook image many had in their minds before birth. The average newborn is 20 inches long and 7½ pounds in weight; boys tend to be slightly longer and heavier than girls. The head is large in relation to the trunk and legs, which are short and bowed. This combination of a large head (with its well-developed brain) and a small body means that human infants learn quickly in the first few months of life. Unlike most mammals, however, they cannot get around on their own until much later.

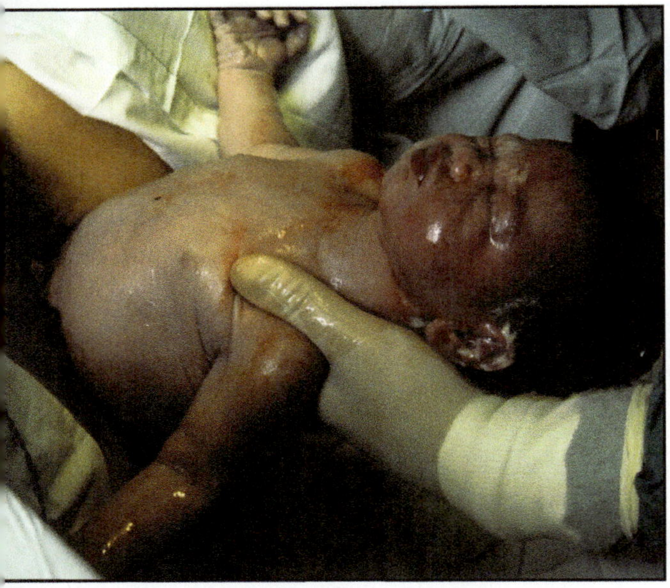

To accommodate the well-developed brain, a newborn's head is large in relation to the trunk and legs. The round face, with chubby cheeks and big eyes, induces adults to approach, pick up, and cuddle the newborn. © SIU/Peter Arnold, Inc.

Even though newborn babies may not match parents' idealized image, some features do make them attractive. Their round faces, chubby cheeks, large foreheads, and big eyes make adults feel like picking them up and cuddling them (Berman, 1980).

Assessing the Newborn's Physical Condition: The Apgar Scale

Infants who have difficulty making the transition to life outside the uterus require special help at once. To assess the baby's physical condition, doctors and nurses use the **Apgar Scale.** As Table 3.9 shows, a rating of 0, 1, or 2 on each of five characteristics is made at 1 minute and again at 5 minutes after birth. A combined Apgar score of 7 or better indicates that the infant is in good physical condition. If the score is between 4 and 6, the baby requires special help in establishing breathing and other vital signs. If the score is 3 or below, the infant is in serious danger and requires emergency medical attention. Two Apgar ratings are given because some babies have trouble adjusting at first but are doing well after a few minutes (Apgar, 1953).

Approaches to Childbirth

Childbirth practices, like other aspects of family life, are molded by the society of which mother and baby are a part. In many village and tribal cultures, expectant mothers are well-acquainted with the childbirth process. For example, the Jarara of South America and the Pukapukans of the Pacific Islands treat birth as a vital part of daily life. The Jarara mother gives birth in full view of the entire community. The Pukapukan girl is so familiar with the events of labor and delivery that she frequently can be seen playing at it. Using a coconut to represent the baby, she stuffs it inside her dress, imitates the mother's pushing, and lets the nut fall at the proper moment. In most nonindustrialized cultures, women are assisted—though often not by medical personnel—during labor and delivery. Among the Mayans of the Yucatán, the mother leans against a woman called the "head helper," who supports her weight and breathes with her during each contraction (Jordan, 1993; Mead & Newton, 1967).

Table 3.9 The Apgar Scale

	Score		
Sign[a]	0	1	2
Heart rate	No heartbeat	Under 100 beats per minute	100 to 140 beats per minute
Respiratory effort	No breathing for 60 seconds	Irregular, shallow breathing	Strong breathing and crying
Reflex irritability (sneezing, coughing, and grimacing)	No response	Weak reflexive response	Strong reflexive response
Muscle tone	Completely limp	Weak movements of arms and legs	Strong movements of arms and legs
Color[b]	Blue body, arms, and legs	Body pink with blue arms and legs	Body, arms, and legs completely pink

[a]To remember these signs, you may find it helpful to use a technique in which the original labels are reordered and renamed as follows: color = **A**ppearance, heart rate = **P**ulse, reflex irritability = **G**rimace, muscle tone = **A**ctivity, and respiratory effort = **R**espiration. Together, the first letters of the new labels spell **Apgar.**

[b]The skin tone of nonwhite babies makes it difficult to apply the "pink" color criterion. However, newborns of all races can be rated for pinkish glow resulting from the flow of oxygen through body tissues.

Source: Apgar, 1953.

In Western nations, childbirth has changed dramatically over the centuries. Before the late 1800s, birth usually took place at home and was a family-centered event. The industrial revolution brought greater crowding to cities, along with new health problems. As a result, childbirth moved from home to hospital, where the health of mothers and babies could be protected. Once doctors assumed responsibility for childbirth, women's knowledge of it declined, and relatives and friends no longer participated (Borst, 1995).

By the 1950s and 1960s, women had begun to question the medical procedures that had come to be used routinely during labor and delivery. Many felt that routine use of strong drugs and delivery instruments had robbed them of a precious experience and was often neither necessary nor safe for the baby. Gradually, a natural childbirth movement arose in Europe and spread to North America. Its purpose was to make hospital birth as comfortable and rewarding for mothers as possible. Today, most hospitals offer birth centers that are family-centered and homelike. *Freestanding birth centers,* which permit greater maternal control over labor and delivery, including choice of delivery positions, presence of family members and friends, and early contact between parents and baby, also exist. However, they offer less backup medical care than hospitals. And a small number of North American women reject institutional birth entirely and choose to have their babies at home.

Natural, or Prepared, Childbirth

Natural, or prepared, childbirth consists of a group of techniques aimed at reducing pain and medical intervention and making childbirth as rewarding an experience as possible. Although many natural childbirth programs exist, most draw on methods developed by Grantly Dick-Read (1959) in England and Ferdinand Lamaze (1958) in France. These physicians recognized that cultural attitudes had taught women to fear the birth experience. An anxious, frightened woman in labor tenses muscles, turning the mild pain that sometimes accompanies strong contractions into intense pain.

In a typical natural childbirth program, the expectant mother and a companion (a partner, a relative, or a friend) participate in three activities:

- *Classes.* The expectant mother and her companion attend a series of classes in which they learn about the anatomy and physiology of labor and delivery. Knowledge about the birth process reduces a mother's fear.
- *Relaxation and breathing techniques.* Expectant mothers are taught relaxation and breathing exercises aimed at counteracting the pain of uterine contractions.
- *Labor coach.* The companion learns how to help during childbirth by reminding the mother to relax and breathe, massaging her back, supporting her body, and offering encouragement and affection.

In Mali, West Africa, a midwife examines a pregnant woman, using an instrument to listen to the fetal heartbeat. The mother will give birth at home, supported by family members throughout labor and delivery. © Giacomo Pirozzi/Panos Pictures

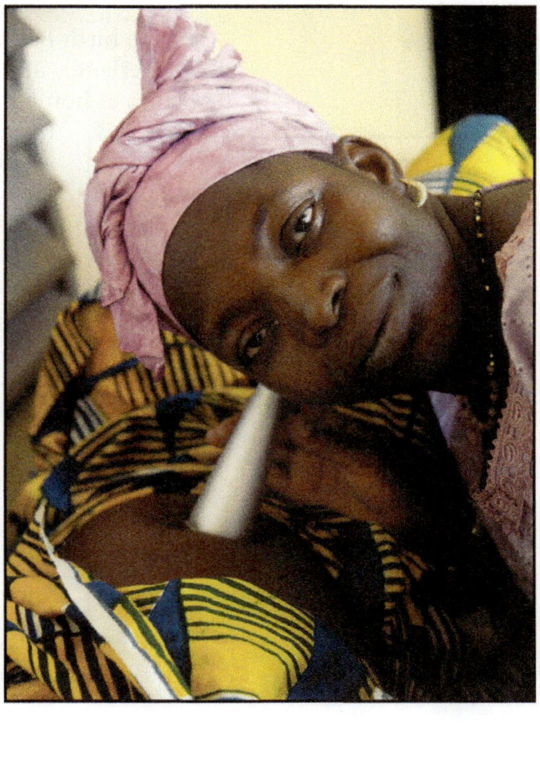

• Social Support and Natural Childbirth Social support is important to the success of natural childbirth techniques. In Guatemalan and American hospitals that routinely isolated patients during childbirth, some mothers were randomly assigned a trained companion who stayed with them throughout labor and delivery, talking to them, holding their hands, and rubbing their backs to promote relaxation. These mothers had fewer birth complications, and their labors were several hours shorter than those of women who did not have supportive companionship. Guatemalan mothers who received support also interacted more positively with their babies after delivery, talking, smiling, and gently stroking (Kennell et al., 1991; Sosa et al., 1980). Other studies indicate that mothers who are supported during labor and delivery less often have cesarean (surgical) deliveries, and their babies' Apgar scores are higher (Sauls, 2002).

The continuous rather than intermittent support of a trained companion during labor and delivery strengthens these outcomes. It is particularly helpful during a first childbirth, when mothers are more

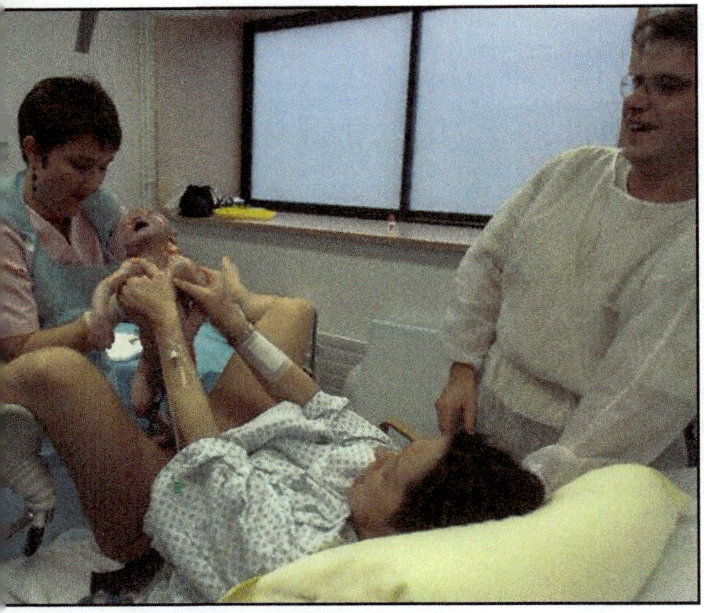

In a hospital birth center, a mother and father welcome their newborn baby, delivered by the midwife. A companion's support is a vital part of natural childbirth, which is associated with shorter labors and fewer birth complications and offers parents a more rewarding birth experience. © Vo Trung Dung/Corbis Sygma

anxious (DiMatteo & Kahn, 1997; Scott, Berkowitz, & Klaus, 1999). And this aspect of natural childbirth makes Western hospital-birth customs more acceptable to women from parts of the world where assistance from family and community members is the norm (Granot et al., 1996).

• Positions for Delivery With natural childbirth, mothers often give birth in the upright, sitting position shown in Figure 3.12 rather than lying flat on their backs with their feet in stirrups (the traditional hospital delivery room practice). Research findings favor the sitting position. When mothers are upright, labor is shortened because pushing is easier and more effective. The baby benefits from a richer supply of oxygen because blood flow to the placenta is increased. Because the mother can see the delivery, she can track the effectiveness of each contraction in pushing the baby out of the birth canal (Kelly, Terry, & Naglieri, 1999). This helps her work with the doctor or midwife to ensure that the baby's head and shoulders emerge slowly, which reduces the chances of tearing the vaginal opening. Compared with those who give birth lying on their backs, women who choose a partner-supported sitting-position birth are less likely to use pain-relieving medication (Eberhard, Stein, & Geissbuehler, 2005).

In another increasingly popular method, water birth, the mother sits in a warm tub of water, which supports her weight, relaxes her, and provides her with the freedom to move into any position she finds most comfortable. Recent evidence indicates that water birth is associated with a shorter labor, a lower rate of episiotomy (incision that increases the size of the vaginal opening), and a greater likelihood of medication-free delivery than either the back-lying or the birthing-stool approach (Eberhard, Stein, & Geissbuehler, 2005; Thoeni et al., 2005). As long as they are carefully managed by health professionals, water births pose no additional risk of infection or safety to mothers or babies.

Home Delivery

Home birth has always been popular in certain industrialized nations, such as England, the Netherlands, and Sweden. The number of North American women choosing to have their babies at home increased during the 1970s and 1980s but remains small, at about 1 percent (Studelska, 2006). These mothers want birth to be an important part of family life. In addition, most want to avoid unnecessary medical procedures. And they want greater control over their own care and that of their babies than hospitals permit (Wickham, 1999). Although some home births are attended by doctors, many more are handled by certified nurse–midwives, who have degrees in nursing and additional training in childbirth management.

Is it just as safe to give birth at home as in a hospital? For healthy women who are assisted by a well-trained doctor or midwife, it seems so because complications rarely occur (Fullerton, Navarro, & Young, 2007; Johnson & Daviss, 2005). However, if attendants are not carefully trained and prepared to handle emergencies, the rate of infant death is high (Mehlmadrona & Madrona, 1997). When mothers are at risk for any kind of complication, the appropriate place for labor and delivery is the hospital, where life-saving treatment is available.

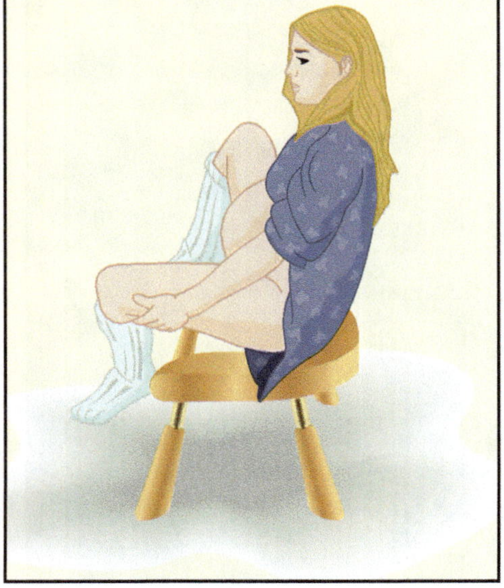

Figure 3.12 **A birthing stool.**

The mother gives birth in an upright posture, which facilitates pushing during the second stage of labor, increases blood flow to the placenta, and permits the mother to see the delivery, enabling her to track the effectiveness of each contraction. Her partner can sit behind, supporting her body.

Labor and Delivery Medication

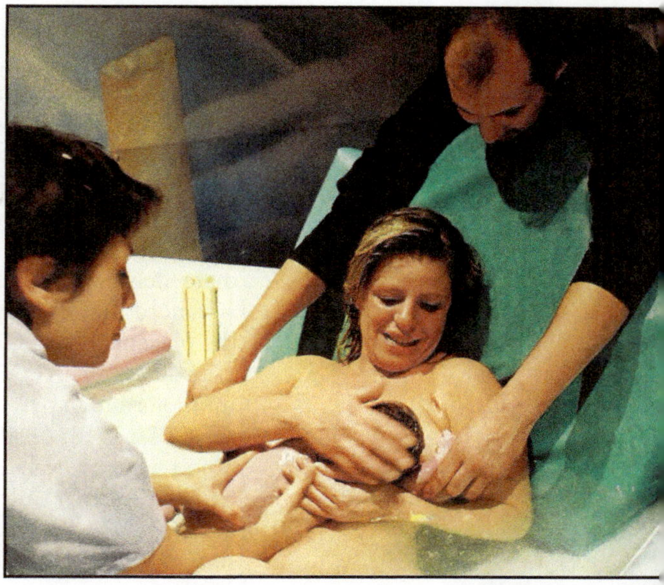

An increasingly popular childbirth option is water birth. Sitting in a warm tub of water relaxes this mother, supports her weight, and gives her the freedom to move into a comfortable position. © France Keyser/In Visu/Corbis

Although natural childbirth techniques lessen or eliminate the need for pain-relieving drugs, some form of medication is used in more than 80 percent of North American births (Sharma & Leveno, 2003). *Analgesics,* drugs used to relieve pain, may be given in mild doses during labor to help a mother relax. *Anesthetics* are a stronger type of painkiller that blocks sensation. Currently, the most common approach to controlling pain during labor is *epidural analgesia,* in which a regional pain-relieving drug is delivered continuously through a catheter into a small space in the lower spine. Unlike older spinal block procedures, which numb the entire lower half of the body, epidural analgesia limits pain reduction to the pelvic region. Because the mother retains the capacity to feel the pressure of the contractions and to move her trunk and legs, she is able to push during the second stage of labor.

Although pain-relieving drugs help women cope with childbirth and enable doctors to perform essential medical interventions, they also cause problems. Epidural analgesia, for example, weakens uterine contractions. As a result, labor is prolonged, and the chances of cesarean (surgical) delivery increase (Klein, 2006). And because drugs rapidly cross the placenta, exposed newborns tend to have lower Apgar scores, to be sleepy and withdrawn, to suck poorly during feedings, and to be irritable when awake (Caton et al., 2002; Eltzschig, Lieberman, & Camann, 2003; Emory, Schlackman, & Fiano, 1996).

Do heavy doses of childbirth medication have a lasting impact on physical and mental development? Some researchers have claimed so (Brackbill, McManus, & Woodward, 1985), but their findings have been challenged (Riordan et al., 2000). Use of medication may be related to other risk factors that could account for long-term consequences in some studies. Nevertheless, the negative impact of these drugs on the newborn's adjustment supports the current trend to limit their use.

Ask Yourself

Review Describe the features and benefits of natural childbirth. What aspect contributes greatly to favorable outcomes, and why?

Apply On seeing her newborn baby for the first time, Caroline exclaimed, "Why is she so out of proportion?" What observations prompted Caroline to ask this question? Explain why her baby's appearance is adaptive.

Connect How might use of epidural analgesia during labor and delivery negatively affect the parent–newborn relationship? Does your answer illustrate bidirectional influences between parent and child? Explain.

Reflect If you were an expectant parent, would you choose home birth? Why or why not?

Birth Complications

We have seen that some babies—in particular, those whose mothers are in poor health, do not receive good medical care, or have a history of pregnancy problems—are especially likely to experience birth complications. Inadequate oxygen, a pregnancy that ends too early, and low birth weight pose serious risks to development that we have touched on many times. Let's look at the impact of each complication on later development.

Oxygen Deprivation

A small number of infants experience *anoxia,* or inadequate oxygen supply, during the birth process. Sometimes the problem results from a failure to start breathing within a few minutes. Healthy newborns can survive periods of little or no oxygen longer than adults can; they reduce their metabolic rate, thereby conserving the limited oxygen available. Nevertheless, brain damage is likely if regular breathing is delayed more than 10 minutes (Kendall & Peebles, 2005).

At other times, anoxia occurs during labor. A common cause is squeezing of the umbilical cord, a condition that is especially likely when infants are in **breech position**—turned in such a way that the buttocks or feet would be delivered first (1 in every 25 births). Because of this danger, breech babies often experience a cesarean (surgical) delivery. An additional cause of oxygen deprivation is *placenta abruptio*, or premature separation of the placenta (complicating about 1 percent of pregnancies), a life-threatening event that requires immediate delivery (Oyelese & Ananth, 2006). Factors related to it include multiple fetuses, advanced maternal age (40 and older), and teratogens that cause abnormal development of the placenta, such as tobacco and cocaine (Oyelese & Ananth, 2006).

Still another condition that can lead to anoxia is **Rh factor incompatibility** between the mother's and baby's blood types. When the mother is Rh negative (lacks the Rh protein) and the father is Rh positive (has the Rh protein), the baby may inherit the father's Rh-positive blood type. If even a little of a fetus's Rh-positive blood crosses the placenta into the Rh-negative mother's bloodstream, she begins to form antibodies to the foreign protein. If these enter the fetus's system, they destroy red blood cells, reducing the supply of oxygen. Mental retardation, miscarriage, heart damage, and infant death can occur. It takes time for the mother to produce antibodies, so firstborn children are rarely affected. The danger increases with each pregnancy. Fortunately, Rh incompatibility can be prevented in most cases. After the birth of each Rh-positive baby, Rh-negative mothers are given a vaccine to prevent the buildup of antibodies.

After initial brain injury from anoxia, another phase of cell death can occur several hours later. Currently, researchers are experimenting with ways to prevent this secondary damage. Compared with routine hospital care, placing anoxic newborns in a head-cooling device shortly after birth for 72 hours substantially reduced brain injury (detected through MRI brain scans) and increased scores on a newborn behavioral assessment (Lin et al., 2006). And in another study, having anoxic newborns lie on a precooled water blanket resulted in an 18 percent reduction in rate of death or disability at 18- to 22-month follow-up (Shankaran et al., 2005).

How do children who experience anoxia during labor and delivery fare as they get older? Research suggests that the greater the oxygen deprivation, the poorer children's cognitive and language skills in early and middle childhood (Hopkins-Golightly, Raz, & Sander, 2003). Although effects of even mild to moderate anoxia often persist, many children improve over time (Bass et al., 2004; Raz, Shah, & Sander, 1996).

This head-cooling device, known as CoolCap, helps prevent brain damage in oxygen-deprived newborns. Olympic Cool-Cap® System. Image courtesy of NATUS Medical Incorporated.

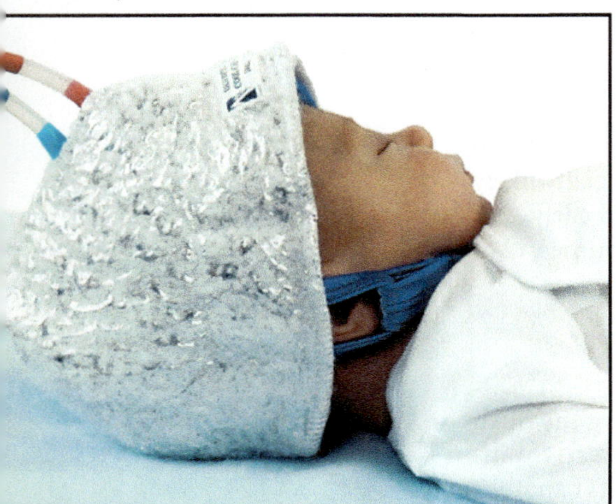

When development is severely impaired, the anoxia was probably extreme. Perhaps it was caused by prenatal insult to the baby's respiratory system or occurred because the infant's lungs were not yet mature enough to breathe. For example, babies born more than six weeks early commonly have *respiratory distress syndrome* (otherwise known as *hyaline membrane disease*). Their tiny lungs are so poorly developed that the air sacs collapse, causing serious breathing difficulties. Today, mechanical respirators keep many such infants alive. In spite of these measures, some babies suffer permanent brain damage from lack of oxygen, and in other cases their delicate lungs are harmed by the treatment itself. Respiratory distress syndrome is only one of many risks for babies born too soon, as we will see in the following section.

Preterm and Low-Birth-Weight Infants

Babies born three weeks or more before the end of a full 38-week pregnancy or who weigh less than 5½ pounds (2,500 grams) have for many years been referred to as "premature." A wealth of research indicates that premature babies are at risk for many problems. Birth weight is the best available predictor of infant survival and healthy development. Many newborns who weigh less than 3½ pounds (1,500 grams) experience difficulties that are not overcome, an effect that becomes stronger as birth weight decreases (Dombrowski, Noonan, & Martin, 2007; Laptook et al., 2005). Frequent illness, inattention, overactivity, sensory impairments, poor motor coordination, language delays, low intelligence test scores, deficits in school learning, and emotional and behavior problems are some of the difficulties that persist through childhood and adolescence and into adulthood (Bayless, 2007; Grunau, Whitfield, & Fay, 2004; Hultman et al., 2007; Lefebvre, Mazurier, & Tessier, 2005).

About 1 in 13 American infants and 1 in 18 Canadian infants are born underweight. Although the problem can strike unexpectedly, it is highest among poverty-stricken women (Statistics Canada, 2007c; U.S. Department of Health and Human Services, 2007a). These mothers, as indicated earlier, are more likely to be undernourished and to be exposed to harmful environmental influences. In addition, they often do not receive adequate prenatal care.

Prematurity is also common when mothers are carrying twins, who are usually born about three weeks early. Because space inside the uterus is restricted, twins gain less weight than singletons after the twentieth week of pregnancy.

• Preterm versus Small for Date Although low-birth-weight infants face many obstacles to healthy development, most go on to lead normal lives; about half of those who weighed only a couple of pounds at birth have no disability (see Figure 3.13). To better understand why some babies do better than others, researchers divide them into two groups. **Preterm infants** are those born several weeks or more before their due date. Although they are small, their weight may still be appropriate, based on time spent in the uterus. **Small-for-date infants** are below their expected weight considering length of the pregnancy. Some small-for-date infants are actually full term. Others are preterm babies who are especially underweight.

Of the two types of babies, small-for-date infants usually have more serious problems. During the first year, they are more likely to die, catch infections, and show evidence of brain damage. By middle childhood, they have lower intelligence test scores, are less attentive, achieve more poorly in school, and are socially immature (Hediger et al., 2002; O'Keefe et al., 2003). Small-for-date infants probably experienced inadequate nutrition before birth. Perhaps their mothers did not eat properly, the placenta did not function normally, or the babies themselves had defects that prevented them from growing as they should. In some of these babies, an abnormally functioning placenta permitted ready transfer of stress hormones from mother to fetus. Consequently, small-for-date infants are especially likely to suffer from prenatal neurological impairments that permanently weaken their capacity to manage stress (Wust et al., 2005).

Even among preterm newborns whose weight is appropriate for length of pregnancy, just seven more days—from 34 to 35 weeks—can contribute greatly to infant health. Compared to babies born at 34 weeks, those born at 35 weeks show substantially reduced rates of illness, costly medical procedures, and lengthy hospital stays, although they need greater medical intervention than full-term babies (Gladstone & Katz, 2004). And despite being relatively low-risk for disabilities, a substantial number of 34-week preterms are well below average in physical growth and mildly to moderately delayed in cognitive development in early and middle childhood (de Haan et al., 2000; Pietz et al., 2004). Yet doctors often induce births several weeks preterm, under the misconception that these babies are developmentally "mature."

■ Figure 3.13 **Incidence of major and minor disabilities by birth weight, obtained from studies of low-birth-weight children at school age.** *Major disabilities* include cerebral palsy, mental retardation, and vision and hearing impairments. *Minor disabilities* include slightly below-average intelligence, learning disabilities (usually in reading, spelling, and math), mild difficulties in motor control, and behavior problems (including poor attention and impulse control, aggressiveness, noncompliance, depression, passivity, anxiety, and difficulty separating from parents). (Adapted from D'Agostino & Clifford, 1998.)

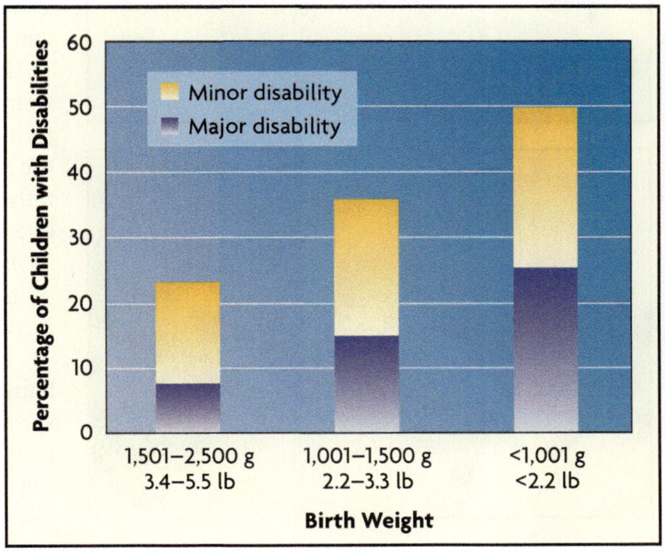

• Consequences for Caregiving Imagine a scrawny, thin-skinned infant whose body is only a little larger than the size of your hand. You try to play with the baby by stroking and talking softly, but he is sleepy and unresponsive. When you feed him, he sucks poorly. During the short, unpredictable periods in which he is awake, he is usually irritable.

The appearance and behavior of preterm babies can lead parents to be less sensitive and responsive in caring for them. Compared to full-term infants, preterm babies—especially those who are very ill at birth—are less often held close, touched, and talked to gently. At times, mothers of these infants resort to interfering pokes and verbal commands, in an effort to obtain a higher level of response from the baby (Barratt, Roach, & Leavitt, 1996; Feldman, 2007a). This may explain why preterm babies as a group are at risk for child abuse. When they are born to isolated, poverty-stricken mothers who cannot provide good nutrition, health care, and parenting, the likelihood of unfavorable outcomes increases. In contrast, parents with stable life circumstances and social supports usually can overcome the stresses of caring for a preterm infant. In these cases, even sick preterm babies have a good chance of catching up in development by middle childhood (Ment et al., 2003).

These findings suggest that how well preterm infants develop has a great deal to do with the parent–child relationship. Consequently, interventions directed at supporting both sides of this tie are more likely to help these infants recover.

Top photo: New mothers in a hospital ward in the Philippines practice skin-to-skin "kangaroo care," which is widely used in developing countries to promote the survival and recovery of preterm babies. Because of its many physical and psychological benefits, kangaroo care has spread to Western nations, where it is used as a supplement to hospital intensive care. *Bottom photo:* A U.S. mother engages in the technique with her fragile newborn. *Top:* REUTERS/Cheryl Ravelo/Landov; *bottom:* Picture Partners/Alamy.

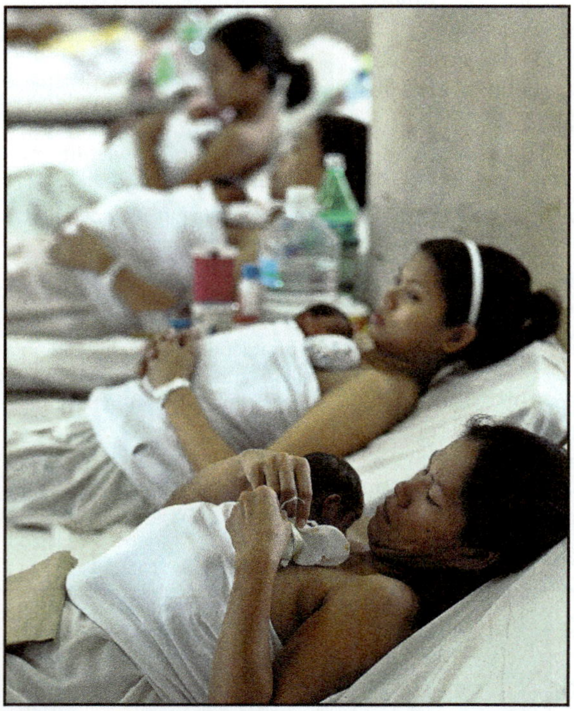

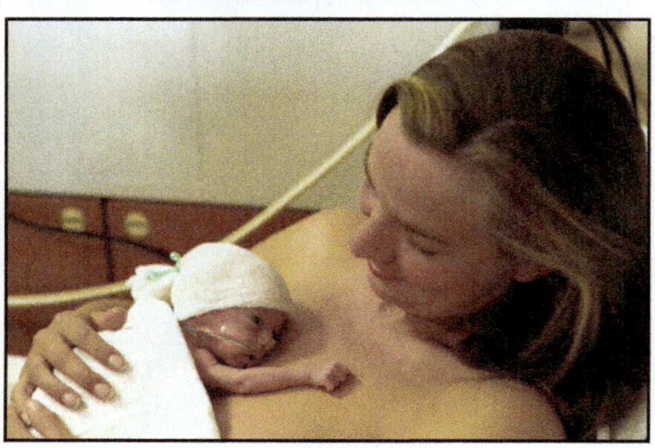

• Interventions for Preterm Infants A preterm baby is cared for in a special Plexiglas-enclosed bed called an *isolette.* Temperature is carefully controlled because these infants cannot yet regulate their own body temperature effectively. To help protect the baby from infection, air is filtered before it enters the isolette. When a preterm infant is fed through a stomach tube, breathes with the aid of a respirator, and receives medication through an intravenous needle, the isolette can be very isolating indeed! Physical needs that otherwise would lead to close contact and other human stimulation are met mechanically.

Special Infant Stimulation. At one time, doctors believed that stimulating such fragile babies could be harmful. Now we know that in proper doses, certain kinds of stimulation can help preterm infants develop. In some intensive care nurseries, preterm babies can be seen rocking in suspended hammocks or lying on waterbeds designed to replace the gentle motion they would have received while still in the mother's uterus. Other forms of stimulation have also been used—for example, an attractive mobile or a tape recording of a heartbeat, soft music, or the mother's voice. These experiences promote faster weight gain, more predictable sleep patterns, and greater alertness (Arnon et al., 2006; Marshall-Baker, Lickliter, & Cooper, 1998; Standley, 1998).

Touch is an especially important form of stimulation. In baby animals, touching the skin releases certain brain chemicals that support physical growth—effects believed to occur in humans as well. When preterm infants were massaged several times each day in the hospital, they gained weight faster and, at the end of the first year, were more advanced in mental and motor development than preterm infants not given this stimulation (Field, 2001; Field, Hernandez-Reif, & Freedman, 2004).

In developing countries where hospitalization is not always possible, skin-to-skin "kangaroo care" is the most readily available intervention for promoting the survival and recovery of preterm babies. It involves placing the infant in a vertical position between the mother's breasts or next to the father's chest (under the parent's clothing) so the parent's body functions as a human incubator. Kangaroo care offers fathers a unique opportunity to increase their involvement in caring for the preterm newborn. Because of its many physical and psychological benefits, the technique is used often in Western nations as a supplement to hospital intensive care.

Kangaroo skin-to-skin contact fosters improved oxygenation of the baby's body, temperature regulation, sleep, feeding, alertness, and infant survival (Feldman & Eidelman, 2003). In addition, the kangaroo position provides the baby with gentle stimulation of all sensory modalities: hearing (through the parent's voice), smell (through proximity of the parent's body), touch (through skin-to-skin contact), and visual (through the upright position). Mothers and fathers practicing kangaroo care feel more confident about caring for their fragile babies, interact more sensitively and affectionately, and feel more attached to them (Dodd, 2005; Feldman et al., 2002, 2003). Together, these factors may explain why preterm babies given many hours of kangaroo care in their early weeks, compared to those given little or no such care, score higher on measures of mental and motor development during the first year (Charpak, Ruiz-Peláez, & Figueroa, 2005; Tessier et al., 2003). Because of its diverse benefits, more than 80 percent of North American nurseries now offer kangaroo care to preterm newborns (Field et al., 2006).

Training Parents in Infant Caregiving Skills. Interventions that support parents of preterm infants generally teach them about the infant's characteristics and promote caregiving skills. For parents with adequate economic and personal resources to care for a preterm infant, just a few sessions of coaching in recognizing and responding to the baby's needs are linked to steady gains in mental test scores that, after several years, resemble those of full-term children (Achenbach et al., 1990).

When preterm infants live in stressed, low-income households, long-term intensive intervention is required to reduce developmental problems. In the Infant Health and Development Program, preterm babies born into poverty received a comprehensive intervention that combined medical follow-up, weekly parent training sessions, and enrollment in cognitively stimulating child care from 1 through 3 years of age. More than four times as many intervention children as no-intervention controls (39 versus 9 percent) were within normal range in intelligence, psychological adjustment, and physical growth (Bradley et al., 1994). In addition, mothers in the intervention group were more affectionate and more often encouraged play and cognitive mastery in their children—one reason their 3-year-olds may have been developing so favorably (McCarton, 1998).

At ages 5 and 8, children who had attended the child-care program regularly—for more than 350 days over the three-year period—continued to show better intellectual functioning. The more they attended, the higher they scored, with greater gains for those whose birth weights were higher—between 4½ and 5½ pounds (2,001 to 2,500 grams) (see Figure 3.14). In contrast, children who attended only sporadically gained little or even lost ground (Hill, Brooks-Gunn, & Waldfogel, 2003). These findings confirm that babies who are both preterm and economically disadvantaged require *intensive* intervention. And special strategies, such as extra adult–child interaction, may be necessary to achieve lasting changes in children with the lowest birth weights.

Figure 3.14 Influence of intensity of early intervention for low-income preterm babies on intellectual functioning at age 8. Infants born preterm received cognitively stimulating child care from 1 through 3 years of age. Those who attended the program sporadically gained little in intellectual functioning (heavier-weight babies) or lost ground (light-weight babies). The more children attended, the greater their intellectual gains. Heavier babies consistently gained more than light babies. But boosting the intensity of intervention above 400 days led to a dramatic increase in the performance of the light-weight group. (Adapted from Hill, Brooks-Gunn, & Waldfogel, 2003.)

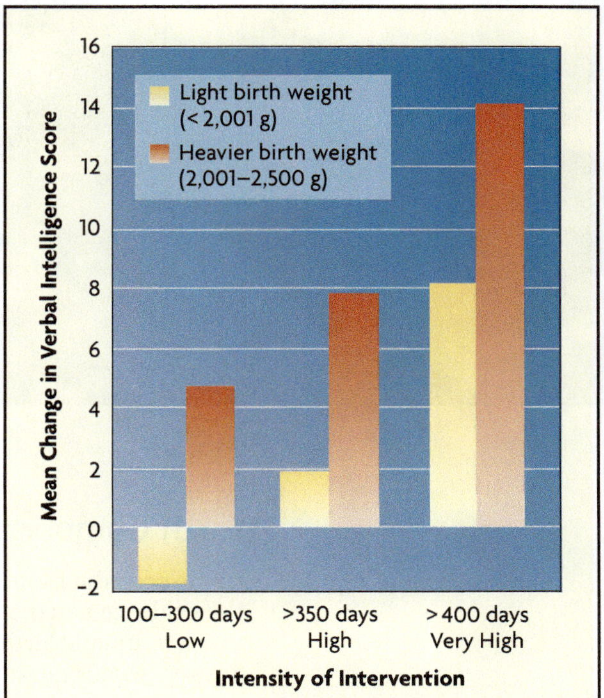

• Very Low Birth Weight, Environmental Advantages, and Long-Term Outcomes

Although very low-birth-weight babies often have lasting problems, in a Canadian study, participants who had weighed between 1 and 2.2 pounds (500 to 1,000 grams) at birth were doing well as young adults (Saigal et al., 2006). At 22 to 25 years of age, they resembled normal-birth-weight individuals in educational attainment, rates of marriage and parenthood, and (for those who had no neurological or sensory impairments) employment status. Researchers believe that home, school, and societal advantages combine to explain these excellent outcomes (Hack & Klein, 2006). Most participants in this study were reared in two-parent middle-SES homes, attended good schools where they received special services, and benefited from Canada's universal health care system.

But even the best environments cannot "fix" the serious biological risks associated with being born severely underweight. An even better course of action would be to prevent this serious threat to infant survival and development. The high rate of underweight babies in the United States—one of the worst in the industrialized world—could be greatly reduced by improving the health and social conditions described in the Social Issues box on pages 116–117.

▪ Social Issues ▪

A Cross-National Perspective on Health Care and Other Policies for Parents and Newborn Babies

Infant mortality—the number of deaths in the first year of life per 1,000 live births—is an index used around the world to assess the overall health of a nation's children. The United States has the most up-to-date health care technology in the world, including a newborn intensive care capacity per number of births far exceeding that of other industrialized nations (Thompson, Goodman, & Little, 2002). Nevertheless, it has made less progress in reducing infant deaths than many other countries. Over the past three decades, it has slipped in the international rankings, from seventh in the 1950s to twenty-sixth in 2006. Members of America's poor ethnic minorities are at greatest risk. African-American and Native-American babies are twice as likely as white infants to die in the first year of life (U.S. Census Bureau, 2007b).

Canada, in contrast, has achieved one of the lowest infant mortality rates in the world. It ranks sixteenth, falling only slightly behind top-ranked countries. Still, infant mortality among Canada's lowest-income groups is much higher than the national figure. First Nations babies die at twice the rate, and Inuit babies at three times the rate, of Canadian babies in general (Statistics Canada, 2005e).

Neonatal mortality, the rate of death within the first month of life, accounts for 67 percent of the infant death rate in the United States and for 80 percent in Canada. Two factors are largely responsible for neonatal mortality. The first is serious physical defects, most of which cannot be prevented. The percentage of babies born with physical defects is about the same in all ethnic and income groups. The second leading cause of neonatal mortality is low birth weight, which is largely preventable. African-American, Native-American, and Canadian-Aboriginal babies are more than twice as likely as white infants to be born early and underweight (Health Canada, 2004; U.S. Census Bureau, 2007b).

Widespread poverty and, in the United States, weak health care programs for mothers and young children are largely responsible for these trends. Unfortunately, 16 percent of pregnant women in the United States wait until after the first trimester to seek prenatal care, and nearly 4 percent receive none at all. Late or no prenatal care is far more common among adolescent and low-income, ethnic minority mothers, many of whom lack health insurance. Although the poorest of these mothers are eligible for government-sponsored health services, many low-income women do not qualify.

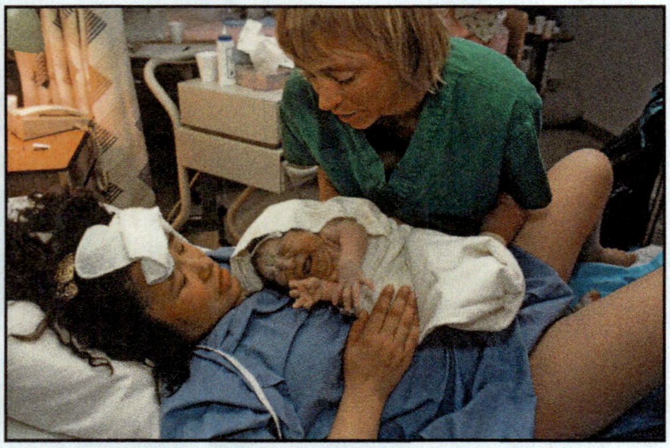

This Inuit mother, from Baffin Island in northernmost Canada, experienced pregnancy complications and had to be flown 190 miles to deliver her son. Limited access to health care and social services in remote areas compromise the futures of many Inuit newborns. © Joanna B. Pinneo/AURORA

Besides financial hardship, some low-income mothers have other reasons for not seeking early prenatal care. They mention a variety of *situational barriers*—difficulty finding a doctor, getting an appointment, and arranging transportation, and insensitive or unsatisfying experiences with clinic staff. Personal barriers—psychological stress, family crises, lack of knowledge about the benefits of prenatal care, and ambivalence about the pregnancy—also stand in the way (Daniels, Noe, & Mayberry, 2006; Maupin et al., 2004).

Each country listed in Figure 3.15 that outranks the United States in birth weight and infant survival provides all its citizens with government-sponsored health care benefits. And each takes extra steps to make sure that pregnant mothers and babies have access to good nutrition, high-quality medical care, and social and economic supports that promote effective parenting.

For example, all Western European nations guarantee women a certain number of prenatal visits at very low or no cost. After a baby is born, a health professional routinely visits the home to provide counseling about infant care and to arrange continuing medical services. Home assistance is especially extensive in the Netherlands. For a token fee, each mother is granted a specially trained maternity helper, who assists with infant care, shopping, housekeeping, meal preparation, and the care of other children during the days after delivery (Bradley & Bray, 1996; Zwart, 2007).

Birth Complications, Parenting, and Resilience

In the preceding sections, we considered a variety of birth complications. Now let's try to put the evidence together. Can any general principles help us understand how infants who survive a traumatic birth are likely to develop? A landmark study carried out in Hawaii provides answers to this question.

■ Figure 3.15 **Infant mortality in 29 nations.** Despite its advanced health care technology, the United States ranks poorly. It is twenty-sixth in the world, with a death rate of 6.6 infants per 1,000 births. Canada, which provides all its citizens government-funded health care, ranks sixteenth. Its infant death rate is 4.8 per 1,000 births. (Adapted from U.S. Census Bureau, 2007a.)

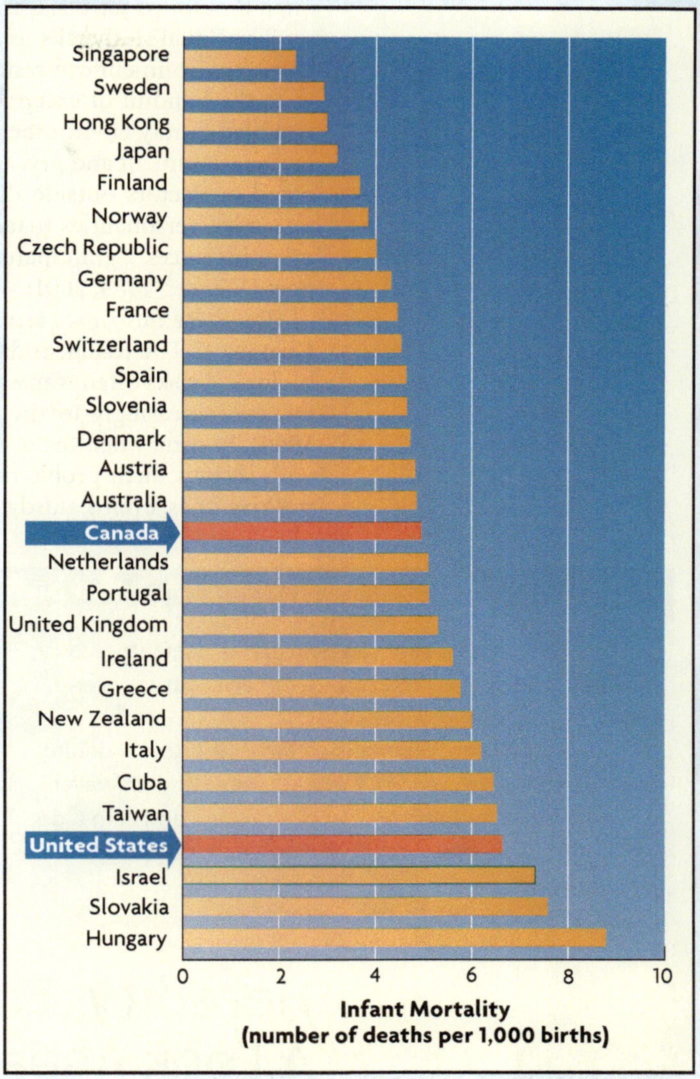

Paid, job-protected employment leave is another vital societal intervention for new parents. Canadian mothers are eligible for a full year of maternity leave at 55 percent of prior earnings (but only up to a maximum of $413 per week), and Canadian mothers or fathers can take an additional year of parental leave at the same rate in certain cases—for example, when a child is ill following birth or adoption. Paid leave is widely available in other industrialized nations as well. Sweden has the most generous parental leave program in the world. Mothers can begin maternity leave 60 days prior to expected delivery, extending it to six weeks after birth, and fathers are granted two weeks of birth leave. In addition, either parent can take full leave until the child reaches age 18 months at 80 percent of prior earnings, followed by an additional three months at a modest flat rate. Each parent is also entitled to another 18 months of unpaid leave. Even less-developed nations offer parental leave benefits. For example, in the People's Republic of China, a new mother is granted three months' leave at regular pay. Furthermore, many countries supplement basic paid leave. In Germany, for example, after a fully paid three-month leave, a parent may take two more years at a flat rate and a third year at no pay (OECD, 2006; Waldfogel, 2001).

Yet in the United States, the federal government mandates *only 12 weeks of unpaid leave* for employees in companies with at least 50 workers. Most women, however, work in smaller businesses, and even those who work in large enough companies may be unable to afford to take unpaid leave (Hewlett, 2003). And because of financial pressures, many new mothers who are eligible for unpaid work leave take far less than 12 weeks, while new fathers tend to take little or none at all (Han & Waldfogel, 2003; OECD, 2006). In 2002, California became the first state to guarantee a mother or father paid leave—up to six weeks at half salary, regardless of the size of the company.

Nevertheless, research indicates that six weeks of childbirth leave (the norm in the United States) is not enough. When a family is stressed by a baby's arrival, a leave of six weeks or less is linked to maternal anxiety, depression, sense of role overload (conflict between work and family responsibilities), and negative interactions with the baby. A longer leave (12 weeks or more) predicts favorable maternal mental health, supportive marital interaction, and sensitive, responsive caregiving (Feldman, Sussman, & Zigler, 2004; Hyde et al., 2001). Single women and their babies are most hurt by the absence of a generous national paid-leave policy. These mothers, who are usually the sole source of support for their families, can least afford to take time from their jobs.

In countries with low infant mortality rates, expectant mothers need not wonder how or where they will get health care and other resources to support their baby's development. The powerful impact of universal, high-quality health care, generous parental leave, and other social services on maternal and infant well-being provides strong justification for these policies.

In 1955, Emmy Werner and Ruth Smith began to follow nearly 700 infants on the island of Kauai who had experienced mild, moderate, or severe birth complications. Each was matched, on the basis of SES and ethnicity, with a healthy newborn (Werner & Smith, 1982). Findings showed that the likelihood of long-term difficulties increased if birth trauma was severe. But among mildly to moderately stressed children, those growing up in stable families did almost as well on measures of intelligence and psychological adjustment as those with no birth problems. Those exposed to poverty, family disorganization, and mentally ill parents often developed serious learning difficulties, behavior problems, and emotional disturbance.

The Kauai study tells us that as long as birth injuries are not overwhelming, a supportive home environment can restore children's growth. But the most intriguing cases in this study were the handful of exceptions. A few children with fairly serious birth complications and troubled family environments grew into competent adults who fared as well as controls in career attainment and psychological adjustment. Werner and Smith found that these children relied on factors outside the family and within themselves to overcome stress. Some had attractive personalities that drew positive responses from relatives, neighbors, and peers. In other instances, a grandparent, aunt, uncle, or babysitter provided the needed emotional support (Werner, 1989, 2001; Werner & Smith, 1992).

Do these outcomes remind you of the characteristics of resilient children, discussed in Chapter 1? The Kauai study and other similar investigations reveal that the impact of early biological risks often wanes as children's personal characteristics and social experiences contribute increasingly to their functioning (Laucht, Esser, & Schmidt, 1997; Resnick et al., 1999). In sum, when the overall balance of life events tips toward the favorable side, children with serious birth problems can develop successfully. And when negative factors outweigh positive ones, even a sturdy newborn can become a lifelong casualty.

Ask Yourself

Review Sensitive care can help preterm infants recover, but they are less likely than full-term newborns to receive such care. Explain why.

Apply Cecilia and Adena each gave birth to a 3-pound baby seven weeks preterm. Cecilia is single and on welfare. Adena and her husband are happily married and earn a good income. Plan an intervention appropriate for helping each baby develop.

Connect List factors discussed in this chapter that increase the chances that an infant will be born underweight. How many of these factors could be prevented by better health care for expectant mothers and babies?

Reflect Many people object to the use of extraordinary medical measures to save extremely low-birth-weight babies because of their high risk of developing serious physical, cognitive, and emotional problems. Do you agree or disagree? Explain.

Heredity, Environment, and Behavior: A Look Ahead

Throughout this chapter, we have discussed a wide variety of genetic and early environmental influences, each of which has the power to alter the course of development. When we consider them together, it may seem surprising that any newborn babies arrive intact. Yet the vast majority—over 90 percent in North America—do. Born healthy and vigorous, these developing members of the human species vary greatly in behavior. Some are outgoing and sociable; others are shy and reserved. By school age, one child loves to read, another is attracted to mathematics, while a third excels at music. **Behavioral genetics** is a field devoted to uncovering the contributions of nature and nurture to this diversity in human traits and abilities. We have already seen that researchers have just begun to understand the genetic and environmental events preceding birth that affect the child's potential. How, then, do they unravel the roots of the many characteristics that emerge later?

All contemporary researchers agree that both heredity and environment are involved in every aspect of development. But for polygenic traits (those due to many genes), such as intelligence and personality, scientists are a long way from knowing the precise hereditary influences involved. Although they are making progress in identifying the multiple variations in DNA sequences associated with complex traits, so far these genetic markers explain only a small amount of variation in human behavior, and a minority of cases of most psychological disorders (Plomin, 2005; Plomin et al., 2003). For the most part, scientists are still limited to investigating the impact of genes on complex characteristics indirectly.

Some believe that it is useful and possible to answer the question of *how much each factor contributes* to differences among children. A growing consensus, however, regards that question as unanswerable. These investigators believe that heredity and environment are inseparable (Gottlieb, Wahlsten, & Lickliter, 2006). The important question, they maintain, is *how nature and nurture work together.* Let's consider each position in turn.

The Question, "How Much?"

To infer the role of heredity in complex human characteristics, researchers use special methods, the most common being the *heritability estimate.* Let's look closely at the information this procedure yields, along with its limitations.

• Heritability **Heritability estimates** measure the extent to which individual differences in complex traits in a specific population are due to genetic factors. We will take a brief look at heritability findings on intelligence and personality here and will return to them in later chapters, when we consider these topics in greater detail. Heritability estimates are obtained from **kinship studies,** which compare the characteristics of family members. The most common type of kinship study compares identical twins, who share all their genes, with fraternal twins, who, on average, share only half. If people who are genetically more alike are also more similar in intelligence and personality, then the researcher assumes that heredity plays an important role.

Kinship studies of intelligence provide some of the most controversial findings in the field of child development. Some experts claim a strong genetic influence, whereas others believe that heredity is barely involved. Currently, most kinship findings support a moderate role for heredity. When many twin studies are examined, correlations between the scores of identical twins are consistently higher than those of fraternal twins. In a summary of more than 10,000 twin pairs, the correlation for intelligence was .86 for identical twins and .60 for fraternal twins (Plomin & Spinath, 2004).

Researchers use a complex statistical procedure to compare these correlations, arriving at a heritability estimate ranging from 0 to 1.00. The value for intelligence is about .50 for child and adolescent samples in Western industrialized nations. This suggests that differences in genetic makeup explain half the variation in intelligence. Adopted children's mental test scores are more strongly related to their biological parents' scores than to those of their adoptive parents, offering further support for the role of heredity (Petrill & Deater-Deckard, 2004).

Heritability research also reveals that genetic factors are important in personality. For frequently studied traits, such as sociability, anxiety, agreeableness, and activity level, heritability estimates obtained on child, adolescent, and young adult twin samples are moderate, in the .40s and .50s (Bouchard, 2004; Caspi & Shiner, 2006; Rothbart & Bates, 2006).

Twin studies of schizophrenia—a psychological disorder involving delusions and hallucinations, difficulty distinguishing fantasy from reality, and irrational and inappropriate behaviors—consistently yield high heritabilities, around .80. The role of heredity in antisocial behavior and major depression (though still apparent) is less strong, with heritabilities in the .30s and .40s (Bouchard, 2004). Again, adoption studies support these results. Biological relatives of schizophrenic, depressed, and antisocial adoptees are more likely than adoptive relatives to share the same disorder (Plomin et al., 2001; Ridenour, 2000; Tienari et al., 2003).

Adriana and Tamara, identical twins born in Mexico, were separated at birth and adopted into different homes in the New York City area. They were unaware of each other's existence until age 20, when they met through a mutual acquaintance. The twins discovered that they were similar in many ways, ranging from academic achievement to a love of dancing. The study of identical twins reared apart reveals that heredity contributes to many psychological characteristics. But generalizing from twin evidence to the population is controversial. © Jacquie Hemmerdinger/The New York Times

• Limitations of Heritability Serious questions have been raised about the accuracy of heritability estimates, which depends on the extent to which the twin pairs studied reflect genetic and environmental variation in the population. Within a population in which all people have very similar home, school, and community experiences, individual differences in intelligence and personality would be largely genetic, and heritability estimates would be close to 1.00. Conversely, the more environments vary, the more likely they are to account for individual differences, yielding lower heritability estimates. In twin studies, most of the twin pairs are reared together under highly similar conditions. Even when separated twins are available for study, social service agencies have often placed them in advantaged homes that are alike in many ways (Rutter et al., 2001). Because the environments of most twin pairs are less diverse than those of the general population, heritability estimates are likely to exaggerate the role of heredity.

Heritability estimates are controversial measures because they can easily be misapplied. For example, high heritabilities have been used to suggest that ethnic differences in intelligence, such as the poorer performance of black children compared to white children, have a genetic basis (Jensen, 1969, 1985, 1998). Yet this line of reasoning is widely regarded as incorrect. Heritabilities computed on mostly white twin samples do not tell us what is responsible for test score differences between ethnic groups. We have already seen that large economic and cultural differences are involved. In Chapter 8, we will discuss research indicating that when black children are adopted into economically advantaged homes at an early age, their mental test scores are well above average and substantially higher than those of children growing up in impoverished families.

Perhaps the most serious criticism of heritability estimates has to do with their limited usefulness. Though interesting, these statistics give us no precise information on how intelligence and personality develop or how children might respond to environments designed to help them develop as far as possible (Rutter, 2002; Wachs, 1999). Indeed, the heritability of intelligence increases as parental education and income increase—that is, as children grow up in conditions that allow them to make the most of their genetic endowment. In disadvantaged environments, children are prevented from realizing their potential. Consequently, enhancing their experiences through interventions—such as increasing parent education and income and providing high-quality preschool or child care—has a greater impact on development (Bronfenbrenner & Morris, 2006; Turkheimer et al., 2003).

According to one group of experts, heritability estimates have too many problems to yield any firm conclusions about the relative strength of nature and nurture (Collins et al., 2000). Although these statistics confirm that heredity contributes to complex traits, they do not tell us how environment can modify genetic influences.

The Question, "How?"

Today, most researchers view development as the result of a dynamic interplay between heredity and environment. How do nature and nurture work together? Several concepts shed light on this question.

• Reaction Range The first of these ideas is **range of reaction,** each person's unique, genetically determined response to the environment (Gottesman, 1963). Let's explore this idea in Figure 3.16. Reaction range can apply to any characteristic; here it is illustrated for intelligence. Notice that when environments vary from extremely unstimulating to highly enriched, Ben's intelligence test score increases steadily, Linda's rises sharply and then falls off, and Ron's begins to increase only after the environment becomes modestly stimulating.

Figure 3.16 **Intellectual ranges of reaction (RR) for three children in environments that vary from extremely unstimulating to highly enriched.** Each child, due to his or her genetic makeup, responds differently as quality of the environment changes. Ben's intelligence test score increases steadily, Linda's rises sharply and then falls off, and Ron's begins to increase only after the environment becomes modestly stimulating. (Adapted from Wahlsten, 1994.)

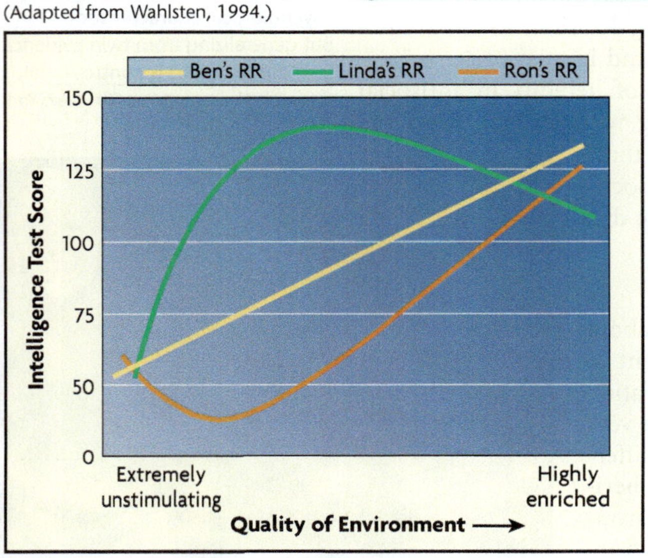

Reaction range highlights two important points. First, it shows that because each of us has a unique genetic makeup, we respond differently to the same environment. Notice in Figure 3.16 how a poor environment results in similarly low scores for all three children. But when the environment provides an intermediate level of stimulation, Linda is by far the best-performing child. And in a highly enriched environment, Ben does best, followed by Ron, both of whom now outperform Linda.

Second, sometimes different genetic–environmental combinations can make two children look the same! For example, if Linda is reared in a minimally stimulating environment, her score will be about 100—average for children in general. Ben and

Ron can also obtain this score, but to do so they must grow up in a fairly enriched home. In sum, range of reaction reveals that unique blends of heredity and environment lead to both similarities and differences in children's behavior (Gottlieb, Wahlsten, & Lickliter, 2006).

• **Canalization** Another way of understanding how heredity and environment combine comes from the concept of **canalization**—the tendency of heredity to restrict the development of some characteristics to just one or a few outcomes. A behavior that is strongly canalized develops similarly in a wide range of environments; only strong environmental forces can change it (Waddington, 1957). For example, infant perceptual and motor development seems to be strongly canalized because all normal human babies eventually roll over, reach for objects, sit up, crawl, and walk. It takes extreme conditions to modify these behaviors or cause them not to appear. In contrast, intelligence and personality are less strongly canalized; they vary much more with changes in the environment.

When we look at behaviors constrained by heredity, we can see that canalization is highly adaptive. Through it, nature ensures that children will develop certain species-typical skills under a wide range of rearing conditions, thereby promoting survival.

• **Genetic–Environmental Correlation** A major problem in trying to separate heredity and environment is that they are often correlated (Plomin et al., 2001; Scarr & McCartney, 1983). According to the concept of **genetic–environmental correlation,** our genes influence the environments to which we are exposed. The way this happens changes with age.

Passive and Evocative Correlation. At younger ages, two types of genetic–environmental correlation are common. The first is called *passive* correlation because the child has no control over it. Early on, parents provide environments influenced by their own heredity. For example, parents who are good athletes emphasize outdoor activities and enroll their children in swimming and gymnastics. Besides being exposed to an "athletic environment," the children may have inherited their parents' athletic ability. As a result, they are likely to become good athletes for both genetic and environmental reasons.

The second type of genetic–environmental correlation is *evocative.* The responses children evoke from others are influenced by the child's heredity, and these responses strengthen the child's original style. For example, an active, friendly baby is likely to receive more social stimulation than a passive, quiet infant. And a cooperative, attentive child probably receives more patient and sensitive interactions from parents than an inattentive, distractible child. In support of this idea, the less genetically alike siblings are, the more their parents treat them differently, in both warmth and negativity. Thus, parents' treatment of identical twins is highly similar, whereas their treatment of fraternal twins and nontwin biological siblings is only moderately so. And little resemblance exists in parents' warm and negative interactions with unrelated stepsiblings (see Figure 3.17) (Reiss, 2003).

Active Correlation. In older children, *active* genetic–environmental correlation becomes common. As children extend their experiences beyond the immediate family and are given the freedom to make more choices, they actively seek environments that fit with their genetic tendencies.

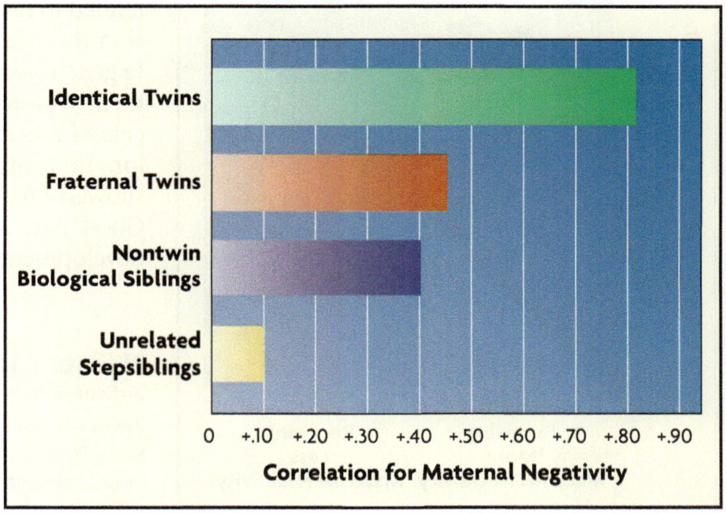

■ **Figure 3.17** **Similarity in mothers' interactions for pairs of siblings differing in genetic relatedness.**

The correlations shown are for maternal negativity. The pattern illustrates evocative genetic–environmental correlation. Identical twins evoke similar maternal treatment because of their identical heredity. As genetic resemblance between siblings declines, the strength of the correlation drops. Mothers vary their interactions as they respond to each child's unique genetic makeup. (Adapted from Reiss, 2003.)

This mother shares her love of running with her daughter, who also may have inherited her mother's athletic ability. When heredity and environment are correlated, they jointly foster the same capacities, and it is impossible to separate the influence of one from the influence of the other.

The well-coordinated, muscular child spends more time at after-school sports, the musically talented youngster joins the school orchestra and practices his violin, and the intellectually curious child is a familiar patron at her local library.

This tendency to actively choose environments that complement our heredity is called **niche-picking** (Scarr & McCartney, 1983). Infants and young children cannot do much niche-picking because adults select environments for them. In contrast, older children and adolescents are much more in charge of their environments. Niche-picking explains why pairs of identical twins reared apart during childhood and later reunited may find, to their surprise, that they have similar hobbies, food preferences, and vocations—a trend that is especially marked when twins' environmental opportunities are similar (Plomin, 1994). Niche-picking also helps us understand why identical twins become somewhat more alike, and fraternal twins and adopted siblings less alike, in intelligence with age (Bouchard, 2004; Loehlin, Horn, & Willerman, 1997).

The influence of heredity and environment is not constant but changes over time. With age, genetic factors may become more important in influencing the environments we experience and choose for ourselves.

• Environmental Influences on Gene Expression Notice how, in the concepts just considered, heredity is granted priority. In range of reaction, it *limits* responsiveness to varying environments. In canalization, it *restricts* the development of certain behaviors. Similarly, some theorists regard genetic–environmental correlation as entirely driven by genetics (Harris, 1998; Rowe, 1994). They believe that children's genetic makeup causes them to receive, evoke, or seek experiences that actualize their inborn tendencies.

Others argue that heredity does not dictate children's experiences or development in a rigid way. In one study, boys with a genetic tendency toward antisocial behavior (based on the presence of a gene on the X chromosome known to predispose both animals and humans to aggression) were no more aggressive than boys without this gene, *unless* they also had a history of severe child abuse (Caspi et al., 2002). Boys with and without the gene did not differ in their experience of abuse, indicating that the "aggressive genotype" did not increase exposure to abuse. And in a large Finnish adoption study, children of schizophrenic mothers reared by healthy adoptive parents showed little mental illness—no more than a control group with healthy biological and adoptive parents. In contrast, schizophrenia and other psychological impairments piled up in adoptees whose biological and adoptive parents were both disturbed (Tienari et al., 2003; Tienari, Wahlberg, & Wynne, 2006).

Furthermore, parents and other caring adults can uncouple adverse genetic–environmental correlations. They often provide children with positive experiences that modify the expression of heredity, yielding favorable outcomes. For example, in a study that tracked the development of 5-year-old identical twins, pair members tended to resemble each other in level of aggression. And the more aggression they displayed, the more maternal anger and criticism they received (a genetic–environmental correlation). Nevertheless, some mothers treated their twins differently. When followed up at age 7, twins who had been targets of more maternal negativity engaged in even more antisocial behavior. In contrast, their better-treated, genetically identical counterparts showed a reduction in disruptive acts (see Figure 3.18) (Caspi et al., 2004). Good parenting protected them from a spiraling, antisocial course of development.

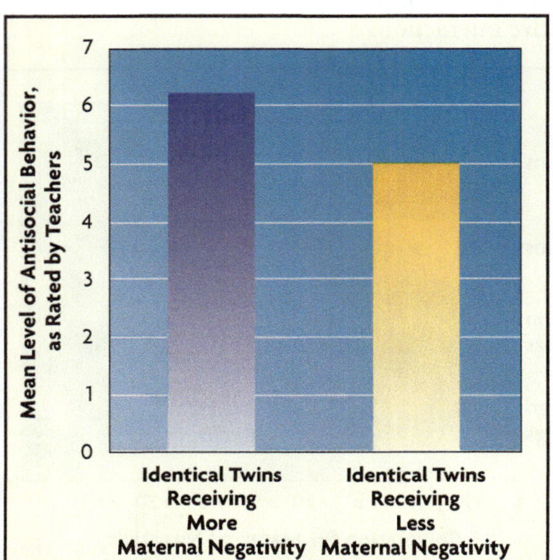

■ Figure 3.18 **Relationship of maternal negativity (criticism and hostility) to antisocial behavior among identical twins.**

Twins who were targets of more maternal negativity at age 5 were rated as more antisocial by their classroom teachers at age 7, after controlling for any behavioral differences between twin-pair members at age 5. (Adapted from Caspi et al., 2004.)

Other research confirms that parents' unequal treatment of siblings is not just the straightforward result of children's heredity but is affected by aspects of family life. In large families, single-parent families, low-income families, and families with unhappy marriages, siblings receive more differential treatment from parents (Jenkins, Rasbash, & O'Connor, 2003). Perhaps parents who are under stress concentrate their limited energies on one child.

Accumulating evidence reveals that the relationship between heredity and environment is not a one-way street, from genes to environment to behavior. Rather, like other system influences considered in this and the previous chapter, it is *bidirectional:* Genes affect children's behavior and experiences, but their experiences and behavior also affect gene expression (Gottlieb, 2000, 2003; Rutter, 2006). Stimulation—both *internal* to the child (activity within the cytoplasm of the cell, release of hormones into the bloodstream) and *external* to the child (home, neighborhood, school, and community)—triggers gene activity.

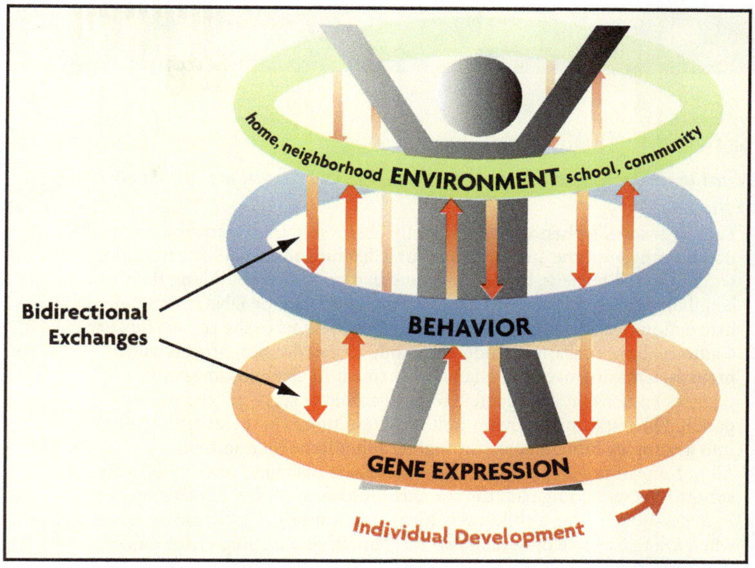

Figure 3.19 **The epigenetic framework.**
Development takes place through ongoing, bidirectional exchanges between heredity and all levels of the environment. Genes affect behavior and experiences. Experiences and behavior also affect gene expression. (Adapted from Gottlieb, 2007.)

Researchers call this view of the relationship between heredity and environment the *epigenetic framework* (Gottlieb, 1998, 2007). It is depicted in Figure 3.19. **Epigenesis** means development resulting from ongoing, bidirectional exchanges between heredity and all levels of the environment. To illustrate, providing a baby with a healthy diet increases brain growth, which translates into new connections between nerve cells, which transform gene expression. This opens the door to new gene–environment exchanges—for example, advanced exploration of objects and interaction with caregivers, which further enhance brain growth and gene expression. These ongoing, bidirectional influences foster cognitive and social development. In contrast, harmful environments can dampen gene expression, at times so profoundly that later experiences can do little to change characteristics (such as intelligence and personality) that were flexible to begin with.

A major reason that researchers are interested in the nature–nurture issue is that they want to improve environments so that children can develop as far as possible. The concept of epigenesis reminds us that development is best understood as a series of complex exchanges between nature and nurture. Although children cannot be changed in any way we might desire, environments can modify genetic influences. The success of any attempt to improve development depends on the characteristics we want to change, the genetic makeup of the child, and the type and timing of our intervention.

Ask Yourself

Review What is epigenesis, and how does it differ from range of reaction and genetic–environmental correlation? Provide an example of epigenesis.

Apply Bianca's parents are accomplished musicians. At age 4, Bianca began taking piano lessons. By age 10, she was accompanying the school choir. At age 14, she asked if she could attend a special music high school. Explain how genetic–environmental correlation promoted Bianca's talent.

Connect Explain how each of the following concepts supports the conclusion that genetic influences on human characteristics are not constant but change over time: somatic mutation (page 79), niche-picking (page 122), and epigenesis (page 123).

Reflect What aspects of your own development—for example, interests, hobbies, college major, or vocational choice—are probably due to niche-picking? Explain.

SUMMARY

Genetic Foundations

What are genes, and how are they transmitted from one generation to the next?

- Each individual's **phenotype,** or directly observable characteristics, is a product of both **genotype** and environment. **Chromosomes,** rodlike structures within the cell nucleus, contain our hereditary endowment. Along their length are **genes,** segments of **deoxyribonucleic acid,** or **DNA,** that send instructions for making a rich assortment of proteins to the cell's cytoplasm.
- **Gametes,** or sex cells, are produced through a cell division process called **meiosis. Crossing over** and chance assortment of chromosomes into gametes ensure that each gamete receives a unique set of genes from each parent. Once sperm and ovum unite, the resulting **zygote** starts to develop into a complex human being through cell duplication, or **mitosis.**
- All but one of the 23 pairs of chromosomes are matching pairs called **autosomes.** The remaining pair, the **sex chromosomes**—XX in females and XY in males—determine a child's sex. **Identical,** or **monozygotic, twins,** develop when a single zygote divides in two early in cell duplication. **Fraternal,** or **dizygotic, twins** result when two ova are released from the ovaries and each is fertilized.

Describe various patterns of genetic inheritance.

- A **homozygous** child inherits the same **allele** from both parents and displays the inherited trait. If the alleles differ, the child is **heterozygous**; relationships between the alleles determine the phenotype. In **dominant–recessive inheritance,** only the dominant allele affects the child's phenotype; a child must inherit two recessive alleles to display the recessive trait. Heterozygous individuals become **carriers** of the recessive trait. In **incomplete dominance,** both alleles are expressed in the phenotype. **Modifier genes** enhance or dilute the effects of other genes.
- In **X-linked inheritance,** a harmful allele is carried on the X chromosome. Males are more likely than females to be affected. In **genomic imprinting,** alleles are *imprinted,* or marked, so only one parent's allele is activated, regardless of its makeup.
- Harmful genes arise from **mutation,** which can either occur spontaneously or be caused by hazardous environmental agents. Human traits that vary on a continuum, such as intelligence and personality, are due to **polygenic inheritance,** meaning influenced by many genes.

Describe major chromosomal abnormalities, and explain how they occur.

© Laura Dwight Photography

- Most chromosomal abnormalities result from errors during meiosis. The most common, Down syndrome, leads to mental retardation, slow motor development, and physical defects. Sex chromosome abnormalities, such as XYY, triple X, Klinefelter, and Turner syndromes, are milder than defects of the autosomes.

Reproductive Choices

What procedures can assist prospective parents in having healthy children?

- **Genetic counseling** helps couples at risk for bearing children with hereditary defects consider appropriate reproductive options. **Prenatal diagnostic methods** permit detection of problems before birth. Reproductive technologies, such as donor insemination, in vitro fertilization, surrogate motherhood, and postmenopausal-assisted childbirth, enable individuals to become parents who otherwise would not, but they also raise serious legal and ethical concerns.

Prenatal Development

List the three periods of prenatal development, and describe the major milestones of each.

- The period of the zygote lasts about two weeks, from fertilization until the blastocyst becomes deeply implanted in the uterine lining. During this time, structures that will support prenatal growth begin to form. The embryonic disk is surrounded by the trophoblast, which forms structures that protect and nourish the organism. The **amnion** fills with amniotic fluid to regulate temperature and cushion against the mother's movements. From the **chorion,** villi emerge that burrow into the uterine wall, and the placenta starts to develop. The developing organism is connected to the **placenta** by the **umbilical cord.**
- During the period of the **embryo,** from implantation through the eighth week of pregnancy, the foundations for all body structures are laid down. The nervous system starts to develop as the neural tube forms and produces neurons. Other organs follow rapidly. At the end of this period, the embryo responds to touch and can move.
- In the period of the **fetus,** from the ninth week until the end of pregnancy, body size increases dramatically and physical structures are completed. The fetus becomes covered with **vernix,** which protects the skin from chapping. White, downy hair called **lanugo** helps the vernix stick to the skin. At the end of the second trimester, most of the brain's neurons are in place.
- The **age of viability** arrives at the beginning of the final trimester, between 22 and 26 weeks. The brain continues to develop rapidly, and new sensory and behavioral capacities emerge. Gradually, the lungs mature, the fetus fills the uterus, and birth draws near.

Prenatal Environmental Influences

Cite factors that influence the impact of teratogens on the developing organism, noting agents that are known teratogens.

© Lennart Nilsson, *A Child Is Born*/Bonniers

- **Teratogens** are environmental agents that cause damage during the prenatal period, in line with the sensitive period concept. The organism is especially vulnerable during the embryonic period, when body structures emerge rapidly.
- The impact of teratogens varies with amount and length of exposure, genetic makeup of mother and fetus, presence or absence of other harmful agents, and age of the organism at time of exposure. Some health consequences appear later in development, and physical defects may have indirect psychological consequences.
- Among medications, known teratogens include thalidomide, diethylstilbestrol (DES), and Accutane. Babies born to users of heroin, methadone, or cocaine are at risk for prematurity, low birth weight, and physical defects and are born drug-addicted. Evidence on long-term effects, however, is mixed.
- Infants whose parents use tobacco are often born underweight and may have attention, learning, and behavior problems in early childhood. Maternal alcohol consumption can lead to **fetal alcohol spectrum disorder (FASD). Fetal alcohol syndrome (FAS)** involves slow physical growth, facial abnormalities, and impairment in mental functioning. Milder forms—**partial fetal alcohol syndrome (p-FAS)** and **alcohol-related neurodevelopmental disorder (ARND)**—affect children whose mothers consumed smaller quantities of alcohol.
- Prenatal exposure to radiation, mercury, lead, and PCBs leads to physical and mental impairments. Among infectious diseases, rubella causes wide-ranging abnormalities. Babies with prenatally transmitted HIV rapidly develop AIDS, leading to brain damage and early death. Cytomegalovirus, herpes simplex 2, and toxoplasmosis can also be devastating to the fetus.

Describe the impact of additional maternal factors on prenatal development.

- In healthy, physically fit women, regular moderate exercise is related to increased birth weight. However, very frequent, vigorous, extended exercise can result in lower birth weight.
- Prenatal malnutrition can lead to low birth weight and central nervous system damage and can suppress development of the immune system. Vitamin–mineral supplementation, including folate, before conception and throughout pregnancy can prevent certain complications.
- Severe emotional stress is associated with many pregnancy complications and may permanently alter fetal neurological functioning. Its impact can be reduced by providing mothers with social support.

- Aside from the risk of chromosomal abnormalities in older women, maternal age through the thirties is not a major cause of prenatal problems. Poor health and environmental risks associated with poverty are the strongest predictors of pregnancy complications in both teenagers and older women.

Childbirth

Describe the three stages of childbirth, the baby's adaptation to labor and delivery, and the newborn baby's appearance.

- In the first stage of childbirth, contractions widen and thin the cervix. In the second stage, the mother feels an urge to push the baby through the birth canal. In the final stage, the placenta is delivered. During labor, infants produce high levels of stress hormones, which help them withstand oxygen deprivation, clear the lungs for breathing, and arouse them into alertness at birth.
- Newborn babies have large heads, small bodies, and facial features that make adults feel like picking them up and cuddling them. The **Apgar Scale** is used to assess the newborn baby's physical condition at birth.

Approaches to Childbirth

Describe natural childbirth and home delivery, and explain the benefits and risks of using pain-relieving drugs during labor and delivery.

- **Natural,** or **prepared, childbirth** involves (1) classes that provide information about labor and delivery, (2) relaxation and breathing techniques to counteract pain, and (3) coaching through labor and childbirth by a companion. Social support, a vital component, reduces the length of labor and the incidence of birth complications.
- Home birth, though uncommon in North America, is as safe as hospital birth for healthy mothers who are assisted by a well-trained doctor or midwife. The use of analgesics and anesthetics during childbirth can prolong labor and cause newborns to be withdrawn and irritable and to feed poorly.

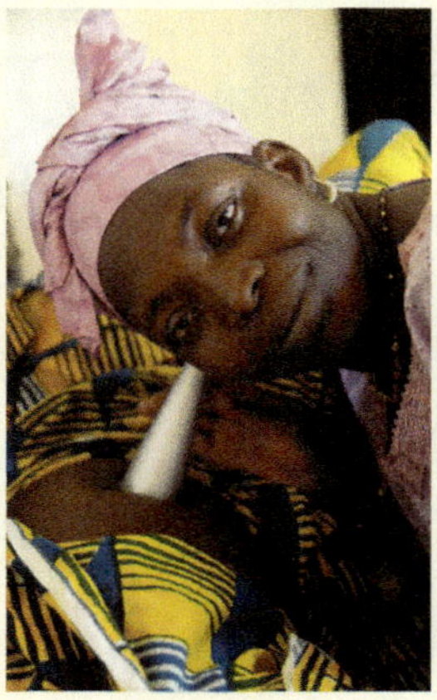

© Giacomo Pirozzi/Panos Pictures

Birth Complications

What risks are associated with oxygen deprivation and with preterm and low-birth-weight infants, and what factors can help infants who survive a traumatic birth develop?

- Anoxia can result when breathing fails to start immediately after delivery, the umbilical cord is squeezed because the baby is in **breech position,** or **Rh factor incompatibility** leads to destruction of the baby's red blood cells. Oxygen deprivation can damage the brain and other organs. Effects of even mild to moderate anoxia often persist, although many children improve over time.
- Low birth weight, a major cause of **neonatal** and **infant mortality** and wide-ranging developmental problems, is most common in infants born to poverty-stricken women and in twins. Compared with **preterm infants,** whose weight is appropriate for time spent in the uterus, **small-for-date infants** usually have longer-lasting difficulties.
- Some interventions provide special stimulation in the intensive care nursery; others teach parents how to care for and interact with their babies. Preterm infants in stressed, low-income households need long-term, intensive intervention.
- When infants experience birth trauma, a supportive family environment or relationships with other caring adults can help restore their growth. Even infants with serious birth complications can recover with the help of positive life events.

Heredity, Environment, and Behavior: A Look Ahead

Explain the various ways heredity and environment may combine to influence complex traits.

- **Behavioral genetics** looks at the contributions of nature and nurture to complex traits. Researchers use **kinship studies** to compute **heritability estimates,** which show that genetic factors contribute to such traits as intelligence and personality. However, their accuracy and usefulness have been challenged.
- According to the concepts of **range of reaction** and **canalization,** heredity influences children's responsiveness to varying environments. **Genetic–environmental correlation** and **niche-picking** describe how children's genes affect the environments to which they are exposed. **Epigenesis** reminds us that development is best understood as a series of complex exchanges between nature and nurture.

IMPORTANT TERMS AND CONCEPTS

age of viability (p. 91)
alcohol-related neurodevelopmental disorder (ARND) (p. 99)
allele (p. 75)
amnion (p. 89)
Apgar Scale (p. 108)
autosomes (p. 74)
behavioral genetics (p. 118)
breech position (p. 112)
canalization (p. 121)
carrier (p. 75)
chorion (p. 89)
chromosomes (p. 72)
crossing over (p. 73)
deoxyribonucleic acid (DNA) (p. 72)
dominant–recessive inheritance (p. 75)
embryo (p. 90)
epigenesis (p. 123)
fetal alcohol spectrum disorder (FASD) (p. 98)
fetal alcohol syndrome (FAS) (p. 98)
fetus (p. 91)
fraternal, or dizygotic, twins (p. 75)
gametes (p. 73)
gene (p. 72)
genetic counseling (p. 82)
genetic–environmental correlation (p. 121)
genomic imprinting (p. 79)
genotype (p. 71)
heritability estimate (p. 119)
heterozygous (p. 75)
homozygous (p. 75)
identical, or monozygotic, twins (p. 74)
incomplete dominance (p. 78)
infant mortality (p. 116)
kinship studies (p. 119)
lanugo (p. 91)
meiosis (p. 73)
mitosis (p. 72)
modifier genes (p. 76)
mutation (p. 79)
natural, or prepared, childbirth (p. 109)
neonatal mortality (p. 116)
niche-picking (p. 122)
partial fetal alcohol syndrome (p-FAS) (p. 98)
phenotype (p. 71)
placenta (p. 89)
polygenic inheritance (p. 80)
prenatal diagnostic methods (p. 82)
preterm infants (p. 113)
range of reaction (p. 120)
Rh factor incompatibility (p. 112)
sex chromosomes (p. 74)
small-for-date infants (p. 113)
teratogen (p. 93)
umbilical cord (p. 89)
vernix (p. 91)
X-linked inheritance (p. 78)
zygote (p. 73)

4

"Dokar—The Cart Pulled by a Horse"

Nathania Caroline Candra
9 years, Indonesia

With wide-eyed eagerness and curiosity, these young children explore a vibrant, enticing world. Research confirms that infants are remarkably capable beings who rapidly make sense of constantly changing sounds, shapes, patterns, and surfaces in their surroundings.

Infancy: Early Learning, Motor Skills, and Perceptual Capacities

Enthralled with their new baby, Yolanda and Jay came to my child development class when Joshua was 4 weeks old to share their reactions to new parenthood. Holding little Joshua over his shoulder while patting him gently, Jay remarked, "When we first saw him—a tiny bundle with his arms and legs all scrunched up, so helpless looking—we worried, 'How will we ever figure out how to meet his needs?' To our surprise, almost immediately, Joshua was able to help us!"

Yolanda demonstrated by speaking softly to Joshua. "Look," she said, "at the sound of our voices, his face perks up, and he turns toward us with rapt attention." She touched his palm and continued, "See how his tiny hand grasps whatever comes near it—our fingers or the folds of our clothing—and how tightly he holds on."

As Joshua snuggled against Jay's chest, Jay noted, "When he's unhappy, we hold him close so he can feel our heartbeats." Joshua whimpered, so Jay began to walk around the room, "When he's bored, we carry him to a new place and sing to him, and often that's enough to quiet him. His cry is becoming a language we can understand."

Jay placed Joshua on his tummy on a blanket-covered table. "See," he announced proudly, "he lifts his head and shows off his strength with shaky half push-ups." When Jay turned Joshua on his back, Joshua stared at Yolanda's bright pink blouse, his face utterly absorbed. Lifting Joshua and giving him a kiss, Jay exclaimed, "We marvel at his determination to master his world!"

As Yolanda's and Jay's observations confirm, our view of infancy—the period of development that spans the first year of life—has changed drastically over the past century. At one time, the newborn, or *neonate,* was considered a passive, incompetent being whose world was, in the words of turn-of-the-twentieth-century psychologist William James, "a blooming, buzzing confusion." Careful observations of infants' behavior and more refined methods enabling researchers to test babies' capacities confirm that, from the outset, infants display many complex abilities.

Infant development proceeds at an astonishing pace. Excited relatives who visit just after the birth and then return a few months later often remark that the baby does not seem like the same individual! Although researchers agree that infants are competent, fervent debates continue over questions like these: What capacities are present from the very beginning? Which mature with the passage of time? And which result from the baby's constant interaction with her physical and social worlds? In this chapter, we explore the infant's early reflexes, ability to learn, motor skills, and perceptual capacities—along with the debates that surround these remarkable competencies.

The Organized Newborn

The newborn baby, as we saw in Chapter 3, is homely looking, with a head that appears too large in relation to the potbellied trunk and bowlegged lower body. In addition, the baby's skin is usually wrinkled and "parboiled" in appearance. Yet a few hours spent with a neonate reveal a wide variety of capacities that are crucial for survival and that evoke care and attention from adults. In relating to their physical and social worlds, babies are active from the very start.

Reflexes

A **reflex** is an inborn, automatic response to a particular form of stimulation. Reflexes are the neonate's most obvious organized patterns of behavior. When a father, changing his newborn baby's diaper, bumps the side of the table, the infant flings her arms wide, then brings them back toward her body. As a mother softly strokes her infant's cheek, the baby turns his head in her direction. **TAKE A MOMENT...** Look at Table 4.1, and see if you can identify the newborn reflexes described here and the ones Joshua displayed in the introduction to this chapter. Then let's consider the meaning and purpose of these curious behaviors.

• **Adaptive Value of Reflexes** Some reflexes have survival value. The rooting reflex helps a breastfed baby find the mother's nipple. Babies display it only when hungry and touched by another person, not when they touch themselves (Rochat & Hespos, 1997). At birth, babies

Table 4.1 Some Newborn Reflexes

Reflex	Stimulation	Response	Age of Disappearance	Function
Eye blink	Shine bright light at eyes, or clap hand near head.	Infant quickly closes eyelids.	Permanent	Protects infant from strong stimulation
Rooting	Stroke cheek near corner of mouth.	Head turns toward source of stimulation.	3 weeks (becomes voluntary head turning at this time)	Helps infant find the nipple
Sucking	Place finger in infant's mouth.	Infant sucks finger rhythmically.	Replaced by voluntary sucking after 4 months	Permits feeding
Swimming[a]	Place infant face down in pool of water.	Baby paddles and kicks in swimming motion.	4–6 months	Helps infant survive if dropped into water
Moro	Hold infant horizontally on back and let head drop slightly, or produce a sudden loud sound against surface supporting infant.	Infant makes an "embracing" motion by arching back, extending legs, throwing arms outward, and then bringing arms in toward the body.	6 months	In human evolutionary past, may have helped infant cling to mother
Palmar grasp	Place finger in infant's hand, and press against palm.	Infant spontaneously grasps finger.	3–4 months	Prepares infant for voluntary grasping
Tonic neck	Turn baby's head to one side while infant is lying awake on back.	Infant lies in a "fencing position." One arm is extended in front of eyes on side to which head is turned, other arm is flexed.	4 months	May prepare infant for voluntary reaching
Stepping	Hold infant under arms, and permit bare feet to touch a flat surface.	Infant lifts one foot after another in stepping response.	2 months in infants who gain weight quickly; sustained in lighter infants	Prepares infant for voluntary walking
Babinski	Stroke sole of foot from toe toward heel.	Toes fan out and curl as foot twists in.	8–12 months	Unknown

[a]Placing infants in a pool of water is dangerous. See discussion on page 130.

Sources: Knobloch & Pasamanick, 1974; Prechtl & Beintema, 1965; Thelen, Fisher, & Ridley-Johnson, 1984.

adjust their sucking pressure to how easily milk flows from the nipple (Craig & Lee, 1999). If sucking were not automatic, our species would be unlikely to survive for a single generation! The swimming reflex helps a baby who is accidentally dropped into water stay afloat, increasing the chances of retrieval by the caregiver.

Other reflexes probably helped babies survive during our evolutionary past. For example, the Moro, or "embracing," reflex is believed to have helped infants cling to their mothers when they were carried about all day. If the baby happened to lose support, the reflex caused the infant to embrace and, along with the powerful grasp reflex (so strong during the first week that it can support the baby's entire weight), regain its hold on the mother's body (Kessen, 1967; Prechtl, 1958).

In the Moro reflex, loss of support or a sudden loud sound causes the baby to extend the legs and throw the arms outward in an "embracing" motion. © Laura Dwight Photography

Several reflexes help parents and infants establish gratifying interaction. A baby who searches for and successfully finds the nipple, sucks easily during feedings, and grasps when her hand is touched encourages parents to respond lovingly and feel competent as caregivers. Reflexes can also help parents comfort the baby because they permit infants to control distress and amount of stimulation. As any new mother who makes sure to bring along a pacifier on an outing with her young baby knows, sucking helps quiet a fussy infant.

• Reflexes and the Development of Motor Skills A few reflexes form the basis for complex motor skills that will develop later. For example, the tonic neck reflex may prepare the baby for voluntary reaching. When babies lie on their backs in this "fencing position," they naturally gaze at the hand in front of their eyes. The reflex may encourage them to combine vision with arm movements and, eventually, reach for objects (Knobloch & Pasamanick, 1974).

Certain reflexes—such as the palmar grasp, swimming, and stepping—drop out of the infants' behavioral repertoire early, but the motor functions involved are renewed later. The stepping reflex, for example, looks like a primitive walking response. Unlike other reflexes, it appears in a wide range of situations—with the newborn's body in a sideways or upside-down position, with feet touching walls or ceilings, and even with legs dangling in the air (Adolph & Berger, 2006). One reason that babies frequently engage in the alternating leg movements of stepping is their ease compared with other movement patterns: Repetitive movement of one leg or of both legs at once requires more effort.

In infants who gain weight quickly in the weeks after birth, the stepping reflex drops out because thigh and calf muscles are not strong enough to lift the baby's increasingly chubby legs. But if the lower part of the infant's body is dipped in water, the reflex reappears because the buoyancy of the water lightens the load on the baby's muscles (Thelen, Fisher, & Ridley-Johnson, 1984). When stepping is exercised regularly, babies display more spontaneous stepping movements and gain muscle strength. Consequently, they tend to walk several weeks earlier than if stepping is not practiced (Zelazo et al., 1993). However, there is no special need for infants to practice the stepping reflex—all normal babies walk in due time.

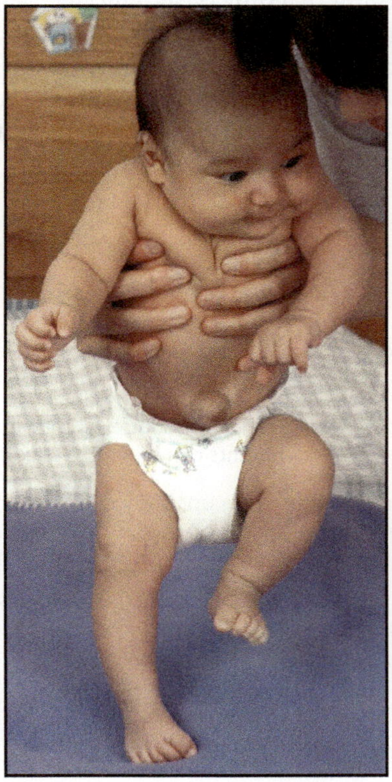

When held upright under the arms, newborn babies show reflexive stepping movements, which form the basis for later walking. © Laura Dwight Photography

The palmar grasp reflex is so strong during the first week after birth that many infants can use it to support their entire weight. © Laura Dwight Photography

In the case of the swimming reflex, trying to build on it is risky. Although young babies placed in a swimming pool will paddle and kick, they swallow large amounts of water. This lowers the concentration of salt in the baby's blood, which can cause brain swelling and seizures. Despite this remarkable reflex, swimming lessons are best postponed until at least 3 years of age.

• **The Importance of Assessing Reflexes** Look at Table 4.1 again, and you will see that most newborn reflexes disappear during the first six months. Researchers believe this is due to a gradual increase in voluntary control over behavior as the cerebral cortex develops. Pediatricians test reflexes carefully, especially if a newborn has experienced birth trauma, because reflexes can reveal the health of the baby's nervous system. Weak or absent reflexes, overly rigid or exaggerated reflexes, and reflexes that persist beyond the point in development when they should normally disappear can signal damage to the cerebral cortex (Schott & Rossor, 2003; Zafeiriou, 2000). However, individual differences in reflexive responses exist that are not cause for concern. An observer must assess newborn reflexes along with other characteristics to distinguish normal from abnormal central nervous system functioning (Touwen, 1984).

States

Throughout the day and night, newborn infants move in and out of five **states of arousal,** or degrees of sleep and wakefulness, described in Table 4.2. During the first month, these states alternate frequently. The most fleeting is quiet alertness, which usually moves quickly toward fussing and crying. Much to the relief of their fatigued parents, newborns spend the greatest amount of time asleep—about 16 to 18 hours a day (Davis, Parker, & Montgomery, 2004).

Between birth and 2 years, the organization of sleep and wakefulness changes substantially. Total sleep time declines slowly—the average 2-year-old still needs 12 to 13 hours per day. But periods of sleep and wakefulness become fewer but longer, and the sleep–wake pattern increasingly conforms to a *circadian rhythm,* or 24-hour schedule. Although newborns sleep more at night than during the day, their sleep–wake cycles are determined mostly by fullness–hunger (Goodlin-Jones, Burnham, & Anders, 2000). By 2 to 3 months, infants respond more to darkness–light. Babies of this age who are exposed to more bright sunlight—for example, through regular early-afternoon stroller rides—sleep better at night (Harrison, 2004). Between 6 and 9 months, daytime sleep typically declines to two naps. By 1½ years, most infants take just one nap. And between 3 and 5 years, napping subsides (Iglowstein et al., 2003).

These changing arousal patterns are due to brain development, but they are also affected by the social environment. In Western nations, many parents try to get their babies to sleep through the night around 4 months of age by offering an evening feeding before putting them down in a

Table 4.2 Infant States of Arousal

State	Description	Daily Duration in Newborn
Regular, or NREM, sleep	The infant is at full rest and shows little or no body activity. The eyelids are closed, no eye movements occur, the face is relaxed, and breathing is slow and regular.	8–9 hours
Irregular, or REM, sleep	Gentle limb movements, occasional stirring, and facial grimacing occur. Although the eyelids are closed, occasional rapid eye movements can be seen beneath them. Breathing is irregular.	8–9 hours
Drowsiness	The infant is either falling asleep or waking up. Body is less active than in irregular sleep but more active than in regular sleep. The eyes open and close; when open, they have a glazed look. Breathing is even but somewhat faster than in regular sleep.	Varies
Quiet alertness	The infant's body is relatively inactive, with eyes open and attentive. Breathing is even.	2–3 hours
Waking activity and crying	The infant shows frequent bursts of uncoordinated body activity. Breathing is very irregular. Face may be relaxed or tense and wrinkled. Crying may occur.	1–4 hours

Source: Wolff, 1966.

separate, quiet room. In this way, they push young infants to the limits of their neurological capacities. Not until the middle of the first year is the secretion of *melatonin,* a hormone within the brain that promotes drowsiness, much greater at night than during the day (Sadeh, 1997).

As the Cultural Influences box on page 132 reveals, isolating infants to promote sleep is rare elsewhere in the world. When babies sleep with their parents, their average sleep period remains constant at three hours from 1 to 8 months of age. Only at the end of the first year, as REM sleep (the state that usually prompts waking) declines, do infants move in the direction of an adultlike sleep–waking schedule (Ficca et al., 1999).

Even after infants sleep through the night, they continue to wake occasionally. In sleep observations and in surveys of parents in Australia, Israel, and the United States, night wakings increased around 6 months and again between 1½ and 2 years (Armstrong, Quinn, & Dadds, 1994; Scher, Epstein, & Tirosh, 2004; Scher et al., 1995). Around the middle of the first year, many infants encounter changes in caregiving routines, such as the mother's return to work. And as Chapters 10 and 11 will reveal, the challenges of toddlerhood—the ability to range farther from the familiar caregiver and increased awareness of the self as separate from others—often prompt anxiety, evident in disturbed sleep and clinginess. When parents offer comfort, these behaviors subside.

Although arousal states become more organized with age, striking individual differences in daily rhythms exist that affect parents' attitudes toward and interactions with the baby. A few infants sleep for long periods at an early age, increasing the energy their well-rested parents have for sensitive, responsive care. Other babies wake frequently and cry often, and their parents must exert great effort to soothe them. If these parents do not succeed, they are likely to feel anxious, less competent, and less positively toward their infant—responses that pose serious risks to parent and family well-being (Sadeh et al., 2007; Smart & Hiscock, 2007).

Arousal patterns also have implications for early cognitive progress. Babies who spend more time quietly alert probably receive more social stimulation and opportunities to explore and, therefore, may be slightly ahead in mental development (Gertner et al., 2002). And as with adults, sleep enhances babies' learning and memory. Fifteen-month-olds who took hour-long naps after listening to short, similarly structured "sentences" of nonsense words were better than their non-napping agemates at recognizing the common structure in new sentences (Gómez, Bootzin, & Nadel, 2006). Napping facilitated memory for higher-order word patterns—a skill essential for language development. Of the states listed in Table 4.2, the two extremes—sleep and crying—have been of greatest interest to researchers. Each tells us something about normal and abnormal early development.

Figure 4.1 Changes in REM sleep, NREM sleep, and the waking state from the prenatal period to middle childhood. REM sleep declines steadily over the prenatal period and the first few years of life. Between 3 and 5 years, it accounts for about the same percentage of sleep time as it does in adulthood. (Adapted from de Weerd & van den Bossche, 2003; Roffwarg, Muzio, & Dement, 1996.)

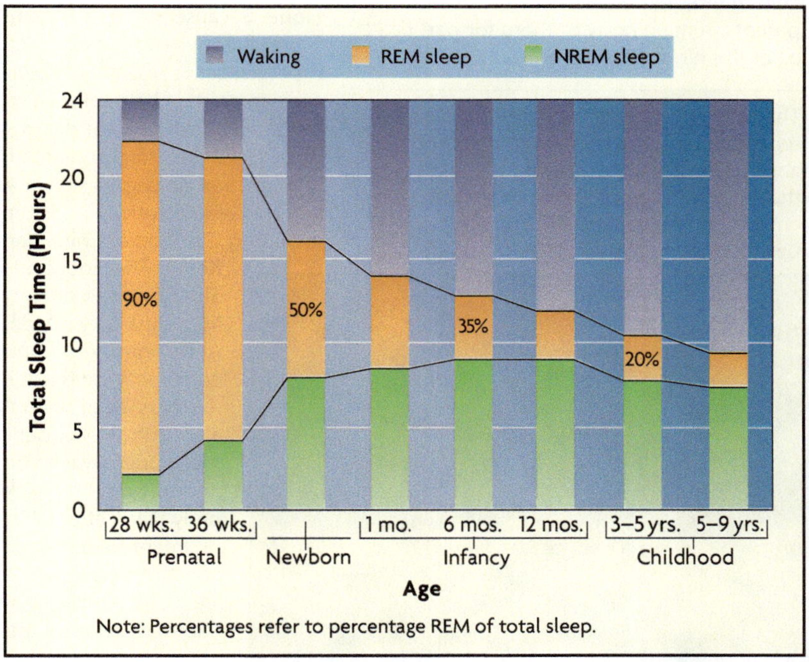

• **Sleep** Sleep is made up of at least two states. The expression "sleeping like a baby" was probably not meant to describe irregular, or **rapid-eye-movement (REM) sleep,** in which electrical brain-wave activity, measured with the EEG, is remarkably similar to that of the waking state. The eyes dart beneath the lids; heart rate, blood pressure, and breathing are uneven; and slight body movements occur. In contrast, during regular, or **non-rapid-eye-movement (NREM) sleep,** the body is almost motionless, and heart rate, breathing, and brain-wave activity are slow and regular.

Like children and adults, newborns alternate between REM and NREM sleep. However, as Figure 4.1 shows, they spend far more time in the REM state than they ever will again. REM sleep accounts for 50 percent of the newborn baby's sleep time. By 3 to 5 years, it has declined to an adultlike level of 20 percent (Louis et al., 1997).

Why do young infants spend so much time in REM sleep? In older children and adults, the REM

Cultural Influences

Cultural Variation in Infant Sleeping Arrangements

While awaiting the birth of a new baby, North American parents typically furnish a bedroom for the infant. For decades, child-rearing experts have strongly encouraged nighttime separation of baby from parent. For example, the most recent edition of Benjamin Spock's *Baby and Child Care* recommends moving babies into their own room by 3 months of age, explaining, "By 6 months, a child who regularly sleeps in her parents' room may become dependent on this arrangement" (Spock & Needlman, 2004, p. 60).

Yet parent–infant "cosleeping" is the norm for approximately 90 percent of the world's population, in cultures as diverse as the Japanese, the rural Guatemalan Maya, the Inuit of northwestern Canada, and the !Kung of Botswana. Japanese and Korean children usually lie next to their mothers in infancy and early childhood, and many continue to sleep with a parent or other family member until adolescence (Takahashi, 1990; Yang & Hahn, 2002). Among the Maya, mother–infant cosleeping continues until the birth of a new baby, when the older child is moved next to the father or to another bed in the same room (Morelli et al., 1992). Cosleeping is also common in some North American groups. African-American children frequently fall asleep with their parents, remaining with them for part or all of the night (Buswell & Spatz, 2006; Brenner et al., 2003). Appalachian children of eastern Kentucky typically sleep with their parents for the first two years (Abbott, 1992).

Cultural values—specifically, *collectivism versus individualism* (see Chapter 1)—strongly influence infant sleeping arrangements. In one study, researchers interviewed Guatemalan Mayan mothers and American middle-SES mothers about their sleeping practices. Mayan mothers stressed a collectivist perspective, explaining that cosleeping builds a close parent–child bond, which children need to learn the ways of people around them. In contrast, American mothers took an individualistic perspective, mentioning the importance of instilling early independence, preventing bad habits, and protecting their own privacy (Morelli et al., 1992).

Over the past 15 years, cosleeping has increased dramatically in North America and other Western nations, perhaps because more mothers are breastfeeding. Today, the rate of bedsharing among U.S. mothers of young babies may be as high as 50 percent (Buswell & Spatz, 2007; Willinger et al., 2003). Research suggests that cosleeping evolved to protect infants' survival and health. During the night, cosleeping babies breastfeed three times as long as infants who sleep alone. Because infants arouse to nurse more often when sleeping next to their mothers, some researchers believe that cosleeping may help safeguard babies at risk for sudden infant death syndrome (SIDS) (see the From Research to Practice box on page 134). In Asian cultures where cosleeping is the norm, including Cambodia, China, Japan, Korea, Thailand, and Vietnam, SIDS is rare (McKenna, 2002; McKenna & McDade, 2005). And contrary to popular belief, cosleeping does not decrease mothers' total sleep time, although they experience more brief awakenings, which permit them to check on their baby (Mao et al., 2004).

Infant sleeping practices affect other aspects of family life. For example, Mayan babies doze off in the midst of ongoing family activities and are carried to bed by their mothers. In contrast, for many North American parents, bedtime involves an elaborate ritual that takes a good part of the evening. Perhaps bedtime struggles, so common in North American homes but rare elsewhere in the world, are related to the stress young children feel when they must fall asleep without assistance (Latz, Wolf, & Lozoff, 1999).

Critics warn that cosleeping children will develop emotional problems, especially excessive dependency. Yet a longitudinal study following children from birth through age 18 showed that young people who had bedshared in the early years were no different from others in any aspect of adjustment (Okami, Weisner, & Olmstead, 2002). Another concern is that infants might become trapped under the parent's body or in soft covers and suffocate. Parents who are obese or who use alcohol, tobacco, or illegal drugs do pose a serious risk to their sleeping babies, as does the use of quilts and comforters or an overly soft mattress (Willinger et al., 2003).

But with appropriate precautions, parents and infants can cosleep safely (Buswell & Spatz, 2007). In cultures where cosleeping is widespread, parents and infants usually sleep with light covering on hard surfaces, such as firm mattresses, floor mats, and wooden planks, or infants sleep in a cradle or hammock next to the parents' bed (McKenna, 2001, 2002). And when sharing the same bed, infants typically lie on their back or side facing the mother—positions that promote frequent, easy communication between parent and baby and arousal if breathing is threatened.

Finally, breastfeeding mothers usually assume a distinctive sleeping posture: They face the infant, with knees drawn up under the baby's feet and arm above the baby's head. Besides facilitating feeding, the position prevents the infant from sliding down under covers or up under pillows (Ball, 2006). Because this posture is also seen in female great apes while sharing sleeping nests with their infants, researchers believe it may have evolved to enhance infant safety.

This Cambodian father and child sleep together, a practice common in their culture and around the globe. Many parents believe that cosleeping helps build a close parent–child bond. © Stephen L. Raymer/National Geographic Image Collection

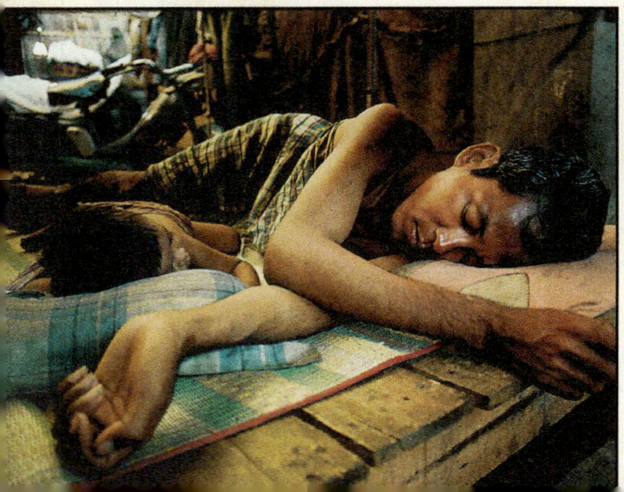

state is associated with dreaming. Babies probably do not dream, at least not in the same way we do. But researchers believe that the stimulation of REM sleep is vital for growth of the central nervous system. Young infants seem to have a special need for this stimulation because they spend so little time in an alert state, when they can get input from the environment. In support of this idea, the percentage of REM sleep is especially great in the fetus and in preterm babies, who are even less able than full-term newborns to take advantage of external stimulation (de Weerd & van den Bossche, 2003; Peirano, Algarin, & Uauy, 2003).

Whereas the brain-wave activity of REM sleep safeguards the central nervous system, the rapid eye movements protect the health of the eye. Eye movements cause the vitreous (gelatin-like substance within the eye) to circulate, thereby delivering oxygen to parts of the eye that do not have their own blood supply. During sleep, when the eye and the vitreous are still, visual structures are at risk for anoxia. As the brain cycles through REM-sleep periods, rapid eye movements stir up the vitreous, ensuring that the eye is fully oxygenated (Blumberg & Lucas, 1996).

Because the normal sleep behavior of the newborn baby is organized and patterned, observations of sleep states can help identify central nervous system abnormalities. In infants who are brain-damaged or who have experienced birth trauma, disturbed REM–NREM sleep cycles are often present. Babies with poor sleep organization are likely to be behaviorally disorganized and, therefore, to have difficulty learning and eliciting caregiver interactions that enhance their development. In follow-ups during the preschool years, they show delayed motor, cognitive, and language development (de Weerd & van den Bossche, 2003; Feldman, 2006; Holditch-Davis, Belyea, & Edwards, 2005). And the brain-functioning problems that underlie newborn sleep irregularities may culminate in sudden infant death syndrome, a major cause of infant mortality (see the From Research to Practice box on page 134).

• **Crying** Crying is the first way that babies communicate, letting parents know that they need food, comfort, and stimulation. During the weeks after birth, all babies have some fussy periods when they are difficult to console. But most of the time, the nature of the cry, combined with the experiences leading up to it, helps guide parents toward its cause. The baby's cry is a complex auditory stimulus that varies in intensity, from a whimper to a message of all-out distress (Gustafson, Wood, & Green, 2000). As early as the first few weeks, infants can be identified by the unique vocal "signature" of their cries, which helps parents locate their baby from a distance (Gustafson, Green, & Cleland, 1994).

Young infants usually cry because of physical needs, most commonly hunger, but babies may also cry in response to temperature change when undressed, a sudden noise, or a painful stimulus. An infant's state also affects proneness to cry. A baby who, when quietly alert, regards a colorful or noise-making object with interest may burst into tears when confronted with the same object while in a state of mild discomfort. And newborns (as well as older infants) often cry at the sound of another crying baby (Dondi, Simion, & Caltran, 1999). Some researchers believe that this response reflects an inborn capacity to react to the suffering of others. Furthermore, as Figure 4.2 shows, crying typically increases during the early weeks, peaks at about 6 weeks, and then declines. Because this trend appears in many cultures with vastly different infant care practices, researchers believe that normal readjustments of the central nervous system underlie it (Barr, 2001).

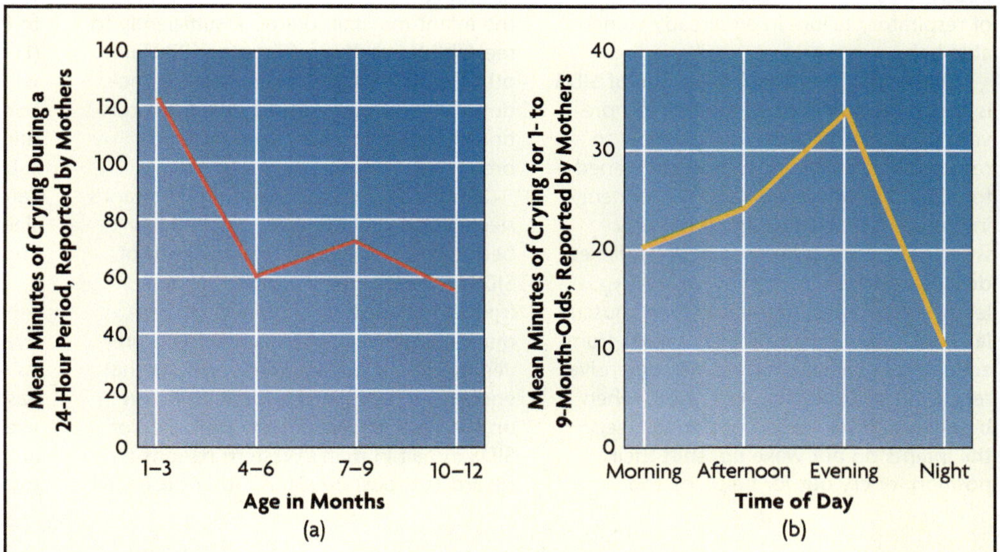

■ **Figure 4.2** **Crying patterns during the first year of life.**
A sample of 400 mothers answered questions about how much time their infants spent crying. (a) Crying was greatest during the first three months but declined with age. The largest drop occurred after three months. (b) During the first nine months, crying peaked in the evening. (Adapted from St James-Roberts & Halil, 1991.)

▪ *From* Research *to* Practice ▪

The Mysterious Tragedy of Sudden Infant Death Syndrome

Millie awoke with a start one morning and looked at the clock. It was 7:30, and Sasha had missed both her night waking and early morning feeding. Wondering if she was all right, Millie and her husband, Stuart, tiptoed into the room. Sasha lay still, curled up under her blanket. She had died silently during her sleep.

Sasha was a victim of **sudden infant death syndrome (SIDS)**, the unexpected death, usually during the night, of an infant younger than 1 year of age that remains unexplained after thorough investigation. In industrialized nations, SIDS is the leading cause of infant mortality between 1 and 12 months, accounting for about 20 percent of these deaths in the United States and Canada. Its incidence peaks between ages 2 and 4 months (Hamilton et al., 2005; Statistics Canada, 2007d, 2007i).

Although the precise cause of SIDS is not known, its victims usually show physical problems from the very beginning. Early medical records of SIDS babies reveal higher rates of prematurity and low birth weight, poor Apgar scores, and limp muscle tone. Abnormal heart rate and respiration and disturbances in sleep–wake activity and in REM–NREM cycles while asleep are also involved (Cornell & Feigenbaum, 2006; Kato et al., 2003). At the time of death, many SIDS babies have a mild respiratory infection (Samuels, 2003). This seems to increase the chances of respiratory failure in an already vulnerable baby.

One hypothesis about the cause of SIDS is that problems in brain functioning prevent these infants from learning how to respond when their survival is threatened—for example, when respiration is suddenly interrupted. Between 2 and 4 months, when SIDS is most likely to occur, reflexes decline and are replaced by voluntary, learned responses. Respiratory and muscular weaknesses may stop SIDS babies from acquiring behaviors that replace defensive reflexes (Lipsitt, 2003). As a result, when breathing difficulties occur during sleep, the infants do not wake up, shift their position, or cry out for help. Instead, they simply give in to oxygen deprivation and death. In support of this interpretation, autopsies reveal that SIDS babies, more often than other infants, show abnormalities in brain centers that control breathing (Paterson et al., 2006).

In an effort to reduce the occurrence of SIDS, researchers are studying environmental factors related to it. Maternal cigarette smoking, both during and after pregnancy, as well as smoking by other caregivers, strongly predicts the disorder. Babies exposed to cigarette smoke have more respiratory infections, arouse less easily from sleep, and are twice as likely as nonexposed infants to die of SIDS (Anderson, Johnson, & Batal, 2005; Shah, Sullivan, & Carter, 2006). Prenatal abuse of drugs that depress central nervous system functioning (opiates and barbiturates) increases the risk of SIDS as much as fifteenfold (Hunt & Hauck, 2006). SIDS babies are also more likely to sleep on their stomachs than on their backs and often are wrapped warmly in clothing and blankets (Hauck et al., 2003).

Researchers suspect that nicotine, depressant drugs, excessive body warmth, and respiratory infection all lead to physiological stress, which disrupts the normal sleep pattern. When sleep-deprived infants experience a sleep "rebound," they sleep more deeply, which results in loss of muscle tone in the airway passages. In at-risk babies, the airway may collapse, and the infant may fail to arouse sufficiently to reestablish breathing (Simpson, 2001). In other cases, healthy babies sleeping face down on soft bedding may die from continually breathing their own exhaled breath.

Quitting smoking, changing an infant's sleeping position, and removing a few bedclothes can reduce the incidence of SIDS. For example, if women refrained from smoking while pregnant, an estimated 30 percent of SIDS would be prevented. Public education campaigns that encourage parents to put babies down on their backs have cut the incidence of SIDS in half in many Western nations (Byard & Krous, 2003). Another protective measure is pacifier use: Sleeping babies who suck arouse more easily in response to breathing and heart-rate irregularities (Li et al., 2006). Nevertheless, compared with white infants, SIDS rates are two to six times as high in poverty-stricken minority groups, where parental stress, substance abuse, reduced access to health care, and lack of knowledge about safe sleep practices are widespread (Pickett, Luo, & Lauderdale, 2005).

When SIDS does occur, surviving family members require a great deal of help to overcome a sudden and unexpected death. As Millie commented six months after Sasha's death, "It's the worst crisis we've ever been through. What's helped us most are the comforting words of others who've experienced the same tragedy."

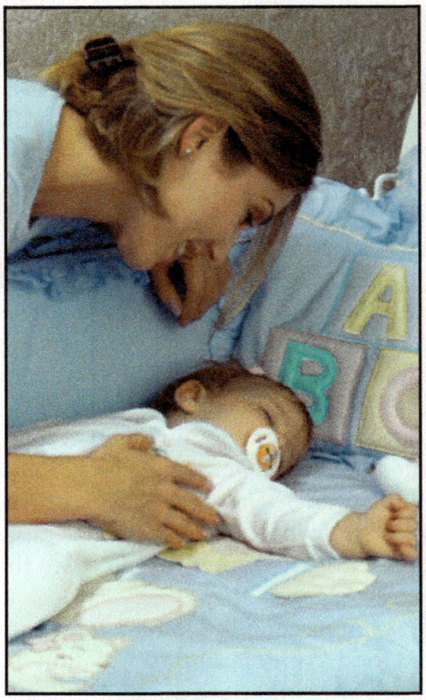

Public education campaigns that encourage parents to place infants on their backs to sleep have reduced the incidence of SIDS by half in many Western nations. Research also confirms the value of using a pacifier: Infants who suck wake from sleep more easily if breathing or heart-rate irregularities occur. © Royalty-Free/CORBIS

Adult Responsiveness to Infant Cries. **TAKE A MOMENT...** The next time you hear a baby cry, notice your own reaction. The sound stimulates strong feelings of arousal and discomfort in men and women, parents and nonparents alike (Murray, 1985). This powerful response is probably innately programmed in all humans to help ensure that babies receive the care and protection they need to survive.

Although parents do not always interpret their baby's cry correctly, their accuracy improves with experience. As babies get older, parents react to more subtle cues in the cry—not just intensity but also whimpering and calling sounds (Thompson & Leger, 1999). These cues, together with the context of the cry, help them figure out what is wrong. If the baby has not eaten for several hours, she is likely to be hungry. If a period of wakefulness and stimulation preceded the cry, the infant may be tired. A sharp, piercing, sustained cry usually means the baby is in pain and prompts caregivers to rush to the infant. Very intense cries are rated as more unpleasant and produce greater physiological arousal in adults (Crowe & Zeskind, 1992). These adaptive reactions help ensure that an infant in danger will quickly get help.

At the same time, parents vary widely in responsiveness. In one laboratory study, parents viewed videotapes of an infant moving from fussing to vigorous crying. Some said they would respond within 20 seconds, whereas others indicated they would wait several minutes. Parents who scored high in empathy (ability to take the perspective of others in distress) and who held "child-centered" attitudes toward infant care (for example, believed that babies cannot be spoiled by being picked up) were more likely to respond quickly to infant crying (Zeifman, 2003). In another study, mothers who believed that they could easily control the crying of an artificial baby (whose quieting was unrelated to the mother's behavior) had difficulty detecting changes in cry sounds, engaged in less sensitive infant care, and had babies who developed into uncooperative toddlers (Donovan, Leavitt, & Walsh, 1997, 2000). The internal state of these mothers—who reacted defensively when they couldn't calm the artificial baby—seemed to interfere with their ability to cope effectively with infant crying.

Soothing a Crying Infant. Fortunately, there are many ways to soothe a crying baby when feeding and diaper changing do not work (see Applying What We Know on page 136). The technique that Western parents usually try first, lifting the infant to the shoulder and rocking or walking, is the most effective. Another common soothing method is swaddling—wrapping the baby snugly in a blanket. The Quechua, who live in the cold, high-altitude desert regions of Peru, dress young babies in several layers of clothing and blankets that cover the head and body. The result—a warm pouch placed on the mother's back that moves rhythmically as she walks—reduces crying and promotes sleep. It also allows the baby to conserve energy for early growth in the harsh Peruvian highlands (Tronick, Thomas, & Daltabuit, 1994).

Will reacting promptly and consistently to infant cries give babies a sense of confidence that their needs will be met and, over time, reduce fussing and complaining? Or will it strengthen crying behavior and produce a miniature tyrant? Answers are contradictory.

According to *ethological theory,* parental responsiveness is adaptive in that it ensures that the infant's basic needs will be met (see Chapter 1, pages 24–25). At the same time, it brings the baby into close contact with the caregiver, who encourages the infant to communicate through means other than crying. In support of this view, two studies showed that mothers who were slow or failed to respond to their young baby's cries had infants who cried more at the end of the first year (Bell & Ainsworth, 1972; Hubbard & van IJzendoorn, 1991). Furthermore, in many tribal and village societies and non-Western developed nations, where babies are in physical contact with their caregivers nearly continuously, infants show shorter bouts of crying than North American babies (Barr, 2001).

To sooth her crying infant, this mother holds her baby upright against her gently moving body. Besides encouraging infants to stop crying, this technique causes them to become quietly alert and attentive to the environment.
© Laura Dwight Photography

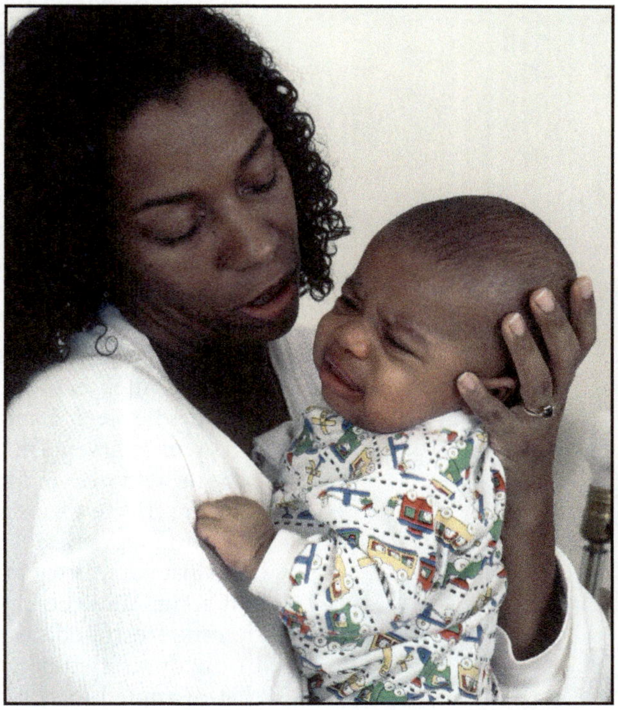

Applying What We Know

Soothing a Crying Baby

Technique	Explanation
Lift the baby to the shoulder and rock or walk.	This combination of physical contact, upright posture, and motion is an effective soothing technique, causing young infants to become quietly alert.
Swaddle the baby.	Restricting movement and increasing warmth often soothe an infant.
Offer a pacifier.	Sucking helps babies control their own level of arousal.
Talk softly, or play rhythmic sounds.	Continuous, monotonous, rhythmic sounds (such as a clock ticking, a fan whirring, or peaceful music) are more effective than intermittent sounds.
Take the baby for a short car ride or a walk in a stroller; swing the baby in a cradle.	Gentle, rhythmic motion of any kind helps lull the baby to sleep.
Massage the baby's body.	Stroking the baby's torso and limbs with continuous, gentle motions relaxes the baby's muscles.
Combine several methods just listed.	Stimulating several of the baby's senses at once is often more effective than stimulating only one.
If these methods do not work, let the baby cry for a short period.	Occasionally, a baby responds well to just being put down and will, after a few minutes, fall asleep.

Sources: Blass, 1999; Campos, 1989; Lester, 1985; Reisman, 1987.

But not all research indicates that rapid parental responsiveness reduces infant crying (van IJzendoorn & Hubbard, 2000). The conditions that prompt crying are complex, and parents must make reasoned choices about what to do on the basis of culturally accepted practices, the suspected reason for the cry, and the context in which it occurs—for example, in the privacy of their own home or while having dinner at a restaurant. Fortunately, with age, crying declines and occurs more often for psychological (demands for attention, expressions of frustration) than physical reasons. Virtually all researchers agree that parents can lessen older babies' need to cry by encouraging more mature ways of expressing their desires, such as gestures and vocalizations.

Abnormal Crying. Like reflexes and sleep patterns, the infant's cry offers a clue to central nervous system distress. The cries of brain-damaged babies and those who have experienced prenatal and birth complications are often shrill, piercing, and shorter in duration than those of healthy infants (Boukydis & Lester, 1998; Green, Irwin, & Gustafson, 2000). Even neonates with a fairly common problem—*colic,* or persistent crying—tend to have high-pitched, harsh-sounding cries (Zeskind & Barr, 1997). Although the cause of colic is unknown, certain newborns, who react especially strongly to unpleasant stimuli, are susceptible. Because their crying is intense, they have more difficulty calming down than other babies. Colic generally subsides between 3 and 6 months (Barr et al., 2005; St James-Roberts et al., 2003).

In an intervention aimed at reducing colic, nurses made periodic home visits, providing parents with help in identifying their baby's early warning signs of becoming overly aroused, in using effective soothing techniques, and in modifying light, noise, and activity in the home to promote predictable sleep–wake cycles (Keefe et al., 2005).

Most parents try to respond to a crying baby's call for help with extra care and attention, but sometimes the cry is so unpleasant and the infant so difficult to soothe that parents become frustrated, resentful, and angry. Preterm and ill babies are more likely to be abused by highly stressed parents, who sometimes mention a high-pitched, grating cry as one factor that disrupted their empathic feelings and caused them to lose control and harm the baby (St James-Roberts, 2007; Zeskind & Lester, 2001). We will discuss a host of additional influences on child abuse in Chapter 14.

Neonatal Behavioral Assessment

This mother of the El Molo people of northern Kenya carries her baby in a sling all day, providing close physical contact, varied stimulation, and ready access to feeding.
© Jeffrey L. Rotman/Corbis

A variety of instruments enable doctors, nurses, and researchers to assess the organized functioning of newborn babies. The most widely used of these tests, T. Berry Brazelton's **Neonatal Behavioral Assessment Scale (NBAS),** evaluates the baby's reflexes, muscle tone, state changes, responsiveness to physical and social stimuli, and other reactions (Brazelton & Nugent, 1995). A recently developed instrument consisting of similar items, the Neonatal Intensive Care Unit Network Neurobehavioral Scale (NNNS), is specially designed for use with newborns at risk for developmental problems because of low birth weight, preterm delivery, prenatal substance exposure, or other conditions (Lester & Tronick, 2004). Scores are used to understand each infant's capacity to initiate caregiver support, to adjust his or her behavior to avoid being overwhelmed by stimulation, and to recommend appropriate interventions.

The NBAS has been given to many infants around the world. As a result, researchers have learned a great deal about individual and cultural differences in newborn behavior and how child-rearing practices can maintain or change a baby's reactions. For example, NBAS scores of Asian and Native-American babies reveal that they are less irritable than Caucasian infants. Mothers in these cultures often encourage their babies' calm dispositions through swaddling, close physical contact, and nursing at the first signs of discomfort (Murett-Wagstaff & Moore, 1989; Small, 1998). In contrast, maternal care quickly changes the poor NBAS scores of undernourished infants in Zambia, Africa. The Zambian mother carries her baby about on her hip all day, providing a rich variety of sensory stimulation. As a result, an unresponsive newborn becomes an alert, contented 1-week-old (Brazelton, Koslowski, & Tronick, 1976).

TAKE A MOMENT... Using these examples, can you explain why a single neonatal assessment score is not a good predictor of later development? Because newborn behavior and parenting styles combine to influence development, *changes in scores* over the first week or two of life (rather than a single score) provide the best estimate of the baby's ability to recover from the stress of birth. NBAS "recovery curves" predict normal brain functioning (as assessed by EEG and fMRI), intelligence, and absence of emotional and behavior problems with moderate success well into the preschool years (Brazelton, Nugent, & Lester, 1987; Ohgi et al., 2003a, 2003b).

In some hospitals, health professionals use the NBAS or the NNNS to help parents get to know their newborns through discussion or demonstration of the capacities assessed by these instruments. Parents of both preterm and full-term newborns who participate in these programs, compared with no-intervention controls, interact more effectively with their babies—more often establishing eye contact, smiling, vocalizing, and soothing in response to infant signals (Browne & Talmi, 2005; Bruschweiler-Stern, 2004). Although lasting effects on development have not been demonstrated, neonatal behavioral assessment interventions are useful in helping the parent–infant relationship get off to a good start.

Learning Capacities

Learning refers to changes in behavior as the result of experience. Babies come into the world with built-in learning capacities that permit them to profit from experience immediately. Infants are capable of two basic forms of learning, which were introduced in Chapter 1: classical and operant conditioning. They learn through their natural preference for novel stimulation. Finally, shortly after birth, babies learn by observing others; they can soon imitate the facial expressions and gestures of adults.

• **Classical Conditioning** Newborn reflexes make **classical conditioning** possible in the young infant. In this form of learning, a neutral stimulus is paired with a stimulus that leads to a reflexive response. Once the baby's nervous system makes the connection between the two stimuli, the new stimulus will produce the behavior by itself. Classical conditioning helps infants recognize which events usually occur together in the everyday world, so they can anticipate what is about to happen next. As a result, the environment becomes more orderly and predictable. Let's take a closer look at the steps of classical conditioning.

Imagine a mother who gently strokes her infant's forehead each time she settles down to nurse the baby. Soon the mother notices that each time the baby's forehead is stroked, he makes active sucking movements. The infant has been classically conditioned. Here is how it happened (see Figure 4.3):

- Before learning takes place, an **unconditioned stimulus (UCS)** must consistently produce a reflexive, or **unconditioned, response (UCR).** In our example, the stimulus of sweet breast milk (UCS) resulted in sucking (UCR).
- To produce learning, a *neutral stimulus* that does not lead to the reflex is presented at about the same time as the UCS. Ideally, the neutral stimulus should occur just before the UCS. The mother stroked the baby's forehead as each nursing period began. The stroking (neutral stimulus) was paired with the taste of milk (UCS).
- If learning has occurred, the neutral stimulus by itself produces a response similar to the reflexive response. The neutral stimulus is then called a **conditioned stimulus (CS)**, and the response it elicits is called a **conditioned response (CR).** We know that the baby has been classically conditioned because stroking his forehead outside the feeding situation (CS) results in sucking (CR).

If the CS is presented alone enough times, without being paired with the UCS, the CR will no longer occur, an outcome called **extinction.** In other words, if the mother repeatedly strokes the infant's forehead without feeding him, the baby will gradually stop sucking in response to stroking.

Young infants can be classically conditioned most easily when the association between two stimuli has survival value. In the feeding situation, they learn quickly because learning which stimuli regularly accompany feeding improves the infant's ability to get food and survive (Blass, Ganchrow, & Steiner, 1984). In contrast, some responses, such as fear, are very difficult to classically condition in young babies. Until infants have the motor skills to escape unpleasant events, they have no biological need to form these associations. After age 6 months, however, fear is easy to condition. **TAKE A MOMENT...** Return to Chapter 1, page 19, to review John Watson's famous experiment in which he conditioned Little Albert to withdraw and cry at the sight of a furry white rat. Then test your knowledge of classical conditioning by identifying the UCS, UCR, CS, and CR in Watson's study. In Chapter 10, we will discuss the development of fear, as well as other emotional reactions.

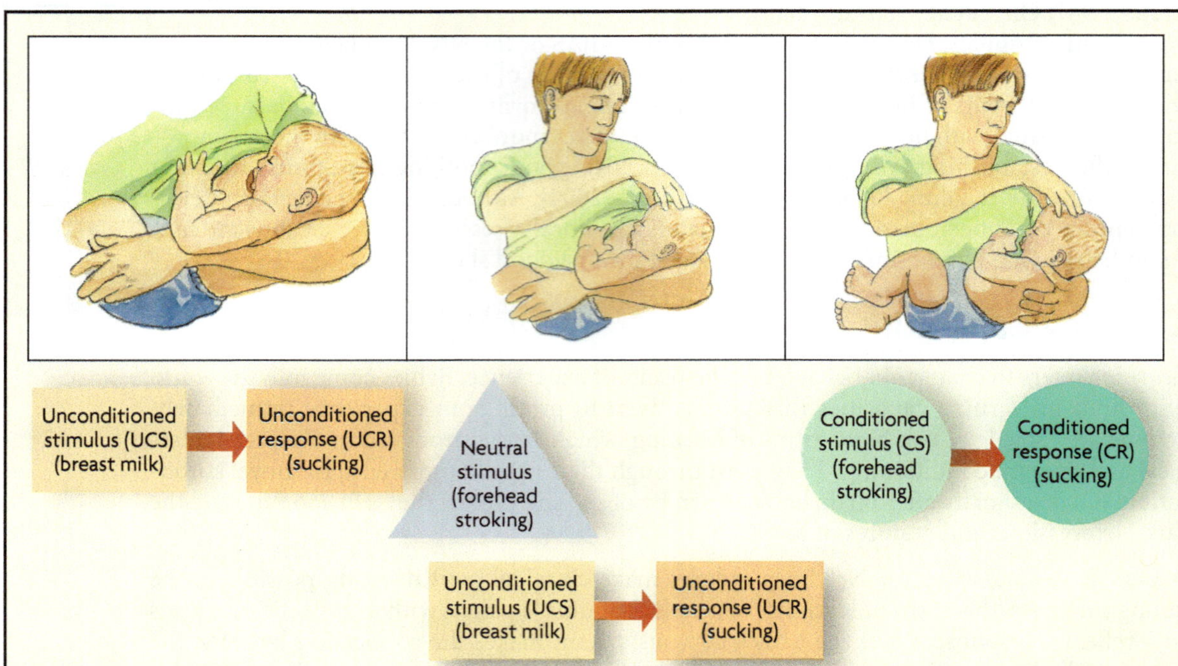

Figure 4.3 **The steps of classical conditioning.** The example here shows how a mother classically conditioned her baby to make sucking movements by stroking his forehead at the beginning of feedings.

• **Operant Conditioning** In classical conditioning, babies build expectations about stimulus events in the environment, but their behavior does not influence the stimuli that occur. In **operant conditioning**, infants act, or *operate*, on the environment, and stimuli that follow their behavior change the probability that the behavior will occur again. A stimulus that increases the occurrence of a response is called a **reinforcer.** For example, sweet liquid *reinforces* the sucking response in newborns. Removing a desirable stimulus or presenting an unpleasant one to decrease the occurrence of a response is called **punishment.** A sour-tasting fluid *punishes* newborns' sucking response, causing them to purse their lips and stop sucking entirely.

Many stimuli besides food can serve as reinforcers of infant behavior. For example, researchers have created special laboratory conditions in which the baby's rate of sucking on a nipple produces a variety of interesting sights and sounds. Newborns will suck faster to see visual designs or to hear music and human voices (Floccia, Christophe, & Bertoncini, 1997). Even preterm babies will seek reinforcing stimulation. In one study, they increased their contact with a soft teddy bear that "breathed" at a rate reflecting the infant's respiration, whereas they decreased their contact with a nonbreathing bear (Thoman & Ingersoll, 1993). As these findings suggest, operant conditioning is a powerful tool for finding out what stimuli babies can perceive and which ones they prefer.

As infants get older, operant conditioning includes a wider range of responses and stimuli. For example, researchers have hung mobiles over the cribs of 2- to 6-month-olds. When the baby's foot is attached to the mobile with a long cord, the infant can, by kicking, make the mobile turn. Under these conditions, it takes only a few minutes for infants to start kicking vigorously. This technique has yielded important information about infant memory. In a series of studies, Carolyn Rovee-Collier found that 3-month-olds remembered how to activate the mobile one week after training. By 6 months, memory increases to two weeks (Rovee-Collier, 1999; Rovee-Collier & Bhatt, 1993). Around the middle of the first year, babies can manipulate switches or buttons to control stimulation. When 6- to 18-month-olds pressed a lever to make a toy train move around a track, duration of memory continued to increase with age; 13 weeks after training, 18-month-olds still remembered how to press the lever (Hartshorn et al., 1998b). Figure 4.4 shows this dramatic rise in retention of operant responses over the first year and a half.

Even after 3- to 6-month-olds forget an operant response, they need only a brief prompt—an adult who shakes the mobile—to reinstate the memory (Hildreth & Rovee-Collier, 2002). And when 6-month-olds are given a chance to reactivate the response themselves for just a couple of minutes—jiggling the mobile by kicking or moving the train by lever-pressing—their memory not only returns but extends dramatically, to about 17 weeks (Hildreth, Sweeney, & Rovee-Collier, 2003). Perhaps permitting the baby to generate the previously learned behavior strengthens memory because it reexposes the child to more aspects of the original learning situation.

At first, infants' memory for operant responses is highly *context dependent.* If 3- to 6-month-olds are not tested in the same situation in which they were trained—with the same mobile and crib bumper and in the same room—they remember poorly (Hayne & Rovee-Collier, 1995; Hayne, 2004). This specificity of infant memory also applies to imitation; young babies will imitate adult-modeled actions on a toy only when given a toy identical in color and features to the one the adult used. After 9 months, the importance of context declines. Older infants and toddlers remember how to push a button to make a toy train move or how to make a toy animal emit a sound even when the toy's features are altered and testing takes place in a different room (Hartshorn et al., 1998a; Hayne, Boniface, & Barr, 2000; Learmonth, Lamberth, & Rovee-Collier, 2004). Crawling is strongly associated with 9-month-olds' formation of an increasingly context-free memory (Herbert, Gross, & Hayne, 2007). As babies move on their own and experience frequent changes in context, they apply learned responses more flexibly, generalizing them to relevant new situations.

As Chapter 6 will make clear, operant conditioning has also been used to study babies' ability to group similar stimuli into categories. It plays a vital role in the formation of social relationships as well. As the baby gazes into the adult's eyes, the adult looks and smiles back, and then

■ **Figure 4.4 Increase in retention of operant responses in two tasks from 2 to 18 months of age.**

Two- to 6-month-olds were trained to make a kicking response that turned a mobile. Six- to 18-month-olds were trained to press a lever that made a toy train move around a track. Six-month-olds learned both responses and retained them for an identical length of time, indicating that the tasks are comparable. Consequently, researchers could plot a single line tracking gains in retention of operant responses from 2 to 18 months of age. The line shows that memory improves dramatically. (From C. Rovee-Collier & R. Barr, 2001, "Infant Learning and Memory," in G. Bremner & A. Fogel, eds., *Blackwell Handbook of Infant Development,* Oxford: Blackwell, p. 150. Reprinted by permission of Blackwell Publishing Ltd.)

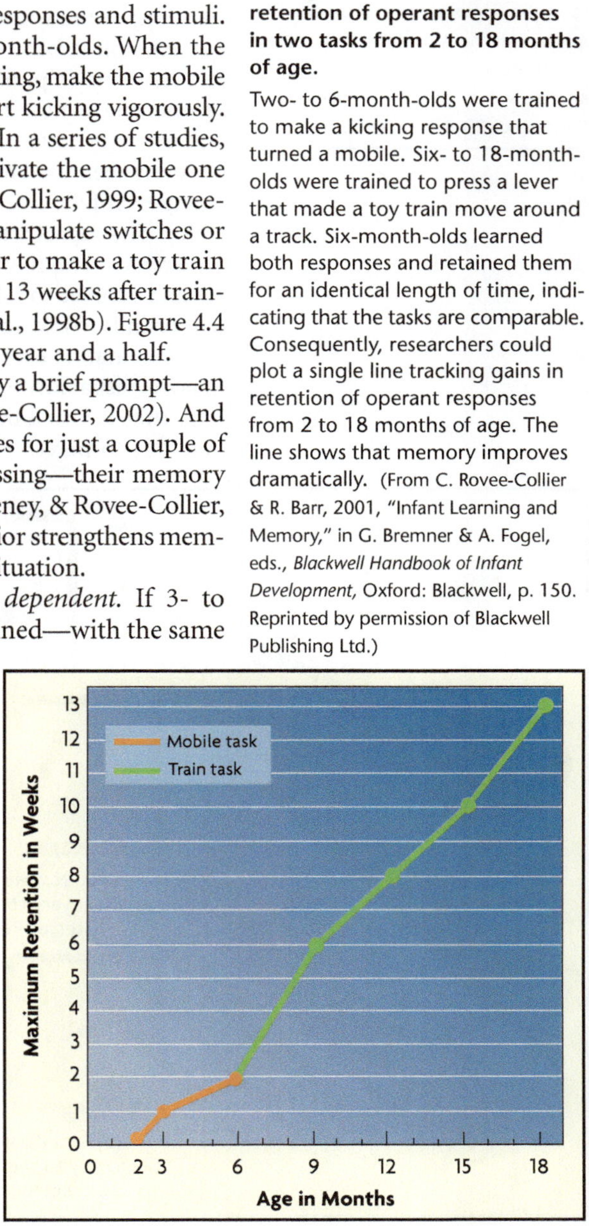

Memory for operant responses improves dramatically over the first 18 months. This 10-month-old has learned to press a lever to make a toy train move around a track—a response he is likely to remember when reexposed to the task after an interval as long as six weeks.
Courtesy of Carolyn Rovee-Collier

the infant looks and smiles again. The behavior of each partner reinforces the other, so that both continue their pleasurable interaction. In Chapter 10, we will see that this contingent responsiveness contributes to the development of infant–caregiver attachment.

• **Habituation** At birth, the human brain is set up to be attracted to novelty. Infants tend to respond more strongly to a new element that has entered their environment, an inclination that ensures that they will continually add to their knowledge base. **Habituation** refers to a gradual reduction in the strength of a response due to repetitive stimulation. Looking, heart rate, and respiration rate may all decline, indicating a loss of interest. Once this has occurred, a new stimulus—a change in the environment—causes the habituated response to return to a high level, an increase called **recovery.** For example, when you walk through a familiar space, you notice things that are new or different—a recently hung picture on the wall or a piece of furniture that has been moved. Habituation and recovery make learning more efficient by focusing our attention on those aspects of the environment we know least about.

Window into Early Attention, Memory, and Knowledge. Researchers studying infants' understanding of the world rely on habituation and recovery more than any other learning capacity. For example, a baby who first *habituates* to a visual pattern (a photo of a baby) and then *recovers* to a new one (a photo of a bald man) appears to remember the first stimulus and perceive the second one as new and different from it. This method of studying infant attention, perception, and memory, illustrated in Figure 4.5a, can be used with newborns, including preterm infants. It has even been used to study the fetus's sensitivity to external stimuli—for example, by measuring changes in fetal heart rate when various repeated sounds are presented (Doherty & Hepper, 2000). The capacity to habituate is evident in the third trimester of pregnancy.

Preterm and newborn babies require a long time—about three or four minutes—to habituate and recover to novel visual stimuli. By 4 or 5 months, however, they need as little as five to ten seconds to take in a complex visual stimulus and recognize it as different from a previous one. Yet a fascinating exception to this trend exists: Two-month-olds actually take longer to habituate to novel visual forms than do newborns and older infants (Colombo, 2002). Later we will see that 2 months is also a time of dramatic gains in visual perception. Perhaps when young babies are first able to perceive certain information, they require more time to take it in. Another factor contributing to the long habituation times of young babies is their difficulty disengaging attention from a stimulus. By 4 months, attention becomes more flexible—a change believed to be due to development of structures in the cerebral cortex controlling eye movements (Blaga & Colombo, 2006; Posner & Rothbart, 2007a). (Nevertheless, as will be apparent shortly, a few babies continue to have trouble shifting attention.)

Recovery to a new stimulus, or *novelty preference,* assesses infants' *recent memory.* **TAKE A MOMENT...** Think about what happens when you return to a place

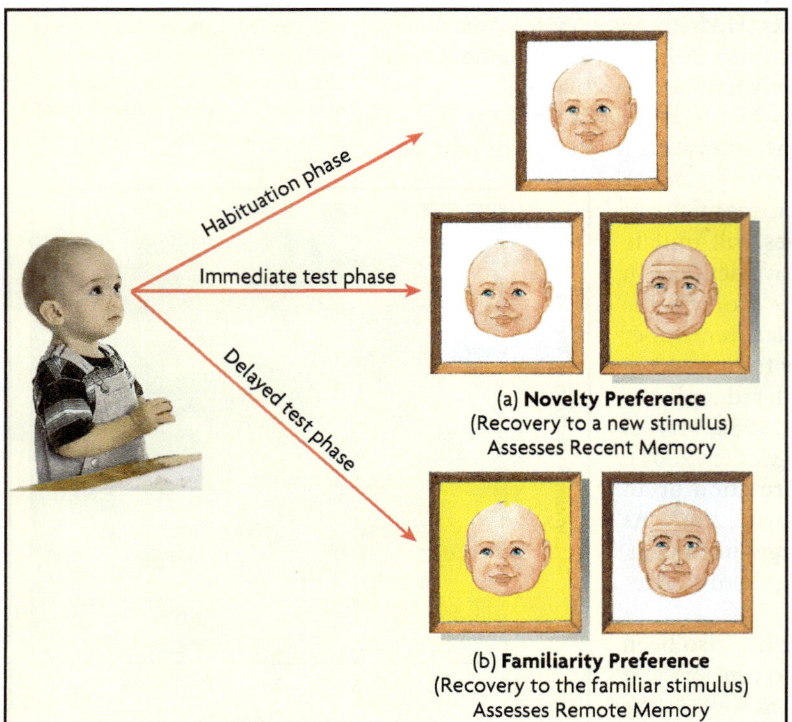

Figure 4.5 Using habituation to study infant memory and knowledge. In the habituation phase, infants view a photo of a baby until their looking declines. In the test phase, infants are again shown the baby photo, but this time it appears alongside a photo of a bald-headed man. (a) When the test phase occurs soon after the habituation phase (within minutes, hours, or days, depending on the age of the infants), participants who remember the baby face and distinguish it from the man's face show a *novelty preference;* they recover to the new stimulus. (b) When the test phase is delayed for weeks or months, infants who continue to remember the baby face shift to a *familiarity preference;* they recover to the familiar baby face rather than to the novel man's face.

you have not seen for a long time. Instead of attending to novelty, you are likely to focus on aspects that are familiar: "I recognize that. I've been here before!" Similarly, with passage of time, infants *shift from a novelty preference to a familiarity preference.* That is, they recover to the familiar stimulus rather than to a novel stimulus (see Figure 4.5b) (Bahrick & Pickens, 1995; Courage & Howe, 1998). By capitalizing on that shift, researchers can use habituation to assess *remote memory*, or memory for stimuli to which infants were exposed weeks or months earlier.

Habituation studies show that infants detect and remember an extraordinarily wide range of stimuli from the constantly changing flow of objects, actions, and events in their surroundings. They are especially attentive to the movements of objects and people, and they retain such information over many weeks. In one study, 5½-month-old babies habituated to a video in which they saw the face of a woman performing an action (either brushing teeth, blowing bubbles, or brushing hair) (Bahrick, Gogate, & Ruiz, 2002). In a test phase one minute later and again after a seven-week delay, infants watched the familiar video next to a novel video, in which the action changed while the woman's face remained the same. As Figure 4.6 indicates, infants clearly remembered the action. At one minute, most showed a *novelty prefer-*

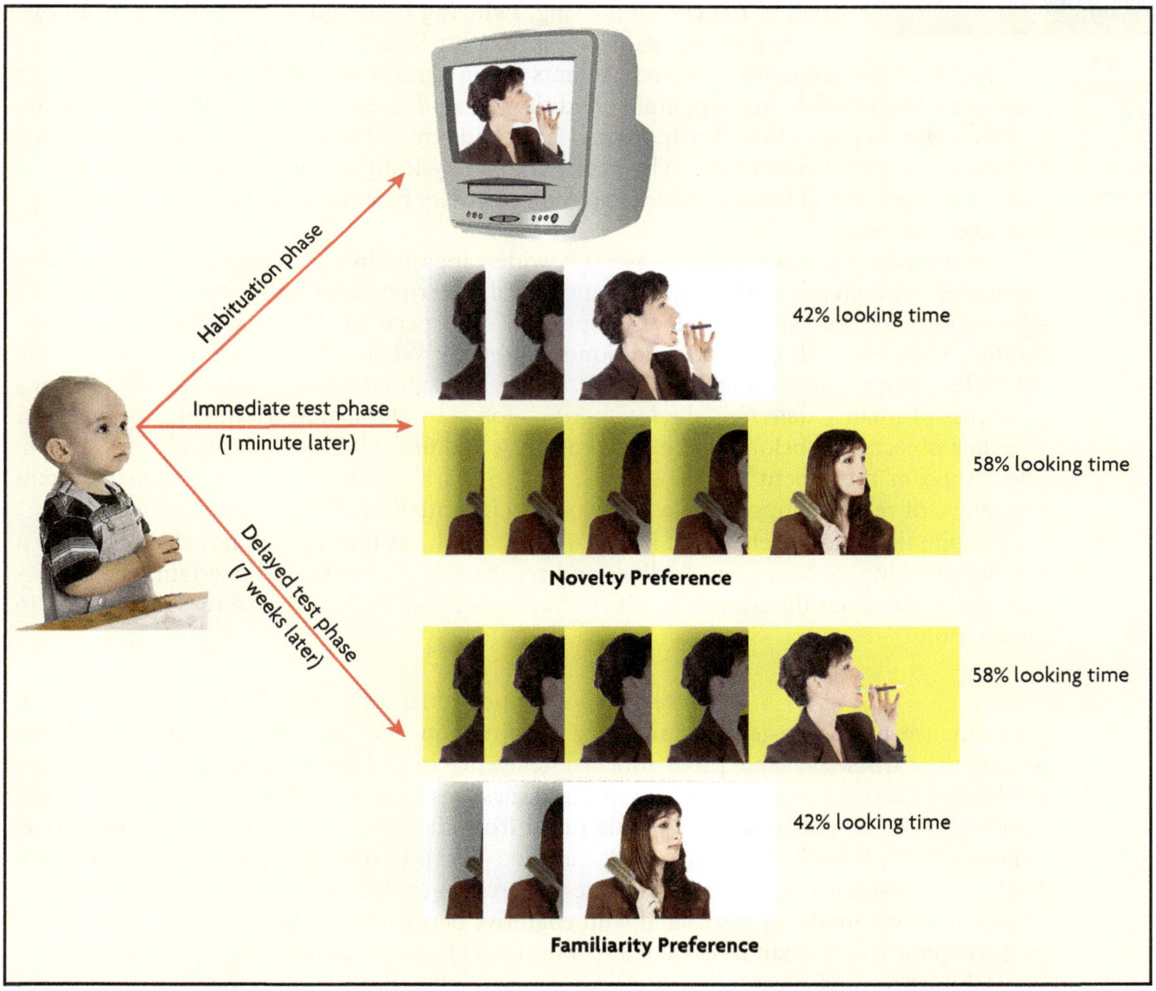

Figure 4.6 **Infants' recent and remote memory for human actions.** Infants 5½ months old habituated to a video that showed the face of a woman while she performed an action, such as brushing teeth. In two test phases, they saw the familiar video next to a novel video, in which the action changed—for example, to brushing hair—while the woman's face remained the same. In the *immediate test phase* (one minute later), which assessed *recent memory*, infants displayed a novelty preference; they looked longer at the novel action than the familiar action. In the delayed test phase (seven weeks later), which assessed *remote memory*, infants showed a *familiarity preference*; they looked longer at the familiar action than the novel action. These findings reveal that young infants remember human actions for an impressively long time. (Adapted from Bahrick, Gogate, & Ruiz, 2002.)

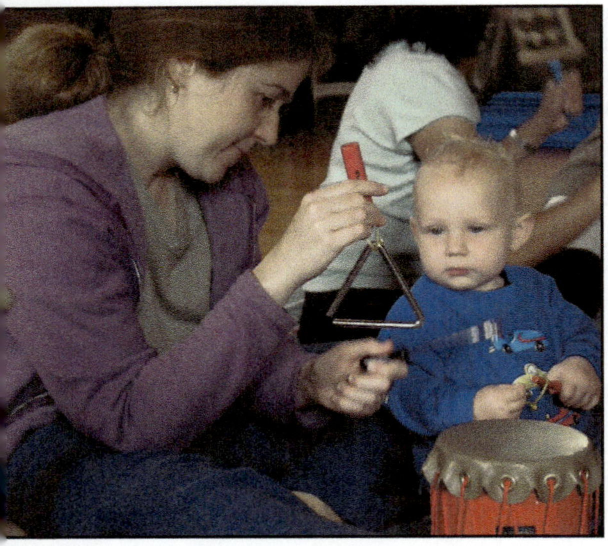
Infants are captivated by people's actions. This baby watches intently as his mother strikes a triangle in an infant music class.
© Geri Engberg/The Image Works

ence, looking longer at the new action than the old action. But at seven weeks, most showed a *familiarity preference,* looking longer at the familiar action than the new action. In fact, the babies were so attentive to the woman's action that they ignored her face! In an additional test phase assessing face recognition in a novel video (the woman's face changed while her original action remained the same), infants showed no facial preference.

These findings, and others in this chapter, confirm that infants find motion so captivating that they attend to and remember an action far better than the features of the person engaging in it! Later we also will see that babies are excellent at discriminating faces in static displays (such as the one in Figure 4.5). However, infants' memory for the faces of unfamiliar people and for other static patterns is short-lived—at 3 months, only about 24 hours, and at the end of the first year, several days to a few weeks (Fagan, 1973; Pascalis, de Haan, & Nelson, 1998). In comparison, 3-month-olds' memory for the unusual movements of objects (such as a metal nut tied to the end of a string, swinging back and forth) persists for at least three months (Bahrick, Hernandez-Reif, & Pickens, 1997).

Note that in habituation research, infants retain certain information over much longer time spans than they do in the operant conditioning studies using the crib mobile (refer again to Figure 4.4 on page 139). Clearly, infants learn and remember a great deal just by watching objects and events around them. They need not be physically active to acquire new information (although, as will become clear later, motor activity facilitates certain aspects of perception and cognition).

Habituation has been used to assess a wide range of infant perceptual and cognitive capacities—speech perception, musical and visual pattern perception, object perception, categorization, and knowledge of many aspects of the social world. These studies reveal yet another disparity with operant conditioning research: When assessed through habituation, infant learning is not as *context dependent.* In this and subsequent chapters, we will see many examples of infants' *detection of relationships*—for example, speech sounds that often occur together, objects that belong to the same category, and the match between an object's rhythm and tempo of movement and its sounds. As early as 3½ months, infants use their current awareness of relationships to make sense of new information (Bahrick, 2002).

Despite the many strengths of habituation research, its findings are not clear-cut. When looking, sucking, or heart rate declines and recovers, it is sometimes uncertain what babies actually know about the stimuli to which they responded. We will return to this difficulty in Chapter 6.

Habituation and Later Mental Development. Individual differences in babies' habituation performance have long-term significance. Habituation and recovery to visual stimuli are among the earliest available predictors of intelligence in childhood, adolescence, and young adulthood. Correlations between the speed of these responses in infancy and the mental test scores of 3- to 21-year-olds consistently range from the .30s to the .60s (Fagan, Holland, & Wheeler, 2007; Kavsek, 2004; McCall & Carriger, 1993). In one study, the speed with which fetal startle reactions in the third trimester of pregnancy declined to a repeatedly presented loud sound was modestly associated with cognitive performance (assessed through recovery to novel photos of human faces) at 6 and 9 months of age (Gaultney & Gingras, 2005).

Habituation and recovery seem to be an especially effective early index of intelligence because they assess memory as well as quickness and flexibility of thinking, which underlie intelligent behavior at all ages. Compared with infants who habituate and recover quickly, infants who are "long lookers" on these tasks have difficulty redirecting their attention from one spot to another. Instead of taking in the overall arrangement of a stimulus followed by its finer details, they get stuck on certain small features and, consequently, process much less information (Colombo, 2002; Colombo et al., 2004). When researchers used a red spotlight to induce 5-month-old long lookers to attend to all parts of a complex design, the babies changed their approach and scanned visual stimuli just as "short lookers" do. As a result, they improved in discrimination and memory for visual stimuli (Jankowski, Rose, & Feldman, 2001). Investigators have yet to explore the impact of such early intervention on intellectual development.

So far, we have considered only one type of memory—*recognition.* It is the simplest form of memory: All the baby has to do is indicate (by looking, kicking, or pressing a lever) whether a new stimulus is identical or similar to a previous one. A second, more challenging form of memory is *recall,* which involves remembering something not present. Can infants engage in recall? By the end of the first year, they can, as indicated by their ability to find hidden objects and imitate the actions of others hours or days after they observed the behavior. We will take up recall in Chapter 7.

• **Newborn Imitation** Newborn babies come into the world with a primitive ability to learn through **imitation**—by copying the behavior of another person. For example, Figure 4.7 shows infants from 2 days to several weeks old imitating two adult facial expressions (Meltzoff & Moore, 1977). The newborn's capacity to imitate extends to certain gestures, such as head and finger movements, and has been demonstrated in many ethnic groups and cultures (Meltzoff & Kuhl, 1994; Nagy et al., 2005). As the figure reveals, even newborn chimpanzees, our closest evolutionary ancestors, imitate some behaviors (Myowa-Yamakoshi et al., 2004).

Although newborns' inclination to imitate is widely accepted, a few studies have failed to reproduce the human findings (see, for example, Anisfeld et al., 2001). And because newborn mouth and tongue movements occur with increased frequency to almost any arousing change in stimulation (such as lively music or flashing lights), some researchers argue that certain newborn "imitative" responses are actually mouthing—a common early exploratory response to interesting stimuli (Jones, 2006). Furthermore, imitation is harder to induce in babies 2 to 3 months old than just after birth. Therefore, skeptics believe that the newborn imitative capacity is little more than an automatic response that declines with age, much like a reflex (Heyes, 2005).

Others claim that newborns imitate a variety of facial expressions and head movements with apparent effort and determination, even after short delays—when the adult is no longer demonstrating the behavior (Hayne, 2002; Meltzoff & Moore, 1999). Furthermore, these investigators argue, imitation—unlike reflexes—does not decline. Human babies several months old often do not imitate an adult's behavior right away because they first try to play social games—mutual gazing, cooing, smiling, and waving their arms. But when an adult models a gesture repeatedly, older human infants soon get down to business and imitate (Meltzoff & Moore, 1994). Similarly, imitation declines in baby chimps around 9 weeks of age, when mother–baby mutual gazing and other face-to-face exchanges increase.

According to Andrew Meltzoff, newborns imitate in much the same way older children and adults do—by actively trying to match body movements they *see* with ones they *feel* themselves make (Meltzoff, 2007; Meltzoff & Decety, 2003). Later we will encounter evidence that young infants are surprisingly good at coordinating

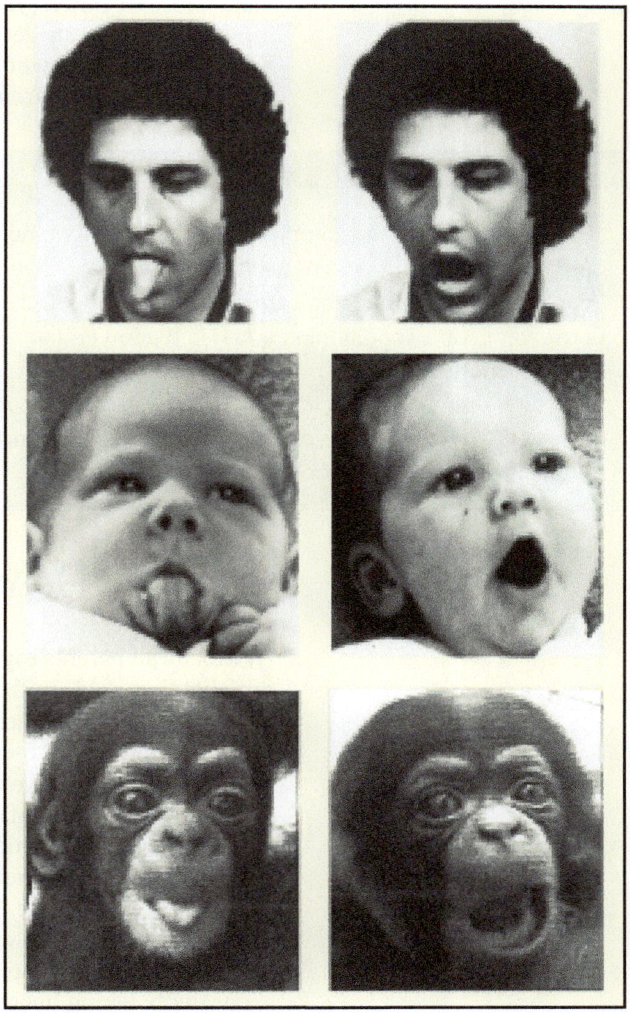

Figure 4.7 **Imitation by human and chimpanzee newborns.** The human infants in the middle row imitating (left) tongue protrusion and (right) mouth opening are 2 to 3 weeks old. The chimpanzee imitating both facial expressions is 2 weeks old. (From A. N. Meltzoff & M. K. Moore, 1977, "Imitation of Facial and Manual Gestures by Human Neonates," *Science,* 198, p. 75; T. M. Field et al., 1992, "Discrimination and Imitation of Facial Expressions by Neonates," *Science,* 218, p.180; and M. Myowa-Yamakoshi et al., 2004, "Imitation in neonatal chimpanzees (Pan troglodytes)," *Developmental Science,* 7, p. 440. Copyright © 1997 and 1982 by AAAS, copyright 2004 by Blackwell Publishing. Reprinted with permission from AAAS, Andrew Meltzoff and Tiffany Field.)

information across sensory systems. Indeed, scientists have identified specialized cells in motor areas of the cerebral cortex in primates—called **mirror neurons**—that underlie these capacities (Rizzolatti & Craighero, 2004). Mirror neurons fire identically when a primate hears or sees an action and when it carries out that action on its own. Brain-imaging studies confirm that human adults have especially elaborate systems of mirror neurons, which enable us to observe another person's behavior (such as smiling or throwing a ball) while simulating the behavior in our own brain. Mirror neurons are believed to be the biological basis of a variety of interrelated, complex social abilities, including imitation, empathic sharing of emotions, and understanding others' intentions (Iocaboni et al., 2005; Schulte-Ruther et al., 2007).

Brain-imaging findings support a functioning mirror-neuron system as early as 6 months of age. Using NIROT, researchers found that the same motor areas of the cerebral cortex were activated in 6-month-olds and in adults when they observed a model engage in a behavior that could be imitated (tapping a box to make a toy pop out) as when they themselves engaged in a motor action (Shimada & Hiraki, 2006). In contrast, when infants and adults observed an object that appeared to move on its own, without human intervention (a ball hanging from the ceiling on a string, swinging like a pendulum), motor areas were not activated.

Still, Meltzoff and Moore's view of newborn imitation as a flexible, voluntary capacity remains controversial. Mirror neurons, although possibly functional at birth, undergo an extended period of development (Bertenthal & Longo, 2007; Lepage & Théoret, 2007). Similarly, as we will see in Chapter 6, the capacity to imitate expands greatly over the first two years. But however limited it is at birth, imitation is a powerful means of learning (Blasi & Bjorklund, 2003). Using imitation, infants explore their social world, getting to know people by matching their behavioral states. As babies notice similarities between their own actions and those of others, they start to learn about themselves. By tapping into infants' ability to imitate, adults can get infants to express desirable behaviors. Finally, caregivers take great pleasure in a baby who imitates their facial gestures and actions, which helps get the infant's relationship with parents off to a good start.

Ask Yourself

Review Provide an example of classical conditioning, of operant conditioning, and of habituation/recovery in young infants. Why is each type of learning useful? Cite differences between operant conditioning and habituation findings on infant memory.

Apply After a difficult birth, 2-day-old Kelly scores poorly on the NBAS. How would you address her mother's concern that Kelly might not develop normally?

Connect How do the diverse capacities of newborn babies contribute to their first social relationships? List as many examples as you can.

Reflect What is your attitude toward parent–infant cosleeping? Is it influenced by your cultural background?

Motor Development in Infancy

Virtually all parents eagerly await mastery of new motor skills, recording with pride when their infants first hold up their heads, reach for objects, sit by themselves, and walk alone. Parents' enthusiasm for these achievements makes perfect sense. With each new motor skill, babies master their bodies and the environment in a new way. For example, sitting upright gives infants a brand-new perspective on the world. Reaching enables babies to find out about objects by acting on them. And when infants can move on their own, their opportunities for exploration multiply.

Babies' motor achievements have a powerful impact on their social relationships. Once infants can crawl, parents start to restrict their activities by saying "no" and expressing mild anger and impatience. Walking often brings the first "testing of wills" (Biringen et al., 1995). Despite her parents' warnings, one newly walking 12-month-old continued to pull items from shelves that were off limits. "I said, 'Don't do that!'" her mother would state firmly, repeatedly taking her toddler by the hand and redirecting her activities.

Milestones

Gross and Fine Motor Development in the First Two Years

Motor Skill	Average Age Achieved	Age Range in Which 90 Percent of Infants Achieve the Skill
When held upright, holds head erect and steady	6 weeks	3 weeks–4 months
When prone, lifts self by arms	2 months	3 weeks–4 months
Rolls from side to back	2 months	3 weeks–5 months
Grasps cube	3 months, 3 weeks	2–7 months
Rolls from back to side	4½ months	2–7 months
Sits alone	7 months	5–9 months
Crawls	7 months	5–11 months
Pulls to stand	8 months	5–12 months
Plays pat-a-cake	9 months, 3 weeks	7–15 months
Stands alone	11 months	9–16 months
Walks alone	11 months, 3 weeks	9–17 months
Builds tower of two cubes	11 months, 3 weeks	10–19 months
Scribbles vigorously	14 months	10–21 months
Walks up stairs with help	16 months	12–23 months
Jumps in place	23 months, 2 weeks	17–30 months
Walks on tiptoe	25 months	16–30 months

Note: These milestones represent overall age trends. Individual differences exist in the precise age at which each milestone is attained.

Sources: Bayley, 1969, 1993, 2005.

Photos: (top) Oote Boe/Alamy; (center and bottom) © Laura Dwight/Corbis

At the same time, parents increase their expressions of affection and playful activities as their independently moving baby seeks them out for greetings, hugs, and a gleeful game of hide-and-seek (Campos, Kermoian, & Zumbahlen, 1992). Certain motor skills, such as reaching and pointing, permit infants to communicate more effectively. Finally, babies' delight—laughing, smiling, and babbling—as they work on new motor competencies triggers pleasurable reactions in others, which encourage infants' efforts further (Mayes & Zigler, 1992). Motor skills, emotional and social competencies, cognition, and language develop together and support one another.

The Sequence of Motor Development

Gross motor development refers to control over actions that help infants get around in the environment, such as crawling, standing, and walking. *Fine motor development* has to do with smaller movements, such as reaching and grasping. The Milestones table above shows the average age at which infants and toddlers achieve a variety of gross and fine motor skills. It also presents the age range during which most babies accomplish each skill, indicating large individual differences exist in *rate* of motor progress. Also, a baby who is a late reacher is not necessarily going to be a late crawler or walker. We would be concerned about a child's development only if many motor skills were seriously delayed.

Look at the table once more, and you will see both organization and direction in infants' motor achievements. A **cephalocaudal trend,** or head-to-tail sequence, is evident: Motor control of the head comes before control of the arms and trunk, which comes before control of the legs. You can also see a **proximodistal trend,** meaning from the center of the body outward: Head, trunk, and arm control precedes coordination of the hands and fingers. Physical growth follows a cephalocaudal and proximodistal course during the prenatal period, infancy, and childhood (see Chapter 5). The similarities between physical and motor development suggest a genetic contribution to motor progress. But as we will see, some motor milestones deviate sharply from these trends.

We must be careful not to think of motor skills as unrelated accomplishments that follow a fixed maturational timetable. Rather, each skill is a product of earlier motor attainments and a contributor to new ones. Furthermore, children acquire motor skills in highly individual ways. For example, most Western babies crawl before they pull to a stand and walk. Yet one infant I know, who disliked being placed on her tummy but enjoyed sitting and being held upright, pulled to a stand and walked before she crawled! Many factors—both internal and external to the child—join together to influence the vast transformations in motor competencies of the first two years. The *dynamic systems perspective,* introduced in Chapter 1 (see page 29), helps us understand how motor development takes place.

Motor Skills as Dynamic Systems

According to **dynamic systems theory of motor development,** mastery of motor skills involves acquiring increasingly complex *systems of action.* When motor skills work as a *system,* separate abilities blend together, each cooperating with others to produce more effective ways of exploring and controlling the environment. For example, control of the head and upper chest combine into sitting with support. Kicking, rocking on all fours, and reaching combine to become crawling. And standing, stepping, and improved upright postural control unite into walking (Thelen, 1989).

Each new skill is a joint product of the following factors: (1) central nervous system development, (2) the body's movement capacities, (3) the goals the child has in mind, and (4) environmental supports for the skill. Change in any element makes the system less stable, and the child starts to explore and select new, more effective motor patterns.

The factors that induce change vary with age. In the early weeks of life, brain and body growth are especially important as infants achieve control over the head, shoulders, and upper torso. Later, the baby's goals (getting a toy or crossing the room) and environmental supports (parental encouragement, objects in the infant's everyday setting) play a greater role. For example, infants with stairs in their home learn to crawl up stairs at an earlier age and also more readily master a back-descent strategy—the safest but also the most challenging position because the baby must turn around at the top, give up visual guidance of her goal, and crawl backward (Berger, Theuring, & Adolph, 2007). Characteristics of the broader physical world also profoundly influence motor skills. If children were reared on the moon, with its reduced gravity, they would prefer jumping to walking or running!

This gleeful, determined baby scales a staircase with a goal in mind—perhaps to take in the panorama of her backyard. Still a novice stair climber, she is likely to repeat the ascent many times, experimenting with the skill until her speed and coordination improve.
© Geri Engberg/The Image Works

When a skill is first acquired, infants must refine it. For example, one baby, just starting to crawl, often collapsed on her tummy and moved backward instead of forward. Soon she figured out how to propel herself forward by alternately pulling with her arms and pushing with her feet. As she experimented, she perfected the crawling motion (Vereijkin & Adolph, 1999). As they attempt a new skill, most babies move back and forth between its presence and absence, and related, previously mastered skills become less secure. A novice walker might take a few steps on Monday, then not do so again until Friday, then not again until the following week. As the baby experiments with the intricate postural adjustments required to balance her body vertically over two small moving feet, balance during sitting may become temporarily less stable (Adolph & Berger, 2006; Chen et al., 2007). In learning to walk, toddlers practice six or more hours a day, traveling the length of 29 football fields! Gradually their small, unsteady steps change to a longer stride, their feet move closer together, their toes point to the front, and their legs become symmetrically coordinated (Adolph, Vereijken, & Shrout, 2003). As movements are repeated thousands of times, they promote new connections in the brain that govern motor patterns.

Look carefully at dynamic systems theory, and you will see why motor development cannot be genetically determined. Because it is motivated by exploration and the desire to master new tasks, heredity can map it out only at a general level. Rather than being *hardwired* into the nervous system, behaviors are *softly assembled,* allowing for different paths to the same motor skill (Adolph & Berger, 2006; Thelen & Smith, 2006).

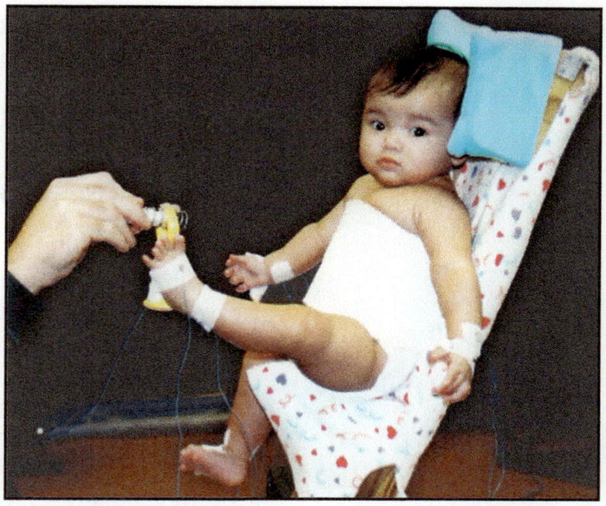

■ Figure 4.8 Reaching "feet first."
When sounding toys were held in front of babies' hands and feet, they reached with their feet as early as 8 weeks of age, a month or more before they reached with their hands—a clear violation of the cephalocaudal pattern. Reduced freedom of movement in the hip joint makes leg movements easier to control than arm movements. This 2½-month-old skillfully explores an object with her foot.

• Dynamic Motor Systems in Action To find out how infants acquire motor capacities, researchers conduct *microgenetic studies* (see Chapter 2, page 63), following babies from their first attempts at a skill until it becomes smooth and effortless. Using this research strategy, James Galloway and Esther Thelen (2004) held sounding toys alternately in front of infants' hands and feet, from the time they first showed interest until they engaged in well-coordinated reaching and grasping. As Figure 4.8 shows, the infants, violating the cephalocaudal trend, first contacted and explored the toys with their feet—as early as 8 weeks of age, at least a month before reaching with their hands!

Why did babies reach "feet first"? Because the hip joint constrains the legs to move less freely than the shoulder constrains the arms, infants could more easily control their leg movements. When they first tried reaching with their hands, their arms actually moved away from the object! Consequently, hand reaching required far more practice than foot reaching. As these findings confirm, rather than following a strict, predetermined cephalocaudal pattern, the order in which motor skills develop depends on the anatomy of the body part being used, the surrounding environment, and the baby's efforts.

• Cultural Variations in Motor Development Cross-cultural research further illustrates how early movement opportunities and a stimulating environment contribute to motor development. Nearly a half-century ago, Wayne Dennis (1960) observed infants in Iranian orphanages who were deprived of the tantalizing surroundings that induce infants to acquire motor skills. These babies spent their days lying on their backs in cribs, without toys to play with. As a result, most did not move on their own until after 2 years of age. When they finally did move, the constant experience of lying on their backs led them to scoot in a sitting position rather than crawl on their hands and knees. Because babies who scoot come up against objects such as furniture with their feet, not their hands, they are far less likely to pull themselves to a standing position in preparation for walking. Indeed, by 3 to 4 years of age, only 15 percent of the Iranian orphans were walking alone.

Cultural variations in infant-rearing practices affect motor development. **TAKE A MOMENT...** Take a quick survey of several parents you know, asking this question: Should sitting, crawling, and walking be deliberately encouraged? Answers vary widely from culture to culture. Japanese mothers and mothers from rural India, for example, believe such efforts are unnecessary. They say that children "just learn" (Seymour, 1999). Among the Zinacanteco Indians of southern Mexico, rapid motor progress is actively discouraged. Babies who walk before they know enough to keep away from cooking fires and weaving looms are viewed as dangerous to themselves and disruptive to others (Greenfield, 1992).

In contrast, among the Kipsigis of Kenya and the West Indians of Jamaica, babies hold their heads up, sit alone, and walk considerably earlier than North American infants. Kipsigi parents deliberately teach these motor skills. In the first few months, babies are seated in holes dug in the ground, and rolled blankets are used to keep them upright. Walking is promoted by frequently bouncing babies on their feet (Hopkins & Westra, 1988; Super, 1981). And as parents in these cultures support babies in upright postures and rarely put them down on the floor, their infants usually skip crawling—a motor skill regarded as crucial in Western nations!

By decreasing exposure to "tummy time," the current Western practice of having babies sleep on their backs to protect them from SIDS (see page 134) delays gross motor milestones of rolling, sitting, and crawling (Majnemer & Barr, 2005; Scrutton, 2005). Regularly exposing babies to the tummy-lying position during waking hours prevents these delays.

Fine Motor Development: Reaching and Grasping

Of all motor skills, reaching may play the greatest role in infant cognitive development. By grasping things, turning them over, and seeing what happens when they are released, infants learn a great deal about the sights, sounds, and feel of objects.

Reaching and grasping, like many other motor skills, start out as gross, diffuse activities and move toward mastery of fine movements. Figure 4.9 illustrates some milestones of reaching over the first nine months. Newborns will actively work to bring their hands into their field of vision: In a dimly lit room, they keep their hand within a narrow beam of light, moving the hand when the light beam moves (van der Meer, 1997). Newborns also make poorly coordinated swipes, called **prereaching,** toward an object in front of them, but because of poor arm and hand control, they rarely contact the object. Nevertheless, they seem to reach to attain a goal: touching things. Like newborn reflexes, prereaching drops out around 7 weeks of age, when babies begin to improve in eye movements involved in tracking and fixating on objects, which is essential for accurate reaching. Yet these early behaviors suggest that babies are biologically prepared to coordinate hand with eye in the act of exploring (Rosander & von Hofsten, 2002; von Hofsten, 2004).

• Development of Reaching and Grasping At about 3 to 4 months, as infants develop the necessary eye, head, and shoulder control, reaching reappears as purposeful, forward arm movements in the presence of a nearby toy and gradually improves in accuracy (Bhat, Heathcock, & Galloway, 2005; Spencer et al., 2000). By 4 months, infants reach for a glowing object in the dark. And at 5 to 6 months, they reach for an object in a room that has been darkened during the reach by switching off the lights—a skill that improves over the next few months (Clifton et al., 1994; McCarty & Ashmead, 1999). These findings indicate that the baby does not need to use vision to guide the arms and hands in reaching. Rather, reaching is largely controlled by *proprioception*—our sense of movement and location in space, arising from stimuli within the body. When vision is freed from the basic act of reaching, it can focus on more complex adjustments, such as fine-tuning actions to fit the distance and shape of objects.

Reaching improves as depth perception advances and as infants gain greater control of body posture and arm and hand movements. Four-month-olds aim their reaches ahead of a moving object so they can catch it (von Hofsten, 1993). Around 5 months, babies reduce their efforts when an object is moved beyond their reach (Robin, Berthier, & Clifton, 1996). By 7 months, the arms become more independent: Infants reach for an object by extending one

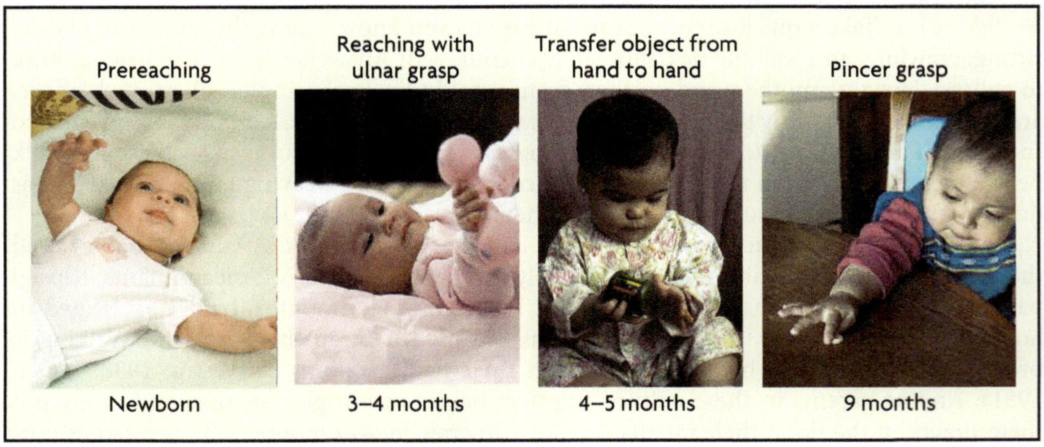

Figure 4.9 Some milestones of reaching.

The average age at which each skill is attained is given. (Ages from Bayley, 1969; Rochat, 1989.)

Photos: (left) © Laura Dwight Photography; (middle left) © Michael Siluk/The Image Works; (middle right) © Laura Dwight Photography; (right) © Elizabeth Crews/The Image Works

arm, rather than both (Fagard & Pezé, 1997). During the next few months, infants become better at reaching for moving objects—ones that spin, change direction, or move closer or farther away (Wentworth, Benson, & Haith, 2000).

Once infants can reach, they modify their grasp. The newborn's grasp reflex is replaced by the **ulnar grasp,** a clumsy motion in which the baby's fingers close against the palm. Still, even 3-month-olds adjust their grasp to the size and shape of an object—a capacity that improves over the first year as infants orient the hand more precisely and do so in advance of contacting the object (Newman, Atkinson, & Braddick, 2001; Witherington, 2005). Around 4 to 5 months, when infants begin to sit up, they no longer need their arms to maintain body balance. This frees both hands to explore objects. Babies of this age can hold an object in one hand while the other scans it with the tips of the fingers, and they frequently transfer objects from hand to hand (Rochat & Goubet, 1995). By the end of the first year, infants use the thumb and index finger opposably in a well-coordinated **pincer grasp.** After that, the ability to manipulate objects greatly expands. The 1-year-old can pick up raisins and blades of grass, turn knobs, and open and close small boxes.

This 2-month-old stares intently at the brightly colored mobile hung over her crib. A moderate amount of stimulation, tailored to her level of visual development, will lead to earlier reaching than either too little or excessive stimulation.
© Jonathan Nourok/PhotoEdit

Between 8 and 11 months, reaching and grasping are well-practiced, freeing attention from the motor skill to events that occur before and after obtaining the object. For example, 10-month-olds easily adjust their reach to anticipate their next action. They reach for a ball faster when they intend to throw it than when they intend to drop it carefully through a narrow tube (Claxton, Keen, & McCarty, 2003). Around this time, too, infants begin to solve simple problems that involve reaching, such as searching for and finding a hidden toy.

Finally, the capacity to reach for and manipulate an object increases infants' attention to the way an adult reaches for and plays with that particular object (Hauf, Aschersleben, & Prinz, 2007; Somerville, Woodward, & Needham, 2004). Perhaps with the aid of mirror neurons (see page 144), babies match their own active experience of reaching to their perception of others' actions. As a result, they broaden their understanding of others' behaviors and—as they watch what others do—of the range of actions that can be performed on various objects.

• Early Experience and Reaching Like other motor milestones, early experience affects reaching. In a well-known study, institutionalized infants given a moderate amount of visual stimulation—at first, simple designs and, later, a mobile hung over their crib—reached for objects six weeks earlier than infants given nothing to look at. A third group given massive stimulation—patterned crib bumpers and mobiles at an early age—also reached sooner than the unstimulated babies. But this heavy enrichment took its toll. These infants looked away and cried a great deal, and they were not as advanced in reaching as the moderately stimulated group (White & Held, 1966). These findings remind us that more stimulation is not necessarily better. Trying to push infants beyond their current readiness to handle stimulation can undermine the development of important motor skills. We will return to this theme at the end of this chapter, and in Chapter 5, where we consider brain development.

Ask Yourself

Review Cite evidence that motor development is not genetically determined but, rather, is a joint product of biological, psychological, and environmental factors.

Apply Roseanne hung mobiles and pictures above her newborn baby's crib, hoping that this would stimulate her infant's motor development. Is Roseanne doing the right thing? Why or why not?

Connect Provide several examples of how motor development influences infants' social experiences. How do social experiences, in turn, influence motor development?

Reflect Do you favor early training of infants in motor skills, such as crawling, standing, walking, and stair climbing? Why or why not?

Perceptual Development in Infancy

TAKE A MOMENT... List research findings in previous sections that illustrate the close link between perception and action in babies' discovery of new skills. To reach for and manipulate objects, maintain balance, or move across various surfaces, infants must continually coordinate their motor behavior with perceptual information. Acting and perceiving are not separate aspects of experience. Instead, motor activity is a vital means for exploring and learning about the world, and improved perception brings about more effective motor activity. The union of perceptual and motor information is basic to our nervous systems, and each domain supports development of the other (Adolph & Berger, 2006; von Hofsten, 2004).

What can young infants perceive with their senses, and how does perception change with age? Researchers have sought answers to these questions for two reasons. First, studies of infant perception reveal in what ways babies are biologically prepared to perceive their world, and how brain development and experience expand their capacities. Second, infant perception sheds light on other aspects of development. For example, because touch, vision, and hearing enable us to interact with others, they are basic to emotional and social development. Through hearing, language is learned. And because knowledge of the world is first gathered through the senses, perception provides the foundation for cognitive development.

Studying infant perception is especially challenging because babies cannot describe their experiences. Fortunately, investigators can make use of a variety of nonverbal responses that vary with stimulation, such as looking, sucking, head turning, facial expressions, and reaching. As noted earlier, researchers also rely on operant conditioning and habituation to find out whether infants can make certain discriminations. And psychophysiological measures—such as stimulus-induced changes in respiration, heart rate, and brain activity (using ERPs and NIROT)—are also used. We will see examples of these methods as we explore the baby's sensitivity to touch, taste, smell, sound, and visual stimulation.

Touch

Touch is a fundamental means of interaction between parents and babies. Within the first few days, mothers can recognize their own newborn by stroking the infant's cheek or hand (Kaitz et al., 1993). Touch helps stimulate early physical growth (see Chapter 3), and it is vital for emotional development. Therefore, it is not surprising that sensitivity to touch is well-developed at birth. The reflexes listed in Table 4.1 on page 128 reveal that the newborn baby responds to touch, especially around the mouth, on the palms, and on the soles of the feet. During the prenatal period, these areas, along with the genitals, are the first to become sensitive to touch (Humphrey, 1978; Streri, 2005).

The *mohel,* a highly trained specialist who performs Jewish circumcisions, prepares to remove the foreskin of this 8-day-old baby with the assistance of a relative. Anesthesia is rarely used in ritual circumcision of very young infants, but the baby is sometimes offered a sweet liquid to reduce the pain of the procedure. © Bojan Brecelj/ CORBIS

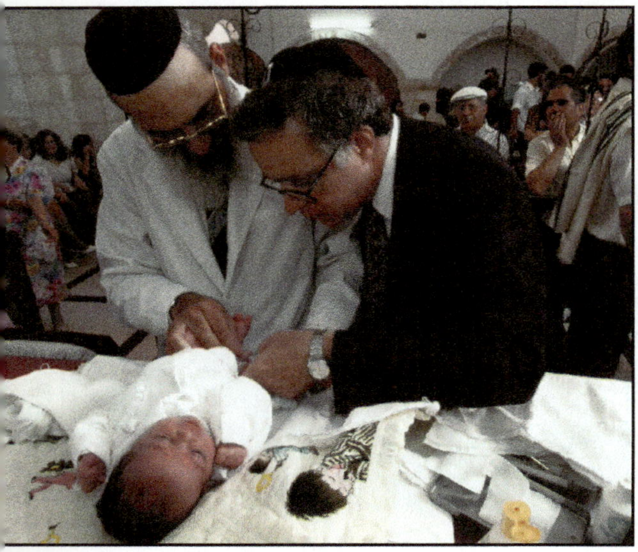

At birth, infants are quite sensitive to pain. If male newborns are circumcised, anesthesia is sometimes not used because of the risks of giving pain-relieving drugs to a very young infant. Babies often respond to pain with a high-pitched, stressful cry and a dramatic rise in heart rate, blood pressure, palm sweating, pupil dilation, and muscle tension (Jorgensen, 1999; Warnock & Sandrin, 2004). Brain-imaging research using NIROT reveals that preterm newborns show intense activation of sensorimotor areas in the cerebral cortex in response to a painful medical injection—a response that is stronger in infants born earlier and in males (Bartocci et al., 2006). Because of central nervous system immaturity, younger preterm and male babies may feel pain especially intensely.

Research establishing the safety of certain local anesthetics for newborns promises to ease the pain of medical procedures. Offering a nipple that delivers a sugar solution is also helpful; it quickly reduces crying and discomfort in young babies, preterm and full-term alike. And combining the sweet liquid with gentle holding by the parent lessens pain even more. Research on infant mammals indicates that physical touch releases *endorphins*—painkilling chemicals in the brain (Axelin, Salanterä, &

Lehtonen, 2006; Gormally et al., 2001). Allowing a baby to endure severe pain overwhelms the nervous system with stress hormones, which can disrupt the child's developing capacity to handle common, everyday stressors. The result is heightened pain sensitivity, sleep disturbances, feeding problems, and difficulty calming down when upset (Mitchell & Boss, 2002).

Gentle touching, in contrast, enhances babies' positive responsiveness to the environment. An adult's soft caresses induce infants to smile and become more attentive to the adult's face (Stack & Muir, 1992). And even newborns use touch to investigate their world. They habituate to an object placed in their palms by reducing their holding and recover to a novel object, indicating that they can use touch to distinguish object shapes (Streri, Lhote, & Dutilleul, 2000). As reaching develops, babies frequently run their lips and tongue over the surface of novel objects, then remove the object to look at it. This exploratory mouthing peaks in the middle of the first year as hand–mouth contact becomes more accurate (Lew & Butterworth, 1997). Then it declines in favor of more elaborate touching with the hands, in which infants turn, poke, and feel the surface of things while looking at them intently (Ruff et al., 1992).

Taste and Smell

Facial expressions reveal that newborns can distinguish several basic tastes. Like adults, they relax their facial muscles in response to sweetness, purse their lips when the taste is sour, and show a distinct archlike mouth opening when it is bitter (Steiner, 1979; Steiner et al., 2001). These reactions are important for survival. The food that best supports the infant's early growth is the sweet-tasting milk of the mother's breast. In contrast, many toxic substances are bitter-tasting. Not until age 4 months do babies prefer a salty taste to plain water, a change that may prepare them to accept solid foods (Mennella & Beauchamp, 1998).

Nevertheless, newborns can readily learn to like a taste that at first evoked either a neutral or a negative response. For example, babies allergic to cow's-milk formula who are given a soy- or other vegetable-based substitute (typically very strong and bitter-tasting) soon prefer it to regular formula. A taste previously disliked can come to be preferred when it is paired with relief of hunger (Harris, 1997).

As with taste, certain odor preferences are present at birth. For example, the smell of bananas or chocolate causes the baby to have a relaxed, pleasant facial expression, whereas the odor of rotten eggs makes the infant frown (Steiner, 1979). During pregnancy, the amniotic fluid is rich in tastes and smells that vary with the mother's diet—early experiences that influence newborns' preferences. In a study carried out in the Alsatian region of France, where anise is frequently used to flavor foods, researchers tested newborns for their reaction to the anise odor (Schaal, Marlier, & Soussignan, 2000). The mothers of some babies had regularly consumed anise-flavored foods and drinks during the last two weeks of pregnancy; the other mothers had never consumed it. When presented with the anise odor on the day of birth, the babies of the anise-consuming mothers spent more time mouthing and turning toward the odor. In contrast, infants of non-anise-consuming mothers were far more likely to turn away with a negative facial expression (see Figure 4.10). These different reactions were still apparent four days later, even though all mothers had refrained from consuming anise during this time.

In many mammals, the sense of smell plays an important role in protecting the young from predators by helping mothers and babies identify each other. Although smell is less well-developed in humans, traces of its survival value remain. Newborns given a choice between the smell of their own mother's amniotic fluid and that of another mother spend more time oriented toward the familiar fluid (Marlier, Schaal, & Soussignan, 1998). The smell of the mother's amniotic fluid is comforting; babies exposed to it cry less than babies who are not (Varendi et al., 1998).

■ Figure 4.10 Examples of facial expressions of newborns exposed to the odor of anise whose mothers differed in anise consumption during late pregnancy.

(a) Babies of anise-consuming mothers spent more time turning toward the odor and mouthing (sucking, licking, and chewing). (b) Babies of non-anise-consuming mothers more often turned away and displayed negative facial expressions—wrinkling their brows and noses, raising their upper lips, lowering the corners of their lips, and closing their eyes. (From B. Schaal, L. Marlier, & R. Soussignan, 2000, "Human Foetuses Learn Odours from Their Pregnant Mother's Diet," *Chemical Senses,* 25, p. 731. Reprinted by permission of Oxford University Press, Inc. and Benoit Schaal.)

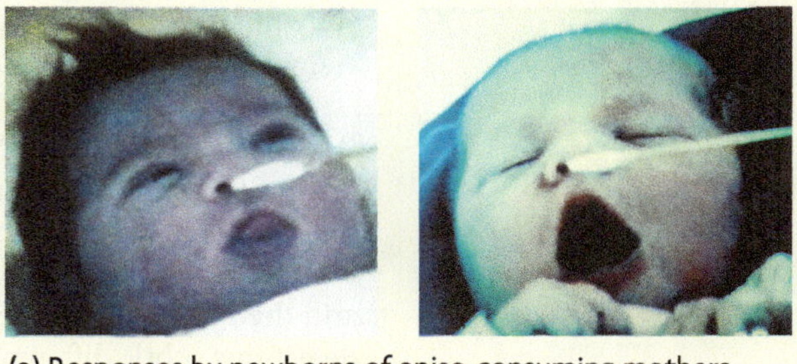

(a) Responses by newborns of anise-consuming mothers

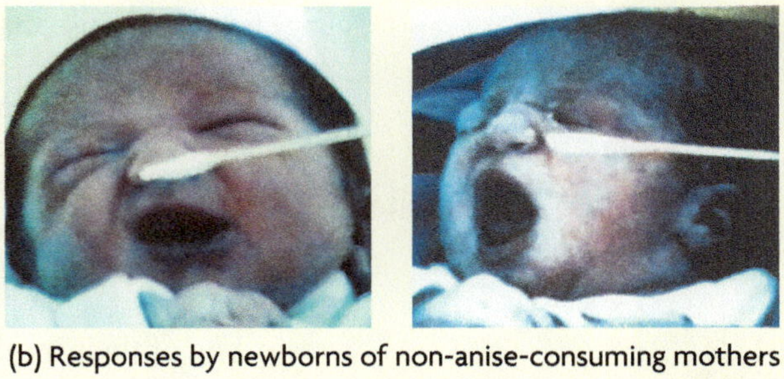

(b) Responses by newborns of non-anise-consuming mothers

Immediately after birth, infants placed face down between their mother's breasts spontaneously latch on to a nipple and begin sucking within an hour. If one breast is washed to remove its natural scent, most newborns grasp the unwashed breast, indicating that they are guided by smell (Varendi & Porter, 2001). At 4 days of age, breastfed babies prefer the smell of their own mother's breast to that of an unfamiliar lactating mother (Cernoch & Porter, 1985). And both breast- and bottle-fed 3- to 4-day-olds orient more and display more mouthing to the smell of unfamiliar human milk than to formula milk, indicating that (even without postnatal exposure) the odor of human milk is more attractive to newborns (Marlier & Schaal, 2005). Newborns' dual attraction to the odor of their mother and to that of breast milk helps them locate an appropriate food source and, in the process, begin to distinguish their caregiver from other people.

Hearing

Although conduction of sound through structures of the ear and transmission of auditory information to the brain are inefficient at birth, newborn infants can hear a wide variety of sounds, and this sensitivity improves greatly over the first few months (Saffran, Werker, & Werner, 2006; Tharpe & Ashmead, 2001). Responsiveness to sound provides support for the young baby's exploration of the environment. Infants as young as 3 days old turn their eyes and head in the general direction of a sound. The ability to identify the precise location of a sound improves greatly over the first six months and shows further gains through the preschool years (Litovsky & Ashmead, 1997).

At birth, infants prefer complex sounds, such as noises and voices, to pure tones. And babies only a few days old can tell the difference between a variety of sound patterns: a series of tones arranged in ascending versus descending order; utterances with two versus three syllables; the stress patterns of words, such as *ma*-ma versus ma-*ma;* happy-sounding speech as opposed to speech with negative or neutral emotional qualities; and even two languages spoken by the same bilingual speaker, as long as those languages differ in their rhythmic features—for example, French from Russian (Mastropieri & Turkewitz, 1999; Ramus, 2002; Sansavini, Bertoncini, & Giovanelli, 1997; Trehub, 2001).

Over the first year, infants organize sounds into increasingly elaborate patterns. Between 4 and 7 months, they show a sense of musical phrasing. They prefer Mozart minuets with pauses between phrases to those with awkward breaks (Krumhansl & Jusczyk, 1990). Around 6 to 7 months, they can distinguish musical tunes on the basis of variations in rhythmic patterns, including beat structure (duple or triple) and accent structure (emphasis on the first note of every beat unit or at other positions) (Hannon & Johnson, 2004). And by the end of the first year, infants recognize the same melody when it is played in different keys (Trehub, 2001). As we will see shortly, 6- to 12-month-olds make comparable discriminations in human speech: They readily detect sound regularities that will facilitate later language learning.

• **Speech Perception** Young infants listen longer to human speech than structurally similar nonspeech sounds (Vouloumanos & Werker, 2004). And they can detect the sounds of any human language. Newborns make fine-grained distinctions between many speech sounds. For example, when given a nipple that turns on the *"ba"* sound, babies suck vigorously for a while and then habituate. When the sound switches to *"ga,"* sucking recovers, indicating that infants detect this subtle difference. Using this method, researchers have found only a few speech sounds that newborns cannot discriminate. Their ability to perceive sounds not found in their own language is more precise than an adult's (Aldridge, Stillman, & Bower, 2001; Jusczyk & Luce, 2002).

TAKE A MOMENT... The next time you talk to a young baby, listen carefully to yourself. You will probably speak in ways that highlight important parts of the speech stream—use a slow, clear, high-pitched, expressive voice with a rising tone at the end of phrases and sentences, and a pause before continuing. Adults probably communicate in this way because they notice that infants are more attentive when they do so. Indeed, shortly after birth, babies prefer human speech with these characteristics, in part because it eases their perceptual learning (Saffran, Werker, & Werner, 2006). In addition, newborns will suck more on a nipple to hear a recording of their mother's voice than that of an unfamiliar woman and to hear their native language as opposed to a foreign language (Moon, Cooper, & Fifer, 1993; Spence & DeCasper,

1987). These preferences may have developed from hearing the muffled sounds of the mother's voice before birth.

Over the first year, infants learn much about the organization of sounds in their native language. As they listen to people talking, they learn to focus on meaningful sound variations. ERP brain-wave recordings reveal that around 5 months, babies become sensitive to syllable stress patterns in their own language (Weber et al., 2004). Between 6 and 8 months, they start to "screen out" sounds not used in their native tongue (Anderson, Morgan, & White, 2003; Polka & Werker, 1994). As the Biology and Environment box on page 154 explains, this increased responsiveness to native-language sounds is part of a general "tuning" process in the second half of the first year—a possible sensitive period in which babies acquire a range of perceptual skills for picking up socially important information.

Soon after, infants focus on larger speech units that are critical to figuring out meaning. They recognize familiar words in spoken passages and listen longer to speech with clear clause and phrase boundaries (Jusczyk & Hohne, 1997; Soderstrom et al., 2003). Around 7 to 9 months, infants extend this sensitivity to speech structure to individual words. They begin to divide the speech stream into wordlike units (Jusczyk, 2002; Saffran, Werker, & Werner, 2006).

• Analyzing the Speech Stream How do infants make such rapid progress in perceiving the structure of language? Research shows that they have an impressive **statistical learning capacity.** By analyzing the speech stream for patterns—regularly occurring sequences of sounds—they acquire a stock of speech structures for which they will later learn meanings, long before they start to talk around age 12 months.

In one set of studies, researchers had 8- and 9-month-olds listen to a continuous sequence of nonsense syllables. Then they gave the babies brief, new syllable sequences; some conformed to the syllable patterns in the original sequence, while others did not. The babies quickly inferred syllable structure: They preferred to listen to new speech that preserved the original syllable patterns. In other words, they listened for statistical regularities, discriminating syllables that often occur together (indicating that they belong to the same word) from syllables that seldom occur together (indicating a word boundary). To cite an English example, consider the word sequence *pretty#baby.* After listening to the speech stream for just one minute (about 60 words), babies can distinguish a word-internal syllable pair *(pretty)* from a word-external syllable pair *(ty#ba)* (Saffran, Aslin, & Newport, 1996; Saffran & Thiessen, 2003). Once infants locate words, they focus on the words and (as we will see in Chapter 9) detect syllable-stress regularities—for example, in English and Dutch, that the onset of a strong syllable (*hap*-py, *rab*-bit) often signals a new word.

Parents often name objects—for example, saying "duck"—while moving the toy and, sometimes, having the toy touch the infant. This multisensory stimulation helps infants associate words with objects. © Simon Jarratt/Corbis

Infants also attend to regularities in word sequences. In a study using nonsense words, 7-month-olds distinguished the ABA structure of "ga ti ga" and "li na li" from the ABB structure of "wo fe fe" and "ta la la" (Marcus et al., 1999). They seemed to detect simple word-order rules—a capacity that may help them figure out the basic grammar of their language. And after extracting these rules, babies generalize them to nonspeech sounds. Seven-month-olds who were exposed to regularities in sequences of nonsense words could identify similar patterns in strings of musical tones and animal sounds. But when presented alone, these stimuli yielded no rule learning (Marcus, Fernandes, & Johnson, 2007). Analyzing the speech stream seems to help babies structure other aspects of their auditory world.

Clearly, babies have a powerful ability to extract regularities from complex, continuous speech. Some researchers believe infants are innately equipped with a general statistical learning capacity for detecting structure in the environment, which they also apply to visual stimulation (Kirkham, Slemmer, & Johnson, 2002). Indeed, because communication is often multisensory (simultaneously verbal, visual, and tactile), infants receive much support from other senses in analyzing speech. When mothers speak to 5- to 8-month-olds, they often provide temporal synchrony between words, object motions, and touch—for example, saying "doll" while moving a doll and, sometimes, having the doll touch the infant (Gogate, Bahrick, & Watson, 2000). In doing so, they create a supportive learning environment: In two studies, 7-month-olds remembered associations between

Biology *and* Environment

"Tuning In" to Familiar Speech, Faces, and Music: A Sensitive Period for Culture-Specific Learning

To share experiences with members of their family and community, babies must become skilled at making perceptual discriminations that are meaningful in their culture. As we have seen, at first babies are sensitive to virtually all speech sounds, but around 6 months, they narrow their focus, limiting the distinctions they make to the language they hear and will soon learn.

The ability to perceive faces shows a similar path of development. After habituating to one member of each pair of faces in Figure 4.11, 6-month-olds were shown the familiar and the novel face side by side. For both pairs, they recovered to (looked longer at) the novel face, indicating that they could discriminate individual faces of both humans and monkeys equally well (Pascalis, de Haan, & Nelson, 2002). But at 9 months, infants no longer showed a novelty preference when viewing the monkey pair. Like adults, they could distinguish only the human faces.

This developmental trend appears again in musical rhythm perception. Western adults are accustomed to the even-beat pattern of Western music—repetition of the same rhythmic structure in every measure of a tune—and easily notice rhythmic changes that disrupt this familiar beat. But present them with music that does not follow this typical Western rhythmic form—Baltic folk tunes, for example—and they fail to pick up on rhythmic-pattern deviations. Six-month-olds, however, can detect such disruptions in both Western and non-Western melodies. But by 12 months, after added exposure to Western music, babies are no longer aware of deviations in foreign musical rhythms, although their sensitivity to Western rhythmic structure remains unchanged (Hannon & Trehub, 2005b).

Several weeks of regular interaction with a foreign-language speaker and of daily opportunities to listen to non-Western music fully restore 12-month-olds' sensitivity to wide-ranging speech sounds and music rhythms (Hannon & Trehub, 2005a; Kuhl, Tsao, & Liu, 2003). Adults given similar extensive experiences, by contrast, show little improvement in perceptual sensitivity.

Taken together, these findings suggest a heightened capacity—or sensitive period—in the second half of the first year, when babies are biologically prepared to "zero in" on socially meaningful perceptual distinctions. Notice how, between 6 and 12 months, learning is especially rapid across several domains (speech, faces, and music) and is easily modified by experience. This suggests a broad neurological change—perhaps a special time of brain development in which babies analyze everyday stimulation of all kinds similarly, in ways that prepare them to participate in their cultural community.

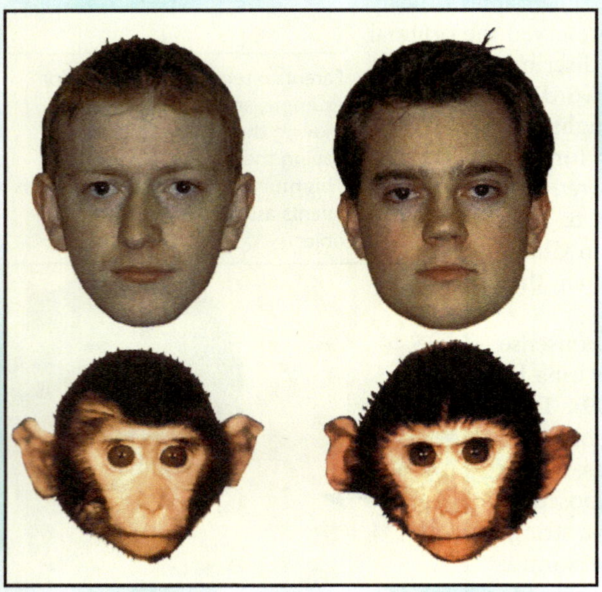

Figure 4.11 **Discrimination of human and monkey faces.** Which of these pairs is easiest for you to tell apart? After habituating to one of the photos in each pair, infants were shown the familiar and the novel face side-by-side. For both pairs, 6-month-olds recovered to (looked longer at) the novel face, indicating that they could discriminate human and monkey faces equally well. By 12 months, babies lost their ability to distinguish the monkey faces. Like adults, they showed a novelty preference only to human stimuli. (From O. Pascalis et al., 2002, "Is Face Processing Species-Specific During the First Year of Life?" *Science, 296*, p. 1322. Copyright © 2002 by AAAS. Reprinted with permission from AAAS.)

sounds and objects only when they heard the sound and saw the object move simultaneously (Gogate & Bahrick, 1998, 2001).

Finally, infants' special responsiveness to speech encourages parents to talk to their baby. Doing so strengthens both the child's readiness for language and the infant–caregiver emotional bond. At first, infants depend on the union of auditory and visual stimuli to pick up emotional information. Three- and 4-month-olds can distinguish happy- from sad-sounding speech, but only while looking at people's faces. Later, babies can discriminate positive from negative emotion in each sensory modality—first voices, then faces (Walker-Andrews, 1997).

Milestones

Development of Touch, Taste, Smell, and Hearing

Age	Touch	Taste and Smell	Hearing
Birth	■ Responds to touch and pain. ■ Distinguishes shape of object placed in palm.	■ Distinguishes sweet, sour, and bitter tastes; prefers sweetness. ■ Distinguishes odors; prefers those of sweet-tasting foods. ■ Prefers smell of own mother's amniotic fluid and the lactating breast.	■ Prefers complex sounds to pure tones. ■ Distinguishes some sound patterns. ■ Makes subtle distinctions between almost all speech sounds, including sounds not found in own language. ■ Turns eyes and head in the general direction of a sound.
1–6 months	■ Frequently engages in exploratory mouthing of objects.	■ Prefers a salty taste to plain water. ■ Readily changes taste preferences through experience.	■ Organizes sounds into increasingly elaborate patterns, such as musical phrases. ■ Identifies location of a sound more precisely. ■ By the end of this period, becomes sensitive to syllable stress patterns in own language.
7–12 months			■ Recognizes the same melody played in different keys. ■ "Screens out" sounds not used in native language. ■ Detects speech units crucial to understanding meaning, including familiar words and regularities in sound and word sequences.

Note: These milestones represent overall age trends. Individual differences exist in the precise age at which each milestone is attained.

Photos: (top) © Ariel Skelley/CORBIS; (middle) © Michael Newman/PhotoEdit; (bottom) © Bananastock/Jupitermages

Before we turn to visual development, consult the Milestones table above for a summary of the perceptual capacities we have just considered.

Vision

For exploring the environment, humans depend on vision more than any other sense. At birth, however, vision is the least developed of the senses. Visual structures in both the eye and the brain are not yet fully formed. For example, cells in the *retina,* the membrane lining the inside of the eye that captures light and transforms it into messages that are sent to the brain, are not as mature or densely packed as they will be in several months. The optic nerve that relays these messages, and visual centers in the brain that receive them, also will not be adultlike for several years. And the muscles of the *lens,* which permit us to adjust our focus to varying distances, are weak (Kellman & Arterberry, 2006).

As a result, newborns cannot focus their eyes well, and their **visual acuity,** or fineness of discrimination, is limited. At birth, infants perceive objects at a distance of 20 feet about as clearly as adults do at 600 feet (Slater, 2001). In addition, unlike adults (who see nearby objects

Figure 4.12 **View of the human face by the newborn and the adult.**

The newborn baby's limited focusing ability and poor visual acuity lead the mother's face, even when viewed from close up, to look more like the fuzzy image in (a) than the clear image in (b). Also, newborn infants have some color vision, although they have difficulty discriminating colors. Researchers speculate that colors probably appear similar, but less intense, to newborns than to older infants and adults. (From Kellman & Arterberry, 2006; Slater, 2001.)

most clearly), newborn babies see unclearly across a wide range of distances (Banks, 1980; Hainline, 1998). As a result, images such as the parent's face, even close up, look like the blurry image in Figure 4.12. And despite their preference for colored over gray stimuli, newborn babies are not yet good at discriminating colors (Kellman & Arterberry, 2006).

The visual system develops rapidly over the first few months. Around 2 months, infants can focus on objects about as well as adults; by 4 months, color discrimination is adultlike (Kellman & Arterberry, 2006). Visual acuity increases steadily, reaching a near-adult level of about 20/20 by 6 months (Slater, 2001).

Although they cannot yet see well, newborns actively explore their environment by scanning it for interesting sights and tracking moving objects. However, their eye movements are slow and inaccurate. Scanning and tracking improve over the first half-year as infants see more clearly and better control their eye movements. In addition, as young infants build an organized perceptual world, they scan more thoroughly and systematically, strategically picking up important information and anticipating with their eye movements what they expect to happen next in a series of events (Haith, 1994; Johnson, Slemmer, & Amso, 2004). Consequently, scanning enhances perception, and—in bidirectional fashion—perception also enhances scanning.

As infants explore the visual field more adeptly, they figure out the characteristics of objects and how they are arranged in space. To understand how they do so, let's examine the development of three aspects of vision: depth, pattern, and object perception.

Depth Perception *Depth perception* is the ability to judge the distance of objects from one another and from ourselves. It is important for understanding the layout of the environment and for guiding motor activity.

Figure 4.13 on page 157 shows the well-known **visual cliff,** designed by Eleanor Gibson and Richard Walk (1960) and used in the earliest studies of depth perception. It consists of a Plexiglas-covered table with a platform at the center, a "shallow" side with a checkerboard pattern just under the glass, and a "deep" side with a checkerboard several feet below the glass. The researchers found that crawling babies readily crossed the shallow side, but most reacted with fear to the deep side. They concluded that around the time that infants crawl, most distinguish deep from shallow surfaces and avoid drop-offs.

The research of Gibson and Walk shows that crawling and avoidance of drop-offs are linked, but not how they are related or when depth perception first appears. Recent research has looked at babies' ability to detect specific depth cues, using methods that do not require that they crawl.

Emergence of Depth Perception. How do we know when an object is near rather than far away? **TAKE A MOMENT...** Try these exercises to find out: Pick up a small object (such as your cup), and move it toward and then away from your face. Did its image grow larger as it approached and smaller as it receded? Next time you take a car or bike ride, notice that nearby objects move past your field of vision more quickly than those far away.

Motion is the first depth cue to which infants are sensitive. Babies 3 to 4 weeks old blink their eyes defensively when an object moves toward their face as if it is going to hit (Nánez & Yonas, 1994). As they are carried about and as people and things turn and move before their eyes, infants learn more about depth. For example, by the time they are 3 months old, motion has helped them figure out that objects are not flat but three-dimensional (Arterberry, Craton, & Yonas, 1993).

Binocular depth cues arise because our two eyes have slightly different views of the visual field. In a process called *stereopsis,* the brain blends these two images, resulting in perception

■ **Figure 4.13** **The visual cliff.**

Plexiglas covers the deep and shallow sides. By refusing to cross the deep side and showing a preference for the shallow side, this infant demonstrates the ability to perceive depth. © Mark Richards/PhotoEdit

of depth. Research in which two overlapping images are projected before the baby, who wears special goggles to ensure that each eye receives only one image, reveals that sensitivity to binocular cues emerges between 2 and 3 months and improves rapidly over the first year (Birch, 1993; Brown & Miracle, 2003). Infants soon make use of binocular cues in their reaching, adjusting arm and hand movements to match the distance of objects from the eyes.

Last to develop are *pictorial depth cues,* the ones artists use to make a painting look three-dimensional—receding lines and line junctions (as in the drawing of a cube) that create the illusion of perspective, changes in texture (nearby textures are more detailed than faraway ones), and overlapping objects (an object partially hidden by another object is perceived to be more distant). Habituation research indicates that 3- to 4-month-olds are sensitive to cues of overlapping lines and line junctions. For example, 4-month-olds discriminate between the structurally "possible" and "impossible" drawings of a cube in Figure 4.14; they look much longer the impossible alternative, as if puzzled by it (Bertin & Bhatt, 2006; Shuwairi, Albert, & Johnson, 2007). Studies in which researchers observe whether babies reach toward closer-appearing parts of images containing pictorial cues reveal that pictorial sensitivity improves sharply between 6 and 7 months (Sen, Yonas, & Knill, 2001; Yonas, Elieff, & Arterberry, 2002; Yonas & Granrud, 2006).

Why does perception of depth cues emerge in the order just described? Researchers speculate that motor development is involved. For example, control of the head during the early weeks of life may help babies notice motion and binocular cues. Around the middle of the first year, the ability to turn, poke, and feel the surface of objects may promote sensitivity to pictorial cues as infants pick up information about size, texture, and shape (Bushnell & Boudreau, 1993). And as we will see next, research shows that one aspect of motor progress—independent movement—plays a vital role in refinement of depth perception.

Independent Movement and Depth Perception. A mother I know described her newly crawling 9-month-old as a "fearless daredevil." "If I put April down in the middle of our bed, she crawls right over the edge," the mother exclaimed. "The same thing's happened by the stairs." Will April become more wary of the side of the bed and the staircase as she becomes a more experienced crawler? Research suggests that she will. Infants with more crawling experience (regardless of when they started to crawl) are far more likely to refuse to cross the deep side of the visual cliff (Campos et al., 2000).

What do infants learn from crawling that promotes this sensitivity to depth information? Research indicates that from extensive everyday experience, babies

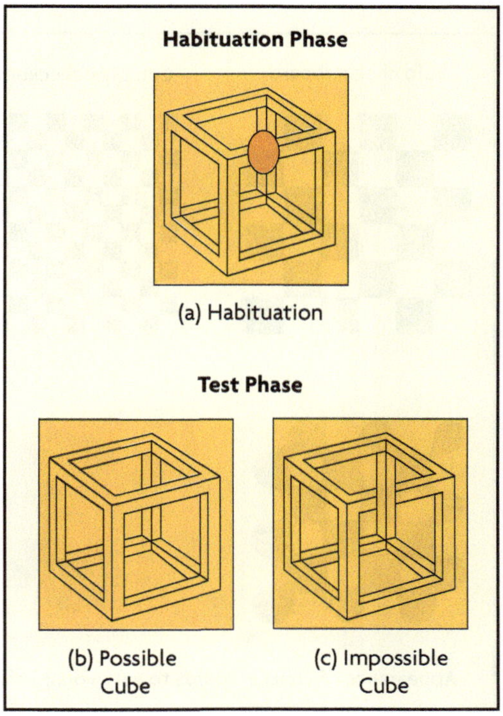

■ **Figure 4.14** **Testing infants' responsiveness to pictorial depth cues—overlapping lines and line junctions.**

(a) Infants were habituated to a line drawing of a cube made to look three-dimensional with overlapping-line and line-junction cues, but with a critical section covered, so looking preference for the makeup of that section could be tested. Next, the infants were shown two test displays in alternation: (b) a structurally "possible" cube and (c) a cube made to look structurally "impossible" by altering the coherence of pictorial cues. Four-month-olds spent much more time looking at the impossible cube, as if puzzled by it—a preference suggesting pictorial-cue sensitivity. (From S. M. Shuwairi, M. K. Albert, & S. P. Johnson, 2007, "Discrimination of Possible and Impossible Objects in Infancy," *Psychological Science,* 18, p. 304. Copyright © 2007 by Blackwell Publishing. Reprinted by permission of Blackwell Publishing Ltd.)

As this baby becomes adept at crawling, she notices how to get from place to place, where objects are in relation to herself and to other objects, and how they appear from different viewpoints. © Myrleen Ferguson Cate/PhotoEdit

gradually figure out how to use depth cues to detect the danger of falling. But because the loss of postural control that leads to falling differs greatly for each body position, babies must undergo this learning separately for each posture. In one study, 9-month-olds, who were experienced sitters but novice crawlers, were placed on the edge of a shallow drop-off that could be widened (Adolph, 2000, 2002). While in the familiar sitting position, infants avoided leaning out for an attractive toy at distances likely to result in falling. But in the unfamiliar crawling posture, they headed over the edge, even when the distance was extremely wide! And newly walking babies, while avoiding sharp drop-offs, careen down slopes and over uneven surfaces without making the necessary postural adjustments, so they fall frequently (Joh & Adolph, 2006; Witherington et al., 2005). As infants discover how to avoid falling in diverse postures and situations, their understanding of depth expands.

Crawling experience promotes other aspects of three-dimensional understanding. For example, seasoned crawlers are better than their inexperienced agemates at remembering object locations and finding hidden objects (Bai & Bertenthal, 1992; Campos et al., 2000). Why does crawling make such a difference? **TAKE A MOMENT...** Compare your own experience of the environment when you are driven from one place to another with what you experience when you walk or drive yourself. When you move on your own, you are much more aware of landmarks and routes of travel, and you take more careful note of what things look like from different points of view. The same is true for infants.

In fact, crawling promotes a new level of brain organization, as indicated by more organized EEG brain-wave activity in the cerebral cortex. Perhaps crawling strengthens certain neural connections, especially those involved in vision and understanding of space (Bell & Fox, 1996). As the Biology and Environment box on page 159 reveals, the link between independent movement and spatial knowledge is also evident in a population with very different perceptual experience: infants with severe visual impairments.

• Pattern Perception Even newborns prefer to look at patterned rather than plain stimuli (Fantz, 1961). As they get older, infants prefer more complex patterns. For example, 3-week-olds look longest at black-and-white checkerboards with a few large squares, whereas 8- and 14-week-olds prefer those with many squares (Brennan, Ames, & Moore, 1966).

Contrast Sensitivity. A general principle, called **contrast sensitivity,** explains early pattern preferences (Banks & Ginsburg, 1985). *Contrast* refers to the difference in the amount of light between adjacent regions in a pattern. If babies *are sensitive to* (can detect) the contrast in two or more patterns, they prefer the one with more contrast. To understand this idea, look at the checkerboards in the top row of Figure 4.15. To us, the one with many small squares has more contrasting elements. Now look at the bottom row, which shows how these checkerboards appear to infants in the first few weeks of life. Because of their poor vision, very young babies cannot resolve the small features in more complex patterns, so they prefer to look at the large, bold checkerboard. Around 2 months, when detection of fine-grained detail has improved, infants become sensitive to the greater contrast in complex patterns and spend more time looking at them. Contrast sensitivity continues to improve during infancy and childhood (Gwiazda & Birch, 2001).

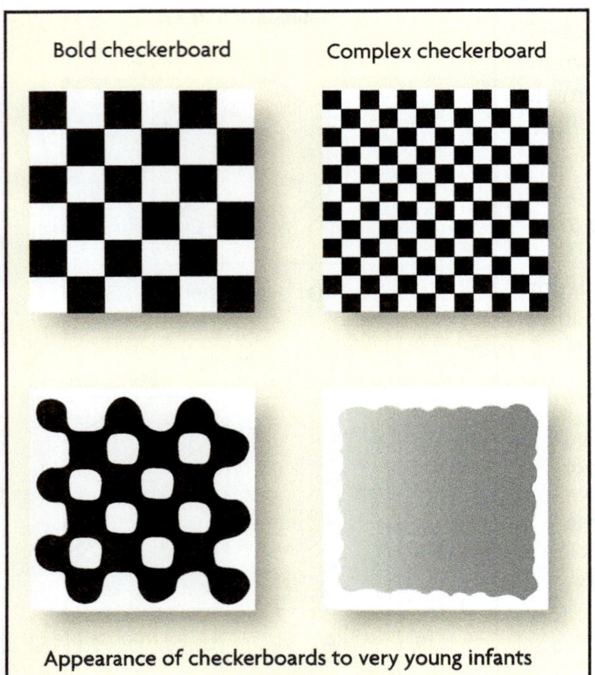

■ Figure 4.15 The way two checkerboards differing in complexity look to infants in the first few weeks of life.

Because of their poor vision, very young infants cannot resolve the fine detail in the *complex checkerboard.* It appears blurred, like a gray field. The large, *bold checkerboard* appears to have more contrast, so babies prefer to look at it. (Adapted from M. S. Banks & P. Salapatek, 1983, "Infant Visual Perception," in M. M. Haith & J. J. Campos [Eds.], *Handbook of Child Psychology: Vol. 2. Infancy and Developmental Psychobiology [4th ed.],* John Wiley & Sons, p. 504. Reprinted with permission of John Wiley & Sons, Inc.)

Biology *and* Environment

Development of Infants with Severe Visual Impairments

Research on infants who can see little or nothing at all dramatically illustrates the interdependence of vision, motor exploration, social interaction, and understanding of the world. In a longitudinal study, infants with a visual acuity of 20/800 or worse—that is, they had only dim light perception or were blind—were followed through the preschool years. Compared to agemates with less severe visual impairments, they showed serious delays in all aspects of development. Motor and cognitive functioning suffered the most; with age, performance in both domains became increasingly distant from that of other children (Hatton et al., 1997).

What explains these profound developmental delays? Minimal or absent vision can alter the child's experiences in at least two crucial, interrelated ways.

Impact on Motor Exploration and Spatial Understanding

Infants with severe visual impairments attain gross and fine motor milestones many months later than their sighted counterparts (Levtzion-Korach et al., 2000). For example, on average, blind infants do not reach for and manipulate objects until 12 months, crawl until 13 months, and walk until 19 months (compare these averages to the norms in the Milestones table on page 145). Why is this so?

Infants with severe visual impairments must rely on sound to identify the whereabouts of objects. But sound does not function as a precise clue to object location until much later than vision—around the middle of the first year (Litovsky & Ashmead, 1997). And because infants who cannot see have difficulty engaging their caregivers, adults may not provide them with rich early exposure to sounding objects. As a result, the baby comes to understand relatively late that there is a world of interesting objects to explore.

Until "reaching on sound" is achieved, infants with severe visual impairments are not motivated to move independently. Because of their own uncertainty coupled with their parents' protectiveness and restraint to prevent injury, blind infants are typically tentative in their movements. These factors delay motor development further.

Motor and cognitive development are closely linked, especially for infants with little or no vision. These babies build an understanding of the location and arrangement of objects in space only after reaching and crawling (Bigelow, 1992). Inability to imitate the motor actions of others presents additional challenges as these children get older, contributing to declines in motor and cognitive progress relative to peers with better vision (Hatton et al., 1997).

Impact on the Caregiver–Infant Relationship

Infants who see poorly have great difficulty evoking stimulating caregiver interaction. They cannot make eye contact, imitate, or pick up nonverbal social cues. Their emotional expressions are muted; for example, their smile is fleeting and unpredictable. And because they cannot gaze in the same direction as a partner, they are greatly delayed in establishing a shared focus of attention on objects as the basis for play (Bigelow, 2003). Consequently, these infants may receive little adult attention and other stimulation vital for all aspects of development.

When a visually impaired child does not learn how to participate in social interaction during infancy, communication is compromised in early childhood. In an observational study of blind children enrolled in preschools with sighted agemates, the blind children seldom initiated contact with peers and teachers. When they did interact, they had trouble interpreting the meaning of others' reactions and responding appropriately (Preisler, 1991, 1993).

Interventions

Parents, teachers, and caregivers can help infants with minimal vision overcome early developmental delays through stimulating, responsive interaction. Until a close emotional bond with an adult is forged, visually impaired babies cannot establish vital links with their environments.

As a result of complications from prematurity, this 2-year-old experienced nearly complete detachment of her retinas and has only minimal light perception. By guiding the child's exploration of a zither through touch and sound, a caregiver helps prevent the developmental delays often associated with severely impaired vision. Courtesy of Rich Kenney, Foundation for Blind Children

Techniques that help infants become aware of their physical and social surroundings include heightened sensory input through combining sound and touch (holding, touching, or bringing the baby's hands to the adult's face while talking or singing), engaging in many repetitions, and consistently reinforcing the infant's efforts to make contact. Manipulative play with objects that make sounds is also vital.

Finally, rich language stimulation can compensate for visual loss (Conti-Ramsden & Pérez-Pereira, 1999). It gives young children a ready means of finding out about objects, events, and behaviors they cannot see. Once language emerges, many children with limited or no vision show impressive rebounds. Some acquire a unique capacity for abstract thinking, and most master social and practical skills that permit them to lead productive, independent lives (Warren, 1994).

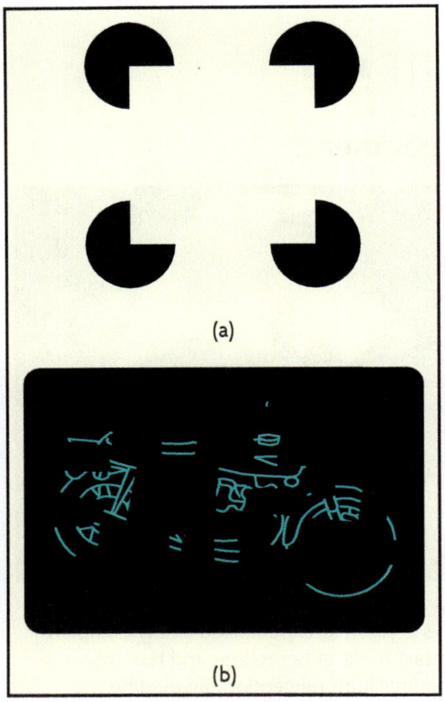

■ **Figure 4.16** **Subjective boundaries in visual patterns.** (a) Do you perceive a square in the middle of the top figure? By 4 months of age, infants do, too. (b) What does the image on the bottom, missing two-thirds of its outline, look like to you? By 12 months, infants detect the image of a motorcycle. After habituating to the incomplete motorcycle image, they were shown an intact motorcycle figure paired with a novel form. Twelve-month-olds recovered to (looked longer at) the novel figure, indicating that they recognized the motorcycle pattern on the basis of very little visual information. (Adapted from Ghim, 1990; Rose, Jankowski, & Senior, 1997.)

Combining Pattern Elements. In the early weeks of life, infants respond to the separate parts of a pattern. They stare at single, high-contrast features and have difficulty shifting their gaze away toward other interesting stimuli (Hunnius & Geuze, 2004a, 2004b). In exploring drawings of human faces, for example, 1-month-olds often limit themselves to the edges of the stimulus and focus on the hairline or chin. At 2 to 3 months, when contrast sensitivity improves and infants can better control their scanning, they thoroughly explore a pattern's internal features, pausing briefly to look at each salient part (Bronson, 1994). (Recall from page 142 that some babies continue to focus on small features and, therefore, take in less information.)

Babies' scanning also varies with pattern characteristics. When exposed to dynamic stimuli, such as the mother's nodding, smiling face, 6-week-olds fixate more on internal features (the mouth and eyes) than on edges. Furthermore, when stimuli are dynamic, development of scanning takes place over a longer period; thorough inspection of the entire stimulus emerges only after 4 months of age (Hunnius & Geuze, 2004b). And when presented with complex stimuli, such as a still frame or a video clip from the TV program *Sesame Street,* babies increase their inspection time over the second half-year as they try to make sense of the image (Courage, Reynolds, & Richards, 2006). Exploring complex patterns, especially those with moving stimuli, is more demanding than exploring simple stationary patterns—a difference we must keep in mind as we examine research on pattern perception, which is based largely on static stimuli.

Once babies take in all aspects of a pattern, they integrate the parts into a unified whole. Around 4 months, they are so good at detecting organization in basic, static patterns that they even perceive subjective boundaries that are not really present. For example, they perceive a square in the center of Figure 4.16a, just as you do (Ghim, 1990). Older infants carry this responsiveness to subjective form even further, applying it to complex, moving stimuli. For example, 9-month-olds look much longer at an organized series of moving lights that resembles a human being walking than at upside-down or scrambled versions (Bertenthal, 1993). At 12 months, infants detect familiar objects represented by incomplete drawings, even when as much as two-thirds of the drawing is missing (see Figure 4.16b) (Rose, Jankowski, & Senior, 1997). As these findings reveal, infants' increasing knowledge of objects and actions supports pattern perception.

• **Face Perception** Infants' tendency to search for structure in a patterned stimulus applies to face perception. Newborns prefer to look at photos and simplified drawings of faces with features arranged naturally (upright) rather than unnaturally (upside down or sideways) (see Figure 4.17a and b) (Cassia, Turati, & Simion, 2004; Mondloch et al., 1999). They also track a facelike pattern moving across their visual field farther than they track other stimuli (Johnson, 1999). And although their ability to distinguish real faces on the basis of inner features is limited, shortly after birth babies prefer photos of faces with eyes open and a direct gaze (Farroni et al., 2002). Yet another amazing capacity is their tendency to look longer at faces judged by adults as attractive, compared with less attractive ones—a preference that may be the origin of the widespread social bias favoring physically attractive people (Slater et al., 2000).

Some researchers claim that these behaviors reflect a built-in capacity to orient toward members of one's own species, just as many newborn animals do (Johnson, 2001; Slater & Quinn, 2001). In support of this view, the upright face preference occurs only when newborns view stimuli in the periphery of their visual field—an area of the retina governed by primitive brain centers (Cassia, Simion, & Umiltá, 2001). Others refute the claim that newborns have a special sensitivity to the facial pattern. Instead, they assert, newborns prefer any stimulus in which the most salient elements are arranged horizontally in the upper part of a pattern—like the "eyes" in Figure 4.17b. Indeed, newborns do prefer nonfacial patterns with these characteristics over other nonfacial arrangements (Simion et al., 2001; Turati, 2004). Possibly, however, a bias favoring the facial pattern promotes such preferences. Still other researchers argue that newborns are exposed to faces more often than to other stimuli—early experiences that could quickly "wire" the brain to detect faces and prefer attractive ones (Nelson, 2001).

Although newborns respond to a general, facelike structure, they cannot discriminate a complex, static image of the human face from other, equally complex configurations (see

Figure 4.17c). Nevertheless, from repeated exposures to their mother's face, they quickly learn to prefer her face to that of an unfamiliar woman, although they are sensitive only to its broad outlines, not its fine-grained features. Babies quickly apply their tendency to search for pattern to face perception. Around 2 months, when they can scan an entire stimulus and combine its elements into an organized whole, they recognize and prefer their mothers' facial features (Bartrip, Morton, & de Schonen, 2001). And they prefer a complex drawing of the human face to other complex stimulus arrangements (Dannemiller & Stephens, 1988).

Around 3 to 4 months, infants make fine distinctions between the features of different faces. For example, as long as eyes gaze directly at them (a characteristic that enhances face processing), 4-month-olds can tell the difference between the photos of two strangers, even when the faces are moderately similar (Farroni et al., 2007). At 5 months—and strengthening over the second half of the first year—infants perceive emotional expressions as meaningful wholes. They treat positive faces (happy or surprised) as different from negative ones (sad or fearful) (Bornstein & Arterberry, 2003; Ludemann, 1991). Around this time, babies rely increasingly on relational information to process faces. When researchers slightly alter the distance among the eyes and mouth in a photo of a face, 5-month olds detect that the face has changed (Hayden et al., 2007).

Experience influences face processing, leading babies to form group biases at a tender age. As early as 3 months, infants prefer and more easily discriminate among female faces than among male faces, probably because they typically spend much more time with female adults (Quinn et al., 2002; Ramsey-Rennels & Langlois, 2006). And 3-month-olds exposed mostly to members of their own race prefer to look at the faces of members of that race and more easily detect differences among those faces (Bar-Haim et al., 2006; Kelly et al., 2007). In contrast, babies who have frequent contact with members of other races show no own-race face preference.

Clearly, extensive face-to-face interaction between infants and their caregivers contributes to the refinement of face perception. As we will see in Chapter 10, babies' developing sensitivity to the human face supports their earliest social relationships and helps regulate exploration of the environment in adaptive ways.

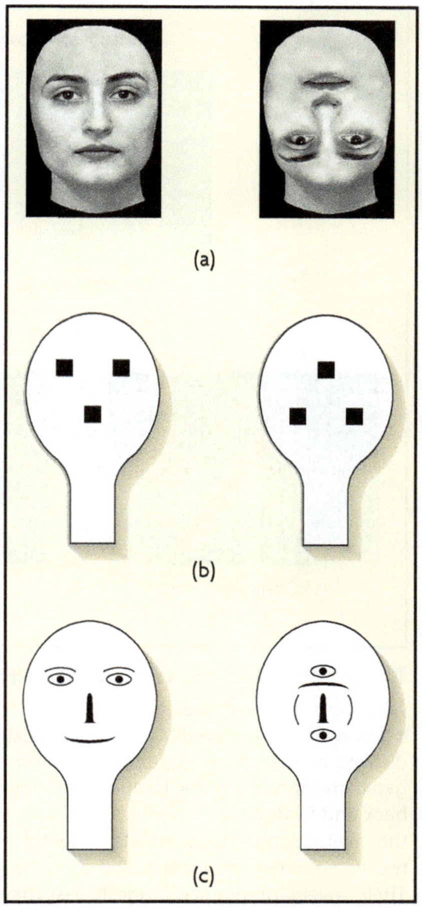

Figure 4.17 **Early face perception.**
(a) Newborns prefer to look at the photo of a face (a) and the simple pattern resembling a face (b) over the upside-down versions.
(c) When the complex drawing of a face on the left and the equally complex, scrambled version on the right are moved across newborns' visual field, they follow the face longer. But if the two stimuli are stationary, infants show no preference for the face until 2 months of age. (From Cassia, Turati, & Simion, 2004; Johnson, 1999; Mondloch et al., 1999.)

• Object Perception

Research on pattern perception involves only two-dimensional stimuli, but our environment is made up of stable, three-dimensional objects. Do young infants perceive a world of independently existing objects—knowledge essential for distinguishing the self, other people, and things?

Size and Shape Constancy. As we move around the environment, the images objects cast on our retina constantly change in size and shape. To perceive objects as stable and unchanging, we must translate these varying retinal images into a single representation.

Size constancy—perception of an object's size as stable, despite changes in the size of its retinal image—is evident in the first week of life. To test for it, researchers habituated infants to a small cube at varying distances from the eye, in an effort to desensitize them to changes in the cube's retinal image size and direct their attention to the object's actual size. When the small cube was presented together with a new, large cube—but at different distances so that they cast retinal images of the same size—all babies recovered to (looked longer at) the novel large cube, indicating that they distinguished objects on the basis of actual size, not retinal image size (Slater, 2001).

Perception of an object's shape as stable, despite changes in the shape projected on the retina, is called **shape constancy.** Habituation research reveals that it, too, is present within the first week of life, long before babies can actively rotate objects with their hands and view them from different angles (Slater & Johnson, 1999).

In sum, both size and shape constancy seem to be built-in capacities that help babies detect a coherent world of objects. Yet they provide only a partial picture of young infants' object perception.

Perception of Object Identity. As adults, we distinguish an object from its surroundings by looking for a regular shape and uniform texture and color. Very young infants, however, are not sensitive to these indicators of an object's boundaries. At first, they rely heavily on motion

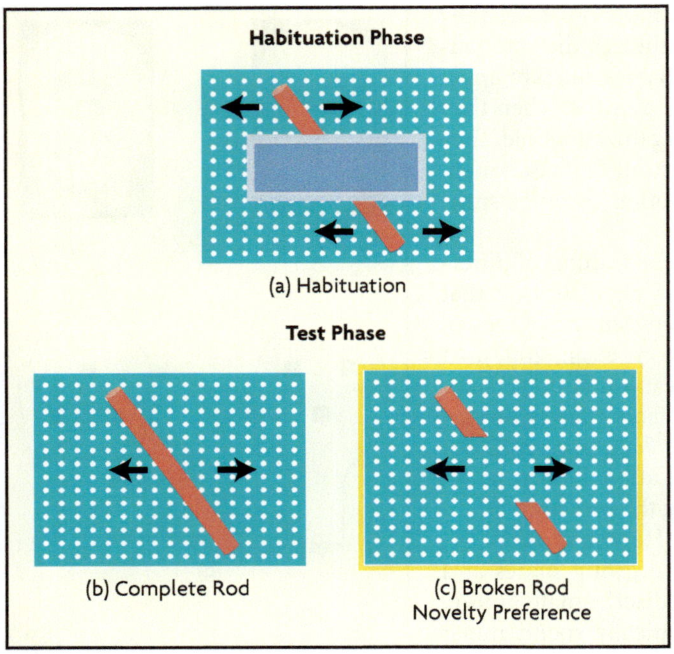

Figure 4.18 **Testing infants' ability to perceive object unity.**
(a) Infants were habituated to a rod moving back and forth behind a box against a textured background. Next, they were shown two test displays in alternation: (b) a complete rod and (c) a broken rod with a gap corresponding to the location of the box. Each stimulus was moved back and forth against the textured background, in the same way as the habituation stimulus. Infants 2 months of age and older typically recovered to (looked longer at) the broken rod than the complete rod. Their novelty preference suggests that they perceive the rod behind the box in the first display as a single unit. (Adapted from Johnson, 1997.)

and spatial arrangement to identify objects (Jusczyk et al., 1999; Spelke & Hermer, 1996). When two objects are touching and either move in unison or stand still, babies younger than 4 months cannot distinguish between them. Infants, as we saw earlier in this chapter, are fascinated by moving objects. As they observe objects' motions, they pick up additional information about objects' boundaries, such as shape, color, and texture.

For example, as Figure 4.18 reveals, around 2 months of age, babies first realize that a moving rod whose center is hidden behind a box is a complete rod rather than two rod pieces. Motion, a textured background, and a small box (so most of the rod is visible) are necessary for young infants to infer object unity. They need all these cues to heighten the distinction between objects in the display because their ability to scan for salient information is still immature (Amso & Johnson, 2006; Johnson et al., 2002).

As infants become familiar with many objects and can integrate each object's diverse features into a unified whole, they rely more on shape, color, and texture and less on motion (Cohen & Cashon, 2001). Babies as young as 4½ months can discriminate two touching objects on the basis of their features in simple, easy-to-process situations. And prior exposure to one of the test objects enhances 4½-month-olds' ability to discern the boundary between two touching objects—a finding that highlights the role of experience (Dueker, Modi, & Needham, 2003; Needham, 2001). In the second half of the first year, the capacity to distinguish objects on the basis of their features extends to increasingly complex displays of objects.

In everyday life, objects frequently move in and out of sight, so infants must keep track of their disappearance and reappearance to perceive their identity. To find out if infants can register an object's path of movement without seeing the entire path, researchers habituated babies to a ball moving back and forth behind a screen (see Figure 4.19). Recovery to test events revealed that as long as the ball was out of view only briefly, 4-month-olds (but not younger infants) perceived the ball's path as continuous rather than broken

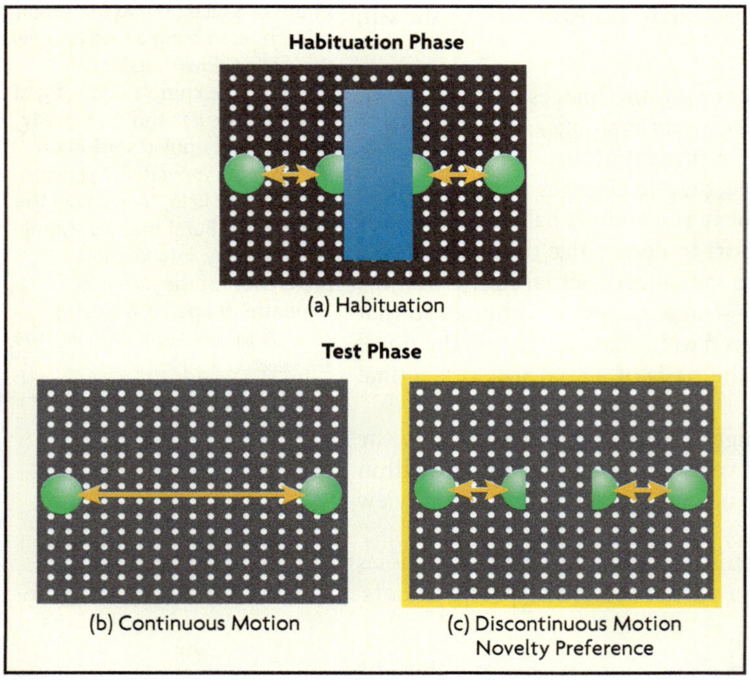

Figure 4.19 **Testing infants' ability to perceive an object's path of movement.**
(a) Infants were habituated to a ball moving back and forth behind a screen. Next, they were shown two test displays in alternation: (b) a ball undergoing continuous back-and-forth motion, with its full trajectory visible, and (c) a ball undergoing discontinuous motion, out of and back into view just as in the habituation stimulus, but without moving behind a visible screen. As long as the ball was out of sight only briefly in the habituation display, 4-month-olds typically recovered to (looked longer at) the discontinuous motion than the continuous motion. Their novelty preference suggests that they perceive the motion of the ball behind the screen in the first display as continuous. (From S. P. Johnson et al., 2003, "Infants' Perception of Object Trajectories," *Child Development,* 74, pp. 98, 101. © The Society for Research in Child Development, Inc. Reprinted by permission of Blackwell Publishing Ltd.)

(Johnson et al., 2003). Once again, experience—in particular, watching objects move in and out of view—contributes to this attainment (Johnson, Amso, & Slemmer, 2003). Between 4 and 5 months, infants can monitor increasingly intricate paths of objects. As indicated by their future-oriented eye movements (looking ahead to where they expect an object to appear from behind a barrier), 5-month-olds even keep track of an object that travels on a curvilinear course at varying speeds (Rosander & von Hofsten, 2004).

Notice that perception of *object unity* in the rod-and-box task (Figure 4.18) is mastered before perception of *an object's continuous path of movement* (Figure 4.19)—a more challenging task. We will revisit these attainments when we take up infants' understanding of object permanence—awareness that an object still exists when hidden—in Chapter 6.

The Milestones table on page 164 provides an overview of the vast changes in visual perception during the first year. Up to this point, we have considered the sensory systems one by one. Now let's examine their coordination.

Intermodal Perception

Our world provides rich, continuous *intermodal stimulation*—simultaneous input from more than one modality, or sensory system. In **intermodal perception,** we make sense of these running streams of light, sound, tactile, odor, and taste information by perceiving them as integrated wholes. We know, for example, that an object's shape is the same whether we see it or touch it; that lip movements are closely coordinated with the sound of a voice; that breaking a glass causes a sharp, crashing sound; and that the patter of footsteps signals the approach of a person.

Recall that in the first few days of life, babies turn in the general direction of a sound and reach for objects in a primitive way. These behaviors suggest that infants expect sight, sound, touch to go together. Research reveals that babies perceive input from different sensory systems in a unified way by detecting **amodal sensory properties**—information that is not specific to a single modality but that overlaps two or more sensory systems, such as rate, rhythm, duration, intensity, temporal synchrony (for vision and hearing), and texture and shape (for vision and touch). Consider, for example, the sight and sound of a bouncing ball or the face and voice of a speaking person. In each event, visual and auditory information are conveyed simultaneously and with the same rate, rhythm, duration, and intensity.

Within the first half-year, infants master a remarkable range of intermodal relationships. This 3-month-old, assisted by her mother, quickly picks up associations between the sights, sounds, and feel of toys.
© Laura Dwight Photography

Even newborns are impressive perceivers of amodal properties. After touching an object (such as a cylinder) placed in their palms, they recognize it visually, distinguishing it from a different-shaped object (Sann & Streri, 2007). And they require just one exposure to learn the association between the sight and sound of a toy, such as a rhythmically jangling rattle (Morrongiello, Fenwick, & Chance, 1998).

Within the first half-year, infants master a remarkable range of intermodal relationships. For example, they match the motions of a wide array of objects with their appropriate sounds. In one such study, 3- and 4-month-olds watched two films side by side—one with two blocks banging and the other with two sponges being squashed together—while hearing the sound track for only one of the films (either a sharp, banging noise or a soft, squishing noise). Infants looked at the film that went with the sound track (Bahrick, 1983). In similar research, infants matched faces with voices on the basis of lip–voice synchrony, emotional expression, and even age and gender of the speaker (Bahrick, Netto, & Hernandez-Reif, 1998; Walker-Andrews, 1997). In addition to detecting amodal properties, babies gradually learn many intermodal associations that are arbitrary, such as the relation between a person's face and the particular sound of his or her voice or between the appearance of an object and its verbal label. The detection of amodal relations precedes and seems to provide the foundation for these more specific intermodal matches (Bahrick, 2001; Bahrick, Hernandez-Reif, & Flom, 2005).

Milestones

Visual Development in Infancy

Age	Acuity, Color Perception, Focusing, and Exploration	Depth Perception	Pattern Perception	Object Perception
Birth–1 month	■ Visual acuity is 20/600. ■ Scans the visual field and tracks moving objects.	■ Responds to motion, blinking defensively when an object moves toward the face.	■ Prefers large, bold patterns. ■ Responds to separate parts of a pattern, focusing on single, high-contrast features. ■ Prefers to look at simplified drawings of facelike patterns and at photos of faces with eyes open and a direct gaze. ■ Shows preference for attractive faces over less attractive ones.	■ Displays size and shape constancy. 
2–3 months	■ Has adultlike focusing ability. ■ Scans more thoroughly and systematically. 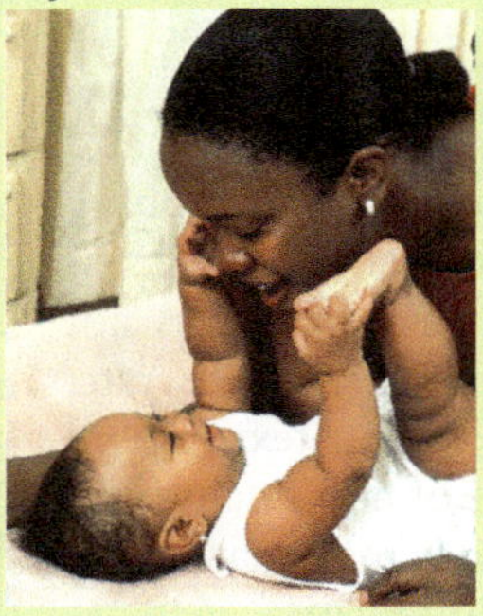	■ Responds to binocular depth cues.	■ Prefers patterns with finer details. ■ Thoroughly scans internal pattern features. ■ Begins to perceive overall pattern structure. ■ Prefers complex drawings of human face to other, equally complex stimulus arrangements. ■ Prefers female to male faces and more easily discriminates among them. ■ Recognizes and prefers mother's face and distinguishes faces of strangers, even when they are moderately similar.	■ Uses motion and spatial arrangement to identify objects. 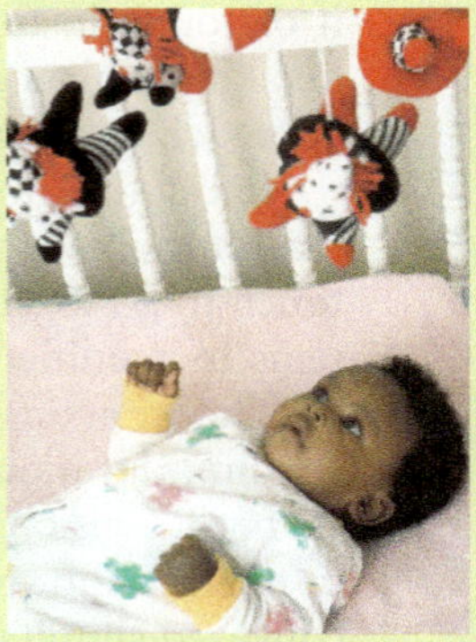
4–5 months	■ Color discrimination is adultlike.	■ Sensitivity to binocular depth cues improves. ■ Begins to respond to pictorial depth cues.	■ Perceives subjective boundaries in simple patterns. ■ Increasingly relies on relational information (such as distance among features) to differentiate faces. ■ Distinguishes emotionally positive from emotionally negative facial expressions.	■ Uses shape, color, and texture to identify objects. ■ Perceives an object's continuous path of movement without seeing the entire path. 
6–9 months	■ Visual acuity improves to near 20/20. ■ Scans the visual field and tracks moving objects more efficiently.	■ Responsiveness to pictorial depth cues improves. 	■ Improves at detecting subjective form in complex patterns. ■ Increasingly perceives facial expressions of emotion as meaningful wholes.	
10–12 months			■ Continues to improve at detecting subjective form: Detects familiar objects represented by incomplete drawings.	

Note: These milestones represent overall age trends. Individual differences exist in the precise age at which each milestone is attained.

Photos: (top) Courtesy of Jamie and Jeremy Friedberg; (second row left) © Laura Dwight Photography; (second row right) © Laura Dwight/PhotoEdit; (bottom left) © Geri Engberg Photography; (bottom right) Laura Dwight

Intermodal sensitivity is crucial for perceptual development. In the early months, infants detect amodal properties only when exposed to intermodal stimulation. For example, 3-month-olds discriminated a change in the rhythm of a toy hammer tapping from an audiovisual display, but not from a purely auditory presentation (just hearing the tapping) or a purely visual presentation (just seeing the hammer move) (Bahrick, Flom, & Lickliter, 2003). Intermodal stimulation makes amodal properties (such as rhythm) stand out. As a result, inexperienced perceivers notice a meaningful unitary event (the hammer's intricate tapping) and are not diverted to momentarily irrelevant aspects of the situation, such as the hammer's color or orientation. In contrast, young infants notice changes in purely visual properties, such as color, orientation, and pattern, only when exposed to purely visual information (Bahrick, Lickliter, & Flom, 2004). With experience, perceptual capacities become more flexible. In the second half of the first year, infants can discriminate amodal properties in both intermodal and unimodal (sights or sounds alone) stimulation. But early on, when much input is unfamiliar and confusing, intermodal stimulation helps babies selectively attend to and make sense of their surroundings.

In addition to easing infants' perception of the physical world, intermodal stimulation facilitates social and language processing, as evidence reviewed earlier in this chapter illustrates. Recall that an adult's gentle touch induces infants to attend to her face (see page 151). And as infants gaze at an adult's face, they initially require both vocal and visual input to distinguish positive from negative emotional expressions. Furthermore, in their earliest efforts to make sense of language, infants profit from temporal synchrony between a speech sound and the motion of an object (see page 153).

In sum, intermodal perception is a fundamental ability that fosters all aspects of psychological development. Early parent–infant interaction presents the baby with a rich context—consisting of many concurrent sights, sounds, touches, and smells—for expanding intermodal knowledge. And when provided with intermodal stimulation, babies process more information, learn faster, and show better memory (Lickliter & Bahrick, 2000). Intermodal perception is yet another capacity that illustrates infants' active efforts to build an orderly, predictable world.

Understanding Perceptual Development

Now that we have reviewed the development of infant perceptual capacities, how can we put together this diverse array of amazing achievements? Widely accepted answers come from the work of Eleanor and James Gibson. According to the Gibsons' **differentiation theory,** infants actively search for **invariant features** of the environment—those that remain stable—in a constantly changing perceptual world. In pattern perception, for example, young babies search for features that stand out and orient toward faces. Soon they explore internal features and notice *stable relationships* between those features. As a result, they detect patterns, such as complex designs and faces. Similarly, babies analyze the speech stream for regularities, detecting words, word-order sequences, and—within words—syllable-stress patterns. The development of intermodal perception also reflects this principle. Babies seek out invariant relationships—first, amodal properties, such as common rate and rhythm, in a voice and face; later, more detailed associations, such as unique voice–face matches.

The Gibsons use the word *differentiation* (where "differentiate" means "analyze" or "break down") because, over time, the baby detects finer and finer invariant features among stimuli. In addition to pattern perception and intermodal perception, differentiation applies to depth and object perception: Recall how, in each, sensitivity to motion precedes detection of fine-grained features. So one way of understanding perceptual development is to think of it as a built-in tendency to seek order and consistency—a capacity that becomes increasingly fine-tuned with age (Gibson, 1970; Gibson, 1979).

Acting on the environment is vital in perceptual differentiation. According to the Gibsons, perception is guided by the discovery of **affordances**—the action possibilities that a situation offers an organism with certain motor capabilities (Gibson, 2000, 2003). By moving

Figure 4.20 Acting on the environment plays a major role in perceptual differentiation. Crawling and walking change the way babies perceive a steeply sloping surface. The newly crawling infant on the left plunges headlong down the incline. He has not yet learned that it affords the possibility of falling. The toddler on the right, who has been walking for more than a month, approaches the slope cautiously. Experience in trying to remain upright but frequently tumbling over has made him more aware of the consequences of his movements. He perceives the incline differently than he did at a younger age.
Courtesy of Karen Adolph, New York University

about and exploring the environment, babies figure out which objects can be grasped, squeezed, bounced, or stroked and whether a surface is safe to cross or presents the possibility of falling. Sensitivity to these affordances means that we spend far less time correcting ineffective actions than we would otherwise because our actions are future-oriented and largely successful rather than reactive and blundering.

To illustrate, recall how infants' changing capabilities for independent movement affect their perception. When babies crawl, and again when they walk, they gradually realize that a steeply sloping surface *affords the possibility* of falling (see Figure 4.20). The more they practice each skill, the more they become hesitant to crawl or walk down a risky incline. Experience in trying to keep their balance on various surfaces seems to make crawlers and walkers more aware of the consequences of their movements. Crawlers come to detect when surface slant places so much body weight on their arms that they will fall forward, and walkers come to sense when an incline shifts body weight so their legs and feet can no longer hold them upright (Adolph & Berger, 2006). Each skill leads infants to perceive surfaces in new ways that guide their movements. As a result, they act more competently. **TAKE A MOMENT...** Can you think of other links between motor milestones and perceptual development described in this chapter?

To be fair, we should note that some researchers believe babies go beyond making sense of experience by searching for invariant features and discovering affordances: They also *impose meaning* on what they perceive, constructing categories of objects and events in the surrounding environment. We have seen the glimmerings of this *cognitive* point of view in this chapter. For example, older babies *interpret* a familiar face as a source of pleasure and affection and a pattern of blinking lights as a moving human being. We will save our discussion of infant cognition for later chapters, acknowledging that this cognitive perspective also offers insight into the achievements of infancy. In fact, many researchers combine these two positions, regarding infant development as proceeding from a perceptual to a cognitive emphasis over the first year of life.

Ask Yourself

Review Using examples, explain why intermodal stimulation is vital for infants' developing understanding of their physical and social worlds.

Apply After several weeks of crawling, Ben learned to avoid going headfirst down a steep incline. Now he has started to walk. Can his mother trust him not to try walking down the steep surface? Explain, using the concept of affordances.

Connect According to differentiation theory, perceptual development reflects infants' active search for invariant features. Provide examples from research on hearing, pattern perception, and intermodal perception.

Reflect Are young infants more competent than you believed before you read this chapter? List the capacities that most surprised you.

Early Deprivation and Enrichment: Is Infancy a Sensitive Period of Development?

Throughout this chapter, we have considered how a variety of early experiences affect the development of motor and perceptual skills. In view of the findings already reviewed, it is not surprising that many investigations have reported that stimulating physical surroundings and warm caregiving that is responsive to infants' self-initiated efforts promote active exploration of the environment and earlier attainment of developmental milestones (see, for example, Belsky & Fearon, 2002; Bendersky & Lewis, 1994).

The powerful effect of early experience is dramatically apparent in infants who lack the rich, varied stimulation of normal homes. Babies reared in severely deprived family situations or in institutions remain substantially below average in physical and psychological development and display emotional and behavior problems throughout childhood (Johnson, 2000). These findings indicate that early experience has a profound impact, but they do not tell us whether infancy is a *sensitive period.* That is, if babies do not experience appropriate stimulation of their senses in the first year or two of life, can they fully recover? This question is controversial. Recall from Chapter 1 that some theorists argue that early experience leaves a lasting imprint on the child's competence. Others believe that most developmental delays resulting from events in the first few years of life can be overcome.

Studies of animals exposed to extreme forms of sensory deprivation provide ample evidence that sensitive periods exist. For example, early, varied visual experiences must occur for the brain's visual centers to develop normally. If a 1-month-old kitten is deprived of light for just three or four days, these areas of the brain degenerate. If the kitten is kept in the dark during the fourth week of life and beyond, the damage is severe and permanent (Crair, Gillespie, & Stryker, 1998). And the general quality of the early environment affects overall brain growth. When animals reared from birth in physically and socially stimulating surroundings are compared with those reared in isolation, the brains of the stimulated animals are larger (Greenough & Black, 1992).

For ethical reasons, we cannot deliberately deprive some infants of normal rearing experiences and observe the impact on their brains and competencies. Instead, we must turn to natural experiments, in which children were victims of deprived early environments that were later rectified. Such studies have revealed some parallels with the animal evidence just described.

For example, when babies are born with cataracts (clouded lenses, preventing clear visual images) in both eyes, those who have corrective surgery within four to six months show rapid improvement in vision, except for subtle aspects of face perception, which require early visual input to the cerebral cortex to preserve structures that enable them to develop later on (Le Grand et al., 2003; Maurer, Mondloch, & Lewis, 2007). The longer cataract surgery is postponed beyond infancy, the less complete the recovery in visual skills. And if surgery is delayed until adulthood, vision is severely and permanently impaired (Maurer et al., 1999).

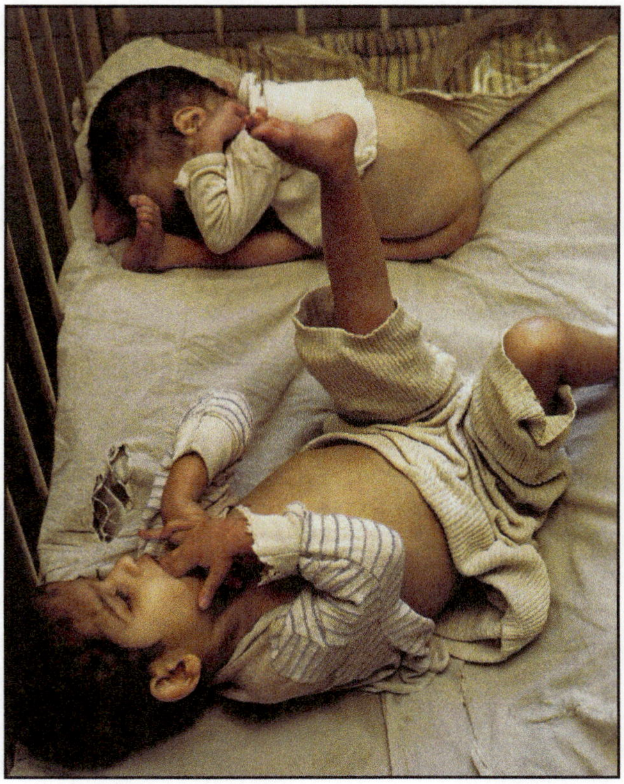

These children in an orphanage in Romania receive very little adult contact or stimulation. The longer they remain in this barren environment, the more they will withdraw and wither, displaying profound impairment in all domains of development. © Andrew Holbrooke/CORBIS

Studies of infants placed in orphanages who were later exposed to family rearing confirm the importance of a generally stimulating physical and social environment for psychological development. In one investigation, researchers followed the progress of a large sample of children transferred between birth and 3½ years from Romanian orphanages to adoptive families in Great Britain (Beckett et al., 2006; O'Connor et al., 2000; Rutter et al., 1998, 2004). On arrival, most were impaired in all domains of development. By the preschool years, catch-up in physical size was dramatic. Cognitive catch-up, assessed at ages 6 and 11, was impressive for children adopted before age 6 months, who attained average mental test scores, performing as well as a comparison group of early-adopted British-born children. But Romanian children who had been institutionalized for more than the first six months showed serious intellectual deficits (see Figure 4.21). Although they improved in mental test scores during middle childhood (perhaps as a result of added time in their adoptive homes and special services at school), they remained substantially below average. And most displayed at least three serious mental health problems, such as inattention, overactivity, and unruly behavior—serious adjustment difficulties seldom seen in children adopted prior to age 6 months (Kreppner et al., 2007).

Among institutionalized infants, abnormal development in one domain often impedes progress in others. For example, adoptive parents of children from orphanages often report visual impairments. A frequent problem is *strabismus* ("crossed eyes"), in which the eyes, because of muscle weakness, do not converge on the same point in space. Untreated infants, for whom strabismus persists longer than a few months, show abnormalities in the brain's visual structures and permanent deficits in visual acuity, depth perception, tracking of moving objects, and perception of the spatial layout of the environment (Tychsen, 2001). Also, the bland, colorless rooms where orphanage infants spend their days, rarely touched or spoken to, lead to deficits in intermodal perception (Cermak & Daunhauer, 1997). Children who have trouble integrating information across modalities tend to be overwhelmed by stimulation, reacting to it with disorganized behavior or withdrawal. As a result, motor, cognitive, and social development suffers.

Unfortunately, many infants reared in underprivileged environments—whether homes or institutions—continue to be affected by disadvantaged conditions during their childhood years. As we will see in later chapters, interventions that break this pattern with warm, stimulating caregiver interaction and environmental enrichment have lasting cognitive and social benefits. One of the most important outcomes is that withdrawn, apathetic babies become

Figure 4.21 **Relationship of age at adoption to mental test scores at ages 6 and 11 among British and Romanian adoptees.**

Children transferred from Romanian orphanages to British adoptive homes in the first six months of life attained average scores and fared as well as British early-adopted children, suggesting that they had fully recovered from extreme early deprivation. Romanian children adopted after 6 months of age performed well below average. And although those adopted after age 2 improved between ages 6 and 11, they continued to show serious intellectual deficits. (Adapted from Beckett et al., 2006.)

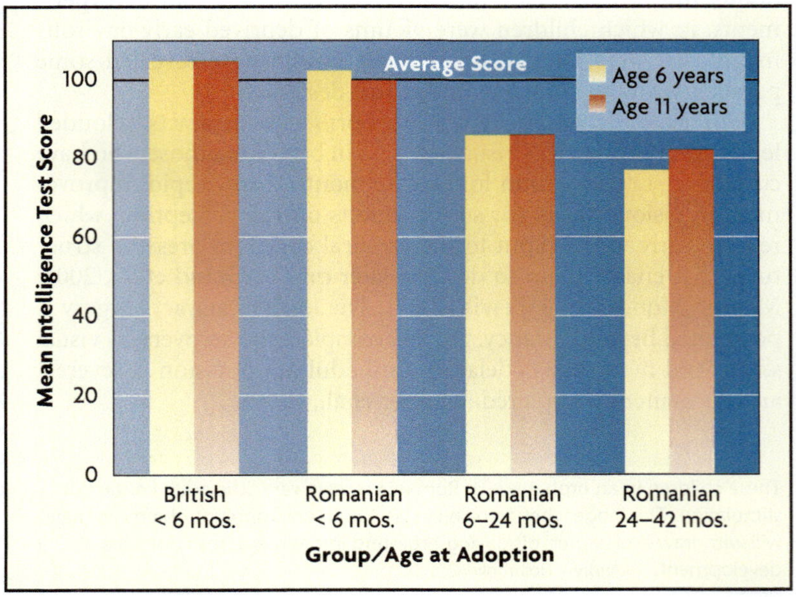

active and alert and, therefore, capable of evoking positive interactions from caregivers and initiating stimulating play and exploration for themselves.

Finally, in addition to impoverished environments, ones that overwhelm children with expectations beyond their current capacities also undermine development. In recent years, expensive early learning centers have sprung up, in which infants are trained with letter and number flash cards, and slightly older toddlers are given a full curriculum of reading, math, science, art, gym, and more. There is no evidence that these programs yield smarter, better "superbabies" (Hirsh-Pasek & Golinkoff, 2003). To the contrary, trying to prime infants with stimulation for which they are not ready can cause them to withdraw, threatening their spontaneous interest and pleasure in learning and creating conditions much like those of stimulus deprivation! We will return to this theme when we take up brain development in Chapter 5.

Ask Yourself

Review Explain why either too much stimulation or too little stimulation over an extended time negatively affects infant development.

Connect What implications do findings on children from Eastern European orphanages have for the controversy over the lasting impact of early experiences on development (see Chapter 1, page 9)?

Reflect Do you think infancy is a sensitive period? Explain, using research evidence.

SUMMARY

The Organized Newborn

Explain the functions of newborn reflexes, and describe changing states of arousal during infancy, emphasizing sleep and crying.

- **Reflexes** are the newborn baby's most obvious organized patterns of behavior. Some have survival value, others help parents and infants establish gratifying interaction, and still others provide the foundation for voluntary motor skills.

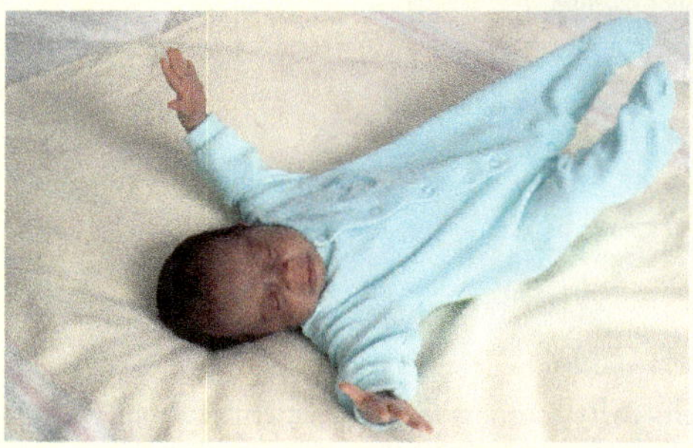
© Jeffrey L. Rotman/Corbis

- Newborns alternate frequently between five **states of arousal,** but spend most of their time asleep. Sleep consists of at least two states: **rapid-eye-movement (REM)** and **non-rapid-eye-movement (NREM) sleep.** Newborns spend more time in REM sleep than they will at any later age. This state provides stimulation essential for central nervous system development and ensures that structures of the eye remain oxygenated during sleep. Individual and cultural differences in sleep–wake patterns are evident in early infancy. Disturbed REM–NREM cycles are a sign of central nervous system abnormalities, which may contribute to **sudden infant death syndrome (SIDS).**

- A baby's crying stimulates strong feelings of discomfort in nearby adults. The intensity of the cry and experiences leading up to it help parents identify what is wrong. Once feeding and diaper changing have been tried, the most effective soothing technique is lifting the baby to the shoulder and rocking or walking; swaddling is also effective. Ethological research indicates that parental responsiveness to infant crying leads to less crying over time. A shrill, piercing cry may signal central nervous system distress.

Why is neonatal behavioral assessment useful?

- The most widely used instrument for assessing the organized functioning of newborn infants is Brazelton's **Neonatal Behavioral Assessment Scale (NBAS).** It helps researchers understand individual and cultural differences in newborn behavior and can also be used to teach parents about their baby's capacities so they interact more confidently and sensitively. The Neonatal Intensive Care Unit Network Neurobehavioral Scale (NNNS) may be used with newborns at risk for developmental problems.

Describe infant learning capacities, the conditions under which they occur, and the unique value of each.

- Through **classical conditioning,** infants recognize which events usually occur together in the everyday world. In this form of learning, a neutral stimulus is paired with an **unconditioned stimulus (UCS)** that produces a reflexive, or **unconditioned, response (UCR).** Once learning has occurred, the neutral stimulus, now called the **conditioned stimulus (CS),** alone elicits a similar response, the **conditioned response (CR). Extinction** occurs when the CS is presented alone enough times to result in a decline of the CR. Young infants are most easily classically conditioned when the association between a UCS and a CS has survival value.

- **Operant conditioning** helps infants explore and control their surroundings. In addition to food, interesting sights and sounds serve as **reinforcers,** increasing the occurrence of a preceding behavior. **Punishment** involves removing a desirable stimulus or presenting an unpleasant one to decrease the occurrence of a response. With age, operant conditioning expands to include a wider range of stimuli and responses. It has yielded important information about infant memory, revealing that retention of operant responses increases dramatically over the first 18 months.
- **Habituation** and **recovery** reveal that at birth, babies are attracted to novelty. With age, infants habituate and recover more quickly. Novelty preference assesses infants' recent memory, whereas familiarity preference assesses their remote memory. Habituation research shows that young infants are especially attracted to motion and remember the movements of objects and people for weeks to months. Speed of habituation and recovery in infancy are among the best early predictors of intelligence in childhood, adolescence, and young adulthood because they assess memory and quickness and flexibility of thinking—basic elements of intelligent behavior.

© Geri Engberg/The Image Works

- Newborn infants have a primitive ability to **imitate** adults' facial expressions and gestures. Some researchers regard newborn imitation as little more than an automatic response to specific stimuli.Others view it as a flexible, voluntary capacity, believing that newborns actively try to match movements they see with those they feel themselves make. Research suggests that **mirror neurons** in primates are the biological basis of imitation and other complex social abilities.

Motor Development in Infancy

Describe the course of gross and fine motor development during the first two years, along with factors that influence it.

- Motor development follows the **cephalocaudal** and **proximodistal trends** with some dramatic exceptions. For example, infants reach with their feet before reaching with their hands. According to **dynamic systems theory of motor development,** new motor skills develop as existing skills combine into increasingly complex systems of action. Each new skill is a joint product of central nervous system development, the body's movement possibilities, the child's goals, and environmental supports for the skill.
- Motor development benefits from movement opportunities and a stimulating environment, as shown by research on infants raised in institutions. Cultural values and child-rearing customs also contribute to development of motor skills.
- The newborn's poorly coordinated **prereaching** eventually drops out. Over the first year, as depth perception and control of body posture and arm and hand movements improve, reaching and grasping become more flexible and accurate. Gradually, the clumsy **ulnar grasp** becomes the well-coordinated **pincer grasp.**

Perceptual Development in Infancy

Describe the newborn baby's senses of touch, taste, smell, and hearing, noting changes during infancy.

- Newborns are highly sensitive to touch and pain, with preterm infants and males showing stronger pain reactions. Newborns prefer a sweet taste and certain sweet odors. Around 4 months, liking for the salty taste emerges and probably supports acceptance of solid foods. Young infants' taste preferences can be easily modified.
- Newborns' odor preferences are influenced by the impact of the pregnant mother's diet on the amniotic fluid. Newborns orient toward the odor of their own mother's amniotic fluid and that of the lactating breast—responses that help them identify their caregiver and locate an appropriate food source.
- Over the first year, infants organize sounds into complex patterns. Between 4 and 7 months, they show a sense of musical phrasing. Around 6 to 7 months, they can distinguish musical tunes on the basis of variations in rhythmic patterns. At the end of the first year, they recognize the same melody when it is played in different keys.
- Newborns can distinguish almost all speech sounds. They prefer listening to slow, clear, high-pitched expressive voices, to their own mother's voice, and to speech in their native language. By the middle of the first year, they become more sensitive to the sounds of their own language.
- Infants' impressive **statistical learning capacity** enables them to analyze the speech stream for patterns. As a result, they acquire many speech structures for which they will later learn meanings. In the second half-year, babies detect word boundaries and, soon after, syllable-stress regularities within words. They also detect simple word-order rules that may help them figure out the basic grammar of their language. Multisensory communication, such as mothers' tendency to label an object while demonstrating, supports infants' language learning.

Describe the development of vision in infancy, with special emphasis on depth, pattern, and object perception.

- Vision is the newborn baby's least developed sense. As the eye and visual centers in the brain develop during the first few months, focusing ability, **visual acuity,** scanning, tracking, and color perception improve rapidly.
- The earliest research on depth perception used the **visual cliff** to investigate babies' ability to distinguish deep from shallow surfaces. Recent research has examined babies' ability to detect specific depth cues. Responsiveness to motion develops first, followed by sensitivity to binocular and then to pictorial depth cues. Experience in crawling facilitates coordination of action with depth information, while also promoting other aspects of three-dimensional understanding and a new level of brain organization.

© Myrleen Ferguson Cate/PhotoEdit

- **Contrast sensitivity** accounts for early pattern preferences. At first, babies stare at single, high-contrast features, often limiting themselves to the edges of a static pattern. At 2 to 3 months, they explore a pattern's internal features and, over time, discriminate increasingly complex, meaningful patterns. By 12 months, they extract a meaningful pattern from an incomplete drawing with as much as two-thirds missing.
- Newborns prefer to look at photos and simplified drawings of faces, at faces with eyes open and a direct gaze, and at faces that adults judge as attractive. But researchers disagree on whether they have a built-in tendency to orient toward human faces. Newborns are sensitive to the broad outlines of their mother's face; at 2 months, they recognize and prefer her facial features. Around 3 to 4 months, infants make fine distinctions between the features of different faces, and at 5 months, they perceive emotional expressions as meaningful wholes. Experience influences face

processing, leading babies to form group biases—for example, a preference for female faces.

- At birth, **size** and **shape constancy** helps infants construct a coherent world of three-dimensional objects. Initially, infants depend on motion and spatial arrangement to identify objects. After 4 months, they rely increasingly on other features, such as distinct color, shape, and texture. Around this time, they register the continuous path of movement of an object that moves in and out of sight and gradually monitor increasingly intricate paths of moving objects.

Describe infants' capacity for intermodal perception, and explain differentiation theory of perceptual development.

- Infants' remarkable capacity to engage in **intermodal perception** enables them to perceive input from different sensory systems in a unified way. Newborns are sensitive to **amodal sensory properties,** such as rate, rhythm, duration, intensity, and temporal synchrony (for vision and hearing) and texture and shape (for vision and touch). They quickly master many intermodal associations. Detection of amodal relations precedes and may provide a basis for detection of other intermodal matches.
- Intermodal stimulation helps young babies selectively attend to meaningful unitary events. It is a fundamental ability that fosters all aspects of psychological development, including perception of the physical world and social and language processing.
- According to **differentiation theory,** perceptual development occurs as infants actively search for increasingly fine-grained **invariant features**—those that remain stable—in a constantly changing perceptual world. Perception is guided by discovery of **affordances**—the action possibilities a situation offers an organism with certain motor capabilities.

Early Deprivation and Enrichment: Is Infancy a Sensitive Period of Development?

How does research on early deprivation and enrichment shed light on the question of whether infancy is a sensitive period of development?

- Evidence that infancy is a sensitive period comes from natural experiments on children born with cataracts in both eyes who later had corrective surgery, and on babies placed in orphanages who were later adopted into families. The later children are removed from deprived rearing conditions, the less favorably they develop. Romanian children who spent their first six months or more in unstimulating institutions displayed serious, persistent intellectual impairments and mental health problems. Environments that overwhelm infants with stimulation beyond their current capacities also undermine development.

IMPORTANT TERMS AND CONCEPTS

5

"My Bicycle"
Nada Fridmanovà
8 years, Czech Republic

This painting of an energetic young bicyclist in dazzling surroundings celebrates the rapid gains in strength, endurance, and coordination of the school years, which support children's expanding activities and relationships.

Physical Growth

On Sabrina's eleventh birthday, her friend Joyce gave her a surprise party, but Sabrina seemed somber during the celebration. Although Sabrina and Joyce had been close friends since third grade, their relationship was faltering. Sabrina was a head taller and some 20 pounds heavier than most girls in her sixth-grade class. Her breasts were well-developed, her hips and thighs had broadened, and she had begun to menstruate. In contrast, Joyce still had the short, lean, flat-chested body of a school-age child.

Ducking into the bathroom while the other girls put candles on the cake, Sabrina looked herself over in the mirror and frowned. "I feel so big and heavy," she whispered. At church youth group on Sunday evenings, Sabrina broke away from Joyce and spent time with the eighth-grade girls. Around them, she didn't feel so large and awkward.

Once a month, parents gathered at Sabrina's and Joyce's school for discussions about child-rearing concerns. Sabrina's parents, Franca and Antonio, attended whenever they could. "How you know they are becoming teenagers is this," volunteered Antonio. "The bedroom door is closed, and they want to be alone. Also, they contradict and disagree. I say something to Sabrina, and the next moment she is arguing with me."

"All our four children were early developers," Franca added. "The three boys, too, were tall by age 12 or 13, but it was easier for them—it made them feel big and important. Sabrina is moody, she doesn't want to be with her old friends, and she thinks about boys instead of her studies. As a little girl, she was skinny, but now she says she is too fat, and she wants to diet. I try to be patient with her," reflected Franca sympathetically.

During the first two decades of life, the human body changes continuously and dramatically. The average individual's height multiplies more than threefold, and weight increases as much as 15- to 20-fold. The top-heavy, chubby infant, whose head represents a quarter of the body's total length, gradually becomes the better-proportioned child and eventually the taller, broader, more muscular teenager. This chapter traces the course of human growth, along with biological and environmental factors that regulate and control it.

As Sabrina's behavior indicates, physical and psychological development are closely linked. But just how the child's transforming body is related to cognitive, emotional, and social changes has puzzled philosophers and scientists for centuries. In particular, they have pondered this question with respect to *puberty*. Ask several parents of young children what they expect their sons and daughters to be like as teenagers, and you are likely to get answers like these: "Rebellious and reckless," "Full of rages and tempers" (Buchanan & Holmbeck, 1998).

This widespread view dates back to eighteenth-century philosopher Jean-Jacques Rousseau (see Chapter 1), who believed that the biological upheaval of puberty triggered heightened emotionality, conflict, and defiance of adults. In the early twentieth century, major theorists picked up this perspective. The most influential was G. Stanley Hall, who described adolescence as a cascade of instinctual passions, a phase of growth so turbulent that it resembled the period in which human beings evolved from savages into civilized beings.

Were Rousseau and Hall correct in seeing adolescence as a period of biologically engendered storm and stress? Or do social and cultural factors combine with biology to influence psychological development? In our discussion, we will see what contemporary research says about this issue.

The Course of Physical Growth

Compared with other animals, primates (including humans) experience a prolonged period of physical growth. Mice and rats develop from birth to puberty in just a few weeks—about 2 percent of the lifespan. By contrast, in chimpanzees, the species most similar to humans genetically, growth takes about seven years, or 16 percent of the lifespan. Physical immaturity is even more exaggerated in humans, who devote about 20 percent of their total years to growing. This prolonged physical immaturity is adaptive: By ensuring that children remain dependent on adults, it gives them added time to acquire the knowledge and skills essential for life in a complex social world.

Changes in Body Size

The most obvious signs of physical growth are changes in overall body size. During infancy, these changes are rapid—faster than at any other time after birth. By the end of the first year, a typical infant's height is 50 percent greater than at birth; by 2 years, it is 75 percent greater. Similarly, birth weight typically doubles by age 5 months, triples by 1 year, and quadruples by age 2. If children kept growing at this rate, by age 10 they would be 10 feet tall and weigh over 200 pounds! Fortunately, growth slows in early and middle childhood, when children add about 2 to 3 inches in height and 5 pounds in weight each year. Then, puberty brings a sharp acceleration. On average, adolescents gain 10 to 11 inches in height and about 50 to 75 pounds in weight.

Two types of growth curves are used to track overall changes in body size. The first, shown in Figure 5.1a, is a **distance curve,** which plots the average size of a sample of children at each

Figure 5.1 Distance and velocity curves for height. (a) The *distance curve* plots average size at each age and shows typical yearly progress toward maturity. (b) The *velocity curve* plots average amount of growth at each yearly interval and reveals the timing of growth spurts. The curves are based on cross-sectional height measurements taken on thousands of U.S. children. Canada does not have a system for collecting nationally representative growth information and commonly relies on the U.S. norms. (Dietitians of Canada et al., 2004; U.S. Department of Health and Human Services, 2000.)

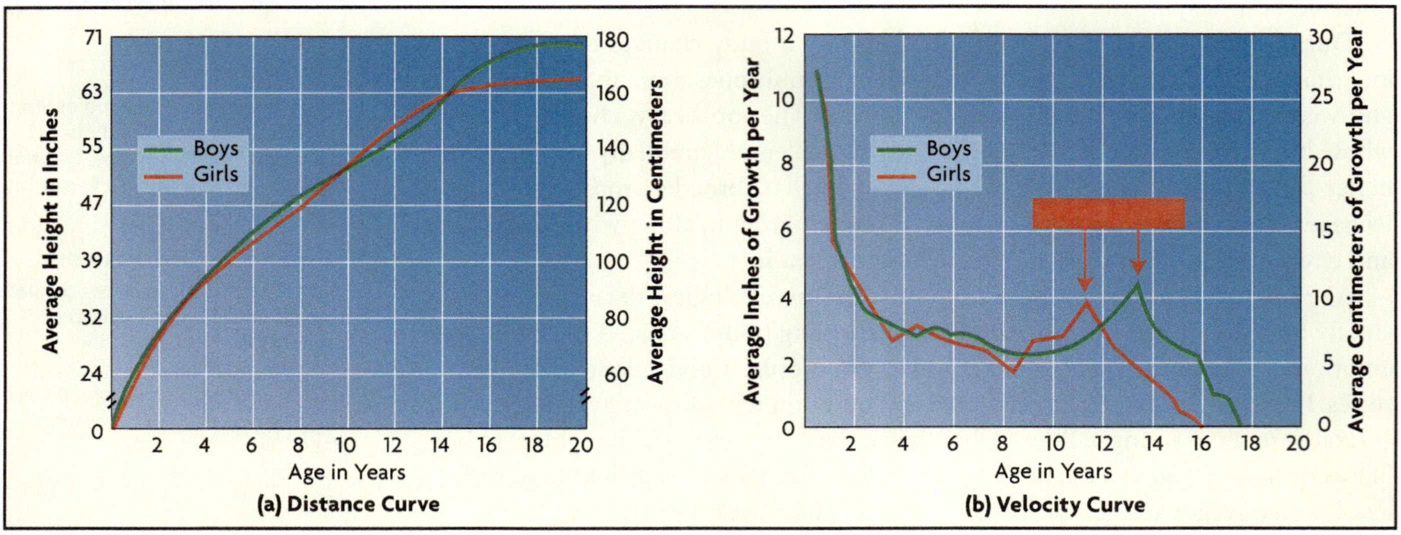

age, indicating typical yearly progress toward maturity. The figure shows gains in height; weight gain follows a similar trend. Notice how during infancy and childhood the two sexes are similar, with the typical girl just slightly shorter (and lighter) than the typical boy. Around age 10 to 11, the typical North American and European girl becomes taller (and heavier) for a time because her pubertal growth spurt takes place two years earlier than the boy's (Archibald, Graber, & Brooks-Gunn, 2006; Bogin, 2001). At age 14, however, she is surpassed by the typical boy, whose growth spurt has now started, whereas hers is almost finished. Growth in height is complete for most North American and European girls by age 16, for boys by age 17½.

Figure 5.1b shows a second type of growth curve, the **velocity curve,** which plots the average amount of growth at each yearly interval, revealing the exact timing of growth spurts. Note the rapid but decelerating growth in infancy; a slower, constant rate during early and middle childhood; and a sharp increase in early adolescence, followed by a swift decrease as the body approaches its adult size.

This comparison between a 4-month-old and a 2-year-old illustrates the dramatic rate of body growth during the first two years. Height increases by 75 percent, and weight quadruples. © Barbara Peacock/CORBIS

Changes in Body Proportions

As the child's overall size increases, parts of the body grow at different rates. Recall from Chapter 3 that during the prenatal period, the head develops first from the primitive embryonic disk, followed by the lower part of the body. After birth, the head and chest continue to have a growth advantage, but the trunk and legs gradually pick up speed. Do you recognize the familiar *cephalocaudal trend,* or head-to-tail sequence, discussed in Chapter 4? Physical growth during infancy and childhood also follows the *proximodistal trend,* from the center of the body outward. The head, chest, and trunk grow first, then the arms and legs, finally the hands and feet.

During puberty, growth proceeds in the reverse direction. The hands, legs, and feet accelerate first, followed by the torso, which accounts for most of the adolescent height gain (Sheehy et al., 1999). This pattern helps explain why young adolescents often appear awkward and out of proportion—long-legged, with giant feet and hands.

In infancy and childhood, girls and boys have similar body proportions. During adolescence, however, large differences appear, caused by the action of sex hormones on the skeleton. Boys' shoulders broaden relative to the hips, whereas girls' hips broaden relative to the shoulders and waist. Of course, boys also end up larger than girls, and their legs are longer in relation to the rest of the body—mainly because boys have two extra years of preadolescent growth, when the legs are growing the fastest.

Changes in Muscle–Fat Makeup

Body fat (most of which lies just beneath the skin) increases in the last few weeks of prenatal life and continues to do so after birth, reaching a peak at about 9 months of age. This early rise in "baby fat" helps the infant keep a constant body temperature. Starting in the second year and continuing into middle childhood, most toddlers slim down (Fomon & Nelson, 2002). At birth, girls have slightly more body fat than boys, a difference that persists into the early school years, then magnifies. Around age 8, girls start to add more fat on their arms, legs, and trunk; they continue to do so throughout puberty, while the arm and leg fat of adolescent boys decreases (Siervogel et al., 2000).

Muscle accumulates slowly throughout infancy and childhood, with a dramatic rise at adolescence. Both sexes gain muscle at puberty, but this increase is 150 percent greater in boys, who develop larger skeletal muscles, hearts, and lung capacity (Rogol, Roemmich, & Clark, 2002). Also, the number of red blood cells—and therefore the ability to carry oxygen from the lungs to the muscles—increases in boys but not in girls. Altogether, boys gain far more muscle strength than girls, contributing to their superior athletic performance during the teenage years (Ramos et al., 1998).

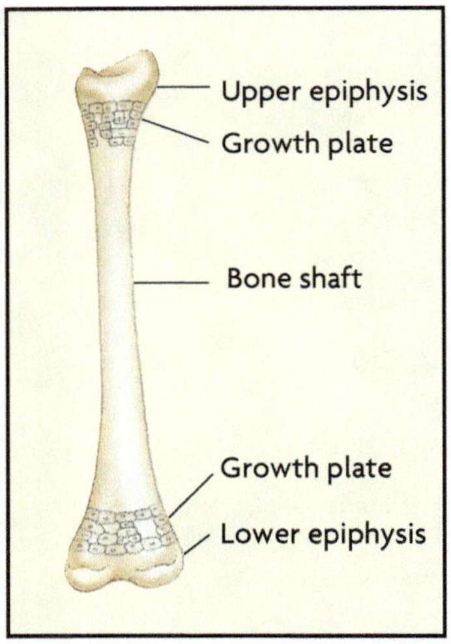

Figure 5.2 **Diagram of a long bone showing upper and lower epiphyses.**

Cartilage cells are produced at the growth plates of the epiphyses and gradually harden into bone. (From J. M. Tanner, *Foetus into Man* [2nd ed.], Cambridge, MA: Harvard University Press, p. 32. Copyright © 1990 by J. M. Tanner. All rights reserved. Reprinted by permission of the publisher and author.)

Skeletal Growth

Because children of the same age differ in *rate* of physical growth, researchers have devised methods for measuring progress toward physical maturity that are useful for studying the causes and consequences of these individual differences. The best estimate of a child's physical maturity is **skeletal age**—a measure of development of the bones of the body. The embryonic skeleton is first formed out of soft, pliable tissue called *cartilage.* In the sixth week of pregnancy, cartilage cells begin to harden into bone, a gradual process that continues throughout childhood and adolescence (Moore & Persaud, 2008).

Just before birth, special growth centers in the bones, called **epiphyses,** appear at the extreme ends of each of the body's long bones (see Figure 5.2). Cartilage cells continue to be produced at the growth plates of these epiphyses, which increase in number throughout childhood and then, as growth continues, get thinner and disappear. After that, no further growth in bone length is possible. As Figure 5.3 shows, skeletal age can be estimated by X-raying the bones to determine the number of epiphyses and the extent to which they are fused.

African-American children tend to be slightly ahead of Caucasian-American children in skeletal age. And girls are considerably ahead of boys—a gap of about four to six weeks at birth, which widens over infancy and childhood (Tanner, Healy, & Cameron, 2001). Girls are advanced in development of other organs as well. This greater physical maturity may contribute to girls' greater resistance to harmful environmental influences. As noted in Chapter 3, girls experience fewer developmental problems than boys and also have lower infant and childhood mortality rates.

Gains in Gross Motor Skills

Changes in size, proportions, and muscle strength support an explosion of new gross motor skills. As the body becomes more streamlined and less top-heavy, the center of gravity shifts downward, toward the trunk. The resulting improvement in balance paves the way for new motor skills involving large muscles.

• **Advances in Early and Middle Childhood** By age 2, preschoolers' gaits become smooth and rhythmic—secure enough that they soon leave the ground, first by running and jumping and then, between 3 and 6 years, by hopping, galloping, and skipping. Eventually, upper and lower body skills combine into more effective actions (Haywood & Getchell, 2005). Whereas 2- and 3-year-olds throw a ball rigidly, using only the arms, 4- and 5-year-olds use a smooth, flexible motion, involving the shoulders, torso, trunk, and legs, that makes the ball travel faster and farther.

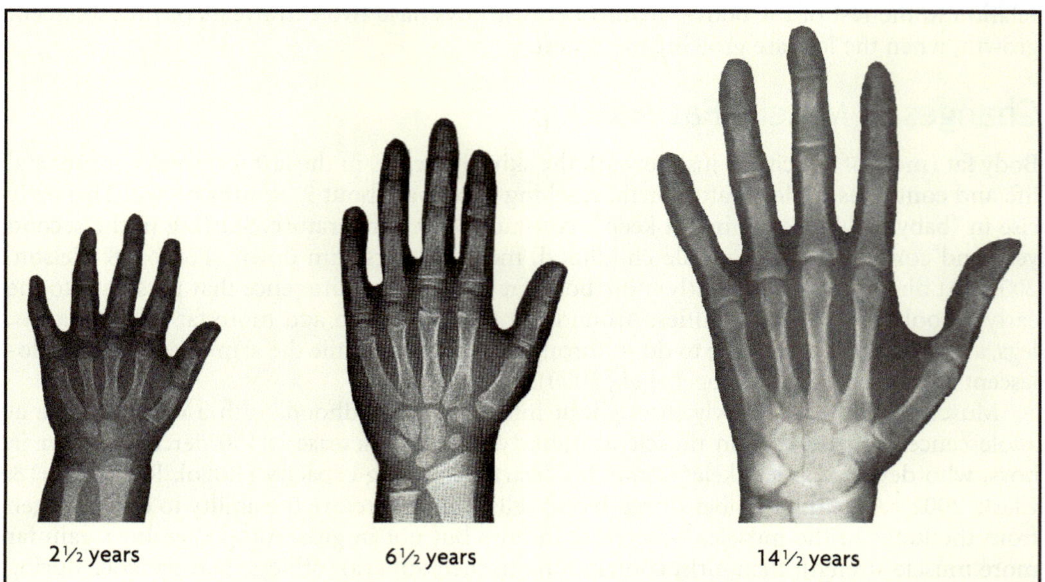

Figure 5.3 **X-rays of a girl's hand, showing skeletal maturity at three ages.**

Notice how, at age 2½, wide gaps exist between the wrist bones and at the ends of the finger and arm bones. By age 6½, these have filled in considerably. At age 14½ (when this girl reached her adult size), the wrist and long bones are completely fused. (Reprinted from J. M. Tanner, M. J. R. Healey, & N. Cameron, 2001, *Assessment of Skeletal Maturity and Predication of Adult Height [TW3 Method], 3rd ed.*, Philadelphia: Saunders, p. 86. Copyright © 2001, with permission from Elsevier.)

Milestones

Gross Motor Development in Early and Middle Childhood

Age	Gross Motor Skills
2–3 years	▪ Walks more rhythmically; hurried walk changes to run ▪ Jumps, hops, throws, and catches with rigid upper body ▪ Pushes riding toy with feet; little steering
3–4 years	▪ Walks up stairs, alternating feet, and down stairs, leading with one foot ▪ Jumps and hops, flexing upper body ▪ Throws and catches with slight involvement of upper body; still catches by trapping ball against chest ▪ Pedals and steers tricycle
4–5 years	▪ Walks down stairs, alternating feet; runs more smoothly ▪ Gallops and skips with one foot ▪ Throws ball with increased body rotation and transfer of weight on feet; catches ball with hands ▪ Rides tricycle rapidly; steers smoothly
5–6 years	▪ Increases running speed to 12 feet per second ▪ Gallops more smoothly; engages in true skipping and sideways stepping ▪ Displays mature, whole-body throwing and catching pattern; increases throwing speed ▪ Rides bicycle with training wheels
7–12 years	▪ Increases running speed to more than 18 feet per second ▪ Displays continuous, fluid skipping and sideways stepping ▪ Increases vertical jump from 4 to 12 inches and broad jump from 3 to over 5 feet; accurately jumps and hops from square to square ▪ Increases throwing and kicking accuracy, distance, and speed ▪ Involves the whole body in batting a ball; batting increases in speed and accuracy ▪ Dribbling changes from awkward slapping of the ball to continuous, relaxed, even stroking

Note: These milestones represent overall age trends. Individual differences exist in the precise age at which each milestone is attained.

Sources: Cratty, 1986; Malina & Bouchard, 1991; Haywood & Getchell, 2005.

Photos: (top) © Lawrence Migdale/Photo Researchers, Inc.; (top middle) © Tony Freeman/PhotoEdit; (bottom middle) © Bob Daemmrich/PhotoEdit; (bottom) © Peter Hvizdak/The Image Works

During the school years, improved balance, strength, agility, and flexibility support refinements in running, jumping, hopping, and ball skills. Children sprint across the playground, play hopscotch in intricate patterns, kick and dribble soccer balls, and swing bats at pitched balls. The Milestones table above summarizes gross motor achievements in early and middle childhood. At adolescence, increased body size and muscle bring continued motor gains.

The same principle that governs motor development during the first two years continues to operate in childhood and adolescence. Children integrate previously acquired skills into more complex, *dynamic systems of action.* (Return to Chapter 4, page 146, to review this concept.) Then they revise each skill as their bodies grow larger and stronger, their central nervous systems become better developed, their interests and goals become clearer, and their environments present new challenges. Sex differences in motor skills, already present in the preschool years, illustrate these multiple influences. Size and strength contribute to boys' superior athletic performance in adolescence but cannot fully account for their childhood advantage. As the From Research to Practice box on pages 178–179 reveals, the social environment plays a prominent role.

▪ *From* Research *to* Practice ▪

Sex Differences in Gross Motor Development

Sex differences in gross motor development are present as early as the preschool years, increase during middle childhood, and are large at adolescence. What underlies this expanding gender gap, and how can we ensure that both boys and girls have opportunities that optimize both skill and enjoyment of athletics?

Early and Middle Childhood

In early childhood, boys are slightly advanced over girls in abilities that emphasize force and power. By age 5, they can broad-jump slightly farther, run slightly faster, and throw a ball about 5 feet farther. During middle childhood, these differences intensify. For example, on average, a 12-year-old boy can throw a ball 43 feet farther than a 12-year-old girl. Boys are also more adept at batting, kicking, dribbling, and catching. Girls have an edge in fine motor skills of handwriting and drawing and in gross motor capacities that depend on balance and agility, such as hopping and skipping (Fischman, Moore, & Steele, 1992; Haywood & Getchell, 2005). Boys' slightly greater muscle mass and, in the case of throwing, slightly longer forearms contribute to their skill advantages. And girls' greater overall physical maturity may be partly responsible for their better balance and precision of movement.

From an early age, boys and girls are usually encouraged into different physical activities. For example, fathers are more likely to play catch with their sons than with their daughters. Differences in motor skills between boys and girls increase with age; however, sex differences in physical capacity remain small throughout childhood, suggesting that social pressures for boys, more than girls, to be active and physically skilled exaggerate small genetically based sex differences. In support of this view, boys can throw a ball much farther than girls only when using their dominant hand. But practice seems to be largely responsible for this advantage: When boys use their nondominant hand, the sex difference is minimal (Williams, Haywood, & Painter, 1996).

Research confirms that parents hold higher expectations for boys' athletic performance—a social message that children absorb at an early age. From first through twelfth grade, girls are less positive than boys about the value of sports and their own sports ability—differences explained in part by parental beliefs (Fredricks & Eccles, 2002). In one study, boys more often stated that it was vital to their parents that they participate in athletics. These attitudes affected children's self-confidence and behavior. Girls saw themselves as less talented at sports and, by sixth grade, devoted less time to athletics than their male classmates (Eccles & Harold, 1991). But girls and older school-age children regard boys' advantage in sports as unjust. They indicate, for example, that coaches should spend equal time with children of each sex and that female sports should command just as much media attention as male sports (Solomon & Bredemeier, 1999).

Adolescence

Not until puberty do sharp sex-related differences in physical size and muscle strength account for large differences in athletic ability. During adolescence, girls' gains in gross motor performance are slow and gradual, leveling off by age 14. In contrast, boys show a dramatic spurt in

With their coach's enthusiastic encouragement, these young softball players are likely to evaluate their own sports ability positively and to continue playing, thereby narrowing the gender gap in athletic participation, skill, and enjoyment. © SW Productions/Brand X/Corbis

Organized Youth Sports Partly because of parents' concerns about safety and the availability and attractions of TV, computer and video games, and the Internet, today's school-age children and adolescents devote less time to outdoor, informal physical play than children in previous generations. At the same time, organized sports, such as Little League baseball and soccer and hockey leagues, have expanded tremendously, filling many hours that children used to spend gathering spontaneously for physical play on sidewalks and playgrounds. About half of North American youngsters—60 percent of boys and 40 percent of girls—participate in organized sports at some time during the school year between ages 6 and 12 (Hanvey, 2006; National Council of Youth Sports, 2005).

For most children, playing on an athletic team is associated with increased self-esteem and social competence (Bowker, 2006; Daniels & Leaper, 2006; Fletcher, Nickerson, & Wright, 2003). And children who view themselves as good at sports are more likely to continue playing on teams in adolescence, which—in turn—predicts greater participation in sports and strength, speed, and endurance that continues through the teenage years, widening the gender gap. By mid-adolescence, few girls perform as well as the average boy in running speed, broad jump, or throwing distance. And practically no boys score as low as the average girl (Haywood & Getchell, 2005; Malina & Bouchard, 1991).

In 1972, the U.S. federal government required schools receiving public funds to provide equal opportunities for males and females in all educational programs, including athletics. Since then, girls' high school extracurricular sports participation has increased in both the United States and Canada. But as Figure 5.4 shows, U.S. girls' involvement still falls short of boys', whereas in Canada, girls and boys now participate equally (Canadian Fitness and Lifestyle Research Institute, 2005; National Federation of State High School Associations, 2006).

By high school, only 54 percent of U.S. students take any physical education, compared with 81 percent of Canadian students. But only a minority in either country—33 percent in the United States, 23 percent in Canada—have a daily physical education class. As with extracurricular sports, Canadian high school boys and girls enroll in physical education at similar rates, whereas U.S. boys exceed girls (60 versus 48 percent) (Canadian Fitness and Lifestyle Research Institute, 2005; U.S. Department of Health and Human Services, 2006c).

For both sexes, physical activity declines with age, a trend that parallels cutbacks (typically to conserve costs) in required school physical education. In the United States, the drop is sharper for girls, two-thirds of whom (compared with just half of boys) take no physical education during their senior year.

Interventions

Besides improving motor performance, sports and exercise influence cognitive and social development. Interschool and intramural athletics provide important lessons in teamwork, problem solving, assertiveness, and competition. And regular, sustained physical activity is associated with healthier dietary habits and improved psychological well-being in adolescence, as indicated by a reduction in use of alcohol, cigarettes, and illegal drugs and in sexual activity (Donnelly & Kidd, 2004; Pate et al., 2000).

Special steps must be taken to raise girls' confidence that they can do well at athletics. Educating parents about the minimal differences between school-age boys' and girls' physical capacities and sensitizing them to unfair biases against promotion of athletic ability among girls may prove helpful. In addition, greater emphasis on skill training for girls, along with increased public attention to their athletic achievements, is likely to improve their participation and performance.

Finally, daily physical education in school, emphasizing enjoyable games and individual exercise rather than competition, is particularly motivating for girls and is associated with lasting positive consequences (Weinberg et al., 2000). In a longitudinal study, participating in team or individual sports at age 14 predicted high rates of physical activity at age 31. Endurance sports such as running and cycling—activities that can easily be performed on one's own time, without expensive equipment or special facilities—were especially likely to carry over into adulthood (Tammelin et al., 2003). The stamina these activities require fosters high *physical self-efficacy*—belief in one's ability to sustain an exercise program (Motl et al., 2002; Telama et al., 2005).

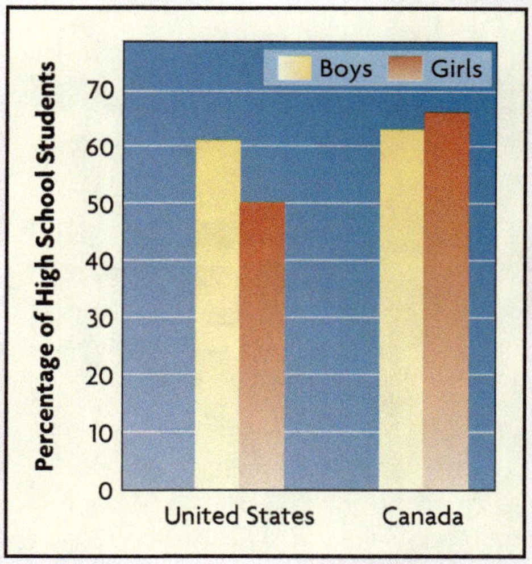

Figure 5.4 Involvement of U.S. and Canadian high school students in extracurricular school sports.
In the United States, boys continue to participate at a higher rate than girls. In Canada, girls' participation now equals boys'. (From Canadian Fitness and Lifestyle Research Institute, 2005; National Federation of State High School Associations, 2006.)

other physical fitness activities in early adulthood (Marsh et al., 2007; McHale et al., 2005). But in some cases, the arguments of critics—that youth sports overemphasize competition and substitute adult control for children's natural experimentation with rules and strategies—are valid. Children who join teams before they are capable of the necessary skills soon lose interest. Coaches and parents who criticize rather than encourage can prompt intense anxiety in some children. Rather than promoting elite performance, high parental pressure to excel at sports and frequent, intense practice are linked to children's emotional difficulties and early athletic dropout (Marsh & Daigneault, 1999; Tofler, Knapp, & Drell, 1998; Wall & Côté, 2007).

Sports-related injuries are another concern. Perhaps because organized sports specify health and safety rules, injuries tend to be infrequent and mild, except in football, which has a high rate of serious injury (Radelet et al., 2002). But excessive practice in any sport can lead to painful "overuse" injuries and to stress-related fractures resulting in premature closure of the epiphyses of the long bones (Lord & Kozar, 1996).

Less than 30 percent of North American school-age children engage in sufficient physical activity for good health, but these girls are fortunate enough to know the pleasure that comes from vigorous exercise. © David Young Wolff/PhotoEdit

When parents and coaches emphasize effort, improvement, and teamwork and permit children to contribute to rules and strategies, young athletes enjoy their chosen sport more, try harder to improve their skills, and perceive themselves as more competent (Ullrich-French & Smith, 2006). This positive emphasis helps promote physical activity, an important factor at a time when less than 30 percent of U.S. and Canadian school-age children and adolescents engage in enough regular, vigorous aerobic activity for good health (Canadian Fitness and Lifestyle Research Institute, 2005; U.S. Department of Health and Human Services, 2006c).

Hormonal Influences on Physical Growth

The endocrine glands control the vast physical changes of childhood and adolescence. They manufacture *hormones,* chemical substances secreted by specialized cells in one part of the body that pass to and influence cells in another.

The most important hormones for human growth are released by the **pituitary gland,** located at the base of the brain near the **hypothalamus,** a structure that initiates and regulates pituitary secretions (see Figure 5.5). Once pituitary hormones enter the bloodstream, they act directly on body tissues to induce growth, or they stimulate the release of other hormones from endocrine glands located elsewhere in the body. The hypothalamus contains special receptors that detect hormone levels in the bloodstream. Through a highly sensitive feedback loop, it instructs the pituitary gland to increase or decrease the amount of each hormone. In this way, growth is carefully controlled. You may find it useful to refer to Figure 5.6 as we review major hormonal influences.

Growth hormone (GH), the only pituitary secretion produced continuously throughout life, affects development of all tissues except the central nervous system and the genitals. GH production doubles during puberty, contributing to tremendous gains in body size, and then decreases after final adult height is reached. It acts directly on the body and also stimulates the liver and epiphyses of the skeleton to release another hormone, *somatomedin,* which triggers cell duplication in the bones. Although GH does not seem to affect prenatal growth, it is necessary for physical development from birth on. Children who lack it attain an average mature height of only 4 feet, 4 inches. When treated early with GH injections, such children show catch-up growth, then grow at a normal rate, becoming much taller than they would have without treatment (Saenger, 2003).

Together, the hypothalamus and pituitary gland prompt the thyroid gland (in the neck) to release **thyroxine,** which is necessary for brain development and for GH to have its full impact on body size. Infants born with a deficiency of thyroxine must receive it at once, or they will be mentally retarded. Once the most rapid period of brain development is complete, thyroxine deficiency no longer affects the central nervous system but still causes children to grow more slowly than average. With prompt treatment, however, they eventually reach normal size (Salerno et al., 2001).

■ Figure 5.5 **Cross-section of the human brain, showing the location of the hypothalamus and pituitary gland.** Also shown are four additional structures—the cerebellum, the reticular formation, the hippocampus, and the corpus callosum—that we will discuss in a later section.

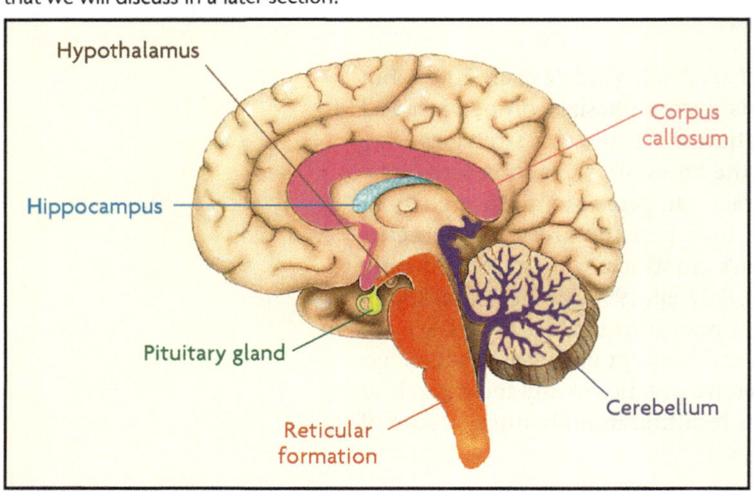

Sexual maturation is controlled by pituitary secretions that stimulate the release of sex hormones. Although we think of **estrogens** as female hormones and **androgens** as male hormones, both types are present in each sex, but in different amounts. The boy's testes release large quantities of the androgen *testosterone,* which leads to muscle growth, body and facial hair, and other male sex characteristics. Androgens (especially testosterone for boys) exert a GH-enhancing effect, contributing greatly to gains in body size. The testes also secrete small amounts of estrogen—the reason that 50 percent of boys experience temporary breast enlargement. In both sexes, estrogens also increase GH secretion, adding to the growth spurt and, in combination

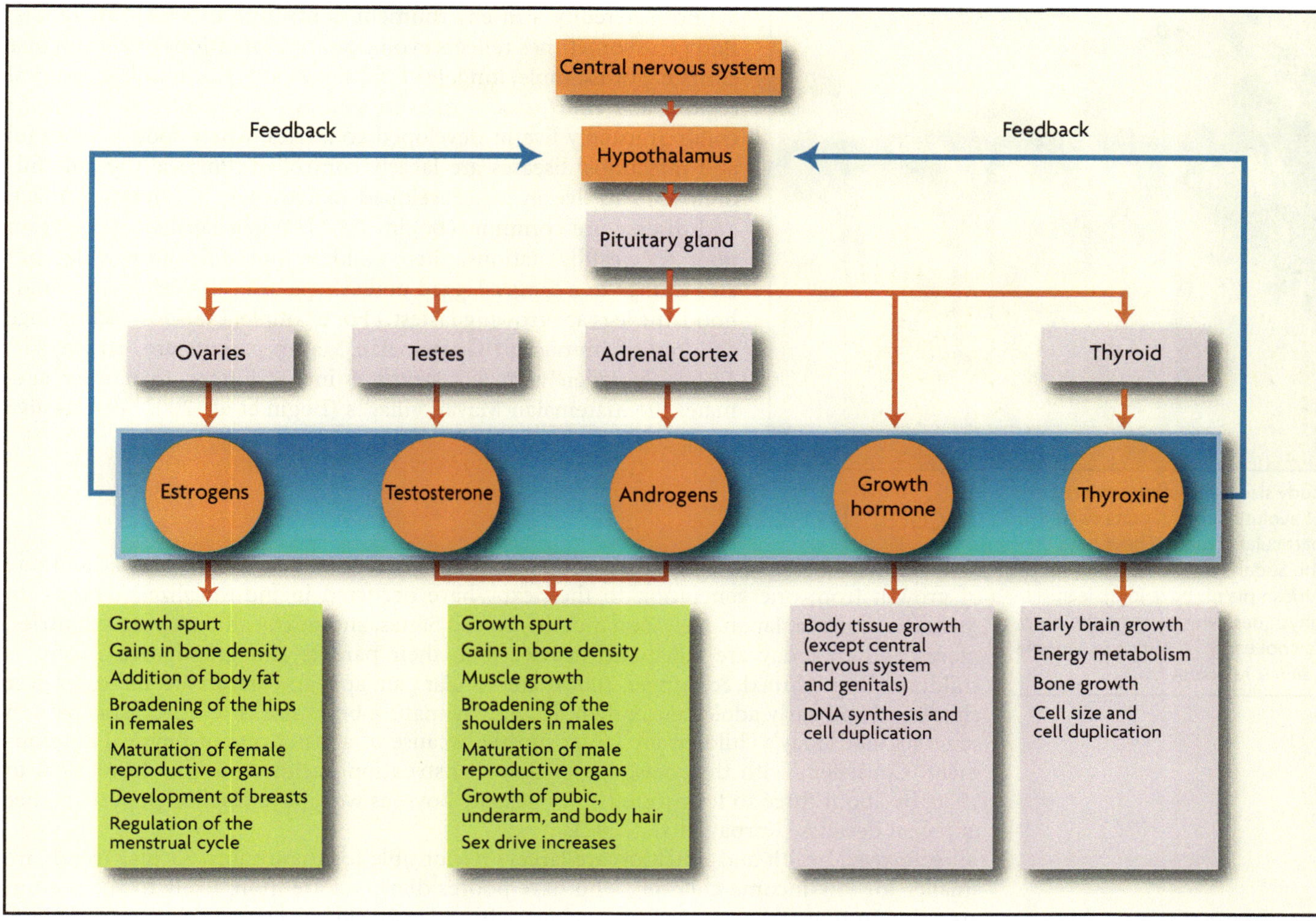

Figure 5.6 Hormonal influences on postnatal growth. The hypothalamus stimulates the pituitary gland to release hormones that either induce growth directly or stimulate other endocrine glands to release growth-inducing hormones (red lines). A highly sensitive feedback loop exists in which the hypothalamus detects hormone levels in the bloodstream and instructs the pituitary gland to increase or decrease the amount of each hormone accordingly (blue lines).

with androgens, stimulating gains in bone density, which continue into early adulthood (Cooper, Sayer, & Dennison, 2006; Styne, 2003).

Estrogens released by girls' ovaries cause the breasts, uterus, and vagina to mature, the body to take on feminine proportions, and fat to accumulate. Estrogens also contribute to regulation of the menstrual cycle. *Adrenal androgens,* released from the adrenal glands located on top of each kidney, influence girls' height spurt and stimulate growth of underarm and pubic hair. They have little impact on boys, whose physical characteristics are influenced mainly by androgen and estrogen secretions from the testes.

Worldwide Variations in Body Size

TAKE A MOMENT... Glance into almost any school classroom, and notice the wide individual differences in children's physical size. This diversity in size is especially apparent when we travel to different nations. Worldwide, a 9-inch gap exists between the smallest and the largest 8-year-olds. The shortest children, found in South America, Asia, the Pacific Islands, and parts of Africa, include such ethnic groups as Colombian, Burmese, Thai, Vietnamese, Ethiopian, and Bantu. The tallest children—living in Australia, northern and central Europe, Canada, and the United States, come from Czech, Dutch, Latvian, Norwegian, Swiss, and African populations (Meredith, 1978; Ruff, 2002).

Ethnic variations in growth rate are also common: African-American and Asian children tend to mature faster than North American Caucasian children, who are slightly ahead of European children (Berkey et al., 1994; Eveleth & Tanner, 1990). These findings remind us that *growth norms* (age-related averages for height and weight) must be applied cautiously, especially in countries with high immigration rates and many ethnic minorities.

Body size is sometimes the result of evolutionary adaptations to a particular climate. These boys of the Sudan, who live on the hot African plains, have long, lean physiques, which permit the body to cool easily. © Betty Press/Woodfin Camp & Associates

Both heredity and environment contribute to these differences. Body size sometimes reflects evolutionary adaptations to a particular climate. For example, long, lean physiques are typical in hot, tropical regions and short, stocky ones in cold, Arctic areas. Also, the tallest children usually live in developed countries, where food is plentiful and infectious diseases are largely controlled. Physically small children tend to live in less-developed regions, where poverty, hunger, and disease are common (Bogin, 2001). When families move from poor to wealthy nations, their children not only grow taller but also change to a longer-legged body shape. (Recall that during childhood, the legs are growing fastest.) For example, U.S.-born school-age children of immigrant Guatemalan Mayan parents are, on average, 4½ inches taller, with legs nearly 3 inches longer, than their agemates in Guatemalan Mayan villages (Bogin et al., 2002; Varela-Silva et al., 2007).

Secular Trends

Over the past 150 years, **secular trends in physical growth**—changes in body size and rate of growth from one generation to the next—have occurred in industrialized nations. In Australia, Canada, Japan, New Zealand, the United States, and nearly all European countries, most children today are taller and heavier than their parents and grandparents were as children (Ong, Ahmed, & Dunger, 2006). The secular gain appears early in life, increases over childhood and early adolescence, then declines as mature body size is reached. This pattern suggests that today's children are larger mostly because of a faster rate of physical development. Consistent with this view, age of first menstruation declined steadily from 1900 to 1970, by about three to four months per decade. Boys, as well, have reached puberty earlier in recent decades (Karpati et al., 2002).

Improved health and nutrition are largely responsible for these gains. Secular trends are smaller for low-income children, who have poorer diets and are more likely to suffer from growth-stunting illnesses. And in regions with widespread poverty, famine, and disease, either no secular change or a secular decrease has occurred (Barnes-Josiah & Augustin, 1995; Cole, 2000).

In most industrialized nations, the secular gain in height has slowed, and—as Figure 5.7 illustrates—the trend toward earlier first menstruation has declined or undergone a slight reversal. However, overweight and obesity have contributed to a continuing secular trend toward earlier first menstruation in North America and a few European countries, such as Denmark, Finland, Germany, and the Netherlands (Parent et al., 2003).

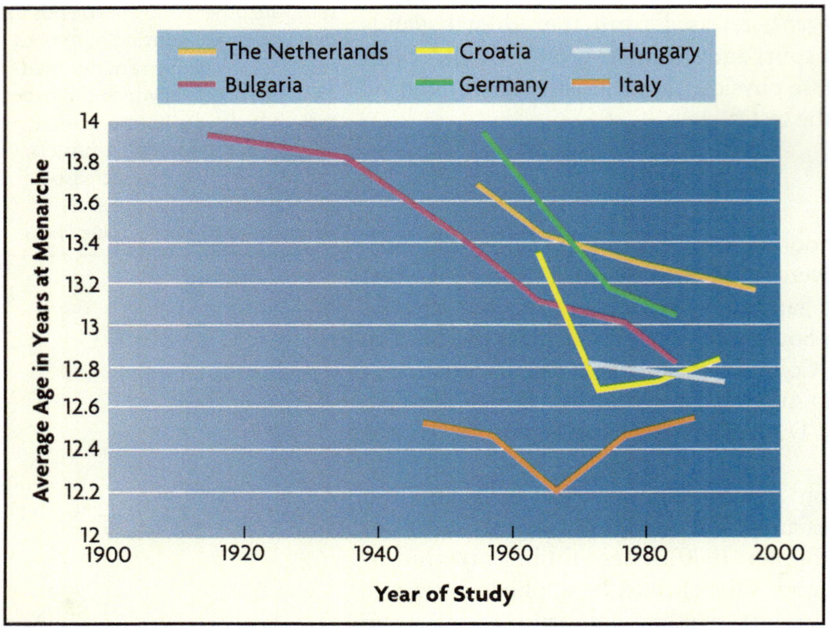

■ **Figure 5.7** **Secular trend in age at menarche in six industrialized nations.**

Age of menarche declined from 1900 to 1970. Thereafter, a few countries showed a modest, continuing decline due to rising rates of overweight and obesity. Others leveled off or underwent a slight reversal. (From S. M. P. F. de Muinck Keizer-Schrama & D. Mul, 2001, "Trends in Pubertal Development in Europe," *Human Reproduction Update,* 7, p. 289. © European Society of Human Reproduction and Embryology. Reproduced by permission of Oxford University Press/Human Reproduction and S. M. P. F. de Muinck Keizer-Schrama.)

Ask Yourself

Review What aspects of physical growth account for the long-legged appearance of many 8- to 12-year-olds?

Apply Nine-year-old Allison dislikes physical education and thinks she isn't good at sports. What strategies can her teacher use to improve her involvement and pleasure in physical activity?

Connect Relate secular trends in physical growth to the concept of cohort effects, discussed on page 61 in Chapter 2.

Reflect In your family, how do members of your generation compare with members of your parents' generation in height and weight? How about your grandparents' generation? Do your observations illustrate secular trends?

Brain Development

The human brain is the most elaborate and effective living structure on earth today. Despite its complexity, it reaches its adult size earlier than any other organ. We can best understand brain growth by looking at it from two vantage points: (1) the microscopic level of individual brain cells, and (2) the larger level of the cerebral cortex, the most complex brain structure and the one responsible for the highly developed intelligence of our species.

Development of Neurons

The human brain has 100 to 200 billion **neurons,** or nerve cells, that store and transmit information, many of which have thousands of direct connections with other neurons. Unlike other body cells, neurons are not tightly packed together. Between them are **synapses**—tiny gaps where fibers from different neurons come close together but do not touch (see Figure 5.8). Neurons send messages to one another by releasing chemicals called **neurotransmitters,** which cross synapses.

The basic story of brain growth concerns how neurons develop and form this elaborate communication system. Figure 5.9 on page 184 summarizes major milestones of brain development. In the prenatal period, neurons are produced in the embryo's primitive neural tube. From there, they migrate to form the major parts of the brain (see Chapter 3, page 90). Once neurons are in place, they differentiate, establishing their unique functions by extending their fibers to form synaptic connections with neighboring cells. During infancy and early childhood, neural fibers grow at an astounding pace (Huttenlocher, 1994; Moore & Persaud, 2008). A surprising aspect of brain growth is **programmed cell death,** which makes space for these connective structures: As synapses form, many surrounding neurons die—20 to 80 percent, depending on the brain region (de Haan & Johnson, 2003b; Stiles, 2001a). Fortunately, during embryonic growth, the neural tube produces far more neurons than the brain will ever need.

■ Figure 5.8 **Neurons and their connective fibers.**
This photograph of several neurons, taken with the aid of a powerful microscope, shows the elaborate synaptic connections that form with neighboring cells. © ASAP/CNRI/Science Source/Photo Researchers, Inc.

As neurons form connections, *stimulation* becomes vital to their survival. Neurons that are stimulated by input from the surrounding environment continue to establish synapses, forming increasingly elaborate systems of communication that support more complex abilities. At first, stimulation results in massive overabundance of synapses, many of which serve identical functions, thereby ensuring that the child will acquire the motor, cognitive, and social skills that our species needs to survive. Neurons that are seldom stimulated soon lose their synapses, a process called **synaptic pruning** that returns neurons not needed at the moment to an uncommitted state so they can support future development. In all, about 40 percent of synapses are pruned during childhood and adolescence (Webb, Monk, & Nelson, 2001). For this process to advance, appropriate stimulation of the child's brain is vital during periods in which the formation of synapses is at its peak (Nelson, Thomas, & de Haan, 2006).

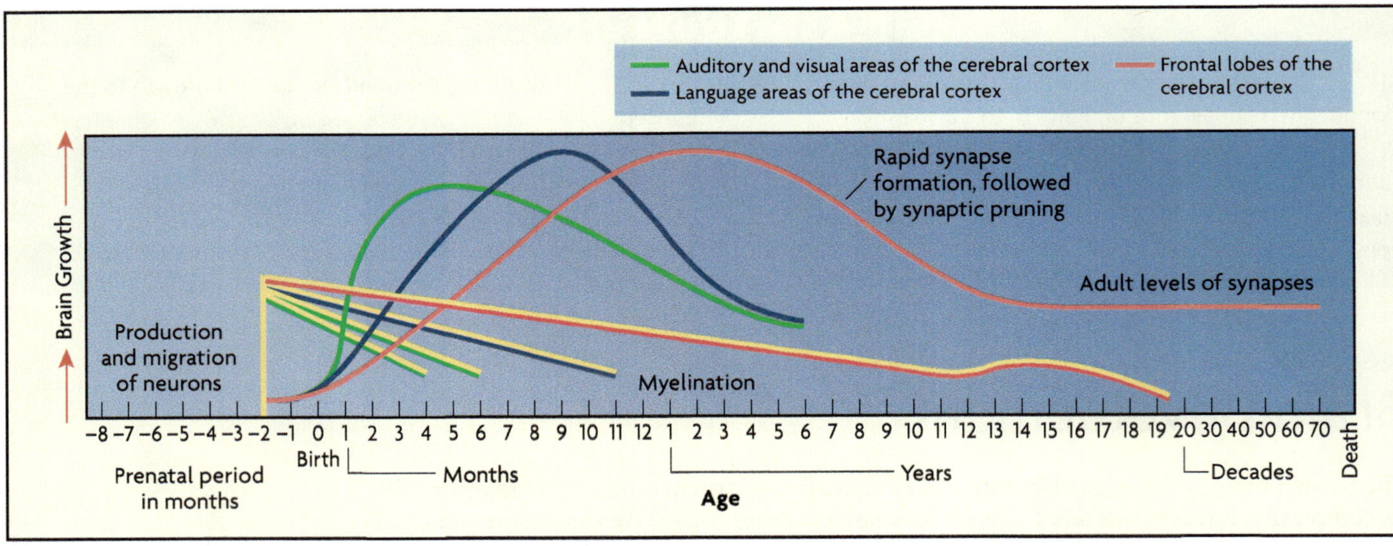

■ **Figure 5.9** **Major milestones of brain development.**
Formation of synapses is rapid during the first two years, especially in the auditory, visual, and language areas of the cerebral cortex. The frontal lobes undergo more extended synaptic growth. In each area, overproduction of synapses is followed by synaptic pruning. The frontal lobes are among the last regions to attain adult levels of synaptic connections—in mid- to late adolescence. Myelination occurs at a dramatic pace during the first two years, more slowly through childhood and adolescence. The multiple yellow lines indicate that the timing of myelination varies among different brain areas. For example, neural fibers continue to myelinate over a longer period in the language areas, and especially in the frontal lobes, than in the visual and auditory areas. (Adapted from Thompson & Nelson, 2001.)

If few new neurons are produced after the prenatal period, what causes the dramatic increase in brain size during infancy and early childhood? About half the brain's volume consists of **glial cells,** which are responsible for **myelination,** the coating of neural fibers with an insulating fatty sheath (called *myelin*) that improves the efficiency of message transfer. Glial cells multiply rapidly from the fourth month of pregnancy through the second year of life, a process that continues at a slower pace through adolescence. Dramatic increases in neural fibers and myelination are responsible for the swift gain in overall brain size. At birth, the brain is 25 percent of its adult weight; by age 2, it reaches 70 percent, and at 6 years, 90 percent (Johnson, 2005; Thatcher et al., 1996).

Brain development can be compared to molding a "living sculpture." First, neurons and synapses are overproduced; then, cell death and synaptic pruning sculpt away excess building material to form the mature brain—a process jointly influenced by genetically programmed events and the child's experiences. The resulting "sculpture" is a set of interconnected regions, each with specific functions—much like countries on a globe that communicate with one another (Johnston et al., 2001). This "geography" of the brain permits researchers to study its organization using psychophysiological methods, such as EEG, ERP, and fMRI (see pages 47–49 in Chapter 2 to review). We will encounter these measures as we turn now to the development of the cerebral cortex.

Development of the Cerebral Cortex

The **cerebral cortex** surrounds the rest of the brain, resembling half of a shelled walnut. It is the largest brain structure—accounting for 85 percent of the brain's weight and containing the greatest number of neurons and synapses. Because it is also the last brain structure to stop growing, it is sensitive to environmental influences for far longer than any other part of the brain.

• **Regions of the Cerebral Cortex** Figure 5.10 shows specific functions of regions of the cerebral cortex, such as receiving information from the senses, instructing the body to move,

Figure 5.10 **The left side of the human brain, showing the cerebral cortex.**
The cortex is divided into different lobes, each containing a variety of regions with specific functions. Some major regions are labeled here.

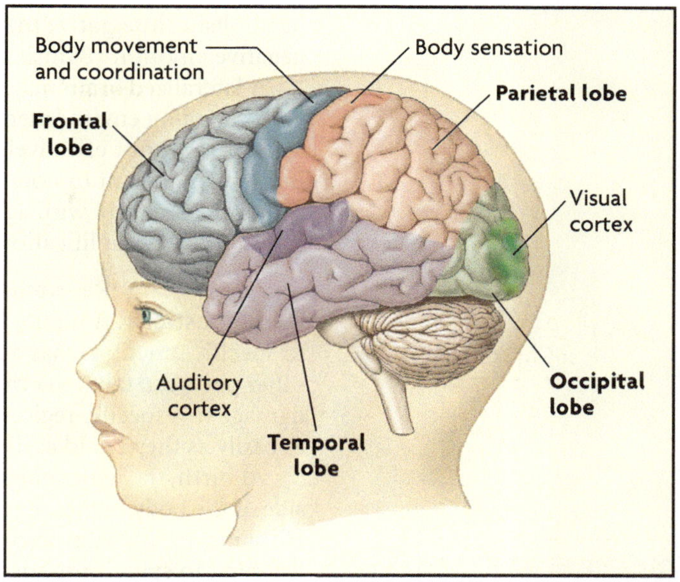

and thinking. The general order in which cortical regions develop corresponds to the emergence of these capacities in the infant and child. For example, ERP and fMRI measures reveal a burst of activity (signifying synaptic growth and myelination) in the auditory and visual cortexes and in areas responsible for body movement over the first year—a period of dramatic gains in auditory and visual perception and mastery of motor skills (Johnson, 2005). Language areas are especially active from late infancy through the preschool years, when language development flourishes (Pujol et al., 2006; Thompson et al., 2000).

The cortical regions with the most extended period of development are the *frontal lobes,* which are responsible for thought—in particular, consciousness, attention, inhibition of impulses, integration of information, and use of memory, reasoning, planning, and problem-solving strategies. From age 2 months on, the frontal lobes function more effectively. But they undergo especially rapid myelination and formation and pruning of synapses during the preschool and school years, followed by another period of accelerated growth in adolescence, when the frontal lobes reach an adult level of synapses (Nelson, 2002; Nelson, Thomas, & de Haan, 2006; Sowell et al., 2002). Furthermore, connections between the frontal lobes and other brain areas expand and attain rapid communication during the teenage years—changes that support diverse cognitive skills, including improved processing speed, attention, memory, planning, and capacity to integrate information (Blakemore & Choudhury, 2006; Keating, 2004; Lenroot & Giedd, 2006).

Because this deaf toddler is learning to communicate in sign language, a spatial skill, she will depend more on the right hemisphere of the cerebral cortex for language processing than will her hearing agemates. © Christina Kennedy/PhotoEdit

Lateralization of the Cerebral Cortex The cerebral cortex has two *hemispheres,* or sides, that differ in their functions. Some tasks are done mostly by the left hemisphere, others by the right. For example, each hemisphere receives sensory information from the side of the body opposite to it and controls only that side.[1] For most of us, the left hemisphere is largely responsible for verbal abilities (such as spoken and written language) and positive emotion (such as joy). The right hemisphere handles spatial abilities (judging distances, reading maps, recognizing geometric shapes) and negative emotion (such as distress) (Banish & Heller, 1998; Nelson & Bosquet, 2000). In left-handed people, this pattern may be reversed—or, more commonly, the cortex may be less clearly specialized than in right-handers.

Why does this specialization of the two hemispheres, called **lateralization,** occur? Studies using fMRI reveal that the left hemisphere is better at processing information in a sequential, analytic (piece-by-piece) way, a good approach for dealing with communicative information—both verbal (language) and emotional (a joyful smile). In contrast, the right hemisphere is specialized for processing information

[1]The eyes are an exception. Messages from the right half of each retina go to the right hemisphere; messages from the left half of each retina go to the left hemisphere. Thus, visual information from *both* eyes is received by *both* hemispheres.

in a holistic, integrative manner, ideal for making sense of spatial information and regulating negative emotion (Banish, 1998).

A lateralized brain may have evolved because it enabled humans to cope more successfully with changing environmental demands (Rogers, 2000). It permits a wider array of functions to be carried out effectively than if both sides processed information exactly the same way. But it is important to note that the two hemispheres communicate and work together, doing so more effectively with age. The popular notion of a "right-brained" or "left-brained" person is an oversimplification.

Brain Plasticity. Researchers study the timing of brain lateralization to learn more about **brain plasticity.** A highly *plastic* cerebral cortex, in which many areas are not yet committed to specific functions, has a high capacity for learning. And if a part of the cortex is damaged, other parts can take over the tasks it would have handled. But once the hemispheres lateralize, damage to a specific region means that the abilities it controls cannot be recovered as fully or as easily as they could earlier.

At birth, the hemispheres have already begun to specialize. Most newborns favor the right side of the body in their head position and reflexive reactions (Grattan et al., 1992; Rönnqvist & Hopkins, 1998). Most also show greater ERP brain-wave activity in the left hemisphere while listening to speech sounds or displaying a positive state of arousal. In contrast, the newborn right hemisphere reacts more strongly to nonspeech sounds and to stimuli (such as a sour-tasting fluid) that evoke negative emotion (Davidson, 1994; Fox & Davidson, 1986).

Nevertheless, research on brain-damaged children and adults offers dramatic evidence for substantial plasticity in the young brain, summarized in the Biology and Environment box on the following page. Furthermore, early experience greatly influences the organization of the cerebral cortex. For example, deaf adults who, as infants and children, learned sign language (a spatial skill) depend more than hearing individuals on the right hemisphere for language processing (Neville & Bavelier, 2002). And toddlers who are advanced in language development show greater left-hemispheric specialization for language than their more slowly developing agemates (Mills, Coffey-Corina, & Neville, 1997; Mills et al., 2005). Similarly, while performing motor and cognitive tasks, children show diffuse fMRI activity in the cerebral cortex relative to adolescents and adults, for whom activity is concentrated in certain cortical areas (Casey et al., 2002; Luna et al., 2001). Apparently, the very process of acquiring motor, cognitive, and language skills promotes lateralization.

In sum, the brain is more plastic during the first few years than it will be ever again. Although the cortex is programmed from the start for hemispheric specialization, experience greatly influences the rate and success of its advancing organization. An overabundance of synaptic connections supports brain plasticity, ensuring that young children will acquire certain capacities even if some areas are damaged. fMRI measures reveal that by age 4, many parts of the cortex have overproduced synapses. Around this time, cerebral blood flow peaks, signifying a high energy need (Huttenlocher, 2002; Nelson, Thomas, & de Haan, 2006). With further stimulation, some neural fibers become more elaborate, synaptic pruning and death of surrounding neurons occur, and brain plasticity declines. By age 8 to 10, energy consumption of most cortical regions drops to near-adult levels (Nelson, 2002).

Lateralization and Handedness. An expanding literature on handedness supports the joint contributions of nature and nurture to brain lateralization. By age 6 months, infants typically display a smoother, more efficient movement when reaching with their right than their left arm—a difference, believed to be biologically based, that may contribute to the right-sided hand preference evident in most babies at age 12 months (Hinojosa, Sheu, & Michel, 2003; Rönnqvist & Domellöf, 2006). Gradually, handedness extends to additional skills, such as eating with utensils, throwing and catching, drawing, and writing.

Handedness reflects the greater capacity of one side of the brain—the individual's **dominant cerebral hemisphere**—to carry out skilled motor action. Other important abilities are generally located on the dominant side as well. For right-handed people—in Western nations, 90 percent of the population—language is housed in the left hemisphere, with hand control. For the left-handed 10 percent, language is occasionally located in the right hemisphere or, more often, shared between the hemispheres (Szaflarski et al., 2002). This indicates

Biology *and* Environment

Brain Plasticity: Insights from Research on Brain-Damaged Children and Adults

In the first few years of life, the brain is highly plastic. It can reorganize areas committed to specific functions in ways that the mature brain cannot. Consistently, adults who suffered brain injuries in infancy and early childhood show fewer cognitive impairments than adults with later-occurring injuries (Holland, 2004; Huttenlocher, 2002). Nevertheless, the young brain is not totally plastic. When it is injured, its functioning is compromised. The extent of plasticity depends on several factors, including age at time of injury, site of damage, and skill area.

Brain Plasticity in Infancy and Early Childhood

In a large study of children with injuries to the cerebral cortex that occurred before birth or in the first six months of life, language and spatial skills were assessed repeatedly into adolescence (Akshoomoff et al., 2002; Stiles, 2001a; Stiles et al., 2005). All the children had experienced early brain seizures or hemorrhages. Brain-imaging techniques—fMRI and PET—revealed the precise site of damage.

Regardless of whether injury occurred in the left or right cerebral hemisphere, the children showed delays in language development that persisted until about 3½ years of age. That damage to either hemisphere affected early language competence indicates that at first, language functioning is broadly distributed in the brain. But by age 5, the children caught up in vocabulary and grammatical skills. Undamaged areas—in either the left or the right hemisphere—had taken over these language functions.

Compared with language, spatial skills were more impaired after early brain injury. When preschool through adolescent-age youngsters were asked to copy designs, those with early right-hemispheric damage had trouble with holistic processing—accurately representing the overall shape. In contrast, those with left-hemispheric damage captured the basic shape but omitted fine-grained details. Nevertheless, the children showed improvement in their drawings with age—gains that do not occur in brain-injured adults (Akshoomoff et al., 2002; Stiles et al., 2003). Clearly, recovery after early brain injury is greater for language than for spatial skills. Why is this so? Researchers speculate that spatial processing is the older of the two capacities in our evolutionary history and, therefore, more lateralized at birth (Stiles, 2001b; Stiles et al., 2002). But early brain injury has far less impact than later injury on *both* language and spatial skills. In sum, the young brain is remarkably plastic.

The Price of High Plasticity in the Young Brain

Despite impressive recovery of language and (to a lesser extent) spatial skills, children with early brain injuries show deficits in a wide variety of complex mental abilities during the school years. Their progress in reading and math is slow, and in telling stories, they produce simpler narratives than agemates without early brain injuries (although many catch up in narrative skills by early adolescence) (Reilly, Bates, & Marchman, 1998; Reilly et al., 2004). Furthermore, the more brain tissue destroyed in infancy or early childhood, the poorer children score on intelligence tests (Anderson et al., 2006).

High brain plasticity, researchers explain, comes at a price. When healthy brain regions take over the functions of damaged areas, a "crowding effect" occurs: Multiple tasks must be done by a smaller than usual volume of brain tissue. Consequently, the brain processes information less quickly and accurately than it would if it were intact. Complex mental abilities of all kinds suffer into middle childhood, and often longer, because performing them well requires considerable space in the cerebral cortex (Huttenlocher, 2002).

Later Plasticity

Brain plasticity is not restricted to early childhood. Though far more limited, reorganization in the brain can occur later, even in adulthood. For example, adult stroke victims often display considerable recovery, especially in response to stimulation of language and motor skills. Brain-imaging techniques reveal that structures adjacent to the permanently damaged area or in the opposite cerebral hemisphere reorganize to support the impaired ability (Bach-y-Rita, 2001; Hallett, 2000).

In infancy and childhood, the goal of brain growth is to form neural connections that ensure mastery of essential skills. Animal research reveals that plasticity is greatest while the brain is forming many new synapses; it declines during synaptic pruning (Kolb & Gibb, 2001). At older ages, specialized brain structures are in place, but after injury they can still reorganize to some degree. The adult brain can produce a small number of new neurons. And when an individual practices relevant tasks, the brain strengthens existing synapses and generates new ones (Nelson, Thomas, & de Haan, 2006). Plasticity seems to be a basic property of the nervous system. Researchers hope to discover how experience and brain plasticity work together throughout life so they can help people of all ages—with and without brain injuries—develop at their best.

This preschooler, who experienced brain damage in infancy, has been spared massive impairments because of high plasticity of the young brain. Here, a teacher guides his hand in drawing shapes to strengthen spatial skills, which remain more impaired than language after early brain injury.

that the brains of left-handers tend to be less strongly lateralized than those of right-handers. Consistent with this idea, many left-handed individuals are *ambidextrous:* They prefer their left hand but may use their right hand skillfully as well (McManus et al., 1988).

Left-handed parents show only a weak tendency to have left-handed children. One genetic theory proposes that most children inherit a gene that *biases* them for right-handedness and a left-dominant cerebral hemisphere, but that this bias is not strong enough to overcome environmental pressures that might sway children toward a left-hand preference (Annett, 2002).

Even prenatal events may profoundly affect handedness. Both identical and fraternal twins are more likely than ordinary siblings to differ in hand preference, probably because twins usually lie in opposite orientations in the uterus (Derom et al., 1996). The orientation of most singleton fetuses—facing toward the left—is believed to promote greater control over movements on the body's right side (Previc, 1991).

Handedness also involves practice. Newborns' bias in head position causes them to spend more time looking at and using one arm and hand, which may contribute to greater skill development (Hinojosa, Sheu, & Michel, 2003). Handedness is strongest for complex skills requiring extensive training, such as eating with utensils, writing, and engaging in athletic activities. And wide cultural differences exist: In Tanzania, Africa, where children are physically restrained and punished for favoring the left hand, less than 1 percent of adults are left-handed (Provins, 1997).

Although left-handedness occurs more frequently among severely retarded and mentally ill people than in the general population, atypical brain lateralization is probably not responsible for these individuals' problems. Rather, early damage to the left hemisphere may have caused their disabilities while also leading to a shift in handedness. In support of this idea, left-handedness is associated with prenatal and birth difficulties that can result in brain damage, including prolonged labor, prematurity, Rh incompatibility, and breech delivery (O'Callaghan et al., 1993; Powls et al., 1996).

Most left-handers, however, have no developmental problems—in fact, unusual lateralization may have certain advantages. Left- and mixed-handed young people are more likely than their right-handed agemates to develop outstanding verbal and mathematical talents (Flannery & Liederman, 1995). More even distribution of cognitive functions across both hemispheres may be responsible.

Other Advances in Brain Development

In addition to the cerebral cortex, several other brain areas make strides during childhood and adolescence. All of these changes involve establishing links between parts of the brain, increasing the coordinated functioning of the central nervous system. (To see where the structures we are about to discuss are located, turn back to Figure 5.5 on page 180.)

At the rear and base of the brain is the **cerebellum,** a structure that aids in balance and control of body movement. Fibers linking the cerebellum to the cerebral cortex grow and myelinate from birth through the preschool years, contributing to dramatic gains in motor coordination: By the time they start school, children can play hopscotch, throw and catch a ball with well-coordinated movements, and print letters of the alphabet. Connections between the cerebellum and the cerebral cortex also support thinking (Diamond, 2000). Children with damage to the cerebellum usually display both motor and cognitive deficits, including problems with memory, planning, and language (Noterdaeme et al., 2002; Riva & Giorgi, 2000).

The **reticular formation,** a structure in the brain stem that maintains alertness and consciousness, generates synapses and myelinates from early childhood into adolescence. Neurons in the reticular formation send out fibers to many other areas of the brain. Many go to the frontal lobes of the cerebral cortex, contributing to improvements in sustained, controlled attention.

An inner-brain structure called the **hippocampus**—which plays a vital role in memory and in images of space that help us find our way—undergoes rapid formation of synapses and myelination in the second half of the first year, when recall memory and independent movement emerge. Over the preschool and school years, the hippocampus and surrounding areas of the cerebral cortex continue to develop swiftly, establishing connections with one another and with the frontal lobes (Nelson, Thomas, & de Haan, 2006). These changes make possible the dramatic gains of early and middle childhood in memory (ability to use strategies to store and retrieve information) and spatial understanding (drawing and reading of maps), which we will take up in Chapters 6 and 7.

The **corpus callosum** is a large bundle of fibers connecting the two cerebral hemispheres. Production of synapses and myelination of the corpus callosum increase at the end of the first year, peak between 3 and 6 years, and continue more slowly through adolescence (Thompson et al., 2000). The corpus callosum supports smooth coordination of movements on both sides of the body and integration of perception, attention, memory, language, problem solving, and other aspects of thinking. The more complex the task, the more essential is communication between the hemispheres.

Finally, in many brain regions, sensitivity of neurons to certain chemical messages readjusts in adolescence. As humans and other mammals become sexually mature, neurons become more responsive to excitatory neurotransmitters. As a result, adolescents react more strongly to stressful events and also experience pleasurable stimuli more intensely (Spear, 2004). These changes probably contribute to teenagers' drive for novel experiences, including drug taking. Alterations in neurotransmitter activity may also be involved in adolescents' increased susceptibility to certain disorders, such as eating disturbances, addressed in a later section, and depression, which we take up in Chapters 11 and 13.

Sensitive Periods in Brain Development

We have seen that stimulation of the brain is vital when it is growing most rapidly. Both animal and human studies, as noted in Chapter 4, reveal that early, extreme sensory deprivation results in permanent brain damage and loss of functions—findings that confirm the existence of sensitive periods in brain development. Recall, also, that research on children adopted from Romanian orphanages indicates that deprived institutional care extending beyond the first six months results in persistent intellectual impairments and mental health problems (see page 168 in Chapter 4).

Much evidence confirms that the brain is particularly spongelike during the first few years, enabling children to acquire new skills easily and quickly. How, then, can we characterize appropriate stimulation during this time? To answer this question, researchers distinguish between two types of brain development. The first, **experience-expectant brain growth,** refers to the young brain's rapidly developing organization, which depends on ordinary experiences—opportunities to see and touch objects, to hear language and other sounds, and to move about and explore the environment. As a result of millions of years of evolution, the brains of all infants, toddlers, and young children *expect* to encounter these experiences and, if they do, grow normally. The second type of brain development, **experience-dependent brain growth,** consists of additional growth and refinement of established brain structures as a result of specific learning experiences that occur throughout our lives, varying widely across individuals and cultures (Greenough & Black, 1992). Reading and writing, playing computer games, weaving an intricate rug, and practicing the violin are examples. The brain of a violinist differs in certain ways from that of a poet because each has exercised different brain regions for a long time (Thompson & Nelson, 2001).

Experience-expectant brain growth takes place naturally, through ordinary, stimulating experiences. As they play in the autumn leaves, these young children enjoy the type of activity that is best for promoting brain development in the early years. © Ariel Skelley/CORBIS

Experience-expectant brain development occurs early and naturally, as caregivers offer babies and preschoolers age-appropriate play materials and engage them in enjoyable daily routines—a shared meal, a game of peek-a-boo, a bath before bed, or a picture book to talk about. The resulting growth provides the foundation for later-occurring, experience-dependent development (Huttenlocher, 2002; Shonkoff & Phillips, 2001). In Chapter 4, we indicated that not just understimulation but also overstimulation—overwhelming children with tasks and expectations for which they are not yet ready—can threaten their development. No evidence exists for a sensitive period in the first five or six years for mastering skills that depend on extensive training, such as reading, musical performance, or gymnastics (Bruer, 1999). To the contrary, rushing early learning harms the brain by overwhelming its neural circuits, thereby reducing the brain's sensitivity to the everyday experiences it needs for a healthy start in life.

Ask Yourself

Review How does stimulation affect early brain development? Cite evidence at the level of neurons and at the level of the cerebral cortex.

Review Lucia experienced damage to the left hemisphere of her cerebral cortex shortly after birth. As a first grader, she shows impressive recovery of language and spatial skills, but her academic progress remains slow relative to her noninjured classmates. What accounts for her recovery of skills? How about her cognitive deficits?

Apply Which infant enrichment program would you choose: one that emphasizes social games and gentle talking and touching, or one that includes reading and number drills and classical music lessons? Explain.

Connect What stance on the nature–nurture issue does evidence on development of handedness support? Document your answer with research findings.

Factors Affecting Physical Growth

Physical growth, like other aspects of development, results from a complex interplay between genetic and environmental factors. Although heredity remains important, environmental factors continue to affect genetic expression. Good nutrition, relative freedom from disease, and emotional well-being are essential to children's healthy development, while environmental pollutants can be a threat. The Biology and Environment box on pages 192–193 considers the extent to which one of the most common pollutants, low-level lead, undermines children's mental and emotional functioning.

Heredity

Because identical twins are much more alike in body size than fraternal twins, we know that heredity is an important contributor to physical growth (Estourgie–van Burk et al., 2006). When diet and health are adequate, height and rate of physical growth (as measured by skeletal age and timing of first menstruation) are largely determined by heredity. In fact, as long as negative environmental influences, such as poor nutrition or illness, are not severe, children and adolescents typically show **catch-up growth**—a return to a genetically influenced growth path once conditions improve. Still, the brain, the heart, the digestive system, and many other internal organs may be permanently compromised (Hales & Ozanne, 2003). (Recall the consequences of inadequate prenatal nutrition for long-term health, discussed on pages 96–97 in Chapter 3.)

Genes influence growth by controlling the body's production of and sensitivity to hormones. Mutations can disrupt this process, leading to deviations in physical size. Occasionally, a mutation becomes widespread in a population. Consider the Efe of the Republic of Congo, who normally grow to an adult height of less than 5 feet. During early childhood, the growth of Efe children tapers off. By age 5, the average Efe child is shorter than over 97 percent of North American 5-year-olds. For genetic reasons, growth hormone (GH) has less effect on Efe youngsters than on other children (Bailey, 1990). The Efe's small size probably evolved because it reduced their caloric requirements in the face of food scarcity in the rain forests of Central Africa and enabled them to move easily through the dense forest underbrush.

Applying What We Know

Reasons to Breastfeed

Nutritional and Health Advantages	Explanation
Provides the correct balance of fat and protein	Compared with the milk of other mammals, human milk is higher in fat and lower in protein. This balance, as well as the unique proteins and fats contained in human milk, is ideal for a rapidly myelinating nervous system.
Ensures nutritional completeness	A mother who breastfeeds need not add other foods to her infant's diet until the baby is 6 months old. The milks of all mammals are low in iron, but the iron contained in breast milk is much more easily absorbed by the baby's system. Consequently, bottle-fed infants need iron-fortified formula.
Helps ensure healthy physical growth	In the first few months, breastfed infants add weight and length slightly faster than bottle-fed infants, who catch up by the end of the first year. One-year-old breastfed babies are leaner (have a higher percentage of muscle to fat); the longer babies are breastfed, the less likely they are to be overweight in early childhood.
Protects against many diseases	Breastfeeding transfers antibodies and other infection-fighting agents from mother to child and enhances functioning of the immune system. As a result, compared with bottle-fed infants, breastfed babies have far fewer allergic reactions and respiratory and intestinal illnesses. Components of human milk that protect against disease can be added to formula, but breastfeeding provides superior immunity.
Protects against faulty jaw development and tooth decay	Sucking the mother's nipple instead of an artificial nipple helps avoid malocclusion, a condition in which the upper and lower jaws do not meet properly. It also protects against tooth decay due to sweet liquid remaining in the mouths of infants who fall asleep while sucking on a bottle.
Ensures digestibility	Because breastfed babies have a different kind of bacteria growing in their intestines than do bottle-fed infants, they rarely suffer from constipation or other gastrointestinal problems.
Smooths the transition to solid foods	Breastfed infants accept new solid foods more easily than bottle-fed infants, perhaps because of their greater experience with a variety of flavors, which pass from the maternal diet into the mother's milk.

Sources: American Academy of Pediatrics, 2005a; Araujo, et al., 2006; Fulhan, Collier, & Duggan, 2003; Kramer et al., 2002, 2003; Wayerman, Rothenbacher, & Brenner, 2006.

Genetic makeup also affects body weight. For example, the weights of adopted children correlate more strongly with those of their biological than of their adoptive parents (Sørensen, Holst, & Stunkard, 1998). At the same time, environment—in particular, nutrition and eating habits—plays an especially important role.

Nutrition

Nutrition is important at any time of development, but it is especially crucial during the first two years because the baby's brain and body are growing so rapidly. Pound for pound, an infant's energy needs are twice those of an adult. Twenty-five percent of babies' total caloric intake is devoted to growth, and infants need extra calories to keep their rapidly developing organs functioning properly (Trahms & Pipes, 1997).

• **Breastfeeding versus Bottle-Feeding** Babies need not only enough food but also the right kind of food. In early infancy, breast milk is ideally suited to their needs, and bottled formulas try to imitate it. Applying What We Know above summarizes major nutritional and health advantages of breast milk.

Because of these benefits, breastfed babies in poverty-stricken regions are much less likely to be malnourished and 6 to 14 times more likely to survive the first year of life. The World Health Organization recommends breastfeeding until age 2 years, with solid foods added at

▪ Biology *and* Environment ▪

Low-Level Lead Exposure and Children's Development

Lead is a highly toxic element that, at blood levels exceeding 60 μg/dL (micrograms per deciliter), causes brain swelling and hemorrhaging. Risk of death rises as blood-lead level exceeds 100 μg/dL. Before 1980, exposure to lead resulted from the use of lead-based paints for the interiors of residences (where infants and young children often ate paint chips that flaked off walls) and from the use of leaded gasoline (car exhaust resulted in a highly breathable form of lead). The passage of laws limiting the lead content of paint and mandating lead-free gasoline led to a sharp decline in children's lead levels, from an average of 15 μg/dL in 1980 to 1.9 μg/dL today (Meyer et al., 2003; U.S. Centers for Disease Control and Prevention, 2005).

But in neighborhoods near industries that use lead production processes, or where lead-based paint remains in older homes, children's blood levels are still markedly elevated. About 16 percent of low-SES children who live in large central cities, and 37 percent of African-American children in these areas, have blood-level levels exceeding 10 μg/dL (the official "level of concern" in the United States and Canada), warranting immediate efforts to reduce exposure (Health Canada, 2006b; U.S. Centers for Disease Control and Prevention, 2005).

How much lead exposure is too much? Is lead contamination a "silent epidemic," impairing children's mental functioning even in small quantities? Until recently, answers were unclear. Studies reporting a negative relationship between children's current lead levels and cognitive performance had serious limitations. Researchers knew nothing about children's history of lead exposure and often failed to control for factors associated with both blood-lead levels and mental test scores (such as SES, home environmental quality, and nutrition) that might account for the findings.

Over the past two decades, seven longitudinal studies of the developmental consequences of lead have been conducted—three in the United States, two in Australia, one in Mexico City, and one in Yugoslavia. Some focused on inner-city, low-SES minority children, others on middle- and upper-middle-SES suburban children, and one on children living close to a lead smelter. Each tracked children's

These children play near a cement factory in Cairo, Egypt, which ranks among the world's most polluted cities in levels of lead and other toxins. Longitudinal studies consistently show lasting negative effects of lead exposure, including learning impairments and behavior problems. AP Images/Mohamed El-Dakhakny

6 months—practices that, if widely followed, would save the lives of more than a million infants annually. Even breastfeeding for just a few weeks offers some protection against respiratory and intestinal infections, which are devastating to young children in developing countries. Also, because a nursing mother is less likely to get pregnant, breastfeeding helps increase spacing between siblings, a major factor in reducing infant and childhood deaths in nations with widespread poverty (Bellamy, 2005). (Note, however, that breastfeeding is not a reliable method of birth control.)

Yet many mothers in the developing world do not know about the benefits of breastfeeding. In Africa, the Middle East, and Latin America, most babies get some breastfeeding, but fewer than 40 percent are exclusively breastfed for the first 6 months, and one-third are fully weaned from the breast before 1 year (Lauer et al., 2004). In place of breast milk, mothers give their babies commercial formula or low-grade nutrients, such as rice water or highly diluted cow or goat milk. Contamination of these foods as a result of poor sanitation is common and often leads to illness and infant death. The United Nations has encouraged all

lead exposure over an extended time and included relevant controls.

Five sites reported negative relationships between lead exposure and children's IQs (Hubbs-Tait et al., 2006). Higher blood levels were also associated with verbal and visual-motor skill deficits, distractibility, overactivity, poor organization, and behavior problems. And an array of findings suggested that persistent childhood lead exposure contributes to antisocial behavior in adolescence (Dietrich et al., 2001; Needleman et al., 2002; Nevin, 2000; Stretesky & Lynch, 2001).

The investigations did not agree on an age period of greatest vulnerability. In some, relationships were strongest in toddlerhood and early childhood; in others, at the most recently studied age—suggesting cumulative effects over time. Still other studies reported a similar susceptibility to lead-related cognitive deficits from infancy through adolescence. Overall, poorer mental test scores associated with lead exposure persisted over time and seemed to be permanent. Children given drugs to induce excretion of lead (chelation) did not improve (Dietrich et al., 2004; Rogan et al., 2001). And negative lead-related cognitive consequences were evident at all levels of exposure—even below 10 μg/dL (Lamphear et al., 2005).

Although the overall impact of low-level lead exposure on all outcomes is modest, in three longitudinal investigations, cognitive consequences were much greater for low-SES than higher-SES children (see, for example, Figure 5.11) (Bellinger, Leviton, & Sloman, 1990; Ris et al., 2004; Tong, McMichael, & Baghurst, 2000). A stressed, disorganized home life seems to heighten lead-induced damage, whereas an organized, stimulating home and school may offset it. Dietary factors can also magnify or reduce lead's toxic effects. Iron deficiency, common in low-SES children, increases lead concentration in the blood, whereas iron supplements decrease it. Similarly, exposed children absorb less lead when their diets contain enough zinc (Noonan et al., 2003; Wolf, Jimenez, & Lozoff, 2003; Wright et al., 2003).

In sum, lead impairs learning and contributes to behavior problems—findings confirmed by rigorous animal experiments (Cory-Slechta, 2003; Delville, 1999; Li et al., 2003). Low-SES children are more likely both to live in lead-contaminated areas and to experience additional risks that magnify lead-induced damage. Because lead is a stable element, its release into the air and soil is difficult to reverse. Therefore, in addition to laws that control lead pollution and limit children's exposure, interventions that reduce the negative impact of lead—through involved parenting, better schools, and dietary enrichment—are vital.

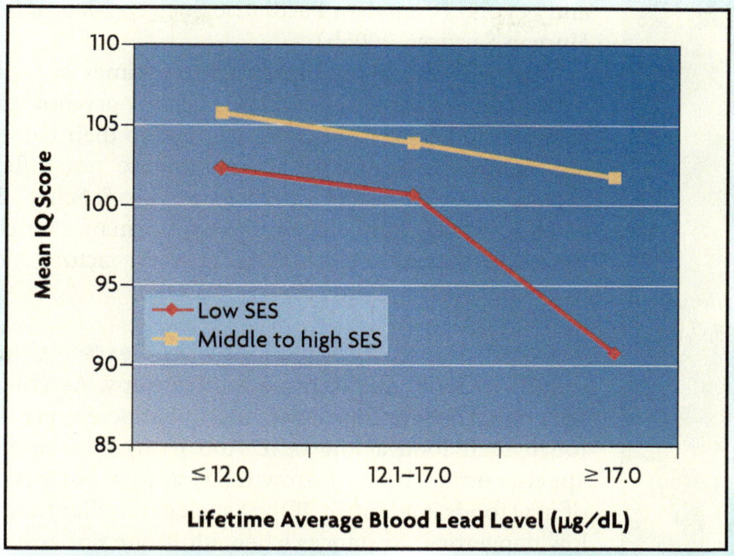

Figure 5.11 **Relationship of lifetime average lead exposure to 11- to 13-year-olds' IQ by SES.**
In this study, conducted in the lead-smelting city of Port Pirie, Australia, blood-lead levels of 375 children were measured repeatedly from birth to age 11 to 13. Among both low-SES and higher-SES participants, increases in lifetime average blood-lead concentrations were associated with poorer mental test scores. But the lead-exposure-related drop in IQ was much greater for low-SES children. (Adapted from Tong, McMichael, & Baghurst, 2000.)

hospitals and maternity units in developing countries to promote breastfeeding as long as mothers do not have viral or bacterial infections (such as HIV or tuberculosis) that can be transmitted to the baby. Today, most developing countries have banned the practice of giving free or subsidized formula to new mothers.

Partly as a result of the natural childbirth movement, breastfeeding has become more common in industrialized nations, especially among well-educated women. Today, 71 percent of American and 75 percent of Canadian mothers breastfeed. However, about two-thirds of breastfeeding U.S. mothers and nearly half of Canadian mothers stop after a few months (Li et al., 2005; Palda et al., 2004). Because breast milk is so easily digestible, a breastfed infant becomes hungry every 1½ to 2 hours, compared to every 3 to 4 hours for a bottle-fed baby, making breastfeeding inconvenient for many employed women. Not surprisingly, mothers who return to work sooner wean their babies from the breast earlier (Kimbro, 2006).

Mothers who cannot be with their babies all the time can still combine breast- and bottle-feeding. U.S. and Canadian national health agencies advise exclusive breastfeeding for the

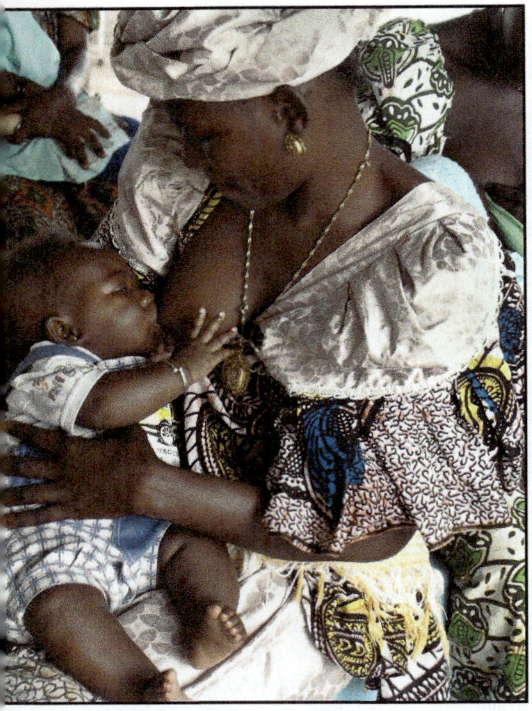

This breastfed baby from Gambia is likely to grow normally during the first year. Breastfeeding is especially important in developing countries, where it helps protect babies against life-threatening infections and early death. © Sean Sprague/The Image Works

first 6 months. In the United States, recommendations also suggest that breast milk be included in the baby's diet until at least 1 year; in Canada, until 2 years and beyond (Canadian Paediatric Society, 2005; U.S. Department of Health and Human Services, 2005b).

Women who do not breastfeed sometimes worry that they are depriving their baby of an experience essential for healthy psychological development. Yet breastfeeding mothers are not more attached to their babies, and breastfed and bottle-fed children in industrialized nations do not differ in emotional adjustment (Fergusson & Woodward, 1999; Wilkinson & Scherl, 2006). Some studies report a small advantage in intelligence test performance for children and adolescents who were breastfed, after controlling for many factors. Most, however, find no cognitive benefits (Der, Batty, & Deary, 2006).

• **Nutrition in Childhood and Adolescence** Around 1 year, infants' diets should include all the basic food groups. As children approach age 2, their appetites become unpredictable. Preschoolers eat well at one meal but barely touch their food at the next. And many become picky eaters. This decline in appetite occurs because growth has slowed. Furthermore, preschoolers' wariness of new foods is adaptive. If they stick to familiar foods, they are less likely to swallow dangerous substances when adults are not around to protect them (Birch & Fisher, 1995). Parents need not worry about variations in amount eaten from meal to meal. Over the course of a day, preschoolers compensate for a meal in which they eat little by eating more at a later meal (Hursti, 1999).

Children tend to imitate the food choices and eating practices of people they admire—adults as well as peers. For example, mothers who drink milk or soft drinks tend to have 5-year-old daughters with a similar beverage preference (Fisher et al., 2001). In Mexico, where children see family members delighting in the taste of peppery foods, preschoolers enthusiastically eat chili peppers, whereas most North American children reject them (Birch, Zimmerman, & Hind, 1980).

Repeated, unpressured exposure to a new food also increases children's acceptance (Fuller et al., 2005). Serving broccoli or tofu increases children's liking for these healthy foods. In contrast, offering sweet fruit or soft drinks promotes "milk avoidance" (Black et al., 2002). Although children's healthy eating depends on a wholesome food environment, too much parental control over eating limits children's opportunities to develop self-control. When parents offer bribes ("Finish your vegetables, and you can have an extra cookie"), children tend to like the healthy food less and the treat more (Birch, Fisher, & Davison, 2003).

Once puberty arrives, rapid body growth leads to a dramatic rise in food intake. This increase in nutritional requirements comes at a time when eating habits are the poorest. Of all age groups, adolescents are the most likely to skip breakfast (a practice linked to obesity), omit nutrient-rich fruits and vegetables from their diets, consume empty calories, and eat on the run (Stockman et al., 2005; Striegel-Moore et al., 2006; Videon & Manning, 2003). Fast-food restaurants—favorite teenage gathering places—have begun to offer some healthful menu options, but adolescents need guidance in choosing these alternatives. Eating fast food and purchases from snack bars and vending machines at school is strongly associated with consumption of high-fat foods and soft drinks (Bowman et al., 2004; Kubik et al., 2003).

The most common nutritional problem of adolescence is iron deficiency, as iron requirements increase to a maximum during the growth spurt and remain high among girls because of iron loss during menstruation. A tired, irritable teenager may be suffering from anemia rather than unhappiness and should have a medical checkup. Most adolescents do not get enough calcium, and they are also deficient in riboflavin (vitamin B_2) and magnesium (both of which support metabolism) (Cavadini, Siega-Riz, & Popkin, 2000).

Frequency of family meals is strongly associated with healthy eating—greater intake of fruits, vegetables, grains, and calcium-rich foods—in teenagers (Neumark-Sztainer et al., 2003). But compared to families with children, those with adolescents eat fewer meals together. Finding ways to arrange family meals, despite busy schedules, can greatly improve teenagers' diets.

Malnutrition In developing countries and war-torn areas, where food resources are limited, malnutrition is widespread. Recent evidence indicates that about one-third of the world's children suffer from malnutrition before age 5 (Bellamy, 2005). The 9 percent who are severely affected suffer from two dietary diseases.

Marasmus is a wasted condition of the body caused by a diet low in all essential nutrients. It usually appears in the first year of life when a baby's mother is too malnourished to produce enough breast milk and bottle-feeding is also inadequate. The starving baby becomes painfully thin and is in danger of dying.

Kwashiorkor is caused by an unbalanced diet very low in protein. The disease usually strikes after weaning, between 1 and 3 years of age. It is common in regions where children get just enough calories from starchy foods, but little protein. In response, the child's body breaks down its own protein reserves. Soon the belly enlarges, the feet swell, the hair falls out, and a skin rash appears. A once bright-eyed, curious youngster becomes irritable and listless.

Children who survive these extreme forms of malnutrition often grow to be smaller in all body dimensions and suffer from lasting damage to the brain, heart, liver, or other organs (Müller & Krawinkel, 2005). When their diets do improve, they tend to gain excessive weight (Branca & Ferrari, 2002; Martins et al., 2004). A malnourished body protects itself by establishing a low basal metabolism rate, which may endure after nutrition improves. Also, malnutrition may disrupt appetite-control centers in the brain, causing the child to overeat when food becomes plentiful.

Learning and behavior are also seriously affected. In one long-term study of marasmic children, an improved diet led to some catch-up growth in height, but not in head size (Stoch et al., 1982). The malnutrition probably interfered with growth of neural fibers and myelination, causing a permanent loss in brain weight. And animal evidence reveals that a deficient diet alters the production of neurotransmitters in the brain—an effect that can disrupt all aspects of development (Haller, 2005). These children score low on intelligence tests, show poor fine motor coordination, and have difficulty paying attention (Galler et al., 1990; Liu et al., 2003). They also display a more intense stress response to fear-arousing situations, perhaps caused by the constant, gnawing pain of hunger (Fernald & Grantham-McGregor, 1998).

Top photo: This baby of Niger, Africa, has marasmus, a wasted condition caused by a diet low in all essential nutrients. *Bottom photo:* The swollen abdomen of this toddler, who lives in a Rwandan refugee camp, is a symptom of kwashiorkor, which results from a diet very low in protein. If they survive, these children are likely to suffer stunted growth, damage to vital organs, and lasting impairments in intellectual and emotional development. © Dominique Derda/France 2/ CORBIS

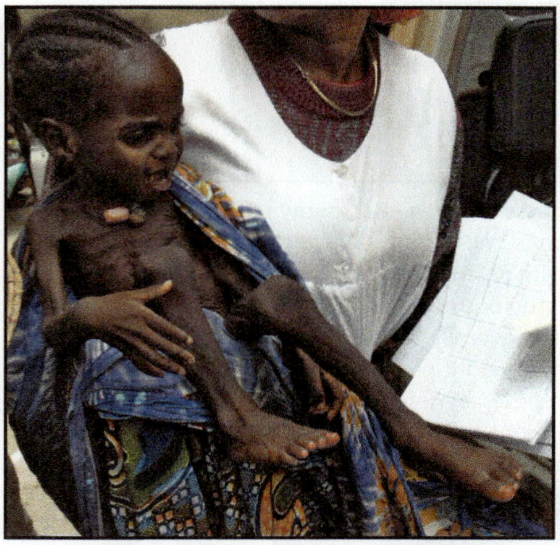

Recall from our discussion of prenatal malnutrition in Chapter 3 that the passivity and irritability of malnourished children worsen the impact of poor diet. These behaviors may appear even when protein-calorie deprivation is only mild to moderate. They also accompany *iron-deficiency anemia,* a condition common among poverty-stricken infants and children that interferes with many central nervous system processes. Withdrawal and listlessness reduce the nutritionally deprived child's ability to pay attention, explore, and evoke sensitive caregiving from parents, whose lives are already disrupted by poverty and stressful living conditions (Corapci, Radan, & Lozoff, 2006; Grantham-McGregor & Ani, 2001). For this reason, interventions for malnourished children must improve the family situation as well as the child's nutrition.

Inadequate nutrition is not confined to developing countries; it is a national and international crisis. Because government-sponsored supplementary food programs do not reach all families in need, an estimated 15 percent of Canadian children and 16 percent of American children suffer from *food insecurity*—uncertain access to enough food for a healthy, active life. Food insecurity is especially high among single-parent families (33 percent) and low-income ethnic minority families—for example, Hispanic and African Americans (22 percent) and Canadian Aboriginals (31 percent) (Statistics Canada, 2005d; U.S. Department of Agriculture, 2005a). Although few of these children have marasmus or kwashiorkor, their physical growth and ability to learn are still affected.

Obesity Today, about one-fourth of North American children and adolescents are overweight, many extremely so. Nearly 8 percent of Canadian and

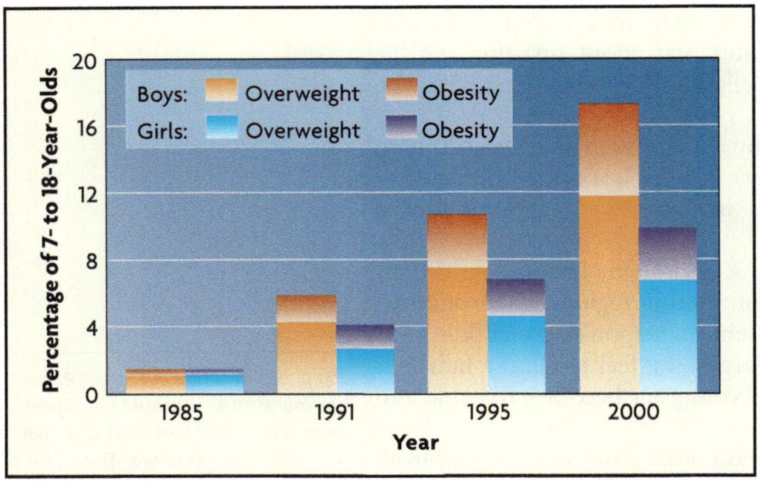

Figure 5.12 **Increase in overweight and obesity among 7- to 18-year-olds in China from 1985 to 2000.**

The trend, though evident in both sexes, is much greater in boys. (From Y. Wu, 2006, "Overweight and Obesity in China," *British Medical Journal*, 333, p. 363. Reprinted by permission of BMJ Publishing Group Ltd.)

10 percent of U.S. youngsters suffer from **obesity,** a greater-than-20-percent increase over healthy weight, based on *body mass index (BMI)*—a ratio of weight to height associated with body fat. (A BMI above the 85th percentile for the child's age and sex is considered overweight, a BMI above the 95th percentile obese.) During the past several decades, a rise in overweight and obesity has occurred in many Western nations, with dramatic escalations in Canada, Finland, Greece, Great Britain, Ireland, New Zealand, and the United States (Ogden et al., 2006; Shields, 2005; U.S. Department of Health and Human Services, 2006b). Smaller increases have occurred in other industrialized nations, including Australia, Germany, Israel, the Netherlands, and Sweden.

Obesity rates are also increasing rapidly in developing countries as urbanization shifts the population toward sedentary lifestyles and diets high in meats and refined foods (Wrotniak et al., 2004). In China, for example, where obesity was nearly nonexistent a generation ago, today 15 percent of children and adolescents are overweight, and 3 percent are obese—a fourfold increase over the past two decades, with boys affected more than girls (see Figure 5.12) (Wu, 2006). Childhood obesity is especially high in Chinese cities, where it has reached 8 percent (McLeod, 2007). In addition to lifestyle changes, a prevailing belief in Chinese culture that excess body fat represents prosperity and health—carried over from a half-century ago, when famine and malnutrition caused millions of deaths—has contributed to this alarming upsurge. High valuing of sons may induce Chinese parents to offer boys especially generous portions of meat, dairy products, and other energy-dense foods that were once scarce but now are widely available.

Overweight rises with age, reaching nearly 30 percent among North American teenagers. And over 80 percent of those affected become overweight adults. Besides serious emotional and social difficulties, obese children are at risk for lifelong health problems. Symptoms that begin to appear in the early school years—high blood pressure, high cholesterol levels, respiratory abnormalities, and insulin resistance—are powerful predictors of heart disease and other circulatory difficulties, type 2 diabetes, gallbladder disease, sleep and digestive disorders, many forms of cancer, and early death (Krishnamoorthy, Hart, & Jelalian, 2006; World Cancer Research Fund/American Institute for Cancer Research, 2007). Indeed, type 2 diabetes—formerly also known as "adult-onset" diabetes because it was rarely seen in childhood—is rising rapidly among overweight children, sometimes leading to early, severe complications, including stroke, kidney failure, and circulatory problems that heighten the risk of eventual blindness and leg amputation (Hannon, Rao, & Arslanian, 2005; National Diabetes Education Program, 2004).

These children at a county fair consume a snack of cheesy fries with joyous abandon. High-calorie, fatty foods are especially prominent in the family diets provided by overweight parents, leaving their children at high risk for excessive weight gain. © Jeff Greenberg/The Image Works

Causes of Obesity. Not all children are equally at risk for excessive weight gain. Overweight children tend to have overweight parents, and concordance for obesity is higher in identical than in fraternal twins. But heredity accounts for only a *tendency* to gain weight (Salbe et al., 2002a). The importance of environment is seen in the consistent relationship of low education and income to overweight and obesity in industrialized nations, especially among certain ethnic minorities, including African-American, Hispanic, Native-American, and Canadian-Aboriginal children and adults (Anand et al., 2001; Ogden et al., 2006). Factors responsible are lack of knowledge about healthy diet; a tendency to buy high-fat, low-cost foods; and family stress, which can prompt overeating. Furthermore, low-income children are more likely to be undernourished in their early years, which—as noted on page 195—can increase the risk of later overweight.

A follow-up of more than 2,000 U.S. 3- to 12-year-olds revealed that children who got less nightly sleep were more likely to be overweight five years later (Snell, Adam, & Duncan, 2007). Reduced sleep may promote weight gain by increasing time available for eating, by leaving children too fatigued for physical activity, or by disrupting the brain's regulation of hunger and metabolism.

Parental feeding practices also contribute to childhood obesity. Overweight children are more likely to eat larger quantities of high-calorie sugary and fatty foods, perhaps because these foods are prominent in the diets offered by their parents, who also tend to be overweight. Interviews with more than 3,000 U.S. parents revealed that many served their 4- to 24-month-olds French fries, pizza, candy, sugary fruit drinks, and soda on a daily basis. On average, infants consumed 20 percent and toddlers 30 percent more calories than they needed (Briefel et al., 2004). Some parents anxiously overfeed, interpreting almost all their child's discomforts as a desire for food. Others pressure their children to eat, a practice common among immigrant parents and grandparents who, as children themselves survived periods of food deprivation. Still other parents are overly controlling, restricting when, what, and how much their child eats and worrying that the child will gain too much weight (Birch, Fisher, & Davison, 2003; Moens, Braet, & Soetens, 2007). In each case, parents fail to help children learn to regulate their own food intake. Also, parents of overweight children often use high-fat, sugary foods to reinforce other behaviors, leading children to attach great value to the treat (Sherry et al., 2004).

Because of these experiences, obese children soon develop maladaptive eating habits. They are more responsive than normal-weight individuals to external stimuli associated with food—taste, sight, smell, time of day, and food-related words—and less responsive to internal hunger cues (Jansen et al., 2003; Temple et al., 2007). They also eat faster and chew their food less thoroughly, a behavior pattern that appears as early as 18 months of age (Drabman et al., 1979).

Overweight children are less physically active than their normal-weight peers, and their parents are similarly inactive (Davison & Birch, 2002). Inactivity is both cause and consequence of excessive weight gain. Research reveals that the rise in childhood obesity is due in part to the many hours North American children spend watching television. In a study that tracked children's TV viewing from ages 4 to 11, the more TV children watched, the more body fat they added, with children who devoted more than 3 hours per day to TV accumulating 40 percent more fat than those devoting less than 1¾ hours (see Figure 5.13) (Proctor et al., 2003). Watching TV greatly reduces time spent in physical exercise, and TV ads encourage children to eat fattening, unhealthy snacks. As children get heavier, they increasingly replace active play with sedentary pursuits—including eating—and gain still more weight (Salbe et al., 2002b). Children permitted to have a TV in their bedroom—a practice linked to especially high TV viewing—are at greater risk for overweight (Adachi-Mejia et al., 2007).

Finally, the broader cultural environment affects the incidence of obesity. Compared with a half-century ago, new communities today are designed for automobile use, with fewer sidewalks and other walkways—a change that has contributed to reduced physical activity (Krishnamoorthy, Hart, & Jelalian, 2006). And over the past two to three decades, the number of families who frequently eat meals outside the home has risen dramatically. Eating the same foods out, as opposed to at home, results in increased consumption—on average, about 200 extra calories per day (French, Story, & Jeffrey, 2001).

Consequences of Obesity. Unfortunately, physical attractiveness is a powerful predictor of social acceptance in Western societies. Both children and adults rate overweight and obese youngsters as less likable than other children, stereotyping them as lazy, sloppy, ugly, stupid, and deceitful (Kilpatrick & Sanders, 1978; Penny & Haddock, 2007; Tiggemann & Anesbury, 2000). In school, obese children are often socially isolated (Strauss & Pollack, 2003). And by middle childhood, they report more

■ Figure 5.13 Relationship of television viewing to gains in body fat from ages 4 to 11. Researchers followed more than 100 children from ages 4 to 11, collecting information on hours per day of television viewing and on body fat, measured in millimeters of skinfold thickness at five body sites (upper arms, shoulders, abdomen, trunk, and thighs). The more TV children watched, the greater the gain in body fat. At ages 10 to 11, the difference between children watching fewer than 1¾ hours and those watching more than 3 hours had become large. (Adapted from M. H. Proctor et al., 2003, "Television Viewing and Change in Body Fat from Preschool to Early Adolescence: The Framingham Children's Study," *International Journal of Obesity, 27,* p. 831. Reprinted by permission from Macmillan Publishers Ltd.)

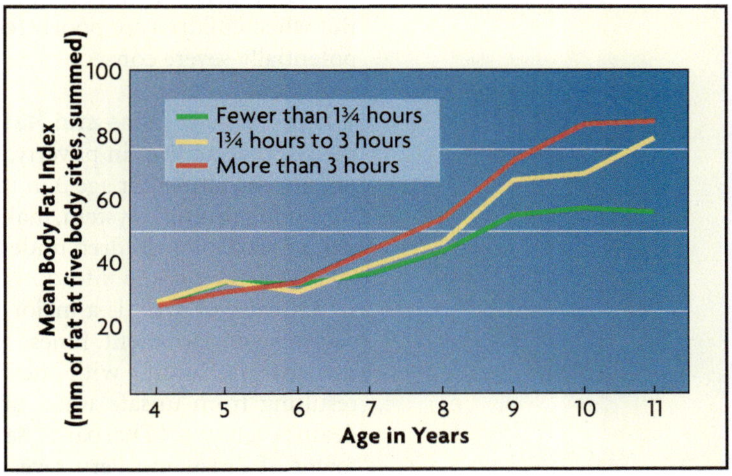

This community program in Dallas, Texas, is addressing the dramatic rise in childhood overweight and obesity by guiding children and their families in developing healthier lifestyles. Here, participating children line up to play a game of kickball. AP Images/Matt Slocum

emotional, social, and school difficulties and display more behavior problems than their normal-weight agemates. Because unhappiness and overeating contribute to each other, the child remains overweight (Zeller & Modi, 2006). Persistent obesity from childhood into adolescence predicts serious disorders, including defiance, aggression, and severe depression (Schwimmer, Burwinkle, & Varni, 2003; Young-Hyman et al., 2006).

The psychological consequences of obesity combine with continuing discrimination to result in reduced life chances. Overweight individuals are less likely than their normal-weight agemates to receive financial aid for college, be rented apartments, find mates, and be offered jobs. And they report frequent mistreatment by family members, peers, co-workers, and health-care professionals (Carr & Friedman, 2005; Rogge, Greenwald, & Golden, 2004).

Treating Obesity. Childhood obesity is difficult to treat because it is a family disorder. In a British study, only one-fourth of overweight parents judged their overweight children to have a weight problem (Jeffrey, 2004). But when parents decide to seek treatment for an obese child, long-term changes in body weight do occur.

The most effective interventions for obesity are family-based and focus on changing behaviors (Kitzmann & Beech, 2006). In one program, both parent and child revised their eating patterns, exercised daily, and reinforced each other with praise and points for progress, which they exchanged for special activities and times together. The more weight parents lost, the more their children lost (Wrotniak et al., 2004). Follow-ups after five and ten years showed that children maintained weight loss more effectively than adults—a finding that underscores the importance of early intervention (Epstein, Roemmich, & Raynor, 2001). Treatment programs that focus on both diet and lifestyle can yield substantial, long-lasting weight reduction among children and adolescents. But these interventions work best when parents' and children's weight problems are not severe (Eliakim et al., 2004; Nemet et al., 2005).

Children consume one-third of their daily energy intake at school. Therefore, schools can help reduce obesity by serving healthier meals and ensuring regular physical activity. Several U.S. states and Canadian provinces have passed obesity-reduction legislation (Cotton et al., 2006). Measures taken include improved nutrition standards and bans on sale of fast foods in schools, additional recess time in the elementary grades, and increased physical education time in all grades. Prohibiting access to fast food at school, however, is unlikely to be effective without attitude change because fast-food restaurants are often located near schools (Tanner, 2005). In some locales, schools are required to offer obesity awareness and weight reduction programs.

Infectious Disease

In well-nourished children, ordinary childhood illnesses have no effect on physical growth. But when children are poorly fed, disease interacts with malnutrition in a vicious spiral, with potentially severe consequences.

• Infectious Disease and Malnutrition In developing nations where a large proportion of the population lives in poverty, illnesses such as measles and chicken pox, which typically do not appear until after age 3 in industrialized nations, occur much earlier. Poor diet depresses the body's immune system, making children far more susceptible to disease. Of the 10 million annual deaths of children under age 5 worldwide, 98 percent are in developing countries and 70 percent are due to infectious diseases (World Health Organization, 2005).

Disease, in turn, is a major contributor to malnutrition, hindering physical growth and cognitive development. Illness reduces appetite and limits the body's ability to absorb foods, especially in children with intestinal infections. In developing countries, widespread diarrhea, resulting from unsafe water and contaminated foods, leads to several million childhood deaths each year (Tharpar & Sanderson, 2004). Studies carried out in the slums and shantytowns of Brazil and Peru reveal that the more persistent diarrhea is in early childhood, the shorter children are in height and the lower they score on mental tests during the school years (Checkley et al., 2003; Niehaus et al., 2002).

Most developmental impairments and deaths due to diarrhea can be prevented with nearly cost-free *oral rehydration therapy (ORT),* in which sick children are given a glucose, salt, and water solution that quickly replaces fluids the body loses. Since 1990, public health workers have taught nearly half the families in the developing world how to administer ORT. Also, supplements of zinc (essential for immune system functioning), which cost only 30 cents for a month's supply, substantially reduce the incidence of severe and prolonged diarrhea (Aggarwal, Sentz, & Miller, 2007). Because of these interventions, the lives of millions of children are saved annually.

Families wait their turn for immunizations at a crowded public health clinic—the only option for people who lack private health insurance. Unfortunately, not all parents have schedules that allow them to endure the long waits, so their children go unvaccinated. AP Images/Damian Dovarganes

• **Immunization** In industrialized nations, childhood diseases have declined dramatically during the past half-century, largely as a result of widespread immunization of infants and young children. Nevertheless, about 20 percent of U.S. infants and toddlers are not fully immunized. Of the 80 percent who receive a complete schedule of vaccinations in the first two years, some do not receive the immunizations they need later, in early childhood. Overall, 24 percent of U.S. preschoolers lack essential immunizations, a rate that rises to 32 percent for poverty-stricken children. Many do not receive full protection until age 5 or 6, when it is required for school entry (U.S. Department of Health and Human Services, 2006c). In contrast, fewer than 10 percent of preschoolers lack immunizations in Denmark and Norway, and fewer than 7 percent in Great Britain, Canada, the Netherlands, and Sweden (United Nations, 2002; UNICEF, 2006).

Why does the United States lag behind these other countries in immunization? In earlier chapters, we noted that many children in the United States lack access to the health care they need. In 1994, all medically uninsured children in the United States were guaranteed free immunizations, a program that has led to a steady improvement in immunization rates.

Inability to pay for vaccines is only one cause of inadequate immunization. Parents with stressful daily lives or without health benefits of their own often fail to schedule vaccination appointments, and those without a primary care physician do not want to endure long waits in crowded U.S. public health clinics. Misconceptions also contribute—for example, the notion that vaccines do not work or that they weaken the immune system (Gellin, Maibach, & Marcuse, 2000). Some parents have been influenced by media reports suggesting a link between the measles–mumps–rubella vaccine and a rise in the number of children diagnosed with autism, although large-scale studies show no association between immunization and autism (Dales, Hammer, & Smith, 2001; Richler et al., 2006; Stehr-Green et al., 2003). In areas where many parents have refused to immunize their children, outbreaks of whooping cough and rubella have occurred, with life-threatening consequences (Tuyen & Bisgard, 2003). Public education programs to increase parental knowledge about the importance and safety of timely immunizations are badly needed.

Emotional Well-Being

We may not associate love and stimulation with healthy physical growth, but they are just as vital as food. **Nonorganic failure to thrive,** a growth disorder resulting from lack of parental love, is usually present by 18 months of age. Infants who have it show all the signs of marasmus—their bodies look wasted, and they are withdrawn and apathetic (Black, 2005). But no organic (or biological) cause can be found for the child's failure to grow. The baby is offered enough food and has no serious illness. The infant's behavior provides a strong clue to this diagnosis: Failure-to-thrive babies keep their eyes on nearby adults, anxiously watching their every move, and they rarely smile at their caregiver (Steward, 2001).

Family circumstances surrounding failure to thrive help explain these typical reactions. During feeding, diaper changing, and play, mothers of these infants seem cold and distant, at other times impatient and hostile (Hagekull, Bohlin, & Rydell, 1997). In response, babies try to protect themselves by keeping track of the threatening adult's whereabouts and, when she approaches, avoiding her gaze. Often an unhappy marriage or parental psychological disturbance contributes to these serious caregiving problems (Drotar, Pallotta, & Eckerle, 1994; Duniz et al., 1996). Sometimes the baby is irritable and displays abnormal feeding behaviors, such as poor sucking or vomiting, that stress the parent–child relationship further (Linscheid, Budd, & Rasnake, 2005). When treated early, by helping parents or placing the baby in a caring foster home, failure-to-thrive infants show quick catch-up growth. But if the disorder is not corrected in infancy, most children remain small and show lasting cognitive and emotional difficulties (Drewett, Corbett, & Wright, 2006; Dykman et al., 2001).

Extreme emotional deprivation can interfere with the production of GH and lead to **psychosocial dwarfism,** a growth disorder that usually appears between 2 and 15 years of age. Typical characteristics include very short stature, decreased GH secretion, immature skeletal age, and serious adjustment problems, which help distinguish psychosocial dwarfism from normal shortness (Doeker et al., 1999; Tarren-Sweeney, 2006). When such children are removed from their emotionally inadequate environments, their GH levels quickly return to normal, and they grow rapidly. But if treatment is delayed, the dwarfism can be permanent.

Ask Yourself

Review Explain why breastfeeding can have lifelong consequences for the development of babies born in poverty-stricken regions of the world.

Apply Ten-month-old Shaun is below average in height and painfully thin. He has one of two serious growth disorders. Name them, and indicate what clues you would look for to tell which one Shaun has.

Connect How are bidirectional influences between parent and child involved in the impact of malnutrition on psychological development?

Reflect In rearing a child, which feeding and other child-rearing practices would you use, and which would you avoid, to prevent overweight and obesity?

Puberty: The Physical Transition to Adulthood

During **puberty,** young people attain an adult-sized body and become capable of producing offspring. Accompanying rapid body growth are changes in physical features related to sexual functioning. Some, called **primary sexual characteristics,** involve the reproductive organs directly (ovaries, uterus, and vagina in females; penis, scrotum, and testes in males). Others, called **secondary sexual characteristics,** are visible on the outside of the body and serve as additional signs of sexual maturity (for example, breast development in females, and the appearance of underarm and pubic hair in both sexes). As the Milestones table on page 201 shows, these characteristics develop in a fairly standard sequence, although the ages at which each begins and is completed vary greatly. Typically, pubertal development takes about four years, but some adolescents complete it in two years, whereas others take five to six years. As you will soon see, puberty profoundly affects psychological development and social relationships.

Sexual Maturation in Girls

The scientific name for first menstruation is **menarche,** from the Greek word *arche,* meaning "beginning." Although most people view menarche as the major sign of puberty in girls, it actually occurs late in the sequence of pubertal events. Female puberty begins with the budding of the breasts, the growth spurt, and the appearance of pubic hair. Typically, menarche occurs around age 12½ for North American girls and age 13 for Western Europeans. But the age range is wide, extending from 10½ to 15½ years. Following menarche, breast and pubic hair growth are completed, and underarm hair appears (Archibald, Graber, & Brooks-Gunn, 2006).

Milestones

Pubertal Development in North American Boys and Girls

Girls	Average Age Attained	Age Range
Breasts begin to "bud"	10	(8–13)
Height spurt begins	10	(8–13)
Pubic hair appears	10.5	(8–14)
Peak strength spurt	11.6	(9.5–14)
Peak height spurt	11.7	(10–13.5)
Menarche (first menstruation) occurs	12.5	(10.5–14)
Peak weight spurt	12.7	(10–14)
Adult stature reached	13	(10–16)
Pubic hair growth completed	14.5	(14–15)
Breast growth completed	15	(10–17)

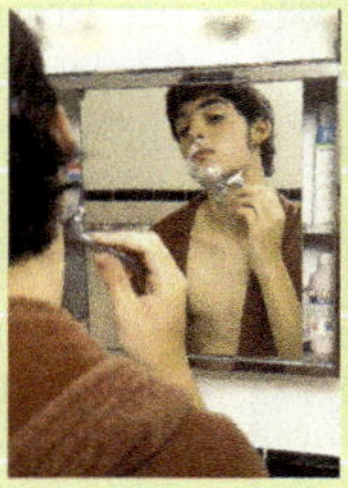

Boys	Average Age Attained	Age Range
Testes begin to enlarge	10	(9–13.5)
Pubic hair appears	12	(10–15)
Penis begins to enlarge	12	(10.5–14.5)
Height spurt begins	12.5	(10.5–16)
Spermarche (first ejaculation) occurs	13.5	(12–16)
Peak height spurt	14	(12.5–15.5)
Peak weight spurt	14	(12.5–15.5)
Facial hair begins to grow	14	(12.5–15.5)
Voice begins to deepen	14	(12.5–15.5)
Penis and testes growth completed	14.5	(12.5–16)
Peak strength spurt	15.3	(13–17)
Adult stature reached	15.5	(13.5–17.5)
Pubic hair growth completed	15.5	(14–17)

Sources: Chumlea et al., 2003; Herman-Giddens, 2006; Rogol, Roemmich, & Clark, 2002; Wu, Mendola, & Buck, 2002.
Photos: (left) © Aaron Haupt/Photo Researchers, Inc.; (right) © Bill Aron/PhotoEdit

Notice in the Milestones table above that nature delays sexual maturity until the girl's body is large enough for childbearing; menarche takes place after the peak of the height spurt. As an extra measure of security, for 12 to 18 months following menarche, the menstrual cycle often occurs without the release of an ovum from the ovaries (Bogin, 2001). This temporary period of sterility, however, does not occur in all girls and cannot be relied on for protection against pregnancy.

Sexual Maturation in Boys

The first sign of puberty in boys is the enlargement of the testes (glands that manufacture sperm), accompanied by changes in the texture and color of the scrotum. Pubic hair emerges soon after, about the same time the penis begins to enlarge (Rogol, Roemmich, & Clark, 2002).

Refer again to the Milestones table, and you will see that the growth spurt occurs much later in the sequence of pubertal events for boys than for girls. Also, boys' height gain is more intense and longer lasting. When it reaches its peak (about age 14), enlargement of the testes and penis is nearly complete, and underarm hair appears soon after. Facial and body hair also emerge just after the peak in body growth and increase gradually for several years. Another landmark of male physical maturity is the deepening of the voice as the larynx enlarges and the vocal cords lengthen. (Girls' voices also deepen slightly.) Voice change usually occurs at the peak of the male growth spurt and often is not complete until puberty is over (Archibald, Graber, & Brooks-Gunn, 2006).

Sex differences in pubertal growth are obvious in these middle school students. Although they are about the same age, the girl is taller and appears far more mature than her dance partner. © José Carillo/PhotoEdit

While the penis is growing, the prostate gland and seminal vesicles (which together produce semen, the fluid containing sperm) enlarge. Then, around age 13½, **spermarche,** or first ejaculation, occurs (Rogol, Roemmich, & Clark, 2002). For a while, the semen contains few living sperm. So, like girls, boys have an initial period of reduced fertility.

Individual and Group Differences in Pubertal Growth

Heredity contributes substantially to the timing of pubertal changes. Identical twins are more similar than fraternal twins in attainment of most pubertal milestones, including growth spurt, menarche, breast development, body hair, and voice change (Eaves et al., 2004; Mustanski et al., 2004). Nutrition and exercise also make a difference. In females, a sharp rise in body weight and fat may trigger sexual maturation. Fat cells release a protein called *leptin,* which is believed to signal the brain that girls' energy stores are sufficient for puberty—a likely reason that breast and pubic hair growth and menarche occur earlier for heavier and, especially, obese girls. In contrast, girls who begin rigorous athletic training at an early age or who eat very little (both of which reduce the percentage of body fat) usually experience later puberty (Anderson, Dallal, & Must, 2003; Delemarre-van de Waal, 2002; Slyper, 2006).

Variations in pubertal growth also exist between regions of the world and between income and ethnic groups. Physical health plays a major role. In poverty-stricken regions where malnutrition and infectious disease are common, menarche is greatly delayed, occurring as late as age 14 to 16 in many parts of Africa. Within developing countries, girls from higher-income families consistently reach menarche 6 to 18 months earlier than those from economically disadvantaged homes (Parent et al., 2003).

But in industrialized nations where food is abundant, the joint roles of heredity and environment in pubertal growth are apparent. For example, breast and pubic hair growth begin, on average, around age 9 in African-American girls—a year earlier than in Caucasian-American girls. And African-American girls reach menarche about six months earlier, around age 12. Although widespread overweight and obesity in the black population contribute, a genetically influenced faster rate of physical maturation is also involved. Black girls usually reach menarche before white girls of the same age and body weight (Anderson, Dallal, & Must, 2003; Chumlea et al., 2003; Herman-Giddens, 2006).

Early family experiences may also contribute to the timing of puberty. One theory suggests that humans have evolved to be sensitive to the emotional quality of their childhood environments. When children's safety and security are at risk, it is adaptive for them to reproduce early. A growing number of studies indicate that girls exposed to parental conflict and separation tend to reach menarche earlier than those with warm, stable family ties (Bogaert, 2005; Ellis, 2004; Mustanski et al., 2004; Romans et al., 2003; Tremblay & Frigon, 2005). But critics claim that the process through which parental behavior affects timing of menarche is unclear. An alternative explanation suggests that mothers who reached puberty early are more likely to bear children earlier, increasing their risk of marital conflict and separation (Mendle et al., 2006). Children of these mothers also may inherit a genetic tendency toward early puberty.

The Psychological Impact of Pubertal Events

TAKE A MOMENT... Think back to your late elementary school and junior high days. As you reached puberty, how did your feelings about yourself and your relationships with others change? Were your reactions similar to those predicted by Rousseau and Hall, described at the beginning of this chapter?

Is Puberty Inevitably a Period of Storm and Stress?

Contemporary research suggests that the notion of adolescence as a biologically determined period of storm and stress is greatly exaggerated. Certain problems, such as eating disorders, depression, suicide (see Chapter 11), and lawbreaking (see Chapter 12), occur more often in adolescence than earlier (Farrington, 2004; Graber, 2004). But the overall rate of serious psychological disturbance rises only slightly (by about 2 percent) from childhood to adolescence, when it is the same as in the adult population—about 20 percent (Costello & Angold, 1995). Although some teenagers encounter serious difficulties, emotional turbulence is not a routine feature.

The first researcher to point out the wide variability in adolescent adjustment was anthropologist Margaret Mead (1928). She returned from the Pacific islands of Samoa with a startling conclusion: Because of the culture's relaxed social relationships and openness toward sexuality, adolescence "is perhaps the pleasantest time the Samoan girl (or boy) will ever know" (p. 308). In Mead's alternative view, the social environment is entirely responsible for the range of teenage experiences, from erratic and agitated to calm and stress-free.

Later researchers found that Samoan adolescence was not as untroubled as Mead had assumed (Freeman, 1983). Still, Mead's work had an enormous impact. Today we know that the experience of adolescence is a product of both biological and social forces. Most tribal and village societies have a briefer transition to adulthood, but adolescence is not absent (Weisfield, 1997). In industrialized nations, where successful participation in economic life requires many years of education, young people face additional years of dependence on parents and postponement of sexual gratification. As a result, adolescence is greatly extended, and teenagers confront a wider array of psychological challenges. In the following sections, we will see many examples of how biological and social forces combine to affect teenagers' adjustment.

Reactions to Pubertal Changes

Two generations ago, menarche was often traumatic. Today, girls commonly react with surprise, undoubtedly due to the sudden onset of the event. Otherwise, they typically report a mixture of positive and negative emotions (DeRose & Brooks-Gunn, 2006). Yet wide individual differences exist, depending on prior knowledge and support from family members. Both are influenced by cultural attitudes toward puberty and sexuality.

For girls who have no advance information, menarche can be shocking and disturbing. In the 1950s, up to 50 percent received no prior warning, and of those who did, many were given negative, "grin-and-bear-it" messages (Costos, Ackerman, & Paradis, 2002; Shainess, 1961). Today, few girls are uninformed, a shift that is probably due to contemporary parents' greater willingness to discuss sexual matters and to the spread of health education classes (Omar, McElderry, & Zakharia, 2003). Almost all girls get some information from their mothers. And some evidence suggests that compared with Caucasian-American families, African-American families may better prepare girls for menarche, treat it as an important milestone, and express less conflict over girls reaching sexual maturity—factors that lead African-American girls to react more favorably (Martin, 1996; Scott et al., 1989).

Like girls' reactions to menarche, boys' reactions to spermarche reflect mixed feelings. Virtually all boys know about ejaculation ahead of time, but many say that no one spoke to them before or during puberty about physical changes (Omar, McElderry, & Zakharia, 2003). Usually they get information from their own reading. Even boys who had advance information often say that their first ejaculation occurred earlier than they expected and that they were unprepared for it. As with girls, boys who feel better prepared tend to react more positively (Stein & Reiser, 1994). But whereas almost all girls tell a friend that they are menstruating, far fewer boys tell anyone about spermarche (DeRose & Brooks-Gunn, 2006; Downs & Fuller, 1991). Overall, boys get much less social support than girls for the physical changes of puberty. This suggests that boys might benefit, especially, from opportunities to ask questions and discuss feelings with a sympathetic parent or health professional.

Many tribal and village societies celebrate physical maturity with an *adolescent initiation ceremony,* a ritualized announcement to the community that marks an important change in

In Hispanic communities, the *quinceañera,* celebrated at age 15, is a rite of passage honoring a girl's journey from childhood to maturity. It usually begins with a mass in which the priest blesses gifts presented to the girl. © Spencer Grant/ PhotoEdit

privilege and responsibility, letting young people know that reaching puberty is valued in their culture. In contrast, Western societies grant little formal recognition to movement from childhood to adolescence or from adolescence to adulthood. Certain ethnic and religious ceremonies, such as the Jewish bar or bat mitzvah and the *quinceañera* in Hispanic communities (celebrating a 15-year-old girl's sexual maturity and marriage availability), resemble initiation ceremonies. But although they carry a meaningful social message within the ethnic group, they do not result in a significant change in social status in the larger society.

Instead, Western adolescents are granted partial adult status at many different ages—an age for starting employment, for driving, for leaving high school, for voting, and for drinking—while in some contexts (at school and at home), they may still be regarded as children. The absence of a single widely accepted marker of physical and social maturity makes the process of becoming an adult especially confusing.

Pubertal Change, Emotion, and Social Behavior

A common belief is that pubertal change triggers adolescent moodiness and a desire for greater physical and psychological separation from parents. What does research say about these relationships?

• **Adolescent Moodiness** Although research reveals that higher sex hormone levels are related to adolescents' experience of negative emotion, these relationships are not strong (Buchanan, Eccles, & Becker, 1992; Graber, Brooks-Gunn, & Warren, 2006). What else might contribute to adolescent moodiness? In several studies, the moods of children, adolescents, and adults were monitored by having them carry electronic pagers. Over a one-week period, they were beeped at random intervals and asked to write down what they were doing, whom they were with, and how they felt.

As expected, adolescents reported less favorable moods than school-age children and adults (Larson et al., 2002; Larson & Lampman-Petraitis, 1989). But negative moods were linked to a greater number of negative life events, such as difficulties getting along with parents, disciplinary actions at school, and breaking up with a boyfriend or girlfriend. Negative events increased steadily from childhood to adolescence, and teenagers also seemed to react to them with greater emotion than children (Larson & Ham, 1993). (Recall that stress reactivity is heightened by changes in brain neurotransmitter activity during adolescence.)

Compared with the moods of older adolescents and adults, those of younger adolescents (ages 12 to 16) were less stable, often varying from cheerful to sad and back again. These mood swings were strongly related to situational changes. High points of adolescents' days were times spent with friends and in self-chosen leisure activities. Low points tended to occur in adult-structured settings—class, job, and religious services. Furthermore teenagers' emotional highs coincided with Friday and Saturday evenings, especially in high school (see Figure 5.14). Going out with friends and romantic partners increases so dramatically during adolescence that it becomes a "cultural script" for what is *supposed* to happen. Teenagers who spend weekend evenings at home often experience profound loneliness (Larson & Richards, 1998).

Yet another contributor to adolescent moodiness is change in sleep schedules. Although teenagers need almost as much sleep as they did in middle childhood (about nine hours), they go to bed much later than they did as children, perhaps because of increased neural sensitivity to evening light. This sleep "phase delay" strengthens with pubertal development. But today's teenagers—with more evening social activities, part-time jobs, and bedrooms equipped with televisions, telephones, computers—get much less sleep than teenagers of previous generations (Carskadon, Acebo, & Jenni, 2004; Carskadon et al., 2002). Sleep-deprived adolescents are more likely to suffer from depressed mood, achieve poorly in school, and engage in high-risk behaviors, including drinking and reckless driving (Dahl & Lewin, 2002; Hansen et al., 2005). Later school start times ease sleep loss but do not eliminate it.

Fortunately, frequent reports of negative mood level off around tenth grade, when teenagers' emotions also become more stable (Larson et al., 2002). Overall, teenagers with supportive family and peer relationships more often report positive and less often negative moods than their agemates with few social supports (Weinstein et al., 2006). In contrast, poorly adjusted young people—with low self-esteem, conduct difficulties, or delinquency—tend to react with stronger negative emotion to unpleasant daily experiences, perhaps compounding their adjustment problems (Schneiders et al., 2006).

In sum, biological and situational forces combine to make adolescence a time of deeper valleys and higher peaks in emotional experience than the periods surrounding it. Notice how this conclusion is consistent with the balanced view presented earlier in this chapter.

Compared with children and adults, adolescents often seem moody. But young people's negative moods are linked to negative life events, which increase from childhood to adolescence. Frequent disagreements with parents might be responsible for this teenager's unhappy frame of mind.
© Don Hammond/Design Pics/CORBIS

• Parent–Child Relationships Recall the observations of Sabrina's father in the introduction to this chapter—that as children enter adolescence, they resist spending time with the family and become more argumentative. Research in cultures as diverse as the United States and Turkey shows that puberty is related to a rise in parent–child conflict. During this time, both parents and teenagers report feeling less close to one another (Gure, Ucanok, & Sayil, 2006; Laursen, Coy, & Collins, 1998; Steinberg & Morris, 2001). Frequency of arguing is surprisingly similar across North American subcultures, occurring as often in families of European descent as in immigrant Asian and Hispanic families whose traditions emphasize respect for parental authority (Fuligni, 1998).

Why should a youngster's more adultlike appearance trigger these disputes? According to an evolutionary view, the association may have adaptive value. Among nonhuman primates, the young typically leave the family around the time of puberty. The same is true in many nonindustrialized cultures (Caine, 1986; Schlegel & Barry, 1991). Departure of young people discourages sexual relations between close blood relatives. But adolescents in industrialized nations, who are still economically dependent on parents, cannot leave the family. Consequently, a modern substitute seems to have emerged: psychological distancing.

As children become physically mature, they demand to be treated in adultlike ways. And as we will see in later chapters, adolescents' new powers of reasoning may also contribute to a rise in family tensions. Parent–adolescent disagreements focus largely on mundane, day-to-day matters—driving, dating partners, curfews, and the like (Adams & Laursen, 2001). But beneath these disputes lie serious concerns: parental efforts to protect teenagers from substance use, auto accidents, and early sex. The larger the gap between parents' and adolescents' views of teenagers' readiness for new responsibilities, the more quarreling (Deković, Noom, & Meeus, 1997).

Parent–daughter conflict tends to be more intense than conflict with sons, perhaps because parents place more restrictions on girls (Allison & Schultz, 2004). This gender disparity varies with culture; for example, it is less evident in Canada than in Italy, where gender-role values are more traditional (Claes et al., 2003). Nevertheless, by late adolescence, only a small minority of families experience continuing friction. Parents and teenagers display both conflict and affection, and they usually agree on important values, such as honesty and education. Although separation from parents is adaptive, both generations benefit from warm, protective family bonds throughout the lifespan.

■ Figure 5.14 Younger and older adolescents' emotional experiences across the week.

Adolescents' reports revealed that emotional high points are on Fridays and Saturdays. Mood drops on Sunday, before returning to school, and during the week, as students spend much time in adult-structured settings in school. (From R. Larson & M. Richards, 1998, "Waiting for the Weekend: Friday and Saturday Night as the Emotional Climax of the Week," in A. C. Crouter & R. Larson [Eds.], *Temporal Rhythms in Adolescence: Clocks, Calendars, and the Coordination of Daily Life*, San Francisco: Jossey-Bass, p. 41. Reprinted by permission of John Wiley & Sons, Inc.)

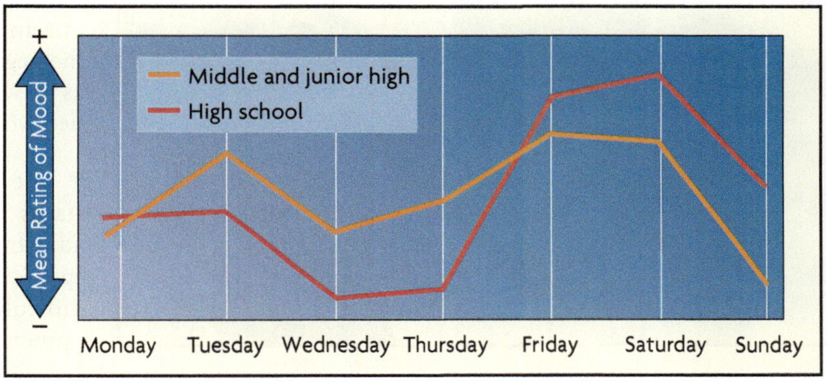

Early versus Late Pubertal Timing

In addition to dramatic physical change, the timing of puberty has a major impact on psychological adjustment. Findings of several studies indicate that both adults and peers viewed early-maturing boys as relaxed, independent, self-confident, and physically attractive. Popular with agemates, they tended to hold leadership positions in school and to be athletic stars. In contrast, both adults and peers viewed late-maturing boys as anxious, overly talkative, and attention-seeking (Brooks-Gunn, 1988; Clausen, 1975). However, early-maturing boys, though viewed as well-adjusted, report slightly more psychological stress and problem behaviors (sexual activity, smoking, drinking, delinquency) than their later-maturing agemates (Ge, Conger, & Elder, 2001b; Huddleston & Ge, 2003).

In contrast, early-maturing girls were unpopular, withdrawn, lacking in self-confidence, anxious, and prone to depression, and they held few leadership positions (Ge, Conger, & Elder, 1996; Graber et al., 1997; Graber, Brooks-Gunn, & Warren, 2006; Jones & Mussen, 1958). They were more involved in deviant behavior (getting drunk, participating in early sexual activity) and achieved less well in school (Caspi et al., 1993; Dick et al., 2000). In contrast, their later-maturing counterparts were especially well off—regarded as physically attractive, lively, sociable, and leaders at school. In one study of several hundred eighth graders, however, negative effects of early pubertal timing were not evident among African-American girls, whose families—and perhaps friends as well—tend to be more unconditionally welcoming of menarche (see page 203) (Michael & Eccles, 2003).

Two factors largely account for the trends just described: (1) how closely the adolescent's body matches cultural ideals of physical attractiveness, and (2) how well young people fit in physically with their agemates.

• **The Role of Physical Attractiveness** TAKE A MOMENT... Flip through the pages of your favorite popular magazine. You will see evidence of our society's view of an attractive female as thin and long-legged and of a good-looking male as tall, broad-shouldered, and muscular. The female image is a girlish shape, favoring the late developer; the male image fits the early-maturing boy.

Research confirms that adolescent girls' **body image**—conception of and attitude toward their physical appearance—declines after they view magazine depictions of female beauty (Clay, Vignoles, & Dittmar, 2005). Early-maturing Caucasian girls tend to report a less positive body image than their on-time and late-maturing agemates. Compared with African-American and Hispanic girls, Caucasian girls are more likely to have internalized the cultural ideal of female attractiveness: Most want to be thinner (Rosen, 2003; Stice, Presnell, & Bearman, 2001; Williams & Currie, 2000). Although findings are less consistent among boys, early, rapid maturers are more likely to be satisfied with their physical characteristics (Alsaker, 1995; Sinkkonen, Anttila, & Siimes, 1998).

Body image is a strong predictor of young people's self-esteem (Clay, Vignoles, & Dittmar, 2005; Harter, 2006). But the negative effects of pubertal timing on body image and—as we will see next—emotional adjustment are greatly amplified when accompanied by other stressors (Stice, 2003).

• **The Importance of Fitting in with Peers** Physical status in relation to peers also explains differences in adjustment between early and late maturers. From this perspective, early-maturing girls and late-maturing boys have difficulty because they fall at the extremes in physical development. Recall that Sabrina felt "out of place" when with

These later-maturing teenagers' slim, girlish appearance fits with cultural ideals of female attractiveness. They are more likely than their early-maturing agemates to be considered physically attractive, lively, sociable, and leaders at school.

her agemates. Not surprisingly, adolescents feel most comfortable with peers who match their own level of biological maturity (Stattin & Magnusson, 1990).

Because few agemates of the same pubertal status are available, early-maturing adolescents of both sexes seek out older companions, sometimes with unfavorable consequences. Older peers often encourage them into activities they are not yet ready to handle emotionally, including sexual activity, drug and alcohol use, and minor delinquent acts (Ge et al., 2002). Perhaps because of such involvements, early maturers of both sexes report feeling emotionally stressed and show declines in academic performance (Graber, 2003; Mendle, Turkheimer, & Emery, 2007). And early-maturing girls are at increased risk for depression (Stice, Presnell, & Bearman, 2001).

At the same time, the young person's context greatly increases the likelihood that early pubertal timing will lead to negative outcomes. In a study of several hundred ethnically diverse urban teenage girls, early maturers engaged in more antisocial acts only if they lived in neighborhoods with high concentrations of poverty (Obeidallah et al., 2004). Early maturers in economically disadvantaged neighborhoods are especially vulnerable to establishing ties with deviant peers, which heightens their defiant, hostile behavior. And because families in such neighborhoods tend to be exposed to chronic, severe stressors and to have few social supports, these early maturers are also more likely to experience harsh, inconsistent parenting, which predicts both deviant peer associations and antisocial behavior (Conger et al., 2002; Ge et al., 2002).

• **Long-Term Consequences** Do the effects of pubertal timing persist? Follow-ups reveal that early-maturing girls, especially, are prone to lasting difficulties. In one study, early-maturing boys' depression subsided by age 13, but depressed early-maturing girls tended to remain depressed (Ge at al., 2003). In another study, which followed young people from ages 14 to 24, early-maturing boys again showed good adjustment. Early-maturing girls, however, reported poorer-quality relationships with family and friends, smaller social networks, and lower life satisfaction into early adulthood than their on-time counterparts (Graber et al., 2004). Similarly, in a Swedish investigation, achievement and substance use difficulties of early-maturing girls lingered, in the form of greater alcohol abuse and lower educational attainment than their agemates (Andersson & Magnusson, 1990; Stattin & Magnusson, 1990).

Impaired social relationships may underlie these long-term negative outcomes (Graber, 2003). Recall that childhood family stress tends to be associated with early menarche (see page 202). Consequently, many early-maturing girls may enter adolescence with emotional and social difficulties. As the stresses of puberty interfere with school performance and lead to unfavorable peer pressures, poor adjustment extends and deepens. Clearly, interventions that target at-risk early-maturing youngsters are needed. These include educating parents and teachers and providing adolescents with counseling and social supports so they will be better prepared to handle the emotional and social challenges of this transition.

Ask Yourself

Review Summarize the impact of pubertal timing on adolescent development.

Apply As a school-age child, Chloe enjoyed leisure activities with her parents. Now, as a 14-year-old, she spends hours in her room and resists going on weekend family excursions. Explain Chloe's behavior.

Connect How might adolescent moodiness contribute to the psychological distancing between parents and children that accompanies puberty? (*Hint:* Think about bidirectional influences in parent–child relationships.)

Reflect Think back to your own reactions to the physical changes of puberty. Are they consistent with research findings? Explain.

Puberty and Adolescent Health

The arrival of puberty is accompanied by new health concerns. Eating disturbances appear in many young people who worry about falling short of their idealized image of attractiveness and fitness. Homosexual teenagers face formidable challenges in forging an open, positive sexual identity. And sexual activity brings the risk of sexually transmitted disease and early pregnancy.

As adolescents attain greater autonomy, their personal decision making becomes important, in health as well as in other areas. Yet none of the health concerns we are about to discuss can be traced to a single cause. Rather, biological, psychological, family, and cultural factors jointly contribute.

Eating Disorders

Girls who reach puberty early, who are very dissatisfied with their body image, and who grow up in homes where concern with weight and thinness is high are at risk for eating problems. Recall from the introduction to this chapter that Sabrina's mother worried about Sabrina's desire to lose weight when she reached puberty. Severe dieting is the strongest predictor of an eating disorder in adolescence (Hetherington, 2000). The two most serious eating disorders are anorexia nervosa and bulimia nervosa.

• Anorexia Nervosa **Anorexia nervosa** is a tragic eating disturbance in which young people starve themselves because of a compulsive fear of getting fat. About 1 percent of North American and Western European teenage girls are affected. During the past half-century, cases have increased sharply, fueled by cultural admiration of female thinness. Anorexia nervosa is equally common in all SES groups, but Asian-American, Caucasian-American, and Hispanic girls are at greater risk than African-American girls, who tend to be more satisfied with their size and shape (Fairburn & Harrison, 2003; Granillo, Jones-Rodriguez, & Carvajal, 2005; Steinhausen, 2006). Boys account for about 10 percent of cases of anorexia; about half of these are homosexual or bisexual young people who are uncomfortable with a strong, muscular appearance (Robb & Dadson, 2002).

Anorexics have an extremely distorted body image. Even after they have become severely underweight, they see themselves as too heavy. Most go on self-imposed diets so strict that they struggle to avoid eating in response to hunger. To enhance weight loss, they exercise strenuously.

In their attempt to reach "perfect" slimness, anorexics lose between 25 and 50 percent of their body weight. Because a normal menstrual cycle requires about 15 percent body fat, either menarche does not occur or menstrual periods stop. Malnutrition causes pale skin, brittle discolored nails, fine dark hairs all over the body, and extreme sensitivity to cold. If it continues, the heart muscle can shrink, the kidneys can fail, and irreversible brain damage and loss of bone mass can occur. About 6 percent of anorexics die of the disorder, as a result of either physical complications or suicide (Katzman, 2005).

Forces within the person, the family, and the larger culture give rise to anorexia nervosa. Identical twins share the disorder more often than fraternal twins, indicating a genetic influence. Abnormalities in neurotransmitters in the brain, linked to anxiety and impulse control, may make some individuals more susceptible (Holtkamp et al., 2005; Kaye et al., 2005). And problem eating behavior in early childhood—persistently refusing to eat or eating very little—is linked to anorexia in adolescence (Rosen, 2003). Many anorexics have extremely high standards for their own behavior and performance, are emotionally inhibited, and avoid intimate ties outside the family. Consequently, these girls are often excellent students who are responsible and well-behaved. But as we have seen, the societal image of "thin is

Aiva, 16, an anorexia nervosa patient, is shown at left on the day she entered treatment. She weighed just 77 pounds—69 percent of her normal body weight. At right, Aiva appears 10 weeks later, on her last day of treatment. Only about 50 percent of young people with anorexia fully overcome the disorder. © Lauren Greenfield/VII Photo

beautiful" contributes to the poor body image of many girls—especially early-maturing girls, who are at greatest risk for anorexia nervosa (Tyrka, Graber, & Brooks-Gunn, 2000).

In addition, parent–adolescent interactions reveal problems related to adolescent autonomy. Often the mothers of these girls have high expectations for physical appearance, achievement, and social acceptance and are overprotective and controlling. Fathers tend to be emotionally distant. Instead of rebelling openly, anorexic girls seem to do so covertly—by fiercely pursuing perfection in achievement, respectable behavior, and thinness (Bruch, 2001). Nevertheless, it remains unclear whether maladaptive parent–child relationships precede the disorder, emerge as a response to it, or both. In a longitudinal study in which 12- to 16-year-old girls were followed for four years, unhealthy eating behaviors led to conflict-ridden interactions with parents, not the reverse (Archibald et al., 2002).

Because anorexic girls typically deny or minimize the seriousness of their disorder, treating it is difficult (Couturier & Lock, 2006). Hospitalization often is necessary to prevent life-threatening malnutrition. The most successful treatment is family therapy plus medication to reduce anxiety and neurotransmitter imbalances (Fairburn, 2005; Patel, Pratt, & Greydanus, 2003; Treasure & Schmidt, 2005). As a supplementary approach, behavior modification—in which hospitalized anorexics are rewarded with praise, social contact, and opportunities for exercise when they eat and gain weight—is helpful. Still, only about 50 percent of anorexics fully recover (Striegel-Moore & Franko, 2006). For many, eating problems continue in less extreme form. About 10 percent show signs of a less severe, but nevertheless debilitating, disorder: bulimia nervosa. And the chronic anxiety associated with both eating disturbances increases girls' risk for major depression in both adolescence and adulthood (Godart et al., 2006).

Cultural admiration of extreme female thinness, evident in the fashion industry, has accompanied the rise in anorexia nervosa over the past half century. This emaciated model encourages young girls to feel dissatisfied with average body weight. AP Images/Stuart Ramson

• **Bulimia Nervosa** In **bulimia nervosa,** young people (again, mainly girls, but gay and bisexual boys are also vulnerable) engage in strict dieting and excessive exercise accompanied by binge eating, often followed by deliberate vomiting and purging with laxatives (Herzog, Eddy, & Beresin, 2006; Wichstrøm, 2006). Bulimia is more common than anorexia nervosa, affecting about 2 to 4 percent of teenage girls, only 5 percent of whom have previously been anorexic.

Twin studies show that bulimia, like anorexia, is influenced by heredity (Klump, Kaye, & Strober, 2001). Overweight and early menarche increase the risk. Some bulimics, like anorexics, are perfectionists. Others lack self-control not just in eating but also in other areas of their lives, engaging in petty shoplifting and alcohol abuse. And although bulimics share with anorexics pathological anxiety about gaining weight, they may have experienced their parents as disengaged and emotionally unavailable rather than overcontrolling (Fairburn & Harrison, 2003).

Unlike anorexics, bulimics feel depressed and guilty about their abnormal eating habits and are desperate to get help. As a result, bulimia is usually easier to treat than anorexia, through support groups, nutrition education, training in changing eating habits, and the use of anti-anxiety, antidepressant, and appetite-control medication.

Sexuality

With the arrival of puberty, hormonal changes—in particular, the production of androgens in young people of both sexes—lead to an increase in sex drive (Halpern, Udry, & Suchindran, 1997). In response, adolescents become very concerned about how to manage sexuality in social relationships. New cognitive capacities involving perspective taking and self-reflection affect their efforts to do so. Yet, like the eating behaviors we have just discussed, adolescent sexuality is heavily influenced by the young person's social context.

• **The Impact of Culture** TAKE A MOMENT... When did you first learn the "facts of life"—and how? Was sex discussed openly in your family, or was the subject treated with secrecy? Exposure to sex, education about it, and efforts to limit the sexual curiosity of children and adolescents vary widely around the world. At one extreme are a number of

Applying What We Know

Communicating with Adolescents About Sexual Issues

Strategy	Explanation
Foster open communication.	Let the teenager know you are a willing and trustworthy resource by stating that you are available when questions arise and will answer fully and accurately.
Use correct terms for body parts.	Correct vocabulary provides the young person with a basis for future discussion and also indicates that sex is not a secretive topic.
Use effective discussion techniques.	Listen, encourage the adolescent to participate, ask open-ended rather than yes/no questions, and give supportive responses. Avoid dominating and lecturing, which cause teenagers to withdraw.
Reflect before speaking.	When the adolescent asks questions or offers opinions about sex, remain nonjudgmental. If you differ with the teenager's views, convey your perspective in a nonthreatening manner, emphasizing that although you disagree, you are not attacking his or her character. Trying to dictate the young person's behavior generally results in alienation.
Keep conversations going.	Many parents regard their job as finished once they have had the "big talk" in early adolescence. But young people are more likely to be influenced by an accumulation of smaller discussions. If open communication is sustained, the teenager is more likely to return with thoughts and questions.

Source: Berkowitz, 2004.

Middle Eastern peoples, who murder girls if they lose their virginity before marriage. At the other extreme are several Asian and Pacific Island groups with highly permissive sexual attitudes and practices. For example, among the Trobriand Islanders of Papua New Guinea, older companions provide children with instruction in sexual practices, and adolescents are expected to engage in sexual experimentation with a variety of partners (Weiner, 1988).

Despite the prevailing image of sexually free adolescents, sexual attitudes in North America are relatively restrictive. Typically, parents provide little or no information about sex, discourage sex play, and rarely talk about sex in children's presence. When young people become interested in sex, only about half report getting information from parents about intercourse, pregnancy prevention, and sexually transmitted disease. Many parents avoid meaningful discussions about sex out of fear of embarrassment or concern that the adolescent will not take them seriously. Yet warm, open give-and-take, as described in Applying What We Know above, is associated with teenagers' adoption of parents' views and with reduced sexual risk taking (Jaccard, Dodge, & Dittus, 2003; Miller, Forehand, & Kotchick, 1999).

Adolescents who do not get information about sex from their parents are likely to learn from friends, books, magazines, movies, TV, and the Internet (Jaccard, Dodge, & Dittus, 2002; Sutton et al., 2002). On prime-time TV shows, which adolescents watch more than other TV offerings, 80 percent of programs contain sexual content. Most depict partners as spontaneous and passionate, taking no steps to avoid pregnancy or sexually transmitted disease, and experiencing no negative consequences (Roberts, Henriksen, & Foehr, 2004).

The Internet is an especially hazardous "sex educator." In a survey of 1,500 U.S. 10- to 17-year-olds, 42 percent said they had viewed online pornographic websites (images of naked people or people having sex) while surfing the Internet in the past 12 months. Of these, 66 percent indicated they had encountered the images accidentally and did not want to view them. Youths who felt depressed, had been bullied by peers, or were involved in delinquent activities had more encounters with Internet pornography, which may have intensified their adjustment problems (Wolak, Mitchell, & Finkelhor, 2007). In other studies of middle and high school students, reports of media exposure to sexual content predicted both current sexual activity and intentions to be sexually active in the future (Friedman, 2006; Pardun, L'Engle, & Brown, 2005).

Consider the contradictory messages young people receive. On one hand, adults emphasize that sex at an early age and outside marriage is wrong. On the other hand, the social environment extols sexual excitement, experimentation, and promiscuity. North American teenagers are left bewildered and poorly informed, with little sound advice on how to conduct their sex lives responsibly.

Adolescence is an especially important time for the development of sexuality, as these two young people demonstrate. But North American teenagers receive contradictory and confusing messages about the appropriateness of sex. © Jeff Greenberg/ PhotoEdit

Adolescent Sexual Attitudes and Behavior Although differences between subcultural groups exist, the sexual attitudes of North American adolescents and adults have become more liberal over the past 40 years. Compared with a generation ago, more people believe that sexual intercourse before marriage is all right, as long as two people are emotionally committed to each other (ABC News, 2004; Michael et al., 1994). During the past decade, a slight swing back toward more conservative sexual beliefs has occurred among adolescents, largely in response to the risk of sexually transmitted disease, especially AIDS, and to teenage sexual abstinence programs sponsored by schools and religious organizations (Ali & Scelfo, 2002; Cope-Farrar & Kunkel, 2002).

Trends in adolescents' sexual behavior are consistent with their attitudes. Rates of extramarital sex among U.S. and Canadian young people rose for several decades but have recently declined (Boyce et al., 2006; U.S. Department of Health and Human Services, 2006d). Nevertheless, as Figure 5.15 reveals, a substantial minority of boys and girls are sexually active by ninth grade or earlier. Boys tend to have their first intercourse earlier than girls. And as the figure suggests, U.S. youths begin sexual activity at younger ages than their Canadian and Western European counterparts (Boyce et al., 2006; U.S. Department of Health and Human Services, 2006d). Because early intercourse is linked to briefer and more sporadic sexual relationships, U.S. teenagers are also more likely to have multiple sexual partners. For example, about 12 percent of adolescent boys in the United States, compared to 8 percent in Canada, have had relations with three or more partners in the past year (Alan Guttmacher Institute, 2004). Most teenagers, however, have had only one or two sexual partners by the end of high school.

Characteristics of Sexually Active Adolescents Early and frequent sexual activity is linked to personal, family, peer, and educational characteristics that include childhood impulsivity, weak sense of personal control over life events, early pubertal timing, parental divorce, single-parent and stepfamily homes, large family size, little or no religious involvement, weak parental monitoring, disrupted parent–child communication, sexually active friends and older siblings, poor school performance, lower educational aspirations, and tendency to engage in norm-violating acts, including alcohol and drug use and delinquency (Crockett, Raffaelli, & Shen, 2006; Manlove et al., 2006; Siebenbruner, Zimmer-Gembeck, & Egeland, 2007; Silver & Bauman, 2006).

Because many of these factors are associated with growing up in a low-income family, it is not surprising that early sexual activity is more common among young people from economically disadvantaged homes. Living in a hazardous neighborhood—one high in physical deterioration, crime, and violence—also increases the likelihood that teenagers will be sexually active (Ge et al., 2002). In such neighborhoods, social ties are weak, adults exert little oversight or control over adolescents' activities, and negative peer influences are widespread. In fact, the high rate of sexual activity among African-American teenagers—68 percent report having had sexual intercourse, compared with 47 percent of all U.S. young people—is largely accounted for by widespread poverty in the black population (Darroch, Frost, & Singh, 2001; U.S. Department of Health and Human Services, 2006d).

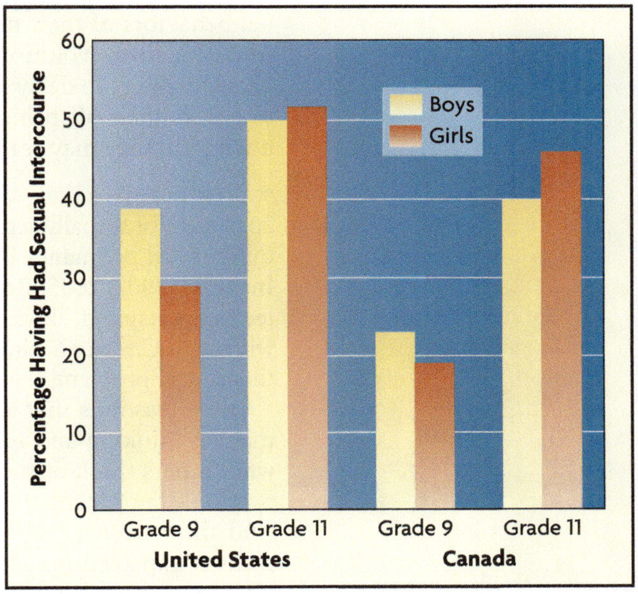

Figure 5.15 **Adolescents in the United States and Canada who report ever having had sexual intercourse.**
Boys tend to have their first intercourse earlier than girls, and U.S. adolescents, compared with Canadian adolescents, begin sexual activity at younger ages. (Adapted from Boyce et al., 2006; U.S. Department of Health and Human Services, 2006d.)

Social Issues

Gay, Lesbian, and Bisexual Youths: Coming Out to Oneself and Others

Cultures vary as much in their acceptance of homosexuality as in their approval of extramarital sex. In North America, homosexuals are stigmatized, as shown by the degrading language often used to describe them. This makes forming a sexual identity a much greater challenge for gay, lesbian, and bisexual youths than for their heterosexual counterparts.

Wide variations in sexual identity formation exist, depending on personal, family, and community factors. Yet interviews with gay and lesbian adolescents and adults reveal that many (though not all) move through a three-phase sequence in coming out to themselves and others.

Feeling Different

Many gay men and lesbians say they felt different from other children when they were young. Typically, this first sense of their biologically determined sexual orientation appears between ages 6 and 12, in play interests more like those of the other gender (Rahman & Wilson, 2003). Boys may find that they are less interested in sports, drawn to quieter activities, and more emotionally sensitive than other boys; girls that they are more athletic and active than other girls.

By age 10, many such children start to engage in *sexual questioning*—wondering why the typical heterosexual orientation does not apply to them. Often, they experience their sense of being different as deeply distressing. They worry about "being normal" and being "found out" by family members and friends. Compared with children confident of their homosexuality, sexual-questioning children report greater anxiety about peer relationships, greater dissatisfaction with their biological gender, and greater gender nonconformity in personal traits and activities over time (Carver, Egan, & Perry, 2004).

Confusion

With the arrival of puberty, feeling different clearly encompasses feeling sexually different. In research on ethnically diverse gay, lesbian, and bisexual youths, awareness of a same-sex physical attraction occurred, on average, between ages 11 and 12 for boys and 14 and 15 for girls, perhaps because adolescent social pressures toward heterosexuality are particularly intense for girls (D'Augelli, 2006; Diamond, 1998).

Realizing that homosexuality has personal relevance generally sparks additional confusion. A few adolescents resolve their discomfort by crystallizing a gay, lesbian, or bisexual identity quickly, with a flash of insight into their sense of being different. But most experience an inner struggle and a deep sense of isolation—outcomes intensified by lack of role models and social support (D'Augelli, 2002; Safren & Pantalone, 2006).

Some throw themselves into activities they have come to associate with heterosexuality. Boys may go out for athletic teams; girls may drop softball and basketball in favor of dance. And many homosexual youths (more females than males) try heterosexual dating, sometimes to hide their sexual orientation and at other times to develop intimacy skills that they later apply to same-sex relationships (D'Augelli, 2006; Dubé, Savin-Williams, & Diamond, 2001). Those who are extremely troubled and guilt-ridden may escape into alcohol, drugs, and suicidal thinking. Suicide attempts are unusually high among gay, lesbian, and bisexual young people (McDaniel, Purcell, & D'Augelli, 2001; Morrow, 2006).

Self-Acceptance

By the end of adolescence, the majority of gay, lesbian, and bisexual teenagers accept their sexual identity. But they face another crossroad: whether to tell others. Powerful

Early and prolonged father absence predicts higher rates of intercourse and pregnancy among adolescent girls, after many family background and personal characteristics are controlled (Ellis et al., 2003). Perhaps father absence exposes young people to the dating and sexual behaviors of their mothers, who serve as models for their physically maturing children. An alternative, evolutionary account proposes that fathers' investment in parenting encourages daughters to delay sexual activity in favor of seeking a similarly committed male partner to ensure their offspring's well-being. Because father-absent girls view male commitment as uncertain, they may readily enter into casual sexual relationships.

Contraceptive Use Although adolescent contraceptive use has increased in recent years, about 20 percent of sexually active teenagers in the United States and 15 percent in Canada are at risk for unintended pregnancy because they do not use contraception consistently (Alan Guttmacher Institute, 2002, 2005; Rotermann, 2005). Why do so many fail to take precautions? Typically, teenagers respond, "I wasn't planning to have sex," or, "I didn't want to spoil the moment." As we will see in Chapter 6, although adolescents can consider multiple possibilities when faced with a theoretical problem, they often fail to apply this advanced reasoning to everyday situations.

One reason is that advances in perspective taking—the capacity to imagine what others may be thinking and feeling—lead teenagers, for a time, to be extremely concerned about what others think of them. Also, in the midst of everyday social pressures, adolescents often overlook the potential consequences of risky behaviors (Beyth-Marom & Fischhoff, 1997). And many teenagers—especially those from troubled, low-income families—do not have realistic expectations about the impact of early parenthood on their current and future lives (Stevens-Simon, Sheeder, & Harter, 2005).

stigma against their sexual orientation leads some to decide that disclosure is impossible: While self-defining as gay, they otherwise "pass" as heterosexual (Savin-Williams, 2001). When homosexual youths do come out, they often are targets of intense hostility. In a study of over 500 gay, lesbian, and bisexual youths in Canada, New Zealand, and the United States, 75 percent reported being verbally abused, and 15 percent being physically attacked, because of their sexual orientation (D'Augelli, 2002).

Nevertheless, many young people eventually acknowledge their sexual orientation publicly, usually by telling trusted friends first. Once teenagers establish a same-sex sexual or romantic relationship, many come out to parents—generally to their mother first, either because she asks or because youths feel closer to her. Few parents respond with severe rejection; most are either positive or slightly negative and disbelieving (Savin-Williams & Ream, 2003). This is an encouraging outcome because parental understanding is the strongest predictor of favorable adjustment among homosexual youths—including reduced *internalized homophobia,* or societal prejudice turned against the self (D'Augelli, Grossman, & Starks, 2005; Savin-Williams, 2003).

When people react positively, coming out strengthens the adolescent's view of homosexuality as a valid, meaningful, and fulfilling identity. Contact with other gays and lesbians is important for reaching this phase, and societal changes permit many adolescents in urban areas to attain it earlier than their counterparts did a decade or two ago. Gay and lesbian communities exist in large cities, along with specialized interest groups, social clubs, religious groups, newspapers, and periodicals. Small towns and rural areas remain difficult places to meet other homosexuals and to find a supportive environment. Teenagers in these locales have a special need for caring adults and peers who can help them find self- and social acceptance.

Gay and lesbian youths who succeed in coming out to themselves and others integrate their sexual orientation into a broader sense of identity, a process we will address in Chapter 11. As a result, they no longer need to focus so heavily on their homosexual self, and energy is freed for other aspects of psychological growth. In sum, coming out can foster many aspects of adolescent development, including self-esteem, psychological well-being, and relationships with family and friends.

Boston-area teenagers participate in the annual Gay/Straight Youth Pride March. When family members and peers react with acceptance, coming out strengthens young people's view of homosexuality as a valid, meaningful, and fulfilling identity. © Marilyn Humphries/The Image Works

As these findings suggest, the social environment also contributes to adolescents' reluctance to use contraception. Those who lack the rewards of meaningful education and work are especially likely to engage in irresponsible sex, sometimes within exploitative relationships. About 11 percent of North American girls and 4 percent of boys say they were pressured to have intercourse when they did not want to (Boyce et al., 2006; U.S. Department of Health and Human Services, 2006d).

In contrast, teenagers who report good relationships with parents and who talk openly with them about sex and contraception are more likely to use birth control (Heinrich et al., 2006; Kirby, 2002a). But few adolescents believe their parents would be understanding and supportive. School sex education classes, as well, often leave teenagers with incomplete or incorrect knowledge. Some do not know where to get birth control counseling and devices; those who do often worry that a doctor or family planning clinic might not keep their visits confidential. About 20 percent of adolescents using health services say that if their parents were notified, they would still have sex, but without contraception (Jones et al., 2005).

• **Sexual Orientation** So far, our discussion has focused only on heterosexual behavior. About 2 to 3 percent of young people identify as lesbian, gay, or bisexual (Bailey, Dunne, & Martin, 2000; Savin-Williams & Diamond, 2004). An unknown number experience same-sex attraction but have not come out to friends or family (see the Social Issues box above). Adolescence is an equally crucial time for the sexual development of these individuals, and societal attitudes, again, loom large in how well they fare.

Heredity makes an important contribution to homosexuality: Identical twins of both sexes are more likely than fraternal twins to share a homosexual orientation; the same is true for biological as opposed to adoptive relatives (Kendler et al., 2000; Kirk et al., 2000).

Furthermore, male homosexuality tends to be more common on the maternal than on the paternal side of families, suggesting that it might be X-linked (see Chapter 3). Indeed, one gene-mapping study found that among 40 pairs of homosexual brothers, 33 (82 percent) had an identical segment of DNA on the X chromosome. One or several genes in that region might predispose males to become homosexual (Hamer et al., 1993).

How might heredity lead to homosexuality? According to some researchers, certain genes affect the level or impact of prenatal sex hormones, which modify brain structures in ways that induce homosexual feelings and behavior (Bailey et al., 1995; LeVay, 1993). Keep in mind, however, that both genetic and environmental factors can alter prenatal hormones. Girls exposed prenatally to very high levels of androgens or estrogens—either because of a genetic defect or from drugs given to the mother to prevent miscarriage—are more likely to become homosexual or bisexual (Meyer-Bahlburg et al., 1995). Homosexual men also tend to be later in birth order and have a higher-than-average number of older brothers (Blanchard & Bogaert, 2004). One possibility is that mothers with several male children sometimes produce antibodies to androgens, reducing the prenatal impact of male sex hormones on the brains of later-born boys.

Widespread stereotypes and misconceptions about homosexuality persist. For example, contrary to common belief, most homosexual adolescents are not "gender-deviant" in dress or behavior. And attraction to members of the same sex is not limited to gay, lesbian, and bisexual teenagers. About 50 to 60 percent of adolescents who report having engaged in homosexual acts identify as heterosexual (Savin-Williams & Diamond, 2004).

Although definitive conclusions await further research, the evidence to date suggests that genetic and prenatal biological influences are largely responsible for homosexuality. In our evolutionary past, homosexuality may have served the adaptive function of reducing aggressive competition for other-sex mates (Rahman & Wilson, 2003).

Sexually Transmitted Disease

Sexually active adolescents, both homosexual and heterosexual, are at risk for sexually transmitted diseases (STDs). Adolescents have the highest incidence of STDs of all age groups. Despite a recent decline in STDs in the United States, one out of six sexually active teenagers contracts one of these illnesses each year—a rate about three times as high as that of Canada and also much higher than in most of Western Europe (Health Canada, 2006c; U.S. Centers for Disease Control and Prevention, 2006). In incidence of the most common STDs, such as chlamydia and herpes, Canada exceeds some Western European nations (Belgium, France, Great Britain) but is considerably lower than others (Denmark, Finland, Norway) (Maticka-Tyndale, 2001; Weinstock, Berman, & Cates, 2004). Left untreated, STDs can lead to sterility and life-threatening complications. Teenagers in greatest danger of contracting STDs are the same ones most likely to engage in irresponsible sexual behavior—poverty-stricken young people who feel a sense of hopelessness (Niccolai et al., 2004).

By far the most serious STD is AIDS. In contrast to Canada, where the incidence of AIDS among people under age 30 is low, one-fifth of U.S. AIDS cases occur in young people between ages 20 and 29. Because AIDS symptoms typically do not emerge until 8 to 10 years after infection with the HIV virus, nearly all these cases originated in adolescence. Drug-abusing teenagers who share needles and male adolescents who have sex with HIV-positive same-sex partners account for most cases, but heterosexual spread of the disease remains high, especially among teenagers with more than one partner in the previous 18 months (Kelley et al., 2003). It is at least twice as easy for a male to infect a female with any STD, including AIDS, as for a female to infect a male. Currently, females account for about 37 percent of new U.S. AIDS cases among adolescents and young adults (Rangel et al., 2006).

As a result of school courses and media campaigns, about 60 percent of middle-school students and 90 percent of high school students in Canada and the United States are aware of basic facts about AIDS. But some hold false beliefs that put them at risk—for example, that birth control pills provide some protection. And most have limited understanding of other STDs and their consequences, underestimate their own susceptibility, and are poorly informed about how to protect themselves (Coholl et al., 2001; Ethier et al., 2003).

Furthermore, high school students report engaging in oral sex much more often than intercourse, and with more partners. Although oral sex is a significant mode of transmission of several STDs, including chlamydia, gonorrhea, herpes, and perhaps AIDS, few teenagers say they consistently use STD protection while engaged in it, and nearly three-fourths never take any precautions (Boyce et al., 2006; Prinstein, Meade, & Cohen, 2003). Clearly, concerted efforts are needed to educate young people about the full range of STDs and risky sexual behaviors.

Early childbearing reduces the chances that teenage mothers will finish high school, marry, and find satisfying, well-paid work. But this high school senior in Hawaii benefits from on-site child care. School programs that provide this service, along with vocational training and instruction in parenting, promote more effective child rearing and more positive long-term outcomes. AP Images/The Honolulu Advertiser, Bruce Asato

Adolescent Pregnancy and Parenthood

An estimated 750,000 to 850,000 teenage girls in the United States—20 percent of those who have had sexual intercourse—become pregnant annually, about 25,000 of them younger than age 15. Despite a steady decline since 1991, the U.S. adolescent pregnancy rate is higher than that of most other industrialized countries (see Figure 5.16). Although the Canadian rate has also declined and is only about half the U.S. rate, teenage pregnancy in Canada remains a problem. Three factors heighten the incidence of adolescent pregnancy: (1) Effective sex education reaches too few teenagers; (2) convenient, low-cost contraceptive services for adolescents are scarce; and (3) many families live in poverty, which encourages young people to take risks without considering the future implications of their behavior.

Because 40 percent of U.S. and 50 percent of Canadian teenage pregnancies end in abortion, the number of North American teenage births is actually lower than it was 35 years ago (Maticka-Tyndale, 2001; U.S. Department of Health and Human Services, 2005a). But teenage parenthood is a much greater problem today because modern adolescents are far less likely to marry before childbirth. In 1960, only 15 percent of teenage births were to unmarried females, compared with 85 percent today (Child Trends, 2006). Increased social acceptance of single motherhood, along with the belief of many teenage girls that a baby might fill a void in their lives, means that very few girls give up their infants for adoption.

• Correlates and Consequences of Adolescent Parenthood Becoming a parent is challenging for anyone, but especially for adolescents, who have not yet established a clear sense of direction for their own lives. Longitudinal research tracking girls from birth through adolescence reveals that life conditions and personal attributes jointly contribute to adolescent childbearing and also interfere with teenage mothers' capacity to parent effectively (Jaffee et al., 2001).

As we have seen, adolescent sexual activity is linked to economic disadvantage. Teenage parents are many times more likely to be poor than their agemates who postpone childbearing. Their backgrounds often include low parental warmth and involvement, domestic violence and child abuse, repeated parental divorce and remarriage, adult models of early unmarried parenthood, and residence in neighborhoods where other adolescents display similar risks. Girls at risk for early pregnancy do poorly in school, engage in alcohol and drug use, have a childhood history of aggressive and antisocial behavior, associate with deviant peers, and experience high rates of depression (Elfenbein & Felice, 2003; Hillis et al., 2004; Luster & Haddow, 2005). A high percentage of out-of-wedlock births are to low-income minority teenagers—African-American, Native-American, Hispanic, and Canadian-Aboriginal. Many of these young people, after unrewarding school experiences, turn to early parenthood as a way to move into adulthood when educational and career avenues are unavailable.

The lives of pregnant teenagers, already troubled in many ways, tend to worsen in several respects after the baby is born:

- *Educational attainment.* Only about 70 percent of U.S. adolescent mothers graduate from high school, compared with 95 percent of girls who wait to become parents (U.S. Department of Education, 2005).

■ Figure 5.16 Pregnancy rates among 15- to 19-year-olds in eight industrialized nations. U.S. teenagers have the highest pregnancy rate. The pregnancy rate in Canada is about half the U.S. rate but much higher than that in Western European nations and Japan. (Adapted from Alan Guttmacher Institute, 2001, 2006.)

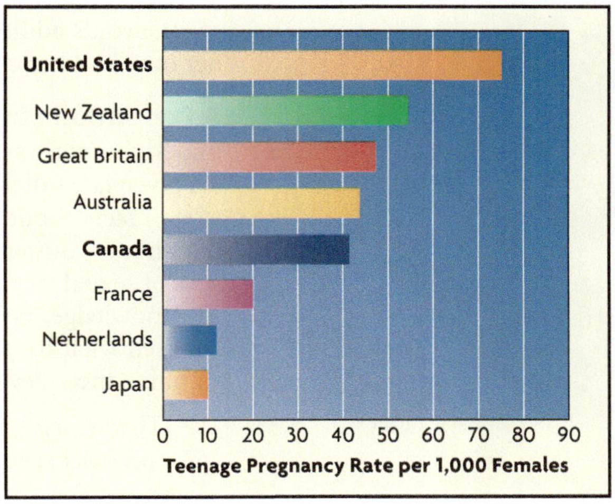

- *Marital patterns.* Teenage motherhood reduces the chances of marriage and, for those who do marry, increases the likelihood of divorce compared with peers who delay childbearing (Moore et al., 1993). Consequently, teenage mothers spend more of their parenting years as single parents. About 35 percent become pregnant again within two years; of these, about half go on to deliver a second child (Child Trends, 2006).
- *Economic circumstances.* Because of low educational attainment, marital instability, and poverty, many teenage mothers are on welfare. If they are employed, their limited education restricts them to unsatisfying, low-paid jobs. Many adolescent fathers, as well, are unemployed or work at unskilled jobs, usually earning too little to provide basic necessities (Bunting & McAuley, 2004). And an estimated 50 percent have committed illegal acts resulting in imprisonment (Elfenbein & Felice, 2003).

Because many pregnant teenage girls have inadequate diets, smoke, use alcohol and other drugs, and do not receive early prenatal care, their babies often experience pregnancy and birth complications—especially low birth weight (Dell, 2001). And compared with adult mothers, adolescent mothers know less about child development, have unrealistically high expectations of infants, perceive their babies as more difficult, interact less effectively with them, and more often engage in child abuse (Moore & Florsheim, 2001; Pomerleau, Scuccimarri, & Malcuit, 2003). Their children tend to score low on intelligence tests, achieve poorly in school, and engage in disruptive social behavior.

Furthermore, adolescent parenthood frequently is repeated in the next generation (Brooks-Gunn, Schley, & Hardy, 2002). In longitudinal studies that followed mothers—some who gave birth as teenagers, others who postponed parenting—and their children for several decades, mothers' age at first childbirth strongly predicted the age at which their offspring, both daughters and sons, became parents (Barber, 2001; Campa & Eckenrode, 2006; Hardy et al., 1998; Manlove, 1997). The researchers found that adolescent parenthood was linked to a set of related, unfavorable family conditions and personal characteristics that negatively influenced development over an extended time and, therefore, often transferred to the next generation.

One important factor was the quality of the home environment: Compared with children in other families, children of unmarried adolescent mothers had families that were less warm, supportive, and stimulating, even after mothers' prebirth education and income were controlled. Younger mothers' cognitive deficits and reduced educational attainment played a part, increasing the likelihood that their children would experience long-term poor-quality home environments. Another factor was father absence: Consistent with findings reported earlier for sexual activity and pregnancy (see page 212), several studies found far greater intergenerational continuity in adolescent parenthood, especially for daughters, when teenage mothers remained unmarried (Barber, 2001; Campa & Eckenrode, 2006; Hardy et al., 1998).

Even when children born to teenage mothers do not become early childbearers, their development is often compromised in terms of likelihood of high school graduation, financial independence in adulthood, and long-term physical and mental health (Moore, Morrison, & Greene, 1997; Pogarsky, Thornberry, & Lizotte, 2006). Still, outcomes for adolescent parents and their children vary widely. If a teenage parent finishes high school, secures gainful employment, avoids additional births, and finds a stable marriage partner, long-term disruptions in her own and her child's development will be less severe.

• Prevention Strategies Preventing teenage pregnancy means addressing the many factors underlying early sexual activity and lack of contraceptive use. Too often, sex education courses are given late (after sexual activity has begun), last only a few sessions, and are limited to a catalog of facts about anatomy and reproduction. Sex education that goes beyond this minimum does not encourage early sex, as some opponents claim (Kirby, 2002c). It does improve awareness of sexual facts—knowledge that is necessary for responsible sexual behavior.

Knowledge, however, is not enough. Sex education must help teenagers build a bridge between what they know and what they do. Today, the most effective sex education programs combine these key elements:

- They teach techniques for handling sexual situations—including refusal skills for avoiding risky sexual behaviors and communication skills for improving contraceptive use—

and offer opportunities to practice these behaviors through role-playing and other activities.

- They deliver clear, accurate messages that are appropriate for participating adolescents' culture and sexual experiences.
- They last long enough to have an impact.
- They provide specific information about contraceptives and ready access to them.

Learning carpentry skills as part of the Summer of Service Teen Volunteer Program in Washington, D.C., will allow these at-risk high school students to play a constructive role in their communities. Building competence through community service reduces rates of adolescent pregnancy and school failure. © Mark Richards/PhotoEdit

Many studies show that sex education including these components can delay the initiation of sexual activity, increase contraceptive use, change attitudes (for example, strengthen future orientation), and reduce pregnancy rates (Kirby, 2002b; Manlove et al., 2006; Thomas & Dimitrov, 2007).

Proposals to increase access to contraceptives are the most controversial aspect of adolescent pregnancy prevention. Many adults argue that placing birth control pills or condoms in the hands of teenagers is equivalent to saying that early sex is OK. Yet sex education programs focusing on abstinence have little or no impact on delaying teenage sexual activity or on preventing pregnancy (Bennett & Assefi, 2005; Underhill, Montgomery, & Operario, 2007). And in Canada and Western Europe, where community- and school-based clinics offer adolescents contraceptives and where universal health insurance helps pay for them, teenage sexual activity is no higher than in the United States—but pregnancy, childbirth, and abortion rates are much lower (Alan Guttmacher Institute, 2001; Schalet, 2007). Radio and TV campaigns promoting contraceptive use—used widely in Africa, Europe, India, and South America—are associated with a reduction in early sexual activity and with an increase in teenagers' use of birth control (Keller & Brown, 2002).

Efforts to prevent adolescent pregnancy and parenthood must go beyond improving sex education and access to contraception; they must build academic and social competence (Allen, Seitz, & Apfel, 2007). In one study, researchers randomly assigned at-risk high school students to either a year-long community service class, called Teen Outreach, or regular classroom experiences in health or social studies. In Teen Outreach, adolescents spent at least 20 hours per week in volunteer work tailored to their interests. They returned to school for discussions that focused on enhancing their community service skills and ability to cope with everyday challenges. At the end of the school year, pregnancy, school failure, and school suspension were substantially lower among participants in Teen Outreach, which fostered social skills, connection to the community, and self-respect (Allen et al., 1997).

Finally, school involvement is linked to delayed initiation of sexual activity and to reduced teenage pregnancy, perhaps because it promotes interaction with and attachment to adults (who discourage risk taking) and belief in a promising future (Lammers et al., 2000). We will take up factors that promote adolescents' commitment to school in Chapter 15.

• Intervening with Adolescent Parents The most difficult and costly way to deal with adolescent parenthood is to wait until it happens. Young mothers need health care, encouragement to stay in school, job training, instruction in parenting and life-management skills, and high-quality, affordable child care. School programs that provide these services reduce the incidence of low-birth-weight babies, increase mothers' educational success, and prevent additional childbearing (Barnet et al., 2004; Seitz & Apfel, 2005).

Adolescent mothers also benefit from relationships with family members and other adults who are sensitive to their developmental needs. Older teenage mothers display more effective parenting when they establish their own residence with the help of relatives—an arrangement that offers a balance of autonomy and support (East & Felice, 1996). In one study, African-American teenage mothers who had a long-term "mentor" relationship—an aunt, neighbor, or teacher who provided emotional support and guidance—were more than three times as likely as those without a mentor to stay in school and graduate (Klaw, Rhodes, & Fitzgerald, 2003).

Programs focusing on fathers are attempting to increase their emotional and financial commitment to the baby (Coley & Chase-Lansdale, 1998). Although nearly half of young fathers visit their children during the first few years after birth, contact usually diminishes. By the time the child starts school, fewer than one-fourth have regular paternal contact. As with teenage mothers, support from family members helps fathers stay involved (Bunting & McAuley, 2004). Teenage mothers who receive financial and child-care assistance and emotional support from the child's father are less distressed and more likely to sustain a relationship with him (Cutrona et al., 1998; Gee & Rhodes, 2003). And infants with lasting ties to their teenage fathers receive warmer, more stimulating caregiving and show better long-term adjustment (Furstenberg & Harris, 1993).

A Concluding Note

The rapid, complex physical and psychological changes of puberty make teenagers vulnerable to certain problems. Yet adolescents' unhealthy behaviors are not an irrational response to inner turmoil, as theorists once believed. Rather, every level of the ecological system affects teenagers' well-being.

Furthermore, we have seen that teenagers with one problem frequently display others—a co-occurrence that you will encounter again when we look at delinquency, depression, suicide, substance abuse, and school underachievement and failure. To design more powerful interventions, researchers must deal with simultaneous risks and the multiple factors that contribute to them. **TAKE A MOMENT...** Think back to the successful intervention efforts discussed in the preceding sections. Notice how they employ several strategies, target multiple behaviors, and involve several contexts.

Finally, adolescence is not only a time of risk but also a time of tremendous opportunity. Teenagers gain a better understanding of how the world works, greater control over their own social contexts, broader access to social support, and increased ability to avoid or alter risky behaviors. Families, schools, communities, and nations must create conditions that enable adolescents to exercise their expanding capacity for positive health practices. This is a theme we will revisit in later chapters.

Ask Yourself

Review Compare risk factors for anorexia nervosa and bulimia nervosa. How do treatments and outcomes differ for the two disorders?

Review Describe unfavorable life experiences and personal attributes associated with early and frequent sexual activity.

Apply At age 17, Veronica gave birth to Ben. When her parents told her they didn't have room for the baby, Veronica dropped out of school and moved in with her boyfriend, Todd. A few months later, Todd left Veronica, saying he couldn't stand being tied down with the baby. Why are Veronica and Ben likely to experience lasting hardships?

Reflect Describe sex education classes that you experienced in school. Did they help you postpone early sex and engage in more responsible sexual behavior? Explain.

SUMMARY

The Course of Physical Growth

Describe the course of physical growth, including changes in body size, proportions, muscle–fat makeup, and skeleton, and their relationship to gains in gross motor skills.

- Compared with other animal species, humans experience a prolonged period of physical growth. **Distance** and **velocity curves** show the overall pattern of change: Gains in height and weight are rapid during infancy, slower during early and middle childhood, and rapid again during puberty.
- In childhood, physical growth follows cephalocaudal and proximodistal trends. During puberty, growth proceeds in the reverse direction, and sex differences in body proportions appear. Body fat is laid down quickly during the first nine months, then rapidly again at adolescence for girls. Muscle accumulates slowly until puberty, when it rises dramatically, especially for boys.
- The best measure of a child's physical maturity is **skeletal age,** which is based on the number of **epiphyses,** or bone growth centers, and the extent to which they are fused. Girls are ahead of boys, a gap that widens over infancy and childhood.

© Peter Hvizdak/The Image Works

- In early childhood, body growth causes the child's center of gravity to shift toward the trunk. Balance improves, paving the way for new gross motor skills. During the school years, improved balance, strength, agility, and flexibility support refinements in running, jumping, hopping, and ball skills. Increased body size and muscle strength lead to continued motor gains in adolescence. As they develop, children integrate previously acquired motor skills into more complex, dynamic systems of action.

- In childhood, boys' advantage over girls in many gross motor skills largely reflects parental expectations and practice. By adolescence, sex differences in size and strength play a greater role.

Describe hormonal influences on physical growth.

- Physical growth is controlled by hormones released by the **pituitary gland,** located at the base of the brain near the **hypothalamus,** which initiates and regulates pituitary secretions.
- **Growth hormone (GH)** affects the development of almost all body tissues. **Thyroxine,** released by the thyroid gland, influences brain development and body size. Sexual maturation is controlled by the sex hormones—**estrogens** and **androgens.**

Discuss factors that contribute to worldwide variations, secular trends, and asynchronies in physical growth.

- Worldwide variations in body size are the combined result of heredity and environment, including evolutionary adaptations to climate, availability of food, and prevalence of disease. **Secular trends in physical growth** have occurred in industrialized nations, where, because of improved health and nutrition, most children are taller and heavier than their ancestors and reach puberty earlier.

Brain Development

Cite major milestones in brain development, at the level of individual brain cells and at the level of the cerebral cortex.

- The human brain reaches its adult size earlier than any other organ. Once **neurons** are in place, they form **synapses** at a rapid rate and communicate by releasing **neurotransmitters,** chemicals that cross the synapses. As the brain grows, **programmed cell death** occurs, making room for growth of neural fibers that form synaptic connections.
- Stimulation determines which neurons will continue to establish new synapses and which will lose their connective fibers through **synaptic pruning. Glial cells,** which are responsible for **myelination,** multiply dramatically through the second year and continue to do so more slowly through adolescence. Myelination contributes greatly to swift gains in brain size.
- Regions of the **cerebral cortex** develop in the order in which various capacities emerge in the infant and child. The frontal lobes have the most extended period of development, reaching an adult level of synapses in adolescence. Although some **lateralization,** or specialization of the cerebral hemispheres, exists at birth, **brain plasticity** remains high for the first few years. Both heredity and early experience contribute to brain organization.
- Handedness, reflecting the individual's **dominant cerebral hemisphere,** first appears in infancy and extends to a wider range of skills—a sign of strengthening lateralization. According to one theory, most children inherit a gene that biases them for right-handedness, but experience can sway them toward a left-hand preference. Body position during the prenatal period and practice can affect handedness.

Describe changes in other brain structures, and discuss evidence on sensitive periods of brain development.

- During infancy and early childhood, connections are established between brain structures. Fibers linking the **cerebellum** to the cerebral cortex myelinate, enhancing balance and motor control and supporting higher cognitive processes. The **reticular formation,** which maintains alertness and consciousness; the **hippocampus,** which plays a vital role in memory and spatial orientation; and the **corpus callosum,** connecting the two cerebral hemispheres, also develop rapidly.
- In many brain regions, sensitivity of neurons to excitatory neurotransmitters readjusts in adolescence, contributing to teenagers' heightened drive for novel experiences, stronger reactions to both stressful and pleasurable stimuli, and susceptibility to certain psychological disorders.
- Animal and human studies reveal the existence of sensitive periods in which appropriate stimulation is necessary for optimal brain development. **Experience-expectant brain growth** depends on ordinary experiences in which caregivers provide age-appropriate play materials and stimulating, enjoyable daily routines. **Experience-dependent brain growth**—additional growth and refinement of established brain structures through specific learning—is a lifelong process, starting later and building on this early learning.

© Ariel Skelley/CORBIS

Factors Affecting Physical Growth

How do heredity, nutrition, infectious disease, and affection and stimulation contribute to physical growth and, as a result, affect other aspects of development?

- Physical growth depends on a complex interplay between heredity and environment. Exposure to environmental pollutants, such as low-level lead, can have a negative impact on children's mental and emotional functioning.
- With adequate diet and health, height and rate of physical growth depend largely on heredity. If negative factors are not severe, children and adolescents who lag in body size show **catch-up growth** when their environment improves.
- Breastfeeding is ideally suited to infants' nutritional needs and is crucial for protecting their health in the developing world. As growth slows around age 2, appetites become unpredictable, and many children become picky eaters. Repeated, unpressured exposure to a new food increases acceptance. During puberty, food intake rises dramatically, but adolescents' eating habits are the poorest. Family mealtimes increase healthy eating.
- Many children in developing countries suffer from **marasmus** and **kwashiorkor,** two diseases caused by malnutrition that can impair body growth and cause lasting damage to the brain, heart, liver, and other organs. Food insecurity affects children even in industrialized countries.
- **Obesity** is a growing problem in both industrialized and developing nations. Although heredity accounts for a tendency to gain weight, environment—including parental feeding practices, maladaptive eating habits, lack of exercise, and poor food choices—is a more powerful influence. Obese children are often socially isolated and display more emotional, social, and school difficulties and behavior problems than their normal-weight peers. Effective treatments for obesity are family-based; schools can also help by serving healthier meals and ensuring physical activity.
- Malnutrition interacts with infectious disease to undermine physical growth. In developing countries, where diarrhea leads to millions of childhood deaths, oral rehydration therapy (ORT) and zinc supplements can save lives. Widespread immunization has led to a dramatic decline in childhood diseases.
- **Nonorganic failure to thrive** and **psychosocial dwarfism** are growth disorders resulting from lack of parental affection and stimulation. Prolonged emotional deprivation can lead to permanent physical, cognitive, and emotional difficulties.

Puberty: The Physical Transition to Adulthood

Describe sexual maturation in girls and boys, noting genetic and environmental influences on pubertal timing.

- At **puberty,** changes in **primary** and **secondary sexual characteristics** accompany rapid body growth. **Menarche** occurs late in the girl's sequence of pubertal events, after the growth spurt, breast growth, and appearance of pubic and underarm hair. In boys, the growth spurt occurs later, preceded by enlargement of the sex organs and **spermarche.** Deepening of the voice occurs at the peak of the growth spurt, followed by growth of facial and body hair.
- Heredity, nutrition, and overall health contribute to the timing of puberty. Menarche is delayed in regions of the world with widespread malnutrition and infectious disease. In industrialized nations, ethnic variations—for example, earlier menarche in African-American than in Caucasian-American girls—reflect both heredity and environment.

The Psychological Impact of Pubertal Events

What factors influence adolescents' reactions to the physical changes of puberty?

- Puberty is not a biologically determined period of storm and stress. Adjustment varies widely and is a product of both biological and social forces.
- Girls typically react to menarche with surprise and mixed emotions. Their feelings lean in a positive direction when they receive advance information and support from family members. Boys, who receive less social support than girls for the physical changes of puberty, react to spermarche with mixed feelings. In Western societies, the absence of a widely accepted marker for physical and social maturity, comparable to the adolescent initiation ceremonies of tribal and village societies, makes the process of becoming an adult especially confusing.

© Don Hammond/Design Pics/Corbis

- Factors associated with adolescent moodiness are higher hormone levels, negative life events, sleep loss, and time spent in adult-structured situations. Psychological distancing between parent and child at puberty may be a modern substitute for physical departure from the family seen in non-human primates and in nonindustrialized human cultures. Parent–adolescent conflict also reflects teenagers' new powers of reasoning and efforts by their parents to protect teenagers from risky situations.

Describe the impact of pubertal timing on adolescent adjustment, noting sex differences.

- Early-maturing boys and late-maturing girls, whose appearance fits cultural standards of physical attractiveness, have a more positive **body image** and usually adjust well in adolescence. In contrast, early-maturing girls and late-maturing boys experience emotional and social difficulties, which—for girls—persist into young adulthood.

Puberty and Adolescent Health

What factors contribute to eating disorders at adolescence?

- In girls who reach puberty early, who are dissatisfied with their body images, and who grow up in families that emphasize thinness, genetic and environmental factors put them at risk for eating disorders. **Anorexia nervosa** typically affects girls who are perfectionists and have overprotective, controlling mothers and emotionally distant fathers. **Bulimia nervosa** is often associated with disengaged parenting. Some bulimics are perfectionists, while others lack self-control in many areas of their lives.

Discuss individual, social, and cultural influences on adolescent sexual attitudes and behavior.

- Social and cultural factors affect how teenagers manage their sexuality. North American attitudes toward adolescent sex remain relatively restrictive, and the social environment—parents, schools, and mass media—delivers contradictory messages. Adolescent sexual attitudes and behavior have become more liberal, with a recent slight swing back toward more conservative views.
- Early, frequent sexual activity is linked to factors associated with economic disadvantage, including a hazardous neighborhood and weak parental monitoring. Early and prolonged father absence predicts sexual activity and pregnancy among adolescent girls.
- Many sexually active teenagers do not practice contraception regularly. Adolescent cognitive processes and lack of social support for responsible sexual behavior, including access to birth control, underlie this failure to take precautions against pregnancy. Those who lack the rewards of meaningful education and work are most likely to engage in irresponsible sex, sometimes in exploitative relationships.

Cite factors involved in the development of homosexuality.

- About 2 to 3 percent of young people identify as lesbian, gay, or bisexual. Research indicates that genetic and prenatal biological influences are largely responsible. Because of widespread stereotypes and prejudice, gay, lesbian, and bisexual teenagers face special challenges in establishing a positive sexual identity.

Discuss factors related to sexually transmitted disease and teenage pregnancy and parenthood, noting prevention and intervention strategies.

- Irresponsible sexual activity puts teenagers at risk for contracting sexually transmitted diseases (STDs), including AIDS—the most serious STD. Drug abusing and homosexual young people account for most cases, but heterosexual spread has increased. Aside from AIDS, most teenagers have limited knowledge about STDs.
- Adolescent pregnancy and parenthood occur at higher rates in the United States than in most other industrialized nations. Teenage pregnancy is a problem in Canada as well. Life conditions linked to economic disadvantage, along with personal attributes, contribute

AP Images/The Honolulu Advertiser, Bruce Asato

to adolescent childbearing. Adolescent parenthood is associated with school dropout, reduced chances of marriage, greater likelihood of divorce, and poverty, jeopardizing the well-being of both parent and child. Children of teenage parents are at risk for carrying irresponsible sexual activity and early childbearing into a second generation.

- Effective sex education, access to contraceptives, and programs that build academic and social competence help prevent early pregnancy. Adolescent mothers need school programs that provide job training, instruction in parenting and life-management skills, and child care. They also benefit when family members and other adults offer guidance and support that are sensitive to their developmental needs. When teenage fathers stay involved, their children develop more favorably.

IMPORTANT TERMS AND CONCEPTS

androgens (p. 180)
anorexia nervosa (p. 208)
body image (p. 206)
brain plasticity (p. 186)
bulimia nervosa (p. 209)
catch-up growth (p. 190)
cerebellum (p. 188)
cerebral cortex (p. 184)
corpus callosum (p. 189)
distance curve (p. 174)
dominant cerebral hemisphere (p. 186)
epiphyses (p. 176)
estrogens (p. 180)
experience-dependent brain growth (p. 189)
experience-expectant brain growth (p. 189)
glial cells (p. 184)
growth hormone (GH) (p. 180)
hippocampus (p. 188)
hypothalamus (p. 180)
kwashiorkor (p. 195)
lateralization (p. 185)
marasmus (p. 195)
menarche (p. 200)
myelination (p. 184)
neurons (p. 183)
neurotransmitters (p. 183)
nonorganic failure to thrive (p. 199)
obesity (p. 196)
pituitary gland (p. 180)
primary sexual characteristics (p. 200)
programmed cell death (p. 183)
psychosocial dwarfism (p. 200)
puberty (p. 200)
reticular formation (p. 188)
secondary sexual characteristics (p. 200)
secular trends in physical growth (p. 182)
skeletal age (p. 176)
spermarche (p. 202)
synapses (p. 183)
synaptic pruning (p. 183)
thyroxine (p. 180)
velocity curve (p. 175)

6

"Clean Waters Forever"
Martin Muzikants
11 years, Latvia

Children make sense of their complex world through their own explorations and the guidance of parents, siblings, and other more expert partners. With the help of an adult, this young fisherman acquires a new skill while becoming increasingly sensitive to the welfare of the environment, in which "clean waters forever" is an important goal.

Cognitive Development: Piagetian, Core Knowledge, and Vygotskian Perspectives

Leslie, a preschool teacher, paused to look around her class of busy 3- and 4-year-olds. "Their minds are such a curious blend of logic, fantasy, and faulty reasoning," she remarked to a visiting parent. "Every day, I'm startled by the maturity and originality of what they say and do. Yet at other times, their thinking seems limited and inflexible."

Leslie's comments sum up the puzzling contradictions of young children's thought. Hearing a loud thunderclap outside, 3-year-old Sammy exclaimed, "A magic man turned on the thunder!" Even after Leslie explained that thunder is caused by lightning, not by a person turning it on or off, Sammy persisted: "Then a magic lady did it."

But in other respects, Sammy's thinking was surprisingly advanced. He could name, categorize, and identify similarities and differences among dozens of dinosaurs in his favorite picture books. "Anatosaurus and Tyrannosaurus walk on their back legs," he told the class during group time. "Then they can use their front legs to pick up food!" But at the snack table, while watching Priti pour her milk from a short, wide carton into a tall, thin glass, Sammy looked at his own identical carton and asked, "How come you got lots of milk, and I got this little bit?" He did not realize that he had just as much—that his carton, though shorter than Priti's glass, was also wider.

Cognition refers to the inner processes and products of the mind that lead to "knowing." It includes all mental activity—attending, remembering, symbolizing, categorizing, planning, reasoning, problem solving, creating, and fantasizing. Indeed, we could easily expand this list, since mental processes make their way into virtually everything human beings do. Our cognitive powers are crucial for survival. To adapt to changing environmental conditions, other species benefit from camouflage, feathers and fur coats, and remarkable speed. Humans, in contrast, rely on thinking, not only adapting to their environments but also transforming them. Among all earthly creatures, we stand out in our extraordinary mental capacities.

This chapter and the two that follow examine cognitive development: how the intellectual capacities of infants change into the capacities of the child, adolescent, and adult. Researchers of cognitive development address three main issues:

- They chart its *typical course,* identifying transformations that most children undergo from birth to maturity. They ask: Do all aspects of cognition develop uniformly, or do some develop at faster rates than others?
- They examine *individual differences.* At every age, some children think more or less maturely, and differently, than others. Chapters 6 and 7 focus primarily on the

general course of cognitive development, Chapter 8 on individual differences. But we will encounter both concerns in all three chapters.

- They uncover the *mechanisms* of cognitive development—how genetic and environmental factors combine to yield particular patterns of change. In this chapter, we address three distinct perspectives on how cognitive development occurs. Two, *Piaget's cognitive-developmental theory* and the *core knowledge perspective,* have a biological emphasis. The third, *Vygotsky's sociocultural theory,* stresses social and cultural contributions to children's thinking.

In considering each of these views, we will see that children move from simpler to more complex cognitive skills, becoming more effective thinkers with age. But we should not view children's immature capacities as merely incomplete, less effective versions of adults'. For children, focusing on a limited amount of information may be adaptive (Bjorklund, 2007). For example, noticing only a few features of an intricate pattern probably protects against overstimulation in young babies whose nervous systems cannot yet handle much complexity. And comparing the amounts of milk in a short, wide carton and a tall, thin glass by attending only to height (not width) may allow preschoolers to develop a thorough grasp of height, in preparation for effectively integrating height with other dimensions.

The adaptiveness of cognitive immaturity has important implications for education. It suggests that hurrying children to higher levels may undermine their progress. Piaget was among the first theorists to stress the importance of *readiness* to learn—presenting appropriately challenging tasks while avoiding overly complex stimulation that may confuse and overwhelm children. Let's begin with Piaget's theory.

Piaget's Cognitive-Developmental Theory

Swiss cognitive theorist Jean Piaget received his education in zoology, and his theory has a distinct biological flavor. According to Piaget, human infants do not start out as cognitive beings. Instead, out of their perceptual and motor activities, they build and refine psychological structures—organized ways of making sense of experience that permit them to adapt more effectively to the environment. Children develop these structures actively, using current structures to select and interpret experiences, then modifying those structures to take into account more subtle aspects of reality. Because Piaget viewed children as discovering, or *constructing,* virtually all knowledge about their world through their own activity, his theory is described as a **constructivist approach** to cognitive development.

Basic Characteristics of Piaget's Stages

Piaget believed that children move through four stages—sensorimotor, preoperational, concrete operational, and formal operational—during which infants' exploratory behaviors transform into the abstract, logical intelligence of adolescence and adulthood. Piaget's stage sequence has three important characteristics:

- The stages provide a *general theory* of development, in which all aspects of cognition change in an integrated fashion, following a similar course.
- The stages are *invariant;* they always occur in a fixed order, and no stage can be skipped.
- The stages are *universal;* they are assumed to characterize children everywhere. (Piaget, Inhelder, & Szeminska, 1948/1960)

Piaget regarded the order of development as rooted in human biology, reflecting the brain's increasing adeptness at analyzing and interpreting experiences common to most children throughout the world. But he emphasized that individual differences in genetic and environmental factors affect the speed with which children move through the stages (Piaget, 1926/1928). Let's consider some of Piaget's central concepts.

According to Piaget's theory, the baby's first schemes are motor action patterns. As this 8-month-old takes apart, turns, and bangs these pots and pans, he discovers that his movements have predictable effects on objects and that objects influence one another in predictable ways. © David Young-Wolff/PhotoEdit

Piaget's Ideas About Cognitive Change

According to Piaget, specific psychological structures called **schemes**—organized ways of making sense of experience—change with age. First schemes are sensorimotor action patterns. Watch a 6-month-old baby catch sight of, grasp, and release objects. Her "dropping scheme" is fairly rigid—she simply lets go of a rattle or teething ring in her hand. By 18 months, her dropping scheme has become deliberate and creative. Given an opportunity, she might toss all sorts of objects down the basement stairs, throwing some up in the air, bouncing others off walls, releasing some gently and others forcefully.

Soon, instead of just acting on objects, the toddler shows evidence of thinking before she acts. For Piaget, this change marks the transition from a sensorimotor approach to the world to a cognitive approach based on **mental representations**—internal depictions of information that the mind can manipulate. Our most powerful mental representations are *images*—mental pictures of objects, people, and spaces—and *concepts,* categories in which similar objects or events are grouped together. We use a mental image to retrace our steps when we've misplaced something or to imitate another's behavior long after observing it. By thinking in concepts and labeling them (for example, *ball* for all rounded, movable objects used in play), we become more efficient thinkers, organizing our diverse experiences into meaningful, manageable, and memorable units.

In Piaget's theory, two processes account for this change from sensorimotor to representational schemes and for further changes in representational schemes from childhood to adulthood: *adaptation* and *organization.*

• **Adaptation** TAKE A MOMENT... Next time you have a chance, notice how infants and children tirelessly repeat actions that lead to interesting effects. They are illustrating a key Piagetian concept. **Adaptation** involves building schemes through direct interaction with the environment. It consists of two complementary activities: *assimilation* and *accommodation.* During **assimilation,** we use our current schemes to interpret the external world. The infant who repeatedly drops objects is assimilating them into his sensorimotor "dropping scheme." And the preschooler who, seeing a camel at the zoo, calls out, "Horse!" has sifted through her conceptual schemes until she finds one that resembles the strange-looking creature. In **accommodation,** we create new schemes or adjust old ones after noticing that our current way of thinking does not capture the environment completely. The baby who drops objects in different ways is modifying his dropping scheme to take account of the varied properties of objects. And the preschooler who calls a camel a "lumpy horse" has noticed that camels differ from horses in certain ways and has revised her scheme accordingly.

According to Piaget, the balance between assimilation and accommodation varies over time. When children are not changing much, they assimilate more than they accommodate—a steady, comfortable state that Piaget called cognitive *equilibrium.* During times of rapid cognitive change, children are in a state of *disequilibrium,* or cognitive discomfort. Realizing that new information does not match their current schemes, they shift from assimilation to accommodation. After modifying their schemes, they move back toward assimilation, exercising their newly changed structures until they are ready to be modified again.

Piaget's term for this back-and-forth movement between equilibrium and disequilibrium is **equilibration.** Each time equilibration occurs, more effective schemes are produced. Because the times of greatest accommodation are the earliest ones, the sensorimotor stage is Piaget's most complex period of development.

• **Organization** Schemes also change through **organization,** a process that occurs internally, apart from direct contact with the environment. Once children form new schemes, they rearrange them, linking them with other schemes to create a strongly interconnected cognitive system. For example, eventually the baby relates "dropping" to "throwing" and to his developing understanding of "nearness" and "farness." According to Piaget, schemes truly reach equilibrium when they become part of a broad network of structures that can be jointly applied to the surrounding world (Piaget, 1936/1952).

In the following sections, we will begin by considering development as Piaget saw it, noting research that supports his observations. Then, for each stage, we will look at more recent evidence, some inspired by Piaget's theory and some that challenges his ideas.

The Sensorimotor Stage: Birth to 2 Years

The **sensorimotor stage** spans the first two years of life. Its name reflects Piaget's belief that infants and toddlers "think" with their eyes, ears, hands, and other sensorimotor equipment. They cannot yet carry out many activities mentally. Yet the advances of the sensorimotor stage are so vast that Piaget divided it into six substages, summarized in Table 6.1. Piaget based this sequence on a very small sample: his own three children. He observed his son and two daughters carefully and presented them with everyday problems (such as hidden objects) that helped reveal their understanding of the world.

According to Piaget, at birth infants know so little about their world that they cannot purposefully explore it. The **circular reaction** provides a special means of adapting their first schemes. It involves stumbling onto a new experience caused by the baby's own motor activity. The reaction is "circular" because, as the infant tries to repeat the event again and again, a sensorimotor response that originally occurred by chance becomes strengthened into a new scheme. Imagine a 2-month-old who accidentally makes a smacking noise after a feeding. Finding the sound intriguing, the baby tries to repeat it until, after a few days, she becomes quite expert at smacking her lips.

The circular reaction initially centers on the infant's own body but later turns outward, toward manipulation of objects. In the second year, it becomes experimental and creative, aimed at producing novel effects in the environment. Infants' difficulty inhibiting new and interesting behaviors may underlie the circular reaction. This immaturity in inhibition seems to be adaptive, helping to ensure that new skills will not be interrupted before they strengthen (Carey & Markman, 1999). Piaget considered revisions in the circular reaction so important that, as Table 6.1 shows, he named the sensorimotor substages after them.

Table 6.1 Summary of Piaget's Sensorimotor Stage

Sensorimotor Substage	Typical Adaptive Behaviors
1. Reflexive schemes (birth–1 month)	Newborn reflexes (see Chapter 4, page 128)
2. Primary circular reactions (1–4 months)	Simple motor habits centered around the infant's own body; limited anticipation of events
3. Secondary circular reactions (4–8 months)	Actions aimed at repeating interesting effects in the surrounding world; imitation of familiar behaviors
4. Coordination of secondary circular reactions (8–12 months)	Intentional, or goal-directed, behavior; ability to find a hidden object in the first location in which it is hidden (object permanence); improved anticipation of events; imitation of behaviors slightly different from those the infant usually performs
5. Tertiary circular reactions (12–18 months)	Exploration of the properties of objects by acting on them in novel ways; imitation of novel behaviors; ability to search in several locations for a hidden object (accurate A–B search)
6. Mental representation (18 months–2 years)	Internal depictions of objects and events, as indicated by sudden solutions to problems; ability to find an object that has been moved while out of sight (invisible displacement); deferred imitation; and make-believe play

Sensorimotor Development

This 3-month-old sees his hands touch, open, and close. He tries to repeat these movements, in a primary circular reaction that helps him gain voluntary control over his behavior. © M. Dominik/zefa/Corbis

Piaget saw newborn reflexes as the building blocks of sensorimotor intelligence. In Substage 1, babies suck, grasp, and look in much the same way, no matter what experiences they encounter. In one amusing example, a mother described how her 2-week-old daughter lay on the bed next to her sleeping father, who suddenly awoke with a start. The baby had latched on and begun to suck on his back!

• Repeating Chance Behaviors Around 1 month, as babies enter Substage 2, they start to gain voluntary control over their actions through the *primary circular reaction,* by repeating chance behaviors largely motivated by basic needs. This leads to some simple motor habits, such as sucking the fist or thumb. Babies in this substage also begin to vary their behavior in response to environmental demands. For example, they open their mouths differently for a nipple than for a spoon. And they start to anticipate events: A hungry 3-month-old is likely to stop crying as soon as his mother enters the room—a signal that feeding time is near.

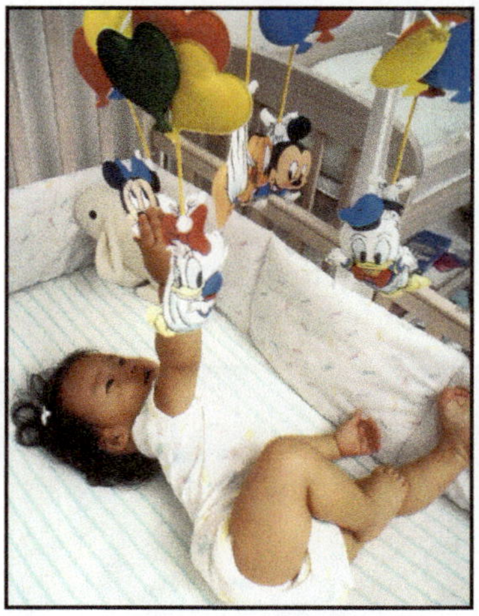

When this 4-month-old accidentally hits a toy hung in front of her, her action causes it to swing. Using the secondary circular reaction, she tries to recapture this interesting swinging effect. In the process, she builds a new "hitting scheme." © Michael Newman/PhotoEdit

During Substage 3, from 4 to 8 months, infants sit up and become skilled at reaching for and manipulating objects—motor achievements that strengthen the *secondary circular reaction,* through which they try to repeat interesting events in the surrounding environment that are caused by their own actions. For example, Piaget (1936/1952) dangled several dolls in front of his 4-month-old son, Laurent. After accidentally knocking them and producing a fascinating swinging motion, Laurent gradually built the sensorimotor scheme of "hitting." Improved control over their own behavior also permits infants to imitate others' behavior more effectively. However, 4- to 8-month-olds cannot adapt flexibly and quickly enough to imitate novel behaviors (Kaye & Marcus, 1981). Although they enjoy watching an adult demonstrate a game of pat-a-cake, they are not yet able to participate.

• Intentional Behavior In Substage 4, 8- to 12-month-olds combine schemes into new, more complex action sequences. Now, behaviors leading to new schemes no longer have a random, hit-or-miss quality—*accidentally* bringing the thumb to the mouth or *happening* to hit the doll. Instead, 8- to 12-month-olds can engage in **intentional, or goal-directed, behavior,** coordinating schemes deliberately to solve simple problems. The clearest example comes from Piaget's famous object-hiding task, in which he shows the baby an attractive toy and then hides it behind his hand or under a cover. Infants in this substage can find the object by coordinating two schemes—"pushing" aside the obstacle and "grasping" the toy. Piaget regarded these *means–end action sequences* as the foundation for all problem solving.

The capacity to find a hidden object emerges between 8 and 12 months, marking a major advance in cognitive development. In coordinating schemes to solve a problem—finding the hidden toy under the pillow—this infant engages in an intentional, goal-directed behavior—the basis of all problem solving. © Laura Dwight Photography

Retrieving hidden objects is evidence that infants have begun to master **object permanence,** the understanding that objects continue to exist when they are out of sight. But this awareness is not yet complete. Babies still make the **A-not-B search error:** If they reach several times for an object at one hiding place (A), then see it moved to another (B), they still search for it in the first hiding place (A). Piaget concluded that the babies do not yet have a clear image of the object as persisting when hidden from view.

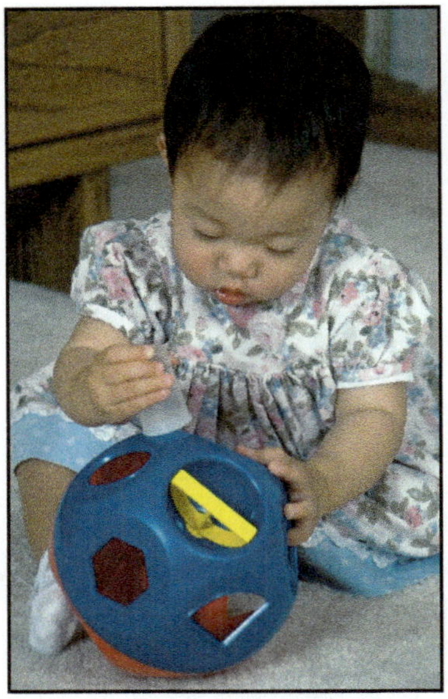

Using a tertiary circular reaction, this baby twists, turns, and pushes until a block fits through its matching hole in her shape sorter. Between 12 and 18 months, toddlers take a deliberately experimental approach to problem solving, repeating behaviors with variation.
© Myrleen Ferguson/PhotoEdit

Infants in Substage 4, who can better anticipate events, sometimes use their capacity for intentional behavior to try to change those events. A 10-month-old might crawl after his mother when she is putting on her coat, whimpering to keep her from leaving. Also, babies can imitate behaviors slightly different from those they usually perform. After watching someone else, they try to stir with a spoon, push a toy car, or drop raisins into a cup. Again, they draw on intentional behavior, purposefully modifying schemes to fit an observed action (Piaget, 1945/1951).

In Substage 5, from 12 to 18 months, the *tertiary circular reaction,* in which toddlers repeat behaviors with variation, emerges. Recall the example on page 225 of the child dropping objects over the basement steps, trying one action after another. This deliberately exploratory approach to the world makes 12- to 18-month-olds better problem solvers. For example, they can figure out how to fit a shape through a hole in a container by turning and twisting it until it falls through, and they can use a stick to obtain a toy that is out of reach. According to Piaget, this capacity to experiment leads to a more advanced understanding of object permanence. Toddlers look for a hidden toy in more than one location, displaying an accurate A–B search. Their more flexible action patterns also permit them to imitate many more behaviors—stacking blocks, scribbling on paper, and making funny faces.

The capacity for mental representation enables this 23-month-old to engage in make-believe play. At first, pretending involves simple schemes that the child has often experienced in everyday life.
© Spencer Grant/PhotoEdit

• **Mental Representation** In Substage 6, sensorimotor development culminates in mental representation. One sign of this capacity is that 18- to 24-month-olds arrive at solutions to problems suddenly rather than through trial-and-error behavior, apparently experimenting with actions inside their heads—evidence that they can mentally represent experiences. Seeing her doll carriage stuck against the wall, Piaget's daughter Lucienne paused for a moment, as if to "think," then immediately turned the toy in a new direction.

Representation also enables older toddlers to solve advanced object-permanence problems involving *invisible displacement*—finding a toy moved while out of sight, such as into a small box while under a cover. Second, it permits **deferred imitation**—the ability to remember and copy the behavior of models who are not present. And it makes possible **make-believe play,** in which children act out everyday and imaginary activities. As the sensorimotor period draws to a close, mental symbols have become major instruments of thinking.

Follow-Up Research on Infant Cognitive Development

Many studies suggest that infants display a variety of understandings earlier than Piaget believed. Recall the operant conditioning research reviewed in Chapter 4, in which newborns sucked vigorously on a nipple to gain access to interesting sights and sounds. This behavior, which closely resembles Piaget's secondary circular reaction, shows that infants explore and control their external world long before 4 to 8 months. In fact, they do so as soon as they are born.

To discover what infants know about hidden objects and other aspects of physical reality, researchers often use the **violation-of-expectation method.** They may *habituate* babies to a physical event (expose them to the event until their looking declines) to familiarize them with a situation in which their knowledge will be tested. Or they may simply show babies an *expected event* (one that follows physical laws) and an *unexpected event* (a variation of the first event that violates physical laws). Heightened attention to the unexpected event suggests that the infant is "surprised" by a deviation from physical reality—and, therefore, is aware of that aspect of the physical world.

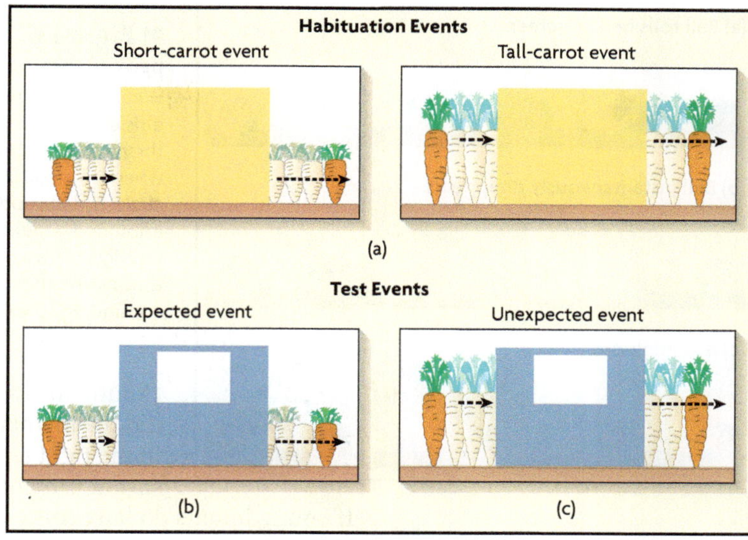

Figure 6.1 **Testing young infants for understanding of object permanence using the violation-of-expectation method.** (a) First, infants were habituated to two events: a short carrot and a tall carrot moving behind a yellow screen, on alternate trials. Next, the researchers presented two test events. The color of the screen was changed to help infants notice its window. (b) In the *expected event,* the carrot shorter than the window's lower edge moved behind the blue screen and reappeared on the other side. (c) In the *unexpected event,* the carrot taller than the window's lower edge moved behind the screen, did not appear in the window, but then emerged intact on the other side. Infants as young as 2½ to 3½ months looked longer at the unexpected event, suggesting that they had some understanding of object permanence. (From R. Baillargeon and J. DeVos, 1991, "Object Permanence in Young Infants: Further Evidence," *Child Development,* 62, p. 1230. © The Society for Research in Child Development. Adapted with permission of Blackwell Publishing.)

The violation-of-expectation method is controversial. Some critics believe that it indicates limited, implicit (nonconscious) awareness of physical events—not the full-blown, conscious understanding that was Piaget's focus in requiring infants to act on their surroundings, as in searching for hidden objects (Munakata, 2001; Thelen & Smith, 1994). Others maintain that the method reveals only babies' perceptual preference for novelty, not their knowledge of the physical world (Bremner & Mareschal, 2004; Hood, 2004). Let's examine this debate in light of recent research on object permanence.

Object Permanence In a series of studies using the violation-of-expectation method, Renée Baillargeon and her collaborators claimed evidence for object permanence in the first few months of life. Figure 6.1 illustrates one of these studies (Aguiar & Baillargeon, 1999, 2002; Baillargeon & DeVos, 1991). After habituating to a short and a tall carrot moving behind a screen, babies were given two test events: (1) an *expected event,* in which the short carrot moved behind a screen, could not be seen in its window, and reappeared on the other side, and (2) an *unexpected event,* in which the tall carrot moved behind a screen, could not be seen in its window (although it was taller than the window's lower edge), and reappeared. Infants as young as 2½ to 3½ months looked longer at the unexpected event, suggesting that they had some awareness that an object moved behind a screen would continue to exist.

Additional violation-of-expectation studies yielded similar results (Baillargeon, 2004; Wang, Baillargeon, & Paterson, 2005). But several researchers using similar procedures failed to confirm some of Baillargeon's findings (Bogartz, Shinskey, & Schilling, 2000; Cashon & Cohen, 2000; Cohen & Marks, 2002; Rivera, Wakeley, & Langer, 1999). Baillargeon and others maintain that these opposing investigations did not include crucial controls. They emphasize that infants look longer at a wide variety of unexpected events involving hidden objects (Newcombe, Sluzenski, & Huttenlocher, 2005; Wang, Baillargeon, & Paterson, 2005). Still, critics question what babies' looking preferences tell us about what they actually know.

But recall the findings on object perception presented in Chapter 4: Four-month-olds can track an object's path of movement as it disappears and reappears from behind a barrier, even gazing ahead to where they expect it to emerge—a behavior suggesting awareness that objects persist when out of view. As further support for such awareness, 5- to 9-month-olds more often engaged in such predictive tracking when a ball viewed on a computer screen gradually rolled behind a barrier than when it disappeared instantaneously or imploded (rapidly decreased in size) at the barrier's edge (see Figure 6.2 on page 230) (Bertenthal, Longo, & Kenny, 2007). Babies seemed to interpret a ball rolling behind a barrier as continued existence, instantaneous disappearance or implosion as disappearance (or at least a discontinuous path of movement). And with age, infants were more likely to fixate on the predicted place of the ball's reappearance and wait for it to emerge—evidence of an increasingly secure grasp of object permanence.

In related research, investigators recorded 6-month-olds' EEG brain-wave activity as the babies watched two events on a computer screen. In one, a black square moved until it covered an object, then moved away to reveal the object (object permanence). In the other event, as a black square began to move across an object, the object disintegrated (object disappearance)

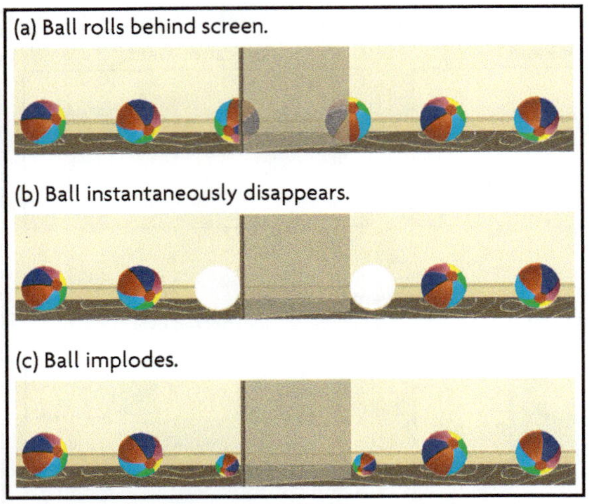

Figure 6.2 **Testing 5- to 9-month-olds for understanding of object permanence using predictive eye tracking.**
When a ball viewed on a computer screen rolled behind a barrier (a), 5- to 9-month-olds engaged in predictive tracking—gazing ahead to the edge of the screen where they expected the ball to emerge. Babies were much less likely to predictively track when (b) a ball instantaneously disappeared on reaching the location of the first white circle and abruptly reappeared at the location of second white circle or (c) a ball imploded—rapidly decreased in size—as it approached the barrier's edge, then rapidly increased in size as it reappeared on the other side. These findings suggest that by the middle of the first year, babies interpret a ball rolling behind a barrier as continuing to exist. (Adapted from Bertenthal, Longo, & Kenny, 2007.)

(Kaufman, Csibra, & Johnson, 2005). Only while watching the first event did the infants display an increase in a particular pattern of EEG activity in the right temporal lobe—the same pattern adults exhibit when told to sustain a mental image of an object.

If young infants do have some notion of object permanence, which strengthens with age, how do we explain Piaget's finding that even babies who are capable of reaching do not try to search for hidden objects? Consistent with Piaget's theory, searching for hidden objects is a true cognitive advance because infants solve some object-hiding tasks before others. Ten-month-olds search for an object placed on a table and covered by a cloth before they search for an object that a hand deposits under a cloth (Moore & Meltzoff, 1999). In the second, more difficult task, infants seem to expect the object to reappear in the hand because that is where the object initially disappeared. When the hand emerges without the object, they conclude that there is no other place the object could be. Not until 14 months can most babies infer that the hand deposited the object under the cloth (see Figure 6.3).

Figure 6.3 **Performance of 10- to 14-month-olds on two types of object-hiding tasks.**
In the hiding-by-cloth task, a hand deposited the object on the table, next to a folded cloth. Then the cloth was unfolded over the object. In the hiding-by-hand task, a hand carried the object toward and under the cloth, deposited the object under the cloth on the table, and emerged empty. Ten-month-olds searched for the object hidden by the cloth before they searched for the object hidden by the hand—a task most toddlers performed successfully only at 14 months. (Adapted from Moore & Meltzoff, 1999.)

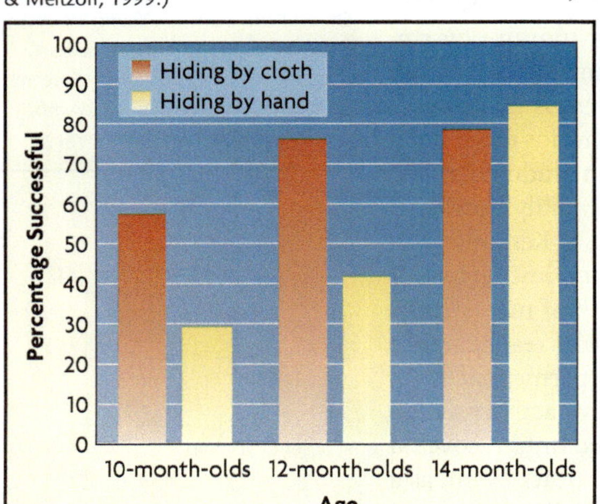

Around this time, toddlers demonstrate a thorough understanding of hidden objects. Fourteen-month-olds know that objects continue to exist in their hidden locations even after the babies have left the location. After seeing an object hidden in a cupboard, on returning the next day the toddlers correctly searched for the specific object in its original location. When exposed to a similar cupboard in a new room, infants behaved just as adults do: They saw no reason to search for an object that had been hidden elsewhere (Moore & Meltzoff, 2004).

• Searching for Objects Hidden in More Than One Location For some years, researchers thought that 8- to 12-month-olds made the A-not-B search error because they had trouble remembering an object's new location after it had been hidden in more than one place. But poor memory cannot fully account for infants' unsuccessful performance. Between 6 and 12 months, infants increasingly *look* at the correct location, even while *reaching* incorrectly (Ahmed & Ruffman, 1998; Hofstadter & Reznick, 1996).

Perhaps babies search at A (where they previously found the object) instead of B (its most recent location) because they have trouble inhibiting a previously rewarded motor response (Diamond, Cruttenden, & Neiderman, 1994). In support of this view, the more prior reaches to A, the greater the likelihood that the infant will reach again toward A when the object is hidden at B. Or perhaps, after finding the object several times at A, babies do not attend closely when it is hidden at B (Ruffman & Langman, 2002). A more comprehensive explanation is that a complex, dynamic system of factors—having built a habit of reaching toward A, continuing to look at A, having the hiding place at B look similar to the one at A, and maintaining a constant body posture—increases the chances that the baby will make the A-not-B search error. Disrupting any one of these factors increases 10-month-olds' accurate searching at B (Thelen et al., 2001).

In sum, mastery of object permanence is a gradual achievement. According to one view, young babies presented with a simple object-hiding task and older babies presented with an A–B search task have a remarkable appreciation of an object's continued existence and location, but at first they have difficulty translating this knowledge into a successful search strategy (Baillargeon, 2000; Berthier et al., 2001). Another view is that babies' understanding becomes increasingly complex with age: They must perceive an object's identity by integrating feature and movement information (see Chapter 4, pages 161–162), distinguish the object from the barrier concealing it, keep track of its whereabouts, and use this knowledge to find it (Cohen & Cashon, 2006; Meltzoff & Moore, 1998; Munakata & Stedron, 2002). Success at simple object search and A–B search tasks coincides with rapid development of the frontal lobes of the cerebral cortex (Bell, 1998). Also crucial are a wide variety of experiences perceiving, acting on, and remembering objects.

• Mental Representation In Piaget's theory, infants lead purely sensorimotor lives, unable to mentally represent experience until about 18 months of age. Yet 8-month-olds' recall of the location of hidden objects after delays of more than a minute, and 14-month olds' recall after delays of a day or more, indicate that babies construct mental representations of objects and their whereabouts (McDonough, 1999; Moore & Meltzoff, 2004). And in studies of deferred imitation, categorization, and problem solving, representational thought is evident even earlier.

Deferred Imitation. Piaget studied imitation by noting when his three children demonstrated it in their everyday behavior. Under these conditions, a great deal must be known about the infant's daily life to be sure that deferred imitation—which requires infants to represent a model's past behavior—has occurred.

Laboratory research suggests that deferred imitation is present at 6 weeks of age! Infants who watched an unfamiliar adult's facial expression imitated it when exposed to the same adult the next day (Meltzoff & Moore, 1994). As motor capacities improve, infants copy actions with objects. In one study, adults showed 6- and 9-month-olds a novel series of actions with a puppet: taking its glove off, shaking the glove to ring a bell inside, and replacing the glove. When tested a day later, infants who had seen the novel actions were far more likely to imitate them. And by merely pairing a second, motionless puppet with the first puppet the day before the demonstration, the researchers induced the infants to generalize the actions to this new, very different-looking puppet (Barr, Marrott, & Rovee-Collier, 2003). Over the second half-year, babies imitate over longer delays and increase the number of novel behaviors they imitate; at 9 months, they copy, on average, three out of six presented by an adult (Collie & Hayne, 1999).

Gains in recall, expressed through deferred imitation, are accompanied by changes in brain-wave activity, as measured by ERPs, during memory tasks. This suggests that improvements in memory storage in the cerebral cortex contribute to these advances (Bauer et al., 2006). Between 12 and 18 months, toddlers use deferred imitation skillfully to enrich their range of schemes. They retain modeled behaviors for at least several months, copy the actions of peers as well as adults, and imitate across a change in context—for example, enact in the home a behavior learned at child care or seen on TV (Barr & Hayne, 1999; Hayne, Boniface, & Barr, 2000; Klein & Meltzoff, 1999). Over the second year, they also gain in ability to imitate an adult's actions on toys in the order in which those actions occurred (Bauer, 2002b, 2006). And when toddlers imitate in correct sequence, they remember more modeled behaviors (Knopf, Kraus, & Kressley-Mba, 2006).

During the second half-year, gains in recall are evident in deferred imitation of others' behaviors over longer delays. After researchers performed a novel series of actions with a puppet, this 6-month-old imitated the actions a day later—at left, removing the glove; at right, shaking the glove to ring a bell inside. Courtesy of Carolyn Rovee-Collier

Toddlers even imitate rationally, by inferring others' intentions! Fourteen-month-olds are more likely to imitate purposeful than accidental behaviors (Carpenter, Akhtar, & Tomasello, 1998). And they adapt their imitative acts to a model's goals. If 12-month-olds see an adult perform an unusual action for fun (make a toy dog enter a miniature house by jumping through the chimney, even though its door is wide open), they copy the behavior. But if the adult engages in the odd behavior because she *must* (she makes the dog go through the chimney only after first trying to use the door and finding it locked), 12-month-olds typically imitate the more efficient action (putting the dog through the door) (Schwier et al., 2006; see also Gergely, Bekkering, & Kiraly, 2003).

Around 18 months, toddlers can imitate actions an adult *tries* to produce, even if these actions are not fully realized (Meltzoff, 1995). On one occasion, a mother attempted to pour some raisins into a bag but missed, spilling them onto the counter. A moment later, her 18-month-old son climbed onto a stool and began dropping the raisins into the bag. He had inferred his mother's intention and used it to guide his imitative actions (Falck-Ytter, Gredebäck, & von Hofsten, 2006). By age 2, children mimic entire social roles—Mommy, Daddy, baby—during make-believe play.

Categorization. Even young infants can *categorize,* grouping similar objects and events into a single representation—an ability that is incompatible with a strictly sensorimotor approach to the world. Categorization helps infants make sense of experience by reducing the enormous amount of new information they encounter every day so they can learn and remember (Cohen, 2003; Oakes & Madole, 2003).

Recall the operant conditioning research in which infants kicked to move a mobile attached to their foot by a long cord (see Chapter 4, page 139). Figure 6.4 illustrates a creative variation of this task, used to investigate infant categorization. Similar studies reveal that in the first few months, babies categorize stimuli on the basis of shape, size, and other physical properties (Wasserman & Rovee-Collier, 2001). By 6 months, they can categorize on the basis of two correlated features—for example, the shape and color of the alphabet letter (Bhatt et al., 2004). This ability to categorize using clusters of features prepares babies for acquiring many complex everyday categories.

Habituation/recovery has also been used to study infant categorization. Researchers show babies a series of pictures belonging to one category, then see whether the babies recover to (look longer at) a picture that does not belong to the category. Findings reveal that 6- to 12-month-olds structure objects into an impressive array of meaningful categories, including food items, furniture, birds, animals, vehicles, kitchen utensils, plants, and spatial location ("above" and "below," "on" and "in") (Casasola, Cohen, & Chiarello, 2003; Mandler & McDonough, 1998; Oakes, Coppage, & Dingel, 1997). Besides organizing the physical world, infants of this age categorize their emotional and social worlds. Their looking responses reveal that they sort people and their voices by gender and age, have begun to distinguish emotional expressions, expect people (but not inanimate objects) to move spontaneously, and can separate people's natural movements from other motions (Bahrick, Netto, & Hernandez-Reif, 1998; Poulin-DuBois et al., 1994; Spelke, Phillips, & Woodward, 1995; see also Chapter 4, pages 160–161).

Babies' earliest categories are *perceptual*—based on similar overall appearance or prominent object part: legs for *animals,* wheels for *vehicles.* By the second half of the

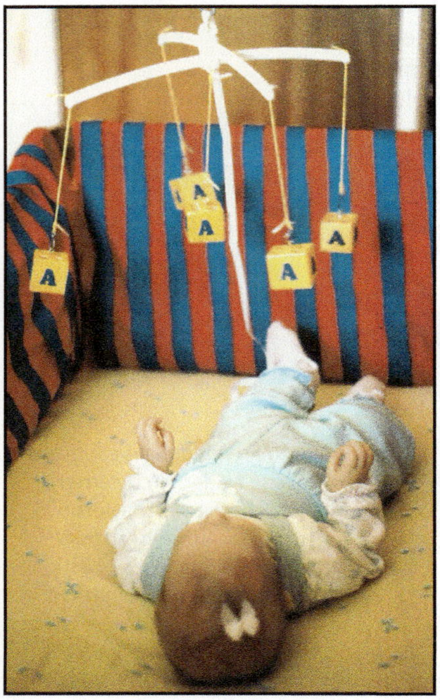

■ Figure 6.4 Investigating infant categorization using operant conditioning.
Three-month-olds were taught to kick to move a mobile made of small blocks, all with the letter *A* on them. After a delay, kicking returned to a high level only if the babies were shown a mobile whose elements were labeled with the same form (the letter *A*). If the form was changed (from an *A* to a *2*), infants no longer kicked vigorously. While making the mobile move, the babies had grouped together its features. They associated the kicking response with the category *A* and, at later testing, distinguished it from the category *2.* (Bhatt, Rovee-Collier, & Weiner, 1994; Hayne, Rovee-Collier, & Perris, 1987.)

first year, more categories are *conceptual*—based on common function and behavior (Cohen, 2003; Mandler, 2004). Older infants can even make categorical distinctions when the perceptual contrast between two categories—animals and vehicles—is minimal (for an illustration, see Figure 6.5). Once infants have formed a variety of object categories, they add event categories involving actions, such as a person walking, an animal drinking, or an object bumping another and causing it to move.

In the second year, toddlers become active categorizers. Around 12 months, they touch objects that go together. As their knowledge of categories and verbal labels expands, toddlers start to categorize flexibly: When 14-month-olds are given four balls and four blocks, some made of soft rubber and some of rigid plastic, their sequence of object touching reveals that after classifying by shape, they can switch to classifying by material (soft versus hard) if an adult calls their attention to the new basis for grouping (Ellis & Oakes, 2006). At 16 months, toddlers can arrange objects into a single category—gathering all the balls together. And around 18 months, they can sort objects into two classes (balls and boxes) (Gopnik & Meltzoff, 1987).

Compared with habituation/recovery, touching, sorting, and other play behaviors better reveal the meanings that children attach to categories by showing how they apply those meanings in their everyday behavior. For example, after watching an experimenter give a toy dog a drink from a cup, 14-month-olds, when shown a rabbit and a motorcycle, usually offer the drink only to the rabbit (Mandler & McDonough, 1998). Their behavior reveals their developing understanding that certain actions are appropriate for some categories of items (animals) but not others (vehicles).

Figure 6.5 **Categorical distinction made by 9- to 11-month-olds.**
After being given an opportunity to examine (by looking or touching) the objects in one category, infants were shown a new object from each category. They recovered to (spent more time looking at or touching) the object from the contrasting category, indicating that they distinguished the birds from the airplanes, despite their perceptual similarity. (Adapted from Mandler & McDonough, 1993.)

Over the second year, toddlers' grasp of the animate–inanimate distinction expands. For example, nonlinear motions are typical of animates (a person or a dog jumping), linear motions of inanimates (a car or a table pushed along a surface). At 18 months, toddlers more often imitate a nonlinear motion with a toy that has animate-like parts (legs), even if it represents an inanimate (a bed). At 22 months, displaying a much fuller understanding, they imitate a nonlinear motion only with toys in the animate category (a cat but not a bed) (Rakison, 2005). They seem to grasp that whereas animates (a cat) are self-propelled and, therefore, have varied paths of movement, inanimates (a bed) move only when acted on, in highly restricted ways (Rakison, 2006).

How does the perceptual-to-conceptual change in categorization occur? Researchers disagree on whether babies learn correlations among perceptually salient physical features and movements of objects that gradually lead to meaningful wholes or whether this shift requires a new approach to analyzing experience (Mandler, 2004; Mareschal & Quinn, 2001; Oakes & Madole, 2003; Rakison & Poulin-Dubois, 2001). But all acknowledge that exploration of objects and expanding knowledge of the world contribute to older infants' capacity to move beyond physical features and group objects by their functions and behaviors. In addition, language both builds on and facilitates categorization. Adult labeling calls babies' attention to commonalities among objects while also promoting vocabulary growth (Waxman & Braun, 2005). Toddlers' advancing vocabulary, in turn, fosters categorization (Gelman & Kalish, 2006; Waxman, 2003).

Variations among languages lead to cultural differences in conceptual development. Korean toddlers, who learn a language in which object names are often omitted from sentences, develop object-grouping skills later than their English-speaking counterparts (Gopnik & Choi, 1990). At the same time, Korean contains a common word, *kkita,* with no English equivalent, referring to a tight fit between objects in contact—a ring on a finger, a cap on a pen, a puzzle piece—and Korean toddlers are advanced in forming the spatial category "tight-fit" (Choi et al., 1999).

Problem Solving. As Piaget indicated, around 7 to 8 months, infants develop intentional means–end action sequences, which they use to solve simple problems, such as pulling on a cloth to obtain a toy resting on its far end (Willatts, 1999). Soon after, infants' representational skills permit more effective problem solving than Piaget's theory suggests.

■ **Figure 6.6** **Analogical problem solving by 10- to 12-month-olds.**

After the parent demonstrated the solution to problem (a), infants solved problems (b) and (c) with increasing efficiency, even though these problems differed from problem (a) in all aspects of their superficial features. (From Z. Chen, R. P. Sanchez, & T. Campbell, 1997, "From Beyond to Within Their Grasp: The Rudiments of Analogical Problem Solving in 10- to 13-Month-Olds," *Developmental Psychology,* 33, p. 792. Copyright © 1997 by the American Psychological Association. Adapted with permission of the American Psychological Association.)

By 10 to 12 months, infants can engage in **analogical problem solving**—applying a solution strategy from one problem to other relevant problems. In one study, babies were given three similar problems, each requiring them to overcome a barrier, grasp a string, and pull it to get an attractive toy. The problems differed in all of their specific features (see Figure 6.6). For the first problem, the parent demonstrated the solution, encouraging the infant to imitate. Babies obtained the toy more readily with each additional problem (Chen, Sanchez, & Campbell, 1997). In another study, 12-month-olds who were repeatedly presented with a spoon in the same orientation (handle to one side) readily adapted their motor actions when the spoon was presented with the handle to the other side, successfully transporting food to their mouths most of the time (McCarty & Keen, 2005). Taken together, these findings suggest that at the end of the first year, infants form flexible mental representations of how to use tools to get objects.

With age, children become better at reasoning by analogy, generalizing across increasingly dissimilar situations (Goswami, 1996). But even in the first year, infants have some ability to move beyond trial-and-error experimentation, represent a solution mentally, and use it in new contexts.

Evaluation of the Sensorimotor Stage

The Milestones table on the following page summarizes the remarkable cognitive attainments we have just considered, along with related milestones that we will take up later in this chapter. **TAKE A MOMENT...** Compare this table with the description of Piaget's account of sensorimotor development on pages 227–228. You will see that infants anticipate events, actively search for hidden objects, master the A–B object search, flexibly vary their sensorimotor schemes, and engage in make-believe play within Piaget's time frame. Yet other capacities—including secondary circular reactions, first signs of object permanence, deferred imitation, categorization, and analogical problem solving—emerge earlier than Piaget expected.

Notice, also, that the cognitive attainments of infancy and toddlerhood do not develop in the neat, stepwise fashion predicted. For example, deferred imitation and the beginnings of analogical problem solving are present long before toddlers can solve Piaget's most advanced object-hiding task. To obtain an object that has been moved while out of sight, infants must go beyond recalling a past event to a more complex form of representation—*imagining an event they have not seen* (Rast & Meltzoff, 1995). Yet Piaget assumed that all representational capacities develop at the same time, at the end of the sensorimotor stage.

Disagreements between Piaget's observations and those of recent research raise controversial questions about how infant development takes place. Consistent with Piaget's ideas, sensorimotor action helps infants construct some forms of knowledge. For example, in Chapter 4 we saw that experience in crawling enhances depth perception and ability to find hidden objects. Yet we have also seen evidence that infants comprehend a great deal before they are capable of the motor behaviors that Piaget assumed led to those understandings. How can we account for babies' amazing cognitive accomplishments?

Most researchers believe that young babies have more built-in cognitive equipment for making sense of experience than granted by Piaget, who thought that

Did this toddler acquire the necessary physical knowledge to build a block structure through repeatedly acting on objects, as Piaget assumed? Or did he begin life with innate knowledge that enabled him to understand objects and their relationships quickly, with little hands-on exploration? © Alistair Berg/Getty Images/Taxi

Milestones

Some Cognitive Attainments of Infancy and Toddlerhood

Approximate Age	Cognitive Attainments
Birth–1 month	■ Secondary circular reactions using limited motor skills, such as sucking a nipple to gain access to interesting sights and sounds
1–4 months	■ Awareness of many physical properties, including object permanence, object solidity, and gravity, as suggested by violation-of-expectation findings ■ Deferred imitation of an adult's facial expression after a short delay (1 day) ■ Categorization of perceptually similar stimuli
4–8 months	■ Improved physical knowledge and basic numerical knowledge ■ Deferred imitation of an adult's novel actions on objects over a short delay (1 day) ■ Categorization of many objects and events conceptually—by similar function and behavior
8–12 months	■ Ability to search for a hidden object after it is covered by a cloth, then when a hand deposits it under a cloth ■ Ability to solve simple sensorimotor problems by analogy to a previous problem
12–18 months	■ Ability to search in several locations for a hidden object (accurate A–B search) ■ Awareness that objects continue to exist in their hidden locations even after the toddler has left the location ■ Deferred imitation of an adult's novel actions on objects after a long delay (at least several months) and across a change in context (from child care to home, from TV to everyday life) ■ Rational imitation, taking into account the model's intentions ■ Active object sorting into a single category
18 months–2 years	■ Ability to find an object moved while out of sight (invisible displacement) ■ Deferred imitation of actions an adult tries to produce, even if these are not fully realized, indicating a capacity to infer others' intentions and perspectives ■ Deferred imitation of everyday behaviors in make-believe play ■ Active object sorting into two categories

Note: These milestones represent overall age trends. Individual differences exist in the precise age at which each milestone is attained. **TAKE A MOMENT...** Which of the capacities listed in this table indicate that mental representation emerges earlier than predicted by Piaget's sensorimotor substages?

Photos: (top left) © Laura Dwight Photography; (top right) © Laura Dwight/CORBIS; (middle left) © Jennie Woodcock/CORBIS; (middle) © David Young Wolff/PhotoEdit; (bottom left) © Myrleen Ferguson Cate/PhotoEdit; (bottom right) © LWA-Dann Tardif/CORBIS

infants constructed all mental representations through sensorimotor activity. But intense disagreement exists over the extent of infants' initial understanding. As we have seen, much evidence on infant cognition rests on the violation-of-expectation method. Researchers who lack confidence in this method argue that babies' cognitive starting point is limited. They believe that newborns begin life with biases for attending to certain information and with general-purpose learning procedures, such as powerful techniques for analyzing complex perceptual information. Together, these capacities enable infants to construct a wide variety of schemes (Bahrick, Lickliter, & Flom, 2004; Huttenlocher, 2002; Kirkham, Slemmer, & Johnson, 2002; Mandler, 2004). Other investigators, convinced by violation-of-expectation findings, argue that infants start life with considerable innate knowledge, which "jump-starts" their cognitive development. This *core knowledge perspective* has gained ground in the past decade. We will discuss its strengths and limitations after considering Piaget's stages of childhood and adolescence.

Ask Yourself

Review Explain Piaget's view of how cognition changes, giving examples of assimilation, accommodation, and organization.

Review Using the text discussion on pages 226–235, construct your own table providing an overview of infant and toddler cognitive development. Which entries are consistent with Piaget's sensorimotor stage? Which ones develop earlier than Piaget anticipated?

Apply Mimi's father holds up her favorite teething biscuit, places it under a napkin, and shows Mimi his empty hand. Ten-month-old Mimi, looking puzzled, fails to search for the biscuit. Why does Mimi find this object-hiding task difficult?

Connect Recall from Chapter 4 (pages 162–163) that around the middle of the first year, infants become adept at identifying objects by their features (shape, color, and texture) and by their paths of movement, even when they cannot observe the entire path. How might these capacities contribute to infants' understanding of object permanence?

The Preoperational Stage: 2 to 7 Years

As children move from the sensorimotor to the **preoperational stage,** which spans ages 2 to 7, the most obvious change is an extraordinary increase in mental representation. Infants have some ability to represent their world. In early childhood, this capacity blossoms.

Advances in Mental Representation

Piaget acknowledged that language is our most flexible means of mental representation. By detaching thought from action, it permits far more efficient thinking than was possible earlier. When we think in words, we can deal with past, present, and future at once. We can also combine concepts in unique ways—imagining a hungry caterpillar eating bananas or monsters flying through the forest at night.

But Piaget did not regard language as the primary ingredient in childhood cognitive change. Instead, he believed that sensorimotor activity leads to internal images of experience, which children then label with words (Piaget, 1936/1952). In support of Piaget's view, children's first words have a strong sensorimotor basis, usually referring to objects that move or can be acted on or to familiar actions (see Chapter 9). And as we have seen, infants acquire an impressive range of categories long before they use words to label them.

Still, Piaget underestimated the power of language to spur children's cognition. Recall, for example, that toddlers' expanding vocabularies enhance their conceptual skills. Research inspired by Vygotsky's theory, which we take up later, confirms that language is a powerful source of cognitive development, not just an indicator of it.

• **Make-Believe Play** Make-believe is another excellent example of the development of representation in early childhood. Piaget believed that through pretending, children practice and strengthen newly acquired representational schemes. Drawing on his ideas, several investigators have traced changes in make-believe play during the preschool years.

Development of Make-Believe Play. **TAKE A MOMENT...** Visit a child-care center or a family with several young children, and compare an 18-month-old's pretending with that of a 2- to 3-year-old. Jot down examples of the following three advances, which reflect the preschool child's growing symbolic mastery:

- *Play increasingly detaches from the real-life conditions associated with it.* In early pretending, toddlers use only realistic objects—a toy telephone to talk into or a cup to drink from. Their earliest pretend acts usually imitate adults' actions and are not yet flexible. Children younger than age 2, for example, will pretend to drink from a cup but refuse to pretend a cup is a hat (Tomasello, Striano, & Rochat, 1999). They have trouble using an object (cup) that already has an obvious use as a symbol for another object (hat).

After age 2, children pretend with less realistic toys (a block for a telephone receiver). Gradually, they can flexibly imagine objects and events, without any support from the real world (O'Reilly, 1995; Striano, Tomasello, & Rochat, 2001).

- *Play becomes less self-centered.* At first, make-believe is directed toward the self; for example, children pretend to feed only themselves. A short time later, children direct pretend actions toward other people or objects, pouring tea for a parent or feeding a doll. Early in the third year, children become detached participants, assigning make-believe intentions to objects—making a doll feed itself or a parent doll feed a baby doll. Make-believe becomes less self-centered as children realize that agents and recipients of pretend actions can be independent of themselves (McCune, 1993).
- *Play includes more complex combinations of schemes.* An 18-month-old can pretend to drink from a cup but does not yet combine pouring and drinking. Later, children combine pretend schemes with those of peers in **sociodramatic play,** the make-believe with others that is under way around age 2 and increases rapidly during the next few years (Haight & Miller, 1993; Kavanaugh, 2006a). By age 4 to 5, children build on one another's play ideas, create and coordinate several roles, and have a sophisticated understanding of story lines (Göncü, 1993).

In sociodramatic play, children not only represent their world but also display *awareness* that make-believe is a representational activity. Between ages 2 and 3, children distinguish make-believe from real experiences and grasp that pretending is a deliberate effort to act out imaginary ideas—an understanding that strengthens steadily over early childhood (Lillard, 2003; Rakoczy, Tomasello, & Striano, 2004; Sobel, 2006). TAKE A MOMENT... Listen closely to a group of preschoolers as they jointly create an imaginary scene. Notice how they assign roles and negotiate make-believe plans: "*You pretend to be* the astronaut, *I'll act like* I'm operating the control tower!" "Wait, *I gotta set up* the spaceship." In communicating about pretend, children think about their own and others' fanciful representations—evidence that they have begun to reason about people's mental activities.

Benefits of Make-Believe Play. Piaget captured an important aspect of make-believe when he underscored its role in exercising representational schemes. He also noted its emotionally integrative function. Young children often revisit anxiety-provoking events, such as a trip to the doctor's office or discipline by a parent, but with roles reversed so the child is in command and can take charge of the unpleasant experience (Piaget, 1945/1951).

These 3- and 4-year-olds coordinate several make-believe roles as they jointly care for a sick baby. Sociodramatic play contributes to cognitive, emotional, and social development. © Laura Dwight Photography

Today, Piaget's view of make-believe as mere practice of representational schemes is regarded as too limited. Play not only reflects but also contributes to children's cognitive and social skills. Sociodramatic play has been studied most thoroughly. In comparison to social nonpretend activities (such as drawing or putting puzzles together), during social pretend preschoolers' interactions last longer, show more involvement, draw larger numbers of children into the activity, and are more cooperative (Creasey, Jarvis, & Berk, 1998).

Not surprisingly, then, preschoolers who spend more time in sociodramatic play are seen as more socially competent by their teachers (Connolly & Doyle, 1984). And many studies reveal that make-believe strengthens a wide variety of mental abilities, including sustained attention, memory, logical reasoning, language and literacy skills, imagination, creativity, understanding of emotions, and the ability to reflect on one's own thinking, inhibit impulses, control one's own behavior, and take another's perspective (Bergen & Mauer, 2000; Berk, 2006; Elias & Berk, 2002; Kavanaugh & Engel, 1998; Lindsey & Colwell, 2003; Ruff & Capozzoli, 2003).

Between 25 and 45 percent of preschoolers and young school-age children spend much time in solitary role play, creating *imaginary companions*—special fantasized friends endowed with humanlike qualities. One preschooler created Nutsy and Nutsy, a pair of boisterous birds living outside her bedroom window who often went along on family outings (Gleason, Sebanc, & Hartup, 2000; Taylor et al.,

Applying What We Know

Enhancing Make-Believe Play in Early Childhood

Strategy	Description
Provide sufficient space and play materials.	Generous space and materials allow for many play options and reduce conflict.
Supervise and encourage children's play without controlling it.	Respond to, guide, and elaborate on preschoolers' play themes when they indicate a need for assistance. Provide open-ended suggestions ("Would the animals like a train ride?"), and talk with the child about play characters' thoughts, motivations, and emotions. Avoid directing the child's play; excessive adult control destroys the creativity and joy of make-believe.
Offer a variety of both realistic materials and materials without clear functions.	Children use realistic materials, such as trucks, dolls, tea sets, dress-up clothes, and toy scenes (house, farm, garage, airport) to act out everyday roles in their culture. Materials without clear functions (such as blocks, cardboard cylinders, paper bags, and sand) inspire fantastic role play, such as "pirate" and "creature from outer space."
Ensure that children have many rich real-world experiences to inspire positive fantasy play.	Opportunities to participate in real-world activities with adults and to observe adult roles in the community provide children with rich social knowledge to integrate into make-believe. Restricting television viewing, especially programs with violent content, limits the degree to which violent themes and aggressive behavior become part of children's play. (See Chapter 15.)
Help children solve social conflicts constructively.	Cooperation is essential for sociodramatic play. Guide children toward positive relationships with agemates by helping them resolve disagreements constructively. For example, ask, "What could you do if you want a turn?" If the child cannot think of possibilities, suggest some options and help the child implement them.

2004). Imaginary companions were once viewed as a sign of maladjustment, but research challenges this assumption. Children with an invisible playmate typically treat it with care and affection and say it offers caring, comfort, and good company, just as their real friendships do (Gleason & Hohmann, 2006; Hoff, 2005). Such children also display more complex and imaginative pretend play, are advanced in understanding others' viewpoints and emotions, and are more sociable with peers (Bouldin, 2006; Gleason, 2002; Taylor & Carlson, 1997).

Refer to Applying What We Know above for ways to enhance preschoolers' make-believe. Later we will return to the origins and consequences of make-believe from an alternative perspective—that of Vygotsky.

• **Drawings** When given crayon and paper, even toddlers scribble in imitation of others. As preschoolers' ability to mentally represent the world expands, marks on the page take on meaning. A variety of cognitive factors influence the development of children's artful representations (Golomb, 2004). These include the realization that pictures can serve as symbols, improved planning and spatial understanding, and the emphasis the child's culture places on artistic expression.

From Scribbles to Pictures. Typically, drawing progresses through the following sequence:

1. *Scribbles.* At first, children's gestures rather than the resulting scribbles contain the intended representation. For example, one 18-month-old took her crayon and hopped it around the page, explaining, as she made a series of dots, "Rabbit goes hop-hop" (Winner, 1986).
2. *First representational forms.* Around age 3, children's scribbles start to become pictures. Often this happens after they make a gesture with the crayon, notice that they have drawn a recognizable shape, and then decide to label it—as with a child who made some random marks on a page and then, noticing that his scribbles resembled noodles, called his creation "chicken pie and noodles" (Winner, 1986).

   Few 3-year-olds spontaneously draw so others can tell what their picture represents. But in a study in which an adult demonstrated how pictures can be used to stand for

Figure 6.7 **Examples of young children's drawings.**
On the left is the universal tadpole-like shape that children use to draw their first picture of a person. The tadpole soon becomes an anchor for greater detail as arms, fingers, toes, and facial features sprout from the basic shape. By the end of the preschool years, children produce more complex, differentiated pictures like the one on the right, drawn by a 6-year-old. (*Left:* From H. Gardner, 1980, *Artful Scribbles: The Significance of Children's Drawing,* New York: Basic Books, p. 64. Copyright © 1980 by Howard Gardner. Reprinted by permission of Basic Books, a member of Perseus Books, LLC. *Right:* From E. Winner, August 1986, "Where Pelicans Kiss Seals," *Psychology Today,* 20[8], p. 35. Used by permission of the author.)

objects in a game, more 3-year-olds drew recognizable forms (Callaghan & Rankin, 2002). When adults draw with children and point out the resemblances between drawings and objects, preschoolers' drawings become more comprehensible and detailed (Braswell & Callanan, 2003).

A major milestone in drawing occurs when children use lines to represent the boundaries of objects, enabling 3- and 4-year-olds to draw their first picture of a person. Fine motor and cognitive limitations lead the preschooler to reduce the figure to the simplest form that still looks human: a circular shape with lines attached—the universal "tadpole" image shown on the left in Figure 6.7. Four-year-olds add features, such as eyes, nose, mouth, hair, fingers, and feet, as the tadpole drawings illustrate.

3. *More realistic drawings.* Greater realism in drawings develops gradually, as perception, language (ability to describe visual details), memory, and fine motor capacities improve (Toomela, 2002). Five- and 6-year-olds create more complex drawings, like the one on the right in Figure 6.7, containing more conventional human and animal figures in which head and body are differentiated and arms and legs appear.

   Older preschoolers' drawings still contain perceptual distortions because they have just begun to represent depth (Braine et al., 1993). Use of depth cues, such as overlapping objects, smaller size for distant than for near objects, diagonal placement, and converging lines, increases during middle childhood (Nicholls & Kennedy, 1992). And instead of depicting objects separately (as in the drawing in Figure 6.7), older school-age children relate them in an organized spatial arrangement (Case & Okamoto, 1996).

Cultural Variations in Development of Drawing. In cultures with rich artistic traditions, children create elaborate drawings that reflect the conventions of their culture. Adults encourage young children in drawing activities by commenting on children's pictures, offering suggestions, and modeling ways to draw (Boyatzis, 2000). Parents and teachers frequently ask children to label their pictures, emphasizing the representational function of drawing. Peers, as well, discuss one another's pictures, copy from one another's artwork, and occasionally critique the realism of one another's products (Braswell, 2006). All of these cultural practices enhance young children's drawing progress.

But in cultures with little interest in art, even older children and adolescents produce only simple forms. In the Jimi Valley, a remote region of Papua New Guinea with no indigenous pictorial art, many children do not attend school and therefore have little opportunity to develop drawing skills. When a Western researcher asked nonschooled Jimi 10- to 15-year-olds to draw a human figure for the first time, most produced nonrepresentational scribbles and shapes or simple "stick" or "contour" images (see Figure 6.8 on page 240) (Martlew & Connolly,

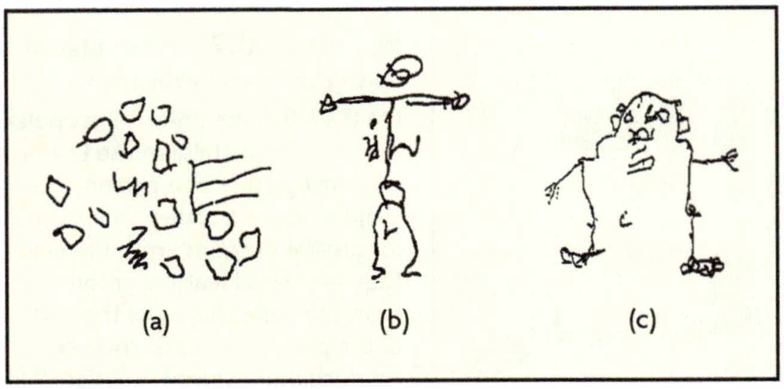

Figure 6.8 **Drawings produced by nonschooled 10- to 15-year-old children of the Jimi Valley of Papua New Guinea when they were asked to draw a human figure for the first time.** Many produced nonrepresentational scribbles and shapes (a), "stick" figures (b), or "contour" figures (c). Compared with the Western tadpole form, the Jimi "stick" and "contour" figures emphasize the hands and feet. Otherwise, the drawings of these older children resemble those of young preschoolers. (From M. Martlew & K. J. Connolly, 1996, "Human Figure Drawings by Schooled and Unschooled Children in Papua New Guinea," *Child Development,* 67, pp. 2750–2751. © The Society for Research in Child Development. Adapted with permission of the Society for Research in Child Development.)

1996). These forms, which resemble those of preschoolers, seem to be a universal beginning in drawing. Once children realize that lines must evoke human features, they find solutions to figure drawing that vary somewhat from culture to culture but, overall, follow the sequence of development described earlier.

• Symbol–Real World Relations To make believe and draw—and to understand other forms of representation, such as photographs, models, and maps—preschoolers must realize that each symbol corresponds to a specific state of affairs in everyday life. When do children comprehend symbol–real world relations?

In one study, 2½- and 3-year-olds watched an adult hide a small toy (Little Snoopy) in a scale model of a room, then were asked to retrieve it. Next, they had to find a larger toy (Big Snoopy) hidden in the room that the model represented. Not until age 3 could most children use the model as a guide to finding Big Snoopy in the real room (DeLoache, 1987). The 2½-year-olds did not realize that the model could be both *a toy room* and *a symbol of another room.* They had trouble with **dual representation**—viewing a symbolic object as both an object in its own right and a symbol. In support of this interpretation, when researchers made the model room less prominent as an object, by placing it behind a window and preventing children from touching it, more 2½-year-olds succeeded at the search task (DeLoache, 2000, 2002b).

Recall a similar limitation in early pretending—that 1½- to 2-year-olds cannot use an object with an obvious use (cup) to stand for another object (hat). Similarly, not until 20 to 22 months do toddlers realize that a toy object (miniature pig) has a real-world counterpart (Younger & Johnson, 2006). Furthermore, 2-year-olds do not yet grasp that a drawing—an object in its own right—represents real-world objects. When an adult held up a drawing indicating which of two objects preschoolers should drop down a chute, 3-year-olds used the drawing as a symbol to guide their behavior, but 2-year-olds did not (Callaghan, 1999).

How do children grasp the dual representation of symbolic objects? When adults point out similarities between models and real-world spaces, 2½-year-olds perform better on the find-Snoopy task (Peralta de Mendoza & Salsa, 2003). Also, insight into one type of symbol–real world relation helps preschoolers master others. For example, children regard photos and pictures in books as symbols early, around 18 months, because a picture's primary purpose is to stand for something; it is not an interesting object in its own right (Preissler & Carey, 2004; Simcock & DeLoache, 2006). And 3-year-olds who can use a model of a room to locate Big Snoopy readily transfer their understanding to a simple map (Marzolf & DeLoache, 1994).

In sum, exposing young children to diverse symbols—picture books, photos, drawings, make-believe, and maps—helps them appreciate that one object can stand for another (DeLoache, 2002a). With age, children come to understand a wide range of symbols that do not bear a strong physical similarity to what they represent (Liben, 1999). As a result, doors open to vast realms of knowledge.

Children who experience a variety of symbols come to understand that one object, such as the birdhouse this daughter and her father are making, can stand for another—a full-sized house that people live in. © Ariel Skelley/CORBIS

Limitations of Preoperational Thought

Aside from gains in representation, Piaget described preschool children in terms of what they *cannot* understand (Beilin, 1992). As the term *pre*operational suggests, he compared preschoolers to older, more competent children who have reached the concrete operational stage. According to Piaget, young children are not capable of **operations**—mental representations of actions that obey logical rules. Rather, their thinking is rigid, limited to one aspect of a situation at a time, and strongly influenced by the way things appear at the moment.

• Egocentric and Animistic Thinking For Piaget, the most fundamental deficiency of preoperational thinking is **egocentrism**—the failure to distinguish others' symbolic viewpoints from one's own. He believed that when children first mentally represent the world, they tend to focus on their own viewpoint and to assume that others perceive, think, and feel the same way they do.

Piaget's most convincing demonstration of egocentrism involves his *three-mountains problem,* described in Figure 6.9. Egocentrism, he pointed out, is responsible for preoperational children's **animistic thinking**—the belief that inanimate objects have lifelike qualities, such as thoughts, wishes, feelings, and intentions (Piaget, 1926/1930). The 3-year-old who charmingly explains that the sun is angry at the clouds and has chased them away is demonstrating this kind of reasoning. According to Piaget, because young children egocentrically assign human purposes to physical events, magical thinking is especially common during the preschool years.

Piaget argued that young children's egocentric bias prevents them from *accommodating,* or reflecting on and revising their faulty reasoning in response to their physical and social worlds. To understand this shortcoming, let's consider some additional tasks that Piaget gave children.

Figure 6.9 Piaget's three-mountains problem. Each mountain is distinguished by its color and by its summit. One has a red cross, another a small house, and the third a snow-capped peak. Children at the preoperational stage respond egocentrically: They cannot select a picture that shows the mountains from the doll's perspective. Instead, they simply choose the photo that reflects their own vantage point.

• **Inability to Conserve** Piaget's famous conservation tasks reveal several deficiencies of preoperational thinking. **Conservation** refers to the idea that certain physical characteristics of objects remain the same, even when their outward appearance changes. For example, in the conservation-of-liquid problem, the child is shown two identical tall glasses of water and asked if they contain equal amounts. Once the child agrees, the water in one glass is poured into a short, wide container, changing the water's appearance but not its amount. Then the child is asked whether the amount of water is the same or has changed. Preoperational children think the quantity has changed. They explain, "There is less now because the water is way down here" (that is, its level is so low) or "There is more because the water is all spread out." Figure 6.10 illustrates other conservation tasks that you can try with children.

The inability to conserve highlights several related aspects of preoperational children's thinking. First, their understanding is *centered,* or characterized by **centration.** They focus on one aspect of a situation, neglecting other important features. In conservation of liquid, the child *centers* on the height of the water, failing to realize that changes in width compensate for the changes in height. Second, children are easily distracted by the *perceptual appearance* of objects. Third, children treat the initial and final *states* of the water as unrelated events, ignoring the *dynamic transformation* (pouring of water) between them.

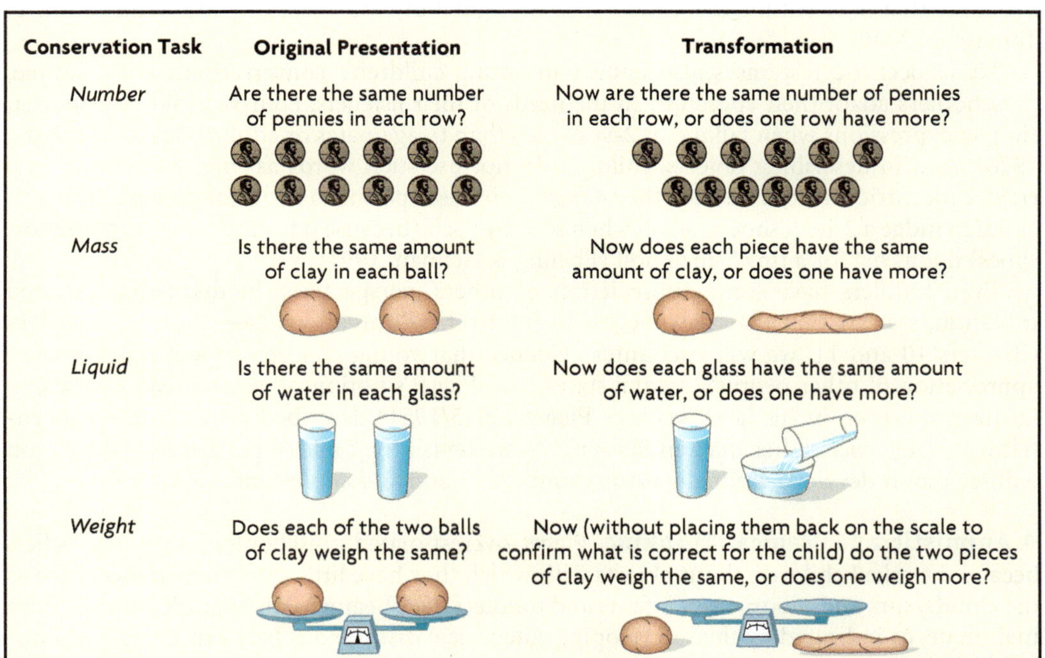

Figure 6.10 Some Piagetian conservation tasks. Children at the preoperational stage cannot yet conserve. These tasks are mastered gradually over the concrete operational stage. Children in Western nations typically acquire conservation of number, mass, and liquid sometime between 6 and 7 years and of weight between 8 and 10 years.

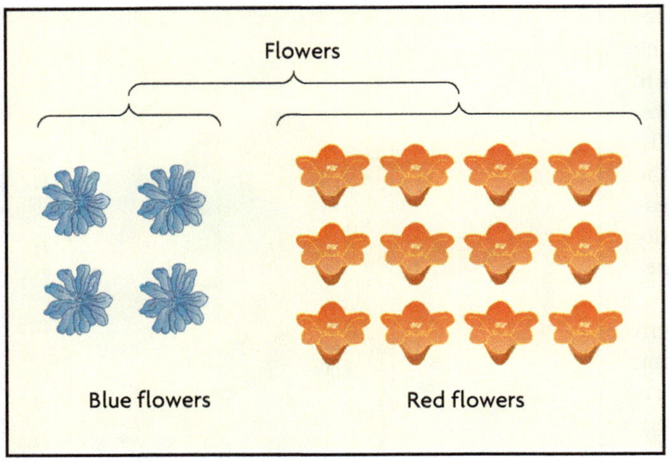

Figure 6.11 **A Piagetian class inclusion problem.** Children are shown 16 flowers, 4 of which are blue and 12 of which are red. Asked, "Are there more red flowers or flowers?" the preoperational child responds, "More red flowers," failing to realize that both red and blue flowers are included in the category "flowers."

The most important illogical feature of preoperational thought is *irreversibility.* **Reversibility**—the ability to go through a series of steps in a problem and then mentally reverse direction, returning to the starting point—is part of every logical operation. In the case of conservation of liquid, the preoperational child cannot imagine the water being poured back into its original container and so fails to see how the amount must remain the same.

• **Lack of Hierarchical Classification** Preoperational children have difficulty with **hierarchical classification**—the organization of objects into classes and subclasses on the basis of similarities and differences. Piaget's famous *class inclusion problem,* illustrated in Figure 6.11, demonstrates this limitation. Preoperational children center on the overriding feature, red. They do not think reversibly, moving from the whole class (flowers) to the parts (red and blue) and back again.

Follow-Up Research on Preoperational Thought

Over the past three decades, researchers have challenged Piaget's account of preschoolers as cognitively deficient. Because many Piagetian problems contain unfamiliar elements or too many pieces of information for young children to handle at once, preschoolers' responses often do not reflect their true abilities. Piaget also missed many naturally occurring instances of effective reasoning by preschoolers. Let's look at some examples.

• **Egocentrism** Do young children really believe that a person standing elsewhere in a room sees exactly what they see? When researchers adapt Piaget's three-mountains problem, including familiar objects and using methods other than picture selection (which is difficult even for 10-year-olds), 4-year-olds show clear awareness of others' vantage points (Borke, 1975; Newcombe & Huttenlocher, 1992). Even 2-year-olds realize that what they see sometimes differs from what another person sees. When asked to help an adult looking for a lost object, 24-month-olds—but not 18-month-olds—handed her a toy resting behind a bucket that was within the child's line of sight but not visible to the adult (Moll & Tomasello, 2006).

Nonegocentric responses also appear in young children's conversations. For example, preschoolers adapt their speech to fit the needs of their listeners. Four-year-olds use shorter, simpler expressions when talking to 2-year-olds than to agemates or adults (Gelman & Shatz, 1978). And in describing objects, children do not use such words as "big" and "little" in a rigid, egocentric fashion. Instead, they *adjust* their descriptions to allow for context. By age 3, children judge a 2-inch shoe as small when seen by itself (because it is much smaller than most shoes) but as big for a tiny 5-inch doll (Ebeling & Gelman, 1994).

Even toddlers have some appreciation of others' perspectives. In discussing deferred imitation, we saw that they have begun to infer others' intentions (see page 232). And in Chapters 10 and 11, we will encounter evidence that young children have a much greater appreciation of other people's mental states than Piaget's notion of egocentrism implies. In fairness, however, in his later writings Piaget (1945/1951) described preschoolers' egocentrism as a *tendency* rather than an inability. As we revisit the topic of perspective taking, you will see that it develops gradually throughout childhood and adolescence.

• **Animistic and Magical Thinking** Piaget overestimated preschoolers' animistic beliefs because he asked children about objects with which they have little direct experience, such as the clouds, sun, and moon. Even infants and toddlers have begun to distinguish animate from inanimate, as indicated by their developing categorical distinctions between living and nonliving things (see pages 232–233).

Is this child convinced that the magician's trick is due to supernatural powers? Most 3- and 4-year-olds believe that magic accounts for events they cannot explain. But they deny that magic can alter their everyday experiences. © Corbis Premium Collection/Alamy

By age 2½, children give psychological explanations ("he likes to"; "she wants to") for people and occasionally for animals, but rarely for objects (Hickling & Wellman, 2001). They do make errors when questioned about certain vehicles, such as trains and airplanes, which (like animate beings) appear to be self-moving and have some lifelike features, such as headlights that resemble eyes (Gelman & Opfer, 2002). But their responses reflect incomplete knowledge, not a belief that inanimate objects are alive.

The same is true for other fantastic beliefs of the preschool years. Most 3- and 4-year-olds believe in the supernatural powers of fairies, goblins, and other enchanted creatures. They think that magic accounts for events they cannot explain, as in 3-year-old Sammy's magical explanation for thunder in the opening to this chapter (Rosengren & Hickling, 2000). But they deny that magic can alter their everyday experiences—for example, turn a picture into a real object (Subbotsky, 1994). Furthermore, older 3-year-olds and 4-year-olds think that violations of physical laws (walking through a wall) and mental laws (turning on the TV just by thinking about it) require magic more than violations of social conventions (taking a bath with shoes on) (Browne & Woolley, 2004). These responses indicate that preschoolers' notions of magic are flexible and appropriate.

Between ages 4 and 8, as children gain familiarity with physical events and principles, their magical beliefs decline. They figure out who is really behind Santa Claus and the Tooth Fairy, and they realize that magicians' feats are due to trickery, not special powers (Subbotsky, 2004). But because children still entertain the possibility that something they imagine might materialize, they may react with anxiety to scary stories and nightmares. In one study, researchers had 4- to 6-year-olds imagine that a monster was inside one empty box, a puppy inside another. Almost all the children approached the "puppy" box, but many avoided putting their finger in the "monster" box, even though they knew that imagination cannot create reality (Harris et al., 1991).

Religion and culture play a role in how quickly children give up certain fantastic ideas. For example, Jewish children are more likely than their Christian agemates to express disbelief in Santa Claus and the Tooth Fairy. Having learned at home that Santa is not real, they seem to generalize this attitude to other magical figures (Woolley, 1997). And cultural myths about wishing—for example, the custom of making a wish before blowing out birthday candles—probably underlie the conviction of most 3- to 6-year-olds that simply by wishing, you can sometimes make your desires come true (Woolley, 2000).

• **Illogical Thought** Many studies have shown that when preschoolers are given tasks that are simplified and made relevant to their everyday lives, they do not display the illogical characteristics that Piaget saw in the preoperational stage. For example, when a conservation-of-number task is scaled down to include only three items instead of six or seven, 3-year-olds perform well (Gelman, 1972). And when preschoolers are asked carefully worded questions about what happens to substances (such as sugar) after they are dissolved in water, they give accurate explanations. Most 3- to 5-year-olds know that the substance is conserved—that it continues to exist, can be tasted, and makes the liquid heavier, even though it is invisible in the water (Au, Sidle, & Rollins, 1993; Rosen & Rozin, 1993).

Preschoolers' ability to reason about transformations is evident on other problems. For example, they can engage in impressive *reasoning by analogy* about physical changes. When presented with the picture-matching problem "Playdough is to cut-up playdough as apple is to . . . ?," even 3-year-olds choose the correct answer from a set of alternatives, several of which (a bitten apple, a cut-up loaf of bread) share physical features with the right choice (Goswami, 1996). These findings indicate that in familiar contexts, preschoolers can overcome appearances and think logically about cause and effect.

Furthermore, preschoolers have a remarkable understanding of diverse cause-and-effect relationships. For example, although they have little detailed biological or mechanical knowledge, they know that the insides of animals differ from the insides of machines and that animals' insides are responsible for certain cause–effect sequences (such as willing oneself to move) that are impossible for nonliving things (Gelman, 2003; Keil & Lockhart, 1999).

Finally, 3- and 4-year-olds use logical, causal expressions, such as *if–then* and *because,* as accurately as adults do (McCabe & Peterson, 1988). Illogical reasoning seems to occur only when they grapple with unfamiliar topics, too much information, or contradictory facts that they have trouble reconciling (Ruffman, 1999).

• Categorization Although preschoolers have difficulty with Piagetian class inclusion tasks, their everyday knowledge is organized into nested categories at an early age. By the second half of the first year, children have formed a variety of global categories—furniture, animals, vehicles, plants, and kitchen utensils—each of which includes objects varying widely in perceptual features (Mandler, 2004). The objects go together because of their common function and behavior, challenging Piaget's assumption that young children's thinking is wholly governed by appearances.

Indeed, 2- to 5-year-olds readily draw inferences about nonobservable characteristics shared by category members. For example, after being told that a bird has warm blood and a stegosaurus (dinosaur) has cold blood, preschoolers infer that a pterodactyl (labeled a dinosaur) has cold blood, even though it closely resembles a bird (Gopnik & Nazzi, 2003). And when shown a set of three characters—two of whom look different but share an inner trait ("outgoing") and two of whom look similar but have different inner traits (one "shy," one "outgoing")—preschoolers rely on the trait category, not physical appearance, to predict similar preferred activities (Heyman & Gelman, 2000).

During the second and third years, and perhaps earlier, children's global categories differentiate. They form many *basic-level categories*—ones at an intermediate level of generality, such as "chairs," "tables," "dressers," and "beds." Performance on object-sorting tasks indicates that by the third or fourth year, preschoolers easily move back and forth between basic-level and *general categories,* such as "furniture" (Blewitt, 1994). They also break down basic-level categories into *subcategories,* such as "rocking chairs" and "desk chairs." In fact, a case study of a highly verbal toddler with a strong interest in birds revealed that by age 2, he had constructed a hierarchical understanding of the bird domain that included such basic-level categories and subcategories as "waterbirds" ("ducks" and "swans"), "landbirds" ("roosters" and "turkeys"), and "other birds" ("bluebirds," "cardinals," and "seagulls") (Mervis, Pani, & Pani, 2003). His category structure, though different from that of many adults, was, indeed, hierarchical. And he used that knowledge to make many correct inferences about category membership—for example, that baby birds and their parents must belong to the same species (both "robins"), even though they look strikingly different.

In early childhood, children form categories based on underlying characteristics rather than perceptual features. Guided by knowledge that "dinosaurs have cold blood," this 4-year-old categorizes the pterodactyl (in the foreground) as a dinosaur rather than a bird, even though pterodactyls have wings and can fly.

Preschoolers' rapidly expanding vocabularies and general knowledge support their impressive skill at categorizing. As they learn more about their world, they devise theories about underlying characteristics shared by category members, which help them identify new instances (Gelman & Kalish, 2006; Gelman & Koenig, 2003). For example, they realize that animals have an inborn potential for certain physical features and behaviors that determine their identity. In categorizing, they look for causal links among these features. In one study, researchers invented two categories of animals—one with horns, armor, and a spiky tail; the other with wings, large ears, long toes, and a monkeylike tail (see Figure 6.12). Four-year-olds who were given a theory that identified an inner cause for the coexistence of the animals' features—animals in the first category "like to fight"; those in the second category "like to hide in trees"—easily classified new examples of animals. But 4-year-olds for whom animal features were merely pointed out or who were given a separate function for each feature could not remember the categories (Krascum & Andrews, 1998).

As this investigation suggests, adults' explanations are a major source of young children's categorical learning (Gelman & Kalish, 2006). An especially rich context for understanding categories is picture-book reading, during which parents are likely to provide information that guides children's inferences about the structure of categories: "Penguins live at the South Pole, swim, and catch fish" or "Fish breathe by taking water into their mouths."

In sum, although preschoolers' category systems are less complex than those of older children and adults, they already have the capacity to classify hierarchically and on the basis of nonobvious properties. And preschoolers use logical, causal reasoning to identify the interrelated features that form the basis of a category and to classify new members.

Figure 6.12 Categories of imaginary animals shown to preschoolers.

When an adult provided a theory about the coexistence of animals' features ("likes to fight" and "likes to hide in trees"), 4-year-olds easily classified new instances of animals with only one or two features. Without the theory, preschoolers could not remember the categories. Theories about underlying characteristics support the formation of many categories in early childhood. (From R. M. Krascum & S. Andrews, 1998, "The Effects of Theories on Children's Acquisition of Family-Resemblance Categories," *Child Development*, 69, p. 336. © The Society for Research in Child Development, Inc. Reprinted by permission.)

• **Appearance versus Reality** As we have seen, preschoolers show some remarkably advanced reasoning when presented with familiar situations and simplified problems. But when they encounter objects that have two identities—a real one and an apparent one—can they distinguish appearance from reality? In a series of studies, John Flavell and his colleagues presented children with objects that were disguised in various ways and asked what each "looks like" and what each "is really and truly." Preschoolers had difficulty. For example, when asked whether a candle that looks like a crayon "is really and truly" a crayon or whether a stone painted to look like an egg "is really and truly" an egg, they often responded "Yes!" Not until age 6 or 7 did children do well on these tasks (Flavell, Green, & Flavell, 1987).

Younger children's poor performance, however, is not due to difficulty in distinguishing appearance from reality, as Piaget suggested. Rather, they have trouble with the *language* of these tasks (Deák, Ray, & Brenneman, 2003). When permitted to solve appearance–reality problems nonverbally, by selecting from an array of objects the one that "really" has a particular identity, most 3-year-olds perform well (Sapp, Lee, & Muir, 2000).

These findings suggest that preschoolers begin to appreciate the appearance–reality distinction sometime during the third year. Note how this involves a capacity we discussed earlier: *dual representation*—the realization that an object can be one thing (a candle) while symbolizing another (a crayon). At first, however, children's understanding is fragile. After putting on a Halloween mask, young preschoolers may be frightened when they see themselves in a mirror. And not until the school years do children fully appreciate the unreality of much that they see on TV. Performing well on verbal appearance–reality tasks signifies a more secure understanding and is related to further progress in representational ability (Bialystok & Senman, 2004).

Evaluation of the Preoperational Stage

The Milestones table on page 246 provides an overview of the cognitive attainments of early childhood just considered. **TAKE A MOMENT...** Compare them with Piaget's description of the preoperational child on pages 240–242. The evidence as a whole indicates that Piaget was partly wrong and partly right about young children's cognitive capacities. When given simplified tasks based on familiar experiences, preschoolers show the beginnings of logical thinking. How can we make sense of the contradictions between Piaget's conclusions and the findings of recent research?

That preschoolers have some logical understanding suggests that they acquire operational reasoning gradually. Over time, children rely on increasingly effective mental approaches to solving problems. For example, children who cannot use counting to compare two sets of items do not conserve number. Rather, they rely on perceptual cues to compare the amounts in two sets of items (Rouselle, Palmers, & Noël, 2004; Sophian, 1995). Once preschoolers can count, they apply this skill to conservation-of-number tasks involving just a few items. As counting improves, they extend the strategy to problems with more items. By age 6, they understand that number remains the same after a transformation as long as nothing is added or taken away. Consequently, they no longer need to count to verify their answer (Halford &

Milestones

Some Cognitive Attainments of Early Childhood

Approximate Age	Cognitive Attainments
2–4 years  	■ Shows a dramatic increase in representational activity, as reflected in the development of language, make-believe play, drawing, understanding of symbol–real world relations (such as photos, drawings, and maps), and categorization ■ Takes the perspective of others in simplified, familiar situations and in everyday, face-to-face communication ■ Distinguishes animate beings from inanimate objects; denies that magic can alter everyday experiences ■ Grasps conservation, notices transformations, reverses thinking, and understands many cause-and-effect relationships in familiar contexts ■ Categorizes objects on the basis of common natural kind, function, and behavior (not just perceptual features) and devises ideas about underlying characteristics that category members share ■ Sorts familiar objects into hierarchically organized categories ■ Distinguishes appearance from reality
4–7 years	■ Becomes increasingly aware that make-believe (and other thought processes) are representational activities ■ Replaces magical beliefs about fairies, goblins, and events that violate expectations with plausible explanations ■ Solves verbal appearance–reality problems, signifying a more secure understanding

Note: These milestones represent overall age trends. Individual differences exist in the precise age at which each milestone is attained.

Photos: (top) © Ellen B. Senisi/The Image Works; (bottom) © Jeff Greenberg/Alamy

Andrews, 2006). Thus, children pass through several steps on the way to a full understanding of relationships among variables in conservation problems, although (as Piaget indicated) they do not fully grasp conservation until the school years.

Evidence that preschool children can be trained to perform well on Piagetian problems also supports the idea that operational thought is not absent at one point in time and present at another (Roazzi & Bryant, 1997; Siegler, 1995; Siegler & Svetina, 2006). Children who possess some understanding would naturally benefit from training, in contrast to those with no understanding at all.

The gradual development of logical operations poses yet another challenge to Piaget's stage concept. Although the minds of young children still have a great deal of developing to do, research shows that they are considerably more capable than Piaget assumed.

Ask Yourself

Review Select two of the following features of Piaget's preoperational stage: egocentrism, a focus on perceptual appearances, difficulty reasoning about transformations, and lack of hierarchical classification. Cite findings that led Piaget to conclude that preschoolers are deficient in those ways. Then present evidence indicating that preschoolers are more capable thinkers than Piaget assumed.

Apply Three-year-old Will understands that his tricycle isn't alive and can't feel or move on its own. But at the beach, watching the sun dip below the horizon, Will exclaimed, "The sun is tired. It's going to sleep!" What explains this apparent contradiction in Will's reasoning?

Connect When do children realize that a scale model of a room represents a real room? When do they first grasp the real and apparent identities of disguised objects (such as a stone painted to look like an egg)? What cognitive capacity underlies both attainments?

Reflect Did you have an imaginary companion as a young child? If so, what was your companion like, and why did you create it? Were your parents aware of your companion? What was their attitude toward it?

The Concrete Operational Stage: 7 to 11 Years

In Piaget's concrete operational stage, school-age children think in a logical, organized fashion about concrete objects. This 8-year-old easily grasps conservation of liquid. © Spencer Grant/PhotoEdit

According to Piaget, the **concrete operational stage,** extending from about 7 to 11 years, marks a major turning point in cognitive development. Thought becomes far more logical, flexible, and organized, more closely resembling the reasoning of adults than that of younger children.

Concrete Operational Thought

Concrete operations are evident in the school-age child's performance on a wide variety of Piagetian tasks. Let's look closely at these diverse accomplishments.

• **Conservation** The ability to pass *conservation tasks* provides clear evidence of *operations.* In conservation of liquid, for example, children state that the amount of liquid has not changed, and they are likely to offer an explanation something like this: "The water's shorter, but it's also wider. Pour it back—you'll see it's the same amount." Notice how the child coordinates several aspects of the task rather than centering on only one. The older child engages in *decentration,* recognizing that a change in one aspect of the water (its height) is compensated for by a change in another aspect (its width). This explanation also illustrates *reversibility*—the capacity to imagine the water being returned to the original container as proof of conservation.

• **Classification** Between ages 7 and 10, children pass Piaget's *class inclusion problem.* This indicates that they are more aware of classification hierarchies and can focus on relations between a general and two specific categories at the same time—that is, on three relations at once (Hodges & French, 1988; Ni, 1998). Collections—stamps, coins, rocks, bottle caps—become common in middle childhood. At age 10, one boy I know spent hours sorting and resorting his large box of baseball cards, grouping them first by league and team membership, then by playing position and batting average. He could separate the players into various classes and subclasses and easily rearrange them.

An improved ability to categorize underlies children's interest in collecting objects during middle-childhood. These older school-age children sort baseball cards into an elaborate structure of categories and subcategories. © Gabe Palmer/Corbis

• **Seriation** The ability to order items along a quantitative dimension, such as length or weight, is called **seriation.** To test for it, Piaget asked children to arrange sticks of different lengths from shortest to longest. Older preschoolers can put the sticks in a row to create the series, but they do so haphazardly, making many errors. In contrast, 6- to 7-year-olds create the series efficiently, moving in an orderly sequence from the smallest stick to the next largest, and so on.

The concrete operational child can also seriate mentally, an ability called **transitive inference.** In a well-known transitive inference problem, Piaget (1967) showed children pairings of sticks of different colors. From observing that stick *A* is longer than stick *B* and that stick *B* is longer than stick *C*, children must infer that *A* is longer than *C*. Like Piaget's class inclusion task, transitive inference requires children to integrate three relations at once: *A–B, B–C, A–C.* When researchers take steps to ensure that children remember the premises (*A–B* and *B–C*), 7-year-olds can grasp transitive inference (Andrews & Halford, 1998; Wright, 2006).

• **Spatial Reasoning** Piaget found that school-age children's understanding of space is more accurate than that of preschoolers. Let's take two related examples—understanding of directions and maps.

Directions. When asked to name an object to the left or right of another person, 5- and 6-year-olds answer incorrectly, applying their own frame of reference. Between 7 and 8 years, children start to perform *mental rotations,* aligning the self's frame to match that of a person in a different orientation, which enables them to identify left and right for positions they do not occupy (Roberts & Aman, 1993). Around 8 to 10 years, children can give clear, well-organized

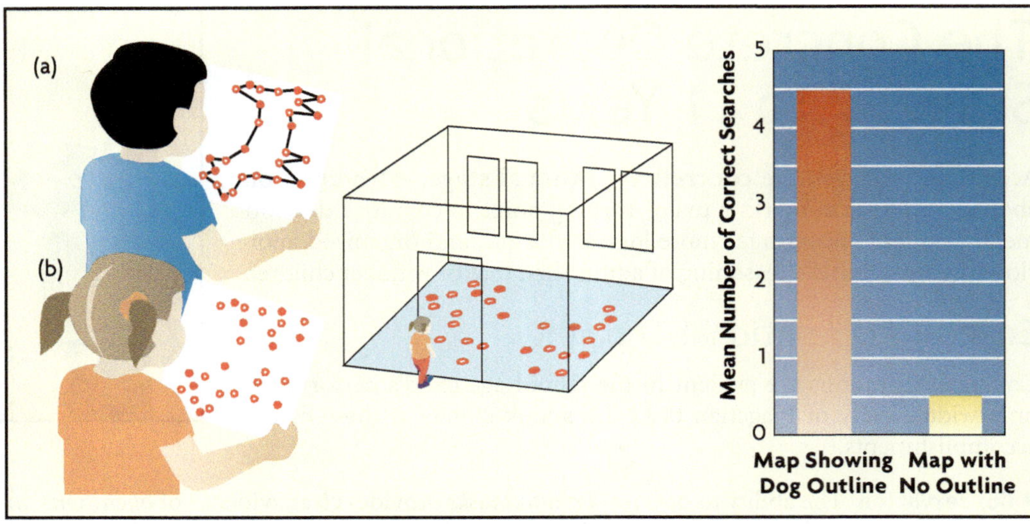

Figure 6.13 Five-year-olds' use of a rotated map to find objects hidden in a room.
In one condition (a), locations on the map were connected to form a meaningful pattern—outline of a dog. In a second condition (b), the locations on the map were not connected. The map showing the dog outline resulted in more correct searches than the map with no outline. The meaningful pattern seemed to help children reason by analogy from the rotated map to locations in the room. (Adapted from Uttal et al., 2001.)

directions for getting from one place to another by using a "mental walk" strategy in which they imagine another person's movements along a route (Gauvain & Rogoff, 1989). Six-year-olds give more organized directions after they walk the route themselves or are specially prompted. Otherwise, they focus on the end point without describing exactly how to get there (Plumert et al., 1994).

Cognitive Maps. Children's mental representations of familiar large-scale spaces, such as their school or neighborhood, are called **cognitive maps.** Drawing a map of a large-scale space requires considerable perspective-taking skill because the child cannot see the entire space at once but must infer its overall layout by relating its separate parts (Piaget & Inhelder, 1948/1956).

Preschoolers and young school-age children include *landmarks* on the maps they draw, but their arrangement is not always accurate. They do better when asked to place stickers showing the location of desks and people on a map of their classroom. But if the map is rotated to a position other than the orientation of the classroom, they have difficulty placing the stickers (Liben & Downs, 1993). Their use of a rotated map to find objects hidden in a room improves when the locations form a meaningful pattern, such as the outline of a dog (see Figure 6.13). Pointing out the pattern on the map helps children *reason by analogy* from the rotated map to corresponding locations in the room (Uttal et al., 2001).

This fourth grader, who is constructing a map that depicts the overall layout of her neighborhood, represents landmarks and routes of travel as interrelated. © David Young-Wolff/PhotoEdit

In the early school grades, children's maps become more coherent. They draw landmarks along an *organized route of travel*—an attainment that resembles their improved direction giving. By the end of middle childhood, children combine landmarks and routes into an overall view of space. And they readily draw and read maps, even when the map's orientation does not match the space it represents (Liben, 1999). Ten- to 12-year-olds also grasp the notion of *scale*—the proportional relation between a space and its representation on a map (Liben, 2006).

Besides cognitive development, cultural frameworks influence children's map making. In many non-Western communities, people rarely use maps for way-finding; instead, they rely on information from neighbors, street vendors, and shopkeepers. Also, non-Western children ride in cars less often and walk more often than their Western agemates, thereby gaining intimate neighborhood knowledge. When a researcher had 12-year-olds in small cities in India and in the United States draw maps of their neighborhoods, the Indian children represented a rich array of landmarks and aspects of social life, such as people and vehicles, in a small area surrounding their home. The U.S. children, in contrast, drew a more formal, extended space, highlighting main streets and key directions (north–south, east–west) but including few landmarks and features (see Figure 6.14) (Parameswaran, 2003). Although the U.S. children's maps scored higher in cognitive maturity, this difference reflected the

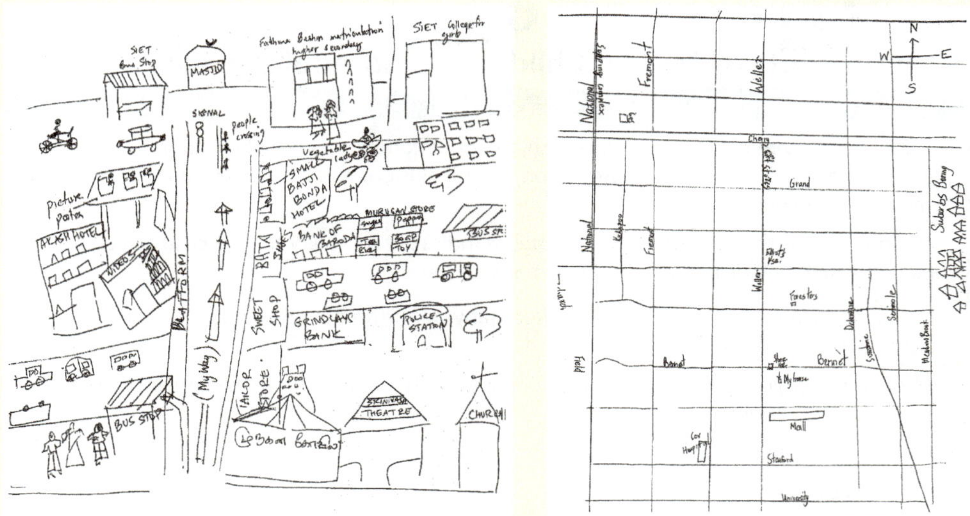

(a) (b)

Figure 6.14 **Maps drawn by 12-year-olds from India and the United States.**
(a) The Indian child depicted many landmarks and features of social life in a small area near her home. (b) The U.S. child drew a more extended space, highlighted main streets and key directions, but included few landmarks and people. (From G. Parameswaran, 2003, "Experimenter Instructions as a Mediator in the Effects of Culture on Mapping One's Neighborhood," *Journal of Environmental Psychology,* 23, pp. 415–416. Copyright © 2003, with permission from Elsevier.)

children's cultural interpretations of the task. When asked to create a map to "help people find their way," the Indian children drew spaces as far-reaching and organized as the U.S. children's.

Limitations of Concrete Operational Thought

As the name of this stage suggests, concrete operational thinking suffers from one important limitation: Children think in an organized, logical fashion only when dealing with concrete information they can perceive directly. Their mental operations work poorly with abstract ideas—ones not apparent in the real world. Consider children's solutions to transitive inference problems. When shown pairs of sticks of unequal length, children 7 years and older readily figure out that if stick *A* is longer than stick *B* and stick *B* is longer than stick *C,* then *A* is longer than *C.* But until age 11 or 12, they have difficulty with a hypothetical version, such as "Susan is taller than Sally and Sally is taller than Mary. Who is the tallest?"

That logical thought is at first tied to immediate situations helps account for a special feature of concrete operational reasoning: School-age children master Piaget's concrete operational tasks step by step, not all at once. For example, they usually grasp conservation of number first, then liquid and mass, and then weight. This *continuum of acquisition* (or gradual mastery) of logical concepts is another indication of the limitations of concrete operational thinking (Fischer & Bidell, 1991). Rather than coming up with general logical principles that they apply to all relevant situations, school-age children seem to work out the logic of each problem separately.

Follow-Up Research on Concrete Operational Thought

According to Piaget, brain development combined with experience in a rich and varied external world should lead children everywhere to reach the concrete operational stage. Yet already we have seen that culture profoundly affects children's task performance, and schooling is influential as well (Rogoff, 2003; Rogoff & Chavajay, 1995).

In tribal and village societies, conservation is often delayed. Among the Hausa of Nigeria, who live in small agricultural settlements and rarely send their children to school, even basic conservation tasks—number, length, and liquid—are not understood until age 11 or later (Fahrmeier, 1978). This suggests that participating in relevant everyday activities helps children master conservation and other Piagetian problems (Light & Perrett-Clermont, 1989). Many children in Western nations, for example, learn to think of "fairness" in terms of equal

Milestones

Some Cognitive Attainments of Middle Childhood and Adolescence

Approximate Age	Cognitive Attainments
Middle childhood 7–11 years 	▪ Thinks in a more organized, logical fashion about concrete information, as indicated by gradual mastery of Piagetian conservation, class inclusion, and seriation problems, including transitive inference ▪ Displays more effective spatial reasoning, as indicated by ability to give clear directions and construct well-organized cognitive maps
Adolescence 11–18 years 	▪ Reasons abstractly in situations that offer many opportunities for hypothetico-deductive reasoning and propositional thought ▪ Grasps the logical necessity of propositional thought, permitting reasoning about premises that contradict reality ▪ Displays imaginary audience and personal fable, which gradually decline ▪ Improves in decision-making strategies

Note: These milestones represent overall age trends. Individual differences exist in the precise age at which each milestone is attained.

Photos: (top) © Cindy Charles/PhotoEdit; (bottom) © Simon Jarratt/Corbis

distribution—a value emphasized in their culture. They frequently divide materials, such as crayons or treats, equally among their friends. Because they often see the same quantity arranged in different ways, they grasp conservation early.

The very experience of going to school seems to promote mastery of Piagetian tasks. When children of the same age are tested, those who have been in school longer do better on transitive inference problems (Artman & Cahan, 1993). Opportunities to seriate objects, to learn about order relations, and to remember the parts of a complex problem are probably responsible.

Yet certain informal, nonschool experiences can also foster operational thought. Brazilian 6- to 9-year-old street vendors, who seldom attend school, do poorly on Piaget's class inclusion tasks. But they perform much better than economically advantaged schoolchildren on versions relevant to street vending—for example, "If you have 4 units of mint chewing gum and 2 units of grape chewing gum, is it better to sell me the mint gum or [all] the gum?" (Ceci & Roazzi, 1994). Similarly, around age 7 to 8, Zinacanteco Indian girls of southern Mexico, who learn to weave elaborately designed fabrics as an alternative to schooling, engage in mental transformations to figure out how a warp strung on a loom will turn out as woven cloth—reasoning expected at the concrete operational stage. North American children of the same age, who do much better than Zinacanteco children on Piagetian tasks, have great difficulty with these weaving problems (Maynard & Greenfield, 2003).

This Zinacanteco Indian girl of southern Mexico learns the centuries-old practice of backstrap weaving. Although North American children perform better on Piaget's tasks, Zinacanteco children are far more adept at the complex mental transformations required to figure out how warp strung on a loom will turn out as woven cloth. © Lauren Greenfield/VII Photo

On the basis of such findings, some investigators have concluded that the forms of logic required by Piagetian tasks do not emerge spontaneously but are heavily influenced by training, context, and cultural conditions. The Milestones table above summarizes the cognitive attainments of middle childhood discussed in the preceding sections, along with those that will follow in adolescence.

Ask Yourself

Review Children's performance on conservation tasks illustrates a continuum of acquisition of logical concepts. Review the preceding sections, and list additional examples of gradual development of operational reasoning.

Apply Nine-year-old Adrienne spends many hours helping her father build furniture in his woodworking shop. How might this experience facilitate Adrienne's advanced performance on Piagetian seriation problems?

Connect Using research on cognitive maps, conservation, and class inclusion, explain how tasks that are not adapted to children's cultural contexts can easily underestimate their cognitive competencies.

Reflect Which aspects of Piaget's description of the concrete operational stage do you accept? Which do you doubt? Explain, citing research evidence.

The Formal Operational Stage: 11 Years and Older

According to Piaget, around age 11 young people enter the **formal operational stage,** in which they develop the capacity for abstract, systematic, scientific thinking. Whereas concrete operational children can "operate on reality," formal operational adolescents can "operate on operations." They no longer require concrete things or events as objects of thought. Instead, they can come up with new, more general logical rules through internal reflection (Inhelder & Piaget, 1955/1958). Let's look at two major features of the formal operational stage.

Hypothetico-Deductive Reasoning

Piaget believed that at adolescence, young people become capable of **hypothetico-deductive reasoning.** When faced with a problem, they start with a *hypothesis,* or prediction about variables that might affect an outcome, from which they *deduce* logical, testable inferences. Then they systematically isolate and combine variables to see which of these inferences are confirmed in the real world. Notice how this form of problem solving begins with possibility and proceeds to reality. In contrast, concrete operational children start with reality—with the most obvious predictions about a situation. If these are not confirmed, they cannot think of alternative ways to solve the problem.

Adolescents' performance on Piaget's famous *pendulum problem* illustrates this new approach. Suppose we present several school-age children and adolescents with strings of different lengths, objects of different weights to attach to the strings, and a bar from which to hang the strings (see Figure 6.15). Then we ask each of them to figure out what influences the speed with which a pendulum swings through its arc.

Formal operational adolescents hypothesize that four variables might be influential: (1) the length of the string, (2) the weight of the object hung on it, (3) the height to which the object is raised before it is released, and (4) the force with which the object is pushed. By varying one factor at a time while holding the other three constant, they test each variable separately and, if necessary, also in combination. Eventually they discover that only string length makes a difference.

In contrast, concrete operational children experiment unsystematically. Because they have difficulty separating the effects of the individual variables, they may test for the effect of string length without holding weight constant—comparing, for example, a short, light pendulum with a long, heavy one. Also, they typically fail to notice variables that are not immediately suggested by the concrete materials of the task—for example, how high the object is raised or how forcefully it is released.

Figure 6.15 **Piaget's pendulum problem.** Adolescents who engage in hypothetico-deductive reasoning think of variables that might possibly affect the speed with which a pendulum swings through its arc. Then they isolate and test each variable, and also test the variables in combination. Eventually they deduce that the weight of the object, the height from which it is released, and how forcefully it is pushed have no effect on the speed with which the pendulum swings through its arc. Only string length makes a difference.

In Piaget's formal operational stage, adolescents engage in propositional thought. As these students discuss problems in a science class, they show that they can reason with symbols that do not necessarily represent objects in the real world.
© Craig Witkowski/Index Stock

Propositional Thought

A second important characteristic of the formal operational stage is **propositional thought**—adolescents' ability to evaluate the logic of propositions (verbal statements) without referring to real-world circumstances. In contrast, children can evaluate the logic of statements only by considering them against concrete evidence in the real world.

In a study of propositional reasoning, researchers showed children and adolescents a pile of poker chips and asked whether some statements about the chips were true, false, or uncertain (Osherson & Markman, 1975). In one condition, the investigator hid a chip in her hand and then presented the following propositions:

"*Either* the chip in my hand is green or it is not green."

"The chip in my hand is green *and* it is not green."

In another condition, the researcher made the same statements while holding either a red or a green chip in full view.

School-age children focused on the concrete properties of the poker chips. When the chip was hidden, they replied that they were uncertain about both statements. When it was visible, they judged both statements to be true if the chip was green and false if it was red. In contrast, adolescents analyzed the logic of the statements. They understood that the "either-or" statement is always true and the "and" statement is always false, regardless of the poker chip's color.

Although Piaget did not view language as playing a central role in cognitive development, he acknowledged its importance in adolescence. Formal operations require language-based and other symbolic systems that do not stand for real things, such as those in higher mathematics. Secondary school students use such systems in algebra and geometry. Formal operational thought also involves verbal reasoning about abstract concepts. Adolescents show that they can think in this way when they ponder the relations among time, space, and matter in physics or wonder about justice and freedom in philosophy.

Consequences of Abstract Thought

The development of increasingly complex, effective thinking leads to dramatic revisions in the way adolescents see themselves, others, and the world in general. But just as adolescents are occasionally awkward in using their transformed bodies, so they initially falter in their abstract thinking. Although teenagers' self-concern, idealism, criticism, and indecisiveness often perplex and worry adults, they usually are beneficial in the long run. Applying What We Know on the following page suggests ways to handle the everyday consequences of teenagers' newfound cognitive capacities.

• **Self-Consciousness and Self-Focusing** Adolescents' ability to reflect on their own thoughts, combined with the physical and psychological changes they are undergoing, means that they think more about themselves. Piaget believed that a new form of egocentrism arises, in which adolescents again have difficulty distinguishing their own and others' perspectives (Inhelder & Piaget, 1955/1958). As a result, followers of Piaget suggest, two distorted images of the relationship between self and others appear.

The first is called the **imaginary audience**—adolescents' belief that they are the focus of everyone else's attention and concern (Elkind & Bowen, 1979). As a result, they become extremely self-conscious, often going to great lengths to avoid embarrassment. The imaginary audience helps explain the long hours adolescents spend inspecting every detail of their appearance. It also accounts for their sensitivity to public criticism. To teenagers, who believe that everyone is monitoring their performance, a critical remark from a parent or teacher can be mortifying.

A second cognitive distortion is the **personal fable.** Because teenagers are sure that others are observing and thinking about them, they develop an inflated opinion of their own importance—a feeling that they are special and unique. Many adolescents view themselves as

Applying What We Know

Handling Teenagers' New Capacity for Abstract Thought

Abstract Thought Expressed as . . .	Suggestion
Sensitivity to public criticism	Refrain from finding fault with the adolescent in front of others. If the matter is important, wait until you can speak to the teenager alone.
Exaggerated sense of personal uniqueness	Acknowledge the adolescent's unique characteristics. At opportune times, encourage a more balanced perspective by pointing out that you had similar feelings as a young teenager.
Idealism and criticism	Respond patiently to the adolescent's grand expectations and critical remarks. Point out positive features of targets of criticism, helping the teenager see that all societies and people are blends of virtues and imperfections.
Difficulty making everyday decisions	Refrain from deciding for the adolescent. Instead, model effective decision making, and offer diplomatic suggestions about the pros and cons of alternatives, the likelihood of various outcomes, and learning from poor choices.

reaching great heights of omnipotence and also as sinking to unusual depths of despair—experiences others cannot possibly understand (Elkind, 1994). One teenager wrote in her diary, "My parents' lives are so ordinary, so stuck in a rut. Mine will be different. I'll realize my hopes and ambitions." Another, upset when a boy failed to return her affections, rebuffed her mother's comforting words: "Mom, you don't know what it's like to be in love!"

Although imaginary-audience and personal-fable ideation is common in adolescence, these distorted visions of the self do not result from egocentrism, as Piaget suggested. Rather, they are partly an outgrowth of advances in perspective taking, which cause young teenagers to be more concerned with what others think (Vartanian & Powlishta, 1996).

In fact, certain aspects of the imaginary audience may serve positive, protective functions. In a study in which adolescents were asked why they worry about the opinions of others, they responded that they do so because others' evaluations have important *real* consequences—for self-esteem, peer acceptance, and social support (Bell & Bromnick, 2003). The idea that others are concerned with their appearance and behavior also has emotional value, helping teenagers maintain a hold on important relationships as they struggle to separate from parents and establish an independent sense of self (Vartanian, 1997).

With respect to the personal fable, in an investigation of sixth through tenth graders, sense of omnipotence predicted self-esteem and overall positive adjustment, perhaps because viewing the self as highly capable and influential helps young people cope with the many challenges of adolescence. Sense of personal uniqueness, in contrast, was modestly associated with depression and suicidal thinking (Aalsma, Lapsley, & Flannery, 2006). Focusing on the distinctiveness of one's own experiences may interfere with forming close, rewarding relationships, which provide social support during stressful times. And when combined with a sensation-seeking personality, the personal fable seems to contribute to adolescent risk taking by reducing teenagers' sense of vulnerability. In one study, young people with high personal-fable and sensation-seeking scores took more sexual risks, more often used drugs, and committed more delinquent acts than their agemates (Greene et al., 2000).

• Idealism and Criticism Because abstract thinking permits adolescents to go beyond the real to the possible, it opens up the world of the ideal and the notion of perfection. Teenagers can imagine alternative family, religious, political, and moral systems, and they want to explore them. They often construct grand visions of a perfect world, with no injustice, discrimination, or tasteless behavior. The disparity between teenagers' idealism and adults' more realistic view creates tension between parent and child. Envisioning a perfect family against which their parents and siblings fall short, adolescents become faultfinding critics.

Overall, however, teenage idealism and criticism are advantageous. Once adolescents come to see other people as having both strengths and weaknesses, they have a much greater capacity to work constructively for social change and to form positive, lasting relationships (Elkind, 1994).

• **Decision Making** Although adolescents handle many cognitive tasks more effectively than they did when younger, when it comes to decision making in everyday life, they often do not think rationally: (1) identifying the pros and cons of each alternative, (2) assessing the likelihood of various possible outcomes, (3) evaluating their choice in terms of whether their goals were met, and, if not, (4) learning from the mistake and making a better future decision. In one study of decision making, researchers gave adolescents and adults hypothetical dilemmas—whether to have cosmetic surgery, whether to participate in an experimental study of a new acne medication, which parent to live with after divorce—and asked them to explain how they would decide. Adults outperformed adolescents, especially the younger ones, more often considering alternatives, weighing the benefits and risks of each, and suggesting advice-seeking, especially in areas (such as medical decisions) where they had little experience (Halpern-Felsher & Cauffman, 2001). Other evidence shows that adolescents are less likely than adults to learn from feedback by revising their decision-making strategies (Byrnes, 2002).

Furthermore, in making decisions, adolescents, more often than adults (who also have difficulty), fall back on well-learned intuitive judgments (Jacobs & Klaczynski, 2002). Consider a hypothetical problem in which you have to choose, on the basis of two arguments, between taking a traditional lecture class and taking a computer-based class. One argument contains large-sample information: course evaluations from 150 students, 85 percent of whom liked the computer class. The other argument contains small-sample personal reports: complaints of two honor-roll students who both hated the computer class and enjoyed the traditional class. Many adolescents, even though they knew that selecting the large-sample argument was "more intelligent," still based their choice on the small-sample argument, which resembled the informal opinions they depend on in everyday life (Klaczynski, 2001).

Why is decision making so challenging for adolescents? As "first-timers" at many experiences, they do not have enough knowledge to consider the pros and cons of many options and to predict how they might react after selecting one over the others. They also face many more complex situations involving competing goals—for example, how to maintain peer approval while avoiding getting drunk at a party. In the heat of the moment and in unfamiliar situations, when making a good decision would require them to inhibit "feel-good" behavior (smoking, overeating, unsafe sex), adolescents are far more likely than adults to emphasize short-term over long-term goals (Amsel et al., 2005; Boyer, 2006; Reyna & Farley, 2006). And after engaging in such behavior without negative consequences, teenagers rate its benefits higher and its risks lower than peers who have not tried it (Halpern-Felsher et al., 2004).

Furthermore, adolescents often feel overwhelmed by their expanding range of options—abundant choices of school courses, extracurricular activities, social events, and material goods. As a result, their efforts to choose frequently break down, and they resort to habit, act on impulse, or postpone decision making. And recall from Chapter 5 that heightened responsiveness to excitatory neurotransmitters in the brain contributes to adolescents' emotional reactivity. High emotional arousal interferes with good decision making.

Over time, young people learn from their successes and failures, gather information from others about factors that affect decision making, and reflect on the decision-making process (Byrnes, 2003; Reyna & Farley, 2006). Consequently, their confidence and performance in decision making improve.

Follow-Up Research on Formal Operational Thought

Research on formal operational thought poses questions similar to those we discussed with respect to Piaget's earlier stages: Does formal operational thinking appear earlier than Piaget expected? And do all individuals reach formal operations during their teenage years?

• **Are Children Capable of Hypothetico-Deductive and Propositional Thinking?** School-age children show the glimmerings of hypothetico-deductive reasoning, although they are less competent at it than adolescents. In simplified situations involving no more than two possible causal variables, 6-year-olds understand that hypotheses must be confirmed by appropriate evidence. They also realize that once it is supported, a hypothesis shapes predictions about what might happen in the future (Ruffman et al., 1993). But school-age children cannot sort out evidence that bears on three or more variables at once. And as we will see when we take up information-processing research on scientific reasoning in Chapter 7, children have difficulty explaining why a pattern of observations supports a hypothesis, even when they recognize the connection between the two.

With respect to propositional thought, when a simple set of premises defies real-world knowledge ("All cats bark. Rex is a cat. Does Rex bark?"), 4- to 6-year-olds can reason logically in make-believe play. In justifying their answer, they are likely to say, "We can pretend cats bark!" (Dias & Harris, 1988, 1990). But in an entirely verbal mode, children have great difficulty reasoning from premises that contradict reality or their own beliefs.

Consider the following set of statements: "If dogs are bigger than elephants and elephants are bigger than mice, then dogs are bigger than mice." Children younger than age 10 judge this reasoning to be false because some of the relations specified do not occur in real life (Moshman & Franks, 1986; Pillow, 2002). They automatically access well-learned knowledge ("Elephants are larger than dogs") that casts doubt on the truthfulness of the premises. Children have more trouble than adolescents inhibiting activation of such knowledge (Klaczynski, Schuneman, & Daniel, 2004; Simoneau & Markovits, 2003). Partly for this reason, they fail to grasp the **logical necessity** of propositional reasoning—that the accuracy of conclusions drawn from premises rests on the rules of logic, not on real-world confirmation.

Furthermore, in reasoning with propositions, school-age children do not think carefully about the major premise and, therefore, violate the most basic rules of logic (Markovits, Schleifer, & Fortier, 1989). For example, when given the following problem, they almost always draw an incorrect conclusion:

Major premise: If Susan hits a tambourine, then she will make a noise.
Second premise: Suppose that Susan does not hit a tambourine.
Question: Did Susan make a noise?
Wrong conclusion: No, Susan did not make a noise.

Notice that the major premise did *not* state that Susan makes a noise *if, and only if,* she hits a tambourine. Adolescents generally detect that Susan could make noise in other ways, partly because they are better at searching their knowledge for examples that contradict wrong conclusions (Klaczynski & Narasimham, 1998b; Markovits & Barrouillet, 2002).

As with hypothetico-deductive reasoning, in early adolescence young people become better at analyzing the *logic* of propositions, regardless of their *content.* And as they get older, they handle problems requiring increasingly complex mental operations. In justifying their reasoning, they move from giving a concrete example ("She could have hit a drum instead of a tambourine") to explaining the logical rules on which it is based ("We can be certain that Susan did not hit a tambourine. But we cannot be certain that Susan did not make a noise; she might have done so in many other ways") (Müller, Overton, & Reese, 2001; Venet & Markovits, 2001). These capacities, however, do not appear suddenly around the time of puberty. Rather, gains occur gradually from childhood on (Keating, 2004; Kuhn & Franklin, 2006; Moshman, 2005).

These adolescents of Irian Jaya province in Indonesia live in highland rainforests where they have little contact with the outside world. Although they would probably have difficulty with Piaget's formal operational tasks, they deftly build a tree house, mentally coordinating multiple variables to ensure that the structure is stable and sturdy. Clearly they are capable of highly complex reasoning in familiar situations. © Anders Ryman/CORBIS

• **Do All Individuals Reach the Formal Operational Stage?** TAKE A MOMENT… Try giving one or two of the formal operational tasks just described to your friends. How well do they do? Even many well-educated adults fail hypothetico-deductive tasks and have trouble reasoning with sets of propositions that contradict real-world facts (Keating, 1979; Markovits & Vachon, 1990).

Why are so many adults not fully formal operational? One reason is that people are most likely to think abstractly and systematically on tasks in which they have had extensive guidance and practice in using such reasoning. This conclusion is supported by evidence that taking college courses leads to improvements in formal reasoning related to course content. Math and science prompt gains in propositional thought, social science in methodological and statistical reasoning (Lehman & Nisbett, 1990). Like concrete reasoning in children, formal operations does not emerge in all contexts at once but is specific to situation and task (Keating, 1990, 2004).

In tribal and village societies, formal operational tasks are rarely mastered (Cole, 1990). People in nonliterate societies often refuse requests to engage in propositional thought. Take this hypothetical proposition: "In the North, where there is snow, all bears are white. Novaya Zemlya is in the Far North, and it always has snow. What color are the bears there?" In response, a Central Asian peasant explains that he must see the event to discern its logical implications. Whereas the interviewer states that truth can be based on ideas alone, the peasant insists on firsthand knowledge. Yet the peasant uses propositions to defend his point of view: "*If* a man . . . had seen a white bear and had told about it, [*then*] he could be believed, *but* I've never seen one and *hence* I can't say" (Luria, 1976, pp. 108–109). Although he rarely displays it in everyday life, the peasant is clearly capable of formal operational thought!

Piaget acknowledged that without the opportunity to solve hypothetical problems, people in some societies might not display formal operations. Still, researchers ask, Does formal operational thinking result largely from children's and adolescents' independent efforts to make sense of their world, as Piaget claimed? Or is it a culturally transmitted way of thinking that is specific to literate societies and is taught in school? In an Israeli study of seventh to ninth graders, after controlling for participants' age, researchers found that years of schooling fully accounted for early adolescent gains in propositional thought (Artman, Cahan, & Avni-Babad, 2006). School tasks, the investigators speculated, provide crucial experiences in setting aside the "if . . . then" logic of everyday conversations that is often used to convey intentions, promises, and threats ("If you don't do your chores, then you won't get your allowance") but that conflicts with the logic of academic reasoning. In school, then, adolescents encounter rich opportunities to realize their neurological potential to think more effectively.

Ask Yourself

Review Using the concepts of hypothetico-deductive reasoning and propositional thought, illustrate the difference between school-age children's cognition and that of adolescents.

Apply Clarissa, age 14, is convinced that no one appreciates how hurt she feels at not being invited to the homecoming dance. Meanwhile, 15-year-old Justine, alone in her room, pantomimes being sworn in as student body president with her awestruck parents, teachers, and peers looking on. Which aspect of the personal fable is each girl displaying? Which girl is more likely to be well-adjusted, which poorly adjusted? Explain.

Connect How does evidence on adolescent decision making help us understand teenagers' risk taking in sexual activity and drug use?

Reflect Do you recall engaging in idealistic thinking or poor decision making as a teenager? Cite examples. How has your thinking changed?

Piaget and Education

Piaget has had a major impact on education, especially during early and middle childhood. Three educational principles derived from his theory continue to have a widespread influence on teacher training and classroom practices:

- *Discovery learning.* In a Piagetian classroom, children are encouraged to discover for themselves through spontaneous interaction with the environment. Instead of presenting ready-made knowledge verbally, teachers provide a rich variety of activities designed to promote exploration and discovery—art, puzzles, table games, dress-up clothing, building blocks, books, measuring tools, natural science tasks, musical instruments, and more. Teachers carefully select and arrange materials so children varying widely in developmental progress can construct more mature understandings.
- *Sensitivity to children's readiness to learn.* Piaget believed that appropriate learning experiences build on children's current thinking. Teachers watch and listen to their students, introducing experiences that permit them to practice newly discovered schemes and that challenge their incorrect ways of viewing the world. But teachers do not try to hasten development by imposing new skills before children indicate interest or readiness—an approach that leads to superficial acceptance of adult formulas rather than true understanding.

- *Acceptance of individual differences.* Piaget's theory assumes that all children go through the same sequence of development, but at different rates. Therefore, teachers must plan activities for individual children and small groups, not just for the class as a whole. In addition, teachers evaluate educational progress in relation to the child's previous development, rather than on the basis of normative standards, or average performance of same-age peers.

Like his stages, educational applications of Piaget's theory have met with criticism, especially for his insistence that young children learn mainly through acting on the environment and his neglect of other important avenues, such as verbal teaching and corrective feedback (Brainerd, 2003). Nevertheless, Piaget's influence on education has been powerful. He gave teachers new ways to observe, understand, and enhance young children's development and offered strong theoretical justification for child-oriented approaches to teaching and learning.

Overall Evaluation of Piaget's Theory

Piaget's contributions to the field of child development are greater than those of any other theorist. He awakened psychologists and educators to a view of children as curious knowledge seekers who contribute actively to their own development. Furthermore, Piaget was among the first to both describe and explain development. His pioneering efforts inspired the current focus on *mechanisms of cognitive change*—precise accounts of biological, psychological, and environmental factors that lead children to modify their thinking, which we will encounter in Chapter 7 (McClelland & Siegler, 2001). Finally, Piaget's theory offers a useful "road map" of cognitive development that is accurate in many respects, though incorrect in others. His milestones of preoperational, concrete operational, and formal operational thought remain powerful aids to understanding emotional, social, and moral development.

Nevertheless, the wealth of research that Piaget's theory inspired has uncovered weaknesses in his theory. Let's consider two major challenges posed by his critics.

Is Piaget's Account of Cognitive Change Clear and Accurate?

Piaget's explanation of cognitive change focused on broad transformations in thinking—in particular, equilibration and its attendant processes of adaptation and organization. But exactly what the child does to equilibrate is vague (Siegler & Ellis, 1996). Recall our description of *organization*—that the structures of each stage form a coherent whole. Piaget was not explicit about how the diverse achievements of each stage are bound together by a single, underlying form of thought—and efforts to confirm this coherence have not succeeded. On a variety of tasks, infants and young children appear more competent, and adolescents and adults less competent, than Piaget assumed. Today, researchers agree that the child's efforts to assimilate, accommodate, and reorganize structures cannot adequately explain these patterns of change.

Furthermore, Piaget's belief that infants and young children must act on the environment to revise their thinking is too narrow a notion of how learning takes place. Without explicit adult teaching, including verbal explanations, children may not always notice or come to understand aspects of a situation necessary for building more effective schemes. With its overemphasis on the child's initiative, Piaget's theory has been of limited practical value in devising teaching strategies that foster children's optimum learning.

Although Piaget insisted that young children learn mainly by acting on the environment, verbal teaching, corrective feedback, and other methods also play important roles. In this hands-on science lesson using microscopes and pond water, children learn in different ways—some looking to the teacher for guidance, some exploring on their own, some writing in journals.
© Ellen Senisi/The Image Works

Does Cognitive Development Take Place in Stages?

We have seen that many cognitive changes proceed slowly and gradually. Few abilities are altogether absent during one period and suddenly present in the next. Also, periods of cognitive equilibrium are rare. Instead, children are constantly modifying structures and acquiring new skills. Today, virtually all experts agree that children's cognition is less broadly stagelike than Piaget believed (Bjorklund, 2005; Flavell, Miller, & Miller, 2002). Further, contemporary researchers disagree on how general or specific cognitive development actually is.

Some theorists agree with Piaget that development is a *general process,* following a similar course across the diverse cognitive domains of physical, numerical, and social knowledge. But they reject the existence of stages, believing instead that thought processes are alike at all ages—just present to a greater or lesser extent—and that variations in children's knowledge and experience largely account for uneven performance across domains. These assumptions form the basis of the *information-processing perspective,* discussed in Chapter 7.

Other researchers think that the stage notion is valid but that it must be modified. They point to strong evidence for certain stagelike changes, such as the flourishing of representation around age 2 and the move toward abstract, systematic thinking in adolescence. Yet they also recognize many smaller developments that lead up to these transformations. In Chapter 7, we will consider a *neo-Piagetian perspective* that combines Piaget's stage approach with information-processing ideas (Case, 1996, 1998; Halford, 2002; Halford & Andrews, 2006). In this view, Piaget's strict definition of stage is modified into a less tightly knit concept, in which related competencies develop over an extended period, depending on brain development and specific experiences.

Still others deny not only Piaget's stages but also his belief that the human mind is made up of general reasoning abilities that can be applied to any cognitive task. They argue that the remarkable competencies of infants and young children indicate that cognitive development begins with far more than sensorimotor reflexes. Rather, infants come into the world with several basic, built-in types of knowledge, each of which jump-starts vital aspects of cognition. We will take up this *core knowledge* perspective in the next section.

Piaget's Legacy

Although Piaget's description of development is no longer fully accepted, researchers are far from consensus on how to modify or replace it. Some have begun to search for points of contact among the alternative perspectives just mentioned. Others blend Piaget's emphasis on the child as an active agent with a stronger role for context—the objects, events, and people in children's lives. For example, followers of Vygotsky's theory are intensively studying social and cultural influences on children's thinking—an area largely neglected by Piaget.

Diverse theories and lines of investigation leave research into children's thinking far more fragmented today than several decades ago, when Piaget's theory held sway. Nevertheless, researchers continue to draw inspiration from Piaget's vision of the child as an active, constructive learner and his lifelong quest to understand how children acquire new capacities. Piaget's findings have served as the starting point for virtually every major contemporary line of research on cognitive development.

Ask Yourself

Review Cite examples of findings that have led contemporary researchers to challenge Piaget's account of cognitive change.

Connect How are educational principles derived from Piaget's theory consistent with his emphasis on an active child who takes responsibility for her own learning?

Reflect Which aspects of Piaget's theory do you accept? Which do you doubt? Explain, citing research evidence.

The Core Knowledge Perspective

According to the **core knowledge perspective,** infants begin life with innate, special-purpose knowledge systems referred to as *core domains of thought.* Each of these "prewired" understandings permits a ready grasp of new, related information and therefore supports early, rapid development of certain aspects of cognition. Each core domain has a long evolutionary history and is essential for survival (Carey & Markman, 1999; Leslie, 2004; Spelke, 2004; Spelke & Kinzler, 2007). Core knowledge theorists argue that infants could not make sense of the multifaceted stimulation around them without having been genetically "set up" in the course of evolution to comprehend its crucial aspects.

Two core domains have been studied extensively in infancy. The first is *physical knowledge*—in particular, understanding of objects and their effects on one another. The second is *numerical knowledge*—the capacity to keep track of multiple objects and to add and subtract small quantities. Physical and numerical knowledge permitted our ancestors to secure food and other resources from the environment.

The core knowledge perspective asserts that an inherited foundation makes possible remarkably advanced knowledge systems in early childhood. In Chapter 9, we will consider a nativist (or inborn) view of preschoolers' amazing language skill that regards *linguistic knowledge* as etched into the structure of the human brain. Furthermore, infants' early orientation toward people (see Chapter 4) provides the foundation for rapid development of *psychological knowledge*—in particular, understanding of people as agents who have mental states (such as emotions, intentions, desires, beliefs, and perspectives) that influence their behavior, which is vital for surviving in human groups. And children demonstrate impressive *biological knowledge,* including ideas about inheritance of characteristics and understanding of bodily processes, such as birth, growth, illness, and death.

Rather than regarding development as a general process, core knowledge theorists see it as *domain-specific* and uneven, with each core domain developing independently. And although initial knowledge is assumed to be innate, that knowledge becomes more elaborate as children explore, play, and interact with others (Geary & Bjorklund, 2000; Leslie, 2004). Children are viewed as *naïve theorists,* building on core knowledge concepts to explain their everyday experiences in the physical, psychological, and biological realms. Let's examine a sampling of findings that shed light on the existence of core domains of thought.

Infancy: Physical and Numerical Knowledge

Do infants display impressive physical and numerical understandings so early that some knowledge must be innate? Again, the violation-of-expectation method has been used to answer this question. Besides research on early awareness of object permanence (see pages 229–230), core knowledge theorists point to evidence indicating that young infants are aware of basic object properties and that they build on this knowledge quickly, acquiring more detailed understandings (Baillargeon, 2004; Luo & Baillargeon, 2005; Spelke & Kinsler, 2007).

For example, 2½-month-olds seem to recognize that one solid object cannot move through another solid object. In one study, some infants saw an object lowered into a container with an opening, whereas others saw an object lowered into a container with no opening (see Figure 6.16 on page 260). Babies in the closed-container condition looked longer, suggesting that this impossible event violated their notions of physical reality (Hespos & Baillargeon, 2001). By 6½ months, infants look longer when an object much wider than an opening appears to pass through that opening than they do at an appropriately sized object passing through (Aguiar & Baillargeon, 2003). And around 7½ months, they spend more time looking at an object too tall to fit inside a container that disappears into the container than they do at an object that is the right height (Hespos & Baillargeon, 2001).

How much does this 5-month-old baby already know about the physical properties of the morsels of cereal in front of her? According to core knowledge researchers, she already has some basic number concepts, in that she can discriminate quantities up to three. © David Young-Wolff/Alamy

Furthermore, in the first half-year, infants are sensitive to basic principles of object support. Babies as young as 4½ months stare intently at a box resting in midair, with nothing to hold it in place (Needham & Baillargeon, 1993). Six- and 7-month-olds' attention increases when an object is placed on top of another object with most of its bottom surface not in contact with the lower object—conditions that would cause the top object to fall (Baillargeon, 1994). And 8-month-olds are sensitive to position of contact: When a large, oblong box rests horizontally on a small, square box, babies expect the large box to be centered over the small box so it is adequately supported (Huettel & Needham, 2000).

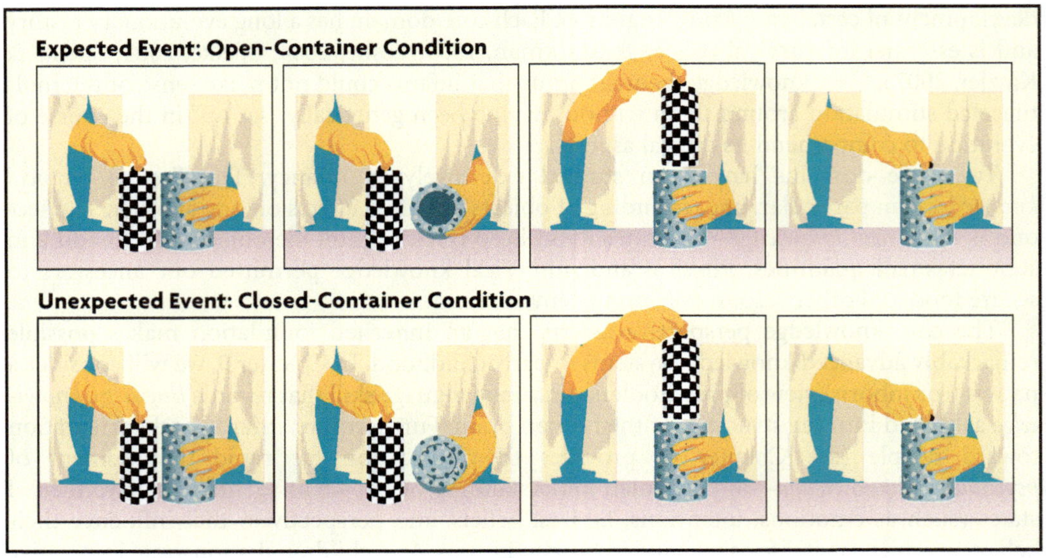

Figure 6.16 **Testing infants for understanding of object solidity using the violation-of-expectation method.**

Infants in the *expected event: open-container condition* saw a tall object and a tall container standing a short distance apart. An adult's right hand grasped a knob attached to the top of the object, while her left hand rotated the container forward so infants could see its opening. After a few seconds, the container was returned to its original position. Then the right hand lifted the object and lowered it into the container. Finally, the hand lifted the object out of the container and set it down. Infants in the *unexpected event: closed-container condition* saw the same event, with one exception: The container's top was closed, so it should have been impossible for the object to be lowered into the container. (In fact, the container had a false, magnetic top that adhered to the bottom of the object, which could be lowered into it.) Five-month-olds looked longer at the unexpected, closed-container event, suggesting awareness of object solidity. (Adapted from R. Baillargeon & J. DeVos, 1991, "Object Permanence in Young Infants: Further Evidence," *Child Development*, 62, p. 1230. © The Society of Research in Child Development. Reprinted by permission.)

Research also suggests that young infants have basic number concepts (Spelke, 2004; Spelke & Kinzler, 2007). In the best-known study, 5-month-olds saw a screen raised to hide a single toy animal, then watched a hand place a second toy behind the screen. Finally the screen was removed to reveal either one or two toys. As Figure 6.17 reveals, infants looked longer at the impossible, one-toy display, suggesting that they kept track of the two objects, which would require them to add one object to another. In additional experiments using this task, 5-month-olds looked longer at three objects than two. These findings and those of similar investigations suggest that babies can discriminate quantities up to three and use that knowledge to perform simple arithmetic—both addition and subtraction (in which two objects are covered and one object is removed) (Kobayashi et al., 2004; Kobayashi, Hiraki, & Hasegawa, 2005; Wynn, Bloom, & Chiang, 2002).

Other research shows that 6-month-olds can distinguish among large sets of items when the difference between those sets is very great—at least a factor of 2. For example, they can tell the difference between 8 and 16 dots but not between 6 and 12 (Lipton & Spelke, 2004; Xu, Spelke, & Goddard, 2005). As a result, some researchers believe that infants can represent approximate large-number values, in addition to the small-number discriminations evident in Figure 6.17.

These findings—like other violation-of-expectation results—are controversial. In other experiments similar to those just described, researchers found that looking preferences were inconsistent (Langer, Gillette, & Arriaga, 2003; Wakeley, Rivera, & Langer, 2000). These investigators note that claims for infants' knowledge of number concepts are surprising, given other research indicating that before 14 to 16 months, toddlers have difficulty with less-than and greater-than relationships between small sets. And as we will see in Chapter 7, not until the preschool years do children add and subtract small sets correctly.

Overall, in some studies, infants display amazing knowledge; in others, they do not. Further, if such knowledge is innate, older children should reason in the same way as infants,

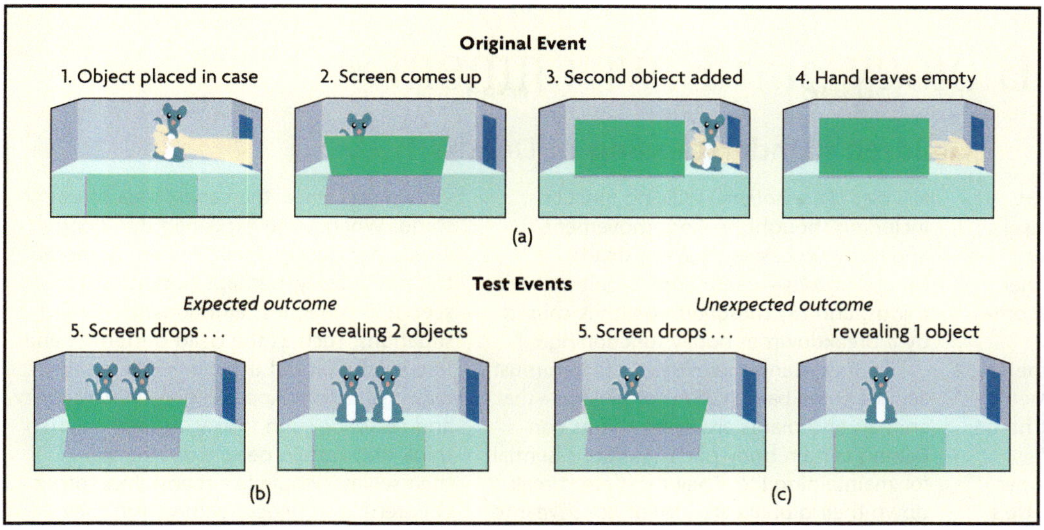

Figure 6.17 **Testing infants for basic number concepts.**

(a) First, infants saw a screen raised in front of a toy animal. Then an identical toy was added behind the screen. Next, the researchers presented two outcomes. (b) In the *expected outcome,* the screen dropped to reveal two toy animals. (c) In the *unexpected outcome,* the screen dropped to reveal one toy animal. Five-month-olds shown the unexpected outcome looked longer than 5-month-olds shown the expected outcome. The researchers concluded that infants can discriminate the quantities "one" and "two" and use that knowledge to perform simple addition: 1 + 1 = 2. A variation of this procedure suggested that 5-month-olds could also do simple subtraction: 2 – 1 = 1. (From K. Wynn, 1992, "Addition and Subtraction by Human Infants," *Nature,* 358, p. 749. Copyright © 1992, Nature Publishing Group. Reprinted by permission from Macmillan Publishers Ltd.)

yet they do not always do so. Core knowledge theorists respond that infant looking behaviors may be a more reliable indicator of understanding than older children's verbal and motor behaviors, which may not always display their true competencies (Wynn, 2002). And ERP brain-wave recordings taken while babies view correct and incorrect solutions to simple arithmetic equations reveal a response pattern identical to the pattern adults show when they detect errors (Berger, Tzur, & Posner, 2006).

Finally, proponents of the core knowledge perspective point to studies of two peoples living in Brazil's remote Amazon regions, whose cultures have no verbal counting routines: the Piraha, whose language lacks number words beyond "two"; and the Munduruku, who have number words only up to "three." Despite this numerical language deprivation (which impedes learning about number through social communication), Piraha and Munduruku adults demonstrate primitive number knowledge that resembles findings on infants: They can accurately discriminate and compare numerical quantities only up to three (Gordon, 2004; Pica et al., 2004). Still, critics continue to argue that such knowledge is not built-in but, rather, constructed over an extended time period.

Children as Naïve Theorists

A growing number of researchers believe that children form naïve theories, or explanations of events, that differ between core domains. According to this **theory theory** (meaning *theory of children as theorists*), after observing an event, children draw on innate concepts to explain, or theorize about, its cause. Then they test their naïve theory against experience, revising it when it cannot adequately account for new information (Gelman, 2003; Gelman & Kalish, 2006; Gopnik & Nazzi, 2003). These revisions often lead to stagelike changes—dramatic, qualitative shifts in the complexity of concepts and explanations. Although this account of cognitive change is similar to Piaget's, theory theorists claim that because children start with innate knowledge, their reasoning advances quickly, with sophisticated cause-and-effect explanations evident much earlier than Piaget proposed.

The most extensively investigated naïve theory is children's *theory of mind*—the psychological knowledge of self and others that forms rapidly during the preschool years, which we will consider in Chapters 7 and 11. Preschoolers also have naïve physical and biological theories. When researchers asked 3- and 4-year-olds to explain events that had either a psychological, a physical, or a biological cause, children reasoned about each event in ways consistent with its core domain. For a child who pours orange juice instead of milk on his cereal, they offered mostly psychological explanations ("He *thought* it was milk"). But for a boy who tries to float in the air by jumping off a stool but falls, they gave mostly physical explanations ("He's too *heavy* to float"). And a girl who tries to hang from a tree branch "forever" but lets go tended to elicit biological explanations ("Her arms got *hurting*"). In everyday conversation,

▪ Biology *and* Environment ▪

Children's Understanding of Death

When 5-year-old Miriam arrived at preschool the day after her dog Pepper died, she didn't join the other children as usual but stayed close to her teacher, Leslie. Noticing Miriam's discomfort, Leslie asked, "What's wrong?"

"Daddy said Pepper was so sick the vet had to put him to sleep." For a moment, Miriam looked hopeful: "When I get home, Pepper might be up."

Leslie answered directly: "No, Pepper won't get up again. He's not asleep. He's dead, and that means he can't sleep, eat, run, or play anymore."

Miriam wandered off. Later, she returned to Leslie and, sobbing, confessed, "I chased Pepper too hard."

Leslie put her arm around Miriam. "Pepper didn't die because you chased him," she explained. "He was very old and sick."

Over the next few days, Miriam asked more questions: "When I go to sleep, will I die?" "Can a tummy ache make you die?" "Will Mommy and Daddy die?"

Development of the Death Concept

An accurate understanding of death is based on five ideas: (1) *permanence*—once a living thing dies, it cannot be brought back to life; (2) *inevitability*—all living things eventually die; (3) *cessation*—all living functions, including thought, feeling, movement, and body processes, cease at death; (4) *applicability*—death applies only to living things; and (5) *causation*—death is caused by a breakdown of bodily functioning.

To understand these ideas, children must acquire some basic notions of biology—that animals and plants are living things containing certain body parts that are essential for maintaining life. They must also break down their global category of *not alive* into *dead, inanimate, unreal,* and *nonexistent* (Carey, 1999). Until children grasp these ideas, they interpret death in terms of familiar experiences—as a change in behavior. Like Miriam, they may believe that they caused the death of a relative or pet, that having a stomachache can cause someone to die, and that death is like sleep. When researchers asked 4- to 6-year-olds whether dead people need food, air, and water, whether they go to the bathroom, whether they sleep and dream, and whether a cut on their body would heal, more than half of those who had not yet started to acquire biological understandings answered yes (Slaughter, Jaakkola, & Carey, 1999).

Most children master the components of the death concept by age 7, starting with *permanence*, the easiest idea to understand. When Leslie explained that Pepper would not get up again, Miriam accepted this fact quickly, perhaps because she had seen it in other, less emotionally charged situations, such as the dead butterflies and beetles she picked up and inspected while playing outside. Appreciation of *inevitability* and *cessation* soon follow. At first, children think that certain people do not die—themselves, people like themselves (other children), and people with whom they have close emotional ties. Also, many pre-schoolers view dead things as retaining living capacities (Kenyon, 2001; Speece & Brent, 1996). *Applicability* and *causation*, the most difficult components to master, require a firm grasp of the biological concepts just noted.

Cultural Influences

Ethnic variations suggest that religious teachings affect children's understanding of death. In a comparison of four ethnic groups in Israel, Druze and Moslem children's death concepts differed from those of Christian and Jewish children (Florian & Kravetz, 1985). The Druze emphasis on reincarnation and the greater religiosity of both Druze and Moslem groups may have led more of their children

too, preschoolers typically offer psychological, physical, or biological explanations that are linked appropriately to the behaviors of humans, animals, and objects (Hickling & Wellman, 2001; Wellman, Hickling, & Schultz, 1997).

Although young children are impressive theorists, their explanations in different domains develop at different rates. Physical and psychological explanations are prevalent at age 2, probably because these understandings originate in infancy. But because grasping biological processes is difficult, young preschoolers frequently use psychological concepts to explain biological events (Carey, 1995, 1999; Inagaki & Hatano, 2002). For example, when asked whether they can tell a pain to go away or a heartbeat to stop, many 3-year-olds say yes!

In contrast, 4-year-olds know that they cannot control biological processes (Inagaki, 1997). And by age 6, children interpret biological processes, especially those of humans, in terms of a "life force" derived from food and water that enables living things to grow, energizes their activity, and prevents them from becoming ill. When asked what will happen if a child eats very little, they are likely to say, "If we don't eat food, we lose energy and die" (Inagaki & Hatano, 2004, p. 359). Nevertheless, psychological accounts of biological events persist into the early school years, as research on children's understanding of death reveals (see the Biology and Environment box above).

Biological knowledge emerges later in children from widely varying cultures, suggesting that unlike other core domains, it may have only a weak innate foundation or, rather than

to deny permanence and nonfunctionality. Similarly, children of U.S. Southern Baptist families, who believe in an afterlife, are less likely to endorse permanence than are children from Unitarian families, who focus on achieving peace and justice in today's world (Candy-Gibbs, Sharp, & Petrun, 1985).

Experiences with death also influence understanding. Children growing up on Israeli kibbutzim (agricultural settlements) who have witnessed terrorist attacks, family members' departure on army tours, and parental anxiety about safety express a full grasp of the death concept by age 5 (Mahon, Goldberg, & Washington, 1999). And experiencing the death of a close relative or friend greatly accelerates appreciation of permanence and inevitability, even among children as young as age 3 (Reilly, Hasazi, & Bond, 1983).

Enhancing Children's Understanding

Parents often worry needlessly that discussing death candidly with children fuels their fears. But children with a good grasp of the facts of death have an easier time accepting it. Direct explanations, like Leslie's, that match the child's capacity to understand, work best. When adults use clichés or make misleading statements, children may take these literally and become confused. For example, when a parent told her 5-year-old daughter, "Grandpa went on a long trip," the child wondered, "Why didn't he take me?" (Wolfelt, 1997). When children ask difficult questions—"Will I die?" "Will you die?"—parents can be both truthful and comforting by taking advantage of children's sense of time. "Not for many, many years," they can say. "First I'm going to enjoy you as a grown-up and be a grandparent."

Another way to foster an accurate appreciation of death is to teach preschoolers about human biology. Three- to 5-year-olds given lessons in the role of the heart, kidneys, lungs, brain, digestion, bones, and muscles in sustaining life have more advanced death concepts than children not given such lessons (Slaughter & Lyons, 2003).

Adult–child discussions should also be culturally sensitive. Rather than presenting scientific evidence as negating religious beliefs, parents and teachers can help children blend the two sources of knowledge. Older children often combine their appreciation of the death concept with religious and philosophical views, which offer solace in times of bereavement. During adolescence, mystical explanations, such as being called by God and existing in a nonmaterial state, increase as young people ponder the nature of existence and grapple with spiritual ideas (Cuddy-Casey & Orvaschel, 1997). Open, honest, and respectful communication about death contributes to both cognitive development and emotional well-being.

This mother comforts her daughter as they bury a family pet in the backyard. Candid, age-appropriate explanations help children gain an accurate appreciation of what happens when living things die.
© Bubbles Photolibrary/Alamy

being innately specified, may depend entirely on a lengthy process of construction based on experience. For example, when told stories about a child born to one parent and raised by another, not until ages 5 to 7 do North American and European children show knowledge of biological inheritance, consistently predicting that an adopted child will resemble her birth parents in physical characteristics (such as hair type and skin color) but resemble her adoptive parents in beliefs and skills (Gimenez & Harris, 2002; Solomon et al., 1996; Weissman & Kalish, 1999).

In some non-Western village societies, this distinction between the influence of biology and that of social learning on human traits is not attained until adolescence or adulthood (Bloch, Solomon, & Carey, 2001; Mahalingham, 1999). The Vezo of Madagascar hold certain folk beliefs that make it harder for their children to grasp biological inheritance—for example, that a pregnant mother who spends much time thinking about another person can cause her baby to look like that person! Because Vezo children do not go to school, they are not exposed to biology lessons that contradict such folk beliefs (Astuti, Solomon, & Carey, 2004). They must, instead, notice and gradually make sense of the fact that children and their biological parents resemble each other physically—a challenging task that is not mastered until ages 14 to 20.

Nevertheless, controversy persists over whether biology is a core domain of thought (Hirschfeld, 1996; Slaughter & Lyons, 2003). Most claim that more evidence is needed to answer this question with certainty.

Evaluation of the Core Knowledge Perspective

Core knowledge theorists offer a fascinating evolutionary account of why certain cognitive skills emerge early and develop rapidly. And more seriously than other perspectives, they have addressed the question, What allows learning to get off the ground? As a result, they have enriched our understanding of infants' and young children's thinking.

Nevertheless, critics take issue with the core knowledge assumption that infants are endowed with *knowledge.* As we have seen, infant looking in violation-of-expectation studies may indicate only a perceptual preference, not the existence of concepts or reasoning. And some skeptics claim that human evolution may not have equipped infants with ready-made knowledge, which might limit their ability to adapt to environmental changes (Haith, 1999). Debate continues over just what babies start out with—domain-specific understandings or minimal perceptual biases that combine with powerful, general learning strategies to permit rapid discovery of various types of knowledge.

While emphasizing native endowment, the core knowledge perspective acknowledges that experience is essential for children to elaborate this initial knowledge. So far, however, it has not offered greater clarity than Piaget's theory about how biology and environment jointly produce cognitive change. It does not tell us just what children do to revise their innate structures. And it says little about which experiences are most important in each domain and how those experiences advance children's thinking. Finally, the core knowledge perspective, like Piaget's theory, views children as building more adequate structures largely through their own activity. It pays little attention to children's learning in interaction with others—the unique strength of Vygotsky's theory, which we take up next. Despite these limitations, the ingenious studies and provocative findings of core knowledge research have sharpened the field's focus on specifying the starting point for human cognition and carefully tracking the changes that build on it.

Ask Yourself

Review What are core domains of thought? Cite an example of infants' innate knowledge in the physical domain and the numerical domain. Why do some researchers question whether infants actually have such knowledge?

Review Why do core knowledge researchers characterize young children as naïve theorists? Cite findings that support the theory theory. Cite evidence that challenges the existence of an innately based biological theory.

Connect Describe similarities and differences between Piaget's theory and the core knowledge perspective.

Vygotsky's Sociocultural Theory

Piaget's theory and the core knowledge perspective emphasize the biological side of cognitive development. Both identify the most important source of cognition as the child himself—a busy, self-motivated explorer who forms ideas and tests them against the world. Lev Vygotsky, while also viewing children as active seekers of knowledge, emphasized the profound effects of rich social and cultural contexts on their thinking.

Early events in Vygotsky's life contributed to his vision of human cognition as inherently social and language-based. As a university student, he was interested primarily in a verbal field—literature. After graduating, he first became a teacher and only later turned to psychology. Because Vygotsky died of tuberculosis at age 37, his theory is not as complete as Piaget's. Nevertheless, the field of child development has experienced a burst of interest in Vygotsky's sociocultural perspective. His appeal lies mainly in his rejection of an individualistic view of the developing child in favor of a socially formed mind (Bakhurst, 2007; Tudge & Scrimsher, 2003).

According to Vygotsky, infants are endowed with basic perceptual, attention, and memory capacities that they share with other animals. These develop during the first two years through direct contact with the environment. Then rapid growth of language leads to a profound change in thinking. It broadens preschoolers' participation in social dialogues with more knowledgeable individuals, who encourage them to master culturally important tasks. Soon young children start to communicate with themselves much as they converse with others. As a result, basic mental capacities are transformed into uniquely human, higher cognitive processes.

This 3-year-old makes a sculpture from playdough and plastic sticks with the aid of private speech. As Vygotsky theorized, preschool children often guide their thinking and behavior by talking to themselves as they play or tackle other challenging tasks. © Laura Dwight Photography

Children's Private Speech

TAKE A MOMENT... Watch preschoolers as they play and explore the environment, and you will see that they frequently talk out loud to themselves. For example, as a 4-year-old worked a puzzle at preschool one day, I heard him say, "Where's the red piece? I need the red one. Now a blue one. No, it doesn't fit. Try it here."

Piaget (1923/1926) called these utterances *egocentric speech,* reflecting his belief that young children have difficulty taking the perspectives of others. For this reason, he said, their talk is often "talk for self" in which they run off thoughts in whatever form they happen to occur, regardless of whether a listener can understand. Piaget believed that cognitive development and certain social experiences eventually bring an end to egocentric speech. Specifically, through repeated disagreements with agemates, children see that others hold viewpoints different from their own. As a result, egocentric speech declines in favor of social speech, in which children adapt what they say to their listeners.

Vygotsky (1934/1986) disagreed strongly with Piaget's conclusions. Because language helps children think about mental activities and behavior and select courses of action, Vygotsky saw it as the foundation for all higher cognitive processes, including controlled attention, deliberate memorization and recall, categorization, planning, problem solving, abstract reasoning, and self-reflection. In Vygotsky's view, children speak to themselves for self-guidance. As they get older and find tasks easier, their self-directed speech is internalized as silent, *inner speech*—the internal verbal dialogues we carry on while thinking and acting in everyday situations.

Over the past three decades, almost all studies have supported Vygotsky's perspective (Berk & Harris, 2003). As a result, children's self-directed speech is now called **private speech** instead of egocentric speech. Research shows that children use more of it when tasks are appropriately challenging (neither too easy nor too hard), after they make errors, or when they are confused about how to proceed. Figure 6.18 shows how 5- and 6-year-olds' private speech increased as researchers made a problem-solving task moderately difficult, then decreased as the task became very difficult (Fernyhough & Fradley, 2005).

With age, as Vygotsky predicted, private speech goes underground, changing into whispers and silent lip movements (Patrick & Abravanel, 2000; Winsler & Naglieri, 2003). Furthermore, children who freely use self-guiding private speech during a challenging activity are more attentive and involved and show better task performance than their less talkative agemates (Al-Namlah, Fernyhough, & Meins, 2006; Berk & Spuhl, 1995; Fernyhough & Fradley, 2005; Winsler, Naglieri, & Manfra, 2006).

Finally, compared with their normally achieving agemates, children with learning and behavior problems engage in higher rates of private speech over a longer period of development (Berk, 2001b; Ostad & Sorensen, 2007; Paladino, 2006; Winsler et al., 2007). They seem to use private speech to help compensate for impairments in cognitive processing and attention that make academic tasks more difficult for them.

■ Figure 6.18 **Relationship of private speech to task difficulty among 5- and 6-year-olds.** Researchers increased the difficulty of a problem-solving task. Private speech rose as the task became moderately difficult, then declined as it became highly difficult. Children are more likely to use private speech for self-guidance when tasks are within their zone of proximal development, or range of mastery. (Adapted from Fernyhough & Fradley, 2005.)

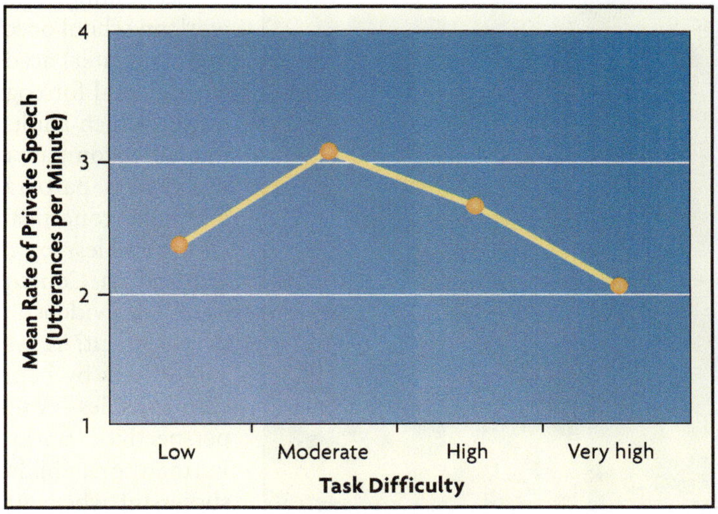

Social Origins of Cognitive Development

Where does private speech come from? Vygotsky (1930–1935/1978) believed that children's learning takes place within the **zone of proximal development**—a range of tasks too difficult for the child to do alone but possible with the help of adults and more skilled peers. Consider the joint activity of 3-year-old Sammy and his mother, who helps him put together a difficult puzzle:

Sammy: I can't get this one in. [*Tries to insert a piece in the wrong place.*]

Mother: Which piece might go down here? [*Points to the bottom of the puzzle.*]

Sammy: His shoes. [*Looks for a piece resembling the clown's shoes but tries the wrong one.*]

Mother: Well, what piece looks like this shape? [*Points again to the bottom of the puzzle.*]

Sammy: The brown one. [*Tries it, and it fits; then attempts another piece and looks at his mother.*]

Mother: Try turning it just a little. [*Gestures to show him.*]

Sammy: There! [*Puts in several more pieces while his mother watches.*]

By questioning, prompting, and suggesting strategies, Sammy's mother keeps the puzzle within his zone of proximal development, at a manageable level of difficulty.

To promote cognitive development, social interaction must have certain features. One is **intersubjectivity,** the process whereby two participants who begin a task with different understandings arrive at a shared understanding (Newson & Newson, 1975). Intersubjectivity creates a common ground for communication, as each partner adjusts to the perspective of the other. Adults try to promote it when they translate their own insights in ways that are within the child's grasp. As the child stretches to understand the adult, she is drawn into a more mature approach to the situation (Rogoff, 1998).

The capacity for intersubjectivity exists early, in parent–infant mutual gaze, exchange of vocal and emotional signals, imitation, and joint play with objects (Feldman, 2007b). Later, language facilitates intersubjectivity. As conversational skills improve, preschoolers increasingly seek others' help and direct that assistance to ensure that it is beneficial (Whitington & Ward, 1999). Between ages 3 and 5, children strive for intersubjectivity in dialogues with peers, as when they affirm a playmate's message, add new ideas, and contribute to ongoing play to sustain it. They may say, "I think [this way]. What do you think?"—evidence for a willingness to share viewpoints (Berk, 2001a). In these ways, children begin to create zones of proximal development for one another.

Another important feature of social interaction is **scaffolding**—adjusting the support offered during a teaching session to fit the child's current level of performance. When the child has little notion of how to proceed, the adult uses direct instruction, breaking the task down into manageable units, suggesting strategies, and offering rationales for using them. As the child's competence increases, effective scaffolders—such as Sammy's mother—gradually and sensitively withdraw support, turning over responsibility to the child. Then children take the language of these dialogues, make it part of their private speech, and use this speech to organize their independent efforts.

As this child works on a puzzle, her mother engages in scaffolding: breaking down the task into manageable units, suggesting and explaining strategies, and gradually turning over responsibility to the child. © SW Productions/Brand X Pictures/Jupiter Images

Scaffolding captures the form of teaching interaction that occurs as children work on school or school-like tasks, such as puzzles, model building, picture matching, and (later) academic assignments. It may not apply to other contexts that are equally vital for cognitive development—for example, play or everyday activities, during which adults usually support children's efforts without deliberately teaching. To encompass children's diverse opportunities to learn through involvement with others, Barbara Rogoff (1998, 2003) suggests the term **guided participation,** a broader concept than scaffolding that refers to shared endeavors between more expert and less expert participants, without specifying the precise features of communication. Consequently, it allows for variations across situations and cultures.

What evidence supports Vygotsky's ideas on the social origins of cognitive development? A wealth of research indicates that when adults establish intersubjectivity by being stimulating, responsive, and supportive, they foster many competencies—attention, language, complex play, and understanding of others' perspectives (Bornstein et al., 1992; Charman et al., 2001; Morales et al., 2000). Furthermore, children of effective scaffolders use more private speech, are more successful when attempting difficult tasks on their own, and are advanced in overall cognitive development (Berk & Spuhl, 1995; Conner & Cross, 2003; Mulvaney et al., 2006). Adult cognitive support—teaching in small steps and offering strategies—predicts children's mature thinking. And adult emotional support—offering encouragement and transferring responsibility to the child—predicts children's effort (Neitzel & Stright, 2003). The result is a winning combination for successful learning.

Vygotsky's View of Make-Believe Play

In accord with his emphasis on social experience and language as vital forces in cognitive development, Vygotsky (1933/1978) regarded make-believe play as a unique, broadly influential zone of proximal development in which *children advance themselves* as they try out a wide variety of challenging skills. In Vygotsky's theory, make-believe is the central source of development during the preschool years, leading development forward in two ways. First, as children create imaginary situations, they learn to act in accord with internal ideas, not just in response to external stimuli. Children's object substitutions are crucial in this process. While pretending, children continually use one object to stand for another—a stick for a horse, a folded blanket for a sleeping baby—and, in the process, change the object's usual meaning. Gradually they realize that thinking (or the meaning of words) is separate from objects and that ideas can be used to guide behavior.

The rule-based nature of make-believe also strengthens children's capacity to think before they act. Pretend play, Vygotsky pointed out, constantly demands that children act against their impulses because they must follow the rules of the play scene (Bodrova & Leong, 2007). For example, a child pretending to go to sleep obeys the rules of bedtime behavior. A child imagining himself as a father and a doll as his child conforms to the rules of parental behavior. Through enacting rules in make-believe, children come to better understand social norms and expectations and strive to follow them.

Much evidence fits with Vygotsky's conclusion that make-believe play serves as a zone of proximal development, supporting the emergence and refinement of many competencies. Turn back to pages 237–238 to review evidence that make-believe enhances a diverse array of cognitive and social skills. Pretend play is also rich in private speech—a finding that supports its role in helping children bring action under the control of thought (Krafft & Berk, 1998). In one study, preschoolers who engaged in more complex sociodramatic play showed greater gains in following classroom rules over a four-month period (Elias & Berk, 2002).

Finally, Vygotsky questioned Piaget's belief that make-believe arises spontaneously in the second year of life. Vygotsky argued that, like other higher cognitive processes, the elaborate pretending of the preschool years has social origins. Research reviewed in the From Research to Practice box on page 268 supports the view that children learn to pretend under the supportive guidance of experts.

Vygotsky and Education

Vygotsky's theory offers new visions of teaching and learning—ones that emphasize the importance of social context and collaboration. Today, educators are eager to use his ideas. Like Piagetian classrooms, Vygotskian classrooms accept individual differences and provide opportunities for children's active participation. Yet a Vygotskian classroom goes beyond independent discovery: It promotes *assisted discovery*. Teachers guide children's learning, tailoring their interventions to each child's zone of proximal development. Assisted discovery is also fostered by *peer collaboration*. Children with varying abilities work in groups, teaching and helping one another.

Vygotsky's educational message for the preschool years is to provide socially rich, meaningful activities in children's zones of proximal development and a wealth of opportunities for make-believe play—the ultimate means of fostering the self-discipline required for later academic learning. Once formal schooling begins, Vygotsky emphasized literacy activities (Scrimsher & Tudge, 2003). As children talk about literature, mathematics, science, and social studies, their teachers inform, correct, and ask them to explain. As a result, children reflect on their own thought processes and shift to a higher level of cognitive activity in which they

om Research to Practice

Social Origins of Make-Believe Play

Ken, … to do with our two sons when they were young was to bake pineapple upside-down cake, a favorite treat. One Sunday afternoon when a cake was in the making, 21-month-old Peter stood on a chair at the kitchen sink, busily pouring water from one cup to another.

"He's in the way, Dad!" complained 4-year-old David, trying to pull Peter away from the sink.

"Maybe if we let him help, he'll give us some room," Ken suggested. As David stirred the batter, Ken poured some into a small bowl for Peter, moved his chair to the side of the sink, and handed him a spoon.

"Here's how you do it, Petey," instructed David, with a superior air. Peter watched David stir, then tried to copy his motion. When it was time to pour the batter, Ken helped Peter hold and tip the small bowl.

"Time to bake it," said Ken.

"Bake it, bake it," repeated Peter, watching Ken slip the pan into the oven.

Several hours later, we observed one of Peter's earliest instances of make-believe play. He got his pail from the sandbox and, after filling it with a handful of sand, carried it into the kitchen and set it on the floor in front of the oven. "Bake it, bake it," Peter called to Ken. Together, father and son pretended to place the make-believe cake inside the oven.

Piaget and his followers concluded that toddlers discover make-believe independently, once they are capable of representational schemes. Vygotsky challenged this view. He believed that society provides children with opportunities to represent culturally meaningful activities in play. Make-believe, like other complex mental activities, is first learned under the guidance of experts (Berk, 2006). In the example just described, Peter extended his capacity to represent daily events when Ken drew him into the baking task and helped him act it out in play.

Current evidence supports the idea that early make-believe is the combined result of children's readiness to engage in it and social experiences that promote it. In one observational study of Caucasian-American toddlers, 75 to 80 percent of make-believe involved mother–child interaction (Haight & Miller, 1993). At 12 months, almost all play episodes were initiated by mothers, but by the end of the second year, half of pretend episodes were initiated by each.

During make-believe (such as pretending to eat a snack), mothers offer toddlers a rich array of cues that signal they are pretending—looking and smiling at the child more, making faster and more exaggerated movements, and using more "we" talk (acknowledging that pretending is a joint endeavor) than they do during the same real-life event (Lillard, 2007b). When adults participate, toddlers' make-believe is more elaborate (O'Reilly & Bornstein, 1993). For example, play themes are more varied. And toddlers are more likely to combine schemes into complex sequences, as Peter did when he put the sand in the bucket ("making the batter"), carried it into the kitchen, and (with Ken's help) pretended to put it in the oven ("baking the cake"). The more parents pretend with their toddlers, the more time their children devote to make-believe. In certain collectivist societies, such as Argentina and Japan, mother–toddler other-directed pretending, as in feeding or putting a doll to sleep, is particularly rich in maternal expressions of affection and praise (Bornstein et al., 1999a).

In some cultures, such as those of Indonesia and Mexico, where extended-family households and sibling caregiving are common, make-believe is more frequent and complex with older siblings than with mothers. As early as age 3 to 4, children provide rich, challenging stimulation to their younger brothers and sisters, take these teaching responsibilities seriously, and, with age, become better at them (Zukow-Goldring, 2002). In a study of Zinacanteco Indian children of southern Mexico, by age 8, sibling teachers were highly skilled at showing 2-year-olds how to play at everyday tasks, such as washing and cooking. They guided toddlers verbally and physically through the task and provided feedback (Maynard, 2002).

In cultures where sibling caregiving is common, make-believe play is more frequent and complex with older siblings than with mothers. As these Venezuelan brothers play with a balsa-wood boat, the older boy provides his younger sibling with rich, challenging stimulation. © David Woodfall/WWI/Peter Arnold, Inc.

In Western middle-SES families, older siblings less often teach deliberately but still serve as influential models of playful behavior. In a study of New Zealand families of Western European descent, when both a parent and an older sibling were available, toddlers more often imitated the actions of the sibling, especially when siblings engaged in make-believe or in routines (like answering the phone or raking leaves) that could inspire pretending (Barr & Hayne, 2003).

Make-believe play is a major means through which children extend their cognitive skills and learn about important activities in their culture. Vygotsky's theory, and the findings that support it, tell us that providing a stimulating environment is not enough to promote early cognitive development. Toddlers also must be invited and encouraged by more skilled members of their culture to participate in the social world around them. Parents and teachers can enhance early make-believe by playing often with toddlers and guiding and elaborating on their make-believe themes.

think about how to symbolize ideas in socially useful ways. Gradually they become proficient in manipulating and controlling the symbol systems of their culture.

Let's look at two Vygotsky-based educational innovations, each of which incorporates assisted discovery and peer collaboration.

Reciprocal Teaching

Originally designed to improve reading comprehension in poorly achieving students, this teaching method has been extended to other subjects and all schoolchildren. In **reciprocal teaching,** a teacher and two to four students form a collaborative group and take turns leading dialogues on the content of a text passage. Within the dialogues, group members apply four cognitive strategies: questioning, summarizing, clarifying, and predicting.

The dialogue leader (at first the teacher, later a student) begins by *asking questions* about the content of the text passage. Students offer answers, raise additional questions, and, in case of disagreement, reread the original text. Next, the leader *summarizes* the passage, and children discuss the summary and *clarify* unfamiliar ideas. Finally, the leader encourages students to *predict* upcoming content based on clues in the passage.

Elementary and middle school students exposed to reciprocal teaching show impressive gains in reading comprehension compared with controls taught in other ways (Lederer, 2000; Rosenshine & Meister, 1994; Takala, 2006). Notice how reciprocal teaching creates a zone of proximal development in which children gradually learn to scaffold one another's progress and assume more responsibility for comprehending text passages (Gillies, 2003). Also, by collaborating with others, children forge group expectations for high-level thinking and acquire skills vital for learning and success in everyday life.

Cooperative Learning

Although reciprocal teaching uses peer collaboration, a teacher guides it, helping to ensure its success. According to Vygotsky, more expert peers can also spur children's development, as long as they adjust the help they provide to fit the less mature child's zone of proximal development. Recall that Piaget, too, thought that peer interaction could contribute to cognitive change. In fact, he regarded discussion with agemates as more valuable than discussion with adults because a child might superficially accept an adult authority's perspective without critically examining it. Piaget also asserted that clashing viewpoints—arguments jarring the child into noticing a peer's viewpoint—were necessary for peer interaction to foster logical thought.

Today, peer collaboration is widely used, but evidence is mounting that it promotes development only under certain conditions. A crucial factor is **cooperative learning,** in which small groups of classmates work toward common goals. Conflict and disagreement seem less important than the extent to which peers achieve intersubjectivity—by resolving differences of opinion, sharing responsibility, and providing one another with sufficiently elaborate explanations to correct misunderstandings (Webb, Troper, & Fall, 1995). And in line with Vygotsky's theory, children profit more when their peer partner is an "expert"—especially capable at the task. When older or more expert students assist younger or less expert students, both benefit in achievement and self-esteem, with stronger effects for low-income, minority students (Ginsburg-Block, Rohrbeck, & Fantuzzo, 2006: Renninger, 1998).

In reciprocal teaching, a Vygotsky-inspired educational innovation, a teacher and two to four students form a cooperative learning group to discuss a text passage. Elementary and middle school students who participate show impressive gains in reading comprehension. © Pearson Learning

Cultural variations exist in students' ability to learn cooperatively. Working in groups comes more easily to children reared in collectivist than in individualistic cultures. For example, Navajo children do so more readily than Caucasian-American children (Ellis & Gauvain, 1992). Japanese classroom practices, in which children solve problems by building on one another's ideas, reflect a larger culture that values interdependence (Hatano, 1994). In contrast, North American cultural-majority children typically regard competition and independent work as natural—a perspective that interferes with their ability to attain intersubjectivity in groups.

Cultural Influences

Children in Village and Tribal Cultures Observe and Participate in Adult Work

In Western societies, children are largely excluded from participating in adult work, which generally occurs in settings beyond the home. The role of equipping children with the skills they need to become competent workers is assigned to school. In early childhood, middle-class parents' interactions with children dwell on preparing children to succeed in school through child-focused activities—especially adult–child conversations and play that enhance language, literacy, and other school-related knowledge. In village and tribal cultures, children receive little or no schooling, spend their days in contact with or participating in adult work, and start to assume mature responsibilities in early childhood (Rogoff et al., 2003). Consequently, parents have little need to rely on conversation and play to teach children.

A study comparing 2- and 3-year-olds' daily lives in four cultures—two U.S. middle-class suburbs, the Efe hunters and gatherers of the Republic of Congo, and a Mayan agricultural town in Guatemala—documented these differences (Morelli, Rogoff, & Angelillo, 2003). In the U.S. communities, young children had little access to adult work and spent much time involved in adult–child conversations and play that catered to children's interests and provided academic lessons. In contrast, the Efe and Mayan children rarely engaged in these child-focused activities. Instead, they spent their day in close proximity to adult work, which often took place in or near the Efe campsite or the Mayan family home. Compared to their U.S. counterparts, Mayan and Efe children spent far more time observing adult work.

An ethnography of a remote Mayan village in Yucatán, Mexico, shows that when young children are legitimate onlookers and participants in a daily life structured around adult work, their competencies differ sharply from those of Western preschoolers (Gaskins, 1999; Gaskins, Haight, & Lancy, 2007). Yucatec Mayan adults are subsistence farmers. Men tend cornfields, aided by sons age 8 and older. Women prepare meals, wash clothes, and care for the livestock and garden, assisted by daughters and by sons too young to work in the fields. From the second year on, children join in these activities to the extent they can. When not participating with adults, they are expected to be self-sufficient. Young children make many nonwork decisions for themselves—how much to sleep and eat, what to wear, when to bathe (as long as they do so every afternoon), and even when to start school. As a result, Yucatec Mayan preschoolers are highly competent at self-care. In contrast, their make-believe play is limited; when it occurs, they usually enact adult work. Otherwise, they watch others—for hours each day.

Yucatec Mayan parents rarely converse or play with preschoolers or scaffold their learning. Rather, when children imitate adult tasks, parents conclude that they are ready for more responsibility. Then they assign chores, selecting tasks the child can do with little help so that adult work is not disturbed. If a child cannot do a task, the adult takes over and the child observes, reengaging when able to contribute.

Expected to be autonomous and helpful, Yucatec Mayan children seldom display attention-getting behaviors or ask others for something interesting to do. From an early age, they can sit quietly, with little fussing, through a lengthy religious service or a three-hour truck ride. And when an adult interrupts their activity and directs them to do a chore, they respond eagerly to the type of command that Western children frequently avoid or resent. By age 5, Yucatec Mayan children spontaneously take responsibility for tasks beyond those assigned.

A Mayan 3-year-old imitates her mother in balancing a basin of water on her head, while her younger sibling prepares to attempt the skill. Children in Yucatec Mayan culture join in the work of their community from an early age, spending many hours observing adults.
© Adrian Lascom/Alamy

For cooperative learning to succeed, Western children usually require extensive guidance. In several studies, groups of three to four students trained in collaborative processes displayed more cooperative behavior, gave higher-level explanations, and enjoyed learning more than did untrained groups (Gillies, 2000, 2003; Terwel et al., 2001). In other research, the quality of children's collaborative discussions predicted gains in diverse cognitive skills that persisted for weeks beyond the cooperative learning experience (Fleming & Alexander, 2001). Teaching through cooperative learning broadens Vygotsky's concept of the zone of proximal development, from a single child in collaboration with an expert partner (adult or peer) to multiple partners with diverse forms of expertise stimulating and encouraging one another.

Evaluation of Vygotsky's Theory

In granting social experience a fundamental role in cognitive development, Vygotsky's theory helps us understand the wide cultural variation in cognitive skills. Whereas Piaget emphasized universal cognitive change, Vygotsky's theory leads us to expect highly diverse paths of development. For example, the reading, writing, and mathematical activities of children who attend school in literate societies generate cognitive capacities different from those in tribal and village cultures, where children receive little formal schooling. But the elaborate spatial skills of Australian Aborigines, whose food-gathering missions require that they find their way through barren desert regions, and the proportional reasoning of Brazilian fishermen, promoted by their navigational experiences, are just as advanced (Carraher, Schliemann, & Carraher, 1988; Kearins, 1981). Each is a unique form of symbolic thinking required by activities that make up that culture's way of life.

Vygotsky's theory also underscores the vital role of teaching in cognitive development. According to Vygotsky (1934/1986), from communicating with more expert partners, children engage in "verbalized self-observation," reflecting on, revising, and controlling their own thought processes. In this way, parents' and teachers' engagement with children prompts profound advances in the complexity of children's thinking.

Vygotsky's theory has not gone unchallenged. Although he acknowledged the role of diverse symbol systems (such as pictures, maps, and mathematical expressions) in the development of higher cognitive processes, he elevated language to highest importance. But in some cultures, verbal dialogues are not the only—or even the most important—means through which children learn. When Western parents help children with challenging tasks, they take much responsibility for children's motivation by frequently giving verbal instructions and conversing with the child. Their communication resembles the teaching that occurs in school, where their children will spend years preparing for adult life. In cultures that place less emphasis on schooling and literacy, parents often expect children to take greater responsibility for acquiring new skills through keen observation and participation in community activities (Rogoff, 2003). The Cultural Influences box on the previous page describes research illustrating this difference.

Finally, in focusing on social and cultural influences, Vygotsky said little about biological contributions to children's cognition. His theory does not address how elementary motor, perceptual, memory, and problem-solving capacities spark changes in children's social experiences, from which more advanced cognition springs. Nor does it tell us just how children internalize social experiences to advance their mental functioning (Miller, 2001; Moll, 1994). Consequently, like the other perspectives addressed in this chapter, Vygotsky's theory is vague in its explanation of cognitive change. It is intriguing to speculate about the broader theory that might exist today had Piaget and Vygotsky—the two twentieth-century giants of cognitive development—had a chance to meet and weave together their extraordinary accomplishments.

Ask Yourself

Review Describe characteristics of social interaction that support children's cognitive development. How does such interaction create a zone of proximal development?

Apply Tanisha's 5-year-old son, Toby, talks aloud to himself while he plays. Tanisha wonders whether she should discourage this behavior. Using Vygotsky's theory and related research, explain why Toby talks to himself. How would you advise Tanisha?

Connect Explain how Piaget's and Vygotsky's theories complement each other. How would classroom practices inspired by these theories be similar? How would they be different?

Reflect When do you use private speech? Does it serve a self-guiding function for you, as it does for children? Explain.

SUMMARY

Piaget's Cognitive-Developmental Theory

According to Piaget, how does cognition develop?

- Piaget's **constructivist approach** assumes that children construct knowledge of their world by acting on the environment, moving through four invariant, universal stages. According to Piaget, newborn infants have little in the way of built-in structures; only at the end of the second year are they capable of a cognitive approach to the world through **mental representations.**
- In Piaget's theory, psychological structures, or **schemes,** change in two ways: through **adaptation,** which consists of two complementary activities—**assimilation** and **accommodation**—and through **organization,** the internal rearrangement of schemes to form a strongly interconnected cognitive system. **Equilibration** describes the changing balance of assimilation and accommodation that gradually leads to more effective schemes.

The Sensorimotor Stage: Birth to 2 Years

Describe the major cognitive attainments of the sensorimotor stage.

- Piaget's **sensorimotor stage** is divided into six substages. Through the **circular reaction,** the newborn baby's reflexes gradually transform into the older infant's more flexible action patterns. In Substage 4, 8- to 12-month-olds first engage in **intentional,** or **goal-directed, behavior** and begin to master **object permanence.** In Substage 5, from 12 to 18 months, toddlers become better problem solvers and no longer make the **A-not-B search error.** In Substage 6, mental representation is evident in sudden solutions to sensorimotor problems, mastery of object permanence problems involving invisible displacement, **deferred imitation,** and **make-believe play.**

What does follow-up research say about the accuracy of Piaget's sensorimotor stage?

- Many studies suggest that infants display various understandings earlier than Piaget believed. Some awareness of object permanence, as revealed by the **violation-of-expectation method,** may be evident in the first few months. Young infants also display deferred imitation, categorization, and **analogical problem solving,** indicating that mental representation develops concurrently with sensorimotor schemes during the first two years.
- Today, investigators believe that newborns have more built-in cognitive equipment for making sense of experience than Piaget assumed, although they disagree on the extent of infants' initial understanding.

The Preoperational Stage: 2 to 7 Years

Describe advances in mental representation and limitations of thinking during the preoperational stage.

- Rapid advances in mental representation, including language, make-believe play, and drawing, occur during the **preoperational stage.** With age, make-believe becomes increasingly complex, evolving into **sociodramatic play** with others. Preschoolers' make-believe not only reflects but also contributes to their cognitive and social development. During the preschool years, drawings progress from scribbles to increasingly detailed and realistic representational forms.
- **Dual representation** improves rapidly during the third year of life as children realize that photographs, drawings, models, and simple maps correspond to circumstances in the real world. Insight into one type of symbol–real-world relation helps preschoolers understand others.

© Ariel Skelley/CORBIS

- Piaget described preschoolers as not yet capable of **operations.** Because **egocentrism** prevents children from accommodating, it contributes to **animistic thinking, centration,** a focus on superficial perceptual appearances, and lack of **reversibility** in problem solving—difficulties that cause preschoolers to fail **conservation** and **hierarchical classification** tasks.

What does follow-up research say about the accuracy of Piaget's preoperational stage?

- When preschoolers are given simplified problems relevant to their everyday lives, their performance appears more mature than Piaget assumed. They recognize differing perspectives, distinguish animate from inanimate objects, and reason about transformations and cause-and-effect relations. Their language reflects accurate causal reasoning and hierarchical classification, and they form many categories based on nonobservable characteristics. They also notice distinctions between appearance and reality, an understanding that improves with age.

© Corbis Premium Collection/Alamy

The Concrete Operational Stage: 7 to 11 Years

What are the major characteristics of the concrete operational stage?

- During the **concrete operational stage,** thought is far more logical and organized than earlier. The ability to conserve indicates that children can engage in decentration and reversibility. They also are better at hierarchical classification and **seriation,** including **transitive inference.**
- School-age children's spatial reasoning improves, as indicated by their ability to give directions, and their **cognitive maps** become more organized and accurate.
- Concrete operational thought is limited in that children have difficulty reasoning about abstract ideas. School-age children's mastery of Piaget's concrete operational tasks takes place gradually, not all at once.

What does follow-up research say about the accuracy of Piaget's concrete operational stage?

- Cultural practices and schooling profoundly affect children's mastery of Piagetian tasks. Concrete operations are greatly influenced by training, context, and cultural conditions.

The Formal Operational Stage: 11 Years and Older

Describe major characteristics of the formal operational stage and their consequences for adolescents' typical reactions.

- In Piaget's **formal operational stage,** abstract, systematic, scientific thinking develops. Adolescents become capable of **hypothetico-deductive reasoning.** When faced with a problem, they start with a hypothesis about variables that might affect an outcome; deduce logical, testable inferences; and systematically isolate and combine variables to see which inferences are confirmed.
- Adolescents also develop **propositional thought**—the ability to evaluate the logic of verbal statements without referring to real-world circumstances.
- With the transition to formal operations, two distorted images of the relation between self and other appear: the **imaginary audience** and the **personal fable.** Research suggests that these visions of the self result not from egocentrism but from advances in perspective taking.
- Because abstract thinking fosters idealism, teenagers become faultfinding critics of their real world. Despite advances in cognition, adolescents are less competent than adults at diverse aspects of decision making.

What does follow-up research say about the accuracy of Piaget's formal operational stage?

- School-age children display the beginnings of hypothetico-deductive reasoning but are less competent than adolescents. They cannot evaluate evidence that bears on three or more variables at once, and they do not grasp the **logical necessity** of propositional reasoning.
- Adolescents and adults are most likely to think abstractly and systematically in situations in which they have had extensive experience. In tribal and village societies, formal operational tasks usually are not mastered at all, suggesting that Piaget's highest stage is promoted by specific learning opportunities made available in school.

Piaget and Education

Describe educational implications of Piaget's theory.

- A Piagetian classroom promotes discovery learning, sensitivity to children's readiness to learn, and acceptance of individual differences.

Overall Evaluation of Piaget's Theory

Summarize contributions and shortcomings of Piaget's theory.

- Piaget awakened psychologists and educators to children's active contributions to their own development and inspired the contemporary focus on mechanisms of cognitive change. His stages, though incorrect in some respects, provide a useful "road map" of cognitive development. However, Piaget's notions of adaptation, organization, and equilibration offer only a vague account of how cognition develops. And children's cognitive attainments are less coherent and more gradual than Piaget's stages indicate.
- Some researchers reject Piaget's stages while retaining his view of cognitive development as an active, constructive process. Others support a less tightly knit stage concept. Still others deny both Piaget's stages and his belief in the existence of general reasoning abilities.

The Core Knowledge Perspective

Explain the core knowledge perspective on cognitive development, noting research that supports its assumptions.

- According to the **core knowledge perspective,** infants begin life with innate, core domains of thought that support early, rapid cognitive development. Each core domain has a long evolutionary history, is essential for survival, and develops independently, resulting in uneven, domain-specific changes. Some violation-of-expectation research suggests that young infants have impressive physical and numerical knowledge, but overall, findings on early, innate knowledge are mixed.

© David Young-Wolff/Alamy

- The **theory theory** regards children as naïve theorists who draw on innate concepts to explain their everyday experiences and then test their theory, revising it to account for new information. In support of this view, children reason about everyday events in ways consistent with the event's core domain. Physical and psychological explanations emerge earlier than biological explanations, suggesting that biological knowledge may have little or no innate foundation.

Summarize the strengths and limitations of the core knowledge perspective.

- Core knowledge researchers are testing intriguing ideas about why certain cognitive skills emerge early and develop rapidly. But critics believe that results of violation-of-expectation studies are not adequate to show that infants are endowed with knowledge. So far, the core knowledge perspective has not offered greater clarity than Piaget's theory on how cognition changes.

Vygotsky's Sociocultural Theory

Explain Vygotsky's view of cognitive development, noting the importance of social experience and language.

- In Vygotsky's sociocultural theory, language development broadens preschoolers' participation in dialogues with more knowledgeable individuals, who encourage them to master culturally important tasks. These social experiences transform basic mental capacities into uniquely human, higher cognitive processes.
- As experts assist children with tasks within their **zone of proximal development,** children integrate the language of these dialogues into their **private speech** and use it for self-guidance. With age and task mastery, children internalize private speech as silent, inner speech.

Describe features of social interaction that promote cognitive development, and discuss Vygotsky's view of the role of make-believe play in development.

- **Intersubjectivity,** which creates a common ground for communication, and **scaffolding,** involving adult assistance adjusted to the child's current level of performance, promote cognitive development. The term **guided participation** recognizes cultural and situational variations in adults' support of children's efforts.
- Vygotsky viewed make-believe play as a unique, broadly influential zone of proximal development in which children learn to act in accord with internal ideas rather than on impulse. Like other higher cognitive processes, make-believe has social origins.

Vygotsky and Education

Describe educational implications of Vygotsky's theory.

- A Vygotskian classroom emphasizes assisted discovery through teachers' guidance and peer collaboration. When formal schooling begins, literacy activities prompt children to shift to a higher level of cognitive activity, in which they proficiently manipulate and control their culture's symbol systems.
- Educational practices inspired by Vygotsky's theory include **reciprocal teaching** and **cooperative learning.** Teaching through cooperative learning broadens Vygotsky's concept of the zone of proximal development to include multiple partners who stimulate and encourage one another.

Evaluation of Vygotsky's Theory

Cite strengths and limitations of Vygotsky's theory.

- Vygotsky's theory helps us understand wide cultural variation in cognitive skills and underscores the vital role of teaching in cognitive development. In some cultures, however, verbal dialogues are not the only or even the most important means through which children learn. Vygotsky said little about biological contributions to children's cognition. He also did not address exactly how children internalize social experiences to advance their thinking.

IMPORTANT TERMS AND CONCEPTS

A-not-B search error (p. 227)
accommodation (p. 225)
adaptation (p. 225)
analogical problem solving (p. 234)
animistic thinking (p. 241)
assimilation (p. 225)
centration (p. 241)
circular reaction (p. 226)
cognitive maps (p. 248)
concrete operational stage (p. 247)
conservation (p. 241)
constructivist approach (p. 224)
cooperative learning (p. 269)
core knowledge perspective (p. 258)
deferred imitation (p. 228)
dual representation (p. 240)
egocentrism (p. 240)
equilibration (p. 225)
formal operational stage (p. 251)
guided participation (p. 266)
hierarchical classification (p. 242)
hypothetico-deductive reasoning (p. 251)
imaginary audience (p. 252)
intentional, or goal-directed, behavior (p. 227)
intersubjectivity (p. 266)
logical necessity (p. 255)
make-believe play (p. 228)
mental representation (p. 225)
object permanence (p. 227)
operations (p. 240)
organization (p. 226)
personal fable (p. 252)
preoperational stage (p. 236)
private speech (p. 265)
propositional thought (p. 252)
reciprocal teaching (p. 269)
reversibility (p. 242)
scaffolding (p. 266)
schemes (p. 225)
sensorimotor stage (p. 226)
seriation (p. 247)
sociodramatic play (p. 237)
theory theory (p. 261)
transitive inference (p. 247)
violation-of-expectation method (p. 229)
zone of proximal development (p. 265)

7

"Tsunami Classroom"

Qanita Qamarani
10 years, Indonesia

Despite the devastation of the Indonesian tsunami visible in the background, these children gather for lessons in a makeshift classroom. During the school years, the capacity to attend to, remember, transform, and use information to solve problems expands greatly.

Cognitive Development: An Information-Processing Perspective

On Fridays in Mr. Sharp's fourth-grade class, the children often played memory games. One day, Mr. Sharp announced, "I'm going to put 12 words on the board and leave them up for 1 minute. Let's see how many you can recall."

Milk, shoe, jug, soup, hand, plate, foot, cake, gloves, sock, head, bowl, Mr. Sharp wrote quickly. Then, after 60 seconds, he erased them.

Victor's hand shot up. "I've got 'em!" he exclaimed, and recited the words perfectly.

"How did you do that, Victor?" asked Mr. Sharp.

"I put all the food together, the kitchen stuff together, and the clothes together," Victor explained. "Then I repeated the words in each group over and over."

Now consider a different scene—a researcher interviewing Kpelle farmers of Liberia about how they would sort familiar objects to remember them (Glick, 1975). Rather than putting all the tools in one pile and the food items in another, adults in this nonliterate culture arranged the objects in pairs—a knife with an orange, a hoe with a potato. The researcher asked the Kpelle adults why they did not use the more effective memorizing techniques typical of Western schoolchildren. "A wise person," many Kpelle replied, "would learn the Kpelle way." "Then how would a fool do it?" the researcher persisted—and immediately got the kinds of object groupings he had first expected!

Information processing is not a unified theory of cognitive development. Rather, it is an approach followed by researchers who thoroughly study specific aspects of cognition in an effort to uncover *mechanisms of change*—how children and adults operate on information, detecting, transforming, storing, accessing, and modifying it further as it makes its way through the cognitive system.

This chapter provides an overview of the information-processing perspective. First, we review models of the human cognitive system that are major forces in child development research. Next, we turn to two basic processes involved in all human thinking: attention and memory. We also consider how children's expanding knowledge of the world and awareness of their own mental activities affect these processes.

As we examine these topics, we will return to a familiar theme: the impact of task demands and cultural context on children's thinking. Comparing Victor's memorizing techniques with those of the Kpelle suggests that culture can greatly influence information processing. We pay special attention to how schooling, with its emphasis on literacy, mathematics, scientific reasoning, and retention of discrete pieces of information, channels cognitive development in culturally specific ways. Although information-processing theorists are especially interested in internal, self-generated cognitive changes, they also want to find out how external influences—teaching techniques, the design of learning environments and tasks, and cultural values and practices—affect children's thinking. We conclude with an evaluation of information processing as a framework for understanding cognitive development.

The Information-Processing Approach

Most information-processing theorists view the mind as a complex symbol-manipulating system through which information from the environment flows, often using the metaphor of a computer. First, information is *encoded*—taken in by the system and retained in symbolic form. Then a variety of internal processes operate on it, *recoding* it, or revising its symbolic structure into a more effective representation, and then *decoding* it, or interpreting its meaning by comparing and combining it with other information in the system. When these cognitive operations are complete, individuals use the information to make sense of their experiences and to solve problems.

Notice the clarity and precision of the computer analogy of human mental functioning. Researchers use computer-like diagrams and flowcharts to try to map the exact series of steps children and adults follow when faced with a task or problem. Some researchers do this in such detail that the same mental operations can be programmed into a computer. Then the researcher conducts *simulations* to see if the computer responds as children and adults do on certain tasks. Other investigators intensively study children's and adults' thinking by tracking eye movements, analyzing error patterns, and examining self-reports of mental activity. Regardless of approach, all share a strong commitment to explicit models of thinking that guide the questions they raise about components of cognitive development and thorough testing of each component.

General Models of Information Processing

The computer-like view of the cognitive system adopted, either directly or indirectly, by most information-processing researchers emerged in the late 1960s and early 1970s. Called the *store model,* it focuses on general units of cognitive functioning, such as sensation and memory (Klahr & MacWhinney, 1998). A second, more recent model, *connectionism*—also computer-based—is part and parcel of cognitive neuroscientists' quest to understand what might be happening in the brain as cognition changes (de Haan & Johnson, 2003a).

The Store Model

The **store model** of the information-processing system assumes that we hold, or store, information in three parts of the mental system for processing: the *sensory register; working,* or *short-term, memory*; and *long-term memory* (see Figure 7.1) (Atkinson & Shiffrin, 1968). As information flows through each, we can use **mental strategies** to operate on and transform it, increasing the chances that we will retain information, use it efficiently, and think flexibly, adapting the information to changing circumstances. To understand this more clearly, let's look at each component of the mental system.

• **Components of the Store Model** First, information enters the **sensory register.** Here, sights and sounds are represented directly and stored briefly. TAKE A MOMENT... Look around you and then close your eyes. An image of what you saw persists for a few seconds but

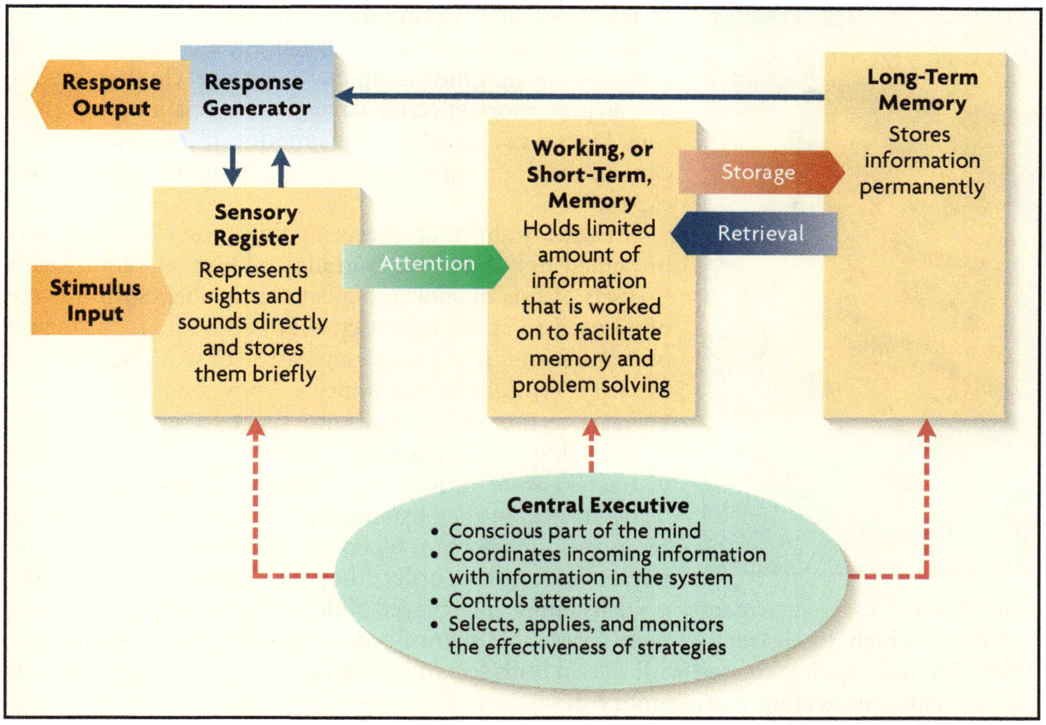

Figure 7.1 Store model of the human information-processing system. Information flows through three parts of the mental system: the *sensory register; working,* or *short-term, memory;* and *long-term memory.* In each, mental strategies can be used to manipulate information, increasing the efficiency and flexibility of thinking and the chances that information will be retained. The *central executive* is the conscious, reflective part of working memory. It coordinates incoming information already in the system, decides what to attend to, and oversees the use of strategies.

then decays, or disappears, unless you use mental strategies to preserve it. For example, by *attending to* some information more carefully than to other information, you increase the chances that it will transfer to the next step of the information-processing system.

In the second part of the mind, **working, or short-term, memory,** we actively apply mental strategies as we "work" on a limited amount of information. For example, if you are studying this book effectively, you are taking notes, repeating information to yourself, or grouping pieces of information together. Why do you apply these strategies? The sensory register, though limited, can take in a wide panorama of information. The capacity of working memory is more restricted. By meaningfully connecting pieces of information into a single representation, we reduce the number of separate pieces we must attend to, thereby making room in working memory for more. Also, the more thoroughly we learn information, the more *automatically* we use it. Automatic processing expands working memory by enabling us to focus on additional information simultaneously.

To manage its complex activities, a special part of working memory—the **central executive**—directs the flow of information. It decides what to attend to, coordinates incoming information with information already in the system, and selects, applies, and monitors strategies (Baddeley, 2000; Pressley & Hilden, 2006). The central executive is the conscious, reflective part of our mental system. It works closely with working memory to direct such complex activities as comprehension, reasoning, and problem-solving. As we will see later, the central executive is sometimes referred to as *metacognition,* meaning awareness and understanding of thought.

The longer we hold information in working memory, the more likely it will transfer to the third and largest storage area—**long-term memory,** our permanent knowledge base, which is unlimited. In fact, we store so much in long-term memory that *retrieval*—getting information back from the system—can be problematic. To aid retrieval, we apply strategies, just as we do in working memory. Information in long-term memory is *categorized* by its contents, much like a library shelving system that allows us to retrieve items easily by following the same network of associations used to store them in the first place.

• Implications for Development When applied to development, the store model suggests that two broad aspects of the cognitive system increase with age: (1) the *basic capacity* of its

While collaborating on a complex quilt-making project, these fourth graders rely on the central executive, a part of working memory that allocates attention, oversees the use of strategies, and coordinates incoming information with information already in the system. © Felicia Martinez/PhotoEdit

stores, especially working memory, and (2) the extent and effectiveness of *strategy use*. Throughout this chapter, we will consider research indicating that, with age, children gradually acquire more effective strategies for retaining information. Does basic capacity—the amount of information that can be held in mind *without* applying strategies—also expand?

In a study aimed at answering this question, researchers presented first- and fourth-grade children and adults with two sets of lists of spoken digits to remember. Such lists are often used to assess **memory span**—the longest sequence of items a person can recall, a measure of working memory capacity. Typically, scores improve from about two digits at 2½ years, to four or five digits at 7 years, to six or seven digits in adolescence and adulthood. In the *attended-to lists*, no distracters were introduced to prevent participants from using strategies; they listened and, when cued by a display on a computer screen, typed as many digits as they could remember, in the order they had heard them. In the *unattended-to lists*, participants, while listening, also played a picture-matching game on the computer, which, by distracting them, prevented them from using strategies (Cowan et al., 1999). Memory span increased with age on both sets of lists, even when participants did not use strategies, indicating that memory development involves expansion of basic working-memory capacity.

With age, children also use their basic mental capacity more efficiently, as research on processing speed demonstrates. Robert Kail (1991, 1993, 1997) gave 7- to 22-year-olds a variety of cognitive tasks in which they had to respond as quickly as possible. For example, in a visual search task, they were shown a single digit and asked to signal if it was among a set of digits that appeared on a screen. In a mental addition task, they were given addition problems and answers, and they had to indicate whether the solutions were correct. On all tasks, processing time decreased with age. More important, rate of change—a fairly rapid decline in processing time, trailing off around age 12—was similar across many activities (see Figure 7.2). This

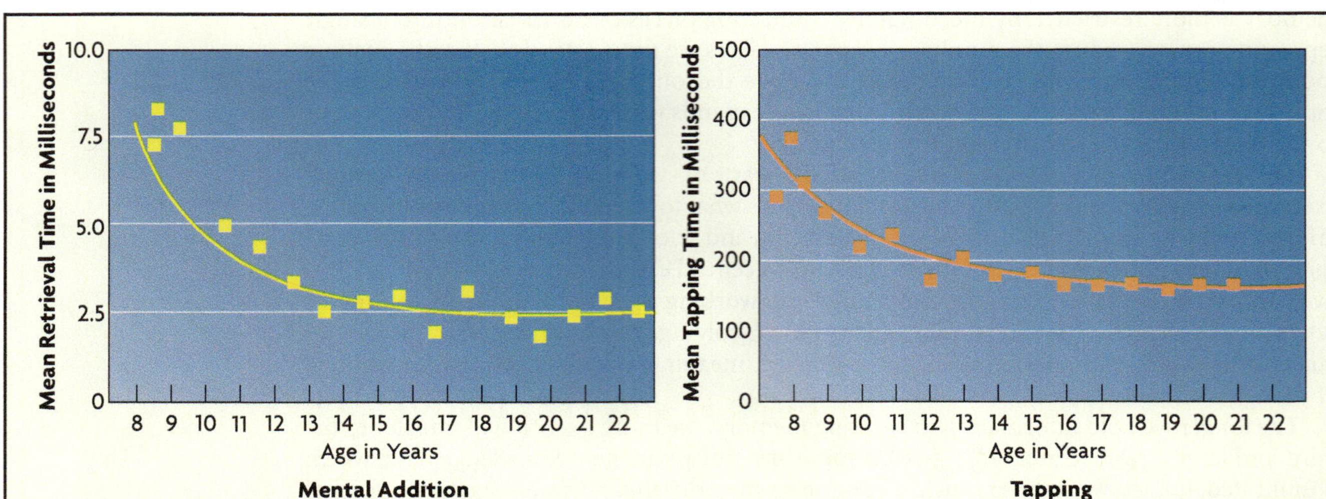

Figure 7.2 **Age-related decline in processing time, illustrated for mental addition and tapping.**
Processing speed improves similarly across many tasks, even perceptual–motor activities such as tapping as fast as possible, which do not rely on mental strategies. This common trend implies an age-related gain in basic processing capacity. (Reprinted from R. Kail, "Developmental Functions for Speeds of Cognitive Processes," *Journal of Experimental Child Psychology,* 45, p. 361, copyright 1988, with permission from Elsevier and Robert V. Kail; and from R. Kail, "Processing Time Declines Exponentially During Childhood and Adolescence," *Developmental Psychology,* 27, p. 265. Copyright © 1991 by the American Psychological Association. Adapted with permission of the American Psychological Association.)

pattern was also evident when participants performed perceptual–motor tasks that do not rely on strategies, such as releasing a button or tapping as fast as possible (Kail, 1991).

The changes in processing speed shown in Figure 7.2 have been found in Canada, Korea, and the United States (Fry & Hale, 1996; Kail & Park, 1992). Similarity in development across diverse tasks in several cultures implies a fundamental change in efficiency of the information-processing system, perhaps due to myelination or synaptic pruning in the brain (see Chapter 5) (Kail, 2003). Increased processing speed enhances working memory (Luna et al., 2004). It enables older children and adults to scan information more quickly, to transform it more rapidly with strategies, and therefore to hold more information in their cognitive systems at once.

Gains in working-memory capacity and in processing speed contribute vitally to children's ability to learn. In middle childhood and adolescence, scores on memory span and speed-of-processing tasks consistently predict academic achievement in language arts, math, and science (Colom et al., 2007; Gathercole et al., 2005; St Clair-Thompson & Gathercole, 2006).

Connectionism

To discover exactly what happens in the brain as children master new skills, researchers in developmental cognitive neuroscience (see Chapter 1, page 24) use computers to devise **connectionist,** or **artificial neural network, models,** which simulate the workings of the most basic information-processing units: neurons and their connections. These models reveal how strengthening of simple connections between units leads to new cognitive capacities, just as strengthening of synaptic connections between neurons promotes development of brain functioning.

An artificial neural network consists of thousands of simple processing units organized into layers, much like the brain's neurological structure. A typical network includes an *input layer,* which encodes the task; one or more *hidden layers,* representing information needed to perform the task; and an *output layer,* which generates a response (Figure 7.3 shows a simplified example). Like neurons, the units send signals when the stimulation they receive from other units reaches a certain strength. Because information is distributed throughout the system—over all the units, acting in parallel (simultaneously)—artificial neural networks are sometimes called *parallel distributed processing systems.*

The connections between units are programmed with a basic learning procedure. For example, the network might be structured to respond to regularities in the movements of objects or in the speech stream. The network is given a task (such as locating hidden objects or identifying words in speech sounds) and receives feedback about the accuracy of its responses. If a response is correct, the connections that produced it strengthen; if incorrect, they weaken. If the network's responses resemble those of individuals of different ages, researchers conclude that the network is a good model of human learning and development.

Connectionists have succeeded in depicting changes in infants' and children's performance on a variety of tasks, including object permanence, responsiveness to native-language speech sounds, early vocabulary growth, mastery of basic grammatical rules, formation of certain concepts, beginning reading of words, attainment of conservation, and problem solving (Jones, Ritter, & Wood, 2000; Mareschal, 2003; Plunkett et al., 1997; Powell, Plaut, & Funnell, 2006; Sirois & Schultz, 2003). Findings reveal that a great deal of inner change in the strength of connections generally occurs before a network—and therefore a child behaving similarly—consistently displays a correct response. Consequently, networks show that gradual, internal learning often precedes changes in behavior that—viewed from outside the system—appear abrupt, or stagelike. For example, recall from Chapter 6 that infants' knowledge of object permanence, assessed through looking preferences in violation-of-expectation studies, precedes knowledge based on reaching. Connectionist models

■ **Figure 7.3** **A simplified example of an artificial neural network.**

Processing units in the computer are organized into layers, much like the brain's neurological structure. Stimulation turns on input units, which encode the task. Hidden units represent information, and output units generate a response. Researchers program connections between units with a basic learning procedure. Connections that lead to correct responses strengthen; those that lead to incorrect responses weaken.

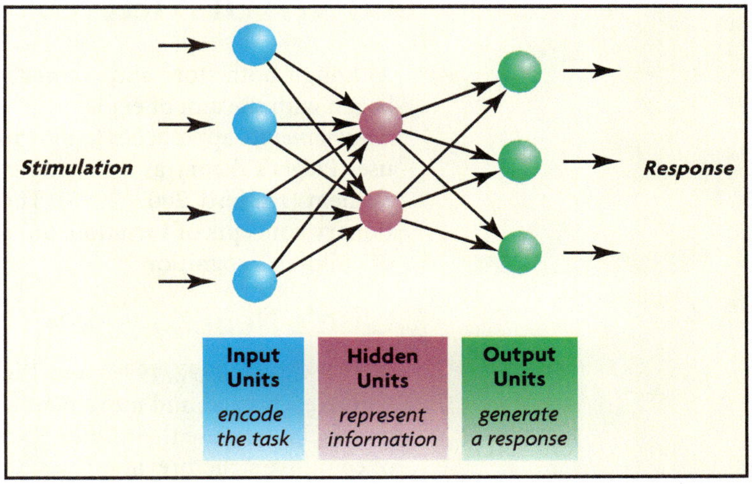

suggest that neural networks are initially weak, sufficient only to support looking. Reaching requires stronger connections—ones that integrate information across regions of the cerebral cortex (Johnson & Mareschal, 2001; Munakata, 2004; Munakata & McClelland, 2003).

In connectionist models, a few built-in procedures get learning started on many types of tasks; the system learns by capturing regularities in diverse environmental inputs. Consequently, connectionists claim that their findings present a powerful argument against the core knowledge perspective, which assumes that infants begin life with innate, special-purpose knowledge systems (see Chapter 6, pages 260–261). Instead, connectionists see the human cognitive system as a general processing device that gradually attains domain-specific competencies as relevant learning opportunities arise (Karmiloff-Smith, 1999; Thelen & Bates, 2003).

Artificial neural networks are still far from duplicating the operation of the human brain. Perhaps because their internal representations are limited to connection strengths, most networks learn slowly, usually requiring many more exposures to a task than children or adults and often failing to reach an adult level of competence. Networks do not construct plans, hypotheses, and propositions, which foster complex, highly efficient human learning (Cowan, 2003). Finally, as we will see when we address strategy choice—a developmental model of information processing—children are great experimenters. To reach the most efficient means of solving a problem, they change their strategies not only after they make errors (as artificial neural networks do) but also after they succeed!

To overcome these deficiencies, connectionists are attempting to devise more complete models of brain functioning. They are experimenting with *constructivist connectionist models,* which add new units and connections in the course of learning a task (just as brain regions gradually become interconnected) and remove units and connections that do not contribute to learning (as in synaptic pruning). Constructivist networks recognize that the brain's structure changes in response to the learner's experiences. Though still imperfect, these models better capture infants' and children's rapid progress on diverse tasks, including visual tracking, language, and problem-solving (Westermann et al., 2006, 2007). They also shed light on how experiences might affect the specialization and coordinated functioning of brain regions, which makes possible more complex, efficient learning.

In sum, connectionist models help us understand the cognitive consequences of changes in neural connections, while reminding us that a full understanding of cognitive development must take into account the operation of its most basic units (Johnson & Mareschal, 2001). More refined connectionist models are currently under way—ones that account for age-related performance on a wider variety of tasks, for sensitive periods in development, and for learning impairments resulting from abnormal brain development and brain injuries (Thomas & Johnson, 2006; Westermann et al., 2006).

Developmental Theories of Information Processing

Although both store and connectionist models have implications for development, neither began with the aim of explaining how children's thinking changes. Next, we will consider two *developmental* approaches to information processing. The first, Case's *neo-Piagetian perspective,* uses Piaget's theory as a starting point for constructing an overall vision of cognitive development (Halford, 2002, 2005). The second, Siegler's *model of strategy choice,* draws on evolutionary concepts of variation and selection to explain the diversity and ever-changing nature of children's cognition.

Case's Neo-Piagetian Theory

Robbie Case's (1992, 1998) **neo-Piagetian theory** accepts Piaget's stages but attributes change within each stage, and movement from one stage to the next, to increases in the efficiency with which children use their limited working memory capacity. Each stage involves a distinct type of cognitive structure: in infancy, sensory input and physical actions; in early childhood, internal representations of events and actions; in middle childhood, simple transformations of representations; and in adolescence, complex transformations of representations. As children become more efficient processors, the amount of information they can hold and combine in working memory expands, making this sequence possible. Three factors contribute to cognitive change:

- *Brain development.* Recall our discussion of synaptic growth, synaptic pruning, and myelination in Chapter 5. These neurological changes improve the efficiency of thought, leading to readiness for each stage. According to Case, biology imposes a system-wide ceiling on cognitive development. At any given time, the child cannot exceed a certain upper limit of processing speed. (Refer back to age-related gains in speed of processing on pages 278–280.)
- *Practice with schemes and automization.* In Case's theory, Piagetian schemes are the child's mental strategies. Through repeated use, the child's schemes become more automatic, freeing working memory for combining existing schemes and generating new ones. Notice how Case's mechanisms of change offer a clarified view of Piaget's concepts of assimilation and accommodation. *Practicing schemes* (assimilation) leads to *automization,* which *releases working memory* for other activities, permitting *scheme combination and construction* (accommodation).
- *Formation of central conceptual structures.* Once the schemes of a Piagetian stage become sufficiently automatic, enough space in working memory is available to consolidate them into an improved representational form. As a result, children generate **central conceptual structures**—networks of concepts and relations that permit them to think about a wide range of situations in more advanced ways. Consequently, processing efficiency expands further (Case, 1996, 1998). When children form new central conceptual structures, they move to the next stage of development.

Let's take a familiar set of tasks—conservation—to illustrate Case's ideas. Imagine a 5-year-old who cannot yet conserve liquid but who has some isolated schemes: (1) After water is poured from a tall glass into a short glass, the height of the water level is reduced. (2) After water is poured from a thin into a wide glass, the width of the water increases. As the child gains experience in transferring liquids from one container to another, these schemes become automatic, and she combines them into a conserving response. A similar sequence occurs in other conservation situations—involving, for example, mass and weight. Eventually the child coordinates several task-specific conserving responses into a new, broadly applicable principle: a central conceptual structure. When this happens, cognition moves from simple to complex transformations of representations, or from concrete to formal operational thought.

As this 6-year-old practices counting money, she will become a more efficient processor, coordinating an increasing number of task dimensions into a central conceptual structure—a general representation that she can apply in many situations. © JGI/Getty Images/Blend Images

Case and his colleagues have applied his theory to many tasks: solving arithmetic word problems, understanding stories, drawing pictures, sight-reading music, handling money, and interpreting social situations (Case, 1992, 1998; Case & Okamoto, 1996). In each case, children coordinate an increasing number of task dimensions with age. In understanding stories, for example, preschoolers grasp only a single story line. By the early school years, they combine two story lines into a single plot. Around age 9 to 11, central conceptual structures integrate multiple dimensions: Children tell coherent stories with a main plot and several subplots. Figure 7.4 on page 282 shows similar changes in children's drawings.

Case's (1998) theory offers an information-processing account of the *continuum of acquisition*—that many understandings appear in specific situations at different times rather than being mastered all at once (see page 260 in Chapter 6). First, different forms of the same logical insight, such as the various conservation tasks, vary in their processing demands; those acquired later require that more information be held and combined in working memory. Second, children's experiences vary widely. A child who often listens to and tells stories but rarely draws pictures displays more advanced central conceptual structures in storytelling. And children who do not show central conceptual structures expected for their age can usually be

Figure 7.4 **Development of central conceptual structures in Case's neo-Piagetian theory.**
Case identified the same general sequence in children's performance on many tasks, here shown for drawings. Children were asked to "draw a picture of a mother and a father holding hands in a park, with their little baby on the grass in front of them, and a tree far off behind." (a) Preschoolers focused on one dimension. They depicted objects separately, ignoring their spatial arrangement. (b) During the early school years, children coordinated two dimensions, showing both features of objects and relationships among objects. (c) Nine- to 11-year-olds integrated multiple dimensions, using perspective to represent several points of reference (near, midway, and far). (From R. Case & Y. Okamoto, 1996, "The Role of Central Conceptual Structures in the Development of Children's Thought," *Monographs of the Society for Research in Child Development,* 61[246, 1–2], p. 106. © The Society for Research in Child Development, Inc. Adapted by permission. Courtesy of Robbie Case.)

trained to attain them (Case, Griffin, & Kelly, 2001). Therefore, Case's theory is better able than Piaget's to account for unevenness in cognitive development. Although Case's ideas remain to be tested with many more tasks, his theory is unique in offering an integrated picture of how children's processing efficiency, practice with strategies, and constructive efforts to reorganize their thinking interact to produce development.

Siegler's Model of Strategy Choice

Robert Siegler's (1996, 2005) **model of strategy choice** is one of several current efforts to apply an evolutionary perspective to children's cognition. When given challenging problems, children generate a *variety* of strategies. With experience, some strategies are *selected;* they become more frequent and "survive." Others become less frequent and "die off." Like physical characteristics, children's mental strategies display *variation* and *selection,* yielding adaptive problem-solving techniques.

To study children's strategy use, Siegler used the microgenetic research design (see Chapter 2, pages 63–64), presenting children with many problems over an extended time period. He found that children experiment with diverse strategies on many types of problems—basic math facts, numerical estimation, conservation, memory for lists of items, reading first words, telling time, spelling, even tic-tac-toe. Consider 5-year-old Darryl, who was adding marbles tucked into pairs of small bags that his kindergarten teacher had set out on a table. As Darryl dealt with each pair, his strategies varied. Sometimes he guessed, not applying any strategy. At other times, he counted from 1 on his fingers. For example, for bags containing 2 + 4 marbles, his fingers popped up one by one as he exclaimed, "1, 2, 3, 4, 5, 6!" Occasionally he started with the lower digit, 2, and "counted on" ("2, 3, 4, 5, 6"). Or he began with the higher digit, 4, and counted on ("4, 5, 6"), a strategy called *min* because it minimizes the work. Sometimes he retrieved the answer from memory.

Siegler found that strategy use for basic math facts—and many other types of problems—follows an *overlapping-waves pattern* (see Figure 7.5). Performance tends to progress from a single incorrect approach, to a highly variable state in which children try different strategies, to use of a more advanced procedure. Even 2-year-olds solving simple problems, such as how to use a tool to obtain an out-of-reach toy, display this sequence (Chen & Siegler, 2000; Siegler, 2007). While trying strategies, children observe which work best, which work less well, and which are ineffective. Gradually they select strategies on the basis of two adaptive criteria: *accuracy* and *speed*—for basic addition, the *min* strategy. As children home in on effective strategies, they learn more about the problems at hand. As a result, correct solutions become more strongly associated with problems, and children display the most efficient strategy—automatic retrieval of the answer.

How do children move from less to more effective strategies? Often they discover faster, more accurate procedures by using more time-consuming techniques. For example, by repeatedly returning to counting on his fingers, Darryl began to recognize the number of fingers he held up. And by alternating between counting from the lower digit and using *min*, Darryl directly observed *min*'s speed and accuracy (Siegler & Jenkins, 1989). Indeed, when given the same problems repeatedly over a short time interval, children regress from more advanced to less advanced approaches on as many as 40 percent of the trials! The more variable their strategies, the better their eventual performance (Siegler, 2007). Even on a single item, children may generate varying procedures, as indicated by occasions in which their words and gestures differ (see the From Research to Practice box on page 284 for the significance of these mismatches for readiness to learn).

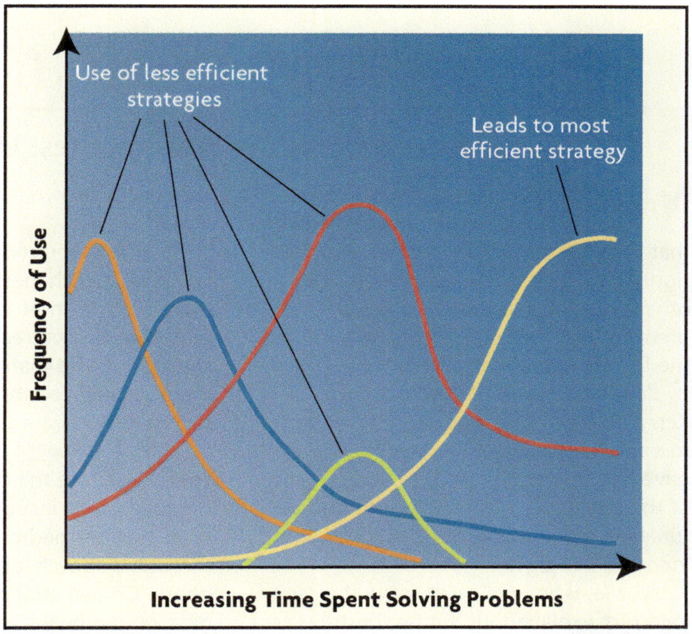

■ **Figure 7.5** **Overlapping-waves pattern of strategy use in problem solving.**
When given challenging problems, a child generates a variety of strategies, each represented by a wave. The waves overlap because the child oscillates among several strategies at a given time. Use of each strategy, depicted by the height of the wave, is constantly changing. As the child observes which strategies work best, which work less well, and which are ineffective, the strategy that results in the most rapid, accurate solutions wins out. (From R. S. Siegler, *Emerging Minds: The Process of Change in Children's Thinking.* Copyright © 1996 by Oxford University Press, Inc. Used by permission of Oxford University Press, Inc.)

Certain problems dramatize the need for a better strategy. When Darryl opened a pair of bags, one containing ten marbles, the other two marbles, he realized that *min* would be best. Reasoning about concepts relevant to the problems at hand also helps (Canobi, Reeve, & Pattison, 1998). First graders more often use *min* after realizing that regardless of the order in which two sets are combined, they yield the same results ($2 + 4 = 6$ and $4 + 2 = 6$). Finally, when children are taught an effective strategy, they usually adopt it, abandoning less successful techniques (Alibali, 1999; Siegler & Booth, 2004). Sometimes, however, children do not immediately take advantage of new, more adaptive strategies. As we will see in later sections, using a new strategy taxes working memory, and children may resist giving up a well-established strategy for a new one because gains in speed of thinking are small at first.

Siegler's model reveals that no child thinks in just one way, even on a single task. A child given the same problem on two occasions often uses different approaches. Strategy variability is vital for devising new, more adaptive ways of thinking, which "evolve" through extensive experience solving problems.

The model of strategy choice offers a powerful image of development that overcomes deficiencies of the stage approach in accounting for both diversity and continuous change in children's thinking. By exploiting the microgenetic method, researchers have captured periods of high variability in children's strategy use that contribute vitally to cognitive advances. Typical cross-sectional and longitudinal studies, which easily miss such periods, make cognitive change appear more abrupt (and therefore stagelike) than it actually is.

Ask Yourself

Review Summarize evidence indicating that both basic capacity and speed of information processing increase with age. In Case's neo-Piagetian theory, how do gains in processing efficiency contribute to development?

Review What is a connectionist, or artificial neural network, model? What challenge do connectionists present to the core knowledge perspective?

Apply Five-year-old Kayla used several strategies to solve conservation-of-number problems involving rows of pennies. On one, she said, "The rows aren't the same." On the next, she said, "The rows have the same number because you didn't add any." On the third, she said, "I counted the pennies. The rows have the same number." Did she move from a more to a less mature strategy? Explain. Why is it beneficial for Kayla to experiment with strategies?

Connect Recall the dynamic systems perspective, which assumes that periods of instability precede a reorganized, more effectively functioning, stable system (see pages 29–30 in Chapter 1 and page 146 in Chapter 4). How are findings on children's strategy development consistent with this idea?

▪ *From* Research *to* Practice ▪

Speech–Gesture Mismatches: Using the Hand to Read the Mind

Mr. Beal introduced his fourth-grade class to the concept of equivalence—that the quantity on one side of an equals sign is the same as the quantity on the other side. Then he watched as several children stepped up to the blackboard to work the following problem: 5 + 3 + 4 = __ + 4.

"I added 5 + 3 + 4 + 4 equals 16," Kerry said, pointing to each number as she mentioned it and then to the blank as she gave her answer, ignoring the placement of the equals sign. Kerry's speech and gestures were consistent: Both revealed an incorrect strategy.

Noelle, who went next, gave the same incorrect explanation. But her gestures sent a different message. As she spoke, she pointed to each number on the left, then touched the equals sign, then the 4 on the right, and finally rested her finger on the blank. Noelle showed a *speech–gesture mismatch:* Her hand movements suggested she knew more than she could say. Over the next few weeks, Noelle mastered equivalence problems more rapidly than Kerry. How can we account for Noelle's faster progress?

According to Susan Goldin-Meadow, children who produce speech–gesture mismatches are in a transitional state. Their behavior indicates that they are considering two contradictory strategies at once, a sign of readiness to learn. In a microgenetic study, the researchers identified two groups of children who did not have a full understanding of addition-based equivalence problems: speech–gesture matched and speech–gesture mismatched. As the children worked more problems, some in each group received feedback on the accuracy of their answers along with instruction explaining the equivalence principle; others received no intervention. Finally, children's learning was assessed as they worked problems on their own (Goldin-Meadow, 2003a, 2006b).

Children who received instruction following a speech–gesture mismatch were more likely than others to move out of that state to a correct answer, based on a speech–gesture match. They also more often generalized their new knowledge to multiplication-based equivalence problems (5 × 3 × 4 = 5 × __). Interestingly, the few speech–gesture match children who improved with instruction generalized what they learned only if they first passed through a speech–gesture mismatch phase. Correct strategies appeared first in gesture and only later in speech.

Children on the verge of learning appear to have strategies that are accessible to gesture but not to speech (Goldin-Meadow, 2002). Perhaps expressing a strategy in gesture that differs from one in speech facilitates awareness of conflicting ideas, encouraging the child to resolve the discrepancy in favor of the more effective strategy. Children in a mismatch state are particularly open to teaching. Speech–gesture mismatches also may indicate that the neural pathways of interest to connectionists are growing stronger and are about to reach a critical juncture.

Parents and teachers can use children's gestures to provide instruction at the most opportune moment. Indeed, many adults are attuned to children's speech–gesture mismatches, and others can be taught to notice them (Goldin-Meadow, 2005a). In one study, adults were more likely to teach a variety of problem-solving strategies to children who displayed mismatches than to children who did not (Goldin-Meadow & Singer, 2003). In doing so, they encouraged the "mismatchers" to try out many strategies, which—as Siegler's model of strategy choice makes clear—facilitates learning.

Finally, children who adopt the gestures a teacher uses are more likely to profit from instruction (Cook & Goldin-Meadow, 2006b). Adults who gesture while teaching encourage students to use their hands to support learning. How might gesturing contribute to advances in understanding? By enabling children (and adults) to represent thoughts they cannot yet express in words, it may lighten demands on working memory (Goldin-Meadow, 2006b). As a result, learners can allocate additional cognitive resources to grappling with the task.

A 7-year-old works on a homework assignment. If her hand gestures indicate that she understands more than she can articulate—a speech–gesture mismatch—this may be an opportune moment for instruction. © Blue Jean Images/Getty Images

Attention

The following sections address children's processing in the major parts of the cognitive system—how children encode information, operate on it in working memory so it will transfer to long-term memory, and retrieve it so they can think and solve problems. We begin with research on the development of attention. Attention is fundamental to human thinking because it determines which information will be considered in any task. Parents and teachers notice that young children spend only a short time involved in a task, have difficulty focusing on details, and are easily distracted. During early and middle childhood, attention improves greatly, becoming more selective, adaptable, and planful.

Sustained, Selective, and Adaptable Attention

During the first year, infants attend to novel and eye-catching events, orienting to them more quickly and tracking their movements more effectively. They also spend more time focused on complex stimuli, such as toys and video clips, and display greater slowing of heart rate while engaged—a physiological indicator of *sustained attention* (Courage, Reynolds, & Richards, 2006). In toddlerhood, children become increasingly capable of intentional, or goal-directed, behavior (see Chapter 6, page 229). Consequently, attraction to novelty declines (but does not disappear), and sustained attention improves further, especially during play. A toddler who engages in goal-directed behavior even in a limited way, such as stacking blocks or putting them in a container, must sustain attention to reach the goal. In a study of toddlers and young preschoolers, sustained attention during play with toys increased sharply between ages 2 and 3½ years (Ruff & Capozzoli, 2003).

Rapid growth of the frontal lobes of the cerebral cortex (see Chapter 5), the capacity to generate increasingly complex play goals (children must concentrate to attain them), and adult scaffolding of attention are jointly responsible for this gain in sustained attention (Ruff & Cappozoli, 2003). When parents help toddlers and young preschoolers maintain a focus of attention by offering suggestions, questions, and comments about the child's current interest, sustained attention improves. More attentive children are better developed, cognitively and socially (Bono & Stifter, 2003; Landry et al., 2000; Murphy et al., 2007). Many skills, including language, exploration, problem solving, academic learning, social interaction, cooperation, and complex play, benefit from an improved ability to concentrate.

As sustained attention increases, children become better at focusing on only those aspects of a situation that are relevant to their goals. To study this increasing selectivity of attention, researchers introduce irrelevant stimuli into a task and see how well children respond to its central elements. For example, they might present a stream of numbers on a computer screen and ask children to press a button whenever a particular sequence of two digits (such as "1" and then "9") appears. Findings show that selective attention improves sharply between ages 6 and 10, with gains continuing into adulthood (Goldberg, Maurer, & Lewis, 2001; Lin, Hsiao, & Chen, 1999; Smith et al., 1998). Tasks tapping everyday requirements for selective attention reveal similar trends. In one study, researchers showed 6- to 11-year-olds computer images of safe and dangerous road-crossing scenes, sometimes with and sometimes without visual and auditory distractors (Tabibi & Pfeffer, 2007). Ability to distinguish safe from dangerous sites increased with age, especially in the presence of distractors (see Figure 7.6), and also correlated positively with scores on laboratory attention tasks.

Older children also flexibly adapt their attention to task requirements. When asked to sort cards with pictures varying in both color and shape, children age 5 and older can switch their basis of sorting from color to shape when asked to do so; younger children persist in sorting in just one way (Brooks et al., 2003; Zelazo, Frye, & Rapus, 1996). Furthermore, with age, children adapt their attention to changes in their own learning. When given lists of items to learn and allowed to select half for further study, first graders do not choose systematically, but third graders select those they had previously missed (Masur, McIntyre, &

■ **Figure 7.6** **Gains in selective attention from age 6 to 11 years on a task requiring children to distinguish safe from dangerous road-crossing scenes.** Children viewed computer images of road-crossing scenes, pushing a green key to indicate a safe scene and a red key to indicate an unsafe scene. On some sets of scenes, researchers introduced visual and auditory distractors, such as a dog barking, a train whistling, or a boy shouting. Accuracy increased with age, even under distracting conditions. (Adapted from Tabibi & Pfeffer, 2007.)

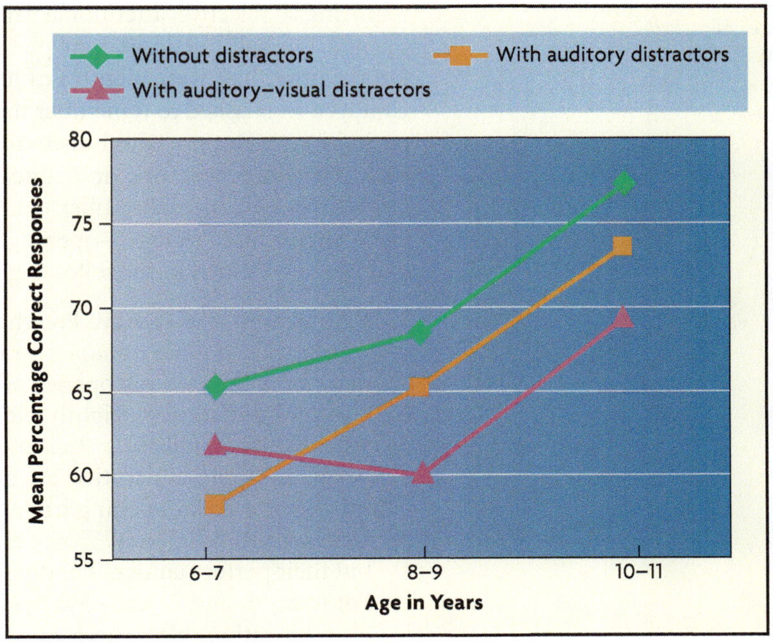

These Japanese schoolchildren cross the street at a busy intersection, where many distracting stimuli tax their capacity to keep track of oncoming vehicles and traffic signals. In middle childhood, children make dramatic gains in selective attention, as indicated by their ability to distinguish safe from dangerous road crossings. © Jeremy Hoare/Alamy

Flavell, 1973). In research presenting complex information, such as prose passages, the ability to allocate attention based on previous performance continues to improve into the college years (Brown, Smiley, & Lawton, 1978).

How do children acquire selective, adaptable attention? Gains in two factors—inhibition and attentional strategies—are important.

• Inhibition Selective attention depends on **inhibition**—the ability to control internal and external distracting stimuli. Individuals who are skilled at inhibition can prevent the mind from straying to alternative attractive thoughts and can keep stimuli unrelated to a current goal from capturing their attention (Dempster & Corkill, 1999). By keeping irrelevant stimuli from cluttering working memory, inhibition supports many information-processing skills (Bjorklund & Harnishfeger, 1995; Handley et al., 2004; Klenberg, Korkman, & Lahti-Nuuttila, 2001). Besides helping children remember, reason, and solve problems, it helps them control behavior in social situations. As we will see in later chapters, to get along with others, children must learn to restrain impulses, keep negative emotions in check, and resist temptation.

The ability to inhibit thoughts and behavior improves from infancy on. Between age 3 and 4 years, for example, preschoolers perform considerably better in situations in which they must follow some commands but not others, as in the game "Simon Says" (Jones, Rothbart, & Posner, 2003). On more complex tasks that involve ignoring distracting stimuli, marked gains in inhibition occur from early to middle childhood and continue into adolescence (Johnson, Im-Bolter, & Pascual-Leone, 2003). These gains are linked to development of the cerebral cortex. ERP and fMRI measures show a steady, age-related increase in activation of diverse cortical regions, especially the frontal lobes, while children and adolescents engage in activities that require suppression of inappropriate responses (Bartgis, Lilly, & Thomas, 2003; Diamond, 2004; Luna et al., 2001). Children and adults whose frontal lobes are damaged usually cannot ignore irrelevant information (Dempster, 1995).

In sum, by clearing unnecessary stimuli, inhibition increases available space in working memory. This, in turn, opens the door to effective strategy use—working more effectively with information held in mind. Can high-quality preschool education enhance inhibition and other aspects of cognitive control? Turn to the Social Issues box on page 288 to find out.

• Attentional Strategies Patricia Miller and her colleagues gave 3- to 9-year-olds a task requiring a selective attentional strategy—a large box with rows of doors that could be opened. On half the doors were pictures of cages, indicating that behind each was an animal. On the other half were pictures of houses, indicating that they contained household objects. Children were asked to remember the location of each object in one group, then given a study period in which they could open any doors they wished. Next they were shown pictures of each relevant object, one at a time, and asked to point to the object's location (DeMarie-Dreblow & Miller, 1988; Miller et al., 1986; Woody-Ramsey & Miller, 1988). The most efficient attentional strategy—opening only doors with relevant pictures on them—emerged and became refined in the following sequence:

1. **Production deficiency.** Preschoolers rarely engage in attentional strategies. In other words, they fail to *produce* strategies when they could be helpful. On the task just described, they simply opened all the doors.
2. **Control deficiency.** Slightly older children sometimes produce strategies, but not consistently. They fail to *control,* or execute, strategies effectively. For example, 5-year-olds began to apply a selective attentional strategy—opening only relevant doors—but, at times, reverted to opening irrelevant doors.
3. **Utilization deficiency.** Young elementary school children execute strategies consistently, but their performance either does not improve or improves less than that of older children. For many 6- and 7-year-olds, opening only the relevant doors did not increase memory for object locations after the pictures were removed from the doors.

4. **Effective strategy use.** By the mid-elementary school years, children use strategies consistently, and performance improves. (Miller, 2000)

As we will soon see, these phases also characterize children's use of memory strategies. Why, when children first use a strategy, does it sometimes not work well? Recall from our discussion of Siegler's model of strategy choice that initially, applying a strategy requires so much effort and attention that little space in working memory remains to perform other parts of the task well (Woody-Dorning & Miller, 2001). Consistent with this interpretation, reducing the demands of the task by having an adult perform the strategy for the child (by opening relevant doors) led to substantial gains in memory for object locations (DeMarie-Dreblow & Miller, 1988).

Another reason a new strategy may not lead to performance gains is that young children are not good at monitoring their task performance (Schneider & Bjorklund, 2003). Because they fail to keep track of how well a strategy is working, they do not apply it consistently or refine it in other ways.

Planning

With age, children's attention changes in another way: It becomes more planful. **Planning** involves thinking out a sequence of acts ahead of time and allocating attention accordingly to reach a goal (Scholnick, 1995). The seeds of effective planning are present in infancy. When researchers showed 2- and 3-month-olds a series of pictures that alternated in a predictable left–right sequence, the babies quickly learned to shift their focus to the location of the next stimulus before it appeared (Wentworth & Haith, 1998). And recall 4-month-olds' ability to engage in predictive tracking of objects' movements (see pages 162–163 in Chapter 4). Even young infants' attention seems to be "future-oriented."

For familiar tasks that are not too complex, preschoolers sometimes generate and follow a plan. For example, by age 4, they search for a lost object in a play yard systematically, looking only in locations between where they last saw the object and where they discovered it missing (Wellman, Somerville, & Haake, 1979). But when asked to compare detailed pictures, preschoolers are less systematic than school-age children in their visual search (Vurpillot, 1968). And on complex tasks, older children make decisions about what to do first and what to do next in a more orderly fashion. When 5- to 9-year-olds were given lists of items to obtain from a play grocery store, older children more often took time to scan the store before shopping and also paused more often to look for each item before moving to get it. Consequently, they followed shorter routes through the aisles (Gauvain & Rogoff, 1989; Szepkouski, Gauvain, & Carberry, 1994).

The development of planning illustrates how attention becomes coordinated with other cognitive processes. To solve problems involving multiple steps, children must postpone action in favor of weighing alternatives, organizing task materials (such as items on a grocery list), and remembering the steps of their plan so they can attend to each one in sequence. Along the way, they must monitor how well the plan works and revise it if necessary. Clearly, planning places heavy demands on working memory. Not surprisingly, even when young children do plan, they often forget important steps.

Children learn much from cultural tools that support planning—directions for playing games, patterns for construction, recipes for cooking—especially when they collaborate with more expert planners. When 4- to 7-year-olds were observed jointly constructing a toy with their mothers, the mothers provided basic information about the usefulness of plans and how to implement specific steps: "Do you want to look at the picture and see what goes where? What piece do you need first?" After working with their mothers, younger children more often referred to the plan when building on their own (Gauvain, 2004; Gauvain, de la Ossa, & Hurtado-Ortiz, 2001).

Having many opportunities to practice planning helps children understand its components and use that knowledge. Parents can foster planning by encouraging it in everyday activities, from loading the dishwasher to planning for a vacation. In one study, parent–child discussions involving planning at ages 4 to 9 predicted planning competence in adolescence (Gauvain & Huard, 1999). The demands of academic tasks—and teachers' explanations of how to plan—also contribute to gains in planning.

This child in Newfoundland, Canada, participates in traditional Viking boat building under the guidance of an expert. By engaging in this complex, multi-step project, he learns important lessons about planning—what to do first and what to do next in an orderly fashion. © Richard T. Nowitz/CORBIS

▪ Social Issues ▪

Enhancing Cognitive Control Through Preschool Education

Cognitive control refers to three core abilities: inhibition, effortfully holding and operating on information in working memory, and flexibly adjusting attention to changes in task requirements. Measured as early as 3 to 5 years of age, good cognitive control skills predict reading and math achievement from kindergarten through high school (Blair & Razza, 2007; Duncan et al., 2007; Gathercole et al., 2005). In contrast, poor cognitive control—often seen in children from stressed low-income homes—is linked to emotional and behavior problems, including ADHD (see pages 290–291) and, in adolescence, drug use and delinquency.

In Tools of the Mind, a preschool curriculum inspired by Vygotsky's theory, scaffolding of cognitive control is woven into virtually all classroom activities. For example:

- Teachers model and encourage private speech as a means of controlling their own thinking and behavior.
- Teachers provide external aids to support attention and memory. In "buddy reading," children pair up and take turns telling a story to go with a picture book. Before they begin, the teacher gives one child a drawing of lips, the other a drawing of an ear, explaining that "ears don't talk, ears listen." The drawing reminds the listener to inhibit talking and to think of a question to ask the reader about the story, which verifies comprehension.
- Teachers lead children in rule-switching games in which regular movement patterns shift often, requiring flexibility of attention.
- Teachers encourage complex make-believe play, guiding children in joint planning of play scenarios before enacting them. Recall that in Vygotsky's view, make-believe play helps children suppress impulses, follow social rules, and use thought to guide behavior. (Bodrova & Leong, 2007)

A 4-year-old who has experienced the Tools curriculum completes the "hearts and flowers" task, which assesses ability to inhibit behavior. © Martin Dee

In an evaluation of the success of Tools of the Mind in enhancing cognitive control, nearly 150 children from low-income families were randomly assigned either to Tools classrooms or to comparison classrooms with similar content and activities but without addressing cognitive control (Diamond et al., 2007). At the end of their preschool experience, children were given two cognitive-control measures.

The first task, illustrated in Figure 7.7a, assessed ability to inhibit behavior: A red heart or flower appeared on the right or left side of a computer screen. On the first set of trials, children were asked to follow a *congruent rule* ("Press the button on the same side as the heart"). On the second set of trials, children had to follow an *incongruent rule,* which required inhibition of the same-side response ("Press the button on the side opposite the flower"). A third set of trials alternated between the congruent and incongruent rules, requiring children to hold both rules in working memory while flexibly shifting attention between them.

The second task measured ability to inhibit distracting stimuli: Children had to focus on a small, central shape, ignoring a larger shape around it, or vice versa (see Figure 7.7b). On *congruent trials,* inner and outer shapes were the same (both circles or both triangles). On *incongruent trials,* the two shapes differed (triangle inside and circle outside, or the reverse). Again, intermixing congruent and incongruent trials tapped effortful working memory and attention flexibility.

Findings revealed no group differences on congruent trials. But on incongruent trials (taxing inhibition), Tools children exceeded their comparison-group peers by 10 percent or more correct responses. On the more demanding mixed trials (taxing all three aspects of cognitive control), Tools children excelled even more (by at least 25 percent correct responses). Incongruent-trial and, especially, mixed-trial scores predicted end-of-year language, literacy, and math progress.

Tools of the Mind—currently being implemented in public preschools in several U.S. states—demonstrates that cognitive control can be taught at an early age, at minimal additional expense. Nurturing cognitive control through the Tools program may prove powerful in early prevention of academic, emotional, and behavior problems, especially among economically disadvantaged children.

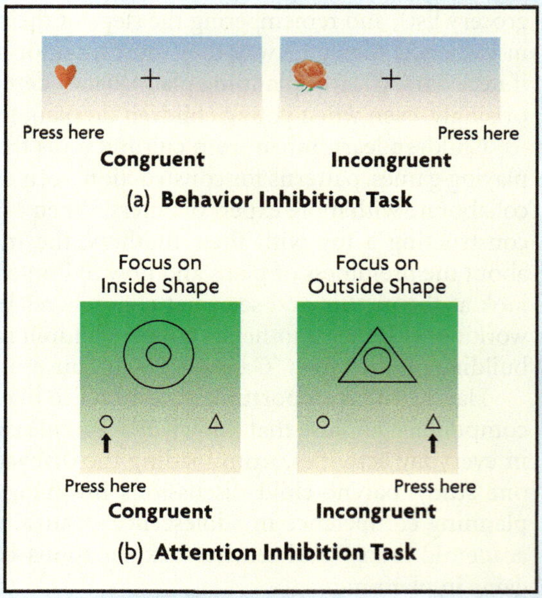

■ **Figure 7.7** **Tasks used to assess cognitive control in Tools of the Mind and comparison preschoolers.**
Mixed trials taxed all three aspects of cognitive control: inhibition, effortful working memory, and attention flexibility. Tools of the Mind preschoolers greatly exceeded comparison-group agemates in cognitive control. (Adapted from Diamond et al., 2007.)

The attentional strategies just considered are crucial for success in school. Unfortunately, some children have great difficulty paying attention. See the Biology and Environment box on pages 290–291 for a discussion of the serious learning and behavior problems of children with attention-deficit hyperactivity disorder.

Ask Yourself

Review What aspect of brain development supports gains in inhibition? How does inhibition support development of attention and other information-processing skills?

Review What advances in information processing contribute to improved planning in middle childhood? What can adults do to promote children's planning skills?

Apply At age 7, Jonah played his piano pieces from beginning to end instead of spending extra time on the hard sections. Around age 8, he devoted more time to sections he knew least well, but his performance did not improve for several months. What explains Jonah's gradual gains in strategy use and performance?

Reflect Describe an instance in which you applied a strategy for the first time but experienced a utilization deficiency. Why do you think the deficiency occurred, and how did you overcome it?

Memory

As attention improves, so do *memory strategies*—deliberate mental activities we use to increase the likelihood of holding information in working memory and transferring it to our long-term knowledge base. In Chapters 4 and 6, we saw that during the first two years, memory for objects, people, and events—as assessed in operant conditioning, habituation, and deferred-imitation studies—undergoes dramatic gains. With age, babies remember more information over longer periods (see pages 139 and 233). But infants and toddlers are not effortful, strategic memorizers. Rather, they remember unintentionally, as part of their ongoing activities (Bjorklund, 2005). And when memory strategies emerge during the preschool years, they are not very successful at first. Not until middle childhood do these techniques take a giant leap forward (Schneider, 2002).

Strategies for Storing Information

Researchers have studied the development of three strategies that enhance memory for new information: rehearsal, organization, and elaboration.

• **Rehearsal, Organization, and Elaboration** TAKE A MOMENT... Next time you have a list of things to learn, such as major cities in your state or country, or items to buy at the supermarket, notice your behavior. You are likely to repeat the information to yourself, a memory strategy called **rehearsal.** And you will probably group related items (for example, all the cities in the same part of the country), a strategy called **organization.**

Why are young children not adept at rehearsal and organization? Memory strategies require extra space in working memory and time and effort to perfect. Even when school-age children use these strategies more often—around age 7 for rehearsal and age 8 for organization—many show *control* and *utilization deficiencies* (Bjorklund & Coyle, 1995). For example, 7- to 8-year-olds often rehearse in a piecemeal fashion. When given the word *cat* in a list of items, they say, "*Cat, cat, cat.*" In contrast, older children combine previous words with each new item, saying "*Desk, man, yard, cat, cat,*" which results in much better memory (Kunzinger, 1985). Similarly, younger children usually organize items by their everyday association: "*hat–head,*" "*carrot–rabbit.*" Older children group such items into *taxonomic categories,* based on common properties—clothing, body parts, food, animals. Placing more items in a few categories permits more efficient organization, dramatically improving recall (Bjorklund et al., 1994).

Biology *and* Environment

Children with Attention-Deficit Hyperactivity Disorder

While the other fifth graders worked quietly at their desks, Calvin squirmed, dropped his pencil, looked out the window, fiddled with his shoelaces, and talked aloud. "Hey Joey," he yelled over the heads of several classmates, "wanna play ball after school?" But the other children weren't eager to play with Calvin, who was physically awkward and failed to follow the rules of the game. He had trouble taking turns at bat. In the outfield, he tossed his mitt in the air and looked elsewhere when the ball came his way. Calvin's desk was a chaotic mess. He often lost his books, pencils, and other school materials, and he had trouble remembering assignments or deadlines.

Symptoms of ADHD

Calvin is one of 3 to 6 percent of school-age children with **attention-deficit hyperactivity disorder (ADHD),** which involves inattention, impulsivity, and excessive motor activity resulting in academic and social problems (American Psychiatric Association, 1994; Barkely, 2006). Boys are diagnosed about four times as often as girls. However, many girls with ADHD seem to be overlooked, either because their symptoms are less flagrant or because of a gender bias: A difficult, disruptive boy is more likely to be referred for treatment (Abikoff et al., 2002; Biederman et al., 2005).

Children with ADHD cannot stay focused on a task requiring mental effort for more than a few minutes. They often act impulsively, ignoring social rules and lashing out with hostility when frustrated. Many, though not all, are *hyperactive,* exhausting parents and teachers and irritating other children with their excessive motor activity. For a child to be diagnosed with ADHD, these symptoms must have appeared before age 7 as a persistent problem.

Because of their difficulty concentrating, children with ADHD score 7 to 15 points lower than other children on intelligence tests (Barkley, 2002). Researchers agree that deficient executive processing (refer to the central executive in Figure 7.1 on page 277) underlies ADHD symptoms. According to one view, children with ADHD are impaired in capacity to inhibit action in favor of thought—a basic difficulty that results in wide-ranging inadequacies in strategic thinking and, therefore, in impulsive, disorganized behavior (Barkley, 2003). Another hypothesis is that ADHD is the direct result of a cluster of executive processing problems that interfere with ability to guide one's own actions (Brown, 2005, 2006). Research confirms that children with ADHD do poorly on tasks requiring sustained attention; find it hard to ignore irrelevant information; have difficulty with memory, planning, reasoning, and problem solving in academic and social situations; and often fail to manage frustration and intense emotion (Barkley, 2003, 2006).

Origins of ADHD

ADHD runs in families and is highly heritable: Identical twins share it much more often than fraternal twins do (Rasmussen et al., 2004; Rietvelt et al., 2004). Children with ADHD show abnormal brain functioning, including reduced electrical and blood-flow activity and structural abnormalities in the *frontal lobes* of the cerebral cortex and in other areas involved in attention, inhibition of behavior, and additional aspects of motor control. These include the *caudate nucleus,* a cortical structure that translates commands from the frontal cortex into motor behavior, and the *cerebellum,* a structure at the rear and base of the brain that supports both motor control and executive processing (see page 188 in Chapter 5) (Mackie et al., 2007; Sowell et al., 2003). Also, the brains of children with ADHD grow more slowly and are about 3 percent smaller in overall volume than those of unaffected agemates (Durston et al., 2004; Shaw et al., 2007). Several genes affecting neurotransmitter and hormone levels have been implicated in the disorder (Biederman & Spencer, 2000; Quist & Kennedy, 2001).

At the same time, ADHD is associated with environmental factors. Prenatal

Experience with materials that form clear categories helps children use organization and apply the strategy to less clearly related materials. In longitudinal research, many young schoolchildren organized inconsistently (a *control deficiency*) and, when they did organize, showed little or no gain in performance (a *utilization deficiency*). Between ages 8 and 10, after realizing the value of organization, most children suddenly began using it regularly, with immediate gains in recall (Schlagmüller & Schneider, 2002; Weinert & Schneider, 1999).

Furthermore, older children are more likely to apply several memory strategies at once, rehearsing, organizing, and stating category names. The more strategies they use, the better they remember (Coyle & Bjorklund, 1997). Although younger children's use of multiple memory strategies has little impact on performance, their tendency to experiment is adaptive, allowing them to discover which strategies work best on different tasks and how to combine them effectively. For example, second to fourth graders know that a good way to study lists is to organize the items first, next rehearse category names, and then rehearse individual

This child frequently engages in disruptive behavior at school. Children with ADHD have great difficulty staying on task and often act impulsively, ignoring social rules. © David Young-Wolff/PhotoEdit

teratogens—particularly those involving long-term exposure, such as illegal drugs, alcohol, and cigarettes—are linked to inattention and hyperactivity (Milberger et al., 1997). Furthermore, children with ADHD are more likely to come from homes in which marriages are unhappy and family stress is high (Bernier & Siegel, 1994). But a stressful home life rarely causes ADHD. Rather, these children's behaviors can contribute to family problems, which intensify the child's preexisting difficulties.

Treating ADHD

Calvin's doctor eventually prescribed stimulant medication, the most common treatment for ADHD. As long as dosage is carefully regulated, these drugs reduce activity level and improve attention, academic performance, and peer relations for about 70 percent of children who take them (Greenhill, Halperin, & Abikoff, 1999). Stimulant medication seems to increase activity in the frontal lobes, thereby improving the child's capacity to sustain attention and to inhibit off-task and self-stimulating behavior.

In 2006, an advisory panel convened by the U.S. Food and Drug Administration warned that stimulants might impair heart functioning, even causing sudden death in a few individuals, and advocated warning labels describing these potential risks. Debate over the safety of medication for ADHD is likely to intensify. In any case, medication is not enough. Drugs cannot teach children to compensate for inattention and impulsivity. The most effective treatment approach combines medication with interventions that model and reinforce appropriate academic and social behavior (American Academy of Pediatrics, 2005a; Smith, Barkley, & Shapiro, 2006).

Family intervention is also important. Inattentive, overactive children strain the patience of parents, who are likely to react punitively and inconsistently—a child-rearing style that strengthens defiant, aggressive behavior. In fact, in 45 to 65 percent of cases, these two sets of behavior problems occur together (Barkley, 2002).

Some media reports suggest that the number of North American children diagnosed with ADHD has increased greatly. But two large surveys yielded similar overall prevalence rates 20 years ago and today. Nevertheless, the incidence of ADHD is much higher in some communities than in others. At times, children are overdiagnosed and unnecessarily medicated because their parents and teachers are impatient with inattentive, active behavior that is actually within normal range. In Hong Kong, where academic success is particularly prized, children are diagnosed at more than twice the rate seen in North America. But in Great Britain, where doctors are hesitant to label children as ADHD and to prescribe medication, children are underdiagnosed and do not receive the treatment they need (Taylor, 2004).

ADHD is usually a lifelong disorder. Affected individuals are at risk for persistent antisocial behavior, depression, alcohol and drug abuse, and other problems (Kessler et al., 2005, 2006). Adults with ADHD continue to need help—in structuring their environments, regulating negative emotion, selecting appropriate careers, and understanding their condition as a biological deficit rather than a character flaw.

items (Hock, Park, & Bjorklund, 1998). Recall from Siegler's model of strategy choice that children experiment with strategies when faced with many cognitive challenges.

By the end of middle childhood, children start to use a third memory strategy, **elaboration.** It involves creating a relationship, or shared meaning, between two or more pieces of information that do not belong to the same category. For example, to learn the words *fish* and *pipe*, you might generate the verbal statement or mental image, "The fish is smoking a pipe." This highly effective memory technique becomes more common during adolescence as young people improve at holding two or more items in mind while generating meaningful associations (Schneider & Pressley, 1997).

• Culture, Schooling, and Memory Strategies People usually employ memory strategies when they need to remember information for its own sake. On many other occasions, memory occurs as an ordinary accompaniment to daily activities (Rogoff, 2003). In a study illustrating

A mother and daughter of the U'wa people, who live in the remote northeastern rainforests of Colombia and have no written tradition, work together in the fields, making cocara leaf hats, which girls wear from puberty until marriage. Although this child demonstrates keen memory for how to select, cut, and assemble the leaves, she is likely to have difficulty recalling isolated bits of information, as school tasks often require. © Paul Smith/Panos Pictures

this idea, 4- and 5-year-olds were told either to *play with* a set of toys or to *remember* them. The play condition produced far better recall because the children engaged in many spontaneous organizations. These included using objects in typical ways (putting a shoe on a doll's foot) and narrating their activities: "I'm squeezing this lemon," or "Fly away in this helicopter, doggie" (Newman, 1990).

These findings help explain why the Kpelle farmers described at the beginning of this chapter viewed grouping by everyday use as "the wise way" to organize familiar objects. People in non-Western cultures who lack formal schooling rarely use or benefit from instruction in memory strategies because they see no practical reason to use these techniques (Rogoff & Mistry, 1985).

Tasks requiring children to remember isolated bits of information, which are common in school, strongly motivate use of memory strategies. In fact, Western children get so much practice with this type of learning that they do not refine techniques relying on cues available in every life, such as spatial location and arrangement of objects (Mistry, 1997). For example, Guatemalan Mayan 9-year-olds do slightly better than their North American agemates when told to remember the placement of 40 familiar objects in a play scene. North American children often rehearse object names when it would be more effective to keep track of spatial relations (Rogoff & Waddell, 1982). Viewed in this way, the development of memory strategies is not just a matter of a more competent information-processing system. It is also a product of task demands and cultural circumstances.

Retrieving Information

Once information enters our long-term knowledge base, we must *retrieve* (or recover) it to use it again. We retrieve information in three ways: through recognition, recall, and reconstruction. As we discuss these approaches to remembering, we will consider how children's expanding knowledge base affects their memory performance. We will also delve into the accuracy of a special type of memory—children's eyewitness accounts in legal proceedings—that can seriously affect their own and others' welfare.

● **Recognition and Recall** TAKE A MOMENT... Show a young child a set of 10 pictures or toys. Then mix them up with some unfamiliar items, and ask the child to point to the ones in the original set. Noticing that a stimulus is identical or similar to one previously experienced is called **recognition.** It is the simplest form of retrieval, since the material to be remembered is fully present during testing to serve as its own retrieval cue.

As seen in the habituation research discussed in Chapters 4 and 6, even young infants are good at recognition. The ability to recognize a larger number of stimuli over longer delays improves steadily with age, reaching a near-adult level during the preschool years. For example, after viewing a series of 80 pictures, 4-year-olds correctly discriminated 90 percent from pictures not in the original set (Brown & Campione, 1972). Because recognition appears early and develops rapidly, it is probably a fairly automatic process. Nevertheless, the ability of older children to apply strategies during storage, such as rehearsal and organization, increases the number of items recognized later (Mandler & Robinson, 1978).

TAKE A MOMENT... Now give the child a more challenging task: Keeping the items out of view, ask the child to name the ones she saw. This requires **recall**—generating a mental representation of an absent stimulus. The beginnings of recall appear in the second half of the first year for memories that are strongly cued. Think back to the rapid gains in deferred imitation under way after age 6 months, discussed in Chapter 6—good evidence for recall. Development of recall lags behind recognition from infancy on. In early childhood, young children's recall in tasks that require retention of pieces of information is far poorer than their recognition. At age 2, children can recall no more than one or two items, at age 4 only about three or four (Perlmutter, 1984).

Improvement in recall over the preschool years is strongly associated with language development, which greatly enhances long-lasting representations of past experiences (Simcock & Hayne, 2003). But even when asked to recall an event that occurred weeks earlier, young children report only part of what could be remembered. In one longitudinal study, sixth graders were asked to tell what happened when they went to an archeological museum in kindergarten. They said less about the experience than when they had been asked the same question as kindergartners, six weeks after the museum trip. But in response to specific retrieval cues, including photos of the event, sixth graders remembered a great deal. And in some respects, their recall was more accurate. For example, they inferred that adults had hidden artifacts in a sandbox for them to find, whereas in kindergarten they simply recalled digging for objects (Hudson & Fivush, 1991).

Compared with recognition, recall shows far greater improvement because older children make use of a wider range of retrieval cues. With age, the long-term knowledge base grows larger and becomes organized into increasingly elaborate, hierarchically structured networks (Bjorklund, 2005; Schneider, 2002). When representations of experiences are interconnected in long-term memory, many internal retrieval cues can be used with little or no effort to recall them later.

• **Reconstruction** When we must remember complex, meaningful material, we do not merely copy material into the system at storage and faithfully reproduce it at retrieval. Instead, we select and interpret information we encounter in our everyday lives in terms of our existing knowledge. Once we have transformed the material, we often have difficulty distinguishing it from the original (Bartlett, 1932). Constructive processing can take place during any phase of information processing. It can occur during storage. In fact, the memory strategies of organization and elaboration are within the province of constructive memory because both involve generating relationships between stimuli. Constructive processing can also involve **reconstruction** of information, or recoding it while it is in the system or being retrieved.

Do children reconstruct stored information? Clearly, they do. When asked to recall and retell a story, children, like adults, condense, integrate, and add information. By age 5 or 6, children recall important features of a story while forgetting unimportant ones, combine information into more tightly knit units, reorder the sequence of events in more logical fashion, and even include new information that fits with a passage's meaning (Bischofshausen, 1985).

Furthermore, when children receive new information related to a story they previously recalled, they reconstruct the story further. In one study, before telling each of three stories, an adult gave kindergartners information about a main character that was positive ("a nice" child), negative ("not a nice" child), or neutral. Children reconstructed the main character's behaviors to fit with prior information (Greenhoot, 2000). Compared with those in the neutral condition, those in the positive condition offered a more positive account, those in the negative condition a more negative account. Seven to ten days later, a fourth story gave children additional information about the main character. In some conditions, the new information was consistent with the original information; in others, it conflicted—for example, the "nice" child was now described as a "mean" child. Children again revised their recollections of the main character's behavior accordingly. And in a further recall session, the children's reconstructions were even more biased in that direction.

In revising information in meaningful ways, children give themselves a wealth of helpful retrieval cues to use during recall. Over time, as originally provided information decays, children make more inferences about actors and actions,

As he tells a story to his grandfather, this child growing up on a Colorado ranch selects and interprets events and details, engaging in the memory process called reconstruction.

adding events and interpretations that help make sense of a story. This process increases the coherence of reconstructed information and, therefore, its memorableness. Gains in working-memory capacity and language skills, which support the organization and complexity of children's recollections, predict the extent to which 9- to 11-year-olds reframe their story recall in response to new information—overriding previously acquired events and viewpoints, elaborating on and integrating old and new details into a coherent picture (Tsethlikai & Greenhoot, 2006). At the same time, as these findings reveal, much information children and adults recall can be inaccurate.

Another View of Reconstruction: Fuzzy-Trace Theory So far, we have emphasized deliberate reconstruction of meaningful material, using new information and the long-term knowledge base to interpret it. According to C. J. Brainerd and Valerie Reyna's (1993, 2001) **fuzzy-trace theory,** when we first encode information, we reconstruct it automatically, creating a vague, fuzzy version called a **gist,** which preserves essential meaning without details and is especially useful for reasoning. Although we can also retain a literal, verbatim version, we have a bias toward gist because it requires less space in working memory, freeing attention for the steps involved in thinking. For example, a person choosing among several recipes to prepare a dish for dinner relies on gist representations, noting which recipes are easier and have low-cost ingredients. But once he has selected a recipe, he needs verbatim information to prepare it. Because he is unlikely to have remembered those details, he consults the cookbook.

Fuzzy-trace theorists take issue with the assumption that all reconstructions are transformations of verbatim memory. Instead, they believe that both verbatim and gist memories are present but are stored separately to be used for different purposes. In support of this idea, shortly after being read a brief story, children can discriminate between sentences they actually heard and ones they did not hear but that are consistent with the story's gist. Over time, as the complete, verbatim memory decays more quickly than the efficiently represented gist, children begin to say that statements consistent with but not actually in the story were ones they heard (Reyna & Kiernan, 1994). Fuzzy-trace theory also helps us understand why children (and adults) often reason effectively without recalling specifics.

With age, children rely less on verbatim memory and more on fuzzy, reconstructed gists. To illustrate, researchers presented children with the following problem: "Farmer Brown owns many animals. He has three dogs, five sheep, seven chickens, nine horses, and eleven cows." Then they asked two types of questions: (1) questions requiring verbatim knowledge ("How many cows does Farmer Brown own, eleven or nine?") and (2) questions requiring only gist information ("Does Farmer Brown have more cows or more horses?"). As Figure 7.8 shows, preschoolers were better at answering verbatim- than gist-dependent questions, whereas the reverse was true for second graders (Brainerd & Gordon, 1994).

Fuzzy-trace theory adds to our understanding of reconstruction by indicating that it can occur immediately, as soon as information is encoded. Fuzzy-trace research reveals that although memory is vital for reasoning, getting bogged down in details (as young children tend to do) can interfere with effective problem solving. And because fuzzy traces are less likely than verbatim memories to be forgotten, gists can serve as enduring retrieval cues, contributing to improved recall of details with age (Brainerd & Reyna, 1995).

In such recall, however, gists heighten the chances of reporting false items consistent with the fuzzy meaning of an experience. After studying a list containing the words *bed, rest, wake, tired, dream, blanket, nap,* and *snooze,* adolescents and adults—who are more skilled gist thinkers—not only recall more items correctly than children but also mention more gist-related words not in the list, such as *sleep.* Children's false reports, in contrast, are frequently unrelated to a just-studied list—for example, *candy* or *fire* following presentation of the *sleep* list (Brainerd, Holliday, & Reyna, 2004; Brainerd et al., 2006). Fuzzy-trace theory helps explain why some memory inaccuracies decrease with age, while others increase.

Figure 7.8 **Preschoolers' and second graders' performance on verbatim and gist memory questions.**

Preschoolers did better on the verbatim than on the gist memory test; for second graders, the reverse was true. (Adapted from Brainerd & Gordon, 1994.)

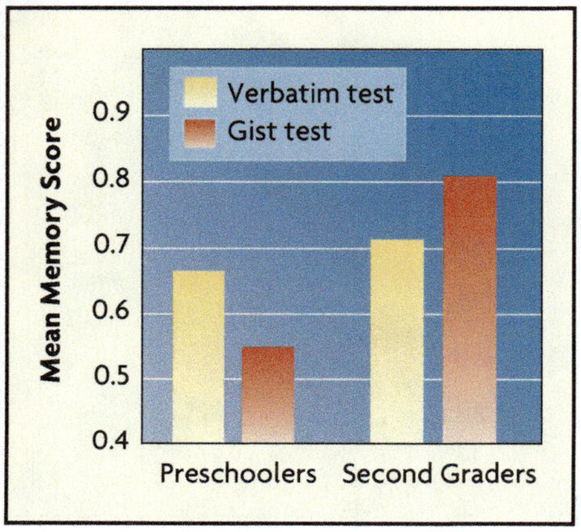

The Knowledge Base and Memory Performance

We have suggested that children's expanding knowledge promotes improved memory by making new, related information more meaningful so that it is easier to store and retrieve. In a landmark study testing this idea, Michelene Chi (1978) looked at how well third- through eighth-grade chess experts could remember complex chessboard arrangements. The children recalled the configurations considerably better than adults who knew how to play chess but were not especially knowledgeable—findings that cannot be explained by the selection of very bright youngsters with exceptional memories. When participants were given a list of numbers, however, the adults did better (see Figure 7.9).

In Chi's study of chess-playing children, better memory was credited to a larger knowledge base. Experts also have more elaborately structured knowledge. In another investigation, researchers classified elementary school children as either experts or novices in knowledge of soccer, then gave both groups lists of soccer and nonsoccer items to learn. As in Chi's study, the experts remembered far more items on the soccer list (but not on the nonsoccer list) than the nonexperts. And during recall, the experts' listing of items was better organized, as indicated by clustering of items into categories (Schneider & Bjorklund, 1992). This greater organization at retrieval suggests that highly knowledgeable children apply memory strategies in their area of expertise with little or no effort—by rapidly associating new items with the large number they already know. This *automatized* recall lets experts devote more working-memory resources to using recalled information to reason and solve problems (Bjorklund & Douglas, 1997).

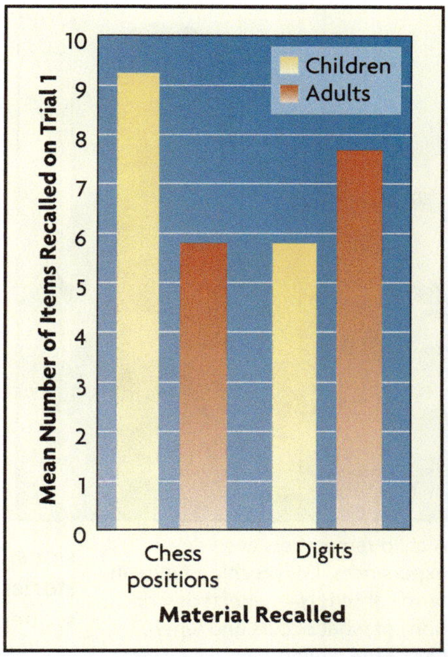

Figure 7.9 **Performance of skilled child chess players and adults on two tasks: memory for complex chessboard arrangements and memory for numerical digits.**
The child chess experts recalled more on the chess task, the adults on the digit task—findings demonstrating that size of the knowledge base contributes to memory performance. (Adapted from Chi, 1978.)

Knowledge, though powerfully influential, is not the only important factor in children's strategic memory processing. Children who are expert in an area are usually highly motivated as well. Faced with new information, they ask themselves, "What can I do to learn this more effectively?" As a result, they not only acquire knowledge more quickly but also *actively use what they know* to add more. In contrast, academically unsuccessful children fail to ask how previously stored information can clarify new material. This, in turn, interferes with the development of a broad knowledge base (Schneider & Bjorklund, 1998). In sum, extensive knowledge and use of memory strategies support one another.

Scripts

Our vast, taxonomically organized and hierarchically structured general knowledge system, often called **semantic memory,** must grow out of the young child's **episodic memory,** or memory for many personally experienced events. How semantic memory emerges from specific, real-world experiences is one of the most puzzling questions about memory development.

Like adults, preschoolers remember familiar events—what you do when you go to child care or get ready for bed—in terms of **scripts,** general descriptions of what occurs and when it occurs in a particular situation. Young children's scripts begin as a structure of main acts. When asked to tell what happens at a restaurant, a 3-year-old might say, "You go in, get the food, eat, and then pay." Although first scripts contain only a few acts,

These middle school chess tournament participants are experts at the game. Their extensive knowledge of chess enables them to recall complex chessboard configurations far more accurately than less knowledgeable adults. © Bob Daemmrich/The Image Works

A child remembers everyday experiences, like brushing teeth, in terms of scripts—general descriptions of what occurs and when. Over time, children provide more elaborate scripts, as in: "You squeeze out the toothpaste and brush your teeth. You rinse your mouth and then your toothbrush."
© Andy Sacks/Getty Images/Riser

young children—even 1- and 2-year-olds, who cannot verbally describe events but can act them out with toys—almost always recall these acts in correct sequence. Still, to obtain young children's scripted reports, adults must work hard, asking questions and prompting (Bauer, 2002a, 2006). With age, scripts become more spontaneous and elaborate, as in this 5-year-old's account of going to a restaurant: "You go in. You can sit in the booths or at a table. Then you tell the waitress what you want. You eat. If you want dessert, you can have some. Then you pay and go home" (Hudson, Fivush, & Kuebli, 1992).

Scripts are a special form of reconstructive memory. When we experience repeated events, we fuse them into the same script representation. Then any specific instance of a scripted experience becomes hard to recall. **TAKE A MOMENT...** Try recalling what you had for dinner two or three days ago. Unless it was out of the ordinary, you probably cannot remember. The same is true for young children. In this way, scripts prevent long-term memory from being cluttered with unimportant information.

Scripts help children (and adults) organize and interpret everyday experiences. Once formed, they can be used to predict what will happen on future similar occasions. Young children rely on scripts in make-believe play and when listening to and telling stories. Scripts also support children's earliest efforts at planning as they represent action sequences leading to desired goals (Hudson, Sosa, & Shapiro, 1997).

Some researchers believe that scripts are the developmental link between early episodic memory and a semantic memory store (Lucariello, 1998). In several studies, preschoolers remembered script-related items (peanut butter, bologna, cheese—lunch foods) in clustered form and recalled them more easily than a list of items belonging to the same taxonomic category (toast, cheese, ice cream—foods) (Lucariello, Kyratzis, & Nelson, 1992; Yu & Nelson, 1993). As children develop an array of script sequences, they may merge objects that share the same function but occur in different scripts (eating toast for breakfast, peanut butter for lunch) into a typical taxonomic category (food).

Although scripts may support children's taxonomic categorization, they are not the exclusive means through which children build their semantic memories. Recall from Chapter 6 that even preschoolers can sort objects into categories at different levels (general, basic, subcategory) and move back and forth between those levels (see page 244). In a series of studies, 3- to 7-year-olds could categorize food items into both script and taxonomic categories. Although the children categorized more accurately with age, they did not shift from script to taxonomic categorization (Nguyen & Murphy, 2003). Nevertheless, when given a choice between matching a food item (bologna) with a script associate (cheese) or a taxonomic associate (ice cream), 3-year-olds showed no preference (both types of categories were just forming), 4-year-olds preferred the script category, and 7-year-olds preferred the taxonomic category.

By age 7, children clearly use script and taxonomic categories for different purposes—the former to group items on the basis of shared everyday situations, the latter to group items on the basis of common properties (Nguyen & Murphy, 2003). Just how children build and structure their semantic memory remains largely unknown. As we saw in Chapter 6, expanding knowledge, vocabulary development, and adult explanations of category memberships are helpful.

Autobiographical Memory

Another type of episodic memory is **autobiographical memory,** representations of one-time events that are long-lasting because they are imbued with personal meaning. Perhaps you recall the day a sibling was born, the first time you took an airplane, or a birthday celebration. How does memory for autobiographical events arise and persist for a lifetime? At least two developments make this possible. First, children must have a sufficiently clear self-image to serve as an anchor for personally significant events. That is, they must be able to encode events as "something that happened to me"—a milestone reached around age 2 years (see Chapter 11) (Howe, 2003). Second, children must integrate their experiences into a meaningful, time-organized life story. They learn to structure personally significant memories in narrative form by conversing about them with adults, especially their parents, who expand on their fragmented recollections (Nelson & Fivush, 2004).

As early as 1½ to 2 years, children start to talk about the past. As cognitive and conversational skills improve in early childhood, parents' conversations about past events become more complex. Gradually, children adopt the narrative thinking of these dialogues: Their independent descriptions of special events become better organized, detailed, enriched with a personal perspective, and related to the larger context of their lives (Fivush, 2001). A young preschooler simply reports, "I went camping." Older preschoolers include specifics: where and when they went and who was present. With age, preschoolers increasingly add subjective information—why, for example, an event was exciting, funny, or sad, or made them feel proud or embarrassed ("I loved sleeping all night in the tent!")—that explains the event's personal significance.

Adults use two styles for prompting children's autobiographical narratives. In the *elaborative style,* they follow the child's lead, discussing topics of interest to the child, asking varied questions, adding information to the child's statements, and volunteering their own recollections and evaluations of events. For example, after visiting the zoo, one parent asked her 4-year-old, "What was the first thing we did?" "Why weren't the parrots in their cages?" "I thought the roaring lion was scary. What did you think?" In this way, the parent helped the child reestablish and reorganize his memory of the outing. In contrast, adults who use the *repetitive style* keep repeating the same questions ("Do you remember the zoo?" "What did we do at the zoo?" "What did we do there?") regardless of the child's interest, providing little additional information. Preschoolers who experience the elaborative style recall more information about past events, and they also produce more organized and detailed personal stories when followed up one to two years later (Cleveland & Reese, 2005; Farrant & Reese, 2000).

As children talk with adults about the past, they not only improve their episodic memory but also create a shared history that strengthens close relationships and self-understanding. In line with these ideas, parents and preschoolers with secure attachment bonds engage in more elaborate reminiscing than those with insecure bonds, who generally limit themselves to the repetitive style (Bost et al., 2006; Fivush & Reese, 2002). And children of elaborative-style parents describe themselves in clearer, more consistent ways (Bird & Reese, 2006). When, in past-event conversations, a child discovers that she finds swimming, running, climbing, getting together with friends, and going to the zoo fun, she can begin to connect these specific experiences into a general understanding of "what I enjoy." The result is a clearer image of herself.

Beginning in the preschool years, girls tend to have better organized and detailed autobiographical memories than boys. And Western children produce narratives with more talk about their own thoughts, emotions, and preferences than do Asian children. These differences fit with variations in parent–child conversations. Parents reminisce in more detail with daughters (Bruce, Dolan, & Phillips-Grant, 2000; Reese, Haden, & Fivush, 1996). And collectivist cultural values lead many Asian parents to discourage children from talking about themselves. Chinese and Chinese-immigrant parents, for example, engage in less detailed and evaluative past-event dialogues with their preschoolers. Rather, they tend to pose pointed questions that emphasize adults' greater knowledge and authority (Fivush & Wang, 2005; Wang, 2004, 2006a). Perhaps because women's early experiences were integrated into more coherent narratives, they report an earlier age of first memory and more vivid early memories than men. And Western adults' autobiographical memories include earlier, more detailed events that focus more on their own roles than do the memories of Asians, who tend to highlight the roles of others (Wang, 2003, 2006b).

Nevertheless, few of us can retrieve events that happened to us before age 3. Yet much evidence shows that we both learned and remembered during our early years. Why do we experience this *infantile amnesia?* Refer to the Biology and Environment box on pages 298–299 for research aimed at answering this question.

As she converses with her father about past experiences, this young child in Shanghai builds an autobiographical memory. Asian parents, reflecting collectivist values, tend to discourage children from talking about themselves. Perhaps as a result, Asian adults' autobiographical memories focus less on their own roles than on the roles of others. © Tina Manley/Children/Alamy

Biology *and* Environment

Infantile Amnesia

If infants and toddlers remember many aspects of their everyday lives, how do we explain **infantile amnesia**—that most of us cannot retrieve events that happened to us before age 3? The reason we forget cannot be merely the passage of time because we can recall many events that happened long ago (Eacott, 1999). At present, several accounts of infantile amnesia exist.

One theory credits brain development, suggesting that vital changes in the hippocampus and the frontal lobes of the cerebral cortex may pave the way for an *explicit* memory system—one in which children remember consciously rather than *implicitly,* without conscious awareness (Boyer & Diamond, 1992). But a growing number of researchers argue that even young infants remember consciously: Their memory processing is not fundamentally different from that of children and adults. For example, as with adults, infant retention is greater with increased training and with training distributed over several sessions rather than massed into one session. And like adults, babies given memory prompts (retrieval cues) readily recover forgotten responses (see page 139 in Chapter 4) (Bauer, 2006; Rovee-Collier, 1999; Rovee-Collier & Barr, 2001).

Another conjecture is that older children and adults often use verbal means for storing information, whereas infants' and toddlers' memory processing is largely nonverbal—an incompatibility that may prevent long-term retention of early experiences. To test this idea, researchers sent two adults to the homes of 2- to 4-year-olds with a highly unusual toy that the children were likely to remember: the Magic Shrinking Machine, depicted in Figure 7.10. One adult showed the child how, after inserting an object in an opening on the top of the machine and turning a crank that activated flashing lights and musical sounds, the child could retrieve a smaller, identical object from behind a door on the front of the machine. (The second adult discreetly dropped the smaller object down a chute leading to the door.) The child was encouraged to participate as the machine "shrank" additional objects.

A day later, the researchers tested the children to see how well they recalled the event. Results revealed that their nonverbal memory—based on acting out the "shrinking" event and recognizing the "shrunken" objects in photos—was excellent. But even when they had the vocabulary, children younger than age 3 had trouble describing features of the "shrinking" experience. Verbal recall increased sharply between ages 3 and 4—the period during which children "scramble over the amnesia barrier" (Simcock & Hayne, 2003, p. 813). In a second study, preschoolers could not translate their nonverbal memory for the game into language after six months to one year had elapsed, their language had improved dramatically, and they viewed a photo of the shrinking machine. Their verbal reports were "frozen in time," reflecting their limited language skill at the time they played the game (Simcock & Hayne, 2002).

These findings help us reconcile infants' and toddlers' remarkable memory skills with infantile amnesia. During the first few years, children remember largely with nonverbal techniques, such as visual images and motor actions. As language develops, preschoolers can use it to refer to preverbal memories. But their ability to do so is fragile, requiring strong contextual supports, such as direct exposure to the physical setting and props of the experience to be recalled (Bauer et al., 2004; Morris & Baker-Ward, 2007). Only after age 3 do children often represent events

Eyewitness Memory

Until recently, children younger than age 5 were rarely asked to testify in court cases, and not until age 10 were they assumed fully competent to do so. As a result of societal reactions to rising rates of child abuse and the difficulty of prosecuting perpetrators, legal requirements for child testimony have been relaxed in the United States and Canada (Sandler, 2006). Children as young as age 3 frequently serve as witnesses.

Compared with preschoolers, school-age children are better able to give accurate, detailed descriptions of past experiences and correctly infer others' motives and intentions. Older children are also more resistant to misleading questions of the sort attorneys may ask when probing for more information or trying to influence the child's response (Roebers & Schneider, 2001). What makes younger children more prone to memory errors? The following factors are involved:

- Responding to interview questions is challenging for children whose language competence is not well-developed. Preschoolers are often unaware when they do not understand, and they answer the question anyway.
- Preschoolers are especially poor at *source-monitoring*—identifying where they got their knowledge, even minutes after they acquired it. They often confuse what they heard or saw on TV with what actually occurred.
- Younger children are less skilled at *inhibition*—ignoring irrelevant information—which contributes to their greater willingness to accept adult suggestions that are inconsistent with experienced events.

verbally and participate in elaborate conversations with adults about them. Once children have encoded one-time events in verbal form, they can use language-based cues to retrieve them, increasing the accessibility of these memories at later ages (Hayne, 2004).

Other findings suggest that the advent of a clear self-image contributes to the end of infantile amnesia. Toddlers who were advanced in development of a sense of self demonstrated better verbal memories a year later while conversing about past events with their mothers (Harley & Reese, 1999). Very likely, both biology and social experience contribute to the decline of infantile amnesia. Brain development and adult–child interaction may jointly foster self-awareness, language, and improved memory, which enable children to talk with adults about significant past experiences (Bauer, 2007; Nelson & Fivush, 2004). As a result, preschoolers begin to construct a long-lasting autobiographical narrative of their lives and enter into the history of their family and community.

Figure 7.10 **The Magic Shrinking Machine, used to test young children's verbal and nonverbal memory of an unusual event.** After being shown how the machine worked, the child participated in selecting objects from a polka-dot bag, dropping them into the top of the machine (a) and turning a crank, which produced a "shrunken" object (b). When tested the next day, 2- to 4-year-olds' nonverbal memory for the event was excellent. But below 36 months, verbal recall was poor, based on the number of features recalled about the game during an open-ended interview (c). Recall improved between 36 and 48 months, the period during which infantile amnesia subsides. (From G. Simcock & H. Hayne, 2003, "Age-Related Changes in Verbal and Nonverbal Memory During Early Childhood," *Developmental Psychology,* 39, pp. 807, 809. Copyright © 2003 by the American Psychological Association. Reprinted with permission of the American Psychological Association and Harlene Hayne.) *Photos:* Ross Coombes/Courtesy of Harlene Hayne.

- When an adult asks a yes-or-no question ("Was he holding a screwdriver?"), younger children are more likely to agree, perhaps out of a desire to please.
- Preschoolers' bias toward verbatim representations (encoding specifics) leads them to forget more easily than older children, whose gist memories persist over time and serve as retrieval cues for details. (But, as noted on page 294, older children are prone to memory inaccuracies consistent with their gists.)
- Because younger children are less competent at using narratives to report their autobiographical memories systematically and completely, they may omit information that they actually remember (Brainerd, Reyna, & Poole, 2000; Poole & Lindsay, 2001; Roberts & Powell, 2005).

Suggestibility Court testimony often involves repeated questioning by adults who have a vested interest in the child's responses. When biased adults repeatedly ask specific questions, some of which suggest incorrect facts or reinforce the child for giving desired answers, they can increase inaccurate reporting by preschool and school-age children alike (Bruck & Ceci, 2004).

In one study, 4- to 5-year-olds and 6- to 7-year-olds were asked to recall details about a visitor who had come to their classroom a week earlier. Half the children received a low-pressure interview containing leading questions that implied abuse ("He took your clothes off, didn't he?"). The other half received a high-pressure interview in which an adult told the child that her friends had said "yes" to the leading questions, praised the child for agreeing ("You're doing great"), and, if the child did not agree, repeated the question. Children in both age groups were far more likely to give false information in the high-pressure condition (Finnilä

When interviewed for their eyewitness accounts, school-age children are better able than preschoolers to give accurate, detailed descriptions and correctly infer others' motives and intentions. This police officer can promote accurate recall by using a warm, supportive tone and avoiding leading questions. © Michael Newman/PhotoEdit

et al., 2003). As these findings illustrate, events that children fabricate can be quite fantastic. Moreover, children who have constructed a false memory often continue to give false reports when later questioned by an impartial interviewer (Garven, Wood, & Malpass, 2000).

By the time children appear in court, weeks, months, or even years have passed since the target events, and memory is likely to have decayed. When a long delay is combined with biased interviewing procedures and with stereotyping of the accused ("He's in jail because he's been bad"), children can easily be misled into giving false information (Ceci, Fitneva, & Gilstrap, 2003; Gilstrap & Ceci, 2005; Quas et al., 2007). The more *distinctive and personally relevant* an event is, the more likely children are to recall it accurately after the passage of time. For example, a year later, even when exposed to misleading information, children correctly reported details of an injury that required emergency room treatment—an event that was both distinctive and emotionally involving (Peterson, Parsons, & Dean, 2004).

In many child sexual abuse cases, anatomically correct dolls are used to prompt children's recall. Although this method helps older children provide more detail about experienced events, it increases the suggestibility of preschoolers, prompting them to report physical and sexual contact that never happened (Goodman et al., 1999).

• **Interventions** Adults must prepare child witnesses so they understand the courtroom process and know what to expect. In some places, "court schools" take children through the setting and give them an opportunity to role-play court activities. Practice interviews—in which children learn to provide the most accurate, detailed information possible and to admit not knowing rather than agreeing or guessing—are helpful (Saywitz, Goodman, & Lyon, 2002). For example, when 3- and 4-year-olds are trained to monitor the source of their memories (recall whether an event occurred in real life or on TV) and to reject misleading source information, they responded more accurately to questions about new events (Thierry & Spence, 2002).

At the same time, legal professionals must use interviewing procedures that increase children's accurate reporting. Unbiased, open-ended questions or statements that prompt children to disclose details—"Tell me what happened" or "You said there was a man; tell me about the man"—reduce the risk of suggestibility (Holliday, 2003). Also, a warm, supportive interview tone fosters accurate recall, perhaps by easing children's fears so they feel freer to counter an interviewer's false suggestions (Ceci, Bruck, & Battin, 2000).

If children are likely to experience emotional trauma or later punishment (as in a family dispute) for answering questions, courtroom procedures can be adapted to protect them. For example, children can testify over closed-circuit TV so they do not have to face an abuser. When it is not wise for a child to participate directly, expert witnesses can provide testimony that reports on the child's psychological condition and includes important elements of the child's story.

Ask Yourself

Review According to fuzzy-trace theory, why do we encode information in gist form? Describe the development of gist and verbatim representations, and explain how gist representations contribute to improved reasoning and more detailed recall—but also to certain memory errors—with age.

Apply When asked what happens at kindergarten, 5-year-old Ali replies, "First, you have center time and circle time. Sometimes you listen to a story. Next you eat your snack and go outdoors." But Ali can't remember what she did during center time two days ago. Explain Ali's memory performance. Why is this type of memory useful?

Connect Using what you have learned about development of autobiographical memory, explain why preschoolers' eyewitness testimony usually is less accurate than that of older children. What situational factors make children's reporting more inaccurate?

Reflect Describe your earliest autobiographical memory. How old were you when the event occurred? Do your responses fit with research on infantile amnesia?

Metacognition

Throughout this chapter, we have mentioned many ways in which cognitive processing becomes more reflective and deliberate with age. These trends suggest that another form of knowledge may influence how well children remember and solve problems: **metacognition**—awareness and understanding of various aspects of thought.

During early and middle childhood, metacognition expands greatly as children construct a naïve **theory of mind,** a coherent understanding of people as mental beings, which they revise as they encounter new evidence. Most investigations into theory of mind address children's "mind reading"—their ability to detect their own and other people's perceptions, feelings, desires, and beliefs. We will take up this aspect when we consider emotional and social understanding in Chapters 10 and 11. A second facet of metacognitive research concerns children's knowledge of mental activity—*what it means to think.* To work most effectively, the information-processing system must be aware of itself. It must arrive at such realizations as "I'd better write that phone number down or I'll forget it" and "This paragraph is complicated; I'll have to read it again to grasp the point."

For metacognitive knowledge to be helpful, children must monitor what they do, calling on what they know about thinking to overcome difficulties. In the following sections, we consider these higher-level, "executive" aspects of information processing.

Metacognitive Knowledge

With age, children become increasingly conscious of their own mental activities, including cognitive capacities, strategies for processing information, and task variables that aid or impede performance.

• **Knowledge of Cognitive Capacities** TAKE A MOMENT... Listen closely to young children's conversations, and you will find early awareness of mental activities. As their vocabularies expand, 2-year-olds' verbs include such words as *want, think, remember,* and *pretend,* which they use appropriately to refer to internal states (Wellman, 2002). By age 3, children realize that thinking takes place inside their heads and that a person can think about something without seeing, talking about, or touching it (Flavell, Green, & Flavell, 1995).

But preschoolers' understanding of the workings of the mind is limited. Three- and 4-year-olds conclude that mental activity stops while people wait, look at pictures, listen to stories, or read books—when no obvious cues indicate that they are thinking (Flavell, Green, & Flavell, 1993, 1995, 2000). Furthermore, children younger than age 6 pay little attention to the *process* of thinking but, instead, focus on outcomes of thought. When asked about subtle distinctions between mental states, such as *know* and *forget,* they express confusion (Lyon & Flavell, 1994). And they often insist that they have always known information they just learned (Taylor, Esbensen, & Bennett, 1994).

School-age children have a more complete grasp of cognitive processes. Six- and 7-year-olds realize, for example, that doing well on a task depends on paying attention—concentrating and exerting effort (Miller & Bigi, 1979). Their understanding of *sources of knowledge* also expands: They realize that people can extend their knowledge not just by directly observing events and talking to others but also by making *mental inferences* (Miller, Hardin, & Montgomery, 2003). And they recognize that when two people view the same object, their trains of thought will differ because of variations in their knowledge, experiences, and other characteristics (Eisbach, 2004).

By age 10, children distinguish mental activities on the basis of *certainty of knowledge.* They are aware that if you "remember," "know," or "understand," you are more certain than if you "guess," "estimate," or "compare." They also grasp the interrelatedness of cognitive processes—for example, that remembering is crucial for understanding and that understanding strengthens memory (Schwanenflugel, Fabricius, & Noyes, 1996; Schwanenflugel, Henderson, & Fabricius, 1998).

How, then, should we describe the difference between younger and older children's understanding of cognitive capacities? Preschoolers view the mind as a passive container of information and thus greatly underestimate the amount of mental activity that goes on in people

School-age children have an improved ability to reflect on their own mental life. This child is aware that external aids to memory are often necessary to ensure that information will be retained.
© Laura Dwight Photography

and have trouble inferring what people know or are thinking about. In view of their limited awareness of how knowledge is acquired, it is not surprising that preschoolers rarely engage in planning or use memory strategies. In contrast, older children regard the mind as an active, constructive agent that selects and transforms information (Flavell, 2000; Kuhn, 2000).

School-age children's capacity for more complex thinking contributes greatly to their more reflective, process-oriented view of the mind. So do relevant experiences. In a study of rural children of Cameroon, Africa, those who attended school had a more advanced awareness of mental activities than those who did not (Vinden, 2002). In school, teachers often call attention to the workings of the mind by reminding children to pay attention, remember mental steps, and evaluate their reasoning. And as children engage in reading, writing, and math, they often use *private speech,* at first speaking aloud and later silently to themselves. As they "hear themselves think," they probably detect many aspects of mental life.

• Knowledge of Strategies Consistent with their more active view of the mind, school-age children are far more conscious of mental strategies than preschoolers. When shown video clips depicting two children using different recall strategies and asked which one is likely to produce better memory, kindergarten and young elementary school children knew that rehearsing or categorizing is better than looking or naming. Older children recognize more subtle differences—that organizing is better than rehearsing (Justice, 1986; Schneider, 1986).

Between third and fifth grade, children develop a much better understanding of how and why strategies work (Alexander et al., 2003). Consequently, fifth graders are considerably better than younger school-age children at discriminating good from bad reasoning, regardless of its outcome (correctness of answer, happiness with a choice). When given examples varying in quality, fifth graders consistently rated "good" reasoning as based on a thoughtful strategy (rather than an arbitrary decision), weighing of alternative possibilities (rather than jumping to conclusions), and gathering of evidence (rather than ignoring important facts)—even if such reasoning led to an unfavorable result (see Figure 7.11) (Amsterlaw, 2006).

Once children become conscious of the many factors that influence mental activity, they combine them into a more effective understanding. By the end of middle childhood, children take account of how *interactions* among multiple variables—age and motivation of the learner, effective use of strategies, and nature and difficulty of the task—affect performance (Wellman, 1990). In this way, metacognition broadens into a more complex theory.

Cognitive Self-Regulation

School-age children and adolescents often have difficulty putting their expanded metacognitive knowledge into action. They are not yet good at

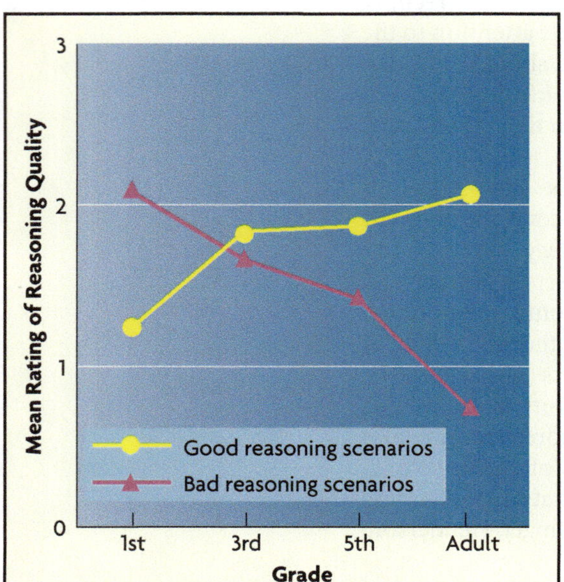

■ Figure 7.11 First through fifth graders' and adults' ability to discriminate good from bad reasoning, regardless of outcome.
Children were given scenarios in which a character engaged in either good or bad reasoning about an everyday problem. In the experimental condition depicted here, scenarios with good reasoning always led to unfavorable outcomes, and scenarios with bad reasoning always led to favorable outcomes. First graders tended to judge reasoning quality on the basis of outcome, giving a low rating to good reasoning and a high rating to bad reasoning. Ability to distinguish good from bad reasoning, regardless of outcome, increased with age, especially after third grade. (From J. Amsterlaw, 2006, "Children's Beliefs About Everyday Reasoning," *Child Development,* 77 (2), p. 454. © The Society for Research in Child Development, Inc. Reprinted by permission of Blackwell Publishing Ltd.)

cognitive self-regulation, the process of continually monitoring progress toward a goal, checking outcomes, and redirecting unsuccessful efforts. For example, most third to sixth graders know that they should group items when memorizing, reread a complicated paragraph to make sure they understand it, and relate new information to what they already know. But they do not always do so. And as we saw in Chapter 6, many teenagers, though aware of the ingredients of good reasoning, fail to engage in effective decision making.

To study cognitive self-regulation, researchers sometimes look at the impact of children's awareness of memory strategies on how well they remember. By second grade, the more children know about memory strategies, the more they recall—a relationship that strengthens over middle childhood (Pierce & Lange, 2000). Furthermore, children who can explain why a memory strategy works use it more effectively, resulting in better memory performance (Justice et al., 1997). Applying a useful strategy consistently, in turn, enhances children's knowledge of strategies, resulting in a bidirectional relationship between metacognition and strategic processing that promotes self-regulation (Schlagmüller & Schneider, 2002).

This student's capacity for cognitive self-regulation is evident as she does a homework assignment. Will she reread complex material and relate new information to existing knowledge? Her parents and teachers can foster her self-regulatory skills by suggesting strategies and explaining why they are effective. © J. Jacquemart/ REX USA

What explains the gradual development of cognitive self-regulation? Monitoring learning outcomes is cognitively demanding, requiring constant evaluation of effort and progress. At first, children's efforts suffer from control and utilization deficiencies (see page 286). By adolescence, cognitive self-regulation is a strong predictor of academic success (Joyner & Kurtz-Costes, 1997). Students who do well in school know whether or not their learning is going well. If they encounter obstacles, they take steps to address them—for example, organize the learning environment, review confusing material, or seek support from more expert adults or peers. This active, purposeful approach contrasts sharply with the passive orientation of students who achieve poorly (Zimmerman & Risemberg, 1997).

Parents and teachers can foster self-regulation. In one study, researchers observed parents helping their children with problem solving during the summer before third grade. Parents who patiently pointed out important features of the task and suggested strategies had children who, in the classroom, more often discussed ways to approach problems and monitored their own performance (Stright et al., 2002). Explaining the effectiveness of strategies—telling children not just what to do but why to do it—is particularly helpful because it provides a rationale for future action.

Applying What We Know on page 304 lists ways to foster children's cognitive self-regulation. Children who acquire effective self-regulatory skills develop a sense of *academic self-efficacy*—confidence in their own ability, which supports future use of self-regulation (Schunk & Pajares, 2005). As we turn to development within academic skill areas, the importance of self-regulation will be evident. But first, consult the Milestones table on page 305, which summarizes the diverse changes in information processing we have considered.

Ask Yourself

Review What evidence indicates that preschoolers view the mind as a passive container of information, whereas school-age children view it as an active, constructive agent?

Apply Although 9-year-old Melody knows she should look over her homework, she nevertheless often turns in assignments with careless mistakes. What might account for the gap between what Melody knows and what she does?

Connect How are the suggestions for fostering cognitive self-regulation above consistent with Vygotsky's emphasis on the social origins of higher cognitive processes?

Applying What We Know

Promoting Children's Cognitive Self-Regulation

Strategy	Description
Stress the importance of planful learning.	Encourage children to analyze the learning task and to plan—by considering a variety of ways to approach the task and by setting appropriate learning goals, including how much time and practice they will need to complete the task.
Suggest effective learning strategies.	Show children how to use effective learning strategies, and explain why those strategies are effective, so children know when and why to use those strategies in the future.
Emphasize monitoring of progress.	Encourage children to check progress toward their learning goals by monitoring themselves, asking such questions as, "Am I staying focused?" "Am I using the strategy, as planned?" "Is the strategy working, or do I need to adjust it?"
Provide for evaluation of strategy effectiveness.	Have children evaluate their performance to improve learning, by answering such questions as, "How well did I perform?" "Were my learning strategies effective?" "What strategies might work better?" "What other tasks might benefit from these strategies?"

Source: Schunk & Zimmerman, 2003.

Applications of Information Processing to Academic Learning

Over the past two decades, fundamental discoveries about the development of information processing have been applied to children's mastery of academic skills. In various academic subjects, researchers are identifying the cognitive ingredients of skilled performance, tracing their development, and pinpointing differences in cognitive skills between good and poor learners. They hope, as a result, to design teaching methods that will improve children's learning. In the following sections, we discuss several of these efforts in reading, mathematics, and scientific reasoning.

Reading

Reading makes use of many skills at once, taxing all aspects of our information-processing system. We must perceive single letters and letter combinations, translate them into speech sounds, recognize the visual appearance of many common words, hold chunks of text in working memory while interpreting their meaning, and combine the meanings of various parts of a text passage into an understandable whole. And because reading is so demanding, most or all of these skills must be done automatically. If one or more are poorly developed, they will compete for space in our limited working memories, and reading performance will decline. Becoming a proficient reader is a complex process that begins in the preschool years.

• **Early Childhood** Preschoolers understand a great deal about written language long before they learn to read and write in conventional ways. This is not surprising: Children in industrialized nations live in a world filled with written symbols. Each day, they observe and participate in activities involving storybooks, calendars, lists, and signs and, while doing so, try to figure out how written symbols convey meaning. Children's active efforts to construct literacy knowledge through informal experiences are called **emergent literacy.**

Milestones

Development of Information Processing

Age	Basic Capacities	Strategies	Knowledge	Metacognition
2–5 years 	■ Basic capacity of the system and processing speed increase. ■ Many processing skills are evident, including attention, recognition, recall, and reconstruction.	■ Attention becomes more focused and sustained. ■ Inhibition improves. ■ Beginnings of memory strategies are present, but they are seldom used spontaneously and have little impact on performance. ■ Variability and adaptive selection among strategies are evident.	■ Knowledge expands and becomes better organized. ■ Familiar events are remembered in scripts, which become more elaborate. ■ Autobiographical memory emerges, takes on narrative organization, and becomes more detailed.	■ Awareness of mental activities is present, but preschoolers view the mind as a passive container of information.
6–10 years	■ Basic capacity of the system and processing speed continue to increase. 	■ Attention becomes more selective, adaptable, and planful. ■ Inhibition continues to improve. ■ Memory strategies of rehearsal and taxonomic organization are used spontaneously and more effectively. ■ Ability to use multiple strategies at once increases. ■ Ability to draw inferences in reconstructive processing improves. ■ Reliance on gist memory for reasoning increases. ■ By the end of this period, memory strategy of elaboration appears.	■ Knowledge continues to expand and become better organized. 	■ View of the mind as an active constructive agent develops. ■ Knowledge of cognitive processes and their relationships grows. ■ Knowledge of the impact of strategies on performance increases. ■ Knowledge of interactions among cognitive processes, strategies, and type of task increases. ■ Cognitive self-regulation improves gradually.
11 years–adulthood	■ Basic capacity of the system and processing speed continue to increase, but at a slower pace.	■ Inhibition and attention and memory strategies continue to improve. 	■ Knowledge expands further and becomes more intricately organized.	■ Metacognitive knowledge and cognitive self-regulation continue to improve.

Note: These milestones represent overall age trends. Individual differences exist in the precise age at which each milestone is attained.

Photos: (top) © Laura Dwight Photography; (middle) © David Young-Wolff/PhotoEdit; (bottom) © Adrian Sherratt/Alamy

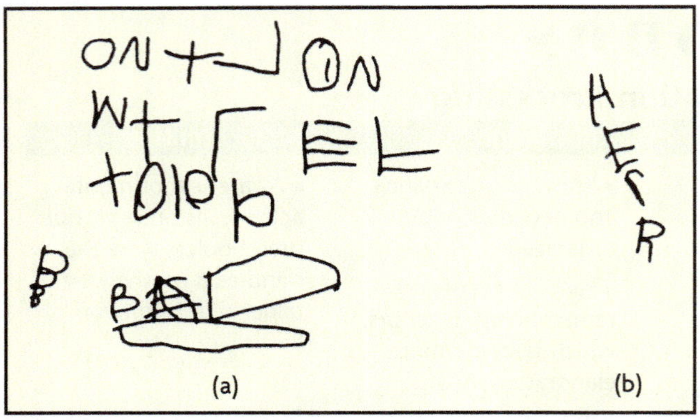

Figure 7.12 **A story (a) and a grocery list (b) written by a 4-year-old child.**
This child's writing has many features of real print. It also reveals an awareness of different kinds of written expression. (From Lea M. McGee & Donald J. Richgels, *Literacy's Beginnings: Supporting Young Readers And Writers, 4/e.* Published by Allyn & Bacon, Boston, MA. Copyright © 2004 by Pearson Education. Reprinted by permission of the publisher.)

Young preschoolers search for units of written language as they "read" memorized versions of stories and recognize familiar signs, such as "PIZZA." But they do not yet understand the symbolic function of the elements of print (Bialystok & Martin, 2003). Many preschoolers think that a single letter stands for a whole word or that each letter in a person's signature represents a separate name. In fact, initially preschoolers do not distinguish between drawing and writing. Around age 4, their writing shows some distinctive features of print, such as separate forms arranged in a line. But they often include picturelike devices, such as writing "sun" by using a yellow marker or a circular shape (Levin & Bus, 2003). They use their understanding of the symbolic function of drawings to make a "drawing of print."

Preschoolers revise these ideas as their cognitive capacities improve, as they encounter writing in many contexts, and as adults help them with written communication. Gradually, they notice more features of written language and depict writing that varies in function, as in the "story" and "grocery list" in Figure 7.12.

Eventually children figure out that letters are parts of words and are linked to sounds in systematic ways, as seen in the invented spellings typical between ages 5 and 7. At first, children rely on sounds in the names of letters: "ADE LAFWTS KRMD NTU A LAVATR" ("eighty elephants crammed into a[n] elevator"). Over time, they grasp sound–letter correspondences and learn that some letters have more than one common sound and that context affects their use (*a* is pronounced differently in *cat* than in *table*) (McGee & Richgels, 2008).

Literacy development builds on a broad foundation of spoken language and knowledge about the world. Over time, children's language and literacy progress facilitate each other (Dickinson et al., 2003). **Phonological awareness**—the ability to reflect on and manipulate the sound structure of spoken language, as indicated by sensitivity to changes in sounds within words, to rhyming, and to incorrect pronunciation—is a strong predictor of emergent literacy knowledge (Dickinson et al., 2003; Paris & Paris, 2006). When combined with sound–letter knowledge, it enables children to isolate speech segments and link them with their written symbols. Vocabulary and grammatical knowledge are also influential. And adult–child narrative conversations enhance diverse language skills essential for literacy progress.

The more informal literacy experiences preschoolers have, the better their language and emergent literacy development and their later reading skills (Dickinson & McCabe, 2001; Speece et al., 2004). Pointing out letter–sound correspondences and playing language-sound games enhance children's awareness of the sound structure of language and its representation in print (Foy & Mann, 2003). *Interactive reading,* in which adults discuss storybook content with preschoolers, promotes many aspects of language and literacy development. Adult-supported writing activities that focus on narrative, such as preparing a letter or a story, also have wide-ranging benefits (Purcell-Gates, 1996; Wasik & Bond, 2001). In longitudinal research, each of these literacy experiences predicted improved reading achievement in middle childhood (Senechal & LeFevre, 2002; Storch & Whitehurst, 2001).

Preschoolers from low-income families have fewer home and preschool language and literacy learning opportunities than economically advantaged agemates—a major reason that they lag behind in reading achievement throughout the school years (Foster et al., 2005; Foster & Miller, 2007). In a program that "flooded" child-care centers with children's books and provided caregivers with training on how to get 3- and 4-year-olds to spend time with books, children showed much greater gains in emergent literacy knowledge than a control group not experiencing the intervention (Neuman, 1999). For ways to support early childhood literacy development, see Applying What We Know on the following page.

Preschoolers acquire literacy knowledge informally through participating in everyday activities involving written symbols. This 4-year-old tries to write his name while a classmate helps by holding up his name card so he can easily see the letters. © Laura Dwight Photography

Applying What We Know

Supporting Emergent Literacy in Early Childhood

Strategy	Explanation
Provide literacy-rich home and preschool environments.	Homes and preschools with abundant reading and writing materials—including a wide variety of children's storybooks, some relevant to children's ethnic backgrounds—open the door to a wealth of language and literacy experiences.
Engage in interactive book reading.	When adults discuss story content, ask open-ended questions about story events, explain the meaning of words, and point out features of print, they promote language development, comprehension of story content, knowledge of story structure, and awareness of units of written language.
Provide outings to libraries, museums, parks, zoos, and other community settings.	Visits to child-oriented community settings enhance children's general knowledge and offer many opportunities to see how written language is used in everyday life. They also provide personally meaningful topics for narrative conversation, which promote many language skills essential for literacy development.
Point out letter–sound correspondences, play rhyming and other language-sound games, and read rhyming poems and stories.	Experiences that help children isolate the sounds in words foster phonological awareness—a powerful predictor of early childhood literacy knowledge and later reading and spelling achievement.
Support children's efforts at writing, especially narrative products.	Assisting children in their efforts to write—especially letters, stories, and other narratives—fosters many language and literacy skills.
Model literacy activities.	When children see adults engaged in reading and writing activities, they better understand the diverse, everyday functions of literacy skills and the knowledge and pleasure that literacy brings. As a result, children's motivation to become literate is strengthened.

Sources: Dickinson & McCabe, 2001; McGee & Richgels, 2008.

• **Middle Childhood** As children make the transition from emergent literacy to conventional reading, phonological awareness continues to predict reading (and spelling) progress. Other information-processing activities also contribute. Gains in processing speed foster school-age children's rapid conversion of visual symbols into sounds—an ability that also distinguishes good from poor readers (Kail, Hall, & Caskey, 1999; McBride-Chang & Kail, 2002). Visual scanning and discrimination are also important and improve with reading experience (Rayner, Pollatsek, & Starr, 2003). Performing all these skills efficiently releases working memory for higher-level activities involved in comprehending the text's meaning.

Until recently, researchers were involved in an intense debate over how to teach children to read. Those who took a **whole-language approach** argued that reading should be taught in a way that parallels natural language learning. From the beginning, children should be exposed to text in its complete form—stories, poems, letters, posters, and lists—so that they can appreciate the communicative function of written language. According to this view, as long as reading is kept meaningful, children will be motivated to discover the specific skills they need (Watson, 1989). Other experts advocated a **phonics approach,** believing that children should first be coached on *phonics*—the basic rules for translating written symbols into sounds. Only after mastering these skills should they get complex reading material (Rayner & Pollatsek, 1989).

Many studies show that, in fact, children learn best with a mixture of both approaches. In kindergarten, first, and second grades, teaching that includes phonics boosts reading scores, especially for children who lag behind in reading progress (Stahl & Miller, 2006; Xue & Meisels, 2004). And when teachers combine real reading and writing with teaching of phonics and engage in other excellent teaching practices—encouraging children to tackle reading

Effective reading instruction involves a complex mix of elements—among them, balancing phonics and whole-language teaching. This first-grade teacher works with a small group, embedding phonics in exposure to interesting stories and challenging writing tasks. © Syracuse Newspapers/The Image Works

challenges and integrating reading into all school subjects—first graders show far greater literacy progress (Pressley et al., 2002).

Why might combining phonics with whole language work best? Learning relations between letters and sounds enables children to *decode,* or decipher, words they have never seen before. Children who enter school low in phonological awareness make far better reading progress when given training in phonics. Soon they detect new letter–sound relations while reading on their own (Goswami, 2000). It is not surprising, then, that phonics training promotes children's belief that they can succeed at challenging reading tasks (Tunmer & Chapman, 2002).

Yet too much emphasis on basic skills may cause children to lose sight of the goal of reading: understanding. Children who read aloud fluently without registering meaning know little about effective reading strategies—for example, that they must read more carefully if they will be tested than if they are reading for pleasure or that explaining a passage in their own words is a good way to assess comprehension. Providing instruction aimed at increasing knowledge and use of reading strategies readily enhances reading performance from third grade on (Paris & Paris, 2006; Van Keer, 2004).

Around age 7 to 8, children make a major shift—from "learning to read" to "reading to learn" (Ely, 2005). As decoding and comprehension skills become efficient, adolescent readers actively engage with the text, adjusting the way they read to fit their current purpose—at times seeking new facts and ideas, at other times questioning, agreeing with, or disagreeing with the writer's viewpoint.

Mathematics

Mathematical reasoning, like reading, builds on informally acquired knowledge. Recall from Chapter 6 that some evidence suggests that infants have basic numerical knowledge (see page 259). Between 14 and 16 months, toddlers display a beginning grasp of **ordinality,** or order relationships between quantities—for example, that 3 is more than 2 and 2 is more than 1—an attainment that serves as the basis for more complex understandings (Starkey, 1992; Strauss & Curtis, 1984).

• **Early Childhood** In the early preschool years, children attach verbal labels (*lots, little, big, small*) to amounts and sizes. Sometime in the third year, they begin to count. By the time children turn 3, most can count rows of about five objects, saying the correct number words, although they do not know exactly what the words mean. For example, when asked for *one,* they give one item, but when asked for *two, three, four,* or *five,* they usually give a larger, but incorrect, amount. Nevertheless, 2½- to 3½-year-olds understand that a number word refers to a unique quantity—that when a number label changes (for example, from *five* to *six*), the number of items should also change (Sarnecka & Gelman, 2004).

By age 3½ to 4, most children have mastered the meaning of numbers up to *ten,* count correctly, and grasp the vital principle of **cardinality**—that the last word in a counting sequence indicates the quantity of items in a set (Geary, 2006a). Mastery of cardinality increases the efficiency of children's counting. By age 4, children use counting to solve arithmetic problems. At first, their strategies are tied to the order of numbers as presented; when given $2 + 4$, they count on from 2 (Bryant & Nunes, 2002). But soon they experiment with other strategies and, as a result, master the *min* strategy, a more efficient approach (refer back to Siegler's model of strategy choice, pages 282–283). Around this time, children realize that subtraction cancels out addition. Knowing, for example, that $4 + 3 = 7$, they infer without counting that $7 - 3 = 4$ (Rasmussen, Ho, & Bisanz, 2003). Grasping this principle, along with other basic rules of addition and subtraction, greatly facilitates rapid computation.

Young children's understanding of basic arithmetic computation makes possible beginning *estimation*—the ability to generate approximate answers, which can be used to evaluate the accuracy of exact answers. After watching several doughnuts being added to or removed from a plate of four to ten doughnuts, 3- and 4-year-olds make sensible predictions of how many doughnuts are on the plate (Zur & Gelman, 2004). Still, children can estimate only just beyond limit of their calculation competence (Dowker, 2003). For example, those who can solve addition problems with sums up to 10 can estimate answers with sums up to about 20. And as with arithmetic operations, children try out diverse estimation strategies, gradually moving to more accurate, efficient techniques.

The arithmetic knowledge just described emerges in many cultures around the world. But children construct these understandings sooner when adults provide frequent occasions for counting, comparing quantities, and talking about number concepts (Benigno & Ellis, 2004; Klibanoff et al., 2006). In a math intervention program for low-income 4-year-olds, teachers included math activities in almost all classroom routines—for example, counting the number of steps needed to get from various locations in the classroom to the play yard and identifying a partner holding a card with a certain number of dots on it. Compared with children in other classrooms, intervention children scored higher in math concepts and enjoyed math activities more (Arnold et al., 2002). Solid, secure early-childhood math knowledge is essential for the wide variety of mathematical skills children will be taught once they enter school.

• **Middle Childhood** Mathematics teaching in elementary school builds on and greatly enriches children's informal knowledge of number concepts and counting. Written notation systems and formal computational techniques enhance children's ability to represent numbers, compute, and estimate. Over the early elementary school years, children acquire basic math facts through a combination of frequent practice, reasoning about number concepts, and teaching that conveys effective strategies. (Return to page 281 for research supporting the importance of both extended practice and a grasp of concepts.) Eventually, children retrieve answers automatically and apply this knowledge to more complex problems.

Arguments about how to teach math resemble those in reading, pitting drill in computing against "number sense," or understanding. Again, a blend of both approaches is most beneficial. In learning basic math, poorly performing students use cumbersome techniques (such as counting all items in an addition problem) or try to retrieve answers from memory too soon. They have not sufficiently experimented with strategies to see which are most effective and to reorganize their observations in logical, efficient ways—for example, noticing that multiplication problems involving 2 (2 × 8) are equivalent to addition doubles (8 + 8). On tasks that reveal their grasp of math concepts, their performance is weak (Canobi, 2004; Canobi, Reeve, & Pattison, 2003). This suggests that encouraging students to apply strategies and making sure they understand why certain strategies work well are essential for solid mastery of basic math.

A similar picture emerges for more complex skills, such as carrying in addition, borrowing in subtraction, and operating with decimals and fractions. Children taught by rote cannot apply the procedure to new problems. Instead, they persistently make mistakes, following a "math rule" that they recall incorrectly because they do not understand it (Carpenter et al., 1999). Look at the following subtraction errors:

$$\begin{array}{r} 427 \\ -138 \\ \hline 311 \end{array} \qquad \begin{array}{r} 7{,}002 \\ -5{,}445 \\ \hline 1{,}447 \end{array}$$

In the first problem, the child consistently subtracts the smaller from the larger digit, regardless of which is on top. In the second, the child skips columns with zeros in a borrowing operation and, whenever there is a zero on top, writes the bottom digit as the answer.

Children who are given rich opportunities to experiment with problem solving, to appreciate the reasons behind strategies, and to evaluate solution techniques seldom make such errors. In one study, second

Preschoolers construct basic arithmetic understandings sooner when they have many opportunities to count, compare quantities, and talk about number concepts. Solid, secure, informally acquired early childhood math knowledge is essential for math skills that will be taught in elementary school. © Sally and Richard Greenhill/Alamy

graders who were taught in these ways not only mastered correct procedures but even invented their own successful strategies—some of them superior to standard, school-taught methods! Consider this solution:

$$\begin{array}{rrrr} ^{3}4 & ^{15}6 & ^{14}\not{5} & ^{12}2 \\ -1 & 9 & 6 & 8 \\ 2 & 6 & 8 & 4 \end{array}$$

In subtracting, the child performed all trades first, flexibly moving either from right to left or from left to right, and then subtracted all four columns—a highly efficient, accurate approach (Fuson & Burghard, 2003).

In a German study, the more teachers emphasized conceptual knowledge—by having children actively construct meanings in word problems before practicing computation and memorizing math facts—the more children gained in math achievement from second to third grade (Staub & Stern, 2002). Children taught in this way draw on their solid knowledge of relationships between operations (for example, that the inverse of division is multiplication) to generate efficient procedures. And because they have been encouraged to estimate answers, if these children take the wrong path in computation, they are usually self-correcting. Furthermore, they appreciate connections between math operations and problem contexts and, when appropriate, can solve a word problem quickly through estimation instead of exact calculation, as in, "If Jesse spent \$3.45 for bananas, \$2.62 for bread, and \$3.55 for peanut butter, can he pay for it all with a \$10 bill?" (De Corte & Verschaffel, 2006).

In Asian countries, students receive a variety of supports for acquiring mathematical knowledge and often excel at both math reasoning and computation. Use of the metric system, which presents ones, tens, hundreds, and thousands values in all areas of measurement, helps Asian children grasp place value. The consistent structure of number words in Asian languages (*ten-two* for 12, *ten-three* for 13) also makes this idea clear (Miura & Okamoto, 2003). And because Asian number words are shorter and more quickly pronounced, more digits can be held in working memory at once, increasing the speed of thinking. Furthermore, in early math lessons, particularly abacus instruction, many Chinese and Japanese children learn to use the number 5 as an anchor, which facilitates efficient computation (Kuriyama & Yoshida, 1995).

Finally, compared with North America (especially the United States), math lessons in Asian classrooms devote more time to exploring math concepts and strategies and less to drill and repetition (Woodward & Ono, 2004; Zhou & Peverly, 2005). As Chapter 15 will reveal, Asian countries consistently score at or near the top in international comparisons of high school achievement in math—and in other subjects as well.

Cultural and language-based factors contribute to Asian children's skill at manipulating multidigit numbers. The abacus supports these Japanese students' understanding of place value. Ones, tens, hundreds, and thousands are each represented by a different column of beads, and calculations are performed by moving the beads to different positions. As children become skilled at using the abacus, they generate mental images that help them solve complex arithmetic problems. © Fiji Foto/The Image Works

Scientific Reasoning

During a free moment in physical education class, 13-year-old Heidi wondered why more of her tennis serves and returns passed the net and dropped in her opponent's court when she used a particular brand of balls. "Is it something about their color or size?" she asked herself. "Hmm . . . or maybe it's their surface texture—that might affect their bounce."

According to Deanna Kuhn, the heart of scientific reasoning is coordinating theories with evidence. A scientist can clearly describe the theory he or she favors, knows what evidence is needed to support it and what would refute it, and can explain how pitting evidence against theories has led to the acceptance of one theory as opposed to others. What evidence would Heidi need to confirm her theory about the tennis balls?

Kuhn (2002) has conducted extensive research into the development of scientific reasoning, using problems that resemble Piaget's tasks in that several variables might affect an outcome. In one series of studies, third, sixth, and ninth graders and adults were first given evidence, sometimes consistent and sometimes conflicting with theories, then questioned about the accuracy of each theory.

■ **Figure 7.13** **Which features of these sports balls—size, color, surface texture, or presence or absence of ridges—influence the quality of a player's serve?**
This set of evidence suggests that color might be important, since light-colored balls are largely in the good-serve basket and dark-colored balls in the bad-serve basket. But the same is true for texture! The good-serve basket has mostly smooth balls, the bad-serve basket rough balls. Since all light-colored balls are smooth and all dark-colored balls are rough, we cannot tell whether color or texture makes a difference. But we can conclude that size and presence or absence of ridges are not important, since these features are equally represented in the good-serve and bad-serve baskets. (Adapted from Kuhn, Amsel, & O'Loughlin, 1988.)

For example, participants were given a problem much like Heidi's: to theorize about which of several features of sports balls—size (large or small), color (light or dark), surface texture (rough or smooth), or presence or absence of ridges on the surface—influences the quality of a player's serve. Next, they were told about the theory of Mr. (or Ms.) S, who believes that the ball's size is important, and the theory of Mr. (or Ms.) C, who thinks color matters. Finally, the interviewer presented evidence, placing balls with certain characteristics into two baskets, one labeled "good serve" and the other "bad serve" (see Figure 7.13).

• **Age-Related Change** Kuhn and her collaborators (1988) found that the capacity to reason like a scientist improved with age. The youngest participants often ignored conflicting evidence or distorted it in ways consistent with their theory. When one third grader, who judged that size was causal (with large balls producing good serves and small balls producing bad serves), was shown incomplete evidence (a single, large, light-colored ball in the good-serve basket and no balls in the bad-serve basket), he still insisted on the accuracy of Mr. S's theory (which was also his own). Asked to explain, he stated flatly, "Because this ball is big . . . the color doesn't really matter" (Kuhn, 1989, p. 677).

These findings, and others like them, suggest that on complex, multivariable tasks, children—instead of viewing evidence as separate from and bearing on a theory—often blend the two into a single representation of "the way things are." Children are especially likely to overlook evidence that does not match their prior beliefs when a causal variable is implausible (like color affecting performance of a sports ball) and when task demands (number of variables to be evaluated) are high (Zimmerman, 2005, 2007). The ability to distinguish theory from evidence and use logical rules to examine their relationship improves from childhood through adolescence, continuing into adulthood (Kuhn & Dean, 2004; Kuhn & Pearsall, 2000).

• **How Scientific Reasoning Develops** What factors support skill at coordinating theory with evidence? Greater working-memory resources, permitting simultaneous comparison of a theory and the effects of several variables, is vital. In addition, participants benefit from exposure to increasingly complex problems and to teaching that highlights critical features of scientific reasoning—for example, pointing out why a scientist's expectations in a particular situation are inconsistent with everyday beliefs and experiences (Chinn & Malhotra, 2002). These findings explain why scientific reasoning is strongly influenced by years of schooling, whether individuals grapple with traditional scientific tasks (like the sports ball problem) or engage in informal reasoning—for example, justifying a theory about what causes children to fail in school (Amsel & Brock, 1996; Kuhn, 1993).

High school students attending an engineering summer camp at the University of Texas attempt to design a catapult for shooting water balloons. Extensive experience coordinating theory with evidence to solve complex problems results in gains in scientific reasoning as teenagers reflect on their strategies and revise them. © Bob Daemmrich/The Image Works

Many researchers believe that sophisticated *metacognitive understanding* is vital for scientific reasoning (Kuhn, 1999; Moshman, 1999). Microgenetic research (see pages 63–64 in Chapter 2) shows that when children regularly pit theory against evidence over many weeks, they experiment with various strategies, reflect on and revise them, and become aware of the nature of logic. Then they apply their abstract appreciation of logic to a wide variety of situations. The ability to *think about* theories, *deliberately isolate* variables, and *actively seek* disconfirming evidence is rarely present before adolescence (Kuhn, 2000; Moshman, 1998).

Though far more competent than children, adolescents and adults vary widely in scientific reasoning skills. Many continue to show a self-serving bias, applying logic more effectively to ideas they doubt than to those they favor (Klaczynski, 1997; Klaczynski & Narasimham, 1998a). Reasoning scientifically requires the metacognitive capacity to evaluate one's objectivity—a disposition to be fair-minded rather than self-serving (Moshman, 1999). As we will see in Chapter 11, this flexible, open-minded approach is not just a cognitive attainment but a personality trait—one that assists teenagers greatly in forming an identity and developing morally.

Children and adolescents develop scientific reasoning skills in a similar step-by-step fashion on different kinds of tasks. In a series of studies, 10- to 20-year-olds were given sets of problems graded in difficulty. One set contained causal-experimental tasks like the sports ball problem in Figure 7.13, another contained quantitative-relational tasks like Piaget's pendulum problem, and still another consisted of verbal propositional tasks (see page 252 in Chapter 6). In each type of task, adolescents mastered component skills in sequential order by expanding their metacognitive awareness (Demetriou et al., 1993, 1996, 2002). For example, on causal-experimental tasks, they first became aware of the many variables—separately and in combination—that could influence an outcome. This enabled them to formulate and test hypotheses. Over time, adolescents combined separate skills into a smoothly functioning system, constructing a general model that they could apply to many instances of a given type of problem.

Do the metacognitive advances just described remind you of the concept of *central conceptual structures* in Robbie Case's neo-Piagetian theory, discussed on page 281? Piaget also underscored the role of metacognition in formal operational thought when he spoke of "operating on operations" (see Chapter 6, page 251). But information-processing findings reveal that scientific reasoning does not result from an abrupt, stagewise change, as Piaget believed. Instead, it develops gradually out of many specific experiences that require children and adolescents to match theory against evidence and reflect on their thinking.

Evaluation of the Information-Processing Approach

A major strength of the information-processing approach is its explicitness and precision in breaking down complex cognitive activities into their components. Information processing has provided a wealth of detailed evidence on how younger versus older and more-skilled versus less-skilled individuals attend, remember, reason, and solve problems. It also offers precise mechanisms of cognitive development; Table 7.1 summarizes the most important of these. **TAKE A MOMENT...** As you review them, think back to theories and findings that illustrate the role of each. Finally, because of its precision, information-processing research has contributed greatly to the design of teaching techniques that advance many aspects of children's thinking.

The principal limitation of the information-processing perspective stems, ironically, from its central strength: By analyzing cognition into its components, information processing has had difficulty reassembling them into a broad, comprehensive theory of development. As we have seen, the neo-Piagetian perspective is one effort to build a general theory by retaining Piaget's stages while drawing on information-processing mechanisms to explain cognitive change.

Furthermore, the computer metaphor, while bringing precision to research on the human mind, has drawbacks. Computer models of cognitive processing, though complex in their own right, do not reflect the richness of real-life learning experiences. They overlook aspects of cognition that are not linear and logical, such as imagination and creativity. Moreover, computers do not have desires, interests, and intentions, nor can they engage in interaction with others, as children do when they learn from parents, teachers, and peers. Perhaps because of the narrowness of the computer metaphor, information processing has not told us much about the links between cognition and other areas of development. In later chapters, we will look at findings of investigators who have applied information-processing assumptions to children's thinking about certain aspects of their social world. But in research on children's social and moral understanding, extensions of Piaget's theory still prevail.

Finally, only recently has information-processing research responded to growing interest in the biological bases of cognitive development. Connectionist theories have begun to fill

Table 7.1 Mechanisms of Cognitive Development from the Information-Processing Perspective

Mechanism	Description
Basic processing capacity	Capacity of the mental system increases, enabling more information to be held in working memory at once.
Processing efficiency	Speed of basic operations increases, freeing up available space in working memory for additional mental activities.
Encoding of information	Encoding, in the form of attention, becomes more thorough and better adapted to task demands.
Inhibition	Ability to prevent internal and external distracting stimuli from capturing attention improves, freeing up working memory for remembering, reasoning, and solving problems.
Strategy execution	Strategies become more effective, improving storage, retrieval, and use of information for reasoning and problem solving.
Knowledge	Amount and structure of the knowledge base increase, making new, related information more meaningful so it is easier to store and retrieve.
Metacognition	Awareness and understanding of cognitive processes expand and self-regulation improves, leading strategies to be applied more effectively in a wider range of situations.

this gap by creating computer simulations that model human information processing at a neural level. Evolutionary ideas, as well, have started to appear in information-processing theories, as Siegler's model of strategy choice illustrates. And currently, the work of developmental cognitive neuroscientists is enlarging our appreciation of how changes in the brain are related to children's processing skills.

Despite its shortcomings, the information-processing approach holds great promise. The near future is likely to bring new breakthroughs in understanding mechanisms of cognitive development and neurological changes that underlie various mental activities, and in identifying teaching techniques that support children's learning.

Ask Yourself

Review Why are gains in metacognition important for the development of scientific reasoning? How can teachers promote the development of scientific reasoning?

Apply Review Heidi's reasoning about the impact of several variables on the bounce of tennis balls on page 310. What features of her thinking suggest that she is beginning to reason scientifically?

Connect Using mechanisms of cognitive development discussed in this chapter, explain why teaching both basic skills and understanding of concepts and strategies is vital for children's progress in reading and mathematics.

Reflect Describe early, informal experiences important for literacy and math development that you experienced while growing up. How do you think those experiences contributed to your academic progress after you started school?

SUMMARY

The Information-Processing Approach

What unique features characterize the information-processing approach to cognitive development?

- Information-processing theorists view the mind as a complex, symbol-manipulating system through which information flows, much like a computer. Researchers use computer-like diagrams and flowcharts to analyze thinking into its components, mapping the precise steps involved in thinking about a task or problem.

General Models of Information Processing

Describe the store and connectionist models, noting implications for cognitive development.

- The **store model** assumes that we hold, or store, information in three parts of the system, where **mental strategies** operate on it so that it can be retained and used efficiently and flexibly. The **sensory register** and **working,** or **short-term, memory** are limited in capacity. Within working memory, the **central executive** directs the flow of information and the use of strategies, influencing the extent to which information is transferred to **long-term memory,** our limitless, permanent knowledge base.
- The store model suggests that two broad aspects of the cognitive system increase with age: (1) the basic capacity of its stores, especially working memory, and (2) the extent and effectiveness of strategy use. Research on **memory span** supports this view. Processing speed also increases, with dramatic gains in middle childhood that enhance working memory and ability to learn.
- Researchers in developmental cognitive neuroscience have devised **connectionist,** or **artificial neural network, models** that use computers to simulate the workings of neurons and their connections. A typical artificial neural network is organized into layers much like the brain's neurological structure. Researchers compare the network's responses with those of individuals of different ages. Findings reveal that gradual, internal learning often

precedes changes in behavior that appear stagelike when viewed from outside the system. Because just a few built-in procedures get learning started on many types of tasks, connectionists claim that the human cognitive system is a general processing device.

- Compared to children and adults, most artificial neural networks learn slowly. Constructivist connectionist models, which add new units and connections and remove those that do not contribute to learning, better capture infants' and children's progress on diverse tasks. They also shed light on how brain structure changes in response to learners' experiences.

Developmental Theories of Information Processing

Describe and evaluate Case's neo-Piagetian theory and Siegler's model of strategy choice.

- Case's **neo-Piagetian theory** accepts Piaget's stages but attributes change within and between stages to greater efficiency in use of working-memory capacity. Brain development, practice with schemes and automization of strategies, and formation of **central conceptual structures** contribute to development. Case's theory provides an information-processing explanation of the continuum of acquisition—that many understandings appear in specific situations at different times—and thus is better able than Piaget's theory to account for unevenness in cognitive development.
- Siegler's **model of strategy choice** applies an evolutionary perspective to children's cognition. Strategy development follows an overlapping-waves pattern. When given challenging problems, children generate a variety of strategies, gradually selecting from them on the basis of accuracy and speed. Siegler's model accounts for both diversity and continuous change in children's thinking.

Attention

Describe the development of attention, including selective, adaptable, and planful strategies.

- Gains in sustained attention depend on rapid growth of the frontal lobes of the cerebral cortex, the capacity to generate increasingly complex play goals, and adult scaffolding of attention. As sustained attention increases, children become more selective—better at focusing on relevant aspects of a task—and better at flexibly adapting attention to task requirements. Selective attention depends on **inhibition,** the ability to control distracting stimuli.
- Development of attentional (and memory) strategies tends to occur in four phases: (1) **production deficiency** (failure to produce the strategy); (2) **control deficiency** (failure to execute the strategy effectively); (3) **utilization deficiency** (consistent use of the strategy, but with little or no performance improvement); and (4) **effective strategy use.**

© Felicia Martinez/PhotoEdit

- During middle childhood, children become better at **planning.** On tasks requiring systematic visual search or the coordination of many acts, school-age children are more likely than preschoolers to proceed in an orderly fashion. Children learn much from cultural tools that support planning, adult guidance and encouragement, and opportunities to practice.
- Deficits in executive processing and inhibition may underlie the serious attentional and impulse-control difficulties of children with **attention-deficit hyperactivity disorder (ADHD).** Children with ADHD have serious academic and social problems.

Memory

Describe the development of memory strategies of rehearsal, organization, and elaboration, noting the influence of task demands and culture.

- Although the beginnings of memory strategies can be seen in the preschool years, young children seldom engage in **rehearsal** or **organization.** As use of these strategies improves, children combine them; the more strategies children use simultaneously, the better they remember. **Elaboration** develops later—at the end of middle childhood—and becomes more common during adolescence.
- School tasks requiring children to memorize isolated bits of information promote deliberate memorization in middle childhood. Like young children, adults in non-Western cultures who lack formal schooling rarely use or benefit from instruction in memory strategies.

Describe the development of three approaches to memory retrieval: recognition, recall, and reconstruction.

- **Recognition,** the simplest form of retrieval, is a fairly automatic process that is highly accurate by the preschool years. **Recall**—generating a mental representation of an absent stimulus—is more difficult, shows much greater improvement with age, and is strongly associated with language development.
- Even young children engage in **reconstruction** when remembering complex, meaningful material. As originally provided information decays and new information is presented, children make more inferences about actors and actions, increasing the coherence of reconstructed information and, therefore, its memorableness. However, much recalled information can be inaccurate.

© Nancy Richmond/The Image Works

- According to **fuzzy-trace theory,** when information is encoded, it is reconstructed automatically into a **gist**—a vague, fuzzy version, stored separately from the verbatim version, that is especially useful for reasoning. With age, children rely less on verbatim memory and more on reconstructed gists, contributing to improved recall of details with age. More skilled gist thinkers, however, are prone to reporting false items consistent with the fuzzy trace.

How do gains in knowledge enhance memory performance?

- Children's expanding knowledge base improves memory by making new, related information easier to store and retrieve. Experts also have more elaborately structured knowledge and show greater organization at retrieval, suggesting that they apply memory strategies in their area of expertise with little or no effort.
- Children differ not only in what they know but also in their motivation to use their knowledge to acquire new information. Extensive knowledge and use of memory strategies support each other.

Describe the development and function of scripts and autobiographical memory.

- Like adults, young children remember familiar experiences in terms of **scripts**—a special form of reconstructive memory that permits them to predict what might happen on future similar occasions. Scripts, which become more elaborate with age, may support the transition from the young child's **episodic memory** to **semantic memory.**
- Research suggests that changes in the frontal lobes of the cerebral cortex, the advent of a clear self-image, and the development of verbal means for storing information contribute to the end of **infantile amnesia** after age 3. As preschoolers talk with adults about personally significant past events, they adopt the narrative thinking generated in these dialogues, forming an **autobiographical memory.** Children whose parents use an elaborative rather than a repetitive conversational style will produce more coherent and detailed personal stories.

How does eyewitness memory change with age, and what factors influence the accuracy of children's reports?

- Compared with preschoolers, school-age children are better able to give accurate, detailed, and complete eyewitness accounts and to resist adults' misleading questions. When a biased adult repeatedly asks leading questions, children are far more likely to give false information. Stereotyping of the accused as "bad" and a long delay between the events and the child's eyewitness report further contribute to inaccurate reporting. Interventions that increase children's accurate recall include practice interviews, open-ended questioning that prompts children to disclose details, and a warm interview tone.

Metacognition

Describe the development of metacognitive knowledge and cognitive self-regulation, and explain why cognitive self-regulation is vital for success on complex tasks.

- **Metacognition** expands greatly as children construct a naïve **theory of mind,** a coherent understanding of people as mental beings. From early to middle childhood, children become increasingly conscious of cognitive capacities and strategies. They come to view the mind as an active, constructive agent rather than a passive container of information. Gradually, children take account of interactions among variables, and metacognition broadens into a more complex theory.
- **Cognitive self-regulation**—continually monitoring progress toward a goal, checking outcomes, and redirecting unsuccessful efforts—develops slowly. The relationship between knowledge of memory strategies and recall strengthens over middle childhood. By adolescence, cognitive self-regulation is a strong predictor of academic success. Parents and teachers can promote self-regulation by suggesting problem-solving strategies and explaining why they are effective.

Applications of Information Processing to Academic Learning

Discuss the development of reading, mathematics, and scientific reasoning, noting the implications of research findings for teaching.

- **Emergent literacy** reveals that young children understand a great deal about written language before they read and write in conventional ways. Preschoolers gradually revise incorrect ideas about the meaning of written symbols as their cognitive capacities improve, as they encounter writing in many contexts, and as adults help them with written communication.
- **Phonological awareness** is a strong predictor of emergent literacy knowledge and of later reading and spelling achievement. Adult–child narrative conversations and informal literacy-related experiences also contribute to literacy development.
- As children make the transition to conventional literacy, phonological awareness, processing speed, and visual scanning and discrimination contribute to reading progress. A combination of **whole-language** and **phonics approaches** is most effective for teaching beginning reading.
- Like reading, mathematical reasoning builds on informally acquired knowledge. Toddlers display a beginning grasp of **ordinality,** which serves as the basis for more complex understandings. As preschoolers gain experience with counting, they grasp **cardinality** and begin to solve simple addition and subtraction problems. When adults provide many occasions for counting and comparing quantities, children acquire basic numerical understandings sooner.

© Sally and Richard Greenhill/Alamy

- During the early school years, children acquire basic math facts through a combination of frequent practice, reasoning about number concepts, and teaching that conveys effective strategies. In attempting to solve more complex problems, they sometimes apply strategies incorrectly because they do not understand the basis for them. The best mathematics instruction combines practice in experimenting with strategies and conceptual understanding.
- The ability to coordinate theory with evidence—the heart of scientific reasoning—improves from childhood to adolescence. Greater working-memory resources and exposure to increasingly complex problems in school contribute to the metacognitive understanding that is vital for reasoning scientifically.

Evaluation of the Information-Processing Approach

Summarize the strengths and limitations of the information-processing approach.

- A major strength of the information-processing approach is its precision in breaking down cognition into its components so that each can be studied thoroughly. Information processing has uncovered mechanisms of cognitive change and has contributed to the design of teaching techniques that advance children's thinking.
- Nevertheless, computer models of cognitive processing do not reflect the richness of real-life learning experiences and have not told us much about the links between cognition and other areas of development. Only recently has information-processing research responded to growing interest in the biological bases of cognitive development; connectionist theories have begun to fill this gap.

IMPORTANT TERMS AND CONCEPTS

8

"Circus"
Oindrila Gupta
12 years, India

Although intelligence tests predict children's academic achievement, they are far less effective at evaluating the analytical understanding, creativity, and practical know-how evident in the feat of these circus aerialists—or in this artist's colorful, dynamic depiction.

Intelligence

James Cleveland is the new president of Jumpstart, a U.S. organization that provides 3- to 5-year-olds from low-income families with several hundred hours per year of one-to-one educational enrichment. Two or three times a week, Jumpstart corps members (college students and older adults) go to a preschool or child-care center, where they read to and converse with a designated child, engage in additional individualized learning activities, and play collaborative games in small groups. Currently, Jumpstart serves more than 13,000 children in over 60 communities across the country.

Stepping into Jumpstart's top leadership position, James wrote to his nationwide staff, expressing his passion and resolve to help ever-increasing numbers of at-risk children start school with the literacy, self-regulation, and social skills they need to succeed. He had an inspiring personal story to tell.

James started public school as a weak, self-doubting reader—the very situation Jumpstart strives to prevent. He struggled with language arts assignments and frequently spent recess sitting in the classroom, barred from participating because he could not do—and soon refused to do—his reading work. "Pressure from my teacher and the embarrassment of being singled out added to my frustration," James recalled.

After weeks without progress, James's teacher called his parents. His father, an African American who had not had the chance to go to college, responded immediately. "He became my inspiration," said James. "He regarded his involvement as vital to my academic success—and to a life path of greater opportunity than his own."

James's father began taking him to the public library regularly. On each visit, he guided James in selecting a book, insisting that he choose a challenging one. Then father and son read together, jointly deciphering difficult passages. If James did not understand a word, they looked it up in the dictionary. "That unlocked the world of reading for me," said James, who went on to become a voracious reader, an excellent student, valedictorian of his high school class, and a graduate of Stanford University.

James summed up: "My dad's involvement taught me firsthand about the power of caring adult intervention. I began believing in myself because I knew my dad believed in me." His father's inspiration led James to dedicate his career to early educational intervention—a topic we consider in depth later in this chapter.

The **psychometric approach** to cognitive development is the basis for the wide variety of intelligence tests available for assessing children's mental abilities. Unlike Piagetian, Vygotskian, and information-processing views, which focus on the *process* of thinking, the psychometric perspective is *product* oriented, largely concerned with outcomes and results—how many and what kinds of questions children of different ages answer correctly. Psychometric researchers ask questions like these:

- What factors, or dimensions, make up intelligence, and how do they change with age?
- How can intelligence be measured so that scores predict future academic achievement, career attainment, and other aspects of intellectual success?
- Are mental test scores largely stable over childhood and adolescence, or can performance change dramatically?
- To what extent do children of the same age differ in intelligence, and what explains those differences?

As we examine these questions, we will quickly become immersed in the long-standing debate over the contribution of nature (heredity) and nurture (environment) to intelligence and the related controversy over whether intelligence tests are biased, or inaccurate, measures of the mental abilities of members of certain ethnic minority groups. We will see how the cognitive perspectives considered in previous chapters, as well as research on environmental contexts—home, school, societal attitudes, and public policies—have contributed to our understanding of children's test performance. We conclude with the development of giftedness, in the form of talent and creativity.

Definitions of Intelligence

TAKE A MOMENT... Jot down a list of behaviors that you regard as typical of highly intelligent people. Does your list contain just one or two items or a great many? In a study in which laypeople and experts completed a similar exercise, both groups viewed intelligence as made up of at least three broad attributes: verbal ability, practical problem solving, and social competence (Sternberg & Detterman, 1986). But respondents differed in their descriptions of these attributes. And contemporary experts showed much less agreement about the makeup of intelligence than did experts in a similar study conducted a half-century earlier! Clearly, most people think of intelligence as a complex combination of attributes, and little consensus exists among experts on its ingredients.

Defining children's intelligence is especially challenging because behaviors reflecting intelligence change with age. To illustrate, researchers asked students in an introductory psychology course to list five traits of intelligent 6-month-olds, 2-year-olds, 10-year-olds, and adults. Table 8.1 lists the students' responses. With age, sensorimotor responsiveness becomes less important, while verbal ability, problem solving, and reasoning become more important. Furthermore, when the students estimated correlations between various abilities, they predicted some close connections but expected others to correlate weakly (Siegler & Richards, 1980). This tension between intelligence as a single ability versus a collection of loosely related skills is ever present in historical and current theories on which mental tests are based.

James Cleveland attributes his academic and career success to his father's involvement in his learning. Today, as president of Jumpstart, James strives to provide the same kind of support to young children growing up in economically disadvantaged communities. © Bear Cieri/Courtesy of Jumpstart

Alfred Binet: A Holistic View

The social and educational climate of the late nineteenth and early twentieth centuries led to the development of the first intelligence tests. With the beginning of universal public education in Europe and North America—allowing all children, not just society's privileged, to enroll in school—educators sought methods to identify students who were unable to benefit from regular classroom instruction. The first

Table 8.1 Five Traits Most Often Mentioned by College Students as Characterizing Intelligence at Different Ages

6-Month-Olds	2-Year-Olds	10-Year-Olds	Adults
1. Recognition of people and objects	1. Verbal ability	1. Verbal ability	1. Reasoning
2. Motor coordination	2. Learning ability	2, 3, 4. Learning ability; problem solving; reasoning (three-way tie)	2. Verbal ability
3. Alertness	3. Awareness of people and environment		3. Problem solving
4. Awareness of environment	4. Motor coordination		4. Learning ability
5. Verbalization	5. Curiosity	5. Creativity	5. Creativity

Source: R. S. Siegler & D. D. Richards, 1980, "College Students' Prototypes of Children's Intelligence." Paper presented at the annual meeting of the American Psychological Association, New York. Adapted by permission of the author.

successful intelligence test, constructed by French psychologist Alfred Binet and his colleague Theodore Simon in 1905, responded to this need.

The French Ministry of Instruction asked Binet to devise an objective method for assigning pupils to special classes—one based on mental ability, not classroom disruptiveness. Other researchers had tried to assess intelligence using simple measures of sensory responsiveness and reaction time (Cattell, 1890; Galton, 1883). In contrast, Binet believed that test items should tap complex mental activities involved in intelligent behavior, such as memory and reasoning. Consequently, Binet and Simon (1908) devised a test of general ability that included a variety of verbal and nonverbal items, each requiring thought and judgment. Their test was also the first to associate items of increasing difficulty with chronological age (Wasserman & Tulsky, 2005). This enabled Binet and Simon to estimate how much a child was behind or ahead of her agemates in intellectual development.

The Binet test was so successful in predicting school performance that it became the basis for new intelligence tests. In 1916, Lewis Terman at Stanford University adapted it for use with English-speaking schoolchildren. Since then, the English version has been known as the *Stanford-Binet Intelligence Scale.* As we will see later, the Stanford-Binet has changed greatly; it no longer provides just a single, holistic measure of intelligence.

The Factor Analysts: A Multifaceted View

To find out whether intelligence is a single trait or an assortment of abilities, researchers used a complicated correlational procedure called **factor analysis,** which identifies sets of test items that cluster together, meaning that test-takers who do well on one item in a cluster tend to do well on the others. Distinct clusters are called *factors.* For example, if vocabulary, verbal comprehension, and verbal analogy items all correlate highly, they form a factor that the investigator might label "verbal ability." Using factor analysis, many researchers tried to identify the mental abilities that contribute to successful intelligence test performance.

• Early Factor Analysts British psychologist Charles Spearman (1927) was the first influential factor analyst. He found that all test items he examined correlated with one another. As a result, he proposed that a common underlying **general intelligence,** called **"g,"** influenced each of them. At the same time, noticing that the test items were not perfectly correlated, Spearman concluded that they varied in the extent to which "g" contributed to them and suggested that each item, or a set of similar items, also measured a **specific intelligence** unique to the task.

Spearman downplayed the significance of specific intelligences, regarding "g" as central and supreme. Because test items that involved forming relationships and applying general principles clustered together especially strongly—and also were the best predictors of cognitive performance outside the testing situation—he inferred that "g" represents abstract reasoning capacity.

American psychologist Louis Thurstone (1938) questioned the importance of "g." His factor analysis of college students' scores on more than 50 intelligence tests indicated that separate, unrelated factors exist. Declaring the supremacy of these factors, Thurstone called them *primary mental abilities.*

• **Contemporary Extensions** Spearman and Thurstone eventually resolved their differences, each acknowledging findings that supported the other's perspective (Wasserman & Tulsky, 2005). Current theorists and test designers, combining both approaches, propose *hierarchical models* of mental abilities. At the highest level is "g," assumed to be present to some degree in all separate factors. These factors, in turn, are measured by *subtests,* groups of related items. Subtest scores provide information about a child's strengths and weaknesses. They also can be combined into a total score representing general intelligence.

Contemporary theorists have extended factor-analytic research. The two most influential are R. B. Cattell and John Carroll. Each offers a unique, multifaceted perspective on intelligence.

Crystallized versus Fluid Intelligence. According to Raymond B. Cattell (1971, 1987), in addition to "g," intelligence consists of two broad factors: **Crystallized intelligence** refers to skills that depend on accumulated knowledge and experience, good judgment, and mastery of social customs—abilities acquired because they are valued by the individual's culture. On intelligence tests, vocabulary, general information, and arithmetic problems are examples of items that emphasize crystallized intelligence. In contrast, **fluid intelligence** depends more heavily on basic information-processing skills—the ability to detect relationships among stimuli, the speed with which the individual can analyze information, and the capacity of working memory. Fluid intelligence, which is assumed to be influenced more by conditions in the brain and less by culture, often works with crystallized intelligence to support effective reasoning, abstraction, and problem solving (Horn & Noll, 1997).

Among children with similar cultural and educational backgrounds, crystallized and fluid intelligence are highly correlated and difficult to distinguish in factor analyses, probably because children high in fluid intelligence acquire information more easily. But in children differing greatly in cultural and educational experiences, the two abilities show little relationship; children with the same fluid capacity may perform quite differently on crystallized tasks (Horn, 1994). As these findings suggest, Cattell's theory has important implications for the issue of *cultural bias* in intelligence testing. Tests aimed at reducing culturally specific content usually emphasize fluid over crystallized items.

The Three-Stratum Theory of Intelligence. Using improved factor-analytic methods, John Carroll (1993, 2005) reanalyzed relationships among items in hundreds of studies. His findings yielded a **three-stratum theory of intelligence** that elaborates the models proposed by Spearman, Thurstone, and Cattell. Carroll represented the structure of intelligence as having three tiers. As Figure 8.1 shows, "g" presides at the top. In the second tier are an array of *broad abilities,* which Carroll considered the basic biological components of intelligence; they are arranged from left to right in terms of decreasing relationship with "g." In the third tier are *narrow abilities*—specific behaviors through which people display the second-tier factors.

Carroll's model is the most comprehensive factor-analytic classification of mental abilities to date. As we will see in the next section, it provides a useful framework for researchers seeking to understand mental-test performance in cognitive-processing terms. It also reminds us of the great diversity of intellectual factors. Currently, no test measures all of Carroll's factors.

Recent Advances in Defining Intelligence

Many researchers believe that factors on intelligence tests have limited usefulness unless we can identify the cognitive processes responsible for those factors. Once we discover exactly what separates individuals who can solve certain mental test items from those who cannot,

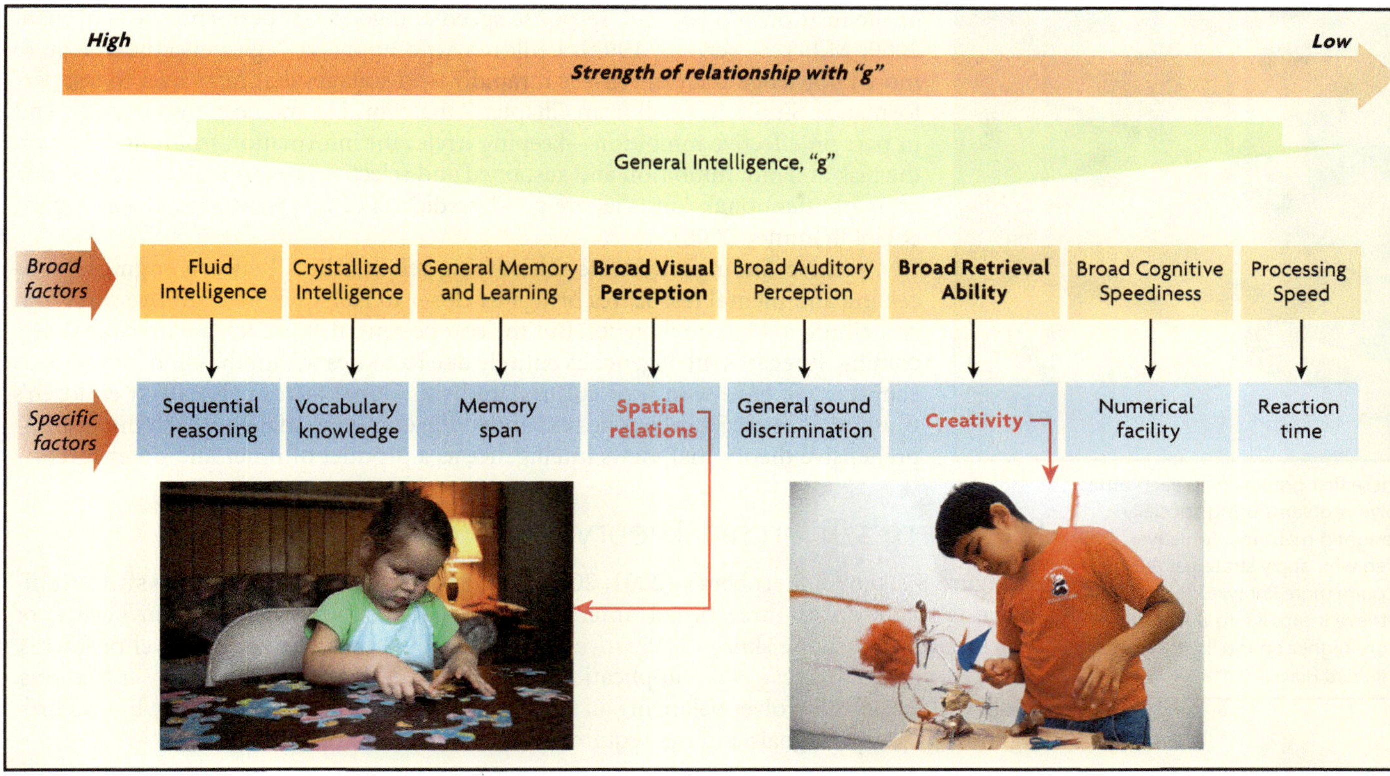

■ **Figure 8.1** **Carroll's hierarchical model of intelligence.**
At the top is general intelligence, or "g." The second tier shows eight broad abilities, or factors, arranged from left to right in terms of decreasing strength of relationship with "g." In the third tier are examples of narrow factors, specific behaviors through which people display the broad abilities. The child on the left is completing a spatial-relations task in which she solves a puzzle—a type of broad visual perception. The child on the right is applying his broad retrieval ability as he uses art materials creatively. Carroll's model reflects the wide array of abilities tapped by mental tests, but no single test includes all of his factors. (Adapted from Carroll, 1993, 2005.) *Photos:* (left) © J Burleson/Alamy; (right) © Jeff Greenberg/PhotoEdit

we will know more about why a particular child does well or poorly and what skills must be strengthened to improve performance.

Combining Psychometric and Information-Processing Approaches

To overcome the limitations of factor analysis, investigators combine psychometric and information-processing approaches. They conduct **componential analyses** of children's test scores, looking for relationships between aspects (or components) of information processing and children's intelligence test performance.

Measures of basic working-memory capacity (such as digit span) correlate well with mental test scores in both school-age children and adults (Conway, Kane, & Engle, 2003; de Ribaupierre & Lecerf, 2006). And processing speed, assessed in terms of reaction time on diverse cognitive tasks, is moderately related to general intelligence and to gains in mental test performance over time (Deary, 2001; Li et al., 2004). Individuals whose central nervous systems function more efficiently, permitting them to take in and manipulate information quickly, appear to have an edge in intellectual skills. In support of this interpretation, fast, strong ERPs (EEG brain waves in response to stimulation) predict both speedy cognitive processing and higher mental test scores (Rijsdijk & Boomsma, 1997; Schmid, Tirsch, & Scherb, 2002). Furthermore, fMRI research reveals that the metabolic rate of the cerebral cortex during complex tasks is lower for high-scoring individuals, suggesting that they require less mental energy for intricate thinking (Vernon et al., 2001).

But other factors, including flexible attention, memory, and reasoning strategies, are as important as basic processing capacity and efficiency in predicting IQ, and they explain some

These first graders help each other solve problems using specially designed math manipulatives. Children who apply strategies effectively acquire more knowledge and can retrieve it rapidly. As a result, they score higher on intelligence tests.
© Richard Hutchings/PhotoEdit

of the relationship between response speed and good test performance (Lohman, 2000; Miller & Vernon, 1992). Children who apply strategies effectively acquire more knowledge and can retrieve it rapidly—advantages that carry over to test performance. Similarly, recall from Chapter 7 that working-memory resources depend in part on effective inhibition—keeping irrelevant information from intruding on the task at hand. Inhibition and sustained and selective attention are among a wide array of attentional skills that are good predictors of IQ (Schweizer, Moosbrugger, & Goldhammer, 2006).

As these findings illustrate, identifying relationships between cognitive processing and mental test scores brings us closer to isolating the cognitive skills that contribute to high intelligence. But the componential approach has a major shortcoming: It regards intelligence as entirely due to causes within the child. In previous chapters, we have seen how cultural and situational factors also affect children's thinking. Robert Sternberg has expanded the componential approach into a comprehensive theory that views intelligence as a product of inner and outer forces.

Sternberg's Triarchic Theory

As Figure 8.2 shows, Sternberg's (2001, 2002, 2005) **triarchic theory of successful intelligence** is made up of three broad, interacting intelligences: (1) *analytical intelligence,* or information-processing skills; (2) *creative intelligence,* the capacity to solve novel problems; and (3) *practical intelligence,* application of intellectual skills in everyday situations. Intelligent behavior involves balancing all three intelligences to achieve success in life, according to one's personal goals and the requirements of one's cultural community.

• **Analytical Intelligence** *Analytical* intelligence consists of the information-processing components that underlie all intelligent acts: applying strategies, acquiring task-relevant and metacognitive knowledge, and engaging in self-regulation. But on mental tests, processing skills are used in only a few of their potential ways, resulting in far too narrow a view of intelligent behavior. As we have seen, children in tribal and village societies do not necessarily perform well on measures of "school" knowledge but thrive when processing information in out-of-school situations that most Westerners would find highly challenging.

■ **Figure 8.2** **Sternberg's triarchic theory of successful intelligence.**
People who behave intelligently balance three interrelated intelligences—analytical, creative, and practical—to achieve success in life.

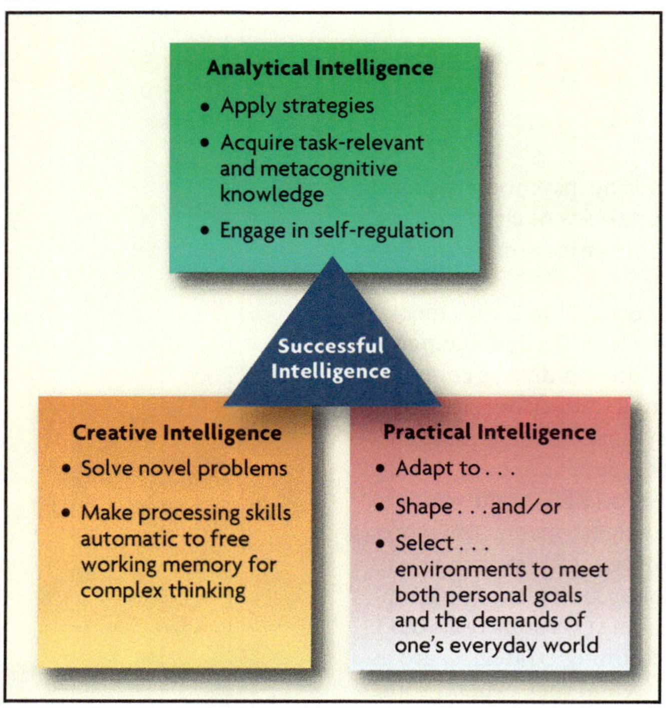

• **Creative Intelligence** In any context, success depends not only on processing familiar information but also on generating useful solutions to new problems. People who are *creative* think more skillfully than others when faced with novelty. Given a new task, they apply their information-processing skills in exceptionally effective ways, rapidly making those skills automatic so that working memory is freed for more complex aspects of the situation. Consequently, they quickly move to high-level performance. Although all of us are capable of some creativity, only a few individuals excel at generating novel solutions. We will address the ingredients of creativity in greater detail at the end of this chapter.

• **Practical Intelligence** Finally, intelligence is a *practical,* goal-oriented activity aimed at one or more of the following purposes: *adapting to, shaping,* or *selecting environments.* Intelligent people skillfully *adapt* their thinking to fit with both their desires and the demands of their everyday worlds. When they cannot adapt to a situation, they try to *shape,* or change, it to meet their needs. If they cannot shape it, they *select* new contexts that better match their skills, values, or goals. Practical intelligence reminds us that intelligent behavior is never culture-free. Because of their backgrounds, some children do well at the behaviors required for success on intelligence tests and adapt easily to the testing conditions and tasks. Others, with different life histories, may misinterpret or reject the testing context. Yet such children often display sophisticated abilities in daily life—for example, telling stories, engaging in complex artistic activities, or interacting skillfully with other people.

To examine the validity of the triarchic theory, Sternberg and his collaborators gave thousands of children and adolescents in Finland, Spain, Russia, and the United States test items that tap analytical, creative, and practical skills. Factor analyses repeatedly indicated that the three intelligences are relatively distinct (Grigorenko & Sternberg, 2001; Sternberg, 2003a; Sternberg et al., 1999, 2001).

The triarchic theory emphasizes the complexity of intelligent behavior and the limitations of current intelligence tests in assessing that complexity. For example, out-of-school, practical forms of intelligence are vital for life success and help explain why cultures vary widely in the behaviors they regard as intelligent (Sternberg et al., 2000). When researchers asked ethnically diverse parents to describe an intelligent first grader, Caucasian Americans mentioned cognitive traits. In contrast, ethnic minorities (Cambodian, Filipino, Vietnamese, and Mexican immigrants) identified noncognitive capacities—motivation, self-management, and social skills (Okagaki & Sternberg, 1993). According to Sternberg, mental tests can easily underestimate, and even overlook, the intellectual strengths of some children, especially ethnic minorities.

Gardner's Theory of Multiple Intelligences

In yet another view of how information-processing skills underlie intelligent behavior, Howard Gardner's (1983, 1993, 2000) **theory of multiple intelligences** defines intelligence in terms of distinct sets of processing operations that permit individuals to solve problems, create products, and discover new knowledge in a wide range of culturally valued activities. Dismissing the idea of general intelligence, Gardner proposes at least eight independent intelligences (see Table 8.2).

Gardner believes that each intelligence has a unique biological basis, a distinct course of development, and different expert, or "end-state," performances. At the same time, he emphasizes that a lengthy process of education is required to transform any raw potential

Table 8.2 Gardner's Multiple Intelligences

Intelligence	Processing Operations	End-State Performance Possibilities
Linguistic	Sensitivity to the sounds, rhythms, and meaning of words and the functions of language	Poet, journalist
Logico-mathematical	Sensitivity to, and capacity to detect, logical or numerical patterns; ability to handle long chains of logical reasoning	Mathematician
Musical	Ability to produce and appreciate pitch, rhythm (or melody), and aesthetic quality of the forms of musical expressiveness	Instrumentalist, composer
Spatial	Ability to perceive the visual-spatial world accurately, to perform transformations on those perceptions, and to re-create aspects of visual experience in the absence of relevant stimuli	Sculptor, navigator
Bodily-kinesthetic	Ability to use the body skillfully for expressive as well as goal-directed purposes; ability to handle objects skillfully	Dancer, athlete
Naturalist	Ability to recognize and classify all varieties of animals, minerals, and plants	Biologist
Interpersonal	Ability to detect and respond appropriately to the moods, temperaments, motivations, and intentions of others	Therapist, salesperson
Intrapersonal	Ability to discriminate complex inner feelings and to use them to guide one's own behavior; knowledge of one's own strengths, weaknesses, desires, and intelligences	Person with detailed, accurate self-knowledge

Sources: Gardner, 1993, 1998a, 2000.

According to Gardner, children are capable of at least eight distinct intelligences. As this 10-year-old notes characteristics of different trees on a school field trip, he enriches his naturalist intelligence.

into a mature social role (Connell, Sheridan, & Gardner, 2003). Cultural values and learning opportunities affect the extent to which a child's strengths are realized and the way they are expressed.

Gardner acknowledges that if tests were available to assess all these abilities, they should show little relationship to one another. But he finds neurological support for their separateness particularly compelling. Research indicating that damage to a certain part of the adult brain influences only one ability (such as linguistic or spatial), while sparing others, suggests that the affected ability is independent. The existence of people with unusual profiles of intelligence also fits with Gardner's belief in distinct abilities. Individuals with *savant syndrome,* who display one area of outstanding strength alongside deficits in many others, provide an illustration. Children with *autism* occasionally show this pattern. Though severely impaired in language and communication, a few individuals with autism have remarkable abilities, always featuring dazzling memory (Treffert & Wallace, 2002). These usually involve numerical and spatial skills—such as effortless calculation, detailed drawing, or performance of long piano pieces after hearing them only once—that are primarily housed in the right hemisphere of the cerebral cortex. Savant syndrome often is associated with damage to the left cerebral hemisphere, which may have caused the right hemisphere to compensate, yielding an "island of strength" (Miller et al., 1998).

Does Gardner's view remind you of the *core knowledge perspective,* discussed in Chapter 6? Indeed, he accepts the existence of innately specified, core domains of thought, present at birth or emerging early in life. Then, as children respond to the demands of their culture, they transform those intelligences to fit the activities they are called on to perform. Gardner's work has been especially helpful in efforts to understand and nurture children's special talents, a topic we address at the end of this chapter.

Critics of Gardner's theory, however, question the independence of his intelligences. They point out that the unusual skills of people with savant syndrome are mechanical and inflexible because those skills are not aided by other abilities. In contrast, excellence in most fields requires a combination of intelligences. A talented musician, for example, uses logico-mathematical intelligence to interpret the score, linguistic intelligence to respond to teaching, spatial intelligence to orient to the keyboard, interpersonal intelligence to react to the audience, and intrapersonal intelligence to play expressively. Furthermore, some exceptionally gifted individuals have abilities that are broad rather than limited to a particular domain (Goldsmith, 2000). Finally, current mental tests do tap several of Gardner's intelligences (linguistic, logico-mathematical, and spatial), and evidence for "g" suggests that they have common features (Visser, Ashton, & Vernon, 2006). Nevertheless, Gardner calls attention to several abilities not measured by intelligence tests. For example, his interpersonal and intrapersonal intelligences include a set of capacities for dealing with people and understanding oneself. As the From Research to Practice box on the following page indicates, researchers are attempting to define and measure these vital abilities.

Ask Yourself

Review Using Sternberg's triarchic theory, explain the limitations of current mental tests in assessing the complexity of human intelligence.

Apply Eight-year-old Charya, an immigrant from Cambodia, had difficulty responding to test items asking for word definitions and general information. But she solved puzzles easily, and she quickly figured out which number comes next in a complex series. How does Charya score in crystallized and fluid intelligence? What might explain the difference?

Connect Describe similarities between Gardner's theory of multiple intelligences and the core knowledge perspective on cognitive development (see Chapter 6, pages 258–259). What questions raised about this view also apply to Gardner's theory?

Reflect Select one of your intellectual strengths from Gardner's multiple intelligences, listed in Table 8.2 on page 323. How do you display that intelligence? What other intelligences contribute to your strong performance?

From Research to Practice

Emotional Intelligence

During recess, Muriel handed a birthday party invitation to every fifth-grade girl except Claire, who looked on sadly as her classmates chattered about the party. But one of Muriel's friends, Jessica, looked troubled. Pulling Muriel aside, she exclaimed, "Why'd you do that? You hurt Claire's feelings—you embarrassed her! If you bring invitations to school, you've got to give everybody one!" And after school, Jessica comforted Claire, saying, "If you aren't invited, I'm not going, either!"

Jessica's IQ is only slightly above average, but she excels at *emotional intelligence*—a term that has captured public attention because of popular books suggesting that it is an overlooked set of skills that can greatly improve life success (Goleman, 1995, 1998). According to one influential definition, **emotional intelligence** is a set of emotional abilities that enable individuals to process and adapt to emotional information (Salovey & Pizarro, 2003). To measure it, researchers have devised items tapping emotional skills that enable people to manage their own emotions and interact competently with others. One test requires individuals to identify and rate the strength of emotions expressed in photographs of faces (perceiving emotions), to reason about emotions in social situations (understanding emotions), and to evaluate the effectiveness of strategies for controlling negative emotions (regulating emotions). Factor analyses of the scores of hundreds of adolescents and young adults identified several emotional capacities as well as a higher-order general factor (Mayer, Salovey, & Caruso, 2003).

Emotional intelligence is modestly related to IQ. And in school-age children, adolescents, and adults, it is positively associated with self-esteem, empathy, prosocial behavior, cooperation, leadership skills, and life satisfaction and negatively related to dependency, depression, and aggressive behavior (Law et al., 2004; Mavroveli et al., 2007; Petrides et al., 2006; Wilhelm, 2005).

Nevertheless, only a few assessments of emotional intelligence are available for children. These require careful training of teachers in observing and recording children's emotional skills during everyday activities, gathering information from parents, and taking into account children's ethnic backgrounds (Denham, 2005; Denham & Burton, 2003). As more and better measures are devised, they may help identify children with weak social and emotional competencies who would profit from intervention (Denham, 2006; Stewart-Brown & Edmunds, 2007). But some researchers worry that emotional ability scores will lead psychologists and educators to make simplistic comparisons, overlooking the fact that the adaptiveness of children's emotional and social behavior often varies across situations (Saarni, 2000).

The concept of emotional intelligence has increased teachers' awareness that providing experiences that meet students' social and emotional needs can improve their adjustment. Lessons that teach emotional understanding, respect and caring for others, strategies for regulating emotion, and resistance to unfavorable peer pressure—using active learning techniques that provide skill practice both in and out of the classroom—are becoming more common (Goetz et al., 2005).

The child on the left displays high emotional intelligence as she accurately interprets her friend's sadness and offers comfort. Because emotional intelligence is positively associated with self-esteem and prosocial behavior, teachers are increasingly providing lessons aimed at promoting emotional and social skills. © David Young-Wolff/PhotoEdit

Measuring Intelligence

Although intelligence tests sample only a narrow range of human cognitive capacities, psychologists and educators give them to school-age children because the scores, as we will see shortly, are modest to good predictors of future success—in school, on the job, and in other aspects of life. The *group-administered tests* given from time to time in classrooms permit large numbers of students to be tested at once and are useful for instructional planning and for identifying students who require more extensive evaluation with *individually administered tests.* Unlike group tests, which teachers can give with minimal training, individually administered tests demand considerable training and experience to give well. The examiner not only considers the child's answers but also carefully observes the child's behavior, noting such reactions as attention to and interest in the tasks and wariness of the adult. These observations provide insights into whether the test results accurately reflect the child's abilities.

Some Commonly Used Intelligence Tests

Two individual tests—the Stanford-Binet and the Wechsler—are most often used to identify highly intelligent children and diagnose those with learning problems. Figure 8.3 provides examples of items that typically appear on intelligence tests for children.

• **The Stanford-Binet Intelligence Scales** The modern descendant of Alfred Binet's first successful intelligence test is the **Stanford-Binet Intelligence Scales, Fifth Edition,** for individuals from age 2 to adulthood. This latest edition measures general intelligence and five intellectual factors: fluid reasoning, quantitative reasoning, knowledge, visual-spatial processing, and working memory (Roid, 2003). Each factor includes both a verbal mode and a nonverbal mode of testing, yielding 10 subtests in all. The nonverbal subtests do not require spoken language and are especially useful when assessing individuals with limited English, hearing impairments, or communication disorders. The quantitative reasoning and knowledge factors emphasize crystallized intelligence (culturally loaded, fact-oriented information), such as vocabulary and arithmetic problems. In contrast, the fluid reasoning, visual-spatial processing, and working-memory factors, which tap fluid intelligence, are assumed to be less culturally biased.

A special edition of the test, the *Stanford-Binet Intelligence Scales for Early Childhood,* includes fewer items and is tailored for assessing children between 2 years of age and 7 years 3 months. This makes the current Stanford-Binet more useful than its previous edition for diagnosing intellectual difficulties in early childhood.

• **The Wechsler Intelligence Scale for Children** The **Wechsler Intelligence Scale for Children–IV (WISC–IV)** is the fourth edition of a widely used test for 6- through 16-year-olds. A downward extension of it, the *Wechsler Preschool and Primary Scale of Intelligence–III (WPPSI–III),* is appropriate for children 2 years 6 months through 7 years 3 months (Wechsler, 2002, 2003). The Wechsler tests offered both a measure of general intelligence and a variety of factor scores long before the Stanford-Binet. As a result, many psychologists and educators came to prefer them.

The WISC–IV includes four broad intellectual factors: verbal reasoning, perceptual reasoning, working memory, and processing speed. Each factor is made up of two or three subtests, yielding 10 separate scores in all. The WISC–IV was designed to downplay crystallized, culture-dependent intelligence, which is emphasized on only one factor (verbal reasoning). The remaining three factors focus on fluid, information-processing skills. According to the test designers, the result is the most theoretically current and "culture-fair" intelligence test available (Williams, Weiss, & Rolfhus, 2003).

The Wechsler tests were the first to use samples representing the total population of the United States, including ethnic minorities, to devise standards for interpreting test scores. The WISC-IV, like previous WISC editions, has been adapted for children in Canada, where both English and French versions are available (Wechsler, 2004).

Aptitude and Achievement Tests

Two other types of tests are closely related to intelligence tests. **Aptitude tests** assess an individual's potential to learn a specialized activity. For example, mechanical aptitude is the capacity to acquire mechanical skills, musical aptitude is the capacity to acquire musical skills, and scholastic aptitude is the capacity to master school tasks. The well-known Scholastic Assessment Test (SAT) and American College Testing Assessment (ACT), which you may have submitted as part of your college application, yield measures of scholastic aptitude. In contrast, **achievement tests** aim to assess not potential to learn but actual knowledge and skill attainment. When a school district assesses fourth-grade reading comprehension or a college professor gives a final exam, an achievement test has been used.

Note, however, that differences among intelligence, aptitude, and achievement tests are not clear-cut. Certain items on each, especially those assessing verbal and math skills, are similar. As this overlap suggests, most tests tap both aptitude and achievement, though in different balances. The three test types do differ in breadth of content. Intelligence tests assess the widest array of skills. Aptitude tests are narrower, focusing on particular skill areas. And achievement tests cover the narrowest range because they are aimed at measuring recent learning, usually in particular school subjects.

Tests for Infants

Accurately measuring infants' intelligence is a challenge because babies cannot answer questions or follow directions. All we can do is present them with stimuli, coax them to respond, and observe their behavior. In addition, these young test-takers are not necessarily cooperative. To compensate for their unpredictable behaviors, some tests depend heavily on information supplied by parents.

Most infant measures emphasize perceptual and motor responses. But increasingly, new tests are being developed that tap early language, cognition, and social behavior, especially with older infants and toddlers. One commonly used test, *The Bayley Scales of Infant and Toddler Development,* is suitable for children between 1 month and 3½ years. The most recent edition, the *Bayley–III,* has three main subtests: (1) the Cognitive Scale, which includes such items as attention to familiar and unfamiliar objects, looking for a fallen object, and pretend play; (2) the Language Scale, which taps understanding and expression of language—for example, recognition of objects and people, following simple directions, and naming objects and pictures; and (3) the Motor Scale, which assesses fine and gross motor skills, such as grasping, sitting, stacking blocks, and climbing stairs (Bayley, 2006).

Two additional Bayley–III scales depend on parental report: (4) the Social-Emotional Scale, which asks caregivers about such behaviors as ease of calming, social responsiveness, and imitation in play, and (5) the Adaptive Behavior Scale, which asks about adaptation to the demands of daily life, including communication, self-control, following rules, and getting along with others.

TYPICAL VERBAL ITEMS

Vocabulary — Tell me what *carpet* means.

General Information — What day of the week comes right after Thursday?

Verbal Comprehension — Why do we need police officers?

Similarities — How are a ship and a train alike?

Arithmetic — If a $60 jacket is 25% off, how much does it cost?

TYPICAL PERCEPTUAL- AND SPATIAL-REASONING ITEMS

Block Design — Make these blocks look just like the picture.

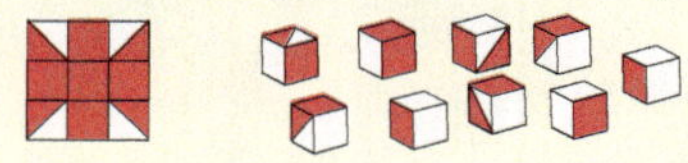

Picture Concepts — Choose one object from each row to make a group of objects that goes together.

Spatial Visualization — Which of the boxes on the right can be made from the pattern on the left?

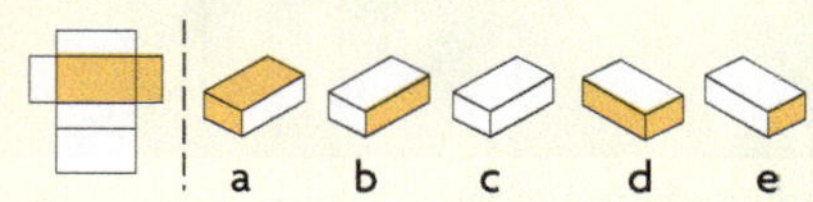

TYPICAL WORKING-MEMORY ITEMS

Digit Span — Repeat these digits in the same order. Now repeat these digits (a similar series) backward.
2, 6, 4, 7, 1, 8

Letter–Number Sequencing — Repeat these numbers and letters, first giving the numbers, then the letters, each in correct sequence.
8 G 4 B 5 N 2

TYPICAL PROCESSING-SPEED ITEM

Symbol Search — If the shape on the left is the same as any of those on the right, mark YES. If the shape is not the same, mark NO. Work as quickly as you can without making mistakes.

■ **Figure 8.3** **Test items like those on commonly used intelligence tests for children.**
The verbal items emphasize culturally loaded, fact-oriented information. The perceptual- and spatial-reasoning, working-memory, and processing-speed items emphasize aspects of information processing and are assumed to assess more biologically based skills.

Despite careful construction, infant tests—including previous editions of the Bayley—are poor predictors of mental ability in childhood. Infants and toddlers easily become distracted, fatigued, or bored during testing, so their scores often do not reflect their true abilities. And infant perceptual and motor items differ from the tasks given to older children, which increasingly emphasize verbal, conceptual, and problem-solving skills. In contrast, the Bayley–III Cognitive and Language Scales, which better dovetail with childhood tests, are good predictors of preschool mental test performance (Albers & Grieve, 2007). But because most infant scores do not tap the same dimensions of intelligence assessed in older children, they are conservatively labeled **developmental quotients (DQs)** rather than IQs.

A trained examiner tests a baby with the Bayley Scales of Infant Development while her mother looks on. Unlike tests for older children, which assess verbal, conceptual, and problem-solving skills, most infant tests emphasize perceptual and motor responses, which predict later intelligence poorly. © Laura Dwight Photography

Infant tests are somewhat better at making long-term predictions for very low-scoring babies. Today, they are largely used for *screening*—helping to identify for further observation and intervention infants who are at risk for future developmental problems.

Recall from Chapter 4 that speed of habituation and recovery to visual stimuli is among the best infant correlates of later intelligence (see page 140). One test, the *Fagan Test of Infant Intelligence,* consists entirely of habituation/recovery items. To take it, the infant sits on the mother's lap and views a series of pictures. After exposure to each, the examiner records looking time toward a novel picture paired with the familiar one. Outside of highly controlled laboratory conditions, however, measures of babies' looking behavior are unreliable, or inconsistent from one occasion to the next. Because of its low test–retest reliability (see Chapter 2, page 54), the Fagan test is less successful than researchers' assessments of infant habituation/recovery in predicting childhood mental test scores. And contradictory findings exist concerning whether Fagan test scores are useful for identifying infants at risk for delays in mental development (Andersson, 1996; Fagan & Detterman, 1992; Tasbihsazan, Nettelbeck, & Kirby, 2003).

Computation and Distribution of IQ Scores

Intelligence tests for infants, children, and adults are scored in the same way—by computing an **intelligence quotient (IQ),** which indicates the extent to which the raw score (number of items passed) deviates from the typical performance of same-age individuals. To make this comparison possible, test designers engage in **standardization**—giving the test to a large, representative sample of individuals, which serves as the *standard* for interpreting scores.

Within the standardization sample, scores at each age level form a **normal distribution** in which most scores cluster around the mean, or average, with progressively fewer falling toward each extreme (see Figure 8.4). This *bell-shaped* distribution results whenever researchers measure individual differences in large samples. When intelligence tests are standardized, the mean IQ is set at 100. An individual's IQ is higher or lower than 100 by an amount reflecting how much his or her test performance deviates from the standardization-sample mean.

Because we know the percentage of people who fall within each unit of the normal curve, we can figure out exactly what any IQ score means. For example, a child with an IQ of 100 performed better than 50 percent of same-age children. A child with an IQ of 85 did better than only 16 percent, whereas a child with an IQ of 130 outperformed 98 percent. The IQs of the great majority of people (96 percent) fall between 70 and 130; only a few achieve higher or lower scores.

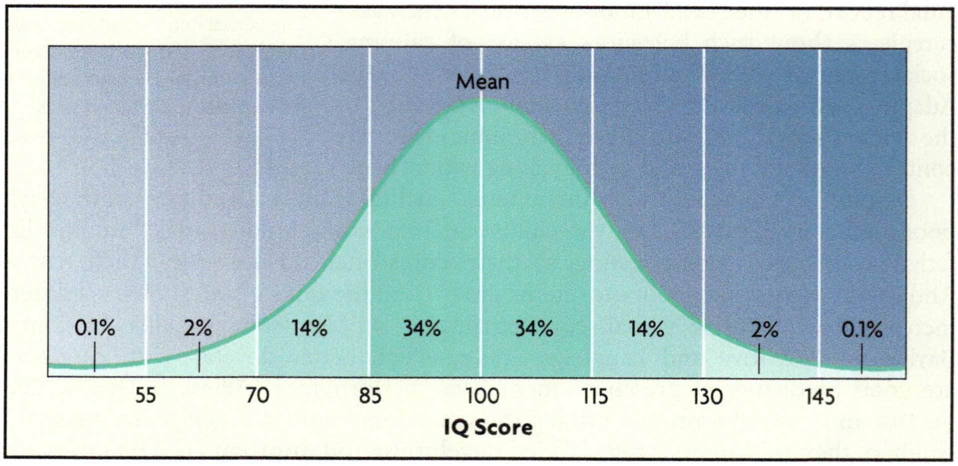

Figure 8.4 **Normal distribution of intelligence test scores.**

To determine the percentage of same-age individuals in the population a person with a certain IQ outperformed, add the figures to the left of that IQ score. For example, an 8-year-old child with an IQ of 115 scored better than 84 percent of the population of 8-year-olds.

Ask Yourself

Review Why are aptitude and achievement tests closely related to intelligence tests and to each other?

Apply Assia's score on the Stanford-Binet Intelligence Scales is 115; Leila's score is 145. Using Figure 8.4, explain how well each child performed in relation to other children her age.

Connect Both the Stanford-Binet and the Wechsler tests provide a measure of general intelligence and an array of subtest scores. What evidence presented earlier in this chapter supports the use of these hierarchical models of intelligence?

What Do Intelligence Tests Predict, and How Well?

Psychologists and educators who use test scores to make decisions about children's educational placement assume that the scores are good indicators of future intelligence and scholastic performance. How well does IQ actually fare as a predictive measure?

Stability of IQ Scores

Stability refers to how effectively IQ at one age predicts itself at the next. Do children who obtain a particular IQ score at age 3 or 4 perform about the same during elementary school and again in high school? To answer this question, researchers rely on longitudinal studies in which the same children are tested repeatedly.

• **Correlational Stability** One way of examining the stability of IQ is to correlate scores obtained at different ages. This tells us whether children who score low or high in comparison to their agemates at one age continue to do so later. Examining these correlations, researchers have identified two generalizations about the stability of IQ:

- *The older the child at time of first testing, the better the prediction of later IQ.* Preschool IQs do not predict school-age scores well; correlations are typically no better than in the .30s. But after age 6, stability improves, with many correlations in the .70s and .80s. Relationships between two testings in adolescence are as high as the .80s and .90s (Hayslip, 1994; Kaufman & Lichtenberger, 2002).
- *The closer in time two testings are, the stronger the relationship between the scores.* In one long-term study, 4-year-old IQ correlated with 5-year-old IQ at .52, but prediction dropped to .46 by age 9 and to .42 by age 12 (Schneider et al., 1999).

Why do preschool scores predict less well than later scores? One reason is that with age, test items focus less on concrete knowledge and more on complex reasoning and problem solving, which require different skills. Another explanation is that during periods of rapid development, children frequently change places in a distribution. One child may spurt ahead and reach a plateau; a second child, progressing slowly and steadily, may eventually overtake the first. Finally, IQ may become more stable after schooling is under way because daily classroom activities and test items become increasingly similar. Then, variations among children in quality of school experiences and in mastery of those experiences may help sustain individual differences in IQ.

• **Stability of Absolute Scores** So far, we have considered IQ stability in terms of how well children maintain their relative standing among agemates. Stability can also be viewed in *absolute* terms—by examining each child's profile of IQ scores over repeated testings. Longitudinal research reveals that the majority of children show substantial IQ fluctuations during childhood and adolescence—typically 10 to 20 points, and sometimes much more (McCall, 1993; Weinert & Hany, 2003).

Children who change the most tend to have orderly profiles, with scores either increasing or decreasing with age. Examining personality traits and life experiences associated with these profiles reveals that gainers tended to be more independent and competitive about doing well in school. Also, their parents were more likely to use warm, rational discipline and encourage them to succeed. In contrast, decliners often had parents who used either very severe or very lax discipline and who offered little intellectual stimulation (Honzik, Macfarlane, & Allen, 1948; McCall, Appelbaum, & Hogarty, 1973; Sontag, Baker, & Nelson, 1958).

When children who live in poverty are selected for special study, many show mental test score declines. According to the **environmental cumulative deficit hypothesis,** the negative effects of underprivileged rearing conditions increase the longer children remain in them. As a result, early cognitive deficits lead to more deficits, which become harder to overcome (Klineberg, 1963). In support of this idea, many studies show that children from economically disadvantaged families fall further and further behind their agemates in both IQ and achievement as they get older, and children who suffer from more stressors (such as parental divorce, job loss, illness, or deaths in the family) experience greater declines (Gutman, Sameroff, & Cole, 2003; Gutman, Sameroff, & Eccles, 2002).

In sum, many children show substantial changes in the absolute value of IQ that are the combined result of personal characteristics, child-rearing practices, and living conditions. Nevertheless, once IQ becomes reasonably stable in a correlational sense, it predicts a variety of important outcomes.

IQ as a Predictor of Academic Achievement

In thousands of studies, correlations between IQ and achievement test scores range from the .40s to the .80s, typically falling between .50 and .60 (Brody, 1997; Deary et al., 2007; Zhu & Weiss, 2005). Students with higher IQs also get better grades and stay in school longer. Beginning at age 7, IQ is moderately correlated with adult educational attainment (McCall, 1977).

Why does IQ predict scholastic performance? Some researchers believe that both IQ and achievement depend on the same abstract reasoning processes that underlie "g." Consistent with this interpretation, IQ correlates best with achievement in the more abstract school subjects, such as English, mathematics, and science (Jensen, 1998). Other researchers disagree, arguing that both IQ and achievement tests draw on the same pool of culturally specific information. From this perspective, an intelligence test is, in fact, partly an achievement test, and a child's past experiences affect performance on both measures. Support for this view comes from evidence that crystallized intelligence (which reflects acquired knowledge) is a better predictor of academic achievement than is its fluid counterpart (Kaufman, Kamphaus, & Kaufman, 1985; Kunina et al., 2007).

A wealth of research indicates that IQ predicts academic achievement. However, other factors, such as motivation and personality characteristics, are also important in accounting for children's learning in school. © Laura Dwight Photography

As you can imagine, researchers who believe that heredity contributes strongly to individual differences in IQ prefer the first of these explanations. Those who favor the power of environment prefer the second. We will delve into this nature–nurture debate shortly, but for now let's note that although IQ predicts achievement better than any other tested measure, the correlation is far from perfect. Other factors, such as motivation and personality characteristics that lead some children to try hard in school, are at least as important as IQ in accounting for individual differences in school performance (Neisser et al., 1996).

IQ as a Predictor of Occupational Attainment

If IQ scores were unrelated to long-term life success, psychologists and educators would probably be less concerned with them.

But research indicates that childhood IQ predicts adult occupational attainment just about as well as it correlates with academic achievement. By second grade, children with the highest IQs are more likely, as adults, to enter prestigious professions, such as engineering, law, medicine, and science (McCall, 1977).

Preparing a meal successfully requires more than just reading a recipe. This child must also organize the ingredients, plan and coordinate the component steps, look for shortcuts, and handle several tasks simultaneously—practical skills not reflected in IQ.
© Laura Dwight Photography

Again, the relationship between IQ and occupational attainment is far from perfect. Factors related to family background, such as parental encouragement, modeling of career success, and connections in the world of work, also predict occupational choice and attainment (Kalil, Levine, & Ziol-Guest, 2005). Furthermore, one reason that IQ is associated with occupational status is that IQ-like tests (the SAT and ACT) affect access to higher education. Educational attainment is a stronger predictor than IQ of occupational success and income (Ceci & Williams, 1997).

Another prominent factor in occupational achievement is personality. Examining seven longitudinal studies spanning one to four decades, researchers found that, after childhood IQ and parents' educational and occupational attainment were controlled, such traits as childhood emotional stability, conscientiousness, and sociability positively predicted career success, whereas belligerence and negative emotionality forecast unfavorable career outcomes, including job instability, reduced occupational prestige, and lower income (Roberts et al., 2007).

Finally, once a person enters an occupation, **practical intelligence**—mental abilities apparent in the real world but not in testing situations—predicts on-the-job performance as well as, and sometimes better than, IQ. Yet mental test performance and practical intelligence require distinctly different capacities. Whereas test items are formulated by others, provide complete information, are often detached from real life, and have only one solution, practical problems are not clearly defined, are embedded in everyday experiences, and generally have several appropriate solutions, each with strengths and limitations (Sternberg et al., 2000). Practical intelligence is evident in the assembly-line worker who discovers the fewest moves needed to complete a product or the business manager who increases productivity by making her subordinates feel valued. Unlike IQ, practical intelligence does not vary with ethnicity. And the two types of intelligence are unrelated and make independent contributions to job success (Cianciolo et al., 2006; Sternberg, 2003a).

In sum, occupational outcomes are a complex function of traditionally measured intelligence, education, family influences, motivation, and practical know-how. Current evidence indicates that IQ, though influential, is not more important than these other factors.

IQ as a Predictor of Psychological Adjustment

IQ is moderately correlated with emotional and social adjustment. For example, higher-IQ children and adolescents tend to be better-liked by their agemates. But the reasons for this association are not clear. Besides IQ, good peer relations are linked to patient but firm child-rearing practices and an even-tempered, sociable personality, both of which are positively correlated with IQ (Hogan, Harkness, & Lubinski, 2000; Scarr, 1997).

Another way of exploring the relationship of IQ to psychological adjustment is to look at the mental test performance of aggressive youths who frequently engage in lawbreaking acts. On average, juvenile delinquents score about 8 points lower in IQ than nondelinquents; persistently aggressive children and adolescents are especially deficient in verbal ability (Coie & Dodge, 1998; Dodge, Coie, & Lynam, 2006). Perhaps similar genetic and environmental factors (such as proneness to impulsivity, parenting, and family functioning) influence both IQ and conduct problems. Alternatively, low IQ (especially verbal scores) may predispose children to conduct difficulties by affecting their ability to make mature moral judgments, evaluate future consequences of their actions, and control their emotions and behavior. Consistent with both interpretations, longitudinal research indicates that low IQ in early and middle childhood is associated with later antisocial behavior only when children also score high in emotional and behavior problems and when their poor intellectual functioning persists (Fergusson, Horwood, & Ridder, 2005; Leech et al., 2003).

Finally, many psychological disorders, such as high anxiety, social withdrawal, and depression, are unrelated to mental test scores. IQ's imperfect prediction of all life success indicators provides strong justification for refusing to rely on IQ alone when forecasting a child's future or making important educational placement decisions.

Ask Yourself

Review Provide two competing explanations for the correlation between IQ and academic achievement.

Apply When 5-year-old Paul had difficulty adjusting to kindergarten, his teacher arranged for special testing. Paul's IQ turned out to be below average, at 95. When discussing Paul's score with his parents and teacher, what should the psychologist say about the stability of IQ?

Connect Describe evidence from previous chapters that non-Western children with little or no formal schooling display considerable practical intelligence, despite poor performance on tasks commonly used to assess Western children's cognitive skills. (*Hint:* See Chapter 6, page 250, and Chapter 7, pages 291–292.)

Reflect How do James's experiences, described in the opening to this chapter, fit with findings on children who show mental test score gains with age?

Ethnic and Socioeconomic Variations in IQ

People in industrialized nations are stratified on the basis of what they do at work and how much they earn for doing it—factors that determine their social position and economic well-being. Researchers assess a family's standing on this continuum through an index called **socioeconomic status (SES),** which combines three interrelated—but not completely overlapping—variables: (1) years of education and (2) the prestige of one's job and the skill it requires, both of which measure social status; and (3) income, which measures economic status.

In searching for the roots of socioeconomic disparities, researchers have compared the IQ scores of SES and ethnic groups because certain ethnicities (for example, African American and Hispanic) are heavily represented at lower SES levels and others (for example, Caucasian and Asian American) at middle and upper SES levels. These findings are responsible for the IQ nature–nurture debate. If group differences in IQ exist, then either heredity varies with SES and ethnicity, or certain groups must have fewer opportunities to acquire the skills needed for successful test performance.

Among these Canadian students, differences in IQ scores may correlate with ethnicity and SES. Research aimed at uncovering the reasons for these associations has generated heated controversy.
© Will Hart/PhotoEdit

In the 1970s, the IQ nature–nurture controversy escalated after psychologist Arthur Jensen (1969) published a controversial monograph in the *Harvard Educational Review* entitled "How Much Can We Boost IQ and Scholastic Achievement?" Jensen's answer was "not much." He claimed—and still maintains—that heredity is largely responsible for individual, ethnic, and SES differences in IQ (Jensen, 1998, 2001; Rushton & Jensen, 2005, 2006). Jensen's work sparked an outpouring of responses and research studies. Scientists also posed ethical challenges, reflecting deep concern that his conclusions would fuel social prejudices. Richard Herrnstein and Charles Murray rekindled the controversy with *The Bell Curve* (1994). Like Jensen, they argued that heredity contributes substantially to individual and SES differences in IQ, and they implied that heredity plays a sizable role in the black–white IQ gap.

As with Jensen's monograph, Herrnstein and Murray's book was praised by some researchers and deplored by others, who underscored its damaging social consequences. But before we consider relevant research, let's look closely at group differences in IQ, which lie at the heart of the controversy.

Differences in General Intelligence

American black children score, on average, 12 to 13 IQ points below American white children. Although the difference has been shrinking over the past several decades, a substantial gap remains (Dickens & Flynn, 2006; Edwards & Oakland, 2006; Hedges & Nowell, 1998). Research comparing adolescents who had emigrated from Zimbabwe to Canada revealed a black–white IQ gap of similar magnitude (Rushton & Jensen, 2003). Hispanic-American children fall midway between black and white children, and Asian Americans score slightly higher than their white counterparts—about 3 points (Ceci, Rosenblum, & Kumpf, 1998).

The gap between middle- and low-SES children—about 9 points—accounts for some of the ethnic differences in IQ, but not all. When black children and white children are matched on parental education and income, the black–white IQ gap is reduced by a third to a half (Brooks-Gunn et al., 2003; Smith, Duncan, & Lee, 2003).

No ethnic differences exist on infant measures of habituation/recovery to visual stimuli, which are good predictors of later IQ (Fagan & Singer, 1983). But before age 3, African-American children lag behind their white peers on other mental tests, a difference that persists into adulthood (Peoples, Fagan, & Drotar, 1995). Still, IQ varies greatly *within* each ethnic and SES group. For example, as Figure 8.5 shows, the IQ distributions of blacks and whites overlap substantially. About 20 percent of blacks score above the white mean, and the same percentage of whites score below the black mean. In fact, ethnicity and SES account for only about one-fourth of the total variation in IQ. Nevertheless, these group differences are large enough and of serious enough consequence that they cannot be ignored.

Differences in Specific Mental Abilities

Are ethnic and SES differences limited to certain kinds of mental abilities? Arthur Jensen believes so. He distinguishes two types of intelligence: (1) *associative*, which emphasizes rote memory and is measured by such items as digit span and recall of basic arithmetic facts; and (2) *conceptual*, which emphasizes abstract reasoning and problem solving and is measured by items strongly correlated with "g," such as vocabulary, verbal comprehension, block design, and spatial visualization. (Turn back to Figure 8.3 on page 327 to review examples of these items.)

According to Jensen, black–white and (to a lesser extent) SES differences in IQ are due to conceptual abilities; the groups are similar in associative intelligence (Jensen, 1998, 2002). Furthermore, Jensen indicated that among the various conceptual abilities, black children do worst on the least culturally loaded, most fluid items (such as block design and spatial visualization) and best on crystallized tasks (such as vocabulary). Therefore, he argued, black–white IQ differences are not caused by cultural bias in the tests. His conclusion—that blacks are less well-endowed than whites with higher-order, abstract forms of intelligence—intensified public outcries over the racist implications of his work.

Is there support for Jensen's theory? In a series of studies, Jensen (2001) found that specific mental abilities strongly correlated with "g" show large black–white gaps, whereas abilities weakly correlated with "g" show little or

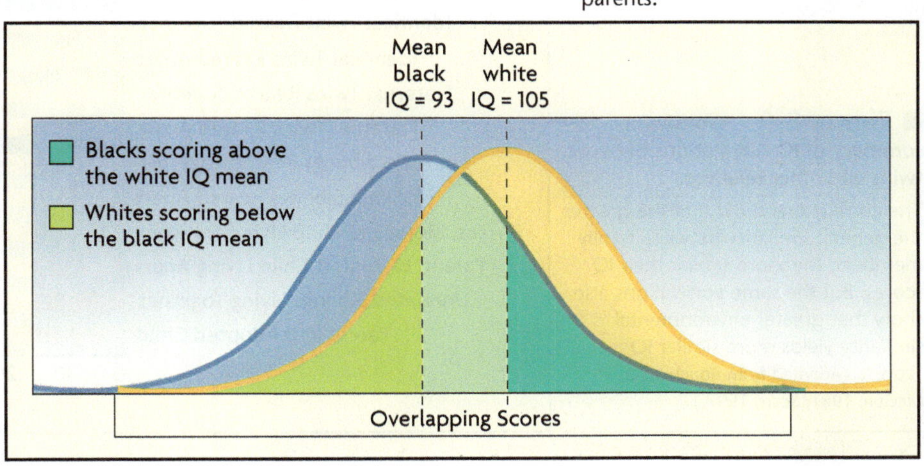

■ Figure 8.5 IQ score distributions for black and for white children.
The means represent approximate values obtained in studies of children reared by their biological parents.

no black–white difference. But other researchers report contrary findings. In a Dutch investigation, IQ differences between cultural-majority children and African-, Caribbean-, and Turkish-immigrant children were better explained by culturally specific knowledge than by "g" (Helms-Lorenz et al., 2003). And in a study of U.S. preschoolers, the black–white gap was far larger in vocabulary than in general intelligence (Smith, Duncan, & Lee, 2003).

At present, findings on specific mental abilities are not consistent enough to favor either a genetic or a cultural-bias explanation of ethnic and SES differences in IQ. To account for individual and group differences in IQ, we must turn to other evidence.

Explaining Individual and Group Differences in IQ

Over the past three decades, researchers have carried out hundreds of studies aimed at explaining individual, ethnic, and SES differences in mental abilities. The research is of three broad types: (1) investigations addressing the importance of heredity, (2) those that look at whether IQ scores are biased measures of the abilities of low-SES and minority children, and (3) those that examine the influence of children's home environments on their mental test performance.

Genetic Influences

Recall from Chapter 3 that behavioral geneticists examine the relative contributions of heredity and environment to complex traits by conducting *kinship studies,* which compare the characteristics of family members. Let's look closely at what they have discovered about IQ.

• **Heritability of Intelligence** In Chapter 3, we introduced the *heritability estimate.* To review briefly, researchers correlate the IQs of family members who vary in the extent to which they share genes. Then, using a complicated statistical procedure to compare the correlations, they arrive at an index of heritability, ranging from 0 to 1, which indicates the proportion of variation in a specific population due to genetic factors.

Figure 8.6 summarizes findings on IQ correlations from more than 100 studies on approximately 50,000 pairs of twins and other relatives (Bouchard & McGue, 1981; Scarr, 1997). The greater the genetic similarity between family members, the more they resemble one another in IQ. In fact, two correlations reveal that heredity is, without question, partially responsible for individual differences in mental test performance. The correlation for identical twins reared apart (.76) is much higher than for fraternal twins reared together (.55).

Age-related changes in these twin correlations provide additional support for the contribution of heredity. As Figure 8.7 shows, correlations for identical twins increase modestly

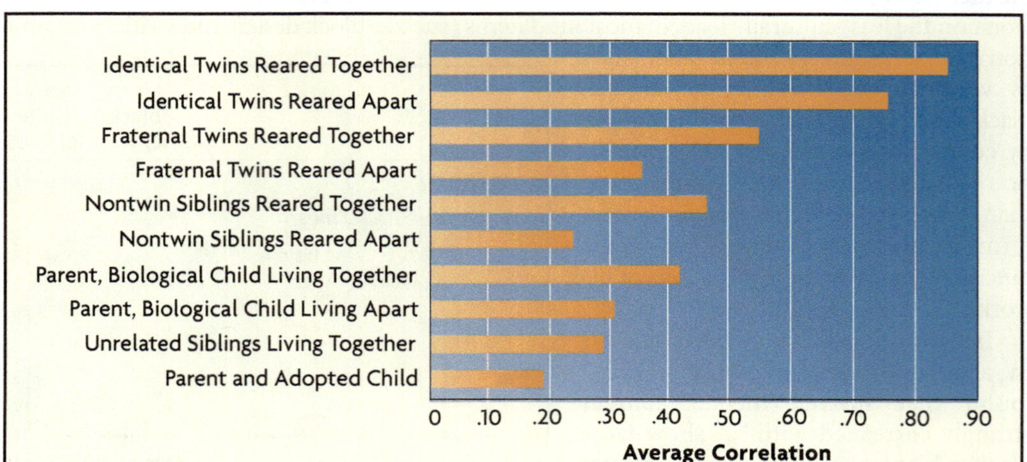

■ **Figure 8.6** **Worldwide summary of IQ correlations between twins and other relatives.**

The correlations show that the greater the genetic similarity between family members, the more similar their IQ scores. But the same correlations also show that greater environmental similarity yields more similar IQ scores. (Adapted from Bouchard & McGue, 1981; Scarr, 1997.)

into adulthood, whereas those for fraternal twins drop sharply at adolescence. Do these trends remind you of the *niche-picking* idea, discussed in Chapter 3? Common rearing experiences support the similarity of fraternal twins during childhood. But as they get older and experience more influences outside their families, each fraternal twin follows a path of development, or finds a niche, that fits with his or her unique genetic makeup. As a result, their IQ scores diverge. In contrast, the genetic likeness of identical twins causes them to seek out similar niches in adolescence and adulthood. Consequently, their IQ resemblance strengthens (Loehlin, Horn, & Willerman, 1997; McGue et al., 1993).

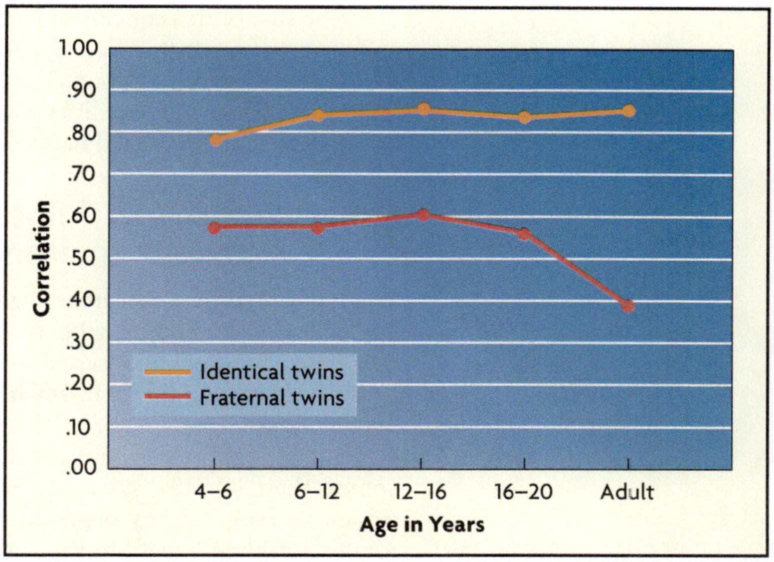

Figure 8.7 **Cross-sectional age-related changes in IQ correlations for identical and fraternal twins.**

Correlations for identical twins increase modestly into adulthood, whereas those for fraternal twins drop sharply at adolescence. Similar trends appear when twins are followed longitudinally. The findings are derived from studies including thousands of twin pairs. (From M. McGue, T. J. Bouchard, Jr., W. G. Iacono, & D. T. Lykken, 1993, "Behavioral Genetics of Cognitive Ability: A Life-Span Perspective," in R. Plomin & G. E. McClearn, Eds., *Nature, Nurture, and Psychology,* 1993, p. 63. Copyright © 1993 by the American Psychological Association. Adapted by permission of the American Psychological Association and M. McGue.)

Although kinship research underscores the importance of heredity, the correlations in Figure 8.6 reveal that environment is clearly involved. Correlations for twin, nontwin sibling, and parent–child pairs living together are stronger than for those living apart. And parents and adopted children, as well as unrelated siblings living together, show low positive correlations, again supporting the influence of environment.

As indicated in Chapter 3, heritability estimates usually are derived from comparisons of identical and fraternal twins. In Western industrialized nations, the typical value is about .50, meaning that half the variation in IQ is due to individual differences in heredity. But the values vary greatly between studies, ranging from the .40s to the .80s (Plomin, 2003).

Furthermore, recall from Chapter 3 that this moderate heritability estimate may be too high because twins reared together often experience very similar overall environments. Even twins reared apart often have been placed in homes that are advantaged and similar in many ways. When the range of environments to which twins are exposed is restricted, heritabilities underestimate the role of environment and overestimate the role of heredity.

In sum, although heritability research offers convincing evidence that genes contribute to IQ, disagreement persists over the extent of heredity's role. And heritability estimates do not reveal the complex processes through which genetic and environmental factors influence intelligence as children develop.

• Do Heritability Estimates Explain Ethnic and SES Variations in IQ? Despite the limitations of the heritability estimate, Jensen (1969, 1998, 2001) relied on it to support the argument that ethnic and SES differences in IQ have a strong genetic basis. This line of reasoning is widely regarded as inappropriate. Heritability estimates computed *within* black and white populations, though similar, provide no direct evidence on what accounts for between-group differences (Plomin et al., 2001; Sternberg, Grigorenko, & Kidd, 2005). Furthermore, recall from Chapter 3 that the heritability of IQ is *higher* under advantaged (higher-SES) than disadvantaged (lower-SES) rearing conditions (Bronfenbrenner & Morris, 2006; Turkheimer et al., 2003). Factors associated with low income and poverty, including weak or absent prenatal care, family stress, low-quality schools, and lack of community supports for effective child rearing, prevent children from attaining their genetic potential.

In a well-known example, geneticist Richard Lewontin (1976, 1995) showed that using within-group heritabilities to account for between-group differences is like comparing different seeds in different soil. Imagine planting a handful of flower seeds in a pot of soil generously enriched with fertilizer and another handful in a pot with very little fertilizer. The plants in each pot vary in height, but those in the first pot grow much taller than those in the second. *Within each group,* individual differences in plant height are largely due to heredity because the growth environments of all plants were about the same. But the average difference in height *between the two groups* is probably environmental because the second group got far less fertilizer.

To be sure of this conclusion, we could design a second study in which we expose the second group of seeds to a full supply of fertilizer and see if they reach an average height that equals that of the first group. Then we would have powerful evidence that environment is responsible for the group difference. As we turn now to adoption research, we will see that researchers have conducted natural experiments of this kind.

Adoption Studies: Joint Influence of Heredity and Environment

In adoption studies, researchers gather two types of information: (1) correlations of the IQs of adopted children with those of their biological and adoptive parents, for insight into genetic and environmental influences; and (2) changes in the absolute value of IQ as a result of growing up in an advantaged adoptive family, for evidence on the power of the environment.

Findings consistently reveal that when young children are adopted into caring, stimulating homes, their IQs rise substantially compared with the IQs of nonadopted children who remain in economically deprived families (van IJzendoorn, Juffer, & Poelhuis, 2005). But adopted children benefit to varying degrees. In one investigation, called the Texas Adoption Project, children of two extreme groups of biological mothers—those with IQs below 95 and those with IQs above 120—were adopted at birth by parents who were well above average in income and education. During the school years, the children of the low-IQ biological mothers scored above average in IQ but did less well than the children of high-IQ biological mothers placed in similar adoptive families (see Figure 8.8). Furthermore, parent–child correlations revealed that as the children grew older, they became more similar in IQ to their biological mothers and less similar to their adoptive parents (Loehlin, Horn, & Willerman, 1997).

The Texas Adoption Project and other similar investigations confirm that *both* environment and heredity contribute to IQ. In fact, children adopted in the early years attain IQs that, on average, match the scores of their adoptive parents' biological children and the scores of nonadopted peers in their schools and communities (van IJzendoorn, Juffer, & Poelhuis, 2005). These outcomes suggest a sizable role for environment in explaining SES variations in mental test scores. At the same time, adoption studies repeatedly reveal stronger correlations between the IQ scores of biological relatives than between those of adoptive relatives—clear evidence for a genetic contribution (Bouchard, 1997; Plomin et al., 2001; Scarr, 1997).

■ Figure 8.8 IQs of adopted children as a function of biological mothers' IQ in the Texas Adoption Project.
Children of both low-IQ and high-IQ biological mothers scored above average in IQ, but those of the high-IQ mothers did better. (Adapted from Loehlin, Horn, & Willerman, 1997.)

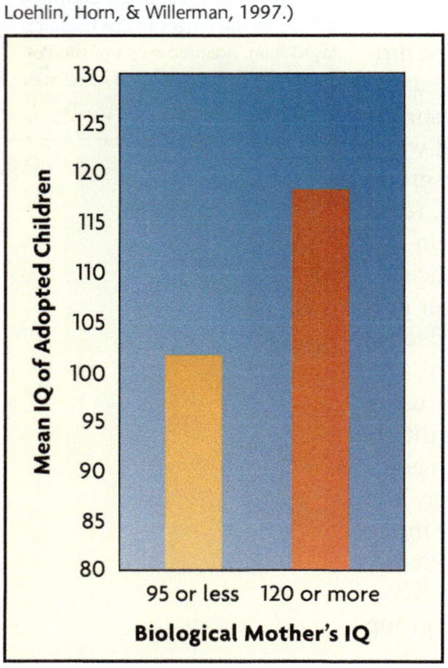

Adoption research also sheds light on the black–white IQ gap. In two studies, African-American children adopted into economically well-off white homes during the first year of life scored high on intelligence tests, attaining mean IQs of 110 and 117 by middle childhood—20 to 30 points higher than the typical scores of children growing up in low-income black communities (Moore, 1986; Scarr & Weinberg, 1983). In one investigation, the IQs of black adoptees declined in adolescence, leading some researchers to claim that the adoptive rearing environments influenced IQ only temporarily, in childhood. But the IQ drop may have resulted from use of different tests at the two ages. Or it may have been caused by the challenges minority adolescents face in forming an ethnic identity that blends birth and rearing backgrounds (DeBerry, Scarr, & Weinberg, 1996; Waldman, Weinberg, & Scarr, 1994). When this process is filled with emotional turmoil, it can affect motivation on intelligence tests.

Adoption findings do not completely resolve questions about ethnic differences in IQ. Still, the IQ gains of black children "reared in the culture of the tests and schools" are consistent with a wealth of evidence indicating that poverty severely depresses the scores of many ethnic minority children (Nisbett, 1998, 2005). Dramatic gains in IQ from one generation to the next further support the conclusion that, given new experiences and opportunities, members of oppressed groups can move far beyond their current test performance. See the Cultural Influences box on the following page to learn about the *Flynn effect.*

Cultural Influences

The Flynn Effect: Massive Generational Gains in IQ

After gathering IQ scores from 20 industrialized nations that had either military mental testing or frequent testing of other large, representative samples, James Flynn (1994, 1999, 2007) reported a finding so consistent and intriguing that it became known as the **Flynn effect:** IQs have increased steadily from one generation to the next. The largest increases have occurred on fluid-ability tests of spatial reasoning—tasks often assumed to be "culture-fair" and, therefore, largely genetically based. Figure 8.9 shows these gains for one such test, administered to military samples consisting of almost all young men in Belgium, Israel, the Netherlands, and Norway. IQ rose, on average, 18 points per generation (30 years).

Consistent with this *secular trend* (see page 182 in Chapter 5 to review this concept), when intelligence tests are revised, the new standardization sample almost always performs better than the previous one. After locating every study in which the same individuals had taken two or more versions of Stanford-Binet or Wechsler tests (a total of 81 samples, with nearly 10,000 participants), Flynn used the data to estimate the rate of IQ change between 1932 and 2002. On average, IQ increased about ⅓ point per year, steadily over time and similarly across all ages, for a total of 22 points over the 46-year period (Flynn, 2007; Flynn & Weiss, 2007). When subtest scores were examined, gains were (again) largest for fluid-ability tasks. The Flynn effect has been reconfirmed in an investigation spanning the years 1986 to 2000 that included over 12,000 nationally representative U.S. youths (Rodgers & Wänström, 2007).

The Flynn effect is environmental: Improved nutrition and education, technological innovations (including TV and computers), more time devoted to cognitively demanding leisure activities (from chess to video games), a generally more stimulating world, and greater test-taking motivation may have contributed to the better reasoning ability of each successive generation (Flynn, 2003; Williams, 1998). Recently, the Flynn effect has slowed or stopped in certain developed nations with especially favorable health, social, and economic conditions (Scandinavia, for example) (Schneider, 2006; Sundet, Barlaug, & Torjussen, 2004). At the same time, it has spread to the developing world. The IQs of rural schoolchildren in Kenya underwent a large increase from 1984 to 1998. During this period, children's diets improved, TV sets appeared in some households, parental education and literacy increased, and family size declined, permitting parents to devote more time and resources to each child (Daley et al., 2003).

Notice that the generational gain in intelligence (18 points) is larger than the black–white IQ gap (about 12 to 13 points), indicating that environmental explanations for ethnic differences in IQ are highly plausible. Flynn argues that large, environmentally induced IQ increases over time present a major challenge to the assumption that black–white and other ethnic variations in IQ are mostly genetic (Dickens & Flynn, 2001; Flynn, 2007).

Figure 8.9 **The Flynn effect: Generational gains in performance on a test of spatial reasoning in four nations.** Findings are based on military testing that includes nearly all young adults in each country. (From J. R. Flynn, 1999, "Searching for Justice: The Discovery of IQ Gains over Time," *American Psychologist,* 54, p. 7. Copyright © 1999 by the American Psychological Association. Adapted with permission from the American Psychological Association and James Flynn.)

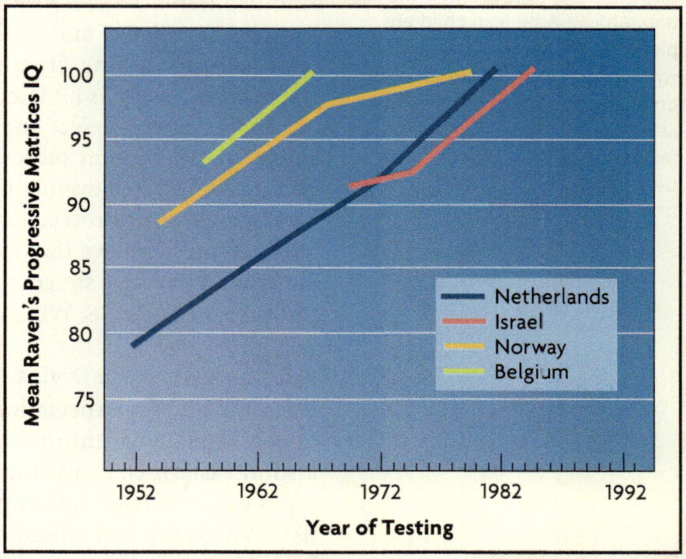

Race and Ethnicity: Genetic or Cultural Groupings?

DNA analyses reveal wide genetic variation *within* races (identified by physical features, such as skin color) and minimal genetic variation *between* them (Lewontin, 2003; Sternberg, Grigorenko, & Kidd, 2005; Templeton, 2002). Members of ethnic groups that have been the focus of the IQ nature–nurture controversy are far more similar in cultural values, experiences, and opportunities than in genetic makeup.

Nevertheless, many people incorrectly assume that genetic, racial differences underlie ethnic group differences in psychological traits. Yet racial labels themselves are often arbitrary. In the United States, "black" designates people with dark skin. In Brazil and Peru, where "black" refers to hair texture, eye color, and stature, many African Americans would be called "white." Asians and the !Kung of Botswana, Africa, could be regarded as one race because they have similarly shaped eyes. Alternatively, Asians, Native Americans, and Swedes might be grouped together because of their similarly shaped teeth (Fish, 2002; Renzetti & Curran, 1998).

Differences in racial designations over time and across nations underscore their unclear boundaries. On the U.S. Census form, ten racial categories appeared in 1930, only five in 1990, and six in 2000, with respondents permitted to check more than one race—all six, if they chose! In Canada, the census form listed 28 categories in 2001; in 2006, it listed 15, ending with "other," and asked respondents to mark as many as appropriate. Many designations encompass enormous cultural, linguistic, and biological diversity: "Black" includes, for example, people from Africa, Haiti, Jamaica, and Somalia: "Hispanic" includes people from Argentina, Costa Rica, Cuba, Guatemala, and Spain. In research as in census surveys, people self-identify, expressing their cultural heritage and sense of group belonging. Finally, in countries as culturally diverse as the United States and Canada, ethnic mixing is extensive. Consider this Hawaiian native's description of his ethnicity: "I'm Asian on my birth certificate and the census form, but I'm really multiracial. My mother's parents were Japanese, my father's mother was Filipino, and my father's father was Irish."

As one scholar of race relations summed up, "Classification of human beings into races is in the end a futile exercise" (Payne, 1998, p. 32). And perpetuating the belief that some ethnic groups are genetically inferior in IQ promotes an ever-present danger: unfair allocation of resources, making an unfounded assumption seem true.

These children, who are brothers, are growing up in the same stimulating, advantaged home. Adoption research supports the view that rearing environment is responsible for the black–white IQ gap. African-American children placed in economically well-off white homes early in life score high on intelligence tests because they are "reared in the culture of the tests and schools." © Ken Chernus/Getty Images/Taxi

Cultural Bias in Testing

Ethnic differences in IQ raise a controversial question: Do they result from *test bias?* If a test samples knowledge and skills that not all groups of children have had equal opportunity to learn, or if the testing situation impairs the performance of some groups but not others, then the resulting score is a biased, or unfair, measure.

Some experts reject the idea that intelligence tests are biased, claiming that they are intended to represent success in the common culture. From this perspective, because IQ predicts academic achievement equally well for majority and minority children, IQ tests are fair to both groups (Brown, Reynolds, & Whitaker, 1999; Edwards & Oakland, 2006; Jensen, 2002). Others believe that lack of exposure to certain communication styles and knowledge, along with negative stereotypes about the test-taker's ethnic group, can undermine children's performance (Ceci & Williams, 1997; Sternberg, 2005). Let's look at the evidence.

• **Communication Styles** Ethnic minority families often foster unique language skills that do not match the expectations of most classrooms and testing situations. Shirley Brice Heath (1982, 1989), an anthropologist who spent many hours observing in low-SES black homes in a southeastern U.S. city, found that African-American adults rarely asked their children the types of knowledge-training questions typical of middle-SES white families ("What color is it?" "What's this story about?"), which resemble the questioning style of tests and classrooms. Instead, the black parents asked only "real" questions, ones they themselves could not answer. Often these were analogy questions ("What's that like?") or story-starter questions ("Didja hear Miss Sally this morning?") that called for elaborate responses about personal experiences and had no "right answer."

Heath and other researchers report that these experiences lead low-SES black children to develop complex verbal skills at home, such as storytelling and exchanging quick-witted remarks. But their language emphasizes emotional and social concerns rather than facts about the world. Not surprisingly, black children may be confused by the "objective" questions they encounter on tests and in classrooms.

Also, African-American children often take a unique approach to storytelling that reflects a culturally specific form of narrative (also see page 297 in Chapter 7 and page 391 in Chapter 9). Instead of the *topic-focused* style of most school-age children, who describe an experience from beginning to end, they use a *topic-associating* style, blending several similar experiences. One African-American 9-year-old, for example, related having a tooth pulled, then described seeing her sister's tooth being pulled, next told how she had removed one of her baby teeth, and concluded, "I'm a pullin' teeth expert . . . call me, and I'll be over'" (McCabe, 1997, p. 164). Yet many teachers criticize this culturally distinctive narrative form as "disorganized," and it is not included in verbal test items. In contrast, mental tests often ask children to rearrange events in consecutive order.

Furthermore, many ethnic minority parents without extensive schooling prefer a *collaborative style of communication* when completing tasks with children. They work together in a coordinated, fluid way, each focused on the same aspect of the problem. This pattern of adult–child engagement has been observed in Native American, Canadian Inuit, Hispanic, and Guatemalan Mayan cultures (Chavajay & Rogoff, 2002; Crago, Annahatak, & Ningiuruvik, 1993; Delgado-Gaitan, 1994). With increasing education, parents establish a *hierarchical style of communication,* more like that of classrooms and tests. The parent directs each child to carry out an aspect of the task, and children work independently (Greenfield, Suzuki, & Rothstein-Fish, 2006). The sharp discontinuity between home and school communication practices may contribute to low-SES minority children's lower IQ and school performance (Greenfield, Quiroz, & Raeff, 2000).

A teacher in an Aboriginal community school in Australia leads an interactive reading lesson. Sensitive, supportive feedback that prompts students to look at challenging tasks in new ways is especially effective in helping these children succeed academically. © Bill Bachman

Indeed, intelligence testing is an extreme of this directive approach. Tasks are presented in only one way, and test-takers get no feedback. When an adult refuses to reveal whether the child is on the right track, minority children may react with "disruptive apprehension"—giving any answer that comes to mind and rejecting the personal relevance of the testing situation (Ferguson, 1998). In one study, Australian Aboriginal 7- to 14-year-olds—who scored far below their Australian European agemates on a typical, paper-and-pencil math skills test—showed dramatic performance gains when given a computerized, interactive version. The computerized test provided immediate feedback about the accuracy of answers and, after an incorrect response, allowed the child to invoke a brief, narrated lesson on how to solve the item (Hippisley, Douglas, & Houghton, 2005). Providing feedback and prompting minority children to look at missed problems in new ways resulted in a more "culture-fair" assessment of their math competencies.

• **Test Content** Many researchers argue that IQ scores are affected by specific information acquired as part of majority-culture upbringing. Consistent with this view, low-SES African-American preschoolers often miss vocabulary words on mental tests that have alternative meanings in their cultural community—for example, interpreting the word *frame* as "physique," *digging* as "liking someone," and *wrapping* as "rapping," a popular style of music (Champion, 2003a).

Unfortunately, attempts to change tests by eliminating verbal, fact-oriented (crystallized) items and relying only on spatial reasoning (fluid) tasks have not raised the scores of ethnic minority children much (Reynolds & Kaiser, 1990). Yet even fluid test items depend on learning opportunities. In one study, children's Block Design scores (see the sample item in Figure 8.3) were related to how often they had played a popular but expensive game that (like the test) required them to arrange blocks to duplicate a design as quickly as possible (Dirks, 1982). Playing video games that require fast responding and mental rotation of visual images also increases success on spatial test items (Maynard, Subrahmanyam, & Greenfield, 2005). Low-income minority children, who often grow up in more "people-oriented" than "object-oriented" homes, may lack opportunities to use games and objects that promote certain intellectual skills.

When same-age children are compared, those who have spent more time in school have higher IQs—clear evidence that exposure to the knowledge and ways of thinking valued in classrooms boosts mental test performance. © Will McIntyre/ Corbis

Furthermore, the sheer amount of time a child spends in school predicts IQ. In comparisons of children who are the same age but in different grades, those who have been in school longer score higher on intelligence tests. Similarly, dropping out of school causes IQ to decline. The earlier young people leave school, the greater

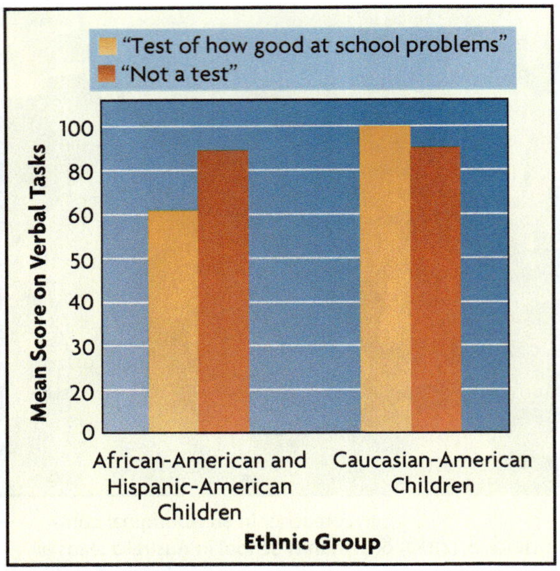

■ **Figure 8.10** **Effect of stereotype threat on test performance.**
Among African-American and Hispanic-American children who were aware of ethnic stereotypes, being told that verbal tasks were a "test of how good children are at school problems" led to far worse performance than being told the tasks "were not a test." These statements had little impact on the performance of Caucasian-American children. (Adapted from McKown & Weinstein, 2003.)

their loss of IQ points (Ceci, 1991, 1999). Taken together, these findings indicate that children's exposure to the factual knowledge and ways of thinking valued in classrooms has a sizable impact on their intelligence test performance.

• **Stereotypes** TAKE A MOMENT... Imagine trying to succeed at an activity when the prevailing attitude is that members of your group are incompetent. What might you be feeling and saying to yourself? **Stereotype threat**—the fear of being judged on the basis of a negative stereotype—can trigger anxiety that interferes with performance (Aronson, 2002; Steele, 1997). Mounting evidence confirms that stereotype threat undermines test taking in both children and adults. For example, researchers gave African-American, Hispanic-American, and Caucasian 6- to 10-year-olds verbal tasks. Some children were told that the tasks were "not a test." Others were informed that they were "a test of how good children are at school problems"—a statement designed to induce stereotype threat in the ethnic minority children. Among children who were aware of ethnic stereotypes (such as "black people aren't smart"), African Americans and Hispanics performed far worse in the "test" condition than in the "not a test" condition. Caucasian children, in contrast, performed similarly in both conditions. The researchers concluded that only under the "not a test" instructions did the minority children do as well as would have been expected on the basis of a prior measure of their verbal ability (see Figure 8.10) (McKown & Weinstein, 2003).

Over middle childhood, children become increasingly conscious of ethnic stereotypes, and those from stigmatized groups are especially mindful of them. By junior high school, many low-SES, minority students start to devalue doing well in school, saying it is unimportant to them (Major et al., 1998; Osborne, 1994). Self-protective disengagement, sparked by stereotype threat, may be responsible. This undermining of motivation can have serious long-term consequences. Research shows that self-discipline—effort and delay of gratification—predicts school performance at least as well as, and sometimes better than, IQ does (Duckworth & Seligman, 2005).

Reducing Cultural Bias in Testing

Although not all experts agree, many acknowledge that IQ scores can underestimate the intelligence of children from ethnic minority groups. A special concern exists about incorrectly labeling minority children as slow learners and assigning them to remedial classes, which are far less stimulating than regular school experiences. To avoid this danger, test scores need to be combined with assessments of children's adaptive behavior—their ability to cope with the demands of their everyday environments. The child who does poorly on an IQ test yet can play a complex game on the playground, figure out how to rewire a broken TV, or care for younger siblings responsibly is unlikely to be mentally deficient.

This teacher uses dynamic assessment, tailoring instruction to students' individual needs—an approach that reveals what a child can learn with social support. © Janine Wiedel Photolibrary/Alamy

In addition, culturally relevant testing procedures enhance minority children's performance. In an approach called **dynamic assessment,** an innovation consistent with Vygotsky's *zone of proximal development,* the adult introduces purposeful teaching into the testing situation to find out what the child can attain with social support (Lidz, 2001; Sternberg & Grigorenko, 2002). Three factors distinguish dynamic assessment from traditional static approaches:

- A focus on the *processes* involved in learning and development (rather than on intellectual products)
- *Feedback* provided after each task (rather than no feedback)
- An *adult–child relationship* based on teaching and help individualized for each child (rather than a neutral relationship that is identical for all children) (Grigorenko & Sternberg, 1998)

Dynamic assessment often follows a pretest–intervene–retest procedure. While intervening, the adult seeks the teaching style best suited to the child and communicates strategies that the child can generalize to new situations.

Research consistently shows that "static" assessments, such as IQ scores, frequently underestimate how well children do on test items after receiving adult assistance. Children's receptivity to teaching and their capacity to transfer what they have learned to novel problems add considerably to the prediction of future performance (Sternberg & Grigorenko, 2002; Tzuriel, 2001). In one study, Ethiopian 6- and 7-year-olds who had recently immigrated to Israel scored well below their Israeli-born agemates on spatial reasoning tasks. The Ethiopian children had little experience with this type of thinking. After several dynamic assessment sessions in which the adult suggested effective strategies, the Ethiopian children's scores rose sharply, nearly equaling those of Israeli-born children (see Figure 8.11). They also transferred their learning to new test items (Tzuriel & Kaufman, 1999).

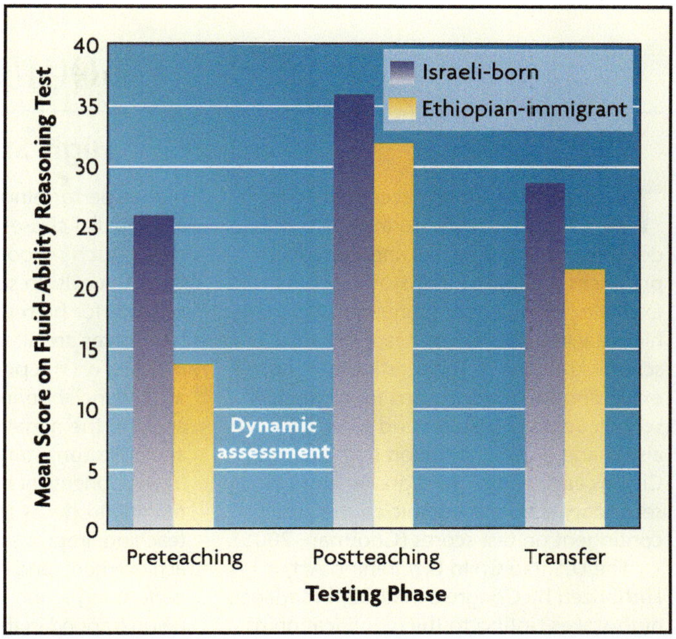

Figure 8.11 **Influence of dynamic assessment on mental test scores of Ethiopian-immigrant and Israeli-born 6- and 7-year-olds.** Each child completed test items in a preteaching phase, a postteaching phase, and a transfer phase, in which they had to generalize their learning to new problems. After dynamic assessment, Ethiopian and Israeli children's scores were nearly equal. Ethiopian children also transferred their learning to new test items, performing much better in the transfer phase than in the preteaching phase. (Adapted from Tzuriel & Kaufman, 1999.)

Dynamic assessment is time-consuming and requires extensive knowledge of minority children's cultural values and practices. As yet the approach has not been more effective than traditional tests in predicting academic achievement (Grigorenko & Sternberg, 1998). Better correspondence may emerge in classrooms where teaching interactions resemble the dynamic testing approach—namely, individualized assistance on tasks carefully selected to help the child move beyond her current level of development.

But rather than adapting testing to support high-quality classroom learning experiences, North American education is placing greater emphasis on traditional test scores. To upgrade the academic achievement of poorly performing students, a *high-stakes testing* movement has arisen, making progress through the school system contingent on test performance. As the Social Issues box on pages 342–343 indicates, this stepped-up emphasis on passing standardized tests has narrowed the focus of instruction in many classrooms to test preparation, and it may widen SES and ethnic group differences in educational attainment.

In view of its many problems, should intelligence testing in schools be suspended? Most experts reject this solution. Without testing, important educational decisions would be based only on subjective impressions, perhaps increasing discrimination in placement of minority children. Intelligence tests are useful when interpreted carefully by psychologists and educators who are sensitive to cultural influences on test performance. And despite their limitations, IQ scores continue to be valid measures of school learning potential for the majority of Western children.

Home Environment and Mental Development

As noted earlier, children of the *same* ethnic and SES background vary greatly in mental test scores. Many studies support the conclusion that factors in the home environment contribute to these differences.

Researchers divide home influences into two broad types: **Shared environmental influences** pervade the general atmosphere of the home and, therefore, *similarly* affect siblings living in it. Examples include the availability of stimulating toys and books and parental modeling of cognitively challenging activities. **Nonshared environmental influences** make siblings *different* from one another. Unique treatment by parents, birth order and spacing, and special events that affect one sibling more than the other (such as moving to a new neighborhood) are examples.

• Shared Environmental Influences Two types of research shed light on the role of shared environmental influences: (1) studies in which researchers observe home environmental

■ Social Issues ■

High-Stakes Testing

To better hold schools accountable for educating students, during the past two decades many U.S. states and Canadian provinces mandated that students pass exams for high school graduation. As these high-stakes achievement tests spread, schools stepped up their testing programs, extending them downward to elementary school. Some U.S. states and school districts also made grade promotion (in New York City, as early as the third grade) and secondary-school academic course credits contingent on test scores (Gootman, 2005).

The U.S. No Child Left Behind Act, authorized by Congress in 2002, broadened high-stakes testing to the identification of "passing" and "failing" schools. The law mandates that each state evaluate every public school's performance through annual achievement testing and publicize the results. Schools that consistently perform poorly (have a high percentage of failing students) must give parents options for upgrading their children's education, such as transfers to nearby higher-performing schools or enrollment in remedial classes. When they lose students, such schools also lose state and federal funds. In some states, schoolwide rewards for high scores and penalties for low scores are already in place. These include, on the positive side, official praise and financial bonuses to school staff and, on the negative side, withdrawal of accreditation, state takeover, and closure.

Proponents of high-stakes testing believe that it introduces greater rigor into classroom teaching, improves student motivation and achievement, and either turns around poor-performing schools or protects students from being trapped in them. But accumulating evidence indicates that high-stakes testing often undermines, rather than upgrades, the quality of education.

For example, in a Canadian study, researchers examined the impact of requiring students to pass British Columbia's high school exit exam on eighth-, tenth-, and twelfth-grade science teaching. Observing classes and interviewing teachers, they found that twelfth-grade teachers narrowed the scope of what they taught to strings of facts to be memorized for the test. As a result, eighth and tenth graders, in some respects, were doing more advanced work than twelfth graders—conducting more experiments, exploring topics in greater depth, and engaging in more critical thinking (Wideen et al., 1997).

Many teachers also express concern that high-stakes testing promotes a one-size-fits-all education that is insensitive to student diversity. And because the main goal is to upgrade the test performance of poorly performing students, low-income and ethnic minority children are especially likely to be exposed to narrowly focused, regimented teaching. Simultaneously, the educational needs of gifted and talented students are neglected (Mondoza, 2006).

An additional concern is that high-stakes testing promotes fear—a poor motivator for upgrading teaching and learning. Principals and teachers worry about losing funding and their jobs if students do

qualities and relate them to IQ; and (2) studies examining the impact of family beliefs about intellectual success on student performance.

Observations of Home Environmental Qualities. The **Home Observation for Measurement of the Environment (HOME)** is a checklist for gathering information about the quality of children's home lives through observation and parental interview (Caldwell & Bradley, 1994). Refer to Applying What We Know on page 344 for factors that HOME measures in infancy and toddlerhood, early childhood, and middle childhood.

Evidence on HOME confirms the findings of decades of research—that stimulation provided by parents is moderately linked to mental development. Regardless of SES and ethnicity, an organized, stimulating physical setting and parental encouragement, involvement, and affection repeatedly predict better language and IQ scores in toddlerhood and early childhood (Espy, Molfese, & DiLalla, 2001; Fuligni, Han, & Brooks-Gunn, 2004; Klebanov et al., 1998; Linver, Martin, & Brooks-Gunn, 2004; Roberts, Burchinal, & Durham, 1999; Tamis-LeMonda et al., 2004). In a study in which researchers controlled for both SES and home environmental quality, the black–white disparity in preschoolers' IQ diminished to just a few points (Smith, Duncan, & Lee, 2003).

The extent to which parents talk to infants and toddlers contributes strongly to early language progress, which, in turn, predicts intelligence and academic achievement in elementary school (Hart & Risley, 1995). Recall from Chapter 7 that knowledge of the sound structure of language (phonological awareness), vocabulary and grammatical development, and wide-ranging general knowledge are vital for learning to read.

The HOME–IQ relationship declines in middle childhood, perhaps because older children spend increasing amounts of time in school and other out-of-home settings (Luster & Dubow,

poorly—punishments that, some experts note, have sparked unprecedented levels of adult cheating and other educationally detrimental behaviors. These range from giving students answers during testing, changing students' scores, and offering students rewards (money, sweets, and expensive toys) for earning high scores to suspending or expelling students likely to perform poorly just before test administration (Nichols & Berliner, 2007).

Furthermore, experts in assessment note that tests measuring achievement at the school or district level are imprecise instruments for making decisions about individuals (Hursh, 2007; Sacks, 1999). Many students who get passing grades on their report cards, even high grades, fail high-stakes exams because a time-limited test with several dozen multiple-choice questions can tap only a small sampling of the skills covered in the classroom.

Students most likely to score poorly are minority youths living in poverty. When they are punished with course failure and grade retention, their self-esteem and motivation drop sharply. A Massachusetts study demonstrated that relying solely on test scores, while ignoring teacher-assigned grades (which take into account effort and a broad range of skills), amplifies achievement gaps between white and black students and between boys and girls in math and science (Brennan et al., 2001). Other research confirms that high-stakes testing requirements in the United States and Canada have contributed to the high dropout rates among inner-city ethnic minority youths (Balfanz et al., 2007; Ferguson et al., 2005; Hursh, 2007).

The trend toward "teaching to tests" induced by high-stakes testing contrasts sharply with the emphasis on teaching for deeper understanding in countries that rank at the top in cross-cultural comparisons of academic achievement (see Chapter 15). Even after devoting hundreds of hours of class time to test preparation, thousands of North American students fail school-exit exams and do not graduate. In 2006–2007, for example, 27,000 students (16 percent of the tenth-grade population) in Ontario, Canada—mostly low-SES minorities, recent immigrants not yet proficient in English, or young people with learning problems—failed the literacy test (Government of Ontario, 2007a, 2007b). Although most retake these exams, some fail repeatedly, with potentially dire long-term consequences.

When classroom instruction is narrowly focused on test preparation, students who test poorly may become inattentive and eventually drop out. © Cleve Bryant/PhotoEdit

Clearly, serious issues remain for lawmakers and educators to resolve about the use of high-stakes tests. These include their ethnic and gender fairness and their questionable power to spark school reforms that make students better learners.

1992). Nevertheless, two middle-childhood HOME scales are especially strong predictors of academic achievement: provision for active stimulation (for example, encouraging hobbies and organizational memberships) and family participation in developmentally stimulating experiences (visiting friends, attending theater performances) (Bradley, Caldwell, & Rock, 1988).

Yet we must interpret these correlational findings cautiously. In all the studies, children were reared by their biological parents, with whom they share not just a common environment but also a common heredity. Parents who are genetically more intelligent may provide better experiences as well as give birth to genetically brighter children, who evoke more stimulation from their parents. Research supports this hypothesis, which refers to *genetic–environmental correlation* (see Chapter 3, page 121). The HOME–IQ correlation is stronger for biological than for adopted children, suggesting that parent–child genetic similarity elevates the relationship (Saudino & Plomin, 1997).

But heredity does not account for the entire association between home environment and mental test scores. Family living conditions—both HOME scores and affluence of the surrounding neighborhood—continue to predict children's IQ beyond the contribution of parental IQ and education (Chase-Lansdale et al., 1997; Klebanov et al., 1998). These findings highlight the vital importance of environmental quality.

Family Beliefs About Intellectual Success. Regardless of SES, newly arrived immigrant parents from Asia and Latin America emphasize the importance of intellectual success, and their children do remarkably well in school. (Return to the Cultural Influences box on pages 52–53 in Chapter 2 to review these findings.) Parental support for achievement is greater in higher-SES families in which both parent and child IQs are higher, making it difficult to isolate the impact of family beliefs on children's performance. Is IQ responsible for immigrant families'

Applying What We Know

Features of a High-Quality Home Life in Infancy and Toddlerhood, Early Childhood, and Middle Childhood: The HOME Subscales

Infancy and Toddlerhood	Early Childhood	Middle Childhood
1. Emotional and verbal responsiveness of the parent	1. Parental pride, affection, and warmth	1. Parental emotional and verbal responsiveness
2. Parental acceptance of the child	2. Avoidance of physical punishment	2. Emotionally positive parent–child relationship
3. Parental involvement with the child	3. Language stimulation	3. Parental encouragement of social maturity
4. Organization of the physical environment	4. Stimulation of academic behavior	4. Provision for active stimulation
5. Provision of appropriate play materials	5. Stimulation through toys, games, and reading material	5. Growth-fostering materials and experiences
6. Opportunities for variety in daily stimulation	6. Parental modeling and encouragement of social maturity	6. Family participation in developmentally stimulating experiences
	7. Opportunities for variety in daily stimulation	7. Parental involvement in child rearing
	8. Physical environment: safe, clean, and conducive to development	8. Physical environment: safe, clean, and conducive to development

Sources: Bradley, 1994; Bradley et al., 2001.

high valuing of intellectual endeavors and their children's superior academic performance? Probably not; recent arrivals are unlikely to be more intelligent than North American–born children whose parents arrived a decade or two earlier. Rather, immigrant parents' belief that education is the surest way to improve life chances seems to play a profound role (Cooper, Dominguez, & Rosas, 2005; Fuligni & Yoshikawa, 2003).

Parental beliefs are also linked to academic performance among nonimmigrant children. In a study of more than 1,300 U.S. Caucasian- and African-American families with school-age children, parental expectations for educational attainment predicted parents' involvement in their children's school activities, supervision of homework, and—two years later—children's reading and math achievement (Zhan, 2005). Similarly, an investigation of Asian-American, Hispanic, and Caucasian-American families revealed that within each group, the more education parents expected their fourth and fifth graders to attain, the higher the children's school grades (Okagaki & Frensch, 1998). Parental expectations were not merely responsive to their child's prior achievements. Rather, regardless of children's grades the previous year, parental beliefs predicted school performance.

A Vietnamese-American immigrant mother attends her second-grader's parent–teacher conference as the child's aunt looks on. When parents place a high value on education, children are more successful in school, beyond the influence of SES or IQ. © Bob Daemmrich/The Image Works

Think back to James's father's conviction that academic success could transform James's life path, described in the opening to this chapter. Warm, appropriately demanding child rearing, cognitively stimulating parent–child activities, and parents' school involvement seem to be the major means through which parents convey such beliefs to their children (Davis-Kean, 2005; Okagaki, 2001). We will consider parenting and achievement further in Chapters 11 and 14.

• **Nonshared Environmental Influences** The experiences of children growing up in the same family, while similar in some ways, differ in others. Parents may favor one child or assign children special roles—for example, one expected to achieve in school, a second to get along with others. Each child also experiences sibling relationships differently.

Kinship research suggests that nonshared environmental factors are more powerful than shared influences on IQ. Turn back to Figure 8.6 on page 334. Notice the relatively low IQ correlations between unrelated siblings living together—a direct estimate of the effect of shared environment. Recall, also, that in adolescence the IQ resemblance between fraternal twins declines (see pages 334–335). This trend, which also characterizes nontwin siblings, is particularly marked for unrelated siblings, whose IQs at adolescence are no longer correlated. These findings indicate that the impact of the shared environment on IQ is greatest in childhood (Finkel & Pedersen, 2001; Loehlin, Horn, & Willerman, 1997). Thereafter, it gives way to nonshared influences, as young people spend more time outside the home, encounter experiences unlike those of their siblings, and seek environments consistent with their genetic makeup.

Nevertheless, few studies have examined nonshared environmental influences on IQ. The most extensively studied factors are sibling birth order and spacing. For years, researchers thought that earlier birth order and wider spacing might grant children more parental attention and stimulation and, therefore, result in higher IQs. But recent evidence indicates that birth order and spacing are unrelated to IQ (Rodgers, 2001; Rodgers et al., 2000; Wichman, Rodgers, & MacCallum, 2006). Why is this so? Parents' differential treatment of siblings appears to be far more responsive to children's personalities, interests, and behaviors than to these family-structure variables.

Finally, some researchers believe the most potent nonshared environmental influences are unpredictable unique events—an inspiring English teacher, a summer at a special camp, or perhaps a period of intense sibling rivalry (McCall, 1993). To understand the role of these nonshared factors in mental development, we will need intensive case studies of children growing up in the same family.

Ask Yourself

Review Why can't heritability estimates explain ethnic differences in IQ? Using research findings, describe environmental factors that contribute to these differences.

Apply Josefina, a Hispanic fourth grader, does well on homework assignments. But when her teacher announces, "It's time for a test to see how much you've learned," Josefina usually does poorly. How might stereotype threat explain this inconsistency?

Connect Explain how dynamic assessment is consistent with Vygotsky's zone of proximal development and with scaffolding (see Chapter 6, pages 265–266).

Reflect Do you think that intelligence tests are culturally biased? What evidence and observations influenced your conclusions?

Early Intervention and Intellectual Development

In the 1960s, as part of the War on Poverty in the United States, many intervention programs for economically disadvantaged preschoolers were initiated. Their goal was to offset the declines in IQ and achievement common among low-SES schoolchildren by addressing learning problems early, before formal schooling begins. The most extensive of these federal programs, **Project Head Start,** began in 1965 and currently includes more than 19,000 Head Start centers serving about 909,000 children (Head Start Bureau, 2007). A typical Head Start center provides children with a year or two of preschool, along with nutritional and health services. Parent involvement is central to the Head Start philosophy. Parents serve on policy councils, contribute to program planning, work directly with children in classrooms, and attend special programs on parenting and child development. They also receive services addressing their own emotional, social, and vocational needs.

Project Head Start provides preschoolers from poverty-stricken families with preschool education and nutritional and health services. High-quality, early educational intervention has benefits lasting into adulthood. © SassyStock/FotoSearch

In 1995, Canada initiated **Aboriginal Head Start** for First Nations, Inuit, and Métis children younger than age 6, 60 percent of whom live in poverty. Like Project Head Start, the program provides children with preschool education and nutritional and health services and encourages parent involvement. It also builds on the children's knowledge of Aboriginal languages and cultures. Currently, Aboriginal Head Start has about 130 sites and serves more than 3,900 children (Public Health Agency of Canada, 2004).

Benefits of Early Intervention

More than two decades of research have established the long-term benefits of early intervention. The most extensive of these studies, coordinated by the Consortium for Longitudinal Studies, combined data from seven interventions implemented by universities or research foundations. Results showed that poverty-stricken children who attended programs had higher IQ and achievement test scores than controls during the first two to three years of elementary school. After that, differences declined (Lazar & Darlington, 1982). But on real-life measures of school adjustment, children and adolescents who received intervention remained ahead. They were less likely to be placed in special education or retained in grade, and a greater number graduated from high school. They also showed lasting benefits in attitudes and motivation: They were more likely to give achievement-related reasons (such as school or job accomplishments) for being proud of themselves.

A separate report on one program, the High/Scope Perry Preschool Project, revealed benefits lasting well into adulthood. More than 100 African-American 3- and 4-year-olds were randomly assigned either to a cognitively enriching two-year preschool program or to no intervention. During weekly visits to the homes of the intervention group, teachers showed parents how to teach and read to their children. Besides improved school adjustment, preschool intervention was associated with increased employment and reduced pregnancy and delinquency rates in adolescence. At age 27, those who had attended preschool were more likely to have graduated from high school, to have enrolled in college, to have higher earnings, and to be married and own their own home. And they were less likely than their no-preschool counterparts to have been arrested, to have spent time in prison, and to have ever been on welfare (see Figure 8.12) (Weikart, 1998). The most recent follow-up, at age 40, revealed that the intervention group sustained its advantage on all measures of life success, including education, income, law-abiding behavior, and family life (Schweinhart et al., 2005).

■ **Figure 8.12** **Some outcomes of the High/Scope Perry Preschool Project on follow-up at age 27.**
Although two years of a cognitively enriching preschool program did not eradicate the effects of growing up in poverty, children who received intervention were advantaged over no-intervention controls on all measures of life success when they reached adulthood. (Adapted from Schweinhart et al., 2005.)

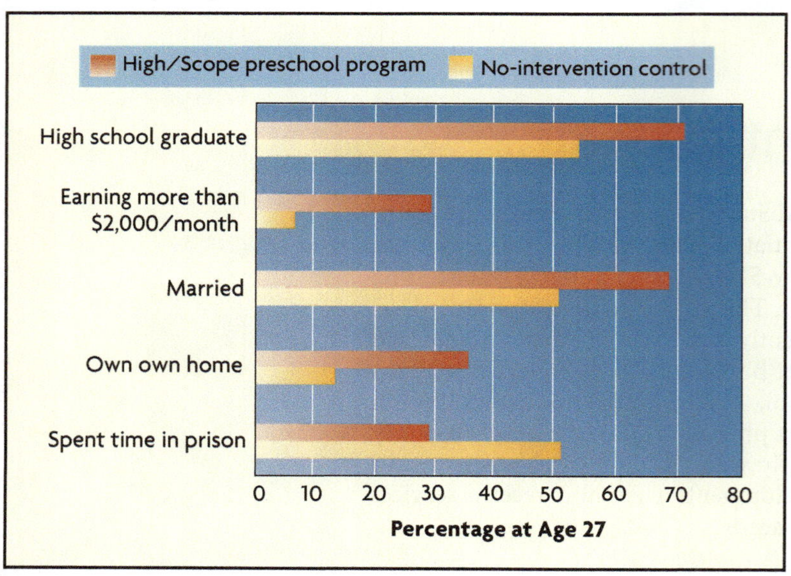

Do the effects on school adjustment of these well-designed and well-delivered interventions generalize to Head Start and other community-based preschool interventions? Gains are similar, though not as strong. Head Start preschoolers, who are more economically disadvantaged than children in other programs, have more severe learning and behavior problems. And quality of services is more variable across community programs (Barnett, 2004; NICHD Early Child Care Research Network, 2001). But interventions of high quality are associated with diverse, long-lasting favorable outcomes, including higher rates of high school graduation and college enrollment and lower rates of adolescent drug use and delinquency (Garces, Thomas, & Currie, 2002; Love et al., 2006; Reynolds & Ou, 2004).

▪ Social Issues ▪

The Carolina Abecedarian Project: A Model of Early Intervention

In the 1970s, an experiment was begun to find out if educational enrichment starting at a very early age could prevent the declines in mental development that affect children born into extreme poverty. In the Carolina Abecedarian Project, more than 100 infants from poverty-stricken families, ranging in age from 3 weeks to 3 months, were randomly assigned to either a treatment group or a control group. Treatment infants were enrolled in full-time, year-round child care through the preschool years. There they received stimulation aimed at promoting motor, cognitive, language, and social skills and, after age 3, literacy and math concepts. Special emphasis was placed on tailoring experiences to children's individual needs and on rich, responsive adult–child verbal communication. All children received nutrition and health services; the primary difference between treatment and controls was the intensive, individualized educational program.

As Figure 8.13 shows, by 12 months of age, the IQs of the two groups diverged. Treatment children sustained their IQ advantage until last tested—at age 21. In addition, throughout their years of schooling, treatment youths achieved considerably better than controls in reading and math. These gains translated into more years of schooling completed, higher rates of college enrollment and employment in skilled jobs, and lower rates of adolescent drug use and parenthood (Campbell et al., 2001, 2002; Ramey & Ramey, 1999).

While the children were in elementary school, the researchers conducted a second experiment to compare the impact of early and later intervention. From kindergarten through second grade, for half the treatment group and half the control group, a resource teacher introduced into the home educational activities addressing the child's specific learning needs. This school-age intervention had no impact on IQ. It did enhance children's academic achievement, but the effects were weaker than for very early intervention (Campbell & Ramey, 1995).

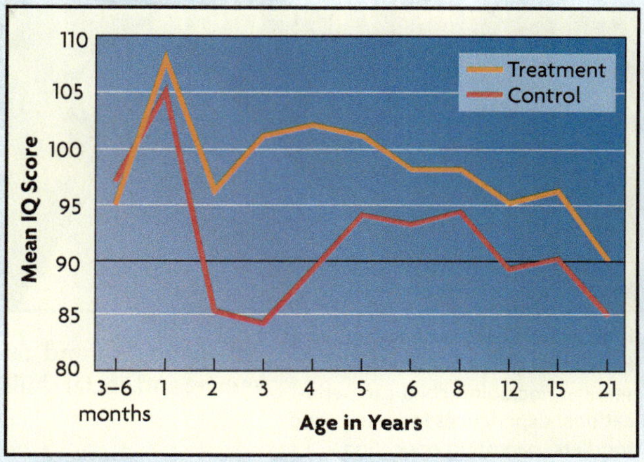

Figure 8.13 **IQ scores of treatment and control children from infancy to 21 years in the Carolina Abecedarian Project.**

At 1 year, treatment children outperformed controls, an advantage consistently maintained through 21 years of age. The IQ scores of both groups declined gradually during childhood and adolescence—a trend probably due to the damaging impact of poverty on mental development. (Adapted from Campbell et al., 2001.)

The Carolina Abecedarian Project shows that providing continuous, high-quality enrichment from infancy through the preschool years reduces the negative impact of poverty on children's mental development. It confirms the conclusions of recent reviews of many programs: The greater the "dose" of educational intervention, the more powerful its effects (Galinsky, 2006; Love, Chazan-Cohen, & Raikes, 2007; Nelson, Westhues, & MacLeod, 2003).

A consistent finding is that gains in IQ and achievement test scores from attending Head Start and other interventions quickly dissolve. These children typically enter inferior public schools in poverty-stricken neighborhoods, an experience that undermines the benefits of preschool education (Brooks-Gunn, 2003; Ramey, Ramey, & Lanzi, 2006). But in the Chicago Child–Parent Centers—a program emphasizing literacy intervention and parent involvement that began at age 3 and continued through third grade—gains in academic achievement were still evident in junior high school (Reynolds & Temple, 1998). And when intensive intervention starts in infancy and extends through early childhood, IQ gains endure into adulthood (see the Social Issues box above).

Recognition of the greater power of intervening as early as possible led the U.S. Congress to provide limited funding for services directed at infants and toddlers, who already have serious developmental problems or who are at risk for problems because of poverty. **Early Head Start,** begun in 1995, currently has 700 sites serving 65,000 low-income families. It offers an array of coordinated services—child care, educational experiences for infants and toddlers, parenting education, family social support, and health care—delivered through a center-based, home-based, or mixed approach, depending on community needs. A recent evaluation,

Intervention programs such as Early Head Start offer coordinated services, including child care, educational experiences for infants and toddlers, parenting education, health care, and social support for families. An evaluation showed that Early Head Start led to warmer, more stimulating parenting, cognitive and language gains, and a decline in harsh discipline and child aggression. © Ellen B. Senisi

conducted when children reached age 3, showed that intervention led to warmer, more stimulating parenting, a reduction in harsh discipline, gains in cognitive and language development, and lessening of child aggression (Love et al., 2005; Love, Chazan-Cohen, & Raikes, 2007). The strongest effects occurred at sites mixing center and home-visiting services—a combination that may intensify educational and family services.

Even when intervention is delayed until age 3 or 4, the improved school adjustment that results from attending a one- or two-year Head Start program is impressive. The comprehensiveness of Head Start—provision of health, nutrition, education, and family social services—along with its emphasis on parent involvement may be responsible. The greater parents' involvement in Head Start, the better their child-rearing practices and the more stimulating their home learning environments. These factors are positively related to preschoolers' independence and task persistence in the classroom and to their year-end academic, language, and social skills (Marcon, 1999b; McLoyd, Aikens, & Burton, 2006; Parker et al., 1999).

The Future of Early Intervention

Excellent early intervention is highly cost effective when compared with the cost of providing special education, treating criminal behavior, and supporting unemployed adults. For example, researchers calculated a \$9 return on each \$1 invested when participants in the High/Scope Perry Preschool Project reached age 27, and a \$17 return on each \$1 invested when they reached age 40 (Temple & Reynolds, 2006). Extrapolating from these figures, the lifetime return to society is more than \$250,000 on an investment of \$15,000 per preschool child—a potential total savings of many billions of dollars if such programs reached every poverty-stricken preschooler in the United States and Canada (Heckman & Masterov, 2004).

What factors contributed to the enduring impact of such outstanding programs as the High/Scope Perry Preschool Project, the Chicago Child–Parent Centers, and the Carolina Abecedarian Project? According to one analysis, they shared the following critical features:

- *Starting early.* The Abecedarian Program began in the first months of life, the High/Scope Perry Preschool Project and the Chicago Child–Parent Centers as early as age 3.
- *Employing well-educated, well-compensated teachers.* Most teachers in the three programs had at least a bachelor's degree in education, and they were paid competitively with public school teachers—factors resulting in low staff turnover and, thus, stability in teacher–child relationships.
- *Maintaining generous teacher–child ratios and small class sizes.* In the Abecedarian Program, the teacher–infant ratio was 1 to 3, the teacher–toddler ratio 1 to 4. Preschool ratios in the three programs ranged from 1 to 5 to 1 to 8.
- *Offering intensive intervention.* Each program included many hours of classroom contact with children in the early years—in the High/Scope Perry Preschool Project and Chicago Child–Parent Centers, full days for up to two school years; in the Abecedarian Project, full days, year-round, for five years.
- *Emphasizing parent involvement, education, and support.* The High/Scope Perry Preschool Project and the Chicago Child–Parent Centers made concerted efforts to involve parents in their children's learning.
- *Focusing on the whole child.* The three programs promoted all aspects of children's development—not just academic skills. They recognized that a child who is ill, hungry, weak in social skills, or suffering from emotional or behavior problems is unable to learn at his or her best.

To achieve lasting favorable results, designers of today's early intervention programs must include these key ingredients (Galinsky, 2006; Love et al., 2006; Zigler & Bishop-Josef, 2006). Also, the number of children served must be greatly expanded. Unfortunately, because of limited funding, many children in need do not receive any intervention. A few supplementary programs—such as Jumpstart, described at the beginning of this chapter—have responded to this shortage by delivering intervention to children in child-care centers, as well as strengthening intervention in Head Start and other preschool classrooms. Evaluations indicate that 3- to 5-year-olds who experience Jumpstart's intensive, one-to-one approach show greater end-of-year gains in language, literacy, task persistence, and social skills than non-Jumpstart controls in the same early childhood settings (Jumpstart Evaluation Team, 2008).

Jumpstart volunteers work closely with individual children, forming a close relationship that promotes gains in social skills and task persistence, as well as in language and literacy. Michael Warren/Courtesy of Jumpstart

Giftedness: Creativity and Talent

Throughout this chapter, we have seen that intelligence includes much more than mental abilities that predict success in school. Today, educators recognize that **gifted** children—those who display exceptional intellectual strengths—have diverse characteristics. Some have IQ scores above 130, the standard definition of giftedness based on intelligence test performance (Gardner, 1998b). High-IQ children, as we have seen, have keen memories and an exceptional capacity to solve challenging academic problems. Yet recognition that intelligence tests do not sample the entire range of human mental skills has led to an expanded conception of giftedness, which includes creativity.

Creativity is the ability to produce work that is *original* yet *appropriate*—something that others have not thought of but that is useful in some way (Lubart, 2003; Sternberg, 2003b). Judgments of creativity reflect not only the quality of the product but also the process of arriving at it. Rather than following established rules, a creative work pulls together previously disparate ideas. Typically, it also involves hard work and the need to overcome obstacles on the way to the final product.

In addition to its value on the job and in daily life, creativity is vital for societal progress. Without it, there would be no new inventions, scientific findings, movements in art, or social programs. Therefore, understanding its ingredients and nurturing them from childhood are of paramount importance. As we will see in the following sections, ideas about creativity have changed radically during the past two decades.

The Psychometric View

Until recently, a purely cognitive perspective dominated research on creativity. Commonly used tests tapped **divergent thinking**—the generation of multiple and unusual possibilities when faced with a task or problem. Divergent thinking contrasts with **convergent thinking,** which involves arriving at a single correct answer and is emphasized on intelligence tests (Guilford, 1985).

Because highly creative children (like high-IQ children) are often better at some types of tasks than others, a variety of tests of divergent thinking are available (Runco, 1992a, 1993; Torrance, 1988). A verbal measure might ask children to name uses for common objects (such as a newspaper). A figural measure might ask them to come up with drawings based on a circular motif (see Figure 8.14 on page 350). A "real-world problem" measure requires students to suggest solutions to everyday problems. Responses to all these tests can be scored for the number of ideas generated and their originality. For example, on a verbal test, saying that

Figure 8.14 **Responses of an 8-year-old who scored high on a figural measure of divergent thinking.** This child was asked to make as many pictures as she could from the circles on the page. The titles she gave her drawings, from left to right, are as follows: "Dracula," "one-eyed monster," "pumpkin," "Hula-Hoop," "poster," "wheelchair," "earth," "moon," "planet," "movie camera," "sad face," "picture," "stoplight," "beach ball," "the letter O," "car," "glasses." Tests of divergent thinking tap only one of the complex cognitive contributions to creativity. (Reprinted by permission of Laura Berk.)

a newspaper can be used "as handgrips for a bicycle" would be more original than saying it can be used "to clean things."

Tests of divergent thinking are known as the *psychometric approach to creativity* because they permit scores to be compared to the performance of standardization samples. Yet critics note that these measures are poor predictors of creative accomplishment in everyday life because they tap only one of the complex cognitive contributions to creativity. And they say nothing about personality traits, motivation, and environmental circumstances that foster creative potential. Still, divergent-thinking tests do tap relevant skills, have been the major focus of research on creativity in children, and (as we will see shortly) have enhanced our understanding of the development of creativity.

A Multifaceted View

Recent theories agree that many elements must converge for creativity to occur (Csikszentmihalyi, 1999; Renzulli, 2006; Runco, 2006). One influential multifaceted approach is Robert Sternberg and Todd Lubart's (1991, 1996) **investment theory of creativity.** According to Sternberg and Lubart, pursuing a novel project (one not being tackled by others) increases the chances of arriving at a creative, highly valued product. But whether a person invests in novelty—initiates an original project and brings it to fruition—depends on that person's cognitive, personality, motivational, and environmental resources, summarized in Table 8.3. Each must be present to catalyze creativity, although strength in one (such as perseverance) can compensate for weakness in another (an environment that is lukewarm toward novel ideas).

Contrary to popular belief, creativity is neither determined at birth nor the prized possession of an elite few. Many people can develop it to varying degrees, and it is likely to reach greater heights when nurtured from an early age. Let's look at the components of creativity and how to strengthen them in children.

• **Cognitive Resources** Creative work brings together a variety of high-level cognitive skills. It requires *problem finding*—detecting a gap in current knowledge, a need for a new product, or a deficiency in existing procedures. Once a problem is found, *the ability to define it*—to move it from a vague to a clearly specified state—becomes important. In both children and adults, the more effort devoted to defining the problem, the more original the final product (Runco & Okuda, 1988; Sternberg, 2003b).

Divergent thinking is essential for generating novel solutions to problems. But the successful creator must also choose the best responses, setting aside fruitless options. Therefore, creativity involves *alternating between divergent and convergent thinking* (Guignard & Lubart, 2006). In narrowing the range of possibilities, creative individuals rely on *insight processes*—combining and restructuring elements in sudden but useful ways. For example, the use of analogies and metaphors to identify unique connections is common among people who have made outstanding creative contributions (Barron, 1988). At an early age, children engage in

Table 8.3 Resources Necessary for Creativity

Cognitive	Personality	Motivational and Environmental
Problem finding	Innovative style of thinking	Settings rich in stimulation
Divergent thinking	Curiosity	Emphasis on intellectual curiosity
Convergent thinking: evaluating competing ideas	Willingness to take intellectual risks	Systematic teaching that builds talent
Insight	Tolerance of ambiguity	Availability of time to reflect on ideas
Knowledge	Courage of one's convictions	Encouragement of original ideas and evaluation of those ideas
		Emphasis on intrinsic motivation

this kind of thinking (see Chapter 6, page 234, and Chapter 9, page 397). Furthermore, *evaluating competing ideas* to select the most promising is vital. School-age children's evaluative ability can be enhanced by instructions to critically assess the originality of ideas (Runco, 1992b).

Finally, extensive *knowledge* is necessary to make a creative contribution to any field. Without it, people cannot recognize or understand new ideas. Consider this cognitive ingredient, and you will see why high creativity is usually manifested as **talent**—outstanding performance in one or a few related fields. Case studies reveal that excellence in such endeavors as creative writing, mathematics, science, music, visual arts, athletics, and leadership have roots in specialized interests and skills that appear in childhood (Moran & Gardner, 2006; Winner, 2003). And research supports the *10-year-rule* in development of master-level creativity—a decade between initial exposure to a field and sufficient expertise to produce a creative work (Simonton, 2000; Winner, 2003). Furthermore, IQ and creativity correlate only modestly, typically around .20 to .40 (Lubart, 2003). Beyond an above-average general intelligence, other factors are necessary for creative giftedness.

• Personality Resources Certain personality characteristics foster the cognitive components of creativity, ensuring that they are applied to best advantage:

- *Innovative style of thinking.* Creative individuals not only see things in new ways but also enjoy doing so. They prefer loosely structured activities involving innovative problem finding rather than already defined tasks.
- *Perseverance and tolerance of ambiguity.* Working toward creative goals brings periods when pieces of the problem do not fit together—prompting many children and adults to give up or pursue the first (but not the best) solution. Creativity requires patience and persistence in the face of obstacles.
- *Willingness to take risks.* Creativity requires a willingness to deviate from the crowd, to undertake challenges when outcomes are uncertain.
- *The courage of one's convictions.* Because their ideas are novel, creators may at times doubt them, especially when criticized by skeptical teachers or peers. People who think creatively often encounter resistance, ranging from puzzlement to hostility. Creative endeavors require independence of judgment and high self-esteem. (Sternberg & Lubart, 1996)

How can we nurture creativity? One approach is to challenge children to generate original solutions to problems. These fourth-graders in Wales collaborate in building a model lighthouse using modular construction materials. © Jeff Morgan Education/Alamy

• Motivational Resources Motivation for creativity must be *task-focused* rather than *goal-focused.* Task-focusing motivators, such as the desire to meet a high standard, energize work and keep attention on the problem. Goal-focusing motivators, in contrast, often impair performance by diverting attention from the task to extrinsic rewards such as grades and prizes. In one study, 7- to 11-year-old girls worked on collages, some competing for prizes and others expecting that the prizes would be raffled off. The products of those in the first group were much less creative (Amabile, 1982).

Extrinsic rewards are not always detrimental to creativity. Teaching children how to engage in divergent thinking on a task and rewarding them for original responses increases the frequency of those responses (Collins & Amabile, 1999). And an occasional reward for a creative product can underscore the social value of creativity and encourage children to embark on innovative projects. But when rewards are overemphasized, children focus only on these goals, and creativity suffers.

• **Environmental Resources** Studies of the backgrounds of talented children and highly accomplished adults often reveal a family life focused on the child's needs—warm, sensitive parents who provide a stimulating home life, are devoted to developing their child's abilities, and provide models of hard work and high achievement. These parents are reasonably demanding but not driving or overambitious (Winner, 1996, 2000). They arrange for caring teachers while the child is young and for more rigorous master teachers as the child's talent develops.

Many gifted children and adolescents are socially isolated, partly because their highly driven, nonconforming, and independent styles leave them out of step with peers and partly because they enjoy solitude, which is necessary to develop their talents. Still, gifted children desire gratifying peer relationships, and some—more often girls than boys—try to become better-liked by hiding their abilities. Compared with their ordinary agemates, gifted youths, especially girls, report more emotional and social difficulties, including low self-esteem and depression (Reis, 2004; Winner, 2000).

Classrooms in which gifted youths can interact with like-minded peers, choose topics for extended projects, take intellectual risks, and reflect on ideas without being rushed to the next assignment foster creativity. In classrooms where knowledge acquisition is stressed over using knowledge originally, children's thinking tends to become *entrenched*—limited to commonplace associations that produce correct answers. Talented students, when not sufficiently challenged, sometimes lose their drive to excel. But when pushed too hard by parents or teachers, by adolescence these students are likely to ask, "Why am I doing this?" If the answer is not "Because it interests me," they may decide not to pursue their gift (Winner, 1997, 2000, p. 166).

Eight-year-old piano prodigy Harris Wang performs in Edmonton, Alberta, in 2004. Parents of highly talented children can best promote their talents by offering warmth, sensitivity, and stimulation and arranging for master teachers as the child's talent develops. But parents should avoid being driving or overambitious. © CP Photo/Edmonton Sun–David Bloom

Refer to Applying What We Know on the following page for ways that parents and teachers can promote children's creativity. Debate about the effectiveness of school programs for the gifted typically focuses on factors irrelevant to creativity—for example, whether to offer enrichment in regular classrooms, pull children out for special instruction (the most common practice), or advance brighter pupils to a higher grade. Overall, gifted children fare well academically and socially within each of these models (Moon & Feldhusen, 1994). At the same time, interventions aimed at protecting students' self-esteem are crucial in selective educational settings. In a study of more than 100,000 students in 26 countries, the more selective the high school, the lower the students' academic self-esteem (Marsh & Hau, 2003). A top student in elementary school who enters a selective secondary school may suddenly find herself average or below average, with potentially detrimental effects on motivation.

Some societies focus so narrowly on high academic achievement as an index of success that they dampen the development of creativity. The collectivism characteristic of Asian cultures often leads teachers to emphasize mastery of knowledge and analytical skills over generating new ideas, which requires students to stand out from the crowd. In one study, Chinese college students' artwork was judged less creative than that of U.S. students by experts from both countries (Niu & Sternberg, 2001). In interventions aimed at promoting creative expression in high school art classes in Beijing, students were asked to make collages. One group received a general instruction to be creative, a second group specific instructions in *how* to be creative ("fold or tear materials so their shapes and sizes do not limit creative expression"), and a control group no creativity instructions. Students in the two creative conditions generated products that were more creative than those produced by students in the control group, with the specific-instruction group performing best (Niu & Sternberg, 2003). A brief prompt—especially, guidance in how to take a creative approach—readily enhanced artistic originality.

Applying What We Know

Promoting Children's Creativity

Suggestion	Description
Encourage idea generation and evaluation.	Offer opportunities for divergent thinking and praise it, even when some ideas are silly or irrelevant. Then engage children in constructive criticism: When an idea has little value, suggest new approaches that include aspects of the child's idea, thereby demonstrating that most ideas must be refined to be useful.
Encourage sensible risk-taking.	Provide assignments and activities that include choices and that have more than one acceptable answer. Avoid praising children mainly for high test scores or papers based on one right answer, which may lead them to avoid new ways of thinking.
Encourage tolerance of ambiguity.	Point out that creative individuals often feel unsure of whether they are on the right track. Encourage children to accept these feelings and to spend time working through uncertainty. Emphasize that doing so will result in better ideas.
Help children believe in their ability to be creative.	Remind children that the value of a creative idea does not depend on teachers' or classmates' approval but, rather, on the idea's originality and usefulness.
Help children find what they love to do.	Encourage children to explore new fields rather than just accepting interests that you value. To help them uncover their true interests, ask each child to demonstrate an ability or talent for the class, and point out the diversity of worthwhile interests.
Model creative thinking.	Balance teaching knowledge with teaching how to think about that knowledge. Help children reason across subjects, pointing out that creative insights often result from integrating material across fields, not from memorizing information.

Source: Sternberg, 2003b.

Gardner's theory of multiple intelligences has inspired several model school programs that provide enrichment to all students in diverse disciplines, so any child capable of high-level, creative performance can manifest it. Meaningful activities, each tapping a specific intelligence or set of intelligences, serve as contexts for assessing strengths and weaknesses and, on that basis, teaching new knowledge and original thinking (Gardner, 1993, 2000). For example, linguistic intelligence might be fostered through storytelling or playwriting; spatial intelligence through drawing, sculpting, or taking apart and reassembling objects; and kinesthetic intelligence through dance or pantomime.

Evidence is still needed on how well these programs nurture children's talents and creativity. But they have already succeeded in one way—by highlighting the strengths of some students who previously had been considered unexceptional or even at risk for school failure (Kornhaber, 2004). Consequently, they may be especially useful in identifying talented low-SES, ethnic minority children, who are often underrepresented in school programs for the gifted (McBee, 2006). How best to maximize the creative resources of the coming generation—the future poet and scientist as well as the everyday citizen—is a challenge for future research.

Ask Yourself

Review Summarize the benefits of early intervention programs, such as Head Start, for poverty-stricken children. What program characteristics might contribute to and strengthen those benefits?

Connect Using what you learned about brain development in Chapter 5 (see pages 183–190), explain why intensive intervention for poverty-stricken children starting in infancy and continuing through early childhood has a greater impact on IQ than intervention starting later.

Connect How is high-stakes testing likely to affect encouragement of creativity in classrooms? Explain.

Reflect Describe several childhood experiences that you believe enhanced your creativity, along with ones that might have discouraged it. In the latter instances, what would you do differently to foster children's creative potential? Use research to justify your recommendations.

SUMMARY

Definitions of Intelligence

Describe changing definitions of intelligence, from Binet's first successful test to the modern factor analysts.

- The **psychometric approach** to cognitive development is the basis for intelligence tests used to assess individual differences in children's mental abilities. The first successful test, developed by Binet in 1905, provided a single, holistic measure of intelligence.
- **Factor analysis** emerged as a way of determining whether intelligence is a single trait or an assortment of abilities. Spearman proposed the existence of an underlying **general intelligence,** or **"g,"** though he acknowledged the existence of various types of **specific intelligence.** Thurstone, in contrast, viewed intelligence as a set of distinct primary mental abilities.
- Contemporary theorists propose hierarchical models of mental abilities. Cattell's identification of two broad factors, **crystallized** and **fluid intelligence,** has influenced attempts to reduce cultural bias in intelligence testing. Carroll's **three-stratum theory of intelligence** is the most comprehensive factor-analytic classification of mental abilities.

© Richard Hutchings/PhotoEdit

Recent Advances in Defining Intelligence

Why have researchers conducted componential analyses of intelligence test scores, and how have Sternberg's triarchic theory and Gardner's theory of multiple intelligences expanded contemporary definitions of intelligence?

- Researchers conducting **componential analyses** of children's test scores have identified relationships between aspects of information processing—including working-memory capacity, processing speed, and flexible attention, memory, and reasoning strategies—and intelligence test performance. Extending these efforts, Sternberg's **triarchic theory of successful intelligence** views intelligence as a complex interaction of analytical intelligence (information-processing skills), creative intelligence (capacity to solve novel problems), and practical intelligence (application of intellectual skills in everyday situations).
- Gardner's **theory of multiple intelligences** identifies at least eight distinct intelligences, each with a unique biological basis and a distinct course of development. It has been influential in efforts to understand and nurture children's special talents. The ability to manage one's own emotions and interact competently with others, to detect others' thoughts and feelings, and to deal effectively with social problems is labeled **emotional intelligence.**

Measuring Intelligence

Cite commonly used intelligence tests for children, and discuss prediction of later IQ from infant tests.

- The **Stanford-Binet Intelligence Scales, Fifth Edition,** and the **Wechsler Intelligence Scale for Children–IV (WISC–IV)** are most often used to identify highly intelligent children and diagnose those with learning problems. Each provides a measure of general intelligence and a profile of subtest scores; each has a downward extension, tailored for assessing the intelligence of preschoolers. Two related types of tests are **aptitude tests,** which assess potential to learn a specialized activity, and **achievement tests,** which assess actual knowledge and skill attainment. Both types of tests include items similar to those found on intelligence tests.
- Most infant tests are poor predictors of childhood mental ability because they emphasize perceptual and motor items, which differ from the tasks given to older children. As a result, infant scores are conservatively labeled **developmental quotients (DQs)** rather than IQs. The Fagan Test of Infant Intelligence consists entirely of habituation/recovery items, a good infant correlate of later intelligence. But its low test–retest reliability makes it less successful than laboratory measures in predicting childhood mental test scores.

How are IQ scores computed and distributed?

- Intelligence tests are scored by computing an **intelligence quotient (IQ).** It compares the test-taker's raw score to the scores of a **standardization** sample of same-age individuals, which form a bell-shaped **normal distribution,** with mean IQ set at 100. IQ reflects the extent to which test performance deviates from the standardization-sample mean.

What Do Intelligence Tests Predict, and How Well?

Discuss the stability of IQ and its prediction of academic achievement, occupational attainment, and psychological adjustment.

- After age 6, IQ scores show substantial correlational stability. The older the child at time of first testing and the closer in time two testings are, the stronger the relationship between the scores. However, most children show substantial fluctuations in the absolute value of IQ. According to the **environmental cumulative deficit hypothesis,** children living in poverty often show declines resulting from the compounding effects of underprivileged rearing conditions.
- IQ is moderately correlated with adult academic achievement, occupational attainment, and emotional and social adjustment, but the underlying causes of these findings are complex. Other traits, including education, family influences, motivation, and **practical intelligence,** also contribute substantially to life success.

Ethnic and Socioeconomic Variations in IQ

Describe ethnic and socioeconomic variations in IQ.

- Black children and children of low socioeconomic status (SES) score lower on intelligence tests than white and middle-SES children, respectively, findings that have kindled the IQ nature–nurture debate. Jensen argues that ethnic differences do not stem from cultural bias but reflect genetic differences in conceptual intelligence, measured by items strongly correlated with "g." However, research has challenged this theory.

© Will Hart/PhotoEdit

Explaining Individual and Group Differences in IQ

Describe and evaluate the contributions of heredity and environment to individual and group differences in IQ.

- Heritability estimates support a moderate role for heredity in IQ individual differences. Kinship studies of identical and fraternal twins indicate that the contribution of heredity strengthens with development. However, heritabilities cannot be used to explain between-group, ethnic, and SES differences in test scores.
- Adoption studies indicate that advantaged rearing conditions can raise the absolute value of children's IQs substantially. But adopted children's scores correlate more strongly with those of their biological than with those of their adoptive relatives, providing support for the influence of heredity. African-American children reared in economically well-off white homes attain above-average IQs by middle childhood. No evidence supports the assumption that heredity underlies the ethnic differences that have been the focus of the IQ nature–nurture debate.
- The **Flynn effect**—consistent gains in IQ from one generation to the next—is the result of environmental factors. It challenges the assumption that black–white and other ethnic variations in IQ are mostly genetic.

Evaluate evidence on whether IQ is a biased measure of the intelligence of ethnic minority children, and discuss efforts to reduce test bias.

- Experts disagree on whether ethnic differences in IQ result from test bias. Although IQ predicts academic achievement equally well for majority and minority children, culturally specific communication styles, lack of familiarity with test content, and **stereotype threat** can lead to test scores that underestimate minority children's intelligence.
- Combining test scores with assessments of children's adaptive behavior can provide a safeguard against underestimating minority children's intelligence. An innovative testing procedure called **dynamic assessment,** which introduces purposeful teaching into the testing situation to measure what the child can attain with social support, enhances minority children's performance.

Summarize the impact of shared and nonshared environmental influences on IQ.

- **Shared** and **nonshared environmental influences** contribute to individual differences in mental development. Research using the **Home Observation for Measurement of the Environment (HOME)** indicates that overall quality of the home—a shared environmental influence—consistently predicts language progress and IQ. Although parent–child genetic similarity plays a part in the HOME–IQ relationship, a warm, stimulating family environment does promote mental ability. Parental belief in the importance of intellectual endeavors also has a powerful impact on academic performance.
- Kinship research suggests that nonshared environmental factors are more powerful than shared influences and strengthen in adolescence and adulthood. Birth order and spacing, once considered influential, are unrelated to IQ. The most potent nonshared factors may be unpredictable, one-time events.

Early Intervention and Intellectual Development

Discuss the impact of early intervention on intellectual development.

- **Project Head Start** is the most extensive federally funded preschool program for low-income children in the United States. In Canada, **Aboriginal Head Start** serves First Nations, Inuit, and Métis preschoolers living in poverty.
- Research on high-quality early interventions implemented by universities or research foundations shows that immediate IQ and achievement score gains decline within a few years, while benefits in school adjustment persist. And one program yielded advantages for preschool intervention children, over no-intervention controls, on adulthood indicators of life success, including education, income, and law-abiding behavior.
- The earlier intervention starts, the longer it lasts, and the more intensive the program, the broader and more enduring the benefits. **Early Head Start** offers coordinated services for infants and toddlers and their families, with positive effects on parenting, cognitive and language development, and lessening of aggression. Early intervention programs are highly cost-effective compared with the cost of providing later services to deal with learning problems, criminal behavior, and unemployment.

Courtesy of Jumpstart

Giftedness: Creativity and Talent

Describe and evaluate evidence on the development of creativity, including the psychometric view and the multifaceted approach of investment theory.

- Recognition that intelligence includes much more than mental abilities that predict school success has expanded conceptions of **giftedness** to include **creativity.** The psychometric approach, emphasizing the distinction between **divergent** and **convergent thinking,** is too narrow to predict real-world creative accomplishment. New, multifaceted approaches, such as Sternberg and Lubart's **investment theory of creativity,** look at a wide variety of intellectual, personality, motivational, and environmental resources that are necessary to initiate creative projects and bring them to fruition.
- Because people usually demonstrate creativity in one or a few related areas, it is usually manifested as **talent.** Highly talented children typically have parents and teachers who nurture their exceptional abilities. However, gifted children may be socially isolated, and they often report emotional and social difficulties. They are best served by educational programs in which they can interact with like-minded peers, take intellectual risks, reflect on ideas, and acquire skills relevant to their talents.
- Asian cultures' collectivism often leads teachers to emphasize mastery of knowledge and analytical skills over generating new ideas. Instructions to be creative can enhance students' originality.

IMPORTANT TERMS AND CONCEPTS

Aboriginal Head Start (p. 346)
achievement test (p. 326)
aptitude test (p. 326)
componential analysis (p. 321)
convergent thinking (p. 349)
creativity (p. 349)
crystallized intelligence (p. 320)
developmental quotient (DQ) (p. 327)
divergent thinking (p. 349)
dynamic assessment (p. 340)
Early Head Start (p. 347)
emotional intelligence (p. 325)
environmental cumulative deficit hypothesis (p. 330)
factor analysis (p. 319)
fluid intelligence (p. 320)
Flynn effect (p. 337)
general intelligence, or "g" (p. 319)
gifted (p. 349)
Home Observation for Measurement of the Environment (HOME) (p. 342)
intelligence quotient (IQ) (p. 328)
investment theory of creativity (p. 350)
nonshared environmental influences (p. 341)
normal distribution (p. 328)
practical intelligence (p. 331)
Project Head Start (p. 345)
psychometric approach (p. 317)
shared environmental influences (p. 341)
socioeconomic status (SES) (p. 332)
specific intelligence (p. 319)
standardization (p. 328)
Stanford-Binet Intelligence Scales, Fifth Edition (p. 326)
stereotype threat (p. 340)
talent (p. 351)
theory of multiple intelligences (p. 323)
three-stratum theory of intelligence (p. 320)
triarchic theory of successful intelligence (p. 322)
Wechsler Intelligence Scale for Children–IV (WISC–IV) (p. 326)

9

"Brother and Me"
Qi Sharlene Seet
6 years, Singapore

A 6-year-old artist conveys her brother's and her own pride and pleasure in learning to read and write—skills that depend on mastery of spoken language. Language is an awesome and distinctly human achievement. How does it develop so rapidly and easily in childhood?

Language Development

"Done!" exclaimed 1-year-old Erin, wriggling in her high chair.

Oscar and Marilyn looked at each other and exclaimed in unison, "Did she say, 'Done'?" Lifting Erin down, Marilyn responded, "Yes! You're done," to her daughter's first clear word. In the next few weeks, more words appeared—among them "Mama," "Dada," "please," "thanks," and "sure."

Marilyn spoke to Erin and her 11-year-old brother, Amos, in English. But Oscar, determined that his second child would become bilingual, used only Spanish, his native tongue. As Erin reached the 18-month mark, her vocabulary grew rapidly, and she mixed words from the two languages. "Book!" she called out, thrusting her favorite picture book toward Oscar in a gesture that meant, "Read this!" As father and daughter "read" together, Erin labeled: "*Nariz*" ("nose"). "*Boca*" ("mouth"). "Head." "*Ojos*" ("eyes"). "Hippo." "*Grande!*" (referring to the size of the hippo). On reaching the last page, she exclaimed, "*Gracias!*" and slipped off Oscar's lap.

By her second birthday, Erin had a vocabulary of several hundred words and often combined them: "So big!" "*Muy grande*" ("very big"), "More cracker," "*Dame galleta*" ("Give me cracker"), and "*No quiero*" ("I don't want to"). Amused by Erin's willingness to imitate almost anything, Amos taught her a bit of slang. During mealtime conversations, Erin would interject, "Geta picture" ("Get the picture"). And when asked a question, she sometimes casually answered, "Whatever."

At age 2½, Erin conversed easily. After a family excursion to the aquarium, Marilyn asked, "What did you see?"

"A big turtle put his head in the shell," Erin replied.

"Why did he do that?"

"He goed away. He's sleepy."

If Amos interrupted, Erin would cleverly recapture her mother's attention. On one occasion, she commanded in a parental tone, "Amos, go do your homework!"

Language—the most awesome of universal human achievements—develops with extraordinary speed in early childhood. At age 1, Erin used single words to name familiar objects and convey her desires. Only a year and a half later, she had a diverse vocabulary and combined words into grammatically correct sentences. Even her mistakes ("goed") revealed an active, rule-oriented approach to language. Before her third birthday, Erin used language creatively to satisfy her desires, converse with others, and experiment with social roles. And she moved easily between her two native tongues, speaking English with her mother and brother and Spanish with her father.

To communicate effectively, these preschoolers must manage principles of sound, meaning, structure, and everyday use. How they accomplish this feat raises puzzling—and fascinating—questions about development.

Children's amazing linguistic accomplishments raise puzzling questions about development. How do children acquire a vast vocabulary and intricate grammatical system in such a short time? Is language a separate capacity, with its own prewired, special-purpose neural system in the brain? Or is it governed by powerful general cognitive abilities that humans also apply to other aspects of their physical and social worlds? Do all children acquire language in the same way, or do individual and cultural differences exist?

Our discussion opens with the fiery theoretical debate of the 1950s between behaviorist B. F. Skinner and linguist Noam Chomsky, which inspired a burst of research on language development. Next we turn to infant preparatory skills that set the stage for the child's first words. Then, to appreciate the diverse linguistic skills children master, we follow the common practice of dividing language into four components. For each, we consider, first, *what* develops, then the more controversial question of *how* children acquire so much in so little time. We conclude with a discussion of the challenges and benefits of bilingualism—mastering two languages—in childhood.

Components of Language

Language consists of several subsystems that have to do with sound, meaning, overall structure, and everyday use. Knowing language entails mastering each of these aspects and combining them into a flexible communication system.

The first component, **phonology,** refers to the rules governing the structure and sequence of speech sounds. If you have ever visited a foreign country where you did not know the language, you probably wondered how anyone could analyze the rapid flow of speech into organized strings of words. Yet in English, you easily apply an intricate set of rules to comprehend and produce complicated sound patterns. How you acquired this ability is the story of phonological development.

Semantics, the second component, involves vocabulary—the way underlying concepts are expressed in words and word combinations. When young children first use a word, it often does not mean the same thing as it does to adults. To build a versatile vocabulary, preschoolers must refine the meanings of thousands of words and connect them into elaborate networks of related terms.

Once mastery of vocabulary is under way, children combine words and modify them in meaningful ways. **Grammar,** the third component of language, consists of two main parts: **syntax,** the rules by which words are arranged into sentences, and **morphology,** the use of grammatical markers indicating number, tense, case, person, gender, active or passive voice, and other meanings (the endings *-s* and *-ed* are examples in English).

Finally, **pragmatics** refers to the rules for engaging in appropriate and effective communication. To converse successfully, children must take turns, stay on the same topic, and state their meaning clearly. They also must figure out how gestures, tone of voice, and context clarify meaning. Furthermore, because society dictates how language should be spoken, pragmatics involves *sociolinguistic knowledge.* Children must acquire certain interaction rituals, such as verbal greetings and leave-takings. They must adjust their speech to mark important social relationships, such as differences in age and status. And they must master their culture's narrative mode of sharing personally meaningful experiences with others.

As we take up the four components of language, you will see that they are interdependent. Acquisition of each facilitates mastery of the others.

Theories of Language Development

During the first half of the twentieth century, research on language development identified milestones that applied to children around the globe: All babbled around 6 months, said their first words at about 1 year, combined words at the end of the second year, and had mastered a vast vocabulary and most grammatical constructions by 4 to 5 years. The regularity of these achievements suggested a process largely governed by maturation. At the same time, language seemed to be learned, not innate: Without exposure to language, children born deaf or severely neglected did not acquire verbal communication. This apparent contradiction set the stage for an intense nature–nurture debate. By the end of the 1950s, two major figures had taken opposing sides.

The Behaviorist Perspective

Behaviorist B. F. Skinner (1957) proposed that language, like any other behavior, is acquired through *operant conditioning.* As the baby makes sounds, parents reinforce those that most resemble words by responding with smiles, hugs, and speech. For example, at 12 months, my older son, David, often babbled something like "book-a-book-a-dook-a-dook-a-book-a-nook-a-book-aaa." One day as he babbled away, I held up his picture book and said, "Book!" Soon David was saying "book-aaa" in the presence of books.

Some behaviorists believe that children rely on *imitation* to acquire complex utterances, such as whole phrases and sentences (Moerk, 2000). And imitation can combine with reinforcement to promote language, as when a parent coaxes, "Say 'I want a cookie,'" and delivers praise and a treat after the toddler responds, "Wanna cookie!"

Although reinforcement and imitation contribute to early language development, few researchers advocate the behaviorist perspective today. Think about the process of language learning just described. Adults would have to engage in intensive tutoring, continuously modeling and reinforcing, to yield the extensive vocabulary and complex sentences of a typical 6-year-old—a physically impossible task. Furthermore, children create novel utterances that are not reinforced by or copied from others, as in Erin's use of "goed" at the beginning of this chapter. And when children do imitate language, they do so selectively, focusing mainly on building their vocabularies (as David did in repeating the word "book") and on refining aspects of language that they are working on at the moment (Owens, 2005).

In sum, the kind of learning described by behaviorists cannot account for language development in young children, who, rather than acquiring specific sentences, develop a working knowledge of language rules. As we will see, however, adults do influence children's language by interacting with them in particular ways.

The Nativist Perspective

Linguist Noam Chomsky (1957) proposed a *nativist* account that regards language as a uniquely human accomplishment, etched into the structure of the brain. He was the first to convince the scientific community that—in contrast to the behaviorist view—children assume much responsibility for their own language learning.

Focusing on grammar, Chomsky reasoned that the rules for sentence organization are too complex to be directly taught to or discovered by even a cognitively sophisticated young child. Children and adults alike readily produce and understand an unlimited range of sentences—often ones they have never said or heard before. To account for this extraordinary facility with language, Chomsky proposed that all children have an innate **language acquisition device (LAD)**—a system that permits them, once they have acquired sufficient vocabulary, to combine words into grammatically consistent, novel utterances and to understand the meaning of sentences they hear.

How can a single LAD account for children's mastery of the world's diverse languages? According to Chomsky (1976, 1997), within the LAD is a **universal grammar,** a built-in storehouse of rules that apply to all human languages. Young children use this knowledge to decipher grammatical categories and relationships in any language to which they are exposed. Because the LAD is specifically suited for language processing, children master the structure of language spontaneously, with only limited language exposure. Therefore, in sharp contrast to the behaviorist view, the nativist perspective regards deliberate training by parents as unnecessary for language development (Pinker, 1994). Instead, the LAD ensures that language, despite its complexity, will be acquired early and swiftly.

Biology *and* Environment

Deaf Children Invent Language

Can children develop complex, rule-based language systems with only minimal language input, or with input so inconsistent that the rules of grammar are not readily apparent? If so, this evidence would provide strong support for Chomsky's idea that humans are born with a biological program for language development (Goldin-Meadow, 2005, 2006a). Research reveals that deaf children can generate an intricate natural language, even when reared in linguistically deficient environments.

Minimal Language Input

In a series of studies, Susan Goldin-Meadow (2003b) and her colleagues followed deaf toddlers and preschoolers whose parents discouraged manual signing and addressed them verbally. None of the children made progress in acquiring spoken language or used even the most common gestures of their nation's sign language. Nevertheless, they spontaneously produced a gestural communication system, called *homesign,* strikingly similar in basic structure to hearing children's verbal language.

The deaf children developed gestural vocabularies with distinct forms for nouns and verbs, each of which stood for a class of objects or a class of actions (for example, a *twist* gesture to request that someone open a jar and to convey that a door knob will not open), similar to the meanings of spoken words. Furthermore, the children combined gestures into novel sentences conforming to basic grammatical rules that were not necessarily those of their parents' spoken language (Goldin-Meadow, Mylander, & Butcher, 1995; Goldin-Meadow et al., 1994). For example, to describe a large bubble he had just blown, one child first pointed at a bubble jar and then used two open palms with fingers spread to denote the act of "blowing up big."

By age 4, the children's gestural sentences were more complex than those of their mothers (Goldin-Meadow & Mylander, 1998). The children seemed to be taking the lead in creating these gesture systems. And they used them for the same diverse purposes as any language—to comment on objects and events, to ask questions, to influence others' actions, to tell stories, to talk about their own and others' signs, and to talk to themselves (Goldin-Meadow, 2003b).

Language becomes a flexible means of communicating when it is used to talk about nonpresent objects and events. In referring to the nonpresent, the deaf children followed the same sequence of development as hearing children—first denoting objects and events in the recent past or anticipated but immediate future, next the more remote past and future, and finally hypothetical and fantasized events (Goldin-Meadow, 1999; Morford & Goldin-Meadow, 1997). Homesigning children conversed in the nonpresent far more often than their parents did. One homesigning child pointed over his shoulder to signify the past, then pointed to a picture of a poodle, and finally pointed to the floor in front of him, saying, "I used to have a poodle!"

In Nicaragua, educators brought deaf children and adolescents together to form a community. Within two decades, they devised a new language—Nicaraguan Sign Language. © Nicaraguan Sign Language Projects, Inc.

Hearing children reach language milestones earlier and acquire a far more complex grammar than children inventing homesign. These findings indicate that a rich language environment with partners who "speak" the same language fosters the attainments just mentioned. But without access to conventional language, deaf children generate their own language system.

• Support for the Nativist Perspective Are children biologically primed to acquire language? Research reviewed in the Biology and Environment box above, suggesting that children have a remarkable ability to invent new language systems, provides some of the most powerful support for this perspective. Three additional sets of evidence—efforts to teach language to animals, localization of language functions in the human brain, and investigations into whether a sensitive period for language development exists—are consistent with Chomsky's view. Let's look at each in turn.

Can Animals Acquire Language? Is the ability to master a grammatically complex language system unique to humans? To find out, many attempts have been made to teach language to animals, including dolphins, parrots, gorillas, orangutans, and chimpanzees. With extensive training, members of each of these species can acquire a vocabulary ranging from several dozen to several hundred symbols and can produce and respond to short, novel sentences, although they do so less consistently than a preschool child (Herman & Uyeyama, 1999; Pepperberg, 2000; Savage-Rumbaugh & Shanker, 1998).

In Nicaragua, educators brought deaf children and adolescents, each with a unique homesign, together to form a community. Although they had no shared language, in less than two decades they developed an elaborate one—Nicaraguan Sign Language—that matched other human languages in structural complexity (Senghas & Coppola, 2001).

Inconsistent Language Input

An unusual study of a rare child whose language environment was not the typical rich form—offering examples of all linguistic structures—also illustrates children's remarkable capacity to invent language. Simon, a deaf child, was born to deaf parents who did not start to learn American Sign Language (ASL) (which is as elaborate as any spoken language) until they were adolescents. As with the deaf children just described, Simon's parents were exposed only to oral language in childhood. They communicated with Simon in ASL from infancy, but because they were late ASL learners, they had not attained the grammatical complexity of native signers, and they used many ASL structures inconsistently. (See the section on a sensitive period for language development on page 363.) Simon has a hearing younger sibling and goes to a school with hearing teachers and children; his only ASL input comes from his parents.

When Simon was 7, Jenny Singleton and Alyssa Newport (2004) gave him a challenging ASL grammar task, which assessed his knowledge of the verb *to move.* In ASL, accurately expressing motion requires up to seven grammatical markers, which indicate (1) the object's path, (2) the object's orientation, (3) the manner in which the object moves (for example, bouncing or rolling), (4) the object's location relative to a secondary object, (5) the position of the secondary object with respect to the path, (6) the features of the moving object (category, size, or shape), and (7) the features of the secondary object. The researchers compared Simon's performance with that of several reference groups: his parents, deaf school-age children of deaf native-signing parents, and deaf native-signing adults.

Findings confirmed that Simon's parents' ASL grammar was much weaker than that of native-signing adults. Yet Simon's language did not mirror his parents' error-ridden input. Instead, he introduced a level of regularity into his language that surpassed his parents' usage. As Figure 9.1 shows, his score on the "to move" task exceeded the average score of native-signing deaf children and approached the performance of native-signing deaf adults. Simon managed to extract the regularities from his parents' imperfect language and magnify them, arriving at a highly systematic grammar that differed substantially from the language to which he was exposed.

Deaf children's remarkable capacity to invent language, despite minimal or inconsistent input, is compatible with the existence of a biologically based language acquisition device. As we will see, however, other theorists claim that nonlinguistic cognitive capacities, applied to the task of communicating, are responsible.

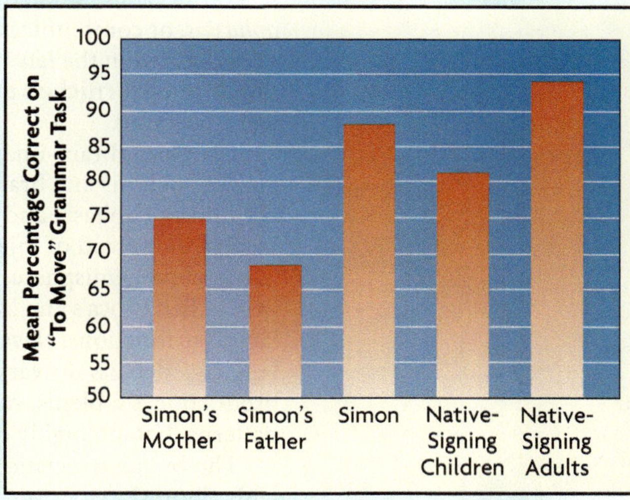

Figure 9.1 **Simon's performance on a challenging ASL grammar task, compared with the performance of his parents and native-signing children and adults.**

Despite inconsistent input from his late–ASL-learning parents, 7-year-old Simon showed excellent mastery of ASL grammar, exceeding the average performance of native-signing deaf children and approaching the performance of native-signing deaf adults. (Adapted from Singleton & Newport, 2004.)

Chimpanzees are closest to humans in the evolutionary hierarchy. Common chimps, the species studied most often, have been taught artificial languages (in which a computer keyboard generates visual symbols) and American Sign Language. Yet even after years of training, common chimps are unable to produce strings of three or more symbols that conform to a rule-based structure. Their language limitations may, in part, reflect a narrow understanding of others' mental states. Common chimps can accurately predict others' goals if those goals are readily apparent in their behavior—for example, whether or not someone is willing to share food with them. But they may not recognize less obvious intentions, including ones that motivate use of language—for example, that others want to exchange knowledge and ideas (Tomasello, Call, & Hare, 2003).

Bonobo chimps are more intelligent and social than common chimps. The linguistic attainments of a bonobo named Kanzi are especially impressive (Savage-Rumbaugh, 2001). While young, Kanzi picked up his mother's artificial language by observing trainers interact with her. To encourage his language development, Kanzi's caregivers communicated both in the artificial language and in English. Kanzi rarely combined words, preferring to join a word to a gesture—for example, "*carry* + [gesture to person]," meaning "you carry Kanzi." But through listening to

Kanzi, a Bonobo chimp, presses keys on a symbol board to communicate with Dr. Sue Savage-Rumbaugh, who is tracking his language development. © FRANS LANTING/Minden Pictures

fluent speech, he acquired remarkable comprehension of English, including the ability to discriminate hundreds of English words and to act out unusual sentences he had not heard before, such as "Put the money in the mushroom." And Kanzi could usually detect the difference between novel, reversed sentences—"Take the potato outdoors" and "Go outdoors and get the potato" (Savage-Rumbaugh et al., 1993; Shanker, Savage-Rumbaugh, & Taylor, 1999).

Still, researchers disagree on Kanzi's linguistic achievements. Some argue that he is a remarkable conversationalist who wants to share information (Greenspan & Shanker, 2004). Others claim that he uses language only to get what he wants (a strawberry to eat), not to share information (talk about strawberries) (Seidenberg & Petitto, 1987). And Kanzi's comprehension of grammar does not exceed that of a human 2-year-old, who (as we will see) is not far along in grammatical development. Overall, the findings support Chomsky's assumption of a uniquely human capacity for an elaborate grammar. No evidence exists that even the brightest animals can comprehend and produce sentences that are both complex *and* novel.

Language Areas in the Brain. Recall from Chapter 5 that for most individuals, language is housed largely in the left hemisphere of the cerebral cortex. Within it are two important language-related structures (see Figure 9.2). To clarify their functions, researchers have, for several decades, studied adults who experienced damage to these structures and display *aphasias,* or communication disorders. The patients' linguistic deficits suggested that **Broca's area,** located in the left frontal lobe, supports grammatical processing and language production, while **Wernicke's area,** located in the left temporal lobe, plays a role in comprehending word meaning.

But recent brain-imaging research suggests more complicated relationships between language functions and brain structures. The impaired pronunciation and grammar of patients with Broca's aphasia and the meaningless speech streams of patients with Wernicke's aphasia involve the spread of injury to nearby cortical areas and widespread abnormal activity in the left cerebral hemisphere, triggered by the brain damage (Bates et al., 2003). Contrary to long-held belief, Broca's and Wernicke's areas are not solely or even mainly responsible for specific language functions. Nevertheless, depending on the site of injury to the adult left hemisphere, language deficits do vary predictably. Damage to frontal-lobe areas usually yields language production problems, damage to the areas in the other lobes comprehension problems—patterns that are highly consistent across individuals (Dick et al., 2004).

The broad association of language functions with left-hemispheric regions is consistent with Chomsky's notion of a brain prepared to process language. But recall from Chapter 5 that at birth, the brain is not fully lateralized; it is highly plastic. Language areas in the cerebral cortex *develop* as children acquire language (Friedrich & Friederici, 2005; Mills & Conboy, 2005). Although the left hemisphere is biased for language processing, if it

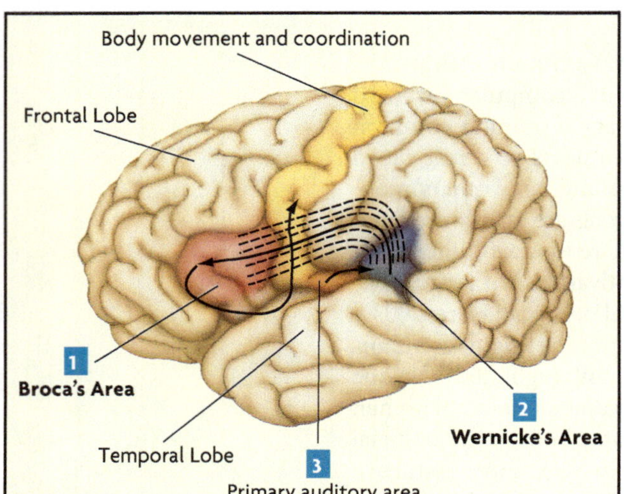

■ **Figure 9.2** **Broca's and Wernicke's areas, in the left hemisphere of the cerebral cortex.**

(1) Broca's area, located in the frontal lobe, supports grammatical processing and language production. (2) Wernicke's area, located in the temporal lobe, is involved in comprehending word meaning. Contrary to what was once believed, however, neither area is solely or even mainly responsible for these functions. Instead, each cooperates with many other regions of the left hemisphere. Wernicke's area and Broca's area communicate through a bundle of nerve fibers represented by dashed lines in the figure. Among the regions from which Wernicke's area receives impulses is (3) the primary auditory area, where sensations from the ears are sent. Broca's area communicates with motor areas involved in speaking.

is injured in the first few years, other regions take over language functions, and most such children eventually attain normal language competence (see page 187 in Chapter 5). Thus, left-hemispheric localization is not necessary for effective language processing. For example, recall from Chapter 5 that deaf adults who as children learned sign language depend more on the right hemisphere. Additional research reveals that many parts of the brain participate in language activities to differing degrees, depending on the language skill and the individual's mastery of that skill (Huttenlocher, 2002; Shafer & Garrido-Nag, 2007).

Grammatical competence, however, may depend more on specific brain structures than the other components of language. When 2- to 2½-year-old children and adults listened to short sentences—some syntactically correct, others with phrase-structure violations—both groups showed similarly distinct ERP brain-wave patterns for each sentence type in the left frontal and temporal lobes (Oberecker & Friederici, 2006; Oberecker, Friedrich, & Friederici, 2005). This suggests that 2½-year-olds process sentence structures with the same neural system as adults do. Furthermore, in studies of adults who had their left hemispheres removed because of disease or abnormalities that caused severe seizures, grammatical abilities suffered much more than semantic or pragmatic abilities, which seem to draw more on right-hemispheric regions (Baynes & Gazzaniga, 1988). Similarly, in older children with left-hemispheric brain damage, grammar is more impaired than other language functions (Stromswold, 2000).

Finally, when the young brain allocates language to the right hemisphere after injury—as a result of left-hemispheric damage or learning of sign language—it localizes it in roughly the same regions that typically support language in the left hemisphere (Mueller et al., 1998; Newman et al., 2002). This suggests that those regions are uniquely disposed for language processing.

A Sensitive Period for Language Development. Erik Lenneberg (1967) first proposed that children must acquire language during the age span of brain lateralization, which he believed to be complete by puberty. Evidence for a sensitive period coinciding with brain lateralization would support the nativist position that language development has unique biological properties.

To test this idea, researchers have examined the language competence of deaf adults who acquired their first language—American Sign Language (ASL)—at different ages. The later learners, whose parents chose to educate them through the oral method, which relies on speech and lip-reading and discourages signing, did not acquire spoken language because of their profound deafness. Consistent with Lenneberg's prediction, those who learned ASL in adolescence or adulthood never became as proficient as those who learned in childhood (recall Simon's parents, in Figure 9.1, who scored lower on a test of complex grammar than he did because they had not acquired ASL until adolescence) (Mayberry, 1994; Newport, 1991; Singleton & Newport, 2004). Furthermore, the typical right-hemispheric localization of ASL functions, which require visual–spatial processing of hand, arm, and facial movements, is greatly reduced in individuals who learned ASL after puberty (Newman et al., 2002). However, a precise age cutoff for a decline in first-language competence has not been established.

Acquiring a second language becomes more difficult with age, but these children attending preschool in Toronto are well within the sensitive period. Those who are learning English as a second language will probably attain the competence of native speakers. The Canadian Press (Frank Gunn)

Is acquiring a second language also harder after a sensitive period has passed? In one study, researchers examined U.S. census data, selecting immigrants from Spanish- and Chinese-speaking countries who had resided in the United States for at least ten years. The census form had asked the immigrants to rate how competently they spoke English, from "not at all" to "very well"—self-reports that correlate strongly with objective language measures. As age of immigration increased from infancy and early childhood into adulthood, English proficiency declined, regardless of respondents' level of education (see Figure 9.3 on page 364) (Hakuta, Bialystok, & Wiley, 2003). Other research confirms an age-related decline beginning around age 5 to 6 in capacity to acquire a second language with a native accent (Flege, Yeni-Komshian, & Liu, 1999; Flege et al., 2006). Furthermore, ERP and fMRI measures of brain activity indicate that second-language processing is less lateralized, and also overlaps less with brain areas devoted to first-language processing, in older than in younger learners (Neville & Bruer, 2001). But second-language competence does not drop sharply at adolescence, as Lenneberg predicted. Rather, a continuous, age-related decrease occurs.

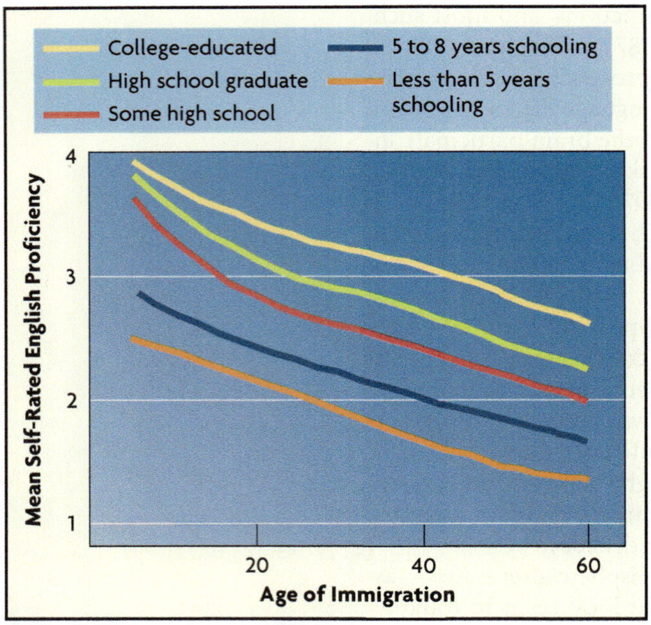

Figure 9.3 Relationship between age of immigration to the United States and self-rated English proficiency, illustrated for native Spanish speakers.

As age of immigration increased, English proficiency decreased for individuals at all levels of education, from a few years of elementary school to a college education. Findings for native Chinese speakers were similar. (From K. Hakuta, E. Bialystok, & E. Wiley, 2003, "Critical Evidence: A Test of the Critical Period Hypothesis for Second-Language Acquisition," *Psychological Science*, 14, p. 37. © 2003 Blackwell Publishing, Ltd. Reprinted by permission.)

What factors underlie the younger-age language-learning advantage? Some researchers assign a key role to the narrowing of speech perception during the second half of the first year—from discrimination among nearly all language sounds to heightened sensitivity to sound distinctions in the language (or languages) the baby hears (see Chapter 4, page 153). As a result, neural networks become dedicated to processing native-language sounds, strengthening native-language learning while weakening capacity to acquire unfamiliar languages. As preliminary evidence for this view, 7-month-olds' skill at perceiving native-language sounds, along with their insensitivity to sound variations in languages they do not hear, predicts rapid vocabulary and grammatical development in the second and third years (Kuhl et al., 2005; Tsao, Liu, & Kuhl, 2004).

In sum, the more "committed" the brain is to native-language patterns, the better children's mastery of their native language and the less effectively they acquire foreign languages (Kuhl, 2006). This neural commitment increases with mastery of language and, thus, with age.

• Limitations of the Nativist Perspective Chomsky's theory has had a major impact on current views of language development. But despite wide acceptance of Chomsky's belief in humans' unique, biologically based capacity to acquire language, his account of development has been challenged on several grounds.

First, researchers have had great difficulty specifying the universal grammar that Chomsky believes underlies the widely varying grammatical systems of human languages. A persistent source of dissatisfaction is the absence of a complete description of these abstract grammatical structures, or even an agreed-on list of how many exist or the best examples of them. Chomsky's critics doubt that one set of rules can account for all grammatical forms (Maratsos, 1998; Tomasello, 2003, 2005). How children manage to link such rules with the strings of words they hear is also unclear.

Second, Chomsky's assumption that grammatical knowledge is innately determined does not fit with certain observations of language development. Once children begin to use an innate grammatical structure, we would expect them to apply it to all relevant instances in their language. But later we will encounter evidence that children refine and generalize many grammatical forms gradually, engaging in much piecemeal learning and making errors along the way (Tomasello, 2000, 2003, 2006). Complete mastery of some forms (such as the passive voice) is not achieved until well into middle childhood (Tager-Flusberg & Zukowski, 2009). This suggests that more experimentation and learning are involved than Chomsky assumed.

Chomsky's theory also lacks comprehensiveness. For example, it cannot explain how children weave statements together into connected discourse and sustain meaningful conversations. Perhaps because Chomsky did not dwell on the pragmatic side of language, his theory grants little attention to the quality of language input or to social experience in supporting language progress. Furthermore, the nativist perspective does not regard children's cognitive capacities as important. Yet in Chapter 6, we saw that cognitive development is involved in children's early vocabulary growth. And studies of children with mental retardation (see the Biology and Environment box on the following page) show that cognitive competence also influences children's grammatical mastery.

The Interactionist Perspective

In recent years, new theories of language development have arisen, replacing the dichotomy of the Skinner–Chomsky debate with an emphasis on *interactions* between inner predispositions and environmental influences. One type of interactionist theory applies the information-processing perspective to language development; a second type emphasizes social interaction.

• Information-Processing Theories The most influential information-processing accounts are derived from research with connectionist, or artificial neural network, models (see Chap-

▪ Biology *and* Environment ▪

Language Development in Children with Williams Syndrome

Williams syndrome, a rare disorder occurring in only one in 7,500 births, results from deletion of genetic material on the seventh chromosome. Affected individuals have facial, heart, and kidney abnormalities and mild to serious mental retardation. With IQ scores typically ranging from 50 to 70, they are just as mentally impaired as individuals with Down syndrome—yet they are far more advanced in language skills (Bellugi et al., 2000; Tager-Flusberg, 2007). For many years, researchers took this apparent "decoupling" of cognition and language as evidence that language is controlled by an innate LAD. But new evidence on language attainments associated with the disorder reveals that this conclusion is not warranted.

Infants with Williams syndrome are strongly oriented toward the social world—extremely gregarious and fascinated by faces and voices (Jones et al., 2000). Their language development, though delayed, is impressive. During the preschool years, children with Williams syndrome have larger vocabularies and produce grammatically more complex sentences than children with Down syndrome (Mervis & Robinson, 2000). For example, the longest sentence of one 3-year-old with Williams syndrome was "Please have some grapes in my cup right now." Her counterpart with Down syndrome said, "Here-ya-go" and "Hold me" (Jarrold, Baddeley, & Hewes, 1998, p. 361). By adolescence, the vocabularies of young people with Williams syndrome contain many unusual words. When asked to name as many animals as possible, one teenager said, "weasel, newt, salamander, Chihuahua, ibex, yak" (Bellugi et al., 1992, p. 11).

Yet affected individuals have trouble with highly challenging grammatical rules. For example, French-speaking adolescents with Williams syndrome do poorly on grammatical gender assignment—matching masculine and feminine articles (such as *un* versus *une*) with nouns by attending to word endings and noting exceptions. Normally developing French children master this gender system by age 4 (Karmiloff-Smith et al., 1997). And a study of English-speaking adults revealed difficulties with subtle verb forms ("He struggle the dog" rather than "He struggled with the dog") (Karmiloff-Smith et al., 1998).

Why does Williams syndrome lead to an uneven language profile—areas of both strength and weakness? Growing evidence indicates that the cognitive deficits of Williams syndrome profoundly alter the course of language development. Children with the disorder are relatively good at memorizing but poor at rule learning (Karmiloff-Smith et al., 2003; Rowe & Mervis, 2006). To compensate, they capitalize on their social strengths, attending closely to faces and voices and acquiring as much language by rote as they can.

In support of this explanation, toddlers with Williams syndrome do not build their early vocabularies on intentional gestures (such as pointing) and advances in categorization, as normally developing children do (Laing et al., 2002). Instead, they more often mimic others, so much so that their parents report that they frequently speak without fully comprehending what they are saying. Working-memory capacity (as measured by digit span) is more strongly correlated with grammatical development in children with Williams syndrome than in typically developing children (Robinson, Mervis, & Robinson, 2003). This suggests, again, a heavy reliance on memory to learn language.

In sum, although the language of individuals with Williams syndrome is impressive in view of their cognitive limitations, it is impaired in significant ways. These findings indicate that language is not as separate from other human mental abilities as Chomsky's LAD assumes.

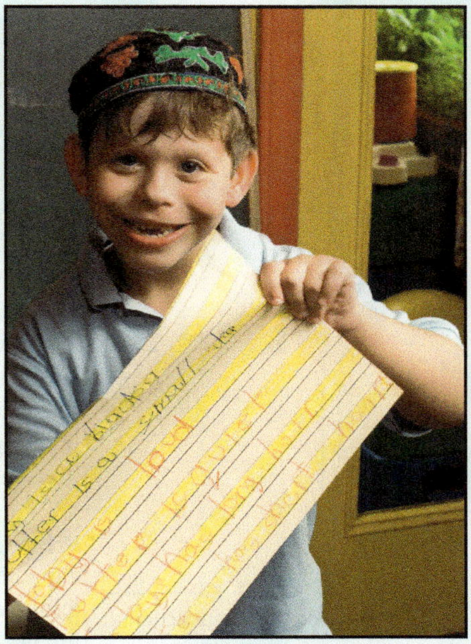

The impish smile and facial features of this child, who has Williams syndrome, suggest that he is strongly oriented toward the social world. Despite mild to serious mental retardation, children with Williams syndrome display impressive language skills. Nevertheless their cognitive deficits limit their ability to master complex language rules. © Laura Dwight Photography

ter 7, page 279, to review). Researchers program computers to simulate the multilayered networks of neural connections in the brain and then expose them to various types of language input. Tests with certain language sounds, words, and basic grammatical forms show that these networks capture children's early errors and gradually detect adult linguistic patterns. In acquiring the past tense, for example, a network first constructed some simple rules—for example, "Retrieve the past-tense form from memory." "Add *-ed* to any verb"—which at times resulted in mistakes. With further experience, the network modified and combined rules to arrive at adult usage: "For frequently used verbs (such as *go*), retrieve the unique past-tense form from memory *(went)*." "For novel or infrequently used verbs, form the past tense by adding *–ed*" (Taatgen & Anderson, 2002). Notice that neural networks are not biased to learn language.

Instead, connectionists assume that children make sense of their complex language environments by applying powerful, analytic cognitive capacities of a general kind rather than capacities especially tuned to language (Bates, 1999; Elman, 2001; Munakata, 2006).

Other theorists blend Chomsky's nativist perspective with the information-processing proposal that the human brain is extraordinarily skilled at detecting patterns. Recall the research presented in Chapter 4 (see pages 152–153), which showed that 8-month-old babies are amazing statistical analyzers of the sound stream, capable of detecting which adjacent sounds often occur together and which do not—a skill that helps them discriminate words in fluent speech. Using this *statistical learning capacity,* infants identify basic language patterns by applying the same strategies they use to make sense of their nonlinguistic experiences. At the same time, researchers recognize that such statistical computations are not sufficient to account for mastery of higher-level aspects of language—for example, intricate grammatical structures that require a grasp of distant relationships between words and phrases (Newport & Aslin, 2000). Currently, statistical learning theorists are investigating how sensitivity to statistical regularities might combine with other general-cognitive and language-specific processing abilities to explain children's acquisition of increasingly complex language structures (Saffran & Thiessen, 2007).

Proponents of information-processing approaches draw on biological evidence, pointing out that regions of the brain housing language also govern other similar perceptual, motor, and cognitive abilities. For example, ERP and fMRI studies reveal that damage to the left hemisphere, including Wernicke's area, results in difficulty comprehending both language and other patterned stimuli, such as music and series of moving lights that depict familiar shapes (Bates et al., 2003; Koelsch et al., 2002; Saygin et al., 2004). Indeed, Wernicke's area—once thought to be language-specific—is actually more strongly associated with comprehension of nonverbal than of verbal sound (Dick et al., 2004).

Information-processing theorists have tested their ideas mostly with simplified language stimuli, presented to artificial neural networks and to children in laboratories. In many instances, they cannot be certain that the learning strategies identified generalize to children's language acquisition in everyday social contexts. Other interactionist theorists believe that children's social skills and language experiences are centrally involved in language development.

• Social Interactionist Theories According to the social interactionist perspective, native capacity, a strong desire to understand others and to be understood by them, and a rich language environment combine to help children discover the functions and regularities of language. An active child, well-endowed for making sense of language, strives to communicate. In doing so, she cues her caregivers to provide appropriate language experiences, which in turn help her relate the content and structure of language to its social meanings (Bohannon & Bonvillian, 2009; Chapman, 2000, 2005).

Among social interactionist theorists, disagreement continues over whether children make sense of their complex language environments by applying general cognitive capacities or capacities specially tuned to language (Lidz, 2007; Shatz, 2007; Tomasello, 2003, 2006). Nevertheless, as we chart the course of language development, we will encounter much support for their central premise—that children's social competencies and language experiences greatly affect language development. At the same time, these ideas have not escaped criticism from contemporary researchers. Social interactionists assume that language grows out of communication, yet large disparities between pragmatics and other aspects of language do exist. In some children with mental retardation, for example, conversational skills lag behind other language achievements (Levy, 1996).

In reality, native endowment, cognitive-processing strategies, and social experience may operate in different balances with respect to each component of language. Today, we still know much more about the course of language development than about precisely how it takes place.

According to the social interactionist perspective, native capacity, a strong desire to communicate, and a rich language environment combine to help this preschooler discover the functions and regularities of language. © José Luis Pelaez/Getty Images/Iconica

Ask Yourself

Review Summarize outcomes of attempts to teach language to animals. Are results consistent with the nativist assumption that human children are uniquely endowed with an LAD? Explain.

Review How do the two types of interactionist theories of language development differ from behaviorist and nativist views and from each other?

Apply Describe evidence for the existence of a sensitive period for language learning. What are the practical implications of these findings for teaching children a second language?

Connect Cite research in this chapter and in Chapter 5 indicating that with age, areas of the cortex become increasingly specialized for language. Relate these findings to the concept of brain plasticity.

Prelinguistic Development: Getting Ready to Talk

From the very beginning, infants are prepared to acquire language. During the first year, sensitivity to language, cognitive and social milestones, and environmental supports pave the way for the onset of verbal communication.

Receptivity to Language

Recall from Chapter 4 that newborns are especially sensitive to the pitch range of the human voice and prefer speech—especially their mother's voice and their native tongue—to other sounds, perhaps because of repeated exposure to their mother speaking during pregnancy. We have also seen that newborns make fine-grained distinctions between virtually any human-language sounds. Because this skill may help them crack the phonological code of their native tongue, let's look at it more closely.

• Learning Native-Language Sound Categories and Patterns As adults, we analyze the speech stream into **phonemes,** the smallest sound units that signal a change in meaning, such as the difference between the consonant sounds in "pa" and "ba." Phonemes are not the same across all languages. For example, "ra" and "la" are distinct sounds to English speakers but sound the same to speakers of Japanese. Similarly, English speakers have trouble perceiving the difference between two "p" sounds—a soft "p" and a sharp "p" with a burst of air—used to distinguish meaning in the Thai language. This tendency to perceive as identical a range of sounds that belong to the same phonemic class is called **categorical speech perception.** Newborns, like adults, are capable of it. But they are sensitive to a much wider range of categories than exists in their own language (Jusczyk, 2003).

As infants listen actively to the talk of people around them, they focus on meaningful sound variations. Between 6 and 8 months, they start to organize speech into the phonemic categories of their own language—that is, they stop attending to sounds that will not be useful in mastering their native tongue (Kuhl et al., 1992; Polka & Werker, 1994). Interestingly, visual language discrimination—by monitoring a speaker's face and lip movements—changes similarly. At 4 to 6 months, infants can distinguish their native language (English) from an unfamiliar language (French) merely by watching silent video clips of adults saying sentences in each language. At 8 months, however, English-learning infants no longer make this visual discrimination. But 8-month-olds from French–English bilingual homes continue to separate the two languages visually—a discrimination that helps them learn two languages at once (see Figure 9.4) (Weikum et al., 2007).

■ Figure 9.4 **Visual language discrimination by English-learning and French/English-learning 8-month-olds.** During habituation, infants watched a series of silent video clips of adults speaking one language (either English or French) until their looking time declined. Then they were tested with the same adults speaking the other language. At 4 to 6 months (not shown), both English- and French/English-learning babies recovered (increased their looking time) following the language switch, indicating that they could visually discriminate the two languages. At 8 months (depicted below), only the babies from French/English bilingual homes recovered and, thus, continued to separate the two languages visually. (From Weikum et al., 2007.)

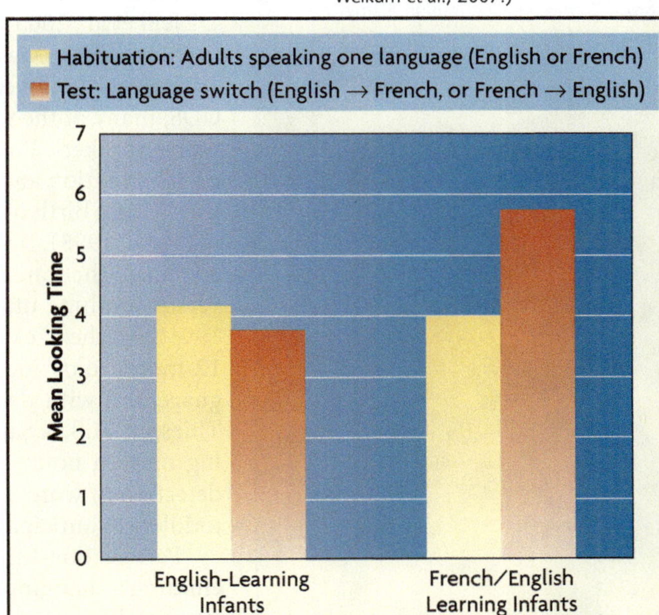

As older infants focus intently on language regularities, they soon recognize familiar words in spoken passages, listen longer to speech with clear clause and phrase boundaries, and divide the speech stream into wordlike units (see Chapter 4, page 153, to review). They also extend their sensitivity to speech structure to individual words. Using phoneme sequences and stress patterns, 7-month-olds can distinguish sounds that typically begin words from those that do not (Jusczyk, Houston, & Newsome, 1999). For example, English and Dutch infant learners often rely on the onset of a strong syllable to indicate a new word, as in "*an*imal" and "*pud*ding." By 10 months, they can detect words that start with weak syllables, such as "sur*prise*" (Jusczyk, 2001). The reverse pattern—earlier detection of words starting with weak syllables—characterizes infants acquiring Canadian French, which includes more words with a weak–strong stress pattern (Polka & Sundara, 2003).

Taken together, these findings reveal that in the second half of the first year, infants have begun to detect the internal structure of sentences and words—information that will be vital for linking speech units with their meanings (Werker & Yeung, 2005). How do babies accomplish these feats? We have seen that 8-month-olds are vigilant *statistical analyzers* of sound patterns; they can distinguish adjacent syllables that frequently occur together (signaling that they belong to the same word) from those that seldom occur together (signaling a word boundary). Research suggests that infants first use these statistical learning abilities to locate words in speech. Then they focus on the words, detecting regular patterns of syllable stress (Saffran & Thiessen, 2007). Furthermore, babies of this age are budding *rule learners.* At 7 months, they can distinguish an ABA from an ABB pattern in the structure of short, nonsense-word sequences—a capacity that may eventually help them grasp basic syntax (Marcus et al., 1999) (see page 153 in Chapter 4).

Do infants actually apply these analytic skills—discovered by presenting them with artificial sound sequences in laboratories—to the language they hear in everyday life? Analyses of maternal speech to English- and Dutch-learning babies indicate that real words can easily be extracted by attending to frequent, co-occurring syllables and to stress patterns (Swingley, 2005). Clearly, infants acquire a great deal of language-specific knowledge before they start to talk around 12 months of age. As we will see, certain features of adult speech greatly assist them in detecting meaningful speech units.

This mother speaks to her baby in short, clearly pronounced sentences with high-pitched, exaggerated intonation. This form of communication, called child-directed speech, eases language learning for infants and toddlers.

• **Adult Speech to Young Language Learners** Adults in many countries speak to infants and toddlers in **child-directed speech (CDS),** a form of communication made up of short sentences with high-pitched, exaggerated expression, clear pronunciation, distinct pauses between speech segments, clear gestures to support verbal meaning, and repetition of new words in a variety of contexts ("See the *ball.*" "The *ball* bounced!") (Fernald et al., 1989; O'Neill et al., 2005). Deaf parents use a similar style of communicating when signing to their babies (Masataka, 1996).

Parents do not seem to be deliberately trying to teach infants to talk when they use CDS; many of the same speech qualities appear when adults communicate with nonnative speakers. Rather, CDS probably arises from adults' desire to hold young children's attention and ease their task of understanding, and it works effectively in these ways. From birth on, infants prefer CDS over other kinds of adult talk (Aslin, Jusczyk, & Pisoni, 1998). By 5 months, they are more emotionally responsive to it and can discriminate the tone quality of CDS with different meanings—for example, approving versus soothing utterances (Moore, Spence, & Katz, 1997; Werker, Pegg, & McLeod, 1994). Mothers' exaggerated pronunciation in CDS is strongly associated with 6- to 12-month-olds' increasing sensitivity to the phonemic categories of their native language and with detection of words in the speech stream (Liu, Kuhl, & Tsao, 2003; Thiessen, Hill, & Saffran, 2005). And in the second year, the short, simple phrases leading up to a noun ("*Where's the* kitty?" "*See the* kitty."), common in CDS, facilitate detection of word meanings (Fernald & Hurtado, 2006). Perhaps these phrases enable toddlers to anticipate that an important word is coming and, thus, listen closely for it.

Parents fine-tune CDS, adjusting the length and content of their utterances to fit children's changing needs. Furthermore, in Chapter 4 we saw that parents combine speech with messages in other modalities (naming an object while moving it, conveying emotion in both speaking tone and facial expression), thereby enabling babies to use their capacity for intermodal matching to make sense of language (see pages 153–154). The more effectively parents modify their verbal input to suit their infants' learning needs, the better toddlers' language comprehension at age 18 months (Murray, Johnson, & Peters, 1990). In addition, toddlers' first words and phrases are usually ones they hear often in their caregivers' CDS (Cameron-Faulkner, Lieven, & Tomasello, 2003).

First Speech Sounds

Around 2 months, babies begin to make vowel-like noises, called **cooing** because of their pleasant "oo" quality. Gradually, consonants are added, and around 6 months **babbling** appears, in which infants repeat consonant–vowel combinations, often in long strings such as "babababababa" and "nananananana."

Babies everywhere (even those who are deaf) start babbling at about the same age and produce a similar range of early sounds. But for babbling to develop further, infants must hear human speech. A baby with impaired hearing will be greatly delayed in babbling and produce a reduced range of sounds. And a deaf infant not exposed to sign language will stop babbling entirely (Oller, 2000).

In one case, a deaf-born 5-month-old who received a cochlear implant—an electronic device inserted into the ear that converts external sounds into a signal to stimulate the auditory nerve—showed typical babbling in infancy and resembled her hearing agemates in language development at 3 to 4 years (Schauwers et al., 2004). But if auditory input is not restored until after age 2 (the usual time for cochlear implant surgery), children remain behind in language development. And if implantation occurs after age 4, language delays are severe and persistent (Govaerts et al., 2002; Svirsky, Teoh, & Neuburger, 2004). These outcomes suggest an early sensitive period in which exposure to speech is essential for the brain to develop the necessary organization for normal speech processing.

Babies initially produce a limited number of sounds, then expand to a much broader range (Oller et al., 1997). Around 7 months, babbling includes consonant–vowel syllables common in spoken languages. By 10 months, it reflects the sound and intonation patterns of children's language community, some of which are transformed into first words ("Mama," "Dada") (Boysson-Bardies & Vihman, 1991). TAKE A MOMENT... The next time you hear an older baby babbling, notice how certain sounds appear in particular contexts—for example, when exploring objects, looking at books, or walking upright (Blake & Boysson-Bardies, 1992). Infants seem to be experimenting with the sound system and meaning of language before they speak in conventional ways. Infants continue babbling for four or five months after they say their first words.

Deaf infants exposed to sign language from birth babble with their hands in much the same way hearing infants do through speech (Petitto & Marentette, 1991). Furthermore, hearing babies who have deaf, signing parents produce babble-like hand motions with the rhythmic patterns of natural sign languages (Petitto et al., 2001, 2004). This sensitivity to language rhythm—evident not just in perception of speech but also in the babbles babies produce, whether in manual or spoken mode—supports both discovery and production of meaningful language units.

Becoming a Communicator

At birth, infants are already prepared for some aspects of conversational behavior. For example, newborns can initiate interaction by making eye contact and terminate it by looking away. By 3 to 4 months, infants start to gaze in the same direction adults are looking—a skill that becomes more accurate at 10 to 11 months. Around this time, babies become sensitive to adults' precise direction of gaze, suggesting that they realize that others' focus provides information about their communicative intentions (Amano, Kezuka, & Yamamoto, 2004; Brooks & Meltzoff, 2005). Adults also follow the baby's line of vision and comment on what the infant sees. This **joint attention,** in which the child attends to the same object or event as the caregiver, who labels it, contributes greatly to early language development. Infants and toddlers who often experience it sustain attention longer, comprehend more language, produce meaningful gestures and words earlier, and show faster vocabulary development (Carpenter, Nagell, & Tomasello, 1998b;

This 1-year-old uses a preverbal gesture to draw his father's attention to the train. His father's verbal response promotes the baby's transition to spoken language.

Flom & Pick, 2003; Silvén, 2001). Gains in joint attention at the end of the first year suggest that infants are beginning to appreciate that other people have goals, just as they themselves do. This enables the child to establish a "common ground" with the adult, through which the child can figure out the meaning of the adult's verbal labels.

Between 4 and 6 months, interactions between caregivers and babies begin to include *give-and-take,* as in pat-a-cake and peekaboo games. At first, the parent starts the game, and the baby is an amused observer. But even 4-month-olds are sensitive to the structure and timing of these interactions, smiling more at an organized than a disorganized peekaboo exchange (Rochat, Querido, & Striano, 1999). By 12 months, babies participate actively, trading roles with the caregiver. As they do so, they practice the turn-taking pattern of human conversation—a vital context for acquiring language and communication skills. Infants' play maturity and vocalizations during games predict advanced language progress in the second year (Rome-Flanders & Cronk, 1995).

Around the first birthday, babies extend their joint attention and social interaction skills: They *point* toward an object or location while looking back toward the caregiver, in an effort to direct the adult's attention and influence their behavior. One-year-olds also grasp the communicative function of others' pointing. They interpret pointing to indicate the location of a hidden toy only when the adult also makes eye contact, not when the adult looks down at his finger (Liszkowski, Carpenter & Tomasello, 2007; Tomasello, Carpenter, & Liszkowski, 2007).

Infant pointing leads to two communicative gestures. The first is the **protodeclarative,** in which the baby points to, touches, or holds up an object while looking at others to make sure they notice. In the second, the **protoimperative,** the baby gets another person to do something by reaching, pointing, and often making sounds at the same time (Carpenter, Nagell, & Tomasello, 1998a). Over time, some of these gestures become explicitly symbolic—much like those in children's early make-believe play (see Chapter 6). For example, a 1- to 2-year-old might flap her arms to indicate "butterfly" or raise her palms to signal "all gone" (Goldin-Meadow, 1999).

Early in the second year, turn-taking and gestural communication come together, especially in situations in which children's messages do not communicate clearly. When adults label toddlers' reaching and pointing gestures ("Oh, you want a cookie!"), toddlers learn that using language quickly leads to desired results. Soon they use gestures to expand their verbal messages, as in pointing to a toy while saying "give" (Capirci et al., 2005). Gradually, gestures recede, and words become dominant. Toddlers' use of preverbal gestures predicts faster vocabulary growth in the second and third years (Blake et al., 2005). And the earlier toddlers form word–gesture combinations the sooner they produce two-word utterances with meanings like those of their word-gesture expressions at the end of the second year (Özçaliskan & Goldin-Meadow, 2005b). Clearly gesture is at the cutting edge of early language development, serving as a steppingstone to more complex constructions.

We have seen that caregivers who respond sensitively and involve infants in dialogue-like exchanges encourage early language progress. Yet in some cultures, such as the Kaluli of Papua New Guinea, the people of Western Samoa, and the Maya of southern Mexico, adults rarely communicate with young children and never play social games with them. Not until infants crawl and walk do siblings take charge, talk to toddlers, and respond to their vocalizations. Yet Kaluli, Samoan, and Mayan children acquire language within the normal time frame (de León, 2000; Ochs, 1988).

These findings suggest that adult molding of communication during the first year is not essential. But by the second year, caregiver–child interaction contributes greatly to the transition to language. In observations of mother–child play at 9 and 13 months, the frequency with which mothers joined in the child's activity, offered verbal prompts, and imitated and expanded on the child's vocalizations predicted how early children attained major language milestones, including first words, a 50-word vocabulary, two-word combinations, and use of language to talk about the past. The relationship of maternal responsiveness to language progress was particularly strong at 13 months (Tamis-LeMonda, Bornstein, & Baumwell, 2001).

As the From Research to Practice box on the following page illustrates, when a child's disability makes it difficult for parents to engage in responsive communication, children show profound delays in both language and cognitive development. For ways that caregivers can support early language learning, see Applying What We Know on page 372.

▪ *From* Research *to* Practice ▪

Parent–Child Interaction: Impact on Language and Cognitive Development of Deaf Children

About one in every 1,000 North American infants is born profoundly or fully deaf (Deafness Research Foundation, 2005). When a deaf child cannot participate fully in communication with caregivers, development is severely compromised. Yet the consequences of deafness for children's language and cognition vary with social context, as revealed by comparing two groups of deaf children: those with hearing parents and those with deaf parents.

Over 90 percent of deaf children have hearing parents who are not fluent in sign language. In toddlerhood and early childhood, these children often are delayed in development of language and make-believe play. In middle childhood, many achieve poorly in school, are deficient in perspective taking and social skills, and display impulse-control problems (Arnold, 1999; Edmondson, 2006). Yet deaf children of deaf parents escape these difficulties! Their language (use of sign), play maturity, and impulse control are on a par with hearing children's. After school entry, deaf children of deaf parents learn easily and get along well with adults and peers (Bornstein et al., 1999b; Spencer & Lederberg, 1997).

These differences can be traced to early parent–child communication. Children with limited and less sensitive parental communication lag behind their age-mates in achieving verbal control over their behavior—in thinking before they act and in planning. Beginning in infancy, hearing parents of deaf children are less positive, less responsive to the child's efforts to communicate, less effective at achieving joint attention and turn-taking, less involved in play, and more directive and intrusive (Spencer, 2000; Spencer & Meadow-Orlans, 1996). In contrast, the quality of interaction between deaf children and deaf parents resembles that of hearing children and hearing parents.

Hearing parents are not to blame for their deaf child's problems. Rather, they lack experience with visual communication, which enables deaf parents to respond readily to a deaf child's needs. Deaf parents know they must wait for the child to turn toward them before interacting (Loots & Devise, 2003). Hearing parents tend to speak or gesture while the child's attention is directed elsewhere—a strategy that works with a hearing but not with a deaf partner. When the child is confused or unresponsive, hearing parents often feel overwhelmed and become overly controlling (Jamieson, 1995).

The impact of deafness on language and cognitive development can best be understood by considering how it affects parents and other significant people in the child's life. Deaf children need access to language models—deaf adults and peers—to experience natural language learning. And their hearing parents benefit from social support along with training in how to interact sensitively with a nonhearing partner.

Screening techniques can now identify deaf babies at birth. Many U.S. states, some Canadian provinces, and an increasing number of Western nations now require that every newborn be tested, enabling immediate enrollment in programs aimed at fostering effective parent–child interaction (Hearing Foundation of Canada, 2006). When children with profound hearing loss start to receive intervention within the first year of life, they show much better language, cognitive, and social development (Yoshinaga-Itano, 2003).

When his mother signs "eat," this 16-month-old, who is deaf, responds with babblelike hand motions, similar to the babbling speech of hearing infants. Babbling, whether spoken or signed, supports production of meaningful language. © David Young-Wolff/PhotoEdit

Ask Yourself

Review Cite findings indicating that both infant capacities and caregiver communication contribute to prelinguistic development.

Apply Fran frequently corrects her 17-month-old son Jeremy's attempts to talk and—fearing that he won't use words—refuses to respond to his gestures. How might Fran be contributing to Jeremy's slow language progress?

Connect Explain how parents' use of child-directed speech illustrates Vygotsky's zone of proximal development (see Chapter 6, pages 265–266).

Reflect Find an opportunity to speak to an infant or toddler. How did your manner of speaking differ from the way you typically speak to an adult? What features of your speech are likely to promote early language development, and why?

Applying What We Know

Supporting Early Language Learning

Strategy	Consequence
Respond to infants' coos and babbles with speech sounds and words.	Encourages experimentation with sounds that can later be blended into first words. Provides experience with the turn-taking pattern of human conversation.
Establish joint attention and comment on what the child sees.	Promotes sustained attention, earlier onset of language, and faster vocabulary development.
Play social games, such as pat-a-cake and peekaboo, with infants and toddlers.	Promotes all aspects of conversational dialogue.
Engage children in frequent conversations.	Promotes faster language development and academic competence during the school years.
Expand slightly on what the child just said, adding new information.	Saying something like, "You want juice? I have some juice. It's apple juice!" to a toddler models use of language just ahead of the child's current level, thereby promoting language progress.
Read to children often, engaging them in dialogues about picture books.	Provides exposure to many aspects of language, including vocabulary, grammar, communication skills, and information about written symbols and story structures important for literacy progress.

Phonological Development

TAKE A MOMENT... Listen in on a 1- to 2-year-old trying out her first handful of words. You will probably hear an assortment of interesting pronunciations ("nana" for "banana," "oap" for "soap," "weddy" for "ready"), as well as some wordlike utterances that do not resemble adult forms—for "translations," you must ask the toddler's parent. Phonological development is a complex process that depends on the child's ability to attend to sound sequences, produce sounds, and combine them into understandable words and phrases. Between 1 and 4 years, children make great progress at this task. In trying to talk like people around them, they draw on their impressive capacity to distinguish the phonemic categories of their native language, which is well developed by the end of the first year. They also adopt temporary strategies for producing sounds that bring adult words within their current range of physical and cognitive capabilities (Menn & Stoel-Gammon, 2009). Let's see how they do so.

The Early Phase

Children's first words are influenced in part by the small number of sounds they can pronounce (Stoel-Gammon & Sosa, 2007; Vihman, 1996). The easiest sound sequences start with consonants, end with vowels, and include repeated syllables, as in "Mama," "Dada," "bye-bye," and "nigh-nigh" (for "night-night"). Sometimes young speakers use the same sound to represent a variety of words, making their speech hard to understand (Ingram, 1999). For example, one toddler substituted "bat" for as many as 12 different words, including "bad," "bark," "bent," and "bite."

Research confirms that toddlers and young preschoolers with more words in their spoken vocabularies can pronounce more speech sounds and syllable structures (Smith, McGregor, & Demille, 2006; Stoel-Gammon, 1998). Fortunately, languages cater to young children's phonological limitations. Throughout the world, sounds resembling "Mama," "Dada," and "Papa" refer to parents, so it is not surprising that these are among the first words produced by children everywhere. Also, in child-directed speech, adults often use simplified words to talk about things of interest to toddlers—"bunny" for rabbit, "choo-choo" for train. These word forms support the child's first attempts to talk.

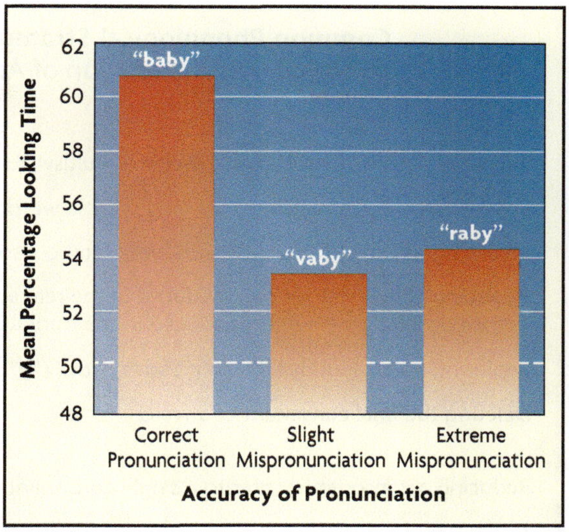

■ **Figure 9.5** **One-year-olds know the correct pronunciation of familiar words.** Babies viewed pairs of familiar objects (such as a baby and a dog) accompanied by a voice speaking the word for one of the objects with either correct pronunciation ("baby"), slight mispronunciation ("vaby"), or considerable mispronunciation ("raby"). They looked longest at the appropriate object when a word was pronounced correctly. Notice that in each condition, time spent looking at the correct object exceeded 50 percent, indicating that babies recognized the words whether or not they were pronounced correctly. (Adapted from Swingley & Aslin, 2002.)

One-year-olds first learning to talk know how familiar words—such as *dog, baby,* and *ball*—are supposed to sound, even when they mispronounce them. Researchers showed 14-month-olds pairs of objects (such as a baby and a dog), accompanied by a voice speaking the word for one of the objects, with either correct pronunciation ("baby"), slight mispronunciation ("vaby"), or considerable mispronunciation ("raby") (Swingley & Aslin, 2002). The toddlers easily detected the correct pronunciation: They looked longer at the appropriate object when a word was pronounced correctly than when it was either mildly or extremely mispronounced (see Figure 9.5).

Toddlers are also sensitive to mispronunciations of new words (Ballem & Plunkett, 2005). Nevertheless, when learning a new word, they often do not pick up the fine details of its sounds—a failure that contributes to their pronunciation errors. In several studies, 14-month-olds were unable to associate two similar-sounding nonsense words ("bih" and "dih") with different objects, despite easily detecting the "b"–"d" contrast in sound discrimination tasks (Fennell & Werker, 2003; Stager & Werker, 1997). Why don't toddlers apply their impressive sensitivity to speech sounds when acquiring new words? Associating words with their referents places extra demands on toddlers' limited working memories. Intent on communicating, they focus on the word–referent pairing while sacrificing the word's sounds, which they encode imprecisely.

As toddlers' vocabularies increase, they become better at using their perceptual abilities to distinguish similar-sounding new words. Once they acquire several sets of words that sound alike, they may be motivated to attend more closely to fine-grained distinctions between others.

Appearance of Phonological Strategies

By the middle of the second year, children move from trying to pronounce whole syllables and words to trying to pronounce each individual sound within a word. As a result, they can be heard experimenting with phoneme patterns. One 21-month-old pronounced "juice" as "du," "ju," "dus," "jus," "sus," "zus," "fus," "tfus," "jusi," and "tfusi" within a single hour (Fee, 1997). This marks an intermediate phase of development in which pronunciation is partly right and partly wrong. Because young children get more practice perceiving and producing phoneme patterns that occur frequently in their language, they pronounce words containing those patterns more accurately and rapidly (Munson, 2001; Zamuner, Gerken, & Hammond, 2004). Unique-sounding words are generally difficult to pronounce. A close look reveals that children apply systematic strategies to challenging words so that these words fit with their pronunciation capacities yet resemble adult utterances. Although individual differences exist in the precise strategies that children adopt (see Table 9.1 on page 374 for examples), they follow a general developmental pattern (Vihman, 1996).

At first, children produce *minimal words,* focusing on the stressed syllable and trying to pronounce its consonant–vowel combination ("du" or "ju" for "juice"). Soon they add ending consonants ("jus"), adjust vowel length ("beee" for "please"), and add unstressed syllables ("mae-do" for "tomato"). Finally, they produce the full word with a correct stress pattern, although they may still need to refine its sounds ("timemba" for "remember," "pagetti" for "spaghetti") (Demuth, 1996; Salidis & Johnson, 1997).

Children's errors are similar across a range of languages, including Cantonese, Czech, English, French, Italian, Quiché (a Guatemalan Mayan language), Spanish, and Swedish. But rate of phonological progress depends on the complexity of a language's sound system and the importance of certain sounds for conveying meaning. Cantonese-speaking children, for example, develop more quickly than English-speaking children.

This toddler growing up in Hong Kong, China, who is learning Cantonese, is likely to make faster progress in mastering language phonology than English-speaking children do. In Cantonese, many words are easy-to-pronounce single syllables. © Tom Owen Edmunds/ CORBIS

Table 9.1 Common Phonological Strategies Used by Young Children to Simplify Pronunciation of Adult Words

Strategy	Example
Repeating the first consonant-vowel in a multisyllable word	"TV" becomes "didi," "cookie" becomes "gege."
Deleting unstressed syllables in a multisyllable word	"Banana" becomes "nana," "giraffe" becomes "raffe."
Replacing fricatives (hissing sounds) with stop consonant sounds	"Sea" becomes "tea," "say" becomes "tay."
Replacing consonant sounds produced in the rear and palate area of the vocal tract with ones produced in the frontal area	"Kid" becomes "tid," "goose" becomes "doose."
Replacing liquid sounds ("l" or "r") with glides ("y" or "w")	"Lap" becomes "yap," "ready" becomes "weddy."
Deleting the final consonant of a word	"Bike" becomes "bai," "more" becomes "muh," "bottom" becomes "bada."
Reducing a consonant cluster to a single consonant	"Clown" becomes "cown," "play" becomes "pay."

Source: Ingram, 1986.

Many Cantonese words are single syllables, but a change in a syllable's tone can change its meaning. Chinese children master this tone system by age 2 (So & Dodd, 1995). Among children acquiring English, "v" is a late-appearing sound, whereas Swedish children master it early. In English, "v" is relatively infrequent; in Swedish, it is common and vital for distinguishing words (Ingram, 1999).

Over the preschool years, children's pronunciation improves greatly. Maturation of the vocal tract and the child's active problem-solving efforts are largely responsible, since children's phonological errors are resistant to adult correction. One father tried repeatedly to get his 2½-year-old daughter to pronounce the word "music," but she persisted with "ju-jic." When her father made one last effort, she replied, "Wait 'til I big. Then I say 'ju-jic,' Daddy!"

Later Phonological Development

Although phonological development is largely complete by age 5, a few syllable stress patterns signaling subtle differences in meaning are not acquired until middle childhood or adolescence. For example, when shown pairs of pictures and asked to distinguish the "greenhouse" from the "green house," most children recognized the correct label by third grade and produced it between fourth and sixth grade (Atkinson-King, 1973). Changes in syllabic stress when certain abstract words take on endings ("humid" to "humidity," "method" to "methodical") are not mastered until adolescence (Camarata & Leonard, 1986).

These late attainments are probably affected by the semantic complexity of the words, in that hard-to-understand words are also more difficult to pronounce. Even at later ages, working simultaneously on the sounds and meaning of a new word may overload the cognitive system, causing children to sacrifice pronunciation temporarily until they better grasp the word's meaning.

Ask Yourself

Review Why do toddlers often fail to pick up the fine details of a new word's sounds, even though they can perceive those sounds?

Apply As his father placed a bowl of pasta on the dinner table, 2-year-old Luke exclaimed, "So 'licious!" Explain Luke's phonological strategy.

Reflect For one week, keep a log of words you mispronounce or do not pronounce fluently (you slow down to say them). Are they words that convey complex concepts or words with sounds that are relatively infrequent in English or in your native tongue? Research indicates that these factors, which affect children's pronunciation, also affect the pronunciation of adults.

Semantic Development

Word comprehension begins in the middle of the first year. When 6-month-olds listened to the words "Mommy" and "Daddy" while looking at side-by-side videos of their parents, they looked longer at the video of the named parent (Tincoff & Jusczyk, 1999). At 9 months, after hearing a word paired with an object, babies looked longer at other objects in the same category than at those in a different category (Balaban & Waxman, 1997). On average, children say their first word around 12 months. By age 6, they have a vocabulary of about 10,000 words (Bloom, 1998). To accomplish this feat, children learn about five new words each day.

As these achievements reveal, children's **comprehension,** the language they understand, develops ahead of **production,** the language they use. For example, toddlers follow many simple directions ("Bring me your book," "Don't touch the lamp") even though they cannot yet express all these words in their own speech. A five-month lag exists between children's comprehension of 50 words (at about 13 months) and production of 50 words (around 18 months) (Menyuk, Liebergott, & Schultz, 1995).

Think back to the distinction made in Chapter 7 between two types of memory—recognition and recall. Comprehension requires only that children *recognize* the meaning of a word. But for production, children must *recall,* or actively retrieve from their memories, not only the word but also the concept for which it stands. Still, the two capacities are related. The speed and accuracy of toddlers' comprehension of spoken language increase dramatically over the second year. And toddlers who are faster and more accurate in comprehension tend to show more rapid growth in words understood and produced as they approach age 2 (Fernald, Perfors, & Marchman, 2006). Quick comprehension frees space in working memory for picking up new words and for the more demanding task of using them to communicate.

The Early Phase

To learn words, children must identify which concept each label picks out in their language community. **TAKE A MOMENT...** Ask several parents to list their toddlers' first words. Notice how the words build on the sensorimotor foundations Piaget described and on categories children form during their first two years (see Chapter 6). Earliest words refer to important people ("Mama," "Dada"), animals ("doggie," "kitty"), objects that move ("ball," "car," "shoe"), foods ("milk," "apple"), familiar actions ("bye-bye," "more," "up"), or outcomes of familiar actions ("dirty," "hot," "wet") (Hart, 2004; Nelson, 1973). As Table 9.2 reveals, in their first 50 words, toddlers rarely name things that just sit there, like "table" or "vase."

Besides cognition, emotion influences early word learning. At first, when acquiring a new word for an object, person, or event, 1½-year-olds say it neutrally. To learn, they need to listen

Table 9.2 Types of Words Appearing in Toddlers' 50-Word Vocabularies

Word Type	Description	Typical Examples	Percentage of Total Words[a]
Object words	Words used to refer to the "thing world"	*Apple, ball, bird, boat, book, car, cookie, Dada, doggie, kitty, milk, Mama, shoe, snow, truck*	66
Action words	Words that describe, demand, or accompany action or that express attention or demand attention	*Bye-bye, go, hi, look, more, out, up*	13
State words (modifiers)	Words that refer to properties or qualities of things or events	*All gone, big, dirty, hot, mine, pretty, outside, red, uh-oh, wet*	9
Personal/social words	Words that express emotional states and social relationships	*No, ouch, please, want, yes, thank you*	8
Function words	Words that fill a solely grammatical function	*For, is, to, what, where*	4

[a]Average percentages are given, based on a sample of 18 American toddlers.

Source: Nelson, 1973.

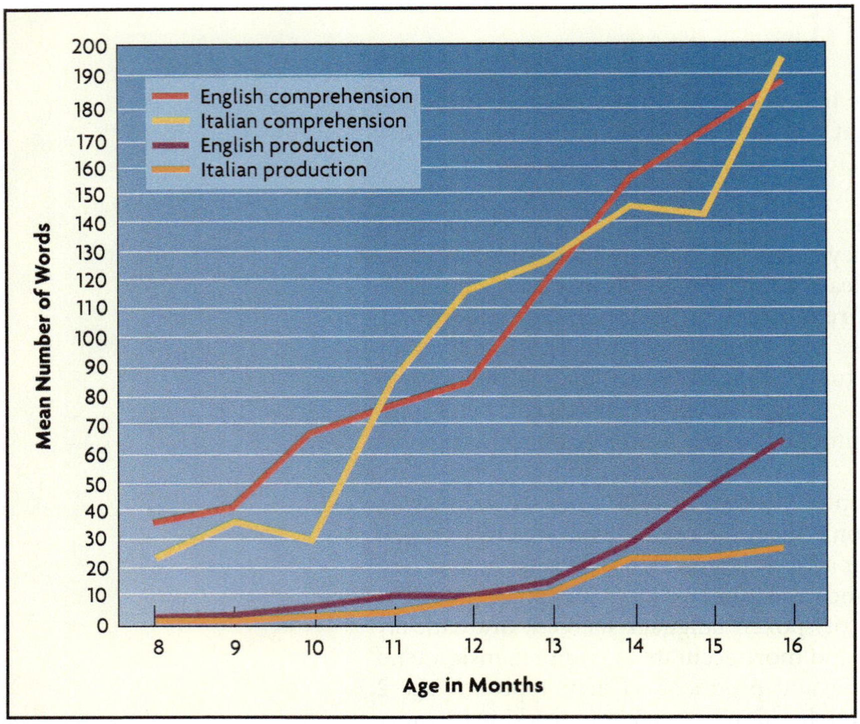

Figure 9.6 **English and Italian learners' vocabulary growth between 8 and 16 months.**

The increase in vocabulary size is far more rapid in comprehension than in production. Rate of word learning gradually accelerates. (From M. C. Caselli et al., 1995, "A Cross-Linguistic Study of Early Lexical Development," *Cognitive Development*, 10, p. 172. Reprinted with permission from Elsevier.)

carefully, and strong emotion would divert their attention. As words become better learned, toddlers integrate talking and expressing feelings (Bloom, 1998). "Shoe!" said an enthusiastic 22-month-old as her mother tied her shoelaces before an outing. At the end of the second year, toddlers label their emotions with words like "happy," "mad," and "sad"—a development we will consider in Chapter 10.

Young toddlers add to their vocabularies slowly, at a pace of one to three words per week. Gradually, the number of words learned accelerates. The increase is much more rapid in comprehension than in production, as illustrated by English and Italian learners' vocabulary growth between 8 and 16 months, shown in Figure 9.6 (Caselli et al., 1995). Because rate of word learning between 18 and 24 months is so impressive (one or two words per day), many researchers concluded that toddlers undergo a *spurt in vocabulary*—a transition between a slow and a faster learning phase once the number of words produced reaches 50 to 100. Recent evidence, however, indicates that only a minority of young children experience a vocabulary spurt (Ganger & Brent, 2004). Most show a steady, continuous increase in rate of word learning that persists through the preschool years, when children add as many as nine new words per day.

How do young children build their vocabularies so quickly? An improved ability to categorize experience (see Chapter 6), recall words, and pronounce new words is involved (Dapretto & Bjork, 2000; Gershoff-Stowe & Smith, 1997). In addition, a better grasp of others' intentions, evident in toddlers' imitation around 18 months (see page 232), supports rapid vocabulary growth because it helps toddlers figure out what others are talking about (Golinkoff & Hirsh-Pasek, 2006; Tomasello, 2003). Furthermore, as toddlers' experiences broaden, they have a wider range of interesting objects and events to label. For example, children approaching age 2 more often mention places to go ("park," "store"). And as they construct a clearer self-image, they add more words that refer to themselves ("me," "mine," "Katy") and to their own and others' bodies and clothing ("eyes," "mouth," "jacket") (Hart, 2004).

Researchers have discovered that children can connect a new word with an underlying concept after only a brief encounter, a process called **fast-mapping.** When an adult labeled an oddly shaped plastic ring with the nonsense word "koob" during a game, children as young as 2 picked up the word's meaning (Dollaghan, 1985). Even 15- to 18-month-olds comprehend new labels remarkably quickly. But they need more repetitions of the word's use across several situations than preschoolers, who better remember and categorize speech-based information (Akhtar & Montague, 1999; Fernald, Perfors, & Marchman, 2006).

Toddlers' understanding of a fast-mapped word is incomplete at first, deepening with repeated exposure. They start to form networks of related concepts and words, which help them fast-map new words, contributing to the age-related increase in rate of word learning. In one study, researchers gave 18-month-olds extended training on a set of novel words in 12 weekly sessions by showing the child pictures and talking about word meanings ("See the *crab.* The *crab* lives in the ocean"). Compared with no-practice controls, trained toddlers acquired a second set of novel words far more rapidly (Gershkoff-Stowe & Hahn, 2007). And preschoolers become adept at fast-mapping two or more new words encountered in the same situation (Wilkinson, Ross, & Diamond, 2003).

• Individual and Cultural Differences Although the average age at which children produce their first word is 12 months, the range is large, from 8 to 18 months—variation due to a complex blend of genetic and environmental influences. Many studies show that girls are slightly ahead of boys in early vocabulary growth up (Fenson et al., 1994). The most common biological explanation is girls' faster rate of physical maturation, which is believed to promote earlier development of the left cerebral hemisphere. Temperament matters, too. Shy toddlers often wait until they understand a great deal before trying to speak. Once they do speak, their vocabularies increase rapidly, although they remain slightly behind their agemates in language skills during the preschool years (Spere et al., 2004). Temperamentally negative toddlers also acquire language more slowly (Salley & Dixon, 2007). Their high emotional reactivity diverts them from processing linguistic information, and their relationships with caregivers are often conflict-ridden and, therefore, poorly suited to promoting language progress.

The surrounding language environment also plays a role. The more words caregivers use, the more children learn (Weizman & Snow, 2001). Mothers talk much more to toddler-age girls than to boys, and parents converse less often with shy than with sociable children (Leaper, Anderson, & Sanders, 1998; Patterson & Fisher, 2002). Low-SES children, who receive less verbal stimulation in their homes than higher-SES children, usually have smaller vocabularies (Hoff, 2004, 2006). In addition to amount and quality of parent–child interaction, limited parent–child storybook reading plays a major role. As Figure 9.7 shows, as early as 2 years of age, quality of children's home literacy experiences strongly predicts vocabulary size (Tamis-Lemonda et al., 2006). On average, a middle-SES child is read to for 1,000 hours between 1 and 5 years, a low-SES child for only 25 hours (Neuman, 2003). By the time they enter kindergarten, low-SES children have vocabularies only one-fourth as large as those of their higher-SES agemates (Lee & Burkam, 2002).

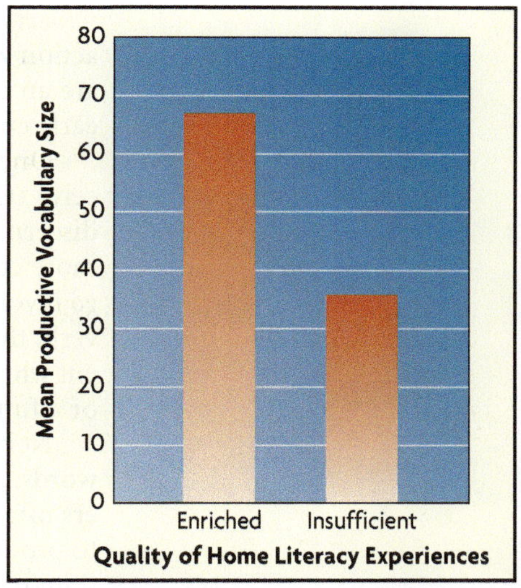

Figure 9.7 Relationship of quality of home literacy experiences to productive vocabulary at age 2. In families diverse in SES, 2-year-olds with rich home literacy experiences (access to many age-appropriate books and frequent participation in joint adult–child book-reading) had vocabularies that were far larger than those of 2-year-olds with insufficient literacy experiences. (Adapted from Tamis-Lemonda et al., 2006.)

Children also have unique styles of early language learning. Most toddlers use a **referential style**; their vocabularies consist mainly of words that refer to objects. A smaller number of toddlers use an **expressive style**; compared with referential children, they produce many more social formulas and pronouns ("thank you," "done," "I want it"), uttered as compressed phrases that sound like single words ("Iwannit"). Recall, from the opening to this chapter, Erin's early use of largely expressive-style words. The language styles reflect early ideas about the functions of language. Referential-style children think words are for naming things, whereas expressive-style children believe words are for talking about people's feelings and needs. The vocabularies of referential-style children grow faster because all languages contain many more object labels than social phrases (Bates et al., 1994).

Why does a toddler use a particular language style? Rapidly developing, referential-style children often have an especially active interest in exploring objects. They also eagerly imitate their parents' frequent naming of objects, and their parents imitate back—a strategy that supports swift vocabulary growth by helping children remember new labels (Masur & Rodemaker, 1999). Expressive-style children tend to be highly sociable, and their parents more often use verbal routines ("How are you?" "It's no trouble") that support social relationships (Goldfield, 1987).

The two language styles are also linked to culture. Object words are particularly common in the vocabularies of English-speaking toddlers, but Chinese, Japanese, and Korean toddlers have more words for social routines. Mothers' speech in each culture reflects this difference: Asian mothers, perhaps because of a cultural emphasis on the importance of group membership, teach social routines as soon as their children begin to speak (Choi & Gopnik, 1995; Fernald & Morikawa, 1993; Tardif, Gelman, & Xu, 1999).

Notice how these findings support the social interactionist perspective: Children's inner dispositions and their linguistic and social worlds combine to influence both rate and makeup of early language progress.

In Western societies, mothers typically emphasize object labels with young language learners. In contrast, this African mother of Ghana focuses on social routines as she converses with her toddler and his two older brothers. © Greenshoots Communications/Alamy

Types of Words Three types of words—object, action, and state—are most common in young children's vocabularies. Each provides important information about the course of semantic development.

Object and Action Words. Young language learners in many cultures have more object than action words in their beginning vocabularies (Bornstein & Cote, 2004; Kern, 2007). If actions are an especially important means through which infants learn about their world, why this early emphasis on naming objects?

One reason is that nouns refer to concepts (such as *table, bird,* or *dog*) that are easy to perceive (Gentner & Namy, 2004). When adults label an object, they frequently help the child discern the word's meaning by showing and repeating the label. In contrast, verbs require more complex understandings—of relationships between objects and actions. For example, *go* involves a person going somewhere, *fix* a person fixing something. And when adults use a verb, the selected action usually is not taking place (Poulin-Dubois & Forbes, 2006). A parent who says the word *move* is probably referring to a past event ("Someone *moved* the bowl") or a future event ("Let's *move* the bowl").

Nevertheless, the linguistic environment affects toddlers' relative use of object and action words. As noted in our discussion of early language-learning styles, English-speaking mothers often name objects for their children. In one study, they rarely prompted 20-month-olds to produce verbs. Rather, they often used verbs to get toddlers to perform actions ("Can you *spin* that wheel?"). Consequently, the toddlers comprehended more verbs than they produced (Goldfield, 2000). In Chinese, Japanese, and Korean, nouns are often omitted entirely from adult sentences, while verbs are stressed. As a result, Asian toddlers' early vocabularies typically include many more verbs than those of their English-speaking counterparts (Kim, McGregor, & Thompson, 2000; Tardif, 2006).

State Words. Between 2 and 2½ years, children's use of *state* (or modifier) words expands to include labels for attributes of objects, such as size and color ("big," "red") and possession ("my toy," "Mommy purse"). Words referring to the functions of objects ("dump truck," "pickup truck") appear soon after (Nelson, 1976).

When state words are related in meaning, general distinctions (which are easier) appear before more specific ones. Thus, among words referring to the size of objects, children first acquire *big–small,* then *tall–short, high–low,* and *long–short,* and finally *wide–narrow* and *deep–shallow.* The same is true for temporal terms. Between ages 3 and 5, children first master *now–then* and *before–after,* followed by *today–yesterday* and *today–tomorrow* (Stevenson & Pollitt, 1987).

State words referring to object location provide additional examples of how cognition influences vocabulary development. Before age 2, children can easily imitate an adult's action in putting an object *in* or *on* another object, but they have trouble imitating the placement of one object *under* another. These terms appear in children's vocabularies in just this order, with all three achieved around age 2½ (Clark, 1983).

Cognitive development influences young children's mastery of state words (modifiers). This child is likely to say "on" the spoon and "in" the cup before she says "under" the sand. Adult labeling of object locations will help her master these terms. © Dennis MacDonald/PhotoEdit

Because state words refer to qualities of objects and actions, children can use them to express a wide variety of concepts. As preschoolers master these words, their language becomes increasingly flexible.

Underextensions and Overextensions When young children first learn words, they often do not use them just as adults do. They may apply words too narrowly, an error called **underextension.** For example, at 16 months, my younger son used the word "bear" to refer only to a special teddy bear to which he had become attached. A more common error between 1 and 2½ years is **overextension**—applying a word to a broader collection of objects and events than is appropriate. For example, a toddler might use the word "car" for buses, trains, trucks, and fire engines.

Toddlers' overextensions reflect their remarkable sensitivity to categorical relations. They apply a new word to a group of similar experiences, such as "dog" for any furry, four-legged animal or "open" to mean opening a door, peeling fruit, and untying shoe laces. Furthermore, the toddler who refers to trucks, trains, and bikes as "cars" is likely to point to these objects correctly when given their names in comprehension tasks (Naigles & Gelman, 1995). This suggests that children often overextend deliberately because they have difficulty recalling or have not acquired a suitable word. In addition, when a word is hard to pronounce, toddlers frequently substitute a related one they can say (Bloom, 2000; Elsen, 1994). As vocabulary and pronunciation improve, overextensions disappear.

● **Word Coinages and Metaphors** Children as young as age 2 fill in for words they have not yet learned by coining new words based on ones they know ("plant-man" for a gardener, "crayoner" for a child using crayons). These early expressions reveal a remarkable, rule-governed approach to language.

Preschoolers also extend language meanings through metaphor. For example, one 3-year-old described a stomachache as a "fire engine in my tummy" (Winner, 1988). Young preschoolers' metaphors are based largely on concrete, sensory comparisons ("clouds are pillows," "leaves are dancers"). As their vocabulary and knowledge of the world expand, they grasp nonsensory comparisons: "Friends are like magnets," "Time flies by" (Keil, 1986; Özçaliskan, 2005). Metaphors permit children to communicate in especially vivid and memorable ways.

Later Semantic Development

Between the start and end of elementary school, vocabulary increases fourfold, eventually exceeding 40,000 words (Anglin, 1993). On average, school-age children learn about 20 new words each day, a rate of growth exceeding that of early childhood (see Figure 9.8). In addition to fast-mapping, older school-age children, especially those with excellent reading comprehension, enlarge their vocabularies by analyzing the structure of complex words. From *happy, decide,* and *leader,* they can derive the meanings of *happiness, decision,* and *leadership* (Larsen & Nippold, 2007). They also figure out many more word meanings from context (Nagy & Scott, 2000).

As at earlier ages, children benefit from engaging in conversation with more expert speakers, especially when their partners use complex words and explain them (Weizman & Snow, 2001). But because written language contains a far more diverse and complex vocabulary than spoken language, reading contributes enormously to vocabulary growth in middle childhood and adolescence. Engaging in as little as 21 minutes of independent reading per day exposes children to nearly 2 million words per year (Cunningham & Stanovich, 1998).

As their knowledge expands and becomes better organized (see Chapter 7), older school-age children think about and use words more precisely: In addition to the verb *fall,* for example, they also use *topple, tumble,* and *plummet* (Berman, 2007). Word definitions also illustrate this change. Five- and 6-year-olds offer concrete descriptions referring to functions or appearance—for example, *knife:* "when you're cutting carrots"; *bicycle:* "it's got wheels, a chain, and handlebars." By the end of elementary school, synonyms and explanations of categorical relationships appear—for example, *knife:* "Something you could cut with. A saw is like a knife. It could also be a weapon" (Wehren, De Lisi, & Arnold, 1981). This advance reflects older children's ability to deal with word meanings on an entirely verbal plane. They can add new words to their vocabulary simply by being given a definition.

School-age children's more reflective and analytical approach to language permits them to appreciate the multiple meanings of words—to recognize, for example, that words such as *cool* or *neat* have psychological as well as physical meanings: "What a cool shirt!" or "That movie was really neat!" This grasp of double meanings permits 8- to 10-year-olds to comprehend subtle metaphors, such as "sharp as a tack" and "spilling the beans" (Nippold, Taylor, & Baker, 1996; Wellman & Hickling, 1994). It also leads to a change in children's humor. Riddles and puns that alternate between different meanings of a key word are common: "Hey, did you take a bath?" "Why, is one missing?" (Ely & McCabe, 1994).

Adolescents add a variety of abstract words—*counterintuitive, revolutionized, philosophy*—to their vocabularies. They also master sarcasm and irony (Pexman & Glenwright, 2007; Winner, 1988). When his mother prepares a dish for dinner that he dislikes, a 13-year-old might quip, "Oh boy, my favorite!" School-age children sometimes realize that a sarcastic remark is insincere if it is said in an exaggerated, mocking tone of voice. But adolescents and adults need only notice the discrepancy between a statement and its context to grasp the intended meaning (Capelli, Nakagawa, & Madden, 1990).

Similarly, grasp of figurative language improves greatly in adolescence. Proverbs—especially those expressing subtle attitudes—are especially challenging. They can be used to comment ("Blood is thicker than water"), interpret ("His bark

Figure 9.8 Estimated increase in vocabulary during the school years.
Vocabulary growth from grades 1 to 5 exceeds that of early childhood. (Adapted from Anglin, 1993.)

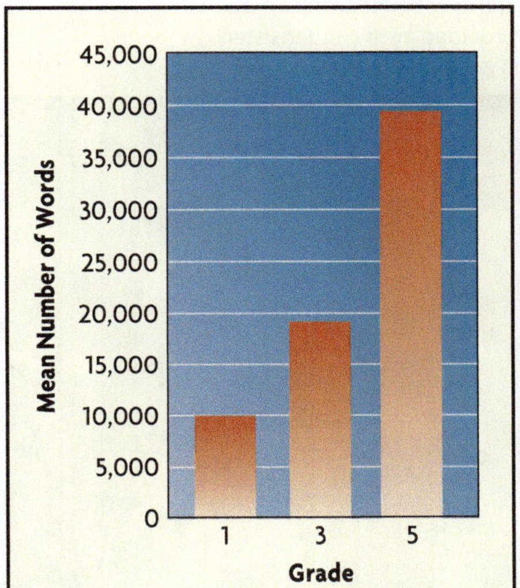

is worse than his bite"), advise ("Humility often gains more than pride"), warn ("Of idleness comes no goodness"), and encourage ("Every cloud has a silver lining"). And they make sense only in certain situations: "Too many cooks spoil the broth" is good advice for balancing a checkbook but bad advice for cleaning up a classroom (Nippold, 2000). As with other aspects of semantic development, reading proficiency fosters understanding of proverbs (Nippold, Allen, & Kirsch, 2001). And a better grasp of figurative language enables teenagers to appreciate adult literary works.

Ideas About How Semantic Development Takes Place

Research shows that adult feedback facilitates semantic development. When adults go beyond correcting and explain ("That's not a car. It's a truck. See, it has a place to put things in"), toddlers are more likely to move toward conventional word meanings (Chapman, Leonard, & Mervis, 1986). Still, adults cannot tell children exactly what concept each new word picks out. If an adult points to a dog and says, "doggie," the word may refer to any four-legged animal, the dog's shaggy ears, or its barking sound. Therefore, the child's cognitive processing must play a major role.

• The Influence of Memory Young children's fast-mapping is supported by a special part of working memory, a **phonological store** that permits us to retain speech-based information. The more rapidly 4-year-olds can recall a just-presented sequence of nonsense words (a measure of phonological memory skill), the larger their current vocabulary and the greater their vocabulary growth over the following year (Gathercole, 1995; Gathercole et al., 1999). This suggests that a child with good phonological memory has a better chance of transferring new words to long-term memory and linking them with relevant concepts.

By the end of the second year, phonological memory is so good that toddlers can recognize familiar words on the basis of their initial sounds. When given only the first two or three phonemes of a familiar word ("ba" for "baby," "daw" for "doggie"), 18- to 24-month-olds looked at the correct object, responding as accurately and quickly as they did to the whole word. Furthermore, toddlers with better verbal recognition scores had larger productive vocabularies (Fernald, Swingley, & Pinto, 2001). Early in development, phonological memory is linked to advanced vocabulary development. Being able to identify a word rapidly on the basis of initial sounds has clear advantages: It frees working memory for other language tasks, such as comprehending longer and more complex strings of words.

But phonological memory does not provide a full account of word learning. After age 5, semantic knowledge influences the speed with which children form phonological traces, and both factors affect vocabulary growth (Gathercole et al., 1997). Even at younger ages (as we will see next), children rely heavily on words they know to detect the meanings of new ones.

• Strategies for Word Learning Young children figure out the meanings of words by contrasting them with words they already know and assigning the new label to a gap in their vocabulary. On hearing a new word in conversation, 2-year-olds repeat the word or acknowledge it with "yeah" or "uh-huh" in their next verbalization more than 60 percent of the time (Clark, 2007). These findings suggest that they assign the word a preliminary meaning and start to use it right away. Over time, they refine the word's meaning, striving to match its conventional use in their language community (Clark, 1990). On learning a new noun, toddlers and preschoolers acquiring diverse languages tend to assume it refers to an object category at the basic level—an intermediate level of generality (see page 244 in Chapter 6). This preference helps young children narrow the range of possible meanings. Once they acquire a basic-level name *(dog)*, they add names at other hierarchical levels, both more general *(animal)* and more specific *(beagle, greyhound)* (Imai & Haryu, 2004; Waxman & Lidz, 2006).

How do children discover which concept each word picks out? This process is not yet fully understood. One speculation is that early in vocabulary growth, children adopt a **mutual exclusivity bias**—the assumption that words refer to entirely separate (nonoverlapping) categories (Markman, 1992). Two-year-olds seem to rely on mutual exclusivity when the objects named are perceptually distinct—for example, differ clearly in shape. After hearing the names for two distinct novel

Young children rely on any useful information available to figure out the meanings of new words. This toddler might be focusing on the distinctive shape of the ice cream, along with social information provided by his older sister.
© Bubbles Photolibrary/Alamy

objects (a clip and a horn), they assign each word correctly, to the whole object and not to a part of it (Waxman & Senghas, 1992).

Indeed, children's first several hundred nouns refer mostly to objects well-organized by shape. Once toddlers have acquired about 75 words, a **shape bias** is clearly evident: Previous learning of nouns based on shape heightens attention to the shape properties of additional objects. As a result, toddlers readily master more names for objects distinguished by shape, and vocabulary accelerates. When toddlers repeatedly played with and heard names for novel objects varying in shape over a nine-week period, they soon formed the generalization that only similarly shaped objects have the same name (Smith et al., 2002). Toddlers with this training added more than three times as many object names to their vocabularies outside the laboratory as did untrained controls. Because shape is a perceptual property relevant to most categories of objects for which they have already acquired names, preschoolers continue to rely heavily on shape when first learning new nouns (Yoshida & Smith, 2003).

Mutual exclusivity and object shape are especially useful when speakers provide few or no cues about a new word's meaning. But they cannot account for young children's remarkably flexible responses when objects have more than one name. By age 3, preschoolers' memory, categorization, and language skills have expanded, and they readily assign multiple labels to many objects (Déak, Yen, & Pettit, 2001). For example, they refer to a sticker of a gray goose as "sticker," "goose," and "gray." Children often call on other components of language for help in these instances. According to one proposal, preschoolers discover many word meanings by observing how words are used in syntax, or the structure of sentences—a hypothesis called **syntactic bootstrapping** (Gleitman et al., 2005; Naigles & Swenson, 2007). Consider an adult who says, "This is a *citron* one," while showing a child a yellow car. Two- and 3-year-olds conclude that a new word used as an adjective for a familiar object (car) refers to a property of that object (Hall & Graham, 1999; Imai & Haryu, 2004). As preschoolers hear the word in various sentence structures ("That lemon is bright *citron*"), they use syntactic information to refine the word's meaning and generalize it to other categories.

Young children also take advantage of the rich social information that adults frequently provide when they introduce new words. For example, they often draw on their expanding ability to infer others' intentions and perspectives (Akhtar & Tomasello, 2000). In one study, an adult performed an action on an object and then used a new label while looking back and forth between the child and the object, as if to invite the child to play. Two-year-olds concluded that the label referred to the action, not the object (Tomasello & Akhtar, 1995). Toddlers can even accurately interpret an adult's ambiguous request for an object ("Where's the ball?") by referring to their recent experience with that adult. They retrieve the particular object the adult had just played with (ball in a red bucket), not an identical object that another adult played with (ball in a blue bucket) (Saylor & Ganea, 2007). And 3-year-olds use information about a speaker's recently expressed desires (recalling which of two novel objects an adult said she liked) to figure out a word referent ("I really want to play with the *riff*") (Saylor & Troseth, 2006).

Adults also inform children directly about word meanings. Parents commonly highlight the meaning of adjectives by using the new label with several objects (a "red car," a "red truck")—information that helps children infer that the word refers to an object property (Hall, Burns, & Pawluski, 2003). And adults often explain which of two or more words to use, saying, for example: "You can call it a sea creature, but it's better to say 'dolphin.'" Parents who provide such clarifying information have preschoolers whose vocabularies grow more quickly (Callanan & Sabbagh, 2004; Deák, 2000).

• Explaining Vocabulary Development Children acquire vocabulary so efficiently and accurately that some theorists believe that they are innately biased to induce word meanings using certain principles, such as mutual exclusivity and syntactic bootstrapping (Lidz, Gleitman, & Gleitman, 2004; Woodward & Markman, 1998). But critics observe that a small set of built-in, fixed principles is not sufficient to account for the varied, flexible manner in which children master vocabulary (Deák, 2000). And many word-learning strategies cannot be innate because children acquiring different languages use different approaches to mastering the same meanings. For example, English-speaking children rely on syntactic bootstrapping to tell the difference between one object ("This is *a dax*"), multiple objects of the same

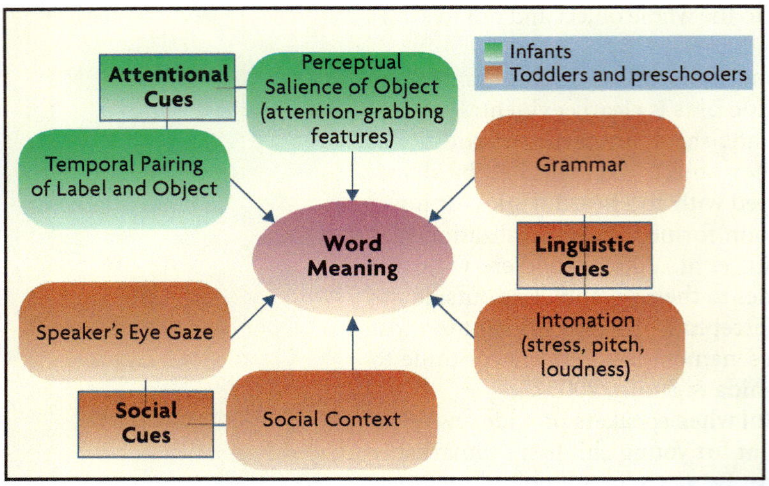

Figure 9.9 **Emergentist coalition model of word-learning strategies.** Children draw on a coalition of cues—perceptual, social, and linguistic—to infer word meanings. With age, these cues shift in importance. Infants rely solely on perceptual cues. While remaining sensitive to perceptual features, toddlers increasingly attend to social cues. And as language develops further, preschoolers add linguistic cues. (From R. M. Golinkoff & K. Hirsh-Paske, 2006, "Baby Wordsmith: From Associationist to Social Sophisticate," *Current Directions in Psychological Science,* 15, p. 31. © 2006 Blackwell Publishing, Ltd. Adapted by permission.)

category ("Those are *daxes*"), and a proper name ("This is *Dax*") (Hall, Lee, & Belanger, 2001). In Japanese, all nouns are treated the same syntactically ("This is *dax*"). But Japanese preschoolers find ways to compensate for the missing syntactic cues, learning just as quickly as their English-speaking agemates (Imai & Haryu, 2001).

An alternative perspective is that vocabulary growth is governed by the same cognitive strategies that children apply to nonlinguistic stimuli. A recent account, called the **emergentist coalition model,** proposes that word-learning strategies *emerge* out of children's efforts to decipher language (Golinkoff & Hirsh-Pasek, 2006). Children draw on a *coalition* of cues—perceptual, social, and linguistic—which shift in importance with age (see Figure 9.9). Infants rely solely on perceptual cues—for example, a parent shaking a toy while naming it. Toddlers, while still sensitive to perceptual features (such as object shape), increasingly attend to social cues—the speaker's direction of gaze and gestures (Hollich, Hirsh-Pasek, & Golinkoff, 2000; Pruden et al., 2006). And as language develops further, linguistic cues—syntax and intonation (stress, pitch, and loudness)—play larger roles.

Preschoolers are most successful at figuring out new word meanings when several kinds of information are available. Researchers have just begun to study the multiple cues they use for different types of words and how their combined strategies change with development (Saylor, Baldwin, & Sabbagh, 2005; Saylor & Sabbagh, 2004). We still have much to discover about how children's inner capacities join with patterns of information in the environment to yield the phenomenal pace of semantic development.

Ask Yourself

Review Using your knowledge of phonological and semantic development, explain why "Mama" and "Dada" are usually among children's first words.

Apply Katy's first words included "see," "give," and "thank you," and her vocabulary grew slowly during the second year. What style of language learning did she display, and what factors might have contributed to it?

Apply At age 20 months, Nathan says "candy" when he sees buttons, pebbles, marbles, cough drops, and chocolate kisses. Are Nathan's naming errors random or systematic? Why are they an adaptive way of communicating?

Connect Explain how children's strategies for word learning support an interactionist perspective on language development.

Grammatical Development

Studying children's grammar requires that they use more than one word in an utterance. Researchers have puzzled over the following questions about grammatical development: Do children build a consistent grammar resembling that of adults relatively easily and quickly, or do they acquire complex forms little by little? Are language-specific strategies, general cognitive strategies, or both involved in children's progress? What is the role of adult teaching—in particular, corrective feedback for grammatical errors? As we chart the course of grammatical development, we will consider evidence on these issues.

First Word Combinations

Sometime between 1½ and 2½ years, as productive vocabulary approaches 200 words, children transition from word–gesture combinations to joining two words: "Mommy shoe," "go car," "more cookie." These two-word utterances are called **telegraphic speech** because, like a telegram, they focus on high-content words and omit smaller, less important ones, such as *can, the,* and *to.* For children learning languages that emphasize word order, such as English and French, endings like *-s* and *-ed* are not yet present. In languages in which word order is flexible and small grammatical markers are stressed, children's first sentences include them from the start (de Villiers & de Villiers, 1999).

Table 9.3 Common Meanings Expressed by Children's Two-Word Utterances

Meaning	Example
Agent–action	"Tommy hit"
Action–object	"Give cookie"
Agent–object	"Mommy truck" (meaning "Mommy, push the truck")
Action–location	"Put table" (meaning "Put X on the table")
Entity–location	"Daddy outside"
Possessor–possession	"My truck"
Attribution–entity	"Big ball"
Demonstrative–entity	"That doggie"
Notice–noticed object	"Hi mommy"; "Hi truck"
Recurrence	"More milk"
Nonexistence–nonexistent or disappeared object	"No shirt"; "No more milk"

Source: Brown, 1973.

Children the world over use two-word utterances to express a wide variety of meanings (see Table 9.3). Are they applying a consistent grammar? According to one view, a more complete, and perhaps adultlike, grammar lies behind these two-word sentences (Gleitman et al., 1988; Lidz, 2007; Valian, 1991, 2005). Indeed, children often use the same construction to express different propositions. For example, a child might say, "Mommy cookie" when he sees his mother eating a cookie and also when he wants her to give him a cookie. Perhaps the more elaborate structures are present in the child's mind, but because of limited space in working memory, he cannot yet produce the longer word string.

Consistent with this idea, children seem more knowledgeable about grammar in comprehension than in production (Lidz, 2007). In one study, 18- and 24-month-olds listened to grammatical sentences in which the article *the* preceded a noun, as well as three types of ungrammatical sentences: *the* was dropped, replaced by a nonsense word *(el),* or replaced by an alternate English word *(and),* as follows: *"Can you see the/and/el ball?"* (Kedar, Casasola, & Lust, 2006). When presented with video images of objects, toddlers of both ages oriented more quickly and more accurately toward the correct object following grammatical sentences. Similarly, when shown two videos—one in which a duck acts on a bunny, the other in which a bunny acts on a duck—2-year-olds looked longer at the video event that correctly matched a sentence containing a novel verb ("The duck *is gorping* the bunny") (see Figure 9.10) (Gertner, Fisher, & Eisengart, 2006). This suggests that 2-year-olds have some awareness of subject-verb-object word order, which they generalize to comprehension of new verbs.

But other researchers emphasize that toddlers' two-word sentences do not follow a consistent, flexible grammar but are largely made up of simple formulas, such as "more + *X*" and "eat + *X*," with many different words inserted in the *X* position. Toddlers rarely make gross word-order errors, such as saying "chair my" instead of "my chair." But their word-order regularities are usually copies of adult word pairings: "How about *more sandwich?*" or "Let's see if you can *eat the berries?*" (Tomasello & Brooks, 1999). When children entering the two-word phase were taught several noun and verb nonsense words (for example, *meek* for a doll and *gop* for a snapping action), they easily combined the new nouns with words they knew well, as in "more meek."

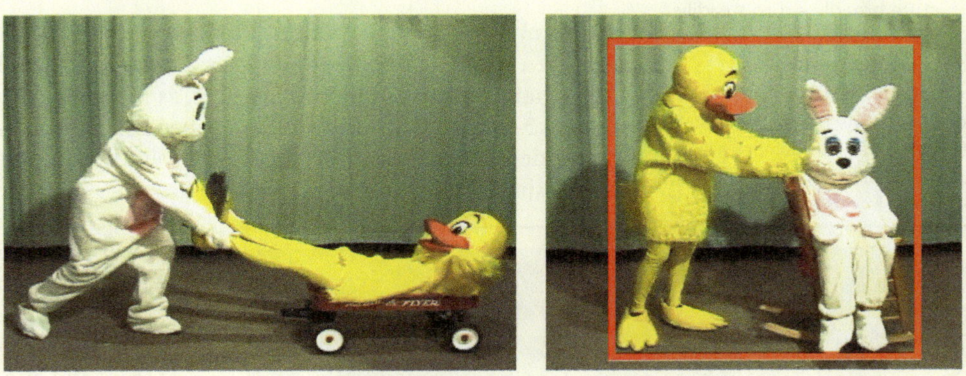

(a) "The duck is gorping the bunny!" (b)

Figure 9.10 Are English-learning 2-year-olds aware of subject–verb–object word order? Two-year-olds viewed two side-by-side videos accompanied by a sentence with a novel verb—for example, "The duck is *gorping* the bunny." They spent more time looking at the event that matched the sentence—in this case, the duck acting on the bunny rather than the bunny acting on the duck. Children as young as 21 months responded similarly, suggesting that they have some awareness of subject–verb–object word order. But because toddlers fail to use verbs flexibly in their earliest word combinations, this conclusion is controversial. (From Y. Gertner, C. Fisher, & J. Eisengart, 2006, "Learning Words and Rules: Abstract Knowledge of Word Order in Early Sentence Comprehension," *Psychological Science, 17,* p. 686. Reprinted by permission.)

But they seldom produced word combinations with the new verbs (Tomasello, 2000; Tomasello et al., 1997).

In contrast to the comprehension findings, toddlers' inability to use verbs flexibly in two-word utterances implies that they do not yet grasp subject–verb and verb–object relations—the foundation of English grammar. According to this alternative view, young children first acquire "concrete pieces of language" from frequent word pairings that they hear. Only gradually do they generalize from those pieces to construct the word-order and other grammatical rules of their native tongue (Tomasello, 2006).

From Simple Sentences to Complex Grammar

In the third year, three-word sentences appear in which English-speaking children clearly follow a subject–verb–object word order. Children learning other languages adopt the word orders of the adult speech to which they are exposed. For example, for "It is broken," a German child says, "*Kaputt ist der*" (literally, "Broken is it"). Between ages 2½ and 3, children create sentences in which adjectives, articles, nouns, verbs, and prepositional phrases start to conform to an adult structure, indicating that they have begun to master the grammatical categories of their language.

Nevertheless, studies of children acquiring diverse languages, including Dutch, English, Hebrew, Inuktitut (spoken by the Inuit of Arctic Canada), Italian, Portuguese, and Russian, reveal that their first use of grammatical rules is piecemeal—applied to only one or a few verbs, not across the board. As children listen for familiar verbs in adult discourse, they expand their own utterances containing those verbs, drawing on adult usage as their model (Allen, 1996; Gathercole, Sebastián, & Soto, 1999; Lieven, Pine, & Baldwin, 1997; Stoll, 1998). One child, for example, added the preposition *with* to the verb *open* ("You open with scissors") but not to the word *hit* ("He hit me stick").

Only gradually do preschoolers refine and generalize their early grammatical forms. In a number of investigations, English-learning children were tested for their ability to produce novel sentences that conformed to basic English syntax. They had to use a new verb in the subject–verb–object form after hearing it in a different construction, such as passive ("Ernie is getting *gorped* by the dog"). The percentage of children who performed well (when asked what the dog was doing, they responded, "He's gorping Ernie") rose steadily with age. But as Figure 9.11 shows, not until 3½ to 4 could the majority of children apply the fundamental subject–verb–object structure broadly, to newly acquired verbs (Tomasello, 2003, 2006).

■ Figure 9.11 Percentage of children in different studies who could use a new verb in the subject–verb–object form after hearing it in another construction. Each dot in the graph represents the findings of one study. The ability to use the new verb—an indicator of the child's capacity to apply the subject–verb–object structure broadly—rose steadily with age. Children mastered this fundamental grammatical construction gradually. (From M. Tomasello, 2000, "Do Young Children Have Adult Syntactic Competence?" *Cognition, 74*, p. 223. Reprinted with permission from Elsevier.)

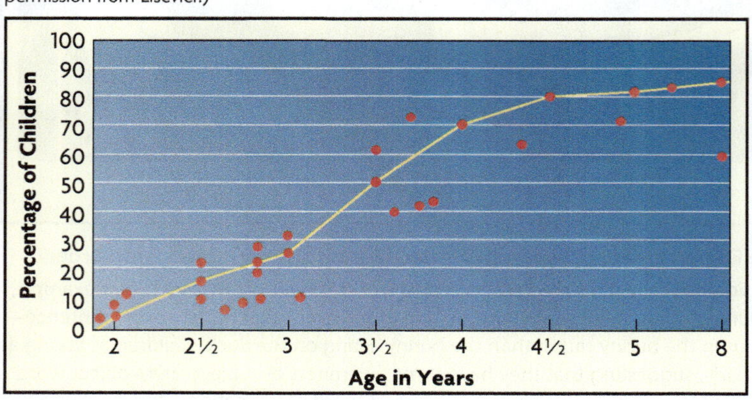

• Development of Grammatical Morphemes As the examples just cited illustrate, once children form three-word sentences, they add **grammatical morphemes**[1]—small markers that change the meaning of sentences, as in "John's dog" and "he *is* eating." English-speaking 2- and 3-year-olds acquire these morphemes in a regular sequence, shown in Table 9.4 (Brown, 1973; de Villiers & de Villiers, 1973). Given the difficulty of the task, however, their errors are surprisingly few (Maratsos, 1998).

What explains this sequence of development? Two characteristics of morphemes play important roles. The first is *structural complexity.* For example, adding the ending *-ing* or *-s* is structurally less complex than using forms of the verb *to be.* In the latter, the child must express correct tense and also make the subject and verb agree ("*I am* coming" versus "*They are* coming"). Second, grammatical morphemes differ in *semantic complexity,* or the number and difficulty of the meanings they express. Adding *-s* to a word requires only one semantic distinction—the difference between one and more than one. In contrast, using *to be* involves many more, including an understanding of person, number, and time of occurrence (Slobin, 1982).

[1]A *morpheme* is the smallest unit of meaning in speech; any further division violates the meaning or produces meaningless units. Both "dog" and "-s" are morphemes; "-s" is a *grammatical morpheme.*

Table 9.4 Order of Acquisition of English Grammatical Morphemes

Morpheme	Example
1. Verb present progressive ending ("-ing")	"He singing."
2. Preposition "on"	"On horsie."
3. Preposition "in"	"In wagon."
4. Noun plural ("-s")	"Cats."
5. Verb irregular past tense	"He ran." "It broke."
6. Noun possessive	"Daddy's hat."
7. Verb uncontractible "be" form used with adjective, preposition, or noun phrase	"Are kitties sleepy?"
8. Articles "a and "the"	"A cookie." "The bunny."
9. Verb regular past tense ending ("-ed")	"He kicked it."
10. Verb present tense, third person singular regular ending	"He likes it."
11. Verb present tense, third person singular irregular ending	"She has [from *have*] a cookie." "He does [from *do*] a good job."
12. Auxiliary verb uncontractible "be" forms	"Are you eating?"
13. Verb contractible "be" forms used with adjective, preposition, or noun phrase	"He's inside." "They're sleepy."
14. Auxiliary verb contractible "be" forms	"He's coming." "Doggie's eating."

Source: Brown, 1973.

Look again at Table 9.4, and you will see that some morphemes with irregular forms are acquired before those with regular forms. For example, children use past-tense irregular verbs, such as *ran* and *broke,* before they acquire the regular *-ed* ending. But once children apply a regular morphological rule, they extend it to words that are exceptions, a type of error called **overregularization.** Expressions like "My toy car *breaked*" and "We each have two *foots*" start to appear between 2 and 3 years of age and persist into middle childhood (Marcus et al., 1992). The extent to which children overregularize varies greatly across words, occurring less often on frequently used verbs. One 2½-year-old nearly always produced the irregular past tenses of *go* and *say*—"I *went* there," "I *said* that." For rarely used verbs, however, the error rate can be higher than 50 percent (Maratsos, 2000). This child frequently overregularized *grow* ("I *growed* tall") and *sing* ("She *singed* 'Jingle Bells'").

Why do children show this inconsistent pattern? Because they hear frequently used irregular forms often in adult speech, they probably learn those by rote memory. For less common irregulars, children alternate between correct and overregularized forms for many months or even several years. According to one view, as children hear more instances in others' speech, the irregular form eventually wins out (Elman, 2003; Maratsos, 2000). Return to page 365, and note how an artificial neural network's mastery of the past tense fits with this explanation. At times, however, preschoolers do overregularize frequently used exceptions, as when they say "ated," "felled," or "feets." In these instances, perhaps their memory for the irregular morpheme fails, so they call on the *–ed* rule, and overregularization results.

Development of Complex Grammatical Forms

Once children master the auxiliary verb *to be,* the door is open to a variety of new expressions. Negatives and questions are examples.

• **Negatives** Three types of negation appear in the following order in 2½- to 3-year-olds learning languages as different as Cantonese, English, and Tamil (spoken in India): (1) *nonexistence,* in which the child remarks on the absence of something ("No cookie," "All gone crackers"); (2) *rejection,* in which the child expresses opposition to something ("No take bath"); and (3) *denial,* in which the child denies the truthfulness of something ("That not my kitty") (Clancy, 1985; Tam & Stokes, 2001; Vaidyanathan, 1991).

These early constructions probably result from imitating parental speech. When parents express nonexistence or rejection, they often put *no* at the beginning of the sentence: "No

This 3-year-old, who is helping her mother sort freshly picked berries, is acquiring Bhoti, the language of her community in the Himalayan mountains of northern India. Like English-speaking preschoolers, she is likely to master yes/no questions before *wh-* questions, which are semantically and structurally more difficult. © Achim Pohl/Peter Arnold Inc.

more cookies" or "No, you can't have another cracker." Around 3 to 3½ years, as children add auxiliary verbs and become sensitive to the way they combine with negatives, correct negative forms appear: "There aren't any more cookies" (nonexistence), "I don't want a bath" (rejection), and "That isn't my kitty" (denial) (Tager-Flusberg & Zukowski, 2009).

• **Questions** Like negatives, questions first appear during the early preschool years and develop in an orderly sequence. English-speaking children, as well as those who speak many other languages, can use rising intonation to convert an utterance into a yes/no question: "Mommy baking cookies?" As a result, they produce such expressions quite early.

Correct question form in English requires that children invert the subject and auxiliary verb. In *wh-* questions—ones that begin with *what, where, which, who, when, why,* and *how*—the *wh-* word must also be placed at the beginning of the sentence. When first creating questions, 2-year-olds use many formulas: "Where's *X*?" "What's *X*?" "Can I *X*?" (Dabrowska, 2000; Tomasello, 1992, 2003). Preschoolers' question asking remains quite variable for a couple of years. A common error is to omit the auxiliary verb ("What he doing?"). Another is to fail to invert the subject and auxiliary verb when asking certain questions ("What she will do?" "Why he can go?") but not others ("How do you like it?" "What do you want?") (Rowland et al., 2005; Rowland & Pine, 2000) The correct expressions tend to be those that occur most often in caregivers' speech. And sometimes children produce errors in subject–auxiliary verb agreement ("Where does the dogs play?") and in subject case ("Where can me sit?"). These diverse errors are difficult to reconcile with the existence of a built-in universal grammar (Rowland, 2007). As with other grammatical constructions, children seem to produce accurate questions piecemeal and gradually.

Among English-, Korean-, and Tamil-speaking preschoolers, correct question form appears first for yes/no and later for *wh-* constructions (Clancy, 1989; Vaidyanathan, 1988). Among *wh-* questions, which are semantically and structurally more difficult, *what, where,* and *who* tend to precede *how, why,* and *when,* which are harder to understand and answer (de Villiers, 2000).

• **Other Complex Constructions** Between ages 3½ and 6, children produce more complex constructions, and their usage increasingly conforms to the rules of their language. First, connectives appear, joining whole sentences ("Mom picked me up, *and* we went to the park") and verb phrases ("I got up *and* ate breakfast"). The most general connective, *and,* is used first, followed by connectives expressing more specific meanings: *then* and *when* for temporal relations, *because* and *so* for causal relations, *if* for conditionals, and *but* for opposition (Bloom et al., 1980).

Later, children produce embedded sentences ("I think *he will come*"), tag questions ("Dad's going to be home soon, *isn't he?*"), indirect object–direct object structures ("He showed *his friend* the present"), and passive sentences ("The dog *was patted by* the girl"). As the preschool years draw to a close, children use most grammatical structures of their native language competently (Tager-Flusberg & Zukowski, 2009).

Later Grammatical Development

During the school years, children's mastery of complex constructions improves. The passive voice is an example. At all ages, children produce more abbreviated passive statements ("It got broken" or "They got lost") than full passives ("The glass was broken by Mary"). During middle childhood and early adolescence, children use the passive voice—including full passive statements—more often (Horgan, 1978).

Older children also apply the passive voice to a wider range of nouns and verbs. Preschoolers comprehend the passive best when the subject of the sentence is an animate being and the verb is an action word ("The *boy is kissed* by the girl"). Over the school years, children extend the passive form to inanimate subjects ("The *hat* was worn by the man") and experiential verbs ("The dog *was seen* by the cat") (Lempert, 1990; Pinker, Lebeaux, & Frost, 1987).

What accounts for this developmental trend? Recall that action is salient to young children in mastering vocabulary, a bias that may affect their mastery of complex grammar as well. But language input is also influential. English-speaking adults rarely use full and experiential passives in everyday conversation. In languages in which adults use these forms often, such as Inuktitut (spoken by the Inuit people), children produce them earlier (Allen & Crago, 1996). And exposure to adult speech containing a variety of passive-sentence types (as opposed to just one type) prompts 4- and 5-year-olds to produce more passive utterances (Savage et al., 2006). Varied input seems to foster a general representation of the passive construction.

Another later grammatical achievement is advanced understanding of infinitive phrases—the difference between "John is eager to please" and "John is easy to please" (Berman, 2007; Chomsky, 1969). Like gains in vocabulary, appreciation of these subtle grammatical distinctions in middle childhood and adolescence is supported by an improved capacity to analyze and reflect on language and to attend to multiple linguistic and situational cues.

Ideas About How Grammatical Development Takes Place

Preschoolers' mastery of most of the grammar of their language is an astounding feat. How to explain it is perhaps the most disputed issue in the study of language development.

• Strategies for Acquiring Grammar Evidence that grammatical development is an extended rather than a sudden process has raised questions about Chomsky's nativist account. Some experts have concluded that grammar is a product of general cognitive development—children's tendency to search for consistencies and patterns of all sorts (Bloom, 1999; MacWhinney, 2005; Maratsos, 1998; Tomasello, 2003). Yet among these theorists, debate continues over just how children master grammar.

According to one view, young children rely on other properties of language to detect basic grammatical regularities. In **semantic bootstrapping,** for example, they use word meanings to figure out sentence structure. Children might begin by grouping together words with "agent qualities" (things that cause actions) as *subjects* and words with "action qualities" as *verbs*. Then they merge these categories with observations of how words are used in sentences (Bates & MacWhinney, 1987; Braine, 1994). In this way, children lay down a basic grammatical framework, which they modify over time to account for exceptions. In some languages, however, semantic categories (such as "agent") and basic grammatical structures (such as "subject") do not match up—a major problem for semantic bootstrapping. In Tagalog, a language spoken in the Philippines, certain agents can be subjects, but others cannot. Yet Tagalog-speaking children acquire the main grammar of their language within a typical time frame (Maratsos, 1998).

Other theorists believe that children master grammar through direct observation of the structure of language: They notice which words appear in the same positions in sentences, take the same morphological endings, and are similarly combined with other words. Over time, they group words into grammatical categories and use them appropriately in sentences (Bloom, 1999; Chang, Dell, & Bock, 2006; Tomasello, 2003).

Still other theorists agree with the essence of Chomsky's position. One idea accepts semantic bootstrapping but proposes that the grammatical categories into which children group word meanings are innate—present at the outset (Pinker, 1989, 1999). Another theory holds that children do not start with innate knowledge but have a special *language-making capacity*—a set of procedures for analyzing the language they hear that supports the discovery of grammatical regularities. Research on children learning more than 40 different languages reveals common patterns, consistent with a basic set of strategies (Slobin, 1985, 1997). Yet controversy persists over whether a universal language-processing device exists or whether children who hear different languages devise unique strategies (Lidz, 2007; Marchman & Thal, 2005).

• Environmental Support for Grammatical Development Besides investigating the child's capacities, researchers have examined features of the language environment that might ease the task of mastering grammar. Previous research reported that although adults frequently correct children's mistaken inferences about word meaning ("That's not a bird, it's a butterfly"), they rarely provide direct feedback about grammar (Brown & Hanlon, 1970). Consequently, some researchers argue that adult instruction about how to correct grammatical errors is so minimal that children must have an innate language acquisition device that guides their acquisition of grammatical rules.

As this preschooler tells her father what she is cooking, he might expand her short sentences and recast them into grammatically correct form. Although researchers differ on the impact of this feedback, it does demonstrate good grammar and may encourage children to experiment with new forms. © Laura Dwight Photography

Yet parents often correct their child's grammatical errors *indirectly*—in ways that inform the child about conventional usage while keeping the conversation going. In a study in which three English-learning and two French-learning children were followed from ages 2 to 4, researchers coded thousands of utterances for errors in pronunciation, word choice, and grammar, along with parents' immediate responses and children's reactions to those responses (Chouinard & Clark, 2003). Findings revealed that parents reformulated as many as two-thirds of children's erroneous expressions—a rate that was similar across the error types and the five children.

Many adult reformulations inform children about grammar through two techniques, often used in combination: **recasts**—restructuring inaccurate speech into correct form; and **expansions**—elaborating on children's speech, increasing its complexity (Bohannon & Stanowicz, 1988). For example, if a child says, "I gotted new red shoes," the parent might respond, "Yes, you got a pair of new red shoes," *recasting* the incorrect features of the child's statement while also *expanding* its complexity. After such corrective input, 2- to 4-year-olds often shift to correct forms—improvements still evident several months later (Saxton, Backley, & Gallaway, 2005).

Other grammatical prompts ask children to clarify what they mean so interaction can continue. For example, when a 2½-year-old said, "I want hugging Ava," his mother queried, "What do you want?" In one study, such error-contingent clarifying questions led 2½-year-olds to shift from an incorrect to a correct form 16 percent of the time, 4-year-olds 34 percent of the time (Saxton, Houston-Price, & Dawson, 2005). Clarifying questions may encourage children to reflect on their utterances and apply what they know about correct grammar more consistently.

Nevertheless, the impact of such feedback has been challenged. The techniques are not used in all cultures and, in a few investigations, had no impact on children's grammar (Strapp & Federico, 2000; Valian, 1999). But in some societies, older siblings may take over the task of providing young children with feedback, and parents may do so in other, culturally prescribed ways. For example, on certain occasions, New Guinean Kaluli and Western Samoan adults tell children what to say by facing the child toward her listener, speaking for the child, and commanding, "*Elema,*" which means, "Say like that" (Ochs, 1988). Low-SES Western parents engage in similar practices (Hart & Risley, 1995).

In sum, virtually all investigators agree that young children are amazing processors of linguistic structure. But the extent to which factors in the language environment help them correct errors and take the next grammatical step forward remains a contested issue in child language research.

Ask Yourself

Review To what extent do children use a consistent grammar in their early two- and three-word utterances? Explain, using research evidence.

Apply Three-year-old Jason's mother told him that the family would take a vacation in Miami. The next morning, Jason announced, "I gotted my bags packed. When are we going to Your-ami?" How do language researchers explain Jason's errors?

Connect Provide several examples of how children's cognitive development influences their mastery of grammar.

Reflect Do you favor a nativist, an information-processing, or a social interactionist account of grammatical development, or some combination? Use research evidence to support your position.

Pragmatic Development

Besides mastering phonology, vocabulary, and grammar, children must learn to use language effectively in social contexts—by taking turns, staying on the same topic, stating their messages clearly, and conforming to cultural rules for interaction. During the preschool years, children make considerable headway in mastering the pragmatics of language.

Acquiring Conversational Skills

Young children are already skilled conversationalists. In face-to-face interaction, they make eye contact, respond appropriately to their partner's remarks, and take turns (Bloom et al., 1996; Pan & Snow, 1999). With age, the number of turns over which children can sustain interaction and their ability to maintain a topic over time increase, but even 2-year-olds converse effectively (Snow et al., 1996).

In early childhood, additional conversational strategies are added. In the **turnabout,** the speaker not only comments on what has just been said but also adds a request to get the partner to respond again. Because 2-year-olds cannot generate many words in each turn, they seldom use turnabouts, but children do so increasingly over the next few years (Goelman, 1986). Between ages 5 and 9, more advanced conversational strategies appear, such as **shading,** in which a speaker initiates a change of topic gradually by modifying the focus of discussion (Wanska & Bedrosian, 1985).

Effective conversation also depends on understanding **illocutionary intent**—what a speaker means to say, even if the form of the utterance is not perfectly consistent with it. By age 3, children comprehend a variety of requests for action not directly expressed as requests: "I need a pencil" or "Why don't you tickle me?" (Garvey, 1974). During middle childhood, illocutionary knowledge develops further. For example, an 8-year-old who has forgotten to do his chores understands that when his mother says, "The garbage is beginning to smell," she really means, "Take that garbage out!" (Ackerman, 1978). Appreciating form–intention pairings like this one requires children to make subtle inferences that are beyond preschoolers' cognitive capacities.

Still, surprisingly advanced conversational abilities are present early, and adults' patient, sensitive interactions with young children encourage and sustain them. Throughout this chapter, we have seen examples of how adult–child conversation fosters language development. Whether observed at home or in preschool, it is consistently related to general measures of language progress (Hart & Risley, 1995; NICHD Early Child Care Research Network, 2006). Dialogues about storybooks are particularly effective. They expose children to great breadth of language knowledge, including how to communicate in a clear, coherent narrative style—a skill that undoubtedly contributes to the association between joint storybook reading and literacy development (see Chapter 7, page 306).

Finally, the presence of a sibling enhances young children's conversational skills. Toddlers closely monitor conversations between their twin or older siblings and parents, and they often try to join in. When they do, these verbal exchanges last longer, with each participant taking more turns (Barton & Strosberg, 1997; Barton & Tomasello, 1991). As they listen to these conversations, younger siblings pick up important skills, such as use of personal pronouns ("I" versus "you"), which are more common in the early vocabularies of later-born than of first-born siblings (Pine, 1995). Furthermore, older siblings' remarks to a younger brother or sister often focus on regulating interaction: "Do you like Kermit?" "OK, your turn" (Oshima-Takane & Robbins, 2003). This emphasis probably contributes to younger siblings' conversational skills.

When this father exclaims, "Look at all these groceries!" his 9-year-old son comprehends the statement as an indirect request to help carry the bags inside. Understanding of illocutionary intent improves in middle childhood. © Peter Samuels/Getty Images/Photodisc

Communicating Clearly

To communicate effectively, we must produce clear verbal messages and must recognize when messages we receive are unclear so we can ask for more information. These aspects of language are called **referential communication skills.**

Typically, laboratory tasks designed to assess children's ability to communicate clearly present them with challenging situations in which they must describe to a listener one object among a group of similar objects. For example, in one study, 3- to 10-year-olds were shown several eight-object arrays. In each, the objects were similar in size, shape, and color. Most 3-year-olds gave ambiguous descriptions. When asked for clarification, they relied heavily on gestures, such as pointing (Deutsch & Pechmann, 1982). The ability to send clear messages improved steadily with age.

When preschoolers are given simpler tasks or engage in face-to-face interaction with familiar people, they adjust their speech to their listener's perspective quite well. **TAKE A MOMENT...** But try engaging a preschooler in conversation on the telephone,

■ **Figure 9.12** **Scene used to test for referential communication skills.**

When an adult instructed, "Put the frog on the book in the box," 4- and 5-year-olds could not resolve the ambiguity between the phrases "on the book" and "in the box." They stuck to their first inference and put one of the frogs on the empty book. Not until middle childhood can children integrate the two competing representations by selecting the frog on the book and placing it in the box. (Adapted from Hurewitz et al., 2000.)

jotting down what you and the child say. Here is an excerpt of one 4-year-old's phone conversation with his grandfather:

Grandfather: How old will you be?
John: Dis many. *[Holding up four fingers.]*
Grandfather: Huh?
John: Dis many. *[Again holding up four fingers.]* (Warren & Tate, 1992, pp. 259–260)

Young children's conversations appear less mature in highly demanding situations in which they cannot see their listeners' reactions or rely on typical conversational aids, such as gestures and objects to talk about. But when asked to tell a listener how to solve a simple puzzle, 3- to 6-year-olds give more specific directions over the phone than in person, indicating that they realize the need for more verbal description on the phone (Cameron & Lee, 1997). Between ages 4 and 8, both conversing and giving directions over the phone improve greatly. Telephone talk provides an excellent example of how preschoolers' communication skills depend on the demands of the situation.

Children's ability to evaluate the adequacy of messages they receive also improves with age. Around age 3, preschoolers start to ask others to clarify ambiguous messages. At first, children recognize when a message provides a poor description of a concrete object (Ackerman, 1993). Only later can they tell when a message contains inconsistencies. For example, when researchers showed 4- and 5-year-olds the scene in Figure 9.12 and instructed, "Put the frog on the book in the box," preschoolers could not resolve the ambiguity. Most put a frog on the empty book rather than in the box, even though they used similar embedded phrases in their own speech ("The frog *on the book* went to Mrs. Squid's house") (Hurewitz et al., 2000).

Notice how this task requires children to *inhibit* their attention from being drawn to the empty book in the scene, which increases the salience of the first part of the directive, "Put the frog *on the book.*" When asked to listen to the instruction with their back to the display, which temporarily blocked the scene's distracting features, almost all 4- and 5-year-olds processed the entire message and responded correctly (Meroni & Crain, 2003).

Narratives

Conversations with adults about past experiences contribute to dramatic gains in children's ability to produce well-organized, detailed, expressive narratives (see page 297 in Chapter 7). When asked to relate a personally important event, 4-year-olds typically produce brief renditions called *leapfrog narratives,* jumping from one event to another in a disorganized fashion. Between 4½ and 5, children start to produce *chronological narratives,* placing events in temporal sequence and building to a high point: "We went to the lake. We fished and waited. Paul waited, and he got a huge catfish." Around age 6, chronological narratives extend into *classic narratives,* in which children add a resolution: "After Dad cleaned the catfish, we cooked it and ate it all up!" (Peterson & McCabe, 1983).

Preschoolers' limited working memories are partly responsible for their restricted narratives. In addition, young children often presume more shared knowledge than their listener has, so they offer little orienting information about events, such as time, place, and participants. Preschoolers' narratives also contain few *evaluations*—comments about how and why events took place or about their own and others' thoughts, feelings, and intentions. During middle childhood, orienting information, detailed descriptions, and connectives that lend coherence to the story ("next," "then," "so," "finally") increase. And evaluative comments rise dramatically, becoming common by age 8 to 9 (Melzi & Ely, 2009; Ukrainetz et al., 2005). When parents use the elaborative strategy discussed in Chapter 7 to help young children construct narratives, preschoolers produce more organized, detailed, and evaluative personal stories (see page 297).

Like narrative, make-believe play requires children to organize events around a plot, constructing a connected, meaningful story line. Pretend-play and narrative competence support each other (Nicolopoulou, 2006). When 4-year-olds created narratives in a make-believe context ("Tell me a story using these toys"), they generated more complex, coherent stories than agemates who were directly prompted (Ilgaz & Aksu-Koç, 2005). The pretend props and actions served as powerful cues for narrative events, reducing memory demands during storytelling. And in a school program, 5- to 7-year-olds who participated in 14 weeks of joint adult–child dramatization of a work of children's literature showed greater gains in narrative development than agemates who merely listened to an adult read the story over 14 sessions, with no playacting (Baumer, Ferholt, & Lecusay, 2005).

Family mealtimes provide rich experiences in listening to and telling personal stories. When families regularly eat meals together, children are advanced in language and literacy development, perhaps because of their mastery of narrative.
© Digital Vision/Alamy Images

Because children pick up the narrative styles of parents and other significant adults in their lives, their narrative forms vary widely across cultures. As noted in Chapter 8, instead of relating a single experience from beginning to end, African-American children often use a *topic-associating style,* blending several similar anecdotes. As a result, their narratives are usually longer and more complex than those of North American white children (Champion, 2003b). Japanese children also connect events with a common theme, using a structure that resembles *haiku,* a culturally valued poetic form (Minami, 1996).

The ability to generate clear oral narratives contributes to literacy development, enhancing reading comprehension and preparing children for producing longer, more explicit written narratives. In families who regularly eat meals together, children are advanced in language and literacy development, perhaps because mealtimes offer many opportunities to listen to and relate personal stories (Beals, 2001).

Sociolinguistic Understanding

As early as the preschool years, children are sensitive to language adaptations to social expectations, known as **speech registers.** In one study, 4- to 7-year-olds were asked to act out roles with hand puppets. Even the youngest children showed that they understood the stereotypic features of different social positions. They used more commands when playing socially dominant and male roles, such as teacher, doctor, and father. When playing less dominant and feminine roles, such as student, patient, and mother, they spoke more politely and used more indirect requests (Andersen, 1992, 2000).

The importance of register adjustments is evident in how often parents teach social routines, such as politeness. Before infants can grasp the gesture's meaning, parents encourage them to wave "bye-bye." By age 2, when children fail to say "please" and "thank you," or "hi" and "good-bye," parents usually model and demand an appropriate response (Becker, 1990).

Some cultures have elaborate systems of polite language. In Japan, for example, politeness affects many aspects of verbal and nonverbal communication, which vary with gender, age, social status, and familiarity of speaker and listener. Japanese mothers and preschool teachers constantly model and teach these expressions, so children acquire a large repertoire of polite forms early in the preschool years (Nakamura, 2001). For example, when greeting customers in a make-believe store, even 1-year-olds use the greeting *"Irasshaimase!"* ("Welcome!"). Two- and 3-year-olds use more complicated polite speech, such as *"Mata oide-kudasai"* ("Please come again"). And 3- and 4-year-olds make considerable headway in acquiring the complex honorific/humble language of Japanese society, which is fully mastered in middle childhood.

As this Vietnamese 8-year-old converses with his grandmother, he uses the elaborate honorific system of his language that he began to master as a preschooler. Speaking deferentially to elders, who are high in social status, is expected in Vietnamese culture.
© blickwinkel/Alamy

Adolescence brings dramatic gains in capacity to adapt language style to social context, in part because teenagers enter many more situations than they did at younger ages. To succeed on the debate team, they must speak in a persuasive, well-organized, rapid-fire fashion. At work, they must respond to customers cheerfully and courteously. On a date, they must communicate with heightened sensitivity and intimacy. Greater skill at reflecting on the features of language and engaging in cognitive self-regulation also supports effective use of speech registers (Obler, 2008). Teenagers are far more likely than school-age children to practice what they want to say in an expected situation, review what they did say, and figure out how they could say it better.

Ask Yourself

Review Summarize findings indicating that adult–child conversations promote preschoolers' pragmatic skills as well as general language progress.

Apply What pragmatic skills are evident in Erin's utterances, presented in the introduction to this chapter? How did Erin's parents and brother encourage her pragmatic development?

Connect What cognitive advances contribute to the development of referential communication?

Reflect List examples of speech registers you use in daily life. What childhood experiences might have influenced your mastery of these registers?

Development of Metalinguistic Awareness

Consider the following exchange between a mother and her 4-year-old child:

Child: What's that?
Mother: It's a typewriter.
Child: [*frowning*] No, you're the typewriter, that's a typewrite. (Karmiloff-Smith et al., 1996)

This preschooler, conscious of word endings, expected *-er* to signify an animate agent, like *baker* or *dancer.* The child shows the beginnings of **metalinguistic awareness**—the ability to think about language as a system. Researchers have been especially interested in when metalinguistic awareness emerges and the role it plays in a variety of language-related accomplishments.

Around age 4, children know that word labels are arbitrary and not part of the objects to which they refer. When asked if an object could be called by a different name in a new language, they say "yes." They can also make some basic syntactic judgments—for example, that a puppet who says, "Nose your touch" or "Dog the pat," is saying his sentences backwards (Chaney, 1992). And by age 5, children have a good sense of the concept of "word." When an adult reading a story stops to ask, "What was the last word I said?" they almost always answer correctly for all parts of speech—they do not say "on-the-floor" instead of "floor" or "is-a" instead of "a" (Karmiloff-Smith et al., 1996). These early metalinguistic understandings are good predictors of vocabulary and grammatical development (Smith & Tager-Flusberg, 1982).

Nevertheless, full flowering of metalinguistic skills does not occur until middle childhood, as cognition advances and teachers point out features of language in reading and writing activities. Between ages 4 and 8, children make great strides in *phonological awareness* (Ehri et al., 2001). Whereas preschoolers are sensitive to rhyme and other changes in word sounds, third graders can identify all the phonemes in a word. Recall from Chapter 7 that phonological awareness strongly predicts reading progress. Around age 8, children can also judge the grammatical correctness of a sentence even if its meaning is false or senseless (Bialystok, 1986). And metalinguistic knowledge is evident in elementary school children's improved ability to define words and appreciate their multiple meanings in puns, riddles, and metaphors—skills that continue to improve in adolescence (Benelli et al., 2006).

As we will see next, bilingual children are advanced in metalinguistic awareness, as well as other cognitive skills. But before we conclude with this topic, refer to the Milestones table on page 394, which provides an overview of language development.

Bilingualism: Learning Two Languages in Childhood

Throughout the world, many children grow up *bilingual,* learning two languages, and sometimes more than two. Recall from Chapter 2 that both the United States and Canada have large immigrant populations. An estimated 15 percent of American children—6 million in all—speak a language other than English at home (U.S. Census Bureau, 2007b). Similarly, 13 percent of Canadian children—nearly 700,000—speak a language at home that is neither English nor French, the country's two official languages. In the French-speaking province of Quebec, 41 percent of the population are French–English bilinguals. In the remaining English-speaking provinces, the French–English bilingualism rate is about 10 percent (Statistics Canada, 2007f).

Children can become bilingual in two ways: (1) by acquiring both languages at the same time in early childhood, as Erin did; or (2) by learning a second language after mastering the first. Children of bilingual parents who teach them both languages in infancy and early childhood show no special problems with language development. From the start, they separate the language systems (see page 367), distinguishing their sounds, mastering equivalent words in each, and attaining early language milestones according to a typical timetable (Conboy & Thal, 2006; Genesee & Nicoladis, 2007; Holowka, Brosseau-Lapré, & Petitto, 2002). Preschoolers acquire normal native ability in the language of their surrounding community and good-to-native ability in the second language, depending on their exposure to it (Genesee, 2001). When school-age children acquire a second language after they already speak a first, they generally take five to seven years to attain verbal and academic skills on a par with those of native-speaking agemates (Paradis, 2007).

Like many bilingual adults, bilingual children sometimes engage in **code switching**—producing an utterance in one language that contains one or more "guest" words from the other—without violating the grammar of either language. Children may engage in code switching because they lack the vocabulary to convey a particular thought in one language, so they use the other. But children who code-switch the most are those whose parents often do so. Bilingual adults frequently code-switch to express cultural identity, and children may follow suit—as when a Korean child speaking English switches to Korean on mentioning her piano teacher, a sign of respect for authority (Chung, 2006).

Until recently, a widespread belief in the United States was that childhood bilingualism led to cognitive and linguistic deficits and a sense of personal rootlessness because the bilingual child was thought to identify only weakly with mainstream culture. This negative attitude has been fueled by ethnic prejudices because bilingualism in the United States is strongly associated with low-SES minority status.

A large body of research now shows that children who become fluent in two languages are actually advanced in cognitive development. Brain-imaging research reveals that individuals who acquire two languages earlier and to greater proficiency develop denser neuronal connections in language areas of the left hemisphere (Mechelli et al., 2004). Bilingual children outperform others on tests of selective attention, analytical reasoning, concept formation, and cognitive flexibility (Bialystok, 2001; Bialystok & Martin, 2004). They are also advanced in certain aspects of metalinguistic awareness, such as detection of errors in grammar and meaning. And children transfer their phonological awareness skills in one language to the other, especially if the two languages share phonological features and letter–sound correspondences, as Spanish and English do (Bialystok, McBride-Chang, & Luk, 2005; Snow & Kang, 2006). These capacities, as noted earlier, enhance reading achievement.

The advantages of bilingualism provide strong justification for bilingual education programs in schools. The Social Issues box on page 395 describes the vastly differing approaches to bilingual education in the United States and Canada. In both countries, however, many immigrant children do not receive support for their native language in classrooms. Currently, some schools are trying a new approach—*two-way bilingual programs,* in which children with limited proficiency in English who speak a common native language and children who are fluent in English are assigned in equal numbers to the same classroom. Teaching is aimed at helping all children become fluent in both languages and at increasing cross-cultural understanding (Padilla, 2006). The goal is to foster the linguistic, cognitive, and cultural enrichment of the entire nation.

Schoolchildren in Alberta, Canada, enjoy a Chinese New Year performance. Several come from Chinese-speaking homes and are bilingual—a capacity that enhances cognitive development and metalinguistic skills. © Edmonton Sun/ The Canadian Press (Darryl Dyck)

Milestones

Language Development

Age	Phonology	Semantics	Grammar	Pragmatics
Birth–1 year	▪ Has categorical speech perception ▪ Coos, then babbles ▪ Organizes speech sounds into phonemic categories of native language ▪ Babbles reflect sound and intonation patterns of native language	▪ Prefers to listen to mother's voice and to native language ▪ Analyzes speech stream for words and syllable stress patterns ▪ Recognizes familiar words ▪ Uses preverbal gestures 	▪ Notices the structure of word sequences, distinguishing ABA from ABB patterns ▪ Develops sensitivity to clause and phrase boundaries	▪ Establishes joint attention ▪ Engages in vocal exchanges and turn-taking games 
1–2 years	▪ Recognizes correct pronunciation of familiar words ▪ Uses systematic strategies to simplify word pronunciation	▪ Says first words ▪ Vocabulary grows to several hundred words	▪ Combines two words in telegraphic speech ▪ As three-word sentences appear, gradually adds grammatical morphemes	▪ Engages in conversational turn taking and topic maintenance
3–5 years	▪ Phonological awareness increases ▪ Pronunciation improves greatly 	▪ Coins words to fill in for words not yet mastered ▪ Understands metaphors based on concrete, sensory comparisons	▪ Gradually generalizes grammatical forms ▪ Continues to add grammatical morphemes in a regular order ▪ Gradually produces complex grammatical structures	▪ Masters additional conversational strategies, such as the turnabout ▪ Begins to grasp illocutionary intent ▪ Adjusts speech to listener's perspective and to social expectations ▪ Asks for clarification of ambiguous messages ▪ Produces chronological narratives
6–10 years	▪ Phonological awareness extends to all phonemes in a word ▪ Masters syllable stress patterns signaling subtle differences in meaning	▪ At school entry, has a vocabulary of about 10,000 words ▪ Grasps meanings of words on the basis of definitions ▪ Appreciates the multiple meanings of words, as indicated by metaphors and humor	 ▪ Refines complex grammatical structures, such as the passive voice and infinitive phrases	▪ Uses advanced conversational strategies, such as shading ▪ Continues to refine understanding of illocutionary intent ▪ Communicates clearly in demanding situations, such as on the telephone ▪ Produces classic narratives rich in orienting information and evaluations
11 years–adulthood	 ▪ Masters syllable stress patterns of abstract words	▪ Has a vocabulary of over 40,000 words that includes many abstract terms. ▪ Understands subtle, nonliteral word meanings, as in sarcasm, irony, and proverbs	▪ Continues to refine complex grammatical structures	▪ Ability to communicate clearly and in accordance with social expectations in diverse situations improves

Note: These milestones represent overall age trends. Individual differences exist in the precise age at which each milestone is attained.

Photos: (top left and middle) © Laura Dwight Photography; (top right) © Laura Dwight/PhotoEdit; (bottom left) © Tony Freeman/PhotoEdit; (bottom right) © Laura Dwight Photography

▪ Social Issues ▪

Two Approaches to Bilingual Education: Canada and the United States

Canadian national education policies actively promote bilingual education. Children with an official minority-language background (French in the English-speaking provinces, English in French-speaking Quebec) have the right to elementary and secondary education in their respective languages. In addition, schools are encouraged to provide programs that maintain the languages and cultures of immigrants to Canada and also to promote First Nations languages. Although such programs are in short supply, funding for them is increasing. Overall, Canada places a high value on bilingual education that enhances minority children's native-language competence.

Nationally, French–English bilingualism has increased by 12 percent since the mid-1990s (Statistics Canada, 2007f). A major reason is Canada's *language immersion programs,* in which English-speaking elementary school children are taught entirely in French for several years. Currently, about 7 percent of Canadian elementary school students are enrolled. The immersion strategy succeeds in developing children who are proficient in both languages, and who, by grade 6, achieve as well in reading, writing, and math as their counterparts in the regular English program (Harley & Jean, 1999; Holobow, Genesee, & Lambert, 1991; Turnbull, Hart, & Lapkin, 2003). The Canadian government is taking steps to expand language immersion opportunities, in hopes of increasing the percentage of 15- to 19-year-olds who speak both English and French from one-fourth to one-half in the coming decade (Government of Canada, 2004).

In this English–Spanish bilingual classroom, children's first and second languages are both integrated into the curriculum. As a result, the children are more involved in learning, participate more actively in class discussions, and acquire the second language more easily. © Robin Sachs/PhotoEdit

In the United States, fierce disagreement exists over how to educate minority children with limited English proficiency. Some believe that time spent communicating in the child's native tongue detracts from English-language achievement, which is crucial for success in the worlds of school and work. Other educators, committed to developing minority children's native language while fostering mastery of English, note that providing instruction in the native tongue lets minority children know that their heritage is respected. It also prevents inadequate proficiency in both languages. Minority children who gradually lose their first language as a result of being taught the second end up limited in both languages for a time (Ovando & Collier, 1998). This circumstance leads to serious academic difficulties and is believed to contribute to the high rates of school failure and dropout among low-SES Hispanic young people, who make up 50 percent of the U.S. language-minority population.

At present, public opinion and educational practice favor English-only instruction. Many U.S. states have passed laws declaring English to be their official language, creating conditions in which schools have no obligation to teach minority students in languages other than English. Yet in classrooms where both languages are integrated into the curriculum, minority children are more involved in learning, participate more actively in class discussions, and acquire the second language more easily. In contrast, when teachers speak only in a language that children can barely understand, minority children display frustration, boredom, and withdrawal (Crawford, 1997).

Supporters of U.S. English-only education often point to the success of Canadian language immersion programs, in which classroom lessons are conducted in the second language. But Canadian parents enroll their children in immersion classrooms voluntarily, and both French and English are majority languages that are equally valued in Canada. Furthermore, teaching in the child's native language is merely delayed, not ruled out. For U.S. non–English-speaking minority children, whose native languages are not valued by the larger society, a different strategy seems necessary: one that promotes children's native-language skills while they learn English.

Ask Yourself

Review Explain why metalinguistic awareness expands greatly in middle childhood. What might account for bilingual children's advanced metalinguistic skills?

Apply Reread the examples of Erin's language at the beginning of this chapter. Were Marilyn and Oscar wise to teach Erin both English and Spanish? Does Erin's mixing of the two languages indicate confusion? Justify your answers with research findings.

Reflect Did you acquire a second language at home or study one in school? If so, when did you begin, and how proficient are you in the second language? Considering research on bilingualism, what changes would you make in your second-language learning, and why?

SUMMARY

Components of Language

What are the four components of language?

- Language consists of four subsystems that children combine into a flexible communication system: (1) **phonology,** the rules governing the structure and sequence of speech sounds; (2) **semantics,** the way underlying concepts are expressed in words; (3) **grammar,** consisting of **syntax,** the rules by which words are arranged in sentences, and **morphology,** markers that vary word meaning; and (4) **pragmatics,** the rules for engaging in appropriate and effective conversation.

Theories of Language Development

Describe and evaluate three major theories of language development.

- The *behaviorist* perspective, which proposes that language is learned through operant conditioning and imitation, has difficulty accounting for the speed of language progress and for children's novel, rule-based utterances.
- Chomsky's *nativist* perspective proposes a **language acquisition device** (LAD) containing a **universal grammar,** or storehouse of rules that apply to all languages. The LAD permits children, once they have sufficient vocabulary, to speak grammatically and comprehend sentences in any language to which they are exposed. Consistent with Chomsky's ideas, chimpanzees' comprehension of grammar does not exceed that of a human 2-year-old; a complex language system is unique to humans.
- The roles of **Broca's area** in grammatical processing and language production and **Wernicke's area** in comprehending word meaning are more complicated than previously assumed. But the broad association of language functions, especially grammatical competence, with left-hemispheric regions of the cerebral cortex is consistent with Chomsky's notion of a brain prepared to process language. Evidence for a sensitive period of language development also supports the nativist view that language has unique biological properties.
- Researchers have challenged the nativist perspective on several grounds, including the difficulty of specifying a universal grammar underlying the widely varying grammatical systems of human languages. Also, children's continuous, gradual mastery of many constructions is inconsistent with the nativist assumption of innately determined grammatical knowledge.
- According to the *interactionist* perspective, language development results from exchanges between inner predispositions and environmental influences. The most influential information-processing accounts are connectionist, or artificial neural network, models, which show that powerful, general cognitive capacities are sufficient to detect certain linguistic patterns. Other evidence confirms that babies are extraordinary statistical analyzers of the sound stream who identify basic language patterns with the same strategies they use to understand nonlinguistic experiences.
- Social interactionist theorists believe that children's social skills and language experiences combine with native capacity to profoundly affect language development. But debate continues over whether children make sense of their complex language environments by applying general cognitive capacities or capacities specially tuned to language.

Prelinguistic Development: Getting Ready to Talk

Describe receptivity to language, development of speech sounds, and conversational skills during infancy.

- From birth, infants are prepared to acquire language. Newborns are capable of **categorical speech perception** but sensitive to a wider range of **phonemes** than children and adults. Between 6 and 8 months, infants start to organize speech into the phonemic categories of their own language. In the second half of the first year, they have begun to analyze the internal structure of sentences and words. Adults' use of **child-directed speech (CDS)** eases children's task of making sense of language.
- Infants begin **cooing** around 2 months, **babbling** around 6 months. Over the first year, the range of babbled sounds expands. Then, as infants get ready to talk, sound and intonation patterns start to resemble those of the child's native language. Certain patterns of babbles appear in particular contexts, suggesting that infants are experimenting with the semantic function of language.
- Conversational behavior emerges in the first few months as infants and caregivers establish **joint attention,** and the adult comments on what the baby sees. Early interactions involve give-and-take; by the end of the first year, babies become active participants in turn-taking games and use two preverbal gestures, the **protodeclarative** and the **protoimperative,** to influence others' behavior. Once words are uttered, gestures diminish as children make the transition to verbal communication. By the second year, caregiver–child interaction contributes greatly to language progress.

Phonological Development

Describe the course of phonological development.

- First words are influenced partly by the sounds children can pronounce. When learning to talk, children experiment with sounds, sound patterns, and speech rhythms. Because associating new words with their referents taxes toddlers' working memories, they tend to miss the fine details of a new word's sounds, which contributes to early pronunciation errors.
- Young children apply systematic phonological strategies to simplify challenging pronunciations. Gradually, they refine minimal words into full words with correct stress patterns. As the vocal tract matures and preschoolers engage in active problem solving, pronunciation improves greatly. But syllable stress patterns signaling subtle differences in meaning are not mastered until middle childhood or adolescence.

Semantic Development

Describe the course of semantic development, noting individual differences.

- Vocabulary increases rapidly in early childhood; language **comprehension** develops ahead of **production.** First words build on early cognitive and emotional foundations. For most children, the pace of vocabulary development increases steadily and continuously from toddlerhood through the preschool years. To build vocabulary quickly, children engage in **fast-mapping.**

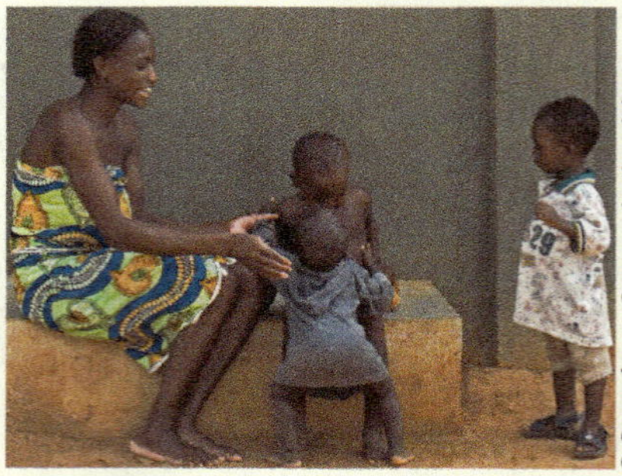

© Greenshoots Communications/Alamy

- Girls show faster early vocabulary growth than boys, and temperamentally shy or negative toddlers acquire language more slowly than other children. Low-SES children, who experience less verbal stimulation, usually have smaller vocabularies. Most toddlers use a **referential style** of language learning; their early words mainly refer to objects. Some use an **expressive style,** producing more social formulas and pronouns.
- Early vocabularies typically emphasize object words; action and state words appear soon after. When first learning words, children make errors of **underextension** and **overextension.** Word coinages and metaphors enable children to expand the range of meanings they can express.
- Reading contributes enormously to vocabulary growth in middle childhood, which exceeds that of early childhood. School-age children can grasp word meanings from definitions, and comprehension of metaphor and humor expands. Adolescents' ability to reason abstractly leads to an enlarged vocabulary and to appreciation of subtle meanings, as in irony, sarcasm, and figurative language.

Discuss ideas about how semantic development takes place, including the influence of memory and strategies for word learning.

- A special part of working memory, a **phonological store** that permits retention of speech-based information, supports young children's vocabulary growth. After age 5, semantic knowledge influences how quickly children form phonological traces, and both factors affect vocabulary.

- Children figure out the meanings of words by contrasting them with words they already know and assigning new words to gaps in their vocabulary. According to one view, a **mutual exclusivity bias** explains how children acquire early words. A **shape bias** is evident in toddlers' learning of nouns. Preschoolers engage in **syntactic bootstrapping,** observing how words are used in syntax to figure out their meanings. They also make use of the rich social information adults provide when introducing new words.
- Intense disagreement exists over whether children are innately biased to detect word meanings or whether they use the same cognitive strategies they apply to nonlinguistic stimuli. The **emergentist coalition model** proposes that word-learning strategies emerge out of children's efforts to decipher language. Children draw on a coalition of cues—perceptual, social, and linguistic—which shift in importance with age.

Grammatical Development

Describe the course of grammatical development.

- Between 1½ and 2½ years, children combine two words to express a variety of meanings—utterances known as **telegraphic speech** because they leave out less important words. These early combinations probably do not follow a consistent grammar. As children generate three-word sentences, they use grammatical rules in a piecemeal fashion, gradually refining and generalizing structures.
- English-speaking children add **grammatical morphemes** in a consistent order that reflects both structural and semantic complexity. Once children acquire a regular morphological rule, they **overregularize,** extending it to words that are exceptions, especially rarely used irregular words. Over time, children master expressions based on auxiliary verbs, such as negatives and questions. Between ages 3½ and 6, they add a variety of complex constructions. Certain forms, such as the passive voice and infinitive phrases, continue to be refined in middle childhood.

Discuss ideas about how grammatical development takes place, including strategies and environmental supports for mastering new structures.

- Some experts believe grammar is a product of general cognitive development. According to one view, children rely on other properties of language to figure out basic grammatical regularities. In **semantic bootstrapping,** they use word meanings to figure out sentence structure. Others believe children master grammar through direct observation of language structure. Still others agree with the essence of Chomsky's theory. One idea accepts semantic bootstrapping but proposes that grammatical categories are innate. Another speculation is that children have a built-in set of procedures for analyzing language, which supports the discovery of grammatical regularities.
- While conversing with children, adults provide indirect feedback about grammatical errors by asking for clarification or by restructuring their speech using **recasts** and **expansions.** However, the impact of such feedback on grammatical development has been challenged.

Pragmatic Development

Describe the course of pragmatic development, including social influences.

- Even 2-year-olds are effective conversationalists—early skills that are fostered by caregiver–child interaction. Strategies that help sustain interaction, such as **turnabout** and **shading,** are added in early and middle childhood. Children's understanding of **illocutionary intent** also improves, and they also acquire more effective **referential communication skills.**

- From the preschool to school years, children produce more organized, detailed, and evaluative narratives, which vary widely in form across cultures. The ability to generate clear oral narratives contributes to literacy development. Preschoolers are already sensitive to **speech registers.** Parents tutor young children in politeness routines, emphasizing the importance of adapting language to social expectations.

Development of Metalinguistic Awareness

Describe the development of metalinguistic awareness, noting its influence on language and literacy skills.

- Preschoolers show the beginnings of **metalinguistic awareness.** Their understandings are good predictors of vocabulary and grammatical development and, in the case of phonological awareness, literacy development. Major advances in metalinguistic skills take place in middle childhood.

Bilingualism: Learning Two Languages in Childhood

What are the advantages of bilingualism in childhood?

- Children who learn two languages in early childhood separate the language systems from the start and acquire each according to a typical timetable. When school-age children acquire a second language after mastering the first, they take five to seven years to attain the competence of native-speaking agemates. Bilingual children sometimes engage in **code switching** between the two languages. Bilingual children are advanced in cognitive development and metalinguistic awareness—advantages that provide strong justification for bilingual education programs in schools.

IMPORTANT TERMS AND CONCEPTS

10

"Astonished Girl"
Jana Stuck
9 years, Germany

School-age children become increasingly aware of subtleties in emotional expression, including the rapid escalation of surprise that culminates in astonishment. Cognitive development and opportunities to talk about feelings contribute to advances in emotional understanding.

Emotional Development

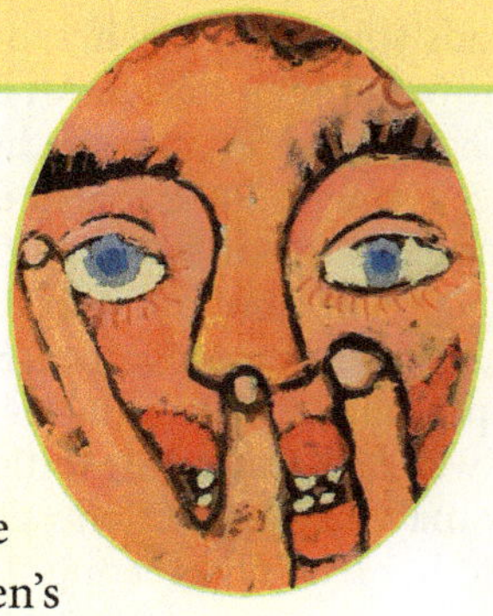

On a spring day, 4-month-old Zach, cradled in his father's arms, arrived at the door of my classroom, which had been transformed into a playroom for the morning. Behind him, led by their mothers, came 13-month-old Emily and 23-month-old Brenda. My students and I spent the next hour watching the three children closely. Especially captivating were the children's emotional reactions to people and objects. Zach grinned gleefully as his dad lifted him in the air, and he responded with an excited giggle to a tickle followed by a lively kiss on the tummy. When I offered Zach a rattle, his brows knit, his face sobered, and he eyed the rattle intently as he mobilized all his energies to reach for it.

Transferred to my arms and then to the laps of several students, Zach remained at ease (although he reserved a particularly broad smile for his father). In contrast, Emily and Brenda were wary of this roomful of strangers. When I held out a toy and coaxed Emily toward it, she pulled back and glanced at her mother, as if to check whether the new adult and tantalizing object were safe to explore. But when her mother encouraged her, Emily approached cautiously and accepted the toy. A greater capacity to understand the situation, along with her mother's explanations, helped Brenda adjust, and soon she was engrossed in play. During the hour, Brenda displayed a wide range of emotions, including embarrassment at seeing chocolate on her chin in a mirror and pride as I remarked on the tall block tower she had built.

Emotional development—formerly overshadowed by cognition—is an exciting, rapidly expanding area of research. Our discussion opens with the functions of emotions in all aspects of human activity. Next, we chart age-related gains in children's emotional expression and understanding. As we do so, we will account for Zach, Emily, and Brenda's expanding emotional capacities. Our attention then turns to individual differences in temperament and personality. We will examine biological and environmental contributions to these differences and their consequences for future development. Finally, we look at attachment to the caregiver, the infant's first affectionate tie. We will see how the feelings of security that grow out of this bond support the child's exploration, sense of independence, and expanding social relationships.

Functions of Emotions

TAKE A MOMENT... Think back over the past day or so. Do you recall feeling happy, sad, fearful, or angry in response to a grade on a test or a conversation with a friend? These events trigger emotion because you care about their outcomes. Your **emotion** is a rapid appraisal of the personal significance of the situation, which prepares you for action. For example, happiness leads you to approach, sadness to passively withdraw, fear to actively move away, and anger to overcome obstacles. An emotion, then, expresses your readiness to establish, maintain, or change your relation to the environment on a matter of importance to you (Campos, Frankel, & Camras, 2004; Saarni et al., 2006).

A number of theorists take a **functionalist approach to emotion,** emphasizing that the broad function of emotions is to energize behavior aimed at attaining personal goals (Barrett & Campos, 1987; Campos, Frankel, & Camras, 2004; Frijda, 2000; Saarni et al., 2006). Events can become personally relevant in several ways. First, you may already have a goal in mind, such as doing well on a test, so the testing situation prompts strong emotion. Second, others' social behavior may alter a situation's significance for you, as when a friend visits and you respond warmly to her friendly greeting. Third, any sensation or state of mind—a sight, sound, taste, smell, touch, memory, or imagining—can become personally relevant and evoke emotion, positive or negative. Your emotional reaction, in turn, affects your desire to repeat the experience.

In each case, emotions arise from ongoing exchanges between the person and the environment, flexibly serving different functions as the individual's circumstances change. Functionalist theorists believe that emotions are central in all our endeavors—cognitive processing, social behavior, and even physical health (Halle, 2003). Let's see how emotions organize and regulate experiences in each domain.

Seventeen-year-old Mao Asada of Japan exemplifies the impact of anxiety on cognitive processing during her winning performance at the 2008 World Figure Skating Championships. She suffered a hard fall from a difficult jump just moments into her program but then arose and skated flawlessly to take the gold medal. She later explained that she fell because she felt "extremely nervous," but the crash reduced her anxiety, enabling her to focus. AP Photo/Ahn Young-Joon

Emotions and Cognitive Processing

Emotional reactions can lead to learning that is essential for survival. For example, a caregiver's highly charged "No!" is sufficient to keep most newly walking toddlers from touching an electric outlet or careening down a staircase. The toddler need not experience a shock or a fall to avoid these dangers.

The emotion–cognition relationship is evident in the impact of anxiety on performance. Among children and adults, very high or very low anxiety impairs thinking, but moderate anxiety can be facilitating (Sarason, 1980). Emotions can also powerfully affect memory. For example, preschool and school-age children who were highly upset by an inoculation at the doctor's office tended to remember the event more clearly than their less stressed agemates (Goodman et al., 1991). Similarly, 3- and 4-year-olds' recall of a hurricane that damaged their home was far more detailed than their recall of a nontraumatic one-time event, such as a family trip to Disney World (Bahrick et al., 1998; Fivush, 1998). And as with the anxiety–performance relationship, children experiencing the storm under moderate stress (trees falling, windows breaking) remembered more than children experiencing high stress (roofs caving in, objects flying) or low stress (little home damage).

The relationship between emotion and cognition is bidirectional—a dynamic interplay already under way in early infancy (Lewis, 1999). In one study, researchers taught 2- to 8-month-olds to pull a string to activate pleasurable sights and sounds. As the infants learned the task, they responded with interest, happiness, and surprise. Then, for a short period, pulling the string no longer turned on the attractive stimuli. The babies' emotional reactions quickly changed—mostly to anger but occasionally to sadness. Once the contingency was restored, the infants who had reacted angrily showed renewed interest and enjoyment, whereas the sad babies turned away (Lewis, Sullivan, & Ramsay, 1992). Emotions were interwoven with cognitive processing, serving as outcomes of mastery and as the energizing force for continued involvement and learning.

Emotions and Social Behavior

Children's emotional signals, such as smiling, crying, and attentive interest, powerfully affect the behavior of others. Similarly, the emotional reactions of others regulate children's social behavior.

Careful analyses of caregiver–infant interaction reveal that by 3 months, a complex communication system is in place in which each partner responds in an appropriate and carefully timed fashion to the other's cues (Weinberg et al., 1999). In several studies, researchers disrupted this exchange of emotional signals by having the parent assume either a still-faced, unreactive pose or a depressed emotional state. Infants tried facial expressions, vocalizations, and body movements to get the parent to respond again. When these efforts failed, they turned away, frowned, and cried (Moore, Cohn, & Campbell, 2001; Papousek, 2007). The still-face reaction occurs only when natural human communication is disrupted (not to a still-faced doll or to the mother wearing a still-faced mask), and it is identical in American, Canadian, and Chinese babies—suggesting that it may be a built-in withdrawal response to caregivers' lack of communication (Kisilevsky et al., 1998; Legerstee & Markova, 2007). Clearly, when engaged in face-to-face interaction, even young infants expect their partners to be emotionally responsive. To learn more about the impact of parental depression on children's emotional and social adjustment, consult the From Research to Practice box on pages 402–403.

With age, emotional expressions become deliberate means through which infants communicate, and babies monitor the emotional expressions of others to assess their intentions and perspectives. For example, mothers initiate nearly all positive emotional exchanges with young babies. But by 9 months, infants become initiators, smiling before their mother smiles (Cohn & Tronick, 1987). Furthermore, recall from Chapter 9 that by the end of the first year, babies become increasingly skilled at *joint attention*—following the caregiver's line of regard (see page 369). In these joint attentional episodes, infants and toddlers pick up not only verbal information but also emotional information. Later in this chapter, we will see that when faced with unfamiliar people, objects, or events, older infants pay close attention to their caregiver's affect, using it as a guide for how to respond. Through this checking of others' emotions, called *social referencing,* young children learn how to behave in a great many everyday situations. One 18-month-old, on first witnessing his newborn sister cry, monitored his mother's reaction. On subsequent occasions, he patted the baby and comforted, "No, no, Peach [her nickname], no tears."

Emotions and Health

Much research indicates that emotions influence children's physical well-being. In Chapter 5, we discussed two childhood growth disorders—*nonorganic failure to thrive* and *psychosocial dwarfism*—that result from emotional deprivation. Many other studies indicate that persistent psychological stress, manifested in anxiety, depressed mood, anger, and irritability, is associated with a variety of health difficulties from infancy to adulthood. For example, stress elevates heart rate and blood pressure and depresses the immune response—reactions that may explain its relationship with cardiovascular disease, infectious illness, and several forms of cancer. Stress also reduces digestive activity as blood flows to the brain, heart, and extremities to mobilize the body for action. Consequently, it can lead to gastrointestinal difficulties, including constipation, diarrhea, colitis, and ulcers (Antoni & Lutgendorf, 2007; Ray, 2004). And stress not only induces illness but results from it—a feedback loop that can cause both to worsen over time.

In a dramatic demonstration of the emotion–health relationship, researchers followed children adopted into Canadian homes who had been exposed to chronic stress as a result of at least 8 months of early rearing in extremely depleted Romanian orphanages, where they lacked adult attention and stimulation and suffered from infectious and dietary diseases—most commonly, intestinal parasites, hepatitis, and anemia. Compared with healthy agemates who had been adopted shortly after birth, these physically ill, emotionally deprived children showed extreme reactivity to stress, as indicated by high concentrations of the stress hormone *cortisol* in their saliva—a physiological response linked to persistent illness and learning and behavior problems, including deficits in concentration and control of anger and other impulses. The longer the children spent in orphanage care, the higher their cortisol levels, even six and a half years after adoption (Gunnar et al., 2001; Gunnar & Cheatham, 2003). In other investigations,

▪ *From* Research *to* Practice ▪

Parental Depression and Child Development

About 8 to 10 percent of women experience *chronic depression*—mild to severe feelings of sadness, distress, and withdrawal that continue for weeks or months. Often, the beginnings of this emotional state cannot be pinpointed; it simply becomes a part of the person's daily life. In other instances, depression emerges or strengthens after childbirth but fails to follow the usual pattern of subsiding as the new mother adjusts to hormonal changes in her body and gains confidence in caring for her baby.

Although less common than maternal depression—and less recognized and studied—fathers, too, experience chronic depression. About 3 to 5 percent report symptoms after the birth of a child (Madsen & Juhl, 2007; Spector, 2006). Either maternal or paternal depression can interfere with effective parenting and seriously impair children's development. Genetic makeup affects an individual's risk of depressive illness, but social and cultural factors are also involved (Swendsen & Mazure, 2000).

Maternal Depression

During Julia's pregnancy, her husband, Kyle, showed so little interest in the baby that Julia worried that having a child might be a mistake. Then, shortly after Lucy was born, Julia's mood plunged. She felt anxious and weepy, overwhelmed by Lucy's needs, and angry that she no longer had control over her own schedule. When Julia approached Kyle about her own fatigue and his unwillingness to help with the baby, he snapped that she was overreacting. Julia's childless friends stopped by just once to see Lucy but did not call again.

Julia's depressed mood quickly affected her baby. In the weeks after birth, infants of depressed mothers sleep poorly, are less attentive to their surroundings, and have elevated levels of the stress hormone cortisol (Field, 1998). The more extreme the depression and the greater the number of stressors in a mother's life (such as marital discord, lack of social support, and poverty), the more the parent–child relationship suffers (Simpson et al., 2003). Julia, for example, rarely smiled at, comforted, or talked to Lucy, who responded to her mother's sad, vacant gaze by turning away, crying, and often looking sad or angry herself (Herrera, Reissland, & Shepherd, 2004; Stanley, Murray, & Stein, 2004). Julia, in turn, felt guilty and inadequate, and her depression deepened. By age 6 months, Lucy showed mental and emotional symptoms common in babies of depressed mothers—delays in

This depressed mother appears overwhelmed and unresponsive to her infant. If her disengagement continues, the baby is likely to become negative and irritable and, eventually, withdrawn. Over time, this disruption in the parent–child relationship leads to serious emotional and behavior problems. © Janine Wiedel PhotoLibrary/Alamy

orphanage children displayed abnormally low cortisol—a blunted physiological stress response that may be the central nervous system's adaptation to earlier, frequent cortisol elevations (Carlson & Earls, 1997; Gunnar & Vasquez, 2000). Extremely low cortisol interferes with release of growth hormone (GH) and, thus, can stunt children's physical growth.

Fortunately, sensitive adult care helps normalize cortisol production in both typically developing and emotionally traumatized infants and young children. Good parenting seems to protect the young brain from the potentially damaging effects of both excessive and inadequate stress-hormone exposure (Gunnar & Quevedo, 2007; Tarullo & Gunnar, 2006). In one study, researchers devised a special intervention for difficult-to-manage preschoolers with disrupted home lives. Over several months, a therapist worked with the children in a weekly playgroup, and their foster parents received extensive social support and coaching in parenting skills. After five weeks, the children's abnormally high cortisol levels declined, as did their behavior problems (Fisher et al., 2000). In contrast, children in regular foster care who received no intervention showed a rise in both cortisol production and difficult behaviors. Over time, adopted orphanage children's cortisol production also moves toward typical levels, and growth and behavior problems lessen (Fisher et al., 1997; Gunnar & Vasquez, 2001). Nevertheless, as we will see later, many institutionalized children adopted after age 6 to 8 months suffer from serious, lasting adjustment difficulties.

Other Features of the Functionalist Approach

In addition to the vital role of emotions in cognitive, social, and physical development, functionalist theorists point out that emotions contribute to the emergence of self-awareness. For

motor and mental development, an irritable mood, and attachment difficulties (Cornish et al., 2005; McMahon et al., 2006).

When maternal depression persists, the parent–child relationship worsens. Depressed mothers view their infants and children more negatively than independent observers do (Forman et al., 2007). And they use inconsistent discipline—sometimes lax, at other times too forceful. As we will see in later chapters, children who experience these maladaptive parenting practices often have serious adjustment problems. Some withdraw into a depressed mood themselves; others, mimicking their parent's anger, become impulsive and aggressive (Hay et al., 2003). In several studies, infants and preschoolers of depressed mothers showed atypical EEG brain-wave patterns—reduced activation of the left hemisphere (which governs positive emotion) and increased activation of the right hemisphere (which governs negative emotion) (see page 185 in Chapter 5). These alterations, a sign of difficulty controlling negative emotional arousal, are associated with increased behavior problems (Dawson et al., 2003; Jones, Field, & Davalos, 2000).

Paternal Depression

Like maternal depression, paternal depression is linked to dissatisfaction with marriage and family life after childbirth and to other life stressors, including job loss and divorce. In fact, it often follows maternal depression (Bielawska-Batorowicz & Kossakowska-Petrycka, 2006).

In a study of a large representative sample of British parents and babies, researchers assessed depressive symptoms of fathers shortly after birth and again the following year. Then they tracked the development of their children into the preschool years. Persistent paternal depression was a strong predictor of child behavior problems—especially overactivity, defiance, and aggression in boys—even after many other factors, including family life and maternal depression, had been controlled (Ramchandani et al., 2005).

Although little is known about the precise effects of paternal depression on parenting, well-adjusted fathers are more positive, attentive, and involved with their babies. At older ages, paternal depression is linked to frequent father–child conflict (Kane & Garber, 2004). Over time, children subjected to parental negativity develop a pessimistic world view—one in which they lack self-confidence and perceive their parents and other people as threatening. Children who constantly feel endangered are especially likely to become overly aroused in stressful situations, easily losing control in the face of cognitive and social challenges (Cummings & Davies, 1994). Although children of depressed parents may inherit a tendency to develop emotional and behavior problems, quality of parenting is a major factor in their adjustment.

Interventions

Early treatment of parental depression is vital to prevent the disorder from spiraling and further harming children's development. Julia's doctor referred her to a therapist, who provided counseling aimed at reducing parenting stress and helping Julia and Kyle with their marital problems. At times, antidepressant medication is prescribed. But treatment aimed at alleviating parental depression usually is not sufficient to improve the parent–child relationship. Therapy that encourages depressed mothers to revise their negative views of their babies and that teaches them to engage in emotionally positive, patient, and responsive caregiving is vital for reducing young children's attachment and other developmental problems (Cicchetti, Toth, & Rogosch, 2004; Forman et al., 2007; Nylen et al., 2006). When a depressed parent does not respond to intervention, a warm relationship with the other parent or another caregiver can safeguard children's development (Mezulis, Hyde, & Clark, 2004).

example, the interest and excitement that babies display when acting on novel objects help them forge a *sense of self-efficacy*—confidence in their own ability to control events in their surroundings (Harter, 2006). By the middle of the second year, when self-awareness is sufficiently developed, children begin to experience a new array of emotions with distinct functions. Recall Brenda's expressions of pride and embarrassment—two feeling states that have to do with evaluating the self's goodness or badness in relation to standards for morality, social behavior, and task mastery (Saarni et al., 2006).

Finally, the functionalist approach emphasizes that to adapt to their physical and social worlds, children must gain control over their emotions, just as they do their motor, cognitive, and social behavior. As part of this increasing *emotional self-regulation*, children must master their culture's rules for when and how to convey emotion. As a result, by late childhood, few emotions are expressed as openly and freely as they were in the early years of life. With these ideas in mind, let's chart the course of emotional development.

Ask Yourself

Review Using research findings, provide an example of the impact of emotions on children's (1) cognitive processing, (2) social behavior, and (3) physical health.

Apply Recently divorced, Jeannine—mother of 3-month-old Jacob—feels lonely, depressed, and anxious about finances. How might Jeannine's emotional state affect Jacob's emotional and social adjustment? What can be done to help Jeannine and Jacob?

Reflect Using one of your own experiences, illustrate the bidirectional relationship between emotion and cognition.

Development of Emotional Expression

Because infants cannot describe their feelings, determining exactly which emotions they are experiencing is a challenge. Although vocalizations and body movements provide some information, researchers have relied most on facial expressions. Cross-cultural evidence reveals that people around the world associate photographs of different facial expressions with emotions in the same way (Ekman, 2003; Ekman & Friesen, 1972). These findings inspired researchers to analyze infants' facial patterns carefully to determine the range of emotions they display at different ages. A commonly used method for doing so, the MAX System, is illustrated in Figure 10.1.

Basic emotions—happiness, interest, surprise, fear, anger, sadness, disgust—are universal in humans and other primates, have a long evolutionary history of promoting survival, and can be directly inferred from facial expressions. Do infants come into the world with the ability to express these basic emotions? Although signs of some emotions are present, babies' earliest emotional life consists of little more than two global arousal states: attraction to pleasant stimulation and withdrawal from unpleasant stimulation (Camras et al., 2003; Fox, 1991; Sroufe, 1979). Only gradually do emotions become clear, well-organized signals.

■ **Figure 10.1** **Which emotions are these babies displaying?**
The MAX (Maximally Discriminative Facial Movement) System is a widely used method for classifying infants' emotional expressions by determining the correspondence between facial muscle movements and basic feeling states. (a) Cheeks raised and corners of the mouth pulled back and up signal happiness. (b) Eyebrows raised, eyes widened, and mouth opened with corners pulled straight back denote fear. (From Izard, 1979.)

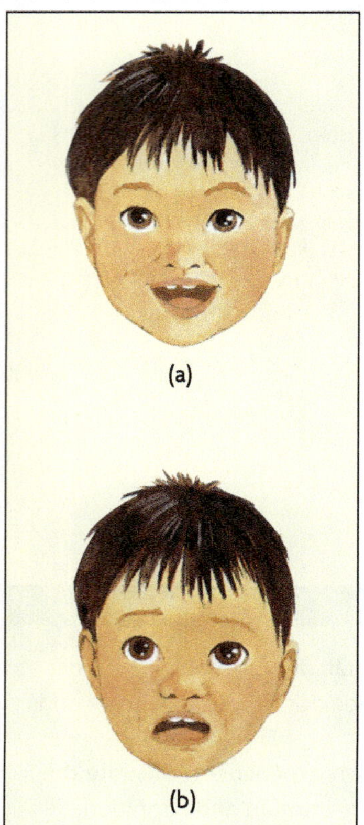

The *dynamic systems perspective* helps us understand how this happens: Children coordinate separate skills into more effective, emotionally expressive systems as the central nervous system develops and the child's goals and experiences change (see Chapter 4). Videotaping the facial expressions of her daughter from 6 to 14 weeks, Linda Camras (1992) found that in the early weeks, the infant displayed a fleeting angry face as she was about to cry and a sad face as her crying waned. These expressions first appeared on the way to or away from full-blown distress and were not clearly linked to the baby's experiences and desires. With age, she was better able to sustain an angry signal when she encountered a blocked goal and a sad signal when she could not overcome an obstacle.

According to one view, sensitive, contingent caregiver communication, in which parents selectively mirror aspects of the baby's diffuse emotional behavior, helps infants construct discrete emotional expressions more similar to those of adults (Gergely & Watson, 1999). Around 6 months, face, gaze, voice, and posture form distinct, organized patterns that vary meaningfully with environmental events. For example, babies typically respond to their parent's playful interaction with a joyful face, pleasant babbling, and a relaxed posture, as if to say, "This is fun!" In contrast, an unresponsive parent often evokes a sad face, fussy vocalizations, and a drooping body (sending the message "I'm despondent") or an angry face, crying, and "pick me up" gestures (as if to say "Change this unpleasant event!"). By the middle of the first year, emotional expressions are organized and specific—and therefore able to tell us a great deal about the infant's internal state (Weinberg & Tronick, 1994; Yale et al., 1999).

Four basic emotions—happiness, anger, sadness, and fear—have received the most research attention. Let's see how they develop.

Happiness

Happiness—expressed first in blissful smiles, later through exuberant laughter—contributes to many aspects of development. When infants achieve new skills, they smile and laugh, displaying delight in motor and cognitive mastery. As the smile encourages caregivers to be affectionate and stimulating, the baby smiles even more (Aksan & Kochanska, 2004). Happiness binds parent and child into a warm, supportive relationship that fosters the infant's developing competence.

During the early weeks, newborn babies smile when full, during REM sleep, and in response to gentle touches and sounds, such as stroking of the skin, rocking, and the mother's soft, high-pitched voice. By the end of the first month, infants smile at dynamic, eye-catching sights, such as a bright object jumping suddenly across their field of vision. And as infants attend to the parent's face, and the parent talks and smiles, babies knit their brows, open their mouths to coo, and move their arms and legs excitedly, gradually becoming more emotionally positive until, between 6 and 10 weeks, the parent's communication evokes a broad grin called the **social smile** (Lavelli & Fogel, 2005; Sroufe & Waters, 1976). These changes parallel the development of infant perceptual capacities—in particular, babies' sensitivity to visual patterns, including the human face (see Chapter 4). And social smiling becomes better organized and stable as babies learn to use it to evoke and sustain pleasurable face-to-face interaction.

Laughter, which appears around 3 to 4 months, reflects faster processing of information than does smiling. But as with smiling, the first laughs occur in response to very active stimuli, such as the parent saying playfully, "I'm gonna get you!" and kissing the baby's tummy. As infants understand more about their world, they laugh at events with subtler elements of surprise, such as a silent game of peekaboo (Sroufe & Wunsch, 1972).

Around the middle of the first year, infants smile and laugh more when interacting with familiar people, a preference that strengthens the parent–child bond. Like adults, 10- to 12-month-olds have several smiles, which vary with context—a broad, "cheek-raised" smile in response to a parent's greeting; a reserved, muted smile for a friendly stranger; and a mouth-open smile during stimulating play (Bolzani et al., 2002; Dickson, Fogel, & Messinger, 1998). At the end of the first year, the smile becomes a deliberate social signal. Between 8 and 10 months, infants more often interrupt their play with an interesting toy to relay their delight to an attentive adult (Venezia et al., 2004).

This Tibetan baby, snuggled in his father's robe, smiles with delight at onlookers. Infants' smiles and laughter encourage caregivers to respond in kind, binding parent and baby in a warm, supportive relationship that promotes all aspects of development. © Alison Wright/Corbis

Anger and Sadness

Newborn babies respond with generalized distress to a variety of unpleasant experiences, including hunger, painful medical procedures, changes in body temperature, and too much or too little stimulation (see Chapter 4). From 4 to 6 months into the second year, angry expressions increase in frequency and intensity. Older infants react with anger in a wider range of situations—when an interesting object or event is removed, their arms are restrained, the caregiver leaves for a brief time, they are put down for a nap, or they cannot control an expected outcome—for example, when they pull a string that previously produced interesting sights and sounds but no longer does so (Camras et al., 1992; Stenberg & Campos, 1990; Sullivan & Lewis, 2003).

Why do angry reactions increase with age? Cognitive and motor development are intimately involved. As infants become capable of intentional behavior (see Chapter 6), they want to control their own actions and the effects they produce (Alessandri, Sullivan, & Lewis, 1990). They are also more persistent about obtaining desired objects and less easily distracted from those goals (Mascolo & Fischer, 2007). Furthermore, older infants are better at identifying the agent of a painful stimulus or a blocked goal. Consequently, their anger is particularly intense when a caregiver from whom they have come to expect warm behavior causes discomfort (Stenberg, Campos, & Emde, 1983). The rise in anger is also adaptive. New motor capacities enable babies to use the energy mobilized by anger to defend themselves or overcome obstacles (Izard & Ackerman, 2000). At the same time, anger motivates caregivers to ease a baby's distress and, in the case of separation, may discourage them from leaving again soon.

Although expressions of sadness also occur in response to pain, removal of an object, and brief separations, they are less common than anger (Alessandri, Sullivan, & Lewis, 1990; Izard, Hembree, & Huebner, 1987; Shiller, Izard, & Hembree, 1986). In contrast, sadness occurs often when infants are deprived of a familiar, loving caregiver or when caregiver–infant communication is seriously disrupted (refer again to the From Research to Practice box on pages 402–403).

Angry reactions increase as babies become capable of intentional behavior and as their ability to identify agents of blocked goals improves. This 8-month-old knows just what toy he wants and who is keeping it from him. © Image Source/Getty Images

Fear

Like anger, fear rises during the second half of the first year. Older infants hesitate before playing with a new toy, and newly crawling infants soon show fear of heights (see Chapter 4). But the most frequent expression of fear is to unfamiliar adults, a reaction called **stranger anxiety.** Many infants and toddlers are quite wary of strangers,

This 1-year-old ventures off confidently as long as her mother remains near as a secure base to which she can return if she becomes uneasy or frightened. The rise in fear after age 6 months restrains infants' compelling urge to set out on their own. © David Young-Wolff/ PhotoEdit

although the reaction does not always occur. It depends on several factors: temperament (some babies are generally more fearful), past experiences with strangers, and the current situation (Thompson & Limber, 1991). When an unfamiliar adult picks up the infant in a new setting, stranger anxiety is likely. But if the adult sits still while the baby moves around and a parent remains nearby, infants often show positive and curious behavior (Horner, 1980). The stranger's style of interaction—expressing warmth, holding out an attractive toy, playing a familiar game, and approaching slowly rather than abruptly—reduces the baby's fear.

Cross-cultural research reveals that infant-rearing practices can modify stranger anxiety. Among the Efe hunters and gatherers of Congo, West Africa, where the maternal death rate is high, infant survival is safeguarded by a collective caregiving system in which, starting at birth, Efe babies are passed from one adult to another. Consequently, Efe infants show little stranger anxiety (Tronick, Morelli, & Ivey, 1992). In contrast, among infants in Israeli kibbutzim (cooperative agricultural settlements), who live in isolated communities vulnerable to terrorist attacks, wariness of strangers is widespread. By the end of the first year, when infants look to others for cues about how to respond emotionally, kibbutz babies display far greater stranger anxiety than their city-reared counterparts (Saarni et al., 2006).

The rise in fear after age 6 months keeps newly mobile babies' enthusiasm for exploration in check. Once wariness develops, infants use the familiar caregiver as a **secure base,** or point from which to explore, venturing into the environment and then returning for emotional support. As part of this adaptive system, encounters with strangers lead to two conflicting tendencies: approach (indicated by interest and friendliness) and avoidance (indicated by fear). The infant's behavior is a balance between the two.

Eventually, as cognitive development permits toddlers to discriminate more effectively between threatening and nonthreatening people and situations, stranger anxiety and other fears decline. This change is adaptive because adults other than caregivers will soon be important in children's development. Fear also wanes as children acquire a wider array of strategies for coping with it, as you will see when we discuss emotional self-regulation.

Self-Conscious Emotions

Besides basic emotions, humans are capable of a second, higher-order set of feelings, including shame, embarrassment, guilt, envy, and pride. These are called **self-conscious emotions** because each involves injury to or enhancement of our sense of self. For example, when we are ashamed or embarrassed, we have negative feelings about our behavior or accomplishments, and we want to retreat so others will no longer notice our failings. We feel guilt when we know that we have harmed someone and we want to relieve the other's suffering and repair the relationship. In contrast, pride reflects delight in the self's achievements, and we are inclined to tell others what we have accomplished and to take on further challenges (Saarni et al., 2006).

Self-conscious emotions appear at the end of the second year, as 18- to 24-month-olds become firmly aware of the self as a separate, unique individual. Toddlers show shame and embarrassment by lowering their eyes, hanging their heads, and hiding their faces with their hands. They show guiltlike reactions, too, like the 22-month-old who returned a toy she had grabbed and patted her upset playmate. Pride also emerges around this time, and envy by age 3 (Barrett, 2005; Garner, 2003; Lewis et al., 1989).

Besides self-awareness, self-conscious emotions require an additional ingredient: adult instruction in when to feel proud, ashamed, or guilty. The situations in which adults encourage self-conscious emotions vary from culture to culture. In Western individualistic nations, most children are taught to feel pride over personal achievement—throwing a ball the farthest, winning a game, and (later on) getting good grades. In collectivist cultures such as China and Japan, calling attention to purely personal success evokes embarrassment and self-effacement. And violating cultural standards by failing to show concern for others—a parent, a teacher, or an employer—sparks intense shame (Akimoto & Sanbonmatsu, 1999; Lewis, 1992).

As their self-concepts develop, children become increasingly sensitive to praise and blame or to the possibility of such feedback from parents, teachers, and other adults who matter to them, often viewing their expectations as obligatory rules ("Dad said you're 'posed to take turns"). By age 3, self-conscious emotions are clearly linked to self-evaluation (Stipek, 1995; Thompson, Meyer, & McGinley, 2006). Preschoolers show much more pride when they succeed in difficult rather than easy tasks and much more shame when they fail simple rather than hard tasks (Lewis, Alessandri, & Sullivan, 1992).

A 2-year-old follows her grandfather's lead, clapping to celebrate her success at completing a puzzle. She is learning to experience pride in personal achievement, as is appropriate in her culture. © Stefanie Felix Photography. All Rights Reserved.

Quality of adult feedback influences these early self-evaluative reactions. When parents repeatedly comment on the worth of the child and her performance ("That's a bad job!" "I thought you were a good girl"), children experience self-conscious emotions intensely—more shame after failure, more pride after success. In contrast, when parents focus on how to improve performance ("You did it this way; now try doing it that way"), they induce moderate, more adaptive levels of shame and pride and greater persistence on difficult tasks (Kelley, Brownell, & Campbell, 2000; Lewis, 1998).

Among Western children, intense shame is associated with feelings of personal inadequacy ("I'm stupid"; "I'm a terrible person") and is linked to maladjustment—withdrawal and depression as well as intense anger and aggression at others who participated in the shame-evoking situation (Lindsay-Hartz, de Rivera, & Mascolo, 1995; Mills, 2005). In contrast, guilt—when it occurs in appropriate circumstances and is not accompanied by shame—is related to good adjustment. Guilt helps children resist harmful impulses, and it motivates a misbehaving child to repair the damage and behave more considerately (Mascolo & Fischer, 2007; Tangney, 2001).

The consequences of shame for children's adjustment, however, may vary across cultures. In Asian collectivist societies, where people define themselves in relation to their social group, shame is viewed as an adaptive reminder of the importance of others' judgments (Bedford, 2004). Chinese parents, for example, believe that it is important for a misbehaving child to feel ashamed. As early as age 2½, they frequently use shame to teach right from wrong, while mindful that excessive shaming could harm the child's self-esteem (Fung, 1999). Not surprisingly, Chinese children add the word *shame* to their vocabularies by age 3, much earlier than their North American counterparts do (Shaver, Wu, & Schwartz, 1992).

As children develop inner standards of excellence and good behavior and a sense of personal responsibility, the circumstances under which they experience self-conscious emotions change. Unlike preschoolers, school-age children experience pride in a new accomplishment or guilt about a transgression even when no adult is present (Harter & Whitesell, 1989). Also, school-age children do not report guilt for any mishap, as they did when younger, but only for intentional wrongdoing, such as ignoring responsibilities, cheating, or lying (Ferguson, Stegge, & Damhuis, 1991). These changes reflect the older child's more mature sense of morality, a topic we will take up in Chapter 12.

Emotional Self-Regulation

Besides expressing a wider range of emotions, children learn to manage their emotional experiences. **Emotional self-regulation** refers to the strategies we use to adjust the intensity or duration of our emotional reactions to a comfortable level so we can accomplish our goals. It requires several cognitive capacities that we discussed in Chapter 7—attention focusing and shifting, the ability to inhibit thoughts and behavior, and planning, or actively taking steps to relieve a stressful situation (Eisenberg & Spinrad, 2004; Thompson & Goodvin, 2007). When you remind yourself that an anxiety-provoking event will be over soon, suppress your anger at a friend's behavior, or decide not to see a scary horror film, you are engaging in emotional self-regulation.

Emotional self-regulation requires voluntary, effortful management of emotions. This *effortful control* improves gradually, as the result of brain development and the assistance of caregivers, who help children manage intense emotion and teach them strategies for doing so

(Fox & Calkins, 2003; Rothbart, Posner, & Kieras, 2006). Individual differences in voluntary control of emotion are evident in infancy and, by early childhood, play such a vital role in children's adjustment that—as we will see later—effortful control is considered a major dimension of temperament. Let's turn now to changes in emotional self-regulation from infancy to adolescence.

• **Infancy** In the early months, infants have only a limited capacity to regulate their emotional states. Although they can turn away from unpleasant stimulation and can mouth and suck when their feelings get too intense, they are easily overwhelmed. They depend on the soothing interventions of caregivers—being lifted to the shoulder, rocked, gently stroked, and talked to softly.

Rapid development of the frontal lobes of the cerebral cortex increases the baby's tolerance for stimulation. Between 2 and 4 months, caregivers build on this capacity by initiating face-to-face play and attention to objects. In these interactions, parents arouse pleasure in the baby while adjusting the pace of their behavior so the infant does not become overwhelmed and distressed. As a result, the baby's tolerance for stimulation increases (Kopp & Neufeld, 2003).

By 4 to 6 months, the ability to shift attention and engage in self-soothing helps infants control emotion. When faced with a highly stimulating novel event (a toy fire truck with siren blaring and lights flashing), babies who more readily turn away or suck their fingers are less prone to distress (Axia, Bonichini, & Benini, 1999; Crockenberg & Leerkes, 2003a). At the end of the first year, crawling and walking enable infants to regulate feelings by approaching or retreating from various stimuli. And further gains in attention permit toddlers to sustain interest in their surroundings and in play activities for a longer time (Rothbart & Bates, 2006).

Infants whose parents read and respond contingently and sympathetically to their emotional cues tend to be less fussy, to express more pleasurable emotion, to be more interested in exploration, and to be easier to soothe (Crockenberg & Leerkes, 2004; Eisenberg, Cumberland, & Spinrad, 1998; Volling et al., 2002). In contrast, parents who respond impatiently or angrily or who wait to intervene until the infant has become extremely agitated reinforce the baby's rapid rise to intense distress. This makes it harder for parents to soothe the baby in the future—and for the baby to learn to calm herself. When caregivers do not regulate stressful experiences for infants, brain structures that buffer stress may fail to develop properly, resulting in an anxious, emotionally reactive child with a reduced capacity for regulating emotion (Crockenberg & Leerkes, 2000; Little & Carter, 2005).

In the second year, gains in representation and language lead to new ways of regulating emotion. As we will see, a vocabulary for talking about feelings develops rapidly after 18 months, but toddlers are not yet good at using language to manage their emotions. Temper tantrums occur because toddlers cannot control the intense anger that often arises when an adult rejects their demands, particularly in situations where they are fatigued or hungry (Mascolo & Fischer, 2007). Toddlers whose parents are emotionally sympathetic but set limits (by not giving in to tantrums), actively distract the child from the prohibited activity (by engaging the child in an acceptable alternative), and later suggest better ways to handle adult refusals acquire more effective anger-regulation strategies and social skills during the preschool years (Laible & Thompson, 2002; Lecuyer & Houck, 2006).

Parents who offer such sensitive support encourage toddlers to describe their internal states. Then, when 2-year-olds feel distressed, they can guide caregivers to help them. For example, while listening to a story about monsters, one 22-month-old whimpered, "Mommy, scary." Her mother put down the book and gave her a consoling hug.

• **Early Childhood** After age 2, children frequently talk about their feelings and actively try to control them. By age 3 to 4, they verbalize a variety of emotional self-regulation strategies. For example, they know they can blunt emotions by restricting sensory input (covering their eyes or ears to block out an unpleasant sight or sound), talking to themselves ("Mommy said she'll be back soon"), or changing their goals (deciding that they don't want to play anyway after being excluded from a game). Children's use of these strategies means fewer emotional outbursts over the preschool years (Thompson & Goodvin, 2007). As the examples suggest,

Applying What We Know

Helping Children Manage Common Fears of Early Childhood

Fear	Suggestion
Monsters, ghosts, and darkness	Reduce exposure to frightening stories in books and on TV until the child is better able to sort out appearance from reality. Make a thorough "search" of the child's room for monsters, showing him that none are there. Leave a night-light burning, sit by the child's bed until he falls asleep, and tuck in a favorite toy for protection.
Preschool or child care	If the child resists going to preschool but seems content once there, then the fear is probably separation. Provide a sense of warmth and caring while gently encouraging independence. If the child fears being at preschool, find out what is frightening—the teacher, the children, or perhaps a crowded, noisy environment. Provide extra support by accompanying the child and gradually lessening the amount of time you are present.
Animals	Do not force the child to approach a dog, cat, or other animal that arouses fear. Let the child move at her own pace. Demonstrate how to hold and pet the animal, showing the child that when treated gently, the animal is friendly. If the child is larger than the animal, emphasize this: "You're so big. That kitty is probably afraid of *you!*"
Intense fears	If a child's fear is intense, persists for a long time, interferes with daily activities, and cannot be reduced in any of the ways just suggested, it has reached the level of a *phobia*. Sometimes phobias are linked to family problems, and counseling is needed to reduce them. At other times, phobias diminish without treatment as the child's capacity for emotional self-regulation improves.

shifting attention away from sources of frustration continues to be an effective strategy for preschoolers to use in managing emotion. Three-year-olds who can distract themselves when frustrated tend to become school-age children whom teachers rate as high in cooperation and low in problem behaviors (Gilliom et al., 2002).

By watching adults handle their own feelings, preschoolers pick up strategies for regulating emotion. Warm, patient parents who use verbal guidance to help children understand and control their feelings, including suggesting and explaining strategies, strengthen the child's capacity to handle stress (Colman et al., 2006; Gottman, Katz, & Hooven, 1997). In contrast, when parents rarely express positive emotion, dismiss their child's feelings as unimportant, and have difficulty controlling their own anger and hostility, children have continuing problems managing emotion that seriously interfere with psychological adjustment (Hill et al., 2006; Katz & Windecker-Nelson, 2004; Owens & Shaw, 2003; Thompson & Meyer, 2007).

These children are conducting a fundraiser to help the thousands of pets who were injured or left homeless by Hurricane Katrina in 2005. Their efforts are an adaptive strategy for managing the intense fear they may have felt after witnessing on television the destructive effects of the hurricane.
© Journal-Courier/Tiffany M. Hermon/ The Image Works

As with infants and toddlers, preschoolers who experience negative emotion intensely have greater difficulty inhibiting their feelings and shifting their attention away from disturbing events. Young children with poor emotion-regulation skills are more likely to be anxious and fearful or to respond with irritation to others' distress, react angrily or aggressively when frustrated, get along poorly with teachers and peers, and have difficulty adjusting to classroom routines (Chang et al., 2003; Denham et al., 2002; Eisenberg et al., 2005). Because these emotionally reactive children become increasingly difficult to rear, they often are targets of ineffective parenting, which compounds their poor emotional self-regulation.

Adults' conversations with preschoolers also foster emotional self-regulation (Thompson, 2006). Parents who prepare children for difficult experiences by describing what to expect and ways to handle anxiety offer strategies that children can apply. Preschoolers' vivid imaginations and incomplete grasp of the distinction between appearance and reality make fears common in early childhood. Consult Applying What We Know above for ways adults can help young children manage fears.

• **Middle Childhood and Adolescence** Rapid gains in emotional self-regulation occur after school entry, as emotion regulation strategies become more varied, sophisticated, and flexible (Raffaelli, Crockett, & Shen, 2005). Between ages 6 and 8—as they become aware of the difference between feeling an emotion and expressing it—children increasingly reserve the full performance of emotional expressions for communicating with others. When alone—although they report experiencing emotions just as intensely—they abbreviate their emotional expressions, representing them internally, just as they internalize their private speech (see page 265 in Chapter 6) (Holodynski, 2004). This emergence of a *mental level* of emotional self-communication helps children reflect on their emotions and, therefore, manage them.

At the same time, school-age children face new challenges in regulating negative emotion, prompted by their developing sense of self-worth and expanding knowledge of the wider world. Common fears of the school years include poor academic performance, rejection by classmates, the possibility of personal harm (being robbed or shot), threats to parental health, and media events (wars and disasters) (Gullone, 2000; Weems & Costa, 2005). School-age children's fears are shaped in part by their culture. For example, in China, where self-restraint and compliance with social standards are highly valued, more children mention failure and adult criticism as salient fears than in Australia or North America. Chinese children, however, are not more fearful overall (Ollendick et al., 1996). The number and intensity of fears they report resemble those of Western children.

By age 10, most children shift adaptively between two general strategies for managing emotion. In **problem-centered coping,** they appraise the situation as changeable, identify the difficulty, and decide what to do about it. If problem solving does not work, they engage in **emotion-centered coping,** which is internal, private, and aimed at controlling distress when little can be done about an outcome (Kliewer, Fearnow, & Miller, 1996; Lazarus & Lazarus, 1994). For example, when faced with an anxiety-provoking test or a friend who is angry at them, older school-age children view problem solving and seeking social support as the best strategies. But when outcomes are beyond their control—for example, after receiving a bad grade—they opt for distraction or try to redefine the situation in ways that help them accept current conditions: "Things could be worse. There'll be another test." Compared with preschoolers, school-age children more often use these internal strategies to regulate emotion, a change due to their improved ability to appraise situations and reflect on thoughts and feelings (Brenner & Salovey, 1997). Consequently, fears gradually decline (Gullone, 2000).

Cognitive development and a wider range of social experiences contribute to flexible, effective coping strategies. When emotional self-regulation has developed well, young people acquire a sense of *emotional self-efficacy*—a feeling of being in control of their emotional experience (Saarni, 2000). This fosters a favorable self-image and an optimistic outlook, which help them face further emotional challenges.

Acquiring Emotional Display Rules

In addition to regulating internal emotional states, children must learn to control what they communicate to others. Young preschoolers have some ability to modify their expressive behavior. For example, when denied a cookie before dinnertime, one 2-year-old paused, picked up her blanket, and walked from the hard kitchen floor to the soft family-room carpet where she could comfortably throw herself down and howl loudly!

At first, children modify emotional expressions to serve personal needs, and they exaggerate their true feelings (as this child did to get attention and a cookie). Soon, they learn to damp down their expressive behavior and substitute other reactions, such as smiling when feeling anxious or disappointed. All societies have **emotional display rules** that specify when, where, and how it is appropriate to express emotions.

As early as the first few months, parents encourage infants to suppress negative emotion by often imitating their expressions of interest, happiness, and surprise and rarely imitating their expressions of anger and sadness. Boys get more of this training than girls, in part because boys have a harder time regulating negative emotion (Else-Quest et al., 2006; Malatesta et al., 1986; Weinberg et al., 1999). As a result, the well-known sex difference—

females as emotionally expressive and males as emotionally controlled—is promoted at a tender age. Perhaps because of greater social pressure to suppress emotion, school-age boys are less accurate than girls in describing their emotions. In a Canadian study, after watching an emotionally arousing video, boys were less likely than girls to report feelings that matched their facial expressions (Strayer & Roberts, 1997). This disconnect between boys' public messages (facial expressions) and verbal acknowledgment of feelings probably contributes to the gender difference in intimacy of close relationships, which we examine in Chapter 13.

Although caregiver shaping of emotional behavior begins early, children only gradually gain the ability to conform to display rules. By age 3, capacity for self-regulation predicts children's skill at portraying an emotion they do not feel—for example, reacting cheerfully after receiving an undesirable gift (Kieras et al., 2005). These emotional "masks" are largely limited to positive feelings of happiness and surprise. Children of all ages (like adults) find it harder to act angry, sad, or disgusted than pleased (Lewis, Sullivan, & Vasen, 1987). These trends reflect social pressures: To foster harmonious relationships, most cultures teach children to communicate positive feelings and inhibit unpleasant emotional displays.

Through interacting with parents, teachers, and peers, children learn how to express negative emotion in ways likely to evoke a desired response from others. School-age children increasingly prefer verbal strategies to crying, sulking, or aggression (Shipman et al., 2003). As these findings suggest, children gradually become consciously aware of display rules. Kindergartners typically say they obey the rules to avoid punishment and gain approval from others. By third grade, children understand the value of display rules in ensuring social harmony (Jones, Abbey, & Cumberland, 1998). School-age children who justify emotional display rules by referring to concern for others' feelings are rated as especially helpful, cooperative, and socially responsive by teachers and as better liked by peers (Garner, 1996; McDowell & Parke, 2000).

Collectivist cultures place particular emphasis on emotional display rules, although they vary in how they teach children to inhibit negative displays. In a striking illustration, researchers studied children in two collectivist subcultures in rural Nepal. In response to stories about emotionally charged situations (such as peer aggression or an unjust parental punishment), Hindu children more often said they would feel angry and would try to mask their feelings. Buddhist children, in contrast, interpreted the situation so they did not experience anger. Saying they would feel "just OK," they explained, "Why be angry? The event already happened" (see Figure 10.2). In line with this difference, Hindu mothers reported that they often teach their children how to control their emotional behavior, whereas Buddhist mothers pointed to the value their religion places on a calm, peaceful disposition (Cole & Tamang, 1998; Cole, Tamang, & Shrestha, 2006). In comparison to both Nepalese groups, U.S. children preferred conveying their anger verbally in these situations—for example, to an unjust punishment, they answered, "If I say I'm angry, he'll stop hurting me!" (Cole, Bruschi, & Tamang, 2002). Notice how this response fits with the Western individualistic emphasis on personal rights and self-expression.

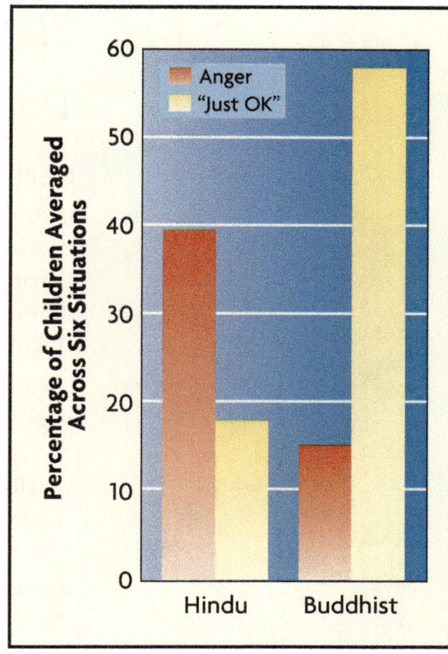

Figure 10.2 **Hindu and Buddhist children's reports of feeling anger and "just OK" in response to emotionally charged situations.**

Hindu children reported that they would feel more anger. Buddhist children, whose religion values a calm, peaceful disposition, more often stated that they would feel "just OK." The children sometimes selected other emotions, such as "happy," "sad," or "scared," but these did not differ between the two subcultures and are not shown. (Adapted from Cole & Tamang, 1998.)

Ask Yourself

Review Why do many infants show stranger anxiety in the second half of the first year? What factors can increase or decrease wariness of strangers?

Apply At age 14 months, Reggie built a block tower and gleefully knocked it down. But at age 2, Reggie called to his mother and pointed proudly to his tall block tower. What explains this change in Reggie's emotional behavior?

Connect Why do children of depressed mothers have difficulty regulating emotion (see pages 402–403)? What implications do their weak self-regulatory skills have for their response to cognitive and social challenges?

Reflect How do you typically manage negative emotion? Describe several recent examples. How might your early experiences and cultural background have influenced your style of emotional self-regulation?

Understanding and Responding to the Emotions of Others

Children's emotional expressiveness is intimately tied to their ability to interpret the emotional cues of others. We have seen that in the first few months, infants match the feeling tone of the caregiver in face-to-face communication. Early on, babies detect others' emotions through a fairly automatic process of *emotional contagion*, just as we tend to feel happy or sad when we sense these emotions in others. Around 3 to 4 months, infants have become sensitive to the structure and timing of face-to-face interactions (see Chapter 9, page 370). When they gaze, smile, or vocalize, they now expect their social partner to respond in kind, and they reply with positive vocal and emotional reactions (Markova & Legerstee, 2006; Rochat, Striano, & Blatt, 2002). Within these exchanges, babies increasingly orient toward their social world and become more aware of the range of emotional expressions (Montague & Walker-Andrews, 2001). According to some researchers, out of this early imitative communication, babies start to view others as "like me"—an awareness believed to lay the foundation for understanding others' thoughts and feelings (Gergely & Watson, 1996; Meltzoff, 2007).

From 5 months on, infants perceive facial expressions as organized patterns, and they can match the emotion in a voice with the appropriate face of a speaking person (see Chapter 4). Babies' responses to emotional expressions as organized wholes indicate that these signals have become meaningful to them. As skill at establishing joint attention improves, infants realize that an emotional expression not only has meaning but is also a meaningful reaction to a specific object or event (Moses et al., 2001; Tomasello, 1999). Once these understandings are in place, infants actively seek emotional information from trusted caregivers.

Social Referencing

By the end of the first year, babies engage in social referencing, using another person's emotional response to evaluate an uncertain situation. Hearing his mother's calm, confident voice, this 1-year-old approaches an unfamiliar dog. © Profimedia International s.r.o./Alamy Images

Social referencing involves relying on another person's emotional reaction to appraise an uncertain situation. Beginning at 8 to 10 months, when infants start to evaluate unfamiliar people, objects, and events in terms of their own safety and security, social referencing occurs often (Mumme et al., 2007). Many studies show that a caregiver's emotional expression (happy, angry, or fearful) influences whether a 1-year-old will be wary of strangers, play with an unfamiliar toy, or cross the deep side of the visual cliff (see Chapter 4, page 156) (de Rosnay et al., 2007; Stenberg, 2003; Striano & Rochat, 2000). The caregiver's voice—either alone or combined with a facial expression—is more effective than a facial expression alone (Mumme, Fernald, & Herrera, 1996; Vaish & Striano, 2004). The voice conveys both emotional and verbal information, and the baby need not turn toward the adult but, instead, can focus on evaluating the novel event.

As recall memory and language skills improve, and as parents' warnings to their newly walking youngsters become more frequent and intense, babies retain these emotional messages over longer time intervals. At 11 months, they respond appropriately after a delay of a few minutes, at 14 months after a delay of an hour or more (Hertenstein & Campos, 2004).

Parents can take advantage of social referencing to teach their youngsters how to react to many everyday events. And around the middle of the second year, as toddlers begin to appreciate that others' emotional reactions may differ from their own, social referencing allows them to compare their own and others' assessments of events. In one study, an adult showed 14- and 18-month-olds broccoli and crackers. In one condition, she acted delighted with the taste of broccoli but disgusted with the taste of crackers. In the other condition, she showed the reverse preference. When asked to share the food, 14-month-olds offered only the type of food they themselves preferred—usually crackers. In contrast, 18-month-olds gave the adult whichever food she appeared to like, regardless of their own preferences (Repacholi & Gopnik, 1997).

In sum, social referencing helps toddlers move beyond simply reacting to others' emotional messages. They use those signals to guide their own actions and to find out about others' intentions, preferences, and desires. These experiences, along with cognitive and language development, help toddlers refine the meanings of emotions of the same valence—for example, happiness versus surprise, anger versus fear—during the second year (Saarni et al., 2006).

Emotional Understanding in Childhood

During the preschool years, children's emotional understanding expands rapidly, as their everyday talk about emotions reveals:

> *Two-year-old:* *[After father shouted at child, she became angry, shouting back]* I'm mad at you, Daddy. I'm going away. Good-bye.
>
> *Two-year-old:* *[Commenting on another child who refused to take a nap and cried]* Mom, Annie cry. Annie sad.
>
> *Six-year-old:* *[In response to mother's comment, "It's hard to hear the baby crying"]* Well, it's not as hard for me as it is for you. *[When mother asked why]* Well, you like Johnny better than I do! I like him a little, and you like him a lot, so I think it's harder for you to hear him cry.
>
> *Six-year-old:* *[Comforting a small boy in church whose mother had gone up to communion]* She'll be right back. Don't be afraid. I'm here. (Bretherton et al., 1986, pp. 536, 540, 541)

• Cognitive Development and Emotional Understanding As these examples show, early in the preschool years, children refer to causes, consequences, and behavioral signs of emotion, and over time their understanding becomes more accurate and complex (Stein & Levine, 1999). By age 4 to 5, they correctly judge the causes of many basic emotions ("He's happy because he's swinging very high"; "He's sad because he misses his mother"). Preschoolers' explanations tend to emphasize external factors over internal states, a balance that changes with age (Levine, 1995). In Chapter 11, we will see that after age 4, children appreciate that both desires and beliefs motivate behavior. As a result, their grasp of how internal factors can trigger emotion expands. Preschoolers can also predict what a playmate expressing a certain emotion might do next. Four-year-olds know that an angry child might hit someone and that a happy child is more likely to share (Russell, 1990). And they realize that thinking and feeling are interconnected—that a person reminded of a previous sad experience is likely to feel sad (Lagattuta, Wellman, & Flavell, 1997). Furthermore, they come up with effective ways to relieve others' negative feelings, such as hugging to reduce sadness (Fabes et al., 1988).

In middle childhood, ability to consider conflicting cues when explaining others' emotions improves. When asked what might be happening in a picture showing a happy-faced child with a broken bicycle, 4- and 5-year-olds tended to rely only on the emotional expression: "He's happy because he likes to ride his bike." By age 8 to 9, children more often reconciled the two cues: "He's happy because his father promised to help fix his broken bike" (Gnepp, 1983; Hoffner & Badzinski, 1989). Similarly, older children recognize that people can experience more than one emotion at a time, each of which may be positive or negative and may differ in intensity (Pons et al., 2003). Preschoolers, by contrast, staunchly deny that two emotions can occur at once, much as they do not integrate two variables (height and width) in a Piagetian conservation-of-liquid task (see Chapter 6, page 241).

An appreciation of mixed emotions helps school-age children realize that people's expressions may not reflect their true feelings (Misailidi, 2006; Saarni, 1999). It also fosters awareness of self-conscious emotions, which are more complex in expression than basic emotions. For example, between ages 6 and 7, children improve sharply in ability to distinguish pride from happiness and surprise (Tracy, Robins, & Lagattuta, 2005). And 8- and 9-year-olds understand that shame combines two feelings: anger at ourselves for a personal inadequacy and sadness at having disappointed another (Harter, 1999). As with

During the preschool years, children's understanding of the causes, consequences, and behavioral signs of emotion expands rapidly. This 4-year-old tries to figure out why his baby brother is crying. Perhaps the menu is not quite right.
© Elizabeth Crews

the development of *metacognition* (thinking about thought), discussed in Chapter 7, striking gains in thinking about emotion occur in middle childhood.

• **Social Experience and Emotional Understanding** The more mothers label emotions, explain them, and express warmth and enthusiasm when conversing with preschoolers, the more "emotion words" children use and the better developed their emotional understanding (Fivush & Haden, 2005; Laible & Song, 2006). Maternal prompting of emotional thoughts ("What makes him afraid?") is a good predictor of 2-year-olds' emotion language. For older preschoolers, explanations ("He's sad because his dog ran away") are more important (Cervantes & Callanan, 1998). Does this remind you of the concept of *scaffolding*, discussed in Chapter 6—that to be effective, adult teaching must adjust to children's increasing competence?

Preschoolers whose parents frequently acknowledge their emotional reactions and explicitly teach them about diverse emotions are better able to judge others' emotions when tested at later ages (Denham & Kochanoff, 2002). Discussions in which family members disagree are particularly helpful. In one study, when mothers explained feelings and negotiated and compromised during conflicts with their 2½-year-olds, their children, at age 3, were advanced in understanding emotion and used similar strategies to resolve disagreements (Laible & Thompson, 2002). Such dialogues seem to help children reflect on the causes and consequences of emotion while modeling mature communication skills. Furthermore, 3- to 5-year-olds who have a warm, relaxed relationship with their mothers (a secure attachment bond) better understand emotion. Secure attachment is related to warmer and more elaborative parent–child narratives, including discussions of feelings that highlight the emotional significance of events (Laible, 2004; Raikes & Thompson, 2006).

As preschoolers learn more about emotion from conversing with adults, they transfer this knowledge to other contexts, engaging in more emotion talk with siblings and friends, especially during sociodramatic play (Brown, Donelan-McCall, & Dunn, 1996; Hughes & Dunn, 1998). Make-believe, in turn, contributes to emotional understanding, especially when children play with siblings (Youngblade & Dunn, 1995). The intense nature of the sibling relationship, combined with frequent acting out of feelings, makes pretending an excellent context for early learning about emotions. And when parents intervene in sibling disputes by reasoning and negotiating, preschoolers gain in sensitivity to their siblings' feelings (Perlman & Ross, 1997). They more often refer to their siblings' emotional perspective ("You get mad when I don't share") and engage in less fighting.

Knowledge about emotions helps children greatly in their efforts to get along with others. As early as 3 to 5 years of age, it is related to friendly, considerate behavior; willingness to make amends after harming another; and constructive responses to disputes with agemates (Brown & Dunn, 1996; Dunn, Brown, & Maguire, 1995; Garner & Estep, 2001). Also, the more preschoolers refer to feelings when interacting with playmates, the better liked they are by their peers (Fabes et al., 2001). Children seem to recognize that acknowledging others' emotions and explaining their own enhance the quality of relationships.

Empathy and Sympathy

In empathy, understanding and expression of emotions are interwoven, since both awareness of the emotions of another and the vicarious experience of those emotions are required for an empathic response. Current theorists agree that **empathy** involves a complex interaction of cognition and affect: the ability to detect different emotions, to take another's emotional perspective, and to *feel with* that person, or respond emotionally in a similar way. Beginning in the preschool years, empathy is an important motivator of **prosocial, or altruistic, behavior**—actions that benefit another person without any expected reward for the self (Eisenberg, Fabes, & Spinrad, 2006; Roberts & Strayer, 2003). Yet in some children, empathizing with an upset adult or peer does not yield acts of kindness and helpfulness but, instead, escalates into *personal distress.* In trying to reduce these feelings, the child focuses on his own anxiety rather than on the person in need. Consequently, empathy does not lead to **sympathy**—feelings of concern or sorrow for another's plight.

• **Development of Empathy** Empathy has roots early in development. Newborn babies tend to cry in response to the cry of another baby (see page 133 in Chapter 4). And earlier we noted young infants' contagious matching of others' emotional expressions. In sensitive, face-to-face communication, infants "connect" emotionally with their caregivers—experiences believed to be the foundation for empathy and concern for others (Zahn-Waxler, 1991).

A 4-year-old tries to comfort a sad classmate. As children's language skills expand and their ability to take the perspective of others improves, empathy also increases, motivating prosocial, or altruistic, behavior. © Ellen Senisi/The Image Works

Like self-conscious emotions, true empathy requires children to understand that the self is distinct from other people. As self-awareness develops, children nearing age 2 years begin to empathize. They not only sense another's unhappiness but often try to relieve it. For example, one 21-month-old reacted to his mother's simulated sadness by offering comforting words, giving her a hug, trying to distract her with a hand puppet, and asking the researcher to help (Zahn-Waxler & Radke-Yarrow, 1990). As language develops, children rely more on words to console others, indicating a more reflective level of empathy (Bretherton et al., 1986). When a 4-year-old received a Christmas gift that she hadn't included on her list for Santa, she assumed it belonged to another little girl and pleaded with her parents, "We've got to give it back—Santa's made a big mistake. I think the girl's crying 'cause she didn't get her present!"

Empathy increases over the elementary school years as children understand a wider range of emotions and take multiple cues into account in assessing others' feelings (Ricard & Kamberk-Kilicci, 1995). During late childhood and adolescence, advances in perspective taking permit an empathic response not just to people's immediate distress but also to their general life condition (Hoffman, 2000). The ability to empathize with the poor, oppressed, and sick requires an advanced form of perspective taking in which the young person understands that people lead continuous emotional lives beyond the current situation.

• Individual Differences Temperament plays a role in whether empathy occurs and whether it prompts sympathetic, prosocial behavior or a personally distressed, self-focused response. Twin studies reveal that empathy is moderately heritable (Zahn-Waxler et al., 2001). Children who are sociable, assertive, and good at regulating emotion are more likely than poor emotion regulators to display sympathy and prosocial behavior, helping, sharing, and comforting others in distress (Bengtson, 2005; Eisenberg et al., 1998; Valiente et al., 2004). Aggressive children's high hostility, weakened capacity to take another's perspective, and impulsive acting out of negative feelings blunt their capacity for empathy and sympathy. Many show a decline—rather than the typical rise—in concern for others during middle childhood (Hastings et al., 2000; Strayer & Roberts, 2004b). And shy children may not display sympathetic concern because they are easily overwhelmed by anxiety when others are distressed (Eisenberg et al., 1996).

Individual differences in empathy and sympathy are evident in children's facial and psychophysiological responses. In a series of studies, children watched videotapes of people in need, such as two children lying on the ground crying. Children who reacted with facial or physiological markers of concern—an interested, caring expression or a decrease in heart rate, suggesting orienting and attention—usually behaved prosocially when offered a chance to help. Those who showed facial and physiological evidence of distress—frowning, lip biting, and a rise in heart rate—were less prosocial (Fabes et al., 1994; Miller et al., 1996). Similarly, empathy is related to EEG brain-wave activity—a mild increase in the left hemisphere (which houses positive emotion) among children showing facial signs of empathy. In contrast, children who do not show these empathic signs often display a sharp EEG increase in the right hemisphere (which houses negative emotion)—an indication that they are overwhelmed by negative emotion (Jones, Field, & Davalos, 2000; Pickens, Field, & Nawrocki, 2001).

Parenting profoundly influences empathy and sympathy. When parents are warm, encourage their children's emotional expressiveness, and show a sensitive, empathic concern for their youngsters' feelings, their children are likely to react in a concerned way to the distress of others—relationships that persist into adolescence and emerging adulthood (Koestner, Franz, & Weinberger, 1990; Michalik et al., 2007; Strayer & Roberts, 2004a). Besides modeling sympathy, parents can help children learn to regulate angry feelings, which disrupt empathy and sympathy. They can also teach children the importance of kindness and can intervene when they display inappropriate emotion—strategies that predict high levels of sympathetic responding (Eisenberg, 2003). And parents can provide opportunities for children to show sympathetic concern through charitable giving and community service activities.

Milestones

Emotional Development

Age	Emotional Expressiveness	Emotional Understanding
Birth–6 months	■ Social smile emerges ■ Laughter appears ■ Expressions of happiness increase when interacting with familiar people ■ Emotional expressions gradually become well-organized patterns that are meaningfully related to environmental events	■ Detects emotions by matching the caregiver's feeling tone in face-to-face communication
7–12 months	■ Anger and fear increase in frequency and intensity ■ Uses caregiver as a secure base ■ Regulates emotion by approaching and retreating from stimulation	■ Detects the meaning of others' emotional signals ■ Engages in social referencing
1–2 years	■ Self-conscious emotions emerge but depend on monitoring and encouragement of adults ■ Begins to use language to assist with emotional self-regulation	■ Begins to appreciate that others' emotional reactions may differ from one's own ■ Acquires a vocabulary of emotional terms ■ Displays empathy
3–6 years	■ Self-conscious emotions are clearly linked to self-evaluation ■ As representation and language improve, uses active strategies for regulating emotion ■ Begins to conform to emotional display rules; can pose a positive emotion he or she does not feel	■ Understanding of causes, consequences, and behavioral signs of emotion improves in accuracy and complexity ■ As language develops, empathy becomes more reflective
7–11 years	■ Self-conscious emotions are integrated with inner standards of excellence and good behavior ■ Uses internal strategies for engaging in emotional self-regulation; shifts adaptively between problem-centered and emotion-centered coping ■ Conformity to and conscious awareness of emotional display rules improve	■ Can reconcile conflicting cues when explaining others' emotions ■ Is aware that people can have mixed feelings and that their expressions may not reflect their true feelings ■ Empathy increases as emotional understanding improves

Note: These milestones represent overall age trends. Individual differences exist in the precise age at which each milestone is attained.

Photos: (top) © Laura Dwight Photography; (middle) © Myrleen Ferguson Cate/PhotoEdit; (bottom) © Ellen B. Senisi/The Image Works

In contrast, angry, punitive parenting disrupts empathy and sympathy at an early age—particularly among children who are poor emotion regulators and, therefore, respond to parental hostility with especially high levels of personal distress (Valiente et al., 2004). In one study, physically abused toddlers at a child-care center rarely expressed concern at a peer's unhappiness but, rather, reacted with fear, anger, and physical attacks (Klimes-Dougan & Kistner, 1990). The children's reactions resembled their parents' insensitive responses to others' suffering.

These findings, like others discussed so far, reveal wide variations in children's emotional dispositions. As we turn now to the topic of temperament, we will encounter additional evidence for the joint contribution of heredity and environment to these differences. But first, consult the Milestones table above for an overview of the emotional attainments just considered.

Ask Yourself

Review What do preschoolers understand about emotion, and how do cognition and social experience contribute to their understanding?

Review Why is good emotional self-regulation vital for empathy to result in sympathy and prosocial behavior?

Apply When 15-month-old Ellen fell down while running, she looked at her mother, who smiled and exclaimed, "Oh, wasn't that a funny tumble!" How is Ellen likely to respond emotionally, and why?

Connect Cite ways that parenting contributes to emotional understanding, self-conscious emotions, empathy, and sympathy. Do you see any patterns? Explain.

Temperament and Development

When we describe one person as cheerful and upbeat, another as active and energetic, and still others as calm, cautious, persistent, or prone to angry outbursts, we are referring to **temperament**—early-appearing, stable individual differences in reactivity and self-regulation. *Reactivity* refers to variations in quickness and intensity of emotional arousal, attention, and motor action. *Self-regulation,* as we have seen, refers to strategies that modify reactivity (Rothbart, 2004; Rothbart & Bates, 2006). Researchers have become increasingly interested in temperamental variations among children because the psychological traits that make up temperament are believed to form the cornerstone of the adult personality.

In 1956, Alexander Thomas and Stella Chess initiated the New York Longitudinal Study, a groundbreaking investigation of the development of temperament that followed 141 children from early infancy well into adulthood. Results showed that temperament increases a child's chances of experiencing psychological problems or, alternatively, may protect a child from the negative effects of a stressful home life. However, Thomas and Chess (1977) also found that parenting practices can modify children's temperaments considerably.

These findings stimulated a growing body of research on temperament, including its stability, biological roots, and interaction with child-rearing experiences. Let's begin to explore these issues by looking at the structure, or makeup, of temperament and how it is measured.

The Structure of Temperament

Thomas and Chess's nine dimensions, listed in Table 10.1 on page 418, served as the first influential model of temperament, inspiring all others that followed. When detailed descriptions of infants' and children's behavior obtained from parent interviews were rated on these dimensions, certain characteristics clustered together, yielding three types of children:

- The **easy child** (40 percent of the sample) quickly establishes regular routines in infancy, is generally cheerful, and adapts easily to new experiences.
- The **difficult child** (10 percent of the sample) has irregular daily routines, is slow to accept new experiences, and tends to react negatively and intensely.
- The **slow-to-warm-up child** (15 percent of the sample) is inactive; shows mild, low-key reactions to environmental stimuli; is negative in mood; and adjusts slowly to new experiences.

Note that 35 percent of the children did not fit any of these categories. Instead, they showed unique blends of temperamental characteristics.

The difficult pattern has sparked the most interest because it places children at high risk for adjustment problems—both anxious withdrawal and aggressive behavior in early and middle childhood (Bates, Wachs, & Emde, 1994; Ramos et al., 2005; Thomas, Chess, & Birch, 1968). Compared with difficult children, slow-to-warm-up children present fewer problems in the early years. However, they tend to show excessive fearfulness and slow, constricted behavior in the late preschool and school years, when they are expected to respond actively and quickly in classrooms and peer groups (Chess & Thomas, 1984; Schmitz et al., 1999).

Table 10.1 Two Models of Temperament

Thomas and Chess

Dimension	*Description*
Activity level	Ratio of active periods to inactive ones
Rhythmicity	Regularity of body functions, such as sleep, wakefulness, hunger, and excretion
Distractibility	Degree to which stimulation from the environment alters behavior—for example, whether crying stops when a toy is offered
Approach/withdrawal	Response to a new object, food, or person
Adaptability	Ease with which child adapts to changes in the environment, such as sleeping or eating in a new place
Attention span and persistence	Amount of time devoted to an activity, such as watching a mobile or playing with a toy
Intensity of reaction	Energy level of response, such as laughing, crying, talking, or gross motor activity
Threshold of responsiveness	Intensity of stimulation required to evoke a response
Quality of mood	Amount of friendly, joyful behavior as opposed to unpleasant, unfriendly behavior

Rothbart

Dimension	*Description*
Reactivity	
Activity level	Level of gross motor activity
Attention span/ persistence	Duration of orienting or interest
Fearful distress	Wariness and distress in response to intense or novel stimuli, including time to adjust to new situations
Irritable distress	Extent of fussing, crying, and distress when desires are frustrated
Positive affect	Frequency of expression of happiness and pleasure
Self-Regulation	
Effortful control	Capacity to voluntarily suppress a dominant, reactive response in order to plan and execute a more adaptive response

Sources: Left: Thomas & Chess, 1977; right: Rothbart, Ahadi, & Evans, 2000; Rothbart & Mauro, 1990.

Table 10.1 also shows a second model of temperament, devised by Mary Rothbart, which combines overlapping dimensions of Thomas and Chess and other researchers. For example, "distractibility" and "attention span and persistence" are considered opposite ends of the same dimension, labeled "attention span/persistence." This model also includes a dimension not identified by Thomas and Chess, "irritable distress," which permits reactivity triggered by frustration to be distinguished from reactivity due to fear. And it deletes overly broad dimensions, such as "rhythmicity," "intensity of reaction," and "threshold of responsiveness" (Rothbart, Ahadi, & Evans, 2000; Rothbart & Mauro, 1990). A child who is rhythmic in sleeping is not necessarily rhythmic in eating or bowel habits. And a child who smiles and laughs intensely is not necessarily intense in fear, irritability, or motor activity.

Rothbart's dimensions are supported by factor analyses of many measures of children's temperament (see page 319 in Chapter 8 to review the concept of factor analysis). Notice how her dimensions represent the three underlying components included in the definition of temperament: (1) *emotion* ("fearful distress," "irritable distress," and "positive affect"), (2) *attention* ("attention span/persistence"), and (3) *action* ("activity level"). According to Rothbart, individuals differ not only in their reactivity on each dimension, but also in their effortful capacity to manage that reactivity. **Effortful control,** the self-regulatory dimension of temperament, involves voluntarily suppressing a dominant response in order to plan and execute a more adaptive response (Rothbart, 2003; Rothbart & Bates, 2006). Variations in effortful control are evident in how effectively a child can focus and shift attention, inhibit impulses, and engage in problem solving to manage negative emotion.

TAKE A MOMENT... Turn back to page 288 in Chapter 7 to review the concept of *cognitive control,* and note its strong resemblance to *effortful control.* As we will see later, researchers assess these capacities in similar ways. Their converging concepts, measures, and findings reveal that the same mental activities lead to effective regulation in both the cognitive and emotional/social domains.

Measuring Temperament

This child reacts negatively and intensely to a new situation—his mother's request for help carrying the clean laundry. Patient, supportive parenting can help him modify his biologically based temperament and become better at managing his reactivity to new stimuli. © Steve Cole/Getty Images/ Photodisc Red

Temperament is often assessed through interviews or questionnaires given to parents. Behavior ratings by pediatricians, teachers, and others familiar with the child, as well as laboratory observations by researchers, have also been used. Parental reports are convenient and take advantage of parents' depth of knowledge of the child across many situations (Gartstein & Rothbart, 2003). But information from parents has been criticized as being biased. Parents' prebirth expectations for their infant's temperament affect their later reports (Diener, Goldstein, & Mangelsdorf, 1995). And mothers who are anxious or depressed tend to view their babies as more difficult (Forman et al., 2003). Nevertheless, parental reports are moderately related to researchers' observations of children's behavior (Mangelsdorf, Schoppe, & Buur, 2000; Majdandžić & van den Boom, 2007). And parent perceptions are vital for understanding the way parents view and respond to their child.

Observations by researchers in the home or laboratory avoid the subjectivity of parental reports but can lead to other inaccuracies. In homes, observers find it hard to capture all relevant information, especially events that are rare but important, such as infants' response to frustration. And in the unfamiliar lab setting, distress-prone children who calmly avoid certain experiences at home may become too upset to complete the session if the lab does not permit avoidance (Wachs & Bates, 2001). Still, researchers can better control children's experiences in the lab. And they can conveniently combine observations of behavior with psychophysiological measures to gain insight into the biological bases of temperament.

Most psychophysiological research has focused on two types of children, who fall at opposite extremes of the positive-affect and fearful-distress dimensions of temperament (refer again to Table 10.1): **inhibited,** or **shy, children,** who react negatively to and withdraw from novel stimuli; and **uninhibited,** or **sociable, children,** who display positive emotion to and approach novel stimuli. As the Biology and Environment box on pages 420–421 reveals, biologically based reactivity—evident in heart rate, hormone levels, and EEG brain waves in the frontal region of the cerebral cortex—differentiate children with inhibited and uninhibited temperaments.

Stability of Temperament

Many studies indicate that young children who score low or high on attention span, irritability, sociability, shyness, or effortful control tend to respond similarly when assessed again several months to a few years later and, occasionally, even into the adult years (Caspi et al., 2003; Kochanska & Knack, 2003; Komsi et al., 2006; Majdandžić & van den Boom, 2007; Rothbart, Ahadi, & Evans, 2000). However, the overall stability of temperament is only low to moderate. Some children remain the same, but many others change.

Why isn't temperament more stable? A major reason is that temperament itself develops with age. To illustrate, let's look at irritability and activity level. Recall from Chapter 4 that most babies fuss and cry in the early months. But as infants better regulate their attention and emotions, many who initially seemed irritable become calm and content. In the case of activity level, the meaning of the behavior changes. At first, an active, wriggling infant tends to be highly aroused and uncomfortable, whereas an inactive baby is often alert and attentive. But as infants move on their own, the reverse is so! An active crawler is usually alert and interested in exploration, whereas a very inactive baby may be fearful and withdrawn.

These inconsistencies help us understand why long-term prediction from early temperament is best achieved after age 3, when the child's system of emotion, attention, and action is better established (Roberts & DelVecchio, 2000). In line with this idea, between ages 2½ and 3, children improve substantially and also perform more consistently across a wide variety of tasks requiring effortful control, such as waiting for a reward, lowering their voice to a whisper, succeeding at games like "Simon Says," and selectively attending to one stimulus while ignoring

Biology *and* Environment

Development of Shyness and Sociability

Two 4-month-old babies, Larry and Mitch, visited the laboratory of Jerome Kagan, who observed their reactions to various unfamiliar experiences. When exposed to new sights and sounds, such as a moving mobile decorated with colorful toys, Larry tensed his muscles, moved his arms and legs with agitation, and began to cry. In contrast, Mitch remained relaxed and quiet, smiling and cooing with apparent pleasure.

As toddlers, Larry and Mitch returned to the laboratory, where each experienced procedures designed to induce uncertainty. Electrodes were placed on their bodies and blood pressure cuffs on their arms to measure heart rate; toy robots, animals, and puppets moved before their eyes; and unfamiliar people entered and behaved in unexpected ways or wore novel costumes. While Larry whimpered and quickly withdrew, Mitch watched with interest, laughed, and approached the toys and strangers.

On a third visit, at age 4½, Larry barely talked or smiled during an interview with an unfamiliar adult. In contrast, Mitch asked questions and communicated his pleasure at each intriguing activity. In a playroom with two unfamiliar peers, Larry pulled back and watched, while Mitch made friends quickly.

In longitudinal research on several hundred Caucasian children, Kagan found that about 20 percent of 4-month-old babies were, like Larry, easily upset by novelty; 40 percent, like Mitch, were comfortable, even delighted, with new experiences. About 20 to 30 percent of these extreme groups retained their temperamental styles as they grew older (Kagan, 2003; Kagan & Saudino, 2001; Kagan et al., 2007). But most children's dispositions became less extreme over time. Biological makeup and child-rearing experiences jointly influenced both stability and change in temperament.

Physiological Correlates of Shyness and Sociability

Kagan believes that individual differences in arousal of the *amygdala,* an inner brain structure that controls avoidance reactions, contribute to these contrasting temperaments. In shy, inhibited children, novel stimuli easily excite the amygdala and its connections to the cerebral cortex and sympathetic nervous system, which prepares the body to act in the face of threat. In sociable, uninhibited children, the same level of stimulation evokes minimal neural excitation (Kagan & Fox, 2006). In support of this theory, while viewing photos of unfamiliar faces, adults who had been classified as inhibited in the second year of life showed greater fMRI activity in the amygdala than adults who had been uninhibited as toddlers (Schwartz et al., 2003). And the two emotional styles are distinguished by additional physiological responses that are known to be mediated by the amygdala:

- *Heart rate.* From the first few weeks of life, the heart rates of shy children are consistently higher than those of sociable children, and they speed up further in response to unfamiliar events (Schmidt et al., 2007; Snidman et al., 1995).
- *Cortisol.* In many studies, saliva concentrations of the stress hormone cortisol tend to be higher overall and to rise more in the face of a stressful event in shy than in sociable young children (Gunnar & Nelson, 1994; Schmidt et al., 1997, 1999). Findings, however, are not entirely consistent: Assertive, socially confident preschoolers also show spiking of cortisol levels in response to social challenges (unfamiliar adults and peers) (Gunnar, 1994). But cortisol elevations are more common in shy children—a

competing stimuli (Kochanska, Murray, & Harlan, 2000; Li-Grining, 2007). Researchers believe that around this time, areas in the frontal lobes involved in suppressing impulses develop rapidly (Gerardi-Caulton, 2000; Rothbart & Bates, 2006). Nevertheless, the ease with which children manage their reactivity in early childhood depends on the type and strength of the reactive emotion involved. Preschoolers who were highly fearful as 2-year-olds tended to score slightly better than their agemates in effortful control as 4-year-olds. In contrast, angry, irritable 2-year-olds were less effective at effortful control at later ages (Kochanska & Knaack, 2003; Kochanska, Murray, & Harlan, 2000).

In sum, many factors affect the extent to which a child's temperament remains stable, including development of the biological systems on which temperament is based, the child's capacity for effortful control, and the success of her efforts, which depend on the quality and intensity of her emotional reactivity. When we consider the evidence as a whole, the low to moderate stability of temperament makes sense. It also confirms that experience can modify biologically based temperamental traits considerably, although children rarely change from one extreme to another—that is, a shy preschooler practically never becomes highly sociable. With these ideas in mind, let's turn to genetic and environmental contributions to temperament and personality.

Genetic and Environmental Influences

The word *temperament* implies a genetic foundation for individual differences in personality. Research indicates that identical twins are more similar than fraternal twins across a wide

pattern that may play a role in sustaining their fearful behavior (Zimmermann & Stansbury, 2004).

- *Pupil dilation, blood pressure, and skin surface temperature.* Compared with sociable children, shy children tend to show greater pupil dilation, rise in blood pressure, and cooling of the fingertips when faced with novelty (Kagan et al., 1999, 2007).

Another physiological correlate of approach–withdrawal to people and objects is the pattern of EEG brain waves in the frontal lobes of the cerebral cortex. Shy infants and preschoolers show greater EEG activity in the right frontal lobe, which is associated with negative emotional reactivity; sociable children show the opposite pattern (Kagan & Snidman, 2004; Kagan et al., 2007). Neural activity in the amygdala, which is transmitted to the frontal lobes, probably contributes to these differences. Inhibited children also show greater generalized activation of the cerebral cortex, an indicator of high emotional arousal and monitoring of new situations for potential threats (Henderson et al., 2004).

Child-Rearing Practices

According to Kagan, extremely shy or sociable children inherit a physiology that biases them toward a particular temperamental style. Yet heritability research indicates that genes contribute only modestly to shyness and sociability (Kagan & Fox, 2006). Experience has a powerful impact.

Child-rearing practices affect the chances that an emotionally reactive baby will become a fearful child. Warm, supportive parenting reduces shy infants' and preschoolers' intense physiological reaction to novelty, whereas cold, intrusive parenting heightens anxiety (Rubin, Burgess, & Hastings, 2002). And if parents protect infants who dislike novelty from minor stresses, they make it harder for the child to overcome an urge to retreat. Parents who make appropriate demands for their baby to approach new experiences help the child overcome fear (Rubin et al., 1997).

When early inhibition persists, it leads to excessive cautiousness, low self-esteem, and loneliness (Fordham & Stevenson-Hinde, 1999; Rubin, Stewart, & Coplan, 1995). In adolescence, persistent shyness increases the risk of severe anxiety, especially social phobia—intense fear of being humiliated in social situations (Kagan & Fox, 2006). For inhibited children to acquire effective social skills, parenting must be tailored to their temperaments—a theme we will encounter again in this and later chapters.

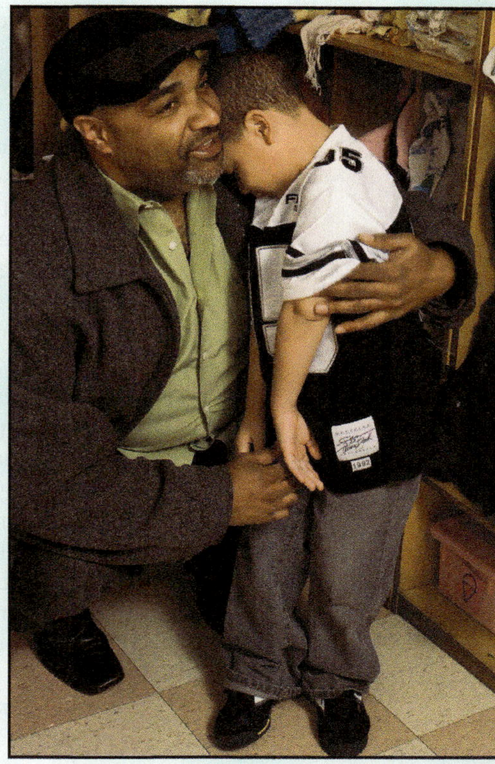

A strong physiological response to uncertain situations prompts this child to cling to his father. With patient but insistent encouragement, the father can help his son overcome his urge to retreat from unfamiliar events.
© Laura Dwight Photography

range of temperamental traits (activity level, attention span, shyness/sociability, irritability, and effortful control) and personality measures (introversion/extroversion, anxiety, agreeableness, curiosity and imaginativeness, and impulsivity) (Bouchard, 2004; Bouchard & Loehlin, 2001; Caspi & Shiner, 2006; Roisman & Fraley, 2006; Saudino & Cherny, 2001). In Chapter 3, we noted that heritability estimates derived from kinship studies suggest a moderate role for genetic factors in temperament and personality: On average, about half of individual differences have been attributed to differences in genetic makeup.

Nevertheless, genetic influences vary with the temperamental trait and the age of the individual being studied. For example, heritability estimates are much higher for expressions of negative emotion than for positive emotion. And the role of heredity is considerably less in infancy than in childhood and later years, when temperament becomes more stable (Wachs & Bates, 2001).

Although genetic influences on temperament are clear, environment is also powerful. For example, persistent nutritional and emotional deprivation profoundly alters temperament, resulting in maladaptive emotional reactivity (Wachs & Bates, 2001). Recall from Chapter 5 that even after dietary improvement, children exposed to severe malnutrition in infancy remain more distractible and fearful than their agemates. Also, higher levels of home noise and crowding are linked to withdrawal and irritability in the second year (Matheny & Phillips, 2001; Wachs, 2006). And earlier in this chapter, we noted that children who spent their infancy in deprived orphanages are easily overwhelmed by stress. Their poor regulation of emotion results in inattention and weak impulse control, including frequent expressions of anger (see page 401).

Other research shows that child rearing has much to do with whether or not infants and young children maintain their temperamental traits. In fact, heredity and environment often jointly contribute to temperament, since a child's approach to the world affects the experiences to which she is exposed. To see how this works, let's look closely at ethnic differences in temperament.

• **Cultural Variations** Compared with North American Caucasian infants, Chinese and Japanese babies tend to be less active, irritable, and vocal, more easily soothed when upset, and better at quieting themselves (Kagan et al., 1994; Lewis, Ramsay, & Kawakami, 1993). Chinese and Japanese toddlers are also more fearful and inhibited, remaining closer to their mothers in an unfamiliar playroom and displaying more anxiety when interacting with a stranger than their North American counterparts (Chen, Wang, & DeSouza, 2006). And some Asian infants are more emotionally restrained. Chinese 1-year-olds, for example, smile and cry less than Caucasian-American babies (Camras et al., 1998).

These variations may have genetic roots, but they are supported by cultural beliefs and practices. Japanese mothers usually say that babies come into the world as independent beings who must learn to rely on their parents through close physical contact. North American mothers typically believe just the opposite—that they must wean the baby away from dependency into autonomy. Consistent with these beliefs, Asian mothers interact gently, soothingly, and gesturally with their babies, whereas Caucasian mothers use a more active, stimulating, verbal approach (Rothbaum et al., 2000b). Also, recall from our discussion of emotional self-regulation that Chinese and Japanese adults discourage babies from expressing strong emotion, which contributes further to their infants' tranquility.

• **Nonshared Environment** In families with several children, an additional influence on temperament is at work. Recall from Chapter 8 that *nonshared environmental influences*—those that make siblings different from one another—play an important role in intelligence. They are also influential in personality development. TAKE A MOMENT... Ask several parents to describe each of their children's personalities. You will see that they often emphasize differences between siblings: "She's a lot more active." "He's more sociable." "She's far more persistent." As a result, parents often regard siblings as more distinct than other observers do. In a large study of 1- to 3-year-old twin pairs, parents rated identical twins as resembling each other less in temperament than researchers' ratings indicated. And whereas researchers rated fraternal twins as moderately similar, parents viewed them as somewhat opposite in temperamental style (see Figure 10.3) (Saudino, 2003).

Figure 10.3 Temperament correlations for identical and fraternal twin pairs, as rated by researchers and parents. Parents rated 1- to 3-year-old identical twins as resembling each other less in temperament than did researchers. And whereas researchers rated fraternal twins as moderately similar, parents rated them as somewhat opposing in temperament. The correlations depicted here are for emotional reactivity. Activity level, shyness, and attention span/persistence yielded a similar pattern of findings. (Adapted from Saudino, 2003.)

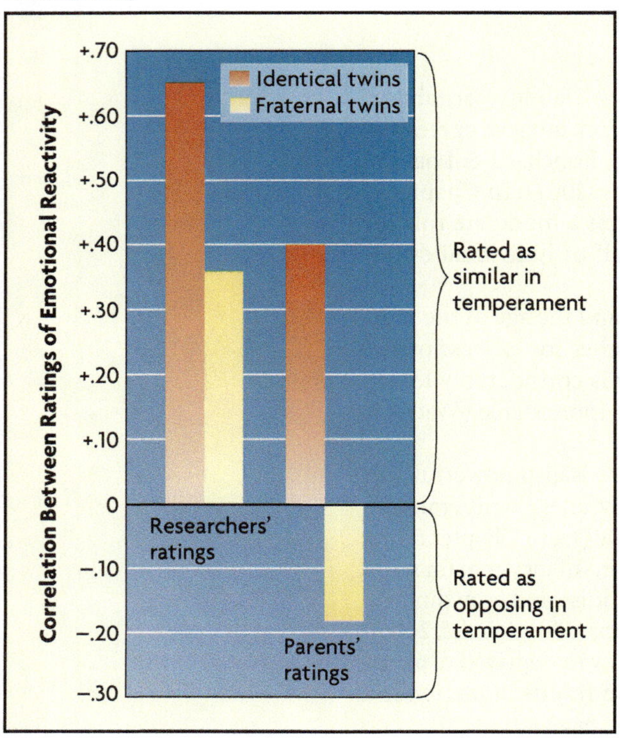

Parents' tendency to emphasize each child's unique qualities affects their child-rearing practices. In a study of 3-year-old identical twins, mothers' differential treatment of each twin predicted differences between twins in psychological adjustment. The pair member who received more warmth and less punitive parenting was more positive in mood and prosocial behavior and less likely to have behavior problems (Deater-Deckard et al., 2001). Each child, in turn, evokes responses from caregivers that are consistent with parental beliefs and the child's developing temperament.

Besides different experiences within the family, siblings have distinct experiences with teachers, peers, and others in their community that affect personality development. And as they get older, siblings often seek ways to differ from one another. For all these reasons, both identical and fraternal twins tend to become increasingly dissimilar in personality with age (Loehlin & Martin, 2001; McCartney, Harris, & Bernieri, 1990). The less contact twins have with each other, the stronger this effect.

Are nonshared factors more important in personality development than *shared environmental influences*—those that affect all siblings similarly? In Chapter 14, we will see that shared factors, such as family stress and child-rearing styles, also affect children's personalities. In sum, we must think of temperament and personality as affected by a complex mix of environmental conditions, some child-specific and others stemming from shared family conditions.

Because parents tend to emphasize their children's unique qualities, this mother may treat her twins differently, giving more warmth and encouragement to one than the other. Such nonshared environmental factors contribute to differences between siblings in development. © Photodisc/Alamy Images

Temperament as a Predictor of Children's Behavior

Research on temperament provides a powerful illustration of the child's contribution to his or her own development. Children's temperamental traits consistently predict their cognitive and social functioning.

Almost as soon as it can be measured, children's attention span forecasts their learning and cognitive development. For example, persistence during the first year correlates with infant mental test scores and preschool IQ (Matheny, 1989). During early and middle childhood, persistence continues to predict IQ, along with literacy and mathematical progress and grades in school. In contrast, distractibility, high activity level, and difficult temperament are linked to poor school performance (Coplan, Barber, & Lagacé-Séguin, 1999; Martin, Olejnik, & Gaddis, 1994; Strelau, Zawadzki, & Piotrowska, 2001).

Temperament is also related to social behavior. Highly active preschoolers tend to be sociable with peers, but they also become involved in more conflict than their less active agemates. Shy, inhibited children often watch classmates and engage in anxious behaviors that discourage interaction, such as hovering around play activities and rarely speaking (Chen, Wang, & DeSouza, 2006; Henderson et al., 2004). And as we will see in Chapter 12, inhibited children's high anxiety leads to more discomfort after wrongdoing and a greater sense of responsibility to others. As a result, early fearfulness protects children against becoming aggressive. In contrast, irritable, impulsive children are at risk for aggressive and antisocial conduct (Sanson, Hemphill, & Smart, 2004; Vitaro et al., 2006).

In some cases, as with shy children, social behavior seems to be a direct result of temperament. In other instances, it reflects the way people respond to the child's emotional style. For example, active, impulsive children often elicit negative interaction, which leads to conflict. As Chapter 12 will make clear, the link between early impulsivity and later lawbreaking and aggressive acts has much to do with the inept parenting often evoked by distractible, headstrong children.

Finally, beginning in the preschool years, children's capacity for effortful control is linked to diverse aspects of competence (Rothbart, Posner, & Kieras, 2006). These include motivation, persistence, task mastery, cooperation, moral maturity (such as concern about wrongdoing and willingness to apologize), empathy, sympathy, and prosocial behaviors of sharing and helpfulness (Eisenberg et al., 2004; Harris et al., 2007; Kochanska & Aksan, 2006; Posner & Rothbart, 2007). Effortful control is also positively related to children's resistance to stress. For example, it buffers them against the negative impact of parental conflict, perhaps because children high in effortful control can shift attention away from their parents' negative behaviors and their own feelings of anxiety to more positive features of their social environments (David & Murphy, 2007). At the same, time, as we will see next, parenting practices can impede or promote children's effortful control, thereby profoundly altering the link between early temperament and development.

Temperament and Child Rearing: The Goodness-of-Fit Model

If a child's disposition interferes with learning or getting along with others, adults must gently but consistently counteract the child's maladaptive style. Thomas and Chess (1977) proposed a **goodness-of-fit model** to explain how temperament and environment together can produce favorable outcomes. Goodness of fit involves creating child-rearing environments that recognize each child's temperament while encouraging more adaptive functioning.

Goodness of fit helps explain why difficult children (who withdraw from new experiences and react negatively and intensely) are at high risk for later adjustment problems. These children

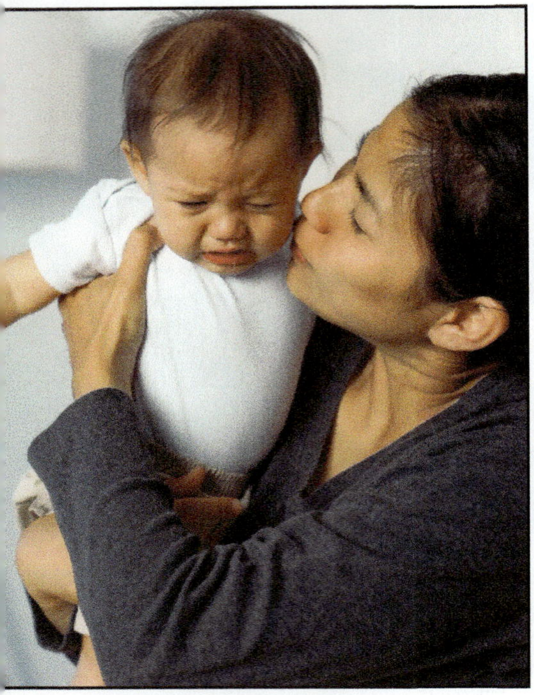

"Goodness of fit" describes the interaction between a child's biologically based temperament and the child-rearing environment. This mother's calm, soothing response will help her child regulate intense emotional reactions and develop more adaptive responses to frustration. © Royalty-Free/Corbis

frequently experience parenting that fits poorly with their dispositions. As infants, they are less likely to receive sensitive caregiving (van den Boom & Hoeksma, 1994). By the second year, parents of difficult children—especially in low-SES families—tend to use angry, punitive discipline, which undermines the development of effortful control. As the child reacts with defiance and disobedience, parents become increasingly stressed (Coplan, Bowker, & Cooper, 2003; Paulussen-Hoogeboom et al., 2007). As a result, they continue their coercive tactics and also discipline inconsistently, sometimes rewarding the child's noncompliance by giving in to it (Calkins, 2002). These practices sustain and even increase the child's irritable, conflict-ridden style.

In contrast, when parents are positive and sensitive, which helps babies regulate emotion, difficultness declines by age 2 to 3 (Feldman, Greenbaum, & Yirmiya, 1999; Raikes et al., 2007). In childhood and adolescence, parental sensitivity, support, and clear expectations reduce the likelihood that difficultness will persist and lead to emotional and social difficulties (Jaffari-Bimmel et al., 2006).

Effective parenting of challenging children, however, depends on life conditions—good parental mental health, marital harmony, and favorable economic conditions (Schoppe-Sullivan et al., 2007). In a comparison of the temperaments of Russian and U.S. babies, Russian infants were more emotionally negative, fearful, and upset when frustrated (Gartstein, Slobodskaya, & Kinsht, 2003). Faced with longer work hours and increased stress resulting from a depressed national economy, Russian parents may have lacked time and energy for the sensitive, patient interaction with their babies that protects against difficultness.

Cultural values also affect the fit between parenting and child temperament, as research in China illustrates. In the past, collectivist values, which discourage self-assertion, led Chinese adults to evaluate shy, withdrawn children positively—as advanced in social maturity. Consistent with this view, several studies showed that compared with North American parents, Chinese parents were more accepting and encouraging and less punitive toward inhibited children. Consequently, shy Chinese youngsters of a decade or two ago appeared well-adjusted, both academically and socially (Chen, Rubin, & Li, 1995; Chen et al., 1998).

But rapid expansion of a market economy in China, which requires assertiveness and sociability for success, may be responsible for a recent change in Chinese parents' and teachers' attitudes toward childhood shyness (Chen, Wang, & DeSouza, 2006; Yu, 2002). Among Shanghai fourth graders, the association between shyness and adjustment also changed over time. Whereas shyness was positively correlated with teacher-rated competence, peer acceptance, leadership, and academic achievement in 1990, these relationships weakened in 1998 and reversed in 2002, when they mirrored findings of Western research (see Figure 10.4) (Chen et al., 2005). Cultural context makes a difference in whether shy children receive support or disapproval and whether they adjust well or poorly.

An effective match between rearing conditions and child temperament is best accomplished early, before unfavorable temperament–environment relationships produce maladjustment. Both difficult and shy children benefit from warm, accepting parenting that makes firm but reasonable demands for mastering new experiences. With reserved, inactive toddlers, highly stimulating parenting—questioning, instructing, and pointing out objects—fosters exploration. Yet for highly active toddlers, these same parental behaviors are too directive, dampening their play and curiosity (Miceli et al., 1998).

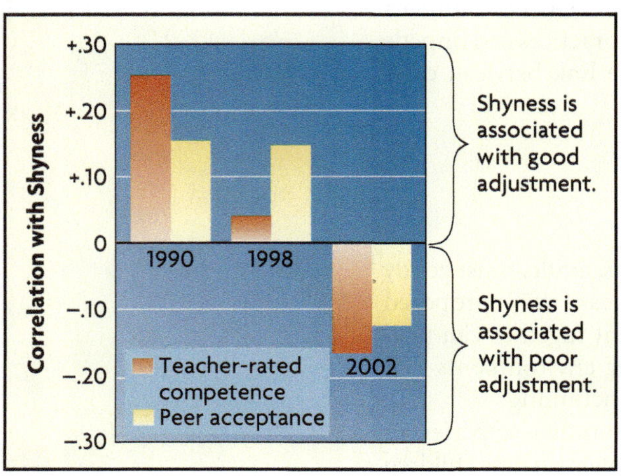

■ **Figure 10.4** **Changes over time in correlations between shyness and adjustment among Chinese fourth graders.**

In 1990, shy Chinese children appeared well-adjusted. But as China's market economy expanded and valuing of self-assertion and sociability increased, the direction of the correlations shifted. In 2002, shyness was negatively associated with adjustment. These findings are for teacher-rated competence and peer acceptance. Those for leadership (holding offices in student organizations) and academic achievement changed similarly. (Adapted from Chen et al., 2005.)

The goodness-of-fit model reminds us that babies have unique dispositions that adults must accept. Parents can neither take full credit for their children's virtues nor be blamed for all their faults. But parents can turn an environment that exaggerates a child's problems into one that builds on the child's strengths. In the following sections, we will see that goodness of fit is also at the heart of infant–caregiver attachment. This first intimate relationship grows out of interaction between parent and baby, to which the emotional styles of both partners contribute.

Ask Yourself

Review How do genetic and environmental factors work together to influence a child's temperament? Cite examples from research on nonshared environmental influences, cultural variations in temperament, and goodness of fit.

Apply Mandy and Jeff are parents of 2-year-old inhibited Sam and 3-year-old difficult Maria. Explain the importance of effortful control to Mandy and Jeff, and suggest ways they can strengthen it in each of their children.

Connect Do findings on ethnic differences in temperament illustrate genetic–environmental correlation, discussed on page 121 in Chapter 3? Explain.

Reflect How would you describe your temperament as a young child? Do you think it has remained stable, or has it changed? What factors might be involved?

Development of Attachment

Attachment is the strong, affectionate tie we have with special people in our lives that leads us to experience pleasure when we interact with them and to be comforted by their nearness in times of stress. By the second half of the first year, infants have become attached to familiar people who have responded to their needs. **TAKE A MOMENT...** Watch how babies of this age single out their parents for special attention. When the mother enters the room, the baby breaks into a broad, friendly smile. When she picks him up, he pats her face, explores her hair, and snuggles against her. When he feels anxious, he crawls into her lap and clings closely.

Freud first suggested that the infant's emotional tie to the mother is the foundation for all later relationships. Contemporary research indicates that, although the parent–infant bond is vitally important, later development is influenced not just by early attachment experiences but also by the continuing quality of the parent–child relationship.

Attachment has also been the subject of intense theoretical debate. Recall from Chapter 1 how the *psychoanalytic perspective* regards feeding as the central context in which caregivers and babies build this close emotional bond. *Behaviorism,* too, emphasizes the importance of feeding, but for different reasons. According to a well-known behaviorist explanation, infants learn to prefer the mother's soft caresses, warm smiles, and tender words because these events are paired with tension relief as she satisfies the baby's hunger.

Although feeding is an important context for building a close relationship, attachment does not depend on hunger satisfaction. In the 1950s, a famous experiment showed that rhesus monkeys reared with terry-cloth and wire-mesh "surrogate mothers" clung to the soft terry-cloth substitute, even though the wire-mesh "mother" held the bottle and infants had to climb on it to be fed (Harlow & Zimmerman, 1959). Human infants, too, become attached to family members who seldom feed them, including fathers, siblings, and grandparents. And toddlers in Western cultures who sleep alone and experience frequent daytime separations from their parents sometimes develop strong emotional ties to cuddly objects, such as blankets or teddy bears, that play no role in infant feeding!

Both psychoanalytic and behaviorist accounts of attachment have another problem: They emphasize the caregiver's contribution to the attachment relationship but pay little attention to the importance of the infant's characteristics.

Baby monkeys reared with "surrogate mothers" preferred to cling to a soft terry-cloth "mother" instead of a wire-mesh "mother" that held a bottle. These findings contradict both psychoanalytic and behaviorist views of feeding as central to building the infant–caregiver attachment bond. © Martin Rogers/Woodfin Camp & Associates

Bowlby's Ethological Theory

Today, **ethological theory of attachment,** which recognizes the infant's emotional tie to the caregiver as an evolved response that promotes survival, is the most widely accepted view. John Bowlby (1969), who first applied this idea to the infant–caregiver bond, was originally a psychoanalyst. His theory retains the psychoanalytic idea that quality of attachment to the caregiver has profound implications for the child's feelings of security and capacity to form trusting relationships.

At the same time, Bowlby was inspired by Konrad Lorenz's studies of imprinting (see Chapter 1). Bowlby believed that the human infant, like the young of other animal species, is endowed with a set of built-in behaviors that keep the parent nearby to protect the infant from danger and to provide support for exploring and mastering the environment (Waters & Cummings, 2000). Contact with the parent also ensures that the baby will be fed, but Bowlby pointed out that feeding is not the basis for attachment. Rather, attachment can best be understood in an evolutionary context in which survival of the species—through ensuring both safety and competence—is of utmost importance.

According to Bowlby, the infant's relationship with the parent begins as a set of innate signals that call the adult to the baby's side. Over time, a true affectionate bond develops, supported by new emotional and cognitive capacities as well as by a history of warm, sensitive care. Attachment develops in four phases:

1. *Preattachment phase* (birth to 6 weeks). Built-in signals—grasping, smiling, crying, and gazing into the adult's eyes—help bring newborn babies into close contact with other humans. Once an adult responds, infants encourage her to remain nearby because closeness comforts them. Babies of this age recognize their own mother's smell, voice, and face (see Chapter 4). But they are not yet attached to her, since they do not mind being left with an unfamiliar adult.
2. *"Attachment-in-the-making" phase* (6 weeks to 6–8 months). During this phase, infants respond differently to a familiar caregiver than to a stranger. For example, the baby smiles, laughs, and babbles more freely with the mother and quiets more quickly when she picks him up. As infants learn that their own actions affect the behavior of those around them, they begin to develop a *sense of trust*—the expectation that the caregiver will respond when signaled—but they still do not protest when separated from her.
3. *"Clear-cut" attachment phase* (6–8 months to 18 months–2 years). Now attachment to the familiar caregiver is evident. Babies display **separation anxiety,** becoming upset when the adult on whom they have come to rely leaves. Like stranger anxiety (see pages 405–406), separation anxiety does not always occur; it depends on infant temperament and the current situation. But in many cultures, separation anxiety increases between 6 and 15 months, suggesting that infants have developed a clear understanding that the caregiver continues to exist when not in view (Kagan, Kearsley, & Zelazo, 1978). Consistent with this idea, babies who have not yet mastered Piagetian object permanence usually do not become anxious when separated from the parent (Lester et al., 1974).

   Besides protesting the parent's departure, older infants and toddlers try hard to maintain her presence. They approach, follow, and climb on her in preference to others. And they use her as a *secure base* from which to explore.
4. *Formation of a reciprocal relationship* (18 months–2 years and on). By the end of the second year, rapid growth in representation and language permits toddlers to understand some of the factors that influence the parent's coming and going and to predict her return. As a result, separation protest declines. Instead, children negotiate with the caregiver, using requests and persuasion to alter her goals. For example, one 2-year-old asked her parents to read a story before leaving her with a babysitter. The extra time with her parents, along with a better understanding of where they were going ("to have dinner with Uncle Charlie") and when they would be back ("right after you go to sleep"), helped this child withstand her parents' absence.

Although separation anxiety increases between 6 and 15 months of age, its occurrence depends on infant temperament, context, and adult behavior. This child shows distress as his mother says goodbye, but because his caregiver is sensitive and supportive, his anxiety will probably be short-lived.

With age, children depend less on caregivers' physical proximity and more on a sense of confidence that they will be accessible and responsive in times of need. According to Bowlby (1980), out of their experiences during these four phases, children construct an enduring affectionate tie that they can use as a secure base in the parents' absence. This image serves as an **internal working model,** or set of expectations about the availability of attachment figures, their likelihood of providing support during times of stress, and the self's interaction with those figures. The internal working model becomes a vital part of personality, serving as a guide for all future close relationships (Bretherton & Munholland, 1999). With age, children continually revise and expand their internal working model as their cognitive, emotional, and social capacities increase and as they interact with parents and form other close bonds with adults, siblings, and friends.

Measuring the Security of Attachment

Although virtually all family-reared babies become attached to a familiar caregiver by the second year, the quality of this relationship differs from child to child. Some infants appear secure in the presence of the caregiver; they know they can count on her for protection and support. Others seem anxious and uncertain.

A widely used laboratory technique for measuring the quality of attachment between 1 and 2 years of age is the **Strange Situation.** In designing it, Mary Ainsworth and her colleagues (1978) reasoned that if the development of attachment has gone well, infants and toddlers should use the parent as a secure base from which to explore an unfamiliar playroom. In addition, when the parent leaves, an unfamiliar adult should be less comforting than the parent. The Strange Situation takes the baby through eight short episodes in which brief separations from and reunions with the caregiver occur (see Table 10.2).

Observing infants' responses to these episodes, researchers have identified a secure attachment pattern and three patterns of insecurity; a few babies cannot be classified (Ainsworth et al., 1978; Barnett & Vondra, 1999; Main & Solomon, 1990; Thompson, 2006). Although separation anxiety varies among the groups, the baby's reunion responses define attachment quality.

- **Secure attachment.** These infants use the parent as a secure base. When separated, they may or may not cry, but if they do, it is because the parent is absent and they prefer her to the stranger. When the parent returns, they actively seek contact, and their crying is reduced immediately. About 60 percent of North American infants in middle-SES families show this pattern. (In low-SES families, a smaller proportion of babies show the secure pattern, with higher proportions falling into the following insecure patterns.)

Table 10.2 Episodes in the Strange Situation

Episode	Events	Attachment Behavior Observed
1	Experimenter introduces parent and baby to playroom and then leaves.	
2	Parent is seated while baby plays with toys.	Parent as a secure base
3	Stranger enters, is seated, and talks to parent.	Reaction to unfamiliar adult
4	Parent leaves room. Stranger responds to baby and offers comfort if baby is upset.	Separation anxiety
5	Parent returns, greets baby, and offers comfort if necessary. Stranger leaves room.	Reaction to reunion
6	Parent leaves room.	Separation anxiety
7	Stranger enters room and offers comfort.	Ability to be soothed by stranger
8	Parent returns, greets baby, offers comfort if necessary, and tries to reinterest baby in toys.	Reaction to reunion

Note: Episode 1 lasts about 30 seconds; each of the remaining episodes lasts about 3 minutes. Separation episodes are cut short if the baby becomes very upset. Reunion episodes are extended if the baby needs more time to calm down and return to play.

Source: Ainsworth et al., 1978.

- **Avoidant attachment.** These infants seem unresponsive to the parent when she is present. When she leaves, they usually are not distressed, and they react to the stranger in much the same way as to the parent. During reunion, they avoid or are slow to greet the parent, and when picked up, they often fail to cling. About 15 percent of North American infants in middle-SES families show this pattern.
- **Resistant attachment.** Before separation, these infants seek closeness to the parent and often fail to explore. When the parent leaves, they are usually distressed, and on her return, they combine clinginess with angry, resistive behavior, struggling when held and sometimes hitting and pushing. Many continue to cry and cling after being picked up and cannot be comforted easily. About 10 percent of North American infants in middle-SES families show this pattern.
- **Disorganized/disoriented attachment.** This pattern reflects the greatest insecurity. At reunion, these infants show confused, contradictory behaviors—for example, looking away while the parent is holding them or approaching the parent with flat, depressed emotion. Most display a dazed facial expression, and a few cry out unexpectedly after having calmed down or display odd, frozen postures. About 15 percent of North American infants in middle-SES families show this pattern.

Infants' reactions in the Strange Situation closely resemble their use of the parent as a secure base and their response to separation and reunion at home (Pederson & Moran, 1996; Pederson et al., 1998). For this reason, the procedure is a powerful tool for assessing attachment security. Researchers have modified Strange Situation procedures to make them appropriate for preschoolers, looking closely at the child's seeking of physical closeness, eye contact, expressions of emotion, and content and style of parent-directed speech—especially during reunion episodes. The resulting preschool attachment classifications are modestly associated with previously obtained infant assessments (Crittenden, 2000; Main & Cassidy, 1988; Moss, Cyr, & Dubois-Comtois, 2004).

The **Attachment Q-Sort,** an alternative method suitable for children between 1 and 4 years of age, permits attachment to be assessed through home observations (Waters et al., 1995). Either the parent or a highly trained observer sorts 90 behaviors—such as "Child greets mother with a big smile when she enters the room," "If mother moves very far, child follows along," and "Child uses mother's facial expressions as a good source of information when something looks risky or threatening"—into nine categories, ranging from "highly descriptive" to "not at all descriptive" of the child. Then a score, ranging from high to low in security, is computed.

This securely attached 1-year-old actively seeks contact and is calmed and comforted by his father's return. In a similar situation, an avoidantly attached toddler would be slow to greet the parent, while a resistantly attached toddler would be both clingy and angry. © Elizabeth Crews

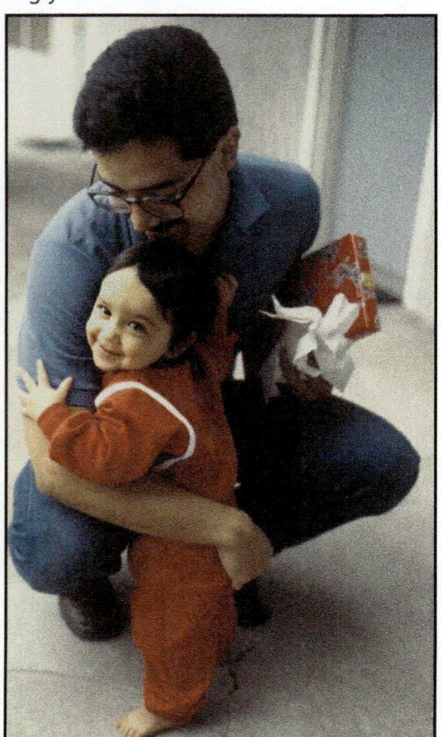

Because the Q-Sort taps a wider array of attachment-related behaviors than the Strange Situation, it may better reflect the parent–infant relationship in everyday life. However, the Q-sort method is time-consuming, requiring a nonparent informant to spend several hours observing the child before sorting the descriptors, and it does not differentiate between types of insecurity. The Q-Sort responses of expert observers correspond well with infants' secure-base behavior in the Strange Situation; more research is needed to verify a correspondence for preschoolers (Posada, 2006). Without careful training, parents' Q-Sort judgments show little relationship with Strange Situation assessments (van IJzendoorn et al., 2004). Parents of insecure children, especially, may lack skills for accurately reporting their child's attachment behaviors.

Stability of Attachment

Research on the stability of attachment patterns between 1 and 2 years of age yields a wide range of findings. In some studies, as many as 70 to 90 percent of babies remain the same in their reactions to parents; in others, only 30 to 40 percent do (Thompson, 2000, 2006). A close look at which babies stay the same and which ones change yields a more consistent picture. Quality of attachment is usually secure and stable for middle-SES babies experiencing favorable life conditions. And infants who move from insecurity to security typically have well-adjusted mothers with positive family and friendship ties. Perhaps many became parents before they were psychologically ready but, with social support, grew into the role. In contrast, in low-SES families with many daily stresses, little social support, and parental psychological problems, attachment status generally moves away from security or changes from one insecure pattern to another (Belsky et al., 1996; Fish, 2004; Vondra, Hommerding, & Shaw, 1999; Vondra et al., 2001).

These findings indicate that securely attached babies more often maintain their attachment status than insecure babies, whose relationship with the caregiver is, by definition, fragile and uncertain. The exception is disorganized/disoriented attachment, an insecure pattern that is as stable as attachment security: Nearly 70 percent retain this classification over the second year (Barnett, Ganiban, & Cicchetti, 1999; Hesse & Main, 2000; Weinfield, Whaley, & Egeland, 2004). As you will see, many disorganized/disoriented infants experience extremely negative caregiving, which may disrupt emotional self-regulation so severely that confused, ambivalent feelings toward parents persist.

Overall, many children show short-term instability in attachment quality. A few studies reveal high long-term stability from infancy to middle childhood and—on the basis of interviews about relationships with parents—into adolescence and emerging adulthood (Hamilton, 2000; Waters et al., 2000). But once again, participants came from middle-SES homes, and most probably had stable family lives. In one poverty-stricken sample, many participants moved from secure attachment in infancy to insecure attachment in young adulthood. Child maltreatment, maternal depression, and poor family functioning in early adolescence distinguished these young people from the few who stayed securely attached. Disorganized/disoriented participants, however, typically remained insecure over the long term, expressing confused, ambivalent feelings toward their parents, many of whom had been abusive (Weinfield, Sroufe, & Egeland, 2000; Weinfield, Whaley, & Egeland, 2004).

Cultural Variations

Cross-cultural evidence indicates that attachment patterns may have to be interpreted differently in certain cultures. For example, as Figure 10.5 reveals, German infants show considerably more avoidant attachment than American babies do. But German parents encourage their infants to be nonclingy and independent, so the baby's behavior may be an intended outcome of cultural beliefs and practices (Grossmann et al., 1985). In contrast, in a study of infants of the Dogon people of Mali, Africa, none showed avoidant attachment to their mothers (True, Pisani, & Oumar, 2001). Even when grandmothers are primary caregivers (as they are with firstborn sons), Dogon mothers remain available to their babies, holding them close and nursing them promptly in response to hunger and distress.

Similarly, Japanese infants rarely show avoidant attachment (refer again to Figure 10.5). Rather, many are resistantly attached—a reaction that may not represent true insecurity. Japanese mothers rarely leave their babies in others' care, so the Strange Situation probably induces greater stress in them than in infants who experience frequent maternal separations (Takahashi, 1990). Also, Japanese parents view the infant clinginess and attention seeking that are part of resistant attachment as normal indicators of infant closeness and dependency (Rothbaum et al., 2000a). Likewise, infants in Israeli kibbutzim seldom show avoidant attachment. For these babies, who can sense the fear of unfamiliar people that is pervasive in their communities (see page 406), the Strange Situation probably induces unusual distress (van IJzendoorn & Sagi, 1999). Despite these cultural variations and others, the secure pattern is still the most common attachment classification in all societies studied to date (van IJzendoorn & Sagi, 1999).

Figure 10.5 **A cross-cultural comparison of infants' reactions in the Strange Situation.** A high percentage of German babies seem avoidantly attached, whereas a substantial number of Japanese and Israeli kibbutz infants appear resistantly attached. Note that these responses may not reflect true insecurity. Instead, they are probably due to cultural differences in child-rearing practices. (Adapted from Sagi et al., 1995; van IJzendoorn & Kroonenberg, 1988.)

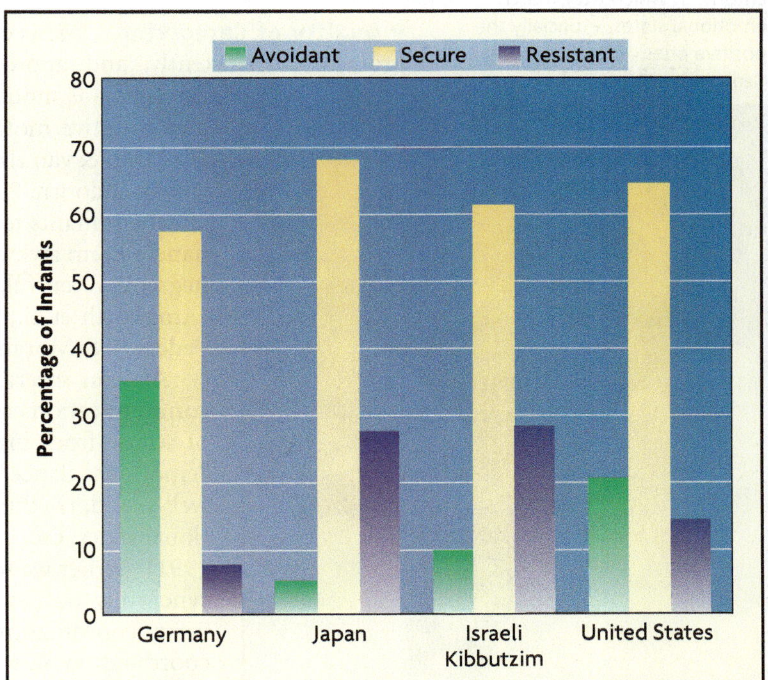

Factors Affecting Attachment Security

What factors might influence attachment security? Researchers have looked closely at four important influences: (1) opportunity to establish a close relationship, (2) quality of caregiving, (3) the baby's characteristics, and (4) family context, including parents' internal working models.

• **Opportunity for Attachment** What happens when a baby does not have the opportunity to establish a close tie to a caregiver? In a series of studies, René Spitz (1946) observed institutionalized infants whose mothers had given them up between 3 and 12 months of age. After being placed in a large ward where each shared a nurse with at least seven others, the babies lost weight, wept, withdrew from their surroundings, and had difficulty sleeping. If a consistent caregiver did not replace the mother, the depression deepened rapidly.

These institutionalized infants had emotional difficulties because they were prevented from forming a bond with one or a few adults (Rutter, 1996). In another study, which supports this conclusion, researchers followed the development of infants in an institution with a good caregiver–child ratio and a rich selection of books and toys—but where staff turnover was so rapid that the average child had 50 different caregivers by the age of 4½! Many of these children became "late adoptees" who were placed in homes after age 4. Most developed deep ties with their adoptive parents, indicating that a first attachment bond can develop as late as 4 to 6 years of age (Hodges & Tizard, 1989; Tizard & Rees, 1975). But these children were also more likely to display attachment difficulties, including an excessive desire for adult attention, "overfriendliness" to unfamiliar adults and peers, failure to check back with the parent in anxiety-arousing situations, and few friendships.

Adopted children who spent their first 6 to 8 months or more in deprived Romanian orphanages often display these same difficulties. Symptoms typically persist and are associated with wide-ranging mental health problems in middle childhood, including cognitive impairments, peer rejection, inattention and hyperactivity, and disruptive behavior (O'Connor et al., 2003; Rutter et al., 2007). Furthermore, as early as 7 months, Romanian orphanage children show reduced ERP brain waves in response to facial expressions of emotion and have trouble discriminating such expressions—outcomes that suggest disrupted formation of neural structures involved in "reading" emotions (Parker et al., 2005). Taken together, the evidence indicates that fully normal emotional development depends on establishing close ties with caregivers early in life.

• **Quality of Caregiving** Dozens of studies report that **sensitive caregiving**—responding promptly, consistently, and appropriately to infants and holding them tenderly and carefully—is moderately related to attachment security in both biological and adoptive mother–infant pairs and in diverse cultures and SES groups (DeWolff & van IJzendoorn, 1997; Posada et al., 2002, 2004; Stams, Juffer, & van IJzendoorn, 2002; van IJzendoorn et al., 2004). In contrast, insecurely attached infants tend to have mothers who engage in less physical contact, handle them awkwardly, behave in a "routine" manner, and are sometimes negative, resentful, and rejecting, particularly in response to infant distress (Ainsworth et al., 1978; Isabella, 1993; McElwain & Booth-LaForce, 2006; Pederson & Moran, 1996).

This mother and baby engage in a sensitively tuned form of communication called interactional synchrony, in which they match emotional states, especially the positive ones. © VCL/Spencer Rowell/Getty Images/Taxi

Also, in several studies of North American infants, a special form of communication called **interactional synchrony** separated the experiences of secure from insecure babies. It is best described as a sensitively tuned "emotional dance," in which the caregiver responds to infant signals in a well-timed, rhythmic, appropriate fashion, and both partners match emotional states, especially the positive ones (Feldman, 2003; Isabella & Belsky, 1991). Earlier we saw that sensitive face-to-face play, in which interactional synchrony occurs, helps infants regulate emotion. But moderate adult–infant coordination is a better predictor of attachment security than "tight" coordination, in which the adult responds to most infant cues (Jaffe et al., 2001). Perhaps warm, sensitive caregivers use a relaxed, flexible style of communication in which they comfortably accept and repair emotional mismatches, returning to a synchronous state.

Cultures vary in their view of sensitivity toward infants. Among the Gusii people of Kenya, for example, mothers rarely cuddle, hug, or interact playfully with their babies, although they are very responsive to their infants' needs. Yet most Gusii infants appear securely attached, using the mother as a secure base (LeVine et al., 1994). This suggests that security depends on attentive caregiving, not necessarily on moment-by-moment contingent interaction. Puerto Rican mothers, who highly value obedience and socially appropriate behavior, often physically direct and limit their babies' actions—a style of caregiving linked to attachment security in Puerto Rican culture (Carlson & Horwood, 2003). Yet in many Western cultures, such physical control is viewed as intrusive and predicts insecurity.

Compared with securely attached infants, avoidant babies tend to receive overstimulating care. Their mothers might, for example, talk energetically to them while they are looking away or falling asleep. By avoiding the mother, these infants try to escape from overwhelming interaction. Resistant infants often experience inconsistent care: Their mothers are unresponsive to infant signals. Yet when the baby begins to explore, these mothers interfere, shifting the infant's attention back to themselves. As a result, the baby is overly dependent as well as angry at the mother's lack of involvement (Cassidy & Berlin, 1994; Isabella & Belsky, 1991).

Among the Dogon people of Mali, Africa, mothers stay close to their babies and respond promptly and gently to infant distress. Dogon mothers are almost never overly stimulating or intrusive—practices linked to avoidant attachment. And none of their infants were avoidantly attached. © Wolfgang Kaehler/Corbis

Highly inadequate caregiving is a powerful predictor of disruptions in attachment. Child abuse and neglect (topics we will consider in Chapter 14) are associated with all three forms of attachment insecurity. Among maltreated infants, disorganized/disoriented attachment is especially high (Barnett, Ganiban, & Cicchetti, 1999; van IJzendoorn, Schuengel, & Bakermans-Kranenburg, 1999). Persistently depressed mothers, mothers with very low marital satisfaction, and parents suffering from a traumatic event, such as serious illness or loss of a loved one, also tend to promote the uncertain behaviors of this pattern (Campbell et al., 2004; Moss et al., 2005b; van IJzendoorn, 1995). Some of these mothers display frightening, contradictory, and unpleasant behaviors, such as looking scared, mocking or teasing the baby, holding the baby stiffly at a distance, roughly pulling the baby by the arm, or seeking reassurance from the upset child (Goldberg et al., 2003; Lyons-Ruth, Bronfman, & Parsons, 1999; Madigan, Moran, & Pederson, 2006; Schuengel, Bakermans-Kranenburg, & van IJzendoorn, 1999). The baby's disorganized behavior seems to reflect his conflicted reaction to the parent, who sometimes comforts but at other times arouses fear.

• **Infant Characteristics** Because attachment is the result of a *relationship* that builds between two partners, infant characteristics should affect how easily it is established. In Chapter 3, we saw that prematurity, birth complications, and newborn illness make caregiving more taxing. In families under stress, these difficulties are linked to attachment insecurity. In one study, the *combination* of preterm birth and maternal depression—but not preterm birth alone—increased the likelihood of insecure attachment at 12 months (Poehlmann & Fiese, 2001). Infants with special needs probably require greater sensitivity, which stressed parents often cannot provide. But when parents have the time and patience to care for a baby with special needs and view their infants positively, at-risk newborns fare quite well in attachment security (Brisch et al., 2005; Cox, Hopkins, & Hans, 2000).

The role of infant temperament in attachment security has been intensely debated. Some researchers believe that irritable, fearful infants may simply react to brief separations with intense anxiety, regardless of the parent's sensitivity to the baby (Kagan, 1998; Kagan & Fox, 2006). Consistent with this view, emotionally reactive, difficult babies are more likely to develop later insecure attachments (van IJzendoorn et al., 2004; Vaughn & Bost, 1999). Again, however, other evidence suggests that caregiving is involved. In a study extending from birth to age 2, difficult infants more often had highly anxious mothers—a combination that, by the second year, often resulted in a "disharmonious relationship" characterized by both maternal insensitivity and attachment insecurity (see Figure 10.6 on page 432) (Symons, 2001). Infant difficultness and maternal anxiety seemed to perpetuate each other, impairing caregiving and the security of the

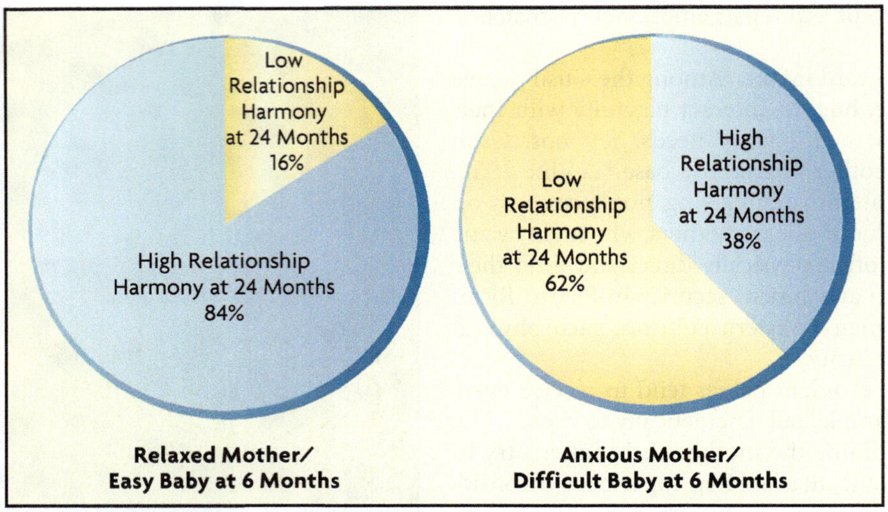

Figure 10.6 **Influence of mother–infant distress at 6 months on relationship harmony at 24 months.**

In a study extending over the first two years, the combination of high maternal anxiety and high infant difficultness frequently impaired caregiving, resulting in many mothers and babies with low relationship harmony—characterized by maternal insensitivity and attachment insecurity—in the second year. (Adapted from Symons, 2001.)

parent–infant bond. In another investigation that focused on disorganized/disoriented babies, negative emotional reactivity increased sharply between 12 and 18 months. Attachment disorganization was not caused by a difficult temperament; rather, it preceded difficultness and seemed to promote it (Barnett, Ganiban, & Cicchetti, 1999).

Indeed, extensive research confirms that caregiving can override the impact of infant characteristics on attachment security. When researchers combined data from more than 1,000 mother–infant pairs, they found that maternal problems—such as mental illness, teenage parenthood, and child abuse—were associated with a sharp rise in attachment insecurity. In contrast, child problems—ranging from prematurity and developmental delays to serious physical disabilities and psychological disorders—had little impact on attachment quality (van IJzendoorn et al., 1992). Indeed, mothers who view their difficult babies as soothable are far more sensitive caregivers than mothers who believe their negative, reactive babies cannot be pacified (Ghera et al., 2006).

Finally, if children's traits alone determined attachment security, we would expect attachment, like temperament, to be at least moderately heritable. Yet twin comparisons reveal that the heritability of attachment is virtually nil (O'Connor & Croft, 2001). Identical twins are no more alike than fraternal twins (or other siblings) in attachment security. About two-thirds of siblings—whether identical twins, fraternal twins, nontwin siblings, unrelated siblings, or foster infants—establish similar attachment patterns with their parent. Yet these siblings often differ in temperament (Cole, 2006; Dozier et al., 2001; van IJzendoorn, 1995). This suggests that the strongest parental influences on attachment security are *nonshared* experiences, reflecting most parents' efforts to adjust their caregiving to each child's individual needs.

At the same time, in a study of twins, mothers who did treat one baby less sensitively reduced the impact of sensitive caregiving on the other infant's attachment security (Fearon et al., 2006). The better-parented baby may have monitored parental insensitivity toward his or her sibling and felt threatened by it. In this way, nonshared parental behaviors may operate in complex ways, affecting attachment patterns of other children in the family.

A major reason that children's characteristics do not show strong relationships with attachment quality is that their influence depends on goodness of fit. From this perspective, *many* child attributes can lead to secure attachment as long as caregivers sensitively adjust their behavior to fit the baby's needs (Seifer & Schiller, 1995; Sroufe, 1985). Interventions that teach parents to interact sensitively with difficult-to-care-for infants are highly successful in enhancing both quality of caregiving and attachment security (Velderman et al., 2006). But when parents' capacity is strained—by their own personalities or by stressful living conditions—then infants with illnesses, disabilities, and difficult temperaments are at risk for attachment problems.

• Family Circumstances As we have indicated in this and previous chapters, quality of caregiving can be fully understood only in terms of the larger context of the parent–child relationship. Job loss, a failing marriage, financial strain, and other stressors can undermine attachment indirectly, by interfering with the sensitivity of parental care. Or these stressors can affect babies' sense of security directly by altering the emotional climate of the family (for example, exposing them to angry adult interactions) or by disrupting familiar daily routines (Raikes & Thompson, 2005; Thompson & Raikes, 2003).

The arrival of a new sibling illustrates how family circumstances can affect attachment quality. In one study, firstborn preschoolers who declined in attachment security after the birth of a baby had mothers who were depressed, anxious, or hostile before the birth. These symptoms were associated with marital friction (which the firstborns probably sensed) as well as with unfavorable mother–firstborn interaction. When mothers had cooperative marriages, coped well with the second birth, and stayed involved with their older child, preschoolers maintained a secure attachment bond (Teti et al., 1996). The availability of social supports, especially parents with a good relationship who assist each other with caregiving, reduces family stress and predicts greater attachment security (Belsky, 2006; Owen & Cox, 1997).

This mother's involvement with both her toddler and her new baby helps sustain secure attachment with the older child. But when a mother is stressed after a second birth, mother–first-born interaction is likely to become negative and undermine the quality of the attachment bond. © PhotoDisc/Getty Images

• **Parents' Internal Working Models** Parents bring to the family context a long history of attachment experiences, out of which they construct internal working models that they apply to the bonds established with their babies. To assess parents' "state of mind" with respect to attachment, Mary Main and her colleagues devised the *Adult Attachment Interview,* which asks adults to recall and evaluate childhood attachment experiences (Main & Goldwyn, 1998).

As Table 10.3 shows, quality of mothers' working models is clearly related to children's attachment security in infancy and early childhood—results replicated in Canada, Germany, Great Britain, the Netherlands, and the United States. Mothers who show objectivity and balance in discussing their childhoods tend to have securely attached infants. In contrast, those who dismiss the importance of early relationships or describe them in angry, confused ways usually have insecurely attached babies (Steele, Steele, & Fonagy, 1996; van IJzendoorn, 1995). Caregiving behavior helps explain these associations. Mothers with autonomous/secure representations are warmer and more sensitive with their babies. They are also more likely to be supportive and to encourage learning and mastery in their older children, who, in turn, are more affectionate and comfortably interactive with them (Pederson et al., 1998; Slade et al., 1999).

But we must be careful not to assume any direct transfer of parents' childhood experiences to quality of attachment with their own children. Parental internal working models are *reconstructed memories* affected by many factors, including relationship experiences over the life course, personality, and current life satisfaction. Longitudinal research reveals that certain negative life events can weaken the link between an individual's own attachment security in infancy and a secure internal working model in adulthood. And insecurely attached babies who become adults with insecure internal working models often have lives that, based on adulthood self-reports, are fraught with family crises (Waters et al., 2000; Weinfield, Sroufe, & Egeland, 2000).

In sum, our early rearing experiences do not destine us to become sensitive or insensitive parents. Rather, the way we *view* our childhoods—our ability to come to terms with negative events, to integrate new information into our working models, and to look back on our own parents in an understanding, forgiving way—is much more influential in how we rear our children than the actual history of care we received (Main, 2000).

Table 10.3 Relationship of Mothers' Internal Working Models to Infant Attachment Security

Type of Maternal Working Model	Description	Infant Attachment Classification[a]
Autonomous/ secure	These mothers show objectivity and balance in discussing their childhood experiences, whether these were positive or negative. They neither idealize their parents nor feel angry about the past. Their explanations are coherent and believable.	Secure
Dismissing	These mothers devalue the importance of their attachment relationships. They tend to idealize their parents without being able to recall specific experiences. What they do recall is discussed intellectually, with little emotion.	Avoidant
Overinvolved	These mothers talk about their childhood experiences with highly charged emotion, sometimes expressing anger toward their parents. They appear overwhelmed and confused about their early attachments and cannot discuss them coherently.	Resistant
Unresolved	These mothers show characteristics of any of the three other patterns. At the same time, they reason in a disorganized and confused way when loss of a loved one or experiences of physical or sexual abuse are discussed.	Disorganized/ disoriented

[a]Correspondences between type of maternal working model and infant attachment classification hold for 60 to 70 percent of mother–infant pairs.

Sources: Benoit & Parker, 1994; Main & Goldwyn, 1994; Pederson et al., 1998.

Multiple Attachments: The Father's Special Role

As we have indicated, babies develop attachments to a variety of familiar people—not just mothers but fathers, siblings, grandparents, and professional caregivers. Although Bowlby (1969) believed that infants are predisposed to direct their attachment behaviors to a single special person, especially when they are distressed, his theory allowed for these multiple attachments. Consistent with this view, when anxious or unhappy, most babies prefer to be comforted by their mother. But this preference declines over the second year. And when babies are not distressed, they approach, vocalize to, and smile equally often at both parents, who in turn are equally responsive to their infants' social bids (Bornstein, 2006; Parke, 2002).

Fathers' sensitive caregiving and interactional synchrony with infants, like mothers', predict attachment security (Lundy, 2003; van IJzendoorn et al., 2004). And fathers of 1- to 5-year-olds enrolled in full-time child care report feeling just as much anxiety as mothers about separating from their child and just as much concern about the impact of these daily separations on the child's well-being (Deater-Deckard et al., 1994). But as infancy progresses, mothers and fathers in the United States, Canada, and many other cultures, including Australia, India, Israel, Italy, and Japan, tend to interact differently with their babies: Mothers devote more time to physical care and expressing affection, fathers to playful interaction (Lamb, 1987; Roopnarine et al., 1990).

Mothers and fathers also play differently. Mothers more often provide toys, talk to infants, and gently play conventional games like pat-a-cake and peekaboo. In contrast, fathers—especially with their infant sons—tend to engage in highly arousing physical play with bursts of excitement that increase as play progresses (Feldman, 2003). This stimulating, surprising play style may help prepare babies to venture confidently into the surrounding world and to approach unfamiliar situations, such as play with peers (Paquette, 2004).

In cultures such as Japan, where long work hours prevent most fathers from sharing in infant caregiving, play is a vital context in which fathers build secure attachments (Hewlett, 2004; Schwalb et al., 2004). In many Western nations, however, a strict division of parental roles—mother as caregiver, father as playmate—has changed over the past quarter century in response to women's workforce participation and to cultural valuing of gender equality. Recent surveys indicate that in dual-earner families, U.S. fathers devote 85 percent as much time, and Canadian fathers 75 percent as much time, to children as mothers do—on average, about 3½ hours per day (Pleck & Masciadrelli, 2004; Sandberg & Hofferth, 2001; Zuzanek, 2000). Paternal availability to children is fairly similar across SES and ethnic groups, with one exception: Hispanic fathers spend more time engaged, probably because of the particularly high value that Hispanic cultures place on family involvement (Cabrera & García-Coll, 2004; Parke et al., 2004).

Mothers in dual-earner families tend to engage in more playful stimulation of their babies than mothers who are at home full-time (Cox et al., 1992). But fathers who are primary caregivers retain their arousing play style (Lamb & Oppenheim, 1989). These highly involved fathers are less gender-stereotyped in their beliefs; have sympathetic, friendly personalities; often had fathers who were more involved in rearing them; and regard parenthood as an especially enriching experience (Cabrera et al., 2000; Levy-Shiff & Israelashvili, 1988).

Fathers' involvement with babies occurs within a complex system of family attitudes and relationships. When both parents believe that men are capable of nurturing infants, fathers devote more time to caregiving (Beitel & Parke, 1998). A warm marital bond supports both parents' sensitivity and involvement with babies, but it is particularly important for fathers (Lamb & Lewis, 2004). See the Cultural Influences box on the following page for cross-cultural evidence documenting this conclusion—and also highlighting the powerful role of paternal warmth in children's development.

Attachment and Later Development

According to psychoanalytic and ethological theories, the inner feelings of affection and security that result from a healthy attachment relationship support all aspects of psychological development. In an extensive longitudinal study consistent with this view, Alan Sroufe and his collaborators found that preschoolers who were securely attached as babies were rated by

Cultural Influences

The Powerful Role of Paternal Warmth in Development

Research in diverse cultures demonstrates that fathers' warmth contributes greatly to children's long-term favorable development. In studies of many societies and ethnic groups around the world, researchers coded paternal expressions of love and nurturance—evident in such behaviors as cuddling, hugging, comforting, playing, verbally expressing love, and praising the child's behavior. Fathers' sustained affectionate involvement predicted later cognitive, emotional, and social competence as strongly as did mothers' warmth—and occasionally more strongly (Rohner & Veneziano, 2001; Veneziano, 2003). And in Western cultures, paternal warmth protected children against a wide range of difficulties, including childhood emotional and behavior problems and adolescent substance abuse and delinquency (Grant et al., 2000; Rohner & Brothers, 1999; Tacon & Caldera, 2001).

In families where fathers devote little time to physical caregiving, they express warmth through play. In a German study, fathers' play sensitivity—accepting toddlers' play initiatives, adapting play behaviors to toddlers' capacities, and responding appropriately to toddlers' expressions of emotion—predicted children's secure internal working models of attachment during middle childhood and adolescence (Grossmann et al., 2002). Through play, fathers seemed to transfer to young children a sense of confidence about parental support, which may strengthen their capacity to master many later challenges.

What factors promote paternal warmth? Cross-cultural research reveals a consistent relationship between the amount of time fathers spend near infants and toddlers and their expressions of caring and affection (Rohner & Veneziano, 2001). Consider the Aka hunters and gatherers of Central Africa, where fathers spend more time in physical proximity to their babies than in any other known society. Observations reveal that Aka fathers are within arm's reach of infants more than half the day. They pick up, cuddle, and play with their babies at least five times as often as fathers in other hunting-and-gathering societies. Why are Aka fathers so involved? The bond between Aka husband and wife is unusually cooperative and intimate. Throughout the day, couples share hunting, food preparation, and social and leisure activities. The more time Aka parents spend together, the greater the father's loving interaction with his baby (Hewlett, 1992).

In Western cultures as well, fathers in gratifying marriages spend more time with and interact more effectively with infants. In contrast, marital dissatisfaction is associated with insensitive paternal care (Grych & Clark, 1999; Lundy, 2002). Clearly, mothers' and fathers' warm interactions with each other and with their babies are closely linked. But paternal warmth promotes long-term favorable development beyond the influence of maternal warmth (Rohner & Veneziano, 2001). Evidence for the power of fathers' affection, reported in virtually every culture and ethnic group studied, may help motivate more men to engage in nurturing care of young children.

This Japanese father engages in the exciting, active play typical of fathers in many cultures. In both Western and non-Western nations, fathers' warmth predicts long-term favorable development. And in Western societies, it protects against a range of adjustment problems in childhood and adolescence.

their teachers as higher in self-esteem, social competence, and empathy than their insecurely attached counterparts. When studied again at age 11 in summer camp, children who had been secure infants had more favorable relationships with peers, closer friendships, and better social skills, as judged by camp counselors. And as these well-functioning school-age children became adolescents and young adults, they continued to benefit from more supportive social networks, formed more stable and gratifying romantic relationships, and attained higher levels of education (Elicker, Englund, & Sroufe, 1992; Sroufe, 2002; Sroufe et al., 2005).

For some researchers, these findings seem to indicate that secure attachment in infancy causes improved cognitive, emotional, and social competence in later years. Yet contrary evidence exists. In other longitudinal studies, secure infants sometimes developed more favorably than insecure infants, but not always (Lewis, 1997; McCartney et al., 2004; Schneider, Atkinson, & Tardif, 2001; Stams, Juffer, & van IJzendoorn, 2002). Disorganized/disoriented attachment, however, is an exception: It is uniformly related to both internalizing problems (fear and anxiety) and externalizing problems (anger and aggression) during the preschool and school years. Disorganized children also show inappropriate role reversals: In an apparent effort to compensate for their parent's confused communication, they use either exaggerated comforting or hostility to try to control the parent's behavior (Lyons-Ruth, 1996; Lyons-Ruth, Easterbrooks, & Cibelli, 1997; Moss et al., 2005a, 2006; Moss, Cyr, & Dubois-Comtois, 2004).

What accounts for the inconsistency in research findings on the consequences of early attachment quality? Mounting evidence indicates that *continuity of caregiving* determines whether attachment security is linked to later development (Lamb et al., 1985; Thompson, 2006). Children whose parents respond sensitively not just in infancy but also in later years are likely to develop favorably. In contrast, children whose parents react insensitively or who, over a long period, are exposed to a negative family climate tend to establish lasting patterns of avoidant, resistant, or disorganized behavior and are at greater risk for developmental difficulties.

A close look at the relationship between parenting and children's adjustment in the first few years supports this interpretation. Recall that parents of disorganized/disoriented infants tend to have serious psychological difficulties and to engage in highly maladaptive caregiving—conditions that usually persist and are strongly linked to poor adjustment in children (Lyons-Ruth, Bronfman, & Parsons, 1999). And when more than 1,000 children were tracked from age 1 to 3 years, those with histories of secure attachment followed by sensitive parenting scored highest in cognitive, emotional, and social outcomes. Those with histories of insecure attachment followed by insensitive parenting scored lowest, while those with mixed histories of attachment and maternal sensitivity scored in between (Belsky & Fearon, 2002). Specifically, insecurely attached infants whose mothers became more positive and supportive in early childhood showed signs of developmental recovery.

Does this trend remind you of our discussion of *resilience* in Chapter 1? A child whose parental caregiving improves or who has other compensating affectionate ties outside the immediate family can bounce back from adversity. In contrast, a child who experiences tender care in infancy but lacks sympathetic ties later on is at risk for problems.

As early as the second year, toddlers have formed attachment-related expectations about parental comfort and support. As Figure 10.7 shows, securely attached 12- to 16-month-olds looked longer at a video of an unresponsive caregiver (inconsistent with their expectations) than a video of a responsive caregiver. Insecurely attached infants, in contrast, did not distinguish between the two (Johnson, Dweck, & Chen, 2007). With cognitive development and continuing experiences with caregivers, this rudimentary internal working model expands into a broader, more complex representation. Recall from page 414 that parents of securely attached preschoolers converse with them in more elaborative ways, especially about emotion. Some researchers believe that these narratives facilitate children's construction of a coherent image of the self in relation to attachment figures (Fivush, 2006). Then, as children encounter new attachment-related experiences, they refine and "update" their internal working model.

■ Figure 10.7 Testing toddlers for internal working models of attachment.

(a) First, 12- to 16-month-olds were habituated to a video of two animated shapes, one large (representing the "caregiver") and one small (representing the "child"). The caregiver traveled halfway up an incline to a plateau, and the child began to "cry," depicted by pulsing and bouncing accompanied by a human infant cry. Next, the researchers presented two test events: (b) In the responsive-caregiver outcome, the caregiver returned to the child. (c) In the unresponsive-caregiver outcome, the caregiver continued up the slope, away from the child. Securely attached toddlers looked longer at the unresponsive outcome, depicting caregiver behavior inconsistent with their attachment-related expectations. Insecurely attached toddlers did not differentiate between the two test events. (Adapted from S. C. Johnson, C. S. Dweck, & F. S. Chen, 2007.)

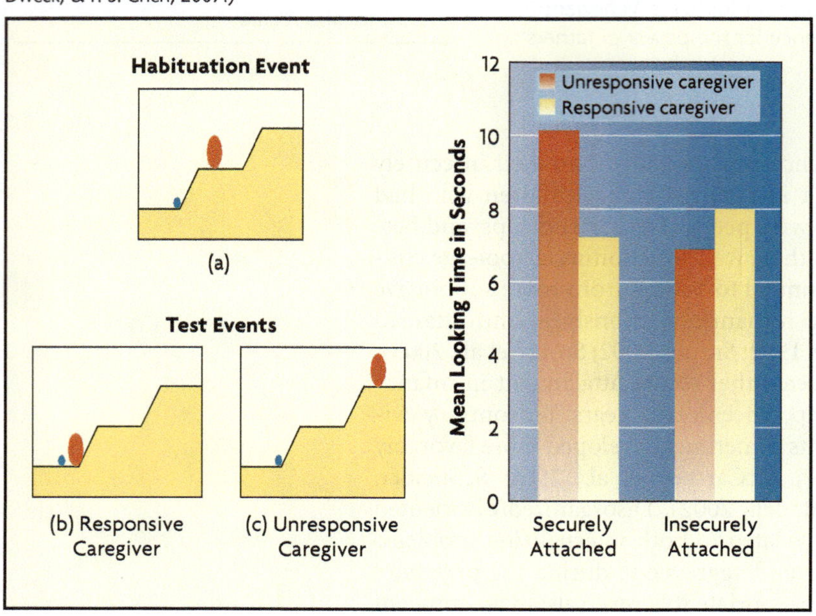

Although a secure attachment in infancy does not guarantee continued good parenting, it does launch the parent–child relationship on a positive path that is likely to continue. Much research shows that an early warm, positive parent–child tie, sustained over time, promotes many aspects of children's development—a more confident and complex self-concept, more advanced emotional understanding, more favorable and supportive relationships with teachers and peers, more effective social skills, a stronger sense of moral responsibility, and higher motivation to achieve in school (Thompson, 2006; Thompson, Easterbrooks, & Padilla-Walker, 2003). But the effects of early attachment security are *conditional*—dependent on the quality of the child's future relationships. Finally, as our discussion has already revealed and as you will see again in future chapters, attachment is only one of the complex influences on children's psychological development.

Ask Yourself

Review What factors explain stability in attachment pattern for some children and change for others? Are these factors also involved in the link between attachment in infancy and later development? Explain.

Apply In evaluating her childhood attachment experiences, Monica recalls her mother as tense and distant. Is Monica's newborn daughter likely to develop an insecure attachment? Explain, using research on adults' internal working models.

Connect Review research on emotional self-regulation on page 408. How do the caregiving experiences of securely attached infants promote development of emotional self-regulation?

Reflect How would you characterize your internal working model? What factors, in addition to your early relationship with your parents, might have influenced it?

Attachment, Parental Employment, and Child Care

Over the past three decades, women have entered the labor force in record numbers. Today, more than 60 percent of North American mothers with a child under age 2 are employed (Statistics Canada, 2003; U.S. Census Bureau, 2007b). In response to this trend, researchers and laypeople alike have raised questions about the impact on the attachment bond of child care and daily separations of infant from parent.

The Social Issues box on page 438 reviews the current controversy over whether child care threatens young children's development. As you will see, the weight of evidence suggests that *quality of care* is crucially important. Infants and young children exposed to long hours of mediocre to poor nonparental care, regardless of whether they come from middle- or low-SES homes, score lower on measures of cognitive and social skills (Hausfather et al., 1997; Kohen et al., 2000; NICHD Early Child Care Research Network, 2000b, 2001, 2003b, 2006).

In contrast, good child care can reduce the negative impact of a stressed, poverty-stricken home life, and it sustains the benefits of growing up in an economically advantaged family (Lamb & Ahnert, 2006; NICHD Early Child Care Research Network, 2003b). In Swedish longitudinal research, entering high-quality child care in infancy and toddlerhood was associated with cognitive, emotional, and social competence in middle childhood and adolescence (Andersson, 1989, 1992; Broberg et al., 1997).

TAKE A MOMENT... Visit several child-care settings, and take notes on what you see. In contrast to most European countries and to Australia and New Zealand, where child care is nationally regulated and funded to ensure its quality, reports on U.S. and Canadian child care are cause for concern. Standards are set by the individual states and provinces and vary widely. In some places, caregivers need no special training in child development, and one adult is permitted to care for 6 to 12 babies at once (Children's Defense Fund, 2006). In studies of child-care quality in each nation, only 20 to 25 percent of child-care centers and family child-care settings (in which a caregiver cares for children in her home) provided infants and toddlers with sufficiently positive, stimulating experiences to promote healthy psychological development. Most settings offered substandard care (Doherty et al., 2000; Goelman et al., 2000; NICHD Early Child Care Research Network, 2000a, 2004c).

Unfortunately, many children from low-income families experience inadequate child care (Brooks-Gunn, 2004). In the United States, however, settings providing the very worst care tend to serve middle-SES families. These parents are especially likely to place their children in for-profit centers, where quality tends to be lowest. Low-SES children more often attend publicly subsidized, nonprofit centers, which have smaller group sizes and better teacher–child ratios (Lamb & Ahnert, 2006). Still, child-care quality for low-SES children varies widely.

Refer to Applying What We Know on page 439 for signs of high-quality child care for infants and toddlers, based on standards for **developmentally appropriate practice.** These standards, devised by the U.S. National Association for the Education of Young Children, specify program characteristics that meet the developmental and individual needs of young children, based on both current research and consensus among experts. When child care meets standards for

Social Issues

Does Child Care in Infancy Threaten Attachment Security and Later Adjustment?

Research suggests that infants placed in full-time child care before 12 months of age are more likely than home-reared babies to display insecure attachment—especially avoidance—in the Strange Situation (Belsky, 2001, 2005). Does this mean that babies who experience daily separations from their employed parents and early placement in child care are at risk for developmental problems? Let's look closely at the evidence.

Attachment Quality

In North American studies reporting an association between child care and attachment quality, the rate of insecurity among child-care infants is somewhat higher than among non-child-care infants—about 36 versus 29 percent (Lamb, Sternberg, & Prodromidis, 1992). But not all investigations report that babies in child care differ in attachment quality from those cared for solely by parents (NICHD Early Child Care Research Network, 1997; Roggman et al., 1994). The relationship between child care and emotional well-being depends on both family and child-care experiences.

Family Circumstances

As we have seen, family conditions affect attachment security. Many employed women find the pressures of handling two full-time jobs—work and motherhood—stressful. Some mothers, fatigued and anxious because they receive little help from the child's father, may respond less sensitively to their babies, thereby risking the infant's security (Stifter, Coulehan, & Fish, 1993). Other employed parents probably value and encourage their infant's independence. Or their babies may be unfazed by the Strange Situation because they are used to separating from their parents. In these cases, avoidance in the Strange Situation may represent healthy autonomy rather than insecurity (Clarke-Stewart, Allhusen, & Goosens, 2001).

Quality and Extent of Child Care

Long periods spent in poor-quality child care may contribute to a higher rate of insecure attachment. In the U.S. National Institute of Child Health and Development (NICHD) Study of Early Child Care—the largest longitudinal study to date, including more than 1,300 infants and their families—child care alone did not contribute to attachment insecurity. But when babies were exposed to combined home and child-care risk factors—insensitive caregiving at home along with insensitive caregiving in child care, long hours in child care, or more than one child-care arrangement—the rate of insecurity increased. Overall, mother–child interaction was more favorable when children attended higher-quality child care and also spent fewer hours in child care (NICHD Early Child Care Research Network, 1997, 1999).

Furthermore, when children in the NICHD sample reached 3 years of age, a history of higher-quality child care predicted better social skills (NICHD Early Child Care Research Network, 2002b). At the same time, at age 4½ to 5, children averaging more than 30 child-care hours per week were somewhat more likely to have behavior problems, especially defiance, disobedience, and aggression (NICHD Early Child Care Research Network, 2003a, 2006). This does not necessarily mean that child care causes behavior problems. Rather, heavy exposure to substandard care, which is widespread in the United States, may promote these difficulties. In Australia, infants enrolled full-time in government-funded, high-quality child care have a higher rate of secure attachment than infants who are informally cared for by relatives, friends, or babysitters. And amount of time in child care is unrelated to Australian preschoolers' behavior problems (Love et al., 2003). In the Canadian province of Quebec, time in high-quality child care is associated with fewer behavior problems (Palacio-Quintin, 2000).

Still, some children may be particularly stressed by long child-care hours. Many infants, toddlers, and preschoolers attending child-care centers for full days show a mild increase in saliva concentrations of the stress hormone cortisol across the day—a pattern that does not occur on days they spend at home. In one study, children rated as highly fearful by their caregivers experienced an especially sharp increase in cortisol levels (Watamura et al., 2003). Inhibited children may find the social context of child care—constantly being in the company of large numbers of peers—particularly stressful.

Conclusions

Taken together, research suggests that some infants may be at risk for attachment insecurity and adjustment problems due to inadequate child care, long hours in child care, and the joint pressures their mothers experience from full-time employment and parenthood. But it is inappropriate to use these findings to justify a reduction in infant child-care services. When family incomes are limited or mothers who want to work are forced to stay at home, children's emotional security is not promoted.

Instead, it makes sense to increase the availability of high-quality child care, to provide paid employment leave so parents can limit the hours their children spend in child care (see page 117), and to educate parents about the vital role of sensitive caregiving and child-care quality in early emotional development. For child care to foster attachment security, the professional caregiver's relationship with the child is vital. When caregiver–child ratios are generous, group sizes are small, and caregivers are educated about child development and child rearing, caregivers' interactions are more positive and children develop more favorably—cognitively, emotionally, and socially (McCartney et al., 2007; NICHD Early Child Care Research Network, 2000a, 2002a, 2006). Child care with these characteristics can become part of an ecological system that relieves rather than intensifies parental and child stress, thereby promoting healthy attachment and development.

At the end of his day in child care, a toddler eagerly greets his mother. High-quality child care and fewer hours in child care are associated with favorable mother–child interaction, which promotes attachment security. © Ellen B. Senisi

Applying What We Know

Signs of Developmentally Appropriate Infant and Toddler Child Care

Program Characteristic	Signs of Quality
Physical setting	Indoor environment is clean, in good repair, well-lighted, and well-ventilated. Fenced outdoor play space is available. Setting does not appear overcrowded when children are present.
Toys and equipment	Play materials are appropriate for infants and toddlers and are stored on low shelves within easy reach. Cribs, highchairs, infant seats, and child-sized tables and chairs are available. Outdoor equipment includes small riding toys, swings, slide, and sandbox.
Caregiver–child ratio	In child-care centers, caregiver–child ratio is no greater than 1 to 3 for infants and 1 to 6 for toddlers. Group size (number of children in one room) is no greater than six infants with two caregivers and 12 toddlers with two caregivers. In family child care, caregiver is responsible for no more than six children; within this group, no more than two are infants and toddlers. Staffing is consistent, so infants and toddlers can form relationships with particular caregivers.
Daily activities	Daily schedule includes times for active play, quiet play, naps, snacks, and meals. It is flexible rather than rigid, to meet the needs of individual children. Atmosphere is warm and supportive, and children are never left unsupervised.
Interactions among adults and children	Caregivers respond promptly to infants' and toddlers' distress; hold, talk to, sing to, and read to them; and interact with them in a manner that respects the individual child's interests and tolerance for stimulation.
Caregiver qualifications	Caregiver has some training in child development, first aid, and safety.
Relationships with parents	Parents are welcome anytime. Caregivers talk frequently with parents about children's behavior and development.
Licensing and accreditation	Child-care setting, whether a center or a home, is licensed by the state or province. In the United States, voluntary accreditation by the NAEYC Academy for Early Childhood Program Accreditation, *www.naeyc.org/academy,* or the National Association for Family Child Care, *www.nafcc.org,* is evidence of an especially high-quality program. Canada has been developing a voluntary accreditation system, under the leadership of the Canadian Child Care Federation, *www.cccf-fcsge.ca.* Accredited programs are available in the provinces of Alberta and Manitoba.

Sources: Bredekamp & Copple, 1997; National Association for the Education of Young Children, 1998.

developmentally appropriate practice, children's learning opportunities and the warmth, sensitivity, and stability of their caregivers are especially high (Helburn, 1995).

Child care in the United States and Canada is affected by a macrosystem of individualistic values and weak government regulation and funding. Furthermore, many parents think that their children's child-care experiences are higher in quality than they really are (Helburn, 1995). Because they are unable to identify good care, many parents do not demand it. In recent years, the U.S. and Canadian federal governments, as well as some states and provinces, have tried to address the child-care crisis by allocating additional funds to subsidize the cost of care, especially for low-income families. Though far from meeting the need, this increase in resources has had a positive impact on child-care quality and accessibility (Canada Campaign 2000, 2003; Children's Defense Fund, 2006). In Canada, the province of Quebec leads the nation with universal, government-supported, good-quality child care for infants and preschoolers, for which every Quebec family pays the same minimal daily fee.

High-quality child care is a cost-effective means of supporting the development of all children, and it can serve as effective early intervention for children whose development is at risk, much like the programs we discussed in Chapter 8. We will revisit the topics of parental employment and child care in Chapter 14, when we focus on their consequences for development during childhood and adolescence.

Ask Yourself

Review Cite evidence that high-quality infant and toddler child care supports development, whereas poor-quality care undermines it.

Apply Randi and Mike are worried that placing their 6-month-old baby, Lucinda, in child care may disrupt Lucinda's sense of security. List steps that Randi and Mike can take to ensure that Lucinda's experiences—at home and in child care—support her emotional and social development.

SUMMARY

Functions of Emotions

Describe the functionalist approach to emotional development.

- The **functionalist approach** emphasizes that the broad function of **emotions** is to energize behavior aimed at attaining personal goals. Emotions are central in all human activity, including cognitive processing, social behavior, and physical health. Emotions also contribute to the emergence of self-awareness, which makes possible new, self-evaluative emotions. Gradually, children gain voluntary control over their emotions.

Development of Emotional Expression

How does the expression of happiness, anger, sadness, and fear change during infancy?

- During the first six months, **basic emotions** become clear, well-organized signals. Happiness promotes a warm, supportive parent–child bond and strengthens motor and cognitive mastery. Between 6 and 10 weeks, the parent's communication evokes the **social smile.** Around 3 to 4 months, laughter emerges.

© Alison Wright/Corbis

- From 4 to 6 months into the second year, with advances in cognitive and motor development, angry expressions increase. Sadness also occurs but is less common than anger. Fear, which rises during the second half of the first year, is most frequently expressed as **stranger anxiety.** Once fear develops, infants use the familiar caregiver as a **secure base** from which to explore.

Describe the development of self-conscious emotions, emotional self-regulation, and conformity to emotional display rules.

- At the end of the second year, self-awareness and adult instruction provide the foundation for **self-conscious emotions,** including shame, embarrassment, guilt, envy, and pride. With age, these emotions become more internally governed. Among Western children, guilt is often related to good adjustment, but intense shame is associated with feelings of personal inadequacy. In collectivist societies, however, shame is an adaptive reminder of the child's relationship to the social group.
- **Emotional self-regulation** emerges as the frontal lobes of the cerebral cortex develop and as caregivers sensitively assist infants in adjusting their emotional reactions. With motor, cognitive, and language development and warm parental guidance in understanding and controlling feelings, children acquire more effective self-regulatory strategies. Children who experience negative emotion intensely find it harder to inhibit feelings and shift attention away from disturbing events.
- In middle childhood, children attain a mental level of emotional self-communication, which helps them reflect on and manage their feelings. By age 10, most children have an adaptive set of techniques for regulating emotion, using **problem-centered coping** or **emotion-centered coping** as the situation requires. Emotionally well-regulated children are optimistic and cooperative and have positive relationships with teachers and peers.
- Young preschoolers start to conform to their culture's **emotional display rules.** From infancy on, parents encourage children—especially boys—to suppress negative emotion. In middle childhood, children understand the value of display rules in ensuring social harmony.

Understanding and Responding to the Emotions of Others

Describe the development of emotional understanding from infancy into adolescence.

- Around the middle of the first year, infants respond to emotional expressions as organized, meaningful wholes. By 8 to 10 months, they often engage in **social referencing** to obtain emotional information from trusted caregivers. By the middle of the second year, toddlers begin to appreciate that others' emotional reactions may differ from their own.
- Preschoolers understand many causes, consequences, and behavioral signs of emotion. The capacity to consider conflicting cues when explaining others' feelings improves in middle childhood, along with an appreciation of mixed emotions. Warm parental conversations about emotions and interactions with siblings and friends, especially sociodramatic play, are excellent contexts for learning about emotions.

Describe the development of empathy from infancy into adolescence, noting individual differences.

- **Empathy** is an important motivator of **prosocial,** or **altruistic, behavior.** But when it escalates into personal distress, it does not lead to **sympathy** and resulting acts of kindness and helpfulness. As toddlers develop self-awareness, they begin to empathize. Gains in language, emotional understanding, and perspective taking support an increase in empathy during childhood and adolescence.
- Children who are sociable, assertive, and good at regulating emotion are more likely than poor emotion regulators to move from empathy to sympathetic, prosocial behavior. Warm parents who encourage emotional expressiveness, show empathic concern, and help their child regulate angry feelings promote development of empathy and sympathy. Angry, punitive parenting disrupts these capacities.

Temperament and Development

What is temperament, and how is it measured?

- Children vary widely in **temperament**—early-appearing, stable individual differences in reactivity and self-regulation. Thomas and Chess's New York Longitudinal Study identified three patterns of temperament: the **easy child,** the **difficult child,** and the **slow-to-warm-up child.** Rothbart's dimensions of temperament represent three underlying components: emotion, attention, and action. Individuals differ not only in their reactivity on each dimension but also in **effortful control,** their ability to regulate that reactivity.

© Laura Dwight Photography

- Temperament is often assessed through parental reports. Although laboratory observations avoid the subjectivity of parental reports and allow researchers to control children's experiences, the unfamiliar setting introduces other inaccuracies. Researchers can combine observations of behavior with psychophysiological measures to distinguish temperamental styles. Most psychophysiological research has focused on **inhibited,** or **shy, children** and **uninhibited,** or **sociable, children.**

Discuss the role of heredity and environment in the stability of temperament, the relationship of temperament to cognitive and social functioning, and the goodness-of-fit model.

- Long-term prediction from early temperament is best achieved after age 3, when styles of responding are better established. Although kinship studies indicate that temperament is moderately heritable, environment also has a powerful effect. Both shared environmental influences and nonshared influences—evident in parents' tendency to emphasize each child's unique qualities—contribute to temperament.
- The **goodness-of-fit model** describes how a child's temperament and environment work together to affect later development. Parenting practices that create a good fit with the child's temperament help difficult, shy, and highly active children achieve more adaptive functioning.

Development of Attachment

What are the unique features of ethological theory of attachment?

- The development of **attachment,** the strong affectionate tie we feel for special people in our lives, has been the subject of intense theoretical debate. The most widely accepted perspective, **ethological theory of attachment,** views babies as biologically prepared to contribute to ties with their caregivers, which promote survival by ensuring both safety and competence.
- In early infancy, a set of built-in behaviors encourages the parent to remain close to the baby. Around 6 to 8 months, **separation anxiety** and use of the parent as a secure base indicate that a clear-cut attachment bond has formed. Separation anxiety declines as preschoolers better understand the parent's coming and going. Out of early caregiving experiences, children construct an **internal working model** that serves as a guide for all future close relationships.

Cite the four attachment patterns assessed by the Strange Situation and the Attachment Q-Sort, and discuss factors that affect the development of attachment.

- Researchers using the **Strange Situation** to measure the quality of attachment between ages 1 and 2 have identified four attachment patterns: **secure, avoidant, resistant,** and **disorganized/disoriented.** The **Attachment Q-Sort,** a home observation method suitable for children between ages 1 and 4 years, yields a score ranging from high to low in security.
- Attachment is usually secure and stable for infants reared in middle-SES families with favorable life conditions. Low SES and serious family problems negatively affect attachment stability and security. Cultural conditions influence the meaning of attachment patterns.
- Infants deprived of affectionate ties with one or a few adults show lasting emotional and social problems. **Sensitive caregiving** is moderately related to secure attachment. **Interactional synchrony** also separates the experiences of secure from insecure babies, but cultures differ in their view of sensitivity and in the importance of interactional synchrony. Caregiving can override the impact of infant characteristics, including temperament, on attachment.

© PhotoDisc/Getty Images

- The strongest parental influences on attachment security are nonshared experiences, in which parents adjust their caregiving to each child's individual needs. Quality of parents' internal working models is related to children's attachment security, but because internal working models are reconstructed memories, the impact of parents' childhood experiences on attachment with their own children is indirect and affected by many factors.

Discuss fathers' attachment relationships with their infants and the role of early attachment quality in later development.

- Like mothers', fathers' sensitive caregiving predicts secure attachment. Fathers in a variety of cultures devote more time than mothers to stimulating, playful interaction, through which they build secure attachments with their babies.
- Continuity of parental care is crucial in determining whether attachment security is linked to later development. Children can recover from an insecure attachment history if caregiving improves. Nevertheless, secure attachment in infancy launches the parent–child relationship on a positive path, increasing the likelihood of continued parental sensitivity.

Attachment, Parental Employment, and Child Care

Discuss the effects of parental employment and child care on attachment security and early psychological development.

- Research on the impact of child care and daily separations of infant from parent suggests that quality of care is crucially important. Spending many hours in mediocre to poor-quality nonparental care contributes to insecure attachment and less favorable cognitive, emotional, and social development.
- When child-care settings meet professionally accepted standards for **developmentally appropriate practice,** children's learning opportunities and the warmth, sensitivity, and stability of their caregivers are especially high. Good child care can also serve as effective early intervention for children whose development is at risk.

IMPORTANT TERMS AND CONCEPTS

attachment (p. 425)
Attachment Q-Sort (p. 428)
avoidant attachment (p. 428)
basic emotions (p. 404)
developmentally appropriate practice (p. 437)
difficult child (p. 417)
disorganized/disoriented attachment (p. 428)
easy child (p. 417)
effortful control (p. 418)
emotion (p. 400)
emotion-centered coping (p. 410)
emotional display rules (p. 410)
emotional self-regulation (p. 407)
empathy (p. 414)
ethological theory of attachment (p. 426)
functionalist approach to emotion (p. 400)
goodness-of-fit model (p. 423)
inhibited, or shy, children (p. 419)
interactional synchrony (p. 430)
internal working model (p. 427)
problem-centered coping (p. 410)
prosocial, or altruistic, behavior (p. 414)
resistant attachment (p. 428)
secure attachment (p. 427)
secure base (p. 406)
self-conscious emotions (p. 406)
sensitive caregiving (p. 430)
separation anxiety (p. 426)
slow-to-warm-up child (p. 417)
social referencing (p. 412)
social smile (p. 405)
Strange Situation (p. 427)
stranger anxiety (p. 405)
sympathy (p. 414)
temperament (p. 417)
uninhibited, or sociable, children (p. 419)

11

"Cosmic Leap"

Nicola Roos
11 years, South Africa

Young people's self-descriptions reflect their expanding abilities, accomplishments, and aspirations. Here, an artist on the cusp of adolescence imagines soaring into space on a fanciful flying horse—an expression of growing awareness of her potential.

Self and Social Understanding

"Grandpa, look at my new shirt!" exclaimed 4-year-old Ellen at her family's annual reunion. "See, it's got a ladybug on it, and a yellow flower, and. . . ."

Ellen's voice trailed off as she realized that all eyes were on her 1-year-old cousin, who was about to take his first steps. As little David tottered forward, the grownups laughed and cheered. No one—not even Grandpa, who was usually so attentive and playful—took note of Ellen and her new shirt.

Ellen retreated to the bedroom, where she threw a blanket over her head. Arms outstretched, she peered through the blanket's loose weave and made her way back to the living room. "Here I come, the scary ghost," announced Ellen, deliberately bumping into David, who toppled over and burst into tears.

Pulling off the blanket, Ellen caught her mother's disapproving glance and protested, "I couldn't see him, Mom! The blanket was over my face."

Ellen's mother insisted that Ellen apologize and help David up. But she couldn't help marveling at Ellen's skillful capacity for trickery.

This chapter addresses the development of **social cognition,** or how children come to understand their multifaceted social world. Like our discussion of cognitive development in Chapters 6 and 7, this chapter is concerned with how children think about and interpret experience. The experience of interest, however, is no longer the child's physical surroundings but the self and other people.

Researchers interested in social cognition seek answers to questions like these: When do infants discover that they are separate beings, distinct from other people and objects? How does children's understanding of their own and others' mental lives change with age? (For example, what new realizations underlie Ellen's creative act of deception?) When children and adolescents are asked to describe their own and others' characteristics, what do they say?

As we answer these and other questions, you will see that the trends identified for cognitive development also apply to children's social understanding:

- Social-cognitive development proceeds *from concrete to abstract.* Children start by noticing observable characteristics—their own and others' appearance and behavior. Soon after, they become aware of internal processes—the existence of desires, beliefs, intentions, abilities, and attitudes.
- Social cognition becomes *better-organized* with age as children integrate separate behaviors into an appreciation of their own and others' personalities and identities.
- Children revise their ideas about the causes of behavior—from *simple, one-sided explanations* to *complex, interacting relationships* that take into account both person and situation.

- Social cognition moves toward *metacognitive understanding.* As children get older, their thinking extends beyond social reality to their own and other people's social thoughts.

Although nonsocial and social cognition share many features, social cognition is more complex. Movements of things—for example, a rolling ball—can be fully explained by the physical forces that act on objects. In contrast, a person's behavior is affected not only by others' actions but also by inner states that we cannot observe directly.

In view of this complexity, we might expect social cognition to develop more slowly than nonsocial cognition. Surprisingly, it does not. Unique features of social experience are probably responsible. First, because people are animated beings and objects of deep emotional investment, they are especially interesting to think about. Second, social experience constantly prompts children to revise their social cognitions by presenting them with discrepancies between the behaviors they expect and those that occur. Finally, because we are all human beings, with the same basic nervous system and a background of similar experiences, interpreting behavior from the self's viewpoint often helps us understand others' actions. When it does not, humans are equipped with a powerful capacity—*perspective taking*—that enables us to infer others' thoughts and feelings.

Our discussion is organized around three aspects of development: thinking about the self, thinking about other people, and thinking about relationships between people. We have already considered some social–cognitive topics—for example, referential communication skills in Chapter 9 and emotional understanding in Chapter 10. Research on moral reasoning, another social–cognitive topic, is so extensive that it merits a chapter of its own. We will consider it in Chapter 12.

Emergence of Self and Development of Self-Concept

Infancy is a rich formative period for development of both physical and social understanding. In Chapter 6, you learned that infants develop an appreciation of the permanence of objects. And in Chapter 10, we saw that over the first year, infants recognize and respond appropriately to others' emotions and distinguish familiar from unfamiliar people. That both objects and people achieve an independent, stable existence for infants implies that knowledge of the self as a separate, permanent entity is also emerging. Self-development begins with the dawning of self-awareness in infancy and gradually evolves into a rich, multifaceted, organized view of the self's characteristics and capacities during childhood and adolescence.

Self-Awareness

As early as the first few months of life, infants smile and return friendly behaviors to their reflection in a mirror. When do they realize that the baby smiling back at them is the self?

• Beginnings of Self-Awareness At birth, infants sense that they are physically distinct from their surroundings. For example, newborns display a stronger rooting reflex in response to external stimulation (an adult's finger touching their cheek) than to self-stimulation (their own hand contacting their cheek) (Rochat & Hespos, 1997). Newborns' remarkable capacity for *intermodal perception* (see page 163 in Chapter 4) supports the beginnings of self-awareness (Rochat, 2003). As they feel their own touch, feel and watch their limbs move, and feel and hear themselves cry, babies experience intermodal matches that differentiate their own body from surrounding bodies and objects.

Over the first few months, infants distinguish their own visual image from other stimuli, although self-awareness is still limited—expressed only in perception and action. When shown two side-by-side video images of their kicking legs—one from their own perspective (camera behind the baby) and one from an observer's perspective (camera in front of the baby)—3-month-olds looked longer at the observer's view (see Figure 11.1a). In another video-image comparison, they looked longer at a reversal of their leg positions than at a normal view (see Figure 11.1b) (Rochat, 1998). By 4 months, infants look and smile more at video images of others than at video images of themselves, indicating that they view another person (as opposed to the self) as a potential social partner (Rochat & Striano, 2002).

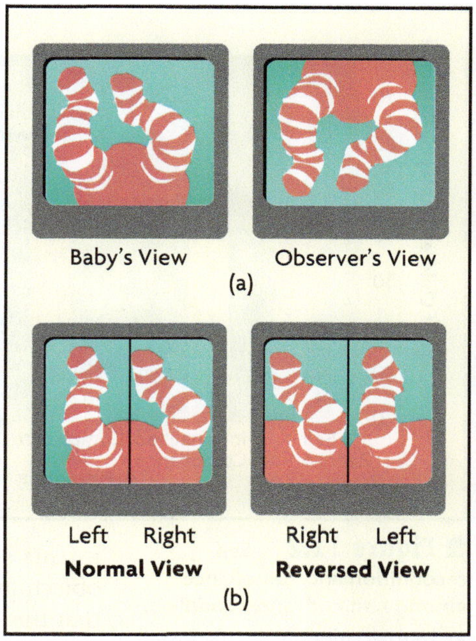

Figure 11.1 **Three-month-olds' emerging self-awareness, as indicated by reactions to video images.**
(a) When shown two side-by-side views of their kicking legs, babies looked longer at the novel, observer's view than at their own view. (b) When shown a normal view of their leg positions alongside a reversed view, infants looked longer at the novel, reversed view. (Adapted from Rochat, 1998.)

Self-Recognition During the second year, toddlers become consciously aware of the self's physical features. In several studies, 9- to 28-month-olds were placed in front of a mirror. Then, under the pretext of wiping the baby's face, each mother rubbed red dye on her child's nose or forehead. Younger babies touched the mirror as if the red mark had nothing to do with themselves. But those older than 20 months rubbed their strange-looking noses or foreheads, indicating awareness of their unique appearance (Bard et al., 2006; Lewis & Brooks-Gunn, 1979). And some toddlers act silly or coy in front of the mirror, playfully experimenting with the way the self looks (Bullock & Lutkenhaus, 1990).

Around age 2, **self-recognition**—identification of the self as a physically unique being—is well under way. Children point to themselves in photos, and almost all refer to themselves by name or with a personal pronoun ("I" or "me") (Lewis & Brooks-Gunn, 1979). Over the third year, children refine their mental representation of their own appearance: They can identify themselves in images with less detail and fidelity than mirrors. Around age 2½, most reach for a sticker surreptitiously placed on top of their heads when shown themselves in a live video, and around age 3, most recognize their own shadow (Cameron & Gallup, 1988; Suddendorf, Simcock, & Nielsen, 2007).

What experiences contribute to self-awareness and self-recognition? During the first year, as infants act on the environment, they notice effects that help them sort out self, other people, and objects (Nadel, Prepin, & Okanda, 2005; Rochat, 2001). For example, batting a mobile and seeing it swing in a pattern different from the infant's own actions informs the baby about the relation between self and physical world. Smiling and vocalizing at a caregiver who smiles and vocalizes back help clarify the relation between self and social world. The contrast between these experiences helps infants build an image of self as separate from, but vitally connected to, external reality.

Sensitive caregiving promotes early self-development. Compared to their insecurely attached agemates, securely attached toddlers—whose parents provide a secure base for exploration—display more complex self-related actions during play, such as making a doll labeled as the self take a drink or kiss a teddy bear. They also show greater knowledge of their own and their parents' physical features—for example, in labeling of body parts (Pipp, Easterbrooks, & Brown, 1993; Pipp, Easterbrooks, & Harmon, 1992). And 18- to 20-month-olds who often establish joint attention with their caregivers are advanced in mirror self-recognition (Nichols, Fox, & Mundy, 2005). Joint attention seems to offer toddlers many opportunities to monitor and compare their own and others' reactions to objects and events, which promotes self-awareness.

This 22-month-old, seeing his changed appearance in a mirror as a result of wearing a new hat, immediately reaches for the hat—a response indicating that he recognizes his unique physical features. He is well aware of himself as a separate being, distinct from other people and objects.

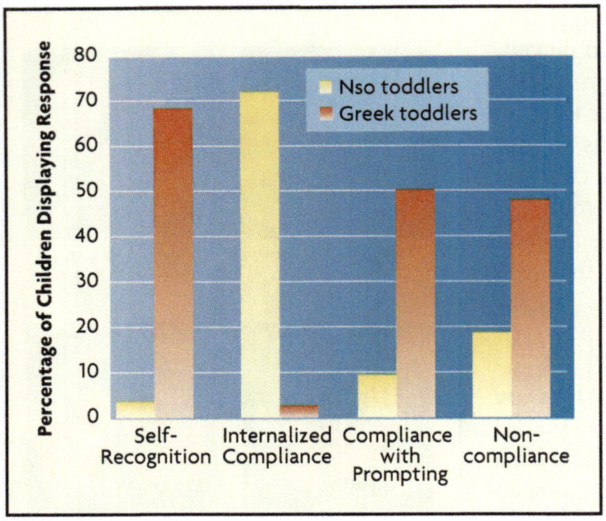

■ **Figure 11.2** **Self-recognition and compliance among Nso and Greek toddlers.** At 18 to 20 months, toddlers were tested for mirror self-recognition and for compliance to an adult's prohibition (they were told not to open a transparent container with an attractive food). Among Greek toddlers, whose culture values independence, many more had attained self-recognition. But Nso toddlers, reared in an interdependent culture, were greatly advanced in compliance. The majority displayed internalized compliance (following directions without prompting), whereas Greek toddlers either needed reminders or did not comply. (Adapted from Keller et al., 2004.)

Cultural variations exist in early self-development. Urban German and Greek toddlers attain mirror self-recognition earlier than toddlers of the Nso people of Cameroon, a collectivist rural farming society that highly values interdependence—social harmony and responsibility to others (Keller et al., 2004, 2005). Compared to their German and Greek counterparts, Nso mothers engage in less face-to-face communication and object stimulation and more body contact and physical stimulation of their babies. The German and Greek practices reflect a *distal parenting style* common in cultures that value independence, the Nso practices a *proximal parenting style* typical in cultures that value interdependence. In line with these differences, Nso proximal parenting predicts later attainment of self-recognition but earlier emergence of toddlers' compliance with adult requests (see Figure 11.2).

• **Self-Awareness and Early Emotional and Social Development** Self-awareness quickly becomes a central part of children's emotional and social lives. In the final months of the first year, as infants start to behave intentionally, they learn that their own goals (touching a breakable object, grabbing a peer's toy) frequently conflict with the goals of others. Soon, they realize that the self can be the focus of others' intentions and emotional reactions. As a result, they become increasingly sensitive to variations in caregivers' emotional messages (Thompson, 2006). This sets the stage for social referencing and, in the middle of the second year, emergence of self-conscious emotions (see pages 406 and 412 in Chapter 10).

Self-awareness also leads to first efforts to understand another's perspective. We have seen in previous chapters that toddlers increasingly appreciate others' intentions, feelings, and desires. They also show the beginnings of empathy (see page 415) and self-conscious behavior: bashfulness and embarrassment. Furthermore, mirror self-awareness precedes the appearance of sustained, mutual peer imitation—a partner banging an object, the toddler copying the behavior, the partner imitating back, and the toddler copying again (Asendorpf, Warkentin, & Baudonniere, 1996). These exchanges indicate that the toddler not only is interested in the playmate but also realizes that the playmate is interested in him or her.

Two-year-olds' self-recognition leads to a sense of ownership. The stronger their self-definitions, the more possessive 2-year-olds tend to be, claiming objects as "Mine!" (Fasig, 2000; Levine, 1983). A firmer sense of self also enables children to cooperate in resolving disputes over objects, playing games, and solving simple problems (Brownell & Carriger, 1990; Caplan et al., 1991). Accordingly, when trying to promote friendly peer interaction, parents and teachers can accept young children's possessiveness as a sign of self-assertion ("Yes, that's your toy") and then encourage compromise ("but in a little while, would you give someone else a turn?"), rather than insisting on sharing.

The Categorical, Remembered, and Enduring Selves

By the end of the second year, language becomes a powerful tool in self-development. Because it permits children to represent and express the self more clearly, it greatly enhances self-awareness. Between 18 and 30 months, children develop a **categorical self** as they classify themselves and others on the basis of age ("baby," "boy," or "man"), sex ("boy" or "girl"), physical characteristics ("big," "strong"), and even goodness and badness ("I good girl." "Tommy mean!"). They also start to refer to the self's competencies ("Did it!" "I can't") (Stipek, Gralinski, & Kopp, 1990).

Recall from Chapter 7 that adult–child conversations about the past lead to an autobiographical memory. This life-story narrative grants the child a **remembered self**—a more coherent portrait than is offered by the isolated, episodic memories of the first few years. By participating in personal storytelling, children come to view the self as a unique, continuously existing individual embedded in a world of others. As early as age 2, parents use these discussions to impart rules, standards, and evaluative information about the child, as when they say, "You added the milk when we made mashed potatoes. That's a very important job!" (Nelson,

Cultural Influences

Cultural Variations in Personal Storytelling: Implications for Early Self-Concept

Preschoolers of many cultural backgrounds participate in personal storytelling with their parents. Striking cultural differences exist in parents' selection and interpretation of events in these early narratives, affecting the way children come to view themselves.

In one study, researchers spent hundreds of hours over a two-year period studying the storytelling practices of six middle-SES Irish-American families in Chicago and six middle-SES Chinese families in Taiwan. From extensive videotapes of adults' conversations with 2½-year-olds, the investigators identified personal stories and coded them for content, quality of their endings, and evaluation of the child (Miller, Fung, & Mintz, 1996; Miller et al., 1997).

Parents in both cultures discussed pleasurable holidays and family excursions in similar ways and with similar frequency. But Chinese parents more often told long stories about the child's misdeeds—using impolite language, writing on the wall, or playing in an overly rowdy way. These narratives were conveyed with warmth and caring, stressed the impact of misbehavior on others ("You made Mama lose face"), and often ended with direct teaching of proper behavior ("Saying dirty words is not good"). By contrast, in the few instances in which Irish-American stories referred to transgressions, parents downplayed their seriousness, attributing them to the child's spunk and assertiveness.

Early narratives about the child seem to launch preschoolers' self-concepts on culturally distinct paths. Influenced by Confucian traditions of strict discipline and social obligations, Chinese parents integrated these values into their personal stories, affirming the importance of not disgracing the family and explicitly conveying expectations in the story's conclusion. Although Irish-American parents disciplined their children, they rarely dwelt on misdeeds in storytelling. Rather, they cast the child's shortcomings in a positive light, perhaps to promote self-esteem.

Whereas most North Americans regard favorable self-esteem as crucial for healthy development, Chinese adults generally see it as unimportant or even negative—as impeding the child's willingness to listen and be corrected (Miller et al., 2002). Consistent with this view, the Chinese parents did little to cultivate their child's individuality. Instead, they used storytelling to guide the child toward socially responsible behavior. Hence, the Chinese child's self-image emphasizes membership in the collective and obligations to others, whereas the North American child's is more autonomous (Wang, 2006b).

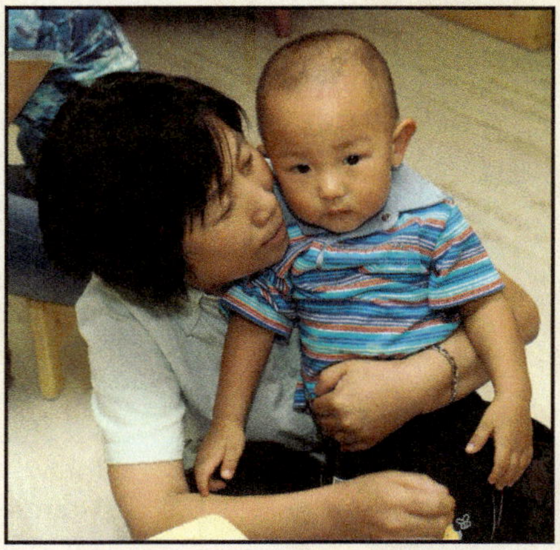

Gently but firmly conveying her expectations for proper behavior, this Chinese mother helps her son develop a view of himself that emphasizes social obligations rather than individuality. © Ellen B. Senisi

2003). As the Cultural Influences box above reveals, these narratives are a major means through which caregivers imbue the young child's sense of self with cultural values.

As they talk about personally significant events and as their cognitive skills advance, preschoolers gradually develop an **enduring self**—a view of themselves as persisting over time. Not until age 4 are children certain that a video image of themselves replayed a few minutes after it was filmed is still "me" (Povinelli, 2001). Similarly, when researchers asked 3- to 5-year-olds to imagine a future event (walking next to a waterfall) and to envision a future personal state by choosing from three items (a raincoat, money, a blanket) the one they would need to bring with them, performance—along with future-state justifications ("I'm gonna get wet")—increased sharply between ages 3 and 4 (Atance & Meltzoff, 2005).

The Inner Self: Young Children's Theory of Mind

As children think more about themselves and others, they form a naïve *theory of mind*—a coherent understanding of their own and others' rich mental lives. Recall from our discussion of metacognition in Chapter 7 that after age 2, children refer to mental states frequently and appropriately in everyday language. Although they confuse certain mental terms (see page 301), young preschoolers are clearly aware of an **inner self** of private thoughts and imaginings.

How does the young child view this inner self, and how does this view change with age? Investigators are interested in this question because ideas about the mind are powerful tools in predicting and explaining our own and others' everyday behavior.

Early Understandings of Mental States Over the first year of life, infants build an implicit appreciation of people as animate beings whose behavior is governed by intentions, desires, and feelings. This sets the stage for the verbalized mental understandings that blossom in early childhood.

In Chapter 10, we saw that 3-month-olds smile more at people than at objects and become upset when a person poses a still face and fails to communicate. By 6 months, when infants see people talk, they expect the talk to be directed at other people, not at inanimate objects (Legerstee, Barna, & DiAdamo, 2000). At the end of the first year, babies view people as intentional beings who can share and influence one another's mental states, a milestone that opens the door to new forms of communication—joint attention, social referencing, preverbal gestures, and language. These interactive skills, in turn, enhance toddlers' mental understandings (Tomasello & Rakoczy, 2003). At the end of the second and continuing over the third year, children display a clearer grasp of people's emotions and desires, evident in their increasing mental-state vocabulary, capacity to empathize, and realization that people often differ from one another and from themselves in likes, dislikes, wants, needs, and wishes ("Mommy likes green beans. Daddy doesn't. He likes carrots. I like carrots, too!") (Cassidy et al., 2005; Rakoczy, Warneken, & Tomasello, 2007).

As language for talking about the mind expands in the third year, children appreciate the connections among perceiving, feeling, and desiring. For example, seeing that a person peeking inside a box is *happy,* 2½-year-olds predict that the box contains a *desirable* rather than an *undesirable* snack. In addition, they often talk about links between perception and desire ("I *want see* beaver") and emotion and desire ("I *like* celery, so I *want* celery"). Occasionally, they link all three ("You *want* to *see* how he *cried*") (Wellman, Phillips, & Rodriguez, 2000). But although 2- to 3-year-olds have started to integrate mental states, their understanding is limited to a simplistic **desire theory of mind:** They think that people always act in ways consistent with their desires and do not understand that less obvious, more interpretive mental states, such as beliefs, also affect behavior (Bartsch & Wellman, 1995).

Development of Belief–Desire Reasoning Between ages 3 and 4, children increasingly refer to their own and others' thoughts and beliefs (Wellman, 2002). And from age 4 on, they exhibit a **belief–desire theory of mind,** a more sophisticated view in which both beliefs and desires determine actions, and they understand the relationship between these inner states (Gopnik & Wellman, 1994; Ziv & Frye, 2003). Turn back to the beginning of this chapter, and notice how 4-year-old Ellen deliberately tries to alter her mother's *belief* about the motive behind her pretending, in hopes of warding off any *desire* on her mother's part to punish her. From early to middle childhood, efforts to alter others' beliefs increase, suggesting that children more firmly realize the power of belief to influence action.

Dramatic evidence for preschoolers' belief–desire reasoning comes from games that test whether they realize that *false beliefs*—ones that do not represent reality accurately—can guide people's behavior. TAKE A MOMENT... Show a child two small closed boxes, one a familiar Band-Aid box and the other a plain, unmarked box (see Figure 11.3). Then say, "Pick the box you think has the Band-Aids in it." Children usually pick the marked container. Next, open the boxes and show the child that, contrary to her own belief, the marked one is empty and the unmarked one contains the Band-Aids. Finally, introduce the child to a hand puppet and explain, "Here's Pam. She has a cut, see? Where do you think she'll look for Band-Aids? Why would she look in there? Before you looked inside, did you think that the plain box contained Band-Aids? Why?" (Bartsch & Wellman, 1995; Gopnik & Wellman, 1994). Only a handful of 3-year-olds can explain Pam's—and their own—false beliefs, but many 4-year-olds can.

Among children of diverse cultural and SES backgrounds, false-belief understanding strengthens gradually after age 3½, becoming more secure

Figure 11.3 **Example of a false-belief task.**

(a) An adult shows a child the contents of a Band-Aid box and an unmarked box. The Band-Aids are in the unmarked container. (b) The adult introduces the child to a hand puppet named Pam and asks the child to predict where Pam would look for the Band-Aids and to explain Pam's behavior. The task reveals whether children understand that without having seen that the Band-Aids are in the unmarked container, Pam will hold a false belief.

(a) (b)

between ages 4 and 6 (Amsterlaw & Wellman, 2006; Callaghan et al., 2005; Flynn, 2006). Mastery of false belief signals a change in representation—the ability to view beliefs as *interpretations,* not just reflections, of reality. Does this remind you of school-age children's more active view of the mind, discussed in Chapter 7? Belief–desire reasoning may mark the beginnings of this overall change.

With the realization that people can increase their knowledge by making *mental inferences* (see page 301 in Chapter 7), school-age children extend false-belief understanding further. In several studies, researchers told children complex stories involving one character's belief about a second character's belief. Then the children answered questions about what the first character thought the second character would do (see Figure 11.4). By age 7, children were aware that people form beliefs about other people's beliefs and that these *second-order beliefs* can also be wrong! Appreciation of *second-order false belief* enables children to pinpoint the reasons that another person arrived at a certain belief (Astington, Pelletier, & Homer, 2002; Harris, 2006). This assists them greatly in understanding others' perspectives.

• Consequences of Belief–Desire Reasoning Once it emerges, the capacity to use both beliefs and desires to predict people's behavior becomes a powerful tool for reflecting on thoughts and emotions and a good predictor of social skills (Harwood & Farrar, 2006; Watson et al., 1999). False-belief understanding predicts gains in 3- and 4-year-olds' sociodramatic play—specifically, the capacity to engage in joint planning, to negotiate pretend roles, and to imagine verbally, without the support of real objects (Jenkins & Astington, 2000). It is also associated with early reading ability, probably because it helps children comprehend story narratives (Astington & Pelletier, 2005). To follow a story line, children generally must link plot actions with characters' motives and beliefs.

Once children grasp the relation between beliefs and behavior, they refine their understanding, applying it to a wider range of situations. For example, children who pass false-belief tasks have more accurate eyewitness memories (Templeton & Wilcox, 2000). They realize that one person can present misinformation to another, which can affect the second individual's beliefs. Consequently, in reporting observed events, such children are more likely to resist attempts to mislead them. Development of a belief–desire theory may be a major reason that children's eyewitness memories become more dependable after age 6, when appreciation of the belief–reality distinction is more secure (see Chapter 7, page 298).

School-age children soon use their grasp of the relation between beliefs and behavior to persuade others. Third graders are more adept than first graders in considering people's beliefs when trying to convince them to do something. They know, for example, that a boy who wants

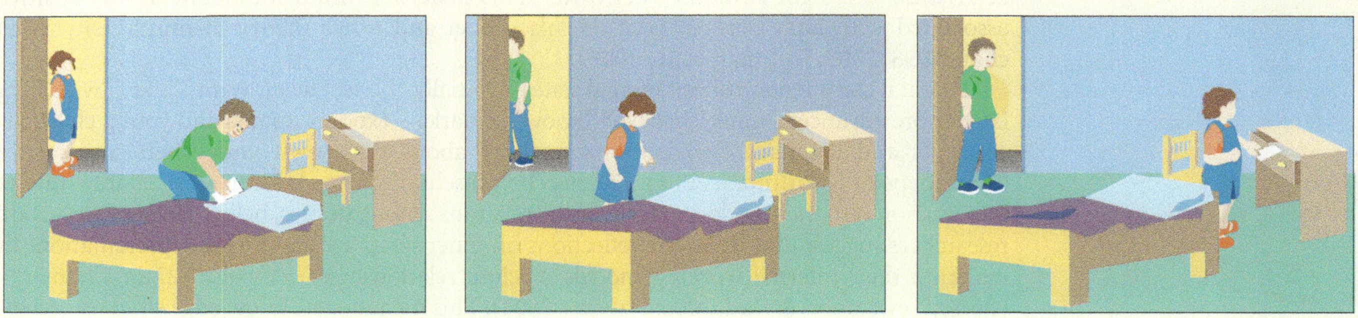

(a) Jason has a letter from a friend. Lisa wants to read the letter, but Jason doesn't want her to. Jason puts the letter under his pillow.

(b) Jason leaves the room to help his mother.

(c) While Jason is gone, Lisa takes the letter and reads it. Jason returns and watches Lisa, but Lisa doesn't see Jason. Then Lisa puts the letter in Jason's desk.

Figure 11.4 **Example of a second-order false-belief task.**

After relating the story in the sequence of pictures, the researcher asks a second-order false-belief question: "Where does Lisa think Jason will look for the letter? Why?" Around age 7, children answer correctly—that Lisa thinks Jason will look under his pillow because Lisa doesn't know that Jason saw her put the letter in the desk. (Adapted from Astington, Pelletier, & Homer, 2002.)

a kitten but whose mother believes that cats scratch furniture should focus on telling his mother that the cat is declawed rather than litter-trained (Bartsch & London, 2000).

In sum, development of a belief–desire theory strengthens children's sensitivity to people's beliefs and promotes their reasoned attempts to change those beliefs. As a result, it contributes to many social competencies.

• Factors Contributing to Young Children's Theory of Mind How do children develop a theory of mind at such a young age? Great controversy surrounds this question, but research suggests that language, cognitive abilities, make-believe play, and social experiences all contribute.

Language. Understanding the mind requires the ability to reflect on thoughts, which language makes possible. Many studies indicate that language ability strongly predicts preschoolers' grasp of false belief (Milligan, Astington, & Dack, 2007). Children who spontaneously use, or are trained to use, complex sentences with mental-state words are especially likely to pass false-belief tasks (de Villiers & de Villiers, 2000; Hale & Tager-Flusberg, 2003). The Quechua village people of the Peruvian highlands refer to mental states such as "think" and "believe" indirectly, because their language lacks mental-state terms. Quechua children have difficulty with false-belief tasks for years after children in industrialized nations have mastered them (Vinden, 1996). In contrast, Chinese languages have verb markers that can label the word "believe" as decidedly false. When adults use those markers within false-belief tasks, Chinese preschoolers perform better (Tardif, Wellman, & Cheung, 2004).

Cognitive Abilities. The ability of 3- and 4-year-olds to inhibit inappropriate responses, think flexibly, and plan predicts current performance on false-belief tasks as well as improvements over time (Hughes, 1998; Sabbagh et al., 2006). Like language, these cognitive skills enhance children's capacity to reflect on their experiences and mental states. Gains in cognitive inhibition, considered in Chapter 7, predict false-belief understanding particularly strongly, perhaps because to do well on false-belief tasks, children must suppress an irrelevant response—namely, the tendency to assume that others' knowledge and beliefs are the same as their own (Birch & Bloom, 2003; Carlson, Moses, & Claxton, 2004).

Security of Attachment and Maternal "Mind-Mindedness." In longitudinal research, mothers of securely attached babies were more likely to comment appropriately on their infants' mental states: "Do you *remember* Grandma?" "You really *like* that swing." These mothers continued to describe their children, when they reached preschool age, in terms of mental characteristics: "She's got a mind of her own!" This maternal "mind-mindedness" was positively associated with later performance on false-belief and other theory-of-mind tasks (Meins et al., 1998, 2003; Ruffman et al., 2006).

Parental commentary about mental states—initially, "desire" talk ("want," "like," "wish") and, later, more advanced "think," believe," "know" remarks—exposes infants and young children to concepts and language that help them think about their own and others' mental lives (Taumoepeau & Ruffman, 2006). During the preschool years, children seem to integrate this information into their understanding of the relations among desires, beliefs, and behavior. Some researchers suggest that children's reflections on inner states are among the representations that make up their internal working models of close relationships (see page 427 in Chapter 10) (Reese, Newcombe, & Bird, 2006; Symons, 2004). This mental-state knowledge emerges earlier—and seems to be more objective and richer—among securely attached children, whose parents frequently refer to and converse with them about desires, intentions, beliefs, and emotions.

Make-Believe Play. Earlier we noted that theory of mind fosters children's sociodramatic play. But make-believe also offers a rich context for thinking about the mind. As children act out roles, they imagine and express the thoughts and emotions of the characters they portray and their implications (Kavanaugh, 2006b). These experiences may increase children's awareness that belief influences behavior. In support of this idea, preschoolers who engage in extensive fantasy role play or who have imaginary companions—and, thus, are deeply absorbed in creating make-believe characters—are advanced in understanding of false belief and other aspects of the mind (Astington & Jenkins, 1995; Lalonde & Chandler, 1995).

Social Interaction. Preschoolers with siblings who are also children (but not infants)—and especially those with older siblings or with two or more siblings—tend to be more aware of false belief. Children with older siblings close in age, and those with more siblings, are exposed to—and participate in—more family talk about thoughts, beliefs, and emotions (Jenkins et al., 2003; McAlister & Peterson, 2006, 2007; Symons, 2004). Similarly, preschool friends who often engage in mental-state talk are advanced in false-belief understanding (de Rosnay & Hughes, 2006). Interacting with more mature members of society also contributes. In a study of Greek preschoolers, daily contact with many adults and older children predicted mastery of false belief (Lewis et al., 1996). In line with Vygotsky's theory, all these encounters offer opportunities for children to observe different viewpoints, talk about inner states, and become increasingly aware of their own and others' mental activities.

Children with siblings—especially older siblings—participate in more family talk about thoughts, beliefs, and emotions. Sibling interaction contributes to preschoolers' theory of mind, including their understanding of false belief. © Ian Shaw/Alamy

Core knowledge theorists (see Chapter 6, page 261) believe that to profit from the social experiences just described, children must be biologically prepared to develop a theory of mind. They claim that children with *autism,* for whom mastery of false belief is either greatly delayed or absent, are deficient in the brain mechanism that enables humans to detect mental states. See the Biology and Environment box on page 452 to find out more about the biological basis of reasoning about the mind.

Self-Concept

As children develop an appreciation of their inner mental world, they think more intently about themselves. During early childhood, knowledge and evaluation of the self's characteristics expands (Harter, 2003, 2006). Children begin to construct a **self-concept,** the set of attributes, abilities, attitudes, and values that an individual believes defines who he or she is.

Preschoolers' self-concepts emphasize observable characteristics. If asked to describe himself, this 5-year-old might say, "I can make a huge snow shield!" In a few years, he will begin to mention personality traits: "I'm friendly and determined." © Steve Mason/Getty Images/PhotoDisc Green

• Early Childhood

Ask a 3- to 5-year-old to tell you about himself, and you are likely to hear something like this: "I'm Tommy. See, I got this new red T-shirt. I'm 4 years old. I can wash my hair all by myself. I have a new Tinker Toy set, and I made this big, big tower." Preschoolers' self-concepts are very concrete. Usually they mention observable characteristics, such as their name, physical appearance, possessions, and everyday behaviors (Harter, 2006; Watson, 1990).

By age 3½, children also describe themselves in terms of typical emotions and attitudes ("I'm happy when I play with my friends"; "I don't like being with grownups"), suggesting a beginning understanding of their unique psychological characteristics (Eder & Mangelsdorf, 1997). As further support for this budding grasp of personality, when given a trait label ("shy," "mean"), 4-year-olds infer appropriate motives and feelings. For example, they know that a shy person doesn't like to be with unfamiliar people (Heyman & Gelman, 1999). But preschoolers do not yet say, "I'm helpful" or "I'm shy." Direct references to personality traits must wait for greater cognitive maturity.

• Middle Childhood

Over time, children organize their observations of typical behaviors and internal states into general dispositions, with a major change occurring between ages 8 and 11. Consider this 11-year-old's self-description:

> My name is A. I'm a human being. I'm a girl. I'm a truthful person. I'm not pretty. I do so-so in my studies. I'm a very good cellist. I'm a very good pianist. I'm a little bit tall for my age. I like several boys. I like several girls. I'm old-fashioned. I play tennis. I am a very good swimmer. I try to be helpful. I'm always ready to be friends with anybody. Mostly I'm good, but I lose my temper. I'm not well liked by some girls and boys. I don't know if I'm liked by boys or not. (Montemayor & Eisen, 1977, pp. 317–318)

Instead of specific behaviors, this child emphasizes competencies: "a very good cellist," "so-so in my studies" (Damon & Hart, 1988). She also describes her personality, mentioning both positive and negative traits: "truthful" but "short-tempered." Older school-age children

Biology *and* Environment

"Mindblindness" and Autism

Michael stood at the water table in Leslie's classroom, repeatedly filling a plastic cup and dumping out its contents—dip-splash, dip-splash—until Leslie came over and redirected his actions. Without looking at Leslie's face, Michael moved to a new repetitive pursuit: pouring water from one cup into another and back again. As other children entered the play space and conversed, Michael hardly noticed.

Michael has autism, the most severe behavior disorder of childhood. The term *autism,* meaning "absorbed in the self," is an apt description of Michael. Like other children with autism, by age 3 he displayed deficits in three core areas of functioning: First, he had only limited ability to engage in nonverbal behaviors required for successful social interaction, such as eye gaze, facial expressions, gestures, and give-and-take. He usually seemed aloof and uninterested in other people. Second, his language was delayed and stereotyped. He used words to echo what others said and to get things he wanted, not to connect socially or exchange ideas, and his verbal utterances were grammatically less complex than those of children with other developmental delays (such as Down syndrome). Third, he engaged in much less make-believe play than other children (Frith, 2003; Walenski, Tager-Flusberg, & Ullman, 2006). And Michael showed another typical feature of autism: His interests were narrow and overly intense. For example, one day he sat for more than an hour spinning a toy Ferris wheel.

Researchers agree that autism stems from abnormal brain functioning, usually due to genetic or prenatal environmental causes. From the first year on, children with the disorder have larger-than-average brains, perhaps due to massive overgrowth of synapses and lack of synaptic pruning, which accompanies normal development of cognitive, language, and communication skills (Courchesne, Carper, & Akshoomoff, 2003). Furthermore, fMRI studies reveal that autism is associated with reduced activity in areas of the cerebral cortex known to mediate emotional and social responsiveness and thinking about mental activities, including mirror neurons, discussed in Chapter 4 (see page 144) (Mundy, 2003; Théoret et al., 2005).

Growing evidence reveals that children with autism have a deficient theory of mind. Long after they reach the intellectual level of an average 4-year-old, they have great difficulty with false belief. Most find it hard to attribute mental states to themselves or others (Steele, Joseph, & Tager-Flusberg, 2003). They rarely use mental-state words, such as *believe, think, know, feel,* and *pretend.*

As early as the second year, children with autism show deficits in social capacities believed to contribute to an understanding of mental life. Compared with other children, they less often establish joint attention, point to share interest in an object or event, engage in social referencing, or imitate an adult's novel behaviors (Mundy & Stella, 2000). Furthermore, they are less sensitive than typically developing children to eye gaze as a cue to what a speaker is talking about. Instead, children with autism often assume that another person's language refers to what they themselves are looking at—a possible reason for their frequent nonsensical expressions (Baron-Cohen, Baldwin, & Crowson, 1997).

Do these findings indicate that autism is due to an impairment in an innate, core brain function, which leaves the child "mindblind" and therefore unable to engage in human sociability? Some researchers think so (Baron-Cohen & Belmonte, 2005; Scholl & Leslie, 2000). But others point out that individuals with mental retardation but not autism also perform poorly on tasks assessing mental understanding (Yirmiya et al., 1998). This suggests that some kind of general intellectual deficit is involved.

One conjecture is that children with autism are impaired in *executive processing* (refer to the *central executive* in the information-processing model on page 277 in Chapter 7). This leaves them deficient in skills involved in flexible, goal-oriented thinking, including shifting attention to address relevant aspects of a situation, inhibiting irrelevant responses, applying strategies to hold information in working memory, and generating plans (Geurts et al., 2004; Joseph & Tager-Flusberg, 2004). Another possibility is that children with autism display a peculiar style of information processing, preferring to process the parts of stimuli over patterns and coherent wholes (Frith & Happé, 1994).

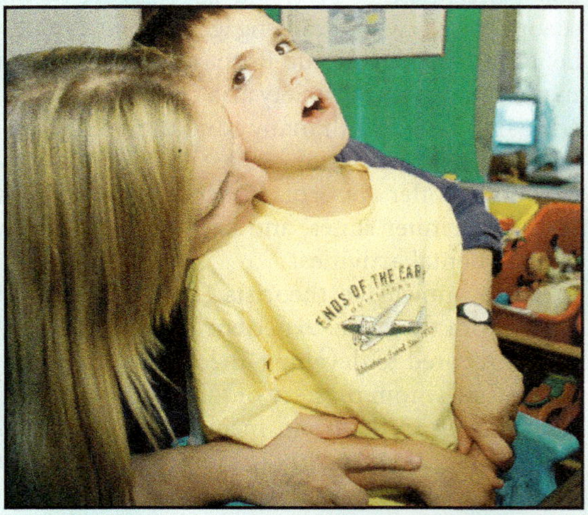

This child, who has autism, is barely aware of his mother's voice or touch as she tries to direct his attention to the computer. Researchers disagree on whether the "mindblindness" of children with autism results from a specific deficit in social understanding or a general intellectual impairment involving executive processing. © Jan Sonnenmair/Aurora & Quanta Productions, Inc.

Performance of children with autism on diverse cognitive tasks supports both of these views. Deficits in thinking flexibly and in holistic processing of stimuli would each interfere with understanding the social world, since social interaction involves quick integration of information from various sources and evaluation of alternative possibilities.

It is not clear which of these hypotheses is correct. In fact, some research suggests that impairments in social awareness, flexible thinking, processing coherent wholes, and verbal ability contribute independently to autism (Morgan, Maybery, & Durkin, 2003; Pellicano et al., 2006). Perhaps several biologically based deficits underlie the tragic social isolation of children like Michael.

are far less likely than younger children to describe themselves in extreme, all-or-none ways (Harter, 2003, 2006).

A major reason for these evaluative self-descriptions is that school-age children often make **social comparisons,** judging their own appearance, abilities, and behavior in relation to those of others. Whereas 4- to 6-year-olds can compare their own performance to that of a single peer, older children can compare multiple individuals, including themselves. Consequently, they conclude that they are "very good" at some things, "so-so" at others, and "not good" at still others (Butler, 1998; Harter, 2006).

• **Adolescence** In early adolescence, the self differentiates further. Teenagers mention a wider array of traits, which vary with social context: self with mother, father, close friends, and romantic partner; self as student, athlete, and employee. As one young teenager commented:

> I'm an extrovert with my friends: I'm talkative, pretty rowdy, and funny. . . . With my parents, I'm more likely to be depressed. I feel sad as well as mad and also hopeless about ever pleasing them. . . . At school, I'm pretty intelligent. I know that because I'm smart when it comes to how I do in classes. I'm curious about learning new things, and I'm also creative when it comes to solving problems. . . . I can be a real introvert around people I don't know well. . . . I worry a lot about what others my age who are not my closest friends must think of me, probably that I'm a total dork. (Harter, 2006, p. 531)

Notice, also, that young adolescents unify separate traits ("smart" and "curious") into more abstract descriptors ("intelligent"). But these generalizations about the self are not interconnected and are often contradictory. For example, 12- to 14-year-olds might mention opposing traits—"intelligent" and "dork," "extrovert" and "introvert." These disparities result from the adolescent's expanded social world, which creates pressure to display different selves in different relationships. As their awareness of these inconsistencies grows, adolescents frequently agonize over "which is the real me" (Harter, 1999, 2003, 2006).

From middle to late adolescence, cognitive changes enable teenagers to combine their traits into an organized system. Their use of qualifiers ("I have a *fairly* quick temper," "I'm not *thoroughly* honest") reveals their awareness that psychological qualities often change from one situation to the next. Older adolescents also add integrating principles, which make sense of formerly troublesome contradictions. "I'm very adaptable," one young person remarked. "When I'm around my friends, who think that what I say is important, I'm very talkative, but around my family I'm quiet because they're never interested enough to really listen to me" (Damon, 1990, p. 88).

Compared with school-age children, teenagers place more emphasis on social virtues, such as being friendly, considerate, kind, and cooperative—traits that reflect adolescents' increasing concern with being viewed positively by others. Among older adolescents, personal and moral values also emerge as key themes. Here is how one 17-year-old described herself:

> I'm a pretty conscientious person. . . . Eventually I want to go to law school, so developing good study habits and getting top grades are both essential. . . . I'd like to be an ethical person who treats other people fairly. That's the kind of lawyer I'd like to be, too. I don't always live up to that standard; that is, sometimes I do something that doesn't feel ethical. When that happens, I get a little depressed because I don't like myself as a person. But I tell myself that it's natural to make mistakes, so I don't really question the fact that deep down inside, the real me is a moral person. (Harter, 2006, pp. 545–546)

This well-integrated account differs from the fragmented, listlike self-descriptions typical of children. As adolescents revise their views of themselves to include enduring beliefs and plans, they move toward the kind of unity of self that is central to identity development.

Cognitive, Social, and Cultural Influences on Self-Concept

What factors account for these revisions in self-concept? Cognitive development certainly affects the changing structure of the self. School-age children, as we saw in Chapter 6, can better coordinate several aspects of a situation in reasoning about their physical world. Similarly, in the social realm, they combine typical experiences and behaviors into stable psychological dispositions, blend positive and negative characteristics, and compare their own characteristics with those of many other peers (Harter, 2003, 2006). In middle childhood, children also gain a clearer understanding of traits as linked to specific desires (a "generous" person *wants* to share) and, therefore, as causes of behavior (Yuill & Pearson, 1998). For this reason, they may mention traits more often. And formal operational thought transforms the adolescent's vision of the self into a complex, well-organized, internally consistent picture (Harter, 1999, 2003).

The changing *content* of the self is a product of both cognitive capacities and feedback from others. Sociologist George Herbert Mead (1934) described the self as a **generalized other**—a blend of what we imagine important people in our lives think of us. He proposed that a psychological self emerges when children adopt a view of the self that resembles others' attitudes toward the child. Mead's ideas indicate that *perspective-taking skills*—in particular, an improved ability to infer what other people are thinking—are crucial for developing a self-concept based on personality traits. During middle childhood and adolescence, young people become better at "reading" messages they receive from others. As school-age children internalize others' expectations, they form an *ideal self* that they use to evaluate their real self. As we will see shortly, a large discrepancy between the two can greatly undermine self-esteem, leading to sadness, hopelessness, and depression.

Parental support contributes vitally to the clarity and optimism of children's self-concepts. In one study, the richness of mothers' emotional communication in narratives about the past—evaluations of positive events and explanations of children's negative feelings and their resolution ("Talking about your teacher moving away helped you feel better")—predicted greater consistency in 5- and 6-year-olds' reports of their personal characteristics (Bird & Reese, 2006). And school-age children with a history of elaborative parent–child conversations construct more positive, detailed personal narratives and thus have more complex, favorable, and coherent self-images (Harter, 2006).

In middle childhood, children also look to more people beyond the family for information about themselves as they enter a wider range of settings in school and community. And self-descriptions now include frequent references to social groups: "I'm a Boy Scout, a paper boy, and a Prairie City soccer player," remarked one 10-year-old. Gradually, as children move into adolescence, their sources of self-definition become more selective. Although parents remain influential, self-concept becomes increasingly vested in feedback from close friends (Oosterwegel & Oppenheimer, 1993).

Keep in mind, however, that the content of self-concept varies from culture to culture. In earlier chapters, we noted that Asian parents stress harmonious interdependence, Western parents separateness and self-assertion (Markus & Kitayama, 1991). Turn back to the Cultural Influences box on page 447, and notice this difference in parents' personal storytelling with their young children. These contrasting values are apparent in school-age children's self-concepts. When asked to recall personally significant past experiences (their last birthday, a time their parent scolded them), U.S. children gave longer accounts including more personal preferences, skills, and opinions. Chinese children, in contrast, more often referred to social interactions and to others. Similarly, in their self-descriptions, U.S. children listed more personal attributes ("I'm smart," "I like hockey"), Chinese children more attributes involving group membership and relationships ("I'm in second grade," "My friends are crazy about me") (Wang, 2004, 2006b).

During the school years, as children spend more time in settings away from home, self-descriptions increasingly make reference to social groups—for example, "I'm a Boy Scout." Participating in a holiday sing-along, these scouts might include friendliness, helpfulness, and cheerfulness in their self-definitions. © Mark Richards/PhotoEdit

In characterizing themselves, children from individualistic cultures seem to be more egoistic and competitive, those from collectivist cultures more concerned with the welfare of others—a finding that underscores the powerful impact of the social environment on self-concept. The Milestones table on the following page summarizes the vast changes in the self from infancy through adolescence.

Milestones

Emergence of Self and Development of Self-Concept

Age	Milestones
1–2 years	▪ Aware of self as physically distinct and as causing people and objects to react in predictable ways. ▪ Recognizes image of self in mirrors and photos and on videotape. ▪ Uses own name or personal pronoun to label image of self.
3–5 years	▪ Forms a categorical self by classifying the self and others on the basis of age, gender, physical characteristics, goodness and badness, and competencies. ▪ Constructs a remembered self, in the form of a life-story narrative. ▪ Desire theory of mind expands into a belief–desire theory, as indicated by understanding of false-belief. ▪ Forms a self-concept consisting of observable characteristics and typical emotions and attitudes.
6–10 years	▪ Emphasizes personality traits and both positive and negative attributes in self-concept. ▪ Makes social comparisons among multiple individuals.
11 years and older	▪ Unifies separate traits, such as "smart" and "talented," into more abstract descriptors, such as "intelligent," in self-concept. ▪ Combines traits making up self-concept into an organized system.

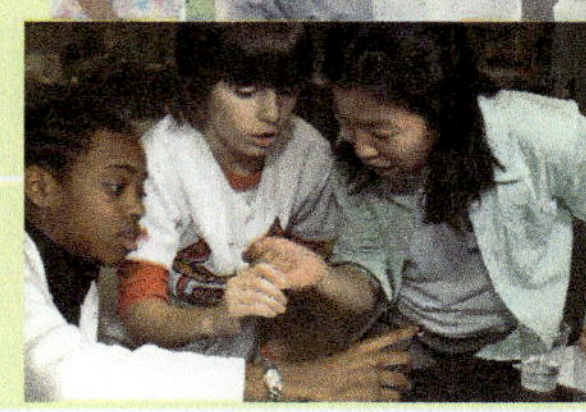

Note: These milestones represent overall age trends. Individual differences exist in the precise age at which each milestone is attained.

Photos: (top) © Laura Dwight Photography; (middle) © RightImage/Alamy Images; (bottom) © Laura Dwight Photography

Ask Yourself

Review What factors contribute to development of a belief–desire theory of mind, and why is each factor influential?

Review How does cognitive development affect changes in self-concept from early childhood to adolescence?

Apply Suggest ways that parents can promote a sturdy sense of self in infants and toddlers.

Connect Recall from Chapter 6 (page 243) that between ages 4 and 8, children figure out who is really behind the activities of Santa Claus and the Tooth Fairy, and they realize that magicians use trickery. How might these understandings be related to their developing theory of mind?

Self-Esteem: The Evaluative Side of Self-Concept

So far, we have focused on how the general structure and content of self-concept change with age. Another component of self-concept is **self-esteem,** the judgments we make about our own worth and the feelings associated with those judgments. High self-esteem implies a realistic evaluation of the self's characteristics and competencies, coupled with an attitude of self-acceptance and self-respect.

Self-esteem ranks among the most important aspects of self-development because evaluations of our own competencies affect emotional experiences, future behavior, and long-term psychological adjustment. As soon as a categorical self with features that can be judged positively or negatively is in place, children become self-evaluative beings. Around age 2, they call a parent's attention to an achievement, such as completing a puzzle, by pointing and saying something like "Look, Mom!" In addition, 2-year-olds are likely to smile when they succeed at a task an adult set for them and to look away or frown when they fail (Stipek, Recchia, & McClintic, 1992). Self-esteem originates early, and its structure becomes increasingly elaborate with age.

The Structure of Self-Esteem

TAKE A MOMENT... Think about your own self-esteem. Besides a global appraisal of your worth as a person, do you have an array of separate self-judgments concerning how well you perform at different activities?

Researchers have studied the multifaceted nature of self-esteem by applying *factor analysis* (see page 319 in Chapter 8) to children's ratings of the extent to which statements like these are true: "I am good at homework." "I'm usually the one chosen for games." "Most kids like me." By age 4, preschoolers have several self-judgments—for example, about learning things in school, making friends, getting along with parents, and feeling physically attractive (Marsh, Ellis, & Craven, 2002). Compared with that of older children, however, their understanding is limited.

The structure of self-esteem depends on evaluative information available to children and their ability to process that information. Around age 6 to 7, children in diverse Western cultures have formed at least four broad self-evaluations: academic competence, social competence, physical/athletic competence, and physical appearance. Within these are more refined categories that become increasingly distinct with age (Marsh, 1990; Marsh & Ayotte, 2003; Van den Bergh & De Rycke, 2003). For example, academic self-esteem divides into performance in language arts, math, and other subjects; social self-esteem into peer and parental relationships; and physical/athletic competence into skill at various sports.

Furthermore, school-age children's newfound ability to view themselves in terms of stable dispositions enables them to combine their separate self-evaluations into a general psychological image of themselves—an overall sense of self-esteem (Harter, 2003, 2006). Consequently, self-esteem takes on the hierarchical structure shown in Figure 11.5. Separate self-esteems, however, do not contribute equally to general self-esteem. Children attach greater importance

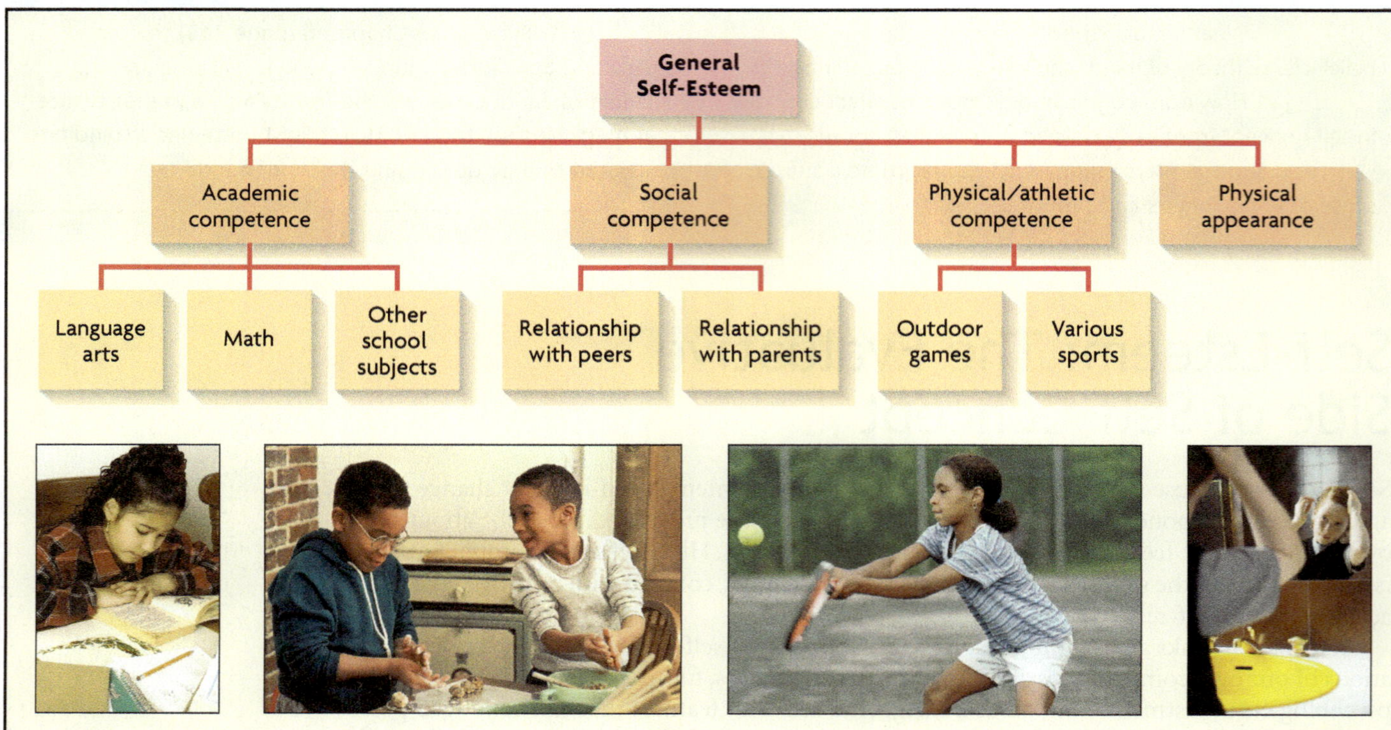

■ Figure 11.5 Hierarchical structure of self-esteem in the mid-elementary school years. From their experiences in different settings, school-age children form at least four separate self-esteems: academic competence, social competence, physical/athletic competence, and physical appearance. These differentiate into additional self-evaluations and combine to form a general sense of self-esteem. *Photos:* (far left) © Laura Dwight Photography; (middle left) © George Disario/CORBIS; (middle right) © Mitch Wojnarowicz/The Image Works; (far right) Radius Images/Photolibrary

to certain self-judgments, giving them more weight in the total picture. Although individual differences exist, during childhood and adolescence perceived physical appearance correlates more strongly with global self-esteem than any other self-esteem factor (Klomsten, Skaalvik, & Espnes, 2004; Shapka & Keating, 2005). Emphasis on appearance—in the media, among peers, and in society—has major implications for satisfaction with the self.

The arrival of adolescence adds several new dimensions of self-esteem—close friendship, romantic appeal, and job competence—that reflect important concerns of this period (Harter, 1999, 2003, 2006). Furthermore, adolescents become more discriminating in the people to whom they look for validation of their self-esteem. Some rely more on parents, others on teachers, and still others on peers—differences that reflect the extent to which teenagers believe that people in each context are interested in and respect them as individuals (Harter, Waters, & Whitesell, 1998).

Changes in Level of Self-Esteem: The Role of Social Comparisons

Because preschoolers have trouble distinguishing between their desired and their actual competence, they usually rate their own ability as extremely high and often underestimate the difficulty of tasks. Over the first few years of elementary school, self-esteem declines (Marsh, Craven, & Debus, 1998; Wigfield et al., 1997). As children increasingly engage in social comparison, they adjust their self-esteem to a more realistic level that matches the opinions of others, as well as objective performance.

To protect their self-esteem, most children eventually balance social comparison information with personal achievement goals (Ruble & Flett, 1988). Perhaps for this reason, the drop in self-esteem in the early school years is seldom harmful. Then, from fourth grade on, self-esteem rises and remains high for the majority of young people, who feel especially good about their peer relationships and athletic capabilities (Cole et al., 2001; Twenge & Campbell, 2001). The main exception is a decline in self-worth for some adolescents after transition to middle and high school. Entry into a new school, accompanied by new teacher and peer expectations, may temporarily interfere with the ability to make realistic judgments about behavior and performance. In Chapter 15, we will examine these school transition effects. For most young people, however, becoming an adolescent leads to feelings of pride and self-confidence.

Influences on Self-Esteem

From middle childhood to adolescence, individual differences in self-esteem become increasingly stable (Trzesniewski, Donnellan, & Robins, 2003). And positive relationships among self-esteem, valuing of various activities, and success at those activities emerge and strengthen with age. For example, academic self-esteem predicts how important, useful, and interesting children and adolescents judge school subjects to be, their willingness to exert effort, and their achievement in those subjects (Denissen, Zarrett, & Eccles, 2007; Valentine, DuBois, & Cooper, 2004). In a Canadian study, academic self-esteem in elementary school was associated with educational attainment ten years later, in young adulthood (Guay, La Rose, & Boivin, 2004). Children with high social self-esteem are consistently better liked by their classmates (Jacobs et al., 2002). And as we saw in Chapter 5, sense of athletic competence is positively associated with investment in and performance at sports.

Furthermore, across age, sex, SES, and ethnic groups, individuals with mostly favorable self-esteem profiles tend to be well-adjusted, sociable, and conscientious. In contrast, low self-esteem in all areas is linked to a wide array of adjustment difficulties (DuBois et al., 1999; Robins et al., 2001). But certain self-esteem factors are more strongly related to

Teenagers perform Scottish highland dancing at a community festival in British Columbia, Canada. The highly intricate dance form requires several years of training and practice to perfect. Self-esteem typically rises during adolescence, as do optimism and pride in new competencies. © Gunter Marx/Alamy Images

A grandmother puts the final touches on her grandchildren's Mardi Gras costumes for a Martin Luther King, Jr., parade in Miami, Florida. Warm extended families may contribute to African-American children's higher self-esteem relative to their Caucasian agemates. © Jeff Greenberg/PhotoEdit

adjustment than others. Adolescents who feel highly dissatisfied with parental relationships often are aggressive and antisocial. Those with poor academic self-esteem tend to be anxious and unfocused. And those who view their peer relationships negatively are likely to be anxious and depressed (Marsh, Parada, & Ayotte, 2004; Rudolph, Caldwell, & Conley, 2005). And although virtually all teenagers become increasingly concerned about others' opinions, those who are overly dependent on social approval place their self-esteem continually "on the line." As a result, they report frequent self-esteem shifts—on average, about once a week (Harter & Whitesell, 2003).

From age 5 on, children realize that self-esteem has important consequences. They say that individuals who like themselves would do better at a challenging task and cope more easily with a peer's rebuff (Daniels, 1998). Because self-esteem is related to individual differences in children's behavior, researchers have been intensely interested in identifying factors that cause it to be high for some children and low for others.

Culture As with self-concept, cultural forces profoundly affect self-esteem. An especially strong emphasis on social comparison in school may underlie the finding that despite their higher academic achievement, Chinese and Japanese children score lower than U.S. children in self-esteem—a difference that widens with age (Harter, 2006; Hawkins, 1994; Twenge & Crocker, 2002). In Asian classrooms, competition is tough, and achievement pressure is high. At the same time, because their culture values modesty and social harmony, Asian children rely less on social comparisons to promote their own self-esteem. Rather, they tend to be reserved about judging themselves positively but generous in their praise of others (Falbo et al., 1997). In addition, certain self-evaluations important to Asian children—willingness to help others, respect for parents' and teachers' authority—are not included on self-esteem questionnaires for North American children (Meredith, Wang, & Zheng, 1993).

Gender-stereotyped expectations also affect self-esteem. In one study, the more 5- to 8-year-old girls talked with friends about the way people look, watched TV shows focusing on physical appearance, and perceived their friends as valuing thinness, the greater their dissatisfaction with their physical self and the lower their overall self-esteem a year later (Dohnt & Tiggemann, 2006). By adolescence, girls feel less confident than boys about their physical appearance and athletic abilities. With respect to academic self-esteem, boys, again, are somewhat advantaged: Whereas girls score higher in language arts self-esteem, boys have higher math, science, and physical/athletic self-esteem—even when children of equal skill levels are compared (Fredericks & Eccles, 2002; Jacobs et al., 2002; Tennenbaum & Leaper, 2003). At the same time, girls exceed boys in self-esteem dimensions of close friendship and social acceptance.

Although only a slight difference exists between boys and girls in overall self-esteem, a widely held assumption is that boys' overall sense of self-worth is much higher than girls' (Marsh & Ayotte, 2003; Young & Mroczek, 2003). Girls may think less well of themselves because they internalize this negative cultural message.

Compared with their Caucasian agemates, African-American children tend to have slightly higher self-esteem, perhaps because of warm extended families and a stronger sense of ethnic pride (Gray-Little & Hafdahl, 2000). Finally, children and adolescents who attend schools or live in neighborhoods where their SES and ethnic groups are well-represented feel a stronger sense of belonging and have fewer self-esteem problems (Gray-Little & Carels, 1997).

Child-Rearing Practices Children and adolescents whose parents are warm and accepting, provide reasonable expectations for mature behavior, and engage in positive problem solving (resolve conflicts by collaborating with the child on a solution) feel especially good about themselves (Carlson, Uppal, & Prosser, 2000; Rudy & Grusec, 2006; Wilkinson, 2004). Warm, positive parenting lets young people know that they are accepted as competent and worthwhile. And firm but appropriate expectations, backed up with explanations, help them make sensible choices and evaluate themselves against reasonable standards.

Controlling parents—those who too often help or make decisions for their child—communicate a sense of inadequacy to children. Having parents who are repeatedly disapproving and insulting is also linked to low self-esteem (Kernis, 2002; Pomerantz & Eaton, 2000). Children subjected to such parenting need constant reassurance, and many rely heavily on peers to affirm their self-worth—a risk factor for adjustment difficulties, including aggression, antisocial behavior, and delinquency (Donnellan et al., 2005).

This mother shows her concern and commitment by sitting close and talking frankly about her expectations. Although this direct approach may make her daughter uncomfortable, it will also help her develop a realistic, credible sense of self-esteem. © Photodisc/Alamy Images

In contrast, overly tolerant, indulgent parenting is linked to unrealistically high self-esteem, which also undermines development. These children tend to lash out at challenges to their overblown self-images and are also likely to have adjustment problems, including meanness and aggression (Hughes, Cavell, & Grossman, 1997).

North American cultural values have increasingly emphasized a focus on the self that may lead parents to indulge children and boost their self-esteem too much. The self-esteem of U.S. youths rose sharply from the 1970s to the 1990s—a period in which much popular parenting literature advised promoting children's self-esteem (Twenge & Campbell, 2001). Yet compared with previous generations, U.S. youths are achieving less well and displaying more antisocial behavior and other adjustment problems (Berk, 2005). Research confirms that children do not benefit from compliments ("You're terrific") that have no basis in real attainment (Damon, 1995). Rather, the best way to foster a positive, secure self-image is to encourage children to strive for worthwhile goals. Over time, a bidirectional relationship between achievement and self-esteem emerges: Achievement fosters self-esteem, which contributes to further effort and gains in performance (Gest, Domitrovich, & Welsh, 2005; Guay, Marsh, & Boivin, 2003).

What can adults do to encourage—and avoid undermining—this mutually supportive relationship between motivation and self-esteem? Some answers come from research on the precise content of adults' messages to children in achievement situations.

Achievement-Related Attributions

Attributions are our common, everyday explanations for the causes of behavior—our answers to the question "Why did I or another person do that?" We group the causes of our own and others' behavior into two broad categories: external, environmental causes and internal, psychological causes. Then we further divide psychological causes into two types: *ability* and *effort.* In assigning a cause, we use certain rules: If a behavior occurs for many people but only in a single situation (for example, the whole class gets A's on Mrs. Apple's French test), we conclude that it is externally caused (the test was easy). In contrast, if an individual displays a behavior in many situations (Sally always gets A's on French tests), we judge the behavior to be internally caused—by ability, effort, or both (Sally is smart and works hard).

Most preschoolers are "learning optimists" who believe they can succeed if they keep trying. Their attributions support initiative in the face of challenging tasks. © Owen Franken/Corbis

In Chapter 8, we showed that although intelligence predicts school achievement, the relationship is far from perfect. Individual differences in **achievement motivation**—the tendency to persist at challenging tasks—are just as important. Today, researchers regard achievement-related attributions as the main reason some children display initiative when faced with obstacles to success, whereas others give up easily.

• **Emergence of Achievement-Related Attributions** Around age 3, children begin making attributions about their successes and failures. These attributions affect their *expectancies of success,* which influence their willingness to try hard in the future.

Many studies show that preschoolers are "learning optimists" who rate their own ability very high, often underestimate task difficulty, and hold positive expectancies of success. When asked to react to a situation in which one person does worse on a task than another, young children indicate that the lower-scoring person can still succeed if she keeps on trying (Schuster, Ruble, & Weinert, 1998). Cognitively, preschoolers cannot yet distinguish the precise causes of their successes and failures. Instead, they view all good things as going together: A person who tries hard is also a smart person who is going to succeed.

Nevertheless, by age 3, some children give up easily when faced with a challenge, expressing shame and despondency after failing at a task. These nonpersisters have a history of parental criticism of their worth and performance. In contrast, their enthusiastic, highly motivated agemates have parents who patiently encourage while offering information about how to succeed (Kelley, Brownell, & Campbell, 2000). When preschool nonpersisters use dolls to act out an adult's reaction to failure, they anticipate disapproval—saying, for example, "He's punished because he can't do the puzzle." Persisters say, "He worked hard but just couldn't finish. He wants to try again" (Burhans & Dweck, 1995). Preschoolers readily internalize adult evaluations. Whereas persisters view themselves as "good," nonpersisters see themselves as "bad" (Heyman, Dweck, & Cain, 1992). Already, nonpersisters seem to base their self-esteem entirely on others' judgments, not on inner standards. Consequently, they show early signs of maladaptive achievement behaviors that become more common during middle childhood.

• Mastery-Oriented versus Learned-Helpless Children As a result of improved reasoning skills and frequent evaluative feedback, school-age children gradually become able to distinguish ability, effort, and external factors in explaining their performance (Dweck, 2002). Those who are high in achievement motivation make **mastery-oriented attributions,** crediting their successes to ability—a characteristic they can improve through trying hard and can count on when faced with new challenges. This **incremental view of ability**—that it can increase through effort—influences the way mastery-oriented children interpret negative events. They attribute failure to factors that can be changed or controlled, such as insufficient effort or a difficult task (Heyman & Dweck, 1998). Whether these children succeed or fail, they take an industrious, persistent approach to learning.

Unfortunately, children who develop **learned helplessness** attribute their failures, not their successes, to ability. When they succeed, they are likely to conclude that external events, such as luck, are responsible. Unlike their mastery-oriented counterparts, they hold an **entity view of ability**—that it cannot be improved by trying hard (Cain & Dweck, 1995). When a task is difficult, these children experience an anxious loss of control. They give up without really trying.

Children's attributions affect their goals. Mastery-oriented children focus on *learning goals*—increasing their ability through effort and seeking information on how to do so. Hence, their performance increases over time (Blackwell, Trzesniewski, & Dweck, 2007). In contrast, learned-helpless children focus on *performance goals*—obtaining positive and avoiding negative evaluations of their fragile sense of ability. Over time, learned-helpless children's ability no longer predicts how well they do. In one study, the more fourth to sixth graders held self-critical attributions, the lower they rated their competence, the less they knew about effective study strategies, the more they avoided challenge, and the poorer their academic performance. These outcomes strengthened their entity view of ability (Pomerantz & Saxon, 2001). Because learned-helpless children fail to connect effort with success, they do not develop the metacognitive and self-regulatory skills necessary for high achievement (see Chapter 7). Lack of effective learning strategies, reduced persistence, low performance, and a sense of loss of control sustain one another in a vicious cycle (Chan & Moore, 2006).

Repeated negative evaluations can cause children to develop learned helplessness. While his classmate focuses intently on the lesson, this boy is completely derailed by his sense of defeat. © Stephanie Maze/ CORBIS

In adolescence, young people attain a fully differentiated understanding of the relationship between ability and effort. They realize that people who vary in ability can achieve the same outcome with different degrees of effort (Butler, 1999). When adolescents view their own ability as fixed and low, they conclude that mastering a challenging task is not worth the cost—extremely high effort. To protect themselves from painful feelings of failure, these learned-helpless young people select less demanding courses and careers. As Figure 11.6 shows, learned helplessness prevents children from realizing their potential.

• Influences on Achievement-Related Attributions What accounts for the different attributions of mastery-oriented and learned-helpless children? As with preschoolers, adult communication plays a key role. When parents hold an entity view of ability,

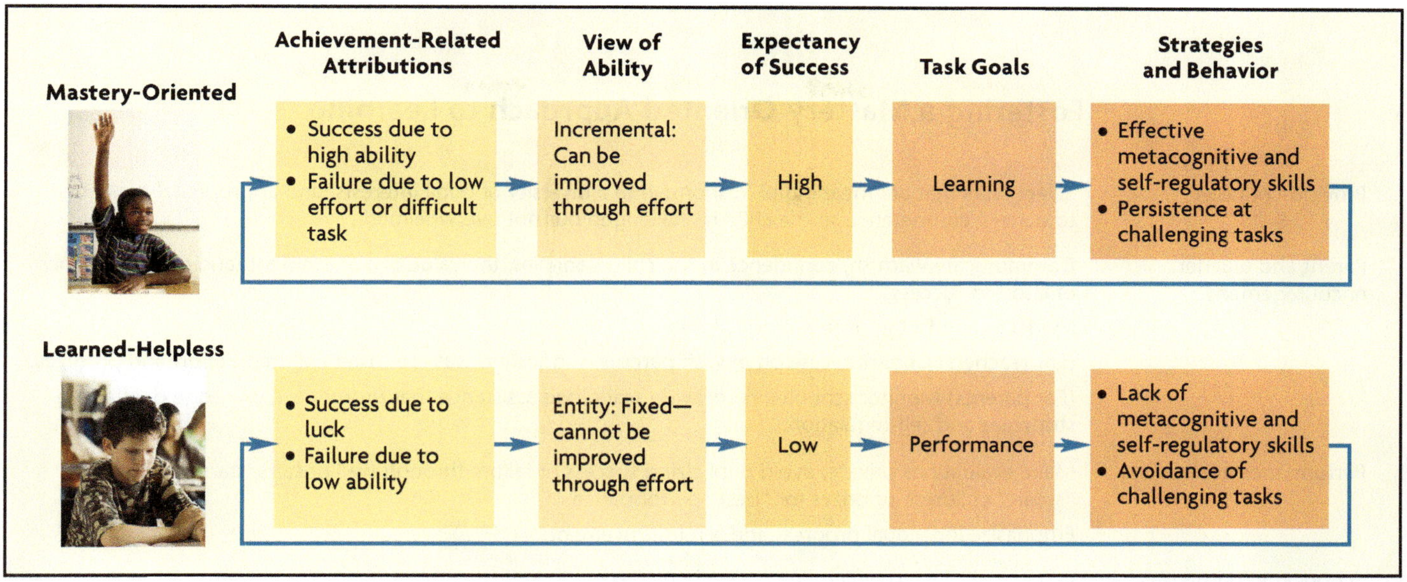

Figure 11.6 **Consequences of mastery-oriented and learned-helpless attributional styles.**

Top: © Michael Newman/PhotoEdit; *bottom:* © Image Source Black/Alamy Images

their children's self-evaluations and school grades conform more closely to parental ability judgments than do those of children whose parents deny that ability is fixed (Pomerantz & Dong, 2006). Parents who believe that little can be done to improve ability may ignore information that is inconsistent with their perceptions, giving their child little opportunity to counteract a negative parental evaluation.

Indeed, children with a learned-helpless style often have parents who believe that their child is not very capable and must work much harder than others to succeed. When the child fails, the adult might say, "You can't do that, can you? It's OK if you quit" (Hokoda & Fincham, 1995). After the child succeeds, the parent might offer feedback evaluating the child's traits ("You're so smart"). Trait statements—even when positive—encourage children to adopt an entity view of ability, leading them to question their competence in the face of setbacks and to retreat from challenge (Mueller & Dweck, 1998).

Teachers' messages also affect children's attributions. Teachers who are caring and helpful and who emphasize learning goals tend to have mastery-oriented students (Anderman et al., 2001; Daniels, Kalkman, & McCombs, 2001). In a study of 1,600 third to eighth graders, students who viewed their teachers as providing positive, supportive learning conditions worked harder and participated more in class—factors that predicted high achievement, which sustained children's belief in the value of effort. In contrast, students with unsupportive teachers regarded their performance as externally controlled (by their teachers or by luck). This attitude predicted withdrawal from learning activities and declining achievement—outcomes that led children to doubt their ability (Skinner, Zimmer-Gembeck, & Connell, 1998).

For some children, performance is especially likely to be undermined by adult feedback. Despite their higher achievement, girls more often than boys attribute poor performance to lack of ability. Girls tend to receive messages from teachers and parents that their ability is at fault when they do not do well, and negative stereotypes (for example, that girls are weak at math) reduce their interest and effort (Bleeker & Jacobs, 2004; Cole et al., 1999). And low-SES, ethnic-minority children often receive less favorable feedback from teachers, especially when assigned to homogeneous groups of poorly achieving students in school—conditions that result in a drop in academic self-esteem and achievement (Harris & Graham, 2007; Ogbu, 1997).

Finally, cultural values affect the likelihood that children will develop learned helplessness. Compared with North Americans, Asian parents and teachers believe that doing well depends much more on effort than on ability and that trying hard is a moral responsibility—messages they transmit to children (Grant & Dweck, 2001). Furthermore, because of the high value their culture places on self-improvement, Asians attend more to failure than to success because failure indicates where corrective action is needed. North Americans, in contrast, focus more on success because it enhances self-esteem. When researchers observed Chinese

Applying What We Know

Fostering a Mastery-Oriented Approach to Learning

Context	Strategies
Provision of tasks	Select tasks that are meaningful, responsive to a diversity of pupil interests, and appropriately matched to current competence so the child is challenged but not overwhelmed.
Parent and teacher encouragement	Communicate warmth, confidence in the child's abilities, the value of achievement, and the importance of effort in success. Model high effort in overcoming failure. (For teachers) Communicate often with parents, suggesting ways to foster children's effort and progress. (For parents) Monitor schoolwork; provide scaffolded assistance that promotes knowledge of effective strategies and self-regulation.
Performance evaluations	Make evaluations private; avoid publicizing success or failure through wall posters, stars, privileges for "smart" children, or prizes for "best" performance. Emphasize individual progress and self-improvement.
School environment	Offer small classes, which permit teachers to provide individualized support for mastery. Provide for cooperative learning and peer tutoring, in which children assist one another; avoid ability grouping, which makes evaluations of children's progress public. Accommodate individual and cultural differences in learning styles. Create an atmosphere that values academics and sends a clear message that all students can learn.

Sources: Hilt, 2004; Wigfield et al., 2006.

and U.S. mothers' responses to their fourth- and fifth-grade children's puzzle solutions, mothers from both cultures were complimentary after children succeeded, but U.S. mothers more so. When children failed, Chinese mothers more often pointed out the child's inadequate performance. And regardless of success or failure, Chinese mothers made more task-relevant statements aimed at ensuring that children exerted sufficient effort to do well ("You concentrated on it"; "You only got 6 out of 12") (see Figure 11.7). When children continued with the task after mothers left the room, the Chinese children showed greater gains in performance (Ng, Pomerantz, & Lam, 2007).

Figure 11.7 Chinese and U.S. mothers' task-relevant statements in response to their fourth-grade child's success or failure on puzzle tasks. Observations revealed that regardless of whether their child had just succeeded or failed, Chinese mothers were more likely than U.S. mothers to make task-relevant statements aimed at ensuring that the child exerted high effort. (Adapted from Ng, Pomerantz, & Lam, 2007.)

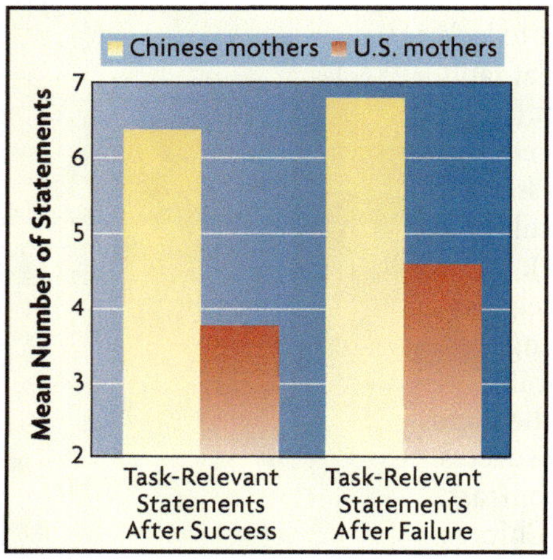

Fostering a Mastery-Oriented Approach Attribution research suggests that well-intended messages from adults sometimes undermine children's competence. An intervention called **attribution retraining** encourages learned-helpless children to believe that they can overcome failure by exerting more effort. Children are given tasks hard enough that they will experience some failure, followed by repeated feedback that helps them revise their attributions: "You can do it if you try harder." After they succeed, children receive additional feedback ("You're really good at this"; "You really tried hard on that one") so that they attribute their success to both ability and effort, not chance. Another approach is to encourage low-effort students to focus less on grades and more on mastering a task for its own sake (Hilt, 2004; Horner & Gaither, 2004). Instruction in effective strategies and self-regulation is also vital, to compensate for development lost in this area and to ensure that renewed effort will pay off (Borkowski & Muthukrisna, 1995; Wigfield et al., 2006).

Attribution retraining is most effective when begun early, before children's views of themselves become hard to change. School-age children with low academic self-esteem whose parents regularly used mastery-oriented practices while helping with homework gained in sense of academic competence, willingness to exert effort on difficult tasks, and experience of positive emotion when assessed six months later (Pomerantz, Ng, & Wang, 2006). The strategies summarized in Applying What We Know above are helpful in preventing learned helplessness. Consult the Milestones table on the following page for an overview of development of self-esteem.

Milestones

Development of Self-Esteem

Age	Milestones
1–2 years	■ Expressions of pleasure in mastery are evident. ■ Sensitivity to adults' evaluations appears.
3–5 years	■ Self-esteem is typically high and consists of several separate self-evaluations. ■ Achievement-related attributions appear but are undifferentiated; for example, a person who tries hard is smart and will succeed.
6–10 years	■ Self-esteem becomes hierarchically organized; separate self-evaluations (academic, social, and physical/athletic competence, physical appearance) are integrated into an overall sense of self-esteem. ■ Self-esteem declines as children make social comparisons, then rises. ■ Achievement-related attributions differentiate into ability, effort, and external factors.
11 years–adulthood	■ New dimensions of self-esteem are added (close friendship, romantic appeal, job competence). ■ Self-esteem continues to rise. ■ Achievement-related attributions reflect full differentiation of ability and effort.

Note: These milestones represent overall age trends. Individual differences exist in the precise age at which each milestone is attained.

Photos: (top) © Nancy Richmond/The Image Works; (middle) © Cindy Charles/PhotoEdit; (bottom) © Barbara Stitzer/PhotoEdit

Ask Yourself

Review Describe and explain changes in the structure and level of self-esteem from early childhood to adolescence.

Apply Should parents try to promote children's self-esteem by telling them they're "smart" or "wonderful"? Are children harmed if they do not feel good about everything they do? Why or why not?

Connect What cognitive changes support the transition to a self-concept emphasizing competencies, personality traits, and social comparisons? (*Hint:* See pages 276–277 in Chapter 7.)

Reflect Recall your own attributions for academic successes and failures when you were in elementary school. What are those attributions like now? What messages from others may have contributed to your attributions?

Constructing an Identity: Who Should I Become?

Adolescents' well-organized self-descriptions and differentiated sense of self-esteem provide the cognitive foundation for forming an **identity,** first recognized by psychoanalyst Erik Erikson (1950, 1968) as a major personality achievement and a crucial step toward becoming a productive, content adult. Constructing an identity involves defining who you are, what you value, and the directions you choose to pursue in life. One expert described it as an explicit theory of oneself as a rational agent—one who acts on the basis of reason, takes responsibility for those actions, and can explain them (Moshman, 2005). This search for what is true and real about the self drives many choices—vocation, interpersonal relationships, community involvement, ethnic-group membership, and expression of one's sexual orientation, as well as moral, political, and religious ideals.

Erikson believed that successful psychosocial outcomes of infancy and childhood pave the way toward a coherent, positive identity. (Return to Chapter 1, page 18, to review Erikson's

As this teenager gathers information about events in the news, he becomes more aware of a diversity of viewpoints. A flexible, open-minded approach to grappling with competing beliefs and values fosters identity development.
© Dwayne Newton/PhotoEdit

stages.) Although the seeds of identity formation are planted early, not until late adolescence and emerging adulthood do young people become absorbed in this task. According to Erikson, in complex societies teenagers experience an *identity crisis*—a temporary period of confusion and distress as they experiment with alternatives before settling on values and goals. Those who go through a process of inner soul-searching eventually arrive at a mature identity. They sift through characteristics that defined the self in childhood and combine them with emerging traits, capacities, and commitments. Then they mold these into a solid inner core that provides a sense of sameness as they move through different roles in daily life. Once formed, identity continues to be refined throughout life as people reevaluate earlier commitments and choices.

Current theorists agree with Erikson that questioning of values, plans, and priorities is necessary for a mature identity, but they no longer describe this process as a "crisis" (Grotevant, 1998; Kroger, 2005). For most young people, identity development is not traumatic or disturbing but, more typically, a process of *exploration* followed by *commitment.* As young people try out life possibilities, they gather important information about themselves and their environment and sort through that information for the purpose of making enduring decisions. In the process, they forge an organized self-structure (Arnett, 2000, 2006; Moshman, 2005).

Erikson described the negative outcome of adolescence as *identity confusion.* If young people's earlier conflicts were resolved negatively or if society limits their choices to ones that do not match their abilities and desires, they may appear shallow, directionless, and unprepared for the psychological challenges of adulthood.

Does research support Erikson's ideas about identity development? In the following sections, we will see that young people go about the task of defining the self in ways that closely match Erikson's description.

Paths to Identity

Using a clinical interviewing procedure devised by James Marcia (1980) or briefer questionnaire measures, researchers evaluate progress in identity development on two key criteria derived from Erikson's theory: *exploration* and *commitment.* Their various combinations yield four *identity statuses,* summarized in Table 11.1: **identity achievement,** commitment to values, beliefs, and goals following a period of exploration; **identity moratorium,** exploration without having reached commitment; **identity foreclosure,** commitment in the absence of exploration; and **identity diffusion,** an apathetic state characterized by lack of both exploration and commitment.

Identity development follows many paths. Some young people remain in one status, whereas others experience many status transitions. And the pattern often varies across *identity domains,* such as sexual orientation, vocation, and religious, political, and other world views. Most young people change from "lower" statuses (foreclosure or diffusion) to "higher" statuses (moratorium or achievement) between their mid-teens and mid-twenties, but some move in the reverse direction (Kroger, 2001, 2005; Meeus, 1996). The number of domains explored and the intensity with which they are examined vary widely. Almost all young people grapple with work, close relationships, and family. Others add political, religious, community, and leisure-time commitments, some of which are more central to their identity than others.

Because attending college provides opportunities to explore career options and lifestyles, college students make more identity progress than they did in high school (Montgomery & Côté, 2003). After college, young people often sample various life experiences through travel or short-term volunteer jobs in such programs as the U.S. Peace Corps or the Canada Corps. Those who go to work immediately after high school graduation often settle on a self-definition earlier. But if they encounter obstacles to realizing their occupational goals because of lack of training or vocational choices, they are at risk for long-term identity foreclosure or diffusion (Cohen et al., 2003; Eccles et al., 2003).

At one time, researchers thought that adolescent girls postponed establishing an identity, focusing instead on Erikson's next stage, intimacy development. Some girls do show more

Table 11.1 The Four Identity Statuses

Identity Status	Description	Example
Identity achievement	Identity-achieved individuals have already explored alternatives and are committed to a clearly formulated set of self-chosen values and goals. They feel a sense of psychological well-being, of sameness through time, and of knowing where they are going.	When asked how willing she would be to give up going into her chosen occupation if something better came along, Lauren responded, "Well, I might, but I doubt it. I've thought long and hard about law as a career. I'm pretty certain it's for me."
Identity moratorium	*Moratorium* means "delay or holding pattern." These individuals have not yet made definite commitments. They are in the process of exploring—gathering information and trying out activities in an effort to find values and goals to guide their lives.	When asked whether he had ever had doubts about his religious beliefs, Ramón said, "Yes, I guess I'm going through that right now. I just don't see how there can be a God and yet so much evil in the world."
Identity foreclosure	Identity-foreclosed individuals have committed themselves to values and goals without exploring alternatives. They accept a ready-made identity chosen for them by authority figures—usually parents but sometimes teachers, religious leaders, or romantic partners.	When asked if she had ever reconsidered her political beliefs, Emily answered, "No, not really, our family is pretty much in agreement on these things."
Identity diffusion	Identity-diffused individuals lack clear direction. They are neither committed to values and goals nor actively trying to reach them. They may never have explored alternatives or may have found the task too threatening and overwhelming.	When asked about his attitude toward nontraditional gender roles, Justin responded, "Oh, I don't know. It doesn't make much difference to me. I can take it or leave it."

sophisticated reasoning in intimacy-related domains, such as sexuality and family versus career priorities. Otherwise, adolescents of both sexes typically make progress on identity concerns before experiencing genuine intimacy in relationships (Berman et al., 2006; Meeus et al., 1999).

Identity Status and Psychological Well-Being

According to identity theorists, individuals who move away from foreclosure and diffusion toward moratorium and achievement build a well-structured identity that integrates various domains. As a result, they experience a gratifying sense of personal continuity and social connection—of being the same person across time and contexts and of becoming a competent member of the adult community (Snarey & Bell, 2003). A wealth of research supports the conclusion that identity achievement and moratorium are psychologically healthy routes to a mature self-definition, whereas long-term foreclosure and diffusion are maladaptive.

Adolescents in moratorium resemble identity-achieved individuals in using an active, information-gathering cognitive style to make personal decisions and solve problems: They seek out relevant information, evaluate it carefully, and critically reflect on and revise their views (Berzonsky, 2003; Berzonsky & Kuk, 2000). Young people who are identity-achieved or exploring have higher self-esteem, feel more in control of their own lives, are more likely to view school and work as feasible avenues for realizing their aspirations, and are more advanced in moral reasoning (Adams & Marshall, 1996; Kroger, 2007; Serafini & Adams, 2002). When asked for a "turning point" narrative (an account of a past event that they view as important in understanding themselves), identity-achieved individuals tell stories containing more sophisticated personal insights and portraying negative life events as followed by good outcomes—personal renewal, improvement, and enlightenment (McLean & Pratt, 2006).

Adolescents stuck in either foreclosure or diffusion are passive in the face of identity concerns and have adjustment difficulties. Foreclosed individuals display a *dogmatic, inflexible cognitive style,* internalizing the values and beliefs of parents and others without deliberate evaluation and resisting information that threatens their position (Berzonsky & Kuk, 2000). Most fear rejection by people on whom they depend for affection and self-esteem. A few foreclosed teenagers who are alienated from their families and society may join cults or other extremist groups, uncritically adopting a way of life that is different from their past.

▪ Social Issues ▪

Adolescent Suicide: Annihilation of the Self

The suicide rate increases over the lifespan. It is lowest in childhood and highest in old age, but it jumps sharply at adolescence. Currently, suicide is the third-leading cause of death among U.S. youths (after motor vehicle collisions and homicides) and the second-leading cause among Canadian youths (after motor vehicle collisions) (Statistics Canada, 2007e; U.S. Census Bureau, 2007b). Perhaps because North American teenagers experience more stresses and fewer supports than they did in the past, the rate of adolescent suicide tripled in both the United States and Canada between the mid-1960s and the mid-1990s, followed by a slight decline (Spirito & Esposito-Smythers, 2006). At the same time, rates of adolescent suicide vary widely among industrialized nations—low in Greece, Italy, the Netherlands, and Spain; intermediate in Australia, Canada, Japan, and the United States; and high in Finland, New Zealand, and Singapore (Bridge, Goldstein, & Brent, 2006). These international differences remain unexplained.

Factors Related to Adolescent Suicide

Striking sex differences in suicidal behavior exist. The number of boys who kill themselves exceeds the number of girls by a ratio of 3 or 4 to 1. Girls make more unsuccessful suicide attempts and use methods from which they are more likely to be revived, such as a sleeping pill overdose. In contrast, boys tend to choose techniques that lead to instant death, such as firearms or hanging. Gender-role expectations may contribute; less tolerance exists for feelings of helplessness and failed efforts in males than in females (Canetto & Sakinofsky, 1998).

Perhaps because of higher levels of support from extended families, African Americans and Hispanics have slightly lower suicide rates than Caucasian Americans. Recently, however, suicide has risen among African-American adolescent males; the current rate approaches that of Caucasian-American males. And Native-American and Canadian Aboriginal youths commit suicide at rates two to six times national averages (Health Canada, 2003; U.S. Census Bureau, 2007b). High rates of profound family poverty, school failure, alcohol and drug use, and depression probably underlie these trends.

Gay, lesbian, and bisexual youths also are at high risk, making suicide attempts at a rate three times as high as other adolescents. Those who have tried to kill themselves report more family conflict over their gender-atypical behavior, inner turmoil about their sexuality, problems in romantic relationships, and peer rejection due to their sexual orientation (D'Augelli et al., 2005).

Suicide tends to occur in two types of young people. The first group includes adolescents who are highly intelligent but solitary, withdrawn, and unable to meet their own standards or those of important people in their lives. Members of a second, larger group show antisocial tendencies and express their despondency through bullying, fighting, stealing, increased risk taking, and drug abuse (Fergusson, Woodward, & Horwood, 2000). Besides being hostile and destructive, they turn their anger and disappointment inward.

Biology and environment jointly contribute to suicidal behavior. A family history of emotional and antisocial disorders and of suicide is often present. In addition, suicidal young people are more likely to have experienced multiple stressful life events, including economic disadvantage, parental separation and divorce, absence of family warmth, frequent parent–child conflict, and abuse and neglect. Stressors typically increase during the period preceding a suicide attempt or completion (Beautrais, 2003; Wagner, Silverman, & Martin, 2003). Triggering events include parental blaming of the teenager for family problems, the breakup of an important peer relationship, or the humiliation of having been caught engaging in irresponsible, antisocial acts.

Public policies resulting in cultural disintegration have amplified suicide rates among Native American and Canadian Aboriginal youths. In both countries, from the late 1800s to the 1960s or 1970s, Native families were forced to enroll their children in government-run residential boarding schools designed to eradicate tribal affiliations. From the moment children arrived, they were not allowed to "be Indian" in any way—culturally, linguistically, artistically, or

Diffused teenagers are the least mature in identity development. They typically use a diffuse-avoidant cognitive style in which they avoid dealing with personal decisions and problems and, instead, allow current situational pressures to dictate their reactions (Berzonsky & Kuk, 2000; Krettenauer, 2005). Taking an "I don't care" attitude, they entrust themselves to luck or fate and tend to go along with the crowd. As a result, they often experience time management and academic difficulties and, of all young people, are the most likely to commit antisocial acts and to use and abuse drugs (Archer & Waterman, 1990; Schwartz et al., 2005). Often at the heart of their apathy and impulsiveness is a sense of hopelessness about the future that puts many at risk for serious depression and suicide (see the Social Issues box above).

Influences on Identity Development

Adolescent identity formation begins a lifelong, dynamic process in which a change in either the individual or the context opens up the possibility of reformulating identity (Kunnen & Bosma, 2003). A wide variety of factors influence identity development.

spiritually (Goldston et al., 2008). These repressive schools left many young people academically unprepared and emotionally scarred, contributing to family and community disorganization in current and succeeding generations—and to associated high youth crime and suicide rates (Barnes, Josefowitz, & Cole, 2006; Howell & Yuille, 2004).

Community powerlessness is yet another source of soaring suicide rates among Native youths. In British Columbia, the incidence of suicide among Canadian Aboriginal adolescents is six times higher in communities without self-government than in those with self-government (Health Canada, 2003). And historically, suicide among the Inuit of Alaska, northern Canada, and Greenland was rare. But between 1960 and 2003, when they were forced off their lands into urban areas with overcrowded housing, poor-quality schools, high unemployment, and widespread ethnic prejudice, youth suicide rose dramatically (Hicks, 2007)

Why does suicide increase in adolescence? One factor seems to be teenagers' improved ability to plan ahead. Although some act impulsively, many young people at risk take purposeful steps toward killing themselves. Other cognitive changes also contribute. Belief in the personal fable (see Chapter 6) leads many depressed young people to conclude that no one could possibly understand their intense pain. As a result, despair, hopelessness, and isolation deepen.

Prevention and Treatment

Picking up on signals from a troubled teenager is a crucial first step in suicide prevention. Parents and teachers must be trained to recognize warning signs. Schools and community settings, such as recreational and religious organizations, can help by strengthening adolescents' connections with their cultural heritage and providing knowledgeable, approachable, and sympathetic adults, peer support groups, and information about telephone hot lines (Goldston et al., 2008; Spirito et al., 2003). Once a teenager takes steps toward suicide, staying with the young person, listening, and expressing compassion and concern until professional help can be obtained are essential.

Juliette Turtle, a resident of the Pikangikum First Nation community in Ontario, has lost seven children to suicide. Public policies leading to community displacement and cultural disintegration have amplified suicide rates among Native Canadian youths. The Canadian Press (John Woods)

Intervention with depressed and suicidal adolescents takes many forms, from antidepressant medication to individual, family, and group therapy. Sometimes hospitalization is necessary to ensure the teenager's safety. Until the adolescent improves, removing weapons, knives, razors, scissors, and drugs from the home is vital. On a broader scale, gun-control legislation limiting adolescents' access to the most frequent and deadly suicide method in the United States would greatly reduce both the number of suicides and the high teenage homicide rate. In Canada and other industrialized nations with strict gun-control policies, teenage deaths due to firearms occur, on average, only one-sixteenth as frequently as in the United States (Fingerhut & Christoffel, 2002).

After a suicide, family and peer survivors need support to help them cope with grief, anger, and guilt over not having been able to help the victim. Teenage suicides often occur in clusters: One such death increases the likelihood of other suicides among depressed peers who knew the young person or heard about the death through the media (Bearman & Moody, 2004; Gould, Jamieson, & Romer, 2003). In view of this trend, an especially watchful eye must be kept on vulnerable adolescents after a suicide happens. Media restraint in reporting teenage suicides also aids prevention.

● **Personality** Identity status, as we have just seen, is both cause and consequence of personality characteristics. Adolescents who assume that absolute truth is always attainable tend to be foreclosed, whereas those who doubt they will ever feel certain about anything are more often identity-diffused. Young people who appreciate that they can use rational criteria to choose among alternatives are more likely to be in a state of moratorium or identity achievement (Berzonsky & Kuk, 2000; Boyes & Chandler, 1992). This flexible, open-minded approach helps them greatly in and pursuing educational, vocational, and other life goals.

● **Family** Teenagers' identity development is enhanced when their families serve as a "secure base" from which they can confidently move out into the wider world. In families of diverse ethnicities, adolescents who feel attached to their parents and say they provide effective guidance, but who also feel free to voice their own opinions, tend to be in a state of moratorium or identity achievement (Berzonsky, 2004; Luyckx et al., 2006; Schwartz et al., 2005). Foreclosed teenagers usually have close bonds with parents but lack opportunities for healthy separation. And diffused young people report the lowest levels of parental support and warm, open communication (Reis & Youniss, 2004; Zimmerman & Becker-Stoll, 2002).

Cultural Influences

Identity Development Among Ethnic Minority Adolescents

Most adolescents are aware of their cultural ancestry but relatively unconcerned about it. But for teenagers who are members of minority groups, **ethnic identity**—a sense of ethnic group membership and attitudes and feelings associated with that membership—is central to the quest for identity, and it presents complex challenges. As they develop cognitively and become more sensitive to feedback from the social environment, minority youths become painfully aware that they are targets of prejudice and discrimination. This discovery complicates their efforts to develop a sense of cultural belonging and a set of personally meaningful goals.

Minority youths often feel caught between the standards of the larger society and the traditions of their culture of origin. In many immigrant families from collectivist cultures, adolescents' commitment to obeying their parents and fulfilling family obligations lessens the longer the family has been in the immigrant-receiving country—a circumstance that induces **acculturative stress**, psychological distress resulting from conflict between the minority and the host culture (Phinney, Ong, & Madden, 2000). When immigrant parents tightly restrict their teenagers through fear that assimilation into the larger society will undermine their cultural traditions, their youngsters often rebel, rejecting aspects of their ethnic background.

Other minority teenagers react to years of shattered self-esteem, school failure, and barriers to success in the mainstream culture by defining themselves in contrast to majority values. A Mexican-American teenager who had given up on school commented, "Mexicans don't have a chance to go on to college and make something of themselves" (Matute-Bianche, 1986, pp. 250–251). At the same time, discrimination can interfere with the formation of a positive ethnic identity. In one study, Mexican-American youths who had experienced more discrimination were less likely to explore their ethnicity and to report feeling good about it. Those with low ethnic pride showed a sharp drop in self-esteem in the face of discrimination (Romero & Roberts, 2003).

With age, some ethnic minority young people progress from ethnic-identity diffusion or foreclosure through moratorium to ethnic-identity achievement. But because the process of forging an ethnic identity can be painful and confusing, others show no change, and still others regress (Seaton, Scottham, & Sellers, 2006). Young people with parents of different ethnicities face extra challenges. In a large survey of high school students, part-black biracial teenagers reported as much discrimination as their monoracial black counterparts, yet they felt less positively about their ethnicity. And compared with monoracial minorities, many biracials—including black–white, black–Asian, white–Asian, black–Hispanic, and white–Hispanic—regarded ethnicity as less central to their identities (Herman, 2004). Perhaps these adolescents encountered fewer opportunities in their homes and communities to forge a strong sense of belonging to either culture.

When family members encourage them to behave proactively by disproving ethnic stereotypes of low achievement or antisocial behavior, adolescents typically surmount the threat that discrimination poses to a favorable ethnic identity. These young people manage experiences of unfair treatment effectively, by seeking

• **Peers** Interaction with diverse peers through school and community activities encourages adolescents to explore values and role possibilities (Barber et al., 2005). And close friends, like parents, can act as a secure base, providing emotional support, assistance, and models of identity development. In one study, 15-year-olds with warm, trusting peer ties were more involved in exploring relationship issues—for example, thinking about what they valued in a life partner (Meeus, Oosterwegel, & Vollebergh, 2002). In another study, college students' attachment to friends predicted progress in choosing a career (Felsman & Blustein, 1999).

• **School, Community, and Culture** Schools and communities can jointly foster identity development. Supportive experiences include classrooms that promote high-level thinking, teachers and counselors who encourage low-SES and ethnic minority students to go to college, extracurricular activities that offer teenagers responsible roles consistent with their interests and talents, and vocational training that immerses adolescents in the real world of adult work (Coatsworth et al., 2005; Cooper, 1998).

Culture strongly influences an aspect of mature identity not captured by the identity-status approach: constructing a sense of self-continuity despite major personal changes. In one study, researchers asked Canadian-Aboriginal and cultural-majority 12- to 20-year-olds to describe themselves in the past and in the present and then to justify why they were the same continuous person (Lalonde & Chandler, 2005). Both groups gave increasingly complex responses with age, but their strategies differed. Most cultural-majority adolescents used an

social support and engaging in direct problem solving (Phinney & Chavira, 1995; Scott, 2003). Also, adolescents whose families taught them the history, traditions, values, and language of their ethnic group and who frequently interact with same-ethnicity peers are more likely to forge a favorable ethnic identity (Hughes et al., 2006; McHale et al., 2006).

How can society help minority adolescents resolve identity conflicts constructively? Here are some relevant approaches:

- Promote effective parenting, in which children and adolescents benefit from family ethnic pride yet are encouraged to explore the meaning of ethnicity in their own lives.
- Ensure that schools respect minority youths' native languages, unique learning styles, and right to a high-quality education.
- Foster contact with peers of the same ethnicity, along with respect between ethnic groups (García Coll & Magnuson, 1997).

A strong, secure ethnic identity is associated with higher self-esteem, optimism, and sense of mastery over the environment, and with more positive attitudes toward one's ethnicity (St. Louis & Liem, 2005; Umana-Taylor & Updegraff, 2007; Worrell & Gardner-Kitt, 2006). For these reasons, adolescents with a positive connection to their ethnic group are better-adjusted. They cope more effectively with stress, show higher achievement in school, and have fewer emotional and behavior problems than agemates who identify only weakly with their ethnicity (Greene, Way, & Pahl, 2006; Seaton, Scottham, & Sellers, 2006; Umana-Taylor & Alfaro, 2006; Yip, Seaton, & Sellers, 2006). For teenagers faced with adversity, ethnic identity is a powerful source of resilience.

These adolescents celebrate their cultural heritage by participating in a Filipino parade in New York City. When minority youths encounter respect for their ethnic heritage in schools and communities, they are more likely to retain ethnic values and customs as an important part of their identity.

Forming a **bicultural identity**—by exploring and adopting values from both the adolescent's subculture and the dominant culture—offers added benefits. Biculturally identified adolescents tend to be achieved in other areas of identity as well and to have especially favorable relations with members of other ethnic groups (Phinney, 2007; Phinney et al., 2001). In sum, achievement of ethnic identity enhances many aspects of psychological development.

individualistic approach: They described an *enduring personal essence,* a core self that remained the same despite change. In contrast, Aboriginal youths took an interdependent approach that emphasized a *constantly transforming self,* resulting from new roles and relationships. They typically constructed a coherent narrative in which they linked together various time slices of their life with a thread explaining how they had changed in meaningful ways.

Finally, societal forces are also responsible for the special challenges faced by gay, lesbian, and bisexual youths (see Chapter 5) and by ethnic minority adolescents in forming a secure identity (see the Cultural Influences box above). For ways in which adults can support healthy identity development in adolescence, consult Applying What We Know on page 470.

Ask Yourself

Review List personal and contextual factors that promote identity development.

Apply Eighteen-year-old Brad's parents worry that he will waste time at college because he is unsure about his major and career goals. Explain why Brad's uncertainty might be advantageous for his identity development.

Connect Explain how changes in self-concept and self-esteem at adolescence pave the way for identity development.

Reflect Does your identity status vary across the domains of sexuality, close relationships, vocation, religious beliefs, and political values? Describe factors that may have influenced your identity development in an important domain.

Applying What We Know

Supporting Healthy Identity Development

Strategy	Explanation
Engage in warm, open communication.	Provides both emotional support and freedom to explore values and goals.
Initiate discussions that promote high-level thinking at home and at school.	Encourages rational and deliberate selection among competing beliefs and values.
Provide opportunities to participate in extracurricular activities and vocational training programs.	Permits young people to explore the real world of adult work.
Provide opportunities to talk with adults and peers who have worked through identity questions.	Offers models of identity achievement and advice on how to resolve identity concerns.
Provide opportunities to explore ethnic heritage and learn about other cultures in an atmosphere of respect.	Fosters identity achievement in all areas and ethnic tolerance, which supports the identity explorations of others.

Thinking About Other People

Children's understanding of other people—the inferences they make about others' personality traits and viewpoints—has much in common with their developing understanding of themselves. These facets of social cognition also become increasingly differentiated and well organized with age.

Person Perception

Person perception refers to the way we size up the attributes of people with whom we are familiar. Researchers study person perception by asking children to describe people they know, using methods similar to those that focus on children's self-concepts. For example, the researcher might ask, "Can you tell me what kind of person ____ is?"

• Understanding People as Personalities Like their self-descriptions, before age 8, children's descriptions of others focus on commonly experienced emotions and attitudes, concrete activities, and behaviors. Over time, children discover consistencies in the actions of people they know, and they mention personality traits.

At first, these references are closely tied to behavior and consist of implied dispositions: "He's always fighting with people" or "She steals and lies" (Rholes, Newman, & Ruble, 1990). Later, children mention traits directly, but they use vague, stereotyped language, such as "good," "nice," or "acts smart." Gradually, sharper trait descriptions appear—"honest," "trustworthy," "generous," "polite," "selfish"—and children become more convinced of the stability of such dispositions (Droege & Stipek, 1993; Ruble & Dweck, 1995).

During adolescence, as abstract thinking becomes better established, inferences about others' personalities are drawn together into organized character sketches (O'Mahoney, 1989). As a result, between ages 14 and 16, teenagers present rich accounts of people they know that integrate physical traits, typical behaviors, and inner dispositions.

• Understanding Ethnicity and Social Class Person perception also includes making sense of diversity and inequality among people. Most 3- and 4-year-olds have formed basic concepts of race and ethnicity, in that they can apply the labels "black" and "white" to pictures, dolls, and people (Aboud, 2003). Although indicators of social class—education and occupational prestige—are not accessible to young children, they can distinguish rich from poor on the basis of physical characteristics, such as clothing, residence, and possessions (Ramsey, 1991).

By the early school years, children absorb prevailing societal attitudes, associating power and privilege with white people and poverty and inferior status with people of color. They do not necessarily acquire these views directly from parents or friends. In one study, although white school-age children assumed that parents' and friends' racial attitudes would resemble their own, no similarities in attitudes emerged (Aboud & Doyle, 1996). Perhaps white parents are reluctant to discuss their racial and ethnic views with children, and friends also say little. Given limited or ambiguous information, children may fill in the gaps with information they encounter in the media and elsewhere in their environments and then infer others' attitudes on the basis of their own.

Consistent with this idea, research indicates that children pick up much information about group status from implicit messages in their surroundings. In one experiment, 7- to 12-year-olds attending a summer school program were randomly assigned to social groups, denoted by colored T-shirts (yellow or blue) that the children wore. The researchers hung posters in the classroom that depicted unfamiliar yellow-group members as having higher status—for example, as having won more athletic and spelling competitions. When teachers recognized the social groups by using them as the basis for seating arrangements, task assignments, and bulletin-board displays, children in the high-status group evaluated their own group more favorably than the other group, and children in the low-status group appeared to view their own group less favorably. When teachers ignored the social groupings, however, no prejudice emerged (Bigler, Brown, & Markell, 2001). These findings indicate that children do not necessarily form stereotypes even when some basis for them exists—in this instance, information on wall posters. But when an authority figure validates a status hierarchy, children do form biased attitudes.

In-Group and Out-Group Biases: Development of Prejudice. Studies in diverse Western nations confirm that by age 5 to 6, white children generally evaluate their own racial group favorably and other racial groups less favorably or negatively—biases that also characterize many adults. *In-group favoritism* emerges first and strengthens until age 7 to 8. Children simply prefer their own group, generalizing from self to similar others (Bennett et al., 2004; Cameron et al., 2001). *Out-group prejudice* requires a more challenging social comparison between in-group and out-group. But it does not take long for white children to acquire negative attitudes toward ethnic minority out-groups, especially when they have little direct experience with them. When white Canadian 4- to 7-year-olds living in a white community and attending nearly all-white schools sorted positive and negative adjectives into boxes labeled as belonging to a white child and a black child, out-group prejudice emerged at age 5 (see Figure 11.8) (Aboud, 2003).

Unfortunately, many ethnic minority children show a reverse pattern: *out-group favoritism,* in which they assign positive characteristics to the privileged ethnic majority and negative characteristics to their own group. In one study, researchers asked African-American 5- to 7-year-olds to recall information in stories either consistent or inconsistent with stereotypes of blacks. The children recalled more stereotypic traits, especially if they agreed with negative cultural views of African Americans or rated their own skin tone as lighter and, therefore, may have identified themselves with the white majority (Averhart & Bigler, 1997). Similarly, Native Canadian second to fourth graders recall more positive attributes about white Canadians and more negative attributes about Native Canadians (Corenblum, 2003). And like their white Canadian agemates, Native Canadian children attributed a white Canadian child's successful task performance to ability or effort but a Native Canadian child's similar success to luck or an easy task (Corenblum, Annis, & Young, 1996). A societal context that devalues people of color makes minority children vulnerable to internalizing those beliefs.

But recall that with age, children pay more attention to inner traits and make finer distinctions between people. The capacity to classify the social world in multiple ways enables school-age children to understand that people can be both "the same" and "different"—those who look different need not think, feel, or act differently (Aboud & Amato, 2001). Consequently, voicing of negative attitudes toward minorities declines. After age 7 to 8, both majority and minority children express in-group favoritism, and white children's prejudice against out-group members often weakens (Nesdale et al.,

Figure 11.8 White Canadian 5-year-olds' expressions of in-group favoritism and out-group prejudice.
When asked to sort positive and negative adjectives into boxes labeled as belonging to a white child and a black child, white Canadian 5-year-olds assigned a greater number of positive adjectives (such as *clean, nice, smart*) to the white child than to the black child—evidence for in-group favoritism. In addition to viewing the black child less positively, the white Canadian 5-year-olds also assigned a greater number of negative adjectives (such as *dirty, naughty, cruel*) to the black child—evidence for *out-group prejudice.* (Adapted from Aboud, 2003.)

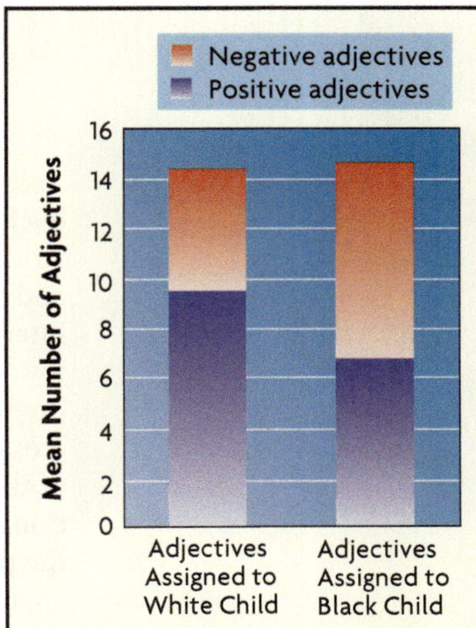

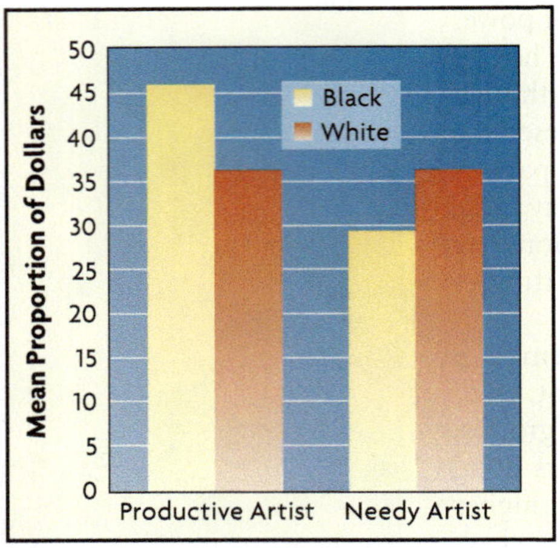

Figure 11.9 **White fourth graders' racially biased distribution of money to child artists.**

When dividing money earned from selling children's art among three child artists—two white and one black—the fourth graders gave more money to a productive black artist (who countered a stereotype) than to a productive white artist and less money to a needy black artist (who conformed to a stereotype) than to a needy white artist. In both instances, the fourth graders seemed to engage in subtle, unintentional prejudice. (From A. V. McGillicuddy-DeLisi, M. Daly, & A. Neal, 2006, "Children's Distributive Justice Judgments: Aversive Racism in Euro-American Children?" *Child Development, 77*, p. 1072. © The Society for Research in Child Development, Inc. Adapted by permission of Blackwell Publishing Ltd.)

2005; Ruble et al., 2004). Most school-age children and adolescents are also quick to verbalize the wrongness of excluding others from peer-group and learning activities on the basis of skin color—discrimination they evaluate as unfair (Killen et al., 2002).

Yet even in children aware of the injustice of discrimination, prejudice may operate subtly, unintentionally, and without awareness—as it does in many white adults (Dovidio et al., 2004; Dunham, Baron, & Banaji, 2006). Consider a study in which white school-age children were asked to divide fairly among three child artists—two white and one black—money that had been earned from selling the children's art. (This task assesses beliefs about *distributive justice*—an aspect of morality we will consider further in Chapter 12.) In each version of the task, one artist was labeled as "productive" (making more art works), one as "the oldest," and one as "poor and needing money for lunch." By age 8 to 9, most children recognize that special consideration is appropriate for children who perform exceptionally or are at a disadvantage. But racial stereotypes interfered with fourth graders' even-handed application of these principles. They gave more money to a productive black artist (who countered the racial stereotype of "low achiever") than to a productive white artist and less money to a needy black artist (who conformed to the racial stereotype of "poor") than to a needy white artist (see Figure 11.9) (McGillicuddy-De Lisi, Daly, & Neal, 2006).

The extent to which children hold ethnic and social-class biases varies, depending on the following personal and situational factors:

- *A fixed view of personality traits.* Children who believe that children's personality traits are fixed rather than changeable often judge others as either "good" or "bad." Ignoring motives and circumstances, they readily form extreme impressions on the basis of limited information. For example, they infer that "a new girl at school who makes up a lie to try to get other kids to like her" is a bad kid, or that "a kid who told a classmate her art work is ugly" goes to a school full of mean kids (Heyman & Dweck, 1998; Levy & Dweck, 1999).
- *Overly high self-esteem.* Children (and adults) with very high self-esteem are more likely to hold racial and ethnic prejudices (Baumeister et al., 2003; Bigler, Brown, & Markell, 2001). These individuals seem to belittle disadvantaged individuals or groups to justify their own extremely favorable self-evaluation. Furthermore, children of diverse backgrounds who say their own ethnicity makes them feel especially "good"—and thus perhaps socially superior—are more likely to display in-group favoritism and out-group prejudice (Pfeifer et al., 2007).
- *A social world in which people are sorted into groups.* The more adults highlight group distinctions, the greater the chances that white children will express in-group favoritism and out-group prejudice (Bigler, Brown, & Markell, 2001; Kowalski & Lo, 1999). And the less interracial contact children experience in their families, schools, and communities, the more white children display subtle prejudices—for example, interpreting an African-American agemate in an ambiguous situation as engaged in bad behavior (cheating, stealing, or harming others) (McGlothlin & Killen, 2006).

Reducing Prejudice. A wealth of research confirms that an effective way to reduce prejudice—in children and adults alike—is through intergroup contact, in which ethnically different individuals have equal status, work toward common goals, and become personally acquainted, and in which authority figures (such as parents and teachers) expect them to engage in such interaction. Schoolchildren assigned to cooperative learning groups, in which they work toward joint goals with peers of diverse backgrounds and characteristics, show low levels of prejudice in their expressions of likability and in their behavior. For example, they form more cross-race friendships than children in typical classrooms (Pettigrew & Tropp, 2005). Sharing of thoughts and feelings with close cross-race friends, in turn, reduces even subtle, unintentional prejudices, which are highly resistant to change (Turner, Hewstone, & Voci, 2007). But the positive effects of cooperative learning seem not to generalize to outgroup members who are not part of these learning teams.

Children perform a Polynesian song on the playground of their culturally diverse school. Collaboration with members of other ethnic groups and traditions can reduce the tendency to classify the social world on the basis of race and ethnicity and to view one's own group positively and other groups negatively. © Michael J. Doolittle/The Image Works

Long-term contact and collaboration among neighborhood, school, and community groups may be the best ways to reduce prejudice. Consistent with this view, white 5- and 6-year-olds attending an ethnically mixed school relied on their everyday experiences to construct generally positive out-group attitudes (Aboud, 2003). Classrooms that expose children to broad ethnic diversity, teach them to understand and value those differences, directly address the damage caused by prejudice and discrimination, and encourage perspective taking and empathy both prevent children from forming negative biases and reduce already acquired biases (Pfeifer, Brown, & Juvonen, 2007).

Finally, inducing children to view others' traits as malleable is a promising approach to reducing prejudice. The more school-age children and adolescents believe that people can change their personalities, the more they report liking, wanting to spend time with, and perceiving themselves as similar to members of disadvantaged out-groups. Furthermore, young people who believe in the malleability of human attributes spend more time volunteering to help the needy—for example, by serving meals to the homeless or reading to poverty-stricken preschoolers (Karafantis & Levy, 2004). Volunteering may, in turn, promote a malleable view of others by inducing young people to imagine themselves in the place of the underprivileged and thus helping them appreciate the social conditions that lead to disadvantage.

Regretfully, despite the 1954 U.S. Supreme Court *Brown v. Board of Education* decision ordering schools to desegregate, school integration in the United States—which increased steadily until the late 1980s—has receded dramatically as courts terminated their desegregation orders and returned this authority to states and cities. Most U.S. white, black, and Hispanic students now attend schools where the majority of their fellow students are of their own race. White students are the most isolated group—typically in schools that are 80 percent white. And when African-American and Hispanic students attend mixed-race schools, they usually do so with other minorities (Frankenberg, Lee, & Orfield, 2003). Consequently, today's U.S. schools seldom offer exposure to the diversity necessary for countering negative racial and ethnic biases but, instead, largely perpetuate prejudices. Ideals and policies promoting interethnic contact and respect yield far more extensive school integration in Canada. Still, in both nations, 30 to 40 percent of Native children (Native American and First Nations) live on reservation lands, where they attend segregated schools (Statistics Canada, 2008; U.S. Census Bureau, 2007b).

Many studies indicate that attending integrated classrooms leads to higher achievement, educational attainment, and occupational aspirations among ethnic minority students—especially when integration begins in the early grades (Hanushek, Kain, & Rivkin, 2002). It also greatly increases the likelihood that young people will lead integrated lives as adults (Schofield, 1995). Environments in which students of diverse ethnicities learn together offer many opportunities to grapple with multiple perspectives, which challenge students to think about their social world in more complex ways. As we will see next, children's developing capacity to take the perspective of others contributes greatly to interpersonal understanding and positive social behavior.

Perspective Taking

In this and previous chapters, we have emphasized that **perspective taking**—the capacity to imagine what other people may be thinking and feeling—is important for a wide variety of social–cognitive achievements: understanding others' emotions (Chapter 10); appreciating false belief; developing referential communication skills (Chapter 9), self-concept, self-esteem, and person perception; and reducing prejudice.

Recall that Piaget regarded *egocentrism* as the major feature responsible for the immaturity of preschoolers' thought, in both the physical and social domains. Yet we have seen that even

As these children participate in an animated debate, they engage in self-reflective perspective taking—viewing their own attitudes toward an issue from another's perspective.
© Tony Freeman/PhotoEdit

toddlers have some capacity for perspective taking as soon as they become consciously self-aware in the second year of life. Nevertheless, Piaget's ideas inspired a wealth of research on children's capacity to take another's perspective, which improves steadily over childhood and adolescence.

Selman's Stages of Perspective Taking Robert Selman devised a five-stage sequence of perspective-taking skill, based on children's and adolescents' responses to social dilemmas in which characters have differing information and opinions about an event. As Table 11.2 indicates, longitudinal and cross-sectional findings reveal that at first children have only a limited idea of what other people might be thinking and feeling. Over time, they become more aware that people can interpret the same event quite differently. Soon they can "step into another person's shoes" and reflect on how that person might regard their own thoughts, feelings, and behavior. (Note the similarity between this level of perspective taking and second-order false belief, described on page 449.) Finally, older children and adolescents can evaluate two people's perspectives simultaneously, at first from the vantage point of a disinterested spectator and later by making reference to societal values, as the following explanation illustrates: "I know why Joey hid the stray kitten in the basement, even though his mom was against keeping it. He believes in not hurting animals. If you put the kitten outside or give it to the pound, it might die" (Gurucharri & Selman, 1982; Selman, 1980).

Cognitive development contributes to advances in perspective taking. Children who fail Piaget's concrete operational tasks tend to be at Selman's Level 0; those who pass concrete but not formal operational tasks tend to be at Levels 1 and 2; and young people who are increasingly formal operational tend to be at Levels 3 and 4 (Keating & Clark, 1980; Krebs & Gillmore, 1982). Furthermore, each set of Piagetian tasks tends to be mastered somewhat earlier than its related perspective-taking level (Walker, 1980). This suggests that additional cognitive and social capacities contribute to gains in perspective taking.

Other Assessments of Perspective Taking According to several theorists, preschoolers' limited capacity to take another's perspective is largely due to their passive view of the mind—their assumption that what a person knows results from observing rather than actively interpreting experience (Chandler & Carpendale, 1998). To explore this idea, researchers have devised gamelike tasks that assess children's realization that people's preexisting knowledge and beliefs affect their viewpoints.

One approach is to see whether children realize that younger, and therefore less knowledgeable, individuals view new information differently than older individuals do. In one study, 4- to 8-year-olds were asked whether a baby and an adult would know the location of an object

Table 11.2 Selman's Stages of Perspective Taking

Stage	Approximate Age Range	Description
Level 0: Undifferentiated perspective taking	3–6	Children recognize that self and other can have different thoughts and feelings, but they frequently confuse the two.
Level 1: Social-informational perspective taking	4–9	Children understand that different perspectives may result because people have access to different information.
Level 2: Self-reflective perspective taking	7–12	Children can "step into another person's shoes" and view their own thoughts, feelings, and behavior from the other person's perspective. They also recognize that others can do the same.
Level 3: Third-party perspective taking	10–15	Children can step outside a two-person situation and imagine how the self and other are viewed from the point of view of a third, impartial party.
Level 4: Societal perspective taking	14–adult	Individuals understand that third-party perspective taking can be influenced by one or more systems of larger societal values.

Sources: Selman, 1976; Selman & Byrne, 1974.

after seeing where it had been placed or, alternatively, being told where it had been placed (Montgomery, 1993). Children of all ages judged correctly that both the baby and the adult would know through directly perceiving. But 4-year-olds—even though they said that babies don't know what most words mean—incorrectly thought that the baby could learn from the verbal message. Not until 6 to 8 years do most children understand that a person's *prior knowledge* affects her ability to understand new information. Around this time, children also realize that people's *preexisting beliefs* can affect their viewpoints and that two people can interpret the same ambiguous information differently (Miller, 2000).

One-Loop Recursion
"The boy is thinking that he is thinking about himself."

Two-Loop Recursion
"The boy is thinking that the girl is thinking of the father thinking of the mother."

Figure 11.10 Cartoon drawings depicting recursive thought.
Not until midadolescence do young people master the complexities of this self-embedded form of perspective taking. (From P. H. Miller, F. S. Kessel, & J. H. Flavell, 1970, "Thinking About People Thinking About People Thinking About . . . : A Study of Social Cognitive Development." *Child Development,* 41, p. 616. © The Society for Research in Child Development, Inc. Reprinted by permission.)

Perspective-taking tasks for older children and adolescents have focused on *recursive thought*—thinking about what another person is thinking. Selman's stages suggest that thinking recursively (Levels 3 and 4) improves from middle childhood to adolescence, a trend that is supported by research. When first through sixth graders were asked to describe cartoons like those in Figure 11.10, only 50 percent of sixth graders succeeded on one-loop recursions, and few could handle two-loop recursions (Miller, Kessel, & Flavell, 1970). Not until midadolescence do young people grasp complex recursive understanding.

Recursive thought makes human interaction truly reciprocal. People often call on it to clear up misunderstandings: "*I thought you would think* I was just kidding when I said that." It is also involved in clever attempts to disguise our real thoughts and feelings: "He'll think I'm jealous if I tell him I don't like his new car, so I'll act like I do." Finally, the capacity to think recursively probably contributes to the intense self-focusing and concern with the imaginary audience common in adolescence (see Chapter 6).

• Perspective Taking and Social Behavior Experiences in which adults and peers explain their viewpoints contribute greatly to children's perspective taking. Good perspective takers, in turn, are more likely to display empathy and sympathy and to handle difficult social situations effectively—among the reasons they are better-liked by peers (Eisenberg, Murphy, & Shepard, 1997; FitzGerald & White, 2003).

Although good perspective taking is crucial for mature social behavior, situational and personal factors determine whether it will lead to prosocial acts. In competitive situations, skilled perspective takers are often as good at defending their own viewpoint as they are at cooperating. Also, even when children appreciate another person's thoughts and feelings, temperament influences their behavior. Recall from Chapter 10 that children who can better regulate negative emotion are more likely to help others in distress and to handle social conflicts constructively.

Finally, children and adolescents with poor social skills—in particular, those with the angry, aggressive styles we will take up in Chapter 12—have great difficulty imagining the thoughts and feelings of others. They often mistreat both adults and peers without experiencing the guilt and remorse prompted by awareness of another's point of view. Interventions that provide coaching and practice in perspective taking help reduce antisocial behavior and increase empathy and prosocial responding (Chalmers & Townsend, 1990).

Ask Yourself

Review What cognitive and social factors contribute to the development of out-group prejudice in children?

Review How does perspective taking contribute to effective social skills?

Apply Ten-year-old Marla says her classmate Bernadette will never get good grades because she's lazy. Jane believes that Bernadette tries but can't concentrate because her parents are divorcing. Why is Marla more likely than Jane to develop prejudices?

Connect What features of concrete operational thought might explain its association with Selman's self-reflective perspective taking? Why is formal operational thought important for third-party and societal perspective taking?

Reflect Describe several efforts by schools, religious institutions, and youth organizations in your community to combat racial and ethnic prejudices in children. What would you do to increase the effectiveness of these efforts?

Thinking About Relations Between People: Understanding Conflict

As children develop, they apply their insights about themselves and others to an understanding of relations between people. Most research on this aspect of social cognition has to do with friendship and conflicts. We will take up friendship in Chapter 15. Here we focus on how children think about and resolve situations in which their goals and the goals of agemates are at odds.

Social Problem Solving

Children, even when they are good friends, sometimes come into conflict. Yet even preschoolers seem to handle most quarrels constructively; only rarely do their disagreements result in hostile encounters. Overall, conflicts are not very frequent when compared with children's friendly, cooperative interactions.

TAKE A MOMENT... At your next opportunity, observe young children's play, noting disputes over objects ("That's mine!" "I had it first!"), entry into and control over play activities ("I'm on your team, Jerry." "No, you're not!"), and disagreements over facts, ideas, and beliefs ("I'm taller than he is." "No, you aren't!"). Children take these matters quite seriously. From the preschool to the school years, conflicts shift from material concerns to mental and social issues (Chen et al., 2001). In Chapter 6, we noted that resolution of conflict, rather than conflict per se, promotes development. Social conflicts provide repeated occasions for **social problem solving**—generating and applying strategies that prevent or resolve disagreements, resulting in outcomes that are both acceptable to others and beneficial to the self. To engage in social problem solving, children must bring together diverse social understandings.

Nicki Crick and Kenneth Dodge (1994) organize the steps of social problem solving into the circular model shown in Figure 11.11. Notice how this flowchart takes an *information-processing approach*, clarifying exactly what a child must do to grapple with and solve a social problem. It enables identification of processing deficits, so intervention can be tailored to meet individual needs.

Social problem solving profoundly affects peer relations. Children who get along well with agemates interpret social cues accurately, formulate goals (being helpful to peers) that enhance relationships, and have a repertoire of effective problem-solving strategies—for

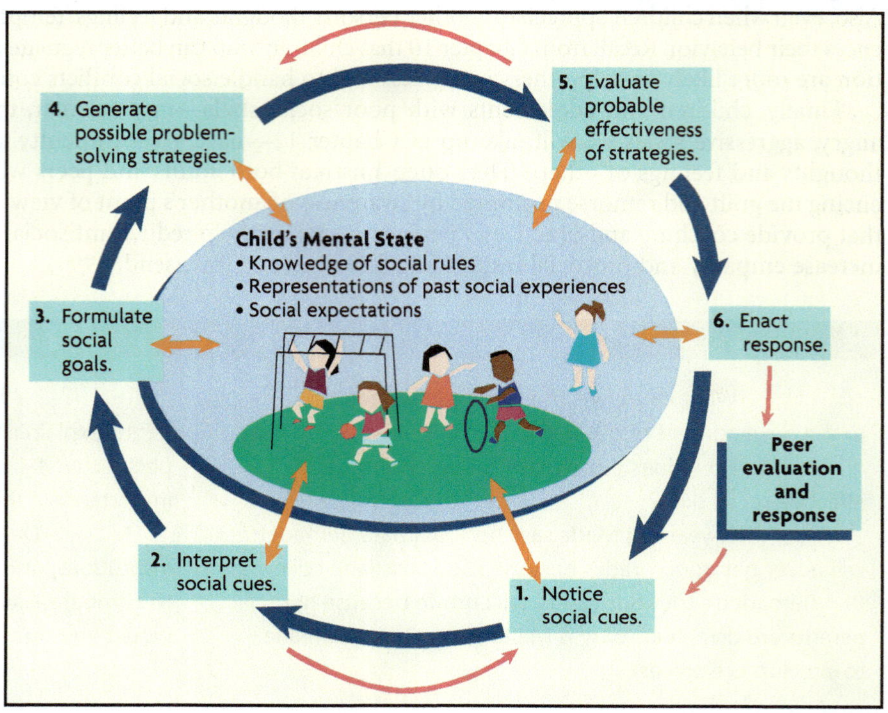

Figure 11.11 **An information-processing model of social problem solving.** The model is circular because children often engage in several information-processing activities at once—for example, interpreting information as they notice it and continuing to consider the meaning of another's behavior while they generate and evaluate problem-solving strategies. The model also takes into account the impact of mental state on social information processing—in particular, children's knowledge of social rules, their representations of past social experiences, and their expectations for future experiences. Peer evaluations and responses to enacted strategies are also important factors in social problem solving. (Adapted from N. R. Crick and K. A. Dodge, 1994, "A Review and Reformulation of Social Information-Processing Mechanisms in Children's Social Adjustment," *Psychological Bulletin*, 115, pp. 74–101, Figure 2 (adapted), p. 76. Copyright © 1994 by the American Psychological Association. Reprinted with permission of the American Psychological Association and Nicki Crick.)

example, politely asking to play and requesting an explanation when they do not understand a peer's behavior. In contrast, children with peer difficulties often hold biased social expectations. Consequently, they attend selectively to social cues (such as hostile acts) and misinterpret others' behavior (view an unintentional jostle as hostile). Their social goals (satisfying an impulse, getting even with or avoiding a peer) often lead to strategies that damage relationships (Dodge, Coie, & Lynam, 2006; Youngstrom et al., 2000). They might barge into a play group without asking, use threats and physical force, or fearfully hover around peers' activities.

Children improve greatly in social problem solving over the preschool and early school years. Instead of grabbing, hitting, or insisting that another child obey, 5- to 7-year-olds tend to rely on friendly persuasion and compromise, to think of alternative strategies when an initial one does not work, and to resolve disagreements without adult intervention (Chen et al., 2001; Mayeux & Cillessen, 2003). Sometimes they suggest creating new, mutual goals, reflecting awareness that how they solve current problems will influence the future of the relationship (Yeates, Schultz, & Selman, 1991). By kindergarten, the accuracy and effectiveness of each component of social problem solving is related to socially competent behavior (Dodge et al., 1986).

Social conflicts give children opportunities to practice social problem solving—for example, resolve disagreements over the rules of a playground game. Children who get along well with peers solve social problems in ways that take into account their playmates' perspectives and goals. © Kayte M. Deioma/PhotoEdit

Training Social Problem Solving

Intervening with children who have weak social problem-solving skills can enhance development in several ways. Besides improving peer relations, effective social problem solving gives children a sense of mastery in the face of stressful life events. It reduces the risk of adjustment difficulties in children from low-SES and troubled families (Goodman, Gravitt, & Kaslow, 1995).

In one widely applied social problem-solving training program, preschoolers and kindergartners discuss how to resolve social problems acted out with puppets in daily sessions over several months. In addition, teachers intervene as conflicts arise in the classroom, point out consequences of children's behavior ("How do you think Johnny feels when you hit him?"), and help children think of alternative strategies ("Can you think of a different way to solve this problem so you both won't be mad?"). In several studies, trained children, in contrast to untrained controls, gained in ability to think about social problems and in teacher-rated adjustment—benefits still evident months after the program ended (Shure & Aberson, 2005). School-age children profit from similar interventions (Gettinger, Doll, & Salmon, 1994).

Generating and evaluating strategies, however, are only two steps of the social problem-solving process. In a comprehensive year-long intervention called Making Choices, third graders diverse in SES received multiple lessons on each social problem-solving component depicted in Figure 11.11 as a supplement to their routine health curriculum. And those in a Making Choices–Plus condition received the intervention plus teacher and family enhancements: Teachers were given guidance in positive classroom discipline and in implementing activities aimed at strengthening emotion regulation, and parents received newsletters offering suggestions for follow-up exercises at home (Fraser et al., 2005). Regardless of SES, intervention children—compared with children in regular health classes—gained in teacher-rated social competence and declined in self-reported aggression over the school year. Children in the Making Choices–Plus condition performed especially well on story-based assessments of knowledge of the various social problem-solving steps.

Practice in enacting responses may strengthen intervention outcomes. Sometimes children know how to solve a social problem effectively but do not apply their knowledge (Rudolph & Heller, 1997). And children who have repeatedly enacted maladaptive responses may need to rehearse alternatives to overcome their habitual behaviors and to spark more adaptive social information processing.

On a final note, social-cognitive training is not the only approach to helping children with social difficulties. Because their parents often model poor social problem-solving skills and use ineffective child-rearing practices, intensive family intervention may be necessary—a topic we will return to several times in later chapters.

Ask Yourself

Review Describe the skills of a 6-year-old who is an effective social problem solver.

Apply Illustrate the influence of temperament on social problem solving by explaining how an impulsive child and a shy, inhibited child, respectively, might respond at each social problem-solving step in Figure 11.11 on page 476.

Connect How might improved perspective taking contribute to gains in social problem solving from early to middle childhood?

Reflect Describe several efforts by schools, religious institutions, and youth organizations in your community to combat racial and ethnic prejudices in children. What would you do to increase the effectiveness of these efforts?

SUMMARY

What is social cognition, and how does it differ from nonsocial cognition?

- **Social cognition** refers to children's understanding of themselves, other people, and relationships between people. Compared with nonsocial cognition, social cognition involves the challenge of comprehending how both inner states and external forces affect people's behavior.

Emergence of Self and Development of Self-Concept

Describe the development of self-awareness in infancy and toddlerhood and its consequences for young children's emotional and social capacities.

- Self-awareness begins at birth, supported by newborns' capacity for intermodal perception. Three- to 4-month-olds' reactions to their own visual image suggest some awareness of being physically distinct from their surroundings.
- By age 2, **self-recognition** is well under way, as indicated by toddlers' responses to their own image in mirrors and photos and in their use of language to refer to themselves. Sensitive caregiving promotes early self-development. Toddlers in collectivist cultures attain self-recognition later but comply with adult requests earlier than their counterparts in individualistic cultures.
- Increasing self-awareness over the first two years sets the stage for social referencing, self-conscious emotions, perspective taking, empathy, sustained imitative play, peer competition for objects, and cooperation.

Describe the development of the categorical, remembered, enduring, and inner selves, and cite consequences of and contributors to preschoolers' belief–desire theory of mind.

- Language development permits young preschoolers to construct a **categorical self** as they classify themselves and others on the basis of age, sex, physical characteristics, and goodness and badness. Adult–child conversations about the past lead to an autobiographical memory that grants the child a **remembered self** and an **enduring self.**
- Awareness of mental states permits young preschoolers to develop an **inner self** of private thoughts and imaginings. As 2- to 3-year-olds talk about mental states, they form a **desire theory of mind,** thinking that people's actions are always consistent with their desires.
- Between ages 3 and 4, children develop a **belief–desire theory of mind;** mastery of false-belief tasks reveals that they understand that both beliefs and desires determine actions. As school-age children realize that people can increase their knowledge by making mental inferences, they grasp second-order false belief.
- False-belief understanding is associated with gains in sociodramatic play, with early reading ability, and with more accurate eyewitness memory. School-age children use their grasp of the relation between beliefs and behavior to persuade others.
- Factors contributing to the development of theory of mind include language development; cognitive abilities (inhibition, flexible thinking, and planning); parent–child conversations about mental states; make-believe play; and social interaction with siblings, friends, and adults.
- Some researchers believe that the human brain is biologically prepared to develop a belief–desire theory. Others think that belief–desire understanding is supported by general cognitive development.

Discuss the development of self-concept from early childhood through adolescence, noting cognitive, social, and cultural influences.

- As children think more intently about themselves, they construct a **self-concept,** or set of beliefs about their own characteristics. In middle childhood, self-concept shifts from a focus on observable characteristics and typical emotions and attitudes to personality traits and **social comparisons.** Adolescents unify separate traits into more abstract descriptors, forming an organized system that emphasizes social virtues and personal and moral values.
- Changes in self-concept are supported by cognitive development, perspective-taking skills (as suggested by Mead's concept of the **generalized other**), and feedback from others. Self-concept varies from culture to culture: Children in individualistic cultures focus on personal characteristics, those in collectivist cultures on group membership and relationships.

© Mark Richards/PhotoEdit

Self-Esteem: The Evaluative Side of Self-Concept

Discuss development of and influences on self-esteem from early childhood through adolescence.

- **Self-esteem**—our judgments about our own worth—differentiates, becomes hierarchically organized, and declines over the first few years of elementary school as children start to make social comparisons. Except for a temporary drop associated with school transition, self-esteem rises from fourth grade on, with new dimensions added in adolescence.
- From middle childhood to adolescence, individual differences in self-esteem become increasingly stable and correlated with everyday behaviors. Generally positive self-esteem profiles are associated with positive adjustment; low self-esteem in all areas is linked to adjustment difficulties. Cultural forces, including relative emphasis on social comparison and gender-stereotyped expectations, affect self-esteem.
- Children whose parents are warm and accepting and who provide reasonable expectations for mature behavior have comparatively high self-esteem. In contrast, excessive parental control is linked to low self-esteem and indulgent parenting to unrealistically high self-esteem.

Discuss the development of achievement-related attributions, and suggest ways to foster a mastery-oriented style.

- Research on achievement-related **attributions** has identified adult messages that affect children's **achievement motivation.** During middle childhood, children begin to distinguish ability, effort, and external factors in their attributions for success and failure. Children who make **mastery-oriented attributions** credit their successes to high ability and their failures to insufficient effort and hold an **incremental view of ability.** In contrast, children who develop **learned helplessness** attribute their successes to external factors, such as luck, and their failures to low ability and hold an **entity view of ability.** Mastery-oriented children focus on learning goals, learned-helpless children on performance goals.
- Children who experience negative feedback about their ability, messages that evaluate their traits, pressure to focus on performance goals, and lack of support from teachers are likely to develop learned helplessness. Caring, helpful teachers who emphasize learning over performance goals and effort and interpersonal harmony in their classrooms foster a mastery orientation.
- **Attribution retraining,** which encourages students to believe they can overcome failure through effort, improves the self-evaluations and task performance of learned-helpless children. Effective approaches include teaching children to focus less on grades and more on mastering tasks for their own sake and providing instruction in effective strategies and self-regulation.

Constructing an Identity: Who Should I Become?

Describe the quest for identity, the four identity statuses, and factors that influence identity development.

- Erikson first recognized formation of an **identity**—a solid self-definition based on self-chosen values and goals—as the major personality achievement of adolescence. In complex societies, **identity achievement** (exploration followed by commitment) and **identity moratorium** (exploration without having reached commitment) are psychologically healthy identity statuses. Long-term **identity foreclosure** (commitment without exploration) and **identity diffusion** (lack of both exploration and commitment) are related to adjustment difficulties. Because attending college provides many opportunities to explore career options and lifestyles, college students make more progress toward formulating an identity than they did in high school.
- Adolescents who take a flexible, open-minded approach to grappling with competing beliefs and values and who feel attached to parents but free to voice their own opinions are likely to be advanced in identity development. Close friends provide support as young people explore options. Schools and communities that offer varied options for exploration also foster identity achievement. Youths whose families are immigrants from collectivist cultures often experience **acculturative stress.** But those who construct a secure **ethnic identity** or a **bicultural identity** are advantaged in emotional and social development.

Thinking About Other People

Discuss gains in children's appreciation of others' personalities and their understanding of ethnicity and social class, including factors that contribute to ethnic prejudices.

- **Person perception** refers to how we size up the attributes of familiar people. Like their self-descriptions, children's descriptions of others increasingly emphasize personality traits and become more organized with age.
- Basic concepts of race, ethnicity, and social class emerge in the preschool years. By the early school years, children absorb prevailing attitudes toward social groups from implicit messages in their environments.
- White children who have had little direct experience with ethnic minorities show in-group favoritism and out-group prejudice by age 5 to 6. Ethnic minority children often absorb their culture's ethnic stereotypes and, as a result, show out-group favoritism. The capacity to classify the social world in multiple ways leads to a decline in overt prejudice in middle childhood, although subtle prejudice may persist. Children who view personality as fixed, have overly high self-esteem, and experience a social world in which people sorted into groups are more likely to harbor ethnic prejudices.
- Long-term intergroup contact and collaboration are highly effective in reducing prejudice. Inducing children to view others' traits as malleable—a perspective encouraged by volunteer activities—may also help. School integration—a powerful basis for combating negative ethnic and racial biases—has receded dramatically in the United States.

© Michael J. Doolittle/The Image Works

Cite major changes in perspective taking from early childhood into adolescence, along with consequences for development.

- **Perspective taking** improves greatly from childhood to adolescence, as Selman's five-stage sequence indicates. Between 6 and 8 years, children understand that prior knowledge affects a person's ability to understand new information and that people's preexisting beliefs can affect their viewpoints. During adolescence, recursive thought is mastered.
- The ability to understand others' viewpoints contributes to many social skills. Angry, aggressive young people have trouble imagining the thoughts and feelings of others. Interventions that teach perspective-taking skills help reduce antisocial behavior and increase prosocial responding.

Thinking About Relations Between People: Understanding Conflict

Describe the components of social problem solving, the development of social problem-solving skills, and ways to help children who are poor social problem solvers.

- Components of **social problem solving**—noticing and interpreting social cues, clarifying social goals, generating and evaluating strategies, and enacting responses—improve over early and middle childhood and predict socially competent behavior. Training in social problem solving leads to gains in social information processing and adjustment.

IMPORTANT TERMS AND CONCEPTS

12

"I Want Peace"
Melisa Bese
12 years, Turkey

This adolescent artist's keen moral sensibilities are apparent in her decorative self-portrait, which expresses her yearning for worldwide peace. Human nature, family, peer, school, and culture all contribute to the cognitive, emotional, and behavioral ingredients of morality.

Moral Development

Three-year-old Leisl grabbed a toy from Ava, a neighbor child who had come to play. "Give it back!" Ava cried. "It's mine!"

Leisl's mother bent down. "Look!" she explained. "Ava's about to cry. She was playing with the teddy bear, and when you took it, you made her sad. Let's give the bear back to Ava." Gently, she freed the toy from Leisl's hands and returned it to Ava. For a moment, Leisl looked hurt, but she soon busied herself with her blocks. A few moments later, Leisl turned to Ava. "Want some of these blocks?" she offered generously, making a pile of blocks for Ava. "We can share!"

Now consider Leisl at age 11, reacting to a newspaper article about an elderly woman, soon to be evicted from her crumbling home because city inspectors judged it a fire and health hazard. "Look at what they're trying to do!" exclaimed Leisl. "They're going to throw this poor lady out of her house. You don't just knock someone's home down! Where're her friends and neighbors? Why aren't they over there fixing up that house?"

Eleven-year-old Leisl has come a long way from the preschool child just beginning to appreciate others' rights and feelings. That beginning, however, is an important one. Preschooler Leisl's prosocial invitation to her visiting playmate is not unique—it is part of an emerging picture. Accompanying gains in self-awareness and representational capacities at the end of the second year is another crowning achievement: The child becomes a moral being. Recall that around this time, empathy and sympathetic concern emerge (Chapter 10), and children soon begin to evaluate their own and others' behavior as "good" or "bad" (Chapter 11). As children's cognition and language develop and their social experiences broaden, they express increasingly elaborate moral thoughts accompanied by intense emotion that—as with 11-year-old Leisl—sometimes escalates to moral outrage.

In all cultures, morality is promoted by an overarching social organization that specifies rules for good conduct. At the same time, morality has roots in each major aspect of our psychological makeup:

- Morality has an *emotional component.* Powerful feelings cause us to empathize with another's distress or to feel guilty when we are the cause of that distress.
- Morality also has an important *cognitive component.* Children's developing social understanding enables them to make increasingly profound judgments about actions they believe to be right or wrong.

- Morality has a vital *behavioral component.* Experiencing morally relevant thoughts and feelings increases the likelihood, but does not guarantee, that people will act in accordance with them.

Traditionally, these three aspects of morality have been studied separately: Biological and psychoanalytic theories focus on emotions, cognitive-developmental theory on moral thought, and social learning theory on moral behavior. Today, a growing body of research reveals that all three facets are interrelated. Still, major theories disagree on which is primary. And as we will see, the aspect a theory emphasizes has major implications for how it conceptualizes the basic trend of moral development: the shift from superficial, or externally controlled, responses to behavior based on inner standards, or moral understanding. Truly moral individuals do not merely do the right thing for the sake of social conformity or to meet the expectations of authority figures. Rather, they have developed compassionate concerns and ideals of good conduct, which they follow in a wide variety of situations.

Our discussion of moral development begins by highlighting the strengths and limitations of the theories just mentioned on the basis of recent research. Next we consider the important related topic of self-control. The development of a personal resolve to keep the self from doing anything it feels like doing is crucial for translating moral commitments into action. We conclude with a discussion of the other side of self-control—the development of aggression.

Morality as Rooted in Human Nature

In the 1970s, biological theories of human social behavior suggested that many morally relevant behaviors and emotions have roots in our evolutionary history (Wilson, 1975). This view was supported by the work of ethologists, who observed animals aiding other members of their species, often at great personal risk. For example, ants, bees, and termites show extremes of self-sacrifice. Large numbers will sting or bite an animal that threatens the hive, a warlike response that often results in their own death. Dogs who breach a master's prohibition by damaging furniture or defecating indoors sometimes display intense regret, expressed as distress and submission (Lorenz, 1983).

Among primates, chimpanzees (who are genetically closest to humans) conform to moral-like rules, which group members enforce in one another. For example, when males attack

Left photo: Chimpanzees conform to moral-like rules. Here a family group gathers to share food, with less powerful members patiently waiting their turn. *Right photo:* Humans' unique capacity to act prosocially is believed to have originated tens of thousands of years ago in small hunting-and-gathering bands, such as these Kalahari Bushmen of northeast Nambia, whose informal systems of social exchange promote group survival. *Left:* © Steve Bloom Images/Alamy; *right:* © Janine Wiedel Photolibrary/Alamy

females, they avoid using their sharp canine teeth. If a male does harm a female, the entire colony responds with a chorus of indignant barks, sometimes followed by a band of females chasing off the aggressor (de Waal, 1996). Chimps also reciprocate favors, generously grooming and sharing food with those who have done the same for them. And they engage in kind and comforting acts. Juveniles sometimes soothe frightened or injured peers, and adult females will adopt a baby that has lost its mother (Goodall, 1990). Furthermore, shortly after a physical fight, former combatants may embrace, hold hands, and groom, intensifying friendly behaviors in an apparent effort to restore their long-term relationship (de Waal, 2001, 2006). On the basis of this evidence, researchers reasoned that evolution must have made similar biologically based provisions for moral acts in humans.

In other species, most self-sacrificing acts occur within family groups, whose members have common reproductive interests. Humans, too, are biased to aid family members—helping that strengthens as genetic relatedness increases and that is particularly strong in life-and-death situations, such as entering a burning building to save a life or donating a kidney for a transplant (Neyer & Lang, 2003). But humans also have an unmatched capacity to make sacrifices for nonrelatives—by investing time and effort in helping the needy in their communities, donating generously to charities, aiding others in emergencies, and giving their lives for their country in wartime (Becker & Eagly, 2004; Van Lange et al., 2007).

Evolutionary theorists speculate that our unique capacity to act prosocially toward genetic strangers originated several million years ago, in the small hunting-and-gathering bands—including both kin and nonkin—in which we spent 95 percent of our evolutionary history. To limit selfishness (which can quickly undermine group functioning), humans developed informal systems of social exchange, in which they acted benevolently toward others with the expectation that others might do the same for them in the future. These reciprocal exchanges (as noted earlier) are seen in other species, especially primates, but they are far more common, varied, and highly developed in humans (Van Vugt & Van Lange, 2006). Willingness of many members of a group to aid others and engage in self-sacrifice ensures that the majority of the group will survive and reproduce. Under these conditions, traits that foster altruism undergo natural selection, becoming increasingly prominent in succeeding generations.

How might genes encourage prosocial acts and, thereby, promote survival of the species? Many researchers believe that prewired emotional reactions are involved (de Waal, 2006; Haidt, 2001, 2003; Hoffman, 2000; Trivers, 1971). In Chapter 10, we noted that newborns cry when they hear another baby cry, a possible precursor of empathy. As Figure 12.1 illustrates, 6-month-olds' reaching behaviors convey a preference for an individual who helps over one who hinders others—an attitude present so early that the investigators speculated it is built in (Hamlin, Wynn, & Bloom, 2007). As toddlers approach age 2, they show clear empathic concern, and they begin experiencing self-conscious emotions, which greatly enhance their responsiveness to social expectations.

Researchers have identified areas within the frontal region of the cerebral cortex (the ventromedial area, located just behind the bridge of the nose, and the orbitofrontal area, resting above the orbits of the eyes) that are vital for emotional responsiveness to the suffering of others and to one's own misdeeds. Functioning of the frontal lobes improves over the first two years, preceding children's increased empathic concern (Hastings, Zahn-Waxler, & McShane, 2006). Furthermore, adults with damage to these areas rarely react with empathy to others' distress,

Figure 12.1 **Infants prefer an individual who helps to one who hinders others.** Researchers exposed 6- and 10-month-olds to a scene in which a climber (red circle) repeatedly tried to climb a hill. After the third attempt, the infants saw alternating instances of helping and hindering events: (a) Either a helper (yellow triangle) aided the climber by pushing it from behind, or (b) a hinderer (blue square) pushed the climber down the hill. Then the infants were presented with the helper and the hinderer and encouraged to choose between the two. The overwhelming majority—100 percent of 6-month-olds and 88 percent of 10-month-olds—reached for the helper. The researchers concluded that babies have a built-in preference for individuals who aid others. Others, however, claim that social experiences during the first six months offer many relevant learning opportunities. (From J. K. Hamlin, K. Wynn, & P. Bloom, 2007, "Social Evaluation by Preverbal Infants," *Nature,* 450, p. 557. Copyright © 2007, Nature Publishing Group. Reprinted by permission from Macmillan Publishers Ltd.)

do poorly on tests of social reasoning, and are relatively unconcerned about conforming to social norms (Barrash, Tranel, & Anderson, 2000; Damasio, 1994; Eslinger et al., 2007). Early-occurring ventromedial and orbitofrontal damage severely disrupts social learning, resulting in extreme antisocial behavior (Anderson et al., 1999; Eslinger, 1998). And EEG and fMRI research reveals that psychopaths, who inflict harm on others without any trace of empathy or guilt, show reduced activity in these areas (Raine, 1997).

Humans' elaborate mirror neuron systems are also believed to support empathic responding (see Chapter 4, page 144). fMRI evidence indicates that self-experienced pain and observations of another's facial reactions to pain activate overlapping areas in the cerebral cortex (Botvinick et al., 2005). Even the intensity of pain experienced by another is reflected in heightened cortical activity—a response that correlates positively with observers' self-reported empathy (Saarela et al., 2007).

But like most other human behaviors, morality cannot be fully explained by its biological foundations. Recall from Chapter 10 that empathy, sympathy, pride, guilt, and other self-conscious emotions require strong caregiving supports to develop, and their mature expression depends on cognitive development. Furthermore, although emotion is one basis for moral action, it is not a complete account. For example, most of us would question the behavior of a parent who decides not to take a sick child to the doctor out of empathy with the child's fear and anxiety over doctor visits.

Still, the biological perspective reminds us of morality's adaptive value. Because of the necessity for group living, humans have evolved an elaborate brain-based moral substrate that counteracts self-centered motives and promotes concern for others.

Morality as the Adoption of Societal Norms

The two perspectives we are about to discuss—psychoanalytic theory and social learning theory—offer different accounts of how children become moral beings. Yet both regard moral development as a matter of **internalization**: adopting societal standards for right action as one's own. In other words, both focus on how morality moves from society to individual—how children acquire norms, or prescriptions for good conduct, widely held by members of their social group.

Our consideration of these theories will reveal that several factors jointly affect the child's willingness to adopt societal standards:

- Parental style of discipline, which varies with the type of misdeed
- The child's characteristics, including age and temperament
- The parent's characteristics
- The child's view of both the misdeed and the reasonableness of parental demands

As this list indicates, internalization results from a combination of influences within the child and the rearing environment. When the process goes well, external forces foster the child's positive inclinations and counteract the child's negative inclinations (Turiel, 2006). In the following sections, we will see many examples of this idea.

Psychoanalytic Theory

According to Sigmund Freud, morality emerges between ages 3 and 6, the period when the well-known Oedipus and Electra conflicts arise. Young children desire to possess the parent of the other sex, but they abandon this wish because they fear punishment and loss of parental love. To maintain their parents' affection, children form a *superego,* or conscience, by *identifying* with the same-sex parent, whose moral standards they adopt. Finally, children turn the hostility previously aimed at the same-sex parent toward themselves, which evokes painful feelings of guilt each time they disobey the superego (Freud, 1925/1961). In Freud's view, moral development is largely complete by age 5 or 6.

Today, most researchers disagree with Freud's ideas about conscience development. First, his view of guilt as a hostile impulse redirected toward the self is no longer accepted. As we will see, high levels of self-blame are not associated with moral internalization. Rather, school-age children experience guilt when they intentionally engage in acts that harm others and feel personally responsible for the outcome (see Chapter 10). Second, Freud assumed that fear of punishment and loss of parental love motivate conscience formation (Tellings, 1999). Yet children whose parents frequently use threats, commands, or physical force tend to violate standards often and feel little guilt, whereas parental warmth and responsiveness predict greater guilt following transgressions (Kochanska et al., 2002, 2005, 2008). And children whose parents withdraw love—for example, refuse to speak to or state a dislike for the child—often respond with high levels of self-blame, thinking "I'm no good" or "Nobody loves me." Eventually, to protect themselves from overwhelming guilt, these children may deny the emotion and, as a result, also develop a weak conscience (Kochanska, 1991; Zahn-Waxler et al., 1990).

• The Power of Inductive Discipline In contrast, conscience formation is promoted by a type of discipline called **induction,** in which an adult helps the child notice others' feelings by pointing out the effects of the child's misbehavior on others, noting especially their distress and making clear that the child caused it. For example, to a young preschool child, the parent might say, "She's crying because you won't give back her teddy bear," as Leisl's mother did in the introduction to this chapter. Later in the preschool years, parents can explain why the child's action was harmful, perhaps by referring to the other person's intentions: "Don't yell at him. That makes him feel sad. He was trying to help you!" And with further cognitive advances, more subtle psychological explanations are possible: "He felt proud of his tower, and you hurt his feelings by knocking it down" (Hoffman, 2000).

When generally warm parents provide explanations that match the child's capacity to understand, while firmly insisting that the child listen and comply, induction is effective as early as age 2. Preschoolers whose parents use this approach are more likely to refrain from wrongdoing, confess and repair damages after misdeeds (as Leisl did when she invited Ava to play with her blocks), and display prosocial behavior—spontaneously offering hugs, toys, and verbal sympathy to others in distress (Kerr et al., 2004; Zahn-Waxler, Radke-Yarrow, & King, 1979).

The success of induction may lie in its power to motivate children's active commitment to moral norms, in the following ways:

- Induction gives children information about how to behave that they can use in future situations.
- By emphasizing the impact of the child's actions on others, induction encourages empathy and sympathetic concern, which motivate prosocial behavior (Krevans & Gibbs, 1996).
- Giving children reasons for changing their behavior encourages them to adopt moral standards because those standards make sense.
- Children who consistently experience induction may form a script for the negative emotional consequences of harming others—child causes harm, inductive message points out harm, child feels empathy for victim, child makes amends—that deters future transgressions (Hoffman, 2000).

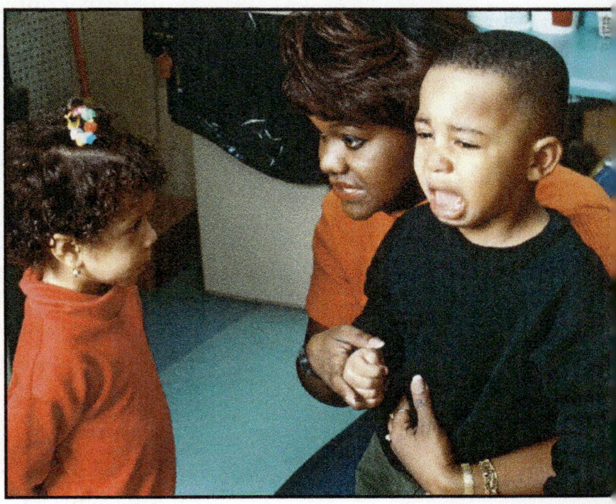

This teacher uses induction to explain to a child how her transgression affects a classmate. Induction supports conscience development by indicating how the child should behave, encouraging empathy and sympathetic concern, and clarifying the reasons behind adult expectations. © Laura Dwight Photography

In contrast, discipline that relies too heavily on threats of punishment or withdrawal of love makes children so anxious and frightened that they cannot think clearly enough to figure out what they should do. As a result, these practices do not get children to internalize moral norms, and—as noted earlier—also interfere with empathy and prosocial responding (Eisenberg, Fabes, & Spirad, 2006). Nevertheless, warnings, disapproval, and commands are sometimes necessary to get an unruly child to listen to an inductive message (Grusec, 2006).

A secure attachment relationship fosters conscience development in fearless, impulsive children. If this father is generally warm and patient, his 5-year-old son is likely to obey his request to "look, but don't touch." © Pixland/Corbis

The Child's Contribution Although good discipline is crucial for conscience development, children's characteristics affect the success of parenting techniques. For example, in Chapter 10 we noted that empathy is moderately heritable. Children who are more empathic require less power assertion and are more responsive to induction.

Temperament is also influential. Mild, patient tactics—requests, suggestions, and explanations—are sufficient to prompt guilt reactions and conscience development in anxious, fearful preschoolers (Kochanska et al., 2002). But with fearless, impulsive children, gentle discipline has little impact. Power assertion also works poorly: It undermines the child's emerging capacity for effortful control, which strongly predicts moral internalization, empathy, sympathy, and prosocial behavior (Kochanska & Aksan, 2006; Kochanska & Knaack, 2003). Parents of impulsive children can foster conscience development by building a warm, affectionate relationship that promotes secure attachment and by combining firm correction of misbehavior with induction (Fowles & Kochanska, 2000; Kochanska, Aksan, & Joy, 2007).

Why is this so? When children are so low in anxiety that parental interventions cause them little discomfort, a close parent–child bond provides an alternative foundation for morality. It motivates children to listen to parents' inductions and follow their rules as a means of preserving an affectionate, supportive relationship. In one longitudinal study, attachment security at 14 months predicted children's eagerness to cooperate with parental demands. Children's cooperative spirit, in turn, increased the likelihood of patient, supportive parenting, which was positively associated with an internalized conscience at age 4½ (Kochanska et al., 2004). In sum, to foster early moral development, parents must tailor their disciplinary strategies to their child's personality. Does this remind you of goodness of fit, discussed in Chapter 10? Return to page 423 to review this idea.

The Role of Guilt Although little support exists for Freudian ideas about conscience development, Freud was correct that guilt is an important motivator of moral action. By the end of toddlerhood, preschoolers' assertions of guilt reveal that they have internalized the parent's moral voice: "Didn't you hear my mommy? We'd better not play with these toys" (Thompson, 2006). Inducing *empathy-based guilt* (expressions of personal responsibility and regret, such as "I'm sorry I hurt him") by explaining that the child's behavior is causing someone distress and has disappointed the parent is a means of influencing children without using coercion. Empathy-based guilt reactions are associated with stopping harmful actions, repairing damage caused by misdeeds, and engaging in future prosocial behavior (Baumeister, 1998). At the same time, parents must help children deal with guilt feelings constructively—by guiding them to make up for immoral behavior rather than minimizing or excusing it (Bybee, Merisca, & Velasco, 1998).

But contrary to what Freud believed, guilt is not the only force that compels us to act morally. Nor is moral development complete by the end of early childhood. Rather, it is a gradual process, beginning in the preschool years and extending into adulthood.

Social Learning Theory

The social learning perspective does not regard morality as a special human activity with a unique course of development. Rather, moral behavior is acquired just like any other set of responses: through reinforcement and modeling.

The Importance of Modeling Operant conditioning—reinforcement for good behavior with approval, affection, and other rewards—is not enough for children to acquire moral responses. To be reinforced, a behavior must first occur spontaneously. Yet many prosocial acts, such as sharing, helping, or comforting an unhappy playmate, occur so rarely at first that reinforcement cannot explain their rapid development in early childhood. Rather, social learning theorists believe that children learn to behave morally largely through *modeling*—observing and imitating adults who demonstrate appropriate behavior (Bandura, 1977; Grusec, 1988).

Once children acquire a moral response, such as sharing or telling the truth, reinforcement in the form of praising the act ("That was a very nice thing to do") or the child's character ("You're a very kind and considerate boy") increases its frequency (Mills & Grusec, 1989).

Many studies show that having helpful or generous models increases young children's prosocial responses. And certain characteristics of the model affect children's willingness to imitate:

- *Warmth and responsiveness.* Preschoolers are more likely to copy the prosocial actions of an adult who is warm and responsive than those of a cold, distant adult (Yarrow, Scott, & Waxler, 1973). Warmth seems to make children more attentive and receptive to the model and is itself an example of a prosocial response.
- *Competence and power.* Children admire and therefore tend to imitate competent, powerful models—especially older peers and adults (Bandura, 1977).
- *Consistency between assertions and behavior.* When models say one thing and do another—for example, announce that "it's important to help others" but rarely engage in helpful acts—children generally choose the most lenient standard of behavior that adults demonstrate (Mischel & Liebert, 1966).

Models of helpful behavior are especially influential in the early years. This 19-month-old watches attentively as her mother demonstrates how to sweep dirt from the kitchen floor. © Elizabeth Crews

Models are most influential in the early years. In one study, toddlers' eager, willing imitation of their mothers' behavior predicted moral conduct (not cheating in a game) and guilt following transgressions at age 3 (Forman, Aksan, & Kochanska, 2004). At the end of early childhood, children who have had consistent exposure to caring adults tend to behave prosocially whether or not a model is present. They have internalized prosocial rules from repeated observations and encouragement by others (Mussen & Eisenberg-Berg, 1977).

• The Effects of Punishment Many parents know that yelling at, slapping, and spanking children for misbehavior are ineffective disciplinary tactics. A sharp reprimand or physical force to restrain or move a child is justified when immediate obedience is necessary—for example, when a 3-year-old is about to run into the street. In fact, parents are most likely to use forceful methods under these conditions. But to foster long-term goals, such as acting kindly toward others, they tend to rely on warmth and reasoning (Kuczynski, 1984). And in response to very serious transgressions, such as lying or stealing, they often combine power assertion with reasoning (Grusec, 2006; Grusec & Goodnow, 1994).

Frequent punishment, however, promotes only immediate compliance, not lasting changes in behavior. Children who are repeatedly criticized, shouted at, or hit are likely to display the unacceptable response again as soon as adults are out of sight. Many studies confirm that the more harsh threats, angry physical control (yanking an object from the child, handling the child roughly), and physical punishment children experience, the more likely they are to develop serious, lasting mental health problems. These include weak internalization of moral rules; depression, aggression, antisocial behavior, and poor academic performance in childhood and adolescence; and depression, alcohol abuse, criminality, and partner and child abuse in adulthood (Afifi et al., 2006; Bender et al., 2007; Gershoff, 2002a; Kochanska, Aksan, & Nichols, 2003; Lynch et al., 2006).

Harsh punishment has several undesirable side effects:

- Parents often insult and spank in response to children's aggression (Holden, Coleman, & Schmidt, 1995). Yet the punishment itself models aggression!
- Harshly treated children react with anger, resentment, and a chronic sense of being personally threatened, which prompts a focus on the self's distress rather than a sympathetic orientation to others' needs (see Chapter 10, page 414).
- Children who are frequently punished soon learn to avoid the punishing adult, who, as a result, has little opportunity to teach desirable behaviors.
- By stopping children's misbehavior temporarily, harsh punishment gives adults immediate relief, reinforcing them for using coercive discipline. For this reason, a punitive adult

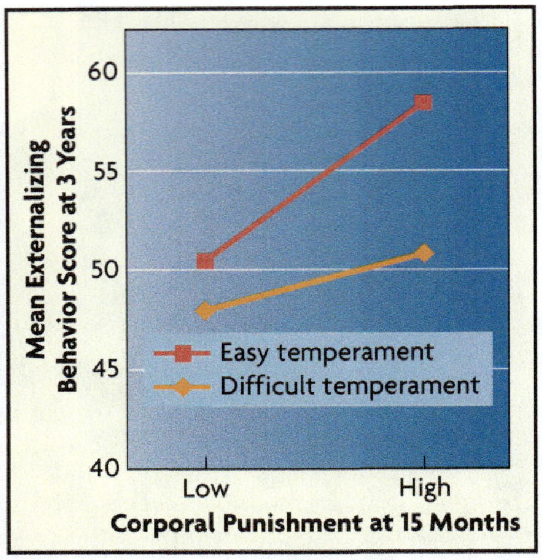

■ **Figure 12.2** **Relationship of parental corporal punishment at age 15 months to externalizing behavior at 3 years, by child temperament.**
Corporal punishment was associated with increased externalizing behavior (anger and aggression) for both easy and difficult children, even after controlling for family and parenting characteristics. The rise in externalizing behavior was greater for difficult children—a difference also present during a follow-up in first grade. (From M. K. Mulvaney & C. J. Mebert, 2007, "Parental Corporal Punishment Predicts Behavior Problems in Early Childhood," *Journal of Family Psychology,* 21, p. 394. Copyright © 2007 by the American Psychological Association. Reprinted with permission of the American Psychological Association.)

is likely to punish with greater frequency over time, a course of action that can spiral into serious abuse.

- School-age children, adolescents, and adults whose parents used corporal punishment—the use of physical force to inflict pain but not injury—are more accepting of such discipline (Bower-Russa, Knutson, & Winebarger, 2001; Deater-Deckard et al., 2003). In this way, use of corporal punishment may transfer to the next generation.

Parents with conflict-ridden marriages and with mental health problems (who are emotionally reactive, depressed, or aggressive) are more likely to be punitive and also to have hard-to-manage children, whose disobedience evokes more parental harshness (Erath et al., 2006; Knafo & Plomin, 2006; Kochanska, Aksan, & Nichols, 2003). These parent–child similarities suggest that heredity contributes to the link between punitive discipline and children's adjustment difficulties. But heredity is not a complete explanation. Return to page 122 in Chapter 3 to review findings indicating that good parenting can shield children who are genetically at risk for aggression and antisocial activity from developing those behaviors. Other research indicates that parental harshness and corporal punishment predict emotional and behavior problems in children of diverse temperaments (O'Connor et al., 1998). As Figure 12.2 shows, negative outcomes are simply more pronounced among children with difficult temperaments (Mulvaney & Mebert, 2007).

In view of these findings, the widespread use of corporal punishment by North American parents is cause for concern. A survey of a nationally representative sample of U.S. households revealed that although corporal punishment increases from infancy to age 5 and then declines, it is high at all ages (see Figure 12.3). An alarming 35 to 50 percent of U.S. infants—who are not yet capable of complying with adult directives—get spanked or hit. Similarly, depending on the survey, 40 percent of Canadian parents of infants, and 50 to 70 percent of Canadian parents of preschoolers, admit to having disciplined with hitting or spanking (Durrant, Broberg, & Rose-Krasnor, 2000; Oldershaw, 2002). Furthermore, about one-fourth of U.S. parents who physically punish their children report having used a hard object, such as a brush or a belt (Gershoff, 2002b).

A prevailing North American belief is that corporal punishment, if implemented by caring parents, is harmless, perhaps even beneficial. But as the Cultural Influences box on the following page reveals, this assumption is valid only under conditions of limited use in certain social contexts. Consistent negative outcomes for most children indicate that parents are wise to refrain from harsh physical discipline.

● **Alternatives to Harsh Punishment** Alternatives to criticism, slaps, and spankings can reduce the side effects of punishment. A technique called **time out** involves removing children from the immediate setting—for example, by sending them to their rooms—until they are ready to act appropriately. When a child is out of control, a few minutes in time out can be enough to change behavior while also giving angry parents time to cool off. Another approach is *withdrawal of privileges,* such as playing outside or watching a favorite TV program. Like time out, removing privileges allows parents to avoid harsh techniques that can easily intensify into violence.

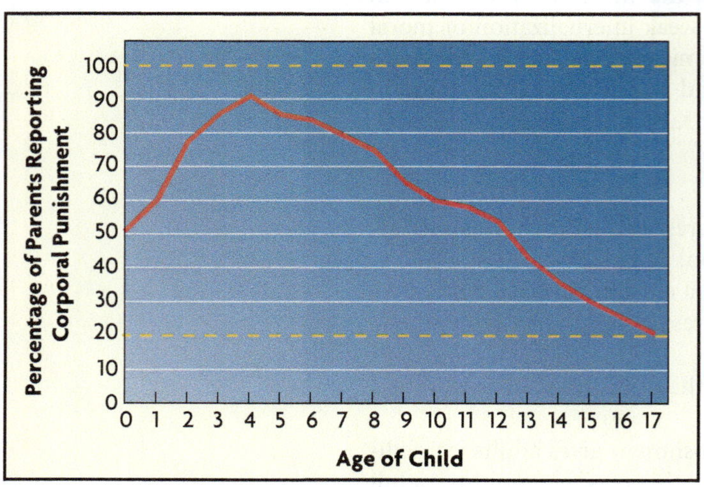

■ **Figure 12.3** **Prevalence of corporal punishment by child's age.**
Estimates are based on the percentage of parents in a nationally representative U.S. sample of nearly 1,000 who reported one or more instances of spanking, slapping, pinching, shaking, or hitting with a hard object in the past year. Physical punishment increases sharply in early childhood and then declines, but it is high at all ages. (From M. A. Straus & J. H. Stewart, 1999, "Corporal Punishment by American Parents: National Data on Prevalence, Chronicity, Severity, and Duration, in Relation to Child and Family Characteristics," *Clinical Child and Family Psychology Review,* 2, p. 59. Adapted with kind permission from Springer Science and Business Media and the author.)

Cultural Influences

Ethnic Differences in the Consequences of Physical Punishment

In an African-American community, six elders, who had volunteered to serve as mentors for parents facing child-rearing challenges, met to discuss parenting issues at a social service agency. Their attitudes toward discipline were strikingly different from those of the white social workers who had brought them together. Each elder argued that successful child rearing required the use of appropriate physical tactics. At the same time, they voiced strong disapproval of screaming or cursing at children, calling such out-of-control parental behavior "abusive." Ruth, the oldest and most respected member of the group, characterized good parenting as a complex combination of warmth, teaching, talking nicely, and disciplining physically. She related how an older neighbor advised her to handle her own children when she was a young parent:

> She said to me says, don't scream at . . . your children . . . you talk to them real nice and sweet and when they do something ugly and you don't like it . . . she say you get a nice little switch and you won't have any trouble with them and from that day I raised my children that's the way I raised 'em.

The others chimed in, emphasizing *mild* punishment: "Just tap 'em a little bit." "When you do things like [get too harsh] you're wronging yourself" (Mosby et al., 1999, pp. 511–512).

Use of physical punishment is highest among low-SES ethnic minority parents, who are more likely than middle-SES white parents to advocate slaps and spankings (Pinderhughes et al., 2000; Straus & Stewart, 1999). And although corporal punishment is linked to a wide array of negative child outcomes, exceptions do exist.

In one longitudinal study, researchers followed several hundred families for 12 years, collecting information from mothers on disciplinary strategies in early and middle childhood and from both mothers and their children on youth problem behaviors in adolescence. Even after many child and family characteristics were controlled, the findings were striking: In Caucasian-American families, physical punishment was positively associated with adolescent aggression and antisocial behavior. In African-American families, by contrast, the more mothers had disciplined physically in childhood, the less their teenagers displayed angry, acting-out behavior and got in trouble at school and with the police (Lansford et al., 2004).

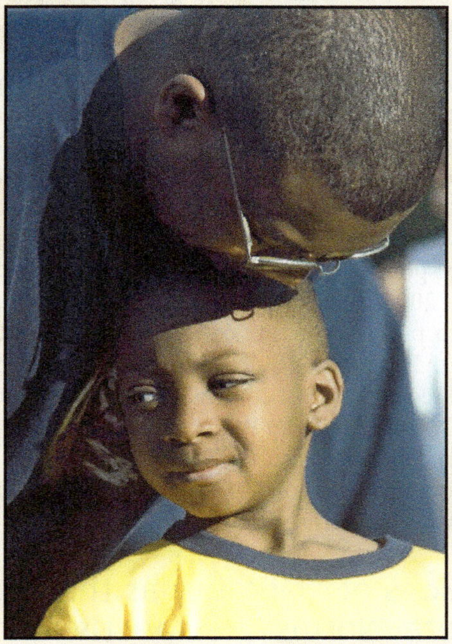

African-American parents often include mild physical punishment among their disciplinary tactics. Because the practice is culturally approved and delivered in an overall context of parental warmth, children may view it as a well-meaning effort to encourage maturity. © Sean Cayton/The Image Works

African-American and Caucasian-American parents seem to mete out physical punishment differently. In black families, such discipline is typically culturally approved, mild, delivered in a context of parental warmth, and aimed at helping children become responsible adults. White parents, in contrast, usually consider physical punishment to be wrong, so when they resort to it, they are often highly agitated and rejecting of the child (Dodge, McLoyd, & Lansford, 2006). As a result, most black children may view spanking as a practice carried out with their best interests in mind, whereas white children may regard it as an "act of personal aggression" (Gunnoe & Mariner, 1997, p. 768).

In support of this view, when several thousand ethnically diverse children were followed from the preschool through the early school years, spanking was associated with a rise in behavior problems if parents were cold and rejecting, not if they were warm and supportive (McLoyd & Smith, 2002). And in research spanning six nations, physical discipline was less strongly associated with child adjustment problems in cultures where mothers and children perceived it as customary and appropriate (Lansford et al., 2005). In another study, spanking predicted depressive symptoms only among a minority of African-American children whose mothers disapproved of the practice and, as a result, tended to use it when they were highly angry and frustrated (McLoyd et al., 2007). These findings are not an endorsement of physical punishment. Other forms of discipline, including time out, withdrawal of privileges, and the positive strategies listed on page 491, are far more effective. But it is noteworthy that the meaning and impact of physical discipline vary sharply with cultural context.

Although its usefulness is limited, punishment can play a valuable role in moral development. Earlier we noted that mild warnings and disapproval are occasionally necessary to get the child to attend to the parent's inductive teaching. When parents do decide to use punishment, they can increase its effectiveness in three ways:

- *Consistency.* Permitting children to act inappropriately on some occasions but scolding them on others confuses them, and the unacceptable act persists (Acker & O'Leary, 1996).

- *A warm parent–child relationship.* Children of involved, caring parents find the interruption in parental affection that accompanies punishment especially unpleasant. They want to regain parental warmth and approval as quickly as possible.
- *Explanations.* Explanations help children recall the misdeed and relate it to expectations for future behavior. Consequently, providing reasons for mild punishment (such as time out) leads to a far greater reduction in misbehavior than using punishment alone (Larzelere et al., 1996).

• Positive Relationships, Positive Discipline The most effective forms of discipline encourage good conduct—by building a mutually respectful bond with the child, letting her know ahead of time how to act, and praising mature behavior (Zahn-Waxler & Robinson, 1995). When sensitivity, cooperation, and shared positive emotion are evident in joint activities between mothers and their toddlers or preschoolers, children show firmer conscience development—expressing empathy after transgressions, behaving responsibly, playing fairly in games, and considering others' welfare (Kochanska et al., 2005, 2008). An early, mutually responsive, pleasurable mother–child tie continues to predict a firmer conscience into the early school years (Kochanska & Murray, 2000). Parent–child closeness leads children to heed parental demands because the child feels a sense of commitment to the relationship.

Consult Applying What We Know on the following page for ways to discipline positively. Parents who use these strategies focus on long-term social and life skills—cooperation, problem solving, and consideration for others. As a result, they greatly reduce the need for punishment.

By cultivating an involved, caring relationship with his daughter, this parent strengthens the effectiveness of his attempts to discipline. When he disapproves of her behavior, she will want to regain his affection by following his directives. © Steve Baccon/Getty Images/Digital Vision

Limitations of "Morality as the Adoption of Societal Norms" Perspective

As previously noted, both psychoanalytic and social learning theories view moral development as a process of adopting societal norms. Personal commitment to societal standards of good conduct is an essential aspect of moral development. Without an internalized, shared moral code and the cultivation of empathy through parental warmth and inductive discipline, people would disregard one another's rights whenever their desires conflicted and would transgress whenever they were unobserved.

But theories that regard morality as entirely a matter of internalizing norms have been criticized because prevailing standards may be at odds with important ethical principles and humanitarian goals. Under these conditions, deliberate violation of norms is not immoral but justifiable and courageous. **TAKE A MOMENT. . .** Think, for a moment, about historical figures who rose to greatness because they refused to accept certain societal norms. Abraham Lincoln's opposition to slavery, Susan B. Anthony's leadership in the crusade for women's suffrage, and Martin Luther King Jr.'s campaign to end racial prejudice are examples. Can you name others?

Parents who engage in positive discipline reduce opportunities for misbehavior. By bringing along toys and joining in his make-believe, this mother helps her young child behave appropriately during a long wait at the airport. © Stock4B/Getty Images

With respect to children, parental concern about internalization of societal norms is often accompanied by other goals. At times, parents may accept noncompliance if the child provides a reasonable justification (Kuczynski & Hildebrandt, 1997). Consider a boy who violates a parental prohibition by cutting a cake reserved for a family celebration and giving a piece to a hungry playmate. As the parent begins to reprimand, the boy explains that the playmate had not eaten all day and that the refrigerator was nearly empty, leaving no alternative. In this instance, many parents would value the morality of the boy's claims along with his reasoning and negotiation skills.

Cognitive-developmental theorists believe that neither identification with parents nor teaching, modeling, and reinforcement are the major means through which children become moral. The cognitive-developmental approach assumes that individuals, rather than internalizing existing rules

Applying What We Know

Practicing Positive Discipline

Practice	Explanation
Use transgressions as opportunities to teach.	When a child engages in harmful or unsafe behavior, intervene firmly, and then use induction, which motivates children to make amends and behave prosocially.
Reduce opportunities for misbehavior.	On a long car trip, bring back-seat activities that relieve children's restlessness. At the supermarket, converse with children and let them help with shopping. In these ways, children learn to occupy themselves constructively when options are limited.
Provide reasons for rules.	When children appreciate that rules are fair to all concerned, not arbitrary, they strive to follow the rules because these are reasonable and rational.
Arrange for children to participate in family routines and duties.	By joining with adults in preparing a meal, washing dishes, or raking leaves, children develop a sense of responsible participation in family and community life and acquire many practical skills.
When children are obstinate, try compromising and problem solving.	When a child refuses to obey, express understanding of the child's feelings ("I know it's not fun to clean up"), suggest a compromise ("You put those away, I'll take care of these"), and help the child think of ways to avoid the problem in the future. Responding firmly but kindly and respectfully increases the likelihood of willing cooperation.
Encourage mature behavior.	Express confidence in children's capacity to learn and appreciation for effort and cooperation: "You gave that your best!" "Thanks for helping!" Adult encouragement fosters pride and satisfaction in succeeding, thereby inspiring children to improve further.
Be sensitive to children's physical and emotional resources.	When children are tired, ill, or bored, they are likely to engage in attention-getting, disorganized, or otherwise improper behavior as a reaction to discomfort. In these instances, meeting the child's needs makes more sense than disciplining.

Sources: Berk, 2001a; Grusec, 2006; Nelson, 1996.

and expectations, develop morally through **construction**—actively attending to and interrelating multiple perspectives on situations in which social conflicts arise and thereby attaining new moral understandings. In other words, children make moral evaluations and decisions on the basis of concepts they construct about justice and fairness. As these concepts become increasingly adequate with age, children arrive at a deeper understanding of morality—as something that *must be true* in the social world, just as conservation *must be true* in the physical world (Gibbs, 1991, 2010).

In sum, the cognitive-developmental position on morality is unique in its view of the child as a thinking moral being who wonders about right and wrong and searches for moral truth. These theorists regard changes in children's reasoning as the heart of moral development.

Ask Yourself

Review Describe evidence indicating that many morally relevant behaviors have roots in our evolutionary history.

Review Summarize the main features of the psychoanalytic and social learning perspectives on moral development. Why has each been criticized?

Apply Alice and Wayne want their two young children to develop a strong, internalized conscience and to become generous, caring individuals. List some parenting practices that would foster these goals, and explain why each is effective.

Reflect Did you display a strong, internalized conscience as a child? How do you think temperament, parenting practices, family living conditions, and cultural background affected your childhood moral maturity?

Morality as Social Understanding

According to the cognitive-developmental perspective, cognitive maturity and social experience lead to advances in moral understanding, from a superficial orientation to physical power and external consequences toward a more profound appreciation of interpersonal relationships, societal institutions, and lawmaking systems (Gibbs, 1995, 2010). As their grasp of social cooperation expands, children's ideas about what ought to be done when the needs and desires of people conflict also change, toward increasingly just, fair, and balanced solutions to moral problems.

Piaget's Theory of Moral Development

Piaget's (1932/1965) early work on children's moral judgments originally inspired the cognitive-developmental perspective. Using open-ended clinical interviews, Piaget questioned 5- to 13-year-old Swiss children about their understanding of rules in the game of marbles. He also told children stories in which characters' intentions to engage in right or wrong action differed from the consequences of their behavior. In the best known of these stories, children were asked which of two boys is naughtier, and why—well-intentioned John, who accidentally breaks 15 cups while on his way to dinner, or ill-intentioned Henry, who breaks a single cup while stealing some jam. From children's responses, Piaget identified two broad stages of moral understanding.

• **Heteronomous Morality (about 5 to 10 Years)** *Heteronomous* means under the authority of another. As the term **heteronomous morality** suggests, children in this first stage view rules as handed down by authorities (God, parents, and teachers), as having a permanent existence, as unchangeable, and as requiring strict obedience. For example, young children state that the rules of the game of marbles cannot be changed, explaining that "God didn't teach [the new rules]," "you couldn't play any other way," or "it would be cheating. . . . A fair rule is one that is in the game" (Piaget, 1932/1965, pp. 58, 59, 63).

According to Piaget, two factors limit children's moral understanding: (1) the power of adults to insist that children comply, which promotes unquestioning respect for rules and those who enforce them; and (2) cognitive immaturity, especially children's limited capacity to imagine other perspectives and their **realism**—tendency to view mental phenomena, including rules, as fixed external features of reality. Together, adult power, egocentrism, and realism result in superficial moral understandings. Younger children think that all people view rules in the same way and that rules are absolutes rather than cooperative principles that can be modified at will. In judging an act's wrongness, they focus on outcomes rather than on intent to do harm. For example, in the story about John and Henry mentioned earlier, they regard John as naughtier, despite his innocent intentions, because he broke more cups.

• **Autonomous Morality, or the Morality of Cooperation (about 10 Years and Older)** Cognitive development, gradual release from adult control, and peer interaction lead children to make the transition to the second stage, **autonomous morality,** in which they no longer view rules as fixed but see them as flexible, socially agreed-on principles that can be revised to suit the will of the majority. Piaget regarded peer disagreements as especially facilitating. Through them, children realize that people's perspectives on moral action can differ and that intentions, not concrete consequences, should serve as the basis for judging behavior.

Furthermore, as children interact as equals with peers, they learn to settle conflicts in mutually beneficial ways. Gradually, they start to use a standard of fairness called *reciprocity,* in which they express the same concern for the welfare of others as they do for themselves. Piaget found that children start with a crude, tit-for-tat understanding of reciprocity: "You scratch my back, and I'll scratch yours." This defines the beginning of the morality of cooperation. Older children and adolescents move beyond this payback morality to a grasp of the importance of mutuality of expectations, called **ideal reciprocity**—the idea expressed in the Golden Rule: "Do unto others as you would have them do unto you." Ideal reciprocity helps young people realize that rules can be reinterpreted and revised to take individual motives and circumstances into account, thereby ensuring just outcomes for all.

Evaluation of Piaget's Theory

Follow-up research indicates that Piaget's theory accurately describes the general direction of change in moral judgment. As children get older, outer features, such as physical damage or getting punished, give way to subtler considerations, such as the actor's intentions or the needs and desires of others. Also, much evidence confirms Piaget's conclusion that moral understanding is supported by cognitive maturity, gradual release from adult control, and peer interaction—findings we will consider when we turn to extensions of Piaget's work by Lawrence Kohlberg and his followers. Nevertheless, several aspects of Piaget's theory have been questioned because they underestimate the moral capacities of young children.

• **Intentions and Moral Judgments** Look back at the story about John and Henry on the previous page. Because bad intentions are paired with little damage and good intentions with a great deal of damage, Piaget's method yields a conservative picture of young children's ability to appreciate intentions. When questioned about moral issues in a way that makes a person's intention as obvious as the harm done, preschool and early school-age children are quite capable of judging ill-intentioned people as naughtier and more deserving of punishment than well-intentioned ones (Helwig, Zelazo, & Wilson, 2001; Jones & Thomson, 2001).

As further evidence, by age 4, children clearly recognize the difference between two morally relevant intentional behaviors: truthfulness and lying. They approve of telling the truth and disapprove of lying, even when a lie remains undetected (Bussey, 1992). And by age 7 to 8—earlier than suggested by Piaget's findings—children integrate their judgments of lying and truth telling with prosocial and antisocial intentions. They rate telling the truth in certain social situations very negatively—for example, bluntly telling a friend that you don't like her drawing (Bussey, 1999). And although both Chinese and Canadian schoolchildren consider lying about antisocial acts "very naughty," Chinese children—influenced by collectivist values—more often rate lying favorably when the intention is modesty (as when a student who has thoughtfully picked up the garbage in the school yard says, "I didn't do it") (Lee et al., 1997, 2001). Similarly, Chinese children are more likely than Canadian children to favor lying to support the group at the expense of the individual (saying you're sick so, as a poor singer, you won't harm your class's chances of winning a singing competition). In contrast, Canadian children more often favor lying to support the individual at the expense of the group (claiming that a friend who is a poor speller is actually a good speller because he wants to represent the class in a spelling competition) (Fu et al., 2007).

Nevertheless, an advanced understanding of the morality of intentions does await autonomous morality. Younger children are more likely to *center,* or focus on, salient features and consequences in their judgments, while neglecting other important information. For example, preschoolers more often than older children evaluate lies as always wrong (Peterson, Peterson, & Seeto, 1983). And although they disapprove of undetected lies, they also judge lies that lead to punishment more negatively than lies that do not (Bussey, 1992).

Furthermore, through the early school years, children generally interpret statements of intention in a rigid, heteronomous fashion. They believe that once you say you will do something, you are obligated to follow through, even if uncontrollable circumstances (such as an accident) make it difficult or impossible to do so. By age 9 or 10, children realize that not keeping your word is much worse in some situations than in others—namely, when you are able to do so and have permitted another person to count on your actions (Mant & Perner, 1988). In sum, Piaget was partly right and partly wrong about this aspect of moral reasoning.

• **Reasoning about Authority** Research on young children's understanding of authority reveals that they do not regard adults with the unquestioning respect Piaget assumed. Even preschoolers judge certain acts, such as hitting and stealing, to be wrong regardless of the opinions of authorities. When asked to explain, 3- and 4-year-olds express concerns about harming other people rather than obeying adult dictates (Smetana, 1981, 1985).

These Korean first graders have been reared in a culture that places a high value on deference to adults. Still, if their teacher directed them to cheat or steal, they would say that her immoral order should not be obeyed. © Jack Stein Grove/ PhotoEdit

By age 4, children have differentiated notions about the legitimacy of authority figures, which they refine during the school years. In several studies, children in kindergarten through sixth grade were asked questions designed to assess their view of how broad an adult's authority should be. Almost all denied that adults have general authority. For example, they rejected a principal's right to set rules and issue directives in settings other than his own school (Laupa, 1995).

With respect to nonmoral concerns, such as the rules of a game, children usually base the legitimacy of authority on a person's knowledge of the situation, not on social position. And when a directive is fair and caring (for example, telling children to stop fighting or to share candy), children view it as right, regardless of who states it—a principal, a teacher, a class president, or another child. Even among Korean children, whose culture places a high value on respect for and deference to adults, 7- to 11-year-olds evaluate negatively a teacher's or principal's order to keep fighting, to steal, or to refuse to share—a response that strengthens with age (Kim, 1998; Kim & Turiel, 1996).

As these findings reveal, adult status is not required for preschool and school-age children to view someone as an authority. Knowledgeable peers or those who act to protect others' rights are regarded as just as legitimate. But in reasoning about authority, preschool and young elementary school children do tend to place greater weight than older children on power, status, and consequences for disobedience.

• **Stagewise Progression** Many children display both heteronomous and autonomous reasoning, raising doubts about whether each Piagetian stage represents a general, unifying organization of moral judgment responses. But to be fair, Piaget (1932/1965) also observed this mixture in children and, therefore, regarded the two moralities as fluid, overlapping phases rather than tightly knit stages.

Finally, moral development is currently viewed as a more extended process than Piaget believed. Kohlberg's six-stage sequence, to which we turn next, identifies three stages beyond the first appearance of autonomous morality. Nevertheless, Kohlberg's theory is a direct continuation of the research begun by Piaget.

Kohlberg's Extension of Piaget's Theory

Like Piaget, Kohlberg used a clinical interviewing procedure to study moral development. But whereas Piaget asked children to judge and explain which of two children in a pair of stories was naughtier, Kohlberg used a more open-ended approach: He presented people with hypothetical moral dilemmas and asked what the main actor should do and why.

• **The Clinical Interview** In Kohlberg's **Moral Judgment Interview,** individuals resolve dilemmas that present conflicts between two moral values and justify their decisions. The best known of these, the "Heinz dilemma," pits the value of obeying the law (not stealing) against the value of human life (saving a dying person):

> In Europe, a woman was near death from cancer. There was one drug that the doctors thought might save her. A druggist in the same town had discovered it, but he was charging ten times what the drug cost him to make. The sick woman's husband, Heinz, went to everyone he knew to borrow the money, but he could only get together half of what it cost. The druggist refused to sell the drug for less or let Heinz pay later. So Heinz got desperate and broke into the man's store to steal the drug for his wife. Should Heinz have done that? Why or why not? (paraphrased from Colby et al., 1983, p. 77)

In addition to explaining their answer, participants are asked to evaluate the conflicting moral values on which the dilemma is based. Scoring of responses is highly intricate and demanding (Gibbs, Basinger, & Grime, 2003; Miller, 1998).

Kohlberg emphasized that it is *the way an individual reasons about the dilemma,* not *the content of the response* (whether or not to steal) that determines moral judgment maturity. Individuals who believe that Heinz should steal the drug and those who think he should not can be found at each of Kohlberg's first four stages. Only at the highest two stages do moral reasoning and content come together in a coherent ethical system, in which individuals agree not only on *why* certain actions are justified but also on *what* people ought to do when facing a moral dilemma. Given a choice between obeying the law and preserving individual rights, the most advanced moral thinkers support individual rights—in the Heinz dilemma, stealing the drug to save a life (Kohlberg, Levine, & Hewer, 1983).

• A Questionnaire Approach For more efficient gathering and scoring of moral reasoning, researchers have devised short-answer questionnaires. The most recent, the **Sociomoral Reflection Measure–Short Form (SRM–SF),** poses 11 questions that, like Kohlberg's clinical interview, ask individuals to evaluate the importance of moral values and to reason about them. Here are four of the 11 questions:

- Let's say a friend of yours needs help and may even die, and you're the only person who can save him or her. How important is it for a person (without losing his or her own life) to save the life of a friend?
- What about saving the life of anyone? How important is it for a person (without losing his or her own life) to save the life of a stranger?
- How important is it for people not to take things that belong to other people?
- How important is it for people to obey the law? (Gibbs, Basinger, & Fuller, 1992, pp. 151–152)

After reading each question, participants rate the importance of the value it addresses (as "very important," "important," or "not important") and write a brief explanation of their rating. The explanations are coded according to a revised rendition of Kohlberg's stages.

The SRM–SF is far less time consuming than the Moral Judgment Interview because it does not require people to read and think about lengthy descriptions of moral dilemmas. Instead, participants merely evaluate moral values and justify their evaluations. Nevertheless, SRM–SF scores correlate well with those obtained from the Moral Judgment Interview and show similar age trends (Basinger, Gibbs, & Fuller, 1995; Gibbs, Basinger, & Grime, 2003). The discovery that moral reasoning can be measured without posing dilemmas has eased the task of conducting moral development research.

• Kohlberg's Stages of Moral Understanding In his initial investigation, Kohlberg (1958) extended the age range Piaget studied, including participants who were well into adolescence (10-, 13-, and 16-year-old boys). Then he followed the participants longitudinally, reinterviewing them at three- to four-year intervals over the next 20 years (Colby et al., 1983). Analyzing age-related changes in the boys' moral judgments, Kohlberg generated his six-stage sequence. As with Piaget's progression of development, Kohlberg's first three stages characterize children as moving from a morality focused on outcomes to one based on ideal reciprocity. Inclusion of older adolescents yielded the fourth stage, in which young people expand their notion of ideal reciprocity to encompass societal rules and laws as vital for ensuring that people treat one another justly. Relying on the moral judgment responses of a small minority of adolescents, Kohlberg extended his sequence further, positing a fifth and sixth stage. As we will see, these stages have remained infrequent in subsequent research.

Kohlberg organized his six stages into three general levels and made stronger claims than Piaget about a fixed order of moral change. In doing so, however, Kohlberg drew on characteristics that Piaget used to describe his cognitive stage sequence:

- Kohlberg regarded his moral stages as invariant and universal—a sequence of steps through which people everywhere move in a fixed order.
- He viewed each new stage as building on reasoning of the preceding stage, resulting in a more logically consistent and morally adequate concept of justice.
- Kohlberg saw each stage as an organized whole—a qualitatively distinct structure of moral thought that a person applies across a wide range of situations (Colby & Kohlberg, 1987).

Furthermore, Kohlberg believed that moral understanding is promoted by the same factors Piaget thought were important for cognitive development: (1) disequilibrium, or actively grappling with moral issues and noticing weaknesses in one's current thinking, and (2) gains

If the child on the right expects a favor in return for carrying her injured friend's backpack, she is at Kohlberg's preconventional level. If she is guided by the Golden Rule, "Do unto others as you would have them do unto you," then she understands ideal reciprocity and has advanced to the conventional level.

in perspective taking, which permit individuals to resolve moral conflicts in increasingly complex and effective ways. **TAKE A MOMENT...** As we examine Kohlberg's developmental sequence and illustrate it with responses to the Heinz dilemma, look for changes in cognition and perspective taking that each stage assumes.

The Preconventional Level. At the **preconventional level,** morality is externally controlled. Children accept the rules of authority figures and judge actions by their consequences. Behaviors that result in punishment are viewed as bad, those that lead to rewards as good.

- *Stage 1: The punishment and obedience orientation.* Children at this stage find it difficult to consider two points of view in a moral dilemma. As a result, they overlook people's intentions. Instead, they focus on fear of authority and avoidance of punishment as reasons for behaving morally.

  Prostealing: "If you let your wife die, you will . . . be blamed for not spending the money to help her, and there'll be an investigation of you and the druggist for your wife's death" (Kohlberg, 1969, p. 381).

  Antistealing: "You shouldn't steal the drug because you'll be caught and sent to jail if you do. If you do get away, [you'd be scared that] the police would catch up with you any minute" (Kohlberg, 1969, p. 381).

- *Stage 2: The instrumental purpose orientation.* Children realize that people can have different perspectives in a moral dilemma, but at first this understanding is concrete. They view right action as flowing from self-interest and understand reciprocity as equal exchange of favors: "You do this for me, and I'll do that for you."

  Prostealing: "[I]f Heinz decides to risk jail to save his wife, it's his life he's risking; he can do what he wants with it. And the same goes for the druggist; it's up to him to decide what he wants to do" (Rest, 1979, p. 26).

  Antistealing: "[Heinz] is running more risk than it's worth [to save a wife who is near death]" (Rest, 1979, p. 27).

The Conventional Level. At the **conventional level,** individuals continue to regard conformity to social rules as important, but not for reasons of self-interest. Rather, they believe that actively maintaining the current social system ensures positive human relationships and societal order.

- *Stage 3: The "good boy–good girl" orientation, or the morality of interpersonal cooperation.* The desire to obey rules because they promote social harmony first appears in the context of close personal ties. Stage 3 individuals want to maintain the affection and approval of friends and relatives by being a "good person"—trustworthy, loyal, respectful, helpful, and nice. The capacity to view a two-person relationship from the vantage point of an impartial, outside observer supports this new approach to morality. At this stage, the individual understands *ideal reciprocity,* as expressed in the Golden Rule.

  Prostealing: "No one will think you're bad if you steal the drug, but your family will think you're an inhuman husband if you don't. If you let your wife die, you'll never be able to look anyone in the face again" (Kohlberg, 1969, p. 381).

  Antistealing: "It isn't just the druggist who will think you're a criminal, everyone else will too. . . . [Y]ou'll feel bad thinking how you brought dishonor on your family and yourself" (Kohlberg, 1969, p. 381).

- *Stage 4: The social-order-maintaining orientation.* At this stage, the individual takes into account a larger perspective—that of societal laws. Moral choices no longer depend on close ties to others. Instead, rules must be enforced in the same evenhanded fashion for everyone, and each member of society has a personal duty to uphold them. The Stage 4 individual believes that laws should be obeyed because they are vital for ensuring societal order and cooperation between individuals.

  Prostealing: "He should steal it. Heinz has a duty to protect his wife's life; it's a vow he took in marriage. But it's wrong to steal, so he would have to take the drug with the idea of paying the druggist for it and accepting the penalty for breaking the law later."

  Antistealing: "It's a natural thing for Heinz to want to save his wife but. . . . Even if his wife is dying, it's still his duty as a citizen to obey the law. . . . If everyone starts breaking the law in a jam, there'd be no civilization, just crime and violence" (Rest, 1979, p. 30).

By participating in this protest against global warming, these young people express a principled level of morality. They evaluate their own society's rules and laws on the basis of how well they serve the interests of the majority. © Jim West/Alamy Images

The Postconventional or Principled Level. Individuals at the **postconventional level** move beyond unquestioning support for the rules and laws of their own society. They define morality in terms of abstract principles and values that apply to all situations and societies.

- *Stage 5: The social-contract orientation.* At Stage 5, individuals regard laws and rules as flexible instruments for furthering human purposes. They can imagine alternatives to their own social order, and they emphasize fair procedures for interpreting and changing the law. When laws are consistent with individual rights and the interests of the majority, each person follows them because of a *social-contract orientation*—free and willing participation in the system because it brings about more good for people than if it did not exist.

  Prostealing: "Although there is a law against stealing, the law wasn't meant to violate a person's right to life. . . . If Heinz is prosecuted for stealing, the law needs to be reinterpreted to take into account situations in which it goes against people's natural right to keep on living."
- *Stage 6: The universal ethical principle orientation.* At this highest stage, right action is defined by self-chosen ethical principles of conscience that are valid for all humanity, regardless of law and social agreement. Stage 6 individuals typically mention such abstract principles as equal consideration of the claims of all human beings and respect for the worth and dignity of each person.

  Prostealing: "It doesn't make sense to put respect for property above respect for life itself. [People] could live together without private property at all. Respect for human life and personality is absolute, and accordingly [people] have a mutual duty to save one another from dying" (Rest, 1979, p. 37).

Research on Kohlberg's Stages

Kohlberg's original research and other longitudinal studies using hypothetical dilemmas provide the most convincing evidence for his stage sequence. With few exceptions, individuals move through the first four stages in the predicted order, without skipping steps or returning to less mature reasoning after attaining a stage (Boom, Wouters, & Keller, 2007; Colby et al., 1983; Dawson, 2002; Walker, 1989; Walker & Taylor, 1991b).

A striking finding is that development of moral reasoning, whether assessed longitudinally or cross-sectionally, with the Moral Judgment Interview or the SRM–SF, and in diverse Western industrialized or non-Western village cultures, is slow and gradual (Colby et al., 1983; Gibbs et al., 2007; Snarey, 1985). Stages 1 and 2 decrease from late childhood to early adolescence, whereas Stage 3 increases, becoming common by the end of the teenage years, when adolescents begin reasoning at Stage 4. Among college-educated young adults, Stage 4 is the typical response; few people move beyond it. As noted earlier, postconventional morality is so rare that no clear evidence exists that Kohlberg's Stage 6 actually follows Stage 5.

• **Are Kohlberg's Stages Organized Wholes?** TAKE A MOMENT... Think about an actual moral dilemma you faced recently. How did you solve it? Did your reasoning fall at the same stage as your thinking about the Heinz dilemma? If each of Kohlberg's stages forms an organized whole, then individuals should use the same level of moral reasoning across many tasks and situations—not just for hypothetical dilemmas but for everyday moral problems as well. In fact, real-life conflicts, such as whether to continue helping a friend who is taking advantage of you, often elicit moral reasoning below a person's actual capacity because they involve practical considerations and mix cognition with intense emotion (Carpendale, 2000; Walker & Moran, 1991). Although adolescents and adults still mention reasoning as their most

Will this 14-year-old accept a peer's offer of a drink? Real-life moral dilemmas bring out the motivational and emotional sides of moral judgment, along with practical considerations involved in resolving conflicts. © Photodisc/Alamy Images

frequent strategy for resolving these dilemmas, they also refer to other strategies—talking through issues with others, relying on intuition, and calling on notions of religious and spiritual ideas. And they report feeling drained, confused, and torn by temptation—an emotional side of moral judgment not tapped by hypothetical situations, which evoke the upper limits of moral thought because they allow reflection without the interference of personal risk (Walker, 2004; Walker et al., 1995, 1999).

The influence of situational factors on moral reasoning suggests that, like Piaget's cognitive and moral stages, Kohlberg's moral stages are loosely organized and overlapping. Rather than developing in a neat, stepwise fashion, people draw on a range of moral responses that vary with context. With age, this range shifts upward as less mature moral reasoning is gradually replaced by more advanced moral thought.

• Cognitive Prerequisites for Moral Reasoning Moral maturity, whether based on Piaget's or Kohlberg's theory, is positively correlated with IQ, performance on Piagetian cognitive tasks, and perspective-taking skill (Lickona, 1976; Walker & Hennig, 1997). Kohlberg (1976) argued that each moral stage requires certain cognitive and perspective-taking capacities, but that these are not enough to ensure moral advances, which also require reorganization of thought unique to the moral domain. In other words, Kohlberg hypothesized that cognitive and perspective-taking attainments are *necessary but not sufficient conditions* for each moral stage.

Research indicates that, consistent with Kohlberg's predictions, children and adolescents at each moral stage score at either an equivalent or a higher stage of cognition and perspective taking, as shown in Table 12.1 (Krebs & Gillmore, 1982; Selman, 1976; Walker, 1980). Still, the domain in which the cognitive ingredients required for more mature moral judgment first emerge—cognitive, social, or moral—remains unclear. In Chapters 6 and 7, we encountered a wealth of evidence indicating that children display more advanced reasoning on tasks with which they have more extensive experience. Young people who frequently grapple with social and moral issues may actually construct the cognitive supports for moral development directly—while reasoning about social or moral concerns (Damon, 1977; Gibbs, 2010).

Table 12.1 Relationships Among Kohlberg's Moral, Piaget's Cognitive, and Selman's Perspective-Taking Stages

Kohlberg's Moral Stage	Description	Piaget's Cognitive Stage	Selman's Perspective-Taking Stage[a]
Punishment and obedience orientation	Fear of authority and avoidance of punishment	Preoperational, early concrete operational	Social-informational
Instrumental purpose orientation	Satisfying personal needs	Concrete operational	Self-reflective
"Good boy–good girl" orientation	Maintaining the affection and approval of friends and relatives	Early formal operational	Third-party
Social-order-maintaining orientation	A duty to uphold laws and rules for their own sake	Formal operational	Societal
Social contract orientation	Fair procedures for changing laws to protect individual rights and the needs of the majority		
Universal ethical principle orientation	Abstract universal principles that are valid for all humanity		

[a]To review these stages, return to Table 11.2 on page 474.

Finally, Kohlberg's stage sequence makes sense to adolescents and adults who have not studied his theory. When Russian high school and Dutch university students were asked to sort statements typical of Kohlberg's stages, they tended to rank reasoning at each consecutive stage as more sophisticated. However, the higher the stage, the more participants disagreed in their rankings because they had difficulty ordering statements beyond their own current stage (Boom, Brugman, & van der Heijden, 2001).

Are There Sex Differences in Moral Reasoning?

As we have seen, real-life moral dilemmas highlight the role of emotion in moral judgment. Return to Leisl's moral reasoning in the opening to this chapter and notice how her argument focuses on caring and commitment to others. Carol Gilligan (1982) is the best known of those who have argued that Kohlberg's theory—originally formulated on the basis of interviews with males—does not adequately represent the morality of girls and women. Gilligan believes that feminine morality emphasizes an "ethic of care" that Kohlberg's system devalues. Leisl's reasoning falls at Kohlberg's Stage 3 because it is based on interpersonal obligations. In contrast, Stages 4 to 6 emphasize justice—an abstract, rational commitment to moral ideals. According to Gilligan, a concern for others is a *different* but no less valid basis for moral judgment than a focus on impersonal rights.

Many studies have tested Gilligan's claim that Kohlberg's approach underestimates the moral maturity of females, and most do not support it (Turiel, 2006; Walker, 2006). On hypothetical dilemmas, everyday moral problems, and the SMR–SF, adolescent and adult females display reasoning at the same stage as their male counterparts and often at a higher stage. Also, themes of justice and caring appear in the responses of both sexes, and when girls do raise interpersonal concerns, they are not downgraded in Kohlberg's system (Jadack et al., 1995; Jaffee & Hyde, 2000; Walker, 1995). Rather, many studies report that girls shift from Stage 2 to Stage 3 reasoning earlier than boys (Gibbs et al., 2007). These findings suggest that although Kohlberg emphasized justice rather than caring as the highest of moral ideals, his theory taps both sets of values.

This teenager cares for and comforts her grandmother, who has Alzheimer's disease. Adolescents, whether male or female, express moral themes of both justice and caring. But some evidence indicates that females place greater emphasis on care, especially when reasoning about real-life dilemmas. © Ole Graf/ZEFA/Corbis

Still, Gilligan makes a powerful claim that research on moral development has been limited by too much attention to rights and justice (a "masculine" ideal) and too little to caring and responsiveness (a "feminine" ideal). Some evidence shows that although the morality of males and females taps both orientations, females do tend to stress care, or empathic perspective taking, whereas males either stress justice or focus equally on justice and care (Jaffe & Hyde, 2000; Wark & Krebs, 1996; Weisz & Black, 2002). This difference in emphasis, which appears more often in real life than in hypothetical dilemmas, may reflect women's greater emotional closeness in friendship and greater involvement in daily activities involving care and concern for others.

Indeed, both cultural and situational contexts profoundly affect use of a care orientation. In one study, U.S. and Canadian 17- to 26-year-old females showed more complex reasoning about care issues than their male counterparts. But Norwegian males were just as advanced as Norwegian females in care-based understanding (Skoe, 1998). Perhaps Norwegian culture, which explicitly endorses gender equality, induces boys and men to think deeply about interpersonal obligations. And in an Australian investigation, researchers presented 18- to 38-year-old university students with one of three versions of a moral dilemma, in which the main character varied in familiarity: (1) a close friend in class, (2) a person "known only vaguely" from class, or (3) a classmate whose relationship was unspecified (Ryan, David, & Reynolds, 2004). When asked whether they would permit the character who was in danger of failing the course to borrow a copy of their recently completed assignment despite risk of cheating, both male and female participants gave more care responses when considering a close friend than a socially distant classmate. As Figure 12.4 on page 500 shows, gender differences emerged only in the unspecified condition, where women—who tend to forge closer relationships—may have assumed greater familiarity.

Collectivist values of Asian cultures explicitly emphasize care and concern for others as a societal norm. In one study, Japanese adolescents almost always integrated care and justice

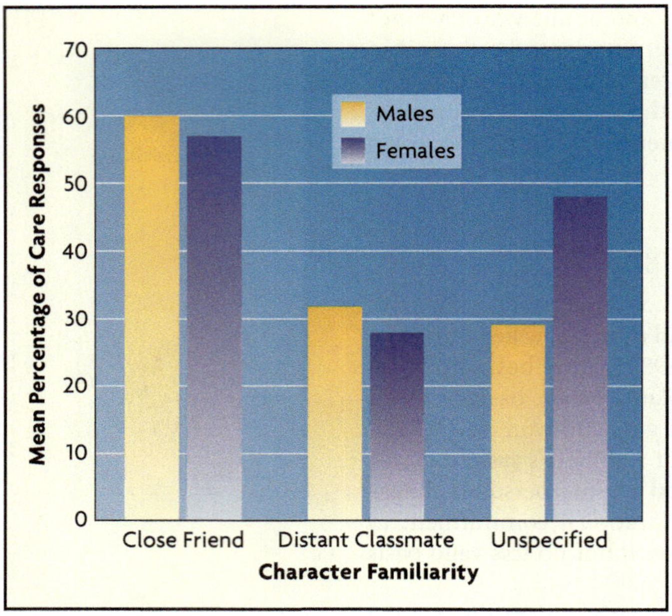

Figure 12.4 **Relationship of familiarity of the main character in a moral dilemma to care responses.**

Australian university students were presented with one of three versions of a moral dilemma in which familiarity of the main character varied: close friend, distant classmate, and unspecified. Both male and female participants gave more care responses when considering a close friend than a distant classmate. Sex differences appeared only in the unspecified condition, where females may have assumed greater familiarity. (From M. K. Ryan, B. David, & K. J. Reynolds, 2004, "Who Cares? The Effect of Gender and Context on the Self and Moral Reasoning," *Psychology of Women Quarterly,* 28, pp. 246–255. Copyright © 2004 by the American Psychological Association. Reprinted with permission of the American Psychological Association.)

reasoning. At the same time, both males and females stressed caring, which they regarded as a communal responsibility. As one boy remarked, *yasashii* (kindness/gentleness) and *omoiyari* (empathy) are "something 'normal' that everyone shows" (Shimizu, 2001).

Although current evidence indicates that justice and caring are not gender-specific moralities, Gilligan's work has expanded our conception of the highly moral person. In several investigations, researchers examined the development of care-based reasoning using dilemmas that ask adolescents and adults to reason about relationships—for example, a lonely parent wanting to move in with an adult child. Findings revealed gradual change from an egocentric focus on the self's needs, to a self-sacrificing focus on others' needs, to balanced consideration of the needs of both self and other, generally paralleling age-related change in justice-based reasoning (Pratt, Skoe, & Arnold, 2004; Skoe & Diessner, 1994). Perhaps Piaget (1932/1965) himself said it best: "Between the more refined forms of justice . . . and love properly so called, there is no longer any real conflict" (p. 324).

Influences on Moral Reasoning

Many factors affect the maturity of moral reasoning, including the young person's personality and a wide range of social experiences—child-rearing practices, peer interaction, schooling, and aspects of culture. Growing evidence suggests that, as Kohlberg believed, these experiences work in two ways: They encourage young people to take the perspective of others, and they induce cognitive disequilibrium by presenting cognitive challenges, which stimulate young people to think about moral problems in more complex ways.

• **Personality** A flexible, open-minded approach to new information and experiences is linked to gains in moral reasoning, just as it is to identity development (Hart et al., 1998; Matsuba & Walker, 1998). Because open-minded young people are more socially skilled, they have more opportunities for social participation. A richer social life enhances exposure to others' perspectives, and open-mindedness helps adolescents derive moral insights from that exposure. In contrast, adolescents who have difficulty adapting to new experiences are less likely to be interested in others' moral ideas and justifications.

• **Child-Rearing Practices** Child-rearing practices associated with mature moral reasoning combine warmth, exchange of ideas, and appropriate demands for maturity. Children and adolescents who gain most in moral understanding in succeeding years are those whose parents engage in moral discussions, encourage prosocial behavior, insist that others be treated respectfully and fairly, and create a supportive atmosphere by listening sensitively, asking clarifying questions, and presenting higher-level reasoning (Pratt, Skoe, & Arnold, 2004; Wyatt & Carlo, 2002). In one study, 11-year-olds were asked what they thought an adult would say to justify a moral rule, such as not lying, stealing, or breaking a promise. Those with warm, demanding, communicative parents were far more likely than their agemates to point to the importance of ideal reciprocity: "I trusted you," "You wouldn't like it if I did it to you" (Leman, 2005). In contrast, when parents lecture, use threats, or make sarcastic remarks, children show little or no change in moral reasoning over time (Walker & Taylor, 1991a). In sum, parents who facilitate moral understanding are affectionate, verbal, and rational and promote a cooperative style of family life. Notice that these are the very characteristics, discussed earlier in this chapter, that foster moral internalization in young children.

• **Schooling** Years of schooling completed is one of the most powerful predictors of moral understanding, and it may account for the positive relationship of SES with stage of moral judgment. Moral reasoning advances in late adolescence and early adulthood only as long as a person remains in school (Dawson et al., 2003; Gibbs et al., 2007; Speicher, 1994). Higher education introduces young people to social issues that extend beyond personal relationships to entire political and cultural groups. Consistent with this idea, college students who report more perspective-taking opportunities (for example, classes that emphasize open discussion of opinions, friendships with others of different cultural backgrounds) and who indicate that they have become more aware of social diversity tend to be advanced in moral reasoning (Comunian & Gielen, 2006; Mason & Gibbs, 1993a, 1993b).

These college students have many opportunities to discuss ideas with culturally diverse peers—experiences that lead to gains in perspective taking and moral understanding.

• **Peer Interaction** Research supports Piaget's belief that interaction among peers who confront one another with differing viewpoints promotes moral understanding. Adolescents who report more close friendships, more often participate in conversations with their friends, and are viewed as leaders by classmates score higher in moral reasoning (Schonert-Reichl, 1999).

As Piaget suggested, peer interaction probably contributes to gains in moral reasoning by making young people more aware of others' perspectives. But as noted in Chapter 6, conflict resolution, rather than conflict per se, may be the feature of peer exchanges that stimulates cognitive development—nonmoral and moral alike. Through engaging in negotiation and compromise, children realize that social life can be based on cooperation between equals rather than on authority relations (Killen & Nucci, 1995). The mutuality and intimacy of friendship, which foster decisions based on consensual agreement, may be particularly important for moral development.

Peer discussions and role-playing of moral problems have provided the basis for interventions aimed at improving high school and college students' moral understanding. For these interventions to be effective, young people must be highly engaged—confronting, critiquing, and attempting to clarify one another's viewpoints (Berkowitz & Gibbs, 1983; Comumian & Gielen, 2006). And because moral development is a gradual process, many peer interaction sessions over weeks or months typically are needed to produce moral change.

• **Culture** Individuals in industrialized nations move through Kohlberg's stages more rapidly and advance to a higher level than individuals in village societies, who rarely move beyond Stage 3. One explanation of these cultural differences is that in village societies, moral cooperation is based on direct relations between people and does not allow for the development of advanced moral understanding (Stages 4 to 6), which depends on appreciating the role of larger social structures, such as laws and government institutions, in resolving moral conflict (Gibbs et al., 2007).

In support of this view, in cultures where young people participate in the institutions of their society at early ages, moral reasoning is advanced. For example, on *kibbutzim,* small but technologically complex agricultural settlements in Israel, children receive training in the governance of their community in middle childhood. By third grade, they mention more concerns about societal laws and rules when discussing moral conflicts than do Israeli city-reared or U.S. children (Fuchs et al., 1986). During adolescence and adulthood, a greater percentage of kibbutz than U.S. individuals reach Kohlberg's Stages 4 and 5 (Snarey, Reimer, & Kohlberg, 1985).

A second possible reason for cultural variation is that responses to moral dilemmas in some cultures cannot always be scored in Kohlberg's scheme (Snarey, 1985, 1995). Recall from Chapter 11 that self-concepts in collectivist cultures (including village societies) are often more other-directed than in Western Europe and North America—a difference that also characterizes moral reasoning (Miller, 2006). In cultures that highly value interdependency, statements portraying the individual as vitally connected to the social group are common. For example, one New Guinea village leader responded to the Heinz dilemma by blaming the entire community, stating, "If I were the judge, I would give him only light punishment

In India, poverty, overcrowding, illiteracy, crime, and shortages of food and medical care are major social problems, affecting hundreds of millions of people. Many East Indians, who highly value interdependency, view relieving injustice as a collective rather than an individual responsibility—reasoning not easily scored in Kohlberg's scheme. Courtesy of Stephen Friedberg

because he asked everybody for help, but nobody helped him" (Tietjen & Walker, 1985, p. 990).

Similarly, members of Asian societies place more weight on obligations to others than do Westerners. East Indians, for example, less often hold individuals accountable for moral transgressions. In their view, the self and social surroundings are inseparable (Miller & Bersoff, 1995). This perspective is evident even among well-educated adults in India, who would be expected to be at Kohlberg's higher stages. In discussing the Heinz dilemma, they resist choosing a course of action, explaining that a moral solution should be the burden of the entire society. As one woman put it,

> The problems that Heinz is up against are not individual problems that are affecting one or two Heinzes of the world. These are social problems. Forget Heinz in Europe, just come to India. . . . Heinz's story is being repeated all around us all the time with wives dying, with children dying, and there is no money to save them. . . . So Heinz in his individual capacity—yes, okay, steal the drug, but it's not going to make any difference on a large scale. . . . I don't think in the final analysis a solution can be worked out on an individual basis. . . . It will probably have to be tackled on a macro level. (Vasudev & Hummel, 1987, p. 110)

These findings raise the question of whether Kohlberg's highest level represents a culturally specific way of thinking—one limited to Western societies that emphasize individual rights and an appeal to an inner, private conscience. At the same time, a common justice morality is clearly evident in the dilemma responses of people from vastly different cultures.

Moral Reasoning and Behavior

A central assumption of the cognitive-developmental perspective is that moral understanding should affect moral motivation. As young people grasp the moral "logic" of human social cooperation, they are upset when this logic is violated. As a result, they realize that behaving in line with one's thinking is vital for creating and maintaining a just social world (Blasi, 1994; Gibbs, 2010). Consistent with this idea, higher-stage adolescents more often act prosocially by helping, sharing, and defending victims of injustice and by volunteering in their communities (Carlo et al., 1996; Comunian & Gielen, 2000, 2006). Also, they less often engage in cheating, aggression, and other antisocial or delinquent behaviors (Gregg, Gibbs, & Fuller, 1994; Raaijmakers, Engels, & Van Hoof, 2005; Stams et al., 2006).

Yet the connection between more mature moral reasoning and action is only modest. As we have seen, moral behavior is influenced by many factors besides cognition, including the emotions of empathy, sympathy, and guilt; individual differences in temperament; and a long history of experiences that affect moral choice and decision making. **Moral self-relevance**—the degree to which morality is central to self-concept—also affects moral behavior (Walker, 2004). When moral goals are personally important, individuals are more likely to feel obligated to act on their moral judgments. In a study of low-SES African-American and Hispanic teenagers, those who emphasized moral traits and goals in their self-descriptions displayed exceptional levels of community service, but they did not differ from their agemates in moral reasoning (Hart & Fegley, 1995). That a synthesis of moral concern with sense of self can motivate moral action is also supported by a study of people who have made outstanding contributions to moral causes, such as civil rights, the fight against poverty, medical ethics, and religious freedom. Interviews with these moral exemplars revealed that their most distinguishing characteristic is "seamless integration" of moral vision with personal identity (Colby & Damon, 1992, p. 309).

Research has yet to identify the origins of moral self-relevance, or just how thought combines with other influences to foster moral commitment. Close relationships with parents, teachers, and friends may play a vital role by modeling prosocial behavior and fostering morally relevant emotions of empathy and guilt, which combine with moral cognition to powerfully motivate moral action (Arsenio, 2006; Hoffman, 2000; Kohlberg & Diessner, 1991). Another possibility is that *just educational environments*—in which teachers guide students in democratic decision making and rule setting, resolving disputes civilly, and taking responsibility for others' welfare—are influential (Atkins, Hart, & Donnelly, 2004). A compassionate and just school climate may be particularly important for poverty-stricken ethnic minority children and adolescents. For many such students, meaningful participation in their school community may be the crucial factor that prevents them from pessimistically concluding that prejudice and diminished opportunity are pervasive in society and, therefore, insurmountable (Hart & Atkins, 2002)

Schools can also expand students' opportunities to experience and explore moral emotions, thoughts, and actions by promoting civic engagement. As the From Research to Practice box on page 504 reveals, encouraging civic responsibility in young people can help them see the connection between their personal interests and the public interest—an insight that may foster all aspects of morality.

Religious Involvement and Moral Development

Recall that in resolving real-life moral dilemmas, many people express notions of religion and spirituality. For these individuals, morality and spirituality are inseparable; their moral values, judgments, and behaviors are deeply embedded in their faith.

Religion is especially important in North American family life. In recent national polls, nearly two-thirds of Americans and about one-half of Canadians reported being religious, compared with one-third of those in Great Britain and Italy and even fewer elsewhere in Europe (Adams, 2003; Jones, 2003). People who are affiliated with a church, synagogue, or mosque and regularly attending religious services include many parents with children. By middle childhood, children have begun to formulate religious and spiritual ideas that are remarkably complex and that serve as moral forces in their lives.

During adolescence, formal religious involvement declines—among U.S. youths, from 55 percent at ages 13 to 15 to 40 percent at ages 17 to 18 (Donahue & Benson, 1995; Kerestes & Youniss, 2003). The drop coincides with increased autonomy and efforts to construct a personally meaningful religious identity—a task usually not complete until the late teens or twenties (Hunsberger, Pratt, & Pancer, 2001).

But adolescents who remain part of a religious community are advantaged in moral values and behavior. Compared with nonaffiliated youths, they are more involved in community service activities aimed at helping the less fortunate (Kerestes, Youniss, & Metz, 2004). And religious involvement promotes responsible academic and social behavior and discourages misconduct (Dowling et al., 2004). It is associated with lower levels of drug and alcohol use, early sexual activity, and delinquency (Regnerus, Smith, & Fritsch, 2003).

This teenager clearly has a warm relationship with the two young girls she teaches at their vacation Bible school. Adolescents who are part of a religious community tend to be advanced in moral development and are more likely to be involved in community service.

A variety of factors probably contribute to these favorable outcomes:

- Religious involvement provides young people with expanded networks of caring adults and peers—conditions that foster moral maturity. In a study of a large sample of inner-city high school students, religiously involved adolescents were more likely to report trusting relationships with parents, adults, and friends who hold similar worldviews. The more activities they shared with this network, the higher they scored in empathic concern and prosocial behavior (King & Furrow, 2004).
- Religious education and youth activities directly teach concern for others and provide opportunities for moral discussions and civic engagement.

From Research to Practice

Development of Civic Responsibility

On Thanksgiving Day, Jill, Todd, and Brett joined their parents at a soup kitchen serving holiday dinners to poverty-stricken people. Throughout the year, Jill and Brett volunteered on Saturday mornings at a nursing home, conversing with bedridden elders. During a congressional election, the three teenagers raised questions about issues at special youth meetings with candidates. At school, Todd and his girlfriend formed an organization devoted to promoting ethnic and racial tolerance.

These young people show a strong sense of *civic responsibility*—a complex combination of cognition, emotion, and behavior that involves knowledge of political issues, a desire to make a difference in the community, and skills for achieving civic goals, such as how to resolve differing views fairly and conduct meetings so all participants have a voice (Flanagan & Faison, 2001).

When young people engage in community service that exposes them to people in need or to public issues, they are especially likely to express a commitment to future service. And youth volunteers—who tend to be advanced in moral reasoning—gain further as a result of participating (Gibbs et al., 2007; Hart, Atkins, & Donnelly, 2006; Reinders & Youniss, 2006). Family, school, and community experiences contribute to adolescents' civic responsibility.

Family Influences

Teenagers whose parents encourage them to form opinions about controversial issues are more knowledgeable about civic issues and better able to see them from more than one perspective (Santoloupo & Pratt, 1994). Also, adolescents whose parents engage in community service and stress compassion tend to hold socially responsible values. When asked what causes unemployment or poverty, they more often mention situational and societal factors (lack of education, government policies, or the state of the economy) than individual factors (low intelligence or personal problems). Youths who endorse situational and societal causes, in turn, have more altruistic life goals, such as working to eradicate poverty or to preserve the earth for future generations (Flanagan & Tucker, 1999).

Young people paint a mural on a wall once filled with graffiti in a low-income, inner-city neighborhood. Family, school, and community experiences contribute to their sense of civic responsibility. © Jim West/The Image Works

School and Community Influences

A democratic climate at school in which teachers promote discussion of controversial issues while insisting that students listen to and respect one another's ideas fosters critical analysis of political issues and commitment to social causes (Flanagan & Faison, 2001). Participation in extracurricular activities and youth organizations is also associated with civic commitment persisting into adulthood (Obradović & Masten, 2007).

Two aspects of these involvements seem to account for their lasting impact. First, they introduce adolescents to the vision and skills required for mature civic engagement. Within student government, clubs, teams, and other groups, young people see how their actions affect the wider school and community. They realize that collectively they can achieve results greater than any one person can achieve alone. And they learn to work together, balancing strong convictions with compromise (Atkins, Hart, & Donnelly, 2004; Youniss, McLellan, & Yates, 1997). Second, while producing a weekly newspaper, participating in a dramatic production, or implementing a service project, young people explore political and moral ideals and, as a result, often redefine their identities to include a responsibility to combat others' misfortunes (Wheeler, 2002).

The power of family, school, and community to promote civic responsibility may lie in discussions, educational practices, and activities that jointly foster moral thought, emotion, and behavior. In a comparison of nationally representative samples of 14-year-olds in 28 nations, North American young people excelled at community service, with 50 percent of students reporting membership in organizations devoted to volunteering (Torney-Purta, 2002).

Currently, 66 percent of U.S. public schools provide students with community service opportunities. Nearly half of these schools have *service-learning programs,* which integrate service activities into the academic curriculum, and about one-third of students enroll. High school students who are required to serve their communities express as strong a desire to remain engaged as do students who volunteer. And when they reach early adulthood, they are equally likely to vote and to participate in community organizations (Hart et al., 2007; Metz & Youniss, 2005).

Still, most principals in U.S. schools offering service learning say that neither their school nor their district has policies encouraging or mandating such programs (Scales & Roehlkepartain, 2004). In Canada, the province of Ontario requires 40 hours of community service for high school graduation. Nevertheless, low-SES, inner-city youths—although they express high interest in social justice and contributing to society—score substantially lower than higher-SES youths in civic knowledge and participation (Balsano, 2005). A broad societal commitment to fostering civic character must pay special attention to supportive school and community experiences for these young people, so their eagerness to make a difference can be realized.

- Adolescents who feel connected to a higher being may develop certain inner strengths—including moral self-relevance and prosocial values—that help them resolve real-life moral dilemmas maturely and translate their thinking into action (Furrow, King, & White, 2004; Hardy & Carlo, 2005).

Because most teenagers, regardless of formal affiliation, identify with a religious denomination and say they believe in a higher being, religious institutions may be uniquely suited to foster moral and prosocial commitments and discourage risky behaviors (Bridges & Moore, 2002). For youths in inner-city neighborhoods with few alternative sources of social support, outreach by religious institutions can lead to life-altering involvement (Jang & Johnson, 2001). An exception is seen in religious cults, where rigid indoctrination into the group's beliefs, suppression of individuality, and estrangement from society all work against moral maturity (Richmond, 2004).

Further Challenges to Kohlberg's Theory

Although there is much support for Kohlberg's theory, it continues to face challenges. The most important of these concern Kohlberg's conception of moral maturity, the applicability of his stage model to moral reasoning and behavior in everyday life, and the appropriateness of his stages for characterizing children's moral reasoning.

A key controversy has to do with Kohlberg's belief that moral maturity is not achieved until the postconventional level. Yet if people had to reach Stages 5 and 6 to be considered truly morally mature, few individuals anywhere would measure up! John Gibbs (1991, 2010) argues that "postconventional morality" should not be viewed as the standard against which other levels are judged immature. Gibbs finds maturity in a revised understanding of Stages 3 and 4 that emphasizes ideal reciprocity. These stages are not "conventional," or based on social conformity, as Kohlberg assumed. Instead, they require profound moral constructions—an understanding of ideal reciprocity as the basis for relationships between people (Stage 3) and for widely accepted moral standards, set forth in rules and laws (Stage 4).

Gibbs (2010) regards "postconventional" moral reasoning as a highly reflective, metacognitive endeavor in which people grapple with existential issues: What is the meaning of life? Why be moral? Most people who contemplate such questions have attained advanced education, usually in philosophy—which sheds light on why Stages 5 and 6 are so rare. Occasionally, however, as a result of soul-searching life crises, life-threatening events, or spiritual awakenings, individuals without formal training in philosophy generate ethical insights into the meaning of existence—transformations that may heighten their resolve to lead a moral life. As a result, Gibbs notes, "postconventional" moral judgment is sometimes seen as early as adolescence, when young people first become capable of the formal operational and perspective-taking capacities needed to engage in it.

A more radical challenge comes from Dennis Krebs and Kathy Denton (2005), who claim that Kohlberg's theory inadequately accounts for morality in everyday life. Pointing to wide variability in maturity of moral reasoning across situations, these researchers favor abandoning Kohlberg's stages for a *pragmatic approach to morality.* They assert that each person makes moral judgments at varying levels of maturity, depending on the individual's current context and motivations: Conflict over a business deal is likely to evoke Stage 2 (instrumental purpose) reasoning, a friendship or marital dispute Stage 3 (ideal reciprocity) reasoning, and a breach of contract Stage 4 (social-order-maintaining) reasoning (Krebs et al., 1991). According to Krebs and Denton, everyday moral judgments—rather than being efforts to arrive at just solutions—are practical tools that people use to achieve their goals. To benefit personally, they often must advocate cooperation with others. But many people act first and then invoke moral judgments to rationalize their actions, regardless of whether the behavior is self-centered or altruistic (Haidt, 2001). People also use moral judgments for immoral purposes—to excuse their transgressions, blame others, or attract unmerited admiration, This pragmatism of moral reasoning, Krebs and Denton argue, is responsible for the lack of a strong association between moral judgment maturity and behavior.

Do people strive to resolve moral dilemmas in the fairest way possible, using the most advanced reasoning of which they are capable, only when presented with hypothetical dilemmas or real-life conflicts in which they are not personally involved? Gibbs (2006) points out that despite their mixed motives in everyday situations, people often rise above self-gratification to support others' rights. For example, moral exemplars in business—rather than yielding to Stage 2 reasoning—endorse the importance of trust, integrity, good faith, and just laws and codes of conduct (Damon, 2004). Furthermore, the pragmatic approach fails to recognize people's awareness of the greater adequacy of higher-stage moral judgments, which some individuals act on despite highly corrupt environments. And people who engage in sudden altruistic action may have previously considered the relevant moral issues so thoroughly that their cognitive structures activate automatically, inducing an immediate response (Pizarro & Bloom, 2003). In these instances, individuals who appear to be engaging in after-the-fact rationalization are actually behaving with great forethought.

Finally, Kohlberg's stages tell us much more about moral understanding in adolescence and adulthood than in early and middle childhood. Nancy Eisenberg created dilemmas relevant to children's everyday lives that pit satisfying one's own desires against acting prosocially—for example, going to a birthday party versus taking time to help an injured peer and missing the party as a result (Eisenberg, 1986; Eisenberg et al., 1991, 1995). She found that children's *prosocial moral reasoning* is more advanced than Kohlberg's stages suggest. Furthermore, empathic perspective taking strengthens prosocial moral thought and its realization in everyday behavior (Eisenberg, Fabes, & Spinrad, 2006; Eisenberg, Zhoe, & Koller, 2001).

In sum, because Kohlberg focused on young children's tendency to center on prominent external features in their social world, he underestimated their potential for deeper moral understanding. In the following sections, we consider additional evidence on both child and adolescent moral reasoning.

The Domain Approach to Moral Understanding

Researchers taking a *domain approach to moral understanding* focus on children's developing capacity to distinguish and coordinate **moral imperatives,** which protect people's rights and welfare, from two other types of social rules and expectations: **social conventions,** customs determined solely by consensus, such as table manners and rituals of social interaction (saying "hello," "please," "thank you"); and **matters of personal choice,** such as choice of friends, hairstyle, and leisure activities, which do not violate rights and are up to the individual (Ardila-Rey & Killen, 2001; Nucci, 1996; Smetana, 2006). According to domain theorists, children construct these systems of social knowledge out of their experiences with three types of regularities in their social world (Turiel, 2006). And research reveals that children arrive at these distinctions early, displaying more advanced moral reasoning than assumed by the externally controlled vision of Kohlberg's preconventional morality.

• **Moral versus Social-Conventional Distinctions** Interviews with 3- and 4-year-olds reveal that they judge moral violations (such as stealing an apple) as more wrong than violations of social conventions (eating ice cream with your fingers). They also say that moral violations are more generalizably wrong—not OK regardless of the setting in which they are committed, such as another country or school. And they indicate that moral (but not a social-conventional) transgressions would still be wrong if authority figures (parents or teachers) did not observe them and no rules existed to prohibit them (Smetana, 2006; Yan & Smetana, 2003).

How do young children arrive at these distinctions? According to Elliott Turiel (2006), they observe that after a moral offense, peers respond with strong negative emotion, describe their own injury or loss, tell another child to stop, or retaliate (Arsenio & Fleiss, 1996). And an adult who intervenes is likely to call attention to the victim's rights and feelings. Violations of social convention elicit less intense peer reactions. And in these situations, adults usually demand obedience without explanation or point to the importance of keeping order.

But while realizing that moral transgressions are worse than social-conventional violations, preschool and young school-age children (as Piaget pointed out) tend to reason rigidly *within* the moral domain, making judgments based on salient features and consequences while neglecting other important information. They claim, for example, that stealing and lying are always wrong, even when a person has a morally sound reason for doing so (Lourenco, 2003). They view inflicting physical damage (breaking a peer's toy) as a more serious transgression than treating others unfairly (not sharing) (Nucci, 2002). And their accounts of having been hurt or having hurt another person tend to feature simple acts of physical harm—for example, "Jack hit me, and he also kicked me" (Wainryb, Brehl, & Matwin, 2005).

These schoolchildren are aware that the social convention of respecting the flag has moral implications. They realize that any public flag-burning would harm others emotionally. At the same time, they acknowledge that destroying a flag is a form of freedom of expression that is warranted in a country that treats its citizens unfairly. © Jeff Greenberg/PhotoEdit

As they construct a flexible appreciation of moral rules, children clarify and link moral imperatives and social conventions. Gradually their understanding becomes more complex, taking into account an increasing number of variables, including the purpose of the rule; people's intentions, knowledge, and beliefs; and the context of people's behavior. School-age children, for example, distinguish social conventions with a clear *purpose* (not running in school hallways to prevent injuries) from ones with no obvious justification (crossing a "forbidden" line on the playground). They regard violations of purposeful conventions as closer to moral transgressions (Buchanan-Barrow & Barrett, 1998). With age, they also realize that people's *intentions* and the *context* of their actions affect the moral implications of violating a social convention. In a Canadian study, many 6-year-olds always disapproved of flag burning, citing its physical consequences. But 8- to 10-year-olds made subtle distinctions, stating that because of a flag's symbolic value, burning it to express disapproval of a country or to start a cooking fire is worse than burning it accidentally. They also stated that public flag burning is worse than private flag burning because it inflicts emotional harm on others. But they recognized that burning a flag is a form of freedom of expression, and most agreed that it would be acceptable in a country that treated its citizens unfairly (Helwig & Prencipe, 1999).

In middle childhood, children also realize that people whose *knowledge* differs may not be equally responsible for moral transgressions. Many 7-year-olds tolerate a teacher's decision to give more snacks to girls than to boys because she thinks (incorrectly) that girls need more food. But when a teacher gives girls more snacks because she holds an *immoral belief* ("It's all right to be nicer to girls than boys"), almost all children judge her actions negatively (Wainryb & Ford, 1998).

• **Relation of Personal and Moral Domains** Preschoolers display a budding awareness of the personal domain, conveyed through such statements as, "I'm gonna wear *this* shirt." As children's grasp of moral imperatives and social conventions strengthens, so does their conviction that certain choices are up to the individual. Early on, children learn that parents and teachers are willing to compromise on personal issues and, at times, on social-conventional matters but not on moral concerns.

Likewise, when children and adolescents challenge adult authority, they typically do so within the personal domain (Nucci, 2001, 2005). At adolescence, as insistence that parents not intrude on the personal arena increases, disputes over personal issues occur more often. Teenagers whose parents frequently intrude into the personal domain report greater psychological stress (Hasebe, Nucci, & Nucci, 2004). In contrast, adolescents typically say that parents have a right to tell them what to do in moral and social-conventional situations and, when these spark disagreements, are less likely to challenge parental authority (Smetana & Daddis, 2002)

Notions of personal choice, in turn, enhance children's moral understanding. As early as age 6, children view freedom of speech and religion as individual rights, even if laws exist that deny those rights (Helwig, 2006). And they regard laws that discriminate against individuals—for example, laws that deny certain people access to medical care or education—as wrong and worthy of violating (Helwig & Jasiobedzka, 2001). In justifying their responses, children appeal to personal privileges and, by the end of middle childhood, to democratic ideals, such as the importance of individual rights for maintaining a fair society.

At the same time, older school-age children place limits on individual choice, depending on circumstances. While they believe that nonacademic matters (such as where to go on field trips) are best decided democratically, they regard the academic curriculum as the province of teachers, based on teachers' superior ability to make such choices (Helwig & Kim, 1999).

As they enlarge the range of issues they regard as personal, adolescents think more intently about conflicts between personal choice and community obligation—whether, and under what conditions, it is permissible to restrict speech, religion, marriage, childbearing, group membership, and other individual rights (Helwig, 1995; Wainryb, 1997). Teenagers display more subtle thinking than school-age children on such issues. For example, when asked if it is OK to exclude a child from a friendship or peer group on the basis of race or gender, fourth graders usually say exclusion is always unfair. But by tenth grade, young people, though increasingly mindful of fairness, indicate that under certain conditions—within friendship more often than peer groups, and on the basis of gender more often than race—exclusion is OK (Killen et al., 2002). In explaining, they mention the right to personal choice as well as concerns about effective group functioning. Justifying her belief that members of an all-boys music club need not let a girl in, one tenth grader said, "It's not nice . . . but it's their club." Another commented, "[The girls and the boys] probably wouldn't relate on very many things" (p. 62).

As adolescents integrate personal rights with ideal reciprocity, they demand that the protections they want for themselves extend to others. Similarly, they are increasingly mindful of the overlap between moral imperatives, social conventions, and personal choice. Eventually they realize that violating strongly held conventions in favor of asserting personal choices—showing up at a wedding in a T-shirt, talking out of turn at a student council meeting—can harm others, either by inducing distress or by undermining fair treatment. Over time, as their grasp of fairness deepens, young people realize that many social conventions have moral implications: They are vital for maintaining a just and peaceful society (Nucci, 2001). Notice how this understanding is central to Kohlberg's Stage 4, which is typically attained as adolescence draws to a close.

• **Culture and Moral, Social-Conventional, and Personal Distinctions** Children and adolescents in diverse Western and non-Western cultures use similar criteria to reason about moral, social-conventional, and personal concerns (Neff & Helwig, 2002; Nucci, 2002, 2005). For example, Chinese and Japanese young people, whose cultures place a high value on respect for authority, nevertheless say that adults have no right to interfere in their personal matters, such as how they spend their free time (Hasebe, Nucci, & Nucci, 2004; Helwig et al., 2003). A Colombian child illustrated this vehement defense of the right to personal control when asked if a teacher had the right to tell a student where to sit during circle time. In the absence of a moral reason from the teacher, the child emphatically declared, "She should be able to sit wherever she wants" (Ardila-Rey & Killen, 2001, p. 249).

Still, certain behaviors are classified differently across cultures. For example, East Indian Hindu children believe it is morally wrong to eat chicken the day after a father's death because, according to Hindu religious teachings, this will prevent the father's soul from reaching salvation. To North American children, in contrast, this practice is an arbitrary convention (Shweder, Mahapatra, & Miller, 1990). But when children are asked about acts that obviously lead to harm or violate rights—breaking promises, destroying another's property, or kicking harmless animals—cross-cultural similarity prevails (Turiel, 2006). We are reminded, once again, that justice considerations are a universal feature of moral thought.

Distributive Justice

In everyday life, children frequently experience situations involving **distributive justice**—beliefs about how to divide material goods fairly. Heated debates arise over how much weekly allowance is appropriate for siblings of different ages, who should sit where on a long car trip, and how six hungry playmates should share an eight-slice pizza. William Damon (1977, 1988) has traced children's changing concepts of distributive justice over early and middle childhood. Findings confirm—once again—more advanced reasoning in familiar contexts than Kohlberg's preconventional level suggests.

Children's ideas about distributive justice—how to divide material goods fairly—develop gradually in middle childhood. The child on the right understands that fairness should include benevolence. He shares with two younger children who do not have access to a special treat. © Mary Kate Denny/ PhotoEdit

Even 4-year-olds recognize the importance of sharing, although their reasons often seem self-serving: "I shared because if I didn't, she wouldn't play with me." In middle childhood, children express more mature notions of distributive justice, which follow a three-step sequence:

1. *Strict equality* (5 to 6 years). Children in the early school grades focus on equality in tangible outcomes. They are intent on making sure that each person gets the same amount of a treasured resource, such as money, turns in a game, or a delicious treat.
2. *Merit* (6 to 7 years). Slightly older children begin to take intangible considerations such as merit into account. They may suggest that extra rewards go to someone who has worked especially hard or otherwise performed in an exceptional way.
3. *Equity and benevolence* (8 to 9 years). Finally, children take into account participants' circumstances. They recognize that special consideration should be given to those at a disadvantage—for example, that a child who cannot produce as much or who does not get any allowance should be given more. Older children also adapt their basis of fairness to fit the situation, relying more on equality when interacting with strangers and more on benevolence when interacting with friends (McGillicuddy-De Lisi, Watkins, & Vinchur, 1994).

According to Damon (1988), the give-and-take of peer interaction makes children more sensitive to others' perspectives, and this supports their developing ideas of justice (Kruger, 1993). Advanced distributive justice reasoning, in turn, is associated with a greater willingness to help, share, and cooperate (Blotner & Bearison, 1984; McNamee & Peterson, 1986).

The research reviewed in the preceding sections reveals the richness and diversity of children's moral understanding. To fully represent the development of moral thought, researchers must examine children's responses to a wide range of problems. Consult the Milestones table on page 510 review changes in moral internalization and construction during childhood and adolescence.

Ask Yourself

Review How does an understanding of ideal reciprocity contribute to moral development? Why might Kohlberg's Stages 3 and 4 be morally mature constructions?

Apply Tam grew up in a small village culture, Lydia in a large industrial city. At age 15, Tam reasons at Kohlberg's Stage 3, Lydia at Stage 4. What factors probably account for the difference?

Connect Return to page 472 in Chapter 11, and note the impact of racial stereotypes on white fourth graders' distributive justice reasoning. How do these findings add to our understanding of contextual influences on moral judgment?

Reflect Do you favor a cognitive-developmental or a pragmatic approach to morality, or both? What research evidence and personal experiences influenced your viewpoint?

Milestones

Internalization of Moral Norms and Development of Moral Understanding

Age	Internalization of Moral Norms	Moral Understanding
2–5 years	▪ Models many morally relevant behaviors ▪ Responds with empathy-based guilt to transgressions 	▪ Tends to focus on salient features and consequences in moral judgment, such as physical damage, getting punished, or an adult's power or status ▪ Begins to show sensitivity to others' intentions in moral judgment ▪ At the end of this period, has a differentiated understanding of authority figures' legitimacy ▪ Distinguishes moral imperatives, social conventions, and matters of personal choice ▪ At the end of this period, bases distributive justice on equality
6–11 years	▪ Internalizes many norms of good conduct, including prosocial standards 	▪ Continues to emphasize superficial factors, including physical consequences and self-interest, in responses to moral dilemmas (Piaget's "heteronomous" and Kohlberg's preconventional Stages 1 and 2 morality) ▪ Gradually understands ideal reciprocity and increasingly emphasizes people's intentions and expectations in moral judgment (Piaget's autonomous and Kohlberg's "conventional" Stage 3 morality) ▪ Clarifies and coordinates moral imperatives, social conventions, and matters of personal choice and, in judging violations, considers more variables—purpose of the rule, people's intentions, and context ▪ Includes merit and, eventually, equity and benevolence in distributive justice reasoning
12 years–adulthood		▪ Increasingly emphasizes ideal reciprocity as the basis for interpersonal relationships and societal laws (Kohlberg's "conventional" Stages 3 and 4 morality) ▪ Highly reflective moral judgments that grapple with existential issues appear among a few individuals, usually with advanced education (Kohlberg's "postconventional" Stages 5 and 6) ▪ Relationship between moral reasoning and behavior strengthens

Note: These milestones represent overall age trends. Individual differences exist in the precise age at which each milestone is attained.

Photos: (top) © Gabe Palmer/Alamy Images; (middle) © Mary Kate Denny/PhotoEdit; (bottom) © Steve Skjold/Alamy Images

Development of Morally Relevant Self-Control

The study of moral judgment tells us what people think they should do, and why, when faced with a moral problem. But people's good intentions often fall short. Whether children and adults act in accord with their beliefs depends in part on characteristics we call willpower, firm resolve, or, more simply, self-control. In Chapter 10, we considered individual differences in the broad temperamental dimension of *effortful control*—the extent to which children can manage their reactivity. Here we focus specifically on self-control in the moral domain: inhibiting urges to act in ways that violate moral standards, sometimes called *resistance to temptation.* Earlier in this book we noted that verbal guidance in managing emotion, inductive discipline, and modeling promote self-controlled behavior in children. But these practices become effective only when children have the ability to resist temptation. When and how does this capacity develop?

Toddlerhood

The beginnings of self-control are supported by achievements of the second year, discussed in earlier chapters. To behave in a self-controlled fashion, children must have some ability to think of themselves as separate, autonomous beings who can direct their own actions. And they must have the representational, memory, and inhibitory skills to recall a caregiver's directive and apply it to their own behavior (Rothbart & Bates, 2006).

As these capacities emerge between 12 and 18 months, the first glimmerings of self-control appear in the form of **compliance.** Toddlers show clear awareness of caregivers' wishes and expectations and can obey simple requests and commands. But at first, self-control depends heavily on caregiver support. According to Vygotsky (1934/1986), children cannot guide their own behavior until they have integrated standards represented in adult–child dialogues into their own self-directed speech (see Chapter 6). Compliance quickly leads to toddlers' first consciencelike verbalizations—for example, correcting the self by saying, "No, can't" before touching a delicate object or jumping on the sofa.

Researchers often study self-control by giving children tasks that, like the situations just mentioned, require **delay of gratification**—waiting for an appropriate time and place to engage in a tempting act. Between ages 1½ and 3, children show an increasing capacity to wait before eating a treat, opening a present, or playing with a toy (Vaughn, Kopp, & Krakow, 1984). Children who are advanced in development of attention and language tend to be better at delaying gratification—findings that help explain why girls are typically more self-controlled than boys (Else-Quest et al., 2006).

Like effortful control in general, young children's capacity to delay gratification is influenced by both biologically based temperament and quality of caregiving (Kochanska & Aksan, 2006; Kochanska & Knaack, 2003). Inhibited children find it easier to wait than angry, irritable children do. But toddlers who experience parental warmth and gentle encouragement are more likely to be cooperative and to resist temptation. Such parenting—which encourages and models patient, nonimpulsive behavior—is particularly important for temperamentally reactive babies. In one study, anger-prone 7-month-olds with gentle, responsive mothers became eagerly compliant 15-month-olds, whereas angry infants with insensitive mothers developed into uncooperative toddlers (Kochanska, Aksan, & Carlson, 2005). As self-control improves, parents gradually increase the range of rules they expect toddlers to follow, from safety and respect for property and people to family routines, manners, and simple chores (Gralinski & Kopp, 1993).

Childhood and Adolescence

Although the capacity for self-control is in place by the third year, it is not complete. Cognitive development—in particular, gains in attention and mental representation—enables children to use a variety of effective self-instructional strategies. As a result, resistance to temptation improves during childhood and adolescence.

How will this 4-year-old resist temptation? If he focuses on the sweetness of the strawberries, he is likely to give in quickly. If he diverts his attention by covering his eyes, engaging in another activity, or imagining the strawberries to be inedible objects, he will be able to wait longer. © José Luis Pelaez/Getty Images/Iconica

• **Strategies for Resisting Temptation** Walter Mischel has studied what children think and say to themselves that promotes resistance to temptation. In several studies, preschoolers were shown two rewards: a highly desirable one that they would have to wait for and a less desirable one that they could have right away (Mischel, 1996; Mischel & Ayduck, 2004). The most self-controlled preschoolers used any technique they could to divert their attention from the desired objects: covering their eyes, singing, even trying to sleep!

In everyday situations, preschoolers find it difficult to keep their minds off tempting activities and objects for long. When their thoughts turn to a prohibited goal, the way they mentally represent it has much to do with their success at self-control. Teaching preschoolers to transform the stimulus in ways that de-emphasize its arousing qualities—an approach that helps children shift attention

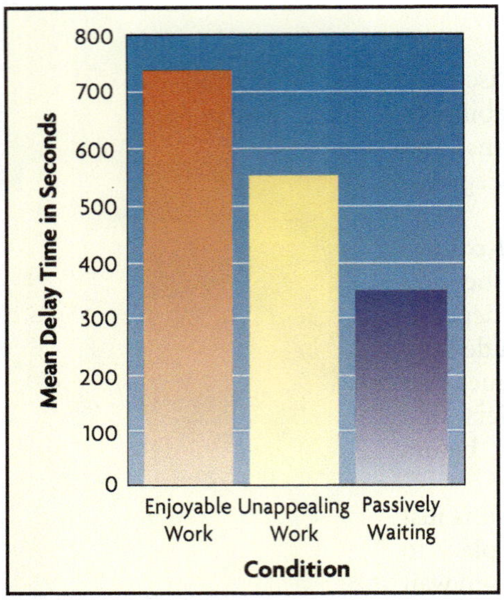

Figure 12.5 **Influence of engaging in a work task on preschoolers' delay of gratification.** Availability of enjoyable work (feeding a "hungry" Baby Bird marbles) greatly increased children's capacity to wait. When the work was unappealing (sorting marbles), preschoolers' attention often strayed to the enticing reward; hence, they were not as successful at waiting. (Adapted from Peake, Hebl, & Mischel, 2002.)

and inhibit emotional reactivity—promotes delay of gratification. In one study, preschoolers who were told to think about marshmallows as "white and puffy clouds" waited much longer before eating a marshmallow reward than those who focused on marshmallows' "sweet and chewy properties" (Mischel & Baker, 1975).

Having something interesting to do while waiting also helps preschoolers divert attention from rewards and resist temptation. In a modified delay-of-gratification task in which 3- to 5-year-olds could engage in enjoyable work (feeding marbles to a colorfully decorated, "hungry" Baby Bird), the amount of time children waited for a nearby, attractive reward more than doubled over simply waiting passively (see Figure 12.5). But when the work was unappealing (sorting marbles), preschoolers were less successful. They often looked up from the boring task, which increased the likelihood that the enticing reward would capture their attention (Peake, Hebl, & Mischel, 2002).

During the school years, children become better at devising their own strategies for resisting temptation. By this time, self-control has become a flexible capacity for **moral self-regulation**—the ability to monitor one's own conduct, constantly adjusting it as circumstances present opportunities to violate inner standards (Kopp & Wyer, 1994; Thompson, Meyer, & McGinley, 2006).

• **Knowledge of Strategies** Recall from Chapter 7 that metacognitive knowledge, or awareness of strategies, contributes to self-regulation. When asked about situational conditions and self-instructions likely to help delay gratification, school-age children suggested a broader array of arousal-reducing strategies with age. But not until the late elementary school years did they mention techniques involving transformations of rewards or their own arousal states. For example, one 11-year-old proposed saying, "The marshmallows are filled with an evil spell." Another said he would tell himself, "I hate marshmallows; I can't stand them. But when the grown-up gets back, I'll tell myself 'I love marshmallows' and eat it" (Mischel & Mischel, 1983, p. 609).

Perhaps awareness of transforming ideation appears late in development because it requires the hypothetical reasoning powers of formal operational thought. But once this advanced metacognitive understanding emerges, it greatly facilitates moral self-regulation (Rodriguez, Mischel, & Shoda, 1989).

Table 12.2 Characteristics of "Hot" and "Cool" Processing Systems in the Development of Self-Control

Hot System	Cool System
Emotional	Cognitive
"Go"	"Know"
Simple	Complex
Reflexive	Reflective
Fast	Slow
Develops early	Develops later
Accentuated by stress	Attenuated by stress
Stimulus control	Self-control

Source: J. Metcalf & W. Mischel, 1999, "A Hot/Cool-System Analysis of Delay of Gratification: Dynamics of Willpower," *Psychological Review,* 106, p. 4. Copyright © 2004 by the American Psychological Association. Reprinted with permission of the American Psychological Association.

Individual Differences

Mischel and his collaborators found that toddlers who could divert their attention and wait patiently while briefly separated from their mother tended to perform better during a delay-of-gratification task at age 5 (Sethi et al., 2000). And in a series of studies, 4-year-olds who were better at delaying gratification were especially adept as adolescents in applying metacognitive skills to their behavior and in inhibiting impulsive responding. In addition, their parents saw them as more responsive to reason, as better at concentrating and planning ahead, and as coping with stress more maturely. When applying to college, those who had been self-controlled preschoolers scored higher on the Scholastic Assessment Test (SAT), although they were no more intelligent than other individuals (Eigsti et al. 2006; Mischel, Shoda, & Peake, 1988; Shoda, Mischel, & Peake, 1990). Furthermore, children who are better at delaying gratification can wait long enough to interpret social cues accurately, which supports effective social problem solving and positive peer relations (Gronau & Waas, 1997).

Mischel proposes that the interaction of two processing systems—*hot* and *cool*—governs the development of self-control and accounts for individual differences (Metcalfe & Mischel, 1999; Mischel & Ayduk, 2004). Table 12.2 displays the characteristics of each. With age,

Milestones

Development of Morally Relevant Self-Control and Aggression

Age	Self-Control	Aggression
1½–5 years	▪ Compliance and delay of gratification emerge and improve. ▪ Benefits from adult-provided strategies for delaying gratification.	▪ Proactive, or instrumental, aggression declines, while reactive (hostile aggression) increases. ▪ Physical aggression declines, while verbal aggression increases. ▪ Relational aggression appears.
6–11 years	▪ Generates an increasing variety of strategies for delaying gratification. ▪ Displays a flexible capacity for moral self-regulation.	▪ Reactive, or hostile, aggression (largely verbal and relational) continues to increase. ▪ Girls' relational aggression becomes increasingly indirect.
12–20 years	▪ Continues to gain in moral self-regulation.	▪ Teacher- and peer-reported aggression declines. ▪ Delinquency rises, then declines.

Note: These milestones represent overall age trends. Individual differences exist in the precise age at which each milestone is attained.

Photos: (left) © STOCK IMAGE/PIXLAND/Alamy; (right) David L. Moore—Lifestyle/Alamy

the emotional, reactive hot system is increasingly subordinated to the cognitive, reflective cool system, as a result of improved functioning of the frontal lobes of the cerebral cortex.

Throughout childhood and adolescence, temperament and parenting jointly influence the extent to which cool-system representations gain control over hot-system reactivity. **TAKE A MOMENT...** Describe evidence from this and previous chapters indicating that power-assertive, inconsistent discipline—especially with temperamentally vulnerable children—results in a poorly functioning cool system, enabling the hot system to prevail. Such children display hostile, unruly behavior and serious deficits in moral conduct. Refer to the Milestones table above for a summary of changes in self-control and aggression—our next topic.

The Other Side of Self-Control: Development of Aggression

Beginning in late infancy, all children display aggression from time to time. As opportunities to interact with siblings and peers increase, aggressive outbursts occur more often (Dodge, Coie, & Lynam, 2006; Tremblay, 2004). Although at times aggression serves prosocial ends (for example, stopping a victimizer from harming others), most human aggressive acts are clearly antisocial.

As early as the preschool years, some children show abnormally high rates of hostility, assaulting others verbally and physically with little or no provocation. If allowed to continue, their belligerent behavior can lead to lasting delays in moral development, deficits in self-control, and ultimately an antisocial lifestyle. To understand this process, let's see how aggression develops during childhood and adolescence.

This preschool boy displays proactive aggression as he grabs his classmate's toy. Proactive aggression declines with age as children's capacity to delay gratification improves. © Ellen Senisi/The Image Works

Emergence of Aggression

In the second half of the first year, infants develop the cognitive capacity to identify sources of anger and frustration and the motor skills to lash out at them (see Chapter 10). By the second year, two general types of aggression emerge. Initially, the most common is **proactive** (or *instrumental*) **aggression,** in which children act to fulfill a need or desire—obtain an object, privilege, space, or social reward, such as adult attention or (in older children) peer admiration—and unemotionally attack a person to achieve their goal. The other type, **reactive** (or *hostile*) **aggression,** is an angry, defensive response to a provocation or a blocked goal and is meant to hurt another person (Dodge, Coie, & Lynam, 2006; Little et al., 2003).

Naturalistic observations of children in classrooms or at play reveal low positive correlations between proactive and reactive aggression (Polman et al., 2007). But when aggression is assessed using parent or teacher reports, proactive and reactive aggression are strongly correlated (Vitaro, Brendgen, & Tremblay, 2002).Thus, the extent to which the two types of aggression represent distinct styles is unclear. At least some, and perhaps many, aggressive children engage in both, and most studies do not distinguish between them.

Proactive and reactive aggression come in three forms, which are the focus of the majority of research:

- **Physical aggression** harms others through physical injury—pushing, hitting, kicking, or punching others, or destroying another's property.
- **Verbal aggression** harms others through threats of physical aggression, name-calling, or hostile teasing.
- **Relational aggression** damages another's peer relationships through social exclusion, malicious gossip, or friendship manipulation.

Although verbal aggression is always direct, physical and relational aggression can be either *direct* or *indirect.* For example, hitting injures a person directly, whereas destroying property indirectly inflicts physical harm. Similarly, saying, "Do what I say, or I won't be your friend," conveys relational aggression directly, while spreading rumors, refusing to talk to a peer, or manipulating friendships by saying behind someone's back, "Don't play with her; she's a nerd," does so indirectly.

Aggression in Early and Middle Childhood

Between ages 3 and 6, physical aggression decreases, whereas verbal aggression increases (Alink et al., 2006; Tremblay et al., 1999). Rapid language development contributes to this change, but it is also due to adults' and peers' strong negative reactions to physical attacks. Furthermore, proactive aggression declines as preschoolers' improved capacity to delay gratification enables them to resist grabbing others' possessions. But reactive aggression in verbal and relational forms tends to rise over early and middle childhood (Côté et al., 2007; Tremblay, 2000). Older children are better able to detect malicious intentions and, as a result, more often respond in hostile ways.

By age 17 months, boys are considerably more physically aggressive than girls—a difference found throughout childhood in many cultures (Baillargeon et al., 2007; Broidy et al., 2003; Dodge, Coie, & Lynam, 2006). As we will see in Chapter 13, when we consider sex differences in aggression in greater detail, biological factors—in particular, the effects of male sex hormones (androgens) and temperamental traits on which boys and girls differ—contribute to the early greater prevalence of physical attacks by boys. Gender-role conformity is also a factor. As soon as 2-year-olds become dimly aware of gender stereotypes—that males and females are expected to behave differently—physical aggression drops off more sharply for girls than for boys (Fagot & Leinbach, 1989).

Although girls have a reputation for being verbally and relationally more aggressive than boys, Chapter 13 will reveal that in most studies sex differences are small (Crick et al., 2004,

2006; Crick, Ostrov, & Werner, 2006). Beginning in the preschool years, girls concentrate most of their aggressive acts in the relational category. Boys inflict harm in more variable ways and, therefore, display overall rates of aggression that are much higher than girls'. At the same time, girls more often use indirect relational tactics that—in disrupting intimate bonds especially important to girls—can be particularly mean. In contrast to physical attacks, which are usually brief, acts of indirect relational aggression may extend for hours, weeks, or even months (Nelson, Robinson, & Hart, 2005; Underwood, 2003). In one instance, a second-grade girl formed a "pretty-girls club" at school and—for nearly an entire school year—convinced its members to exclude several classmates by saying they were "ugly and smelly." At least in childhood, then, it may not be meaningful to describe one sex as more aggressive than the other.

Aggression and Delinquency in Adolescence

Although most young people decline in teacher- and peer-reported aggression in adolescence, the teenage years are accompanied by a rise in delinquent acts. Although North American youth crime has declined since the mid-1990s, U.S. and Canadian 12- to 17-year-olds account for a substantial proportion of police arrests—16 to 17 percent, although they constitute only 8 percent of the population in each nation (Statistics Canada, 2007b; U.S. Department of Justice, 2007). When asked directly and confidentially about lawbreaking, almost all teenagers admit to having committed some sort of offense—usually a minor crime, such as petty stealing or disorderly conduct (Flannery et al., 2003).

Both police arrests and self-reports show that delinquency rises over the early teenage years, remains high during middle adolescence, then declines (Farrington, 2004; U.S. Department of Justice, 2007). What accounts for this trend? Among young teenagers, antisocial behavior increases as a result of desire for peer approval. Over time, peers become less influential, decision making and moral reasoning improve, and young people enter social contexts (such as higher education, work, career, and marriage) that are less conducive to lawbreaking.

For most adolescents, a brush with the law does not forecast long-term antisocial behavior. But repeated arrests are cause for concern. Teenagers are responsible for 13 percent of violent crimes in the United States and for 15 percent in Canada (Statistics Canada, 2007b; U.S. Department of Justice, 2007). A small percentage become recurrent offenders, who commit most of these crimes, and some enter a life of crime.

In adolescence, the gender gap in physical aggression widens (Chesney-Lind, 2001). Although girls account for about one in five adolescent arrests for violent crimes—a larger proportion than a decade ago—their offenses are largely limited to simple assault (such as pushing), the least serious category. Once labeled status offenses (noncriminal behavior), today these acts are more likely to lead to arrests, especially in physical exchanges with parents, who may report the youth's behavior to the police (Chesney-Lind & Belknap, 2004). Serious violent crime, however, continues to be mostly the domain of boys (Dahlberg & Simon, 2006). Although SES and ethnicity are strong predictors of arrests, they are only mildly related to teenagers' self-reports of antisocial acts. The difference is due to the tendency to arrest, charge, and punish low-SES ethnic minority youths more often than their higher-SES white and Asian counterparts (Farrington, 2004; U.S. Department of Justice, 2007).

Delinquency rises during the early teenage years and remains high during middle adolescence. Although most of the time it involves petty stealing and disorderly conduct, a small percentage of young people engage in repeated, serious offenses and are at risk for a life of crime.
© ACE STOCK LIMITED/Alamy

Stability of Aggression

Children high in either physical or relational aggression relative to their agemates tend to remain so over time (Côté et al., 2007; Vaillancourt et al., 2003). Following more than 1,000 Canadian, New Zealand, and U.S. boys from ages 6 to 15, researchers identified four main patterns of change,

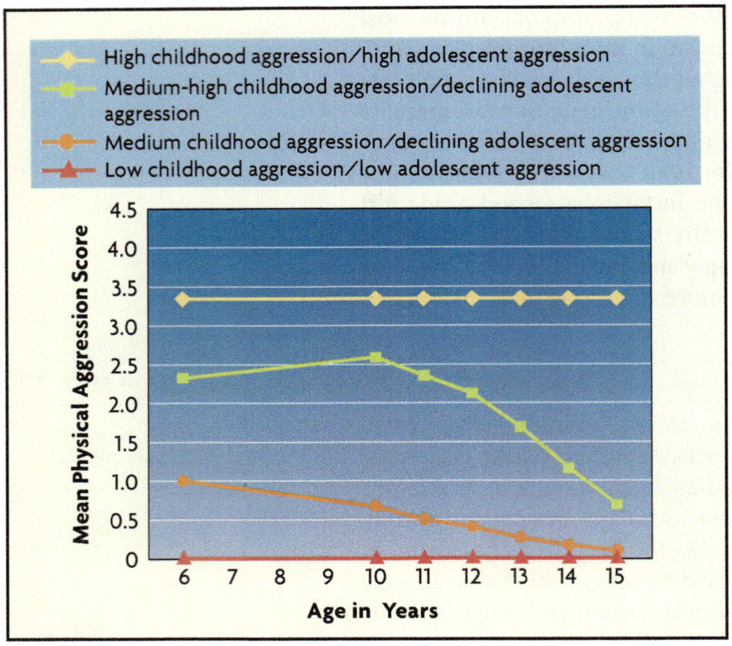

Figure 12.6 **Longitudinal trends in boys' physical aggression from 6 to 15 years of age.** The patterns are based on a sample of more than 1,000 boys from Canada, New Zealand, and the United States. Boys with high-level childhood physical aggression were especially likely to sustain their aggressive style. In contrast, boys with medium-high and medium levels of aggression usually declined in aggressive responding. And boys who rarely displayed aggression in childhood typically remained nonaggressive. (From R. E. Tremblay, 2000, "The Development of Aggressive Behaviour During Childhood: What Have We Learned in the Past Century?," *International Journal of Behavioral Development,* 24, p. 136. Reprinted by permission of Sage Publications Ltd.)

shown in Figure 12.6. Kindergarten boys high in physical aggression (4 percent of the sample) were especially likely to move to high-level adolescent aggression, becoming involved in violent delinquency. In contrast, kindergarten boys who were moderately physically aggressive usually declined in aggression over time. And boys who rarely physically aggressed in early childhood typically remained nonaggressive. However, a small number of boys high in oppositional behavior (such as disobedience and inconsiderateness) but not in physical aggression were prone to less violent forms of adolescent delinquency (such as theft) (Brame, Nagin, & Tremblay, 2001; Nagin & Tremblay, 1999).

Girls who consistently engage in disruptive, disobedient behavior in childhood are also more likely to have continuing conduct problems (Coté et al., 2001). And for both boys and girls, persistently high physical or relational aggression predicts later internalizing and externalizing difficulties and social skills deficits, including loneliness, anxiety, depression, poor-quality friendships, and antisocial activity (Campbell et al., 2006; Crick, Ostrov, & Werner, 2006).

As the Biology and Environment box on pages 518–519 confirms, aggressive behavior that emerges in childhood and persists is far more likely to translate into long-term adjustment difficulties than aggression that first appears in adolescence. Although some children—especially those who are irritable, fearless, impulsive, and overactive—are at risk for aggression, whether or not they become aggressive largely depends on child-rearing conditions. Most 2-year-olds who are high in angry reactivity respond with empathy to others' distress—a powerful deterrent to aggressive acts (Gill & Calkins, 2003). But by the end of the preschool years, aggression and empathy are negatively related (Hastings et al., 2000). Strife-ridden families, poor parenting practices, aggressive peers, and televised violence strongly predict both antisocial activity and reduced sensitivity to others' suffering. In this chapter, we focus on family and peer influences, reserving TV influences for Chapter 15. We will also see that community and cultural influences can heighten or reduce children's risk of sustaining a hostile interpersonal style.

The Family as Training Ground for Aggressive Behavior

The same parenting behaviors that undermine moral internalization and self-control—love withdrawal, power assertion, negative comments and emotions, physical punishment, and inconsistent discipline—are linked to aggression from early childhood through adolescence in diverse cultures, with most of these practices predicting both physical and relational forms (Bradford et al., 2003; Casas et al., 2006; Côté et al., 2007; Nelson & Crick, 2002; Nelson et al., 2006a; Rubin et al., 2003; Yang et al., 2004).

Home observations of aggressive children reveal that anger and punitiveness quickly create a conflict-ridden family atmosphere and an "out-of-control" child. As Figure 12.7 shows, the pattern begins with forceful discipline, which occurs more often with stressful life experiences (such as economic hardship or an unhappy marriage), a parent with an unstable personality, or a temperamentally difficult child (Dodge, Coie, & Lynam, 2006). Typically, the parent threatens, criticizes, and punishes, and the child whines, yells, and refuses until the parent gives in. At the end of each exchange, both parent and child get relief from stopping the other's unpleasant behavior, so the behaviors repeat and escalate (Patterson, 1995, 1997).

As these cycles become more frequent, they generate anxiety and irritability among other family members, who soon join in the hostile interactions. Compared with siblings in typical families, preschool siblings who have critical, punitive parents are more aggressive toward one another. Physically, verbally, and relationally destructive sibling conflict, in turn, quickly spreads to peer relationships, contributing to poor impulse control and antisocial behavior by the early school years (Garcia et al., 2000; Ostrov, Crick, & Stauffacher, 2006).

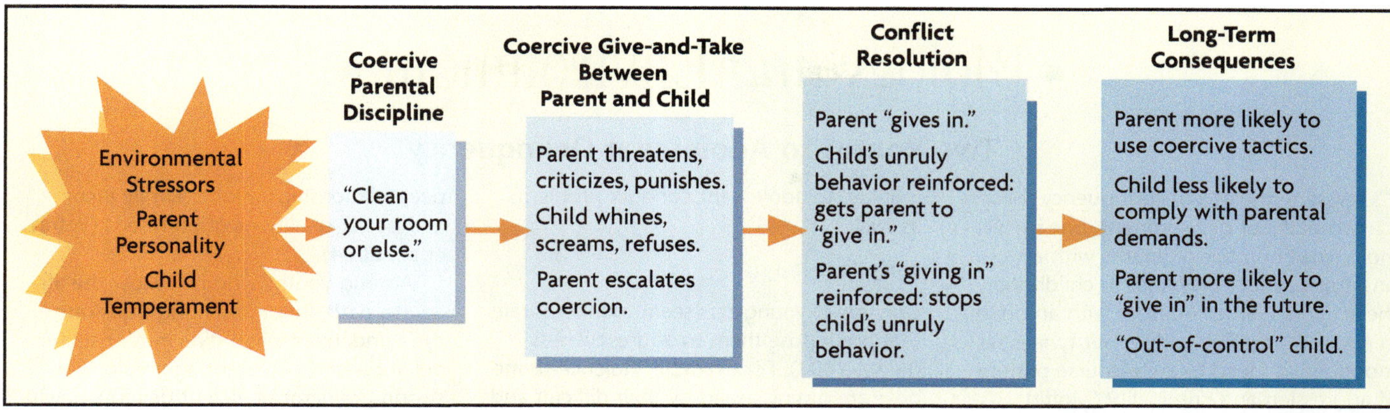

Figure 12.7 Coercive interaction pattern that promotes and sustains aggression between family members.

Boys are more likely than girls to be targets of harsh, inconsistent discipline because they are more active and impulsive and therefore harder to control. When children who are extreme in these characteristics are exposed to emotionally negative, inept parenting, their capacity for emotional self-regulation is disrupted, and they lash out when disappointed or frustrated (Chang et al., 2003; NICHD Early Child Care Research Network, 2004c). As a result, aggression persists (refer again to the Biology and Environment box).

Besides fostering aggression directly, parents can encourage it indirectly, through poor supervision of children (Vitaro, Brendgen, & Tremblay, 2000). Unfortunately, children from conflict-ridden homes who already display serious antisocial tendencies are most likely to experience inadequate parental monitoring. As a result, few if any limits are placed on out-of-home activities and association with antisocial friends, who encourage their hostile style of responding.

Social-Cognitive Deficits and Distortions

Children who are products of the family processes just described soon acquire a violent and callous view of the social world. Those who are high in reactive aggression often see hostile intent where it does not exist—in situations where a peer's intentions are unclear, where harm is accidental, and even where a peer is trying to be helpful (Dodge & Coie, 1987; Lochman & Dodge, 1998; Orobio de Castro et al., 2002). When such children feel threatened (for example, a researcher tells them that a peer they will work with is in a bad mood and might pick a fight), they are especially likely to interpret accidental mishaps as hostile (Williams et al., 2003). As a result, they make many unprovoked attacks, which trigger aggressive retaliations.

High proactive aggression is linked to different social-cognitive deficits. Compared with their nonaggressive agemates, these children believe there are more benefits and fewer costs for engaging in destructive acts (Dodge et al., 1997). And they are more likely to think that aggression "works," producing tangible rewards and reducing others' unpleasant behaviors (Goldstein & Tisak, 2004; Perry, Perry, & Rasmussen, 1986). When tempted to aggress, they are more concerned about achieving control and less concerned about causing suffering or being disliked by peers (Boldizar, Perry, & Perry, 1989).

Another biased social-cognitive attribute of proactively aggressive children is overly high self-esteem, even in the face of academic and social failings. When their arrogant, cocky behavior prompts others to challenge their inflated but vulnerable self-image, they lash out angrily at others (Baumeister, Smart, & Boden, 1996; Costello & Dunaway, 2003; Orobio de Castro et al., 2007). Furthermore, aggressive young people may neutralize their basic biological capacity for empathy by using such cognitive distortion techniques as blaming their victims. As a result, they retain a positive self-evaluation after behaving aggressively (Liau, Barriga, & Gibbs, 1998; McCrady et al., 2008). Looking back on his burglaries, one delinquent reflected, "If I started feeling bad, I'd say to myself, 'Tough rocks for him. He should have had his house locked better and the alarm on'" (Samenow, 1984, p. 115).

Antisocial adolescents are delayed in maturity of moral judgment, and they tend to view aggression as within the social conventional and personal domains rather than the moral

Biology *and* Environment

Two Routes to Adolescent Delinquency

Persistent adolescent delinquency follows two paths of development, one involving a small number of youths with an onset of conduct problems in childhood, the second a larger number with an onset in adolescence. The early-onset type is far more likely to lead to a life-course pattern of aggression and criminality (Moffitt, 2006). In contrast, the late-onset type usually does not persist beyond the transition to early adulthood.

Both childhood-onset and adolescent-onset youths engage in serious offenses; associate with deviant peers; participate in substance abuse, unsafe sex, and dangerous driving; and spend time in correctional facilities. Why does antisocial activity more often persist and escalate into violence in the first group than in the second? Longitudinal studies yield similar answers to this question. So far, the findings are clearest for boys, who are the focus of most research. But several investigations report that girls who were physically aggressive in childhood are also at risk for later problems—occasionally violent delinquency but more often other norm-violating behaviors and psychological disorders (Broidy et al., 2003; Chamberlain, 2003). And early relational aggression is linked to adolescent conduct problems as well.

Early-Onset Type

Early-onset youngsters seem to inherit traits that predispose them to aggressiveness (Pettit, 2004). For example, violence-prone boys are distinguished by their difficult and fearless temperamental styles; they are emotionally negative, restless, willful, and physically aggressive as early as age 2. They also show subtle deficits in cognitive functioning that seem to contribute to disruptions in development of language, memory, and cognitive and emotional self-regulation (Moffitt, 2006; Shaw et al., 2003). Some have attention-deficit hyperactivity disorder (ADHD), which compounds their learning and self-control problems (see Chapter 7, pages 290–291).

Yet these biological risks are not sufficient to sustain antisocial behavior: Most early-onset boys decline in aggression over time and do not display serious delinquency followed by adult criminality. Those who avoid the life-course path benefit from better reading achievement in first grade and an interrelated set of protective factors in middle school—parental monitoring, avoidance of deviant peer relationships, higher family income, and better-quality neighborhoods (Petras et al., 2004).

Among youths who do follow the life-course path, inept parenting transforms their undercontrolled style into hostility, defiance, and persistent aggression—a strong predictor of violent delinquency in adolescence (Brame, Nagin, & Tremblay, 2001; Broidy et al., 2003). As they fail academically and are rejected by peers, they befriend other deviant youths, who facilitate one another's violent behavior while relieving loneliness (see Figure 12.8) (Lacourse et al., 2003). Early-onset teenagers' limited cognitive and social skills result in high rates of school dropout and unemployment, contributing further to their antisocial involvements. Often these boys experience their first arrest before age 14, a good indicator that they will be chronic offenders by age 18 (Patterson & Yoerger, 2002).

Preschoolers high in relational aggression also tend to be hyperactive and frequently in conflict with peers and adults (Willoughby, Kupersmidt, & Bryant, 2001). As these behaviors trigger peer rejection, relationally aggressive girls befriend other girls high in relational hostility, and their

domain (Harvey, Fletcher, & French, 2001; Tisak, Tisak, & Goldstein, 2006). They are also low in moral self-relevance. In a study of 16- to 19-year-olds, those with immature moral reasoning and low moral self-relevance were prone to self-serving cognitive distortions (such as blaming the victim or minimizing the harm done), which predicted high levels of acting-out behavior. Compared with boys, girls scored higher in moral self-relevance and lower in self-serving cognitive distortions—likely contributors to their lower rates of antisocial activity (Barriga et al., 2001).

Finally, although aggressive children are typically impaired in social cognition and social skills, some—called *bistrategic controllers*—combine proactively aggressive and positive social tactics to access desirable resources, such as the best role in a school activity or the attentions of peers. Bistrategic controllers view themselves as both aggressive and socially skilled, and their classmates agree. They are also adept at perspective taking and social problem solving and are knowledgeable about moral norms—social-cognitive strengths that they use to manipulate others to get what they want while concealing their aggression from adults (Hawley, 2003a, 2003b). Because they maneuver themselves into positions of influence, bistrategic controllers attract considerable peer admiration. Agemates rate friendships with them as among the highest in intimacy, companionship, and fun but also as highly physically and relationally aggressive (Hawley, Little, & Card, 2007). Little is known about the long-term development of these children, who combine selfish motives with impressive social savvy. Although they appear well adjusted, their morality may be limited to helping others only when motivated by self-interest.

relational aggression rises (Werner & Crick, 2004). Adolescents high in relational aggression are often angry, vengeful, and defiant of adult rules. Among teenagers who combine physical and relational hostility, these oppositional reactions intensify, increasing the likelihood of serious antisocial activity (Harachi et al., 2006; Prinstein, Boergers, & Vernberg, 2001).

Late-Onset Type

Other youths first display antisocial behavior around the time of puberty, gradually increasing their involvement. Their conduct problems arise from the peer context of early adolescence, not from biological deficits and a history of unfavorable development. For some, quality of parenting may decline for a time, perhaps as a result of family stresses or the challenges of disciplining an unruly teenager (Moffitt, 2006). But when age brings gratifying adult privileges, these youths draw on prosocial skills mastered before adolescence and abandon their antisocial ways.

A few late-onset youths do continue to engage in antisocial acts. The seriousness of their adolescent offenses seems to trap them in situations that close off opportunities for responsible behavior. Being employed or in school and forming positive, close relationships predict an end to criminal offending by age 20 to 25 (Clingempeel & Henggeler, 2003; Stouthamer-Loeber et al., 2004). In contrast, the longer antisocial young people spend in prison, the more likely they are to sustain a life of crime.

These findings suggest a need for a fresh look at policies aimed at stopping youth crime. Keeping youth offenders locked up for many years disrupts their vocational lives and access to social support during a crucial period of development, condemning them to a bleak future.

Figure 12.8 **Path to chronic delinquency for adolescents with childhood-onset antisocial behavior.** Difficult temperament and cognitive deficits characterize many of these youths in early childhood; some have attention-deficit hyperactivity disorder. Inept parenting transforms biologically based self-control difficulties into hostility and defiance.

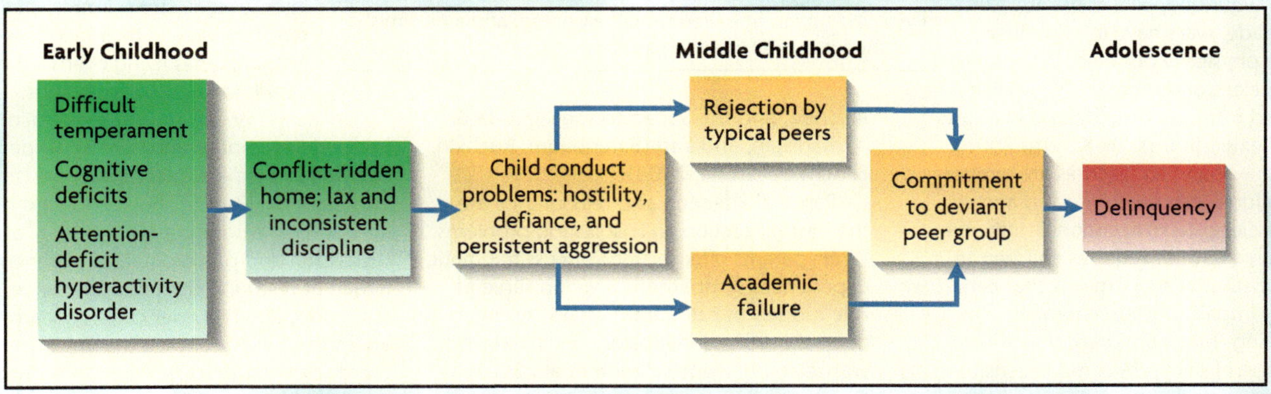

Community and Cultural Influences

Young people's tendency to engage in destructive, injurious behavior increases under certain environmental conditions. In a tense, competitive peer-group atmosphere, hostility is more likely (DeRosier et al., 1994). These group characteristics are more common in poverty-stricken neighborhoods with a wide range of stressors, including poor-quality schools, limited recreational and employment opportunities, and high adult criminality (Kroneman, Loeber, & Hipwell, 2004).

Such neighborhoods predict aggression beyond family influences (Farrington & Loeber, 2000). Children and adolescents have easy access to deviant peers, drugs, and (in the United States) firearms, all of which are linked to violence. And youths are especially likely to be recruited into antisocial gangs, whose members commit the vast majority of violent delinquent acts (Thornberry & Krohn, 2001). Furthermore, schools in these locales typically fail to meet students' developmental needs (Flannery et al., 2003). Large classes, weak instruction, and rigid rules are associated with higher rates of lawbreaking, even after other influences are controlled.

Ethnic and political prejudices further magnify the risk of angry, combative responses. In inner-city ghettos and in war-torn areas of the world, large numbers of children live in the midst of constant danger, chaos, and deprivation. As the Cultural Influences box on page 520 reveals, these youngsters are at risk for severe emotional stress, deficits in moral reasoning, and behavior problems.

Cultural Influences

Impact of Ethnic and Political Violence on Children

Today, half of all casualties of worldwide conflict are children. Around the world, many children live with armed conflict, terrorism, and other acts of violence stemming from ethnic and political tensions. Some children may participate in fighting, either because they are forced or because they want to please adults. Others are kidnapped, assaulted, and tortured. Those who are bystanders often come under direct fire and may be killed or physically maimed. And many watch in horror as family members, friends, and neighbors flee, are wounded, or die. In the past decade, wars have left 6 million children physically disabled, 20 million homeless, and more than 1 million separated from parents (Ursano & Shaw, 2007; Wexler, Branski, & Kerem, 2006).

An Iraqi child runs past burning tires following a terrorist attack in Baghdad. Because of exposure to chronic danger, she is at risk for severe and lasting problems, including desensitization to violence, terrifying memories, impaired moral reasoning, and a pessimistic view of the future. AP Images/Karim Kadim

When war and social crises are temporary, most children can be comforted and do not show long-term emotional difficulties. But chronic danger requires children to make substantial adjustments that can seriously impair their psychological functioning. Many children of war lose their sense of safety, become desensitized to violence, are haunted by terrifying memories, struggle with moral reasoning, and adopt a pessimistic view of the future. Anxiety and depression increase, as do aggression and antisocial behavior (Joshi et al., 2006; Klingman, 2006). These outcomes appear to be culturally universal, appearing among children from every war zone studied—from Bosnia, Angola, Rwanda, and the Sudan to the West Bank, Afghanistan, and Iraq (Barenbaum, Ruchkin, & Schwab-Stone, 2004).

Parental affection and reassurance are the best protection against lasting problems. When parents offer security, discuss traumatic experiences sympathetically, and serve as role models of calm emotional strength, most children can withstand even extreme war-related violence (Smith et al., 2001). Children who are separated from parents must rely on help from their communities. Orphans in Eritrea who were placed in residential settings where they could form a close emotional tie with an adult showed less emotional stress five years later than orphans placed in impersonal settings (Wolff & Fesseha, 1999). Education and recreation programs are powerful safeguards, too, providing children with consistency in their lives along with teacher and peer supports.

With the September 11, 2001, terrorist attacks on the World Trade Center and the Pentagon, some U.S. children experienced extreme wartime violence firsthand. Children in Public School 31 in Brooklyn, New York, for example, watched through classroom windows as the planes struck the towers and were engulfed in flames and as the towers crumbled. Many worried about the safety of family members, and some lost them. In the aftermath, most expressed intense fears—for example, that terrorists were in their neighborhood or that planes flying overhead might smash into nearby buildings.

Unlike many war-traumatized children in the developing world, P.S. 31 students received immediate intervention—a "trauma curriculum" in which they expressed their emotions through writing, drawing, and discussion and participated in experiences aimed at restoring trust and tolerance (Lagnado, 2001). Older children learned about the feelings of their Muslim classmates, the dire condition of children in Afghanistan, and ways to help victims as a means of overcoming a sense of helplessness.

When wartime drains families and communities of resources, international organizations must step in and help children. Efforts to preserve children's physical, psychological, and educational well-being may be the best way to stop transmission of violence to the next generation.

Helping Children and Parents Control Aggression

Treatment for aggressive children must break the cycle of hostilities between family members and promote effective ways of relating to others. Interventions with preschool and school-age children have been most successful. Once antisocial patterns persist into adolescence, so many factors act to sustain them that treatment is far more difficult.

• **Coaching, Modeling, and Reinforcing Alternative Behaviors** Parent training programs based on social learning theory have been devised to interrupt destructive family interaction. A therapist observes inept parenting behaviors, models alternatives, and has parents practice them. Parents learn not to give in to an acting-out child and not to escalate forceful attempts to control misbehavior. In addition, they are taught to pair commands with reasons and to replace verbal insults and harsh punishment with more effective strategies, such as time out and withdrawal of privileges. After several weeks of such training, children's aggression declines, and parents view their children more positively—benefits still evident one to four years later (Kazdin, 2003; Patterson & Fisher, 2002)

On the child's side, teaching nonaggressive ways of resolving conflict is helpful. Sessions in which children model and role-play cooperation and sharing and see that these behaviors lead to rewarding social outcomes reduce aggression and increase positive social behavior. Many aggressive children also need help with language delays and deficits that interfere with development of self-control. Encouraging parents to converse with their young children, especially about how to regulate strong negative emotion, helps children develop internalized controls. Once aggressive children begin to change, parents must be reminded to give them attention and approval for prosocial acts (Kazdin, 2000). The coercive cycles of parents and aggressive children are so pervasive that these children often are punished even when they do behave appropriately.

Many North American schools—lacking resources for effective intervention—also focus only on punishment. *Zero tolerance policies*—which severely punish all disruptive and threatening behaviors, major and minor, usually with suspension or expulsion—have become increasingly common. Yet often they are implemented inconsistently: Low-SES minority students are two to three times as likely to be punished, especially for minor misbehaviors (Goode & Goode, 2007; Skiba & Rausch, 2006). No evidence exists that zero tolerance achieves its objective of reducing youth aggression and other forms of misconduct (Stinchcomb, Bazemore, & Riestenberg, 2006). To the contrary, some studies find that by excluding students from school, zero tolerance heightens high school dropout and antisocial behavior.

• **Social-Cognitive Interventions** The social-cognitive deficits and distortions of aggressive children prevent them from empathizing with another person's pain and suffering. And because aggressive children have few opportunities to witness family members acting in sensitive, caring ways, they miss early experiences that are vital for promoting empathy and sympathy (see Chapter 10). In such children, these responses may have to be directly taught.

Social-cognitive treatments focus on teaching children and adolescents to attend to relevant, nonhostile social cues, to seek additional information before acting, and to evaluate the likely effectiveness of potential responses. These interventions increase skill in solving social problems, decrease endorsement of beliefs supporting aggression, reduce hostile behaviors, and improve relationships with teachers and peers (Guerra & Slaby, 1990; Webster-Stratton, Reid, & Hammond, 2001). Training in perspective taking also helps (see Chapter 11) by promoting more accurate interpretation of social cues, empathy, and sympathetic concern for others.

• **Comprehensive Approaches** According to some researchers, effective treatment for antisocial youths must be multifaceted, encompassing parent training, social understanding, relating to others, and self-control. A program called EQUIP uses positive peer culture—an adult-guided but adolescent-conducted small group approach aimed at creating a prosocial climate. By themselves, peer-culture groups do not reduce antisocial behavior. Rather, they sometimes perpetuate deviant peer influences (Dodge, Dishion, & Lansford, 2006). But in EQUIP, the approach is supplemented with training in social skills, anger management, correction of cognitive distortions, and moral reasoning (DiBiase, Gibbs, & Potter, 2005; Gibbs et al., 2009). Delinquents who participated in EQUIP displayed improved social skills and conduct during the following year compared with controls receiving no intervention. Also, the more advanced moral reasoning that emerged during group meetings seemed to have a long-term impact on antisocial youths' ability to inhibit lawbreaking behavior (Leeman, Gibbs, & Fuller, 1993).

Yet even multidimensional treatments can fall short if young people remain embedded in hostile home lives, poor-quality schools, antisocial peer groups, and violent neighborhoods. In another program, called *multisystemic therapy*, counselors trained parents in communication, monitoring, and discipline skills; integrated violent youths into positive school, work, and leisure activities; and disengaged them from deviant peers. Compared with conventional services or individual therapy, the intervention led to improved parent–child relations and a dramatic drop in arrests over a four-year period (Huey & Henggeler, 2001). Efforts to create nonaggressive environments—at the family, community, and cultural levels—are needed to help delinquent youths and to foster healthy development of all young people.

Ask Yourself

Review Cite factors that contribute to an improved ability to delay gratification from early to middle childhood.

Review Explain how heredity and environment jointly contribute to persistent aggression.

Apply Zeke had been well behaved in elementary school, but around age 13 he started spending time with the "wrong crowd." At 16, he was arrested for property damage. Is Zeke likely to become a long-term offender? Why or why not?

Connect Reread the section on adolescent parenthood in Chapter 5 (pages 215–218) and the section on adolescent suicide in Chapter 11 (pages 466–467). What factors do these problems have in common with chronic antisocial behavior?

Reflect Describe a recent instance in which your cool processing system dominated your hot-system reactivity, resulting in resistance to temptation. What did your cool processing system do to gain control?

SUMMARY

Morality as Rooted in Human Nature

Describe and evaluate the biological perspective on morality.

- The biological perspective assumes that morality is grounded in our genetic heritage, perhaps through prewired emotional reactions. We share many morally relevant behaviors with other species, and the ventromedial and orbitofrontal areas of the frontal region of the cerebral cortex are vital for emotional responsiveness to others' suffering. However, mature expression of moral emotions requires strong caregiving supports and cognitive attainments.

Morality as the Adoption of Societal Norms

Describe and evaluate the psychoanalytic perspective on moral development.

- Both psychoanalytic and social learning theories regard moral development as a process of **internalization** of societal standards. According to Freud, morality emerges between ages 3 and 6, when the Oedipus and Electra conflicts are resolved with formation of the superego. The child adopts the moral standards of the same-sex parent and redirects hostile impulses toward the self in the form of guilt.
- Although guilt is an important motivator of moral action, Freud's view of it is no longer widely accepted. Fear of punishment and loss of parental love do not foster conscience development. **Induction** is far more effective in motivating children's active commitment to moral norms.

© Pixland/Corbis

- Mild, patient parenting tactics are sufficient to promote conscience development in anxious, fearful preschoolers. For fearless, impulsive children, a secure attachment relationship motivates children to respond to firm parental correction of misbehavior and to listen to parental inductions.
- Contrary to Freud's belief, moral development is not complete by the end of early childhood. Rather, it proceeds gradually, extending into adulthood.

Describe and evaluate the social learning perspective on moral development, including the importance of modeling, the effects of punishment, and alternatives to harsh discipline.

- Social learning theory views moral behavior as acquired like other responses: through reinforcement and modeling. Effective models are warm, responsive, competent, and powerful, and display consistency between assertions and behavior. By middle childhood, children have internalized prosocial rules.
- Frequent harsh punishment results in weak moral internalization and wide-ranging adjustment problems, models aggressive behavior, and can spiral into serious abuse. Alternatives, such as **time out** and withdrawal of privileges, can reduce these undesirable side effects, as long as parents apply them consistently, maintain a warm relationship with the child, and offer explanations for punishment.
- The most effective forms of discipline encourage good conduct. Children whose parents build a positive relationship with them heed parental demands because they feel a sense of commitment to the relationship.

Morality as Social Understanding

Describe Piaget's theory of moral development, and evaluate its accuracy.

- Piaget's work inspired the cognitive-developmental perspective, which assumes that morality develops through **construction**—actively thinking about situations in which social conflicts arise and attaining new moral understandings.
- Piaget identified two stages of moral understanding: **heteronomous morality,** in which children view moral rules in terms of **realism,** as fixed dictates of authorities, and **autonomous morality,** in which children regard rules as flexible, socially agreed-on principles and base fairness on **ideal reciprocity.**
- Piaget's theory describes the general direction of moral development but underestimates young children's moral capacities. Preschool and early school-age children consider intentions when making moral judgments, although they interpret intentions rigidly. They also have differentiated notions about the legitimacy of authority figures. For nonmoral concerns, they base authority on knowledge, not social position. When a directive is fair and caring, they view it as right, regardless of whether an authority endorses it.

Describe Kohlberg's extension of Piaget's theory, methods for assessing moral reasoning, and evidence on the accuracy of his stages.

- Kohlberg viewed moral development as a gradual process extending into adolescence and adulthood. Using his **Moral Judgment Interview,** he constructed a sequence of moral reasoning based on responses to hypothetical dilemmas. Short-answer questionnaires for assessing moral understanding include the **Sociomoral Reflection Measure–Short Form (SRM–SF).**
- Kohlberg concluded that moral reasoning advances through six stages, organized into three levels: (1) the **preconventional level,** in which morality is viewed as externally controlled and actions are judged by their consequences; (2) the **conventional level,** in which conformity to laws and rules is regarded as necessary for societal order; and (3) the **postconventional level,** in which morality is defined in terms of abstract, universal principles and values.
- Most individuals move through Kohlberg's first four stages slowly, gradually, and in the predicted order. Kohlberg's hypothetical moral dilemmas, however, do not address the whole range of strategies people use to resolve real-life moral problems. Because situational factors affect moral reasoning, Kohlberg's stages are best viewed as loosely organized and overlapping.

- Piaget's cognitive and Selman's perspective-taking stages are related to advances in moral reasoning. However, the domain in which the cognitive prerequisites for mature moral reasoning first emerge—cognitive, social, or moral—remains unclear.
- Contrary to Gilligan's claim, Kohlberg's theory does not underestimate the moral maturity of females. Females' tendency to emphasize care over justice appears more often in real-life than in hypothetical dilemmas and also varies across cultures and situations.

Describe influences on moral reasoning, its relationship to moral behavior, and continuing challenges to Kohlberg's theory.

- A flexible, open-minded approach to new information and experiences is linked to gains in moral reasoning. Experiences that contribute include warm, rational child-rearing practices, years of schooling, and peer interactions involving conflict resolution through negotiation and compromise.

© James Marshall/The Image Works

- Village societies, where moral cooperation is based on direct relations between people, do not allow for development beyond Kohlberg's Stage 3. In collectivist cultures, which are more other-directed than Western societies, responses to moral dilemmas cannot always be scored in Kohlberg's scheme. Nevertheless, a common justice morality is evident in vastly different cultures.
- Maturity of moral reasoning is modestly related to a wide variety of moral behaviors. Other factors influencing moral action include emotions, temperament, a history of morally relevant experiences, and **moral self-relevance**—the degree to which morality is central to self-concept.
- Although formal religious involvement declines in adolescence, young people who remain part of a religious community are advantaged in moral values and behavior. Religious affiliation is linked to community service, responsible academic and social behavior, and avoidance of misconduct.
- In a revised conception of moral development, moral maturity is achieved at Kohlberg's Stages 3 and 4, when young people grasp ideal reciprocity—attainments that are not "conventional" but, rather, require profound moral constructions. Some critics of Kohlberg's theory favor a pragmatic approach in which moral judgments are viewed as practical tools that people use to achieve their goals.

Explain how children distinguish moral imperatives from social conventions and matters of personal choice, and trace changes in their understanding from childhood into adolescence.

- Researchers taking a domain approach to moral understanding report that even preschoolers show a rudimentary grasp of justice, distinguishing **moral imperatives** from **social conventions** and **matters of personal choice.** Through actively making sense of people's everyday social experiences and emotional reactions, young children conclude that moral transgressions (but not social conventions) are wrong in any context, regardless of whether rules or authorities prohibit them.
- School-age children gradually clarify and link moral imperatives and social conventions, taking into account more variables, including the purpose of the rule; people's intentions, knowledge, and beliefs; and the context of people's behavior. The conviction that certain matters are up to the individual strengthens with age, especially in adolescence. Notions of personal choice foster moral understanding of individual rights.

Describe the development of distributive justice reasoning, noting factors that foster mature understanding.

- Children's concepts of **distributive justice** change over middle childhood, from equality to merit to equity and benevolence. Peer interaction supports children's developing ideas of fair distribution.

Development of Morally Relevant Self-Control

Trace the development of morally relevant self-control from early childhood into adolescence, noting implications of individual differences for cognitive and social competencies.

- The emergence of self-control is supported by self-awareness and by the representational, memory, and inhibitory skills of the second year. Self-control first appears as **compliance.** The capacity for **delay of gratification** increases steadily between ages 1½ and 3 years. Language development and warm, supportive parenting foster self-control.
- Preschoolers benefit when adults provide delay-of-gratification strategies. Over middle childhood, children produce an increasing variety of strategies and become aware of which ones work well and why, leading to a flexible capacity for **moral self-regulation.**
- Individual differences in delay of gratification predict diverse cognitive and social competencies, including effective social problem solving and positive peer relations. As self-control develops, an emotionally reactive "hot" system is subordinated to a cognitive, reflective "cool" system.

The Other Side of Self-Control: Development of Aggression

Discuss the development of aggression from infancy into adolescence, noting individual, family, community, and cultural influences, and describe successful interventions.

- Aggression first appears by the second year. Over early and middle childhood, **proactive aggression** declines, while **reactive aggression** increases. Proactive and reactive aggression come in at least three forms: **physical aggression, verbal aggression,** and **relational aggression.**
- During early childhood, physical aggression decreases, while verbal aggression increases. By age 17 months, boys are more physically aggressive than girls. Sex differences in verbal and relational aggression are small. Teacher- and peer-reported aggression declines in adolescence, but delinquent acts increase, especially for boys.
- Children high in physical or relational aggression tend to remain so over time. Irritable, fearless, impulsive, and overactive children are at risk for aggression, but whether or not they become so depends on child-rearing conditions. Strife-ridden families and harsh, inconsistent discipline promote self-perpetuating cycles of aggressive behavior.
- Children who are products of these family processes develop social-cognitive deficits and distortions that contribute to long-term maintenance of aggression. Widespread poverty, harsh living conditions, and inadequate schools increase antisocial acts among children and adolescents.
- Training parents in effective discipline and teaching children alternative ways of resolving conflict are helpful in reducing aggression. Social-cognitive interventions that focus on improving social information processing and perspective taking are also beneficial. The most effective approaches address the multiple factors that sustain antisocial behavior.

IMPORTANT TERMS AND CONCEPTS

13

"Two Skater Friends"
Melika Rabiei
8 years, Iran

This artist depicts "two skater friends" with distinct gender-related attributes. The male leaps boldly aloft, while the female glides gently alongside him.

Development of Sex Differences and Gender Roles

On a typical morning, in our university laboratory preschool, 4-year-old Jenny eagerly entered the housekeeping corner and put on a frilly long dress and high heels. Karen, setting the table nearby, produced whimpering sound effects for the baby doll in the crib. Jenny lifted the doll, sat down in the rocking chair, gently cradled the baby in her arms, and whispered, "You're hungry, aren't you?" A moment later, Jenny announced, "This baby won't eat. I think she's sick. Ask Rachel if she'll be the nurse." Karen ran off to find Rachel, who was coloring at the art table.

Meanwhile, Nathan called to Tommy, "Wanna play traffic?" Both boys dashed energetically toward the cars and trucks in the block corner. Soon David joined them. "I'll be policeman first!" announced Nathan, climbing onto a chair. "Green light, go!" shouted the young police officer. With this signal, Tommy and David scurried on all fours around the chair, each pushing a large wooden truck. "Red light!" exclaimed Nathan, and the trucks screeched to a halt.

"My truck beat yours," Tommy informed David.

"Only 'cause I need gas," David responded.

"Let's build a runway for the trucks," suggested Nathan. The three construction engineers began gathering large blocks for the task.

At an early age, children adopt many gender-linked standards of their culture. Jenny, Karen, and Rachel use dresses, dolls, and household props to act out a stereotypically feminine scene of nurturance. In contrast, Nathan, Tommy, and David's play is active, competitive, and masculine in theme. And both boys and girls interact more with agemates of their own sex.

Why do young children's play and social preferences become so strongly gender-typed, and how do these attitudes and behaviors change with age? Do societal expectations affect children's view of themselves as masculine or feminine beings, thereby limiting their potential? To what extent do widely held beliefs about the characteristics of males and females reflect reality? Is it true that the average boy is aggressive and competitive, with good spatial and mathematical skills, whereas the average girl is passive and nurturant, with superior verbal skills? How large are differences between the sexes, and in what ways do heredity and environment contribute to them? These are the central questions asked by researchers studying gender typing. In this chapter, we will answer each of them.

Perhaps more than any other area of child development, the study of gender typing has responded to societal change. Until the early 1970s, psychologists regarded the adoption of gender-typed beliefs and behaviors as essential for healthy adjustment. Since then, this view has changed, largely because of progress in women's rights. Today, many people recognize that some gender-typed characteristics, such as extreme aggressiveness and competitiveness on the part of males and passivity and conformity on the part of females, are serious threats to mental health.

Consistent with this realization, the study of gender typing has undergone theoretical revision. Major current approaches are social learning theory, with its emphasis on modeling and reinforcement, and cognitive-developmental theory, with its focus on children as active thinkers about their social world. But neither is sufficient by itself. An information-processing view, *gender schema theory,* combines elements of both theories to explain how children acquire gender-typed knowledge.

Central to our discussion is a set of special terms. Two involve the public face of gender in society. **Gender stereotypes** are widely held beliefs about characteristics deemed appropriate for males and females. **Gender roles** are the reflection of these stereotypes in everyday behavior. A third, **gender identity,** is the private face of gender—perception of the self as relatively masculine or feminine in characteristics. Finally, **gender typing** refers broadly to any association of objects, activities, roles, or traits with biological sex in ways that conform to cultural stereotypes of gender and, therefore, encompasses all the gender-linked responses just mentioned (Liben & Bigler, 2002). As we explore each facet of gender typing in children and adolescents, you will see that biological, cognitive, and social factors are involved.

Gender Stereotypes and Gender Roles

Gender stereotypes have appeared in religious, philosophical, and literary works for centuries. Consider the following excerpts, from ancient times to the present:

- "Woman is more compassionate than man and has a greater propensity to tears. . . . But the male . . . is more disposed to give assistance in danger, and is more courageous than the female." (Aristotle, cited in Miles, 1935)
- "A man will say what he knows, a woman says what will please." (Jean-Jacques Rousseau, *Emile,* 1762/1955)
- "Man with the head and woman with the heart; Man to command and woman to obey; All else confusion." (Alfred, Lord Tennyson, *Home They Brought Her Warrior,* 1842)
- "Love is a mood—no more—to a man, And love to a woman is life or death." (Ella Wheeler Wilcox, *Blind,* 1882)
- "Women ask: How do you get a man to open up? Men ask: Why does she always want to talk about the relationship?" (Gray, *Mars and Venus on a Date,* 1997)

Although the past four decades have brought a new level of awareness about the wide range of roles possible for each gender, strong beliefs about sex differences remain. In the 1960s, researchers began asking people what personality characteristics they consider typical of men and women. Widespread agreement emerged in many studies. As Table 13.1 illustrates, **instrumental traits,** reflecting competence, rationality, and assertiveness, were regarded as masculine; **expressive traits,** emphasizing warmth, caring, and sensitivity, were viewed as feminine. Despite intense political activism promoting gender equality in the 1970s and 1980s, these stereotypes have remained essentially unchanged (Lueptow, Garovich, & Lueptow, 2001; Ruble, Martin, & Berenbaum, 2006; Vonk & Ashmore, 2003). Furthermore, cross-cultural research conducted in 30 nations reveals that the instrumental–expressive dichotomy is a widely held stereotype around the world (Williams & Best, 1990).

Besides personality traits, other gender stereotypes exist. These include physical characteristics (tall, strong, and sturdy for men; soft, dainty, and graceful for women), occupations (truck driver, insurance agent, and chemist for men; elementary school teacher, secretary, and nurse for women), and activities or behaviors (good at fixing things and at leading groups for men; good at child care and decorating the home for women) (Biernat, 1991; Powlishta et al., 2001).

The variety of attributes consistently identified as masculine or feminine, their broad acceptance, and their stability over time suggest that gender stereotypes are deeply ingrained patterns of thinking. What's more, they cast men in a generally positive light and women in a generally negative light. The traits, activities, and roles associated with the male gender are more numerous, diverse, and desirable than those associated with the female gender. For example, in Western cultures, stereotypically masculine occupations are far more numerous than feminine occupations (Liben & Bigler, 2002). And only a few masculine attributes, such as "aggressive" and "criminal," are negative; the overwhelming majority are advantageous and high-status. Feminine attributes, in contrast, are mostly unfavorable and low-status.

Adults apply gender stereotypes to children with a special intensity. In a study in which 20- to 40-year-olds were shown photos of children and adults and asked to rate each on "masculine," "feminine," and "neutral" personality traits, adults differentiated boys from girls more sharply than they did men from women (see Figure 13.1) (Powlishta, 2000). Given that many adults view children through a gender-biased lens, perhaps it is not surprising that by the second year, children have begun to absorb these messages.

Table 13.1 Personality Traits Regarded as Stereotypically Masculine or Feminine

Masculine Traits	Feminine Traits
Active	Aware of others' feelings
Acts as a leader	Considerate
Adventurous	Cries easily
Aggressive	Devotes self to others
Ambitious	Emotional
Competitive	Excitable in a major crisis
Doesn't give up easily	Feelings hurt easily
Dominant	Gentle
Feels superior	Home-oriented
Holds up well under pressure	Kind
Independent	Likes children
Makes decisions easily	Neat
Not easily influenced	Needs approval
Outspoken	Passive
Rough	Tactful
Self-confident	Understanding of others
Takes a stand	Warm in relations with others

Gender Stereotyping in Early Childhood

Recall from Chapter 11 that between 18 months and 3 years, children label their own and others' sex, using such words as *boy* and *girl* and *woman* and *man*. As children sort out what these categories mean in terms of activities and behaviors, gender stereotypes appear and expand rapidly. Before age 2, children have begun to acquire subtle associations with gender that most of us hold—men as rough and sharp, women as soft and round. In one study, 18-month-olds linked such items as fir trees and hammers with males, although they had not yet learned comparable feminine associations (Eichstedt et al., 2002). Preschoolers associate toys, articles of clothing, tools, household items, games, occupations, colors (pink and blue), and behaviors (relational and physical aggression) with one sex or the other (Giles & Heyman, 2005; Poulin-Dubois et al., 2002; Ruble, Martin, & Berenbaum, 2006). They have even acquired gender-stereotyped metaphors—"bears are for boys"; "butterflies are for girls" (Leinbach, Hort, & Fagot, 1997).

During early childhood, gender-stereotyped beliefs strengthen—so much so that many children apply them as blanket rules rather than flexible guidelines. When children were asked whether gender stereotypes could be violated, half or more of 3- and 4-year-olds answered "no" to clothing, hairstyle, and play with certain toys (such as Barbie dolls and G.I. Joes) (Blakemore, 2003). Furthermore, most 3- to 6-year-olds are firm about not wanting to be friends with a child who violates a gender stereotype (a boy who wears nail polish, a girl who plays with trucks) or to attend a school where such violations are allowed (Ruble et al., 2007).

Striking evidence that young children view their world in strongly gender-stereotyped terms also comes from studies in which researchers labeled a target child as a boy or a girl and then provided either gender-typical or gender-atypical information about the target's characteristics. Then they asked children to rate the target on additional gender-stereotypic attributes. Preschoolers usually relied only on the gender label in making

Figure 13.1 **Adults' ratings of photos of adults and children for "masculine" personality traits.**
Adults perceived little difference in the adult photos but a sharp difference in the child photos, rating boys as far more "masculine" in personality traits than girls. Ratings for "feminine" personality traits were similar: Adults reported a much greater difference between boys and girls than between men and women. (Adapted from Powlishta, 2000.)

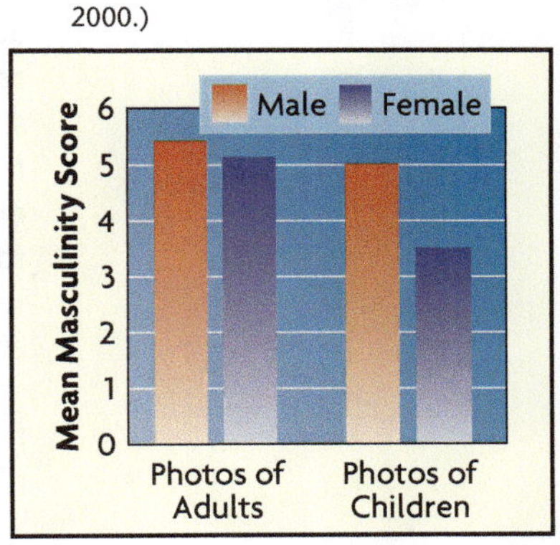

Gender-stereotyped game and toy choices are present before age 2 and strengthen over the preschool years. Already, these 3-year-olds play in highly gender-stereotyped ways. © E. Zuckerman/PhotoEdit

judgments, ignoring the specific information. For example, when told, "Tommy is a boy. Tommy's best friend is a girl, and Tommy likes to play house," children under age 6 nevertheless said that Tommy would much rather play with cars and train engines than with sewing machines and dolls (Biernat, 1991; Martin, 1989).

The rigidity of preschoolers' gender stereotypes helps us understand some commonly observed everyday behaviors. Shown a picture of a Scottish bagpiper wearing a kilt, 4-year-olds are likely to say, "Men don't wear skirts!" During free play, they exclaim that girls can't be police officers and boys can't take care of babies. These one-sided judgments are a joint product of gender stereotyping in the environment and young children's cognitive limitations—in particular, their difficulty coordinating conflicting sources of information. Most preschoolers do not yet realize that characteristics *associated with* being male or female—activities, toys, occupations, hairstyle, and clothing—do not *determine* a person's sex. They have trouble understanding that males and females can be different in terms of their bodies but similar in many other ways.

Gender Stereotyping in Middle Childhood and Adolescence

By age 5, gender stereotyping of activities and occupations is well-established. During middle childhood and adolescence, knowledge of stereotypes increases in the less obvious areas of personality traits and achievement (Serbin, Powlishta, & Gulko, 1993; Signorella, Bigler, & Liben, 1993). At the same time, because older children realize that gender-stereotypic attributes are associated—but not defining—features of gender, their beliefs about possible male and female characteristics and capacities become more flexible (Martin, Ruble, & Szkrybalo, 2002).

• **Personality Traits** To assess stereotyping of personality traits, researchers ask children to assign "masculine" adjectives ("tough," "rational," "cruel") and "feminine" adjectives ("gentle," "affectionate," "dependent") to either a male or a female stimulus figure. Recall from Chapter 11 that not until middle childhood are children good at sizing up people's dispositions. This same finding carries over to awareness of gender stereotypes.

Research in many countries reveals that stereotyping of personality traits increases steadily in middle childhood, becoming adultlike around age 11 (Best, 2001; Heyman & Legare, 2004). A large Canadian study examined the pattern of children's trait learning and found that the stereotypes acquired first reflected *in-group favoritism.* Kindergartners through second graders had greatest knowledge of trait stereotypes that portrayed their own gender in a positive light. Once trait stereotyping was well under way, elementary school students were most familiar with "positive feminine" traits and "negative masculine" traits (Serbin, Powlishta, & Gulko, 1993). In addition to learning specific traits, children of both sexes seemed to pick up a widely held general impression—that of girls as "sugar and spice and everything nice" and of boys as "snakes and snails and puppy dog tails."

• **Achievement Areas** Shortly after entering elementary school, children figure out which academic subjects and skill areas are "masculine" and which are "feminine." They often regard reading, spelling, art, and music as more for girls and mathematics, athletics, and mechanical skills as more for boys (Eccles, Jacobs, & Harold, 1990; Jacobs & Weisz, 1994). These stereotypes influence children's preferences for and sense of competence at certain subjects. For example, in both Asian and Western nations, boys tend to feel more competent than girls at math, science, and athletics, and girls feel more competent than boys at language arts—even when children of equal skill level are compared (Bhanot & Jovanovic, 2005; Freedman-Doan et al., 2000; Hong, Veach, & Lawrenz, 2003).

Furthermore, girls often adopt a more general stereotype of males as smarter than females, which they apply to themselves. In a study of over 2,000 second to sixth graders from diverse cultures (Eastern and Western Europe, Japan, Russia, and the United States), girls consistently had higher school grades than boys. Yet despite being aware of their better performance, they did not report stronger beliefs in their own ability but, compared with boys, discounted their talent (Stetsenko et al., 2000). Recall from Chapter 11 that when girls have difficulty with school tasks, parents and teachers are likely to attribute their difficulties to lack of ability. Apparently, gender stereotyping of academic talent occurs in many parts of the world.

One encouraging sign is that some children's gender-stereotyped beliefs about achievement areas may be changing. In a recent investigation, U.S. elementary school girls from economically advantaged homes regarded children of each gender as equally good at math. But when the girls were asked about adults, their judgments reverted to the stereotype—that men were better than women (see Figure 13.2). Boys, in contrast, held stereotyped views of math ability for both children and adults (Steele, 2003).

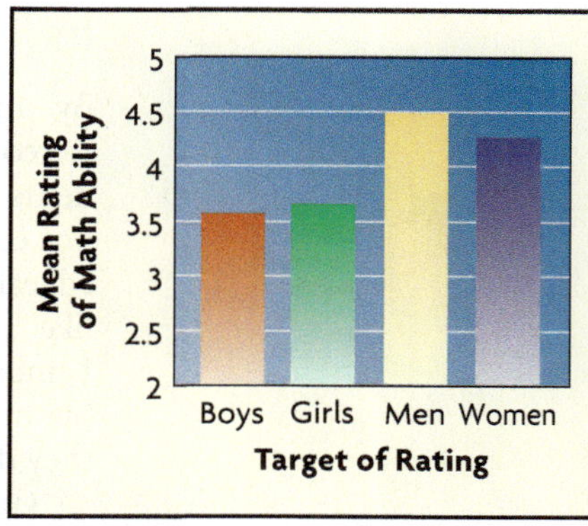

Figure 13.2 **School-age girls' ratings of the math ability of children and adults.**
The girls regarded children of each gender as equally good at math. Their ratings of adults, however, reverted to the stereotype that men were better at math than women. (Adapted from Steele, 2003.)

• Toward Greater Flexibility Clearly, school-age children are knowledgeable about a wide variety of gender stereotypes. At the same time, they develop a more open-minded view of what males and females *can do,* a trend that continues into adolescence.

In studying gender stereotyping, researchers usually ask children whether or not both genders can display a personality trait or activity—a response that measures **gender-stereotype flexibility,** or overlap in the characteristics of males and females. In a German study that followed children from ages 5 to 10, regardless of the degree of early gender-stereotype rigidity, flexibility increased dramatically from age 7 on (Trautner et al., 2005). As Figure 13.3 shows, the early period of rigidity was short-lived, and children differing in strength of rigidity became equally flexible in middle childhood. Gender stereotype flexibility rises as children develop the cognitive capacity to integrate conflicting social cues. As they realize that a person's sex is not a certain predictor of his or her personality traits, activities, and behavior, they no longer rely on a gender label alone to predict what a person will be like—they also consider the individual's unique characteristics.

Accompanying this change is a tendency to view gender typing as socially rather than biologically influenced. In one study, 4- to 10-year-olds and adults were told stories about hypothetical boy and girl babies reared on an island by members either of their own sex or of the other sex. Then they were asked what "masculine" and "feminine" properties each child would develop. Preschool and younger school-age children believed that gender-stereotyped characteristics would emerge, regardless of rearing environment. But by the end of middle childhood, children thought that a child reared by the other sex would be nonstereotyped in many ways (Taylor, 1996).

Nevertheless, acknowledging that boys and girls *can* cross gender lines does not mean that children always *approve* of doing so. They tend to take a harsh view of certain violations—boys playing with dolls and wearing girls' clothing, girls acting noisily and roughly. They are especially intolerant when boys engage in these "cross-gender" acts, which children regard as nearly as bad as moral transgressions (Blakemore, 2003; Levy, Taylor, & Gelman, 1995). Clearly, evaluations of certain male deviations from gender roles are negative at all ages, a finding that reflects greater social pressure on boys and men to conform to gender stereotypes. As we will see later when we take up gender identity, children's disapproval of gender-role violations can seriously affect the adjustment of peers who are targets of their criticism.

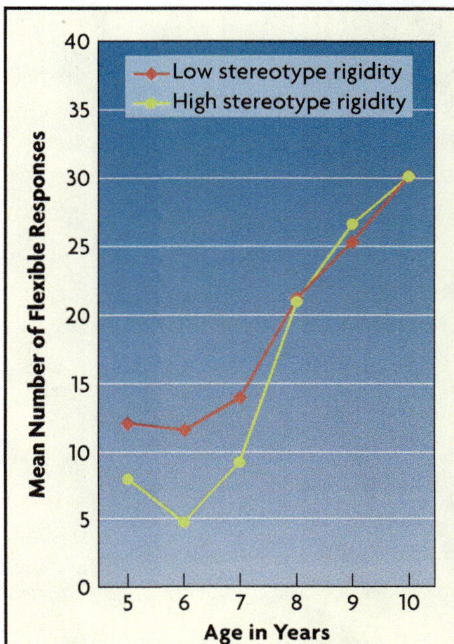

Figure 13.3 **Changes in gender-stereotype flexibility between ages 5 and 10.**
In a longitudinal study, German schoolchildren responded annually to a questionnaire assessing the flexibility of their gender-stereotyped beliefs (whether they thought both genders could display a personality trait or activity). Children differing in degree of gender-stereotype rigidity at age 5 eventually became equally flexible. Findings support the powerful role of cognitive changes in inducing flexibility, since early individual differences in rigidity were not sustained. (From H. M. Trautner et al., 2005, "Rigidity and Flexibility of Gender Stereotypes in Childhood: Developmental or Differential?", *Infant and Child Development,* 14, p. 371. Copyright © 2005 John Wiley & Sons Limited. Reprinted with permission.)

Individual and Group Differences in Gender Stereotyping

By middle childhood, almost all children have acquired extensive knowledge of gender stereotypes. But they vary widely in the makeup of their understanding. The various components of gender stereotyping—activities, behaviors, occupations, and personality traits—do not correlate highly: A child may be very knowledgeable in one area without being knowledgeable in the others (Serbin, Powlishta, & Gulko, 1993). This suggests that gender typing is like "an intricate puzzle that the child pieces together in a rather idiosyncratic way" (Hort, Leinbach, & Fagot, 1991, p. 196). To build a coherent notion of gender, children must assemble many elements. The precise pattern in which they acquire the pieces, the rate at which they do so, and the flexibility of their beliefs vary greatly from child to child.

Group differences in gender stereotyping also exist. The strongest of these is sex-related: Boys hold more rigid gender-stereotyped views than girls throughout childhood and adolescence (Steele, 2003; Turner, Gervai, & Hinde, 1993). A few studies, however, report no sex differences (Serbin, Powlishta, & Gulko, 1993; Taylor, 1996). And in one study, adolescents of both sexes, responding to vignettes about hypothetical high-achieving peers, expressed greater liking for the high-achieving girls (Quatman, Sokolik, & Smith, 2000). One heartening possibility is that older boys, at least, are beginning to view gender roles as encompassing more varied possibilities.

The limited evidence available on ethnic minorities suggests that African-American children hold less stereotyped views of females than do Caucasian-American children (Bardwell, Cochran, & Walker, 1986). Perhaps this is a response to the less traditional gender roles seen in African-American families—for example, more employed mothers and mother-headed households (U.S. Census Bureau, 2007b). In adolescence and adulthood, higher-SES individuals tend to hold more flexible gender-stereotyped views than their lower-SES counterparts (Lackey, 1989; Serbin, Powlishta, & Gulko, 1993). Years of schooling and a wider array of life options may contribute to this difference.

Gender Stereotyping and Gender-Role Adoption

Does gender-stereotyped thinking influence children's gender-role adoption, thereby restricting their experiences and potential? The evidence is mixed. Gender-typed preferences and behaviors increase sharply over the preschool years—the same period in which children rapidly acquire stereotypes. And boys—the more stereotyped of the two sexes—show greater conformity to their gender role (Bussey & Bandura, 1992; Ruble, Martin, & Berenbaum, 2006).

But these parallel patterns do not tell us whether gender stereotyping shapes children's behavior. In some cases, a reverse direction of influence may operate because certain gender-role preferences are acquired long before children know much about stereotypes. For example, by the middle of the second year, boys and girls favor different toys. When researchers showed toddlers paired photos of vehicles and dolls, 18-month-old boys looked longer than girls at the vehicles, whereas 18-month-old girls looked longer than boys at the dolls (see Figure 13.4) (Serbin et al., 2001).

Furthermore, children who are well-versed in gender-related expectations are sometimes highly gender-typed, and sometimes not, in their everyday activities (Downs & Langlois, 1988; Serbin, Powlishta, & Gulko, 1993; Weinraub et al., 1984). Why might this be so? First, we have seen that children master the components of gender-stereotyped knowledge in diverse ways, each of which may have different implications for their

Children well-versed in gender stereotypes do not always behave consistently with their knowledge. Perhaps because this boy has observed his father engaged in infant caregiving, in play he enacts a similar role. © Michael Newman/PhotoEdit

behavior. Second, by middle childhood, virtually all children know a great deal about gender stereotypes—knowledge so universal that it cannot predict variations in their behavior.

Rather than stereotype knowledge, stereotype flexibility is a good predictor of children's gender-role adoption in middle childhood. Children who believe that many stereotyped characteristics are appropriate for both sexes (for example, that playing with trucks is OK for girls) are more likely to cross gender lines in their own choices of activities, playmates, and occupational roles (Liben, Bigler, & Krogh, 2002; Serbin, Powlishta, & Gulko, 1993; Signorella, Bigler, & Liben, 1993). This suggests that gender stereotypes affect behavior only when children incorporate those beliefs into their gender identities—self-perceptions of what they can and should do at play, in school, and as future participants in society. Now let's turn to various influences that promote children's gender-typed beliefs and behaviors.

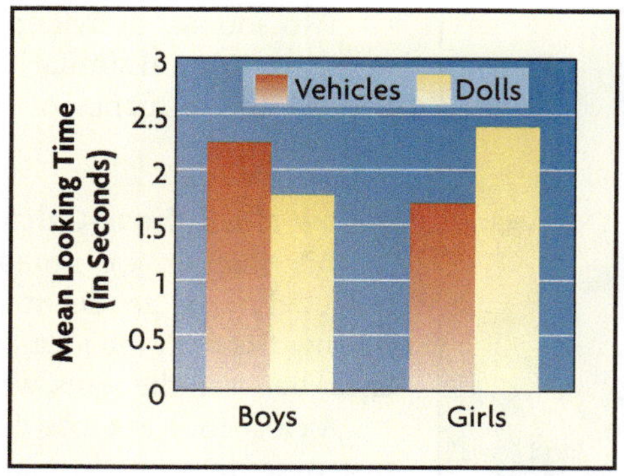

Figure 13.4 Eighteen-month-old girls' and boys' looking times at vehicles and dolls. Already, gender-role preferences are evident: Boys looked longer at the vehicles, whereas girls looked longer at the dolls. (Adapted from Serbin et al., 2001.)

Ask Yourself

Review Explain how young children's cognitive limitations combine with the social environment to contribute to rigid gender stereotyping in early childhood.

Review What factors allow for flexibility in gender stereotyping in middle childhood and adolescence? How is gender-stereotype flexibility related to gender-typed preferences and behavior?

Apply Dennis is the top student in his seventh-grade cooking class. His friends Tom and Bill tease him relentlessly. Cite evidence that explains this negative reaction to Dennis's "cross-gender" behavior.

Connect Describe parallels between the development of gender and ethnic attitudes (see Chapter 11, pages 470–472).

Influences on Gender Stereotyping and Gender-Role Adoption

According to social learning theorists, gender-stereotyped knowledge and behaviors are transmitted to children through direct teaching. As we will see shortly, much research is consistent with this view. Others argue, however, that biological makeup leads each sex to be uniquely suited to particular roles and that most societies do little more than encourage gender differences that are genetically based. Is there evidence to support this idea?

The Case for Biology

Although practically no contemporary theorist would argue that "biology is destiny," serious questions about biological influences on gender typing remain. According to an evolutionary perspective, the adult life of our male ancestors was largely oriented toward competing for mates, that of our female ancestors toward rearing children. Therefore, males became genetically primed for dominance and females for intimacy, responsiveness, and cooperativeness. These sex differences in behavior exist in 97 percent of mammalian species, including chimpanzees, our closest evolutionary relative (de Waal, 1993, 2001). Evolutionary theorists claim that family and cultural forces can influence the intensity of biologically based sex differences, leading some individuals to be more gender-typed than others. But experience cannot eradicate aspects of gender typing that served adaptive functions in human history (Geary, 1999; Maccoby, 2002).

A Bangladeshi girl breaks bricks with her mother after the capital city, Dhaka, was ravaged by floods. Current conditions may alter the extent to which a culture promotes instrumental traits in boys and expressive traits in girls. © RAFIQUR RAHMAN/Reuters/Corbis

Two sources of evidence have been used to support the role of biology: (1) cross-cultural similarities in gender stereotypes and gender-role adoption and (2) the influence of hormones on gender-role behavior. Let's examine each in turn.

How Much Cross-Cultural Similarity Exists in Gender Typing? Earlier in this chapter, we noted that the instrumental–expressive dichotomy is reflected in the gender stereotyping of many national groups. Although this finding fits with the idea that social influences simply build on genetic differences between the sexes, we must be cautious in drawing this conclusion.

A close look at cross-cultural findings reveals that most societies promote instrumental traits in males and expressive traits in females, although great diversity exists in the magnitude of this difference (Munroe & Romney, 2006; Whiting & Edwards, 1988b). For example, in Nyansongo, a small agricultural settlement in Kenya, mothers work four to five hours a day in the gardens, while older siblings care for young children, tend the cooking fire, and wash dishes. Because these duties are assigned to children of both sexes, girls do not have total responsibility for "feminine" tasks and have more time to interact with agemates. Their greater freedom and independence lead them to score higher than girls of other tribal and village cultures in dominance, assertiveness, and playful roughhousing. In contrast, boys' caregiving responsibilities mean that they often display help-giving and emotional support (Whiting & Edwards, 1988a). Among industrialized nations, Sweden is widely recognized as a society in which traditional gender-linked beliefs and behaviors are considerably reduced (see the Cultural Influences box on the following page).

These examples indicate that experience can profoundly influence gender typing. Nevertheless, reversals of traditional gender roles are rare. Because cross-cultural findings are inconclusive, scientists have turned to a more direct test of the importance of biology: the impact of sex hormones on gender typing.

Sex Hormones and Gender Typing In Chapters 3 and 5, we discussed how genetic makeup, mediated by hormones, regulates sexual development and body growth. Sex hormones also affect brain development and neural activity in many animal species, and they do so in humans as well (Hines & Green, 1991). Are hormones, which so pervasively affect body structures, also important in gender-role adoption?

Play Styles and Preference for Same-Sex Peers. Experiments with animals reveal that prenatally administered androgens (male sex hormones) increase active play in both male and female mammals. Androgens also promote male-typical sexual behavior and aggression and suppress maternal caregiving in a wide variety of species (Lephart et al., 2001; Sato et al., 2004).

Eleanor Maccoby (1998) argues that at least some of these hormonal effects extend to humans. Recall from the introduction to this chapter that as early as the preschool years, children seek out playmates of their own sex—a preference observed in many mammalian species and cultures (Beatty, 1992; Munroe & Romney, 2006). At age 4, children spend three times as much time with same-sex as with other-sex playmates. By age 6, this ratio has climbed to 11 to 1 (Martin & Fabes, 2001). Throughout the school years, children continue to show a strong preference for same-sex peers.

Why is gender segregation so widespread and persistent? According to Maccoby, early on, hormones affect play styles, leading to rough, noisy movements among boys and to calm, gentle actions among girls. Then, as children interact with peers, they choose partners whose interests and behaviors are compatible with their own. By age 2, girls appear overwhelmed by boys' rambunctious behavior. When a girl and a boy are paired in a laboratory play session, the girl is likely to stand idly by while the boy explores the toys (Benenson, Apostoleris, & Parnass, 1997). Nonhuman primates react similarly. When a male juvenile initiates rough, physical play, male peers join in, whereas females withdraw (Beatty, 1992).

During the preschool years, girls increasingly seek out other girls and like to play in pairs because of a common preference for quieter activities involving cooperative roles. Boys come to prefer larger-group play with other boys, who share a desire to run, climb, play-fight,

Cultural Influences

Sweden's Commitment to Gender Equality

Among all nations in the world, Sweden is unique in the value it places on gender equality. More than a century ago, Sweden's ruling political party adopted equality as a central goal. One social class was not to exploit another, nor one gender another. In the 1960s, Sweden's expanding economy attracted women into the labor force in large numbers, raising the question of who would help sustain family life. Calling on the principle of equality, the Swedish people responded: fathers, just like mothers (Plantin, Mansson, & Kearney, 2003).

The Swedish "equal roles family model" maintains that husband and wife should have the same opportunity to pursue a career and should be equally responsible for housework and child care. To support this goal, Swedish fathers have had the right to paid parental employment leave longer than fathers in any other nation—since 1974. In addition, Sweden made child-care centers available, so toddlers and preschoolers could be cared for outside the home. Otherwise, a class of less privileged women might be exploited for caregiving and domestic work—an outcome that would contradict the principle of equality. And because full-time employment for both parents often strains a family with young children, Sweden mandated that mothers and fathers with children younger than age 8 could reduce the length of their working day to six hours, with a corresponding reduction in pay but not in benefits (Sandqvist, 1992).

According to several indicators, Sweden's family model is very successful. Child-care centers are numerous, of high quality, and heavily subsidized by the government. Over 80 percent of mothers of infants and preschoolers are employed, and although Swedish fathers do not yet share housework and child care equally with mothers, they are more involved than fathers in North America and in other Western European nations. Today, 90 percent of Swedish fathers take at least some parental employment leave—more than in any other nation in the world. And more than half make work adjustments—reducing work hours, turning down promotions, and refusing overtime—so they can spend additional time with children (Haas, 2003; Anders, Chronholm, & Hwang, 2006).

Has Sweden's progressive family policy affected the gender beliefs and behaviors of its population? A study of Swedish and American adolescents found that valuing of the "masculine" over the "feminine" role was less pronounced in Sweden than in the United States. Swedish young people regarded each gender as a blend of instrumental and expressive traits, and they more often viewed gender roles as a matter of learned tasks and domains of expertise than as inborn traits or rights and duties (Intons-Peterson, 1988). Similarly, large nationally representative surveys in Western European countries revealed that Swedish adults held more favorable attitudes toward maternal employment. For example, more Swedish than British and Norwegian respondents agreed that "a working mother could establish just as warm and secure a relationship with her children as a mother who does not work" (Knudsen & Waerness, 2003).

Traditional gender typing has not been eradicated in Sweden. But great progress has been made as a result of steadfastly pursuing a program of gender equality for several decades.

In Sweden, which places a high value on gender equality, fathers are more involved in housework and child care than they are in North America and other Western European nations. This father enjoys a paid 18-month paternity leave (see Chapter 3, page 117). © Mikael Svensson/Alamy

compete, and build up and knock down (Fabes, Martin, & Hanish, 2003). Social pressures for "gender-appropriate" play and cognitive factors—in particular, gender stereotyping, the tendency to evaluate members of one's own sex more positively, and expectations of negative reactions from others for play with other-sex children—also contribute to gender segregation (Ruble, Martin, & Berenbaum, 2006). But sex hormones are involved, a conclusion supported by studies of exceptional sexual development in humans.

Exceptional Sexual Development. For ethical reasons, we cannot experimentally manipulate hormones to see how they affect human behavior. But we can consider cases in which hormone levels varied naturally or were modified for medical reasons.

Congenital adrenal hyperplasia (CAH) is a disorder in which a genetic defect causes the adrenal system to produce unusually high levels of androgens from the prenatal period onward. Although the physical development of boys remains unaffected, girls with CAH are

Sex hormones are believed to influence children's play styles, prompting preschoolers to choose same-sex partners who share their interests and behaviors. Calm, gentle play in pairs is typical among girls, noisy roughhousing in large groups among boys. But social pressure for "gender-appropriate" play also promotes gender segregation. *Left:* © Michael Newman/ PhotoEdit; *right:* © Blend Images/ SuperStock

usually born with masculinized external genitals. Most undergo surgical correction in infancy, followed by continuous drug therapy to overcome the hormone imbalance.

Interview and observational studies support the conclusion that prenatal androgen exposure influences certain aspects of "masculine" gender-role behavior. Compared with other girls, girls with CAH tend to be higher in activity level; to like cars, trucks, and blocks better than dolls; to prefer boys as playmates; and to be more interested in "masculine" careers, such as truck driver, soldier, or pilot (Cohen-Bendahan, van de Beek, & Berenbaum, 2005; Hines, 2004; Meyer-Bahlburg et al., 2004). When women with CAH look back on their childhoods, they recall preferring "masculine play" and feeling dissatisfied with their female identity (Hines, Brook, & Conway, 2004). The greater CAH girls' exposure to prenatal androgens, the more "masculine" their play and career interests (Hall et al., 2004; Servin et al., 2003). Furthermore, although girls with CAH receive more parental encouragement to play with girls' toys than do their unaffected sisters, they nevertheless prefer boys' toys—whether playing alone or in the presence of their mother or father (Pasterski et al., 2005). Even normal variation in prenatal androgen exposure is linked to gender-typed play behavior in girls (Hines, 2003).

Fewer studies are available on genetic males with abnormally low early androgen exposure. In *androgen insensitivity syndrome,* the testes produce normal levels of androgens, but androgen receptors in body cells are partially or completely impaired. In other conditions, androgen production by the testes is reduced. Depending on the extent of impairment, physical outcomes range from predominantly male to typically female urogenital tract and external genitals. In one study of such children, degree of reduction in prenatal androgen exposure predicted feminine gender-typed behavior, including toy choices, play behaviors, and preference for girl playmates (Jürgensen et al., 2007). Nevertheless, all children with complete androgen insensitivity syndrome were reared as girls. And children with partial androgen effects reared as girls displayed more feminine behavior than those reared as boys—findings suggesting a role for child rearing.

Other research on individuals reared as members of the other sex because they had ambiguous genitals indicates that sexual identity (comfort with being male or female) is usually consistent with gender of rearing, regardless of genetic sex (Zucker, 2001). But in these cases, children's biological sex and prenatal hormone exposure (which caused the ambiguous genitals) are discrepant—circumstances that might permit successful assignment to either gender. What about children whose genetic sex and prenatal hormone exposure match but whose genitals are ambiguous as a result of injury? Refer to the Biology and Environment box on the following page for a case study of David, a boy who experienced serious sexual-identity and adjustment problems because his biological makeup and sex of rearing were at odds.

Taken together, research indicates that sex hormones influence gender typing, with the most consistent findings involving activity level and associated preferences for "gender-appropriate" play, toys, and careers. But we must be careful not to minimize the role of experience. As we will see next, environmental forces build on genetic influences to promote children's awareness of and conformity to gender roles.

▪ Biology *and* Environment ▪

David: A Boy Who Was Reared as a Girl

As a married man and father in his mid-thirties, David Reimer talked freely about his everyday life—his problems at work and the challenges of child rearing. But when asked about his first 15 years, he distanced himself, speaking as if the child of his early life were another person. In essence, she was.

David—named Bruce at birth—underwent the first infant sex reassignment ever reported on a genetically and hormonally normal child. To find out about David's development, researchers interviewed him intensively and studied his medical and psychotherapy records (Colapinto, 2001; Diamond & Sigmundson, 1999).

When Bruce was 8 months old, his penis was accidentally severed during circumcision. Soon afterward, his desperate parents heard about psychologist John Money's success in assigning a sex to children born with ambiguous genitals. They traveled from their home in Canada to Johns Hopkins University in Baltimore, where, under Money's oversight, 22-month-old Bruce had surgery to remove his testicles and sculpt his genitals to look like those of a girl. The operation complete, Bruce's parents named their daughter Brenda.

Brenda's upbringing was tragic. From the outset, she resisted her parents' efforts to steer her in a "feminine" direction. Brian (Brenda's identical twin brother) recalled that Brenda looked like a delicate, pretty girl—until she moved or spoke: "She walked like a guy. She talked about guy things. . . . She played with my toys: Tinkertoys, dump trucks" (Colapinto, 2001, p. 57).

At school, Brenda's boyish behavior led classmates to taunt and tease her. When she played with girls, she tried organizing large-group, active games, but they weren't interested. Friendless and uncomfortable as a girl, Brenda increasingly displayed behavior problems. During periodic medical follow-ups, she drew pictures of herself as a boy and refused additional surgery to create a vagina.

As adolescence approached, Brenda's parents moved her from school to school and from therapist to therapist in an effort to help her fit in socially and accept a female identity—pressures that increased Brenda's anxiety and conflict with her parents. At puberty, when Brenda's shoulders broadened and her body added muscle, her parents insisted that she begin estrogen therapy to feminize her appearance. Soon she grew breasts and added fat around her waist and hips. Repelled by her feminizing shape, Brenda began overeating to hide it. Her classmates reacted to her confused appearance with stepped-up brutality.

At last, Brenda was transferred to a therapist who recognized her despair and encouraged her parents to tell her about her infancy. When Brenda was 14, her father explained the circumcision accident. David recalled reacting with relief. Deciding to return to his biological sex immediately, he chose for himself the name David, after the biblical lad who slew a giant and overcame adversity. David soon started injections of the androgen hormone testosterone to masculinize his body, and he underwent surgery to remove his breasts and to construct a penis. Although his adolescence continued to be troubled, in his twenties he fell in love with Jane, a single mother of three children, and married her.

David's case confirms the impact of genetic sex and prenatal hormones on a person's sense of self as male or female. His gender reassignment failed because his male biology overwhelmingly demanded a consistent sexual identity. At the same time, his childhood highlights the importance of experience. David expressed outrage at adult encouragement of dependency in girls—after all, he had experienced it firsthand.

Although David tried to surmount his tragic childhood, the troubled life that sprang from it persisted. When he was in his mid-thirties, his twin brother, Brian, committed suicide. Then, after David had lost his job and had been swindled out of his life savings in a shady investment deal, his wife left him, taking the children with her. Grief-stricken, David sank into a deep depression. On May 4, 2004, at age 38, he shot himself.

Because of a medical accident when he was a baby, David Reimer underwent the first sex reassignment on a genetically and hormonally normal baby: He was reared as a girl. His story illustrates the overwhelming impact of biology on gender identity. David is seen here at age 36, a married man and father. Two years later, the troubled life that sprang from his childhood ended tragically, in suicide.
Courtesy of David Reimer

The Case for Environment

A wealth of evidence reveals that environmental factors provide powerful support for gender-role development. Adults view boys and girls differently and treat them differently. In addition, children's social contexts—home, school, and community—offer many opportunities to observe males and females behaving in gender-stereotyped ways. And as soon as children enter the peer group, their agemates promote vigorous gender typing.

• **Perceptions and Expectations of Adults** When adults are asked to observe neutrally dressed infants who are labeled as either boy or girl, they "see" qualities that fit with the baby's artificially assigned sex. In research of this kind, adults tend to rate infants' physical features and (to a lesser extent) their personality traits in a gender-stereotyped fashion (Stern & Karraker, 1989; Vogel et al., 1991). Boys, for example, are viewed as firmer, larger, better-coordinated, and hardier, girls as softer, finer-featured, more delicate, and less alert.

During childhood and adolescence, parents continue to hold different perceptions and expectations of their sons and daughters. They want their preschoolers to play with "gender-appropriate" toys and, with respect to child-rearing values, describe achievement, competition, and control of emotion as important for sons and warmth, "ladylike" behavior, and closely supervised activities as important for daughters (Brody, 1999; Turner & Gervai, 1995). Furthermore, when asked about attitudes toward "cross-gender" behavior, parents of preschoolers responded more negatively to the idea of boys than of girls crossing gender lines. And they predicted that "cross-gender" children of both sexes would grow up to be slightly less well-adjusted than "typical" children (Sandnabba & Ahlberg, 1999).

• **Treatment by Parents** Do adults actually treat children in accord with stereotypical beliefs? A combined analysis of many studies reported that on the whole, differences in the way parents socialize boys and girls are small (Lytton & Romney, 1991). This does not mean that parental treatment is unimportant. It simply indicates that if we generalize across age periods, contexts, and behaviors, we find only a few clear trends. When the evidence is examined closely, however, consistent effects emerge. Younger children receive more direct training in gender roles than older children—a finding that is not surprising, since gender typing occurs especially rapidly during early childhood (Fagot & Hagan, 1991). And wide variation from study to study suggests that some parents practice differential treatment far more intensely than others.

Infancy and Early Childhood. In infancy and early childhood, parents encourage a diverse array of gender-specific play activities and behaviors. As early as the first few months of life—before children can express their own preferences—parents create different environments for boys and girls. Bedrooms are decorated with distinct colors and themes. Parents give their sons toys that stress action and competition (such as guns, cars, tools, and footballs), while giving their daughters toys that emphasize nurturance, cooperation, and physical attractiveness (dolls, tea sets, jump ropes, and jewelry) (Leaper, 1994; Leaper & Friedman, 2007).

Parents also actively reinforce independence in boys and closeness and dependency in girls. For example, parents react more positively when a son plays with cars and trucks, demands attention, runs and climbs, or tries to take toys from others. In contrast, when interacting with daughters, they more often direct play activities, provide help, encourage participation in household tasks, engage in conversation, make supportive statements (approval, praise, and agreement), and refer to emotions (Clearfield & Nelson, 2006; Fagot & Hagan, 1991; Kuebli, Butler, & Fivush, 1995). Furthermore, mothers more often *label emotions* when talking to girls. In doing so, they seem to teach daughters to "tune in" to others' feelings. In contrast, when talking to boys, mothers more often *explain emotions*, noting causes and consequences—an approach that emphasizes why it is important to control the expression of emotion (Cervantes & Callanan, 1998). Gender-typed play contexts amplify these communication differences. For example, when playing housekeeping, mothers engage in high rates of supportive emotional talk with girls (Leaper, 2000).

As these findings suggest, language is a powerful *indirect* means for teaching children about gender stereotypes and gender roles. Earlier in this chapter, we saw that most young children hold rigid beliefs about gender. Although their strict views are due in part to cognitive limitations, they also draw on relevant social experiences to construct these views. Like ethnic biases discussed in Chapter 11 (see page 471), young children's gender biases often bear little resemblance to those of their parents (Tenenbaum & Leaper, 2002). But even parents who believe strongly in gender equality unconsciously use language that highlights gender distinctions and informs children about traditional gender roles. **TAKE A MOMENT...** Watch several parents conversing with their preschoolers about picture books. Do your observations match findings reported in the From Research to Practice box on pages 538–539?

Early in development, then, parents provide many experiences—through play materials and social interaction—that promote assertiveness, exploration, engagement with the physical world, and emotional control in boys and imitation, reliance on others, and emotional sensitivity in girls. These experiences, in turn, give young children a rich array of cues for constructing a view of the world that emphasizes stereotypical gender distinctions.

Middle Childhood and Adolescence. As children's skills expand during the school years, issues of achievement become more salient to parents. Observations of mothers and fathers interacting with their youngsters in teaching situations reveal that parents continue to demand greater independence from boys. For example, when a child requests help, parents are more likely to ignore or refuse to respond to a son but to help a daughter right away. In helping a child with a task, parents behave in a more mastery-oriented fashion with sons, pointing out important features of tasks and setting higher standards—particularly during gender-typed pursuits, such as science activities (Crowley et al., 2001; Tenenbaum & Leaper, 2003). For example, when asked to play with magnets with their 5- and 9-year-olds, mothers engaged in more talk about scientific concepts and principles and more often suggested how to use the magnets imaginatively (for construction and in make-believe play) with sons than with daughters (see Figure 13.5). Mothers' scientific talk at age 9 predicted children's reading comprehension of science text two years later, in sixth grade (Tenenbaum et al., 2005).

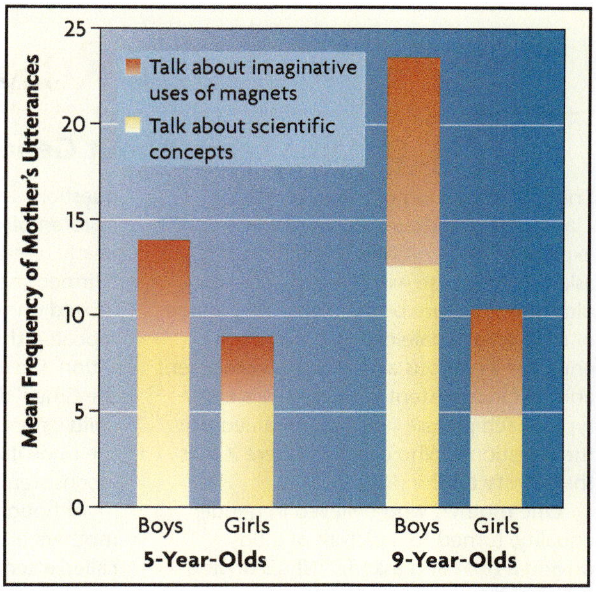

Figure 13.5 Mothers' science-related talk while playing with magnets with their 5- and 9-year-old children.
Mothers and children were given a powerful magnet and some small metal and plastic objects and asked to play with them. At both ages, mothers engaged in more talk about scientific concepts and imaginative uses of magnets with boys than with girls. This difference was especially large at age 9, when mothers' scientific talk predicted children's reading comprehension of science two years later, in sixth grade. (Adapted from Tenenbaum et al., 2005.)

Consistent with their interaction patterns, parents hold gender-differentiated perceptions of and expectations for children's competencies in various school subjects. In longitudinal research, mothers of sixth graders rated sons as more competent than daughters at math, regardless of their child's actual performance. Mothers' gender-typed judgments, in turn, influenced children's self-perceptions of math ability, the effort children devoted to math, and their later math achievement (Eccles et al., 2000; Jacobs & Eccles, 1992). When the participants were followed up two years after high school graduation and again at age 24 to 25, mothers' early perceptions no longer predicted sons' outcomes. But they continued to predict daughters' self-perceptions and also their career choices. Young women whose mothers had regarded them as highly capable at math were far more likely to choose a physical science career (Bleeker & Jacobs, 2004). Yet mothers rarely made such optimistic judgments, with long-term negative implications for girls' math-related accomplishments. Indeed, women's progress in entering such fields as engineering, mathematics, and physics has been slow. In the United States, only 10 percent of engineers and physicists are women. Women's representation is somewhat better in Canada, where they make up 22 percent of those in physical and life-science occupations (which include physicists, chemists, engineers, mathematicians, biologists, and computer scientists) (Statistics Canada, 2007k; U.S. Census Bureau, 2007b).

Parents' differential treatment of boys and girls extends to the freedom granted children in their everyday lives. Parents use more directive speech (imperatives and specific suggestions) with girls than with boys (Leaper, Anderson, & Sanders, 1998). Furthermore, when insisting that children meet their daily responsibilities, mothers of sons more often pair control with autonomy granting. Whereas they usually ask boys to make decisions ("When do you think would be a good time for you to do your music practice?"), for girls, parents tend to decide ("Do your practicing right after dinner") (Pomerantz & Ruble, 1998b). Although school-age children interpret parental control without autonomy granting as well-intentioned guidance, they also say it makes them feel incompetent (Pomerantz & Ruble, 1998a).

A father encourages his son's sense of mastery in operating a riding mower. Parents tend to provide boys with experiences that promote autonomy, assertiveness, and exploration beyond the home, girls with experiences that foster imitation, adult closeness, and reliance on others.

▪ *From* Research *to* Practice ▪

Children Learn About Gender Through Mother–Child Conversations

In an investigation of the potential for language to shape children's beliefs and expectations about gender, mothers were asked to converse with their 2- to 6-year-olds about picture books containing images of male and female children and adults engaged in various activities, half consistent and half inconsistent with gender stereotypes. Each picture was accompanied by the question, "Who can X?" where X was the activity on the page.

One mother, who believed in gender equality, turned to a picture of a boy driving a boat and asked, "Who's driving the boat?"

Her 4-year-old son replied, "A sail-man."

The mother affirmed, "A sail-man. Yup, a sailor." Then she asked, "Who can be a sailor? Boys and girls?"

"Boys," the child replied.

"Boys . . . OK," the mother again affirmed.

The child stated more decisively, "Only boys."

Again the mother agreed, "Only boys," and turned the page (Gelman, Taylor, & Nguyen, 2004, p. 104).

A detailed analysis of picture-book conversations revealed that mothers' directly expressed attitudes about gender stereotypes were neutral, largely because, like this mother, they typically posed questions to their children. But by age 4, children often voiced stereotypes, and—nearly one-third of the time—mothers affirmed them! Some mothers either moved on with the conversation or repeated the question, as in the conversation above, but rarely—just 2 percent of the time—did they explicitly counter a child's stereotype, and usually only when the book itself included stereotype-inconsistent pictures.

Although the researchers did not ask mothers to discuss gender, the mothers called attention to it even when they did not have to do so. In the English language, many nouns referring to people convey age-related information *(kid, baby, 2-year-old, preschooler, teenager, grownup, senior),* whereas only a few encode gender *(male, female, sister, brother, aunt, uncle).* Yet when using a noun to refer to a person, mothers explicitly called attention to gender more than half the time, even though the people shown in the books varied as much in age (children versus adults) as in gender. Mothers labeled gender, either with nouns or with pronouns (which in English always refer to gender), especially often when conversing with 2-year-olds: "Is that a he or a she?" "That's a boy." "There's a girl." Such statements encourage toddlers to sort their social world into gender categories, even when the statements themselves do not explicitly convey stereotypes.

While reading, this mother may unconsciously teach her child to see the world in gender-linked terms—by referring to gender when she does not need to or making generic gender statements ("Most girls prefer X"; "Boys usually don't like X"). © DCA Productions/Getty Images/Taxi

Other signs of boys' greater freedom are evident in parental willingness to let them range farther from home without supervision and in assignment of chores. In many cultures, girls are given tasks such as food preparation, cleaning, and baby-sitting that keep them close to home, whereas boys are given responsibilities that take them into the surrounding world, such as yard work and errands (Whiting & Edwards, 1988a). As noted earlier, when cultural circumstances require children to perform "cross-gender" chores (as in Nyansongo), the range of behaviors practiced expands.

Do these findings suggest that children in Western cultures should be assigned more "cross-gender" tasks? The consequences of doing so are not straightforward. Research shows that when fathers hold stereotypical views yet their sons engage in "feminine" housework, boys experience strain in the father–child relationship, feel stressed by their responsibilities, and judge themselves as less competent (McHale et al., 1990). In contrast, a match between parental values and nontraditional child-rearing practices leads to a reduction in children's gender stereotyping and gender-role behavior and to an increase in girls' nontraditional career aspirations (Tenenbaum & Leaper, 2002; Turner & Gervai, 1995; Weisner & Wilson-Mitchell, 1990). Furthermore, in homes where fathers devote as much or more time to child care as mothers, children tend to be less gender-typed in emotional expression—sons more emotionally sensitive, daughters more self-confident (Brody, 1997).

Furthermore, both mothers and children frequently expressed *generic utterances*—ones that were broad in scope, referring to many, or nearly all, males and females: "Boys can be sailors." "Most girls don't like trucks." Even generics that were gender-neutral ("Lots of girls in this book") or denied a stereotype ("Boys can be ballet dancers, too.") prompted children to view individuals of the same gender as alike and to ignore exceptions. Other research indicates that generics promote gender-role conformity. Later in this chapter, we will see that statements such as "This toy is for girls" induce children to prefer the toy labeled for their own sex and to avoid the toy labeled for the other sex.

As Figure 13.6 shows, mothers' and children's use of generics increased sharply between ages 2 and 6, a period in which gender stereotyping and gender-role conformity rise dramatically. Initially, the mothers led the way in generic talk; at age 2, they introduced these category-wide generalizations nearly three times as often as children. By age 6, however, children were producing generics more often than mothers. In addition, mother–child pairs produced more generics about males than about females, and generics were especially common in speech to and from boys, who are the more gender typed of the two sexes.

Even though these mothers overwhelmingly believed in gender equality, they did little to instill those ideas in their children. To the contrary, their most common response to children's stereotypical comments was to affirm them! In this way, even without directly teaching stereotypes, parents—through language—provide a wealth of implicit cues that enable children to readily construct them.

Adults can combat stereotypical thinking in children through concerted efforts to avoid gendered language. Here are some suggestions:

- Refrain from labeling gender when it is unnecessary to do so, substituting *child, friend, adult,* or *person* for *boy, girl, man,* or *woman.*
- Substitute references to individuals ("That person wants to be a firefighter") for generic expressions, or use qualifiers ("Some boys and some girls want to be firefighters").
- Monitor their own inclination to affirm children's stereotypical claims, countering these as often as possible.
- Discuss gender biases in language with children, pointing out how words can shape inappropriate beliefs and expectations and asking children to avoid using gender labels and generics in their own conversations.

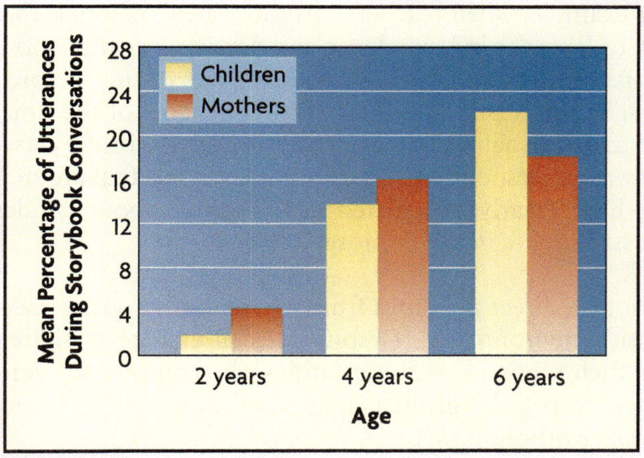

Figure 13.6 Mothers' and children's use of generic references to gender during storybook conversations.
Generic utterances were broad in scope, encouraging children to view individuals of the same gender as alike. Mothers' and children's use of generics increased dramatically between ages 2 and 6. At age 2, mothers produced more generics than children. By age 6, children produced more generics than mothers. (From S. A. Gelman, M. G. Taylor, & S. P. Nguyen, "Mother-Child Conversations About Gender," *Monographs of the Society for Research in Child Development,* 69 [1, Serial No. 275], p. 46. Reprinted with permission of the Society for Research in Child Development.)

Mothers versus Fathers. In most aspects of differential treatment of boys and girls, fathers discriminate the most. For example, in Chapter 10 we saw that fathers tend to engage in more physically stimulating play with their infant sons than daughters, whereas mothers tend to play more quietly with babies of both sexes. In childhood, fathers more than mothers encourage "gender-appropriate" behavior, and they place more pressure to achieve on sons than on daughters (Gervai, Turner, & Hinde, 1995; Wood, Desmarais, & Gugula, 2002).

Parents also seem especially committed to ensuring the gender typing of children of their own sex. While mothers go on shopping trips and bake cookies with their daughters, fathers play catch, help coach Saturday morning soccer games, and take their sons fishing. In addition to spending more time with children of their own sex, parents are more vigilant about monitoring the activities of same-sex children while the children are away from home (Leaper, 2002; Tucker, McHale, & Crouter, 2003). This pattern of greater involvement with same-sex children is another aspect of gender-role training that is more pronounced for fathers (Parke, 1996).

• Treatment by Teachers In some ways, preschool and elementary school teachers reinforce children of both sexes for "feminine" rather than "masculine" behavior. In classrooms, men and women teachers alike usually value obedience and discourage assertiveness (Fagot, 1985a). This "feminine bias" is believed to promote discomfort for boys in school, but it may

Teachers may reinforce gender roles learned at home—for example, by praising boys for their knowledge and girls for their obedience.
© Michael Newman/PhotoEdit

be as harmful—or even more so—for girls, who willingly conform, with possible long-term negative consequences for their sense of independence and self-esteem.

Teachers also act in ways that maintain and even extend gender roles taught at home. They often emphasize gender distinctions, as when they say, "Will the girls line up on one side and the boys on the other?" or "Boys, I wish you'd quiet down like the girls!"—labeling that promotes gender stereotyping, in-group favoritism, and out-group prejudice in children (Bigler, 1995). At the same time, teachers interrupt girls more than boys during conversation, thereby promoting boys' social dominance and girls' passivity. By age 4, children respond in kind: Boys interrupt their female teachers more than girls do (Hendrick & Stange, 1991).

At older ages, teachers praise boys for their knowledge, girls for their obedience. And although they discourage unruliness in all children, teachers do so more frequently and forcefully with boys. When girls misbehave, teachers are more likely to negotiate, coming up with a joint plan to improve their conduct (Erden & Wolfgang, 2004). Teachers' more frequent use of disapproval and controlling discipline with boys seems to result from an expectation that boys will misbehave more often than girls—a belief based partly on boys' actual behavior and partly on gender stereotypes. When teachers reprimand girls, it is usually for giving a wrong answer (Good & Brophy, 2003).

Just as teachers can promote gender typing, they can counteract it by modifying the way they communicate with children. For example, when teachers introduce new materials in a non-gender-biased fashion, praise all students for independence and persistence, and ignore attention seeking and dependency, children's activity choices and behaviors change accordingly (Serbin, Connor, & Citron, 1978; Serbin, Connor, & Iler, 1979). But most of the time, such changes are short-lived. As soon as the usual interaction patterns resume in the classroom, children return to their former ways of responding. Like families, schools that are successful in modifying gender typing have clearly articulated philosophies about gender equality that pervade all aspects of classroom life (Gash & Morgan, 1993).

• Observational Learning In addition to direct pressures from adults, numerous gender-typed models are available in children's environments. Despite societal changes, children continue to encounter many people in their schools and communities who conform to traditional gender roles—women as teachers (especially in the early grades) and men as school principals, women as nurses, men as police officers.

Reflections of gender in the media are also stereotyped. As we will see in Chapter 15, portrayal of gender roles in television programs has changed little in recent years. And gender stereotypes are especially prevalent in cartoons, music television (MTV), TV commercials, and video games (Calvert et al., 2003; Dietz, 1998; Pike & Jennings, 2005). In addition, despite an increase in gender-equitable storybooks and textbooks, many children read older books in which males are main characters, take center stage in exciting plot activities, and display assertiveness and creativity, while females are submissive, dependent, and passive (Tepper & Cassidy, 1999; Turner-Bowker, 1996). And in a study of recently published, award-winning picture books for young children, fathers were represented only half as often as mothers and, when they were included, rarely expressed affection or participated in caregiving but, instead, seemed disengaged from the parenting role (Anderson & Hamilton, 2005).

When children are exposed to nonstereotyped models, they are less traditional in their beliefs and behaviors. Children who often see their parents cross traditional gender lines—mothers who are employed or who do "masculine" household tasks (repairing appliances, washing the car), fathers who do "feminine" household tasks (ironing, cooking, child care)—less often endorse gender stereotypes (Turner & Gervai, 1995; Updegraff, McHale, & Crouter, 1996). Girls with career-oriented mothers show special benefits. They are more likely to engage in typically masculine activities (such as physically active play), have higher educational aspirations, and hold nontraditional career goals (Hoffman, 2000).

Furthermore, among children of divorced parents, boys in father-absent homes and girls in mother-absent homes are less gender typed, perhaps because they have fewer opportunities to observe traditional gender roles than in a two-parent household (Brenes, Eisenberg, & Helmstadter, 1985; Williams, Radin, & Allegro, 1992). And compared with agemates in two-parent families, children from single-parent homes are more likely to have at least one other-sex friend (Kovacs, Parker, & Hoffman, 1996).

• **Peers** Because most children associate almost exclusively with peers of their own sex, the peer context is an especially potent source of gender-role learning. In a study in which researchers followed preschoolers and kindergartners over the school year, children who spent more time playing with same-sex partners in the fall showed greater gains in gender typing—in terms of toy choices, activity level, aggression, and extent of play near adults—in the spring (Martin & Fabes, 2001).

Gender-Role Learning in Gender-Segregated Peer Groups. By age 3, same-sex peers positively reinforce one another for "gender-appropriate" play by praising, imitating, or joining in. In contrast, when preschoolers engage in "cross-gender" activities—for example, when boys play with dolls or girls with cars and trucks—peers criticize them. Boys are especially intolerant of "cross-gender" play in other boys (Fagot, 1984). A boy who frequently crosses gender lines is likely to be ignored by other boys, even when he does engage in "masculine" activities!

Children also develop different styles of social influence in gender-segregated peer groups. To get their way in large-group play, boys often rely on commands, threats, and physical force. Girls' preference for playing in pairs leads to greater concern with a partner's needs, evident in girls' use of polite requests, persuasion, and acceptance. Girls soon find that these gentle tactics succeed with other girls but not with boys, who ignore their courteous overtures (Leaper, 1994; Leaper, Tenenbaum, & Shaffer, 1999). And boys' unresponsiveness gives girls another reason to stop interacting with them.

Over time, children come to believe in the "correctness" of gender-segregated play, which further strengthens gender segregation and stereotyped activities. In one study, 3- to 6-year-olds believed that peers would be more likely to approve of their behavior if they played with same-sex agemates—a conviction that predicted children's association with same-sex peers (Martin et al., 1999). As boys and girls separate, in-group favoritism becomes another factor that sustains the separate social worlds of boys and girls, resulting in "two distinct subcultures" of shared knowledge, beliefs, interests, and behaviors (Maccoby, 2002).

Some educators believe that forming mixed-sex activity groups in classroom and recreational settings is a vital means of reducing gender stereotyping and broadening developmental possibilities for both sexes. To be successful, however, interventions may have to modify the styles of social influence typically learned in same-sex peer relations. Otherwise, boys are likely to dominate and girls to react passively, thereby strengthening traditional gender roles and the stereotypes each sex holds of the other.

The majority of North American children and adolescents regard excluding an agemate from a peer-group activity (such as a music club) on the basis of the individual's gender as unfair. But between fourth and seventh grade, more young people—especially boys—say it is OK to exclude on the basis of gender than on ethnicity (see Figure 13.7). When asked to explain, they point to concerns about group functioning that often are based on sex differences in interests and communication styles. As two 14-year-olds noted, "But boys, they talk about stuff, that you know, girls just don't like." "They [boys and girls] probably wouldn't relate on very many things" (Killen et al., 2002, p. 56).

Figure 13.7 **Percentage of children and adolescents saying "It's OK" to exclude an agemate from a peer-group activity on the basis of gender and ethnicity.**

When asked about excluding an other-sex or other-ethnicity peer from a peer-group activity (a music club in which members trade CDs), many more young people said that it is OK to do so on the basis of gender than on the basis of ethnicity. Willingness to exclude on the basis of gender increased with age. (Adapted from Killen et al., 2002.)

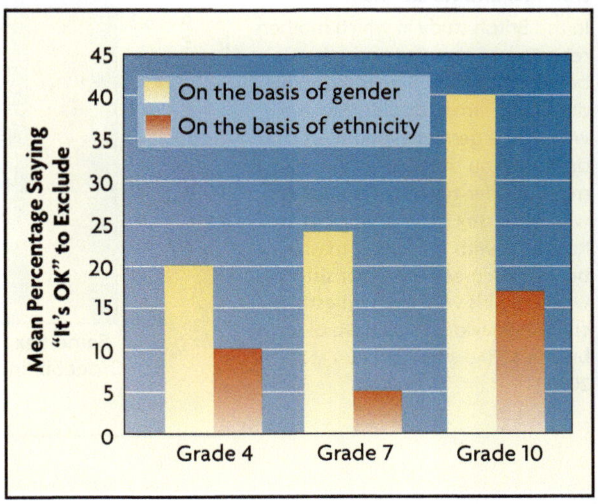

Cultural Variations. Although gender segregation is pervasive, cultures and subcultures differ in the extent of gender-typed communication within those groups. African-American and Hispanic-American lower-SES girls, for example, are generally more assertive and independent in their interactions with one another and with boys than are Caucasian-American girls (Goodwin, 1998). A comparison of Chinese and American preschoolers' play revealed similar differences. Chinese 5-year-old girls used more direct commands, complaints, and critical statements when interacting with both same- and other-sex peers than their American counterparts did. And Chinese boys frequently combined commands with warning, appeasing, and justifying statements, which reduced dominance relations in boys' playgroups ("Better not open that. You'll spill it." "I'll do it. I'm here to help you!") (Kyratzis & Guo, 2001).

In collectivist societies where group cohesion is highly valued, children may not feel a need to work as hard at maintaining same-sex peer relations through traditional interaction patterns. In addition to reducing children's ethnic prejudices (see Chapter 11), ethnically integrated classrooms might reduce gender-typed peer communication as the "cross-gender" influence attempts of some children "rub off" on others.

• **Siblings** Growing up with siblings of the same or the other sex also affects gender typing. But sibling effects are more complex than peer influences because they depend on birth order and family size (McHale, Crouter, & Whiteman, 2003). Whereas younger siblings have little impact on older siblings' gender typing, older siblings serve as powerful models for younger siblings. In a British study, more than 5,000 mothers provided information on the play and other behaviors of their 3-year-old children, each of whom had either one older sibling or no siblings. As Figure 13.8 shows, children with same-sex siblings were more gender-typed than children with no siblings, who in turn were more gender-typed than children with other-sex older siblings (Rust et al., 2000). During the school years, older siblings' influence expands, affecting younger siblings' sex-stereotyped attitudes, personality traits, and leisure pursuits (McHale et al., 2001).

Curiously, however, other research contradicts these findings, indicating that children with same-sex siblings are less stereotyped in their interests and personality traits than those from mixed-sex families (Grotevant, 1978; Tauber, 1979). How can we explain these conflicting results? Recall from Chapter 10 that siblings often strive to be different from one another. This effect is strongest when children are of the same sex and come from large families, in which they may feel a greater need to stand out. A close look reveals that studies reporting a *modeling and reinforcement effect* (an increase in gender typing among same-sex siblings) focus on children from two-child families. In contrast, those reporting a *differentiation effect* often include children from larger families.

In addition, parents whose children are all of the same sex sometimes relax pressures toward gender typing. For example, mothers were more willing to give their child a gender-atypical toy as a gift when the child had an older, same-sex sibling (Stoneman, Brody, &

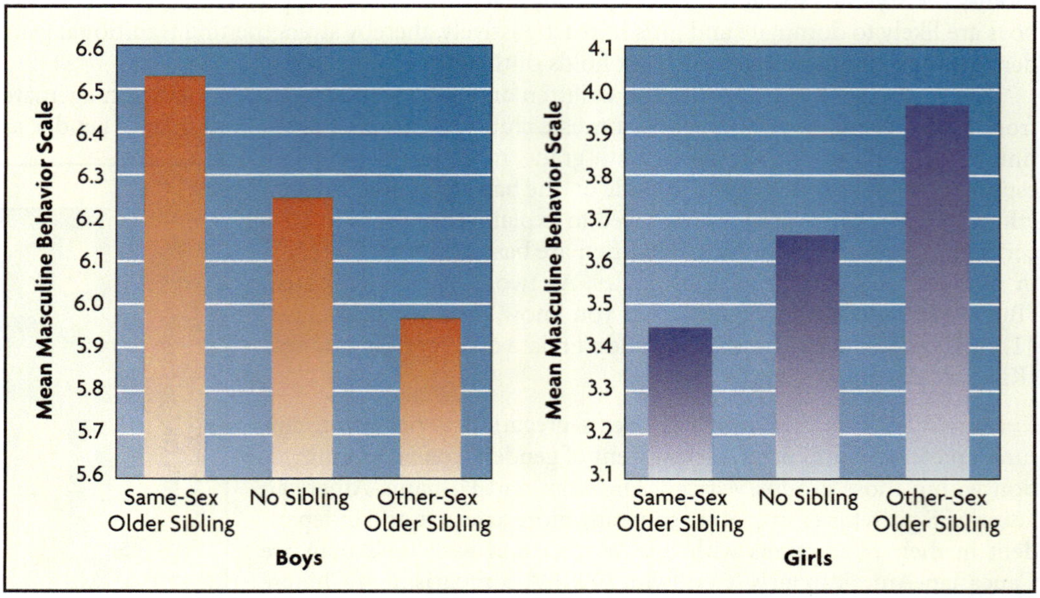

■ **Figure 13.8** **"Masculine" behavior scores for preschool boys and girls with same-sex older siblings, other-sex older siblings, and no siblings.**
In this British study in which mothers reported on the play and other behaviors of their 3-year-olds, children with same-sex older siblings were more gender-typed than children with no siblings, who were more gender-typed than children with other-sex older siblings. Notice how boys with the lowest masculine behavior scores have older sisters, whereas girls with the highest masculine behavior scores have older brothers. (Adapted from Rust et al., 2000.)

These brothers share a typically "feminine" task. When siblings are the same sex, they are more likely to be assigned "cross-gender" chores. © Corbis Super RF/Alamy

MacKinnon, 1986). Also, in all-girl and all-boy families, children are more likely to be assigned "cross-gender" chores because no "gender-appropriate" child is available to do the job. Therefore, families with all same-sex siblings may provide some special opportunities to step out of traditional gender roles.

In sum, older siblings are influential models in young children's gender typing. But aspects of the family context, including family size and parental pressures, can alter this modeling effect.

Ask Yourself

Review Summarize parent, peer, and sibling influences on gender-role adoption. Why are sibling influences more complex than parent and peer influences?

Apply List findings indicating that language and communication—between parents and children, between teachers and children, and between peers—powerfully affect children's gender stereotyping and gender-role behavior. What recommendations would you make to counteract these influences?

Connect Using research in this chapter and in Chapter 11 (see page 461), explain why girls are more susceptible than boys to learned helplessness in achievement situations.

Reflect In early and middle childhood, did you play mostly with peers of your own sex? What gender-linked attitudes and behaviors were emphasized in your peer associations? How did you view members of the other sex?

Gender Identity

Besides biological and environmental influences, another factor eventually affects gender stereotyping and gender-role behavior: *gender identity,* a person's perception of the self as relatively masculine or feminine in characteristics. In middle childhood, as self-concepts emphasize psychological dispositions over concrete behaviors (see Chapter 11), researchers can measure gender identity by asking children to rate themselves on personality traits. A child or adult with a "masculine" identity scores high on traditionally masculine items (*ambitious, competitive,* and *self-sufficient*) and low on traditionally feminine items (*affectionate, cheerful,* and *soft-spoken*). Someone with a "feminine" identity does the reverse. Although most people view themselves in gender-typed terms, a substantial minority (especially females) have a gender identity called **androgyny,** scoring high on *both* masculine and feminine personality characteristics.

Gender identity is a good predictor of psychological adjustment. "Masculine" and androgynous children and adults have higher self-esteem than "feminine" individuals (Boldizar, 1991; Harter, 2006). In line with their flexible self-definitions, androgynous individuals are more adaptable—able to show masculine independence or feminine sensitivity, depending on the situation (Huyck, 1996; Taylor & Hall, 1982).

A close look at these findings, however, reveals that the masculine component of androgyny is largely responsible for the superior psychological health of androgynous women over those with traditional identities. Feminine women seem to have adjustment difficulties because many of their attributes are not valued highly by society (Bronstein, 2006; Taylor & Hall, 1982). Nevertheless, the existence of an androgynous identity demonstrates that children can acquire a mixture of positive qualities traditionally associated with each gender—an orientation that may best help them realize their potential. In a future society in which feminine traits are socially rewarded to the same extent as masculine traits, androgyny may very well represent the ideal personality.

Emergence of Gender Identity

How do children develop a gender identity? According to *social learning theory,* behavior comes before self-perceptions. Preschoolers first acquire gender-typed responses through modeling and reinforcement; only later do they organize these behaviors into gender-linked ideas about themselves. In contrast, *cognitive-developmental theory* maintains that self-perceptions come before behavior. Over the preschool years, children acquire a cognitive appreciation of the permanence of their sex. They develop **gender constancy**—a full understanding of the biologically based permanence of their gender, which combines three understandings: *gender labeling, gender stability,* and *gender consistency.* Then children use this knowledge to guide their behavior. Let's trace the development of gender constancy during the preschool years.

• Development of Gender Constancy Lawrence Kohlberg (1966) proposed that before age 6 or 7, children cannot maintain the constancy of their gender, just as they cannot pass Piagetian conservation problems. They attain this understanding only gradually, by moving through the following stages of development:

1. **Gender labeling.** During the early preschool years, children can label their own sex and that of others correctly. But when asked such questions as "When you [a girl] grow up, could you ever be a daddy?" or "Could you be a boy if you wanted to?" young children freely answer yes (Slaby & Frey, 1975). And when shown a doll whose hairstyle and clothing are transformed before their eyes, children indicate that the doll's sex has changed (Chauhan, Shastri, & Mohite, 2005; Fagot, 1985b).
2. **Gender stability.** At this stage, children have a partial understanding of the permanence of sex, in that they grasp its stability over time. But even though they know that male and female babies will eventually become boys and girls, and then men and women, they continue to insist that changing hairstyle, clothing, or "gender-appropriate" activities will also change a person's sex (Fagot, 1985b; Slaby & Frey, 1975).
3. **Gender consistency.** During the late preschool and early school years, children understand that sex is biologically based and remains the same even if a person dresses in "cross-gender" clothes or engages in nontraditional activities (Emmerich, 1981; Ruble et al., 2007).

If this 4-year-old saw a boy wearing feminine dress-up clothes, she might insist that he had become a girl. She has not yet attained gender consistency—the understanding that sex is biologically based and permanent. © Bob Ebbesen/Alamy

Many studies confirm that the development of gender constancy follows this sequence. As Kohlberg assumed, mastery of gender constancy is associated with attainment of conservation (De Lisi & Gallagher, 1991). It is also strongly related to the ability to pass verbal appearance–reality tasks (see page 245 in Chapter 6) (Trautner, Gervai, & Nemeth, 2003). Indeed, gender consistency tasks can be considered a type of appearance–reality problem because they require children to distinguish between what a person looks like and who he or she really is.

In many cultures, young children do not have access to basic biological knowledge about gender because they rarely see members of the other sex naked. Therefore, they distinguish males and females using the only information they do have: hairstyle, clothing, and behavior. But giving children information about genital differences does not result in gender constancy. Preschoolers who have such knowledge usually say that changing a doll's clothing or hairstyle will not change their sex, but when asked to justify their responses, they do not refer to sex as an innate, unchanging quality of people (Szkrybalo & Ruble, 1999). This suggests that cognitive immaturity, not social experience, is largely responsible for young children's difficulty grasping the permanence of sex.

• **How Well Does Gender Constancy Predict Gender-Role Adoption?** Is cognitive-developmental theory correct that gender constancy is responsible for children's gender-typed behavior? Evidence for this assumption is weak. "Gender-appropriate" behavior appears so early in the preschool years that modeling and reinforcement must contribute to its initial appearance, as social learning theory suggests.

Although gender constancy does not initiate gender-role conformity, the cognitive changes that lead up to it do seem to facilitate gender typing. Preschoolers who reach the stage of gender labeling early show especially rapid development of "gender-appropriate" play preferences and are more knowledgeable about gender stereotypes than their late-labeling peers (Fagot, Leinbach, & O'Boyle, 1992). Similarly, understanding of gender stability prompts increased gender stereotyping, preference for same-sex playmates, choice of "gender-appropriate" toys, and identification with one's gender group (Martin & Little, 1990; Ruble et al., 2007). These findings suggest that as soon as children form basic gender categories, they use them to acquire gender-relevant information about their social world and about themselves.

The stage of gender consistency, in contrast, functions differently. Although outcomes are not entirely consistent, the realization that sex does not change despite superficial transformations in clothing or behavior seems to contribute to increasing gender-stereotype flexibility in the early school years (Ruble et al., 2007). But overall, the impact of gender constancy on gender typing is not great. As we will see next, gender-role adoption is more powerfully affected by children's beliefs about how tight the connection must be between their own gender and their behavior.

Gender Identity in Middle Childhood

During middle childhood, boys' and girls' gender identities follow different paths. Self-ratings on personality traits reveal that from third to sixth grade, boys strengthen their identification with the "masculine" role, while girls' identification with "feminine" characteristics declines. Although girls still lean toward the "feminine" side, they are the more androgynous of the sexes—more likely than boys to describe themselves as having "other-gender" characteristics (Serbin, Powlishta, & Gulko, 1993). This difference is also evident in children's activities. Whereas boys usually stick to "masculine" pursuits, girls experiment with a wider range of options. Besides cooking, sewing, and baby-sitting, they join organized sports teams and work on science projects. And girls are more likely than boys to consider future work roles stereotyped for the other gender, such as firefighter or astronomer (Liben & Bigler, 2002).

During middle childhood, girls feel freer than boys to engage in "cross-gender" activities. This 9-year-old perfects her wood-carving skills.

These changes are due to a mixture of cognitive and social forces. School-age children of both sexes are aware that society attaches greater prestige to "masculine" characteristics. For example, they rate "masculine" occupations as having higher status than "feminine" occupations. And by age 11, they regard a novel job (such as *clipster,* "a person who tests batteries") as higher in status when it is portrayed with a male worker than with a female worker (see Figure 13.9 on page 546) (Liben, Bigler, & Krogh, 2001). In view of the strong association of males' activities with high status, it is not surprising that girls start to identify with "masculine" traits and are attracted to some typically masculine activities.

As school-age children make social comparisons and characterize themselves in terms of stable dispositions, their gender identity expands to include the following self-evaluations, which greatly affect their adjustment:

- *Gender typicality*—the degree to which the child feels similar to others of the same gender, based on his or her own personal evaluation. Children can feel gender-typical for different reasons. For example, one boy might derive this feeling from excelling at math, another from being a good athlete. Children need not be highly gender-typed

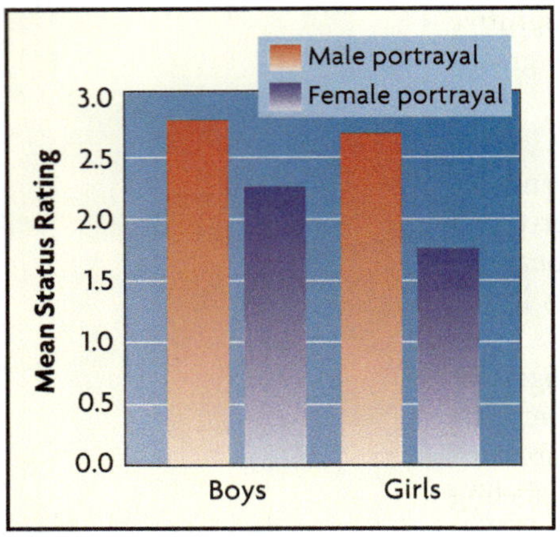

Figure 13.9 **Eleven-year-olds' status ratings of novel jobs portrayed with male and female workers.**
Although children had no prior knowledge of these jobs and therefore had not previously stereotyped them as "masculine" or "feminine," simply portraying the job with a male worker resulted in higher status ratings. (Adapted from Liben, Bigler, & Krogh, 2001.)

to judge themselves as gender-typical, but psychological well-being depends on feeling, at least to some degree, that they "fit in" with their same-sex peers (Egan & Perry, 2001).

- *Gender contentedness*—the degree to which the child feels satisfied with his or her gender assignment. Like gender typicality, gender contentedness promotes happiness and satisfaction with oneself.
- *Felt pressure to conform to gender roles*—the degree to which the child feels parents and peers disapprove of his or her gender-related traits. Because such pressure reduces the likelihood that children will explore options related to their interests and talents, children who feel strong gender-typed pressure are likely to be distressed and dissatisfied.

In a longitudinal study of third through seventh graders, *gender-typical* and *gender-contented* children gained in self-esteem over the following year. In contrast, children who were *gender-atypical* and *gender-discontented* declined in self-worth. Furthermore, gender-atypical children who reported *intense pressure to conform to gender roles* experienced serious difficulties, in the form of withdrawal, sadness, disappointment, and anxiety (Yunger, Carver, & Perry, 2004).

Clearly, how children feel about themselves in relation to their gender group becomes vitally important in middle childhood, and those who experience rejection because of their gender-atypical traits suffer profoundly. **TAKE A MOMENT...** Return to the Biology and Environment box on page 535, and note how David's dissatisfaction with his gender assignment, together with severe peer condemnation, severely impaired his adjustment.

Currently, researchers and therapists are engaged in a heated debate over how best to help children who feel gender-atypical. Some advocate making them more gender-typical, through therapy that reinforces such children for engaging in traditional gender-role activities so they will feel more compatible with same-sex peers (see, for example, Zucker, 2006). Others oppose this approach on grounds that it promotes a pathological view of gender atypicality, is likely to heighten felt pressure to conform (which predicts maladjustment), and—for children who fail to change—may result in parental rejection. These experts advocate modifying parents' and peers' attitudes, through interventions that help them become more accepting of children's gender-atypical interests and behaviors (Bigler, 2007; Conway, 2007; Crawford, 2003). **TAKE A MOMENT...** In view of what you have learned in this chapter, which approach do you think would be more successful, and why?

Gender Identity in Adolescence

The arrival of adolescence is typically accompanied by **gender intensification**—increased gender stereotyping of attitudes and behavior, and movement toward a more traditional gender identity (Basow & Rubin, 1999; Galambos, Almeida, & Petersen, 1990). Both sexes experience gender intensification, but it is stronger for early-adolescent girls, who were more androgynous during middle childhood. Girls continue to be less gender-typed than boys but feel less free to experiment with "other-gender" activities and behaviors than they did earlier (Huston & Alvarez, 1990).

In early adolescence, young people, especially girls, move toward more traditional gender identities. But by their late teens, these girls may shift toward greater gender-role flexibility, moving beyond a stereotypically feminine focus on appearance and popularity. © LWA-Dann Tardif/CORBIS

What accounts for gender intensification? Biological, social, and cognitive factors are involved. Puberty magnifies sex differences in appearance, causing adolescents to spend more time thinking about themselves in gender-linked ways. Pubertal changes also prompt gender-typed pressures from others. Parents—especially those with traditional gender-role beliefs—may encourage "gender-appropriate" activities and behavior to a greater extent than they did in middle childhood (Crouter, Manke, & McHale, 1995). And when adolescents start to date, they often become more gender-typed as a way of increasing their attractiveness (Maccoby, 1998). For example, in encounters with boys, girls frequently use disclaimers ("I may be wrong" or "sort of")—a tentative speech style their male partners prefer (Carli, 1995). Finally, cognitive changes—in particular, greater concern with what others think—make young teenagers more responsive to gender-role expectations.

As young people move toward a mature personal identity, they become less concerned with others' opinions of them and more involved in finding meaningful values to include in their self-definitions (see Chapter 11). As a result, highly stereotypical self-perceptions decline, especially when parents and teachers encourage adolescents to question the value of gender stereotypes for themselves and their society. Thus, the social environment is a major force in promoting gender-role flexibility in adolescence, just as it was at earlier ages.

Gender Schema Theory

Gender schema theory is an information-processing approach that explains how environmental pressures and children's cognitions work together to shape gender typing (Martin & Halverson, 1987; Martin, Ruble, & Szkrybalo, 2002). It also integrates the various elements of gender typing—gender stereotyping, gender identity, and gender-role adoption—into a unified picture of how masculine and feminine orientations emerge and are often strongly maintained.

At an early age, children pick up gender-typed preferences and behaviors from others. At the same time, they organize experiences into *gender schemas,* or masculine and feminine categories, that they use to interpret their world. As soon as preschoolers can label and grasp the stability of their own gender, they select gender schemas consistent with it ("Only boys can be doctors" or "Cooking is a girl's job") and apply those categories to themselves. Their self-perceptions then become gender-typed and serve as additional schemas that children use to process information and guide their own behavior.

We have seen that individual differences exist in the extent to which children endorse gender-typed views. Figure 13.10 shows different cognitive pathways for children who often apply gender schemas to their experiences and those who rarely do (Liben & Bigler, 2002). Consider Billy, who encounters a doll. If Billy is a *gender-schematic child,* his *gender-salience filter* immediately makes gender highly relevant. Drawing on his prior learning, he asks himself, "Should boys play with dolls?" If he answers "yes" and the toy interests him, he will approach it, explore it, and learn more about it. If he answers "no," he will respond by avoiding the "gender-inappropriate" toy. But if Billy is a *gender-aschematic child*—one who seldom views the world in gender-linked terms—he simply asks himself, "Do I like this toy?" and responds on the basis of his interests.

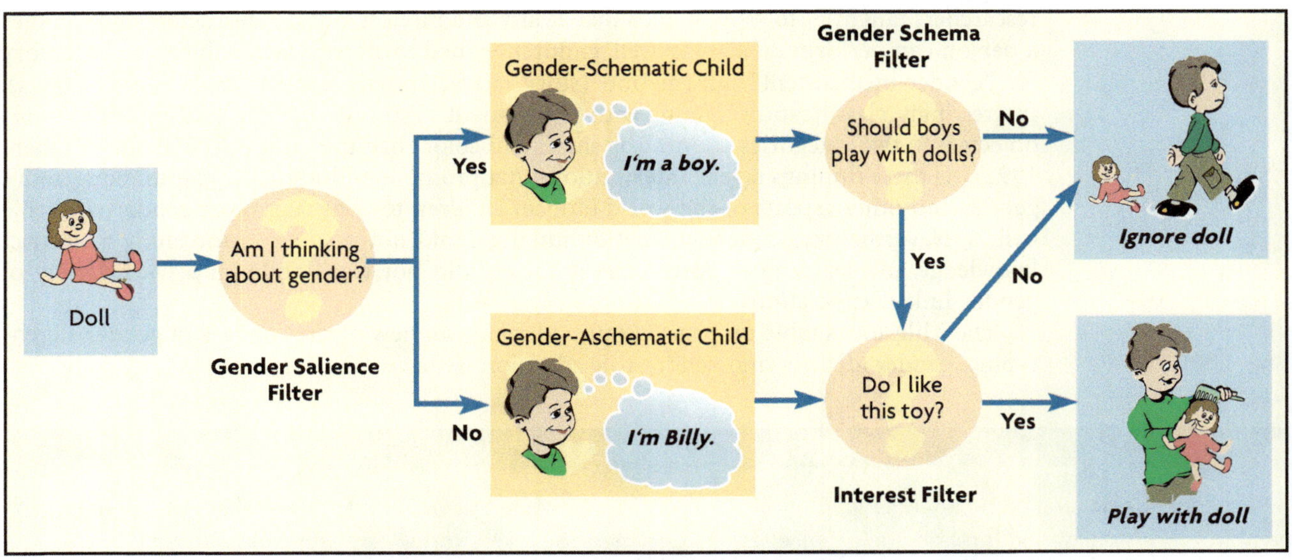

Figure 13.10 **Cognitive pathways for gender-schematic and gender-aschematic children.** In *gender-schematic children,* the gender-salience filter immediately makes gender highly relevant: Billy sees a doll and thinks, "I'm a boy. Should boys play with dolls?" Drawing on his experiences, he answers "yes" or "no." If he answers "yes" and the doll interests him, he plays with the doll. If he answers "no," he avoids the "gender-inappropriate" toy. *Gender-aschematic children* rarely view the world in gender-linked terms: Billy simply asks, "Do I like this toy?" and responds on the basis of his interests. (Drawing by Lynn Liben, The Pennsylvania State University and Rebecca Bigler, University of Texas, Austin. Reprinted by permission of Rebecca Bigler.)

Would these children continue playing if an adult labeled cards as "a boys' game" or "a girls' game"? If children believe a toy or game is for the other gender, powerful gender schemas lead them to like it less. © Image Source/Alamy

To examine the consequences of gender-schematic processing, researchers showed 4- and 5-year-olds toys that were "gender-neutral" and that varied in attractiveness. An adult labeled some as boys' toys and others as girls' toys, leaving a third group unlabeled. Most children engaged in gender-schematic reasoning, preferring toys labeled for their gender and predicting that same-sex peers would also like those toys. Highly attractive toys, especially, lost their appeal when they were labeled as for the other gender (Martin, Eisenbud, & Rose, 1995). And because gender-schematic preschoolers typically conclude, "What I like, children of my own sex will also like," they often use their own preferences to add to their gender biases! For example, a girl who dislikes oysters may declare, "Only boys like oysters!" even though she has never actually been given information supporting such a stereotype (Liben & Bigler, 2002).

Gender-schematic thinking is so powerful that when children see others behaving in "gender-inconsistent" ways, they often cannot remember the behavior or distort their memory to make it "gender-consistent"—for example, when shown a picture of a male nurse, remembering him as a doctor (Liben & Signorella, 1993; Marin & Ruble, 2004). Over time, children learn much more about people, objects, and events that fit with their gender schemas than they do about "cross-gender" activities and behaviors.

Training school-age children in cognitive skills that counteract gender-biased social messages reduces their tendency to view the world in gender-schematic terms. When researchers taught 5- to 10-year-olds that ability and interest, not gender, determine whether a person can perform an activity well, children gained in stereotype flexibility and memory for "gender-inconsistent" information (story characters engaged in "cross-gender" tasks). Interestingly, classification training with gender-neutral stimuli that required children to sort objects into two categories at once (by shape and color) had the same effect (Bigler & Liben, 1992). As these findings reveal, interventions that promote multidimensional thinking about gender and other aspects of the world induces children to construct more gender-equitable beliefs. Nevertheless, gender-schematic thinking could not operate so forcefully to restrict knowledge and learning opportunities if society did not teach children a wide variety of gender-linked associations.

The Milestones table on page 549 provides an overview of the changes in gender stereotyping, gender identity, and gender-role adoption we have considered.

Ask Yourself

Review Describe the general path of gender identity development, from early childhood through adolescence, noting differences between boys and girls.

Apply While looking at a book, 4-year-old Roger saw a picture of a boy cooking at a stove. Later, he recalled the person in the picture as a girl. Using gender schema theory, explain Roger's memory error.

Connect What gains in perspective taking lead young teenagers to be very concerned with what others think and, therefore, probably contribute to gender intensification? (See page 474 in Chapter 11.)

Reflect In early adolescence, did you and your friends display gender intensification? Describe examples. When did this concern with gender appropriateness decline?

Milestones

Gender Typing

Age	Gender Stereotyping and Gender-Role Adoption	Gender Identity
1–5 years	■ "Gender-appropriate" toy preferences emerge and strengthen. ■ Gender stereotyping of activities, occupations, and behaviors expands. ■ Gender segregation in peer interaction emerges and strengthens. ■ Girls' preference for play in pairs, boys' for play in larger groups, appears.	■ Gender constancy develops in a three-stage sequence: gender labeling, gender stability, and gender consistency. 
6–11 years	■ Gender-stereotyped knowledge expands, especially for personality traits and achievement areas. ■ Gender stereotyping becomes more flexible. 	■ "Masculine" gender identity strengthens among boys; girls' gender identity becomes more androgynous. 
12–18 years	■ Gender-role conformity increases in early adolescence and then declines. ■ Gender segregation becomes less pronounced.	■ Gender identity becomes more traditional in early adolescence; gradually, highly stereotypical self-perceptions decline.

Note: These milestones represent overall age trends. Individual differences exist in the precise age at which each milestone is attained and in the extent of gender typing.

Photos: (top) © David Young-Wolff/PhotoEdit; (middle) © Kevin Dodge/Corbis; (bottom) © LWA-Dann Tardif/Corbis

To What Extent Do Boys and Girls *Really* Differ in Gender-Stereotyped Attributes?

So far, we have examined the relationship of biological, social, and cognitive factors to children's gender-typed preferences and behavior. But we have said little about the extent to which boys and girls actually differ in mental abilities and personality traits. Over the past several decades, thousands of studies have measured sex differences in these characteristics. At the heart of these efforts is the age-old nature–nurture debate. Researchers have looked for stable differences between males and females and, from there, have searched for the biological and environmental roots of each variation.

To avoid basing conclusions on single studies and small, potentially biased samples, researchers often use a technique called *meta-analysis,* in which they reanalyze the data of many investigations together. Besides telling us whether a sex difference exists, this method provides an estimate of its size. Table 13.2 on page 550 summarizes differences between boys and girls in mental abilities and personality traits, based on current evidence. The majority of findings listed in the table are small to moderate. Furthermore, as Figure 13.11 shows, the distributions for males and females usually overlap greatly. Sex differences usually account for no more than 5 to 10 percent of individual differences, leaving most to be explained by other factors. Consequently, males and females are actually more alike than different in developmental potential. Nevertheless, as we will see shortly, a few sex differences are considerable.

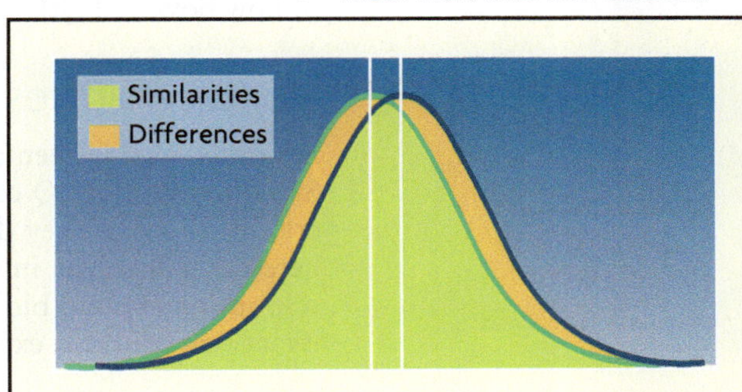

■ **Figure 13.11 Typical distributions of scores in studies comparing males and females on mental abilities and personality traits.**

For most characteristics, the distributions overlap greatly. This means that males and females are actually much more alike than different.

Table 13.2 Sex Differences in Mental Abilities and Personality Traits

Characteristic	Sex Difference
Verbal abilities	Girls are advantaged in early language development and in reading and writing achievement throughout the school years. On tests of verbal ability, girls outperform boys, more so when tests are heavily weighted with writing.
Spatial abilities	Beginning in early childhood, boys outperform girls in certain spatial skills, a difference that persists throughout the lifespan.
Mathematical abilities	In the early school grades, girls do better than boys in math computation. As young people progress through school, boys do better than girls on complex problems involving abstract reasoning and geometry. The difference is greatest among high-achieving students.
School achievement	Girls get better grades than boys in all academic subjects in elementary school, after which the difference declines. In junior high school, boys start to show an advantage in mathematics and physical sciences.
Achievement motivation	Sex differences in achievement motivation are linked to type of task. Boys perceive themselves as more competent and have higher expectations for success in "masculine" achievement areas, such as mathematics, sports, and mechanical skills. Girls have higher expectations and set higher standards for themselves in "feminine" areas, such as reading, writing, literature, and art.
Emotional sensitivity	Girls score higher than boys in emotional understanding and on self-report measures of empathy and sympathy. Girls' advantage in prosocial behavior is greatest for kindness and considerateness, less apparent for helping behavior.
Fear, timidity, and anxiety	Girls are more fearful and timid than boys, a difference that is present in the first year of life. In school, girls are more anxious about failure and try harder to avoid it. Boys are greater risk takers, a difference reflected in their higher injury rates throughout childhood and adolescence.
Effortful control	Compared with boys, girls display greater effortful control, including capacity to inhibit impulses and shift attention away from irrelevant or emotionally arousing stimuli—traits that contribute to girls' better school performance and reduced incidence of behavior problems.
Compliance and dependency	Girls comply more readily with directives from adults and peers. They also seek help from adults more often and score higher in dependency on personality tests.
Activity level	Boys are more active than girls.
Depression	Adolescent girls are more likely than boys to report depressive symptoms.
Aggression	Boys are more physically aggressive than girls and, in adolescence, are far more likely to become involved in antisocial behavior and violent crime. The sex difference favoring girls in relational aggression is small.
Developmental problems	Problems more common among boys than girls include speech and language disorders, reading disabilities, and behavior problems such as hyperactivity, hostile acting-out behavior, and emotional and social immaturity. More boys are born with genetic disorders, physical disabilities, and mental retardation.

Keep in mind that sex differences can change over time. For example, over the past several decades, the gender gap has narrowed in all areas of mental ability for which differences have been identified (Halpern, 2000, 2004). This trend is a reminder that the general picture of how boys and girls differ may not be the same in a few decades as it is today.

Mental Abilities

Sex differences in mental abilities have sparked almost as much controversy as the ethnic and SES differences in IQ considered in Chapter 8. Although boys and girls do not differ in general intelligence, they do vary in specific mental abilities. Many researchers, believing that heredity is involved in these disparities, have attempted to identify the biological processes responsible. But no biological factor operates in a social and cultural vacuum. For each ability we will consider, experience plays a major role.

• **Verbal Abilities** Early in development, girls are ahead of boys in language progress. They begin to talk earlier and show faster vocabulary growth during the second year (see Chapter 9).

Throughout the school years, girls attain higher scores in reading achievement and account for a lower percentage of children referred for remedial reading instruction. Girls also score slightly to moderately higher on tests of verbal ability in middle childhood and adolescence in every country in which assessments have been conducted (Bussiére, Knighton, & Pennock, 2007; Halpern, 2000, 2004; Mullis et al., 2003). And when verbal tests are heavily weighted with writing, girls' advantage is large (Halpern et al., 2007).

A special concern is that the gender gap in reading and writing achievement increases over adolescence, with boys doing especially poorly in writing—trends evident in the United States, Canada, and other industrialized nations (OECD, 2005; Statistics Canada, 2006d; U.S. Department of Education, 2006, 2007). These differences are believed to be major contributors to a widening gender difference in college enrollments. Whereas 30 years ago, males accounted for 60 percent of North American undergraduate students, today they are in the minority, at 42 percent (Statistics Canada, 2006f; U.S. Department of Education, 2007).

Recall from Chapter 9 that girls show a biological advantage in earlier development of the left hemisphere of the cerebral cortex, where language is usually localized. But mothers also talk considerably more to girls than to boys. From the preschool years through adolescence, mother–daughter narratives about past experiences are more organized and elaborative than mother–son narratives, and girls' and boys' independently generated narratives differ similarly (Peterson & Roberts, 2003). Furthermore, we have seen that children tend to view language arts as a "feminine" subject, that parents rate daughters as more competent at it, and that elementary school classrooms are feminine-biased settings in which boys' higher activity level and greater tendency toward noncompliance elicit more teacher disapproval. And, as noted in Chapter 8, as a result of the high-stakes testing movement, students today spend much time at their desks being taught in a regimented, uniform way—an approach particularly at odds with boys' higher activity level, assertiveness, and incidence of learning problems.

Finally, high rates of divorce and births to single mothers mean that more children today grow up without the continuous presence of a father, who models and encourages good work habits and skill at reading and writing. Both maternal and paternal involvement contributes to the achievement and educational attainment of young people of both sexes, but fathers' involvement in their children's home and school lives may be especially important for boys (Flouri & Buchanan, 2004; Le Menestrel, 1999). In one investigation, high-achieving African-American boys were particularly likely to come from homes where fathers are warm, verbally communicative, and demanding of achievement (Grief, Hrabowski, & Maton, 1998). Clearly, reversing boys' weakening literacy skills is a high priority—one that requires a concerted effort on the part of families, schools, and supportive communities.

• Mathematical Abilities Studies of mathematical abilities in the early school grades are inconsistent. Some find no sex differences, others slight disparities depending on the math skill assessed (Lachance & Mazzocco, 2006). Girls tend to be advantaged in arithmetic computation, perhaps because of their better verbal skills and more methodical approach to problem solving. And whereas girls more often rely on concrete manipulatives to solve basic math problems, boys more often mentally represent numbers and retrieve answers rapidly from memory (Carr & Jessup, 1997; Fennema et al., 1998). But around early adolescence, when math concepts become more abstract and spatial, boys start to outperform girls. The difference is especially evident on tests of complex reasoning and geometry (Bielinski & Davison, 1998). In science achievement, too, boys' advantage increases as problems become more difficult (Penner, 2003).

When all adolescents are considered, this male advantage is evident in virtually every country where males and females have equal access to secondary education. At the same time, the gap is small, and it has diminished over the past 30 years (Bussiére, Knighton, & Pennock, 2007; Halpern, Wai, & Saw, 2005; U.S. Department of Education, 2006). Among the most capable, however, the gender gap is greater. In widely publicized research on more than 100,000 bright seventh and eighth graders invited to take the Scholastic Assessment Test (SAT), boys outscored girls on the mathematics subtest year after year. Yet even this disparity has been shrinking. A quarter-century ago, 13 times as many boys as girls scored over 700 (out of a possible 800) on the math portion of the SAT;

Girls, especially, benefit from applied, hands-on learning experiences, which reduce the gender gap in math and science achievement. These high school students deepen their understanding of chemical reactions by simulating an erupting volcano in their chemistry lab. © LWA-Dann Tardif/Corbis

Biology *and* Environment

Sex Differences in Spatial Abilities

Spatial skills are a key focus in researchers' efforts to explain sex differences in mathematical reasoning. The gender gap favoring males is large for *mental rotation tasks,* in which individuals must rotate a three-dimensional figure rapidly and accurately inside their heads (see Figure 13.12). Males also do considerably better on *spatial perception tasks,* in which people must determine spatial relationships by considering the orientation of the surrounding environment. Sex differences on *spatial visualization tasks,* involving analysis of complex visual forms, are weak or nonexistent. Because many different strategies can be used to solve these tasks, both sexes may come up with effective procedures (Collaer & Hill, 2006; Voyer, Voyer, & Bryden, 1995).

Sex differences in spatial abilities emerge in early childhood and persist throughout the lifespan (Levine et al., 1999). The pattern is consistent enough to suggest a biological explanation. One hypothesis is that heredity, perhaps through exposure to androgen hormones, enhances right hemispheric functioning, giving males a spatial advantage. (Recall that for most people, spatial skills are housed in the right hemisphere of the cerebral cortex.) In support of this idea, girls and women whose prenatal androgen levels were abnormally high show superior performance on spatial rotation tasks (Berenbaum, 2001; Halpern & Collaer,

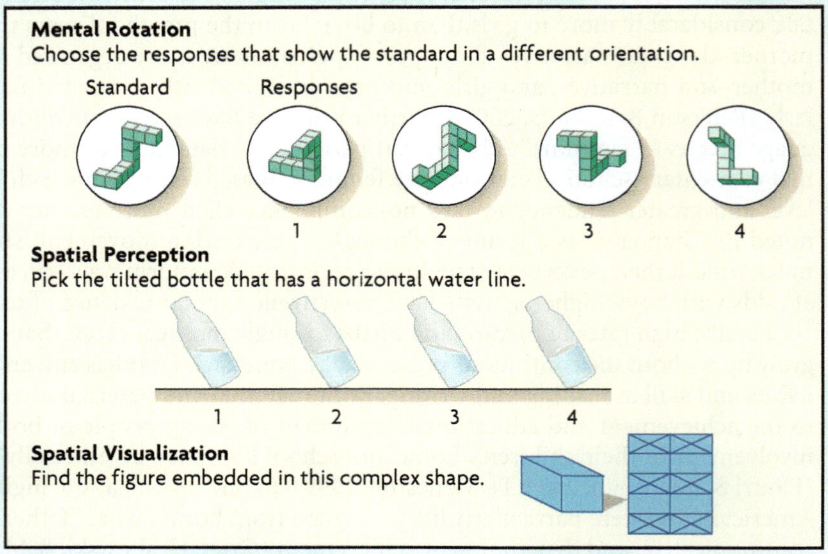

Figure 13.12 **Types of spatial tasks.**
Large sex differences favoring males appear on mental rotation, and males do considerably better than females on spatial perception. In contrast, sex differences on spatial visualization are weak or nonexistent. (From M. C. Linn & A. C. Petersen, 1985, "Emergence and Characterization of Sex Differences in Spatial Ability: A Meta-Analysis," *Child Development,* 56, pp. 1482, 1483, 1485. © The Society for Research in Child Development, Inc. Reprinted by permission.)

today, the ratio is 2.8 to 1 (Benbow & Stanley, 1983; Lubinski & Benbow, 1994; Monastersky, 2005).

Some researchers believe that heredity contributes substantially to the gender gap in math, especially to the tendency for more boys to be extremely talented. Accumulating evidence indicates that boys' advantage originates in two skill areas. First, boys' more rapid numerical memory permits them to devote more energy to complex mental operations. Second, boys' superior spatial reasoning enhances their mathematical problem solving (Geary et al., 2000; Halpern et al., 2007). See the Biology and Environment box above for further consideration of this issue.

Social pressures are also influential. We have seen that children often view math as a "masculine" subject. Also, many parents think boys are better at it—an attitude that encourages girls to view themselves as having to work harder at math to do well, to blame their errors on lack of ability, and to regard math as less useful for their future lives. These beliefs reduce girls' self-efficacy at doing math, which undermines their performance on math achievement tests and their willingness to consider math- or science-related careers in college (Bhanot & Jovanovic, 2005; Bleeker & Jacobs, 2004; Kenney-Benson et al., 2006). Furthermore, *stereotype threat*—the fear of being judged on the basis of a negative stereotype (see page 340 in Chapter 8)—causes girls to do worse than their abilities allow on difficult math problems (Ben-Zeev et al., 2005; Muzzatti & Agnoli, 2007). As a result of all these influences, girls—even those who are highly talented—are less likely to develop effective math reasoning skills.

Gains in spatial skills that accrue from experience often exceed the gender gap in spatial performance. Here an absorbed preschooler experiments with the Sommer Cube, a construction toy with wide-ranging mental-rotation possibilities, invented by systems engineer Michael Sommer. Each cube has four tunnels through which to roll a ball so it exits onto the table. Adding cubes greatly increases the complexity of possible paths, thereby challenging players of any age and spatial-skill level. © Michael S. Sommer/sommercube.com

2005). And in some studies, spatial performance varies with daily and annual androgen levels in both men and women (Temple & Carney, 1995; Van Goozen et al., 1995).

Why might a biologically based sex difference in spatial abilities exist? Evolutionary theorists point out that mental rotation skill predicts rapid, accurate map drawing and interpretation, areas in which boys and men do better than girls and women. Over the course of human evolution, the cognitive abilities of males became adapted for hunting, which required generating mental representations of large-scale spaces to find one's way (Choi & Silverman, 2003; Jones, Braithwaite, & Healy, 2003). But this explanation is controversial: Critics point out that female gatherers also needed to travel long distances to find fruits and vegetables that ripened in different seasons of the year (Newcombe, 2007).

Although biology is involved, experience also contributes to males' superior spatial performance. Children who engage in manipulative activities, such as block play, model building, and carpentry, do better on spatial tasks (Baenninger & Newcombe, 1995). Furthermore, playing video games that require rapid mental rotation of visual images enhances spatial scores (Subrahmanyam & Greenfield, 1996; Terlecki & Newcombe, 2005). Boys spend far more time than girls at these pursuits.

Research confirms that superior spatial skills contribute to the greater ease with which boys solve complex math problems. In studies of middle and high school students, *both* spatial ability and self-efficacy at doing math were related to performance on complex math problems, with spatial skills being the stronger predictor (Casey, Nuttall, & Pezaris, 1997, 2001). Boys are advantaged in both spatial abilities and math self-confidence. Still, spatial skills respond readily to training, with improvements in performance often larger than the sex differences themselves. But because boys and girls show similar training effects, sex differences persist (Newcombe & Huttenlocher, 2006). In sum, biology and environment *jointly* explain variations in spatial and math performance—both within and between the sexes.

A positive sign is that today, North American boys and girls reach advanced levels of high school math and science study in equal proportions—a crucial factor in reducing sex differences in knowledge and skill (Gallagher & Kaufman, 2005). Still, extra steps must be taken to promote girls' interest in and confidence at math and science. Adolescent daughters whose parents hold nonstereotyped beliefs are less likely to avoid math and science and more likely to achieve well (Updegraff, McHale, & Crouter, 1996). And a math curriculum beginning in kindergarten that teaches children how to apply effective spatial strategies—drawing diagrams, mentally manipulating visual images, searching for numerical patterns, and graphing—is vital (Nuttall, Casey, & Pezaris, 2005). Because girls are biased toward verbal processing, they may not realize their math and science potential unless they are specifically taught how to think spatially. Girls also respond especially positively to math and science taught from an applied, hands-on perspective: Secondary school laboratory experiences improve girls' achievement relative to boys', thereby reducing the gender gap (Burkam, Lee, & Smerdon, 1997). Exposure to successful women as role models is likely to add further to girls' belief in their own capacity to succeed.

Personality Traits

Sex differences in personality are in line with gender stereotypes. The traits most often studied include emotional sensitivity, compliance and dependency, depression, and aggression.

Cultural expectations are largely responsible for gender differences in emotional sensitivity. In certain situations—for example, when interacting with a cherished pet—boys are just as caring and affectionate as girls. © Tony Freeman/PhotoEdit

Emotional Sensitivity Females are more emotionally sensitive than males, a difference that appears early. Beginning in the preschool years, girls perform slightly better when asked to infer others' emotional states and the causes of those states. Relative to boys, girls are especially adept at understanding the more complex, self-conscious emotions—an advantage that extends into adulthood (Bosacki & Moore, 2004; Brown & Dunn, 1996; Bybee, 1998). Except for anger, girls also express their feelings more freely and intensely in everyday interaction (Chaplin, Cole, & Zahn-Waxler, 2005; Geary, 1998). And girls are better at identifying their feelings. When researchers observed children's facial expressions of emotion as they watched emotionally arousing videotapes and then asked them how they felt, girls' verbal reports matched their expressed emotion far more often than boys' (Strayer & Roberts, 1997).

It would be reasonable to expect these differences in emotional sensitivity to extend to empathy, sympathy, and prosocial behavior, but the evidence is mixed. On self-report measures, girls and women score higher than boys and men. When they are observed for behavioral signs, however, the gender difference is less consistent. Girls show a slight advantage in prosocial responding that is mostly evident in kindness and considerateness, less apparent in helping behavior (Eisenberg & Fabes, 1998; Eisenberg, Fabes, & Spinrad, 2006). When asked to describe the prosocial acts of their peers, adolescents reported many as-yet-unstudied examples that require self-confidence and assertiveness and, therefore, might be especially common among boys (Bergin, Talley, & Hamer, 2003). These include helping others develop skills (giving tips on how to play basketball), providing physical assistance (volunteering to mow a neighbor's lawn), and confronting others for harmful or otherwise inappropriate behavior.

As with other attributes, both biological and environmental explanations for sex differences in emotional sensitivity exist. According to one evolutionary account, females are genetically primed to be more emotionally sensitive as a way of ensuring their effectiveness as caregivers. Yet research suggests that girls are not naturally more nurturant. Before age 5, boys and girls spend equal amounts of time talking to and playing with babies (Fogel et al., 1987). In middle childhood, Caucasian boys' willingness to relate to infants declines. Yet African-American school-age boys, who endorse fewer gender stereotypes, smile, touch, and look at babies just as much as girls do (Reid & Trotter, 1993). Furthermore, sex differences in emotional sensitivity are not evident in mothers' and fathers' interactions with their babies. In Chapter 10, we saw that fathers are just as affectionate and competent at caregiving as mothers. And in Chapter 4, we noted that men and women react similarly to the sound of a crying baby.

Cultural expectations that girls be warm and expressive and boys be distant and self-controlled seem largely responsible for the gender gap in emotional sensitivity. In infancy, mothers respond more often to a girl's happiness and distress than to a boy's (Malatesta et al., 1986). Similarly, during the preschool years, both fathers and mothers attend more to girls' than boys' sadness and anxiety, and this parental attentiveness predicts greater expression of these emotions by children two years later (Chaplin, Cole, & Zahn-Waxler, 2005). Also, parents are more likely to use inductive discipline (which promotes sympathetic concern) with girls and to pressure girls to be thoughtful and caring (Zahn-Waxler, Cole, & Barrett, 1991). In addition, recall that parents spend more time talking about emotions when conversing with daughters. Taken together, these findings suggest that girls receive far more encouragement than boys to express and reflect on feelings.

Compliance and Dependency As early as toddlerhood and the preschool years, girls are more compliant than boys—a difference partly due to girls' more rapid language development and greater effortful control, including capacity to inhibit impulses (Else-Quest et al., 2006; Lahey et al., 2006). Girls also seek help and information from adults more often and score higher in dependency on personality tests (Feingold, 1994). But these variations in behavior patterns have much to do with the activity environments in which boys and girls spend their time.

From an early age, girls are encouraged into adult-structured activities both at home and at school. Consequently, they spend more time near adults. In contrast, boys are attracted to activities in which adults are minimally involved or entirely absent (Carpenter, 1983;

Powlishta, Serbin, & Moller, 1993). Compliance and bids for help and attention appear more often in adult-structured contexts, whereas assertiveness, leadership, and creative use of materials occur more often in unstructured pursuits.

Ideally, a balance of adult-structured and unstructured activities is best, enabling children to develop both the capacity to be assertive and the ability to comply with others' directives. In one study, assigning preschool boys and girls to classroom activities differing in adult structure readily modified their assertive and compliant tendencies (Carpenter, Huston, & Holt, 1986).

Depression Depression—feeling sad, frustrated, and hopeless about life, accompanied by loss of pleasure in most activities and disturbances in sleep, appetite, concentration, and energy—is the most common psychological problem of adolescence. Among North American teenagers, 20 to 50 percent experience mild to moderate feelings of depression, bouncing back after a short time. More worrisome are the 15 to 20 percent who have had one or more major depressive episodes, a rate comparable to that of adults. From 2 to 8 percent are chronically depressed—gloomy and self-critical for many months and sometimes years. Even in childhood, depression is not absent: Serious depression afflicts about 1 to 2 percent of children, many of whom (especially girls) remain depressed in adolescence (Dekker et al., 2007; Nolen-Hoeksema, 2002). In addition, depression increases sharply from ages 12 to 16 in industrialized nations, with many more girls than boys displaying adolescent onset of symptoms. Teenage girls are twice as likely as boys to experience persistent depressed mood—a difference sustained throughout the lifespan (Dekker et al., 2007; Hankin & Abela, 2005; Saluja et al., 2004). If allowed to continue, depression seriously impairs social, academic, and vocational functioning.

The precise combination of biological and environmental factors leading to depression varies from one individual to the next. Kinship studies reveal that heredity plays an important role (Glowinski et al., 2003). Genes can induce depression by affecting the balance of neurotransmitters in the brain, the development of brain regions involved in inhibiting negative emotion, or the body's hormonal response to stress (Kaufman & Charney, 2003).

But experience can also activate depression, promoting any of these biological changes. A high incidence of depression and other psychological disorders is seen in parents of depressed children and adolescents. Although a genetic risk may be passed from parent to child, in earlier chapters we also saw that depressed or otherwise stressed parents often form insecure attachments with their children and engage in maladaptive parenting. As a result, their child's emotional self-regulation, attachment, and self-esteem may be impaired, with serious consequences for many cognitive and social skills (Abela et al., 2005; Margolese, Markiewicz, & Doyle, 2005). Depressed youths usually display a learned-helpless attributional style, viewing positive academic and social outcomes as beyond their control (Graber, 2004). In a vulnerable young person, numerous negative life events can spark depression—for example, failing at something important, parental divorce, the end of a close friendship or romantic partnership, or the challenges of school transition.

In industrialized nations, stressful life events and gender-typed coping styles—passivity, dependency, and rumination—make adolescent girls more susceptible to depression than boys. © David Grossman/The Image Works

Why are girls more prone to depression than boys? Biological changes associated with puberty cannot be a major factor because the gender difference is limited to industrialized nations. In developing countries, rates of depression are similar for males and females and occasionally higher in males (Culbertson, 1997). Even when females do exceed males in depression, the size of the difference varies. For example, it is smaller in China than in North America, perhaps because of decades of efforts by the Chinese government to eliminate gender inequalities (Greenberger et al., 2000).

Instead, stressful life events and gender-typed coping styles seem to be responsible. Early-maturing girls are especially prone to depression, particularly when they also face other stressful life events (Ge, Conger, & Elder, 2001a). And the gender intensification of early adolescence often strengthens girls' passivity, dependency, and tendency to ruminate on (repetitively mull over) their anxieties and problems—maladaptive approaches to tasks expected of teenagers in complex cultures. Consistent with this explanation, adolescents who identify strongly with "feminine" traits ruminate more and are more depressed, regardless of their sex

(Broderick & Korteland, 2004; Papadakis et al., 2006). Girls who repeatedly feel overwhelmed develop an overly reactive physiological stress response and cope more poorly with challenges in the future (Nolen-Hoeksema, 2002, 2006). In this way, stressful experiences and stress reactivity feed on one another, sustaining depression. In contrast, girls with either an androgynous or a "masculine" gender identity show low rates of depressive symptoms, no different from that of masculine-identified boys (Wilson & Cairns, 1988).

Unfortunately, the stereotypical view of adolescence as a period of "storm and stress" leads many adults to minimize the seriousness of adolescents' depression, seeing it as just a passing phase. Yet without intervention that improves coping strategies and reduces high reactivity to stress, adolescent depression is likely to evolve into a lifelong pattern.

Aggression Aggression has attracted more research attention than any other sex difference. In Chapter 12, we noted that by the second year, boys are more *physically aggressive* than girls. But sex differences in *verbal aggression* (threats of physical harm, name-calling, and hostile teasing) and *relational aggression* (aimed at damaging another's social relationships) are less clear.

Although many people assume that girls more often harm one another with words, the evidence is inconsistent: Some studies indicate that boys are more verbally aggressive, whereas others show no sex difference (Kashani & Shepperd, 1990; Salmivalli, Kaukiainen, & Lagerspetz, 2000). Similarly, a common assumption is that girls are far more likely to engage in the rumor spreading, social exclusion, and other types of relationship manipulation that make up relational aggression. But once again, a growing number of studies reveal that the sex difference favoring girls is small (Crick et al., 2004; Crick, Ostrov, & Werner, 2006; Underwood, 2003). Girls often *appear* much more relationally aggressive than boys because many girls use relational tactics nearly exclusively. Boys, by contrast, draw on a diversity of means to inflict harm—whatever works at the moment.

Although children of both sexes report that relational aggression is very hurtful, girls find it especially so, reporting more distress when they are targets and judging it to be more unjust than boys do (Galen & Underwood, 1997; Murray-Close, Crick, & Galotti, 2006). Because girls place a high value on close relationships, harming a friendship is a powerful way to hurt a peer. There are other reasons, too, that relational aggression may account for the large majority of girls' hostile acts. First, girls spend more time in close proximity to adults and are more sensitive to adult approval. They may emphasize relational aggression because it is hard for adults to detect and, therefore, to punish. Second, as Chapter 15 will make clear, dominance relations are less clear in girls' than in boys' peer groups. As a result, girls may jockey for social position frequently, engaging in relationship manipulation to protect their own status (Underwood, 2003).

The sex difference favoring girls in relational aggression is small. But because of the value they place on close relationships, girls find relational aggression to be especially hurtful. © JUPITERIMAGES/ BananaStock/Alamy

Our discussion of the origins of sex differences in aggression focuses on physical aggression. At present, much less is known about factors that contribute to relational aggression.

Biological Influences. Because males' greater physical aggression is evident early in life, generalizes across cultures, and is found in many animal species, most researchers believe that biology is involved. Androgen hormones are related to aggression in animals and are also believed to play a role in humans. But children with CAH, who were exposed prenatally to abnormally high androgen levels, are not consistently more aggressive (Berenbaum & Resnick, 1997; Pasterski et al., 2007). This suggests that in humans, androgen exposure results in only a tendency to aggress. That is, androgens may promote certain behaviors that, in some circumstances, increase the likelihood of aggressive outcomes.

One possibility is that prenatal androgens promote physical activity and competitiveness—behaviors likely to change into aggression in certain situations (Dodge, Coie, & Lynam, 2006). For example, an active, competitive child who often participates in large-group activities might become more aggressive than a child who prefers small-group pursuits. To explore this idea, researchers brought kindergartners and first graders to a laboratory where they played a game, some in same-sex pairs and others in same-sex tetrads (groups of four). In the game, children rolled a die, which indicated how many beads they could take from either a common pile (a noncompetitive move) or another player (a competitive move). Group size had no impact on girls' competitive moves, but boys displayed nearly twice as many competitive moves in tetrads as in dyads (Benenson et al., 2001). Recall that compared with girls, boys spend more time playing in large groups—an attraction, according to evolutionary theorists, adapted to preparing them for the competitive adult life of their male ancestors. Large groups, in turn, serve as contexts in which competition and striving for social dominance may promote aggression.

Another hypothesis is that sex hormones influence brain functioning in ways that affect emotional reactions. According to this view, hormone levels induce more frequent displays of excitement, anger, or anxiety, which make aggression more likely under certain conditions. Consistent with this prediction, adolescent boys with high androgen levels are more dominant and, therefore, more likely to respond with aggression when provoked by peers (Olweus et al., 1988; Tremblay et al., 1997). In one study, higher estrogen and androgen levels were related to adolescent girls' expressions of anger in a discussion session with their parents (Inoff-Germain et al., 1988).

Although more research is needed, current evidence indicates that multiple pathways exist between sex hormones and physical aggression. Clearly, too, environmental conditions have much to do with whether or not hormonally induced emotions and behaviors are channeled into aggressive acts.

During the school years, boys report feeling more hostile than girls after observing adults' angry exchanges. This boy attempts to minimize the effect by blocking out his parents' argument. © David Young-Wolff/PhotoEdit

Environmental Influences. In Chapter 12, we showed how coercive child-rearing practices and strife-ridden families promote aggressive behavior. For several reasons, boys are more likely than girls to be affected. Parents more often use physical punishment with boys, which encourages them to adopt the same tactics in their own relationships. Also, arguing between husband and wife, though stimulating aggression among all family members, more often triggers hostility in boys. In a study in which 2-year-olds overheard angry verbal exchanges between adults while playing with a familiar peer in a laboratory, girls tended to show fearful, withdrawing reactions, such as freezing in place and covering or hiding their faces. In contrast, boys engaged in more aggression, lashing out at their playmates (Cummings, Iannotti, & Zahn-Waxler, 1985). After observing adults' angry exchanges, boys report feeling more hostile than girls (Hennessy, Rabideau, & Cicchetti, 1994).

At the same time, parents and teachers respond differently to boys' and girls' physical aggression. They often give boys positive attention or relax rules, coaxing, begging, or ignoring rather than using clear, firm prohibitions. In contrast, they usually respond negatively to girls' assertive and aggressive acts (Arnold, McWilliams, & Harvey-Arnold, 1998; Kerig, Cowan, & Cowan, 1993; Radke-Yarrow & Kochanska, 1990). The stereotypical view that "boys will be boys" may lead many adults to overlook or tolerate boys' hostility unless it is extreme, so that boys receive tacit approval for physical aggression, whereas girls suppress it. It is not surprising, then, that school-age boys expect less parental disapproval and report feeling less guilty for aggression than girls (Perry, Perry, & Weiss, 1989).

Gender-segregated peer groups extend adults' lessons about expressing aggression, with boys often engaging in high rates of bossy, rough, aggressive acts while girls encourage one another to refrain from physical fighting. In one study, emotionally reactive preschool and kindergarten boys who mostly played with other boys showed an increase in teacher-reported problem behaviors ("starts fights," "is defiant to adults") over the school year. Among emotionally reactive girls who often played with other girls, incidence of problem behaviors decreased (Fabes et al., 1997). Perhaps these girls begin to vent their anger indirectly. By middle childhood, girls' relational aggression is more malicious than boys' and more likely to be directed at close friends (Simmons, 2002).

In sum, early experiences tend to promote physical aggression in boys but to dampen it in girls, encouraging them to find covert, relational outlets for their hostility. Overall, biological predispositions and social encouragement jointly contribute to sex differences in aggression.

Developing Non-Gender-Stereotyped Children

We have seen that children's developmental possibilities can be seriously limited by persistent gender stereotypes in their culture. Despite wide recognition of the importance of rearing children who feel free to express their human qualities without fear of violating gender-role expectations, no easy recipe exists for accomplishing this difficult task. It must be tackled on many fronts—at home, at school, and in the wider society.

Biology clearly affects children's gender typing, channeling boys toward active, competitive play and girls toward quieter, more intimate interaction—a difference that leads each sex, on average, to seek out activities and social experiences consistent with those predispositions. But substantial revisions in gender roles and in relationships between males and females—along with wide individual, family, and cultural variations—reveal that most aspects of gender typing are not built into human nature (Maccoby, 2000b). Furthermore, a long human childhood ensures that experiences can greatly influence biologically based sex differences (Ruble, Martin, & Berenbaum, 2006).

Throughout our discussion, we have mentioned strategies for reducing gender stereotyping and gender-role conformity. These are summarized in Applying What We Know on page 559. But even children fortunate enough to grow up in homes and schools that minimize stereotyping will eventually encounter it in the media and in the typical roles of men and women in their communities. Consequently, children need early experiences that repeatedly counteract their readiness to absorb our culture's extensive network of gender-linked associations.

Because preschoolers' cognitive limitations lead them to assume that cultural practices determine gender, Sandra Bem (1993, 1998) suggests that parents and teachers make a concerted effort to delay young children's learning of gender-stereotyped messages. Adults can begin by eliminating traditional gender roles from their own behavior and from the alternatives they provide for children. For example, mothers and fathers can take turns making dinner, bathing children, and driving the family car and can provide sons and daughters with both trucks and dolls, both pink and blue clothing. Teachers can make sure that all children spend some time each day in both adult-structured and unstructured activities. Adults can also avoid using language that conveys gender stereotypes and can shield children from media presentations that do the same.

Once children notice the wide array of gender stereotypes in their society, parents and teachers can point out exceptions. For example, they can arrange for children to see men and women pursuing nontraditional careers, and they can explain that interests and skills, not sex, should determine a person's occupation. With older children, adults can discuss the historical roots and current consequences of gender inequalities—why, for example, there have been few female presidents and prime ministers, why fathers rarely stay home with

Applying What We Know

Reducing Children's Gender Stereotyping and Gender-Role Conformity

Strategy	Explanation
Permit children to choose among diverse toys and activities.	Encouraging children to select toys and activities on the basis of their interests, not "gender appropriateness," counters gender stereotypes while also giving children a broader array of experiences.
Avoid transmitting gender stereotypes of achievement areas; point out that high effort improves competence in all areas.	Conveying gender stereotypes about what boys and girls are "good at" reduces children's sense of competence at, interest in, and motivation to achieve in areas stereotyped for the other gender, thereby preventing children from realizing their academic potential.
Teach children to appreciate differences among individuals.	Emphasizing individual differences (for example, one woman saying about another, "She's so interesting because she's different from me!") reduces the pressure children feel to adopt stereotypical attitudes and behaviors associated with their own gender group.
Avoid unnecessary references to gender and gender stereotypes in your language.	Avoiding gender labels and generic utterances ("The boys aren't paying attention." "Most girls like art.") by referring, instead, to individuals ("Mark, Sam, and Jenny aren't paying attention." "Susie likes art.") prevents children from viewing same-sex individuals as alike and from accepting gender stereotypes.
Provide non-gender-stereotyped models.	Exposure to adults engaged in nonstereotyped activities and occupations promotes children's awareness that multiple choices—not just gender-stereotyped ones—are available to them.
Stress the complexity of gender groups.	Comments like "Some boys are good at math, and some girls are good at math," or "Some boys like sports, and some boys don't like sports," teach children that ability and interest, not gender, determine how well a person performs an activity.
Arrange for mixed-sex interaction.	Children who have opportunities to engage in joint endeavors with other-sex peers are less likely to form stereotypes about the other gender.
Discuss gender biases with children.	Discussing why certain social roles (such as president or prime minister) are linked to only one gender helps children to appreciate environmental causes of bias and to reject explanations based on innate sex differences.

young children, and why stereotyped views of men and women are hard to change. Research shows that school-age children who hold flexible beliefs about what boys and girls can do are more likely to notice instances of gender discrimination (Brown & Bigler, 2004). As children build concepts of themselves and their social world that are not limited by a masculine–feminine dichotomy, they contribute to the transformation of societal values, bringing us closer to a time when people will be released from the constraints of traditional gender roles.

Ask Yourself

Review Cite evidence that both biological and environmental factors contribute to girls' advantage in verbal abilities and to boys' advantage in mathematical reasoning.

Review Explain the *indirect* link between androgen hormones and boys' greater physical aggression, noting the influence of both family and peer-group experiences.

Apply Thirteen-year-old Donna, who has a "feminine" gender identity, reached puberty early and is unhappy with her physical appearance. Explain why Donna is at risk for depression.

Connect Using Bronfenbrenner's ecological systems theory (see Chapter 1, page 26), describe steps that can be taken at each level of the environment to reduce gender stereotyping in children.

SUMMARY

Explain how the study of gender typing has responded to societal change.

- Largely because of progress in women's rights, **gender typing** is no longer regarded as essential for healthy psychological development. Current research focuses on how biological, cognitive, and social factors influence development of **gender stereotypes, gender roles,** and **gender identity,** and on how to free children from gender-based societal expectations that limit their potential.

Gender Stereotypes and Gender Roles

Describe the development of gender stereotyping from early childhood into adolescence.

- Children begin acquiring gender stereotypes and gender roles early in the preschool years. By middle childhood, they are aware of stereotypes for activities, behaviors, occupations, achievement areas, and—for personality—**instrumental** and **expressive traits.** Cognitive limitations contribute to preschoolers' rigid gender stereotypes. Gains in **gender-stereotype flexibility** occur in middle childhood and adolescence, but children still may disapprove of violations of gender-role expectations, especially by males.

Cite individual and group differences in gender stereotyping, and discuss the relationship of gender stereotyping to gender-role adoption.

- Children acquire gender stereotypes in idiosyncratic ways, yielding wide individual differences in the makeup of their understanding. Boys hold more rigid gender-stereotyped views than girls, white children more than black children. Higher-SES adolescents and adults hold more flexible views than their lower-SES counterparts.
- Awareness of gender stereotypes is only weakly related to gender-role adoption. Stereotype flexibility, however, is a good predictor of school-age children's willingness to cross gender lines.

Influences on Gender Stereotyping and Gender-Role Adoption

Discuss the role of biology in gender stereotyping and gender-role adoption, including cross-cultural evidence and the influence of hormones.

- According to an evolutionary perspective, males are genetically primed for dominance and females for intimacy, responsiveness, and cooperation. Cross-cultural similarities in gender typing have been used to support the role of biology. However, cultures vary widely in the extent to which they promote gender-role conformity.

© RAFIQUR RAHMAN/Reuters/Corbis

- Prenatal androgen levels contribute to sex differences in play styles and to preference for same-sex peers. Research on children with congenital adrenal hyperplasia (CAH) and androgen insensitivity syndrome supports the role of androgens in "masculine" gender-role adoption. For children reared as members of the other sex because of ambiguous genitals caused by prenatal hormone imbalance, gender typing is usually consistent with sex of rearing. When biological makeup and sex of rearing are at odds, children experience serious adjustment problems.

Discuss environmental influences on gender stereotyping and gender-role adoption, including expectations and treatment by parents, teachers, and peers; observational learning; and the impact of siblings.

- Beginning in infancy, adults hold gender-stereotyped perceptions and expectations of children. By the preschool years, parents reinforce "gender-appropriate" play activities and behaviors and often use language that highlight gender distinctions.
- In middle childhood, parents demand higher achievement from boys and hold gender-stereotyped beliefs about children's academic abilities, with consequences for achievement and later career choices. In most aspects of gender typing, fathers differentiate between boys and girls more than mothers.
- Teachers reinforce children of both sexes for "feminine" behavior while also promoting traditional gender roles. Children also learn through observation of gender-typed models in the surrounding environment.

© Michael Newman/PhotoEdit

- Interaction with same-sex peers further reinforces children's "gender-appropriate" activity choices and promotes gender-typed styles of social influence. Boys rely more on commands, threats, and physical force, girls on polite requests and persuasion—differences that strengthen gender segregation.
- The impact of siblings on gender typing varies with birth order and family size. In two-child families, younger children tend to imitate their older sibling's gender-role behavior. In larger families, same-sex siblings often strive to be different from one another and are likely to be less stereotyped.

Gender Identity

Explain the meaning of androgyny, and describe and evaluate the accuracy of social learning and cognitive-developmental views of the development of gender identity in early childhood.

- Most children and adults have traditional identities in self-ratings of "masculine" and "feminine" personality traits, but some score high on both masculine and feminine characteristics. At present, the masculine component of **androgyny** is largely responsible for its association with superior psychological adjustment.
- According to social learning theory, preschoolers first acquire gender-typed responses through modeling and reinforcement and later organize them into cognitions about themselves. Cognitive-developmental theory suggests that **gender constancy** must precede gender-typed behavior.
- Children master gender constancy in three stages: **gender labeling, gender stability,** and **gender consistency.** Understanding of gender constancy is associated with attainment of conservation and the appearance–reality distinction. Contrary to cognitive-developmental predictions, "gender-appropriate" behavior is acquired long before gender constancy. Whereas

gender labeling and gender stability strengthen early gender-role adoption, gender consistency seems to contribute to gender-stereotype flexibility.

What changes in gender identity occur in middle childhood and adolescence?

- In middle childhood, boys strengthen their identification with the "masculine" role, while girls become more androgynous. Gender identities expand to include self-evaluations of gender typicality, gender contentedness, and felt pressure to conform to gender roles—each of which affects psychological well-being.
- Early adolescence is a period of **gender intensification**: Gender identities become more traditional. Biological, social, and cognitive changes, as well as parental and peer pressures, play a role. As young people construct a mature personal identity, highly stereotypical self-perceptions decline.

Explain how gender schema theory accounts for the persistence of gender stereotypes and gender-role preferences.

- **Gender schema theory** is an information-processing approach that explains how environmental pressures and children's cognitions jointly shape gender typing. As they learn gender-typed preferences and behaviors, children form masculine and feminine gender schemas. Highly gender-schematic children, in contrast to gender-aschematic children, view themselves and the world in gender-linked terms and, as a result, learn more about "gender-appropriate" than "gender-inappropriate" activities and behaviors.

© Image Source/Alamy

To What Extent Do Boys and Girls Really Differ in Gender-Stereotyped Attributes?

Describe sex differences in mental abilities and personality traits, noting factors that contribute to those differences.

- Most sex differences in mental abilities and personality traits are small to moderate. Girls are advantaged in language development, reading and writing, math computation, and emotional understanding. Boys are better at certain spatial skills and at complex mathematical reasoning. Although boys display more physical aggression, sex differences in relational aggression are minimal.
- Biological factors, adult encouragement, and learning opportunities contribute to sex differences in language, spatial, and math skills. Girls' greater emotional sensitivity, compliance, and dependency are largely due to gender-stereotyped expectations and child-rearing practices.
- The higher rate of depression in adolescent girls in industrialized nations is the combined result of the challenges of adolescence and gender-typed coping styles. Gender intensification in early adolescence strengthens girls' passivity and dependency, which interfere with their ability to master challenging tasks and cope with stressful life events.
- Androgen hormones contribute to greater physical aggression in males, but, in humans, may exert their effects indirectly by influencing activity level, emotional reactions, or dominance. Parents and teachers are more likely to encourage physical aggression in boys while suppressing it in girls—lessons reinforced by gender-segregated peer groups.

Developing Non-Gender-Stereotyped Children

Cite ways to reduce gender stereotyping in children.

- Parents and teachers can counteract young children's readiness to absorb gender-linked associations by eliminating traditional gender roles from their own behavior and from the alternatives they provide for children. Once children notice gender stereotypes, adults can point out exceptions and discuss the arbitrariness of many gender inequalities.

IMPORTANT TERMS AND CONCEPTS

androgyny (p. 543)
expressive traits (p. 526)
gender consistency (p. 544)
gender constancy (p. 544)
gender identity (p. 526)
gender intensification (p. 546)
gender labeling (p. 544)
gender roles (p. 526)
gender schema theory (p. 547)
gender stability (p. 544)
gender-stereotype flexibility (p. 529)
gender stereotypes (p. 526)
gender typing (p. 526)
instrumental traits (p. 526)

14

"An Orphan at Christmas"
Claudia Suteu
15 years, Romania

Of all contexts influencing children's development, the family is the most powerful. In this image of an orphaned child exuberantly joining a kind, elderly caregiver for Christmas dinner, the artist portrays a poignant theme: the yearnings of a child who has no parents.

The Family

"I don't remember much family togetherness when I was a kid," 19-year-old Hannah reflected over dinner with Aunt Eva and Uncle Charlie. "Our parents couldn't talk things out with each other, and they weren't very open with us. We almost never sat down to a meal or went anywhere together. I went to Girl Scouts and to summer camp. I liked the activities, and I made good friends, but they couldn't make up for the lack of warm family time."

When Hannah was 9, her parents divorced, and she moved across the country with her mother. At first, her father arranged visits every few months; he would take Hannah out to eat, to the movies, and to the amusement park and would buy her whatever she wanted. Back home, when Hannah objected to her mother's rules and demands, her mother would rail at her father, calling him a "Disneyland Dad" who focused on fun and took no responsibility for Hannah's upbringing. As these arguments flared repeatedly, the visits trailed off, and eventually Hannah's father seldom made contact.

To make ends meet, Hannah's mother, an accountant, extended her work hours to evenings and weekends. Hannah would make a box of macaroni and cheese for dinner, eat by herself, and then—neglecting her homework—spend hours watching TV or just daydreaming. She found it hard to concentrate, and her grades suffered. In high school, stormy relationships with boyfriends left Hannah feeling depressed and rejected. Aimless and "at sea," she was convinced she couldn't do anything.

At 16, Hannah got her driver's license and began visiting Aunt Eva and Uncle Charlie, who lived in a neighboring city. They took time to listen to Hannah, encourage her, and help her with time management, academic, and relationship problems. Longing for a sense of family togetherness, Hannah spent more and more time with her aunt and uncle. Two years later, when Hannah graduated from high school with plans to enter a university, she attributed her turnabout in motivation and self-confidence to her aunt and uncle's warmth, involvement, and guidance.

The family is the child's first, and longest-lasting, context for development. Compared with other species, human children develop slowly, requiring years of support and teaching before they are ready to be independent. This gradual journey to maturity has left an imprint on human social organization everywhere: Families are pervasive, and parenting is universally important in children's lives. Children who lack a satisfying, supportive family life are likely to crave it. Some, like Hannah, find what they seek in extended family or another special adult.

Of course, other contexts also mold children's development, but none equals the family in power and breadth of influence. The attachments children form with parents and siblings usually last a lifetime, and they serve as models for relationships in the wider world of neighborhood and school. Within the family, children experience their first social conflicts. Discipline by parents and arguments with siblings provide important lessons in compliance and cooperation and opportunities to learn how to influence the behavior of others. Finally, within the family, children learn the language, skills, and social and moral values of their culture.

We begin our discussion of the family by examining why this social unit came into being and has survived for thousands of years. Then we describe the current view of the family as a *social system* with many interacting influences on the child. Next, we look closely at the family as the core socializing agency of society by considering child-rearing styles, the factors that influence them, and their consequences for children's development. We also address recent social changes that have led to great diversity in family lifestyles. Finally, recognizing that the contemporary family is especially vulnerable to a breakdown in protective, emotionally supportive parent–child relationships, we consider the origins and consequences of child maltreatment.

Origins and Functions of the Family

The family in its most common form—a lifelong commitment between a man and woman who feed, shelter, and nurture their children until they reach maturity—arose tens of thousands of years ago among our hunting-and-gathering ancestors. From an evolutionary perspective, the human family pattern—in which a man and a woman assumed special responsibility for their own children—enhanced survival by ensuring a relatively even balance of male hunters and female gatherers within a social group, thereby providing protection against starvation at times when game was scarce (Lancaster & Whitten, 1980).

An extended relationship between a man and a woman also increased male certainty that a newborn baby was actually *his* offspring, motivating him to provide mother and child with food and shelter and to invest in child rearing in order to increase the odds of child survival (Bjorklund, Yunger, & Pellegrini, 2002; Geary, 2000). Larger kin networks that included grandparents, aunts, uncles, and cousins formed, increasing the chances of successful competition with other humans for vital resources and providing assistance with child rearing. And because economic and social obligations among family members were essential for survival, strong emotional bonds evolved to foster long-term commitment among parents, children, and other relatives (Nesse, 1990; Williams, 1997).

The most common family structure—a lifelong commitment between a man and a woman who care for their young until maturity—arose tens of thousands of years ago because it enhanced survival. *Left photo:* This Belgian couple balances work and child rearing, enjoying both. The mother hosts a TV program for young parents, drawing inspiration from her own family. *Right photo:* A Chinese couple and their only child share a home with the husband's younger brother and parents. While the younger adults run a small family farm, the grandparents look after their grandson. © Uwe Ommer/ Families/Taschen edition

Besides promoting survival of its members, the family unit of our evolutionary ancestors performed the following vital services for society:

- *Reproduction.* Replacing dying members.
- *Economic services.* Producing and distributing goods and services.
- *Social order.* Devising procedures for reducing conflict and maintaining order.
- *Socialization.* Training the young to become competent, participating members of society.
- *Emotional support.* Helping others surmount emotional crises and fostering in each person a sense of commitment and purpose.

As societies became more complex, the demands placed on the family became too much for it to sustain alone. Other institutions developed to assist with some of these functions, and families became linked to larger social structures (Parke & Kellam, 1994). For example, political and legal institutions assumed responsibility for ensuring societal order, and schools and religious institutions extended the family's socialization function.

Although some family members still carry out economic tasks together (as in family-run farms and businesses), this function has largely been taken over by institutions that make up the world of work. The contemporary family consumes far more goods and services than it produces. Consequently, whereas children formerly contributed to families' economic well-being, today they are economic liabilities. According to a conservative estimate, today's new parents will spend about $200,000 in the United States and $170,000 in Canada to rear a child from birth to age 18, and many will incur substantial additional expense for higher education—a reality that has contributed to the declining birth rate in industrialized nations (Child Care Advocacy Association of Canada, 2004; U.S. Department of Agriculture, 2007).

Despite sharing some functions with other institutions, the family continues to assume primary responsibility for three important ones especially concerned with children: reproduction, socialization, and emotional support. Researchers interested in finding out how families fulfill these functions take a **social systems perspective,** viewing the family as a complex set of interacting relationships influenced by the larger social context.

The Family as a Social System

The social systems perspective on family functioning grew out of researchers' efforts to describe and explain the complex patterns of interaction between family members. As you will see, it has much in common with Bronfenbrenner's *ecological systems theory,* discussed in Chapter 1. Family systems theorists recognize that parents do not mechanically shape their children. Rather, as you already know from earlier chapters, *bidirectional influences* exist, whereby family members mutually influence one another. The very term *family system* implies a network of interdependent relationships (Bornstein & Sawyer, 2006; Parke & Buriel, 2006). These system influences operate both directly and indirectly.

Direct Influences

Recently, as I passed through the checkout counter at the supermarket, I witnessed two episodes, each an example of how parents and children directly influence each other:

- Four-year-old Danny looked longingly at the tempting rows of candy as his mother lifted groceries from her cart onto the counter. "Pleeeease, can I have it, Mom?" Danny begged, holding up a large package of bubble gum. "Do you have a dollar? Just one?"

  "No, not today," his mother answered. "Remember, we picked out your special cereal. That's what I need the dollar for." Gently taking the bubble gum from his hand, Danny's mother handed him the box of cereal. "Here, let's pay," she said, lifting Danny so he could see the checkout counter.
- Three-year-old Meg was sitting in the shopping cart while her mother transferred groceries to the counter. Suddenly Meg turned around, grabbed a bunch of bananas, and started pulling them apart.

"Stop it, Meg!" shouted her mother, snatching the bananas from Meg's hand. But as she turned her attention to swiping her debit card, Meg reached for a chocolate bar from a nearby display. "Meg, how many times have I told you, *don't touch!*" Prying the candy from Meg's tight little fist, Meg's mother slapped her hand. Meg's face turned red with anger as she began to wail.

These observations fit with a wealth of research on the family system. Studies of families of diverse ethnicities show that when parents are firm but warm (like Danny's mother), children tend to comply with their requests. And when children cooperate, their parents are likely to be warm and gentle in the future. In contrast, parents who discipline with harshness and impatience (like Meg's mother) tend to have children who resist and rebel. Because children's misbehavior is stressful for parents, they may increase their use of punishment, leading to more unruliness by the child (Stormshak et al., 2000; Whiteside-Mansell et al., 2003). In each case, the behavior of one family member helps sustain a form of interaction in another that either promotes or undermines children's well-being.

Indirect Influences

The impact of family relationships on child development becomes even more complicated when we consider that interaction between any two family members is affected by others present in the setting. Recall from Chapter 1 that Bronfenbrenner called these indirect influences the effect of *third parties.* Researchers have become intensely interested in how a range of relationships—mother with father, parent with sibling, grandparent with parent—modify the child's direct experiences in the family. In fact, as the From Research to Practice box on the following page reveals, a child's birth can have a third-party impact on parents' interaction that may affect the child's development and well-being.

Third parties can serve as supports for development, or they can undermine it. For example, when parents' marital relationship is warm and considerate, mothers and fathers are more likely to engage in effective **coparenting,** mutually supporting each other's parenting behaviors. Such parents have more secure attachment relationships with their babies, and they praise and stimulate their children more and nag and scold them less. In contrast, parents whose marriage is tense and hostile often interfere with one another's child-rearing efforts, are less responsive to children's needs, and are more likely to criticize, express anger, and punish (Caldera & Lindsey, 2006; Cox, Paley, & Harter, 2001; McHale et al., 2002). Children who are chronically exposed to angry, unresolved parental conflict show myriad problems related to disrupted emotional security and emotional self-regulation (Harold et al., 2004). These include both internalizing difficulties (especially among girls), such as blaming themselves, feeling worried and fearful, and trying to repair their parents' relationship; and externalizing difficulties (especially among boys), including anger and aggression (Davies & Lindsay, 2004). Furthermore, in research carried out in nations as diverse as Bangladesh, China, Bosnia, and the United States, parental conflict consistently undermined good parenting by increasing criticism and belittling of adolescents and decreasing monitoring of their whereabouts and activities (Bradford et al., 2003). These parenting practices, in turn, heightened youth behavior problems.

Yet even when parental arguments strain children's adjustment, other family members may help restore effective interaction. Grandparents, for example, can promote children's development both directly, by responding warmly to the child and helping with caregiving, and indirectly, by providing parents with child-rearing advice, models of child-rearing skill, and sometimes financial assistance. Of course, as with any indirect influence, grandparents can sometimes be harmful. When quarrelsome relations exist between grandparents and parents, children may suffer.

Adapting to Change

Think back to the *chronosystem* in Bronfenbrenner's theory (see page 29 in Chapter 1). The interplay of forces within the family is dynamic and ever-changing, as each member adapts to the development of other members.

▪ *From* Research *to* Practice ▪

The Transition to Parenthood

The early weeks after a baby enters the family are full of profound changes—constant caregiving, added financial responsibilities, and less time for couples to devote to each other. These demands usually cause the gender roles of husband and wife to become more traditional, even for couples strongly committed to gender equality (Cowan & Cowan, 2000; Salmela-Aro et al., 2000). Typically, mothers spend more time at home with the baby, whereas fathers focus more on their provider role.

For most new parents, the arrival of a baby does not cause significant marital strain. Marriages that are gratifying and supportive tend to remain so, resembling childless marriages in overall happiness (Feeney et al., 2001; Miller, 2000). But troubled marriages usually become more distressed after a baby is born. In a study of newlyweds who were interviewed annually for six years, the husband's affection, expression of "we-ness" (values and goals similar to his wife's), and awareness of his wife's daily life predicted mothers' stable or increasing marital satisfaction after childbirth. In contrast, the husband's negativity and the couple's out-of-control conflict predicted a drop in mothers' satisfaction (Shapiro, Gottman, & Carrere, 2000).

Also, violated expectations about division of labor in the home affect new parents' well-being. In dual-earner marriages, the larger the difference between men's and women's caregiving responsibilities, the greater the decline in marital satisfaction after childbirth, especially for women—with negative consequences for parent–infant interaction. In contrast, sharing caregiving tasks predicts greater sensitivity by both parents to their baby (Feldman, 2002; McHale et al., 2004). An exception exists, however, for employed lower-SES women who endorse traditional gender roles. When their husbands take on considerable child-care responsibilities, these mothers tend to report more distress, perhaps because they feel disappointed at being unable to fulfill their desire to do most of the caregiving (Goldberg & Perry-Jenkins, 2003).

Postponing childbearing until the late twenties or thirties, as more couples do today, eases the transition to parenthood. Waiting permits couples to pursue occupational goals, gain life experience, and strengthen their relationship. Under these circumstances, men are more enthusiastic about becoming fathers and therefore more willing to participate. And women whose careers are well under way are more likely to encourage their husbands to share housework and child care (Lee & Doherty, 2007; Saginak & Saginak, 2005).

A second birth typically requires that fathers take an even more active role in parenting—by caring for the first-born while the mother is recuperating and by sharing in the high demands of tending to both a baby and a young child. Consequently, well-functioning families with a newborn second child typically pull back from the traditional division of responsibilities that occurred after the first birth. In a study that tracked parents from the end of pregnancy through the first year after their second child's birth, fathers' willingness to place greater emphasis on the parenting role was strongly linked to mothers' adjustment after the arrival of a second baby (Stewart, 1990). And the support and encouragement of family, friends, and spouse are crucial for fathers' well-being.

Special interventions exist to ease the transition to parenthood. For those who are not at high risk for problems, counselor-led parenting groups are highly effective (Glade, Bean, & Vira, 2005). In one program, first-time expectant couples gathered once a week for six months to discuss their dreams for the family and changes in relationships sparked by the baby's arrival. Eighteen months after the program ended, participating fathers described themselves as more involved with their child than did fathers in a no-intervention condition. Perhaps because of fathers' caregiving assistance, participating mothers maintained their prebirth satisfaction with family and work roles. Three years after the birth, the marriages of all participating couples were still intact and just as happy as they had been before parenthood. In contrast, 15 percent of couples receiving no intervention had divorced (Cowan & Cowan, 1997, 2000).

These first-time parents, just home from the hospital, delight in their newborn. In a warm, gratifying marriage, sharing caregiving tasks is related to greater sensitivity toward the baby.
© Rick Gomez/Corbis

High-risk parents struggling with poverty or the birth of a child with disabilities need more intensive interventions. Programs in which a trained intervener visits the home and enhances both social support and parenting skills have resulted in improved parent–infant interaction and benefits for children's cognitive and social development up to five years after the intervention (Meisels, Dichtelmiller, & Liaw, 1993).

Generous paid employment leave—widely available in industrialized nations but not in the United States—is crucial for easing the transition to parenthood (see Chapter 3, page 117). Flexible work hours are also helpful. When favorable workplace policies exist and couples try to support each other's needs, the stress caused by the birth of a baby remains manageable. Family relationships are worked out after a few months, and most infants flourish, bringing great satisfaction to their parents and making the sacrifices of this period worthwhile.

For example, as children acquire new skills, parents adjust the way they treat their more competent youngsters. To cite just one example, turn back to Chapter 4, page 145, and review how babies' mastery of crawling leads parents to engage in more game playing and expressions of affection, as well as restriction of the child's activities. These changes in child rearing pave the way for new achievements and further revisions in family relationships. **TAKE A MOMENT...** Can you think of other illustrations of this idea, discussed in earlier chapters?

Parents' development affects children as well. As we will see later, the mild increase in parent–child conflict that often occurs in early adolescence is not solely due to teenagers' striving for independence. This is a time when most parents have reached middle age and—conscious that their children will soon leave home and establish their own lives—are reconsidering their own commitments (Steinberg & Silk, 2002). While the adolescent presses for greater autonomy, the parent presses for more togetherness. This imbalance promotes friction, which parent and teenager gradually resolve by accommodating to changes in each other. Indeed, no social unit other than the family is required to adjust to such vast changes in its members.

The Family System in Context

The social systems perspective, as we noted earlier, views the family as affected by surrounding social contexts. As the *mesosystem* and *exosystem* in Bronfenbrenner's model make clear, connections to the neighborhood and the larger community—both *formal organizations,* such as school, workplace, recreation center, child-care center, and religious institution, and *informal social networks* of relatives, friends, and neighbors—influence parent–child relationships.

In several studies, low-SES families were randomly assigned vouchers to move out of public housing into neighborhoods varying widely in affluence. Compared with their peers who remained in poverty-stricken areas, children and youths who moved into low-poverty neighborhoods showed substantially better physical and mental health and school achievement (Goering, 2003; Leventhal & Brooks-Gunn, 2003).

Unstable inner-city neighborhoods with dilapidated housing; schools, parks, and playgrounds in disarray; and lack of community centers introduce stressors that undermine parental warmth, involvement, and monitoring and increase parental harshness and inconsistency. When a run-down, impoverished neighborhood combines with poor parenting, rates of problem behaviors in children and antisocial activity among youths are especially high (Brody et al., 2003; Kohen et al., 2002). In contrast, strong family ties to the surrounding social context—as indicated by contact with friends and relatives, organized youth activities, and regular church, synagogue, or mosque attendance—reduce youth adjustment problems (Garbarino & Kostelny, 1993; Magnuson & Duncan, 2002).

How do links between family and community reduce stress and promote child development? One answer lies in their provision of social support, which leads to the following benefits:

At a block party in an inner-city neighborhood, children participate in a doughnut-eating contest while their parents watch with amusement. According to the social systems perspective, ties to the community are essential for families to function at their best.
AP Images/Muscatine Journal, Connie Street

- *Parental interpersonal acceptance.* A neighbor or relative who listens and tries to relieve a parent's concern enhances her self-esteem. The parent, in turn, is likely to interact in a more sensitive and involved manner with her children.
- *Parental access to valuable information and services.* A friend who suggests where a parent might find a job or housing or who cares for children while the parent attends to other pressing needs helps make the multiple roles of spouse, provider, and caregiver easier to fulfill.
- *Child-rearing controls and role models.* Friends, relatives, and other community members may encourage and demonstrate effective ways of interacting with children and discourage ineffective practices.
- *Direct assistance with child rearing.* As children and adolescents participate in their parents' social networks and in youth-oriented community activities, other adults can influence children directly through warmth, stimulation, and exposure to a wider array of competent models. In this way, family–neighborhood ties can reduce the impact of ineffective parenting (Silk et al., 2004). Nearby adults can also intervene when they see young people skipping school or behaving antisocially.

The Better Beginnings, Better Futures Project of Ontario, Canada, is a government-sponsored set of pilot programs aimed at preventing the dire consequences of neighborhood poverty. The most successful of these efforts, using a local elementary school as its base, provided children with in-class, before- and after-school, and summer enrichment activities. Workers also visited each child's parents regularly, informed them about community resources, and encouraged their involvement in the child's school and neighborhood life (Peters, 2005; Peters, Petrunka, & Arnold, 2003). An evaluation after four years revealed wide-ranging benefits—gains in neighborhood satisfaction, family functioning, effective parenting, and children's reading skills, together with a reduction in emotional and behavior problems.

No researcher could possibly study all aspects of the social systems perspective on the family at once. But throughout this chapter, we will continually see examples of how its interlocking parts combine to influence development.

Ask Yourself

Review Links between family and community are essential for children's well-being. Provide examples and research findings that support this idea.

Apply At the mall, you see a father getting angry with his young son. Using the social systems perspective, list as many factors as you can that might account for the father's behavior.

Connect How does the goodness-of-fit model, discussed in Chapter 10 (see page 423), illustrate central features of the social systems perspective on family functioning?

Reflect Did any third parties—grandparents, aunts or uncles, or others—influence your relationship with your parents when you were a child? Describe how they affected interactions within your family.

Socialization Within the Family

Among the family's functions, socialization centers on children's development. Parents start to socialize their children in earnest during the second year, when toddlers are first able to comply with their directives (see Chapter 12). As children get older, parents gradually step up socialization pressures, but they vary greatly in how they go about the task. In previous chapters, we have seen how parents can foster children's competence—by building a parent–child relationship based on affection and cooperation, by serving as models and reinforcers of mature behavior, by using reasoning and inductive discipline, and by guiding and encouraging children's mastery of new skills. Now let's combine these elements into an overall view of effective parenting.

Styles of Child Rearing

Child-rearing styles are combinations of parenting behaviors that occur over a wide range of situations, creating an enduring child-rearing climate. In a landmark series of studies, Diana Baumrind gathered information on child rearing by watching parents interact with their preschoolers (Baumrind, 1971; Baumrind & Black, 1967). Her findings, and those of others who have extended her work, reveal three features that consistently differentiate an effective style from less effective ones: (1) *acceptance* of the child and *involvement* in the child's life, which establishes an emotional connection with the child; (2) *control* of the child, which promotes more mature behavior; and (3) *autonomy granting,* which encourages self-reliance (Barber & Olsen, 1997; Gray & Steinberg, 1999; Hart, Newell, & Olsen, 2003). Table 14.1 on page 570 compares child-rearing styles on the basis of how they differ on these features. Let's discuss each style in turn.

• **Authoritative Child Rearing** The **authoritative child-rearing style**—the most successful approach—involves high acceptance and involvement, adaptive control techniques, and appropriate autonomy granting. Authoritative parents are warm, attentive, and sensitive to their child's needs. They establish an enjoyable, emotionally fulfilling parent–child relationship that draws the child into close connection. At the same time, authoritative parents exercise

Table 14.1 Comparing Features of Child-Rearing Styles

Child-Rearing Style	Acceptance and Involvement	Control	Autonomy Granting
Authoritative	Is warm, responsive, attentive, patient, and sensitive to the child's needs	Makes reasonable demands for maturity and consistently enforces and explains them	Permits the child to make decisions in accord with readiness Encourages the child to express thoughts, feelings, and desires When parent and child disagree, engages in joint decision making when possible
Authoritarian	Is cold and rejecting and frequently degrades the child	Makes many demands coercively, using force and punishment Often engages in psychological control, withdrawing love and intruding on the child's individuality	Makes decisions for the child Rarely listens to the child's point of view
Permissive	Is warm but overindulgent or inattentive	Makes few or no demands	Permits the child to make many decisions before the child is ready
Uninvolved	Is emotionally detached and withdrawn	Makes few or no demands	Is indifferent to the child's decision making and point of view

firm, reasonable control: They insist on appropriate maturity, give reasons for their expectations, use disciplinary encounters as "teaching moments" to promote the child's self-regulation, and monitor their child's whereabouts and activities. Finally, authoritative parents engage in gradual, appropriate *autonomy granting,* allowing the child to make decisions in areas where he is ready to make choices. They also place a premium on communication, encouraging the child to express her thoughts, feelings, and desires. And when parent and child disagree, authoritative parents engage in joint decision making when possible. Their willingness to accommodate to the child's perspective increases the likelihood that the child will listen to their perspective in situations where compliance is vital (Kuczynski & Lollis, 2002; Russell, Mize, & Bissaker, 2004).

Throughout childhood and adolescence, authoritative parenting is linked to many aspects of competence—an upbeat mood, self-control, task persistence, cooperativeness, high self-esteem, responsiveness to parents' views, social and moral maturity, and favorable school performance (Amato & Fowler, 2002; Aunola, Stattin, & Nurmi, 2000; Gonzalez & Wolters, 2006; Mackey, Arnold, & Pratt, 2001; Milevsky et al., 2007; Steinberg, Darling, & Fletcher, 1995).

These 10-year-olds bundling newspapers for delivery have assumed responsibility for a task they must complete daily, on time. By granting children autonomy appropriate to their age and abilities, authoritative parents promote competence and maturity. © Kraig Scarbinsky/Getty Images/Digital Vision

• Authoritarian Child Rearing The **authoritarian child-rearing style** is low in acceptance and involvement, high in coercive control, and low in autonomy granting. Authoritarian parents appear cold and rejecting; they frequently degrade their child by mocking and putting her down. To exert control, they yell, command, criticize, and threaten. "Do it because I said so!" is their attitude. They make decisions for their child and expect the child to accept their word unquestioningly. If the child does not, authoritarian parents resort to force and punishment.

Children of authoritarian parents are anxious, unhappy, and low in self-esteem and self-reliance. When frustrated, they tend to react with hostility and, like their parents, resort to force when they do not get their way. Boys, especially, show high rates of anger and defiance. Although girls also engage in acting-out behavior, they are more likely to be dependent, lacking interest in exploration, and overwhelmed by challenging tasks (Hart et al., 2004; Nix et al., 1999; Thompson, Hollis, & Richards, 2003). Children and adolescents exposed to the authoritarian style typically do poorly in school. However, because of their parents' concern with controlling their behavior, they tend to achieve better and to commit fewer antisocial acts than peers with undemanding parents—that is, those whose parents use one of the two styles we will consider next (Steinberg, Blatt-Eisengart, & Cauffman, 2006).

Notice how the authoritarian style suppresses children's self-expression and independence. In addition to unwarranted direct control ("Do what I say!"), authoritarian parents engage in a more subtle type called **psychological control**—behaviors that intrude on and manipulate children's verbal expressions, individuality, and attachments to parents. In an attempt to decide virtually everything for the child, these parents frequently interrupt or put down the child's ideas, decisions, and choice of friends. When they are dissatisfied, they withdraw love, making their affection or attention contingent on the child's compliance. They also hold excessively high expectations that do not fit the child's developing capacities. Children and adolescents subjected to psychological control exhibit adjustment problems involving both anxious, withdrawn and defiant, aggressive behaviors (Barber & Harmon, 2002; Silk et al., 2003). And having had few opportunities for exploration, they are impaired in identity development once they reach early adulthood (Luyckx et al., 2007).

Authoritarian parents often engage in psychological control, belittling the child and using withdrawal of love as a punishment. In response, children become either anxious and withdrawn or defiant and aggressive. © SW Productions/Getty Images/Photodisc

• **Permissive Child Rearing** The **permissive child-rearing style** is warm and accepting but uninvolved. Permissive parents are either overindulgent or inattentive and, thus, engage in little *control*. Instead of gradually granting autonomy, they allow children to make many decisions for themselves at an age when they are not yet capable of doing so. Their children can eat meals and go to bed whenever they wish and can watch as much television as they want. They do not have to learn good manners or do household chores. Although some permissive parents truly believe in this approach, many others simply lack confidence in their ability to influence their child's behavior (Oyserman et al., 2005).

Children of permissive parents are impulsive, disobedient, and rebellious. Compared with children whose parents exert more control, they are also overly demanding and dependent on adults, and they show less persistence on tasks, poorer school achievement, and more antisocial behavior. The link between permissive parenting and dependent, nonachieving, rebellious behavior is especially strong for boys (Barber & Olsen, 1997; Baumrind, 1971; Steinberg, Blatt-Eisengart, & Cauffman, 2006).

• **Uninvolved Child Rearing** The **uninvolved child-rearing style** combines low acceptance and involvement with little control and general indifference to issues of autonomy. Often these parents are emotionally detached and depressed, so overwhelmed by life stress that they have little time or energy for children. They may respond to the child's immediate demands for easily accessible objects while failing to engage in strategies to promote long-term goals, such as establishing and enforcing rules about homework and social behavior, listening to the child's point of view, providing guidance about appropriate choices, and monitoring the child's whereabouts and activities.

At its extreme, uninvolved parenting is a form of child maltreatment called *neglect*. Especially when it begins early, it disrupts virtually all aspects of development (see Chapter 10, pages 402–403). Even with less extreme parental disengagement, children and adolescents display many problems—poor emotional self-regulation, school achievement difficulties, and antisocial behavior (Aunola, Stattin, & Nurmi, 2000; Kurdek & Fine, 1994).

What Makes the Authoritative Style Effective?

Table 14.2 on page 572 summarizes outcomes associated with each child-rearing style just considered. As with other correlational findings, the relationship between the authoritative style and children's competence is open to interpretation. Perhaps parents of well-adjusted children are authoritative because their youngsters have especially cooperative dispositions. Children's characteristics do contribute to the ease with which parents can apply the authoritative style. Recall from earlier chapters that temperamentally fearless, impulsive children and emotionally negative, difficult children are more likely to evoke coercive, inconsistent discipline. At the same time, extra warmth and firm control succeed in modifying these

Table 14.2 Relationship of Child-Rearing Styles to Development and Adjustment

Child-Rearing Style	Outcomes: Childhood	Outcomes: Adolescence
Authoritative	Upbeat mood; high self-esteem, self-control, task persistence, and cooperativeness	High self-esteem, social and moral maturity, and academic achievement
Authoritarian	Anxious, withdrawn, and unhappy mood; hostile when frustrated; poor school performance	Less well-adjusted than agemates reared with the authoritative style, but somewhat better school performance and less antisocial behavior than agemates reared with permissive or uninvolved styles
Permissive	Impulsive, disobedient, and rebellious; demanding and dependent on adults; poor persistence at tasks and school performance	Poor self-control and school performance; defiance and antisocial behavior
Uninvolved	Deficits in attachment, cognition, play, and emotional and social skills	Poor emotional self-regulation; low academic self-esteem and school performance; antisocial behavior

children's maladaptive styles (Hart, Newell, & Olson, 2003; Pettit et al., 2007). And with fearful, inhibited children, parents must suppress their tendency to overprotect and take over solving the child's social problems—practices that, as we saw in Chapter 10, worsen the shy child's difficulties. Instead, inhibited children benefit from extra encouragement to be assertive and to express their autonomy (Nelson et al., 2006; Rubin, Burgess, & Coplan, 2002).

Longitudinal research indicates that authoritative child rearing promotes maturity and adjustment in children of diverse temperaments. As the findings just mentioned illustrate, some children, because of their dispositions, require "heavier doses" of certain authoritative features (Hart, Newell, & Olsen, 2003, p. 764). Over time, the relationship between parenting and children's attributes becomes increasingly bidirectional as each participant modifies the actions of the other and, on the basis of past interactions, forms expectancies for the other's behavior (Kuczynski, 2003). Consider an investigation of the consequences of parental monitoring that followed adolescents from ages 14 to 18. The more parents knew about their child's whereabouts and activities, the greater the decline in delinquent acts over time. And the greater the decline in delinquency, the greater the increase in parents' knowledge of their child's daily life (Laird et al., 2003).

What explains these bidirectional associations, in which parental monitoring promotes responsible youth behavior, which in turn leads to gains in parental knowledge? Parents who exert appropriate oversight are likely to parent effectively in other ways as well, giving teenagers both less opportunity and less reason to engage in delinquency. And parents who take proactive steps to intervene in their child's antisocial behavior set the stage for a more positive parent–child relationship, in which teenagers are more willing to provide them with information. In contrast, when monitoring is lax and delinquency rises, parent–child interaction may become increasingly negative. As a result, parents may further disengage from parenting, both to avoid unpleasant parent–child exchanges and to reduce contact with a child whom they have come to dislike.

Most children and adolescents seem to view the affection, appropriate control, and respect for self-determination that make up authoritative child rearing as a well-intentioned parental effort to increase their competence. As a result, even hard-to-rear youngsters gradually respond to authoritativeness with cooperation and maturity, which promote parents' pleasure and approval of the child, sense of self-efficacy at child rearing, and likelihood of continuing to be authoritative. In sum, authoritative child rearing seems to create a *positive emotional context* for parental influence in the following ways:

- Children are far more likely to comply with and internalize control that appears fair and reasonable, not arbitrary (see Chapter 12).
- Warm, involved parents who are secure in the standards they hold for their children provide models of caring concern as well as confident, self-controlled behavior. Perhaps for

this reason, their children are advanced in emotional and social understanding and self-regulation—factors linked to social competence (Lindsey & Mize, 2000).

- Parents who combine warmth with rational and reasonable control are likely to be more effective reinforcing agents, praising children for striving to meet their expectations and making good use of disapproval, which works best when applied by an adult who has been warm and caring (see Chapter 12).
- By making demands and engaging in autonomy granting that fit with children's ability to take responsibility for their own behavior, authoritative parents let children know that they are competent individuals who can do things successfully for themselves. In this way, parents foster favorable self-esteem and cognitive and social maturity (see Chapter 11).
- Supportive aspects of the authoritative style, including parental acceptance, involvement, and rational control, are a powerful source of resilience, protecting children from the negative effects of family stress and poverty (Beyers et al., 2003).

Still, a few theorists remain convinced that parenting has little impact on children's development. They claim that because parents and children share genes, parents provide children with genetically influenced child rearing that does little more than enhance children's built-in propensities. But as the Biology and Environment box on pages 574–575 reveals, a host of findings demonstrate that parenting does contribute vitally to children's competence.

Adapting Child Rearing to Children's Development

Because authoritative parents continually adapt to children's increasing competence, their practices change with children's age. A gradual lessening of control and increase in autonomy granting support development.

• **Parenting in Middle Childhood: Coregulation** In middle childhood, the amount of time children spend with parents declines dramatically. Children's growing independence means that parents must deal with new issues. As one mother described it, "I've struggled with how many chores to assign, how much allowance to give, whether their friends are good influences, and what to do about problems at school. And then there's the challenge of keeping track of them when they're out—or even when they're home and I'm not there to see what's going on."

Despite these new concerns, child rearing becomes easier for those who established an authoritative style during the early years. Reasoning is more effective with school-age children because of their greater capacity for logical thinking and their increased respect for parents' expert knowledge (Collins, Madsen, & Susman-Stillman, 2002). As children demonstrate that they can manage daily activities and responsibilities, effective parents gradually shift control from adult to child. They do not let go entirely but, rather, engage in **coregulation,** a form of supervision in which parents exercise general oversight while letting children take charge of moment-by-moment decision making. Coregulation grows out of a warm, cooperative relationship between parent and child based on give-and-take and mutual respect. Parents must guide and monitor from a distance and effectively communicate expectations when they are with their children. And children must inform parents of their whereabouts, activities, and problems so parents can intervene when necessary (Maccoby, 1984). Coregulation supports and protects children while preparing them for adolescence, when they will make many important decisions themselves.

An 11-year-old on an outing with friends checks in with her parents by phone. During middle childhood, parents who engage in coregulation—permitting children to take charge of daily activities while monitoring them from a distance—prepare them for greater independence in adolescence.

Although school-age children often press for greater independence, they also know how much they need their parents' support. In one study, fifth and sixth graders described parents as the most influential people in their lives, often turning to them for affection, advice, enhancement of self-worth, and assistance with everyday problems (Furman & Buhrmester, 1992).

• **Parenting in Adolescence: Fostering Autonomy** During adolescence, striving for **autonomy**—a sense of oneself as a separate, self-governing individual—becomes a salient task. Autonomy has two vital aspects: (1) an *emotional component*—relying more on oneself and less on parents for

■ Biology *and* Environment ■

Does Parenting Really Matter?

Several highly publicized reviews of research have concluded that parents are only minor players in children's development—that their impact is overshadowed by the effects of children's genetic makeup and the peer culture (Harris, 1998, 2002). These claims are largely based on evidence that siblings reared in the same family show little resemblance in parent-rated temperament (see Chapter 10, page 422, to review), a finding interpreted to mean that parenting is merely a reaction to children's genetic dispositions and does not change children in any appreciable way. No wonder, then, say proponents of this position, that many studies report only a weak to moderate parenting effect on children's development. A related contention is that children and adolescents resemble their friends more strongly than their siblings. Therefore, peers must be far more powerful than parents in influencing children's behavior.

A host of researchers have refuted these assertions, offering evidence that parents—though not the sole influence—exert a profound impact (Berk, 2005; Collins et al., 2000; Hart, 2007; Hart, Newell, & Olsen, 2003; Maccoby, 2000a; Steinberg, 2001). Let's look at their findings:

A wealth of research confirms that parents profoundly affect children's development. When warm parents provide rich, varied experiences, they foster children's positive capacities.
© JUPITERIMAGES/BananaStock/Alamy

- *Well-designed research reveals that the relation between parenting and children's development is sometimes substantial.* For example, in one large-scale study, the correlation between authoritative parenting and adolescents' social responsibility was .76 for mothers, .49 for fathers (Hetherington et al., 1999). Similarly, when parents engage in joint problem solving with their adolescent youngsters; establish firm, consistent control; and monitor the adolescent's whereabouts, research shows strong negative relationships with antisocial behavior (Patterson & Forgatch, 1995).
- *Parenting often has different effects on different children.* When weak associations between parenting and children's development are found, they are not necessarily due to the feeble impact of parenting. Rather, some child-rearing practices affect different children in different ways (Hart, 2007). Much evidence indicates that parents respond differently to children with different temperaments. But the relationship is not just a reactive one. **TAKE A MOMENT...** Cite ways, considered in this and in previous chapters, that parents can modify the behavior of impulsive, difficult, and shy children. As Eleanor Maccoby (2000a) concluded, "The idea that in a long-standing relation such as one between parent and child, the child would be influencing the parent

support and guidance—and (2) a *behavioral component*—making decisions independently by carefully weighing one's own judgment and the suggestions of others to arrive at a well-reasoned course of action (Collins & Laursen, 2004; Steinberg & Silk, 2002). Autonomy is closely related to adolescents' quest for identity. Young people who successfully construct personally meaningful values and life goals are autonomous. They have given up childish dependency on parents for a more mature, responsible relationship.

A variety of changes within the adolescent support autonomy. In Chapter 5, we saw that puberty triggers psychological distancing from parents. In addition, as young people look more mature, parents give them more independence and responsibility. Cognitive development also paves the way for autonomy. Abstract thinking permits teenagers to solve problems and to foresee the consequences of their actions more effectively. And an improved ability to reason about social relationships leads adolescents to *deidealize* their parents, viewing them as "just people." Consequently, they no longer bend as easily to parental authority as they did when younger.

TAKE A MOMENT... Think back to what we said in earlier chapters about the type of parenting that fosters achievement motivation, identity formation, and moral maturity. You will find a common theme: Effective parenting of adolescents strikes a balance between *connection* and *separation.* In diverse ethnic groups, SES levels, nationalities, and family structures (including single-parent, two-parent, and stepparent), warm, supportive parent–adolescent ties that permit young people to explore ideas and social roles foster adolescent autonomy—predicting high self-reliance, effortful control, work orientation, academic achievement, favorable self-esteem, social competence, and ease of separating in the transition

but the parent would not be influencing the child is absurd" (p. 18).

- *Longitudinal research suggests that parenting affects children's development.* Many longitudinal studies indicate that the influence of parenting on diverse aspects of children's development holds even after controlling for children's earlier characteristics (see, for example, Carlson, 1998; D'Onofrio et al., 2006; Laird et al., 2003; Pettit, Bates, & Dodge, 1997). These findings suggest that parents' influence is profound and lasting.
- *Parenting interventions show that when child rearing improves, children's development changes accordingly.* The most powerful evidence that parents matter comes from intervention experiments. In one study, recently divorced single mothers of school-age sons were randomly assigned to a year of parent training and support. Compared to no-intervention controls, the mothers reduced their use of coercive discipline over time; at the conclusion of the intervention, their sons showed fewer behavior problems (Forgatch & DeGarmo, 1999). In another similar program, school-age children whose divorcing mothers attended an 11-week parenting skills class not only showed better immediate adjustment than youths whose parents did not attend, but the children were still functioning more favorably at a six-year follow-up (Wolchick et al., 2003). Furthermore, recall from Chapter 12 that training programs targeting parenting skills can break cycles of parent–child hostility, thereby reducing children's aggressive behavior (see pages 520–521).
- *Parents influence children's peer relations.* Children and adolescents resemble their friends because young people choose friends who are similar to themselves. But beginning in the preschool years, parents propel children toward certain peers by managing their social activities. And as we will see in Chapter 15, authoritative child rearing affects the values and inclinations children and adolescents bring to the peer situation and, therefore, their choice of friends and their peer interactions and activities (Furman et al., 2002; Laird et al., 2003; Zhou et al., 2002).
- *Some parenting influences cannot be measured easily.* Many people report memorable moments with parents that made a lasting impression. In contrast, a parent's broken promise or discovered deception can destroy parent–child trust and change the impact of future parenting.

In sum, parenting effects combine in complex ways with many other factors, including heredity and peers. Indeed, the contribution of each factor cannot be partitioned neatly from the others, just as nature and nurture are interwoven throughout development.

In view of current evidence, what can parents do to ensure the best outcomes for children? Craig Hart (1999) offers four recommendations:

- Teach moral values, to help children make wise choices in the face of their genetic inclinations and pressures from peers.
- Adapt parenting to help children overcome unfavorable dispositions. Using coercive control instead of rational firmness with an impulsive child, or overprotection instead of encouragement with an inhibited youngster, worsens maladaptive behavior.
- Foster children's positive capacities through rich, varied experiences—academic, social, athletic, artistic, musical, and spiritual.
- Engage in authoritative child rearing, a style that consistently predicts positive outcomes for children and adolescents.

to college (Bean, Barber, & Crane, 2007; Eisenberg et al., 2005; Vazsonyi, Hibbert, & Snider, 2003; Wang, Pomerantz, & Chen, 2007).

Conversely, parents who are coercive or psychologically controlling interfere with the development of autonomy. These tactics breed intense, emotionally negative exchanges between parent and teenager (Caples & Barrera, 2006; Kim et al., 2001). And they are linked to low self-esteem, depression, substance use, and antisocial behavior—outcomes that often persist into adulthood (Barber, Stolz, & Olsen, 2005; Bronte-Tinkew, Moore, & Carrano, 2006; Wissink, Deković, & Meijer, 2006).

Nevertheless, parents often report that living with teenagers is stressful. Earlier we described the family as a *system* that must adapt to changes in its members. The rapid physical and psychological changes of adolescence trigger conflicting expectations in parent–child relationships. In Chapter 12, we noted that interest in making choices about personal matters strengthens in adolescence. Yet parents and teenagers—especially young teenagers—differ sharply on the appropriate age for granting certain privileges, such as control over clothing, school courses, going out with friends, and dating (Smetana, 2002). Parents typically say that the young person is not yet ready for these signs of independence at a point when the teenager thinks they should have been granted long ago! Consistent parental monitoring of the young person's daily activities, through a cooperative relationship in which the adolescent willingly discloses information, predicts favorable adjustment. Besides preventing delinquency, it is linked to other positive outcomes—a reduction in sexual activity and delinquency, improved school performance, and positive psychological well-being (Crouter & Head, 2002; Jacobson & Crockett, 2000).

This teenager and his father share an affectionate moment. Adolescents may resist parental authority, especially in matters of personal choice such as dress. But most maintain close family ties, particularly when parents give them the freedom to explore ideas and social roles. © Dex Images/Corbis

Parents' own development can also lead to friction with teenagers. While their children face a boundless future and a wide array of choices, middle-aged parents must come to terms with the fact that their own possibilities are narrowing (Holmbeck, 1996). Often parents can't understand why the adolescent wants to skip family activities to be with peers. And teenagers fail to appreciate that parents want the family to be together as often as possible because an important period in their adult life—child rearing—will soon end.

Immigrant parents from cultures that place a high value on family closeness and obedience to authority have greater difficulty adapting to their teenagers' push for autonomy. Compared with nonimmigrant parents, they often react more strongly to adolescent disagreement. When they do, their youngsters are more dissatisfied with daily life (Phinney & Ong, 2001). Furthermore, over time, adolescents' growing exposure to the host culture's language and individualistic values may prompt parental criticism and a drop in youths' reliance on the family network for social support. The resulting *acculturative stress* (see page 468 in Chapter 11) is associated with a rise in deviant behavior—for example, increasing alcohol use among Hispanic adolescents and delinquency among Chinese youths (Crane et al., 2005; de la Rosa et al., 2005; Gil, Wagner, & Vega, 2000; Warner et al., 2006).

Throughout adolescence, the quality of the parent–child relationship is the single most consistent predictor of mental health. In well-functioning families, young people remain attached to parents and seek their advice, but they do so in a context of greater freedom (Collins & Steinberg, 2006; Steinberg, 2001). The mild conflict that typically arises facilitates adolescent identity and autonomy by helping family members learn to express and tolerate disagreement. Conflicts also inform parents of adolescents' changing needs and expectations, signaling a need for adjustments in the parent–child relationship.

By middle to late adolescence, most parents and children achieve this mature, mutual relationship, and harmonious interaction is on the rise. The reduced time that Western teenagers spend with their families—for U.S. youths, a drop from 33 percent of waking hours in fifth grade to 14 percent in twelfth grade—has little to do with conflict (Larson et al., 1996). Rather, it results from the large amount of unstructured time available to teenagers in North America and Western Europe—on average, nearly half their waking hours (Larson, 2001). Young people tend to fill these free hours with activities that take them away from home—part-time jobs, a growing array of leisure and volunteer pursuits, and time with friends.

But this drop in family time is not universal. In one study, urban low- and middle-SES African-American youths showed no decline from childhood to adolescence in hours spent at home with family—a typical pattern in cultures with collectivist values (Larson et al., 2001). Furthermore, teenagers living in risky neighborhoods tend to have warmer, more trusting relationships with parents and adjust more favorably when their parents maintain tighter control and pressure them not to engage in worrisome behaviors (McElhaney & Allen, 2001). In harsh surroundings, young people seem to interpret more measured granting of autonomy as a sign of parental caring.

Socioeconomic and Ethnic Variations in Child Rearing

Study after study confirms that the authoritative style predicts favorable development in children and adolescents varying widely in SES and culture (Crouter & Head, 2002; Slicker & Thornberry, 2002; Vazaonyi, Hibbert, & Snider, 2003). At the same time, SES and ethnic differences in parenting do exist.

• **Socioeconomic Status** As SES rises and falls, parents and children face changing circumstances that affect family functioning, with each component of SES (educational attainment, occupational prestige and skill, and income) contributing. Researchers have yet to unravel these specific influences. Education and earnings exert substantial influence, with occupation playing a lesser but nevertheless important role (Duncan & Magnusson, 2003).

SES is linked to timing of parenthood and to family size. People who work in skilled and semiskilled manual occupations (for example, construction workers, truck drivers, and custodians) tend to marry and have children earlier, as well as give birth to more children, than people in professional and technical occupations. The two groups also differ in child-rearing values and expectations. When asked about personal qualities they desire for their children, lower-SES parents tend to emphasize external characteristics, such as obedience, politeness, neatness, and cleanliness. In contrast, higher-SES parents emphasize psychological traits, such as curiosity, happiness, self-direction, and cognitive and social maturity (Duncan & Magnusson, 2003; Hoff, Laursen, & Tardiff, 2002; Tudge et al., 2000).

These differences are reflected in family interaction. Parents higher in SES talk to, read to, and otherwise stimulate their babies and preschoolers more (see Chapter 9, page 377). With older children, they set higher developmental goals and use more warmth, explanations, inductive discipline, and verbal praise. Commands ("Do that because I told you to"), criticism, and physical punishment all occur more often in low-SES households (Bradley & Corwyn, 2003).

Education contributes substantially to these differences. Higher-SES parents' interest in providing verbal stimulation and nurturing inner traits is supported by years of schooling, during which they learned to think about abstract, subjective ideas (Uribe, LeVine, & LeVine, 1994). Greater economic security permits higher-SES parents to devote more time, energy, and material resources to nurturing their children's psychological characteristics. In contrast, high levels of stress sparked by economic insecurity, along with a stronger belief in the value of physical punishment, contribute to low-SES parents' greater use of coercive discipline (Conger & Donnellan, 2007; Pinderhughes et al., 2000).

Furthermore, many lower-SES parents feel powerless in their relationships beyond the home. At work, for example, they must obey the rules of others in positions of power and authority. When they get home, their parent–child interaction seems to duplicate these experiences—but now they are in authority. Higher-SES parents, in contrast, typically have more control over their own lives. At work, they are used to making independent decisions and convincing others of their point of view. At home, they are more likely to teach these skills to their children (Greenberger, O'Neil, & Nagel, 1994).

• Affluence Despite their advanced education and greater material wealth, affluent parents—those in prestigious occupations with six-figure annual incomes—too often fail to engage in family interaction and parenting that promote healthy development. In several studies, researchers tracked youths growing up in high-SES suburbs through the adolescent years (Luthar & Latendresse, 2005a). By seventh grade, many showed serious problems, which worsened in high school. Their school grades were poor, and they were more likely than low-SES youths to engage in alcohol and drug use and to report high levels of anxiety and depression (Luthar & Becker, 2002). Furthermore, among affluent (but not low-SES) teenagers, substance use was correlated with anxiety and depression, suggesting that wealthy youths took drugs to self-medicate—a practice that predicts persistent abuse (Luthar & Sexton, 2004).

Why are so many affluent youths troubled? Compared to their better-adjusted counterparts, poorly adjusted affluent young people report less emotional closeness and supervision from their parents, who lead professionally and socially demanding lives. As a group, wealthy parents are nearly as physically and emotionally unavailable to their youngsters as parents coping with serious financial strain. At the same time, these parents often make excessive demands for achievement (Luthar & Becker, 2002). Adolescents whose parents value their accomplishments more than their character are more likely to have academic and emotional problems.

For both affluent and low-SES youths, a simple routine—eating dinner with parents—is associated with a reduction in adjustment difficulties, even after many other aspects of parenting are controlled (see Figure 14.1) (Luthar & Latendresse, 2005b). Interventions that make wealthy parents aware of the high costs of a competitive, overscheduled lifestyle and minimal family time are badly needed.

• Poverty When families slip into poverty, effective parenting and children's development are profoundly threatened. Consider the case

Figure 14.1 **Relationship of regularly eating dinner with parents to affluent youths' adjustment problems.**

Compared with sixth graders who often ate dinner with their parents, those who rarely did so were far more likely to display anxiety and depression, delinquency and substance use, and poor school grades, even after many other aspects of parenting were controlled. In this study, frequent family mealtimes also protected inner-city youths from delinquency and substance use and from classroom learning problems. (Adapted from Luthar & Latendresse, 2005b.)

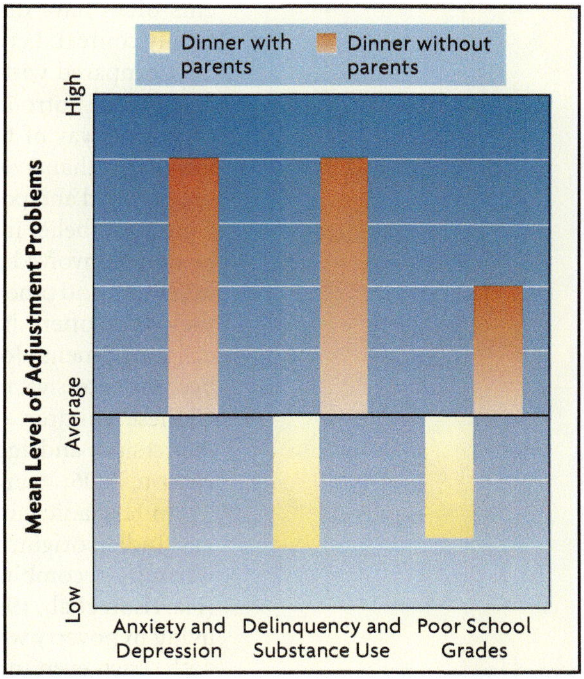

This family, already struggling financially, became homeless after a trailer park fire. Poverty is accompanied by persistent stressors that weaken the family system, with profoundly negative consequences for children's well-being. AP Images/ The Decatur Daily/Jonathan Palmer

of Zinnia Mae, who grew up in a close-knit black community located in a small southeastern American city (Heath, 1990). As unemployment struck in the 1980s and citizens moved away, 16-year-old Zinnia Mae caught a ride to Atlanta. Two years later, she was the mother of a daughter and twin boys, and she had moved into high-rise public housing.

All of Zinnia Mae's days were much the same. She worried constantly about scraping together enough money to put food on the table, finding babysitters so she could go to the laundry or grocery, freeing herself from growing debt, and finding the twins' father, who had stopped sending money. To relieve loneliness and anxiety, she watched TV and talked with a few friends on the phone. Her most frequent words were, "I'm so tired." The children had only one set meal (breakfast); otherwise, they ate whenever they were hungry or bored. Their play space was limited to the living-room sofa and a mattress on the floor. Toys consisted of scraps of a blanket, spoons and food cartons, a small rubber ball, a few plastic cars, and a roller skate abandoned in the building.

At the researcher's request, Zinnia Mae agreed to tape record her interactions with her children. Cut off from family and community ties and overwhelmed by financial strain and feelings of helplessness, she found herself unable to join in activities with her children. In 500 hours of tape, she started a conversation with her children only 18 times.

The constant stressors that accompany poverty gradually weaken the family system. Poor families have many daily hassles—bills to pay, the car breaking down, loss of welfare and unemployment payments, something stolen from the house, to name just a few. When daily crises arise, parents become depressed, irritable, and distracted; hostile interactions increase; and children's development suffers (Conger & Donnellan, 2007; Evans, 2006; Mistry et al., 2004). Negative outcomes are especially severe in single-parent families, in families who must live in poor housing and dangerous neighborhoods, and in homeless families—conditions that make everyday existence even more difficult, while reducing social supports that assist in coping with economic hardship (Leventhal & Brooks-Gunn, 2003).

Besides stress and conflict, reduced parental involvement and depleted home learning environments (like that of Zinnia Mae) profoundly affect poor children's cognitive and emotional well-being. As noted in earlier chapters, poverty that begins early and persists has devastating effects on children's physical and mental health, intelligence, and school achievement.

• **Ethnicity** Although authoritative parenting is broadly advantageous, ethnic minority parents often have distinct child-rearing beliefs and practices that reflect cultural values and family context. Let's take some examples.

Compared with Western parents, Chinese parents describe their parenting as less warm and more controlling. They are more directive in teaching and scheduling their children's time, as a way of fostering self-control and high achievement. Chinese parents may appear less warm than Western parents because they withhold praise, which they believe results in self-satisfied and poorly motivated children (Chao, 1994; Chen, 2001). High control reflects the Confucian belief in strict discipline, respect for elders, and socially desirable behavior, taught by deeply involved parents. Chinese parents report expressing affection and concern and using induction and other reasoning-oriented discipline as much as North American parents do, but they more often shame a misbehaving child (see Chapter 10), withdraw love, and use physical punishment (Jose et al., 2000; Schwalb et al., 2004; Wu et al., 2002). When these practices become excessive, resulting in an authoritarian style high in psychological or coercive control, Chinese children display the same negative outcomes seen in Western children: anxiety, depression, and aggressive behavior (Bradford et al., 2003; Nelson et al., 2005, 2006a, 2006b; Nelson, 2006; Wang, Pomerantz, & Chen, 2007).

In Hispanic families, Asian Pacific Island families, and Caribbean families of African and East Indian origin, firm insistence on respect for parental authority is paired with high parental warmth—a combination suited to promoting competence and strong feelings of family loyalty (Harrison et al., 1994; Roopnarine & Evans, 2007). In one study, Mexican-American mothers living in poverty who adhered strongly to their cultural traditions tended to combine warmth with strict, even somewhat harsh, control—a style that served a protective function, in that it was associated with reduced child and adolescent conduct problems (Hill, Bush, & Roosa, 2003). Although at one time viewed as coercive, contemporary Hispanic-American fathers typically spend much time with their children and are warm and sensitive (Cabrera & Garcia Coll, 2004; Jambunathan, Burts, & Pierce, 2000). In Caribbean families that have immigrated to the United States, fathers' authoritativeness—but not mothers'—predicted preschoolers' literacy and math skills, probably because Caribbean fathers take a larger role in guiding their children's academic progress (Roopnarine et al., 2006).

Some ethnic minority groups pair respect for parental authority with high parental warmth. This combination promotes competence and strong family loyalty, which are associated with fewer child and adolescent conduct problems.

Although wide variation exists, low-SES African-American parents tend to expect immediate obedience. But consistent with findings just reported for Mexican Americans, when African-American families live in depleted, crime-ridden neighborhoods and have few social supports, strict control may have a positive effect, preventing antisocial involvements. Other research suggests that black parents use firm control for broader reasons—to promote self-reliance, self-regulation, and a watchful attitude in risky surroundings, which protects children from becoming victims of crime. Consistent with this view, low-SES African-American parents who use more controlling strategies tend to have more cognitively and socially competent children (Brody & Flor, 1998; Brody, Stoneman, & Flor, 1996a, 1996b). Recall, also, that a childhood history of physical punishment is associated with a reduction in antisocial behavior among African-American adolescents but with an increase among Caucasian-American adolescents (see page 489 in Chapter 12). Most African-American parents who use strict, "no-nonsense" discipline use physical punishment sparingly and combine it with warmth and reasoning.

The family structure and child-rearing customs of many minorities buffer the stress and disorganization caused by poverty. As the Cultural Influences box on page 580 illustrates, the **extended-family household,** in which one or more adult relatives live with the parent–child **nuclear family unit,** is a vital feature of ethnic minority family life that has enabled many families to rear children successfully, despite severe economic deprivation and prejudice. Extended family ties provide yet another example of the remarkable capacity of families to mobilize cultural traditions to safeguard children's development under conditions of high life stress.

Ask Yourself

Review Explain why authoritative parenting is linked to favorable academic and social outcomes among children and adolescents. Is the concept of authoritative parenting useful for understanding effective parenting across cultures? Explain.

Apply Prepare a short talk for a parent–teacher organization, maintaining that parents matter greatly in children's lives. Support each of your points with research evidence.

Connect Explain how factors that promote autonomy in adolescence also foster identity development. (To review the influence of parenting on identity, see page 467 in Chapter 11.)

Reflect How would you classify your parents' child-rearing styles? What factors might have influenced their approach to child rearing?

Family Lifestyles and Transitions

Families in industrialized nations have become more diverse. Today, there are fewer births per family unit, more adults who want to adopt, more lesbian and gay parents who are open about their sexual orientation, and more never-married parents. Further, high rates of divorce, remarriage, and maternal employment have reshaped the family system.

In the following sections, we discuss these changes in the family, emphasizing how each affects family relationships and children's development. **TAKE A MOMENT...** As you consider this array of family forms, think back to the social systems perspective. Note how children's well-being, in each instance, depends on the quality of family interaction, which is sustained by supportive ties to kin and community and by favorable public policies.

Cultural Influences

The African-American Extended Family

The African-American extended family can be traced to the African heritage of most black Americans. In many African societies, newly married couples do not start their own households. Instead, they live with a large extended family, which assists its members with all aspects of daily life. This tradition of maintaining a broad network of kinship ties traveled to North America during the period of slavery. Since then, it has served as a protective shield against the destructive impact of poverty and racial prejudice on African-American family life. Today, more black than white adults have relatives other than their own children living in the same household. African-American parents also live closer to kin, often establish family-like relationships with friends and neighbors, see more relatives during the week, and perceive relatives as more important in their lives (Boyd-Franklin, 2006; Kane, 2000).

By providing emotional support and sharing income and essential resources, the African-American extended family helps reduce the stress of poverty and single parenthood. Extended-family members often help with child rearing, and adolescent mothers living in extended families are more likely to complete high school and get a job and less likely to be on welfare than mothers living on their own—factors that in turn benefit children's well-being (Gordon, Chase-Lansdale, & Brooks-Gunn, 2004; Trent & Harlan, 1994).

A grandmother shares a photo album chronicling family history with her son and grandchildren. Strong bonds with extended family members have helped protect many African-American children against the destructive impact of poverty and racial prejudice. © Richard Lord/The Image Works

For single mothers who were very young at the time of their child's birth, extended-family living continues to be associated with more positive mother–child interaction during the preschool years. Otherwise, establishing an independent household with the help of nearby relatives is related to improved child rearing. Perhaps this arrangement permits the more mature teenage mother who has developed effective parenting skills to implement them (Chase-Lansdale, Brooks-Gunn, & Zamsky, 1994). In families rearing adolescents, kinship support increases the likelihood of effective parenting, which is related to adolescents' self-reliance, emotional well-being, and reduced antisocial behavior (Hamilton, 2005; Simons et al., 2006).

Finally, the extended family plays an important role in transmitting African-American culture. Compared with nuclear family households, extended-family arrangements place more emphasis on cooperation and moral and religious values. And older black adults, such as grandparents and great-grandparents, regard educating children about their African heritage as especially important (Mosley-Howard & Evans, 2000; Taylor, 2000). Family reunions—sometimes held in grandparents' and great-grandparents' hometowns in the South—are especially common among African Americans, giving young people a strong sense of their roots (Boyd-Franklin, 2006). These influences strengthen family bonds, protect children's development, and increase the chances that the extended-family lifestyle will carry over to the next generation.

From Large to Small Families

In 1960, the average number of children per North American couple was 3.1. Currently, it is 1.8 in the United States and Canada, compared with 1.7 in Australia, Great Britain, and Sweden; 1.4 in Japan and Germany; and 1.3 in Italy (Statistics Canada, 2007g; U.S. Census Bureau, 2007b, 2008). In addition to more effective birth control, a major reason for this decline is that a family size of one or two children is more compatible with a woman's decision to divide her energies between family and work. The tendency of many couples to delay having children until they are well-established professionally and secure economically (see Chapter 3) also contributes to smaller family size. Finally, marital instability plays a role: More couples today get divorced before their childbearing plans are complete.

• **Family Size and Child Development** Popular advice to prospective parents often recommends limiting family size in the interests of "child quality"—more parental affection,

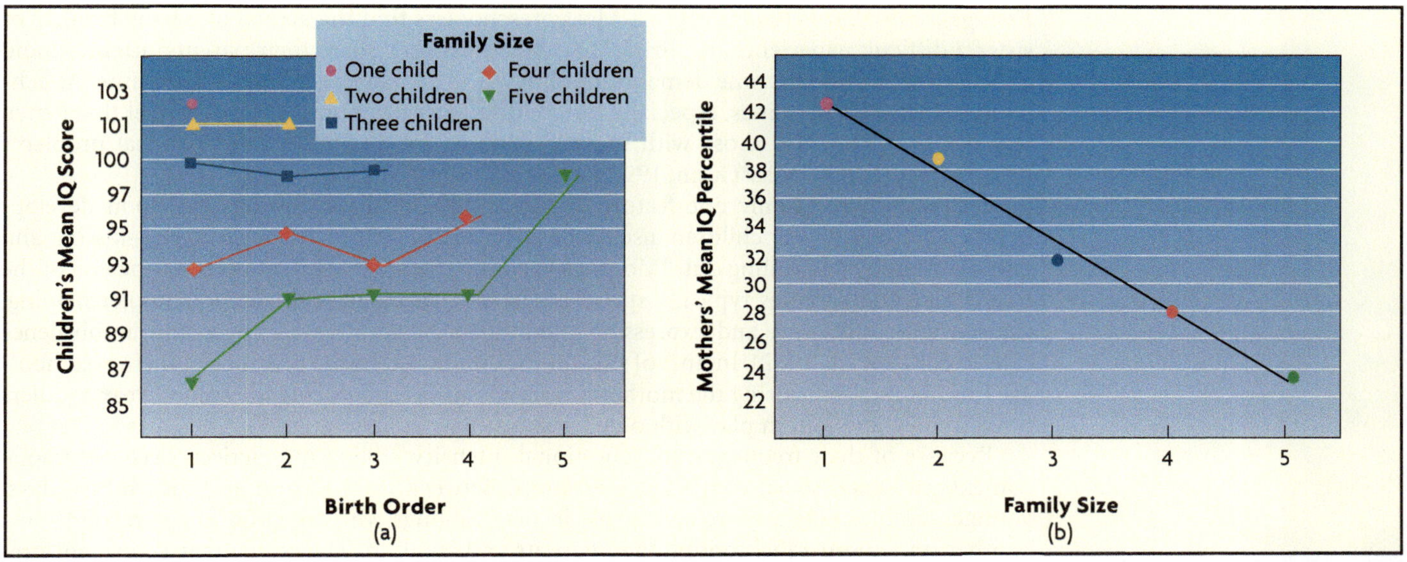

■ **Figure 14.2** **Do large families make less intelligent children?**

Findings of the U.S. National Longitudinal Survey of Youth answer this question with certainty: No. (a) Horizontal lines show that children's IQs did not decline with later birth order, as would be predicted if large families diluted the quality of children's experiences. To the contrary, in the largest families, the youngest children tended to score higher than their siblings. But notice the differences among the lines, which indicate that the larger the family, the lower the IQs of all siblings. (b) The link between family size and children's IQ can be explained by the strong trend for mothers with lower IQs to have larger families. (From J. L. Rodgers, H. H. Cleveland, E. van den Oord, & D. C. Rowe, 2000, "Resolving the Debate Over Birth Order, Family Size, and Intelligence," *American Psychologist*, 55, pp. 607, 609. Copyright © 2000 by the American Psychological Association. Reprinted with permission of the American Psychological Association.)

attention, and material resources per child, which are said to enhance children's intellectual development. Do large families make less-intelligent children, as prevailing attitudes suggest? Or do less-intelligent parents—as a result of heredity, environment, or both—tend to have larger families? For decades, researchers could not resolve this issue because they had access only to samples of unrelated children growing up in different homes, in which comparisons of first-born and later-born children were confounded with other family characteristics, such as SES (which declines as family size increases).

Starting in 1972, the U.S. National Longitudinal Survey of Youth (NLSY) followed a representative sample of more than 3,000 U.S. 14- to 22-year-olds; in 1986 the children of the original participants were added to the investigation. Because both cohorts took intelligence tests, researchers could (1) examine the relationship of sibling birth order within families to IQ, to determine whether having more children depresses children's intellectual functioning; and (2) correlate maternal IQ with family size, for insight into whether mothers who score poorly are prone to have larger families.

As the horizontal lines in Figure 14.2a reveal, children's IQs did not decline with later birth order—a finding that contradicts the assumption that large families make less-intelligent children. At the same time, the differences among the lines show that the larger the family, the lower the scores of all siblings. And as Figure 14.2b indicates, the link between family size and children's IQ can be explained by the strong trend for mothers lower in intelligence to give birth to more children (Rodgers et al., 2000). In other NLSY research, among children of bright, economically advantaged mothers, the family size–IQ correlation disappeared (Guo & VanWey, 1999).

Although many good reasons exist for limiting family size, the concern that additional births will reduce children's intelligence and life chances is not warranted. Instead, young people with lower mental test scores—many of whom dropped out of school, live in poverty, lack hope for their future, and fail to engage in family planning—are most likely to have large families. For adolescents with these risk factors, educational and family planning interventions are crucial (see Chapter 5, page 217).

• **Growing Up with Siblings** Despite a declining family size, 80 percent of North American and European children still grow up with at least one sibling (Dunn, 2004b). Siblings influence development both directly, through relationships with one another, and indirectly, through the impact of an additional child on parents' behavior. In previous chapters, we examined some consequences of having brothers and sisters, including effects on early language development, personality, self- and social understanding, and gender typing. Now let's look closely at the quality of the sibling relationship.

Emergence of Sibling Relationships. Most preschoolers find the arrival of a baby brother or sister a difficult experience. Realizing that they must now share their parents' attention and affection, they often become demanding, clingy, and deliberately naughty for a time. Attachment security also declines, especially for children over age 2 (old enough to feel threatened and displaced) and for those with mothers stressed by marital or psychological problems (Baydar, Greek, & Brooks-Gunn, 1997; Teti et al., 1996).

Yet resentment is only one feature of a rich emotional relationship that soon develops between siblings. Older children also show affection and sympathetic concern—kissing and patting the baby and calling out, "Mom, he needs you" when the infant cries. By the end of the baby's first year, siblings typically spend much time together, with the preschooler helping, sharing toys, imitating, and expressing friendliness in addition to anger and ambivalence (Dunn & Kendrick, 1982). Infants of this age are comforted by the presence of their preschool-age brother or sister during the mother's short absences. And during the second year, toddlers often imitate and join in play with older siblings (Barr & Hayne, 2003).

Because of their frequency and emotional intensity, sibling interactions become unique contexts in which social competence expands. Between their second and fourth birthdays, younger siblings take a more active role in play. Siblings who are close in age relate to one another on a more equal footing than parents and children. They often engage in joint pretend, talk about feelings, tease, deceive, and—when conflicts arise—call attention to their own wants and needs. The skills acquired during sibling interaction contribute to understanding of emotions and other mental states, perspective taking, moral maturity, and competence in relating to other children. Consistent with these outcomes, positive sibling ties predict favorable adjustment, even among hostile children at risk for social difficulties (Modry-Mandell, Gamble, & Taylor, 2007; Stormshak et al., 1996).

Nevertheless, individual differences in sibling relationships emerge soon after the new baby's arrival. In Chapter 10, we noted that certain temperamental traits—high emotional reactivity or activity level—increase the chances of sibling conflict. Parenting is also influential: Maternal warmth toward both children is related to positive sibling interaction and to preschoolers' support of a distressed younger sibling (Volling, 2001; Volling & Belsky, 1992). And mothers who frequently play with their children and head off potential conflicts by explaining the toddler's wants and needs to the preschool sibling foster sibling cooperation. In contrast, maternal harshness and lack of involvement result in increasingly antagonistic sibling relationships (Howe, Aquan-Assee, & Bukowski, 2001).

Finally, a good marriage is linked to preschool siblings' capacity to cope adaptively with jealousy and conflict (Volling, McElwain, & Miller, 2002). Perhaps good communication between parents serves as a model of effective problem solving. It may also foster a generally happy family environment, giving children less reason to feel jealous.

Although sibling rivalry tends to increase in middle childhood, siblings also provide each other with emotional support and help with difficult tasks. © Michael Newman/PhotoEdit

Sibling Relationships in Middle Childhood. Sibling rivalry tends to increase in middle childhood. As children participate in a wider range of activities, parents often compare siblings' traits and accomplishments. The child who gets less parental affection, more disapproval, or fewer material resources is likely to be resentful and to show poorer adjustment over time (Dunn, 2004b; Tamrouti-Makkink et al., 2004).

For same-sex siblings who are close in age, parental comparisons are more frequent, resulting in more quarreling, antagonism, and adjustment difficulties. This effect is particularly strong when parenting is cold or harsh (Feinberg & Hetherington, 2001). A survey of a nationally representative sample of nearly 23,000 Canadian children revealed that differential treatment of siblings increased when parents were under stress as a result of financial worries, marital conflict, the pressures of caring for several children, or single parenthood (Jenkins, Rasbash, & O'Connor, 2003). Parents whose energies are drained become less careful about being fair. Children react especially intensely when fathers prefer one child. Perhaps because fathers, overall, spend less time with children, their favoritism is more noticeable and triggers greater anger (Brody, Stoneman, & McCoy, 1992).

Although conflict rises, most school-age siblings continue to rely on one another for companionship and assistance. When researchers asked siblings about shared daily activities, children mentioned that older siblings often helped younger siblings with academic and peer challenges. And both members of sibling pairs offered each other help with family issues (Tucker, McHale, & Crouter, 2001).

For siblings to reap these benefits, parental encouragement of warm, considerate sibling ties is vital. The more positive their relationship, the more siblings resolve disagreements constructively and turn to one another for emotional support (Howe et al., 2001; Ram & Ross, 2001). Providing parents with training in mediation—how to get siblings to lay down ground rules, identify points of contention and common ground, and discuss goals, feelings, and possible solutions—increases siblings' awareness of one another's perspectives and reduces negativity (Smith & Ross, 2007). When siblings get along well, the older sibling's academic and social competence tends to "rub off on" the younger sibling, fostering higher achievement and more positive peer relations (Brody & Murry, 2001; Lamarche et al., 2006). But older siblings with conflict-ridden peer relations tend to transmit their physically or relationally aggressive styles to their younger brothers and sisters (Ostrov, Crick, & Stauffacher, 2006).

Sibling Relationships in Adolescence. Like parent–child relationships, sibling interactions adapt to development at adolescence. As younger siblings become more self-sufficient, they accept less direction from their older brothers and sisters. Consequently, siblings relate to one another on a more equal footing. Furthermore, as adolescents become more involved in friendships and romantic relationships, they invest less time and energy in their siblings, who are part of the family from which they are trying to establish autonomy. As a result, sibling relationships often become less intense, in both positive and negative feelings (Hetherington, Henderson, & Reiss, 1999; Kim et al., 2006).

Despite a drop in companionship, attachment between siblings, like closeness to parents, remains strong for most young people. Consistent with the high value girls place on emotional closeness, sisters report greater intimacy with their siblings than brothers do, and sister–sister pairings tend to be the closest (Kim et al., 2006). But overall, siblings who established a positive bond in early childhood continue to display greater affection and caring during the teenage years—an outcome linked to more favorable emotional and social adjustment (Branje et al., 2004; Kim et al., 2007). Older siblings frequently offer useful advice as their younger teenage brothers and sisters face challenges in romantic relationships, schoolwork, and decisions about the future.

Sibling interaction at adolescence continues to be affected by other relationships, and vice versa. Teenagers whose parents are warm and supportive and who have a history of caring friendships have more positive sibling ties (Bussell et al., 1999; Kramer & Kowal, 2005). And in bidirectional fashion, warm adolescent sibling relationships contribute to more gratifying friendships (Yeh & Lempers, 2004). Finally, mild sibling differences in perceived parental affection no longer trigger jealousy but, instead, predict increasing sibling warmth (Feinberg et al., 2003). Perhaps adolescents interpret a unique relationship with parents, as long as it is generally accepting, as a gratifying sign of their own individuality.

Limiting family size is a basic national policy in the People's Republic of China. In urban areas, the majority of couples have no more than one child. © Paul Conklin/ PhotoEdit

One-Child Families

Although sibling relationships bring many benefits, they are not essential for healthy development. Contrary to popular belief, only children are not spoiled. In some respects, they are even advantaged. North American children growing up in one-child families are higher in self-esteem and achievement motivation, do better in school, and attain higher levels of education (Falbo, 1992). One reason may be that only children have somewhat closer relationships with parents, who may exert more pressure for mastery and accomplishment. Furthermore, only children have just as many close, high-quality friendships as children with siblings. However, they tend to be less well-accepted in the peer group, perhaps because they have not had opportunities to learn effective conflict-resolution strategies through sibling interactions (Kitzmann, Cohen, & Lockwood, 2002).

Favorable development also characterizes only children in China, where, for more than two decades, a one-child family policy has been strictly enforced in urban areas to control population growth (Yang, 2008). Compared with agemates who have siblings, Chinese only children

Will this adopted girl develop an identity that is a healthy blend of her birth and rearing backgrounds? The answer depends on the extent to which her adoptive parents expose her to her African-American heritage. © Corbis

are advanced in cognitive development and academic achievement. They also feel more emotionally secure, perhaps because government disapproval promotes tension in families with more than one child (Falbo & Poston, 1993; Jiao, Ji, & Jing, 1996; Yang et al., 1995). Chinese mothers usually ensure that their children have regular contact with first cousins (who are considered siblings). Perhaps as a result, Chinese only children do not differ from agemates with siblings in social skills and peer acceptance (Hart, Newell, & Olsen, 2003). The next generation of Chinese only children, however, will have no first cousins.

Adoptive Families

Adults who are infertile, who are likely to pass along a genetic disorder, or who are older and single but want a family are turning to adoption in increasing numbers. Those who have children by birth, too, sometimes choose to expand their families through adoption. Adoption agencies try to ensure a good fit by seeking parents of the same ethnic and religious background as the child and, where possible, trying to choose parents who are the same age as typical biological parents. Because the availability of healthy babies has declined (fewer young unwed mothers give up their babies than in the past), more people in North America and Western Europe are adopting from other countries or accepting children who are past infancy or who have known developmental problems (Schweiger & O'Brien, 2005).

Adopted children and adolescents—whether or not they were born in their adoptive parents' country—have more learning and emotional difficulties than other children, a difference that increases with the child's age at time of adoption (Brodzinsky & Pinderhughes, 2002; Nickman et al., 2005; van IJzendoorn, Juffer, & Poelhuis, 2005). There are many possible reasons for adoptees' more problematic childhoods. The biological mother may have been unable to care for the child because of problems believed to be partly genetic, such as alcoholism or severe depression, and may have passed this tendency to her offspring. Or perhaps she experienced stress, poor diet, or inadequate medical care during pregnancy. Furthermore, children adopted after infancy are more likely than their nonadopted peers to have a preadoptive history of conflict-ridden family relationships, lack of parental affection, neglect and abuse, or deprived institutional rearing. Finally, adoptive parents and children, who are genetically unrelated, are less alike in intelligence and personality than are biological relatives—differences that may threaten family harmony.

Despite these risks, most adopted children fare well, and those with preexisting problems usually make rapid progress (Bimmel et al., 2003; Johnson, 2002). In a Swedish longitudinal study, researchers followed more than 600 infant adoption candidates into adolescence. Some were adopted shortly after birth; some were reared in foster homes; and some were reared by their biological mothers, who initially gave up their babies and then changed their minds and took them back. As Figure 14.3 shows, adoptees developed much more favorably than children growing up in foster families or returned to their birth mothers (Bohman & Sigvardsson, 1990). And in a study of internationally adopted children in the Netherlands, sensitive maternal care and secure attachment in infancy predicted cognitive and social competence at age 7 (Stams, Juffer, & van IJzendoorn, 2002). So even when children are not genetically related to their parents, an early warm, trusting parent–child relationship fosters development. Children with troubled family histories who are adopted at older ages also develop feelings of trust and affection for their adoptive parents as they come to feel loved and supported in their new families (Veríssimo & Salvaterra, 2006).

■ **Figure 14.3** **Relationship of type of rearing to maladjustment among a sample of Swedish adolescents who had been candidates for adoption at birth.** Compared with the other two groups, adopted youths were rated by teachers as having far fewer problems, including anxiety, withdrawal, aggression, inability to concentrate, peer difficulties, and poor school motivation. (Adapted from Bohman & Sigvardsson, 1990.)

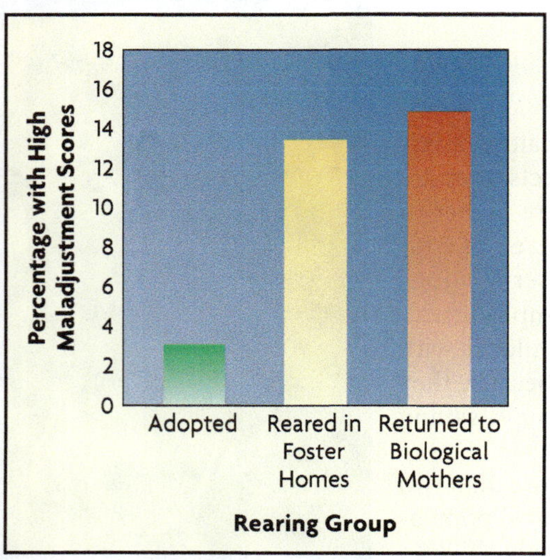

By adolescence, adoptees' lives are often complicated by unresolved curiosity about their roots. Some have difficulty accepting the possibility that they may never know their birth parents. Others worry about what they would do if their birth parents suddenly reappeared (Grotevant & Kohler, 1999). Despite concerns about their origins, most adoptees appear optimistic and well-adjusted as adults. And as long as their parents took steps to help them learn about their heritage in childhood, young people adopted into a different ethnic group or culture generally develop identities that are healthy blends of their birth and rearing backgrounds (Nickman et al., 2005; Thomas, & Tessler, 2007).

Clearly, adoption is a satisfying family alternative for most parents and children who experience it. Good outcomes can be promoted by careful pairing of children with parents and provision of guidance to adoptive families by well-trained social service professionals.

Gay and lesbian parents are as committed to and effective at child rearing as heterosexual parents. Their children are well-adjusted, and the large majority develop a heterosexual orientation. © Creatas Images/Jupiter Images

Gay and Lesbian Families

Several million American and tens of thousands of Canadian gay men and lesbians are parents, most through previous heterosexual marriages, some through adoption, and a growing number through reproductive technologies (Ambert, 2005; Patterson, 2002). In the past, because of laws assuming that homosexuals could not be adequate parents, those who divorced a heterosexual partner lost custody of their children. Today, some U.S. states and the nation of Canada hold that sexual orientation by itself is irrelevant to custody. A few U.S. states, however, ban gay and lesbian adoptions (Laird, 2003).

Most research on homosexual families is limited to volunteer samples. Findings of these investigations indicate that gay and lesbian parents are as committed to and effective at child rearing as heterosexual parents and sometimes more so (Bos et al., 2007; Tasker, 2005). Also, whether born to or adopted by their parents or conceived through donor insemination, the children of homosexuals did not differ from the children of heterosexuals in mental health, peer relations, or gender identity (Allen & Burrell, 1996; Flaks et al., 1995; Golombok & Tasker, 1996). Two additional studies, which surmounted the potential bias associated with a volunteer sample by including all lesbian-mother families who had conceived children at a fertility clinic, also reported that children were developing favorably (Brewaeys et al., 1997; Chan, Raboy, & Patterson, 1998). Likewise, among participants drawn from a representative sample of British mothers and their 7-year-olds, children reared in lesbian-mother families did not differ from children reared in heterosexual families in adjustment and gender-role preferences (Golombok et al., 2003).

Virtually all studies have concluded that children of homosexual parents do not differ from other children in sexual orientation: The large majority are heterosexual (Tasker, 2005). But some evidence suggests that more adolescents from homosexual families experiment for a time with partners of both sexes, perhaps as a result of being reared in families and communities highly tolerant of nonconformity and difference (Bos, van Balen, & van den Boom, 2004; Stacey & Biblarz, 2001).

A major concern of gay and lesbian parents is that their children will be stigmatized by their parents' sexual orientation. Most studies indicate that incidents of teasing and bullying are rare because parents and children carefully manage the information they reveal to others (Tasker, 2005). But in an Australian study, even though most third to tenth graders were guarded about discussing their parents' relationship with peers, nearly half reported harassment (Ray & Gregory, 2001). Overall, children of gay and lesbian parents can be distinguished from other children mainly by issues related to living in a nonsupportive society.

Never-Married Single-Parent Families

About 10 percent of American children and 8 percent of Canadian children live with a single parent who has never married and does not have a partner. Of these parents, 85 to 90 percent are mothers, 10 to 15 percent fathers (Statistics Canada, 2007l; U.S. Census Bureau, 2007b). In recent years, more single women over age 30 in high-status occupations have become parents. However, they are still few in number, and little is known about their children's development.

In the United States, the largest group of never-married parents is African-American young women. Over 60 percent of births to black mothers in their twenties are to women without a partner, compared with 13 percent of births to white women (U.S. Census Bureau, 2007b). African-American women postpone marriage more and childbirth less than women in other U.S. ethnic groups. Job loss, persistent unemployment, and consequent lack of opportunities for many black men to provide economically for their families have contributed to the number of African-American never-married, single-mother families.

Never-married black mothers tap the extended family, especially their own mothers and sometimes male relatives, for help in rearing their children (Gasden, 1999; Jayakody & Kalil, 2002). For about one-third, marriage—not necessarily to the child's biological father—occurs within nine years after birth of the first child (Wu, Bumpass, & Musick, 2001). These couples function much like other first-marriage parents. Their children are often unaware that the father is a stepfather, and parents do not report the child-rearing difficulties usually associated with remarriage that we will discuss shortly (Ganong & Coleman, 1994).

Still, single mothers find it harder to overcome poverty. Nearly 50 percent of white mothers and 60 percent of black mothers have a second child while unmarried. And they are far less likely than divorced mothers to receive paternal child support payments. Consequently, many children in single-mother homes display adjustment problems associated with economic hardship (Kotchick, Dorsey, & Heller, 2005). Furthermore, children of never-married mothers who lack a father's warmth and involvement achieve less well in school and engage in more antisocial behavior than children in low-SES, first-marriage families (Coley, 1998). But marriage to the child's biological father benefits children only when the father is a reliable source of economic and emotional support. For example, when a mother pairs up with an antisocial father, her child is at far greater risk for conduct problems than if she had reared the child alone (Jaffee et al., 2003). Overall, strengthening social support, education, and employment opportunities for low-income parents would greatly enhance the well-being of unmarried mothers and their children.

Divorce

Between 1960 and 1985, divorce rates in Western nations rose dramatically before stabilizing in most countries. The United States has the highest divorce rate in the world, Canada the sixth highest (see Figure 14.4). Of the 45 percent of American and 30 percent of Canadian marriages that end in divorce, half involve children. At any given time, one-fourth of American and one-fifth of Canadian children live in single-parent households. Although most reside with their mothers, the percentage in father-headed households has increased steadily, to about 12 percent in both nations (Federal Interagency Forum on Child and Family Statistics, 2006; Statistics Canada, 2005b).

■ **Figure 14.4** **Divorce rates in ten industrialized nations.** The U.S. divorce rate is the highest in the industrialized world, far exceeding divorce rates in other countries. The Canadian divorce rate is the sixth highest. (Adapted from U.S. Census Bureau, 2007b; United Nations, 2002.)

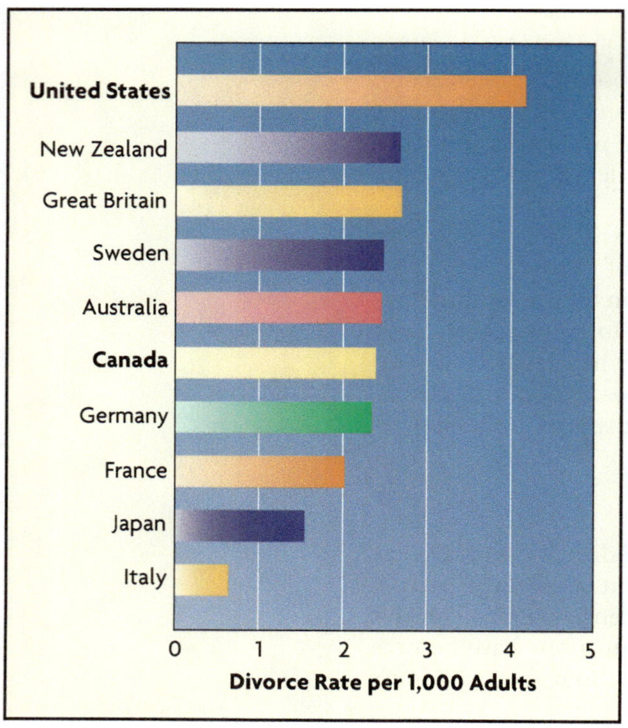

Children of divorce spend an average of five years in a single-parent home—almost a third of childhood. For many, divorce leads to new family relationships. About two-thirds of divorced parents marry again. Half of their children eventually experience a third major change—the end of their parents' second marriage (Hetherington & Kelly, 2002).

These figures reveal that divorce is not a single event in the lives of parents and children. Instead, it is a transition that leads to a variety of new living arrangements, accompanied by changes in housing, income, and family roles and responsibilities. Since the 1960s, many studies have reported that marital breakup is stressful for children. But research also reveals great individual differences (Hetherington, 2003). How well children fare depends on many factors: the custodial parent's psychological health, the child's characteristics, and social supports within the family and surrounding community.

• **Immediate Consequences** Family conflict often rises around the time of divorce as parents try to settle disputes over children and possessions. Once one parent moves out, additional events threaten supportive interactions between parents and children. Mother-headed households typically experience a sharp drop in income. In the United States and Canada, the majority of divorced mothers with young children live in poverty, getting less than the full amount of child support from the absent father or none at all (Children's Defense Fund, 2006; Statistics Canada, 2007l). They often have to move to lower-cost housing, reducing supportive ties to neighbors and friends.

Compared with girls, boys are at slightly greater risk for academic, emotional, and behavior problems following divorce. Fortunately, this child benefits from the continued support and involvement of his noncustodial father—a major predictor of positive adjustment. © Gareth Brown/Corbis

The transition from marriage to divorce typically leads to high maternal stress, depression, and anxiety and to a disorganized family situation. Declines in well-being are greatest for mothers of young children (Hope, Power, & Rodgers, 1999; Williams & Dunne-Bryant, 2006). Predictable events and routines—meals and bedtimes, household chores, and joint parent–child activities—usually disintegrate. As children react with distress and anger to their less secure home lives, discipline may become harsh and inconsistent. Contact with noncustodial fathers decreases over time (Hetherington & Kelly, 2002). Fathers who see their children only occasionally are inclined to be permissive and indulgent, making the mother's task of managing the child even more difficult.

The more parents argue and fail to provide children with warmth, involvement, and consistent guidance, the poorer children's adjustment. About 20 to 25 percent of children in divorced families display severe problems, compared with about 10 percent in nondivorced families (Gerard, Krishnakumar, & Buehler, 2006; Greene et al., 2003; Pruett et al., 2003; Strohschein, 2005). At the same time, reactions vary with children's age, temperament, and sex.

Children's Age. The cognitive immaturity of preschool and early school-age children makes it difficult for them to grasp the reasons behind their parents' separation. Younger children often blame themselves and take the marital breakup as a sign that both parents may abandon them (Lansford et al., 2006). As a result, they are more likely to display both anxious, fearful and angry, defiant reactions than older children and adolescents, who can better understand the reasons for their parents' divorce.

Still, many school-age and adolescent youngsters also react strongly, experiencing depressed mood and escaping into undesirable peer activities, such as running away, truancy, and early sexual activity, particularly when family conflict is high and parental supervision is low (D'Onofrio et al., 2006; Hetherington & Stanley-Hagan, 1999). And as academic pressures in school rise and preoccupied parents reduce their involvement and support, poor school achievement is common (Lansford et al., 2006). But some older children—especially the oldest child in the family—display more mature behavior, willingly taking on family and household tasks, care and protection of younger siblings, and emotional support of a depressed, anxious mother. But if these demands are too great, these children may eventually become resentful, withdraw from the family, and engage in angry, acting-out behavior (Hetherington, 1999).

Children's Temperament and Sex. Exposure to stressful life events and inadequate parenting magnifies the problems of temperamentally difficult children (Lengua et al., 2000). Easy children, who are less often targets of parental anger, also cope better with adversity.

These findings help explain sex differences in response to divorce. Girls sometimes respond with internalizing reactions—crying, self-criticism, and withdrawal. More often, children of both sexes show demanding, attention-getting, acting-out behavior. But in mother-custody families, boys are at slightly greater risk for academic, emotional, and behavior problems (Amato, 2001). Recall from Chapter 13 that boys are more active and noncompliant—behaviors that increase with exposure to parental conflict and inconsistent discipline. Research reveals that long before the marital breakup, sons of divorcing couples display higher rates of impulsivity, defiance, and aggression—behaviors that may have been caused by their parents' marital problems and also contributed to them (Hetherington, 1999; Shaw, Winslow, & Flanagan, 1999; Strohschein, 2005). As a result, many boys enter the period of turmoil surrounding divorce with reduced capacity to cope with stress.

Perhaps because their behavior is so unruly, boys of divorcing parents tend to receive less emotional support from mothers, teachers, and peers. Furthermore, the cycles of coercive interaction between angry, defiant sons and their divorced mothers soon spread to sibling relations, compounding adjustment difficulties (Hetherington & Kelly, 2002; Sheehan et al., 2004). After divorce, children who are challenging to rear generally get worse (Hanson, 1999).

• Long-Term Consequences The majority of children show improved adjustment by two years after divorce. Yet overall, children and adolescents of divorced parents continue to score slightly lower than children of continuously married parents in academic achievement, self-esteem, social competence, and emotional and behavior problems (Amato, 2001). Children with difficult temperaments who were entrenched in family conflict are more likely to drop out of school, to be depressed, and to engage in antisocial behavior in adolescence. And divorce is linked to problems with sexuality and development of intimate ties. Young people who experienced parental divorce, especially more than once, display higher rates of early sexual activity and adolescent parenthood (Wolfinger, 2000). Some experience other lasting difficulties—reduced educational attainment, troubled romantic relationships and marriages, divorce in adulthood, and unsatisfying parent–child relationships (Amato, 2006; Amato & Cheadle, 2005; Wallerstein & Lewis, 2004).

The overriding factor in positive adjustment following divorce is effective parenting—in particular, how well the custodial parent handles stress and shields the child from family conflict, and the extent to which each parent uses authoritative child rearing (Leon, 2003; Wolchik et al., 2000). Where the custodial parent is the mother, contact with fathers is also important. The more paternal contact and the warmer the father–child relationship, the less children of divorce react with defiance and aggression (Dunn et al., 2004). For girls, a good father–child relationship protects against early sexual activity and unhappy romantic involvements (Clarke-Stewart & Hayward, 1996; McLanahan, 1999). High father-child contact, however, is more often seen in families where the mother–child relationship is positive and divorced parents coparent effectively, communicating and supporting each other in their parenting roles (Dunn, 2004a).

Several studies report that outcomes for sons are better when the father is the custodial parent (Clarke-Stewart & Hayward, 1996; McLanahan, 1999). Fathers' greater economic security and image of authority seem to help them engage in effective parenting with sons. And boys in father-custody families may benefit from greater involvement of both parents because noncustodial mothers participate more in their children's lives than noncustodial fathers.

Although divorce is painful for children, remaining in an intact but high-conflict family is worse than making the transition to a low-conflict single-parent household (Greene et al., 2003; Strohschein, 2005). However, more parents today are divorcing because they are moderately (rather than extremely) dissatisfied with their relationship. Research suggests that children in these low-discord homes are especially puzzled and upset. Perhaps these youngsters' inability to understand the marital breakup and grieve over the loss of a seemingly happy home life explain why the adjustment problems of children of divorce have intensified over time (Amato, 2001; Reifman et al., 2001).

Figure 14.5 **Relationship of child-rearing styles to children's adjustment following divorce.** High parental acceptance and consistency in discipline are associated with a low level of behavior problems. As child rearing diminished in quality, behavior problems increased. When both parental acceptance and consistency in discipline were low, behavior problems were severe. All 8- to 15-year-olds in this study had experienced a highly stressful divorce. (Adapted from Wolchik et al., 2000.)

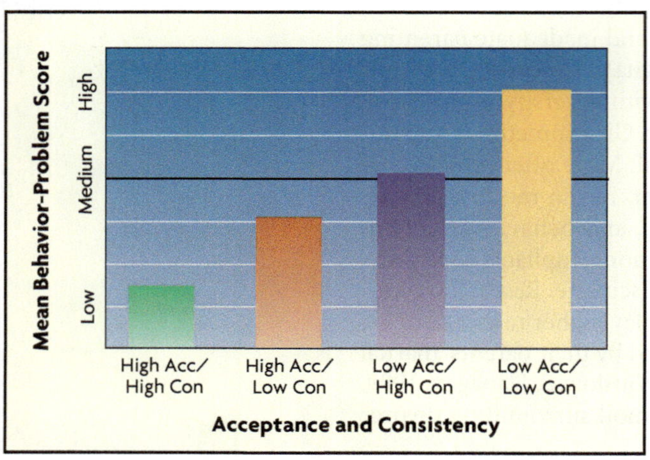

Regardless of the extent of their friction, parents who set aside their disagreements and cooperate in child rearing greatly increase the chances that their children will grow up competent, stable, and happy. As Figure 14.5 shows, in a study of 8- to 15-year-olds, young people who experienced both high parental acceptance and high consistency of discipline had the lowest levels of adjustment problems (Wolchik et al., 2000). Caring extended-family members, teachers, siblings, and friends also reduce the likelihood that divorce will result in long-term difficulties (Hetherington, 2003; Lussier et al., 2002).

• Divorce Mediation, Joint Custody, and Child Support Awareness that divorce is highly stressful for parents and children has led to community-based services aimed at helping them through this difficult time. One such service is *divorce mediation,* a series of meetings between divorcing couples and a trained professional aimed at reducing family conflict, including legal battles over property division and child custody. Where child custody is in dispute, some U.S. states require mediation. Canadian divorce law mandates that lawyers inform divorcing couples about mediation and encourage it. Research reveals that mediation increases out-of-court settlements, effective coparenting, sustained involvement of both parents in their children's lives, and parents' and children's feelings of well-being (Emery, Sbarra, & Grover, 2005). In one study, parents who had resolved disputes through mediation were still more involved in their children's lives 12 years later (Emery et al., 2001).

To further encourage parents to resolve their disputes, parent education programs are becoming common. During several sessions, professionals teach parents about the impact of conflict on children and emphasize the importance of mutual support in child rearing. Because of its demonstrated impact on parental cooperation, parent education prior to filing for divorce is increasingly becoming mandatory across Canada (Department of Justice Canada, 2006). In many U.S. states, the court may require parents to attend a program.

Joint custody, which grants divorced parents equal say in important decisions about the child's upbringing, is becoming increasingly common. Children usually reside with one parent and see the other on a fixed schedule, similar to the typical sole-custody situation. But in some cases, parents share physical custody, and children move between homes and sometimes schools and peer groups. These transitions can be especially hard on some children. Joint-custody parents report little conflict—fortunately so, since the success of the arrangement depends on parental cooperation. And their children, regardless of living arrangements, tend to be better-adjusted than their counterparts in sole maternal-custody homes (Bauserman, 2002).

Finally, many single-parent families depend on child support from the absent parent to relieve financial strain. All U.S. states and Canadian provinces have procedures for withholding wages from parents who fail to make these court-ordered payments. Although child support is usually not enough to lift a single-parent family out of poverty, it can ease the burden substantially. Noncustodial fathers who have generous visitation schedules and see their children often are more likely to pay child support regularly (Amato & Sobolewski, 2004). Applying What We Know on page 590 summarizes ways to help children adjust to their parents' divorce.

Blended Families

Life in a single-parent family often is temporary. About 60 percent of divorced parents remarry within a few years. Others *cohabit,* or share a sexual relationship and a residence with a partner outside of marriage. Parent, stepparent, and children form a new family structure called the **blended,** or **reconstituted, family.** For some children, this expanded family network is positive, bringing greater adult attention. But most have more problems than children in stable, first-marriage families. Switching to stepparents' new rules and expectations can be stressful, and children often regard steprelatives as intruders. How well they adapt is, again, related to the overall quality of family functioning (Hetherington & Kelly, 2002). This depends on which parent forms a new relationship, the child's age and sex, and the complexity of blended-family relationships. As we will see, older children and girls seem to have the hardest time.

Adapting to life in a blended family is stressful for children. When stepparents build warm relationships with children before moving into their parenting role and cooperate with their partner to provide consistency in child rearing, they ease children's adjustment.
© Royalty-Free/Corbis

• **Mother–Stepfather Families** Because mothers generally retain custody of children, the most common form of blended family is a mother–stepfather arrangement. Boys tend to adjust quickly, welcoming a stepfather who is warm, who refrains from exerting his authority too quickly, and who offers relief from coercive cycles of mother–son interaction. Mothers' friction with sons also declines as a result of greater economic security, another adult to share household tasks, and an end to loneliness (Visher, Visher, & Pasley, 2003). Stepfathers who marry rather than cohabit are more involved in parenting, perhaps because men who choose to marry a mother with children are more interested in and skilled at child rearing (Hofferth & Anderson, 2003). Girls, however, often have difficulty

Applying What We Know

Helping Children Adjust to Their Parents' Divorce

Suggestion	Explanation
Shield children from conflict.	Witnessing intense parental conflict is very damaging to children. If one parent insists on expressing hostility, children fare better if the other parent does not respond in kind.
Provide children with as much continuity, familiarity, and predictability as possible.	Children adjust better during the period surrounding divorce when their lives have some stability—for example, the same school, bedroom, baby-sitter, playmates, and daily schedule.
Explain the divorce, and tell children what to expect.	Children are more likely to develop fears of abandonment if they are not prepared for their parents' separation. They should be told that their mother and father will not be living together anymore, which parent will be moving out, and when they will be able to see that parent. If possible, mother and father should explain the divorce together. Parents should provide a reason for the divorce that the child can understand and assure children that they are not to blame.
Emphasize the permanence of the divorce.	Fantasies of parents getting back together can prevent children from accepting the reality of their current life. Children should be told that the divorce is final and that they cannot change this fact.
Respond sympathetically to children's feelings.	Children need a supportive and understanding response to their feelings of sadness, fear, and anger. For children to adjust well, their painful emotions must be acknowledged, not denied or avoided.
Engage in authoritative parenting.	Parents should provide children with affection and acceptance as well as reasonable demands for mature behavior and consistent, rational discipline. Parents who do so greatly reduce their children's risk of maladjustment following divorce.
Promote a continuing relationship with both parents.	When parents disentangle their lingering hostility toward the former spouse from the child's need for a continuing relationship with the other parent, children adjust well. Grandparents and other extended-family members can help by not taking sides.

Source: Teyber, 2001.

with their custodial mother's remarriage. Stepfathers disrupt the close ties many girls have established with their mothers, and girls often react with sulky, resistant behavior (Bray, 1999).

Note, however, that age affects these findings. Older school-age children and adolescents of both sexes display more irresponsible, acting-out, and antisocial behavior than their peers not in stepfamilies (Hetherington & Stanley-Hagan, 2000). Parenting in stepfamilies—particularly those with stepsiblings—is highly challenging. Some parents are warmer and more involved with their biological children than with their stepchildren. Older children are more likely to notice and challenge unfair treatment. And adolescents often view the new stepparent as a threat to their freedom, especially if they experienced little parental monitoring in the single-parent family. But when teenagers have affectionate, cooperative relationships with their mothers, many eventually develop good relationships with their stepfathers—a circumstance linked to more favorable adolescent well-being (Yuan & Hamilton, 2006).

Father–Stepmother Families Remarriage of noncustodial fathers often leads to reduced contact with their biological children, as these fathers tend to withdraw from their "previous" families (Dunn, 2002). When fathers have custody, however, children typically react negatively to remarriage. One reason is that children living with fathers often start out with more problems. Perhaps the biological mother could no longer handle the difficult child (usually a boy), so the father and his new partner are faced with a youngster who has behavior problems. In other instances, the father has custody because of a very close relationship with the child, and his remarriage disrupts this bond (Buchanan, Maccoby, & Dornbusch, 1996). Also, many fathers quickly turn over child-rearing responsibilities to stepmothers, triggering resentment in children.

Girls, especially, have a hard time getting along with their stepmothers, either because the remarriage threatens the girl's bond with her father or because she becomes entangled in loyalty conflicts between the two mother figures. But the longer girls live in father–stepmother households, the more positive their interaction with stepmothers becomes (Hetherington & Jodl, 1994). With time and patience, most girls eventually benefit from the support of a second mother figure.

• **Support for Blended Families** Family life education and counseling can help parents and children in blended families adapt to the complexities of their new circumstances. Effective approaches encourage stepparents to move into their new roles gradually by first building a friendly relationship with the child. Only when a warm bond has formed between stepparents and stepchildren is more active parenting possible (Visher, Visher, & Pasley, 2003). In addition, counselors can help couples form a "parenting coalition" to limit loyalty conflicts and provide consistency in child rearing. This allows children to benefit from the increased diversity that stepparent relationships bring to their lives.

Unfortunately, the divorce rate for second marriages is even higher than that for first marriages. Parents with antisocial tendencies and poor child-rearing skills are particularly likely to have several divorces and remarriages. The more marital transitions children experience, the greater their difficulties (Dunn, 2002). These families usually require prolonged, intensive therapy.

Maternal Employment and Dual-Earner Families

Today, North American single and married mothers are in the labor force in nearly equal proportions, and more than three-fourths of those with school-age children are employed. This figure rises from about 70 percent during the preschool years to 78 percent in middle childhood (Statistics Canada, 2007m; U.S. Census Bureau, 2007b). In Chapter 10, we saw that the impact of maternal employment on early development depends on the quality of child care and the continuing parent–child relationship. This same is true in later years. In addition, the mother's work satisfaction, the support she receives from her partner, and the child's sex have a bearing on how children fare.

• **Maternal Employment and Child Development** Children whose mothers enjoy their work and remain committed to parenting show favorable adjustment—higher self-esteem, more positive family and peer relations, less gender-stereotyped beliefs, and better grades in school. Girls, especially, profit from the image of female competence. Regardless of SES, daughters of employed mothers perceive women's roles as involving more freedom of choice and satisfaction and are more achievement- and career-oriented (Hoffman, 2000).

Parenting practices contribute to these benefits. Employed mothers who value their parenting role are more likely to use authoritative child rearing and coregulation (see page 573). Also, children in dual-earner households devote more daily hours to doing homework under parental guidance and participate more in household chores. And maternal employment often leads fathers—especially those who believe in the importance of the paternal role and who feel successful at rearing children—to take on greater child-care responsibilities, with a small but increasing number staying home full-time (Gottfried, Gottfried, & Bathurst, 2002; Jacobs & Kelley, 2006). Paternal involvement is associated with higher intelligence and achievement, more mature social behavior, greater gender-stereotype flexibility in childhood and adolescence, and generally better mental health in adulthood (Coltrane, 1996; Pleck & Masciadrelli, 2004).

Employed mothers who enjoy their work while remaining committed to parenting tend to have children who show higher self-esteem, less gender-stereotyped beliefs, and better school performance. © Tony Freeman/PhotoEdit

But when employment places heavy demands on a mother's or a father's schedule or is stressful for other reasons, children are at risk for ineffective parenting. Working many hours or experiencing a negative interpersonal workplace atmosphere is associated with reduced parental sensitivity, fewer joint parent–child activities, lessened sense of family togetherness, and poorer cognitive development in children from the preschool through adolescent years (Brooks-Gunn, Han, & Waldfogel, 2002; Bumpus, Crouter, & McHale, 2006; Strazdins et al., 2006). Negative consequences are magnified when low-SES mothers must spend long days at low-paying, menial, or physically taxing jobs—conditions linked to maternal depression, frustration, and fatigue and to use of harsh, inconsistent discipline (Raver, 2003). In contrast, part-time employment and flexible work schedules are associated with parents' enhanced satisfaction with family life and good adjustment in children and adolescents (Frederiksen-Goldsen & Sharlach, 2000; Hill et al., 2006). By preventing work–family role conflict, these arrangements help parents meet children's needs.

• **Support for Employed Parents and Their Families** In dual-earner families, the father's willingness to share child-care responsibilities is a crucial factor. If he helps little or not at all, the mother carries a double load, at home and at work, leading to fatigue, distress, and little time and energy for children.

Employed mothers and dual-earner parents need assistance from work settings and communities in their child-rearing roles. Part-time employment, flexible schedules, job sharing, and paid leave when children are ill help parents juggle the demands of work and child rearing. Equal pay and equal employment opportunities for women also are important. Because these policies enhance financial status and morale, they improve the way mothers feel and behave when they return home at the end of the working day.

Child Care

Over the past several decades, the number of North American young children in child care has steadily increased to more than 60 percent in the United States and over half in Canada (Bushnik, 2006; U.S. Census Bureau, 2007b). As Figure 14.6 shows, most are cared for in child-care centers or family child-care homes or are looked after informally by a relative. But nearly one-fourth of preschoolers, most from low-income families, experience several types of care at once, transitioning between two—and sometimes more than two—settings each day. In addition to a changing cast of caregivers, children in multiple care settings must cope with longer hours in child care (Federal Interagency Forum on Child and Family Statistics, 2007; NICHD Early Child Care Research Network, 2006; Statistics Canada, 2005a).

With age, children typically shift from home-based to center care. Children of higher-income parents and children of very low-income parents are especially likely to be in center care. Many lower-income working parents rely on care by relatives because they are not eligible for public preschool or government-subsidized center child care (Bainbridge et al., 2005; Meyers et al., 2004).

• **Child-Care Quality and Children's Development** Recall from Chapter 8 that early intervention can enhance the development of economically disadvantaged children. As noted in Chapters 1 and 10, however, much North American child care is of poor quality. Refer to Chapter 10, pages 437–438, for a discussion of the negative consequences of exposing infants and toddlers to substandard child care and to many weekly hours of child care. Preschoolers, as well, suffer when placed in poor-quality child care, especially for long hours, scoring lower in cognitive and social skills and higher in behavior problems (Belsky, 2006b; Lamb & Ahnert, 2006; NICHD Early Childhood Research Network, 2003b, 2006). Psychological well-being also declines when children experience the instability of several child-care settings. The emotional problems of temperamentally difficult preschoolers worsen considerably (De Schipper, van IJzendoorn, & Tavecchio, 2004; De Schipper et al., 2004).

In contrast, good child care enhances cognitive, language, and social development, especially for low-SES children—effects that persist into the early school years (Lamb & Ahnert, 2006; NICHD Early Child Care Research Network, 2006;

Figure 14.6 **Who's minding North American young children?**
The percentages refer to settings in which infants and preschoolers spend most time during their mother's absence. In the United States, more children are in preschools or child-care centers than in family child-care homes; in Canada, the two forms of care have similar enrollments. A great many children experience more than one type of care, and with age, they tend to shift from home-based to center programs—facts not reflected in the figure. (Adapted from Bushnik, 2006; Federal Interagency Forum on Child and Family Statistics, 2006.)

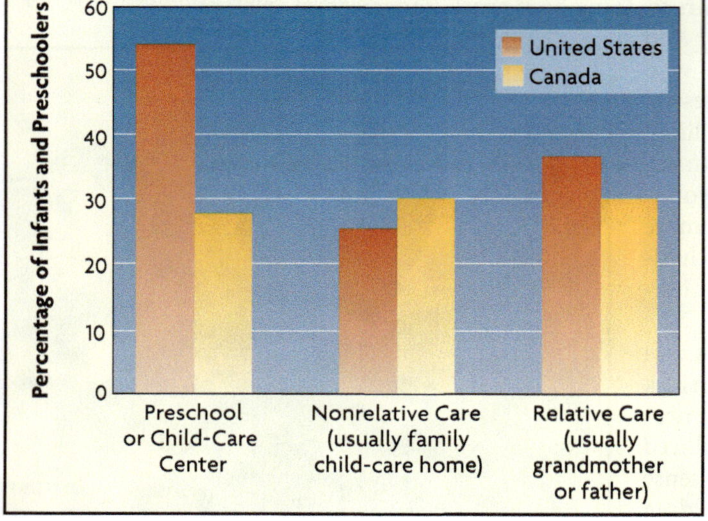

Applying What We Know

Signs of Developmentally Appropriate Early Childhood Programs

Program Characteristic	Signs of Quality
Physical setting	Indoor environment is clean, in good repair, and well-ventilated. Classroom space is divided into richly equipped activity areas, including make-believe play, blocks, science, math, games and puzzles, books, art, and music. Fenced outdoor play space is equipped with swings, climbing equipment, tricycles, and sandbox.
Group size	In preschools and child-care centers, group size is no greater than 18 to 20 children with two teachers.
Caregiver–child ratio	In child-care centers, teacher is responsible for no more than 8 to 10 children. In child-care homes, caregiver is responsible for no more than 6 children.
Daily activities	Children mainly work individually or in small groups, selecting many of their own activities and learning through experiences relevant to their own lives. Teachers facilitate children's involvement, accept individual differences, and adjust expectations to children's developing capacities.
Interactions between adults and children	Teachers move among groups and individuals, asking questions, offering suggestions, and adding more complex ideas. Teachers use positive guidance techniques, such as modeling and encouraging expected behavior and redirecting children to more acceptable activities.
Teacher qualifications	Teachers have college-level specialized preparation in early childhood development, early childhood education, or a related field.
Relationships with parents	Parents are encouraged to observe and participate. Teachers talk frequently with parents about children's behavior and development.
Licensing and accreditation	Child-care setting, whether a center or a home, is licensed by the state or province. In the United States, voluntary accreditation by the NAEYC Academy for Early Childhood Program Accreditation, *www.naeyc.org/academy,* or the National Association for Family Child Care, *www.nafcc.org,* is evidence of an especially high-quality program. Canada has been developing a voluntary accreditation system under the leadership of the Canadian Child Care Federation, *www.cccf-fcsge.ca.* Accredited programs are available in the provinces of Alberta and Manitoba.

Sources: Bredekamp & Copple, 1997; National Association for the Education of Young Children, 1998.

Peisner-Feinberg et al., 2001). In one study of more than 200 2- to 4-year-olds from very low-income families, the more time spent in high-quality child-care centers, the less likely children were to display emotional and behavior problems, even after many family characteristics were controlled (Votruba-Drzal, Coley, & Chase-Lansdale, 2004). And in another investigation, which followed 400 very low-income children over the preschool years, center-based care was more strongly associated with cognitive gains than were other child-care arrangements, probably because child-care centers are more likely to provide a systematic educational program. At the same time, better-quality experiences in all types of child care predicted modest improvements in cognitive, emotional, and social development (Loeb et al., 2004).

What are the ingredients of high-quality child care for preschoolers? Large-scale studies identify several important factors: group size (number of children in a single space), caregiver–child ratio, caregivers' educational preparation, and caregivers' personal commitment to learning about and caring for children. When these characteristics are favorable, adults are more verbally stimulating and sensitive to children's needs (Lamb & Ahnert, 2006). Children of diverse ethnicities and SES levels, in turn, develop favorably—effects that persist into the early school years (Burchinal et al., 2000; Burchinal & Cryer, 2003).

Applying What We Know above summarizes characteristics of high-quality early childhood programs, based on standards devised by the U.S. National Association for the Education of Young Children. Unfortunately, much North American child care is substandard: too often staffed by underpaid adults without specialized educational preparation, overcrowded with children, and (in the case of family child care) unlicensed and therefore not monitored for quality. And in both the United States and Canada, child care is expensive: It consumes from 5 to 25 percent of the average earnings of a single parent with two children,

In this high-quality after-school program in Los Angeles, a community volunteer assists children with learning and completing homework. Children who attend such programs have better work habits and school grades and fewer behavior problems. © Amy Etra/ PhotoEdit

depending on the family's eligibility for government subsidies (Children's Defense Fund, 2006; Statistics Canada, 2006c).

In contrast, in Australia and Western Europe, child care that meets rigorous standards is widely available, and caregivers are paid on the same salary scale as elementary school teachers. Regardless of family income, in Denmark, up to 80 percent of child-care costs are government supported; in Sweden, nearly 90 percent; and in France, 100 percent (Waldfogel, 2001). Because the United States and Canada do not have national child-care policies, they lag behind other industrialized nations in supply, quality, and affordability of child care.

Self-Care

High-quality child care is vital for parents' peace of mind and children's well-being, even during middle childhood. An estimated 2.4 million 5- to 13-year-olds in the United States and several hundred thousand in Canada are **self-care children,** who regularly look after themselves during after-school hours. Self-care rises dramatically with age, from 3 percent of 5- to 7-year-olds to 33 percent of 11- to 13-year-olds. It also rises with SES, perhaps because of the greater safety of higher-income suburban neighborhoods. But when lower-SES parents must use self-care because they lack alternatives, their children spend more hours on their own (Casper & Smith, 2002).

Some studies report that self-care children suffer from low self-esteem, antisocial behavior, poor academic achievement, and fearfulness. Others show no such effects. Children's maturity and the way they spend their time seem to explain these contradictions. Among younger school-age children, those who spend more hours alone have more adjustment difficulties (Vandell & Posner, 1999). As children become old enough to look after themselves, those who have a history of authoritative child rearing, are monitored by parental telephone calls, and have regular after-school chores appear responsible and well-adjusted. In contrast, children left to their own devices are more likely to bend to peer pressures and engage in antisocial behavior (Coley, Morris, & Hernandez, 2004; Steinberg, 1986).

Before age 8 or 9, most children need supervision because they are not yet competent to handle emergencies (Galambos & Maggs, 1991). Also, throughout middle childhood and early adolescence, attending after-school programs with well-trained staffs, generous adult–child ratios, positive adult–child communication, and stimulating activities is linked to better emotional and social adjustment (Pierce, Hamm, & Vandell, 1999). And as early as kindergarten, participation in after-school enrichment activities (sports, music and art lessons, and clubs) predicts higher academic achievement the following year, after many factors (including prior achievement) are controlled (NICHD Early Child Care Research Network, 2004a).

Low-SES children and children whose parents work long hours are less likely to be enrolled in such activities. But when lessons and scouting are included in "after-care" programs, low-SES children show special benefits, including better work habits, higher school grades, and fewer behavior problems (Posner & Vandell, 1994; Vandell, 1999). Unfortunately, good after-care is in especially short supply in inner-city neighborhoods (Shann, 2001). A special need exists for well-planned programs in these areas—ones that provide safe environments, enjoyable skill-building activities, and warm relationships with adults.

Ask Yourself

Review Describe and explain changes in sibling relationships from early childhood to adolescence. What can parents do to promote positive sibling ties?

Apply Steve and Marissa are in the midst of an acrimonious divorce. Their 9-year-old son, Dennis, has become hostile and defiant. How can Steve and Marissa help Dennis adjust?

Connect Review research on resilience in Chapter 1 (see pages 10–11). Are factors that foster resilience similar to those that promote favorable adjustment to parental divorce and blended families? Explain.

Reflect What after-school child-care arrangements did you experience in elementary school? How do you think they influenced your development?

Vulnerable Families: Child Maltreatment

Throughout our discussion of family transitions, we have considered many factors, both within and outside the family, that contribute to parents' capacity to be warm, consistent, and appropriately demanding. As we turn to the topic of child maltreatment, we will see that when these vital supports for effective child rearing break down, children—and their parents—can suffer terribly.

Incidence and Definitions

Child maltreatment is as old as human history, but only recently has the problem been widely acknowledged and research aimed at understanding it. Perhaps public concern has increased because child maltreatment is especially common in large industrialized nations. In the most recently reported year, 905,000 U.S. children (12 out of every 1,000) and 115,000 Canadian children (19 out of every 1,000) were identified as victims (Trocmé et al., 2005; U.S. Department of Health and Human Services, 2008). Because most cases go unreported, the true figures are much higher.

Child maltreatment takes the following forms:

- *Physical abuse.* Assaults, such as kicking, biting, shaking, punching, or stabbing, that inflict physical injury
- *Sexual abuse.* Fondling, intercourse, exhibitionism, commercial exploitation through prostitution or production of pornography, and other forms of sexual exploitation
- *Neglect.* Failure to provide for a child's basic needs for food, clothing, medical attention, education, or supervision
- *Emotional abuse.* Acts that could cause serious mental or behavioral disorders, including social isolation, repeated unreasonable demands, ridicule, humiliation, intimidation, or terrorizing

Neglect accounts for about 60 percent of reported cases, physical abuse for 20 percent, emotional abuse for 10 percent, and sexual abuse for 10 percent (U.S. Department of Health and Human Services, 2008; Whipple, 2006). But these figures are only approximate, as many children experience more than one form.

Parents commit more than 80 percent of abusive incidents. Other relatives account for about 7 percent. The remainder are perpetrated by parents' unmarried partners, school officials, camp counselors, and other adults. Mothers engage in neglect more often than fathers, whereas fathers engage in sexual abuse more often than mothers. Maternal and paternal rates of physical and emotional abuse are fairly similar. And in an especially heartrending 18 percent of cases, parents jointly commit the abusive acts. Infants and young preschoolers are at greatest risk for neglect, preschool and school-age children for physical, emotional, and sexual abuse. But each type occurs at every age (Trocmé & Wolfe, 2002; U.S. Department of Health and Human Services, 2008).

Origins of Child Maltreatment

Early findings suggested that child maltreatment was rooted in adult psychological disturbance (Kempe et al., 1962). But although child maltreatment is more common among disturbed parents, it soon became clear that a single "abusive personality type" does not exist. Parents who were abused as children do not necessarily become abusers (Buchanan, 1996; Simons et al., 1991). And sometimes even "normal" parents harm their children!

For help in understanding child maltreatment, researchers turned to the social systems perspective on family functioning. They discovered that many interacting variables—at the family, community, and cultural levels—contribute. Table 14.3 on page 596 summarizes factors associated with physical and emotional abuse and neglect. For a discussion of child sexual abuse, see the Social Issues box on page 597.

Table 14.3 Factors Related to Child Maltreatment

Factor	Description
Parent characteristics	Psychological disturbance; alcohol and drug abuse; history of abuse as a child; belief in harsh, physical discipline; desire to satisfy unmet emotional needs through the child; unreasonable expectations for child behavior; young age (most under 30); low educational level
Child characteristics	Premature or very sick baby; difficult temperament; inattentiveness and overactivity; other developmental problems
Family characteristics	Low income; poverty; homelessness; marital instability; social isolation; physical abuse of mother by husband or boyfriend; frequent moves; large families with closely spaced children; overcrowded living conditions; disorganized household; lack of steady employment; other signs of high life stress
Community	Characterized by violence and social isolation; few parks, child-care centers, preschool programs, recreation centers, or churches to serve as family supports
Culture	Approval of physical force and violence as ways to solve problems

Sources: Wekerle & Wolfe, 2003; Whipple, 2006.

The Family Within the family, children whose characteristics make them more challenging to rear are more likely to become targets of abuse. These include premature or very sick babies and children who are temperamentally difficult, are inattentive or overactive, or have other developmental problems. Child factors, however, only slightly increase the risk of abuse (Sidebotham et al., 2003). Whether such children are maltreated largely depends on parents' characteristics.

Maltreating parents are less skillful than other parents in handling discipline confrontations and getting children to cooperate in working toward common goals. They also suffer from biased thinking about their child. For example, they often evaluate transgressions as worse than they are, attribute their child's misdeeds to a stubborn or bad disposition, and feel powerless in parenting—perspectives that lead them to move quickly toward physical force (Bugental & Happaney, 2004; Haskett et al., 2003).

Once abuse begins, it quickly becomes part of a self-sustaining relationship. The small irritations to which abusive parents react—a fussy baby, a preschooler who knocks over her milk, or a child who will not mind immediately—soon become bigger ones. Then the harshness increases. By the preschool years, abusive and neglectful parents seldom interact with their children. When they do, they rarely express pleasure and affection; the communication is almost always negative (Wolfe, 2005).

Most parents have enough self-control not to respond with abuse to their children's misbehavior or developmental problems. Other factors combine with these conditions to prompt an extreme response. Unmanageable parental stress is strongly associated with maltreatment. Abusive parents respond to stressful situations with high emotional arousal. And such stressors as low income and education (less than a high-school diploma), unemployment, young maternal age, alcohol and drug use, marital conflict, domestic violence, health problems, overcrowded living conditions, frequent moves, and extreme household disorganization are common in abusive homes (Wekerle & Wolfe, 2003; Wekerle et al., 2007). These conditions increase the chances that parents will be too overwhelmed to meet basic child-rearing responsibilities or will vent their frustrations by lashing out at their children.

The Community The majority of abusive and neglectful parents are isolated from both formal and informal social supports. This social isolation has at least two causes. First, because of their own life histories, many of these parents have learned to mistrust and avoid others. They do not have the skills necessary for establishing and maintaining positive relationships. Second, maltreating parents are more likely to live in unstable, run-down neighborhoods that provide few links between family and community, such as parks, child-care centers, preschool programs, recreation centers, and religious institutions (Coulton et al., 2007; Zielinski & Bradshaw, 2006). For these reasons, they lack "lifelines" to others and have no one to turn to for help during stressful times.

▪ Social Issues ▪

Child Sexual Abuse

Until recently, child sexual abuse was considered rare, and adults often dismissed children's claims of abuse. In the 1970s, efforts by professionals and media attention led to recognition of child sexual abuse as a serious and widespread problem. About 80,000 cases in the United States and 3,200 cases in Canada were confirmed in the most recently reported year (Department of Justice Canada, 2006; U.S. Department of Health and Human Services, 2008).

Characteristics of Abusers and Victims

Sexual abuse is committed against children of both sexes, but more often against girls. Most cases are reported in middle childhood, but sexual abuse also occurs at younger and older ages. For some victims, the abuse begins early in life and continues for many years (Hoch-Espada, Ryan, & Deblinger, 2006; Trickett & Putnam, 1998).

Typically, the abuser is a male, either a parent or someone the parent knows well—a father, stepfather, live-in boyfriend, or, somewhat less often, an uncle or older brother. But in about 25 percent of cases, mothers are the offenders, more often with sons (Boroughs, 2004). If the abuser is a nonrelative, the person is usually someone the child has come to know and trust. However, the Internet and mobile phones have become avenues through which other adults commit sexual abuse—for example, by exposing children and adolescents to pornography and online sexual advances as a way of "grooming" them for sexual acts offline (Wolak et al., 2008).

Abusers make the child comply in a variety of distasteful ways, including deception, bribery, verbal intimidation, and physical force. You may wonder how any adult—especially a parent or close relative—could possibly violate a child sexually. Many offenders deny their own responsibility, blaming the abuse on the willing participation of a seductive youngster. Yet children are not capable of making a deliberate, informed decision to enter into a sexual relationship! Even older children and adolescents are not free to say yes or no. Rather, the responsibility lies with abusers, who tend to have characteristics that predispose them toward sexual exploitation of children. They have great difficulty controlling their impulses and may suffer from psychological disorders, including alcohol or drug addiction. Often they pick out children who are unlikely to defend themselves or to be believed—those who are physically weak, emotionally deprived, socially isolated, or affected by disabilities such as blindness, deafness, or mental retardation (Bolen, 2001).

Reported cases of child sexual abuse are linked to poverty, marital instability, and resulting weakening of family ties. Children who live in homes with a constantly changing cast of characters—repeated marriages, separations, and new partners—are especially vulnerable. But children in economically advantaged, stable families are also victims, although their abuse is more likely to escape detection (Putnam, 2003).

Consequences of Sexual Abuse

The adjustment problems of child sexual abuse victims—including anxiety, depression, low self-esteem, mistrust of adults, and anger and hostility—are often severe and can persist for years after the abusive episodes. Younger children frequently react with sleep difficulties, loss of appetite, and generalized fearfulness. Adolescents may run away and show suicidal reactions, substance abuse, and delinquency. At all ages, persistent abuse accompanied by force, violence, and a close relationship to the perpetrator (incest) has a greater impact (Tricket et al., 2001; Wolfe, 2006). And repeated sexual abuse, like physical abuse, is associated with central nervous system damage (Cicchetti, 2007).

Sexually abused children frequently display precocious sexual knowledge and behavior. They have learned from their abusers that sexual overtures are acceptable ways to get attention and rewards. In adolescence, abused young people often become promiscuous, and as adults, they show increased arrest rates for sex crimes (mostly against children) and prostitution (Salter et al., 2003; Whipple, 2006). Furthermore, women who were sexually abused are likely to choose partners who abuse them and their children. As mothers, they often engage in irresponsible and coercive parenting, including child abuse and neglect (Pianta, Egeland, & Erickson, 1989). In these ways, the harmful impact of sexual abuse is transmitted to the next generation.

Prevention and Treatment

Treating child sexual abuse is difficult. The reactions of family members—anxiety about harm to the child, anger toward the abuser, and sometimes hostility toward the victim for telling—can increase children's distress. Because sexual abuse typically appears in the midst of other serious family problems, long-term therapy with children and parents is usually needed (Olafson & Boat, 2000). The best way to reduce the suffering of victims is to prevent sexual abuse from continuing. Today, courts are prosecuting abusers more vigorously and taking children's testimony more seriously (see Chapter 7).

Educational programs that teach children to recognize inappropriate sexual advances and whom to turn to for help reduce the risk of abuse (Hebert & Tourigny, 2004). Yet because of controversies over educating children about sexual abuse, few schools offer these interventions. New Zealand is the only country with a national, school-based prevention program targeting sexual abuse. In Keeping Ourselves Safe, children and adolescents learn that abusers are rarely strangers. Parent involvement ensures that home and school work together in teaching children self-protection skills. Evaluations reveal that virtually all New Zealand parents and children support the program and that it has helped many children avoid or report abuse (Briggs, 2002).

In Keeping Ourselves Safe, New Zealand's national school-based child abuse prevention program, teachers and police officers collaborate in teaching children to recognize abusive adult behaviors so children can protect themselves. Courtesy of the New Zealand Police

Furthermore, the stressors associated with living in a violent neighborhood seem to heighten violent responses to conflict in the home (Tolan, Gorman-Smith, & Henry, 2006). In a study carried out at a summer day camp, school-age children who reported hearing about, experiencing, or witnessing a greater number of neighborhood violent acts (such as shootings, stabbings, and sexual assaults) were more likely to have been physically abused or severely neglected (Lynch & Cicchetti, 1998).

• **The Larger Culture** Cultural values, laws, and customs profoundly affect the chances that child maltreatment will occur when parents feel overburdened. Societies that view violence as an appropriate way to solve problems set the stage for child abuse. Although the United States and Canada have laws to protect children from maltreatment, parental use of corporal punishment is widespread, as we saw in Chapter 12. Many countries—including Austria, Croatia, Cyprus, Denmark, Finland, Germany, Israel, Italy, Latvia, Norway, and Sweden—have outlawed physical punishment, a measure that dampens both physical discipline and abuse (Bugental & Grusec, 2006).

Furthermore, every industrialized nation except the United States and Canada now prohibits corporal punishment in schools (Center for Effective Discipline, 2005). The U.S. Supreme Court has twice upheld the right of school officials to use physical discipline. Likewise, the Canadian federal criminal code permits corporal punishment of children by caregivers and teachers, as long as such force is "reasonable under the circumstances." This vague definition may encourage adults to assault children while providing a ready defense for those who do so (Justice for Children and Youth, 2003). Indeed, Canadian courts have deemed hard spankings, slaps to the head and face, and hitting of the buttocks and legs with belts and sticks to be consistent with the criminal code. Fortunately, some U.S. states and Canadian provinces have passed laws banning corporal punishment.

Consequences of Child Maltreatment

The family circumstances of maltreated children impair the development of emotional self-regulation, empathy and sympathy, self-concept, social skills, and academic motivation. Over time, these youngsters show serious learning and adjustment difficulties, including academic failure, severe depression, aggressive behavior, peer difficulties, substance abuse, and delinquency, including violent crime (Cicchetti & Toth, 2006; Shonk & Cicchetti, 2001; Wolfe et al., 2001). Emotional and behavior problems often persist in adulthood (Kaplow & Widom, 2007).

How do these damaging consequences occur? Think back to our discussion in Chapter 12 of the effects of hostile cycles of parent–child interaction. For abused children, these are especially severe. Indeed, a family characteristic strongly associated with child abuse is partner abuse (Cox, Kotch, & Everson, 2003). Clearly, the home lives of abused children overflow with opportunities to learn to use aggression as a way of solving problems.

Furthermore, demeaning parental messages, in which children are ridiculed, humiliated, rejected, or terrorized, result in low self-esteem, high anxiety, self-blame, depression, and efforts to escape from extreme psychological pain—at times severe enough to lead to attempted suicide in adolescence (Wolfe, 2005). At school, maltreated children present serious discipline problems. Their noncompliance, poor motivation, and cognitive immaturity interfere with academic achievement—an outcome that further undermines their chances for life success (Wekerle & Wolfe, 2003).

Finally, repeated abuse is associated with central nervous system damage, including abnormal EEG brain-wave activity, fMRI-detected reduced size and impaired functioning of the cerebral cortex and corpus callosum, and atypical production of the stress hormone cortisol—initially too high but, after months of abuse, often too low. Over time, the massive trauma of persistent abuse seems to blunt children's normal physiological response to stress (Cicchetti, 2007; Teicher et al., 2004; Watts-English et al., 2006). These effects increase the chances that abused children's cognitive and emotional problems will endure.

Preventing Child Maltreatment

Because child maltreatment is embedded in families, communities, and society as a whole, efforts to prevent it must be directed at each of these levels. Many approaches have been suggested, including teaching high-risk parents effective child-rearing strategies, providing

Each year, fourth to sixth graders across Los Angeles County enter a poster contest to celebrate Child Abuse Prevention Month. This 2008 winner is a stirring appeal to parents to treat children with warmth and caring. Lisa Valicente and Madeline Zauss, 6th Grade, Jefferson Elementary School, Redondo Beach, CA. Courtesy ICAN Associates, Los Angeles Counter Inter-Agency Council on Child Abuse & Neglect, ican4kids.org.

direct experience with children in high school child development courses, and broad social programs aimed at bettering economic conditions for low-SES families.

We have seen that providing social supports to families is highly effective in easing parental stress. This approach sharply reduces child maltreatment as well (Azar & Wolfe, 1998). A trusting relationship with another person is the most important factor in preventing mothers with childhood histories of abuse from repeating the cycle with their own youngsters (Egeland, Jacobvitz, & Sroufe, 1988). Parents Anonymous, a North American organization that has as its main goal helping child-abusing parents learn constructive parenting practices, does so largely through social supports. Its local chapters offer self-help group meetings, daily phone calls, and regular home visits to relieve social isolation and teach responsible child-rearing skills.

Early intervention aimed at strengthening both child and parent competencies can reduce child maltreatment substantially (Reynolds & Robertson, 2003). Healthy Families America, a program begun in Hawaii that has spread to 430 sites across the United States and Canada, identifies families at risk for maltreatment during pregnancy or at birth. Each receives three years of home visitation, in which a trained worker helps parents manage crises, encourages effective child rearing, and puts parents in touch with community services to meet their own and their children's needs (PCA America, 2006). In an evaluation in which over 600 families were randomly assigned to either intervention or control groups, Healthy Families home visitation alone reduced only neglect, not abuse (Duggan et al., 2004). But adding a *cognitive component* to home visitation dramatically increases its impact. When home visitors helped parents change negative appraisals of their children—by countering inaccurate interpretations (for example, that the baby is behaving with malicious intent), and working on solving child-rearing problems—physical punishment and abuse dropped sharply by the end of one year of intervention (see Figure 14.7) (Bugental et al., 2002). Positive effects were greatest for parents of difficult-to-care-for babies who had experienced birth complications.

Figure 14.7 Impact of a home visitation program with a cognitive component on preventing physical abuse of young children.

In an enhanced home visitation condition, home visitors not only provided social support, encouraged effective child rearing, and connected families with community resources but also helped at-risk parents change their negative appraisals of their babies and solve child-rearing problems. After one year of intervention, this cognitive component sharply reduced physical abuse of babies (hitting, shaking, beating, kicking, biting) compared with an unenhanced home visitation condition and a no-intervention control. (Adapted from Bugental et al., 2002.)

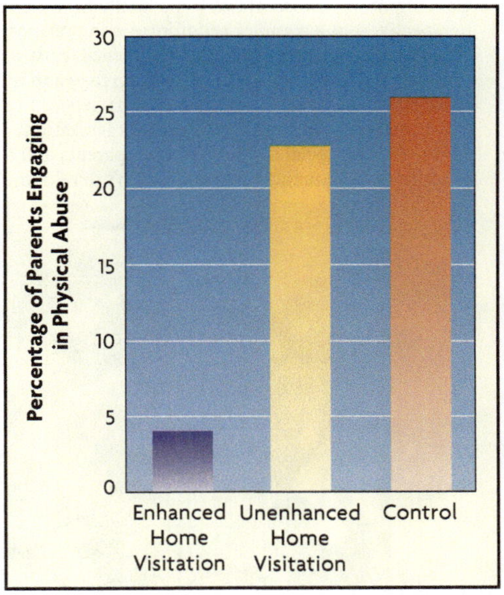

Still, many experts believe that child maltreatment cannot be eliminated as long as violence is widespread and harsh physical punishment is regarded as acceptable. In addition, combating poverty and its diverse correlates—family stress and disorganization, inadequate food and medical care, teenage parenthood, low-birth-weight babies, and parental hopelessness—would protect many children.

Although more cases reach the courts than in decades past, child maltreatment remains a crime that is difficult to prove. Most of the time, the only witnesses are the child victims or other loyal family members. Even in court cases in which the evidence is strong, judges hesitate to impose the ultimate safeguard against further harm: permanently removing the child from the family. There are several reasons for their reluctance. First, in the United States and Canada, government intervention into family life is viewed as a last resort. Second, despite destructive family relationships, maltreated children and their parents are usually attached to one another. Most of the time, neither desires separation. Finally, U.S. and Canadian legal systems tend to regard children as parental property rather than as human beings in their own right, and this also has stood in the way of court-ordered protection.

Even with intensive treatment, some adults persist in their abusive acts. An estimated 1,500 U.S. children, most of them infants and preschoolers, die from maltreatment each year (U.S. Department of Health and Human Services, 2008). When parents are unlikely to change their behavior, the drastic step of separating parent from child and legally terminating parental rights is the only justifiable course of action.

Child maltreatment is a distressing and horrifying topic. When we consider how often it occurs in nations that claim to place a high value on the dignity and worth of the individual, it is even more appalling. But there is reason to be optimistic. Great strides have been made over the past several decades in understanding and preventing child maltreatment.

Ask Yourself

Review Explain how personal and situational factors that contribute to child maltreatment illustrate the social systems perspective on family functioning.

Apply Claire told her 6-year-old daughter to be careful never to talk to or take candy from strangers. Why is Claire's directive not adequate to protect her daughter from sexual abuse?

Connect After reviewing factors linked to adolescent parenthood (Chapter 5, pages 215–216), explain why it places children at risk for abuse and neglect.

Reflect Describe a challenging time for your family during your childhood. What aspects of the experience increased stress? What factors helped you and your parents cope with adversity?

SUMMARY

Origins and Functions of the Family

Discuss the evolutionary origins of the family, and cite functions contemporary families perform for society.

- The human family pattern, which arose among our hunting-and-gathering ancestors, enhanced survival by ensuring a relatively even balance of male hunters and female gatherers within a social group. Larger kin networks, linked by strong emotional bonds, increased the chances of successful competition with other humans for resources and provided assistance with child rearing.
- As societies became more complex, institutions developed to assist families with educating children, ensuring societal order, and producing goods and services. Contemporary families retain primary responsibility for three functions: reproduction, socialization, and emotional support.

The Family as a Social System

Describe the social systems perspective on family functioning.

- Contemporary researchers view the family from a **social systems perspective**—as a complex set of interacting relationships affected by the larger social context. Bidirectional influences exist whereby family members mutually influence one another, both directly and indirectly. Effective **coparenting** depends on mutual support between parents. Connections to the community, through both formal organizations and informal social networks, provide social support for both parents and children, promoting effective family interaction and children's development.

AP Images/Muscatine Journal, Connie Street

Socialization Within the Family

Discuss the features that differentiate major child-rearing styles, and explain how effective parents adapt child rearing to children's growing competence during middle childhood and adolescence.

- Three features differentiate major **child-rearing styles**: (1) acceptance of the child and involvement in the child's life to establish emotional connection; (2) control of the child to promote mature behavior; and (3) autonomy granting to encourage self-reliance. The **authoritative child-rearing style** is high in acceptance and involvement, emphasizes firm control with explanations, and includes gradual, appropriate autonomy granting. It promotes cognitive, emotional, and social competence from early childhood into adolescence.
- The **authoritarian child-rearing style** is low in acceptance and involvement, high in both coercive and **psychological control**, and low in autonomy granting. It is associated with anxious, withdrawn, dependent child behavior, especially among girls, and with high rates of anger, defiance, and aggression, especially among boys. The **permissive child-rearing style** is high in acceptance, low in control, and lax in autonomy granting. Children reared permissively are typically impulsive, disobedient, rebellious, demanding, and dependent. The **uninvolved child-rearing style** combines low acceptance and involvement with little control and indifference to autonomy issues. At its extreme, it constitutes neglect, disrupting virtually all aspects of development.
- Authoritative child rearing promotes maturity and adjustment in children of diverse temperaments. Over time, the authoritative style creates a positive emotional context for parental influence as the relationship between parenting and children's attributes becomes increasingly bidirectional.
- In middle childhood, effective parents engage in **coregulation,** exerting general oversight while permitting children to take charge of moment-by-moment decision making. During adolescence, mature **autonomy** is fostered by parenting that strikes a balance between connection and separation.

Describe socioeconomic and ethnic variations in child rearing, including the impact of affluence and poverty.

- Although the authoritative style predicts favorable development regardless of SES, ethnicity, or family structure, consistent variations in child rearing exist. Higher-SES parents are more verbal and stimulating, relying more on warmth and explanations; low-SES parents use more commands, criticism, and physical punishment.
- Many affluent parents fail to engage in family interaction and parenting that promote healthy development. By adolescence, their children tend to have substance abuse and emotional and academic problems. Excessive achievement pressures and isolation from adults underlie their difficulties.

- Poverty is linked to persistent stressors that leave parents depressed, irritable, and distracted and, as a result, less involved in child rearing. Daily hassles, hostile family interactions, and depleted home learning environments negatively affect children's cognitive and emotional well-being.
- Chinese, Hispanic, Asian Pacific Island, and low-SES African-American parents tend to be highly controlling. When combined with warmth, high control can be adaptive. But excessive control, resulting in an authoritarian child-rearing style, impairs children's adjustment.
- **Extended-family households,** in which one or more adult relatives live with the parent–child **nuclear family unit,** are common among ethnic minorities. Extended family support helps protect children from the stress and disorganization of poverty.

Family Lifestyles and Transitions

Describe the influence of family size on child rearing, and explain how sibling relationships change with age and affect development.

- Contrary to a widespread assumption, larger family size and later birth order do not dilute children's experiences or depress their intelligence. Rather, the link between family size and children's IQ reflects the fact that mothers with low IQs bear more children.
- Despite declining family size, most children grow up with at least one sibling. Because of their frequency and emotional intensity, sibling interactions are unique contexts for expanding social competence. Parental warmth fosters sibling cooperation; harsh, uninvolved parenting promotes sibling antagonism. Sibling rivalry tends to increase in middle childhood, when parental comparisons become more frequent. In adolescence, sibling relationships become less intense as young people strive for autonomy, but attachment to siblings typically remains strong.
- Only children are as well-adjusted as children with siblings, and they are advantaged in self-esteem, academic achievement, and educational attainment.

How do children fare in adoptive families, gay and lesbian families, and never-married single-parent families?

- Adopted children have more learning and emotional difficulties than other children, and by adolescence, their lives are often complicated by unresolved curiosity about their roots. By adulthood, however, most adoptees are well-adjusted. When parents help them learn about their heritage, young people adopted into a different ethnic group or culture typically develop identities that are healthy blends of their birth and rearing backgrounds.

© Corbis

- Research indicates that children of gay and lesbian parents do not differ from children of heterosexual parents in mental health, peer relations, gender identity, or sexual orientation. During adolescence, more youths from homosexual families experiment with partners of both sexes.
- Many children of never-married mothers display adjustment problems associated with economic hardship. Those who lack a father's warmth and involvement achieve less well in school and engage in more antisocial behavior than children in low-SES, first-marriage families.

What factors influence children's adjustment to divorce and blended-family arrangements?

- Although all children experience painful emotional reactions during the period surrounding divorce, children with difficult temperaments and boys are at greater risk for adjustment problems. Over time, children of divorce show improved functioning, but they continue to score slightly lower than children of continuously married parents on a variety of adjustment indicators. Problems with adolescent sexuality, early parenthood, and development of intimate ties surface at later ages.
- The overriding factor in positive adjustment following divorce is effective parenting. Contact with noncustodial fathers is important for children of both sexes, and outcomes for sons tend to be better when fathers have custody. Divorce mediation and parent education programs that help divorcing parents resolve disputes and cooperate in child rearing can help children adjust.
- When divorced parents enter new relationships through cohabitation or remarriage, children must adapt to a **blended, or reconstituted, family.** Girls, older children, and children in father–stepmother families have more adjustment problems. Stepparents can help children adjust by moving into their roles gradually and forming a "parenting coalition" with the child's parent.

How do maternal employment and life in dual-earner families affect children's development?

- Children whose mothers enjoy their work and remain committed to parenting show favorable adjustment—higher self-esteem, more positive family and peer relations, less gender-stereotyped beliefs, and better grades in school. But when employment is stressful because of time demands or other reasons, children are at risk for ineffective parenting and adjustment difficulties.
- In dual-earner families, the father's willingness to share child rearing is linked to many positive outcomes for children. Workplace supports, such as part-time employment, flexible schedules, and paid parental leave, help parents meet the demands of work and child rearing.

Discuss the influence of child-care quality on preschoolers' development and the impact of self-care on school-age children's adjustment.

- Preschoolers exposed to poor-quality care, especially for long hours, score lower in cognitive and social skills and higher in behavior problems. The instability of several child-care settings also impairs young children's adjustment.
- Key ingredients of high-quality child care for preschoolers include small group size, generous caregiver–child ratio, and caregivers who are well-educated and personally committed to learning about and caring for children. High-quality care promotes favorable development in children of diverse ethnicities and SES levels. Because the United States and Canada do not have national child-care policies, they lag behind other industrialized nations in supply, quality, and affordability of child care.
- **Self-care children** who are old enough to look after themselves, are monitored by parental telephone calls, have a history of authoritative parenting, and have regular after-school chores appear responsible and well-adjusted. But children left to their own devices are at risk for antisocial behavior. Involvement in high-quality after-school programs is linked to emotional, social, and academic benefits.

Vulnerable Families: Child Maltreatment

Discuss the multiple origins of child maltreatment, its consequences for development, and prevention strategies.

- Maltreating parents use ineffective discipline and hold negative biases toward their child. Unmanageable parental stress, social isolation, and neighborhood disintegration and violence increase the chances that abuse and neglect will occur. Societal approval of the use of force and violence to solve problems, including support for corporal punishment, promotes child abuse.
- Maltreated children are impaired in development of emotional self-regulation, empathy and sympathy, self-concept, social skills, and academic motivation. Repeated abuse is associated with abnormal brain-wave activity and a blunted physiological response to stress. Successful prevention of child maltreatment requires efforts by families, communities, and society, including programs that strengthen both child and parent competencies and that reduce societal violence and poverty.

IMPORTANT TERMS AND CONCEPTS

authoritarian child-rearing style (p. 570)
authoritative child-rearing style (p. 569)
autonomy (p. 573)
blended, or reconstituted, family (p. 589)
child-rearing styles (p. 569)
coparenting (p. 566)
coregulation (p. 573)
extended-family household (p. 579)
nuclear family unit (p. 579)
permissive child-rearing style (p. 571)
psychological control (p. 571)
self-care children (p. 594)
social systems perspective (p. 565)
uninvolved child-rearing style (p. 571)

15

"Blindfolding a Friend"
Unknown
10 years, Vietnam

The scene depicted by this artist is universal and timeless: children playing with friends. Peer relationships are vital sources of support, contributing greatly to all aspects of development.

Peers, Media, and Schooling

Stu and Pete became friends in their school's Connections program, which smooths the transition to middle school by assigning small groups of sixth graders to the same classes and lunch hour, so they feel "connected" in their new, large-school environment. During an end-of-year discussion in health class, Ms. Stevens asked what their new-school experiences had been like.

"Well," Stu began, "at the beginning of the year, it wasn't so easy. It was like people were bouncing around, trying to find friends they felt comfortable with. I wasn't sure I was going to fit in. In the past few weeks, though, Pete and I just sort of clicked."

"Same with Katy and me," Jessamyn chimed in. "I used to have another group of friends in fifth grade, but I lost interest. I mean, when they got here, they were trying too hard to be popular."

"Can you explain that a little?" Ms. Stevens asked.

"Well, every time they talked to someone, they acted like a different person—kinda two-faced. It was annoying."

"How do you know someone's going to be a good friend?" asked Mrs. Stevens.

"You've gotta have the same interests, and Stu and me, we've kinda got the same personality," replied Pete. "We both like computer stuff like playing games and instant messaging. Also, a friend has to be somebody who makes you feel good about yourself. I wouldn't be friends with someone who's always making me feel bad."

"Yeah," Katy agreed. "I know kids who'll say they're a friend but they're real nasty. They don't show any kindness or understanding. Mostly, everyone dislikes them."

Beyond the family, what forces strongly influence children and adolescents? The answer is clear: peers, with whom they share countless play, classroom, and extracurricular activities; media—especially television and computers, which consume large amounts of their free time; and school, which helps the family transmit culturally valued knowledge to the next generation.

In the first part of this chapter, we look closely at the development of peer sociability, friendship, and peer acceptance, along with their profound significance for psychological adjustment. Next we consider the impact of television and computers on cognitive and social skills. Finally, we turn to the school—how class and school size, educational philosophy, teacher–student interaction, and grouping of students affect educational experiences and learning. We conclude with a look at schooling and achievement in international perspective, with special attention to how well North American schools prepare young people for productive work lives.

Importance of Peer Relations

Are peer relations crucial for development, and how do they add to children's experiences with caring adults? To find out for sure, we would need to study a group of children reared only by parents and compare them to children growing up under typical conditions. In humans, these circumstances rarely occur naturally and are unethical to arrange experimentally. But studies with nonhuman primates reveal that peer bonds are vital for social competence. For example, maternally reared rhesus monkeys with no peer contact show immature play, excessive aggression and fearfulness, and less cooperation at maturity (Harlow, 1969).

Parent and peer relations complement one another. Parental affection and guidance grant children the security and social skills they need to enter the world of peers. Peer interaction, in turn, enables children to expand their social skills. Peers can also stand in, to some extent, for the early parent–child bond. After rearing rhesus monkeys in groups without adults, researchers let them choose between their preferred peer (the one they sought closeness to during rearing), a familiar peer, and an unfamiliar peer. The monkeys spent most time near their preferred peer, who served as a source of security (Higley et al., 1992). Nevertheless, peer-only-reared monkeys do not fare as well as monkeys with typical upbringing. In novel environments, they spend much time anxiously clinging to their preferred agemate. And as they get older, they display behavior problems—including dominance or submission rather than friendly interaction—with unfamiliar peers (Goy & Goldfoot, 1974).

Do these findings generalize to human children? A unique human parallel to peer-only rearing suggests that in large measure, they do. In the 1940s, Anna Freud and Sophie Dann (1951) studied six young German-Jewish orphans whose parents had been murdered in the Nazi gas chambers shortly after the children's birth. For several years, the children remained together in a concentration camp, without close ties to adults. When World War II ended, they were brought to England and cared for as a group. Observations revealed that they were passionately attached, becoming upset whenever separated. They also were intensely prosocial, freely sharing, comforting, and helping one another. Nevertheless, they displayed many anxious symptoms, including intense thumb sucking, restlessness, immature play, and both aggression toward and excessive dependency on their caregivers. As they built trusting relationships with adults, the children's play, language, and exploration developed rapidly.

In sum, peers serve as vital sources of support in threatening situations and contribute greatly to development. But they do so more effectively when children also have warm, supportive ties to parents.

Development of Peer Sociability

In cultures where agemates have regular contact during the first year of life, peer sociability begins early, gradually evolving into the complex, well-coordinated exchanges of childhood and adolescence. Development of peer sociability is supported by and contributes greatly to cognitive, emotional, and social milestones discussed in previous chapters.

Infant and Toddler Beginnings

When pairs of infants are brought together in a laboratory, looking accompanied by touching is present at 3 to 4 months, peer-directed smiles and babbles by 6 months. These isolated social acts increase until, by the end of the first year, an occasional reciprocal exchange occurs in which babies grin, gesture, or otherwise imitate a playmate's behavior (Vandell & Mueller, 1995). Between 1 and 2 years, as toddlers begin to appreciate that others have intentions, desires, and emotions distinct from their own, they increasingly see other children as playmates (Brownell & Kopp, 2007). As a result, coordinated interaction occurs more often, largely in the form of mutual imitation involving jumping, chasing, or banging a toy. These imitative, turn-taking games create joint understandings that aid verbal communication.

Around age 2, toddlers use words to share meanings and establish joint play goals, as when they say, "Let's play chase," and, after the game gets going, "Hey, good running!" (Eckerman & Peterman, 2001; Eckerman & Whitehead, 1999). Reciprocal play and positive emotion are especially frequent in toddlers' interactions with familiar agemates, suggesting that they are building true peer relationships (Ross et al., 1992).

Peer sociability begins in infancy with touches, smiles, and babbles that gradually develop into coordinated interaction in the second year. A warm, sensitive caregiver–child bond fosters early peer sociability. © Geri Engberg/ The Image Works

Though quite limited, peer sociability is present in the first two years and is promoted by the early caregiver–child bond. From interacting with sensitive adults, babies learn how to send and interpret emotional signals in their first peer associations (Trevarthen, 2003). Consistent with this idea, toddlers who have a warm parental relationship or who attend high-quality child care with a small group size and a generous caregiver–child ratio—features that promote warm, stimulating caregiving—engage in more positive and extended peer exchanges. These children, in turn, display more socially competent behavior as preschoolers (Deynoot-Schaub & Riksen-Walraven, 2006a, 2006b; Howes & Matheson, 1992).

The Preschool Years

As children become increasingly self-aware, more effective at communicating, and better at understanding others' thoughts and feelings, their skill at interacting with peers improves greatly. Mildred Parten (1932), one of the first to study peer sociability among 2- to 5-year-olds, noticed a dramatic increase with age in the ability to engage in joint, interactive play. She concluded that social development proceeds in a three-step sequence. It begins with **nonsocial activity**—unoccupied, onlooker behavior and solitary play. Then it shifts to a limited form of social participation called **parallel play,** in which a child plays near other children with similar materials but does not try to influence their behavior. At the highest level are two forms of true social interaction. In **associative play,** children engage in separate activities but exchange toys and comment on one another's behavior. Finally, in **cooperative play,** a more advanced type of interaction. children orient toward a common goal, such as acting out a make-believe theme.

Longitudinal evidence indicates that these play forms emerge in the order suggested by Parten but that later-appearing forms do not replace earlier ones in a developmental sequence (Rubin, Bukowski, & Parker, 2006). Rather, all types coexist during the preschool years. **TAKE A MOMENT ...** Watch children move from one play type to another in a playgroup or preschool classroom, and you will see that they often transition from onlooker to parallel to cooperative play and back again (Robinson et al., 2003). Preschoolers seem to use parallel play as a way station—a respite from the high demands of complex social interaction and a crossroad to new activities. And although nonsocial activity declines with age, it is still the most frequent form among 3- to 4-year-olds. Even among kindergartners it continues to occupy about one-third of children's free-play time. Also, both solitary and parallel play

These 3-year-olds engage in parallel play, which often serves as a respite from the demands of complex social interaction. © Laura Dwight Photography

Table 15.1 Developmental Sequence of Cognitive Play Categories

Play Category	Description	Examples
Functional play	Simple, repetitive motor movements with or without objects. Especially common during the first two years of life.	Running around a room, rolling a car back and forth, kneading clay with no intent to make something
Constructive play	Creating or constructing something. Especially common between 3 and 6 years.	Making a house out of toy blocks, drawing a picture, putting together a puzzle
Make-believe play	Acting out everyday and imaginary roles. Especially common between 2 and 6 years.	Playing house, school, or police officer; acting out storybook or television characters
Games with rules	Understanding and following rules in play activities.	Playing board games, cards, hopscotch, baseball

Source: Rubin, Fein, & Vandenberg, 1983.

remain fairly stable from 3 to 6 years, accounting for as much of the young child's play as highly social, cooperative interaction (Rubin, Fein, & Vandenberg, 1983).

We now understand that it is the *type,* not the amount, of solitary and parallel play that changes during early childhood. In studies of preschoolers' play in Taiwan and the United States, researchers rated the *cognitive maturity* of nonsocial, parallel, and cooperative play by applying the categories shown in Table 15.1. Within each of Parten's play types, older children engaged in more cognitively mature behavior than younger children (Pan, 1994; Rubin, Watson, & Jambor, 1978).

Often parents wonder whether a child who spends large amounts of time playing alone is developing normally. But only *certain types* of nonsocial activity—aimless wandering, hovering near peers, and functional play involving immature, repetitive motor action—are cause for concern. Children who behave reticently, by watching peers without playing, usually are temperamentally inhibited—high in social fearfulness (Coplan et al., 2004; Rubin, Burgess, & Hastings, 2002). And children who engage in solitary, repetitive behavior (banging blocks, making a doll jump up and down) tend to be immature, impulsive youngsters who find it difficult to regulate anger and aggression (Coplan et al., 2001). In the classroom, both reticent and impulsive children are at risk for peer ostracism.

But most preschoolers with low rates of peer interaction are not socially anxious or impulsive. They simply like to play alone, and their solitary activities are positive and constructive. Teachers encourage such play by setting out art materials, books, puzzles, and building toys. Children who frequently choose these pursuits usually are well-adjusted youngsters who, when they do play with peers, show socially skilled behavior (Coplan et al., 2004; Rubin & Coplan, 1998). Still, a few preschoolers do seem to retreat into solitary activities, such as looking at books or drawing pictures, when they would rather play with others. Their social behavior, for reasons not yet clear, causes classmates to rebuff them. Perhaps because quiet play is less consistent with the "masculine" than the "feminine" gender role, boys who engage in it are at greater risk for negative reactions from both parents and peers and, eventually, for adjustment problems (Coplan et al., 2001, 2004).

As noted in Chapter 6, *sociodramatic play*—an advanced form of cooperative play—becomes especially common during the preschool years and supports cognitive, emotional, and social development (Göncü, Patt, & Kouba, 2004). In joint make-believe, preschoolers act out and respond to one another's pretend feelings. They also explore and gain control of fear-arousing experiences when they play doctor or pretend to search for monsters in a magical forest. As a result, they can better understand others' feelings and regulate their own (Smith, 2003). Finally, to create and manage complex plots, preschoolers must resolve their disputes through negotiation and compromise.

Middle Childhood and Adolescence

When formal schooling begins, children are exposed to agemates who vary in many ways, including achievement, ethnicity, religion, interests, and personality. Contact with a diversity of peers contributes to school-age children's increasing awareness that others have viewpoints different from their own (see Chapter 11). Peer communication, in turn, profits from improved perspective taking. Children of this age can better interpret others' emotions and intentions and take them into account in peer dialogues. They also are aware of the value of emotional display rules in facilitating social interaction (see Chapter 10) (Denham et al., 2004). In addition, school-age children's ability to understand the complementary roles of several players in relation to a set of rules permits the transition to rule-oriented games (refer again to Table 15.1).

This father and sons engage in rough-and-tumble play, which is distinguished from aggression by its good-natured quality. In our evolutionary past, rough-and-tumble may have been important for the development of fighting skill and dominance relations.
© Ed Bock/Corbis

School-age children apply their emotional and social knowledge to peer communication. Recall from Chapter 12 that sharing, helping, and other prosocial acts increase in middle childhood. In addition, younger and older children differ in how they help agemates. Kindergartners move right in and give assistance, regardless of whether it is desired. In contrast, school-age children offer to help and wait for a peer to accept before behaving prosocially. In adolescence, agemates work on tasks more cooperatively—staying on task, freely exchanging ideas, asking for opinions, and acknowledging one another's contributions (Azmitia, 1996).

Another form of peer interaction emerges in the preschool years and peaks during middle childhood, when it accounts for 10 percent of free-play behavior. **TAKE A MOMENT...** While watching children at play in a city park or a schoolyard, notice how they occasionally wrestle, roll, hit, and run after one another, alternating roles while smiling and laughing. This friendly chasing and play-fighting, known as **rough-and-tumble play,** is a good-natured, sociable activity, quite distinct from aggressive fighting. Children in many cultures engage in it with peers whom they like especially well. After a rough-and-tumble episode, they continue interacting rather than separating, as they do after an aggressive encounter (Pellegrini, 2004).

Children's rough-and-tumble play resembles the social behavior of many other young mammals. It seems to originate in parents' physical play with babies, especially fathers' play with sons (see Chapter 10). And it is more common among boys, probably because prenatal exposure to androgens (male sex hormones) predisposes boys toward active play (see Chapter 13). Boys' rough-and-tumble largely consists of playful wrestling, restraining, and hitting, whereas girls tend to engage in running and chasing, with only brief physical contact (Boulton, 1996).

In our evolutionary past, rough-and-tumble play may have been important for the development of fighting skill (Boulton & Smith, 1992). It also may help children establish a **dominance hierarchy**—a stable ordering of group members that predicts who will win when conflict arises. Observations of arguments, threats, and physical attacks between children reveal a consistent lineup of winners and losers that becomes increasingly stable in middle childhood and adolescence, especially among boys. Many children seem to use these encounters to evaluate their own and others' strength in a safe venue before challenging a peer's dominance. Over time, children increasingly choose rough-and-tumble partners who resemble themselves in dominance status (Pellegrini & Smith, 1998).

As with nonhuman animals, dominance relations among children serve the adaptive function of limiting aggression. Once a dominance hierarchy is established, hostility is rare (Roseth et al., 2007). As adolescents reach physical maturity and individual differences in strength become clear, rough-and-tumble play declines. When it does occur, its meaning changes: Adolescent boys' rough-and-tumble is linked to aggression (Pellegrini, 2003). After becoming embroiled in a bout, players "cheat" and hurt their opponent. When asked to explain the episode, boys often respond that they are retaliating, apparently to reestablish dominance among their peers. And boy–girl rough-and-tumble, though infrequent, rises slightly at adolescence, perhaps serving as a means through which teenagers playfully initiate heterosexual interaction (Pellegrini, 2006).

Over middle childhood, children interact increasingly often with peers until, by midadolescence, they spend more time with peers than with any other social partners. Common interests, novel play activities, and opportunities to interact on an equal footing make peer interaction highly gratifying. As adolescence draws to a close, most young people are proficient in many complex social behaviors.

Influences on Peer Sociability

Children first acquire skills for interacting with peers within the family. Parents influence children's peer sociability both *directly,* through attempts to influence children's peer relations, and *indirectly,* through their child-rearing practices and play behaviors (Ladd & Pettit, 2002). Situational factors that adults can influence, such as the age mix of children, also make a difference, as do cultural values.

• **Direct Parental Influences** Outside preschool and child care, young children depend on parents to help them establish rewarding peer associations. Preschoolers whose parents frequently arrange informal peer play activities tend to have larger peer networks and to be more socially skilled (Ladd, LeSieur, & Profilet, 1993). In providing play opportunities, parents show children how to initiate peer contacts and encourage them to be good "hosts" who consider their playmates' needs.

Parents also influence children's peer interaction skills by offering guidance on how to act toward others. Their skillful suggestions for managing conflict, discouraging teasing, and entering a play group are associated with preschoolers' social competence and peer acceptance (Mize & Pettit, 1997; Parke et al., 2004). As children get older and acquire effective social skills, they need less parental advice. In middle childhood, heavy provision of parental guidance is usually aimed at children with peer-relationship problems (McDowell, Parke, & Wang, 2004).

Recall from Chapter 14 that during middle childhood and adolescence, parental monitoring of their child's activities protects school-age children and adolescents from antisocial involvements. Young people's disclosure of information is vital for successful monitoring. The extent to which adolescents tell parents about their whereabouts and companions is an especially strong predictor of adjustment (Stattin & Kerr, 2000). Such disclosure, however, depends on a history of consistent monitoring and a well-functioning parent–child relationship, which (as we will see) also promotes positive peer relations.

Parents influence children's peer interaction skills by offering advice, guidance, and examples of how to behave. These boys receive a gentle lesson in how to greet a friend by shaking hands.
© Michael Newman/PhotoEdit

• **Indirect Parental Influences** Many child-rearing variables not directly aimed at promoting peer sociability nevertheless spill over into peer relations. For example, inductive discipline and authoritative parenting offer a firm foundation for competence in relating to agemates. In contrast, coercive psychological control and harsh physical punishment engender poor social skills and aggressive behavior (see Chapters 12 and 14).

Furthermore, secure attachments to parents are linked to more responsive, harmonious peer interactions, larger peer networks, and warmer, more supportive friendships throughout childhood and adolescence (Coleman, 2003; Laible, 2007; Lucas-Thompson & Clarke-Stewart, 2007; Wood, Emmerson, & Cowan, 2004). The sensitive, emotionally expressive parental communication that underlies secure attachment may be responsible. In one study, researchers observed parent–child conversations and rated them for the strength of the mother–child bond, as indicated by exchanges of positive emotion and parental sensitivity to the child's statements and feelings. Kindergartners who were more emotionally "connected" to their mothers displayed more empathy and prosocial behavior toward their classmates. This empathic orientation, in turn, was linked to more positive peer ties (Clark & Ladd, 2000).

Parent–child play seems to be a particularly effective context for promoting peer-interaction skills. During play, parents interact with their child on a "level playing field," much as peers do (Russell, Pettit, & Mize, 1998). Highly involved, emotionally positive, and cooperative play between parents and preschoolers is associated with more positive peer relations. And perhaps because parents play more with children of their own sex, mothers' play is more strongly linked to daughters' competence, fathers' play to sons' competence (Lindsey & Mize, 2000; Pettit et al., 1998).

Finally, the quality of parents' social networks is associated with children's social competence. In one study, parents who reported high-quality friendships had school-age children who interacted more favorably with friends. This relationship was stronger for girls, perhaps because girls spend more time near parents and have more opportunity to observe their parents' friends (Simpkins & Parke, 2001). Furthermore, overlap between parents' and adolescents' social networks—frequent contact among teenagers' friends, their parents, and their friends' parents—is related to better school achievement and low levels of antisocial behavior (Parke et al., 2004). Under these conditions, other adults in parents' networks may promote parents' values and goals and monitor teenagers in their parents' absence.

• **Age Mix of Children** When observed in age-graded settings, such as child-care centers, schools, and summer camps, children typically interact with others close in age. Yet in cultures where children are not segregated by age for schooling and recreation, cross-age interaction is common.

The theories of Piaget and Vygotsky, discussed in Chapter 6, suggest different benefits from same- versus mixed-age interaction. Piaget emphasized experiences with children equal in status who challenge one another's viewpoints, thereby promoting cognitive, social, and moral development. In contrast, Vygotsky believed that children profit from interacting with older, more capable peers, who model and encourage more advanced skills.

Among preschoolers, younger children's play is more cognitively and socially mature in mixed-age classrooms than in single-age classrooms. Furthermore, as early as age 3 or 4, children can modify their behavior to fit the needs of a less advanced child, simplifying their communication and assuming more responsibility for a joint activity (Brody, Graziano, & Musser, 1983; Howes & Farver, 1987). Nevertheless, the oldest school-age children in mixed-age settings prefer same-age companions, perhaps because they have more compatible interests and experience more cooperative interaction. Younger children's interaction with same-age partners is also more intense and harmonious, but they often turn to older peers because of their superior knowledge and exciting play ideas.

Children clearly profit from both same-age and mixed-age relationships. From interacting with equals, they learn to cooperate and resolve conflicts, and they develop vital moral understandings of reciprocity and justice (see Chapters 11 and 12). In mixed-age settings, younger children acquire new competencies from their older companions. And when more mature youngsters help their less mature counterparts, they practice nurturance, guidance, and other prosocial behaviors.

These cousins, who live in central India, play an intricate hand-clapping game called "Chapte." They clap in unison to a jingle with eleven verses that take them through their lifespan, concluding with their transformation into ghosts. The game reflects the value their culture places on group harmony. © Doranne Jacobson

• **Cultural Values** Peer sociability in collectivist societies, which stress group harmony, differs from that in Western individualistic cultures. For example, children in India generally play in large groups that require high levels of cooperation. Much of their behavior is imitative, occurs in unison, and involves close physical contact. In a game called Bhatto Bhatto, children act out a script about a trip to the market, touching one another's elbows and hands as they pretend to cut and share a tasty vegetable (Roopnarine et al., 1994).

Furthermore, unlike North American preschoolers, who tend to reject reticent classmates, Chinese preschoolers are more willing to include a quiet, reserved child in play (Chen et al., 2006). In Chapter 10, we saw that until recently, collectivist values, which discourage self-assertion, led to a positive attitude toward shyness in China (see page 424). Apparently, this benevolent attitude is still evident in the play behaviors of Chinese young children.

Cultural beliefs about the importance of play also affect early peer associations. Caregivers who view play as mere entertainment are less likely to provide props or to encourage pretend than those who value its cognitive and social benefits (Farver & Wimbarti, 1995a, 1995b). Preschool children of Korean-American parents, who emphasize task persistence as crucial for learning, spend less time than Caucasian-American children in joint make-believe and more time unoccupied and in parallel play (Farver, Kim, & Lee, 1995).

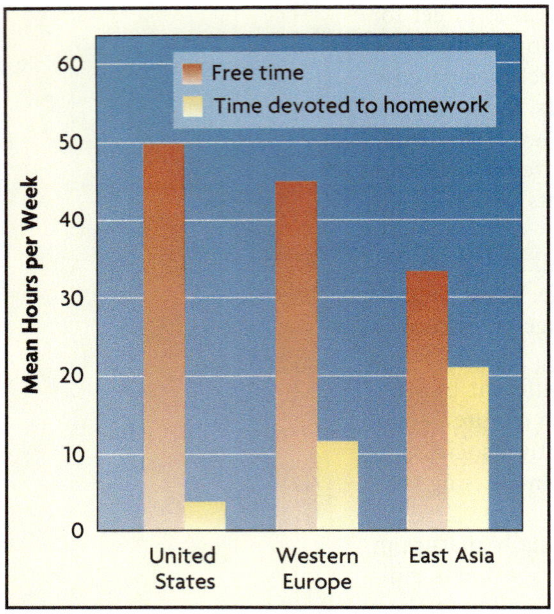

■ **Figure 15.1** **Weekly free time and time devoted to homework by adolescents in the United States, Europe, and East Asia.**
Figures are averages of those reported in many studies. U.S. teenagers have more free time available to spend with peers than their European and, especially, Asian counterparts, a difference largely explained by U.S. adolescents spending far less time doing homework. (Adapted from Larson, 2001.)

Return to the description of the daily lives of children growing up in village and tribal cultures on page 270 in Chapter 6. Mayan parents, for example, do not promote children's play. Yet even though they spend little time pretending, Mayan children are socially competent (Gaskins, 2000). Western-style sociodramatic play, with its elaborate materials and wide-ranging themes, may be more important for social development in societies where child and adult worlds are distinct than it is when children participate in adult activities from an early age.

Peer contact rises in adolescence in all societies but especially in industrialized nations, where young people spend most of each weekday with agemates in school. Teenagers also spend much out-of-class time together, more in some cultures than in others. For example, adolescents in the United States have about 50 hours of free time per week, those in Western Europe about 45 hours, and those in Asian nations (such as China, Japan, and Korea) about 33 hours (Larson, 2001). As Figure 15.1 reveals, factors that account for this difference include a shorter school year coupled with less demanding academic standards, which lead U.S. youths to spend far less time than Western European and Asian youths on schoolwork (especially homework).

Ask Yourself

Review Among children who spend much time playing alone, what factors distinguish those who are likely to have adjustment difficulties from those who are well-adjusted and socially skilled?

Apply Three-year-old Ben lives in the country, with no other preschoolers nearby. His parents wonder whether it is worth driving Ben into town once a week to participate in a peer play group. What advice would you give Ben's parents, and why?

Connect What aspects of parent–child interaction probably account for the relationship between attachment security and children's peer sociability? (*Hint:* See Chapter 10, pages 430–431 and 434.)

Reflect What did your parents do, directly and indirectly, that might have influenced your peer relationships in childhood and adolescence?

Friendship

Children have encounters and relationships with many peers, but they prefer some peers over others as playmates. Beginning in early childhood, they form **friendships**—close relationships involving companionship in which each partner wants to be with the other. Observations of 1- and 2-year-olds reveal that they initiate play, exchange expressions of positive emotion, and engage in more complex interactions with selected, familiar peers (Howes, 1998). These early mutual relationships may lay the groundwork for deeper, more meaningful friendships in childhood and adolescence.

To study friendship, researchers ask the child or a knowledgeable adult to name friends, then check whether nominated friends return the choice. They also observe friendship interactions, comparing these with other peer relationships. And they interview children about what friendship means. Findings reveal that with age, children's ideas about friendship change, as do certain features of friendships (Hartup, 2006). From the preschool years on, friendship contributes uniquely to children's psychological adjustment.

Thinking About Friendship

TAKE A MOMENT... Jot down a description of what *friendship* means to you. You probably pictured a consensual relationship involving companionship, sharing, understanding each other's thoughts and feelings, and caring for and comforting each other in times of need. In addition, mature friendships endure over time and survive occasional conflicts. But to a child, friendship begins as something far more concrete, based on pleasurable activity. With age, friendship evolves into a relationship based on mutual consideration and psychological satisfaction (Damon, 1988; Hartup & Abecassis, 2004). Children's changing ideas about friendship follow a three-stage sequence, confirmed by both longitudinal and cross-sectional research.

• **1. Friendship as a Handy Playmate (About 4 to 7 Years)** Preschoolers understand something about the uniqueness of friendship. They say that a friend is someone "who likes you," with whom you spend a lot of time playing, and with whom you share toys. But friendship does not yet have a long-term, enduring quality. Children at this stage say that a friendship can dissolve when one partner refuses to share, hits, or is not available to play. A 5-year-old's answer to the question "What makes a good friend?" sums up the young child's view of friendship: "Boys play with boys, trucks play with trucks, dogs play with dogs." When the interviewer probed, "Why does that make them good friends?" the child replied, "Because they do the same things" (Selman, 1980, p. 136).

• **2. Friendship as Mutual Trust and Assistance (About 8 to 10 Years)** In middle childhood, friendship becomes more complex and psychologically based. Consider the following 8-year-old's ideas:

> *Why is Shelly your best friend?* Because she helps me when I'm sad, and she shares. . . . *What makes Shelly so special?* I've known her longer, I sit next to her and got to know her better. . . . *How come you like Shelly better than anyone else?* She's done the most for me. She never disagrees, she never eats in front of me, she never walks away when I'm crying, and she helps me on my homework. . . . *How do you get someone to like you?* . . . If you're nice to [your friends], they'll be nice to you. (Damon, 1988, pp. 80–81)

As these responses show, friendship has become a mutually agreed-on relationship in which children like each other's personal qualities and respond to each other's needs and desires. Because friendship requires that both children want to be together, getting it started takes more time and effort than it did at younger ages.

Once a friendship forms, *trust* becomes its defining feature. School-age children state that a good friendship is based on acts of kindness signifying that each person can be counted on to support the other. Consequently, older children regard violations of trust, such as not helping a friend who needs help, breaking promises, and gossiping behind a friend's back, as serious breaches of friendship—as Katy did in the chapter introduction. And rifts cannot be patched up simply by playing nicely after a conflict, as younger children do. Instead, apologies and explanations are necessary (Damon, 1977; Selman, 1980).

During middle childhood, concepts of friendship become more psychologically based. These boys share an interest in cooking, but they want to spend time together because they like each other's personal qualities. © George Disario/Corbis

• **3. Friendship as Intimacy, Mutual Understanding, and Loyalty (11 to 15 Years and Older)** When asked about the meaning of friendship, teenagers stress three characteristics. The most important is *intimacy,* or psychological closeness, which is supported by *mutual understanding* of each other's values, beliefs, and feelings. In addition, more than younger children, teenagers want their friends to be *loyal*—to stick up for them and not to leave them for somebody else (Collins & Madsen, 2006).

As friendship takes on these deeper features, adolescents regard it as formed over time by "getting to know someone." In addition, they view friends as important in relieving psychological distress, such as loneliness, sadness, and fear. Because true mutual understanding implies forgiveness, only an extreme falling out can terminate a friendship. Here is how one teenager described his best friendship:

> Well, you need someone you can tell anything to, all kinds of things that you don't want to spread around. That's why you're someone's friend. *Is that why Jimmy is your friend? Because he can keep a secret?* Yes, and we like the same kinds of things. We speak the same language. My mother says we're two peas in a pod. . . . *Do you ever get mad at Jimmy?* Not really. *What if he did something that got you really mad?* He'd still be my best friend. I'd tell him what he did wrong and maybe he'd understand. I could be wrong too, it depends. (Damon, 1977, p. 163)

Characteristics of Friendships

Changes in children's thinking about friendships are linked to characteristics of their real friendships. Let's look closely at friendship stability, interaction, and resemblance.

• **Friendship Selectivity and Stability** As mutual trust and loyalty become more important in their friendship expectations, school-age children grow more selective about their friendships. Preschoolers say they have lots of friends—sometimes, everyone in their class! But by age 8 or 9, children name only a handful of good friends. As teenagers focus on friendship quality, this narrowing continues. Number of best friends declines from four to six in early adolescence to only one or two in emerging adulthood (Hartup & Stevens, 1999). Girls, who demand greater closeness than boys, are more exclusive in their friendships (Markovits, Benenson, & Dolenky, 2001).

Although friendship stability increases with age, friendships are remarkably stable at all ages. For younger children, however, stability is largely a function of the constancy of social environments, such as school and neighborhood. From fourth grade through high school, when friendships become psychologically based, about 50 to 70 percent endure over the course of a school year, and some for several years, although they often undergo temporary shifts in the strength of each partner's commitment (Berndt, 2004; Degirmencioglu et al., 1998). In middle or junior high school, varying rates of pubertal development, encounters with new peers, and romantic interests often lead to a temporary period of greater change in choice of friends (Hardy, Bukowski, & Sippola, 2002).

• **Interaction Between Friends** At all ages, friends have special ways of interacting. Preschoolers, for example, give twice as much reinforcement—greetings, praise, and compliance—to children they identify as friends, and they also receive more from them. Friends are more emotionally expressive, talking, laughing, and looking at one another more often than nonfriends do (Hartup, 1996, 2006; Vaughn et al., 2001). Spontaneity, intimacy, and sensitivity characterize rewarding friendships very early, although children are not able to express these ideas until much later.

A more mature understanding of friendship seems to spark greater prosocial behavior between friends. When working on a task together, school-age friends help, share, refer to each other's comments, and spend more time focused than preschool friends do (Hartup, 1996; Newcomb & Bagwell, 1995). Cooperation, generosity, mutual affirmation, and self-disclosure (see Figure 15.2) continue to rise into adolescence—trends that may reflect greater effort and skill at preserving the relationship and increased sensitivity to a friend's needs (Phillipsen, 1999). Teenagers are also less possessive of their friends than they were in childhood. They recognize that friends need a certain degree of autonomy—something they also desire for themselves (Rubin, Bukowski, & Parker, 1998).

Friends not only behave more prosocially but also disagree and compete with each other more than nonfriends. Because children regard friendship as based on equality, they seem especially concerned about losing a contest to a friend. Also, when children hold differing opinions, friends are more likely to voice them. At the same time, school-age and adolescent friends use negotiation to resolve conflicts more often than nonfriends do. Friends seem to realize that close relationships can survive disagreements if both parties are secure in their liking for each other (Fonzi et al., 1997; Hartup, 2006; Rose & Asher, 1999). Adolescent girls' friendships are more likely to endure when friends are "up front" about tensions in the relationship rather than dismissing them as "no big deal"—a coping strategy that works better for boys (Bowker, 2004). Because girls highly value sharing feelings, passive responses to conflict may restore surface harmony while the underlying discontent lingers. Clearly, friendship provides an important context in which children learn to tolerate criticism and resolve disputes.

The impact that friendships have on children's development depends on the nature of those friends. Children who bring kindness and compassion to their friendships strengthen one another's prosocial tendencies and form more lasting ties. But when aggressive children make friends, the relationship is often riddled with hostile interaction and is at risk for breakup, especially when just one member of the pair is aggressive (Ellis & Zarbatany, 2007). Friendships of aggressive girls are high in self-disclosure but full of relational hostility, including jealousy, conflict, and betrayal—techniques used to manipulate associations with others. Aggressive boys' friendships involve frequent expressions of anger, coercive statements, physical attacks, and enticements to rule-breaking behavior, as well as relational aggression (Bagwell & Coie, 2004; Crick & Nelson, 2002; Dishion, Andrews, & Crosby, 1995). These findings indicate that the social problems of aggressive children operate within their closest peer ties.

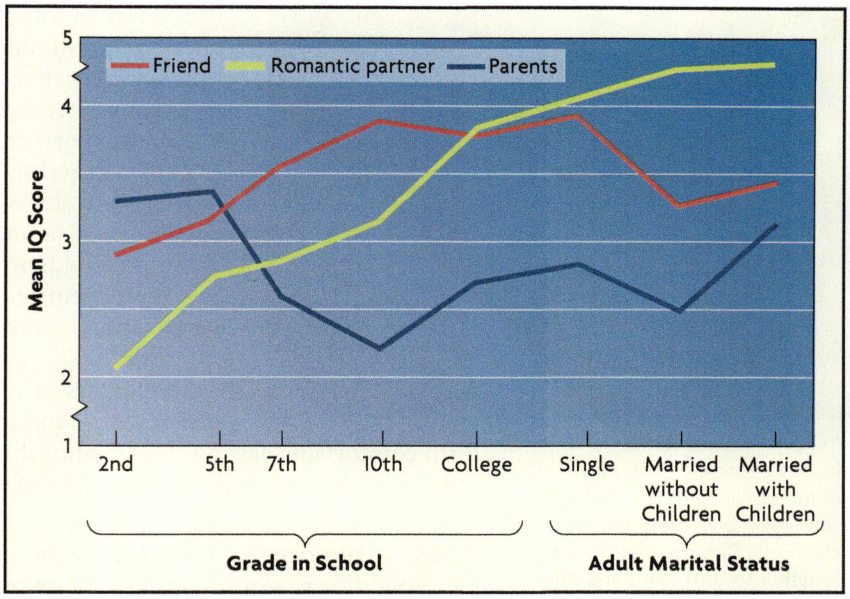

Figure 15.2 **Age changes in reported self-disclosure to parents and peers, based on data from several studies.**

Self-disclosure to friends increases steadily during adolescence, reflecting intimacy as a major basis of friendship. Self-disclosure to romantic partners also rises, but it does not surpass intimacy with friends until the college years. Self-disclosure to parents declines in early adolescence, a time of mild parent–child conflict. As family relationships readjust to the young person's increasing autonomy, self-disclosure to parents rises. (From D. Buhrmester, 1996, "Need Fulfillment, Interpersonal Competence, and the Developmental Contexts of Early Adolescent Friendship," in W. M. Bukowski, A. F. Newcomb, & W. W. Hartup, Eds., *The Company They Keep: Friendship in Childhood and Adolescence*, New York: Cambridge University Press, p. 168. Reprinted with permission of Cambridge University Press.)

Resemblance Between Friends The value adolescents attach to feeling "in sync" with their friends suggests that friends will become increasingly similar in attitudes and values with age. Actually, the attributes on which friends are most alike throughout childhood and adolescence are age, sex, ethnicity, and SES. But from middle childhood on, friends also resemble one another in personality (sociability, aggression, and depression), popularity, academic achievement, prosocial behavior, and judgments (including biased perceptions) of other people (Hartup, 2006; Haselager et al., 1998; Mariano & Harton, 2005). And in adolescence, friends tend to be alike in identity status, educational aspirations, political beliefs, and willingness to try drugs and engage in lawbreaking acts (Akers, Jones, & Coyl, 1998).

Children and adolescents probably choose companions like themselves to increase the supportiveness of friendship. And as we saw in Chapters 11 and 13, school-age children often hold outgroup prejudices, negatively evaluating peers of other ethnicities and the other gender. How do children identify peers who are similar to themselves in other ways? According to some researchers, they go on "shopping expeditions" in their social networks, trying out relationships and sustaining those that "feel right" (Hartup & Abecassis, 2004). As friends spend more time together, they socialize one another, becoming increasingly alike in attitudes, values, school grades, and social behavior (Berndt & Keefe, 1995).

Nevertheless, as young people enter a wider range of school and community settings, they choose some friends who differ from themselves. For a time, young teenagers sacrifice similarity in favor of admiration for superficial features—whether a potential friend is popular, physically attractive, or athletically skilled. And early adolescents of both sexes are attracted to high-status, aggressive boys as friends, a trend that contributes to a rise in antisocial behavior and, for girls, can lead to negative experiences in their first dating relationships (Bukowski, Sippola, & Newcomb, 2000). In other instances, a friend's favorable traits are influential. In one study, low-achieving 9- to 11-year-olds who befriended a high-achieving classmate declined in academic self-esteem (because of social comparison) but nevertheless improved in academic performance (Altermatt & Pomerantz, 2005).

In adolescence, intimacy and loyalty become defining features of friendship. Girls place a higher value than boys on emotional closeness. Girls more often get together to "just talk," and they engage in more self-disclosure and mutually supportive statements with friends. © Tim O'Hara/Corbis

The task of forging a personal identity at times leads adolescents to seek friends with differing attitudes and values, as a means of exploring new perspectives within the security of a compatible relationship. Furthermore, teenagers often judge commonality in certain attributes as more important than in others. For example, compared with Caucasian-American friends, African-American friends place greater emphasis on shared ethnicity and less on similarity in academic achievement (Hamm, 2000; Tolson & Urberg, 1993).

Finally, children and adolescents are more likely to form friendships with agemates of other ethnicities when they attend ethnically diverse schools and live in integrated neighborhoods (Quillian & Campbell, 2003). Cross-ethnic friendships in childhood are among the best predictors of reduction in ethnic prejudice—a relationship that persists into adulthood (Ellison & Powers, 1994). As young people form comfortable, lasting close relationships, they come to view ethnically different peers as individuals instead of through the lens of stereotypes (Carlson, Wilson, & Hargrave, 2003).

• Sex Differences in Friendships In middle childhood, children start to report a consistent sex difference in friendships: Emotional closeness is more common between girls than between boys (Markovits, Benenson, & Dolenszky, 2001). Girls frequently get together to "just talk," and their exchanges contain more self-disclosure (sharing of innermost thoughts and feelings) and mutually supportive statements. In contrast, boys more often gather for an activity—usually sports or other competitive games. Boys' discussions usually focus on recognition and mastery issues, such as achievements in sports and school, and involve more competition and conflict (Brendgen et al., 2001; Rubin, Bukowski, & Parker, 2006).

Because of gender-role expectations, girls' friendships typically focus on communal concerns, boys' on achievement and status. Boys do form close friendship ties, but the quality of their friendships is more variable than for girls. Gender identity plays a role: Androgynous boys are as likely as girls to form intimate same-sex ties, whereas boys who identify strongly with the "masculine" role are less likely to do so (Jones & Dembo, 1989).

Friendship closeness has costs as well as benefits. When friends focus on their deeper thoughts and feelings, they tend to *coruminate,* or repeatedly mull over problems and negative emotions. Corumination, while contributing to high friendship quality, also triggers anxiety and depression—symptoms more common among girls than among boys (Rose, Carlson, & Waller, 2007). And when conflicts arise among intimate friends, more potential exists for one party to harm the other through relational aggression—for example, by divulging sensitive personal information to outsiders. For this reason, girls' closest same-sex friendships tend to be of shorter duration than boys' (Benenson & Christakos, 2003).

In early adolescence, young people who are either very popular or very unpopular are more likely to have other-sex friends. Teenagers who are not accepted by their own sex sometimes look to the other sex for friendships. Boys have more other-sex friends than girls, whose desire for closeness leads them to prefer same-sex friendships (Sippola, Bukowski, & Noll, 1997). Among boys without same-sex friends, having an other-sex friend is associated with feelings of competence. Among girls who lack same-sex friends, however, other-sex friendships are linked to less positive well-being (Bukowski, Sippola, & Hoza, 1999). Perhaps these girls are especially likely to befriend boys with negative traits, such as aggression.

Friendship and Adjustment

Warm, gratifying childhood and adolescent friendships are related to many aspects of psychological health and competence into early adulthood (Bagwell et al., 2001; Bukowski, 2001), for several reasons:

- *Close friendships provide opportunities to explore the self and develop a deep understanding of another.* Through open, honest communication, friends become sensitive to each other's strengths and weaknesses, needs and desires. They get to know both themselves and their friend especially well, a process that supports the development of self-concept, perspective taking, and identity.

- *Close friendships provide a foundation for future intimate relationships.* Look again at Figure 15.2, and you will see that self-disclosure to friends precedes disclosure to romantic partners. Lengthy, often emotionally laden psychological discussions between adolescent friends appear to prepare the young person for love relationships (Sullivan, 1953). Sexuality and romance are common topics of discussion between teenage friends—conversations that, along with the intimacy of friendship itself, may help adolescents establish and work out problems in romantic partnerships (Connolly & Goldberg, 1999).
- *Close friendships help young people deal with the stresses of everyday life.* By enhancing sensitivity to and concern for another, supportive, prosocial friendships promote empathy, sympathy, and positive social behavior. As a result, they contribute to involvement in constructive youth activities, avoidance of antisocial acts, and psychological well-being (Lansford et al., 2003; Wentzel, Barry, & Caldwell, 2004). A rewarding friendship helps protect shy children from developing emotional and behavior problems (Laursen et al., 2007). And adolescents experiencing family stress who have close friends show as high a level of well-being as children from better-functioning families (Gauze et al., 1996).
- *Close friendships can improve attitudes toward and involvement in school.* Close friendship ties promote good school adjustment in both middle- and low-SES students (Berndt & Murphy, 2002; Wentzel, Barry, & Caldwell, 2004). Children and adolescents who enjoy interacting with friends at school may begin to view all aspects of school life more positively.

Some friendships, however, interfere with well-being. Beginning in the preschool years, the conflict-ridden interactions that occur between physically, verbally, and relationally aggressive friends are associated with poor adjustment (Sebanc, 2003). Longitudinal research reveals that children with aggressive friends increase in antisocial behavior over time (Dishion, Poulin, & Burraston, 2001).

Finally, children who have no friends usually have undesirable personalities: They may be easily angered, shy and anxious, or self-centered (less caring and honest) (Bowker et al., 2006; Ladd, 1999). Without supportive friendship as a context for acquiring more adaptive social behaviors, the maladaptive behaviors of these children tend to persist.

Ask Yourself

Review Describe unique qualities of interaction between close friends, and explain how they contribute to development.

Review Why are aggressive children's friendships likely to magnify their antisocial behavior?

Apply Ralph, a high school junior of Irish Catholic background, befriended Jonathan, a Chinese-American of Buddhist faith. Both boys are from middle-SES homes and are good students. Why might Ralph seek out a friend both similar to and different from himself?

Connect Cite similarities in development of self-concept, described in Chapter 11 (pages 451–453), and ideas about friendship. Explain how the discussion among Stu, Pete, Jessamyn, and Katy in the introduction to this chapter reflects friendship expectations that typically emerge at adolescence.

Peer Acceptance

Peer acceptance refers to likability—the extent to which a child is viewed by a group of agemates, such as classmates, as a worthy social partner. Unlike friendship, peer acceptance is not a mutual relationship but, rather, a one-sided perspective, involving the group's view of an individual. Nevertheless, certain social skills that contribute to friendship also enhance peer acceptance. Better-accepted children tend to have more friends and more positive relationships with them (Gest, Graham-Bermann, & Hartup, 2001; Lansford et al., 2006). As with friendship, peer acceptance contributes uniquely to children's adjustment.

To assess peer acceptance, researchers usually use self-reports called **sociometric techniques,** which measure *social preferences.* For example, children and adolescents may be asked to nominate several classmates whom they especially like or dislike, to indicate for all possible pairs of classmates which one they prefer to spend time with, or to rate each peer on a scale from "like very much" to "like very little" (Hymel et al., 2004). Another approach is to assess **peer reputation**—young people's judgments of the peers most of their classmates admire, which identify peers high in *social prominence.* The classmates school-age children and adolescents identify as prominent—looked up to by many others—show only moderate correspondence with the classmates they say they personally prefer to be with on sociometric measures (Lafontana & Cillessen, 1999; Prinstein & Cillessen, 2003).

Sociometric techniques yield four general categories of peer acceptance:

- **Popular children,** who get many positive votes (are well-liked)
- **Rejected children,** who get many negative votes (are disliked)
- **Controversial children,** who get a large number of positive and negative votes (are both liked and disliked)
- **Neglected children,** who are seldom mentioned, either positively or negatively.

About two-thirds of students in a typical elementary school classroom fit one of these categories (Coie, Dodge, & Coppotelli, 1982). The remaining one-third, who do not receive extreme scores, are *average* in peer acceptance.

Peer acceptance is a powerful predictor of current and later psychological adjustment. Rejected children, especially, are anxious, unhappy, disruptive, poorly achieving children with low self-esteem. Both teachers and parents view them as having a wide range of emotional and social problems. Peer rejection in middle childhood is also strongly associated with poor school performance, absenteeism, dropping out, substance use, depression, antisocial behavior, and delinquency in adolescence and with criminality in emerging adulthood (Ladd, 2005; Laird et al., 2001; Parker et al., 1995; Rubin, Bukowski, & Parker, 2006).

However, earlier influences—children's characteristics combined with parenting practices—may largely explain the link between peer acceptance and psychological adjustment. School-age children with peer-relationship problems are more likely to have experienced family stress due to low income, insensitive child rearing, and coercive discipline (Cowan & Cowan, 2004). Nevertheless, as we will see, rejected children evoke reactions from peers that contribute to their unfavorable development. Peer rejection, in turn, adds to the risk of maladjustment, beyond rejected children's maladaptive behavioral styles (Ladd, 2006).

Origins of Acceptance in the Peer Situation

Why is one child liked while another is rejected? A wealth of research reveals that social behavior plays a powerful role.

• Popular Children Although many popular children are kind and considerate, others are admired for their socially sophisticated yet belligerent behavior. Two subtypes of popular children exist:

- **Popular-prosocial children.** The majority of popular children combine academic and social competence. They are good students who communicate with peers in sensitive, friendly, and cooperative ways and who solve social problems constructively. If they disagree with a play partner in a game, they go beyond voicing their displeasure and suggest what the other child could do instead. When they want to enter an ongoing play group, they adapt their behavior to the flow of the activity (Cillessen & Bellmore, 2004; Newcomb, Bukowski, & Pattee, 1993).
- **Popular-antisocial children.** This smaller subtype, which emerges in late childhood and early adolescence, consists of aggressive youngsters. Some are "tough" boys who are athletically skilled but poor students who cause trouble and defy adult authority. Others are relationally aggressive boys and girls who enhance their own status by ignoring, excluding, and spreading rumors about other children (Cillessen & Mayeux, 2004; Rodkin et al., 2000; Rose, Swenson, & Waller, 2004). Despite their aggressiveness, peers view these youths as "cool," perhaps because of their athletic ability and sophisticated but devious social skills. Antisocial youths are especially likely to be popular in classrooms with many

aggressive children—conditions that produce a peer culture that highly values aggressive behavior (Stormshak et al., 1999).

Although peer admiration gives popular-antisocial children some protection against lasting adjustment difficulties, their antisocial acts require intervention (Prinstein & La Greca, 2004; Rodkin et al., 2006). With age, peers like these high-status, aggressive youths less and less, a trend that is stronger for relationally aggressive girls. The more socially prominent and controlling these girls become, the more they engage in relational aggression (Cillessen & Mayeux, 2004). Eventually peers condemn their nasty tactics and reject them.

• Rejected Children Rejected children display a wide range of negative social behaviors. But as with popular children, not all of these disliked children look the same. At least two subtypes exist:

- **Rejected-aggressive children,** the largest subgroup, show severe conduct problems—high rates of conflict, physical and relational aggression, and hyperactive, inattentive, and impulsive behavior. These children also are deficient in social understanding and regulation of negative emotion. For example, they are more likely than others to be poor perspective takers, to misinterpret the innocent behaviors of peers as hostile, to blame others for their social difficulties, and to act on their angry feelings (Crick, Casas, & Nelson, 2002; Hoza et al., 2005; Rubin, Bukowski, & Parker, 2006). Compared with popular-aggressive children, rejected-aggressive children are more extremely antagonistic (Prinstein & Cillessen, 2003). Rather than using aggression skillfully to attain status, rejected-aggressive children display blatantly hostile, acting-out behavior, which triggers scorn and avoidance in their peers.
- **Rejected-withdrawn children,** a smaller subgroup, are passive and socially awkward. These timid children are overwhelmed by social anxiety, hold negative expectations for treatment by peers, and fear being scorned and attacked. Like their aggressive counterparts, they typically feel like retaliating rather than compromising in peer conflicts, although they less often act on those feelings (Hart et al., 2000; Ladd & Burgess, 1999; Troop-Gordon & Asher, 2005).

Rejected children are excluded by peers as early as kindergarten. Rejection, in turn, further impairs these children's biased social information processing, heightening their hostility (Dodge et al., 2003). Soon rejected children's classroom participation declines, their feelings of loneliness rise, their academic achievement falters, and they want to avoid school (Buhs & Ladd, 2001). Rejected-aggressive and rejected-withdrawn children typically befriend other rejected agemates. Most have few friends, and their closest friendship bonds tend to be low in mutual support and effective conflict resolution (Rubin, Bukowski, & Parker, 2006; Rubin et al., 2006). Some rejected children have no friends—a circumstance linked to low self-esteem, mistrust of peers, and severe adjustment difficulties (Ladd & Troop-Gordon, 2003).

Both rejected-aggressive and rejected-withdrawn children are at risk for peer harassment. But as the Social Issues box on page 000 reveals, rejected-aggressive children also act as bullies, and rejected-withdrawn children are especially likely to be victimized because of their inept, submissive style of interaction (Putallaz et al., 2007; Sandstrom & Cillessen, 2003).

• Controversial Children Consistent with the mixed peer opinion they engender, controversial children display a blend of positive and negative social behaviors. They are hostile and disruptive, but they also engage in high rates of positive, prosocial acts. Even though some peers dislike them, controversial children have qualities that protect them from exclusion. They have as many friends as popular children and are happy with their peer relationships (Newcomb, Bukowski, & Pattee, 1993). But, like their popular-antisocial and rejected-aggressive counterparts, they often bully agemates to get their way and engage in calculated relational aggression to sustain their social dominance (DeRosier & Thomas, 2003; Putallaz et al., 2007). The social status of controversial children often changes over time as agemates react to their mixed behavior.

• Neglected Children Perhaps the most surprising finding on peer acceptance is that neglected children, once thought to be in need of treatment, are usually well-adjusted. Although they engage in low rates of interaction and are considered shy by their classmates, they are not less socially skilled than average children. They do not report feeling lonely or unhappy about their social life, and when they want to, they can break away from their usual pattern of

Social Issues

Bullies and Their Victims

Follow the activities of aggressive children over a school day, and you will see that they reserve their hostilities for certain peers. A particularly destructive form of interaction is **peer victimization,** in which certain children become targets of verbal and physical attacks or other forms of abuse. What sustains these repeated assault–retreat cycles between pairs of children?

About 10 to 20 percent of children are bullies, while 15 to 30 percent are repeatedly victimized. Most bullies are boys who use physically, verbally, and relationally aggressive tactics, but girls sometimes bombard a vulnerable classmate with verbal and relational hostility (Rigby, 2004). In addition to other forms of bullying, gender harassment increases in early adolescence—powerful youths (more often boys) delivering insults of a sexual nature against weaker age-mates, heterosexual youths targeting sexual minority peers (Felix & McMahon, 2006; Pepler et al., 2006). And many adolescent bullies amplify their attacks through electronic means (Raskauskas & Stoltz, 2007). In a study of several hundred middle school students, about one in four reported experiencing "cyberbullying" through cell-phone text messages, e-mail, or other electronic tools (Li, 2006).

Although some bullies are high-status youngsters who may be liked for their leadership or athletic abilities, most are disliked—or eventually become so—because of their cruelty (Vaillancourt, Hymel, & McDougall, 2003). Nevertheless, peers rarely intervene to help victims, and about 20 to 30 percent of onlookers encourage bullies, even joining in (Salmivalli & Voeten, 2004).

Chronic victims tend to be passive when active behavior is expected. On the playground, they hang around chatting or wander on their own. When bullied, they reinforce perpetrators by giving in to their demands, crying, and assuming defensive postures (Boulton, 1999). Biologically based traits—an inhibited temperament and a frail physical appearance—contribute to victimization. But victims also have histories of resistant attachment, overly controlling child rearing, and maternal overprotection—parenting that prompts anxiety, low self-esteem, and dependency, resulting in a fearful demeanor that marks these children as vulnerable (Snyder et al., 2003). Persistent bullying, in turn, engenders social-cognitive deficits (poor perspective taking, viewing peers as generally hostile), further impairing victims' emotional self-regulation and social skills—outcomes that heighten victimization (Hoglund & Leadbeater, 2007; Rosen, Milich, & Harris, 2007). As early as kindergarten, victimization leads to adjustment difficulties that may include depression, loneliness, poor school performance, disruptive behavior, and school avoidance (Kochenderfer-Ladd & Wardrop, 2001; Paul & Cillessen, 2003).

Aggression and victimization are not polar opposites. One-third to one-half of victims are also aggressive. Occasionally, they strike back at powerful bullies, who respond by abusing them again—a cycle that sustains their victim status (Kochenderfer-Ladd, 2003). Among rejected children, bully/victims are the most despised. They often have histories of extremely maladaptive parenting, including child abuse. This combination of highly negative home and peer experiences places them at severe risk for maladjustment (Schwartz, Proctor, & Chien, 2001).

Interventions that change victimized children's negative opinions of themselves and that teach them to respond in non-reinforcing ways to their attackers are helpful. Another way to assist victimized children is to help them acquire the social skills needed to form and maintain a gratifying friendship. When children have a close friend whom they can turn to for help, bullying episodes typically end quickly. Anxious, withdrawn children with a prosocial best friend have fewer adjustment problems than victims with no close friends (Bollmer et al., 2005; Fox & Boulton, 2006).

Although modifying victimized children's behavior can help, this does not mean that they are to blame. The best way to reduce bullying is to change youth environments (school, sports programs, recreation centers, and neighborhoods), promoting prosocial attitudes and behaviors. Effective approaches include developing school and community codes against bullying, teaching child bystanders to intervene, enlisting parents' assistance in changing bullies' behaviors, and (if necessary) moving socially prominent bullies to another class or school (Leadbeater & Hoglund, 2006; Smith, Ananiadou, & Cowie, 2003).

In Canada, government leaders, national organizations, community groups, and schools are collaborating in the Canadian Initiative for the Prevention of Bullying, *www.bullying.org*—a nationwide effort to create safe, respectful environments for children and adolescents. The U.S. Department of Health and Human Services has launched a media campaign, Stop Bullying Now, *www.stopbullyingnow.hrsa.gov*, which raises awareness of the harmfulness of bullying through TV and radio public service announcements and provides parents, teachers, and students with information on prevention.

Children who are physically weak, rejected by peers, and afraid to defend themselves tend to be targeted by bullies. Most bullies are boys who use both physical and relational aggression, but some are girls, who bombard their victims with relational hostility. © Jennie Woodcock/Reflections PhotoLibrary/Corbis

playing by themselves (Harrist et al., 1997; Ladd & Burgess, 1999). Probably for this reason, neglected status (like controversial status) is usually temporary. Neglected children remind us that an outgoing, gregarious personality style is not the only path to emotional well-being.

Helping Rejected Children

A variety of interventions exist to improve the peer relations and psychological adjustment of rejected children. Most involve coaching, modeling, and reinforcing positive social skills, such as how to initiate interaction with a peer, cooperate in play, and respond to another child with friendly emotion and approval. Several of these programs have produced gains in social competence and peer acceptance still present from several weeks to a year later (Asher & Rose, 1997; DeRosier, 2007). Combining social-skills training with other treatments increases their effectiveness. Rejected children often are poor students, and their low academic self-esteem magnifies their negative reactions to teachers and classmates (O'Neil et al., 1997). Intensive academic tutoring improves both school achievement and social acceptance (Coie & Krehbiel, 1984).

Still another approach focuses on training in perspective taking and social problem solving (see Chapter 11). Many rejected-aggressive children are unaware of their own social ineffectiveness and do not take responsibility for their social failures (Mrug, Hoza, & Gerdes, 2001). Rejected-withdrawn children, in contrast, are likely to develop a *learned-helpless* approach to peer difficulties. They tend to conclude, after repeated rebuffs, that they will never be liked (Wichmann, Coplan, & Daniels, 2004). Both types of rejected children need help attributing their peer difficulties to internal, changeable causes.

Finally, because rejected children's socially incompetent behaviors often originate in a poor fit between the child's temperament and parenting practices, treatments focusing on the child alone may not be sufficient. As early as the preschool years, rejected children engage in similarly inept communication with parents and peers (Black & Logan, 1995; Guralnick et al., 2007). Without interventions directed at improving the quality of parent–child interaction, rejected children will continue to practice poor interpersonal skills at home and, as a result, may soon return to their old behavior patterns.

Ask Yourself

Review Why are rejected children at risk for maladjustment? What experiences with peers probably contribute to their serious, long-term adjustment problems?

Apply Each day on the school bus and during recess, Jodee—a quiet, sensitive fifth grader—was pushed, pelted with gravel, and showered with insults by her classmates. Following the advice of her well-meaning parents, she tried to ignore her tormentors. What factors made Jodee susceptible to peer victimization? How can it be prevented?

Connect Cite parenting influences on children's social skills, and explain why interventions that focus only on the rejected child are unlikely to produce lasting changes in peer acceptance (see pages 608–609). What changes in parent–child relationships are probably necessary?

Reflect Name several classmates from your high school days who were high in *social prominence*—admired by many peers. Describe these classmates' attributes. Were they also *socially preferred*—that is, peers whom you and your friends liked personally? Explain.

Peer Groups

TAKE A MOMENT... Watch children in the schoolyard or neighborhood, and notice how groups of three to a dozen or more often gather. In what ways are members of the same group noticeably alike?

By the end of middle childhood, children display a strong desire for group belonging. They form **peer groups,** collectives that generate unique values and standards for behavior and a social structure of leaders and followers. Whereas friendships contribute to the development of trust, sensitivity, and intimacy, peer groups provide practice in cooperation, leadership, followership, and loyalty to collective goals. Through these experiences, children experiment with and learn about the functioning of social organizations.

Peer groups first form in middle childhood. These girls have probably established a social structure of leaders and followers as they gather for joint activities. Their relaxed body language and similar way of dressing suggest their strong sense of group belonging. © Philip & Karen Smith/ Getty Images/Iconica

First Peer Groups

Peer groups organize on the basis of proximity (being in the same classroom) and similarity in sex, ethnicity, academic achievement, popularity, and aggression (Rubin, Bukowski, & Parker, 2006). When groups are tracked for three to six weeks, membership changes very little. When they are followed for a year or longer, substantial change can occur, depending on whether children are reshuffled into different classrooms. When children remain together, 50 to 70 percent of groups consist mostly of the same children from year to year (Cairns, Xie, & Leung, 1998).

The practices of these informal groups lead to a "peer culture" that typically involves a specialized vocabulary, dress code, and place to "hang out" during leisure hours. As children develop these exclusive associations, the codes of dress and behavior that grow out of them become more broadly influential. Schoolmates who deviate—by "kissing up" to teachers, wearing the wrong kind of shoes, or tattling on classmates—are often rebuffed, becoming targets of critical glances and comments. These customs bind peers together, creating a sense of group identity.

School-age children evaluate a group's decision to exclude a peer in complex ways. Most view exclusion as wrong, even when they see themselves as different from the excluded child. And with age, children are less likely to endorse excluding someone because of unconventional appearance or behavior. Girls, especially, regard exclusion as unjust, perhaps because they experience it more often than boys (Killen, Crystal, & Watanabe, 2002). But when a peer threatens group functioning, by acting disruptively or by lacking skills to participate in a valued group activity (such as sports), both boys and girls say that exclusion is justified—a perspective that strengthens with age (Killen & Stangor, 2001).

Despite these sophisticated understandings, as we have seen here and in previous chapters, children do exclude unjustly, often using relationally aggressive tactics. Peer groups—at the instigation of their leaders, who can be skillfully aggressive—frequently oust no-longer-"respected" children. Some, whose own previous hostility toward outsiders reduces their chances of being included elsewhere, turn to other low-status peers with poor social skills (Werner & Crick, 2004). Socially anxious children, when ousted, often become increasingly peer-avoidant and thus more isolated (Gazelle & Rudolph, 2004). In either case, opportunities to acquire socially competent behavior diminish.

As excluded children's class participation declines, their academic achievement suffers (Buhs, Ladd, & Herald, 2006). And some aggressive children—especially popular boys—link up with popular, nonaggressive agemates (Bagwell et al., 2000; Farmer et al., 2002). In these groups, mild-mannered children may accept and even support the antisocial acts of their dominant, antisocial associates, who pick fights with other groups or bully weaker children. To reduce peer aggression, teachers and counselors must target both antisocial and mixed peer groups.

School-age children's desire for group belonging also can be satisfied through formal group ties such as scouting, 4-H, and religious youth groups, where adult involvement holds in check the negative behaviors associated with children's informal peer groups. And through working on joint projects and helping in their communities, children gain in social and moral maturity (Killen & Nucci, 1995; Vandell & Shumow, 1999).

Cliques and Crowds

The peer groups of the early teenage years are more tightly structured than those of middle childhood. They are organized into **cliques,** groups of about five to seven members who are friends and, therefore, tend to resemble one another in family background, attitudes, values, and interests. In early adolescence, cliques are limited to same-sex members. Among girls but not boys, being in a clique predicts academic and social competence. Clique membership is more important to girls, who use it as a context for expressing emotional closeness (Henrich et al., 2000). By mid-adolescence, mixed-sex cliques become common.

Often several cliques with similar values form a larger, more loosely organized group called a **crowd.** Unlike the more intimate clique, membership in a crowd is based on reputation and stereotype, granting the adolescent an identity within the larger social structure of the school. Prominent crowds in a typical high school might include "brains" (nonathletes who enjoy academics), "jocks" (who are very involved in sports), "populars" (class leaders who are highly social and involved in activities), "partyers" (who value socializing but care little about schoolwork), "nonconformists" (who like unconventional clothing and music), "burnouts"(who cut school and get into trouble), and "normals" (average to good students who get along with most other peers) (Kinney, 1999; Stone & Brown, 1999).

These high school cheerleaders form a crowd. Unlike the more intimate clique, the larger, more loosely organized crowd grants adolescents an identity within the larger social structure of the school.
© Peter Hvizdak/The Image Works

What influences the sorting of adolescents into cliques and crowds? Crowd affiliations are linked to strengths in their self-concepts, which reflect their abilities and interests (Prinstein & La Greca, 2004). Family factors are important, too. In a study of 8,000 ninth to twelfth graders, adolescents who described their parents as authoritative tended to be members of "brain," "jock," and "popular" groups that accepted both adult and peer reward systems. In contrast, boys with permissive parents aligned themselves with "partyers" and "burnouts," suggesting lack of identification with adult reward systems (Durbin et al., 1993).

These findings indicate that many peer group values are extensions of ones acquired at home. Once adolescents join a clique or crowd, it can modify their beliefs and behaviors. In research on the relationship between crowd affiliation and health-risk behaviors, brains were the lowest risk takers, populars and jocks were intermediate, and nonconformists and burnouts were the highest, often engaging in unhealthy eating, substance use, and unprotected sex and agreeing that they would "do anything on a dare" (LaGreca, Prinstein, & Fetter, 2001; Mackey & La Greca, 2007). But the positive impact of having competent, self-controlled peers is greatest for teenagers whose own parents are authoritative. And the negative impact of associating with antisocial, drug-using agemates is strongest for teenagers whose parents use less effective child-rearing styles (Mounts & Steinberg, 1995). In sum, family experiences affect the extent to which adolescents become like their peer associates over time.

As interest in dating increases, boys' and girls' cliques come together. Mixed-sex cliques provide boys and girls with models for how to interact with the other sex and a chance to do so without having to be intimate (Connolly et al., 2004). Gradually, the larger group divides into couples, several of whom spend time going out together. By late adolescence, when boys and girls feel comfortable enough about approaching each other directly, the mixed-sex clique disappears (Connolly & Goldberg, 1999).

Crowds also decline in importance. As adolescents settle on personal values and goals, they no longer feel a need to broadcast, through dress, language, and preferred activities, who they are. From tenth to twelfth grade, about half of young people switch crowds, mostly in favorable directions. "Brains" and "normal" crowds grow and deviant crowds lose members as teenagers focus more on their future (Strouse, 1999). Rewarding prosocial friendships and gains in self-esteem are associated with these changes.

Dating

The hormonal changes of puberty increase sexual interest (see Chapter 5), but cultural expectations determine when and how dating begins. Asian youths start dating later and have fewer dating partners than young people in Western societies, which tolerate and even encourage early romantic involvements from middle school on (see Figure 15.3 on page 622). At age 12 to 14, these relationships last, on average, only five months, but at age 16 and older, they

■ **Figure 15.3** **Increase in romantic relationships during adolescence.**
More than 16,000 American youths responded to an interview in which they indicated whether they had been involved in a romantic relationship during the past 18 months. Romantic involvements increased steadily with age. At age 12, about one-fourth of young people reported them, a figure that rose to about three-fourths at age 18. (Adapted from Carver, Joyner, & Udry, 2003.)

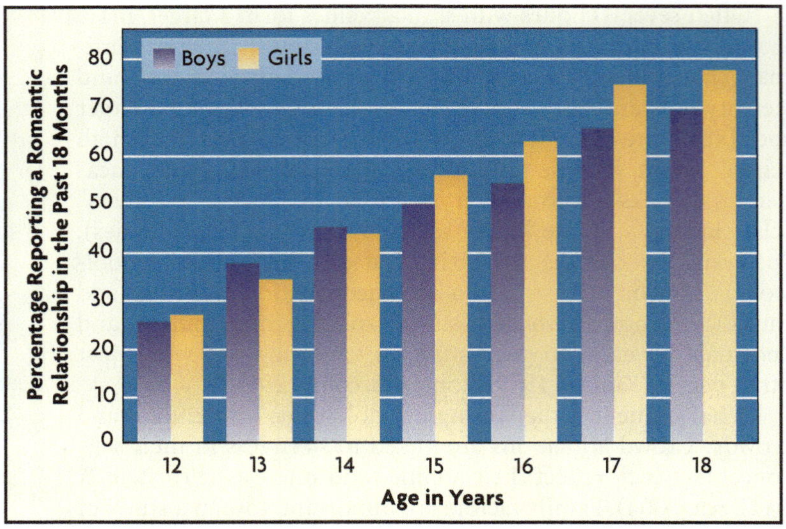

continue for nearly two years (Carver, Joyner, & Udry, 2003). This change reflects transformations in teenagers' dating goals: Early adolescents date largely for superficial reasons—recreation, peer status, and exploration of sexuality. By late adolescence, young people are ready for greater psychological intimacy and seek dating partners who offer personal compatibility, companionship, affection, and social support (Brown, 2004; Collins & Van Dulmen, 2006a).

Achievement of intimacy between dating partners typically lags behind that of friends. And positive relationships with parents and friends contribute to the development of warm romantic ties, whereas conflict-ridden parent–adolescent and peer relationships forecast hostile dating interactions (Connolly, Furman, & Konarski, 2000; Linder & Collins, 2005). Recall from Chapter 10 that, according to ethological theory, early attachment bonds lead to an *internal working model,* or set of expectations about attachment figures, that guides later close relationships. Consistent with this idea, secure attachment to parents in infancy and childhood—together with recollections of that security in adolescence—predicts quality of teenagers' and young adults' friendships and romantic ties (Collins & Van Dulmen, 2006b; Weimer, Kerns, & Oldenburg, 2004). In a study of high school seniors, supportive interactions with parents, and secure models of attachment to parents, predicted adolescents' warm interaction with friends and secure models of friendship. Teenagers' images of friendship security, in turn, were related to their images of security in romantic relationships (Furman et al., 2002).

As long as dating does not begin too soon, it extends the benefits of adolescent friendships, promoting sensitivity, empathy, intimacy, self-esteem, identity development, and capacity to compromise. © Nico Kai/Getty Images/Iconica

Perhaps because early adolescent dating relationships are shallow and stereotyped, they do not foster social maturity. To the contrary, early, frequent dating is related to drug use, delinquency, and poor academic achievement (Eaton et al., 2007; Zimmer-Gembeck, Siebenbruner, & Collins, 2001). These factors, along with a history of uninvolved parenting and aggression in family and peer relationships, increase the likelihood of dating violence (Arriaga & Foshee, 2004; Cyr, McDuff, & Wright, 2006). About 10 to 20 percent of adolescents are physically or sexually abused by dating partners, with both boys and girls equally likely to report being victims and violence by one partner often returned by the other. Mental health consequences are severe, including increased anxiety, depression, suicide attempts, risky sexual behavior, and—in girls—unhealthy weight control (vomiting and use of laxatives) (Silverman et al., 2001; Werkele & Avgoustis, 2003). Furthermore, whereas early-adolescent boys who date gain in status among same-sex peers, girls often experience conflict due to competition and jealousy of other girls. For all these reasons, sticking with group activities, such as parties and dances, before becoming involved with a steady boyfriend or girlfriend is best for young teenagers.

Gay and lesbian youths face special challenges in initiating and maintaining visible romances. Their first dating relationships seem to be short-lived and to involve little emotional commitment for different reasons than those of heterosexuals: They fear peer harassment and rejection (Diamond & Lucas, 2004). Recall from Chapter 5 that because of intense prejudice, gay and lesbian adolescents often retreat into heterosexual dating. In addition, many have difficulty finding a same-sex partner because their homosexual peers have not yet come out. Often their first contacts with other sexual minority youths occur in support groups, where they are free to date publicly and can discuss concerns about coming out (Diamond, 2003).

When it does not begin too soon, dating provides lessons in cooperation, etiquette, and dealing with people in a wide range of situations. Among older teenagers, close romantic ties promote sensitivity, empathy, intimacy, self-esteem, and identity development. In addition, teenagers' increasing capacity for interdependence and compromise within dating probably enhances the quality of other peer relationships (Collins, 2003; Furman & Shaffer, 2003).

Still, first romances usually serve as practice for later, more mature bonds. About half of heterosexual romances do not survive graduation, and those that do usually become less satisfying (Shaver, Furman, & Buhrmester, 1985). Because young people are still forming their identities, high school couples often find that they have little in common later. Nevertheless, warm, caring romantic ties in adolescence can have long-term implications. In a German study, they were positively related to gratifying, committed relationships in early adulthood (Seiffge-Krenke, 2003).

Peer Pressure and Conformity

Conformity to peer pressure is greater in adolescence than in childhood or early adulthood—a finding that is not surprising when we consider how much time teenagers spend together. But contrary to popular belief, adolescence is not a period in which young people blindly do what their peers ask. Peer conformity is a complex process that varies with the adolescent's age, current situation, need for social approval, and culture.

A study of several hundred U.S. middle and high school students revealed that adolescents felt greatest pressure to conform to the most obvious aspects of the peer culture—dress, grooming, and participation in social activities. Peer pressure to engage in proadult behavior, such as cooperating with parents and getting good grades, was also strong (Brown, Lohr, & McClenahan, 1986). Many teenagers said that their friends actively discouraged antisocial acts. In similar research conducted in Singapore, a culture that emphasizes family loyalty, outcomes were much the same, except that peer pressure to meet family and school obligations exceeded pressure to join in peer-culture pursuits (Sim & Koh, 2003). As these findings reveal, adults and peers often act in concert, toward desirable ends!

These teenagers conform to peer expectations in matters of dress and grooming. In more important areas, such as values and educational plans, their parents are probably more influential. © Jack Hollingsworth/Corbis

Perhaps because of greater concern with what their friends think of them, early adolescents are more likely than younger or older individuals to give in to peer pressure to engage in drug taking and delinquent acts (Brown, Clasen, & Eicher, 1986; McIntosh, MacDonald, & McKeganey, 2006). Yet when parents and peers disagree, even young teenagers do not consistently rebel against the family. Whereas peers exert more influence on teenagers' day-to-day personal choices, such as dress, music, and friendships, parents have more impact on basic life values and educational plans. Adolescents' personal characteristics also make a difference (Crockett, Raffaelli, & Shen, 2006; Steinberg, 2001). Young people who feel competent and worthwhile, who score lower in sensation-seeking, and who are more effective decision makers are less likely to fall in line with peers who engage in early sex, delinquency, and frequent drug use (see the From Research to Practice box on pages 624–625).

▪ *From* Research *to* Practice ▪

Adolescent Substance Use and Abuse

In industrialized nations, teenage alcohol and drug use is pervasive, rising steadily over adolescence. According to the most recent nationally representative survey of U.S. high school students, by tenth grade, 40 percent of U.S. young people have tried smoking, 63 percent drinking, and 38 percent at least one illegal drug (usually marijuana). At the end of high school, 17 percent smoke cigarettes regularly, 28 percent have engaged in heavy drinking during the past two weeks, and over 40 percent have experimented with illegal drugs. About 20 percent have tried at least one highly addictive and toxic substance, such as amphetamines, cocaine, phencyclidine (PCP), Ecstasy (MDMA), inhalants, heroin, sedatives (including barbiturates), or OxyContin (a narcotic painkiller). Canadian rates of teenage alcohol and drug use are similar (Johnson et al., 2006; Public Health Agency of Canada, 2007a, 2007b; Statistics Canada, 2006a).

These figures represent a substantial decline in overall drug use since the mid-1990s, probably resulting from greater societal focus on the hazards of drug taking. But use of inhalants, sedatives, and OxyContin has risen in recent years (Johnson et al., 2006). And certain drugs, such as LSD, PCP, and Ecstasy, have made a comeback as adolescents' knowledge of their risks faded.

In part, drug taking reflects the sensation seeking of the teenage years. But adolescents also live in drug-dependent cultural contexts. They see adults using caffeine to wake up in the morning, alcohol and cigarettes to cope with daily hassles, and other remedies to relieve stress, depression, and physical discomfort. And compared to a decade or two ago, today doctors more often prescribe—and parents frequently seek—medication to treat children's problems (Brody, 2006). When these young people reach adolescence, they may readily "self-medicate" in the face of stress.

Most teenagers who dabble in alcohol, tobacco, and marijuana are not headed for a life of addiction. Rather, these *minimal experimenters* are usually psychologically healthy, sociable, curious young people (Shedler & Block, 1990). As Figure 15.4 shows, tobacco and alcohol use is somewhat greater among European than among U.S. adolescents, perhaps because European adults more often smoke and drink. But illegal drug use is far more prevalent among U.S. teenagers (Hibell, 2001). A greater percentage of American young people live in poverty, which is linked to family and peer contexts that promote illegal drug use. At the same time, use of diverse drugs is lower among African Americans than among Hispanic and Caucasian Americans; Native-American and Canadian-Aboriginal youths rank highest in drug taking (RHS National Team, 2007; van der Woerd & Cox, 2001; Wallace et al., 2003). Researchers have yet to explain these variations.

Regardless of type of drug, adolescent drug experimentation should not be taken lightly. Because most drugs impair perception and thought processes, a single heavy dose can lead to permanent injury or death. And a worrisome minority of teenagers move from substance *use* to *abuse*—taking drugs regularly, requiring increasing amounts to achieve the same effect, moving to harder substances, and using enough to impair their ability to meet school, work, or other responsibilities.

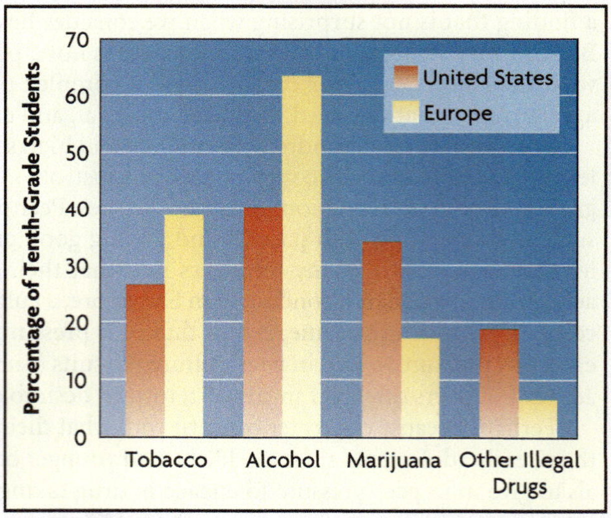

Figure 15.4 **Tenth-grade students in the United States and Europe who have used various substances.**
Rates for tobacco and alcohol are based on any use in the past 30 days. Rates for marijuana and other illegal drugs are based on any lifetime use. Tobacco use and alcohol use are greater for European adolescents, whereas illegal drug use is greater for American adolescents. (Adapted from Hibell, 2001; Johnson et al., 2006.)

Finally, authoritative child rearing is related to resistance to peer pressure. When their parents are supportive and exert appropriate oversight, teenagers respect them—an attitude that fosters mature autonomy and that acts as an antidote to unfavorable peer pressure under conditions of high life stress, such as poverty or divorce (Dorius et al., 2004). In contrast, adolescents who experience extremes of parental behavior—either too much or too little control—tend to be highly peer-oriented. Youths who bend easily to peer influence display wide-ranging problems, including unstable friendships, drug taking, aggression, delinquency,

Correlates and Consequences of Adolescent Substance Abuse

Unlike experimenters, drug abusers are seriously troubled young people who are impulsive, deficient in cognitive and emotional self-regulation, and inclined to express their unhappiness through antisocial acts. Longitudinal evidence reveals that their impulsive, disruptive, hostile styles often are evident during the preschool years. And compared with other young people, their drug taking starts earlier and may have genetic roots (Chassin et al., 2004; Ellickson et al., 2005). But environmental factors—low SES, family mental health problems, parental and older sibling drug abuse, lack of parental warmth and involvement, physical and sexual abuse, and poor school performance—also promote it. Especially among teenagers with family difficulties, encouragement from friends who use and provide access to drugs increases substance abuse and other antisocial behaviors (Goldstein, Davis-Kean, & Eccles, 2005; Prinstein, Boergers, & Spirito, 2001).

When teenagers depend on alcohol and hard drugs to deal with daily stresses, they fail to learn responsible decision-making skills and alternative coping techniques. They show serious adjustment problems, including chronic anxiety, depression, and antisocial behavior, that are both cause and consequences of heavy drug taking (Kassel et al., 2005; Simons-Morton & Haynie, 2003). And they often enter into marriage, childbearing, and the work world prematurely and fail at them—painful outcomes that further promote addictive behavior.

Prevention and Treatment

School and community programs that reduce drug experimentation typically combine several components:

- Promoting effective parenting, including monitoring of teenagers' activities
- Teaching adolescents skills for resisting peer pressure
- Reducing the social acceptability of drug taking by emphasizing health and safety risks
- Getting adolescents to commit to not using drugs (Cuijpers, 2002; Griffin et al., 2003).

But because some drug taking seems inevitable, interventions that prevent teenagers from harming themselves and others when they do experiment are essential. Many communities offer weekend on-call transportation services that any young person can contact for a safe ride home, with no questions asked. Providing appealing substitute activities, such as drug-free video arcades, dances, and sports activities, is also helpful.

Because drug abuse has different causes than occasional use, different prevention strategies are required. One approach is to work with parents early, reducing family adversity and improving child-rearing skills, before children are old enough for drug involvement (Velleman, Templeton, & Copello, 2005). Programs that teach at-risk teenagers effective strategies for handling life stressors and that build competence through community service reduce alcohol and drug abuse, just as they reduce teenage pregnancy (see Chapter 5).

When an adolescent becomes a drug abuser, family and individual therapy are generally needed to treat maladaptive parent–child relationships, impulsivity, low-self-esteem, anxiety, and depression. Academic and vocational training to improve life success also makes a difference. But even comprehensive programs have alarmingly high relapse rates—from 35 to 85 percent (Brown & Ramo, 2005; Waldron, Turner, & Ozechowski, 2005). One recommendation is to start treatment gradually, beginning with support-group sessions that focus on reducing drug taking. Within the group, interveners can address teenagers' low motivation to change and resistance to adult referral, which they often view as an infringement on their personal freedom. Such brief interventions lessen drug taking in the short term (Myers et al., 2001). Modest improvement may boost the young person's sense of self-efficacy for behavior change and, as a result, increase motivation to make longer-lasting changes through intensive treatment.

Peer encouragement is one environmental factor that predicts teenagers' alcohol and drug use. As a result, interventions that teach skills for resisting peer pressure reduce experimentation. © Bob Daemmrich/The Image Works

and declining peer popularity and increasing depressive symptoms over time (Allen, Porter, & McFarland, 2006). Under conditions of high life stress, such as poverty or divorce, supportive ties to parents or other caring, involved adults serve as a powerful antidote to unfavorable peer pressures (Masten, 2001).

Before we turn to the impact of media on children and adolescents, you may find it helpful to examine the Milestones table on page 626, which summarizes the development of peer relations.

Milestones

Development of Peer Relations

Age	Peer Sociability	Friendship	Peer Groups
Birth–2 years	■ Isolated social acts increase and are gradually replaced by coordinate interaction.	■ Mutual relationships with familiar peers emerge.	
2½–6 years	■ Parallel play appears, remains stable, and becomes more cognitively mature. ■ Cooperative play increases, especially sociodramatic play. ■ Rough-and-tumble play emerges.	■ Friendship is viewed concretely, in terms of play and sharing toys. 	
7–11 years	■ Peer communication skills improve as a result of increased awareness of others' perspectives and of emotional display rules. ■ Ability to understand the complementary roles of several players improves, permitting the transition to rule-oriented games. ■ Peer interaction becomes more prosocial. ■ Rough-and-tumble play increases.	■ Friendship is based on mutual trust and assistance. ■ Interaction between friends becomes more prosocial. ■ Number of close friends declines. ■ Friends increasingly resemble one another in personality, popularity, academic achievement, and prosocial behavior.	■ Peer groups emerge. 
12–18 years	■ Peer interaction becomes more cooperative. ■ Rough-and-tumble play declines. ■ Time spent with peers increases, exceeding that with any other social partners. 	■ Friendship is based on intimacy, mutual understanding, and loyalty. ■ Friends tend to be alike in identity status, educational aspirations, political beliefs, and deviant behavior. ■ Young people choose some friends who differ from themselves. ■ Number of close friends declines further.	■ Peer groups become more tightly structured, organized around cliques. ■ Cliques with similar values form crowds. ■ As interest in dating increases, mixed-sex cliques form. ■ Romantic relationships emerge and gradually last longer. ■ Conformity to peer pressure increases, then declines.

Note: These milestones represent overall age trends. Individual differences exist in the precise age at which each milestone is attained.

Photos: (left) © Brand X Pictures/Getty Images; (middle) © Stock Connection Distribution/Alamy; (top right) © Richard Hutchings/PhotoEdit; (bottom right) © Michael Newman/PhotoEdit

Ask Yourself

Review Describe the distinct positive functions of friendships, cliques, and crowds. What factors lead some friendships and peer-group ties to be harmful?

Apply Thirteen-year-old Mattie's parents are warm, firm in their expectations, and consistent in monitoring her activities. At school, Mattie met some girls who want her to tell her parents that she's going to a friend's house and then, instead, to join them at the beach for a party. Is Mattie likely to comply? Explain.

Connect How might gender intensification, discussed on page 546 in Chapter 13, contribute to the shallow quality of early adolescent dating relationships?

Reflect How did family experiences influence your crowd membership in high school? How did your crowd membership influence your behavior?

Media

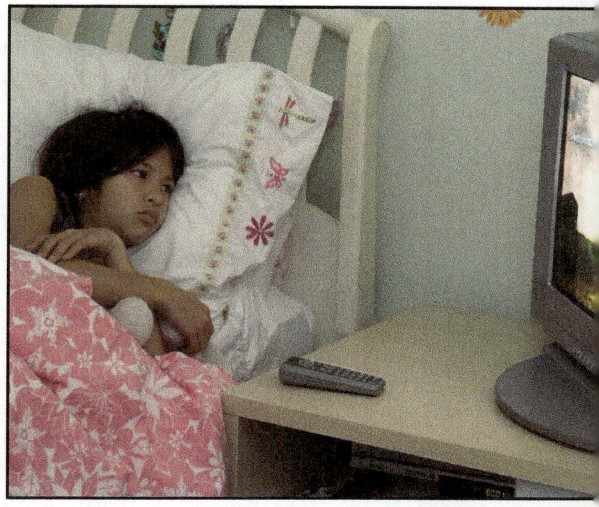

Children with a television set in their bedroom spend considerably more time watching TV. Their parents have less opportunity to monitor and control both the quantity and the quality of their viewing time. © David Young-Wolff/ PhotoEdit

During the past half-century. the role of media in the lives of children and adolescents has undergone "revolutionary change" (Comstock & Scharrer, 2006; Roberts & Foehr, 2004). Although television remains the dominant form of youth media, computers now exist in most North American homes and in virtually all school classrooms. A burgeoning research literature addresses the wide-ranging impact of media on development.

Television

Exposure to television is almost universal in the industrialized world. Nearly all homes have at least one television set, and most have two or more. Average time spent watching is remarkably similar across developed nations, and young people in the developing world are not far behind (Comstock & Scharrer, 2001; Scharrer & Comstock, 2003).

Widespread concern about television's impact on children's development is certainly warranted. In an unusual investigation, residents of a small Canadian town were studied just before TV reception became available in their community and again two years later. Striking changes occurred: In school-age children, a decline in reading ability and creative thinking, a rise in gender-stereotyped beliefs, and an increase in verbal and physical aggression during play; in adolescents, a sharp drop in community participation (Williams, 1986).

But television has equal potential for good. If the content of TV programming were improved and adults capitalized on it to enhance children's interest in their everyday worlds, television could be a powerful, cost-effective means of strengthening cognitive, emotional, and social development.

• **How Much Television Do Children View?** Large surveys reveal that North American children first become viewers in early infancy. About 40 percent of U.S. 3-month-olds regularly watch either TV, videos, or DVDs, a figure that rises to 90 percent by age 2, a period during which average viewing increases from just under an hour to 1½ hours a day (Zimmerman, Christakis, & Meltzoff, 2007). Between 2 and 6 years, the typical North American preschooler watches from 1½ to 2⅔ hours a day, depending on the survey. In middle childhood, viewing increases to an average of 3½ hours a day for U.S. children and 2½ hours for Canadian children. Then, in adolescence, viewing declines, to 2¾ hours in the United States and just under 2 hours in Canada (Rideout & Hamel, 2006; Scharrer & Comstock, 2003; Statistics Canada, 2005f, 2006e).

These figures reveal that each week, U.S. school-age children devote about 24 hours to TV, Canadian children 17½ hours. When we add the time the set is on during school holidays and summer vacations, children and adolescents spend more time with television than in most other waking activities, including parent and peer interaction, physical activity, computer use, homework, and reading (see Figure 15.5).

Figure 15.5 Time spent watching TV compared with time spent engaged in other pursuits by U.S. 8- to 18-year-olds. In this survey of a nationally representative sample of more than 2,000 U.S. school-age children and adolescents, TV emerged as the dominant activity. Despite the rise of the Internet, TV consumed far more time than recreational computer use. (Adapted from Roberts, Foehr, & Rideout, 2005.)

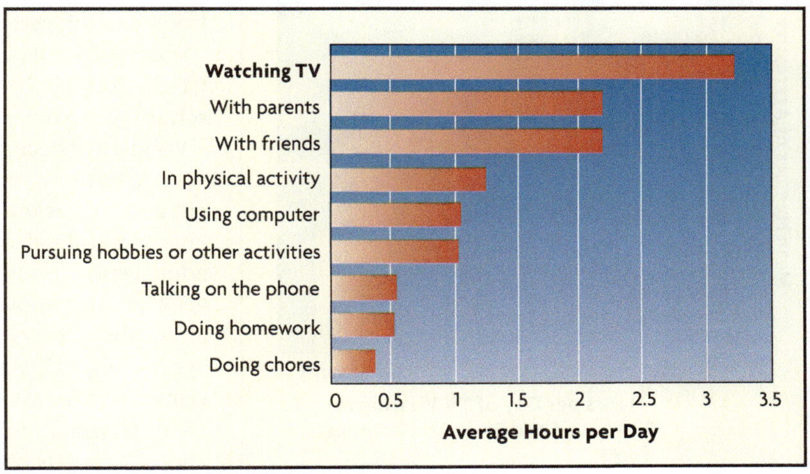

Children vary in their attraction to television. From early childhood on, boys watch slightly more than girls. Low-SES children also are more frequent viewers, perhaps because few alternative forms of entertainment are available in their neighborhoods or are affordable for their families. Also, parents with limited education are more likely to engage in practices that heighten TV viewing, including eating family meals in front of the set and failing to limit children's TV access (Hesketh et al., 2007). About one-third of U.S. preschoolers and two-thirds of school-age children and adolescents have a TV set in their bedroom; these children spend from 40 to 90 more minutes per day watching than agemates without one. And if parents watch a lot of

TV, their children usually do, too (Rideout & Hamel, 2006; Roberts, Foehr, & Rideout, 2005). Extensive TV viewing is associated with family and peer difficulties, perhaps because highly stressed parents and children use it as an escape (Anderson et al., 1996).

• Children's Understanding of Televised Information Even young preschoolers have some awareness that a TV image can represent reality. In several studies, 24-month-olds could use a video of an object being hidden to find that object in a real room (Schmitt & Anderson, 2002; Suddendorf, 2003). But this understanding is fragile: In another investigation, 2- and 3-year-olds said that a bowl of popcorn on TV would spill if the TV were turned upside down and that people could reach in and pick up the objects shown on the screen (Flavell et al., 1990). By age 4, children realize that TV is symbolic. But in judging whether TV images correspond to real-world events, they consider all human actors "real" and all cartoon characters "unreal." Around age 5, they make finer discriminations, saying that news and documentaries depict real events, while fictional programs are "just for TV." Not until age 7 do children fully grasp the unreality of TV fiction—that characters are following a script and do not retain their roles in real life (Wright et al., 1994).

Before age 8, children have difficulty connecting separate TV scenes into a meaningful story line. Consequently, they often fail to detect motives or consequences and may judge villains and their aggressive actions favorably (Collins, 1983). Preschool and young elementary school children's incomplete grasp of televised information and inability to critically evaluate it increase the chances that they will believe and imitate what they see.

• Television and Social Learning Since the 1950s, researchers and public citizens have been concerned about television's influence on the attitudes and behaviors of young viewers. Most studies address the impact of TV violence. Others focus on the power of TV to teach undesirable gender and ethnic stereotypes and consumerism. At the same time, research confirms TV's potential for enhancing children's prosocial behavior.

Aggression. In the United States, 57 percent of TV programs between 6 A.M. and 11 P.M. contain violent scenes, often portraying repeated aggressive acts that go unpunished. Victims of TV violence are rarely seen experiencing serious harm, and few programs condemn violence or depict other ways of solving problems. Violent content is 9 percent above average in children's programming, and cartoons are the most violent (Center for Communication and Social Policy, 1998). Although Canadian broadcasters follow a code that sharply restricts televised violence, English-speaking Canadians devote two-thirds of their viewing time to U.S. channels (Statistics Canada, 2005f). French-speaking Canadians, however, tune to U.S. channels less than one-third of the time (Statistics Canada, 2006e). Consequently, children in the province of Québec view substantially less TV violence than other Canadian children.

Reviewers of thousands of studies—using a wide variety of research designs, methods, and participants—have concluded that television violence increases the likelihood of hostile thoughts and emotions and of verbally, physically, and relationally aggressive behavior (Anderson et al., 2003; Comstock & Scharrer, 2006; Ostrov, Gentile, & Crick, 2006). Although young people of all ages are susceptible, preschool and young school-age children are especially likely to imitate TV violence because of their tendency to accept televised messages.

Violent programming not only creates short-term difficulties in parent and peer relations but also has lasting, negative consequences. In several longitudinal studies, time spent watching TV in childhood and early adolescence predicted aggressive behavior (including seriously violent acts) in later adolescence and adulthood—a relationship that persisted after other factors linked to TV viewing (such as prior child and parent aggression, IQ, parent education, family income, and neighborhood crime) were controlled (see Figure 15.6) (Graber et al., 2006; Huesmann, 1986; Huesmann et al., 2003; Johnson et al., 2002). Aggressive children and adolescents have a greater appetite for TV and other media violence.

■ Figure 15.6 Relationship of television viewing in childhood and early adolescence to aggressive acts in adolescence and early adulthood. Interviews with more than 700 parents and youths revealed that the more TV watched in childhood and early adolescence, the greater the annual number of aggressive acts committed by the young person, as reported in follow-up interviews at ages 16 and 22. (Adapted from Johnson et al., 2002.)

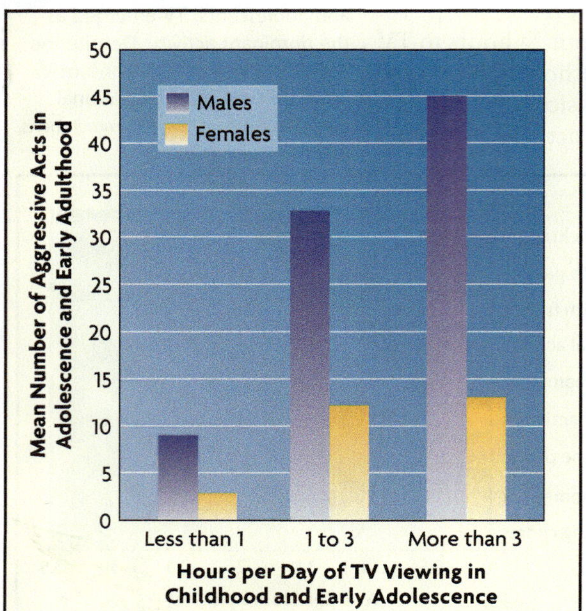

And boys devote more time to violent media than girls, in part because of male-oriented themes of conquest and adventure and use of males as lead characters. Even in nonaggressive children, violent TV sparks hostile thoughts and behavior; its impact is simply less intense (Bushman & Huesmann, 2001).

Furthermore, television violence "hardens" children to aggression, making them more willing to tolerate it in others (Anderson et al., 2003). Heavy viewers believe that much more violence occurs in society than is actually the case—an effect that is especially strong for children who perceive televised aggression to be relevant to their own lives (Donnerstein, Slaby, & Eron, 1994). As these responses indicate, violent television modifies children's attitudes toward social reality so that they increasingly match TV.

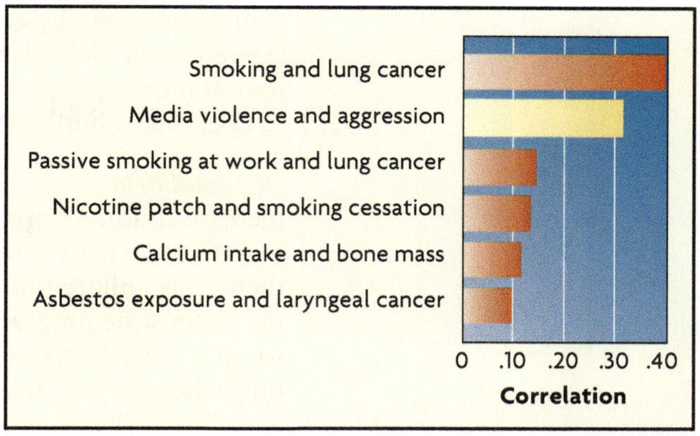

Figure 15.7 Comparison of the consequences of the media violence–aggression relationship with other widely accepted health effects. The correlation between media violence and aggression is almost as strong as the correlation between smoking and lung cancer. It is stronger than the correlation between other health behaviors and outcomes. (Adapted from B. J. Bushman & C. A. Anderson, 2001, "Media Violence and the American Public," *American Psychologist*, 56, p. 481. Reprinted by permission of B. J. Bushman and C. A. Anderson.)

The television industry has contested these findings, claiming that they are weak. But the correlation between media violence and aggression is nearly as high as the correlation between smoking and lung cancer, and higher than correlations between other widely accepted health factors and outcomes (see Figure 15.7). Because exposure to violent TV is so widespread, its impact can be profound even if only a small percentage of viewers are affected. Laboratory research shows that 15 minutes of mildly violent programming increases aggression in at least one-fourth of viewers (Anderson & Bushman, 2002).

Ethnic and Gender Stereotypes. Although educational programming for children is sensitive to issues of equity and diversity, commercial entertainment TV conveys ethnic and gender stereotypes. African Americans, Hispanics, and other ethnic minorities are underrepresented. When minorities do appear, they are more likely than whites to be depicted in secondary or lower-status roles, such as domestic workers or unskilled laborers, and as lawbreakers (Dixon & Azocar, 2006; Scharrer & Comstock, 2003). Similarly, women appear less often than men, especially as main characters. Compared with two decades ago, today's female characters are more often involved in careers. But they continue to be portrayed as young, attractive, caring, emotional, victimized, and in romantic and family contexts. In contrast, men are depicted as dominant and powerful (Signorielli, 2001). Gender stereotypes are especially prevalent in cartoons, music television (MTV), and other entertainment programs for children and youths.

TV viewing is linked to gender-stereotyped attitudes and behaviors in children and adolescents, including beliefs about men's and women's roles, career aspirations, body-image dissatisfaction, and girls' disordered eating (Cole & Daniel, 2005; Rivadeneyra & Ward, 2005). But nonstereotypic TV images reduce these biases. Positive portrayals of women and ethnic minorities lead to more favorable views and greater willingness to form ethnically diverse friendships (Calvert et al., 2003; Graves, 1993).

Consumerism. The marketing industry aimed at selling products to youths—toys, games, foods, clothing, and a host of other items—has exploded, tripling in corporate expenditures during the past decade, including funds devoted to TV advertising. On average, U.S. school-age children and adolescents watch about 30,000 TV commercials per year, Canadian children 23,000 (Gantz et al., 2007; Linn, 2004).

By age 3, children can distinguish an obvious TV ad from regular programming by its loudness, fast-paced action, and sound effects. But because many children's shows contain characters and props that are themselves products (dolls, puppets, action figures, and their accessories), the boundary between programs and commercials is blurred, making it impossible for young children to separate them. Furthermore, preschoolers and young elementary school children seldom grasp the selling purpose of TV ads; they think that commercials are meant to help viewers. Around age 8 or 9, most children understand that commercials are meant to sell, and by age 11, they realize that advertisers will resort to clever techniques to achieve their goals (Kunkel, 2001).

Nevertheless, even older children and adolescents find many commercials alluring. Research suggests that the heavy bombardment of children with advertising contributes to a variety of child and youth problems, including family stress, overweight and obesity, materialism, and substance use. In recent surveys of adults that included many parents, over 90 percent reported that youth-directed ads greatly increase children's nagging of parents to buy items, giving rise to family conflict (Linn, 2005). Furthermore, the greater adolescents' exposure to cigarette and alcohol ads—often designed to appeal to them through youthful characters, upbeat music, and party scenes—the more likely they are to smoke and drink (Austin, Chen, & Grube, 2006; Smith & Atkin, 2003).

Prosocial Behavior. Television that includes acts of cooperating, helping, and comforting can increase children's prosocial behavior. In one study, researchers asked more than 500 second to sixth graders to name their favorite educational TV shows and say what they learned from them. The children not only named many prosocial programs but also accurately described the lessons the programs conveyed (Calvert & Kotler, 2003). Much TV, however, mixes prosocial and antisocial messages. Prosocial programs promote children's kind and helpful acts only when they are free of violent content (Hearold, 1986).

• **Television, Academic Learning, and Imagination** Since the early days of television, educators have been interested in its potential for strengthening academic skills, especially among low-SES children. *Sesame Street,* especially, was created to foster children's learning. It uses lively visual and sound effects to stress basic literacy and number concepts and puppet and human characters to teach general knowledge, emotional and social understanding, and social skills. Today, *Sesame Street* is broadcast in more than 120 countries, making it the most widely viewed children's program in the world (Sesame Workshop, 2008).

Time devoted to watching children's educational programs is associated with gains in early literacy and math skills and to academic progress in elementary school (Ennemoser & Schneider, 2007; Linebarger et al., 2004; Wright et al., 2001). Consistent with these findings, the more children watch *Sesame Street,* the higher they score on tests designed to measure the program's learning goals (Fisch, Truglio, & Cole, 1999). One study reported a link between preschool viewing of *Sesame Street* and similar educational programs and getting higher grades, reading more books, placing more value on achievement, and scoring higher on a divergent-thinking test (a measure of creativity) in high school (Anderson et al., 2001). In recent years, *Sesame Street* has modified its rapid-paced format in favor of more leisurely episodes with a clear story line (Truglio, 2000). Watching children's programs with slow-paced action and easy-to-follow narratives, such as *Mr. Rogers' Neighborhood* and *Barney and Friends,* leads to more elaborate make-believe play than viewing programs that present quick, disconnected bits of information (Singer & Singer, 2005).

Does watching entertainment TV take children away from worthwhile activities? Some evidence suggests that it does. The more preschool and school-age children watch prime-time shows and cartoons, the less time they spend reading and interacting with others and the poorer their performance on tests of academic skills (Ennemoser & Schneider, 2007; Huston et al., 1999; Wright et al., 2001). In sum, whereas educational programs can be beneficial, watching entertainment TV—especially heavy viewing—detracts from children's school success and social experiences.

Computers

Unlike TV, computers offer *interactive* media forms, through a wide range of learning, entertainment, and communication tools (Greenfield & Yan, 2007). About 85 percent of North American children and adolescents live in homes with one or more computers, two-thirds of which have an Internet connection, usually a high-speed link. And virtually all U.S. and Canadian public schools have integrated computers into their instructional programs and can access the Internet—trends also evident in other industrialized nations (Statistics Canada, 2006d; U.S. Census Bureau, 2007b). Although higher-SES homes are more likely to have computers, 70 percent of lower-SES families in the United States and 55 percent in Canada now have them, often with Internet access (Judge, Puckett, & Bell, 2006; Statistics Canada, 2006b). Still, only a minority of poverty-stricken families have a home computer.

A survey of a nationally representative sample of more than 2,000 U.S. 8- to 18-year-olds revealed that children and adolescents, on average, used the computer a half-hour a day for schoolwork and an hour for pleasure—surfing the Web, communicating by e-mail or instant messaging, and accessing music, video, and computer games. Computer time rose with age and SES. More than half the respondents report being "media multitaskers" who engage in two or more media activities some or most of the time—having several computer activities going, using the computer while watching TV or listening to music, or doing all three at once (Media Awareness Network, 2001; Roberts, Foehr, & Rideout, 2005). Media multitasking greatly increases media exposure, but its impact on learning and behavior is not yet known.

Most parents say they purchased a computer to enrich their child's education; about one-third of North American children and adolescents have a computer in their bedroom. At the same time, parents express great concern about the influence of violent computer games and of the Internet (Media Awareness Network, 2001; Rideout & Hamel, 2006; Roberts, Foehr, & Rideout, 2005).

Regardless of the extent of their Internet use, not until ages 10 to 11 do children acquire an adult-level understanding of the technical complexity of the Internet as a networklike system in which computing centers link with many computers (see Figure 15.8). This technical grasp is important, as it precedes and probably contributes to sophisticated knowledge of social risks of the Internet (exposure to pornography, theft of personal information, attacks by hackers) and of protection strategies (firewalls, filtering programs, password protection), which is attained around ages 12 to 13 (Yan, 2006). Let's see how computers affect academic and social development.

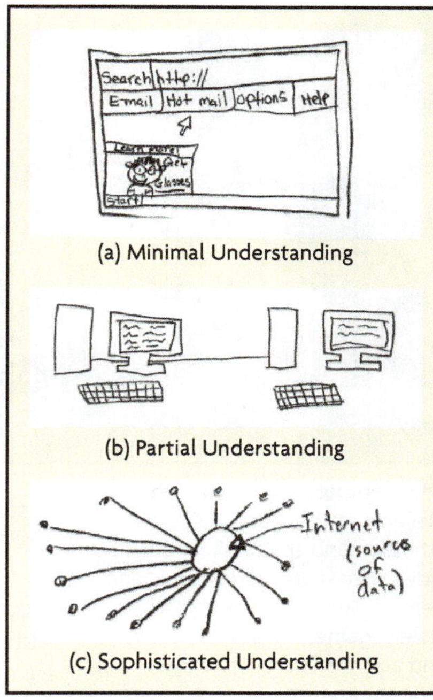

Figure 15.8 **Three children's drawings of the Internet, reflecting increased technical understanding with age.** When elementary school children were asked to describe and then to draw a picture of the Internet, their depictions revealed an age-related gain in appreciation of the Internet's technical complexity. Most children younger than age 10 had either a minimal understanding (viewed the Internet as one computer) or a partial understanding (viewed the Internet as a few computers with simple connections). Ten- and 11-year-olds usually had a sophisticated understanding (pictured the Internet as a network-like system in which computing centers link with multiple computers). (From Z. Yan, 2006, "What Influences Children's and Adolescents' Understanding of the Complexity of the Internet?" *Developmental Psychology*, 42, p. 421. Copyright © 2006 by the American Psychological Association. Reprinted with permission of the American Psychological Association.)

• **Computers and Academic Learning** Computers can have rich educational benefits. As early as age 3, children enjoy computer activities and are able to use the mouse and type simple keyboard commands. In classrooms, small groups often gather around computers, and children more often collaborate in computer activities than in other pursuits (Svensson, 2000).

In childhood and adolescence, nongame computer use is associated with literacy progress (Calvert et al., 2005; Statistics Canada and OECD, 2005). As soon as children begin to read and write, they can use the computer for word processing. It enables them to write freely, experimenting with letters and words without having to struggle with handwriting. Because they can revise their text's meaning and style and also check their spelling, they worry less about making mistakes. As a result, their written products tend to be longer and of higher quality. Often children jointly plan, compose, and revise text, learning from one another (Clements & Sarama, 2003).

As children get older, they increasingly use the computer for schoolwork, mostly to search the Web for information needed for school projects and to prepare written assignments—activities linked to improved academic achievement (Attewell, 2001; Judge, Puckett, & Bell, 2006). In one study, the more low-SES 13-year-olds used their home computers to access the Internet for information gathering (either for school or for personal interests), the better their subsequent reading achievement and school grades (Jackson et al., 2006). Perhaps youths who often search the Web also devote more time to reading, given that many Web pages are heavily text-based.

But despite their learning advantages, computers also raise concerns about a "digital divide" between gender and SES groups. Poverty-stricken children, whose academic performance is often below average, are least likely to have home computers and Internet access. And low-SES children who do have access devote less time to Internet use than their higher-SES counterparts (Jackson et al., 2006). Furthermore, in a Canadian survey of a nationally representative sample of 1,200 15- and 16-year-olds, boys more often than girls engaged in writing computer programs, analyzing data, and using spreadsheets and graphics programs. And many more boys than girls rated their computer skills as "excellent" (Looker & Thiessen, 2003). Schools need to ensure that girls and low-SES students have many opportunities to benefit from the cognitively enriching aspects of computer technology—not simply by equipping classrooms with more technology but also by providing the intensive teacher guidance and encouragement necessary to educate equitably and effectively with computers (Attewell, 2001).

• **Computers and Social Learning** Children and adolescents make extensive use of home computers for entertainment purposes, including games (especially among boys) and surfing the Web. Communicating electronically with friends rises sharply in adolescence, when instant messaging accounts for one-fourth of recreational computer time for boys and nearly one-third for girls (Roberts, Foehr, & Rideout, 2005).

These enthusiastic video game players may benefit in selective attention and spatial skills. But video games are full of ethnic and gender stereotypes, and playing violent games increases hostility and aggression. © OJO Images/SuperStock

Computer Games. Most computer games emphasize speed and action in violent plots in which children advance by shooting at and evading enemies. Children also play complex exploratory and adventure games, generally with themes of conquest and aggression, and sports games, such as football and soccer. And they enjoy simulation games in which players role-play characters in a virtual reality.

Speed-and-action computer games foster selective attention and spatial skills in boys and girls alike (Okagaki & Frensch, 1996; Subrahmanyam & Greenfield, 1996). Yet most game software is unappealing to girls because of its emphasis on violence and male-dominated sports. And an increasing number of studies show that playing violent games, like watching violent TV, increases hostility and aggression (Anderson, 2004). Furthermore, video games are full of ethnic and gender stereotypes (Dietz, 1998). Much less is known about the consequences of children's experiences in computerized virtual realities. Researchers speculate that depending on their content, some virtual-reality games may foster complex narrative skills and imagination, whereas others promote uncooperativeness, callousness, and antisocial acts (Singer & Singer, 2005).

Compared with infrequent users, "passionate" game players tend to be withdrawn young people who use games to escape from unpleasant family and school experiences. A few become addicted: They spend several hours a day playing, constantly think about playing when they are not, and believe they play too much but cannot cut back or stop (Salguero & Morán, 2002). Excessive playing of simulation games can blur the distinction between virtual and real life (Turkle, 1995). When such games are violent, they may contribute—along with disengaged parents, antisocial peers, and alienation from school—to commission of heinous acts by at-risk young people. Columbine High School teenage murderers Eric Harris and Dylan Klebold were obsessed with a game called *Doom,* in which players try to rack up the most kills (Subrahmanyam et al., 2001).

The Internet and Communication. Using the computer to communicate is a popular activity among adolescents. Instant messaging—teenagers' preferred means of online interaction—seems to support friendship closeness. Young people's "cyber slang," developed to facilitate communication and protect its privacy, has become a familiar part of popular culture—"gg" (gotta go), "mwah" (kiss), "lol" (laugh out loud), "brb" (be right back), "yt" (you there?), "pos" (parents over shoulder). As amount of instant messaging between preexisting friends increases, so do young people's perceptions of intimacy in the relationship and their feelings of well-being (Hu et al., 2004; Valkenburg & Peter, 2007a, 2007b).

Although mostly communicating with friends they know, adolescents also use the Internet to meet new people, largely through chat rooms, blogs, and message boards (Lenhart, Madden, & Hitlin, 2005). As they strive for autonomy and identity, teenagers are drawn to establishing relationships in cyberspace, which opens up a vast array of possibilities beyond their families, schools, and communities. Through these online ties, young people explore central adolescent issues—sexuality, challenges in parent and peer relationships, and attitudes and values—in contexts that grant anonymity and, thus, may feel less threatening than similar conversations in the real world (Subrahmanyam, Greenfield, & Tynes, 2004; Subrahmanyam, Smahel, & Greenfield, 2006). Online interactions with strangers also offer some teenagers vital sources of support. Socially anxious youths, for example, may engage in Internet communication to relieve loneliness while practicing and improving their social skills. And teenagers suffering from depression, eating disorders, and other problems can access message boards where participants provide informal mutual assistance, including a sense of group belonging and acceptance (Whitlock, Powers, & Eckenrode, 2006).

For these young teenagers at a sleepover, sending text messages to friends adds to their fun and can support feelings of friendship closeness. © Katja Zimmermann/Getty Images/Taxi

But online communication also poses dangers. In unmonitored chat rooms, teenagers are likely to encounter degrading racial and ethnic slurs and sexually obscene and harassing remarks (Subrahmanyam, Smahel, & Greenfield, 2006; Tynes, Reynolds, & Greenfield, 2004). Furthermore, in a survey of a nationally representative sample of U.S. 10- to 17-year-old

Internet users, 14 percent said they had online close friendships or romances. Although some well-adjusted adolescents formed such bonds, many were youths who reported high levels of conflict with parents, peer victimization, depression, and delinquency, and who spent extensive time on the Internet (see Figure 15.9). They also more often had been asked by online friends for face-to-face meetings and had attended those meetings—without telling their parents (Wolak, Mitchell, & Finkelhor, 2003).

As these findings illustrate, troubled youths who use Internet communication to relieve feelings of isolation and rejection are especially vulnerable to exploitation. Adolescents who lack protective networks—family and friends with whom to discuss online encounters and appropriate and inappropriate online behaviors—may be overly trusting and may also find deceptions and harassment in Internet relationships particularly painful. Under these circumstances, Internet relationships may worsen their problems.

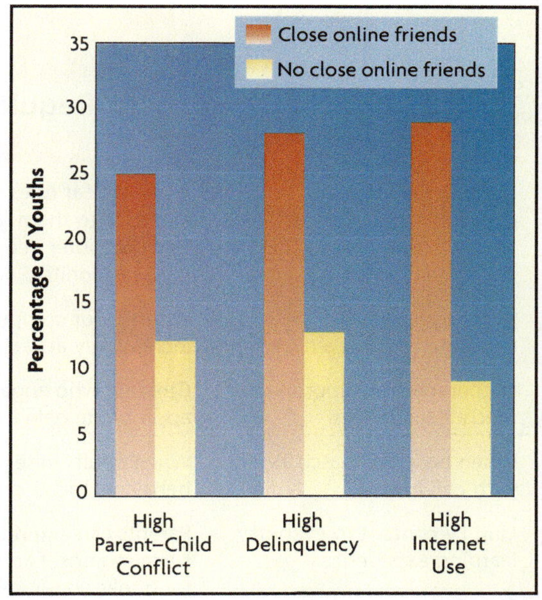

■ **Figure 15.9** **Association of close online friendships with parent–child conflict, delinquency, and high Internet use.** In this survey of a nationally representative sample of 1,500 U.S. Internet-using 10- to 17-year-olds, those who reported that they had formed close online friendships or romances were more likely to be troubled youths who spent much time on the Internet. (Adapted from Wolak, Mitchell, & Finkelhor, 2003.)

Regulating Media Use

The potential for TV and computer media to negatively affect children's cognitive and social development has led to strong public pressures to improve media content. In the United States, the First Amendment right to free speech has hampered these efforts. At present, U.S. television is only minimally regulated to protect children. Broadcasters must provide three hours per week of educational and informational programming for children and must limit commercials in certain children's shows to 10½ minutes per hour (Children's Television Act, 1990). All programs must be rated for violent and sexual content, and manufacturers must build the V-chip (violence chip) into new TV sets to allow parents to block undesired material.

Canada mandates both the V-chip and program ratings. The province of Québec also prohibits commercial advertising directed at children (CRTC, 2007a). And Canada's nationwide broadcasting code bans from children's shows realistic scenes of violence that minimize consequences and cartoons with violence as the central theme. Further, violent programming intended for adults cannot be shown on Canadian channels before 9 P.M. (CRTC, 2007b). (As noted earlier, however, Canadian children can access violent TV fare on U.S. channels.)

At present, parents bear most responsibility for regulating their children's exposure to inappropriate media content. As with the V-chip for TV, parents can control children's Internet access by using filters or programs that monitor website visits. Yet surveys of U.S. parents and youths indicate that 20 to 30 percent of U.S. preschoolers, 40 percent of school-age children, and more than 50 percent of early adolescents experience no limits on TV or computer use at home. Some U.S. children begin accessing Internet websites without parental supervision as early as age 4 (Rideout & Hamel, 2006; Roberts, Foehr, & Rideout, 2005; Varnhagen, 2007). In contrast, most Canadian parents and youths report computer-use rules of some type—more often directed at regulating Internet access than at curbing hours of use (Spears, Seydegart, & Zulinov, 2005). Applying What We Know on page 000 lists strategies parents can use to protect their children from undesirable TV and computer fare.

Ask Yourself

Review Describe research findings on the academic and social benefits of television and computer use.

Apply Thirteen-year-old Tommy spends hours each afternoon surfing the Web, instant messaging with online friends he has never met, and playing computer games. Explain why his parents should intervene.

Connect Which subtypes of popular and rejected children, described on pages 000–000, are most likely to be attracted to violent TV? Explain.

Reflect How much and what kinds of television viewing and computer use did you engage in as a child and adolescent? Did your parents have rules about watching TV and using the computer, and did they enforce those rules? How do you think your home media environment influenced your development?

Applying What We Know

Regulating TV and Computer Use

Strategy	Explanation
Limit TV viewing and computer use.	Provide clear rules limiting what children and adolescents can view on TV and do on the computer—and stick to them. Avoid using the TV or the computer as a baby-sitter for children. Do not place a TV or a computer in a child's bedroom; doing so substantially increases use and makes the child's activity hard to monitor.
Avoid using TV or computer time as a reward.	When TV or computer access is used as a reward or withheld as a punishment, children become increasingly attracted to it.
Encourage child-appropriate media experiences.	Children who engage in TV and computer activities that are educational, prosocial, and age-appropriate gain in cognitive and social skills.
When possible, watch TV with children.	When adults raise questions about realism in TV depictions, express disapproval of on-screen behavior, and encourage discussion, they help children understand and evaluate TV content.
Link TV content to everyday learning experiences.	Parents can extend TV learning in ways that encourage children to engage actively with their surroundings. For example, a program on animals might spark a trip to the zoo, a visit to the library for books about animals, or new ways of observing and caring for the family pet.
Model good TV and computer practices.	Parents' media behavior—avoiding excessive TV and computer use and limiting exposure to harmful content—influences their children's media behavior.
Explain Internet technology and safety practices to school-age children and adolescents.	Children and adolescents who view the Internet as a networklike system are more likely to understand its social risks. They also benefit from instruction in appropriate online behavior and in the dangers of Internet communication, with emphasis on the greatest safety risks: revealing personal information and getting together with people they have "met" online. For online safety information for teenagers and parents, consult *Teen Safety on the Information Highway,* available at *www.safeteens.com.*
Use an authoritative approach to child rearing.	Children of warm, involved parents who make reasonable demands for mature behavior prefer media experiences with educational and prosocial content and are less likely to use the TV or computer as an escape.

Schooling

Unlike the informal world of peer relations, the school is a formal institution designed to transmit the knowledge and skills children need to become productive members of society. By high school graduation, children in the developed world have spent, on average, about 14,000 hours in school. As noted in earlier chapters, schools are vital forces in children's development, affecting their motivation to learn and modes of remembering, reasoning, problem solving, and social and moral understanding. How do schools exert such a powerful impact? Research looking at schools as complex social systems—class and student body size, educational philosophies, transitions from one school level to the next, teacher–student relationships, and grouping practices—provides important insights.

Class and Student Body Size

The physical plants of all schools tend to be similar: Each has classrooms, hallways, a playground, and a lunchroom. But they also vary widely in number of students in each class and in the school as a whole.

Is there an optimal class size? In a large field experiment, more than 6,000 Tennessee kindergartners were randomly assigned to three class types: "small" (13 to 17 students), "regular" (22 to 25 students) with only a teacher, and regular with a teacher plus a full-time teacher's aide. These arrangements continued into third grade. Small-class students—especially ethnic minority children—scored higher in reading and math achievement each year (Mosteller, 1995). Placing teachers' aides in regular-size classes had no impact. Rather, being in small classes from kindergarten through third grade predicted substantially higher achievement from fourth through ninth grades, after children had returned to regular-size classes. It also predicted greater likelihood of graduating from high school, particularly for low-income students (Finn, Gerber, & Boyd-Zaharias, 2005; Nye, Hedges, & Konstantopoulos, 2001).

Why is small class size beneficial? With fewer children, teachers spend less time disciplining and more time teaching and giving individual attention. Also, children who learn in smaller groups show better concentration, higher-quality class participation, and more favorable attitudes toward school (Blatchford et al., 2003, 2007; Blatchford, Bassett, & Brown, 2005). The impact of small class size on children's social behavior, however, is inconsistent and may depend on the extent to which teachers include social goals in their daily plans (NICHD Early Child Care Research Network, 2004b).

Once students reach secondary school, where they move from class to class and have access to many activities outside classroom instruction, the relevant physical context is the school as a whole. Student body size profoundly affects school life. Members of smaller schools consistently report more social support and caring. As one teacher at a large high school commented, "A huge problem here is our size. It breeds anonymity. It breeds disconnection. . . . There is no sense of identification" (Lee et al., 2000, p. 159).

Furthermore, schools with 500 to 700 students or less have fewer people to ensure that clubs, sports events, and social activities will function. As a result, young people enter a greater number and variety of activities and hold more positions of responsibility and leadership. In large schools, where plenty of students are available to fill activity slots, a smaller percentage—typically an elite who compete successfully for positions—are genuinely active (Barker & Gump, 1964; Feldman & Matjasko, 2007).

In view of these findings, it is not surprising that adolescents in small schools report a greater sense of personal responsibility, competence, and challenge from their extracurricular experiences. Participation focusing on the arts, community service, and vocational development promotes diverse aspects of adjustment, including improved academic performance, reduced antisocial behavior, more favorable self-esteem and initiative, and greater peer acceptance and concern for others (Fredricks & Eccles, 2005, 2006; Mahoney, 2000). Benefits extend into adult life (see also research on youth civic responsibility, Chapter 12, page 504). Young adults who were more involved in high school clubs and organizations achieved more in their occupations and engaged in more community service, after other possibly explanatory factors (including SES, IQ, and academic performance) were controlled (Obradović & Masten, 2007).

Adolescents with academic, emotional, and social problems are especially likely to profit from extracurricular pursuits that require them to take on meaningful roles and responsibilities (Mahoney & Cairns, 1997; Marsh & Kleitman, 2002). A special advantage of small schools is that potential dropouts are far more likely to join in activities, gain recognition, and remain until graduation. In large schools, reorganizations that create smaller "schools within schools" can have the same effect.

Educational Philosophies

Each teacher brings to the classroom an educational philosophy that plays a major role in children's learning. Two philosophical approaches have received most research attention. They differ in what children are taught, in the way they are believed to learn, and in how their progress is evaluated.

• Traditional versus Constructivist Classrooms In a **traditional classroom,** the teacher is the sole authority for knowledge, rules, and decision making and does most of the talking. Students are relatively passive—listening, responding when called on, and completing teacher-assigned tasks. Their progress is evaluated by how well they keep pace with a uniform set of standards for their grade.

▪ Social Issues ▪

School Recess—A Time to Play, a Time to Learn

When 7-year-old Whitney's family moved to a new city, she left a school with three daily recess periods for one with just a single 15-minute break per day, which her second-grade teacher cancelled if any child misbehaved. Whitney, who had previously enjoyed school, complained daily of headaches and an upset stomach. Her mother, Jill, thought, "My child is stressing out because she can't move all day!" After Jill and other parents successfully appealed to the school board to add a second recess period, Whitney's symptoms vanished (Rauber, 2006).

In recent years, recess—with its rich opportunities for child-organized play and peer interaction—has diminished or disappeared in many U.S. and Canadian elementary schools (Pellegrini, 2005; Pellegrini & Holmes, 2006). Under the assumption that extra time for academics will translate into achievement gains, 7 percent of U.S. schools no longer provide recess to students as young as second grade. And over half of schools that do have recess now schedule it just once a day (U.S. Department of Education, 2007).

Yet rather than subtracting from classroom learning, recess periods boost it! Research dating back more than a century confirms that distributing cognitively demanding tasks over a longer time by introducing regular breaks, rather than consolidating intensive effort within one period, enhances attention and performance at all ages. Such breaks are particularly important for children. In a series of studies, elementary school students were more attentive in the classroom after recess than before it—an effect that was greater for second than fourth graders (Pellegrini, Huberty, & Jones, 1995).

For school-age children, recess offers regular opportunities for unstructured play and games that promote academic achievement and social competence. © Toronto Star/FirstLight

In other research, kindergartners' and first graders' engagement in peer conversation and games during recess predicted gains in academic achievement, even after other factors that might explain the relationship (such as previous achievement) were controlled (Pellegrini, 1992; Pellegrini et al., 2002). Recall that children's social maturity contributes substantially to academic competence. Recess is one of the few remaining contexts devoted to child-organized games that provide practice in vital social skills—cooperation, leadership, followership, and inhibition of aggression—under adult supervision rather than adult direction. As children transfer these skills to the classroom, they may participate in discussions, collaborate, follow rules, and enjoy academic pursuits more—factors that enhance motivation and achievement.

A **constructivist classroom,** in contrast, encourages students to *construct* their own knowledge. Although constructivist approaches vary, many are grounded in Piaget's view of children as active agents who reflect on and coordinate their own thoughts, rather than absorbing those of others. A glance inside a constructivist classroom reveals richly equipped learning centers, small groups and individuals solving self-chosen problems, and a teacher providing guidance and support in response to children's needs. Students are evaluated by considering their progress in relation to their own prior development.

In North America, the pendulum has swung back and forth between these two views. In the 1960s and early 1970s, constructivist classrooms gained in popularity. Then, as concern arose over the academic progress of children and youths, especially in the United States, a "back to basics" movement arose. Classrooms returned to traditional instruction—a style increasingly emphasized today as a result of the rise in high-stakes testing (see page 342 in Chapter 8). To devote even more time to academic instruction, many schools have cut back on recess, despite its contribution to all domains of development (see the Social Issues box above).

The combined results of many studies reveal that older elementary school children in traditional classrooms have a slight edge in achievement test scores. But constructivist settings are associated with many other benefits—gains in academic motivation, critical thinking, social and moral maturity, and positive attitudes toward school (DeVries, 2001; Rathunde & Csikszentmihalyi, 2005; Walberg, 1986).

Despite grave concerns about its appropriateness, even preschool and kindergarten teachers have felt increased pressure to stress teacher-directed, academic training. Young children who spend much time passively sitting and doing worksheets, as opposed to being actively engaged in learning centers, display more stress behaviors (such as wiggling and rocking), have less confidence in their abilities, prefer less challenging tasks, and are less advanced in motor, academic, language, and social skills at the end of the school year (Marcon, 1999a; Stipek, 1995). Follow-ups reveal lasting effects through elementary school in poorer study habits and achievement (Burts et al., 1992; Hart et al., 1998, 2003). These outcomes are strongest for low-SES children, with whom teachers more often use an academic approach—a disturbing trend in view of its negative impact on motivation and emotional well-being (Stipek, 2004; Stipek & Byler, 1997).

In contrast, low-SES children experiencing *Montessori education*—a constructivist method devised a century ago by Italian physician Maria Montessori—reap many benefits. Features of Montessori schooling include multiage classrooms, teaching materials specially designed to promote exploration and discovery, long time periods for individual and small-group learning in child-chosen activities, and equal emphasis on academic and social development (Lillard, 2007b). In an evaluation of Montessori public preschools serving mostly urban minority children in Milwaukee, researchers compared students assigned by random lottery to Montessori classrooms with those in other classrooms (Lillard & Else-Quest, 2006). Five-year-olds who had completed two years of Montessori education outperformed controls on tests of literacy and math skills, cognitive flexibility, understanding of false belief, and social problem solving. On the playground, Montessori children more often engaged in positive joint play with classmates.

Nevertheless, the heavy emphasis on knowledge absorption as early as kindergarten has contributed to a growing trend among parents to delay their child's school entry. Traditional teaching may also increase the incidence of grade retention. For research on these issues, see the From Research to Practice box on page 638.

• New Philosophical Directions New approaches to education, grounded in Vygotsky's sociocultural theory, capitalize on the rich social context of the classroom to spur children's learning. In these **social-constructivist classrooms,** children participate in a wide range of challenging activities with teachers and peers, with whom they jointly construct understandings. As children *appropriate* (take for themselves) the knowledge and strategies generated from working together, they become competent, contributing members of their classroom community and advance in cognitive and social development (Bodrova & Leong, 2007; Palincsar, 2003). Vygotsky's emphasis on the social origins of complex mental activities has inspired the following educational themes:

- *Teachers and children as partners in learning.* A classroom rich in both teacher–child and child–child collaboration transfers culturally valued ways of thinking to children.
- *Experience with many types of symbolic communication in meaningful activities.* As children master reading, writing, and mathematics, they become aware of their culture's communication systems, reflect on their own thinking, and bring it under voluntary control.
- *Teaching adapted to each child's zone of proximal development.* Assistance that both responds to current understandings and encourages children to take the next step helps ensure that each student will make the best progress possible.

In Chapter 6, we considered two Vygotsky-inspired collaborative practices: reciprocal teaching and cooperative learning (see pages 269–271). Recognizing that collaboration requires a supportive context to be most effective, another Vygotsky-based innovation makes it a schoolwide value. Classrooms become **communities of learners** where teachers guide the overall process of learning but no other distinction is made between adult and child contributors: All participate in joint endeavors and have the authority to define and resolve problems. This approach is based on the assumption that different people have different expertises that can benefit the community and that students, too, may become experts (Sullivan & Glanz, 2006). Classroom activities are often long-term projects addressing complex, real-world problems. In working toward project goals, children and teachers draw on the expertises of one another and of others within and outside the school.

In social-constructivist classrooms grounded in Vygotsky's sociocultural theory, children engage in rich literacy activities with teachers and peers. Through jointly constructing understandings, students advance in cognitive and social development. © Lindfors Photography

From Research to Practice

School Readiness and Grade Retention

While waiting to pick up their sons from preschool, Susan and Vicky struck up a conversation about kindergarten enrollment. "Freddy will be 5 in August," Susan announced. "He's a month older than the cutoff date."

"But he'll be one of the youngest in the class," Vicky countered. "Better check into what kids have to do in kindergarten these days. Have you asked his teacher what she thinks?"

As he says good-bye on the first day of school, this father may wonder if his son is ready for classroom learning. Yet delaying kindergarten entry for a year has no demonstrated academic or social benefits. © Ariel Skelley/Corbis

"Well," Vicky admitted, "she did say Freddy was a bit young."

Since the 1980s, more parents have been delaying their child's kindergarten entry, a trend that has accelerated recently as academic expectations of kindergartners have increased. Aware that boys lag behind girls in development, parents most often hold out sons whose birth dates are close to the cutoff for enrolling in kindergarten. Is delaying kindergarten entry beneficial? Although some teachers and principals recommend it, research has not revealed any advantages. Younger children make just as much academic progress as older children in the same grade (Cameron & Wilson, 1990; Graue & DiPerna, 2000). And younger first graders reap academic gains from on-time enrollment, outperforming same-age children a year behind them (Stipek & Byler, 2001). Furthermore, a large longitudinal survey tracking U.S. students through high school and young adulthood showed that delaying kindergarten entry had no long-term academic or social benefits, in terms of achievement test scores, high school or college graduation, extracurricular participation, or prevention of behavior problems (Lincove & Painter, 2006).

A related dilemma concerns whether to retain a student for a second year in kindergarten or in one of the primary grades. A wealth of research reveals no learning benefits and suggests negative consequences for self-esteem, peer relations, school attitudes, academic motivation, and achievement (Hong & Raudenbush, 2005; Jimerson et al., 2006; Silberglitt et al., 2006). In a Canadian study, students retained between kindergarten and second grade—regardless of the academic and social skills they brought to the situation—showed worsening academic performance, anxiety, and (among boys) disruptiveness throughout elementary school (Pagani et al., 2001). These unfavorable trends did not characterize nonretained students.

As an alternative to kindergarten retention, some school districts place poorly performing children in a "transition" class—a way station between kindergarten and first grade. Transition classes, however, are a form of homogeneous grouping. As with other "low groups," teachers may have reduced expectations and may teach transition children in a less stimulating fashion than other children (Dornbusch, Glasgow, & Lin, 1996).

Each of these options is based on the view that school readiness results largely from biological maturation. An alternative perspective, based on Vygotsky's sociocultural theory, is that children acquire the knowledge, skills, and attitudes for school success through the assistance of parents and teachers. The U.S. National Association for the Education of Young Children recommends that all children of legal age start kindergarten and be provided with classroom experiences that foster their individual progress. Research confirms that school readiness is not something to wait for; it can be cultivated.

In one classroom, students studied animal–habitat relationships in order to design an animal of the future, suited to environmental changes. The class formed small research groups, each of which selected a subtopic—for example, defense against predators, protection from the elements, reproduction, or food getting. Each group member assumed responsibility for part of the subtopic, consulting diverse experts and preparing teaching materials. Then group members taught one another, assembled their contributions, and brought them to the community as a whole so the knowledge gathered could be used to solve the problem (Brown, 1997; Stone, 2005). The result was a multifaceted understanding of the topic that would have been too difficult and time-consuming for any learner to accomplish alone.

School Transitions

Besides size and educational philosophy, an additional structural feature of schooling contributes to student achievement and adjustment: the timing of transitions from one school level to the next. Entering kindergarten is a major milestone. Children must accommodate to new physical settings, adult authorities, daily schedules, peer companions, and academic challenges.

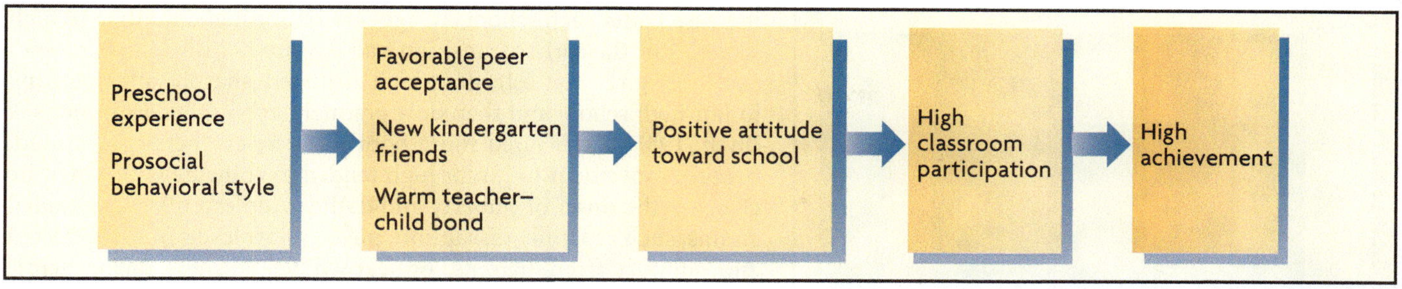

Figure 15.10 Factors linked to favorable adaptation to kindergarten.

• Early Adjustment to School In longitudinal research extending over the kindergarten year, children with more preschool experience scored higher on school readiness tests and showed increasingly positive school attitudes. Liking for school predicted greater classroom participation, which in turn predicted higher achievement. Furthermore, children with friendly, prosocial styles more easily made new friends, gained peer acceptance, and formed a warm bond with their teacher. These favorable relationships also predicted high achievement, perhaps by energizing cooperation and initiative in the classroom (Birch & Ladd, 1997; Ladd, Birch, & Buhs, 1999; Ladd, Buhs, & Seid, 2000; Ladd, Kochenderfer, & Coleman, 1997).

In contrast, kindergartners with argumentative, aggressive styles tended to establish conflict-ridden relationships with teachers and peers, which impaired their liking for school, classroom participation, and achievement. And peer-avoidant kindergartners often became overly dependent on teachers, clinging and asking for help they did not really need (Birch & Ladd, 1998). These early poor-quality teacher–child relationships predicted academic and behavior problems through elementary school (Hamre & Pianta, 2001).

Figure 15.10 summarizes factors linked to favorable adaptation to kindergarten. In a follow-up of more than 900 4-year-olds, children of average intelligence but with above-average social skills fared better in academic achievement in first grade than children of equal mental ability who were socially below average (Konold & Pianta, 2005). Because social maturity in early childhood contributes to later academic performance, a growing number of experts propose that readiness for kindergarten be assessed in terms of not just academic skills but also social skills, including capacity to form supportive bonds with teachers and peers, to participate actively and positively in interactions with classmates, and to behave prosocially (Ladd, Herald, & Kochel, 2006). Preschool interventions, too, should attend to these vital social prerequisites.

• School Transitions in Adolescence Early adolescence is another important period of school transition: Students typically move from an intimate, self-contained elementary school classroom to a much larger, impersonal secondary school where they must shift between classes. With each school change—from elementary to middle or junior high and then to high school—adolescents' grades decline. The drop is partly due to tighter academic standards. At the same time, the transition to secondary school often brings less personal attention, more whole-class instruction, and less chance to participate in classroom decision making (Seidman, Aber, & French, 2004).

In view of these changes, it is not surprising that students rate their middle or junior-high school learning experiences less favorably than their elementary school experiences (Wigfield & Eccles, 1994). They also report that their teachers care less about them, are less friendly, grade less fairly, and stress competition more and mastery and improvement less. Consequently, many young people feel less academically competent, and their liking for school and motivation decline (Barber & Olsen, 2004; Gutman & Midgley, 2000; Otis, Grouzet, & Pelletier, 2005).

Inevitably, students must readjust their feelings of self-confidence and self-worth as they encounter revised academic expectations and a more complex social world. A study following more than 300 students from sixth to tenth grade revealed that grade point average declined and feelings of anonymity

Moving from a small, self-contained elementary school classroom to a large, impersonal secondary school is stressful for adolescents. As this crowded hallway suggests, feelings of anonymity increase. Also, school attitudes and grades often decline.

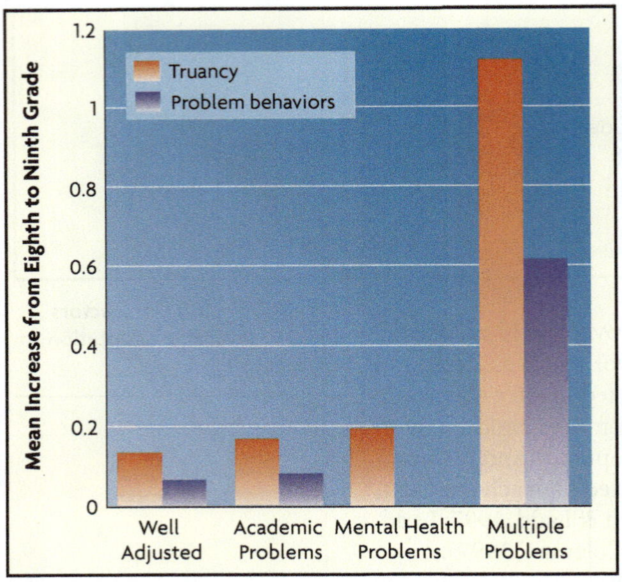

Figure 15.11 **Increase in truancy and out-of-school problem behaviors across the transition to high school in four groups of students.** Well-adjusted students, students with only academic problems, and students with only mental health problems showed little change. (Good students with mental health problems actually declined in problem behaviors, so no purple bar is shown for them.) In contrast, multiple-problem students—with both academic and mental health difficulties—increased sharply in truancy and problem behaviors after changing schools from eighth to ninth grade. (Adapted from Roeser, Eccles, & Freedman-Doan, 1999.)

increased after each school change—to junior high and then to high school. But the earlier transition had a more negative impact, especially on girls' self-esteem, which dropped sharply after starting junior high school and then only gradually rebounded (Simmons & Blyth, 1987). Girls fared more poorly, the researchers conjectured, because movement to junior high tended to coincide with other life changes: the onset of puberty and dating. Adolescents facing added strains, such as family disruption, poverty, low levels of involvement and support from parents, or learned helplessness on academic tasks, are at greatest risk for self-esteem and academic difficulties (de Bruyn, 2005; Rudolph et al., 2001; Seidman et al., 2003).

Distressed young people whose school performance either remains low or drops sharply after school transition often show a persisting pattern of poor self-esteem, motivation, and achievement. In another study, researchers compared "multiple-problem" youths (those having both academic and mental health problems), youths having difficulties in just one area (either academic or mental health), and well-adjusted youths (those doing well in both areas) across the transition to high school. Although all groups declined in grade point average, well-adjusted students continued to get high marks and multiple-problem youths low marks, with the others falling in between. And as Figure 15.11 shows, the multiple-problem youths showed a far greater rise in truancy and out-of-school problem behaviors, such as doing something dangerous for the thrill of it, damaging public property, or getting drunk (Roeser, Eccles, & Freedman-Doan, 1999). For some, school transition initiates a downward spiral in academic performance and school involvement that leads to dropping out.

• **Helping Adolescents Adjust to School Transitions** As these findings reveal, school transitions often lead to environmental changes that fit poorly with adolescents' developmental needs (Eccles, 2004). They disrupt close relationships with teachers at a time when adolescents need adult support. They emphasize competition during a period of heightened self-focusing. They reduce decision making and choice as the desire for autonomy is increasing. And they interfere with peer networks as young people become more concerned with peer acceptance.

Support from parents, teachers, and peers eases the strain of school transition. Parental involvement, monitoring, autonomy granting, and emphasis on mastery rather than merely good grades are associated with better adjustment (Grolnick et al., 2000; Gutman, 2006). Adolescents with close friends are more likely to sustain these friendships across the transition, which increases social integration and academic motivation in the new school (Aikens, Bierman, & Parker, 2005). Forming smaller units within large schools promotes closer relations with both teachers and peers and greater extracurricular involvement (Seidman, Aber, & French, 2004).

Other, less extensive changes are also effective. In the first year after a school transition, homerooms can be provided in which teachers offer academic and personal counseling and work closely with parents to promote favorable school adjustment. Assigning students to classes with several familiar peers or a constant group of new peers strengthens emotional security and social support. In schools that took these steps, students were less likely to decline in academic performance and to display other serious adjustment problems (Felner et al., 2002).

Finally, teenagers' perceptions of the sensitivity and flexibility of their school learning environments contribute substantially to successful school transitions. When schools minimize competition and differential treatment based on ability, middle school students are less likely to feel angry and depressed, to be truant, or to show declines in academic values, self-esteem, and achievement (Roeser, Eccles, & Sameroff, 2000). School rules that strike young people as fair rather than punitive also foster satisfaction with school life (Eccles et al., 1993).

Teacher–Student Interaction

The classroom is a complex social system in which teachers engage in as many as 1,000 exchanges with students each day (Jackson, 1968). Extensive research exists on teacher–student interaction, most focusing on its significance for academic achievement.

Elementary and secondary school students describe good teachers as caring, helpful, and stimulating—behaviors associated with gains in motivation, achievement, and favorable peer relations (Hughes & Kwok, 2006, 2007; Hughes, Zhang, & Hill, 2006; O'Connor & McCartney, 2007). But too many U.S. teachers emphasize repetitive drill over higher-level thinking, such as grappling with ideas and applying knowledge to new situations (Sacks, 2005). In a longitudinal investigation of more than 5,000 seventh graders, those in more stimulating, academically demanding classrooms showed better attendance and larger gains in math achievement over the following two years (Phillips, 1997).

As we have seen, teachers do not interact in the same way with all children. Well-behaved, high-achieving students typically get more encouragement and praise, whereas unruly students have more conflicts with teachers and receive more criticism from them (Henricsson & Rydell, 2004). Caring teacher–student relationships have an especially strong impact on the achievement and social behavior of low-SES minority students and other children at risk for learning difficulties (Baker, 2006; Crosno, Kirkpatrick, & Elder, 2004). But overall, higher-SES students—who tend to be higher-achieving and to have fewer learning and behavior problems—have more sensitive and supportive relationships with teachers (Pianta, Hamre, & Stuhlman, 2003).

Unfortunately, once teachers' attitudes toward students are established, they can become more extreme than students' behavior warrants. A special concern is **educational self-fulfilling prophecies:** Children may adopt teachers' positive or negative views and start to live up to them.[1] As early as first grade, teachers' beliefs in children's ability to learn predict students' year-end achievement progress after controlling for students' beginning-of-year performance. This effect is particularly strong when teachers emphasize competition and publicly compare children, regularly favoring the best students (Kuklinski & Weinstein, 2001; Weinstein, 2002).

Teacher expectations have a greater impact on low achievers than high achievers (Madon, Jussim, & Eccles, 1997). High-achieving students have less room to improve when teachers think well of them, and when a teacher is critical, they can fall back on their history of success. Low-achieving students' sensitivity to self-fulfilling prophecies can be beneficial when teachers believe in them, but unfortunately, biased teacher judgments usually have a negative slant. In one study, African-American children were especially responsive to negative teacher expectations in reading, and girls were especially responsive to negative teacher expectations in math (McKown & Weinstein, 2002). Recall our discussion of *stereotype threat* in Chapter 8. A child in the position of confirming a negative stereotype may respond with anxiety and reduced motivation, increasing the likelihood of a negative self-fulfilling prophecy.

Grouping Practices

Many schools group students by ability or track them into classes in which students of similar achievement levels are taught together. The goal is to reduce the need for individual teachers to meet a wide range of academic needs.

• **Grouping in Elementary School** *Homogeneous* groups or classes can be a potent source of self-fulfilling prophecies. Low-group students—who as early as first grade are disproportionately low-SES, minority, and male—get more drill on basic facts and skills, engage in less discussion, and progress at a slower pace. Gradually, they may be viewed by themselves and others as "not smart" and decline in academic self-esteem and motivation (Chorzempa & Graham, 2006; Condron, 2007; Trautwein et al., 2006). Not surprisingly, homogeneous grouping widens the gap between high and low achievers (Dornbusch, Glasgow, & Lin, 1996; Ross & Harrison, 2006).

Partly because of this finding, some schools have increased the *heterogeneity* of student groups by combining two or three adjacent

[1]Most research on self-fulfilling prophecies focuses on teacher–student relationships, but the effect can occur in other social contexts, such as parent–child and peer relationships.

Second and third graders learn together during a visit to their school library. Compared to the typical single-grade arrangement, multigrade classrooms are associated with higher academic achievement and self-esteem, and more positive attitudes toward school.

grades. In *multigrade classrooms,* academic achievement, self-esteem, and attitudes toward school are usually more favorable than in the single-grade arrangement, perhaps because multigrade classrooms often decrease competition and increase harmony (Lloyd, 1999; Ong, Allison, & Haladyna, 2000). The opportunity that mixed-age grouping affords for peer tutoring may also contribute to its favorable outcomes. When older or more expert students teach younger or less expert students, both tutors and tutees benefit in achievement and self-esteem, with stronger effects for low-SES minority students and students in grades 1 to 3 (Ginsburg-Block, Rohrbeck, & Fantuzzo, 2006; Renninger, 1998).

However, small heterogeneous groups of students working together often engage in poorer-quality interaction (less accurate explanations and answers) than homogeneous groups of above-average students (Webb, Nemer, & Chizhik, 1998). In Chapter 6, we noted that for collaboration between heterogeneous peers to succeed, children often need extensive guidance (see page 270). When teachers provide this assistance, heterogeneous classrooms are desirable into middle or junior high school, effectively supporting the motivation and achievement of students who vary widely in academic progress (Gilles, 2003; Gillies & Ashman, 1996).

• **Grouping in High School** By high school, some homogeneous grouping is unavoidable because certain aspects of education must dovetail with the young person's educational and vocational plans. In the United States and Canada, high school students are counseled into college preparatory, vocational, or general education tracks. Unfortunately, low-SES minority students are assigned in large numbers to noncollege tracks, perpetuating educational inequalities of earlier years.

Longitudinal research following thousands of U.S. students from eighth to twelfth grade reveals that assignment to a college track accelerates academic progress, whereas assignment to a vocational or general education track decelerates it (Hallinan & Kubitschek, 1999). Even in secondary schools without an overarching tracking program, low-SES minority students tend to be assigned to lower course levels in most or all academic subjects, resulting in *de facto* (unofficial) *tracking* (Lucas & Behrends, 2002).

Compared to students in higher tracks, students in low tracks exert substantially less effort, in part because their classes are less stimulating (Carbonaro, 2005). When capable students (as indicated by achievement test scores) end up in low tracks, they "sink" to their trackmates' performance level. Furthermore, teachers of non-college-track classes are less likely to communicate with parents about ways they can support their adolescent's learning. Many minority parents, in turn, do not understand the tracking system, are unaware of their child's low placement, and therefore do not intervene on behalf of their child (Dornbusch & Glasgow, 1997).

High school students are separated into academic and vocational tracks in virtually all industrialized nations. But in China, Japan, and most Western European countries, high school track placement is determined by a national exam, which usually establishes the young person's future possibilities. In North America, educational decisions are more fluid: Students who are not assigned to a college preparatory track or who do poorly in high school can still get a college education. But ultimately, many young people do not benefit from this more open system. By adolescence, SES differences in quality of education and academic achievement have already sorted students more drastically than occurs in other countries. Compared with other Western nations, both the United States and Canada have a higher percentage of young people—about 10 percent—who regard themselves as educational failures and drop out of high school (Statistics Canada, 2005f; U.S. Department of Education, 2007).

This student in a lower-level high school English course daydreams through class. Assignment to a vocational or general education track is associated with less stimulating teaching, poorer parent–teacher communication, decelerating academic progress, and increased risk of dropping out. © image100/Corbis

Teaching Students with Special Needs

So far, we have seen that effective teachers flexibly adjust their teaching strategies to accommodate students with a wide range of characteristics. These adjustments, however, are especially challenging when children have learning difficulties.

The girl in the blue shirt, who has mild mental retardation, is fully included in this regular classroom. She is likely to do well if she receives support from a special education teacher and if her classroom teacher minimizes comparisons with classmates and encourages cooperative learning—as in this card game.
© Paul Conklin/PhotoEdit

• **Children with Learning Difficulties** U.S. and Canadian legislation mandates that schools place children who require special supports for learning in the "least restrictive" (as close to normal as possible) environments that meet their educational needs. In **inclusive classrooms,** students with learning difficulties learn alongside typical students in the regular educational setting for part or all of the school day—a practice designed to prepare them for participation in society and to combat prejudices against individuals with disabilities that lead to social exclusion (Kugelmass & Ainscow, 2004). Largely as the result of parental pressures, an increasing number of students experience *full inclusion*—full-time placement in regular classrooms.

Some students in inclusive classrooms have *mild mental retardation:* Their IQs fall between 55 and 70, and they also show problems in adaptive behavior, or skills of everyday living (American Psychiatric Association, 1994). But the largest number—5 to 10 percent of school-age children—have **learning disabilities,** great difficulty with one or more aspects of learning, usually reading. As a result, their achievement is considerably behind what would be expected on the basis of their IQ. Sometimes, deficits express themselves in other ways—for example, as severe inattention, which depresses both IQ and achievement test scores. The problems of students with learning disabilities cannot be traced to any obvious physical or emotional difficulty or to environmental disadvantage. Instead, subtle deficits in brain functioning are involved (Berninger, 2006). Some disorders run in families, and in certain cases, specific genes have been identified that contribute to the problem (Miller, Sanchez, & Hynd, 2003; Raskind et al., 2005). In many instances, the cause is unknown.

• **How Effective Are Inclusive Classrooms?** Do inclusive classrooms provide these students with appropriate learning experiences and integrated participation in classroom life? Although some included students benefit academically, many do not. Achievement gains depend on both the severity of the disability and the support services available (Klingner et al., 1998). Furthermore, children with disabilities are often rejected by regular-classroom peers. Students with mental retardation are overwhelmed by the social skills of their classmates; they cannot interact adeptly in a conversation or game. And the processing deficits of some students with learning disabilities lead to problems in social awareness and responsiveness (Kelly & Norwich, 2004; Sridhar & Vaughn, 2001).

Does this mean that children with special needs cannot be served in regular classrooms? Not necessarily. Many children do best when they receive instruction in a resource room for part of the day and in the regular classroom for the remainder—an arrangement that the majority of school-age children with learning disabilities say they prefer (Vaughn & Klingner, 1998; Weiner & Tardif, 2004). In the resource room, a special education teacher works with students on an individual and small-group basis. Then, depending on their progress, children join regular classmates for different subjects and amounts of time.

Special steps must be taken to promote positive peer relations in inclusive classrooms. Cooperative learning and peer-tutoring experiences in which teachers guide children with learning difficulties and their classmates in working together lead to friendly interaction, improved peer acceptance, and achievement gains (Fuchs et al., 2002a, 2002b). Teachers can also prepare their class for the arrival of a student with special needs. Under these conditions, inclusion may foster emotional sensitivity and prosocial behavior among regular classmates.

Parent–School Partnerships

Regardless of students' age, abilities, gender, SES, or ethnicity, parent involvement in education—keeping tabs on the child's progress, communicating often with teachers, and ensuring that the child is enrolled in challenging, well-taught classes—promotes academic motivation and achievement (Hill & Taylor, 2004; Jeynes, 2005). When parents are in frequent contact with the school, they send a message to their child about the value of education, model constructive solutions to academic problems, and (as children get older) promote wise educational decisions. Involved parents also learn from other parents about which classes and teachers are the best and how to handle difficult situations. And teachers and parents are more likely to give students consistent messages about academic and behavioral expectations.

Families living in low-income, high-risk neighborhoods face daily stresses that reduce their energy for school involvement (Bowen, Bowen, & Ware, 2002). Yet stronger home–school links could relieve some of this stress. Schools can build parent–school partnerships by strengthening personal relationships between teachers and parents, showing parents how to support their child's education at home, building bridges between minority home cultures and the culture of the school, tapping parents' talents to improve the quality of school programs, and including parents in school governance so they remain invested in school goals.

How Well-Educated Are North American Young People?

Our discussion has focused largely on how teachers can support the education of children and adolescents. Yet we have also seen in this and previous chapters that many factors—both within and outside schools—affect children's learning. Societal values, school resources, quality of teaching, and parental encouragement all play important roles. These multiple influences are especially apparent when we examine schooling in cross-cultural perspective.

Cross-National Research on Academic Achievement

In international studies of reading, mathematics, and science achievement, young people in Hong Kong, Korea, Japan, and Taiwan are consistently top performers. Among Western nations, Canada is also in the top tier, but U.S. students typically perform at the international average, and sometimes below it (see Figure 15.12) (Programme for International Student Assessment, 2003, 2006).

Figure 15.12 **Average mathematics scores of 15-year-olds by country.** The Programme for International Student Assessment assessed achievement in many nations around the world. Japan, Hong Kong, Korea, Taiwan, and Canada were among the top performers in mathematics, whereas the United States performed below the international average. Similar outcomes occurred in reading and science. (Adapted from Programme for International Student Assessment, 2006.)

	Country	Average Math Achievement Score
High-Performing Nations	Taiwan	549
	Finland	548
	Hong Kong	547
	Korea, Republic of	547
	Netherlands	531
	Switzerland	530
	Canada	**527**
	Macao, China	525
	Japan	523
	New Zealand	522
	Belgium	520
	Australia	520
Intermediate-Performing Nations	Denmark	513
	Czech Republic	510
	Iceland	506
	Austria	505
	Germany	504
	Sweden	502
	Ireland	501
International Average = 498		
	France	496
	United Kingdom	495
	Poland	495
	Hungary	491
	Luxembourg	491
	Norway	490
	Spain	480
	United States	**474**
Low-Performing Nations	Portugal	466
	Italy	462
	Greece	459
	Turkey	424

Why do U.S. students fall behind in academic accomplishments? International comparisons reveal that instruction in the United States is less challenging and focused than in other countries. In the Programme for International Student Assessment, which periodically assesses the academic achievement of 15-year-olds in many countries, students were asked about their study habits. Compared with students in top-achieving nations, many more U.S. students reported studying by memorizing rather than by relating information to previously acquired knowledge. And achievement varies much more among U.S. schools, suggesting that the United States is less equitable in the quality of education it provides (Programme for International Student Assessment, 2005).

Researchers have conducted in-depth research on learning environments in Asian nations, such as Japan, Korea, and Taiwan, to clarify the factors that support high achievement. Except for the influence of language on early counting skills (see Chapter 7, page 310), Asian students do not start school with cognitive advantages. Rather, a variety of social forces combine to foster a strong commitment to learning in Asian families and schools:

- *Cultural valuing of academic achievement.* Compared to Western countries, Japan, Korea, and Taiwan invest more in education, including higher salaries for teachers. In these countries, where natural resources are limited, progress in science and technology is essential for economic well-being (United Nations Development Programme, 2002).

- *Emphasis on effort.* North American parents and teachers tend to regard native ability as the key to academic success. In contrast, Japanese, Korean, and Taiwanese parents and teachers believe that all children can succeed academically with enough effort. Asian parents devote many more hours to helping their children with homework (Stevenson, Lee, & Mu, 2000). And Asian youths, influenced by collectivist values, typically view striving to achieve as a moral obligation—a responsibility to family and community. In contrast, North American young people see working hard in individualistic terms—as a matter of personal choice (Bempchat & Drago-Severson, 1999).
- *High-quality education for all.* Ability grouping is absent from Japanese, Korean, and Taiwanese elementary schools. All students receive the same nationally mandated, high-quality education. Academic lessons are particularly well-organized and presented in ways that capture children's attention and encourage high-level thinking (Grow-Maienza, Hahn, & Joo, 2001). Topics in mathematics are treated in greater depth, with less repetition of previously taught material. And Japanese elementary school teachers are three times as likely as U.S. teachers to work outside class with students who need additional help (Woodward & Ono, 2004).
- *More time devoted to instruction.* In Japan, Hong Kong, and Taiwan, the school year is more than 50 days longer than in the United States and about 30 days longer than in Canada (World Education Services, 2007). Also, on a day-to-day basis, Asian teachers devote much more time to academic pursuits (Stevenson, Lee, & Mu, 2000). Yet Asian schools are not regimented: An eight-hour school day allows time for extra recesses as well as field trips and extracurricular activities. Frequent breaks may increase Asian children's capacity to learn (Pellegrini & Smith, 1998).

A longer school day in Japanese schools permits frequent alternation of academic instruction with pleasurable activity, an approach that fosters learning. During a break, Japanese elementary-school children enjoy a calligraphy class.
© Cameramann/The Image Works

The Asian examples underscore the need for families, schools, and the larger society to work together to upgrade education. Currently, the United States is investing more tax dollars in elementary and secondary education and strengthening teacher preparation. In addition, many schools are taking steps to increase parent involvement. Results of these efforts can be seen in recent national assessments of educational progress (U.S. Department of Education, 2003, 2005). After two decades of decline, U.S. students' overall academic achievement has risen, though not enough to enhance their standing internationally.

Effective educational change must take into account students' life backgrounds and future goals. As we will see next, besides improving academic instruction, special efforts are needed in vocational education to help non-college-bound youths prepare for productive work roles.

Making the Transition from School to Work

Approximately one-third of North American young people graduate from high school without plans to go to college. Although they are more likely to find employment than those who drop out, they have fewer work opportunities than high school graduates of several decades ago. About 10 percent of Canadian and 20 percent of U.S. recent high school graduates who do not continue their education are unemployed (Statistics Canada, 2007k; U.S. Department of Education, 2007). When they do find work, most hold low-paid, unskilled jobs. In addition, they have few alternatives for vocational counseling and job placement as they transition from school to work (Shanahan, Mortimer, & Krüger, 2002).

North American employers regard recent high school graduates as poorly prepared for skilled business and industrial occupations and manual trades. And there is some truth to this impression. In high school, almost half of U.S. adolescents are employed—a greater percentage than in other developed countries (Bowlby & McMullen, 2002; Children's Defense Fund, 2006). But most are middle-SES students in pursuit of spending money rather than vocational exploration and training. Low-income teenagers who need to contribute to family income find it harder to get jobs (U.S. Department of Education, 2007).

Furthermore, the jobs adolescents hold are typically low-level, repetitive tasks that provide little contact with adult supervisors. A heavy

Teenagers' employment opportunities are typically limited to menial tasks that do little to extend their knowledge or skills. Students with a heavy time commitment to such jobs are less likely to participate in extracurricular activities and more likely to drop out of school.
© Robin Nelson/PhotoEdit

High school students on site in a home-construction course learn energy-efficient building techniques from an expert. The success of apprenticeship programs in several European countries suggest that similar programs would improve the transition from school to work in the United States and Canada. AP Images/Robert E. Klein

commitment to such jobs is actually harmful. The more hours students work, the poorer their school attendance, the lower their grades, the less likely they are to participate in extracurricular activities, and the more likely they are to drop out (Marsh & Kleitman, 2005). Students who spend many hours at such jobs also tend to feel more distant from their parents and report more drug and alcohol use and delinquent acts (Kouvonen & Kivivuori, 2001; Staff & Uggen, 2003).

When work experiences are specially designed to meet educational and vocational goals, outcomes are different. Participation in work–study programs or other jobs that provide academic and vocational learning opportunities is related to positive school and work attitudes, achievement, and reduced delinquency (Hamilton & Hamilton, 2000; Staff & Uggen, 2003). Yet high-quality vocational preparation for non-college-bound North American adolescents is scarce. Unlike some European nations, the United States and Canada have no widespread training systems to prepare youths for skilled business and industrial occupations and manual trades (Heinz, 1999a).

In Germany, adolescents who do not go to a *Gymnasium* (college-preparatory high school) have access to one of the most successful work–study apprenticeship systems in the world for entering business and industry. About two-thirds of German youths participate. After completing full-time schooling at age 15 or 16, they spend the remaining two years of compulsory education in the *Berufsschule*, combining part-time vocational courses with an apprenticeship that is jointly planned by educators and employers. Students train in work settings for more than 400 blue- and white-collar occupations. Apprentices who complete the program and pass a qualifying examination are certified as skilled workers and earn union-set wages. Businesses provide financial support because they know that the program guarantees a competent, dedicated work force (Heinz, 1999b; Kerckhoff, 2002). Many apprentices are hired into well-paid jobs by the firms that train them.

The success of the German system—and of similar systems in Austria, Denmark, Switzerland, and several Eastern European countries—suggests that a national apprenticeship program would improve the transition from high school to work for North American young people. The many benefits of bringing together the worlds of schooling and work include helping non-college-bound young people establish productive lives right after graduation, motivating at-risk youths to stay in school, and contributing to the nation's economic growth. Nevertheless, implementing an apprenticeship system poses major challenges: overcoming the reluctance of employers to assume part of the responsibility for vocational training, ensuring cooperation between schools and businesses, and preventing low-SES youths from being concentrated in the lowest-skilled apprenticeship placements, an obstacle that Germany itself has not yet fully overcome (Hamilton & Hamilton, 2000).

Currently, small-scale school-to-work projects in the United States and Canada are attempting to solve these problems and build bridges between learning and working. Young people who are well-prepared for an economically and personally satisfying work life are much more likely to become productive citizens, devoted family members, and contented adults. The support of families, schools, businesses, communities, and society as a whole can contribute greatly to a positive outcome.

Ask Yourself

Review List educational practices that promote positive attitudes toward school, academic motivation, and achievement, and explain why each is effective.

Apply Ray is convinced that his 5-year-old son Trip would learn more in school if only Trip's kindergarten would provide more teacher-directed lessons and worksheets and reduce the time devoted to learning-center activities. Is Ray correct? Explain.

Connect What common factors contribute to the high academic achievement of students in Asian nations and to the academic success of immigrant youths, discussed on page 00 in Chapter 2?

Reflect Describe your experiences in making the transition to middle or junior high school and then to high school. What made these transitions stressful? What helped you adjust?

SUMMARY

Importance of Peer Relations

Discuss evidence indicating that both parental and peer relationships are vital for children's development.

- Research on both humans and nonhuman primates suggests that the parent–child bond gives children the security to enter the world of peers, which permits children to expand their social skills. Although peer relations can substitute to some extent for the early parent–child bond, peer support is more effective when children also have warm ties to parents.

Development of Peer Sociability

Trace the development of peer sociability from infancy into adolescence.

- Peer sociability begins in infancy with isolated social acts, followed by coordinated exchanges in the second year. During the preschool years, play moves from **nonsocial activity** to **parallel play,** then to **associative** and **cooperative play,** with all types coexisting. Sociodramatic play becomes especially frequent, supporting cognitive, emotional, and social development.
- In middle childhood, improved perspective taking permits peer interaction to become more prosocial and cooperative and to transition to rule-oriented games. **Rough-and-tumble play**—important in our evolutionary past for developing fighting skill and establishing **dominance hierarchies**—also becomes common, especially among boys.

How do parental encouragement, age mix of children, and cultural values influence peer sociability?

- Parents influence children's social competence both directly, by providing guidance and opportunities for peer contact, and indirectly, through secure attachment, authoritative child rearing, inductive discipline, emotionally positive and cooperative parent–child play, and the quality of parents' own social networks.
- Same-age peers engage in more intense and harmonious exchanges, but mixed-age interaction offers older children practice in prosocial behavior and younger children opportunities to learn from older companions.
- In collectivist societies, large-group, imitative play is common. Sociodramatic play is particularly important for social development in societies where child and adult worlds are distinct.

Friendship

Describe children's developing concepts of friendship, characteristics of friendships in childhood and adolescence, and implications of friendship for psychological adjustment.

- For preschool and young school-age children, **friendship** is a concrete relationship based on shared activities. During middle childhood, children form friendships based on mutual trust. Teenagers' friendships are based on intimacy, mutual understanding, and loyalty.
- With age, friendships become more selective, stable, and prosocial, providing contexts in which children learn to tolerate criticism and resolve disputes. For aggressive children, friendships often magnify antisocial tendencies.
- Friends tend to be alike in age, sex, ethnicity, and SES—and, from middle childhood on, in personality, popularity, achievement, and prosocial behavior. Adolescent friends resemble one another in identity status, educational aspirations, political beliefs, and deviance. But to explore new perspectives, they also befriend agemates with differing attitudes and values. Ethnically diverse schools and integrated neighborhoods foster cross-ethnic friendships.
- Girls, more than boys, emphasize emotional closeness in friendships. Very popular and very unpopular early adolescents are more likely to have other-sex friends.
- Gratifying friendships foster self-concept, perspective taking, and identity development; provide a foundation for intimate relationships; offer support in dealing with everyday stresses; and promote good school adjustment. Aggressive friendships, however, seriously undermine development.

Peer Acceptance

Describe major categories of peer acceptance, the relationship of social behavior to likability, and ways to help rejected children.

- Researchers usually assess **peer acceptance** using **sociometric techniques,** which measure social preferences. Another approach is to assess **peer reputation,** or social prominence—children's judgments of whom their classmates most admire. Sociometric techniques identify four categories of peer acceptance: **popular children, rejected children, controversial children,** and **neglected children.** Rejected children often experience lasting adjustment problems.
- **Popular-prosocial children** are academically and socially competent; **popular-antisocial children** are aggressive but admired by peers for their sophisticated social skills. **Rejected-aggressive children** display severe conduct problems, in contrast to **rejected-withdrawn children,** who are passive, socially awkward, and at high risk for **peer victimization.** Controversial children blend positive and negative behaviors. Neglected children, though often choosing to play alone, are usually socially competent and well-adjusted.
- Interventions for rejected children include coaching in social skills, intensive academic tutoring, and training in perspective taking and social problem solving. Treatments must also address maladaptive parent–child interaction.

Peer Groups

Describe peer groups in middle childhood and adolescence and their consequences for development.

- By the end of middle childhood, **peer groups**—based on proximity and similarity in sex, ethnicity, academic achievement, popularity, and aggression—emerge. Within them, children practice cooperation, leadership, followership, and loyalty to collective goals.

© Peter Hvizdak/The Image Works

- Early-adolescent peer groups are organized around **cliques** with common attitudes and values. Several cliques may form a loosely organized **crowd,** granting adolescents an identity within the school's social structure. Peer group values extend those acquired at home. Mixed-sex cliques provide a supportive context for learning to interact with the other sex, disappearing by late adolescence.

Dating

Discuss dating relationships in adolescence.

- Intimacy in dating lags behind that in friendships; early, frequent dating is linked to adjustment problems. Positive relationships with parents and friends contribute to warm romantic ties, which provide practice for more mature bonds.

Peer Pressure and Conformity

What factors influence conformity to peer pressure?

- Peer conformity rises in early adolescence, but most peer pressure focuses on obvious aspects of peer culture, such as dress and musical taste, rather than basic life values. Authoritative parenting promotes resistance to peer pressure.

Media

Discuss the influence of television on children's development.

- Television is the dominant form of youth media. Boys and low-SES children tend to be more frequent viewers. Extensive TV watching is associated with family and peer difficulties. Preschool and young school-age children's incomplete grasp of televised information and inability to critically evaluate it increase the chances that they will believe and imitate what they see.
- Televised violence promotes hostile thoughts and emotions, aggression, and a violent worldview. TV also conveys ethnic and gender stereotypes. Heavy bombardment of children with advertising contributes to many problems, including family stress, overweight and obesity, materialism, and substance use.

- Educational television can promote children's cognitive and academic skills, emotional and social understanding, and prosocial behavior. Slow-paced programs with easy-to-follow story lines foster more elaborate make-believe play. But heavy viewing of entertainment TV detracts from academic success and social experiences.

Discuss computer use by children and adolescents, noting benefits and concerns.

- Computers' educational benefits include word processing for writing and online information-gathering—activities that promote literacy progress and reading achievement. However, girls and low-SES students are disadvantaged in computer opportunities and skills.
- Boys' attraction to speed-and-action computer games fosters selective attention and spatial skills, but violent games promote hostility and aggression. "Passionate" players tend to use games to escape from family and school problems.
- Communicating through instant messaging promotes closeness between adolescent friends. Using the Internet to interact with strangers can offer vital sources of social support, but teenagers who form Internet romances tend to be troubled young people who are at risk for exploitation.

Schooling

How do class and student body size and teachers' educational philosophies affect academic and social development?

- Smaller classes in the early elementary grades promote lasting gains in academic achievement. In small high schools, students are more involved in extracurricular activities, which foster a sense of responsibility, competence, and challenge. Also, "marginal" students are more likely to participate and graduate.
- Older students in **traditional classrooms** have a slight edge in academic achievement over those in **constructivist classrooms,** who gain in academic motivation, critical thinking, social and moral maturity, and positive attitudes toward school. Young children in traditional classrooms display poorer study habits and achievement through elementary school.
- Students in **social-constructivist classrooms** benefit both cognitively and socially from collaboration with teachers and peers. In classrooms organized as **communities of learners,** teachers and students draw on one another's expertises to work on complex projects with real-world meaning.

Cite factors that influence adjustment following school transitions in early childhood and in adolescence.

- Factors predicting favorable kindergarten adjustment include preschool experience, a friendly, prosocial style, and supportive ties to peers and teachers. Kindergartners with antisocial and peer-avoidant styles tend to establish poor-quality relationships with teachers, which predict academic and behavior problems.
- School transitions in adolescence bring larger, more impersonal school environments, in which both grades and feelings of competence decline. Girls experience more adjustment difficulties after the transition to middle or junior high school, which coincides with other life changes (puberty and the beginning of dating). Distressed young people with poor school performance are at risk for continuing academic difficulties and eventual dropout.

Discuss the role of teacher–student interaction and grouping practices in academic achievement.

- Patterns of teacher–student interaction affect children's academic progress. Instruction that encourages higher-level thinking is associated with greater student interest and achievement. **Educational self-fulfilling prophecies** are particularly strong in classrooms emphasizing competition and public evaluation, and they have a greater impact on low achievers.

© Guy Cali/The Stock Connection

- Homogeneous grouping in elementary school is linked to poorer-quality instruction and declines in self-esteem and academic achievement for children in low-ability groups. In contrast, multigrade classrooms promote achievement, self-esteem, and positive school attitudes. Teacher guidance is essential for successful collaboration between heterogeneous peers.
- By high school, some homogeneous grouping is educationally necessary, but in North America, high school tracking extends earlier educational inequalities. Low-SES students are at risk for unfair placement in noncollege tracks.

Under what conditions is placement of students with mild mental retardation and learning disabilities in regular classrooms successful, and how can schools increase parent involvement in education?

- Effective placement of students with mild mental retardation and **learning disabilities** in **inclusive classrooms** depends on learning experiences tailored to children's academic needs and promotion of positive peer relations.
- Schools can increase parent involvement by fostering personal parent–teacher relationships, building bridges between minority home cultures and the school culture, and involving parents in school governance.

How Well-Educated Are North American Young People?

How well are North American young people achieving, compared with their counterparts in other industrialized nations, and what prevents North American non-college-bound youths from making an effective school-to-work transition?

- In international studies, young people in Asian nations are consistently top performers, and Canada is also in the top tier. But U.S. students typically score at or below the international average. A strong commitment to learning in families and schools underlies Asian students' success.
- Unlike their European counterparts, non-college-bound adolescents in the United States and Canada have no widespread vocational training system to help them prepare for skilled business and industrial occupations and manual trades.

IMPORTANT TERMS AND CONCEPTS

associative play (p. 605)
clique (p. 620)
community of learners (p. 637)
constructivist classroom (p. 636)
controversial children (p. 616)
cooperative play (p. 605)
crowd (p. 620)
dominance hierarchy (p. 607)
educational self-fulfilling prophecy (p. 641)
friendship (p. 610)
inclusive classroom (p. 643)
learning disability (p. 643)
neglected children (p. 616)
nonsocial activity (p. 605)
parallel play (p. 605)
peer acceptance (p. 615)
peer group (p. 619)
peer reputation (p. 616)
peer victimization (p. 618)
popular children (p. 616)
popular-antisocial children (p. 616)
popular-prosocial children (p. 616)
rejected children (p. 616)
rejected-aggressive children (p. 617)
rejected-withdrawn children (p. 617)
rough-and-tumble play (p. 607)
social-constructivist classroom (p. 637)
sociometric techniques (p. 615)
traditional classroom (p. 635)

Glossary

A

Aboriginal Head Start A Canadian federal early intervention program that provides First Nations, Inuit, and Métis children younger than age 6 with educational, nutritional, and health services and that encourages parent involvement in program planning and children's learning and development. (p. 346)

accommodation In Piaget's theory, that part of adaptation in which new schemes are created or old ones adjusted to produce a better fit with the environment. Distinguished from *assimilation.* (p. 225)

acculturative stress Psychological distress resulting from conflict between an individual's minority culture and the host culture. (p. 468)

achievement motivation The tendency to persist at challenging tasks. (p. 459)

achievement test A test that assesses actual knowledge and skill attainment. Distinguished from *aptitude test.* (p. 326)

adaptation In Piaget's theory, the process of building schemes through direct interaction with the environment. Consists of two complementary activities: *assimilation* and *accommodation.* (p. 225)

affordances The action possibilities that a situation offers an organism with certain motor capabilities. Discovery of affordances plays a major role in perceptual differentiation. (p. 165)

age of viability The age at which the fetus can first survive if born early. Occurs sometime between 22 and 26 weeks. (p. 91)

alcohol-related neurodevelopmental disorder (ARND) The least severe form of fetal alcohol spectrum disorder, involving brain injury but with typical physical growth and absence of facial abnormalities. (p. 99)

allele Each of two or more forms of a gene located at the same place on the chromosomes. (p. 75)

amnion The inner membrane that encloses the prenatal organism in amniotic fluid, which helps keep temperature constant and provides a cushion against jolts caused by the mother's movement. (p. 89)

amodal sensory properties Information that is not specific to a single modality but that overlaps two or more sensory systems, such as rate, rhythm, duration, intensity, temporal synchrony (for vision and hearing), and texture and shape (for vision and touch). (p. 163)

analogical problem solving Taking a solution strategy from one problem and applying it to other relevant problems. (p. 234)

androgens Hormones released chiefly by boys' testes, and in smaller amounts by the adrenal glands, that influence the pubertal growth spurt and stimulate muscle growth, body and facial hair, and male sex characteristics. (p. 180)

androgyny The gender identity held by individuals who score high on both traditionally masculine and traditionally feminine personality characteristics. (p. 543)

animistic thinking The belief that inanimate objects have lifelike qualities, such as thoughts, wishes, feelings, and intentions. (p. 241)

anorexia nervosa An eating disorder in which young people, mainly females, starve themselves because of a compulsive fear of getting fat and an extremely distorted body image. (p. 208)

A-not-B search error The error made by 8- to 12-month-olds who, after an object is moved from hiding place A to hiding place B, search for it incorrectly in the first hiding place (A). (p. 227)

Apgar Scale A rating system used to assess a newborn baby's physical condition immediately after birth on the basis of five characteristics: heart rate, respiratory effort, reflex irritability, muscle tone, and color. (p. 108)

aptitude test A test that assesses an individual's potential to learn a specialized activity. Distinguished from *achievement test.* (p. 326)

assimilation In Piaget's theory, that part of adaptation in which the external world is interpreted in terms of current schemes. Distinguished from *accommodation.* (p. 225)

associative play A form of social interaction in which children engage in separate activities but interact by exchanging toys and commenting on one another's behavior. Distinguished from *nonsocial activity, parallel play,* and *cooperative play.* (p. 605)

attachment The strong, affectionate tie that humans have with special people in their lives, which leads them to feel pleasure when interacting with those people and to be comforted by their nearness in times of stress. (p. 425)

Attachment Q-Sort A method for assessing the quality of attachment between ages 1 and 4 years through home observations of a variety of attachment-related behaviors. (p. 428)

attention-deficit hyperactivity disorder (ADHD) A childhood disorder involving inattention, impulsivity, and excessive motor activity. Often leads to academic and social problems. (p. 290)

attribution retraining An intervention that uses adult feedback to encourage learned-helpless children to believe that they can overcome failure through effort. (p. 462)

attributions Common, everyday explanations for the causes of behavior. (p. 459)

authoritarian child-rearing style A child-rearing style that is low in acceptance and involvement, high in coercive and psychological control, and low in autonomy granting. Distinguished from *authoritative, permissive,* and *uninvolved child-rearing styles.* (p. 570)

authoritative child-rearing style A child-rearing style that is high in acceptance and involvement, emphasizes firm control with explanations, and includes gradual, appropriate autonomy granting. Distinguished from *authoritarian, permissive,* and *uninvolved child-rearing styles.* (p. 569)

autobiographical memory Representations of one-time events that are long-lasting because they are imbued with personal meaning. (p. 296)

autonomous morality Piaget's second stage of moral development, in which children view rules as flexible, socially agreed-on principles that can be revised to suit the will of the majority. (p. 492)

autonomy In adolescence, a sense of oneself as a separate, self-governing individual. Involves relying more on oneself and less on parents for support and guidance and engaging in careful, well-reasoned decision making. (p. 573)

autosomes The 22 matching chromosome pairs in each human cell. (p. 74)

avoidant attachment The attachment pattern characterizing infants who seem unresponsive to the parent when she is present, are usually not distressed when she leaves, and avoid the parent when she returns. Distinguished from *secure, resistant,* and *disorganized/disoriented attachment.* (p. 428)

B

babbling Repetition of consonant–vowel combinations in long strings, beginning around 6 months of age. (p. 369)

basic emotions Emotions such as happiness, interest, surprise, fear, anger, sadness, and disgust that are universal in humans and other primates, have a long evolutionary history of promoting survival, and can be directly inferred from facial expressions. (p. 404)

behavior modification Procedures that combine conditioning and modeling to eliminate undesirable behaviors and increase desirable responses. (p. 20)

behavioral genetics A field devoted to uncovering the contributions of nature and nurture to the diversity in human traits and abilities. (p. 118)

behaviorism An approach that regards directly observable events—stimuli and responses—as the appropriate focus of study and that views the development of behavior as taking place through classical and operant conditioning. (p. 19)

belief–desire theory of mind The more sophisticated theory of mind that emerges around age 4, in which children understand that both beliefs and desires determine behavior. (p. 447)

biased sampling Failure to select participants who are representative of the population of interest in a study. (p. 61)

bicultural identity The identity constructed by individuals who explore and adopt values from both their family's subculture and the dominant culture. (p. 469)

blended, or **reconstituted, family** A family structure resulting from cohabitation or remarriage that includes parent, child, and steprelatives. (p. 589)

body image Conception of and attitude toward one's physical appearance. (p. 206)

brain plasticity The capacity of various parts of the cerebral cortex to take over functions of damaged regions. Declines as hemispheres of the cerebral cortex lateralize. (p. 186)

breech position A position of the baby in the uterus that would cause the buttocks or feet to be delivered first. (p. 112)

Broca's area A structure located in the left frontal lobe of the cerebral cortex that supports grammatical processing and language production. (p. 362)

bulimia nervosa An eating disorder in which individuals, mainly girls but also including some gay and bisexual boys, engage in strict dieting and excessive exercise accompanied by binge eating, often followed by deliberate vomiting and purging with laxatives. (p. 209)

C

canalization The tendency of heredity to restrict the development of some characteristics to just one or a few outcomes. (p. 121)

cardinality The principle stating that the last word in a counting sequence indicates the quantity of items in the set. (p. 308)

carrier A heterozygous individual who can pass a recessive trait to his or her offspring. (p. 75)

catch-up growth A return to a genetically influenced growth path once negative environmental conditions improve. (p. 190)

categorical self Classification of the self according to prominent ways in which people differ, such as age, sex, physical characteristics, and goodness and badness. Develops between 18 and 30 months. (p. 446)

categorical speech perception The tendency to perceive as identical a range of sounds that belong to the same phonemic class. (p. 367)

central conceptual structures In Case's neo-Piagetian theory, networks of concepts and relations that permit children to think about a wide range of situations in more advanced ways. Generated once the schemes of a Piagetian stage become sufficiently automatic, freeing space in working memory to consolidate them into an improved representational form. (p. 282)

central executive In information processing, the conscious, reflective part of working memory that directs the flow of information through the mental system by deciding what to attend to, coordinating incoming information with information already in the system, and selecting, applying, and monitoring strategies. (p. 277)

centration In Piaget's theory, the tendency to focus on one aspect of a situation and neglect other important features. (p. 241)

cephalocaudal trend An organized pattern of physical growth and motor control that proceeds from head to tail. (p. 146)

cerebellum A brain structure that aids in balance and control of body movement. (p. 188)

cerebral cortex The largest, most complex structure of the human brain, and the one that contains the greatest number of neurons and synapses and that makes possible the unique intelligence of our species. (p. 184)

child development A field devoted to understanding constancy and change from conception through adolescence. (p. 4)

child-directed speech (CDS) A form of language adults use to speak to infants and toddlers, consisting of short sentences with high-pitched, exaggerated expression, clear pronunciation, distinct pauses between speech segments, clear gestures to support verbal meaning, and repetition of new words in a variety of contexts. (p. 368)

child-rearing styles Combinations of parenting behaviors that occur over a wide range of situations, creating an enduring child-rearing climate. (p. 569)

chorion The outer membrane that forms a protective covering around the prenatal organism. It sends out tiny hairlike villi, from which the placenta begins to develop. (p. 89)

chromosomes Rodlike structures in the cell nucleus that store and transmit genetic information. (p. 72)

chronosystem In ecological systems theory, temporal changes in children's environments, which produce new conditions that affect development. These changes can be imposed externally or arise from within the child. Distinguished from *microsystem, mesosystem, exosystem,* and *macrosystem.* (p. 29)

circular reaction In Piaget's theory, a means of adapting schemes in which babies try to repeat a chance event caused by their own motor activity. (p. 226)

classical conditioning A form of learning that involves associating a neutral stimulus with a stimulus that leads to a reflexive response. Once the nervous system makes the connection between the two stimuli, the new stimulus will produce the behavior by itself. (p. 137)

clinical interview An interview method in which the researcher uses a flexible, conversational style to probe for the participant's point of view. (p. 46)

clinical, or case study, method A research method in which the aim is to obtain as complete a picture as possible of one child's psychological functioning by bringing together a wide range of information, including interviews, observations, test scores, and sometimes psychophysiological measures. (p. 49)

clique A group of about five to seven members who are friends and, therefore, tend to resemble one another in family background, attitudes, values, and interests. (p. 620)

code switching A strategy in which bilingual individuals produce an utterance in one language that contains one or more "guest" words from the other, without violating the grammar of either language. (p. 393)

cognitive-developmental theory An approach introduced by Piaget that views children as actively constructing knowledge as they manipulate and explore their world and that regards cognitive development as taking place in stages. (p. 20)

cognitive maps Mental representations of familiar large-scale spaces, such as school or neighborhood. (p. 248)

cognitive self-regulation The process of continuously monitoring progress toward a goal, checking outcomes, and redirecting unsuccessful efforts. (p. 303)

cohort effects The effects of cultural–historical change on the accuracy of longitudinal and cross-sectional findings. Results based on one cohort—children developing in the same time period who are influenced by particular cultural and historical conditions—may not apply to other cohorts. (p. 61)

collectivist societies Societies in which people define themselves as part of a group and stress group goals over individual goals. Distinguished from *individualistic societies.* (p. 34)

community of learners A classroom in which both teachers and students have the authority to define and resolve problems, drawing on the expertise of one another and of others as they work toward project goals, which often address complex real-world issues. (p. 637)

compliance Voluntary obedience to adult requests and commands. (p. 511)

componential analysis Research that combines the psychometric and information-processing approaches in an effort to identify relationships between aspects (or components) of information processing and children's intelligence test performance. (p. 321)

comprehension In language development, the words children understand. Distinguished from *production.* (p. 375)

concrete operational stage Piaget's third stage, extending from about 7 to 11 years, during which thought becomes logical, flexible, and organized in its application to concrete information. (p. 247)

conditioned response (CR) In classical conditioning, a response similar to the reflexive response evoked by the unconditioned stimulus (UCS) that, following learning, is produced by a conditioned stimulus (CS). (p. 138)

conditioned stimulus (CS) In classical conditioning, a neutral stimulus that, through pairing with an unconditioned stimulus (UCS), leads to a new, conditioned response (CR). (p. 138)

confounding variables Variables so closely associated that their effects on an outcome cannot be distinguished. (p. 57)

connectionist, or artificial neural network, models Models of mental functioning that focus on the most basic information-processing units, using computer simulations to imitate the workings of neurons and their connections in the brain. If the network's responses resemble those of individuals of different ages, then researchers conclude that the network is a good model of human learning and development. (p. 279)

conservation The understanding that certain physical characteristics of objects remain the same, even when their outward appearance changes. (p. 241)

construction In moral development, the process of actively attending to and interrelating multiple perspectives on situations in which social conflicts arise and thereby attaining new moral understandings. (p. 491)

constructivist approach Piaget's view of cognitive development, in which children discover, or construct, virtually all knowledge about their world through their own activity. (p. 224)

constructivist classroom A classroom in which students are active learners who are encouraged to construct their own knowledge, the teacher guides and supports in response to children's needs, and students are evaluated by considering their progress in relation to their own prior development. Often grounded in Piaget's theory. Distinguished from *traditional classrooms* and *social constructivist classrooms.* (p. 636)

contexts Unique combinations of personal and environmental circumstances that can result in different paths of development. (p. 8)

continuous development The view that development is a process of gradually adding more of the same types of skills that were there to begin with. Distinguished from *discontinuous development.* (p. 7)

contrast sensitivity A general principle accounting for early pattern preferences, which states that if babies can detect a difference in contrast between two or more patterns, they will prefer the one with more contrast. (p. 158)

control deficiency Inability to execute a mental strategy effectively. Distinguished from *production deficiency, utilization deficiency,* and *effective strategy use.* (p. 286)

controversial children Children who get many votes, both positive and negative, on sociometric measures of peer acceptance and, thus, are both liked and disliked. Distinguished from *popular, rejected,* and *neglected children.* (p. 616)

conventional level Kohlberg's second level of moral development, in which moral understanding is based on conforming to social rules to ensure positive human relationships and maintain societal order. (p. 496)

convergent thinking Thinking that involves arriving at a single correct answer to a problem; the type of thinking emphasized on intelligence tests. Distinguished from *divergent thinking.* (p. 349)

cooing Pleasant vowel-like noises made by infants, beginning around 2 months of age. (p. 369)

cooperative learning Collaboration on a task by a small group of peers who resolve differences, share responsibility, and work toward common goals. (p. 269)

cooperative play A form of social interaction in which children orient toward a common goal, such as acting out a make-believe theme or working on a project together. Distinguished from *nonsocial activity, parallel play,* and *associative play.* (p. 605)

coparenting Parents' mutual support for each other's parenting behaviors. (p. 566)

core knowledge perspective A perspective that states that infants begin life with innate, special-purpose knowledge systems, or core domains of thought, each of which permits a ready grasp of new, related information and therefore supports early, rapid development of certain aspects of cognition. (p. 258)

coregulation A form of supervision in which parents exercise general oversight while permitting children to take charge of moment-by-moment decision making. (p. 573)

corpus callosum The large bundle of fibers connecting the two hemispheres. (p. 189)

correlation coefficient A number, ranging from +1.00 to −1.00, that describes the strength and direction of the relationship between two variables. (p. 56)

correlational design A research design in which the investigator gathers information on individuals without altering their experiences and then examines relationships between participants' characteristics and their behavior or development. Does not permit inferences about cause and effect. (p. 55)

creativity The ability to produce work that is original yet appropriate—something that others have not thought of but that is useful in some way. (p. 349)

crossing over During meiosis, the exchange of genes between chromosomes next to each other. (p. 73)

cross-sectional design A research design in which groups of participants of different ages are studied at the same point in time. Distinguished from *longitudinal design.* (p. 62)

crowd A large, loosely organized social group consisting of several cliques, with membership based on reputation and stereotype. (p. 620)

crystallized intelligence In Cattell's theory, a form of intelligence involving skills that depend on accumulated knowledge and experience, good judgment, and mastery of social customs. Distinguished from *fluid intelligence.* (p. 320)

D

debriefing Providing a full account and justification of research activities to participants in a study in which deception was used. (p. 68)

deferred imitation The ability to remember and copy the behavior of models who are not present. (p. 228)

delay of gratification Ability to wait for an appropriate time and place to engage in a tempting act. (p. 511)

deoxyribonucleic acid (DNA) Long, double-stranded molecules that make up chromosomes. (p. 72)

dependent variable The variable the researcher expects to be influenced by the independent variable in an experiment. (p. 57)

desire theory of mind The theory of mind of 2- to 3-year-olds, who assume that people always act in ways consistent with their desires but do not understand the influence on behavior of interpretive mental states, such as beliefs. (p. 447)

developmental cognitive neuroscience An area of investigation that brings together researchers from psychology, biology, neuroscience, and medicine to study the relationship between changes in the brain and the developing child's cognitive processing and behavior patterns. (p. 24)

developmental quotient (DQ) A score on an infant intelligence test, computed in the same manner as an IQ but labeled more conservatively because it does not tap the same dimensions of intelligence measured in older children and predicts childhood mental abilities poorly. (p. 327)

developmental science An interdisciplinary field devoted to the study of all changes humans experience throughout the lifespan. (p. 4)

developmentally appropriate practice Research-based standards devised by the National Association for the Education of Young Children that specify program characteristics that meet the developmental and individual needs of young children of varying ages. (p. 437)

differentiation theory The view that perceptual development involves the detection of increasingly fine-grained, invariant features in the environment. (p. 165)

difficult child A child whose temperament is characterized by irregular daily routines, slow acceptance of new experiences, and a tendency to react negatively and intensely. Distinguished from *easy child* and *slow-to-warm-up child.* (p. 417)

discontinuous development The view that development is a process in which new ways of understanding and responding to the world emerge at specific times. Distinguished from *continuous development.* (p. 7)

disorganized/disoriented attachment The attachment pattern reflecting the greatest insecurity, characterizing infants who show confused, contradictory behaviors when reunited with the parent after a separation. Distinguished from *secure, avoidant,* and *resistant attachment.* (p. 428)

distance curve A growth curve that plots the average size of a sample of children at each age, indicating typical yearly progress toward maturity. Distinguished from *velocity curve.* (p. 174)

distributive justice Beliefs about how to divide material goods fairly. (p. 508)

divergent thinking Thinking that involves generating multiple and unusual possibilities when faced with a task or problem; associated with creativity. Distinguished from *convergent thinking.* (p. 349)

dominance hierarchy A stable ordering of group members that predicts who will win when conflict arises. (p. 607)

dominant cerebral hemisphere The hemisphere of the cerebral cortex responsible for skilled motor action and where other important abilities are located. In right-handed individuals, the left hemisphere is dominant. (p. 186)

dominant–recessive inheritance A pattern of inheritance in which, under heterozygous conditions, the influence of only one allele is apparent. (p. 75)

dual representation The ability to view a symbolic object as both an object in its own right and a symbol. (p. 240)

dynamic assessment An approach to testing consistent with Vygotsky's zone of proximal development in which an adult introduces purposeful teaching into the testing situation to find out what the child can attain with social support. (p. 340)

dynamic systems perspective A view that regards the child's mind, body, and physical and social worlds as a *dynamic, integrated system.* A change in any part of the system leads the child to reorganize his behavior so the components of the system work together again but in a more complex and effective way. (p. 29)

dynamic systems theory of motor development A theory that views new motor skills as reorganizations of previously mastered skills, which lead to more effective ways of exploring and controlling the environment. Each new skill is a joint product of central nervous system development, the body's movement possibilities, the child's goals, and environmental supports for the skill. (p. 146)

E

Early Head Start A U.S. federal program that provides infants and toddlers from low-income families with intervention involving coordinated services, including child care, educational experiences, parenting education, family social support, and health care. (p. 347)

easy child A child whose temperament is characterized by establishment of regular routines in infancy, general cheerfulness, and easy adaptation to new experiences. Distinguished from *difficult child* and *slow-to-warm-up child.* (p. 417)

ecological systems theory Bronfenbrenner's approach, which views the child as developing within a complex *system* of relationships affected by multiple levels of the surrounding environment, from immediate settings of family and school to broad cultural values and programs. (p. 26)

educational self-fulfilling prophecies Teachers' positive or negative views of individual children, who tend to adopt and start to live up to those views. (p. 641)

effective strategy use Consistent use of a mental strategy, leading to improved performance. Distinguished from *production deficiency, control deficiency,* and *utilization deficiency.* (p. 287)

effortful control The self-regulatory dimension of temperament, involving voluntary suppression of a dominant response in order to plan and execute a more adaptive response. (p. 418)

egocentrism Failure to distinguish others' symbolic viewpoints from one's own. (p. 240)

elaboration A memory strategy that involves creating a relationship, or shared meaning, between two or more pieces of information that do not belong to the same category. (p. 291)

embryo The prenatal organism from 2 to 8 weeks after conception—the period when the groundwork for all body structures and internal organs is laid down. (p. 90)

emergent literacy Children's active efforts to construct literacy knowledge through informal experiences. (p. 304)

emergentist coalition model The view that word-learning strategies *emerge* out of children's efforts to decipher language, during which they draw on a *coalition* of perceptual, social, and linguistic cues that shift in importance with age. (p. 382)

emotion A rapid appraisal of the personal significance of a situation, which prepares the individual for action. (p. 400)

emotion-centered coping A general strategy for managing emotion that is internal, private, and aimed at controlling distress when little can be done to change an outcome. Distinguished from *problem-centered coping.* (p. 410)

emotional display rules A society's rules specifying when, where, and how it is appropriate to express emotions. (p. 410)

emotional intelligence A set of emotional abilities that enable individuals to process and adapt to emotional information, measured by tapping emotional skills that enable people to manage their own emotions and interact competently with others. (p. 325)

emotional self-regulation Strategies for adjusting our emotional state to a comfortable level of intensity so we can accomplish our goals. (p. 407)

empathy The ability to take another individual's emotional perspective and to "feel with" that person, or respond emotionally in a similar way. (p. 414)

enduring self A view of the self as persisting over time. (p. 446)

entity view of ability The view that ability is a fixed characteristic that cannot be improved through effort; associated with learned helplessness. Distinguished from *incremental view of ability.* (p. 460)

environmental cumulative deficit hypothesis The view that the negative effects of underprivileged rearing conditions increase the longer children remain in them, making early cognitive deficits harder to overcome. (p. 330)

epigenesis Development resulting from ongoing, bidirectional exchanges between heredity and all levels of the environment. (p. 123)

epiphyses Growth centers in the bones where new cartilage cells are produced and gradually harden. (p. 176)

episodic memory Memory for personally experienced events. (p. 295)

equilibration In Piaget's theory, the back-and-forth movement between equilibrium and disequilibrium that produces more effective schemes. (p. 225)

estrogens Hormones released by girls' ovaries that cause the breasts, uterus, and vagina to mature, the body to take on feminine proportions, and fat to accumulate. Estrogens also contribute to regulation of the menstrual cycle. (p. 180)

ethnic identity A sense of ethnic group membership, and attitudes and feelings associated with that membership, as an enduring aspect of the self. (p. 468)

ethnography A method in which the researcher attempts to understand the unique values and social processes of a culture or a distinct social group through participant observation—living with its members and taking field notes for an extended period. (p. 51)

ethological theory of attachment A theory formulated by Bowlby that recognizes the infant's emotional tie to the caregiver as an evolved response that promotes survival. (p. 426)

ethology An approach concerned with the adaptive, or survival, value of behavior and its evolutionary history. (p. 24)

event sampling An observational procedure in which the researcher records all instances of a particular behavior during a specified time period. (p. 45)

evolutionary developmental psychology An approach that seeks to understand the adaptive value of species-wide cognitive, emotional, and social competencies as those competencies change with age. (p. 25)

exosystem In ecological systems theory, social settings that do not contain children but that affect children's experiences in immediate settings. Examples are parents' workplace, health and welfare services in the community, and parents' social networks. Distinguished from *microsystem, mesosystem, macrosystem,* and *chronosystem.* (p. 28)

expansions Adult responses that elaborate on children's speech, increasing its complexity. (p. 388)

experience-dependent brain growth Growth and refinement of established brain structures as a result of specific learning experiences that vary widely across individuals and cultures. Distinguished from *experience-expectant brain growth.* (p. 189)

experience-expectant brain growth The young brain's rapidly developing organization, which depends on ordinary experiences—opportunities to see and touch objects, to hear language and other sounds, and to move about and explore the environment. Distinguished from *experience-dependent brain growth.* (p. 189)

experimental design A research design in which the investigator randomly assigns participants to treatment conditions and studies the effect that manipulating an independent variable has on a dependent variable. Permits inferences about cause and effect. (p. 57)

expressive style A style of early language learning in which toddlers use language mainly to talk about their own and others' feelings and needs, with an initial vocabulary emphasizing social formulas and pronouns. Distinguished from *referential style.* (p. 377)

expressive traits Personality traits emphasizing warmth, caring, and sensitivity, regarded as feminine. Distinguished from *instrumental traits.* (p. 526)

extended-family household A household in which one or more adult relatives live with the parent–child nuclear family unit. (p. 579)

external validity The degree to which researchers' findings generalize to settings and participants outside the original study. Distinguished from *internal validity.* (p. 55)

extinction In classical conditioning, decline of the conditioned response (CR) as a result of presenting the conditioned stimulus (CS) enough times, without being paired with the unconditioned stimulus (UCS). (p. 138)

F

factor analysis A complicated correlational procedure that identifies sets of test items that cluster together. Used to investigate whether intelligence is one trait or an assortment of abilities. (p. 319)

fast-mapping Children's ability to connect a new word with an underlying concept after only a brief encounter. (p. 376)

fetal alcohol spectrum disorder (FASD) A range of physical, mental, and behavioral outcomes caused by prenatal alcohol exposure. (p. 98)

fetal alcohol syndrome (FAS) The most severe form of fetal alcohol spectrum disorder, distinguished by slow physical growth, facial abnormalities, and brain injury; usually seen in children whose mothers consumed large amounts of alcohol during most or all of pregnancy. (p. 98)

fetus The prenatal organism from the ninth week to the end of pregnancy—the period when body structures are completed and dramatic growth in size occurs. (p. 91)

field experiment A research design in which participants are randomly assigned to treatment conditions in natural settings. (p. 57)

fluid intelligence In Cattell's theory, a form of intelligence that depends primarily on basic information-processing skills—ability to detect relationships among stimuli, speed of analyzing information, and capacity of working memory. Distinguished from *crystallized intelligence.* (p. 320)

Flynn effect An increase in IQ from one generation to the next. (p. 337)

formal operational stage Piaget's highest stage, beginning around age 11, in which adolescents develop the capacity for abstract, systematic, scientific thinking. (p. 251)

fraternal, or **dizygotic, twins** Twins resulting from the release and fertilization of two ova. They are genetically no more alike than ordinary siblings. Distinguished from *identical,* or *monozygotic, twins.* (p. 75)

friendship A close relationship involving companionship in which each partner wants to be with the other. (p. 610)

functionalist approach to emotion A perspective emphasizing that the broad function of emotions is to energize behavior aimed at attaining personal goals. (p. 400)

fuzzy-trace theory A theory proposing that when we first encode information, we automatically reconstruct it into a gist—a fuzzy version that preserves essential meaning without details and is especially useful for reasoning. (p. 294)

G

gametes Sex cells, or sperm and ova, which contain half as many chromosomes as regular body cells. (p. 73)

gender consistency Kohlberg's final stage of gender understanding, in which children in the late preschool and early school years understand that sex is biologically based and remains the same even if a person dresses in "cross-gender" clothes or engages in nontraditional activities. (p. 544)

gender constancy A full understanding of the biologically based permanence of gender, which combines three understandings: *gender labeling, gender stability,* and *gender consistency.* (p. 544)

gender identity A perception of oneself as relatively masculine or feminine in characteristics. (p. 526)

gender intensification The increased gender stereotyping of attitudes and behavior and movement toward a more traditional gender identity, typical of early adolescence. (p. 546)

gender labeling Kohlberg's first stage of gender understanding, in which children in the early preschool years can correctly label their own sex and that of others but do not understand that sex is biologically based and permanent. (p. 544)

gender roles The reflection of gender stereotypes in everyday behavior. (p. 526)

gender schema theory An information-processing approach to gender typing that explains how environmental pressures and children's cognitions work together to shape gender-role development. (p. 547)

gender stability Kohlberg's second stage of gender understanding, in which preschoolers grasp the stability of sex over time. (p. 544)

gender-stereotype flexibility The belief that both males and females can display a gender-stereotyped personality trait or activity. (p. 529)

gender stereotypes Widely held beliefs about characteristics deemed appropriate for males and females. (p. 526)

gender typing Any association of objects, activities, roles, or traits with biological sex in ways that conform to cultural stereotypes of gender. (p. 526)

gene A segment of a DNA molecule that contains hereditary instructions. (p. 72)

general intelligence, or **"g"** In Spearman's theory, a common underlying intelligence that represents abstract reasoning capacity and that influences, in varying degrees, performance on all types of test items. Distinguished from *specific intelligence.* (p. 319)

generalized other A blend of what we imagine important people in our lives think of us, crucial to developing a self-concept based on personality traits. (p. 454)

genetic counseling A communication process designed to help couples assess their chances of giving birth to a baby with a hereditary disorder and choose the best course of action in view of risks and family goals. (p. 82)

genetic–environmental correlation The idea that heredity influences the environments to which individuals are exposed. (p. 121)

genomic imprinting A pattern of inheritance in which alleles are imprinted, or chemically marked, in such a way that one pair member is activated, regardless of its makeup. (p. 79)

genotype An individual's genetic makeup. Distinguished from *phenotype.* (p. 71)

gifted Displaying exceptional intellectual strengths. Includes high IQ, creativity, and talent. (p. 349)

gist In fuzzy-trace theory, a vague, fuzzy representation of information that preserves essential content without details and is especially useful for reasoning. (p. 294)

glial cells Cells that are responsible for myelination of neural fibers, improving the efficiency of message transfer. (p. 184)

goodness-of-fit model Thomas and Chess's model, which states that an effective match, or "good fit," between a child's temperament and the child-rearing environment leads to more adaptive functioning, whereas a "poor fit" results in adjustment problems. (p. 423)

grammar The component of language concerned with *syntax,* the rules by which words are arranged into sentences, and *morphology,* the use of grammatical markers indicating number, tense, case, person, gender, active or passive voice, and other meanings. (p. 358)

grammatical morphemes In language development, small markers that change the meaning of sentences, as in "John*'s* dog" and "he *is* eating." (p. 384)

growth hormone (GH) A pituitary hormone that affects the development of all body tissues except the central nervous system and the genitals. (p. 180)

guided participation Shared endeavors between more expert and less expert participants, regardless of the precise features of communication. A broader concept than *scaffolding.* (p. 266)

H

habituation A gradual reduction in the strength of a response due to repetitive stimulation. (p. 140)

heritability estimate A statistic that measures the extent to which individual differences in complex traits in a specific population are due to genetic factors. (p. 119)

heteronomous morality Piaget's first stage of moral development, in which children view rules as handed down by authorities, as having a permanent existence, as unchangeable, and as requiring strict obedience. (p. 492)

heterozygous Having two different alleles at the same place on a pair of chromosomes. Distinguished from *homozygous.* (p. 75)

hierarchical classification The organization of objects into classes and subclasses on the basis of similarities and differences. (p. 242)

hippocampus An inner-brain structure that plays a vital role in memory and in images of space we use to help us find our way. (p. 188)

Home Observation for Measurement of the Environment (HOME) A checklist for gathering information about the quality of children's home lives through observation and parental interview. (p. 342)

homozygous Having two identical alleles at the same place on a pair of chromosomes. Distinguished from *heterozygous.* (p. 75)

hypothalamus A structure located at the base of the brain that initiates and regulates pituitary secretions. (p. 180)

hypothesis A prediction drawn from a theory. (p. 42)

hypothetico-deductive reasoning A formal operational problem-solving strategy that begins with a hypothesis, from which logical inferences can be deduced and then tested by systematically isolating and combining variables. (p. 251)

I

ideal reciprocity A standard of fairness based on mutuality of expectations, as expressed in the Golden Rule: "Do unto others as you would have them do unto you." (p. 492)

identical, or monozygotic, twins Twins that result when a zygote, during early cell duplication, divides in two. They have the same genetic makeup. Distinguished from *fraternal,* or *dizygotic, twins.* (p. 74)

identity A well-organized conception of the self that defines who one is, what one values, and what directions one wants to pursue in life. (p. 463)

identity achievement The identity status of individuals who have explored and committed themselves to self-chosen values and goals. Distinguished from *identity moratorium, identity foreclosure,* and *identity diffusion.* (p. 464)

identity diffusion The identity status of individuals who do not engage in exploration and are not commited to values and goals. Distinguished from *identity achievement, identity moratorium,* and *identity foreclosure.* (p. 464)

identity foreclosure The identity status of individuals who do not engage in exploration but, instead, are committed to ready-made values and goals chosen for them by authority figures. Distinguished from *identity achievement, identity moratorium,* and *identity diffusion.* (p. 464)

identity moratorium The identity status of individuals who are exploring, but not yet committed to, self-chosen values and goals. Distinguished from *identity achievement, identity foreclosure,* and *identity diffusion.* (p. 464)

illocutionary intent In conversation, what a speaker means to say, even if the form of the utterance is not perfectly consistent with it. (p. 389)

imaginary audience Adolescents' belief that they are the focus of others' attention and concern. (p. 252)

imitation Learning by copying the behavior of another person. Also called *modeling* or *observational learning.* (p. 143)

inclusive classroom A classroom in which students with learning difficulties learn alongside typical students in a regular educational setting for part or all of the school day. (p. 643)

incomplete dominance A pattern of inheritance in which both alleles are expressed in the phenotype, resulting in a combined trait, or one that is intermediate between the two. (p. 78)

incremental view of ability The view that ability can be improved through effort; associated with mastery-oriented attributions. Distinguished from *entity view of ability.* (p. 460)

independent variable The variable the researcher expects to cause changes in another variable in an experiment. Distinguished from *dependent variable.* (p. 57)

individualistic societies Societies in which people think of themselves as separate entities and are largely concerned with their own personal needs. Distinguished from *collectivist societies.* (p. 34)

induction A type of discipline in which the adult helps make the child aware of others' feelings by pointing out the effects of the child's misbehavior on others, noting especially their distress and making clear that the child caused it. (p. 485)

infant mortality The number of deaths in the first year of life per 1,000 live births. (p. 116)

infantile amnesia The inability of most older children and adults to retrieve from long-term memory events that happened to them before age 3. (p. 298)

information processing An approach that views the human mind as a symbol-manipulating system through which information flows and that regards cognitive development as a continuous process. (p. 22)

informed consent The right of research participants, including children, to have explained to them, in language they can understand, all aspects of a study that might affect their willingness to participate. (p. 66)

inhibited, or shy, child A child who tends to react negatively to and withdraw from novel stimuli. Distinguished from *uninhibited,* or *sociable, child.* (p. 419)

inhibition The ability to control internal and external distracting stimuli, which helps children remember, reason, solve problems, and control behavior in social situations. (p. 286)

inner self Awareness of the self's private thoughts and imaginings. (p. 447)

instrumental traits Personality traits reflecting competence, rationality, and assertiveness, regarded as masculine. Distinguished from *expressive traits.* (p. 526)

intelligence quotient (IQ) A score that indicates the extent to which an individual's raw score (number of items passed) on an intelligence test deviates from the typical performance of same-age individuals. (p. 328)

intentional, or goal-directed, behavior A sequence of actions in which schemes are deliberately coordinated to solve a problem. (p. 227)

interactional synchrony A form of communication in which the caregiver responds to infant signals in a well-timed, rhythmic, appropriate fashion and both partners match emotional states, especially positive ones. (p. 430)

intermodal perception Perception that combines simultaneous input from more than one modality, or sensory system, resulting in an integrated whole. (p. 163)

internal validity The degree to which conditions internal to the design of a research study permit an accurate test of the researcher's hypothesis or question. Distinguished from *external validity.* (p. 55)

internal working model A set of expectations about the availability of attachment figures, their likelihood of providing support during times of stress, and the self's interaction with those figures, which becomes a guide for all future close relationships. (p. 427)

internalization In moral development, the process of adopting societal standards for right action as one's own. (p. 484)

intersubjectivity The process whereby two participants who begin a task with different understandings arrive at a shared understanding. (p. 266)

invariant features Features that remain stable in a constantly changing perceptual world. (p. 165)

investment theory of creativity Sternberg and Lubart's theory, in which an individual's investment in novel projects depends on diverse cognitive, personality, motivational, and environmental resources, each of which must be present to catalyze creativity. (p. 350)

J

joint attention A state in which child and caregiver attend to the same object or event and the caregiver labels what the child sees, which contributes to language development. (p. 369)

K

kinship studies Studies comparing the characteristics of family members to estimate the importance of heredity in complex human characteristics. (p. 119)

kwashiorkor A disease caused by a diet low in protein that usually appears after weaning, between 1 and 3 years of age, with symptoms including an enlarged belly, swollen feet, hair loss, skin rash, and irritable, listless behavior. (p. 195)

L

laboratory experiment An experiment conducted in the laboratory, permitting the maximum possible control over treatment conditions. (p. 57)

language acquisition device (LAD) In Chomsky's theory, an innate system containing a universal grammar, or set of rules common to all languages, that permits children, once they have acquired sufficient vocabulary, to understand and speak in a rule-oriented fashion. (p. 359)

lanugo White, downy hair that covers the entire body of the fetus, helping the vernix stick to the skin. (p. 91)

lateralization Specialization of functions in the two hemispheres of the cerebral cortex. (p. 185)

learned helplessness The view that success is due to external factors, such as luck, while failure is due to low ability, which cannot be improved by trying hard. Distinguished from *mastery-oriented attributions.* (p. 460)

learning disability Great difficulty with one or more aspects of learning, usually reading, which causes students' achievement to be considerably behind what would be expected on the basis of IQ. (p. 643)

logical necessity The idea that the accuracy of conclusions drawn from premises rests on the rules of logic, not on real-world confirmation. A basic property of propositional thought. (p. 255)

longitudinal design A research design in which one group of participants is studied repeatedly at different ages. Distinguished from *cross-sectional design.* (p. 60)

long-term memory In information processing, the largest storage area of the mental system, containing our permanent knowledge base. (p. 277)

M

macrosystem In ecological systems theory, cultural values, laws, customs, and resources that influence experiences and interactions at inner levels of the environment. Distinguished from *microsystem, mesosystem, exosystem,* and *chronosystem.* (p. 28)

make-believe play A type of play in which children act out everyday and imaginary activities. (p. 228)

marasmus A disease usually appearing in the first year of life, caused by a diet low in all essential nutrients, that leads to a wasted condition of the body. (p. 195)

mastery-oriented attributions Attributions that credit success to ability, which can be improved by trying hard, and that credit failure to insufficient effort. Distinguished from *learned helplessness.* (p. 460)

matching A research procedure in which participants are measured ahead of time on the factor in question, enabling investigators to assign participants with similar characteristics in equal numbers to each treatment condition in an experiment. Ensures that groups will be equivalent on factors likely to distort the results. (p. 57)

matters of personal choice Concerns that do not violate rights or others' welfare and are up to the individual. Distinguished from *moral imperatives* and *social conventions.* (p. 506)

maturation A genetically determined, naturally unfolding course of growth. (p. 12)

meiosis The process of cell division through which gametes are formed and in which the number of chromosomes in each cell is halved. (p. 73)

memory span The longest sequence of items a person can recall; a measure of working-memory capacity. (p. 278)

menarche Scientific name for first menstruation, from the Greek word *arche* ("beginning"). (p. 200)

mental representation An internal depiction of information that the mind can manipulate, including images and concepts. (p. 225)

mental strategies Procedures for operating on and transforming information, thereby increasing the chances that the information will be retained and used efficiently and flexibly. (p. 276)

mesosystem In ecological systems theory, connections between children's immediate settings, or microsystems. Distinguished from *microsystem, exosystem, macrosystem,* and *chronosystem.* (p. 27)

metacognition Awareness and understanding of various aspects of thought. (p. 301)

metalinguistic awareness The ability to think about language as a system. (p. 392)

microgenetic design A research design in which investigators present children with a novel task and follow their mastery over a series of closely spaced sessions. (p. 63)

microsystem In ecological systems theory, the innermost level of the environment, consisting of activities and interaction patterns in the child's immediate surroundings. Distinguished from *mesosystem, exosystem, macrosystem,* and *chronosystem.* (p. 26)

mirror neurons Specialized cells in motor areas of the cerebral cortex in primates that fire identically when a primate hears or sees an action and when it carries out that action on its own. (p. 144)

mitosis The process of cell duplication, in which each new cell receives an exact copy of the original chromosomes. (p. 72)

model of strategy choice An attempt to apply an evolutionary perspective to children's mental strategies by analyzing how, when given challenging problems, children first generate a variety of strategies and then select the most accurate, efficient strategies, which "survive," while others become less frequent and "die off." Analogous to variation and selection of physical characteristics. (p. 282)

modifier genes Genes that enhance or dilute the effects of other genes. (p. 76)

moral imperatives Standards that protect people's rights and welfare. Distinguished from *social conventions* and *matters of personal choice.* (p. 506)

Moral Judgment Interview A clinical interviewing procedure for assessing moral understanding in which individuals resolve hypothetical dilemmas that present conflicts between two moral values and justify their decisions. (p. 494)

moral self-regulation The ability to monitor one's own conduct, constantly adjusting it as circumstances present opportunities to violate inner standards. (p. 512)

moral self-relevance The degree to which morality is central to an individual's self-concept. (p. 502)

morphology The use of grammatical markers indicating number, tense, case, person, gender, active or passive voice, and other meanings. (p. 358)

mutation A sudden but permanent change in a segment of DNA. (p. 79)

mutual exclusivity bias Children's assumption in early vocabulary growth that words refer to entirely separate (nonoverlapping) categories. (p. 380)

myelination The coating of neural fibers with an insulating fatty sheath, *myelin,* that improves the efficiency of message transfer. (p. 184)

N

natural, or **prepared, childbirth** A group of techniques aimed at reducing pain and medical intervention and making childbirth as rewarding an experience as possible. Typically includes classes that provide information about the birth process, relaxation and breathing techniques to counteract the pain of uterine contractions, and a labor coach who provides encouragement and affection. (p. 109)

natural, or **quasi-, experiment** A research design in which the investigator compares treatments that already exist in natural settings by carefully selecting groups of participants with similar characteristics. (p. 58)

naturalistic observation A research method in which the investigator goes into the natural environment to observe the behavior of interest. Distinguished from *structured observation.* (p. 43)

nature–nurture controversy Disagreement among theorists about whether genetic or environmental factors are more important influences on development. (p. 8)

neglected children Children who are seldom chosen, either positively or negatively, on sociometric measures of peer acceptance. Distinguished from *popular, rejected,* and *controversial children.* (p. 616)

Neonatal Behavioral Assessment Scale (NBAS) A test used to assess the behavioral status of the newborn by evaluating the baby's reflexes, muscle tone, state changes, responsiveness to physical and social stimuli, and other reactions. (p. 137)

neonatal mortality The rate of death within the first month of life. (p. 116)

neo-Piagetian theory A reinterpretation of Piaget's stages within an information-processing framework. For example, Case's theory attributes change within each stage, and movement from one stage to the next, to increases in the efficiency with which children use their limited working memory capacity. (p. 280)

neurons Nerve cells that store and transmit information. (p. 183)

neurotransmitters Chemicals released by neurons that cross the synapse to send messages to other neurons. (p. 183)

niche-picking A type of genetic–environmental correlation in which individuals actively choose environments that complement their heredity. (p. 122)

noble savage Rousseau's view of the child as naturally endowed with a sense of right and wrong and an innate plan for orderly, healthy growth. (p. 12)

nonorganic failure to thrive A growth disorder, usually present by 18 months of age, that is caused by lack of affection and stimulation. Infants show signs of marasmus despite the absence of an organic cause. (p. 199)

non-rapid-eye-movement (NREM) sleep A "regular" sleep state in which the body is almost motionless and heart rate, breathing, and brain-wave activity are slow and regular. Distinguished from *rapid-eye-movement (REM) sleep.* (p. 131)

nonshared environmental influences Environmental influences that make siblings living in the same home different from one another. Distinguished from *shared environmental influences.* (p. 341)

nonsocial activity Unoccupied, onlooker behavior and solitary play. Distinguished from *parallel play, associative play,* and *cooperative play.* (p. 605)

normal distribution A bell-shaped distribution that results when individual differences are measured in large samples. (p. 328)

normative approach An approach in which measures of behavior are taken on large numbers of individuals, and age-related averages are computed to represent typical development. (p. 13)

nuclear family unit A family unit consisting of parents and their dependent children living in one household. (p. 579)

O

obesity A greater-than-20-percent increase over healthy body weight, based on body mass index, a ratio of weight to height associated with body fat. (p. 196)

object permanence The understanding that objects continue to exist when they are out of sight. (p. 227)

observer bias The tendency of observers who are aware of the purposes of a study to see and record what they expect to see rather than what participants actually do. (p. 45)

observer influence The tendency of participants in a study to behave in unnatural ways in the presence of an observer. (p. 45)

operant conditioning A form of learning in which a spontaneous behavior is followed by a stimulus that changes the probability that the behavior will occur again. (p. 139)

operations In Piaget's theory, mental representations of actions that obey logical rules. (p. 240)

ordinality Order relationships (more than and less than) between quantities. (p. 308)

organization In Piaget's theory, the internal rearrangement and linking together of schemes so that they form a strongly interconnected cognitive system. In information processing, a memory strategy that involves grouping related information to improve recall. (pp. 226, 289)

overextension An early vocabulary error in which a word is applied too broadly, to a wider collection of objects and events than is appropriate. Distinguished from *underextension.* (p. 378)

overregularization Extension of regular morphological rules to words that are exceptions. (p. 385)

P

parallel play A form of limited social participation in which a child plays near other children with similar materials but does not try to influence their behavior. Distinguished from *nonsocial activity, associative play,* and *cooperative play.* (p. 605)

partial fetal alcohol syndrome (p-FAS) A form of fetal alcohol spectrum disorder characterized by facial abnormalities and brain injury, but less severe than fetal alcohol syndrome; usually seen in children whose mothers drank alcohol in smaller quantities during pregnancy. (p. 98)

peer acceptance Likeability, or the extent to which a child is viewed by a group of agemates, such as classmates, as a worthy social partner. (p. 615)

peer group A collective of peers who generate unique values and standards for behavior and a social structure of leaders and followers. (p. 619)

peer reputation Judgments by children and adolescents of the peers most of their classmates admire, yielding an assessment of peer acceptance in terms of *social prominence.* (p. 616)

peer victimization A destructive form of peer interaction in which certain children become frequent targets of verbal and physical attacks or other forms of abuse. (p. 618)

permissive child-rearing style A child-rearing style that is high in acceptance but overindulging or inattentive, low in control, and lenient rather than appropriate in autonomy granting. Distinguished from *authoritative, authoritarian,* and *uninvolved child-rearing styles.* (p. 571)

person perception The way individuals size up the attributes of people with whom they are familiar. (p. 470)

personal fable Adolescents' inflated opinion of their own importance—the belief that they are special and unique, which leads them to conclude that others cannot possibly understand their thoughts and feelings. (p. 252)

perspective taking The capacity to imagine what other people may be thinking and feeling. (p. 473)

phenotype An individual's directly observable physical and behavioral characteristics, which are determined by both genetic and environmental factors. Distinguished from *genotype.* (p. 71)

phonemes The smallest sound units that signal a change in meaning. (p. 367)

phonics approach An approach to beginning reading instruction that emphasizes coaching children on phonics—the basic rules for translating written symbols into sounds—before exposing them to complex reading material. Distinguished from *whole-language approach.* (p. 307)

phonological awareness The ability to reflect on and manipulate the sound structure of spoken language, as indicated by sensitivity to changes in sounds within words, to rhyming, and to incorrect pronunciation—a strong predictor of emergent literacy. (p. 306)

phonological store A special part of working memory that permits retention of speech-based information and, thus, supports early vocabulary development. (p. 380)

phonology The component of language concerned with the rules governing the structure and sequence of speech sounds. (p. 358)

physical aggression A form of reactive aggression that harms others through physical injury to themselves or their property. Distinguished from *verbal aggression* and *relational aggression.* (p. 514)

pincer grasp The well-coordinated grasp that emerges at the end of the first year, involving thumb and index finger opposition. (p. 149)

pituitary gland A gland located at the base of the brain that releases hormones affecting physical growth. (p. 180)

placenta The organ that permits exchange of nutrients and waste products between the bloodstreams of the mother and the embryo, while also preventing the mother's and embryo's blood from mixing directly. (p. 89)

planning Thinking out a sequence of acts ahead of time and allocating attention accordingly to reach a goal. (p. 287)

polygenic inheritance A pattern of inheritance in which many genes determine a characteristic that varies on a continuum among people. (p. 80)

popular children Children who get many positive votes on sociometric measures of peer acceptance and, thus, are high in likability. Distinguished from *rejected, controversial,* and *neglected children.* (p. 616)

popular-antisocial children A subtype of popular children consisting of "tough," athletically skilled but defiant, trouble-causing boys and of relationally aggressive boys and girls who are admired for their sophisticated but devious social skills. Distinguished from *popular-prosocial children.* (p. 616)

popular-prosocial children A subtype of popular children who combine academic and social competence. Distinguished from *popular-antisocial children.* (p. 616)

postconventional level Kohlberg's highest level of moral development, in which individuals define morality in terms of abstract principles and values that apply to all situations and societies. (p. 497)

practical intelligence Mental abilities apparent in the real world but not in testing situations. (p. 331)

practice effects Changes in participants' natural responses as a result of repeated testing. (p. 61)

pragmatics The component of language concerned with the rules for engaging in appropriate and effective communication. (p. 358)

preconventional level Kohlberg's first level of moral development, in which morality is externally controlled—based on rewards, punishments, and the power of authority figures. (p. 496)

prenatal diagnostic methods Medical procedures that permit detection of developmental problems before birth. (p. 82)

preoperational stage Piaget's second stage, spanning ages 2 to 7, characterized by an extraordinary increase in mental representation, although thought is not yet logical. (p. 236)

prereaching The poorly coordinated, primitive reaching movements of newborn babies. (p. 148)

preterm infants Infants born several weeks or more before their due date. (p. 113)

primary sexual characteristics Physical features involving the reproductive organs (ovaries, uterus, and vagina in females; penis, scrotum, and testes in males). Distinguished from *secondary sexual characteristics.* (p. 200)

private speech Self-directed speech that children use to guide their own thinking and behavior. (p. 265)

proactive aggression Aggression in which children act to fulfill a need or desire—obtain an object, privilege, space, or social reward—and unemotionally attack a person to achieve their goal. Also called *instrumental* aggression. Distinguished from *reactive aggression.* (p. 514)

problem-centered coping A general strategy for managing emotion in which the individual appraises the situation as changeable, identifies the difficulty, and decides what to do about it. Distinguished from *emotion-centered coping.* (p. 410)

production In language development, the words and word combinations that children use. Distinguished from *comprehension.* (p. 375)

production deficiency Failure to produce a mental strategy when it could be helpful. Distinguished from *control deficiency, utilization deficiency,* and *effective strategy use.* (p. 286)

programmed cell death Death of many surrounding neurons as neural fibers and their synapses increase rapidly, which makes room for these connective structures. (p. 183)

Project Head Start A U.S. federal early intervention program that provides children from low-income families with a year or two of preschool education, along with nutritional and health services, and that encourages parent involvement in program planning and children's learning and development. (p. 345)

propositional thought A type of formal operational reasoning involving the ability to evaluate the logic of propositions (verbal statements) without referring to real-world circumstances. (p. 252)

prosocial, or **altruistic, behavior** Actions that benefit another person without any expected reward for the self. (p. 414)

protection from harm The right of research participants to be protected from physical or psychological harm. (p. 66)

protodeclarative A preverbal communicative gesture in which the baby points to, touches, or holds up an object while looking at others to make sure they notice. (p. 370)

protoimperative A preverbal communicative gesture in which the baby gets another person to do something by reaching, pointing, and often making sounds at the same time. (p. 370)

proximodistal trend An organized pattern of physical growth and motor control that proceeds from the center of the body outward. (p. 146)

psychoanalytic perspective An approach to personality development introduced by Freud, in which children move through a series of stages in which they confront conflicts between biological drives and social expectations. The way these conflicts are resolved determines the person's ability to learn, to get along with others, and to cope with anxiety. (p. 16)

psychological control Parental behaviors that intrude on and manipulate children's verbal expressions, individuality, and attachments to parents. (p. 571)

psychometric approach An approach to cognitive development that focuses on the construction of tests to assess mental abilities. (p. 317)

psychophysiological methods Research methods that measure the relationship between physiological processes and behavior. Among the most common are measures of autonomic nervous system activity (such as heart rate, respiration, and stress hormone levels) and measures of brain functioning (such as the *electroencephalogram [EEG], event-related potentials [ERPs], positron emission tomography [PET], functional magnetic resonance imaging [fMRI],* and *near-infrared optical topography [NIROT]*). (pp. 47–49)

psychosexual theory Freud's theory, which emphasizes that how parents manage their child's sexual and aggressive drives in the first few years is crucial for healthy personality development. (p. 16)

psychosocial dwarfism A growth disorder, usually appearing between 2 and 15 years of age and caused by extreme emotional deprivation, characterized by very short stature, decreased growth hormone secretion, immature skeletal age, and serious adjustment problems, which help distinguish psychosocial dwarfism from normal shortness. (p. 200)

psychosocial theory Erikson's theory, which emphasizes that at each Freudian stage, individuals not only develop a unique personality but also acquire attitudes and skills that help them become active, contributing members of their society. Recognizes the lifespan nature of development and the impact of culture. (p. 17)

puberty Biological changes at adolescence that lead to an adult-sized body and sexual maturity. (p. 200)

public policy Laws and government programs aimed at improving current conditions. (p. 32)

punishment In operant conditioning, removal of a desirable stimulus or presentation of an unpleasant stimulus, either of which decreases the occurrence of a response. (p. 139)

R

random assignment An evenhanded procedure for assigning participants to treatment groups, such as drawing numbers out of a hat or flipping a coin. Increases the chances that participants' characteristics will be equally distributed across treatment conditions in an experiment. (p. 57)

range of reaction Each person's unique, genetically determined response to a range of environmental conditions. (p. 120)

rapid-eye-movement (REM) sleep An "irregular" sleep state in which electrical brain-wave activity is similar to that of the waking state; eyes dart beneath the lids; heart rate, blood pressure, and breathing are uneven; and slight body movements occur. Distinguished from *non-rapid-eye-movement (NREM) sleep.* (p. 131)

reactive aggression An angry, defensive response to a provocation or a blocked goal; intended to hurt another person. Also called *hostile* aggression. Distinguished from *proactive aggression.* (p. 514)

realism In Piaget's heteronomous stage of moral development, the child's tendency to view rules, like other mental phenomena, as fixed external features of reality rather than as cooperative principles that can be modified at will. (p. 492)

recall The type of memory that involves generating a mental representation of an absent stimulus. Distinguished from *recognition.* (p. 292)

recasts Adult responses that restructure children's grammatically inaccurate speech into correct form. (p. 388)

reciprocal teaching A teaching method in which a teacher and two to four students form a cooperative group, within which dialogues occur that create a zone of proximal development. (p. 269)

recognition The simplest form of memory, which involves noticing that a stimulus is identical or similar to one previously experienced. Distinguished from *recall.* (p. 292)

reconstruction The type of memory that involves recoding information while it is in the system or being retrieved. (p. 293)

recovery Following habituation, an increase in responsiveness to a new stimulus. (p. 140)

referential communication skills The ability to produce clear verbal messages and to recognize when the meaning of others' messages in unclear. (p. 389)

referential style A style of early language learning in which toddlers use language mainly to label objects. Distinguished from *expressive style.* (p. 377)

reflex An inborn, automatic response to a particular form of stimulation. (p. 128)

rehearsal A memory strategy that involves repeating information to oneself. (p. 289)

reinforcer In operant conditioning, a stimulus that increases the occurrence of a response. (p. 139)

rejected children Children who get many negative votes on sociometric measures of peer acceptance and, thus, are actively disliked. Distinguished from *popular, controversial,* and *neglected children.* (p. 616)

rejected-aggressive children A subtype of rejected children who show severe conduct problems—high rates of conflict, physical and relational aggression, and hyperactive, inattentive, and impulsive behavior. Distinguished from *rejected-withdrawn children.* (p. 617)

rejected-withdrawn children A subtype of rejected children who are passive, socially awkward, and overwhelmed by social anxiety. Distinguished from *rejected-aggressive children.* (p. 617)

relational aggression A form of reactive aggression that damages another's peer relationships through social exclusion, malicious gossip, or friendship manipulation. Distinguished from *physical aggression* and *verbal aggression.* (p. 514)

reliability The consistency, or repeatability, of measures of behavior. (p. 54)

remembered self The child's life-story narrative, or autobiographical memory, constructed from conversations with adults about the past. (p. 446)

resilience The ability to adapt effectively in the face of threats to development. (p. 10)

resistant attachment The quality of insecure attachment characterizing infants who seek closeness to the parent before her departure, are usually distressed when she leaves, and combine clinginess with angry, resistive behavior when she returns. Distinguished from *secure, avoidant,* and *disorganized/disoriented attachment.* (p. 428)

reticular formation A structure in the brain stem that maintains alertness and consciousness. (p. 188)

reversibility The ability to go through a series of steps in a problem and then mentally reverse direction, returning to the starting point. In Piaget's theory, part of every logical operation. (p. 242)

Rh factor incompatibility A condition that arises when the Rh protein is present in the fetus's blood but not in the mother's, causing the mother to build up antibodies. If these enter the fetus's system, they destroy red blood cells, reducing the oxygen supply to organs and tissues. (p. 112)

risks-versus-benefits ratio A comparison of the costs of a research study to participants in terms of inconvenience and possible psychological or physical injury against the study's value for advancing knowledge and improving conditions of life. Used in assessing the ethics of research. (p. 66)

rough-and-tumble play A form of peer interaction involving friendly chasing and play-fighting that, in our evolutionary past, may have been important for the development of fighting skill. (p. 607)

S

scaffolding Adjusting the assistance offered during a teaching session to fit the child's current level of performance. As competence increases, the adult gradually and sensitively withdraws support, turning responsibility over to the child. (p. 266)

schemes In Piaget's theory, specific psychological structures, or organized ways of making sense of experience, that change with age. (p. 225)

scripts General representations of what occurs and when it occurs in a particular situation, used to organize and interpret repeated events. (p. 295)

secondary sexual characteristics Features visible on the outside of the body that serve as signs of sexual maturity but do not involve the reproductive organs, including breast development in females and the appearance of underarm and pubic hair in both sexes. Distinguished from *primary sexual characteristics.* (p. 200)

secular trends in physical growth Changes in body size and rate of growth from one generation to the next. (p. 182)

secure attachment The attachment pattern characterizing infants who use the parent as a secure base from which to explore and who are easily comforted by the parent on being reunited after a separation. Distinguished from *avoidant, resistant,* and *disorganized/disoriented attachment.* (p. 427)

secure base The baby's use of the familiar caregiver as the point from which to explore the environment and to return to for emotional support. (p. 406)

selective attrition Selective loss of participants during an investigation, resulting in a biased sample. (p. 61)

self-care children Children who regularly look after themselves during after-school hours. (p. 594)

self-concept The set of attributes, abilities, attitudes, and values that an individual believes defines who he or she is. (p. 451)

self-conscious emotions Emotions—such as shame, embarrassment, guilt, envy, and pride—that involve injury to or enhancement of the sense of self. (p. 406)

self-esteem The aspect of self-concept that involves judgments about one's own worth and the feelings associated with those judgments. (p. 455)

self-recognition Identification of the self as a physically unique being, distinct from other people and objects. (p. 445)

semantic bootstrapping In language development, children's reliance on semantics, or word meanings, to figure out sentence structure. (p. 387)

semantic memory The vast, taxonomically organized and hierarchically structured general knowledge system. (p. 295)

semantics The component of language that involves vocabulary—the way underlying concepts are expressed in words and word combinations. (p. 358)

sensitive caregiving Caregiving that involves responding promptly, consistently, and appropriately to infant signals and holding infants tenderly and carefully. (p. 430)

sensitive period A time that is optimal for certain capacities to emerge and in which the individual is especially responsive to environmental influences. (p. 24)

sensorimotor stage Piaget's first stage, spanning the first two years of life, in which infants and toddlers "think" with their eyes, ears, hands, and other sensorimotor equipment. (p. 226)

sensory register The part of the information-processing system in which sights and sounds are represented directly and stored briefly before they decay or are transferred to working memory. (p. 276)

separation anxiety An infant's distressed reaction to the departure of the familiar caregiver. (p. 426)

sequential design A research design in which several similar cross-sectional or longitudinal studies (called sequences) are conducted at varying times. (p. 63)

seriation The ability to arrange items along a quantitative dimension, such as length or weight. (p. 247)

sex chromosomes The twenty-third pair of chromosomes, which determines the sex of the child. In females, this pair is called XX; in males, it is called XY. (p. 74)

shading A conversational strategy in which a speaker initiates a change of topic gradually by modifying the focus of discussion. (p. 389)

shape bias In early language development, children's tendency to rely heavily on shape as a distinguishing property when learning names for objects. (p. 381)

shape constancy Perception of an object's shape as stable, despite changes in the shape projected on the retina. (p. 161)

shared environmental influences Environmental influences that pervade the general atmosphere of the home and, therefore, similarly affect siblings living in it. Distinguished from *nonshared environmental influences*. (p. 341)

size constancy Perception of an object's size as stable, despite changes in the size of its retinal image. (p. 161)

skeletal age An estimate of physical maturity based on development of the bones of the body. (p. 176)

slow-to-warm-up child A child whose temperament is characterized by inactivity; mild, low-key reactions to environmental stimuli; negative mood; and slow adjustment to new experiences. Distinguished from *easy child* and *difficult child*. (p. 417)

small-for-date infants Infants, either full-term or preterm, whose birth weight is below normal considering length of the pregnancy. (p. 113)

social cognition Thinking about the characteristics of the self and of other people. (p. 443)

social comparisons Evaluations of one's own abilities, behavior, and appearance in relation to those of others. (p. 453)

social-constructivist classroom A classroom in which children participate in a wide range of challenging activities with teachers and peers, with whom they jointly construct understandings. Grounded in Vygotsky's sociocultural theory. Distinguished from *traditional classrooms* and *constructivist classrooms*. (p. 637)

social conventions Customs, such as table manners and rituals of social interaction, that are determined solely by consensus. Distinguished from *moral imperatives* and *matters of personal choice*. (p. 506)

social learning theory A theory that emphasizes the role of modeling, otherwise known as imitation or observational learning, in the development of behavior. Its most recent revision stresses the importance of thinking in social learning and is called *social-cognitive theory*. (p. 19)

social policy Any planned set of actions by a group, institution, or governing body directed at attaining a social goal. (p. 32)

social problem solving Generating and applying strategies that prevent or resolve disagreements, resulting in outcomes that are both acceptable to others and beneficial to the self. (p. 476)

social referencing Relying on another person's emotional reaction to appraise an uncertain situation. (p. 412)

social smile The smile evoked by the stimulus of the human face. First appears between 6 and 10 weeks. (p. 405)

social systems perspective A view of the family as a complex set of interacting relationships influenced by the larger social context. (p. 565)

sociocultural theory Vygotsky's theory, in which children acquire the ways of thinking and behaving that make up a community's culture through cooperative dialogues with more knowledgeable members of society. (p. 25)

sociodramatic play The make-believe play with other children that is under way around age 2 and increases rapidly during the next few years. (p. 237)

socioeconomic status (SES) A measure of a family's social position and economic well-being that combines three related variables: years of education, the prestige of and skill required by one's job, and income. (p. 332)

sociometric techniques Self-reports that measure peer acceptance in terms of social preferences—the extent to which children or adolescents like, or prefer to spend time with, particular peers. (p. 615)

Sociomoral Reflection Measure–Short Form (SRM–SF) A short-answer questionnaire that assesses moral understanding by asking individuals to rate the importance of moral values posed by 11 brief questions and to write a brief explanation of their ratings. More efficient than Kohlberg's Moral Judgment Interview. (p. 495)

specific intelligence In Spearman's theory, a mental ability that is unique to a test item. Distinguished from *general intelligence*, or *"g."* (p. 319)

speech registers Language adaptations to social expectations. (p. 391)

spermarche Scientific name for first ejaculation. (p. 202)

stage A qualitative change in thinking, feeling, and behaving that characterizes a specific period of development. (p. 8)

standardization The practice of giving a newly constructed test to a large, representative sample of individuals, which serves as the standard for interpreting individual scores. (p. 328)

Stanford-Binet Intelligence Scales, Fifth Edition An individually administered intelligence test, appropriate for individuals age 2 to adulthood, that is the modern descendent of Alfred Binet's first successful test for children. Measures general intelligence and five intellectual factors: fluid reasoning, quantitative reasoning, knowledge, visual-spatial processing, and working memory. (p. 326)

states of arousal Different degrees of sleep and wakefulness. (p. 130)

statistical learning capacity Infants' ability to analyze the speech stream for regularly occurring sound sequences, through which they acquire a stock of speech structures for which they will later learn meanings. (p. 153)

stereotype threat The fear of being judged on the basis of a negative stereotype, which can trigger anxiety that interferes with performance. (p. 340)

store model An information-processing model that assumes that we hold, or store, information in three parts of the mental system for processing: the sensory register; working, or short-term, memory; and long-term memory. (p. 276)

Strange Situation A laboratory technique for assessing the quality of infant–caregiver attachment between 1 and 2 years of age by observing the baby's responses to eight short episodes, in which brief separations from and reunions with the caregiver occur in an unfamiliar playroom. (p. 427)

stranger anxiety Expression of fear in response to unfamiliar adults, which appears in many babies in the second half of the first year. (p. 405)

structured interview An interview method in which each participant is asked the same questions in the same way. (p. 46)

structured observation A method in which the researcher sets up a laboratory situation that evokes the behavior of interest so that every participant has an equal opportunity to display the response. Distinguished from *naturalistic observation*. (p. 44)

sudden infant death syndrome (SIDS) The unexpected death, usually during the night, of an infant under 1 year of age that remains unexplained after thorough investigation. (p. 134)

sympathy Feelings of concern or sorrow for another's plight. (p. 414)

synapses The gaps between neurons, across which chemical messages are sent. (p. 183)

synaptic pruning Loss of synapses by seldom-stimulated neurons, thereby returning them to an uncommitted state so they can support future development. (p. 183)

syntactic bootstrapping In language development, children's discovery of word meanings by observing how words are used in syntax, or the structure of sentences. (p. 381)

syntax The rules by which words are arranged into sentences. (p. 358)

T

tabula rasa Locke's view of the child as a "blank slate" whose character is shaped by experience. (p. 12)

talent Outstanding performance in one or a few related fields. (p. 351)

telegraphic speech Young children's two-word utterances that, like a telegram, focus on high-content words while omitting smaller, less important ones. (p. 383)

temperament Early appearing, stable individual differences in reactivity and self-regulation. Reactivity refers to variations in quickness and intensity of emotional arousal, attention, and motor action. Self-regulation refers to strategies that modify reactivity. (p. 417)

teratogen Any environmental agent that causes damage during the prenatal period. (p. 93)

theory An orderly, integrated set of statements that describes, explains, and predicts behavior. (p. 6)

theory of mind A coherent understanding of people as mental beings, which children revise as they encounter new evidence. (p. 301)

theory of multiple intelligences Gardner's theory, which identifies at least eight intelligences, defined in terms of distinct sets of processing operations applied in culturally valued activities: linguistic, logico-mathematical, musical, spatial, bodily-kinesthetic, naturalist, interpersonal, and intrapersonal. (p. 323)

theory theory A theory that assumes that children draw on innate concepts to form naïve theories, or explanations of everyday events in each core domain of thought. Then they test their theory against experience, revising it when it cannot adequately account for new information. (p. 261)

three-stratum theory of intelligence Carroll's factor-analytic theory, which represents the structure of intelligence in three tiers, with "g" at the top; an array of biologically based abilities in the second tier; and specific behaviors in the third tier. The most comprehensive factor-analytic classification of mental abilities to date. (p. 320)

thyroxine A hormone released by the thyroid gland that is necessary for brain development and for growth hormone (GH) to have its full impact on body size. (p. 180)

time out A form of mild punishment in which children are removed from the immediate setting until they are ready to act appropriately. (p. 488)

time sampling An observational procedure in which the researcher records whether certain behaviors occur during a sample of short intervals. (p. 45)

traditional classroom A classroom in which the teacher is the sole authority for knowledge, rules, and decision making and students are relatively passive learners who are evaluated in relation to a uniform set of standards. Distinguished from *constructivist classroom* and *social-constructivist classroom.* (p. 635)

transitive inference The ability to seriate, or arrange items along a quantitative dimension, mentally. (p. 247)

triarchic theory of successful intelligence Sternberg's theory, which states that intelligent behavior involves balancing analytical intelligence, creative intelligence, and practical intelligence to achieve success in life, according to one's personal goals and the requirements of one's cultural community. (p. 322)

turnabout A conversational strategy in which the speaker, after commenting on what has just been said, also adds a request to get the partner to respond again. (p. 389)

U

ulnar grasp The clumsy grasp of the young infant, in which the fingers close against the palm. (p. 149)

umbilical cord The long cord connects the prenatal organism to the placenta, delivering nutrients and removing waste products. (p. 89)

unconditioned response (UCR) In classical conditioning, a reflexive response that is produced by an unconditioned stimulus (UCS). (p. 138)

unconditioned stimulus (UCS) In classical conditioning, a stimulus that leads to a reflexive response. (p. 138)

underextension An early vocabulary error in which a word is applied too narrowly, to a smaller number of objects or events than is appropriate. Distinguished from *overextension.* (p. 378)

uninhibited, or **sociable, child** A child who tends to display positive emotion to and approach novel stimuli. Distinguished from *inhibited,* or *shy, child.* (p. 419)

uninvolved child-rearing style A parenting style that combines low acceptance and involvement with little control and general indifference to issues of autonomy. Distinguished from *authoritarian, authoritative,* and *permissive child-rearing styles.* (p. 571)

universal grammar In Chomsky's theory of language development, a built-in storehouse of grammatical rules that applies to all human languages. (p. 359)

utilization deficiency Consistent use of a mental strategy, with little or no improvement in performance. Distinguished from *production deficiency, control deficiency,* and *effective strategy use.* (p. 286)

V

validity The extent to which methods in a research study accurately measure what the investigator set out to measure. (p. 54)

velocity curve A growth curve that plots the average amount of growth at each yearly interval for a sample of children, revealing the exact timing of growth spurts. Distinguished from *distance curve.* (p. 175)

verbal aggression A form of reactive aggression that harms others through threats of physical aggression, name-calling, or hostile teasing. Distinguished from *physical aggression* and *relational aggression.* (p. 514)

vernix A white, cheeselike substance covering the fetus, preventing the skin from chapping due to constant exposure to amniotic fluid. (p. 91)

violation-of-expectation method A method in which researchers show babies an expected event (one that follows physical laws) and an unexpected event (a variation of the first event that violates physical laws). Heightened attention to the unexpected event suggests that the infant is "surprised" by a deviation from physical reality and, therefore, is aware of that aspect of the physical world. (p. 229)

visual acuity Fineness of visual discrimination. (p. 155)

visual cliff An apparatus used to study depth perception in infants. Consists of a Plexiglas-covered table and a central platform, from which babies are encouraged to crawl. Checkerboard patterns placed beneath the glass create the appearance of a shallow and a deep side. (p. 156)

W

Wechsler Intelligence Scale for Children–IV (WISC–IV) An individually administered intelligence test, appropriate for ages 6 through 16, that measures general intelligence and four broad intellectual factors: verbal reasoning, perceptual reasoning, working memory, and processing speed. (p. 326)

Wernicke's area A language structure located in the left temporal lobe of the cerebral cortex that plays a role in comprehending word meaning. (p. 362)

whole-language approach An approach to beginning reading instruction that parallels natural language learning by exposing children to text in its complete form, using reading materials that are whole and meaningful. Distinguished from *phonics approach.* (p. 307)

working, or **short-term, memory** The part of the information-processing system where we "work" on a limited amount of information, actively applying mental strategies to ensure that information will be retained and used effectively to comprehend, reason, and solve problems. (p. 277)

X

X-linked inheritance A pattern of inheritance in which a recessive gene is carried on the X chromosome. Males are more likely to be affected. (p. 78)

Z

zone of proximal development In Vygotsky's theory, a range of tasks too difficult for the child to do alone but possible with the help of adults and more skilled peers. (p. 265)

zygote The newly fertilized cell formed by the union of sperm and ovum at conception. (p. 73)

References

Aalsma, M., Lapsley, D. K., & Flannery, D. J. (2006). Personal fables, narcissism, and adolescent adjustment. *Psychology in the Schools, 43,* 481–491.

Abbott, S. (1992). Holding on and pushing away: Comparative perspectives on an eastern Kentucky child-rearing practice. *Ethos, 20,* 33–65.

ABC News. (2004). *The American Sex Survey: A peek beneath the sheets.* Retrieved from abcnews.go.com/images/Politics/959a1AmericanSexSurvey.pdf

Abel, E. (2004). Paternal contribution to fetal alcohol syndrome. *Addiction Biology, 9,* 127–133.

Abela, J. R. Z., Hankin, B. L., Haigh, E. A. P., Adams, P., Vinokuroff, T., & Trayhern, L. (2005). Interpersonal vulnerability to depression in high-risk children: The role of insecure attachment and reassurance seeking. *Journal of Clinical Child and Adolescent Psychology, 34,* 182–192.

Aber, J. L., Jones, S. M., & Raver, C. C. (2007). Poverty and child development: New perspectives on a defining issue. In J. L. Aber, S. J. Bishop-Josef, S. M. Jones, K. T. McLearn, & D. Phillips (Eds.), *Child development and social policy: Knowledge for action* (pp. 149–166). Washington, DC: American Psychological Association.

Abikoff, H. B., Jensen, P. S., Arnold, L. L. E., Hoza, B., et al. (2002). Observed classroom behavior of children with ADHD: Relationship to gender and comorbidity. *Journal of Abnormal Child Psychology, 30,* 349–359.

Aboud, F. E. (2003). The formation of in-group favoritism and out-group prejudice in young children: Are they distinct attitudes? *Developmental Psychology, 39,* 48–60.

Aboud, F. E., & Amato, M. (2001). Developmental and socialization influences on intergroup bias. In R. Brown & S. Gaertner (Eds.), *Blackwell handbook of social psychology: Intergroup processes.* Oxford, UK: Blackwell.

Aboud, F. E., & Doyle, A. (1996). Parental and peer influences on children's racial attitudes. *International Journal of Intercultural Relations, 20,* 371–383.

Achenbach, T. M., Phares, V., Howell, C. T., Rauh, V. A., & Nurcombe, B. (1990). Seven-year outcome of the Vermont intervention program for low-birthweight infants. *Child Development, 61,* 1672–1681.

Acker, M. M., & O'Leary, S. G. (1996). Inconsistency of mothers' feedback and toddlers' misbehavior and negative affect. *Journal of Abnormal Child Psychology, 24,* 703–714.

Ackerman, B. P. (1978). Children's understanding of speech acts in unconventional frames. *Child Development, 49,* 311–318.

Ackerman, B. P. (1993). Children's understanding of the speaker's meaning in referential communication. *Journal of Experimental Child Psychology, 55,* 56–86.

Adachi-Mejia, A. M., Longacre, M. R., Gibson, J. J., Beach, M. L., Titus-Ernstoff, L. T., & Dalton, M. A. (2007). Children with a TV in their bedroom at higher risk for being overweight. *International Journal of Obesity, 31,* 644–651.

Adams, G. R., & Marshall, S. (1996). A developmental social psychology of identity: Understanding the person in context. *Journal of Adolescence, 19,* 429–442.

Adams, M. (2003). *Fire and ice: The United States, Canada, and the myth of converging values.* Toronto: Penguin.

Adams, R., & Laursen, B. (2001). The organization and dynamics of adolescent conflict with parents and friends. *Journal of Marriage and the Family, 63,* 97–110.

Adolph, K. (2002). Learning to keep balance. In R. V. Kail (Ed.), *Advances in child development and behavior* (Vol. 30, pp. 1–40). Boston: Academic Press.

Adolph, K. E. (2000). Specificity of learning: Why infants fall over a veritable cliff. *Psychological Science, 11,* 290–295.

Adolph, K. E., & Berger, S. E. (2006). Motor development. In D. Kuhn & R. Siegler (Eds.), *Handbook of child psychology: Vol. 2. Cognition, perception, and language* (6th ed., pp. 161–213). Hoboken, NJ: Wiley.

Adolph, K. E., Vereijken, B., & Shrout, P. E. (2003). What changes in infant walking and why. *Child Development, 74,* 475–497.

Afifi, T. O., Brownridge, D. A., Cox, B. J., & Sareen J. (2006). Physical punishment, childhood abuse and psychiatric disorders. *Child Abuse and Neglect, 30,* 1093–1103.

Aggarwal, R., Sentz, J., & Miller, M. A. (2007). Role of zinc administration in prevention of childhood diarrhea and respiratory illnesses: A meta-analysis. *Pediatrics, 119,* 1120–1130.

Aguiar, A., & Baillargeon, R. (1999). 2.5-month-old infants' reasoning about when objects should and should not be occluded. *Cognitive Psychology, 39,* 116–157.

Aguiar, A., & Baillargeon, R. (2002). Developments in young infants' reasoning about occluded objects. *Cognitive Psychology, 45,* 267–336.

Aguiar, A., & Baillargeon, R. (2003). Perseverative responding in a violation-of-expectation task in 6.5-month-old infants. *Cognition, 88,* 277–316.

Ahlgren, M., Melbye, M., Wohlfahrt, J., & Sørensen, T. I. (2004). Growth patterns and the risk of breast cancer in women. *New England Journal of Medicine, 351,* 1619–1626.

Ahmed, A., & Ruffman, T. (1998). Why do infants make A not B errors in a search task, yet show memory for the location of hidden objects in a nonsearch task? *Developmental Psychology, 34,* 441–453.

Aikens, J. W., Bierman, K. L., & Parker, J. G. (2005). Navigating the transition to junior high school: The influence of pre-transition friendship and self-system characteristics. *Social Development, 14,* 42–60.

Ainsworth, M. D. S., Blehar, M., Waters, E., & Wall, S. (1978). *Patterns of attachment.* Hillsdale, NJ: Erlbaum.

Akers, J. F., Jones, R. M., & Coyl, D. D. (1998). Adolescent friendship pairs: Similarities in identity status development, behaviors, attitudes, and intentions. *Journal of Adolescent Research, 13,* 178–201.

Akhtar, N., & Montague, L. (1999). Early -lexical acquisition: The role of cross-situational learning. *First Language, 19,* 347–358.

Akhtar, N., & Tomasello, M. (2000). The social nature of words and word learning. In R. Golinkoff & K. Hirsh-Pasek (Eds.), *Becoming a word learner: A debate on lexical acquisition.* Oxford, UK: Oxford University Press.

Akimoto, S. A., & Sanbonmatsu, D. M. (1999). Differences in self-effacing behavior between European and Japanese Americans: Effect on competence evaluations. *Journal of Cross-Cultural Psychology, 30,* 159–177.

Aksan, N., & Kochanska, G. (2004). Heterogeneity of joy in infancy. *Infancy, 6,* 79–94.

Akshoomoff, N. A., Feroleto, C. C., Doyle, R. E., & Stiles, J. (2002). The impact of early unilateral brain injury on perceptual organization and visual memory. *Neuropsychologia, 40,* 539–561.

Alan Guttmacher Institute. (2001). *Can more progress be made? Teenager sexual and reproductive behavior in developed countries.* New York: Author. Retrieved from www.guttmacher.org

Alan Guttmacher Institute. (2002). Teen sex and pregnancy. Retrieved from www.agi-usa.org/pubs/ib_teensex.html

Alan Guttmacher Institute. (2004). Teen sexuality: Stats & facts. Retrieved from www.fotf.ca/familyfacts/issues/teensexuality/stats.html

Alan Guttmacher Institute. (2005). *Facts in brief: Contraceptive use.* Retrieved from www.guttmacher.org/pubs/fb_contr_use.html

Alan Guttmacher Institute. (2006). *U.S. teenage pregnancy statistics: National and state trends and trends by race and ethnicity.* New York: Author. Retrieved from www.guttmacher.org/pubs/2006/09/12/USTPstats.pdf

Albers, C. A., & Grieve, A. J. (2007). Test review: Bayley, N. (2006). Bayley Scales of Infant and Toddler Development–Third Edition. San Antonio, TX: Harcourt Assessment. *Journal of Psychoeducational Assessment, 25,* 180–190.

Aldridge, M. A., Stillman, R. D., & Bower, T. G. R. (2001). Newborn categorization of vowel-like sounds. *Developmental Science, 4,* 220–232.

Alessandri, S. M., Sullivan, M. W., & Lewis, M. (1990). Violation of expectancy and frustration in early infancy. *Developmental Psychology, 26,* 738–744.

Alexander, J. M., Fabricius, W. V., Fleming, V. M., Zwahr, M., & Brown, S. A. (2003). The development of metacognitive causal explanations. *Learning and Individual Differences, 13,* 227–238.

Alexandre-Bidon, K. L., & Lett, D. (1997). *Les enfants au Moyen Age, Ve–XVe siecles.* Paris: Hachette.

Ali, L., & Scelfo, J. (2002, December 9). Choosing virginity. *Newsweek,* pp. 60–65.

Alibali, M. W. (1999). How children change their minds: Strategy change can be gradual or abrupt. *Developmental Psychology, 35,* 127–145.

Alink, L. R. A., Mesman, J., van Zeijl, J., Stolk, M. N., Juffer, F., & Koot, H. M. (2006). The early childhood aggression curve: Development of physical aggression in 10- to 50-month-old children. *Child Development, 77,* 954–966.

Allen, J. P., Philliber, S., Herrling, S., & Kuperminc, G. P. (1997). Preventing teen pregnancy and academic failure: Experimental evaluation of a developmentally based approach. *Child Development, 64,* 729–742.

Allen, J. P., Porter, M. R., & McFarland, F. C. (2006). Leaders and followers in adolescent close friendships: Susceptibility to peer influence as a predictor of risky behavior, friendship instability, and depression. *Development and Psychopathology, 18,* 155–172.

Allen, J. P., Seitz, V., & Apfel, N. H. (2007). The sexually mature teen as a whole person. In J. L. Aber, S. J. Bishop-Josef, S. M. Jones, K. T. McLearn, & D. A. Phillips (Eds.), *New directions in prevention and intervention for teen pregnancy and parenthood* (pp. 185–199). Washington, DC: American Psychological Association.

Allen, M., & Burrell, N. (1996). Comparing the impact of homosexual and heterosexual parents on children: Meta-analysis of existing research. *Journal of Homosexuality, 32,* 19–35.

Allen, S. E. M. (1996). *Aspects of argument structure acquisition in Inuktitut.* Amsterdam: Benjamins.

Allen, S. E. M., & Crago, M. B. (1996). Early passive acquisition in Inukitut. *Journal of Child Language, 23,* 129–156.

Allison, B. N., & Schultz, J. B. (2004). Parent–adolescent conflict in early adolescence. *Adolescence, 39,* 101–119.

Al-Namlah, A. S., Fernyhough, C., & Meins, E. (2006). Sociocultural influences on the development of verbal mediation: Private speech and phonological recoding in Saudi Arabian and British samples. *Developmental Psychology, 42,* 117–131.

Alsaker, F. D. (1995). Timing of puberty and reactions to pubertal changes. In M. Rutter (Ed.), *Psychosocial disturbances in young people* (pp. 37–82). New York: Cambridge University Press.

Altermatt, E. R., & Pomerantz, E. M. (2005). The implications of having high-achieving versus low-achieving friends: A longitudinal analysis. *Social Development, 14,* 61–81.

Amabile, T. M. (1982). Children's artistic creativity: Detrimental effects of competition in a field setting. *Personality and Social Psychology Bulletin, 8,* 573–578.

Amano, S., Kezuka, E., & Yamamoto, A. (2004). Infant shifting attention from an adult's face to an adult's hand: A precursor of joint attention. *Infant Behavior and Development, 27,* 64–80.

Amato, P. R. (2001). Children of divorce in the 1990s: An update of the Amato and Keith (1991) meta-analysis. *Journal of Family Psychology, 15,* 355–370.

Amato, P. R. (2006). Marital discord, divorce, and children's well-being: Results from a 20-year longitudinal study of two generation. In A. Clarke-Stewart & J. Dunn (Eds.), *Families count: Effects on child and adolescent development* (pp. 179–202). New York: Cambridge University Press.

Amato, P. R., & Cheadle, J. (2005). The long reach of divorce: Divorce and child well-being across three generations. *Journal of Marriage and Family, 67,* 191–206.

Amato, P. R., & Fowler, F. (2002). Parenting practices, child adjustment, and family diversity. *Journal of Marriage and the Family, 64,* 703–716.

Amato, P. R., & Sobolewski, J. M. (2004). The effects of divorce on fathers and children: Nonresidential fathers and stepfathers. In M. E. Lamb (Ed.), *The role of the father in child development* (4th ed., pp. 341–367). Hoboken, NJ: Wiley.

Ambert, A.-M. (2005). *Same-sex couples and same-sex parent families: Relationships, parenting, and issues of marriage.* Ontario: Vanier Institute of the Family. Retrieved from www.vifamily.ca/library/publications/samesexd.html

American Academy of Pediatrics. (2005a). Breastfeeding and the use of human milk. *Pediatrics, 115,* 496–506.

American Academy of Pediatrics, Subcommittee on Attention-Deficit Hyperactivity Disorder. (2005b). Treatment of attention-deficit hyperactivity disorder. *Pediatrics, 115,* e749–e757.

American Academy of Pediatrics. (2006). Folic acid for the prevention of neural tube defects. *Pediatrics, 104,* 325–327.

American Psychiatric Association. (1994). *Diagnostic and statistical manual of mental disorders* (4th ed.). Washington, DC: Author.

American Psychological Association. (2002). Ethical principles of psychologists and code of conduct. *American Psychologist, 57,* 1060–1073.

Amsel, E., & Brock, S. (1996). The development of evidence evaluation skills. *Cognitive Development, 11,* 523–550.

Amsel, E., Cottrell, J., Sullivan, J., & Bowden, T. (2005). Anticipating and avoiding regret as a model of adolescent decision-making. In J. Jacobs & P. Kaczynski (Eds.), *The development of judgment and decision-making in children and adolescents* (pp. 119–154). Mahwah, NJ: Erlbaum.

Amso, D., & Johnson, S. P. (2006). Learning by selection: Visual search and object perception in young infants. *Developmental Psychology, 42,* 1236–1245.

Amsterlaw, J. (2006). Children's beliefs about everyday reasoning. *Child Development, 77,* 443–464.

Amsterlaw, J., & Wellman, H. M. (2006). Theories of mind in transition: A microgenetic study of the development of false belief understanding. *Journal of Cognition and Development, 7,* 139–172.

Anand, S. S., Yusuf, S., Jacobs, R., Davis, A. D., Yi, Q., & Gerstein, H. (2001). Risk factors, arteriosclerosis, and cardiovascular disease among Aboriginal people in Canada: The study of health assessment and risk evaluation in Aboriginal peoples (SHARE-AP). *Lancet, 358,* 1147–1153.

Anderman, E. M., Eccles, J. S., Yoon, K. S., Roeser, R., Wigfield, A., & Blumenfeld, P. (2001). Learning to value mathematics and reading: Relations to mastery and performance-oriented instructional practices. *Contemporary Educational Psychology, 26,* 76–95.

Andersen, E. (1992). *Speaking with style: The sociolinguistic skills of children.* New York: Routledge.

Andersen, E. (2000). Exploring register knowledge: The value of "controlled improvisation." In L. Menn & N. B. Ratner (Eds.), *Methods for studying language production* (pp. 225–248). Mahwah, NJ: Erlbaum.

Anderson, C. A. (2004). An update on the effects of violent video games. *Journal of Adolescence, 27,* 113–122.

Anderson, C. A., Berkowitz, L., Donnerstein, E., Huesmann, R., Johnson, J. D., Linz, D., Malamuth, N. M., & Wartella, E. (2003). The influence of media violence on youth. *Psychological Science in the Public Interest, 4*(3), 81–106.

Anderson, C. A., & Bushman, B. J. (2002). The effects of media violence on society. *Science, 295,* 2377–2379.

Anderson, D. A., & Hamilton, M. (2005). Gender role stereotyping of parents in children's picture books: The invisible father. *Sex Roles, 52,* 145–151.

Anderson, D. M., Huston, A. C., Schmitt, K. L., Linebarger, D. L., & Wright, J. C. (2001). Early childhood television viewing and adolescent behavior. *Monographs of the Society for Research in Child Development, 66*(1, Serial No. 264).

Anderson, D. R., Collins, P. A., Schmitt, K. L., & Jacobvitz, R. S. (1996). Stressful life events and television viewing. *Communication Research, 23,* 243–260.

Anderson, J. L., Morgan, J. L., & White, K. S. (2003). A statistical basis for speech sound discrimination. *Language and Speech, 46,* 155–182.

Anderson, M. E., Johnson, D. C., & Batal, H. A. (2005). Sudden infant death syndrome and prenatal maternal smoking: Rising attributed risk in the Back to Sleep era. *BMC Medicine, 3,* 4.

Anderson, S. E., Dallal, G. E., & Must, A. (2003). Relative weight and race influence average age at menarche: Results from two nationally representative surveys of U.S. girls studied 25 years apart. *Pediatrics, 111,* 844–850.

Anderson, S. W., Bechara, A., Damasio, H., Tranel, D., & Damasio, A. R. (1999). Impairment of social and moral behavior related to early damage in human prefrontal cortex. *Nature Neuroscience, 2,* 1032–1037.

Anderson, V. A., Catroppa, C., Dudgeon, P., Morse, S. A., Haritou, F., & Rosenfeld, J. V. (2006). Understanding predictors of functional recovery and outcome 30 months following early childhood head injury. *Neuropsychology, 20,* 42–57.

Andersson, B.-E. (1989). Effects of public day care—A longitudinal study. *Child Development, 60,* 857–866.

Andersson, B.-E. (1992). Effects of day-care on cognitive and socioemotional competence of thirteen-year-old Swedish schoolchildren. *Child Development, 63,* 20–36.

Andersson, H. (1996). The Fagan Test of Infant Intelligence: Predictive validity in a random sample. *Psychological Reports, 78,* 1015–1026.

Andersson, S. W., Bengtsson, C., Hallberg, L., Lapidus, L., Niklasson, A., Wallgren, A., & Huthén, L. (2001). Cancer risk in Swedish women: The relation to size at birth. *British Journal of Cancer, 84,* 1193–1198.

Andersson, T., & Magnusson, D. (1990). Biological maturation in adolescence and the development of drinking habits and alcohol abuse among young males: A prospective longitudinal study. *Journal of Youth and Adolescence, 19,* 33–41.

Andresen, M. (2006). Accutane registry compulsory in U.S., but not Canada. *Canadian Medical Association Journal, 174,* 1701.

Andrews, G., & Halford, G. S. (1998). Children's ability to make transitive inferences: The importance of premise integration and structural complexity. *Cognitive Development, 13,* 479–513.

Anglin, J. M. (1993). Vocabulary development: A morphological analysis. *Monographs of the Society for Research in Child Development, 58*(10, Serial No. 238).

Anisfeld, M., Turkewitz, G., Rose, S. A., Rosenberg, F. R., Shelber, F. J., Couturier-Fagan, D. A., Ger, J. S., & Sommer, I. (2001). No compelling evidence that newborns imitate oral gestures. *Infancy, 2,* 111–122.

Annett, M. (2002). *Handedness and brain asymmetry:* The right shift theory. Hove, UK: Psychology Press.

Antoni, M. H., & Lutgendorf, S. (2007). Psychosocial factors and disease progression in cancer. *Current Directions in Psychological Science, 16,* 42–46.

Antshel, K. M. (2003). Timing is everything: Executive functions in children exposed to elevated levels of phenylalanine. *Neuropsychology, 17,* 458–468.

Apgar, V. (1953). A proposal for a new method of evaluation in the newborn infant. *Current Research in Anesthesia and Analgesia, 32,* 260–267.

Araujo, C. L., Victora, C. G., Hallal, P. C., & Gigante, D. P. (2006). Breastfeeding and overweight in childhood: Evidence from the Pelotas 1993 birth cohort study. *International Journal of Obesity, 30,* 500–506.

Archer, S. L., & Waterman, A. S. (1990). Varieties of identity diffusions and foreclosures: An exploration of subcategories of the identity statuses. *Journal of Adolescent Research, 5,* 96–111.

Archibald, A. B., Graber, J. A., & Brooks-Gunn, J. (2006). Pubertal processes and physiological growth in adolescence. In G. R. Adams & M. D. Berzonsky (Eds.), *Blackwell handbook of adolescence* (pp. 24–48). Malden, MA: Blackwell.

Archibald, A. B., Linver, M. R., Graber, J. A., & Brooks-Gunn, J. (2002). Parent–adolescent relationships and girls' unhealthy eating: Testing reciprocal effects. *Journal of Research on Adolescence, 12,* 451–461.

Ardila-Rey, A., & Killen, M. (2001). Middle-class Colombian children's evaluations of personal, moral, and social-conventional interactions in the classroom. *International Journal of Behavioral Development, 25,* 246–255.

Armstrong, K. L., Quinn, R. A., & Dadds, M. R. (1994). The sleep patterns of normal children. *Medical Journal of Australia, 161,* 202–206.

Arnett, J. J. (2000). Emerging adulthood: A theory of development from the late teens through the twenties. *American Psychologist, 55,* 469–480.

Arnett, J. J. (2003). Conceptions of the transition to adulthood among emerging adults in American ethnic groups. In J. J. Arnett & N. L. Galambos (Eds.), *Exploring cultural conceptions of the transition to adulthood (New directions for child and adolescent development,* No. 100, pp. 63–75). San Francisco: Jossey-Bass.

Arnett, J. J. (2006). Emerging adulthood: Understanding the new way of coming of age. In J. J. Arnett & J. L. Tanner (Eds.), *Emerging adults in America: Coming of age in the 21st century* (pp. 3–19). Washington, DC: American Psychological Association.

Arnett, J. J., & Tanner, J. L. (Eds.). (2006). *Emerging adults in America: Coming of age in the 21st century.* Washington, DC: American Psychological Association.

Arnold, D. H., Fisher, P. H., Doctoroff, G. L., & Dobbs, J. (2002). Accelerating math development in Head Start classrooms. *Journal of Educational Psychology, 94,* 762–770.

Arnold, D. H., McWilliams, L., & Harvey-Arnold, E. (1998). Teacher discipline and child misbehavior in daycare: Untangling causality with correlational data. *Developmental Psychology, 34,* 276–287.

Arnold, P. (1999). Emotional disorders in deaf children. In V. L. Schwean & D. H. Saklofske (Eds.), *Handbook of psychosocial characteristics of exceptional children* (pp. 493–522). New York: Kluwer.

Arnon, S., Shapsa, A., Forman, L., Regev, R., Bauer, S., & Litmanovitz, I. (2006). Live music is beneficial to preterm infants in the neonatal intensive care unit. *Birth, 33,* 131–136.

Aronson, J. M. (Ed.). (2002). *Improving academic achievement: Impact of psychological factors in education.* San Diego, CA: Academic Press.

Arriaga, X. B., & Foshee, V. A. (2004). Adolescent dating violence: Do adolescents follow in their friends' or their parents' footsteps? *Journal of Interpersonal Violence, 19,* 162–184.

Arsenio, W. F. (2006). Happy victimizers and moral responsibility: Sociocultural and developmental considerations. In M. Schleifer & C. Martiny (Eds.), *Talking to children about responsibility and control of emotions* (pp. 49–69). Calgary, Canada: Detselig Enterprises.

Arsenio, W., & Fleiss, K. (1996). Typical and behaviourally disruptive children's understanding of the emotional consequences of socio-moral events. *British Journal of Developmental Psychology, 14,* 173–186.

Arterberry, M. E., Craton, L. G., & Yonas, A. (1993). Infants' sensitivity to motion-carried information for depth and object properties. In C. E. Granrud (Ed.), *Visual perception and cognition in infancy* (pp. 215–234). Hillsdale, NJ: Erlbaum.

Artman, L., & Cahan, S. (1993). Schooling and the development of transitive inference. *Developmental Psychology, 29,* 753–759.

Artman, L., Cahan, S., & Avni-Babad, D. (2006). Age, schooling, and conditional reasoning. *Cognitive Development, 21,* 131–145.

Asakawa, K. (2001). Family socialization practices and their effects on the internationalization of educational values for Asian and white American adolescents. *Applied Developmental Science, 5,* 184–194.

Asendorpf, J. B., Warkentin, V., & Baudonniere, P. (1996). Self-awareness and other-awareness II: Mirror self-recognition, social contingency awareness, and synchronic imitation. *Developmental Psychology, 32,* 313–321.

Asher, S. R., & Rose, A. J. (1997). Promoting children's social-emotional adjustment with peers. In P. Salovey & D. J. Sluyter (Eds.), *Emotional development and emotional intelligence* (pp. 193–195). New York: Basic Books.

Aslin, R. N., Jusczyk, P. W., & Pisoni, D. B. (1998). Speech and auditory processing during infancy: Constraints on and precursors to language. In D. Kuhn & R. S. Siegler (Eds.), *Handbook of child psychology: Vol. 2. Cognition, perception, and language* (5th ed., pp. 147–198). New York: Wiley.

Astington, J. W., & Jenkins, J. M. (1995). Theory of mind development and social understanding. *Cognition and Emotion, 9,* 151–165.

Astington, J. W., & Pelletier, J. (2005). Theory of mind, language, and learning in the early years: Developmental origins of school readiness. In B. D. Homer & C. S. Tamis-LeMonda (Eds.), *The development of social cognition and communication* (pp. 205–230). Mahwah, NJ: Erlbaum.

Astington, J. W., Pelletier, J., & Homer, B. (2002). Theory of mind and epistemological development: The relation between children's second-order false belief understanding and their ability to reason about evidence. *New Ideas in Psychology, 20,* 131–144.

Astuti, R., Solomon, G. E. A., & Carey, S. (2004). Constraints on conceptual development: A case study of the acquisition of folkbiological and folksociological knowledge in Madagascar. *Monographs of the Society for Research in Child Development, 69*(3, Serial No. 277).

Atance, C. M., & Meltzoff, A. N. (2005). My future self: Young children's ability to anticipate and explain future states. *Cognitive Development, 20,* 341–361.

Atkins, R., Hart, D., & Donnelly, T.M. (2004). Moral identity development and school attachment. In D. Narvaez & D. Lapsley (Eds.), *Morality, self and identity* (pp. 65–82). Mahwah, NJ: Erlbaum.

Atkinson, R. C., & Shiffrin, R. M. (1968). Human memory: A proposed system and its control processes. In K. W. Spence & J. T. Spence (Eds.), *Advances in the psychology of learning and motivation* (Vol. 2, pp. 90–195). New York: Academic Press.

Atkinson-King, K. (1973). Children's acquisition of phonological stress contrasts. *UCLA Working Papers in Phonetics,* 25.

Attewell, P. (2001). The first and second digital divides. *Sociology of Education, 74,* 252–259.

Au, T. K., Sidle, A. L., & Rollins, K. B. (1993). Developing an intuitive understanding of conservation and contamination: Invisible particles as a plausible mechanism. *Developmental Psychology, 29,* 286–299.

Aunola, K., Stattin, H., & Nurmi, J.-E. (2000). Parenting styles and adolescents' achievement strategies. *Journal of Adolescence, 23,* 205–222.

Austin, E. W., Chen, M.-J., & Grube, J. W. (2006). How does alcohol advertising influence underage drinking? The role of desirability, identification and skepticism. *Journal of Adolescent Health, 38,* 376–384.

Averhart, C. J., & Bigler, R. S. (1997). Shades of meaning: Skin tone, racial attitudes, and constructive memory in African-American children. *Journal of Experimental Child Psychology, 67,* 368–388.

Axelin, A., Salanterä, S., & Lehtonen, L. (2006). 'Facilitated tucking by parents' in pain management of preterm infants—a randomized crossover trial. *Early Human Development, 82,* 241–247.

Axia, G., Bonichini, S., & Benini, F. (1999). Attention and reaction to distress in infancy: A longitudinal study. *Developmental Psychology, 35,* 500–504.

Azar, S. T., & Wolfe, D. A. (1998). Child physical abuse and neglect. In E. J. Mash & R. A. Barkley (Eds.), *Treatment of childhood disorders* (2nd ed., pp. 501–504). New York: Guilford.

Azmitia, M. (1996). Peer interactive minds: Developmental, theoretical, and methodological issues. In P. B. Baltes & U. M. Staudinger (Eds.), *Interactive minds: Life-span perspectives on the social foundations of cognition* (pp. 133–162). New York: Cambridge University Press.

Bacallao, M. L., & Smokowski, P. R. (2007). The costs of getting ahead: Mexican family system changes after immigration. *Family Relations, 56,* 52–66.

Bach-y-Rita, P. (2001). Theoretical and practical considerations in the restoration of function after stroke. *Topics in Stroke Rehabilitation, 8,* 1–15.

Baddeley, A. (2000). Short-term and working memory. In E. Tulving & R. I. M. Craik (Eds.), *The Oxford handbook of memory* (pp. 77–92). New York: Oxford University Press.

Baenninger, M., & Newcombe, N. (1995). Environmental input to the development of sex-related differences in spatial and mathematical ability. *Learning and Individual Differences, 7,* 363–379.

Baer, J. (2002). Is family cohesion a risk or protective factor during adolescent development? *Journal of Marriage and Family, 64,* 668–675.

Bagwell, C. L., & Coie, J. D. (2004). The best friendships of aggressive boys: Relationship quality, conflict management, and rule-breaking behavior. *Journal of Experimental Child Psychology, 88,* 5–24.

Bagwell, C. L., Coie, J. D., Terry, R. A., & Lochman, J. E. (2000). Peer clique participation and social status in preadolescence. *Merrill-Palmer Quarterly, 46,* 280–305.

Bagwell, C. L., Schmidt, M. E., Newcomb, A. F., & Bukowski, W. M. (2001). Friendship and peer rejection as predictors of adult adjustment. In D. W. Nangle & C. A. Erdley (Eds.), *The role of friendship in psychological adjustment* (pp. 25–49). San Francisco: Jossey-Bass.

Bahrick, L. E. (1983). Infants' perception of substance and temporal synchrony in multimodal events. *Infant Behavior and Development, 6,* 429–451.

Bahrick, L. E. (2001). Increasing specificity in perceptual development: Infants' detection of nested levels of multimodal stimulation. *Journal of Experimental Child Psychology, 79,* 253–270.

Bahrick, L. E. (2002). Generalization of learning in three-and-a-half-month-old infants on the basis of amodal relations. *Child Development, 73,* 667–681.

Bahrick, L. E., Flom, R., & Lickliter, R. (2003). Intersensory redundancy facilitates discrimination of tempo in 3-month-old infants. *Developmental Psychobiology, 41,* 352–363.

Bahrick, L. E., Gogate, L. J., & Ruiz, I. (2002). Attention and memory for faces and actions in infancy: The salience of actions over faces in dynamic events. *Child Development, 73,* 1629–1643.

Bahrick, L. E., Hernandez-Reif, M., & Flom, R. (2005). The development of infant learning about specific face–voice relations. *Developmental Psychology, 41,* 541–552.

Bahrick, L. E., Hernandez-Reif, M., & Pickens, J. N. (1997). The effect of retrieval cues on visual preferences and memory in infancy: Evidence for a four-phase attention function. *Journal of Experimental Child Psychology, 67,* 1–20.

Bahrick, L. E., Lickliter, R., & Flom, R. (2004). Intersensory redundancy guides the development of selective attention, perception, and cognition in infancy. *Current Directions in Psychological Science, 13,* 99–102.

Bahrick, L. E., Netto, D., & Hernandez-Reif, M. (1998). Intermodal perception of adult and child faces and voices by infants. *Child Development, 69,* 1263–1275.

Bahrick, L. E., Parker, J. F., Fivush, R., & Levitt, M. (1998). The effects of stress on young children's memory for a natural disaster. *Journal of Experimental Psychology: Applied, 4,* 301–331.

Bahrick, L. E., & Pickens, J. N. (1995). Infant memory for object motion across a period of three months: Implications for a four-phase attention function. *Journal of Experimental Child Psychology, 59,* 343–371.

Bai, D. L., & Bertenthal, B. I. (1992). Locomotor status and the development of spatial search skills. *Child Development, 63,* 215–226.

Bailey, J. M., Bobrow, D., Wolfe, M., & Mikach, S. (1995). Sexual orientation of adult sons of gay fathers. *Developmental Psychology, 31,* 124–129.

Bailey, J. M., Dunne, M. P., & Martin, N. G. (2000). Genetic and environmental influences on sexual orientation and its correlates in an Australian twin sample. *Journal of Personality and Social Psychology, 78,* 524–536.

Bailey, R. C. (1990). Growth of African pygmies in early childhood. *New England Journal of Medicine, 323,* 1146.

Baillargeon, R. (1994). Physical reasoning in infancy. In M. S. Gazzaniga (Ed.), *The cognitive neurosciences* (pp. 181–204). Cambridge, MA: MIT Press.

Baillargeon, R. (2000). Reply to Bogartz, Shinskey, and Schilling; Schilling; and Cashon and Cohen. *Infancy, 1,* 447–462.

Baillargeon, R. (2004). Infants' reasoning about hidden objects: Evidence for event-general and event-specific expectations. *Developmental Science, 7,* 391–424.

Baillargeon, R., & DeVos, J. (1991). Object permanence in young infants: Further evidence. *Child Development, 62,* 1227–1246.

Baillargeon, R. H., Zoccolillo, M., Keenan, K., Côté, S., Pérusse, D., Wu, H.-X., & Boivin, M. (2007). Gender differences in physical aggression: A prospective population-based survey of children before and after 2 years of age. *Developmental Psychology, 43,* 13–26.

Bainbridge, J., Meyers, M. K., Tanaka, S., & Waldfogel, J. (2005). Who gets an early education? Family income and the enrollment of three- to five-year-olds from 1968 to 2000. *Social Science Quarterly, 86,* 724–745.

Bakeman, R., Adamson, L. B., Konner, M., & Barr, R. G. (1990). !Kung infancy: The social context of object exploration. *Child Development, 61,* 794–809.

Baker, J. A. (2006). Contributions of teacher–child relationships to positive school adjustment during elementary school. *Journal of School Psychology, 44,* 211–229.

Bakhurst, D. (2007). Vygotsky's demons. In H. Daniels, M. Cole, & J. V. Wertsch (Eds.), *The Cambridge companion to Vygotsky* (pp. 50–74). New York: Cambridge University Press.

Balaban, M. T., & Waxman, S. R. (1997). Do words facilitate object categorization in 9-month-old infants? *Journal of Experimental Child Psychology, 64,* 3–26.

Baldwin, J. M. (1895). *Mental development in the child and the race: Methods and processes.* New York: Macmillan.

Baldwin, J. M. (1897). *Social and ethnic interpretations in mental development: A study in social psychology.* New York: Macmillan.

Balfanz, R., Legters, N., West, T. C., & Weber, L. M. (2007). Are NCLB's measures, incentives, and improvement strategies the right ones for the nation's low-performing high schools? *American Educational Research Journal, 44,* 559–593.

Ball, H. (2006). Parent–infant bed-sharing behavior: Effects of feeding type and presence of father. *Human Nature, 17,* 301–318.

Ballem, K., & Plunkett, K. (2005). Phonological specificity in children at 1;2. *Journal of Child Language, 32,* 159–173.

Balsano, A. B. (2005). Youth civic engagement in the United States: Understanding and addressing the impact of social impediments on positive youth and community development. *Applied Developmental Science, 9,* 188–201.

Bandura, A. (1977). *Social learning theory.* Englewood Cliffs, NJ: Prentice-Hall.

Bandura, A. (1992). Perceived self-efficacy in cognitive development and functioning. *Educational Psychologist, 28,* 117–148.

Bandura, A. (1999). Social cognitive theory of personality. In L. A. Pervin & O. P. John (Eds.), *Handbook of personality: Theory and research* (2nd ed., pp. 154–196). New York: Guilford.

Bandura, A. (2001). Social cognitive theory: An agentic perspective. *Annual Review of Psychology, 52,* 1–26.

Banish, M. T. (1998). Integration of information between the cerebral hemispheres. *Current Directions in Psychological Science, 7,* 32–37.

Banish, M. T., & Heller, W. (1998). Evolving perspectives on lateralization of function. *Current Directions in Psychological Science, 7,* 1–2.

Banks, M. S. (1980). The development of visual accommodation during early infancy. *Child Development, 51,* 646–666.

Banks, M. S., & Ginsburg, A. P. (1985). Early visual preferences: A review and new theoretical treatment. In H. W. Reese (Ed.), *Advances in child development and behavior* (Vol. 19, pp. 207–246). New York: Academic Press.

Banks, M. S., & Salapatek, P. (1983). Infant visual perception. In M. M. Haith & J. J. Campos (Eds.), *Handbook of child psychology: Vol. 2. Infancy and developmental psychobiology* (4th ed., pp. 436–571). New York: Wiley.

Barber, B. K., & Harmon, E. L. (2002). Violating the self: Parental psychological control of children and adolescents. In

B. K. Barber (Ed.), *Intrusive parenting: How psychological control affects children and adolescents* (pp. 15–52). Washington, DC: American Psychological Association.

Barber, B. K., & Olsen, J. A. (1997). Socialization in context: Connection, regulation, and autonomy in the family, school, and neighborhood, and with peers. *Journal of Adolescent Research, 12,* 287–315.

Barber, B. K., & Olsen, J. A. (2004). Assessing the transitions to middle and high school. *Journal of Adolescent Research, 19,* 3–30.

Barber, B. K., Stolz, H. E., & Olsen, J. A. (2005). Parental support, psychological control, and behavioral control: Assessing relevance across time, culture, and method. *Monographs of the Society for Research in Child Development, 70*(4, Serial No. 282).

Barber, B. L., Stone, M. R., Hunt, J. E., & Eccles, J. S. (2005). Benefits of activity participation: The roles of identity affirmation and peer group norm sharing. In J. L. Mahoney, R. W. Larson, & J. S. Eccles (Eds.), *Organized activities as contexts of development: Extracurricular activities, after-school and community programs* (pp. 185–210). Mahwah, NJ: Erlbaum.

Barber, J. S. (2001). The intergenerational transmission of age at first birth among married and unmarried men and women. *Social Sciences Research, 30,* 219–247.

Bard, K. A., Todd, B. K., Bernier, C., Love, J., & Leavens, D. A. (2006). Self-awareness in human and chimpanzee infants: What is measured and what is meant by the mark and mirror test? *Infancy, 9,* 191–219.

Bardwell, J. R., Cochran, S. W., & Walker, S. (1986). Relationship of parental education, race, and gender to sex role stereotyping in five-year-old kindergartners. *Sex Roles, 15,* 275–281.

Barenbaum, J., Ruchkin, V., & Schwab-Stone, M. (2004). The psychosocial aspects of children exposed to war: Practice and policy initiatives. *Journal of Child Psychology and Psychiatry, 45,* 41–62.

Bar-Haim, Y., Ziv, T., Lamy, D., & Hodes, R. M. (2006). Nature and nurture in own-race face processing. *Psychological Science, 17,* 159–163.

Barker, D. J. P., Eriksson, J. G., Forsén, T., & Osmond, C. (2002). Fetal origins of adult disease: Strength of effects and biological basis. *International Journal of Epidemiology, 31,* 1235–1239.

Barker, R. G., & Gump, P. V. (1964). *Big school, small school: High school size and student behavior.* Stanford, CA: Stanford University Press.

Barkley, R. A. (2002). Psychosocial treatments of attention-deficit/hyperactivity disorder in children. *Journal of Clinical Psychology, 63*(Suppl. 12), 36–43.

Barkley, R. A. (2003). Issues in the diagnosis of attention-deficit hyperactivity disorder in children. *Brain and Development, 25,* 77–83.

Barkley, R. A. (2006). Attention-deficit/hyperactivity disorder. In R. A. Barkley, D. A. Wolfe, & E. J. Mash (Eds.), *Behavioral and emotional disorders in adolescents: Nature, assessment, and treatment* (pp. 91–152). New York: Guilford.

Barnes, R., Josefowitz, N., & Cole, E. (2006). Residential schools: Impact on Aboriginal students' academic and cognitive development. *Canadian Journal of School Psychology, 21,* 18–32.

Barnes-Josiah, D., & Augustin, A. (1995). Secular trend in the age at menarche in Haiti. *American Journal of Human Biology, 7,* 357–362.

Barnet, B., Arroyo, C., Devoe, M., & Duggan, A. K. (2004). Reduced school dropout rates among adolescent mothers receiving school-based prenatal care. *Archives of Pediatric and Adolescent Medicine, 158,* 262–268.

Barnett, D., & Vondra, J. I. (1999). Atypical patterns of early attachment: Theory, research, and current directions. In J. I. Vondra & D. Barnett (Eds.), Atypical attachment in infancy and early childhood among children at developmental risk. *Monographs of the Society for Research in Child Development, 64*(3, Serial No. 258), 1–24.

Barnett, D., Ganiban, J., & Cicchetti, D. (1999). Maltreatment, negative expressivity, and the development of Type D attachments from 12 to 24 months of age. In J. I. Vondra & D. Barnett (Eds.), Atypical attachment in infancy and early childhood among children at developmental risk. *Monographs of the Society for Research in Child Development, 64*(3, Serial No. 258), 97–118.

Barnett, W. S. (2004). Does Head Start have lasting cognitive effects? The myth of fade-out. In E. Zigler & S. J. Styfco (Eds.), *The Head Start debates* (pp. 221–250). Baltimore: Brookes.

Baron-Cohen, S., Baldwin, D. A., & Crowson, M. (1997). Do children with autism use the speaker's direction of gaze strategy to crack the code of language? *Child Development, 68,* 48–57.

Baron-Cohen, S., & Belmonte, M. K. (2005). Autism: A window onto the development of the social and the analytic brain. *Annual Review of Neuroscience, 28,* 109–126.

Barr, H. M., Bookstein, F. L., O'Malley, K. D., Connor, P. D., Huggins, J. E., & Streissguth, A. P. (2006). Binge drinking during pregnancy as a predictor of psychiatric disorders on the structured clinical interview for DSM-IV in young adult offspring. *American Journal of Psychiatry, 163,* 1061–1065.

Barr, H. M., Streissguth, A. P., Darby, B. L., & Sampson, P. D. (1990). Prenatal exposure to alcohol, caffeine, tobacco, and aspirin: Effects on fine and gross motor performance in 4-year-old children. *Developmental Psychology, 26,* 339–348.

Barr, R., & Hayne, H. (1999). Developmental changes in imitation from television during infancy. *Child Development, 70,* 1067–1081.

Barr, R., & Hayne, H. (2003). It's not what you know, it's who you know: Older siblings facilitate imitation during infancy. *International Journal of Early Years Education, 11,* 7–21.

Barr, R., Marrott, H., & Rovee-Collier, C. (2003). The role of sensory preconditioning in memory retrieval by preverbal infants. *Learning and Behavior, 31,* 111–123.

Barr, R. G. (2001). "Colic" is something infants do, rather than a condition they "have": A developmental approach to crying phenomena patterns, pacification and (patho)genesis. In R. G. Barr, I. St James-Roberts, & M. R. Keefe (Eds.), *New evidence on unexplained infant crying* (pp. 87–104). St. Louis: Johnson & Johnson Pediatric Institute.

Barr, R. G., Paterson, J. A., MacMartin, L. M., & Lehtonen, L. (2005). Prolonged and unsoothable crying bouts in infants with and without colic. *Journal of Developmental and Behavioral Pediatrics, 26,* 14–23.

Barrash, J., Tranel, D., & Anderson, S. W. (2000). Acquired personality disturbances associated with bilateral damage to the ventromedial prefrontal region. *Developmental Neuropsychology, 18,* 355–381.

Barratt, M. S., Roach, M. A., & Leavitt, L. A. (1996). The impact of low-risk prematurity on maternal behaviour and toddler outcomes. *International Journal of Behavioral Development, 19,* 581–602.

Barrett, K. C. (2005). The origins of social emotions and self-regulation in toddlerhood: New evidence. *Cognition and Emotion, 19,* 953–979.

Barrett, K. C., & Campos, J. J. (1987). Perspectives on emotional development II: A functionalist approach to emotions. In J. D. Osofsky (Ed.), *Handbook of infant development* (2nd ed., pp. 555–578). New York: Wiley.

Barriga, A. Q., Morrison, E. M., Liau, A. K., & Gibbs, J. C. (2001). Moral cognition: Explaining the gender difference in antisocial behavior. *Merrill-Palmer Quarterly, 47,* 532–562.

Barron, F. (1988). Putting creativity to work. In R. J. Sternberg (Ed.), *The nature of creativity: Contemporary psychological perspectives* (pp. 76–98). New York: Cambridge University Press.

Bartgis, J., Lilly, A. R., & Thomas, D. G. (2003). Event-related potential and behavioral measures of attention in 5-, 7-, and 9-year-olds. *Journal of General Psychology, 130,* 311–335.

Bartlett, F. C. (1932). *Remembering.* Cambridge: Cambridge University Press.

Bartocci, M., Berggvist, L. L., Lagercrantz, H., & Anand, K. J. (2006). Pain activates cortical areas in the preterm newborn brain. *Pain, 122,* 109–117.

Barton, M. E., & Strosberg, R. (1997). Conversational patterns of two-year-old twins in mother–twin–twin triads. *Journal of Child Language, 24,* 257–269.

Barton, M. E., & Tomasello, M. (1991). Joint attention and conversation in mother-infant-sibling triads. *Child Development, 62,* 517–529.

Bartrip, J., Morton, J., & de Schonen, S. (2001). Responses to mother's face in 3-week to 5-month-old infants. *British Journal of Developmental Psychology, 19,* 219–232.

Bartsch, K., & London, K. (2000). Children's use of mental state information in selecting persuasive arguments. *Developmental Psychology, 36,* 352–365.

Bartsch, K., & Wellman, H. M. (1995). *Children talk about the mind.* New York: Oxford University Press.

Basinger, K. S., Gibbs, J. C., & Fuller, D. (1995). Context and the measurement of moral judgment. *International Journal of Behavioral Development, 18,* 537–556.

Basow, S. A., & Rubin, L. R. (1999). Gender influences on adolescent development. In N. G. Johnson & M. C. Roberts (Eds.), *Beyond appearance: A new look at adolescent girls* (pp. 25–52). Washington, DC: American Psychological Association.

Bass, J. L., Corwin, M., Gozal, D., Moore, C., Nishida, H., Parker, S., Schonwald, A., Wilker, R. E., Stehle, S., & Kinane, T. B. (2004). The effect of chronic or intermittent hypoxia on cognition in childhood: A review of the evidence. *Pediatrics, 114,* 805–816.

Bates, E. (1999). Plasticity, localization, and language development. In S. H. Broman & J. M. Fletcher (Eds.), *The changing nervous system: Neurobehavioral consequences of early brain disorders* (pp. 214–247). New York: Oxford University Press.

Bates, E., & MacWhinney, B. (1987). Competition, variation, and language learning. In B. MacWhinney (Ed.), *Mechanisms of language acquisition* (pp. 157–193). Hillsdale, NJ: Erlbaum.

Bates, E., Wilson, S. M., Saygin, A. P., Dick, F., Sereno, M. I., Knight, R. T., & Dronkers, N. F. (2003). Voxel-based lesion-symptom mapping. *Nature Neuroscience, 6,* 448–450.

Bates, J. E., Wachs, T. D., & Emde, R. N. (1994). Toward practical uses for biological concepts. In J. E. Bates & T. D. Wachs (Eds.), *Temperament: Individual differences at the interface of biology and behavior* (pp. 275–306). Washington, DC: American Psychological Association.

Bauer, C. R., Langer, J. C., Shakaran, S., Bada, H. S., & Lester, B. (2005). Acute neonatal effects of cocaine exposure during pregnancy. *Archives of Pediatrics and Adolescent Medicine, 159,* 824–834.

Bauer, P. J. (2002a). Early memory development. In U. Goswami (Ed.), *Blackwell handbook of child cognitive development* (pp. 127–150). Malden, MA: Blackwell.

Bauer, P. J. (2002b). Long-term recall memory: Behavioral and neuro-developmental changes in the first 2 years of life. *Current Directions in Psychological Science, 11,* 137–141.

Bauer, P. J. (2006). Event memory. In D. Kuhn & R. S. Siegler (Eds.), *Handbook of child psychology: Vol. 2. Cognition, perception, and language* (6th ed., pp. 373–425). Hoboken, NJ: Wiley.

Bauer, P. J. (2007). Recall in infancy: A neurodevelopmental account. *Current Directions in Psychological Science, 16,* 142–146.

Bauer, P. J., Van Abbema, D. L., Wiebe, S. A., Cary, M. S., Phill, C., & Burch, M. M. (2004). Props, not pictures, are worth a thousand words: Verbal accessibility of early memories under different conditions of contextual support. *Applied Cognitive Psychology, 18,* 373–392.

Bauer, P. J., Wiebe, S. A., Carver, L. J., Lukowski, A. F., Haight, J. C., Waters, J. M., & Nelson, C. A. (2006). Electrophysiological indexes of encoding and behavioral indexes of recall: Examining relations and developmental change late in the first year of life. *Developmental Neuropsychology, 29,* 293–320.

Baumeister, R. F. (1998). Inducing guilt. In J. Bybee (Ed.), *Guilt and children* (pp. 185–213). San Diego: Academic Press.

Baumeister, R. F., Campbell, J. D., Krueger, J. I., & Vohs, K. D. (2003). Does high self-esteem cause better performance, interpersonal success, happiness, or healthier lifestyles? *Psychological Science in the Public Interest, 4*(1), 1–44.

Baumeister, R. F., Smart, L., & Boden, J. M. (1996). Relation of threatened egotism to violence and aggression: The dark side of high self-esteem. *Psychological Review, 103,* 5–33.

Baumer, S., Ferholt, B., & Lecusay, R. (2005). Promoting narrative competence through adult–child joint pretense: Lessons from the Scandinavian educational practice of playworld. *Cognitive Development, 20,* 576–590.

Baumrind, D. (1971). Current patterns of parental authority. *Developmental Psychology Monograph, 4*(1, Pt. 2).

Baumrind, D., & Black, A. E. (1967). Socialization practices associated with dimensions of competence in preschool boys and girls. *Child Development, 38,* 291–327.

Bauserman, R. (2002). Child adjustment in joint-custody versus sole-custody arrangements: A meta-analytic review. *Journal of Family Psychology, 16,* 91–102.

Baydar, N., Greek, A., & Brooks-Gunn, J. (1997). A longitudinal study of the effects of the birth of a sibling during the first 6 years of life. *Journal of Marriage and the Family, 59,* 939–956.

Bayless, S. (2007). Executive functions in school-age children born very prematurely. *Early Human Development, 83,* 247–254.

Bayley, N. (1969). *Bayley Scales of Infant Development.* New York: Psychological Corporation.

Bayley, N. (1993). *Bayley Scales of Infant Development* (2nd ed.). New York: Psychological Corporation.

Bayley, N. (2005). *Bayley Scales of Infant and Toddler Development* (3rd ed.). (Bayley III). San Antonio, TX: Harcourt Assessment.

Bayley, N. (2006). *Bayley Scales of Infant and Toddler Development–Third Edition.* San Antonio, TX: Harcourt Assessment.

Baynes, K., & Gazzaniga, M. S. (1988). Right hemisphere language: Insights into normal language mechanisms. In F. Plum (Ed.), *Language, communication, and the brain* (pp. 117–126). New York: Raven.

Beals, D. E. (2001). Eating and reading: Links between family conversations with preschoolers and later language literacy. In D. K. Dickinson & P. O. Tabors (Eds.), *Beginning literacy with language: Young children's learning at home and school* (pp. 75–92). Baltimore, MD: Paul H. Brookes.

Bean, R. A., Barber, B. K., & Crane, D. R. (2007). Parental support, behavioral control, and psychological control among African American youth: The relationships to academic grades, delinquency, and depression. *Journal of Family Issues, 27,* 1335–1355.

Bearman, P. S., & Moody, J. (2004). Suicide and friendships among American adolescents. *American Journal of Public Health, 94,* 89–95.

Beatty, W. W. (1992). Gonadal hormones and sex differences in nonreproductive behaviors. In A. A. Gerall, H. Moltz, & I. L. Ward (Eds.), *Handbook of behavioral neurobiology: Vol. 11. Sexual differentiation* (pp. 85–128). New York: Plenum.

Beautrais, A. L. (2003). Life course factors associated with suicidal behaviors in young people. *American Behavioral Scientist, 46,* 1137–1156.

Becker, J. (1990). Processes in the acquisition of pragmatic competence. In G. Conti-Ramsden & C. Snow (Eds.), *Children's language* (Vol. 7, pp. 7–24). Hillsdale, NJ: Erlbaum.

Becker, S., & Eagly, A. H. (2004). The heroism of women and men. *American Psychologist, 59,* 163–178.

Beckett, C., Maughan, B., Rutter, M., Castle, J., Colvert, E., & Groothues, C. (2006). Do the effects of early severe deprivation on cognition persist into early adolescence? Findings from the English and Romanian adoptees study. *Child Development, 77,* 696–711.

Bedford, O. A. (2004). The individual experience of guilt and shame in Chinese culture. *Culture and Psychology, 10,* 29–52.

Behnke, M., Eyler, F. D., Garvan, C. W., & Wobie, K. (2001). The search for congenital malformations in newborns with fetal cocaine exposure. *Pediatrics, 107,* E74.

Behnke, M., Eyler, F. D., Warner, T. D., Garvan, C. W., Hou, W., & Wobie, K. (2006). Outcome from a prospective, longitudinal study of prenatal cocaine use: Preschool development at 3 years of age. *Journal of Pediatric Psychology, 31,* 41–49.

Beilin, H. (1992). Piaget's enduring contribution to developmental psychology. *Developmental Psychology, 28,* 191–204.

Beitel, A. H., & Parke, R. D. (1998). Paternal involvement in infancy: The role of maternal and paternal attitudes. *Journal of Family Psychology, 12,* 268–288.

Bell, J. H., & Bromnick, R. D. (2003). The social reality of the imaginary audience: A grounded theory approach. *Adolescence, 38,* 205–219.

Bell, M. A. (1998). Frontal lobe function during infancy: Implications for the development of cognition and attention. In J. E. Richards (Ed.), *Cognitive neuroscience of attention: A developmental perspective* (pp. 327–362). Mahwah, NJ: Erlbaum.

Bell, M. A., & Fox, N. A. (1996). Crawling experience is related to changes in cortical organization during infancy: Evidence from EEG coherence. *Developmental Psychobiology, 29,* 551–561.

Bell, S. M., & Ainsworth, M. D. S. (1972). Infant crying and maternal responsiveness. *Child Development, 43,* 1171–1190.

Bellamy, C. (2005). *The state of the world's children 2005.* New York: UNICEF.

Bell-Dolan, D. J., Foster, S. L., & Sikora, D. M. (1989). Effects of sociometric testing on children's behavior and loneliness in school. *Developmental Psychology, 25,* 306–311.

Bell-Dolan, D. J., & Wessler, A. E. (1994). Ethical administration of sociometric measures: Procedures in use and suggestions for impovement. *Professional Psychology—Research and Practice, 25,* 23–32.

Bellinger, D. C. (2005). Teratogen update: Lead and pregnancy. *Birth Defects Research: Part A, Clinical and Molecular Teratology, 73,* 409–420.

Bellinger, D. C., Leviton, A., & Sloman, J. (1990). Antecedents and correlates of improved cognitive performance in children exposed in utero to low levels of lead. *Environmental Health Perspectives, 89,* 5–11.

Bellugi, U., Bihrle, A., Neville, H., Jernigan, T., & Doherty, S. (1992). Language, cognition, and brain organization in a neurodevelopmental disorder. In M. Gunnar & C. Nelson (Eds.), *Developmental behavioral neuroscience* (pp. 201–232). Hillsdale, NJ: Erlbaum.

Bellugi, U., Lichtenberger, L., Jones, W., Lai, Z., & St. George, M. (2000). The neurocognitive profile of Williams syndrome: A complex pattern of strengths and weaknesses. *Journal of Cognitive Neuroscience, 12,* 1–29.

Belsky, J. (2001). Emanuel Miller Lecture: Developmental risks (still) associated with early child care. *Journal of Child Psychology and Psychiatry, 42,* 845–859.

Belsky, J. (2005). Attachment theory and research in ecological perspective: Insights from the Pennsylvania Infant and Family Development Project and the NICHD Study of Early Child Care. In K. E. Grossmann, K. Grossmann, & E. Waters (Eds.), *Attachment from infancy to adulthood: The major longitudinal studies* (pp. 71–97). New York: Guilford.

Belsky, J. (2006a). Determinants and consequences of parent–infant attachment. In L. Balter & C. S. Tamis-LeMonda (Eds.), *Child psychology: A handbook of contemporary issues* (2nd ed., pp. 53–77). New York: Psychology Press.

Belsky, J. (2006b). Early child care and early child development: Major findings of the NICHD Study of Early Child Care. *European Journal of Developmental Psychology, 3,* 95–110.

Belsky, J., Campbell, S. B., Cohn, J. F., & Moore, G. (1996). Instability of infant–parent attachment security. *Developmental Psychology, 32,* 921–924.

Belsky, J., & Fearon, R. M. P. (2002). Early attachment security, subsequent maternal sensitivity, and later child development: Does continuity in development depend on caregiving? *Attachment and Human Development, 4,* 361–387.

Bem, S. L. (1977). On the utility of alternative procedures for assessing psychological androgyny. *Journal of Consulting and Clinical Psychology, 45,* 196–205.

Bem, S. L. (1993). *The lenses of gender: Transforming the debate on sexual inequality.* New Haven, CT: Yale University Press.

Bem, S. L. (1998). *An unconventional family.* New Haven, CT: Yale University Press.

Bempechat, J., & Drago-Severson, E. (1999). Cross-national differences in academic achievement: Beyond etic conceptions of children's understandings. *Review of Educational Research, 69,* 287–314.

Benarroch, F., Hirsch, H. J., Genstil, L., Landau, Y. E., & Gross-Tsur, V. (2007). Prader-Willi syndrome: Medical prevention and behavioral challenges. *Child and Adolescent Psychiatric Clinics of North America, 16,* 695–708.

Benbow, C. P., & Stanley, J. C. (1983). Sex differences in mathematical reasoning: More facts. *Science, 222,* 1029–1031.

Bender, H. L., Allen, J. P., McElhaney, K. B., Antonishak, J., Moore, C. M., Kelly, H. L., & Davis, S. M. (2007). Use of harsh physical discipline and developmental outcomes in adolescence. *Development and Psychopathology, 19,* 227–242.

Bendersky, M., & Lewis, M. (1994). Environmental risk, biological risk, and developmental outcome. *Developmental Psychology, 30,* 484–494.

Benelli, B., Belacchi, C., Gini, G., & Luccangeli, D. (2006). 'To define means to say what you know about things': The development of definitional skills as metalinguistic acquisition. *Journal of Child Language, 33,* 71–97.

Benenson, J. F., & Christakos, A. (2003). The greater fragility of females' versus males' closest same-sex friendships. *Child Development, 74,* 1123–1129.

Benenson, J. F., Apostoleris, N. H., & Parnass, J. (1997). Age and sex differences in dyadic and group interaction. *Developmental Psychology, 33,* 538–543.

Benenson, J. F., Nicholson, C., Waite, A., Roy, R., & Simpson, A. (2001). The influence of group size on children's competitive behavior. *Child Development, 72,* 921–928.

Bengtson, H. (2005). Children's cognitive appraisal of others' distressful and positive experiences. *International Journal of Behavioral Development, 29,* 457–466.

Benigno, J. P., & Ellis, S. (2004). Two is greater than three: Effects of older siblings on parental support of preschoolers' counting in middle-income families. *Early Childhood Research Quarterly, 19,* 4–20.

Bennett, M., Barrett, M., Karakozov, R., Kipiani, G., Lyons, E., Pavlenko, V., & Riazanova, T. (2004). Young children's evaluations of the ingroup and outgroups: A multi-national study. *Social Development, 13,* 124–141.

Bennett, S. E., & Assefi, N. P. (2005). School-based teenage pregnancy prevention programs: A systematic review of randomized controlled trials. *Journal of Adolescent Health, 36,* 72–81.

Benoit, D., & Parker, K. C. H. (1994). Stability and transmission of attachment across three generations. *Child Development, 65,* 1444–1456.

Benson, P. L., Scales, P. C., Hamilton, S. F., & Sesma, A., Jr. (2006). Positive youth development: Theory, research, and applications. In R. M. Lerner (Ed.), *Handbook of child psychology: Vol. 1. Theoretical models of human development* (6th ed., pp. 894–941). Hoboken, NJ: Wiley.

Ben-Zeev, T., Carrasquillo, C. M., Ching, A. M. L., Patton, G. E., Stewart, T. D., & Stoddard, T. (2005). "Math is hard!" (Barbie™, 1994): Responses of threat vs. challenge-mediated arousal to stereotypes alleging intellectual inferiority. In A. M. Gallagher & J. C. Kaufman (Eds.), *Gender differences in mathematics: An integrative psychological approach* (pp. 189–206). New York: Cambridge University Press.

Berenbaum, S. A. (2001). Cognitive function in congenital adrenal hyperplasia. *Endocrinology and Metabolism Clinics of North America, 30,* 173–192.

Berenbaum, S. A., & Resnick, S. M. (1997). Early androgen effects on aggression in children and adults with congenital adrenal hyperplasia. *Psychoneuroendocrinology, 22,* 505–515.

Bergen, D., & Mauer, D. (2000). Symbolic play, phonological awareness, and literacy skills at three age levels. In K. A. Roskos & J. F. Christie (Eds.), *Play and literacy in early childhood: Research from multiple perspectives* (pp. 45–62). Mahwah, NJ: Erlbaum.

Berger, A., Tzur, G., & Posner, M. I. (2006). Infant brains detect arithmetic errors. *Proceedings of the National Academy of Sciences, 103,* 12649–12653.

Berger, S. E., Theuring, C., & Adolph, K. E. (2007). How and when infants learn to climb stairs. *Infant Behavior and Development, 30,* 36–49.

Bergin, C., Talley, S., & Hamer, L. (2003). Prosocial behaviours of young adolescents: A focus group study. *Journal of Adolescence, 26,* 13–32.

Berk, L. E. (2001a). *Awakening children's minds: How parents and teachers can make a difference.* New York: Oxford University Press.

Berk, L. E. (2001b). Private speech and self-regulation in children with impulse-control difficulties: Implications for research and practice. *Journal of Cognitive Education and Psychology, 2,* 1–21.

Berk, L. E. (2004). *Awakening children's minds: How parents and teachers can make a difference.* New York: Oxford University Press.

Berk, L. E. (2005). Why parenting matters. In S. Olfman (Ed.), *Childhood lost: How American culture is failing its children* (pp. 19–53). New York: Praeger.

Berk, L. E. (2006). Make-believe play: Wellspring for development of self-regulation. In D. Singer, K. Hirsh-Pasek, & R. Golinkoff (Eds.), *Play = learning*. New York: Oxford University Press.

Berk, L. E., & Harris, S. (2003). Vygotsky, Lev. In L. Nadel (Ed.), *Encyclopedia of cognitive science*. London: Macmillan.

Berk, L. E., & Spuhl, S. T. (1995). Maternal interaction, private speech, and task performance in preschool children. *Early Childhood Research Quarterly, 10*, 145–169.

Berkey, C. S., Wang, X., Dockery, D. W., & Ferris, B. G., Jr. (1994). Adolescent height growth of U.S. children. *Annals of Human Biology, 21*, 435–442.

Berkowitz, C. M. (2004). *Talking to your kids about sex*. Somerville, NJ: Somerset Medical Center. Retrieved from www.somersetmedicalcenter.com/1817.cfm

Berkowitz, M. W., & Gibbs, J. C. (1983). Measuring the developmental features of moral discussion. *Merrill-Palmer Quarterly, 29*, 399–410.

Berkowitz, R. L., Roberts, J., & Minkoff, H. (2006). Challenging the strategy of maternal age-based prenatal genetic counseling. *Journal of the American Medical Association, 295*, 1446–1448.

Berman, P. (1980). Are women more responsive than men to the young? A review of developmental and situational variables. *Psychological Bulletin, 88*, 668–695.

Berman, R. A. (2007). Developing linguistic knowledge and language use across adolescence. In K. Hirsh-Pasek & R. M. Golinkoff (Eds.), *Action meets word: How children learn verbs* (pp. 347–367). New York: Oxford University Press.

Berman, S. L., Weems, C. F., Rodriguez, E. T., & Zamora, I. J. (2006). The relation between identity status and romantic attachment style in middle and late adolescence. *Journal of Adolescence, 29*, 737–748.

Berndt, T. J. (2004). Children's friendships: Shifts over a half-century in perspectives on their development and effects. *Merrill-Palmer Quarterly, 50*, 206–223.

Berndt, T. J., & Keefe, K. (1995). Friends' influence on adolescents' adjustment to school. *Child Development, 66*, 1312–1329.

Berndt, T. J., & Murphy, L. M. (2002). Influences of friends and friendships: Myths, truths, and research recommendations. In R. V. Kail (Ed.), *Advances in child development and behavior* (Vol. 30, pp. 275–310). San Diego, CA: Academic Press.

Bernier, J. C., & Siegel, D. H. (1994). Attention-deficit hyperactivity disorder: A family ecological systems perspective. *Families in Society, 75*, 142–150.

Bernier, L., & Grégoire, D. (2004). Reproductive and therapeutic cloning, germline therapy, and purchase of gametes and embryos: Comments on Canadian legislation governing reproduction technologies. *Journal of Medical Ethics, 30*, 527–532.

Berninger, V. W. (2006). A developmental approach to learning disabilities. In K. A. Renninger & I. E. Sigel (Eds.), *Handbook of child psychology: Vol. 4. Child psychology in practice* (6th ed., pp. 420–452). Hoboken, NJ: Wiley.

Bertenthal, B. I. (1993). Infants' perception of biomechanical motions: Instrinsic image and knowledge-based constraints. In C. Granrud (Ed.), *Visual perception and cognition in infancy* (pp. 175–214). Hillsdale, NJ: Erlbaum.

Bertenthal, B. I., & Longo, M. R. (2007). Is there evidence of a mirror neuron system from birth? *Developmental Science, 10*, 513–523.

Bertenthal, B. I., Longo, M. R., & Kenny, S. (2007). Phenomenal permanence and the development of predictive tracking in infancy. *Child Development, 78*, 350–363.

Berthier, N. E., Bertenthal, B. I., Seaks, J. D., Sylvia, M. R., Johnson, R. L., & Clifton, R. K. (2001). Using object knowledge in visual tracking and reaching. *Infancy, 2*, 257–284.

Bertin, E., & Bhatt, R. S. (2006). Three-month-olds' sensitivity to orientation cues in the three-dimensional depth plane. *Journal of Experimental Child Psychology, 93*, 45–62.

Berzonsky, M. D. (2003). Identity style and well-being: Does commitment matter? *Identity: An International Journal of Theory and Research, 3*, 131–142.

Berzonsky, M. D. (2004). Identity style, parental authority, and identity commitment. *Journal of Youth and Adolescence, 33*, 213–220.

Berzonsky, M. D., & Kuk, L. S. (2000). Identity status, identity processing style, and the transition to university. *Journal of Adolescent Research, 15*, 81–98.

Best, D. L. (2001). Gender concepts: Convergence in cross-cultural research and methodologies. *Cross-cultural Research: The Journal of Comparative Social Science, 35*, 23–43.

Beyers, J. M., Bates, J. E., Pettit, G. S., & Dodge, K. A. (2003). Neighborhood structure, parenting processes, and the development of youths' externalizing behaviors: A multilevel analysis. *American Journal of Community Psychology, 31*, 35–53.

Beyth-Marom, R., & Fischhoff, B. (1997). Adolescents' decisions about risks: A cognitive perspective. In J. Schulenberg, J. L. Maggs, & K. Hurrelmann (Eds.), *Health risks and developmental transitions during adolescence* (pp. 110–135). New York: Cambridge University Press.

Bhagavath, B., & Layman, L. C. (2007). The genetics of hypogonadotropic hypogonadism. *Seminars in Reproductive Medicine, 25*, 272–286.

Bhanot, R., & Jovanovic, J. (2005). Parents' academic gender stereotypes influence whether they intrude on their children's work. *Sex Roles, 52*, 597–607.

Bhat, A., Heathcock, J., & Galloway, J. C. (2005). Toy-oriented changes in hand and joint kinematics during the emergence of purposeful reaching. *Infant Behavior and Development, 28*, 445–465.

Bhatt, R. S., Rovee-Collier, C., & Weiner, S. (1994). Developmental changes in the interface between perception and memory retrieval. *Developmental Psychology, 30*, 151–162.

Bhatt, R. S., Wilk, A., Hill, D., & Rovee-Collier, C. (2004). Correlated attributes and categorization in the first half-year of life. *Developmental Psychobiology, 44*, 103–115.

Bialystok, E. (1986). Factors in the growth of linguistic awareness. *Child Development, 57*, 498–510.

Bialystok, E. (2001). *Bilingualism in development: Language, literacy, and cognition.* New York: Cambridge University Press.

Bialystok, E., & Martin, M. M. (2003). Notation to symbol: Development in children's understanding of print. *Journal of Experimental Child Psychology, 86*, 223–243.

Bialystok, E., & Martin, M. M. (2004). Attention and inhibition in bilingual children: Evidence from the dimensional change card sort task. *Developmental Science, 7*, 325–339.

Bialystok, E., McBride-Chang, C., & Luk, G. (2005). Bilingualism, language proficiency, and learning to read in two writing systems. *Journal of Educational Psychology, 97*, 580–590.

Bialystok, E., & Senman, L. (2004). Executive processes in appearance–reality tasks: The role of inhibition of attention and symbolic representation. *Child Development, 75*, 562–579.

Bianchi, D. W. (2005). Prenatal genetic diagnosis. In H. W. Taeusch, R. A. Ballard, & C. A. Gleason (Eds.), *Avery's diseases of the newborn* (pp. 57–70). Philadelphia: Saunders.

Bianco, A., Stone, J., Lynch, L., Lapinski, R., Berkowitz, G., & Berkowitz, R. L. (1996). Pregnancy outcome at age 40 and older. *Obstetrics and Gynecology, 87*, 917–922.

Biederman, J., Kwon, A., Aleardi, M., Chouinard, V.-A., Marino, T., & Cole, H. (2005). Absence of gender effects on attention-deficit hyperactivity disorder: Findings in nonreferred subjects. *American Journal of Psychiatry, 162*, 1083–1089.

Biederman, J., & Spencer, T. J. (2000). Genetics of childhood disorders: XIX. ADHD, part 3: Is ADHD a noradrenergic disorder? *Journal of the American Academy of Child and Adolescent Psychiatry, 39*, 1330–1333.

Bielawska-Batorowicz, E., & Kossakowska-Petrycka, K. (2006). Depressive mood in men after the birth of their offspring in relation to a partner's depression, social support, fathers' personality and prenatal expectations. *Journal of Reproductive and Infant Psychology, 24*, 21–29.

Bielinski, J., & Davison, M. L. (1998). Gender differences by item difficulty interactions in multiple-choice mathematics items. *American Educational Research Journal, 35*, 455–476.

Biernat, M. (1991). A multi-component, developmental analysis of sex-typing. *Sex Roles, 24*, 567–586.

Bigelow, A. (1992). Locomotion and search behavior in blind infants. *Infant Behavior and Development, 15*, 179–189.

Bigelow, A. E. (2003). The development of joint attention in blind infants. *Development and Psychopathology, 15*, 259–275.

Bigler, R. S. (1995). The role of classification skill in moderating environmental influences on children's gender stereotyping: A study of the functional use of gender in the classroom. *Child Development, 66*, 1072–1087.

Bigler, R. S. (2007, June). Personal communication.

Bigler, R. S., Brown, C. S., & Markell, M. (2001). When groups are not created equal: Effects of group status on the formation of intergroup attitudes in children. *Child Development, 72*, 1151–1162.

Bigler, R. S., & Liben, L. S. (1992). Cognitive mechanisms in children's gender stereotyping: Theoretical and educational implications of a cognitive-based intervention. *Child Development, 63*, 1351–1363.

Bimmel, N., Juffer, F., van IJzendoorn, M. H., & Bakermans-Kranenburg, M. J. (2003). Problem behavior of internationally adopted adolescents: A review and meta-analysis. *Harvard Review of Psychiatry, 11*, 64–77.

Binet, A., & Simon, T. (1908). Le développement de l'intelligence chez les enfants. *L'Année Psychologique, 14*, 1–94.

Bioethics Consultative Committee. (2003). *Comparison of ethics legislation in Europe.* Retrieved from www.synapse.net.mt/bioethics/euroleg1.htm

Birch, E. E. (1993). Stereopsis in infants and its developmental relation to visual acuity. In K. Simons (Ed.), *Early visual development: Normal and abnormal* (pp. 224–236). New York: Oxford University Press.

Birch, L. L., & Fisher, J. A. (1995). Appetite and eating behavior in children. *Pediatric Clinics of North America, 42*, 931–953.

Birch, L. L., Fisher, J. O., & Davison, K. K. (2003). Learning to overeat: Maternal use of restrictive feeding practices promotes girls' eating in the absence of hunger. *American Journal of Clinical Nutrition, 78*, 215–220.

Birch, L. L., Zimmerman, S., & Hind, H. (1980). The influence of social-affective context on preschool children's food preferences. *Child Development, 51*, 856–861.

Birch, S. A. J., & Bloom, P. (2003). Children are cursed: An asymmetric bias in mental-state attribution. *Psychological Science, 14*, 283–285.

Birch, S. H., & Ladd, G. W. (1997). The teacher–child relationship and children's early school adjustment. *Journal of School Psychology, 35*, 61–79.

Birch, S. H., & Ladd, G. W. (1998). Children's interpersonal behaviors and the teacher–child relationship. *Developmental Psychology, 34*, 934–946.

Bird, A., & Reese, E. (2006). Emotional reminiscing and the development of an autobiographical self. *Developmental Psychology, 42*, 613–626.

Biringen, Z., Emde, R. N., Campos, J. J., & Appelbaum, M. I. (1995). Affective reorganization in the infant, the mother, and the dyad: The role of upright locomotion and its timing. *Child Development, 66*, 499–514.

Birney, D. P., Citron-Pousty, J. H., Lutz, D. J., & Sternberg, R. J. (2005). The development of cognitive and intellectual abilities. In M. H. Bornstein & M. E. Lamb (Eds.), *Developmental science: An advanced textbook* (5th ed., pp. 327–358). Mahwah, NJ: Erlbaum.

Bischofshausen, S. (1985). Developmental differences in schema dependency for temporally ordered story events. *Journal of Psycholinguistic Research, 14*, 543–556.

Bjorklund, D. F. (2005). *Children's thinking: Cognitive development and individual differences* (4th ed.). Belmont, CA: Wadsworth.

Bjorklund, D. F. (2007). *Why youth is not wasted on the young.* Hoboken, NJ: Wiley.

Bjorklund, D. F., & Blasi, C. (2005). Evolutionary developmental psychology. In D. Buss (Ed.), *Handbook of evolutionary psychology* (pp. 828–850). Hoboken, NJ: Wiley.

Bjorklund, D. F., & Coyle, T. R. (1995). Utilization deficiencies in the development of memory strategies. In F. E. Weinert & W. Schneider (Eds.), *Research on memory development: State of the art and future directions* (pp. 161–180). Hillsdale, NJ: Erlbaum.

Bjorklund, D. F., & Douglas, R. N. (1997). The development of memory strategies. In N. Cowan (Ed.), *The development of mem-*

ory in childhood (pp. 83–111). Hove, UK: Psychology Press.

Bjorklund, D. F., & Harnishfeger, K. K. (1995). The evolution of inhibition mechanisms and their role in human cognition and behavior. In M. L. Howe & R. Pasnak (Eds.), *Emerging themes in cognitive development: Vol. 1. Foundations* (pp. 141–173). New York: Springer-Verlag.

Bjorklund, D. F., Schneider, W., Cassel, W. S., & Ashley, E. (1994). Training and extension of a memory strategy: Evidence for utilization deficiencies in high- and low-IQ children. *Child Development, 65,* 951–965.

Bjorklund, D. F., Yunger, J. L., & Pellegrini, A. D. (2002). The evolution of parenting and evolutionary approaches to childrearing. In M. H. Bornstein (Ed.), *Handbook of parenting: Vol. 2. Biology and Ecology of Parenting* (2nd ed., pp. 3–30). Mahwah, NJ: Erlbaum.

Black, B., & Logan, A. (1995). Links between communication patterns in mother–child, father–child, and child–peer interactions and children's social status. *Child Development, 66,* 255–271.

Black, M. M. (2005). Failure to thrive. In M. C. Roberts (Ed.), *Handbook of pediatric psychology and psychiatry* (3rd ed., pp. 499–511). New York: Guilford.

Black, R. E., Williams, S. M., Jones, I. E., & Goulding, A. (2002). Children who avoid drinking cow milk have low dietary calcium intakes and poor bone health. *American Journal of Clinical Nutrition, 76,* 675–680.

Blackwell, L. S., Trzesniewski, K. H., & Dweck, C. S. (2007). Implicit theories of intelligence predict achievement across an adolescent transition: A longitudinal study and an intervention. *Child Development, 78,* 246–263.

Blaga, O. M., & Colombo, J. (2006). Visual processing and infant ocular latencies in the overlap paradigm. *Developmental Psychology, 42,* 1069–1076.

Blair, C., & Razza, R. P. (2007). Relating effortful control, executive function, and false belief understanding to emerging math and literacy ability in kindergarten. *Developmental Psychology, 78,* 647–663.

Blake, J., & Boysson-Bardies, B. de (1992). Patterns in babbling: A cross-linguistic study. *Journal of Child Language, 19,* 51–74.

Blake, J., Vitale, G., Osborne, P., & Olshansky, E. (2005). A cross-cultural comparison of communicative gestures in human infants during the transition to language. *Gesture, 5,* 201–217.

Blakemore, J. E. O. (2003). Children's beliefs about violating gender norms: Boys shouldn't look like girls, and girls shouldn't act like boys. *Sex Roles, 48,* 411–419.

Blakemore, S.-J., & Choudhury, S. (2006). Development of the adolescent brain: Implications for executive function and social cognition. *Journal of Child Psychology and Psychiatry, 47,* 296–312.

Blanchard, R., & Bogaert, A. F. (2004). Proportion of homosexual men who owe their sexual orientation to fraternal birth order: An estimate based on two national probability samples. *American Journal of Human Biology, 16,* 151–157.

Blasi, A. (1994). Bridging moral cognition and moral action: A critical review of the literature. In B. Puka (Ed.), *Fundamental research in moral development: A compendium* (Vol. 2, pp. 123–167). New York: Garland.

Blasi, C. H., & Bjorklund, D. F. (2003). Evolutionary developmental psychology: A new tool for better understanding human ontogeny. *Human Development, 46,* 259–281.

Blass, E M. (1999). Savoring sucrose and suckling milk: Easing pain, saving calories, and learning about mother. In M. Lewis & D. Ramsay (Eds.), *Soothing and stress* (pp. 79–107). Mahwah, NJ: Erlbaum.

Blass, E. M., Ganchrow, J. R., & Steiner, J. E. (1984). Classical conditioning in newborn humans 2–48 hours of age. *Infant Behavior and Development, 7,* 223–235.

Blatchford, P., Bassett, P., & Brown, P. (2005). Teachers' and pupils' behavior in large and small classes: A systematic observation study of pupils aged 10 and 11 years. *Journal of Educational Psychology, 97,* 454–467.

Blatchford, P., Bassett, P., Goldstein, H., & Martin, C. (2003). Are class size differences related to pupils' educational progress and classroom processes? Findings from the Institute of Education Class Size Study of Children Aged 5–7 Years. *British Educational Research Journal, 29,* 709–730.

Blatchford, P., Russell, A., Bassett, P., Brown, P., & Martin, C. (2007). The effect of class size on the teaching of pupils aged 7–11 years. *School Effectiveness and School Improvement, 18,* 147–172.

Bleeker, M. M., & Jacobs, J. E. (2004). Achievement in math and science: Do mothers' beliefs matter 12 years later? *Journal of Educational Psychology, 96,* 97–109.

Blewitt, P. (1994). Understanding categorical hierarchies: The earliest levels of skill. *Child Development, 65,* 1279–1298.

Bloch, M. E. F., Solomon, G. E. A., & Carey, S. (2001). An understanding of what is passed on from parents to children: A cross-cultural investigation. *Journal of Cognition and Culture, 1,* 43–68.

Bloom, L. (1998). Language acquisition in its developmental context. In D. Kuhn & R. S. Siegler (Eds.), *Handbook of child psychology: Vol. 2. Cognition, perception, and language* (5th ed., pp. 309–370). New York: Wiley.

Bloom, L. (2000). The intentionality model of language development: How to learn a word, any word. In R. Golinkoff, K. Hirsh-Pasek, N. Akhtar, L. Bloom, G. Hollich, L. Smith, M. Tomasello, & A. Woodward (Eds.), *Becoming a word learner: A debate on lexical acquisition.* New York: Oxford University Press.

Bloom, L., Lahey, M., Liften, K., & Fiess, K. (1980). Complex sentences: Acquisition of syntactic connections and the semantic relations they encode. *Journal of Child Language, 7,* 235–256.

Bloom, L., Margulis, C., Tinker E., & Fujita, N. (1996). Early conversations and word learning: Contributions from child and adult. *Child Development, 67,* 3154–3175.

Bloom, P. (1999). The role of semantics in solving the bootstrapping problem. In R. Jackendoff & P. Bloom (Eds.), *Language, logic, and concepts* (pp. 285–309). Cambridge, MA: MIT Press.

Blotner, R., & Bearison, D. J. (1984). Developmental consistencies in socio-moral knowledge: Justice reasoning and altruistic behavior. *Merrill-Palmer Quarterly, 30,* 349–367.

Blumberg, M. S., & Lucas, D. E. (1996). A developmental and component analysis of active sleep. *Developmental Psychobiology, 29,* 1–22.

Blumenfeld, P. C., Marx, R. W., & Harris, C. J. (2006). Learning environments. In K. A. Renninger & I. E. Sigel (Eds.), *Handbook of child psychology: Vol. 4. Child psychology in practice* (6th ed., pp. 297–342). Hoboken, NJ: Wiley.

Bodrova, E., & Leong, D. J. (2007). *Tools of the mind: The Vygotskian approach to early childhood education* (2nd ed.). Upper Saddle River, NJ: Merrill/Prentice Hall.

Bogaert, A. F. (2005). Age at puberty and father absence in a national probability sample. *Journal of Adolescence, 28,* 541–546.

Bogartz, R. S., Shinskey, J. L., & Schilling, T. H. (2000). Object permanence in five-and-a-half-month-old infants. *Infancy, 1,* 403–428.

Bogin, B. (2001). *The growth of humanity.* New York: Wiley-Liss.

Bogin, B., Smith, P., Orden, A. B., Varela, S., & Loucky, J. (2002). Rapid change in height and body proportions of Maya American children. *American Journal of Human Biology, 14,* 753–761.

Bohannon, J. N., & Bonvillian, J. D. (2009). Theoretical approaches to language acquisition. In J. B. Gleason & B. Ratner (Ed.), *The development of language* (7th ed., pp. 227–284). Boston: Allyn and Bacon.

Bohannon, J. N., III, & Stanowicz, L. (1988). The issue of negative evidence: Adult responses to children's language errors. *Developmental Psychology, 24,* 684–689.

Bohman, M., & Sigvardsson, S. (1990). Outcome in adoption: Lessons from longitudinal studies. In D. M. Bordzkinsky & M. D. Schechter (Eds.), *The psychology of adoption* (pp. 93–106). New York: Oxford University Press.

Bohnert, A. M., Crnic, K., & Lim, K. G. (2003). Emotional competence and aggressive behavior in school-age children. *Journal of Abnormal Child Psychology, 31,* 79–91.

Boldizar, J. P. (1991). Assessing sex typing and androgyny in children: The children's sex role inventory. *Developmental Psychology, 27,* 505–515.

Boldizar, J. P., Perry, D. G., & Perry, L. C. (1989). Outcome values and aggression. *Child Development, 60,* 571–579.

Bolen, R. M. (2001). *Child sexual abuse.* New York: Kluwer Academic.

Bollmer, J. M., Milich, R., Harris, M. J., & Maras, M. A. (2005). A friend in need: The role of friendship quality as a protective factor in peer victimization and bullying. *Journal of Interpersonal Violence, 20,* 701–712.

Bolzani, L. H., Messinger, D. S., Yale, M., & Dondi, M. (2002). Smiling in infancy. In M. H. Abel (Ed.), *An empirical reflection on the smile* (pp. 111–136). Lewiston, NY: Edwin Mellen Press.

Bono, M. A., & Stifter, C. A. (2003). Maternal attention-directing strategies and infant focused attention during problem solving. *Infancy, 4,* 235–250.

Boom, J., Brugman, D., & van der Heijden, P. G. M. (2001). Hierarchical structure of moral stages assessed by a sorting task. *Child Development, 72,* 535–548.

Boom, J., Wouters, H., & Keller, M. (2007). A cross-cultural validation of stage development: A Rasch re-analysis of longitudinal socio-moral reasoning data. *Cognitive Development, 22,* 213–229.

Borke, H. (1975). Piaget's mountains revisited: Changes in the egocentric landscape. *Developmental Psychology, 11,* 240–243.

Borkowski, J. G., & Muthukrisna, N. (1995). Learning environments and skill generalization: How contexts facilitate regulatory processes and efficacy beliefs. In F. Weinert & W. Schneider (Eds.), *Memory performances and competence: Issues in growth and development* (pp. 283–300). Hillsdale, NJ: Erlbaum.

Bornstein, M. H. (1989). Sensitive periods in development: Structural characteristics and causal interpretations. *Psychological Bulletin, 105,* 179–197.

Bornstein, M. H. (2006). Parenting science and practice. In K. Renninger & I. E. Sigel (Eds.), *Handbook of child psychology: Vol. 4. Child psychology in practice* (6th ed., pp. 893–949). Hoboken, NJ: Wiley.

Bornstein, M. H., & Arterberry, M. E. (2003). Recognition, discrimination, and categorization of smiling by 5-month-old infants. *Developmental Science, 6,* 585–599.

Bornstein, M. H., & Cote, L. R. (2004). Cross-linguistic analysis of vocabulary in young children: Spanish, Dutch, French, Hebrew, Italian, Korean, and American English. *Child Development, 75,* 1115–1139.

Bornstein, M. H., Haynes, O. M., Pascual, L., Painter, K. M., & Galperin, C. (1999). Play in two societies: Pervasiveness of process, specificity of structure. *Child Development, 70,* 317–331.

Bornstein, M. H., & Sawyer, J. (2006). Family systems. In K. McCartney & D. Phillips (Eds.), *Blackwell handbook of early childhood development* (pp. 381–398). Malden, MA: Blackwell.

Bornstein, M. H., Selmi, A. M., Haynes, O. M., Painter, K. M., & Marx, E. S. (1999). Representational abilities and the hearing status of child/mother dyads. *Child Development, 70,* 833–852.

Bornstein, M. H., Vibbert, M., Tal, J., & O'Donnell, K. (1992). Toddler language and play in the second year: Stability, covariation, and influences of parenting. *First Language, 12,* 323–338.

Boroughs, D. S. (2004). Female sexual abusers of children. *Children and Youth Services Review, 26,* 481–487.

Borst, C. G. (1995). *Catching babies: The professionalization of childbirth, 1870–1920.* Cambridge, MA: Harvard University Press.

Bos, H. M. W., van Balen, F., & van den Boom, D. C. (2004). Experience of parenthood, couple relationship, social support, and child-rearing goals in planned lesbian mother families. *Journal of Child Psychology and Psychiatry, 25,* 755–764.

Bos, H. M. W., van Balen, F., & van den Boom, D. C. (2007). Child adjustment and parenting in planned lesbian-parent families. *American Journal of Orthopsychiatry, 77,* 38–48.

Bosacki, S. L., & Moore, C. (2004). Preschoolers' understanding of simple and complex emotions: Links with gender and language. *Sex Roles, 50,* 659–675.

Bost, K. K., Shin, N., McBride, B. A., Brown, G. L., Vaughn, B. E., & Coppola, G. (2006). Maternal secure base scripts, children's attachment security, and mother–child narrative styles. *Attachment and Human Development, 8,* 241–260.

Botvinick, M., Jha, A. P., Bylsma, L. M., Fabian, S. A., Solomon, P. E., & Prkachin, K. M. (2005). Viewing facial expressions of pain engages cortical areas involved in the direct experience of pain. *Neuroimage, 25,* 312–319.

Bouchard, T. J. (2004). Genetic influence on human psychological traits: A survey. *Current Directions in Psychological Science, 13,* 148–151.

Bouchard, T. J., & Loehlin, J. C. (2001). Genes, evolution, and personality. *Behavior Genetics, 31,* 243–274.

Bouchard, T. J., Jr. (1997). IQ similarity in twins reared apart: Findings and responses to critics. In R. J. Sternberg & E. L. Grigorenko (Eds.), *Intelligence, heredity, and environment* (pp. 126–160). New York: Cambridge University Press.

Bouchard, T. J., Jr., & McGue, M. (1981). Familial studies of intelligence: A review. *Science, 212,* 1055–1058.

Bouchard, T. J., Jr., & McGue, M. (2003). Genetic and environmental influences on human psychological differences. *Journal of Neurobiology, 54,* 4–45.

Boukydis, C. F. Z., & Lester, B. M. (1998). Infant crying, risk status and social support in families of preterm and term infants. *Early Development and Parenting, 7,* 31–39.

Bouldin, P. (2006). An investigation of the fantasy predisposition and fantasy style of children with imaginary companions. *Journal of Genetic Psychology, 167,* 17–29.

Boulton, M. J. (1996). A comparison of 8- and 11-year-old girls' and boys' participation in specific types of rough-and-tumble play and aggressive fighting: Implications for functional hypotheses. *Aggressive Behavior, 22,* 271–287.

Boulton, M. J. (1999). Concurrent and longitudinal relations between children's playground behavior and social preference, victimization, and bullying. *Child Development, 70,* 944–954.

Boulton, M. J., & Smith, P. K. (1992). The social nature of play-fighting and play-chasing: Mechanisms and strategies underlying cooperation and compromise. In J. H. Barkow, L. Cosmides, & J. Tooby (Eds.), *The adapted mind* (pp. 429–444). New York: Oxford University Press.

Bowen, N. K., Bowen, G. L., & Ware, W. B. (2002). Neighborhood social disorganization, families, and the educational behavior of adolescents. *Journal of Adolescent Research, 17,* 468–490.

Bower-Russa, M. E., Knutson, J. F., & Winebarger, A. (2001). Disciplinary history, adult disciplinary attitudes, and risk for abusive parenting. *Journal of Community Psychology, 29,* 219–240.

Bowker, A. (2003). The relationship between sports participation and self-esteem during early adolescence. *Canadian Journal of Behavioural Science, 38,* 214–229.

Bowker, A. (2004). Predicting friendship stability during early adolescence. *Journal of Early Adolescence, 24,* 85–112.

Bowker, A. (2006). The relationship between sports participation and self-esteem during early adolescence. *Canadian Journal of Behavioural Science, 38,* 214–229.

Bowker, J. C. W., Rubin, K. H., Burgess, K. B., Booth-LaForce, C., & Rose-Krasnor, L. (2006). Behavioral characteristics associated with stable and fluid best friendship patterns in middle childhood. *Merrill-Palmer Quarterly, 52,* 671–693.

Bowlby, J. (1969). *Attachment and loss: Vol. 1. Attachment.* New York: Basic Books.

Bowlby, J. (1980). *Attachment and loss: Vol. 3. Loss.* New York: Basic Books.

Bowlby, J. W., & McMullen, K. (2002). *At a crossroads: First results for the 18- to 20-year-old cohort of the Youth in Transition Survey.* Ottawa, Canada: Human Resources Development Canada.

Bowman, S. A., Gortmaker, S. L., Ebbeling, C. B., Pereira, M. A., & Ludwig, D. S. (2004). Effects of fast-food consumption on energy intake and diet quality among children in a national household survey. *Pediatrics, 113,* 112–118.

Boyatzis, C. J. (2000). The artistic evolution of mommy: A longitudinal case study of symbolic and social processes. In C. J. Boyatzis & M. W. Watson (Eds.), *Symbolic and social constraints on the development of children's artistic style* (pp. 5–29). San Francisco: Jossey-Bass.

Boyce, W., Doherty-Poirier, M., MacKinnon, D., Fortin, C., Saab, H., King, M., & Gallupe, O. (2006). Sexual health of Canadian youth: Findings from the Canadian Youth, Sexual Health and HIV/AIDS Study. *Canadian Journal of Human Sexuality, 15,* 59–68.

Boyd-Franklin, N. (2006). *Black families in therapy* (2nd ed.). New York: Guilford.

Boyer, K., & Diamond, A. (1992). Development of memory for temporal order in infants and young children. In A. Diamond (Ed.), *Development and neural bases of higher cognitive function* (pp. 267–317). New York: New York Academy of Sciences.

Boyer, T. W. (2006). The development of risk-taking: A multi-perspective review. *Developmental Review, 26,* 291–345.

Boyes, M. C., & Chandler, M. (1992). Cognitive development, epistemic doubt, and identity formation in adolescence. *Journal of Youth and Adolescence, 21,* 277–304.

Boysson-Bardies, B. de, & Vihman, M. M. (1991). Adaptation to language: Evidence from babbling and first words in four languages. *Language, 67,* 297–319.

Brackbill, Y., McManus, K., & Woodward, L. (1985). *Medication in maternity: Infant exposure and maternal information.* Ann Arbor: University of Michigan Press.

Bradford, K., Barber, B. K., Olsen, J. A., Maughan, S. L., Erickson, L. D., Ward, D., & Stolz, H. E. (2003). A multi-national study of interparental conflict, parenting, and adolescent functioning: South Africa, Bangladesh, China, India, Bosnia, Germany, Palestine, Colombia, and the United States. *Marriage and Family Review, 35,* 107–137.

Bradley, P. J., & Bray, K. H. (1996). The Netherlands' Maternal–Child Health Program: Implications for the United States. *Journal of Obstetric, Gynecologic, and Neonatal Nursing, 25,* 471–475.

Bradley, R. H. (1994). The HOME Inventory: Review and reflections. In H. W. Reese (Ed.), *Advances in child development and behavior* (Vol. 25, pp. 241–288). San Diego, CA: Academic Press.

Bradley, R. H., Caldwell, B. M., & Rock, S. L. (1988). Home environment and school performance: A ten-year follow-up and examination of three models of environmental action. *Child Development, 59,* 852–867.

Bradley, R. H., & Corwyn, R. F. (2003). Age and ethnic variations in family process mediators of SES. In M. H. Bornstein & R. H. Bradley (Eds.), *Socioeconomic status, parenting, and child development* (pp. 161–188). Mahwah, NJ: Erlbaum.

Bradley, R. H., Corwyn, R. F., McAdoo, H. P., & Garcia Coll, C. (2001). The home environments of children in the United States. Part I: Variations by age, ethnicity, and poverty status. *Child Development, 72,* 1844–1867.

Bradley, R. H., Whiteside, L., Mundfrom, D. J., Casey, P. H., Kelleher, K. J., & Pope, S. K. (1994). Contribution of early intervention and early caregiving experiences to resilience in low-birthweight, premature children living in poverty. *Journal of Clinical Child Psychology, 23,* 425–434.

Bradshaw, R. A., & Burlingame, A. L. (2005). From proteins to proteomics. *IUBMB Life, 57,* 267–272.

Braine, L G., Schauble, L., Kugelmass, S., & Winter, A. (1993). Representation of depth by children: Spatial strategies and lateral biases. *Developmental Psychology, 29,* 466–479.

Braine, M. D. S. (1994). Is nativism sufficient? *Journal of Child Language, 21,* 1–23.

Brainerd, C. J. (2003). Jean Piaget, learning, research, and American education. In B. J. Zimmerman (Ed.), *Educational psychology: A century of contributions* (pp. 251–287). Mahwah, NJ: Erlbaum.

Brainerd, C. J., Forrest, T. J., Karibian, D., & Reyna, V. F. (2006). Development of the false-memory illusion. *Developmental Psychology, 42,* 962–979.

Brainerd, C. J., & Gordon, L. L. (1994). Development of verbatim and gist memory for numbers. *Developmental Psychology, 30,* 163–177.

Brainerd, C. J., Holliday, R. E., & Reyna, V. F. (2004). Behavioral measurement of remembering phenomenologies. *Child Development, 75,* 505–522.

Brainerd, C. J., & Reyna, V. F. (1993). Memory independence and memory interference in cognitive development. *Psychological Review, 100,* 42–67.

Brainerd, C. J., & Reyna, V. F. (1995). Learning rate, learning opportunities, and the development of forgetting. *Developmental Psychology, 31,* 251–262.

Brainerd, C. J., & Reyna, V. F. (2001). Fuzzy-trace theory: Dual processes in memory, reasoning, and cognitive neuroscience. In H. W. Reese (Ed.), *Advances in child development and behavior* (Vol. 28). San Diego, CA: Academic Press.

Brainerd, C. J., Reyna, V. F., & Poole, D. A. (2000). Fuzzy-trace theory and false memory: Memory theory in the courtroom. In D. F. Bjorklund (Ed.), *Research and theory in false-memory creation in children and adults* (pp. 93–127). Mahwah, NJ: Erlbaum.

Brame, B., Nagin, D. S., & Tremblay, R. E. (2001). Developmental trajectories of physical aggression from school entry to late adolescence. *Journal of Child Psychology and Psychiatry, 42,* 503–512.

Branca, F., & Ferrari, M. (2002). Impact of micronutrient deficiencies on growth: The stunting syndrome. *Annals of Nutrition and Metabolism, 46*(Suppl. 1), 8–17.

Branje, S. J. T., van Lieshout, C. F. M., van Aken, M. A. G., & Haselager, G. J. T. (2004). Perceived support in sibling relationships and adolescent adjustment. *Journal of Child Psychology and Psychiatry, 45,* 1385–1396.

Braswell, G. S. (2006). Sociocultural contexts for the early development of semiotic production. *Psychological Bulletin, 132,* 877–894.

Braswell, G. S., & Callanan, M. A. (2003). Learning to draw recognizable graphic representations during mother–child interactions. *Merrill-Palmer Quarterly, 49,* 471–494.

Bray, J. H. (1999). From marriage to remarriage and beyond: Findings from the Developmental Issues in Stepfamilies Research Project. In E. M. Hetherington (Ed.), *Coping with divorce, single parenting, and remarriage: A risk and resiliency perspective* (pp. 295–319). Mahwah, NJ: Erlbaum.

Brazelton, T. B., Koslowski, B., & Tronick, E. Z. (1976). Neonatal behavior among urban Zambians and Americans. *Journal of the American Academy of Child Psychiatry, 15,* 97–107.

Brazelton, T. B., & Nugent, J. K. (1995). *Neonatal Behavioral Assessment Scale.* London: Mac Keith Press.

Brazelton, T. B., Nugent, J. K., & Lester, B. M. (1987). Neonatal Behavioral Assessment Scale. In J. D. Osofsky (Ed.), *Handbook of infant development* (2nd ed., pp. 780–817). New York: Wiley.

Bredekamp, S., & Copple, C. (Eds.). (1997). *Developmentally appropriate practice in early childhood programs* (rev. ed.). Washington, DC: National Association for the Education of Young Children.

Bremner, A. J., & Mareschal, D. (2004). Reasoning ... what reasoning? *Developmental Science, 7,* 419–421.

Brendgen, M., Markiewicz, D., Doyle, A. B., & Bukowski, W. M. (2001). The relations between friendship quality, ranked-friendship preference, and adolescents' behavior with their friends. *Merrill-Palmer Quarterly, 47,* 395–415.

Brenes, M. E., Eisenberg, N., & Helmstadter, G. C. (1985). Sex role development of preschoolers from two-parent and one-parent families. *Merrill-Palmer Quarterly, 31,* 33–46.

Brennan, R. T., Kim, J., Wenz-Gross, M., & Siperstein, G. N. (2001). The relative equitability of high-stakes testing versus teacher-assigned grades: An analysis of the Massachusetts Comprehensive Assessment System (MCAS). *Harvard Educational Review, 71,* 173–216.

Brennan, W. M., Ames, E. W., & Moore, R. W. (1966). Age differences in infants' attention to patterns of different complexities. *Science, 151,* 354–356.

Brenner, E., & Salovey, P. (1997). Emotion regulation during childhood: Developmental, interpersonal, and individual considerations. In P. Salovey & D. Sluyter (Eds.), *Emotional literacy and emotional development* (pp. 168–192). New York: Basic Books.

Brenner, R. A., Simons-Morton, B. G., Bhaskar, B., Revenis, M., Das, A., & Clemens, J. D. (2003). Infant–parent bed sharing in an inner-city population. *Archives of Pediatrics and Adolescent Medicine, 157,* 33–39.

Bretherton, I., Fritz, J., Zahn-Waxler, C., & Ridgeway, D. (1986). Learning to talk about emotions: A functionalist perspective. *Child Development, 57,* 529–548.

Bretherton, I., & Munholland, K. A. (1999). Internal working models in attachment relationships: A construct revisited. In J. Cassidy & P. R. Shaver (Eds.), *Handbook of attachment* (pp. 89–111). New York: Guilford.

Brewaeys, A., Ponjaert, I., Van Hall, E. V., & Golombok, S. (1997). Donor insemination: Child development and family functioning in lesbian mother families. *Human Reproduction, 12,* 1349–1359.

Bridge, J. A., Goldstein, T. R., & Brent, D. A. (2006). Adolescent suicide and suicidal

behavior. *Journal of Child Psychology and Psychiatry, 47,* 372–394.
Bridges, L. J., & Moore, K. A. (2002). Religious involvement and children's well-being: What research tells us (and what it doesn't). *Child Trends Research Brief.* Retrieved from www.childtrends.org
Briefel, R. R., Reidy, K., Karwe, V., & Devaney, B. (2004). Feeding Infants and Toddlers Study: Improvements needed in meeting infant feeding recommendations. *Journal of the American Dietetic Association, 104*(Suppl. 1), s31–s37.
Briggs, F. (2002). *To what extent can Keeping Ourselves Safe protect children?* Wellington, NZ: New Zealand Police.
Brisch, K. H., Bechinger, D., Betzler, S., Heineman, H., Kachele, H., Pohlandt, F., Schmucker, G., & Buchheim, A. (2005). Attachment quality in very low-birth-weight premature infants in relation to maternal attachment representations and neurological development. *Parenting: Science and Practice, 5,* 11–32.
British Columbia Reproductive Care Program. (2003). Guidelines for perinatal care manual: Perinatal cocaine use: Care of the newborn. Retrieved from http://mdm.ca/cpgsnew/cpgs-f/search/french/help/2bcrcp.htm
Broberg, A. G., Wessels, H., Lamb, M. E., & Hwang, C. P. (1997). Effects of day care on the development of cognitive abilities in 8-year-olds: A longitudinal study. *Developmental Psychology, 33,* 62–69.
Broderick, P. C., & Korteland, C. (2004). A prospective study of rumination and depression in early adolescence. *Clinical Child Psychology and Psychiatry, 9,* 383–394.
Brody, G. H., & Flor, D. L. (1998). Maternal resources, parenting practices, and child competence in rural, single-parent African American families. *Child Development, 69,* 803–816.
Brody, G. H., Ge, X., Kim, S. Y., Murry, V. M., Simons, R. L., & Gibbons, F. X. (2003). Neighborhood disadvantage moderates associations of parenting and older sibling problem attitudes and behavior with conduct disorders in African American children. *Journal of Consulting and Clinical Psychology, 71,* 211–222.
Brody, G. H., Graziano, W. G., & Musser, L. M. (1983). Familiarity and children's behavior in same-age and mixed-age peer groups. *Developmental Psychology, 19,* 568–576.
Brody, G. H., & Murry, V. M. (2001). Sibling socialization of competence in rural, single-parent African American families. *Journal of Marriage and Family, 63,* 996–1008.
Brody, G. H., Stoneman, Z., & Flor, D. (1996a). Family wages, family processes, and youth competence in rural married African American families. In E. M. Hetherington & E. A. Blechman (Eds.), *Stress, coping, and resiliency in children and families: Family research consortium* (pp. 173–188). Mahwah, NJ: Erlbaum.
Brody, G. H., Stoneman, Z., & Flor, D. (1996b). Parental religiosity, family processes, and youth competence in rural, two-parent African-American families. *Developmental Psychology, 32,* 696–706.
Brody, G. H., Stoneman, Z., McCoy, J. K., & Forehand, R. (1992). Contemporaneous and longitudinal associations of sibling conflict with family relationship assessments and family discussions about sibling problems. *Child Development, 63,* 391–400.
Brody, L. (1999). *Gender, emotion, and the family.* Cambridge, MA: Harvard University Press.
Brody, L. R. (1997). Gender and emotion: Beyond stereotypes. *Journal of Social Issues, 53,* 369–393.
Brody, M. (2006). Child psychiatry, drugs, and the corporation. In S. Olfman (Ed.), *No child left different* (pp. 89–105). Westport, CT: Praeger.
Brodzinsky, D. M., & Pinderhughes, E. (2002). Parenting and child development in adoptive families. In M. H. Borstein (Ed.), *Handbook of parenting: Vol. 1* (2nd ed., pp. 279–311). Mahwah, NJ: Erlbaum.
Broidy, L. M., Nagin, D. S., Tremblay, R. E., Bates, J. E., Brame, B., Dodge, K. A., Fergusson, D., Horwood, J. L., Loeber, R., Laird, R., Lynam, D. R., Moffitt, T. E., Pettit, G. S., & Vitaro, F. (2003). Developmental trajectories of childhood disruptive behaviors and adolescent delinquency: A six-site, cross-national study. *Developmental Psychology, 39,* 222–245.
Bronfenbrenner, U. (Ed.). (2005). *Making human beings human.* Thousand Oaks, CA: Sage.
Bronfenbrenner, U., & Morris, P. A. (2006). The bioecological model of human development. In R. M. Lerner (Ed.), *Handbook of child psychology: Vol. 1. Theoretical models of human development* (6th ed., pp. 297–342). Hoboken, NJ: Wiley.
Bronson, G. W. (1994). Infants' transitions toward adult-like scanning. *Child Development, 65,* 1243–1261.
Bronstein, P. (2006). The family environment: Where gender role socialization begins. In J. Worell & C. D. Goodheart (Eds.), *Handbook of girls' and women's psychological health: Gender and well-being across the lifespan* (pp. 262–271). New York: Oxford University Press.
Bronte-Tinkew, J., Moore, K. A., & Carrano, J. (2006). The father–child relationship, parenting styles, and adolescent risk behaviors in intact families. *Journal of Family Issues, 27,* 850–881.
Brooks, P. J., Hanauere, J. B., Padowska, B., & Rosman, H. (2003). The role of selective attention in preschoolers' rule use in a novel dimensional card sort. *Cognitive Development, 18,* 195–215.
Brooks, R., & Meltzoff, A. N. (2005). The development of gaze following and its relation to language. *Developmental Science, 8,* 535–543.
Brooks-Gunn, J. (1988). Antecedents and consequences of variations in girls' maturational timing. *Journal of Adolescent Health Care, 9,* 365–373.
Brooks-Gunn, J. (2003). Do you believe in magic? What we can expect from early childhood intervention programs. *Social Policy Report of the Society for Research in Child Development, 27*(1).
Brooks-Gunn, J. (2004). Intervention and policy as change agents for young children. In P. L. Chase-Lansdale, K. Kiernan, & R. J. Friedman (Eds.), *Human development across lives and generations: The potential for change* (pp. 293–340). New York: Cambridge University Press.
Brooks-Gunn, J., Han, W.-J., & Waldfogel, J. (2002). Maternal employment and child cognitive outcomes in the first three years of life: The NICHD study of early child care. *Child Development, 73,* 1052–1072.
Brooks-Gunn, J., Klebanov, P. K., Smith, J., Duncan, G. J., & Lee, K. (2003). The black–white test score gap in young children. Contributions of test and family characteristics. *Applied Developmental Science, 7,* 239–252.
Brooks-Gunn, J., Schley, S., & Hardy, J. (2002). Marriage and the baby carriage: Historical change and intergenerational continuity in early parenthood. In L. J. Crockett & R. K. Sibereisen (Eds.), *Negotiating adolescence in times of social change* (pp. 36–57). New York: Cambridge University Press.
Brown, A. L. (1997). Transforming schools into communities of thinking and learning about serious matters. *American Psychologist, 52,* 399–413.
Brown, A. L., & Campione, J. C. (1972). Recognition memory for perceptually similar pictures in preschool children. *Journal of Experimental Psychology, 95,* 55–62.
Brown, A. L., Smiley, S. S., & Lawton, S. Q. C. (1978). The effects of experience on the selection of suitable retrieval cues for studying texts. *Child Development, 49,* 829–835.
Brown, A. M., & Miracle, J. A. (2003). Early binocular vision in human infants: Limitations on the generality of the Superposition Hypothesis. *Vision Research, 43,* 1563–1574.
Brown, A. S. (2006). Prenatal infection as a risk factor for schizophrenia. *Schizophrenia Bulletin, 32,* 200–202.
Brown, B. (2004). Adolescents' relationships with peers. In R. Lerner & L. Steinberg (Eds.), *Handbook of adolescent psychology* (2nd ed., pp. 363–394). Hoboken, NJ: Wiley.
Brown, B. B., Clasen, D., & Eicher, S. (1986). Perception of peer pressure, peer conformity, dispositions, and self-reported behavior among adolescents. *Developmental Psychology, 22,* 521–530.
Brown, B. B., Lohr, M. J., & McClenahan, E. L. (1986). Early adolescents' perceptions of peer pressure. *Journal of Early Adolescence, 6,* 139–154.
Brown, C. S., & Bigler, R. S. (2002). Effects of minority status in the classroom on children's intergroup attitudes. *Journal of Experimental Child Psychology, 83,* 77–110.
Brown, C. S., & Bigler, R. S. (2004). Children's perceptions of gender discrimination. *Developmental Psychology, 40,* 714–726.
Brown, J. R., Donelan-McCall, N., & Dunn, J. (1996). Why talk about mental states? The significance of children's conversations with friends, siblings and mothers. *Child Development, 67,* 836–849.
Brown, J. R., & Dunn, J. (1996). Continuities in emotion understanding from 3 to 6 years. *Child Development, 67,* 789–802.
Brown, R. (1973). *A first language: The early stages.* Cambridge, MA: Harvard University Press.
Brown, R., & Hanlon, C. (1970). Derivational complexity and order of acquisition in child speech. In J. R. Hayes (Ed.), *Cognition and the development of language* (pp. 11–53). New York: Wiley.
Brown, R. T., Reynolds, C. R., & Whitaker, J. S. (1999). Bias in mental testing since *Bias in Mental Testing. School Psychology Quarterly, 14,* 208–238.
Brown, S. A., & Ramo, D. E. (2005). Clinical course of youth following treatment for alcohol and drug problems. In. H. A. Liddle & C. L. Rowe (Eds.), *Adolescent substance abuse: Research and clinical advances* (pp. 79–103). Cambridge, UK: Cambridge University Press.
Brown, T. E. (2005). *Attention deficit disorder: The unfocused mind in children and adults.* New Haven, CT: Yale University Press.
Brown, T. E. (2006). Executive functions and attention deficit hyperactivity disorder: Implications of two conflicting views. *International Journal of Disability, Development and Education, 53,* 35–46.
Browne, C. A., & Woolley, J. D. (2004). Preschoolers' magical explanations for violations of physical, social, and mental laws. *Journal of Cognition and Development, 5,* 239–260.
Browne, J. V., & Talmi, A. (2005). Family-based intervention to enhance infant–parent relationships in the neonatal intensive care unit. *Journal of Pediatric Psychology, 30,* 667–677.
Brownell, C. A., & Carriger, M. S. (1990). Changes in cooperation and self-other differentiation during the second year. *Child Development, 61,* 1164–1174.
Brownell, C. A., & Kopp, C. B. (2007). Transitions in toddler socioemotional development: Behavior, understanding, relationships. In C. A. Brownell & C. B. Kopp (Eds.), *Socioemotional development in the toddler years: Transitions and transformations* (pp. 1–40). New York: Guilford.
Bruce, D., Dolan, A., & Phillips-Grant, K. (2000). On the transition from childhood amnesia to recall of personal memories. *Psychological Science, 11,* 360–364.
Bruch, H. (2001). *The golden cage: The enigma of anorexia nervosa.* Cambridge, MA: Harvard University Press.
Bruck, M., & Ceci, S. J. (2004). Forensic developmental psychology: Unveiling four common misconceptions. *Current Directions in Psychological Science, 13,* 229–232.
Bruer, J. T. (1999). *The myth of the first three years.* New York: Free Press.
Bruschweiler-Stern, N. (2004). A multifocal neonatal intervention. In A. J. Sameroff, S. C. McDonough, & K. L. Rosenblum (Eds.), *Treating parent–infant relationship problems* (pp. 188–212). New York: Guilford.
Bruzzese, J.-M., & Fisher, C. B. (2003). Assessing and enhancing the research consent capacity of children and youth. *Applied Developmental Science, 7,* 13–26.
Bryant, P., & Nunes, T. (2002). Children's understanding of mathematics. In U. Goswami (Ed.), *Blackwell handbook of childhood cognitive development* (pp. 412–439). Malden, MA. Blackwell.
Buchanan, A. (1996). *Cycles of child maltreatment.* Chichester, UK: Wiley.
Buchanan, C. M., Eccles, J. S., & Becker, J. B. (1992). Are adolescents the victims of raging hormones? Evidence for activational effects of hormones on moods and behavior at adolescence. *Psychological Bulletin, 111,* 62–107.
Buchanan, C. M., & Holmbeck, G. N. (1998). Measuring beliefs about adolescent personality and behavior. *Journal of Youth and Adolescence, 27,* 609–629.
Buchanan, C. M., Maccoby, E. E., & Dornbusch, S. M. (1996). *Adolescents after divorce.* Cambridge, MA: Harvard University Press.
Buchanan-Barrow, E., & Barrett, M. (1998). Children's rule discrimination within the context of the school. *British Journal of Developmental Psychology, 16,* 539–551.
Bugental, D. B., Ellerson, P. C., Lin, E. K., Rainey, B., & Kokotovic, A. (2002). A cognitive approach to child abuse prevention. *Journal of Family Psychology, 16,* 243–258.

Bugental, D. B., & Grusec, J. E. (2006). Socialization processes. In N. Eisenberg (Ed.), *Handbook of child psychology: Vol. 3. Social, emotional, and personality development* (6th ed., pp. 366–428). Hoboken, NJ: Wiley.

Bugental, D. B., & Happaney, K. (2004). Predicting infant maltreatment in low-income families: The interactive effects of maternal attributions and child status at birth. *Developmental Psychology, 40,* 234–243.

Buhrmester, D. (1996). Need fulfillment, interpersonal competence, and the developmental contexts of early adolescent friendship. In W. M. Bukowski, A. F. Newcomb, & W. W. Hartup (Eds.), *The company they keep: Friendship in childhood and adolescence* (pp. 158–185). New York: Cambridge University Press.

Buhrmester, D., & Furman, W. (1990). Perceptions of sibling relationships during middle childhood and adolescence. *Child Development, 61,* 1387–1398.

Buhs, E. S., & Ladd, G. W. (2001). Peer rejection as antecedent of young children's school adjustment: An examination of mediating processes. *Developmental Psychology, 37,* 550–560.

Buhs, E. S., Ladd, G. W., & Herald, S. L. (2006). Peer exclusion and victimization: Processes that mediate the relation between peer group rejection and children's classroom engagement and achievement. *Journal of Educational Psychology, 98,* 1–13.

Bukowski, W. M. (2001). Friendship and the worlds of childhood. In D. W. Nangle & C. A. Erdley (Eds.), *The role of friendship in psychological adjustment* (pp. 93–105). San Francisco: Jossey-Bass.

Bukowski, W. M., Sippola, L. K., & Hoza, B. (1999). Same and other: Interdependency between participation in same- and other-sex friendships. *Journal of Youth and Adolescence, 28,* 439–459.

Bukowski, W. M., Sippola, L. K., & Newcomb, A. F. (2000). Variations in patterns of attraction of same- and other-sex peers during early adolescence. *Developmental Psychology, 36,* 147–154.

Bullock, M., & Lutkenhaus, P. (1990). Who am I? The development of self-understanding in toddlers. *Merrill-Palmer Quarterly, 36,* 217–238.

Bumpus, M. F., Crouter, A. C., & McHale, S. M. (2006). Linkages between negative work-to-family spillover and mothers' and fathers' knowledge of their young adolescents' daily lives. *Journal of Early Adolescence, 26,* 36–59.

Bunting, L., & McAuley, C. (2004). Teenage pregnancy and parenthood: The role of fathers. *Child and Family Social Work, 9,* 295–303.

Burchinal, M. R., & Cryer, D. (2003). Diversity, child care quality, and developmental outcomes. *Early Childhood Research Quarterly, 18,* 401–426.

Burchinal, M. R., Peisner-Feinberg, E., Bryant, D. M., & Clifford, R. (2000). Children's social and cognitive development and child-care quality: Testing for differential associations related to poverty, gender, or ethnicity. *Applied Developmental Science, 4,* 149–165.

Burden, M. J., Jacobson, S. W., & Jacobson, J. L. (2005). Relation of prenatal alcohol exposure to cognitive processing speed and efficiency in childhood. *Alcoholism: Clinical and Experimental Research, 29,* 1473–1483.

Burhans, K. K., & Dweck, C. S. (1995). Helplessness in early childhood: The role of contingent worth. *Child Development, 66,* 1719–1738.

Burkam, D. T., Lee, V. E., & Smerdon, B. A. (1997). Gender and science learning early in high school: Subject matter and laboratory experiences. *American Educational Research Journal, 34,* 297–331.

Burts, D. C., Hart, C. H., Charlesworth, R., Fleege, P. O., Mosley, J., & Thomasson, R. H. (1992). Observed activities and stress behaviors of children in developmentally appropriate and inappropriate kindergarten classrooms. *Early Childhood Research Quarterly, 7,* 297–318.

Bushman, B. J., & Anderson, C. A. (2001). Media violence and the American public: Scientific facts versus media misinformation. *American Psychologist, 56,* 477–489.

Bushman, B. J., & Huesmann, L. R. (2001). Effects of televised violence on aggression. In D. G. Singer & J. L. Singer (Eds.), *Handbook of children and the media* (pp. 223–254). Thousand Oaks, CA: Sage.

Bushnell, E. W., & Boudreau, J. P. (1993). Motor development and the mind: The potential role of motor abilities as a determinant of aspects of perceptual development. *Child Development, 64,* 1005–1021.

Bushnik, T. (2006). *Child care in Canada.* Children and Youth Research Paper Series, Statistics Canada, Catalogue no. 89-599-MIE. Retrieved from www.statcan.ca/bsolc/english/bsolc?catno=89-599-MIE2006003

Bushnik, T., Barr-Telford, L., & Bussiére, P. (2004). *In and out of high school: First results from the second cycle of the Youth in Transition Survey, 2002.* Ottawa, ON: Statistics Canada.

Bussell, D. A., Neiderhiser, J. M., Pike, A., Plomin, R., Simmens, S., Howe, G. W., Hetherington, E. M., Carroll, E., & Reiss, D. (1999). Adolescents' relationships to siblings and mothers: A multivariate genetic analysis. *Developmental Psychology, 35,* 1248–1259.

Bussey, K. (1992). Lying and truthfulness: Children's definitions, standards, and evaluative reactions. *Child Development, 63,* 129–137.

Bussey, K. (1999). Children's categorization and evaluation of different types of lies and truths. *Child Development, 70,* 1338–1347.

Bussey, K., & Bandura, A. (1992). Self-regulatory mechanisms governing gender development. *Child Development, 63,* 1236–1250.

Bussiére, P., Knighton, T., & Pennock, D. (2007). *Measuring up: Canadian results of the OECD PISA Study: The performance of Canada's youth in science, reading, and mathematics: 2006.* First results for Canadians aged 15. Catalogue No. 81-590-XPE—No. 3. Ottawa: Human Resources and Social Development Canada, Council of Ministers of Education, Canada and Statistics Canada. Retrieved from www.statcan.ca/english/freepub/81-590-XIE/81-590-XIE2007001.htm

Buswell, S. D., & Spatz, D. L. (2007). Parent–infant co-sleeping and its relationship to breastfeeding. *Journal of Pediatric Health Care, 21,* 22–28.

Butler, M., & Meaney, J. (Eds.). (2005). *Genetics of developmental disabilities.* Boca Raton, FL: Taylor & Francis.

Butler, R. (1998). Age trends in the use of social and temporal comparison for self-evaluation: Examination of a novel developmental hypothesis. *Child Development, 69,* 1054–1073.

Butler, R. (1999). Information seeking and achievement motivation in middle childhood and adolescence: The role of conceptions of ability. *Developmental Psychology, 35,* 146–163.

Byard, R. W., & Krous, H. F. (2003). Sudden infant death syndrome: Overview and update. *Perspectives on Pediatric Pathology, 6,* 112–127.

Bybee, J. (Ed.). (1998). *Guilt and children.* San Diego, CA: Academic Press.

Bybee, J., Merisca, R., & Velasco, R. (1998). The development of reactions to guilt-producing events. In J. Bybee (Ed.), *Guilt and children* (pp. 185–213). San Diego: Academic Press.

Byrnes, J. P. (2002). The development of decision-making. *Journal of Adolescent Health, 31,* 208–215.

Byrnes, J. P. (2003). Cognitive development during adolescence. In G. R. Adams & M. D. Berzonsky (Eds.), *Blackwell handbook of adolescence* (pp. 227–246). Malden, MA: Blackwell.

Cabrera, N. J., & Garcia-Coll, C. (2004). Latino fathers: Uncharted territory in need of much exploration. In M. E. Lamb (Ed.), *The role of the father in child development* (4th ed., pp. 98–120). Hoboken, NJ: Wiley.

Cabrera, N. J., Tamis-LeMonda, C. S., Bradley, R. H., Hoferth, S., & Lamb, M. E. (2000). Fatherhood in the twenty-first century. *Child Development, 71,* 127–136.

Cain, K. M., & Dweck, C. S. (1995). The relation between motivational patterns and achievement cognitions through the elementary school years. *Merrill-Palmer Quarterly, 41,* 25–52.

Caine, N. (1986). Behavior during puberty and adolescence. In G. Mitchell & J. Erwin (Eds.), *Comparative primate biology: Vol. 2A. Behavior, conservation, and ecology* (pp. 327–361). New York: Alan R. Liss.

Cairns, R., Xie, H., & Leung, M.-C. (1998). The popularity of friendship and the neglect of social networks: Toward a new balance. In W. M. Bukowski & A. H. Cillessen (Eds.), *Sociometry then and now: Building on six decades of measuring children's experiences with the peer group* (pp. 25–53). San Francisco: Jossey-Bass.

Cairns, R. B. (1998). The making of developmental psychology. In R. M. Lerner (Ed.), *Handbook of child psychology: Vol. 1. Theoretical models of human development* (5th ed., pp. 25–105). New York: Wiley.

Cairns, R. B., & Cairns, B. D. (2006). The making of developmental psychology. In R. M. Lerner (Ed.), *Handbook of child psychology: Vol. 1. Theoretical models of human development* (6th ed., pp. 89–165). Hoboken, NJ: Wiley.

Caldera, Y. M., & Lindsey, E. W. (2006). Coparenting, mother–infant interaction, and infant–parent attachment relationships in two-parent families. *Journal of Family Psychology, 20,* 275–283.

Caldwell, B. M., & Bradley, R. H. (1994). Environmental issues in developmental follow-up research. In S. L. Friedman & H. C. Haywood (Eds.), *Developmental follow-up* (pp. 235–256). San Diego: Academic Press.

Calkins, S. D. (2002). Does aversive behavior during toddlerhood matter? The effects of difficult temperament on maternal perceptions and behavior. *Infant Mental Health Journal, 23,* 381–402.

Callaghan, T., Rochat, P., Lillard, A., Claux, M. L., Odden, H., Itakura, S., Tapanya, S., & Singh, S. (2005). Synchrony in the onset of mental-state reasoning: Evidence from five cultures. *Psychological Science, 16,* 378–384.

Callaghan, T. C. (1999). Early understanding and production of graphic symbols. *Child Development, 70,* 1314–1324.

Callaghan, T. C., & Rankin, M. P. (2002). Emergence of graphic symbol functioning and the question of domain specificity: A longitudinal training study. *Child Development, 73,* 359–376.

Callanan, M. A., & Sabbagh, M. A. (2004). Multiple labels for objects in conversations with young children: Parents' language and children's developing expectations about word meanings. *Developmental Psychology, 40,* 746–763.

Calvert, S. L., & Kotler, J. A. (2003). Lessons from children's television: The impact of the Children's Television Act on children's learning. *Applied Developmental Psychology, 24,* 275–335.

Calvert, S. L., Kotler, J. A., Zehnder, S. M., & Shockey, E. M. (2003). Gender stereotyping in children's reports about educational and informational television programs. *Media Psychology, 5,* 139–162.

Calvert, S. L., Rideout, V. J., Woolard, J. L., Barr, R. F., & Strouse, G. A. (2005). Age, ethnicity, and socioeconomic patterns in early computer use: A national survey. *American Behavioral Scientist, 48,* 590–607.

Camarata, S., & Leonard, L. B. (1986). Young children pronounce object words more accurately than action words. *Journal of Child Language, 13,* 51–65.

Cameron, C. A., & Lee, K. (1997). The development of children's telephone communication. *Journal of Applied Developmental Psychology, 18,* 55–70.

Cameron, J. A., Alvarez, J. M., Ruble, D. N., & Fuligni, A. J. (2001). Children's lay theories about in-groups and out-groups: Reconceptualizing research on prejudice. *Personality and Social Psychology Review, 5,* 118–128.

Cameron, M. B., & Wilson, B. J. (1990). The effects of chronological age, gender, and delay of entry on academic achievement and retention: Implications for academic redshirting. *Psychology in the Schools, 27,* 260–263.

Cameron, P. A., & Gallup, G. G. (1988). Shadow recognition in human infants. *Infant Behavior and Development, 11,* 465–471.

Cameron-Faulkner, T., Lieven, E., & Tomasello, M. (2003). A construction based analysis of child-directed speech. *Cognitive Science, 27,* 843–873.

Campa, M. J., & Eckenrode, J. J. (2006). Pathways to intergenerational adolescent childbearing in a high-risk sample. *Journal of Marriage and Family, 68,* 558–572.

Campbell, F. A., Pungello, E. P., Miller-Johnson, S., Burchinal, M., & Ramey, C. T. (2001). The development of cognitive and academic abilities: Growth curves from an early childhood educational experiment. *Developmental Psychology, 37,* 231–242.

Campbell, F. A., & Ramey, C. T. (1995). Cognitive and school outcomes for high-risk African-American students at middle adolescence: Positive effects of early intervention. *American Educational Research Journal, 32,* 743–772.

Campbell, F. A., Ramey, C. T., Pungello, E. P., Sparling, J., & Miller-Johnson, S. (2002). Early childhood education: Young adult outcomes from the Abecedarian Project. *Applied Developmental Science, 6,* 42–57.

Campbell, S. B., Brownell, C. A., Hungerford, A., Spieker, S. J., Mohan, R., & Blessing, J. S. (2004). The course of maternal depressive symptoms and maternal sensitivity as predictors of attachment security at 36 months. *Development and Psychopathology, 16,* 231–252.

Campbell, S. B., Spieker, S., Burchinal, M., Poe, M. D., & the NICHD Early Child Care Research Network. (2006). Trajectories of aggression from toddlerhood to age 9 predict academic and social functioning through age 12. *Journal of Child Psychology and Psychiatry, 47,* 791–800.

Campos, J. J., Anderson, D. I., Barbu-Roth, M. A., Hubbard, E. M., Hertenstein, J. J., & Witherington, D. (2000). Travel broadens the mind. *Infancy, 1,* 149–219.

Campos, J. J., Frankel, C. B., & Camras, L. (2004). On the nature of emotion regulation. *Child Development, 75,* 377–394.

Campos, J. J., Kermoian, R., & Zumbahlen, M. R. (1992). Socioemotional transformation in the family system following infant crawling onset. In N. Eisenberg & R. A. Fabes (Eds.), *New directions for child development* (No. 55, pp. 25–40). San Francisco: Jossey-Bass.

Campos, R. G. (1989). Soothing pain-elicited distress in infants with swaddling and pacifiers. *Child Development, 60,* 781–792.

Camras, L. A. (1992). Expressive development and basic emotions. *Cognition and Emotion, 6,* 267–283.

Camras, L. A., Oster, H., Campos, J. J., & Bakeman, R. (2003). Emotional facial expressions in European-American, Japanese, and Chinese infants. *Annals of the New York Academy of Sciences, 1000,* 1–17.

Camras, L. A., Oster, H., Campos, J., Campos, R., Ujie, T., Miyake, K., Wang, L., & Meng, Z. (1998). Production of emotional and facial expressions in European American, Japanese, and Chinese infants. *Developmental Psychology, 34,* 616–628.

Camras, L. A., Oster, H., Campos, J. J., Miyake, K., & Bradshaw, D. (1992). Japanese and American infants' responses to arm restraint. *Developmental Psychology, 28,* 578–583.

Canada Campaign 2000. (2003). *Diversity or disparity? Early childhood education and care in Canada (ECEC).* Retrieved from www.campaign2000.ca

Canada Campaign 2000. (2007). *Oh Canada! Too many children in poverty for too long . . . 2006 Report Card on Child and Family Poverty in Canada.* Retrieved from www.campaign2000.ca

Canadian Diabetes Association. (2007). The prevalence and costs of diabetes. Retrieved from www.diabetes.ca/Section_About/prevalence.asp

Canadian Fitness and Lifestyle Research Institute. (2005). *Physical activity and sport: Encouraging children to be active.* Retrieved from www.cflri.ca/eng/statistics/surveys/pam2005.php

Canadian Paediatric Society, Dietitians of Canada and Health Canada. (2005). *Nutrition for Healthy Term Infants.* Ottawa, Canada: Minister of Public Works and Government Services. Available on the web at http://www.hc-sc.gc.ca/fn-an/pubs/infant-nourrisson/nut_infant_nourrisson_term_e.html

Canadian Psychological Association. (2000). *Canadian code of ethics for psychologists.* Ottawa, ON: Author. Retrieved from www.cpa.ca/ethics2000.html

Candy-Gibbs, S., Sharp, K., & Petrun, C. (1985). The effects of age, object, and cultural/religious background on children's concepts of death. *Omega, 15,* 329–345.

Canetto, S. S., & Sakinofsky, I. (1998). The gender paradox in suicide. *Suicide and Life-Threatening Behavior, 28,* 1–23.

Canobi, K. H. (2004). Individual differences in children's addition and subtraction knowledge. *Cognitive Development, 19,* 81–93.

Canobi, K. H., Reeve, R. A., & Pattison, P. E. (1998). The role of conceptual understanding in children's addition problem solving. *Developmental Psychology, 34,* 882–891.

Canobi, K. H., Reeve, R. A., & Pattison, P. E. (2003). Patterns of knowledge in children's addition. *Developmental Psychology, 39,* 521–534.

Capelli, C. A., Nakagawa, N., & Madden, C. M. (1990). How children understand sarcasm: The role of context and intonation. *Child Development, 61,* 1824–1841.

Capirci, O., Contaldo, A., Caselli, M. C., & Volterra, V. (2005). From action to language through gesture. *Gesture, 5,* 155–177.

Caplan, M., Vespo, J., Pedersen, J., & Hay, D. F. (1991). Conflict and its resolution in small groups of one- and two-year-olds. *Child Development, 62,* 1513–1524.

Caples, H. S., & Barrera, M., Jr. (2006). Conflict, support and coping as mediators of the relation between degrading parenting and adjustment. *Journal of Youth and Adolescence, 35,* 603–615.

Carbonaro, W. (2005). Tracking, students' effort, and academic achievement. *Sociology of Education, 78,* 27–49.

Carey, S. (1995). On the origins of causal understanding. In D. Sperber, D. Premack, & A. J. Premack (Eds.), *Causal cognition* (pp. 268–308). Oxford, UK: Clarendon Press.

Carey, S. (1999). Sources of conceptual change. In E. K. Scholnick, K. Nelson, S. A. Gelman, & P. H. Miller (Eds.), *Conceptual development: Piaget's legacy* (pp. 293–326). Mahwah, NJ: Erlbaum.

Carey, S., & Markman, E. M. (1999). Cognitive development. In B. M. Bly & D. E. Rumelhart (Eds.), *Cognitive science* (pp. 201–254). San Diego: Academic Press.

Carli, L. L. (1995). No: Biology does not create gender differences in personality. In M. R. Walsh (Ed.), *Women, men, and gender.* New Haven, CT: Yale University Press.

Carlo, G., Koller, S. H., Eisenberg, N., Da Silva, M., & Frohlich, C. (1996). A cross-national study on the relations among prosocial moral reasoning, gender-role orientations, and prosocial behaviors. *Developmental Psychology, 32,* 231–240.

Carlson, C., Uppal, S., & Prosser, E. (2000). Ethnic differences in processes contributing to the self-esteem of early adolescent girls. *Journal of Early Adolescence, 20,* 44–67.

Carlson, C. I., Wilson, K. D., & Hargrave, J. L. (2003). The effect of school racial composition on Hispanic intergroup relations. *Journal of Social and Personal Relationships, 20,* 203–220.

Carlson, E. A. (1998). A prospective longitudinal study of attachment disorganization/disorientation. *Child Development, 4,* 1107–1128.

Carlson, M., & Earls, F. (1997). Psychological and neuroendocrinological sequelae of early social deprivation in institutionalized children in Romania. *Annals of the New York Academy of Sciences, 807,* 419–428.

Carlson, S. M., Moses, L. J., & Claxton, S. J. (2004). Individual differences in executive functioning and theory of mind: An investigation of inhibitory control and planning ability. *Journal of Experimental Child Psychology, 87,* 299–319.

Carlson, V. J., & Horwood, R. L. (2003). Attachment, culture, and the caregiving system: The cultural patterning of everyday experiences among Anglo and Puerto Rican mother–infant pairs. *Infant Mental Health Journal, 24,* 53–73.

Carmichael, S. L., & Shaw, G. M. (2000). Maternal life stress and congenital anomalies. *Epidemiology, 11,* 30–35.

Carpendale, J. I. M. (2000). Kohlberg and Piaget on stages and moral reasoning. *Developmental Review, 20,* 181–205.

Carpenter, C. J. (1983). Activity structure and play: Implications for socialization. In M. Liss (Ed.), *Social and cognitive skills: Sex roles and children's play* (pp. 117–145). New York: Academic Press.

Carpenter, C. J., Huston, A. C., & Holt, W. (1986). Modification of preschool sex-typed behaviors by participation in adult-structured activities. *Sex Roles, 14,* 603–615.

Carpenter, M., Akhtar, N., & Tomasello, M. (1998). Fourteen- through 18-month-old infants differentially imitate intentional and accidental actions. *Infant Behavior and Development, 21,* 315–330.

Carpenter, M., Nagel, K., & Tomasello, M. (1998). Social cognition, joint attention, and communicative competence. *Monographs of the Society for Research in Child Development, 63*(4, Serial No. 255).

Carpenter, T. P., Fennema, E., Fuson, K., Hiebert, J., Human, P., & Murray, H. (1999). Learning basic number concepts and skills as problem solving. In E. Fennema & T. A. Romberg (Eds.), *Mathematics classrooms that promote understanding: Studies in mathematical thinking and learning series* (pp. 45–61). Mahwah, NJ: Erlbaum.

Carr, D., & Friedman, M. A. (2005). Is obesity stigmatizing? Body weight, perceived discrimination, and psychological well-being in the United States. *Journal of Health and Social Behavior, 46,* 244–256.

Carr, J. (2002). Down syndrome. In P. Howlin & O. Udwin (Eds.), *Outcomes in neurodevelopmental and genetic disorders* (pp. 169–197). New York: Cambridge University Press.

Carr, M., & Jessup, D. L. (1997). Gender differences in first-grade mathematics strategy use: Social and metacognitive influences. *Journal of Educational Psychology, 89,* 318–328.

Carraher, T., Schliemann, A. D., & Carraher, D. W. (1988). Mathematical concepts in everyday life. In G. B. Saxe & M. Gearhart (Eds.), *New directions for child development* (Vol. 41, pp. 71–87). San Francisco: Jossey-Bass.

Carroll, J. B. (1993). *Human cognitive abilities: A survey of factor-analytic studies.* New York: Cambridge University Press.

Carroll, J. B. (2005). The three-stratum theory of cognitive abilities. In D. P. Flanagan & P. L. Harrison (Eds.), *Contemporary intellectual assessment: Theories, tests, and issues* (2nd ed., pp. 69–76). New York: Guilford.

Carskadon, M. A., Acebo, C., & Jenni, O. G. (2004). Regulation of adolescent sleep: Implications for behavior. In R. E. Dahl & L. P. Spear (Eds.), *Adolescent brain development: Vulnerabilities and opportunities* (pp. 276–291). New York: New York Academy of Sciences.

Carskadon, M. A., Harvey, K., Duke, P., Anders, T. F., Litt, I. F., & Dement, W. C. (2002). Pubertal changes in daytime sleepiness. *Sleep, 25,* 525–605.

Carver, K., Joyner, K., & Udry, J. R. (2003). National estimates of adolescent romantic relationships. In P. Florsheim (Ed.), *Adolescent romantic relations and sexual behavior: Theory, research, and practical implications* (pp. 23–56). Mahwah, NJ: Erlbaum.

Carver, P. R., Egan, S. K., & Perry, D. G. (2004). Children who question their heterosexuality. *Developmental Psychology, 40,* 43–53.

Casas, J. F., Weigel, S. M., Crick, N. R., Ostrov, J. M., Woods, K. E., Yeh, E. A. J., & Huddleston-Casas, C. A. (2006). Early parenting and children's relational and physical aggression in the preschool and home contexts. *Applied Developmental Psychology, 27,* 209–227.

Casasola, M., Cohen, L. B., & Chiarello, E. (2003). Six-month-old infants' categorization of containment spatial relations. *Child Development, 74,* 679–693.

Case, R. (1992). *The mind's staircase.* Hillsdale, NJ: Erlbaum.

Case, R. (1996). Introduction: Reconceptualizing the nature of children's conceptual structures and their development in middle childhood. In R. Case & Y. Okamoto (Eds.), The role of central conceptual structures in the development of children's thought. *Monographs of the Society for Research in Child Development, 61*(1–2, Serial No. 246), pp. 1–26.

Case, R. (1998). The development of central conceptual structures. In D. Kuhn & R. Siegler (Eds.), *Handbook of child psychology: Vol. 2. Cognition, perception, and language* (5th ed., pp. 745–800). New York: Wiley.

Case, R., Griffin, S., & Kelly, W. M. (2001). Socioeconomic differences in children's early cognitive development and their readiness for schooling. In S. L. Golbeck (Ed.), *Psychological perspectives on early education* (pp. 37–63). Mahwah, NJ: Erlbaum.

Case, R., & Okamoto, Y. (Eds.). (1996). The role of central conceptual structures in the development of children's thought. *Monographs of the Society for Research in Child Development, 61*(1–2, Serial No. 246).

Caselli, M. C., Bates, E., Casadio, P., Fenson, J., Fenson, L., Sanderl, L., & Weir, J. (1995). A cross-linguistic study of early lexical development. *Cognitive Development, 10,* 159–199.

Casey, B. J., Thomas, K. M., Davidson, M. C., Kunz, K., & Franzen, P. L. (2002). Dissociating striatal and hippocampal function developmentally with a stimulus-response compatibility task. *Journal of Cognitive Neuroscience, 22,* 8647–8652.

Casey, M. B., Nuttall, R. L., & Pezaris, E. (1997). Mediators of gender differences in mathematics college entrance test scores: A comparison of spatial skills with internalized beliefs and anxieties. *Developmental Psychology, 33,* 669–680.

Casey, M. B., Nuttall, R. L., & Pezaris, E. (2001). Spatial-mechanical reasoning skills versus mathematics self-confidence as mediators of gender differences on mathematics subtests using cross-national gender-based items. *Journal for Research in Mathematics Education, 32,* 28–57.

Cashon, C. H., & Cohen, L. B. (2000). Eight-month-old infants' perceptions of possible and impossible events. *Infancy, 1,* 429–446.

Casper, L. M., & Smith, K. E. (2002). Dispelling the myths: Self-care, class, and race. *Journal of Family Issues, 23,* 716–727.

Caspi, A. (2000). The child is father of the man: Personality continuities from childhood to adulthood. *Journal of Personality and Social Psychology, 78,* 158–172.

Caspi, A., Elder, G. H., Jr., & Bem, D. J. (1987). Moving against the world: Life-course patterns of explosive children. *Developmental Psychology, 23,* 308–313.

Caspi, A., Elder, G. H., Jr., & Bem, D. J. (1988). Moving away from the world: Life-course patterns of shy children. *Developmental Psychology, 24,* 824–831.

Caspi, A., Harrington, H., Milne, B., Amell, J. W., Theodore, R. F., & Moffitt, T. E. (2003). Children's behavioral styles at age 3 are linked to their adult personality traits at age 26. *Journal of Personality, 71,* 495–513.

Caspi, A., Lynam, D., Moffitt, T. E., & Silva, P. A. (1993). Unraveling girls' delinquency: Biological, dispositional, and contextual contributions to adolescent misbehavior. *Developmental Psychology, 29,* 19–30.

Caspi, A., McClay, J., Moffitt, T. E., Mill, J., Martin, J., & Craig, I. W. (2002). Role of genotype in the cycle of violence in maltreated children. *Science, 297,* 851–854.

Caspi, A., Moffitt, T. E., Morgan, J., Rutter, M., Taylor, A., Kim-Cohen, J., & Polo-Tomas, M. (2004). Maternal expressed emotion predicts children's antisocial behavior problems: Using monozygotic-twin differences to identify environmental effects on behavioral development. *Developmental Psychology, 40,* 149–161.

Caspi, A., & Roberts, B. W. (2001). Personality development across the life course: The argument for change and continuity. *Psychological Inquiry, 12,* 49–66.

Caspi, A., & Shiner, R. L. (2006). Personality development. In N. Eisenberg (Ed.), *Handbook of child psychology: Vol. 3. Social, emotional, and personality development* (6th ed., pp. 300–365). Hoboken, NJ: Wiley.

Cassia, V. M., Simion, F., & Umiltá, C. (2001). Face preference at birth: The role of an orienting mechanism. *Developmental Science, 4,* 101–108.

Cassia, V. M., Turati, C., & Simion, F. (2004). Can a nonspecific bias toward top-heavy patterns explain newborns' face preference? *Psychological Science, 15,* 379–383.

Cassidy, J., & Berlin, L. J. (1994). The insecure/ambivalent pattern of attachment: Theory and research. *Child Development, 65,* 971–991.

Cassidy, K., Adamek-Griggs, R., Cosetti, M., Meier, V., Kelton, E., & Richman, L. (2005). Preschool children's understanding of conflicting desires. *Journal of Cognition and Development, 6,* 427–454.

Catalano, R., Bruckner, T., Anderson, E., & Gould, J. B. (2005). Fetal death sex ratios: A test of the economic stress hypothesis. *International Journal of Epidemiology, 34,* 944–948.

Catalano, R. A. (2003). Sex ratios in the two Germanies: A test of the economic stress hypothesis. *Human Reproduction, 18,* 1972–1975.

Caton, D., Corry, M. P., Frigoletto, F. D., Hokins, D. P., Liberman, E., & Mayberry, L. (2002). The nature and management of labor pain: Executive summary. *American Journal of Obstetrics and Gynecology, 186,* S1–S15.

Cattell, J. M. (1890). Mental tests and measurements. *Mind, 15,* 373–381.

Cattell, R. B. (1971). *Abilities: Their structure, growth and action.* Boston: Houghton Mifflin.

Cattell, R. B. (1987). *Intelligence: Its structure, growth and action.* Amsterdam: North-Holland.

Cavadini, C., Siega-Riz, A. M., & Popkin, B. M. (2000). U.S. adolescent food intake trends from 1965 to 1996. *Archives of Diseases in Childhood, 83,* 18–24.

Ceci, S. J. (1991). How much does schooling influence general intelligence and its cognitive components? A reassessment of the evidence. *Developmental Psychology, 27,* 703–722.

Ceci, S. J. (1999). Schooling and intelligence. In S. J. Ceci & W. M. Williams (Eds.), *The nature–nurture debate: The essential readings* (pp. 168–175). Oxford: Blackwell.

Ceci, S. J., Bruck, M., & Battin, D. B. (2000). The suggestibility of children's testimony. In D. F. Bjorklund (Ed.), *False-memory creation in children and adults* (pp. 169–201). Mahwah, NJ: Erlbaum.

Ceci, S. J., Fitneva, S. A., & Gilstrap, L. L. (2003). Memory development and eyewitness testimony. In A. Slater & G. Bremner (Eds.), *An introduction to developmental psychology* (pp. 283–310). Malden, MA: Blackwell.

Ceci, S. J., & Roazzi, A. (1994). The effects of context on cognition: Postcards from Brazil. In R. J. Sternberg (Ed.), *Mind in context* (pp. 74–101). New York: Cambridge University Press.

Ceci, S. J., Rosenblum, T. B., & Kumpf, M. (1998). The shrinking gap between high- and low-scoring groups: Current trends and possible causes. In U. Neisser (Ed.), *The rising curve* (pp. 287–302). Washington, DC: American Psychological Association.

Ceci, S. J., & Williams, W. M. (1997). Schooling, intelligence, and income. *American Psychologist, 52,* 1051–1058.

Center for Communication and Social Policy. (Ed.). (1998). *National television violence study* (Vol. 2). Newbury Park, CA: Sage.

Center for Effective Discipline. (2005). *Worldwide bans on corporal punishment.* Retrieved from www.stophitting.com/disatschool/facts.php

Cermak, S. A., & Daunhauer, L. A. (1997). Sensory processing in the post-institutionalized child. *American Journal of Occupational Therapy, 51,* 500–507.

Cernoch, J. M., & Porter, R. H. (1985). Recognition of maternal axillary odors by infants. *Child Development, 56,* 1593–1598.

Cervantes, C. A., & Callanan, M. A. (1998). Labels and explanations in mother–child emotion talk: Age and gender differentiation. *Developmental Psychology, 34,* 88–98.

Chalmers, J. B., & Townsend, M. A. R. (1990). The effects of training in social perspective taking on socially maladjusted girls. *Child Development, 61,* 178–190.

Chamberlain, P. (2003). Antisocial behavior and delinquency in girls. In P. Chamberlain (Ed.), *Treating chronic juvenile offenders* (pp. 109–127). Washington, DC: American Psychological Association.

Champion, T. B. (2003a). "A matter of vocabularly": Performances of low-income African-American Head Start children on the Peabody Picture Vocabulary Test. *Communication Disorders Quarterly, 24,* 121–127.

Champion, T. B. (2003b). *Understanding storytelling among African-American children: A journey from Africa to America.* Mahwah, NJ: Erlbaum.

Chan, L. K. S., & Moore, P. J. (2006). Development of attributional beliefs and strategic knowledge in years 5–9: A longitudinal analysis. *Educational Psychology, 26,* 161–185.

Chan, R. W., Raboy, B., & Patterson, C. J. (1998). Psychosocial adjustment among children conceived via donor insemination by lesbian and heterosexual mothers. *Child Development, 69,* 443–457.

Chandler, M. J., & Carpendale, J. I. (1998). Inching toward a mature theory of mind. In M. Ferrari & R. J. Sternberg (Eds.), *Self-awareness: Its nature and development* (pp. 148–190). New York: Guilford.

Chandra, R. K. (1991). Interactions between early nutrition and the immune system. In *Ciba Foundation Symposium* (No. 156, pp. 77–92). Chichester, UK: Wiley.

Chaney, C. (1992). Language development, metalinguistic skills, and print awareness in 3-year-old children. *Applied Psycholinguistics, 13,* 485–514.

Chang, F., Dell, G. S., & Bock, K. (2006). Becoming syntactic. *Psychological Review, 113,* 234–272.

Chang, L., Schwartz, D., Dodge, K. A., & McBride-Chang, C. (2003). Harsh parenting in relation to child emotion regulation and aggression. *Journal of Family Psychology, 17,* 598–606.

Channon, S., Mockler, C., & Lee, P. (2005). Executive functioning and speed of processing in phenylkentonuria. *Neuropsychology, 19,* 679–686.

Chao, R. K. (1994). Beyond parental control and authoritarian parenting style: Understanding Chinese parenting through the cultural notion of training. *Child Development, 65,* 1111–1119.

Chaplin, T. M., Cole, P. M., & Zahn-Waxler, C. (2005). Parental socialization of emotion expression: Gender differences and relations to child adjustment. *Emotion, 5,* 80–88.

Chapman, K. L., Leonard, L. B., & Mervis, C. B. (1986). The effect of feedback on young children's inappropriate word usage. *Journal of Child Language, 13,* 101–117.

Chapman, R. S. (2000). Children's language learning: An interactionist perspective. *Journal of Child Psychology and Psychiatry, 41,* 33–54.

Chapman, R. S. (2006). Children's language learning: An interactionist perspective. In R. Paul (Ed.), *Language disorders from a developmental perspective* (pp. 1–53). Mahwah, NJ: Erlbaum.

Charman, T., Baron-Cohen, S., Swettenham, J., Baird, G., Cox, A., & Drew, A. (2001). Testing joint attention, imitation, and play as infancy precursors to language and theory of mind. *Cognitive Development, 15,* 481–498.

Charpak, N., Ruiz-Peláez, J. G., & Figueroa, Z. (2005). Influence of feeding patterns and other factors on early somatic growth of healthy preterm infants in home-based kangaroo mother care: A cohort study. *Journal of Pediatric Gastroenterology and Nutrition, 41,* 430–437.

Chase-Lansdale, P. L., Brooks-Gunn, J., & Zamsky, E. S. (1994). Young African-American multigenerational families in poverty: Quality of mothering and grandmothering. *Child Development, 65,* 373–393.

Chase-Lansdale, P. L., Gordon, R., Brooks-Gunn, J., & Klebanov, P. K. (1997). Neighborhood and family influences on the intellectual and behavioral competence of preschool and early school-age children. In J. Brooks-Gunn, G. Duncan, & J. L. Aber (Eds.), *Neighborhood poverty: Context and consequences for development* (pp. 79–118). New York: Russell Sage Foundation.

Chassin, L., Hussong, A., Barrera, M., Jr., Molina, B. S. G., Trim, R., & Ritter, J. (2004). Adolescent substance use. In R. M. Lerner & L. Steinberg (Eds.), *Handbook of adolescent psychology* (2nd ed., pp. 665–696). Hoboken, NJ: Wiley.

Chauhan, G. S., Shastri, J., & Mohite, P. (2005). Development of gender constancy in preschoolers. *Psychological Studies, 50,* 62–71.

Chavajay, P., & Rogoff, B. (2002). Schooling and traditional collaborative social organization of problem solving by Mayan mothers and children. *Developmental Psychology, 38,* 55–66.

Checkley, W., Epstein, L. D., Gilman, R. H., Cabrera, L., & Black, R. E. (2003). Effects of acute diarrhea on linear growth in Peruvian children. *American Journal of Epidemiology, 157,* 166–175.

Chen, L.-C., Metcalfe, J. S., Jeka, J. J., & Clark, J. E. (2007). Two steps forward and one back: Learning to walk affects infants' sitting posture. *Infant Behavior and Development, 30,* 16–25.

Chen, M. (2003). Wombs for rent: An examination of prohibitory and regulatory approaches to governing preconception arrangements. *Health Law in Canada, 23,* 33–50.

Chen, X. (2001). Growing up in a collectivistic culture: Socialization and socioemotional development in Chinese children. In A. L. Comunian & U. P. Gielen (Eds.), *Human development in cross-cultural perspective.* Padua, Italy: Cedam.

Chen, X., Cen, G., Li, D., & He, Y. (2005). Social functioning and adjustment in Chinese children: The imprint of historical time. *Child Development, 76,* 182–195.

Chen, X., DeSouza, A. T., Chen, H., & Wang, L. (2006). Reticent behavior and experiences in peer interactions in Chinese and Canadian children. *Developmental Psychology, 42,* 656–665.

Chen, X., Hastings, P. D., Rubin, K. H., Chen, H., Cen, G., & Stewart, S. L. (1998). Child-rearing attitudes and behavioral inhibition in Chinese and Canadian toddlers: A cross-cultural study. *Developmental Psychology, 34,* 677–686.

Chen, X., Rubin, K. H., & Li, D. (1995). Social functioning and adjustment in Chinese children: A longitudinal study. *Developmental Psychology, 31,* 531–539.

Chen, X., Wang, L., & DeSouza, A. (2006). Temperament, socioemotional functioning, and peer relationships in Chinese and North American children. In X. Chen, D. C. French, & B. H. Schneider (Eds.), *Peer relationships in cultural context* (pp. 123–147). New York: Cambridge University Press

Chen, X., Wu, H., Chen, H., Wang, L., & Cen, G. (2001). Parenting practices and aggressive behavior in Chinese children. *Parenting: Science and Practice, 1,* 159–184.

Chen, Y.-C., Yu, M.-L., Rogan, W., Gladen, B., & Hsu, C.-C. (1994). A 6-year follow-up of behavior and activity disorders in the Taiwan Yu-cheng children. *American Journal of Public Health, 84,* 415–421.

Chen, Y.-J., & Hsu, C.-C. (1994). Effects of prenatal exposure to PCBs on the neurological function of children: A neuropsychological and neurophysiological study. *Developmental Medicine and Child Neurology, 36,* 312–320.

Chen, Z., & Siegler, R. S. (2000). Across the great divide: Bridging the gap between understanding of toddlers' and older children's thinking. *Monographs of the Society for Research in Child Development, 65*(2, Serial No. 261).

Chen, Z., Sanchez, R. P., & Campbell, T. (1997). From beyond to within their grasp: The rudiments of analogical problem solving in 10- to 13-month-olds. *Developmental Psychology, 33,* 790–801.

Chesney-Lind, M. (2001). Girls, violence, and delinquency: Popular myths and persistent problems. In S. O. White (Ed.), *Handbook of youth and justice* (pp. 135–158). New York: Kluwer Academic.

Chesney-Lind, M., & Belknap, J. (2004). Trends in delinquent girls' aggression and violent behavior. In M. Putallaz & K. L. Bierman (Eds.), *Aggression, antisocial behavior, and violence among girls: A developmental perspective* (pp. 203–220). New York: Guilford.

Chess, S., & Thomas, A. (1984). *Origins and evolution of behavior disorders.* New York: Brunner/Mazel.

Chi, M. T. H. (1978). Knowledge structures and memory development. In R. S. Siegler (Ed.), *Children's thinking: What develops?* (pp. 73–96). Hillsdale, NJ: Erlbaum.

Child Care Advocacy Association of Canada. (2004). *Family living costs in Manitoba, 2004, and cost of raising a child.* Retrieved from www.action.web.ca/home/ccaac/alerts/shtm?x=67753

Child Trends. (2006). *Facts at a glance.* Washington, DC: Author.

Children's Defense Fund. (2005). *The state of America's children: Yearbook 2005.* Washington, DC: Author.

Children's Defense Fund. (2006). *Annual report 2006.* Washington, DC: Author.

Children's Television Act. (1990). Public Law No. 101-437, 104 Stat. 996-1000, codified at 47 USC Sections 303a, 303b, 394.

Chinn, C. A., & Malhotra, B. A. (2002). Children's responses to anomalous scientific data: How is conceptual change impeded? *Journal of Educational Psychology, 94,* 327–343.

Choi, J., & Silverman, I. (2003). Processes underlying sex differences in route-learning strategies in children and adolescents. *Personality and Individual Differences, 34,* 1153–1166.

Choi, S., & Gopnik, A. (1995). Early acquisition of verbs in Korean: A cross-linguistic study. *Journal of Child Language, 22,* 497–529.

Choi, S., McDonough, L., Bowerman, M., & Mandler, J. M. (1999). Early sensitivity to language-specific spatial categories in English and Korean. *Cognitive Development, 14,* 241–268.

Chomsky, C. (1969). *The acquisition of syntax in children from 5 to 10.* Cambridge, MA: MIT Press.

Chomsky, N. (1957). *Syntactic structures.* The Hague: Mouton.

Chomsky, N. (1976). *Reflections on language.* London: Temple Smith.

Chomsky, N. (1997). Language and mind: Current thoughts on ancient problems (Part 1). Retrieved from http://fccl.ksu.ru/papers/chomsky1.htm

Chorzempa, B. F., & Graham, S. (2006). Primary-grade teachers' use of within-class ability grouping in reading. *Journal of Educational Psychology, 98,* 529–541.

Chouinard, M. M., & Clark, E. V. (2003). Adult reformulations of child errors as negative evidence. *Journal of Child Language, 30,* 637–669.

Christ, S. E., Steiner, R. D., Grange, D. K., Abrams, R. A., & White, D. A. (2006). Inhibitory control in children with phenylketonuria. *Developmental Neuropsychology, 30,* 845–864.

Christian, P. (2003). Micronutrients and reproductive health issues: An international perspective. *Journal of Nutrition, 133,* 1969S–1973S.

Chudley, A. E., Conry, J., Cook, J. L., Loock, C., Rosales, T., & LeBlanc, N. (2005). Fetal alcohol spectrum disorder: Canadian guidelines for diagnosis. *Canadian Medical Association Journal, 172,* S1–S21.

Chumlea, W. C., Schubert, C. M., Roche, A. F., Kulin, H. E., Lee, P. A., Himes, J. H., & Sun, S. S. (2003). Age at menarche and racial comparisons in U.S. girls. *Pediatrics, 111,* 110–113.

Chung, H. H. (2006). Code switching as a communicative strategy: A case study of Korean–English bilinguals. *Bilingual Research Journal, 30,* 293–307.

Cianciolo, A. T., Matthew, C., Sternberg, R. J., & Wagner, R. K. (2006). Tacit knowledge, practical intelligence, and expertise. In K. A. Cricsson, N. Charness, P. J. Feltovich, & R. R. Hoffman (Eds.), *The Cambridge handbook of expertise and expert performance* (pp. 613–632). New York: Cambridge University Press.

Cicchetti, D. (2007). Intervention and policy implications of research on neurobiological functioning in maltreated children. In J. L. Aber, S. J. Bishop-Josef, S. M. Jones, K. T. McLearn, & D. A. Phillips (Eds.), *Child development and social policy* (pp. 167–184). Washington, DC: American Psychological Association.

Cicchetti, D., & Toth, S. L. (2006). Developmental psychopathology and preventive intervention. In K. A. Renninger & I. E. Sigel (Eds.), *Handbook of child psychology: Vol. 4. Child psychology in practice* (6th ed., pp. 497–547). Hoboken, NJ: Wiley.

Cicchetti, D., Toth, S. L., & Rogosch, F. A. (2004). Toddler–parent psychotherapy for depressed mothers and their offspring: Implications for attachment theory. In L. Atkinson & S. Goldberg (Eds.), *Attachment issues in psychotherapy and intervention* (pp. 229–275). Mahwah, NJ: Erlbaum.

Cillessen, A. H. N., & Bellmore, A. D. (2004). Social skills and interpersonal perception in early and middle childhood. In P. K. Smith & C. H. Hart (Eds.), *Blackwell handbook of childhood social development* (pp. 355–374). Malden, MA: Blackwell.

Cillessen, A. H. N., & Mayeux, L. (2004). From censure to reinforcement: Developmental changes in the association between aggression and social status. *Child Development, 75,* 147–163.

Claes, M., Lacourse, E., Bouchard, C., & Perucchini, P. (2003). Parental practices in late adolescence, a comparison of three countries: Canada, France and Italy. *Journal of Adolescence, 26,* 387–399.

Clancy, P. (1985). Acquisition of Japanese. In D. I. Slobin (Ed.), *The crosslinguistic study of language acquisition: Vol. 1. The data* (pp. 323–524). Hillsdale, NJ: Erlbaum.

Clancy, P. (1989). Form and function in the acquisition of Korean wh- questions. *Journal of Child Language, 16,* 323–347.

Clapp, J. F., III, Kim, H., Burciu, B., Schmidt, S., Petry, K., & Lopez, B. (2002). Continuing regular exercise during pregnancy: Effect of exercise volume on fetoplacental growth. *American Journal of Obstetrics and Gynecology, 186,* 142–147.

Clark, E. V. (1983). Meanings and concepts. In P. H. Mussen (Ed.), *Handbook of child psychology: Vol. 3. Cognitive development* (pp. 787–840). New York: Wiley.

Clark, E. V. (1990). On the pragmatics of contrast. *Journal of Child Language, 17,* 417–431.

Clark, E. V. (2007). Young children's uptake of new words in conversation. *Language in Society, 36,* 157–182.

Clark, K. E., & Ladd, G. W. (2000). Connectedness and autonomy support in parent–child relationships: Links to children's socioemotional orientation and peer relationships. *Developmental Psychology, 36,* 485–498.

Clarke-Stewart, A., Allhusen, V., & Goosens, F. (2001). Day care and the Strange Situation. In A. Göncü & E. L. Klein (Eds.), *Children in play, story, and school* (pp. 241–266). New York: Guilford.

Clarke-Stewart, K. A. (1998). Historical shifts and underlying themes in ideas about rearing young children in the United States: Where have we been? Where are we going? *Early Development and Parenting, 7,* 101–117.

Clarke-Stewart, K. A., & Hayward, C. (1996). Advantages of father custody and contact for the psychological well-being of school-age children. *Journal of Applied Developmental Psychology, 17,* 239–270.

Clarkson, T. W., Magos, L., & Myers, G. J. (2003). The toxicology of mercury—current exposures and clinical manifestations. *New England Journal of Medicine, 349,* 1731–1737.

Clausen, J. A. (1975). The social meaning of differential physical and sexual maturation. In S. E. Dragastin & G. H. Elder (Eds.), *Adolescence in the life cycle: Psychological change and the social context* (pp. 25–47). New York: Halsted.

Claxton, L. J., Keen, R., & McCarty, M. E. (2003). Evidence of motor planning in infant reaching behavior. *Psychological Science, 14,* 354–356.

Clay, D., Vignoles, V. L., & Dittmar, H. (2005). Body image and self-esteem among adolescent girls: Testing the influence of sociocultural factors. *Journal of Research on Adolescence, 15,* 451–477.

Clearfield, M. W., & Nelson, N. M. (2006). Sex differences in mothers' speech and play behavior with 6-, 9-, and 14-month-old infants. *Sex Roles, 54,* 127–137.

Clements, D. H., & Sarama, J. (2003). Young children and technology: What does the research say? *Young Children, 58*(6), 34–40.

Cleveland, E. S., & Reese, E. (2005). Maternal structure and autonomy support in conversations about the past: Contributions to children's autobiographical memory. *Developmental Psychology, 41,* 376–388.

Clifton, R. K., Rochat, P., Robin, D. J., & Berthier, N. E. (1994). Multimodal perception in the control of infant reaching. *Journal of Experimental Psychology: Human Perception and Performance, 20,* 876–886.

Clingempeel, W. G., & Henggeler, S. W. (2003). Aggressive juvenile offenders transitioning into emerging adulthood: Factors discriminating persistors and desistors. *American Journal of Orthopsychiatry, 73,* 310–323.

Coatsworth, J. D., Sharp, E. H., Palen, L., Darling, N., Cumsille, P., & Marta, M. (2005). Exploring adolescent self-defining leisure activities and identity experiences across three countries. *International Journal of Behavioral Development, 29,* 361–370.

Cohen, L. B. (2003). Commentary on Part I: Unresolved issues in infant categorization. In D. H. Rakison & L. M. Oakes (Eds.), *Early category and concept development: Making sense of the blooming, buzzing confusion* (pp. 193–209). New York: Oxford University Press.

Cohen, L. B., & Cashon, C. H. (2001). Infant object segregation implies information integration. *Journal of Experimental Child Psychology, 78,* 75–83.

Cohen, L. B., & Cashon, C. H. (2006). Infant cognition. In D. Kuhn & R. Siegler (Eds.), *Handbook of child psychology: Vol. 2. Cognition, perception, and language* (6th ed., pp. 214–251). Hoboken, NJ: Wiley.

Cohen, L. B., & Marks, K. S. (2002). How infants process addition and subtraction events. *Developmental Science, 5,* 186–201.

Cohen, P., Kasen, S., Chen, H., Harmrk, C., & Gordon, K. (2003). Variations in patterns of developmental transitions in the emerging adulthood period. *Developmental Psychology, 39,* 657–669.

Cohen-Bendahan, C. C. C., van de Beek, C., & Berenbaum, S. A. (2005). Prenatal sex hormones effects on child and adult sex-typed behavior: Methods and findings. *Neuroscience and Biobehavioral Reviews, 29,* 353–384.

Cohn, J., & Tronick, E. Z. (1987). Mother–infant face-to-face interaction: The sequencing of dyadic states at 3, 6, and 9 months. *Developmental Psychology, 23,* 68–77.

Coholl, A., Kassotis, J., Parks, R., Vaughan, R., Bannister, H., & Northridge, M. (2001). Adolescents in the age of AIDS: Myths, misconceptions, and misunderstandings regarding sexually transmitted diseases. *Journal of the National Medical Association, 93,* 64–69.

Coie, J. D., & Dodge, K. A. (1998). Aggression and antisocial behavior. In N. Eisenberg (Ed.), *Handbook of child psychology: Vol. 3. Social, emotional, and personality development* (5th ed., pp. 779–862). New York: Wiley.

Coie, J. D., Dodge, K. A., & Coppotelli, H. (1982). Dimensions and types of social status: A cross-age perspective. *Developmental Psychology, 18,* 557–570.

Coie, J. D., & Krehbiel, G. (1984). Effects of academic tutoring on the social status of low-achieving, socially rejected children. *Child Development, 55,* 1465–1478.

Colapinto, J. (2001). *As nature made him: The boy who was raised as a girl.* New York: Perennial.

Colby, A., & Damon, W. (1992). *Some do care: Contemporary lives of moral commitment.* New York: Free Press.

Colby, A., & Kohlberg, L. (1987). *The measurement of moral judgment: Theoretical foundations and research validation* (Vol. 1). Cambridge, UK: Cambridge University Press.

Colby, A., Kohlberg, L., Gibbs, J. C., & Lieberman, M. (1983). A longitudinal study of moral judgment. *Monographs of the Society for Research in Child Development, 48*(1–2, Serial No. 200).

Cole, D. A., Martin, J. M., Peeke, L. A., Seroczynski, A. D., & Fier, J. (1999). Children's over- and underestimation of academic competence: A longitudinal study of gender differences, depression, and anxiety. *Child Development, 70,* 459–473.

Cole, E., & Daniel, J. (Ed.). (2005). *Featuring females: Feminist analyses of media.* Washington, DC: American Psychological Association.

Cole, M. (1990). Cognitive development and formal schooling: The evidence from cross-cultural research. In L. C. Moll (Ed.), *Vygotsky and education* (pp. 89–110). New York: Cambridge University Press.

Cole, M. (2005). Culture in development. In M. H. Bornstein & M. E. Lamb (Ed.), *Developmental science: An advanced textbook* (5th ed., pp. 45–102). Mahwah, NJ: Erlbaum.

Cole, M. (2006). Culture and cognitive development in phylogenetic, historical, and ontogenetic perspective. In R. M. Lerner (Ed.), *Handbook of child psychology: Vol. 1. Theoretical models of human development* (6th ed., pp. 636–685). Hoboken, NJ: Wiley.

Cole, P. M., Bruschi, C. J., & Tamang, B. L. (2002). Cultural differences in children's emotional reactions to difficult situations. *Child Development, 73,* 983–996.

Cole, P. M., & Tamang, B. L. (1998). Nepali children's ideas about emotional displays in hypothetical challenges. *Developmental Psychology, 34,* 640–646.

Cole, P. M., Tamang, B. L., & Shrestha, S. (2006). Cultural variations in the socialization of young children's anger and shame. *Child Development, 77,* 1237–1251.

Cole, S. A. (2006). Building secure relationships: Attachment in kin and unrelated foster caregiver–infant relationships. *Families in Society, 87,* 497–508.

Cole, T. J. (2000). Secular trends in growth. *Proceedings of the Nutrition Society, 59,* 317–324.

Coleman, P. K. (2003). Perceptions of parent–child attachment, social self-efficacy, and peer relationships in middle childhood. *Infant and Child Development, 12,* 351–368.

Coley, R. L. (1998). Children's socialization experiences and functioning in single-mother households: The importance of fathers and other men. *Child Development, 69,* 219–230.

Coley, R. L., & Chase-Lansdale, P. L. (1998). Adolescent pregnancy and parenthood: Recent evidence and future directions. *American Psychologist, 53,* 152–166.

Coley, R. L., Morris, J. E., & Hernandez, D. (2004). Out-of-school care and problem behavior trajectories among low-income adolescents: Individual, family, and neighborhood characteristics as added risks. *Child Development, 75,* 948–965.

Collaer, M. L., & Hill, E. M. (2006). Large sex difference in adolescents on a timed line judgment task: Attentional contributors and task relationship to mathematics. *Perception, 35,* 561–572.

Collie, R., & Hayne, H. (1999). Deferred imitation by 6- and 9-month-old infants: More evidence for declarative memory. *Developmental Psychobiology, 35,* 83–90.

Collins, M. A., & Amabile, T. M. (1999). Motivation and creativity. In R. J. Sternberg (Ed.), *Handbook of creativity* (pp. 297–312). Cambridge, UK: Cambridge University Press.

Collins, W. A. (1983). Children's processing of television content: Implications for prevention of negative effects. *Prevention in Human Services, 2,* 53–66.

Collins, W. A. (2003). More than myth: The developmental significance of romantic relationships during adolescence. *Journal of Research on Adolescence, 13,* 1–24.

Collins, W. A., & Laursen, B. (2004). Parent–adolescent relationships and influences. In R. M. Lerner & L. Steinberg (Eds.), *Handbook of adolescent psychology* (2nd ed., pp. 331–361). New York: Wiley.

Collins, W. A., Maccoby, E. E., Steinberg, L. D., Hetherington, E. M., & Bornstein, M. H. (2000). Contemporary research on parenting: The case for nature and nurture. *American Psychologist, 55,* 218–232.

Collins, W. A., & Madsen, S. D. (2006). Personal relationships in adolescence and early adulthood. In A. L. Vangelisti & D. Perlman (Eds.), *Cambridge handbook of personal relationships* (pp. 191–209). New York: Cambridge University Press.

Collins, W. A., Madsen, S. D., & Susman-Stillman, A. (2002). Parenting during middle childhood. In M. H. Bornstein (Ed.), *Handbook of parenting: Vol. 1. Children and parenting* (2nd ed., pp. 73–101). Mahwah, NJ: Erlbaum.

Collins, W. A., & Van Dulmen, M. (2006a). Friendships and romantic relationships in emerging adulthood: Continuities and discontinuities. In J. J. Arnett & J. Tanner (Eds.), *Emerging adults in America: Coming of age in the 21st century* (pp. 219–234). Washington, DC: American Psychological Association.

Collins, W. A., & Van Dulmen, M. (2006b). "The course of true love(s) . . .": Origins and pathways in the development of romantic relationships. In A. Booth & A. Crouter (Eds.), *Romance and sex in adolescence and emerging adulthood: Risks and opportunities* (pp. 63–86). Mahwah, NJ: Erlbaum.

Collins, W. K., & Steinberg, L. (2006). Adolescent development in interpersonal context. In N. Eisenberg (Ed.), *Handbook of child psychology: Vol. 3. Social, emotional, and personality development* (6th ed., pp. 1003–1067). Hoboken, NJ: Wiley.

Colman, R. A., Hardy, S. A., Albert, M., Raffaelli, M., & Crockett, L. (2006). Early predictors of self-regulation in middle childhood. *Infant and Child Development, 15,* 421–437.

Colom, R., Escorial, S., Shih, P. C., & Privado, J. (2007). Fluid intelligence, memory span, and temperament difficulties predict academic performance of young adolescents. *Personality and Individual Differences, 42,* 1503–1514.

Colombo, J. (2002). Infant attention grows up: The emergence of a developmental cognitive neuroscience perspective. *Current Directions in Psychological Science, 11,* 196–199.

Colombo, J., Shaddy, D. J., Richman, W. A., Maikranz, J. M., & Blaga, O. M. (2004). The developmental course of habituation in infancy and preschool outcome. *Infancy, 5,* 1–38.

Coltrane, S. (1996). *Family man.* New York: Oxford University Press.

Comstock, G. A., & Scharrer, E. (2001). The use of television and other film-related media. In D. G. Singer & J. L. Singer (Eds.), *Handbook of children and the media* (pp. 47–72). Thousand Oaks, CA: Sage.

Comstock, G., & Scharrer, E. (2006). Media and popular culture. In K. A. Renninger & I. E. Sigel (Eds.), *Handbook of child psychology: Vol. 4. Child psychology in practice* (6th ed., pp. 817–863). Hoboken, NJ: Wiley.

Comunian, A. L, & Gielen, U. P. (2000). Sociomoral reflection and prosocial and antisocial behavior: Two Italian studies. *Psychological Reports, 87,* 161–175.

Comunian, A. L., & Gielen, U. P. (2006). Promotion of moral judgment maturity through stimulation of social role-taking and social reflection: An Italian intervention study. *Journal of Moral Education, 35,* 51–69.

Conboy, B. T., & Thal, D. J. (2006). Ties between the lexicon and grammar: Cross-sectional and longitudinal studies of bilingual toddlers. *Child Development, 77,* 712–735.

Condron, D. J. (2007). Stratification and educational sorting: Explaining ascriptive inequalities in early childhood reading group placement. *Social Problems, 54,* 139–160.

Conger, R., Wallace, L., Sun, Y., Simons, L., McLoyd, V., & Brody, G. (2002). Economic pressure in African American families: A replication and extension of the family stress model. *Developmental Psychology, 38,* 179–193.

Conger, R. D., & Conger, K. J. (2002). Resilience in Midwestern families: Selected findings from the first decade of a prospective, longitudinal study. *Journal of Marriage and the Family, 64,* 361–373.

Conger, R. D., & Donnellan, M. B. (2007). An interactionist perspective on the socioeconomic context of human development. *Annual Review of Psychology, 58,* 175–199.

Connell, M. W., Sheridan, K., & Gardner, H. (2003). On abilities and domains. In R. J. Sternberg & E. Grigorenko (Eds.), *Perspectives on the psychology of abilities, competencies, and expertise* (pp. 126–155). New York: Cambridge University Press.

Conner, D. B., & Cross, D. R. (2003). Longitudinal analysis of the presence, efficacy, and stability of maternal scaffolding during informal problem-solving interactions. *British Journal of Developmental Psychology, 21,* 315–334.

Connolly, J., Craig, W., Goldberg, A., & Pepler, D. (2004). Mixed-gender groups, dating, and romantic relationships in early adolescence. *Journal of Research on Adolescence, 14,* 185–207.

Connolly, J., Furman, W., & Konarski, R. (2000). The role of peers in the emergence of romantic relationships in adolescence. *Child Development, 71,* 1395–1408.

Connolly, J. A., & Doyle, A. B. (1984). Relations of social fantasy play to social competence in preschoolers. *Developmental Psychology, 20,* 797–806.

Connolly, J. A., & Goldberg, A. (1999). Romantic relationships in adolescence: The role of friends and peers in their emergence and development. In W. Furman, B. B. Brown, & C. Feiring (Eds.), *The development of romantic relationships in adolescence* (pp. 266–290). Cambridge, UK: Cambridge University Press.

Connor, P. D., Sampson, P. D., Streissguth, A. P., Bookstein, F. L., & Barr, H. M. (2006). Effects of prenatal alcohol exposure on fine motor coordination and balance: A study of two adult samples. *Neuropsychologia, 44,* 744–751.

Conti-Ramsden, G., & Pérez-Pereira, M. (1999). Conversational interactions between mothers and their infants who are congenitally blind, have low vision, or are sighted. *Journal of Visual Impairment and Blindness, 93,* 691–703.

Conway, A. R. A., Kane, M. J., & Engle, R. W. (2003). Working memory capacity and its relation to general intelligence. *Trends in Cognitive Sciences, 7,* 547–552.

Conway, L. (2007, April 5). Drop the Barbie: Ken Zucker's reparatist treatment of gender-variant children. *Trans News Updates.* Retrieved from ai.eecs.umich.edu/people/conway/TS/News/Drop%20the%20Barbie.htm

Conyers, C., Miltenberger, R., Maki, A., Barenz, R., Jurgens, M., Sailer, A., Haugen, M., & Kopp, B. (2004). A comparison of response cost and differential reinforcement of other behaviors to reduce disruptive behavior in a preschool classroom. *Journal of Applied Behavior Analysis, 37,* 411–415.

Cook, S. W., & Goldin-Meadow, S. (2006). The role of gesture in learning: Do children use their hands to change their minds? *Journal of Cognition and Development, 7,* 211–232.

Cooper, C., Sayer, A. A., & Dennison, E. M. (2006). The developmental environment: Clinical perspectives on effects on the musculoskeletal system. In P. Gluckman & M. Hanson (Eds.), *Developmental origins of health and disease* (pp. 392–405). Cambridge, UK: Cambridge University Press.

Cooper, C. R. (1998). *The weaving of maturity: Cultural perspectives on adolescent development.* New York: Oxford University Press.

Cooper, C. R., Dominguez, E., & Rosas, S. (2005). Soledad's dream: How immigrant children bridge their multiple worlds and build pathways to college. In C. R. Cooper, C. T. Carcia Coll, W. T. Bartko, H. Davis, & C. Chatman (Eds.), *Developmental pathways through middle childhood: Rethinking contexts and diversity as resources* (pp. 235–260). Mahwah, NJ: Erlbaum.

Cope-Farrar, K. M., & Kunkel, D. (2002). Sexual messages in teens' favorite prime-time television programs. In J. D. Brown, J. R. Steele, & K. Walsh-Childers (Eds.), *Sexual teens, sexual media* (pp. 59–78). Mahwah, NJ: Erlbaum.

Coplan, R. J., Barber, A. M., & Lagacé-Séquin, D. G. (1999). The role of child temperament as a predictor of early literacy and numeracy skills in preschoolers. *Early Childhood Research Quarterly, 14,* 537–553.

Coplan, R. J., Bowker, A., & Cooper, S. M. (2003). Parenting daily hassles, child temperament, and social adjustment in preschool. *Early Childhood Research Quarterly, 18,* 376–395.

Coplan, R. J., Gavinsky-Molina, M. H., Lagace-Seguin, D., & Wichmann, C. (2001). When girls versus boys play alone: Nonsocial play and adjustment in kindergarten. *Developmental Psychology, 37,* 464–474.

Coplan, R. J., Prakash, K., O'Neil, K., & Armer, M. (2004). Do you "want" to play? Distinguishing between conflicted shyness and social disinterest in early childhood. *Developmental Psychology, 40,* 244–258.

Corapci, F., Radan, A. E., & Lozoff, B. (2006). Iron deficiency in infancy and mother–child interaction at 5 years. *Journal of Developmental and Behavioral Pediatrics, 27,* 371–378.

Corenblum, B. (2003). What children remember about ingroup and outgroup peers: Effects of stereotypes on children's processing of information about group members. *Journal of Experimental Child Psychology, 86,* 32–66.

Corenblum, B., Annis, R., & Young, S. (1996). Effects of own group success or failure on judgments of task performance by children of different ethnicities. *European Journal of Social Psychology, 26,* 1996.

Cornish, A. M., McMahon, C. A., Ungerer, J. A., Barnett, B., Kowalenko, N., & Tennant, C. (2005). Postnatal depression and infant cognitive and motor development in the second postnatal year: The impact of depression chronicity and infant gender. *Infant Behavior and Development, 28,* 407–417.

Cornwell, A. C., & Feigenbaum, P. (2006). Sleep biological rhythms in normal infants and those at high risk for SIDS. *Chronobiology International, 23,* 935–961.

Cory-Slechta, D. A. (2003). Lead-induced impairments in complex cognitive function: Offerings from experimental studies. *Child Neuropsychology, 9,* 64–75.

Cosden, M., Peerson, S., & Elliott, K. (1997). Effects of prenatal drug exposure on birth outcomes and early child development. *Journal of Drug Issues, 27,* 525–539.

Costello, B. J., & Dunaway, R. G. (2003). Egotism and delinquent behavior. *Journal of Interpersonal Violence, 18,* 572–590.

Costello, E. J., & Angold, A. (1995). Developmental epidemiology. In D. Cicchetti & D. Cohen (Eds.), *Developmental psychopathology: Vol. 1. Theory and method* (pp. 23–56). New York: Wiley.

Costos, D., Ackerman, R., & Paradis, L. (2002). Recollections of menarche: Communication between mothers and daughters regarding menstruation. *Sex Roles, 46,* 49–59.

Côté, S., Zoccolillo, M., Tremblay, R., Nagin, D., & Vitaro, F. (2001). Predicting girls' conduct disorder in adolescence from childhood trajectories of disruptive behaviors. *Journal of the American Academy of Child and Adolescent Psychiatry, 40,* 678–684.

Côté, S. M., Vaillancourt, T., Barker, E. D., Nagin, D., & Tremblay, R. E. (2007). The joint development of physical and indirect aggression: Predictors of continuity and change during childhood. *Development and Psychopathology, 19,* 37–55.

Cotinot, C., Pailhoux, E., Jaubert, F., & Fellous, M. (2002). Molecular genetics of sex determination. *Seminars in Reproductive Medicine, 20,* 157–168.

Cotton, A., Stanton, K. R., Acs, Z. J., & Lovegrove, M. (2006). *The UB Obesity Report Card: An overview.* Retrieved from www.ubalt.edu/experts/obesity

Coulton, C. J., Crampton, D. S., Irwin, M., Spilsbury, J. C., & Korbin, J. E. (2007). How neighborhoods influence child maltreatment: A review of the literature and alternative pathways. *Child Abuse and Neglect, 31,* 1117–1142.

Courage, M. L., & Howe, M. L. (1998). The ebb and flow of infant attentional preferences: Evidence for long-term recognition memory in 3-month-olds. *Journal of Experimental Child Psychology, 18,* 98–106.

Courage, M. L., Reynolds, G. D., & Richards, J. E. (2006). Infants' attention to patterned stimuli: Developmental change from 3 to 12 months of age. *Child Development, 77,* 680–695.

Courchesne, E., Carper, R., & Akshoomoff, N. (2003). Evidence of brain overgrowth in the first year of life in autism. *Journal of the American Medical Association, 290,* 337–344.

Couturier, J. L., & Lock, J. (2006). Denial and minimization in adolescents with anorexia nervosa. *International Journal of Eating Disorders, 39,* 212–216.

Covington, C. Y., Nordstrom-Klee, B., Ager, J., Sokol, R., & Delaney-Black, V. (2002). Birth to age 7 growth of children prenatally exposed to drugs: A prospective cohort study. *Neurotoxicology and Teratology, 24,* 489–496.

Cowan, C. P., & Cowan, P. A. (1997). Working with couples during stressful transitions. In S. Dreman (Ed.), *The family on the threshold of the 21st century* (pp. 17–47). Mahwah, NJ: Erlbaum.

Cowan, C. P., & Cowan, P. A. (2000). *When partners become parents.* Mahwah, NJ: Erlbaum.

Cowan, N. (2003). Comparisons of developmental modeling frameworks and levels of analysis in cognition: Connectionist and dynamic systems theories deserve attention. *Developmental Science, 6,* 440–447.

Cowan, N., Nugent, L. D., Elliott, E. M., Ponomarev, I., & Saults, J. S. (1999). The role of attention in the development of short-term memory: Age differences in the verbal span of apprehension. *Child Development, 70,* 1082–1097.

Cowan, P. A., & Cowan, C. P. (2004). From family relationships to peer rejection to antisocial behavior in middle childhood. In J. B. Kupersmidt & K. A. Dodge (Eds.), *Children's peer relations: From development to intervention* (pp. 159–177). Washington, DC: American Psychological Association.

Cox, C. E., Kotch, J. B., & Everson, M. D. (2003). A longitudinal study of modifying influences in the relationship between domestic violence and child maltreatment. *Journal of Family Violence, 18,* 5–17.

Cox, M. J., Owen, M. T., Henderson, V. K., & Margand, N. A. (1992). Prediction of infant–father and infant–mother attachment. *Developmental Psychology, 28,* 474–483.

Cox, M. J., Paley, B., & Harter, K. (2001). Interparental conflict and parent–child relationships. In J. H. Grych & F. D. Fincham (Eds.), *Interparental conflict and child development: Theory, research, and applications* (pp. 249–272). New York: Cambridge University Press.

Cox, S. M., Hopkins, J., & Hans, S. L. (2000). Attachment in preterm infants and their mothers: Neonatal risk status and maternal representations. *Infant Mental Health Journal, 21,* 464–480.

Coyle, T. R., & Bjorklund, D. F. (1997). Age differences in, and consequences of, multiple- and variable-strategy use on a multitrial sort-recall task. *Developmental Psychology, 33,* 372–380.

Crago, M. B., Annahatak, B., & Ningiuruvik, L. (1993). Changing patterns of language socialization in Inuit homes. *Anthropology and Education Quarterly, 24,* 205–223.

Craig, C. M., & Lee, D. N. (1999). Neonatal control of sucking pressure: Evidence for an intrinsic tau-guide. *Experimental Brain Research, 124,* 371–382.

Craig, W. M., Pepler, D., & Atlas, R. (2000). Observations of bullying in the playground and in the classroom. *School Psychology International, 21,* 22-36.

Crain, W. (2005). *Theories of development* (5th ed.). Upper Saddle River, NJ: Prentice-Hall.

Crair, M. C., Gillespie, D. C., & Stryker, M. P. (1998). The role of visual experience in the development of columns in the cat visual cortex. *Science, 279,* 566–570.

Crane, D. R., Ngai, S. W., Larson, J. H., & Hafen, M., Jr. (2005). The influence of family functioning and parent–adolescent acculturation on North American Chinese adolescent outcomes. *Family Relations, 54,* 400–410.

Cratty, B. J. (1986). *Perceptual and motor development in infants and children* (3rd ed.). Englewood Cliffs, NJ: Prentice-Hall.

Crawford, J. (1997). *Best evidence: Research foundations of the Bilingual Education Act.* Washington, DC: National Clearinghouse for Bilingual Education.

Crawford, N. (2003, September). Understanding children's atypical gender behavior. *APA Monitor,* p. 40.

Creasey, G. L., Jarvis, P. A., & Berk, L. E. (1998). Play and social competence. In O. N. Saracho & B. Spodek (Eds.), *Multiple perspectives on play in early childhood education* (pp. 116–143). Albany: State University of New York Press.

Crick, N. R., Casas, J. F., & Nelson, D. A. (2002). Toward a more comprehensive understanding of peer maltreatment: Studies of relational victimization. *Current Directions in Psychological Science, 11,* 98–101.

Crick, N. R., & Dodge, K. A. (1994). A review and reformulation of social information-processing mechanisms in children's social adjustment. *Psychological Bulletin, 115,* 74–101.

Crick, N. R., & Nelson, D. A. (2002). Relational and physical victimization within friendships: Nobody told me there'd be friends like these. *Journal of Abnormal Child Psychology, 30,* 599–607.

Crick, N. R., Ostrov, J. M., Appleyard, K., Jansen, E., & Casas, J. F. (2004). Relational aggression in early childhood: You can't come to my birthday party unless. . . . In M. Putallaz & K. Bierman (Eds.), *Aggression, antisocial behavior, and violence among girls: A developmental perspective* (pp. 71–89). New York: Guilford.

Crick, N. R., Ostrov, J. M., Burr, J. E., Cullerton-Sen, C., Jansen-Yeh, E., & Ralston, P. (2006). A longitudinal study of relational and physical aggression in preschool. *Journal of Applied Developmental Psychology, 27,* 254–268.

Crick, N. R., Ostrov, J. M., & Werner, N. E. (2006). A longitudinal study of relational aggression, physical aggression, and social-psychological adjustment. *Journal of Abnormal Child Psychology, 34,* 131–142.

Crittenden, P. (2000). A dynamic-maturational approach to continuity and change in patterns of attachment. In P. Crittenden & A. Claussen (Eds.), *The organization of attachment relationships* (pp. 343–358). New York: Cambridge University Press.

Crockenberg, S., & Leerkes, E. (2000). Infant social and emotional development in family context. In C. H. Zeanah, Jr. (Ed.), *Handbook of infant mental health* (2nd ed., pp. 60–90). New York: Guilford.

Crockenberg, S., & Leerkes, E. (2003a). Infant negative emotionality, caregiving, and family relationships. In A. C. Crouter & A. Booth (Eds.), *Children's influence on family dynamics* (pp. 57–78). Mahwah, NJ: Erlbaum.

Crockenberg, S. C., & Leerkes, E. M. (2003b). Parental acceptance, postpartum depression, and maternal sensitivity: Mediating and moderating processes. *Journal of Family Psychology, 17,* 80–93.

Crockenberg, S. C., & Leerkes, E. M. (2004). Infant and maternal behaviors regulate infant reactivity to novelty at 6 months. *Developmental Psychology, 40,* 1123–1132.

Crockett, L. J., Raffaelli, M., & Shen, Y.-L. (2006). Linking self-regulation and risk proneness to risky sexual behavior: Pathways through peer pressure and early substance use. *Journal of Research on Adolescence, 16,* 503–525.

Crosno, R., Kirkpatrick, M., & Elder, G. H., Jr. (2004). Intergenerational bonding in school: The behavioral and contextual correlates of student–teacher relationships. *Sociology of Education, 77,* 60–81.

Crouter, A. C., & Head, M. R. (2002). Parental monitoring and knowledge of children. In M. H. Bornstein (Ed.), *Handbook of parenting: Vol. 3. Being and becoming a parent* (2nd ed., pp. 461–483). Mahwah, NJ: Erlbaum.

Crouter, A. C., Manke, B. A., & McHale, S. M. (1995). The family context of gender intensification in early adolescence. *Child Development, 66,* 317–329.

Crowe, H. P., & Zeskind, P. S. (1992). Psychophysiological and perceptual responses to infant cries varying in pitch: Comparison of adults with low and high scores on the child abuse potential inventory. *Child Abuse and Neglect, 16,* 19–29.

Crowley, K., Callanan, M. A., Tenenbaum, H. R., & Allen, E. (2001). Parents explain more often to boys than to girls during shared scientific thinking. *Psychological Science, 12,* 258–261.

CRTC (Canadian Radio-Television and Telecommunications Commission). (2007a). *Children's advertising.* Retrieved from www.crtc.gc.ca/eng/INFO_SHT/b300.htm

CRTC (Canadian Radio-Television and Telecommunications Commission). (2007b). *TV violence.* Retrieved from www.crtc.gc.ca/eng/INFO_SHT/b317.htm

Csikszentmihalyi, M. (1999). Implications of a systems perspective for the study of creativity. In R. J. Sternberg (Ed.), *Handbook of creativity* (pp. 313–335). Cambridge, UK: Cambridge University Press.

Cuddy-Casey, M., & Orvaschel, H. (1997). Children's understanding of death in relation to child suicidality and homicidality. *Clinical Psychology Review, 17,* 33–45.

Cuijpers, P. (2002). Effective ingredients of school-based drug prevention programs: A systematic review. *Addictive Behaviors, 27,* 1009–1023.

Culbertson, F. M. (1997). Depression and gender: An international review. *American Psychologist, 52,* 25–51.

Culnane, M., Fowler, M. G., Lee, S. S., McSherry, G., Brady, M., & O'Donnell, K. (1999). Lack of long-term effects of in utero exposure to zidovudine among uninfected children born to HIV-infected women. *Journal of the American Medical Association, 281,* 151–157.

Cummings, E. M., & Davies, P. T. (1994). Maternal depression and child development. *Journal of Child Psychology and Psychiatry, 35,* 73–112.

Cummings, E. M., Iannotti, R. J., & Zahn-Waxler, C. (1985). Influence of conflict between adults on the emotions and aggression of young children. *Developmental Psychology, 21,* 495–507.

Cunningham, A. E., & Stanovich, K. E. (1998, Spring/Summer). What reading does for the mind. *American Educator,* 8–15.

Cutrona, C. E., Hessling, R. M., Bacon, P. L., & Russell, D. W. (1998). Predictors and correlates of continuing involvement with the baby's father among adolescent mothers. *Journal of Family Psychology, 12,* 369–387.

Cutter, W. J., Daly, E. M., Robertson, D. M. W., Chitnis, X. A., van Amelsvoort, T. A. M. J., & Simmons, A. (2006). Influence of X chromosome and hormones on human brain development: A magnetic resonance imaging and proton magnetic resonance spectroscopy study of Turner syndrome. *Biological Psychiatry, 59,* 273–283.

Cyr, M., McDuff, P., & Wright, J. (2006). Prevalence and predictors of dating violence among adolescent female victims of child sexual abuse. *Journal of Interpersonal Violence, 21,* 1000–1017.

Dabrowska, E. (2000). From formula to schema: The acquisition of English questions. *Cognitive Linguistics, 11,* 1–20.

D'Agostino, J. A., & Clifford, P. (1998). Neurodevelopmental consequences associated with the premature neonate. *AACN Clinical Issues, 9,* 11–24.

Dahl, R. E., & Lewin, D. S. (2002). Pathways to adolescent healthy sleep regulation and behavior. *Journal of Adolescent Health, 31,* 175–184.

Dahl, R. E., Scher, M. S., Williamson, D. E., Robles, N., & Day, N. (1995). A longitudinal study of prenatal marijuana use. Effects on sleep and arousal at age 3 years. *Archives of Pediatric and Adolescent Medicine, 149,* 145–150.

Dahlberg, L. L., & Simon, T. R. (2006). Predicting and preventing youth violence: Developmental pathways and risk. In L. L. Dahlberg & T. R. Simon (Eds.), *Preventing violence: Research and evidence-based intervention strategies* (pp. 97–124). Washington, DC: American Psychological Association.

Dales, L., Hammer, S. J., & Smith, N. J. (2001). Time trends in autism and MMR immunization coverage in California. *Journal of the American Medical Association, 285,* 1183–1185.

Daley, T. C., Whaley, S. E., Sigman, M. D., Espinosa, M. P., & Neumann, C. (2003). IQ on the rise: The Flynn effect in rural Kenyan children. *Psychological Science, 14,* 215–219.

Damasio, A. R. (1994). *Descartes' error: Emotion, reason, and the human brain.* New York: Putnam.

Damon, W. (1977). *The social world of the child.* San Francisco: Jossey-Bass.

Damon, W. (1988). *The moral child.* New York: Free Press.

Damon, W. (1990). Self-concept, adolescent. In R. M. Lerner, A. C. Petersen, & J. Brooks-Gunn (Eds.), *The encyclopedia of adolescence* (Vol. 2, pp. 67–91). New York: Garland.

Damon, W. (1995). *Greater expectations: Overcoming the culture of indulgence in America's homes and schools.* New York: Free Press.

Damon, W. (2004). *The moral advantage: How to succeed in business by doing the right thing.* San Francisco: Berrett-Koehler.

Damon, W., & Hart, D. (1988). *Self-understanding in childhood and adolescence.* New York: Cambridge University Press.

Daniels, D. H. (1998). Age differences in concepts of self-esteem. *Merrill-Palmer Quarterly, 44,* 234–259.

Daniels, D. H., Kalkman, D. L., & McCombs, B. L. (2001). Young children's perspectives on learning and teacher practices in different classroom contexts: Implications for motivation. *Early Education and Development, 12,* 253–273.

Daniels, E., & Leaper, C. (2006). A longitudinal investigation of sport participation, peer acceptance, and self-esteem among adolescent girls and boys. *Sex Roles, 55,* 875–880.

Daniels, P., Noe, G. F., & Mayberry, R. (2006). Barriers to prenatal care among black women of low socioeconomic status. *American Journal of Health Behavior, 30,* 188–198.

Dannemiller, J. L., & Stephens, B. R. (1988). A critical test of infant pattern preference models. *Child Development, 59,* 210–216.

Dapretto, M., & Bjork, E. L. (2000). The development of word retrieval abilities in the second year and its relation to early vocabulary growth. *Child Development, 71,* 635–648.

Darroch, J. E., Frost, J. J., & Singh, S. (2001). *Teenage sexual and reproductive behavior in developed countries: Can more progress be made?* New York: Alan Guttmacher Institute.

Darwin, C. (1877). Biographical sketch of an infant. *Mind, 2,* 285–294.

Das, D. A., Grimmer, D. A., Sparnon, A. L., McRae, S. E., & Thomas, B. H. (2005). The efficacy of playing a virtual reality game in modulating pain for children with acute burn injuries: A randomized controlled trial. *BMC Pediatrics, 5*(1), 1–10.

D'Augelli, A. R. (2002). Mental health problems among lesbian, gay, and bisexual youths ages 14 to 21. *Clinical Child Psychology and Psychiatry, 7,* 433–456.

D'Augelli, A. R. (2006). Developmental and contextual factors and mental health among lesbian, gay, and bisexual youths. In A. M. Omoto & H. S. Howard (Eds.), *Sexual orientation and mental health: Examining identity and development in lesbian, gay, and bisexual people* (pp. 37–53). Washington, DC: American Psychological Association.

D'Augelli, A. R., Grossman, A. H., Salter, N. P., Vasey, J. J., Starks, M. T., & Sinclair, K. O. (2005). Predicting the suicide attempts of lesbian, gay, and bisexual youth. *Suicide and Life-Threatening Behavior, 35,* 646–660.

D'Augelli, A. R., Grossman, A. H., & Starks, M. T. (2005). Parents' awareness of lesbian, gay, and bisexual youths' sexual orientation. *Journal of Marriage and Family, 67,* 474–482.

David, K. M., & Murphy, B. C. (2007). Interparental conflict and preschoolers' peer relations: The moderating roles of temperament and gender. *Social Development, 16,* 1–23.

Davidson, M. C., Thomas, K. M., & Casey, B. J. (2003). Imaging the developing brain with fMRI. *Mental Retardation and Developmental Disabilities Research Reviews, 9,* 161–167.

Davidson, R. J. (1994). Asymmetric brain function, affective style, and psychopathology: The role of early experience and plasticity. *Development and Psychopathology, 6,* 741–758.

Davies, P. A., & Lindsay, L. L. (2004). Everyday marital conflict and child aggression. *Journal of Abnormal Child Psychology, 32,* 191–202.

Davis, K. F., Parker, K. P., & Montgomery, G. L. (2004). Sleep in infants and young children. Part 1: Normal sleep. *Journal of Pediatric Health Care, 18,* 65–71.

Davis-Kean, P. E. (2005). The influence of parent education and family income on child achievement: The indirect role of parental expectations and the home environment. *Journal of Family Psychology, 19,* 294–304.

Davison, K. K., & Birch, L. L. (2002). Obesigenic families: Parents' physical activity and dietary intake patterns predict girls' risk of overweight. *International Journal of Obesity and Related Metabolic Disorders, 26,* 1186–1193.

Dawson, G., Ashman, S. B., Panagiotides, H., Hessl, D., Self, J., Yamada, E., & Embry, L. (2003). Preschool outcomes of children of depressed mothers: Role of maternal behavior, contextual risk, and children's brain activity. *Child Development, 74,* 1158–1175.

Dawson, T. L. (2002). New tools, new insights: Kohlberg's moral judgment stages revisited. *International Journal of Behavioral Development, 26,* 154–166.

Deafness Research Foundation. (2005). Hear us: Incidence of deafness in newborns. Retrieved from www.hearinghealth.com

Deák, G. O. (2000). Hunting the fox of word learning: Why "constraints" fail to capture it. *Developmental Review, 20,* 29–80.

Deák, G. O., Ray, S. D., & Brenneman, K. (2003). Children's perseverative appearance–reality errors are related to emerging language skills. *Child Development, 74,* 944–964.

Deák, G. O., Yen, L., & Pettit, J. (2001). By any other name: When will preschoolers produce several labels for a reference? *Journal of Child Language, 28,* 787–804.

Dearing, E., McCartney, K., & Taylor, B. A. (2006). Within-child associations between family income and externalizing and internalizing problems. *Developmental Psychology, 42,* 237–252.

Deary, I. J. (2001). *g* and cognitive elements of information processing: An agnostic view. In R. J. Sternberg & E. L. Girgorenko (Eds.), *The general factor of intelligence: How general is it?* (pp. 447–479). Mahwah, NJ: Erlbaum.

Deary, I. J., Strand, S., Smith, P., & Fernandes, C. (2007). Intelligence and educational achievement. *Intelligence, 35,* 13–21.

Deater-Deckard, K., Lansford, J. E., Dodge, K. A., Pettit, G. S., & Bates, J. E. (2003). The development of attitudes about physical punishment: An 8-year longitudinal study. *Journal of Family Psychology, 17,* 351–360.

Deater-Deckard, K., Pike, A., Petrill, S. A., Cutting, A. L., Hughes, C., & O'Connor, T. G. (2001). Nonshared environmental processes in social-emotional development: An observational study of identical twin differences in the preschool period. *Developmental Science, 4,* F1–F6.

Deater-Deckard, K., Scarr, S., McCartney, K., & Eisenberg, M. (1994). Paternal separation anxiety: Relationships with parenting stress, child-rearing attitudes, and maternal anxieties. *Psychological Science, 5,* 341–346.

DeBerry, K. M., Scarr, S., & Weinberg, R. (1996). Family racial socialization and ecological competence: Longitudinal assessments of African-American transracial adoptees. *Child Development, 67,* 2375–2399.

Debes, F., Budtz-Jorgensen, E., Weihe, P., White, R. F., & Grandjean, P. (2006). Impact of prenatal methylmercury exposure on neurobehavioral function at age 14 years. *Neurotoxicology and Teratology, 28,* 536–547.

DeBoer, T., Scott, L. S., & Nelson, C. A. (2007). Methods for acquiring and analyzing infant event-related potentials. In M. de Haan (Ed.), *Infant EEG and event-related potentials* (pp. 5–37). New York: Psychology Press.

de Bruyn, E. H. (2005). Role strain, engagement and academic achievement in early adolescence. *Educational Studies, 31,* 15–27.

DeCasper, A. J., & Spence, M. J. (1986). Prenatal maternal speech influences newborns' perception of speech. *Infant Behavior and Development, 9,* 133–150.

DeCasper, A. J., & Spence, M. J. (1988). Prenatal maternal speech influences newborns' perception of speech sounds. In S. Chess, A. Thomas, & M. Hertzig (Eds.), *Annual progress in child psychiatry and child development* (Vol. 12, pp. 5–25). Philadelphia, PA: Brunner/Mazel.

De Corte, E., & Verschaffel, L. (2006). Mathematical thinking and learning. In K. A. Renninger & I. E. Sigel (Eds.), *Handbook of child psychology: Vol. 4. Child psychology in practice* (6th ed., pp. 103–152). Hoboken, NJ: Wiley.

Degirmencioglu, S. M., Urberg, K. A., Tolson, J. M., & Richard, P. (1998). Adolescent friendship networks: Continuity and change over the school year. *Merrill-Palmer Quarterly, 44,* 313–337.

de Haan, M., Bauer, P. J., Georgieff, M. K., & Nelson, C. A. (2000). Explicit memory in low-risk infants aged 19 months born between 27 and 42 weeks of gestation. *Developmental Medicine and Child Neurology, 42,* 304–312.

de Haan, M., & Johnson, M. H. (2003a). Introduction. In M. de Haan & M. H. Johnson (Eds.), *The cognitive neuroscience of development* (pp. xv–xx). New York: Psychology Press.

de Haan, M., & Johnson, M. H. (2003b). Mechanisms and theories of brain development. In M. de Haan & M. H. Johnson (Eds.), *The cognitive neuroscience of development* (pp. 1–18). Hove, UK: Psychology Press.

Dekker, M. C., Ferdinand, R. F., van Lang, D. J., Bongers, I. L., van der Ende, J., & Verhulst, F. C. (2007). Developmental trajectories of depressive symptoms from early childhood to late adolescence: Gender differences and adult outcome. *Journal of Child Psychology and Psychiatry, 48,* 657–666.

Deković, M., Noom, M. J., & Meeus, W. (1997). Expectations regarding development during adolescence: Parent and adolescent perceptions. *Journal of Youth and Adolescence, 26,* 253–271.

de la Rosa, M. R., Holleran, L. K., Rugh, D., & MacMaster, S. A. (2005). Substance abuse among U.S. Latinos: A review of the literature. *Journal of Social Work Practice in the Addictions, 5,* 1–20.

de León, L. (2000). The emergent participant: Interactive patterns in the socialization of Tzotzil (Mayan) infants. *Journal of Linguistic Anthropology, 8,* 131–161.

Delemarre-van de Waal, H. A. (2002). Regulation of puberty. *Best Practice and Research Clinical Endocrinology and Metabolism. 16,* 1–12.

Delgado-Gaitan, C. (1994). Socializing young children in Mexican-American families: An intergenerational perspective. In P. Greenfield & R. Cocking (Eds.),

Cross-cultural roots of minority child development (p. 55–86). Hillsdale, NJ: Erlbaum.

De Lisi, R., & Gallagher, A. M. (1991). Understanding gender stability and constancy in Argentinean children. *Merrill-Palmer Quarterly, 37,* 483–502.

Dell, C., & Roberts, G. (2005). *Research update: Alcohol use and pregnancy: An important Canadian public health and social issue.* Ottawa: Public Health Agency of Canada. Retrieved from www.phac-aspc.gc.ca/publicat/fasd-ru-ectaf-pr-06/index.html

Dell, D. L. (2001). Adolescent pregnancy. In N. L. Stotland & D. E. Stewart (Eds.), *Psychological aspects of women's health care* (pp. 95–116). Washington, DC: American Psychiatric Association.

DeLoache, J. S. (1987). Rapid change in symbolic functioning of very young children. *Science, 238,* 1556–1557.

DeLoache, J. S. (2002a). Early development of the understanding and use of symbolic artifacts. In U. Goswami (Ed.), *Blackwell handbook of child cognitive development* (pp. 206–226). Malden, MA: Blackwell.

DeLoache, J. S. (2002b). The symbol-mindedness of young children. In W. Hartup & R. A. Weinberg (Eds.), *Minnesota Symposia on Child Psychology* (Vol. 32, pp. 73–101). Mahwah, NJ: Erlbaum.

Delville, Y. (1999). Exposure to lead during development alters aggressive behavior in golden hamsters. *Neurotoxicology and Teratology, 21,* 445–449.

DeMarie-Dreblow, D., & Miller, P. H. (1988). The development of children's strategies for selective attention: Evidence for a transitional period. *Child Development, 59,* 1504–1513.

Demetriou, A., Christou, C., Spanoudis, G., & Platsidou, M. (2002). The development of mental processing: Efficiency, working memory, and thinking. *Monographs of the Society for Research in Child Development, 67*(1, Serial No. 268).

Demetriou, A., Efklides, A., Papadaki, M., Papantoniou, G., & Economou, A. (1993). Structure and development of causal–experimental thought: From early adolescence to youth. *Developmental Psychology, 29,* 480–497.

Demetriou, A., Pachaury, A., Metallidou, Y., & Kazi, S. (1996). Universals and specificities in the structure and development of quantitative-relational thought: A cross-cultural study in Greece and India. *International Journal of Behavioral Development, 19,* 255–290.

Dempster, F. N. (1995). Interference and inhibition in cognition: An historical perspective. In F. N. Dempster & C. J. Brainerd (Eds.), *Interference and inhibition in cognition* (pp. 3–26). San Diego: Academic Press.

Dempster, F. N., & Corkill, A. J. (1999). Interference and inhibition in cognition and behavior: Unifying themes for educational psychology. *Educational Psychology Review, 11,* 1–88.

Demuth, K. (1996). The prosodic structure of early words. In J. Morgan & K. Demuth (Eds.), *From signal to syntax* (pp. 171–184). Mahwah, NJ: Erlbaum.

Denham, S. A. (2005). Emotional competence counts: Assessment as support for school readiness. In K. Hirsh-Pasek, A. Kochanoff, N. S. Newcombe, & J. de Villiers (Eds.), Using scientific knowledge to inform preschool assessment. *Social Policy Report of the Society for Research in Child Development, 19*(No.1), 12.

Denham, S. A. (2006). Emotional competence: Implications for social functioning. In J. L. Luby (Ed.), *Handbook of preschool mental health: Development, disorders, and treatment* (pp. 23–44). New York: Guilford.

Denham, S. A., Blair, K., Schmidt, M., & DeMulder, E. (2002). Compromised emotional competence: Seeds of violence sown early? *American Journal of Orthopsychiatry, 72,* 70–82.

Denham, S. A., & Burton, R. (2003). *Social and emotional prevention and intervention programming for preschoolers.* New York: Kluwer-Plenum.

Denham, S. A., & Kochanoff, A. T. (2002). Parental contributions to preschoolers' understanding of emotion. *Marriage and Family Review, 34,* 311–343.

Denham, S. A., von Salisch, M., Olthof, T., Kochanoff, A., & Caverly, S. (2004). Emotional and social development in childhood. In P. K. Smith & C. H. Hart (Eds.), *Blackwell handbook of childhood social development* (pp. 307–328). Malden, MA: Blackwell.

Denissen, J. J. A., Zarrett, N. R., & Eccles, J. S. (2007). I like to do it, I'm able, and I know I am: Longitudinal couplings between domain-specific achievement, self-concept, and interest. *Child Development, 78,* 430–447.

Dennis, T., Bendersky, M., Ramsay, D., & Lewis, M. (2006). Reactivity and regulation in children prenatally exposed to cocaine. *Developmental Psychology, 42,* 688–697.

Dennis, W. (1960). Causes of retardation among institutionalized children: Iran. *Journal of Genetic Psychology, 96,* 47–59.

Department of Justice Canada. (2006). *Parenting after divorce.* Retrieved from www.justice.gc.ca/en/ps/pad/resources/index.html

Der, G., Batty, G. D., & Deary, I. J. (2006). Effect of breastfeeding on intelligence in children: Prospective study, sibling pairs analysis, and meta-analysis. *British Medical Journal, 333,* 945.

deRegnier, R., Long, J. D., Georgieff, M. K., & Nelson, C. A. (2007). Using event-related potentials to study perinatal nutrition and brain development in infants of diabetic mothers. *Developmental Neuropsychology, 31,* 379–396.

deRegnier, R.-A. (2005). Neurophysiologic evaluation of early cognitive development in high-risk infants and toddlers. *Mental Retardation and Developmental Disabilities, 11,* 317–324.

de Ribaupierre, A., & Lecerf, T. (2006). Relationships between working memory and intelligence from a developmental perspective: Convergent evidence from a neo-Piagetian and a psychometric approach. *European Journal of Cognitive Psychology, 18,* 109–137.

Derom, C., Thiery, E., Vlietinck, R., Loos, R., & Derom, R. (1996). Handedness in twins according to zygosity and chorion type: A preliminary report. *Behavior Genetics, 26,* 407–408.

DeRose, L. M., & Brooks-Gunn, J. (2006). Transition into adolescence: The role of pubertal processes. In L. Balter & C. S. Tamis-LeMonda (Eds.), *Child psychology: A handbook of contemporary issues* (2nd ed., pp. 385–414). New York: Psychology Press.

DeRosier, M. E. (2007). Peer-rejected and bullied children: A safe schools initiative for elementary school students. In J. E. Zins, M. J. Elias, & C. A. Maher (Eds.), *Bullying, victimization, and peer harassment* (pp. 257–276). New York: Haworth.

DeRosier, M. E., Cillessen, A. H. N., Coie, J. D., & Dodge, K. A. (1994). Group social context and children's aggressive behavior. *Child Development, 65,* 1068–1079.

DeRosier, M. E., & Thomas, J. M. (2003). Strengthening sociometric prediction: Scientific advances in the assessment of children's peer relations. *Child Development, 75,* 1379–1392.

de Rosnay, M., Cooper, P. J., Tsigaras, N., & Murray, L. (2006). Transmission of social anxiety from mother to infant: An experimental study using a social referencing paradigm. *Behaviour Research and Therapy, 44,* 1165–1175.

de Rosnay, M., & Hughes, C. (2006). Conversation and theory of mind: Do children talk their way to socio-cognitive understanding? *British Journal of Developmental Psychology, 24,* 7–37.

De Schipper, J. C., Tavecchio, L. W. C., van IJzendoorn, M. H., & van Zeijl, J. (2004). Goodness-of-fit in center day care: Relations of temperament, stability, and quality of care with the child's adjustment. *Early Childhood Research Quarterly, 19,* 257–272.

De Schipper, J. C., van IJzendoorn, M. H., & Tavecchio, L. W. C. (2004). Stability in center day care: Relations with children's well-being and problem behavior in day care. *Social Development, 13,* 531–550.

deUngria, M., Rao, R., Wobken, J. D., Luciana, M., & Georgieff, M. K. (2000). Neurophysiologic evaluation of auditory recognition memory in healthy newborn infants and infants of diabetic mothers. *Journal of Pediatrics, 137,* 777–784.

Deutsch, W., & Pechmann, T. (1982). Social interaction and the development of definite descriptions. *Cognition, 11,* 159–184.

de Villiers, J. G. (2000). Language and theory of mind: What are the developmental relationships? In S. Baron-Cohen, H. Tager-Flusberg, & D. J. Cohen (Eds.), *Understanding other minds; Perspectives from developmental cognitive neuroscience* (2nd ed.). Oxford: Oxford University Press.

de Villiers, J. G., & de Villiers, P. A. (1973). A cross-sectional study of the acquisition of grammatical morphemes in child speech. *Journal of Psycholinguistic Research, 2,* 267–278.

de Villiers, J. G., & de Villiers, P. A. (1999). Language development. In M. H. Bornstein & M. E. Lamb (Eds.), *Developmental psychology: An advanced textbook* (4th ed., pp. 313–373). Mahwah, NJ: Erlbaum.

de Villiers, J. G., & de Villiers, P. A. (2000). Linguistic determinism and the understanding of false beliefs. In P. Mitchell & K. J. Riggs (Eds.), *Children's reasoning and the mind* (pp. 87–99). Hove, UK: Psychology Press.

DeVries, R. (2001). Constructivist education in preschool and elementary school: The sociomoral atmosphere as the first educational goal. In S. L. Golbeck (Ed.), *Psychological perspectives on early childhood education* (pp. 153–180). Mahwah, NJ: Erlbaum.

de Waal, F. (1996). *Good natured: The origins of right and wrong in humans and other animals.* Cambridge, MA: Harvard University Press.

de Waal, F. (2006). *Primates and philosophers: How morality evolved.* Princeton, NJ: Princeton University Press.

de Waal, F. B. M. (1993). Sex differences in chimpanzee (and human) behavior: A matter of social values? In M. Hechter, L. Nadel, & R. E. Michod (Eds.), *The origin of values* (pp. 285–303). New York: Aldine de Gruyter.

de Waal, F. B. M. (2001). *Tree of origin.* Cambridge, MA: Harvard University Press.

de Weerd, A. W., & van den Bossche, A. S. (2003). The development of sleep during the first months of life. *Sleep Medicine Reviews, 7,* 179–191.

de Weerth, C., & Buitelaar, J. K. (2005). Physiological stress reactivity in human pregnancy—a review. *Neuroscience and Biobehavioral Reviews, 29,* 295–312.

De Wolff, M. S., & van IJzendoorn, M. H. (1997). Sensitivity and attachment: A meta-analysis on parental antecedents of infant attachment. *Child Development, 68,* 571–591.

Deynoot-Schaub, M. J. G., & Riksen-Walraven, J. M. (2006a). Peer contacts of 15-month-olds in childcare: Links with child temperament, parent–child interaction and quality of childcare. *Social Development 15,* 709–729.

Deynoot-Schaub, M. J. G., & Riksen-Walraven, J. M. (2006b). Peer interaction in child care centres at 15 and 23 months: Stability and links with children's socio-emotional adjustment. *Infant Behavior and Development, 29,* 276–288.

Diamond, A. (2000). Close interrelation of motor development and cognitive development and of the cerebellum and prefrontal cortex. *Child Development, 71,* 44–56.

Diamond, A. (2004). Normal development of the prefrontal cortex from birth to young adulthood: Cognitive functions, anatomy, and biochemistry. In D. T. Stuff & R. T. Knight (Eds.), *Principles of frontal lobe function* (pp. 466–503). New York: Oxford University Press.

Diamond, A., Barnett, W. S., Thomas, J., & Munro, S. (2007). Preschool program improves cognitive control. *Science, 318,* 1387–1388.

Diamond, A., Cruttenden, L., & Neiderman, D. (1994). AB with multiple wells: 1. Why are multiple wells sometimes easier than two wells? 2. Memory or memory + inhibition. *Developmental Psychology, 30,* 192–205.

Diamond, L. M. (1998). Development of sexual orientation among adolescent and young adult women. *Developmental Psychology, 34,* 1085–1095.

Diamond, L. M. (2003). Love matters: Romantic relationships among sexual-minority adolescents. In P. Florsheim (Ed.), *Adolescent romantic relations and sexual behavior* (pp. 85–108). Mahwah, NJ: Erlbaum.

Diamond, L. M., & Lucas, S. (2004). Sexual-minority and heterosexual youths' peer relationships: Experiences, expectations, and implications for well-being. *Journal of Research on Adolescence, 14,* 313–340.

Diamond, M., & Sigmundson, H. K. (1999). Sex reassignment at birth. In S. J. Ceci & W. M. Williams (Eds.), *The nature–nurture debate* (pp. 55–75). Malden, MA: Blackwell.

Dias, M. G., & Harris, P. (1988). The effect of making-believe play on deductive reasoning. *British Journal of Developmental Psychology, 8,* 305–318.

Dias, M. G., & Harris, P. (1990). The influence of the imagination on reasoning by young children. *British Journal of Developmental Psychology, 8,* 305–318.

DiBiase, A., Gibbs, J. C., & Potter, G. B. (2005). *EQUIP for educators: Teaching youth (grades 5–8) to think and act responsibly.* Champaign, IL: Research Press.

Dick, D. M., Rose, R. J., Viken, R. J., & Kaprio, J. (2000). Pubertal timing and substance use: Associations between and within families across late adolescence. *Developmental Psychology, 36,* 180–189.

Dick, F., Dronkers, N. F., Pizzamiglio, L., Saygin, A. P., Small, S. L., & Wilson, S. (2004). Language and the brain. In M. Tomasello & D. I. Slobin (Eds.), *Beyond nature–nurture: Essays in honor of Elizabeth Bates* (pp. 237–260). Mahwah, NJ: Erlbaum.

Dickens, W. T., & Flynn, J. R. (2001). Heritability estimates versus large environmental effects: The IQ paradox resolved. *Psychological Review, 108,* 346–369.

Dickens, W. T., & Flynn, J. R. (2006). Black Americans reduce the racial IQ gap: Evidence from standardization samples. *Psychological Science, 17,* 913–920.

Dickinson, D. K., & McCabe, A. (2001). Bringing it all together: The multiple origins, skills, and environmental supports of early literacy. *Learning Disabilities Research and Practice, 16,* 186–202.

Dickinson, D. K., McCabe, A., Anastasopoulos, L., Peisner-Feinberg, E. S., & Poe, M. D. (2003). The comprehensive language approach to early literacy: The interrelationships among vocabulary, phonological sensitivity, and print knowledge among preschool-age children. *Journal of Educational Psychology, 95,* 465–481.

Dick-Read, G. (1959). *Childbirth without fear.* New York: Harper & Brothers.

Dickson, K. L., Fogel, A., & Messinger, D. (1998). The development of emotion from a social process view. In M. F. Mascolo (Ed.), *What develops in emotional development?* (pp. 253–271). New York: Plenum.

Diener, M. L., Goldstein, L. H., & Mangelsdorf, S. C. (1995). The role of prenatal expectations in parents' reports of infant temperament. *Merrill-Palmer Quarterly, 41,* 172–190.

Dieticians of Canada, Canadian Paediatric Society, the College of Family Physicians of Canada, & Community Health Nurses Association of Canada. (2004). The use of growth charts for assessing and monitoring growth in Canadian infants and children. *Paediatrics and Child Health, 9,* 171–180.

Dietrich, K. N., Ris, M. D., Succop, P. A., Berger, O. G., & Bornschein, R. L. (2001). Early exposure to lead and juvenile delinquency. *Neurotoxicology and Teratology, 23,* 511–518.

Dietrich, K. N., Ware, J. H., Salganik, M., Radcliffe, J., Rogan, W. J., & Rhoads, G. C. (2004). Effect of chelation therapy on the neuropsychological and behavioral development of lead-exposed children after school entry. *Pediatrics, 114,* 19–26.

Dietz, T. L. (1998). An examination of violence and gender role portrayals in video games: Implications for gender socialization and aggressive behavior. *Sex Roles, 38,* 425–442.

Dildy, G. A., Jackson, G. M., Fowers, G. K., Oshiro, B. T., Varner, M. W., & Clark, S. L. (1996). Very advanced maternal age. Pregnancy after age 45. *American Journal of Obstetrics and Gynecology, 175,* 668–674.

DiMatteo, M. R., & Kahn, K. L. (1997). Psychosocial aspects of childbirth. In S. J. Gallant, G. P. Keita, & R. Royak-Schaler (Eds.), *Health care for women: Psychological, social, and behavioral influences* (pp. 175–186). Washington, DC: American Psychological Association.

DiPietro, J. A., Bornstein, M. H., Costigan, K. A., Pressman, E. K., Hahn, C.-S., & Painter, K. (2002). What does fetal movement predict about behavior during the first two years of life? *Developmental Psychobiology, 40,* 358–371.

DiPietro, J. A., Caulfield, L. E., Irizarry, R. A., Chen, P., Merialdi, M., & Zavaleta, N. (2006). Prenatal development of intrafetal and maternal–fetal synchrony. *Behavioral Neuroscience, 120,* 687–701.

DiPietro, J. A., Hodgson, D. M., Costigan, K. A., & Hilton, S. C. (1996). Fetal neurobehavioral development. *Child Development, 67,* 2553–2567.

Dirks, J. (1982). The effect of a commercial game on children's Block Design scores on the WISC-R test. *Intelligence, 6,* 109–123.

Dishion, T. J., Andrews, D. W., & Crosby, L. (1995). Antisocial boys and their friends in early adolescence: Relationship characteristics, quality, and interactional processes. *Child Development, 66,* 139–151.

Dishion, T. J., Poulin, F., & Burraston, B. (2001). Peer group dynamics associated with iatrogenic effects in group interventions with high-risk young adolescents. In D. W. Nangle & C. A. Erdley (Eds.), *The role of friendship in psychological adjustment* (pp. 79–92). San Francisco: Jossey-Bass.

Dixon, T. L., & Azocar, C. I. (2006). The representation of juvenile offenders by race on Los Angeles area television news. *Howard Journal of Communications, 17,* 143–161.

Dodd, V. L. (2005). Implications of kangaroo care for growth and development in preterm infants. *JOGNN, 34,* 218–232.

Dodge, K. A., & Coie, J. D. (1987). Social-information-processing factors in reactive and proactive aggression in children's peer groups. *Journal of Abnormal and Social Psychology, 53,* 1146–1158.

Dodge, K. A., Coie, J. D., & Lynam, D. (2006). Aggression and antisocial behavior in youth. In N. Eisenberg (Ed.), *Handbook of child psychology: Vol. 3. Social, emotional, and personality development* (6th ed., pp. 719–788). New York: Wiley.

Dodge, K. A., Dishion, T. J., & Lansford, J. E. (2006). Deviant peer influences in intervention and public policy for youth. *Social Policy Report of the Society for Research in Child Development, 20*(1), 3–19.

Dodge, K. A., Lansford, J. E., Burks, V. S., Bates, J. E., Pettit, G. S., Fontaine, R., & Price, J. M. (2003). Peer rejection and social information-processing factors in the development of aggressive behavior problems in children. *Child Development, 74,* 374–393.

Dodge, K. A., Lochman, J. E., Harnish, J. D., Bates, J. E., & Pettit, G. S. (1997). Reactive and proactive aggression in school children and psychiatrically impaired chronically assaultive youth. *Journal of Abnormal Psychology, 106,* 37–51.

Dodge, K. A., McLoyd, V. C., & Lansford, J. E. (2006). The cultural context of physically disciplining children. In V. C. McLoyd, N. E. Hill, & K. A. Dodge (Eds.), *African-American family life: Ecological and cultural diversity* (pp. 245–263). New York: Guilford.

Dodge, K. A., Pettit, G. S., McClaskey, C. L., & Brown, M. M. (1986). Social competence in children. *Monographs of the Society for Research in Child Development, 51*(2, Serial No. 213).

Doeker, N., Simic-Schleicher, A., Hauffa, B. P., & Andler, W. (1999). Psychosozialer Kleinwuchs maskiert als Wachstumshormonmangel. [Psychosocially stunted growth masked as growth hormone deficiency.] *Klinische Pädiatrie, 211,* 394–398.

Doherty, G., Lero, D. S., Goelmjan, H., Tougas, J., & LaGrange, A. (2000). *You bet I care! Caring and learning environments: Quality in regulated family child care across Canada.* Guelph, ON: Centre for Families, Work and Well-Being, University of Guelph.

Doherty, N. N., & Hepper, P. G. (2000). Habituation in fetuses of diabetic mothers. *Early Human Development, 59,* 85–93.

Dohnt, H., & Tiggemann, M. (2006). The contribution of peer and media influences to the development of body satisfaction and self-esteem in young girls: A prospective study. *Developmental Psychology, 42,* 929–936.

Dollaghan, C. (1985). Child meets word: "Fast mapping" in preschool children. *Journal of Speech and Hearing Research, 28,* 449–454.

Dombrowski, S. C., Noonan, K., & Martin, R. P. (2007). Low birth weight and cognitive outcomes: Evidence for a gradient relationship in an urban, poor, African American birth cohort. *School Psychology Quarterly, 22,* 26–43.

Donahue, M. J., & Benson, P. L. (1995). Religion and the well-being of adolescents. *Journal of Social Issues, 51,* 145–160.

Dondi, M., Simion, F., & Caltran, G. (1999). Can newborns discriminate between their own cry and the cry of another newborn infant? *Developmental Psychology, 35,* 418–426.

Donnellan, M. B., Trzesniewski, K. H., Robins, R. W., Moffitt, T. E., & Caspi, A. (2005). Low self-esteem is related to aggression, antisocial behavior, and delinquency. *Psychological Science, 16,* 328–335.

Donnelly, P., & Kidd, B. (2004). *Realizing the expectations: Youth, character, and community in Canadian sport.* Ottawa: Canadian Centre for Ethics in Sport. Retrieved from www.cces.ca/pdfs/CCES-PAPER-Kidd-Donnelly-E.pdf

Donnerstein, E., Slaby, R. G., & Eron, L. D. (1994). The mass media and youth aggression. In L. D. Eron, J. H. Gentry, & P. Schlegel (Eds.), *Reason to hope: A psychosocial perspective on violence and youth* (pp. 219–250). Washington, DC: American Psychological Association.

D'Onofrio, B. M., Turkheimer, E., Emery, R. E., Slutske, W. S., Heath, A. C., Madden, P. A., & Martin, N. G. (2006). A genetically informed study of the processes underlying the association between parental marital instability and offspring adjustment. *Developmental Psychology, 42,* 486–499.

Donovan, W. L., Leavitt, L. A., & Walsh, R. O. (1997). Cognitive set and coping strategy affect mothers' sensitivity to infant cries: A signal detection approach. *Child Development, 68,* 760–772.

Donovan, W. L., Leavitt, L. A., & Walsh, R. O. (2000). Maternal illusory control predicts socialization strategies and toddler compliance. *Developmental Psychology, 36,* 402–411.

Dorius, C. J., Bahr, S. J., Hoffman, J. P., Harmon, E. L. (2004). Parenting practices as moderators of the relationship between peers and adolescent marijuana use. *Journal of Marriage and Family, 66,* 163–178.

Dornbusch, S. M., & Glasgow, K. L. (1997). The structural context of family–school relations. In A. Booth & J. F. Dunn (Eds.), *Family–school links: How do they affect educational outcomes?* (pp. 35–55). Mahwah, NJ: Erlbaum.

Dornbusch, S. M., Glasgow, K. L., & Lin, I.-C. (1996). The social structure of schooling. *Annual Review of Psychology, 47,* 401–427.

Dorris, M. (1989). *The broken cord.* New York: Harper & Row.

dos Santos Silva, I., De Stavola, B. L., Hardy, R. J., Kuh, D. J., McCormack, V. A., & Wadsworth, M. E. J. (2004). Is the association of birth weight with premenopausal breast cancer risk mediated through childhood growth? *British Journal of Cancer, 91,* 519–524.

Dovidio, J. F., Gaertner, S. L., Nier, J. A., Kawakami, K., & Hodson, G. (2004). Contemporary racial bias: When good people do bad things. In G. A. Miller (Ed.), *The social psychology of good and evil* (pp. 141–167). New York: Guilford.

Dowker, A. (2003). Younger children's estimates for addition: The zone of partial knowledge and understanding. In A. J. Baroody & A. Dowker (Eds.), *The development of arithmetic concepts and skills: Constructing adaptive expertise* (pp. 243–265). Mahwah, NJ: Erlbaum.

Dowling, E. M., Gestsdottir, S., Anderson, P. M., von Eye, A., Almerigi, J., & Lerner, R. M. (2004). Structural relations among spirituality, religiosity, and thriving in adolescence. *Applied Developmental Psychology, 8,* 7–16.

Downs, A. C., & Fuller, M. J. (1991). Recollections of spermarche: An exploratory investigation. *Current Psychology: Research and Reviews, 10,* 93–102.

Downs, A. C., & Langlois, J. H. (1988). Sex typing: Construct and measurement issues. *Sex Roles, 18,* 87–100.

Dozier, M., Stovall, K. C., Albus, K. E., & Bates, B. (2001). Attachment for infants in foster care: The role of caregiver state of mind. *Child Development, 72,* 1467–1477.

Drabman, R. S., Cordua, G. D., Hammer, D., Jarvie, G. J., & Horton, W. (1979). Developmental trends in eating rates of normal and overweight preschool children. *Child Development, 50,* 211–216.

Draper, P., & Cashdan, E. (1988). Technological change and child behavior among the !Kung. *Ethnology, 27,* 339–365.

Drewett, R. F., Corbett, S. S., & Wright, C. M. (2006). Physical and emotional development, appetite and body image in adolescents who failed to thrive as infants. *Journal of Child Psychology and Psychiatry, 47,* 524–531.

Driscoll, M. C. (2007). Sickle cell disease. *Pediatrics in Review, 28,* 259–268.

Droege, K. L., & Stipek, D. J. (1993). Children's use of dispositions to predict classmates' behavior. *Developmental Psychology, 29,* 646–654.

Drotar, D., Overholser, J. C., Levi, R., Walders, N., Robinson, J. R., Palermo, T. M., & Riekert, K. A. (2000). Ethical issues in conducting research with pediatric and clinical child populations in applied settings.

In D. Drotar (Ed.), *Handbook of research in pediatric and clinical child psychology* (pp. 305–326). New York: Kluwer.

Drotar, D., Pallotta, J., & Eckerle, D. (1994). A prospective study of family environments of children hospitalized for nonorganic failure-to-thrive. *Developmental and Behavioral Pediatrics, 15,* 78–85.

Dubé, E. M., Savin-Williams, R. C., & Diamond, L. M. (2001). Intimacy development, gender, and ethnicity among sexual-minority youths. In A. R. D'Augelli & C. J. Patterson (Eds.), *Lesbian, gay, and bisexual identities and youth* (pp. 129–152). New York: Oxford University Press.

DuBois, D. L., Felner, R. D., Brand, S., & George, G. R. (1999). Profiles of self-esteem in early adolescence: Identification and investigation of adaptive correlates. *American Journal of Community Psychology, 27,* 899–932.

Duckworth, A. L., & Seligman, M. E. P. (2005). Self-discipline outdoes IQ in predicting academic performance of adolescents. *Psychological Science, 12,* 939–944.

Dueker, G. L., Modi, A., & Needham, A. (2003). 4.5-month-old infants' learning, retention and use of object boundary information. *Infant Behavior and Development, 26,* 588–605.

Duggan, A., McFarlane, E., Fuddy, L., Burrell, L., Higman, S. M., Windham, A., & Sia, C. (2004). Randomized trial of a statewide home visiting program: Impact in preventing child abuse and neglect. *Child Abuse and Neglect, 28,* 597–622.

Duncan, G. J., & Brooks-Gunn, J. (2000). Family poverty, welfare reform, and child development. *Child Development, 71,* 188–196.

Duncan, G. J., Dowsett, C. J., Claessens, A., Magnuson, K., Huston, A. C., Klebanov, P., et al. (2007). School readiness and later achievement. *Developmental Psychology, 43,* 1428–1446.

Duncan, G. J., & Magnuson, K. A. (2003). Off with Hollingshead: Socioeconomic resources, parenting, and child development. In M. H. Bornstein & R. H. Bradley (Eds.), *Socioeconomic status, parenting, and child development* (pp. 83–106). Mahwah, NJ: Erlbaum.

Dunham, Y., Baron, A. S., & Banaji, M. R. (2006). From American city to Japanese village: A cross-cultural investigation of implicit race attitudes. *Child Development, 77,* 1129–1520.

Dunifon, R., Kalil, A., & Danziger, S. K. (2003). Maternal work behavior under welfare reform: How does the transition from welfare to work affect child development? *Children and Youth Services Review, 25,* 55–82.

Duniz, M., Scheer, P. J., Trojovsky, A., Kaschnitz, W., Kvas, E., & Macari, S. (1996). *European Child and Adolescent Psychiatry, 5,* 93–100.

Dunn, J. (2002). Sibling relationships. In P. K. Smith & C. H. Hart (Eds.), *Blackwell handbook of childhood social development* (pp. 223–237). Malden, MA: Blackwell.

Dunn, J. (2004a). Annotation: Children's relationships with their nonresident fathers. *Journal of Child Psychology and Psychiatry, 45,* 659–671.

Dunn, J. (2004b). Sibling relationships. In P. K. Smith & C. H. Hart (Eds.), *Handbook of childhood social development* (pp. 223–237). Malden, MA: Blackwell.

Dunn, J., & Kendrick, C. (1982). *Siblings: Love, envy and understanding.* Cambridge, MA: Harvard University Press.

Dunn, J., Brown, J. R., & Maguire, M. (1995). The development of children's moral sensibility: Individual differences and emotion understanding. *Developmental Psychology, 31,* 649–659.

Dunn, J., Cheng, H., O'Connor, T. G., & Bridges, L. (2004). Children's perspectives on their relationships with their nonresident fathers: Influences, outcomes and implications. *Journal of Child Psychology and Psychiatry, 45,* 553–566.

Dunn, J., Slomkowski, C., & Beardsall, L. (1994). Sibling relationships from the preschool period through middle childhood and early adolescence. *Developmental Psychology, 30,* 315–324.

Durbin, D. L., Darling, N., Steinberg, L. D., & Brown, B. B. (1993). Parenting style and peer group membership among European-American adolescents. *Journal of Research on Adolescence, 3,* 87–100.

Durlach, J. (2004). New data on the importance of gestational Mg deficiency. *Journal of the American College of Nutrition, 23,* 694S-700S.

Durrant, J., Broberg, A., & Rose-Krasnor, L. (2000). Predicting use of physical punishment during mother–child conflicts in Sweden and Canada. In P. Hastings & C. Piotrowski (Eds.), *Conflict as a context for understanding maternal beliefs about child rearing and children's misbehavior: New directions for child development.* San Francisco: Jossey-Bass.

Durston, S., Pol, H. E. H., Schnack, H. G., Buitelaar, J. K., Steenhuis, M. P., & Minderaa, R. B. (2004). Magnetic resonance imaging of boys with attention-deficit/hyperactivity disorder and their unaffected siblings. *Journal of the American Academy of Child and Adolescent Psychiatry, 43,* 332–340.

Dweck, C. S. (2002). Messages that motivate: How praise molds students' beliefs, motivation, and performance (in surprising ways). In J. Aronson (Ed.), *Improving academic achievement: Impact of psychological factors on education* (pp. 37–60). San Diego, CA: Academic Press.

Dykman, R., Casey, P. H., Ackerman, P. T., & McPherson, W. B. (2001). Behavioral and cognitive status in school-aged children with a history of failure to thrive during early childhood. *Clinical Pediatrics, 40,* 63–70.

Dzurova, D., & Pikhart, H. (2005). Down syndrome, paternal age and education: Comparison of California and the Czech Republic. *BMC Public Health, 5,* 69.

Eacott, M. J. (1999). Memory for the events of early childhood. *Current Directions in Psychological Science, 8,* 46–48.

East, P. L., & Felice, M. E. (1996). *Adolescent pregnancy and parenting: Findings from a racially diverse sample.* Mahwah, NJ: Erlbaum.

Eaton, D. K., Davis, K. S., Barrios, L., Brener, N. D., & Noonan, R. K. (2007). Associations of dating violence victimization with lifetime participation, co-occurrence, and early initiation of risk behaviors among U.S. high school students. *Journal of Interpersonal Violence, 22,* 585–602.

Eaves, L., Silberg, J., Foley, D., Bulik, C., Maes, H., & Erkanli, A. (2004). Genetic and environmental influences on the relative timing of pubertal change. *Twin Research, 7,* 471–481.

Ebeling, K. S., & Gelman, S. A. (1994). Children's use of context in interpreting "big" and "little." *Child Development, 65,* 1178–1192.

Eberhard, J., Stein, S., & Geissbuehler, V. (2005). Experience of pain and analgesia with water and land births. *Journal of Psychosomatic Obstetrics and Gynecology, 26,* 127–133.

Eberhart-Phillips, J. E., Frederick, P. D., & Baron, R. C. (1993). Measles in pregnancy: A descriptive study of 58 cases. *Obstetrics and Gynecology, 82,* 797–801.

Eccles, J. S. (2004). Schools, academic motivation, and stage–environment fit. In R. M. Lerner & L. Steinberg (Eds.), *Handbook of adolescent psychology* (2nd ed., pp. 125–154). Hoboken, NJ: Wiley.

Eccles, J. S., Freedman-Doan, C., Frome, P., Jacobs, J., & Yoon, K. S. (2000). Gender-role socialization in the family: A longitudinal approach. In T. Eckes & H. M. Trautner (Eds.), *The developmental social psychology of gender* (pp. 333–360). Mahwah, NJ: Erlbaum.

Eccles, J. S., & Harold, R. D. (1991). Gender differences in sport involvement: Applying the Eccles' expectancy-value model. *Journal of Applied Sport Psychology, 3,* 7–35.

Eccles, J. S., Jacobs, J. E., & Harold, R. D. (1990). Gender-role stereotypes, expectancy effects, and parents' role in the socialization of gender differences in self-perceptions and skill acquisition. *Journal of Social Issues, 46,* 183–201.

Eccles, J. S., Templeton, J., Barber, B., & Stone, M. (2003). Adolescence and emerging adulthood: The critical passage ways to adulthood. In M. H. Bornstein, L. Davidson, C. L., Keyes, K. A. Moore, & the Center for Child Well-Being (Eds.), *Well-being: Positive development across the life course* (pp. 383–406). Mahwah, NJ: Erlbaum.

Eccles, J. S., Wigfield, A., Harold, R. D., & Blumfeld, P. B. (1993). Age and gender differences in children's self- and task perceptions during elementary school. *Child Development, 64,* 830–847.

Eckerman, C. O., & Peterman, K. (2001). Peers and infant social/communicative development. In G. Bremner & A. Fogel (Eds.), *Blackwell handbook of infant development* (pp. 326–350). Malden, MA: Blackwell.

Eckerman, C. O., & Whitehead, H. (1999). How toddler peers generate coordinated action: A cross-cultural exploration. *Early Education and Development, 10,* 241–266.

Eder, R. A., & Mangelsdorf, S. C. (1997). The emotional basis of early personality development: Implications for the emergent self-concept. In R. Hogan, J. Johnson, & S. Briggs (Eds.), *Handbook of personality psychology* (pp. 209–240). San Diego, CA: Academic Press.

Edmondson, P. (2006). Deaf children's understanding of other people's thought processes. *Educational Psychology in Practice, 22,* 159–169.

Edwards, O. W., & Oakland, T. D. (2006). Factorial invariance of Woodcock-Johnson III scores for African Americans and Caucasian Americans. *Journal of Psychoeducational Assessment, 24,* 358–366.

Egan, S. K., & Perry, D. G. (2001). Gender identity: A multidimensional analysis with implications for psychosocial adjustment. *Developmental Psychology, 37,* 451–463.

Egeland, B., Jacobvitz, D., & Sroufe, L. A. (1988). Breaking the cycle of abuse. *Child Development, 59,* 1080–1088.

Ehri, L. C., Nunes, S. R., Willows, D. M., Schuster, B. V., Yaghoub-Zadeh, Z., & Shanahan, T. (2001). Phonemic awareness instruction helps children learn to read: Evidence from the National Reading Panel's meta-analysis. *Reading Research Quarterly, 36,* 250–287.

Eichstedt, J. A., Serbin, L. A., Poulin-Dubois, D., & Sen, M. G. (2002). Of bears and men: Infants' knowledge of conventional and metaphorical gender stereotypes. *Infant Behavior and Development, 25,* 296–310.

Eigsti, I.-M., Zayas, V., Mischel, W., Shoda, Y., Ayduk, O., Dadlani, M. B., Davidson, M. C., Aber, J. L., & Casey, B. J. (2006). Predicting cognitive control from preschool to late adolescence and young adulthood. *Psychological Science, 17,* 478–484.

Eisbach, A. O. (2004). Children's developing awareness of diversity in people's trains of thought. *Child Development, 75,* 1694–1707.

Eisenberg, N. (1986). *Altruistic emotion, cognition, and behavior.* Hillsdale, NJ: Erlbaum.

Eisenberg, N. (2003). Prosocial behavior, empathy, and sympathy. In M. H. Bornstein & L. Davidson (Eds.), *Well-being: Positive development across the life course* (pp. 253–265). Mahwah, NJ: Erlbaum.

Eisenberg, N., Carlo, G., Murphy, B., & Van Court, P. (1995). Prosocial development in late adolescence: A longitudinal study. *Child Development, 66,* 1179–1197.

Eisenberg, N., Cumberland, A., & Spinrad, T. L. (1998). Parental socialization of emotion. *Psychological Inquiry, 9,* 241–273.

Eisenberg, N., & Fabes, R. A. (1998). Prosocial development. In N. Eisenberg (Ed.), *Handbook of child psychology: Vol. 3. Social, emotional, and personality development* (5th ed., pp. 701–778). New York: Wiley.

Eisenberg, N., Fabes, R., Murphy, B., Karbon, M., Smith, M., & Maszk, P. (1996). The relations of children's dispositional empathy-related responding to their emotionality, regulation, and social functioning. *Developmental Psychology, 32,* 195–209.

Eisenberg, N., Fabes, R. A., Shepard, S. A., Murphy, B. C., Jones, S., & Guthrie, I. K. (1998). Contemporaneous and longitudinal prediction of children's sympathy from dispositional regulation and emotionality. *Developmental Psychology, 34,* 910–924.

Eisenberg, N., Fabes, R. A., & Spinrad, T. L. (2006). Prosocial development. In N. Eisenberg (Ed.), *Handbook of child psychology: Vol. 3. Social, emotional, and personality development* (6th ed., pp. 646–718). Hoboken, NJ: Wiley.

Eisenberg, N., Miller, P. A., Shell, R., McNalley, S., & Shea, C. (1991). Prosocial development in adolescence: A longitudinal study. *Developmental Psychology, 27,* 849–857.

Eisenberg, N., Murphy, B. C., & Shepard, S. (1997). The development of empathic accuracy. In W. Ickes (Ed.), *Empathic accuracy* (pp. 73–116). New York: Guilford.

Eisenberg, N., Sadovsky, A., Spinrad, T. L., Fabes, R. A., Losoya, S., & Valiente, C. (2005). The relations of problem behavior status to children's negative emotionality, effortful control, and impulsivity: Concurrent relations and prediction of change. *Developmental Psychology, 41,* 193–211.

Eisenberg, N., Smith, C. L., Sadovsky, A., & Spinrad, T. L. (2004). Effortful control: Relations with emotion regulation, adjustment, and socialization in childhood. In

R. Baumeister & K. D. Vohs (Eds.), *Handbook of self-regulation: Research, theory, and applications* (pp. 259–282). New York: Guilford.

Eisenberg, N., & Spinrad, T. L. (2004). Emotion-related regulation: Sharpening the definition. *Child Development, 75,* 334–339.

Eisenberg, N., Zhoe, Q., & Koller, S. (2001). Brazilian adolescents' prosocial moral judgment and behavior: Relations to sympathy, perspective taking, gender-role orientation, and demographic characteristics. *Child Development, 72,* 518–534.

Eisenberg, N., Zhou, Q., Spinrad, T. L., Valiente, C., Fabes, R. A., & Liew, J. (2005). Relations among positive parenting, children's effortful control, and externalizing problems: A three-wave longitudinal study. *Child Development, 76,* 1055–1071.

Ekman, P. (2003). *Emotions revealed.* New York: Times Books.

Ekman, P., & Friesen, W. (1972). Constants across culture in the face of emotion. *Journal of Personality and Social Psychology, 17,* 124–129.

Elfenbein, D. S., & Felice, M. E. (2003). Adolescent pregnancy. *Pediatric Clinics of North America, 50,* 781–800.

Eliakim, A., Friedland, O., Kowen, G., Wolach, B., & Nemet, D. (2004). Parental obesity and higher pre-intervention BMI reduce the likelihood of a multidisciplinary childhood obesity program to succeed: A clinical observation. *Journal of Pediatric Endocrinology and Metabolism, 17,* 1055–1061.

Elias, C. L., & Berk, L. E. (2002). Self-regulation in young children: Is there a role for sociodramatic play? *Early Childhood Research Quarterly, 17,* 1–17.

Elicker, J., Englund, M., & Sroufe, L. A. (1992). Predicting peer competence and peer relationships in childhood from early parent–child relationships. In R. D. Parke & G. W. Ladd (Eds.), *Family–peer relationships: Modes of linkage* (pp. 77–106). Hillsdale, NJ: Erlbaum.

Elkind, D. (1994). *A sympathetic understanding of the child: Birth to sixteen* (3rd ed.). Boston: Allyn and Bacon.

Elkind, D., & Bowen, R. (1979). Imaginary audience behavior in children and adolescence. *Developmental Psychology, 15,* 33–44.

Ellickson, P. L., D'Amico, E. J., Collins, R. L., & Klein, D. J. (2005). Marijuana use and later problems: When frequency of recent use explains age of initiation effects. *Substance Use and Misuse, 40,* 343–359.

Elliott, D. S., Wilson, W. J., Huizinga, D., Sampson, R. J., Elliott, A., & Rankin, B. (1996). The effects of neighborhood disadvantage on adolescent development. *Journal of Research in Crime and Delinquency, 33,* 389–426.

Ellis, A. E., & Oakes, L. M. (2006). Infants flexibly use different dimensions to categorize objects. *Developmental Psychology, 42,* 1000–1011.

Ellis, B. J. (2004). Timing of pubertal maturation in girls: An integrated life history approach. *Psychological Bulletin, 130,* 920–958.

Ellis, B. J., Bates, J. E., Dodge, K. A., Fergusson, D. M., Horwood, L. J., Pettit, G. S., & Woodward, L. (2003). Does father absence place daughters at special risk for early sexual activity and teenage pregnancy? *Child Development, 74,* 801–821.

Ellis, S., & Gauvain, M. (1992). Social and cultural influences on children's collaborative interactions. In L. T. Winegar & J. Valsiner (Eds.), *Children's development within social context* (Vol. 2, pp. 155–180). Hillsdale, NJ: Erlbaum.

Ellis, W. E., & Zarbatany, L. (2007). Explaining friendship formation and friendship stability: The role of children's and friends' aggression and victimization. *Merrill-Palmer Quarterly, 53,* 79–104.

Ellison, C. G., & Powers, D. A. (1994). The contact hypothesis and racial attitudes among black Americans. *Social Science Quarterly, 75,* 385–400.

Elman, J. (2003). Development: It's about time. *Developmental Science, 6,* 430–433.

Elman, J. L. (2001). Connectionism and language acquisition. In M. Tomasello & E. Bates (Eds.). *Language development* (pp. 295–306). Oxford, UK: Blackwell.

Elsen, H. (1994). Phonological constraints and overextensions. *First Language, 14,* 305–315.

Else-Quest, N. M., Hyde, J. S., Goldsmith, H. H., & Van Hulle, C. A. (2006). Gender differences in temperament: A meta-analysis. *Psychological Bulletin, 132,* 33–72.

El-Sheikh, M., Cummings, E. M., & Reiter, S. (1996). Preschoolers' responses to ongoing interadult conflict: The role of prior exposure to resolved versus unresolved arguments. *Journal of Abnormal Child Psychology, 24,* 665–679.

Eltzschig, H. K., Lieberman, E. S., & Camann, W. R. (2003). Regional anesthesia and analgesia for labor and delivery. *New England Journal of Medicine, 384,* 319–332.

Ely, R. (2005). Language and literacy in the school years. In J. B. Gleason (Ed.), *The development of language* (6th ed., pp. 395–443). Boston: Allyn and Bacon.

Ely, R., & McCabe, A. (1994). The language play of kindergarten children. *First Language, 14,* 19–35.

Emery, R. E., Laumann-Billings, L., Waldron, M. C., Sbarra, D. A., & Dillon, P. (2001). Child custody mediation and litigation: Custody, contact, and coparenting 12 years after initial dispute resolution. *Journal of Consulting and Clinical Psychology, 69,* 323–332.

Emery, R. E., Sbarra, D., & Grover, T. (2005). Divorce mediation: Research and reflections. *Family Court Review, 43,* 22–37.

Emmerich, W. (1981). Non-monotonic developmental trends in social cognition: The case of gender constancy. In S. Strauss (Ed.), *U-shaped behavioral growth* (pp. 249–269). New York: Academic Press.

Emory, E. K., Schlackman, L. J., & Fiano, K. (1996). Drug–hormone interactions on neurobehavioral responses in human neonates. *Infant Behavior and Development, 19,* 213–220.

Ennemoser, M., & Schneider, W. (2007). Relations of television viewing and reading: Findings from a 4-year longitudinal study. *Journal of Educational Psychology, 99,* 349–368.

Epstein, L. H., Roemmich, J. N., & Raynor, H. A. (2001). Behavioral therapy in the treatment of pediatric obesity. *Pediatric Clinics of North America, 48,* 981–983.

Erath, S. A., Bierman, K. L., & the Conduct Problems Prevention Research Group. (2006). Aggressive marital conflict, maternal harsh punishment, and child aggressive-disruptive behavior: Evidence for direct and mediate relations. *Journal of Family Psychology, 20,* 217–226.

Erden, F., & Wolfgang, C. H. (2004). An exploration of the differences in prekindergarten, kindergarten, and first-grade teachers' beliefs related to discipline when dealing with male and female students. *Early Child Development and Care, 174,* 3–11.

Erikson, E. H. (1950). *Childhood and society.* New York: Norton.

Erikson, E. H. (1968). *Identity, youth, and crisis.* New York: Norton.

Eslinger, P. J. (1998). Neurological and neuropsychological bases of empathy. *European Neurology, 39,* 193–199.

Eslinger, P. J., Moore, P., Troiani, V., Antani, S., Cross, K., Kwok, S., & Grossman, M. (2007). Oops! Resolving social dilemmas in frontotemporal dementia. *Journal of Neurology, Neurosurgery, and Psychiatry, 78,* 457–460.

Espy, K. A., Molfese, V. J., & DiLalla, L. F. (2001). Effects of environmental measures on intelligence in young children: Growth curve modeling of longitudinal data. *Merrill-Palmer Quarterly, 47,* 42–73.

Estourgie-van Burk, G. F., Bartels, M., van Beijsterveldt, T. C., Delemarre-van de Waal, H. A., & Boomsma, D. I. (2006). Body size in five-year-old twins: Heritability and comparison to singleton standards. *Twin Research and Human Genetics, 9,* 646–655.

Evans, G. W. (2004). The environment of child poverty. *American Psychologist, 59,* 77–92.

Evans, G. W. (2006). Child development and the physical environment. *Annual Review of Psychology, 57,* 424–451.

Eveleth, P. B., & Tanner, J. M. (1990). *Worldwide variation in human growth* (2nd ed.). Cambridge, UK: Cambridge University Press.

Everman, D. B., & Cassidy, S. B. (2000). Genetics of childhood disorders: XII. Genomic imprinting: Breaking the rules. *Journal of the American Academy of Child and Adolescent Psychiatry, 38,* 386–389.

Fabes, R. A., Eisenberg, N., Hanish, L. D., & Spinrad, T. L. (2001). Preschoolers' spontaneous emotion vocabulary: Relations to likability. *Early Education and Development, 12,* 11–27.

Fabes, R. A., Eisenberg, N., Karbon, M., Troyer, D., & Switzer, G. (1994). The relations of children's emotion regulation to their vicarious emotional responses and comforting behavior. *Child Development, 65,* 1678–1693.

Fabes, R. A., Eisenberg, N., McCormick, S. E., & Wilson, M. S. (1988). Preschoolers' attributions of the situational determinants of others' naturally occurring emotions. *Developmental Psychology, 24,* 376–385.

Fabes, R. A., Martin, C. L., & Hanish, L. D. (2003). Young children's play qualities in same-, other-, and mixed-sex peer groups. *Child Development, 74,* 921–932.

Fabes, R. A., Shepard, S. A., Guthrie, I. K., & Martin, C. L. (1997). Roles of temperamental arousal and gender-segregated play in young children's social adjustment. *Developmental Psychology, 33,* 693–702.

Fagan, J. F., Holland, C. R., & Wheeler, K. (2007). The prediction, from infancy, of adult IQ and achievement. *Intelligence, 35,* 225–231.

Fagan, J. F., III. (1973). Infant's delayed recognition memory and forgetting. *Journal of Experimental Child Psychology, 16,* 424–450.

Fagan, J. F., III, & Detterman, D. K. (1992). The Fagan Test of Infant Intelligence: A technical summary. *Journal of Applied Developmental Psychology, 13,* 173–193.

Fagan, J. F., III, & Singer, L. T. (1983). Infant recognition memory as a measure of intelligence. In L. P. Lipsitt (Ed.), *Advances in infancy research* (Vol. 2, pp. 31–78). Norwood, NJ: Ablex.

Fagard, J., & Pezé, A. (1997). Age changes in interlimb coupling and the development of bimanual coordination. *Journal of Motor Behavior, 29,* 199–208.

Fagot, B. I. (1984). The child's expectations of differences in adult male and female interactions. *Sex Roles, 11,* 593–600.

Fagot, B. I. (1985a). Beyond the reinforcement principle: Another step toward understanding sex role development. *Developmental Psychology, 21,* 1097–1104.

Fagot, B. I. (1985b). Changes in thinking about early sex role development. *Developmental Review, 5,* 83–98.

Fagot, B. I., & Hagan, R. I. (1991). Observations of parent reactions to sex-stereotyped behaviors: Age and sex effects. *Child Development, 62,* 617–628.

Fagot, B. I., & Leinbach, M. D. (1989). The young child's gender schema: Environmental input, internal organization. *Child Development, 60,* 663–672.

Fagot, B. I., Leinbach, M. D., & O'Boyle, C. (1992). Gender labeling, gender stereotyping, and parenting behaviors. *Developmental Psychology, 28,* 225–230.

Fahrmeier, E. D. (1978). The development of concrete operations among the Hausa. *Journal of Cross-Cultural Psychology, 9,* 23–44.

Fairburn, C. G. (2005). Evidence-based treatment of anorexia nervosa. *International Journal of Eating Disorders, 37,* S26–S30.

Fairburn, C. G., & Harrison, P. J. (2003). Eating disorders. *Lancet, 361,* 407–416.

Falbo, T. (1992). Social norms and the one-child family: Clinical and policy implications. In F. Boer & J. Dunn (Eds.), *Children's sibling relationships* (pp. 71–82). Hillsdale, NJ: Erlbaum.

Falbo, T., & Poston, D. L., Jr. (1993). The academic, personality, and physical outcomes of only children in China. *Child Development, 64,* 18–35.

Falbo, T., Poston, D. L., Jr., Triscari, R. S., & Zhang, X. (1997). Self-enhancing illusions among Chinese schoolchildren. *Journal of Cross-Cultural Psychology, 28,* 172–191.

Falck-Ytter, T., Gredebäck, G., & von Hofsten, C. (2006). Infants predict other people's action goals. *Nature Neuroscience, 9,* 878–879.

Fantz, R. L. (1961). The origin of form perception. *Scientific American, 204,* 66–72.

Farmer, T. W., Leung, M., Pearl, R., Rodkin, P. C., Cadwallader, T. W., & Van Acker, R. (2002). Deviant or diverse peer groups? The peer affiliations of aggressive elementary students. *Journal of Educational Psychology, 94,* 611–620.

Farrant, K., & Reese, E. (2000). Maternal style and children's `participation in reminiscing: Stepping stones in children's autobiographical memory development. *Journal of Cognition and Development, 1,* 193–225.

Farrington, D. P. (2004). Conduct disorder, aggression, and delinquency. In R. M. Lerner & L. Steinberg (Eds.), *Handbook of adolescent psychology* (2nd ed., pp. 627–664). New York: Wiley.

Farrington, D. P., & Loeber, R. (2000). Epidemiology of juvenile violence. *Juvenile Violence, 9,* 733–748.

Farroni, T., Csibra, G., Simion, F., & Johnson, M. H. (2002). Eye contact detection in humans from birth. *Proceedings of the*

National Academy of Sciences, 99, 9602–9605.

Farroni, T., Massaccesi, S., Menon, E., & Johnson, M. H. (2007). Direct gaze modulates face recognition in young infants. *Cognition, 102,* 396–404.

Farver, J. M., & Branstetter, W. H. (1994). Preschoolers' prosocial responses to their peers' distress. *Developmental Psychology, 30,* 334–341.

Farver, J. M., & Wimbarti, S. (1995a). Indonesian toddlers' social play with their mothers and older siblings. *Child Development, 66,* 1493–1503.

Farver, J. M., & Wimbarti, S. (1995b). Paternal participation in toddlers' pretend play. *Social Development, 4,* 19–31.

Farver, J. M., Kim, Y. K., & Lee, Y. (1995). Cultural differences in Korean- and Anglo-American preschoolers' social interaction and play behaviors. *Child Development, 66,* 1088–1099.

Fasig, L. G. (2000). Toddlers' understanding of ownership: Implications for self-concept development. *Social Development, 9,* 370–382.

Fattibene, P., Mazzei, R., Nuccetelli, C., & Risica, S. (1999). Prenatal exposure to ionizing radiation: Sources, effects, and regulatory aspects. *Acta Paediatrica, 88,* 693–702.

Fearon, R. M. P., van IJzendoorn, M. H., Fonagy, P., Bakermans-Kranenburg, M. J., Schuengel, C., & Bokhorst, C. L. (2006). In search of shared and nonshared environmental factors in security of attachment: A behavior-genetic study of the association between sensitivity and attachment security. *Developmental Psychology, 42,* 1026–1040.

Federal Interagency Forum on Child and Family Statistics. (2006). *Family structure and children's living arrangements.* Retrieved from www.childstats.gov/americaschildren06/tables/pop6b.asp

Federal Interagency Forum on Child and Family Statistics. (2007). *America's children: Key national indicators of well-being, 2007.* Retrieved from www.childstats.gov/americaschildren/tables.asp

Federenko, I. S., & Wadhwa, P. D. (2004). Women's mental health during pregnancy influences fetal and infant developmental and health outcomes. *CNS Spectrums, 9,* 198–206.

Fee, E. J. (1997). The prosodic framework for language learning. *Topics in Language Disorders, 17,* 53–62.

Feeney, J. A., Hohaus, L., Noller, P., & Alexander, R. P. (2001). *Becoming parents: Exploring the bonds between mothers, fathers, and their infants.* New York: Cambridge University Press.

Feinberg, M. E., & Hetherington, E. M. (2001). Differential parenting as a within-family variable. *Journal of Family Psychology, 51,* 22–37.

Feinberg, M. E., McHale, S. M., Crouter, A. C., & Cumsille, P. (2003). Sibling differentiation: Sibling and parent relationship trajectories in adolescence. *Child Development, 74,* 1261–1274.

Feingold, A. (1994). Gender differences in personality: A meta-analysis. *Psychological Bulletin, 116,* 429–456.

Feldman, A. F., & Matjasko, J. L. (2007). Profiles and portfolios of adolescent school-based extracurricular activity participation. *Journal of Adolescence, 30,* 313–332.

Feldman, D. H. (2004). Child prodigies: A distinctive form of giftedness. In R. J. Sternberg (Ed.), *Definitions and conceptions of giftedness* (pp. 133–144). Thousand Oaks, CA: Corwin Press.

Feldman, R. (2002). Parents' convergence on sharing and marital satisfaction, father involvement, and parent–child relationship in the transition to parenthood. *Infant Mental Health Journal, 21,* 176–191.

Feldman, R. (2003). Infant–mother and infant–father synchrony: The coregulation of positive arousal. *Infant Mental Health Journal, 24,* 1–23.

Feldman, R. (2006). From biological rhythms to social rhythms: Physiological precursors of mother–infant synchrony. *Developmental Psychology, 42,* 175–188.

Feldman, R. (2007a). Maternal versus child risk and the development of parent–child and family relationships in five high-risk populations. *Development and Psychopathology, 19,* 293–312.

Feldman, R. (2007b). Parent–infant synchrony and the construction of shared timing; Physiological precursors, developmental outcomes, and risk conditions. *Journal of Child Psychology and Psychiatry, 48,* 329–354.

Feldman, R., & Eidelman, A. I. (2003). Skin-to-skin contact (kangaroo care) accelerates autonomic and neurobehavioral maturation in preterm infants. *Developmental Medicine and Child Neurology, 45,* 274–281.

Feldman, R., Eidelman, A., Sirota, L., & Weller, A. (2002). Comparison of skin-to-skin (kangaroo) and traditional care: Parenting outcomes and preterm infant development. *Pediatrics, 110,* 16–26.

Feldman, R., Greenbaum, C. W., & Yirmiya, N. (1999). Mother–infant affect synchrony as an antecedent of the emergence of self-control. *Developmental Psychology, 35,* 223–231.

Feldman, R., & Klein, P. S. (2003). Toddlers' self-regulated compliance to mothers, caregivers, and fathers: Implications for theories of socialization. *Developmental Psychology, 39,* 680–692.

Feldman, R., Sussman, A. L., & Zigler, E. (2004). Parental leave and work adaptation at the transition to parenthood: Individual, marital, and social correlates. *Journal of Applied Developmental Psychology, 25,* 459–479.

Feldman, R., Weller, A., Sirota, L., & Eidelman, A. I. (2003). Testing a family intervention hypothesis: The contribution of mother–infant skin-to-skin contact (kangaroo care) to family interaction, proximity, and touch. *Journal of Family Psychology, 17,* 94–107.

Felix, E. D., & McMahon, S. D. (2006). Gender and multiple forms of peer victimization: How do they influence adolescent psychosocial adjustment? *Violence and Victims, 21,* 707–724.

Felner, R. D., Favazza, A., Shim, M., Brand, S., Gu, K., & Noonan, N. (2002). Whole school improvement and restructuring as prevention and promotion: Lessons from STEP and the Project on High Performance Learning Communities. *Journal of School Psychology, 39,* 177–202.

Felsman, D. E., & Blustein, D. L. (1999). The role of peer relatedness in late adolescent career development. *Journal of Vocational Behavior, 54,* 279–295.

Feng, Q. (2005). Postnatal consequences of prenatal cocaine exposure and myocardial apoptosis: Does cocaine in utero imperil the adult heart? *British Journal of Pharmacology, 144,* 887–888.

Fennell, C. T., & Werker, J. F. (2003). Early word learners' ability to access phonetic detail in well-known words. *Language and Speech, 46,* 245–264.

Fennema, E., Carpenter, T. P., Jacobs, V. R., Franke, M. L., & Levi, L. W. (1998). A longitudinal study of gender differences in young children's mathematical thinking. *Educational Researcher, 27,* 6–11.

Fenson, L., Dale, P. S., Reznick, J. S., Bates, E., Thal, D. J., & Pethick, S. J. (1994). Variability in early communicative development. *Monographs of the Society for Research in Child Development, 59*(5, Serial No. 242).

Ferguson, B., Tilleczek, K., Boydell, K., Rummens, J., Edney, D., Michaud, J., & the Community Health Systems Resource Group, The Hospital for Sick Children. (2005). *Early School Leavers: Understanding the Lived Reality of Student Disengagement from Secondary School: Final Report.* Ontario Ministry of Education and Training, Special Education Branch. Toronto, Canada. Retrieved from www.edu.gov.on.ca/eng/parents/schoolleavers.pdf

Ferguson, R. F. (1998). Teachers' perceptions and expectations and the black–white test score gap. In C. Jencks & M. Phillips (Eds.), *The black–white test score gap* (pp. 273–317). Washington, DC: Brookings Institution.

Ferguson, T. J., Stegge, H., & Damhuis, I. (1991). Children's understanding of guilt and shame. *Child Development, 62,* 827–839.

Fergusson, D. M., & Horwood, J. (2003). Resilience to childhood adversity: Results of a 21-year study. In S. S. Luthar (Ed.), *Resilience and vulnerability* (pp. 130–155). New York: Cambridge University Press.

Fergusson, D. M., Horwood, L. J., & Ridder, E. M. (2005). Show me the child at seven II: Childhood intelligence and later outcomes in adolescence and young adulthood. *Journal of Child Psychology and Psychiatry, 46,* 850–858.

Fergusson, D. M., & Woodward, L. J. (1999). Breast-feeding and later psychosocial adjustment. *Paediatric and Perinatal Epidemiology, 13,* 144–157.

Fergusson, D. M., Woodward, L. J., & Horwood, L. J. (2000). Risk factors and life processes associated with the onset of suicidal behaviour during adolescence and early adulthood. *Psychological Medicine, 30,* 23–39.

Fernald, A., & Hurtado, N. (2006). Names in frames: Infants interpret words in sentence frames faster than words in isolation. *Developmental Science, 9,* F33–F40.

Fernald, A., & Morikawa, H. (1993). Common themes and cultural variations in Japanese and American mothers' speech to infants. *Child Development, 64,* 637–656.

Fernald, A., Perfors, A., & Marchman, V. A. (2006). Picking up speed in understanding: Speech processing efficiency and vocabulary growth across the 2nd year. *Developmental Psychology, 42,* 98–116.

Fernald, A., Swingley, D., & Pinto, J. P. (2001). When half a word is enough: Infants can recognize spoken words using partial phonetic information. *Child Development, 72,* 1003–1015.

Fernald, A., Taeschner, T., Dunn, J., Papousek, M., Boysson-Bardies, B., & Fukui, I. (1989). A cross-language study of prosodic modifications in mothers' and fathers' speech to preverbal infants. *Journal of Child Language, 16,* 477–502.

Fernald, L. C., & Grantham-McGregor, S. M. (1998). Stress response in school-age children who have been growth-retarded since early childhood. *American Journal of Clinical Nutrition, 68,* 691–698.

Fernyhough, C., & Fradley, E. (2005). Private speech on an executive task: Relations with task difficulty and task performance. *Cognitive Development, 20,* 103–120.

Ficca, G., Fagioli, I., Giganti, F., & Salzarulo, P. (1999). Spontaneous awakenings from sleep in the first year of life. *Early Human Development, 55,* 219–228.

Field, T. (1998). Massage therapy effects. *American Psychologist, 53,* 1270–1281.

Field, T. (2001). Massage therapy facilitates weight gain in preterm infants. *Current Directions in Psychological Science, 10,* 51–54.

Field, T., Diego, M., Hernandez-Reif, M., Figueiredo, B., Schanberg, S., & Kuhn, C. (2007). Sleep disturbances in depressed pregnant women and their newborns. *Infant Behavior and Development, 30,* 127–133.

Field, T., Hernandez-Reif, M., Feijo, L., & Freedman, J. (2006). Prenatal, perinatal and neonatal stimulation: A survey of neonatal nurseries. *Infant Behavior and Development, 29,* 24–31.

Field, T., Hernandez-Reif, M., & Freedman, J. (2004). Stimulation programs for preterm infants. *Social Policy Report of the Society for Research in Child Development, 18*(1).

Fingerhut, L. A., & Christoffel, K. K. (2002). Firearm-related death and injury among children and adolescents. *Future of Children, 12,* 25–37.

Finkel, D., & Pedersen, N. L. (2001). Sources of environmental influence on cognitive abilities in adulthood. In E. L. Grigorenko & R. J. Sternberg (Eds.), *Family environment and intellectual functioning: A life-span perspective* (pp. 173–194). Mahwah, NJ: Erlbaum.

Finn, J. D., Gerber, S. B., & Boyd-Zaharias, J. (2005). Small classes in the early grades, academic achievement, and graduating from high school. *Journal of Educational Psychology, 97,* 214–233.

Finnilä, K., Mahlberga, N., Santtilia, P., & Niemib, P. (2003). Validity of a test of children's suggestibility for predicting responses to two interview situations differing in degree of suggestiveness. *Journal of Experimental Child Psychology, 85,* 32–49.

Fisch, H., Hyun, G., Golden, R., Hensle, T. W., Olsson, C. A., & Liberson, G. L. (2003). The influence of paternal age on Down syndrome. *Journal of Urology, 169,* 2275–2278.

Fisch, S. M., Truglio, R. T., & Cole, C. (1999). The impact of Sesame Street on preschool children: A review and synthesis of 30 years' research. *Media Psychology, 1,* 165–190.

Fischer, K., & Bidell, T. (1991). Constraining nativist inferences about cognitive capacities. In S. Carey & R. Gelman (Eds.), *The epigenesis of mind: Essays on biology and cognition* (pp. 199–235). Hillsdale, NJ: Erlbaum.

Fischer, K. W., & Bidell, T. R. (2006). Dynamic development of action and thought. In R. M. Lerner (Ed.), *Handbook of child psychology: Vol. 1. Theoretical models of human development* (6th ed., pp. 313–399). Hoboken, NJ: Wiley.

Fischman, M. G., Moore, J. B., & Steele, K. H. (1992). Children's one-hand catching as a function of age, gender, and ball location. *Research Quarterly for Exercise and Sport, 63,* 349–355.

Fish, J. M. (2002). *Race and intelligence: Separating science from myth.* Mahwah, NJ: Erlbaum.

Fish, M. (2004). Attachment in infancy and preschool in low socioeconomic status rural Appalachian children: Stability and change and relations to preschool and kindergarten competence. *Development and Psychopathology, 16,* 293–312.

Fisher, C. B. (1993, Winter). Integrating science and ethics in research with high-risk children and youth. *Social Policy Report of the Society for Research in Child Development, 4*(4).

Fisher, C. B. (2005). Deception research involving children: Ethical practices and paradoxes. *Ethics & Behavior, 15,* 271–287.

Fisher, J. O., Mitchell, D. S., Smiciklas-Wright, H., & Birch, L. L. (2001). Maternal milk consumption predicts the tradeoff between milk and soft drinks in young girls' diets. *Journal of Nutrition, 131,* 246–250.

Fisher, L., Ames, E., Chisholm, K., & Savoie, L. (1997). Problems reported by parents of Romanian orphans adopted to British Columbia. *International Journal of Behavioral Development, 20,* 67–82.

Fisher, M., Barkley, R. A., Smallish, L., & Fletcher, K. (2002). Young adult follow-up of hyperactive children: Self-reported psychiatric disorders, comorbidity, and the role of childhood conduct problems and teen CD. *Journal of Abnormal Child Psychology, 39,* 463–475.

Fisher, P. A., Gunnar, M. R., Chamberlain, P., & Reid, J. B. (2000). Preventive intervention for maltreated preschool children: Impact on children's behavior, neuroendocrine activity, and foster parent functioning. *Journal of the American Academy of Child and Adolescent Psychiatry, 39,* 1356–1364.

FitzGerald, D. P., & White, K. J. (2003). Linking children's social worlds: Perspective-taking in parent–child and peer contexts. *Social Behavior and Personality, 31,* 509–522.

Fivush, R. (1998). Children's recollections of traumatic and nontraumatic events. *Development and Psychopathology, 10,* 699–716.

Fivush, R. (2001). Owning experience: Developing subjective perspective in autobiographical narratives. In C. Moore & K. Lemmon (Eds.), *The self in time: Developmental perspectives* (pp. 35–52). Mahwah, NJ: Erlbaum.

Fivush, R. (2006). Scripting attachment: Generalized event representations and internal working models. *Attachment and Human Development, 8,* 283–289.

Fivush, R., & Haden, C. A. (2005). Parent–child reminiscing and the construction of a subjective self. In B. D. Homer & C. S. Tamis-LeMonda (Eds.), *The development of social cognition and communication* (pp. 315–336). Mahwah, NJ: Erlbaum.

Fivush, R., & Reese, E. (2002). Reminiscing and relating: The development of parent–child talk about the past. In J. D. Webster & B. K. Haight (Eds.), *Critical advances in reminiscence work: From theory to application* (pp. 109–122). New York: Springer.

Fivush, R., & Wang, Q. (2005). Emotion talk in mother–child conversations of the shared past: The effects of culture, gender, and event valence. *Journal of Cognition and Development, 6,* 489–506.

Flake, A. W. (2003). Surgery in the human fetus: The future. *Journal of Physiology, 547,* 45–51.

Flaks, D. K., Ficher, I., Masterpasqua, F., & Joseph, G. (1995). Lesbians choosing motherhood: A comparative study of lesbian and heterosexual parents and their children. *Developmental Psychology, 31,* 105–114.

Flanagan, C. A., & Faison, N. (2001). Youth civic development: Implications of research for social policy and programs. *Social Policy Report of the Society for Research in Child Development, 15*(1).

Flanagan, C. A., & Tucker, C. J. (1999). Adolescents' explanations for political issues: Concordance with their views of self and society. *Developmental Psychology, 35,* 1198–1209.

Flannery, D. J., Hussey, D. L., Biebelhausen, L., & Wester, K. L. (2003). Crime, delinquency, and youth gangs. In G. R. Adams & M. D. Berzonsky (Eds.), *Blackwell handbook of adolescence* (pp. 502–522). Malden, MA: Blackwell.

Flannery, K. A., & Liederman, J. (1995). Is there really a syndrome involving the co-occurrence of neurodevelopmental disorder, talent, nonright handedness and immune disorder among children? *Cortex, 31,* 503–515.

Flavell, J. H. (2000). Development of children's knowledge about the mental world. *International Journal of Behavioral Development, 24,* 15–23.

Flavell, J. H., Flavell, E. R., Green, F. L., & Korfmacher, J. E. (1990). Do young children think of television images as pictures or real objects? *Journal of Broadcasting and Electronic Media, 34,* 399–419.

Flavell, J. H., Green, F. L., & Flavell, E. R. (1987). Development of knowledge about the appearance–reality distinction. *Monographs of the Society for Research in Child Development, 51*(1, Serial No. 212).

Flavell, J. H., Green, F. L., & Flavell, E. R. (1993). Children's understanding of the stream of consciousness. *Child Development, 64,* 387–398.

Flavell, J. H., Green, F. L., & Flavell, E. R. (1995). Young children's knowledge about thinking. *Monographs of the Society for Research in Child Development, 60*(1, Serial No. 243).

Flavell, J. H., Green, F. L., & Flavell, E. R. (2000). Development of children's awareness of their own thoughts. *Journal of Cognition and Development, 1,* 97–112.

Flavell, J. H., Miller, P. H., & Miller, S. A. (2002). *Cognitive development* (4th ed.). Upper Saddle River, NJ: Prentice Hall.

Flege, J. E., Birdsong, D., Bialystok, E., Mack, M., Sung, H., & Tsukada, K. (2006). Degree of foreign accent in English sentences produced by Korean children and adults. *Journal of Phonetics, 34,* 153–175.

Flege, J. E., Yeni-Komshian, G. H., & Liu, S. (1999). Age constraints on second-language acquisition. *Journal of Memory and Language, 41,* 78–104.

Fleming, V., M., & Alexander, J. M. (2001). The benefits of peer collaboration: A replication with a delayed posttest. *Contemporary Educational Psychology, 26,* 588–601.

Floccia, C., Christophe, A., & Bertoncini, J. (1997). High-amplitude sucking and newborns: The quest for underlying mechanisms. *Journal of Experimental Child Psychology, 64,* 175–198.

Flom, R., & Pick, A. D. (2003). Verbal encouragement and joint attention in 18-month-old infants. *Infant Behavior and Development, 26,* 121–134.

Florian, V., & Kravetz, S. (1985). Children's concepts of death: A cross-cultural comparison among Muslims, Druze, Christians, and Jews in Israel. *Journal of Cross-Cultural Psychology, 16,* 174–179.

Flouri, E., & Buchanan, A. (2004). Early father's and mother's involvement and child's later educational outcomes. *British Journal of Educational Psychology, 74,* 141–153.

Flynn, E. (2006). A microgenetic investigation of stability and continuity in theory of mind development. *British Journal of Developmental Psychology, 24,* 631–654.

Flynn, J. R. (1994). IQ gains over time. In R. J. Sternberg (Ed.), *The encyclopedia of human intelligence* (pp. 617–623). New York: Macmillan.

Flynn, J. R. (1999). Searching for justice: The discovery of IQ gains over time. *American Psychologist, 54,* 5–20.

Flynn, J. R. (2003). Movies about intelligence: The limitations of *g. Current Directions in Psychological Science, 12,* 95–99.

Flynn, J. R. (2007). *What is intelligence? Beyond the Flynn effect.* New York: Cambridge University Press.

Flynn, J. R., & Weiss, L. G. (2007). American IQ gains from 1932 to 2002: The WISC subtests and educational progress. *International Journal of Testing, 7,* 209–224.

Fogel, A., & Garvey, A. (2007). Alive communication. *Infant Behavior and Development, 30,* 251–257.

Fogel, A., Melson, G. F., Toda, S., & Mistry, T. (1987). Young children's responses to unfamiliar infants. *International Journal of Behavioral Development, 10,* 1071–1077.

Fomon, S. J., & Nelson, S. E. (2002). Body composition of the male and female reference infants. *Annual Review of Nutrition, 22,* 1–17.

Fonzi, A., Schneider, B. H., Tani, F., & Tomada, G. (1997). Predicting children's friendship status from their dyadic interaction in structured situations of potential conflict. *Child Development, 68,* 496–506.

Fordham, K., & Stevenson-Hinde, J. (1999). Shyness, friendship quality, and adjustment during middle childhood. *Journal of Child Psychology and Psychiatry, 40,* 757–768.

Forgatch, M. S., & DeGarmo, D. S. (1999). Parenting through change: An effective prevention program for single mothers. *Journal of Consulting and Clinical Psychology, 67,* 711–724.

Forman, D. R., Aksan, N., & Kochanska, G. (2004). Toddlers' responsive imitation predicts preschool-age conscience. *Psychological Science, 15,* 699–704.

Forman, D. R., O'Hara, M. W., Larsen, K., Coy, K. C., Gorman, L. L., & Stewart, S. (2003). Infant emotionality: Observational methods and the validity of maternal reports. *Infancy, 4,* 541–565.

Forman, D. R., O'Hara, M. W., Stuart, S., Gorman, L. L., Larsen, K. E., & Coy, K. C. (2007). Effective treatment for postpartum depression is not sufficient to improve the developing mother–child relationship. *Development and Psychopathology, 19,* 585–602.

Foster, M. A., Lambert, R., Abbott-Shim, M., McCarty, F., & Franze, S. (2005). A model of home learning environment and social risk factors in relation to children's emergent literacy and social outcomes. *Early Childhood Research Quarterly, 20,* 13–36.

Foster, W. A., & Miller, M. (2007). Development of the literacy achievement gap: A longitudinal study of kindergarten through third grade. *Language, Speech, and Hearing Services in Schools, 38,* 173–181.

Fowden, A. L., Giussani, D. A., & Forhead, A. J. (2005). Endocrine and metabolic programming during intrauterine development. *Early Human Development, 81,* 723–734.

Fowles, D. C., & Kochanska, G. (2000). Temperament as a moderator of pathways to conscience in children: The contribution of electrodermal activity. *Psychophysiology, 37,* 788–795.

Fox, C. L., & Boulton, M. J. (2006). Friendship as a moderator of the relationship between social skills problems and peer victimization. *Aggressive Behavior, 32,* 110–121.

Fox, N. A. (1991). If it's not left, it's right: Electroencephalograph asymmetry and the development of emotion. *American Psychologist, 46,* 863–872.

Fox, N. A., & Calkins, S. D. (2003). The development of self-control of emotion: Intrinsic and extrinsic influences. *Motivation and Emotion, 27,* 7–26.

Fox, N. A., & Card, J. A. (1998). Psychophysiological measures in the study of attachment. In J. Cassidy & P. Shaver (Eds.), *Handbook of attachment: Theory, research, and clinical applications* (pp. 226–245). New York: Guilford.

Fox, N. A., & Davidson, R. J. (1986). Taste-elicited changes in facial signs of emotion and the asymmetry of brain electrical activity in newborn infants. *Neuropsychologia, 24,* 417–422.

Foy, J. G., & Mann, V. (2003). Home literacy environment and phonological awareness in preschool children: Differential effects for rhyme and phoneme awareness. *Applied Psycholinguistics, 24,* 59–88.

Franco, P., Chabanski, S., Szliwowski, H., Dramaiz, M., & Kahn, A. (2000). Influence of maternal smoking on autonomic nervous system in healthy infants. *Pediatric Research, 47,* 215–220.

Franco, P., Danias, A. P., Akamine, E. H., Kawamoto, E. M., Fortes, Z. B., Scavone, C., & Tostes, R. C. (2002). Enhanced oxidative stress as a potential mechanism underlying the programming of hypertension in utero. *Journal of Cardiovascular Pharmacology, 40,* 501–509.

Frank, D. A., Rose-Jacobs, R., Beeghly, M., Wilbur, M., Bellinger, D., & Cabral, H. (2005). Level of prenatal cocaine exposure and 48-month IQ: Importance of preschool enrichment. *Neurotoxicology and Teratology, 27,* 15–28.

Frankenberg, E., Lee, C., & Orfield, G. (2003). *A multiracial society with segregated schools: Are we losing the dream?* Cambridge, MA: The Civil Rights Project, Harvard University.

Fraser, M. W., Galinsky, M. J., Smokowski, P. R., Day, S. H., Terzian, M. A., Rose, R. A., & Guo, S. (2005). Social information-processing skills training to promote social competence and prevent aggressive behavior in third grade. *Journal of Consulting and Clinical Psychology, 73,* 1045–1055.

Frederiksen-Goldsen, K. I., & Sharlach, A. E. (2000). *Families and work: New directions in the twenty-first century.* New York: Oxford University Press.

Fredricks, J. A., & Eccles, J. S. (2002). Children's competence and value beliefs from childhood through adolescence: Growth trajectories in two male-sex-typed domains. *Developmental Psychology, 38,* 519–533.

Fredricks, J. A., & Eccles, J. S. (2005). Developmental benefits of extracurricular involvement: Do peer characteristics mediate the link between activities and youth outcomes? *Journal of Youth and Adolescence, 34,* 507–520.

Fredricks, J. A., & Eccles, J. S. (2006). Is extracurricular participation associated with beneficial outcomes? Concurrent and longitudinal relations. *Developmental Psychology, 42,* 698–713.

Freedman-Doan, C., Wigfield, A., Eccles, J. S., Blumenfeld, P., Arbreton, A., & Harold, R. D. (2000). What am I best at? Grade and gender differences in children's beliefs about ability improvement. *Journal of Applied Developmental Psychology, 21,* 379–402.

Freeman, D. (1983). *Margaret Mead and Samoa: The making and unmaking of an anthropological myth.* Cambridge, MA: Harvard University Press.

French, S. A., Story, M., & Jeffrey, R. W. (2001). Environmental influences on eating and physical activity. *Annual Review of Public Health, 22,* 309–335.

Freud, A., & Dann, S. (1951). An experiment in group upbringing. *Psychoanalytic Study of the Child, 6,* 127–168.

Freud, S. (1961). Some psychological consequences of the anatomical distinction between the sexes. In J. Strachey (Ed.), *Standard edition of the complete psychological works of Sigmund Freud* (Vol. 19, pp. 248–258). London: Hogarth Press. (Original work published 1925)

Freud, S. (1973). *An outline of psychoanalysis.* London: Hogarth. (Original work published 1938)

Freud, S. (1974). *The ego and the id.* London: Hogarth. (Original work published 1923)

Fried, P. A. (1993). Prenatal exposure to tobacco and marijuana: Effects during pregnancy, infancy, and early childhood. *Clinical Obstetrics and Gynecology, 36,* 319–337.

Fried, P. A., Watkinson, B., & Gray, R. (2003). Differential effects on cognitive functioning in 13- to 16-year-olds prenatally exposed to cigarettes and marijuana. *Neurotoxicology and Teratology, 25* 427–436.

Friedman, J. M. (1996). *The effects of drugs on the fetus and nursing infant: A handbook for health care professionals.* Baltimore: Johns Hopkins University Press.

Friedman, J. M. (2006). *The effects of drugs on the fetus and nursing infant: A handbook for health care professionals.* Baltimore: Johns Hopkins University Press.

Friedrich, M., & Friederici, A. D. (2005). Phonotactic knowledge and lexical–semantic processing in one-year-olds: Brain responses to words and nonsense words in picture contexts. *Journal of Cognitive Neuroscience, 17,* 1785–1802.

Frijda, N. (2000). The psychologist's point of view. In M. Lewis & J. M. Haviland-Jones (Eds.), *Handbook of emotions* (pp. 59–74). New York: Guilford.

Frith, L. (2001). Gamete donation and anonymity: The ethical and legal debate. *Human Reproduction, 16,* 818–824.

Frith, U. (2003). *Autism: Explaining the enigma* (2nd ed.). Malden, MA: Blackwell.

Frith, U., & Happé, F. (1994). Autism: Beyond "theory of mind." *Cognition, 50,* 115–132.

Fry, A. F., & Hale, S. (1996). Processing speed, working memory, and fluid intelligence: Evidence for a developmental cascade. *Psychological Science, 7,* 237–241.

Fu, G., Xu, F., Cameron, C. A., Heyman, G., & Lee, K. (2007). Cross-cultural differences in children's choices, categorizations, and evaluations of truths and lies. *Developmental Psychology, 43,* 278–293.

Fuchs, I., Eisenberg, N., Hertz-Lazarowitz, R., & Sharabany, R. (1986). Kibbutz, Israeli city, and American children's moral reasoning about prosocial moral conflicts. *Merrill-Palmer Quarterly, 32,* 37–50.

Fuchs, L. S., Fuchs, D., Mathes, P. G., Martinez, E. A. (2002a). Preliminary evidence on the standing of students with learning disabilities in PALS and No-PALS classrooms. *Learning Disabilities Research and Practice, 17,* 205–215.

Fuchs, L. S., Fuchs, D., Yazkian, L., & Powell, S. R. (2002b). Enhancing first-grade children's mathematical development with peer-assisted learning strategies. *School Psychology Review, 31,* 569–583.

Fulhan, J., Collier, S., & Duggan, C. (2003). Update on pediatric nutrition: Breastfeeding, infant nutrition, and growth. *Current Opinion in Pediatrics, 15,* 323–332.

Fuligni, A. J. (1998). Authority, autonomy, and parent–adolescent conflict and cohesion: A study of adolescents from Mexican, Chinese, Filipino, and European backgrounds. *Developmental Psychology, 34,* 782–792.

Fuligni, A. J. (2004). The adaptation and acculturation of children from immigrant families. In U. P. Gielen & J. Roopnarine (Eds.), *Childhood and adolescence: Cross-cultural perspectives* (pp. 297–318). Westport, CT: Praeger.

Fuligni, A. J., & Yoshikawa, H. (2003). Socioeconomic resources, parenting, and child development among immigrant families. In M. H. Bornstein & R. H. Bradley (Eds.), *Socioeconomic status, parenting, ad child development* (pp. 107–124). Mahwah, NJ: Erlbaum.

Fuligni, A. J., Yip, T., & Tseng, V. (2002). The impact of family obligation on the daily activities and psychological well-being of Chinese-American adolescents. *Child Development, 73,* 302–314.

Fuligni, A. S., Han, W.-J., & Brooks-Gunn, J. (2004). The Infant-Toddler HOME in the 2nd and 3rd years of life. *Parenting: Science and Practice, 4,* 139–159.

Fuller, C., Keller, L., Olson, J., Plymale, A., & Gottesman, M. (2005). Helping preschoolers become healthy eaters. *Journal of Pediatric Health Care, 19,* 178–182.

Fullerton, J. T., Navarro, A. M., & Young, S. H. (2007). Outcomes of planned home birth: An integrative review. *Journal of Midwifery and Women's Health, 52,* 323–333.

Fung, H. (1999). Becoming a moral child: The socialization of shame among Chinese children. *Ethos, 27,* 180–209.

Furman, W., & Buhrmester, D. (1992). Age and sex differences in perceptions of networks of personal relationships. *Child Development, 63,* 103–115.

Furman, W., & Shaffer, L. (2003). The role of romantic relationships in adolescent development. In P. Florsheim (Ed.), *Adolescent romantic relations and sexual behavior* (pp. 3–22). Mahwah, NJ: Erlbaum.

Furman, W., Simon, V. A., Shaffer, L., & Bouchey, H. A. (2002). Adolescents' working models and styles for relationships with parents, friends, and romantic partners. *Child Development, 73,* 241–255.

Furrow, J. L., King, P. E., & White, K. (2004). Religion and positive youth development: Identity, meaning, and prosocial concerns. *Applied Developmental Science, 8,* 17–26.

Furstenberg, F. F., Jr., & Harris, K. M. (1993). When and why fathers matter: Impact of father involvement on children of adolescent mothers. In R. I. Lerman & T. J. Ooms (Eds.), *Young unwed fathers* (pp. 117–138). Philadelphia: Temple University Press.

Fuson, K. C., & Burghard, B. H. (2003). Multidigit addition and subtraction methods invented in small groups and teacher support of problem solving and reflection. In A. J. Baroody & A. Dowker (Eds.), *The development of arithmetic concepts and skills* (pp. 267–304). Mahwah, NJ: Erlbaum.

Galambos, N. L., Almeida, D. M., & Petersen, A. C. (1990). Masculinity, femininity, and sex role attitudes in early adolescence: Exploring gender intensification. *Child Development, 61,* 1904–1914.

Galambos, N. L., & Maggs, J. L. (1991). Children in self-care: Figures, facts, and fiction. In J. V. Lerner & N. L. Galambos (Eds.), *Employed mothers and their children* (pp. 131–157). New York: Garland.

Galen, B. R., & Underwood, M. K. (1997). A developmental investigation of social aggression among children. *Developmental Psychology, 33,* 589–600.

Galinsky, E. (2006). *The economic benefits of high-quality early childhood programs: What makes the difference?* Washington, DC: Committee for Economic Development.

Gallagher, A. M., & Kaufman, J. C. (2005). Gender differences in mathematics: What we know and what we need to know. In A. M. Gallagher & J. C. Kaufman (Eds.), *Gender differences in mathematics: An integrative psychological approach* (pp. 316–331). New York: Cambridge University Press.

Galler, J. R., Ramsey, C. F., Morley, D. S., Archer, E., & Salt, P. (1990). The long-term effects of early kwashiorkor compared with marasmus. IV. Performance on the National High School Entrance Examination. *Pediatric Research, 28,* 235–239.

Galloway, J., & Thelen, E. (2004). Feet first: Object exploration in young infants. *Infant Behavior and Development, 27,* 107–112.

Galton, F. (1883). *Inquiries into human faculty and its development.* London: Macmillan.

Ganger, J., & Brent, M. R. (2004). Reexamining the vocabulary spurt. *Developmental Psychology, 40,* 621–632.

Ganong, L. H., & Coleman, M. (1994). *Remarried family relationships.* Thousand Oaks, CA: Sage.

Gantz, W., Schwartz, N., Angelini, J., & Rideout, V. (2007). *Food for thought: Television food advertising to children in the United States.* Kaiser Family Foundation. Retrieved from www.kff.org/entmedia/7618.cfm

Garbarino, J., & Bedard, C. (2002). *Parents under siege: Why you are the solution and not the problem in your child's life.* New York: Touchstone

Garbarino, J., & Kostelny, K. (1993). Neighborhood and community influences on parenting. In T. Luster & L. Okagaki (1993), *Parenting: An ecological perspective* (pp. 203–226). Hillsdale, NJ: Erlbaum.

Garces, E., Thomas, D., & Currie, J. (2002). Longer-term effects of Head Start. *American Economic Review, 92,* 999–1012.

Garcia, M. M., Shaw, D. S., Winslow, E. B., & Yaggi, K. E. (2000). Destructive sibling conflict and the development of conduct problems in young boys. *Developmental Psychology, 36,* 44–53.

García-Coll, C., & Magnuson, K. (1997). The psychological experience of immigration: A developmental perspective. In A. Booth, A. C. Crouter, & N. Landale (Eds.), *Immigration and the family* (pp. 91–131). Mahwah, NJ: Erlbaum.

Gardner, H. (1980). *Artful scribbles: The significance of children's drawings.* New York: Basic Books.

Gardner, H. (1983). *Frames of mind.* New York: Basic Books.

Gardner, H. (1993). *Multiple intelligences: The theory in practice.* New York: Basic Books.

Gardner, H. E. (1998a). Are there additional intelligences? The case of the naturalist, spiritual, and existential intelligences. In J. Kane (Ed.), *Educational information and transformation.* Upper Saddle River, NJ: Prentice-Hall.

Gardner, H. E. (1998b). Extraordinary cognitive achievements (ECA): A symbol systems approach. In W. Damon & R. M. Lerner (Eds.), *Handbook of child psychology: Vol. 1. Theoretical models of human development* (5th ed., pp. 415–466). New York: Wiley.

Gardner, H. E. (2000). *Intelligence reframed: Multiple intelligences for the twenty-first century.* New York: Basic Books.

Garmezy, N. (1993). Children in poverty: Resilience despite risk. *Psychiatry, 56,* 127–136.

Garner, P. W. (1996). The relations of emotional role taking, affective/moral attributions, and emotional display rule knowledge to low-income school-age children's social competence. *Journal of Applied Developmental Psychology, 17,* 19–36.

Garner, P. W. (2003). Child and family correlates of toddlers' emotional and behavioral responses to a mishap. *Infant Mental Health Journal, 24,* 580–596.

Garner, P. W., & Estep, K. (2001). Emotional competence, emotion socialization, and young children's peer-related social competence. *Early Education and Development, 12,* 29–48.

Gartstein, M. A., & Rothbart, M. K. (2003). Studying infant temperament via the revised infant behavior questionnaire. *Infant Behavior and Development, 26,* 64–86.

Gartstein, M. A., Slobodskaya, H. R., & Kinsht, I. A. (2003). Cross-cultural differences in temperament in the first year of life: United States of America (U.S.) and Russia. *International Journal of Behavioral Development, 27,* 316–328.

Garven, S., Wood, J. M., & Malpass, R. S. (2000). Allegations of wrongdoing: The effects of reinforcement on children's mundane and fantastic claims. *Journal of Applied Psychology, 85,* 38–49.

Garvey, C. (1974). Requests and responses in children's speech. *Journal of Child Language, 2,* 41–60.

Gasden, V. (1999). Black families in intergenerational and cultural perspective. In M. E. Lamb (Ed.), *Parenting and child development in "nontraditional" families* (pp. 221–246). Mahwah, NJ: Erlbaum.

Gash, H., & Morgan, M. (1993). School-based modifications of children's gender-related beliefs. *Journal of Applied Developmental Psychology, 14,* 277–287.

Gaskins, S. (1999). Children's daily lives in a Mayan village: A case study of culturally constructed roles and activities. In R. Göncü (Ed.), *Children's engagement in the world: Sociocultural perspectives* (pp. 25–61). Cambridge, UK: Cambridge University Press.

Gaskins, S. (2000). Children's daily activities in a Mayan village: A culturally grounded description. *Cross-Cultural Research, 34,* 375–389.

Gaskins, S., Haight, W., & Lancy, D. F. (2007). The cultural construction of play. In A. Göncü & S. Gaskins (Eds.), *Play and development: Evolutionary, sociocultural, and functional perspectives* (pp. 179–202). Mahwah, NJ: Erlbaum.

Gathercole, S. E. (1995). Is nonword repetition a test of phonological memory or long-term knowledge? It all depends on the nonwords. *Memory and Cognition, 23,* 83–94.

Gathercole, S. E., Hitch, G. J., Service, E., & Martin, A. J. (1997). Phonological short-term memory and new word learning in children. *Developmental Psychology, 33,* 966–979.

Gathercole, S. E., Service, E., Hitch, G. J., Adams, A., & Martin, A. J. (1999). Phonological short-term memory and vocabulary development: Further evidence on the nature of the relationship. *Applied Cognitive Psychology, 13,* 65–77.

Gathercole, S. E., Tiffany, C., Briscoe, J., Thorn, A., & ALSPAC Team. (2005). Developmental consequences of poor phonological short-term memory function in childhood: A longitudinal study. *Journal of Child Psychology and Psychiatry, 46,* 598–611.

Gathercole, V., Sebastián, E., & Soto, P. (1999). The early acquisition of Spanish verbal morphology: Across-the-board or piecemeal knowledge? *International Journal of Bilingualism, 3,* 133–182.

Gaultney, J. F., & Gingras, J. L. (2005). Fetal rate of behavioral inhibition and preference for novelty during infancy. *Early Human Development, 81,* 379–386.

Gauvain, M. (2004). Bringing culture into relief: Cultural contributions to the development of children's planning skills. In R. V. Kail (Ed.), *Advances in child development and behavior* (pp. 39–71). San Diego, CA: Elsevier.

Gauvain, M., de la Ossa, J. L., & Hurtado-Ortiz, M. T. (2001). Parental guidance as children learn to use cultural tools: The case of pictorial plans. *Cognitive Development, 16,* 551–575.

Gauvain, M., & Huard, R. D. (1999). Family interaction, parenting style, and the development of planning: A longitudinal analysis using archival data. *Journal of Family Psychology, 13,* 75–92.

Gauvain, M., & Rogoff, B. (1989). Collaborative problem solving and children's planning skills. *Developmental Psychology, 25,* 139–151.

Gauze, C., Bukowski, W. M., Aquan-Assee, J., & Sippola, L. K. (1996). Interactions between family environment and friendship and associations with self-perceived well-being during early adolescence. *Child Development, 67,* 2201–2216.

Gazelle, H., & Rudolph, K. D. (2004). Moving toward and away from the world: Social approach and avoidance trajectories in anxious and solitary youth. *Child Development, 75,* 829–849.

Ge, X., Brody, G. H., Conger, R. D., Simons, R. L., & Murry, V. (2002). Contextual amplification of the effects of pubertal transition on African American children's deviant peer affiliation and externalized behavioral problems. *Developmental Psychology, 38,* 42–54.

Ge, X., Conger, R. D., & Elder, G. H., Jr. (1996). Coming of age too early: Pubertal influences on girls' vulnerability to psychological distress. *Child Development, 67,* 3386–3400.

Ge, X., Conger, R. D., & Elder, G. H., Jr. (2001a). Pubertal transition, stressful life events, and the emergence of gender differences in adolescent depressive symptoms. *Developmental Psychology, 37,* 404–417.

Ge, X., Conger, R. D., & Elder, G. H., Jr. (2001b). The relation between puberty and psychological distress in adolescent boys. *Journal of Research on Adolescence, 11,* 49–70.

Ge, X., Kim, I. J., Brody, G. H., Conger, R. D., & Simons, R. L. (2003). It's about timing and change: Pubertal transition effects on symptoms of major depression among African American youths. *Developmental Psychology, 39,* 430–439.

Geary, D. C. (1998). *Male, female: The evolution of human sex differences.* Washington, DC: American Psychological Association.

Geary, D. C. (1999). Evolution and developmental sex differences. *Current Directions in Psychological Science, 8,* 115–120.

Geary, D. C. (2000). Evolution and proximate expression of human paternal investment. *Psychological Bulletin, 126,* 55–77.

Geary, D. C. (2006a). Development of mathematical understanding. In D. Kuhn & R. Siegler (Eds.), *Handbook of child psychology: Vol. 2. Cognition, perception, and language* (pp. 777–810). Hoboken, NJ: Wiley.

Geary, D. C. (2006b). Evolutionary developmental psychology: Current status and future directions. *Developmental Review, 26,* 113–119.

Geary, D. C., & Bjorklund, D. F. (2000). Evolutionary developmental psychology. *Child Development, 71,* 57–65.

Geary, D. C., Saults, J. S., Liu, F., & Hoard, M. K. (2000). Sex differences in spatial cognition, computational fluency, and arithmetic reasoning. *Journal of Experimental Child Psychology, 77,* 337–353.

Gee, C. B., & Rhodes, J. E. (2003). Adolescent mothers' relationship with their children's biological fathers: Social support, social strain, and relationship continuity. *Journal of Family Psychology, 17,* 370–383.

Geerts, M., Steyaert, J., & Fryns, J. P. (2003). The XYY syndrome: A follow-up study on 38 boys. *Genetic Counseling, 14,* 267–279.

Gellin, B. G., Maibach, E. W., & Marcuse, E. K. (2000). Do parents understand immunizations? A national telephone survey. *Pediatrics, 106,* 1097–1102.

Gelman, R. (1972). Logical capacity of very young children: Number invariance rules. *Child Development, 43,* 75–90.

Gelman, R., & Koenig, M. A. (2003). Theory-based categorization in early childhood. In D. H. Rakison & L. M. Oakes (Eds.), *Early category and concept development* (pp. 330–359). New York: Oxford University Press.

Gelman, R., & Shatz, M. (1978). Appropriate speech adjustments: The operation of conversational constraints on talk to two-year-olds. In M. Lewis & L. A. Rosenblum (Eds.), *Interaction, conversation, and the development of language* (pp. 27–61). New York: Wiley.

Gelman, S. A. (2003). *The essential child.* New York: Oxford University Press.

Gelman, S. A., & Kalish, C. W. (2006). Conceptual development. In D. Kuhn & R. Siegler (Eds.), *Handbook of child psychology: Vol. 2. Cognition, perception, and language* (6th ed., pp. 687–733). Hoboken, NJ: Wiley.

Gelman, S. A., & Opfer, J. E. (2002). Development of the animate–inanimate distinction. In U. Goswami (Ed.), *Blackwell handbook of childhood cognitive development* (pp. 151–166). Malden, MA: Blackwell.

Gelman, S. A., Taylor, M. G., & Nguyen, S. P. (2004). Mother–child conversations about gender. *Monographs of the Society for Research in Child Development, 69*(1, Serial No. 275), pp. 1–127.

Genesee, F. (2001). Portrait of the bilingual child. In V. Cook (Ed.), *Portraits of the second language user.* Clevedon, UK: Multilingual Matters.

Genesee, F., & Nicoladis, E. (2007). Bilingual first language acquisition. In E. Hoff & M. Shatz (Eds.), *Blackwell handbook of language development* (pp. 324–342). Malden, MA: Blackwell.

Gennetian, L. A., & Morris, P. A. (2003). The effects of time limits and make-work-pay strategies on the well-being of children: Experimental evidence from two welfare reform programs. *Children and Youth Services Review, 25,* 17–54.

Gentner, D., & Namy, L. L. (2004). The role of comparison in children's early word learning. In D. G. Hall & S. R. Waxman (Eds.), *Weaving a lexicon* (pp. 533–568). Cambridge, MA: MIT Press.

Gerard, J. M., Krishnakumar, A., & Buehler, C. (2006). Marital conflict, parent–child relations, and youth maladjustment: A longitudinal investigation of spillover effects. *Journal of Family Issues, 27,* 951–975.

Gerardi-Caulton, G. (2000). Sensitivity to spatial conflict and the development of self-regulation in children 24–36 months of age. *Developmental Science, 3,* 397–404.

Gergely, G., Bekkering, H., & Király, I. (2003). Rational imitation in preverbal infants. *Nature, 415,* 755.

Gergely, G., & Watson, J. (1999). Early socio-emotional development: Contingency perception and the social-biofeedback model. In P. Rochat (Ed.), *Early social cognition: Understanding others in the first months of life* (pp. 101–136). Mahwah, NJ: Erlbaum.

Gergely, G., & Watson, J. S. (1996). The social biofeedback theory of parental affect-mirroring: The development of emotional self-awareness and self-control in infancy. *International Journal of Psychoanalysis, 77,* 1181–1212.

Gershoff, E. T. (2002a). Corporal punishment by parents and associated child behaviors and experiences: A meta-analytic and theoretical review. *Psychological Bulletin, 128,* 539–579.

Gershoff, E. T. (2002b). Corporal punishment, physical abuse, and the burden of proof: Reply to Baumrind, Larzelere, and Cowan (2002), Holden (2002), and Parke (2002). *Psychological Bulletin, 128,* 602–611.

Gershoff, E. T., & Aber, J. L. (2006). Neighborhoods and schools: Contexts and consequences for the mental health and risk behaviors of children and youth. In L. Balter & C. S. Tamis-LeMonda (Eds.), *Child psychology: A handbook of contemporary issues* (2nd ed., pp. 611–645). New York: Psychology Press.

Gershoff-Stowe, L., & Hahn, E. R. (2007). Fast mapping skills in the developing lexicon. *Journal of Speech, Language, and Hearing Research, 50,* 682–697.

Gershoff-Stowe, L., & Smith, L. B. (1997). A curvilinear trend in naming errors as a function of early vocabulary growth. *Cognitive Psychology, 34,* 37–71.

Gertner, S., Greenbaum, C. W., Sadeh, A., Dolfin, Z., Sirota, L., & Ben-Nun, Y. (2002). Sleep-wake patterns in preterm infants and 6 month's home environment: Implications for early cognitive development. *Early Human Development, 68,* 93–102.

Gertner, Y., Fisher, C., & Eisengart, J. (2006). Learning words and rules: Abstract knowledge of word order in early sentence comprehension. *Psychological Science, 17,* 684–691.

Gervai, J., Turner, P. J., & Hinde, R. A. (1995). Gender-related behaviour, attitudes, and personality in parents of young children in England and Hungary. *International Journal of Behavioral Development, 18,* 105–126.

Gesell, A. (1933). Maturation and patterning of behavior. In C. Murchison (Ed.), *A handbook of child psychology.* Worcester, MA: Clark University Press.

Gest, S. D., Domitrovich, C. E., & Welsh, J. A. (2005). Peer academic reputation in elementary school: Associations with changes in self-concept and academic skills. *Journal of Educational Psychology, 97,* 337–346.

Gest, S. D., Graham-Bermann, S. A., & Hartup, W. W. (2001). Peer experience: Common and unique features of number of friendships, social network centrality, and sociometric status. *Social Development, 10,* 23–40.

Gettinger, M., Doll, B., & Salmon, D. (1994). Effects of social problem solving, goal setting, and parent training on children's peer relations. *Journal of Applied Developmental Psychology, 15,* 141–163.

Geurts, H. M., Verte, S., Oosterlaan, J., Roeyers, H., Sergeant, J. A., & Geurts, H. M. (2004). How specific are executive functioning deficits in attention-deficit hyperactivity disorder and autism? *Journal of Child Psychology and Psychiatry, 45,* 836–854.

Ghera, M. M., Hane, A. A., Malesa, E. E., & Fox, N. A. (2006). The role of infant soothability in the relation between infant negativity and maternal sensitivity. *Infant Behavior and Development, 29,* 289–293.

Ghim, H. R. (1990). Evidence for perceptual organization in infants: Perception of subjective contours by young infants. *Infant Behavior and Development, 13,* 221–248.

Gibbons, A. (1998). Which of our genes make us human? *Science, 281,* 1432–1434.

Gibbons, R., Dugaiczyk, L. J., Girke, T., Duistermars, B., Zielinski, R., & Dugaiczyk, A. (2004). Distinguishing humans from great apes with AluYb8 repeats. *Journal of Molecular Biology, 339,* 721–729.

Gibbs, J. C. (1991). Toward an integration of Kohlberg's and Hoffman's theories of morality. In W. M. Kurtines & J. L. Gewirtz (Eds.), *Handbook of moral behavior and development* (Vol. 1, pp. 183–222). Hillsdale, NJ: Erlbaum.

Gibbs, J. C. (1995). The cognitive developmental perspective. In W. M. Kurtines & J. L. Gewirtz (Eds.), *Moral development: An introduction* (pp. 27–48). Boston: Allyn and Bacon.

Gibbs, J. C. (2004). Moral reasoning training. In A. P. Goldstein, R. Nensen, B. Daleflod, & M. Kalt (Eds.), *New perspectives on aggression replacement training* (pp. 51–72). West Sussex, UK: Wiley.

Gibbs, J. C. (2006). Should Kohlberg's cognitive developmental approach to morality be replaced with a more pragmatic approach? Comment on Krebs and Denton (2005). *Psychological Review, 113,* 666–671.

Gibbs, J. C. (2010). *Moral development and reality: Beyond the theories of Kohlberg and Hoffman* (2nd ed.). Boston: Pearson Allyn & Bacon.

Gibbs, J. C., Basinger, K. S., & Fuller, D. (1992). *Moral maturity: Measuring the development of sociomoral reflection.* Hillsdale, NJ: Erlbaum.

Gibbs, J. C., Basinger, K. S., & Grime, R. L. (2003). Moral judgment maturity: From clinical to standard measures. In S. J. Lopez & C. R. Snyder (Eds.), *Handbook of positive psychological assessment* (pp. 361–373). Washington, DC: American Psychological Association.

Gibbs, J. C., Basinger, K. S., Grime, R. L., & Snarey, J. R. (2007). Moral judgment development across cultures: Revisiting Kohlberg's universality claims. *Developmental Review, 24,* 443–500.

Gibbs, J. C., Potter, G. B., DiBiase, A.-M., & Devlin, R. (2009). The EQUIP program: Social perspective-taking for responsible thought and behavior. In B. Glick (Ed.), *Cognitive behavioral interventions for at-risk youth* (2nd ed.). Kingston, NJ: Civic Research Institute.

Gibson, E. J. (1970). The development of perception as an adaptive process. *American Scientist, 58,* 98–107.

Gibson, E. J. (2000). Perceptual learning in development: Some basic concepts. *Ecological Psychology, 12,* 295–302.

Gibson, E. J. (2003). The world is so full of a number of things: On specification and perceptual learning. *Ecological Psychology, 15,* 283–287.

Gibson, E. J., & Walk, R. D. (1960). The "visual cliff." *Scientific American, 202,* 64–71.

Gibson, J. J. (1979). *The ecological approach to visual perception.* Boston: Houghton Mifflin.

Gil, A. G., Wagner, E. F., & Vega, W. A. (2000). Acculturation, familism and alcohol use among Latino adolescent males: Longitudinal relations. *Journal of Community Psychology, 28,* 443–458.

Giles, J. W., & Heyman, G. D. (2005). Young children's beliefs about the relationship between gender and aggressive behavior. *Child Development, 76,* 107–121.

Gill, K. L., & Calkins, S. D. (2003). Do aggressive/destructive toddlers lack concern for others? Behavioral and physiological indicators of empathic responding in 2-year-old children. *Development and Psychopathology, 15,* 55–71.

Gillies, R. M. (2000). The maintenance of cooperative and helping behaviours in cooperative groups. *British Journal of Educational Psychology, 70,* 97–111.

Gillies, R. M. (2003). The behaviors, interactions, and perceptions of junior high school students during small-group learning. *Journal of Educational Psychology, 95,* 137–147.

Gillies, R. M., & Ashman, A. F. (1996). Teaching collaborative skills to primary school children in classroom-based workgroups. *Learning and Instruction, 6,* 187–200.

Gilligan, C. F. (1982). *In a different voice.* Cambridge, MA: Harvard University Press.

Gilliom, M., Shaw, D. S., Beck, J. E., Schonberg, M. A., & Lukon, J. L. (2002). Anger regulation in disadvantaged preschool boys: Strategies, antecedents, and the development of self-control. *Developmental Psychology, 38,* 222–235.

Gilstrap, L. L., & Ceci, S. J. (2005). Reconceptualizing children's suggestibility: Bidirectional and temporal properties. *Child Development, 76,* 40–53.

Gimenez, M., & Harris, P. L. (2002). Understanding constraints on inheritance: Evidence for biological thinking in early childhood. *British Journal of Developmental Psychology, 20,* 307–324.

Ginsburg, H. P. (1997). *Entering the child's mind: The clinical interview in psychological research and practice.* New York: Cambridge University Press.

Ginsburg-Block, M. D., Rohrbeck, C. A., & Fantuzzo, J. W. (2006). A meta-analytic review of social, self-concept, and behavioral outcomes of peer-assisted learning. *Journal of Educational Psychology, 98,* 732–749.

Glade, A. C., Bean, R. A., & Vira, R. (2005). A prime time for marital/relational intervention: A review of the transition to parenthood literature with treatment recommendations. *American Journal of Family Therapy, 33,* 319–336.

Gladstone, I. M., & Katz, V. L. (2004). The morbidity of the 34- to 35-week gestation: Should we reexamine the paradigm? *American Journal of Perinatology, 21,* 9–13.

Gleason, T. R. (2002). Social provisions of real and imaginary relationships in early childhood. *Developmental Psychology, 38,* 979–992.

Gleason, T. R., & Hohmann, L. M. (2006). Concepts of real and imaginary friendships in early childhood. *Social Development, 15,* 128–144.

Gleason, T. R., Sebanc, A. M., & Hartup, W. W. (2000). Imaginary companions of preschool children. *Developmental Psychology, 36,* 419–428.

Gleitman, L. R., Cassidy, K., Nappa, R., Papfragou, A., & Trueswell, J. C. (2005). Hard words. *Language Learning and Development, 1,* 23–64.

Gleitman, L., Gleitman, H., Landau, B., & Wanner, E. (1988). Where learning begins: Initial representations for language learning. In F. Newmeyer (Ed.), *Language: Psychological and biological aspects* (Vol. 3, pp. 150–193). Cambridge, UK: Cambridge University Press.

Glick, J. (1975). Cognitive development in cross-cultural perspective. In F. Horowitz (Ed.), *Review of child development research* (Vol. 4, pp. 595–654). Chicago: University of Chicago Press.

Glowinski, A. L., Madden, P. A. F., Bucholz, K. K., Lynskey, M. T., & Heath, A. C. (2003). Genetic epidemiology of self-reported lifetime DSM-IV major depressive disorder in a population-based twin sample of female adolescents. *Journal of Child Psychology and Psychiatry and Allied Disciplines, 44,* 988–996.

Gnepp, J. (1983). Children's social sensitivity: Inferring emotions from conflicting cues. *Developmental Psychology, 19,* 805–814.

Godart, N. T., Perdereau, F., Curt, F., Rein, Z., Lang, F., & Venisse, J. L. (2006). Is major depressive episode related to anxiety disorders in anorexics and bulimics? *Comprehensive Psychiatry, 47,* 91–98.

Godfrey, K. M., & Barker, D. J. (2000). Fetal nutrition and adult disease. *American Journal of Clinical Nutrition, 71,* 1344S–1352S.

Goelman, H. (1986). The language environments of family day care. In S. Kilmer (Ed.), *Advances in early education and day care* (Vol. 4, pp. 153–179). Greenwich, CT: JAI Press.

Goelman, H., Doherty, G., Lero, D. S., LaGrange, A., & Tougas, J. (2000). *You bet I care! Caring and learning environments: Quality in child care centres across Canada.* Guelph, ON: Centre for Families, Work and Well-Being, University of Guelph.

Goering, J. (Ed.). (2003). *Choosing a better life? How public housing tenants selected a HUD experiment to improve their lives and those of their children: The Moving to Opportunity Demonstration Program.* Washington, DC: Urban Institute Press.

Goetz, T., Frenzel, A. C., Pekrun, R., & Hall, N. (2005). Emotional intelligence in the context of learning and achievement. In R. Schulze & R. D. Roberts (Eds.), *Emotional intelligence: An international handbook* (pp. 233–253). Göttingen, Germany: Hogrefe & Huber.

Gogate, L. J., & Bahrick, L. E. (1998). Intersensory redundancy facilitates learning of arbitrary relations between vowel sounds and objects in seven-month-old infants. *Journal of Experimental Child Psychology, 69,* 133–149.

Gogate, L. J., & Bahrick, L. E. (2001). Intersensory redundancy and 7-month-old infants' memory for arbitrary syllable–object relations. *Infancy, 2,* 219–231.

Gogate, L. J., Bahrick, L. E., & Watson, J. D. (2000). A study of multimodal motherese: The role of temporal synchrony between verbal labels and gestures. *Child Development, 71,* 878–894.

Goldberg, A. E., & Perry-Jenkins, M. (2003). Division of labor and working-class women's well-being across the transition to parenthood. *Journal of Family Psychology, 18,* 225–236.

Goldberg, M. C., Maurer, D., & Lewis, T. L. (2001). Developmental changes in attention: The effects of endogenous cueing and of distracters. *Developmental Science, 4,* 209–219.

Goldberg, S., Benoit, D., Blokland, K., & Madigan, S. (2003). Atypical maternal behavior, maternal representations, and infant disorganized attachment. *Development and Psychopathology, 15,* 239–257.

Goldbloom, R. B. (2004). *Screening for hemoglobinopathies in Canada.* Hamilton, Ontario: McMaster University Medical Centre.

Goldenberg, C., Gallimore, R., Reese, L., & Garnier, H. (2001). Cause or effect? Immigrant Latino parents' aspirations and expectations, and their children's school performance. *American Educational Research Journal, 38,* 547–582.

Goldfield, B. A. (1987). The contributions of child and caregiver to referential and expressive language. *Applied Psycholinguistics, 8,* 267–280.

Goldfield, B. A. (2000). Nouns before verbs in comprehension vs. production: The view from pragmatics. *Journal of Child Language, 27,* 501–520.

Goldin-Meadow, S. (1999). The development of gesture with and without speech in hearing and deaf children. In L. S. Messing & R. Campbell (Eds.), *Gesture, speech, and sign* (pp. 117–132). New York: Oxford University Press.

Goldin-Meadow, S. (2002). Constructing communication by hand. *Cognitive Development, 17,* 1385–1405.

Goldin-Meadow, S. (2003a). *Hearing gesture: How our hands help us think.* Cambridge, MA: Harvard University Press.

Goldin-Meadow, S. (2003b). *The resilience of language.* New York: Psychology Press.

Goldin-Meadow, S. (2005a). Gesture in social interactions: A mechanism for cognitive change. In B. D. Homer & C. S. Tamis-LeMonda (Eds.), *The development of social cognition and communication* (pp. 259–283). Mahwah, NJ: Erlbaum.

Goldin-Meadow, S. (2005b). What language creation in the manual modality tells us about the foundations of language. *Linguistic Review, 22,* 199–225.

Goldin-Meadow, S. (2006a). Nonverbal communication: The hand's role in talking and thinking. In D. Kuhn & R. Siegler (Eds.), *Handbook of child psychology: Vol. 2. Cognition, perception, and language* (6th ed., pp. 336–369). Hoboken, NJ: Wiley.

Goldin-Meadow, S. (2006b). Talking and thinking with our hands. *Current Directions in Psychological Science, 15,* 34–39.

Goldin-Meadow, S., & Mylander, C. (1998). Spontaneous sign systems created by deaf children in two cultures. *Nature, 391,* 279–281.

Goldin-Meadow, S., Butcher, C., Mylander, C., & Dodge, M. (1994). Nouns and verbs in a self-styled gesture system: What's in a name? *Cognitive Psychology, 27,* 259–319.

Goldin-Meadow, S., Mylander, C., & Butcher, C. (1995). The resilience of combinatorial structure at the word level: Morphology in self-styled gesture systems. *Cognition, 56,* 88–96.

Goldin-Meadow, S., & Singer, M. A. (2003). From children's hands to adults' ears: Gesture's role in the learning process. *Developmental Psychology, 39,* 509–520.

Goldschmidt, L., Richardson, G. A., Cornelius, M. D., & Day, N. L. (2004). Prenatal marijuana and alcohol exposure and academic achievement at age 10. *Neurotoxicology and Teratology, 26,* 521–532.

Goldsmith, L. T. (2000). Tracking trajectories of talent: Child prodigies growing up. In R. C. Friedman & B. M. Shore (Eds.), *Talents unfolding: Cognition and development* (pp. 89–122). Washington, DC: American Psychological Association.

Goldstein, S. E., Davis-Kean, P. E., & Eccles, J. S. (2005). Parents, peers, and problem behavior: A longitudinal investigation of the impact of relationship perceptions and characteristics on the development of adolescent problem behavior. *Developmental Psychology, 41,* 401–413.

Goldstein, S. E., & Tisak, M. S. (2004). Adolescents' outcome expectancies about relational aggression within acquaintanceships, friendships, and dating relationships. *Journal of Adolescence, 27,* 283–302.

Goldston, D. B., Molock, S. D., Whitbeck, L. B., Murakami, J. L., Zayas, L. H., & Hall, G. C. N. (2008). Cultural considerations in adolescent suicide prevention and psychosocial treatment. *American Psychologist, 63,* 14–31.

Goleman, D. (1995). *Emotional intelligence.* New York: Bantam.

Goleman, D. (1998). *Working with emotional intelligence.* New York: Bantam.

Golinkoff, R. M., & Hirsh-Pasek, K. (2006). Baby wordsmith: From associationist to social sophisticate. *Current Directions in Psychological Science, 15,* 30–33.

Golomb, C. (2004). *The child's creation of a pictorial world* (2nd ed.). Mahwah, NJ: Erlbaum.

Golombok, S., & MacCallum, F. (2003). Practitioner review: Outcomes for parents and children following non-traditional conception: What do clinicians need to know? *Journal of Child Psychology and Psychiatry, 44,* 303–315.

Golombok, S., Perry, B., Burston, A., Murray, C., Mooney-Somers, J., Stevens, M., & Golding, J. (2003). Children with lesbian parents: A community study. *Developmental Psychology, 39,* 20–33.

Golombok, S., & Tasker, F. L. (1996). Do parents influence the sexual orientation of their children? Findings from a longitudinal study of lesbian families. *Developmental Psychology, 32,* 3–11.

Gómez, R. L., Bootzin, R. R., & Nadel, L. (2006). Naps promote abstraction in language-learning infants. *Psychological Science, 17,* 670–674.

Göncü, A. (1993). Development of intersubjectivity in the dyadic play of preschoolers. *Early Childhood Research Quarterly, 8,* 99–116.

Göncü, A., Patt, M. B., & Kouba E. (2004). Understanding young children's pretend play in context. In P. K. Smith & C. H. Hart (Eds.), *Blackwell handbook of childhood social development* (pp. 418–437). Malden, MA: Blackwell.

Gonzales, N. A., Cauce, A. M., Friedman, R. J., & Mason, C. A. (1996). Family, peer, and neighborhood influences on academic achievement among African-American adolescents: One-year prospective effects. *American Journal of Community Psychology, 24,* 365–387.

Gonzalez, A.-L., & Wolters, C. A. (2006). The relation between perceived parenting practices and achievement motivation in mathematics. *Journal of Research in Childhood Education, 21,* 203–217.

Good, T. L., & Brophy, J. (2003). *Looking in classrooms* (9th ed.). Boston: Allyn and Bacon.

Goodall, J. (1990). *Through a window: My thirty years with the chimpanzees of Gombe.* Boston: Houghton Mifflin.

Goode, V., & Goode, J. D. (2007). De facto zero tolerance: An exploratory study of race and safe school violations. In J. L. Kincheloe & K. Hayes (Eds.), *Teaching city kids: Understanding and appreciating them* (pp. 85–96). New York: Peter Lang.

Goodlin-Jones, B. L., Burnham, M. M., & Anders, T. F. (2000). Sleep and sleep disturbances: Regulatory processes in infancy. In A J. Sameroff, M. Lewis, & S. M. Miller (Eds.), *Handbook of developmental psychology* (2nd ed., pp. 309–325). New York: Kluwer.

Goodlin-Jones, B. L., Tassone, F., Gane, L. W., & Hagerman, R. J. (2004). Autistic spectrum disorder and the fragile X permutation. *Journal of Developmental and Behavioral Pediatrics, 25,* 392–398.

Goodman, G. S., Hirschman, J. E., Hepps, D., & Rudy, L. (1991). Children's memory for stressful events. *Merrill-Palmer Quarterly, 37,* 109–158.

Goodman, G. S., Quas, J. A., Bulkley, J., & Shapiro, C. (1999). Innovations for child witnesses: A national survey. *Psychology, Public Policy,* and *Law, 5,* 255–281.

Goodman, S. H., Gravitt, G. W., Jr., & Kaslow, N. J. (1995). Social problem solving: A moderator of the relation between negative life stress and depression symptoms in children. *Journal of Abnormal Child Psychology, 23,* 473–485.

Goodwin, M. H. (1998). Games of stance: Conflict and footing in hopscotch. In S. Hoyle & C. T. Adger (Eds.), *Language practices of older children* (pp. 23–46). New York: Oxford University Press.

Gootman, E. (2005, January 16). New York City: The politics of promotion. *New York Times.* Retrieved from www.nytimes.com/2005/01/16/education/edlife/EDGOOT.html

Gopnik, A., & Choi, S. (1990). Do linguistic differences lead to cognitive differences? A cross-linguistic study of semantic and cognitive development. *First Language, 11,* 199–215.

Gopnik, A., & Meltzoff, A. N. (1987). The development of categorization in the second year and its relation to other cognitive and linguistic developments. *Child Development, 58,* 1523–1531.

Gopnik, A., & Nazzi, T. (2003). Words, kinds, and causal powers: A theory theory perspective on early naming and categorization. In D. H. Rakison & L. M. Oakes (Eds.), *Early category and concept development: Making sense of the blooming, buzzing confusion* (pp. 303–329). New York: Oxford University Press.

Gopnik, A., & Wellman, H. M. (1994). The 'theory' theory. In L. A. Hirschfeld & S. A. Gelman (Eds.), *Mapping the mind: Domain specificity in cognition and culture* (pp. 257–293). Cambridge, UK: Cambridge University Press.

Gordon, B. N., Baker-Ward, L., & Ornstein, P. A. (2001). Children's testimony: A review of research on memory for past experiences. *Clinical Child and Family Psychology Review, 4,* 157–181.

Gordon, P. (2004). Numerical cognition without words: Evidence from Amazonia. *Science, 306,* 496–499.

Gordon, R. A., Chase-Lansdale, P. L., & Brooks-Gunn, J. (2004). Extended households and the life course of young mothers: Understanding the associations using a sample of mothers with premature, low-birth-weight babies. *Child Development, 75,* 1013–1038.

Gormally, S., Barr, R. G., Wertheim, L., Alkawaf, R., Calinoui, N., & Young, S. N. (2001). Contact and nutrient caregiving effects on newborn infant pain responses. *Developmental Medicine and Child Neurology, 43,* 28–38.

Goswami, U. (1996). Analogical reasoning and cognitive development. In H. Reese (Ed.), *Advances in child development and behavior* (Vol. 26, pp. 91–138). New York: Academic Press.

Goswami, U. (2000). Phonological and lexical processes. In M. L. Kamil & P. B. Mosenthal (Eds.), *Handbook of reading research* (Vol. 3, pp. 251–284). Mahwah, NJ: Erlbaum.

Gottesman, I. I. (1963). Genetic aspects of intelligent behavior. In N. R. Ellis (Ed.), *Handbook of mental deficiency* (pp. 253–296). New York: McGraw-Hill.

Gottfried, A. E., Gottfried, A. W., & Bathurst, K. (2002). Maternal and dual-earner employment status and parenting. In M. H. Bornstein (Ed.), *Handbook of parenting: Vol. 3. Being and becoming a parent* (2nd ed., pp. 207–230). Mahwah, NJ: Erlbaum.

Gottlieb, G. (1998). Normally occurring environmental and behavioral influences on gene activity: From central dogma to probabilistic epigenesis. *Psychological Review, 105,* 792–802.

Gottlieb, G. (2000). Environmental and behavioral influences on gene activity. *Current Directions in Psychological Science, 9,* 93–97.

Gottlieb, G. (2003). On making behavioral genetics truly developmental. *Human Development, 46,* 337–355.

Gottlieb, G. (2007). Probabilistic epigenesis. *Developmental Science, 10,* 1–11.

Gottlieb, G., Wahlsten, D., & Lickliter, R. (2006). The significance of biology for human development: A developmental psychobiological systems view. In R. M. Lerner (Ed.), *Handbook of child psychology: Vol. 1. Theoretical models of human development* (6th ed., pp. 210–257). Hoboken, NJ: Wiley.

Gottman, J. M., Katz, L. F., & Hooven, C. (1997). *Meta-emotion: How families communicate emotionally.* Mahwah, NJ: Erlbaum.

Gould, J. L., & Keeton, W. T. (1996). *Biological science* (6th ed.). New York: Norton.

Gould, M., Jamieson, P., & Romer, D. (2003). Media contagion and suicide among the young. *American Behavioral Scientist, 46,* 1269–1284.

Govaerts, P. J., De Beukelaer, C., Daemers, K., De Ceulaer, G., Yperman, M., Somers, T., Schatteman, I., & Offeciers, F. E. (2002). Outcome of cochlear implantation at different ages from 0 to 6 years. *Otology and Neurotology, 23,* 885–890.

Government of Canada. (2004). Action Plan for Official Languages. Retrieved from www.wd.gc.ca/rpts/strategies/ola/2004/1_e.asp

Government of Ontario, Ministry of Education (2007a). *Ontario District School Board Progress Reports.* Retrieved from www.edu.gov.on.ca/eng/bpr/indicators.asp

Government of Ontario, Ministry of Education (2007b). *Education Facts.* Retrieved from www.edu.gov.on.ca/eng/educationFacts.html

Goy, R. W., & Goldfoot, D. A. (1974). Experiential and hormonal factors influencing development of sexual behavior in the male rhesus monkey. In R. O. Schmitt & F. G. Worden (Eds.), *The neurosciences* (pp. 571–581). Cambridge, MA: MIT Press.

Graber, J. A. (2003). Puberty in context. In C. Hayward (Ed.), *Gender differences at puberty* (pp. 307–325). New York: Cambridge University Press.

Graber, J. A. (2004). Internalizing problems during adolescence. In R. M. Lerner & L. Steinberg (Eds.), *Handbook of adolescent psychology* (2nd ed., pp. 587–626). Hoboken, NJ: Wiley.

Graber, J. A., Brooks-Gunn, J., & Warren, M. P. (2006). Pubertal effects on adjustment in girls: Moving from demonstrating effects to identifying pathways. *Journal of Youth and Adolescence, 35,* 413–423.

Graber, J. A., Lewinsohn, P. M., Seeley, J. R., & Brooks-Gunn, J. (1997). Is psychopathology associated with the timing of pubertal development? *Journal of the American Academy of Child and Adolescent Psychiatry, 36,* 1768–1776.

Graber, J. A., Nichols, T., Lynne, S. D., Brooks-Gunn, J., & Botwin, G. J. (2006). A longitudinal examination of family, friend, and media influences on competent versus problem behaviors among urban minority youth. *Applied Developmental Science, 10,* 75–85.

Graber, J. A., Seeley, J. R., Brooks-Gunn, J., & Lewinsohn, P. M. (2004). Is pubertal timing associated with psychopathology in young adulthood? *Journal of the American Academy of Child and Adolescent Psychiatry, 43,* 718–726.

Graham, Y. P., Heim, C., Goodman, S. H., Miller, A. H., & Nemeroff, C. B. (1999). The effects of neonatal stress on brain development: Implications for psychopathology. *Development and Psychopathology, 11,* 545–565.

Gralinski, J. H., & Kopp, C. B. (1993). Everyday rules for behavior: Mothers' requests to young children. *Developmental Psychology, 29,* 573–584.

Granic, I., Hollenstein, T., Dishion, T. J., & Patterson, G. R. (2003). Longitudinal analysis of flexibility and reorganization in early adolescence: A dynamic systems study of family interactions. *Developmental Psychology, 39,* 606–617.

Granier-Deferre, C., Bassereau, S., Ribeiro, A., Jacquet, A.-Y., & Lecanuet, J.-P. (2003). *Cardiac "orienting" response in fetuses and babies following in utero melody-learning.* Paper presented at the 11th European Conference on Developmental Psychology, Milan, Italy.

Granillo, T., Jones-Rodriguez, G., & Carvajal, S. C. (2005). Prevalence of eating disorders in Latina adolescents: Associations with substance use and other correlates. *Journal of Adolescent Health, 36,* 214–220.

Granot, M., Spitzer, A., Aroian, K. J., Ravid, C., Tamir, B., & Noam, R. (1996). Pregnancy and delivery practices and beliefs of Ethiopian immigrant women in Israel. *Western Journal of Nursing Research, 18,* 299–313.

Grant, H., & Dweck, C. S. (2001). Cross-cultural response to failure: Considering outcome attributions with different goals. In F. Salili & C. Chiu (Eds.), *Student motivation: The culture and context of learning* (pp. 203–219). New York: Plenum.

Grant, K., O'Koon, J., Davis, T., Roache, N., Poindexter, L., & Armstrong, M. (2000). Protective factors affecting low-income urban African American youth exposed to stress. *Journal of Early Adolescence, 20,* 388–418.

Grantham-McGregor, S., & Ani, C. (2001). A review of studies on the effect of iron deficiency on cognitive development in children. *Journal of Nutrition, 131,* 649S–668S.

Grantham-McGregor, S., Powell, C., Walker, S., Chang, S., & Fletcher, P. (1994). The long-term follow-up of severely malnourished children who participated in an intervention program. *Child Development, 65,* 428–439.

Grantham-McGregor, S., Schofield, W., & Powell, C. (1987). Development of severely malnourished children who received psychosocial stimulation: Six-year follow-up. *Pediatrics, 79,* 247–254.

Grattan, M. P., De Vos, E., Levy, J., & McClintock, M. K. (1992). Asymmetric action in the human newborn: Sex differences in patterns of organization. *Child Development, 63,* 273–289.

Graue, M. E., & DiPerna, J. (2000). Redshirting and early retention: Who gets the "gift of time" and what are its outcomes? *American Educational Research Journal, 37,* 509–534.

Graves, S. B. (1993). Television, the portrayal of African Americans, and the development of children's attitudes. In G. L. Berry & J. K. Asamen (Eds.), *Children and television* (pp. 179–190). Newbury Park, CA: Sage.

Gray, J. (1997). *Mars and Venus on a date.* New York: HarperCollins.

Gray, K. A., Day, N. L., Leech, S., & Richardson, G. A. (2005). Prenatal marijuana exposure: Effect on child depressive symptoms at ten years of age. *Neurotoxicology and Teratology, 27,* 439–448.

Gray, M. R., & Steinberg, L. D. (1999). Unpacking authoritative parenting: Reassessing a multidimensional construct. *Journal of Marriage and the Family, 61,* 574–587.

Gray-Little, B., & Carels, R. (1997). The effects of racial and socioeconomic consonance on self-esteem and achievement in elementary, junior high, and high school students. *Journal of Research on Adolescence, 7,* 109–131.

Gray-Little, B., & Hafdahl, A. R. (2000). Factors influencing racial comparisons of self-esteem: A quantitative review. *Psychological Bulletin, 126,* 26–54.

Green, G. E., Irwin, J. R., & Gustafson, G. E. (2000). Acoustic cry analysis, neonatal status and long-term developmental outcomes. In R. G. Barr, B. Hopkins, & J. A. Green (Eds.), *Crying as a sign, a symptom, and a signal* (pp. 137–156). Cambridge, UK: Cambridge University Press.

Greenberger, E., Chen, C., Tallym, S. R., & Dong, Q. (2000). Family, peer, and individual correlates of depressive symptomology among U. S. and Chinese adolescents. *Journal of Consulting and Clinical Psychology, 68,* 209–219.

Greenberger, E., O'Neil, R., & Nagel, S. K. (1994). Linking workplace and homeplace: Relations between the nature of adults' work and their parenting behaviors. *Developmental Psychology, 30,* 990–1002.

Greene, K., Krcmar, M., Walters, L. H., Rubin, D. L., Hale, J., & Hale, L. (2000). Targeting adolescent risk-taking behaviors: The contributions of egocentrism and sensation-seeking. *Journal of Adolescence, 23,* 439–461.

Greene, M. L., Way, N., & Pahl, K. (2006). Trajectories of perceived adult and peer discrimination among Black, Latino, and Asian American adolescents: Patterns and psychological correlates. *Developmental Psychology, 42,* 218–238.

Greene, S. M., Anderson, E., Hetherington, E. M., Forgath, M. S., & DeGarmo, D. S. (2003). Risk and resilience after divorce. In R. Walsh (Ed.), *Normal family processes* (pp. 96–120). New York: Guilford.

Greenfield, P. (1992, June). *Notes and references for developmental psychology.* Conference on Making Basic Texts in Psychology More Culture-Inclusive and Culture-Sensitive, Western Washington University, Bellingham, WA.

Greenfield, P. M. (2004). *Weaving generations together: Evolving creativity in the Maya of Chiapas.* Santa Fe, NM: School of American Research.

Greenfield, P. M., Maynard, A. E., & Childs, C. P. (2000). History, culture, learning, and development. *Cross-Cultural Research, 34,* 351–374.

Greenfield, P. M., Quiroz, B., & Raeff, C. (2000). Cross-cultural conflict and harmony in the social construction of the child. In S. Harkness, C. Raeff, & C. M. Super (Eds.), *Variability in the social construction of the child* (pp. 93–108). San Francisco: Jossey-Bass.

Greenfield, P. M., Suzuki, L. K., & Rothstein-Fish, C. (2006). Cultural pathways through human development. In K. A. Renninger & I. E. Sigel (Eds.), *Handbook of child psychology: Vol. 4. Child psychology in practice* (6th ed., pp. 655–699). Hoboken, NJ: Wiley.

Greenfield, P., & Yan, Z. (2007). Children, adolescents, and the Internet: A new field of inquiry in developmental psychology. *Developmental Psychology, 42,* 391–394.

Greenhill, L. L., Halperin, J. M., & Abikoff, H. (1999). Stimulant medications. *Journal of the American Academy of Child and Adolescent Psychiatry, 38,* 503–512.

Greenhoot, A. F. (2000). Remembering and understanding: The effects of changes in underlying knowledge on children's recollections. *Child Development, 71,* 1309–1328.

Greenough, W. T., & Black, J. E. (1992). Induction of brain structure by experience: Substrates for cognitive development. In M. R. Gunnar & C. A. Nelson (Eds.), *Minnesota Symposia on Child Psychology* (pp. 155–200). Hillsdale, NJ: Erlbaum.

Greenspan, S. I., & Shanker, S. G. (2004). *The first idea: How symbols, language, and intelligence evolved from our primate ancestors to modern humans.* Cambridge, MA: Da Capo Press.

Gregg, V., Gibbs, J. C., & Fuller, D. (1994). Patterns of developmental delay in moral judgment by male and female delinquents. *Merrill-Palmer Quarterly, 40,* 538–553.

Grief, G. L., Hrabowski, F. A., Maton, K. I. (1998). African-American fathers of high-achieving sons: Using outstanding members of an at-risk population to guide intervention. *Families in Society, 79,* 45–52.

Griffin, K. W., Botwin, G. J., Nichols, T. R., & Doyle, M. M. (2003). Effectiveness of a universal drug abuse prevention approach for youth at high risk for substance use initiation. *Preventive Medicine, 36,* 1–7.

Grigorenko, E. L., & Sternberg, R. J. (2001). Analytical, creative, and practical intelligence as predictors of self-reported adaptive functioning: A case study in Russia. *Intelligence, 29,* 57–73.

Grolnick, W. S., Kurowski, C. O., Dunlap, K. G., & Hevey, C. (2000). Parental resources and the transition to junior high. *Journal of Research on Adolescence, 10,* 465–488.

Gronau, R. C., & Waas, G. A. (1997). Delay of gratification and cue utilization: An examination of children's social information processing. *Merrill-Palmer Quarterly, 43,* 305–322.

Groome, L. J., Swiber, M. J., Holland, S. B., Bentz, L. S., Atterbury, J. L., & Trimm, R. F., III. (1999). Spontaneous motor activity in the perinatal infant before and after birth: Stability in individual differences. *Developmental Psychobiology, 35,* 15–24.

Grossmann, K., Grossmann, K. E., Fremmer-Bombik, E., Kindler, H., Scheuerer-Englisch, H., & Zimmermann, P. (2002). The uniqueness of the child–father attachment relationship: Fathers' sensitive and challenging play as a pivotal variable in a 16-year longitudinal study. *Social Development, 11,* 307–331.

Grossmann, K., Grossmann, K. E., Spangler, G., Suess, G., & Unzner, L. (1985). Maternal sensitivity and newborns' orientation responses as related to quality of attachment in Northern Germany. In I. Bretherton & E. Waters (Eds.), Growing points of attachment theory and research. *Monographs of the Society for Research in Child Development, 50* (1–2, Serial No. 209).

Grotevant, H. D. (1978). Sibling constellations and sex-typing of interests in adolescence. *Child Development, 49,* 540–542.

Grotevant, H. D. (1998). Adolescent development in family contexts. In N. Eisenberg (Ed.), *Handbook of child psychology: Vol. 3. Social, emotional, and personality development* (5th ed., pp. 1097–1149). New York: Wiley.

Grotevant, H. D., & Kohler, J. K. (1999). Adoptive families. In M. E. Lamb (Ed.), *Parenting and child development in "nontraditional" families* (pp. 161–190). Mahwah, NJ: Erlbaum.

Grow-Maienza, J., Hahn, D.-D., & Joo, C.-A. (2001). Mathematics instruction in Korean primary schools: Structures, processes, and a linguistic analysis of questioning. *Journal of Educational Psychology, 93,* 363–376.

Gruendel J., & Aber, J. L. (2007). Bridging the gap between research and child policy change: The role of strategic communications in policy advocacy. In J. L. Aber, S. J. Bishop-Josef, S. M. Jones, K. T. McLearn, & D. Phillips (Eds.), *Child development and social policy: Knowledge for action* (pp. 43–58). Washington, DC: American Psychological Association.

Grunau, R. E., Whitfield, M. F., & Fay, T. B. (2004). Psychosocial and academic characteristics of extremely low birth weight (<or=800g) adolescents who are free of major impairment compared with term-born control subjects. *Pediatrics, 114,* E725–E732.

Grusec, J. E. (1988). *Social development: History, theory, and research.* New York: Springer-Verlag.

Grusec, J. E. (2006). The development of moral behavior and conscience from a socialization perspective. In M. Killen & J. Smetana (Eds.), *Handbook of moral development* (pp. 243–265). Philadelphia: Erlbaum.

Grusec, J. E., & Goodnow, J. J. (1994). Impact of parental discipline methods on the child's internalization of values: A reconceptualization of current points of view. *Developmental Psychology, 30,* 4–19.

Grych, J. H., & Clark, R. (1999). Maternal employment and development of the father–infant relationship in the first year. *Developmental Psychology, 35,* 893–903.

Guay, F., LaRose, S., & Boivin, M. (2004). Academic self-concept and educational attainment level: A ten-year longitudinal study. *Self and Identity, 3,* 53–68.

Guay, F., Marsh, H. W., & Boivin, M. (2003). Academic self-concept and academic achievement: Developmental perspectives on their causal ordering. *Journal of Educational Psychology, 95,* 124–136.

Guerra, N. G., & Slaby, R. G. (1990). Cognitive mediators of aggression in adolescent offenders: 2. Intervention. *Developmental Psychology, 26,* 269–277.

Guignard, J.-H., & Lubart, T. (2006). Is it reasonable to be creative? In J. C. Kaufman & J. Baer (Eds.), *Creativity and reason in cognitive development* (pp. 269–281). New York: Cambridge University Press.

Guilford, J. P. (1985). The structure-of-intellect model. In B. B. Wolman (Ed.), *Handbook of intelligence* (pp. 225–266). New York: Wiley.

Gullone, E. (2000). The development of normal fear: A century of research. *Clinical Psychology Review, 20,* 429–451.

Gunnar, M. R. (1994). Psychoendocrine studies of temperament and stress in early childhood: Expanding current models. In J. E. Bates & T. D. Wachs (Eds.), *Temperament: Individual differences at the interface of biology and behavior* (pp. 175–198). Washington, DC: American Psychological Association.

Gunnar, M. R., & Cheatham, C. L. (2003). Brain and behavior interfaces: Stress and the developing brain. *Infant Mental Health Journal, 24,* 195–211.

Gunnar, M. R., Morison, S. J., Chisholm, K., & Schuder, M. (2001). Salivary cortisol levels in children adopted from Romanian orphanages. *Development and Psychopathology, 13,* 611–628.

Gunnar, M. R., & Nelson, C. A. (1994). Event-related potentials in year-old infants: Relations with emotionality and cortisol. *Child Development, 65,* 80–94.

Gunnar, M., & Quevedo, K. (2007). The neurobiology of stress and development. *Annual Review of Psychology, 58,* 145–173.

Gunnar, M. R., & Vasquez, D. M. (2001). Low cortisol and a flattening of expected daytime rhythm: Potential indices of risk in human development. *Development and Psychopathology, 13,* 515–538.

Gunnoe., M. L., & Mariner, C. L. (1997). Toward a developmental-contextual model of the effects of parental spanking on children's aggression. *Archives of Pediatrics and Adolescent Medicine, 151,* 768–775.

Guo, G., & VanWey, L. K. (1999). Sibship size and intellectual development: Is the relationship causal? *American Sociological Review, 64,* 169–187.

Guralnick, M. J., Neville, B., Hammond, M. A., & Connor, R. T. (2007). Linkages between delayed children's social interactions with mothers and peers. *Child Development, 78,* 459–473.

Gure, A., Ucanok, Z., & Sayil, M. (2006). The associations among perceived pubertal timing, parental relations and self-perception in Turkish adolescents. *Journal of Youth and Adolescence, 35,* 541–550.

Gurucharri, C., & Selman, R. L. (1982). The development of interpersonal understanding during childhood, preadolescence, and adolescence: A longitudinal follow-up study. *Child Development, 53,* 924–927.

Gustafson, G. E., Green, J. A., & Cleland, J. W. (1994). Robustness of individual identity in the cries of human infants. *Developmental Psychobiology, 27,* 1–9.

Gustafson, G. E., Wood, R. M., & Green, J. A. (2000). Can we hear the causes of infants' crying? In R. G. Barr, B. Hopkins, & J. A. Green (Eds.), *Crying as a sign, a symptom, and a signal* (pp. 8–22). New York: Cambridge University Press.

Gutman, L. M. (2006). How student and parent goal orientations and classroom goal structures influence the math achievement of African Americans during the high school transition. *Contemporary Educational Psychology, 31,* 44–63.

Gutman, L. M., & Midgley, C. (2000). The role of protective factors in supporting the academic achievement of poor African-American students during the middle school transition. *Journal of Youth and Adolescence, 29,* 223–248.

Gutman, L. M., Sameroff, A. J., & Cole, R. (2003). Academic growth curve trajectories from 1st grade to 12th grade: Effects of multiple social risk factors and preschool child factors. *Developmental Psychology, 39,* 777–790.

Gutman, L. M., Sameroff, A. J., & Eccles, J. S. (2002). The academic achievement of African-American students during early adolescence: An examination of multiple risk, promotive, and protective factors. *American Journal of Community Psychology, 39,* 367–399.

Gutteling, B. M., de Weerth, C., Zandbelt, N., Mulder, E. J. H., Visser, G. H. A., & Buitelaar, J. K. (2006). Does maternal prenatal stress adversely affect the child's learning and memory at age six? *Journal of Abnormal Child Psychology, 34,* 789–798.

Gwiazda, J., & Birch, E. E. (2001). Perceptual development: Vision. In E. B. Goldstein (Ed.), *Blackwell handbook of perception* (pp. 636–668). Oxford: Blackwell.

Haas, L. (2003). Women in Sweden. In L. Walter (Ed.), *The Greenwood encyclopedia of women's issues worldwide: Europe.* Westport, CT: Greenwood Press.

Haas, L., Chronholm, A., & Hwang, P. (2006). Sweden. In P. Moss & M. O'Brien (Eds.), *International review of leave policies and related research, 2006* (pp. 205–216). London: Department of Trade and Industry.

Hack, M., & Klein, N. (2006). Young adult attainments of preterm infants. *Journal of the American Medical Association, 295,* 695–696.

Hagekull, B., Bohlin, G., & Rydell, A. (1997). Maternal sensitivity, infant temperament, and the development of early feeding problems. *Infant Mental Health Journal, 18,* 92–106.

Haidt, J. (2001). The emotional dog and its rational tail: A social intuitionist approach to moral judgment. *Psychological Review, 108,* 814–834.

Haidt, J. (2003). The moral emotions. In R. J. Davidson, K. R. Scherer, & H. H. Goldsmith (Eds.), *Handbook of affective sciences* (pp. 852–870). New York: Oxford University Press.

Haight, W. L., & Miller, P. J. (1993). *Pretending at home: Early development in a sociocultural context.* Albany, NY: SUNY Press.

Hainline, L. (1998). The development of basic visual abilities. In A. Slater (Ed.), *Perceptual development: Visual, auditory, and speech perception in infancy* (pp. 37–44). Hove, UK: Psychology Press.

Haith, M. M. (1994). Visual expectation as the first step toward the development of future-oriented processes. In M. M. Haith, J. B. Benson, R. J. Roberts, Jr., & B. Pennington (Eds.), *The development of future-oriented processes* (pp. 11–38). Chicago: University of Chicago Press.

Haith, M. M. (1999). Some thoughts about claims for innate knowledge and infant physical reasoning. *Developmental Science, 2,* 153–156.

Hakuta, K., Bialystok, E., & Wiley, E. (2003). Critical evidence: A test of the critical period hypothesis for second-language acquisition. *Psychological Science, 14,* 31–38.

Hale, C. M., & Tager-Flusberg, H. (2003). The influence of language on theory of mind: A training study. *Developmental Science, 6,* 346–359.

Hales, C. N., & Ozanne, S. E. (2003). The dangerous road of catch-up growth. *Journal of Physiology, 547,* 5–10.

Halfon, N., & McLearn, K. T. (2002). Families with children under 3: What we know and implications for results and policy. In N. Halfon & K. T. McLearn (Eds.), *Child rearing in America: Challenges facing parents with young children* (pp. 367–412). New York: Cambridge University Press.

Halford, G. S. (2002). Information-processing models of cognitive development. In U. Goswami (Ed.), *Blackwell handbook of childhood cognitive development* (pp. 555–574). Malden, MA: Blackwell.

Halford, G. S. (2005). Development of thinking. In K. J. Holyoak & R. G. Morrison (Eds.), *The Cambridge handbook of thinking and reasoning* (pp. 529–558). New York: Cambridge University Press.

Halford, G. S., & Andrews, G. (2006). Reasoning and problem solving. In D. Kuhn & R. Siegler (Eds.), *Handbook of child psychology: Vol. 2. Cognition, perception, and language* (6th ed., pp. 557–608). Hoboken, NJ: Wiley.

Hall, C. M., Jones, J. A., Meyer-Bahlburg, H. F. L., Dolezal, C., Coleman, M., & Foster, P. (2004). Behavioral and physical masculinization are related to genotype in girls with congenital adrenal hyperplasia. *Journal of Clinical Endocrinology and Metabolism, 89,* 419–424.

Hall, D. G., & Graham, S. A. (1999). Lexical form class information guides word-to-object mapping in preschoolers. *Child Development, 70,* 78–91.

Hall, D. G., Burns, T., & Pawluski, J. (2003). Input and word learning: Caregivers' sensitivity to lexical category distinctions. *Journal of Child Language, 30,* 711–729.

Hall, D. G., Lee, S. C., & Belanger, J. (2001). Young children's use of syntactic cues to learn proper names and count nouns. *Developmental Psychology, 37,* 298–307.

Hall, G. S. (1904). *Adolescence* (Vols. 1–2). New York: Appleton-Century-Crofts.

Hall, J. G. (2003). Twinning. *Lancet, 362,* 735–743.

Halle, T. G. (2003). Emotional development and well-being. In M. H. Bornstein, L. Davidson, C. L. M. Keyes, K. A. Moore, & The Center for Child Well-Being (Eds.), *Well-being: Positive development across the life course* (pp. 125–138). Mahwah, NJ: Erlbaum.

Haller, J. (2005). Vitamins and brain function. In H. R. Lieberman, R. B. Kanarek, & C. Prasad (2005). *Nutritional neuroscience* (pp. 207–233). Philadelphia: Taylor & Francis.

Hallett, M. (2000). Brain plasticity and recovery from hemiplegia. *Journal of Medical Speech-Language Pathology, 9,* 107–115.

Halliday, J. L., Watson, L. F., Lumley, J., Danks, D. M., & Sheffield, L. S. (1995). New estimates of Down syndrome risks at chorionic villus sampling, amniocentesis, and live birth in women of advanced maternal age from a uniquely defined population. *Prenatal Diagnosis, 15,* 455–465.

Hallinan, M. T., & Kubitschek, W. N. (1999). Curriculum differentiation and high school achievement. *Social Psychology of Education, 3,* 41–62.

Halpern, C. T., Udry, J. R., & Suchindran, C. (1997). Testosterone predicts initiation of coitus in adolescent females. *Psychosomatic Medicine, 59,* 161–171.

Halpern, D. F. (2000). *Sex differences in cognitive abilities* (3rd ed.). Mahwah, NJ: Erlbaum.

Halpern, D. F. (2004). A cognitive-process taxonomy for sex differences in cognitive abilities. *Current Directions in Psychological Science, 13,* 135–139.

Halpern, D. F., Benbow, C. P., Geary, D. C., Gur, R. C., Hyde, J. S., & Gernsbacher, M. A. (2007). The science of sex differences in science and mathematics. *Psychological Science in the Public Interest, 8,* 1–51.

Halpern, D. F., & Collaer, M. L. (2005). Sex differences in visuospatial abilities: More than meets the eye. In P. Shah & A. Miyake (Eds.), *Handbook of visuospatial thinking* (pp. 170–212). New York: Cambridge University Press.

Halpern, D. F., Wai, J., & Saw, A. (2005). A psychobiosocial model: Why females are sometimes greater than and sometimes less than males in math achievement. In D. F. Halpern, J. Wai, & A. Saw (Eds.), *Gender differences in mathematics: An integrative psychological approach* (pp. 48–72). New York: Cambridge University Press.

Halpern-Felsher, B. L., Biehl, M., Kropp, R. Y., & Rubinstein, M. L. (2004). Perceived risks and benefits of smoking: Differences among adolescents with different smoking experiences and intentions. *Preventive Medicine, 39,* 559–567.

Halpern-Felsher, B. L., & Cauffman, E. (2001). Costs and benefits of a decision: Decision-making competence in adolescents and adults. *Journal of Applied Developmental Psychology, 22,* 257–273.

Hamer, D. H., Hu, S., Magnuson, V. L., Hu, N., & Pattatucci, A. M. L. (1993). A linkage between DNA markers on the X chromosome and male sexual orientation. *Science, 261,* 321–327.

Hamilton, B. E., Ventura, S. J., Martin, J. A., & Sutton, P. D. (2005). Preliminary births for 2004. *Health E-Stats.* Retrieved from www.cdc.gov/nchs/products/pubs/pubd/hestats/prelim_births/prelim_births04.htm

Hamilton, C. E. (2000). Continuity and discontinuity of attachment from infancy through adolescence. *Child Development, 71,* 690–694.

Hamilton, H. A. (2005). Extended families and adolescent well-being. *Journal of Adolescent Health, 36,* 260–266.

Hamilton, S. F., & Hamilton, M. A. (2000). Research, intervention, and social change: Improving adolescents' career opportunities. In L. J. Crockett & R. K. Silbereisen (Eds.), *Negotiating adolescence in times of social change* (pp. 267–283). New York: Cambridge University Press.

Hamlin, J. K., Wynn, K., & Bloom, P. (2007). Social evaluation by preverbal infants. *Nature, 450,* 557–559.

Hamm, J. V. (2000). Do birds of a feather flock together? The variable bases for African American, Asian American, and European American adolescents' selection of similar friends. *Developmental Psychology, 36,* 209–219.

Hammes, B., & Laitman, C. J. (2003). Diethylstilbestrol (DES) update: Recommendations for the identification and management of DES-exposed individuals. *Journal of Midwifery and Women's Health, 48,* 19–29.

Hamre, B. K., & Pianta, R. C. (2001). Early teacher–child relationships and the trajectory of children's school outcomes through eighth grade. *Child Development, 72,* 625–638.

Han, W.-J., & Waldfogel, J. (2003). Parental leave: The impact of recent legislation on parents' leave taking. *Demography, 40,* 191–200.

Hanawalt, B. A. (1993). *Growing up in medieval London: The experience of childhood in history.* New York: Oxford University Press.

Hanawalt, B. A. (2003). The child in the Middle Ages and the Renaissance. In W. Koops & M. Zuckerman (Eds.), *Beyond the century of childhood: Cultural history and developmental psychology.* Philadelphia: University of Pennsylvania Press.

Handley, S. J., Capon, A., Beveridge, M., Dennis, I., & Evans, J. St. B. T. (2004). Working memory, inhibitory control and the development of children's reasoning. *Thinking and Reasoning, 10,* 175–195.

Hanke, W., Sobala, W., & Kalinka, J. (2004). Environmental tobacco smoke exposure among pregnant women: Impact on fetal biometry at 20-24 weeks of gestation and newborn child's birth weight. *International Archives of Occupational and Environmental Health, 77,* 47–52.

Hankin, B. L., & Abela, J. R. Z. (2005). Depression from childhood through adolescence and adulthood: A developmental vulnerability and stress perspective. In B. L. Hankin & J. R. Z. Abela (Eds.), *Development of psychopathology: A vulnerability-stress perspective* (pp. 245–288). Thousand Oaks, CA: Sage.

Hannon, E. E., & Johnson, S. P. (2004). Infants use meter to categorize rhythms and melodies: Implications for musical structure learning. *Cognitive Psychology, 50,* 354–377.

Hannon, E. E., & Trehub, S. E. (2005a). Metrical categories in infancy and adulthood. *Psychological Science, 16,* 48–55.

Hannon, E. E., & Trehub, S. E. (2005b). Tuning in to musical rhythms: Infants learn more readily than adults. *Proceedings of the National Academy of Sciences, 102,* 12639–12643.

Hannon, T. S., Rao, G., & Arslanian, S. A. (2005). Childhood obesity and type 2 diabetes mellitus. *Pediatrics, 116,* 473–480.

Hansen, M., Janssen, I., Schiff, A., Zee, P. C., & Dubocovich, M. L. (2005). The impact of school daily schedule on adolescent sleep. *Pediatrics, 115,* 1555–1561.

Hanson, T. L. (1999). Does parental conflict explain why divorce is negatively associated with child welfare? *Social Forces, 77,* 1283–1316.

Hanson, T. N., Corbet, A., & Ballard, R. A. (2005). Disorders of the chest wall, pleural cavity, and diaphragm. In H. W. Taeusch, R. A. Ballard, & C. A. Gleason (Eds.), *Avery's diseases of the newborn* (pp. 57–70). Philadelphia: Saunders.

Hanushek, E., Kain, J., & Rivkin, S. (2002). *New evidence about Brown v. Board of Education: The complex effects of school racial composition on achievement.* Working Paper 8741. Cambridge, MA: National Bureau of Economic Research.

Hanvey, L. (2006). *Issues affecting the well-being of Canadian children in the middle years—6 to 12: A discussion paper.* Literature review prepared for the Middle Childhood Initiative of the Canadian National Children's Alliance. Ottawa: National Children's Alliance.

Hanvey, L., & Kunz, J. L. (2000). *Immigrant youth in Canada.* Toronto, ON: Canadian Council on Social Development.

Harachi, T. W., Fleming, C. B., White, H. R., Ensminger, M. E., Abbott, R. D., Catalano, R. F., & Haggerty, K. P. (2006). Aggressive behavior among girls and boys during middle childhood: Predictors and sequelae of trajectory group membership. *Aggressive Behavior, 32,* 279–293.

Hardy, C. L., Bukowski, W. M., & Sippola, L. K. (2002). Stability and change in peer relationships during the transition to middle-level school. *Journal of Early Adolescence, 22,* 117–142.

Hardy, J. B., Astone, N. M., Brooks-Gunn, J., Shapiro, S., & Miller, T. L. (1998). Like mother, like child: Intergenerational patterns of age at first birth and associations with childhood and adolescent characteristics and adult outcomes in the second generation. *Developmental Psychology, 34,* 1220–1232.

Hardy, S. A., & Carlo, G. (2005). Religiosity and prosocial behaviours in adolescence: The mediating role of prosocial values. *Journal of Moral Education, 34,* 231–249.

Harley, B., & Jean, G. (1999). Vocabulary skills of French immersion students in their second language. *Zeitschrift für Interkulterellen Fremdsprachenunterricht, 4*(2). Retrieved from www.ualberta.ca

Harley, K., & Reese, E. (1999). Origins of autobiographical memory. *Developmental Psychology, 35,* 1338–1348.

Harlow, H. F. (1969). Age-mate or peer affectional system. In D. S. Lehrman, R. A. Hinde, & E. Shaw (Eds.), *Advances in the study of behavior* (Vol. 2, pp. 333–383). New York: Academic Press.

Harlow, H. F., & Zimmerman, R. (1959). Affectional responses in the infant monkey. *Science, 130,* 421–432.

Harold, G. T., Shelton, K. H., Goeke-Morey, M. C., & Cummings, E. M. (2004). Marital conflict, child emotional security about family relationships and child adjustment. *Social Development, 13,* 350–376.

Harris, G. (1997). Development of taste perception and appetite regulation. In G. Bremner, A. Slater, & G. Butterworth (Eds.), *Infant development: Recent advances* (pp. 9–30). East Sussex, UK: Erlbaum.

Harris, J. R. (1998). *The nurture assumption: Why children turn out the way they do.* New York: Free Press.

Harris, J. R. (2002). Beyond the nurture assumption: Testing hypotheses about the child's environment. In J. G. Borkowski & S. L. Ramey (Eds.), *Parenting and the child's world* (pp. 3–20). Mahwah, NJ: Erlbaum.

Harris, P. L. (2006). Social cognition. In D. Kuhn & R. S. Siegler (Eds.), *Handbook of child psychology: Vol. 2: Cognition, perception, and language* (6th ed., pp. 811–858). Hoboken, NJ: Wiley.

Harris, P. L., Brown, E., Marriott, C., Whitall, S., & Harmer, S. (1991). Monsters, ghosts and witches: Testing the limits of the fantasy–reality distinction in young children. *British Journal of Developmental Psychology, 9,* 105–123.

Harris, R. C., Robinson, J. B., Chang, F., & Burns, B. M. (2007). Characterizing preschool children's attention regulation in parent–child interactions: The roles of effortful control and motivation. *Journal of Applied Developmental Psychology, 28,* 25–39.

Harris, Y. R., & Graham, J. A. (2007). *The African American child: Development and challenges.* New York: Springer.

Harrison, A. O., Wilson, M. N., Pine, C. J., Chan, S. Q., & Buriel, R. (1994). Family ecologies of ethnic minority children. In G. Handel & G. G. Whitchurch (Eds.), *The psychosocial interior of the family* (pp. 187–210). New York: Aldine De Gruyter.

Harrison, Y. (2004). The relationship between daytime exposure to light and night-time sleep in 6–12-week-old infants. *Journal of Sleep Research, 13,* 345–352.

Harrist, A. W., Zaia, A. F., Bates, J. E., Dodge, K. A., & Pettit, G. S. (1997). Subtypes of social withdrawal in early childhood: Sociometric status and social–cognitive differences across four years. *Child Development, 68,* 278–294.

Hart, B. (2004). What toddlers talk about. *First Language, 24,* 91–106.

Hart, B., & Risley, T. R. (1995). *Meaningful differences in the everyday experience of young American children.* Baltimore: Paul H. Brookes.

Hart, C. H. (1999, November). *Combating the myth that parents don't matter.* Address presented at the World Congress of Families II, Geneva, Switzerland.

Hart, C. H. (2007). Why are parents important? Linking parenting to childhood social skills in Australia, China, Japan, Russia, and the United States. In A. S. Loveless & T. B. Holman (Eds.), *The family in the new millennium: World voices supporting the "natural" clan: Vol. 1. The place of family in human society* (pp. 227–247). Westport, CT: Praeger.

Hart, C. H., Burts, D. C., Durland, M. A., Charlesworth, R., DeWolf, M., & Fleege, P. O. (1998). Stress behaviors and activity type participation of preschoolers in more and less developmentally appropriate classrooms: SES and sex differences. *Journal of Research in Childhood Education, 13,* 176–196.

Hart, C. H., Newell, L. D., & Olsen, S. F. (2003). Parenting skills and social–communicative competence in childhood. In J. O. Greene & B. R. Burleson (Eds.), *Handbook of communication and social interaction skills* (pp. 753–797). Mahwah, NJ: Erlbaum.

Hart, C. H., Yang, C., Charlesworth, R., & Burts, D. C. (2003, April). *Kindergarten teaching practices: Associations with later child academic and social/emotional adjustment to school.* Paper presented at the biennial meeting of the Society for Research in Child Development, Tampa, FL.

Hart, C. H., Yang, C., Nelson, L. J., Robinson, C. C., Olsen, J. A., & Nelson, D. A. (2000). Peer acceptance in early childhood and subtypes of socially withdrawn behavior in China, Russia, and the United States. *International Journal of Behavioral Development, 24,* 73–81.

Hart, D., & Atkins, R. (2002). Civic competence in urban youth. *Applied Developmental Science, 6,* 227–236.

Hart, D., Atkins, R., & Donnelly, T. M. (2006). Community service and moral development. In M. Killen & J. G. Smetana (Eds.), *Handbook of moral development* (pp. 633–656). Philadelphia: Erlbaum.

Hart, D., Donnelly, T. M., Youniss, J., & Atkins, R. (2007). High school community service as a predictor of adult voting and volunteering. *American Educational Research Journal, 44,* 197–219.

Hart, D., & Fegley, S. (1995). Prosocial behavior and caring in adolescence: Relations to self-understanding and social judgment. *Child Development, 66,* 1346–1359.

Harter, S. (1999). *The construction of self: A developmental perspective.* New York: Guilford.

Harter, S. (2006). The self. In N. Eisenberg (Ed.), *Handbook of child psychology: Vol. 3. Social, emotional, and personality development* (6th ed., pp. 505–570). Hoboken, NJ: Wiley.

Harter, S., Waters, P., & Whitesell, N. R. (1998). Relational self-worth: Differences in perceived worth as a person across interpersonal contexts among adolescents. *Child Development, 69,* 756–766.

Harter, S., & Whitesell, N. R. (1989). Developmental changes in children's understanding of simple, multiple, and blended emotion concepts. In C. Saarni & P. Harris (Eds.), *Children's understanding of emotion* (pp. 81–116). Cambridge, UK: Cambridge University Press.

Harter, S., & Whitesell, N. R. (2003). Beyond the debate: Why some adolescents report stable self-worth over time and situation, whereas others report changes in self-worth. *Journal of Personality, 71,* 1027–1058.

Hartshorn, K., Rovee-Collier, C., Gerhardstein, P., Bhatt, R. S., Klein, P. J., Aaron, F., Wondoloski, T. L., & Wurtzel, N. (1998a). Developmental changes in the specificity of memory over the first year of life. *Developmental Psychobiology, 33,* 61–68.

Hartshorn, K., Rovee-Collier, C., Gerhardstein, P., Bhatt, R. S., Wondoloski, T. L., Klein, P., Gilch, J., Wurtzel, N., & Campos-de-Carvalho, M. (1998b). The ontogeny of long-term memory over the first year-and-a-half of life. *Developmental Psychobiology, 32,* 69–89.

Hartup, W. W. (1996). The company they keep: Friendships and their developmental significance. *Child Development, 67,* 1–13.

Hartup, W. W. (2006). Relationships in early and middle childhood. In A. L. Vangelisti & D. Perlman (Eds.), *Cambridge handbook of personal relationships* (pp. 177–190). New York: Cambridge University Press.

Hartup, W. W., & Abecassis, M. (2004). Friends and enemies. In P. K. Smith & C. H. Hart (Eds.), *Blackwell handbook of childhood social development* (pp. 285–306). Malden, MA: Blackwell.

Hartup, W. W., & Stevens, N. (1999). Friendships and adaptation across the life span. *Current Directions in Psychological Science, 8,* 76–79.

Harvey, R. J., Fletcher, J., & French, D. J. (2001). Social reasoning: A source of influence on aggression. *Clinical Psychology, Review, 21,* 447–469.

Harwood, M. D., & Farrar, M. J. (2006). Conflicting emotions: The connection between affective perspective taking and theory of mind. *British Journal of Developmental Psychology, 24,* 401–418.

Hasebe, Y., Nucci, L., & Nucci, M. S. (2004). Parental control of the personal domain and adolescent symptoms of psychopathology: A cross-national study in the United States and Japan. *Child Development, 75,* 815–828.

Haselager, J. T., Hartup, W. W., van Lieshout, C. F. M., & Riksen-Walraven, J. M. A. (1998). Similarities between friends and nonfriends in middle childhood. *Child Development, 69,* 1198–1208.

Haskett, M. E., Scott, S. S., Grant, R., Ward, C. S., & Robinson, C. (2003). Child-related cognitions and affective functioning of physically abusive and comparison parents. *Child Abuse and Neglect, 27,* 663–686.

Hastings, P. D., Zahn-Waxler, C. R., Robinson, J., Usher, B., & Bridges, D. (2000). The development of concern for others in children with behavior problems. *Developmental Psychology, 36,* 531–546.

Hastings, P. D., Zahn-Waxler, C., & McShane, K. (2006). We are, by nature, moral creatures: Biological bases of concern for others. In M. Killen & J. G. Smetana (Eds.), *Handbook of moral development* (pp. 483–516). Philadelphia: Erlbaum.

Hastings, P. D., Zahn-Waxler, C., & Usher, B. A. (2007). Cardiovascular and affective responses to social stress in adolescents with internalizing and externalizing problems. *International Journal of Behavioral Development, 31,* 77–87.

Hastings, P. D., Zahn-Waxler, C., Usher, B., Robinson, J. L., & Bridges, D. (2000). The development of concern for others in children with behavior problems. *Developmental Psychology, 36,* 531–546.

Hatano, G. (1994). Introduction: Conceptual change—Japanese perspectives. *Human Development, 37,* 189–197.

Hatton, D. D., Bailey, D. B., Jr., Burchinal, M. R., & Ferrell, K. A. (1997). Developmental growth curves of preschool children with vision impairments. *Child Development, 68,* 788–806.

Hauck, F. R., Herman, S. M., Donovan, M., Iyasu, S., Merrick Moore, C., & Donoghue, E. (2003). Sleep environment and the risk of sudden infant death syndrome in an urban population: The Chicago Infant Mortality Study. *Pediatrics, 111,* 1207–1214.

Hauf, P., Aschersleben, G., & Prinz, W. (2007). Baby do–baby see! How action production influences action perception in infants. *Cognitive Development, 22,* 16–32.

Hausfather, A., Toharia, A., LaRoche, C., & Engelsmann, F. (1997). Effects of age of entry, day-care quality, and family characteristics on preschool behavior. *Journal of Child Psychology and Psychiatry, 38,* 441–448.

Hawkins, J. N. (1994). Issues of motivation in Asian education. In H. F. O'Neil, Jr., & M. Drillings (Eds.), *Motivation: Theory and research* (pp. 101–115). Hillsdale, NJ: Erlbaum.

Hawley, P. A. (2003a). Prosocial and coercive configurations of resource control in early adolescence: A case for the well-adapted Machiavellian. *Merrill-Palmer Quarterly, 49,* 279–309.

Hawley, P. A. (2003b). Strategies of control, aggression, and morality in preschoolers: An evolutionary perspective. *Journal of Experimental Child Psychology, 85,* 213–235.

Hawley, P. H., Little, T. D., & Card, N. A. (2007). The allure of a mean friend: Relationship quality and processes of aggressive adolescents with prosocial skills. *International Journal of Behavioral Development, 31,* 170–180.

Hay, D. F., Pawlby, S., Angold, A., Harold, G. T., & Sharp, D. (2003). Pathways to violence in the children of mothers who were depressed postpartum. *Developmental Psychology, 39,* 1983–1094.

Hayden, A., Bhatt, R. S., Reed, A., Corbly, C. R., & Joseph, J. E. (2007). The development of expert face processing: Are infants sensitive to normal differences in second-order relational information? *Journal of Experimental Child Psychology, 97,* 85–98.

Hayne, H. (2002). Thoughts from the crib: Meltzoff and Moore (1994) alter our views of mental representation during infancy. *Infant Behavior and Development, 25,* 62–64.

Hayne, H. (2004). Infant memory development: Implications for childhood amnesia. *Developmental Review, 24,* 33–73.

Hayne, H., Boniface, J., & Barr, R. (2000). The development of declarative memory in human infants: Age-related changes in deferred imitation. *Behavioral Neuroscience, 114,* 77–83.

Hayne, H., & Rovee-Collier, C. K. (1995). The organization of reactivated memory in infancy. *Child Development, 66,* 893–906.

Hayne, H., Rovee-Collier, C. K., & Perris, E. E. (1987). Categorization and memory retrieval by three-month-olds. *Child Development, 58,* 750–767.

Hayslip, B., Jr. (1994). Stability of intelligence. In R. J. Sternberg (Ed.), *Encyclopedia of human intelligence* (Vol. 2, pp. 1019–1026). New York: Macmillan.

Haywood, K. M., & Getchell, N. (2005). *Life span motor development* (4th ed.). Champaign, IL: Human Kinetics.

Head Start Bureau. (2007). *Head Start Program fact sheet.* Retrieved from www.acf.hhs.gov/programs/ohs/about/fy2007.html

Health Canada. (2003). *Acting on what we know: Preventing youth suicide in First Nations.* Ottawa, Canada: Author.

Health Canada. (2004). *Canadian perinatal health report 2004.* Ottawa: Minister of Public Works and Government Services.

Health Canada. (2005). Pregnancy. *Healthy living.* Retrieved from www.hc-sc.gc.ca/hl-vs/tobac-tabac/body-corps/preg-gros/index_e.html

Health Canada. (2006a). *Canada Prenatal Nutrition Program (CPNP).* Retrieved from www.phac-aspc.gc.ca/dca-dea/programs-mes/cpnp_main_e.html

Health Canada. (2006b), *Lead information package.* Retrieved from www.hc-sc.gc.ca/ewh-semt/contaminants/lead-plomb/index_e.html

Health Canada. (2006c). *Sexually transmitted infections surveillance and epidemiology.* Retrieved from www.phac-aspc.gc.ca/sti-its-surv-epi/surveillance_e.html

Hearing Foundation of Canada. (2006). *Newborn screening.* Retrieved from www.thfc.ca/NewbornScreening.asp

Hearold, S. (1986). A synthesis of 1,043 effects of television on social behavior. In G. Comstock (Ed.), *Public communications and behavior* (Vol. 1, pp. 65–133). New York: Academic Press.

Heath, S. B. (1982). Questioning at home and at school: A comparative study. In G. Spindler (Ed.), *Doing the ethnography of schooling: Educational anthropology in action* (pp. 102–127). New York: Holt.

Heath, S. B. (1989). Oral and literate traditions among black Americans living in poverty. *American Psychologist, 44,* 367–373.

Heath, S. B. (1990). The children of Trackton's children: Spoken and written language and social change. In J. Stigler, G. Herdt, & R. A. Shweder (Eds.), *Cultural psychology: Essays on comparative human development* (pp. 496–519). New York: Cambridge University Press.

Hebert, M., & Tourigny, M. (2004). Child sexual abuse prevention: A review of evaluative studies and recommendations for program development. In S. P. Serge (Ed.), *Advances in psychology research* (Vol. 29, pp. 123–155). Hauppauge, NY: Nova Science Publishers.

Heckman, J. J., & Masterov, D. V. (2004). *The productivity argument for investing in young children.* Working Paper 5, Invest in Kids Working Group, Committee for Economic Development. Retrieved from jenni.uchicago.edu/Invest

Hedges, L. V., & Nowell, A. (1995). Sex differences in mental test scores: Variability and numbers of high-scoring individuals. *Science, 269,* 41–45.

Hediger, M. L., Overpeck, M. D., Ruan, W. J., & Troendle, J. F. (2002). Birthweight and gestational age effects on motor and social development. *Paediatric and Perinatal Epidemiology, 16,* 33–46.

Heinz, W. R. (1999a). Introduction: Transitions to employment in a cross-national perspective. In W. R. Heinz (Ed.), *From education to work: Cross-national perspectives* (pp. 1–21). New York: Cambridge University Press.

Heinz, W. R. (1999b). Job-entry patterns in a life-course perspective. In W. R. Heinz (Ed.), *From education to work: Cross-national perspectives* (pp. 214–231). New York: Cambridge University Press.

Helburn, S. W. (Ed.). (1995). *Cost, quality and child outcomes in child care centers.* Denver: University of Colorado.

Helms-Lorenz, M., Van de Vijver, F. J. R., & Poortinga, Y. H. (2003). Cross-cultural differences in cognitive performance and Spearman's hypothesis: g or c? *Intelligence, 31,* 9–29.

Helwig, C. C. (1995). Adolescents' and young adults' conceptions of civil liberties: Freedom of speech and religion. *Child Development, 66,* 152–166.

Helwig, C. C. (2006). Rights, civil liberties, and democracy across cultures. In M. Killen & J. G. Smetana (Eds.), *Handbook of moral development* (pp. 185–210). Philadelphia: Erlbaum.

Helwig, C. C., Arnold, M. L., Tan, D., & Boyd, D. (2003). Chinese adolescents' reasoning about democratic and authority-based decision making in peer, family, and school contexts. *Child Development, 74,* 783–800.

Helwig, C. C., & Jasiobedzka, U. (2001). The relation between law and morality: Children's reasoning about socially beneficial and unjust laws. *Child Development, 72,* 1382–1393.

Helwig, C. C., & Kim, S. (1999). Children's evaluations of decision-making procedures in peer, family, and school contexts. *Child Development, 70,* 502–512.

Helwig, C. C., & Prencipe, A. (1999). Children's judgments of flags and flag-burning. *Child Development, 70,* 132–143.

Helwig, C. C., Zelazo, P. D., & Wilson, M. (2001). Children's judgments of psychological harm in normal and noncanonical situations. *Child Development, 72,* 66–81.

Henderson, H. A., Marshall, P. J., Fox, N. A., & Rubin, K. H. (2004). Psychophysiological and behavioral evidence for varying forms and functions of nonsocial behavior in preschoolers. *Child Development, 75,* 251–263.

Hendrick, J., & Stange, T. (1991). Do actions speak louder than words? An effect of the functional use of language on dominant sex role behavior in boys and girls. *Early Childhood Research Quarterly, 6,* 565–576.

Hennessy, K. D., Rabideau, G. J., & Cicchetti, D. (1994). Responses of physically abused and nonabused children to different forms of interadult anger. *Child Development, 65,* 815–828.

Henrich, C. C., Brookmeyer, K. A., Shrier, L. A., & Shahar, G. (2006). Supportive relationships and sexual risk behavior in adolescence: An ecological–transactional approach. *Journal of Pediatric Psychology, 31,* 286–297.

Henrich, C. C., Kuperminc, G. P., Sack, A., Blatt, S. J., & Leadbeater, B. J. (2000). Characteristics and homogeneity of early adolescent friendship groups: A comparison of male and female clique and nonclique members. *Applied Developmental Science, 4,* 15–26.

Henricsson, L., & Rydell, A.-M. (2004). Elementary school children with behavior problems: Teacher–child relations and self perception. A prospective study. *Merrill-Palmer Quarterly, 50,* 111–138.

Henry, B., Moffitt, T. E., Caspi, A., Langley, J., & Silva, P. A. (1994). On the "remembrance of things past": A longitudinal evaluation of the retrospective method. *Psychological Assessment, 6,* 92–101.

Herbert, J., Gross, J., & Hayne, H. (2007). Crawling is associated with more flexible memory retrieval by 9-month-old infants. *Developmental Science, 10,* 183–189.

Herman, L. M., & Uyeyama, R. K. (1999). The dolphin's grammatical competency: Comments on Kako. *Animal Learning and Behavior, 27,* 18–23.

Herman, M. R. (2004). Forced to choose: Some determinants of racial identification in multiracial adolescents. *Child Development, 75,* 730–748.

Herman-Giddens, M. E. (2006). Recent data on pubertal milestones in United States children: The secular trend toward earlier development. *International Journal of Andrology, 29,* 241–246.

Herrera, E., Reissland, N., & Shepherd, J. (2004). Maternal touch and maternal child-directed speech: Effects of depressed mood in the postnatal period. *Journal of Affective Disorders, 81,* 29–39.

Herrnstein, R. J., & Murray, C. (1994). *The bell curve: Intelligence and class structure in American life.* New York: Free Press.

Hertenstein, M. J., & Campos, J. J. (2004). The retention effects of an adult's emotional displays on infant behavior. *Child Development, 75,* 595–613.

Herzog, D. B., Eddy, K. T., & Beresin, E. V. (2006). Anorexia and bulimia nervosa. In M. K. Dulcan & J. M. Wiener (Eds.), *Essentials of child and adolescent psychiatry* (pp. 527–560). Washington, DC: American Psychiatric Publishing.

Hesketh, K., Ball, K., Crawford, D., Campbell, K., & Salmon, J. (2007). Mediators of the relationship between maternal education and children's TV viewing. *American Journal of Preventive Medicine, 33,* 41–47.

Hespos, S. J., & Baillargeon, R. (2001). Reasoning about containment events in very young infants. *Cognition, 78,* 207–245.

Hesse, E., & Main, M. (2000). Disorganized infant, child, and adult attachment: Collapse in behavioral and attentional strategies. *Journal of the American Psychoanalytic Association, 48,* 1097–1127.

Hetherington, E. M. (1999). Social capital and the development of youth from nondivorced, divorced, and remarried families. In A. Collins (Ed.), *Minnesota Symposia on Child Psychology* (Vol. 29, pp. 177–209). Mahwah, NJ: Erlbaum.

Hetherington, E. M. (2003). Social support and the adjustment of children in divorced and remarried families. *Childhood, 10,* 237–254.

Hetherington, E. M., Henderson, S. H., & Reiss, D. (1999). Adolescent siblings in stepfamilies: Family functioning and adolescent adjustment. *Monographs of the Society for Research in Child Development, 64*(4, Serial No. 259).

Hetherington, E. M., & Jodl, K. M. (1994). Stepfamilies as settings for child development. In A. Booth & J. Dunn (Eds.), *Stepfamilies: Who benefits? Who does not?* (pp. 55–79). Hillsdale, NJ: Erlbaum.

Hetherington, E. M., & Kelly, J. (2002). *For better or worse: Divorce reconsidered.* New York: Norton.

Hetherington, E. M., & Stanley-Hagan, M. (1999). The adjustment of children with divorced parents: A risk and resiliency perspective. *Journal of Child Psychology and Psychiatry, 40,* 129–140.

Hetherington, E. M., & Stanley-Hagan, M. (2000). Diversity among stepfamilies. In D. H. Demo, K. R. Allen, & M. A. Fine (Eds.), *Handbook of family diversity* (pp. 173–196). New York: Oxford University Press.

Hetherington, M. (2000). Eating disorders: Diagnosis, etiology, and treatment. *Nutrition, 16,* 547–551.

Hewlett, B. S. (1992). Husband–wife reciprocity and the father–infant relationship among Aka pygmies. In B. S. Hewlett (Ed.), *Father–child relations: Cultural and biosocial contexts* (pp. 153–176). New York: Aldine De Gruyter.

Hewlett, B. S. (2004). Fathers in forager, farmer, and pastoral cultures. In M. E. Lamb (Ed.), *The role of the father in child development* (4th ed., pp. 182–195). Hoboken, NJ: Wiley.

Hewlett, S. (2003). *Creating a life.* New York: Miramax.

Heyes, C. (2005). Imitation by association. In S. Hurley & N. Chater (Eds.), *From neuroscience to social science: Vol. 1. Mechanisms of imitation and imitation in animals* (pp. 157–177). Cambridge, MA: MIT Press.

Heyman, G. D., & Dweck, C. S. (1998). Children's thinking about traits: Implications for judgments of the self and others. *Child Development, 69,* 391–403.

Heyman, G. D., Dweck, C. S., & Cain, K. M. (1992). Young children's vulnerability to self-blame and helplessness: Relationship to beliefs about goodness. *Child Development, 63,* 401–415.

Heyman, G. D., & Gelman, S. A. (1999). The use of trait labels in making psychological inferences. *Child Development, 70,* 604–619.

Heyman, G. D., & Gelman, S. A. (2000). Preschool children's use of trait labels to make inductive inferences. *Journal of Experimental Child Psychology, 77,* 1–19.

Heyman, G. D., & Legare, C. H. (2004). Children's beliefs about gender differences in the academic and social domains. *Sex Roles, 50,* 227–239.

Hibell, B. (2001). *European School Survey Project on Alcohol and Drugs.* Stockholm: Swedish Council for Information on Alcohol and Other Drugs.

Hickling, A. K., & Wellman, H. M. (2001). The emergence of children's causal explanations and theories: Evidence from everyday conversation. *Developmental Psychology, 37,* 668–683.

Hicks, J. (2007, April). The social determinants of elevated rates of suicide among Inuit youth. *Indigenous Affairs,* pp. 30–37. Retrieved from www.iwgia.org/graphics/

Synkron-Library/Documents/publications/Downloadpublications/IndigenousAffairs/IA%204_07.pdf

Higley, J. D., Hopkins, W. D., Thompson, W. W., Byrne, E. A., Hirsch, R. M., & Suomi, S. J. (1992). Peers as primary attachment sources in yearling rhesus monkeys (*Macaca mulatta*). *Developmental Psychology, 28,* 1163–1171.

Hildreth, K., & Rovee-Collier, C. (2002). Forgetting functions of reactivated memories over the first year of life. *Developmental Psychobiology, 41,* 277–288.

Hildreth, K., Sweeney, B., & Rovee-Collier, C. (2003). Differential memory-preserving effects of reminders at 6 months. *Journal of Experimental Child Psychology, 84,* 41–62.

Hill, A. L., Degnan, K. A., Calkins, S. D., & Keane, S. P. (2006). Profiles of externalizing behavior problems for boys and girls across preschool: The roles of emotion regulation and inattention. *Developmental Psychology, 42,* 913–928.

Hill, E. J., Mead, N. T., Dean, L. R., Hafen, D. M., Gadd, R., Palmer, A. A., & Ferris, M. S. (2006). Researching the 60-hour dual-earner workweek: An alternative to the "opt-out revolution." *American Behavioral Scientist, 49,* 1184–1203.

Hill, J. L., Brooks-Gunn, J., & Waldfogel, J. (2003). Sustained effects of high participation in an early intervention for low-birth-weight premature infants. *Developmental Psychology, 39,* 730–744.

Hill, N. E., Bush, K. R., & Roosa, M. W. (2003). Parenting and family socialization strategies and children's mental health: Low-income Mexican-American and Euro-American mothers and children. *Child Development, 74,* 189–204.

Hill, N. E., & Taylor, L. C. (2004). Parental school involvement and children's academic achievement: Pragmatics and issues. *Current Directions in Psychological Science, 13,* 161–164.

Hillis, S. D., Anda, R. F., Dube, S. R., Felitti, V. J., Marchbanks, P. A., & Marks, J. S. (2004). The association between adverse childhood experiences and adolescent pregnancy, long-term psychosocial consequences, and fetal death. *Pediatrics, 113,* 320–327.

Hilt, L. M. (2004). Attribution retaining for therapeutic change: Theory, practice, and future directions. *Imagination, Cognition, and Personality, 23,* 289–307.

Hinde, R. A. (1992). Ethological relationships and approaches. In R. Vasta (Ed.), *Six theories of child development* (pp. 251–285). Philadelphia, PA: Jessica Kingsley.

Hines, M. (2003). Sex steroids and human behavior: Prenatal androgen exposure and sex-typical play behavior in children. *Annals of the New York Academy of Sciences, 1007,* 272–282.

Hines, M. (2004). *Brain gender.* New York: Oxford University Press.

Hines, M., Brook, C., & Conway, G. S. (2004). Androgen and psychosexual development: Core gender identity, sexual orientation, and recalled childhood gender role behavior in women and men with congenital adrenal hyperplasia (CAH). *Journal of Sex Research, 41,* 75–81.

Hines, M., & Green, R. (1991). Human hormonal and neural correlates of sex-typed behaviors. *Review of Psychiatry, 10,* 536–555.

Hinojosa, T., Sheu, C.-F., & Michel, G. F. (2003). Infant hand-use preference for grasping objects contributes to the development of a hand-use preference for manipulating objects. *Developmental Psychobiology, 43,* 328–334.

Hippisley, J., Douglas, G., & Houghton, S. (2005). A cross-cultural comparison of numeracy skills using a written and an interactive arithmetic text. *Educational Research, 47,* 205–215.

Hirschfeld, L. A. (1995). Do children have a theory of race? *Cognition, 54,* 209–252.

Hirschfeld, L. A. (1996). *Race in the making: Cognition, culture, and the child's construction of human kinds.* Cambridge, MA: MIT Press.

Hirsh-Pasek, K., & Burchinal, M. (2006). Mother and caregiver sensitivity over time: Predicting language and academic outcomes with variable- and person-centered approaches. *Merrill-Palmer Quarterly, 52,* 449–485.

Hirsh-Pasek, K., & Golinkoff, R. M. (2003). *Einstein never used flash cards.* New York: Rodale.

Hoch-Espada, A., Ryan, E., & Deblinger, E. (2006). Child sexual abuse. In J. E. Fisher & W. T. O'Donohue (Eds.), *Practitioner's guide to evidence-based psychotherapy* (pp. 177–188). New York: Springer.

Hock, H. S., Park, C. L., & Bjorklund, D. F. (1998). Temporal organization in children's strategy formation. *Journal of Experimental Child Psychology, 70,* 187–206.

Hodges, J., & Tizard, B. (1989). Social and family relationships of ex-institutional adolescents. *Journal of Child Psychology and Psychiatry, 30,* 77–97.

Hodges, R. M., & French, L. A. (1988). The effect of class and collection labels on cardinality, class-inclusion, and number conservation tasks. *Child Development, 59,* 1387–1396.

Hodgson, J., & Spriggs, M. (2005). A practical account of autonomy: Why genetic counseling is especially well suited to the facilitation of informed autonomous decision making. *Journal of Genetic Counseling, 14,* 89–97.

Hoff, E. (2003). The specificity of environmental influence: Socioeconomic status affects early vocabulary development via maternal speech. *Child Development, 74,* 1368–1378.

Hoff, E. (2004). The specificity of environmental influence: Socioeconomic status affects early vocabulary development via maternal speech. *Child Development, 74,* 1368–1378.

Hoff, E. (2006). How social contexts support and shape language development. *Developmental Review, 26,* 55–88.

Hoff, E., & Naigles, L. (2002). How children use input to acquire a lexicon. *Child Development, 73,* 418–433.

Hoff, E., Laursen, B., & Tardiff, T. (2002). Socioeconomic status and parenting. In M. H. Bornstein (Ed.), *Handbook of parenting: Vol. 2. Biology and ecology of parenting* (2nd ed., 231–252). Mahwah, NJ: Erlbaum.

Hoff, E. V. (2005). A friend living inside me: The forms and functions of imaginary companions. *Imagination, Cognition and Personality, 24,* 151–189.

Hofferth, S. L., & Anderson, K. G. (2003). Are all dads equal? Biology versus marriage as a basis for paternal investment. *Journal of Marriage and the Family, 65,* 213–232.

Hoffman, L. W. (2000). Maternal employment: Effects of social context. In R. D. Taylor & M. C. Wang (Eds.), *Resilience across contexts: Family, work, culture, and community* (pp. 147–176). Mahwah, NJ: Erlbaum.

Hoffman, M. L. (2000). *Empathy and moral development.* New York: Cambridge University Press.

Hoffman, S., & Hatch, M. C. (1996). Stress, social support and pregnancy outcome: A reassessment based on research. *Paediatric and Perinatal Epidemiology, 10,* 380–405.

Hoffmann, W. (2001). Fallout from the Chernobyl nuclear disaster and congenital malformations in Europe. *Archives of Environmental Health, 56,* 478–483.

Hoffner, C., & Badzinski, D. M. (1989). Children's integration of facial and situational cues to emotion. *Child Development, 60,* 411–422.

Hofstadter, M., & Reznick, J. S. (1996). Response modality affects human infant delayed-response performance. *Child Development, 67,* 646–658.

Hogan, R. T., Harkness, A. R., & Lubinski, D. (2000). Personality and individual differences. In K. Pawlik & M. R. Rosensweig (Eds.), *International handbook of psychology* (pp. 283–304). London: Sage.

Hoglund, W. L., & Leadbeater, B. J. (2007). Managing threat: Do social-cognitive processes mediate the link between peer victimization and adjustment problems in early adolescence? *Journal of Research on Adolescence, 17,* 525–540.

Hokoda, A., & Fincham, F. D. (1995). Origins of children's helpless and mastery achievement patterns in the family. *Journal of Educational Psychology, 87,* 375–385.

Holden, G. W., Coleman, S. M., & Schmidt, K. L. (1995). Why 3-year-old children get spanked: Determinants as reported by college-educated mothers. *Merrill-Palmer Quarterly, 41,* 431–452.

Holditch-Davis, D., Belyea, M., & Edwards, L. J. (2005). Prediction of 3-year developmental outcomes from sleep development over the preterm period. *Infant Behavior and Development, 79,* 49–58.

Holland, A. L. (2004). Plasticity and development. *Brain and Language, 88,* 254–255.

Hollich, G. J., Hirsh-Pasek, K., & Golinkoff, R. M. (2000). Breaking the language barrier: An emergentist coalition model for the origins of word learning. *Monographs of the Society for Research in Child Development, 65*(3, Serial No. 262).

Holliday, R. E. (2003). Reducing misinformation effects in children with cognitive interviews: Dissociating recollection and familiarity. *Child Development, 74,* 728–751.

Holmbeck, G. N. (1996). A model of family relational transformations during the transition to adolescence: Parent–adolescent conflict and adaptation. In J. A. Graber, J. Brooks-Gunn, & A. C. Petersen (Eds.), *Transitions through adolescence* (pp. 167–199). Mahwah, NJ: Erlbaum.

Holobow, N., Genesee, F., & Lambert, W. (1991). The effectiveness of a foreign language immersion program for children from different ethnic and social class backgrounds: Report 2. *Applied Psycholinguistics, 12,* 179–198.

Holodynski, M. (2004). The miniaturization of expression in the development of emotional self-regulation. *Developmental Psychology, 40,* 16–28.

Holowka, S., Brosseau-Lapré, F., & Petitto, L. A. (2002). Semantic and conceptual knowledge underlying bilingual babies' first signs and words. *Language Learning, 52,* 205–262.

Holtkamp, K., Muller, B., Heussen, N., Remschmidt, H., & Herpertz-Dahlmann, B. (2005). Depression, anxiety, and obsessionality in long-term recovered patients with adolescent-onset anorexia nervosa. *European Child and Adolescent Psychiatry, 14,* 106–110.

Homae, F., Watanabe, H., Nakano, T., Asakawa, K., & Taga, G. (2006). The right hemisphere of sleeping infant perceives sentential prosody. *Neuroscience Research, 54,* 276–280.

Honein, M. A., Paulozzi, L. J., & Erickson, J. D. (2001). Continued occurrence of Accutane-exposed pregnancies. *Teratology, 64,* 142–147.

Hong, G., & Raudenbush, S. W. (2005). Effects of kindergarten retention policy on children's cognitive growth in reading and mathematics. *Educational Evaluation and Policy Analysis, 27,* 205–224.

Hong, Z.-R., Veach, P. M., & Lawrenz, F. (2003). An investigation of the gender stereotyped thinking of Taiwanese secondary school boys and girls. *Sex Roles, 48,* 495–504.

Honzik, M. P., Macfarlane, J. W., & Allen, L. (1948). The stability of mental test performance between two and eighteen years. *Journal of Experimental Education, 17,* 309–329.

Hood, B. M. (2004). Is looking good enough or does it beggar belief? *Developmental Science, 7,* 415–417.

Hope, S., Power, C., & Rodgers, B. (1999). Does financial hardship account for elevated psychological distress in lone mothers? *Social Science and Medicine, 29,* 381–389.

Hopkins, B., & Westra, T. (1988). Maternal handling and motor development: An intracultural study. *Genetic, Social and General Psychology Monographs, 14,* 377–420.

Hopkins-Golightly, T., Raz, S., & Sander, C. J. (2003). Influence of slight to moderate risk for birth hypoxia on acquisition of cognitive and language function in the preterm infant: A cross-sectional comparison with preterm-birth controls. *Neuropsychology, 17,* 3–13.

Horgan, D. (1978). The development of the full passive. *Journal of Child Language, 5,* 65–80.

Horn, J. L. (1994). Theory of fluid and crystallized intelligence. In R. J. Sternberg (Ed.), *Encyclopedia of intelligence* (pp. 443–451). New York: Macmillan.

Horn, J. L., & Noll, J. (1997). Human cognitive capabilities: Gf-Gc theory. In D. P. Flanagan & J. L. Genshaft (Eds.), *Contemporary intellectual assessment: Theories, tests, and issues* (pp. 53–91). New York: Guilford.

Horner, S. L., & Gaither, S. M. (2004). Attribution retraining instruction with a second-grade class. *Early Childhood Education Journal, 31,* 165–170.

Horner, T. M. (1980). Two methods of studying stranger reactivity in infants: A review. *Journal of Child Psychology and Psychiatry, 21,* 203–219.

Hort, B. E., Leinbach, M. D., & Fagot, B. I. (1991). Is there coherence among the cognitive components of gender acquisition? *Sex Roles, 24,* 195–207.

Houlihan, J., Kropp, T., Wiles, R., Gray, S., & Campbell, C. (2005). *Body burden: The pollution in newborns.* Washington, DC: Environmental Working Group.

Hoven, C. W., Duarte, C. S., Lucas, C. P., Wu, P., Mandell, D. J., & Goodwin, R. D.

(2005). Psychopathology among New York City school children 6 months after September 11. *Archives of General Psychiatry, 62,* 545–552.

Howe, M. L. (2003). Memories from the cradle. *Current Directions in Psychological Science, 12,* 62–65.

Howe, N., Aquan-Assee, J., & Bukowski, W. M. (2001). Predicting sibling relations over time: Synchrony between maternal management styles and sibling relationship quality. *Merrill-Palmer Quarterly, 47,* 121–141.

Howell, K. K., Lynch, M. E., Platzman, K. A., Smith, G. H., & Coles, C. D. (2006). Prenatal alcohol exposure and ability, academic achievement, and school functioning in adolescence: A longitudinal follow-up. *Journal of Pediatric Psychology, 31,* 116–126.

Howell, T. M., & Yuille, J. C. (2004). Healing and treatment of Aboriginal offenders: A Canadian example. *American Journal of Forensic Psychology, 22,* 53–76.

Howes, C. (1998). The earliest friendships. In W. M. Bukowski, A. F. Newcomb, & W. W. Hartup (Eds.), *The company they keep: Friendship in childhood and adolescence* (pp. 66–86). New York: Cambridge University Press.

Howes, C., & Farver, J. (1987). Social pretend play in 2-year-olds: Effects of age of partner. *Early Childhood Research Quarterly, 2,* 305–314.

Howes, C., & Matheson, C. C. (1992). Sequences in the development of competent play with peers: Social and social pretend play. *Developmental Psychology, 28,* 961–974.

Hoza, B., Gerdes, A. C., Hinshaw, S. P., Bukowski, W. M., Gold, J. A., Kraemer, H. C., Pelham, W. E., Jr., Wigal, T., & Arnold, L. E. (2005). What aspects of peer relationships are impaired in children with attention-deficit/hyperactivity disorder? *Journal of Consulting and Clinical Psychology, 73,* 411–423.

Hu, Y., Wood, J. F., Smith, V., & Westbrook, N. (2004). Friendships through IM: Examining the relationship between instant messaging and intimacy. *Journal of Computer-Mediated Communication, 10*(1). Retreived from jcmc.indiana.edu/vol10/issue1

Hubbard, F. O. A., & van IJzendoorn, M. H. (1991). Maternal unresponsiveness and infant crying across the first 9 months: A naturalistic longitudinal study. *Infant Behavior and Development, 14,* 299–312.

Hubbs-Tait, L., Nation, J. R., Krebs, N. F., & Bellinger, D. C. (2005). Nuerotoxicants, micronurtrients, and social environments: Individual and combined effects on children's development. *Psychological Science in the Public Interest, 6,* 57–121.

Huddleston, J., & Ge, X. (2003). Boys at puberty: Psychosocial implications. In C. Hayward (Ed.), *Gender differences at puberty* (pp. 113–134). New York: Cambridge University Press.

Hudson, J. A., & Fivush, R. (1991). As time goes by: Sixth graders remember a kindergarten experience. *Applied Cognitive Psychology, 5,* 347–360.

Hudson, J. A., Fivush, R., & Kuebli, J. (1992). Scripts and episodes: The development of event memory. *Applied Cognitive Psychology, 6,* 483–505.

Hudson, J. A., Sosa, B. B., & Shapiro, L. R. (1997). Scripts and plans: The development of preschool children's event knowledge and event planning. In S. L. Friedman & E. K. Scholnick (Eds.), *The developmental psychology of planning: Why, how, and when do we plan?* (pp. 77–102). Mahwah, NJ: Erlbaum.

Huesmann, L. R. (1986). Psychological processes promoting the relation between exposure to media violence and aggressive behavior by the viewer. *Journal of Social Issues, 42,* 125–139.

Huesmann, L. R., Moise-Titus, J., Podolski, C., & Eron, L. D. (2003). Longitudinal relations between children's exposure to TV violence and their aggressive and violent behavior in young adulthood: 1977–1992. *Developmental Psychology, 39,* 201–221.

Huettel, S. A., & Needham, A. (2000). Effects of balance relations between objects on infants' object segregation. *Developmental Science, 3,* 415–427.

Huey, S. J., Jr., & Henggeler, S. W. (2001). Effective community-based interventions for antisocial and delinquent adolescents. In J. N. Hughes & A. M. La Greca (Eds.), *Handbook of psychological services for children and adolescents* (pp. 301–322). London: Oxford University Press.

Hughes, C., & Dunn, J. (1998). Understanding mind and emotion: Longitudinal associations with mental-state talk between young friends. *Developmental Psychology, 34,* 1026–1037.

Hughes, D., Rodriguez, J., Smith, E. P., Johnson, D. J., Stevenson, H. C., & Spicer, P. (2006). Parents' ethnic-racial socialization practices: A review of research and directions for future study. *Developmental Psychology, 42,* 747–770.

Hughes, F. P. (1998). Play in special populations. In O. N. Saracho & B. Spodek (Eds.), *Multiple perspectives on play in early childhood education* (pp. 171–193). Albany: State University of New York Press.

Hughes, J. N., Cavell, T. A., & Grossman, P. B. (1997). A positive view of self: Risk or protection for aggressive children? *Development and Psychopathology, 9,* 75–94.

Hughes, J. N., & Kwok, O. (2006). Classroom engagement mediates the effect of teacher–student support on elementary students' peer acceptance. *Journal of School Psychology, 43,* 465–480.

Hughes, J. N., & Kwok, O. (2007). Influence of student–teacher and parent–teacher relationships on lower achieving readers' engagement and achievement in the primary grades. *Journal of Educational Psychology, 99,* 39–51.

Hughes, J. N., Zhang, D., & Hill, C. R. (2006). Peer assessments of normative and individual teacher–student support predict social acceptance and engagement among low-achieving children. *Journal of School Psychology, 43,* 447–463.

Huijbregts, S. C. J., Séguin, J. R., Zelazo, P. D., Parent, S., Japel, C., & Tremblay, R. E. (2006). Interrelations between maternal smoking during pregnancy, birth weight and sociodemographic factors in the prediction of early cognitive abilities. *Infant and Child Development, 15,* 593–607.

Huizink, A. C., & Mulder, E. J. (2006). Maternal smoking, drinking or cannabis use during pregnancy and neurobehavioral and cognitive functioning in human offspring. *Neuroscience and Biobehavioral Reviews, 30,* 24–41.

Hultman, C. M., Torrang, A., Tuvblad, C., Cnattingius, S., Larsson, J.-O., & Lichtenstein, P. (2007). Birth weight and attention-deficit/hyperactivity symptoms in childhood and early adolescence: A prospective Swedish twin study. *Journal of the American Academy of Child and Adolescent Psychiatry, 46,* 370–377.

Humphrey, T. (1978). Function of the nervous system during prenatal life. In U. Stave (Ed.), *Perinatal physiology* (pp. 651–683). New York: Plenum.

Hunnius, S., & Geuze, R. H. (2004a). Developmental changes in visual scanning of dynamic faces and abstract stimuli in infants: A longitudinal study. *Infancy, 6,* 231–255.

Hunnius, S., & Geuze, R. H. (2004b). Gaze shifting in infancy: A longitudinal study using dynamic faces and abstract stimuli. *Infant Behavior and Development, 27,* 397–416.

Hunsberger, B., Pratt, M., & Pancer, S. M. (2001). Adolescent identity formation: Religious exploration and commitment. *Identity, 1,* 365–386.

Hunt, C. E., & Hauck, F. R. (2006). Sudden infant death syndrome. *Canadian Medical Association Journal, 174,* 1861–1869.

Huotilainen, M., Kujala, A., Hotakainen, M., Parkkonen, L., Taulu, S., & Simola, J. (2005). Short-term memory functions of the human fetus recorded with magnetoencephalography. *Neuroreport, 16,* 81–84.

Hurewitz, F., Brown-Schmidt, S., Thorpe, K., Gleitman, L. R., & Trueswell, J. C. (2000). One frog, two frog, red frog, blue frog: Factors affecting children's syntactic choices in production and comprehension. *Journal of Psycholinguistic Research, 29,* 597–626.

Hursh, D. (2007). Assessing No Child Left Behind and the rise of neoliberal education policies. *American Educational Research Journal, 44,* 493–518.

Hursti, U. K. (1999). Factors influencing children's food choice. *Annals of Medicine, 31,* 26–32.

Hurt, H., Brodsky, N. L., Roth, H., Malmud, E., & Giannetta, J. M. (2005). School performance of children with gestational cocaine exposure. *Neurotoxicology and Teratology, 27,* 203–211.

Huston, A. C., & Alvarez, M. M. (1990). The socialization context of gender role development in early adolescence. In R. Montemayor, G. R. Adams, & T. P. Gullotta (Eds.), *From childhood to adolescence: A transitional period?* (pp. 156–179). Newbury Park, CA: Sage.

Huston, A. C., Wright, J. C., Marquis, J., & Green, S. B. (1999). How young children spend their time: Television and other activities. *Developmental Psychology, 35,* 912–925.

Huttenlocher, P. R. (1994). Synaptogenesis in human cerebral cortex. In G. Dawson & K. W. Fischer (Eds.), *Human behavior and the developing brain* (pp. 137–152). New York: Guilford.

Huttenlocher, P. R. (2002). *Neural plasticity: The effects of environment on the development of the cerebral cortex.* Cambridge, MA: Harvard University Press.

Huyck, M. H. (1996). Continuities and discontinuities in gender identity in midlife. In V. L. Bengtson (Ed.), *Adulthood and aging* (pp. 98–121). New York: Springer-Verlag.

Hyde, J. S., Essex, M. J., Clark, R., & Klein, M. H. (2001). Maternity leave, women's employment, and marital incompatibility. *Journal of Family Psychology, 15,* 476–491.

Hymel, S., Vaillancourt, T., McDougall, P., & Renshaw, P. D. (2004). Peer acceptance and rejection in childhood. In P. K. Smith & C. H. Hart (Eds.), *Blackwell handbook of childhood social development* (pp. 265–284). Malden, MA: Blackwell.

Hyppönen, E., Power, C., & Smith, G. D. (2003). Prenatal growth, BMI, and risk of type 2 diabetes by early midlife. *Diabetes Care, 26,* 2512–2517.

Iglowstein, I., Jenni, O. G., Molinari, L., & Largo, R. H. (2003). Sleep duration from infancy to adolescence: Reference values and generational trends. *Pediatrics, 111,* 302–307.

Ilgaz, H., & Aksu-Koç, A. (2005). Episodic development in preschool children's play-prompted and direct-elicited narratives. *Cognitive Development, 20,* 526–544.

Imai, M., & Haryu, E. (2001). Learning proper nouns and common nouns without clues from syntax. *Child Development, 72,* 787–802.

Imai, M., & Haryu, E. (2004). The nature of word-learning biases and their roles for lexical development: From a cross-linguistic perspective. In D. G. Hall & S. R. Waxman (Eds.), *Weaving a lexicon* (pp. 411–444). Cambridge, MA: MIT Press.

Inagaki, K. (1997). Emerging distinctions between naïve biology and naïve psychology. In H. M. Wellman & K. Inagaki (Eds.), *The emergence of core domains of thought: New directions for child development #75,* (pp. 27–44). San Francisco: Jossey-Bass.

Inagaki, K., & Hatano, G. (2002). *Young children's naïve thinking about the biological world.* New York: Psychology Press.

Inagaki, K., & Hatano, G. (2004). Vitalistic causality in young children's naïve biology. *Trends in Cognitive Sciences, 8,* 356–362.

Ingram, D. (1986). Phonological development: Production. In P. Fletcher & M. Garman (Eds.), *Language acquisition* (2nd ed., pp. 223–239). Cambridge: Cambridge University Press.

Ingram, D. (1999). Phonological acquisition. In M. Barrett (Ed.), *The development of language* (pp. 73–97). Philadelphia: Psychology Press/Taylor & Francis.

Inhelder, B., & Piaget, J. (1958). *The growth of logical thinking from childhood to adolescence: An essay on the construction of formal operational structures.* New York: Basic Books. (Original work published 1955)

Inoff-Germain, G., Arnold, G. S., Nottelman, E. D., Susman, E. J., Cutler, G. B., Jr., & Crousos, G. P. (1988). Relations between hormone levels and observational measures of aggressive behavior of young adolescents in family interactions. *Developmental Psychology, 24,* 129–139.

International Human Genome Sequencing Consortium. (2004). Finishing the euchromatic sequence of the human genome. *Nature, 21,* 931–945.

Intons-Peterson, M. J. (1988). *Gender concepts of Swedish and American youth.* Hillsdale, NJ: Erlbaum.

Iocaboni, M., Molnar-Szakacs, I., Gallese, V., Buccino, G., & Mazziotta, J. C. (2005). Grasping the intentions of others with one's own mirror neuron system. *Public Library of Science: Biology, 3*(3), e79.

Isabella, R. A. (1993). Origins of attachment: Maternal interactive behavior across the first year. *Child Development, 64,* 605–621.

Isabella, R. A., & Belsky, J. (1991). Interactional synchrony and the origins of infant–mother attachment: A replication study. *Child Development, 62,* 373–384.

Itti, E., Gaw, G. I. T., Pawlikowska-Haddal, A., Boone, K. B., Mlikotic, A., & Itti, L. (2006). The structural brain correlates of cognitive deficits in adults with Klinefelter's syndrome. *Journal of Clinical Endocrinology and Metabolism, 91,* 1423–1427.

Izard, C. E. (1979). *The maximally discriminative facial movement scoring system.* Unpublished manuscript, University of Delaware.

Izard, C. E., & Ackerman, B. P. (2000). Motivational, organizational, and regulatory functions of discrete emotions. In M. Lewis & J. M. Haviland-Jones (Eds.), *Handbook of emotions* (2nd ed., pp. 253–264). New York: Guilford.

Izard, C. E., Hembree, E. A., & Huebner, R. R. (1987). Infants' emotion expressions to acute pain. *Developmental Psychology, 23,* 105–113.

Jaakkola, J. J., & Gissler, M. (2004). Maternal smoking in pregnancy, fetal development, and childhood asthma. *American Journal of Public Health, 94,* 136–140.

Jaccard, J., Dodge, T., & Dittus, P. (2002). Parent–adolescent communication about sex and birth control: A conceptual framework. In S. S. Feldman & D. A. Rosenthal (Eds.), *Talking sexuality: Parent–adolescent communication* (pp. 9–41). San Francisco: Jossey-Bass.

Jaccard, J., Dodge, T., & Dittus, P. (2003). Maternal discussions about pregnancy and adolescents' attitudes toward pregnancy. *Journal of Adolescent Health, 33,* 84–87.

Jackson, L. A., von Eye, A., Biocca, F. A., Barbatsis, G., Zhao, Y., & Fitzgerald, H. E. (2006). Does home Internet use influence the academic performance of low-income children? *Developmental Psychology, 42,* 429–435.

Jackson, P. W. (1968). *Life in classrooms.* New York: Holt, Rinehart & Winston.

Jackson, R. A., Gibson, K. A., & Wu, Y. W. (2004). Perinatal outcomes in singletons following in vitro fertilization: A meta-analysis. *Obstetrics and Gynecology, 103,* 551–563.

Jacobs, J. E., & Eccles, J. S. (1992). The impact of mothers' gender-role stereotypic beliefs on mothers' and children's ability perceptions. *Journal of Personality and Social Psychology, 63,* 932–944.

Jacobs, J. E., & Klaczynski, P. A. (2002). The development of judgment and decision making during childhood and adolescence. *Current Directions in Psychological Science, 11,* 145–149.

Jacobs, J. E., Lanza, S., Osgood, D. W., Eccles, J. S., & Wigfield, A. (2002). Changes in children's self-competence and values: Gender and domain differences across grades one through twelve. *Child Development, 73,* 509–527.

Jacobs, J. E., & Weisz, V. (1994). Gender stereotypes: Implications for gifted education. *Roeper Review, 16,* 152–155.

Jacobs, J. N., & Kelley, M. L. (2006). Predictors of paternal involvement in childcare in dual-earner families with young children. *Fathering, 4,* 23–47.

Jacobson, J. L., & Jacobson, S. W. (2003). Prenatal exposure to polychlorinated biphenyls and attention at school age. *Journal of Pediatrics, 143,* 780–788.

Jacobson, K. C., & Crockett, L. J. (2000). Parental monitoring and adolescent adjustment: An ecological perspective. *Journal of Research on Adolescence, 10,* 65–97.

Jacobson, S. W., Jacobson, J. L., Sokol, R. J., Chiodo, L. M., & Corobana, R. (2004). Maternal age, alcohol abuse history, and quality of parenting as moderators of the effects of prenatal alcohol exposure on 7.5-year intellectual function. *Alcoholism: Clinical and Experimental Research, 28,* 1732–1745.

Jacquet, P. (2004). Sensitivity of germ cells and embryos to ionizing radiation. *Journal of Biological Regulators and Homeostatic Agents, 18,* 106–114.

Jadack, R. A., Hyde, J. S., Moore, C. F., & Keller, M. L. (1995). Moral reasoning about sexually transmitted diseases. *Child Development, 66,* 167–177.

Jaffari-Bimmel, N., Juffer, F., van IJzendoorn, M. H., Bakermans-Kranenburg, M. J., & Mooijaart, A. (2006). Social development from infancy to adolescence: Longitudinal and concurrent factors in an adoption sample. *Developmental Psychology, 42,* 1143–1153.

Jaffee, S. R., Caspi, A., Moffitt, T. E., Belsky, J., & Silva, P. (2001). Why are children born to teen mothers at risk for adverse outcomes in young adulthood? Results of a 20-year longitudinal study. *Development and Psychopathology, 13,* 377–397.

Jaffee, S. R., & Hyde, J. S. (2000). Gender differences in moral orientation: A meta-analysis. *Psychological Bulletin, 126,* 703–706.

Jaffee, S. R., Moffitt, T. E., Caspi, A., & Taylor, A. (2003). Life with (or without) father: The benefits of living with two biological parents depend on the father's antisocial behavior. *Child Development, 74,* 109–126.

Jambunathan, S., Burts, D. C., & Pierce, S. (2000). Comparisons of parenting attitudes among five ethnic groups in the United States. *Journal of Comparative Family Studies, 31,* 395–406.

Jamieson, J. R. (1995). Interactions between mothers and children who are deaf. *Journal of Early Intervention, 19,* 108–117.

Jang, S. J., & Johnson, B. R. (2001). Neighborhood disorder, individual religiosity, and adolescent use of illicit drugs: A test of multilevel hypotheses. *Criminology, 39,* 109–143

Jankowski, J. J., Rose, S. A., & Feldman, J. F. (2001). Modifying the distribution of attention in infants. *Child Development, 72,* 339–351.

Jansen, A., Theunissen, N., Slechten, K., Nederkoorn, C., Boon, B., Mulkens, S., & Roefs, A. (2003). Overweight children overeat after exposure to food cues. *Eating Behaviors, 4,* 197–209.

Jarrold, C., Baddeley, A. D., & Hewes, A. K. (1998). Verbal and nonverbal abilities in the Williams syndrome phenotype: Evidence for diverging developmental trajectories. *Journal of Child Psychology and Psychiatry, 39,* 511–523.

Jayakody, R., & Kalil, A. (2002). Social fathering in low-income, African-American families with preschool children. *Journal of Marriage and the Family, 64,* 504–516.

Jeffrey, J. (2004, November). Parents often blind to their kids' weight. *British Medical Journal Online, 1.* Retrieved from http://content.health.msn.com/content/article/97/104292.htm

Jenkins, J. M., & Astington, J. W. (2000). Theory of mind and social behavior: Causal models tested in a longitudinal study. *Merrill-Palmer Quarterly, 46,* 203–220.

Jenkins, J. M., Rasbash, J., & O'Connor, T. G. (2003). The role of the shared family context in differential parenting. *Developmental Psychology, 39,* 99–113.

Jenkins, J. M., Turrell, S. L., Kogushi, Y., Lollis, S., & Ross, H. S. (2003). A longitudinal investigation of the dynamics of mental state talk in families. *Child Development, 74,* 905–920.

Jensen, A. R. (1969). How much can we boost IQ and scholastic achievement? *Harvard Educational Review, 39,* 1–123.

Jensen, A. R. (1985). The nature of the black–white difference on various psychometric tests: Spearman's hypothesis. *Behavioral and Brain Sciences, 8,* 193–219.

Jensen, A. R. (1998). *The g factor: The science of mental ability.* New York: Praeger.

Jensen, A. R. (2001). Spearman's hypothesis. In J. M. Collis & S. Messick (Eds.), *Intelligence and personality: Bridging the gap in theory and measurement* (pp. 3–24). Mahwah, NJ: Erlbaum.

Jensen, A. R. (2002). Galton's legacy to research on intelligence. *Journal of Biosocial Science, 34,* 145–172.

Jeynes, W. H. (2005). A meta-analysis of the relation of parental involvement to urban elementary school student academic achievement. *Urban Education, 40,* 237–269.

Jiao, S., Ji, G., & Jing, Q. (1996). Cognitive development of Chinese urban only children and children with siblings. *Child Development, 67,* 387–395.

Jimerson, S. R., Graydon, K., Fletcher, S. M., Schnurr, B., Kundert, D., & Nickerson, A. (2006). Grade retention and promotion. In G. G. Bear & K. M. Minke (Eds.), *Children's needs III: Development, prevention, and intervention* (pp. 601–613). Washington, DC: National Association of School Psychologists.

Joh, A. S., & Adolph, K. E. (2006). Learning from falling. *Child Development, 77,* 89–102.

Johnson, D. E. (2000). Medical and developmental sequelae of early childhood institutionalization in Eastern European adoptees. In C. A. Nelson (Ed.), *Minnesota Symposia on Child Psychology* (Vol. 31, pp. 113–162). Mahwah, NJ: Erlbaum.

Johnson, D. E. (2002). Adoption and the effect on children's development. *Early Human Development, 68,* 39–54.

Johnson, J., Im-Bolter, N., & Pascual-Leone, J. (2003). Development of mental attention in gifted and mainstream children: The role of mental capacity, inhibition, and speed of processing. *Child Development, 74,* 1594–1614.

Johnson, J. G., Cohen, P., Smailes, E. M., Kasen, S., & Brook, J. S. (2002). Television viewing and aggressive behavior during adolescence and adulthood. *Science, 295,* 2468–2471.

Johnson, K. C., & Daviss, B.-A. (2005). Outcomes of planned home births with certified professional midwives: Large prospective study in North America. *British Medical Journal, 330,* 1416.

Johnson, L. D., O'Malley, P. M., Bachman, J. G., & Schulenberg, J. E. (2006). *Monitoring the Future national survey results on drug use, 1975–2005: Vol. 1, Secondary school students* (NIH Publication No. 06-5883). Bethesda, MD: National Institute on Drug Abuse.

Johnson, M. H. (1999). Ontogenetic constraints on neural and behavioral plasticity: Evidence from imprinting and face processing. *Canadian Journal of Experimental Psychology, 55,* 77–90.

Johnson, M. H. (2001). The development and neural basis of face recognition: Comment and speculation. *Infant and Child Development, 10,* 31–33.

Johnson, M. H. (2005). Developmental neuroscience, psychophysiology, and genetics. In M. H. Bornstein & M. E. Lamb (Eds.), *Developmental science: An advanced textbook* (5th ed., pp. 187–222). Mahwah, NJ: Erlbaum.

Johnson, M. H., & Mareschal, D. (2001). Cognitive and perceptual development during infancy. *Current Opinion in Neurobiology, 11,* 213–218.

Johnson, S. C., Dweck, C. S., & Chen, F. S. (2007). Evidence for infants' internal working models of attachment. *Psychological Science, 18,* 501–502.

Johnson, S. P. (1997). Young infants' perception of object unity: Implications for development of attentional and cognitive skills. *Current Directions in Psychological Science, 6,* 5–11.

Johnson, S. P., Amso, D., & Slemmer, J. A. (2003). Development of object concepts in infancy: Evidence for early learning in an eye-tracking paradigm. *Proceedings of the National Academy of Sciences, 100,* 10568–10753.

Johnson, S. P., Bremner, J. G., Slater, A. M., Mason, U. C., & Foster, K. (2002). Young infants' perception of unity and form in occlusion displays. *Journal of Experimental Child Psychology, 81,* 358–374.

Johnson, S. P., Bremner, J. G., Slater, A., Mason, U., Foster, K., & Cheshire, A. (2003). Infants' perception of object trajectories. *Child Development, 74,* 94–108.

Johnson, S. P., Slemmer, J. A., & Amso, D. (2004). Where infants look determines how they see: Eye movements and object perception performance in 3-month-olds. *Infancy, 6,* 185–201.

Johnston, M. V., Nishimura, A., Harum, K., Pekar, J., & Blue, M. E. (2001). Sculpting the developing brain. *Advances in Pediatrics, 48,* 1–38.

Jones, C. M., Braithwaite, V. A., & Healy, S. D. (2003). The evolution of sex differences in spatial ability. *Behavioral Neuroscience, 117,* 403–411.

Jones, D. C., Abbey, B. B., & Cumberland, A. (1998). The development of display rule knowledge: Linkages with family expressiveness and social competence. *Child Development, 69,* 1209–1222.

Jones, E. F., & Thomson, N. R. (2001). Action perception and outcome valence: Effects on children's inferences of intentionality and moral and liking judgments. *Journal of Genetic Psychology, 162,* 154–166.

Jones, F. (2003). Religious commitment in Canada, 1997 and 2000. *Religious Commitment Monograph No. 3.* Ottawa, Canada: Christian Commitment Research Institute.

Jones, G., Ritter, F. E., & Wood, D. J. (2000). Using a cognitive architecture to examine what develops. *Psychological Science, 11,* 93–100.

Jones, G. P., & Dembo, M. H. (1989). Age and sex role differences in intimate friendships during childhood and adolescence. *Merrill-Palmer Quarterly, 35,* 445–462.

Jones, H. E. (2006). Drug addiction during pregnancy: Advances in maternal treatment and understanding child outcomes. *Current Directions in Psychological Science, 15,* 126–130.

Jones, J., Lopez, A., & Wilson, M. (2003). Congenital toxoplasmosis. *American Family Physician, 67,* 2131–2137.

Jones, L. B., Rothbart, M. K., & Posner, M. I. (2003). Development of executive attention in preschool children. *Developmental Science, 6,* 498–504.

Jones, M. C., & Mussen, P. H. (1958). Self-conceptions, motivations, and interpersonal attitudes of early- and late-maturing girls. *Child Development, 29,* 491–501.

Jones, N. A., Field, T., & Davalos, M. (2000). Right frontal EEG asymmetry and lack of empathy in preschool children of depressed mothers. *Child Psychiatry and Human Development, 30,* 189–204.

Jones, R. K., Purcell, A., Singh, S., & Finer, L. B. (2005). Adolescents' reports of parental knowledge of adolescents' use of sexual health services and their reactions to mandated parental notification for prescription contraceptives. *Journal of the American Medical Association, 293,* 340–348.

Jones, S. S. (2006). Exploration or imitation? The effect of music on 4-week-old infants' tongue protrusions. *Infant Behavior and Development, 29,* 126–130.

Jones, W., Bellugi, U., Lai, Z., Chiles, M., Reilly, J., Lincoln, A., & Adolphs, R. (2000). Hypersociability in Williams syndrome. *Journal of Cognitive Neuroscience, 12,* 30–46

Jongbloet, P. H., Zielhuis, G. A., Groenewoud, H. M., & Paster-De Jong, P. C. (2001). The secular trends in male:female ratio at birth in postwar industrialized countries. *Environmental Health Perspectives, 109,* 749–752.

Jordan, B. (1993). *Birth in four cultures.* Prospect Heights, IL: Waveland.

Jorgensen, K. M. (1999). Pain assessment and management in the newborn infant. *Journal of PeriAnesthesia Nursing, 14,* 349–356.

Jose, P., Huntsinger, C., Huntsinger, P., & Liaw, F.-R. (2000). Parental values and practices relevant to young children's social development in Taiwan and the United States. *Journal of Cross-Cultural Psychology, 31,* 677–702.

Joseph, R. M., & Tager-Flusberg, H. (2004). The relationship of theory of mind and executive functions to symptom type and severity in children with autism. *Development and Psychopathology, 16,* 137–155.

Joshi, P. T., O'Donnell, D. A., Cullins, L. M., & Lewin, S. (2006). Children exposed to war and terrorism. In M. M. Feerick & G. B. Silverman (Eds.), *Children exposed to violence* (pp. 53–84). Baltimore: Paul H. Brookes.

Joyner, M. H., & Kurtz-Costes, B. (1997). Metamemory development. In W. Schneider & F. E. Weinert (Eds.), *Memory performance and competencies: Issues in growth and development* (pp. 275–300). Hillsdale, NJ: Erlbaum.

Judge, S., Puckett, K., & Bell, S. M. (2006). Closing the digital divide: Update from the Early Childhood Longitudinal Study. *Journal of Educational Research, 100,* 52–60.

Jumpstart Evaluation Team. (2008, April). *Influence of Jumpstart implementation quality on child outcomes.* Paper presented at the annual meeting of the American Educational Research Association, New York.

Jürgensen, M., Hiort, O., Holterhus, P.-M., & Thyen, U. (2007). Gender role behavior in children with XY karyotype and disorders of sex development. *Hormones and Behavior, 51,* 443–453.

Jusczyk, P. W. (2001). In the beginning, was the word . . . In F. Lacerda & C. von Hofsten (Eds.), *Emerging cognitive abilities in early infancy* (pp. 173–192). Mahwah, NJ: Erlbaum.

Jusczyk, P. W. (2002). Some critical developments in acquiring native language sound organization. *Annals of Otology, Rhinology and Laryngology, 189,* 11–15.

Jusczyk, P. W. (2003). The role of speech perception capacities in early language acquisition. In M. T. Banich & M. Mack (Eds.). *Mind, brain, and language: Multidisciplinary perspectives* (pp. 61–83). Mahwah, NJ: Erlbaum.

Jusczyk, P. W., & Hohne, E. A. (1997). Infants' memory for spoken words. *Science, 277,* 1984–1986.

Jusczyk, P. W., Houston, D. M., & Newsome, M. (1999). The beginnings of word segmentation in English-learning infants. *Cognitive Psychology, 39,* 159–207.

Jusczyk, P. W., & Luce, P. A. (2002). Speech perception. In H. Pashler & S. Yantis (Eds.), *Steven's handbook of experimental psychology: Vol. 1. Sensation and perception* (3rd ed., pp. 493–536). New York: Wiley.

Justice for Children and Youth. (2003). *Corporal punishment.* Toronto: Canadian Foundation for Children, Youth, and the Law. Retrieved from www.jfcy.org/corporalp/corporalp.html

Justice, E. M. (1986). Developmental changes in judgments of relative strategy effectiveness. *British Journal of Developmental Psychology, 4,* 75–81.

Justice, E. M., Baker-Ward, L., Gupta, S., & Jannings, L. R. (1997). Means to the goal of remembering: Developmental changes in awareness of strategy use–performance relations. *Journal of Experimental Child Psychology, 65,* 293–314.

Kabakus, N., Aydin, M., Haluk, A., Balci, T. A., Kurt, A., & Kekilli, E. (2006). Fragile X syndrome and cerebral perfusion abnormalities: Single-photon emission computed tomographic study. *Journal of Child Neurology, 21,* 1040–1046.

Kagan, J. (1998). Biology and the child. In N. Eisenberg (Ed.), *Handbook of child psychology: Vol. 3. Social, emotional, and personality development* (5th ed., pp. 177–236). New York: Wiley.

Kagan, J. (2003). Behavioral inhibition as a temperamental category. In R. J. Davidson, K. R. Scherer, & H. H. Goldsmith (Eds.), *Handbook of affective science* (pp. 320–331). New York: Oxford University Press.

Kagan, J. (2006). Biology's useful contribution: A comment. *Human Development, 49,* 310–314.

Kagan, J., Arcus, D., Snidman, N., Feng, W. Y., Hendler, J., & Greene, S. (1994). Reactivity in infants: A cross-national comparison. *Developmental Psychology, 30,* 342–345.

Kagan, J., & Fox, N. A. (2006). Biology, culture, and temperamental biases. In N. Eisenberg (Ed.), *Handbook of child psychology: Vol. 3. Social, emotional, and personality development* (6th ed., pp. 167–225). Hoboken, NJ: Wiley.

Kagan, J., Kearsley, R. B., & Zelazo, P. R. (1978). *Infancy: Its place in human development.* Cambridge, MA: Harvard University Press.

Kagan, J., & Saudino, K. J. (2001). Behavioral inhibition and related temperaments. In R. N. Emde & J. K. Hewitt (Eds.), *Infancy to early childhood: Genetic and environmental influences on developmental change* (pp. 111–119). New York: Oxford University Press.

Kagan, J., & Snidman, N. (2004). *The long shadow of temperament.* Cambridge, MA: Belknap Press.

Kagan, J., Snidman, N., Kahn, V., & Towsley, S. (2007). The preservation of two infant temperaments into adolescence. *Monographs of the Society for Research in Child Development, 72*(2, Serial No. 287).

Kagan, J., Snidman, N., Zentner, M., & Peterson, E. (1999). Infant temperament and anxious symptoms in school-age children. *Development and Psychopathology, 11,* 209–224.

Kail, R. (1988). Developmental functions for speeds of cognitive processes. *Journal of Experimental Child Psychology, 45,* 339–364.

Kail, R. (1991). Processing time declines exponentially during childhood and adolescence. *Developmental Psychology, 27,* 259–266.

Kail, R. (1993). The role of a global mechanism in developmental change in speed of processing. In M. L. Howe & R. Pasnak (Eds.), *Emerging themes in cognitive development: Vol. 1. Foundations.* New York: Springer-Verlag.

Kail, R. (1997). Processing time, imagery, and spatial memory. *Journal of Experimental Child Psychology, 64,* 67–78.

Kail, R., & Park, Y. (1992). Global developmental change in processing time. *Merrill-Palmer Quarterly, 38,* 525–541.

Kail, R., Hall, L. K., & Caskey, B. J. (1999). Processing speed, exposure to print, and naming speed. *Applied Psycholinguistics, 20,* 303–314.

Kail, R. V. (2003). Information processing and memory. In M. H. Bornstein, L. Davidson, C. L. M. Keyes, K. A. Moore, and The Center for Child Well-Being (Eds.), *Well-being: Positive development across the life course* (pp. 269–280). Mahwah, NJ: Erlbaum.

Kaitz, M., Meirov, H., Landman, I., & Eidelman, A. I. (1993). Infant recognition by tactile cues. *Infant Behavior and Development, 16,* 333–341.

Kalil, A., Levine, J. A., & Ziol-Guest, K. M. (2005). Following in their parents' footsteps: How characteristics of parental work predict adolescents' interest in parents' jobs. In B. Schneider & L. J. Waite (Eds.), *Being together, working apart: Dual-career families and the work–life balance* (pp. 422–442). New York: Cambridge University Press.

Kane, C. M. (2000). African-American family dynamics as perceived by family members. *Journal of Black Studies, 30,* 691–702.

Kane, P., & Garber, J. (2004). The relations among depression in fathers, children's psychopathology, and father–child conflict: A meta-analysis. *Clinical Psychology Review, 24,* 339–360.

Kaplow, J. B., & Widom, C. S. (2007). Age of onset of child maltreatment predicts long-term mental health outcomes. *Journal of Abnormal Psychology, 116,* 176–187.

Karafantis, D. M., & Levy, S. R. (2004). The role of children's lay theories about the malleability of human attributes in beliefs about volunteering for disadvantaged groups. *Child Development, 75,* 236–250.

Karmiloff-Smith, A. (1999). The connectionist infant: Would Piaget turn in his grave? In A. Slater & D. Muir (Eds.), *The Blackwell reader in developmental psychology* (pp. 43–52). Malden, MA: Blackwell.

Karmiloff-Smith, A., Brown, J. H., Grice, S., & Paterson, S. (2003). Dethroning the myth: Cognitive dissociations and innate modularity in Williams syndrome. *Developmental Neuropsychology, 23,* 227–242.

Karmiloff-Smith, A., Grant, J., Berthoud, I., Davies, M., Howlin, P., & Udwin, O. (1997). Language and Williams syndrome: How intact is "intact"? *Child Development, 68,* 246–262.

Karmiloff-Smith, A., Grant, J., Sims, K., Jones, M., & Cuckle, P. (1996). Rethinking metalinguistic awareness: Representing and accessing knowledge about what counts as a word. *Cognition, 58,* 197–219.

Karmiloff-Smith, A., Tyler, L. K., Voice, K., Sims, K., Udwin, O., Howlin, P., & Davies, M. (1998). Linguistic dissociations in Williams syndrome: Evaluating receptive syntax in on-line and off-line tasks. *Neuropsychologia, 36,* 343–351.

Karpati, A. M., Rubin, C. H., Kieszak, S. M., Marcus, M., & Troiano, R. P. (2002). Stature and pubertal stage assessment in American boys: The 1988–1994 Third National Health and Nutrition Examination Survey. *Journal of Adolescent Health, 30,* 205–212.

Kashani, J. H., & Shepperd, J. A. (1990). Aggression in adolescents: The role of social support and personality. *Canadian Journal of Psychiatry, 35,* 311–315.

Kasmauski, K., & Jaret, P. (2003). *Impact: On the frontlines of global health.* Washington, DC: National Geographic.

Kassel, J. D., Weinstein, S., Skitch, S. A., Veilleux, J., & Mermelstein, R. (2005). The development of substance abuse in adolescence: Correlates, causes, and consequences. In J. D. Kassel, S. Weinstein, S. A. Skitch, J. Veilleux, & R. Mermelstein (Eds.), *Development of psychopathology: A vulnerability-stress perspective* (pp. 355–384). Thousand Oaks, CA: Sage.

Kato, I., Franco, P., Groswasser, J., Scaillet, S., Kelmanson, I., Togari, H., & Kahn, A. (2003). Incomplete arousal processes in infants who were victims of sudden death. *American Journal of Respiratory and Critical Care, 168,* 1298–1303.

Katz, L. F., & Windecker-Nelson, B. (2004). Parental meta-emotion philosophy in families with conduct-problem children: Links with peer relations. *Journal of Abnormal Child Psychology, 32,* 385–398.

Katzman, D. K. (2005). Medical complications in adolescents with anorexia nervosa: A review of the literature. *International Journal of Eating Disorders, 37,* S52–S59.

Kaufman, A. S., & Lichtenberger, E. O. (2002). *Assessing adolescent and adult intelligence* (2nd ed.). Boston: Allyn and Bacon.

Kaufman, A. S., Kamphaus, R. W., & Kaufman, N. L. (1985). New directions in intelligence testing: The Kaufman Assessment Battery for Children (K-ABC). In B. B. Wolman (Ed.), *Handbook of intelligence* (pp. 663–698). New York: Wiley.

Kaufman, J., & Charney, D. (2003). The neurobiology of child and adolescent depression: Current knowledge and future directions. In D. Cicchetti & E. Walker (Eds.), *Neurodevelopmental mechanisms in psychopathology* (pp. 461–490). New York: Cambridge University Press.

Kaufman, J., Csibra, G., & Johnson, M. H. (2005). Oscillatory activity in the infant brain reflects object maintenance. *Proceedings of the National Academy of Sciences, 102,* 15271–15274.

Kavanaugh, R. D. (2006a). Pretend play. In B. Spodek & O. N. Saracho (Eds.), *Handbook of research on the education of young chil-*

dren (2nd ed., pp. 269–278). Mahwah, NJ: Erlbaum.

Kavanaugh, R. D. (2006b). Pretend play and theory of mind. In L. Balter & C. S. Tamis-LeMonda (Eds.), *Child psychology: A handbook of contemporary issues* (2nd ed., pp. 153–166). New York: Psychology Press.

Kavanaugh, R. D., & Engel, S. (1998). The development of pretense and narrative in early childhood. In O. N. Saracho & B. Spodek (Eds.), *Multiple perspectives on play in early childhood education* (pp. 80–99). Albany: State University of New York Press.

Kavsek, M. (2004). Predicting later IQ from infant visual habituation and dishabituation: A meta-analysis. *Journal of Applied Developmental Psychology, 25,* 369–393.

Kaye, K., & Marcus, J. (1981). Infant imitation: The sensory-motor agenda. *Developmental Psychology, 17,* 258–265.

Kaye, W. H., Frank, G. K., Bailer, U. F., & Henry, S. E. (2005). Neurobiology of anorexia nervosa: Clinical implications of alterations of the function of serotonin and other neuronal systems. *International Journal of Eating Disorders, 37,* S15–S19.

Kazdin, A. E. (2000). Treatments for aggressive and antisocial children. *Child and Adolescent Psychiatric Clinics of North America, 9,* 841–858.

Kazdin, A. E. (2003). Problem-solving skills training and parent management training for conduct disorder. In A. E. Kazdin & J. R. Weisz (Eds.), *Evidence-based psychotherapies for children and adolescents* (pp. 241–262). New York: Guilford.

Kearins, J. M. (1981). Visual spatial memory in Australian aboriginal children of desert regions. *Cognitive Psychology, 13,* 434–460.

Keating, D. (1979). Adolescent thinking. In J. Adelson (Ed.), *Handbook of adolescent psychology* (pp. 211–246). New York: Wiley.

Keating, D. (1990). Adolescent thinking. In S. S. Feldman & G. R. Elliott (Eds.), *At the threshold* (pp. 54–89). Cambridge, MA: Harvard University Press.

Keating, D., & Clark, L. V. (1980). Development of physical and social reasoning in adolescence. *Developmental Psychology, 16,* 23–30.

Keating, D. P. (2004). Cognitive and brain development. In R. M. Lerner & L. Steinberg (Eds.), *Handbook of adolescent psychology* (2nd ed., pp. 45–84). Hoboken, NJ: Wiley.

Kedar, Y., Casasola, M., & Lust, B. (2006). Getting there faster: 18- and 24-month-old infants' use of function words to determine reference. *Child Development, 77,* 325–338.

Keefe, M. R., Barbosa, G. A., & Froese-Fretz, A., Kotzer, A. M., & Lobo, M. (2005). An intervention program for families with irritable infants. *American Journal of Maternal/Child Nursing, 30,* 230–236.

Keil, F. C. (1986). Conceptual domains and the acquisition of metaphor. *Cognitive Development, 1,* 72–96.

Keil, F. C., & Lockhart, K. L. (1999). Explanatory understanding in conceptual development. In E. K. Scholnick, K. Nelson, S. A. Gelman, & P. H. Miller (Eds.), *Conceptual development: Piaget's legacy* (pp. 103–130). Mahwah, NJ: Erlbaum.

Keller, H., Borke, Y. J., Kärtner, J., Jensen, H., & Papaligoura, Z. (2004). Developmental consequences of early parenting experiences: Self-recognition and self-regulation in three cultural communities. *Child Development, 75,* 1745–1760.

Keller, H., Kärtner, J., Borke, J., Yovsi, R., & Kleis, A. (2005). Parenting styles and the development of the categorical self: A longitudinal study on mirror self-recognition in Cameroonian Nso and German families. *International Journal of Behavioral Development, 29,* 496–504.

Keller, S. N., & Brown, J. D. (2002). Media interventions to promote responsible sexual behavior. *Journal of Sex Research, 39,* 67–72.

Kelley, S. A., Brownell, C. A., & Campbell, S. B. (2000). Mastery motivation and self-evaluative affect in toddlers: Longitudinal relations with maternal behavior. *Child Development, 71,* 1061–1071.

Kelley, S. S., Borawski, E. A., Flocke, S. A., & Keen, K. J. (2003). The role of sequential and concurrent sexual relationships in the risk of sexually transmitted diseases among adolescents. *Journal of Adolescent Health, 32,* 296–305.

Kellman, P. J., & Arteberry, M. E. (2006). Infant visual perception. In D. Kuhn & R. Siegler (Eds.), *Handbook of child psychology: Vol. 2. Cognition, perception, and language* (6th ed., pp. 109–160). Hoboken, NJ: Wiley.

Kelly, D. J., Liu, S., Ge, L., Quinn, P. C., Slater, A. M., Lee, K., Liu, Q., & Pascalis, O. (2007). Cross-race preferences for same-race faces extend beyond the African versus Caucasian contrast in 3-month-old infants. *Infancy, 11,* 87–95.

Kelly, F. W., Terry, R., & Naglieri, R. (1999). A review of alternative birthing positions. *Journal of the American Osteopathic Association, 99,* 470–474.

Kelly, N., & Norwich, B. (2004). Pupils' perceptions of self and of labels: Moderate learning difficulties in mainstream and special schools. *British Journal of Educational Psychology, 74,* 411–435.

Kempe, C. H., B. F., Steele, P. W., Droegemueller, P. W., & Silver, H. K. (1962). The battered-child syndrome. *Journal of the American Medical Association, 181,* 17–24.

Kendall, G., & Peebles, D. (2005). Acute fetal hypoxia: The modulating effect of infection. *Early Human Development, 81,* 27–34.

Kendler, K. S., Thornton, L. M., Gilman, S. E., & Kessler, R. C. (2000). Sexual orientation in a U.S. national sample of twin and nontwin sibling pairs. *American Journal of Psychiatry, 157,* 1843–1846.

Kennell, J., Klaus, M., McGrath, S., Robertson, S., & Hinkley, C. (1991). Continuous emotional support during labor in a U.S. hospital. *Journal of the American Medical Association, 265,* 2197–2201.

Kenney-Benson, G. A., Pomerantz, E. M. Ryan, A. M., & Patrick, H. (2006). Sex differences in math performance: The role of children's approach to schoolwork. *Developmental Psychology, 42,* 11–26.

Kenyon, B. L. (2001). Current research in children's conceptions of death: A critical review. *Omega, 43,* 63–91.

Kerckhoff, A. C. (2002). The transition from school to work. In J. T. Mortimer & R. Larson (Eds.), *The changing adolescent experience* (pp. 52–87). New York: Cambridge University Press.

Kerestes, M., & Youniss, J. E. (2003). Rediscovering the importance of religion in adolescent development. In R. M. Lerner, F. Jacobs, & D. Wertlieb (Eds.), *Handbook of applied developmental science* (Vol. 1, pp. 165–184). Thousand Oaks, CA: Sage.

Kerestes, M., Youniss, J., & Metz, E. (2004). Longitudinal patterns of religious perspective and civic integration. *Applied Developmental Science, 8,* 39–46.

Kerig, P. K., Cowan, P. A., & Cowan, C. P. (1993). Marital quality and gender differences in parent–child interactions. *Developmental Psychology, 29,* 931–939.

Kern, S. (2007). Lexicon development in French-speaking infants. *First Language, 27,* 227–250.

Kernis, M. H. (2002). Self-esteem as a multifaceted construct. In T. M. Brinthaupt & R. P. Lipka (Eds.), *Understanding early adolescent self and identity* (pp. 57–88). Albany, NY: State University of New York Press.

Kerr, D. C. R., Lopez, N. L., Olson, S. L., & Sameroff, A. J. (2004). Parental discipline and externalizing behavior problems in early childhood: The roles of moral regulation and child gender. *Journal of Abnormal Child Psychology, 32,* 369–383.

Kesler, S. R. (2007). Turner syndrome. *Child and Adolescent Psychiatric Clinics of North America, 16,* 709–722.

Kessen, W. (1967). Sucking and looking: Two organized congenital patterns of behavior in the human newborn. In H. W. Stevenson, E. H. Hess, & H. L. Rheingold (Eds.), *Early behavior: Comparative and developmental approaches* (pp. 147–179). New York: Wiley.

Kessler, R. C., Adler, L. A., Barkley R., Biederman, J., Conners, C. K., & Demler, O. (2006). The prevalence and correlates of adult ADHD in the United States: Results from the National Comorbidity Survey Replication. *American Journal of Psychiatry, 163,* 716–723.

Kessler, R. C., Adler, L. A., Barkley, R., Biederman, J., Conners, C. K., & Faraone, S. V. (2005). Patterns and predictors of attention-deficit/hyperactivity disorder persistence into adulthood: Results from the National Comorbidity Survey Replication. *Biological Psychiatry, 57,* 1442–1451.

Kieras, J. E., Tobin, R. M., Graziano, W. G., & Rothbart, M. K. (2005). You can't always get what you want: Effortful control and children's responses to undesirable gifts. *Psychological Science, 16,* 391–396.

Killen, M., Crystal, D., & Watanabe, H. (2002). The individual and the group: Japanese and American children's evaluations of peer exclusion, tolerance of difference, and prescriptions for conformity. *Child Development, 73,* 1788–1802.

Killen, M., Lee-Kim, J., McGlothlin, H., & Stangor, C. (2002). How children and adolescents evaluate gender and racial exclusion. *Monographs of the Society for Research in Child Development, 67*(4, Serial No. 271).

Killen, M., & Nucci, L. P. (1995). Morality, autonomy, and social conflict. In M. Killen & D. Hart (Eds.), *Morality in everyday life: Developmental perspectives* (pp. 52–86). Cambridge: Cambridge University Press.

Killen, M., & Stangor, M. (2001). Children's social reasoning about inclusion and exclusion in gender and race peer group contexts. *Child Development, 72,* 174–186.

Kilpatrick, S. W., & Sanders, D. M. (1978). Body image stereotypes: A developmental comparison. *Journal of Genetic Psychology, 132,* 87–95.

Kim, J. M. (1998). Korean children's concepts of adult and peer authority and moral reasoning. *Developmental Psychology, 34,* 947–955.

Kim, J. M., & Turiel, E. (1996). Korean children's concepts of adult and peer authority. *Social Development, 5,* 310–329.

Kim, J.-Y., McHale, S. M., Crouter, A. C., & Osgood, D. W. (2007). Longitudinal linkages between sibling relationships and adjustment from middle childhood through adolescence. *Developmental Psychology, 43,* 960–973.

Kim, J.-Y., McHale, S. M., Osgood, D. W., & Crouter, A. C. (2006). Longitudinal course and family correlates of sibling relationships from childhood through adolescence. *Child Development, 77,* 1746–1761.

Kim, K. J., Conger, R. D., Lorenz, F. O., & Elder, G. H., Jr. (2001). Parent–adolescent reciprocity in negative affect and its relation to early adult social development. *Developmental Psychology, 37,* 775–790.

Kim, M., McGregor, K. K., & Thompson, C. K. (2000). Early lexical development in English- and Korean-speaking children: Language-general and language-specific patterns. *Journal of Child Language, 27,* 225–254.

Kimbro, R. T. (2006). On-the-job moms: Work and breastfeeding initiation and duration for a sample of low-income women. *Maternal and Child Health Journal, 10,* 19–26.

King, P. E., & Furrow, J. L. (2004). Religion as a resource for positive youth development: Religion, social capital, and moral outcomes. *Developmental Psychology, 40,* 703–713.

Kinney, D. (1999). From "headbangers" to "hippies": Delineating adolescents' active attempts to form an alternative peer culture. In J. A. McLellan & M. J. V. Pugh (Eds.), *The role of peer groups in adolescent social identity: Exploring the importance of stability and change* (pp. 21–35). San Francisco: Jossey-Bass.

Kirby, D. (2002a). Antecedents of adolescent initiation of sex, contraceptive use, and pregnancy. *American Journal of Health Behavior, 26,* 473–485.

Kirby, D. (2002b). Effective approaches to reducing adolescent unprotected sex, pregnancy, and childbearing. *Journal of Sex Research, 39,* 51–57.

Kirby, D. (2002c). The impact of schools and school programs upon adolescent sexual behavior. *Journal of Sex Research, 39,* 27–33.

Kirk, K. M., Bailey, J. M., Dunne, M. P., & Martin, N. G. (2000). Measurement models for sexual orientation in a community twin sample. *Behavior Genetics, 30,* 345–356.

Kirkham, N. Z., Slemmer, J. A., & Johnson, S. P. (2002). Visual statistical learning in infancy: Evidence for a domain general learning mechanism. *Cognition, 83,* B35–B42.

Kisilevsky, B. S., Hains, S. M. J., Lee, K., Muir, D. W., Xu, F., Fu, G., Zhao, Z. Y., & Yang, R. L. (1998). The still-face effect in Chinese and Canadian 3- to 6-month-old infants. *Developmental Psychology, 34,* 629–639.

Kisilevsky, B. S., Hains, S. M. J., Lee, K., Xie, X., Huang, H., Ye, H. H., Zhang, K., & Wang, Z. (2003). Effects of experience on fetal voice recognition. *Psychological Science, 14,* 220–224.

Kisilevsky B. S., & Low, J. A. (1998). Human fetal behavior: 100 years of study. *Developmental Review, 18,* 1–29.

Kitzmann, K. M., & Beech, B. M. (2006). Family-based interventions for pediatric obesity: Methodological and conceptual challenges from family psychology. *Journal of Family Psychology, 20,* 175–189.

Kitzmann, K. M., Cohen, R., & Lockwood, R. L. (2002). Are only children missing out? Comparison of the peer-related social competence of only children and siblings. *Journal of Social and Personal Relationships, 19,* 299–316.

Klaczynski, P. A. (1997). Bias in adolescents' everyday reasoning and its relationships with intellectual ability, personal theories, and self-serving motivation. *Developmental Psychology, 33,* 273–283.

Klaczynski, P. A. (2001). Analytic and heuristic processing influences on adolescent reasoning and decision-making. *Child Development, 72,* 844–861.

Klaczynski, P. A., & Narasimham, G. (1998a). Development of scientific reasoning biases: Cognitive versus ego-protective explanations. *Developmental Psychology, 34,* 175–187.

Klaczynski, P. A., & Narasimham, G. (1998b). Representations as mediators of adolescent deductive reasoning. *Developmental Psychology, 34,* 865–881.

Klaczynski, P. A., Schuneman, M. J., & Daniel, D. B. (2004). Theories of conditional reasoning: A developmental examination of competing hypotheses. *Developmental Psychology, 40,* 559–571.

Klahr, D., & MacWhinney, B. (1998). Information processing. In D. Kuhn & R. S. Siegler (Eds.), *Handbook of child psychology: Vol. 2. Cognition, perception, and language* (5th ed., pp. 631–678). New York: Wiley.

Klahr, D., & Nigam, M. (2004). The equivalence of learning paths in early science instruction: Effects of direct instruction and discovery learning. *Psychological Science, 15,* 661–667.

Klaw, E. L., Rhodes, J. E., & Fitzgerald, L. F. (2003). Natural mentors in the lives of African-American adolescent mothers: Tracking relationships over time. *Journal of Youth and Adolescence, 32,* 223–232.

Klebanoff, M. A., Levine, R. J., Clemens, J. D., & Wilkins, D. G. (2002). Maternal serum caffeine metabolites and small-for-gestational-age birth. *American Journal of Epidemiology, 155,* 32–37.

Klebanov, P. K., Brooks-Gunn, J., McCarton, C., & McCormick, M. C. (1998). The contribution of neighborhood and family income to developmental test scores over the first three years of life. *Child Development, 69,* 1420–1436.

Klein, M. C. (2006). Does epidural analgesia increase rate of cesarean section? *Canadian Family Physician, 52,* 419–421.

Klein, P. J., & Meltzoff, A. N. (1999). Long-term memory, forgetting, and deferred imitation in 12-month-old infants. *Developmental Science, 2,* 102–113.

Klenberg, L., Korkman, M., & Lahti-Nuuttila, P. (2001). Differential development of attention and executive functions in 3- to 12-year-old Finnish children. *Developmental Neuropsychology, 20,* 407–428.

Klesges, L. M., Johnson, K. C., Ward, K. D., & Barnard, M. (2001). Smoking cessation in pregnant women. *Obstetrics and Gynecology Clinics of North America, 28,* 269–282.

Klibanoff, R. S., Levine, S. C., Huttenlocher, J., Vasilyeva, M., & Hedges, L. V. (2006). Preschool children's mathematical knowledge: The effect of teacher "math talk." *Developmental Psychology, 42,* 59–69.

Kliegman, R. M., Behrman, R. E., Jenson, H. B., & Stanton, B. F. (Eds.). (2008). *Nelson textbook of pediatrics e-dition.* Philadelphia: Saunders.

Kliewer, W., Fearnow, M. D., & Miller, P. A. (1996). Coping socialization in middle childhood: Tests of maternal and paternal influences. *Child Development, 67,* 2339–2357.

Klimes-Dougan, B., & Kistner, J. (1990). Physically abused preschoolers' responses to peers' distress. *Developmental Psychology, 26,* 599–602.

Klineberg, O. (1963). Negro–white differences in intelligence test performance: A new look at an old problem. *American Psychologist, 18,* 198–203.

Klingman, A. (2006). Children and war trauma. In K. A. Renninger & I. E. Sigel (Eds.), *Handbook of child psychology: Vol. 4. Child psychology in practice* (6th ed., pp. 619–652). Hoboken, NJ: Wiley.

Klingner, J. K., Vaughn, S., Hughes, M. T., Schumm, J. S., & Elbaum, B. (1998). Outcomes for students with and without learning disabilities in inclusive classrooms. *Learning Disabilities Research and Practice, 13,* 153–161.

Klomsten, A. T., Skaalvik, E. M., & Espnes, G. A. (2004). Physical self-concept and sports: Do gender differences exist? *Sex Roles, 50,* 119–127.

Klump, K. L., Kaye, W. H., & Strober, M. (2001). The evolving foundations of eating disorders. *Psychiatric Clinics of North America, 24,* 215–225.

Knafo, A., & Plomin, R. (2006). Parental discipline and affection and children's prosocial behavior: Genetic and environmental links. *Journal of Personality and Social Psychology, 90,* 147–164.

Knobloch, H., & Pasamanick, B. (Eds.). (1974). *Gesell and Amatruda's Developmental Diagnosis.* Hagerstown, MD: Harper & Row.

Knopf, M., Kraus, U., & Kressley-Mba, R. A. (2006). Relational information processing of novel unrelated actions by infants. *Infant Behavior and Development, 29,* 44–53.

Knudsen, K., & Waerness, K. (2003). National context, individual characteristics, and attitudes on mothers' employment: A comparative analysis of Great Britain, Sweden, and Norway. *Acta Sociologica, 44,* 67–97.

Kobayashi, T., Hiraki, K., & Hasegawa, T. (2005). Auditory-visual intermodal matching of small numerosities in 6-month-old infants. *Developmental Science, 8,* 409–419.

Kobayashi, T., Kazuo, H., Ryoko, M., & Hasegawa, T. (2004). Baby arithmetic: One object plus one tone. *Cognition, 91,* B23–B34.

Kochanska, G. (1991). Socialization and temperament in the development of guilt and conscience. *Child Development, 62,* 1379–1392.

Kochanska, G., & Aksan, N. (2006). Children's conscience and self-regulation. *Journal of Personality, 74,* 1587–1617.

Kochanska, G., Aksan, N., & Carlson, J. J. (2005). Temperament, relationships, and young children's receptive cooperation with their parents. *Developmental Psychology, 41*(4), 648–660.

Kochanska, G., Aksan, N., & Joy, M. E. (2007). Children's fearfulness as a moderator of parenting in early socialization: Two longitudinal studies. *Developmental Psychology, 43,* 222–237.

Kochanska, G., Aksan, N., Knaack, A., & Rhines, H. M. (2004). Maternal parenting and children's conscience: Early security as moderator. *Child Development, 75,* 1229–1242.

Kochanska, G., Aksan, N., & Nichols, K. E. (2003). Maternal power assertion in discipline and moral discourse contexts: Commonalities, differences, and implications for children's moral conduct and cognition. *Developmental Psychology, 39,* 949–963.

Kochanska, G., Aksan, N., Prisco, T. R., & Adams, E. E. (2008). Mother–child and father–child mutually responsive orientation in the first 2 years and children's outcomes at preschool age: Mechanisms of influence. *Child Development, 79,* 30–44.

Kochanska, G., Forman, D. R., Aksan, N., & Dunbar, S. B. (2005). Pathways to conscience: Early mother–child mutually responsive orientation and children's moral emotion, conduct, and cognition. *Journal of Child Psychology and Psychiatry, 46,* 19–34.

Kochanska, G., Gross, J. N., Lin, M.-H., & Nichols, K. E. (2002). Guilt in young children: Development, determinants, and relations with broader system standards. *Child Development, 73,* 461–482.

Kochanska, G., & Knaack, A. (2003). Effortful control as a personality characteristic of young children: Antecedents, correlates, and consequences. *Journal of Personality, 71,* 1087–1112.

Kochanska, G., & Murray, K. T. (2000). Mother–child mutually responsive orientation and conscience development: From toddler to early school age. *Child Development, 71,* 417–431.

Kochanska, G., Murray, K. T., & Harlan, E. T. (2000). Effortful control in early childhood: Continuity and change, antecedents, and implications for social development. *Developmental Psychology, 36,* 220–232.

Kochenderfer-Ladd, B. (2003). Identification of aggressive and asocial victims and the stability of their peer victimization. *Merrill-Palmer Quarterly, 49,* 401–425.

Kochenderfer-Ladd, B., & Wardrop, J. L. (2001). Chronicity and instability of children's peer victimization experiences as predictors of loneliness and social satisfaction trajectories. *Child Development, 72,* 134–151.

Koelsch, S., Gunter, T., von Cramon, D., Zysset, S., Lohmann, G., & Friederici, A. (2002). Bach speaks: A cortical "language-network" serves the processing of music. *NeuroImage, 17,* 956–966.

Koestner, R., Franz, C., & Weinberger, J. (1990). The family origins of empathic concern: A 26-year longitudinal study. *Journal of Personality and Social Psychology, 58,* 709–717.

Kohen, D., Hunter, T., Pence, A., & Goelman, H. (2000). The Victoria Day Care Research Project: Overview of a longitudinal study of child care and human development in Canada. *Canadian Journal of Research in Early Childhood Education, 8,* 49–54.

Kohen, D. E., Brooks-Gunn, J., Leventhal, T., & Hertzman, C. (2002). Neighborhood income and physical and social disorder in Canada: Associations with young children's competencies. *Child Development, 73,* 1844–1860.

Kohlberg, L. (1958). *The development of modes of moral thinking and choice in the years ten to sixteen.* Unpublished doctoral dissertation, University of Chicago.

Kohlberg, L. (1966). A cognitive-developmental analysis of children's sex-role concepts and attitudes. In E. E. Maccoby (Ed.), *The development of sex differences* (pp. 82–173). Stanford, CA: Stanford University Press.

Kohlberg, L. (1969). Stage and sequence: The cognitive-developmental approach to socialization. In D. A. Goslin (Ed.), *Handbook of socialization theory and research* (pp. 347–480). Chicago: Rand McNally.

Kohlberg, L. (1976). Moral stages and moralization: The cognitive-developmental approach. In T. Lickona (Ed.), *Moral development and behavior: Theory, research, and social issues* (pp. 31–53). New York: Holt.

Kohlberg, L., & Diessner, R. (1991). A cognitive-developmental approach to moral attachment. In W. M. Kurtines (Ed.), *Intersections with attachment* (pp. 229–246). Hillsdale, NJ: Erlbaum.

Kohlberg, L., Levine, C., & Hewer, A. (1983). *Moral stages: A current formulation and a response to critics.* Basel: Karger.

Kolb, B., & Gibb, R. (2001). Early brain injury, plasticity, and behavior. In C. A. Nelson & M. Luciana (Eds.), *Handbook of developmental cognitive neuroscience* (pp. 175–190). Cambridge, MA: MIT Press.

Kolominsky, Y., Igumnov, S., & Drozdovitch, V. (1999). The psychological development of children from Belarus exposed in the prenatal period to radiation from the Chernobyl atomic power plant. *Journal of Child Psychology and Psychiatry, 40,* 299–305.

Komsi, N., Räikkönen, K., Pesonen, A.-K., Heinonen, K., Keskivaara, P., Järvenpää, A.-L., & Strandberg, T. E. (2006). Continuity of temperament from infancy to middle childhood. *Infant Behavior and Development, 29,* 494–508.

Kon, A. A., & Klug, M. (2006). Methods and practices of investigators for determining participants' decisional capacity and comprehension of protocols. *Journal of empirical Research on Human Research Ethics, 1,* 61–68.

Konold, T. R., & Pianta, R. C. (2005). Empirically-derived, person-oriented patterns of school readiness in typically developing children: Description and prediction to first-grade achievement. *Applied Developmental Science, 9,* 174–187.

Kontic-Vucinic, O., Sulovic, N., & Radunovic, N. (2006). Micronutrients in women's reproductive health: II. Minerals and trace elements. *International Journal of Fertility and Women's Medicine, 51,* 116–124.

Kopp, C. B., & Neufeld, S. J. (2003). Emotional development during infancy. In R. Davidson, K. R. Scherer, & H. H. Goldsmith (Eds.), *Handbook of affective sciences* (pp. 347–374). Oxford, UK: Oxford University Press.

Kopp, C. B., & Wyer, N. (1994). Self-regulation in normal and atypical development. In D. Cicchetti & S. L. Toth (Eds.), *Disorders and dysfunctions of the self. Rochester Symposium on Developmental Psychopathology* (Vol. 5, pp. 31–56). Rochester, NY: University of Rochester Press.

Korkman, M., Kettunen, S., & Autti-Raemoe, I. (2003). Neurocognitive impairment in early adolescence following prenatal alcohol exposure of varying duration. *Child Neurology, 9,* 117–128.

Kornhaber, M. L. (2004). Using multiple intelligences to overcome cultural barriers to identification for gifted education. In D. Boothe & J. C. Stanley (Eds.), *In the eyes of the beholder: Critical issues for diversity in gifted education* (pp. 215–225). Waco, TX: Prufrock Press.

Kotchick, B. A., Dorsey, S., & Heller, L. (2005). Predictors of parenting among African-American single mothers: Personal and contextual factors. *Journal of Marriage and Family, 67,* 448–460.

Kouvonen, A., & Kivivuori, J. (2001). Part-time jobs, delinquency, and victimization among Finnish adolescents. *Journal of Scandinavian Studies in Criminology and Crime Prevention, 2,* 191–212.

Kovacs, D. M., Parker, J. G., & Hoffman, L. W. (1996). Behavioral, affective, and social correlates of involvement in cross-sex friendship in elementary school. *Child Development, 67,* 2269–2286.

Kowalski, K., & Lo, Y. (1999, April). *The influence of perceptual features and sociocultural information on the development of ethnic/racial bias in young children.* Paper presented at the biennial meeting of the Society for Research in Child Development, Albuquerque, NM.

Kozer, E., Costei, A. M., Boskovic, R., Nulman, I., Nikfar, S., & Koren, G. (2003). Effects of aspirin consumption during pregnancy on pregnancy outcomes: Meta-analysis. *Birth Defects Research, Part B, Developmental and Reproductive Toxicology, 68,* 70–84.

Kozulin, A. (Ed.). (2003). *Vygotsky's educational theory in cultural context.* Cambridge, U.K.: Cambridge University Press.

Krafft, K., & Berk, L. E. (1998). Private speech in two preschools: Significance of open-ended activities and make-believe play for verbal self-regulation. *Early Childhood Research Quarterly, 13,* 637–658.

Kramer, L., & Kowal, A. K. (2005). Sibling relationship quality from birth to adolescence: The enduring contributions of friends. *Journal of Family Psychology, 19,* 503–511.

Kramer, M. S., Guo, T., Platt, R. W., Sevkovskaya, Z., Dzikovich, I., & Collet, J. P. (2003). Infant growth and health outcomes associated with 3 compared with 6 mo. of exclusive breastfeeding. *American Journal of Clinical Nutrition, 78,* 291–295.

Kramer, M. S., Guo, T., Platt, R. W., Shapiro, S., Collet, J. P., & Chalmers, B. (2002). Breastfeeding and infant growth: Biology or bias? *Pediatrics, 110,* 343–347.

Krascum, R. M., & Andrews, S. (1998). The effects of theories on children's acquisition of family-resemblance categories. *Child Development, 69,* 333–346.

Krebs, D., & Denton, K. (2005). Toward a more pragmatic approach to morality: A critical evaluation of Kohlberg's model. *Psychological Review, 112,* 629–649.

Krebs, D., & Gillmore, J. (1982). The relationship among the first stages of cognitive development, role-taking abilities, and moral development. *Child Development, 53,* 877–886.

Krebs, D. L., Vermeulen, S. C., Carpendale, J. I., & Denton, K. (1991). Structural and situational influences on moral judgment: The interaction between stage and dilemma. In W. Kurtines & J. Gewirtz (Eds.), *Handbook of moral behavior and development: Theory, research, and application* (pp. 139–169). Hillsdale, NJ: Erlbaum.

Kreppner, J. M., Rutter, M., Beckett, C., Castle, J., Colvert, E., Groothues, C., Hawkins, A., & O'Connor, T. G. (2007). Normality and impairment following profound early institutional deprivation: A longitudinal follow-up into early adolescence. *Developmental Psychology, 43,* 931–946.

Krettenauer, T. (2005). The role of epistemic cognition in adolescent identity formation: Further evidence. *Journal of Youth and Adolescence, 34,* 185–198.

Krevans, J., & Gibbs, J. C. (1996). Parents' use of inductive discipline: Relations to children's empathy and prosocial behavior. *Child Development, 67,* 3263–3277.

Krishnamoorthy, J. S., Hart, C., & Jelalian, E. (2006). The epidemic of childhood obesity: Review of research and implications for public policy. *Social Policy Report of the Society for Research in Child Development, 9*(2).

Kroger, J. (2001). What transits in an identity status transition: A rejoinder to commentaries. *Identity, 3,* 291–304.

Kroger, J. (2005). *Identity in adolescence: The balance between self and other.* New York: Routledge.

Kroger, J. (2007). *Identity development: Adolescence through adulthood* (2nd ed.). Thousand Oaks, CA: Sage.

Kroneman, L., Loeber, R., & Hipwell, A. E. (2004). Is neighborhood context differently related to externalizing problems and delinquency for girls compared with boys? *Clinical Child and Family Psychology Review, 7,* 109–122.

Kruger, A. C. (1993). Peer collaboration: Conflict, cooperation, or both? *Social Development, 2,* 165–182.

Krumhansl, C. L., & Jusczyk, P. W. (1990). Infants' perception of phrase structure in music. *Psychological Science, 1,* 70–73.

Kubik, M. Y., Lytle, L. A., Hannan, P. J., Perry, C. L., & Story, M. (2003). The association of the school food environment with dietary behaviors of young adolescents. *American Journal of Public Health, 93,* 1168–1173.

Kuczynski, L. (1984). Socialization goals and mother–child interaction: Strategies for long-term and short-term compliance. *Developmental Psychology, 20,* 1061–1073.

Kuczynski, L. (2003). Beyond bidirectionality. In L. Kuczynski (Ed.), *Handbook of dynamics in parent–child relations* (pp. 3–24). Thousand Oaks, CA: Sage.

Kuczynski, L., & Hildebrandt, N. (1997). Models of conformity and resistance in socialization theory. In J. E. Grusec & L. Kuczynski (Eds.), *Parenting and children's internalization of values* (pp. 227–256). New York: Wiley.

Kuczynski, L., & Lollis, S. (2002). Four foundations for a dynamic model of parenting. In J. R. M. Gerris (Eds.), *Dynamics of parenting.* Hillsdale, NJ: Erlbaum.

Kuebli, J., Butler, S., & Fivush, R. (1995). Mother–child talk about past emotions: relations of maternal language and child gender over time. *Cognition and Emotion, 9,* 265–283.

Kugelmass, J., & Ainscow, M. (2004). Leadership for inclusion: A comparison of international practices. *Journal of Research in Special Educational Needs, 4,* 133–141.

Kuhl, P. K. (2006). A new view of language acquisition. In H. Luria, D. M. Seymour, & T. Smoke (2006), *Language and linguistics in context: Readings and applications for teachers* (pp. 29–42). Mahwah, NJ: Erlbaum.

Kuhl, P. K., Conboy, B. T., Padden, D., Nelson, T., & Pruitt, J. (2005). Early speech perception and later language development: Implications for the "critical period." *Language Learning and Development, 1,* 237–264.

Kuhl, P. K., Tsao, F.-M., & Liu, H.-M. (2003). Foreign-language experience in infancy: Effects of short-term exposure and social interaction on phonetic learning. *Proceedings of the National Academy of Sciences, 100,* 9096–9101.

Kuhl, P. K., Williams, K. A., Lacerda, F., Stevens, K. N., & Lindblom, B. (1992). Linguistic experience alters phonetic perception in infants by 6 months of age. *Science, 255,* 606–608.

Kuhn, D. (1989). Children and adults as intuitive scientists. *Psychological Review, 96,* 674–689.

Kuhn, D. (1993). Connecting scientific and informal reasoning. *Merrill-Palmer Quarterly, 39,* 74–103.

Kuhn, D. (1995). Microgenetic study of change: What has it told us? *Psychological Science, 6,* 133–139.

Kuhn, D. (1999). Metacognitive development. *Current Directions in Psychological Science, 9,* 178–181.

Kuhn, D. (2000). Why development does (and does not) occur: Evidence from the domain of inductive reasoning. In R. Siegler & J. McClelland (Eds.), *Mechanisms of cognitive development* (pp. 221–249). Mahwah, NJ: Erlbaum.

Kuhn, D. (2002). What is scientific thinking, and how does it develop? In U. Goswami (Ed.), *Blackwell handbook of childhood cognitive development* (pp. 371–393). Malden, MA: Blackwell.

Kuhn, D., Amsel, E., & O'Loughlin, M. (1988). *The development of scientific thinking* skills. Orlando, FL: Academic Press.

Kuhn, D., & Dean, D., Jr. (2004). Connecting scientific reasoning and causal inference. *Journal of Cognition and Development, 5,* 261–288.

Kuhn, D., & Franklin, S. (2006). The second decade: What develops (and how)? In D. Kuhn & R. S. Siegler (Eds.), *Handbook of child psychology: Vol. 2. Cognition, perception, and language* (6th ed., pp. 953–994). Hoboken, NJ: Wiley.

Kuhn, D., & Pearsall, S. (2000). Developmental origins of scientific thinking. *Journal of Cognition and Development, 1,* 113–129.

Kuklinski, M. R., & Weinstein, R. S. (2001). Classroom and developmental differences in a path model of teacher expectancy effects. *Child Development, 72,* 1554–1578.

Kumar, S., & O'Brien, A. (2004). Recent developments in fetal medicine. *British Medical Journal, 328,* 1002–1006.

Kunina, O., Wilhelm, O., Formazin, M., Jonkmann, K., & Schroeders, U. (2007). Extended criteria and predictors in college admission: Exploring the structure of study success and investigating the validity of domain knowledge. *Psychology Science, 49,* 88–114.

Kunkel, D. (2001). Children and television advertising. In D. G. Singer & J. L. Singer (Eds.), *Handbook of children and the media* (pp. 375–393). Thousand Oaks, CA: Sage.

Kunnen, E. S., & Bosma, H. A. (2003). Fischer's skill theory applied to identity development: A response to Kroger. *Identity, 3,* 247–270.

Kunzinger, E. L., III. (1985). A short-term longitudinal study of memorial development during early grade school. *Developmental Psychology, 21,* 642–646.

Kurdek, L. A., & Fine, M. A. (1994). Family acceptance and family control as predictors of adjustment in young adolescents: Linear, curvilinear, or interactive effects? *Child Development, 65,* 1137–1146.

Kuriyama, K., & Yoshida, H. (1995). Representational structure of numbers in mental addition. *Japanese Journal of Educational Psychology, 43,* 402–410.

Kyratzis, A., & Guo, J. (2001). Preschool girls' and boys' verbal conflict strategies in the United States and China. *Research on Language and Social Interaction, 34,* 45–74.

Lachance, J. A., & Mazzocco, M. M. M. (2006). A longitudinal analysis of sex differences in math and spatial skills in primary school age children. *Learning and Individual Differences, 16,* 195–216.

Lackey, P. N. (1989). Adults' attitudes about assignments of household chores to male and female children. *Sex Roles, 20,* 271–281.

Lacourse, E., Nagin, D., Tremblay, R. E., Vitaro, F., & Claes, M. (2003). Developmental trajectories of boys' delinquent group membership and facilitation of violent behaviors during adolescence. *Development and Psychopathology, 15,* 183–197.

Ladd, G. W. (1999). Peer relationships and social competence during early and middle childhood. *Annual Review of Psychology, 50,* 333–359.

Ladd, G. W. (2005). *Children's peer relationships and social competence: A century of progress.* New Haven, CT: Yale University Press.

Ladd, G. W. (2006). Peer rejection, aggressive or withdrawn behavior, and psychological maladjustment from ages 5 to 12: An examination of four predictive models. *Child Development, 77,* 822–846.

Ladd, G. W., Birch, S. H., & Buhs, E. S. (1999). Children's social and scholastic lives in kindergarten: Related spheres of influence? *Child Development, 70,* 1373–1400.

Ladd, G. W., Buhs, E. S., & Seid, M. (2000). Children's initial sentiments about kindergarten: Is school liking an antecedent of early classroom participation and achievement? *Merrill-Palmer Quarterly, 46,* 255–279.

Ladd, G. W., & Burgess, K. B. (1999). Charting the relationship trajectories of aggressive, withdrawn, and aggressive/withdrawn children during early grade school. *Child Development, 70,* 910–929.

Ladd, G. W., Herald, S. L., & Kochel, K. P. (2006). School readiness: Are there social prerequisites? *Early Education and Development, 17,* 115–150.

Ladd, G. W., Kochenderfer, B. J., & Coleman, C. C. (1997). Classroom peer acceptance, friendship, and victimization: Distinct relational systems that contribute uniquely to children's school adjustment? *Child Development, 68,* 1181–1197.

Ladd, G. W., LeSieur, K., & Profilet, S. M. (1993). Direct parental influences on young children's peer relations. In S. Duck (Ed.), *Learning about relationships* (Vol. 2, pp. 152–183). London: Sage.

Ladd, G. W., & Pettit, G. S. (2002). Parenting and the development of children's peer relationships. In M. Bornstein (Ed.), *Handbook of parenting* (2nd ed.). Mahwah, NJ: Erlbaum.

Ladd, G. W., & Troop-Gordon, W. (2003). The role of chronic peer difficulties in the development of children's psychological adjustment problems. *Child Development, 74,* 1344–1367.

LaFontana, K. M., & Cillessen, A. H. N. (1999). Children's interpersonal perceptions as a function of sociometric and peer perceived popularity. *Journal of Genetic Psychology, 160,* 225–242.

Lagattuta, K. H., Wellman, H. M., & Flavell, J. H. (1997). Preschoolers' understanding of the link between thinking and feeling: Cognitive cuing and emotional change. *Child Development, 68,* 1081–1104.

Lagercrantz, H., & Slotkin, T. A. (1986). The "stress" of being born. *Scientific American, 254,* 100–107.

Lagnado, L. (2001, November 2). Kids confront Trade Center trauma. *The Wall Street Journal,* pp. B1, B6.

La Greca, A. M., Prinstein, M. J., & Fetter, M. D. (2001). Adolescent peer crowd affiliation: Linkages with health-risk behaviors and close friendships. *Journal of Pediatric Psychology, 26,* 131–143.

Lahey, B. B., Van Hulle, C. A., Waldman, I. D., Rodgers, J. L., D'Onofrio, B. M., Pedlow, S., Rathouz, P., & Keenan, K. (2006). Testing descriptive hypotheses regarding sex differences in the development of conduct problems and delinquency. *Journal of Abnormal Child Psychology, 34,* 737–755.

Laible, D. (2004). Mother–child discourse in two contexts: Links with child temperament, attachment security, and socioemotional competence. *Developmental Psychology, 40,* 979–992.

Laible, D. (2007). Attachment with parents and peers in late adolescence: Links with emotional competence and social behavior. *Personality and Individual Differences, 43,* 1185–1197.

Laible, D., & Song, J. (2006). Constructing emotional and relational understanding: The role of affect and mother–child discourse. *Merrill-Palmer Quarterly, 52,* 44–69.

Laible, D. J., & Thompson, R. A. (2002). Mother–child conflict in the toddler years: Lessons in emotion, morality, and relationships. *Child Development, 73,* 1187–1203.

Laing, E., Butterworth, G., Ansari, D., Gsödl, M., Longhi, E., Panagiotaki, G., Paterson, S., & Karmiloff-Smith, A. (2002). Atypical development of language and social communication in toddlers with Williams syndrome. *Developmental Science, 5,* 233–246.

Laird, J. (2003). Lesbian and gay families. In F. Walsh (Ed.), *Normal family processes* (pp. 176–209). New York: Guilford.

Laird, R. D., Jordan, K. Y., Dodge, K. A., Pettit, G. S., & Bates, J. E. (2001). Peer rejection in childhood, involvement with antisocial peers in early adolescence, and the development of externalizing behavior problems. *Development and Psychopathology, 13,* 337–354.

Laird, R. D., Pettit, G. S., Bates, J. E., & Dodge, K. A. (2003). Parents' monitoring-relevant knowledge and adolescents' delinquent behavior: Evidence of correlated developmental changes and reciprocal influences. *Child Development, 74,* 752–768.

Lalonde, C. E., & Chandler, M. J. (1995). False-belief understanding goes to school: On the social-emotional consequences of coming early or late to a first theory of mind. *Cognition and Emotion, 9,* 167–185.

Lalonde, C. E., & Chandler, M. J. (2005). Culture, selves, and time: Theories of personal persistence in native and non-native youth. In C. Lightfoot, C. Lalonde, & M. Chandler (Eds.), *Changing conceptions of psychological life* (pp. 207–229). Mahwah, NJ: Erlbaum.

Lamarche, V., Brendgen, M., Boivin, M., Vitaro, F., Perusse, D., & Dionne, G. (2006). Do friendships and sibling relationships provide protection against peer victimization in a similar way? *Social Development, 15,* 373–393.

Lamaze, F. (1958). *Painless childbirth.* London: Burke.

Lamb, M. E. (1987). *The father's role: Cross-cultural perspectives.* Hillsdale, NJ: Erlbaum.

Lamb, M. E., & Ahnert, L. (2006). Nonparental child care: Context, concepts, correlates, and consequences. In K. A. Renninger & I. E. Sigel (Eds.), *Handbook of child psychology: Vol. 4. Child psychology in practice* (6th ed., pp. 700–778). Hoboken, NJ: Wiley.

Lamb, M. E., & Lewis, C. (2004). The development and significance of father–child relationships in two-parent families. In M. E. Lamb (Ed.), *The role of the father in child development* (4th ed., pp. 272–306). Hoboken, NJ: Wiley.

Lamb, M. E., & Oppenheim, D. (1989). Fatherhood and father–child relationships: Five years of research. In S. H. Cath, A. Gurwitt, & L. Gunsberg (Eds.), *Fathers and their families* (pp. 11–26). Hillsdale, NJ: Erlbaum.

Lamb, M. E., Sternberg, K. J., & Prodromidis, M. (1992). Nonmaternal care and the security of infant–mother attachment: A reanalysis of the data. *Infant Behavior and Development, 15,* 71–83.

Lamb, M. E., Thompson, R. A., Gardner, W., Charnov, E. L., & Connell, J. P. (1985). *Infant–mother attachment: The origins and developmental significance of individual differences in Strange Situation behavior.* Hillsdale, NJ: Erlbaum.

Lammers, C., Ireland, M., Resnick, M., & Blum, R. (2000). Influences on adolescents' decisions to postpone onset of sexual intercourse: A survival analysis of virginity among youths aged 13 to 18 years. *Journal of Adolescent Health, 26,* 42–48.

Lamphear, B. P., Hornung, R., Khoury, J., Yolton, K., Baghurst, P., & Bellinger, D. C. (2005). Low-level environmental lead exposure and children's intellectual function: An international pooled analysis. *Environmental Health Perspectives, 113,* 894–899.

Lancaster, J. B., & Whitten, P. (1980). Family matters. *The Sciences, 20,* 10–15.

Landry, S. H., Smith, K. E., Swank, P. R., & Miller-Loncar, C. L. (2000). Early maternal and child influences on children's later independent cognitive and social functioning. *Child Development, 71,* 358–375.

Langer, J., Gillette, P., & Arriaga, R. I. (2003). Toddlers' cognition of adding and subtracting objects in action and in perception. *Cognitive Development, 18,* 233–246.

Lansford, J. E., Chang, L., Dodge, K. A., Malone, P. S., Oburu, P., & Palmerus, K. (2005). Physical discipline and children's adjustment: Cultural normativeness as a moderator. *Child Development, 76,* 1234–1246.

Lansford, J. E., Criss, M. M., Pettit, G. S., Dodge, K. A., & Bates, J. E. (2003). Friendship quality, peer group affiliation, and peer antisocial behavior as moderators of the link between negative parenting and adolescent externalizing behavior. *Journal of Research on Adolescence, 13,* 161–184.

Lansford, J. E., Malone, P. S., Castellino, D. R., Dodge, K. A., Pettit, G., & Bates, J. E. (2006). Trajectories of internalizing, externalizing, and grades for children who have and have not experienced their parents' divorce or separation. *Journal of Family Psychology, 20,* 292–301.

Lansford, J. E., Putallaz, M., Grimes, C. L., Schiro-Osman, K. A., Kupersmidt, J. B., & Coie, J. D. (2006). Perceptions of friendship quality and observed behaviors with friends: How do sociometrically rejected, average, and popular girls differ? *Merrill-Palmer Quarterly, 52,* 694–720.

Laptook, A. R., O'Shea, T. M., Shankaran, S., & Bhaskar, B. (2005). Adverse neurodevelopmental outcomes among extremely low birth weight infants with a normal head ultrasound: Prevalence and antecedents. *Pediatrics, 115,* 673–680.

Larsen, J. A., & Nippold, M. A. (2007). Morphological analysis in school-age children: Dynamic assessment of a word learning strategy. *Language, Speech, and Hearing Services in Schools, 38,* 201–212.

Larson, R. W. (2001). How U.S. children and adolescents spend time: What it does (and doesn't) tell us about their development. *Current Directions in Psychological Science, 10,* 160–164.

Larson, R. W., & Ham, M. (1993). Stress and "storm and stress" in early adolescence: The relationship of negative events with dysphoric affect. *Developmental Psychology, 29,* 130–140.

Larson, R. W., & Lampman-Petraitis, C. (1989). Daily emotional states as reported by children and adolescents. *Child Development, 60,* 1250–1260.

Larson, R. W., Moneta, G., Richards, M. H., & Wilson, S. (2002). Continuity, stability, and change in daily emotional experience across adolescence. *Child Development, 73,* 1151–1165.

Larson, R. W., & Richards, M. (1998). Waiting for the weekend: Friday and Saturday night as the emotional climax of the week. In A. C. Crouter & R. Larson (Eds.), *Temporal rhythms in adolescence: Clocks, calendars, and the coordination of daily life* (pp. 37–51). San Francisco: Jossey-Bass.

Larson, R. W., Richards, M. H., Moneta, G., Holmbeck, G., & Duckett, E. (1996). Changes in adolescents' daily interactions with their families from ages 10 to 18: Disengagement and transformation. *Developmental Psychology, 32,* 744–754.

Larson, R. W., Richards, M. H., Sims, B., & Dworkin, J. (2001). How urban African-American young adolescents spend their time: Time budgets for locations, activities, and companionship. *American Journal of Community Psychology, 29,* 565–597.

Larzelere, R. E., Schneider, W. N., Larson, D. B., & Pike, P. L. (1996). The effects of discipline responses in delaying toddler misbehavior recurrences. *Child and Family Behavior Therapy, 18,* 35–57.

Lashley, F. R. (2007). Essentials of clinical genetics in nursing practice. New York: Springer.

Latz, S., Wolf, A. W., & Lozoff, B. (1999). Sleep practices and problems in young children in Japan and the United States. *Archives of Pediatric and Adolescent Medicine, 153,* 339–346.

Laucht, M., Esser, G., & Schmidt, M. H. (1997). Developmental outcome of infants born with biological and psychosocial risks. *Journal of Child Psychology and Psychiatry, 38,* 843–853.

Lauer, J. A., Betrán, A. P., Victora, C. G., de Onís, M., & Barros, A. J. (2004). Breastfeeding patterns and exposure to suboptimal breastfeeding among children in developing countries: Review and analysis of nationally representative surveys. *BMC Medicine, 2,* 26.

Laupa, M. (1995). "Who's in charge?" Preschool children's concepts of authority. *Early Childhood Research Quarterly, 9,* 1–7.

Laursen, B., Bukowski, W. M., Aunola, K., & Nurmi, J.-E. (2007). Friendship moderates prospective associations between social isolation and adjustment problems in young children. *Child Development, 78,* 1395–1404.

Laursen, B., Coy, K. C., & Collins, W. A. (1998). Reconsidering changes in parent–child conflict across adolescence: A meta-analysis. *Child Development, 69,* 817–832.

Lavelli, M., & Fogel, A. (2005). Developmental changes in the relationship between the infant's attention and emotion during early face-to-face communication: The 2-month transition. *Developmental Psychology, 41,* 265–280.

Law, K. L., Stroud, L. R., Niaura, R., LaGasse, L. L., Liu, J., & Lester, B. M. (2003). Smoking during pregnancy and newborn neurobehavior. *Pediatrics, 111,* 1318–1323.

Law, K. S., Wong, C.-S., Song, L. J., & Law, K. S. (2004). The construct and criterion validity of emotional intelligence and its potential utility for management studies. *Journal of Applied Psychology, 89,* 483–496.

Lawrence, K., Kuntsi, J., Coleman, M., Campbell, R., & Skuse, D. (2003). Face and emotion recognition deficits in Turner syndrome: A possible role for X-linked genes in amygdala development. *Neuropsychology, 17,* 39–49.

Lazar, I., & Darlington, R. (1982). Lasting effects of early education: A report from the Consortium for Longitudinal Studies. *Monographs of the Society for Research in Child Development, 47*(2–3, Serial No. 195).

Lazarus, R. S., & Lazarus, B. N. (1994). *Passion and reason.* New York: Oxford University Press.

Leadbeater, B., & Hoglund, W. (2006). Changing the social texts of peer victimization. *Journal of the Canadian Academy of Child and Adolescent Psychiatry, 15,* 21–26.

Leaper, C. (1994). Exploring the correlates and consequences of gender segregation: Social relationships in childhood, adolescence, and adulthood. In C. Leaper (Ed.), *New directions for child development* (No. 65, pp. 67–86). San Francisco: Jossey-Bass.

Leaper, C. (2000). Gender, affiliation, assertion, and the interactive context of parent–child play. *Developmental Psychology, 36,* 381–393.

Leaper, C. (2002). Parenting girls and boys. In M. H. Bornstein (Ed.), *Handbook of parenting: Vol. 1. Children and parenting* (pp. 127–152). Mahwah, NJ: Erlbaum.

Leaper, C., Anderson, K. J., & Sanders, P. (1998). Moderators of gender effects on parents' talk to their children: A meta-analysis. *Developmental Psychology, 34,* 3–27.

Leaper, C., & Friedman, C. K. (2007). The socialization of gender. In J. E. Grusec & P. D. Hastings (Eds.), *Handbook of socialization: theory and research* (pp. 561–587). New York: Guilford.

Leaper, C., Tenenbaum, H. R., & Shaffer, T. G. (1999). Communication patterns of African-American girls and boys from low-income, urban backgrounds. *Child Development, 70,* 1489–1503.

Learmonth, A. E., Lamberth, R., & Rovee-Collier, C. (2004). Generalization of deferred imitation during the first year of life. *Journal of Experimental Child Psychology, 88,* 297–318.

Lecanuet, J.-P., Granier-Deferre, C., & DeCasper, A. (2005). Are we expecting too much from prenatal sensory experiences? In B. Hopkins & S. P. Johnson (Eds.), *Prenatal development of postnatal functions* (pp. 31–49). Westport, CT: Praeger.

Lecanuet, J.-P., Granier-Deferre, C., Jacquet, A.-Y., Capponi, I., & Ledru, L. (1993). Prenatal discrimination of a male and female voice uttering the same sentence. *Early Development and Parenting, 2,* 217–228.

Lecuyer, E., & Houck, G. M. (2006). Maternal limit-setting in toddlerhood: Socialization strategies for the development of self-regulation. *Infant Mental Health Journal, 27,* 344–370.

Lederer, J. M. (2000). Reciprocal teaching of social studies in inclusive elementary classrooms. *Journal of Learning Disabilities, 33,* 91–106.

Lee, C.-Y. S., & Doherty, W. J. (2007). Marital satisfaction and father involvement during the transition to parenthood. *Fathering, 5,* 75–96.

Lee, K., Cameron, C., Xu, F., Fu, G., & Board, J. (1997). Chinese and Canadian children's evaluations of lying and truth telling: Similarities and differences in the context of pro- and antisocial behaviors. *Child Development, 68,* 924–934.

Lee, K., Xu, F., Fu, G., Cameron, C. A., & Chen, S. (2001). Taiwan and Mainland Chinese and Canadian children's categorization and evaluation of lie- and truth-telling: A modesty effect. *British Journal of Developmental Psychology, 19,* 525–542.

Lee, S. J., Ralston, H. J., Partridge, J. C., & Rosen, M. A. (2005). Fetal pain: A systematic multidisciplinary review of the evidence. *Journal of the American Medical Association, 294,* 947–954.

Lee, V. E., & Burkam, D. T. (2002). *Inequality at the starting gate.* Washington, DC: Economic Policy Institute.

Lee, V. E., Smerdon, B. A., Alfeld-Liro, C., & Brown, S. L. (2000). Inside large and small high schools: Curriculum and social relations. *Educational Evaluation and Policy Analysis, 22,* 147–171.

Leech, S. L., Day, N. L., Richardson, G. A., & Goldschmidt, L. (2003). Predictors of self-reported delinquent behavior in a sample of young adolescents. *Journal of Early Adolescence, 23,* 78–106.

Leeman, L. W., Gibbs, J. C., & Fuller, D. (1993). Evaluation of a multicomponent group treatment program for juvenile delinquents. *Aggressive Behavior, 19,* 281–292.

Lefebvre, F., Mazurier, E., & Tessier, R. (2005). Cognitive and educational outcomes in early adulthood for infants weighing 1000 grams or less at birth. *Acta Paediatria, 94,* 733–740.

Legerstee, M., Barna, J., & DiAdamo, C. (2000). Precursors to the development of intention at 6 months: Understanding people and their actions. *Developmental Psychology, 36,* 627–634.

Legerstee, M., & Markova, G. (2007). Intentions make a difference: Infant responses to still-face and modified still-face conditions. *Infant Behavior and Development, 30,* 232–250.

Le Grand, R., Mondloch, C. J., Maurer, D., & Brent, H. P. (2003). Expert face processing requires input to the right hemisphere during infancy. *Nature Neuroscience, 6,* 1108–1112.

Lehman, D. R., & Nisbett, R. E. (1990). A longitudinal study of the effects of undergraduate training on reasoning. *Developmental Psychology, 26,* 952–960.

Leiferman, J. A., & Evenson, K. R. (2003). The effect of regular leisure physical activity on birth outcomes. *Maternal and Child Health Journal, 7,* 59–64.

Leinbach, M. D., Hort, B. E., & Fagot, B. I. (1997). Bears are for boys: Metaphorical associations in young children's gender stereotypes. *Cognitive Development, 12,* 107–130.

Leman, P. J. (2005). Authority and moral reasons: Parenting style and children's perceptions of adult rule justifications. *International Journal of Behavioral Development, 29,* 265–270.

Le Menestrel, S. (1999). What do fathers contribute to children's well-being? *Child Trends Research Brief.* Retrieved from www.eric.ed.gov/ERICWebPortal/custom/portlets/recordDetails/detailmini.jsp?_nfpb=true&_&ERICExtSearch_SearchValue_0=ED442551&ERICExtSearch_SearchType_0=no&accno=ED442551

Lempert, H. (1990). Acquisition of passives: The role of patient animacy, salience, and lexical accessibility. *Journal of Child Language, 17,* 677–696.

Lengua, L. J., Wolchik, S., Sandler, I. N., & West, S. G. (2000). The additive and interactive effects of parenting and temperament in predicting problems of children of divorce. *Journal of Clinical Psychology, 29,* 232–244.

Lenhart, A., Madden, M., & Hitlin, P. (2005, July 27). *Teens and technology: Youth are leading the transition to a fully wired and mobile nation.* Retrieved from www.pewInternet.org/pdfs/PIP_Teens_Tech_July2005web.pdf

Lenneberg, E. H. (1967). *Biological foundations of language.* New York: Wiley.

Lenroot, R. K., & Giedd, J. N. (2006). Brain development in children and adolescents: Insights from anatomical magnetic resonance imaging. *Neuroscience and Biobehavioral Reviews, 30,* 718–729.

Leon, K. (2003). Risk and protective factors in young children's adjustment to parental divorce: A review of the research. *Family Relations, 52,* 258–270.

Lepage, J.-F., & Théoret, H. (2007). The mirror neuron system: Grasping others' actions from birth? *Developmental Science, 10,* 513–523.

Lephart, E. D., Call, S. B., Rhees, R. W., Jacobson, N. A., Weber, K. S., Bledsoe, J., & Teuscher, C. (2001). Neuroendocrine regulation of sexually dimorphic brain structure and associated sexual behavior in male rats is genetically controlled. *Biological Reproduction, 64,* 571–578.

Lerner, R. M. (2006). Developmental science, developmental systems, and contemporary theories of human development. In R. M. Lerner (Ed.), *Handbook of child psychology: Vol. 1. Theoretical models of human development* (6th ed., pp. 1–17). Hoboken, NJ: Wiley.

Lerner, R. M., Fisher, C. B., & Weinberg, R. A. (2000). Toward a science for and of the people: Promoting civil society through the application of developmental science. *Child Development, 71,* 11–20.

Leslie, A. M. (2004). Who's for learning? *Developmental Science, 7,* 417–419.

Lester, B. M. (1985). Introduction: There's more to crying than meets the ear. In B. M. Lester & C. F. Z. Boukydis (Eds.), *Infant crying* (pp. 1–27). New York: Plenum.

Lester, B. M., Kotelchuck, M., Spelke, E., Sellers, M. J., & Klein, R. E. (1974). Separation protest in Guatemalan infants: Cross-cultural and cognitive findings. *Developmental Psychology, 10,* 79–85.

Lester, B. M., LaGasse, L., Seifer, R., Tronick, E. Z., Bauer, C., & Shankaran, S. (2003). The maternal lifestyle study (MLS): Effects of prenatal cocaine and/or opiate exposure on auditory brain response at one month. *Journal of Pediatrics, 142,* 279–285.

Lester, B. M., Masten, A. S., & McEwen, B. (Eds.). (2006). *Resilience in children.* New York: Annals of the New York Academy of Sciences.

Lester, B. M., & Tronick, E. Z. (2004). *NICU Network Neurobehavioral Scale (NNNS).* Baltimore, MD: Brookes.

Lett, D. (1997). *L'enfant des miracles: Enfance et société au Moyen Ages, XIIe–XIIIe siecles.* Paris: Aubier.

LeVay, S. (1993). *The sexual brain.* Cambridge, MA: MIT Press.

Leventhal, T., & Brooks-Gunn, J. (2003). Children and youth in neighborhood contexts. *Current Directions in Psychological Science, 12,* 27–31.

Levin, I., & Bus, A. G. (2003). How is emergent writing based on drawing? Analyses of children's products and their sorting by children and mothers. *Developmental Psychology, 39,* 891–905.

Levine, L. E. (1983). Mine: Self-definition in 2-year-old boys. *Developmental Psychology, 19,* 544–549.

Levine, L. J. (1995). Young children's understanding of the causes of anger and sadness. *Child Development, 66,* 697–709.

LeVine, R. A., Dixon, S., LeVine, S., Richman, A., Leiderman, P. H., Keefer, C. H., & Brazelton, T. B. (1994). *Child care and culture: Lessons from Africa.* New York: Cambridge University Press.

Levine, S. C., Huttenlocher, J., Taylor, A., & Langrock, A. (1999). Early sex differences in spatial skill. *Developmental Psychology, 35,* 940–949.

Levtzion-Korach, O., Tennenbaum, A., Schnitzer, R., & Ornoy, A. (2000). Early motor development of blind children. *Journal of Paediatric and Child Health, 36,* 226–229.

Levy, G. D., Taylor, M. G., & Gelman, S. A. (1995). Traditional and evaluative aspects of flexibility in gender roles, social conventions, moral rules, and physical laws. *Child Development, 66,* 515–531.

Levy, S. R., & Dweck, C. S. (1999). The impact of children's static vs. dynamic conceptions of people on stereotype formation. *Child Development, 70,* 1163–1180.

Levy, Y. (1996). Modularity of language reconsidered. *Brain and Language, 55,* 240–263.

Levy-Shiff, R., & Israelashvili, R. (1988). Antecedents of fathering: Some further exploration. *Developmental Psychology, 24,* 434–440.

Lew, A. R., & Butterworth, G. (1997). The development of hand–mouth coordination in 2- to 5-month-old infants: Similarities with reaching and grasping. *Infant Behavior and Development, 20,* 59–69.

Lewis, C., Freeman, N. H., Kyriadidou, C., Maridakikassotaki, K., & Berridge, D. M. (1996). Social influences on false belief access—specific sibling influences or general apprenticeship? *Child Development, 67,* 2930–2947.

Lewis, M. (1992). *Shame: The exposed self.* New York: Free Press.

Lewis, M. (1997). *Altering fate: Why the past does not predict the future.* New York: Guilford.

Lewis, M. (1998). Emotional competence and development. In D. Pushkar, W. M. Bukowski, A. E. Schwartzman, E. M. Stack, & D. R. White (Eds.), *Improving competence across the lifespan* (pp. 27–36). New York: Plenum.

Lewis, M. (1999). The role of the self in cognition and emotion. In T. Dalgleish & M. J. Power (Eds.), *Handbook of cognition and emotion* (pp. 125–142). Chichester, UK: Wiley.

Lewis, M., Alessandri, S. M., & Sullivan, M. W. (1992). Differences in shame and pride as a function of children's gender and task difficulty. *Child Development, 63,* 630–638.

Lewis, M., & Brooks-Gunn, J. (1979). *Social cognition and the acquisition of self.* New York: Plenum.

Lewis, M., & Ramsay, D. S. (2002). Cortisol response to embarrassment and shame. *Child Development, 73,* 1034–1045.

Lewis, M., Ramsay, D. S., & Kawakami, K. (1993). Differences between Japanese infants and Caucasian American infants in behavioral and cortisol response to inoculation. *Child Development, 64,* 1722–1731.

Lewis, M., Sullivan, M. W., & Ramsay, D. S. (1992). Individual differences in anger and sad expressions during extinction: Antecedents and consequences. *Infant Behavior and Development, 15,* 443–452.

Lewis, M., Sullivan, M. W., Stanger, C., & Weiss, M. (1989). Self development and self-conscious emotions. *Child Development, 60,* 146–156.

Lewis, M., Sullivan, M. W., & Vasen, A. (1987). Making faces: Age and emotion differences in the posing of emotional expressions. *Developmental Psychology, 23,* 690–697.

Lewis, M. D. (2000). The promise of dynamic systems approaches for an integrated account of human development. *Child Development, 71,* 36–43.

Lewontin, R. (1976). Race and intelligence. In N. J. Block & G. Dworkin (Eds.), *The IQ controversy* (pp. 78–92). New York: Pantheon Books.

Lewontin, R. (1995). *Human diversity.* New York: Freeman.

Lewontin, R. (2003). *Race: The power of an illusion.* Alexandria, VA: Public Broadcasting System. Retrieved from www.pbs.org/race

Li, D.-K., Willinger, M., Petitti, D. B., Odouli, R., Liu, L., & Hoffman, H. J. (2006). Use of a dummy (pacifier) during sleep and risk of sudden infant death syndrome (SIDS): Population based case-control study. *British Medical Journal, 332,* 18–21.

Li, Q. (2006). Cyberbullying in schools: A research of gender differences. *School Psychology International, 27,* 157–170.

Li, R., Darling, N., Maurice, E., Barker, L., & Grummer-Strawn, L. M. (2005). Breastfeeding rates in the United States by characteristics of the child, mother, or family:

The 2002 National Immunization Survey. *Pediatrics, 115,* e31–e37.

Li, S.-C., Lindenberger, U., Hommel, B., Aschersleben, G., Prinz, W., & Baltes, P. B. (2004). Transformation in the couplings among intellectual abilities and constituent cognitive processes across the life span. *Psychological Science, 15,* 155–163.

Li, W., Han, S., Gregg, T. R., Kemp, F. W., Davidow, A. L., & Louria, D. B. (2003). Lead exposure potentiates predatory attack behavior in the cat. *Environmental Research, 92,* 197–206.

Liau, A. K., Barriga, A. Q., & Gibbs, J. C. (1998). Relations between self-serving cognitive distortion and overt vs. covert antisocial behavior in adolescents. *Aggressive Behavior, 24,* 335–346.

Liben, L. (2006). Education for spatial thinking. In K. A. Renninger & I. E. Sigel (Eds.), *Handbook of child psychology: Vol. 4. Child psychology in practice* (6th ed., pp. 197–247). Hoboken, NJ: Wiley.

Liben, L. S. (1999). Developing an understanding of external spatial representations. In I. E. Sigel (Ed.), *Development of mental representation* (pp. 297–321). Mahwah, NJ: Erlbaum.

Liben, L. S., & Bigler, R. S. (2002). The developmental course of gender differentiation: Conceptualizing, measuring, and evaluating constructs and pathways. *Monographs of the Society for Research in Child Development, 67*(2, Serial No. 269).

Liben, L. S., Bigler, R. S., & Krogh, H. R. (2001). Pink and blue collar jobs: Children's judgments of job status and job aspirations in relation to sex of worker. *Journal of Experimental Child Psychology, 79,* 346–363.

Liben, L. S., Bigler, R. S., & Krogh, H. R. (2002). Language at work: Children's gendered interpretations of occupational titles. *Child Development, 73,* 810–828.

Liben, L. S., & Downs, R. M. (1993). Understanding person-space-map relations: Cartographic and developmental perspectives. *Developmental Psychology, 29,* 739–752.

Liben, L. S., & Signorella, M. L. (1993). Gender-schematic processing in children: The role of initial interpretations of stimuli. *Developmental Psychology, 29,* 141–149.

Lickliter, R., & Bahrick, L. E. (2000). The development of infant intersensory perception: Advantages of a comparative convergent-operations approach. *Psychological Bulletin, 126,* 260–280.

Lickona, T. (1976). Research on Piaget's theory of moral development. In T. Lickona (Ed.), *Moral development and behavior* (pp. 219–240). New York: Holt, Rinehart & Winston.

Lidz, C. S. (2001). Multicultural issues and dynamic assessment. In L. A. Suzuki & J. G. Ponterotto (Eds.), *Handbook of multicultural assessment: Clinical, psychological, and educational applications* (2nd ed., pp. 523–539). San Francisco: Jossey-Bass.

Lidz, J. (2007). The abstract nature of syntactic representations. In E. Hoff & M. Shatz (Eds.), *Blackwell handbook of language development* (pp. 277–303). Malden, MA: Blackwell.

Lidz, J., Gleitman, H., & Gleitman, L. (2004). Kidz in the 'hood: Syntactic bootstrapping and the mental lexicon. In D. G. Hall & S. R. Waxman (Eds.), *Weaving a lexicon* (pp. 603–636). Cambridge, MA: MIT Press.

Lieven, E., Pine, J., & Baldwin, G. (1997). Lexically based learning and early grammatical development. *Journal of Child Language, 24,* 187–220.

Light, P., & Perrett-Clermont, A. (1989). Social context effects in learning and testing. In A. R. H. Gellatly, D. Rogers, & J. Sloboda (Eds.), *Cognition and social worlds* (pp. 99–112). Oxford: Clarendon Press.

Li-Grining, C. P. (2007). Effortful control among low-income preschoolers in three cities: Stability, change, and individual differences. *Developmental Psychology, 43,* 208–221.

Lillard, A. (2003). Pretend play and cognitive development. In U. Goswami (Ed.), *Blackwell handbook of childhood cognitive development* (pp. 189–205). Malden, MA: Blackwell.

Lillard, A. (2007a). Guided participation: How mothers structure and children understand pretend play. In A. Göncü & S. Gaskins (Eds.), *Play and development: Evolutionary, sociocultural, and functional perspectives* (pp. 131–153). Mahwah, NJ: Erlbaum.

Lillard, A. (2007b). *Montessori: The science behind the genius.* New York: Oxford University Press.

Lillard, A., & Else-Quest, N. (2006). Evaluating Montessori education. *Science, 313,* 1893–1894.

Lin, C. C., Hsiao, C. K., & Chen, W. J. (1999). Development of sustained attention assessed using the continuous performance test among children 6–15 years. *Journal of Abnormal Child Psychology, 27,* 403–412.

Lin, Z. L., Yu, H. M., Chen, S. Q., Liang, Z. Q., & Zhang, Z. Y. (2006). Mild hypothermia via selective head cooling as neuroprotective therapy in term neonates with perinatal asphyxia: An experience from a single neonatal intensive care unit. *Journal of Perinatology, 26,* 180–184.

Linares, T. J., Singer, L. T., Kirchner, H., Lester, H., Short, E. J., & Min, M. O. (2006). Mental health outcomes of cocaine-exposed children at 6 years of age. *Journal of Pediatric Psychology, 31,* 85–97.

Lincove, J. A., & Painter, G. (2006). Does the age that children start kindergarten matter? Evidence of long-term educational and social outcomes. *Educational Evaluation and Policy Analysis, 28,* 153–179.

Linder, J. R., & Collins, W. A. (2005). Parent and peer predictors of physical aggression and conflict management in romantic relationships in early adulthood. *Journal of Family Psychology, 19,* 252–262.

Lindsay-Hartz, J., de Rivera, J., & Mascolo, M. F. (1995). Differentiating guilt and shame and their effects on motivation. In J. P. Tangney & K. W. Fischer (Eds.), *Self-conscious emotions* (pp. 274–300). New York: Guilford.

Lindsey, D., & Martin, S. K. (2003). Deepening child poverty: The not so good news about welfare reform. *Children and Youth Services Review, 25,* 165–173.

Lindsey, E. W., & Colwell, M. J. (2003). Preschoolers' emotional competence: Links to pretend and physical play. *Child Study Journal, 33,* 39–52.

Lindsey, E. W., & Mize, J. (2000). Parent–child physical and pretense play: Links to children's social competence. *Merrill-Palmer Quarterly, 46,* 565–591.

Linebarger, D. L., Kosanic, A. Z., Greenwood, C. R., & Doku, N. S. (2004). Effects of viewing the television program *Between the Lions* on the emergent literacy skills of young children. *Journal of Educational Psychology, 96,* 297–308.

Linn, M. C., & Petersen, A. C. (1985). Emergence and characterization of sex differences in spatial ability: A meta-analysis. *Child Development, 56,* 1479–1498.

Linn, S. (2004). *Consuming kids: The hostile takeover of childhood.* New York: New Press.

Linn, S. (2005). The commercialization of childhood. In S. Olfman (Ed.), *Childhood lost: How American culture is failing our kids* (pp. 107–122). Westport, CT: Praeger.

Linscheid, T. R., Budd, K. S., & Rasnake, L. K. (2005). Pediatric feeding problems. In M. C. Roberts (Ed.), *Handbook of pediatric psychology and psychiatry* (3rd ed., pp. 481–488). New York: Guilford.

Linver, M. R., Martin, A., & Brooks-Gunn, J. (2004). Measuring infants' home environment: The IT-HOME for infants between birth and 12 months in four national data sets. *Parenting: Science and Practice, 4,* 115–137.

Lipsitt, L. P. (2003). Crib death: A biobehavioral phenomenon? *Psychological Science, 12,* 164–170.

Lipton, J., & Spelke, E. (2004). Discrimination of large and small numerosities by human infants. *Infancy, 5,* 271–290.

Liszkowski, U., Carpenter, M., & Tomasello, M. (2007). Pointing out new news, old news, and absent referents at 12 months of age. *Developmental Science, 10,* F1–F7.

Litovsky, R. Y., & Ashmead, D. H. (1997). Development of binaural and spatial hearing in infants and children. In R. H. Gilkey & T. R. Anderson (Eds.), *Binaural and spatial hearing in real and virtual environments* (pp. 571–592). Mahwah, NJ: Erlbaum.

Little, C., & Carter, A. S. (2005). Negative emotional reactivity and regulation in 12-month-olds following emotional challenge: Contributions of maternal–infant emotional availability in a low-income sample, *Infant Mental Health Journal, 26,* 354–368.

Little, T. D., Jones, S. M., Henrich, C. C., & Hawley, P. H. (2003). Disentangling the "whys" from the "whats" of aggressive behavior. *International Journal of Behavioral Development, 27,* 122–133.

Liu, H.-M., Kuhl, P. K., & Tsao, F. M. (2003). An association between mothers' speech clarity and infants' speech discrimination skills. *Developmental Science, 6,* F1–F10.

Liu, J., Raine, A., Venables, P. H., Dalais, C., & Mednick, S. A. (2003). Malnutrition at age 3 years and lower cognitive ability at age 11 years. *Archives of Paediatric and Adolescent Medicine, 157,* 593–600.

Lloyd, L. (1999). Multi-age classes and high ability students. *Review of Educational Research, 69,* 187–212.

Lochman, J. E., & Dodge K. A. (1998). Distorted perceptions in dyadic interactions of aggressive and nonaggressive boys: Effects of prior expectations, context, and boys' age. *Development and Psychopathology, 10,* 495–512.

Locke, J. (1892). Some thoughts concerning education. In R. H. Quick (Ed.), *Locke on education* (pp. 1–236). Cambridge, UK: Cambridge University Press. (Original work published 1690)

Lockhart, R. S., & Craik, F. I. M. (1990). Levels of processing: A retrospective commentary on a framework for memory research. *Canadian Journal of Psychology, 44,* 87–112.

Loeb, S., Fuller, B., Kagan, S. L., & Carrol, B. (2004). Child care in poor communities: Early learning effects of type, quality, and stability. *Child Development, 75,* 47–65.

Loehlin, J. C., Horn, J. M., & Willerman, L. (1997). Heredity, environment, and IQ in the Texas Adoption Project. In R. J. Sternberg & E. L. Grigorenko (Eds.), *Intelligence, heredity, and environment* (pp. 105–125). New York: Cambridge University Press.

Loehlin, J. C., & Martin, N. G. (2001). Age changes in personality traits and their heritabilities during the adult years: Evidence from Australian twin registry samples. *Personality and Individual Differences, 30,* 1147–1160.

Loganovskaja, T. K., & Loganovsky, K. N. (1999). EEG, cognitive and psychopathological abnormalities in children irradiated in utero. *International Journal of Psychophysiology, 34,* 211–224.

Lohman, D. F. (2000). Measures of intelligence: Cognitive theories. In A. E. Kazdin (Ed.), *Encyclopedia of psychology: Vol. 5* (pp. 147–150). Washington, DC: American Psychological Association.

Loock, C., Conry, J., Cook, J. L., Chudley, A. E., & Rosales, T. (2005). Identifying fetal alcohol spectrum disorder in primary care. *Canadian Medical Association Journal, 172,* 628–630.

Looker, D., & Thiessen, V. (2003). *The digital divide in Canadian schools: Factors affecting student access to and use of information technology.* Ottawa: Statistics Canada, Catalogue no. 81-597-XIE. Retrieved from www.statcan.ca/bsolc/english/bsolc?catno=81-597-X

Loots, G., & Devise, I. (2003). The use of visual–tactile communication strategies by deaf and hearing fathers and mothers of deaf infants. *Journal of Deaf Studies and Deaf Education, 8,* 31–42.

Lord, R. H., & Kozar, B. (1996). Overuse injuries in young athletes. In F. L. Smoll & R. E. Smith (Eds.), *Children and youth in sport: A biopsychological perspective* (pp. 281–294). Dubuque, IA: Brown & Benchmark.

Lorenz, K. Z. (1952). *King Solomon's ring.* New York: Crowell.

Lorenz, K. Z. (1983). *So Kam der Mensch auf den Hund.* Munich: DTV.

Louie, V. (2001). Parents' aspirations and investment: The role of social class in the educational experiences of 1.5- and second generation Chinese Americans. *Harvard Educational Review, 71,* 438–474.

Louis, J., Cannard, C., Bastuji, H., & Challamel, M.-J. (1997). Sleep ontogenesis revisited: A longitudinal 24-hour home polygraphic study on 15 normal infants during the first two years of life. *Sleep, 20,* 323–333.

Lourenco, O. (2003). Making sense of Turiel's dispute with Kohlberg: The case of the child's moral competence. *New Ideas in Psychology, 21,* 43–68.

Love, J. M., Chazan-Cohen, R., & Raikes, H. (2007). Forty years of research knowledge and use: From Head Start to Early Head Start and beyond. In J. L. Aber, S. J. Bishop-Josef, S. M. Jones, K. T. McLearn, & D. Phillips (Eds.), *Child development and social policy: Knowledge for action* (pp. 79–95). Washington, DC: American Psychological Association.

Love, J. M., Harrison, L., Sagi-Schwartz, A., van IJzendoorn, M. H., Ross, C., & Ungerer, J. A. (2003). Child care quality matters: How conclusions may vary with context. *Child Development, 74,* 1021–1033.

Love, J. M., Kisker, E. E., Ross, C., Raikes, H., Constantine, J., Boller, K., & Brooks-Gunn, J. (2005). The effectiveness of Early Head Start for 3-year-old children and their parents: Lessons for policy and programs. *Developmental Psychology, 41,* 885–901.

Love, J. M., Tarullo, L. B., Raikes, H., & Chazan-Cohen, R. (2006). Head Start: What do we know about its effectiveness? What do we need to know? In K. McCartney & D. Phillips (2006). *Blackwell handbook of early childhood development* (pp. 550–575). Malden, MA: Blackwell.

Lubart, T. I. (2003). In search of creative intelligence. In R. J. Sternberg, J. Lautrey, & T. I. Lubart (Eds.), *Models of intelligence: International perspectives* (pp. 279–292). Washington, DC: American Psychological Association.

Lubinski, D., & Benbow, C. P. (1994). The study of mathematically precocious youth: The first three decades of a planned 50-year study of intellectual talent. In R. F. Subotnik & K. D. Arnold (Eds.), *Beyond Terman: Contemporary longitudinal studies of giftedness and talent* (pp. 255–281). Norwood, NJ: Ablex.

Lucariello, J. (1998). Together wherever we go: The ethnographic child and the developmentalist. *Child Development, 69,* 355–358.

Lucariello, J., Kyratzis, A., & Nelson, K. (1992). Taxonomic knowledge: What kind and when? *Child Development, 63,* 978–998.

Lucas, S. R., & Behrends, M. (2002). Sociodemographic diversity, correlated achievement, and de facto tracking. *Sociology of Education, 75,* 328–348.

Lucas-Thompson, R., & Clarke-Stewart, K. A. (2007). Forecasting friendship: How marital quality, maternal mood, and attachment security are linked to children's peer relationships. *Journal of Applied Developmental Psychology, 28,* 499–514.

Ludemann, P. M. (1991). Generalized discrimination of positive facial expressions by seven- and ten-month-old infants. *Child Development, 62,* 55–67.

Lueptow, L. B., Garovich, L., & Lueptow, M. B. (2001). Social change and the persistnce of sex typing: 1974–1997. *Social Forces, 80,* 1–36.

Luna, B., Garvger, K. E., Urban, T. A., Lazar, N. A., & Sweeney, J. A. (2004). Maturation of cognitive processes from late childhood to adulthood. *Child Development, 75,* 1357–1372.

Luna, B., Thulborn, K. R., Monoz, D. P., Merriam, E. P., Garver, K. E., Minshew, N. J., Keshavan, M. S., Genovese, C. R., Eddy, W. F., & Sweeney, J. A. (2001). Maturation of widely distributed brain function subserves cognitive development. *Neuroimage, 13,* 786–793.

Lundy, B. L. (2002). Paternal socio-psychological factors and infant attachment: The mediating role of synchrony in father–infant interactions. *Infant Behavior and Development, 25,* 221–236.

Lundy, B. L. (2003). Father- and mother-infant face-to-face interactions: Differences in mind-related comments and infant attachment? *Infant Behavior and Development, 26,* 200–212.

Luo, Y., & Baillargeon, R. (2005). When the ordinary seems unexpected: Evidence for incremental physical knowledge in young infants. *Cognition, 95,* 297–328.

Luria, A. R. (1976). *Cognitive development: Its cultural and social foundations.* Cambridge, MA: Harvard University Press.

Lussier, G., Deater-Deckard, K., Dunn, J., & Davies, L. (2002). Support across two generations: Children's closeness to grandparents following parental divorce and remarriage. *Journal of Family Psychology, 16,* 363–376.

Luster, T., & Dubow, E. (1992). Home environment and maternal intelligence as predictors of verbal intelligence: A comparison of preschool and school-age children. *Merrill-Palmer Quarterly, 38,* 151–175.

Luster, T., & Haddow, J. L. (2005). Adolescent mothers and their children: An ecological perspective. In T. Luster & J. L. Haddow (Eds.), *Parenting: An ecological perspective* (2nd ed., pp. 73–101). Mahwah, NJ: Erlbaum.

Luthar, S. S. (2006). Resilience in development: A synthesis of research across five decades. In D. Cicchetti & D. J. Cohen (Eds.), *Developmental psychopathology. Vol. 3: Risk, disorder, and adaptation* (2nd ed., pp. 739–795). Hoboken, NJ: Wiley.

Luthar, S. S., & Becker, B. E. (2002). Privileged but pressured: A study of affluent youth. *Child Development, 73,* 1593–1610.

Luthar, S. S., & Latendresse, S. J. (2005a). Children of the affluent: Challenges to well-being. *Current Directions in Psychological Science, 14,* 49–53.

Luthar, S. S., & Latendresse, S. J. (2005b). Comparable "risks" at the socioeconomic status extremes: Preadolescents' perceptions of parenting. *Development and Psychopathology, 17,* 207–230.

Luthar, S. S., & Sexton, C. (2004). The high price of affluence. In R. V. Kail (Ed.), *Advances in child development* (Vol. 32, pp. 126–162). San Diego, CA: Academic Press.

Luxembourg Income Study. (2005). *Household income surveys, 2000.* Retrieved from www.lisproject.org

Luyckz, K., Goosens, L., Soenens, B., & Beyers, W. (2006). Unpacking commitment and exploration. Preliminary validation of an integrative model of late adolescent identity formation. *Journal of Adolescence, 29,* 361–378.

Luyckz, K., Soenens, B., Vansteenkiste, M., Goossens, L., & Berzonsky, M. D. (2007). Parental psychological control and dimensions of identity formation in emerging adulthood. *Journal of Family Psychology, 21,* 546–550.

Lynch, M., & Cicchetti, D. (1998). An ecological-transactional analysis of children and contexts: The longitudinal interplay among child maltreatment, community violence, and children's symptomatology. *Development and Psychopathology, 10,* 235–257.

Lynch, S. K., Turkheimer, E., D'Onofrio, B. M., Mendle, J., Emery, R. E., Slutske, W. S., & Martin, N. G. (2006). A genetically informed study of the association between harsh punishment and offspring behavioral problems. *Journal of Family Psychology, 20,* 190–198.

Lyon, T. D., & Flavell, J. H. (1994). Young children's understanding of "remember" and "forget." *Child Development, 65,* 1357–1371.

Lyons-Ruth, K. (1996). Attachment relationships among children with aggressive behavior problems: The role of disorganized early attachment patterns. *Journal of Consulting and Clinical Psychology, 64,* 64–73.

Lyons-Ruth, K., Bronfman, E., & Parsons, E. (1999). Maternal frightened, frightening, or atypical behavior and disorganized infant attachment patterns. *Monographs of the Society for Research in Child Development, 64*(3, Serial No. 258), 67–96.

Lyons-Ruth, K., Easterbrooks, A., & Cibelli, C. (1997). Infant attachment strategies, infant mental lag, and maternal depressive symptoms: Predictors of internalizing and externalizing problems at age 7. *Developmental Psychology, 33,* 681–692.

Lytton, H., & Romney, D. M. (1991). Parents' sex-related differential socialization of boys and girls: A meta-analysis. *Psychological Bulletin, 109,* 267–296.

Maberly, G. F., Haxton, D. P., & van der Haar, F. (2003). Iodine deficiency: Consequences and progress toward elimination. *Food and Nutrition Bulletin, 24,* S91–S98.

Maccoby, E. E. (1984). Socialization and developmental change. *Child Development, 55,* 317–328.

Maccoby, E. E. (1998). *The two sexes: Growing up apart, coming together.* Cambridge, MA: Belknap/Harvard University Press.

Maccoby, E. E. (2000a). Parenting and its effects on children: On reading and misreading behavior genetics. *Annual Review of Psychology, 51,* 1–27.

Maccoby, E. E. (2000b). Perspectives on gender development. *International Journal of Behavioral Development, 24,* 398–406.

Maccoby, E. E. (2002). Gender and group process: A developmental perspective. *Current Directions in Psychological Science, 11,* 54–58.

Machin, G. A. (2005). Multiple birth. In H. W. Taeusch, R. A. Ballard, & C. A. Gleason (Eds.), *Avery's disease of the newborn* (8th ed., pp. 57–62). Philadelphia: Saunders.

Mackey, E. R., & La Greca, A. M. (2007). Adolescents' eating, exercise, and weight control behaviors: Does peer crowd affiliation play a role? *Journal of Pediatric Psychology, 32,* 13–23.

Mackey, K., Arnold, M. L., & Pratt, M. W. (2001). Adolescents' stories of decision making in more and less authoritative families: Representing the voices of parents in narrative. *Journal of Adolescent Research, 16,* 243–268.

Mackie, S., Show, P., Lenroot, R., Pierson, R., Greenstein, D. K., & Nugent, T. F., III. (2007). Cerebellar development and clinical outcome in attention deficit hyperactivity disorder. *American Journal of Psychiatry, 164,* 647–655.

MacWhinney, B. (2005). Language development. In M. H. Bornstein & M. E. Lamb (Eds.), *Developmental science: An advanced textbook* (5th ed., pp. 359–387). Mahwah, NJ: Erlbaum.

Madigan, S., Moran, G., & Pederson, D. R. (2006). Unresolved states of mind, disorganized attachment relationships, and disrupted interactions of adolescent mothers and their infants. *Developmental Psychology, 42,* 293–304.

Madon, S., Jussim, L., & Eccles, J. (1997). In search of the powerful self-fulfilling prophecy. *Journal of Personality and Social Psychology, 72,* 791–809.

Madsen, S. A., & Juhl, T. (2007). Paternal depression in the postnatal period assessed with traditional and male depression scales. *Journal of Men's Health and Gender, 4,* 26–31.

Magnuson, K. A., & Duncan, G. J. (2002). Parents in poverty. In M. H. Bornstein (Ed.), *Handbook of parenting: Vol. 4. Social conditions and applied parenting* (2nd ed., pp. 95–122). Mahwah, NJ: Erlbaum.

Mahalingham, R. (1999). Essentialism, power, and representation of caste: A developmental study. *Dissertation Abstracts International, 60*(2–B), 856.

Mahon, M. M., Goldberg, E. Z., & Washington, S. K. (1999). Concept of death in a sample of Israeli kibbutz children. *Death Studies, 23,* 43–59.

Mahoney, J. L. (2000). Participation in school extracurricular activities as a moderator in the development of antisocial patterns. *Child Development, 71,* 502–516.

Mahoney, J. L., & Cairns, R. B. (1997). Do extracurricular activities protect against early school dropout? *Developmental Psychology, 33,* 241–253.

Main, M. (2000). The organized categories of infant, child, and adult attachment: Flexible vs. inflexible attention under attachment-related stress. *Journal of the American Psychoanalytic Association, 48,* 1055–1096.

Main, M., & Cassidy, J. (1988). Categories of response to reunion with the parent at age 6: Predictable from infant attachment classifications and stable over a 1-month period. *Developmental Psychology, 24,* 415–426.

Main, M., & Goldwyn, R. (1994). *Interview-based adult attachment classifications: Related to infant–mother and infant–father attachment.* Unpublished manuscript, University of California, Berkeley.

Main, M., & Goldwyn, R. (1998). *Adult attachment classification system.* London: University College.

Main, M., & Solomon, J. (1990). Procedures for identifying infants as disorganized/disoriented during the Ainsworth Strange Situation. In M. Greenberg, D. Cicchetti, & M. Cummings (Eds.), *Attachment in the preschool years: Theory, research, and intervention* (pp. 121–160). Chicago: University of Chicago Press.

Majdanžić, M., & van den Boom, D. C. (2007). Multimethod longitudinal assessment of temperament in early childhood. *Journal of Personality, 75,* 121–167.

Majnemer, A., & Barr, R. G. (2005). Influence of supine sleep positioning on early motor milestone acquisition. *Developmental Medicine and Child Neurology, 47,* 370–376.

Major, B., Spencer, S., Schmader, T., Wolfe, C., & Crocker, J. (1998). Coping with negative stereotypes about intellectual performance: The role of psychological disengagement. *Personality and Social Psychology Bulletin, 24,* 34–50.

Makin, J. W., Fried, P. A., & Watkinson, B. (1991). A comparison of active and passive smoking during pregnancy: Long-term effects. *Neurotoxicology and Teratology, 13,* 5–12.

Malatesta, C. Z., Grigoryev, P., Lamb, C., Albin, M., & Culver, C. (1986). Emotion socialization and expressive development in preterm and full-term infants. *Child Development, 57,* 316–330.

Malina, R. M., & Bouchard, C. (1991). *Growth, maturation, and physical activity.* Champaign, IL: Human Kinetics.

Mandler, J. M. (2004). *The foundations of mind: Origins of conceptual thought.* New York: Oxford University Press.

Mandler, J. M., & McDonough, L. (1993). Concept formation in infancy. *Cognitive Development, 8,* 291–318.

Mandler, J. M., & McDonough, L. (1998). On developing a knowledge base in infancy. *Developmental Psychology, 34,* 1274–1288.

Mandler, J. M., & Robinson, C. A. (1978). Developmental changes in picture recognition. *Journal of Experimental Child Psychology, 26,* 122–136.

Mange, E. J., & Mange, A. P. (1998). *Basic human genetics* (2nd ed.). Sunderland, MA: Sinauer Associates.

Mangelsdorf, S. C., Schoppe, S. J., & Buur, H. (2000). The meaning of parental reports: A contextual approach to the study of temperament and behavior problems. In V. J. Molfese & D. L. Molfese (Eds.), *Temperament and personality across the life span* (pp. 121–140). Mahwah, NJ: Erlbaum.

Manlove, J. (1997). Early motherhood in an intergenerational perspective: The experiences of a British cohort. *Journal of Marriage and the Family, 59,* 263–279.

Manlove, J. S., Terry-Humen, E., Ikramullah, E. N., & Moore, K. A. (2006). The role of parent religiosity in teens' transitions to sex and contraception. *Journal of Adolescent Health, 39,* 578–587.

Mann, T., Braswell, G., & Berk, L. E. (2005, April). *A community children's museum as a context for parent–child engagement.* Poster presented at the biennial meeting of the Society for Research in Child Development, Atlanta, GA.

Mant, C. M., & Perner, J. (1988). The child's understanding of commitment. *Developmental Psychology, 24,* 343–351.

Mao, A., Burnham, M. M., Goodlin-Jones, B. L., Gaylor, E. E., & Anders, T. F. (2004). A comparison of the sleep–wake patterns of cosleeping and solitary-sleeping infants. *Child Psychiatry and Human Development, 35,* 95–105.

Maratsos, M. (1998). The acquisition of grammar. In D. Kuhn & R. S. Siegler (Eds.), *Handbook of child psychology: Vol. 2. Cognition, perception and language* (5th ed., pp. 421–466). New York: Wiley.

Maratsos, M. (2000). More overregularizations after all: New data and discussion on Marcus, Pinker, Ullman, Hollander, Rosen, & Xu. *Journal of Child Language, 27,* 183–212.

Marchman, V. A., & Thal, D. J. (2005). Words and grammar. In M. Tomasello & D. I. Slobin (Eds.), *Beyond nature–nurture: Essays in honor of Elizabeth Bates* (pp. 141–164). Mahwah, NJ: Erlbaum.

Marcia, J. E. (1980). Identity in adolescence. In J. Adelson (Ed.), *Handbook of adolescent psychology* (pp. 159–187). New York: Wiley.

Marcon, R. A. (1999a). Differential impact of preschool models on development and early learning of inner-city children: A three-cohort study. *Developmental Psychology, 35,* 358–375.

Marcon, R. A. (1999b). Positive relationships between parent–school involvement and public school inner-city preschoolers' development and academic performance. *School Psychology Review, 28,* 395–412.

Marcus, G. F., Fernandes, K. J., & Johnson, S. P. (2007). Infant rule learning facilitated by speech. *Psychological Science, 18,* 387–391.

Marcus, G. F., Pinker, S., Ullman, M., Hollander, M., Rosen, T. J., & Xu, F. (1992). Overregularization in language acquisition. *Monographs of the Society for Research in Child Development, 57*(4, Serial No. 228).

Marcus, G. F., Vijayan, S., Rao, S. B., & Vishton, P. M. (1999). Rule learning by seven-month-old infants. *Science, 283,* 77–80.

Mardh, P. A. (2002). Influence of infection with *Chlamydia trachomatis* on pregnancy outcome, infant health and lifelong sequelae in infected offspring. *Best Practices in Clinical Obstetrics and Gynecology, 16,* 847–964.

Mareschal, D. (2003). The acquisition and use of implicit categories in early development. In D. H. Rakison & L. M. Oakes (Eds.), *Early category and concept development* (pp. 360–383). New York: Oxford University Press.

Mareschal, D., & Quinn, P. C. (2001). Categorization in infancy. *Trends in Cognitive Sciences, 5,* 443–450.

Margolese, S. K., Markiewicz, D., & Doyle, A. B. (2005). Attachment to parents, best friend, and romantic partner: Predicting different pathways to depression in adolescence. *Journal of Youth and Adolescence, 34,* 637–650.

Mariano, K. A., & Harton, H. C. (2005). Similarities in aggression inattention/hyperactivity, depression, and anxiety in middle childhood friendships. *Journal of Social and Clinical Psychology, 24,* 471–496.

Markman, E. M. (1992). Constraints on word learning: Speculations about their nature, origins, and domain specificity. In M. R. Gunnar & M. P. Maratsos (Eds.), *Minnesota Symposia on Child Psychology* (Vol. 25, pp. 59–101). Hillsdale, NJ: Erlbaum.

Markova, G., & Legerstee, M. (2006). Contingency, imitation, and affect sharing: Foundations of infants' social awareness. *Developmental Psychology, 42,* 132–141.

Markovits, H., & Barrouillet, P. (2002). The development of conditional reasoning: A Piagetian reformulation of mental models theory. *Merrill-Palmer Quarterly, 39,* 131–158.

Markovits, H., Benenson, J., & Dolensky, E. (2001). Evidence that children and adolescents have internal models of peer interactions that are gender differentiated. *Child Development, 72,* 879–886.

Markovits, H., Schleifer, M., & Fortier, L. (1989). Development of elementary deductive reasoning in young children. *Developmental Psychology, 25,* 787–793.

Markovits, H., & Vachon, R. (1990). Conditional reasoning, representation, and level of abstraction. *Developmental Psychology, 26,* 942–951.

Markus, H. R., & Kitayama, S. (1991). Culture and the self: Implications for cognition, emotion, and motivation. *Psychological Review, 98,* 224–253.

Marlier, L., & Schaal, B. (2005). Human newborns prefer human milk: Conspecific milk odor is attractive without postnatal exposure. *Child Development, 76,* 155–168.

Marlier, L., Schaal, B., & Soussignan, R. (1998). Neonatal responsiveness to the odor of amniotic and lacteal fluids: A test of perinatal chemosensory continuity. *Child Development, 69,* 611–623.

Marosi, E., Bazan, O., Yanez, G., Bernal, J., Fernandez, T., & Rodriguez, M. (2002). Narrow-band spectral measurements of EEG during emotional tasks. *International Journal of Neuroscience, 112,* 871–891.

Marsh, H. W. (1990). The structure of academic self-concept: The Marsh/Shavelson model. *Journal of Educational Psychology, 82,* 623–636.

Marsh, H. W., & Ayotte, V. (2003). Do multiple dimensions of self-concept become more differentiated with age? The differential distinctiveness hypothesis. *Journal of Educational Psychology, 95,* 687–706.

Marsh, H. W., Craven, R., & Debus, R. (1998). Structure, stability, and development of young children's self-concepts: A multicohort-multioccasion study. *Child Development, 69,* 1030–1053.

Marsh, H. W., Ellis, L. A., & Craven, R. G. (2002). How do preschool children feel about themselves? Unraveling measurement and multidimensional self-concept structure. *Developmental Psychology, 38,* 376–393.

Marsh, H. W., Gerlach, E., Trautwein, U., Lüdtke, O., & Brettschneider, W.-D. (2007). Longitudinal study of predadolescent sport self-concept and performance: Reciprocal effects and causal ordering. *Child Development, 78,* 1640–1656.

Marsh, H. W., & Hau, K.-T. (2003). Big-fish–little-pond effect on academic self-concept: A cross-cultural (26-country) test of the negative effects of academically selective schools. *American Psychologist, 58,* 364–376.

Marsh, H. W., & Kleitman, S. (2002). Extracurricular school activities: The good, the bad, and the non-linear. *Harvard Educational Review, 72,* 464–514.

Marsh, H. W., & Kleitman, S. (2005). Consequences of employment during high school: Character building, subversion of academic goals, or a threshold? *American Educational Research Journal, 42,* 331–369.

Marsh, J. S., & Daigneault, J. P. (1999). The young athlete. *Current Opinion in Pediatrics, 11,* 84–88.

Marsh, M. W., Parada, R. H., & Ayotte, V. (2004). A multidimensional perspective of relations between self-concept (Self Description Questionnaire II) and adolescent mental health (Youth Self Report). *Psychological Assessment, 16,* 27–41.

Marshall-Baker, A., Lickliter, R., & Cooper, R. P. (1998). Prolonged exposure to a visual pattern may promote behavioral organization in preterm infants. *Journal of Perinatal and Neonatal Nursing, 12,* 50–62.

Martin, C. L. (1989). Children's use of gender-related information in making social judgments. *Developmental Psychology, 25,* 80–88.

Martin, C. L., Eisenbud, L., & Rose, H. (1995). Children's gender-based reasoning about toys. *Child Development, 66,* 1453–1471.

Martin, C. L., & Fabes, C. A. (2001). The stability and consequences of young children's same-sex peer interactions. *Developmental Psychology, 37,* 431–446.

Martin, C. L., Fabes, R. A., Evans, S. M., & Wyman, H. (1999). Social cognition on the playground: Children's beliefs about playing with girls versus boys and their relations to sex segregated play. *Journal of Social and Personal Relationships, 16,* 751–771.

Martin, C. L., & Halverson, C. F., Jr. (1987). The role of cognition in sex role acquisition. In D. B. Carter (Ed.), *Current conceptions of sex roles and sex typing: Theory and research* (pp. 123–137). New York: Praeger.

Martin, C. L., & Little, J. K. (1990). The relation of gender understanding to children's sex-typed preferences and gender stereotypes. *Child Development, 61,* 1427–1439.

Martin, C. L., & Ruble, D. (2004). Children's search for gender cues: Cognitive perspectives on gender development. *Current Directions in Psychological Science, 13,* 67–70.

Martin, C. L., Ruble, D. N., & Szkrybalo, J. (2002). Cognitive theories of early gender development. *Psychological Bulletin, 128,* 903–933.

Martin, G. L., & Pear, J. (2007). *Behavior modification: What it is and how to do it* (8th ed.). Upper Saddle River, NJ: Prentice-Hall.

Martin, K. A. (1996). *Puberty, sexuality and the self: Girls and boys at adolescence.* New York: Routledge.

Martin, R. P., Olejnik, S., & Gaddis, L. (1994). Is temperament an important contributor to schooling outcomes in elementary school? Modeling effects of temperament and scholastic ability on academic achievement. In W. B. Carey & S. C. McDevitt (Eds.), *Prevention and early intervention* (pp. 59–68). New York: Brunner/Mazel.

Martinez-Frias, M. L., Bermejo, E., Rodríguez-Pinilla, E., & Frías, J. L. (2004). Risk for congenital anomalies associated with different sporadic and daily doses of alcohol consumption during pregnancy: A case-control study. *Birth Defects Research, Part A, Clinical and Molecular Teratology, 70,* 194–200.

Martins, P. A., Hoffman, D. J., Fernandes, M. T., Nascimento, C. R., Roberts, S. B., Sesso, R., & Sawaya, A. L. (2004). Stunted children gain less lean body mass and more fat mass than their non-stunted counterparts: A prospective study. *British Journal of Nutrition, 92,* 819–825.

Martlew, M., & Connolly, K. J. (1996). Human figure drawings by schooled and unschooled children in Papua New Guinea. *Child Development, 67,* 2743–2762.

Martyn, C. N., Barker, D. J. P., & Osmond, C. (1996). Mothers' pelvic size, fetal growth, and death from stroke and coronary heart disease in men in the UK. *Lancet, 348,* 1264–1268.

Marzolf, D. P., & DeLoache, J. S. (1994). Transfer in young children's understanding of spatial representations. *Child Development, 65,* 1–15.

Masataka, N. (1996). Perception of motherese in a signed language by 6-month-old deaf infants. *Developmental Psychology, 32,* 874–879.

Mascolo, M. F., & Fischer, K. W. (2007). The codevelopment of self and sociomoral emotions during the toddler years. In C. A. Brownell & C. B. Kopp (Eds.), *Socioemotional development in the toddler years: Transitions and transformations* (pp. 66–99). New York: Guilford.

Mason, M. G., & Gibbs, J. C. (1993a). Role-taking opportunities and the transition to advanced moral judgment. *Moral Education Forum, 18,* 1–12.

Mason, M. G., & Gibbs, J. C. (1993b). Social perspective taking and moral judgment among college students. *Journal of Adolescent Research, 8,* 109–123.

Masten, A. S. (2001). Ordinary magic: Resilience processes in development. *American Psychologist, 56,* 227–238.

Masten, A. S., Coatsworth, J. D., Neemann, J., Gest, S. D., Tellegen, A., & Garmezy, N. (1995). The structure and coherence of competence from childhood through adolescence. *Child Development, 66,* 1635–1659.

Masten, A. S., & Gewirtz, A. H. (2006). Vulnerability and resilience in early child development. In K. McCartney & D.

Phillips (Eds.), *Blackwell handbook of early childhood development* (pp. 22–43). Malden, MA: Blackwell.

Masten, A. S., & Powell, J. L. (2003). A resilience framework for research, policy, and practice. In S. S. Luthar (Ed.), *Resilience and vulnerability* (pp. 1–25). New York: Cambridge University Press.

Masten, A. S., & Reed, M. J. (2002). Resilience in development. In C. R. Snyder & S. J. Lopez (Eds.), *Handbook of positive psychology* (pp. 74–88). New York: Oxford University Press.

Masten, A. S., & Shaffer, A. (2006). How families matter in child development: Reflections from research on risk and resilience. In A. S. Masten & A. Shaffer (Eds.), *Families count: Effects on child and adolescent development* (pp. 5–25). New York: Cambridge University Press.

Mastropieri, D., & Turkewitz, G. (1999). Prenatal experience and neonatal responsiveness to vocal expressions of emotion. *Developmental Psychobiology, 35,* 204–214.

Masur, E. F., McIntyre, C. W., & Flavell, J. H. (1973). Developmental changes in apportionment of study time among items in a multi-trial free recall task. *Journal of Experimental Child Psychology, 15,* 237–246.

Masur, E. F., & Rodemaker, J. E. (1999). Mothers' and infants' spontaneous vocal, verbal, and action imitation during the second year. *Merrill-Palmer Quarterly, 45,* 392–412.

Matheny, A. P., Jr. (1989). Temperament and cognition: Relations between temperament and mental test scores. In G. A. Kohnstamm, J. E. Bates, & M. K. Rothbart (Eds.), *Temperament in childhood* (pp. 263–282). New York: Wiley.

Matheny, A., & Phillips, K. (2001). Temperament and context: Correlates of home environment with temperament continuity and change. In T. D. Wachs & G. Kohnstamm (Eds.), *Temperament in context* (pp. 81–102). Mahwah, NJ: Erlbaum.

Mathiesen, K. S., & Prior, M. (2006). The impact of temperament factors and family functioning on resilience processes from infancy to school age. *European Journal of Developmental Psychology, 3,* 357–387.

Maticka-Tyndale, E. (2001). Sexual health and Canadian youth: How do we measure up? *Canadian Journal of Human Sexuality, 10*(1–2), 1–17.

Matsuba, M. K., & Walker, L. J. (1998). Moral reasoning in the context of ego functioning. *Merrill-Palmer Quarterly, 44,* 464–483.

Mattson, S. N., Calarco, K. E., & Lang, A. R. (2006). Focused and shifting attention in children with heavy prenatal alcohol exposure. *Neuropsychology, 20,* 361–369.

Matute-Bianchi, M. E. (1986). Ethnic identities and patterns of school success and failure among Mexican-descent and Japanese-American students in a California high school: An ethnographic analysis. *American Journal of Education, 95,* 233–255.

Maupin, R., Lyman, R., Fatsis, J., Prystowiski, E., Nguyen, A., & Wright, C. (2004). Characteristics of women who deliver with no prenatal care. *Journal of Maternal-Fetal and Neonatal Medicine, 16,* 45–50.

Maurer, D., Lewis, T. L., Brent, H. P., & Levin, A. V. (1999). Rapid improvement in the acuity of infants after visual input. *Science, 286,* 108–110.

Maurer, D., Mondloch, C. J., & Lewis, T. L. (2007). Sleeper effects. *Developmental Science, 10,* 40–47.

Mavroveli, S., Petrides, K. V., Rieffe, C., & Bakker, F. (2007). Trait emotional intelligence, psychological well-being and peer-rated social competence in adolescence. *British Journal of Developmental Psychology, 25,* 263–275.

Mayberry, R. I. (1994). The importance of childhood to language acquisition: Evidence from American Sign Language. In J. C. Goodman & H. C. Nusbaum (Eds.), *The development of speech perception: The transition from speech sounds to spoken words* (pp. 57–90). Cambridge, MA: MIT Press.

Mayeux, L., & Cillessen, A. H. N. (2003). Development of social problem solving in early childhood: Stability, change, and associations with social competence. *Journal of Genetic Psychology, 164,* 153–173.

Mayer, J. D., Salovey, P., & Caruso, D. R. (2003). *Mayer–Salovey–Caruso Emotional Intelligence Test (MSCEIT): User's manual.* Toronto, Canada: Multi-Health Systems.

Mayes, L. C. (1999). Reconsidering the concept of vulnerability in children using the model of prenatal cocaine exposure. In T. B. Cohen & E. M. Hossein (Eds.), *The vulnerable child* (Vol. 3, pp. 35–54). Madison, CT: International Universities Press.

Mayes, L. C., & Zigler, E. (1992). An observational study of the affective concomitants of mastery in infants. *Journal of Child Psychology and Psychiatry, 33,* 659–667.

Maynard, A. E. (2002). Cultural teaching: The development of teaching skills in Maya sibling interactions. *Child Development, 73,* 969–982.

Maynard, A. E., & Greenfield, P. M. (2003). Implicit cognitive development in cultural tools and children: Lessons from Maya Mexico. *Cognitive Development, 18,* 489–510.

Maynard, A. E., Subrahmanyam, K., & Greenfield, P. M. (2005). Technology and the development of intelligence: From the loom to the computer. In R. J. Sternberg & D. D. Preiss (Eds.), *Intelligence and technology: The impact of tools in the nature and development of human abilities* (pp. 29–53). Mahwah, NJ: Erlbaum.

McAlister, A., & Peterson, C. C. (2006). Mental playmates: Siblings, executive functioning and theory of mind. *British Journal of Developmental Psychology, 24,* 733–751.

McAlister, A., & Peterson, C. C. (2007). A longitudinal study of child siblings and theory of mind development. *Cognitive Development, 22,* 258–270.

McBee, M. T. (2006). A descriptive analysis of referral sources for gifted identification screening by race and socioeconomic status. *Journal of Secondary Gifted Education, 17,* 103–111.

McBride-Chang, C., & Kail, R. V. (2002). Cross-cultural similarities in the predictors of reading acquisition. *Child Development, 73,* 1392–1407.

McCabe, A. (1997). Developmental and cross-cultural aspects of children's narration. In M. Bamberg (Ed.), *Narrative development: Six approaches* (pp. 137–174). Mahwah, NJ: Erlbaum.

McCabe, A., & Peterson, C. (1988). A comparison of adults' versus children's spontaneous use of *because* and *so. Journal of Genetic Psychology, 149,* 257–268.

McCall, R. B. (1977). Childhood IQs as predictors of adult educational and occupational status. *Science, 197,* 482–483.

McCall, R. B. (1993). Developmental functions for general mental performance. In D. K. Detterman (Ed.), *Current topics in human intelligence* (Vol. 3, pp. 3–29). Norwood, NJ: Ablex.

McCall, R. B., Appelbaum, M. I., & Hogarty, P. S. (1973). Developmental changes in mental performance. *Monographs of the Society for Research in Child Development, 38*(3, Serial No. 150).

McCall, R. B., & Carriger, M. S. (1993). A meta-analysis of infant habituation and recognition memory performance as predictors of later IQ. *Child Development, 64,* 57–79.

McCartney, K., Dearing, E., Taylor, B., & Bub, K. (2007). Quality child care supports the achievement of low-income children: Direct and indirect pathways through caregiving and the home environment. *Journal of Applied Developmental Psychology, 28,* 411–426.

McCartney, K., Harris, M. J., & Bernieri, F. (1990). Growing up and growing apart: A developmental meta-analysis of twin studies. *Psychological Bulletin, 107,* 226–237.

McCartney, K., Owen, M., Booth, C., Clarke-Stewart, A., & Vandell, D. (2004). Testing a maternal attachment model of behavior problems in early childhood. *Journal of Child Psychology and Psychiatry, 45,* 765–778.

McCarton, C. (1998). Behavioral outcomes in low birth weight infants. *Pediatrics, 102,* 1293–1297.

McCarty, M. E., & Ashmead, D. H. (1999). Visual control of reaching and grasping in infants. *Developmental Psychology, 35,* 620–631.

McCarty, M. E., & Keen, R. (2005). Facilitating problem-solving performance among 9- and 12-month-old infants. *Journal of Cognition and Development, 6,* 209–228.

McClelland, J. L., & Siegler, R. S. (Eds.). (2001). *Mechanisms of cognitive development: Behavioral and neural perspectives.* Mahwah, NJ: Erlbaum.

McCormack, V. A., dos Santos Silva, I., Koupil, I., Leon, D. A., & Lithell, H. O. (2005). Birth characteristics and adult cancer incidence: Swedish cohort of over 11,000 men and women. *International Journal of Cancer, 115,* 611–617.

McCrady, F., Kaufman, K., Vasey, M. W., Barriga, A. Q., Devlin, R. S., & Gibbs, J. C. (2008). It's all about me: A brief report of adolescent sex offenders' generic and sex-specific cognitive distortions. *Sexual Abuse, 20.*

McCune, L. (1993). The development of play as the development of consciousness. In M. H. Bornstein & A. O'Reilly (Eds.), *New directions for child development* (No. 59, pp. 67–79). San Francisco: Jossey-Bass.

McDaniel, J., Purcell, D., & D'Augelli, A. R. (2001). The relationship between sexual orientation and risk for suicide: Research findings and future directions for research and prevention. *Suicide and Life-Threatening Behavior, 31,* 84–105.

McDonough, L. (1999). Early declarative memory for location. *British Journal of Developmental Psychology, 17,* 381–402.

McDowell, D. J., & Parke, R. D. (2000). Differential knowledge of display rules for positive and negative emotions: Influences from parents, influences on peers. *Social Development, 9,* 415–432.

McDowell, D. J., Parke, R. D., & Wang, S. J. (2004). Differences between mothers' and fathers' advice-giving style and content: Relations with social competence and psychological functioning in middle childhood. *Merrill-Palmer Quarterly, 49,* 55–76.

McElhaney, K. B., & Allen, J. (2001). Autonomy and adolescent social functioning: The moderating effect of risk. *Child Development, 72,* 220–235.

McElwain, N. L., & Booth-LaForce, C. (2006). Maternal sensitivity to infant distress and nondistress as predictors of infant–mother attachment security. *Journal of Family Psychology, 20,* 247–255.

McGee, G. (1997). Legislating gestation. *Human Reproduction, 12,* 407–408.

McGee, L. M., & Richgels, D. J. (2008). *Literacy's beginnings: Supporting young readers and writers* (5th ed.). Boston: Allyn and Bacon.

McGillicuddy-De Lisi, A. V., Daly, M., & Neal, A. (2006). Children's distributive justice judgments: Aversive racism in Euro-American children? *Child Development, 77,* 1063–1080.

McGillicuddy-De Lisi, A. V., Watkins, C., & Vinchur, A. J. (1994). The effect of relationship on children's distributive justice reasoning. *Child Development, 65,* 1694–1700.

McGlothlin, H., & Killen, M. (2006). Intergroup attitudes of European American children attending ethnically homogeneous schools. *Child Development, 77,* 1375–1386.

McGue, M., Bouchard, T. J., Jr., Iacono, W. G., & Lykken, D. T. (1993). Behavioral genetics of cognitive ability: A life-span perspective. In R. Plomin & G. E. McClearn (Eds.), *Nature, nurture, and psychology* (pp. 59–76). Washington, DC: American Psychological Association.

McHale, J. P., Kazali, C., Rotman, T., Talbot, J., Carleton, M., & Lieberson, R. (2004). The transition to coparenthood: Parents' prebirth expectations and early coparental adjustment at 3 months postpartum. *Development and Psychopathology, 16,* 711–733.

McHale, J. P., Lauretti, A., Talbot, J., & Pouquette, C. (2002). Retrospect and prospect in the psychological study of coparenting and family group process. In J. P. McHale & W. S. Grolnick (Eds.), *Retrospect and prospect in the psychological study of families* (pp. 127–165). Mahwah, NJ: Erlbaum.

McHale, J. P., Vinden, P. G., Bush, L., Richer, D., Shaw, D., & Smith, B. (2005). Patterns of personal and social adjustment among sport-involved and noninvolved urban middle-school children. *Sociology of Sport Journal, 22,* 119–136.

McHale, S. M., Bartko, W. T., Crouter, A. C., & Perry-Jenkins, M. (1990). Children's housework and psychosocial functioning: The mediating effects of parents' sex-role behaviors and attitudes. *Child Development, 61,* 68–81.

McHale, S. M., Crouter, A. C., Kim, J.-Y., Burton, L. M., Davis, K. D., Dotterer, A. M., & Swanson, D. P. (2006). Mothers' and fathers' racial socialization in African-American families: Implications for youth. *Child Development, 77,* 1387–1402.

McHale, S. M., Crouter, A. C., & Whiteman, S. D. (2003). The family contexts of gender development in childhood and adolescence. *Social Development, 12,* 125–148.

McHale, S. M., Updegraff, K. A., Helms-Erikson, H., & Crouter, A. C. (2001).

Sibling influences on gender development in middle childhood and early adolescence: A longitudinal study. *Developmental Psychology, 37,* 115–125.

McIntosh, J., MacDonald, F., & McKeganey, N. (2006). Why do children experiment with illegal drugs? The declining role of peer pressure with increasing age. *Addiction Research and Theory, 14,* 275–287.

McKelvie, P., & Low, J. (2002). Listening to Mozart does not improve children's spatial ability: Final curtains for the Mozart effect. *British Journal of Developmental Psychology, 20,* 241–258.

McKenna, J. J. (2001). Why we never ask "Is it safe for infants to sleep alone?" *Academy of Breast Feeding Medicine News and Views, 7*(4), 32, 38.

McKenna, J. J. (2002, September/October). Breastfeeding and bedsharing still useful (and important) after all these years. *Mothering, 114.* Retrieved from www.mothering.com/articles/new_baby/sleep/mckenna.html

McKenna, J. J., & McDade, T. (2005). Why babies should never sleep alone: A review of the co-sleeping controversy in relation to SIDS, bedsharing, and breastfeeding. *Paediatric Respiratory Reviews, 6,* 134–152.

McKown, C., & Weinstein, R. S. (2002). Modeling the role of child ethnicity and gender in children's differential response to teacher expectations. *Journal of Applied Social Psychology, 32,* 159–184.

McKown, C., & Weinstein, R. S. (2003). The development and consequences of stereotype consciousness in middle childhood. *Child Development, 74,* 498–515.

McKusick, V. A. (2007). *Online mendelian inheritance in man.* Retrieved from www.ncbi.nlm.nih.gov/sites/entrez?db=omim

McLanahan, S. (1999). Father absence and the welfare of children. In E. M. Hetherington (Ed.), *Coping with divorce, single parenting, and remarriage: A risk and resiliency perspective* (pp. 117–145). Mahwah, NJ: Erlbaum.

McLean, K. C., & Pratt, M. W. (2006). Life's little (and big) lessons: identity statuses and meaning-making in the turning point narratives of emerging adults. *Developmental Psychology, 42,* 714–722.

McLeod, C. (2007). *Obesity of China's kids stuns officials.* Retrieved from www.usatoday.com/news/world/2007-01-08-chinese-obesity_x.htm

McLoyd, V. C., Aikens, N. L., & Burton, L. M. (2006). Child poverty, policy, and practice. In K. A. Renninger & I. E. Sigel (Eds.), *Handbook of child psychology: Vol. 4. Child psychology in practice* (6th ed., pp. 700–778). Hoboken, NJ: Wiley.

McLoyd, V. C., Kaplan, R., Hardaway, C. R., & Wood, D. (2007). Does endorsement of physical discipline matter? Assessing moderating influences on the maternal and child psychological correlates of physical discipline in African-American families. *Journal of Family Psychology, 21,* 165–175.

McLoyd, V. C., & Smith, J. (2002). Physical discipline and behavior problems in African-American, European-American, and Hispanic children: Emotional support as a moderator. *Journal of Marriage and the Family, 64,* 40–53.

McMahon, C. A., Barnett, B., Kowalenko, N. M., & Tennant, C. C. (2006). Maternal attachment state of mind moderates the impact of postnatal depression on infant attachment. *Journal of Child Psychology and Psychiatry, 47,* 660–669.

McManus, I. C., Sik, G., Cole, D. R., Mellon, A. F., Wong, J., & Kloss, J. (1988). The development of handedness in children. *British Journal of Developmental Psychology, 6,* 257–273.

McNamee, S., & Peterson, J. (1986). Young children's distributive justice reasoning, behavior, and role taking: Their consistency and relationship. *Journal of Genetic Psychology, 146,* 399–404.

MCR Vitamin Study Research Group. (1991). Prevention of neural tube defects: Results of the Medical Research Council Vitamin Study. *Lancet, 338,* 131–137.

Mead, G. H. (1934). *Mind, self, and society.* Chicago: University of Chicago Press.

Mead, M. (1928). *Coming of age in Samoa.* Ann Arbor, MI: Morrow.

Mead, M., & Newton, N. (1967). Cultural patterning of perinatal behavior. In S. Richardson & A. Guttmacher (Eds.), *Childbearing: Its social and psychological aspects* (pp. 142–244). Baltimore: Williams & Wilkins.

Mechelli, A., Crinion, J. T., Noppeney, U., O'Doherty, J., Ashburner, J., Frackowiak, R. S., & Price, C. J. (2004). Structural plasticity in the bilingual brain: Proficiency in a second language and age at acquisition affect grey-matter density. *Nature, 431,* 757.

Media Awareness Network. (2001). Parental awareness of Canadian children's Internet use. Retrieved from www.media-awareness.ca

Meek, J. (2002). Basic principles of optical imaging and application to the study of infant development. *Developmental Science, 5,* 371–380.

Meeus, W. (1996). Studies on identity development in adolescence: An overview of research and some new data. *Journal of Youth and Adolescence, 25,* 569–598.

Meeus, W., Iedema, J., Helsen, M., & Vollebergh, W. (1999). Patterns of adolescent identity development: Review of literature and longitudinal analysis. *Developmental Review, 19,* 419–461.

Meeus, W., Oosterwegel, A., & Vollebergh, W. (2002). Parental and peer attachment and identity development in adolescence. *Journal of Adolescence, 25,* 93–106.

Mehlmadrona, L., & Madrona, M. M. (1997). Physician- and midwife-attended home births—effects of breech, twin, and post-dates outcome data on mortality rates. *Journal of Nurse-Midwifery, 42,* 91–98.

Meins, E., Fernyhough, C., Russell, J., & Clark-Carter, D. (1998). Security of attachment as a predictor of symbolic and mentalizing abilities: A longitudinal study. *Social Development, 7,* 1–24.

Meins, E., Fernyhough, C., Wainwright, R., Clark-Carter, D., Gupta, M. D., Fradley, E., & Tucker, M. (2003). Pathways to understanding mind: Construct validity and predictive validity of maternal mind-mindedness. *Child Development, 74,* 1194–1211.

Meisels, S. J., Dichtelmiller, M., & Liaw, F. R. (1993). A multidimensional analysis of early childhood intervention programs. In C. H. Zeanah (Ed.), *Handbook of infant mental health* (pp. 361–385). New York: Guilford.

Melton, G. B. (2005). Treating children like people: A framework for research and advocacy. *Journal of Clinical Child and Adolescent Psychology, 34,* 646–657.

Meltzoff, A. N. (1995). Understanding the intentions of others: Re-enactment of intended acts by 18-month-old children. *Developmental Psychology, 31,* 838–850.

Meltzoff, A. N. (2007). 'Like me': A foundation for social cognition. *Developmental Science, 10,* 126–134.

Meltzoff, A. N., & Decety, J. (2003). What imitation tells us about social cognition: A rapprochement between developmental psychology and cognitive neuroscience. *Philosophical Transactions of the Royal Society of London, Series B, Biological Sciences, 358,* 491–500.

Meltzoff, A. N., & Kuhl, P. K. (1994). Faces and speech: Intermodal processing of biologically relevant signals in infants and adults. In D. J. Lewkowicz & R. Lickliter (Eds.), *The development of intersensory perception: Comparative perspectives* (pp. 335–369). Hillsdale, NJ: Erlbaum.

Meltzoff, A. N., & Moore, M. K. (1977). Imitation of facial and manual gestures by human neonates. *Science, 198,* 75–78.

Meltzoff, A. N., & Moore, M. K. (1994). Imitation, memory, and the representation of persons. *Infant Behavior and Development, 17,* 83–99.

Meltzoff, A. N., & Moore, M. K. (1998). Object representation, identity, and paradox of early permanence: Steps toward a new framework. *Infant Behavior and Development, 21,* 201–235.

Meltzoff, A. N., & Moore, M. K. (1999). Persons and representations: Why infant imitation is important for theories of human development. In J. Nadel & G. Butterworth (Eds.), *Imitation in infancy* (pp. 9–35). Cambridge, UK: Cambridge University Press.

Melzi, G., & Ely, R. (2009). Language development in the school years. In J. B. Gleason & N. B. Ratner (Eds.), *The development of language* (7th ed., pp. 391–435). Boston: Allyn and Bacon.

Mendle, J., Turkheimer, E., & Emery, R. E. (2007). Detrimental psychological outcomes associated with early pubertal timing in adolescent girls. *Developmental Review, 27,* 151–171.

Mendle, J., Turkheimer, E., D'Onofrio, B. M., Lynch, S., Emery, R. E., & Slutske, W. S. (2006). Family structure and age at menarche: A children-of-twins approach. *Developmental Psychology, 42,* 533–542.

Menendez, M. (2005). Down syndrome, Alzheimer's disease, and seizures. *Brain and Development, 27,* 246–252.

Menn, L., & Stoel-Gammon, C. (2009). Phonological development: Learning sounds and sound patterns. In J. B. Gleason & B. Ratner (Eds.), *The development of language* (7th ed., pp. 58–103). Boston: Allyn and Bacon.

Mennella, J. A., & Beauchamp, G. K. (1998). Early flavor experiences: Research update. *Nutrition Reviews, 56,* 205–211.

Ment, L. R., Vohr, B., Allan, W., Katz, K. H., Schneider, K. C., Westerveld, M., Cuncan, C. C., & Makuch, R. W. (2003). Change in cognitive function over time in very low-birth-weight infants. *Journal of the American Medical Association, 289,* 705–711.

Menyuk, P., Liebergott, J. W., & Schultz, M. C. (1995). *Early language development in full-term and premature infants.* Hillsdale, NJ: Erlbaum.

Meredith, N. V. (1978). *Human body growth in the first ten years of life.* Columbia, SC: State Printing.

Meredith, W. H., Wang, A., & Zheng, F. M. (1993). Determining constructs of self-perception for children in Chinese cultures. *School Psychology International, 14,* 371–380.

Meroni, L., & Crain, S. (2003). On not being led down the kindergarten path. *Proceedings of the 25th annual Boston University Conference on Language Development.* Somerville, MA: Cascadilla Press.

Mervis, C. B., Pani, J. R., & Pani, A. M. (2003). Transaction of child cognitive-linguistic abilities and adult input in the acquisition of lexical categories at the basic and subordinate levels. In D. H. Rakison & L. M. Oakes (Ed.), *Early category and concept development* (pp. 242–274). New York: Oxford University Press.

Mervis, C. B., & Robinson, B. F. (2000). Expressive vocabulary ability of toddlers with Williams syndrome or Down syndrome: A comparison. *Developmental Neuropsychology, 17,* 111–126.

Metcalfe, J., & Mischel, W. (1999). A hot/cool system analysis of delay of gratification: Dynamics of willpower. *Psychological Review, 106,* 3–19.

Metz, E. C., & Youniss, J. (2005). Longitudinal gains in civic development through school-based required service. *Political Psychology, 26,* 413–437.

Meyer, P. A., Pivetz, T., Dignam, T. A., Hma, D. M., Schoonover, J., & Brody, D. (2003). Surveillance for elevated blood lead levels among children—United States, 1997–2001. *Morbidity and Mortality Weekly Report, 52*(No. SS-10), 1–21.

Meyer-Bahlburg, H. F. L., Dolezal, C., Baker, S. W., Carlson, A. D., Obeid, J. S., & New, M. I. (2004). Prenatal androgenization affects gender-related behavior but not gender identity in 5- to 12-year-old girls with congenital adrenal hyperplasia. *Archives of Sexual Behavior, 33,* 97–104.

Meyer-Bahlburg, H. F. L., Ehrhardt, A. A., Rosen, L. R., Gruen, R. S., Veridiano, N. P., Vann, F. H., & Neuwalder, H. F. (1995). Prenatal estrogens and the development of homosexual orientation. *Developmental Psychology, 31,* 12–21.

Meyers, C., Adam, R., Dungan, J., & Prenger, V. (1997). Aneuploidy in twin gestations: When is maternal age advanced? *Obstetrics and Gynecology, 89,* 248–251.

Meyers, M. K., Rosenbaum, D., Ruhm, C., & Waldfogel, J. (2004). Inequality in early childhood education and care: What do we know? In K. Neckerman (Ed.), *Social inequality.* New York: Russell Sage Foundation.

Mezulis, A. H., Hyde, J. S., & Clark, R. (2004). Father involvement moderates the effect of maternal depression during a child's infancy on child behavior problems in kindergarten. *Journal of Family Psychology, 18,* 575–588.

Miceli, P. J., Whitman, T. L., Borkowski, J. G., Braungart-Riekder, J., & Mitchell, D. W. (1998). Individual differences in infant information processing: The role of temperamental and maternal factors. *Infant Behavior and Development, 21,* 119–136.

Michael, A., & Eccles, J. S. (2003). When coming of age means coming undone: Links between puberty and psychosocial adjustment among European American and African American girls. In C. Hayward (Ed.), *Gender differences at puberty* (pp. 277–303). New York: Cambridge University Press.

Michael, R. T., Gagnon, J. H., Laumann, E. O., & Kolata, G. (1994). *Sex in America.* Boston: Little, Brown.

Michalik, N. M., Eisenberg, N., Spinrad, T. L., Ladd, B., Thompson, M., & Valiente, C. (2007). Longitudinal relations among parental emotional expressivity and sympathy and prosocial behavior in adolescence. *Social Development, 16,* 286–309.

Milberger, S., Biederman, J., Faraone, S. V., Guite, J., & Tsuang, M. T. (1997). Pregnancy, delivery and infancy complications and attention deficit hyperactivity disorder: Issues of gene–environment interaction. *Biological Psychiatry, 41,* 65–75.

Miles, C. (1935). Sex in social psychology. In C. Murchison (Ed.), *Handbook of social psychology* (pp. 699–704). Worcester, MA: Clark University Press.

Milevsky, A., Schlechter, M., Netter, S., & Keehn, D. (2007). Maternal and paternal parenting styles in adolescents: Associations with self-esteem, depression, and life satisfaction. *Journal of Child and Family Studies, 16,* 39–47.

Miller, B., Cummings, J., Mishkin, F., Boone, K., Prince, F., Ponton, M., & Cotman, C. (1998). Emergence of artistic talent in frontotemporal dementia. *Neurology, 51,* 978–982.

Miller, C. J., Sanchez, J., & Hynd, G. W. (2003). Neurological correlates of reading disabilities. In H. L. Swanson, K. R. Harris, & S. Graham (Eds.), *Handbook of learning disabilities* (pp. 242–255). New York: Guilford.

Miller, J. G. (2006). Insights into moral development from cultural psychology. In M. Killen & J. Smetana (Eds.), *Handbook of moral development* (pp. 375–398). Philadelphia: Erlbaum.

Miller, J. G., & Bersoff, D. M. (1995). Development in the context of everyday family relationships: Culture, interpersonal morality, and adapation. In M. Killen & D. Hart (Eds.), *Morality in everyday life: Developmental perspectives* (pp. 259–282). Cambridge, UK: Cambridge University Press.

Miller, K. S., Forehand, R., & Kotchick, B. (1999). Adolescent sexual behavior in two ethnic minority samples: The role of family variables. *Journal of Marriage and the Family, 61,* 85–98.

Miller, L. T., & Vernon, P. A. (1992). The general factor in short-term memory, intelligence, and reaction time. *Intelligence, 16,* 5–29.

Miller, P. A., Eisenberg, N., Fabes, R. A., & Shell, R. (1996). Relations of moral reasoning and vicarious emotion to young children's prosocial behavior toward peers and adults. *Developmental Psychology, 32,* 210–219.

Miller, P. H. (2000). How best to utilize a deficiency. *Child Development, 71,* 1013–1017.

Miller, P. H. (2001). *Theories of developmental psychology.* New York: Worth.

Miller, P. H., & Bigi, L. (1979). The development of children's understanding of attention. *Merrill-Palmer Quarterly, 25,* 235–250.

Miller, P. H., Haynes, V. F., DeMarie-Dreblow, D., & Woody-Ramsey, J. (1986). Children's strategies for gathering information in three tasks. *Child Development, 57,* 1429–1439.

Miller, P. H., Kessel, F. S., & Flavell, J. H. (1970). Thinking about people thinking about people thinking about . . . : A study of social cognitive development. *Child Development, 41,* 613–623.

Miller, P. J., Fung, H., & Mintz, J. (1996). Self-construction through narrative practices: A Chinese and American comparison of early socialization. *Ethos, 24,* 1–44.

Miller, P. J., Hengst, J. A., & Wang, S. (2003). Ethnographic methods: Applications from developmental cultural psychology. In P. M. Camic & J. E. Rhodes (Eds.), *Qualitative research in psychology* (pp. 219–242). Washington, DC: American Psychological Association.

Miller, P. J., Wang, S., Sandel, T., & Cho, G. E. (2002). Self-esteem as folk theory: A comparison of European American and Taiwanese mothers' beliefs. *Parenting: Science and Practice, 2,* 209–239.

Miller, P. J., Wiley, A. R., Fung, H., & Liang, C.-H. (1997). Personal storytelling as a medium of socialization in Chinese and American families. *Child Development, 68,* 557–568.

Miller, R. B. (2000). Do children make a marriage unhappy? *Family Science Review, 13,* 60–73.

Miller, S. A. (1998). *Developmental research methods* (2nd ed.). Englewood Cliffs, NJ: Prentice-Hall.

Miller, S. A. (2007). *Developmental research methods* (3rd ed.). Thousand Oaks, CA: Sage.

Miller, S. A., & Davis, T. L. (1992). Beliefs about children: A comparative study of mothers, teachers, peers, and self. *Child Development, 63,* 1251–1265.

Miller, S. A., Hardin, C. A., & Montgomery, D. E. (2003). Young children's understanding of the conditions for knowledge acquisition. *Journal of Cognition and Development, 4,* 325–356.

Milligan, K., Astington, J. W., & Dack, L. A. (2007). Language and theory of mind: Meta-analysis of the relation between language ability and false-belief understanding. *Child Development, 78,* 622–646.

Mills, D., & Conboy, B. T. (2005). Do changes in brain organization reflect shifts in symbolic functioning? In L. Namy (Ed.), *Symbol use and symbolic representation* (pp. 123–153). Mahwah, NJ: Erlbaum.

Mills, D., Plunkett, K., Prat, C., & Schafer, G. (2005). Watching the infant brain learn words: Effects of language and experience. *Cognitive Development, 20,* 19–31.

Mills, D. L., Coffey-Corina, S., & Neville, H. J. (1997). Language comprehension and cerebral specialization from 13 to 20 months. *Developmental Neuropsychology, 13,* 397–445.

Mills, R. S. L. (2005). Taking stock of the developmental literature on shame. *Developmental Review, 25,* 26–63.

Mills, R., & Grusec, J. E. (1989). Cognitive, affective, and behavioral consequences of praising altruism. *Merrill-Palmer Quarterly, 35,* 299–326.

Minami, M., (1996). Japanese preschool children's narrative development. *First Language, 16,* 339–363.

Misailidi, P. (2006). Young children's display rule knowledge: Understanding the distinction between apparent and real emotions and the motives underlying the use of display rules. *Social Behavior and Personality, 34,* 1285–1296.

Mischel, H. N., & Liebert, R. M. (1966). Effects of discrepancies between observed and imposed reward criteria on their acquisition and transmission. *Journal of Personality and Social Psychology, 3,* 45–53.

Mischel, H. N., & Mischel, W. (1983). The development of children's knowledge of self-control strategies. *Child Development, 54,* 603–619.

Mischel, W. (1996). From good intentions to willpower. In P. M. Gollwitzer & J. A. Bargh (Eds.), *The psychology of action* (pp. 197–218). New York: Guilford.

Mischel, W., & Ayduck, O. (2004). Willpower in a cognitive–affective processing system: The dynamics of delay of gratification. In R. F. Baumeister & K. D. Vohs (Eds.), *Handbook of self-regulation* (pp. 99–129). New York: Guilford.

Mischel, W., & Baker, N. (1975). Cognitive appraisals and transformations in delay behavior. *Journal of Personality and Social Psychology, 31,* 254–261.

Mischel, W., Shoda, Y., & Peake, P. K. (1988). The nature of adolescent competencies predicted by preschool delay of gratification. *Journal of Personality and Social Psychology, 54,* 687–696.

Mishna, F., Antle, B. J., & Regehr, C. (2004). Tapping the perspectives of children. *Qualitative Social Work, 3,* 449–468.

Mistry, J. (1997). The development of remembering in cultural context. In N. Cowan (Ed.), *The development of memory in childhood* (pp. 343–368). Hove, UK: Psychology Press.

Mistry, R. S., Biesanz, J. C., Taylor, L. C., Burchinal, M., & Cox, M. J. (2004). Family income and its relation to preschool children's adjustment for families in the NICHD Study of Early Child Care. *Developmental Psychology, 40,* 727–745.

Mitchell, A., & Boss, B. J. (2002). Adverse effects of pain on the nervous systems of newborns and young children: A review of the literature. *Journal of Neuroscience Nursing, 34,* 228–235.

Miura, I. T., & Okamoto, Y. (2003). Language supports for mathematics understanding and performance. In A. J. Baroody & A. Dowker (Eds.), *The development of arithmetic concepts and skills* (pp. 229–242). Mahwah, NJ: Erlbaum.

Mize, J., & Pettit, G. S. (1997). Mothers' social coaching, mother–child relationship style, and children's peer competence: Is the medium the message? *Child Development, 68,* 312–332.

Modry-Mandell, K. L., Gamble, W. C., & Taylor, A. R. (2007). Family emotional climate and sibling relationship quality: Influences on behavioral problems and adaptation in preschool-aged children. *Journal of Child and Family Studies, 16,* 61–73.

Moens, E., Braet, C., & Soetens, B. (2007). Observation of family functioning at mealtime: A comparison between families of children with and without overweight. *Journal of Pediatric Psychology, 32,* 52–63.

Moerk, E. L. (2000). *The guided acquisition of first language skills.* Westport, CT: Ablex.

Moffitt, T. E. (2006). A review of research on the taxonomy of life-course persistent versus adolescence-limited antisocial behavior. In F. T. Cullen, J. P. Wright, & K . Blevins (Eds.), *Taking stock: The status of criminological theory* (pp. 277–311). New Brunswick, NJ: Transaction Publishers.

Moll, H., & Tomasello, M. (2006). Level I perspective-taking at 24 months of age. *British Journal of Developmental Psychology, 24,* 603–613.

Moll, I. (1994). Reclaiming the natural line in Vygotsky's theory of cognitive development. *Human Development, 37,* 333–342.

Monastersky, R. (2005, March 4). Primed for numbers: Are boys born better at math? Experts try to divide the influences of nature and nurture. *Chronicle of Higher Education.* pp. A1, A12–A14.

Mondloch, C. J., Lewis, T., Budreau, D. R., Maurer, D., Dannemillier, J. L., Stephens, B. R., & Kleiner-Gathercoal, K. A. (1999). Face perception during early infancy. *Psychological Science, 10,* 419–422.

Mondoza, C. (2006). Inside today's classrooms: Teacher voices on No Child Left Behind and the education of gifted children. *Roeper Review, 29,* 28–31.

Monk, C., Fifer, W. P., Myers, M. M., Sloan, R. P., Trien, L., & Hurtado, A. (2000). Maternal stress responses and anxiety during pregnancy: Effects on fetal heart rate. *Developmental Psychobiology, 36,* 67–77.

Monk, C., Myers, M. M., Sloan, R. P., Ellman, L. M., & Fifer, W. P. (2003). Effects of women's stress-elicited physiological activity and chronic anxiety on fetal heart rate. *Journal of Developmental and Behavioral Pediatrics, 24,* 32–38.

Monk, C., Sloan, R., Myers, M. M., Ellman, L., Werner, E., Jeon, J., Tager, F., & Fifer, W. P. (2004). Fetal heart rate reactivity differs by women's psychiatric status: An early marker for developmental risk? *Journal of the American Academy of Child and Adolescent Psychiatry, 43,* 283–290.

Montague, D. P. F., & Walker-Andrews, A. S. (2001). Peekaboo: A new look at infants' perception of emotion expressions. *Developmental Psychology, 37,* 826–838.

Montemayor, R., & Eisen, M. (1977). The development of self-conceptions from childhood to adolescence. *Developmental Psychology, 13,* 314–319.

Montgomery, D. E. (1993). Young children's understanding of interpretive diversity between different-aged listeners. *Developmental Psychology, 29,* 337–345.

Montgomery, M. J., & Côté, J. E. (2003). The transition to college: Adjustment, development, and outcomes. In G. R. Adams & M. D. Berzonsky (Eds.), *Blackwell handbook of adolescence* (pp. 179–194). Malden, MA: Blackwell.

Moon, C., Cooper, R. P., & Fifer, W. P. (1993). Two-day-old infants prefer their native language. *Infant Behavior and Development, 16,* 495–500.

Moon, S. M., & Feldhusen, J. F. (1994). The Program for Academic and Creative Enrichment (PACE): A follow-up study ten years later. In R. F. Subotnik & K. D. Arnold (Eds.), *Beyond Terman: Contemporary longitudinal studies of giftedness and talent* (pp. 375–400). Norwood, NJ: Ablex.

Moore, D. R., & Florsheim, P. (2001). Interpersonal processes and psychopathology among expectant and nonexpectant adolescent couples. *Journal of Consulting and Clinical Psychology, 69,* 101–113.

Moore, D. S., Spence, M. J., & Katz, G. S. (1997). Six-month-olds' categorization of natural infant-directed utterances. *Developmental Psychology, 33,* 980–989.

Moore, E. G. J. (1986). Family socialization and the IQ test performance of traditionally and transracially adopted black children. *Developmental Psychology, 22,* 317–326.

Moore, G. A., Cohn, J. E., & Campbell, S. B. (2001). Infant affective responses to mother's still face at 6 months differentially predict externalizing and internalizing behaviors at 18 months. *Developmental Psychology, 37,* 706–714.

Moore, K. A., Morrison, D. R., & Greene, A. D. (1997). Effects on the children born to adolescent mothers. In R. A. Maynard (Ed.), *Kids having kids* (pp. 145–180). Washington, DC: Urban Institute.

Moore, K. A., Myers, D. E., Morrison, D. R., Nord, C. W., Brown, B., & Edmonston, B. (1993). Age at first childbirth and later poverty. *Journal of Research on Adolescence, 3,* 393–422.

Moore, K. L., & Persaud, T. V. N. (2003). *Before we are born* (6th ed.). Philadelphia: Saunders.

Moore, K. L., & Persaud, T. V. N. (2008). *Before we are born* (7th ed.). Philadelphia: Saunders.

Moore, M. K., & Meltzoff, A. N. (1999). New findings on object permanence: A developmental difference between two types of occlusion. *British Journal of Developmental Psychology, 17,* 563–584.

Moore, M. K., & Meltzoff, A. N. (2004). Object permanence after a 24-hr delay and leaving the locale of disappearance: The role of memory, space, and identity. *Developmental Psychology, 40,* 606–620.

Morales, M., Mundy, P., Delgado, C. E. F., Yale, M., Messinger, D., Neal, R., & Schwartz, H. K. (2000). Responding to joint attention across the 6- through 24-month age period and early language acquisition. *Journal of Applied Developmental Psychology, 21,* 283–298.

Moran, G. F., & Vinovskis, M. A. (1986). The great care of godly parents: Early childhood in Puritan New England. In A. B. Smuts & J. W. Hagen (Eds.), History and research in child development. *Monographs of the Society for Research in Child Development, 50*(4–5, Serial No. 211), pp. 24–37.

Moran, S., & Gardner, H. (2006). Extraordinary achievements: A developmental and systems analysis. In D. Kuhn & R. Siegler (Eds.), *Handbook of child psychology: Vol. 2. Cognition, perception, and language* (6th ed., pp. 905–949). Hoboken, NJ: Wiley.

Morelli, G. A., Rogoff, B., & Angelillo, C. (2003). Cultural variation in young children's access to work or involvement in specialized child-focused activities. *International Journal of Behavioral Development, 27,* 264–274.

Morelli, G. A., Rogoff, B., Oppenheim, D., & Goldsmith, D. (1992). Cultural variation in infants' sleeping arrangements: Questions of independence. *Developmental Psychology, 28,* 604–613.

Morford, J. P., & Goldin-Meadow, S. (1997). From here and now to there and then: The development of displaced reference in homesign and English. *Child Development, 68,* 420–435.

Morgan, B., Maybery, M., & Durkin, K. (2003). Weak central coherence, poor joint attention, and low verbal ability: Independent deficits in early autism. *Developmental Psychology, 28,* 604–613.

Morgane, P. J., Austin-LaFrance, R., Bronzino, J., Tonkiss, J., Diaz-Cintra, S., Cintra, L., Kemper, T., & Galler, J. R. (1993). Prenatal malnutrition and development of the brain. *Neuroscience and Biobehavioral Reviews, 17,* 91–128.

Morris, G., & Baker-Ward, L. (2007). Fragile but real: Children's capacity to use newly acquired words to convey preverbal memories. *Child Development, 78,* 448–458.

Morrongiello, B. A., Fenwick, K. D., & Chance, G. (1998). Crossmodal learning in newborn infants: Inferences about properties of auditory-visual events. *Infant Behavior and Development, 21,* 543–554.

Morrow, D. F. (2006). Gay, lesbian, and transgender adolescents. In D. F. Morrow & L. Messinger (Eds.), *Sexual orientation and gender expression in social work practice* (pp. 177–195). New York: Columbia University Press.

Mosby, L., Rawls, A. W., Meehan, A. J., Mays, E., & Pettinari, C. J. (1999). Troubles in interracial talk about discipline: An examination of African American child rearing narratives. *Journal of Comparative Family Studies, 30,* 489–521.

Mosely-Howard, G. S., & Evans, C. B. (2000). Relationships and contemporary experiences of the African-American family: An ethnographic case study. *Journal of Black Studies, 30,* 428–451.

Moses, L. J., Baldwin, D. A., Rosicky, J. G., & Tidball, G. (2001). Evidence for referential understanding in the emotions domain at twelve and eighteen months. *Child Development, 72,* 718–735.

Moshman, D. (1998). Cognitive development beyond childhood. In D. Kuhn & R. S. Siegler (Eds.), *Handbook of child psychology: Vol. 2. Cognition, perception, and language* (5th ed., pp. 947–978). New York: Wiley.

Moshman, D. (1999). *Adolescent psychological development: Rationality, morality, and identity.* Mahwah, NJ: Erlbaum.

Moshman, D. (2005). *Adolescent psychological development: Rationality, morality, and identity* (2nd ed.). Mahwah, NJ: Erlbaum.

Moshman, D., & Franks, B. A. (1986). Development of the concept of inferential validity. *Child Development, 57,* 153–165.

Moss, E., Cyr, C., Bureau, J.-F., Tarabulsy, G. M., & Dubois-Comtois, K. (2005b). Stability of attachment during the preschool period. *Developmental Psychology, 41,* 773–783.

Moss, E., Cyr, C., & Dubois-Comtois, K. (2004). Attachment at early school age and developmental risk: Examining family contexts and behavior problems of controlling-caregiving, controlling-punitive, and behaviorally disorganized children. *Developmental Psychology, 40,* 519–532.

Moss, E., Smolla, N., Guerra, I., Mazzarello, T., Chayer, D., & Berthiaume, C. (2006). Attachment and self-reported internalizing and externalizing behavior problems in a school period. *Canadian Journal of Behavioural Science, 38,* 142–157.

Moss, E., St.-Laurent, D., Dubois-Comtois, K., & Cyr, C. (2005a). Quality of attachment at school age: Relations between child attachment behavior, psychosocial functioning, and school performance. In K. A. Kerns & R. A. Richardson (Eds.), *Attachment in middle childhood* (pp. 189–211). New York: Guilford.

Mosteller, F. (1995). The Tennessee Study of Class Size in the Early School Grades. *Future of Children, 5*(2), 113–127.

Motl, R. W., Dishman, R. K., Saunders, R. P., Dowda, M., Felton, G., Ward, D. S., & Pate, R. R. (2002). Examining social–cognitive determinants of intention and physical activity among black and white adolescent girls using structural equation modeling. *Health Psychology, 21,* 459–467.

Mounts, N. S., & Steinberg, L. D. (1995). An ecological analysis of peer influence on adolescent grade point average and drug use. *Developmental Psychology, 31,* 915–922.

Mrug, S., Hoza, B., & Gerdes, A. C. (2001). Children with attention-deficit/hyperactivity disorder: Peer relationships and peer-oriented interventions. In D. W. Nangle & C. A. Erdley (Eds.), *The role of friendship in psychological adjustment* (pp. 51–77). San Francisco: Jossey-Bass.

Mueller, C. M., & Dweck, C. S. (1998). Intelligence praise can undermine motivation and performance. *Journal of Personality and Social Psychology, 75,* 33–52.

Mueller, R. A., Rothermel, R., Behen, M., Muzik, O., Mangner, T., & Chugani, H. (1998). Differential patterns of language and motor reorganization following early left hemisphere injury. *Archives of Neurology, 55,* 1113–1119.

Muenchow, S., & Marsland, K. W. (2007). Beyond baby steps: Promoting the growth and development of U.S. child-care policy. In J. L. Aber, S. J. Bishop-Josef, S. M. Jones, K. T. McLearn, & D. Phillips (Eds.), *Child development and social policy: Knowledge for action* (pp. 97–112). Washington, DC: American Psychological Association.

Mulder, E. J. H., Robles de Medina, P. G., Huizink, A. C., Van den Bergh, B. R. H., Buitelaar, J. K., & Visser, G. H. A. (2002). Prenatal maternal stress: Effects on pregnancy and the (unborn) child. *Early Human Development, 70,* 3–14.

Müller, O., & Krawinkel, M. (2005). Malnutrition and health in developing countries. *Canadian Medical Association Journal, 173,* 279–286.

Müller, U., Overton, W. F., & Reese, K. (2001). Development of conditional reasoning: A longitudinal study. *Journal of Cognition and Development, 2,* 27–49.

Mullis, I. V. S., Martin, M. O., Gonzales, E. J., & Kennedy, A. M. (2003). *PIRLS 2001 international report: IEA's study of reading literacy achievement in primary schools.* Chestnut Hill, MA: Boston College. Retrieved from timss.bc.edu/pirls2001.html

Mulvaney, M. K., & Mebert, C. J. (2007). Parental corporal punishment predicts behavior problems in early childhood. *Journal of Family Psychology, 21,* 389–397.

Mulvaney, M. K., McCartney, K., Bub, K. L., & Marshall, N. L. (2006). Determinants of dyadic scaffolding and cognitive outcomes in first graders. *Parenting: Science and Practice, 6,* 297–310.

Mumme, D. L., Bushnell, E. W., DiCorcia, J. A., & Lariviere, L. A. (2007). Infants' use of gaze cues to interpret others' actions and emotional reactions. In R. Flom, K. Lee, & D. Muir (Eds.), *Gaze-following: Its development and significance* (pp. 143–170). Mahwah, NJ: Erlbaum.

Mumme, D. L., Fernald, A., & Herrera, C. (1996). Infants' responses to facial and vocal emotional signals in a social referencing paradigm. *Child Development, 67,* 3219–3237.

Munakata, Y. (2001). Task-dependency in infant behavior: Toward an understanding of the processes underlying cognitive development. In F. Lacerda, C. von Hofsten, & M. Heimann (Eds.), *Emerging cognitive abilities in early infancy* (pp. 29–52). Mahwah, NJ: Erlbaum.

Munakata, Y. (2004). Computational cognitive neuroscience of early memory development. *Developmental Review, 24,* 133–153.

Munakata, Y. (2006). Information processing approaches to development. In D. Kuhn & R. S. Siegler (Eds.), *Handbook of child psychology: Vol. 3. Cognition, perception, and language* (6th ed., pp. 426–463). Hoboken, NJ: Wiley.

Munakata, Y., Casey, B. J., & Diamond, A. (2004). Developmental cognitive neuroscience: Progress and potential. *Trends in Cognitive Sciences, 8,* 122–128.

Munakata, Y., & McClelland, J. L. (2003). Connectionist models of development. *Developmental Science, 6,* 413–429.

Munakata, Y., & Stedron, J. M. (2002). Modeling infants' perception of object unity: What have we learned? *Developmental Science, 5,* 176.

Mundy, P. (2003). The neural basis of social impairments in autism: The role of the dorsal medial-frontal cortex and anterior cingulate system. *Journal of Child Psychology and Psychiatry and Allied Disciplines, 44,* 793–809.

Mundy, P., & Stella, J. (2000). Joint attention, social orienting, and nonverbal communication in autism. In A. M. Wetherby & B. M. Prizant (Eds.), *Autism spectrum disorders* (Vol. 9, pp. 55–77). Baltimore, MD: Paul H. Brookes.

Munroe, R. L., & Romney, A. K. (2006). Gender and age differences in same-sex aggregation and social behavior. *Journal of Cross-Cultural Psychology, 37,* 3–19.

Munson, B. (2001). Phonological pattern frequency and speech production in adults and children. *Journal of Speech, Language, and Hearing Research, 44,* 778–792.

Murett-Wagstaff, S., & Moore, S. G. (1989). The Hmong in America: Infant behavior and rearing practices. In J. K. Nugent, B. M. Lester, & T. B. Brazelton (Eds.), *Biology, culture, and development* (Vol. 1, pp. 319–339). Norwood, NJ: Ablex.

Murphy, L. M. B., Laurie-Rose, C., Brinkman, T. M., & McNamara, K. A. (2007). Sustained attention and social competence in typically developing preschool-aged children. *Early Child Development and Care, 177,* 133–149.

Murray, A. D. (1985). Aversiveness is in the mind of the beholder. In B. M. Lester & C. F. Z. Boukydis (Eds.), *Infant crying* (pp. 217–239). New York: Plenum.

Murray, A. D., Johnson, J., & Peters, J. (1990). Fine-tuning of utterance length to preverbal infants: Effects on later language development. *Journal of Child Language, 17,* 511–525.

Murray-Close, D., Crick, N. R., & Galotti, K. M. (2006). Children's moral reasoning regarding physical and relational aggression. *Social Development, 15,* 345–372.

Mussen, P. H., & Eisenberg-Berg, N. (1977). *Roots of caring, sharing, and helping.* San Francisco: Freeman.

Mustanski, B. S., Viken, R. J., Kaprio, J., Pulkkinen, L., & Rose, R. J. (2004). Genetic and environmental influences on pubertal development: Longitudinal data from Finnish twins at ages 11 and 14. *Developmental Psychology, 40,* 1188–1198.

Muzzatti, B., & Agnoli, F. (2007). Gender and mathematics: Attitudes and stereotype threat susceptibility in Italian children. *Developmental Psychology, 43,* 747–759.

Myers, M. G., Brown, S. A., Tate, S., Abrantes, A., & Tomlinson, K. (2001). *Adolescents, alcohol, and substance abuse* (pp. 275–296). New York: Guilford.

Myowa-Yamakoshi, M., Tomonaga, M., Tanaka, M., & Matsuzawa, T. (2004). Imitation in neonatal chimpanzees *(Pan troglodytes). Developmental Science, 7,* 437–442.

Nadel, J., Prepin, K., & Okanda, M. (2005). Experiencing contingency and agency:

First step toward self-understanding in making a mind? *Interaction Studies, 6,* 447–462.

Nagin, D., & Tremblay, R. E. (1999). Trajectories of boys' physical aggression, opposition, and hyperactivity on the path to physically violent and nonviolent juvenile delinquency. *Child Development, 70,* 1181–1196.

Nagy, E., Compagne, H., Orvos, H., Pal, A., Molnar, P., & Janszky, I. (2005). Index finger movement imitation by human neonates: Motivation, learning, and left-hand preference. *Pediatric Research, 58,* 749–753.

Nagy, W. E., & Scott, J. A. (2000). Vocabulary processes. In M. L. Kamil & P. B. Mosenthal (Eds.), *Handbook of reading research* (Vol. 3, pp. 269–284). Mahwah, NJ: Erlbaum.

Naigles, L. G., & Gelman, S. A. (1995). Overextensions in comprehension and production revisited: Preferential-looking in a study of dog, cat, and cow. *Journal of Child Language, 22,* 19–46.

Naigles, L. R., & Swenson, L. D. (2007). Syntactic supports for word learning. In E. Hoff & M. Shatz (Eds.), *Blackwell handbook of language development* (pp. 212–231). Malden, MA: Blackwell.

Nakamura, K. (2001). The acquisition of polite language by Japanese children. In K. E. Nelson, A. Aksu-Koc, & C. E. Johnson (Eds.), *Children's language: Vol. 10. Developing narrative and discourse competence* (pp. 93–112). Mahwah, NJ: Erlbaum.

Nánez, J., Sr., & Yonas, A. (1994). Effects of luminance and texture motion on infant defensive reactions to optical collision. *Infant Behavior and Development, 17,* 165–174.

National Association for the Education of Young Children. (1998). *Accreditation criteria and procedures of the National Academy of Early Childhood Programs* (2nd ed.). Washington, DC: Author.

National Coalition on Health Care. (2007). *Health insurance coverage.* Retreived from www.nchc.org/facts/coverage.shtml

National Council of Youth Sports. (2005). *Report on trends and participation in youth sports.* Stuart, FL: Author.

National Diabetes Education Program, Diabetes in Children and Adolescents Work Group. (2004). An update on type 2 diabetes in youth from the National Diabetes Education Program. *Pediatrics, 114,* 259–263.

National Federation of State High School Associations. (2006). *High school athletic participation survey.* Kansas City, MO: Author.

National Forum on Welfare to Work. (2004). *Welfare to work: The next generation. A national forum.* St. John's, Newfoundland: Author. Retrieved from www.envision.ca

National Institutes of Health. (2007). *Genes and disease.* Retrieved from www.ncbi .nlm.nih.gov/disease

Navarrete, C., Martinez, I., & Salamanca, F. (1994). Paternal line of transmission in chorea of Huntington with very early onset. *Genetic Counseling, 5,* 175–178.

Needham, A. (2001). Object recognition and object segregation in 4.5-month-old infants. *Journal of Experimental Child Psychology, 78,* 3–24.

Needham, A., & Baillargeon, R. (1993). Intuitions about support in 4.5-month-old infants. *Cognition, 47,* 121–148.

Needleman, H. L., MacFarland, C., Ness, R. B., Reinberg, S., & Tobin, M. J. (2002). Bone lead levels in adjudicated delinquents: A case control study. *Neurotoxicology and Teratology, 24,* 711–717.

Neff, K. D., & Helwig, C. C. (2002). A constructivist approach to understanding the development of reasoning about rights and authority within cultural contexts. *Cognitive Development, 17,* 1429–1450.

Neisser, U., Boodoo, G., Bouchard, T. J., Jr., Boykin, A. W., Brody, N., Ceci, S. J., Halpern, D. F., Loehlin, J. C., Perloff, R., Sternberg, R. J., & Urbina, S. (1996). Intelligence: Knowns and unknowns. *American Psychologist, 51,* 77–101.

Neitzel, C., & Stright, A. D. (2003). Mothers' scaffolding of children's problem solving: Establishing a foundation of academic self-regulatory competence. *Journal of Family Psychology, 17,* 147–159.

Nelson, C. A. (2000). Neural plasticity and human development: The role of early experience sculpting memory systems. *Developmental Science, 3,* 115–130.

Nelson, C. A. (2001). The development and neural bases of face recognition. *Infant and Child Development, 10,* 3–18.

Nelson, C. A. (2002). Neural development and lifelong plasticity. In R. M. Lerner, F. Jacobs, & D. Wertlieb (Eds.), *Handbook of applied developmental science* (Vol. 1, pp. 31–60). Thousand Oaks, CA: Sage.

Nelson, C. A. (2007). A developmental cognitive neuroscience approach to the study of atypical development: A model system involving infants of diabetic mothers. In D. Coch, G. Dawson, & K. W. Fischer (Eds.), *Human behavior, learning, and the developing brain: Atypical development* (pp. 1–27). New York: Guilford.

Nelson, C. A., & Bosquet, M. (2000). Neurobiology of fetal and infant development: Implications for infant mental health. In C. H. Zeanah, Jr. (Ed.), *Handbook of infant mental health* (2nd ed., pp. 37–59). New York: Guilford.

Nelson, C. A., Thomas, K. M., & de Haan, M. (2006). Neural bases of cognitive development. In D. Kuhn & R. Siegler (Eds.), *Handbook of child psychology: Vol. 2. Cognition, perception, and language* (6th ed., pp. 3–57). Hoboken, NJ: Wiley.

Nelson, C. A., Wewerka, S., Borscheid, A. J., deRegnier, R., & Georgieff, M. K. (2003). Electrophysiologic evidence of impaired cross-modal recognition memory in 8-month-old infants of diabetic mothers. *Journal of Pediatrics, 142,* 575–582.

Nelson, C. A., Wewerka, S., Thomas, K. M., Tribby-Walbridge, S., deRegnier, R., & Georgieff, M. K. (2000). Neurocognitive sequelae of infants of diabetic mothers. *Behavioral Neuroscience, 114,* 950–956.

Nelson, D. A., & Crick, N. R. (2002). Parental psychological control: Implications for childhood physical and relational aggression. In B. K. Barber (Ed.), *Intrusive parenting: How psychological control affects children and adolescents* (pp. 168–189). Washington, DC: American Psychological Association.

Nelson, D. A., Hart, C. H., Yang, C., Olsen, J. A., & Jin, S. (2006a). Aversive parenting in China: Associations with child physical and relational aggression. *Child Development, 77,* 554–572.

Nelson, D. A., Nelson, L. J., Hart, C. H., Yang, C., & Jin, S. (2006b). Parenting and peer-group behavior in cultural context. In X. Chen, D. French, & B. Schneider (Eds.), *Peer relations in cultural context* (pp. 213–246). New York: Cambridge University Press.

Nelson, D. A., Nelson, L. J., Hart, C. H., Yang, C., & Jin, S. (2005). Parenting and peer-group behavior in cultural context. In X. Chen, B. Schneider, & D. French (Eds.), *Peer relations in cultural context.* New York Cambridge University Press.

Nelson, D. A., Robinson, C. C., & Hart, C. H. (2005). Relational and physical aggression of preschool-age children: Peer status linkages across informants. *Early Education and Development, 16,* 115–139.

Nelson, G., Westhues, A., & MacLeod, J. (2003). A meta-analysis of longitudinal research on preschool prevention programs for children. *Prevention and Treatment, 6.* Retrieved from www.apa.org

Nelson, K. (1973). Structure and strategy in learning to talk. *Monographs of the Society for Research in Child Development, 38*(1–2, Serial No. 149).

Nelson, K. (1976). Some attributes of adjectives used by young children. *Cognition, 4,* 13–30.

Nelson, K. (2003). Narrative and the emergence of a consciousness of self. In G. D. Fireman & T. E. McVay, Jr. (2003). *Narrative and consciousness: Literature, psychology, and the brain* (pp. 17–36). London: Oxford University Press.

Nelson, K., & Fivush, R. (2004). The emergence of autobiographical memory: A social cultural developmental theory. *Developmental Review, 111,* 486–511.

Nelson, W. E. (Ed.). (1996). *Nelson textbook of pediatrics.* Philadelphia: Saunders.

Nemet, D., Barkan, S., Epstein, Y., Friedland, O., Kowen, G., & Eliakim, A. (2005). Short- and long-term beneficial effects of a combined dietary–behavioral–physical activity intervention for the treatment of childhood obesity. *Pediatrics, 115,* e443–e449.

Nesdale, D., Durkin, K., Maas, A., & Griffiths, J. (2005). Threat, group identification, and children's ethnic prejudice. *Social Development, 14,* 189–205.

Nesse, R. M. (1990). Evolutionary explanations of emotions. *Human Nature, 1,* 261–289.

Neuman, S. B. (1999). Books make a difference: A study of access to literacy. *Reading Research Quarterly, 34,* 286–311.

Neuman, S. B. (2003). From rhetoric to reality: The case for high-quality compensatory prekindergarten programs. *Phi Delta Kappan, 85*(4), pp. 286–291.

Neumark-Sztainer, D., Hannan, P. J., Story, M., Croll, J., & Perry, C. (2003). Family meal patterns: Associations with sociodemographic characteristics and improved dietary intake among adolescents. *Journal of the American Dietetic Association, 103,* 317–322.

Neville, H. J., & Bavelier, D. (2002). Human brain plasticity: Evidence from sensory deprivation and altered language experience. In M. A. Hofman, G. J. Boer, A. J. G. D. Holtmaat, E. J. W. van Someren, J. Berhaagen, & D. F. Swaab (Eds.), *Plasticity in the adult brain: From genes to neurotherapy* (pp. 177–188). Amsterdam: Elsevier Science.

Neville, H. J., & Bruer, J. T. (2001). Language processing: How experience affects brain organization. In D. B. Bailey, Jr., J. T. Bruer, F. J. Symons, & J. W. Lichtman (Eds.), *Critical thinking about critical periods* (pp. 151–172). Baltimore: Paul H. Brookes.

Nevin, R. (2000). How lead exposure relates to temporal changes in IQ, violent crime, and unwed pregnancy. *Environmental Research, 83,* 1–22.

Newcomb, A. F., & Bagwell, C. (1995). Children's friendship relations: A meta-analytic review. *Psychological Bulletin, 117,* 306–347.

Newcomb, A. F., Bukowski, W. M., & Pattee, L. (1993). Children's peer relations: A meta-analytic review of popular, rejected, neglected, controversial, and average sociometric status. *Psychological Bulletin, 113,* 99–128.

Newcombe, N., & Huttenlocher, J. (1992). Children's early ability to solve perspective-taking problems. *Developmental Psychology, 28,* 635–643.

Newcombe, N. S. (2007). Taking science seriously: Straight thinking about spatial sex differences. In S. J. Ceci & W. M. Williams (Eds.), *Why aren't more women in science?* (pp. 69–77). Washington, DC: American Psychological Association.

Newcombe, N. S., & Huttenlocher, J. (2006). Development of spatial cognition. In D. Kuhn & R. Siegler (Eds.), *Handbook of child psychology: Vol. 2. Cognition, perception, and language* (6th ed., pp. 734–776). Hoboken, NJ: Wiley.

Newcombe, N. S., Sluzenski, J., & Huttenlocher, J. (2005). Preexisting knowledge versus on-line learning: What do young infants really know about spatial location? *Psychological Science, 16,* 222–227.

Newman, A. J., Bavelier, D., Corina, D., Jezzard, P., & Neville, H. J. (2002). A critical period for right hemisphere recruitment in American sign language processing. *Nature Neuroscience, 5,* 76–80.

Newman, C., Atkinson, J., & Braddick, O. (2001). The development of reaching and looking preferences in infants to objects of different sizes. *Developmental Psychology, 37,* 561–572.

Newman, L. S. (1990). Intentional and unintentional memory in young children: Remembering vs. playing. *Journal of Experimental Child Psychology, 50,* 243–258.

Newport, E. L. (1991). Contrasting conceptions of the critical period for language. In S. Carey & R. Gelman (Eds.), *The epigenesis of mind: Essays on biology and cognition* (pp. 111–130). Hillsdale, NJ: Erlbaum.

Newport, E. L., & Aslin, R. N. (2000). Innately constrained learning: Blending old and new approaches to language acquisition. In S. C. Howell, S. A. Fish, & T. Keith-Lucas (Eds.), *Proceedings of the 24th Annual Boston University Conference on Language Development* (pp. 1–21). Somerville, MA: Cascadilla Press.

Newson, J., & Newson, E. (1975). Intersubjectivity and the transmission of culture: On the social origins of symbolic functioning. *Bulletin of the British Psychological Society, 28,* 437–446.

Neyer, F. J., & Lang, F. R. (2003). Blood is thicker than water: Kinship orientation across adulthood. *Journal of Personality and Social Psychology, 84,* 310–321.

Ng, F. F., Pomerantz, E. M., & Lam, S. (2007). European American and Chinese parents' responses to children's success and failure: Implications for children's responses. *Developmental Psychology, 43,* 1239–1255.

Nguyen, S. P., & Murphy, G. L. (2003). An apple is more than just a fruit: Cross-classification in children's concepts. *Child Development, 74,* 1783–1806.

Ni, Y. (1998). Cognitive structure, content knowledge, and classificatory reasoning.

Journal of Genetic Psychology, 159, 280–296.

Niccolai, L. M., Ethier, K. A., Kershaw, T. S., Lewis, J. B., Meade, C. S., & Ickovics, J. R. (2004). New sex partner acquisition and sexually transmitted disease risk among adolescent females. *Journal of Adolescent Health, 34,* 216–223.

NICHD (National Institute of Child Health and Human Development) Early Child Care Research Network. (1997). The effects of infant child care on infant–mother attachment security: Results of the NICHD Study of Early Child Care. *Child Development, 68,* 860–879.

NICHD (National Institute of Child Health and Human Development) Early Child Care Research Network. (1999). Child care and mother–child interaction in the first 3 years of life. *Developmental Psychology, 35,* 1399–1413.

NICHD (National Institute of Child Health and Human Development) Early Child Care Research Network. (2000a). Characteristics and quality of child care for toddlers and preschoolers. *Applied Developmental Science, 4,* 116–135.

NICHD (National Institute of Child Health and Human Development) Early Child Care Research Network. (2000b). The relation of child care to cognitive and language development. *Child Development, 71,* 960–980.

NICHD (National Institute of Child Health and Human Development) Early Child Care Research Network. (2001, April). *Early child care and children's development prior to school entry.* Symposium presented at the biennial meeting of the Society for Research in Child Development, Minneapolis, MN.

NICHD (National Institute of Child Health and Human Development) Early Child Care Research Network. (2002a). Child-care structure → process → outcome: Direct and indirect effects of child-care quality on young children's development. *Psychological Science, 13,* 199–206.

NICHD (National Institute of Child Health and Human Development) Early Child Care Research Network. (2002b). The interaction of child care and family risk in relation to child development at 24 and 36 months. *Applied Developmental Science,* 6, 144–156

NICHD (National Institute of Child Health and Human Development) Early Child Care Research Network. (2003a). Does amount of time spent in child care predict socioemotional adjustment during the transition to kindergarten? *Child Development, 74,* 976–1005.

NICHD (National Institute of Child Health and Human Development) Early Child Care Research Network. (2003b). Does quality of child care affect child outcomes at age 4½? *Developmental Psychology, 39,* 451–469.

NICHD (National Institute of Child Health and Human Development) Early Child Care Research Network. (2004a). Are child development outcomes related to before- and after-school care arrangements? Results from the NICHD Study of Early Child Care. *Child Development, 75,* 280–295.

NICHD (National Institute of Child Health and Human Deveopment) Early Child Care Research Network. (2004b). Does class size in first grade relate to children's academic and social performance or observed classroom processes? *Developmental Psychology, 40,* 651–664.

NICHD (National Institute of Child Health and Human Development) Early Child Care Research Network. (2004c). Trajectories of physical aggression from toddlerhood to middle childhood. *Monographs of the Society for Research in Child Development, 69*(4, Serial No. 278).

NICHD (National Institute of Child Health and Human Development) Early Child Care Research Network. (2006). Child-care effect sizes for the NICHD Study of Early Child Care and Youth Development. *American Psychologist, 61,* 99–116.

Nicholls, A. L., & Kennedy, J. M. (1992). Drawing development: From similarity of features to direction. *Child Development, 63,* 227–241.

Nichols, K. E., Fox, N., & Mundy, P. (2005). Joint attention, self-recognition, and neurocognitive function in toddlers. *Infancy, 7,* 35–51.

Nichols, S. L., & Berliner, D. C. (2007). The pressure to cheat in a high-stakes testing environment. In E. M. Anderman & T. B. Murdock (Eds.), *Psychology of academic cheating* (pp. 289–311). San Francisco: Jossey-Bass.

Nickman, S. L., Rosenfeld, A. A., Fine, P., MacIntyre, J. C., Pilowsky, D. J., & Howe, R.-A. (2005). Children in adoptive families: Overview and update. *Journal of the American Academy of Child and Adolescent Psychiatry, 44,* 987–995.

Nicolopoulou, A. (2006). The interplay of play and narrative in children's development: Theoretical reflections and concrete examples. In A. Göncü & S. Gaskins (Eds.), *Play and development: Evolutionary, sociocultural, and functional perspectives* (pp. 247–276). Hillsdale, NJ: Erlbaum.

Niehaus, M. D., Moore, S. R., Patrick, P. D., Derr, L. L., Lorntz, B., Lima, A. A., & Gurerrant, R. L. (2002). Early childhood diarrhea is associated with diminished cognitive function 4 to 7 years later in children in a northeast Brazilian shantytown. *American Journal of Tropical Medicine and Hygiene, 66,* 590–593.

Nigg, J. T., & Breslau, N. (2007). Prenatal smoking exposure, low birth weight, and disruptive behavior disorders. *Journal of the American Academy of Child and Adolescent Psychiatry, 46,* 362–369.

Nippold, M. A. (2000). Language development during the adolescent years: Aspects of pragmatics, syntax, and semantics. *Topics in Language Disorders, 20,* 15–28.

Nippold, M. A., Allen, M. M., & Kirsch, D. I. (2001). Proverb comprehension as a function of reading proficiency in preadolescents. *Language, Speech and Hearing Services in the Schools, 32,* 90–100.

Nippold, M. A., Taylor, C. L., & Baker, J. M. (1996). Idiom understanding in Australian youth: A cross-cultural comparison. *Journal of Speech and Hearing Research, 39,* 442–447.

Nisbett, R. E. (1998). Race, genetics, and IQ. In C. Jencks & M. Phillips (Eds.), *The black–white test score gap* (pp. 86–102). Washington, DC: Brookings Institution.

Nisbett, R. E. (2005). Heredity, environment, and race differences in IQ: A commentary on Rushton and Jensen (2005). *Psychology, Public Policy, and Law, 11,* 302–310.

Niu, W., & Sternberg, R. (2001). Cultural influence of artistic creativity and its evaluation. *International Journal of Psychology, 36,* 225–241.

Niu, W., & Sternberg, R. J. (2003). Societal and school influences on student creativity: The case of China. *Psychology in the Schools, 40,* 103–114.

Nix, R. L., Pinderhughes, E. E., Dodge, K. A., Bates, J. E., Pettit, G. S., & McFadyen-Ketchum, S. A. (1999). The relation between mothers' hostile attribution tendencies and children's externalizing behavior problems: The mediating role of mothers' harsh discipline practices. *Child Development, 70,* 896–909.

Noland, J. S., Singer, L. T., Short, E. J., Minnes, S., Arendt, R. E., & Krichner, H. L. (2005). Prenatal drug exposure and selective attention in preschoolers. *Neurotoxicology and Teratology, 27,* 429–438.

Nolen-Hoeksema, S. (2002). Gender differences in depression. In I. H. Gotlib & C. L. Hammen (Eds.), *Handbook of depression* (pp. 492–509). New York: Guilford.

Nolen-Hoeksema, S. (2006). The etiology of gender differences in depression. In C. M. Mazure & G. Puryear (Eds.), *Understanding depression in women: Applying empirical research to practice and policy* (pp. 9–43). Washington, DC: American Psychological Association.

Noonan, C. W., Kathman, S. J., Sarasua, S. M., & White, M. C. (2003). Influence of environmental zinc on the association between environmental and biological measures of lead in children. *Journal of Exposure Analysis and Environmental Epidemiology, 13,* 318–323.

Noterdaeme, M., Mildenberger, K., Minow, F., & Amorosa, H. (2002). Evaluation of neuromotor deficits in children with autism and children with a specific speech and language disorder. *European Child and Adolescent Psychiatry, 11,* 219–225.

Nucci, L. P. (1996). Morality and the personal sphere of action. In E. Reed, E. Turiel, & T. Brown (Eds.), *Values and knowledge* (pp. 41–60). Hillsdale, NJ: Erlbaum.

Nucci, L. P. (2001). *Education in the moral domain.* New York: Cambridge University Press.

Nucci, L. P. (2002). The development of moral reasoning. In U. Goswami (Ed.), *Blackwell handbook of childhood cognitive development* (pp. 303–325). Malden, MA: Blackwell.

Nucci, L. P. (2005). Culture, context, and the psychological sources of human rights concepts. In W. Edelstein & G. Nunner-Winkler (Eds.), *Morality in context* (pp. 365–394). Amsterdam, Netherlands: Elsevier.

Nuttall, R. L., Casey, M. B., & Pezaris, E. (2005). Spatial ability as a mediator of gender differences on mathematics tests: A biological–environmental framework. In A. M. Gallagher & C. J. Kaufman (Eds.), *Gender differences in mathematics: An integrated psychological approach* (pp. 121–142). New York: Cambridge University Press.

Nye, B., Hedges, L. V., & Konstantopoulos, S. (2001). Are effects of small classes cumulative? Evidence from a Tennessee experiment. *Journal of Educational Research, 94,* 336–345.

Nylen, K. J., Moran, T. E., Franklin, C. L., & O'Hara, M. W. (2006). Maternal depression: A review of relevant treatment approaches for mothers and infants. *Infant Mental Health Journal, 27,* 327–343.

Oakes, L. M., Coppage, D. J., & Dingel, A. (1997). By land or by sea: The role of perceptual similarity in infants' categorization of animals. *Developmental Psychology, 33,* 396–407.

Oakes, L. M., & Madole, K. L. (2003). Principles of developmental change in infants' category formation. In D. H. Rakison & L. M. Oakes (Eds.), *Early category and concept development: Making sense of the blooming, buzzing confusion* (pp. 132–158). New York: Oxford University Press.

Obeidallah, D., Brennan, R. T., Brooks-Gunn, J., & Earls, F. (2004). Links between pubertal timing and neighborhood contexts: Implications for girls' violent behavior. *Journal of the American Academy of Child and Adolescent Psychiatry, 43,* 1460–1468.

Oberecker, R., & Friederici, A. D. (2006). Syntactic event-related potential components in 24-month-olds' sentence comprehension. *Neuroreport, 17,* 1017–1021.

Oberecker, R., Friedrich, M., & Friederici, A. D. (2005). Neural correlates of syntactic processing in two-year-olds. *Journal of Cognitive Neuroscience, 17,* 1667–1678.

Oberlander, T. F., Warburton, W., Misri, S., Jaafar, A., & Hertzman, C. (2006). Neonatal outcomes after prenatal exposure to selective serotonin reuptake inhibitor antidepressants and maternal depression using population-based linked health data. *Archives of General Psychiatry, 63,* 898–906.

Obler, L. K. (2008). Developments in the adult years. In J. B. Gleason & B. Ratner (Eds.), *The development of language* (7th ed., pp. 436–464). Boston: Allyn and Bacon.

Obradović, J., & Masten, A. S. (2007). Developmental antecedents of young adult civic engagement. *Applied Developmental Science, 11,* 2–19.

O'Callaghan, M. J., Burn, Y. R., Mohay, H. A., Rogers, Y., & Tudehope, D. I. (1993). The prevalence and origins of left hand preference in high-risk infants, and its implications for intellectual, motor, and behavioral performance at four and six years. *Cortex, 29,* 617–627.

Ochs, E. (1988). *Culture and language development: Language acquisition and language socialization in a Samoan village.* Cambridge, UK: Cambridge University Press.

O'Connor, E., & McCartney, K. (2007). Examining teacher–child relationships and achievement as part of an ecological model of development. *American Educational Research Journal, 44,* 340–369.

O'Connor, T. G., & Croft, C. M. (2001). A twin study of attachment in preschool children. *Child Development, 72,* 1501–1511.

O'Connor, T. G., Deater-Deckard, K., Fulker, D., Rutter, M., & Plomin, R. (1998). Genotype–environment correlations in late childhood and early adolescence: Antisocial behavioral problems and coercive parenting. *Developmental Psychology, 34,* 970–981.

O'Connor, T. G., Marvin, R. S., Rutter, M., Olrich, J. T., Britner, P. A., & the English and Romanian Adoptees Study Team. (2003). Child–parent attachment following early institutional deprivation. *Development and Psychopathology, 15,* 19–38.

O'Connor, T. G., Rutter, M., Beckett, C., Keaveney, L., Dreppner, J. M., & the English and Romanian Adoptees Study Team. (2000). The effects of global severe privation on cognitive competence: Extension and longitudinal follow-up. *Child Development, 71,* 376–390.

OECD (Organisation for Economic Cooperation and Development). (2005). *Education at a glance: OECD indicators 2005.* Paris: Author.

OECD (Organisation for Economic Cooperation and Development). (2006). *Starting strong II: Early childhood education and care.* Paris: OECD Publishing. Retrieved from www.sourceoecd.org/education/9264035451

Ogden, C. L., Carroll, M. D., McDowell, M., Tabak, C. J., & Flegal, K. M. (2006). Prevalence of overweight and obesity in the United States, 1999–2004. *Journal of the American Medical Association, 295,* 1549–1555.

Ohgi, S., Arisawa, K., Takahashi, T., Kusumoto, T., Goto, Y., Akiyama, T., & Saito, H. (2003a). Neonatal Behavioral Assessment Scale as a predictor of later developmental disabilities of low-birth-weight and/or premature infants. *Brain and Development, 25,* 313–321.

Ohgi, S., Takahashi, T., Nugent, J. K., Arisawa, K., & Akiyama, T. (2003b). Neonatal behavioral characteristics and later behavioral problems. *Clinical Pediatrics, 42,* 679–686.

Okagaki, L. (2001). Parental beliefs, parenting style, and children's intellectual development. In E. L. Grigorenko & R. J. Sternberg (Eds.), *Family environment and intellectual functioning: A life-span perspective* (pp. 141–172). Mahwah, NJ: Erlbaum.

Okagaki, L., & Frensch, P. A. (1996). Effects of video game playing on measures of spatial performance: Gender effects in late adolescence. In P. M. Greenfield & R. R. Cocking (Eds.), *Interacting with video* (pp. 115–140). Norwood, NJ: Ablex.

Okagaki, L., & Frensch, P. A. (1998). Parenting and children's school achievement: A multi-ethnic perspective. *American Educational Research Journal, 35,* 123–144.

Okagaki, L., & Sternberg, R. J. (1993). Parental beliefs and children's school performance. *Child Development, 64,* 36–56.

Okami, P., Weisner, T., & Olmstead, R. (2002). Outcome correlates of parent–child bedsharing: An eighteen-year longitudinal study. *Developmental and Behavioral Pediatrics, 23,* 244–253.

O'Keefe, M. J., O'Callaghan, M., Williams, G. M., Najman, J. M., & Bor, W. (2003). Learning, cognitive, and attentional problems in adolescents born small for gestational age. *Pediatrics, 112,* 301–307.

Olafson, E., & Boat, B. W. (2000). Long-term management of the sexually abused child: Considerations and challenges. In R. M. Reece (Ed.), *Treatment of child abuse: Common ground for mental health, medical, and legal practitioners* (pp. 14–35). Baltimore: Johns Hopkins University Press.

Oldershaw, L. (2002). *A national survey of parents of young children.* Toronto: Invest in Kids.

Ollendick, T. H., Yang, B., King, N. J., Dong, Q., & Akande, A. (1996). Fears in American, Australian, Chinese, and Nigerian children and adolescents: A cross-cultural study. *Journal of Child Psychology and Psychiatry, 37,* 213–220.

Oller, D. K. (2000). *The emergence of the speech capacity.* Mahwah, NJ: Erlbaum.

Oller, D. K., Eilers, R. E., Urbano, R., & Cobo-Lewis, A. B. (1997). Development of precursors to speech in infants exposed to two languages. *Journal of Child Language, 24,* 407–425.

Olweus, D., Mattison, A., Schalling, D., & Low, H. (1988). Circulating testosterone levels and aggression in adolescent males: A causal analysis. *Psychosomatic Medicine, 50,* 261–272.

O'Mahoney, J. F. (1989). Development of thinking about things and people: Social and nonsocial cognition during adolescence. *Journal of Genetic Psychology, 150,* 217–224.

Omar, H., McElderry, D., & Zakharia, R. (2003). Educating adolescents about puberty: What are we missing? *International Journal of Adolescent Medicine and Health, 15,* 79–83.

Ondrusek, N., Abramovitch, R., Pencharz, P., & Koren, G. (1998). Empirical examination of the ability of children to consent to clinical research. *Journal of Medical Ethics, 24,* 158–165.

O'Neil, R., Welsh, M., Parke, R. D., Wang, S., & Strand, C. (1997). A longitudinal assessment of the academic correlates of early peer acceptance and rejection. *Journal of Clinical Child Psychology, 26,* 290–303.

O'Neill, M., Bard, K. A., Kinnell, M., & Fluck, M. (2005). Maternal gestures with 20-month-old infants in two contexts. *Developmental Science, 8,* 352–359.

Ong, K. K., Ahmed, M. L., & Dunger, D. B. (2006). Lessons from large population studies on timing and tempo of puberty (secular trends and relation to body size): the European trend. *Molecular and Cellular Endocrinology, 254–255,* 8–12.

Ong, W., Allison, J., & Haladyna, T. M. (2000). Student achievement of third graders in comparable single-age and multiage classrooms. *Journal of Research in Childhood Education, 14,* 205–215.

Oosterwegel, A., & Oppenheimer, L. (1993). *The self-system: Developmental changes between and within self-concepts.* Hillsdale, NJ: Erlbaum.

O'Rahilly, R., & Müller, F. (2001). *Human embryology and teratology.* New York: Wiley-Liss.

O'Reilly, A. W. (1995). Using representations: Comprehension and production of actions with imagined objects. *Child Development, 66,* 999–1010.

O'Reilly, A. W., & Bornstein, M. H. (1993). Caregiver–child interaction in play. In M. H. Bornstein & A. W. O'Reilly (Eds.), *New directions for child development* (No. 59, pp. 55–66). San Francisco: Jossey-Bass.

Orobio de Castro, B., Brendgen, M., Van Boxtel, H., Vitaro, F., & Schaepers, L. (2007). "Accept me, or else. . .": Disputed overestimation of social competence predicts increases in proactive aggression. *Journal of Abnormal Child Psychology, 35,* 165–178.

Orobio de Castro, B., Veerman, J. W., Koops, W., Bosch, J. D., & Monshouwer, H. J. (2002). Hostile attribution of intent and aggressive behavior: A meta-analysis. *Child Development, 73,* 916–934.

Osborne, J. (1994). Academics, self-esteem, and race: A look at the underlying assumption of the disidentification hypothesis. *Personality and Social Psychology Bulletin, 21,* 449–455.

Osherson, D. N., & Markman, E. M. (1975). Language and the ability to evaluate contradictions and tautologies. *Cognition, 2,* 213–226.

Oshima-Takane, Y., & Robbins, M. (2003). Linguistic environment of secondborn children. *First Language, 23,* 21–40.

Ostad, S. A., & Sorensen, P. M. (2007). Private speech and strategy-use patterns: Bidirectional comparisons of children with and without mathematical difficulties in a developmental perspective. *Journal of Learning Disabilities, 40,* 2–14.

Ostrov, J. M., Crick, N. R., & Stauffacher, K. (2006). Relational aggression in sibling and peer relationships during early childhood. *Applied Developmental Psychology, 27,* 241–253.

Ostrov, J. M., Gentile, D. A., & Crick, N. R. (2006). Media exposure, aggression, and prosocial behavior during early childhood: A longitudinal study. *Social Development, 15,* 612–627.

Otis, N., Grouzet, F. M. E., & Pelletier, L. G. (2005). Latent motivational change in an academic setting: A three-year longitudinal study. *Journal of Educational Psychology, 97,* 170–183.

Ovando, C. J., & Collier, V. P. (1998). *Bilingual and ESL classrooms: Teaching in multicultural contexts.* Boston: McGraw-Hill.

Owen, M. T., & Cox, M. J. (1997). Marital conflict and the development of infant–parent attachment relationships. *Journal of Family Psychology, 11,* 152–164.

Owens, E. B., & Shaw, D. S. (2003). Predicting growth curves of externalizing behavior across the preschool years. *Journal of Abnormal Child Psychology, 31,* 575–590.

Owens, R. E. (2005). *Language development: An introduction* (6th ed.). Boston: Allyn and Bacon.

Oyelese, Y., & Ananth, C. V. (2006). Placental abruption. *Obstetrics and Gynecology, 108,* 1005–1016.

Oyserman, D., Bybee, D., Mowbray, C., & Hart-Johnson, T. (2005). When mothers have serious mental health problems: Parenting as a proximal mediator. *Journal of Adolescence, 28,* 443–463.

Özçaliskan, S. (2005). On learning to draw the distinction between physical and metaphorical motion: Is metaphor an early emerging cognitive and linguistic capacity? *Journal of Child Language, 32,* 291–318.

Özçaliskan, S., & Goldin-Meadow, S. (2005). Gesture is at the cutting edge of early language development. *Cognition, 96,* B101–B113.

Padilla, A. M. (2006). Second language learning: Issues in research and teaching. In P. A. Alexander & P. H. Winne (Eds.), *Handbook of educational psychology* (pp. 571–591). Mahwah, NJ: Erlbaum.

Pagani, L., Tremblay, R. E., Vitaro, F., Boulerice, B., & McDuff, P. (2001). Effects of grade retention on academic performance and behavioral development. *Development and Psychopathology, 13,* 297–315.

Palacio-Quintin, E. (2000). Les services de garde et le développement de l'enfant [The impact of day care on child development]. *ISUMA: Canadian Journal of Policy Research, 1*(2), 25–30.

Paladino, J. (2006). *Private speech in children with autism: Developmental course and functional utility.* Unpublished doctoral dissertation, Illinois State University.

Palda, V., Guise, J.-M., & Wathen, N., with the Canadian Task Force on Preventive Health Care. (2004). Interventions to promote breast-feeding: Applying the evidence in clinical practice. *Canadian Medical Association Journal, 170,* 976–978.

Palincsar, A. S. (2003). Advancing a theoretical model of learning and instruction. In B. J. Zimmerman (Ed.), *Educational psychology: A century of contributions* (pp. 459–475). Mahwah, NJ: Erlbaum.

Palmer, J. R., Hatch, E. E., Rao, R. S., Kaufman, R. H., Herbst, A. L., & Noller, K. L. (2001). Infertility among women exposed prenatally to diethylstilbestrol. *American Journal of Epidemiology, 154,* 316–321.

Pan, B. A., & Snow, C. E. (1999). The development of conversation and discourse skills. In M. Barrett (Ed.), *The development of language* (pp. 229–249). Hove, UK: Psychology Press.

Pan, H. W. (1994). Children's play in Taiwan. In J. L. Roopnarine, J. E. Johnson, & F. H. Hooper (Eds.), *Children's play in diverse cultures* (pp. 31–50). Albany, NY: SUNY Press.

Papadakis, A. A., Prince, R. P., Jones, N. P., & Strauman, T. J. (2006). Self-regulation, rumination, and vulnerability to depression in adolescent girls. *Development and Psychopathology, 18,* 815–829.

Papousek, M. (2007). Communication in early infancy: An arena of intersubjective learning. *Infant Behavior and Development, 30,* 258–266.

Paquette, D. (2004). Theorizing the father–child relationship: Mechanisms and developmental outcomes. *Human Development, 47,* 193–219.

Paradis, J. (2007). Second language acquisition in childhood. In E. Hoff & M. Shatz (Eds.), *Blackwell handbook of language development* (pp. 387–405). Malden, MA: Blackwell.

Parameswaran, G. (2003). Experimenter instructions as a mediator in the effects of culture on mapping one's neighborhood. *Journal of Environmental Psychology, 23,* 409–417.

Pardun, C. J., L'Engle, K. L., & Brown, J. D. (2005). Linking exposure to outcomes: Early adolescents' consumption of sexual content in six media. *Mass Communication and Society, 87,* 75–91.

Parent, A., Teilmann, G., Juul, A., Skakkebaek, N. E., Toppari, J., & Bourguingnon, J. (2003). The timing of normal puberty and the age limits of sexual precocity: Variations around the world, secular trends, and changes after migration. *Endocrine Reviews, 24,* 668–693.

Paris, S. G., & Paris, A. H. (2006). Assessments of early reading. In K. A. Renninger & I. E. Sigel (Eds.), *Handbook of child psychology: Vol. 4. Child psychology in practice* (6th ed., pp. 48–74). Hoboken, NJ: Wiley.

Parke, R. D. (1996). *Fatherhood.* Cambridge, MA: Cambridge University Press.

Parke, R. D. (2002). Fathers and families. In M. H. Bornstein (Ed.), *Handbook of parenting: Vol. 3* (2nd ed., pp. 27–73). Mahwah, NJ: Erlbaum.

Parke, R. D., & Buriel, R. (2006). Socialization in the family: Ethnic and ecological perspectives. In N. Eisenberg (Ed.), *Handbook of child psychology: Vol. 3. Social, emotional, and personality development* (6th ed., pp. 429–504). Hoboken, NJ: Wiley.

Parke, R. D., Coltrane, S., Fabricius, W., Powers, J., & Adams, M. (2004). Assessing father involvement in Mexican-American families. In R. Day & M. E. Lamb (Eds.), *Conceptualizing and measuring paternal involvement* (pp. 17–38). Mahwah, NJ: Erlbaum.

Parke, R. D., & Kellam, S. G. (Eds.) (1994). *Exploring family relationships with other social contexts.* Hillsdale, NJ: Erlbaum.

Parke, R. D., Simpkins, S. D., McDowell, D. J., Kim, M., Killian, C., Dennis, J., Flyr, M. L., Wild, M., & Rah, Y. (2004). Relative contributions of families and peers to children's social development. In P. K. Smith & C. H. Hart (Eds.), *Blackwell handbook of childhood social development* (pp. 156–177). Malden, MA: Blackwell.

Parker, F. L., Boak, A. Y., Griffin, K. W., Ripple, C., & Peay, L. (1999). Parent–child relationship, home learning environment, and school readiness. *School Psychology Review, 28,* 413–425.

Parker, J. G., Rubin, K. H., Price, J., & DeRosier, M. E. (1995). Peer relationships, child development, and adjustment: A developmental psychopathology perspective. In D. Cicchetti & D. Cohen (Eds.), *Developmental psychopathology: Vol. 2. Risk, disorder, and adaptation* (pp. 96–161). New York: Wiley.

Parker, S. W., Nelson, C. A., & the Bucharest Early Intervention Project Core Group. (2005). The impact of early institutional rearing on the ability to discriminate facial expressions of emotion: An event-related potential study. *Child Development, 76,* 54–72.

Parten, M. (1932). Social participation among preschool children. *Journal of Abnormal and Social Psychology, 27,* 243–269.

Pascalis, O., de Haan, M., & Nelson, C. A. (1998). Long-term recognition memory for faces assessed by visual paired comparison in 3- and 6-month-old infants. *Journal of Experimental Psychology: Learning, Memory, and Cognition, 24,* 249–260.

Pascalis, O., de Haan, M., & Nelson, C. A. (2002). Is face processing species-specific during the first year of life? *Science, 296,* 1321–1323.

Pasterski, V. L., Geffner, M. E., Brain, C., Hindmarsh, P., & Brook, C. (2005). Prenatal hormones and postnatal socialization by parents as determinants of male-typical toy play in girls with congenital adrenal hyperplasia. *Child Development, 76,* 264–278.

Pasterski, V., Hindmarsh, P., Geffner, M., Brook, C., Brain, C., & Hines, M. (2007). Increased aggression and activity level in 3- to 11-year-old girls with congenital adrenal hyperplasia (CAH). *Hormones and Behavior, 52,* 368–374.

Pate, R. R., Trost, S. G., Levin, S., & Dowda, M. (2000). Sports participation and health-related behaviors among U.S. youth. *Archives of Pediatric and Adolescent Medicine, 154,* 904–911.

Patel, D. R., Pratt, H. D., & Greydanus, D. E. (2003). Treatment of adolescents with anorexia nervosa. *Journal of Adolescent Research, 18,* 244–260.

Paterson, D. S., Trachtenberg, F. L., Thompson, E. G., Belliveau, R. A., Beggs, A. H., & Darnall, R. (2006). Multiple serotonergic brainstem abnormalities in sudden infant death syndrome. *Journal of the American Medical Association, 296,* 2124–2132.

Patrick, E., & Abravanel, E. (2000). The self-regulatory nature of preschool children's private speech in a naturalistic setting. *Applied Psycholinguistics, 21,* 45–61.

Pattenden, S., Antova, T., Neuberger, M., Nikiforov, B., De Sario, M., Grize, L., & Heinrich, J. (2006). Parental smoking and children's respiratory health: Independent effects of prenatal and postnatal exposure. *Tobacco Control, 15,* 294–301.

Patterson, C. J. (2002). Lesbian and gay parenthood. In M. H. Bornstein (Ed.), *Handbook of parenting: Vol. 3. Being and becoming a parent* (2nd ed., pp. 317–338). Mahwah, NJ: Erlbaum.

Patterson, G. R. (1995). Coercion—A basis for early age of onset for arrest. In J. McCord (Ed.), *Coercion and punishment in long-term perspective* (pp. 81–105). New York: Cambridge University Press.

Patterson, G. R. (1997). Performance models for parenting: A social interactional perspective. In J. E. Grusec & L. Kuczynski (Eds.), *Parenting and children's internalization of values* (pp. 193–226). New York: Wiley.

Patterson, G. R., & Fisher, P. A. (2002). Recent developments in our understanding of parenting: Bidirectional effects, causal models, and the search for parsimony. In M. H. Bornstein (Ed.), *Handbook of parenting: Vol. 5. Practical issues in parenting* (2nd ed., pp. 59–88). Mahwah, NJ: Erlbaum.

Patterson, G. R., & Forgatch, M. (1995). Predicting future clinical adjustment from treatment outcome and process variables. *Psychological Assessment, 7,* 275–285.

Patterson, G. R., & Yoerger, K. (2002). A developmental model for early- and late-onset delinquency. In J. B. Reid & G. R. Patterson (Eds.), *Antisocial behavior in children and adolescents* (pp. 147–172). Washington, DC: American Psychological Association.

Paul, J. J., & Cillessen, A. H. N. (2003). Dynamics of peer victimization in early adolescence: Results from a four-year longitudinal study. *Journal of Applied School Psychology, 19,* 25–43.

Paulussen-Hoogeboom, M. C., Stams, G. J. J. M., Hermanns, J. M. A., & Peetsma, T. T. D. (2007). Child negative emotionality and parenting from infancy to preschool: A meta-analytic review. *Developmental Psychology, 43,* 438–453.

Payne, R. J. (1998). *Getting beyond race: The changing American culture.* Boulder, CO: Westview.

PCA America. (2006). *Healthy Families America FAQ.* Retrieved from www.healthyfamiliesamerica.org/about_us/faq.shtml

Peake, P. K., Hebl, M., & Mischel, W. (2002). Strategic attention deployment for delay of gratification in working and waiting situations. *Developmental Psychology, 38,* 313–326.

Pederson, D. R., Gleason, K. E., Moran, G., & Bento, S. (1998). Maternal attachment representations, maternal sensitivity, and the infant–mother attachment relationship. *Developmental Psychology, 34,* 925–933.

Pederson, D. R., & Moran, G. (1996). Expressions of the attachment relationship outside of the Strange Situation. *Child Development, 67,* 915–927.

Peirano, P., Algarin, C., & Uauy, R. (2003). Sleep–wake states and their regulatory mechanisms throughout early human development. *Journal of Pediatrics, 143,* S70–S79.

Peisner-Feinberg, E. S., Burchinal, M. R., Clifford, R. M., Culkin, M. L., Howes, C., Kagan, S. L., & Yazijian, N. (2001). The relation of preschool child-care quality to children's cognitive and social developmental trajectories through second grade. *Child Development, 72,* 1534–1553.

Pellegrini, A. D. (1992). Kindergarten children's social cognitive status as a predictor of first grade success. *Early Childhood Research Quarterly, 7,* 565–577.

Pellegrini, A. D. (2003). Perceptions and functions of play and real fighting in early adolescence. *Child Development, 74,* 1522–1533.

Pellegrini, A. D. (2004). Rough-and-tumble play from childhood through adolescence: Development and possible functions. In P. K. Smith & C. H. Hart (Eds.), *Blackwell handbook of childhood social development* (pp. 438–453). Malden, MA: Blackwell.

Pellegrini, A. D. (2005). *Recess: Its role in development and education.* Mahwah, NJ: Erlbaum.

Pellegrini, A. D. (2006). The development and function of rough-and-tumble play in childhood and adolescence: A sexual selection theory. In A. Göncü & S. Gaskins (Eds.), *Play and development: Evolutionary, sociocultural, and functional perspectives* (pp. 77–98). Mahwah, NJ: Erlbaum.

Pellegrini, A. D., & Holmes, R. M. (2006). The role of recess in primary school. In D. G. Singer, R. M. Golinkoff, & K. Hirsh-Pasek (Eds.), *Play = learning* (pp. 36–53). New York: Oxford University Press.

Pellegrini, A. D., Huberty, P. D., & Jones, I. (1995). The effects of recess timing on children's playground and classroom behaviors. *American Educational Research Journal, 32,* 845–864.

Pellegrini, A. D., Kato, K., Blatchford, P., & Baines, E. (2002). A short-term longitudinal study of children's playground games across the first year of school: Implications for social competence and adjustment to school. *American Educational Research Journal, 39,* 991–1015.

Pellegrini, A. D., & Smith, P. K. (1998). Physical activity play: The nature and function of a neglected aspect of play. *Child Development, 69,* 577–598.

Pellicano, E., Maybery, M., Durkin, K., & Maley, A. (2006). Multiple cognitive capabilities/deficits in children with an autism spectrum disorder: "Weak" central coherence and its relationship to theory of mind and executive control. *Development and Psychopathology, 18,* 77–98.

Penner, A. M. (2003). International gender item difficulty interactions in mathematics and science achievement tests. *Journal of Educational Psychology, 95,* 650–655.

Penny, H., & Haddock, G. (2007). Anti-fat prejudice among children: The 'mere proximity' effect in 5–10 year olds. *Journal of Experimental Social Psychology, 43,* 678–683.

Peoples, C. E., Fagan, J. F., III, & Drotar, D. (1995). The influence of race on 3-year-old children's performance on the Stanford-Binet: Fourth Edition. *Intelligence, 21,* 69–82.

Pepler, D. J., Craig, W. M., Connolly, J. A., Yuile, A., McMaster, L., & Jiang, D. (2006). A developmental perspective on bullying. *Aggressive Behavior, 32,* 376–384.

Pepperberg, I. M. (2000). *The Alex studies: Cognitive and communicative abilities of grey parrots.* Cambridge, MA: Harvard University Press.

Peralta de Mendoza, O. A., & Salsa, A. M. (2003). Instruction in early comprehension and use of a symbol–referent relation. *Cognitive Development, 18,* 269–284.

Perie, M., Sherman, J. D., Phillips, G., & Riggan, M. (2000). Elementary and secondary education: An international perspective. *Education Statistics Quarterly.* Retrieved from http://nces.ed.gov/pubs2000/quarterly/summer/5int/q51.html

Perlman, M., & Ross, H. S. (1997). The benefits of parent intervention in children's disputes: An examination of concurrent changes in children's fighting styles. *Child Development, 64,* 690–700.

Perlmutter, M. (1984). Continuities and discontinuities in early human memory: Paradigms, processes, and performances. In R. V. Kail, Jr., & N. R. Spear (Eds.), *Comparative perspectives on the development of memory* (pp. 253–287). Hillsdale, NJ: Erlbaum.

Perry, D. G., Perry, L. C., & Rasmussen, P. (1986). Cognitive social learning mediators of aggression. *Child Development, 57,* 700–711.

Perry, D. G., Perry, L. C., & Weiss, R. J. (1989). Sex differences in the consequences that children anticipate for aggression. *Developmental Psychology, 25,* 171–184.

Peshkin, A. (1978). *Growing up American: Schooling and the survival of the community.* Chicago: University of Chicago Press.

Peshkin, A. (1997). *Places of memory: Whiteman's schools and native American communities.* Mahwah, NJ: Erlbaum.

Peters, R. D. (2005). A community-based approach to promoting resilience in young children, their families, and their neighborhoods. In R. D. Paters, B. Leadbeater, & R. J. McMahon (Eds.), *Resilience in children, families, and communities: Linking context to practice and policy* (pp. 157–176). New York: Kluwer Academic.

Peters, R. D., Petrunka, K., & Arnold, R. (2003). The Better Beginnings, Better Futures Project: A universal, comprehensive, community-based prevention approach for primary school children and their families. *Journal of Clinical Child and Adolescent Psychology, 32,* 215–227.

Peterson, C., & McCabe, A. (1983). *Developmental psycholinguistics: Three ways of looking at a child's narrative.* New York: Plenum.

Peterson, C., & Roberts, C. (2003). Like mother, like daughter: Similarities in narrative style. *Developmental Psychology, 39,* 551–562.

Peterson, C., Parsons, T., & Dean, M. (2004). Providing misleading and reinstatement information a year after it happened: Effects on long-term memory. *Memory, 12,* 1–13.

Peterson, C. C., Peterson, J. L., & Seeto, D. (1983). Developmental changes in ideas about lying. *Child Development, 54,* 1529–1535.

Petitto, L. A., Holowka, S., Sergio, L. E., Levy, B., & Ostry, D. J. (2004). Baby hands that move to the rhythm of language: Hearing babies acquiring sign languages babble silently on the hands. *Cognition, 93,* 43–73.

Petitto, L. A., Holowka, S., Sergio, L. E., & Ostry, D. (2001). Language rhythms in babies' hand movements. *Nature, 413,* 35–36.

Petitto, L. A., & Marentette, P. F. (1991). Babbling in the manual mode: Evidence for the ontogeny of language. *Science, 251,* 1493–1496.

Petras, H., Schaeffer, C. M., Ialongo, N., Hubbard, S., Muthén, B., & Lambert, S. F. (2004). When the course of aggressive behavior in childhood does not predict antisocial outcomes in adolescence and young adulthood: An examination of potential explanatory variables. *Development and Psychopathology, 16,* 919–941.

Petrides, K. V., Sangareau, Y., Furnham, A., & Fredrickson, N. (2006). Trait emotional intelligence and children's peer relations at school. *Social Development, 15,* 537–547.

Petrill, S. A., & Deater-Deckard, K. (2004). The heritability of general cognitive ability: A within-family adoption design. *Intelligence, 32,* 403–409.

Pettigrew, T. F., & Tropp, L. R. (2005). Allport's intergroup contact hypothesis: its history and influence. In J. F. Dovidio, P. Glick, & L. Rudman (Eds.), *Reflecting on the nature of prejudice: Fifty years after Allport* (pp. 262–277). Malden, MA: Blackwell.

Pettit, G. S. (2004). Violent children in developmental perspective. *Current Directions in Psychological Science, 13,* 194–197.

Pettit, G. S., Bates, J. E., & Dodge, K. A. (1997). Supportive parenting, ecological context, and children's adjustment: A seven-year longitudinal study. *Child Development, 68,* 908–923.

Pettit, G. S., Brown, E. G., Mize, J., & Lindsey, E. (1998). Mothers' and fathers' socializing behaviors in three contexts: Links with children's peer competence. *Merrill-Palmer Quarterly, 44,* 173–193.

Pettit, G. S., Keiley, M. K., Laird, R. D., Bates, J. E., & Dodge, K. A. (2007). Predicting the developmental course of mother-reported monitoring across childhood and adolescence from early proactive parenting, child temperament, and parents' worries. *Journal of Family Psychology, 21,* 206–217.

Pexman, P. M., & Glenwright, M. (2007). How do typically developing children grasp the meaning of verbal irony? *Journal of Neurolinguistics, 20,* 178–196.

Pfeffer, C. R., Altemus, M., Heo, M., & Jiang, H. (2007). Salivary cortisol and psychopathology in children bereaved by the September 11, 2001 terror attacks. *Biological Psychiatry, 61,* 957–965.

Pfeifer, J. H., Brown, C. S., & Juvonen, J. (2007). Teaching tolerance in schools: lessons learned since Brown v. Board of Education about the development and reduction of children's prejudice. *Social Policy Report of the Society for Research in Child Development, 22*(2).

Pfeifer, J. H., Ruble, D. N., Bachman, M. A., Alvarez, J. M., Cameron, J. A., & Fuligni, A. J. (2007). Social identities and intergroup bias in immigrant and nonimmigrant children. *Developmental Psychology, 43,* 496–507.

Phillips, D., & Styfco, S. J. (2007). Child development research and public policy: Triumphs and setbacks on the way to maturity. In J. L. Aber, S. J. Bishop-Josef, S. M. Jones, K. T. McLearn, & D. Phillips (Eds.), *Child development and social policy: Knowledge for action* (pp. 11–27). Washington, DC: American Psychological Association.

Phillips, M. (1997). What makes schools effective? A comparison of the relationships of communitarian climate and academic climate to mathematics achievement and attendance during middle school. *American Educational Research Journal, 34,* 633–662.

Phillipsen, L. C. (1999). Associations between age, gender, and group acceptance and three components of friendship quality. *Journal of Early Adolescence, 19,* 438–464.

Phinney, J. S. (2007). Ethnic identity exploration in emerging adulthood. In J. J. Arnett & J. L. Tanner (Eds.), *Emerging adults in America: Coming of age in the 21st century* (pp. 117–134). Washington, DC: American Psychological Association.

Phinney, J. S., & Chavira, V. (1995). Parental ethnic socialization and adolescent outcomes in ethnic minority families. *Journal of Research on Adolescence, 5,* 31–53.

Phinney, J. S., Horenczyk, G., Liebkind, K., & Vedder, P. (2001). Ethnic identity, immigration, and well-being: An interactional perspective. *Journal of Social Issues, 57,* 493–510.

Phinney, J. S., & Ong, A. (2001). *Family obligations and life satisfaction among adolescents from immigrant and non-immigrant families: Direct and moderated effects.* Unpublished manuscript, California State University.

Phinney, J. S., Ong, A., & Madden, T. (2000). Cultural values and intergenerational value discrepancies in immigrant and non-immigrant families. *Child Development, 71,* 528–539.

Piaget, J. (1926). *The language and thought of the child.* New York: Harcourt, Brace & World. (Original work published 1923)

Piaget, J. (1928). *Judgment and reasoning in the child.* New York: Harcourt, Brace & World. (Original work published 1926)

Piaget, J. (1930). *The child's conception of the world.* New York: Harcourt, Brace & World. (Original work published 1926)

Piaget, J. (1951). *Play, dreams, and imitation in childhood.* New York: Norton. (Original work published 1945)

Piaget, J. (1952). *The origins of intelligence in children.* New York: International Universities Press. (Original work published 1936)

Piaget, J. (1965). *The moral judgment of the child.* New York: Free Press. (Original work published 1932)

Piaget, J. (1967). *Six psychological studies.* New York: Vintage.

Piaget, J. (1971). *Biology and knowledge.* Chicago: University of Chicago Press.

Piaget, J., & Inhelder, B. (1956). *The child's conception of space.* London: Routledge & Kegan Paul. (Original work published 1948)

Piaget, J., Inhelder, B., & Szeminska, A. (1960). *The child's conception of geometry.* New York: Basic Books. (Original work published 1948)

Pianta, R. C., Egeland, B., & Erickson, M. F. (1989). The antecedents of maltreatment: Results of the Mother–Child Interaction Research Project. In D. Cicchetti & V. Carlson (Eds.), *Child maltreatment* (pp. 203–253). New York: Cambridge University Press.

Pianta, R. C., Hamre, B., & Stuhlman, M. (2003). Relationships between teachers and children. In W. M. Reynolds & G. E. Miller (Eds.), *Handbook of psychology: Educational psychology* (Vol. 7, pp. 199–234). New York: Wiley.

Pica, P., Lerner, C., Izard, V., & Dehaene, S. (2004). Exact and approximate arithmetic in an Amazonian indigene group. *Science, 306,* 499–503.

Pickens, J., Field, T., & Nawrocki, T. (2001). Frontal EEG asymmetry in response to emotional vignettes in preschool age children. *International Journal of Behavioral Development, 25,* 105–112.

Pickett, K. E., Luo, Y., & Lauderdale, D. S. (2005). Widening social inequalities in risk for sudden infant death syndrome. *American Journal of Public Health, 95,* 1976–1981.

Pierce, K. M., Hamm, J. V., & Vandell, D. L. (1999). Experiences in after-school programs and children's adjustment in first-grade classrooms. *Child Development, 70,* 756–767.

Pierce, S. H., & Lange, G. (2000). Relationships among metamemory, motivation and memory performance in young school-age children. *British Journal of Developmental Psychology, 18,* 121–135.

Pietz, J., Peter, J., Graf, R., Rauterberg, R. I., Rupp, A., & Sontheimer, D. (2004). Physical growth and neurodevelopmental outcome of nonhandicapped low-risk children born preterm. *Early Human Development, 79,* 131–143.

Pike, J. J., & Jennings, N. A. (2005). The effects of commercials on children's perceptions of gender appropriate toy use. *Sex Roles, 52,* 83–91.

Pillow, B. (2002). Children's and adults' evaluation of the certainty of deductive inferences, inductive inferences, and guesses. *Child Development, 73,* 779–792.

Pinderhughes, E. E., Dodge, K. A., Bates, J. E., Pettit, G. S., & Zelli, A. (2000). Discipline responses: Influences of parents' socioeconomic status, ethnicity, beliefs about parenting, stress, and cognitive-emotional processes. *Journal of Family Psychology, 14,* 380–400.

Pine, J. M. (1995). Variation in vocabulary development as a function of birth order. *Child Development, 66,* 272–281.

Pinker, S. (1989). *Learnability and cognition.* Cambridge, MA: MIT Press.

Pinker, S. (1994). *The language instinct: How the mind creates language.* New York: William Morrow.

Pinker, S. (1999). *Words and rules: The ingredients of language.* New York: Basic Books.

Pinker, S., Lebeaux, D. S., & Frost, L. A. (1987). Productivity and constraints in the acquisition of the passive. *Cognition, 26,* 195–267.

Pinter, J. D., Eliez, S., Schmitt, J. E., Capone, G. T., & Reiss, A. L. (2001). Neuroanatomy of Down's syndrome: A high-resolution MRI study. *American Journal of Psychiatry, 158,* 1659–1665.

Pipp, S., Easterbrooks, M. A., & Brown, S. R. (1993). Attachment status and complexity of infants' self- and other-knowledge when tested with mother and father. *Social Development, 2,* 1–14.

Pipp, S., Easterbrooks, M. A., & Harmon, R. J. (1992). The relation between attachment and knowledge of self and mother in one-year-old infants to three-year-old infants. *Child Development, 63,* 738–750.

Pivarnik, J. M. (1998). Potential effects of maternal physical activity on birth weight: Brief review. *Medicine and Science in Sports and Exercise, 30,* 407–414.

Pizarro, D. A., & Bloom, P. (2003). The intelligence of the moral intuitions: Comment on Haidt (2001). *Psychological Review, 110,* 193–196.

Plantin, L., Mansson, S.-A., & Kearney, J. (2003). Talking and doing fatherhood: On fatherhood and masculinity in Sweden and England. *Fathering, 1,* 3–26.

Pleck, J. H., & Masciadrelli, B. P. (2004). Paternal involvement by U.S. residential fathers: Levels, sources, and consequences. In M. E. Lamb (Ed.), *The role of the father in child development* (4th ed., pp. 222–271). Hoboken, NJ: Wiley

Plomin, R. (1994). *Genetics and experience: The interplay between nature and nurture.* Thousand Oaks, CA: Sage.

Plomin, R. (2003). General cognitive ability. In R. Plomin & J. C. DeFries (Eds.), *Behavioral genetics in the postgenomic era* (pp. 183–201). Washington, DC: American Psychological Association.

Plomin, R. (2005). Finding genes in child psychology and psychiatry: When are we going to be there? *Journal of Child Psychology and Psychiatry, 46,* 1030–1038.

Plomin, R., DeFries, J. C., Craig, I. W., & McGuffin, P. (2003). Behavioral genomics. In R. Plomin, J. C. DeFries, I. W. Craig, & P. McGuffin (Eds.), *Behavioral genetics in the postgenomic era* (pp. 531–540). Washington, DC: American Psychological Association.

Plomin, R., DeFries, J. C., McClearn, G. E., & McGuffin, P. (2001). *Behavioral genetics* (4th ed.). New York: Worth.

Plomin, R., & Spinath, F. M. (2004). Intelligence: Genetics, genes, and genomics. *Journal of Personality and Social Psychology, 86,* 112–129.

Plumert, J. M., Pick, H. L., Jr., Marks, R. A., Kintsch, A. S., & Wegesin, D. (1994). Locating objects and communicating about locations: Organizational differences in children's searching and direction-giving. *Developmental Psychology, 30,* 443–453.

Plunkett, K., Karmiloff-Smith, A., Bates, E., Elman, J. L., & Johnson, M. H. (1997). Connectionism and developmental psychology. *Journal of Child Psychology and Psychiatry, 38,* 53–80.

Poehlmann, J., & Fiese, B. H. (2001). The interaction of maternal and infant vulnerabilities on developing attachment relationships. *Development and Psychopathology, 13,* 1–11.

Pogarsky, G., Thornberry, T. P., & Lizotte, A. J. (2006). Developmental outcomes for children of young mothers. *Journal of Marriage and Family, 68,* 332–344.

Pohl, R. (2002). *Poverty in Canada.* Ottowa: Innercity Ministries.

Polka, L., & Sundara, M. (2003). Word segmentation in monolingual and bilingual infant learners of English and French. In *Proceedings of the 15th International Congress of Phonetic Sciences* (Vol. 1, pp. 1021–1024). Barcelona, Spain: University Autonoma Barcelona.

Polka, L., & Werker, J. F. (1994). Developmental changes in perception of nonnative vowel contrasts. *Journal of Experimental Psychology: Human Perception and Performance, 20,* 421–435.

Pollitt, E. (1996). A reconceptualization of the effects of undernutrition on children's biological, psychosocial, and behavioral development. *Social Policy Report of the Society for Research in Child Development, 10*(5).

Pollock, L. (1987). *A lasting relationship: Parents and children over three centuries.* Hanover, NH: University Press of New England.

Polman, H., Orobio de Castro, B., Koops, W., van Boxtel, H. W., & Merk, W. W. (2007). A meta-analysis of the distinction between reactive and proactive aggression in children and adolescents. *Journal of Abnormal Child Psychology, 35,* 522–535.

Pomerantz, E. M., & Dong, W. (2006). Effects of mothers' perceptions of children's competence: The moderating role of mothers' theories of competence. *Developmental Psychology, 42,* 950–961.

Pomerantz, E. M., & Eaton, M. M. (2000). Developmental differences in children's conceptions of parental control: "They love me, but they make me feel incompetent." *Merrill-Palmer Quarterly, 46,* 140–167.

Pomerantz, E. M., Ng, F. F., & Wang, Q. (2006). Mothers' mastery-oriented involvement in children's homework: Implications for the well-being of children with negative perceptions of competence. *Journal of Educational Psychology, 98,* 99–111.

Pomerantz, E. M., & Ruble, D. N. (1998a). The multidimensional nature of control: Implications for the development of sex differences in self-evaluation. In J. Heckhausen & C. S. Dweck (Eds.), *Motivation and self-regulation across the life span* (pp. 159–184). New York: Cambridge University Press.

Pomerantz, E. M., & Ruble, D. N. (1998b). The role of maternal control in the development of sex differences in child self-evaluative factions. *Child Development, 69,* 458–478.

Pomerantz, E. M., & Saxon, J. L. (2001). Conceptions of ability as stable and self-evaluative processes: A longitudinal examination. *Child Development, 72,* 152–173.

Pomerleau, A., Scuccimarri, C., & Malcuit, G. (2003). Mother–infant behavioral interactions in teenage and adult mothers during the first six months postpartum: Relations with infant development. *Infant Mental Health Journal, 24,* 495–509.

Pons, F., Lawson, J., Harris, P. L., & de Rosnay, M. (2003). Individual differences in children's emotion understanding: Effects of age and language. *Scandinavian Journal of Psychology, 44,* 347–353.

Poole, D. A., & Lindsay, D. S. (2001). Children's eyewitness reports after exposure to misinformation from parents. *Journal of Experimental Psychology: Applied, 7,* 27–50.

Portes, A., & Rumbaut, R. G. (2005), Introduction: The second generation and the Children of Immigrants Longitudinal Study. *Ethnic and Racial Studies, 28,* 983–999.

Posada, G. (2006). Assessing attachment security at age three: Q-sort home observations and the MacArthur Strange Situation adaptation. *Social Development, 15,* 644–658.

Posada, G., Carbonell, O. A., Alzate, G., & Plata, S. J. (2004). Through Colombian lenses: Ethnographic and conventional analyses of maternal care and their associations with secure base behavior. *Developmental Psychology, 40,* 508–518.

Posada, G., Jacobs, A., Richmond, M. K., Carbonell, O. A., Alzate, G., Bustamante, M. R., & Quiceno, J. (2002). Maternal caregiving and infant security in two cultures. *Developmental Psychology, 38,* 67–78.

Posner, J. K., & Vandell, D. L. (1994). Low-income children's after-school care: Are there beneficial effects of after-school programs? *Child Development, 64,* 440–456.

Posner, M. I., & Rothbart, M. K. (2007a). *Educating the human brain.* Washington, DC: American Psychological Association.

Posner, M. I., & Rothbart, M. K. (2007b). Temperament and learning. In M. I. Posner & M. K. Rothbart (Eds.), *Educating the human brain* (pp. 121–146). Washington, DC: American Psychological Association.

Poudevigne, M., & O'Connor, P. J. (2006). A review of physical activity patterns in pregnant women and their relationship to psychological health. *Sports Medicine, 36,* 19–38.

Poulin-Dubois, D., & Forbes, J. N. (2006). Word, intention, and action: A two-tiered model of action word learning. In K. Hirsh-Pasek & R. M. Golinkoff (Eds.), *Action meets word: How children learn verbs* (pp. 262–285). New York: Oxford University Press.

Poulin-Dubois, D., Serbin, L. A., Eichstedt, J. A., Sen, M. G., & Beissel, C. F. (2002). Men don't put on make-up.: Toddlers' knowledge of the gender stereotypes of household activities. *Social Development, 11,* 166–181.

Poulin-Dubois, D., Serbin, L. A., Kenyon, B., & Derbyshire, A. (1994). Infants' intermodal knowledge about gender. *Developmental Psychology, 30,* 436–442.

Povinelli, D. J. (2001). The self: Elevated in consciousness and extended in time. In C. Moore & K. Lemmon (Eds.), *The self in time: Developmental perspectives* (pp. 75–95). Mahwah, NJ: Erlbaum.

Powell, D., Plaut, D., & Funnell, E. (2006). Does the PMSP connectionist model of single word reading learn to read in the same way as a child? *Journal of Research in Reading, 29,* 229–250.

Powlishta, K. K. (2000). The effect of target age on the activation of gender stereotypes. *Sex Roles, 42,* 271–282.

Powlishta, K. K., Sen, M. G., Serbin, L. A., Poulin-Dubois, D., & Eichstedt, J. A. (2001). From infancy through middle childhood: The role of cognitive and social factors in becoming gendered. In R. K. Unger (Ed.), *Handbook of the psychology of women and gender* (pp. 116–132). New York: Wiley.

Powlishta, K. K., Serbin, L. A., & Moller, L. C. (1993). The stability of individual differences in gender typing: Implications for understanding gender segregation. *Sex Roles, 29,* 723–737.

Powls, A., Botting, N., Cooke, R. W. I., & Marlow, N. (1996). Handedness in very-low-birthweight (VLBW) children at 12 years of age: Relation to perinatal and outcome variables. *Developmental Medicine and Child Neurology, 38,* 594–602.

Pratt, M. W., Skoe, E. E., & Arnold, M. L. (2004). Care reasoning development and family socialization patterns in later adolescence: A longitudinal analysis. *International Journal of Behavioral Development, 28,* 139–147.

Prechtl, H. F. R. (1958). Problems of behavioral studies in the newborn infant. In D. S. Lehrmann, R. A. Hinde, & E. Shaw (Eds.), *Advances in the study of behavior* (Vol. 1, pp. 75–98). New York: Academic Press.

Prechtl, H. F. R., & Beintema, D. (1965). *The neurological examination of the full-term newborn infant.* London: William Heinemann Medical Books.

Preisler, G. M. (1991). Early patterns of interaction between blind infants and their sighted mothers. *Child: Care, Health and Development, 17,* 65–90.

Preisler, G. M. (1993). A descriptive study of blind children in nurseries with sighted children. *Child: Care, Health and Development, 19,* 295–315.

Preissler, M. A., & Carey, S. (2004). Do both pictures and words function as symbols for 18- and 24-month-old children? *Journal of Cognition and Development, 5,* 185–212.

Pressley, M., & Hilden, D. (2006). Cognitive strategies. In D. Kuhn & R. Siegler (Eds.), *Handbook of child psychology: Vol. 2. Cognition, perception, and language* (6th ed., pp. 511–556). Hoboken, NJ: Wiley.

Pressley, M., Wharton-McDonald, R., Raphael, L. M., Bogner, K., & Roehrig, A. (2002). Exemplary first-grade teaching. In B. M. Taylor & P. D. Pearson (Eds.), *Teaching reading: Effective schools, accomplished teachers* (pp. 73–88). Mahwah, NJ: Erlbaum.

Previc, F. H. (1991). A general theory concerning the prenatal origins of cerebral lateralization. *Psychological Review, 98,* 299–334.

Preyer, W. (1888). *The mind of the child* (2 vols.). New York: Appleton. (Original work published 1882)

Primus, W., Rawlings, L., Larin, K., & Porter, K. (1999). *Initial impacts of welfare reform on the incomes of single-mother families.* Washington, DC: Center on Budget and Policy Priorities.

Prinstein, M. J., Boergers, J., & Spirito, A. (2001). Adolescents' and their friends' health-risk behavior: Factors that alter or add to peer influence. *Journal of Pediatric Psychology, 26,* 287–298.

Prinstein, M. J., Boergers, J., & Vernberg, E. M. (2001). Overt and relational aggression in adolescents: Social–psychological adjustment of aggressors and victims. *Journal of Clinical Child Psychology, 30,* 479–491.

Prinstein, M. J., & Cillessen, A. H. N. (2003). Forms and functions of adolescent peer aggression associated with high levels of peer status. *Merrill-Palmer Quarterly, 49,* 310–342.

Prinstein, M. J., & La Greca, A. M. (2004). Childhood peer rejection and aggression as predictors of adolescent girls' externalizing and health risk behaviors: A 6-year longitudinal study. *Journal of Consulting and Clinical Psychology, 72,* 103–112.

Prinstein, M. J., Meade, C. S., & Cohen, G. L. (2003). Adolescent oral sex, peer popularity, and perceptions of best friends' sexual behavior. *Journal of Pediatric Psychology, 28,* 243–249.

Proctor, M. H., Moore, L. L., Gao, D., Cupples, L. A., Bradlee, M. L., Hood, M. Y., & Ellison, R. C. (2003). Television viewing and change in body fat from preschool to early adolescence: The Framingham Children's Study. *International Journal of Obesity, 27,* 827–833.

Programme for International Student Assessment. (2003). *Learning for tomorrow's world: First results from Programme for International Student Assessment 2003.* Retrieved from www.pisa.oecd.org

Programme for International Student Assessment. (2005). *School factors related to quality and equity.* Retrieved from www.pisa.oecd.org

Programme for International Student Assessment. (2006). *PISA 2006: Science competencies for tomorrow's world.* Retrieved from www.oecd.org

Provins, K. A. (1997). Handedness and speech: A critical reappraisal of the role of genetic and environmental factors in the cerebral lateralization of function. *Psychological Review, 104,* 554–571.

Pruden, S. M., Hirsh-Pasek, K., Golinkoff, R. M., & Hennon, E. A. (2006). The birth of words: Ten-month-olds learn words through perceptual salience. *Child Development, 77,* 266–280.

Pruett, M. K., Williams, T. Y., Insabella, G., & Little, T. D. (2003). Family and legal indicators of child adjustment to divorce among families with young children. *Journal of Family Psychology, 17,* 169–180.

Prysak, M., Lorenz, R. P., & Kisly, A. (1995). Pregnancy outcome in nulliparous women 35 years and older. *Obstetrics and Gynecology, 85,* 65–70.

Public Agenda. (2002). *A lot easier said than done: Parents talk about raising children in today's America.* Retrieved from www.publicagenda.org/specials/parents/parents.htm

Public Health Agency of Canada (2004). *Aboriginal Head Start.* Retrieved from http://www.phac-aspc.gc.ca/dca-dea/programs-mes/ahs_overview_e.html#allocation

Public Health Agency of Canada. (2007a). *Table 110-0089—Health behaviour in school-aged children 2002,* Student response to question: Have you ever used or taken cannabis?, every 4 years (percent). CANSIM database. Retrieved from cansim2.statcan.ca

Public Health Agency of Canada. (2007b). *Table 110-0090—Health behaviour in school-aged children 2002,* Student response to question: Have you ever used or taken one or several of these substances in your life?, every 4 years (percent). CANSIM database. Retrieved from cansim2.statcan.ca

Pujol, J., Soriano-Mas, C., Ortiz, H., Sebastián-Gallés, N., Losilla, J. M., & Deus, J. (2006). Myelination of language-related areas in the developing brain. *Neurology, 66,* 339–343.

Punamaki, R.-L. (2006). Ante- and perinatal factors and child characteristics predicting parenting experience among formerly infertile couples during the child's first year: A controlled study. *Journal of Family Psychology, 20,* 670–679.

Purcell-Gates, V. (1996). Stories, coupons, and the TV Guide: Relationships between home literacy experiences and emergent literacy knowledge. *Reading Research Quarterly, 31,* 406–428.

Putallaz, M., Grimes, C. L., Foster, K. J., Kupersmidt, J. B., Coie, J. D., & Dearing, K. (2007). Overt and relational aggression and victimization: Multiple perspectives within the school setting. *Journal of School Psychology, 45,* 523–547.

Putnam, F. W. (2003). Ten-year research update review: Child sexual abuse. *Journal of the American Academy of Child and Adolescent Psychiatry, 42,* 269–278.

Pyeritz, R. E. (1998). Sex: What we make of it. *Journal of the American Medical Association, 279,* 269.

Quas, J. A., Malloy, L. C., Melinder, A., Goodman, G. S., & D'Mello, M. (2007). Developmental differences in the effects of repeated interviews and interviewer bias on young children's event memory and false reports. *Developmental Psychology, 43,* 823–837.

Quatman, T., Sokolik, E., & Smith, K. (2000). Adolescent perception of peer success: A gendered perspective over time. *Sex Roles, 43,* 61–84.

Quillian, L., & Campbell, M. E. (2003). Beyond black and white: The present and future of multiracial friendship segregation. *American Sociological Review, 68,* 540–566.

Quinn, P. C., Yahr, J., Kuhn, A., Slater, A. M., & Pascalis, O. (2002). Representation of the gender of human faces by infants: A preference for female. *Perception, 31,* 1109–1121.

Quinn, T. C., & Overbaugh, J. (2005). HIV/AIDS in women: An expanding epidemic. *Science,* 308, 1582–1583.

Quist, J. R., & Kennedy, J. L. (2001). Genetics of childhood disorders: XXIII. ADHD, part 7: The serotonin system. *Journal of the American Academy of Child and Adolescent Psychiatry, 40,* 253–256.

Raaijmakers, Q. A. W., Engels, R. C. M. E., & Van Hoof, A. (2005). Delinquency and moral reasoning in adolescence and young adulthood. *International Journal of Behavioral Development, 29,* 247–258.

Radelet, M. A., Lephart, S. M., Rubinstein, E. N., & Myers, J. B. (2002). Survey of the injury rate for children in community sports. *Pediatrics, 110,* e28.

Radke-Yarrow, M., & Kochanska, G. (1990). Anger in young children. In N. L. Stein, B. Leventhal, & T. Trabasso (Eds.), *Psychological and behavioral approaches to emotion* (pp. 297–310). Hillsdale, NJ: Erlbaum.

Raffaelli, M., Crockett, L. J., & Shen, Y.-L. (2005). Developmental stability and change in self-regulation from childhood to adolescence. *Journal of Genetic Psychology, 166,* 54–75.

Rahman, Q., & Wilson, G. D. (2003). Born gay? The psychobiology of human sexual orientation. *Personality and Individual Differences, 34,* 1337–1382.

Raikes, H. A., & Thompson, R. A. (2005). Links between risk and attachment security: Models of influence. *Journal of Applied Developmental Psychology, 26,* 440–455.

Raikes, H. A., & Thompson, R. A. (2006). Family emotional climate, attachment security, and young children's emotion knowledge in a high-risk sample. *British Journal of Developmental Psychology, 24,* 89–104.

Raikes, H. A., Robinson, J. L., Bradley, R. H., Raikes, H. H., & Ayoub, C. C. (2007). Developmental trends in self-regulation among low-income toddlers. *Social Development, 16,* 128–149.

Raine, A. (1997). Antisocial behavior and psychophysiology: A biosocial perspective and a prefrontal dysfunction hypothesis. In D. M. Stoff, J. Breiling, & J. D. Maser (Eds.), *Handbook of antisocial behavior* (pp. 289–304). New York: Wiley.

Rakison, D. H. (2005). Developing knowledge of objects' motion properties in infancy. *Cognition, 96,* 183–214.

Rakison, D. H. (2006). Make the first move: How infants learn about self-propelled objects. *Developmental Psychology, 42,* 900–912.

Rakison, D. H., & Poulin-Dubois, D. (2001). Developmental origin of the animate–inanimate distinction. *Psychological Bulletin, 127,* 209–228.

Rakoczy, H., Tomasello, M., & Striano, T. (2004). Young children know that trying is not pretending: A test of the "behaving-as-if" construal of children's early concept of pretense. *Developmental Psychology, 40,* 388–399.

Rakoczy, H., Warneken, F., & Tomasello, M. (2007). "This way!" "No! That way!"—3-year-olds know that two people can have mutually incompatible desires. *Cognitive Development, 22,* 47–68.

Ram, A., & Ross, H. S. (2001). Problem-solving, contention, and struggle: How siblings resolve a conflict of interest. *Child Development, 72,* 1710–1722.

Ramchandani, P., Stein, A., Evan, J., O'Connor, T. G., & the ALSPAC Study Team. (2005). Paternal depression in the postnatal period and child development: A prospective population study. *Lancet, 365,* 2201–2205.

Ramey, C. T., Ramey, S. L., & Lanzi, R. G. (2006). Children's health and education. In K. A. Renninger & I. E. Sigel (Eds.), *Handbook of child psychology: Vol. 4. Child psychology in practice* (6th ed., pp. 864–892). Hoboken, NJ: Wiley.

Ramey, S. L., & Ramey, C. T. (1999). Early experience and early intervention for children "at risk" for developmental delay and mental retardation. *Mental Retardation and Developmental Disabilities, 5,* 1–10.

Ramos, E., Frontera, W. R., Llorpart, A., & Feliciano, D. (1998). Muscle strength and hormonal levels in adolescents: Gender related differences. *International Journal of Sports Medicine, 19,* 526–531.

Ramos, M. C., Guerin, D. W., Gottfried, A. W., Bathurst, K., & Oliver, P. H. (2005). Family conflict and children's behavior problems: The moderating role of child temperament. *Structural Equation Modeling, 12,* 278–298.

Ramsey, P. G. (1991). Young children's awareness and understanding of social class differences. *Journal of Genetic Psychology, 152,* 71–82.

Ramsey-Rennels, J. L., & Langlois, J. H. (2006). Differential processing of female and male faces. *Current Directions in Psychological Science, 15,* 59–62.

Ramus, F. (2002). Language discrimination by newborns: Teasing apart phonotactic, rhythmic, and intonational cues. *Annual Review of Language Acquisition, 2,* 85–115.

Rangel, M. C., Gavin, L., Reed, C., Fowler, M. G., & Lee, L. M. (2006). Epidemiology of HIV and AIDS among adolescents and young adults in the United States. *Journal of Adolescent Health, 39,* 156–163.

Raskauskas, J., & Stoltz, A. D. (2007). Involvement in traditional and electronic bullying among adolescents. *Developmental Psychology, 43,* 564–575.

Raskind, W. H., Igo, R. P., Jr., Chapman, N. H., Berninger, V. W., Thomson, J. B., Jatsushita, M., & Brkanac, Z. (2005). A genome scan in multigenerational families with dyslexia: Identification of a novel locus on chromosome 2q that contributions to phonological decoding efficiency. *Molecular Psychiatry, 10,* 699–711.

Rasmussen, C., Ho, E., & Bisanz, J. (2003). Use of the mathematical principle of inversion in young children. *Journal of Experimental Child Psychology, 85,* 89–102.

Rasmussen, E. R., Neuman, R. J., Heath, A. C., Levy, F., Hay, D. A., & Todd, R. D. (2004). Familial clustering of latent class and *DSM-IV* defined attention-deficit hyperactivity disorder (ADHD) subtypes. *Journal of Child Psychology and Psychology, 45,* 589–598.

Rast, M., & Meltzoff, A. N. (1995). Memory and representation in young children with Down syndrome: Exploring deferred imitation and object permanence. *Development and Psychopathology, 7,* 393–407.

Rathunde, K., & Csikszentmihalyi, M. (2005). The social context of middle school: Teachers, friends, and activities in Montessori and traditional school environments. *Elementary School Journal, 106,* 59–79.

Rauber, M. (2006, May 18). Parents aren't sitting still as recess disappears. *Parents in Action.* Retrieved from http://healthyschoolscampaign.org/news/media/food/2006-05_recess_disappears.php

Rauscher, F. H., Shaw, G. L., & Ky, K. N. (1993). Music and spatial task performance. *Nature, 365,* 611.

Raver, C. C. (2003). Does work pay psychologically as well as economically? The role of employment in predicting depressive symptoms and parenting among low-income families. *Child Development, 74,* 1720–1736.

Ray, N., & Gregory, R. (2001). School experiences of the children of lesbian and gay parents. *Family Matters, 59,* 28–35.

Ray, O. (2004). How the mind hurts and heals the body. *American Psychologist, 59,* 29–40.

Rayner, K., & Pollatsek, A. (1989). *The psychology of reading.* Englewood Cliffs, NJ: Prentice-Hall.

Rayner, K., Pollatsek, A., & Starr, M. S. (2003). Reading. In A. F. Healy & R. W. Proctor (Eds.). (2003). *Handbook of psychology: Experimental psychology* (Vol. 4, pp. 549–574). New York: Wiley.

Raz, S., Shah, F., & Sander, C. J. (1996). Differential effects of perinatal hypoxic risk on early developmental outcome: A twin study. *Neuropsychology, 10,* 429–436.

Reese, E., Haden, C. A., & Fivush, R. (1996). Mothers, fathers, daughters and sons: Gender differences in autobiographical reminiscing. *Research on Language and Social Interaction, 29*(1), 27–56.

Reese, E., Newcombe, R., & Bird, G. M. (2006). The emergence of autobiographical memory: Cognitive, social, and emotional factors. In C. M. Flinn-Fletcher & G. M. Haberman (Eds.), *Cognition and language: Perspectives from New Zealand* (pp. 177–189). Bowen Hills, Australia: Australian Academic Press.

Regnerus, M., Smith, C., & Fritsch, M. (2003). *Religion in the lives of American adolescents: A review of the literature.* Chapel Hill, NC: National Study of Youth and Religion.

Reid, P. T., & Trotter, K. H. (1993). Children's self-presentations with infants: Gender and ethnic comparisons. *Sex Roles, 29,* 171–181.

Reifman, A., Villa, L. C., Amans, J. A., Rethinam, V., & Telesca, T. Y. (2001). Children of divorce in the 1990s: A meta-analysis. *Journal of Divorce and Remarriage, 36,* 27–36.

Reilly, J. S., Bates, E. A., & Marchman, V. A. (1998). Narrative discourse in children with early focal brain injury. *Brain and Language, 61,* 335–375.

Reilly, J. S., Losh, M., Bellugi, U., & Wulfeck, B. (2004). "Frog, where are you?" Narratives in children with specific language impairment, early focal brain injury, and Williams syndrome. *Brain and Language, 88,* 229–247.

Reilly, T. P., Hasazi, J. E., & Bond, L. A. (1983). Children's concepts of death and personal mortality. *Journal of Paediatric Psychology, 8,* 21–31.

Reinders, H., & Youniss, J. (2006). School-based required community service and civic development in adolescents. *Applied Developmental Science, 10,* 2–12.

Reis, O., & Youniss, J. (2004). Patterns in identity change and development in relationships with mothers and friends. *Journal of Adolescent Research, 19,* 31–44.

Reis, S. M. (2004). We can't change what we don't recognize: Understanding the special needs of gifted females. In S. Baum (Ed.), *Twice-exceptional and special populations of gifted students* (pp. 67–80). Thousand Oaks, CA: Corwin Press.

Reisman, J. E. (1987). Touch, motion, and proprioception. In P. Salapatek & L. Cohen (Eds.), *Handbook of infant perception: Vol. 1. From sensation to perception* (pp. 265–303). Orlando, FL: Academic Press.

Reiss, A. L., & Dant, C. C. (2003). The behavioral neurogenetics of fragile X syndrome: Analyzing gene–brain– behavior relationships in child developmental psychopathologies. *Development and Psychopathology, 15,* 927–968.

Reiss, D. (2003). Child effects on family systems: Behavioral genetic strategies. In A. C. Crouter & A. Booth (Eds.), *Children's influence on family dynamics: The neglected side of family relationships* (pp. 3–36). Mahwah, NJ: Erlbaum.

Relph, K., Harrington, K., & Pandha, H. (2004). Recent developments and current status of gene therapy using viral vectors in the United Kingdom. *British Medical Journal, 329,* 839–842.

Renninger, K. A. (1998). Developmental psychology and instruction: Issues from and for practice. In I. Sigel & K. A. Renninger (Eds.), *Handbook of child psychology: Vol. 4. Child psychology and practice* (pp. 211–274). New York: Wiley.

Renzetti, C. M., & Curran, D. J. (1998). *Living sociology.* Boston: Allyn and Bacon.

Renzulli, J. S. (2006). Swimming upstream in a small river: Changing conceptions and practices about the development of giftedness. In M. A. Constas & R. J. Sternberg (Eds.), *Translating theory and research into educational practice* (pp. 223–254). Mahwah, NJ: Erlbaum.

Repacholi, B. M., & Gopnik, A. (1997). Early reasoning about desires: Evidence from 14- and 18-month-olds. *Developmental Psychology, 33,* 12–21.

Resnick, M. B., Gueorguieva, R. V., Carter, R. L., Ariet, M., Sun, Y., Roth, J., Bucciarelli, R. L., Curran, J. S., & Mahan, C. S. (1999). The impact of low birth weight, perinatal conditions, and sociodemographic factors on educational outcome in kindergarten. *Pediatrics, 104,* e74.

Rest, J. R. (1979). *Development in judging moral issues.* Minneapolis: University of Minnesota Press.

Resta, R., Biesecker, B. B., Bennett, R. L., Blum, S., Hahn, S. E., Strecker, M. N., & Williams, J. L. (2006). A new definition of genetic counseling: National Society of Genetic Counselors' Task Force Report. *Journal of Genetic Counseling, 15,* 77–83.

Reyna, V. F., & Farley, F. (2006). Risk and rationality in adolescent decision making: Implications for theory, practice, and public policy. *Psychological Science in the Public Interest, 7,* 1–44.

Reyna, V. F., & Kiernan, B. (1994). Development of gist versus verbatim memory in sentence recognition: Effects of lexical familiarity, semantic content, encoding instructions, and retention interval. *Developmental Psychology, 30,* 178–191.

Reynolds, A. J., & Ou, S.-R. (2004). Alterable predictors of child well-being in the Chicago longitudinal study. *Children and Youth Services Review, 26,* 1–14.

Reynolds, A. J., & Robertson, D. L. (2003). School-based early intervention and later child maltreatment in the Chicago Longitudinal Study. *Child Development, 74,* 3–26.

Reynolds, A. J., & Temple, J. A. (1998). Extended early childhood intervention and school achievement: Age thirteen findings from the Chicago Longitudinal Study. *Child Development, 69,* 231–246.

Reynolds, C. R., & Kaiser, S. M. (1990). Test bias in psychological assessment. In T. B. Gutkin & C. R. Reynolds (Eds.), *The handbook of school psychology* (pp. 487–525). New York: Wiley.

Reynolds, M. A., Schieve, L. A., Martin, J. A., Meng, G., & Macaluso, M. (2003). Trends in multiple births conceived using assisted reproductive technology, United States, 1997–2000. *Pediatrics, 111,* 1159–1162.

Rholes, W. S., Newman, L. S., & Ruble, D. N. (1990). Understanding self and others: Developmental and motivational aspects of perceiving persons in terms of invariant dispositions. In E. Higgins & R. Sorrentino (Eds.), *Handbook of motivation and cognition: Foundations of social behavior* (Vol. 2, pp. 369–407). New York: Guilford.

RHS National Team (2007). *First Nations Regional Longitudinal Health Survey (RHS) 2002/03: Results for adults, youth and children living in First Nations communities.* Available from http://rhs-ers.ca/english/ or from the Canadian Centre on Substance Abuse, www.ccsa.ca/CCSA/EN/Topics/Populations/AboriginalPeoples.htm

Ricard, M., & Kamberk-Kilicci, M. (1995). Children's empathic responses to emotional complexity. *International Journal of Behavioral Development, 18,* 211–225.

Richards, M. (2004). Assisted reproduction, genetic technologies, and family life. In J. Scott, J. Treas, & M. Richards (Eds.), *The Blackwell companion to the sociology of families* (pp. 478–498). Malden, MA: Blackwell.

Richler, J., Luyster, R., Risi, S., Hsu, W.-L., Dawson, G., & Bernier, R. (2006). Is there a 'regressive phenotype' of autism spectrum disorder associated with the measles-mumps-rubella vaccine? A CPEA study. *Journal of Autism and Developmental Disorders, 36,* 299–316.

Richmond, L. J. (2004). When spirituality goes awry: Students in cults. *Professional School Counseling, 7,* 367–375.

Ridenour, T. A. (2000). Genetic epidemiology of antisocial behavior. In D. H. Fishbein (Ed.), *The science, treatment, and prevention of antisocial behaviors* (pp. 7.1–7.24). Kingston, NJ: Civic Research Institute.

Rideout, V., & Hamel, E. (2006). *The media family: Electronic media in the lives of infants, toddlers, preschoolers and their parents.* Menlo Park, CA: Henry J. Kaiser Family Foundation.

Rietvelt, M. J. H., Hudziak, J. J., Bartels, M., van Beijsterveldt, C. E. M., & Boomsma, D. I. (2004). Heritability of attention problems in children: Longitudinal results from a study of twins, age 3 to 12. *Journal of Child Psychology and Psychiatry, 45,* 577–588.

Rigby, K. (2004). Bullying in childhood. In P. K. Smith & C. H. Hart (Eds.), *Blackwell handbook of childhood social development* (pp. 549–568). Malden, MA: Blackwell.

Rijsdijk, F. V., & Boomsma, D. I. (1997). Genetic mediation of the correlation between peripheral nerve conduction velocity and IQ. *Behavior Genetics, 27,* 87–98.

Riley, E. P., McGee, C. L., & Sowell, E. R. (2004). Teratogenic effects of alcohol: A decade of brain imaging. *American Journal of Medical Genetics: Part C, Seminars in Medical Genetics, 127,* 35–41.

Riordan, J., Gross, A., Angeron, J., Drumwiede, B., & Melin, J. (2000). The effect of labor pain relief medication on neonatal suckling and breastfeeding duration. *Journal of Human Lactation, 16,* 7–12.

Ripple, C. H., & Zigler, E. (2003). Research, policy, and the federal role in prevention initiatives for children. *American Psychologist, 58,* 482–490.

Ris, M. D., Dietrich, K. N., Succop, P. A., Berger, O. G., & Bornschein, R. L. (2004). Early exposure to lead and neuropsychological outcome in adolescence. *Journal of the International Neuropsychological Society, 10,* 261–270.

Riva, D., & Giorgi, C. (2000). The cerebellum contributes to higher functions during development: Evidence from a series of children surgically treated for posterior fossa tumours. *Brain, 123,* 1051–1061.

Rivadeneyra, R., & Ward, L. M. (2005). From Ally McBeal to Sábado Gigante: Contributions of television viewing to the gender role attitudes of Latino adolescents. *Journal of Adolescent Research, 20,* 453–475.

Rivera, S. M., Wakeley, A., & Langer, J. (1999). The drawbridge phenomenon: Representational reasoning or perceptual preference? *Developmental Psychology, 35,* 427–435.

Rivkees, S. A. (2003). Developing circadian rhythmicity in infants. *Pediatrics, 112,* 373–381.

Rizzo, T. A., Metzger, B. E., Dooley, S. L., & Cho, N. H. (1997). Early malnutrition and child neurobehavioral development: Insights from the study of children of diabetic mothers. *Child Development, 68,* 26–38.

Rizzolatti, G., & Craighero, L. (2004). The mirror-neuron system. *Annual Review of Neuroscience, 27,* 169–192.

Roazzi, A., & Bryant, P. (1997). Explicitness and conservation: Social class differences. *International Journal of Behavioral Development, 21,* 51–70.

Robb, A. S., & Dadson, M. J. (2002). Eating disorders in males. *Child and Adolescent Psychiatric Clinics of North America, 11,* 399–418.

Roberts, B. W., & DelVecchio, W. F. (2000). The rank-order consistency of personality traits from childhood to old age: A quantitative review of longitudinal studies. *Psychological Bulletin, 126,* 3–25.

Roberts, B. W., Kuncel, N. R., Shiner, R., Caspi, A., & Goldberg, L. R. (2007). The power of personality: The comparative validity of personality traits, socioeconomic status, and cognitive ability for predicting important life outcomes. *Perspectives on Psychological Science, 2,* 313–345.

Roberts, D. F., & Foehr, U. G. (2004). *Kids and media in America.* New York: Cambridge University Press.

Roberts, D. F., Foehr, U. G., & Rideout, V. (2005). *Generation M: Media in the lives of 8–18 year olds.* Menlo Park, CA: Henry J. Kaiser Family Foundation.

Roberts, D. F., Henriksen, L., & Foehr, U. G. (2004). Adolescents and media. In R. M. Lerner & L. Steinberg (Eds.), *Handbook of adolescent psychology* (2nd ed., pp. 627–664). Hoboken, NJ: Wiley.

Roberts, J. E., Burchinal, M. R., & Durham, M. (1999). Parents' report of vocabulary and grammatical development of American preschoolers: Child and environment associations. *Child Development, 70,* 92–106.

Roberts, K. P., & Powell, M. B. (2005). The relation between inhibitory control and children's eyewitness memory. *Applied Cognitive Psychology, 19,* 1003–1018.

Roberts, R. J., Jr., & Aman, C. J. (1993). Developmental differences in giving directions: Spatial frames of reference and mental rotation. *Child Development, 64,* 1258–1270.

Roberts, W., & Strayer, J. (2003, April). Towards, away, and against: Emotions and prosocial behavior. In K. Kokko & S. Côté (Chairs), *Prosocial and Aggressive Behaviors over the Life Course.* Symposium presented at the biennial meeting of the Society for Research in Child Development, Tampa, Florida. Retrieved from www.tru.ca/faculty/wlroberts

Robin, D. J., Berthier, N. E., & Clifton, R. K. (1996). Infants' predictive reaching for moving objects in the dark. *Developmental Psychology, 32,* 824–835.

Robins, R. W., Tracy, J. L., Trzesniewski, K., Potter, J., & Gosling, S. D. (2001). Personality correlates of self-esteem. *Journal of Research in Personality, 35,* 463–482.

Robinson, B. F., Mervis, C. B., & Robinson, B. W. (2003). The roles of verbal short-term memory in the acquisition of grammar by children with Williams syndrome. *Developmental Neuropsychology, 23,* 13–31.

Robinson, C. C., Anderson, G. T., Porter, C. L., Hart, C. H., & Wouden-Miller, M. (2003). Sequential transition patterns of preschoolers' social interactions during child-initiated play: Is parallel-aware play a bi-directional bridge to other play states? *Early Childhood Research Quarterly, 18,* 3–21.

Robinson, J. L., Lee, B. E., Preiksaitis, J. K., Plitt, S., & Tipplies, G. A. (2006). Prevention of congenital rubella syndrome—What makes sense in 2006? *Epidemiologic Reviews, 28,* 81–87.

Rochat, P. (1989). Object manipulation and exploration in 2- to 5-month-old infants. *Developmental Psychology, 25,* 871–884.

Rochat, P. (1998). Self-perception and action in infancy. *Experimental Brain Research, 123,* 102–109.

Rochat, P. (2001). *The infant's world.* Cambridge, MA: Harvard University Press.

Rochat, P. (2003). Five levels of self-awareness as they unfold early in life. *Consciousness and Cognition, 12,* 717–731.

Rochat, P., & Goubet, N. (1995). Development of sitting and reaching in 5- to 6-month-old infants. *Infant Behavior and Development, 18,* 53–68.

Rochat, P., & Hespos, S. J. (1997). Differential rooting response by neonates: Evidence for an early sense of self. *Early Development and Parenting, 6,* 105–112.

Rochat, P., Querido, J. G., & Striano, T. (1999). Emerging sensitivity to the timing and structure of protoconversation. *Developmental Psychology, 35,* 950–957.

Rochat, P., & Striano, T. (2002). Who's in the mirror? Self–other discrimination in specular images by four- and nine-month-old infants. *Infant and Child Development, 11,* 289–303.

Rochat, P., Striano, T., & Blatt, L. (2002). Differential effects of happy, neutral, and sad still-faces on 2-, 4-, and 6-month-old infants. *Infant and Child Development, 11,* 289–303.

Rodgers, J. L. (2001). The confluence model: An academic "tragedy of the commons"? In E. L. Grigorenko & R. J. Sternberg (Eds.), *Family environment and intellectual functioning: A life-span perspective* (pp. 71–95). Mahwah, NJ: Erlbaum.

Rodgers, J. L., Cleveland, H. H., van den Oord, E., & Rowe, D. C. (2000). Resolving the debate over birth order, family size, and intelligence. *American Psychologist, 55,* 599–612.

Rodgers, J. L., & Wänström, L. (2007). Identification of a Flynn effect in the NLSY: Moving from the center to the boundaries. *Intelligence, 35,* 187–196.

Rodkin, P. C., Farmer, T. W., Pearl, R., & Van Acker, R. (2000). Resolving the debate over birth order, family size, and intelligence. *American Psychologist, 55,* 599–612.

Rodkin, P. C., Farmer, T. W., Pearl, R., & Van Acker, R. (2006). They're cool: Social status and peer group supports for aggressive boys and girls. *Social Development, 15,* 175–204.

Rodriguez, M. L., Mischel, W., & Shoda, Y. (1989). Cognitive and personality variables in the delay of gratification of older children at risk. *Journal of Personality and Social Psychology, 57,* 358–367.

Roebers, C. M., & Schneider, W. (2001). Individual differences in children's eyewitness recall: The influence of intelligence and shyness. *Applied Developmental Science, 5,* 9–20.

Roelfsema, N. M., Hop, W. C., Boito, S. M., & Wladimiroff, J. W. (2004). Three-dimensional sonographic measurement of normal fetal brain volume during the second half of pregnancy. *American Journal of Obstetrics and Gynecology, 190,* 275–280.

Roeser, R. W., Eccles, J. S., & Freedman-Doan, C. (1999). Academic functioning and mental health in adolescence: Patterns, progressions, and routes from childhood. *Journal of Adolescent Research, 14,* 135–174.

Roeser, R. W., Eccles, J. S., & Sameroff, A. J. (2000). School as a context of early adolescents' academic and social-emotional development: A summary of research findings. *Elementary School Journal, 100,* 443–471.

Roffwarg, H. P., Muzio, J. N., & Dement, W. C. (1966). Ontogenetic development of the human sleep-dream cycle. *Science, 152,* 604–619.

Rogan, W. J., Dietrich, K. N., Ware, J. H., Dockery, D. W., Salganik, M., & Radcliffe, J. (2001). The effect of chelation therapy with succimer on neuropsychological development in children exposed to lead. *New England Journal of Medicine, 344,* 1421–1426.

Rogers, L. J. (2000). Evolution of hemispheric specialization: Advantages and disadvantages. *Brain and Language, 73,* 236–253.

Rogge, M. M., Greenwald, M., & Golden, A. (2004). Obesity, stigma, and civilized oppression. *Advances in Nursing Science, 27,* 301–315.

Roggman, L. A., Langlois, J. H., Hubbs-Tait, L., & Rieser-Danner, L. A. (1994). Infant day-care, attachment, and the "file drawer problem." *Child Development, 65,* 1429–1443.

Rogler, L. H. (2002). Historical generations and psychology. *American Psychologist, 57,* 1013–1023.

Rogoff, B. (1998). Cognition as a collaborative process. In D. Kuhn & R. S. Siegler (Eds.), *Handbook of child psychology: Vol. 2. Cognition, perception, and language* (5th ed., pp. 679–744). New York: Wiley.

Rogoff, B. (2003). *The cultural nature of human development.* New York: Oxford University Press.

Rogoff, B., & Chavajay, P. (1995). What's become of research on the cultural basis of cognitive development? *American Psychologist, 50,* 859–877.

Rogoff, B., & Mistry, J. (1985). Memory development in cultural context. In M. Pressley & C. Brainerd (Eds.), *Cognitive learning and memory in children* (pp. 117–142). New York: Springer-Verlag.

Rogoff, B., Paradise, R., Arauz, R. M., Correa-Chávez, M., & Angelillo, C. (2003). Firsthand learning through intent participation. *Annual Review of Psychology, 54,* 175–203.

Rogoff, B., & Waddell, K. J. (1982). Memory for information organized in a scene by children from two cultures. *Child Development, 53,* 1224–1228.

Rogol, A. D., Roemmich, J. N., & Clark, P. A. (2002). Growth at puberty. *Journal of Adolescent Health, 31,* 192–200.

Rohner, R. P., & Brothers, S. A. (1999). Perceived parental rejection, psychological maladjustment, and borderline personality disorder. *Journal of Emotional Abuse, 1,* 81–95.

Rohner, R. P., & Veneziano, R. A. (2001). The importance of father love: History and contemporary evidence. *Review of General Psychology, 5,* 382–405.

Roid, G. (2003). *The Stanford-Binet Intelligence Scales, Fifth Edition, Interpretive Manual.* Itasca, IL: Riverside Publishing.

Roisman, R., & Fraley, C. (2006). The limits of genetic influence: A behavior-genetic analysis of infant–caregiver relationship quality and temperament. *Child Development, 77,* 1656–1667.

Roizen, N. J., & Patterson, D. (2003). Down's syndrome. *Lancet, 361,* 1281–1289.

Romans, S. E., Martin, M., Gendall, K., & Herbison, G. P. (2003). Age of menarche: The role of some psychosocial factors. *Psychological Medicine, 33,* 933–939.

Rome-Flanders, T., & Cronk, C. (1995). A longitudinal study of infant vocalizations during mother–infant games. *Journal of Child Language, 22,* 259–274.

Romero, A. J., & Roberts, R. E. (2003). The impact of multiple dimensions of ethnic identity on discrimination and adolescents' self-esteem. *Journal of Applied Social Psychology, 33,* 2288–2305.

Rönnqvist, L., & Domellöf, E. (2006). Quantitative assessment of right and left reaching movements in infants: A longitudinal study from 6 to 36 months. *Developmental Psychobiology, 48,* 444–459.

Rönnqvist, L., & Hopkins, B. (1998). Head position preference in the human newborn: A new look. *Child Development, 69,* 13–23.

Roopnarine, J. L., & Evans, M. E. (2007). Family structural organization, mother–child and father–child relationships and psychological outcomes in English-speaking African Caribbean and Indo Caribbean families. In M. Sutherland (Ed.), *Psychological of development in the Caribbean.* Kingston, Jamaica: Ian Randle.

Roopnarine, J. L., Hossain, Z., Gill, P., & Brophy, H. (1994). Play in the East Indian context. In J. L. Roopnarine, J. E. Johnson, & F. H. Hooper (Eds.), *Children's play in diverse cultures* (pp. 9–30). Albany, NY: SUNY Press.

Roopnarine, J. L., Krishnakumar, A., Metindogan, A., & Evans, M. (2006). Links between parenting styles, parent–child academic interaction, parent–school interaction, and early academic skills and social behaviors in young children of English-speaking Caribbean immigrants. *Early Childhood Research Quarterly, 21,* 238–252.

Roopnarine, J. L., Talukder, E., Jain, D., Joshi, P., & Srivastave, P. (1990). Characteristics of holding, patterns of play, and social behaviors between parents and infants in New Delhi, India. *Developmental Psychology, 26,* 667–673.

Rosander, K., & von Hofsten, C. (2002). Development of gaze tracking of small and large objects. *Experimental Brain Research, 146,* 257–264.

Rosander, K., & von Hofsten, C. (2004). Infants' emerging ability to represent occluded object motion. *Cognition, 91,* 1–22.

Rose, A. J., & Asher, S. R. (1999). Children's goals and strategies in response to conflicts within a friendship. *Developmental Psychology, 35,* 69–79.

Rose, A. J., Carlson, W., & Waller, E. M. (2007). Prospective associations of co-rumination with friendship and emotional adjustment: Considering the socioemotional trade-offs of co-rumination. *Developmental Psychology, 43,* 1019–1031.

Rose, A. J., Swenson, L. P., & Waller, E. M. (2004). Overt and relational aggression and perceived popularity: Developmental differences in concurrent and prospective relations. *Developmental Psychology, 40,* 378–387.

Rose, S. A., Jankowski, J. J., & Senior, G. J. (1997). Infants' recognition of contour-deleted figures. *Journal of Experimental Psychology: Human Perception and Performance, 23,* 1206–1216.

Roseboom, T., de Rooij, S., & Painter, R. (2006). The Dutch famine and its long-term consequences for adult health. *Early Human Development, 82,* 485–491.

Rosen, A. B., & Rozin, P. (1993). Now you see it, now you don't: The preschool child's conception of invisible particles in the context of dissolving. *Developmental Psychology, 29,* 300–311.

Rosen, D. (2003). Eating disorders in children and young adolescents: Etiology, classification, clinical features, and treatment. *Adolescent Medicine: State of the Art Reviews, 14,* 49–59.

Rosen, P. J., Milich, R., & Harris, M. J. (2007). Victims of their own cognitions: Implicit social cognitions, emotional distress, and peer victimization. *Journal of Applied Developmental Psychology, 28,* 211–226.

Rosenberg, D. R., Sweeney, J. A., Gillen, J. S., Kim, J., Varanelli, M. J., O'Hearn, K. M., & Erb, P. A. (1997). Magnetic resonance imaging of children without sedation: Preparation with simulation. *Journal of the American Academy of Child and Adolescent Psychiatry, 36,* 853–859.

Rosengren, K. S., & Hickling, A. K. (2000). The development of children's thinking about possible events and plausible mechanisms. In K. S. Rosengren, C. N. Johnson, & P. L. Harris (Eds.), *Imagining the impossible* (pp. 75–98). Cambridge, UK: Cambridge University Press.

Rosenshine, B., & Meister, C. (1994). Reciprocal teaching: A review of nineteen experimental studies. *Review of Educational Research, 64,* 479–530.

Roseth, C. J., Pellegrini, A. D., Bohn, C. M., van Ryzin, M., & Vance, N. (2007). Preschoolers' aggression, affiliation, and social dominance relationships: An observational, longitudinal study. *Journal of School Psychology, 45,* 479–497.

Ross, C. M., & Harrison, P. L. (2006). Ability grouping. In G. G. Bear & K. M. Minke (Eds.), *Children's needs III: Development, prevention, and intervention* (pp. 579–588). Washington, DC: National Association of School Psychologists.

Ross, H. S., Conant, C., Cheyne, J. A., & Alevizos, E. (1992). Relationships and alliances in the social interactions of kibbutz toddlers. *Social Development, 1,* 1–17.

Rotermann, M. (2005). Sex, condoms and STDs among young people. *Health Reports* (Statistics Canada, Catalogue 82-003), *16*(3), 39–46.

Rothbart, M. K. (2003). Temperament and the pursuit of an integrated developmental psychology. *Merrill-Palmer Quarterly, 50,* 492–505.

Rothbart, M. K. (2004). Emotion-related regulation: Sharpening the definition. *Child Development, 75,* 334–339.

Rothbart, M. K., Ahadi, S. A., & Evans, D. E. (2000). Temperament and personality: Origins and outcome. *Journal of Personality and Social Psychology, 78,* 122–135.

Rothbart, M. K., & Bates, J. E. (2006). Temperament. In N. Eisenberg (Ed.), *Handbook of child psychology: Vol. 3. Social, emotional, and personality development* (6th ed., pp. 99–166). Hoboken, NJ: Wiley.

Rothbart, M. K., & Mauro, J. A. (1990). Questionnaire approaches to the study of infant temperament. In J. W. Fagen & J. Colombo (Eds.), *Individual differences in infancy: Reliability, stability, and prediction* (pp. 411–429). Hillsdale, NJ: Erlbaum.

Rothbart, M. K., Posner, M. I., & Kieras, J. (2006). Temperament, attention, and the development of self-regulation. In K. McCartney & D. Phillips (Eds.), *Blackwell handbook of early childhood development* (pp. 338–357). Malden, MA: Blackwell.

Rothbaum, F., Pott, M., Azuma, H., Miyake, K., & Weisz, J. (2000b). The development of close relationships in Japan and the United States: Paths of symbiotic harmony and generative tension. *Child Development, 71,* 1121–1142.

Rothbaum, F., Weisz, J., Pott, M., Miyake, K., & Morelli, G. A. (2000a). Attachment and culture: Security in the United States and Japan. *American Psychologist, 55,* 1093–1104.

Rouselle, L., Palmers, E., & Noël, M.-P. (2004). Magnitude comparison in preschoolers: What counts? Influence of perceptual variables. *Journal of Experimental Child Psychology, 87,* 57–84.

Rousseau, J. J. (1955). *Emile.* New York: Dutton. (Original work published 1762)

Rovee-Collier, C. K. (1999). The development of infant memory. *Current Directions in Psychological Science, 8,* 80–85.

Rovee-Collier, C. K., & Bhatt, R. S. (1993). Evidence of long-term memory in infancy. *Annals of Child Development, 9,* 1–45.

Rovee-Collier, C., & Barr, R. (2001). Infant learning and memory. In G. Bremner & A. Fogel (Eds.), *Blackwell handbook of infant development* (p. 139–168). Oxford, UK: Blackwell.

Rowe, D. C. (1994). *The limits of family influence: Genes, experience, and behavior.* New York: Guilford.

Rowe, M. L., & Mervis, C. B. (2006). Working memory in Williams syndrome. In T. P. Alloway & S. E. Gathercole (Eds.), *Working memory and neurodevelopmental disorders* (pp. 267–293). New York: Psychology Press.

Rowe, S., & Wertsch, J. V. (2002). Vygotsky's model of cognitive development. In G. Bremner & A. Fogel (Eds.), *Blackwell handbook of infant development* (pp. 538–554). Oxford, UK: Blackwell.

Rowland, C. F. (2007). Explaining errors in children's questions. *Cognition, 104,* 106–134.

Rowland, C. F., Pine, J. M., Lieven, E. V. M., & Theakston, A. L. (2005). The incidence of error in young children's wh- questions. *Journal of Speech, Language, and Hearing Research, 48,* 384–404.

Rowland, C., & Pine, J. M. (2000). Subject-auxiliary inversion errors and wh-question acquisition: "What children do know?" *Journal of Child Language, 27,* 157–181.

Rubel, E. W., & Ryals, B. M. (1982). Patterns of hair cell loss in chick basilar papilla after intense auditory stimulation: Exposure duration and survival time. *Acta Otolaryngologica, 93,* 31–41.

Rubel, E. W., & Ryals, B. M. (1983). Development of the place principle: Acoustical trauma. *Science, 219,* 512–514.

Rubin, K. H., Bukowski, W., & Parker, J. G. (1998). Peer interactions, relationships, and groups. In N. Eisenberg (Ed.), *Handbook of child psychology: Vol. 3. Social, emotional, and personality development* (5th ed., pp. 619–700). New York: Wiley.

Rubin, K. H., Bukowski, W. M., & Parker, J. G. (2006). Peer interactions, relationships, and groups. In N. Eisenberg (Ed.), *Handbook of child psychology: Vol. 3. Social, emotional, and personality development* (6th ed., pp. 571–645). Hoboken, NJ: Wiley.

Rubin, K. H., Burgess, K. B., & Coplan, R. (2002). Social withdrawal and shyness. In P. K. Smith & C. H. Hart (Eds.), *Blackwell handbook of child social development* (pp. 329–352). Oxford, UK: Blackwell.

Rubin, K. H., Burgess, K. B., Dwyer, K. M., & Hastings, P. D. (2003). Predicting preschoolers' externalizing behaviors from toddler temperament, conflict, and maternal negativity. *Developmental Psychology, 39,* 164–176.

Rubin, K. H., Burgess, K. B., & Hastings, P. D. (2002). Stability and social-behavioral consequences of toddlers' inhibited temperament and parenting behaviors. *Child Development, 73,* 483–495.

Rubin, K. H., & Coplan, R. J. (1998). Social and nonsocial play in childhood: An individual differences perspective. In O. N. Saracho & B. Spodek (Eds.), *Multiple perspectives on play in early childhood education* (pp. 144–170). Albany, NY: State University of New York Press.

Rubin, K. H., Fein, G. G., & Vandenberg, B. (1983). Play. In E. M. Hetherington (Ed.), *Handbook of child psychology: Vol. 4. Socialization, personality, and social development* (4th ed., pp. 693–744). New York: Wiley.

Rubin, K. H., Hastings, P. D., Stewart, S. L., Henderson, H. A., & Chen, X. (1997). The consistency and concomitants of inhibition: Some of the children, all of the time. *Child Development, 68,* 467–483.

Rubin, K. H., Stewart, S. L., & Coplan, R. J. (1995). Social withdrawal in childhood: Conceptual and empirical perspectives. In T. H. Ollendick & R. J. Prinz (Eds.), *Advances in clinical child psychology* (Vol. 17, pp. 157–196). New York: Plenum.

Rubin, K. H., Watson, K. S., & Jambor, T. W. (1978). Free-play behaviors in preschool and kindergarten children. *Child Development, 49,* 534–536.

Rubin, K. H., Wojslawowicz, J. C., Rose-Krasnor, L., Booth-LaForce, C., & Burgess, K. B. (2006). The best friendships of shy/withdrawn children: Prevalence, stability, and relationship quality. *Journal of Abnormal Child Psychology, 34,* 143–157.

Ruble, D. N., Alvarez, J., Bachman, M., Cameron, J., Fuligni, A., Garcia Coll, C., & Rhee, E. (2004). The development of a sense of "we": The emergence and implications of children's collective identity. In M. Bennett & F. Sani (Eds.), *The development of the social self* (pp. 29–76). Hove, UK: Psychology Press.

Ruble, D. N., & Dweck, C. S. (1995). Self-conceptions, person conceptions, and their development. In N. Eisenberg (Ed.), *Social development* (pp. 109–139). Thousand Oaks, CA: Sage.

Ruble, D. N., & Flett, G. L. (1988). Conflicting goals in self-evaluative information seeking: Developmental and ability level analyses. *Child Development, 59,* 97–106.

Ruble, D. N., Martin, C. L., & Berenbaum, S. A. (2006). Gender development. In N. Eisenberg (Ed.), *Handbook of child psychology: Vol. 3. Social, emotional, and personality development* (6th ed., pp. 226–299). Hoboken, NJ: Wiley.

Ruble, D. N., Taylor, L. J., Cyphers, L., Greulich, F. K., Lurye, L. E., & Shrout, P. E. (2007). The role of gender constancy in early gender development. *Child Development, 78,* 1121–1136.

Rudolph, D. K., & Heller, T. L. (1997). Interpersonal problem solving, externalizing behavior, and social competence in preschoolers: A knowledge-performance discrepancy? *Journal of Applied Developmental Psychology, 18,* 107–117.

Rudolph, D. K., Lambert, S. F., Clark, A. G., & Kurlakowsky, K. D. (2001). Negotiating the transition to middle school: The role of self-regulatory processes. *Child Development, 72,* 929–946.

Rudolph, K. D., Caldwell, M. S., & Conley, C. S. (2005). Need for approval and children's well-being. *Child Development, 76,* 309–323.

Rudy, D., & Grusec, J. E. (2006). Authoritarian parenting in individualist and collectivist groups: Associations with maternal emotion and cognition and children's self-esteem. *Journal of Family Psychology, 20,* 68–78.

Ruff, C. (2002). Variation in human body size and shape. *Annual Review of Anthropology, 31,* 211–232.

Ruff, H. A., & Capozzoli, M. C. (2003). Development of attention and distractibility in the first 4 years of life. *Developmental Psychology, 39,* 877–890.

Ruff, H. A., Saltarelli, L. M., Capozzoli, M., & Dubiner, K. (1992). The differentiation of activity in infants' exploration of objects. *Developmental Psychology, 28,* 851–861.

Ruffman, T. (1999). Children's understanding of logical inconsistency. *Child Development, 70,* 872–886.

Ruffman, T., & Langman, L. (2002). Infants' reaching in a multi-well A not B task. *Infant Behavior and Development, 25,* 237–246.

Ruffman, T., Perner, J., Olson, D. R., & Doherty, M. (1993). Reflecting on scientific thinking: Children's understanding of the hypothesis–evidence relation. *Child Development, 64,* 1617–1636.

Ruffman, T., Slade, L., Devitt, K., & Crowe, E. (2006). What mothers say and what they do: The relation between parenting, theory of mind, language, and conflict/cooperation. *British Journal of Developmental Psychology, 24,* 105–124.

Runco, M. A. (1992a). Children's divergent thinking and creative ideation. *Developmental Review, 12,* 233–264.

Runco, M. A. (1992b). The evaluative, valuative, and divergent thinking of children. *Journal of Creative Behavior, 25,* 311–319.

Runco, M. A. (1993). Divergent thinking, creativity, and giftedness. *Gifted Child Quarterly, 37,* 16–22.

Runco, M. A. (2006). The development of children's creativity. In B. Spodek & O. N. Saracho (Eds.), *Handbook of research on the education of young children* (2nd ed., pp. 121–131). Mahwah, NJ: Erlbaum.

Runco, M. A., & Okuda, S. M. (1988). Problem, discovery, divergent thinking, and the creative process. *Journal of Youth and Adolescence, 17,* 211–220.

Rushton, J. P., & Jensen, A. R. (2003). African–white IQ differences from Zimbabwe on the Wechsler Intelligence Scale for Children–Revised are mainly on the g factor. *Personality and Individual Differences, 34,* 177–183.

Rushton, J. P., & Jensen, A. R. (2005). Thirty years of research on race differences in cognitive ability. *Psychology, Public Policy, and Law, 11,* 235–294.

Rushton, J. P., & Jensen, A. R. (2006). The totality of available evidence shows the race IQ gap still remains. *Psychological Science, 17,* 921–924.

Russell, A., Mize, J., & Bissaker, K. (2004). Parent–child relationships. In P. K. Smith & C. H. Hart (Eds.), *Blackwell handbook of childhood social development* (pp. 204–222). Malden, MA: Blackwell.

Russell, A., Pettit, G. S., & Mize, J. (1998). Horizontal qualities in parent–child relationships: Parallels with and possible consequences for children's peer relationships. *Developmental Review, 18,* 313–352.

Russell, J. A. (1990). The preschooler's understanding of the causes and consequences of emotion. *Child Development, 61,* 1872–1881.

Russell, R. B., Petrini, J. R., Damus, K., Mattison, D. R., & Schwarz, R. H. (2003). The changing epidemiology of multiple births in the United States. *Obstetrics and Gynecology, 101,* 129–135.

Rust, J., Golombok, S., Hines, M., Johnston, K., Golding, J., & the ALSPAC Study Team. (2000). The role of brothers and sisters in the gender development of preschool children. *Journal of Experimental Child Psychology, 77,* 292–303.

Rutter, M. (1996). Maternal deprivation. In M. H. Bornstein (Ed.), *Handbook of parenting: Vol. 4. Applied and practical parenting* (pp. 3–31). Mahwah, NJ: Erlbaum.

Rutter, M. (2002). Nature, nurture, and development: From evangelism through science toward policy and practice. *Child Development, 73,* 1–21.

Rutter, M. (2006). *Genes and behavior: Nature–nurture interplay explained.* Malden, MA: Blackwell.

Rutter, M. (2007). Gene–environment interdependence. *Developmental Science, 10,* 12–18.

Rutter, M., Colvert, E., Kreppner, J., Beckett, C., Castle, J., & Groothues, C. (2007). Early adolescent outcomes for institutionally deprived and non-deprived adoptees. I: Disinhibited attachment. *Journal of Child Psychology and Psychiatry, 48,* 17–30.

Rutter, M., & the English and Romanian Adoptees Study Team. (1998). Developmental catch-up, and deficit, following adoption after severe global early privation. *Journal of Child Psychology and Psychiatry, 39,* 465–476.

Rutter, M., O'Connor, T. G., and the English and Romanian Adoptees Study Team. (2004). Are there biological programming effects for psychological development? Findings from a study of Romanian adoptees. *Developmental Psychology, 40,* 81–94.

Rutter, M., Pickles, A., Murray, R., & Eaves, L. (2001). Testing hypotheses on specific environmental causal effects on behavior. *Psychological Bulletin, 127,* 291–324.

Ryan, M. K., David, B., & Reynolds, K. J. (2004). Who cares? The effect of gender and context on the self and moral reasoning. *Psychology of Women Quarterly, 28,* 246–255.

Ryan, R. M., Fauth, R. C., & Brooks-Gunn, J. (2006). Childhood poverty: Implications for school readiness and early childhood education In B. Spodek & O. N. Saracho (Eds.), *Handbook of research on the education of young children* (2nd ed., pp. 323–346). Mahwah, NJ: Erlbaum.

Saarela, M. V., Hlushchuk, Y., Williams, A. C. de C., Schürmann, M., Kalso, E., & Hari, R. (2007). The compassionate brain: Humans detect intensity of pain from another's face. *Cerebral Cortex, 17,* 230–237.

Saarni, C. (1999). *The development of emotional competence.* New York: Guilford.

Saarni, C. (2000). Emotional competence: A developmental perspective. In R. Bar-On & J. D. A. Parker (Eds.), *Handbook of emotional intelligence* (pp. 68–91). San Francisco: Jossey-Bass.

Saarni, C., Campos, J. J., Camras, L. A., & Witherington, D. (2006). Emotional development: Action, communication, and understanding. In N. Eisenberg (Ed.), *Handbook of child psychology: Vol. 3. Social, emotional, and personality development* (6th ed., pp. 226–299). Hoboken, NJ: Wiley.

Sabbagh, M. A., Xu, F., Carlson, S. M., Moses, L. J., & Lee, K. (2006). The development of executive functioning and theory of mind: A comparison of Chinese and U.S. preschoolers. *Psychological Science, 17,* 74–81.

Sacks, P. (1999). *Standardized minds: The high price of America's testing culture and what we can do to change it.* Cambridge, MA: Perseus.

Sacks, P. (2005). "No child left": What are schools for in a democratic society? In S. Olfman (Ed.), *Childhood lost: How American culture is failing our kids* (pp. 185–202). Westport, CT: Praeger.

Sadeh, A. (1997). Sleep and melatonin in infants: A preliminary study. *Sleep, 20,* 185–191.

Sadeh, A., Flint-Ofir, E., Tirosh, T., & Tikotzky, L. (2007). Infant sleep and parental sleep-related cognitions. *Journal of Family Psychology, 21,* 74–87.

Sadler, T. W. (2000). *Langman's medical embryology* (8th ed.). Baltimore: Williams & Wilkins.

Sadler, T. W. (2006). *Langman's medical embryology* (10th ed.). Baltimore: Williams & Wilkins.

Saenger, P. (2003). Dose effects of growth hormone during puberty. *Hormone Research, 60*(Suppl. 1), 52–57.

Saffran, J. R., Aslin, R. N., & Newport, E. L. (1996). Statistical learning by 8-month-old infants. *Science, 274,* 1926–1928.

Saffran, J. R., & Thiessen, E. D. (2003). Pattern induction by infant language learners. *Developmental Psychology, 39,* 484–494.

Saffran, J. R., & Thiessen, E. D. (2007). Domain-general learning capacities. In E. Hoff & M. Shatz (Eds.), *Blackwell handbook of language development* (pp. 68–86). Malden, MA: Blackwell.

Saffran, J. R., Werker, J. F., & Werner, L. A. (2006). The infant's auditory world: Hearing, speech, and the beginnings of language. In D. Kuhn & R. Siegler (Eds.), *Handbook of child psychology: Vol. 2. Cognition, perception, and language* (6th ed., pp. 58–108). Hoboken, NJ: Wiley.

Safren, S. A., & Pantalone, D. W. (2006). Social anxiety and barriers to resilience among lesbian, gay, and bisexual adolescents. In A. M. Omoto & H. S. Kurtzman (Eds.), *Sexual orientation and mental health: Examining identity and development in lesbian, gay, and bisexual young people* (pp. 55–71). Washington, DC: American Psychological Association.

Sagi, A., van IJzendoorn, M. H., Aviezer, O., Donnell, F., Koren-Karie, N., Joels, T., & Harel, Y. (1995). Attachments in a multiple-caregiver and multiple-infant environment: The case of the Israeli kibbutzim. In E. Waters, B. E. Vaughn, G. Posada, & K. Kondo-Ikemura (Eds.), Caregiving, cultural, and cognitive perspectives on secure-base behavior and working models: New growing points in attachment theory and research. *Monographs of the Society for Research in Child Development, 60*(1, Serial No. 244), 71–91.

Saginak, K. A., & Saginak, M. A. (2005). Balancing work and family: Equity, gender, and marital satisfaction. *Counseling and Therapy for Couples and Families, 13,* 162–166.

Saigal, S., Stoskopf, B., Streiner, D., Boyle, M., Pinelli, J., & Paneth, N. (2006). Transition of extremely low-birth-weight infants from adolescence to young adulthood. *Journal of the American Medical Association, 295,* 667–675.

Saitta, S. C., & Zackai, E. H. (2005). Specific chromosome disorders in newborns. In H. W. Taeusch, R. A. Ballard, & C. A. Gleason (Eds.), *Avery's diseases of the newborn* (8th ed., pp. 204–215). Philadelphia: Saunders.

Salbe, A. D., Weyer, C., Harper, I., Lindsay, R. S., Ravussin, E., & Tataranni, P. A. (2002b). Assessing risk factors for obesity between childhood and adolescence: II. Energy metabolism and physical activity. *Pediatrics, 110,* 307–314.

Salbe, A. D., Weyer, C., Lindsay, R. S., Ravussin, E., & Tataranni, P. A. (2002a). Assessing risk factors for obesity between childhood and adolescence: I. Birth weight, childhood adiposity, parental obesity, insulin, and leptin. *Pediatrics, 110,* 299–306.

Salerno, M., Micillo, M., Di Maio, S., Capalbo, D., Ferri, P., & Lettiero, T. (2001). Longitudinal growth, sexual maturation and final height in patients with congenital hypothyroidism detected by neonatal screening. *European Journal of Endocrinology, 145,* 377–383.

Salguero, R. A. T., & Morán, R. M. B. (2003). Measuring problem video game playing in adolescents. *Addiction, 97,* 1601–1606.

Salidis, J., & Johnson, J. S. (1997). The production of minimal words: A longitudinal case study of phonological development. *Language Acquisition, 6,* 1–36.

Salihu, H. M., Shumpert, M. N., Slay, M., Kirby, R. S., & Alexander, G. R. (2003). Childbearing beyond maternal age 50 and fetal outcomes in the United States. *Obstetrics and Gynecology, 102,* 1006–1014.

Salley, B. J., & Dixon, W. E., Jr. (2007). Temperamental and joint attentional predictors of language development. *Merrill-Palmer Quarterly, 53,* 131–154.

Salmela-Aro, K., Nurmi, J.-E., Saisto, T., & Halmesmaki, E. (2000). Women's and men's personal goals during the transition to parenthood. *Journal of Family Psychology, 14,* 171–186.

Salmivalli, C., Kaukiainen, A., & Lagerspetz, K. (2000). Aggression and sociometric status of adolescents' self-concept and its relation to their social behavior. *Journal of Research on Adolescence, 8,* 333–354.

Salmivalli, C., & Voeten, M. (2004). Connections between attitudes, group norms, and behaviour in bullying situations. *International Journal of Behavioral Development, 28,* 246–258.

Salovey, P., & Pizarro, D. A. (2003). The value of emotional intelligence. In R. J. Sternberg, J. Lautrey, & T. I. Lubart (Eds.), *Models of intelligence: International perspectives* (pp. 263–278). Washington, DC: American Psychological Association.

Salter, D., McMillan, D., Richards, M., Talbot, T., Hodges, J., Bentovim, A., & Hastings, R. (2003). Development of sexually abusive behavior in sexually victimized males: A longitudinal study. *Lancet, 361,* 471–476.

Saluja, G., Iachan, R., Scheidt, P. C., Overpeck, M. D., Sun, W., & Giedd, J. N. (2004). Prevalence of and risk factors for depressive symptoms among young adolescents. *Archives of Pediatrics and Adolescent Medicine, 158,* 760–765.

Samenow, S. E. (1984). *Inside the criminal mind.* New York: Random House.

Sameroff, A. (2006). Identifying risk and protective factors for healthy child development. In A. Clarke-Stewart & J. Dunn (Eds.), *Families count: Effects on child and adolescent development* (pp. 53–76). New York: Cambridge University Press.

Sameroff, A. J., & MacKenzie, M. J. (2003). Research strategies for capturing transactional models of development: The limits of the possible. *Development and Psychopathology, 15,* 613–640.

Samuels, M. (2003). Viruses and sudden infant death. *Peaediatric Respiratory Review, 4,* 178–183.

Sandberg, J. F., & Hofferth, S. L. (2001). Changes in children's time with parents: United States, 1981–1997. *Demography, 38,* 423–436.

Sandler, J. C. (2006). Alternative methods of child testimony: A review of law and research. In C. R. Bartol & A. M. Bartol (Eds.), *Current perspectives in forensic psychology and criminal justice* (pp. 203–212). Thousand Oaks, CA: Sage.

Sandnabba, N. K., & Ahlberg, C. (1999). Parents' attitudes and expectations about children's cross-gender behavior. *Sex Roles, 40,* 249–263.

Sandqvist, K. (1992). Sweden's sex-role scheme and commitment to gender equality. In S. Lewis, D. N. Izraeli, & H. Hottsmans (Eds.), *Dual-earner families: International perspectives.* London: Sage.

Sandstrom, M. J., & Cillessen, A. H. N. (2003). Sociometric status and children's peer experiences: Use of the daily diary method. *Merrill-Palmer Quarterly, 49,* 427–452.

Sann, C., & Streri, A. (2007). Perception of object shape and texture in human newborns: Evidence from cross-modal transfer tasks. *Developmental Science, 10,* 399–410.

Sansavini, A., Bertoncini, J., & Giovanelli, G. (1997). Newborns discriminate the rhythm of multisyllabic stressed words. *Developmental Psychology, 33,* 3–11.

Sanson, A., Hemphill, S. A., & Smart, D. (2004). Connections between temperament and social development: A review. *Social Development, 13,* 142–170.

Santoloupo, S., & Pratt, M. (1994). Age, gender, and parenting style variations in mother–adolescent dialogues and adolescent reasoning about political issues. *Journal of Adolescent Research, 9,* 241–261.

Sapp, F., Lee, K., & Muir, D. (2000). Three-year-olds' difficulty with the appearance–reality distinction: Is it real or is it apparent? *Developmental Psychology, 36,* 547–560.

Sarason, I. G. (1980). *Test anxiety: Theory, research, and applications.* Hillsdale, NJ: Erlbaum.

Sarnecka, B. W., & Gelman, S. A. (2004). Six does not just mean a lot: Preschoolers see number words as specific. *Cognition, 92,* 329–352.

Sato, T., Matsumoto, T., Kawano, H., Watanabe, T., Uematsu, Y., & Semine, K. (2004). Brain masculinization requires androgen receptor function. *Proceedings of the National Academy of Sciences, 101,* 1673–1678.

Saucier, J. F., Sylvestre, R., Doucet, H., Lambert, J., Frappier, J. Y., Charbonneau, L., & Malus, M. (2002). Cultural identity and adaptation to adolescence in Montreal. In F. J. C. Azima & N. Grizenko (Eds.), *Immigrant and refugee children and their families: Clinical, research, and training issues* (pp. 133–154). Madison, WI: International Universities Press.

Saudino, K. J. (2003). Parent ratings of infant temperament: Lessons from twin studies. *Infant Behavior and Development, 26,* 100–107.

Saudino, K. J., & Cherny, S. S. (2001). Sources of continuity and change in observed temperament. In R. N. Emde & J. K. Hewitt (Eds.), *Infancy to early childhood: Genetic and environmental influences on developmental change* (pp. 89–110). New York: Oxford University Press.

Saudino, K. J., & Plomin, R. (1997). Cognitive and temperamental mediators of genetic contributions to the home environment during infancy. *Merrill-Palmer Quarterly, 43,* 1–23.

Sauls, D. J. (2002). Effects of labor support on mothers, babies, and birth outcomes. *Journal of Obstetric, Gynecologic, and Neonatal Nursing, 31,* 733–741.

Savage, C., Lieven, E., Theakston, A., & Tomasello, M. (2006). Structural priming as implicit learning in language acquisition: The persistence of lexical and structural priming in 4-year-olds. *Language Learning and Development, 2,* 27–49.

Savage-Rumbaugh, E. S. (2001). *Apes, language, and the human mind.* New York: Oxford University Press.

Savage-Rumbaugh, E. S., Murphy, J., Sevcik, R. A., Brakke, K. E., Williams, S. L., & Rumbaugh, D. M. (1993). Language comprehension in ape and child. *Monographs of the Society for Research in Child Development, 58*(3–4, Serial No. 233).

Savage-Rumbaugh, S., & Shanker, S. (1998). *Apes, language, and the human mind.* New York: Oxford University Press.

Savin-Williams, R. C. (2001). A critique of research on sexual minority youths. *Journal of Adolescence, 24,* 5–13.

Savin-Williams, R. C. (2003). Lesbian, gay, and bisexual youths' relationships with their parents. In L. D. Garnets & D. C. Kimmel (Eds.), *Psychological perspectives on lesbian, gay, and bisexual experiences* (2nd ed., pp. 299–326). New York: Columbia University Press.

Savin-Williams, R. C., & Diamond, L. M. (2004). Sex. In R. M. Lerner & L. Steinberg (Eds.), *Handbook of adolescent development* (2nd ed., pp. 189–231). Hoboken, NJ: Wiley.

Savin-Williams, R. C., & Ream, G. L. (2003). Suicide attempts among sexual-minority male youth. *Journal of Clinical Child and Adolescent Psychology, 32,* 509–522.

Saxe, G. B. (1988, August–September). Candy selling and math learning. *Educational Researcher, 17*(6), 14–21.

Saxton, M., Backley, P., & Gallaway, C. (2005). Negative input for grammatical errors: Effects after a lag of 12 weeks. *Journal of Child Language, 32,* 643–672.

Saxton, M., Houston-Price, C., & Dawson, N. (2005). The prompt hypothesis: Clarification requests as corrective input for grammatical errors. *Applied Psycholinguistics, 26,* 393–414.

Saygin, A. P., Wilson, S. M., Dronkers, N. F., & Bates, E. (2004). Action comprehension in aphasia: Linguistic and non-linguistic deficits and their lesion correlates. *Neuropsychologia, 42,* 1788–1804.

Saylor, C. F., Cowart, B. L., Lipovsky, J. A., Jackson, C., & Finch, A. J., Jr. (2003). Media exposure to September 11: Elementary school students' experiences and posttraumatic symptoms. *American Behavioral Scientist, 46,* 1622–1642.

Saylor, M. M., Baldwin, D. A., & Sabbagh, M. A. (2005). Word learning: A complex product. In G. Hall & S. Waxman (Eds.), *Weaving a lexicon.* Cambridge, MA: MIT Press.

Saylor, M. M., & Ganea, P. (2007). Infants interpret ambiguous requests for absent objects. *Developmental Psychology, 43,* 696–704.

Saylor, M. M., & Sabbagh, M. A. (2004). Different kinds of information affect word learning in the preschool years: The case of part-term learning. *Child Development, 75,* 395–408.

Saylor, M. M., Sabbagh, M. A., & Baldwin, D. A. (2002). Children use whole–part juxtaposition as a pragmatic cue to word meaning. *Developmental Psychology, 38,* 993–1003.

Saylor, M. M., & Troseth, G. L. (2006). Preschoolers use information about speakers' desires to learn new words. *Cognitive Development, 21,* 214–231.

Saywitz, K. J., Goodman, G. S., & Lyon, T. D. (2002). Interviewing children in and out of court: Current research and practice implications. In J. E. B. Myers & L. Berliner (Eds.), *The APSAC handbook on child maltreatment* (2nd ed., pp. 349–377). Thousand Oaks, CA: Sage.

Scales, P. C., & Roehlkepartain, E. C. (2004). *Community service and service learning in U.S. public schools, 2004. Findings from a national survey.* St. Paul, MN: National Youth Leadership Council.

Scarr, S. (1997). Behavior-genetic and socialization theories of intelligence: Truce and reconciliation. In R. J. Sternberg & E. L. Grigorenko (Eds.), *Intelligence, heredity, and environment* (pp. 3–41). New York: Cambridge University Press.

Scarr, S., & McCartney, K. (1983). How people make their own environments: A theory of genotype environment effects. *Child Development, 54,* 424–435.

Scarr, S., & Weinberg, R. A. (1983). The Minnesota Adoption Studies: Genetic differences and malleability. *Child Development, 54,* 260–267.

Schaal, B., Marlier, L., & Soussignan, R. (2000). Human foetuses learn odours from their pregnant mother's diet. *Chemical Senses, 25,* 729–737.

Schalet, A. (2007). Adolescent sexuality viewed through two different cultural lenses. In M. S. Tepper & A. F. Owens (Eds.), *Sexual health: Vol. 3. Moral and cultural foundations* (pp. 365–387). Westport, CT: Praeger.

Scharrer, E., & Comstock, G. (2003). Entertainment televisual media: Content patterns and themes. In E. L. Palmer & B. M. Young (Eds.), *The faces of televisual media: Teaching, violence, selling to children* (pp. 161–193). Mahwah, NJ: Erlbaum.

Schauwers, K., Gillis, S., Daemers, K., De Beukelaer, C., De Ceulaer, G., Yperman, M., & Govaerts, P. J. (2004). Normal hearing and language development in a deaf-born child: Cochlear implants. *Otology and Neurotology, 25,* 924–929.

Schellenberg, E. G. (2004). Music lessons enhance IQ. *Psychological Science, 15,* 511–514.

Schellenberg, E. G., Nakata, T., Hunter, P. G., & Tamoto, S. (2007). Exposure to music and cognitive performance: Tests of children and adults. *Psychology of Music, 35,* 5–19.

Scher, A., Epstein, R., & Tirosh, E. (2004). Stability and changes in sleep regulation: A longitudinal study from 3 months to 3 years. *International Journal of Behavioral Development, 28,* 268–274.

Scher, A., Tirosh, E., Jaffe, M., Rubin, L., Sadeh, A., & Lavie, P. (1995). Sleep patterns of infants and young children in Israel. *International Journal of Behavioral Development, 18,* 701–711.

Schlagmüller, M., & Schneider, W. (2002). The development of organizational strategies in children: Evidence from a microgenetic longitudinal study. *Journal of Experimental Child Psychology, 81,* 298–319.

Schlegel, A., & Barry, H., III. (1991). *Adolescence: An anthropological inquiry.* New York: Free Press.

Schmid, R. G., Tirsch, W. S., & Scherb, H. (2002). Correlation between spectral EEG parameters and intelligence test variables in school-age children. *Clinical Neurophysiology, 113,* 1647–1656.

Schmidt, L. A., Fox, N. A., Rubin, K. H., Sternberg, E. M., Gold, P. W., & Smith, C. C. (1997). Behavioral and neuroendocrine responses in shy children. *Developmental Psychobiology, 35,* 119–135.

Schmidt, L. A., Fox, N. A., Schulkin, J., & Gold, P. W. (1999). Behavioral and psychophysiological correlates of self-presentation in temperamentally shy children. *Developmental Psychobiology, 30,* 127–140.

Schmidt, L. A., Santesso, D. L., Schulkin, J., & Segalowitz, S. J. (2007). Shyness is a necessary but not sufficient condition for high salivary cortisol in typically developing 10-year-old children. *Personality and Individual Differences, 43,* 1541–1551.

Schmitt, K. L., & Anderson, D. R. (2002). Television and reality: Toddlers' use of visual information from video to guide behavior. *Media Psychology, 4,* 51–76.

Schmitz, S., Fulker, D. W., Plomin, R., Zahn-Waxler, C., Emde, R. N., & DeFries, J. C. (1999). Temperament and problem behaviour during early childhood. *International Journal of Behavioural Development, 23,* 333–355.

Schneider, B. H., Atkinson, L., & Tardif, C. (2001). Child–parent attachment and children's peer relations: A quantitative review. *Developmental Psychology, 37,* 86–100.

Schneider, D. (2006). Smart as we can get? *American Scientist, 94,* 311–312.

Schneider, W. (1986). The role of conceptual knowledge and metamemory in the development of organizational processes in memory. *Journal of Experimental Child Psychology, 42,* 218–236.

Schneider, W. (2002). Memory development in childhood. In U. Goswami (Ed.), *Blackwell handbook of childhood cognitive development* (pp. 236–256). Malden, MA: Blackwell.

Schneider, W., & Bjorklund, D. F. (1992). Expertise, aptitude, and strategic remembering. *Child Development, 63,* 461–473.

Schneider, W., & Bjorklund, D. F. (1998). Memory. In D. Kuhn & R. S. Siegler (Eds.), *Handbook of child psychology: Vol. 2. Cognition, perception, and language* (5th ed., pp. 467–521). New York: Wiley.

Schneider, W., & Bjorklund, D. F. (2003). Memory and knowledge development. In J. Valsiner & K. Connolly (Eds.), *Handbook of developmental psychology.* London: Sage.

Schneider, W., & Pressley, M. (1997). *Memory development between two and twenty* (2nd ed.). Mahwah, NJ: Erlbaum.

Schneider, W., Perner, J., Bullock, M., Stefanek, J., & Ziegler, A. (1999). Development of intelligence and thinking. In F. E. Weinert & W. Schneider (Eds.), *Individual development from 3 to 12: Findings from the Munich Longitudinal Study* (pp. 9–28). Cambridge, UK: Cambridge University Press.

Schneiders, J., Nicolson, N. A., Berkhof, J., Feron, F. J., van Os, J., & deVries, M. W. (2006). Mood reactivity to daily negative events in early adolescence: Relationship to risk for psychopathology. *Developmental Psychology, 42,* 543–554.

Schofield, J. W. (1995). Review of research on school desegregation's impact on elementary and secondary students. In J. Banks & C. M. Banks (Eds.), *Handbook of research on multicultural education* (pp. 597–617). New York: Simon & Schuster.

Scholl, B. J., & Leslie, A. M. (2000). Minds, modules, and meta-analysis. *Child Development, 72,* 696–701.

Scholl, T. O., Hediger, M. L., & Belsky, D. (1996). Prenatal care and maternal health during adolescent pregnancy: A review and meta-analysis. *Journal of Adolescent Health, 15,* 444–456.

Scholnick, E. K. (1995, Fall). Knowing and constructing plans. *SRCD Newsletter,* pp. 1–2, 17.

Schonert-Reichl, K. A. (1999). Relations of peer acceptance, friendship adjustment, and social behavior to moral reasoning during early adolescence. *Journal of Early Adolescence, 19,* 249–279.

Schoppe-Sullivan, S. J., Mangelsdorf, S. C., Brown, G. L., & Sokolowski, M. S. (2007). Goodness-of-fit in family context: Infant temperament, marital quality, and early coparenting behavior. *Infant Behavior and Development, 30,* 82–96.

Schott, J. M., & Rossor, M. N. (2003). The grasp and other primitive reflexes. *Journal of Neurological and Neurosurgical Psychiatry, 74,* 558–560.

Schuengel, G., Bakermans-Kranenburg, M. J., & van IJzendoorn, M. H. (1999). Attachment and loss: Frightening maternal behavior linking unresolved loss and disorganized infant attachment. *Journal of Consulting and Clinical Psychology, 67,* 54–63.

Schuetze, P., & Eiden, R. D. (2006). The association between maternal cocaine use during pregnancy and physiological regulation in 4- to 8-week-old infants: An examination of possible mediators and moderators. *Journal of Pediatric Psychology, 31,* 15–26,

Schull, W. J. (2003). The children of atomic bomb survivors: A synopsis. *Journal of Radiological Protection, 23,* 369–384.

Schulte-Ruther, M., Markowitsch, H. J., Fink, G. R., & Piefke, M. (2007). Mirror neuron and theory of mind mechanisms involved in face-to-face interactions: A functional magnetic resonance imaging approach to empathy. *Journal of Cognitive Neuroscience, 19,* 1354–1372.

Schunk, D. H., & Pajares, F. (2005). Competence perceptions and academic functioning. In A. J. Andrew & C. S. Dweck (Eds.), *Handbook of competence and motivation* (pp. 85–104). New York: Guilford.

Schunk, D. H., & Zimmerman, B. J. (2003). Self-regulation and learning. In W. M. Reynolds & G. E. Miller (Eds.), *Handbook of psychology* (Vol. 7, pp. 59–78). New York: Wiley.

Schuster, B., Ruble, D. N., & Weinert, F. E. (1998). Causal inferences and the positivity bias in children: The role of the covariation principle. *Child Development, 69,* 1577–1596.

Schwalb, D. W., Nakazawa, J., Yamamoto, T., & Hyun, J.-H. (2004). Fathering in Japanese, Chinese, and Korean cultures: A review of the literature. In M. E. Lamb (Ed.), *The role of the father in child development* (4th ed., pp. 146–181). Hoboken, NJ: Wiley.

Schwanenflugel, P. J., Fabricius, W. V., & Noyes, C. R. (1996). Developing organization of mental verbs: Evidence for the development of a constructivist theory of mind in middle childhood. *Cognitive Development, 11,* 265–294.

Schwanenflugel, P. J., Henderson, R. L., & Fabricius, W. V. (1998). Develping organisation of mental verbs and theory of mind in middle childhood: Evidence from extensions. *Developmental Psychology, 34,* 514–524.

Schwartz, C. E., Wright, C. I., Shin, L. M., Kagan, J., & Raugh, S. L. (2003). Inhibited and uninhibited infants "grown up": Adult amygdalar response to novelty. *Science, 300,* 1952–1953.

Schwartz, D., Proctor, L. J., & Chien, D. H. (2001). The aggressive victim of bullying: Emotional and behavioral dysregulation as a pathway to victimization by peers. In J. Juonen & S. Graham (Eds.), *Peer harassment in school: The plight of the vulnerable and victimized* (pp. 147–174). New York: Guilford.

Schwartz, S. J., Pantin, H., Prado, G., Sullivan, S., & Szapocznik, J. (2005). Family functioning, identity, and problem behavior: Immigrant early adolescents. *Journal of Early Adolescence, 25,* 392–420.

Schwarz, N. (1999). Self-reports: How the questions shape the answers. *American Psychologist, 54,* 93–105.

Schweiger, W. K., & O'Brien, M. (2005). Special needs adoption: An ecological systems approach. *Family Relations, 54,* 512–522.

Schweinhart, L. J., Montie, J., Xiang, Z., Barnett, W. S., Belfield, C. R., & Nores, M. (2005). *Lifetime effects: The High/Scope Perry Preschool Study through age 40.* Ypsilanti, MI: High/Scope Press.

Schweizer, K., Moosbrugger, H., & Gold hammer, F. (2006). The structure of the relationship between attention and intelligence. *Intelligence, 33,* 589–611.

Schwier, C., van Maanen, C., Carpenter, M., & Tomasello, M. (2006). Rational imitation in 12-month-old infants. *Infancy, 10,* 303–311.

Schwimmer, J. B., Burwinkle, T. M., & Varni, J. W. (2003). Health-related quality of life of severely obese children and adolescents. *Journal of the American Medical Association, 289,* 1813–1819.

Scott, C. S., Arthur, D., Owen, R., & Panizo, M. I. (1989). Black adolescents' emotional response to menarche. *Journal of the National Medical Association, 81,* 285–290.

Scott, K. D., Berkowitz, G., & Klaus, M. (1999). A comparison of intermittent and continuous support during labor: A meta-analysis. *American Journal of Obstetrics and Gynecology, 180,* 1054–1059.

Scott, L. D. (2003). The relation of racial identity and racial socialization to coping with discrimination among African Americans. *Journal of Black Studies, 20,* 520–538.

Scrimsher, S., & Tudge, J. (2003). The teaching/learning relationship in the first years of school: Some revolutionary implications of Vygotsky's theory. *Early Education and Development, 14,* 293–312.

Scrutton, D. (2005). Influence of supine sleeping positioning on early motor milestone acquisition. *Developmental Medicine and Child Neurology, 47,* 364.

Seaton, E. K., Scottham, K. M., & Sellers, R. M. (2006). The status model of racial identity development in African American adolescents: Evidence of structure, trajectories, and well-being. *Child Development, 77,* 1416–1426.

Sebanc, A. (2003). The friendship features of preschool children: Links with prosocial behavior and aggression. *Social Development, 12,* 249–268.

Seidenberg, M. S., & Petitto, L. A. (1987). Communication, symbolic communication, and language: Comment on Savage-Rumbaugh, McDonald, Sevcik, Hopkins, and Rupert. *Journal of Experimental Psychology: General, 116, 279–287.*

Seidman, E., Aber, J. L., & French, S. E. (2004). Assessing the transitions to middle and high school. *Journal of Adolescent Research, 19,* 3–30.

Seidman, E., Lambert, L. E., Allen, L., & Aber, J. L. (2003). Urban adolescents' transition to junior high school and protective family transactions. *Journal of Early Adolescence, 23,* 166–193.

Seifer, R., & Schiller, M. (1995). The role of parenting sensitivity, infant temperament, and dyadic interaction in attachment theory and assessment. In E. Waters, B. E. Vaughn, G. Posada, & K. Kondo-Ikemura (Eds.), Caregiving, cultural, and cognitive perspectives on secure-base behavior and working models: New growing points of attachment theory and research. *Monographs of the Society for Research in Child Development, 60*(2–3, Serial No. 244).

Seiffge-Krenke, I. (2003). Testing theories of romantic development from adolescence to young adulthood: Evidence of a developmental sequence. *International Journal of Behavioral Development, 27,* 519-531.

Seitz, V., & Apfel, N. H. (2005). Creating effective school-based interventions for pregnant teenagers. In R. DeV. Peters, B. Leadbeater, & R. J. McMahon (Eds.), *Resilience in children, families, and communities: Linking context to practice and policy* (pp. 65–82). New York: Kluwer Academic.

Selman, R. L. (1976). Social-cognitive understanding: A guide to educational and clinical practice. In T. Lickona (Ed.), *Moral development and behavior: Theory, research, and social issues* (pp. 299–316). New York: Holt, Rinehart & Winston.

Selman, R. L. (1980). *The growth of interpersonal understanding.* New York: Academic Press.

Selman, R. L., & Byrne, D. F. (1974). A structural-developmental analysis of levels of role taking in middle childhood. *Child Development, 45,* 803–806.

Sen, M. G., Yonas, A., & Knill, D. C. (2001). Development of infants' sensitivity to surface contour information for spatial layout. *Perception, 30,* 167–176.

Senechal, M., & LeFevre, J. (2002). Parental involvement in the development of children's reading skill: A five-year longitudinal study. *Child Development, 73,* 445–460.

Senghas, A., & Coppola, M. (2001). Children creating language: How Nicaraguan sign language acquired a spatial grammar. *Psychological Science, 12,* 323–328.

Serafini, T. E., & Adams, G. R. (2002). Functions of identity: Scale construction and validation. *Identity: An International Journal of Theory and Research, 2,* 361–389.

Serbin, L. A., Connor, J. M., & Citron, C. C. (1978). Environmental control of independent and dependent behaviors in preschool girls and boys: A model for early independence training. *Sex Roles, 4,* 867–875.

Serbin, L. A., Connor, J. M., & Iler, I. (1979). Sex-stereotyped and nonstereotyped introductions of new toys in the preschool classroom: An observational study of teacher behavior and its effects. *Psychology of Women Quarterly, 4,* 261–265.

Serbin, L. A., Poulin-Dubois, D., Colburne, K. A., Sen, M. G., & Eichstedt, J. A. (2001). Gender stereotyping in infancy: Visual preferences for and knowledge of gender-stereotyped toys in the second year. *International Journal of Behavioral Development, 25,* 7–15.

Serbin, L. A., Powlishta, K. K., & Gulko, J. (1993). The development of sex typing in middle childhood. *Monographs of the Society for Research in Child Development, 58*(2, Serial No. 232).

Sermon, K., Van Steirteghem, A., & Liebaers, I. (2004). Preimplantation genetic diagnosis. *Lancet, 363,* 1633–1641.

Service Canada. (2005). *Canadian youth: Who are they and what do they want?* Retrieved from www.youth.gc.ca

Servin, A., Nordenström, A., Larssonk, A., & Bohlin, G. (2003). Prenatal androgens and gender-typed behavior: A study of girls with mild and severe forms of congenital hyperplasia. *Developmental Psychology, 39,* 440–450.

Sesame Workshop. (2008). *Sesame Street season 37 press kit.* Retrieved from www.sesameworkshop.org/aboutus/pressroom/presskits/season37/sesame_street.php

Sesame Workshop. (2005). Sesame workshop. Retrieved from www.sesameworkshop.org

Sethi, A., Mischel, W., Aber, J. L., Shoda, Y., & Rodriguez, M. L. (2000). The role of strategic attention deployment in development of self-regulation: Predicting preschoolers' delay of gratification from mother–toddler interactions. *Developmental Psychology, 36,* 767–777.

Seymour, S. C. (1999). *Women, family, and child care in India.* Cambridge, UK: Cambridge University Press.

Shafer, V. L., & Garrido-Nag, K. (2007). The neurodevelopmental bases of language. In E. Hoff & M. Shatz (Eds.), *Blackwell handbook of language development* (pp. 21–45). Malden, MA: Blackwell.

Shafer, V. L., Shucard, D. W., & Jaeger, J. J. (1999). Electrophysiological indices of cerebral specialization and the role of prosody in language acquisition in 3-month-old infants. *Developmental Neuropsychology, 15,* 73–109.

Shah, T., Sullivan, K., & Carter, J. (2006). Sudden infant death syndrome and reported maternal smoking during pregnancy. *American Journal of Public Health, 96,* 1757–1759.

Shahar, S. (1990). *Childhood in the Middle Ages.* London: Routledge & Kegan Paul.

Shainess, N. (1961). A re-evaluation of some aspects of femininity through a study of menstruation: A preliminary report. *Comparative Psychiatry, 2,* 20–26.

Shanahan, M. L., Mortimer, J. T., & Krüger, H. (2002). Adolescence and adult work in the twenty-first century. *Journal of Research on Adolescence, 12,* 99–120.

Shankaran, S., Laptook, A. R., Ehrenkranz, R. A., Tyson, J. E., McDonald, S. A., & Donovan, E. F. (2005). Whole-body hypothermia for neonates with hypoxic–ischemic encephalopathy. *New England Journal of Medicine, 353,* 1574–1584.

Shanker, S. G., Savage-Rumbaugh, S., & Taylor, T. J. (1999). Kanzi: A new beginning. *Animal Learning and Behavior, 27,* 24–25.

Shapiro, A. F., Gottman, J. M., & Carrere, S. (2000). The baby and the marriage: Identifying factors that buffer against decline in marital satisfaction after the first baby arrives. *Journal of Family Psychology, 14,* 59–70.

Shapka, J. D., & Keating, D. P. (2005). Structure and change in self-concept during adolescence. *Canadian Journal of Behavioural Science, 37,* 83–96.

Sharma, S. K., & Leveno, K. J. (2003). Regional analgesia and progress of labor. *Clinical Obstetrics and Gynecology, 46,* 633–645.

Shatz, M. (2007). On the development of the field. In E. Hoff & M. Shatz (Eds.), *Blackwell handbook of language development* (pp. 1–20). Malden, MA: Blackwell.

Shaver, P., Furman, W., & Buhrmester, D. (1985). Transition to college: Network changes, social skills, and loneliness. In S. Duck & D. Perlman (Eds.), *Understanding personal relationships: An interdisciplinary approach* (pp. 193–219). London: Sage.

Shaver, P. R., Wu, S., & Schwartz, J. C. (1992). Cross-cultural similarities and differences in emotion and its representation: A prototype approach. In M. S. Clark (Ed.), *Review of personality and social psychology* (Vol. 13, pp. 175–212). Newbury Park, CA: Sage.

Shaw, D. S., Gilliom, M., Ingoldsby, E. M., & Nagin, D. S. (2003). Trajectories leading to school-age conduct problems. *Developmental Psychology, 39,* 189–200.

Shaw, D. S., Winslow, E. B., & Flanagan, C. (1999). A prospective study of the effects of marital status and family relations on young children's adjustment among African-American and European-American families. *Child Development, 70,* 742–755.

Shaw, P., Eckstrand, K., Sharp, W., Blumenthal, J., Lerch, J. P., & Greenstein, D. (2007, November 16). Attention-deficit/hyperactivity disorder is characterized by a delay in cortical maturation. *Proceedings of the National Academy of Sciences Online.* Retrieved from www.pnas.org/cgi/content/abstract/0707741104v1

Shedler, J., & Block, J. (1990). Adolescent drug use and psychological health: A longitudinal inquiry. *American Psychologist, 45,* 612–630.

Sheehan, G., Darlington, Y., Noller, P., & Feeney, J. (2004). Children's perceptions of their sibling relationships during parental separation and divorce. *Journal of Divorce and Remarriage, 41,* 69–94.

Sheehy, A., Gasser, T., Molinari, L., & Largo, R. H. (1999). An analysis of variance of the pubertal and midgrowth spurts for length and width. *Annals of Human Biology, 26,* 309–331.

Sherman, S. L., Freeman, S. B., Allen, E. G., & Lamb, N. E. (2005). Risk factors for nondisjunction of trisomy 21. *Cytogenetic Genome Research, 111,* 273–280.

Sherry, B., McDivitt, J., Birch, L. L., Cook, F. H., Sanders, S., Prish, J. L., Francis, L. A., & Scanlon, K. S. (2004). Attitudes, practices, and concerns about child feeding and child weight status among socioeconomically diverse white, Hispanic, and African-American mothers. *Journal of the American Dietetic Association, 104,* 215–221.

Shields, A., Ryan, R. M., & Cicchetti, D. (2001). Narrative representations of caregivers and emotion dysregulation as predictors of maltreated children's rejection by peers. *Developmental Psychology, 37,* 321–337.

Shields, M. (2005). *Overweight Canadian children and adolescents.* Nutrition: Findings from the Canadian Community Health Survey. Statistics Canada Catalogue No. 82-620-MWE2005001. Retrieved from www.statcan.ca/english/research/82-620-MIE/2005001/pdf/cobesity.pdf

Shiller, V., Izard, C. E., & Hembree, E. A. (1986). Patterns of emotion expression during separation in the Strange Situation. *Developmental Psychology, 22,* 378–382.

Shimada, S., & Hiraki, K. (2006). Infant's brain responses to live and televised action. *NeuroImage, 32,* 930–939.

Shimizu, H. (2001). Japanese adolescent boys' senses of empathy (omoiyari) and Carol Gilligan's perspectives on the morality of care: A phenomenological approach. *Culture and Psychology, 7,* 453–475.

Shinn, M. W. (1900). *The biography of a baby.* Boston: Houghton Mifflin.

Shipman, K. L., Zeman, J., Nesin, A. E., & Fitzgerald, M. (2003). Children's strategies for displaying anger and sadness: What works with whom? *Merrill-Palmer Quarterly, 49,* 100–122.

Shoda, Y., Mischel, W., & Peake, P. K. (1990). Predicting adolescent cognitive and self-regulatory competencies from preschool delay of gratification: Identifying diagnostic conditions. *Developmental Psychology, 26,* 978–986.

Shonk, S. M., & Cicchetti, D. (2001). Maltreatment, competency deficits, and risk for academic and behavioral maladjustment. *Developmental Psychology, 37,* 3–17.

Shonkoff, J., & Phillips, D. (Eds.). (2001). *Neurons to neighborhoods: The science of early childhood development.* Washington, DC: National Academy Press.

Shure, M. B., & Aberson, B. (2005). Enhancing the process of resilience through effective thinking. In S. Goldstein & R. B. Brooks (Eds.), *Handbook of resilience in children* (pp. 373–394). New York: Kluwer Academic.

Shuwairi, S. M., Albert, M. K., & Johnson, S. P. (2007) Discrimination of possible and impossible objects in infancy. *Psychological Science, 18,* 303–307.

Shweder, R. A., Goodnow, J. J., Hatano, G., LeVine, R. A., Markus, H. R., & Miller, P. J. (2006). The cultural psychology of development: One mind, many mentalities. In R. M. Lerner (Ed.), *Handbook of child psychology: Vol. 1. Theoretical models of human development* (6th ed., pp. 716–792). Hoboken, NJ: Wiley.

Shweder, R. A., Mahapatra, M., & Miller, J. G. (1990). Culture and moral development. In J. Stigler, R. A. Shweder, & G. Herdt (Eds.), *Cultural psychology: Essays on comparative human development* (pp. 130–204). New York: Cambridge University Press.

Sidappa, A., Georgieff, M. K., Wewerka, S., Worwa, C., Nelson, C. A., & deRegnier, R. (2004). Iron deficiency alters auditory recognition memory in newborn infants of diabetic mothers. *Pediatric Research, 55,* 1034–1041.

Sidebotham, P., Heron, J., & the ALSPAC Study Team. (2003). Child maltreatment in the "children of the nineties": The role of the child. *Child Abuse and Neglect, 27,* 337–352.

Siebenbruner, J., Zimmer-Gembeck, M. J., & Egeland, B. (2007). Sexual partners and contraceptive use: A 16-year prospective study predicting abstinence and risk behavior. *Journal of Research on Adolescence, 17,* 179–206.

Siegler, R. S. (1995). How does change occur? A microgenetic study of number conservation. *Cognitive Psychology, 28,* 225–273.

Siegler, R. S. (1996). *Emerging minds: The process of change in children's thinking.* New York: Oxford University Press.

Siegler, R. S. (2002). Microgenetic studies of self-explanation. In N. Granott & J. Parziale (Eds.), *Microdevelopment: Transition processes in development and learning* (pp. 31–58). New York: Cambridge University Press.

Siegler, R. S. (2005). Children's learning. *American Psychologist, 60,* 769–778.

Siegler, R. S. (2006). Microgenetic analyses of learning. In D. Kuhn & R. Siegler (Eds.), *Handbook of child psychology: Vol. 2. Cognition, perception, and language* (6th ed., pp. 464–510). Hoboken, NJ: Wiley.

Siegler, R. S. (2007). Cognitive variability. *Developmental Science, 10,* 104–109.

Siegler, R. S., & Alibali, M. W. (2005). *Children's thinking* (4th ed.). Upper Saddle River, NJ: Prentice-Hall.

Siegler, R. S., & Booth, J. L. (2004). Development of numerical estimation in young children. *Child Development, 75,* 428–444.

Siegler, R. S., & Crowley, K. (1991). The microgenetic method: A direct means for studying cognitive development. *American Psychologist, 46,* 606–620.

Siegler, R. S., & Ellis, S. (1996). Piaget on childhood. *Psychological Science, 7,* 211–215.

Siegler, R. S., & Jenkins, E. (1989). *How children discover new strategies.* Hillsdale, NJ: Erlbaum.

Siegler, R. S., & Richards, D. D. (1980). *College students' prototypes of children's intelligence.* Paper presented at the annual meeting of the American Psychological Association, New York.

Siegler, R. S., & Svetina, M. (2006). What leads children to adopt new strategies? A microgenetic/cross-sectional study of class inclusion. *Child Development, 77,* 997–1015.

Siervogel, R. M., Maynard, L. M., Wisemandle, W. A., Roche, A. F., Guo, S. S., Chumlea, W. C., & Towne, B. (2000). Annual changes in total body fat and fat-free mass in children from 8 to 18 years in relation to changes in body mass index: The Fels Longitudinal Study. *Annals of the New York Academy of Sciences, 904,* 420–423.

Signorella, M. L., Bigler, R. S., & Liben, L. S. (1993). Developmental differences in children's gender schemata about others: A meta-analytic review. *Developmental Review, 13,* 147–183.

Signorielli, N. (2001). Television's gender-role images and contribution to stereotyping. In D. G. Singer & J. L. Singer (Eds.), *Handbook of children and the media* (pp. 341–358). Thousand Oaks, CA: Sage.

Silberglitt, B., Appleton, J. J., Burns, M. K., & Jimerson, S. R. (2006). Examining the effects of grade retention on student reading performance: A longitudinal study. *Journal of School Psychology, 44,* 255–270.

Silk, J. S., Morris, A. S., Kanaya, T., & Steinberg, L. D. (2003). Psychological control and autonomy granting: Opposite ends of a continuum or distinct constructs? *Journal of Research on Adolescence, 13,* 113–128.

Silk, J. S., Sessa, F. M., Morris, A. S., & Steinberg, L. D. (2004). Neighborhood cohesion as a buffer against hostile maternal parenting. *Journal of Family Psychology, 18,* 135–146.

Silvén, M. (2001). Attention in very young infants predicts learning of first words. *Infant Behavior and Development, 24,* 229–237.

Silver, E. J., & Bauman, L. J. (2006). The association of sexual experience with attitudes, beliefs, and risk behaviors of inner-city adolescents. *Journal of Research on Adolescence, 16,* 29–45.

Silverman, B. E., Goodine, W. M., Ladouceur, M. G., & Quinn, J. (2001). Learning needs of nurses working in Canada's First Nations communities. *Journal of Continuing Education in Nursing, 32,* 38–45.

Silverman, D. (2006). *Interpreting qualitative data: Methods for analyzing talk, text, and interaction.* Thousand Oaks, CA: Sage.

Silverman, J. G., Raj, A., Mucci, L. A., & Hathaway, J. E. (2001). Dating violence against adolescent girls and associated substance use, unhealthy weight control, sexual risk behavior, pregnancy, and suicidality. *Journal of the American Medical Association, 286,* 572–579.

Sim, T. N., & Koh, S. F. (2003). A domain conceptualization of adolescent susceptibility to peer pressure. *Journal of Research on Adolescence, 13,* 57–80.

Simcock, G., & DeLoache, J. (2006). Get the picture? The effects of iconicity on toddlers' reenactment from picture books. *Developmental Psychology, 42,* 1352–1357.

Simcock, G., & Hayne, H. (2002). Breaking the barrier? Children fail to translate their preverbal memories into language. *Psychological Science, 13,* 225–231.

Simcock, G., & Hayne, H. (2003). Age-related changes in verbal and nonverbal memory during early childhood. *Developmental Psychology, 39,* 805–814.

Simion, F., Cassia, V. M., Turati, C., & Valenza, E. (2001). The origins of face perception: Specific versus non-specific mechanisms. *Infant and Child Development, 10,* 59–65.

Simmons, R. (2002). *Odd girl out: The hidden culture of aggression in girls.* New York: Harcourt.

Simmons, R. G., & Blyth, D. A. (1987). *Moving into adolescence.* New York: Aldine De Gruyter.

Simoneau, M., & Markovits, H. (2003). Reasoning with premises that are not empirically true: Evidence for the role of inhibition and retrieval. *Developmental Psychology, 39,* 964–975.

Simons, L. G., Chen, Y.-F., Simons, R. L., Brody, G., & Cutrona, C. (2006). Parenting practices and child adjustment in different types of households: A study of African-American families. 803–825.

Simons, R. L., Whitbeck, L. B., Conger, R. D., & Chyi-In, W. (1991). Intergenerational transmission of harsh parenting. *Developmental Psychology, 27,* 159–171.

Simons-Morton, B. G., & Haynie, D. L. (2003). Growing up drug free: A developmental challenge. In M. H. Bornstein, L. Davidson, C. L. M. Keyes, K. A. Moore, & the Center for Child Well-Being (Eds.), *Well-being: Positive development across the life course* (pp. 109–122). Mahwah, NJ: Erlbaum.

Simonton, D. K. (2000). Creativity: Cognitive, personal, developmental, and social aspects. *American Psychologist, 55,* 151–158.

Simpkins, S. D., & Parke, R. D. (2001). The relations between parental friendships and children's friendships: Self-reports and observational analysis. *Child Development, 72,* 569–582.

Simpson, J. A., Rholes, W. S., Campbell, L., Tran, S., & Wilson, C. L. (2003). Adult attachment, the transition to parenthood, and depressive symptoms. *Journal of Personality and Social Psychology, 84,* 1172–1187.

Simpson, J. L., de la Cruz, F., Swerdloff, R. S., Samango-Sprouse, C., Skakkebaek, N. E., & Graham, J. M., Jr. (2003). Klinefelter syndrome: Expanding the phenotype and identifying new research directions. *Genetic Medicine, 5,* 460–468.

Simpson, J. M. (2001). Infant stress and sleep deprivation as an aetiological basis for the sudden infant death syndrome. *Early Human Development, 61,* 1–43.

Singer, D. G., & Singer, J. L. (2005). *Imagination and play in the electronic age.* Cambridge, MA: Harvard University Press.

Singer, L. T., Minnes, S., Short, E., Arendt, R., Farkas, K., Lewis, B., & Klein, N. (2004). Cognitive outcomes of preschool children with prenatal cocaine exposure. *Journal of the American Medical Association, 291,* 2448–2456.

Singleton, J. L., & Newport, E. L. (2004). When learners surpass their models: The acquisition of American Sign Language from inconsistent input. *Cognitive Psychology, 49,* 370–407.

Sinkkonen, J., Anttila, R., & Siimes, M. A. (1998). Pubertal maturation and changes in self-image in early adolescent Finnish boys. *Journal of Youth and Adolescence, 27,* 209–218.

Sippola, L., Bukowski, W. M., & Noll, R. B. (1997). Age differences in children's and early adolescents' liking for same-sex and other-sex peers. *Merrill-Palmer Quarterly, 43,* 547–561.

Sirois, S., & Shultz, T. R. (2003). A connectionist perspective on Piagetian development. In P. T. Quinlan (Ed.), *Connectionist models of development: Developmental processes in real and artificial neural networks* (pp. 13–41). New York: Psychology Press.

Skiba, R. J., & Rausch, M. K. (2006). Zero tolerance, suspension, and expulsion: Questions of equity and effectiveness. In C. M. Evertson & C. S. Weinstein (Eds.), *Handbook of classroom management: Research, practice, and contemporary issues* (pp. 1063–1089). Mahwah, NJ: Erlbaum.

Skinner, B. F. (1957). *Verbal behavior.* New York: Appleton-Century-Crofts.

Skinner, E. A., Zimmer-Gembeck, M. J., & Connell, J. P. (1998). Individual differences and the development of perceived control. *Monographs of the Society for Research in Child Development, 63*(2–3, Serial No. 254).

Skoe, E. E. A. (1998). The ethic of care: Issues in moral development. In E. E. A. Skoe & A. L. von der Lippe (Eds.), *Personality development in adolescence* (pp. 143–171). London: Routledge.

Skoe, E. E., & Diessner, R. (1994). Ethic of care, justice, identity and gender: An extension and replication. *Merrill-Palmer Quarterly, 40,* 102–119.

Slaby, R. G., & Frey, K. S. (1975). Development of gender constancy and selective attention to same-sex models. *Child Development, 46,* 849–856.

Slack, K. S., Holl, J. L., Yoo, J., Amsden, L. B., Collins, E., & Bolger, K. (2007). Welfare, work, and health care access predictors of low-income children's physical health outcomes. *Children and Youth Services Review, 29,* 782–801.

Slade, A., Belsky, J., Aber, J. L., & Phelps, J. L. (1999). Mothers' representations of their relationships with their toddlers: Links to adult attachment and observed mothering. *Developmental Psychology, 35,* 611–619.

Slater, A. (2001). Visual perception. In G. Bremner & A. Fogel (Eds.), *Blackwell handbook of infant development* (pp. 5–34). Malden, MA: Blackwell.

Slater, A., Bremner, G., Johnson, S. P., Sherwood, P., Hayes, R., & Brown, E. (2000). Newborn infants' preference for attractive faces: The role of internal and external facial features. *Infancy, 1,* 265–274.

Slater, A., & Johnson, S. P. (1999). Visual sensory and perceptual abilities of the newborn: Beyond the blooming, buzzing confusion. In A. Slater & S. P. Johnson (Eds.), *The development of sensory, motor and cognitive capacities in early infancy* (pp. 121–141). Hove, UK: Sussex Press.

Slater, A., & Quinn, P. C. (2001). Face recognition in the newborn infant. *Infant and Child Development, 10,* 21–24.

Slaughter, V., Jaakkola, R., & Carey, S. (1999). Constructing a coherent theory: Children's biological understanding of life and death. In M. Siegel & C. C. Petersen (Eds.), *Children's understanding of biology and health* (pp. 71–96). Cambridge, UK: Cambridge University Press.

Slaughter, V., & Lyons, M. (2003). Learning about life and death in early childhood. *Cognitive Psychology, 46,* 1–30.

Slicker, E. K., & Thornberry, I. (2002). Older adolescent well-being and authoritative parenting. *Adolescent and Family Health, 3,* 9–10.

Slobin, D. I. (1982). Universal and particular in the acquisition of language. In L. R. Gleitman & H. E. Wanner (Eds.), *Language acquisition: The state of the art* (pp. 128–170). Cambridge, UK: Cambridge University Press.

Slobin, D. I. (1985). Crosslinguistic evidence for the language-making capacity. In D. I. Slobin (Ed.), *The crosslinguistic study of language acquisition: Vol. 2. Theoretical issues* (pp. 1157–1256). Hillsdale, NJ: Erlbaum.

Slobin, D. I. (Ed.). (1997). *The crosslinguistic study of language acquisition: Vol. 5. Expanding the contexts* (pp. 265–324). Mahwah, NJ: Erlbaum.

Slonims, V., & McConachie, H. (2006). Analysis of mother-infant interaction in infants with Down syndrome and typically developing infants. *American Journal of Mental Retardation, 111,* 273–289.

Slyper, A. H. (2006). The pubertal timing controversy in the USA, and a review of possible causative factors for the advance in timing of onset of puberty. *Clinical Endocrinology, 65,* 1–8.

Small, M. (1998). *Our babies, ourselves.* New York: Anchor.

Smart, J., & Hiscock, H. (2007). Early infant crying and sleeping problems: A pilot study of impact on parental well-being and parent-endorsed strategies for management. *Journal of Paediatrics and Child Health, 43,* 284–290.

Smetana, J. G. (1981). Preschool children's conceptions of moral and social rules. *Child Development, 52,* 1333–1336.

Smetana, J. G. (1985). Preschool children's conceptions of transgressions: Effects of varying moral and conventional domain-related attributes. *Developmental Psychology, 21,* 18–29.

Smetana, J. G. (2002). Culture, autonomy, and personal jurisdiction in adolescent–parent relationships. In R. V. Kail & H. W. Reese (Eds.), *Advances in child development and behavior* (Vol. 29, pp. 51–87). San Diego, CA: Academic Press.

Smetana, J. G. (2006). Social-cognitive domain theory: Consistencies and variations in children's moral and social judgments. In M. Killen & J. G. Smetana (Eds.), *Handbook of moral development* (pp. 119–154). Mahwah, NJ: Erlbaum.

Smetana, J., & Daddis, C. (2002). Domain-specific antecedents of parental psychological control and monitoring: The role of parenting beliefs and practices. *Child Development, 73,* 563–580.

Smith, B. H., Barkley, R. A., & Shapiro, C. J. (2006). Attention-deficit/hyperactivity disorder. In E. J. Mash & R. A. Barkley (Eds.), *Treatment of childhood disorders* (3rd ed., pp. 65–136). New York: Guilford.

Smith, B. L., McGregor, K. K., & Demille, D. (2006). Phonological development in lexically precocious 2-year-olds. *Applied Psycholinguistics, 27,* 355–375.

Smith, C. L., Calkins, S. D., Keane, S. P., Anastopoulos, A. D., & Shelton, T. L. (2004). Predicting stability and change in toddler behavior problems: Contributions of maternal behavior and child gender. *Developmental Psychology, 40,* 29–42.

Smith, C. L., & Tager-Flusberg, H. (1982). Metalinguistic awareness and language development. *Journal of Experimental Child Psychology, 34,* 449–468.

Smith, J., Duncan, G. J., & Lee, K. (2003). The black–white test score gap in young children: Contributions of test and family characteristics. *Applied Developmental Science, 7,* 239–252.

Smith, J., & Ross, H. (2007). Training parents to mediate sibling disputes affects children's negotiation and conflict understanding. *Child Development, 78,* 790–805.

Smith, J. R., Brooks-Gunn, J., Kohen, D., & McCarton, C. (2001). Transitions on and off AFDC: Implications for parenting and children's cognitive development. *Child Development, 72,* 1512–1533.

Smith, K. E., Landry, S. H., Swank, P. R., Baldwin, C. D., Denson, S. E., & Wildin, S. (1996). The relation of medical risk and maternal stimulation with preterm infants' development of cognitive, language and daily living skills. *Journal of Child Psychology and Psychiatry, 37,* 855–864.

Smith, L. B., Jones, S. S., Landau, B., Gershkoff-Stowe, L., & Samuelson, L. (2002). Object name learning provides on-the-job training for attention. *Psychological Science, 13,* 13–19.

Smith, L. B., Quittner, A. L., Osberger, M. J., & Miyamoto, R. (1998). Audition and visual attention: The developmental trajectory in deaf and hearing populations. *Developmental Psychology, 34,* 840–850.

Smith, P., Perrin, S., Yule, W., & Rabe-Hesketh, S. (2001). War exposure and maternal reactions in the psychological adjustment of children from Bosnia-Hercegovina. *Journal of Child Psychology and Psychiatry and Allied Disciplines, 42,* 395–404.

Smith, P. K. (2003). Play and peer relations. In A. Slater & G. Bremner (Eds.), *An introduction to developmental psychology* (pp. 311–333). Malden, MA: Blackwell.

Smith, P. K., Ananiadou, K., & Cowie, H. (2003). Interventions to reduce school bullying. *Canadian Journal of Psychiatry, 48,* 591–599.

Smith, S. L., & Atkin, C. (2003). Television advertising and children: Examining the intended and unintended effects. In E. L. Palmer & B. M. Young (Eds.), *The faces of televisual media: Teaching, violence, selling to children* (pp. 301–326). Mahwah, NJ: Erlbaum.

Snarey, J. (1985). The cross-cultural universality of social-moral development: A critical review of Kohlbergian research. *Psychological Bulletin, 97,* 202–232.

Snarey, J. R. (1995). In a communitarian voice: The sociological expansion of Kohlbergian theory, research, and practice.

In W. M. Kurtines & J. L. Gewirtz (Eds.), *Moral development: An introduction* (pp. 109–134). Boston: Allyn and Bacon.

Snarey, J. R., & Bell, D. (2003). Distinguishing structural and functional models of human development: A response to "What transits in an identity status transition?" *Identity, 3,* 221–230.

Snarey, J. R., Reimer, J., & Kohlberg, L. (1985). The development of social-moral reasoning among kibbutz adolescents: A longitudinal cross-cultural study. *Developmental Psychology, 20,* 3–17.

Snell, E. K., Adam, E. K., & Duncan, G. J. (2007). Sleep and the body mass index and overweight status of children and adolescents. *Child Development, 78,* 309–323.

Snidman, N., Kagan, J., Riordan, L., & Shannon, D. C. (1995). Cardiac function and behavioral reactivity. *Psychophysiology, 32,* 199–207.

Snow, C. E., & Kang, J. Y. (2006). Becoming bilingual, biliterate, and bicultural. In K. A. Renninger & I. E. Sigel (Eds.), *Handbook of child psychology: Vol. 4. Child psychology in practice* (6th ed., pp. 75–102). Hoboken, NJ: Wiley.

Snow, C. E., Pan, B. A., Imbens-Bailey, A., & Herman, J. (1996). Learning how to say what one means: A longitudinal study of children's speech act use. *Social Development, 5,* 56–84.

Snyder, J., Brooker, M., Patrick, M. R., Snyder, A., Schrepferman, L., & Stoolmiller, M. (2003). Observed peer victimization during early elementary school: Continuity, growth, and relation to risk for child antisocial and depressive behavior. *Child Development, 74,* 1881–1898.

So, L. K. H., & Dodd, B. J. (1995). The acquisition of phonology by Cantonese-speaking children. *Journal of Child Language, 22,* 473–495.

Sobel, D. M. (2006). How fantasy benefits young children's understanding of pretense. *Developmental Science, 9,* 63–75.

Society for Research in Child Development. (1993). Ethical standards for research with children. In *Directory of Members* (pp. 337–339). Ann Arbor, MI: Author.

Soderstrom, M., Seidl, A., Nelson, D. G. K., & Jusczyk, P. W. (2003). The prosodic bootstrapping of phrases: Evidence from prelinguistic infants. *Journal of Memory and Language, 49,* 249–267.

Solomon, G. B., & Bredemeier, B. J. L. (1999). Children's moral conceptions of gender stratification in sport. *International Journal of Sport Psychology, 30,* 350–368.

Solomon, G. E. A., Johnosn, S. C., Zaitchik, D., & Carey, S. (1996). Like father, like son: Children's understanding of how and why offspring resemble their parents. *Child Development, 67,* 151–171.

Somerville, J. A., Woodward, A. L., & Needham, A. (2004). Action experience alters 3-month-old infants' perception of others' actions. *Cognition, 96,* B1–B11.

Sondergaard, C., Henriksen, T. B., Obel, C., & Wisborg, K. (2002). Smoking during pregnancy and infantile colic. *Journal of the American Academy of Child and Adolescent Psychiatry, 41,* 147.

Sontag, C. W., Baker, C. T., & Nelson, V. L. (1958). Mental growth and personality development: A longitudinal study. *Monographs of the Society for Research in Child Development, 23*(2, Serial No. 68).

Sophian, C. (1995). Representation and reasoning in early numerical development: Counting, conservation, and comparisons between sets. *Child Development, 66,* 559–577.

Sørensen, T. I., Holst, C., & Stunkard, A. J. (1998). Adoption study of environmental modifications of the genetic influences on obesity. *International Journal of Obesity and Related Metabolic Disorders, 22,* 73–81.

Sosa, R., Kennell, J., Klaus, M., Robertson, S., & Urrutia, J. (1980). The effect of a supportive companion on perinatal problems, length of labor, and mother–infant interaction. *New England Journal of Medicine, 303,* 597–600.

Sowell, E. R., Thompson, P. M., Welcome, S. E., Henkenius, A. L., Toga, A. W., & Peterson, B. S. (2003). Cortical abnormalities in children and adolescents with attention-deficit hyperactivity disorder. *Lancet, 362,* 1699–1707.

Sowell, E. R., Trauner, D. A., Camst, A., & Jernigan, T. (2002). Development of cortical and subcortical brain structures in childhood and adolescence: A structural MRI study. *Developmental Medicine and Child Neurology, 44,* 4–16.

Spadoni, A. D., McGee, C. L., Frayer, S. L., & Riley, E. P. (2007). Neuroimaging and fetal alcohol spectrum disorders. *Neuroscience and Biobehavioral Reviews, 31,* 239–245.

Spear, L. P. (2004). Adolescent brain development and animal models. In R. E. Dahl & L. P. Spear (Eds.), *Adolescent brain development: Vulnerabilities and opportunities* (pp. 23–26). New York: New York Academy of Sciences.

Spearman, C. (1927). *The abilities of man: Their nature and measurement.* New York: Macmillan.

Spears G., Seydegart, K., & Zulinov, P. (2005). *Young Canadians in a Wired World–Phase II, Student Survey.* Media Awareness Network. Retrieved from www.media-awareness.ca/english/research/YCWW/index.cfm

Spector, A. Z. (2006). Fatherhood and depression: A review of risks, effects, and clinical application. *Issues in Mental Health Nursing, 27,* 867–883.

Speece, D. L., Ritchey, K. D., Cooper, D. H., Roth, F. P., & Schatschneider, C. (2004). Growth in early reading skills from kindergarten to third grade. *Contemporary Educational Psychology, 29,* 312–332.

Speece, M. W., & Brent, S. B. (1996). The development of children's understanding of death. In C. A. Corr & D. M. Corr (Eds.), *Handbook of childhood death and bereavement* (pp. 29–50). New York: Springer.

Speicher, B. (1994). Family patterns of moral judgment during adolescence and early adulthood. *Developmental Psychology, 30,* 624–632.

Spelke, E. S. (2004). Core knowledge. In N. Kanwisher & J. Duncan (Eds.), *Attention and performance* (Vol. 20, pp. 29–56). Oxford, UK: Oxford University Press.

Spelke, E. S., & Hermer, L. (1996). Early cognitive development: Objects and space. In R. Gelman & T. K. Au (Eds.), *Perceptual and cognitive development* (pp. 71–114). San Diego: Academic Press.

Spelke, E. S., & Kinzler, K. D. (2007). Core knowledge. *Developmental Science, 10,* 89–96.

Spelke, E. S., Phillips, A. T., & Woodward, A. L. (1995). Infants' knowledge of object motion and human action. In A. Premack (Ed.), *Causal understanding in cognition and culture* (pp. 4–78). Oxford, UK: Clarendon Press.

Spence, M. J., & DeCasper, A. J. (1987). Prenatal experience with low-frequency maternal voice sounds influences neonatal perception of maternal voice samples. *Infant Behavior and Development, 10,* 133–142.

Spencer, J. P., & Schöner, G. (2003). Bridging the representational gap in the dynamic systems approach to development. *Developmental Science, 6,* 392–412.

Spencer, J. P., Verejiken, B., Diedrich, F. J., & Thelen, E. (2000). Posture and the emergence of manual skills. *Developmental Science, 3,* 216–233.

Spencer, P. E. (2000). Looking without listening: Is audition a prerequisite for normal development of visual attention in infancy? *Journal of Deaf Studies and Education, 5,* 291–302.

Spencer, P. E., & Lederberg, A. (1997). Different modes, different models: Communication and language of young deaf children and their mothers. In L. B. Adamson & M. Romski (Eds.), *Communication and language acquisition: Discoveries from atypical development* (pp. 203–230). Baltimore, MD: Paul H. Brookes.

Spencer, P. E., & Meadow-Orlans, K. P. (1996). Play, language, and maternal responsiveness: A longitudinal study of deaf and hearing infants. *Child Development, 67,* 3176–3191.

Spere, K. A., Schmidt, L. A., Theall-Honey, L. A., & Martin-Chang, S. (2004). Expressive and receptive language skills of temperamentally shy preschoolers. *Infant and Child Development, 13,* 123–133.

Spirito, A., & Esposito-Smythers, C. (2006). Attempted and completed suicide. *Annual Review of Clinical Psychology, 2,* 237–266.

Spirito, A., Valeri, S., Boergers, J., & Donaldson, D. (2003). Predictors of continued suicidal behavior in adolescents following a suicide attempt. *Journal of Clinical Child and Adolescent Psychology, 32,* 284–289.

Spitz, R. A. (1946). Anaclitic depression. *Psychoanalytic Study of the Child, 2,* 313–342.

Spock, B., & Needlman, R. (2004). *Dr. Spock's baby and child care* (8th ed.). New York: Pocket.

Sridhar, D., & Vaughn, S. (2001). Social functioning of students with learning disabilities. In D. P. Hallahan & B. K. Keogh (Eds.), *Research and global perspectives in learning disabilities* (pp. 65–91). Mahwah, NJ: Erlbaum.

Sroufe, L. A. (1979). The ontogenesis of emotion. In J. D. Osofsky (Ed.), *Handbook of infant development* (pp. 462–516). New York: Wiley.

Sroufe, L. A. (1985). Attachment classification from the perspective of infant–caregiver relationships and infant temperament. *Child Development, 56,* 1–14.

Sroufe, L. A. (2002). From infant attachment to promotion of adolescent autonomy: Prospective, longitudinal data on the role of parents in development. In J. G. Borkowski & S. L. Ramey (Eds.), *Parenting and the child's world* (pp. 187–202). Mahwah, NJ: Erlbaum.

Sroufe, L. A. (2005). Attachment and development: A prospective, longitudinal study from birth to adulthood. *Attachment and Human Development, 7,* 349–367.

Sroufe, L. A., Egeland, B., Carlson, E., & Collins, W. (2005). *Minnesota Study of Risk and Adaptation from birth to maturity: The development of the person.* New York: Guilford.

Sroufe, L. A., & Waters, E. (1976). The ontogenesis of smiling and laughter: A perspective on the organization of development in infancy. *Psychological Review, 83,* 173–189.

Sroufe, L. A., & Wunsch, J. P. (1972). The development of laughter in the first year of life. *Child Development, 43,* 1324–1344.

St Clair-Thompson, H. L., & Gathercole, S. E. (2006). Executive functions and achievements in school: Shifting, updating, inhibition, and working memory. *Quarterly Journal of Experimental Psychology, 59,* 745–759.

St James-Roberts, I. (2007). Helping parents to manage infant crying and sleeping: A review of the evidence and its implications for services. *Child Abuse Review, 16,* 47–69.

St James-Roberts, I., Goodwin, J., Peter, B., Adams, D., & Hunt, S. (2003). Individual differences in responsivity to a neurobehavioural examination predict crying patterns of 1-week-old infants at home. *Developmental Medicine and Child Neurology, 45,* 400–407.

St James-Roberts, I., & Halil, T. (1991). Infant crying patterns in the first year: Normal community and clinical findings. *Journal of Child Psychology and Psychiatry, 32,* 951–968.

St. Louis, G. R., & Liem, J. H. (2005). Ego identity, ethnic identity, and the psychosocial well-being of ethnic minority and majority college students. *Identity, 5,* 227–246.

Stacey, J., & Biblarz, T. (2001). (How) Does the sexual orientation of parents matter? *American Sociological Review, 66,* 159–183.

Stack, D. M., & Muir, D. W. (1992). Adult tactile stimulation during face-to-face interactions modulates five-month-olds' affect and attention. *Child Development, 63,* 1509–1525.

Staff, J., & Uggan, C. (2003). The fruits of good work: Early work experiences and adolescent deviance. *Journal of Research in Crime and Delinquency, 40,* 263–290.

Stager, C. L., & Werker, J. F. (1997). Infants listen for more phonetic detail in speech perception than in word-learning tasks. *Nature, 388,* 381–382.

Stahl, S. A., & Miller, P. D. (2006). Whole language and language experience approaches for beginning reading: A quantitative research synthesis. In D. A. Dougherty Stahl & M. C. McKenna (Eds.), *Reading research at work: Foundations of effective practice* (pp. 9–35). New York: Guilford.

Stams, G. J., Brugman, D., Deković, M., van Rosmalen, L., van der Laan, P., & Gibbs, J. C. (2006). The moral judgment of juvenile delinquents: A meta-analysis. *Journal of Abnormal Child Psychology, 34,* 697–713.

Stams, G. J. M., Juffer, R., & van IJzendoorn, M. H. (2002). Maternal sensitivity, infant attachment, and temperament in early childhood predict adjustment in middle childhood: The case of adopted children and their biologically unrelated parents. *Developmental Psychology, 38,* 806–821.

Standley, J. M. (1998). The effect of music and multimodal stimulation on responses of premature infants in neonatal intensive care. *Pediatric Nursing, 24,* 532–538.

Stanley, C., Murray, L., & Stein, A. (2004). The effect of postnatal depression on mother–infant interaction, infant response to the still-face perturbation, and performance on an instrumental learning task.

Development and Psychopathology, 16, 1–18.

Stanovich, K. E. (2004). *How to think straight about psychology* (7th ed.). Boston: Allyn and Bacon.

Starkey, P. (1992). The early development of numerical reasoning. *Cognition, 43,* 93–126.

Statistics Canada. (2003). *Women in Canada: Work chapter updates.* Retrieved from www.statcan.ca/cgi-bin/downpub/freepub.cgi

Statistics Canada. (2004, July 8). Household Internet use survey. *The Daily.* Retrieved from www.statcan.ca/Daily/English/040708/d040708a.htm

Statistics Canada. (2005a, February 7). Child care. *The Daily.* Retrieved from www.statcan.ca/Daily/English/050207/d050207b.htm

Statistics Canada. (2005b). *Divorces.* Retrieved from www.statcan.ca

Statistics Canada. (2005c, December 16). Education matters: Trends in dropout rates among the provinces. *The Daily.* Retrieved from www.statcan.ca/Daily/English/050721/d050721a.htm

Statistics Canada. (2005d, May 3). Food insecurity in Canadian households. *The Daily.* Retrieved from www.statcan.ca/Daily/English/050503/d050503b.htm

Statistics Canada. (2005e). *Infant mortality rates.* Retrieved from www.statcan.ca/english/Pgdb/health21.htm

Statistics Canada. (2005f). *Statistics Canada data bank and analysis of television viewing in Canada.* Retrieved from www.statcan.ca/english/freepub/87-008-GIE/sect/tvmain.htm

Statistics Canada. (2006a). *Canadian Community Health Survey: Public use microdata file, cycle 3.1 (2005).* Retrieved from www.statcan.ca/bsolc/english/bsolc?catno=82M0013XCB

Statistics Canada. (2006b, August 15). Canadian Internet Use Survey. *The Daily.* Retrieved from www.statcan.ca/Daily/English/060815/d060815b.htm

Statistics Canada. (2006c). Detailed average household expenditure by household type, Canada, 2005 (Detailed Table 4). *Survey of Household Spending, 2005.* Statistics Canada Catalogue no. 62F0034XDB.

Statistics Canada. (2006d). *Education indicators in Canada: Report of the Pan-Canadian Education Indicators Program 2005.* Retrieved from www.statcan.ca/english/freepub/81-582-XIE/81-582-XIE2006001.htm

Statistics Canada. (2006e). *Television viewing data bank, fall 2004: Television viewing data tables.* Catalogue no. 87F0006XIE .Retrieved from www.statcan.ca/bsolc/english/bsolc?catno=87F0006X&CHROPG=1

Statistics Canada. (2006f, November 7). University enrolment. *The Daily.* Retrieved from www.statcan.ca/Daily/English/061107/d061107a.htm

Statistics Canada. (2007a). *Aboriginal peoples of Canada; 2001 census.* Retrieved from www12.statcan.ca/english/census01/Products/standard/themes/DataProducts.cfm?S=1&T=45&ALEVEL=2&FREE=0

Statistics Canada. (2007b). *Adult and youth charged, by detailed offences for Canada, provinces and territories, annual (number), 1977–2006.* Table 252-0014. Retrieved from www.cansim2.statcan.ca

Statistics Canada. (2007c). *Births—2005.* Retrieved from www.statcan.ca/english/freepub/84F0210XIE/84F0210XIE2005001.htm

Statistics Canada. (2007d). *Deaths, by cause, Chapter XVIII: Symptoms, signs and abnormal clinical and laboratory findings, not elsewhere classified (R00 to R99), age group and sex, Canada, annual (number).* CANSIM Table 102-0538. Retrieved from www.cansim2.statcan.ca/cgi-win/cnsmcgi.exe?CANSIMFile=CII/CII_1_E.HTM&RootDir=CII/&LANG=E

Statistics Canada. (2007e). *Deaths, by selected grouped causes, age group and sex, Canada, provinces and territories, annual, 2002–2004.* CANSIM Table 102-0551. Retrieved from www40.statcan.ca/l01/cst01/hlth66a.htm

Statistics Canada. (2007f). *Detailed mother tongue (103), knowledge of official languages (5), age groups (17A) and sex (3) for the population of Canada, provinces, territories, census divisions and census subdivisions, 2006 census—20% sample data.* Retrieved from www.statcan.ca/bsolc/english/bsolc?catno=97-555-XWE2006016

Statistics Canada. (2007g). *Family portrait: Continuity and change in Canadian families and households in 2006: National portrait: Households.* Retrieved from www12.statcan.ca/english/census06/analysis/famhouse/pdf/97-553-XIE2006001.pdf

Statistics Canada. (2007h). *Income in Canada, 2005.* Retrieved from www.statcan.ca/english/freepub/75-202-XIE/75-202-XIE2005000.pdf

Statistics Canada. (2007i). *Infant mortality by age group and sex, Canada, annual (2004). CANSIM Table 102-05061.* Retrieved from cansim2.statcan.ca/cgi-win/cnsmcgi.exe?CANSIMFile=CII/CII_1_E.HTM&RootDir=CII/&LANG=E

Statistics Canada. (2007j). *Labour force survey estimates (LFS), by educational attainment, sex and age group, annual* (persons unless otherwise noted). Table 282-0004. CANSIM database. Retrieved from cansim2.statcan.ca

Statistics Canada. (2007k). *Labour force survey estimates (LFS), by National Occupational Classification for Statistics (NOC-S) and sex, annual.* CANSIM Table 282-0010. Retrieved from estat.statcan.ca

Statistics Canada. (2007l). *Marital status, common-law status, families, dwellings and households, 2001—Provinces and territories in Canada (table), 2001 census of population (provinces, census divisions, municipalities)* (database). Retrieved from estat.statcan.ca.ezproxy.tru.ca/cgi-win/cnsmcgi.exe?Lang=E&ESTATFile=EStat\English\E-Main.htm

Statistics Canada. (2007m). *Women in Canada: Work chapter updates, 2006.* Catalogue no. 89F0133XIE. Retrieved from www.statcan.ca/english/freepub/89F0133XIE/89F0133XIE2006000.pdf

Statistics Canada. (2008). *Aboriginal peoples in Canada in 2006: Inuit, Métis, and First Nations, 2006 census: Findings.* Retrieved from www12.statcan.ca/english/census06/analysis/aboriginal/index.cfm

Statistics Canada & OECD (Organisation for Economic Cooperation and Development). (2005). *Learning a living: First results of the Adult Literacy and Life Skills Survey.* Retrieved from http://www.statcan.ca/english/freepub/89-603-XIE/89-603-XIE2005001

Stattin, H., & Kerr, M. (2000). Parental monitoring: A reinterpretation. *Child Development, 71,* 1072–1085.

Stattin, H., & Magnusson, D. (1990). *Pubertal maturation in female development.* Hillsdale, NJ: Erlbaum.

Staub, F. C., & Stern, E. (2002). The nature of teachers' pedagogical content beliefs matters for students' achievement gains: Quasi-experimental evidence from elementary mathematics. *Journal of Educational Psychology, 94,* 344–355.

Steele, C. M. (1997). A threat in the air: How stereotypes shape intellectual identity and performance. *American Psychologist, 52,* 613–629.

Steele, H., Steele, M., & Fonagy, P. (1996). Associations among attachment classifications of mothers, fathers, and their infants. *Child Development, 67,* 541–555.

Steele, J. (2003). Children's gender stereotypes about math: The role of stereotype stratification. *Journal of Applied Social Psychology, 33,* 2587–2606.

Steele, S., Joseph, R. M., & Tager-Flusberg, H. (2003). Developmental change in theory of mind abilities in children with autism. *Journal of Austism and Developmental Disorders, 33,* 461–467.

Stehr-Green, P., Tull, P., Stellfeld, M., Mortenson, P. B., & Simpson, D. (2003). Autism and thimerosal-containing vaccines: Lack of consistent evidence for an association. *American Journal of Preventive Medicine, 25,* 101–106.

Stein, J. H., & Reiser, L. W. (1994). A study of white middle-class adolescent boys' responses to "semenarche" (the first ejaculation). *Journal of Youth and Adolescence, 23,* 373–384.

Stein, N., & Levine, L. J. (1999). The early emergence of emotional understanding and appraisal: Implications for theories of development. In T. Dalgleish & M. J. Power (Eds.), *Handbook of cognition and emotion* (pp. 383–408). Chichester, UK: Wiley.

Stein, Z., Susser, M., Saenger, G., & Marolla, F. (1975). *Famine and human development: The Dutch hunger winter of 1944–1945.* New York: Oxford University Press.

Steinberg, L. D. (1986). Latchkey children and susceptibility to peer pressure: An ecological analysis. *Developmental Psychology, 22,* 433–439.

Steinberg, L. D. (2001). We know some things: Parent–adolescent relationships in retrospect and prospect. *Journal of Research on Adolescence, 11,* 1–19.

Steinberg, L., Blatt-Eisengart, I., & Cauffman, E. (2006). Patterns of competence and adjustment among adolescents from authoritative, authoritarian, indulgent, and neglectful homes: A replication in a sample of serious juvenile offenders. *Journal of Research on Adolescence, 16,* 47–58.

Steinberg, L. D. (2004). *The ten basic principles of good parenting.* New York: Simon & Schuster.

Steinberg, L. D., Darling, N. E., & Fletcher, A. C. (1995). Authoritative parenting and adolescent development: An ecological journey. In P. Moen, G. H. Elder, & K. Luscher (Eds.), *Examining lives in context* (pp. 423–466). Washington, DC: American Psychological Association.

Steinberg, L. D., & Morris, A. S. (2001). Adolescent development. *Annual Review of Psychology, 52,* 83–110.

Steinberg, L. D., & Silk, J. S. (2002). Parenting adolescents. In M. H. Bornstein (Ed.), *Handbook of parenting: Vol. 1. Children and parenting* (2nd ed., pp. 103–134). Mahwah, NJ: Erlbaum.

Steiner, J. E. (1979). Human facial expression in response to taste and smell stimulation. In H. W. Reese & L. P. Lipsitt (Eds.), *Advances in child development and behavior* (Vol. 13, pp. 257–295). New York: Academic Press.

Steiner, J. E., Glaser, D., Hawilo, M. E., & Berridge, D. C. (2001). Comparative expression of hedonic impact: Affective reactions to taste by human infants and other primates. *Neuroscience and Biobehavioral Review, 25,* 53–74.

Steinhausen, C. (2006). Eating disorders: Anorexia nervosa and bulimia nervosa. In C. Gillberg, R. Harrington, & H. Steinhausen (Eds.), *A clinician's handbook of child and adolescent psychiatry* (pp. 272–303). New York: Cambridge University Press.

Stenberg, C., & Campos, J. (1990). The development of anger expressions in infancy. In N. Stein, B. Leventhal, & T. Trabasso (Eds.), *Psychological and biological approaches to emotion* (pp. 247–282). Hillsdale, NJ: Erlbaum.

Stenberg, C., Campos, J., & Emde, R. (1983). The facial expression of anger in seven-month-old infants. *Child Development, 54,* 178–184.

Stenberg, G. (2003). Effects of maternal inattentiveness on infant social referencing. *Infant and Child Development, 12,* 399–419.

Stern, M., & Karraker, K. H. (1989). Sex stereotyping of infants: A review of gender labeling studies. *Sex Roles, 20,* 501–522.

Sternberg, R. J. (2001). Beyond g: The theory of successful intelligence. In R. J. Sternberg & E. L. Grigorenko (Eds.), *The general factor of intelligence: How general is it?* (pp. 447–479). Mahwah, NJ: Erlbaum.

Sternberg, R. J. (2002). Intelligence is not just inside the head: The theory of successful intelligence. In J. Aronson (Ed.), *Improving academic achievement* (pp. 227–244). San Diego, CA: Academic Press.

Sternberg, R. J. (2003a). A broad view of intelligence: The theory of successful intelligence. *Consulting Psychology Journal: Practice and Research, 55,* 139–154.

Sternberg, R. J. (2003b). The development of creativity as a decision-making process. In R. K. Sawyer, V. John-Steiner, S. Moran, R. J. Sternberg, D. H. Feldman, J. Nakamura, & M. Csikszentmihalyi (Eds.), *Creativity and development* (pp. 91–138). New York: Oxford University Press.

Sternberg, R. J. (2005). The triarchic theory of successful intelligence. In D. P. Flanagan & P. L. Harrison (Eds.), *Contemporary intellectual assessment: Theories, tests, and issues* (pp. 103–119). New York: Guilford.

Sternberg, R. J., Castejaon, J. L., Prieto, M. D., Hautaméaki, J., & Grigorenko, E. L. (2001). Confirmatory factor analysis of the Sternberg Triarchic Abilities Test (multiple-choice items) in three international samples: An empirical test of the triarchic theory of intelligence. *European Journal of Psychological Assessment, 17,* 1–16.

Sternberg, R. J., & Detterman, D. K. (1986). *What is intelligence?* Norwood, NJ: Ablex.

Sternberg, R. J., Forsythe, G. B., Hedlund, J., Horvath, J. A., Wagner, R. K., Williams, W. M., Snook, S. A., & Grigorenko, E. L. (2000). *Practical intelligence in everyday life.* Cambridge, UK: Cambridge University Press.

Sternberg, R. J., & Grigorenko, E. L. (2002). *Dynamic testing.* New York: Cambridge University Press.

Sternberg, R. J., Grigorenko, E. L., Ferrari, M., & Clinkenbeard, P. (1999). A triarchic analysis of an aptitude-treatment interaction. *European Journal of Psychological Assessment, 15,* 1–11.

Sternberg, R. J., Grigorenko, E. L., & Kidd, K. K. (2005). Intelligence, race, and genetics. *American Psychologist, 60,* 46–59.

Sternberg, R. J., & Jarvin, L. (2003). Alfred Binet's contributions as a paradigm for impact in psychology. In R. J. Sternberg (Ed.), *The anatomy of impact: What makes the great works of psychology great?* (pp. 89–107). Washington, DC: American Psychological Association.

Sternberg, R. J., & Lubart, T. I. (1991). An investment theory of creativity and its development. *Human Development, 34,* 1–31.

Sternberg, R. J., & Lubart, T. I. (1996). Investing in creativity. *American Psychologist, 51,* 677–688.

Stetsenko, A., Little, T. D., Gordeeva, T., Grassof, M., & Oettingen, G. (2000). Gender effects in children's beliefs about school performance: A cross-cultural study. *Child Development, 71,* 517–527.

Stevenson, H. W., Lee, S., & Mu, X. (2000). Successful achievement in mathematics: China and the United States. In C. F. M. van Lieshout & P. G. Heymans (Eds.), *Developing talent across the lifespan* (pp. 167–183). Philadelphia: Psychology Press.

Stevenson, R., & Pollitt, C. (1987). The acquisition of temporal terms. *Journal of Child Language, 14,* 533–545.

Stevens-Simon, C., Sheeder, J., & Harter, S. (2005). Teen contraceptive decisions: Childbearing intentions are the tip of the iceberg. *Women and Health, 42,* 55–73.

Steward, D. K. (2001). Behavioral characteristics of infants with nonorganic failure to thrive during a play interaction. *American Journal of Maternal Child Nursing, 26,* 79–85.

Stewart, P., Reihman, J., Lonky, E., Darvill, T., & Pagano, J. (2000). Prenatal PCB exposure and neonatal behavioral assessment scale (NBAS) performance. *Neurotoxicology and Teratology, 22,* 21–29.

Stewart, R. B., Jr. (1990). *The second child: Family transition and adjustment.* Newbury Park, CA: Sage.

Stewart-Brown, S., & Edmunds, L. (2007). *Educating people to be emotionally intelligent* (pp. 241–257). Westport, CT: Praeger.

Stice, E. (2003). Puberty and body image. In C. Hayward (Ed.), *Gender differences at puberty* (pp. 61–76). New York: Cambridge University Press.

Stice, E., Presnell, K., & Bearman, S. K. (2001). Relation of early menarche to depression, eating disorders, substance abuse, and comorbid psychopathology among adolescent girls. *Developmental Psychology, 37,* 608–619.

Stifter, C. A., Coulehan, C. M., & Fish, M. (1993). Linking employment to attachment: The mediating effects of maternal separation anxiety and interactive behavior. *Child Development, 64,* 1451–1460.

Stiles, J. (2001a). Neural plasticity in cognitive development. *Developmental Neuropsychology, 18,* 237–272.

Stiles, J. (2001b). Spatial cognitive development. In C. A. Nelson & M. Luciana (Eds.), *Handbook of developmental cognitive neuroscience* (pp. 399–414). Cambridge, MA: MIT Press.

Stiles, J., Bates, E. A., Thal, D., Trauner, D. A., & Reilly, J. (2002). Linguistic and spatial cognitive development in children with pre- and perinatal focal brain injury: A ten-year overview from the San Diego longitudinal project. In M. H. Johnson & Y. Munakata (Eds.), *Brain development and cognition: A reader* (2nd ed., pp. 272–291). Malden, MA: Blackwell.

Stiles, J., Moses, P., Roe, K., Akshoomoff, N. A., Trauner, D., & Hesselink, J. (2003). Alternative brain organization after prenatal cerebral injury: Convergent fMRI and cognitive data. *Journal of the International Neuropsychological Society, 9,* 604–622.

Stiles, J., Reilly, J., Paul, B., & Moses, P. (2005). Cognitive development following early brain injury: Evidence for neural adaptation. *Trends in Cognitive Sciences, 9,* 136–143.

Stinchcomb, J. B., Bazemore, G., & Riestenberg, N. (2006). Beyond zero tolerance: Restoring justice in secondary schools. *Youth Violence and Juvenile Justice, 4,* 123–147.

Stipek, D. (1995). The development of pride and shame in toddlers. In J. P. Tangney & K. W. Fischer (Eds.), *Self-conscious emotions* (pp. 237–252). New York: Guilford.

Stipek, D. (2004). Teaching practices in kindergarten and first grade: Different strokes for different folks. *Early Childhood Research Quarterly, 19,* 548–568.

Stipek, D. J., & Byler, P. (1997). Early childhood education teachers: Do they practice what they preach? *Early Childhood Research Quarterly, 12,* 305–326.

Stipek, D. J., & Byler, P. (2001). Academic achievement and social behaviors associated with age of entry into kindergarten. *Journal of Applied Developmental Psychology, 22,* 175–189.

Stipek, D. J., Gralinski, J. H., & Kopp, C. B. (1990). Self-concept development in the toddler years. *Developmental Psychology, 26,* 972–977.

Stipek, D. J., Recchia, S., & McClintic, S. (1992). Self-evaluation in young children. *Monographs of the Society for Research in Child Development, 57*(1, Serial No. 226).

Stoch, M. B., Smythe, P. M., Moodie, A. D., & Bradshaw, D. (1982). Psychosocial outcome and CT findings after growth undernourishment during infancy: A 20-year developmental study. *Developmental Medicine and Child Neurology, 24,* 419–436.

Stocker, C. J., Arch, J. R., & Cawthorne, M. A. (2005). Fetal origins of insulin resistance and obesity. *Proceedings of the Nutrition Society, 64,* 143–151.

Stockman, N. K. A., Schenkel, T. C., Brown, J. N., & Duncan, A. M. (2005). Comparison of energy and nutrient intakes among meals and snacks of adolescent males. *Preventive Medicine, 41,* 203–210.

Stoel-Gammon, C. (1998). The role of babbling and phonology in early linguistic development. In A. M. Wetherby, S. F. Warren, & J Reichle (Eds.), *Transitions in prelinguistic communication* (pp. 87–110). Baltimore, MD: Paul H. Brookes.

Stoel-Gammon, C., & Sosa, A. V. (2007). Phonological development. In E. Hoff & M. Shatz (Eds.), *Blackwell handbook of language development* (pp. 238–256). Malden, MA: Blackwell.

Stoll, S. (1998). The role of Aktionsart in the acquisition of Russian aspect. *First Language, 18,* 351–378.

Stone, M. R., & Brown, B. B. (1999). Identity claims and projections: Descriptions of self and crowds in secondary school. In J. A. McLellan & M. J. V. Pugh (Eds.), *The role of peer groups in adolescent social identity: Exploring the importance of stability and change* (pp. 7–20). San Francisco: Jossey-Bass.

Stone, R. (2005). *Best classroom management practices for reaching all learners: What award-winning classroom teachers do.* Thousand Oaks, CA: Corwin Press.

Stoneman, Z., Brody, G. H., & MacKinnon, C. E. (1986). Same-sex and cross-sex siblings: Activity choices, roles, behavior, and gender stereotypes. *Sex Roles, 15,* 495–511.

Storch, S. A., & Whitehurst, G. J. (2001). The role of family and home in the literacy development of children from low-income backgrounds. In P. R. Britto & J. Brooks-Gunn (Eds.), *New directions for child and adolescent development* (No. 92, pp. 53–71). San Francisco: Jossey-Bass.

Stormshak, E. A., Bellanti, C. J., Bierman, K. L., & Conduct Problems Prevention Research Group. (1996). The quality of sibling relationships and the development of social competence and behavioral control in aggressive children. *Developmental Psychology, 32,* 79–89.

Stormshak, E. A., Bierman, K. L., Bruschi, C., Dodge, K. A., & Coie, J. D. (1999). The relation between behavior problems and peer preference in different classroom contexts. *Child Development, 70,* 169–182.

Stormshak, E. A., Bierman, K. L., McMahon, R. J., Lengua, L. J., and the Conduct Problems Prevention Research Group. (2000). Parenting practices and child disruptive behavior problems in early elementary school. *Journal of Clinical Child Psychology, 29,* 17–29.

Stouthamer-Loeber, M., Wei, E., Loeber, R., & Masten, A. S. (2004). Desistance from persistent serious delinquency in the transition to adulthood. *Development and Psychopathology, 16,* 897–918.

Strapp, C. M., & Federico, A. (2000). Imitations and repetitions: What do children say following recasts? *First Language, 20,* 273–290.

Straus, M. A., & Stewart, J. H. (1999). Corporal punishment by American parents: National data on prevalence, chronicity, severity, and duration in relation to child and family characteristics. *Clinical Child and Family Psychology Review, 2,* 55–70.

Strauss, M. S., & Curtis, L. E. (1984). Development of numerical concepts in infancy. In C. Sophian (Ed.), *The 18th annual Carnegie Symposium on Cognition: Origins of cognitive skills* (pp. 131 – 155). Hillsdale, NJ: Erlbaum.

Strauss, R. S., & Pollack, H. A. (2003). Social marginalization of overweight children. *Archives of Pediatric and Adolescent Medicine, 157,* 746–752.

Strayer, J., & Roberts, W. (1997). Facial and verbal measures of children's emotions and empathy. *International Journal of Behavioral Development, 20,* 627–649.

Strayer, J., & Roberts, W. (2004a). Children's anger, emotional expressiveness, and empathy: Relations with parents' empathy, emotional expressiveness, and parenting practices. *Social Development, 13,* 229–254.

Strayer, J., & Roberts, W. (2004b). Empathy and observed anger and aggression in five-year-olds. *Social Development, 13,* 1–13.

Strazdins, L., Clements, M. S., Korda, R. J., Broom, D. H., & D'Souza, R. M. (2006). Unsociable work? Nonstandard work schedules, family relationships, and children's well-being. *Journal of Marriage and Family, 68,* 394–410.

Streissguth, A. P., Bookstein, F. L., Barr, H. M., Sampson, P. D., O'Malley, K., & Young, J. K. (2004). Risk factors for adverse life outcomes in fetal alcohol syndrome and fetal alcohol effects. *Journal of Developmental and Behavioral Pediatrics, 25,* 228–238.

Streissguth, A. P., Treder, R., Barr, H. M., Shepard, T., Bleyer, W. A., Sampson, P. D., & Martin, D. (1987). Aspirin and acetaminophen use by pregnant women and subsequent child IQ and attention decrements. *Teratology, 35,* 211–219.

Strelau, J., Zawadzki, B., & Piotrowska, A. (2001). Temperament and intelligence: A psychometric approach to the links between both phenomena. In J. M. Collis & Messick (Eds.), *Intelligence and personality* (pp. 61–78). Mahwah, NJ: Erlbaum.

Streri, A. (2005). Touching for knowing in infancy: The development of manual abilities in very young infants. *European Journal of Developmental Psychology, 2,* 325–343.

Streri, A., Lhote, M., & Dutilleul, S. (2000). Haptic perception in newborns. *Developmental Science, 3,* 319–327.

Stretesky, P. B., & Lynch, M. J. (2001). The relationship between lead exposure and homicide. *Archives of Pediatrics and Adolescent Medicine, 155,* 579–582.

Striano, T., & Rochat, P. (2000). Emergence of selective social referencing in infancy. *Infancy, 1,* 253–264.

Striano, T., Tomasello, M., & Rochat, P. (2001). Social and object support for early symbolic play. *Developmental Science, 4,* 442–455.

Striegel-Moore, R. H., & Franko, D. L. (2006). Adolescent eating disorders. In R. H. Striegel-Moore & D. L. Franko (Eds.), *Child and adolescent psychopathology: Theoretical and clinical implications* (pp. 160–183). New York: Routledge.

Striegel-Moore, R. H., Thompson, D. R., Affenito, S. G., Franko, D. L., Barton, B. A., Schreiber, G. B., Daniels, S. R., Schmidt, M., & Crawford, P. B. (2006). Fruit and vegetable intake: Few adolescent girls meet national guidelines. *Preventive Medicine, 42,* 223–228.

Stright, A. D., Neitzel, C., Sears, K. G., & Hoke-Sinex, L. (2002). Instruction begins in the home: Relations between parental instruction and children's self-regulation in the classroom. *Journal of Educational Psychology, 93,* 456–466.

Strohschein, L. (2005). Parental divorce and child mental health trajectories. *Journal of Marriage and Family, 67,* 1286–1300.

Stromswold, K. (2000). The cognitive neuroscience of language acquisition. In M. S. Gazzaniga (Ed.*), The new cognitive neurosciences* (pp. 909–932). Boston: MIT Press.

Strouse, D. L. (1999). Adolescent crowd orientations: A social and temporal analysis. In J. A. McLellan & M. J. V. Pugh (Eds.), *The role of peer groups in adolescent social identity: Exploring the importance of stability and change* (pp. 37–54). San Francisco: Jossey-Bass.

Studelska, J. V. (2006, Spring). At home in birth. *Midwifery Today,* pp. 32–33.

Styne, D. M. (2003). The regulation of pubertal growth. *Hormone Research, 60*(Suppl.1), 22–26.

Suárez-Orozco, C., & Suárez-Orozco, M. M. (2001). *Children of immigration.*

Cambridge, MA: Harvard University Press.

Suárez-Orozco, C., Todorova, I., & Qin, D. B. (2006). The well-being of immigrant adolescents: A longitudinal perspective on risk and protective factors. In F. A. Villarruel & T. Luster (Eds.), *The crisis in youth mental health: Critical issues and effective programs: Vol. 2. Disorders in adolescence* (pp. 53–83). Westport, CT: Praeger.

Subbotsky, E. V. (1994). Early rationality and magical thinking in preschoolers: Space and time. *British Journal of Developmental Psychology, 12,* 97–108.

Subbotsky, E. V. (2004). Magical thinking in judgments of causation: Can anomalous phenomena affect ontological causal beliefs in children and adults? *British Journal of Developmental Psychology, 22,* 123–152.

Subrahmanyam, K., & Greenfield, P. M. (1996). Effect of video game practice on spatial skills in girls and boys. In P. M. Greenfield & R. R. Cocking (Eds.), *Interacting with video* (pp. 95–114). Norwood, NJ: Ablex.

Subrahmanyam, K., Greenfield, P., Kraut, R., & Gross, E. (2001). The impact of computer use on children's and adolescents' development. *Applied Developmental Psychology, 22,* 7–30.

Subrahmanyam, K., Greenfield, P. M., & Tynes, B. (2004). Constructing sexuality and identity in an online teen chat room. *Applied Developmental Psychology, 25,* 651–666.

Subrahmanyam, K., Smahel, D., & Greenfield, P. (2006). Connecting developmental constructions to the Internet: Identity presentation and sexual exploration in online teen chat rooms. *Developmental Psychology, 42,* 395–406.

Suddendorf, T. (2003). Early representational insight: Twenty-four-month-olds can use a photo to find an object in the world. *Child Development, 74,* 896–904.

Suddendorf, T., Simcock, G., & Nielsen, M. (2007). Visual self-recognition in mirrors and live videos: Evidence for a developmental asynchrony. *Cognitive Development, 22,* 185–196.

Sullivan, H. S. (1953). *The interpersonal theory of psychiatry.* New York: Norton.

Sullivan, M. W., & Lewis, M. (2003). Contextual determinants of anger and other negative expressions in young infants. *Developmental Psychology, 39,* 693–705.

Sullivan, S., & Glanz, J. (2006). *Building effective learning communities: Strategies for leadership, learning, and collaboration.* Thousand Oaks, CA: Corwin Press.

Sundet, J. M., Barlaug, D. G., & Torjussen, T. M. (2004). The end of the Flynn effect? A study of secular trends in mean intelligence test scores of Norwegian conscripts during half a century. *Intelligence, 32,* 349–362.

Super, C. M. (1981). Behavioral development in infancy. In R. H. Monroe, R. L. Monroe, & B. B. Whiting (Eds.), *Handbook of cross-cultural human development* (pp. 181–270). New York: Garland.

Sutcliffe, A. G. (2002). Health risks in babies born after assisted reproduction. *British Medical Journal, 325,* 117–118.

Sutton, M. J., Brown, J. D., Wilson, K. M., & Klein, J. D. (2002). Shaking the tree of forbidden fruit: Where adolescents learn about sexuality and contraception. In J. D. Brown, J. R. Steele, & K. Walsh-Childers (Eds.), *Sexual teens, sexual media* (pp. 25–55). Mahwah, NJ: Erlbaum.

Svensson, A. (2000). Computers in school: Socially isolating or a tool to promote collaboration? *Journal of Educational Computing Research, 22,* 437–453.

Svirsky, M. A., Teoh, S. W., & Neuburger, H. (2004). Development of language and speech perception in congenitally profoundly deaf children as a function of age at cochlear implantation. *Audiology and Neuro-Otology, 9,* 224–233.

Swendsen, J. D., & Mazure, C. M. (2000). Life stress as a risk factor for postpartum depression: Current research and methodological issues. *Clinical Psychology—Science and Practice, 7,* 17–31.

Swingley, D. (2005). Statistical clustering and the contents of the infant vocabulary. *Cognitive Psychology, 50,* 86–132.

Swingley, D., & Aslin, R. N. (2002). Lexical neighborhoods and the word-form representations of 14-month-olds. *Psychological Science, 13,* 480–484.

Symons, D. K. (2001). A dyad-oriented approach to distress and mother–child relationship outcomes in the first 24 months. *Parenting: Science and Practice, 1,* 101–122.

Symons, D. K. (2004). Mental state discourse, theory of mind, and the internalization of self–other understanding. *Developmental Review, 24,* 159–188.

Szaflarski, J. P., Binder, J. R., Possing, E. T., McKiernan, K. A., Ward, B. D., & Hammeke, T. A. (2002). Language lateralization in left-handed and ambidextrous people: fMRI data. *Neurology, 59,* 238–244.

Szepkouski, G. M., Gauvain, M., & Carberry, M. (1994). The development of planning skills in children with and without mental retardation. *Journal of Applied Developmental Psychology, 15,* 187–206.

Szkrybalo, J., & Ruble, D. N. (1999). "God made me a girl": Sex-category constancy judgments and explanations revisited. *Developmental Psychology, 35,* 392–402.

Taatgen, N. A., & Anderson, J. R. (2002). Why do children learn to say "broke"? A model of learning the past tense without feedback. *Cognition, 86,* 123–155.

Tabibi, Z., & Pfeffer, K. (2007). Finding a safe place to cross the road: The effect of distractors and the role of attention in children's identification of safe and dangerous road-crossing sites. *Infant and Child Development, 16,* 193–206.

Tacon, A., & Caldera, Y. (2001). Attachment and parental correlates in late adolescent Mexican American women. *Hispanic Journal of Behavioral Sciences, 23,* 71–88.

Taga, G., Asakawa, K., Maki, A., Konishi, Y., & Koizumi, H. (2003). Brain imaging in awake infants by near-infrared optical topography. *Proceedings of the National Academy of Sciences, 100,* 10722–10727.

Tager-Flusberg, H. (2007). Atypical language development: Autism and other neurodevelopmental disorders. In E. Hoff & M. Shatz (Eds.), *Blackwell handbook of language development* (pp. 432–453). Malden, MA: Blackwell.

Tager-Flusberg, H., & Zukowski, A. (2009). Putting words together: Morphology and syntax in the preschool years. In J. B. Gleason & B. Ratner (Ed.), *The development of language* (7th ed., pp. 139–191). Boston: Allyn and Bacon.

Takahashi, K. (1990). Are the key assumptions of the "Strange Situation" procedure universal? A view from Japanese research. *Human Development, 33,* 23–30.

Takala, M. (2006). The effects of reciprocal teaching on reading comprehension in mainstream and special (SLI) education. *Scandinavian Journal of Educational Research, 50,* 559–576.

Tam, C. W., & Stokes, S. F. (2001). Form and function of negation in early developmental Cantonese. *Journal of Child Language, 28,* 373–391.

Tamis-LeMonda, C. S., Bornstein, M. H., & Baumwell, L. (2001). Maternal responsiveness and children's achievement of language milestones. *Child Development, 72,* 748–767.

Tamis-LeMonda, C. S., Cristofaro, T. N., Rodriguez, E. T., & Bornstein, M. H. (2006). Early language development: Social influences in the first years of life. In L. Balter & C. S. Tamis-LeMonda (Eds.), *Child psychology: A handbook of contemporary issues* (pp. 79–108). New York: Psychology Press.

Tamis-LeMonda, C. S., Shannon, J. D., Cabrera, N. J., & Lamb, M. E. (2004). Fathers and mothers at play with their 2- and 3-year-olds: Contributions to language and cognitive development. *Child Development, 75,* 1806–1820.

Tammelin, T., Näyhä, S., Hills, A. P., & Järvelin, M. (2003). Adolescent participation in sports and adult physical activity. *American Journal of Preventive Medicine, 24,* 22–28.

Tamrouti-Makkink, I. D., Dubas, J. S., Gerris, J. R. M., & van Aken, A. G. (2004). The relation between the absolute level of parenting and differential parental treatment with adolescent siblings' adjustment. *Journal of Child Psychology and Psychiatry, 45,* 1397–1406.

Tangney, J. P. (2001). Constructive and destructive aspects of shame and guilt. In A. C. Bohart & D. J. Stipek (Eds.), *Constructive and destructive behavior* (pp. 127–145). Washington, DC: American Psychological Association.

Tanner, J. M. (1990). *Foetus into man* (2nd ed.). Cambridge, MA: Harvard University Press.

Tanner, J., M., Healy, M., & Cameron, N. (2001). *Assessment of skeletal maturity and prediction of adult height (TW3 method)* (3rd ed.). Philadelphia: Saunders.

Tanner, L. (2005). *Study finds more fast food near schools.* Health Studies at University College, Toronto. Retrieved from www.utoronto.ca/healthstudies/newsitems/08.23.05fastfoodnearschools.html

Tardif, T. (2006). But are they really verbs? Chinese words for action. In K. Hirsh-Pasek & R. M. Golinkoff (Eds.), *Action meets word: How children learn verbs* (pp. 477–498). New York: Oxford University Press.

Tardif, T., Gelman, S. A., & Xu, F. (1999). Putting the "noun bias" in context: A comparison of English and Mandarin. *Child Development, 70,* 620–635.

Tardif, T., Wellman, H. M., & Cheung, K. M. (2004). False belief understanding in Cantonese-speaking children. *Journal of Child Language, 31,* 779–800.

Tarren-Sweeney, M. (2006). Patterns of aberrant eating among preadolescent children in foster care. *Journal of Abnormal Child Psychology, 34,* 623–634.

Tarullo, A. R., & Gunnar, M. R. (2006). Child maltreatment and the developing HPA axis. *Hormones and Behavior, 50,* 632–639.

Tasbihsazan, R., Nettelbeck, T., & Kirby, N. (2003). Predictive validity of the Fagan Test of Infant Intelligence. *British Journal of Developmental Psychology, 21,* 585–597.

Tasker, F. (2005). Lesbian mothers, gay fathers, and their children: A review. *Developmental and Behavioral Pediatrics, 26,* 224–240.

Tauber, M. A. (1979). Parental socialization techniques and sex differences in children's play. *Child Development, 50,* 225–234.

Taumoepeau, M., & Ruffman, T. (2006). Mother and infant talk about mental states relates to desire language and emotion understanding. *Child Development, 77,* 465–481.

Taylor, E. (2004). ADHD is best understood as a cultural construct: Against, *British Journal of Psychiatry, 184,* 9.

Taylor, M. (1996). The development of children's beliefs about the social and biological aspects of gender differences. *Child Development, 67,* 1555–1571.

Taylor, M., & Carlson, S. M. (1997). The relation between individual differences in fantasy and theory of mind. *Child Development, 68,* 436–455.

Taylor, M., & Carlson, S. M. (2000). The influence of religious beliefs on parental attitudes about children's fantasy behavior. In K. S. Rosengren, C. N. Johnson, & P. L. Harris (Eds.), *Imagining the impossible* (pp. 247–268). New York: Cambridge University Press.

Taylor, M., Carlson, S. M., Maring, B. L., Gerow, L., & Charley, C. M. (2004). The characteristics and correlates of fantasy in school-age children: Imaginary companions, impersonation, and social understanding. *Developmental Psychology, 40,* 1173–1187.

Taylor, M., Esbensen, B. M., & Bennett, R. T. (1994). Children's understanding of knowledge acquisition: The tendency for children to report that they have always known what they have just learned. *Child Development, 65,* 1581–1604.

Taylor, M. C., & Hall, J. A. (1982). Psychological androgyny: Theories, methods, and conclusions. *Psychological Bulletin, 92,* 347–366.

Taylor, R. L. (2000). Diversity within African-American families. In D. H. Demo & K. R. Allen (Eds.), *Handbook of family diversity* (pp. 232–251). New York: Oxford University Press.

Teicher, M. H., Dumont, N. L., Ito, Y., Vaituzis, C., Giedd, J., & Andersen, S. L. (2004). Childhood neglect is associated with reduced corpus callosum area. *Biological Psychiatry, 56,* 80–85.

Telama, R., Yang, X., Viikari, J., Valimaki, I., Wanne, O., & Raitakari, O. (2005). Physical activity from childhood to adulthood: A 21-year tracking study. *American Journal of Preventive Medicine, 28,* 267–273.

Tellings, A. (1999). Psychoanalytical and genetic-structuralistic approaches of moral development: Incompatible views? *Psychoanalytic Review, 86,* 903–914.

Temple, C. M., & Carney, R. A. (1995). Patterns of spatial functioning in Turner's syndrome. *Cortex, 31,* 109–118.

Temple, J. A., & Reynolds, A. J. (2006). Economic returns of investments in preschool education. In E. Zigler & S. Jones (Eds.), *A vision for universal prekindergarten* (pp. 37–68). New York: Cambridge University Press.

Temple, J. L., Giacomelli, A. M., Roemmich, J. N., & Epstein, L. H. (2007). Overweight children habituate slower than non-

overweight children to food. *Physiology and Behavior, 9,* 250–254.
Templeton, A. R. (2002). The genetic and evolutionary significance of human races. In J. M. Fish (Ed.), *Race and intelligence* (pp. 31–56). Mahwah, NJ: Erlbaum.
Templeton, L. M., & Wilcox, S. A. (2000). A tale of two representations: The misinformation effect and children's developing theory of mind. *Child Development, 71,* 402–416.
Tenenbaum, H. R., & Leaper, C. (2002). Are parents' gender schemas related to their children's gender-related cognitions? A meta-analysis. *Developmental Psychology, 38,* 615–630.
Tenenbaum, H. R., & Leaper, C. (2003). Parent–child conversations about science: The socialization of gender inequities? *Developmental Psychology, 39,* 34–47.
Tenenbaum, H. R., Snow, C. E., Roach, K. A., & Kurland, B. (2005). Talking and reading science: Longitudinal data on sex differences in mother–child conversations in low-income families. *Journal of Applied Developmental Psychology, 26,* 1–19.
Tepper, C. A., & Cassidy, K. W. (1999). Gender differences in emotional language in children's picture books. *Sex Roles, 40,* 265–280.
Terlecki, M. S., & Newcombe, N. S. (2005). How important is the digital divide? The relations of computer and videogame usage to gender differences in mental rotation ability. *Sex Roles, 53,* 433–441.
Terwel, J., Gillies, R. M., van den Eeden, P., & Hoek, D. (2001). Cooperative learning processes of students: A longitudinal multilevel perspective. *British Journal of Educational Psychology, 71,* 619–645.
Tessier, R., Cristo, M., Velez, S., Giron, M., Nadeau, L., & Figueroa, Z. (2003). Kangaroo mother care: A method of protecting high-risk premature infants against developmental delay. *Infant Behavior and Development, 26,* 384–397.
Teti, D. M., Saken, J. W., Kucera, E., & Corns, K. M. (1996). And baby makes four: Predictors of attachment security among preschool-age firstborns during the transition to siblinghood. *Child Development, 67,* 579–596.
Teyber, E. (2001). *Helping children cope with divorce* (rev. ed.). San Francisco: Jossey-Bass.
Thapar, A., Fowler, T., Rice, F., Scourfield, J., van den Bree, M., Thomas, H., Harold, G., & Hay, D. (2003). Maternal smoking during pregnancy and attention deficit hyperactivity disorder symptoms in offspring. *American Journal of Psychiatry, 160,* 1985–1989.
Thapar, N., & Sanderson, I. R. (2004). Diarrhea in children: An interface between developing and developed countries. *Lancet, 363,* 641–653.
Tharpe, A. M., & Ashmead, D. H. (2001). A longitudinal investigation of infant auditory sensitivity. *American Journal of Audiology, 10,* 104–112.
Thatcher, R. W., Lyon, G. R., Rumsey, J., & Krasnegor, J. (1996). *Developmental neuroimaging.* San Diego, CA: Academic Press.
Thelen, E. (1989). The (re)discovery of motor development: Learning new things from an old field. *Developmental Psychology, 25,* 946–949.
Thelen, E., & Adolph, K. E. (1992). Arnold Gesell: The paradox of nature and nurture. *Developmental Psychology, 28,* 368–380.
Thelen, E., & Bates, E. (2003). Connectionism and dynamic systems: Are they really different? *Developmental Science, 6,* 378–391.
Thelen, E., & Corbetta, D. (2002). Microdevelopment and dynamic systems: Applications to infant motor development. In N. Granott & J. Parziale (Eds.), *Microdevelopment: Transition processes in development and learning* (pp. 59–79). New York: Cambridge University Press.
Thelen, E., Fisher, D. M., & Ridley-Johnson, R. (1984). The relationship between physical growth and a newborn reflex. *Infant Behavior and Development, 7,* 479–493.
Thelen, E., Schöner, G., Scheier, C., & Smith, L. B. (2001). The dynamics of embodiment: A field theory of infant perseverative reaching. *Behavioral and Brain Sciences, 24,* 1–34.
Thelen, E., & Smith, L. B. (1994). *A dynamic systems approach to the development of cognition and action.* Cambridge, MA: Cambridge University Press.
Thelen, E., & Smith, L. B. (1998). Dynamic systems theories. In R. M. Lerner (Ed.), *Handbook of child psychology: Vol. 1. Theoretical models of human development* (5th ed., pp. 563–634). New York: Wiley.
Thelen, E., & Smith, L. B. (2006). Dynamic systems theories. In R. M. Lerner (Ed.), *Handbook of child psychology: Vol. 1. Theoretical models of human development* (6th ed., pp. 258–312). Hoboken, NJ: Wiley.
Théoret, H., Halligan, E., Kobayashi, M., Fregni, F., Tager-Flusberg, H., & Pascual-Leone, A. (2005). Impaired motor facilitation during action observation in individuals with autism spectrum disorder. *Current Biology, 15,* R84–R85.
Thierry, K. L., & Spence, M. J. (2002). Source-monitoring training facilitates preschoolers' eyewitness memory performance. *Developmental Psychology, 38,* 428–437.
Thiessen, E. D., Hill, E. A., & Saffran, J. R. (2005). Infant-directed speech facilitates word segmentation. *Infancy, 7,* 53–71.
Thoeni, A., Zech, N., Moroder, L., & Ploner, F. (2005). Review of 1600 water births. Does water birth increase the risk of neonatal infection? *Journal of Maternal-Fetal and Neonatal Medicine, 17,* 357–361.
Thoman, E. B., & Ingersoll, E. W. (1993). Learning in premature infants. *Developmental Psychology, 29,* 692–700.
Thomas, A., & Chess, S. (1977). *Temperament and development.* New York: Brunner/Mazel.
Thomas, A., Chess, S., & Birch, H. G. (1968). *Temperament and behavior disorders in children.* New York: New York University Press.
Thomas, C. L., & Dimitrov, D. M. (2007). Effects of a teen pregnancy prevention program on teens' attitudes toward sexuality: A latent trait modeling approach. *Developmental Psychology, 43,* 173–185.
Thomas, K. A., & Tessler, R. C. (2007). Bicultural socialization among adoptive families: Where there is a will, there is a way. *Journal of Family Issues, 28,* 1189–1219.
Thomas, M. S. C., & Johnson, M. H. (2006). The computational modeling of sensitive periods. *Developmental Psychobiology, 48,* 337–344.
Thomas, R. M. (2000). *Comparing theories of child development* (5th ed.). Belmont, CA: Wadsworth.
Thomas, R. M. (2005). *Comparing theories of child development* (6th ed.). New York: New York University Press.
Thompson, A., Hollis, C., & Richards, D. (2003). Authoritarian parenting attitudes as a risk for conduct problems: Results of a British national cohort study. *European Child and Adolescent Psychiatry, 12,* 84–91.
Thompson, L. A., Goodman, D. C., & Little, G. A. (2002). Is more neonatal intensive care always better? Insights from a cross-national comparison of reproductive care. *Pediatrics, 109,* 1036–1043.
Thompson, P. M., Giedd, J. N., Woods, R. P., MacDonald, D., Evans, A. C., & Toga, A. W. (2000). Growth patterns in the developing brain detected by using continuum mechanical tensor maps. *Nature, 404,* 190–192.
Thompson, R. A. (1990). Vulnerability in research: A developmental perspective on research risk. *Child Development, 61,* 1–16.
Thompson, R. A. (1992). Developmental changes in research risk and benefit: A changing calculus of concerns. In B. Stanley & J. E. Sieber (Eds.), *Social research on children and adolescents: Ethical issues* (pp. 31–64). Newbury Park, CA: Sage.
Thompson, R. A. (2006). The development of the person: Social understanding, relationships, conscience, self. In N. Eisenberg (Ed.), *Handbook of child psychology: Vol. 3. Social, emotional, and personality development* (6th ed., pp. 24–98). Hoboken, NJ: Wiley.
Thompson, R. A., Easterbrooks, M. A., & Padilla-Walker, L. M. (2003). Social and emotional development in infancy. In R. M. Lerner & M. A. Easterbrooks (Eds.), *Social and emotional development in infancy* (pp. 91–112). New York: Wiley.
Thompson, R. A., & Goodvin, R. (2007). Taming the tempest in the teapot. In C. A. Brownell & C. B. Kopp (Eds.), *Socioemotional development in the toddler years: Transitions and transformations* (pp. 320–341). New York: Guilford.
Thompson, R. A., & Leger, D. W. (1999). From squalls to calls: The cry as a developing socioemotional signal. In B. Lester, J. Newman, & F. Pedersen, (Eds.), *Biological and social aspects of infant crying.* New York: Plenum.
Thompson, R. A., & Limber, S. (1991). "Social anxiety" in infancy: Stranger wariness and separation distress. In H. Leitenberg (Ed.), *Handbook of social and evaluation anxiety* (pp. 85–137). New York: Plenum.
Thompson, R. A., & Meyer, S. (2007). Socialization of emotion regulation in the family. In J. J. Gross (Ed.), *Handbook of emotion regulation* (pp. 249–268). New York: Guilford.
Thompson, R. A., Meyer, S., & McGinley, M. (2006). Understanding values in relationships: The development of conscience. In M. Killen & J. G. Smetana (Eds.), *Handbook of moral development* (pp. 267–298). Mahwah, NJ: Erlbaum.
Thompson, R. A., & Nelson, C. A. (2001). Developmental science and the media: Early brain development. *American Psychologist, 56,* 5–15.
Thompson, R. A., & Raikes, H. A. (2003). Toward the next quarter-century: Conceptual and methodological challenges for attachment theory. *Development and Psychopathology, 15,* 691–718.
Thornberry, T., & Krohn, M. D. (2001). The development of delinquency: An interactional perspective. In S. O. White (Ed.), *Handbook of youth and justice* (pp. 289–305). Dordrecht, Netherlands: Kluwer.
Thornton, S. (1999). Creating conditions for cognitive change: The interaction between task structures and specific strategies. *Child Development, 70,* 588–603.
Thurstone, L. L. (1938). *Primary mental abilities.* Chicago: University of Chicago Press.
Tienari, P., Wahlberg, K.-E., & Wynne, L. C. (2006). Finnish adoption study of schizophrenia: Implications for family interventions. *Families, Systems, and Health, 24,* 442–451.
Tienari, P., Wynne, L. C., Laksy, K., Moring, J., Nieminen, P., & Sorri, A. (2003). Genetic boundaries of the schizophrenia spectrum: Evidence from the Finnish adoptive family study of schizophrenia. *American Journal of Psychiatry, 160,* 1587–1594.
Tietjen, A., & Walker, L. (1985). Moral reasoning and leadership among men in a Papua, New Guinea village. *Developmental Psychology, 21,* 982–992.
Tiggemann, M., & Anesbury, T. (2000). Negative stereotyping of obesity in children: The role of controllability beliefs. *Journal of Applied Social Psychology, 30,* 1977–1993.
Tinbergen, N. (1973). *The animal in its world: Explorations of an ethologist, 1932–1972.* Cambridge, MA: Harvard University Press.
Tincoff, R., & Jusczyk, P. W. (1999). Some beginnings of word comprehension in 6-month-olds. *Psychological Science, 10,* 172–175.
Tisak, M. S. (1995). Domains of social reasoning and beyond. In R. Vasta (Ed.), *Annals of child development* (Vol. 11, pp. 95–130). London: Jessica Kingsley.
Tisak, M. S., Tisak, J., & Goldstein, S. E. (2006). Aggression, delinquency, and morality A social-cognitive perspective. In M. Killen & J. G. Smetana (Eds.), *Handbook of moral development* (pp. 611–629). Philadelphia: Erlbaum.
Tizard, B., & Rees, J. (1975). The effect of early institutional rearing on the behaviour problems and affectional relationships of four-year-old children. *Journal of Child Psychology and Psychiatry, 16,* 61–73.
Tofler, I. R., Knapp, P. K., & Drell, M. J. (1998). The achievement by proxy spectrum in youth sports: Historical perspective and clinical approach to pressured and high-achieving children and adolescents. *Adolescent Psychiatric Clinics of North America, 7,* 803–820.
Tolan, P., Gorman-Smith, D., & Henry, D. (2006). Family violence. *Annual Review of Psychology, 57,* 557–583.
Tolson, J. M., & Urberg, K. A. (1993). Similarity between adolescent best friends. *Journal of Adolescent Research, 8,* 274–288.
Tomasello, M. (1992). *First verbs: A case study of early grammatical development.* New York: Cambridge University Press.
Tomasello, M. (1999). Having intentions, understanding intentions, and understanding communicative intentions. In P. D. Zelazo, J. W. Astington, & J. Wilde (Eds.), *Developing theories of intention: Social understanding and self-control* (pp. 63–75). Mahwah, NJ: Erlbaum.
Tomasello, M. (2000). Do young children have adult syntactic competence? *Cognition, 74,* 209–253.
Tomasello, M. (2003). *Constructing a language: A usage-based theory of language acquisition.* Cambridge, MA: Harvard University Press.
Tomasello, M. (2005). Beyond formalities: The case of language acquisition. *Linguistic Review, 22,* 183–197.

Tomasello, M. (2006). Acquiring linguistic constructions. In D. Kuhn & R. Siegler (Eds.), *Handbook of child psychology: Vol. 2: Cognition, perception, and language* (6th ed., pp. 255–298). Hoboken, NJ: Wiley.

Tomasello, M., & Akhtar, N. (1995). Two-year-olds use pragmatic cues to differentiate reference to objects and actions. *Cognitive Development, 10,* 201–224.

Tomasello, M., Akhtar, N., Dodson, K., & Rekau, L. (1997). Differential productivity in young children's use of nouns and verbs. *Journal of Child Language, 24,* 373–387.

Tomasello, M., & Brooks, P. (1999). Early syntactic development: A construction grammar approach. In M. Barrett (Ed.), *The development of language* (pp. 161–190). London: UCL Press.

Tomasello, M., Call, J., & Hare, B. (2003). Chimpanzees understand psychological states—the question is which ones and to what extent. *Trends in Cognitive Sciences, 7,* 153–156.

Tomasello, M., Carpenter, M., & Liszkowski, U. (2007). A new look at infant pointing. *Child Development, 78,* 705–722.

Tomasello, M., & Rakoczy, H. (2003). What makes human cognition unique? From individual to shared to collective intentionality. *Mind and Language, 18,* 121–147.

Tomasello, M., Striano, T., & Rochat, P. (1999). Do young children use objects as symbols? *British Journal of Developmental Psychology, 17,* 563–584.

Tong, S., McMichael, A. J., & Baghurst, P. A. (2000). Interactions between environmental lead exposure and sociodemographic factors on cognitive development. *Archives of Environmental Health, 55,* 330–335.

Toomela, A. (2002). Drawing as a verbally mediated activity: A study of relationships between verbal, motor, visuospatial skills and drawing in children. *International Journal of Behavioral Development, 26,* 234–247.

Torney-Purta, J. (2002). The school's role in developing civic engagement: A study of adolescents in twenty-eight countries. *Applied Developmental Science, 6,* 203–212.

Torrance, E. P. (1988). The nature of creativity as manifest in its testing. In R. J. Sternberg (Ed.), *The nature of creativity: Contemporary psychological perspectives* (pp. 43–75). New York: Cambridge University Press.

Touwen, B. C. L. (1984). Primitive reflexes—conceptual or semantic problem? In H. F. R. Prechtl (Ed.), *Continuity of neural functions from prenatal to postnatal life* (Clinics in Developmental Medicine, No. 94, pp. 115–125). Philadelphia: Lippincott.

Tracy, J. L., Robins, R. W., & Lagattuta, K. H. (2005). Can children recognize pride? *Emotion, 5,* 251–257.

Trahms, C. M., & Pipes, P. L. (1997). *Nutrition in infancy and childhood* (6th ed.). New York: McGraw-Hill.

Trautner, H. M., Gervai, J., & Nemeth, R. (2003). Appearance–reality distinction and development of gender constancy understanding in children. *International Journal of Behavioral Development, 27,* 275–283.

Trautner, H. M., Ruble, D. N., Cyphers, L., Kirsten, B., Behrendt, R., & Hartmann, P. (2005). Rigidity and flexibility of gender stereotypes in childhood: Developmental or differential? *Infant and Child Development, 14,* 365–381.

Trautwein, U., Ludtke, O., Marsh, H. W., Koller, O., & Baumert, J. (2006). Tracking, grading, and student motivation: Using group composition and status to predict self-concept and interest in ninth-grade mathematics. *Journal of Educational Psychology, 98,* 788–806.

Treasure, J., & Schmidt, U. (2005). Anorexia nervosa. *Clinical Evidence, 13,* 1148–1157.

Treffert, D. A., & Wallace, G. L. (2002, June). Islands of genius. *Scientific American,* pp. 76–85.

Trehub, S. E. (2001). Musical predispositions in infancy. *Annals of the New York Academy of Sciences, 930,* 1–16.

Tremblay, L., & Frigon, J.-Y. (2005). Precocious puberty in adolescent girls: A biomarker of later psychosocial adjustment problems. *Child Psychiatry and Human Development, 36,* 73–94.

Tremblay, R. E. (2000). The development of aggressive behaviour during childhood: What have we learned in the past century? *International Journal of Behavioral Development, 24,* 129–141.

Tremblay, R. E. (2004). Decade of behavior distinguished lecture: Development of physical aggression during infancy. *Infant Mental Health Journal, 25,* 399–407.

Tremblay, R. E., Japel, C., Perusse, D., Voivin, M., Zoccolillo, M., Montplaisir, J., & McDuff, P. (1999). The search for the age of "onset" of physical aggression: Rousseau and Bandura revisited. *Criminal Behavior and Mental Health, 9,* 8–23.

Tremblay, R. E., Schaal, B., Boulerice, B., Arseneault, L., Soussignan, R., & Perusse, D. (1997). Male physical aggression, social dominance, and testosterone levels at puberty: A developmental perspective. In A. Raine & P. A. Brennan (Eds.), *Biosocial bases of violence. NATO ASI Series: Series A: Life sciences* (Vol. 292, pp. 271–291). New York: Plenum.

Trent, K., & Harlan, S. L. (1994). Teenage mothers in nuclear and extended households. *Journal of Family Issues, 15,* 309–337.

Trevarthen, C. (2003). Infant psychology is an evolving culture. *Human Development, 46,* 233–246.

Triandis, H. C. (1995). *Individualism and collectivism.* Boulder, CO: Westview Press.

Triandis, H. C. (1998, May). *Cross-cultural versus cultural psychology: A synthesis?* Colloquium presented at Illinois Wesleyan University, Bloomington, IL.

Trickett, P. K., Noll, J., Reiffman, A., & Putnam, F. (2001). Variants of intrafamilial sexual abuse experiences: Implications for short- and long-term development. *Development and Psychopathology, 13,* 1001–1019.

Trickett, P. K., & Putnam, F. W. (1998). Developmental consequences of child sexual abuse. In P. K. Trickett & C. J. Schellenbach (Eds.), *Violence against children in the family and community* (pp. 39–56). Washington, DC: American Psychological Association.

Trivers, R. L. (1971). The evolution of reciprocal altruism. *Quarterly Review of Biology, 46,* 35–57.

Trocomé, N., Fallon, B., MacLaurin, B., Daciuk, J., Felstiner, C., Black, T., Tonmyr, L., Blackstock, C., Barter, K., Turcotte, D., & Cloutier, R. (2005). *Canadian Incidence Study of Reported Child Abuse and Neglect—Major findings—2003.* Minister of Public Works and Government Services, Canada. Retrieved from www.phac-aspc.gc.ca/cm-vee/csca-ecve/index.html

Trocomé, N., & Wolfe, D. (2002). *Child maltreatment in Canada: The Canadian Incidence Study of Reported Child Abuse and Neglect.* Retrieved from www.hc-sc.gc.ca/pphb-dgspsp/cm-vee

Tronick, E. Z., Morelli, G. A., & Ivey, P. (1992). The Efe forager infant and toddler's pattern of social relationships: Multiple and simultaneous. *Developmental Psychology, 28,* 568–577.

Tronick, E. Z., Thomas, R. B., & Daltabuit, M. (1994). The Quechua manta pouch: A caretaking practice for buffering the Peruvian infant against the multiple stressors of high altitude. *Child Development, 65,* 1005–1013.

Troop-Gordon, W., & Asher, S. R. (2005). Modifications in children's goals when encountering obstacles to conflict resolution. *Child Development, 76,* 568–582.

True, M. M., Pisani, L., & Oumar, F. (2001). Infant–mother attachment among the Dogon of Mali. *Child Development, 72,* 1451–1466.

Truglio, R. (2000, April). *Research guides "Sesame Street."* Public lecture presented as part of the Consider the Children program, Illinois State University, Normal, IL.

Trzesniewski, K. H., Donnellan, M. B., & Robins, R. W. (2003). Stability of self-esteem across the life span. *Journal of Personality and Social Psychology, 84,* 205–220.

Tsao, F.-M., Liu, H.-M., & Kuhl, P. K. (2004). Speech perception in infancy predicts language development in the second year of life: A longitudinal study. *Child Development, 75,* 1067–1084.

Tsethlikai, M., & Greenhoot, A. F. (2006). The influence of another's perspective on children's recall of previously misconstrued events. *Developmental Psychology, 42,* 732–745.

Tucker, C. J., McHale, S. M., & Crouter, A. C. (2001). Conditions of siblings support in adolescence. *Journal of Family Psychology, 15,* 254–271.

Tucker, C. J., McHale, S. M., & Crouter, A. C. (2003). Dimensions of mothers' and fathers' differential treatment of siblings: Links with adolescents' sex-typed personal qualities. *Family Relations, 52,* 82–89.

Tudge, J. R. H., Hogan, D. M., Snezhkova, I. A., Kulakova, N. N., & Etz, K. E. (2000). Parents' child-rearing values and beliefs in the United States and Russia: The impact of culture and social class. *Infant and Child Development, 9,* 105–121.

Tudge, J. R. H., and Scrimsher, S. (2003). Lev S. Vygotsky on education: A cultural-historical, interpersonal, and individual approach to development. In B. J. Zimmerman & D. H. Schunk (Eds.), *Educational psychology: A century of contributions* (pp. 207–228). Mahwah, NJ: Erlbaum.

Tunmer, W. E., & Chapman, J. W. (2002). The relation of beginning readers' reported word identification strategies to reading achievement, reading-related skills, and academic self-perceptions. *Reading and Writing, 15,* 341–358.

Turati, C. (2004). Why faces are not special to newborns: An account of the face preference. *Current Directions in Psychological Science, 13,* 5–8.

Turiel, E. (2006). The development of morality. In N. Eisenberg (Ed.), *Handbook of child psychology: Vol. 3. Social, emotional, and personality development* (6th ed., pp. 789–857). Hoboken, NJ: Wiley.

Turkheimer, E., Haley, A., Waldron, M., D'Onofrio, B., & Gottesman, I. I. (2003). Socioeconomic status modifies heritability of IQ in young children. *Psychological Science, 14,* 623–628.

Turkle, S. (1995). *Life on the screen: Identity in the age of the Internet.* New York: Simon & Schuster.

Turnbull, M., Hart, D., & Lapkin, S. (2003). Grade 6 French immersion students' performance on large-scale reading, writing, and mathematics tests: Building explanations. *Alberta Journal of Educational Research, 49,* 6–23.

Turner, P. J., & Gervai, J. (1995). A multidimensional study of gender typing in preschool children and their parents: Personality, attitudes, preferences, behavior, and cultural differences. *Developmental Psychology, 31,* 759–772.

Turner, P. J., Gervai, J. & Hinde, R. A. (1993). Gender typing in young children: Preferences, behaviour and cultural differences. *British Journal of Developmental Psychology, 11,* 323–342.

Turner, R. N., Hewstone, M., & Voci, A. (2007). Reducing explicit and implicit outgroup prejudice via direct and extended contact: The mediating role of self-disclosure and intergroup anxiety. *Journal of Personality and Social Psychology, 93,* 369–388.

Turner-Bowker, D. M. (1996). Gender stereotyped descriptors in children's picture books: Does "Curious Jane" exist in the literature? *Sex Roles, 35,* 461–488.

Tuyen, J. M., & Bisgard, K. (2003). Community setting: Pertussis outbreak. Atlanta, GA: U.S. Centers for Disease Control and Prevention. Retrieved from www.cdc.gov/nip/publications/pertussis/chapter10.pdf

Twenge, J. M., & Campbell, W. K. (2001). Age and birth cohort differences in self-esteem: A cross-temporal meta-analysis. *Personality and Social Psychology Review, 5,* 321–344.

Twenge, J. M., & Crocker, J. (2002). Race and self-esteem: Meta-analyses comparing whites, blacks, Hispanics, Asians, and America Indians and comment on Gray-Little and Hafdahl (2000). *Psychological Bulletin, 128,* 371–408.

Tychsen, L. (2001). Critical periods for development of visual acuity, depth perception, and eye tracking. In D. B. Bailey, Jr., J. T. Bruer, F. J. Symons, & J. W. Lichtman (Eds.), *Critical thinking about critical periods* (pp. 67–82). Baltimore: Paul H. Brookes.

Tynes, B., Reynolds, L., & Greenfield, P. M. (2004). Adolescence, race and ethnicity on the Internet: A comparison of discourse in monitored vs. unmonitored chat rooms. *Journal of Applied Developmental Psychology, 25,* 667–684.

Tyrka, A. R., Graber, J. A., & Brooks-Gunn, J. (2000). The development of disordered eating: Correlates and predictors of eating problems in the context of adolescence. In A. J. Sameroff & M. Lewis (Eds.), *Handbook of developmental psychopathology* (2nd ed., pp. 607–624). New York: Kluwer.

Tzuriel, D. (2001). *Dynamic assessment of young children.* New York: Kluwer Academic.

Tzuriel, D., & Kaufman, R. (1999). Mediated learning and cognitive modifiability: Dynamic assessment of young Ethiopian immigrant children to Israel. *Journal of Cross-Cultural Psychology, 30,* 359–380.

Ukrainetz, T. A., Justice, L. M., Kaderavek, J. N., Eisenberg, S. L., Gillam, R., & Harm, H. M. (2005). The development of expressive elaboration in fictional narratives. *Journal of Speech, Language, and Hearing Research, 48,* 1363–1377.

Ullrich-French, S., & Smith, A. L. (2006). Perceptions of relationships with parents and peers in youth sport: Independent and combined prediction of motivational outcomes. *Psychology of Sport and Exercise, 7,* 193–214.

Umana-Taylor, A. J., & Alfaro, E. C. (2006). Ethnic identity among U.S. Latino adolescents: Measurement and implications for well-being. In F. A. Villarruel & T. Luster (Eds.), *The crisis in youth mental health: Critical issues and effective programs: Vol. 2. Disorders in adolescence* (pp. 195–211). Westport, CT: Praeger.

Umana-Taylor, A. J., & Updegraff, K. A. (2007). Latino adolescents' mental health: Exploring the interrelations among discrimination, ethnic identity, cultural orientation, self-esteem, and depressive symptoms. *Journal of Adolescence, 30,* 549–567.

Underhill, K., Montgomery, P., & Operario, D. (2007). Sexual abstinence only programmes to prevent HIV infection in high-income countries: Systematic review. *British Medical Journal, 335,* 248.

Underwood, M. K. (2003). *Social aggression among girls.* New York: Guilford.

UNICEF (United Nations Children's Emergency Fund). (2001). *Teenage births in rich nations. Innocenti Report Card No. 3.* Florence, Italy: UNICEF Innocenti Research Centre.

UNICEF (United Nations Children's Emergency Fund). (2006). *Immunization Summary 2006.* Geneva, Switzerland: World Health Organization.

United Nations. (2001). *World social situation.* New York: Author.

United Nations. (2002). *Human Development Report 2001.* New York: Author.

United Nations. (2006). *Preventing HIV in women and infants.* Retrieved from www.unfpa.org/hiv/transmission.htm

United Nations Development Programme. (2002). *Human development report 2002.* New York: Author.

U.S. Census Bureau. (2007a). International data base. Retrieved from http://www.census.gov/ipc/www/idb/

U.S. Census Bureau. (2007b). *Statistical abstract of the United States* (126th ed.). Washington, DC: U.S. Government Printing Office.

U.S. Census Bureau. (2008). *International data base.* Retrieved from http://www.census.gov/ipc/www/idb/

U.S. Centers for Disease Control and Prevention. (2005). *Preventing lead poisoning in young children.* Atlanta: Author.

U.S. Centers for Disease Control and Prevention. (2006). *Sexually transmitted disease (STD) surveillance.* Retrieved from www.cdc.gov/std

U.S. Department of Agriculture. (2005a). *Food insecurity in households with children.* Washington, DC: Author.

U.S. Department of Agriculture. (2005b). *Frequently asked questions about the Special Supplemental Nutrition Program for Women, Infants, and Children (WIC).* Retrieved from www.ers.usda.gov/Briefing/WIC

U.S. Department of Agriculture. (2007). *Expenditures on children by families. Miscellaneous Publication No. 1528-2007.* Washington, DC: U.S. Government Printing Office.

U.S. Department of Education. (2003). *The Nation's Report Card: National Assessment of Educational Progress: 2003 results.* Retrieved from nces.ed.gov/nationsreportcard/mathematics

U.S. Department of Education. (2005). *The condition of education, 2000–2005.* Washington, DC: U.S. Government Printing Office.

U.S. Department of Education. (2006). Long-term trend: Trends in average reading scale scores by race/ethnicity. *The Nation's Report Card.* Retrieved from nces.ed.gov/nationsreportcard/ltt/results2005/sub_reading_race2.asp

U.S. Department of Education. (2007). *Digest of educational statistics, 2006.* Washington, DC: U.S. Government Printing Office.

U.S. Department of Health and Human Services. (2000). 2000 CDC growth charts. Retrieved from www.cdc.gov/growthcharts

U.S. Department of Health and Human Services. (2004). Birth defects. Retrieved from www.cdc.gov/ncbddd

U.S. Department of Health and Human Services. (2005a). Abortion Surveillance—United States, 2002. Retrieved from www.cdc.gov/mmwr/preview/mmwrhtml/ss5407a1.htm

U.S. Department of Health and Human Services. (2005b). *Breastfeeding—Best for baby, best for mom.* Retrieved from www.womenshealth.gov/breastfeeding/index.cfm?page=home

U.S. Department of Health and Human Services. (2006a). Births: Final data for 2004. *National Vital Statistics Report, 55*(1). Retrieved from www.cdc.gov/nchs/data/nvsr/nvsr55/nvsr55_01.pdf

U.S. Department of Health and Human Services. (2006b). *Health, United States, 2006, with chartbook on trends in the health of Americans.* Retrieved from www.cdc.gov/nchs/data/hus/hus06.pdf

U.S. Department of Health and Human Services. (2006c, September 15). National, state, and urban area vaccination levels among children aged 19 to 35 months: United States, 2005. *Morbidity and Mortality Weekly Report, 55,* 988–993.

U.S. Department of Health and Human Services. (2006d). Youth risk behavior surveillance—United States, 2005. *Morbidity and Mortality Weekly Report, 55*(No. SS-5).

U.S. Department of Health and Human Services. (2007a). *Births: Preliminary data for 2005.* Retrieved from www.cdc.gov/nchs/products/pubs/pubd/hestats/prelimbirths05/prelimbirths05.htm

U.S. Department of Health and Human Services. (2007b). *National diabetes fact sheet, United States, 2007.* Retrieved from www.diabetes.org/uedocuments/NationalDiabetesFactSheetRev.pdf

U.S. Department of Health and Human Services. (2007c). *Prenatal care.* Retrieved from www.cdc.gov/nchs/fastats/prenatal.htm

U.S. Department of Health and Human Services. (2007d). *Results from the 2006 National Survey on Drug Use and Health: National findings.* Retrieved from oas.amhsa.gov/nsduh/2k6nsduh/2k6Results.pdfs

U.S. Department of Health and Human Services. (2008). *Child maltreatment, 2006.* Retrieved from www.acf.hhs.gov/programs/cb/pubs/cm06/index.htm

U.S. Department of Justice. (2007). *Uniform crime reports: Preliminary report, 2006.* Retrieved from www.fbi.gov/urc.htm

Updegraff, K. A., McHale, S. M., & Crouter, A. C. (1996). Gender roles in marriage: What do they mean for girls' and boys' school achievement? *Journal of Youth and Adolescence, 25,* 73–88.

Uribe, F. M. T., LeVine, R. A., & LeVine, S. E. (1994). Maternal behavior in a Mexican community: The changing environments of children. In P. M. Greenfield & R. R. Cocking (Eds.), *Cross-cultural roots of minority child development* (pp. 41–54). Hillsdale, NJ: Erlbaum.

Ursano, R. J., & Shaw, J. A. (2007). Children of war and opportunities for peace. *Journal of the American Medical Association, 298,* 567.

Uttal, D. H., Gregg, V. H., Tan, L. S., Chamberlin, M. H., & Sines, A. (2001). Connecting the dots: Children's use of a systematic figure to facilitate mapping and search. *Developmental Psychology, 37,* 338–350.

Vaidyanathan, R. (1988). Development of forms and functions of interrogatives in children: A language study of Tamil. *Journal of Child Language, 15,* 533–549.

Vaidyanathan, R. (1991). Development of forms and functions of negation in the early stages of language acquisition: A study of Tamil. *Journal of Child Language, 18,* 51–66.

Vaillancourt, T., Brendgen, M., Boivin, M., & Tremblay, R. E. (2003). A longitudinal confirmatory factor analysis of indirect physical aggression: Evidence of two factors over time? *Child Development, 74,* 1628–1638.

Vaillancourt, T., Hymel, S., & McDougall, P. (2003). Bullying is power: Implications for school-based intervention strategies. *Journal of Applied Social Psychology, 19,* 157–176.

Vaish, A., & Striano, T. (2004). Is visual reference necessary? Contributions of facial versus vocal cues in 12-month-olds' social referencing behavior. *Developmental Science, 7,* 261–269.

Valdés, G. (1998). The world outside and inside schools: Language and immigrant children. *Educational Researcher, 27*(6), 4–18.

Valentine, J. C., DuBois, D. L., & Cooper, H. (2004). The relation between self-beliefs and academic achievement: A meta-analytic review. *Educational Psychologist, 39,* 111–133.

Valian, V. (1999). Input and language acquisition. In W. C. Ritchie & T. K. Bhatia (Eds.), *Handbook of child language acquisition* (pp. 497–530). San Diego: Academic Press.

Valian, V. (2005). When opportunity knocks twice: Two-year-olds' repetition of sentence subjects. *Journal of Child Language, 32,* 617–641.

Valian, V. V. (1991). Syntactic subjects in the early speech of American and Italian children. *Cognition, 40,* 21–81.

Valiente, C., Eisenberg, N., Fabes, R. A., Shepard, S. A., Cumberland, A., & Losoya, S. H. (2004). Prediction of children's empathy-related responding from their effortful control and parents' expressivity. *Developmental Psychology, 40,* 911–926.

Valkenburg, P. M., & Peter, J. (2007a). Internet communication and its relation to well-being: Identifying some underlying mechanisms. *Media Psychology, 9,* 43–58.

Valkenburg, P. M., & Peter, J. (2007b). Preadolescents' and adolescents' online communication and their closeness to friends. *Developmental Psychology, 43,* 267–277.

Vandell, D. L. (1999). When school is out: Analysis and recommendations. *The Future of Children, 9*(2). Retrieved from www.futureofchildren.org

Vandell, D. L., & Mueller, E. C. (1995). Peer play and friendships during the first two years. In H. C. Foot, A. J. Chapman, & J. R. Smith (Eds.), *Friendship and social relations in children* (pp. 181–208). New Brunswick, NJ: Transaction.

Vandell, D. L., & Posner, J. K. (1999). Conceptualization and measurement of children's after-school environments. In S. L. Friedman & T. D. Wachs (Eds.), *Measuring environment across the life span* (pp. 167–196). Washington, DC: American Psychological Association.

Vandell, D. L., & Shumow, L. (1999). After-school child care programs. *Future of Children, 9*(2), 64–80.

Van den Bergh, B. R. H. (2004). High antenatal maternal anxiety is related to ADHD symptoms, externalizing problems, and anxiety in 8- and 9-year-olds. *Child Development, 75,* 1085–1097.

Van den Bergh, B. R. H., & De Rycke, L. (2003). Measuring the multidimensional self-concept and global self-worth of 6- to 8-year-olds. *Journal of Genetic Psychology, 164,* 201–225.

van den Boom, D. C., & Hoeksma, J. B. (1994). The effect of infant irritability on mother–infant interaction: A growth-curve analysis. *Developmental Psychology, 30,* 581–590.

van der Meer, A. L. (1997). Keeping the arm in the limelight: Advanced visual control of arm movements in neonates. *European Journal of Paediatric Neurology, 4,* 103–108.

van der Woerd, K. A., & Cox, D. N. (2001, August). *Assessing academic competence and the well-being of Aboriginal students in British Columbia.* Poster presented at the annual meeting of the American Psychological Association, Atlanta.

Vandivere, S., Gallagher, M., & Moore, K. A. (2004). *Changes in children's well-being and family environments. Snapshots of America's Families III,* No. 18. New York: Urban Institute. Retrieved from www.urban.org/url.cfm?ID=310912

Van Goozen, S. H. M., Cohen-Kettenis, P. T., Gooren, I. J. G., Frijda, N. H., & Van De Poll, N. E. (1995). Gender differences in behaviour: Activating effects of cross-sex hormones. *Psychoneuroendocrinology, 20,* 171–177.

van IJzendoorn, M. H. (1995). Adult attachment representations, parental responsiveness, and infant attachment: A meta-analysis on the predictive validity of the adult attachment interview. *Psychological Bulletin, 117,* 387–403.

van IJzendoorn, M. H., Goldberg, S., Kroonenberg, P. M., & Frenkel, O. J. (1992). The relative effects of maternal and child problems on the quality of attachment: A meta-analysis of attachment in clinical samples. *Child Development, 63,* 840–858.

van IJzendoorn, M. H., & Hubbard, F. O. A. (2000). Are infant crying and maternal responsiveness during the first year related to infant–mother attachment at 15 months? *Attachment and Human Development, 2,* 371–391.

van IJzendoorn, M. H., Juffer, F., & Poelhuis, C. W. K. (2005). Adoption and cognitive development: A meta-analytic comparison of adopted and nonadopted children's IQ and school performance. *Psychological Bulletin, 131,* 301–316.

van IJzendoorn, M. H., & Kroonenberg, P. M. (1988). Cross-cultural patterns of attachment: A meta-analysis of the Strange Situation. *Child Development, 59,* 147–156.

van IJzendoorn, M. H., & Sagi, A. (1999). Cross-cultural patterns of attachment. In J. Cassidy & P. R. Shaver (Eds.), *Handbook of attachment: Theory, research, and clinical applications* (pp. 713–734). New York: Guilford.

van IJzendoorn, M. H., Schuengel, C., & Bakermans-Kranenburg, M. J. (1999). Disorganized attachment in early childhood: Meta-analysis of precursors, concomitants, and sequelae. *Development and Psychopathology,* 11, 225–249.

van IJzendoorn, M. H., Vereijken, C. M. J. L., Bakermans-Kranenburg, M. J., & Riksen-Walraven, J. M. (2004). Assessing attachment security with the Attachment Q-Sort: Meta-analytic evidence for the validity of the observer AQS. *Child Development, 75,* 1188–1213.

Van Keer, H. (2004). Fostering reading comprehension in fifth grade by explicit instruction in reading strategies and peer tutoring. *British Journal of Educational Psychology, 74,* 37–70.

Van Lange, P. A. M., Bekkers, R., Schuyt, T. N. M., & Van Vugt, M. (2007). From games to giving: Social value orientation predicts donations to noble causes. *Basic and Applied Social Psychology, 29,* 375–384.

Van Vugt, M., & Van Lange, P. A. M. (2006). The altruism puzzle: Psychological adaptations for prosocial behavior. In M. Schaller, J. A. Simpson, & D. T. Kenrick (Eds.), *Evolution and social psychology* (pp. 237–261). New York: Psychology Press.

Varela-Silva, M. I., Frisancho, A. R., Bogin, B., Chatkoff, D., Smith, P. K., Dickinson, F., & Winham, D. (2007). Behavioral, environmental, metabolic, and intergenerational components of early life undernutrition leading to later obesity in developing nations and in minority groups in the U.S.A. *Collegium Antropologicum, 31,* 39–46.

Varendi, H., Christensson, K., Porter, R. H., & Winberg, J. (1998). Soothing effect of amniotic fluid smell in newborn infants. *Early Human Development, 51,* 47–55.

Varendi, H., & Porter, R. H. (2001). Breast odour as the only maternal stimulus elicits crawling toward the odour source. *Acta Paediactrica, 90,* 372–375.

Varnhagen, C. (2007). Children and the Internet. In J. Gackenbach (Ed.), *Psychology and the Internet* (2nd ed., pp, 37–54). Amsterdam: Elsevier.

Vartanian, L. R. (1997). Separation–individuation, social support, and adolescent egocentrism: An exploratory study. *Journal of Early Adolescence, 17,* 245–270.

Vartanian, L. R., & Powlishta, K. K. (1996). A longitudinal examination of the social-cognitive foundations of adolescent egocentrism. *Journal of Early Adolescence, 16,* 157–178.

Vasudev, J., & Hummel, R. C. (1987). Moral stage sequence and principled reasoning in an Indian sample. *Human Development, 30,* 105–118.

Vatten, L. J., Maehle, B. O., Lund, N. T., Treti, S., Hsieh, C. C., Trichopoulos, D., & Stuver, S. O. (2002). Birth weight as a predictor of breast cancer: A case-control study in Norway. *British Journal of Cancer, 86,* 89–91.

Vaughn, B. E., & Bost, K. K. (1999). Attachment and temperament: Redundant, independent, or interacting influences on interpersonal adaptation and personality development? In J. Cassidy & P. Shaver (Eds.), *Handbook of attachment: Theory, research, and clinical applications* (pp. 265–286). New York: Guilford.

Vaughn, B. E., Colvin, T. N., Azria, M. R., Caya, L., & Krzysik, L. (2001). Dyadic analyses of friendship in a sample of preschool-age children attending Head Start: Correspondence between measures and implications for social competence. *Child Development, 72,* 862–878.

Vaughn, B. E., Kopp, C. B., & Krakow, J. B. (1984). The emergence and consolidation of self-control from eighteen to thirty months of age: Normative trends and individual differences. *Child Development, 55,* 990–1004.

Vaughn, S., & Klingner, J. K. (1998). Students' perceptions of inclusion and resource room settings. *Journal of Special Education, 32,* 79–88.

Vazsonyi, A. T., Hibbert, J. R., & Snider, J. B. (2003). Exotic enterprise no more? Adolescent reports of family and parenting processes from youth in four countries. *Journal of Research on Adolescence, 13,* 129–160.

Velderman, M. K., Bakermans-Kranenburg, M. J., Juffer, F., & van IJzendoorn, M. H. (2006). Effects of attachment-based interventions on maternal sensitivity and infant attachment: Differential susceptibility of highly reactive infants. *Journal of Family Psychology, 20,* 266–274.

Velleman, R. D. B., Templeton, L. J., & Copello, A. G. (2005). The role of the family in preventing and intervening with substance use and misuse: A comprehensive review of family interventions, with a focus on young people. *Drug and Alcohol Review, 24,* 93–109.

Venet, M., & Markovits, H. (2001). Understanding uncertainty with abstract conditional premises. *Merrill-Palmer Quarterly, 47,* 74–99.

Venezia, M., Messinger, D. S., Thorp, D., & Mundy, P. (2004). The development of anticipatory smiling. *Infancy, 6,* 397–406.

Veneziano, R. A. (2003). The importance of paternal warmth. *Cross-Cultural Research, 37,* 265–281.

Vereijken, B., & Adolph, K. E. (1999). Transitions in the development of locomotion. In G. J. P. Savelsbergh, H. L. J. van der Maas, & P. C. L. van Geert (Eds.), *Nonlinear analyses of developmental processes* (pp. 137–149). Amsterdam: Elsevier.

Veríssimo, M., & Salvaterra, F. (2006). Maternal secure-base scripts and children's attachment security in an adopted sample. *Attachment and Human Development, 8,* 261–273.

Vernon, P. A., Wickett, J. C., Bazana, G., & Stelmack, R. M. (2001). The neuropsychology and psychophysiology of human intelligence. In R. J. Sternberg (Ed.), *Handbook of intelligence* (pp. 245–264). Cambridge, UK: Cambridge University Press.

Videon, T. M., & Manning, C. K. (2003). Influences on adolescent eating patterns: The importance of family meals. *Journal of Adolescent Health, 32,* 365–373.

Vihman, M. M. (1996). *Phonological development.* London: Blackwell.

Vik, T., Bakketeig, L. S., Trygg, K. U., Lund-Larsen, K., & Jacobsen, G. (2003). High caffeine consumption in the third trimester of pregnancy: Gender-specific effects on fetal growth. *Paediatric and Perinatal Epidemiology, 17,* 324–331.

Vinden, P. G. (1996). Junín Quechua children's understanding of mind. *Child Development, 67,* 1707–1716.

Vinden, P. G. (2002). Understanding minds and evidence for belief: A study of Mofu children in Cameroon. *International Journal of Behavioral Development, 26,* 445–452.

Visher, E. B., Visher, J. S., & Pasley, K. (2003). Remarriage families and stepparenting. In F. Walsh (Ed.), *Normal family processes* (pp. 153–175). New York: Guilford.

Visser, B. A., Ashton, M. C., & Vernon, P. A. (2006). Beyond g: Putting multiple intelligences theory to the test. *Intelligence, 34,* 487–502.

Vitaro, F., Barker, E. D., Boivin, M., Brendgen, M., & Tremblay, R. E. (2006). Do early difficult temperament and harsh parenting differentially predict reactive and proactive aggression? *Journal of Abnormal Child Psychology, 34,* 685–695.

Vitaro, F., Brendgen, M., & Tremblay, R. E. (2000). Influence of deviant friends on delinquency: Searching for moderator variables. *Journal of Abnormal Child Psychology, 28,* 313–325.

Vitaro, F., Brendgen, M., & Tremblay, R. E. (2002). Reactive and proactive aggression: Antecedent and subsequent correlates. *Journal of Child Psychology and Psychiatry, 43,* 495–505.

Vogel, D. A., Lake, M. A., Evans, S., & Karraker, H. (1991). Children's and adults' sex-stereotyped perceptions of infants. *Sex Roles, 24,* 605–616.

Volling, B. L. (2001). Early attachment relationships as predictors of preschool children's emotion regulation with a distressed sibling. *Early Education and Development, 12,* 185–207.

Volling, B. L., & Belsky, J. (1992). Contribution of mother–child and father–child relationships to the quality of sibling interaction: A longitudinal study. *Child Development, 63,* 1209–1222.

Volling, B. L., McElwain, N. L., & Miller, A. L. (2002). Emotion regulation in context: The jealousy complex between young siblings and its relations with child and family characteristics. *Child Development, 73,* 581–600.

Volling, B. L., McElwain, N. L., Notaro, P. C., & Herrera, C. (2002). Parents' emotional availability and infant emotional competence: Predictors of parent–infant attachment and emerging self-regulation. *Journal of Family Psychology, 16,* 447–465.

Vondra, J. I., Hommerding, K. D., & Shaw, D. S. (1999). Stability and change in infant attachment in a low-income sample. In J. I Vondra & D. Barnett (Eds.), Atypical attachment in infancy and early childhood among children at developmental risk. *Monographs of the Society for Research in Child Development, 64*(3, Serial No. 258), 119–144.

Vondra, J. I., Shaw, D. S., Searingen, L., Cohen, M., & Owens, E. B. (2001). Attachment stability and emotional and behavioral regulation from infancy to preschool age. *Development and Psychopathology, 13,* 13–33.

von Hofsten, C. (1993). Prospective control: A basic aspect of action development. *Human Development, 36,* 253–270.

von Hofsten, C. (2004). An action perspective on motor development. *Trends in Cognitive Sciences, 8,* 266–272.

Vonk, R., & Ashmore, R. D. (2003). Thinking about gender types: Cognitive organization of female and male types. *British Journal of Social Psychology, 42,* 257–280.

Votruba-Drzal, E., Coley, R. L., & Chase-Lansdale, P. L. (2004). Child care and low-income children's development: Direct and moderated effects. *Child Development, 75,* 296–312.

Vouloumanos, A., & Werker, J. F., (2004). Tuned to the signal: The privileged status of speech for young infants. *Developmental Science, 7,* 270–276.

Voyer, D., Voyer, S., & Bryden, M. P. (1995). Magnitude of sex differences in spatial abilities: A meta-analysis and consideration of critical variables. *Psychological Bulletin, 117,* 250–270.

Vurpillot, E. (1968). The development of scanning strategies and their relation to visual differentiation. *Journal of Experimental Child Psychology, 6,* 632–650.

Vygotsky, L. S. (1978). *Mind in society: The development of higher mental processes.* Cambridge, MA: Harvard University Press. (Original works published 1930, 1933, and 1935)

Vygotsky, L. S. (1986). *Thought and language* (A. Kozulin, Trans.). Cambridge, MA: MIT Press. (Original work published 1934)

Vygotsky, L. S. (1987). Thinking and speech. In R. W. Rieber, A. S. Carton (Eds.), & N. Minick (Trans.), *The collected works of L. S. Vygotsky: Vol. 1. Problems of general psychology* (pp. 37–285). New York: Plenum. (Original work published 1934)

Wachs, T. D. (1999). The what, why, and how of temperament: A piece of the action. In L. Balter & C. S. Tamis-LeMonda (Eds.), *Child psychology: A handbook of contemporary issues* (pp. 23–44). Philadelphia: Psychology Press.

Wachs, T. D. (2006). The nature, etiology, and consequences of individual differences in temperament. In L. Balter & C. S. Tamis-LeMonda (Eds.), *Child psychology: A handbook of contemporary issues* (pp. 27–52). New York: Psychology Press.

Wachs, T. D., & Bates, J. E. (2001). Temperament. In G. Bremner & A. Fogel (Eds.), *Blackwell handbook of infant development* (pp. 465–501). Oxford, UK: Blackwell.

Waddington, C. H. (1957). *The strategy of the genes.* London: Allen and Unwin.

Wadhwa, P. D., Sandman, C. A., & Garite, T. J. (2001). The neurobiology of stress in human pregnancy: Implications for prematurity and development of the fetal central nervous system. *Progress in Brain Research, 133,* 131–142.

Wagner, B. M., Silverman, M. A. C., & Martin, C. E. (2003). Family factors in youth suicidal behaviors. *American Behavioral Scientist, 46,* 1171–1191.

Wahlsten, D. (1994). The intelligence of heritability. *Canadian Psychology, 35,* 244–259.

Wainryb, C. (1997). The mismeasure of diversity: Reflections on the study of cross-cultural differences. In H. D. Saltzstein (Ed.), *New directions for child development* (No. 76, pp. 51–65). San Francisco: Jossey-Bass.

Wainryb, C., Brehl, B. A., & Matwin, S. (2005). Being hurt and hurting others: Children's narrative accounts and moral judgments of their own interpersonal conflicts. *Monographs of the Society for Research in Child Development, 70*(3, Serial No. 281).

Wainryb, C., & Ford, S. (1998). Young children's evaluations of acts based on beliefs different from their own. *Merrill-Palmer Quarterly, 44,* 484–503.

Wakeley, A., Rivera, S., & Langer, J. (2000). Can young infants add and subtract? *Child Development, 71,* 1477–1720.

Walberg, H. J. (1986). Synthesis of research on teaching. In M. C. Wittrock (Ed.), *Handbook of research on teaching* (3rd ed., pp. 214–229). New York: Macmillan.

Waldfogel, J. (2001). International policies toward parental leave and child care. *Future of Children 11,* 52–61.

Waldman, I. D., Weinberg, R. A., & Scarr, S. (1994). Racial-group differences in IQ in the Minnesota Transracial Adoption Study: A reply to Levin and Lynn. *Intelligence, 19,* 29–44.

Waldron, H. B., Turner, C. W., & Ozechowski, T. J. (2005). Profiles of change in behavioral and family interventions for adolescent substance abuse and dependence. In H. A. Liddle & C. L. Rowe (Eds.), *Adolescent substance abuse: Research and clinical advances* (pp. 357–374). Cambridge, UK: Cambridge University Press.

Walenski, M., Tager-Flusberg, H., & Ullman, M. T. (2006). Language in autism. In S. O. Moldin & J. L. R. Rubenstein (Eds.), *Understanding autism: From basic neuroscience to treatment* (pp. 175–203). Boca Raton, FL: CRC Press.

Walker, A., Rosenberg, M., & Balaban-Gil, K. (1999). Neurodevelopmental and neurobehavioral sequelae of selected substances of abuse and psychiatric medications in utero. *Neurological Disorders: Developmental and Behavioral Sequelae, 8,* 845–867.

Walker, L. J. (1980). Cognitive and perspective-taking prerequisites for moral development. *Child Development, 51,* 131–139.

Walker, L. J. (1989). A longitudinal study of moral reasoning. *Child Development, 60,* 157–166.

Walker, L. J. (1995). Sexism in Kohlberg's moral psychology? In W. M. Kurtines & J. L. Gewirtz (Eds.), *Moral development: An introduction* (pp. 83–107). Boston: Allyn and Bacon.

Walker, L. J. (2004). Progress and prospects in the psychology of moral development. *Merrill-Palmer Quarterly, 50,* 546–557.

Walker, L. J. (2006). Gender and morality. In M. Killen & J. G. Smetana (Eds.), *Handbook of moral development* (pp. 93–118). Philadelphia: Erlbaum.

Walker, L. J., & Hennig, K. H. (1997). Moral development in the broader context of personality. In S. Hala (Ed.), *The development of social cognition* (pp. 297–327). Hove, UK: Psychology Press.

Walker, L. J., & Moran, T. J. (1991). Moral reasoning in a communist Chinese society. *Journal of Moral Education, 20,* 139–155.

Walker, L. J., Pitts, R. C., Hennig, K. H., & Matsuba, M. K. (1995). Reasoning about morality and real-life moral problems. In M. Killen & D. Hart (Eds.), *Morality in everyday life* (pp. 37–407). New York: Cambridge University Press.

Walker, L. J., Pitts, R. C., Hennig, K. H., & Matsuba, M. K. (1999). Reasoning about morality and real-life moral problems. In M. Killen & D. Hart (Eds.), *Morality in everyday life* (pp. 371–407). New York: Cambridge University Press.

Walker, L. J., & Taylor, J. H. (1991a). Family interactions and the development of moral reasoning. *Child Development, 62,* 264–283.

Walker, L. J., & Taylor, J. H. (1991b). Stage transitions in moral reasoning: A longitudinal study of developmental processes. *Developmental Psychology, 27,* 330–337.

Walker-Andrews, A. S. (1997). Infants' perception of expressive behaviors: Differentiation of multimodal information. *Psychological Bulletin, 121,* 437–456.

Walkowiak, J., Wiener, J., Fastabend, A., Heinzow, B., Krämer, U., & Schmidt, E. (2001). Environmental exposure to polychlorinated biphenyls and quality of the home environment: Effects on psychodevelopment in early childhood. *Lancet, 358,* 1602–1607.

Wall, M., & Côté, J. (2007). Developmental activities that lead to dropout and investment in sport. *Physical Education and Sport Pedagogy, 12,* 77–87.

Wallace, J. M., Jr., Bachman, J. G., O'Malley, P. M., Schulenberg, J. E., Cooper, S. M., & Johnston, L. D. (2003). Gender and ethnic differences in smoking, drinking, and illicit drug use among American 8th, 10th, and 12th grade students, 1976–2000. *Addiction, 98,* 225–234.

Wallerstein, J. S., & Lewis, J. M. (2004). The unexpected legacy of divorce: Report of a 25-year study. *Psychoanalytic Psychology, 21,* 353–370.

Wang, Q. (2003). Infantile amnesia reconsidered: A cross-cultural analysis. *Memory, 11,* 65–80.

Wang, Q. (2004). The emergence of cultural self-construct: Autobiographical memory and self-description in American and Chinese children. *Developmental Psychology, 40,* 3–15.

Wang, Q. (2006a). Earliest recollections of self and others in European American and Taiwanese young adults. *Psychological Science, 17,* 708–714.

Wang, Q. (2006b). Relations of maternal style and child self-concept to autobiographical memories in Chinese, Chinese immigrant, and European American 3-year-olds. *Child Development, 77,* 1794–1809.

Wang, Q., Pomerantz, E. M., & Chen, H. (2007). The role of parents' control in early adolescents' psychological functioning: A longitudinal investigation in the United States and China. *Child Development, 78,* 1592–1610.

Wang, S., Baillargeon, R., & Paterson, S. (2005). Detecting continuity violations in infancy: A new account and new evidence from covering and tube events. *Cognition, 95,* 129–173.

Wanska, S. K., & Bedrosian, J. L. (1985). Conversational structure and topic performance in mother–child interaction. *Journal of Speech and Hearing Research, 28,* 579–584.

Wark, G. R., & Krebs, D. L. (1996). Gender and dilemma differences in real-life moral judgment. *Developmental Psychology, 32,* 220–230.

Warner, L. A., Valdez, A., Vega, W. A., de la Rosa, M., Turner, R. J., & Canino, G. (2006). Hispanic drug abuse in an evolving cultural context: An agenda for research. *Drug and Alcohol Dependence, 84* (Suppl. 1), S8–S16.

Warnock, F., & Sandrin, D. (2004). Comprehensive description of newborn distress behavior in response to acute pain (newborn male circumcision). *Pain, 107,* 242–255.

Warren, A. R., & Tate, C. S. (1992). Egocentrism in children's telephone conversations. In R. M. Diaz & L. E. Berk (Eds.), *Private speech: From social interaction to self-regulation* (pp. 245–264). Hillsdale, NJ: Erlbaum.

Warren, D. H. (1994). *Blindness and children: An individual difference approach.* New York: Cambridge University Press.

Waschbusch, D. A., Daleiden, E., & Drabman, R. S. (2000). Are parents accurate reporters of their child's cognitive abilities? *Journal of Psychopathology and Behavioral Assessment, 22,* 61–77.

Wasik, B. A., & Bond, M. A. (2001). Beyond the pages of a book: Interactive book reading and language development in preschool classrooms. *Journal of Educational Psychology, 93,* 243–250.

Wasserman, E. A., & Rovee-Collier, C. (2001). Pick the flowers and mind your As and 2s! Categorization by pigeons and infants. In M. E. Carroll & J. B. Overmier (Eds.), *Animal research and human health: Advancing human welfare through behavioral science* (pp. 263–279). Washington, DC: American Psychological Association.

Wasserman, J. D., & Tulsky, D. S. (2005). A history of intelligence assessment. In D. P. Flanagan & P. L. Harrison (Eds.), *Contemporary intellectual assessment: Theories, tests, and issues* (2nd ed., pp. 3–22). New York: Guilford.

Watamura, S. E., Donzella, B., Alwin, J., & Gunnar, M. R. (2003). Morning-to-afternoon increases in cortisol concentrations for infants and toddlers at child care: Age differences and behavioral correlates. *Child Development, 74,* 1006–1020.

Waters, E., & Cummings, E. M. (2000). A secure base from which to explore close relationships. *Child Development, 71,* 164–172.

Waters, E., Merrick, S., Treboux, D., Crowell, J., & Albersheim, L. (2000). Attachment security in infancy and early adulthood: A twenty-year longitudinal study. *Child Development, 71,* 684–689.

Waters, E., Vaughn, B. E., Posada, G., & Kondo-Ikemura K. (Eds.). (1995). Caregiving, cultural, and cognitive perspectives on secure-base behavior and working models: New growing points of attachment theory and research. *Monographs of the Society for Research in Child Development, 60*(2–3, Serial No. 244).

Watson, A. C., Nixon, C. L., Wilson, A., & Capage, L. (1999). Social interaction skills and theory of mind in young children. *Developmental Psychology, 35,* 386–391.

Watson, D. J. (1989). Defining and describing whole language. *Elementary School Journal, 90,* 129–141.

Watson, J. B., & Raynor, R. (1920). Conditioned emotional reactions. *Journal of Experimental Psychology, 3,* 1–14.

Watson, M. (1990). Aspects of self development as reflected in children's role playing. In D. Cicchetti & M. Beeghly (Eds.), *The self in transition: Infancy to childhood* (pp. 281–307). Chicago: University of Chicago Press.

Watts-English, T., Fortson, B. L., Gibler, N., Hooper, S. R., & De Bellis, M. D. (2006). The psychobiology of maltreatment in childhood. *Journal of Social Issues, 62,* 717–736.

Waxman, S., & Lidz, J. L. (2006). Early word learning. In D. Kuhn & R. Siegler (Eds.), *Handbook of child psychology: Vol. 2. Cognition, perception, and language* (6th ed., pp. 464–510). Hoboken, NJ: Wiley.

Waxman, S. R. (2003). Links between object categorization and naming: Origins and emergence in human infants. In D. H. Rakison & L. M. Oakes (Eds.), *Early category and concept development: Making sense of the blooming, buzzing confusion* (pp. 193–209). New York: Oxford University Press.

Waxman, S. R., & Braun, I. (2005). Consistent (but not variable) names as invitations to form object categories: New evidence from 12-month-old infants. *Cognition, 95,* B59–B68.

Waxman, S. R., & Senghas, A. (1992). Relations among word meanings in early lexical development. *Developmental Psychology, 28,* 862–873.

Wayermann, M., Rothenbacher, D., & Brenner, H. (2006). Duration of breastfeeding and risk of overweight in childhood: A prospective birth cohort study from Germany. *International Journal of Obesity, 30,* 1281–1287.

Webb, N. M., Nemer, K. M., & Chizhik, A. W. (1998). Equity issues in collaborative group assessment: Group composition and performance. *American Educational Research Journal, 35,* 607–651.

Webb, N. M., Troper, J., & Fall, R. (1995). Constructive activity and learning in collaborative small groups. *Journal of Educational Psychology, 87,* 406–423.

Webb, S. J., Monk, C. S., & Nelson, C. A. (2001). Mechanisms of postnatal neurobiological development: Implications for human development. *Developmental Neuropsychology, 19,* 147–171.

Weber, C., Hahne, A., Friedrich, M., & Friederici, A. (2004). Discrimination of word stress in early infant perception: Electrophysiological evidence. *Cognitive Brain Research, 18,* 149–161.

Webster-Stratton, C., Reid, J., & Hammond, M. (2001). Social skills and problem-solving training for children with early-onset conduct problems: Who benefits? *Journal of Child Psychology and Psychiatry, 42,* 943–952.

Wechsler, D. (2002). *WPPSI-III: Wechsler Preschool and Primary Scale of Intelligence* (3rd ed.). San Antonio, TX: Psychological Corporation.

Wechsler, D. (2003). *WISC-IV: Wechsler Intelligence Scale for Children* (4th ed.). San Antonio, TX: Psychological Corporation.

Wechsler, D. (2004). *WISC-IV Canadian manual.* Toronto: Harcourt Assessment.

Weems, C. F., & Costa, N. M. (2005). Developmental differences in the expression of childhood anxiety symptoms and fears. *Journal of the American Academy of Child and Adolescent Psychiatry, 44,* 656–663.

Wehren, A., De Lisi, R., & Arnold, M. (1981). The development of noun definition. *Journal of Child Language, 8,* 165–175.

Weikart, D. P. (1998). Changing early childhood development through educational intervention. *Preventive Medicine, 27,* 233–237.

Weikum, W. M., Vouloumanos, A., Navarra, J., Soto-Faraco, S., Sebastián-Gallés, N., & Werker, J. F. (2007). Visual language discrimination in infancy. *Science, 316,* 1159.

Weimer, B. L., Kerns, K. A., & Oldenburg, C. M. (2004). Adolescents' interactions with a best friend: Associations with attachment style. *Journal of Experimental Child Psychology, 88,* 102–120.

Weinberg, M. K., & Tronick, E. Z. (1994). Beyond the face: An empirical study of infant affective configurations of facial, vocal, gestural, and regulatory behaviors. *Child Development, 65,* 1503–1515.

Weinberg, M. K., Tronick, E. Z., Cohn, J. F., & Olson, K. L. (1999). Gender differences in emotional expressivity and self-regulation during early infancy. *Developmental Psychology, 35,* 175–188.

Weinberg, R., Tenenbaum, G., McKenzie, A., Jackson, S., Anshel, M., Grove, R., & Fogarty, G. (2000). Motivation for youth participation in sport and physical activity: Relationships to culture, self-reported activity levels, and gender. *International Journal of Sport Psychology, 31,* 321–346.

Weiner, A. (1988). *The Trobrianders of Papua New Guinea.* New York: Holt.

Weiner, J., & Tardif, C. (2004). Social and emotional functioning of children with learning disabilities: Does special education placement make a difference? *Learning Disabilities Research and Practice, 19,* 20–32.

Weinert, F. E., & Hany, E. A. (2003). The stability of individual differences in intellectual development: Empirical evidence, theoretical problems, and new research questions. In R. J. Sternberg, J. Lautrey, & T. I. Lubart (Eds.), *Models of intelligence: International perspectives* (pp. 169–181). Washington, DC: American Psychological Association.

Weinert, F. E., & Schneider, W. (Eds.). (1999). *Individual development from 3 to 12: Findings from the Munich Longitudinal Study.* Cambridge, UK: Cambridge University Press.

Weinfield, N. S., Sroufe, L. A., & Egeland, B. (2000). Attachment from infancy to early adulthood in a high-risk sample: Continuity, discontinuity, and their correlates. *Child Development, 71,* 695–702.

Weinfield, N. S., Whaley, G. J. L., & Egeland, B. (2004). Continuity, discontinuity, and coherence in attachment from infancy to late adolescence: Sequelae of organization and disorganization. *Attachment and Human Development, 6,* 73–97.

Weinraub, M., Clemens, L. P., Sockloff, A., Ethridge, T., Gracely, E., & Myers, B. (1984). The development of sex-role stereotypes in the third year: Relationships to gender labeling, gender identity, sex-typed toy preference, and family characteristics. *Child Development, 55,* 1493–1503.

Weinstein, R. S. (2002). *Reaching higher: The power of expectations in schooling.* Cambridge, MA: Harvard University Press.

Weinstein, S. M., Mermelstein, R. J., Hedeker, D., Hankin, B. L., & Flay, B. R. (2006). The time-varying influences of peer and family support on adolescent daily positive and negative affect. *Journal of Clinical Child and Adolescent Psychology, 35,* 420–430.

Weinstock, H., Berman, S., & Cates, W., Jr. (2004). Sexually transmitted diseases among American youth: Incidence and prevalence estimates, 2000. *Perspectives on Sexual and Reproductive Health, 36,* 6–10.

Weisfield, G. E. (1997). Puberty rites as clues to the nature of human adolescence. *Cross-Cultural Research, 31,* 27–54.

Weisner, T. S., & Wilson-Mitchell, J. E. (1990). Nonconventional family life-styles and sex typing in six-year-olds. *Child Development, 61,* 1915–1933.

Weiss, K. M. (2005). Cryptic causation of human disease: Reading between the germ lines. *Trends in Genetics, 21,* 82–88.

Weissman, M. D., & Kalish, C. (1999). The inheritance of desired characteristics: Children's view of the role of intention in parent–offspring resemblance. *Quarterly Journal of Experimental Child Psychology, 73,* 245–265.

Weisz, A. N., & Black, B. M. (2002). Gender and moral reasoning: African American youths respond to dating dilemmas. *Journal of Human Behavior in the Social Environment, 6,* 17–34.

Weizman, Z. O., & Snow, C. E. (2001). Lexical output as related to children's vocabulary acquisition: Effects of sophisticated exposure and support for meaning. *Developmental Psychology, 37,* 265–279.

Wekerle, C., & Avgoustis, E. (2003). Child maltreatment, adolescent dating, and adolescent dating violence. In P. Florsheim (Ed.), *Adolescent romantic relations and sexual behavior: Theory, research, and practical implications* (pp. 213–242). Mahwah, NJ: Erlbaum.

Wekerle, C., Wall, A.-M., Leung, E., & Trocmé, N. (2007). Cumulative stress and substantiated maltreatment: The importance of caregiver vulnerability and adult partner violence. *Child Abuse and Neglect, 31,* 427–443.

Wekerle, C., & Wolfe, D. A. (2003). Child maltreatment. In E. J. Mash & R. A. Barkley (Eds.), *Child psychopathology* (2nd ed., pp. 632–684). New York: Guilford.

Wellman, H. M. (1990). *The child's theory of mind.* Cambridge, MA: MIT Press.

Wellman, H. M. (2002). Understanding the psychological world: Developing a theory of mind. In U. Goswami (Ed.), *Blackwell handbook of child cognitive development* (pp. 167–187). Malden, MA: Blackwell.

Wellman, H. M., & Hickling, A. K. (1994). The mind's "I": Children's conception of the mind as an active agent. *Child Development, 65,* 1564–1580.

Wellman, H. M., Hickling, A. K., & Schultz, C. A. (1997). Young children's psychological, physical, and biological explanations. In H. M. Wellman & K. Inagaki (Eds.), *The emergence of core domains of thought: New directions for child development #75* (pp. 7–25). San Francisco: Jossey-Bass.

Wellman, H. M., Phillips, A. T., & Rodriquez, T. (2000). Young children's understanding of perception, desire, and emotion. *Child Development, 71,* 895–912.

Wellman, H. M., Somerville, S. C., & Haake, R. J. (1979). Development of search procedures in real-life spatial environments. *Developmental Psychology, 15,* 530–542.

Wentworth, N., Benson, J. B., & Haith, M. M. (2000). The development of infants' reaches for stationary and moving targets. *Child Development, 71,* 576–601.

Wentworth, N., & Haith, M. M. (1998). Infants' acquisition of spatiotemporal expectations. *Developmental Psychology, 24,* 247–257.

Wentzel, K. R., Barry, C. M., & Caldwell, K. A. (2004). Friendships in middle school: Influences on motivation and school adjustment. *Journal of Educational Psychology, 96,* 195–203.

Werker, J. F., Pegg, J. E., & McLeod, P. (1994). A cross-language investigation of infant preference for infant-directed communication. *Infant Behavior and Development, 17,* 323–333.

Werker, J. F., & Yeung, H. H. (2005). Infant speech perception bootstraps word learning. *Trends in Cognitive Sciences, 9,* 519–527.

Werner, E. E. (1989). Children of the Garden Island. *Scientific American, 260*(4), 106–111.

Werner, E. E. (2001). *Journeys from childhood to midlife: Risk, resilience, and recovery.* Ithaca, NY: Cornell University Press.

Werner, E. E. (2005). What can we learn about resilience from large-scale longitudinal studies? In S. Goldstein & R. B. Brooks (Eds.), *Handbook of resilience in children* (pp. 91–105). New York: Kluwer Academic.

Werner, E. E., & Smith, R. S. (1982). *Vulnerable but invincible.* New York: McGraw-Hill.

Werner, E. E., & Smith, R. S. (1992). *Overcoming the odds: High risk children from birth to adulthood.* Ithaca, NY: Cornell University Press.

Werner, N. E., & Crick, N. R. (2004). Maladaptive peer relationships and the development of relational and physical aggression during middle childhood. *Social Development, 13,* 495–514.

Westermann, G., Mareschal, D., Johnson, M. H., Sirois, S., Spratling, M. W., & Thomas, M. S. C. (2007). Neuroconstructivism. *Developmental Science, 10,* 75–83.

Westermann, G., Sirois, S., Shultz, T. R., & Mareschal, D. (2006). Modeling developmental cognitive neuroscience. *Trends in Cognitive Sciences, 10,* 227–232.

Wexler, I. D., Branski, D., & Kerem, E. (2006). War and children. *Journal of the American Medical Association, 296,* 579–581.

Wheeler, W. (2002). Youth leadership for development: Civic activism as a component of youth development programming and a strategy for strengthening civil society. In R. M. Lerner, F. Jacobs, & D. Wertlieb (Eds.), *Handbook of applied developmental science: Vol. 2* (pp. 491–506). Thousand Oaks, CA: Sage.

Whipple, E. E. (2006). Child abuse and neglect: Consequences of physical, sexual, and emotional abuse of children. In H. E. Fitzgerald, B. M. Lester, & B. Zuckerman (Eds.), *The crisis in youth mental health: Critical issues and effective programs: Vol. 1. Childhood disorders* (pp. 205–229). Westport, CT: Praeger.

White, B., & Held, R. (1966). Plasticity of sensorimotor development in the human infant. In J. F. Rosenblith & W. Allinsmith (Eds.), *The causes of behavior* (pp. 60–70). Boston: Allyn and Bacon.

Whiteman, S. D., & Loken, E. (2006). Comparing analytic techniques to classify dyadic relationships: an example using siblings. *Journal of Marriage and Family, 68,* 1370–1382.

Whiteside-Mansell, L., Bradley, R. H., Owen, M. T., Randolph, S. M., & Cauce, A. M. (2003). Parenting and children's behavior at 36 months: Equivalence between African-American and European-American mother–child dyads. *Parenting: Science and Practice, 3,* 197–234.

Whiting, B., & Edwards, C. P. (1988a). *Children of different worlds.* Cambridge, MA: Harvard University Press.

Whiting, B., & Edwards, C. P. (1988b). A cross-cultural analysis of sex differences in the behavior of children aged 3 through 11. In G. Handel (Ed.), *Childhood socialization* (pp. 281–297). New York: Aldine De Gruyter.

Whitington, V., & Ward, C. (1999). Intersubjectivity in caregiver–child communication. In L. E. Berk (Ed.), *Landscapes of development* (pp. 109–120). Belmont, CA: Wadsworth.

Whitlock, J. L., Powers, J. L., & Eckenrode, J. (2006). The virtual cutting edge: The Internet and adolescent self-injury. *Developmental Psychology, 42,* 407–417.

Wichman, A. L., Rodgers, J. L., & MacCallum, R. C. (2006). A multilevel approach to the relationship between birth order and intelligence. *Personality and Social Psychology Bulletin, 32,* 117–127.

Wichmann, C., Coplan, R. J., & Daniels, T. (2004). The social cognitions of socially withdrawn children. *Social Development, 13,* 377–392.

Wichstrøm, L. (2006). Sexual orientation as a risk factor for bulimic symptoms. *International Journal of Eating Disorders, 39,* 448–453.

Wickham, S. (1999, Summer). Homebirth: What are the issues? *Midwifery Today, 50,* 16–18.

Wideen, M. F., O'Shea, T., Pye, I., & Ivany, G. (1997). High-stakes testing and the teaching of science. *Canadian Journal of Education, 22,* 428–444.

Wigfield, A., & Eccles, J. S. (1994). Children's competence beliefs, achievement values, and general self-esteem change across elementary and middle school. *Journal of Early Adolescence, 14,* 107–138.

Wigfield, A., Eccles, J. S., Schiefele, U., Roeser, R. W., & Davis-Kean, P. (2006). Development of achievement motivation. In N. Eisenberg (Ed.), *Handbook of child psychology: Vol. 3. Social, emotional, and personality development* (6th ed., pp. 933–1002). Hoboken, NJ: Wiley.

Wigfield, A., Eccles, J. S., Yoon, K. S., Harold, R. D., Arbreton, A. J., Freedman-Doan, C., & Blumenfeld, P. C. (1997). Changes in children's competence beliefs and subjective task values across the elementary school years: A three-year study. *Journal of Educational Psychology, 89,* 451–469.

Wilcox, A. J., Weinberg, C. R., & Baird, D. D. (1995). Timing of sexual intercourse in relation to ovulation: Effects on the probability of conception, survival of the pregnancy, and sex of the baby. *New England Journal of Medicine, 333,* 1517–1519.

Wilhelm, O. (2005). Measures of emotional intelligence: Practice and standards. In R. Schulze & R. D. Roberts (Eds.), *Emotional intelligence: An international handbook* (pp. 131–154). Göttingen, Germany: Hogrefe & Huber.

Wilkinson, K., Ross, E., & Diamond, A. (2003). Fast mapping of multiple words: Insights into when "the information provided" does and does not equal "the information perceived." *Applied Developmental Psychology, 24,* 739–762.

Wilkinson, R. B. (2004). The role of parental and peer attachment in the psychological health and self-esteem of adolescents. *Journal of Youth and Adolescence, 33,* 479–493.

Wilkinson, R. B., & Scherl, F. B. (2006). Psychological health, maternal attachment and attachment style in breast- and formula-feeding mothers: A preliminary study. *Journal of Reproductive and Infant Psychology, 24,* 5–19.

Willatts, P. (1999). Development of means–end behavior in young infants: Pulling a support to retrieve a distant object. *Developmental Psychology, 35,* 651–667.

Wille, M. C., Weitz, B., Kerper, P., & Frazier, S. (2004). Advances in preconception genetic counseling. *Journal of Perinatal and Neonatal Nursing, 18,* 28–40.

Williams, C. (2006). Dilemmas in fetal medicine: Premature application of technology or responding to women's choice? *Sociology of Health and Illness, 28,* 1–20.

Williams, E., Radin, N., & Allegro, T. (1992). Sex-role attitudes of adolescents reared primarily by their fathers: An 11-year follow-up. *Merrill-Palmer Quarterly, 38,* 457–476.

Williams, G. C. (1997). Review of *Adaptation,* edited by Michael R. Rose and George V. Lauder. *Copeia,* No. 3, 645–647.

Williams, J. E., & Best, D. L. (1990). *Measuring sex stereotypes: A multination study.* Newbury Park, CA: Sage.

Williams, J. M., & Currie, C. (2000). Self-esteem and physical development in early adolescence: Pubertal timing and body image. *Journal of Early Adolescence, 20,* 129–149.

Williams, K., & Dunne-Bryant, A. (2006). Divorce and adult psychological well-being: Clarifying the role of gender and age. *Journal of Marriage and Family, 68,* 1178–1196.

Williams, K., Haywood, K. I., & Painter, M. (1996). Environmental versus biological influences on gender differences in the overarm throw for force: Dominant and nondominant arm throws. *Women in Sport and Physical Activity Journal, 5,* 29–48.

Williams, P. E., Weiss, L. G., & Rolfhus, E. (2003). *WICS-IV: Theoretical model and test blueprint.* San Antonio, TX: Psychological Corporation.

Williams, S. C., Lochman, J. E., Phillips, N. C., & Barry, T. D. (2003). Aggressive and nonaggressive boys' physiological and cognitive processes in response to peer provocations. *Journal of Clinical Child and Adolescent Psychology, 32,* 568–576.

Williams, T. M. (1986). *The impact of television: A natural experiment in three communities.* Orlando, FL: Academic Press.

Williams, W. M. (1998). Are we raising smarter children today? School- and home-related influences on IQ. In U. Neisser (Ed.), *The rising curve: Long-term gains in IQ and related measures* (pp. 125–154). Washington, DC: American Psychological Association.

Willinger, M., Ko, C. W., Hoffman, H. J., Kessler, R. C., & Corwin, M. J. (2003). Trends in infant bed sharing in the United States, 1993–2000: The National Infant Sleep Position Study. *Archives of Pediatric and Adolescent Medicine, 157,* 43–49.

Willoughby, J., Kupersmidt, J. B., & Bryant, D. (2001). Overt and covert dimensions of antisocial behavior. *Journal of Abnormal Child Psychology, 29,* 177–187.

Wilson, E. O. (1975). *Sociobiology: The new synthesis.* Cambridge, MA: Harvard University Press.

Wilson, R., & Cairns, E. (1988). Sex-role attributes, perceived competence, and the development of depression in adolescence. *Journal of Child Psychology and Psychiatry, 29,* 635–650.

Winner, E. (1986, August). Where pelicans kiss seals. *Psychology Today, 20* (8), 25–35.

Winner, E. (1988). *The point of words: Children's understanding of metaphor and irony.* Cambridge, MA: Harvard University Press.

Winner, E. (1996). *Gifted children: Myths and realities.* New York: Basic Books.

Winner, E. (1997). Exceptionally high intelligence and schooling. *American Psychologist, 52,* 1070–1081.

Winner, E. (2000). The origins and ends of giftedness. *American Psychologist, 55,* 159–169.

Winner, E. (2003). Creativity and talent. In M. H. Bornstein, L. Davidson, C. L. M. Keyes, K. A. Moore, & The Center for Child Well-Being (Eds.), *Well-being: Positive development across the life course* (pp. 371–380). Mahwah, NJ: Erlbaum.

Winsler, A., Abar, B., Feder, M. A., Rubio, D. A., & Schunn, C. D. (2007). Private speech and executive functioning among high-functioning children with autistic spectrum disorders. *Journal of Autism and Developmental Disorders, 37,* 1617–1635.

Winsler, A., & Naglieri, J. (2003). Overt and covert verbal problem-solving strategies: Developmental trends in use, awareness, and relations with task performance in children aged 5 to 17. *Child Development, 74,* 659–678.

Winsler, A., Naglieri, J., & Manfra, L. (2006). Children's search strategies and accompanying verbal and motor strategic behavior: Developmental trends and relations with task performance among children age 5 to 17. *Cognitive Development, 21,* 232–248.

Wissink, I. B., Deković, M., & Meijer, A. M. (2006). Parenting behavior, quality of the parent–adolescent relationship, and adolescent functioning in four ethnic groups. *Journal of Early Adolescence, 26,* 133–159.

Witherington, D. C. (2005). The development of prospective grasping control between 5 and 7 months: A longitudinal study. *Infancy, 7,* 143–161.

Witherington, D. C., Campos, J. J., Anderson, D. I., Lejeune, L., & Seah, E. (2005). Avoidance of heights on the visual cliff in newly walking infants. *Infancy, 7,* 285–298.

Wolak, J., Finkelhor, D., Mitchell, K. J., & Ybarra, M. L. (2008). Online "predators" and their victims: Myths, realities, and implications for prevention and treatment. *American Psychologist, 63,* 111–128.

Wolak, J., Mitchell, K. J., & Finkelhor, D. (2003). Escaping or connecting? Characteristics of youth who form close online relationships. *Journal of Adolescence, 26,* 105–119.

Wolak, J., Mitchell, K., & Finkelhor, D. (2007). Unwanted and wanted exposure to online pornography in a national sample of youth Internet users. *Pediatrics, 119,* 247–257.

Wolchik, S. A., Sandler, I. N., Millsap, R. E., Plummer, B. A., Greene, S. M., & Anderson, E. R. (2003). Six-year follow-up of preventive interventions for children of divorce: A randomized controlled trial. *Journal of the American Medical Association, 288,* 1874–1881.

Wolchik, S. A., Wilcox, K. L., Tein, J.-Y., & Sandler, I. N. (2000). Maternal acceptance and consistency of discipline as buffers of divorce stressors on children's psychological adjustment problems. *Journal of Abnormal Child Psychology, 28,* 87–102.

Wolf, A. W., Jimenez, E., & Lozoff, B. (2003). Effects of iron therapy on infant blood lead levels. *Journal of Pediatrics, 143,* 789–795.

Wolfe, D. A. (2005). *Child abuse* (2nd ed.) Thousand Oaks: Sage.

Wolfe, D. A., Scott, K., Wekerle, C., & Pittman, A. (2001). Child maltreatment: Risk of adjustment problems and dating violence in adolescence. *Journal of the American Academy of Child and Adolescent Psychiatry, 40,* 282–289.

Wolfe, V. V. (2006). Child sexual abuse. In E. J. Mash & R. A. Barkley (Eds.), *Treatment of childhood disorders* (3rd ed., pp. 647–727). New York: Guilford.

Wolfelt, A. D. (1997). Death and grief in the school setting. In T. N. Fairchild (Ed.), *Crisis intervention strategies for school-based helpers* (2nd ed., pp. 199–244). Springfield, IL: Charles C. Thomas.

Wolff, P. H. (1966). The causes, controls and organization of behavior in the neonate. *Psychological Issues, 5*(1, Serial No. 17).

Wolff, P. H., & Fesseha, G. (1999). The orphans of Eritrea: A five-year follow-up study. *Journal of Child Psychology and Psychiatry and Allied Disciplines, 40,* 1231–1237.

Wolfinger, N. H. (2000). Beyond the intergenerational transmission of divorce: Do people replicate the patterns of marital instability they grew up with? *Journal of Family Issues, 21,* 1061–1086.

Wong, M. M., Nigg, J. T., Zucker, R. A., Puttler, L. I., Fitzgerald, H. E., Jester, J. M., Glass, J. M., & Adams, K. (2006). Behavioral control and resiliency in the onset of alcohol and illicit drug use: A prospective study from preschool to adolescence. *Child Development, 77,* 1016–1033.

Wood, E., Desmarais, S., & Gugula, S. (2002). The impact of parenting experience on gender stereotyped toy play of children. *Sex Roles, 47,* 39–49.

Wood, J. J., Emmerson, N. A., & Cowan, P. A. (2004). Is early attachment security carried forward into relationships with preschool peers? *British Journal of Developmental Psychology, 22,* 245–253.

Woodward, A. L., & Markman, E. M. (1998). Early word learning. In D. Kuhn & R. S. Siegler (Eds.), *Handbook of child psychology: Vol. 2. Cognition, perception, and language* (5th ed., pp. 371–420). New York: Wiley.

Woodward, J., & Ono, Y. (2004). Mathematics and academic diversity in Japan. *Journal of Learning Disabilities, 37,* 74–82.

Woody-Dorning, J., & Miller, P. H. (2001). Children's individual differences in capacity: Effects on strategy production and utilization. *British Journal of Developmental Psychology, 19,* 543–557.

Woody-Ramsey, J., & Miller, P. H. (1988). The facilitation of selective attention in preschoolers. *Child Development, 59,* 1497–1503.

Woolley, J. D. (1997). Thinking about fantasy: Are children fundamentally different thinkers and believers from adults? *Child Development, 68,* 991–1011.

Woolley, J. D. (2000). The development of beliefs about direct mental–physical causality in imagination, magic, and religion. In K. S. Rosengren, C. N. Johnson, & P. L. Harris (Eds.), *Imagining the impossible* (pp. 99–129). New York: Cambridge University Press.

World Cancer Research Fund/American Institute for Cancer Research. (2007). *Food, nutrition, physical activity, and the prevention of cancer: A global perspective.* Washington, DC: American Institute for Cancer Research.

World Education Services. (2007). *World education database.* Retrieved from www.wes.org

World Health Organization. (2005). *The world health report, 2005.* Geneva, Switzerland: Author.

Worrell, F. C., & Gardner-Kitt, D. L. (2006). The relationship between racial and ethnic identity in black adolescents: The cross-racial identity scale and the multigroup ethnic identity measure. *Identity, 6,* 293–315.

Wright, B. C. (2006). On the emergence of the discriminative mode for transitive inference. *European Journal of Cognitive Psychology, 18,* 776–800.

Wright, J. C., Huston, A. C., Murphy, K. C., St. Peters, M., Pinon, M., Scantlin, R., & Kotler, J. (2001). The relations of early television viewing to school readiness and vocabulary of children from low-income families: The Early Window Project. *Child Development, 72,* 1347–1366.

Wright, J. C., Huston, A. C., Reitz, A. L., & Piemyat, S. (1994). Young children's perceptions of television reality: Determinants and developmental differences. *Developmental Psychology, 30,* 229–239.

Wright, R. O., Tsaih, S. W., Schwartz, J., Wright, R. J., & Hu, H. (2003). Associations between iron deficiency and blood lead level in a longitudinal analysis of children followed in an urban primary care clinic. *Journal of Pediatrics, 142,* 9–14.

Wright, V. C., Schieve, L. A., Reynolds, M. A., Jeng, G., & Kissin, D. (2004). Assisted reproductive technology surveillance—United States 2001. *Morbidity and Mortality Weekly Report, 53,* 1–20.

Wrotniak, B. H., Epstein, L. H., Raluch, R. A., & Roemmich, J. N. (2004). Parent weight change as a predictor of child weight change in family-based behavioral obesity treatment. *Archives of Pediatric and Adolescent Medicine, 158,* 342–347.

Wu, G., Bazer, F. W., Cudd, T. A., Meininger, C. J., & Spencer, T. E. (2004). Maternal nutrition and fetal development. *Journal of Nutrition, 134,* 2169–2172.

Wu, L. L., Bumpass, L. L., & Musick, K. (2001). Historical and life course trajectories of nonmarital childbearing. In L. L. Wu & B. Wolfe (Eds.), *Out of wedlock: Causes and consequences of nonmarital fertility* (pp. 3–48). New York: Russell Sage Foundation.

Wu, P., Robinson, C. C., Yang, C., Hart, C. H., Olsen, S. F., Porter, C. L., Jin, S., Wo, J., & Wu, X. (2002). Similarities and differences in mothers' parenting of preschoolers in China and the United States. *International Journal of Behavioral Development, 26,* 481–491.

Wu, T., Mendola, P., & Buck, G. M. (2002). Ethnic differences in the presence of secondary sex characteristics and menarche among U.S. girls: The Third National Health and Nutrition Examination Survey, 1988–1994. *Pediatrics, 110,* 752–757.

Wu, Y. (2006). Overweight and obesity in China. *British Medical Journal, 333,* 362–363.

Wust, S., Entringer, S., Federenko, I. S., Schlotz, W., Helhammer, D. H. (2005). Birth weight is associated with salivary cortisol responses to psychosocial stress in adult life. *Psychoneuroendocrinology, 30,* 591–598.

Wyatt, J. M., & Carlo, G. (2002). What will my parents think? Relations among adolescents' expected parental reactions, prosocial moral reasoning and prosocial and antisocial behaviors. *Journal of Adolescent Research, 17,* 646–666.

Wynn, K. (1992). Addition and subtraction by human infants. *Nature, 358,* 749–750.

Wynn, K. (2002). Do infants have numerical expectations or just perceptual preferences? Comment. *Developmental Science, 5,* 207–209.

Wynn, K., Bloom, P., & Chiang, W.-C. (2002). Enumeration of collective entities by 5-month-old infants. *Cognition, 83,* B55–B62.

Xu, F., Spelke, E., & Goddard, S. (2005). Number sense in human infants. *Developmental Science, 8,* 88–101.

Xue, Y., & Meisels, S. J. (2004). Early literacy instruction and learning in kindergarten: Evidence from the early childhood longitudinal study—kindergarten class of 1998–1999. *American Educational Research Journal, 41,* 191–229.

Yale, M. E., Messinger, D. S., Cobo-Lewis, A. B., Oller, D. K., & Eilers, R. E. (1999). An event-based analysis of the coordination of early infant vocalizations and facial actions. *Developmental Psychology, 35,* 505–513.

Yan, J., & Smetana, J. G. (2003). Conceptions of moral, social-conventional, and personal events among Chinese preschoolers in Hong Kong. *Child Development, 74,* 647–658.

Yan, Z. (2006). What influences children's and adolescents' understanding of the complexity of the Internet? *Developmental Psychology, 42,* 418–428.

Yang, B., Ollendick, T. H., Dong, Q., Xia, Y., & Lin, L. (1995). Only children and children with siblings in the People's Republic of China: Levels of fear, anxiety, and depression. *Child Development, 66,* 1301–1311.

Yang, C. (2008, April). *The influence of one-child policy on child rearing, family, and society in post-Mao China.* Invited address, Illinois State University.

Yang, C., Hart, C. H., Nelson, D. A., Porter, C. L., Olsen, S. F., Robinson, C. C., & Jin, S. (2004). Fathering in a Beijing Chinese sample: Associations with boys' and girls' negative emotionality and aggression. In R. D. Day & M. E. Lamb (Eds.), *Conceptualizing and measuring father involvement* (pp. 185–215). Mahwah, NJ: Erlbaum.

Yang, C.-K., & Hahn, H.-M. (2002). Cosleeping in young Korean children. *Developmental and Behavioral Pediatrics, 23,* 151–157.

Yarrow, M. R., Campbell, J. D., & Burton, R. V. (1970). Recollections of childhood: A study of the retrospective method. *Monographs of the Society for Research in Child Development, 35*(5, Serial No. 138).

Yarrow, M. R., Scott, P. M., & Waxler, C. Z. (1973). Learning concern for others. *Developmental Psychology, 8,* 240–260.

Yeates, K. O., Schultz, L. H., & Selman, R. L. (1991). The development of interpersonal negotiation strategies in thought and action: A social-cognitive link to behavioral adjustment and social status. *Merrill-Palmer Quarterly, 37,* 369–405.

Yeh, H.-C., & Lempers, J. D. (2004). Perceived sibling relationships and adolescent development. *Journal of Youth and Adolescence, 33,* 133–147.

Yehuda, R., Engel, S. M., Brand, S. R., Seckl, J., Marcus, S. M., & Berkowitz, G. S. (2005). Transgenerational effects of posttraumatic stress disorder in babies of mothers exposed to the World Trade Center attacks during pregnancy. *Journal of Clinical Endocrinology and Metabolism, 90,* 4115–4118.

Yip, T., Seaton, E. K., & Sellers, R. M. (2006). African-American racial identity across the lifespan: Identity status, identity content, and depressive symptoms. *Child Development, 77,* 1504–1517.

Yirmiya, N., Erel, O., Shaked, M., & Solomonica-Levi, D. (1998). Meta-analyses comparing theory of mind abilities of individuals with autism, individuals with mental retardation, and normally developing individuals. *Psychological Bulletin, 124,* 283–307.

Yonas, A., Elieff, C., & Arterberry, M. E. (2002). Emergence of sensitivity to pictorial depth cues: Charting development in individual infants. *Infant Behavior and Development, 25,* 295–314.

Yonas, A., & Granrud, C. E. (2006). Infants' perception of depth from cast shadows. *Perception and Psychophysics, 68,* 154–160.

Yoshida, H., & Smith, L. B. (2003). Known and novel noun extensions: Attention at two levels of abstraction. *Child Development, 74,* 564–577.

Yoshinaga-Itano, C. (2003). Early intervention after universal neonatal hearing screening: Impact on outcomes. *Mental Retardation and Developmental Disabilities Research Reviews, 9,* 252–266.

Young, J. F., & Mroczek, D. K. (2003). Predicting intraindividual self-concept trajectories during adolescence. *Journal of Adolescence, 26,* 589–603.

Young, K. T. (1990). American conceptions of infant development from 1955 to 1984: What the experts are telling parents. *Child Development, 61,* 17–28.

Youngblade, L. M., & Dunn, J. (1995). Individual differences in young children's pretend play with mother and sibling: Links to relationships and understanding of other people's feelings and beliefs. *Child Development, 66,* 1472–1492.

Younger, B. A., & Johnson, K. E. (2006). Infants' developing appreciation of similarities between model objects and their real-world referents. *Child Development, 77,* 1680–1697.

Young-Hyman, D., Tanofsky-Kraff, M., Yanovski, S. Z., Keil, M., Cohen, M. L., & Peyrot, M. (2006). Psychological status and weight-related distress in overweight or at-risk-for-overweight children. *Obesity, 14,* 2249–2258.

Youngstrom, E., Wolpaw, J. M., Kogos, J. L., Schoff, K., Ackerman, B., & Izard, C. (2000). Interpersonal problem solving in preschool and first grade: Developmental change and ecological validity. *Journal of Clinical Child Psychology, 29,* 589–602.

Youniss, J., McLellan, J. A., & Yates, M. (1997). What we know about engendering civic identity. *American Behavioral Scientist, 40,* 620–631.

Yu, R. (2002). On the reform of elementary school education in China. *Educational Exploration, 129,* 56–57.

Yu, Y., & Nelson, K. (1993). Slot-filler and conventional category organization in young Korean children. *International Journal of Behavioral Development, 16,* 1–14.

Yuan, A. S. V., & Hamilton, H. A. (2006). Stepfather involvement and adolescent well-being: Do mothers and nonresidential fathers matter? *Journal of Family Issues, 27,* 1191–1213.

Yuill, N., & Pearson, A. (1998). The developmental bases for trait attribution: Children's understanding of traits as causal mechanisms based on desire. *Developmental Psychology, 34,* 574–576.

Yunger, J. L., Carver, P. R., & Perry, D. G. (2004). Does gender identity influence children's psychological well-being? *Developmental Psychology, 40,* 572–582.

Zafeiriou, D. I. (2000). Plantar grasp reflex in high-risk infants during the first year of life. *Pediatric Neurology, 22,* 75–76.

Zahn-Waxler, C. (1991). The case for empathy: A developmental review. *Psychological Inquiry, 2,* 155–158.

Zahn-Waxler, C., Cole, P. M., & Barrett, K. C. (1991). Guilt and empathy: Sex differences and implications for the development of depression. In J. Garber & K. A. Dodge (Eds.), *The development of emotion regulation and dysregulation* (pp. 243–272). Cambridge, UK: Cambridge University Press.

Zahn-Waxler, C., Kochanska, G., Krupnick, J., & McKnew, D. (1990). Patterns of guilt in children of depressed and well mothers. *Developmental Psychology, 26,* 51–59.

Zahn-Waxler, C., & Radke-Yarrow, M. (1990). The origins of empathic concern. *Motivation and Emotion, 14,* 107–130.

Zahn-Waxler, C., Radke-Yarrow, M., & King, R. M. (1979). Childrearing and children's prosocial initiations toward victims of distress. *Child Development, 50,* 319–330.

Zahn-Waxler, C., & Robinson, J. (1995). Empathy and guilt: Early origins of feelings of responsibility. In J. P. Tangney & K. W. Fischer (Eds.), *Self-conscious emotions* (pp. 143–173). New York: Guilford.

Zahn-Waxler, C., Schiro, K., Robinson, J. L., Emde, R. N., & Schmitz, S. (2001). Empathy and prosocial patterns in young MZ and DZ twins: Development and genetic and environmental influences. In R. N. Emde & J. K. Hewitt (Eds.), *Infancy to early childhood: Genetic and environmental influences on developmental change* (pp. 141–162). New York: Oxford University Press.

Zamuner, T. S., Gerken, L., & Hammond, M. (2004). Phonotactic probabilities in young children's speech production. *Journal of Child Language, 31,* 515–536.

Zeifman, D. M. (2003). Predicting adult responses to infant distress: Adult characteristics associated with perceptions, emotional reactions, and timing of intervention. *Infant Mental Health Journal, 24,* 597–612.

Zelazo, N. A., Zelazo, P. R., Cohen, K. M., & Zelazo, P. D. (1993). Specificity of practice effects on elementary neuromotor patterns. *Developmental Psychology, 29,* 686–691.

Zelazo, P. D., Frye, D., & Rapus, T. (1996). An age-related dissociation between knowing rules and using them. *Cognitive Development, 11,* 37–63.

Zeller, M. H., & Modi, A. C. (2006). Predictors of health-related quality of life in obese youth. *Obesity Research, 14,* 122–130.

Zeskind, P. S., & Barr, R. G. (1997). Acoustic characteristics of naturally occurring cries of infants with "colic." *Child Development, 68,* 394–403.

Zeskind, P. S., & Lester, B. M. (2001). Analysis of infant crying. In L. T. Singer & P. S. Zeskind (Eds.), *Biobehavioral assessment of the infant* (pp. 149–166). New York: Guilford.

Zhan, M. (2005). Assets, parental expectations and involvement, and children's educational performance. *Children and Youth Services Review, 28,* 961–975.

Zhou, M., & Bankston, C. L. (1998). *Growing up American: How Vietnamese children adapt to life in the United States.* New York: Russell Sage Foundation.

Zhou, M., & Xiong, S. (2005). The multifaceted American experiences of the children of Asian immigrants: Lessons for segmented assimilation. *Ethnic and Racial Studies, 28,* 1119–1152.

Zhou, Q., Eisenberg, N., Lousoya, S. H., Fabes, R. A., Reiser, M., Guthrie, I. K., Murphy, B. C., Cumberland, A. J., & Shepard, S. A. (2002). The relations of parental warmth and positive expressiveness to children's empathy-related responding and social functioning: A longitudinal study. *Child Development, 73,* 893–915.

Zhou, Z., & Peverly, S. T. (2005). Teaching addition and subtraction to first graders: A Chinese perspective. *Psychology in the Schools, 42,* 259–272.

Zhu, J., & Weiss, L. (2005). The Wechsler Scales. In D. P. Flanagan & P. L. Harrison (Eds.), *Contemporary intellectual assessment* (2nd ed., pp. 297–324). New York: Guilford.

Zielinski, D. S., & Bradshaw, C. P. (2006). Ecological influences on the sequelae of child maltreatment: A review of the literature. *Child Maltreatment, 11,* 49–62.

Zigler, E. F., & Bishop-Josef, S. J. (2006). The cognitive child versus the whole child: Lessons from 40 years of Head Start. In D. G. Singer, R. M. Golinkoff, & K. Hirsh-Pasek (Eds.), *Play = learning* (pp. 15–35). New York: Oxford University Press.

Zimmer-Gembeck, M. J., Siebenbruner, J., & Collins, W. A. (2001). Diverse aspects of dating: Associations with psychosocial functioning from early to middle adolescence. *Journal of Adolescence, 24,* 3 13–336.

Zimmerman, B. J., & Risemberg, R. (1997). Self-regulatory dimensions of academic learning and motivation. In G. D. Phye (Ed.), *Handbook of academic learning: Construction of knowledge* (pp. 105–125). San Diego: Academic Press.

Zimmerman, C. (2005). *The development of scientific reasoning skills: What psychologists contribute to an understanding of elementary science learning.* Report to the National Research Council, Committee on Science Learning Kindergarten through Eighth Grade. Normal, IL: Illinois State University.

Zimmerman, C. (2007). The development of scientific thinking skills in elementary and middle school. *Developmental Review, 27,* 172–223.

Zimmerman, F. J., Christakis, D. A., & Meltzoff, A. N. (2007). Television and DVD/video viewing in children younger than 2 years. *Archives of Pediatrics and Adolescent Medicine, 161,* 473–479.

Zimmerman, L. K., & Stansbury, K. (2004). The influence of emotion regulation, level of shyness, and habituation on the neuroendocrine response of three-year-old children. *Psychoneuroendocrinology, 29,* 973–982.

Zimmerman, P., & Becker-Stoll, F. (2002). Stability of attachment representations during adolescence: The influence of ego-identity status. *Journal of Adolescence, 25,* 107–124.

Ziv, M., & Frye, D. (2003). The relation between desire and false belief in children's theory of mind: No satisfaction? *Developmental Psychology, 39,* 859–876.

Zucker, K. J. (2001). Biological influences on psychosexual differentiation. In R. K. Unger (Ed.), *Handbook of the psychology of women and gender* (pp. 101–115). New York: Wiley.

Zucker, K. J. (2006). "I'm half-boy, half-girl": Play psychotherapy and parent counseling for gender identity disorder. In R. L. Spitzer, M. B. First, J. B. W. Williams, & M. Gibbon (Eds.), *DSM-IV-TR Casebook: Vol. 2. Experts tell how they treated their own patients* (pp. 322–334). Washington, DC: American Psychiatric Publishing.

Zukow-Goldring, P. (2002). Sibling caregiving. In M. H. Bornstein (Ed.), *Handbook of parenting: Vol. 3* (2nd ed., pp. 253–286). Hillsdale, NJ: Erlbaum.

Zur, O., & Gelman, R. (2004). Young children can add and subtract by predicting and checking. *Early Childhood Research Quarterly, 19,* 121–137.

Zuzanek, J. (2000). *The effects of time use and time pressure on child–parent relationships.* Waterloo, ON: Otium.

Zwart, M. (2007). The Dutch system of perinatal care. *Midwifery Today with International Midwife, 81* (Spring), 46.

Name Index

Italic "n" following page number indicates caption or note accompanying figure, illustration, or table.

D

G

H

I

J

Q

R

S

T

X

Y

Z

Subject Index

A

B

D

E

F

G

H

I

J

K

N

O

P

Q

R

S